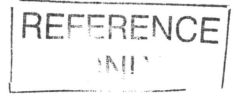

HALSBURY'S
Laws of England

FIFTH EDITION
2017

Volume 56

This is volume 56 of the Fifth Edition of Halsbury's Laws of England, containing the title HOUSING.

The title HOUSING replaces the title of the same name contained in volume 56 (2011). Upon receipt of volume 56 (2017), volume 56 (2011) may be archived.

For a full list of volumes comprised in a current set of Halsbury's Laws of England please see overleaf.

Fifth Edition volumes:

1 (2008), 2 (2017), 3 (2011), 4 (2011), 5 (2013), 6 (2011), 7 (2015), 8 (2015), 9 (2017), 10 (2017), 11 (2015), 12 (2015), 12A (2015), 13 (2009), 14 (2016), 15 (2016), 15A (2016), 16 (2011), 17 (2011), 18 (2009), 19 (2011), 20 (2014), 21 (2016), 22 (2012), 23 (2016), 24 (2010), 25 (2016), 26 (2016), 27 (2015), 28 (2015), 29 (2014), 30 (2012), 31 (2012), 32 (2012), 33 (2013), 34 (2011), 35 (2015), 36 (2015), 37 (2013), 38 (2013), 38A (2013), 39 (2014), 40 (2014), 41 (2014), 41A (2014), 42 (2011), 43 (2011), 44 (2011), 45 (2010), 46 (2010), 47 (2014), 47A (2014), 48 (2015), 49 (2015), 50 (2016), 50A (2016), 51 (2013), 52 (2014), 53 (2014), 54 (2017), 54A (2017), 55 (2012), 56 (2017), 57 (2012), 58 (2014), 58A (2014), 59 (2014), 59A (2014), 60 (2011), 61 (2010), 62 (2016), 63 (2016), 64 (2016), 65 (2015), 66 (2015), 67 (2016), 68 (2016), 69 (2009), 70 (2012), 71 (2013), 72 (2015), 73 (2015), 74 (2011), 75 (2013), 76 (2013), 77 (2016), 78 (2010), 79 (2014), 80 (2013), 81 (2010), 82 (2010), 83 (2010), 84 (2013), 84A (2013), 85 (2012), 86 (2013), 87 (2012), 88 (2012), 88A (2013), 89 (2011), 90 (2011), 91 (2012), 92 (2015), 93 (2008), 94 (2008), 95 (2017), 96 (2012), 97 (2015), 97A (2014), 98 (2013), 99 (2012), 100 (2009), 101 (2009), 102 (2016), 103 (2016), 104 (2014)

Consolidated Index and Tables:

2016 Consolidated Index (A–E), 2016 Consolidated Index (F–O), 2016 Consolidated Index (P–Z), 2017 Consolidated Table of Statutes, 2017 Consolidated Table of Statutory Instruments, etc, 2017 Consolidated Table of Cases (A–G), 2017 Consolidated Table of Cases (H–Q), 2017 Consolidated Table of Cases (R–Z, ECJ Cases)

Updating and ancillary materials:

2017 annual Cumulative Supplement; monthly Noter-up; annual Abridgments 1974–2016

May 2017

HALSBURY'S
Laws of England

Volume 56

2017

Members of the LexisNexis Group worldwide

United Kingdom	RELX (UK) Ltd, trading as LexisNexis, 1–3 Strand, London WC2N 5JR and 9–10 St Andrew Square, Edinburgh EH2 2AF
Australia	Reed International Books Australia Pty Ltd trading as LexisNexis, Chatswood, New South Wales
Austria	LexisNexis Verlag ARD Orac GmbH & Co KG, Vienna
Benelux	LexisNexis Benelux, Amsterdam
Canada	LexisNexis Canada, Markham, Ontario
China	LexisNexis China, Beijing and Shanghai
France	LexisNexis SA, Paris
Germany	LexisNexis GmbH, Dusseldorf
Hong Kong	LexisNexis Hong Kong, Hong Kong
India	LexisNexis India, New Delhi
Italy	Giuffrè Editore, Milan
Japan	LexisNexis Japan, Tokyo
Malaysia	Malayan Law Journal Sdn Bhd, Kuala Lumpur
New Zealand	LexisNexis New Zealand Ltd, Wellington
Singapore	LexisNexis Singapore, Singapore
South Africa	LexisNexis, Durban
USA	LexisNexis, Dayton, Ohio

FIRST EDITION	*Published in 31 volumes between 1907 and 1917*
SECOND EDITION	*Published in 37 volumes between 1931 and 1942*
THIRD EDITION	*Published in 43 volumes between 1952 and 1964*
FOURTH EDITION	*Published in 56 volumes between 1973 and 1987, with reissues between 1988 and 2008*
FIFTH EDITION	*Published between 2008 and 2014, with reissues from 2014*

ISBN 978-1-4743-0598-3

9 781474 305983

ISBN for the set: 9781405734394
ISBN for this volume: 9781474305983

Typeset by LexisNexis
Printed and bound by CPI Group (UK) Ltd, Croydon, CR0 4YY

Visit LexisNexis at www.lexisnexis.co.uk

CONSULTANT EDITOR

JAMES DRISCOLL, LLB, LLM,
a Solicitor of the Senior Courts of England and Wales;
Emeritus Professor of Property Law, London South Bank University;
Judge, First-tier Tribunal (Property Chamber)

The law stated in this volume is in general that in force on 1 April 2017, although subsequent changes have been included wherever possible.

Any future updating material will be found in the Noter-up and annual Cumulative Supplement to Halsbury's Laws of England.

TABLE OF CONTENTS

HOW TO USE HALSBURY'S LAWS OF ENGLAND

Volumes

Each text volume of Halsbury's Laws of England contains the law on the titles contained in it as at a date stated at the front of the volume (the operative date).

Information contained in Halsbury's Laws of England may be accessed in several ways.

First, by using the tables of contents.

Each volume contains both a general Table of Contents, and a specific Table of Contents for each title contained in it. From these tables you will be directed to the relevant part of the work.

Readers should note that the current arrangement of titles can be found in the Noter-up.

Secondly, by using tables of statutes, statutory instruments, cases or other materials.

If you know the name of the Act, statutory instrument or case with which your research is concerned, you should consult the Consolidated Tables of statutes, cases and so on (published as separate volumes) which will direct you to the relevant volume and paragraph.

(Each individual text volume also includes tables of those materials used as authority in that volume.)

Thirdly, by using the indexes.

If you are uncertain of the general subject area of your research, you should go to the Consolidated Index (published as separate volumes) for reference to the relevant volume(s) and paragraph(s).

(Each individual text volume also includes an index to the material contained therein.)

Updating publications

The text volumes of Halsbury's Laws should be used in conjunction with the annual Cumulative Supplement and the monthly Noter-up.

The annual Cumulative Supplement

The Supplement gives details of all changes between the operative date of the text volume and the operative date of the Supplement. It is arranged in the same volume, title and paragraph order as the text volumes. Developments affecting particular points of law are noted to the relevant paragraph(s) of the text volumes.

For narrative treatment of material noted in the Cumulative Supplement, go to the annual Abridgment volume for the relevant year.

Destination Tables

In certain titles in the annual *Cumulative Supplement*, reference is made to Destination Tables showing the destination of consolidated legislation. Those Destination Tables are to be found either at the end of the titles within the annual *Cumulative Supplement*, or in a separate *Destination Tables* booklet provided from time to time with the *Cumulative Supplement*.

The Noter-up

The Noter-up is issued monthly and notes changes since the publication of the annual Cumulative Supplement. Also arranged in the same volume, title and paragraph order as the text volumes, the Noter-up follows the style of the Cumulative Supplement.

For narrative treatment of material noted in the Noter-up, go to the annual Abridgment volume for the relevant year.

REFERENCES AND ABBREVIATIONS

ACT	Australian Capital Territory
A-G	Attorney General
Admin	Administrative Court
Admlty	Admiralty Court
Adv-Gen	Advocate General
affd	affirmed
affg	affirming
Alta	Alberta
App	Appendix
art	article
Aust	Australia
B	Baron
BC	British Columbia
C	Command Paper (of a series published before 1900)
c	chapter number of an Act
CA	Court of Appeal
CAC	Central Arbitration Committee
CA in Ch	Court of Appeal in Chancery
CB	Chief Baron
CCA	Court of Criminal Appeal
CCR	County Court Rules 1981 (as subsequently amended)
CCR	Court for Crown Cases Reserved
CJEU	Court of Justice of the European Union
C-MAC	Courts-Martial Appeal Court
CO	Crown Office
COD	Crown Office Digest
CPR	Civil Procedure Rules
Can	Canada
Cd	Command Paper (of the series published 1900–18)
Cf	compare
Ch	Chancery Division
ch	chapter
cl	clause
Cm	Command Paper (of the series published 1986 to date)
Cmd	Command Paper (of the series published 1919–56)
Cmnd	Command Paper (of the series published 1956–86)
Comm	Commercial Court

Comr	Commissioner
Court Forms (2nd Edn)	Atkin's Encyclopaedia of Court Forms in Civil Proceedings, 2nd Edn. See note 2 post.
CrimPR	Criminal Procedure Rules
DC.............................	Divisional Court
DPP...........................	Director of Public Prosecutions
EAT............................	Employment Appeal Tribunal
EC	European Community
ECJ	Court of Justice of the European Community (before the Treaty of Lisbon (OJ C306, 17.12.2007, p 1) came into force on 1 December 2009); European Court of Justice (after the Treaty of Lisbon (OJ C306, 17.12.2007, p 1) came into force on 1 December 2009)
EComHR	European Commission of Human Rights
ECSC.........................	European Coal and Steel Community
ECtHR Rules of Court	Rules of Court of the European Court of Human Rights
EEC............................	European Economic Community
EFTA	European Free Trade Association
EGC	European General Court
EWCA Civ	Official neutral citation for judgments of the Court of Appeal (Civil Division)
EWCA Crim	Official neutral citation for judgments of the Court of Appeal (Criminal Division)
EWHC	Official neutral citation for judgments of the High Court
Edn	Edition
Euratom.....................	European Atomic Energy Community
EU	European Union
Ex Ch	Court of Exchequer Chamber
ex p..........................	ex parte
Fam...........................	Family Division
Fed...........................	Federal
Forms & Precedents (5th Edn)	Encyclopaedia of Forms and Precedents other than Court Forms, 5th Edn. See note 2 post
GLC	Greater London Council
HC............................	High Court
HC............................	House of Commons
HK............................	Hong Kong
HL............................	House of Lords
IAT	Immigration Appeal Tribunal
ILM...........................	International Legal Materials
INLR	Immigration and Nationality Law Reports

IRC	Inland Revenue Commissioners
Ind	India
Int Rels	International Relations
Ir	Ireland
J	Justice
JA	Judge of Appeal
Kan	Kansas
LA	Lord Advocate
LC	Lord Chancellor
LCC	London County Council
LCJ	Lord Chief Justice
LJ	Lord Justice of Appeal
LoN	League of Nations
MR	Master of the Rolls
Man	Manitoba
n.	note
NB	New Brunswick
NI	Northern Ireland
NS	Nova Scotia
NSW	New South Wales
NY	New York
NZ	New Zealand
OHIM	Office for Harmonisation in the Internal Market
OJ	The Official Journal of the European Union published by the Publications Office of the European Union
Ont	Ontario
P.	President
PC	Judicial Committee of the Privy Council
PEI	Prince Edward Island
Pat	Patents Court
q.	question
QB	Queen's Bench Division
QBD	Queen's Bench Division of the High Court
Qld	Queensland
Que	Quebec
r	rule
RDC	Rural District Council
RPC	Restrictive Practices Court
RSC	Rules of the Supreme Court 1965 (as subsequently amended)
reg	regulation
Res	Resolution
revsd	reversed

Rly	Railway
s	section
SA	South Africa
S Aust	South Australia
SC	Supreme Court
SI	Statutory Instruments published by authority
SR & O	Statutory Rules and Orders published by authority
SR & O Rev 1904	Revised Edition comprising all Public and General Statutory Rules and Orders in force on 31 December 1903
SR & O Rev 1948	Revised Edition comprising all Public and General Statutory Rules and Orders and Statutory Instruments in force on 31 December 1948
SRNI	Statutory Rules of Northern Ireland
STI	Simon's Tax Intelligence (1973–1995); Simon's Weekly Tax Intelligence (1996-current)
Sask	Saskatchewan
Sch	Schedule
Sess	Session
Sing	Singapore
TCC	Technology and Construction Court
TS	Treaty Series
Tanz	Tanzania
Tas	Tasmania
UDC	Urban District Council
UKHL	Official neutral citation for judgments of the House of Lords
UKPC	Official neutral citation for judgments of the Privy Council
UN	United Nations
V-C	Vice-Chancellor
Vict	Victoria
W Aust	Western Australia
Zimb	Zimbabwe

NOTE 1. A general list of the abbreviations of law reports and other sources used in this work can be found at the beginning of the Consolidated Table of Cases.

NOTE 2. Where references are made to other publications, the volume number precedes and the page number follows the name of the publication; eg the reference '12 Forms & Precedents (5th Edn) 44' refers to volume 12 of the Encyclopaedia of Forms and Precedents, page 44.

NOTE 3. An English statute is cited by short title or, where there is no short title, by regnal year and chapter number together with the name by which it is commonly known or a description of its subject matter and date. In the case of a foreign statute, the mode of citation generally follows the style of citation in use in the country concerned with the addition, where necessary, of the name of the country in parentheses.

NOTE 4. A statutory instrument is cited by short title, if any, followed by the year and number, or, if unnumbered, the date.

TABLE OF STATUTES

TABLE
OF STATUTORY INSTRUMENTS

TABLE OF PROCEDURE

Civil Procedure

Civil Procedure Rules 1998, SI 1998/3132 (CPR)

Practice Directions relating to Civil Procedure

TABLE OF CASES

PARA

D

PARA

HOUSING

1. THE LEGISLATION AND ADMINISTRATION

(1) SCOPE OF THE TITLE AND SUMMARY OF LEGISLATION

1. Scope of the title. This title is concerned with the administration by local authorities, the Social Housing Regulator in England, registered social landlords in Wales and other bodies, of the legislation concerning social housing[1]. This includes the provision and management of houses[2] and housing finance[3], the right to buy[4], and certain disposals and transfers of housing land and housing stock[5]. Housing benefit[6], landlord and tenant matters in relation to secure tenancies[7] and the former right of the private sector to acquire dwelling houses subject to secure tenancies[8] are, however, dealt with elsewhere in this work.

Local authority powers and duties in relation to housing conditions and the enforcement of housing standards[9], including the provision of grants for repair and improvement[10] and other assistance for owners of defective housing[11], the prevention of overcrowding[12], and certain energy efficiency provisions[13] fall within the scope of this title. However, building regulations[14] and planning controls[15] are discussed elsewhere in this work.

Residential care homes[16] and children's homes[17] do not fall within the scope of this title.

The duty of a local authority under the Equality Act 2010, when making decisions of a strategic nature about how to exercise its functions in relation, inter alia, to premises, to have due regard to the desirability of exercising them in a way that is designed to reduce the inequalities of outcome which result from socio-economic disadvantage, is dealt with elsewhere in this work[18].

1   For a summary of the main legislation see PARAS 2–4; and as to local administration see PARA 10 et seq. As to the control of housing associations and housing action trusts see PARA 24 et seq; as to the regulation of social housing in England see PARA 51 et seq; as to registered social landlords in Wales see PARA 166 et seq; and as to the ombudsman service see PARAS 9, 130 et seq.
2   See PARA 401 et seq.
3   See PARA 354 et seq.
4   Ie under the Housing Act 1985 Pt V (ss 118–188): see PARA 230 et seq.
5   Ie under the Housing Act 1985 Pt II (ss 8–57) (see PARA 520 et seq) or to housing action trusts (see PARA 537 et seq).
6   See WELFARE BENEFITS AND STATE PENSIONS vol 104 (2014) PARA 318 et seq.
7   Ie under the Housing Act 1985 Pt IV (ss 79–117): see LANDLORD AND TENANT vol 63 (2016) PARA 1037 et seq.
8   Ie under the Housing Act 1988 Pt IV (ss 93–114) (repealed with savings).
9   See PARA 562 et seq.
10   See PARA 835 et seq.
11   See PARA 928 et seq.
12   See PARA 649 et seq.
13   See PARA 896 et seq.
14   Ie regulations made under the Building Act 1984: see BUILDING.
15   See PLANNING.
16   As to residential care homes see SOCIAL SERVICES vol 95 (2017) PARA 3 et seq.
17   As to children's homes see CHILDREN AND YOUNG PERSONS vol 10 (2017) PARA 1002 et seq.
18   See the Equality Act 2010 s 1; and DISCRIMINATION vol 33 (2013) PARAS 289, 290. Part 4 (ss 32–38) deals with matters such as the disposal and management of premises: see DISCRIMINATION vol 33 (2013) PARAS 99–103.

2. Housing legislation generally. Modern housing legislation stems from the Housing of the Working Classes Act 1890, which was repealed in 1925 and was the first public general Act relating to housing[1] and was followed by consolidating legislation in 1925, 1936 and 1957[2]. The Housing Act 1980 introduced a new code of rights for public sector tenants, including the right to buy their homes and security of tenure[3]; altered the powers under which local authorities disposed of houses[4]; introduced new provisions regarding the rate of interest charged by local authorities on mortgages[5]; strengthened and extended to the Housing Corporation the power to indemnify building societies against losses on their housing advances and made amendments to the option mortgage scheme[6]; introduced a new scheme of subsidies for housing authorities[7]; provided for further assistance towards the improvement and repair of existing homes, including grants for tenants and grants for repairs[8]; and amended the law relating to housing associations and the Housing Corporation[9].

The legislation relating to housing was consolidated in 1985, with four statutes which came into operation on 1 April 1986. The principal Act was the Housing Act 1985, while the former provisions relating to housing associations and the Housing Corporation were incorporated into a separate statute, the Housing Associations Act 1985. The Landlord and Tenant Act 1985 is primarily concerned with landlord and tenant matters and falls outside the scope of this title[10]. Finally, the Housing (Consequential Provisions) Act 1985 made provision for repeals, consequential amendments, transitional matters and savings in connection with the other three consolidation Acts.

Following the 1985 consolidation, the Housing Act 1985 and the Housing Associations Act 1985 have been extensively amended and supplemented by later legislation including provisions of the Housing and Planning Act 1986, the Housing Act 1988, the Local Government and Housing Act 1989, the Leasehold Reform, Housing and Urban Development Act 1993, the Housing Act 1996 and the Housing Grants, Construction and Regeneration Act 1996. Part VI of the Local Government and Housing Act 1989[11] established a new financial regime for local authority housing with effect from 1 April 1990. Part I of the Housing Act 1996[12] introduced new terminology whereby a registered housing association became a 'registered social landlord'; Part V[13] enabled a local housing authority or housing action trust to operate an introductory tenancy regime[14]; Part VI[15] changed the rules on allocation of tenancies[16]; and Part VII[17] replaced provisions relating to homelessness[18]. Part I of the Housing Grants, Construction and Regeneration Act 1996[19] brought in new provisions relating to grants by local housing authorities towards the cost of the improvement or repair of dwellings[20]. Provisions relating to houses in multiple occupation[21] were amended by Part II of the Housing Act 1996[22].

Local authorities were given powers under Part V of the Housing Act 1996[23] to deal with anti-social behaviour by tenants[24], which should be considered in conjunction with, inter alia, the powers of environmental health officers to serve on occupiers of dwellings noise abatement notices under the Noise Act 1996[25]. These powers were augmented by amendments made by the Anti-social Behaviour Act 2003, which have now been replaced by provisions of the Anti-social Behaviour, Crime and Policing Act 2014[26].

More recently, extensive changes were made to housing law by the Housing Act 2004, which both enacts new provisions and amends existing legislation[27], and by the Housing and Regeneration Act 2008, which inter alia abolished the Housing Corporation and created a new scheme for the regulation of social housing for England[28]. The Housing and Regeneration Act 2008 created the Homes and Communities Agency ('HCA') to take over the investment powers of the Housing Corporation[29], and the Office for Tenants and Social Landlords (now abolished), whose operating name was the Tenant Services Authority ('TSA')[30].

With the change of government in 2010, housing policy underwent a further extensive review and legislation was enacted to reform the housing revenue account system, to provide for a new form of flexible tenure for social housing tenants, to allow local authorities to discharge their duties to homeless people by using private rented accommodation, to give local authorities the power to limit who can apply for social housing within their areas, to abolish the Tenant Services Authority and provide for a transfer of functions to the Homes and Communities Agency, to amend the way in which a social tenant can make a complaint about his landlord and to improve the ability of social tenants to move to different areas[31].

The Welfare Reform and Work Act 2016 makes provision for the reduction of social housing rents[32].

Housing is now largely dealt with separately by legislation in England and in Wales, and the position of tenants is now different in England from their position in Wales. Separate provision in relation to housing in Wales has been made by the Housing (Wales) Measure 2011[33], the Housing (Wales) Act 2014[34] and the Renting Homes (Wales) Act 2016[35].

The most recent statement from the government sets out a broad range of reforms that it plans to introduce to help reform the housing market and increase the supply of new homes[36].

1 Note that in *Westminster City Council v Duke of Westminster* (1992) 24 HLR 572, CA, it was held that a covenant which required premises to be used as 'dwellings for the working classes' did not impose a valid, enforceable and continuing obligation on the landlord to use the premises as dwellings for working class people only and for no other purpose. See also *Dano Ltd v Earl Cadogan* [2003] EWCA Civ 782, [2003] HLR 1011, [2004] 1 P & CR 169 (covenant unenforceable). The term 'working classes' continued to be used as late as the Housing Act 1957: see ss 5, 127, 128 (all repealed).
2 See the Housing Act 1925; the Housing Act 1936; and Housing Act 1957 (all repealed).
3 See the Housing Act 1980 Pt I (ss 1–50) (repealed). As to the right to buy see now the Housing Act 1985 Pt V (ss 118–188); and PARA 230 et seq. As to security of tenure see Pt IV (ss 79–117); and LANDLORD AND TENANT vol 63 (2016) PARA 1037 et seq.
4 Ie under the Housing Act 1957 Pt V (repealed).
5 See the Housing Act 1980 s 110 (repealed).
6 See the Housing Act 1980 ss 111–116 (repealed).
7 See the Housing Act 1980 Pt VI (ss 96–105) (repealed).
8 See the Housing Act 1980 ss 106–109 (repealed).
9 See the Housing Act 1980 Pt VIII (ss 120–133) (repealed). The Housing Corporation has been abolished: see the Housing and Regeneration Act 2008 s 64(1), (2); and the Housing Corporation (Dissolution) Order 2009, SI 2009/484. As to housing associations see PARA 13.
10 As to landlord and tenant matters generally see LANDLORD AND TENANT.
11 Ie the Local Government and Housing Act 1989 Pt VI (ss 74–88): see PARA 356 et seq.
12 Ie the Housing Act 1996 Pt I (ss A1–64): see PARA 166 et seq.
13 Ie the Housing Act 1996 Pt V (ss 124–158): see PARA 471.
14 As to the meaning of 'introductory tenancy' see PARA 472.
15 Ie the Housing Act 1996 Pt VI (ss 159–174): see PARA 420 et seq.
16 For cases where the new provisions about allocation do not apply see the Housing Act 1996 s 160; and PARA 423.
17 Ie the Housing Act 1996 Pt VII (ss 175–218): see PARA 477 et seq.
18 A major change is that a person may not now fall within the provisions relating to homelessness if he has accommodation available in jurisdictions outside the United Kingdom: see the Housing Act 1996 s 175(1); and PARA 481.
19 Ie the Housing Grants, Construction and Regeneration Act 1996 Pt I (ss 1–103): see PARA 835 et seq.
20 See the Housing Grants, Construction and Regeneration Act 1996 Pt I Ch I (ss 1–59); and PARA 835 et seq.
21 Ie the Housing Act 1985 Pt XI (ss 345–400) (repealed).
22 Ie by the Housing Act 1996 Pt II (ss 65–80) (repealed). See now PARA 666 et seq.
23 See the Housing Act 1996 Pt V Ch III (ss 152–158); and PARA 472.

24 As to the purpose of these provisions see 574 HL Official Report (5 series) cols 429–430. As to the provisions for introductory tenancies see the text and notes 13–14.

25 See the Noise Act 1996 ss 1–8; and NUISANCE; ENVIRONMENTAL QUALITY AND PUBLIC HEALTH vol 46 (2010) PARA 848 et seq.

26 See the Housing Act 1996 ss 153A–153E (repealed); and PARA 473.

27 See further PARA 3.

28 See further PARA 4.

29 As to the HCA see PARA 57 et seq; and PLANNING vol 83 (2010) PARA 1454 et seq.

30 The Localism Act 2011 provided for the abolition of the Office for Tenants and Social Landlords ('the Office'), the creation of the Regulation Committee of the HCA, and the transfer of the functions of the Office to the HCA acting through the Committee. See PARAS 53, 57 et seq. As to the transfer of functions from the Office for Tenants and Social Landlords to the Homes and Communities Agency see the Localism Act 2011 s 178, Sch 16. The Localism Act 2011 Sch 24 makes tax provision in relation to the transfer of property, rights and liabilities from the Office for Tenants and Social Landlords and enables the Treasury to make tax regulations in relation to transfers to permitted authorities under s 17.

31 The Localism Act 2011, which introduces these changes among others, received the royal assent on 15 November 2011 and comes into force in accordance with s 240. The provisions of Pt 7 (ss 145–185):

   (1) amend the Housing Act 1996 Pt VI (ss 159–174) (see PARA 420 et seq) and Pt VII (ss 175–218) (see PARA 477 et seq) in respect of allocation of housing and homelessness;

   (2) require a local housing authority in England to prepare and publish a tenancy strategy (see the Localism Act 2011 ss 150–151; and PARA 421), and amend the Housing and Regeneration Act 2008 s 197 (see PARA 105) and the Homelessness Act 2002 s 3 (see PARA 479);

   (3) amend the Housing and Regeneration Act 2008 s 180 (see PARA 102);

   (4) abolish housing revenue account subsidy in England (see PARA 374), and make provision for settlement payments and to limit the indebtedness of each local housing authority in England that keeps a housing revenue account;

   (5) promote housing mobility by providing for standards facilitating exchange of tenancies and assisting tenants of social landlords to become home owners, amending the Housing and Regeneration Act 2008 s 122 (see PARA 73), s 193 (see PARA 105) and s 197 (see PARA 105);

   (6) provide for the transfer of functions from the Office for Tenants and Social Landlords ('the Office') to the Homes and Communities Agency ('the HCA'), amending the Housing and Regeneration Act 2008 to abolish the Office, create the Regulation Committee of the HCA, and transfer the functions of the Office to the HCA acting through the Committee, and making consequential amendments;

   (7) require complaints to the housing ombudsman to be referred by designated person, and transfer functions to the housing ombudsman, allowing complaints to be made against a local authority in England which is a registered provider of social housing and for collaborative working by a housing ombudsman with a local commissioner for administration, amending the Housing Act 1996 s 51(2), Sch 2 (see PARA 131 et seq) and the Housing and Regeneration Act 2008 s 239(2) (see PARA 114).

32 See the Welfare Reform and Work Act 2016 ss 23–33, Sch 2; and PARA 55.

33 See PARAS 6, 185 et seq.

34 See PARAS 6, 193 et seq, 466 et seq.

35 See PARA 6.

36 See the White Paper *Fixing our broken housing market* (Cm 9352) (Department for Communities and Local Government, 7 February 2017).

3. The Housing Act 2004. The Housing Act 2004[1] made extensive changes to housing law. It establishes a new system for assessing housing conditions and enforcing housing standards in place of the former provisions as to fitness of housing for habitation[2]. It provides for the licensing of houses in multiple occupation[3] and for selective licensing of other private residential accommodation[4], and introduces a scheme to allow the making of interim and final management orders in relation to any house which should be licensed[5], to protect the health, safety or welfare of persons occupying the house or persons occupying or having an estate or interest in any premises in the vicinity and to ensure the proper management of the house[6]. It also makes provision as to overcrowding in relation to houses in multiple occupation[7]. In respect of empty dwellings, the Housing Act 2004 introduces a scheme of interim and final empty dwelling management orders for the purpose of securing that an empty dwelling becomes and continues to be occupied[8]. Provision was also made for residential property tribunals to be established to deal with matters relating, inter alia, to housing[9].

1 As to the commencement of the Housing Act 2004, and for transitional provisions, see s 270; the Housing Act 2004 (Commencement No 1) (England) Order 2005, SI 2005/326; the Housing Act 2004 (Commencement No 2) (England) Order 2005, SI 2005/1120; the Housing Act 2004 (Commencement No 3) (England) Order 2005, SI 2005/1451; the Housing Act 2004 (Commencement No 4 and Transitional Provisions) (England) Order 2005, SI 2005/1729; the Housing Act 2004 (Commencement No 5 and Transitional Provisions and Savings) (England) Order 2006, SI 2006/1060; the Housing Act 2004 (Commencement No 6) (England) Order 2006, SI 2006/3191; the Housing Act 2004 (Commencement No 7) (England) Order 2007, SI 2007/1068; the Housing Act 2004 (Commencement No 8) (England and Wales) Order 2007, SI 2007/1668; the Housing Act 2004 (Commencement No 9) (England and Wales) Order 2007, SI 2007/2471; the Housing Act 2004 (Commencement No 10) (England and Wales) Order 2007, SI 2007/3308; the Housing Act 2004 (Commencement No 11) (England and Wales) Order 2008, SI 2008/898; the Housing Act 2004 (Commencement No 1) (Wales) Order 2005, SI 2005/1814; the Housing Act 2004 (Commencement No 2) (Wales) Order 2005, SI 2005/3237; the Housing Act 2004 (Commencement No 3 and Transitional Provisions and Savings) (Wales) Order 2006, SI 2006/1535; the Housing Act 2004 (Commencement No 4) (Wales) Order 2007, SI 2007/305; and the Housing Act 2004 (Commencement No 5) (Wales) Order 2007, SI 2007/3232. The majority of the provisions of the Housing Act 2004 that are relevant to this title, if not already in force, came into force on 6 April 2006 in relation to England (see the Housing Act 2004 (Commencement No 5 and Transitional Provisions and Savings) (England) Order 2006, SI 2006/1060) and, in relation to Wales, on 16 June 2006 (see the Housing Act 2004 (Commencement No 3 and Transitional Provisions and Savings) (Wales) Order 2006, SI 2006/1535). See also Driscoll *Housing: the New Law, A Guide to the Housing Act 2004* (2007).
2 See the Housing Act 2004 Pt 1 (ss 1–54); and PARA 563 et seq.
3 See the Housing Act 2004 Pt 2 (ss 55–78); and PARA 674 et seq.
4 See the Housing Act 2004 Pt 3 (ss 79–100); and PARA 704 et seq.
5 Ie under the Housing Act 2004 Pt 2 or Pt 3.
6 See the Housing Act 2004 Pt 4 Ch 1 (ss 101–131); and PARA 745 et seq.
7 See the Housing Act 2004 Pt 4 Ch 3 (ss 139–144); and PARA 698 et seq.
8 See the Housing Act 2004 Pt 4 Ch 2 (ss 132–138); and PARA 781 et seq.
9 See the Housing Act 2004 ss 229–231, Sch 13; and PARA 34 et seq. These provisions now apply only in relation to Wales.

4. The Housing and Regeneration Act 2008. The Housing and Regeneration Act 2008, which received the Royal Assent on 22 July 2008 but is not entirely in force[1], establishes the Homes and Communities Agency[2] and provides for the abolition of the Housing Corporation[3]. Part 2 of the Act[4] is concerned with the regulation of social housing[5] and creates a Regulator of Social Housing[6] and a system of registered social housing[7] for England while restricting the registered social landlord system to Wales[8]. Part 3[9] makes provision relating to housing finance and homelessness[10] and deals with a number of matters, including sustainability certificates for new residential property[11] and various landlord and tenant matters[12], which are outside the scope of this title.

1 As to the commencement of the Housing and Regeneration Act 2008 see s 325; and the Housing and Regeneration Act 2008 (Commencement No 1 and Transitional Provision) Order 2008, SI 2008/2358; the Housing and Regeneration Act 2008 (Commencement No 2 and Transitional, Saving and Transitory Provisions) Order 2008, SI 2008/3068; the Housing and Regeneration Act 2008 (Commencement No 3) Order 2009, SI 2009/363; the Housing and Regeneration Act 2008 (Commencement No 1 and Saving Provisions) Order 2009, SI 2009/415; the Housing and Regeneration Act 2008 (Commencement No 1) (Wales) Order 2009, SI 2009/773; the Housing and Regeneration Act 2008 (Commencement No 4 and Transitory Provisions) Order 2009, SI 2009/803; the Housing and Regeneration Act 2008 (Commencement No 5) Order 2009, SI 2009/1261; the Housing and Regeneration Act 2008 (Commencement No 6 and Transitional and Savings Provisions) Order 2009, SI 2009/2096; the Housing and Regeneration Act 2008 (Commencement No 7 and Transitional and Saving Provisions) Order 2010, SI 2010/862; the

Housing and Regeneration Act 2008 (Commencement No 8 and Transitional, Transitory and Saving Provisions) Order 2011, SI 2011/1002; the Housing and Regeneration Act 2008 (Commencement No 2) (Wales) Order 2011, SI 2011/1863; and the Housing and Regeneration Act 2008 (Commencement No 3 and Transitional, Transitory and Saving Provisions) (Wales) Order 2013, SI 2013/1469. Most of the provisions of the Housing and Regeneration Act 2008 relevant to this title came into force on 8 September 2008 or 1 April 2010: see the Housing and Regeneration Act 2008 (Commencement No 1 and Transitional Provision) Order 2008, SI 2008/2358, arts 1(2), 3; and the Housing and Regeneration Act 2008 (Commencement No 7 and Transitional and Saving Provisions) Order 2010, SI 2010/862.

2 See the Housing and Regeneration Act 2008 Pt 1 (ss 1–58), Schs 1–4, 6–8; PARAS 125–128; and PLANNING vol 83 (2010) PARA 1454 et seq.

3 See the Housing and Regeneration Act 2008 ss 64–67, Schs 6–7; the Housing Corporation (Dissolution) Order 2009, SI 2009/484; and PARA 51. The Urban Regeneration Agency and the Commission for New Towns are also abolished: see the Housing and Regeneration Act 2008 ss 49–53, Sch 5; and PLANNING vol 83 (2010) PARA 1452.

4 Ie the Housing and Regeneration Act 2008 ss 59–278A.

5 See the Housing and Regeneration Act 2008 Pt 2 Ch 1 (ss 59–80); and PARAS 51–53.

6 See the Housing and Regeneration Act 2008 Pt 2 Ch 2 (ss 81–109); and PARAS 57–60.

7 See the Housing and Regeneration Act 2008 Pt 2 Ch 3–Ch 8 (ss 110–278A), Sch 9; and PARAS 70–124.

8 See the Housing and Regeneration Act 2008 ss 61–63; and PARAS 52 note 3, 166 et seq.

9 Ie the Housing and Regeneration Act 2008 ss 279–319.

10 See the Housing and Regeneration Act 2008 Pt 3 Ch 3 (ss 313–319), Sch 15; which amend existing statutory provisions.

11 See the Housing and Regeneration Act 2008 Pt 3 Ch 1 (ss 279–293), Sch 10; and BUILDING.

12 See the Housing and Regeneration Act 2008 Pt 3 Ch 2 (ss 294–312), Schs 11–14; and LANDLORD AND TENANT.

5. The Housing and Planning Act 2016. The Housing and Planning Act 2016 (which was passed on 12 May 2016 but is not fully in force)[1] makes various changes to housing law in England and also deals with other matters including planning and compulsory purchase. Chapter 1 of Part 1[2] makes provision intended to promote the supply of starter homes in England[3]. Part 2[4] deals with rogue landlords and property agents in England, providing for banning orders[5] and a database of rogue landlords and property agents[6] as well as making new provision as to rent repayment orders[7]. Part 4[8] deals with social housing in England. Chapter 1 of Part 4[9] provides for the implementation of the right to buy on a voluntary basis by empowering the Secretary of State and the Greater London Authority to make grants to private registered providers in respect of right to buy discounts[10]. Chapter 2[11] enables the Secretary of State to require local housing authorities which are required to keep a housing revenue account to make a payment to the Secretary of State calculated by reference to the market value of the higher value vacant housing owned by the authority[12]. Chapter 3[13] provides for rents for high income social tenants, implementing a 'pay to stay' policy[14].

Chapter 4[15] is concerned with reducing the regulation of private registered providers of social housing, principally by amendment of existing legislation[16] and by reducing local authority influence over private registered providers[17]. Provision as to the insolvency of registered providers of social housing is made by Chapter 5[18], which introduces housing administration orders and imposes restrictions on other insolvency procedures[19]. Prospective amendments are made[20] to the Housing Act 2004 to allow financial penalties to be imposed as an alternative to prosecution for certain offences[21].

1 The following come into force on the day on which the Housing and Planning Act 2016 was passed: Pt 4 Ch 2 (ss 69–79); ss 136, 137 and Sch 10; ss 139, 140, 149, 151, 152(1) and 157; ss 161–168; and Pt 9 (ss 212–217): s 216(1). The following come into force at the end of the period of two months beginning with the day on which the Act was passed: s 124; s 130; and ss 150(1)–(3), 153: s 216(2). The other provisions of the Act come into force on such day as the

The functions of the Secretary of State, so far as exercisable in relation to Wales, have generally been transferred, first, to the National Assembly for Wales and subsequently to the Welsh Ministers[2].

Statutory functions relating to housing are therefore exercisable by the Secretary of State (in relation to England) and the Welsh Ministers (in relation to Wales). The functions exercisable by the Welsh Ministers are:

(1)   functions originally transferred to the National Assembly for Wales[3] by Order in Council and subsequently transferred to the Welsh Ministers[4];

(2)   functions originally conferred on the National Assembly for Wales by enactments made after the establishment of that body and subsequently transferred[5] to the Welsh Ministers[6];

(3)   functions transferred to the Welsh Ministers by Order in Council[7]; and

(4)   functions conferred on the Welsh Ministers by enactments made after the establishment of the Welsh Assembly Government[8].

Furthermore, with the creation of separate statutory regimes for the regulation of social housing in England and Wales[9], specific amendments have been made to legislation formerly applying to both England and Wales to refer specifically to the Welsh Ministers in the case of legislation applying only to Wales[10].

Legislation enacted following the establishment of the Welsh Assembly Government which confers functions on the Secretary of State and the Welsh Ministers often refers to those bodies collectively as 'the appropriate national authority'[11], and that expression is used throughout this title to cover any situation where the function in question is exercised in relation to England by the Secretary of State and in relation to Wales by the Welsh Ministers, and also where functions may be carried out jointly.

The appropriate national authority may by regulations prescribe: (a) anything which by the Housing Act 1985 is to be prescribed; or (b) the form of any notice, advertisement, statement or other document which is required or authorised to be used under or for the purposes of that Act[12], but this power is not exercisable where specific provision for prescribing a thing, or the form of a document, is made elsewhere[13].

The appropriate national authority may dispense with the publication of advertisements or the service of notices required to be published or served by a local authority under the Housing Act 1985 if it is satisfied that there is reasonable cause for dispensing with the publication or service[14].

For the purposes of the execution of the powers and duties of the appropriate national authority under the Housing Act 1985, the appropriate national authority may cause such local inquiries to be held as it may think fit[15].

The appropriate national authority may, for the purposes of the execution of any of the authority's functions under the Housing Act 2004, cause such local inquiries to be held as the authority considers appropriate[16].

1   Ie one of Her Majesty's Principal Secretaries of State: see the Interpretation Act 1978 s 5, Sch 1. The office of Secretary of State is a unified office, and generally in law each Secretary of State is capable of performing the functions of all or any of them: see CONSTITUTIONAL AND ADMINISTRATIVE LAW vol 20 (2014) PARA 153. In practice, at the date at which this volume states the law, housing matters in relation to England are the responsibility of the Secretary of State for Communities and Local Government, under whom serves the Minister for Housing and Local Government.

2   As to the National Assembly for Wales and the Welsh Ministers see CONSTITUTIONAL AND ADMINISTRATIVE LAW vol 20 (2014) PARA 375.

3   Ie by Order in Council under the Government of Wales Act 1998 s 22 (now repealed): see CONSTITUTIONAL AND ADMINISTRATIVE LAW vol 20 (2014) PARA 351.

Functions under the following provisions have been so transferred: the Housing Act 1980, the Housing Act 1985, the Housing Associations Act 1985, the Housing Act 1988, the Local Government Act 1988, the Local Government and Housing Act 1989, the Leasehold Reform, Housing and Urban Development Act 1993, the Home Energy Conservation Act 1995 (now repealed in relation to energy conservation authorities in Wales), the Housing Act 1996 and the Housing Grants, Construction and Regeneration Act 1996: see the National Assembly for Wales (Transfer of Functions) Order 1999, SI 1999/672, art 2, Sch 1. Functions of the Treasury were also transferred, so that in general provisions requiring the consent of the Treasury no longer apply in relation to Wales. Functions under the Social Security Act 1990 were not so transferred, but the functions under s 15 (see PARA 897) were made exercisable by the Assembly concurrently with the Secretary of State and exercisable by the Assembly free from the requirement for Treasury consent: see the National Assembly for Wales (Transfer of Functions) Order 1999, SI 1999/672, Sch 1.

For provisions as to the exercise of transferred functions see the Government of Wales Act 2006 Sch 3, Sch 11 paras 33–35; and STATUTES AND LEGISLATIVE PROCESS vol 96 (2012) PARA 1035.

4　Ie by the operation of the Government of Wales Act 2006 Sch 11 paras 26, 30 (see STATUTES AND LEGISLATIVE PROCESS vol 96 (2012) PARA 1035), which provide that instruments transferring functions to the National Assembly for Wales under the Government of Wales Act 1998 s 22 (repealed) (see note 3) continue to have effect following the transfer of the Assembly's executive functions to the Welsh Ministers as conferring those functions on those Ministers.

5　Ie by the operation of the Government of Wales Act 2006 Sch 11 para 30 (see STATUTES AND LEGISLATIVE PROCESS vol 96 (2012) PARA 1035).

6　Functions were conferred on the National Assembly for Wales by the Warm Homes and Energy Conservation Act 2000, the Sustainable Energy Act 2003 and the Housing Act 2004, and these functions have been transferred to the Welsh Ministers by operation of the Government of Wales Act 2006 Sch 11 para 30 (see STATUTES AND LEGISLATIVE PROCESS vol 96 (2012) PARA 1035).

7　Ie by Order in Council under the Government of Wales Act 2006 s 58 (see CONSTITUTIONAL AND ADMINISTRATIVE LAW vol 20 (2014) PARA 380). At the date at which this volume states the law no functions relating to housing had been transferred to the Welsh Ministers by Order in Council under s 58.

8　Functions have been specifically conferred on the Welsh Ministers by the Housing and Regeneration Act 2008.

9　See PARA 166 et seq.

10　Ie by the Housing and Regeneration Act 2008 ss 61–63.

11　See eg the Housing Act 2004 s 261(1); and PARA 389 note 1.

12　Housing Act 1985 s 614(1). The regulations must be made by statutory instrument which is subject to annulment in pursuance of a resolution of either House of Parliament or, as appropriate, the National Assembly for Wales: s 614(2).

13　Housing Act 1985 s 614(3).

14　Housing Act 1985 s 615(1). A dispensation may be given by the appropriate national authority: (1) either before or after the time at which the advertisement is required to be published or the notice is required to be served; and (2) either unconditionally or upon such conditions, as to the publication of other advertisements or the service of other notices or otherwise, as the appropriate national authority thinks fit, due care being taken by it to prevent the interests of any persons being prejudiced by the dispensation: s 615(2).

15　Housing Act 1985 s 616.

16　Housing Act 2004 s 253.

8. The 'relevant authority'. For the purposes of the Housing Act 1985, 'the relevant authority' means the Regulator of Social Housing (now the Homes and Communities Agency ('HCA'))[1], the Welsh Ministers[2] or Scottish Homes[3].

In relation to a housing association which is a registered charity[4] whose address is in Wales for the purposes of registration by the Charity Commission, or which is a registered society within the meaning of the Co-operative and Community Benefit Societies Act 2014 which has its registered office for the purposes of that Act in Wales, or which is a company registered under the Companies Act 2006 which has its registered office for the purposes of that Act in Wales, 'the relevant authority' is the Welsh Ministers[5]. In relation to a housing association which is a registered society within the meaning of the Co-operative and Community Benefit Societies Act 2014 which has its registered office for the purposes of that Act in

Scotland, 'the relevant authority' is Scottish Homes[6]. In relation to any other housing association which is a registered charity, a registered society within the meaning of the Co-operative and Community Benefit Societies Act 2014 or a company registered under the Companies Act 2006, 'the relevant authority' is the Regulator of Social Housing[7].

In Part VII of the Housing Act 1996[8] 'the relevant authority' means a local housing authority or a social services authority[9].

1 As to the Regulator of Social Housing see PARA 57 et seq. As to the HCA see PARA 57 et seq; and PLANNING vol 83 (2010) PARA 1454 et seq.
2 As to references to the Welsh Ministers see PARA 7 note 4.
3 Housing Act 1985 s 6A(1) (s 6A added by the Housing Act 1988 s 140(1), Sch 17 Pt II and substituted by SI 1996/2325; and the Housing Act 1985 s 6A(1) amended by the Government of Wales Act 1998 s 140, Sch 16 paras 5, 7; and by SI 2010/866). The Housing Act 1985 s 6A is subject to any provision made elsewhere in that Act: s 6A(4A) (added by SI 2008/3002).
4 For the purposes of the Housing Act 1985 s 6A, 'registered charity' means a charity which is registered in accordance with the Charities Act 2011 s 30 (see CHARITIES vol 8 (2015) PARA 307 et seq): Housing Act 1985 s 6A(5) (as added and substituted (see note 3); and amended by the Charities Act 2006 s 75(1), (2), Sch 8 para 77(1), (3), Sch 9; and the Charities Act 2011 s 354(1), Sch 7 para 43).
5 Housing Act 1985 s 6A(2) (as added and substituted (see note 3); and amended by the Government of Wales Act 1998 Sch 16 paras 5, 7; the Charities Act 2006 Sch 8 para 77(2); the Co-operative and Community Benefit Societies Act 2014 s 151(1), Sch 4 paras 32, 34; and SI 2009/1941). Previously, functions were exercised in relation to Wales by Housing for Wales, which was abolished as from 31 March 1999 (see the Housing for Wales (Abolition) Order 1999, SI 1999/781); its functions were transferred to the Secretary of State (see the Government of Wales Act 1998 ss 140–143, 152, Sch 16, Sch 18 Pt VI), and are now exercised by the Welsh Ministers (see the National Assembly for Wales (Transfer of Functions) Order 1999, SI 1999/672, art 2, Sch 1; the Government of Wales Act 2006 s 162, Sch 11 para 30; and PARAS 7, 142).
6 Housing Act 1985 s 6A(3) (as added and substituted (see note 3); and amended by the Government of Wales Act 1998 Sch 16 para 5; and the Co-operative and Community Benefit Societies Act 2014 Sch 4 paras 32, 34).
7 Housing Act 1985 s 6A(4) (as added and substituted (see note 3); and amended by the Government of Wales Act 1998 Sch 16 para 5; the Co-operative and Community Benefit Societies Act 2014 Sch 4 paras 32, 34; and by SI 2009/1941 and SI 2010/866).
8 Ie the Housing Act 1996 Pt VII (ss 175–218): see PARA 477 et seq.
9 Housing Act 1996 s 217(1).

9. Ombudsmen. The Housing Ombudsman Service has been established to deal with complaints made by tenants of social landlords in England[1].

In addition to making a complaint to the local authority's housing department or to a local councillor[2], local authority tenants who were dissatisfied with the service they were receiving could formerly make use of the commissioners for local administration (usually referred to as the 'local government ombudsmen') who had jurisdiction to investigate complaints of maladministration by an authority[3]. The local government ombudsmen could not, however, investigate complaints by tenants of registered social landlords, and now the Housing Ombudsman Service has been extended to cover complaints against a local authority in England which is a registered provider of social housing, in relation to its housing activities so far as they relate to the provision or management of social housing[4].

In relation to Wales, the various ombudsman services were combined as from 1 April 2006 and their functions, including those of the former Social Housing Ombudsman for Wales, are now carried out by the Public Services Ombudsman for Wales[5].

1 See PARA 130 et seq. Complaints may also be made by tenants of certain private landlords and management agents who are registered with the Housing Ombudsman Service.
2 As to local councillors see generally LOCAL GOVERNMENT vol 69 (2009) PARA 126 et seq.

3 See the Local Government Act 1974 Pt III (ss 23–34); and CONSTITUTIONAL AND
   ADMINISTRATIVE LAW vol 20 (2014) PARA 638; LOCAL GOVERNMENT vol 69 (2009)
   PARA 839 et seq. A significant proportion of complaints dealt with by the local government
   ombudsmen related to housing matters.
4 See the Local Government Act 1974 Sch 5 paras 5A, 5B (added by the Localism Act 2011
   s 181(1)(a)). As to the register of social landlords see PARA 167.
5 See the Public Services Ombudsman (Wales) Act 2005; and LOCAL GOVERNMENT vol 69 (2009)
   PARA 267.

(ii) Local Authorities and other Housing Providers

10. Introduction. Local authorities have a number of statutory powers and
duties as regards housing, which are exercisable by local housing authorities[1]. A
local housing authority may enter into a management agreement under which
another person exercises certain of the authority's management functions[2], or
there may be a large scale voluntary transfer of some or all of the
authority's housing stock[3]. Housing action trusts[4] may be formed to take over
local authority housing functions within a defined area under provisions
contained in Part III of the Housing Act 1988[5], but these provisions have not been
widely used in practice[6].

Housing functions are also carried out by housing associations and similar
bodies[7]. Where such bodies are registered with the relevant authority[8] they are
known in Wales as registered social landlords[9].

Housing may, of course, also be provided by private developers who may
receive a grant[10].

1 As to local housing authorities see PARA 11.
2 See PARA 457 et seq. A company set up by a local authority to manage some or all of its housing
   stock is often referred to as an arm's length management organisation (or 'ALMO').
3 As to large scale voluntary transfers see PARA 520 et seq.
4 As to the meaning of 'housing action trust' see PARA 12 head (6).
5 See the Housing Act 1988 Pt III (ss 60–92); and PARA 537 et seq.
6 See Kahn *Remodelling a HAT* in Malpass and Means *Implementing Housing Policy* (1993).
7 As to housing associations see PARA 13.
8 Ie under the Housing Act 1996 Pt I (ss A1–64). As to the relevant authority see PARA 8.
9 See PARA 166 et seq.
10 See eg PARA 151.

11. Local housing authorities. Most of the provisions governing local housing
authorities are contained in the Housing Act 1985[1]. For the purposes of that Act,
'local housing authority' means:
  (1)   a district council[2];
  (2)   a London borough council[3];
  (3)   the Common Council of the City of London[4];
  (4)   a Welsh county council or county borough council[5]; or
  (5)   the Council of the Isles of Scilly[6].
References in the Housing Act 1985 to the district of a local authority are
references to the area of the council concerned, that is, to the district, the London
borough, the City of London, the Welsh county or county borough, or the Isles of
Scilly, as the case may be[7]. References in relation to land to a local housing
authority are references to the local housing authority in whose district the land
is situated[8].

A local housing authority is an 'exempt landlord' for the purposes of the
Landlord and Tenant Act 1987[9], and this affects the rights of its tenants (such as

the right to apply to the First-tier Tribunal (Property Chamber) for a manager to be appointed)[10].

1 Ie the Housing Act 1985 Pt I (ss 1–7). Local authorities and certain other authorities must keep a register of individuals and associations of individuals seeking land for self-build and custom housebuilding projects, and have regard to such registers when carrying out their functions relating to housing and regeneration: see the Self-build and Custom Housebuilding Act 2015; and LOCAL GOVERNMENT.

2 As to local government areas and authorities in England see LOCAL GOVERNMENT vol 69 (2009) PARA 24 et seq.

3 As to the London boroughs and their councils see LONDON GOVERNMENT vol 71 (2013) PARAS 15, 20–22, 55 et seq.

4 As to the Common Council of the City of London see LONDON GOVERNMENT vol 71 (2013) PARA 23 et seq.
    The Common Council of the City of London may appoint a committee, consisting of so many persons as the Council thinks fit, for any purposes of the Housing Act 1985, the Housing Associations Act 1985 or the Housing Act 1996 which in its opinion may be better regulated and managed by means of a committee: Housing Act 1985 s 618(1); Housing Act 1996 s 224(1). A committee so appointed consists as to a majority of its members of members of the Council; it is not authorised to borrow money or to make a rate, and is subject to any regulations and restrictions which may be imposed by the Council: Housing Act 1985 s 618(2); Housing Act 1996 s 224(2). A person is not, by reason only of the fact that he occupies a house at a rental from the Council, disqualified from being elected or being a member of that Council or any committee of that Council; but no person may vote as a member of that Council, or any such committee, on a resolution or question which is proposed or arises in pursuance of the Housing Act 1985, the Housing Associations Act 1985 or the Housing Act 1996 and relates to land in which he is beneficially interested: Housing Act 1985 s 618(3); Housing Act 1996 s 224(3). A person who votes in contravention of these provisions commits a summary offence and is liable on conviction to a fine not exceeding level 4 on the standard scale; but the fact of his giving the vote does not invalidate any resolution or proceeding of the authority: Housing Act 1985 s 618(4) (amended by the Housing and Planning Act 1986 s 24(1), Sch 5 para 6); Housing Act 1996 s 224(4). As to the powers of magistrates' courts to issue fines on summary conviction see SENTENCING vol 92 (2015) PARA 176.

5 As to local government areas and authorities in Wales see LOCAL GOVERNMENT vol 69 (2009) PARA 37 et seq.

6 Housing Act 1985 s 1 (amended by the Local Government (Wales) Act 1994 s 22(2), Sch 8 para 5(1)). As to the Council of the Isles of Scilly see LOCAL GOVERNMENT vol 69 (2009) PARA 36.
    This definition of 'local housing authority' is applied by eg the Housing Act 1988 s 129(7)(a), the Local Government Act 1988 s 24(6), the Local Government and Housing Act 1989 ss 88(1)(a), 169(9), the Housing Act 1996 s 230, the Homelessness Act 2002 s 4, the Local Government Act 2003 s 87(4), the Housing and Regeneration Act 2008 s 275, the Localism Act 2011 s 175 and the Housing and Planning Act 2016 ss 56, 79, 91, 123. For the definition of 'local housing authority' for the purposes of the Housing Act 2004 see PARA 380 note 1.

7 Housing Act 1985 s 2(1) (amended by the Local Government (Wales) Act 1994 s 22(2), Sch 8 para 5(2)). Where a building is situated partly in the district of one local housing authority and partly in the district of another, the authorities may agree that: (1) the building; or (2) the building, its site and any yard, garden, outhouses and appurtenances belonging to the building or usually enjoyed with it, are to be treated as situated in such one of the districts as is specified in the agreement: Housing Act 1985 s 3(1). Whilst such an agreement is in force the enactments relating to housing have effect accordingly: s 3(2).

8 Housing Act 1985 s 2(2).

9 See the Landlord and Tenant Act 1987 s 58(1); and LANDLORD AND TENANT vol 63 (2016) PARA 639.

10 See LANDLORD AND TENANT vol 64 (2016) PARAS 1514 et seq, 1553 et seq.

12. Other descriptions of authorities. For the purposes of the Housing Act 1985:
  (1)   a 'housing authority' means a local housing authority[1], or a new town corporation[2];
  (2)   a 'new town corporation' means a development corporation or the new towns residuary body[3];

(3) a 'development corporation' means a development corporation established by an order made, or having effect as if made, under the New Towns Act 1981[4];

(4) an 'urban development corporation' means an urban development corporation established under Part XVI of the Local Government, Planning and Land Act 1980[5];

(5) a 'local authority' generally means a county, county borough, district or London borough council, the Common Council of the City of London or the Council of the Isles of Scilly[6];

(6) a 'housing action trust' means a housing action trust established under Part III of the Housing Act 1988[7];

(7) a 'new towns residuary body' means: (a) in relation to England, the Homes and Communities Agency so far as exercising functions in relation to anything transferred (or to be transferred)[8] to it or the Greater London Authority[9] so far as exercising its new towns and urban development functions; and (b) in relation to Wales, the Welsh Ministers so far as exercising functions in relation to anything transferred (or to be transferred)[10] to them[11].

1 As to the meaning of 'local housing authority' see PARA 11.
2 See head (2) in the text.
3 See heads (3), (7) in the text.
4 As to the establishment of development corporations see the New Towns Act 1981 s 3, Sch 3; and PLANNING vol 83 (2010) PARA 1499 et seq. See also PARA 18.
5 Ie the Local Government, Planning and Land Act 1980 Pt XVI (ss 134–172). As to the establishment of urban development corporations see s 135, Sch 26; and PLANNING vol 83 (2010) PARA 1581 et seq.
6 For the purposes of the Housing Act 1985 ss 43, 44, 232, 'local authority' also includes the Broads Authority; for the purposes of ss 438, 441–443, 458, it includes the Broads Authority, a joint authority established by the Local Government Act 1985 Pt IV (ss 23–42) (see LOCAL GOVERNMENT vol 69 (2009) PARA 47), an economic prosperity board, a combined authority and the London Fire and Emergency Planning Authority; and for the purposes of the Housing Act 1985 ss 45(2)(b), 50(2), 51(6), 80(1), 157(1), 171(2), 573(1), Sch 1 para 2(1), Sch 2 grounds 7, 12, Sch 3 ground 5, Sch 4 para 7(1), Sch 5 para 5(1)(b), Sch 16, it includes the Broads Authority, a police and crime commissioner, a joint authority established by the Local Government Act 1985 Pt IV, an economic prosperity board, a combined authority and the London Fire and Emergency Planning Authority: Housing Act 1985 s 4(1)(e) (s 4(1) numbered as such by the Local Government and Public Involvement in Health Act 2007 Sch 13 para 41(1); and amended by the Norfolk and Suffolk Broads Act 1988 s 21, Sch 6 para 25; the Education Reform Act 1988 s 237, Sch 13 Pt I; the Greater London Authority Act 1999 ss 325, 328, 423, Sch 27 para 51, Sch 29 para 42, Sch 34 Pt VIII; the Police and Magistrates' Courts Act 1994 ss 43, 93, Sch 4 para 58, Sch 9 Pt I; the Police Act 1997 s 134(1), Sch 9 para 49; the Criminal Justice and Police Act 2001 ss 128(1), 137, Sch 6 para 67, Sch 7 Pt 5(1); the Police Reform Act 2002 ss 100(1), 107(2), Sch 8; the Local Government and Public Involvement in Health Act 2007 s 209(2), Sch 13 para 41(2); the Local Democracy, Economic Development and Construction Act 2009 s 119, Sch 6 para 68(1), (2); the Police Reform and Social Responsibility Act 2011 s 99, Sch 16 para 168; and the Deregulation Act 2015 s 59, Sch 13 para 6(1), (19)(a)).
     'Combined authority' means a combined authority established under the Local Democracy, Economic Development and Construction Act 2009 s 103 (see TRADE AND INDUSTRY vol 97 (2015) PARA 1092 et seq); and 'economic prosperity board' means an economic prosperity board established under s 88 of that Act (see TRADE AND INDUSTRY vol 97 (2015) PARA 1086 et seq): Housing Act 1985 s 4(2) (added by the Local Government and Public Involvement in Health Act 2007 Sch 13 para 41(3); substituted by the Local Democracy, Economic Development and Construction Act 2009 s 119, Sch 6 para 68(1), (3); and amended by the Deregulation Act 2015 Sch 13 para 6(1), (19)(b)). As to the Broads Authority see WATER AND WATERWAYS vol 101 (2009) PARA 734. As to the London Fire and Emergency Planning Authority see FIRE AND RESCUE SERVICES vol 51 (2013) PARA 17. As to police and crime commissioners see POLICE AND INVESTIGATORY POWERS vol 84 (2013) PARA 56 et seq.
7 Ie the Housing Act 1988 Pt III (ss 60–92): see PARA 537 et seq.
8 Ie as mentioned in the Housing and Regeneration Act 2008 s 52(1)(a)–(d): see PLANNING vol 83 (2010) PARA 1455.

9 As to the Greater London Authority see LONDON GOVERNMENT vol 71 (2013) PARA 67 et seq.
10 Ie as mentioned in the New Towns Act 1981 s 36(1)(a)(i)–(iii): see PLANNING vol 83 (2010) PARA 1562.
11 See the Housing Act 1985 s 4(1) (as so numbered (see note 6); amended by the Housing Act 1988 s 62(7); the Local Government (Wales) Act 1994 s 22(2), Sch 8 para 5(3); the Government of Wales Act 1998 ss 129, 152, Sch 15 para 7, Sch 18 Pt IV; and the Localism Act 2011 s 195(1), Sch 19 paras 10, 11; and by SI 2008/3002; and modified by the Waste Regulation and Disposal (Authorities) Order 1985, SI 1985/1884, art 10, Sch 3).

13. Housing associations. A 'housing association' means a society, a body of trustees or a company:

(1)   which is established for the purpose of, or amongst whose objects and powers are included those of, providing, constructing, improving or managing, or facilitating or encouraging the construction or improvement of, housing accommodation[1]; and

(2)   which does not trade for profit[2] or whose constitution or rules prohibit the issue of capital with interest or dividend exceeding such rate as may be prescribed by the Treasury, whether with or without differentiation as between share and loan capital[3].

'Fully mutual', in relation to a housing association, means that the rules of the housing association restrict membership to persons who are tenants or prospective tenants of the association and preclude the granting or assignment of tenancies to persons other than members; and 'co-operative housing association' means a fully mutual housing association which is a registered society within the meaning of the Co-operative and Community Benefit Societies Act 2014[4].

'Self-build society' means a housing association whose object is to provide, for sale to or occupation by its members, dwellings built or improved principally with the use of its members' own labour[5].

Housing associations in Wales which are registered under the Housing Act 1996[6] are known as registered social landlords[7], although that term is no longer used as such in Part I of that Act[8].

A registered social landlord or a fully mutual housing association which is not a registered social landlord is an 'exempt landlord' for the purposes of the Landlord and Tenant Act 1987[9], and this affects the rights of its tenants (such as the right to apply to the First-tier Tribunal (Property Chamber) for a manager to be appointed)[10].

A local housing authority[11] in Wales may promote and assist housing associations[12].

A local housing authority may sell or supply under a hire-purchase agreement[13] furniture to the occupants of houses provided by a housing association, and may buy furniture for that purpose[14].

1 'Housing accommodation' includes flats, lodging-houses and hostels: Housing Act 1985 s 56(1) (numbered as such by SI 2010/844). 'Lodging-houses' means houses not occupied as separate dwellings: Housing Act 1985 s 56(1) (as so renumbered).
2 The activities of a body may be carried on otherwise than for profit although profits are made: see *National Deposit Friendly Society Trustees v Skegness UDC* [1959] AC 293, [1958] 2 All ER 601, HL. There is authority for saying that the making of profits is irrelevant if it is only a subsidiary object, ie only a means whereby the main object of the body in question can be furthered or achieved: see *National Deposit Friendly Society Trustees v Skegness UDC* [1959] AC 293, [1958] 2 All ER 601, HL, per Lord Denning. See also *Hummingbird Entertainment Ltd v Birmingham City Council* [1991] RA 165.
3 Housing Act 1985 s 5(1); Housing Associations Act 1985 s 1(1). The Treasury function under s 1(1)(b) (head (1) in the text) has not been transferred to the Welsh Ministers: see the National Assembly for Wales (Transfer of Functions) Order 1999, SI 1999/672, art 2, Sch 1. As to the Treasury see CONSTITUTIONAL AND ADMINISTRATIVE LAW vol 20 (2014) PARA 262 et seq. This definition is applied for the purposes of the Housing Act 1996 (see s 230).

The National Federation of Housing Associations represents member housing associations, and promotes training and best practice.

4   Housing Act 1985 s 5(2) (amended by the Co-operative and Community Benefit Societies Act 2014 s 151(1), Sch 4 paras 32, 33); Housing Associations Act 1985 s 1(2) (amended by the Co-operative and Community Benefit Societies Act 2014 Sch 4 para 36; and by SI 1996/2325). This definition is applied for the purposes of the Housing Act 1996 Pt I (ss A1–64) (see PARA 166 et seq): see s 63(1).

5   Housing Act 1985 s 5(3); Housing Associations Act 1985 s 1(3).

6   Ie in the register maintained under the Housing Act 1996 s 1, now applicable only in Wales: see PARA 167.

7   Housing Act 1985 s 5(4) (substituted by SI 2010/866). In the Housing Act 1985, references to registered social landlords include, where the context so permits, references to housing associations registered in the register maintained by Scottish Homes under the Housing Associations Act 1985 s 3 (repealed in relation to England and Wales): Housing Act 1985 s 5(5) (added by SI 1996/2325).

8   See PARA 167.

9   See the Landlord and Tenant Act 1987 s 58(1)(ga), (gb); and LANDLORD AND TENANT vol 63 (2016) PARA 639.

10 See further LANDLORD AND TENANT vol 63 (2016) PARA 562 et seq and LANDLORD AND TENANT vol 64 (2016) PARAS 1514 et seq, 1553 et seq.

11 As to local housing authorities see PARA 11.

12 As to promotion and assistance in relation to registered social landlords see the Housing Act 1996 s 22; and PARA 166. As to promotion and assistance in relation to housing associations which are not registered social landlords see the Housing Associations Act 1985 s 58 (substituted by SI 1996/2325; and amended by SI 2010/866).

13 'Hire-purchase agreement' means a hire-purchase agreement or conditional sale agreement within the meaning of the Consumer Credit Act 1974 (see CONSUMER CREDIT vol 21 (2016) PARA 40): Housing Associations Act 1985 s 61(2).

14 Housing Associations Act 1985 s 61(1). Section 61 does not apply where the housing association is: (1) a private registered provider of social housing; or (2) a registered social landlord (for which corresponding provision is made by the Housing Act 1996 s 22: see PARA 166): Housing Associations Act 1985 s 61(3) (added, in relation to England and Wales, by SI 1996/2325; and amended by SI 2010/866). As to the meaning of 'private registered provider of social housing' see PARA 53.

14.   Housing trusts. For the purposes of the Housing Act 1985 and the Housing Associations Act 1985, a 'housing trust' means a corporation or body of persons which:

(1)   is required by the terms of its constituent instrument to use the whole of its funds, including any surplus which may arise from its operations, for the purpose of providing housing accommodation[1]; or

(2)   is required by the terms of its constituent instrument to devote the whole, or substantially the whole, of its funds for charitable purposes[2] and in fact uses the whole, or substantially the whole, of its funds for the purposes of providing housing accommodation[3].

A housing trust is registrable as a registered social landlord[4].

A housing trust which is a charity is an 'exempt landlord' for the purposes of the Landlord and Tenant Act 1987[5], and this affects the rights of its tenants (such as the right to apply to the First-tier Tribunal (Property Chamber) for a manager to be appointed)[6].

1   As to the meaning of 'housing accommodation' see PARA 13 note 1.

2   'Charity' in the legal sense comprises four principal divisions: trusts for the relief of poverty, trusts for the advancement of education, trusts for the advancement of religion, and trusts for other purposes beneficial to the community not falling under any of the preceding heads: see *Income Tax Special Purposes Comrs v Pemsel* [1891] AC 531 at 583, HL, per Lord Macnaghten. See further CHARITIES vol 8 (2015) PARA 1 et seq.

3   Housing Act 1985 s 6; Housing Associations Act 1985 s 2.

4   As to registered social landlords (in Wales) see PARA 166 et seq.

5   See the Landlord and Tenant Act 1987 s 58(1)(f); and LANDLORD AND TENANT vol 63 (2016) PARA 639.

6   Tenants of such a trust have no statutory right of first refusal under the Landlord and Tenant Act
    1987 Pt I (ss 1–20) (see LANDLORD AND TENANT vol 64 (2016) PARA 1514 et seq) on the
    disposal of the premises (s 1(4)), no right to apply to a tribunal under Pt II (ss 21–24) (see
    LANDLORD AND TENANT vol 63 (2016) PARA 562 et seq) for the appointment of managers
    (s 21(3) (amended by the Housing and Regeneration Act 2008 s 56, Sch 8 paras 37, 38), and no
    right of compulsory acquisition under the Landlord and Tenant Act 1987 Pt III (ss 25–34) (see
    LANDLORD AND TENANT vol 64 (2016) PARA 1553 et seq) of the landlord's interest (s 25(5)).

15.   Reserve powers of county councils to provide housing accommodation. A
county council in England has the following reserve powers in relation to the
provision of housing accommodation[1]:

(1)   it may undertake any activity for the purposes of, or incidental to,
        establishing the needs of the whole or a part of the county with respect
        to the provision of housing accommodation[2];

(2)   if requested to do so by one or more local housing authorities[3] for
        districts[4] within the county, it may, with the consent of the Secretary
        of State[5], undertake on behalf of the authority or authorities the
        provision of housing accommodation in any manner in which it or they
        might do so[6];

(3)   with the approval of the Secretary of State given on an application made
        by it, it may undertake the provision of housing accommodation in any
        manner in which a local housing authority for a district within the
        county might do so[7].

The Secretary of State must not give his consent under head (2) or his approval
under head (3) except after consultation with the local housing authorities who
appear to him to be concerned; and his consent or approval may be made subject
to such conditions and restrictions as he may from time to time specify and, in
particular, may include conditions with respect to:

(a)   the transfer of the ownership and management of housing
        accommodation provided by the county council to the local housing
        authority; and

(b)   the recovery by the county council from local housing authorities of
        expenditure incurred by the county council in providing
        accommodation[8].

Before a county council exercises outside the county by virtue of head (2) or
head (3) any specified statutory power[9] it must give notice to the council of the
county in which it proposes to exercise the power; but failure to give notice does
not invalidate the exercise of the power[10].

1   Housing Act 1985 s 28(1) (amended by the Local Government (Wales) Act 1994 s 22(2), Sch 8
    para 5(6)). As to the meaning of 'housing accommodation' see PARA 13 note 1.
2   Housing Act 1985 s 28(2).
3   As to the meaning of 'local housing authority' see PARA 11.
4   As to the meaning of 'district' see PARA 11.
5   As to the Secretary of State see PARA 7.
6   Housing Act 1985 s 28(3).
7   Housing Act 1985 s 28(4).
8   Housing Act 1985 s 28(5).
9   Ie any power the Housing Act 1985 Pt II (ss 8–57): see PARA 401 et seq.
10 Housing Act 1985 s 28(6).

16.   Provision of accommodation for employees of county councils. A county
council may provide houses[1] for persons employed or paid by, or by a statutory
committee of, the council[2]. For that purpose, the council may acquire or
appropriate land in the same way as a local housing authority[3] may acquire or
appropriate land for the statutory purposes related to the provision of housing

accommodation[4]; and land so acquired or appropriated may be disposed of by the county council in the same way as land held for those purposes[5].

1   As to the meaning of 'house' see PARA 405 note 6.
2   Housing Act 1985 s 29(1).
3   As to the meaning of 'local housing authority' see PARA 11.
4   Ie for the purposes of the Housing Act 1985 Pt II (ss 8–57): see PARA 401 et seq.
5   Housing Act 1985 s 29(2).

17.   Service of notices by local housing authority. Where under any provision of the Housing Act 1985 it is the duty of a local housing authority[1] to serve a document on a person who is to the knowledge of the authority:

(1)   a person having control of premises, however defined; or
(2)   a person managing premises, however defined; or
(3)   a person having an estate or interest in premises, whether or not restricted to persons who are owners or lessees or mortgagees or to any other class of those having an estate or interest in premises,

the authority must take reasonable steps to identify the person or persons coming within the description in that provision[2].

A person having an estate or interest in premises may for the purposes of any provision of the Housing Act 1985 give notice to the local housing authority of his interest in the premises and the authority must enter the notice in its records[3].

A document required or authorised by this Act to be served on a person as being a person having control of premises (however defined) may, if it is not practicable after reasonable inquiry to ascertain name or address of that person, be served by:

(a)   addressing it to him by the description of 'person having control of' the premises (naming them) to which it relates; and
(b)   delivering it to some person on the premises or, if there is no person on the premises to whom it can be delivered, by affixing it, or a copy of it, to some conspicuous part of the premises[4].

Where under any provision of the Housing Act 1985 a document is to be served on:

(i)   the person having control of premises, however defined; or
(ii)   the person managing premises, however defined; or
(iii)   the owner of premises, however defined,

and more than one person comes within the description in the enactment, the document may be served on more than one of those persons[5].

1   As to the meaning of 'local housing authority' see PARA 11.
2   Housing Act 1985 s 617(1).
3   Housing Act 1985 s 617(2).
4   Housing Act 1985 s 617(3).
5   Housing Act 1985 s 617(4).

(iii) New Towns Administration

18.   In general. A new town corporation (that is, a development corporation or the new towns residuary body)[1] has power to provide houses under its general powers of acquiring, managing and disposing of land and carrying on building operations[2]. Special provision is made for the transfer of new town housing stock[3] and for the payment of housing subsidy to new town corporations[4]. Rent rebate subsidy is also payable to a new town corporation[5].

No new towns are being created under the relevant legislation and the existing provision is being phased out[6].

1   See PARA 12.
2   See PLANNING vol 83 (2010) PARA 1500.
3   See the Local Government and Housing Act 1989 ss 172, 173; and PARAS 19–20.
4   See the Housing Act 1985 ss 421–427A; and PARAS 372–373.
5   See WELFARE BENEFITS AND STATE PENSIONS vol 104 (2014) PARA 333.
6   See PLANNING vol 83 (2010) PARAs 1452–1453, 1558.

19.   Transfer of new town housing stock. Subject to the provisions below, the appropriate national authority[1] may by regulations make provision for requiring and authorising each new town corporation[2] to take such steps as may be prescribed[3] for making and giving effect to proposals for disposing of its housing stock[4], either by transferring it as a whole to a prescribed person or by transferring different parts of it to different prescribed persons[5]. Any such regulations may not require a new town corporation to transfer any dwelling or associated property, rights, liabilities or obligations[6] to any person other than:

(1)   the district council[7] within whose area the dwelling is situated; or
(2)   a person approved for the purposes of, and in accordance with, the regulations by the Regulator of Social Housing[8].

Nor may any such regulations require a new town corporation to give effect to a proposal for the transfer of any dwelling if the dwelling is one in respect of which a notice of a claim to exercise the right to buy[9] has been served before the prescribed time and such other conditions as may be prescribed are satisfied[10].

A new town corporation may not, in pursuance of any such regulations, transfer any dwellings, or any associated property, rights, liabilities or obligations, to any person except with the consent of the appropriate national authority; and the appropriate national authority may not give its consent to a proposed transfer unless it is satisfied:

(a)   that there has been compliance with all such requirements with respect to the publication of information about the proposal and matters connected with its implementation, and with respect to consultation about the proposal, as are prescribed;
(b)   that all such steps have been taken as are prescribed for the purpose of protecting the interests of the occupiers of the dwellings or the interests of the occupiers of any dwellings excluded from the proposal[11] or any such consultation; and
(c)   that the terms on which the transfer is made:
         (i)   require such price to be paid for the property transferred as appears to the appropriate national authority to be the price which, on the prescribed assumptions, it would realise if sold on the open market by a willing vendor; and
         (ii)   include all such other terms as are prescribed[12].

These provisions replaced Part III of the New Towns Act 1981 (relating to the transfer of dwellings and associated property to district councils), which ceased to have effect, but without: (A) affecting the operation after the time when the repeal came into force of so much of any transfer scheme made under Part III before that time as contains management arrangements with respect to land in which a new town corporation has an interest; or (B) affecting the application after that time of the provision of that Act as to financial arrangements[13] in relation to any transfer scheme made under Part III before that time; or (C) preventing the appropriate national authority from exercising its power to make grants[14] to a district council[15] in respect of defects in transferred dwellings where the grants are paid before 1 April 1990 or such later date as the appropriate national authority may by order made by statutory instrument appoint in relation to that council[16].

1 Ie the Secretary of State or, where statutory functions have been transferred in relation to Wales, the Welsh Ministers: see PARA 7.

2 'New town corporation' means a development corporation within the meaning of the New Towns Act 1981 (see PLANNING vol 83 (2010) PARA 1499 et seq): Local Government and Housing Act 1989 s 172(8) (amended by the Government of Wales Act 1998 s 152, Sch 18 Pt IV; and the Housing and Regeneration Act 2008 ss 56, 321(1), Sch 8 para 51, Sch 16).

3 'Prescribed' means prescribed by or determined under regulations under the Local Government and Housing Act 1989 s 172(1): s 172(8).

4 'Housing stock', in relation to a new town corporation, means: (1) the dwellings (whether or not in the area of a particular new town) which are vested in that corporation and were erected, adapted or acquired for occupation as dwellings; and (2) except so far as may be prescribed, any associated property, rights, liabilities and obligations of that corporation: Local Government and Housing Act 1989 s 172(8). 'Dwelling' means any building or part of a building occupied, or erected or adapted for occupation, as a dwelling or as a hostel (including any land belonging to it or usually enjoyed with it): s 172(8).

5 Local Government and Housing Act 1989 s 172(1). Regulations under s 172(1) may contain such incidental provision and such supplemental, consequential and transitional provision in connection with their other provisions as the appropriate national authority considers appropriate, including, without prejudice to the generality of the foregoing, provision corresponding to the Housing Act 1988 Sch 12 para 2(2), (3) (matters relating to registration of title): Local Government and Housing Act 1989 s 172(5). The following regulations have been made under s 172(1): the New Towns (Transfer of Housing Stock) Regulations 1990, SI 1990/1700; the New Towns (Transfer of Housing Stock) (Amendment) Regulations 1990, SI 1990/2366; the New Towns (Transfer of Housing Stock) (Amendment) Regulations 1991, SI 1991/1281; the Development Board for Rural Wales (Transfer of Housing Stock) Regulations 1993, SI 1993/1808 (lapsed); and the Development Board for Rural Wales (Transfer of Housing Stock) (Amendment) Regulations 1994, SI 1994/1005 (lapsed).

6 'Liabilities and obligations', in relation to a new town corporation, includes liabilities and obligations which, apart from the regulations, would not be capable of being assigned or transferred by the corporation, including liabilities and obligations under the Housing Act 1985 Pt V (ss 118–188) (right to buy: see PARA 230 et seq): Local Government and Housing Act 1989 s 172(8). For the purposes of s 172, the following property, rights, liabilities and obligations of a new town corporation are to be treated as associated with any dwellings comprised in its housing stock:

    (1)   any interest of the corporation in any land occupied or set aside for occupation or use with the dwellings (s 172(9)(a));

    (2)   any interest of the corporation in land in the vicinity of the dwellings which is held by it for the benefit or use of the persons living in those dwellings (rather than the inhabitants of a new town as a whole) or for providing facilities for the persons living in those dwellings, and any other property and any rights of the corporation so held (s 172(9)(b));

    (3)   any property and rights held by the corporation:

        (a)   for the administration of an estate comprising the dwellings or any associated property (s 172(9)(c)(i));

        (b)   for the maintenance or service of the dwellings or any associated property (s 172(9)(c)(ii)); or

        (c)   otherwise in connection with any such property (s 172(9)(c)(iii));

    (4)   any rights, liabilities and obligations which the corporation has in connection with any of the dwellings or any associated property or in connection with any dwellings which were previously part of its housing stock (s 172(9)(d));

    (5)   any interest of the corporation in land set aside by it as an open space for the use or enjoyment of persons living in the dwellings (rather than for the use of the inhabitants of a new town as a whole) (s 172(9)(e)).

7 Or Welsh county council or county borough council. As to local government areas and authorities in England and Wales see LOCAL GOVERNMENT vol 69 (2009) PARA 22 et seq.

8 Local Government and Housing Act 1989 s 172(2) (amended by the Local Government (Wales) Act 1994 s 22(2), Sch 8 para 10(3); the Government of Wales Act 1998 ss 140, 152, Sch 16 para 75, Sch 18 Pt VI; and SI 2010/866). As to the Regulator of Social Housing see PARA 57 et seq.

9 Ie under the Housing Act 1985 s 122: see PARA 273.

10 Local Government and Housing Act 1989 s 172(3).

11 Ie by virtue of the Local Government and Housing Act 1989 s 172(3): see the text and note 10.

12 Local Government and Housing Act 1989 s 172(4).

13 Ie the New Towns Act 1981 s 50 (repealed).

14 Ie under the New Towns Act 1981 s 51A (repealed).

15 See note 7.

16 Local Government and Housing Act 1989 s 172(6), (7) (s 172(7) amended by the Local Government (Wales) Act 1994 Sch 8 para 10(3)). A statutory instrument containing an order under these provisions is subject to annulment in pursuance of a resolution of either House of Parliament: Local Government and Housing Act 1989 s 172(7). See the New Towns (Defects Grants) (Payments to District Councils) (Extensions of Time) Order 1990, SI 1990/456; and the New Towns (Defects Grants) (Payments to District Councils) (Extensions of Time) (Amendment) Order 1992, SI 1992/78 (both made under the Local Government and Housing Act 1989 s 172(7)(c)).

20. Consent for subsequent disposals. Where a dwelling[1] which is for the time being subject to a secure tenancy[2] is transferred[3] to a person approved for the purpose[4] (an 'approved person'), that person may not dispose[5] of it except with the consent of the appropriate authority[6] (which may be given either unconditionally or subject to conditions) or by an exempt disposal[7]. Such a transfer of a dwelling to an approved person is referred to as an 'initial transfer'[8].

Where an estate or interest in a dwelling of the approved person who acquired it on the initial transfer has been mortgaged or charged, the above prohibition applies also to a disposal by the mortgagee or chargee in exercise of a power of sale or leasing, whether or not the disposal is in the name of the approved person[9]. In any case where, by operation of law or by virtue of an order of a court, the dwelling which has been acquired on the initial transfer passes or is transferred from the approved person to another person, and that passing or transfer does not constitute a disposal for which consent is required under these provisions, these provisions (including, where there is more than one such passing or transfer, this provision) apply as if the other person to whom the dwelling passes or is transferred were the approved person[10].

Where the restriction on disposal applies, the new town corporation[11] by which the initial transfer is made must furnish to the approved person a copy of the consent of the appropriate national authority[12] and the instrument by which the initial transfer is effected must contain a statement in a form approved by the Chief Land Registrar that the requirement of these provisions as to consent applies to a subsequent disposal of the dwelling by the approved person[13]. Before giving any consent required by virtue of these provisions, the appropriate authority must satisfy itself that the person who is seeking the consent has taken appropriate steps to consult every tenant of any dwelling proposed to be disposed of, and must have regard to the responses of any such tenants to that consultation[14].

Where the title of the new town corporation to the dwelling which is transferred by the initial transfer is not registered, and the initial transfer is a transfer or grant falling within the provisions as to compulsory registration of title[15]:

(1)   the corporation must give the approved person a certificate in a form approved by the Chief Land Registrar stating that the corporation is entitled to make the transfer subject only to such incumbrances, rights and interests as are stated in the instrument by which the initial transfer is effected or summarised in the certificate; and

(2)   for the purpose of registration of title, the Chief Land Registrar must accept such a certificate as evidence of the facts stated in it, but if as a result he has to meet a claim against him under the Land Registration Act 2002 the corporation by which the initial transfer was made is liable to indemnify him[16].

Where the Chief Land Registrar approves an application for registration of a disposition of registered land, or a person's title under a disposition of unregistered land, and the instrument effecting the initial transfer contains the statement as to the requirement of consent[17], he must enter in the register a restriction reflecting the limitation under these provisions on subsequent disposal[18].

1 For these purposes, 'dwelling' has the same meaning as in the Local Government and Housing Act 1989 s 172 (see PARA 19 note 4): s 173(10)(a).
2 'Secure tenancy' has the meaning assigned by the Housing Act 1985 s 79 (see LANDLORD AND TENANT vol 63 (2016) PARA 1037): Local Government and Housing Act 1989 s 173(10)(b).
3 Ie under the Local Government and Housing Act 1989 s 172: see PARA 19.
4 Ie as mentioned in the Local Government and Housing Act 1989 s 172(2)(b): see PARA 19 head (2).
5 For the purposes of the Local Government and Housing Act 1989 s 173 the grant of an option to purchase the fee simple or any other interest in a dwelling is a disposal and a consent given to such a disposal extends to a disposal made in pursuance of the option: s 173(4).
6 For these purposes, 'the appropriate authority' means: (1) in relation to a disposal of land in England, the Secretary of State; and (2) in relation to a disposal of land in Wales, the Welsh Ministers: Local Government and Housing Act 1989 s 173(1A) (added by the Housing and Regeneration Act 2008 s 191(4)(b); amended by the Housing and Planning Act 2016 s 92, Sch 4 para 5(1), (3)). As from 6 April 2017, the Local Government and Housing Act 1989 s 173(1) does not apply to a disposal of land by a private registered provider of social housing: s 173(1ZA) (added by the Housing and Planning Act 2016 Sch 4 para 5(1), (2)); Housing and Planning Act 2016 (Commencement No 4 and Transitional Provisions) Regulations 2017, SI 2017/75, reg 4.
   As to the Secretary of State see PARA 7. As to the transfer of functions, so far as they are exercisable in relation to Wales, to the Welsh Ministers see PARA 7. As to the meaning of 'private registered provider of social housing' see PARA 53.
7 Local Government and Housing Act 1989 s 173(1)(a), (b) (s 173(1)(a) amended by the Housing and Regeneration Act 2008 s 191(4)(a)). The text refers to an exempt disposal as defined in the Housing Act 1988 s 81(8) (see PARA 556).
8 Local Government and Housing Act 1989 s 173(1).
9 Local Government and Housing Act 1989 s 173(2).
10 Local Government and Housing Act 1989 s 173(2).
11 'New town corporation' has the same meaning as in the Local Government and Housing Act 1989 s 172 (see PARA 19 note 2): s 173(10)(a).
12 Ie under the Local Government and Housing Act 1989 s 172(4): see PARA 19.
13 Local Government and Housing Act 1989 s 173(3). As to the Chief Land Registrar see REAL PROPERTY AND REGISTRATION vol 87 (2012) PARA 562.
14 Local Government and Housing Act 1989 s 173(5) (amended by the Housing and Regeneration Act 2008 s 191(4)(c), (d)). Consent is not required under the Housing Act 1996 s 9 (see PARA 217) or s 42 (see PARA 209) or the Housing Associations Act 1985 s 9 (see PARA 24) for any disposal in respect of which consent is given under the Local Government and Housing Act 1989 s 173: s 173(7) (amended by the Government of Wales Act 1998 s 140, Sch 16 para 76(3); the Housing and Planning Act 2016 Sch 4 para 5(1), (4); and SI 1996/2325).
15 Ie a transfer or grant of a description mentioned in the Land Registration Act 2002 s 4: see REAL PROPERTY AND REGISTRATION vol 87 (2012) PARA 345.
16 Local Government and Housing Act 1989 s 173(8) (amended by the Land Registration Act 1997 s 4(2), Sch 2 Pt I; and the Land Registration Act 2002 s 133, Sch 11 para 24(1), (2)).
17 Ie the statement required by the Local Government and Housing Act 1989 s 173(3): see the text to note 13.
18 Local Government and Housing Act 1989 s 173(9) (substituted by the Land Registration Act 2002 Sch 11 para 24(3)).

(iv) Grants to Housing Associations

21. Recovery of certain grants. Where a grant[1] has been made to a relevant housing association[2], the powers described below are exercisable in such events ('relevant events') as the appropriate authority[3] may from time to time determine[4]. The appropriate authority may:

(1)   reduce the amount of, or of any payment in respect of, the grant;

(2)   suspend or cancel any instalment of the grant; or

(3)   direct the association to apply or appropriate for such purposes as the appropriate authority may specify, or to pay to the appropriate authority, an amount equal to the whole, or such proportion as it may specify, of the amount of any payment made to the association in respect of the grant,

and a direction under head (3) may require the application, appropriation or payment of an amount with interest in accordance with the relevant statutory provisions[5]. Where, after such a grant has been made to an association, a relevant event occurs, the association must notify the appropriate authority and, if so required by written notice of the appropriate authority, must furnish it with such particulars of and information relating to the event as are specified in the notice[6].

Where such a grant has been made to a housing association, and at any time property to which the grant relates becomes vested in, or is leased for a term of years to, or reverts to, some other relevant housing association, or trustees for some other such association, these provisions have effect after that time as if the grant, or a proportion of it[7], had been made to that other association[8].

1   Ie under the Housing Act 1988 s 50 or s 51 (both repealed in relation to England and Wales), or under the Housing Associations Act 1985 s 41 (repealed) or any enactment replaced by that provision: see the Housing Act 1988 s 52(1)(a), (b).

2   'Relevant housing association', in the Housing Act 1988 ss 52–54, means:

    (1)   a housing association which is a registered provider of social housing ('an English relevant housing association'); and

    (2)   a housing association which is a registered social landlord ('a Welsh relevant housing association'): s 52(9A) (s 52(9A), (9B) added, in relation to England and Wales, by the Housing and Regeneration Act 2008 s 56, Sch 8 paras 44, 47(1), (4)).

As to the meaning of 'housing association' see PARA 13 (definition applied by the Housing Act 1988 s 59(1A) (added, in relation to England and Wales, by SI 1996/2325; amended by the Housing Act 2004 s 218, Sch 11 paras 2, 6; the Housing and Regeneration Act 2008 Sch 8 paras 44, 50; and SI 2010/866)). A reference to registration as a provider of social housing, so far as the context permits, is to be construed as including, in relation to times, circumstances and purposes before the commencement of the Housing and Regeneration Act 2008 s 111, a reference to registration under the Housing Act 1996 Pt I (ss A1–64), the Housing Associations Act 1985 Pt I (ss 1–40), or any corresponding earlier enactment: Housing Act 1988 s 52(9B) (as so added). The Housing and Regeneration Act 2008 s 111 came into force on 1 April 2010: see the Housing and Regeneration Act 2008 (Commencement No 7 and Transitional and Saving Provisions) Order 2010, SI 2010/862, art 2.

3   In the Housing Act 1988 ss 52–54, 'the appropriate authority': (1) in relation to an English relevant housing association and property outside Greater London, means the Homes and Communities Agency; (2) in relation to an English relevant housing association and property in Greater London, means the Greater London Authority; and (3) in relation to a Welsh relevant housing association, means the Welsh Ministers: s 52(9A) (as added (see note 2); amended by the Localism Act 2011 s 195(1), Sch 19 paras 25, 28). As to the Homes and Communities Agency see PARA 57 et seq; and PLANNING vol 83 (2010) PARA 1454 et seq. As to the Greater London Authority see LONDON GOVERNMENT vol 71 (2013) PARA 67 et seq. As to the Welsh Ministers see PARA 7.

4   Housing Act 1988 s 52(1) (amended, in relation to England and Wales, by the Housing and Regeneration Act 2008 Sch 8 para 47(2), (3)).

5   Housing Act 1988 s 52(2) (amended by the Housing Act 2004 ss 218, 266, Sch 11 paras 2, 4, Sch 16; and, in relation to England and Wales, by the Government of Wales Act 1998 s 140, Sch 16 para 61; and the Housing and Regeneration Act 2008 Sch 8 para 47(1), (2)). A direction under head (3) in the text requiring the application, appropriation or payment of an amount with interest must specify, in accordance with the Housing Act 1988 s 52(9):

    (1)   the rate or rates of interest (whether fixed or variable) which is or are applicable;

    (2)   the date from which interest is payable, being not earlier than the date of the relevant event; and

    (3)   any provision for suspended or reduced interest which is applicable,

and in head (3): (a) the reference to a provision for suspended interest is a reference to a provision whereby, if the principal amount is applied, appropriated or paid before a date specified in the direction, no interest will be payable for any period after the date of the direction; and (b) the reference to a provision for reduced interest is a reference to a provision whereby, if the principal amount is so applied, appropriated or paid, any interest payable will be payable at a rate or rates lower than the rate or rates which would otherwise be applicable: s 52(7), (8) (amended, in relation to England and Wales, by the Housing Act 1996 s 28(3)). The matters specified in a direction as mentioned in heads (1)–(3) must be either: (i) such as the appropriate authority, acting in accordance with such principles as it may from time to time determine, specifies as being appropriate; or (ii) such as the appropriate authority may determine to be appropriate in the particular case: Housing Act 1988 s 52(9) (amended, in relation to England and Wales, by the Housing and Regeneration Act 2008 Sch 8 para 47(2)).

6   Housing Act 1988 s 52(3) (amended by the Government of Wales Act 1998 Sch 16 para 61).
7   Ie such proportion as is specified or determined under the Housing Act 1988 s 52(6). The proportion is that which, in the circumstances of the particular case: (1) the appropriate authority, acting in accordance with such principles as it may from time to time determine, may specify as being appropriate; or (2) the appropriate authority may determine to be appropriate: s 52(6) (amended, in relation to England and Wales, by the Housing and Regeneration Act 2008 Sch 8 para 47(2)).
8   Housing Act 1988 s 52(5) (amended, in relation to England and Wales, by the Housing and Regeneration Act 2008 Sch 8 para 47(3)).

22.   Tax relief grants. If a housing association[1] makes a claim[2] to the appropriate national authority in respect of a period and satisfies it that throughout the period it was a housing association to which these provisions apply[3] and its functions either:

(1)   consisted exclusively of the function of providing or maintaining housing accommodation[4] for letting[5] or hostels[6] and activities incidental to that function; or

(2)   included that function and activities incidental to that function, the appropriate national authority may make grants to the association for affording relief from tax chargeable[7] on the association[8].

A grant may be made:

(a)   in a case falling within head (1), for affording relief from any tax chargeable on the association for the period in respect of which the claim is made; and

(b)   in a case falling within head (2), for affording relief from such part of any tax so chargeable as the appropriate national authority considers appropriate having regard to the other functions of the association[9].

In any case a grant is to be of such amount, to be made at such times and to be subject to such conditions as the appropriate national authority thinks fit[10].

1   As to the meaning of 'housing association' see PARA 13 (definition applied by the Housing Act 1988 s 59(1A) (added, in relation to England and Wales, by SI 1996/2325; amended by the Housing Act 2004 s 218, Sch 11 paras 2, 6; the Housing and Regeneration Act 2008 Sch 8 paras 44, 50; and SI 2010/866)).
2   A claim under the Housing Act 1988 s 54 must be made in such manner and be supported by such evidence as the appropriate national authority may direct: s 54(6). As to the appropriate national authority, ie the Secretary of State or, where statutory functions have been transferred in relation to Wales, the Welsh Ministers, see PARA 7.
3   Ie the Housing Act 1988 s 54, which applies to a housing association at any time if, at that time: (1) it is a relevant housing association; (2) it does not trade for profit; and (3) it is not approved for the purposes of the Corporation Tax Act 2010 Pt 13 Ch 7 (ss 642–649) (tax treatment of co-operative housing associations): Housing Act 1988 s 54(2) (amended by the Housing and Regeneration Act 2008 Sch 8 para 49; the Corporation Tax Act 2010 s 1177, Sch 1 para 211; and SI 1996/2325). As to the meaning of 'relevant housing association' see PARA 21 note 2.
4   As to the meaning of 'housing accommodation' see PARA 164 note 2 (definition applied by the Housing Act 1988 s 59(1A) (as added and amended: see note 1)).
5   'Letting' includes the grant of a shared ownership lease or a licence to occupy: Housing Act 1988 s 54(8).

6 As to the meaning of 'hostel' see PARA 164 note 2 (definition applied by the Housing Act 1988 s 59(1A) (as added and amended: see note 1)).

7 References in the Housing Act 1988 s 54 to tax chargeable on an association are to income tax (other than income tax which the association is entitled to deduct on making any payment) and corporation tax: s 54(3).

8 Housing Act 1988 s 54(1). The Commissioners for Revenue and Customs and their officers may disclose to the appropriate national authority such particulars as it may reasonably require for determining whether a grant should be made on a claim or whether a grant should be repaid or the amount of such grant or repayment: s 54(7) (amended by virtue of the Commissioners for Revenue and Customs Act 2005 s 50(1), (7)). The Commissioners for Her Majesty's Revenue and Customs are appointed under the Commissioners for Revenue and Customs Act 2005 s 1 and have taken over the functions of the former Commissioners of Inland Revenue and Commissioners of Customs and Excise: see INCOME TAXATION vol 58 (2014) PARAS 33–34.

9 Housing Act 1988 s 54(4)(a), (b).

10 Housing Act 1988 s 54(4). The conditions may include conditions for securing the repayment in whole or in part of a grant made to an association: (1) in the event of tax in respect of which it was made being found not to be chargeable; or (2) in such other events (including the association beginning to trade for profit) as the appropriate national authority may determine: s 54(5).

23. General determinations by the Homes and Communities Agency. A general determination[1] may either make the same provision for all cases, or make different provision for different cases or descriptions of cases, including different provision for different areas or for different descriptions of housing associations[2] or housing activities[3]. For these purposes descriptions may be framed by reference to any matters whatever, including in particular, in the case of housing activities, the manner in which they are financed[4]. The Homes and Communities Agency[5] must not make a general determination except with the approval of the Secretary of State[6].

Before making a general determination, the appropriate authority[7] must consult such bodies appearing to it to be representative of housing associations as it considers appropriate[8]. After making such a determination, the appropriate authority must publish the determination in such manner as it considers appropriate for bringing the determination to the notice of the associations concerned[9].

1 For these purposes, 'general determination' means a determination under the Housing Act 1988 s 52 (see PARA 23), other than a determination relating solely to a particular case: s 53(4) (amended, in relation to England and Wales, by the Housing and Regeneration Act 2008 s 56, Sch 8 paras 44, 48(1), (4)).

2 As to the meaning of 'housing association' see PARA 13 (definition applied by the Housing Act 1988 s 59(1) (amended by SI 1996/2325)).

3 Housing Act 1988 s 53(1). As to the meaning of 'housing activities' see PARA 168 note 25 (definition applied by s 59(1A) (added, in relation to England and Wales, by SI 1996/2325; amended by the Housing Act 2004 s 218, Sch 11 paras 2, 6; the Housing and Regeneration Act 2008 Sch 8 paras 44, 50; and SI 2010/866)). However, in relation to times, circumstances and purposes before the commencement of the Housing Act 1996 s 1 (the register of social landlords), 'housing activities' has the same meaning as in the Housing Associations Act 1985 (definition repealed by SI 1996/2325): Housing Act 1988 s 59(1B) (added, in relation to England and Wales, by SI 1996/2325).

4 Housing Act 1988 s 53(1).

5 As to the Homes and Communities Agency see PARA 57 et seq; and PLANNING vol 83 (2010) PARA 1454 et seq.

6 Housing Act 1988 s 53(2) (substituted, in relation to England and Wales, by the Housing Act 1996 s 28(4); and amended by the Housing and Regeneration Act 2008 Sch 8 para 48(1), (2)). As to the Secretary of State see PARA 7.

7 As to the meaning of 'appropriate authority' see PARA 21 note 3.

8 Housing Act 1988 s 53(3) (amended, in relation to England and Wales, by the Housing and Regeneration Act 2008 Sch 8 para 48(3)).

9 Housing Act 1988 s 53(3) (as amended: see note 8).

(v) Property of Housing Associations and Housing Trusts

24. Control of dispositions of land by housing associations. The consent[1] of the relevant regulator is required for any disposition[2] of grant-aided land[3] by an unregistered housing association[4]; and for this purpose 'the relevant regulator' means, if the land is in England, the Regulator of Social Housing[5], and if the land is in Wales, the Welsh Ministers[6]. Consent may be so given either generally to all housing associations or to a particular housing association or description of association, and either in relation to particular land or in relation to a particular description of land, and may be given subject to conditions[7].

A disposition by a housing association which requires such consent is, however, valid[8] in favour of a person claiming under the association notwithstanding that that consent has not been given; and a person dealing with the association, or with a person claiming under the association, is not to be concerned to see or inquire whether any such consent has been given[9]. However, a disposal of a house[10] by a housing association made without the consent so required is void unless the disposal is to an individual, or to two or more individuals, and the disposal does not extend to any other house[11].

A disposition by an unregistered housing association which is a charity[12] is not within the above restrictions if it cannot[13] be made without an order of the court or the Charity Commission, but before making an order in such a case the Charity Commission must consult, in the case of dispositions of land in England, the Regulator of Social Housing, and, in the case of dispositions of land in Wales, the Welsh Ministers[14]. Nor are certain lettings[15] by an unregistered housing association which is a housing trust[16] within those restrictions[17]. The grant by an unregistered housing association which does not satisfy the landlord condition[18] of a lease[19] for a term ending within the period of seven years and three months beginning on the date of the grant is not within those restrictions unless there is conferred on the lessee (by the lease or otherwise) an option for renewal for a term which, together with the original term, would expire outside that period, or the lease is granted wholly or partly in consideration of a fine[20].

1 Consent under the Housing Associations Act 1985 s 9 must be in writing: s 9(6) (added by the Housing Act 1988 s 59, Sch 6 paras 2, 7; and substituted by the Housing and Regeneration Act 2008 s 277, Sch 9 paras 8, 9(1), (3)). Consents may be general or specific. As to consent see also PARA 217.

2 For these purposes, 'disposition' means sale, lease, mortgage, charge or any other disposal: Housing Associations Act 1985 s 9(5).

3 'Grant-aided land' means land:
    (1)   in respect of which a payment of a specified description falls or fell to be made in respect of a period ending after 24 January 1974; or
    (2)   on which is, or has been, secured a loan of a specified description in respect of which a repayment (by way of principal or interest or both) falls or fell to be made after that date: Housing Associations Act 1985 s 9(1A), Sch 1 para 1 (s 9(1A) added by the Housing Act 1988 Sch 6 paras 2, 7; the Housing Associations Act 1985 Sch 1 para 1 amended by the Government of Wales Act 1998 s 152, Sch 18 Pt VI; and by SI 1996/2325).
The specified payments are:
    (a)   payments by way of annual grants or exchequer contributions under the Housing Act 1949 s 31(3), the Housing (Financial Provisions) Act 1958 s 12(1) or s 15, the Housing Subsidies Act 1967 s 12(6) or the Housing Act 1964 s 62 (all repealed), or under corresponding Scottish legislation;
    (b)   payments by way of annual grant under the Housing Act 1969 s 21(8) (repealed); or
    (c)   payments by way of subsidy under the Housing Finance Act 1972 s 72, 73, 75 or 92 (all repealed) or corresponding Scottish legislation or under the Housing Associations Act 1985 ss 69, 71, Sch 5 Pts I, II, VI and VII (basic or special residual subsidy, new building or improvement subsidy, hostel subsidy (all now superseded)): Sch 1 para 2.
The specified loans are:

    (i)   loans under the Housing Act 1957 s 119 (repealed), the Housing Associations Act 1985 s 58 or corresponding Scottish legislation;

    (ii)   loans to housing associations under the Housing (Financial Provisions) Act 1958 s 47 (repealed), the Housing Associations Act 1985 s 67 (repealed) or corresponding Scottish legislation;

    (iii)   advances made under the Housing Act 1961 s 7 (repealed) or corresponding Scottish legislation;

    (iv)   loans under the Housing Act 1964 s 2 (repealed): Housing Associations Act 1985 Sch 1 para 3.

4   Housing Associations Act 1985 s 9(1A) (as added (see note 3); amended by the Housing and Regeneration Act 2008 Sch 9 para 9(2)(a)). As to the meaning of 'housing association' see PARA 13. 'Unregistered', in relation to a housing association, means: (1) not registered as a provider of social housing under the Housing and Regeneration Act 2008 Pt 2 (ss 59–278A) (see PARA 51 et seq); (2) not registered as a social landlord under the Housing Act 1996 Pt I (ss A1–64) (see PARA 166 et seq); and (3) not registered as a social landlord under the Housing (Scotland) Act 2010 Pt 2 (ss 20–30): Housing Associations Act 1985 s 2B (added by SI 1996/2325; definition substituted, in relation to England and Wales, by SI 2010/866; and amended, in relation to England and Wales, by SI 2012/700).

5   As to the Regulator of Social Housing see PARA 57 et seq.

6   Housing Associations Act 1985 s 9(1A) (as added (see note 3); amended by the Housing and Regeneration Act 2008 Sch 9 para 9(2)(b)).

7   Housing Associations Act 1985 s 9(2) (amended by SI 1996/2325).

8   Ie subject to the Housing Associations Act 1985 s 12: see the text and notes 10–11.

9   Housing Associations Act 1985 s 9(3) (amended by the Housing Act 1988 Sch 6 para 7).

10 'House' includes: (1) any part of a building which is occupied or intended to be occupied as a separate dwelling; (2) any yard, garden, outhouses and appurtenances belonging to the house or usually enjoyed with it: Housing Associations Act 1985 s 106(1).

11 Housing Associations Act 1985 s 12.

12 As to the meaning of 'charity' see CHARITIES vol 8 (2015) PARA 1.

13 Ie by virtue of the Charities Act 2011 ss 117–121, 124: see CHARITIES vol 8 (2015) PARAS 401, 404.

14 See the Housing Associations Act 1985 s 10(1) (amended by the Housing Act 1988 Sch 6 para 8(1); the Charities Act 2006 s 75(1), Sch 8 para 78; the Housing and Regeneration Act 2008 Sch 9 para 10(1), (2); and the Charities Act 2011 s 354(1), Sch 7 para 45).

15 The lettings referred to in the text are:

    (1)   a letting of land under a secure tenancy; or

    (2)   a letting of land under what would be a secure tenancy but for any of the Housing Act 1985 s 79, Sch 1 paras 2–12 or the Housing (Scotland) Act 1987 Sch 2 paras 1–8 (tenancies excepted from being secure tenancies for reasons other than that they are long leases: see LANDLORD AND TENANT vol 63 (2016) PARA 1042 et seq); or

    (3)   a letting of land under an assured tenancy or an assured agricultural occupancy; or

    (4)   a letting of land in England or Wales under what would be an assured tenancy or an assured agricultural occupancy but for any of the Housing Act 1988 s 1(2), Sch 1 paras 4–8 (see LANDLORD AND TENANT vol 63 (2016) PARAS 836–840): Housing Associations Act 1985 s 10(2) (amended by the Housing and Planning Act 1986 s 24(1)(j), Sch 5 para 10(6), (9); the Housing (Scotland) Act 1987 s 339, Sch 23 para 31(2); the Housing (Scotland) Act 1988 s 72(2), Sch 9 para 6; the Housing Act 1988 Sch 6 para 8(2); the Housing and Regeneration Act 2008 ss 277, 321(1), Sch 9 para 10(3), Sch 16; and SI 1996/2325).

16 As to the meaning of 'housing trust' see PARA 14.

17 Housing Associations Act 1985 s 10(2) (as amended: see note 15).

18 Ie the condition in the Housing Act 1985 s 80 (bodies which are capable of granting secure tenancies): see LANDLORD AND TENANT vol 63 (2016) PARA 1037.

19 For these purposes, 'lease' includes an agreement for a lease and a licence to occupy; and 'grant' and 'term' are to be construed accordingly: Housing Associations Act 1985 s 10(4).

20 Housing Associations Act 1985 s 10(3).

25. Provision of land by county councils. Where a housing association[1] wishes to erect houses[2] in England which in the opinion of the Secretary of State[3] are required and the local housing authority[4] in whose district[5] the houses are proposed to be built is unwilling to acquire land with a view to selling or leasing it to the association, the county council, on the application of the association, may acquire land for that purpose[6]. For that purpose, the county council may exercise all the powers of a local housing authority under Part II of the Housing Act 1985[7] in regard to the acquisition and disposal of land; and the provisions of that Act as to the acquisition of land by local housing authorities for the purposes of that Part apply accordingly[8].

1 As to the meaning of 'housing association' see PARA 13.
2 As to the meaning of 'house' see PARA 24 note 10.
3 As to the Secretary of State see PARA 7.
4 As to the meaning of 'local housing authority' see PARA 11.
5 As to the meaning of 'district' see PARA 11.
6 Housing Associations Act 1985 s 34(1) (amended by the Local Government (Wales) Act 1994 s 22(2), Sch 8 para 6(1)).
7 Ie the Housing Act 1985 Pt II (ss 8–57): see PARA 401 et seq.
8 Housing Associations Act 1985 s 34(2).

26. Power of a housing trust to transfer housing to a local housing authority. A housing trust[1] may sell or lease to the local housing authority[2] the houses[3] provided by the trust, or make over to the authority the management of the houses[4]. So far as this provision confers power to dispose of land, however, it does not apply to private registered providers of social housing[5], or to registered social landlords[6] (on whom power to dispose of land is conferred by other statutory provisions[7]); and it has effect subject to the statutory requirement for consent[8] where the housing trust is an unregistered housing association[9] and the land is grant-aided land[10], and subject to the statutory restrictions on dispositions of charity land[11] where the housing trust is a charity[12].

1 As to the meaning of 'housing trust' see PARA 14.
2 As to the meaning of 'local housing authority' see PARA 11 (definition applied by the Housing Associations Act 1985 s 104(1)).
3 As to the meaning of 'house' see PARA 24 note 10.
4 Housing Associations Act 1985 s 35(1).
5 As to the meaning of 'private registered provider of social housing' see PARA 53.
6 As to the meaning of 'registered social landlord' see PARA 13.
7 Ie by the Housing and Regeneration Act 2008 s 171 and the Housing Act 1996 s 8 respectively: see PARAS 100, 216.
8 Ie subject to the Housing Associations Act 1985 s 9: see PARA 24.
9 As to the meaning of 'housing association' see PARA 13.
10 Ie within the meaning of the Housing Associations Act 1985 s 9(1A), Sch 1: see PARA 24 note 3.
11 Ie subject to the Charities Act 2011 ss 117–121, 124: see CHARITIES vol 8 (2015) PARAS 401, 404.
12 Housing Associations Act 1985 s 35(2) (amended by the Government of Wales Act 1998 s 152, Sch 18 Pt VI; the Charities Act 2011 s 354(1), Sch 7 para 46; SI 1996/2325; and SI 2010/866).

27. Functions of the appropriate national authority with respect to legal proceedings. If it appears to the appropriate national authority[1] that the institution of legal proceedings is requisite or desirable with respect to any property belonging to a housing trust[2], or that the expediting of any such legal proceedings is requisite or desirable, it may certify the case to the Attorney General, who may institute legal proceedings, or intervene in legal proceedings already instituted in such manner as he thinks proper in the circumstances[3]. Before preparing a scheme with reference to property belonging to a housing trust, the court or body which is responsible for making the scheme must communicate with the appropriate national authority and consider any recommendations made by it with reference to the proposed scheme[4].

1 Ie the Secretary of State or, where statutory functions have been transferred in relation to Wales, the Welsh Ministers: see PARA 7.
2 As to the meaning of 'housing trust' see PARA 14.
3 Housing Associations Act 1985 s 36(1).
4 Housing Associations Act 1985 s 36(2).

(vi) Landlords' Policies and Procedures in relation to Anti-social Behaviour

28. Policies and procedures about anti-social behaviour. The provisions set out below on anti-social behaviour apply to the following landlords:

(1)   a local housing authority[1];

(2)   a housing action trust[2];

(3)   a non-profit registered provider of social housing[3];

(4)   a registered social landlord[4].

The landlord must prepare a policy in relation to anti-social behaviour[5] and procedures for dealing with occurrences of anti-social behaviour[6] and must publish[7] a statement of the policy and procedures so prepared[8].

The landlord must from time to time keep the policy and procedures under review and, when it thinks appropriate, publish a revised statement[9]. In preparing and reviewing the policy and procedures the landlord must have regard to guidance issued:

(a)   by the Secretary of State[10] in the case of a local housing authority or a housing action trust;

(b)   by the Regulator of Social Housing[11] in the case of a non-profit registered provider of social housing;

(c)   by the Welsh Ministers[12] in the case of a registered social landlord[13].

A copy of a statement or revised statement so published must be available for inspection at all reasonable hours at the landlord's principal office and must be provided on payment of a reasonable fee to any person who requests it[14]. The landlord must also prepare a summary of its current policy and procedures and provide a copy of the summary, without charge, to any person who requests it[15].

1   As to the meaning of 'local housing authority' for these purposes see PARA 11 (definition applied by the Housing Act 1996 s 230).
2   As to the meaning of 'housing action trust' see PARA 12 head (6).
3   As to private registered providers of social housing see PARA 53.
4   Housing Act 1996 s 218A(1) (s 218A added by the Anti-social Behaviour Act 2003 s 12(1); the Housing Act 1996 s 218A(1) amended by SI 2010/866). As to the meaning of 'registered social landlord' see PARA 13.
5   For these purposes, anti-social behaviour is: (1) conduct that is capable of causing nuisance or annoyance to some person (who need not be a particular identified person) and that directly or indirectly relates to or affects the landlord's housing management functions; or (2) conduct that consists of or involves using or threatening to use housing accommodation owned or managed by the landlord for an unlawful purpose: Housing Act 1996 s 218A(8) (substituted by the Anti-social Behaviour, Crime and Policing Act 2014 s 181(1), Sch 11 para 23). As to the powers of local housing authorities and certain other social landlords to deal with housing-related anti-social behaviour see PARA 471 et seq.
6   Housing Act 1996 s 218A(2) (as added: see note 4).
7   The statement was to be published not later than six months after the commencement of the Anti-social Behaviour Act 2003 s 12 (ie 30 June 2004 in relation to England and 30 April 2005 in relation to Wales): see the Housing Act 1996 s 218A(3) (as added: see note 4).
8   Housing Act 1996 s 218A(3) (as added: see note 4).
9   Housing Act 1996 s 218A(4) (as added: see note 4).
10 As to the Secretary of State see PARA 7.
11 As to the Regulator of Social Housing see PARA 57.
12 Ie under the Housing Act 1996 s 36: see PARA 164. As to the Welsh Ministers see PARAS 7, 141.
13 Housing Act 1996 s 218A(7) (as added (see note 4); amended by SI 2010/866).
14 See the Housing Act 1996 s 218A(5) (as added: see note 4).
15 Housing Act 1996 s 218A(6) (as added: see note 4).

(vii) Powers of Appropriate National Authority in respect of Service Charges and Covenants

29. Directions as to certain charges by social landlords. The appropriate national authority[1] may give directions to local authorities and other social landlords[2] in relation to long residential leases about the making of service charges (payable by the long leaseholders)[3] in respect of works of repair, maintenance or improvement:

(1)   requiring or permitting the waiver or reduction of charges where relevant assistance[4] is given by the appropriate national authority[5]; and

(2)   permitting the waiver or reduction of charges in such other circumstances as may be specified in the directions[6].

A direction must not require the waiver or reduction of charges by reference to assistance for which application was made before the date on which the direction was given, but subject to that directions may relate to past charges or works to such extent as appears to the appropriate national authority to be appropriate[7]. Directions which require or permit the waiver or reduction of charges have corresponding effect:

(a)   in relation to charges already demanded so as to require or permit the non-enforcement of the charges[8]; and

(b)   in relation to charges already paid so as to require or permit a refund[9].

Directions may make different provision for different cases or descriptions of case[10]. This includes power to make:

(i)   different provision for different social landlords or descriptions of social landlords[11]; and

(ii)   different provision for different areas[12].

Directions requiring the reduction of a service charge may specify the amount (or proportion) of the reduction or provide for its determination in such manner as may be specified[13]. Directions permitting the waiver or reduction of a service charge may specify criteria to which the social landlord is to have regard in deciding whether to do so or to what extent[14]. The appropriate national authority must publish any direction relating to all social landlords or any description of social landlords in such manner as it considers appropriate for bringing it to the notice of the landlords concerned[15].

1   Ie the Secretary of State or, where statutory functions have been transferred in relation to Wales, the Welsh Ministers: see PARA 7.

2   Ie where the authority or social landlord is the freeholder. For the purposes of the Housing Act 1996 s 219, 'social landlord' means: (1) an authority or body within the Housing Act 1985 s 80(1) (the landlord condition for secure tenancies), other than the Homes and Communities Agency, the Greater London Authority, the Welsh Ministers and a housing co-operative; (2) a private registered provider of social housing; or (3) a registered social landlord: Housing Act 1996 s 219(4) (amended by the Localism Act 2011 s 195(1), Sch 19 paras 33, 35; and by SI 2008/3002 and SI 2010/866). A direction may be given to a social landlord which is a profit-making private registered provider of social housing only in relation to charges relating to its social housing (within the meaning of the Housing and Regeneration Act 2008 Pt 2 (ss 59–278A)): Housing Act 1996 s 219(4A) (added by SI 2010/866). As to the meaning of 'private registered provider of social housing' see PARA 53; as to the meaning of 'registered social landlord' see PARA 13. As to the Homes and Communities Agency see PARA 57 et seq; and PLANNING vol 83 (2010) PARA 1454 et seq. As to the Greater London Authority see LONDON GOVERNMENT vol 71 (2013) PARA 67 et seq.

3   For the purposes of the Housing Act 1996 s 219, 'service charge' means an amount payable by a lessee of a dwelling: (1) which is payable, directly or indirectly, for repairs, maintenance or improvements; and (2) the whole or part of which varies or may vary according to the relevant costs: ss 219(6), 220(5). Cf the definition in the Landlord and Tenant Act 1985 s 18: see LANDLORD AND TENANT vol 63 (2016) PARA 614. The relevant costs are the costs or estimated

costs incurred or to be incurred by or on behalf of the social landlord, or a superior landlord, in connection with the matters for which the service charge is payable: Housing Act 1996 s 220(6). For this purpose, costs are relevant costs in relation to a service charge whether they are incurred, or to be incurred, in the period for which the service charge is payable or in an earlier or later period: s 220(6). For the purposes of s 220, 'costs' includes overheads; and 'dwelling' means a building or part of a building occupied or intended to be occupied as a separate dwelling: s 220(7). As to the meanings of 'landlord' and 'lessee' see PARA 168 note 16.

4 In the Housing Act 1996 s 219, 'assistance' means grant or other financial assistance of any kind; and directions may specify what assistance is relevant for these purposes, and to what buildings or other land any assistance is to be regarded as relevant: s 219(5).

5 Housing Act 1996 s 219(1)(a). See the Social Landlords Mandatory Reduction of Service Charges (England) Directions 1997; and the Social Landlords Discretionary Reduction of Service Charges (England) Directions 1997.

6 Housing Act 1996 s 219(1)(b).

7 Housing Act 1996 s 219(2).

8 Housing Act 1996 s 219(3)(a).

9 Housing Act 1996 s 219(3)(b). The provisions of s 220 (see note 3 and the text and notes 10–15) supplement s 219: s 219(6).

10 Housing Act 1996 s 220(1).

11 Housing Act 1996 s 220(1)(a).

12 Housing Act 1996 s 220(1)(b).

13 Housing Act 1996 s 220(2).

14 Housing Act 1996 s 220(3).

15 Housing Act 1996 s 220(4).

30. Enforcement of covenants against owner for the time being. Provision is made to secure certain controls to a local housing authority over a housing estate which it has disposed of. Where:

(1)   a local housing authority[1] has disposed of land held by the authority for any of the purposes of the Housing Act 1985 and the person to whom the disposal was made has entered into a covenant with the authority concerning the land; or

(2)   an owner[2] of any land has entered into a covenant with the local housing authority concerning the land for the purposes of any of those provisions,

the authority may enforce the covenant against the persons deriving title under the covenantor, even though the authority is not in possession of or interested in any land for the benefit of which the covenant was entered into[3]. These controls can be exercised in like manner and to the like extent as if the authority had been possessed of or interested in such land[4].

1 As to the meaning of 'local housing authority' see PARA 11.

2 'Owner', in relation to premises: (1) means a person (other than a mortgagee not in possession) who is for the time being entitled to dispose of the fee simple absolute in the premises, whether in possession or in reversion; and (2) includes also a person holding or entitled to the rents and profits of the premises under a lease of which the unexpired term exceeds three years: Housing Act 1985 s 623(1).

3 Housing Act 1985 s 609.

4 Housing Act 1985 s 609. Apart from this provision, such restrictive covenants could not be enforced against subsequent purchasers: see *LCC v Allen* [1914] 3 KB 642, CA. The Housing Act 1985 s 609 does not permit the enforcement of positive covenants against a subsequent purchaser of the freehold: *Cantrell v Wycombe District Council* [2008] EWCA Civ 866, [2009] 1 P & CR 277, [2009] PTSR 96.

(viii) Power to Authorise Conversion of House into Flats

31. Power of court to authorise conversion of house into flats. The local housing authority[1], or a person interested in any premises, may apply to the County Court where:

(1) owing to changes in the character of the neighbourhood[2] in which the premises are situated, they cannot readily be let[3] as a single dwelling house, but could readily be let for occupation if converted into two or more dwelling houses; or

(2) planning permission has been granted[4] for the use of the premises as converted into two or more separate dwelling houses instead of as a single dwelling house,

and the conversion is prohibited or restricted by the provisions of the lease[5] of the premises, or by a restrictive covenant affecting the premises, or otherwise[6]. The court may, after giving any person interested an opportunity of being heard, vary the terms of the lease or other instrument imposing the prohibition or restriction, subject to such conditions and upon such terms as the court may think just[7].

1 As to the meaning of 'local housing authority' see PARA 11.
2 As to the meaning of 'changes in the character of the neighbourhood' see *Alliance Economic Investment Co v Berton* (1923) 92 LJKB 750, CA.
3 In the Housing Act 1985, 'lease' and 'tenancy' have the same meaning; both expressions include a sublease or subtenancy and an agreement for a lease or tenancy or sublease or a subtenancy; and the expressions 'lessor' and 'lessee' and 'landlord' and 'tenant', and references to letting, to the grant of a lease or to covenants or terms are to be construed accordingly: s 621(1)–(3).
4 Ie under the Town and Country Planning Act 1990 Pt III (ss 55–106C) (general planning control): see PLANNING vol 81 (2010) PARA 288 et seq.
5 As to the meaning of 'lease' see note 3.
6 Housing Act 1985 s 610(1) (amended by the Local Government and Housing Act 1989 s 165(1), Sch 9 para 88; and the Planning (Consequential Provisions) Act 1990 s 4, Sch 2 para 71(5)). As to the meaning of 'conversion' see *Josephine Trust Ltd v Champagne* [1963] 2 QB 160, [1962] 3 All ER 136, CA. Although the underlying policy of the Housing Act 1985 s 610 appears to be to facilitate the more intensive use of large dwelling houses the Act does not create any presumption in favour of the variation of a restrictive covenant where planning permission has been granted; the court has to take account of all relevant factors and to carry out a balancing exercise, giving such weight as it judges appropriate to the various factors in the exercise of its discretion: see *Lawntown Ltd v Camenzuli* [2007] EWCA Civ 949, [2008] 1 All ER 446, [2008] 1 WLR 2656.
7 Housing Act 1985 s 610(2).

(3) TRIBUNALS

(i) Constitution and Powers of Tribunals

32. England: First-tier Tribunal and Upper Tribunal. The functions of rent assessment committees[1] for areas in England have been transferred to the First-tier Tribunal or, where determined by or under Tribunal Procedure Rules[2] in relation to any particular case, the Upper Tribunal[3]. Rent assessment committees for areas in England have been abolished[4].

The First-tier Tribunal or the Upper Tribunal has jurisdiction in a large number of matters[5] and in appeals[6] relating to housing in England. The tribunal also has jurisdiction over landlord and tenant matters such as rents for assured and protected tenancies[7], service charges[8] and other leasehold matters[9], and enfranchisement and new lease claims for both houses and flats[10].

1 As to rent assessment committees exercising the jurisdiction of residential property tribunals see PARAS 34–35.
2 As to Tribunal Procedure Rules see COURTS AND TRIBUNALS vol 24 (2010) PARAS 918–920. As to transfer to the Upper Tribunal see the Tribunal Procedure (First-tier Tribunal) (Property Chamber) Rules 2013, SI 2013/1169, r 25; and the Tribunal Procedure (Upper Tribunal) (Lands Chamber) Rules 2010, SI 2010/2600, rr 44A, 45 (r 44A added by SI 2013/1188).

3   See the Transfer of Tribunal Functions Order 2013, SI 2013/1036, art 2(1). As to the First-tier Tribunal and the Upper Tribunal see COURTS AND TRIBUNALS vol 24 (2010) PARA 864 et seq. As to procedure in the First-tier Tribunal and the Upper Tribunal see PARA 36 et seq.

4   See the Transfer of Tribunal Functions Order 2013, SI 2013/1036, art 2(2).

5   Eg, in relation to property in England, determining any question arising under the Housing Act 1985 Sch 5 para 11 (right to buy excluded for certain dwelling houses for elderly persons: see PARA 252); proceedings to determine or vary a lease where a prohibition order has become operative (see PARA 603); proceedings relating to expenses incurred by a local housing authority in executing a demolition order (see PARA 625); proceedings to determine or vary a lease where a demolition order has become operative (see PARA 647); making rent repayment orders in relation to HMOs (see PARA 694); making rent repayment orders in relation to unlicensed Part 3 houses (see PARA 717); making banning orders under the Housing and Planning Act 2016 Pt 2 (ss 13–56) (see PARAS 719–720); revoking or varying banning orders (see PARA 721); making rent repayment orders under the Housing and Planning Act 2016 Pt 2 Ch 4 (ss 40–52) (see PARA 727); applications to authorise interim management orders (see PARAS 746, 747); applications to enforce management schemes (see PARA 761); authorising the making of an interim empty dwelling management order (see PARAS 782, 783); applications relating to breach of management schemes (see PARA 796); applications to determine a lease or licence where an empty dwelling management order is in force (see PARA 801); applications for compensation to third parties where an interim empty dwelling management order is in force (see PARA 805).

6   Eg, in relation to property in England, appeals against a final notice imposing a financial penalty (see PARA 398); appeals relating to improvement notices (see PARAS 580–583); appeals relating to the recovery of expenses incurred in taking enforcement action without agreement (see PARA 587); appeals relating to prohibition orders (see PARAS 598–600); appeals relating to emergency measures (see PARA 616); appeals against demolition orders (see PARA 622); appeals relating to HMO declarations (see PARAS 672, 673); appeals relating to temporary exemptions from the licensing requirement under the Housing Act 2004 Pt 2 (ss 55–78) or Pt 3 (ss 79–100) in England (see PARAS 680, 710); appeals against licence decisions (see PARA 691); appeals relating to overcrowding notices (see PARAS 702, 703); appeals under the Housing and Planning Act 2016 Pt 4 (see PARAS 723, 724, 726); appeals relating to expenditure by a local housing authority where an interim management order has been made (see PARA 752); appeals relating to interim or final management orders (see PARAS 770–773, 776); appeals relating to financial arrangements when an interim empty dwelling management order is in force (see PARA 788); appeals against decisions relating to empty dwelling management orders (see PARAS 806–811); appeals relating to sanctions imposed, or other action taken, by the Secretary of State in relation to the Green Deal (see PARA 890).

7   See LANDLORD AND TENANT vol 63 (2016) PARA 908.

8   See LANDLORD AND TENANT vol 63 (2016) PARA 638.

9   Eg variation of a lease under the Landlord and Tenant Act 1987: see LANDLORD AND TENANT vol 62 (2016) PARA 141 et seq.

10   See LANDLORD AND TENANT vol 64 (2016) PARAS 1304, 1513. As to jurisdiction in landlord and tenant matters generally see LANDLORD AND TENANT vol 62 (2016) PARA 61.

33. Additional powers of First-tier Tribunal and Upper Tribunal. The First-tier Tribunal and Upper Tribunal[1] exercising any jurisdiction conferred by or under the Caravan Sites and Control of Development Act 1960, the Mobile Homes Act 1983, the Housing Act 1985 or the Housing Act 2004 has, in addition to any specific powers exercisable by them in exercising that jurisdiction, the following general power[2]. The tribunal's general power is a power to give such directions as the tribunal considers necessary or desirable for securing the just, expeditious and economical disposal of the proceedings or any issue in or in connection with them[3].

When exercising jurisdiction under the Housing Act 2004, the directions which may be given by the tribunal under its general power include (where appropriate)

(1)   directions requiring a licence to be granted under Part 2[4] or 3[5] of that Act;

(2)   directions requiring any licence so granted to contain such terms as are specified in the directions;

(3)   directions requiring any order made under Part 4[6] of that Act to contain such terms as are so specified;

(4)   directions that any building or part of a building so specified is to be treated as if an HMO declaration[7] had been served in respect of it on such date as is so specified[8];

(5)   directions requiring the payment of money by one party to the proceedings to another by way of compensation, damages or otherwise[9].

When exercising jurisdiction under the Caravan Sites and Control of Development Act 1960, the directions which may be given by a tribunal under its general power include (where appropriate) directions requiring the payment of money by one party to the proceedings to another by way of compensation, damages or otherwise[10].

When exercising jurisdiction under the Mobile Homes Act 1983, the directions which may be given by the tribunal under its general power include (where appropriate):

(a)   directions requiring the payment of money by one party to the proceedings to another by way of compensation, damages or otherwise;

(b)   directions requiring the arrears of pitch fees or the recovery of overpayments of pitch fees[11] to be paid in such manner and by such date as may be specified in the directions;

(c)   directions requiring cleaning, repairs, restoration, re-positioning or other works to be carried out in connection with a mobile home[12], pitch[13] or protected site[14] in such manner as may be specified in the directions;

(d)   directions requiring the establishment, provision or maintenance of any service or amenity in connection with a mobile home, pitch or protected site in such manner as may be specified in the directions[15].

1   As to the First-tier Tribunal and the Upper Tribunal see COURTS AND TRIBUNALS vol 24 (2010) PARA 864 et seq. As to the transfer of the functions of residential property tribunals for areas in England to the First-tier Tribunal and the Upper Tribunal see PARA 32.
2   Housing Act 2004 s 231A(1) (s 231A added by SI 2013/1036; the Housing Act 2004 s 231A(1) amended by SI 2014/1900).
3   Housing Act 2004 s 231A(2) (as added: see note 2).
4   Ie the Housing Act 2004 Pt 2 (ss 55–78) (licensing of houses in multiple occupation): see PARA 674 et seq.
5   Ie the Housing Act 2004 Pt 3 (ss 79–100) (selective licensing of other residential accommodation): see PARA 704 et seq.
6   Ie the Housing Act 2004 Pt 4 (ss 101–147) (additional control provisions in relation to residential accommodation): see PARA 745 et seq.
7   As to HMO declarations see PARA 672.
8   Such a direction is to be an excluded decision for the purposes of the Tribunals, Courts and Enforcement Act 2007 ss 11(1), 13(1) (see COURTS AND TRIBUNALS vol 24 (2010) PARAS 928–929): Housing Act 2004 s 231A(3)(d) (as added: see note 2).
9   Housing Act 2004 s 231A(3) (as added: see note 2).
10 Housing Act 2004 s 231A(3A) (added by SI 2014/1900).
11 'Pitch fee' has the meaning given in the Mobile Homes Act 1983 Sch 1 Pt I Ch 2 para 29, Ch 3 para 13 or Ch 4 para 27 (as the case may be): Housing Act 2004 s 231A(5) (as added: see note 2).
12 'Mobile home' has the same meaning as in the Mobile Homes 1983 (see s 5): Housing Act 2004 s 231A(5) (as added: see note 2).
13 'Pitch' has the meaning given by the Mobile Homes Act 1983 Sch 1 Pt I Ch 1 para 1(4): Housing Act 2004 s 231A(5) (as added: see note 2).
14 'Protected site' has the same meaning as in the Mobile Homes 1983 (see s 5): Housing Act 2004 s 231A(5) (as added: see note 2).
15 Housing Act 2004 s 231A(4) (as added: see note 2).

34.   Wales: residential property tribunals. In Wales, any jurisdiction conferred on a residential property tribunal by or under any enactment[1] is exercisable by a rent assessment committee[2]. When so constituted for exercising any such jurisdiction, a rent assessment committee is known as a residential property tribunal[3]. The National Assembly for Wales may by order make provision for and in connection with conferring on residential property tribunals, in relation to such matters as are specified in the order, such jurisdiction as is so specified[4].

Residential property tribunals have jurisdiction in a large number of matters[5] and in appeals[6] relating to housing in Wales.

1 In the Housing Act 2004 s 229, 'enactment' includes an enactment comprised in subordinate legislation (within the meaning of the Interpretation Act 1978: see STATUTES AND LEGISLATIVE PROCESS vol 96 (2012) PARA 609): Housing Act 2004 s 229(5).

2 Ie a rent assessment committee constituted in accordance with the Rent Act 1977 s 65, Sch 10 (see LANDLORD AND TENANT vol 63 (2016) PARA 737): Housing Act 2004 s 229(1). Residential property tribunals are now only constituted in Wales and rent assessment committees for areas in England have been abolished: see PARA 32.

3 Housing Act 2004 s 229(2). As to the powers of residential property tribunals see PARA 35; as to their procedure see PARA 39 et seq; as to appeals from tribunals see PARA 50.

4 Housing Act 2004 s 229(3) (amended by SI 2013/1036). An order under the Housing Act 2004 s 229(3) may modify an enactment (including the Housing Act 2004): s 229(4).

5 Eg, in relation to property in Wales, proceedings to determine or vary a lease where a prohibition order has become operative in Wales (see PARA 603); proceedings relating to expenses incurred by a local housing authority in executing a demolition order in Wales (see PARA 625); proceedings to determine or vary a lease where a demolition order has become operative in Wales (see PARA 647); making rent repayment orders in relation to HMOs in Wales (see PARA 694); making rent repayment orders in relation to unlicensed Part 3 houses in Wales (see PARA 717); making rent stopping orders and rent repayment orders under the Housing (Wales) Act 2014 Pt 1 (ss 1–49) (see PARAS 741, 742); applications to authorise interim management orders (see PARAS 746, 747); applications to enforce management schemes (see PARA 761); authorising the making of an interim empty dwelling management order (see PARAS 782, 783); applications relating to breach of management schemes (see PARA 796); applications to determine a lease or licence where an empty dwelling management order is in force (see PARA 801); applications for compensation to third parties where an interim empty dwelling management order is in force (see PARA 805).

6 Eg, in relation to property in Wales, appeals relating to improvement notices (see PARAS 580–583); appeals relating to the recovery of expenses incurred in taking enforcement action without agreement (see PARA 587); appeals relating to prohibition orders (see PARAS 598–600); appeals relating to emergency measures (see PARA 616); appeals against demolition orders (see PARA 622); appeals relating to HMO declarations (see PARAS 672, 673); appeals relating to temporary exemptions from the licensing requirement under the Housing Act 2004 Pt 2 (ss 55–78) or Pt 3 (ss 79–100) (see PARAS 680, 710); appeals against licence decisions (see PARA 691); appeals relating to overcrowding notices (see PARAS 702, 703); appeals under the Housing (Wales) Act 2014 Pt 1 (see PARAS 735, 738); appeals relating to expenditure by a local housing authority where an interim management order has been made (see PARA 752); appeals relating to interim or final management orders (see PARAS 770–773, 776); appeals relating to financial arrangements when an interim empty dwelling management order is in force (see PARA 788); appeals against decisions relating to empty dwelling management orders (see PARAS 806–811).

35. Powers of residential property tribunals in Wales. A residential property tribunal[1] exercising any jurisdiction in respect of premises situated in Wales by virtue of any enactment[2] has, in addition to any specific powers exercisable by it in exercising that jurisdiction in respect of premises situated in Wales, the following general power[3]. The tribunal's general power is a power by order to give such directions as the tribunal considers necessary or desirable for securing the just, expeditious and economical disposal of the proceedings or any issue raised in or in connection with them[4].

In deciding whether to give directions under its general power a tribunal must have regard to:

(1)   the matters falling to be determined in the proceedings;

(2)   any other circumstances appearing to the tribunal to be relevant; and

(3)   the provisions of the enactment by virtue of which it is exercising jurisdiction and of any other enactment appearing to it to be relevant[5].

A tribunal may give directions under its general power whether or not they were originally sought by a party to the proceedings[6].

When exercising jurisdiction under the Housing Act 2004, the directions which may be given by a tribunal under its general power include (where appropriate):

(a)   directions requiring a licence to be granted under Part 2[7] or Part 3[8] of that Act;

(b)   directions requiring any licence so granted to contain such terms as are specified in the directions;

(c)   directions requiring any order made under Part 4[9] of that Act to contain such terms as are so specified;

(d)   directions that any building or part of a building so specified is to be treated as if an HMO declaration[10] had been served in respect of it on such date as is so specified (without there being any right to appeal against it[11]);

(e)   directions requiring the payment of money by one party to the proceedings to another by way of compensation, damages or otherwise[12].

When exercising jurisdiction under the Caravan Sites and Control of Development Act 1960 or Part 2 of the Mobile Homes (Wales) Act 2013[13], the directions which may be given by a tribunal under its general power include (where appropriate) directions requiring the payment of money by one party to the proceedings to another by way of compensation, damages or otherwise[14]. When exercising jurisdiction under the Mobile Homes Act 1983 or Part 4 of the Mobile Homes (Wales) Act 2013[15], the directions which may be given by a tribunal under its general power include (where appropriate):

(i)   directions requiring the payment of money by one party to the proceedings to another by way of compensation, damages or otherwise;

(ii)   directions requiring the arrears of pitch fees[16] or the recovery of overpayments of pitch fees to be paid in such manner and by such date as may be specified in the directions;

(iii)   directions requiring cleaning, repairs, restoration, re-positioning or other works to be carried out in connection with a mobile home[17], pitch[18] or the protected site[19] in such manner as may be specified in the directions;

(iv)   directions requiring the establishment, provision or maintenance of any service or amenity in connection with a mobile home, pitch or protected site in such manner as may be specified in the directions[20].

1   As to the constitution of residential property tribunals see PARA 34.
2   As to the meaning of 'enactment' see PARA 34 note 1 (definition applied by the Housing Act 2004 s 230(8)).
3   Housing Act 2004 s 230(1) (amended by virtue of SI 2013/1036). Nothing in any enactment conferring specific powers on a residential property tribunal is to be regarded as affecting the operation of the Housing Act 2004 s 230(1)–(5B): s 230(6).
4   Housing Act 2004 s 230(2).
5   Housing Act 2004 s 230(3).
6   Housing Act 2004 s 230(4).
7   Ie the Housing Act 2004 Pt 2 (ss 55–78) (licensing of houses in multiple occupation): see PARA 674 et seq.
8   Ie the Housing Act 2004 Pt 3 (ss 79–100) (selective licensing of other residential accommodation): see PARA 704 et seq.
9   Ie the Housing Act 2004 Pt 4 (ss 101–147) (additional control provisions in relation to residential accommodation): see PARA 745 et seq.
10   As to HMO declarations see the Housing Act 2004 s 255; and PARA 672.
11   Ie under the Housing Act 2004 s 255(9): see PARA 672.

12 Housing Act 2004 s 230(5).

13 Ie the Mobile Homes (Wales) Act 2013 Pt 2 (ss 4–39) (licensing of mobile home sites etc).

14 Housing Act 2004 s 230(5ZA) (added by the Mobile Homes Act 2013 s 7(1), (2); and amended by the Mobile Homes (Wales) Act 2013 s 58(1), Sch 4 para 9(1), (2)(a)).

15 Ie the Mobile Homes (Wales) Act 2013 Pt 4 (ss 48–55) (mobile home agreements).

16 'Pitch fee' has the meaning given in the Mobile Homes Act 1983 Sch 1 Pt I Ch 2 para 29, Ch 3 para 13 or Ch 4 para 27 (as the case may be) or the Mobile Homes (Wales) Act 2013 s 60: Housing Act 2004 s 230(5B) (s 230(5A), (5B) added in relation to England by SI 2011/1005 and in relation to Wales by SI 2012/899; the Housing Act 2004 s 230(5B) amended by the Mobile Homes (Wales) Act 2013 s 58(1), Sch 4 para 9(1), (2)(c)).

17 'Mobile home' has the same meaning as in the Mobile Homes 1983 (see s 5) or the Mobile Homes (Wales) Act 2013 (see ss 2, 60): Housing Act 2004 s 230(5B) (as added and amended: see note 16).

18 'Pitch' has the meaning given by the Mobile Homes Act 1983 Sch 1 Pt I Ch 1 para 1(4) or the Mobile Homes (Wales) Act 2013 s 55: Housing Act 2004 s 230(5B) (as added and amended: see note 16).

19 'Protected site' has the same meaning as in the Mobile Homes 1983 (see s 5) or the Mobile Homes (Wales) Act 2013 (see ss 2, 60): Housing Act 2004 s 230(5B) (as added and amended: see note 16).

20 Housing Act 2004 s 230(5A) (as added (see note 16); amended by the Mobile Homes (Wales) Act 2013 Sch 4 para 9(1), (2)(b)).

(ii) Procedure

A. IN ENGLAND

36. Proceedings in First-tier Tribunal and Upper Tribunal. Proceedings relating to residential property are allocated to the Property Chamber of the First-tier Tribunal and in the Upper Tribunal to the Lands Chamber[1]. The practice and procedure to be followed in the First-tier Tribunal and the Upper Tribunal is governed by procedure rules[2].

1 See COURTS AND TRIBUNALS vol 24 (2010) PARAS 876 et seq, 883 et seq. As to the Upper Tribunal (Lands Chamber) see also COMPULSORY ACQUISITION OF LAND vol 18 (2009) PARA 720 et seq.

2 As to procedure in the First-tier Tribunal and the Upper Tribunal see COURTS AND TRIBUNALS vol 24 (2010) PARA 905 et seq. As to rules and practice directions see COURTS AND TRIBUNALS vol 24 (2010) PARA 918 et seq; and the Tribunal Procedure (First-tier Tribunal) (Property Chamber) Rules 2013, SI 2013/1169 (amended by SI 2014/2128), which govern the practice and procedure to be followed in the First-tier Tribunal in matters including residential property matters. Nothing in those Rules overrides any specific provision that is contained in an enactment which confers jurisdiction on the Tribunal: r 2.

The overriding objective of the Rules is to enable the tribunal to deal with cases fairly and justly, and parties must help the tribunal to further the overriding objective and co-operate with the tribunal generally: see r 3. Alternative dispute resolution is encouraged: see r 4. As to the power to delegate to staff see r 5. As to case management see r 6. As to the procedure for applying for and giving directions see r 7, and as to failure to comply with rules, practice directions or tribunal directions see r 8. As to the power to strike out a party's case see r 9. As to the addition, substitution and removal of parties see r 10 and as to representatives of parties see r 14. As to the payment of fees see r 11. As to orders for costs, reimbursement of fees and interest on costs see r 13. As to calculating time see r 15. As to providing documents see r 16 and as to prevention of disclosure or publication of documents and information see r 17. As to disclosure, evidence and submissions see r 18, as to expert evidence see r 19 and as to witnesses see r 20. As to site inspections see r 21. As to withdrawal of a case see r 22. For guidance on the power of the tribunal under r 13(1)(b), to award costs against a party on account of their unreasonable behaviour in bringing, defending or conducting proceedings before it, see *Willow Court Management Co (1985) Ltd v Alexander* [2016] UKUT 290 (LC).

If two or more cases have been started before the tribunal, in each such case the tribunal has not made a decision disposing of the proceedings and the cases give rise to common or related issues, the tribunal may direct that one or more such cases be specified as a lead case, and stay the other cases: see rr 23, 24.

As to transfer of cases to the Upper Tribunal see r 25. See also the Tribunal Procedure (Upper Tribunal) (Lands Chamber) Rules 2010, SI 2010/2600, rr 44A, 45 (r 44A added by SI 2013/1188).

As to starting proceedings and time limits see the Tribunal Procedure (First-tier Tribunal) (Property Chamber) Rules 2013, SI 2013/1169, rr 26, 27. As to referred and transferred cases see r 28. As to notice to respondents and respondents' response see rr 29, 30.

As to decision with or without a hearing see r 31. As to hearings see rr 32–34. As to consent orders see r 35. As to decisions see r 36.

As to urgent cases see rr 44, 46. As to the making of interim orders see r 47 (amended by SI 2014/2128). As to cases where a mobile home is having a detrimental effect on the amenity of the site the Tribunal Procedure (First-tier Tribunal) (Property Chamber) Rules 2013, SI 2013/1169, r 48.

See also the Tribunal Procedure (Upper Tribunal) (Lands Chamber) Rules 2010, SI 2010/2600 (amended by SI 2012/500, SI 2013/1188 and SI 2014/514).

As to the fees payable in such proceedings see the First-tier Tribunal (Property Chamber) Fees Order 2013, SI 2013/1179 (amended by SI 2013/2302, SI 2014/182, SI 2014/1900, SI 2016/211 and SI 2016/807). The application fee, where no other fee is specified, on filing an application to commence proceedings in a residential property case is £100; on filing an application under the Mobile Homes Act 1983 Sch 1 Pt I Ch 2 para 15(b) (determination of the amount of the pitch fee other than on local authority and county council gypsy and traveller sites) is £20; on filing an application under Sch 1 Pt I Ch 2 para 18(1)(a)(iii) (determination to take into account sums expended by the owner since the last review date on improvements) is £20; on filing an application under Sch 1 Pt I Ch 4 para 14(b) (determination of the amount of the pitch fee on local authority or county council gypsy and traveller sites) is £20; on filing an application under Sch 1 Pt I Ch 4 para 16(1)(a)(iii) (determination to take into account sums expended by the owner since the last review date on improvements) is £20: see the First-tier Tribunal (Property Chamber) Fees Order 2013, SI 2013/1179, art 4, Sch 1 fees 1.1, 1.3–1.6 (art 4 amended, Sch 1 substituted by SI 2016/807). Where an application is made under two or more provisions, the fee payable in respect of the application is the highest fee which would have been payable if a separate application had been made under each of the provisions: First-tier Tribunal (Property Chamber) Fees Order 2013, SI 2013/1179, Sch 1 (as so substituted).

The hearing fee payable on receiving notice of a hearing date is £200: Sch 1 Fee 2.1 (as so substituted). Fee 2.1 only applies to an application which attracts fee 1.1 or 1.2. Where a number of applications are joined together for the purposes of a hearing, fee 2 is payable only once in respect of that hearing: Sch 1 Fee 2 (as so substituted).

As to the fees payable in the Upper Tribunal see the Upper Tribunal (Lands Chamber) Fees Order 2009, SI 2009/1114 (amended by SI 2010/2601, SI 2013/1199, SI 2013/2302, SI 2014/590, SI 2016/211 and SI 2016/434). As to tribunal fees generally see COURTS AND TRIBUNALS vol 24 (2010) PARA 871.

37.   Transfer of certain proceedings from court to First-tier Tribunal. Where, in any proceedings before a court, there falls for determination a question which the First-tier Tribunal or the Upper Tribunal[1] would have jurisdiction to determine on an appeal or application to the tribunal in connection with the Mobile Homes Act 1983[2], the Housing Act 1985 or the Housing Act 2004[3], the court:

(1)   may by order transfer to the First-tier Tribunal so much of the proceedings as relate to the determination of that question;

(2)   may then dispose of all or any remaining proceedings pending the determination of that question by the First-tier Tribunal or the Upper Tribunal, as it thinks fit[4].

Where the First-tier Tribunal or the Upper Tribunal has determined the question, the court may give effect to the determination in an order of the court[5].

Rules of court may prescribe the procedure to be followed in a court in connection with or in consequence of a transfer under these provisions[6].

Nothing in the Housing Act 2004, in the Caravan Sites and Control of Development Act 1960[7] or in the Mobile Homes Act 1983 affects any power of a court to make an order that could be made by the tribunal (such as an order quashing a licence granted or order made by a local housing authority) in a case where:

(a)   the court has not made a transfer under these provisions; and

(b)   the order is made by the court in connection with disposing of any proceedings before it[8].

1   As to the First-tier Tribunal and the Upper Tribunal see COURTS AND TRIBUNALS vol 24 (2010) PARA 864 et seq. As to the transfer of the functions of residential property tribunals for areas in England to the First-tier Tribunal and the Upper Tribunal see PARA 32.
2   As to the jurisdiction of the First-tier Tribunal and the Upper Tribunal under the Mobile Homes Act 1983 see LANDLORD AND TENANT vol 64 (2016) PARA 1765.
3   As to the jurisdiction of the First-tier Tribunal and the Upper Tribunal under the Housing Act 1985 and the Housing Act 2004 see PARA 32.
4   Housing Act 2004 s 231B(1) (s 231B added by SI 2013/1036).
5   Housing Act 2004 s 231B(2) (as added: see note 2).
6   Housing Act 2004 s 231B(3) (as added: see note 2).
7   As to the Caravan Sites and Control of Development Act 1960 see PLANNING vol 83 (2010) PARA 1210 et seq.
8   Housing Act 2004 s 231B(4) (as added (see note 2); amended by SI 2014/1900).

38.   Enforcement. Any decision of the First-tier Tribunal or Upper Tribunal[1] under or in connection with the Caravan Sites and Control of Development Act 1960, the Mobile Homes Act 1983, the Housing Act 1985 or the Housing Act 2004, other than a decision ordering the payment of a sum[2], is to be enforceable with the permission of the County Court in the same way as orders of such court[3].

1   As to the First-tier Tribunal and the Upper Tribunal see COURTS AND TRIBUNALS vol 24 (2010) PARA 864 et seq; COMPULSORY ACQUISITION OF LAND vol 18 (2009) PARA 720 et seq. As to the transfer of the functions of residential property tribunals for areas in England to the First-tier Tribunal and the Upper Tribunal see PARA 32.
2   As to enforcement of such a decision see the Tribunals, Courts and Enforcement Act 2007 s 27 (enforcement); and COURTS AND TRIBUNALS vol 24 (2010) PARA 924.
3   Housing Act 2004 s 231D (added by SI 2013/1036; and amended by SI 2014/1900).

B.   IN WALES

39.   Procedure regulations; commencement and parties. The Housing Act 2004 makes provision for the procedure of residential property tribunals in respect of premises situated in Wales[1]. The Welsh Ministers[2] may make regulations about the procedure of residential property tribunals[3].

Procedure regulations[4] may include provision in relation to applications to tribunals:

(1)   about the form of such applications and the particulars to be contained in them;

(2)   requiring the service of notices of such applications; and

(3)   in the case of specified applications[5], requiring the service of copies of the draft orders submitted with the applications[6].

Procedure regulations may include provision in relation to appeals to tribunals:

(a)   about the form of notices of appeal and the particulars to be contained in them; and

(b)   requiring the service of copies of such notices[7].

Procedure regulations may include provision dispensing with the service of the notices of application or copies of the notice of appeal in such cases of urgency as are specified in the regulations[8].

Procedure regulations may include provision enabling persons to be joined as parties to the proceedings[9], and may include provision enabling persons who are not parties to proceedings before a tribunal to make oral or written representations to the tribunal[10].

1   See the Housing Act 2004 s 230(7), Sch 13; and PARA 40 et seq. Note that the time limits for bringing an appeal to a residential property tribunal vary; for example, an appeal against an improvement notice must be brought within 21 days (see PARA 580), whereas an appeal against

revocation or variation of an improvement notice must be brought within 28 days (see PARA 581). As to the constitution of residential property tribunals see PARA 34.

2 As to the Welsh Ministers see PARA 7.

3 Housing Act 2004 Sch 13 para 1(1) (amended by SI 2013/1036). Nothing in the other provisions of the Housing Act 2004 Sch 13 affects the generality of Sch 13 para 1(1): Sch 13 para 1(2).

As to the regulations that have been made see the Residential Property Tribunal Procedures and Fees (Wales) Regulations 2016, SI 2016/1110. When a tribunal exercises any power under those Regulations or interprets any regulation, it must seek to give effect to the overriding objective of dealing fairly and justly with applications which it is to determine, and parties must help the tribunal to further the overriding objective and co-operate with the tribunal generally: see reg 3. As to requests for extension of time to make an application see reg 4. As to applications see regs 5–13, Schedule. As to fees see regs 14, 44–51; and PARA 46. As to representatives see reg 15. As to the supplying of information and documents see regs 16–19, 39; and PARA 41. As to determination without a hearing see reg 20; and PARA 45. As to interim orders see reg 21; and PARA 43. As to directions see reg 22; and as to case management see regs 25, 26; and PARA 42. As to inspections see reg 23; and as to expert evidence see reg 24. As to hearings see regs 27–32. As to the tribunal's decision see reg 33. As to costs see reg 34; and PARA 47. As to withdrawal of an application see reg 35. As to enforcement see reg 36; and PARA 48. As to permission to appeal see reg 37; and PARA 50. As to assistance to participants see reg 38. As to time see reg 40. As to the power to dismiss frivolous and vexatious applications see reg 41. As to irregularities see reg 42. As to signature of documents see reg 43.

4 'Procedure regulations' means regulations under the Housing Act 2004 Sch 13 para 1 (see note 3): Sch 13 para 1(3).

5 Ie under the Housing Act 2004 s 102(4) or (7) (interim management orders: see PARA 746) or s 133(1) (interim empty dwelling management orders: see PARA 782).

6 Housing Act 2004 Sch 13 para 2(1).

7 Housing Act 2004 Sch 13 para 2(2).

8 Housing Act 2004 Sch 13 para 2(3).

9 Housing Act 2004 Sch 13 para 4(1).

10 Housing Act 2004 Sch 13 para 4(2).

40. Transfers. The following provisions apply where, in any proceedings before a court, there falls for determination a question which a tribunal[1] would have jurisdiction to determine on an application or appeal to the tribunal[2]. The court:

(1)   may by order transfer to the tribunal so much of the proceedings as relate to the determination of that question; and

(2)   may then dispose of all or any remaining proceedings, or adjourn the disposal of all or any remaining proceedings pending the determination of that question by the tribunal, as it thinks fit[3].

When the tribunal has determined the question, the court may give effect to the determination in an order of the court[4]. Nothing in the Housing Act 2004[5], the Caravan Sites and Control of Development Act 1960[6], the Mobile Homes Act 1983[7] or the Mobile Homes (Wales) Act 2013[8] affects any power of a court to make an order that could be made by a tribunal (such as an order quashing a licence granted or order made by a local housing authority) in a case where the court has not made a transfer under these provisions and the order is made by the court in connection with disposing of any proceedings before it[9].

Rules of court may prescribe the procedure to be followed in a court in connection with or in consequence of a transfer under these provisions[10], and procedure regulations[11] may prescribe the procedure to be followed in a tribunal consequent on such a transfer[12].

1 'Tribunal' means a residential property tribunal: Housing Act 2004 s 230(7), Sch 13 para 1(3). As to the constitution of residential property tribunals see PARA 34.

2 Housing Act 2004 Sch 13 para 3(1).

3 Housing Act 2004 Sch 13 para 3(2).

4 Housing Act 2004 Sch 13 para 3(3).

5 As to the jurisdiction of the tribunal under the Housing Act 2004 see PARA 34.

6 As to the jurisdiction of the tribunal under the Mobile Homes Act 1983 see LANDLORD AND TENANT vol 64 (2016) PARA 1765.

7　As to the Caravan Sites and Control of Development Act 1960 see PLANNING vol 83 (2010) PARA 1210 et seq.
8　As to the Mobile Homes (Wales) Act 2013 see LANDLORD AND TENANT vol 64 (2016) PARA 1762.
9　Housing Act 2004 Sch 13 para 3(6) (amended by the Mobile Homes Act 2013 s 7(1), (3)(a); and the Mobile Homes (Wales) Act 2013 s 58(1), Sch 4 para 9(1), (3)(a); and, in relation to England, by SI 2011/1005 and, in relation to Wales by SI 2012/899).
10　Housing Act 2004 Sch 13 para 3(4).
11　As to procedure regulations see PARA 39.
12　Housing Act 2004 Sch 13 para 3(5).

41.　Information. Procedure regulations[1] may include provision relating to the supply of information and documents by a party to the proceedings, and in particular any provision authorised by the following provisions[2]. The regulations may include provision for requiring, or empowering a residential property tribunal[3] to require a party to proceedings before the tribunal:

(1)　to supply to the tribunal information or documents specified, or of a description specified, in the regulations or in an order made by the tribunal;

(2)　to supply to any other party copies of any information or documents supplied to the tribunal;

(3)　to supply any such information, documents or copies by such time as is specified in or determined in accordance with the regulations or order[4].

The regulations may also include provision:

(a)　for granting a party to the proceedings such disclosure or inspection of documents, or such right to further information, as might be granted by the County Court[5];

(b)　for requiring persons to attend to give evidence and produce documents;

(c)　for authorising the administration of oaths to witnesses[6].

The regulations may include provision empowering a tribunal to dismiss, or allow, the whole or part of an appeal or application in a case where a party to the proceedings has failed to comply with a requirement imposed by regulations made by virtue of these provisions, or an order of the tribunal made by virtue of any such regulations[7].

1　As to procedure regulations see PARA 39. See, in particular, the Residential Property Tribunal Procedures and Fees (Wales) Regulations 2016, SI 2016/1110, regs 16–19, 39.
2　Housing Act 2004 s 230(7), Sch 13 para 5(1).
3　See PARA 40 note 1.
4　Housing Act 2004 Sch 13 para 5(2).
5　As to disclosure, inspection etc see CIVIL PROCEDURE vol 12 (2015) PARA 621 et seq.
6　Housing Act 2004 Sch 13 para 5(3) (amended by the Crime and Courts Act 2013 s 17(5), Sch 9 para 52(1)(b), (2)).
7　Housing Act 2004 Sch 13 para 5(4).

42.　Pre-trial reviews etc. Procedure regulations[1] may include provision for the holding of a pre-trial review (on the application of a party to the proceedings or on the residential property tribunal's[2] own initiative)[3]. Procedure regulations may provide for functions of a tribunal in relation to, or at, a pre-trial review, and other functions as to preliminary or incidental matters, to be exercised by a single qualified member[4] of the panel[5].

1　As to procedure regulations see PARA 39.
2　See PARA 40 note 1.
3　Housing Act 2004 s 230(7), Sch 13 para 6(1). See the Residential Property Tribunal Procedures and Fees (Wales) Regulations 2016, SI 2016/1110, reg 25.
4　For this purpose, a person is a qualified member of the panel if he was appointed to it by the Lord Chancellor; and 'the panel' means the panel provided for in the Rent Act 1977 s 65, Sch 10 (see LANDLORD AND TENANT vol 63 (2016) PARA 737): Housing Act 2004 Sch 13 para 6(4). As to

the modification of the role of the Lord Chancellor, and the consequent transfer of various functions, see eg No 10 Downing Street press release *Modernising Government* (12 June 2003); and the Constitutional Reform Act 2005. As to the Lord Chancellor generally see CONSTITUTIONAL AND ADMINISTRATIVE LAW vol 20 (2014) PARA 256 et seq.

5   Housing Act 2004 Sch 13 para 6(2), (3). See the Residential Property Tribunal Procedures and Fees (Wales) Regulations 2016, SI 2016/1110, reg 25(6).

43. Interim orders and additional relief. Procedure regulations[1] may include provision empowering residential property tribunals[2] to make orders, on an interim basis:

(1)   suspending, in whole or in part, the effect of any decision, notice, order or licence which is the subject matter of proceedings before them;

(2)   granting any remedy which they would have had power to grant in their final decisions[3].

Procedure regulations may include provision as to any additional relief[4] which tribunals may grant in respect of proceedings before them and the grounds on which such relief may be granted[5].

1   As to procedure regulations see PARA 39. See, in particular, the Residential Property Tribunal Procedures and Fees (Wales) Regulations 2016, SI 2016/1110, reg 21.
2   See PARA 40 note 1.
3   Housing Act 2004 s 230(7), Sch 13 para 7.
4   'Additional relief' means relief additional to any relief specifically authorised by any provision of Housing Act 2004 Pts 1–4 (ss 1–147) or any provision of the Caravan Sites and Control of Development Act 1960, any provision of the Mobile Homes Act 1983 or any provision of the Mobile Homes (Wales) Act 2013: Housing Act 2004 Sch 13 para 8(2) (amended by virtue of the Mobile Homes Act 2013 s 7(1), (3)(b); by the Mobile Homes (Wales) Act 2013 s 58(1), Sch 4 para 9(1), (3)(b); and, in relation to England, by SI 2011/1005 and, in relation to Wales, by SI 2012/899).
5   Housing Act 2004 Sch 13 para 8(1).

44. Dismissal. Procedure regulations[1] may include provision empowering residential property tribunals[2] to dismiss applications, appeals or transferred proceedings, in whole or in part, on the ground that they are frivolous or vexatious, or otherwise an abuse of process[3].

1   As to procedure regulations see PARA 39.
2   See PARA 40 note 1.
3   Housing Act 2004 s 230(7), Sch 13 para 9. See the Residential Property Tribunal Procedures and Fees (Wales) Regulations 2016, SI 2016/1110, reg 41.

45. Determination without a hearing. Procedure regulations[1] may include provision for the determination of applications, appeals or transferred proceedings without an oral hearing[2]. Such regulations may include provision enabling a single qualified member of the panel[3] to decide whether an oral hearing is appropriate in a particular case[4], and for a single qualified member of the panel to make determinations without an oral hearing[5].

1   As to procedure regulations see PARA 39. See, in particular, the Residential Property Tribunal Procedures and Fees (Wales) Regulations 2016, SI 2016/1110, reg 20.
2   Housing Act 2004 s 230(7), Sch 13 para 10(1).
3   For this purpose, a person is a qualified member of the panel if he was appointed to it by the Lord Chancellor; and 'the panel' means the panel provided for in the Rent Act 1977 s 65, Sch 10 (see LANDLORD AND TENANT vol 63 (2016) PARA 737): Housing Act 2004 Sch 13 para 10(4). As to the modification of the role of the Lord Chancellor, and the consequent transfer of various functions, see eg No 10 Downing Street press release *Modernising Government* (12 June 2003); and the Constitutional Reform Act 2005. As to the Lord Chancellor generally see CONSTITUTIONAL AND ADMINISTRATIVE LAW vol 20 (2014) PARA 256 et seq.
4   Housing Act 2004 Sch 13 para 10(2).
5   Housing Act 2004 Sch 13 para 10(3).

46. Fees. Procedure regulations[1] may include provision requiring the payment of fees in respect of applications, appeals or transfers of proceedings to, or oral hearings by, residential property tribunals[2]. The fees payable are to be such as are specified in or determined in accordance with procedure regulations[3]; but the fee (or, where fees are payable in respect of both an application, appeal or transfer and an oral hearing, the aggregate of the fees) payable by a person in respect of any proceedings must not exceed £500 or such other amount as may be specified in procedure regulations[4].

Procedure regulations may empower a tribunal to require a party to proceedings before it to reimburse another party to the proceedings the whole or any part of any fees paid by him[5]. Procedure regulations may provide for the reduction or waiver of fees by reference to the financial resources of the party by whom they are to be paid or met[6], and if they do so they may apply, subject to such modifications as may be specified in the regulations, any other statutory means-testing regime as it has effect from time to time[7].

1   As to procedure regulations see PARA 39. As to the regulations that have been made see the Residential Property Tribunal Procedures and Fees (Wales) Regulations 2016, SI 2016/1110, regs 14, 44–51. Where a fee which is payable under Pt 3 (regs 44–52) is not paid within a period of 14 days from the date on which the application is received, the application is treated as withdrawn unless the tribunal is satisfied that there are reasonable grounds not to do so: reg 14. See reg 44 (prescribing a fee of £155 for applications under the Housing Act 1985 s 269(1) (demolition orders: see PARA 622) or s 318(1) (authorising execution of works on unfit premises or for improvement) (see PARA 647)); the Residential Property Tribunal Procedures and Fees (Wales) Regulations 2016, SI 2016/1110, reg 45 (prescribing a fee of £155 for certain appeals and applications under the Housing Act 2004); the Residential Property Tribunal Procedures and Fees (Wales) Regulations 2016, SI 2016/1110, reg 46 (prescribing a fee of £155 for applications under the Mobile Homes (Wales) Act 2013); the Residential Property Tribunal Procedures and Fees (Wales) Regulations 2016, SI 2016/1110, reg 47 (prescribing a fee of £155 for applications under the Housing (Wales) Act 2014); the Residential Property Tribunal Procedures and Fees (Wales) Regulations 2016, SI 2016/1110, reg 48 (prescribing a fee of £155 for applications made under the Consumer Rights Act 2015 Sch 9 para 5 (see AGENCY)). See also the Residential Property Tribunal Procedures and Fees (Wales) Regulations 2016, SI 2016/1110, reg 49 as to payment of fees.

2   Housing Act 2004 s 230(7), Sch 13 para 11(1). As to tribunals see PARA 40 note 1.
3   Housing Act 2004 Sch 13 para 11(2).
4   Housing Act 2004 Sch 13 para 11(3).
5   Housing Act 2004 Sch 13 para 11(4). See the Residential Property Tribunal Procedures and Fees (Wales) Regulations 2016, SI 2016/1110, reg 51.
6   Housing Act 2004 Sch 13 para 11(5). See the Residential Property Tribunal Procedures and Fees (Wales) Regulations 2016, SI 2016/1110, reg 50.
7   Housing Act 2004 Sch 13 para 11(6).

47. Costs. A residential property tribunal[1] may determine that a party to proceedings before it is to pay the costs incurred by another party in connection with the proceedings in any of the following circumstances[2], namely where:

(1)   he has failed to comply with an order made by the tribunal;

(2)   in accordance with regulations[3], the tribunal dismisses, or allows, the whole or part of an application or appeal by reason of his failure to comply with a requirement imposed by regulations as to the provision of information[4];

(3)   in accordance with regulations[5], the tribunal dismisses the whole or part of an application or appeal made by him to the tribunal;

(4)   he has, in the opinion of the tribunal, acted frivolously, vexatiously, abusively, disruptively or otherwise unreasonably in connection with the proceedings[6].

The amount which a party to proceedings may be ordered to pay in the proceedings by a determination under these provisions must not exceed: (a) £500 or, in the case of an application to a tribunal under the Mobile Homes Act 1983, £5,000; or (b) such other amount as may be specified in procedure regulations[7]. A person may not be required to pay costs incurred by another person in connection with proceedings before a tribunal, except: (i) by a determination under these provisions; or (ii) in accordance with provision made by any enactment[8] other than these provisions[9].

1 See PARA 40 note 1.
2 Housing Act 2004 s 230(7), Sch 13 para 12(1). The tribunal must not make a determination under Sch 13 para 12 in respect of a party without first giving that party an opportunity of making representations to the tribunal: Residential Property Tribunal Procedures and Fees (Wales) Regulations 2016, SI 2016/1110, reg 34(1).
3 Ie regulations made by virtue of the Housing Act 2004 Sch 13 para 5(4): see PARA 41.
4 Ie regulations made by virtue of the Housing Act 2004 Sch 13 para 5: see PARA 41.
5 Ie regulations made by virtue of the Housing Act 2004 Sch 13 para 9: see PARA 44.
6 Housing Act 2004 Sch 13 para 12(2).
7 Housing Act 2004 Sch 13 para 12(3) (amended, in relation to England, by SI 2011/1005 and, in relation to Wales, by SI 2012/899). As to procedure regulations see PARA 39. In respect of an application to the tribunal under the Mobile Homes (Wales) Act 2013 or the Mobile Homes (Site Rules) (Wales) Regulations 2014, SI 2014/1764, the amount which a party to proceedings may be ordered to pay in the proceedings by a determination made under the Housing Act 2004 Sch 13 para 12 must not exceed £10,000: Residential Property Tribunal Procedures and Fees (Wales) Regulations 2016, SI 2016/1110, reg 34(3).
8 As to the meaning of 'enactment' see PARA 34 note 1 (definition applied by the Housing Act 2004 s 230(8)).
9 Housing Act 2004 Sch 13 para 12(4).

48. Enforcement. Procedure regulations[1] may provide for decisions of residential property tribunals[2] to be enforceable, with the permission of the County Court, in the same way as orders of that court[3].

1 As to procedure regulations see PARA 39.
2 See PARA 40 note 1.
3 Housing Act 2004 s 230(7), Sch 13 para 13 (amended by the Crime and Courts Act 2013 s 17(5), Sch 9 para 52(1)(b), (2)). See the Residential Property Tribunal Procedures and Fees (Wales) Regulations 2016, SI 2016/1110, reg 36. As to the enforcement of County Court orders see CIVIL PROCEDURE vol 12A (2015) PARA 1270 et seq; COURTS AND TRIBUNALS.

(iii) Appeals

49. Appeals from First-tier Tribunal and Upper Tribunal (England). Any party has a right of appeal to the Upper Tribunal on any point of law arising from a decision made by the First-tier Tribunal[1] other than an excluded decision[2]. That right may be exercised only with permission given by the First-tier Tribunal or the Upper Tribunal on an application by the party[3].

A person aggrieved by a decision of the First-tier Tribunal made under or in connection with the Caravan Sites and Control of Development Act 1960[4], the Mobile Homes Act 1983[5], the Housing Act 1985[6] or the Housing Act 2004[7] may appeal to the Upper Tribunal[8]. An appeal may not be brought under this provision in relation to a decision on a point of law[9], or if the decision is set aside[10] on a review[11].

An appeal may be brought under this provision only if, on an application made by the person concerned, the First-tier Tribunal or Upper Tribunal has given its permission for the appeal to be brought[12].

Any party has a right of appeal to the Court of Appeal on any point of law arising from a decision made by the Upper Tribunal other than an excluded decision[13]. The right of appeal may be exercised only with permission given by the

Upper Tribunal, or the Court of Appeal (if permission has been refused by the Upper Tribunal), on an application by the party[14].

1 As to the jurisdiction of the First-tier Tribunal and the Upper Tribunal see PARA 32. As to the First-tier Tribunal and the Upper Tribunal see COURTS AND TRIBUNALS vol 24 (2010) PARAS 864 et seq, 886.

2 See the Tribunals, Courts and Enforcement Act 2007 s 11(1), (2); and COURTS AND TRIBUNALS vol 24 (2010) PARA 928. 'Excluded decisions' include: (1) a decision of the First-tier Tribunal: (a) to review, or not to review, an earlier decision of the tribunal; (b) to take no action, or not to take any particular action, in the light of a review of an earlier decision of the tribunal; (c) to set aside an earlier decision of the tribunal; or (d) to refer, or not to refer, a matter to the Upper Tribunal; (2) a decision of the First-tier Tribunal that is set aside (including a decision set aside after proceedings on an appeal have been begun); and (3) any decision of the First-tier Tribunal that is of a description specified in an order made by the Lord Chancellor: see s 11(5); and COURTS AND TRIBUNALS vol 24 (2010) PARA 928.

3 See the Tribunals, Courts and Enforcement Act 2007 s 11(3), (4); and COURTS AND TRIBUNALS vol 24 (2010) PARA 928.

4 As to the Caravan Sites and Control of Development Act 1960 see PLANNING vol 83 (2010) PARA 1210 et seq.

5 As to the jurisdiction of the First-tier Tribunal and the Upper Tribunal under the Mobile Homes Act 1983 see LANDLORD AND TENANT vol 64 (2016) PARA 1765.

6 Other than one made under the Housing Act 1985 Sch 5 para 11: see PARA 252.

7 As to the jurisdiction of the First-tier Tribunal and the Upper Tribunal under the Housing Act 1985 and the Housing Act 2004 see PARA 32.

8 Housing Act 2004 s 231C(1) (s 231C added by SI 2013/1036; the Housing Act 2004 s 231C(1) amended by SI 2014/1900). In any case where the Upper Tribunal is determining an appeal under the Housing Act 2004 s 231C(1), the provisions of the Tribunals, Courts and Enforcement Act 2007 s 12(2)–(4) (proceedings on appeal to the Upper Tribunal: see COURTS AND TRIBUNALS vol 24 (2010) PARA 928) apply: Housing Act 2004 s 231C(5) (as so added). As to the procedure on appeals see the Tribunal Procedure (First-tier Tribunal) (Property Chamber) Rules 2013, SI 2013/1169, Pt 6 (rr 49–56); and the Tribunal Procedure (Upper Tribunal) (Lands Chamber) Rules 2010, SI 2010/2600, Pts 3, 4 (rr 21–25) (r 21 amended by SI 2014/514; the Tribunal Procedure (Upper Tribunal) (Lands Chamber) Rules 2010, SI 2010/2600, r 24 amended by SI 2012/500). See also COMPULSORY ACQUISITION OF LAND vol 18 (2009) PARA 720 et seq.

9 Housing Act 2004 s 231C(2) (as added: see note 6). As to such appeals see the Tribunals, Courts and Enforcement Act 2007 s 11 (right of appeal to Upper Tribunal); and COURTS AND TRIBUNALS vol 24 (2010) PARA 928.

10 Ie under the Tribunals, Courts and Enforcement Act 2007 s 9: see COURTS AND TRIBUNALS vol 24 (2010) PARA 926.

11 Housing Act 2004 s 231C(3) (as added: see note 6).

12 Housing Act 2004 s 231C(4) (as added: see note 6).

13 See the Tribunals, Courts and Enforcement Act 2007 s 13(1), (2); and COURTS AND TRIBUNALS vol 24 (2010) PARA 929. For these purposes, 'excluded decisions' include:
    (1)   any decision of the Upper Tribunal on an application for permission to appeal;
    (2)   a decision of the Upper Tribunal: (a) to review, or not to review, an earlier decision of the tribunal; (b) to take no action, or not to take any particular action, in the light of a review of an earlier decision of the tribunal; or (c) to set aside an earlier decision of the tribunal;
    (3)   a decision of the Upper Tribunal that is set aside (including a decision set aside after proceedings on an appeal have been begun); and
    (4)   any decision of the Upper Tribunal that is of a description specified in an order made by the Lord Chancellor: see s 13(8); and COURTS AND TRIBUNALS vol 24 (2010) PARA 929.

14 See the Tribunals, Courts and Enforcement Act 2007 s 13(3)–(5); and COURTS AND TRIBUNALS vol 24 (2010) PARA 929.

50. Appeals from residential property tribunals (Wales).

A party to proceedings before a residential property tribunal in Wales[1] may appeal to the Upper Tribunal[2] from a decision of the residential property tribunal[3]. The appeal may only be made, however, with the permission of the residential property tribunal or the Upper Tribunal[4]. On the appeal:
    (1)   the Upper Tribunal may exercise any power which was available to the residential property tribunal; and

(2)   a decision of the Upper Tribunal may be enforced in the same way as a decision of the residential property tribunal[5].

The statutory provision allowing appeals from certain tribunals to the High Court[6] does not apply to any decision of a residential property tribunal[7]. Appeals from decisions of the Upper Tribunal lie to the Court of Appeal[8].

1   As to the constitution of residential property tribunals see PARA 34.
2   Ie the Upper Tribunal (Lands Chamber), the successor to the Lands Tribunal, part of the Tribunals Service. As to appeals to the Upper Tribunal (Lands Chamber) see COMPULSORY ACQUISITION OF LAND vol 18 (2009) PARA 720 et seq; and see COURTS AND TRIBUNALS vol 24 (2010) PARA 886.
3   Housing Act 2004 s 231(1) (amended by SI 2009/1307).
4   Housing Act 2004 s 231(2) (substituted by SI 2009/1307). See the Residential Property Tribunal Procedures and Fees (Wales) Regulations 2016, SI 2016/1110, reg 37.
5   Housing Act 2004 s 231(3) (amended by SI 2009/1307). As to enforcement see PARA 48. As to costs of proceedings before the Upper Tribunal (Lands Chamber) see COMPULSORY ACQUISITION OF LAND vol 18 (2009) PARA 746. As to appeals from a decision of the Upper Tribunal (Lands Chamber) to the Court of Appeal see COMPULSORY ACQUISITION OF LAND vol 18 (2009) PARAS 751–752.
6   Ie the Tribunals and Inquiries Act 1992 s 11(1).
7   Housing Act 2004 s 231(4) (substituted by SI 2013/1036).
8   See the Tribunals, Courts and Enforcement Act 2007 s 13; and COURTS AND TRIBUNALS vol 24 (2010) PARA 929.

(4) REGULATION OF SOCIAL HOUSING

(i) Social Housing in England

A.   INTRODUCTION

51. Preliminary. The Housing and Regeneration Act 2008 was part of the government's drive to deliver new affordable homes and safeguard higher housing standards for social housing tenants, and to promote regeneration of communities based on the government's regeneration framework, 'Transforming Places; Changing Lives'. The Act was intended to help address the shortage of affordable housing for first-time buyers and families through the establishment of the Homes and Communities Agency ('HCA'); to give social housing tenants a better deal with the creation of the Tenants Services Authority ('TSA'), a new watchdog for social tenants; and to make new housing greener to tackle climate change[1].

The purpose of Part 2[2] of the Housing and Regeneration Act 2008 is to regulate the provision of social housing[3] by English bodies[4]. Part 2 of the Act replaces the system of 'registered social landlords' under Part I[5] of the Housing Act 1996[6], but that Part continues to apply in relation to Wales[7], and certain provisions of it are applied in relation to England by Part 2 of the Housing and Regeneration Act 2008[8] or are preserved[9] although they apply to England only[10].

The Secretary of State[11] was required by order to make provision for the dissolution of the Housing Corporation[12] and enabled by order to make consequential amendment of enactments referring to the Housing Corporation[13]. The Secretary of State was empowered make one or more schemes for the transfer of the Housing Corporation's property, rights or liabilities to:

(1)   the regulator[14];
(2)   the Homes and Communities Agency ('the HCA')[15]; or
(3)   the Secretary of State[16].

The Secretary of State could by order transfer functions of the Housing Corporation to:

(a)   the regulator;

(b)   the HCA; or

(c)   the regulator and the HCA jointly or concurrently[17].

The Local Democracy, Economic Development and Construction Act 2009 aimed to further citizens' involvement in local decision-making, and local authorities' involvement in regional economic development[18]. It also makes provision for the establishment of a body to represent the interests of housing tenants in England at a regional level. Under the 2009 Act, the Secretary of State may:

(i)   establish a body with the functions specified below;

(ii)   give financial or other assistance to any person for the purpose of establishing a body with those functions;

(iii)   give financial or other assistance to any body appearing to the Secretary of State to have those functions for the purpose of the carrying out by the body of any or all of those functions[19].

Those functions are:

(A)   that of representing, or facilitating the representation of, the views and interests of tenants[20] of social housing in England or tenants of social housing and other residential property in England[21];

(B)   that of conducting or commissioning research into issues affecting tenants of social housing in England or tenants of social housing and other residential property in England[22];

(C)   that of promoting the representation by other bodies of tenants of social housing in England or any part of England or tenants of social housing and other residential property in England or any part of England[23].

Assistance may be given in such form (including financial assistance by way of grant, loan or guarantee) as the Secretary of State considers appropriate[24]. Assistance may be given on such terms as the Secretary of State considers appropriate[25], and the terms on which assistance may be given include, in particular, provision as to the circumstances in which it must be repaid or otherwise made good to the Secretary of State and the manner in which that must be done[26]. A person or body to whom assistance is given must comply with any terms on which it is given[27].

The Housing and Planning Act 2016 (which is not fully in force) makes various changes to housing law in England. Chapter 1 of Part 1[28] makes provision intended to promote the supply of starter homes[29]. Part 4[30] deals with social housing in England. Chapter 1 of Part 4[31] provides for the implementation of the right to buy on a voluntary basis by empowering the Secretary of State and the Greater London Authority to make grants to private registered providers in respect of right to buy discounts[32]. Under Chapter 2[33] the Secretary of State is enabled to require local housing authorities which are required to keep a housing revenue account to make a payment to the Secretary of State calculated by reference to the market value of the higher value vacant housing owned by the authority[34]. Chapter 3[35] allows the Secretary of State to make provision by regulations as to the levels of rent which an English local housing authority must charge high income tenants of social housing in England[36]. Chapter 4[37] is concerned with reducing the regulation of private registered providers of social housing, principally by the amendment of existing legislation[38] and by reducing local authority influence over private registered providers[39]. Chapter 5[40], concerning the insolvency of registered providers of social housing, introduces housing administration orders and imposes restrictions on other insolvency procedures[41].

Prospective amendments are made[42] to the Housing Act 2004 to allow financial penalties to be imposed as an alternative to prosecution for certain offences[43].

1 See the Department for Communities and Local Government press release, dated 23 July 2008. As to the abolition of the TSA see PARA 2 note 30.
2 Ie the Housing and Regeneration Act 2008 Pt 2 (ss 59–278A). The content of Pt 2 is described in s 60(4) Table (amended by the Localism Act 2011 s 178, Sch 16 paras 1, 12; and SI 2010/844; and the Housing and Planning Act 2016 s 92, Sch 4 paras 7, 8).
3 Ie as defined in the Housing and Regeneration Act 2008 ss 68–77: see PARA 52.
4 Housing and Regeneration Act 2008 s 59. English bodies are as defined in s 79: see PARA 53.
5 Ie the Housing Act 1996 Pt I (ss A1–64).
6 Housing and Regeneration Act 2008 s 60(1).
7 Housing and Regeneration Act 2008 s 60(2). See ss 61–63; and PARA 166 et seq.
8 See the Housing and Regeneration Act 2008 s 179 (repealed).
9 See the Housing and Regeneration Act 2008 s 124; and PARA 131 et seq.
10 Housing and Regeneration Act 2008 s 60(3).
11 As to the Secretary of State see PARA 7. As to orders by the Secretary of State see PARA 54.
12 Housing and Regeneration Act 2008 s 64(1). See the Housing Corporation (Dissolution) Order 2009, SI 2009/484.
13 Housing and Regeneration Act 2008 s 64(2).
14 As to the meaning of 'the regulator' see PARA 57; and as to the regulator see PARAS 53, 57 et seq.
15 'The HCA' means the Homes and Communities Agency: Housing and Regeneration Act 2008 s 275. As to the Homes and Communities Agency see PARA 57 et seq; and PLANNING vol 83 (2010) PARA 1454 et seq.
16 See the Housing and Regeneration Act 2008 s 65(1). The Secretary of State could by notice require the Housing Corporation to provide staff, premises, facilities or other assistance to the regulator or the HCA: s 66. On the transfer date, the designated property, rights or liabilities are transferred and vest in accordance with the scheme: s 65(2). 'The transfer date' means the date specified by a scheme as the date on which the scheme is to have effect, and 'designated', in relation to a scheme, means specified in or determined in accordance with the scheme: s 65(4). As to schemes see Sch 6 and as to the tax implications of schemes see Sch 7 (amended by SI 2008/3002): Housing and Regeneration Act 2008 s 65(3), (5). Sections 65–67, Schs 6, 7 are in force as they apply in relation to, or make provision about the tax implications of, schemes under s 65: see the Housing and Regeneration Act 2008 (Commencement No 1 and Transitional Provision) Order 2008, SI 2008/2358, arts 1(2), 2(1), 3(1).
17 Housing and Regeneration Act 2008 s 67(1). Such an order could make provision in relation to English registered social landlords which is similar to any provision made by Pt 2 in relation to registered providers: s 67(2). 'English registered social landlord' means a body: (1) which is registered as a social landlord under the Housing Act 1996 Pt I (ss A1–64) (see PARA 166 et seq); and (2) which does not fall within s 56(2)(a)–(c) of that Act (Welsh bodies): Housing and Regeneration Act 2008 s 67(3). As to registered social landlords in Wales see PARA 166 et seq. See further s 67(4)–(6); the Transfer of Housing Corporation Functions (Modifications and Transitional Provisions) Order 2008, SI 2008/2839 (revoked); and the Housing and Regeneration Act 2008 (Consequential Provisions) (No 2) Order 2010, SI 2010/671.
18 These provisions were repealed by the Localism Act 2011 ss 45, 237, Sch 25 Pt 6 as from 15 January 2012.
19 Local Democracy, Economic Development and Construction Act 2009 s 25(1). It is immaterial for the purposes of s 25(1) that a body may also have other functions: s 25(5). No such body appears to have been established.
20 'Tenant', in relation to social housing, has the meaning given by the Housing and Regeneration Act 2008 s 275 (see PARA 52 note 9); and 'social housing' has the meaning given by s 68 (see PARA 52): Local Democracy, Economic Development and Construction Act 2009 s 25(10).
21 Local Democracy, Economic Development and Construction Act 2009 s 25(2).
22 Local Democracy, Economic Development and Construction Act 2009 s 25(3).
23 Local Democracy, Economic Development and Construction Act 2009 s 25(4).
24 Local Democracy, Economic Development and Construction Act 2009 s 25(6).
25 Local Democracy, Economic Development and Construction Act 2009 s 25(7).
26 Local Democracy, Economic Development and Construction Act 2009 s 25(8).
27 Local Democracy, Economic Development and Construction Act 2009 s 25(9).
28 Ie the Housing and Planning Act 2016 Pt 1 Ch 1 (ss 1–8).

29 See PARAS 906–907.
30 Ie the Housing and Planning Act 2016 Pt 4 (ss 64–121).
31 Ie the Housing and Planning Act 2016 Pt 4 Ch 1 (ss 64–68). These provisions came into force on 26 May 2016: see the Housing and Planning Act 2016 (Commencement No 1) Regulations 2016, SI 2016/609.
32 See PARA 238.
33 Ie the Housing and Planning Act 2016 Pt 4 Ch 2 (ss 69–79). These provisions came into force on 12 May 2016: see s 216(1)(b).
34 See PARA 356 et seq.
35 Ie the Housing and Planning Act 2016 Pt 4 Ch 3 (ss 80–91). These provisions came into force on 1 October 2016: see the Housing and Planning Act 2016 (Commencement No 3) Regulations 2016, SI 2016/956, reg 2(a).
36 See PARAS 441–445.
37 Ie the Housing and Planning Act 2016 Pt 4 Ch 4 (ss 92–94), Sch 4. These provisions came into force on 6 April 2017: see the Housing and Planning Act 2016 (Commencement No 4 and Transitional Provisions) Regulations 2017, SI 2017/75, reg 4.
38 See PARAS 51–52, 72, 100 et seq, 532, 556, 337.
39 See the Housing and Planning Act 2016 s 93; and PARA 56.
40 Ie the Housing and Planning Act 2016 Pt 4 Ch 5 (ss 95–117). These provisions are to come into force as from a day to be appointed: see s 216(3). At the date at which this volume states the law, no such day had been appointed.
41 See PARA 90 et seq.
42 Ie by the Housing and Planning Act 2016 s 126, Sch 9.
43 See PARA 373.

52. Social housing. In Part 2 of the Housing and Regeneration Act 2008[1] 'social housing' means:

(1)   low cost rental accommodation[2]; and

(2)   low cost home ownership accommodation[3].

Accommodation which becomes 'social housing' by satisfying head (1) or (2) remains 'social housing' for the purposes of Part 2 unless and until a specified event[4] occurs[5]. Accommodation which is both low cost rental accommodation and low cost home ownership accommodation is to be treated as the latter and not as the former (in other words, a shared ownership lease under which the leaseholder owns a share of the equity and pays a rent is to be treated as low cost home ownership)[6]. The Secretary of State may make regulations providing that specified property, or a specified class of property, is or is not to be treated as social housing for the purposes of Part 2[7].

A dwelling[8] ceases to be social housing if:

(a)   it is sold to the tenant[9];

(b)   the provider holds a leasehold interest in the dwelling and the leasehold interest expires[10];

(c)   it is: (i) disposed of[11] with the Secretary of State's consent[12]; (ii) appropriated with the Secretary of State's consent[13]; or (iii) disposed of by a local authority[14] with the Secretary of State's consent in accordance with any other enactment[15].

A dwelling ceases to be social housing if a private registered provider of social housing[16] owns the freehold or a leasehold interest and transfers it to a person who is not a registered provider of social housing[17]. This does not apply, however, if and for so long as the private registered provider has a right to have the interest transferred back to it[18], nor where low cost home ownership accommodation is transferred to the 'buyer' under equity percentage arrangements or to the trustees under a shared ownership trust[19].

The regulator may direct that a specified dwelling is to cease to be social housing[20]. The regulator may make a direction only on the application of the provider[21] and a direction may not be made if the provider is a local authority[22].

1 Ie the Housing and Regeneration Act 2008 Pt 2 (ss 59–278A).
2 Accommodation is low cost rental accommodation if: (1) it is made available for rent; (2) the rent is below the market rate; and (3) the accommodation is made available in accordance with rules designed to ensure that it is made available to people whose needs are not adequately served by the commercial housing market: Housing and Regeneration Act 2008 s 69. 'Rent' includes payments under a licence to occupy accommodation: s 275.
3 Housing and Regeneration Act 2008 s 68(1). Accommodation is low cost home ownership accommodation if the following conditions are satisfied: s 70(1). Condition 1 is that the accommodation is occupied, or made available for occupation, in accordance with: (1) shared ownership arrangements; (2) equity percentage arrangements; or (3) shared ownership trusts: s 70(2). Condition 2 is that the accommodation is made available in accordance with rules designed to ensure that it is made available to people whose needs are not adequately served by the commercial housing market: s 70(3). 'Shared ownership arrangements' means arrangements under a lease which: (a) is granted on payment of a premium calculated by reference to a percentage of either the value of the accommodation or the cost of providing it; and (b) provides that the tenant (or the tenant's personal representatives) will or may be entitled to a sum calculated by reference to the value of the accommodation: s 70(4). 'Equity percentage arrangements' means arrangements under which: (i) the owner of a freehold or leasehold interest in residential property ('the seller') conveys it to an individual ('the buyer'); (ii) the buyer, in consideration for the conveyance: (A) pays the seller a sum (the 'initial payment') expressed to represent a percentage of the value of the interest at the time of the conveyance; and (B) agrees to pay the seller other sums calculated by reference to a percentage of the value of the interest at the time when each sum is to be paid; and (iii) the liability to make any payment required by the arrangements (apart from the initial payment) is secured by a mortgage: s 70(5). 'Conveyance' includes grant, assignment and any other instrument: s 275. 'Shared ownership trusts' has the same meaning as in the Finance Act 2003 Sch 9 (stamp duty land tax: see STAMP TAXES vol 96 (2012) PARA 471): Housing and Regeneration Act 2008 s 70(6). The Secretary of State may make regulations amending the definition of 'low cost home ownership accommodation' and the definition of any of the sub-categories specified in that definition: s 70(7). As to the Secretary of State see PARA 7. As to the making of regulations under the Housing and Regeneration Act 2008 see s 320; and PARA 54.
    Section 77 makes transitional provision as a result of which certain accommodation is to be treated as 'social housing' whether or not it satisfies head (1) or (2) in the text: s 68(3). It applies to property owned by a registered social landlord within the meaning of the Housing Act 1996 Pt I (ss A1–64) (see PARA 166 et seq) before the coming into force of the Housing and Regeneration Act 2008 s 61: s 77(1). Section 61 came into force on 1 April 2010: see the Housing and Regeneration Act 2008 (Commencement No 7 and Transitional and Saving Provisions) Order 2010, SI 2010/862, art 2. Property to which the Housing and Regeneration Act 2008 s 77 applies is social housing whether or not it satisfies s 68(1)(a) or (b) (heads (1), (2) in the text) and unless and until an event specified in ss 73–76 (see the text and notes 8–19) occurs: s 77(2). However, property to which any of the exceptions below applies when s 61 came into force is social housing only if the purchase, construction or renovation of the property was funded by means of a grant under s 19 (financial assistance by the HCA: see PLANNING), the Housing Act 1996 s 18 (social housing grant: see PARA 166) or any of the Housing Act 1988 s 50 (repealed in relation to England and Wales), the Housing Associations Act 1985 s 41 (repealed) or the Housing Act 1974 s 29 or 29A (both repealed) (housing association grant): Housing and Regeneration Act 2008 s 77(3). Exception 1 is accommodation let on the open market: s 77(4). Exception 2 is accommodation made available only to students in full-time education or training: s 77(5). Exception 3 is a care home (within the meaning of the Care Standards Act 2000: see SOCIAL SERVICES vol 95 (2017) PARA 3) in which nursing is provided: Housing and Regeneration Act 2008 s 77(6). Exception 4 is accommodation provided in response to a request by the Secretary of State under the Immigration and Asylum Act 1999 s 100 (support for asylum seekers: see IMMIGRATION AND ASYLUM vol 57 (2012) PARA 356): Housing and Regeneration Act 2008 s 77(7). Exception 5 is property of a kind specified by regulations made by the Secretary of State: s 77(8). As to the meaning of 'HCA' see PARA 51 note 15.
4 Ie specified in the Housing and Regeneration Act 2008 ss 73–76: see the text and notes 8–19.
5 Housing and Regeneration Act 2008 s 68(2).
6 Housing and Regeneration Act 2008 s 71.
7 Housing and Regeneration Act 2008 s 72(1). As to regulations by the Secretary of State see PARA 54. The regulations may provide for property to be social housing despite not satisfying s 68(1)(a) or (b) where the Secretary of State thinks the property is of a kind, or is provided in

circumstances, that serve the needs of a group whose needs are not adequately served by the commercial housing market: s 72(2). The regulations: (1) may override s 68(2); (2) are subject to ss 68(3), 77; and (3) are subject to ss 69, 70 (but may clarify doubt about the application of those sections): s 72(3). The regulations may make provision by reference to the opinion of the regulator or another specified person and may make provision by reference to designation, agreement or other action by the regulator or another specified person: s 72(4). As to the meaning of 'the regulator' see PARA 57.

8 'Dwelling' means a house, flat or other building or part of a building occupied or intended to be occupied as a separate dwelling and includes any garden, yard, outhouse or other appurtenance belonging to, or usually enjoyed with, the dwelling: Housing and Regeneration Act 2008 s 275.

9 Housing and Regeneration Act 2008 s 73(1). 'Tenant' in relation to social housing includes other occupiers: s 275. Low cost rental accommodation is 'sold to the tenant' when the tenant exercises a statutory or contractual right and as a result becomes the owner of: (1) the freehold interest in the property; or (2) the leasehold interest previously owned by the person providing the social housing: s 73(2). Low cost home ownership accommodation of the shared ownership kind is 'sold to the tenant' when the tenant exercises a statutory or contractual right and as a result becomes the owner of: (a) the freehold interest in the property; or (b) the leasehold interest previously owned by the person providing the social housing: s 73(3). Low cost home ownership accommodation of the equity percentage kind is 'sold to the tenant' when the 'buyer' (see s 70(5)(a); and note 3) exercises a statutory or contractual right as a result of which the equity percentage arrangements (see s 70(5)) come to an end: s 73(4). Low cost home ownership accommodation of the shared ownership trust kind comes to an end when the 'purchaser' (see the Finance Act 2003 Sch 9 para 7(4)(a); and STAMP TAXES vol 96 (2012) PARA 471) exercises a statutory or contractual right as a result of which the trust comes to an end: Housing and Regeneration Act 2008 s 73(5).

10 Housing and Regeneration Act 2008 s 74(1). A lease from an associate or subsidiary of the provider is disregarded for the purposes of s 74(1): s 74(2). 'Associate' of a provider means: (1) a body of which the provider is a subsidiary; and (2) any other subsidiary of that body: s 271(6). A company is a 'subsidiary' of a person if any of the following conditions is satisfied: s 271(1). Condition 1 is that the person: (a) is a member of the company; and (b) has power, independent of any other person, to appoint or remove all or a majority of the board of directors: s 271(2). Condition 2 is that the person holds more than half in nominal value of the company's equity share capital: s 271(3). Condition 3 is that the company is a subsidiary, within the meaning of the Companies Act 2006 (see COMPANIES vol 14 (2016) PARA 22) or the Co-operative and Community Benefit Societies Act 2014 Pt 7 (ss 75–102) (see FINANCIAL INSTITUTIONS vol 48 (2015) PARA 1009), of a company which is a subsidiary of the person by virtue of Condition 1 or 2: Housing and Regeneration Act 2008 s 271(4) (amended by the Co-operative and Community Benefit Societies Act 2014 s 151(1), Sch 4 paras 121, 135). In relation to a company which is a registered society a reference to the board of directors is a reference to the committee of management: Housing and Regeneration Act 2008 s 271(5) (amended by the Co-operative and Community Benefit Societies Act 2014 Sch 4 paras 121, 122). 'Registered society' has the same meaning as in the Co-operative and Community Benefit Societies Act 2014 (see FINANCIAL INSTITUTIONS vol 48 (2015) PARA 881 et seq); and 'committee', in relation to a registered society, means the committee of management or other directing body of the society (including any person co-opted to serve on the committee, whether a member of the society or not): Housing and Regeneration Act 2008 s 275 (amended by the Co-operative and Community Benefit Societies Act 2014 Sch 4 paras 121, 122, 136(b)).

11 In the Housing and Regeneration Act 2008 Pt 2, a reference to disposing of property is a reference to: (1) selling it; (2) leasing it; (3) mortgaging it; (4) making it subject to a charge; and (5) disposing of it, or of any interest in it, in any other way: s 273(1). Granting an option to require a disposal is to be treated as making a disposal: s 273(2).

12 Ie in accordance with the Housing Act 1985 s 32 or 43 (disposals by local authorities: see PARAS 522, 531).

13 Ie in accordance with the Housing Act 1985 s 19(2) (appropriation by local authorities for some other purpose: see PARA 418).

14 'Local authority' has the same meaning as in the Housing Associations Act 1985 (see PARA 12): Housing and Regeneration Act 2008 s 275.

15 Housing and Regeneration Act 2008 s 75(1A) (added by SI 2010/844). The Housing and Regeneration Act 2008 s 75(1A) does not apply to a disposal in pursuance of shared ownership arrangements or equity percentage arrangements: s 75(2) (amended by the Housing and Planning Act 2016 s 92, Sch 4 paras 7, 10(1), (3)). Nor does that provision apply if the consent is conditional upon the dwelling continuing to be low cost rental accommodation or low cost home ownership accommodation: Housing and Regeneration Act 2008 s 75(3) (amended by the Housing and Planning Act 2016 Sch 4 paras 7, 10(1), (3)). A condition of that kind must include provision for determining when the dwelling ceases to be social housing: Housing and Regeneration Act 2008 s 75(4).

16 As to the meaning of 'private registered provider of social housing' see PARA 53.
17 Housing and Regeneration Act 2008 s 74A(1) (s 74A added by the Housing and Planning Act 2016 Sch 4 paras 7, 9).
18 Housing and Regeneration Act 2008 s 74A(2) (as added: see note 17).
19 Housing and Regeneration Act 2008 s 74A(3) (as added: see note 17).
20 Housing and Regeneration Act 2008 s 76(1).
21 Housing and Regeneration Act 2008 s 76(2).
22 Housing and Regeneration Act 2008 s 76(3) (added by SI 2010/844).

53. Other key concepts in the Housing and Regeneration Act 2008. A definition of 'English body' is provided. For the purposes of Part 2 of the Housing and Regeneration Act 2008[1], 'English body' means:

(1) a registered charity[2] whose address for the purposes of registration by the Charity Commission[3] is in England;

(2) a registered society[4] whose registered office for the purposes of the Co-operative and Community Benefit Societies Act 2014 is in England;

(3) a registered company[5] which has its registered office in England;

(4) a community land trust[6] which owns land in England; and

(5) any other person (whether or not a body corporate registered under the law of the United Kingdom) which: (a) is not a Welsh body[7] or a local authority[8] in Wales; and (b) makes available, or intends to make available, accommodation in England[9].

A register of providers of social housing has been established[10]. Persons listed in the register may be referred to in an enactment or other instrument as 'registered providers of social housing' and are referred to in Part 2 of the Housing and Regeneration Act 2008 as 'registered providers'[11]. Persons listed in the register who are not local authorities may be referred to in an enactment or other instrument as 'private registered providers of social housing' and are referred to in Part 2 of the Housing and Regeneration Act 2008 as 'private registered providers'[12].

1 Ie the Housing and Regeneration Act 2008 Pt 2 (ss 59–278A).
2 'Registered charity' means a charity registered under the Charities Act 2011: Housing and Regeneration Act 2008 s 275 (definition amended by the Charities Act 2011 s 354(1), Sch 7 para 135(b)).
3 'The Charity Commission' means the Charity Commission for England and Wales: Housing and Regeneration Act 2008 s 275.
4 As to the meaning of 'registered society' see PARA 52 note 10.
5 'Registered company' means a company within the meaning of the Companies Act 2006 (see COMPANIES): Housing and Regeneration Act 2008 s 275.
6 'Community land trust' means a body corporate which satisfies the conditions below: Housing and Regeneration Act 2008 s 79(2). In those conditions 'local community' means the individuals who live or work, or want to live or work, in a specified area: s 79(3). Condition 1 is that the body is established for the express purpose of furthering the social, economic and environmental interests of a local community by acquiring and managing land and other assets in order: (1) to provide a benefit to the local community; and (2) to ensure that the assets are not sold or developed except in a manner which the trust's members think benefits the local community: s 79(4). Condition 2 is that the body is established under arrangements which are expressly designed to ensure that: (a) any profits from its activities will be used to benefit the local community (otherwise than by being paid directly to members); (b) individuals who live or work in the specified area have the opportunity to become members of the trust (whether or not others can also become members); and (c) the members of the trust control it: s 79(5).
7 Ie within the meaning of the Housing Act 1996 s 1A: see PARA 168 note 1.
8 As to the meaning of 'local authority' see PARA 149 note 4 (definition applied by the Housing and Regeneration Act 2008 s 275).
9 Housing and Regeneration Act 2008 s 79(1) (amended by the Co-operative and Community Benefit Societies Act 2014 s 151(1), Sch 4 paras 121, 122, 124; and by SI 2010/844).

10 See the Housing and Regeneration Act 2008 Pt 2 Ch 3 (ss 110–121); and PARA 70 et seq: s 80(2). In Pt 2 Ch 2, a reference to the provider of social housing is to be construed as follows. The provider of social housing is: (1) in the case of low cost rental accommodation, the landlord; (2) in the case of low cost home ownership accommodation: shared ownership, the landlord; (3) in the case of low cost home ownership accommodation: equity percentage, the 'seller' within the meaning of s 70(5)(a); (4) in the case of low cost home ownership accommodation: shared ownership trust, the 'social landlord' within the meaning of the Finance Act 2003 Sch 9 para 7(3): Housing and Regeneration Act 2008 s 80(1). As to the categories of accommodation see PARA 52 note 3.
11 Housing and Regeneration Act 2008 s 80(2).
12 Housing and Regeneration Act 2008 s 80(3) (added by SI 2010/844).

54. Orders and regulations under the Housing and Regeneration Act 2008. The power of the Secretary of State[1], the Treasury or the Welsh Ministers[2] to make orders or regulations under the Housing and Regeneration Act 2008:

(1)   is exercisable by statutory instrument;

(2)   may be exercised so as to make provision generally or subject to exceptions or only in relation to specified cases or circumstances or descriptions of case;

(3)   may be exercised so as to make different provision for different cases or descriptions of case, different circumstances, different purposes or different areas; and

(4)   includes power to make supplementary, incidental, consequential, transitional, transitory or saving provision[3].

An instrument containing an order under specified provisions[4] may not be made unless a draft of the instrument has been laid before, and approved by a resolution of, each House of Parliament[5].

If a draft of an instrument containing a designation order[6] would, apart from this provision, be treated as a hybrid instrument for the purposes of the standing orders of either House of Parliament[7], it is to proceed in that House as if it were not a hybrid instrument[8].

An instrument containing an order amending the Homes and Communities Agency's (the 'HCA's') borrowing limit[9] may not be made unless a draft of the instrument has been laid before, and approved by a resolution of, the House of Commons[10].

An instrument containing orders under specified provisions[11] is subject to annulment in pursuance of a resolution of either House of Parliament[12].

An instrument containing regulations as to the tax consequences of transfers to the HCA, of designated property, rights or liabilities of a specified public body[13] is subject to annulment in pursuance of a resolution of the House of Commons[14].

An instrument containing certain orders and regulations of the Welsh Ministers[15] may not be made unless a draft of the instrument has been laid before, and approved by a resolution of, the National Assembly for Wales[16].

An instrument containing certain orders and regulations of the Welsh Ministers[17] is subject to annulment in pursuance of a resolution of the National Assembly for Wales[18].

1   As to the Secretary of State see PARA 7.
2   As to the Welsh Ministers see PARA 7.
3   Housing and Regeneration Act 2008 s 320(1). This does not apply to orders under Sch 3 para 3 (extinguishment of rights of way: see PLANNING vol 83 (2010) PARA 1463) or Sch 4 (powers in relation to, and for, statutory undertakers: see PLANNING vol 83 (2010) PARA 1465 et seq): s 320(2).
4   Ie: (1) an order under the Housing and Regeneration Act 2008 s 13, 114, 122 or 229; (2) an order of the Secretary of State under s 321 (consequential amendments and repeals); (3) an order of the Secretary of State under Sch 11 para 19(4), 21(2) or (4) or 24; (4) regulations under s 70 or 72; or (5) regulations of the Secretary of State under s 280(3) or 291.

5 Housing and Regeneration Act 2008 s 320(3) (amended by the Localism Act 2011 s 179, Sch 17 paras 1, 18(a)). This does not apply to an instrument containing an order under the Housing and Regeneration Act 2008 s 321 if the order does not amend or repeal a provision of a public general Act: s 320(4).
6 Ie under the Housing and Regeneration Act 2008 s 13: see PLANNING vol 83 (2010) PARA 1470.
7 As to hybrid instruments see STATUTES AND LEGISLATIVE PROCESS vol 96 (2012) PARA 1057.
8 Housing and Regeneration Act 2008 s 320(5).
9 Ie under the Housing and Regeneration Act 2008 s 23: see PLANNING vol 83 (2010) PARA 1475. As to the HCA see PARA 57 et seq; and PLANNING vol 83 (2010) PARA 1454 et seq.
10 Housing and Regeneration Act 2008 s 320(6).
11 Ie: (1) an order under the Housing and Regeneration Act 2008 s 36 or Pt 2 (ss 59–278A) (excluding ss 114, 122, 229); (2) an order of the Secretary of State under s 321 to which s 320(3) (see the text and note 5) does not apply; (3) an order of the Secretary of State under Sch 11 para 16(7), 18(4), 22(2) or 23(2); (4) regulations under s 53A(2); (5) regulations under Pt 2 (excluding ss 70, 72); (6) regulations of the Secretary of State under Pt 3 Ch 1 (ss 279–293) (including Sch 10 but excluding ss 280(3), 291); (7) regulations of the Secretary of State under s 298; or (8) regulations under Sch 3 Pt 3.
12 Housing and Regeneration Act 2008 s 320(7) (amended by the Infrastructure Act 2015 s 31(1), (4)(a); and the Localism Act 2011 Sch 17 paras 1, 18(b)).
13 Ie under the Housing and Regeneration Act 2008 s 53B: see PLANNING.
14 Housing and Regeneration Act 2008 s 320(7A) (added by the Infrastructure Act 2015 s 31(1), (4)(b)).
15 Ie: (1) an order of the Welsh Ministers under the Housing and Regeneration Act 2008 s 321 (consequential amendments and repeals); (2) an order of the Welsh Ministers under Sch 11 para 19(4), 21(2) or (4) or 24; or (3) regulations of the Welsh Ministers under s 280(3) or 291.
16 Housing and Regeneration Act 2008 s 320(8). This does not apply to an instrument containing an order under s 321 if the order does not amend or repeal a provision of a public general Act: s 320(9).
17 Ie: (1) an order of the Welsh Ministers under the Housing and Regeneration Act 2008 s 321 to which s 320(8) (see the text and note 14) does not apply; (2) an order of the Welsh Ministers under Sch 11 para 16(7), 18(4), 22(2) or 23(2); (3) regulations of the Welsh Ministers under Pt 3 Ch 1 (including Sch 10 but excluding s 280(3) or 291); or (4) regulations of the Welsh Ministers under s 298.
18 Housing and Regeneration Act 2008 s 320(10).

55. Reduction in social housing rents. The Welfare Reform and Work Act 2016 has amongst other matters made provision for the reduction in rents paid for accommodation provided by social landlords. The purpose of this change is to reduce the amounts spent in paying housing benefit to tenants in the social rented sector[1].

In relation to each relevant year[2], registered providers of social housing must secure that the amount of rent payable in respect of that relevant year by a tenant[3] of their social housing in England is at least 1 per cent less than the amount of rent that was payable by the tenant in respect of the preceding 12 months (the 'rent reduction requirement')[4]. The rent reduction requirement does not apply if:

(1)   the accommodation is low cost home ownership accommodation[5];
(2)   the accommodation is both low cost rental accommodation[6] and low cost home ownership accommodation[7]; or
(3)   the property is subject to a mortgage[8] and:
  (a)   the mortgagee[9] is in possession of the interest in the property or the part of the property that includes the social housing, in the exercise of the mortgagee's powers to enforce the mortgage[10];
  (b)   a receiver has been appointed in relation to the interest in the property or the part of the property that includes the social housing by: (i) the mortgagee, in the exercise of the mortgagee's powers to enforce the mortgage; or (ii) the court, in connection with enforcing the mortgage, and that appointment is in force[11]; or

(4)   a person has been appointed by the mortgagee, in the exercise of the
        mortgagee's powers to enforce the mortgage[12], to exercise powers that
        include a power to sell or otherwise dispose of the interest in the
        property or the part of the property that includes the social housing and
        that appointment is in force[13].

If a registered provider's interest in property that consists of or includes social
housing was made subject to a mortgage, and the interest in the property, or the
interest in the part that includes the social housing, is sold or otherwise disposed
of after the coming into force of the rent reduction requirement[14] by the
mortgagee, in the exercise of the mortgagee's powers to enforce the mortgage, a
receiver appointed by the mortgagee or by the court as described in head (3)(b),
or a person appointed by the mortgagee as described in head (3)(c), the rent
reduction requirement ceases to apply in relation to that social housing at the time
of that sale or other disposal[15].

In addition, the Secretary of State may by regulations provide for the rent
reduction requirement not to apply in cases prescribed by the regulations[16].

The Regulator of Social Housing[17] in England may, by direction, exempt a
private registered provider from the rent reduction requirement where the
following conditions are satisfied and the Secretary of State consents[18]. The
conditions are:
(i)   that the regulator considers that complying with the rent reduction
        requirement would jeopardise the financial viability of the private
        registered provider[19]; or
(ii)   that the circumstances of the private registered provider satisfy
        requirements prescribed in regulations made by the Secretary of State[20].

The regulator may publish a document about the measures that the regulator
considers could be taken by a private registered provider to comply with the rent
reduction requirement and to avoid jeopardising its financial viability[21].

The Secretary of State may, by direction, exempt a local authority[22] from the
rent reduction requirement where the following conditions are satisfied and the
Secretary of State consents[23]. The conditions are:
(A)   that the Secretary of State considers that the local authority would be
        unable to avoid serious financial difficulties if it were to comply with the
        rent reduction requirement[24]; or
(B)   that the circumstances of the local authority satisfy requirements
        prescribed in regulations made by the Secretary of State[25].

The Secretary of State may publish a document about the measures that the
Secretary of State considers could be taken by a local authority to comply with the
rent reduction requirement and to avoid serious financial difficulties[26].

Further provision is made about the maximum amount of rent that registered
providers must secure is payable in respect of a relevant year or part of a relevant
year by a tenant of their social housing, and for exceptions and exemptions in
relation to such provision[27]. The Secretary of State may make regulations
regarding the maximum amount of rent payable to a registered provider by a
tenant of social housing in relation to whom specified exceptions[28] apply[29].

A lease or other agreement by virtue of which a person is a tenant of a
registered provider contains an implied term enabling the registered provider to
reduce the amount of rent payable by the tenant, without giving prior notice,
where the reduction is made for the purpose of complying with a rent reduction
requirement[30], notwithstanding any express provision in a lease or other
agreement[31].

If particular social housing of a registered provider becomes social housing of another registered provider ('the transferee') and the social housing is subject to a tenancy that began before the social housing became the transferee's social housing, the relevant provisions[32] have effect in relation to the amount of rent payable by the tenant under the tenancy as if the transferee's relevant years were the same as the initial registered provider's relevant years[33] and rent payable by the tenant before the social housing became the transferee's social housing were rent payable to the transferee in respect of such earlier periods[34].

1   See the official guidance: Welfare Reform and Work Act 2016 — social rent reduction (Department for Communities and Local Government, 21 March 2016). It states that the Secretary of State has issued a general consent which enables registered providers of social housing in England who had not implemented their 2015 to 2016 rent increase on 8 July 2015 to use a permitted review day — generally 31 March 2016 except in the case of re-lets of Affordable Rent housing where the permitted review day is the day the new tenancy agreement starts. This is to ensure that all landlords have a 2015 to 2016 baseline for the reductions. The baseline rent and rents in the four relevant years are calculated in the same way as the above, save that it is the rate of rent on the permitted review day (not 8 July 2015) which forms the basis of the calculation. See The General Social Housing Rents Permitted Review Day Consent 2016 (Department for Communities and Local Government, 21 March 2016).

2   For these purposes, a relevant year, in relation to a registered provider, is: (1) in the case of a private registered provider whose practice as regards the greater number of its tenancies is to change rent payable no more than once a year and with effect from a single date other than 1 April ('the review date'): (a) a year beginning on the first review date to occur after 1 April 2016; or (b) a year beginning on the first, second or third anniversary of that date; (2) in any other case, a year beginning on 1 April 2016, 1 April 2017, 1 April 2018 or 1 April 2019: Welfare Reform and Work Act 2016 s 23(6). For the purposes of s 23(6), a private registered provider's practice as regards its tenancies is to be determined by reference to its practice as regards the tenancies of its social housing in the year ending with 31 March 2016 (and a private registered provider which has no tenancies of its social housing in that year is to be regarded as having no practice as regards its tenancies): s 23(7). A private registered provider whose practice is as described in head (1) is to be regarded as having complied with s 23(1)–(7) if it treats tenants in its social housing as if its relevant years were the years mentioned in head (2): s 23(8).
        'Registered provider' means a registered provider within the meaning of the Housing and Regeneration Act 2008 (see s 80; and PARA 53) of social housing within the meaning of that Act (see ss 68, 72; and PARA 52): Welfare Reform and Work Act 2016 s 33(1). 'Private registered provider' means a private registered provider of social housing within the meaning of the Housing and Regeneration Act 2008 (see s 80; and PARA 53): Welfare Reform and Work Act 2016 s 33(1). 'Rent' includes payments under a licence to occupy: s 33(1).

3   The amount of rent payable to the registered provider by the tenant in respect of the 12 months preceding the first relevant year is to be treated for the purposes of the Welfare Reform and Work Act 2016 s 23(1) as having been the greater of the following amounts: (1) the amount of rent that would have been payable in respect of those 12 months if the rate of rent applicable at the beginning of 8 July 2015 had applied during those 12 months; and (2) if the Secretary of State consents to the use by the registered provider of a different day ('the permitted review day'), the amount of rent that would have been payable in respect of those 12 months if the rate of rent applicable at the beginning of the permitted review day had applied during those 12 months: s 23(3). A consent given for the purposes of s 23(3) may be a consent given for a particular case or for a description of cases: s 23(4). If a tenancy existing in the first relevant year began at or before the beginning of 8 July 2015 but less than 12 months before the beginning of the first relevant year, the tenancy is to be treated for the purposes of s 23(1) as having begun at least 12 months before the first relevant year (and s 23(3) is to have effect accordingly): s 23(5). As to the Secretary of State see PARA 7.

4   Welfare Reform and Work Act 2016 s 23(1). If: (1) the tenancy of particular social housing comes to an end after part of a relevant year has elapsed; or (2) s 23 ceases to apply in relation to the tenancy of particular social housing after part of a relevant year has elapsed, the requirement in s 23(1) has effect in relation to the part of the relevant year falling before that time with a proportionate reduction in the maximum amount of rent payable to the registered provider by the tenant: s 23(2). Section 23 is subject to s 27 (provision about excepted cases: see the text and notes 28–29) and Sch 2 (further provision about social housing rents): s 23(9). Transitional provision is made by s 31.

5 Welfare Reform and Work Act 2016 s 24(1)(a). As to the meaning of 'low cost home ownership accommodation' see PARA 52 note 3; definition applied by the Welfare Reform and Work Act 2016 s 33(1).

6 As to the meaning of 'low cost rental accommodation' see PARA 52 note 2; definition applied by the Welfare Reform and Work Act 2016 s 33(1).

7 Welfare Reform and Work Act 2016 s 24(1)(b).

8 'Mortgage' includes a charge or other security: Welfare Reform and Work Act 2016 s 24(4).

9 'Mortgagee' includes a person who is entitled to take steps to enforce a charge or other security: Welfare Reform and Work Act 2016 s 24(4).

10 Welfare Reform and Work Act 2016 s 24(2)(a).

11 Welfare Reform and Work Act 2016 s 24(2)(b).

12 Including, in the case of a floating charge which relates to the interest in the property, the power under the Insolvency Act 1986 Sch B1 para 14 (see COMPANY AND PARTNERSHIP INSOLVENCY vol 16 (2011) PARA 175 et seq).

13 Welfare Reform and Work Act 2016 s 24(2)(c).

14 Ie 1 April 2016: see the Welfare Reform and Work Act 2016 s 36(5)(b); and the Welfare Reform and Work Act 2016 (Commencement No 1) Regulations 2016, SI 2016/394, reg 4.

15 Welfare Reform and Work Act 2016 s 24(3).

16 Welfare Reform and Work Act 2016 s 24(5). Regulations under s 24(5) may in particular make provision about: (1) tenants of a description prescribed by the regulations; (2) tenancies of a description prescribed by the regulations; (3) accommodation of a description prescribed by the regulations; (4) accommodation which satisfies conditions prescribed by the regulations, including conditions relating to the funding of its building or refurbishment; (5) events of a description prescribed by the regulations: s 24(6). Regulations made by virtue of s 24(6)(a) (head (1) above) may include provision about tenants whose income exceeds, or whose household's incomes exceed, an amount prescribed by the regulations during a period prescribed by the regulations: s 24(7). Regulations made by virtue of s 24(6)(e) (head (5) above) may include provision about periods during a tenancy when the rent payable is temporarily reduced or waived: s 24(8). Regulations under s 24 must be made by statutory instrument (s 24(9)), and a statutory instrument containing regulations under s 24 is subject to annulment in pursuance of a resolution of either House of Parliament (s 24(10)). See the Social Housing Rents (Exceptions and Miscellaneous Provisions) Regulations 2016, SI 2016/390 (amended by SI 2017/91).

17 Welfare Reform and Work Act 2016 s 33. As to the Regulator of Social Housing see PARA 57 et seq.

18 Welfare Reform and Work Act 2016 s 25(1). The direction may be: (1) a direction that s 23 does not apply in relation to a private registered provider specified in the direction; (2) a direction that s 23 is to have effect in relation to a private registered provider specified in the direction as if in s 23(1) for 'at least 1% less than' there were substituted 'no more than'; (3) a direction that s 23 is to have effect in relation to a private registered provider specified in the direction as if s 23(1) required at least the lesser reduction specified in the direction; (4) a direction that s 23 is to have effect in relation to a private registered provider specified in the direction as if s 23(1) required the private registered provider to secure that the amount of rent payable by a tenant of its social housing increased by no more than the percentage specified in the direction: s 25(2). The regulator may specify in a direction: (a) the period during which it is to have effect; and (b) the social housing in relation to which it is to have effect: s 25(3).

19 Welfare Reform and Work Act 2016 s 25(4).

20 Welfare Reform and Work Act 2016 s 25(5). Regulations under s 25 must be made by statutory instrument (s 25(13)) and a statutory instrument containing regulations under s 25 is subject to annulment in pursuance of a resolution of either House of Parliament (s 25(14)).

21 Welfare Reform and Work Act 2016 s 25(6).

22 As to the meaning of 'local authority' see PARA 12; definition applied by the Welfare Reform and Work Act 2016 s 33(1).

23 Welfare Reform and Work Act 2016 s 25(7). The direction may be: (1) a direction that s 23 does not apply in relation to a local authority specified in the direction; (2) a direction that s 23 is to have effect in relation to a local authority specified in the direction as if in s 23(1) for 'at least 1% less than' there were substituted 'no more than'; (3) a direction that s 23 is to have effect in relation to a local authority specified in the direction as if s 23(1) required at least the lesser reduction specified in the direction; (4) a direction that s 23 is to have effect in relation to a local authority specified in the direction as if s 23(1) required the authority to secure that the amount of rent payable by a tenant of its social housing increased by no more than the percentage specified in the direction: s 25(8). The Secretary of State may specify in a direction: (a) the period during which it is to have effect; and (b) the social housing in relation to which it is to have effect: s 25(9).

24 Welfare Reform and Work Act 2016 s 25(10).

25 Welfare Reform and Work Act 2016 s 25(11). As to regulations under s 25 see note 20.
26 Welfare Reform and Work Act 2016 s 25(12).
27 See the Welfare Reform and Work Act 2016 s 26, Sch 2. See also the Social Housing Rents (Exceptions and Miscellaneous Provisions) Regulations 2016, SI 2016/390 (amended by SI 2017/91).
28 Ie: (1) in respect of a relevant year, or a part of a relevant year, by a tenant of social housing in relation to whom: (a) the Welfare Reform and Work Act 2016 s 23 does not apply because of an exception in regulations under s 24; (b) a provision about levels of rent in Sch 2 Pt 1 does not apply because of an exception in regulations under Sch 2 para 5 (s 27(1)(a), (b)); (2)(a) in respect of the part of the relevant year after an exception in regulations under s 24 ceases to apply; (b) in respect of the part of the relevant year after an exception in regulations under Sch 2 para 5 ceases to apply; (c) in respect of the following relevant year (if any) (s 27(2)(a)–(c)).
29 Welfare Reform and Work Act 2016 s 27(1), (2). Regulations under s 27(1) or (2) may, in particular, require registered providers to secure that the maximum amount of rent payable in respect of a relevant year, or part of a relevant year, is an amount determined as specified in the regulations: s 27(3). Regulations made by virtue of s 27(3) may, in particular, provide for s 23 or Sch 2 Pt 1 to have effect with modifications: s 27(4). The modifications that may be made by virtue of s 27(4) include (but are not limited to) modifications that:
   (1)   provide for the maximum amount of rent to be increased from year to year by no more than a percentage specified in the regulations;
   (2)   provide for the maximum amount of rent to be determined by disregarding the effect of a temporary reduction or waiver of rent;
   (3)   provide for the maximum amount of rent to be determined by reference to a different period;
   (4)   provide for s 23(1) or Sch 2 para 1(4)(c) or (5)(c) or 3(5) to have effect as if it referred to a different percentage;
   (5)   provide for Sch 2 para 1, 2 or 3 to have effect as if the social rent rate were uplifted by a percentage specified in the regulations;
   (6)   provide for Sch 2 para 3(2) or (3) to have effect as if Sch 2 para 3(2)(a)(ii) or (4)(a)(ii) referred to a different percentage;
   (7)   provide for the maximum amount of rent to be determined by reference to what would have been the amount if an exception in regulations under s 24 or Sch 2 para 5(5) (including an exception making such provision as is described in s 24(7) or Sch 2 para 5(7)) had not applied: s 27(5).
   Regulations made by virtue of s 27(5)(d) (head (4) above) may not provide for a higher percentage to have effect: s 27(6). Regulations made by virtue of s 27(5)(e) (head (5) above) may, in particular, make provision in relation to cases where an exception in regulations under Sch 2 para 5(5) making provision about social housing which satisfies conditions prescribed by the regulations as to design, facilities, use or the provision of support to tenants applies: s 27(7). Regulations under s 27(1) may not provide for a maximum amount of rent payable by a tenant of social housing in respect of a relevant year, or a part of a relevant year, which is less than the amount that would be payable by the tenant in respect of that period if the rent was payable at the social rent rate in that period, in a case where an exception in regulations under Sch 2 para 5(5) applies: s 27(8). Regulations under s 27(1) or (2) may make provision about disapplying or modifying a requirement in the regulations as it relates to a registered provider: s 27(9). Regulations made by virtue of s 27(9) may, in particular, enable the Secretary of State or the regulator to issue a direction that disapplies or modifies a requirement as it relates to a registered provider: s 27(10). Regulations made by virtue of s 27(10) may provide for a direction to specify: (a) the period during which it has effect; (b) the social housing in relation to which it has effect: s 27(11). Regulations made by virtue of s 27(10) may: (i) provide for conditions to be satisfied before a direction is issued; (ii) provide for the regulator to obtain the consent of the Secretary of State before issuing a direction: s 27(12). Regulations under s 27 must be made by statutory instrument (s 27(13)) and a statutory instrument containing regulations under s 27 is subject to annulment in pursuance of a resolution of either House of Parliament (s 27(14)).
   For regulations made under s 27 see the Social Housing Rents (Exceptions and Miscellaneous Provisions) Regulations 2016, SI 2016/390 (amended by SI 2017/91).
30 Ie imposed by or under the Welfare Reform and Work Act 2016 s 23 or s 27 or Sch 2 Pt 1.
31 Welfare Reform and Work Act 2016 s 28(1), (2). The Housing Act 1985 s 102 (variation of terms of a secure tenancy: see LANDLORD AND TENANT vol 63 (2016) PARA 1082) has effect subject to the Welfare Reform and Work Act 2016 s 28(1): s 28(3).
32 Ie the Welfare Reform and Work Act 2016 ss 23–27, Sch 2.
33 'Initial registered provider', in relation to a tenancy of social housing, means the first registered provider which: (1) was subject to a requirement imposed by or under the Welfare Reform and

Work Act 2016 s 23 or 27 or Sch 2 Pt 1 as regards the tenancy; or (2) would have been so subject but for its being disapplied: (a) by or under s 24 or Sch 2 para 5; or (b) by a direction under s 25 or Sch 2 para 6 or under s 27(9): s 29(6). In s 29 a reference to a relevant year of an initial registered provider includes, in the case of an initial registered provider that has ceased to exist, a reference to what would have been a relevant year of an initial registered provider if it had not ceased to exist: s 29(5).

34 Welfare Reform and Work Act 2016 s 29(1), (2). Section 29(4) applies if, immediately before the social housing became the transferee's social housing, a requirement imposed by or under s 23 or 27 or Sch 2 Pt 1 was disapplied or modified as regards the social housing: (1) by a direction under s 25 or Sch 2 para 6; or (2) under s 27(9): s 29(3). In such a case, if the social housing becomes the transferee's social housing otherwise than at the beginning of a relevant year of the initial registered provider, the requirement continues not to apply or continues to apply as modified (as the case may be) until: (a) the relevant year of the initial registered provider current when the social housing becomes the transferee's social housing comes to an end; or (b) if earlier, the tenancy comes to an end: s 29(4).

56. Reducing local authority influence over private registered providers. Under the Housing and Planning Act 2016 there are provisions to reduce the regulation of social housing, which came into force on 3 February 2017[1]. The Secretary of State[2] may by regulations make provision for the purpose of limiting or removing the ability of local authorities[3] to exert influence over private registered providers[4] through:

(1)   appointing[5] or removing officers[6] of private registered providers;

(2)   exercising or controlling voting rights[7].

The regulations may in particular:

(a)   limit the number of officers that a local authority may appoint;

(b)   prohibit a local authority from appointing officers;

(c)   confer power on a private registered provider to remove officers appointed by a local authority;

(d)   prohibit a local authority from doing things that would result in it obtaining voting rights in a private registered provider;

(e)   require a local authority to take steps to reduce or get rid of any voting rights that it has in a private registered provider[8].

Regulations under these provisions may override or modify any contractual or other rights (whenever created) or anything in a private registered provider's constitution[9]. Such regulations may:

(i)   confer a power to amend the constitution of a private registered provider in consequence of provision made by the regulations;

(ii)   make provision about the procedure for exercising that power[10].

1   See the Housing and Planning Act 2016 (Commencement No 4 and Transitional Provisions) Regulations 2017, SI 2017/75, reg 3(a).
2   As to the Secretary of State see PARA 7.
3   'Local authority' has the meaning given by the Housing Associations Act 1985 s 106 (see PARA 149 note 4): Housing and Planning Act 2016 s 93(5).
4   'Private registered provider' means a private registered provider of social housing: Housing and Planning Act 2016 s 93(5).
5   'Appointing', in relation to an officer, includes nominating or otherwise influencing the selection of the officer: Housing and Planning Act 2016 s 93(5).
6   'Officer', in relation to a private registered provider, has the meaning given by the Housing and Regeneration Act 2008 s 270 (see PARA 78 note 6): Housing and Planning Act 2016 s 93(5).
7   Housing and Planning Act 2016 s 93(1).
8   Housing and Planning Act 2016 s 93(2).
9   Housing and Planning Act 2016 s 93(3). 'Constitution' includes rules: s 93(5).
10 Housing and Planning Act 2016 s 93(4).

B.   THE REGULATOR AND THE REGULATION COMMITTEE

(A)   The Regulator

57. Regulation functions of the Homes and Communities Agency. In Part 2 of the Housing and Regeneration Act 2008[1], 'the regulator' means the Homes and Communities Agency ('the HCA')[2]; and in any other enactment or instrument 'the Regulator of Social Housing' means the HCA[3]. The HCA deals with the registration of landlords and it has enforcement powers[4].

The HCA is established under Part 1 of the Housing and Regeneration Act 2008[5], which provides for its powers and duties[6], and makes provision as to its membership, staff, procedure, the establishment of committees and delegation, and as to reports and accounts[7]. The Secretary of State is given certain supervisory powers over the HCA[8].

The HCA must exercise its housing functions through a committee known as the Regulation Committee[9].

1   Ie the Housing and Regeneration Act 2008 Pt 2 (ss 59–278A).
2   Housing and Regeneration Act 2008 s 92A(1) (ss 92A, 92B added by the Localism Act 2011 s 178, Sch 16 paras 1, 26).
3   Housing and Regeneration Act 2008 s 92A(2) (as so added).
4   See PARAS 58–60. As to the HCA generally see PLANNING vol 83 (2010) PARA 1454 et seq. See also www.gov.uk/government/organisations/homes-and-communities-agency.
5   Ie the Housing and Regeneration Act 2008 Pt 1 (ss 1–58): see s 1(1); and PLANNING vol 83 (2010) PARA 1454.
6   See the Housing and Regeneration Act 2008 ss 2–45; and PLANNING vol 83 (2010) PARA 1455 et seq.
7   See the Housing and Regeneration Act 2008 Sch 1; and PLANNING vol 83 (2010) PARA 1454. The Tailored Review of the Homes and Communities Agency (Department for Communities and Local Government, 30 November, 2016) has recommended the separation of the social housing regulator into a new standalone non-departmental public body, to address the potential conflict of interest that arises from the Agency's current configuration. The government has sought public consultation on the matter: see Social housing regulation: using a Legislative Reform Order to establish the Regulator as a stand-alone body (Department for Communities and Local Government, 30 November, 2016).
8   See the Housing and Regeneration Act 2008 ss 46–48; and PLANNING vol 83 (2010) PARAS 1485–1486.
9   See the Housing and Regeneration Act 2008 s 92B; and PARA 61 et seq.

58. Powers. The regulator[1] may do anything it thinks necessary or expedient for the purpose of or in connection with the performance of a function of the regulator[2]. The regulator may carry out or commission studies designed to improve the economy, effectiveness and efficiency of registered providers[3] and may publish a report on a study[4].

The regulator may, where it thinks it advances a fundamental objective (that is, the economic regulation objective or the consumer regulation objective)[5], give financial assistance to a person in connection with:

(1)   undertaking research;
(2)   preparing guidance;
(3)   developing and publicising best practice; or
(4)   facilitating the management of social housing by tenants[6].

The regulator may, where it thinks it advances a fundamental objective, give financial assistance to a private registered provider[7] by: (a) lending money to or in respect of the registered provider; or (b) giving a guarantee or indemnity in respect of the registered provider[8]. Any such financial assistance may be given on conditions (which may include provision for repayment, with or without interest)[9].

In considering whether to exercise a power under Part 2 of the Housing and Regeneration Act 2008[10] the regulator may have regard to information or opinions from any source including, in particular, from tenants, bodies representing tenants, local housing authorities or the Commission for Local Administration in England or an ombudsman[11].

The regulator may for the purpose of advancing its fundamental objectives: (i) publish ideas or information; (ii) undertake research in relation to social housing; (iii) provide guidance, advice, education or training[12].

The regulator must: (A) promote awareness of the regulator's functions among tenants of social housing; (B) where the regulator thinks it appropriate, consult them about the exercise of its functions (for example, by holding meetings); and (C) where the regulator thinks it appropriate, involve them in the exercise of its functions (for example, by appointing them to committees or sub-committees)[13]. The regulator must from time to time publish a statement about how it proposes to comply with heads (A) to (C)[14]. Before publishing a statement, the regulator must consult such persons as it thinks appropriate[15].

1 As to the meaning of 'the regulator' see PARA 57.
2 Housing and Regeneration Act 2008 s 93(1) (amended by the Localism Act 2011 s 178, Sch 16 paras 1, 27). In particular, the regulator may do anything it thinks appropriate for advancing its fundamental objectives: Housing and Regeneration Act 2008 s 93(2). As to the meaning of 'function' see PARA 61 note 4.
3 Housing and Regeneration Act 2008 s 94(1). As to the meaning of 'registered provider' see PARA 53. Nothing in s 93(1) permits the regulator, in relation to local authorities, to carry out or commission studies about the performance of housing functions other than their functions as a provider of social housing: s 94(3) (added by SI 2010/844). As to the meaning of 'local authority' see PARA 149 note 4 (definition applied by the Housing and Regeneration Act 2008 s 275); and as to the meaning of 'social housing' see PARA 52.
4 Housing and Regeneration Act 2008 s 94(2).
5 As to fundamental objectives see PARA 59.
6 Housing and Regeneration Act 2008 s 95(1). As to the meaning of 'tenant' see PARA 52 note 9. Financial assistance under s 95(1) may be given: (1) by way of grant; (2) by way of loan; (3) by defraying expenditure on behalf of a person; or (4) in any other way except purchasing loan or share capital of a body corporate or giving a guarantee or indemnity: s 95(2).
7 As to the meaning of 'private registered provider' see PARA 53.
8 Housing and Regeneration Act 2008 s 95(3) (amended by SI 2010/844). Financial assistance may be given under the Housing and Regeneration Act 2008 s 95(3) only with the consent of the Secretary of State (given with the approval of the Treasury): s 95(4). As to the Secretary of State see PARA 7.
9 Housing and Regeneration Act 2008 s 95(5).
10 Ie the Housing and Regeneration Act 2008 Pt 2 (ss 59–278A).
11 Housing and Regeneration Act 2008 s 96 (amended by SI 2010/844). As to the Commission for Local Administration in England see LOCAL GOVERNMENT vol 69 (2009) PARA 839 et seq. As to an ombudsman appointed by virtue of the Housing and Regeneration Act 2008 s 124 see PARA 130 et seq.
12 Housing and Regeneration Act 2008 s 97(1). The regulator may for that purpose: (1) arrange for another person to do anything within s 97(1)(a)–(c) (heads (i)–(iii) in the text); (2) act jointly with, cooperate with or assist another person doing anything within s 97(1)(a)–(c): s 97(2). The persons to whom advice may be given under s 97(1) include: (a) unregistered housing associations (as defined by the Housing Associations Act 1985 s 2B (see PARA 24 note 4)); and (b) persons who may be forming a housing association (within the meaning of s 1(1) of that Act (see PARA 13)): Housing and Regeneration Act 2008 s 97(3).
13 Housing and Regeneration Act 2008 s 98(1). As to committees and sub-committees see PARA 65.
14 Housing and Regeneration Act 2008 s 98(2).
15 Housing and Regeneration Act 2008 s 98(3).

59. Fundamental objectives. The regulator[1] must perform its functions[2] with a view to achieving (so far as is possible):
(1)   the economic regulation objective, and
(2)   the consumer regulation objective[3].
The economic regulation objective is:

(a)   to ensure that registered providers of social housing[4] are financially viable and properly managed, and perform their functions efficiently and economically;

(b)   to support the provision of social housing sufficient to meet reasonable demands (including by encouraging and promoting private investment in social housing);

(c)   to ensure that value for money is obtained from public investment in social housing;

(d)   to ensure that an unreasonable burden is not imposed (directly or indirectly) on public funds; and

(e)   to guard against the misuse of public funds[5].

The consumer regulation objective is:

(i)   to support the provision of social housing that is well-managed and of appropriate quality;

(ii)   to ensure that actual or potential tenants[6] of social housing have an appropriate degree of choice and protection;

(iii)   to ensure that tenants of social housing have the opportunity to be involved in its management and to hold their landlords to account; and

(iv)   to encourage registered providers of social housing to contribute to the environmental, social and economic well-being of the areas in which the housing is situated[7].

The objectives are referred to in Part 2 of the Housing and Regeneration Act 2008[8] as the regulator's fundamental objectives[9]. The regulator must exercise its functions in a way that: (A) minimises interference; and (B) (so far as is possible) is proportionate, consistent, transparent and accountable[10].

1   As to the meaning of 'the regulator' see PARA 57.
2   As to the meaning of 'function' see PARA 61 note 4.
3   Housing and Regeneration Act 2008 s 92K(1) (s 92K added by the Localism Act 2011 s 178, Sch 16 paras 1, 26).
4   As to the meaning of 'registered provider' see PARA 53; and as to the meaning of 'social housing' see PARA 52.
5   Housing and Regeneration Act 2008 s 92K(2) (as added: see note 3).
6   As to the meaning of 'tenant' see PARA 52 note 9.
7   Housing and Regeneration Act 2008 s 92K(3) (as added: see note 3).
8   Ie the Housing and Regeneration Act 2008 Pt 2 (ss 59–278A).
9   Housing and Regeneration Act 2008 s 92K(4) (as added: see note 3).
10 Housing and Regeneration Act 2008 s 92K(5) (as added: see note 3).

60.   Collection and disclosure of information. The regulator[1] may for a purpose connected with its functions require a person to provide documents or information which it has reason to believe is or may be in the person's possession and which relates to:

(1)   the financial or other affairs of a registered provider[2];

(2)   activities which are or may be carried out by: (a) a person who is, or who has applied to become, a registered provider; or (b) a local authority[3] in England which the regulator thinks may be, or may become, a provider of social housing[4].

A requirement may specify: (i) the form and manner in which a document or information is to be provided (which may include the provision of a legible copy of information stored electronically); (ii) when and where it is to be provided[5]. The regulator may copy or record documents or information provided[6].

Failure to comply with a requirement without reasonable excuse is an offence[7]. Intentionally altering, suppressing or destroying a document or information to which a requirement relates is also an offence[8]. If a person fails to comply with a requirement the High Court may, on an application by the regulator, make an order for the purpose of remedying the failure[9].

A public authority[10] may disclose information to the regulator if the authority thinks that the disclosure is necessary for a purpose connected with the regulator's functions[11]. The regulator may disclose information to a public authority if the regulator thinks that the disclosure is necessary for a purpose connected with the regulator's functions or for a purpose connected with the authority's functions[12]. The regulator may disclose information to a person acting on its behalf for a purpose connected with the regulator's functions[13]. The power to disclose information under these provisions of the Housing and Regeneration Act 2008 is subject to any express restriction on disclosure imposed by another enactment (ignoring any restriction which allows disclosure if authorised by an enactment)[14]. A disclosure may be subject to restrictions on further disclosure[15], and disclosure in contravention of such a restriction is an offence[16].

1 As to the meaning of 'the regulator' see PARA 57.
2 As to the meaning of 'registered provider' see PARA 53.
3 As to the meaning of 'local authority' see PARA 149 note 4 (definition applied by the Housing and Regeneration Act 2008 s 275).
4 Housing and Regeneration Act 2008 s 107(1) (amended by SI 2010/844). As to the meaning of 'social housing' see PARA 52. A requirement may be imposed on a person other than the body to which the document or information relates only if: (1) the body has been required to provide the document or information but has failed to do so; or (2) the regulator thinks that the body is unable to provide it: Housing and Regeneration Act 2008 s 107(2). A requirement does not require a person to disclose anything which the person would be entitled to refuse to disclose on grounds of legal professional privilege in proceedings in the High Court: s 108(1). As to legal professional privilege generally see CIVIL PROCEDURE vol 12 (2015) PARAS 647–662. A requirement does not require a banker to breach a duty of confidentiality owed to a person who is not: (a) the registered provider to whose affairs or activities the documents or information relates; (b) a subsidiary of the registered provider; or (c) an associate of the registered provider: s 108(2). As to the meanings of 'subsidiary' and 'associate' see PARA 52 note 10. As to a banker's duty of confidentiality see FINANCIAL INSTITUTIONS vol 48 (2015) PARA 229.
5 Housing and Regeneration Act 2008 s 107(3).
6 Housing and Regeneration Act 2008 s 107(4).
7 Housing and Regeneration Act 2008 s 107(5). Proceedings for an offence under s 107(5) or (6) (see the text and note 8) may be brought only by or with the consent of the regulator or the Director of Public Prosecutions: s 108(5). A person guilty of an offence under s 107(5) is liable on summary conviction to a fine not exceeding level 5 on the standard scale: s 108(3). As to the powers of magistrates' courts to issue fines on summary conviction see SENTENCING vol 92 (2015) PARA 176. As to the Director of Public Prosecutions see CRIMINAL PROCEDURE vol 27 (2015) PARAS 25, 30 et seq.
8 Housing and Regeneration Act 2008 s 107(6). See note 7. A person guilty of an offence under s 107(6) is liable: (1) on summary conviction, to a fine not exceeding the statutory maximum; (2) on conviction on indictment, to imprisonment for a term not exceeding two years or a fine or both: s 108(4). As to the powers of magistrates' courts to issue fines on summary conviction see SENTENCING vol 92 (2015) PARA 176.
9 Housing and Regeneration Act 2008 s 107(7). An order under s 107(7) may include provision about costs: s 108(6).
10 'Public authority' means a person having functions of a public nature (whether or not in the United Kingdom): Housing and Regeneration Act 2008 s 109(8). 'United Kingdom' means Great Britain and Northern Ireland: Interpretation Act 1978 s 5, Sch 1. 'Great Britain' means England, Scotland and Wales: Union with Scotland Act 1706, preamble art I; Interpretation Act 1978 s 22(1), Sch 2 para 5(a). Neither the Channel Islands nor the Isle of Man is within the United Kingdom. See further CONSTITUTIONAL AND ADMINISTRATIVE LAW vol 20 (2014) PARA 3.
11 Housing and Regeneration Act 2008 s 109(1).
12 Housing and Regeneration Act 2008 s 109(2).
13 Housing and Regeneration Act 2008 s 109(3).
14 Housing and Regeneration Act 2008 s 109(5).
15 Housing and Regeneration Act 2008 s 109(4).
16 Housing and Regeneration Act 2008 s 109(6). A person guilty of such an offence is liable on summary conviction to a fine not exceeding level 3 on the standard scale: s 109(7).

(B)   The Regulation Committee

61. The Regulation Committee. The Homes and Communities Agency ('the HCA')[1] was required to establish a committee to be known as the Regulation Committee[2]. The functions conferred on the HCA as the regulator by virtue of Part 2 of the Housing and Regeneration Act 2008[3], or as the Regulator of Social Housing by virtue of any other enactment or instrument, are exercisable by the HCA acting through its Regulation Committee[4]. Those functions cannot be exercised by the HCA in any other way[5]. These provisions are subject to any express provision to the contrary in Part 2 or in the enactment or instrument in question[6].

1   As to the HCA see PARA 57; and PLANNING vol 83 (2010) PARA 1454 et seq.
2   Housing and Regeneration Act 2008 s 92B(1) (s 92B added by the Localism Act 2011 s 178, Sch 16 paras 1, 26). As to the Committee see PARA 62 et seq.
3   Ie the Housing and Regeneration Act 2008 Pt 2 (ss 59–278A).
4   Housing and Regeneration Act 2008 s 92B(2) (as added: see note 2). References in Pt 2 to the functions of the regulator are to the functions mentioned in s 92B(2): s 92B(5) (as so added). References in any enactment or instrument to the social housing functions of the HCA or the Regulator of Social Housing are to the functions mentioned in s 92B(2): s 92B(6) (as so added).
5   Housing and Regeneration Act 2008 s 92B(3) (as added: see note 2).
6   Housing and Regeneration Act 2008 s 92B(4) (as added: see note 2).

62. Membership of the Regulation Committee. The Regulation Committee[1] consists of: (1) a person appointed by the Secretary of State[2] to chair the Committee ('the chair'); and (2) not less than four and not more than six other members appointed by the Secretary of State[3]. The chair of the Committee must not be a member of the Homes and Communities Agency ('the HCA') immediately prior to the chair's appointment as such, but becomes a member of the HCA on appointment[4]. One other member of the Committee may be a member of the HCA[5], and such a member is referred to in Part 2 of the Housing and Regeneration Act 2008[6] as the internal member[7]. The remaining members of the Committee must be neither a member nor a member of staff of the HCA[8], and such a member is referred to in Part 2 as an external member[9].

The Secretary of State must consult the chair before appointing the other members[10]. In appointing a person to be a member, the Secretary of State must have regard to the desirability of appointing a person who has experience of, and has shown some capacity in, a matter relevant to the exercise of the functions of the regulator[11]. In appointing a person to be a member, the Secretary of State must be satisfied that the person will have no financial or other interest likely to affect prejudicially the exercise of the person's functions as a member[12]. The Secretary of State may require any person whom the Secretary of State proposes to appoint as a member to provide such information as the Secretary of State considers necessary for this purpose[13].

1   As to the establishment of the Committee see PARA 61.
2   As to the Secretary of State see PARA 7.
3   Housing and Regeneration Act 2008 s 92C(1) (s 92C added by the Localism Act 2011 s 178, Sch 16 paras 1, 26).
4   Housing and Regeneration Act 2008 s 92C(2) (as added: see note 3). As to the HCA see PARA 57; and PLANNING vol 83 (2010) PARA 1454 et seq.
5   Housing and Regeneration Act 2008 s 92C(3) (as added: see note 3).
6   Ie the Housing and Regeneration Act 2008 Pt 2 (ss 59–278A).
7   Housing and Regeneration Act 2008 s 92C(4) (as added: see note 3).
8   Housing and Regeneration Act 2008 s 92C(5) (as added: see note 3).
9   Housing and Regeneration Act 2008 s 92C(6) (as added: see note 3).
10 Housing and Regeneration Act 2008 s 92C(7) (as added: see note 3).

11 Housing and Regeneration Act 2008 s 92C(8) (as added: see note 3). As to the meaning of 'the regulator' see PARA 57; and as to the meaning of 'function' see PARA 61 note 4.
12 Housing and Regeneration Act 2008 s 92C(9) (as added: see note 3).
13 Housing and Regeneration Act 2008 s 92C(10) (as added: see note 3).

63. Terms of appointment of members. A member of the Regulation Committee[1] holds office in accordance with the member's terms of appointment[2]. A member may resign by serving notice on the Secretary of State[3]. A person ceases to be the chair[4] if the person resigns that office by serving notice on the Secretary of State or ceases to be a member of the Committee[5]. If a person ceases to be the chair, the person ceases to be a member of the Committee and ceases to be a member of the Homes and Communities Agency ('the HCA')[6]. A person ceases to be the internal member if the person ceases to be a member of the HCA[7].

A person who ceases to be a member or the chair is eligible for re-appointment[8]. The Secretary of State may remove a member who:

(1) has been absent from meetings of the Committee without its permission for more than six months;

(2) has become bankrupt or has made an arrangement with the member's creditors;

(3) the Secretary of State thinks has failed to comply with the member's terms of appointment; or

(4) the Secretary of State thinks is otherwise unable, unfit or unsuitable to exercise the functions of that member[9].

1 As to the establishment of the Committee see PARA 61; and as to membership see PARA 62.
2 Housing and Regeneration Act 2008 s 92D(1) (s 92D added by the Localism Act 2011 s 178, Sch 16 paras 1, 26).
3 Housing and Regeneration Act 2008 s 92D(2) (as added: see note 2). As to the Secretary of State see PARA 7.
4 As to the chair see PARA 62.
5 Housing and Regeneration Act 2008 s 92D(3) (as added: see note 2).
6 Housing and Regeneration Act 2008 s 92D(4) (as added: see note 2). As to the HCA see PARA 57; and PLANNING vol 83 (2010) PARA 1454 et seq.
7 Housing and Regeneration Act 2008 s 92D(5) (as added: see note 2). As to the meaning of 'internal member' see PARA 62.
8 Housing and Regeneration Act 2008 s 92D(6) (as added: see note 2). This is subject to s 92C (see PARA 62): s 92D(6) (as so added).
9 Housing and Regeneration Act 2008 s 92D(7) (as added: see note 2).

64. Remuneration etc of members. The Secretary of State[1] may require the Homes and Communities Agency ('the HCA')[2] to pay to the chair[3] such additional remuneration and allowances as the Secretary of State may decide[4]. The Secretary of State may require the HCA to pay to the external members of the Regulation Committee[5] such remuneration and allowances as the Secretary of State may decide[6]. The Secretary of State may require the HCA to: (1) pay such pensions, allowances or gratuities as the Secretary of State may decide to or in respect of any external member or former external member; (2) pay such sums as the Secretary of State may decide towards provision for the payment of pensions, allowances or gratuities to or in respect of any external member or former external member[7]. If: (a) a person ceases to be an external member; and (b) the Secretary of State considers that there are special circumstances that make it appropriate for the person to receive compensation, the Secretary of State may require the HCA to pay the person such amount as the Secretary of State may decide[8].

1 As to the Secretary of State see PARA 7.

2 As to the HCA see PARA 57; and PLANNING vol 83 (2010) PARA 1454 et seq.
3 As to the chair see PARA 62.
4 Housing and Regeneration Act 2008 s 92E(1) (s 92E added by the Localism Act 2011 s 178, Sch 16 paras 1, 26).
5 As to the establishment of the Committee see PARA 61. As to the meaning of 'external member' see PARA 62.
6 Housing and Regeneration Act 2008 s 92E(2) (as added: see note 4).
7 Housing and Regeneration Act 2008 s 92E(3) (as added: see note 4).
8 Housing and Regeneration Act 2008 s 92E(4), (5) (as added: see note 4).

65.   Sub-committees. The Regulation Committee[1] may establish one or more sub-committees[2]. A sub-committee may include persons who are not members of the Committee[3]. The Secretary of State[4] may require the Homes and Communities Agency ('the HCA')[5] to pay such remuneration and allowances as the Secretary of State may decide to any person who: (1) is a member of a sub-committee; but (2) is not a member of the Committee[6]. The HCA may dissolve a sub-committee[7].

1 As to the establishment of the Committee see PARA 61.
2 Housing and Regeneration Act 2008 s 92F(1) (s 92F added by the Localism Act 2011 s 178, Sch 16 paras 1, 26).
3 Housing and Regeneration Act 2008 s 92F(2) (as added: see note 2). As to membership of the Committee see PARA 62.
4 As to the Secretary of State see PARA 7.
5 As to the HCA see PARA 57; and PLANNING vol 83 (2010) PARA 1454 et seq.
6 Housing and Regeneration Act 2008 s 92F(3) (as added: see note 2).
7 Housing and Regeneration Act 2008 s 92F(4) (as added: see note 2).

66.   Procedure   of   the   Committee   and   its   sub-committees.   The Regulation Committee[1] may decide: (1) its own procedure[2]; and (2) the procedure of any of its sub-committees[3]. Subject to this, a sub-committee may decide its own procedure[4]. The validity of proceedings of the Committee or of any of its sub-committees is not affected by: (a) any vacancy in its membership; (b) any defect in the appointment of a member; or (c) any contravention of the provisions[5] as to members' interests[6].

1 As to the establishment of the Committee see PARA 61.
2 For these purposes, 'procedure' includes quorum: Housing and Regeneration Act 2008 s 92G(4) (s 92G added by the Localism Act 2011 s 178, Sch 16 paras 1, 26).
3 Housing and Regeneration Act 2008 s 92G(1) (as added: see note 2). As to sub-committees see PARA 65.
4 Housing and Regeneration Act 2008 s 92G(2) (as added: see note 2).
5 Ie the Housing and Regeneration Act 2008 s 92H: see PARA 67.
6 Housing and Regeneration Act 2008 s 92G(3) (as added: see note 2).

67.   Members' interests. A member of the Regulation Committee[1] who is directly or indirectly interested in any matter arising at a meeting of the Committee must disclose the nature of that interest to the meeting[2]. A member of a sub-committee of the Committee who is directly or indirectly interested in any matter arising at a meeting of the sub-committee must disclose the nature of that interest to the meeting[3]. Where either of these provisions applies: (1) the member must not take part in any deliberation or decision about the matter if it is a contract or agreement of any description; but (2) may otherwise take part in any deliberation or decision about the matter unless at least one-third of the other members at the meeting decide that the interests disclosed might prejudicially affect the member's consideration of the matter[4].

1 As to the establishment of the Committee see PARA 61; and as to membership see PARA 62.
2 Housing and Regeneration Act 2008 s 92H(1) (s 92H added by the Localism Act 2011 s 178, Sch 16 paras 1, 26).

3 Housing and Regeneration Act 2008 s 92H(2) (as added: see note 2). As to sub-committees see PARA 65.
4 Housing and Regeneration Act 2008 s 92H(3) (as added: see note 2).

68. Exercise of functions. The Regulation Committee[1] may delegate any of the functions of the regulator[2] to: (1) any of its members[3]; (2) any of its sub-committees[4]; or (3) any member of staff of the Homes and Communities Agency ('the HCA')[5]. A sub-committee of the Committee may delegate any function conferred on it to any member of staff of the HCA[6]. A power of the HCA that is a function of the regulator: (a) may be exercised separately or together with, or as part of, another such power; (b) does not limit the scope of another such power[7].

1 As to the establishment of the Committee see PARA 61.
2 As to the meaning of 'function' see PARA 61 note 4; as to the meaning of 'the regulator' see PARA 57.
3 As to membership of the Committee see PARA 62.
4 As to sub-committees see PARA 65.
5 Housing and Regeneration Act 2008 s 92I(1) (s 92I added by the Localism Act 2011 s 178, Sch 16 paras 1, 26). As to the HCA see PARA 57; and PLANNING vol 83 (2010) PARA 1454 et seq.
6 Housing and Regeneration Act 2008 s 92I(2) (as added: see note 5).
7 Housing and Regeneration Act 2008 s 92I(3) (as added: see note 5).

69. Recommendations to Homes and Communities Agency. The Regulation Committee[1] may make recommendations to the Homes and Communities Agency ('the HCA')[2] about the exercise of the HCA's functions[3]. The HCA must publish, in such manner as it thinks fit: (1) a recommendation received from the Regulation Committee under these provisions; and (2) the HCA's response to it[4].

1 As to the establishment of the Committee see PARA 61.
2 As to the HCA see PARA 57; and PLANNING vol 83 (2010) PARA 1454 et seq.
3 Housing and Regeneration Act 2008 s 92J(1) (s 92J added by the Localism Act 2011 s 178, Sch 16 paras 1, 26). In the Housing and Regeneration Act 2008 s 92J the reference to the HCA's functions does not include the functions of the regulator: s 92J(3) (as so added). As to the meaning of 'function' see PARA 61 note 4; as to the meaning of 'the regulator' see PARA 57.
4 Housing and Regeneration Act 2008 s 92J(2) (as added: see note 3).

C. REGISTRATION

70. Introduction. Chapter 3 of Part 2 of the Housing and Regeneration Act 2008[1] provides for the establishment of a register of providers of social housing[2]. The regulator[3] must maintain a register of providers of social housing[4] and it must make the register available for inspection by the public[5].

1 Ie the Housing and Regeneration Act 2008 Pt 2 Ch 3 (ss 110–121).
2 Housing and Regeneration Act 2008 s 110. As to the meaning of 'social housing' see PARA 52.
3 As to the meaning of 'the regulator' see PARA 57.
4 Housing and Regeneration Act 2008 s 111(1). As to eligibility for registration see PARA 71 and as to the registration procedure see PARA 72. The regulator must include in the register under s 111 on its establishment anyone: (1) who was registered under the Housing Act 1996 s 1 (register of social landlords: see PARA 167) immediately before the Housing and Regeneration Act 2008 s 61 (restriction of 'registered social landlord' system to Wales) came into force (ie 1 April 2010: see PARA 52 note 3); and (2) in relation to whom the Relevant Authority was the Housing Corporation (in accordance with the Housing Act 1996 s 56): Housing and Regeneration Act 2008 s 278(1). A person registered under s 278 is to be designated as a non-profit organisation: s 278(2).
5 Housing and Regeneration Act 2008 s 111(2).

71. Eligibility for registration. An English body[1] is eligible for voluntary registration as a provider of social housing[2] if it satisfies the following two conditions and it does not fall within the specified exceptions[3]. Condition 1 is that the body is a provider of social housing in England or intends to become a provider of social housing in England[4]. Condition 2 is that the body satisfies any relevant criteria set by the regulator[5] as to its financial situation, its constitution[6] and other arrangements for its management[7].

The exceptions to eligibility for registration are: (1) a local housing authority[8]; and (2) a county council[9]. However, the Secretary of State may by order require the regulator to register: (a) a specified local authority; or (b) a specified class of local authority[10].

A local authority in England which is not subject to compulsory registration[11] must notify the regulator as soon as it becomes subject to compulsory registration[12].

Each entry in the register must designate the body registered as either a non-profit organisation or a profit-making organisation[13]. If the regulator thinks that what was a profit-making organisation has become a non-profit organisation or vice versa, the regulator must change the registered designation accordingly[14].

1 As to the meaning of 'English body' see PARA 53.
2 As to the meaning of 'social housing' see PARA 52.
3 Housing and Regeneration Act 2008 s 112(1). Section 114 deals with bodies falling within the exceptions in s 113: s 112(5) (added by SI 2010/844). See the text and notes 9–10.
4 Housing and Regeneration Act 2008 s 112(2).
5 As to the meaning of 'the regulator' see PARA 57. Before setting criteria the regulator must consult: (1) the Greater London Authority; (2) one or more bodies appearing to it to represent the interests of private registered providers; (3) any body for the time being nominated under the Housing and Regeneration Act 2008 s 278A; and (4) one or more other bodies appearing to it to represent the interests of tenants: s 112(4) (amended by the Local Democracy, Economic Development and Construction Act 2009 s 26(1), (3); the Localism Act 2011 ss 178, 195(1), 237, Sch 16 paras 1, 36, Sch 19 paras 46, 48; Sch 25 Pt 26; and SI 2010/844). The Secretary of State may for the purposes of the Housing and Regeneration Act 2008 s 112(4) nominate a body appearing to the Secretary of State to represent the interests of tenants of social housing in England: s 278A(1)(a) (s 278A added by the Local Democracy, Economic Development and Construction Act 2009 s 26(1), (2)). The Secretary of State must notify the regulator of any nomination (or withdrawal of any nomination) under the Housing and Regeneration Act 2008 s 278A: s 278A(2) (as so added). See further the Local Democracy, Economic Development and Construction Act 2009 s 25 (establishment and assistance of bodies representing tenants); and PARA 51.
    As to the meaning of 'private registered provider' see PARA 53; and as to the meaning of 'tenant' see PARA 52 note 9. As to the Secretary of State see PARA 7. As to the Greater London Authority see LONDON GOVERNMENT vol 71 (2013) PARA 67 et seq.
6 'Constitution' includes rules: Housing and Regeneration Act 2008 s 275.
7 Housing and Regeneration Act 2008 s 112(3).
8 'Local housing authority' has the same meaning as in the Housing Act 1985 (see PARA 11): Housing and Regeneration Act 2008 s 275.
9 Housing and Regeneration Act 2008 s 113 (amended by SI 2010/844). The Secretary of State may by order repeal the Housing and Regeneration Act 2008 s 113 or amend it so as to permit the registration of specified classes of local authority: s 114(1). For the purposes of s 114, 'local authority' means an authority or person to whom s 113 applies or has applied: s 114(5)(a). Section 114 is in force for certain purposes in relation to Wales, and for all purposes in force in relation to England: see the Housing and Regeneration Act 2008 (Commencement No 2 and Transitional, Saving and Transitory Provisions) Order 2008, SI 2008/2358, arts 1(2), 3(1); and the Housing and Regeneration Act 2008 (Commencement No 6 and Transitional and Savings Provisions) Order 2009, SI 2009/2096, art 2(1).
10 Housing and Regeneration Act 2008 s 114(2); and see note 8. As to orders by the Secretary of State see PARA 54. Registration under s 114(2): (1) takes effect in accordance with any provision of the order about timing or other procedural or incidental matters; (2) does not require an application for registration; and (3) may apply to a local authority whether or not it is eligible for registration by virtue of s 114(1): s 114(3). If the Secretary of State thinks it necessary or desirable in connection with the registration of local authorities, the Secretary of State may by order: (a) provide for a provision of Pt 2 (ss 59–278A) or any other enactment not to apply in relation to registered local authorities; (b) provide for a provision of Pt 2 or any other enactment to apply with specified modifications in relation to registered local authorities; (c) amend a provision of Pt 2 or any other enactment: s 114(4). 'Registered local authorities' means authorities or persons who are registered, registrable or to be registered as a result of an order under s 114(1) or (2): s 114(5)(b).

Before making an order under s 114 the Secretary of State must consult any authority or person likely to be affected by it and such other persons as the Secretary of State thinks fit: s 114(6). As to an order made under s 114 see the Housing and Regeneration Act 2008 (Registration of Local Authorities) Order 2010, SI 2010/844.

11 For these purposes, an authority is subject to compulsory registration if it is a provider of social housing or it intends to become a provider of social housing: Housing and Regeneration Act 2008 s 114A(2) (s 114A added by SI 2010/844).

12 Housing and Regeneration Act 2008 s 114A(1) (as added: see note 11).

13 Housing and Regeneration Act 2008 s 115(1). This does not apply to the entry of a local authority in the register (and, accordingly, references to 'profit-making' and 'non-profit' in connection with a registered provider do not refer to a local authority): s 115(10) (added by SI 2010/844). As to the meaning of 'registered provider' see PARA 53. A body is a non-profit organisation if it is a registered or non-registrable charity: Housing and Regeneration Act 2008 s 115(2). A body is also a non-profit organisation if it satisfies the following conditions: s 115(3). Condition 1 is that the body: (1) does not trade for profit; or (2) is prohibited by its constitution from issuing capital with interest or dividend at a rate exceeding that prescribed under the Housing Associations Act 1985 s 1(1)(b) (see PARA 13): Housing and Regeneration Act 2008 s 115(4). Condition 2 is that a purpose of the body is the provision or management of housing: s 115(5). Condition 3 is that any other purposes of the body are connected with or incidental to the provision of housing: s 115(6). The Secretary of State may make regulations providing that a specified purpose is to be, or not to be, treated as connected with or incidental to the provision of housing: s 115(7). As to regulations by the Secretary of State see PARA 54. A body which is not a non-profit organisation under s 115(2) or (3) is a profit-making organisation: s 115(8). As to the meaning of 'registered charity' see PARA 53 note 2. 'Non-registrable charity' means a charity which is not required to be registered, in accordance with the Charities Act 2011 s 30: Housing and Regeneration Act 2008 s 275 (definition amended by the Charities Act 2011 s 354(1), Sch 7 para 135(a)). As to registered and non-registrable charities see CHARITIES vol 8 (2015) PARA 307 et seq.

14 Housing and Regeneration Act 2008 s 115(9) (amended by the Housing and Planning Act 2016 s 92, Sch 4 paras 22, 23).

72. Procedure for registration. The regulator[1] must register anyone who is eligible for registration as a provider of social housing[2], and who applies to be registered[3]. The regulator may make provision about: (1) the form of an application; (2) the information to be contained in it, or provided with it; (3) the manner in which an application is to be submitted; and (4) the consequences of failure to comply with provision under heads (1) to (3)[4].

The regulator may charge: (a) a fee for initial registration; and (b) an annual fee for continued registration[5]. Except in the case of a local authority[6], the regulator may make initial or continued registration conditional upon payment of the fee[7]. The regulator must prescribe the amount of a fee and make provision about the periods during which and in respect of which annual fees are payable[8]. The regulator may set different fees, and make different provision, for different cases or circumstances[9]. Fees must be set in accordance with principles which the regulator prepares and publishes and which are designed to ensure that so far as is reasonably practicable: (i) fee income matches expenditure on the performance of the regulator's functions; (ii) each fee is reasonable and proportionate to the costs to which it relates; and (iii) actual or potential registered providers[10] can see the relationship between the amount of a fee and the costs to which it relates[11]. The Homes and Communities Agency's ('the HCA's') accounts must show fees received and fees outstanding[12].

Once entered in the register[13] a body remains registered unless and until removed[14] from it[15]. It is to be presumed for all purposes that a person entered in the register under these provisions is eligible for registration while the registration lasts (irrespective of whether and why the person is later removed from the register)[16].

The regulator may remove from the register a private registered provider[17] which the regulator thinks: (A) is no longer eligible for registration; (B) has ceased to carry out activities; or (C) has ceased to exist as an entity[18].

A private registered provider may ask the regulator to remove it from the register[19]. The regulator may comply with a request: (I) on the grounds that the registered provider no longer is or intends to be a provider of social housing in England; (II) on the grounds that the registered provider is subject to regulation by another authority whose control is likely to be sufficient; or (III) on the grounds that the registered provider meets any relevant criteria for de-registration set by the regulator[20]. Before deciding whether or not to comply, the regulator must consult such local authorities in whose area the registered provider acts as it thinks appropriate[21]. The regulator must not comply with a request by a non-profit registered provider[22] if it thinks that removal is sought with a view to enabling the registered provider to distribute assets to members[23]. In deciding whether or not to comply, the regulator must (in particular) have regard to any conditions imposed in connection with financial assistance given to the registered provider under any enactment[24]. Having decided whether or not to remove the registered provider the regulator must notify the provider and any authority consulted[25].

As soon as is reasonably practicable after registering or de-registering a body the regulator must notify, in the case of a registered charity, the Charity Commission[26], in the case of a registered society[27], the Financial Conduct Authority, in the case of a registered company[28] (whether or not also a registered charity), the registrar of companies for England and Wales and, in the case of a local authority, the Secretary of State[29].

Except in the case of a local authority, a notice of registration must specify whether the person registered is designated as a non-profit or profit-making organisation[30]. If the designation changes, the regulator must notify any person notified of the registration[31]. A person to whom notice is given under these provisions must keep a record of it[32].

A body may appeal to the High Court against a decision of the regulator to refuse to register it, to de-register it or to refuse to de-register it[33]. The regulator must not de-register a body while an appeal is pending[34]. The Secretary of State may by order provide for the First-tier Tribunal to have jurisdiction instead of the High Court[35].

1 As to the meaning of 'the regulator' see PARA 57.
2 Ie under the Housing and Regeneration Act 2008 s 112(1): see PARA 71. As to the meaning of 'social housing' see PARA 52.
3 Housing and Regeneration Act 2008 s 116(1) (amended by SI 2010/844). The Housing and Regeneration Act 2008 s 116 is subject to s 117 (fees: see the text and notes 5–12): s 116(3). Section 116 deals with voluntary registration; as to the registration of local housing authorities and county councils, see s 114; and PARA 71: s 116(6) (added by SI 2010/844).
4 Housing and Regeneration Act 2008 s 116(2).
5 Housing and Regeneration Act 2008 s 117(1) (amended by SI 2010/844).
6 As to the meaning of 'local authority' see PARA 149 note 4 (definition applied by the Housing and Regeneration Act 2008 s 275).
7 Housing and Regeneration Act 2008 s 117(2) (substituted by SI 2010/844).
8 Housing and Regeneration Act 2008 s 117(3).
9 Housing and Regeneration Act 2008 s 117(4).
10 As to the meaning of 'registered provider' see PARA 53.
11 Housing and Regeneration Act 2008 s 117(5) (amended by the Localism Act 2011 s 178, Sch 16 paras 1, 37(1), (2)). The principles: (1) must provide for the Housing and Regeneration Act 2008 s 95(3) (financial assistance: see PARA 58) to be disregarded for the purpose of s 117(5)(a); and (2) may provide for specified expenditure or potential expenditure under s 95 or otherwise to be disregarded for the purpose of s 117(5)(a): s 117(6). Principles do not have effect until approved by the Secretary of State: s 117(7). In preparing (or revising) the principles the regulator must consult persons appearing to the regulator to represent the interests of fee-payers: s 117(8). As to the Secretary of State see PARA 7.

12 Housing and Regeneration Act 2008 s 117(9) (amended by the Localism Act 2011 Sch 16 paras 1, 37(1), (3)). The functions of billing for and receiving the payment of fees under the Housing and Regeneration Act 2008 s 117 are exercisable by the HCA rather than by the HCA acting through its Regulation Committee: s 117(10) (added by the Localism Act 2011 Sch 16 paras 1, 37(1), (4)). As to the HCA see PARA 57 et seq; and PLANNING vol 83 (2010) PARA 1454 et seq; as to the Regulation Committee see PARA 61 et seq.

13 Ie under the Housing and Regeneration Act 2008 s 116.

14 Ie under the Housing and Regeneration Act 2008 s 118 or s 119. See the text and notes 17–26.

15 Housing and Regeneration Act 2008 s 116(4) (amended by SI 2010/844).

16 Housing and Regeneration Act 2008 s 116(5) (amended by SI 2010/844).

17 As to the meaning of 'private registered provider' see PARA 53.

18 Housing and Regeneration Act 2008 s 118(1) (amended by SI 2010/844). Before removing a body under head (A) or (B) in the text the regulator must: (1) take all reasonable steps to give the body at least 14 days' notice; and (2) consider any representations it makes in that period: Housing and Regeneration Act 2008 s 118(2). After removing a body under head (A) or (B) in the text the regulator must take all reasonable steps to notify the body: s 118(3). The regulator must remove a local authority from the register if the regulator becomes aware that the authority: (a) is no longer a provider of social housing; or (b) no longer intends to become a provider of social housing (in the case of an authority which intended to become one but did not in fact do so): s 118(4) (added by SI 2010/844). 'Representations' means written representations: Housing and Regeneration Act 2008 s 275.

19 Housing and Regeneration Act 2008 s 119(1) (amended by SI 2010/844).

20 Housing and Regeneration Act 2008 s 119(2). The regulator must publish criteria set for the purposes of head (cc) in the text: s 119(7).

21 Housing and Regeneration Act 2008 s 119(3).

22 As to when a body is a non-profit organisation see PARA 71 note 13.

23 Housing and Regeneration Act 2008 s 119(4).

24 Housing and Regeneration Act 2008 s 119(5) (amended by the Housing and Planning Act 2016 s 92, Sch 4 paras 7, 11).

25 Housing and Regeneration Act 2008 s 119(6).

26 As to the meaning of 'registered charity' and 'Charity Commission' see PARA 53 notes 2, 3.

27 As to the meaning of 'registered society' see PARA 52 note 10.

28 As to the meaning of 'registered company' see PARA 53 note 5.

29 Housing and Regeneration Act 2008 s 120(1) (amended by the Co-operative and Community Benefit Societies Act 2014 s 151(1), Sch 4 paras 121, 122; and by SI 2010/844 and SI 2013/496).

30 Housing and Regeneration Act 2008 s 120(2) (amended by SI 2010/844).

31 Housing and Regeneration Act 2008 s 120(3).

32 Housing and Regeneration Act 2008 s 120(4).

33 Housing and Regeneration Act 2008 s 121(1).

34 Housing and Regeneration Act 2008 s 121(2).

35 Housing and Regeneration Act 2008 s 121(3). As to the First-tier Tribunal see COURTS AND TRIBUNALS vol 24 (2010) PARA 864 et seq; and PARA 32 et seq. As to orders by the Secretary of State see PARA 54.

D.   REGISTERED PROVIDERS

(A)   *In general*

73. Gifts and payments. The making of gifts, and the payment of dividends and bonuses, by a non-profit registered provider[1] are restricted to: (1) a member or former member of the registered provider; (2) a member of the family[2] of a member or former member; (3) a company which has as a director a person within head (1) or (2)[3]. A gift may be made, and a dividend or bonus may be paid, only if it falls within one of the following permitted classes[4].

Class 1 is payments which are in accordance with the constitution[5] of the registered provider and are due as interest on capital lent to the provider or subscribed in its shares[6].

Class 2 is payments which: (a) are paid by a fully mutual housing association[7]; (b) are paid to former members of the association; and (c) are due under either tenancy agreements with the association or agreements under which the former members became members of the association[8].

Class 3 is payments which are in accordance with the constitution of the registered provider making the payment ('the payer') and are made to a registered provider which is a subsidiary or associate of the payer[9].

Class 4 is payments which: (i) are in accordance with the constitution of the registered provider; (ii) are paid for the benefit of tenants of the provider; and (iii) are in any particular case paid to assist the tenant to obtain other accommodation by acquiring a freehold, or long-leasehold, interest in a dwelling[10].

If a registered company[11] or a registered society[12] contravenes these provisions: (A) it may recover the wrongful gift or payment as a debt from the recipient; and (B) the regulator may require it to take action[13] to recover the gift or payment[14].

1   As to the meaning of 'registered provider' see PARA 53. As to when a body is a non-profit organisation see PARA 71 note 13.
2   For the purposes of the Housing and Regeneration Act 2008 Pt 2 (ss 59–278A), one person is a member of the family of another if: (1) they are, or live together as if they were, spouses or civil partners; or (2) one is the parent, grandparent, child, grandchild, brother, sister, uncle, aunt, nephew or niece of the other: s 272(1). For those purposes: (a) a relationship by marriage or civil partnership is to be treated as a relationship by blood (and, in particular, P's stepchild is to be treated as P's child); and (b) a relationship by half-blood is to be treated as a relationship by whole blood: s 272(2). 'Spouse' includes a person who is married to a person of the same sex: see the Marriage (Same Sex Couples) Act 2013 s 11, Sch 3 para 1(1)(c), (2), (3); and MATRIMONIAL AND CIVIL PARTNERSHIP LAW vol 72 (2015) PARA 1 et seq.
3   Housing and Regeneration Act 2008 s 122(1). Provision is made about disposal of property by private registered providers in Pt 2 Ch 5 (ss 170–191): s 123 (amended by SI 2010/844); and see PARA 100 et seq.
4   Housing and Regeneration Act 2008 s 122(2). The Secretary of State may by order amend s 122 for the purpose of: (1) adding to the permitted classes; or (2) modifying or removing a permitted class added by order under s 122(7): s 122(7) (s 122(7), (8) added by the Localism Act 2011 s 179, Sch 17 paras 1, 2). Before making such an order, the Secretary of State must consult: (a) the Charity Commission; (b) the regulator; and (c) one or more bodies appearing to the Secretary of State to represent the interests of registered providers: Housing and Regeneration Act 2008 s 122(8) (as so added). As to the Secretary of State see PARA 7. As to orders by the Secretary of State see PARA 54. As to the meaning of 'Charity Commission' see PARA 53 note 3. As to the meaning of 'the regulator' see PARA 57.
5   As to the meaning of 'constitution' see PARA 71 note 6.
6   Housing and Regeneration Act 2008 s 122(3).
7   Ie within the meaning of the Housing Associations Act 1985 s 1(2): see PARA 13.
8   Housing and Regeneration Act 2008 s 122(4).
9   Housing and Regeneration Act 2008 s 122(5). As to the meanings of 'subsidiary' and 'associate' see PARA 52 note 10.
10 Housing and Regeneration Act 2008 s 122(5A) (s 122(5A), (5B) added by the Localism Act 2011 s 177). For the purposes of the Housing and Regeneration Act 2008 s 122(5A), 'long-leasehold interest', in relation to a dwelling, means the lessee's interest under a lease of the dwelling granted, for a premium, for a term certain exceeding 21 years; and 'acquiring', in relation to a long-leasehold interest in a dwelling, includes acquiring by grant and acquiring by assignment: s 122(5B) (as so added).
11 As to the meaning of 'registered company' see PARA 53 note 5.
12 As to the meaning of 'registered society' see PARA 52 note 10.
13 'Action' includes inaction, proposed action and decision: Housing and Regeneration Act 2008 s 275.
14 Housing and Regeneration Act 2008 s 122(6) (amended by the Co-operative and Community Benefit Societies Act 2014 s 151(1), Sch 4 paras 121, 123).

74. Undertakings. A registered provider[1] may give the regulator[2] an undertaking in respect of any matter concerning social housing[3]. The regulator may prescribe a procedure to be followed in giving an undertaking[4]. When exercising a regulatory or enforcement power[5] the regulator must have regard to any undertaking offered or given[6]. The regulator may found a decision about whether to exercise a regulatory or enforcement power wholly or partly on the extent to which an undertaking has been honoured[7].

1 As to the meaning of 'registered provider' see PARA 53.
2 As to the meaning of 'the regulator' see PARA 57.
3 Housing and Regeneration Act 2008 s 125(1). As to the meaning of 'social housing' see PARA 52.
4 Housing and Regeneration Act 2008 s 125(2).
5 Ie under the Housing and Regeneration Act 2008 Pt 2 Ch 6 (ss 192–217) or Ch 7 (ss 218–269B): see PARAS 104–110, 111–124.
6 Housing and Regeneration Act 2008 s 125(3).
7 Housing and Regeneration Act 2008 s 125(7).

(B)   Accounts

75. Accounts in general. The regulator[1] may give directions to private registered providers[2] about the preparation of their accounts[3]. A direction may be given to a profit-making registered provider[4] only in so far as its accounts relate to social housing activities[5]. The power must be exercised with a view to ensuring that accounts: (1) are prepared in proper form; and (2) present a true and fair view of: (a) the state of affairs of each registered provider in relation to its social housing activities; and (b) the disposition of funds and assets which are, or have been, in its hands in connection with those activities[6]. The regulator must make arrangements for bringing a direction to the attention of every registered provider to which it applies[7].

Each private registered provider must send a copy of its accounts to the regulator within the period of six months beginning with the end of the period to which the accounts relate[8]. The accounts must be accompanied by an auditor's report or, in the case of accounts that by virtue of an enactment are not subject to audit, any report that is required to be prepared in respect of the accounts by virtue of an enactment[9]. The report must specify whether the accounts comply with any relevant directions[10].

Each local authority[11] which is a registered provider must send copies of the following documents to the regulator so far as they relate to the provision of social housing: (i) any public interest report under the Local Audit and Accountability Act 2014[12] in relation to its accounts; (ii) its audited accounts, accompanied by any report made under that Act at the conclusion of the audit[13]. The local authority must send the copies to the regulator as soon as the authority receives them[14].

A person who has received information while acting as auditor of a private registered provider or as a reporting accountant[15] in relation to a private registered provider may disclose[16] the information to the regulator for a purpose connected with the regulator's functions despite any duty of confidentiality and whether or not the regulator requests the information[17].

1 As to the meaning of 'the regulator' see PARA 57.
2 As to the meaning of 'private registered provider' see PARA 53.
3 Housing and Regeneration Act 2008 s 127(1) (amended by SI 2010/844). The provisions dealt with in this paragraph broadly replicate the effect of the Housing Act 1996 Sch 1 Pt III (paras 16–19A) (see PARA 193). As to accounts of companies exempt from audit see PARA 76; as to accounts of registered societies and charities see PARA 77; and as to offences in connection with accounts see PARA 78.
4 As to the meaning of 'registered provider' see PARA 53. As to when a body is a profit-making organisation see PARA 71 note 13.
5 Housing and Regeneration Act 2008 s 127(2). As to the meaning of 'social housing' see PARA 52.
6 Housing and Regeneration Act 2008 s 127(3). A direction may require a registered charity to use a specified method for distinguishing in its accounts between matters relating to its social housing activities and other matters: s 127(4). As to the meaning of 'registered charity' see PARA 53 note 2. A direction: (1) may make provision that applies generally or only to specified cases,

circumstances or registered providers; and (2) may make different provision for different cases, circumstances or registered providers: s 127(5). A direction that relates to more than one registered provider may be given only after consulting one or more bodies appearing to the regulator to represent the interests of private registered providers: s 127(6) (amended by SI 2010/844).

7 Housing and Regeneration Act 2008 s 127(7).

8 Housing and Regeneration Act 2008 s 128(1) (amended by SI 2010/844).

9 Housing and Regeneration Act 2008 s 128(2).

10 Housing and Regeneration Act 2008 s 128(3).

11 As to the meaning of 'local authority' see PARA 149 note 4 (definition applied by the Housing and Regeneration Act 2008 s 275).

12 Ie made under the Local Audit and Accountability Act 2014 Sch 7 para 1 (public interest reports): see LOCAL GOVERNMENT.

13 Housing and Regeneration Act 2008 s 128(4) (added by SI 2010/844; and amended by the Local Audit and Accountability Act 2014 s 45, Sch 12 paras 89, 91).

14 Housing and Regeneration Act 2008 s 128(5) (added by SI 2010/844).

15 'Reporting accountant' means a person who is appointed to prepare a report which, by virtue of any enactment, has to be prepared in respect of accounts that are not subject to audit: Housing and Regeneration Act 2008 s 143(4).

16 The reference to disclosing information includes expressing an opinion on it: Housing and Regeneration Act 2008 s 143(3).

17 Housing and Regeneration Act 2008 s 143(1), (2).

76. Accounts of companies which are exempt from audit. The following provisions apply in relation to a registered provider[1] which: (1) is a registered company[2] other than a charity; and (2) is exempt from the audit requirements of the Companies Act 2006 by virtue of the exemption[3] for small companies[4]. The directors of the company must cause a report to be prepared[5] and made to the company's members in respect of the company's individual accounts[6] for any year in which the company takes advantage of its exemption from audit[7].

The required report must be prepared by a person ('the reporting accountant') who is eligible[8] for such appointment[9]. The report must state whether the individual accounts are in accordance with the company's accounting records kept under the Companies Act 2006[10]. On the basis of the information contained in the accounting records the report must also state whether: (a) the accounts comply with Part 15 of the Companies Act 2006[11]; (b) the company is entitled to exemption from audit[12] for the year in question[13]. The report must give the name of the reporting accountant and be signed[14] and dated[15]. Specified provisions of the Companies Act 2006[16] apply to the reporting accountant and to a reporting accountant's report as they apply to an auditor of the company and an auditor's report on the company's accounts (with any necessary modifications)[17].

Where a company appoints a reporting accountant to prepare a report in respect of its accounts for any year[18], the regulator[19] may require the company to: (i) cause a qualified auditor[20] to audit its accounts and balance sheet for that year; and (ii) send a copy of the report to the regulator by a specified date[21]. A requirement may not be imposed before the end of the financial year to which it relates[22].

1 As to the meaning of 'registered provider' see PARA 53.

2 As to the meaning of 'registered company' see PARA 53 note 5.

3 Ie under the Companies Act 2006 s 477: see COMPANIES vol 15 (2016) PARA 986.

4 Housing and Regeneration Act 2008 s 129(1). As to offences in connection with accounts see PARA 78.

5 Ie in accordance with the Housing and Regeneration Act 2008 s 130: see the text and notes 9–15.

6 'Individual accounts' has the same meaning as in the Companies Act 2006 s 396 (see COMPANIES vol 15 (2016) PARA 803): Housing and Regeneration Act 2008 s 129(3).

7 Housing and Regeneration Act 2008 s 129(2).

8 Ie under the Housing and Regeneration Act 2008 s 131. A person is eligible for appointment by a company as a reporting accountant under s 130 if: (1) either of the following conditions is satisfied; and (2) the person would not be prohibited from acting as auditor of the company by

virtue of the Companies Act 2006 s 1214 (see COMPANIES vol 15 (2016) PARA 1088): Housing and Regeneration Act 2008 s 131(1). Condition 1 is satisfied if the person is a member of a body listed in s 131(4) and under its rules the person: (a) is entitled to engage in public practice; and (b) is not ineligible for appointment as a reporting accountant: s 131(2). Condition 2 is satisfied if the person: (i) is subject to the rules of a body listed in s 131(4) in seeking appointment or acting as a statutory auditor under the Companies Act 2006 Pt 42 (ss 1209–1264) (see COMPANIES vol 15 (2016) PARA 1086); and (ii) under those rules, is eligible for appointment as a statutory auditor under that Part: Housing and Regeneration Act 2008 s 131(3).

The bodies mentioned in s 131(2), (3) are: (A) the Institute of Chartered Accountants in England and Wales; (B) the Institute of Chartered Accountants of Scotland; (C) the Institute of Chartered Accountants in Ireland; (D) the Association of Chartered Certified Accountants; (E) the Association of Authorised Public Accountants; (F) the Association of Accounting Technicians; (G) the Association of International Accountants; (H) the Chartered Institute of Management Accountants; and (I) the Institute of Chartered Secretaries and Administrators: s 131(4). The Secretary of State may by order amend the list of bodies in s 131(4): s 131(5). As to the Secretary of State see PARA 7. As to orders by the Secretary of State see PARA 54.

References in s 131 to the rules of a body are to rules (whether or not laid down by the body itself) which the body has power to enforce and which are relevant for the purposes of the Companies Act 2006 Pt 42 (statutory auditors) or the Housing and Regeneration Act 2008 s 131; and this includes rules relating to the admission and expulsion of members of the body so far as relevant for the purposes of that Part or the Housing and Regeneration Act 2008 s 131: s 131(6).

An individual or a firm may be appointed as a reporting accountant; and the Companies Act 2006 s 1216 (see COMPANIES vol 15 (2016) PARA 1089) applies to the appointment of a partnership constituted under the law of England and Wales, Northern Ireland or any other country or territory in which a partnership is not a legal person: Housing and Regeneration Act 2008 s 131(7). In ss 130–132, 'firm' has the meaning given by the Companies Act 2006 s 1173(1) (see COMPANIES vol 14 (2016) PARA 1): Housing and Regeneration Act 2008 s 130(6).

9   Housing and Regeneration Act 2008 s 130(1).
10   Housing and Regeneration Act 2008 s 130(2). The accounting records referred to in the text are those kept under the Companies Act 2006 s 386, as to which see COMPANIES vol 15 (2016) PARA 782.
11   Ie the Companies Act 2006 Pt 15 (ss 380–474): see COMPANIES vol 15 (2016) PARA 765 et seq.
12   Ie under the Companies Act 2006 s 477 (small companies' exemption): see COMPANIES vol 15 (2016) PARA 986.
13   Housing and Regeneration Act 2008 s 130(3).
14   The report must be signed: (1) where the reporting accountant is an individual, by that individual; and (2) where the reporting accountant is a firm, for and on behalf of the firm by an individual authorised to do so: Housing and Regeneration Act 2008 s 130(5).
15   Housing and Regeneration Act 2008 s 130(4).
16   Ie the Companies Act 2006 ss 423–425 (duty to circulate copies of annual accounts), ss 431, 432 (right of member or debenture holder to demand copies of accounts), s 434–436 (requirements in connection with publication of accounts), ss 441–444A (duty to file accounts with registrar of companies), s 454(4)(b) and regulations made under that provision (functions of auditor in relation to revised accounts), ss 499–502 (auditor's right to information) and ss 505, 506 (name of auditor to be stated in published copies of report): Housing and Regeneration Act 2008 s 132(2). In the Companies Act 2006 ss 505, 506 as they apply by virtue of the Housing and Regeneration Act 2008 s 132 in a case where the reporting accountant is a firm, any reference to the senior statutory auditor is to be read as a reference to the person who signed the report on behalf of the firm: s 132(3).
17   Housing and Regeneration Act 2008 s 132(1).
18   Ie in accordance with the Housing and Regeneration Act 2008 s 129.
19   As to the meaning of 'the regulator' see PARA 57.
20   'Qualified auditor', in relation to a company, means a person who: (1) is eligible for appointment as a statutory auditor of the company under the Companies Act 2006 Pt 42 (statutory auditors: see COMPANIES vol 15 (2016) PARA 1059 et seq); and (2) is not prohibited from acting as statutory auditor of the company by virtue of s 1214 (independence requirement: see COMPANIES vol 15 (2016) PARA 1088): Housing and Regeneration Act 2008 s 133(4).
21   Housing and Regeneration Act 2008 s 133(1), (2).
22   Housing and Regeneration Act 2008 s 133(3).

77. Accounts of registered societies and charities. The regulator[1] may require a registered provider[2] which is a registered society[3] to: (1) appoint a qualified auditor[4] to audit the society's accounts and balance sheet for any year of account[5] in respect of which the audit requirements of the Co-operative and Community Benefit Societies Act 2014[6] did not apply[7]; and (2) send a copy of the auditor's report to the regulator by a specified date[8]. Such a requirement may be imposed only during the year of account following the year to which the accounts relate[9].

A non-profit registered provider[10] which is a registered charity[11] must: (a) keep proper accounting records of its transactions and its assets and liabilities in relation to its housing activities; and (b) maintain a satisfactory system of control of those records, its cash holdings and its receipts and remittances in relation to those activities[12]. For each period of account[13] the charity must prepare: (i) a revenue account giving a true and fair view of the charity's income and expenditure during the period, so far as relating to its housing activities; and (ii) a balance sheet giving a true and fair view of the state of affairs of the charity as at the end of the period[14]. The revenue account and balance sheet must be signed by at least two directors or trustees[15].

In relation to the accounts of a charity prepared as above[16], if Condition 1 or 2 is met, the charity must cause a qualified person[17] to audit the accounts and report[18] on them, and if neither Condition is met, the charity must cause a qualified person ('the reporting accountant') to report[19] on the accounts[20]. Condition 1 is met if the accounts relate to a period during which the charity's gross income[21] arising in connection with its housing activities was greater than the specified[22] sum[23]. Condition 2 is met if: (A) the accounts relate to a period during which the charity's gross income arising in connection with its housing activities was greater than the accounts threshold[24]; and (B) at the end of the period the aggregate value of its assets (before deduction of liabilities) in respect of its housing activities was greater than the specified[25] sum[26].

An auditor appointed[27] in respect of a charity's accounts must make a report to the charity in accordance with the following provisions[28]. The report must state whether the revenue account gives a true and fair view of the charity's income and expenditure, so far as relating to its housing activities, and whether the balance sheet gives a true and fair view of the state of affairs of the charity as at the end of the period to which the accounts relate[29]. The report must give the name of the auditor and be signed[30]. The auditor must, in preparing the report, carry out such investigations as are necessary to form an opinion as to whether the charity has complied with the statutory requirements[31] during the period to which the accounts relate and whether the accounts are in accordance with accounting records kept under the relevant statutory provision[32]. If the auditor thinks that the charity has not complied with the statutory requirements or that the accounts are not in accordance with its accounting records, that must be stated in the report[33]. If the auditor fails to obtain all the information and explanations which the auditor thinks necessary for the purposes of the audit, that must be stated in the report[34].

A reporting accountant appointed[35] in respect of a charity's accounts must make a report to the charity in accordance with the following provisions[36]. The report must state whether the accounts are in accordance with accounting records kept under the relevant statutory provision[37]. On the basis of the information in the accounting records the report must also state whether the accounts comply with the requirements of the Charities Act 2011 and whether the charity was required to appoint a reporting accountant[38] in respect of the accounts[39]. The report must give the name of the reporting accountant and be signed[40]. If the reporting accountant fails to obtain all the information and explanations which the reporting accountant thinks necessary for the purposes of preparing the report, that must be stated in the report[41].

Where a charity appoints a reporting accountant to prepare a report in respect of any accounts[42], the regulator may require the charity to cause a qualified person[43] to audit the accounts and prepare a report on them[44], and send a copy of the report to the regulator by a specified date[45]. Such a requirement may be imposed only during the period of account[46] following the period to which the accounts relate[47].

Where a person is appointed by a charity to audit or report on accounts[48], the charity must grant the person access to its documents, if or in so far as they relate to its housing activities[49]. An officer of the charity must provide such information or explanations as the person thinks necessary[50].

1   As to the meaning of 'the regulator' see PARA 57.
2   As to the meaning of 'registered provider' see PARA 53.
3   As to the meaning of 'registered society' see PARA 52 note 10.
4   'Qualified auditor' has the same meaning as in the Co-operative and Community Benefit Societies Act 2014 Pt 7 (ss 75–102): Housing and Regeneration Act 2008 s 134(5) (substituted by the Co-operative and Community Benefit Societies Act 2014 s 151(1), Sch 4 paras 121, 125(1), (4)). See FINANCIAL INSTITUTIONS vol 48 (2015) PARA 1004.
5   'Year of account' has the same meaning as in the Co-operative and Community Benefit Societies Act 2014 Pt 7 (ss 75–102) (see ss 77, 78; and FINANCIAL INSTITUTIONS vol 48 (2015) PARA 1002): Housing and Regeneration Act 2008 s 134(5) (as substituted: see note 4).
6   Ie the Co-operative and Community Benefit Societies Act 2014 s 83: see FINANCIAL INSTITUTIONS vol 48 (2015) PARA 1004.
7   Ie because of a resolution under the Co-operative and Community Benefit Societies Act 2014 s 84: see FINANCIAL INSTITUTIONS vol 48 (2015) PARA 1004.
8   Housing and Regeneration Act 2008 s 134(1), (3) (amended by the Co-operative and Community Benefit Societies Act 2014 Sch 4 paras 121, 122, 125(1), (3)). The Co-operative and Community Benefit Societies Act 2014 s 85 (see FINANCIAL INSTITUTIONS vol 48 (2015) PARA 1007) applies to the society as if s 85(1)(b) were omitted (accountant's report required only where turnover exceeds specified sum): Housing and Regeneration Act 2008 s 134(2) (substituted by the Co-operative and Community Benefit Societies Act 2014 Sch 4 paras 121, 125(1), (2)). As to offences in connection with accounts see PARA 78.
9   Housing and Regeneration Act 2008 s 134(4).
10   As to when a body is a non-profit organisation see PARA 71 note 13.
11   As to the meaning of 'registered charity' see PARA 53 note 2.
12   Housing and Regeneration Act 2008 s 135(1), (2). Section 135 does not affect any obligation under the Charities Act 2011 Pt 8 (ss 130–176) (charity accounts: see CHARITIES vol 8 (2015) PARA 341 et seq): Housing and Regeneration Act 2008 s 135(6) (amended by the Charities Act 2011 s 354(1), Sch 7 para 131). As to offences in connection with accounts see PARA 78.
13   'Period of account' means: (1) a period of 12 months; or (2) such other period not less than six months nor more than 18 as the charity may, with the consent of the regulator, determine: Housing and Regeneration Act 2008 s 135(5).
14   Housing and Regeneration Act 2008 s 135(3).
15   Housing and Regeneration Act 2008 s 135(4).
16   Ie under the Housing and Regeneration Act 2008 s 135(3).
17   'Qualified person' means a person professionally qualified as an accountant: Housing and Regeneration Act 2008 s 136(7).
18   Ie in accordance with the Housing and Regeneration Act 2008 s 137.
19   Ie in accordance with the Housing and Regeneration Act 2008 s 138.
20   Housing and Regeneration Act 2008 s 136(1)–(3).
21   'Gross income' has the same meaning as in the Charities Act 2011 s 144 (see CHARITIES vol 8 (2015) PARA 356): Housing and Regeneration Act 2008 s 136(6) (amended by the Charities Act 2011 Sch 7 para 132(d)).
22   Ie in the Charities Act 2011 s 144(1)(a): see CHARITIES vol 8 (2015) PARA 356.
23   Housing and Regeneration Act 2008 s 136(4) (amended by the Charities Act 2011 Sch 7 para 132(a)).
24   Ie as defined by the Charities Act 2011 s 144(1) (see CHARITIES vol 8 (2015) PARA 356).
25   Ie in the Charities Act 2011 s 144(1)(b): see CHARITIES vol 8 (2015) PARA 356.

26 Housing and Regeneration Act 2008 s 136(5) (amended by the Charities Act 2011 Sch 7 para 132(b), (c)).

27 Ie for the purposes of the Housing and Regeneration Act 2008 s 136(2) or 139(2).

28 Housing and Regeneration Act 2008 s 137(1).

29 Housing and Regeneration Act 2008 s 137(2).

30 Housing and Regeneration Act 2008 s 137(3).

31 Ie with the Housing and Regeneration Act 2008 s 135(2): see the text and notes 10–12.

32 Housing and Regeneration Act 2008 s 137(4). The text refers to accounting records kept under s 135(2)(a).

33 Housing and Regeneration Act 2008 s 137(5).

34 Housing and Regeneration Act 2008 s 137(6).

35 Ie for the purposes of the Housing and Regeneration Act 2008 s 136(3).

36 Housing and Regeneration Act 2008 s 138(1).

37 Housing and Regeneration Act 2008 s 138(2). The text refers to accounting records kept under s 135(2)(a).

38 Ie whether the Housing and Regeneration Act 2008 s 136(3) applied.

39 Housing and Regeneration Act 2008 s 138(3) (amended by the Charities Act 2011 Sch 7 para 133).

40 Housing and Regeneration Act 2008 s 138(4).

41 Housing and Regeneration Act 2008 s 138(5).

42 Ie in accordance with the Housing and Regeneration Act 2008 s 136(3).

43 'Qualified person' has the meaning given by the Housing and Regeneration Act 2008 s 136(7) (see note 17): s 139(4).

44 Ie in accordance with the Housing and Regeneration Act 2008 s 137.

45 Housing and Regeneration Act 2008 s 139(1), (2).

46 'Period of account' has the meaning given by the Housing and Regeneration Act 2008 s 135(5) (see note 13): s 139(4).

47 Housing and Regeneration Act 2008 s 139(3).

48 Ie for the purposes of the Housing and Regeneration Act 2008 s 136(2) or (3) or s 139(2).

49 Housing and Regeneration Act 2008 s 140(1), (2).

50 Housing and Regeneration Act 2008 s 140(3).

78. Offences. A private registered provider[1] commits an offence if it fails, without reasonable excuse, to comply with: (1) a direction[2] about the preparation of its accounts; (2) a specified provision[3] of the Housing and Regeneration Act 2008; or (3) a requirement imposed under a specified provision[4] of that Act[5].

If a private registered provider fails to comply with a direction, provision or requirement mentioned in heads (1) to (3) above, every officer[6] of the private registered provider is guilty of an offence[7]. It is a defence for an officer to show that the officer did everything that could reasonably have been expected to ensure compliance by the private registered provider[8].

Proceedings for an offence may be brought only by or with the consent of the regulator or the Director of Public Prosecutions[9].

If a private registered provider fails to comply with a direction, provision or requirement mentioned in heads (1) to (3), the High Court may on the application of the regulator make an order for the purpose of remedying the failure[10].

1 As to the meaning of 'private registered provider' see PARA 53.

2 Ie under the Housing and Regeneration Act 2008 s 127: see PARA 75.

3 The specified provisions are: (1) the Housing and Regeneration Act 2008 s 128 (submission of accounts to regulator: see PARA 75); (2) s 129 (accounts of companies exempt from audit: see PARA 76); (3) s 135 (accounts of charities: see PARA 77); (4) s 136 (audit of charity accounts: see PARA 77): s 141(2).

4 The specified provisions are: (1) the Housing and Regeneration Act 2008 s 133 (extraordinary audit of exempt companies: see PARA 76); (2) s 134 (accounts of registered societies: see PARA 77); (3) s 139 (extraordinary audit of charities: see PARA 77): s 141(3).

5 Housing and Regeneration Act 2008 s 141(1) (amended by SI 2010/844). A person guilty of an offence under the Housing and Regeneration Act 2008 s 141 is liable on summary conviction to a fine not exceeding level 5 on the standard scale: s 141(6). As to the powers of magistrates' courts to issue fines on summary conviction see SENTENCING vol 92 (2015) PARA 176.

6 In relation to private registered providers, 'officer' means: (1) in the case of a registered charity which is not a registered company, a trustee, secretary or treasurer; (2) in the case of a registered

society, an 'officer' within the meaning given by the Co-operative and Community Benefit Societies Act 2014 s 149 (including a person co-opted to serve on the society's committee) (see FINANCIAL INSTITUTIONS vol 48 (2015) PARA 497); (3) in the case of a registered company, an 'officer' within the meaning given by the Companies Act 2006 s 1173 (see COMPANIES vol 15 (2016) PARA 679): Housing and Regeneration Act 2008 s 270 (amended by the Co-operative and Community Benefit Societies Act 2014 s 151(1), Sch 4 paras 121, 123, 134; and by virtue of SI 2010/844). As to the meaning of 'registered charity' see PARA 53 note 2; as to the meaning of 'registered company' see PARA 53 note 5; and as to the meaning of 'registered society' and 'committee' see PARA 52 note 10.

7 Housing and Regeneration Act 2008 s 141(4) (amended by SI 2010/844). As to the penalty see note 5.

8 Housing and Regeneration Act 2008 s 141(5) (amended by SI 2010/844).

9 Housing and Regeneration Act 2008 s 141(7). As to the Director of Public Prosecutions see CRIMINAL PROCEDURE vol 27 (2015) PARAS 25, 30 et seq.

10 Housing and Regeneration Act 2008 s 142(1) (amended by SI 2010/844). An order may include provision about costs: Housing and Regeneration Act 2008 s 142(2).

(C) Insolvency

79. Preparatory steps. The provisions of the Housing and Regeneration Act 2008 relating to the insolvency of registered providers[1] do not apply to local authorities[2]. They deal with cases where a registered provider is facing insolvency.

Certain specified steps have effect only if the person specified has given the regulator[3] notice, as follows[4]. In the case of any step of a kind prescribed for these purposes by the Secretary of State by order[5], to enforce a security over land held by a private registered provider[6], notice must be given by the person taking the step[7].

In the case of presenting a petition for the winding up of a registered provider which is a registered company[8] or a registered society[9], notice must be given by the petitioner[10].

In the case of the passing of a resolution for the winding up of a registered provider which is a registered company or a registered society, notice must be given by the registered provider[11].

Where an administration application[12] is made in respect of a registered provider which is a registered company, notice must be given by the applicant[13].

Where an administrator is appointed[14] in respect of a registered provider which is a registered company, notice must be given by the person making the appointment[15].

Where a copy of a notice of intention to appoint a person as an administrator[16] is filed with the court in respect of a registered provider which is a registered company, notice must be given by the person filing the notice[17].

1 Ie the Housing and Regeneration Act 2008 ss 144–159. As to the meaning of 'registered provider' see PARA 53. Those provisions broadly replicate the effects of the Housing Act 1996 ss 39–45, as to which see PARAS 207–211.

2 Housing and Regeneration Act 2008 s 143A (added by SI 2010/844). As to the meaning of 'local authority' see PARA 149 note 4 (definition applied by the Housing and Regeneration Act 2008 s 275).

3 As to the meaning of 'the regulator' see PARA 57.

4 Housing and Regeneration Act 2008 s 144. Section 144 is repealed, as from a day to be appointed, by the Housing and Planning Act 2016 s 115, Sch 6 paras 1, 2; at the date at which this volume states the law, no such day had been appointed). As to housing administration orders see PARA 90 et seq. 'Notice' means written notice (and to 'notify' means to give written notice): Housing and Regeneration Act 2008 s 275.

5 As to the Secretary of State see PARA 7. As to orders by the Secretary of State see PARA 54.

6 As to the meaning of 'private registered provider' see PARA 53.

7 Housing and Regeneration Act 2008 s 144 Table (amended by SI 2010/844; and prospectively repealed (see note 4)). As to the steps prescribed see the Housing and Regeneration Act 2008 (Moratorium) (Prescribed Steps) Order 2010, SI 2010/660. Any step to enforce security over land

held by a registered provider of social housing is a prescribed step for the purposes of the Housing and Regeneration Act 2008 s 144: Housing and Regeneration Act 2008 (Moratorium) (Prescribed Steps) Order 2010, SI 2010/660, art 2.

8 As to the meaning of 'registered company' see PARA 53 note 5.
9 As to the meaning of 'registered society' see PARA 52 note 10.
10 Housing and Regeneration Act 2008 s 144 Table (amended by the Co-operative and Community Benefit Societies Act 2014 s 151(1), Sch 4 paras 121, 122; and prospectively repealed (see note 4)). This does not apply in the case of the presenting of a petition by the regulator under the Housing and Regeneration Act 2008 s 166 (see PARA 87): s 144 Table.
11 Housing and Regeneration Act 2008 s 144 Table (as amended (see note 10); and prospectively repealed (see note 4)). This does not apply to the passing of a resolution for winding up where the regulator's consent is required under s 162 or 164 (see PARAS 85, 86): s 144 Table.
12 Ie in accordance with the Insolvency Act 1986 s 8, Sch B1 para 12: see COMPANY AND PARTNERSHIP INSOLVENCY vol 16 (2011) PARA 163.
13 Housing and Regeneration Act 2008 s 144 Table (prospectively repealed (see note 4)).
14 Ie in accordance with the Insolvency Act 1986 Sch B1 para 14 or Sch B1 para 22: see COMPANY AND PARTNERSHIP INSOLVENCY vol 16 (2011) PARAS 175, 183.
15 Housing and Regeneration Act 2008 s 144 Table (prospectively repealed (see note 4)).
16 Ie under the Insolvency Act 1986 Sch B1 para 14 or Sch B1 para 22.
17 Housing and Regeneration Act 2008 s 144 Table (prospectively repealed (see note 4)).

80. Moratorium. If a step specified below is taken in respect of a private registered provider[1]: (1) a moratorium on the disposal of land by the provider begins[2]; and (2) the person specified must give the regulator[3] notice as soon as is reasonably practicable[4]. If the notice is not given the step is not invalidated (but the end of the moratorium depends on the notice being given)[5]. Where the private registered provider owns land in Greater London, the regulator must give the Greater London Authority[6] a copy of any notice received under these provisions[7].

In the case of any step of a kind prescribed for these purposes by the Secretary of State[8] by order, to enforce a security over land held by a private registered provider, notice must be given by the person taking the step[9].

In the case of the presenting of a petition for winding up a registered provider which is a registered company[10] or a registered society[11], notice must be given by the petitioner[12].

In the case of the passing of a resolution for the winding up of a registered provider which is a registered company or a registered society, notice must be given by the registered provider[13].

In the case of a decision by the directors or other governing body of a registered provider to present a petition for winding up where the registered provider is a registered company or a registered society, notice must be given by the directors or governing body[14].

In the case of the making of an administration order[15] in respect of a registered provider which is a registered company, notice must be given by the person who applied for the order[16].

In the case of the appointment of an administrator[17] in respect of a registered provider which is a registered company, notice must be given by the person making the appointment[18].

The moratorium begins when the step specified above is taken[19]. The moratorium ends (unless extended or cancelled) with the period of 28 working days[20] beginning with the day on which the regulator receives notice under head (2)[21].

The provisions described above apply until a day to be appointed; as from such day, a moratorium on the disposal of land by a private registered provider begins if a notice is given to the regulator under any of certain specified provisions[22] of the Housing and Planning Act 2016[23]. The moratorium begins when such notice is given[24]. The moratorium ends when one of the following occurs: (a) the expiry of the relevant period[25]; (b) the making of a housing administration order[26] in relation to the registered provider; or (c) the cancellation[27] of the moratorium[28].

During the period of a moratorium the regulator may extend it (or further extend it) for a specified period, with the consent[29] of each secured creditor[30] of the registered provider whom the regulator is able to locate after making reasonable inquiries[31]. If the regulator extends a moratorium it must notify: (i) the registered provider; and (ii) any liquidator, administrator, administrative receiver or receiver appointed in respect of the registered provider or its land[32]. If the regulator extends a moratorium in respect of a private registered provider who owns land in Greater London, the regulator must also notify the Greater London Authority[33].

During the period of a moratorium the regulator may cancel it if satisfied that it is unnecessary to make proposals[34] about the future ownership and management of the registered provider's land[35]. Until a day to be appointed, before cancelling a moratorium the regulator must consult the person who took the step that triggered it[36]. When a moratorium ends the regulator must give notice, and (except in the case of cancellation) an explanation of the statutory provision relating to a further moratorium[37], to the registered provider and such of its secured creditors as the regulator is able to locate after making reasonable inquiries[38]. When a moratorium in respect of a private registered provider who owns land in Greater London ends, the regulator must also give notice to the Greater London Authority[39].

Until a day to be appointed, taking a further step during a moratorium does not either start a new moratorium or alter the existing moratorium's duration[40]. Prospectively, if a notice to the regulator[41] is given during a moratorium, that does not start a new moratorium or alter the existing moratorium's duration[42].

If a moratorium in respect of a private registered provider ends otherwise than by cancellation and a further step specified above is taken in relation to the provider within the period of three years beginning with the end of the moratorium, the further step does not automatically trigger a further moratorium, but the regulator may impose a further moratorium for a specified period. It may do this if each secured creditor of the registered provider whom the regulator is able to locate after making reasonable inquiries consents[43]. If the regulator imposes a new moratorium it must notify: (A) the registered provider; and (B) any liquidator, administrator, administrative receiver or receiver appointed in respect of the registered provider or any of its land[44]. If the regulator imposes a new moratorium in respect of a private registered provider who owns land in Greater London, the regulator must also notify the Greater London Authority[45].

During a moratorium neither the Homes and Communities Agency' ('the HCA') nor the Greater London Authority may give the registered provider a direction[46] in relation to social housing assistance or take steps to enforce such a direction against the registered provider[47]. During a moratorium a disposal of the registered provider's land[48] requires the regulator's prior consent[49]. Consent may be given before the moratorium begins and may be subject to conditions[50]. These provisions do not prevent a liquidator from disclaiming land as onerous property during a moratorium[51].

A purported disposal by a registered provider is void if such a disposal requires the regulator's consent[52] and the regulator has not given consent[53]. This does not apply, however, to a disposal by a non-profit registered provider[54] to one or more individuals ('the buyer') if the disposal is of a single dwelling and the registered provider reasonably believes at the time of the disposal that the buyer intends to use the property as the buyer's principal residence[55].

During a moratorium the regulator may appoint an interim manager of the registered provider[56]. An appointment may relate to the registered provider's affairs generally or to the affairs which are specified in the appointment[57]. Such an appointment is to be on terms and conditions (including as to remuneration) specified in, or determined in accordance with, the appointment[58]. An appointment comes to an end with the earliest of the following: (I) the end of the moratorium; (II) the agreement of proposals[59] about the future ownership and management of the registered provider's land; or (III) a date specified in the appointment[60]. An interim manager has any power specified in the appointment and any other power in relation to the registered provider's affairs required by the manager for the purposes specified in the appointment (including the power to enter into agreements and take other action[61] on behalf of the registered provider)[62]. But an interim manager may not dispose of land or grant security over land held by the registered provider[63].

1   As to the meaning of 'registered provider' see PARA 53. As to the disapplication of the Housing and Regeneration Act 2008 ss 144–159 to local authorities see PARA 79.
2   Housing and Regeneration Act 2008 s 145(1) (amended by SI 2010/844). As to the meaning of 'disposal' see PARA 52 note 11.
3   As to the meaning of 'the regulator' see PARA 57.
4   Housing and Regeneration Act 2008 s 145(2) (amended by SI 2010/844). As to the meaning of 'notice' see PARA 79 note 4.
5   Housing and Regeneration Act 2008 s 145(3). See s 146(2); and the text and notes 20–21.
6   As to the Greater London Authority see LONDON GOVERNMENT vol 71 (2013) PARA 67 et seq.
7   Housing and Regeneration Act 2008 s 145(5) (added by the Localism Act 2011 s 195(1), Sch 19 paras 46, 49).
8   As to the Secretary of State see PARA 7. As to orders by the Secretary of State see PARA 54.
9   Housing and Regeneration Act 2008 s 145 Table (amended by SI 2010/844). As to the steps prescribed see the Housing and Regeneration Act 2008 (Moratorium) (Prescribed Steps) Order 2010, SI 2010/660. Any step to enforce security over land held by a registered provider of social housing is a prescribed step for the purposes of the Housing and Regeneration Act 2008 s 145: Housing and Regeneration Act 2008 (Moratorium) (Prescribed Steps) Order 2010, SI 2010/660, art 2.
10 As to the meaning of 'registered company' see PARA 53 note 5.
11 As to the meaning of 'registered society' see PARA 52 note 10.
12 Housing and Regeneration Act 2008 s 145 Table (amended by the Co-operative and Community Benefit Societies Act 2014 s 151(1), Sch 4 paras 121, 122). This does not apply to the presenting of a petition by the directors or other governing body of the registered provider or by the regulator under the Housing and Regeneration Act 2008 s 166 (see PARA 87): s 145 Table.
13 Housing and Regeneration Act 2008 s 145 Table (as amended: see note 12).
14 Housing and Regeneration Act 2008 s 145 Table (as amended: see note 12).
15 Ie in accordance with the Insolvency Act 1986 s 8, Sch B1 para 13: see COMPANY AND PARTNERSHIP INSOLVENCY vol 16 (2011) PARA 173.
16 Housing and Regeneration Act 2008 s 145 Table.
17 Ie in accordance with the Insolvency Act 1986 Sch B1 para 14 or Sch B1 para 22: see COMPANY AND PARTNERSHIP INSOLVENCY vol 16 (2011) PARAS 175, 183.
18 Housing and Regeneration Act 2008 s 145 Table.
19 Housing and Regeneration Act 2008 s 146(1).
20 'Working day' means a day other than: (1) a Saturday or Sunday; (2) Christmas Day or Good Friday; or (3) a day which is a bank holiday in England and Wales under the Banking and Financial Dealings Act 1971: Housing and Regeneration Act 2008 s 275.
21 Housing and Regeneration Act 2008 s 146(2).
22 Ie the Housing and Planning Act 2016 s 104(2)(a) (notice of winding up petition); s 105(4)(a) (notice of application for permission to pass a resolution for voluntary winding up); s 106(3)(a) (notice of ordinary administration application); s 107(4)(a) (notice of appointment of ordinary administrator); s 108(2)(a) (notice of intention to enforce security). See PARA 94.

23 Housing and Regeneration Act 2008 s 145 (substituted, as from a day to be appointed, by the Housing and Planning Act 2016 s 115, Sch 6 paras 1, 3; at the date at which this volume states the law, no such day had been appointed).

24 Housing and Regeneration Act 2008 s 146(1) (s 146(1), (2) substituted, s 146(2A) added, as from a day to be appointed, by the Housing and Planning Act 2016 Sch 6 paras 1, 4(1), (2); at the date at which this volume states the law, no such day had been appointed).

25 The 'relevant period' is: (1) the period of 28 days beginning with the day on which the notice mentioned in the Housing and Regeneration Act 2008 s 145 is given; plus (2) any period by which that period is extended under s 146(3): s 146(2A) (as added: see note 24).

26 Ie under the Housing and Planning Act 2016 Pt 4 Ch 5 (ss 95–117): see PARA 90 et seq.

27 Ie under the Housing and Regeneration Act 2008 s 146(5).

28 Housing and Regeneration Act 2008 s 146(2) (as substituted: see note 24).

29 'Consent' means written consent: Housing and Regeneration Act 2008 s 275.

30 'Secured creditor' means a creditor who holds a mortgage or charge (including a floating charge) over: (1) land held by a registered provider; or (2) a present or future interest of a registered provider in rents or other receipts from land: s 275.

31 Housing and Regeneration Act 2008 s 146(3).

32 Housing and Regeneration Act 2008 s 146(4) (amended by the Localism Act 2011 ss 178, 237, Sch 16 paras 1, 39(1), (2), Sch 25 Pt 26).

33 Housing and Regeneration Act 2008 s 146(4A) (added by the Localism Act 2011 s 195(1), Sch 19 paras 46, 50(1), (2)).

34 Ie under the Housing and Regeneration Act 2008 s 152: see PARA 81.

35 Housing and Regeneration Act 2008 s 146(5).

36 Housing and Regeneration Act 2008 s 146(6) (repealed, as from a day to be appointed, by the Housing and Planning Act 2016 Sch 6 paras 1, 4(1), (3); at the date at which this volume states the law, no such day had been appointed).

37 Ie the Housing and Regeneration Act 2008 s 147: see the text and notes 43–45.

38 Housing and Regeneration Act 2008 s 146(7).

39 Housing and Regeneration Act 2008 s 146(8A) (added by the Localism Act 2011 Sch 19 paras 46, 50(1), (3)).

40 Housing and Regeneration Act 2008 s 146(9).

41 Ie under the Housing and Regeneration Act 2008 s 145: see the text to notes 22–23.

42 Housing and Regeneration Act 2008 s 146(9) (substituted, as from a day to be appointed, by the Housing and Planning Act 2016 Sch 6 paras 1, 4(1), (4); at the date at which this volume states the law, no such day had been appointed).

43 Housing and Regeneration Act 2008 s 147(1)–(3) (s 147(1) amended by SI 2010/844). The Housing and Regeneration Act 2008 ss 143A–159 apply to a further moratorium as to a first moratorium (except for s 146(2)): s 147(5).

44 Housing and Regeneration Act 2008 s 147(4) (amended by the Localism Act 2011 Sch 16 paras 1, 40(1), (2), Sch 25 Pt 26).

45 Housing and Regeneration Act 2008 s 147(4A) (added by the Localism Act 2011 Sch 19 paras 46, 51).

46 Ie under the Housing and Regeneration Act 2008 s 32(4): see PARA 126. As to the meaning of 'social housing' see PARA 52.

47 Housing and Regeneration Act 2008 s 148(1) (amended by the Localism Act 2011 Sch 19 paras 46, 52, Sch 25 Pt 31). As to the HCA see PARA 57 et seq; and PLANNING vol 83 (2010) PARA 1454 et seq.

48 In the Housing and Regeneration Act 2008 s 148 'land' includes a present or future interest in rent or other receipts arising from land: s 148(6). As to the meaning of 'rent' see PARA 52 note 2.

49 Housing and Regeneration Act 2008 s 148(2). Exceptions to s 148(2) are set out in s 149: s 148(3). The regulator's consent is not required under s 148 for the following exceptions: s 149(1). Exception 1 is a letting under: (1) an assured tenancy; or (2) an assured agricultural occupancy: s 149(2). Exception 2 is a letting under what would be an assured tenancy or an assured agricultural occupancy but for any of the Housing Act 1988 Sch 1 paras 4–8, 12(1)(h), 12ZA–12B (tenancies which cannot be assured tenancies: see LANDLORD AND TENANT vol 63 (2016) PARA 832 et seq): Housing and Regeneration Act 2008 s 149(3). Exception 3 is a letting under a secure tenancy: s 149(4). Exception 4 is a letting under what would be a secure tenancy but for any of the Housing Act 1985 Sch 1 paras 2–12 (tenancies which are not secure tenancies: see LANDLORD AND TENANT vol 63 (2016) PARA 1042 et seq): Housing and Regeneration Act 2008 s 149(5). Exception 5 is a disposal under the Housing Act 1985 Pt V (ss 118–188) (right to buy: see PARA 239 et seq): Housing and Regeneration Act 2008 s 149(7) (amended by the Housing and Planning Act 2016 s 92, Sch 4 paras 7, 12(b)). Exception 6 is a disposal under the right conferred by the Housing and Regeneration Act 2008 s 180 (see PARA 102) or the Housing Act 1996 s 16

(tenant's right to acquire social housing in Wales: see PARA 226; and PARAS 242–243): Housing and Regeneration Act 2008 s 149(8) (amended by the Housing and Planning Act 2016 Sch 4 paras 7, 12(c)).

'Assured tenancy' and 'assured agricultural occupancy' have the same meanings as in the Housing Act 1988 Pt I (ss 1–45) (see LANDLORD AND TENANT vol 63 (2016) PARA 825; LANDLORD AND TENANT vol 64 (2016) PARA 1747); and 'secure tenancy' has the same meaning as in the Housing Act 1985 Pt IV (ss 79–117) (see LANDLORD AND TENANT vol 63 (2016) PARA 1037): Housing and Regeneration Act 2008 s 275.

50 Housing and Regeneration Act 2008 s 148(4).
51 Housing and Regeneration Act 2008 s 148(5).
52 Ie under the Housing and Regeneration Act 2008 s 148.
53 Housing and Regeneration Act 2008 s 150(1).
54 As to when a body is a non-profit organisation see PARA 71 note 13.
55 Housing and Regeneration Act 2008 s 150(2).
56 Housing and Regeneration Act 2008 s 151(1).
57 Housing and Regeneration Act 2008 s 151(2).
58 Housing and Regeneration Act 2008 s 151(3).
59 Ie under the Housing and Regeneration Act 2008 s 152: see PARA 81.
60 Housing and Regeneration Act 2008 s 151(4).
61 As to the meaning of 'action' see PARA 73 note 13.
62 Housing and Regeneration Act 2008 s 151(5).
63 Housing and Regeneration Act 2008 s 151(6).

81.   Proposals. During a moratorium[1] the regulator[2] may make proposals about the future ownership and management of the registered provider's land[3], with a view to ensuring that the property will be properly managed by a registered provider[4]. In making proposals the regulator must: (1) have regard to the interests of the registered provider's creditors as a whole; and (2) so far as is reasonably practicable avoid worsening the position of unsecured creditors[5]. Proposals may provide for the appointment of a manager[6] to implement all or part of the proposals[7]. Proposals may not include anything which would result in: (a) a preferential debt being paid otherwise than in priority to a non-preferential debt; (b) an ordinary preferential debt being paid otherwise than in priority to a secondary preferential debt; (c) a preferential creditor (PC1) being paid a smaller proportion of an ordinary preferential debt than another preferential creditor (PC2) (unless PC1 consents); or (d) a preferential creditor (PC1) being paid a smaller proportion of a secondary preferential debt than another preferential creditor (PC2) (unless PC2 consents)[8]. Proposals relating to a registered provider which is a charity (C1) may not require it to act outside the terms of its trusts and may provide for the disposal of accommodation only to another charity whose objects the regulator thinks are similar to those of C1[9].

Before making such proposals the regulator must consult: (i) the registered provider; (ii) its tenants[10] (so far as is reasonably practicable); (iii) if the registered provider is a registered society[11], the Financial Conduct Authority; and (iv) if the registered provider is a registered charity[12], the Charity Commission[13]. The regulator must send a copy of proposals to: (A) the registered provider and its officers[14]; (B) such of its secured creditors[15] as the regulator is able to locate after making reasonable inquiries; and (C) any liquidator, administrator, administrative receiver or receiver appointed in respect of the registered provider or any of its land[16]. The regulator must also make arrangements for bringing proposals to the attention of the registered provider's members, its tenants and its unsecured creditors[17].

If each secured creditor to whom proposals were sent agrees to the proposals by giving notice[18] to the regulator, the proposals will have effect[19]. Proposals may be agreed with modifications if each secured creditor to whom the proposals were sent consents by notice to the regulator and the regulator consents[20]. The regulator must send a copy of agreed proposals to: (I) the registered provider and its officers; (II) its secured creditors to whom the original proposals were sent; (III) any liquidator, administrator, administrative receiver or receiver appointed in respect of the registered provider or any of its land; (IV) if the registered provider is a registered society, the Financial Conduct Authority; and (V) if the registered provider is a registered charity, the Charity Commission[21]. The regulator must also make arrangements for bringing the agreed proposals to the attention of the registered provider's members, its tenants and its unsecured creditors[22].

These proposals may be amended by agreement between the secured creditors to whom the original proposals were sent and the regulator; and all the provisions set out above[23] apply to an amendment as to the original proposals[24].

The following are obliged to implement agreed proposals: the regulator, the registered provider, its creditors and any liquidator, administrator, administrative receiver or receiver appointed in respect of the registered provider or any of its land[25]. The following must co-operate with implementation of agreed proposals: in the case of a charitable trust, its trustees[26]; in the case of a registered society, its committee members[27]; and, in the case of a registered company[28], its directors[29].

1 As to moratoria see PARA 80.
2 As to the meaning of 'the regulator' see PARA 57.
3 As to the meaning of 'registered provider' see PARA 53.
4 Housing and Regeneration Act 2008 s 152(1). As to the disapplication of ss 144–159 to local authorities see PARA 79.
5 Housing and Regeneration Act 2008 s 152(2).
6 In accordance with the Housing and Regeneration Act 2008 s 155: see PARA 82.
7 Housing and Regeneration Act 2008 s 152(3).
8 Housing and Regeneration Act 2008 s 152(4) (amended by SI 2014/3486). 'Preferential creditor', 'preferential debt', 'ordinary preferential debt' and 'secondary preferential debt' have the same meanings as in the Insolvency Act 1986 (see COMPANY AND PARTNERSHIP INSOLVENCY vol 17 (2011) PARA 721): Housing and Regeneration Act 2008 s 275 (definition amended by virtue of SI 2014/3486). As to the meaning of 'consent' see PARA 80 note 29.
9 Housing and Regeneration Act 2008 s 152(5).
10 As to the meaning of 'tenant' see PARA 52 note 9.
11 As to the meaning of 'registered society' see PARA 52 note 10.
12 As to the meaning of 'registered charity' see PARA 53 note 2.
13 Housing and Regeneration Act 2008 s 153(1) (amended by the Co-operative and Community Benefit Societies Act 2014 s 151(1), Sch 4 paras 121, 122; and by SI 2013/496). As to the meaning of 'Charity Commission' see PARA 53 note 3.
14 As to the meaning of 'officer' see PARA 78 note 6.
15 As to the meaning of 'secured creditor' see PARA 80 note 30.
16 Housing and Regeneration Act 2008 s 153(2).
17 Housing and Regeneration Act 2008 s 153(3).
18 As to the meaning of 'notice' see PARA 79 note 4.
19 Housing and Regeneration Act 2008 s 153(4).
20 Housing and Regeneration Act 2008 s 153(5).
21 Housing and Regeneration Act 2008 s 153(6) (amended by the Co-operative and Community Benefit Societies Act 2014 Sch 4 paras 121, 122; and by SI 2013/496).
22 Housing and Regeneration Act 2008 s 153(7).
23 Ie the Housing and Regeneration Act 2008 ss 152, 153.
24 Housing and Regeneration Act 2008 s 153(8).
25 Housing and Regeneration Act 2008 s 154(1).
26 Also, prospectively, in the case of a charitable incorporated organisation (see the Charities Act 2011 Pt 11 (ss 244–250); and see CHARITIES vol 8 (2015) PARA 226 et seq), its charity trustees (as defined by the Charities Act 2011 s 177: see CHARITIES vol 8 (2015) PARA 255): Housing and Regeneration Act 2008 s 154(2)(aa) (added, as from a day to be appointed, by the Housing and Planning Act 2016 s 115, Sch 6 paras 1, 6; at the date at which this volume states the law, no such day had been appointed).
27 As to the meaning of 'committee' see PARA 52 note 10.
28 As to the meaning of 'registered company' see PARA 53 note 5.

29 Housing and Regeneration Act 2008 s 154(2) (amended by the Co-operative and Community Benefit Societies Act 2014 Sch 4 paras 121, 122). This does not require or permit a breach of a fiduciary or other duty: Housing and Regeneration Act 2008 s 154(3).

82. Manager. Where agreed proposals[1] provide for the appointment of a manager, they must provide for the manager to be paid reasonable remuneration and expenses[2]. The regulator[3] must appoint the manager[4]. The regulator may give the manager directions (general or specific)[5]. The manager may apply to the High Court for directions (and directions of the regulator are subject to directions of the High Court)[6]. If the registered provider is a charity, the regulator must notify the Charity Commission[7] that a manager has been appointed[8]. The regulator may appoint a new manager in place of a person who ceases to be manager (in accordance with terms of appointment specified in the proposals or determined by the regulator)[9].

A manager:

(1)   may do anything necessary for the purpose of the appointment;

(2)   acts as the registered provider's[10] agent (and is not personally liable on a contract); and

(3)   has ostensible authority to act for the registered provider (so that a person dealing with the manager in good faith and for value need not inquire into the manager's powers)[11].

In particular, the terms of a manager's appointment may confer power:

(a)   to sell or otherwise dispose[12] of land by public auction or private contract;

(b)   to raise or borrow money;

(c)   to grant security over land;

(d)   to grant or accept surrender of a lease;

(e)   to take a lease;

(f)   to take possession of property;

(g)   to appoint a solicitor, accountant or other professional to assist the manager;

(h)   to appoint agents and staff (and to dismiss them);

(i)   to make payments;

(j)   to bring or defend legal proceedings;

(k)   to refer a question to arbitration;

(l)   to make any arrangement or compromise;

(m)   to carry on the business of the registered provider;

(n)   to carry out works and do other things in connection with the management or transfer of land;

(o)   to take out insurance;

(p)   to use the registered body's seal;

(q)   to execute in the name and on behalf of the registered provider any deed, receipt or other document;

(r)   to do anything incidental to a power in heads (a) to (q)[13].

A manager must so far as is reasonably practicable consult and inform the registered provider's tenants[14] about an exercise of powers likely to affect them[15].

The appointment of a manager appointed to implement proposals relating to a registered society[16] may confer on the manager power to make and execute on behalf of the society: (i) an instrument providing for the amalgamation of the society with another registered society[17]; or (ii) an instrument transferring its engagements[18]. A copy of the instrument must be sent to and registered by the Financial Conduct Authority[19]. An instrument does not take effect until the copy is registered[20].

1　As to proposals see PARA 81.
2　Housing and Regeneration Act 2008 s 155(1), (2). As to the disapplication of ss 144–159 to local authorities see PARA 79.
3　As to the meaning of 'the regulator' see PARA 57.
4　Housing and Regeneration Act 2008 s 155(3).
5　Housing and Regeneration Act 2008 s 155(4).
6　Housing and Regeneration Act 2008 s 155(5).
7　As to the meaning of 'Charity Commission' see PARA 53 note 3.
8　Housing and Regeneration Act 2008 s 155(6).
9　Housing and Regeneration Act 2008 s 155(7).
10　As to the meaning of 'registered provider' see PARA 53.
11　Housing and Regeneration Act 2008 s 156(1).
12　As to the meaning of 'disposal' see PARA 52 note 11.
13　Housing and Regeneration Act 2008 s 156(2).
14　As to the meaning of 'tenant' see PARA 52 note 9.
15　Housing and Regeneration Act 2008 s 156(3).
16　As to the meaning of 'registered society' see PARA 52 note 10.
17　An instrument providing for the amalgamation of a society ('S1') with another has the same effect as a resolution by S1 under the Co-operative and Community Benefit Societies Act 2014 s 109 (see FINANCIAL INSTITUTIONS vol 48 (2015) PARA 1053): Housing and Regeneration Act 2008 s 157(3) (amended by virtue of the Co-operative and Community Benefit Societies Act 2014 s 151(1), Sch 4 paras 121, 126(1), (2)).
18　Housing and Regeneration Act 2008 s 157(1), (2) (amended by the Co-operative and Community Benefit Societies Act 2014 Sch 4 paras 121, 122, 123). An instrument transferring engagements has the same effect as a transfer of engagements under the Co-operative and Community Benefit Societies Act 2014 s 110 or s 112 (see FINANCIAL INSTITUTIONS vol 48 (2015) PARA 1054): Housing and Regeneration Act 2008 s 157(4) (amended by virtue of the Co-operative and Community Benefit Societies Act 2014 Sch 4 paras 121, 126(1), (3)).
19　Housing and Regeneration Act 2008 s 157(5) (amended by SI 2013/496). The copy must be sent for registration during the period of 14 days beginning with the date of execution; but a copy registered after that period is valid: Housing and Regeneration Act 2008 s 157(7). As to the Financial Conduct Authority in relation to registered societies see FINANCIAL INSTITUTIONS vol 48 (2015) PARA 898.
20　Housing and Regeneration Act 2008 s 157(6).

83. Assistance by regulator. The regulator[1] may give financial or other assistance to the registered provider[2] for the purpose of preserving its position pending the agreement of proposals[3]. The regulator may give financial or other assistance to the registered provider or a manager[4] to facilitate the implementation of agreed proposals[5]. In particular, the regulator may:

(1)　lend staff;
(2)　arrange payment of the manager's remuneration and expenses[6].

The regulator may do the following only with the Secretary of State's consent[7]:

(a)　make grants;
(b)　make loans;
(c)　indemnify a manager;
(d)　make payments in connection with secured loans; and
(e)　guarantee payments in connection with secured loans[8].

1　As to the meaning of 'the regulator' see PARA 57.
2　As to the meaning of 'registered provider' see PARA 53.
3　Housing and Regeneration Act 2008 s 158(1) (amended by SI 2010/844). As to proposals see PARA 81. As to the disapplication of ss 144–159 to local authorities see PARA 79.
4　Ie a manager appointed under the Housing and Regeneration Act 2008 s 155: see PARA 82.
5　Housing and Regeneration Act 2008 s 158(2) (amended by SI 2010/844).
6　Housing and Regeneration Act 2008 s 158(3).

7 Housing and Regeneration Act 2008 s 158(4). As to the Secretary of State see PARA 7. As to the meaning of 'consent' see PARA 80 note 29.
8 Housing and Regeneration Act 2008 s 158(4)(a)–(e).

84. Applications to court. A private registered provider[1] may apply to the High Court where it thinks that action[2] taken by a manager[3] is not in accordance with the agreed proposals[4]. A creditor of a private registered provider may also apply to the High Court where the creditor thinks that action taken by a manager is not in accordance with the agreed proposals[5]. The High Court may: (1) confirm, annul or modify an act of the manager; (2) give the manager directions; (3) make any other order[6].

If a person bound by agreed proposals (P1) thinks that action by another person (P2) breaches the statutory requirements as to the implementation of proposals[7], P1 may apply to the High Court[8]. The High Court may: (a) confirm, annul or modify the action; (b) grant relief by way of injunction, damages or otherwise[9].

1 As to the meaning of 'private registered provider' see PARA 53.
2 As to the meaning of 'action' see PARA 73 note 13.
3 Ie a manager appointed under the Housing and Regeneration Act 2008 s 155: see PARA 82.
4 Housing and Regeneration Act 2008 s 159(1) (amended by SI 2010/844). As to proposals see PARA 81. As to the disapplication of ss 144–159 to local authorities see PARA 79.
5 Housing and Regeneration Act 2008 s 159(2) (amended by SI 2010/844).
6 Housing and Regeneration Act 2008 s 159(3).
7 Ie the Housing and Regeneration Act 2008 s 154: see PARA 81.
8 Housing and Regeneration Act 2008 s 159(4).
9 Housing and Regeneration Act 2008 s 159(5).

(D) Restructuring and Dissolution

85. Companies. The provisions of the Housing and Regeneration Act 2008 relating to the restructuring and dissolution of registered providers[1] do not apply to local authorities[2]. The following provisions apply to a non-profit registered provider[3] which is a registered company[4]. The registered provider must notify the regulator[5] of any voluntary arrangement under Part I of the Insolvency Act 1986[6]. The registered provider must notify the regulator of any order of the court[7] sanctioning a compromise or arrangement[8]. Such an order does not take effect until the registered provider has confirmed to the registrar of companies that the regulator has been notified[9]. The registered provider must notify the regulator of any order of the court[10] to facilitate reconstruction or amalgamation[11]. The requirement[12] to send a copy of the order to the registrar of companies is satisfied only if the copy is accompanied by confirmation that the regulator has been notified[13].

The registered provider must notify the regulator of any resolution[14] for converting the registered provider into a registered society[15]. The registrar of companies may register such a resolution only if the registered provider has confirmed to the registrar that the regulator has been notified[16]. The regulator must decide whether the new body is eligible for registration[17] as a provider of social housing[18]. If the new body is eligible for registration, the regulator must register it and designate it as a non-profit organisation[19]. If the new body is not eligible for registration, the regulator must notify it of that fact[20]. Pending registration, or notification that it is not eligible for registration, the new body is to be treated as if it were registered and designated as a non-profit organisation[21].

The following provisions apply until a day to be appointed to a non-profit registered provider which is a registered company[22]. A special resolution for the voluntary winding up of the company under the Insolvency Act 1986[23] is effective only if the regulator has first consented to it[24]. The statutory requirement[25] to send a copy of the resolution to the registrar is satisfied only if the copy is accompanied by a copy of the regulator's consent[26].

1 Ie the Housing and Regeneration Act 2008 ss 160–169. These provisions re-enact the powers of the Housing Corporation in the Housing Act 1996 Sch 1 paras 12–14 as powers of the regulator: see PARAS 180–182. As to the meaning of 'registered provider' see PARA 53.
2 Housing and Regeneration Act 2008 s 159A (added by SI 2010/844). As to the meaning of 'local authority' see PARA 149 note 4 (definition applied by the Housing and Regeneration Act 2008 s 275).
3 As to when a body is a non-profit organisation see PARA 71 note 13.
4 Housing and Regeneration Act 2008 ss 160(1), 161(1) (ss 160, 161 substituted by the Housing and Planning Act 2016 s 92, Sch 4 paras 22, 24, 25 respectively). As to the meaning of 'registered company' see PARA 53 note 5.
5 As to the meaning of 'the regulator' see PARA 57.
6 Housing and Regeneration Act 2008 s 160(2) (as substituted: see note 4). As to directions about notification see PARA 89. As to voluntary arrangements under the Insolvency Act 1986 Pt I (ss 1–7B) see COMPANY AND PARTNERSHIP INSOLVENCY vol 16 (2011) PARA 83 et seq.
7 Ie an order under the Companies Act 2006 s 899: see COMPANIES vol 15A (2016) PARA 1611.
8 Housing and Regeneration Act 2008 s 160(3) (as substituted: see note 4).
9 Housing and Regeneration Act 2008 s 160(4) (as substituted: see note 4).
10 Ie an order under the Companies Act 2006 s 900: see COMPANIES vol 15A (2016) PARA 1614.
11 Housing and Regeneration Act 2008 s 160(5) (as substituted: see note 4).
12 Ie in the Companies Act 2006 s 900(6): see COMPANIES vol 15A (2016) PARA 1616.
13 Housing and Regeneration Act 2008 s 160(6) (as substituted: see note 4).
14 Ie under the Co-operative and Community Benefit Societies Act 2014 s 115: see FINANCIAL INSTITUTIONS vol 48 (2015) PARA 905.
15 Housing and Regeneration Act 2008 s 161(2) (as substituted: see note 4). As to the meaning of 'registered society' see PARA 52 note 10.
16 Housing and Regeneration Act 2008 s 161(3) (as substituted: see note 4).
17 Ie under the Housing and Regeneration Act 2008 s 112: see PARAS 70–72.
18 Housing and Regeneration Act 2008 s 161(4) (as substituted: see note 4).
19 Housing and Regeneration Act 2008 s 161(5) (as substituted: see note 4).
20 Housing and Regeneration Act 2008 s 161(6) (as substituted: see note 4).
21 Housing and Regeneration Act 2008 s 161(7) (as substituted: see note 4).
22 Housing and Regeneration Act 2008 s 162(1) (s 162 repealed, as from a day to be appointed, by the Housing and Planning Act 2016 s 115, Sch 6 paras 1, 7; at the date at which this volume states the law, no such day had been appointed).
23 As to voluntary winding up see COMPANY AND PARTNERSHIP INSOLVENCY vol 17 (2011) PARA 898 et seq.
24 Housing and Regeneration Act 2008 s 162(2) (prospectively repealed: see note 22). As to the meaning of 'consent' see PARA 80 note 29.
25 Ie under the Companies Act 2006 s 30: see COMPANIES vol 14 (2016) PARA 230.
26 Housing and Regeneration Act 2008 s 162(3) (prospectively repealed: see note 22).

86. Registered societies. The following provisions apply to a non-profit registered provider[1] which is a registered society[2]. The registered provider must notify the regulator[3] of any resolution passed by the society for the purposes of the statutory restructuring provisions[4]. The Financial Conduct Authority[5] may register the resolution only if the registered provider has confirmed to the Financial Conduct Authority that the regulator has been notified[6]. The regulator must decide whether the body created or to whom engagements are transferred ('the new body') is eligible for registration[7]. If the new body is eligible for registration, the regulator must register it and designate it as a non-profit organisation[8]. If the new body is not eligible for registration, the regulator must notify it of that fact[9]. Pending registration, or notification that it is not eligible for registration, the new body is to be treated as if it were registered and designated as a non-profit organisation[10].

Where a non-profit registered provider which is a registered society is to be dissolved by instrument of dissolution[11], the registered provider must notify the regulator[12]. The Financial Conduct Authority may register the instrument[13], or cause notice of the dissolution to be advertised[14], only if the registered provider has confirmed to the Financial Conduct Authority that the regulator has been notified[15].

The following provisions apply, until a day to be appointed, to a non-profit registered provider which is a registered society[16]. A resolution for the voluntary winding up of the society under the Insolvency Act 1986[17] is effective only if the regulator has first consented[18]. The statutory requirement[19] to send a copy of the resolution to the Financial Conduct Authority is satisfied only if the copy is accompanied by a copy of the regulator's consent[20].

1   As to the meaning of 'registered provider' see PARA 53. As to when a body is a non-profit organisation see PARA 71 note 13.
2   Housing and Regeneration Act 2008 ss 163(1), 165(1)(a) (s 163 substituted by the Housing and Planning Act 2016 s 92, Sch 4 paras 22, 26; the Housing and Regeneration Act 2008 s 165(1)(a) amended by the Co-operative and Community Benefit Societies Act 2014 s 151(1), Sch 4 paras 121, 122). As to the meaning of 'registered society' see PARA 52 note 10. As to the disapplication of the Co-operative and Community Benefit Societies Act 2014 ss 160–169 to local authorities see PARA 85.
3   As to the meaning of 'the regulator' see PARA 57.
4   Housing and Regeneration Act 2008 s 163(2) (as substituted: see note 2). The following provisions of the Co-operative and Community Benefit Societies Act 2014 are the restructuring provisions: (1) s 109 (amalgamation of societies); (2) s 110 (transfer of engagements between societies); and (3) s 112 (conversion of society into a company etc): Housing and Regeneration Act 2008 s 163(4) (as so substituted). See FINANCIAL INSTITUTIONS vol 48 (2015) PARAS 1052–1055.
5   As to the Financial Conduct Authority see FINANCIAL SERVICES REGULATION vol 50 (2016) PARAS 5, 6 et seq.
6   Housing and Regeneration Act 2008 s 163(3) (as substituted: see note 2).
7   Housing and Regeneration Act 2008 s 163(5) (as substituted: see note 2). As to registration see s 112; and PARAS 70–72.
8   Housing and Regeneration Act 2008 s 163(6) (as substituted: see note 2).
9   Housing and Regeneration Act 2008 s 163(7) (as substituted: see note 2).
10 Housing and Regeneration Act 2008 s 163(8) (as substituted: see note 2).
11 Ie in accordance with the Co-operative and Community Benefit Societies Act 2014 s 119: Housing and Regeneration Act 2008 s 165(1)(b) (amended by the Co-operative and Community Benefit Societies Act 2014 Sch 4 paras 121, 130(1), (2)).
12 Housing and Regeneration Act 2008 s 165(2) (substituted by the Housing and Planning Act 2016 Sch 4 paras 22, 27).
13 Ie under the Co-operative and Community Benefit Societies Act 2014 s 121: see FINANCIAL INSTITUTIONS vol 48 (2015) PARA 1063.
14 Ie under the Co-operative and Community Benefit Societies Act 2014 s 122: see FINANCIAL INSTITUTIONS vol 48 (2015) PARA 1063.
15 Housing and Regeneration Act 2008 s 165(3) (added by the Housing and Planning Act 2016 Sch 4 paras 22, 27).
16 Housing and Regeneration Act 2008 s 164(1) (s 164 repealed, as from a day to be appointed, by the Housing and Planning Act 2016 s 115, Sch 6 paras 1, 8; at the date at which this volume states the law, no such day had been appointed).
17 As to voluntary winding up see COMPANY AND PARTNERSHIP INSOLVENCY vol 17 (2011) PARA 898 et seq.
18 Housing and Regeneration Act 2008 s 164(2) (prospectively repealed: see note 16). As to the meaning of 'consent' see PARA 80 note 29.
19 Ie in the Companies Act 2006 s 30, as applied by the Co-operative and Community Benefit Societies Act 2014 s 123 and the Insolvency Act 1986 s 84(3): see FINANCIAL INSTITUTIONS vol 48 (2015) PARA 1058.
20 Housing and Regeneration Act 2008 s 164(3) (amended by the Co-operative and Community Benefit Societies Act 2014 Sch 4 paras 121, 129; and by SI 2013/496; prospectively repealed (see note 16)).

87. Petition and property. The following provisions apply to a non-profit registered provider[1] which is either a registered company[2] or a registered society[3].

Where a non-profit registered provider which is a registered society is dissolved[4] or a non-profit registered provider which is a registered company is wound up under the Insolvency Act 1986[5], any surplus property that is available after satisfying the registered provider's liabilities must be transferred: (1) to the regulator[6]; or (2) if the regulator directs, to a specified non-profit registered provider[7]. If land belonging to the registered provider needs to be sold to satisfy its liabilities, the regulator may discharge those liabilities so as to ensure that the land is instead transferred in accordance with the above provisions[8]. Where the registered provider dissolved or wound up is a charity, a registered provider may be specified[9] only if it is a charity whose objects the regulator thinks are similar to those of the original charity[10].

1 As to the meaning of 'registered provider' see PARA 53. As to when a body is a non-profit organisation see PARA 71 note 13.
2 As to the meaning of 'registered company' see PARA 53 note 5.
3 Housing and Regeneration Act 2008 s 167(1) (amended by the Co-operative and Community Benefit Societies Act 2014 s 151(1), Sch 4 paras 121, 122); but see note 7. As to the meaning of 'registered society' see PARA 52 note 10. As to the disapplication of the Housing and Regeneration Act 2008 ss 160–169 to local authorities see PARA 85.
4 Ie in accordance with the Co-operative and Community Benefit Societies Act 2014 s 119 or s 123 (see FINANCIAL INSTITUTIONS vol 48 (2015) PARA 1058): Housing and Regeneration Act 2008 s 167(1)(a) (as amended (see note 3); and amended by virtue of the Co-operative and Community Benefit Societies Act 2014 Sch 4 paras 121, 131(1), (2)).
5 Housing and Regeneration Act 2008 s 167(1)(b).
6 As to the meaning of 'the regulator' see PARA 57. Where property is transferred to the regulator in accordance with the Housing and Regeneration Act 2008 s 167(2)(a), the regulator may dispose of the property only to a non-profit registered provider: s 168(1), (2). Where the registered provider wound up or dissolved was a charity, the regulator may dispose of the property only to a registered provider: (1) which is a charity; and (2) whose objects the regulator thinks are similar to those of the original charity: s 168(3). If the property includes land subject to a mortgage or charge, the regulator may dispose of the land: (a) subject to that mortgage or charge; or (b) subject to a new mortgage or charge in favour of the regulator: s 168(4). As to the meaning of 'disposal' see PARA 52 note 11.
7 Housing and Regeneration Act 2008 s 167(2). Section 167 has effect despite anything in the Insolvency Act 1986, the Companies Act 2006, the Co-operative and Community Benefit Societies Act 2014 or the constitution of a registered provider: Housing and Regeneration Act 2008 s 167(5) (amended by the Co-operative and Community Benefit Societies Act 2014 Sch 4 paras 121, 131(1), (3)). As to the meaning of 'constitution' see PARA 71 note 6. The Secretary of State may by regulations provide for the Housing and Regeneration Act 2008 ss 167, 168 to apply in relation to a registered provider which is a charity but not a registered company: (1) in specified circumstances; and (2) with specified modifications: s 169. As to the Secretary of State see PARA 7. As to regulations by the Secretary of State see PARA 54.
8 Housing and Regeneration Act 2008 s 167(3).
9 Ie under the Housing and Regeneration Act 2008 s 167(2)(b) (head (2) in the text).
10 Housing and Regeneration Act 2008 s 167(4).

88. Notification of constitutional changes. A non-profit registered provider[1] that is a registered society[2] must notify the regulator[3] of any change to the society's rules[4]. The trustees of a registered charity[5] that is a non-profit registered provider must notify the regulator of any amendment to the charity's objects[6]. A non-profit registered provider that is a registered company[7] must notify the regulator of: (1) any amendment of the company's articles of association; (2) any change to its name or registered office[8].

1 As to the meaning of 'registered provider' see PARA 53. As to when a body is a non-profit organisation see PARA 71 note 13.
2 As to the meaning of 'registered society' see PARA 52 note 10.
3 As to the meaning of 'the regulator' see PARA 57.
4 Housing and Regeneration Act 2008 s 169A (ss 169A–169C added by the Housing and Planning Act 2016 s 92, Sch 4 paras 22, 29). As to directions about notification see PARA 89.
5 As to the meaning of 'registered charity' see PARA 53 note 2.
6 Housing and Regeneration Act 2008 s 169B (as added: see note 4).

7   As to the meaning of 'registered company' see PARA 53 note 5.
8   Housing and Regeneration Act 2008 s 169C (as added: see note 4).

89. Directions about notifications. The regulator[1] may give directions about: (1) the period within which notifications relating to restructuring or dissolution[2] or to constitutional changes[3] must be given by private registered providers[4]; (2) the content of those notifications[5].

The regulator may give directions dispensing with such notification requirements[6]. A direction dispensing with a notification requirement may include conditions[7].

A direction may be: (a) general; or (b) specific (whether as to particular registered providers, particular kinds of notification requirement or in any other way)[8].

The regulator must make arrangements for bringing a direction to the attention of every registered provider to which it applies[9].

1   As to the meaning of 'the regulator' see PARA 57.
2   Ie under the Housing and Regeneration Act 2008 ss 160–165 (see PARAS 85–86).
3   Ie under the Housing and Regeneration Act 2008 ss 169A–169C (see PARA 88).
4   As to the meaning of 'registered provider' see PARA 53.
5   Housing and Regeneration Act 2008 s 169D(1) (s 169D added by the Housing and Planning Act 2016 s 92, Sch 4 paras 22, 29).
6   Housing and Regeneration Act 2008 s 169D(2) (as added: see note 5).
7   Housing and Regeneration Act 2008 s 169D(4) (as added: see note 5).
8   Housing and Regeneration Act 2008 s 169D(3) (as added: see note 5).
9   Housing and Regeneration Act 2008 s 169D(5) (as added: see note 5).

(E)   Housing Administration Orders etc

90. Housing administration orders. The following provisions apply as from a day to be appointed. Under Chapter 5 of Part 4 of the Housing and Planning Act 2016[1] there are new provisions dealing with the insolvency of registered providers. It introduces a special administration regime for private registered providers of social housing that are at risk of entering insolvency proceedings. It sets out the remit for the different types of private registered providers.

A housing administration may only be commenced by an order of the court[2]. Such an order appoints a person (called the 'housing administrator') to manage the affairs, business and property of a company, registered society or charitable incorporated organisation that is a registered provider of social housing for the duration of the housing administration.

A 'housing administration order' is an order which:

(1)   is made by the court in relation to a private registered provider of social housing[3] that is a company, a registered society within the meaning of the Co-operative and Community Benefit Societies Act 2014[4] or a charitable incorporated organisation within the meaning of Part 11 of the Charities Act 2011[5]; and

(2)   directs that, while the order is in force, the provider's affairs, business and property[6] are to be managed by a person appointed by the court[7].

The person appointed for the purposes of the housing administration order is referred to in the relevant provisions of the Housing and Planning Act 2016[8] as the 'housing administrator'[9].

A housing administrator has two objectives[10]:

(a)   Objective 1: normal administration[11]; and

(b)   Objective 2: keeping social housing in the regulated sector[12]. Objective 1 takes priority over Objective 2 (but the housing administrator must, so far as possible, work towards both objectives)[13].

It follows that, in pursuing Objective 2, the housing administrator must not do anything that would result in a worse distribution to creditors than would be the case if the administrator did not need to pursue Objective 2[14].

Objective 1 is to:

(i)   rescue the registered provider as a going concern;

(ii)   achieve a better result for the registered provider's creditors as a whole than would be likely if the registered provider were wound up (without first being in housing administration); or

(iii) realise property in order to make a distribution to one or more secured or preferential creditors[15].

The housing administrator must aim to achieve Objective 1(i) unless the housing administrator thinks: (A) that it is not reasonably practicable to achieve it; or (B) that Objective 1(ii) would achieve a better result for the registered provider's creditors as a whole[16]. The housing administrator may aim to achieve Objective 1(iii) only if: (I) the housing administrator thinks that it is not reasonably practicable to achieve Objective 1(i) or (ii); and (II) the housing administrator does not unnecessarily harm the interests of the registered provider's creditors as a whole[17]. In pursuing Objective 1(i), (ii) or (iii) the housing administrator must act in the interests of the registered provider's creditors as a whole so far as consistent with that Objective[18].

Objective 2 is to ensure that the registered provider's social housing remains in the regulated housing sector[19]. For this purpose, social housing remains in the regulated housing sector for so long as it is owned by a private registered provider[20].

1   The Housing and Planning Act 2016 Pt 4 Ch 5 (ss 95–117) is to come into force as from a day to be appointed under s 216(3); at the date at which this volume states the law, no such day had been appointed except in relation to s 102(2)–(6) (see note 9), which is in force from 3 February 2017: see the Housing and Planning Act 2016 (Commencement No 4 and Transitional Provisions) Regulations 2017, SI 2017/75, reg 3(c). See further PARAS 91–99.

2   See the Housing and Planning Act 2016 s 95(1)(a). 'The court', in relation to a company or registered society, means the court having jurisdiction to wind up the company or registered society: s 116(1). 'Company' means: (1) a company registered under the Companies Act 2006; or (2) an unregistered company; and 'unregistered company' means a company that is not registered under the Companies Act 2006: Housing and Planning Act 2016 s 116(1). 'Registered society' has the same meaning as in the Co-operative and Community Benefit Societies Act 2014: Housing and Planning Act 2016 s 116(1).

3   'Private registered provider' means a private registered provider of social housing; and 'registered provider' means a registered provider of social housing (see the Housing and Regeneration Act 2008 s 80; and PARA 53): Housing and Planning Act 2016 s 116(1).

4   See FINANCIAL INSTITUTIONS vol 48 (2015) PARA 881 et seq.

5   Ie the Charities Act 2011 Pt 11 (ss 244–250): see CHARITIES vol 8 (2015) PARA 226 et seq.

6   'Business' and 'property' have the same meaning as in the Insolvency Act 1986 (see COMPANY AND PARTNERSHIP INSOLVENCY vol 16 (2011) PARAS 159, 439): Housing and Planning Act 2016 s 116(1). References in Pt 4 Ch 5 (ss 95–117) to a provision of the Insolvency Act 1986 (except the references in the Housing and Planning Act 2016 s 116(2) (see note 9): (1) in relation to a company, are to that provision without the modifications made by the Housing and Planning Act 2016 Sch 5 Pt 1; (2) in relation to a registered society, are to that provision as it applies to registered societies otherwise than by virtue of regulations under s 102 (see note 9) (if at all); and (3) in relation to a charitable incorporated organisation (see note 9), are to that provision as it applies to charitable incorporated organisations otherwise than by virtue of regulations under s 102 (if at all): s 116(7).

7   Housing and Planning Act 2016 s 95(1); applied to Pt 4 Ch 5 by s 116(1). In relation to a housing administration order applying to a registered provider that is a foreign company, the reference in head (2) in the text to the provider's affairs, business and property is a reference to its UK affairs, business and property: s 95(3). 'Foreign company' means a company incorporated outside the United Kingdom: s 116(1). 'UK affairs, business and property', in relation to a company, means: (1) its affairs and business so far as carried on in the United Kingdom; and (2) its property in the United Kingdom: s 116(1). As to the meaning of 'United Kingdom' see PARA 60 note 10.

8 Ie the Housing and Planning Act 2016 Pt 4 Ch 5 (ss 95–117).

9 Housing and Planning Act 2016 ss 95(2), 116(1). In Pt 4 Ch 5 references to the housing administrator of a registered provider: (1) include a person appointed under the Insolvency Act 1986 Sch B1 para 91 or 103, as applied by the Housing and Planning Act 2016 Sch 5 Pt 1 or regulations under s 102, to be the housing administrator of the registered provider; and (2) if two or more persons are appointed as the housing administrator of the registered provider, are to be read in accordance with the provision made under s 101 (see PARA 93): s 116(2). As to housing administrators see further PARA 93.

Schedule 5 contains provision applying the provisions of the Insolvency Act 1986 Sch B1, and certain other legislation, to housing administration orders in relation to companies: Housing and Planning Act 2016 s 102(1). The Secretary of State may by regulations provide for any provision of the Insolvency Act 1986 Sch B1 or any other insolvency legislation to apply, with or without modifications, to cases where a housing administration order is made in relation to a registered society or a charitable incorporated organisation: Housing and Planning Act 2016 s 102(2) (in force: see note 1). The Secretary of State may by regulations modify any insolvency legislation as it applies in relation to a registered society or a charitable incorporated organisation if the Secretary State considers the modifications are appropriate in connection with any provision made by or under Pt 4 Ch 5: s 102(3) (in force: see note 1). 'Charitable incorporated organisation' means a charitable incorporated organisation within the meaning of the Charities Act 2011 Pt 11 (see CHARITIES vol 8 (2015) PARA 226 et seq): Housing and Planning Act 2016 s 116(1). In s 102(3) 'insolvency legislation' means: (a) the Insolvency Act 1986; or (b) any other legislation (whenever passed or made) that relates to insolvency or makes provision by reference to anything that is or may be done under the Insolvency Act 1986: Housing and Planning Act 2016 s 102(4) (in force: see note 1). 'Legislation' includes provision made by or under: (i) an Act; (ii) an Act of the Scottish Parliament; (iii) Northern Ireland legislation; or (iv) a Measure or Act of the National Assembly for Wales: Housing and Planning Act 2016 s 116(1). As to the Secretary of State see PARA 7.

The power to make rules under the Insolvency Act 1986 s 411 (see COMPANY AND PARTNERSHIP INSOLVENCY vol 17 (2011) PARA 1002) is to apply for the purpose of giving effect to the Housing and Planning Act 2016 Pt 4 Ch 5 as it applies for the purpose of giving effect to the Insolvency Act 1986 Pts I–VII (ss 1–251)) (and, accordingly, as if references in s 411 to Pts I–VII included references to the Housing and Planning Act 2016 Pt 4 Ch 5): s 102(5) (in force: see note 1). The Insolvency Act 1986 s 413(2) (duty to consult the Insolvency Rules Committee about rules: see COMPANY AND PARTNERSHIP INSOLVENCY vol 17 (2011) PARA 1002) does not apply to rules made under s 411 as a result of the Housing and Planning Act 2016 s 102: s 102(6) (in force: see note 1).

10 Housing and Planning Act 2016 s 96(1). A reference in Pt 4 Ch 5 to the objectives of a housing administration is to the objectives to be pursued by the housing administrator: ss 96(4), 116(1).

11 Housing and Planning Act 2016 s 96(1)(a). See s 97; and the text to notes 15–18.

12 Housing and Planning Act 2016 s 96(1)(b). See s 98; and the text to notes 19–20.

13 Housing and Planning Act 2016 s 96(2).

14 Housing and Planning Act 2016 s 96(3).

15 Housing and Planning Act 2016 s 97(1).

16 Housing and Planning Act 2016 s 97(2).

17 Housing and Planning Act 2016 s 97(3).

18 Housing and Planning Act 2016 s 97(4).

19 Housing and Planning Act 2016 s 98(1).

20 Housing and Planning Act 2016 s 98(2).

91. Applications for housing administration orders. The following provisions apply as from a day to be appointed[1]. An application for a housing administration order[2] may be made only: (1) by the Secretary of State[3]; or (2) with the consent of the Secretary of State, by the Regulator of Social Housing[4].

The applicant for a housing administration order in relation to a registered provider[5] must give notice of the application to: (a) every person who has appointed an administrative receiver[6] of the provider; (b) every person who is or may be entitled to appoint an administrative receiver of the registered provider; (c) every person who is or may be entitled to make an appointment in relation to the registered provider as the holder of a floating charge[7]; and (d) any other persons specified by housing administration rules[8]. The notice must be given as soon as possible after the making of the application[9].

1 See PARA 90 note 1.

2   As to the meaning of 'housing administration order' see PARA 90.

3   Housing and Planning Act 2016 s 99(1)(a). As to the Secretary of State see PARA 7.

4   Housing and Planning Act 2016 s 99(1)(b). 'Regulator of Social Housing' has the meaning given by the Housing and Regeneration Act 2008 s 92A (see PARA 57): Housing and Planning Act 2016 s 116(1). As to the powers of the court on hearing an application see PARA 92.

5   As to the meaning of 'registered provider' see PARA 90 note 3.

6   In the Housing and Planning Act 2016 s 99, 'administrative receiver' means: (1) an administrative receiver within the meaning given by the Insolvency Act 1986 s 251 for the purposes of Pts I–VII (ss 1–251) (see COMPANIES vol 15A (2016) PARA 1519; see also PARA 90 note 6); or (2) in relation to a foreign company, a person whose functions are equivalent to those of an administrative receiver and relate only to its UK affairs, business and property: Housing and Planning Act 2016 s 99(4). As to the meaning of 'foreign company' and 'UK affairs, business and property' see PARA 90 note 7.

7   Ie under the Insolvency Act 1986 Sch B1 para 14: see COMPANY AND PARTNERSHIP INSOLVENCY vol 16 (2011) PARA 175 et seq. See also PARA 90 note 6.

8   Housing and Planning Act 2016 s 99(2). 'Housing administration rules' means rules made under the Insolvency Act 1986 s 411 as a result of the Housing and Planning Act 2016 s 102 (see PARA 90 note 9): s 116(1).

9   Housing and Planning Act 2016 s 99(3).

92. Powers of court on application for housing administration order. The following provisions apply as from a day to be appointed[1]. On hearing an application for a housing administration order[2], the court[3] has the following powers[4]:

(1)   it may make the order[5];

(2)   it may dismiss the application[6];

(3)   it may adjourn the hearing conditionally or unconditionally[7];

(4)   it may make an interim order[8];

(5)   it may treat the application as a winding-up petition and make any order the court could make[9] on hearing a winding-up petition[10]; and

(6)   it may make any other order which it thinks appropriate[11].

The court may make a housing administration order in relation to a registered provider[12] only if it is satisfied:

(a)   that the registered provider is unable, or is likely to be unable, to pay its debts[13]; or

(b)   that, on a petition by the Secretary of State[14], it would be just and equitable (disregarding the objectives of the housing administration[15]) to wind up the registered provider in the public interest[16].

The court may not make a housing administration order on the ground set out in head (b) unless the Secretary of State has certified to the court that the case is one in which the Secretary of State considers (disregarding the objectives of the housing administration) that it would be appropriate to petition[17] to wind up the registered provider in the public interest[18].

The court has no power to make a housing administration order in relation to a registered provider which: (i) is in administration[19]; or (ii) has gone into liquidation[20].

A housing administration order comes into force either at the time appointed by the court or, if no time is appointed by the court, when the order is made[21].

1   See PARA 90 note 1.

2   As to the meaning of 'housing administration order' see PARA 90. As to applications see PARA 91.

3   As to the meaning of 'the court' see PARA 90 note 2.

4   Housing and Planning Act 2016 s 100(1).

5   Housing and Planning Act 2016 s 100(1)(a).

6   Housing and Planning Act 2016 s 100(1)(b).

7   Housing and Planning Act 2016 s 100(1)(c).

8   Housing and Planning Act 2016 s 100(1)(d). An interim order under s 100(1)(d) may, in particular: (1) restrict the exercise of a power of the registered provider or of its relevant officers; or (2) make

provision conferring a discretion on a person qualified to act as an insolvency practitioner in relation to the registered provider: s 100(6). In s 100(6)(a) (head (1) above) 'relevant officer': (a) in relation to a company, means a director; (b) in relation to a registered society, means a member of the management committee or other directing body of the society; and (c) in relation to a charitable incorporated organisation, means a charity trustee (as defined by the Charities Act 2011 s 177: see CHARITIES vol 8 (2015) PARA 255): Housing and Planning Act 2016 s 100(7). In the case of a foreign company, s 100(6)(a) is to be read as a reference to restricting the exercise of a power of the registered provider or of its directors: (i) within the United Kingdom; or (ii) in relation to the company's UK affairs, business or property: s 100(8).

References in Pt 4 Ch 5 (ss 95–117) to a person qualified to act as an insolvency practitioner in relation to a registered provider are to be read in accordance with the Insolvency Act 1986 Pt XIII (ss 388–391T) (see COMPANY AND PARTNERSHIP INSOLVENCY vol 16 (2011) PARA 9 et seq), but as if references in that Part to a company included a company registered under the Companies Act 2006 in Northern Ireland: Housing and Planning Act 2016 s 116(3). See also PARA 90 note 6.

As to the meaning of 'company' and 'registered society' see PARA 90 note 2. As to the meaning of 'foreign company' and 'UK affairs, business or property' see PARA 90 note 7. As to the meaning of 'United Kingdom' see PARA 60 note 10.

9   Ie under the Insolvency Act 1986 s 125: see COMPANY AND PARTNERSHIP INSOLVENCY vol 16 (2011) PARA 426. See also PARA 90 note 6.
10 Housing and Planning Act 2016 s 100(1)(e).
11 Housing and Planning Act 2016 s 100(1)(f).
12 As to the meaning of 'registered provider' see PARA 90 note 3.
13 Housing and Planning Act 2016 s 100(2)(a). For the purposes of s 100 a registered provider is unable to pay its debts if: (1) it is deemed to be unable to pay its debts under the Insolvency Act 1986 s 123 (see COMPANY AND PARTNERSHIP INSOLVENCY vol 16 (2011) PARA 394); or (2) it is an unregistered company which is deemed, as a result of any of ss 222–224 (see COMPANY AND PARTNERSHIP INSOLVENCY vol 17 (2011) PARA 1114), to be so unable for the purposes of s 221, or which would be so deemed if it were an unregistered company for the purposes of those sections: Housing and Planning Act 2016 s 100(9). See also PARA 90 note 6. As to the meaning of 'unregistered company' see PARA 90 note 2.
14 Ie under the Insolvency Act 1986 s 124A: see COMPANY AND PARTNERSHIP INSOLVENCY vol 16 (2011) PARA 392. See also PARA 90 note 6. As to the Secretary of State see PARA 7.
15 As to the meaning of 'objectives of the housing administration' see PARA 90 note 10.
16 Housing and Planning Act 2016 s 100(2)(b).
17 Ie under the Insolvency Act 1986 s 124A.
18 Housing and Planning Act 2016 s 100(3).
19 Ie under the Insolvency Act 1986 Sch B1: see COMPANY AND PARTNERSHIP INSOLVENCY vol 16 (2011) PARA 158 et seq. See also PARA 90 note 6.
20 Housing and Planning Act 2016 s 100(4). The text refers to liquidation within the meaning of the Insolvency Act 1986 s 247(2): see COMPANY AND PARTNERSHIP INSOLVENCY vol 16 (2011) PARA 10. See also PARA 90 note 6.
21 Housing and Planning Act 2016 s 100(5).

93. Housing administrators. The following provisions apply as from a day to be appointed[1]. The housing administrator[2] of a registered provider[3]: (1) is an officer of the court[4]; and (2) in carrying out functions in relation to the registered provider, is to be treated as the registered provider's agent[5]. The housing administrator of a registered provider must aim to achieve the objectives of the housing administration[6] as quickly and as efficiently as is reasonably practicable[7]. A person is not to be the housing administrator of a registered provider unless qualified to act as an insolvency practitioner[8] in relation to the registered provider[9].

If the court appoints two or more persons as the housing administrator of a registered provider, the appointment must set out: (a) which (if any) of the functions of a housing administrator are to be carried out only by the appointees acting jointly; (b) the circumstances (if any) in which functions of a housing administrator are to be carried out by one of the appointees, or by particular appointees, acting alone; and (c) the circumstances (if any) in which things done in relation to one of the appointees, or in relation to particular appointees, are to be treated as done in relation to all of them[10].

If the housing administrator of a registered provider disposes of[11] land that is the subject of a planning obligation[12] that contains relevant terms[13], the relevant terms are not binding on the person to whom the land is disposed of or any successor in title[14].

1　See PARA 90 note 1.
2　As to the meaning of 'housing administrator' see PARA 90.
3　As to the meaning of 'registered provider' see PARA 90 note 3.
4　As to the meaning of 'the court' see PARA 90 note 2.
5　Housing and Planning Act 2016 s 101(1).
6　As to the meaning of 'objectives of the housing administration' see PARA 90 note 10.
7　Housing and Planning Act 2016 s 101(2).
8　As to the meaning of 'qualified to act as an insolvency practitioner' see PARA 92 note 8.
9　Housing and Planning Act 2016 s 101(3).
10　Housing and Planning Act 2016 s 101(4).
11　In the Housing and Planning Act 2016 s 103, 'disposes of', in relation to land, means sells a freehold or leasehold interest in the land or grants a lease of the land: s 103(2).
12　'Planning obligation' means a planning obligation under the Town and Country Planning Act 1990 s 106 (see PLANNING vol 81 (2010) PARA 335) (whether entered into before or after the Housing and Planning Act 2016 s 103 comes into force): s 103(2).
13　'Relevant terms' in relation to a planning obligation, means any restrictions or requirements imposed by the planning obligation that are expressed not to apply in the event that the land is disposed of by a mortgagee: Housing and Planning Act 2016 s 103(2).
14　Housing and Planning Act 2016 s 103(1).

94. Restrictions on other insolvency procedures. The following provisions apply as from a day to be appointed[1] if a person other than the Secretary of State[2] petitions for the winding-up of a registered provider[3] that is: (1) a company[4]; (2) a registered society within the meaning of the Co-operative and Community Benefit Societies Act 2014[5]; or (3) a charitable incorporated organisation within the meaning of Part 11 of the Charities Act 2011[6]. The court[7] may not exercise its powers on a winding-up petition[8] unless: (a) notice of the petition has been given to the Regulator of Social Housing[9] and a period of at least 28 days has elapsed since that notice was given; or (b) the Regulator of Social Housing has waived the notice requirement in head (a)[10].

The Regulator of Social Housing must give the Secretary of State a copy of any notice given under head (a)[11]. The Regulator of Social Housing may waive the notice requirement under head (a) only with the consent of the Secretary of State[12].

If an application for a housing administration order[13] in relation to the registered provider is made to the court[14] before a winding-up order is made on the petition, the court may exercise its powers on such an application[15] (instead of exercising its powers on the petition)[16].

The following provisions apply to a private registered provider that is: (i) a company; (ii) a registered society within the meaning of the Co-operative and Community Benefit Societies Act 2014; or (iii) a charitable incorporated organisation within the meaning of Part 11 of the Charities Act 2011[17]. The registered provider has no power to pass a resolution for voluntary winding up[18] without the permission of the court[19]. Permission may be granted by the court only on an application made by the registered provider[20]. The court may not grant permission unless: (A) notice of the application has been given to the Regulator of Social Housing and a period of at least 28 days has elapsed since that notice was given; or (B) the Regulator of Social Housing has waived the notice requirement in head (A)[21].

The Regulator of Social Housing must give the Secretary of State a copy of any notice given under head (A)[22]. The Regulator of Social Housing may waive the notice requirement under head (A) only with the consent of the Secretary of State[23].

If an application for a housing administration order in relation to the registered provider is made to the court[24] after an application for permission under these provisions has been made and before it is granted, the court may exercise its powers[25] on an application for a housing administration order[26].

The following provisions apply if a person other than the Secretary of State makes an ordinary administration application[27] in relation to a private registered provider that is a company or a charitable incorporated organisation within the meaning of Part 11 of the Charities Act 2011[28]. The court must dismiss the application if a housing administration order is in force in relation to the registered provider or a housing administration order has been made in relation to the registered provider but is not yet in force[29]. If this does not apply, the court, on hearing the application, must not exercise its powers on such an application[30] (other than its power of adjournment) unless: (I) either notice of the application has been given to the Regulator of Social Housing and a period of at least 28 days has elapsed since that notice was given, or the Regulator of Social Housing has waived the notice requirement; and (II) there is no application for a housing administration order which is outstanding[31].

The Regulator of Social Housing must give the Secretary of State a copy of any notice given under head (I)[32]. The Regulator of Social Housing may waive the notice requirement only with the consent of the Secretary of State[33].

The provisions of the Insolvency Act 1986 relating to an interim moratorium[34] do not prevent, or require the permission of the court for, the making of an application for a housing administration order[35].

On the making of a housing administration order in relation to a registered provider, the court must dismiss any ordinary administration application made in relation to the registered provider which is outstanding[36].

1   See PARA 90 note 1.
2   As to the Secretary of State see PARA 7.
3   As to the meaning of 'registered provider' see PARA 90 note 3.
4   As to the meaning of 'company' see PARA 90 note 2.
5   See FINANCIAL INSTITUTIONS vol 48 (2015) PARA 881 et seq.
6   Housing and Planning Act 2016 s 104(1). As to charitable incorporated organisations within the meaning of the Charities Act 2011 Pt 11 (ss 244–250): see CHARITIES vol 8 (2015) PARA 226 et seq.
7   As to the meaning of 'the court' see PARA 90 note 2.
8   References in the Housing and Planning Act 2016 s 104 to the court's powers on a winding-up petition are to: (1) its powers under the Insolvency Act 1986 s 125 (other than its power of adjournment) (see COMPANY AND PARTNERSHIP INSOLVENCY vol 16 (2011) PARA 426 et seq); and (2) its powers under s 135 (see COMPANY AND PARTNERSHIP INSOLVENCY vol 16 (2011) PARA 441 et seq): Housing and Planning Act 2016 s 104(6). See also PARA 90 note 6.
9   As to the meaning of 'Regulator of Social Housing' see PARA 91 note 4.
10 Housing and Planning Act 2016 s 104(2).
11 Housing and Planning Act 2016 s 104(4).
12 Housing and Planning Act 2016 s 104(5).
13 As to the meaning of 'housing administration order' see PARA 90.
14 Ie in accordance with the Housing and Planning Act 2016 s 99: see PARA 91.
15 Ie under the Housing and Planning Act 2016 s 100: see PARA 92.
16 Housing and Planning Act 2016 s 104(3).
17 Housing and Planning Act 2016 s 105(1).
18 In the Housing and Planning Act 2016 s 105, 'a resolution for voluntary winding up' has the same meaning as in the Insolvency Act 1986 (see COMPANY AND PARTNERSHIP INSOLVENCY vol 17 (2011) PARA 898): Housing and Planning Act 2016 s 105(8). See also PARA 90 note 6.

19 Housing and Planning Act 2016 s 105(2).
20 Housing and Planning Act 2016 s 105(3).
21 Housing and Planning Act 2016 s 105(4).
22 Housing and Planning Act 2016 s 105(6).
23 Housing and Planning Act 2016 s 105(7).
24 Ie in accordance with the Housing and Planning Act 2016 s 99: see PARA 91.
25 Ie under the Housing and Planning Act 2016 s 100: see PARA 92.
26 Housing and Planning Act 2016 s 105(5).
27 In the Housing and Planning Act 2016 s 106, 'ordinary administration application' means an application in accordance with the Insolvency Act 1986 Sch B1 para 12 (see COMPANY AND PARTNERSHIP INSOLVENCY vol 16 (2011) PARA 168): Housing and Planning Act 2016 s 106(8). See also PARA 90 note 6.
28 Housing and Planning Act 2016 s 106(1).
29 Housing and Planning Act 2016 s 106(2).
30 Ie under the Insolvency Act 1986 Sch B1 para 13: see COMPANY AND PARTNERSHIP INSOLVENCY vol 16 (2011) PARA 173. See also PARA 90 note 6.
31 Housing and Planning Act 2016 s 106(3). For the purposes of Pt 4 Ch 5 (ss 95–117), an application made to the court is outstanding if it: (1) has not yet been granted or dismissed; and (2) has not been withdrawn: s 116(4). An application is not to be taken as having been dismissed if an appeal against the dismissal of the application, or a subsequent appeal, is pending: s 116(5). An appeal is to be treated as pending for this purpose if: (a) an appeal has been brought and has not been determined or withdrawn; (b) an application for permission to appeal has been made but has not been determined or withdrawn; or (c) no appeal has been brought and the period for bringing one is still running: s 116(6).
32 Housing and Planning Act 2016 s 106(4).
33 Housing and Planning Act 2016 s 106(7).
34 Ie the Insolvency Act 1986 Sch B1 para 44: see COMPANY AND PARTNERSHIP INSOLVENCY vol 16 (2011) PARA 171. See also PARA 90 note 6.
35 Housing and Planning Act 2016 s 106(5).
36 Housing and Planning Act 2016 s 106(6).

95. Restriction on appointment of administrator by creditors. The following provisions apply as from a day to be appointed[1] to make provision about appointments[2] of administrators in relation to a private registered provider[3] that is:

(1)   a company[4]; or
(2)   a charitable incorporated organisation within the meaning of Part 11 of the Charities Act 2011[5].

If in any case:

(a)   a housing administration order[6] is in force in relation to the registered provider;
(b)   a housing administration order has been made in relation to the registered provider but is not yet in force; or
(c)   an application for a housing administration order in relation to the registered provider is outstanding[7],

a person may not take any step to make an appointment[8].

In any other case, an appointment takes effect only if each of the following conditions are met[9]. The conditions are:

(i)   either:
          (A)   that notice of the appointment has been given to the Regulator of Social Housing[10], accompanied by a copy of every document in relation to the appointment that is filed or lodged with the court[11] and that a period of 28 days has elapsed since that notice was given; or
          (B)   that the Regulator of Social Housing has waived the notice requirement in head (i)(A)[12];

(ii)   that there is no outstanding application to the court for a housing administration order in relation to the registered provider[13]; and

(iii)   that the making of an application for a housing administration order in relation to the registered provider has not resulted in the making of a housing administration order which is in force or is still to come into force[14].

The Regulator of Social Housing must give the Secretary of State a copy of any notice given under head (i) (and a copy of the accompanying documents)[15]. The Regulator of Social Housing may waive the notice requirement under head (i)(A) only with the consent of the Secretary of State[16].

The provision of the Insolvency Act 1986 relating to an interim moratorium[17] do not prevent, or require the permission of the court for, the making of an application for a housing administration order at any time before the appointment takes effect[18].

1   See PARA 90 note 1.
2   Ie under the Insolvency Act 1986 Sch B1 para 14 or Sch B1 para 22: see COMPANY AND PARTNERSHIP INSOLVENCY vol 16 (2011) PARAS 175, 183. See also PARA 90 note 6.
3   As to the meaning of 'private registered provider' see PARA 90 note 3.
4   As to the meaning of 'company' see PARA 90 note 2.
5   Housing and Planning Act 2016 s 107(1). As to charitable incorporated organisations within the meaning of the Charities Act 2011 Pt 11 (ss 244–250) see CHARITIES vol 8 (2015) PARA 226 et seq.
6   As to the meaning of 'housing administration order' see PARA 90. See also PARAS 91–92.
7   As to when an application is outstanding see PARA 94 note 31.
8   Housing and Planning Act 2016 s 107(2).
9   Housing and Planning Act 2016 s 107(3).
10 As to the meaning of 'Regulator of Social Housing' see PARA 91 note 4.
11 Ie in accordance with the Insolvency Act 1986 Sch B1 para 18 or Sch B1 para 29: see COMPANY AND PARTNERSHIP INSOLVENCY vol 16 (2011) PARAS 179, 188. See also PARA 90 note 6. As to the meaning of 'the court' see PARA 90 note 2.
12 Housing and Planning Act 2016 s 107(4)(a).
13 Housing and Planning Act 2016 s 107(4)(b).
14 Housing and Planning Act 2016 s 107(4)(c).
15 Housing and Planning Act 2016 s 107(5).
16 Housing and Planning Act 2016 s 107(6). As to the Secretary of State see PARA 7.
17 Ie the Insolvency Act 1986 Sch B1 para 44: see COMPANY AND PARTNERSHIP INSOLVENCY vol 16 (2011) PARA 171. See also PARA 90 note 6.
18 Housing and Planning Act 2016 s 107(7).

96. Restriction on enforcement of security. The following provisions apply as from a day to be appointed[1] in relation to a private registered provider[2] that is: (1) a company[3]; (2) a registered society within the meaning of the Co-operative and Community Benefit Societies Act 2014[4]; or a charitable incorporated organisation within the meaning of Part 11 of the Charities Act 2011[5].

A person may not take any step to enforce a security[6] over property[7] of the registered provider unless: (a) notice of the intention to do so has been given to the Regulator of Social Housing[8] and a period of at least 28 days has elapsed since the notice was given; or (b) the Regulator of Social Housing has waived the notice requirement in head (a)[9].

The Regulator of Social Housing must give the Secretary of State a copy of any notice given under head (a)[10]. The Regulator of Social Housing may waive the notice requirement only with the consent of the Secretary of State[11].

1   See PARA 90 note 1.
2   As to the meaning of 'private registered provider' see PARA 90 note 3.
3   As to the meaning of 'company' see PARA 90 note 2.
4   See FINANCIAL INSTITUTIONS vol 48 (2015) PARA 881 et seq.

5 Housing and Planning Act 2016 s 108(1). As to charitable incorporated organisations within the meaning of the Charities Act 2011 Pt 11 (ss 244–250) see CHARITIES vol 8 (2015) PARA 226 et seq.
6 'Security' has the same meaning as in the Insolvency Act 1986 (see COMPANY AND PARTNERSHIP INSOLVENCY vol 16 (2011) PARA 121): Housing and Planning Act 2016 s 116(1). See also PARA 90 note 6.
7 In the case of a company which is a foreign company, the reference to the property of the company is to its property in the United Kingdom: Housing and Planning Act 2016 s 108(3). As to the meaning of 'foreign company' and 'property' see PARA 90 note 7.
8 As to the meaning of 'Regulator of Social Housing' see PARA 91 note 4.
9 Housing and Planning Act 2016 s 108(2).
10 Housing and Planning Act 2016 s 108(4). As to the Secretary of State see PARA 7.
11 Housing and Planning Act 2016 s 108(5).

97. Financial support for registered providers in housing administration. The following provisions apply as from a day to be appointed[1]. If a housing administration order[2] has been made in relation to a registered provider[3], the Secretary of State[4] may make grants or loans to the registered provider of such amounts as appear to the Secretary of State appropriate for achieving the objectives of the housing administration[5]. Such a grant may be made on any terms and conditions the Secretary of State considers appropriate (including provision for repayment, with or without interest)[6].

1 See PARA 90 note 1.
2 As to the meaning of 'housing administration order' see PARA 90. See also PARAS 91–92.
3 As to the meaning of 'registered provider' see PARA 90 note 3.
4 As to the Secretary of State see PARA 7.
5 Housing and Planning Act 2016 s 109(1). As to the meaning of 'objectives of the housing administration' see PARA 90 note 10.
6 Housing and Planning Act 2016 s 109(2).

98. Indemnities where housing administration order is made. The following provisions apply as from a day to be appointed[1]. If a housing administration order[2] has been made in relation to a registered provider[3], the Secretary of State[4] may agree to indemnify persons in respect of one or both of the following: (1) liabilities incurred in connection with the carrying out of functions by the housing administrator[5]; and (2) loss or damage sustained in that connection[6]. The agreement may be made in whatever manner, and on whatever terms, the Secretary of State considers appropriate[7]. As soon as practicable after agreeing to indemnify persons under these provisions, the Secretary of State must lay a statement of the agreement before Parliament[8].

The power of the Secretary of State to agree to indemnify persons: (a) is confined to a power to agree to indemnify persons in respect of liabilities, loss and damage incurred or sustained by them as relevant persons[9]; but (b) includes power to agree to indemnify persons (whether or not they are identified or identifiable at the time of the agreement) who subsequently become relevant persons[10].

The following provisions apply where a sum is paid out by the Secretary of State in consequence of an indemnity agreed to[11] in relation to the housing administrator of a registered provider[12]. The registered provider must pay the Secretary of State: (i) such amounts in or towards the repayment to the Secretary of State of that sum as the Secretary of State may direct; and (ii) interest on any such amounts outstanding at such rates as the Secretary of State may direct[13]. The payments must be made by the registered provider at such times and in such manner as the Secretary of State may determine[14].

The Secretary of State must lay before Parliament a statement, relating to the sum paid out in consequence of the indemnity: (A) as soon as practicable after the end of the financial year[15] in which the sum is paid out; and (B) if heads (i) and (ii) apply to the sum, as soon as practicable after the end of each subsequent financial year in relation to which the repayment condition has not been met[16]. The repayment condition is met in relation to a financial year if: (I) the whole of the sum has been repaid to the Secretary of State before the beginning of the year; and (II) the registered provider was not at any time during the year liable to pay interest on amounts that became due in respect of the sum[17].

1   See PARA 90 note 1.
2   As to the meaning of 'housing administration order' see PARA 90. See also PARAS 91–92.
3   As to the meaning of 'registered provider' see PARA 90 note 3.
4   As to the Secretary of State see PARA 7.
5   As to the meaning of 'housing administrator' see PARA 90.
6   Housing and Planning Act 2016 s 110(1). As to repayment of sums paid by the Secretary of State in consequence of an indemnity agreed to under s 110, see s 111; and the text to notes 11–17: s 110(4).
7   Housing and Planning Act 2016 s 110(2).
8   Housing and Planning Act 2016 s 110(3).
9   The following are relevant persons for these purposes: (1) the housing administrator; (2) an employee of the housing administrator; (3) a partner or employee of a firm of which the housing administrator is a partner; (4) a partner or employee of a firm of which the housing administrator is an employee; (5) a partner of a firm of which the housing administrator was an employee or partner at a time when the order was in force; (6) a body corporate which is the employer of the housing administrator; (7) an officer, employee or member of such a body corporate; and (8) a Scottish firm which is the employer of the housing administrator or of which the housing administrator is a partner: Housing and Planning Act 2016 s 110(6). For the purposes of s 110(6): (a) references to the housing administrator are to be read, where two or more persons are appointed as the housing administrator, as references to any one or more of them; and (b) references to a firm of which a person was a partner or employee at a particular time include a firm which holds itself out to be the successor of a firm of which the person was a partner or employee at that time: s 110(7). 'Member' has the same meaning as in the Insolvency Act 1986 (see COMPANY AND PARTNERSHIP INSOLVENCY vol 16 (2011) PARA 84): Housing and Planning Act 2016 s 116(1). See also PARA 90 note 6. 'Scottish firm' means a firm constituted under the law of Scotland: s 116(1).
10   Housing and Planning Act 2016 s 110(5).
11   Ie under the Housing and Planning Act 2016 s 110.
12   Housing and Planning Act 2016 s 111(1).
13   Housing and Planning Act 2016 s 111(2). This does not apply in the case of a sum paid by the Secretary of State for indemnifying a person in respect of a liability to the registered provider: s 111(4).
14   Housing and Planning Act 2016 s 111(3).
15   'Financial year' means a period of 12 months ending with 31 March: Housing and Planning Act 2016 s 116(1).
16   Housing and Planning Act 2016 s 111(5).
17   Housing and Planning Act 2016 s 111(6).

99. Guarantees where housing administration order is made. The following provisions apply as from a day to be appointed[1]. If a housing administration order[2] has been made in relation to a registered provider[3], the Secretary of State[4] may guarantee:

(1)   the repayment of any sum borrowed by the registered provider while that order is in force;

(2)   the payment of interest on any sum borrowed by the registered provider while that order is in force; and

(3)   the discharge of any other financial obligation of the registered provider in connection with the borrowing of any sum while that order is in force[5].

The Secretary of State may give the guarantees in whatever manner, and on whatever terms, the Secretary of State considers appropriate[6]. As soon as practicable after giving a guarantee under these provisions, the Secretary of State must lay a statement of the guarantee before Parliament[7].

Where a sum is paid out by the Secretary of State under a guarantee given by the Secretary of State[8] in relation to a registered provider, the registered provider must pay the Secretary of State:

(a)   such amounts in or towards the repayment to the Secretary of State of that sum as the Secretary of State may direct; and

(b)   interest on amounts outstanding under these provisions at such rates as the Secretary of State may direct[9].

The payments must be made by the registered provider at such times, and in such manner, as the Secretary of State may from time to time direct[10]. The Secretary of State must lay before Parliament a statement, relating to the sum paid out under the guarantee: (i) as soon as practicable after the end of the financial year[11] in which the sum is paid out; and (ii) as soon as practicable after the end of each subsequent financial year in relation to which the repayment condition has not been met[12]. The repayment condition is met in relation to a financial year if: (A) the whole of the sum has been repaid to the Secretary of State before the beginning of the year; and (B) the registered provider was not at any time during the year liable to pay interest on amounts that became due in respect of the sum[13].

1   See PARA 90 note 1.
2   As to the meaning of 'housing administration order' see PARA 90. See also PARAS 91–92.
3   As to the meaning of 'registered provider' see PARA 90 note 3.
4   As to the Secretary of State see PARA 7.
5   Housing and Planning Act 2016 s 112(1). As to repayment of sums paid by the Secretary of State under a guarantee given under s 112 see s 113; and the text to notes 9–13: s 112(4).
6   Housing and Planning Act 2016 s 112(2).
7   Housing and Planning Act 2016 s 112(3).
8   Ie under the Housing and Planning Act 2016 s 112.
9   Housing and Planning Act 2016 s 113(1), (2).
10   Housing and Planning Act 2016 s 113(3).
11   As to the meaning of 'financial year' see PARA 98 note 15.
12   Housing and Planning Act 2016 s 113(4).
13   Housing and Planning Act 2016 s 113(5).

E.   DISPOSAL OF PROPERTY BY PRIVATE REGISTERED PROVIDERS

100.   Introduction. Chapter 5 of Part 2 of the Housing and Regeneration Act 2008[1] makes provision about the disposal[2] of property by private registered providers[3]. A private registered provider may dispose of land[4], but a non-profit registered provider[5] may dispose of the landlord's interest under a secure tenancy[6] only to another non-profit registered provider or to a local authority[7] which is a registered provider[8].

1   Ie the Housing and Regeneration Act 2008 Pt 2 Ch 5 (ss 170–191): see PARA 100 et seq.
2   As to the meaning of 'disposal' see PARA 52 note 11.
3   Housing and Regeneration Act 2008 s 170 (amended by SI 2010/844). As to the meaning of 'private registered provider' see PARA 53.
4   Housing and Regeneration Act 2008 s 171(1) (amended by SI 2010/844). The Housing and Regeneration Act 2008 s 171(1) is subject to ss 172–191: s 171(3) (amended by the Housing and Planning Act 2016 s 92, Sch 4 paras 7, 13); see PARA 101 et seq.
5   As to when a body is a non-profit organisation see PARA 71 note 13.
6   As to the meaning of 'secure tenancy' see PARA 80 note 49.
7   As to the meaning of 'local authority' see PARA 149 note 4 (definition applied by the Housing and Regeneration Act 2008 s 275).
8   Housing and Regeneration Act 2008 s 171(2) (amended by SI 2010/844).

101.   Notification to regulator. The following provisions apply as from 6 April 2017[1]. If a private registered provider[2] disposes of a dwelling[3] that is social housing[4] it must notify the regulator[5]. If a non-profit registered provider[6] disposes of land other than a dwelling it must also notify the regulator[7].

The regulator may give directions about: (1) the period within which notifications must be given; (2) the content of those notifications[8]. The regulator may give directions dispensing with the notification requirement[9]. A direction may be: (a) general; or (b) specific (whether as to particular registered providers, as to particular property, as to particular forms of disposal or in any other way)[10]. A direction dispensing with a notification requirement: (i) may be expressed by reference to a policy for disposals submitted by a registered provider; (ii) may include conditions[11]. The regulator must make arrangements for bringing a direction under these provisions to the attention of every registered provider to which it applies[12].

1 See the Housing and Planning Act 2016 (Commencement No 4 and Transitional Provisions) Regulations 2017, SI 2017/75, reg 4. The Housing and Regeneration Act 2008 ss 172–175, which required the regulator's consent to the disposal of a dwelling by a private registered provider if the dwelling was social housing, are repealed by the Housing and Planning Act 2016 s 92, Sch 4 para 15 as from that date. On the coming into force of that repeal, the Regulator of Social Housing is deemed to have consented to any purported disposal of property made before that date which would have required consent under the Housing and Regeneration Act 2008 s 172: see the Housing and Planning Act 2016 (Commencement No 4 and Transitional Provisions) Regulations 2017, SI 2017/75, reg 6.
2 As to the meaning of 'private registered provider' see PARA 53.
3 As to the meaning of 'dwelling' see PARA 52 note 8.
4 As to the meaning of 'social housing' see PARA 52.
5 Housing and Regeneration Act 2008 s 176(1) (substituted by the Housing and Planning Act 2016 s 92, Sch 4 paras 7, 16). This continues to apply to any land of a private registered provider even if it has ceased to be a dwelling: Housing and Regeneration Act 2008 s 176(3) (as so substituted). As to the meaning of 'the regulator' see PARA 57.
6 As to when a body is a non-profit organisation see PARA 71 note 13.
7 Housing and Regeneration Act 2008 s 176(2) (as substituted: see note 5).
8 Housing and Regeneration Act 2008 s 176(4) (as substituted: see note 5).
9 Housing and Regeneration Act 2008 s 176(5) (as substituted: see note 5).
10 Housing and Regeneration Act 2008 s 176(6) (as substituted: see note 5).
11 Housing and Regeneration Act 2008 s 176(7) (as substituted: see note 5).
12 Housing and Regeneration Act 2008 s 176(8) (as substituted: see note 5).

102. Right to acquire. The tenant[1] of a dwelling[2] in England has a right to acquire the dwelling if: (1) the landlord is a private registered provider[3] or a registered social landlord[4]; (2) the tenancy is: (a) an assured tenancy[5], other than a long tenancy[6]; or (b) a secure tenancy[7]; (3) the provision of the dwelling was publicly funded[8]; (4) the dwelling has remained in the social rented sector[9] ever since that provision; and (5) the tenant satisfies any applicable[10] qualifying conditions[11].

1 As to the meaning of 'tenant' see PARA 52 note 9.
2 As to the meaning of 'dwelling' see PARA 52 note 8.
3 As to the meaning of 'private registered provider' see PARA 53. The reference in the text to a private registered provider includes: (1) a person who provided the dwelling in fulfilment of a condition imposed by the Homes and Communities Agency ('HCA') when giving assistance to the person; (2) a person who provided the dwelling wholly or partly by means of a grant under the Housing Act 1996 s 27A (see PARA 151): Housing and Regeneration Act 2008 s 180(3) (amended by SI 2010/844). As to the HCA see PARA 57 et seq; and PLANNING vol 83 (2010) PARA 1454 et seq. The HCA gives 'assistance' to a person if it: (a) transfers housing or other land to the person; (b) provides infrastructure to the person; or (c) gives financial assistance to the person, and for this purpose 'infrastructure' has the same meaning as in Pt 1 (ss 1–58) (see PLANNING vol 83 (2010) PARA 1455): s 183(1), (2). A person provides a dwelling if the person: (i) acquires, constructs, converts, improves or repairs housing or other land for use as a dwelling; or (ii) ensures such acquisition, construction, conversion, improvement or repair by another: s 183(6).

4 References to a 'registered social landlord' are to a body which, at the time to which the reference relates, was a registered social landlord within the meaning of the Housing Act 1996 Pt I (ss A1–64) as it then had effect (see PARA 166): Housing and Regeneration Act 2008 s 183(1), (3).

5 As to the meaning of 'assured tenancy' see PARA 80 note 49. The Secretary of State may by regulations provide that an assured shorthold tenancy of a description specified in the regulations is not a tenancy within the Housing and Regeneration Act 2008 s 180(2): s 180(2A) (added by the Localism Act 2011 s 165(1), (3), (4)). See the Transfer of Tenancies and Right to Acquire (Exclusion) Regulations 2012, SI 2012/696. See also PARA 240 note 7. As to the Secretary of State see PARA 7.

6 'Long tenancy' has the same meaning as in the Housing Act 1985 Pt V (ss 118–188): Housing and Regeneration Act 2008 s 183(1), (5). See PARA 270.

7 As to the meaning of 'secure tenancy' see PARA 80 note 49.

8 The provision of a dwelling was publicly funded if any of the following conditions is satisfied: Housing and Regeneration Act 2008 s 181(1).

    Condition 1 is that: (1) the dwelling was provided by a person in fulfilment of a condition imposed by the HCA when giving assistance to the person; and (2) before giving the assistance the HCA notified the person that if it did so the provision of the dwelling would be regarded as publicly funded: s 181(2).

    Condition 2 is that: (a) the dwelling was provided wholly or partly by a person using an amount for purposes for which the amount was required to be used by an HCA direction under s 32(4); and (b) before giving the direction the HCA notified the person that any dwelling so provided would be regarded as publicly funded: s 181(2A) (added by the Housing and Planning Act 2016 s 92, Sch 4 paras 32, 34(1), (2)).

    Condition 3 is that the dwelling was provided wholly or partly by using sums in the disposal proceeds fund of: (i) a private registered provider; or (ii) a registered social landlord: s 181(3) (amended by the Housing and Planning Act 2016 Sch 4 paras 32, 34(1), (3); and by SI 2010/844). In relation to a private registered provider, the reference in the Housing and Regeneration Act 2008 s 181(3) to its disposal proceeds fund is to its disposal proceeds fund before the abolition of that fund by the Housing and Planning Act 2016 Sch 4 Pt 3: Housing and Regeneration Act 2008 s 181(3A) (added by the Housing and Planning Act 2016 Sch 4 paras 32, 34(1), (4)). The fund was abolished as from 6 April 2017: see the Housing and Planning Act 2016 (Commencement No 4 and Transitional Provisions) Regulations 2017, SI 2017/75, reg 4.

    Condition 4 is that: (A) the dwelling was acquired by a private registered provider, or a registered social landlord, on a disposal by a public sector landlord; (B) the disposal was made on or after 1 April 1997; and (C) at the time of the disposal the dwelling was capable of being let as a separate dwelling: Housing and Regeneration Act 2008 s 181(4) (amended by the Housing and Planning Act 2016 Sch 4 paras 32, 34(1), (5); and by SI 2010/844). Condition 4 is not satisfied if the dwelling was acquired in pursuance of a contract made, or option created, before 1 April 1997: Housing and Regeneration Act 2008 s 181(5) (amended by the Housing and Planning Act 2016 Sch 4 paras 32, 34(1), (5)).

    Condition 5 is that: (I) the dwelling was provided wholly or partly by means of a grant under the Housing Act 1996 s 18 or s 27A (see PARAS 166, 151); and (II) when the grant was made the recipient was notified under s 16(4) of that Act (see PARA 242) that the dwelling was to be regarded as funded by means of such a grant: Housing and Regeneration Act 2008 s 181(6) (amended by the Housing and Planning Act 2016 Sch 4 paras 32, 34(1), (6)).

    'Public sector landlord' means anyone falling within the Housing Act 1985 s 80(1) (see LANDLORD AND TENANT vol 63 (2016) PARA 1037): Housing and Regeneration Act 2008 s 183(1), (7).

9 The Housing and Regeneration Act 2008 s 182 applies for the purposes of determining whether a dwelling has remained in the social rented sector: s 182(1). A dwelling is to be treated as having remained in the social rented sector for any period during which: (1) the freeholder was a person within s 182(3); and (2) each leaseholder was either a person within s 182(3) or an individual holding otherwise than under a long tenancy: s 182(2). A person is within s 182(3) if the person is: (a) a private registered provider; (b) a registered social landlord; or (c) a public sector landlord: s 182(3) (amended by SI 2010/844). A dwelling provided wholly or partly by means of a grant under the Housing Act 1996 s 27A (see PARA 151) is also to be treated as having remained in the social rented sector for any period during which it was used exclusively for permitted purposes by the recipient of the grant or any person treated as the recipient by virtue of s 27B (see PARA 152): Housing and Regeneration Act 2008 s 182(4). 'Permitted purposes' are purposes for which the grant was made and any other purposes agreed by the Housing Corporation or the HCA: s 182(5). 'Leaseholder' does not include a mortgagee: s 183(1), (4).

    Where a lease of a dwelling has been granted to a former freeholder in pursuance of the Leasehold Reform, Housing and Urban Development Act 1993 Sch 9 para 3 (mandatory leaseback to former freeholder on collective enfranchisement: see LANDLORD AND TENANT vol 64 (2016)

PARA 1428) the reference in the Housing and Regeneration Act 2008 s 182(2)(a) (head (1) above) to the freeholder is to be construed as a reference to the leaseholder under that lease: s 182(6). (Note that s 182(6) refers to s 182(1)(a) but it is submitted that a reference to s 182(2)(a) was intended.)

10 Ie applicable under the Housing Act 1985 Pt V (as it applies by virtue of s 184): see PARA 231.
11 Housing and Regeneration Act 2008 s 180(1), (2) (s 180(1) amended by SI 2010/844; the Housing and Regeneration Act 2008 s 180(2) amended by the Localism Act 2011 ss 165(1), (2), 237, Sch 25 Pt 23). See further PARAS 240–241. The Housing Act 1996 s 17 (right to acquire: supplemental: see PARA 243) applies in relation to the right to acquire under the Housing and Regeneration Act 2008 s 180 with the modifications set out below: s 184(1). The modifications are as follows: (1) references to the right to acquire under the Housing Act 1996 s 16 are to be treated as references to the right to acquire under the Housing and Regeneration Act 2008 s 180; (2) references to the Welsh Ministers are to be treated as references to the Secretary of State; (3) the reference to registered social landlords is to be treated as a reference to private registered providers; and (4) the reference to a resolution of the National Assembly for Wales is to be treated as a reference to a resolution of either House of Parliament: s 184(2) (amended by SI 2010/844). As to the Secretary of State and the Welsh Ministers see PARA 7. Consequential amendments are made by the Housing and Regeneration Act 2008 s 185.

103. Administrative provisions. Where a person ceases to be a private registered provider[1], specified provisions of the Housing and Regeneration Act 2008 relating to disposal of property[2] continue to apply in respect of any property owned by the person at any time when it was registered[3].

The requirement for trustees to obtain the best price[4] does not apply to the disposal of land by a private registered provider[5].

Nothing in Chapter 5 of Part 2 of the Housing and Regeneration Act 2008[6] authorises a charity to effect a disposal which it would not otherwise have power to effect[7].

1 As to the meaning of 'private registered provider' see PARA 53.
2 Ie the Housing and Regeneration Act 2008 ss 171, 176 (apart from s 176(2)): see PARAS 100, 101.
3 Housing and Regeneration Act 2008 s 186 (amended by the Housing and Planning Act 2016 s 92, Sch 4 paras 7, 18; and by SI 2010/844).
4 Ie the Settled Land Act 1925 s 39: see SETTLEMENTS vol 91 (2012) PARAS 729–731.
5 Housing and Regeneration Act 2008 s 188 (amended by SI 2010/844).
6 Ie the Housing and Regeneration Act 2008 Pt 2 Ch 5 (ss 170–191): see PARA 100 et seq.
7 Housing and Regeneration Act 2008 s 189. As to charities' powers see CHARITIES vol 8 (2015) PARA 384 et seq.

F. REGULATORY POWERS

104. Overview. Chapter 6 of Part 2 of the Housing and Regeneration Act 2008[1]: (1) allows the regulator[2] to set standards for the provision of social housing[3]; (2) gives the regulator powers to monitor compliance[4]; (3) requires the regulator to give guidance about the submission of information and opinions relating to registered providers and about the use of its regulatory and enforcement powers[5]; and (4) allows the regulator to arrange for the accreditation[6] of managers of social housing[7].

1 Ie the Housing and Regeneration Act 2008 Pt 2 Ch 6 (ss 192–217): see PARAS 106–110.
2 As to the meaning of 'the regulator' see PARA 57. As to the prospective transfer of social housing regulation to the Homes and Communities Agency see PARA 57 note 1.
3 Housing and Regeneration Act 2008 s 192(a) (amended by the Localism Act 2011 s 179, Sch 17 paras 1, 3(1), (2)). See the Housing and Regeneration Act 2008 ss 193–198B; and PARA 105. As to the meaning of 'social housing' see PARA 52.
4 Housing and Regeneration Act 2008 s 192(b). See ss 199–210; and PARA 107.
5 Housing and Regeneration Act 2008 s 192(d) (amended by the Localism Act 2011 Sch 17 paras 1, 3(1), (3)). The text refers to the regulator's powers under the Housing and Regeneration Act 2008 Pt 2 Ch 6 and Pt 2 Ch 7 (ss 218–269B): see ss 215, 216; and PARA 109.
6 See the Housing and Regeneration Act 2008 s 217; and PARA 110.
7 Housing and Regeneration Act 2008 s 192(e).

105.   Standards. The regulator[1] may set standards for registered providers[2] as to the nature, extent and quality of accommodation, facilities or services provided by them in connection with social housing[3]. In setting standards, the regulator must have regard to the desirability of registered providers being free to choose how to provide services and conduct business[4].

The regulator may set standards for private registered providers in matters relating to their financial and other affairs[5]. In respect of profit-making registered providers[6], standards may be made in relation to the management of their affairs only so far as relating to the provision of social housing[7]. The regulator may set standards for registered providers requiring them to comply with specified rules about their levels of rent (and the rules may, in particular, include provision for minimum or maximum levels of rent or levels of increase or decrease of rent)[8]. In setting standards, the regulator must have regard to the desirability of registered providers being free to choose how to provide services and conduct business[9].

The regulator may issue a code of practice which:

(1)   relates to a matter addressed by a standard relating to economic matters[10]; and

(2)   amplifies the standard[11]. In considering whether such standards have been met the regulator may have regard to a code of practice[12].

The regulator may revise or withdraw a code of practice[13] and must make arrangements for bringing a code of practice to the attention of registered providers[14].

Before setting standards, or issuing, revising or withdrawing a code of practice, the regulator must consult the following or ensure that they have been consulted[15]:

(a)   one or more bodies appearing to it to represent the interests of registered providers[16];

(b)   one or more bodies appearing to it to represent the interests of secured creditors[17] of registered providers[18];

(c)   any body for the time being nominated[19] to represent the interests of tenants[20];

(d)   one or more other bodies appearing to it to represent the interests of tenants of social housing[21];

(e)   one or more bodies appearing to it to represent the interests of local housing authorities[22];

(f)   the Greater London Authority[23]; and

(g)   the Secretary of State[24].

Before setting a standard which would apply to charities, or issuing, revising or withdrawing a code of practice which applies or would apply to charities, the regulator must consult the Charity Commission[25].

The Secretary of State may direct the regulator:

(i)   to set a standard about the provision of social housing by registered providers[26];

(ii)   about the content of such standards; or

(iii)   to have regard to specified objectives when setting standards[27] about the provision of social housing by registered providers or the management of private registered providers[28].

The Secretary of State may give a direction under head (i) or (ii) only if it relates, in the Secretary of State's opinion, to quality of accommodation, tenure, rent, involvement by tenants in the management by registered providers of accommodation or methods of assisting tenants to exchange tenancies[29]. In deciding whether to give a direction the Secretary of State must, in particular, have regard to the regulator's fundamental objectives[30].

Before giving a direction the Secretary of State must consult the following[31]:

(A)   the regulator[32];

(B)   the Greater London Authority[33];

(C)   one or more bodies appearing to the Secretary of State to represent the interests of local housing authorities[34];

(D)   any body for the time being nominated[35] to represent the interests of tenants[36];

(E)   one or more other bodies appearing to the Secretary of State to represent the interests of tenants of social housing[37]; and

(F)   one or more bodies appearing to the Secretary of State to represent the interests of registered providers[38].

Before giving a direction about a standard which would apply to charities the Secretary of State must consult the Charity Commission[39].

The regulator must comply with any direction[40]. The Secretary of State must publish each proposed direction that is the subject of a consultation, each response to a consultation and each direction[41].

The regulator must make arrangements for bringing standards to the attention of registered providers[42]. The regulator may revise or withdraw standards[43]. Standards may be expressed by reference to documents prepared by others[44]. Standards may make provision generally or only in relation to specified cases, circumstances or areas and may make different provision for different cases, circumstances or areas[45].

1   As to the meaning of 'the regulator' see PARA 57.

2   As to the meaning of 'registered provider' see PARA 53.

3   Housing and Regeneration Act 2008 s 193(1). As to the meaning of 'social housing' see PARA 52. As to failure to meet such standards see PARA 106. Standards under s 193(1) may, in particular, require registered providers to comply with specified rules about: (1) criteria for allocating accommodation; (2) terms of tenancies; (3) maintenance; (4) procedures for addressing complaints by tenants against landlords; (5) methods for consulting and informing tenants; (6) methods of enabling tenants to influence or control the management of their accommodation and environment; (7) methods of assisting tenants to exchange tenancies; (8) policies and procedures required by the Housing Act 1996 s 218A in connection with anti-social behaviour (see PARA 28); (9) landlords' contribution to the environmental, social and economic well-being of the areas in which their property is situated; and (10) estate management: Housing and Regeneration Act 2008 s 193(2) (amended by the Localism Act 2011 ss 176(1), 179, 237, Sch 17 paras 1, 4(1), (3), Sch 25 Pt 27). 'Maintenance' includes repair: Housing and Regeneration Act 2008 s 275. As to the meaning of 'tenant' see PARA 52 note 9.

4   Housing and Regeneration Act 2008 s 193(3).

5   Housing and Regeneration Act 2008 s 194(1) (amended by the Localism Act 2011 Sch 17 paras 1, 5(1), (3), Sch 25 Pt 27; and by SI 2010/844). Standards under the Housing and Regeneration Act 2008 s 194(1) may, in particular, require private registered providers to comply with specified rules about: (1) the management of their financial and other affairs; and (2) their efficiency in carrying on their financial and other affairs: s 194(1A) (added by the Localism Act 2011 Sch 17 paras 1, 5(1), (4)). As to failure to meet such standards see PARA 106.

6   As to when a body is a profit-making organisation see PARA 71 note 13.

7   Housing and Regeneration Act 2008 s 194(2). As to the meaning of 'social housing' see PARA 52.

8   Housing and Regeneration Act 2008 s 194(2A) (added by the Localism Act 2011 Sch 17 paras 1, 5(1), (5)). This is subject to the Welfare Reform and Work Act 2016 ss 23–25, 27, 29 and Sch 2: s 32. See PARA 55.

9   Housing and Regeneration Act 2008 s 194(3).

10 Ie a standard under the Housing and Regeneration Act 2008 s 194.

11 Housing and Regeneration Act 2008 s 195(1) (amended by the Localism Act 2011 Sch 17 paras 1, 6(1), (2)).

12 Housing and Regeneration Act 2008 s 195(2) (amended by the Localism Act 2011 Sch 17 paras 1, 6(1), (3)).

13 Housing and Regeneration Act 2008 s 195(3).

14 Housing and Regeneration Act 2008 s 195(3).
15 Housing and Regeneration Act 2008 s 196(1).
16 Housing and Regeneration Act 2008 s 196(1)(a).
17 As to the meaning of 'secured creditor' see PARA 80 note 30.
18 Housing and Regeneration Act 2008 s 196(1)(b).
19 Ie under the Housing and Regeneration Act 2008 s 278A: see PARA 71 note 5.
20 Housing and Regeneration Act 2008 s 196(1)(ba) (added by the Local Democracy, Economic
   Development and Construction Act 2009 s 26(1), (4)(a)).
21 Housing and Regeneration Act 2008 s 196(1)(c) (amended by the Local Democracy, Economic
   Development and Construction Act 2009 s 26(1), (4)(b)).
22 Housing and Regeneration Act 2008 s 196(1)(e). As to the meaning of 'local housing authority' see
   PARA 11 (definition applied by s 275).
23 Housing and Regeneration Act 2008 s 196(1)(ea) (added by the Localism Act 2011 s 195(1),
   Sch 19 paras 46, 55). As to the Greater London Authority see LONDON GOVERNMENT vol 71
   (2013) PARA 67 et seq.
24 Housing and Regeneration Act 2008 s 196(1)(g). As to the Secretary of State see PARA 7.
25 Housing and Regeneration Act 2008 s 196(2). As to the meaning of 'Charity Commission' see
   PARA 53 note 3.
26 Ie under the Housing and Regeneration Act 2008 s 193 or s 194.
27 Ie under the Housing and Regeneration Act 2008 s 193 or s 194.
28 Housing and Regeneration Act 2008 s 197(1) (amended by the Localism Act 2011 Sch 17 paras 1,
   7). A direction may disapply the requirement to consult under the Housing and Regeneration Act
   2008 s 196 in relation to specified matters: s 197(6).
29 Housing and Regeneration Act 2008 s 197(2) (amended by the Localism Act 2011 ss 152, 176(2),
   237, Sch 25 Pt 26).
30 Housing and Regeneration Act 2008 s 197(3). As to the regulator's fundamental objectives see
   PARA 59.
31 Housing and Regeneration Act 2008 s 197(4).
32 Housing and Regeneration Act 2008 s 197(4)(a).
33 Housing and Regeneration Act 2008 s 197(4)(aa) (added by the Localism Act 2011 s 195(1),
   Sch 19 paras 46, 56).
34 Housing and Regeneration Act 2008 s 197(4)(d).
35 Ie under the Housing and Regeneration Act 2008 s 278A: see PARA 71 note 5.
36 Housing and Regeneration Act 2008 s 197(4)(da) (added by the Local Democracy, Economic
   Development and Construction Act 2009 s 26(1), (5)(a)).
37 Housing and Regeneration Act 2008 s 197(4)(e) (amended by the Local Democracy, Economic
   Development and Construction Act 2009 s 26(1), (5)(b)).
38 Housing and Regeneration Act 2008 s 197(4)(f).
39 Housing and Regeneration Act 2008 s 197(5).
40 Housing and Regeneration Act 2008 s 197(7).
41 Housing and Regeneration Act 2008 s 197(8).
42 Housing and Regeneration Act 2008 s 198(2).
43 Housing and Regeneration Act 2008 s 198(3). Section 196 (see the text and notes 15–25) applies
   to revising or withdrawing standards as to setting standards: s 198(3). Section 198(3) is subject to
   the Welfare Reform and Work Act 2016 ss 23–25, 27, 29 and Sch 2: s 32. See PARA 55.
44 Housing and Regeneration Act 2008 s 198(4).
45 Housing and Regeneration Act 2008 s 198(5).

106. Failure to meet standards. Failure by a registered provider[1] to meet a
standard relating to consumer matters[2] set by the regulator[3] is a ground for
exercising either a regulatory power[4] or an enforcement power[5] under the
Housing and Regeneration Act 2008[6]. However, a power under specified
provisions[7] may be exercised on that ground only if the regulator thinks there are
reasonable grounds to suspect that: (1) the failure has resulted in a serious
detriment to the registered provider's tenants[8] or potential tenants; or (2) there is
a significant risk that, if no action is taken by the regulator, the failure will result
in a serious detriment to the registered provider's tenants or potential tenants[9].

The risk that, if no action is taken by a registered provider or the regulator, the
registered provider will fail to meet a standard relating to consumer matters is a
ground for exercising a regulatory power[10]. However, a regulatory power may be

exercised on that ground only if the regulator thinks there are reasonable grounds to suspect that, if the failure occurs: (a) the failure will result in a serious detriment to the registered provider's tenants or potential tenants; or (b) there will be a significant risk that, if no action is taken by the regulator, the failure will result in a serious detriment to the registered provider's tenants or potential tenants[11].

In considering whether to exercise a power within the provisions above on the ground mentioned therein, the regulator must have regard to any information it has received from any of the following[12]: (i) the Commission for Local Administration in England[13]; (ii) a housing ombudsman appointed in accordance with an approved[14] scheme[15]; (iii) any body appearing to the regulator to represent the interests of tenants of social housing in England[16]; (iv) a county council in England, a district council, a London borough council, the Common Council of the City of London in its capacity as a local authority, the Council of the Isles of Scilly or a parish council[17]; (v) a member of any of the bodies listed in head (iv)[18]; (vi) the Greater London Authority[19]; (vii) a Member of Parliament[20]; (viii) a fire and rescue authority under the Fire and Rescue Services Act 2004[21]; (ix) the Health and Safety Executive[22]; (x) the Secretary of State[23].

Failure by a registered provider to meet a standard relating to economic matters[24] is a ground for exercising a regulatory power or an enforcement power under the Housing and Regeneration Act 2008 (if the power is otherwise exercisable in relation to a registered provider of that kind)[25]. The risk that, if no action is taken by a registered provider or the regulator, the registered provider will fail to meet such a standard is a ground for exercising a regulatory power[26].

1 As to the meaning of 'registered provider' see PARA 53.
2 Ie a standard under the Housing and Regeneration Act 2008 s 193: see PARA 105.
3 As to the meaning of 'the regulator' see PARA 57.
4 Ie a power under the Housing and Regeneration Act 2008 Pt 2 Ch 6 (ss 192–217).
5 Ie a power under the Housing and Regeneration Act 2008 Pt 2 Ch 7 (ss 218–269B). See PARA 111 et seq.
6 Housing and Regeneration Act 2008 s 198A(1) (ss 198A, 198B added by the Localism Act 2011 s 179, Sch 17 paras 1, 9).
7 The Housing and Regeneration Act 2008 s 198A(2) applies to the powers conferred by any of the following: (1) s 199 (surveys: see PARA 107); (2) s 201 (inspections: see PARA 107); (3) s 206 (inquiries: see PARA 108); (4) s 220 (enforcement notices: see PARA 112); (5) s 227 (penalties: see PARA 113); (6) s 237 (compensation: see PARA 113); (7) s 247 (management tender: see PARA 115); (8) s 251 (appointment of manager: see PARA 118): s 198A(3) (as added: see note 6).
8 As to the meaning of 'tenant' see PARA 52 note 9.
9 Housing and Regeneration Act 2008 s 198A(2) (as added: see note 6).
10 Housing and Regeneration Act 2008 s 198A(4) (as added: see note 6).
11 Housing and Regeneration Act 2008 s 198A(5) (as added: see note 6).
12 Housing and Regeneration Act 2008 s 198A(6) (as added: see note 6).
13 Housing and Regeneration Act 2008 s 198A(6)(a) (as added: see note 6). As to the Commission for Local Administration in England see LOCAL GOVERNMENT vol 69 (2009) PARA 839 et seq.
14 Ie under the Housing Act 1996 Sch 2: see PARA 131 et seq.
15 Housing and Regeneration Act 2008 s 198A(6)(b) (as added: see note 6).
16 Housing and Regeneration Act 2008 s 198A(6)(c) (as added: see note 6). As to the meaning of 'social housing' see PARA 52.
17 Housing and Regeneration Act 2008 s 198A(6)(d) (as added: see note 6).
18 Housing and Regeneration Act 2008 s 198A(6)(e) (as added: see note 6).
19 Housing and Regeneration Act 2008 s 198A(6)(f) (as added: see note 6). As to the Greater London Authority see LONDON GOVERNMENT vol 71 (2013) PARA 67 et seq.
20 Housing and Regeneration Act 2008 s 198A(6)(g) (as added: see note 6).
21 Housing and Regeneration Act 2008 s 198A(6)(h) (as added: see note 6).
22 Housing and Regeneration Act 2008 s 198A(6)(i) (as added: see note 6).
23 Housing and Regeneration Act 2008 s 198A(6)(j) (as added: see note 6). As to the Secretary of State see PARA 7.
24 Ie a standard under the Housing and Regeneration Act 2008 s 194: see PARA 105.

25 Housing and Regeneration Act 2008 s 198B(1) (as added: see note 6).
26 Housing and Regeneration Act 2008 s 198B(2) (as added: see note 6).

107. Monitoring: survey and inspections. Where the regulator[1] suspects that a registered provider[2] may be failing to maintain premises in accordance with required standards[3], the regulator may arrange for a survey of the condition of the premises by an authorised person (that is a person appointed by the regulator)[4]. An authorised person may enter the premises at any reasonable time and carry out the survey[5]. A registered provider, or an officer of a registered provider, who obstructs an authorised person in exercising a power in relation to a survey[6] commits an offence[7]. Before carrying out the survey an authorised person must give the registered provider at least 28 days' notice[8]. A registered provider who receives notice of a survey must give each occupier of the premises at least seven days' notice[9]. After carrying out a survey an authorised person must produce a written report[10], and the regulator must give the registered provider a copy of the report[11].

The regulator may arrange for a person to inspect: (1) a registered provider's performance of its functions in relation to the provision of social housing[12]; or (2) the financial or other affairs of a registered provider[13]. The person may be a member of the regulator's staff if the Secretary of State consents[14]. The regulator may direct a person carrying out an inspection to discontinue it[15].

After carrying out an inspection[16] the person carrying out the inspection must produce a written report[17]. The regulator must give the registered provider a copy of the report and may publish the report and related information[18]. The person who carried out the inspection may publish the report and related information (whether or not the regulator has done so)[19]. The Secretary of State may by order[20] authorise the regulator to charge fees for inspections[21] and an inspected registered provider must pay any fee charged[22]. The regulator must prescribe a scale of fees for inspections, having consulted: (a) the Secretary of State; and (b) one or more bodies appearing to the regulator to represent the interests of registered providers[23].

An inspector[24] may by notice require a person to provide specified documents or information[25]. An inspector may at any reasonable time: (i) enter premises occupied by the registered provider which is being inspected; and (ii) inspect, copy or take away documents found there[26]. The power to inspect documents includes the power to inspect any computer or electronic storage device on which they have been created or stored[27]. An inspector may require any person on the premises to provide such facilities or assistance as the inspector reasonably requests[28]. It is an offence for a person without reasonable excuse to obstruct an inspector exercising the powers[29] outlined above[30].

1 As to the meaning of 'the regulator' see PARA 57.
2 As to the meaning of 'registered provider' see PARA 53.
3 Ie under the Housing and Regeneration Act 2008 s 193: see PARA 105.
4 Housing and Regeneration Act 2008 s 199(1), (2). 'Authorised person' means a member of the regulator's staff, or another person, authorised in writing by the regulator for the purposes of s 199: s 199(3).
5 Housing and Regeneration Act 2008 s 199(4). An authorised person carrying out a survey, or seeking to enter premises in order to carry out a survey, must produce a copy of the authorisation on request by an occupier: s 200(1).
6 Ie a power under the Housing and Regeneration Act 2008 s 199.
7 Housing and Regeneration Act 2008 s 200(4). A person guilty of an offence under s 200 is liable on summary conviction to a fine not exceeding level 3 on the standard scale: s 200(5). As to the powers of magistrates' courts to issue fines on summary conviction see SENTENCING vol 92 (2015)

PARA 176. Proceedings for an offence under s 200 may be brought only by or with the consent of: (1) the regulator; or (2) the Director of Public Prosecutions: s 200(6). As to the meaning of 'consent' see PARA 80 note 29. As to the Director of Public Prosecutions see CRIMINAL PROCEDURE vol 27 (2015) PARAS 25, 30 et seq.

8 Housing and Regeneration Act 2008 s 199(5).

9 Housing and Regeneration Act 2008 s 199(6). A registered provider who fails without reasonable excuse to comply with s 199(6) commits an offence: s 200(3). As to offences under s 200 see note 7.

10 Housing and Regeneration Act 2008 s 199(7).

11 Housing and Regeneration Act 2008 s 199(8). The regulator may require the registered provider to pay some or all of the costs of the survey and report: s 200(2).

12 As to the meaning of 'social housing' see PARA 52.

13 Housing and Regeneration Act 2008 s 201(1). An inspection may be general or specific: s 201(5).

14 Housing and Regeneration Act 2008 s 201(2) (substituted by the Localism Act 2011 s 179, Sch 17 paras 1, 10(1), (2)). Such consent may be general or specific: Housing and Regeneration Act 2008 s 201(2A) (added by the Localism Act 2011 Sch 17 paras 1, 10(1), (2)). As to the Secretary of State see PARA 7.

15 Housing and Regeneration Act 2008 s 201(4).

16 Ie under the Housing and Regeneration Act 2008 s 201.

17 Housing and Regeneration Act 2008 s 202(1).

18 Housing and Regeneration Act 2008 s 202(2).

19 Housing and Regeneration Act 2008 s 202(3).

20 As to orders by the Secretary of State see PARA 54.

21 Housing and Regeneration Act 2008 s 202(4). Before making an order the Secretary of State must consult: (1) the regulator; (2) one or more bodies appearing to the Secretary of State to represent the interests of registered providers; and (3) such other persons as the Secretary of State thinks appropriate: s 202(6) (amended by the Localism Act 2011 ss 127, 237, Sch 17 paras 1, 11(1), (2), Sch 25 Pt 27).

22 Housing and Regeneration Act 2008 s 202(5). The functions of billing for and receiving the payment of fees under s 202 are exercisable by the Homes and Communities Agency ('HCA') rather than by the HCA acting through its Regulation Committee: s 202(8) (added by the Localism Act 2011 s 178, Sch 16 paras 1, 44). As to the HCA see PARA 57 et seq; and PLANNING vol 83 (2010) PARA 1454 et seq. As to the Regulation Committee see PARA 61 et seq.

23 Housing and Regeneration Act 2008 s 202(7) (amended by the Localism Act 2011 Sch 17 paras 1, 11(1), (3), Sch 25 Pt 27).

24 For these purposes, 'inspector' means a person authorised in writing by the regulator to exercise the powers under the Housing and Regeneration Act 2008 s 203 for the purposes of an inspection under s 201: s 203(12) (substituted by the Localism Act 2011 Sch 17 paras 1, 12).

25 Housing and Regeneration Act 2008 s 203(1). Sections 107(3)–(7), 108 (see PARA 60) apply for the purposes of s 203(1) (with any necessary modifications): s 203(3). The power under s 203(1) may be exercised only in relation to documents and information of a kind in respect of which the regulator can impose a requirement under s 107: s 203(2).

26 Housing and Regeneration Act 2008 s 203(4). The reference to documents found on premises includes: (1) documents stored on computers or electronic storage devices on the premises; and (2) documents stored elsewhere which can be accessed by computers on the premises: s 203(5).

27 Housing and Regeneration Act 2008 s 203(6).

28 Housing and Regeneration Act 2008 s 203(7). For the purposes of s 203(5), (6) an inspector may require any person having charge of a computer to provide such assistance as the inspector reasonably requests: s 203(8).

29 Ie the powers conferred by the Housing and Regeneration Act 2008 s 203(4)–(8).

30 Housing and Regeneration Act 2008 s 203(9). A person guilty of an offence is liable on summary conviction to a fine not exceeding level 3 on the standard scale: s 203(10). As to the powers of magistrates' courts to issue fines on summary conviction see SENTENCING vol 92 (2015) PARA 176. Proceedings for an offence may be brought only by or with the consent of: (1) the regulator; or (2) the Director of Public Prosecutions: s 203(11). As to the meaning of 'consent' see PARA 80 note 29.

108. Monitoring: inquiry. If the regulator[1] suspects that the affairs of a registered provider[2] may have been mismanaged[3], the regulator may hold an inquiry[4]. The regulator must appoint one or more individuals to conduct the inquiry[5]. An individual is eligible for appointment only if the individual is independent of the regulator[6].

The individual or individuals conducting an inquiry ('the inquirer') must determine its procedure[7]. The inquirer may consider the affairs of profit-making organisations[8] and local authorities[9] only so far as relating to social housing[10]. The inquirer may consider affairs of a body which at the material time was a subsidiary or associate[11] of the registered provider[12]. The inquirer may make interim reports[13]. The inquirer must make a final report on matters specified by the regulator[14]. The regulator may arrange for the publication of all or part of an interim or final report[15]. A local authority may contribute to the regulator's expenses in connection with an inquiry[16].

The inquirer may by notice[17] require a person to provide specified documents or information[18]. The notice may, in particular, require evidence to be given on oath (and the inquirer may administer oaths for that purpose)[19].

An inquiry may be held in relation to a registered charity[20] only if it has received public assistance[21]. An inquiry in relation to a registered charity may only relate to its activities relating to housing[22]. If an inquiry is held in relation to a registered charity the regulator must notify the Charity Commission[23].

Where an inquiry in respect of a private registered provider is being held, or has been held[24], the regulator may require the registered provider to allow its accounts and balance sheet to be audited by a qualified auditor[25] appointed by the regulator[26]. On completion of the audit, the auditor must report to the regulator about such matters and in such form as the regulator determines[27]. The revenue accounts of a registered charity may be audited under this provision only in so far as they relate to its housing activities[28]. The registered provider must pay the costs of the audit (including the auditor's remuneration)[29].

Where an inquiry in respect of a local authority is being held, or has been held[30], the regulator may require the local authority to allow its accounts[31], so far as they relate to the provision of social housing, to be audited by a local auditor[32] appointed by the regulator[33]. On completion of the audit, the local auditor must report to the regulator about such matters and in such form as the regulator determines[34]. The local authority must pay the costs of the audit (including the local auditor's remuneration)[35].

1   As to the meaning of 'the regulator' see PARA 57.
2   As to the meaning of 'registered provider' see PARA 53.
3   'Mismanagement', in relation to the affairs of a registered provider, means managed in breach of any legal requirements (imposed by or under an Act or otherwise): Housing and Regeneration Act 2008 s 275 (definition substituted by the Housing and Planning Act 2016 s 92, Sch 4 paras 36, 38).
4   Housing and Regeneration Act 2008 s 206(1).
5   Housing and Regeneration Act 2008 s 206(2).
6   Housing and Regeneration Act 2008 s 206(3). Individuals are independent of the regulator if they and the members of their family: (1) are not members, employees or consultants of the regulator; and (2) have not been members or employees of the regulator within the previous five years: s 206(4). 'Consultant' means an individual providing services to the regulator otherwise than by virtue of employment with the regulator or an appointment under s 206: s 206(5). As to the meaning of 'family' see PARA 73 note 2.
7   Housing and Regeneration Act 2008 s 207(1).
8   As to when a body is a profit-making organisation see PARA 71 note 13.
9   As to the meaning of 'local authority' see PARA 149 note 4 (definition applied by the Housing and Regeneration Act 2008 s 275).
10 Housing and Regeneration Act 2008 s 207(2) (substituted by SI 2010/844).
11 As to the meanings of 'subsidiary' and 'associate' see PARA 52 note 10.
12 Housing and Regeneration Act 2008 s 207(3).
13 Housing and Regeneration Act 2008 s 207(4).
14 Housing and Regeneration Act 2008 s 207(5).
15 Housing and Regeneration Act 2008 s 207(6).
16 Housing and Regeneration Act 2008 s 207(7).

17 As to the meaning of 'notice' see PARA 79 note 4.
18 Housing and Regeneration Act 2008 s 208(1). The power under s 208(1) may be exercised only in relation to documents and information of a kind in respect of which the regulator can impose a requirement under s 107: s 208(3). Sections 107(3)–(7), 108 (see PARA 60) apply for the purposes of s 208 (with any necessary modifications): s 208(4).
19 Housing and Regeneration Act 2008 s 208(2).
20 As to the meaning of 'registered charity' see PARA 53 note 2.
21 Housing and Regeneration Act 2008 s 209(1). For the purposes of Pt 2 a registered charity has received public assistance if at least one of the following conditions is satisfied: s 274(1). Condition 1 is that the charity has received financial assistance from the Homes and Communities Agency ('HCA') under s 19 (see PLANNING vol 83 (2010) PARA 1474): s 274(2). Condition 2 is that the charity has received financial assistance under the Local Government Act 1988 s 24 (assistance for privately let housing accommodation: see PARA 378): Housing and Regeneration Act 2008 s 274(3). Condition 3 is that the charity has had housing transferred to it pursuant to: (1) a large scale disposal, within the meaning of the Housing Act 1985 s 34 (see PARA 524), for which consent was required under s 32 or 43 (see PARAS 522, 531); or (2) a qualifying disposal that was made under the Leasehold Reform, Housing and Urban Development Act 1993 s 135 (repealed): Housing and Regeneration Act 2008 s 274(4). Condition 4 is that the charity has received a grant or loan under: (a) the Housing Act 1996 s 18 (social housing grants: see PARA 166); (b) s 22 of that Act (assistance from local authorities: see PARA 166); (c) the Housing Associations Act 1985 s 58 (grants or loans by local authorities: see PARA 13); (d) the Housing Act 1988 s 50 (repealed in relation to England and Wales), the Housing Associations Act 1985 s 41 (repealed) or any enactment replaced by that section (housing association grant); (e) the Housing Act 1988 s 51 (repealed in relation to England and Wales) or the Housing Associations Act 1985 s 54 or 55 (both repealed) (revenue deficit grant or hostel deficit grant); (f) the Housing Associations Act 1985 s 79 (loans by the Welsh Ministers: see PARA 145); (g) the Housing Act 1974 s 31 (repealed) (management grants); or (h) any enactment mentioned in the Housing Associations Act 1985 Sch 1 para 2 or Sch 1 para 3 (pre-1974 grants and certain loans): Housing and Regeneration Act 2008 s 274(5). As to the HCA see PARA 57 et seq; and PLANNING vol 83 (2010) PARA 1454 et seq.
22 Housing and Regeneration Act 2008 s 209(2).
23 Housing and Regeneration Act 2008 s 209(3). As to the meaning of 'Charity Commission' see PARA 53 note 3.
24 Ie under the Housing and Regeneration Act 2008 s 206: see PARA 108.
25 'Qualified auditor' means a person eligible for appointment as auditor of the registered provider's ordinary accounts: Housing and Regeneration Act 2008 s 210(2).
26 Housing and Regeneration Act 2008 s 210(1) (amended by SI 2010/844).
27 Housing and Regeneration Act 2008 s 210(3).
28 Housing and Regeneration Act 2008 s 210(4).
29 Housing and Regeneration Act 2008 s 210(5).
30 Ie under the Housing and Regeneration Act 2008 s 206: see PARA 108.
31 'Accounts' has the meaning given by the Local Audit and Accountability Act 2014 s 4 (see LOCAL GOVERNMENT): Housing and Regeneration Act 2008 s 210A(5) (s 210A added by SI 2010/844; the Housing and Regeneration Act 2008 s 210A(5) substituted by the Local Audit and Accountability Act 2014 s 45, Sch 12 paras 89, 95(1), (6)).
32 'Local auditor' means a person who is eligible for appointment under or by virtue of the Local Audit and Accountability Act 2014 as an auditor of the local authority's accounts: Housing and Regeneration Act 2008 s 210A(5) (as added and substituted: see note 31). The regulator may not appoint a local auditor to audit the accounts of a local authority if that person: (1) is the person (or one of the persons) appointed under or by virtue of the Local Audit and Accountability Act 2014 to audit the authority's accounts; or (2) was the person (or one of the persons) who carried out the most recent completed audit of the authority's accounts under or by virtue of that Act: Housing and Regeneration Act 2008 s 210A(1A) (s 210A(1A)–(1C) added by the Local Audit and Accountability Act 2014 Sch 12 paras 89, 95(1), (3)).
33 Housing and Regeneration Act 2008 s 210A(1) (as added (see note 31); amended by the Local Audit and Accountability Act 2014 Sch 12 paras 89, 95(1), (2)). The Local Audit and Accountability Act 2014 ss 20(1), (2), (5), (6), 22 and 23 (local auditors' general duties and right to documents etc) apply in relation to an audit under the Housing and Regeneration Act 2008 s 210A as they apply in relation to an audit of the local authority under or by virtue of the Local Audit and Accountability Act 2014: Housing and Regeneration Act 2008 s 210A(1B) (as added: see note 32).
34 Housing and Regeneration Act 2008 s 210A(1C) (as added: see note 32).
35 Housing and Regeneration Act 2008 s 210A(4) (as added (see note 31); amended by the Local Audit and Accountability Act 2014 Sch 12 paras 89, 95(1), (5)).

109. Guidance. The regulator[1] must publish: (1) guidance about the submission of information to the regulator about the performance of registered providers[2]; and (2) guidance about how it uses and intends to use regulatory and enforcement powers[3] under the Housing and Regeneration Act 2008[4]. Guidance under head (1) must, in particular, specify how the regulator will deal with the submissions it receives[5]. Guidance under head (2) must, in particular, specify how the regulator applies and intends to apply the tests[6] as to failure or potential failure to comply with standards relating to consumer matters[7]. The regulator must have regard to guidance under these provisions[8].

Before giving guidance the regulator must consult the following[9]: (a) the Secretary of State[10]; (b) one or more bodies appearing to it to represent the interests of registered providers[11]; (c) any body for the time being nominated[12] to represent the interests of tenants[13]; (d) one or more other bodies appearing to it to represent the interests of tenants[14]; (e) the Greater London authority[15]; (f) one or more bodies appearing to it to represent the interests of local housing authorities[16].

1 As to the meaning of 'the regulator' see PARA 57.
2 As to the meaning of 'registered provider' see PARA 53.
3 Ie powers under the Housing and Regeneration Act 2008 Pt 2 Ch 6 (ss 192–217) and Pt 2 Ch 7 (ss 218–269): see PARAS 104–110, 111–124.
4 Housing and Regeneration Act 2008 s 215(1) (amended by the Localism Act 2011 s 179, Sch 17 paras 1, 15(1), (2)).
5 Housing and Regeneration Act 2008 s 215(2) (amended by the Localism Act 2011 Sch 17 paras 1, 15(1), (3)).
6 Ie the tests in the Housing and Regeneration Act 2008 s 198A: see PARA 106.
7 Housing and Regeneration Act 2008 s 215(2A) (added by the Localism Act 2011 Sch 17 paras 1, 15(1), (4)).
8 Housing and Regeneration Act 2008 s 215(3).
9 Housing and Regeneration Act 2008 s 216.
10 Housing and Regeneration Act 2008 s 216(za) (added by the Localism Act 2011 Sch 17 paras 1, 16(a)). As to the Secretary of State see PARA 7.
11 Housing and Regeneration Act 2008 s 216(a).
12 Ie under the Housing and Regeneration Act 2008 s 278A: see PARA 71 note 5.
13 Housing and Regeneration Act 2008 s 216(aa) (added by the Local Democracy, Economic Development and Construction Act 2009 s 26(1), (6)(a)). As to the meaning of 'tenant' see PARA 52 note 9.
14 Housing and Regeneration Act 2008 s 216(b) (amended by the Local Democracy, Economic Development and Construction Act 2009 s 26(1), (6)(b)).
15 Housing and Regeneration Act 2008 s 216(ba) (added by the Localism Act 2011 s 195(1), Sch 19 paras 46, 57). As to the Greater London Authority see LONDON GOVERNMENT vol 71 (2013) PARA 67 et seq.
16 Housing and Regeneration Act 2008 s 216(c). As to the meaning of 'local housing authority' see PARA 11 (definition applied by s 275).

110. Accreditation of managers of social housing. The regulator[1] may operate a scheme for the purpose of accrediting persons who provide services in connection with the management of social housing[2]. The regulator may approve a scheme operated by someone else for that purpose[3]. Approval may be withdrawn[4].

A scheme may include provision about: (1) eligibility for accreditation; (2) standards to be met by accredited persons[5]; (3) monitoring compliance; (4) complaints against accredited persons; (5) renewal, suspension and withdrawal of accreditation[6]. Accreditation, or continued accreditation, may be conditional on the payment of fees[7].

1 As to the meaning of 'the regulator' see PARA 57.
2 Housing and Regeneration Act 2008 s 217(1). As to the meaning of 'social housing' see PARA 52.
3 Housing and Regeneration Act 2008 s 217(2).
4 Housing and Regeneration Act 2008 s 217(3).

5 These may operate by reference to standards under the Housing and Regeneration Act 2008 s 193 (see PARA 105): s 217(4)(b). Standards under s 193 may refer to accreditation under s 217: s 217(6).
6 Housing and Regeneration Act 2008 s 217(4).
7 Housing and Regeneration Act 2008 s 217(5).

G. ENFORCEMENT POWERS

(A) In general

111. Exercise of enforcement powers. Chapter 7 of Part 2 of the Housing and Regeneration Act 2008[1] makes provision with respect to enforcement powers in relation to registered providers[2].

Where the regulator[3] is deciding: (1) whether to exercise a power under that Chapter; (2) which power under that Chapter to exercise; or (3) how to exercise a power under that Chapter, the regulator must consider: (a) the desirability of registered providers[4] being free to choose how to provide services and conduct business; (b) the speed with which the failure or other problem needs to be addressed[5].

Where the regulator is making a decision in relation to the exercise of a power under that Chapter[6] in relation to failure to meet a standard relating to consumer matters[7], the regulator must consider: (i) whether the failure or other problem concerned is serious or trivial; (ii) whether the failure or other problem is a recurrent or isolated incident[8].

1 Ie the Housing and Regeneration Act 2008 Pt 2 Ch 7 (ss 218–269B).
2 See below and PARA 112 et seq.
3 As to the meaning of 'the regulator' see PARA 57.
4 As to the meaning of 'registered provider' see PARA 53.
5 Housing and Regeneration Act 2008 s 218(1), (2) (amended by the Localism Act 2011 ss 179, 237, Sch 17 paras 1, 17(1)–(3), Sch 25 Pt 27).
6 Ie: (1) the exercise, on a ground other than one specified in the Housing and Regeneration Act 2008 198A(1) (failure to meet standard under s 193: see PARA 106), of a power under Pt 2 Ch 7 that is listed in s 198A(3) (see PARA 106 note 7); or (2) the exercise of a power under Pt 2 Ch 7 that is not listed in s 198A(3).
7 Ie a standard under the Housing and Regeneration Act 2008 s 193: see PARA 105.
8 Housing and Regeneration Act 2008 s 218(3), (4) (added by the Localism Act 2011 Sch 17 paras 1, 17(1), (4)).

(B) Enforcement Notice

112. Enforcement notice to resolve specified failure. The provisions noted in this paragraph[1] allow the regulator[2] to require a registered provider[3] to take specified action[4] to resolve a specified failure or other problem[5].

The regulator may give an enforcement notice to a registered provider if the regulator is satisfied that: (1) any of the following cases applies; and (2) giving an enforcement notice is appropriate (whether it is likely to be sufficient in itself, or a prelude to further action)[6].

Case 1 is where the registered provider has failed to meet a standard applicable[7] to it[8].

Case 2 is where the affairs of the registered provider have been mismanaged[9].

Case 3 is where the registered provider has failed to comply with an earlier enforcement notice[10].

Case 4 is where the registered provider has failed to publish information in accordance with a requirement[11] to do so[12].

Case 5 is where the interests of tenants[13] of the registered provider require protection[14].

Case 6 is where the registered provider is a private registered provider[15] and its assets require protection[16].

Case 7 is where the registered provider has given an undertaking[17] and failed to comply with it[18].

Case 8 is where the registered provider has failed to pay: (a) in the case of a private registered provider, an annual fee[19] for continued registration; or (b) in the case of a local authority[20], an initial fee[21] or an annual fee[22] for continued registration[23].

Case 9 is where an offence under Part 2 of the Housing and Regeneration Act 2008[24] has been committed by the registered provider[25].

Case 10 is where the registered provider has failed to comply with an order made by a duly appointed[26] ombudsman[27].

Case 11 is where the registered provider has failed to comply with certain provisions of the Welfare Reform and Work Act 2016 or regulations thereunder relating to the reduction in social housing rents[28].

An enforcement notice must: (i) specify the grounds on which it is given; (ii) specify the action the regulator wants the registered provider to take in response to the notice; (iii) specify when the action is to be taken (which may be immediately on receipt of the notice); and (iv) explain the effect of the statutory provisions[29] as to appeal against the notice, withdrawal of the notice and sanctions[30]. The action specified in an enforcement notice may include publishing the notice in a specified manner[31].

If the regulator gives such an enforcement notice it must send a copy, in the case of an enforcement notice given to a registered provider who owns land in Greater London, the Greater London Authority and, in the case of an enforcement notice given to a local authority, to the Secretary of State[32].

A registered provider who is given an enforcement notice may appeal against it to the High Court[33].

The regulator may withdraw an enforcement notice by giving notice to the registered provider[34].

If a registered provider does not comply with an enforcement notice the regulator must consider exercising another power[35]. In the case of an enforcement notice given to a person other than the registered provider[36], the regulator may only: (A) exercise the power to issue a penalty notice to the person[37]; or (B) take steps to have the person prosecuted for the offence by reference to which the enforcement notice was given[38]. A person to whom an enforcement notice is given on the ground in Case 9 may not be prosecuted for the offence by reference to which the enforcement notice was given unless the person fails to comply with the enforcement notice[39].

1　Ie the Housing and Regeneration Act 2008 ss 219–225.
2　As to the meaning of 'the regulator' see PARA 57.
3　As to the meaning of 'registered provider' see PARA 53.
4　As to the meaning of 'action' see PARA 73 note 13.
5　Housing and Regeneration Act 2008 s 219.
6　Housing and Regeneration Act 2008 s 220(1).
7　Ie under the Housing and Regeneration Act 2008 s 193 or 194: see PARA 105.
8　Housing and Regeneration Act 2008 s 220(2) (amended by SI 2010/844).
9　Housing and Regeneration Act 2008 s 220(3). As to the meaning of 'mismanagement' see PARA 108 note 3.
10　Housing and Regeneration Act 2008 s 220(4).
11　Ie under the Housing and Regeneration Act 2008 s 228(3) or 240(3): see PARAS 113, 114.
12　Housing and Regeneration Act 2008 s 220(5).
13　As to the meaning of 'tenant' see PARA 52 note 9.

14 Housing and Regeneration Act 2008 s 220(6).
15 As to the meaning of 'private registered provider' see PARA 53.
16 Housing and Regeneration Act 2008 s 220(7) (amended by SI 2010/844).
17 Ie under the Housing and Regeneration Act 2008 s 125: see PARA 74.
18 Housing and Regeneration Act 2008 s 220(8).
19 Ie under the Housing and Regeneration Act 2008 s 117(1)(b): see PARA 72.
20 As to the meaning of 'local authority' see PARA 149 note 4 (definition applied by the Housing and Regeneration Act 2008 s 275).
21 Ie under the Housing and Regeneration Act 2008 s 117(1)(a): see PARA 72.
22 Ie under the Housing and Regeneration Act 2008 s 117(1)(b): see PARA 72.
23 Housing and Regeneration Act 2008 s 220(9) (substituted by SI 2010/844).
24 Ie the Housing and Regeneration Act 2008 Pt 2 (ss 59–278A).
25 Housing and Regeneration Act 2008 s 220(10). Where the regulator is satisfied that an offence under Pt 2 has been committed in respect of a registered provider but by another person (such as a member, employee or agent of the registered provider), Case 9 applies, the regulator may give an enforcement notice to the other person and Pt 2 Ch 7 (ss 218–269B) applies with the substitution of references to that other person for references to the registered provider: s 220(12).
26 Ie an ombudsman appointed by virtue of the Housing and Regeneration Act 2008 s 124: see PARA 130 et seq.
27 Housing and Regeneration Act 2008 s 220(11).
28 Housing and Regeneration Act 2008 s 220(11A) (added by the Welfare Reform and Work Act 2016 s 30(1), (2)). The provisions referred to in the text are the Welfare Reform and Work Act 2016 s 23, regulations under s 27, and Sch 2 Pt 1: see PARA 55.
29 Ie the Housing and Regeneration Act 2008 ss 223–225: see the text and notes 33–39.
30 Housing and Regeneration Act 2008 s 221(1).
31 Housing and Regeneration Act 2008 s 221(2).
32 Housing and Regeneration Act 2008 s 222 (substituted by SI 2010/844; and amended by the Localism Act 2011 ss 178, 195(1), 237, Sch 16 paras 1, 46, Sch 19 paras 46, 58, Sch 25 Pt 26). As to the Greater London Authority see LONDON GOVERNMENT vol 71 (2013) PARA 67 et seq. As to the Secretary of State see PARA 7.
33 Housing and Regeneration Act 2008 s 223.
34 Housing and Regeneration Act 2008 s 224.
35 Housing and Regeneration Act 2008 s 225(1). Ie another power under Pt 2 Ch 6 (ss 192–217) (see PARA 104 et seq) or Pt 2 Ch 7 (ss 218–269B).
36 Ie by virtue of the Housing and Regeneration Act 2008 s 220(12): see note 25.
37 Ie in accordance with the Housing and Regeneration Act 2008 ss 226–235: see PARA 113.
38 Housing and Regeneration Act 2008 s 225(2).
39 Housing and Regeneration Act 2008 s 225(3).

(C) Penalty

113. Imposition of fines in respect of failures by private registered providers. The provisions noted in this paragraph[1] allow the regulator[2] to penalise failures on the part of private registered providers[3] by the imposition of fines[4].

The regulator may require a private registered provider to pay a penalty if the regulator is satisfied that: (1) any of the following cases applies; and (2) the imposition of a penalty is appropriate (whether or not as part of a response including other action)[5].

Case 1 is where the registered provider has failed to meet a standard[6] as to the provision of social housing or the registered provider's management[7].

Case 2 is where the affairs of the registered provider have been mismanaged[8].

Case 3 is where the registered provider has failed to comply with an enforcement notice[9].

Case 4 is where the registered provider has given an undertaking[10] and failed to comply with it[11].

Case 5 is where the registered provider has failed to pay an annual fee[12] for continued registration[13].

Case 6 is where an offence under Part 2 of the Housing and Regeneration Act 2008[14] has been committed by the registered provider[15].

Case 7 is where the registered provider has failed to comply with certain provisions of the Welfare Reform and Work Act 2016 or regulations thereunder relating to the reduction in social housing rents[16].

A penalty is imposed by the regulator giving notice (a 'penalty notice') to the registered provider[17]. The notice must specify: (a) the grounds on which the penalty is imposed; (b) the amount of the penalty; (c) how the penalty must be paid; (d) a period within which it must be paid; and (e) any interest or additional penalty which is payable[18] in the event of late payment[19]. The notice may require the registered provider to publish information about the penalty in a specified manner[20]. The notice must explain the effect of the statutory provisions for enforcement[21] and as to the right of appeal[22] against the notice[23].

Before giving a penalty notice to a registered provider the regulator must give the provider a notice (a 'pre-penalty warning'): (i) specifying grounds on which the regulator thinks a penalty could be imposed; (ii) warning the provider that the regulator is considering imposing a penalty; (iii) including any indication that the regulator is able to give of the likely amount of any penalty; and (iv) explaining the effect of the statutory provisions as to the right to make representations[24], as to enforcement[25] and as to the right of appeal[26] against the notice[27]. When the regulator gives a pre-penalty warning it must send a copy to the Greater London Authority (if the pre-penalty warning is given to a registered provider who owns land in Greater London) and to any other persons it thinks appropriate[28]. A pre-penalty warning must refer to the statutory provision as to voluntary undertakings[29] and indicate whether or to what extent the regulator would accept a voluntary undertaking instead of, or in mitigation of, a penalty[30]. A pre-penalty warning may be combined with notice under one or more other provisions[31] of the Housing and Regeneration Act 2008[32].

A pre-penalty warning must specify a period during which the registered provider may make representations[33] to the regulator[34]. The period must be a period of at least 28 days and begin with the date on which the registered provider receives the pre-penalty warning[35]. Representations may concern: (A) whether a penalty should be imposed; (B) the amount of any penalty that may be imposed[36]. After the end of the specified period the regulator must consider any representations made and decide whether to impose a penalty[37].

If the regulator imposes a penalty on a registered provider who owns land in Greater London, it must send a copy of the penalty notice to the Greater London Authority[38].

Where the regulator receives money by way of penalty, the regulator may deduct a sum which represents the direct costs to the regulator of imposing and enforcing the penalty and a reasonable share of expenditure by the regulator which is indirectly referable to the imposition and enforcement of the penalty[39], and any excess must be paid to the Homes and Communities Agency ('HCA'), to be used for purposes which appear to it to amount to investment in social housing[40].

A penalty is to be treated as a debt owed to the regulator[41]. The Treasury may make regulations authorising the regulator to charge interest on penalty not paid during the period specified[42] and to impose one or more additional penalties where a penalty is not paid during that period[43]. Interest and additional penalty are to be treated as penalty[44]. A penalty notice may include provision allowing a discount if the penalty is paid on or before a date specified in the notice[45]. A person to whom a penalty notice is given on the ground in Case 6 may not be prosecuted for the offence by reference to which the penalty notice was given[46].

A registered provider who is given a penalty notice may appeal to the High Court against the imposition of the penalty, or its amount, or both[47].

1 Ie the Housing and Regeneration Act 2008 ss 226–235.
2 As to the meaning of 'the regulator' see PARA 57.
3 As to the meaning of 'private registered provider' see PARA 53.
4 Housing and Regeneration Act 2008 s 226 (amended by SI 2010/844).
5 Housing and Regeneration Act 2008 s 227(1) (amended by SI 2010/844). As to the meaning of 'action' see PARA 73 note 13.
6 Ie under the Housing and Regeneration Act 2008 s 193 or 194: see PARA 105.
7 Housing and Regeneration Act 2008 s 227(2).
8 Housing and Regeneration Act 2008 s 227(3). As to the meaning of 'mismanagement' see PARA 108 note 3.
9 Housing and Regeneration Act 2008 s 227(4). As to enforcement notices see PARA 112.
10 Ie under the Housing and Regeneration Act 2008 s 125: see PARA 74.
11 Housing and Regeneration Act 2008 s 227(5).
12 Ie under the Housing and Regeneration Act 2008 s 117(1)(b): see PARA 72.
13 Housing and Regeneration Act 2008 s 227(6) (amended by SI 2010/844).
14 Ie the Housing and Regeneration Act 2008 Pt 2 (ss 59–278A).
15 Housing and Regeneration Act 2008 s 227(7). In order to rely on Case 6, the regulator must be satisfied beyond reasonable doubt that it applies: s 227(9). As to satisfaction beyond reasonable doubt see CRIMINAL PROCEDURE vol 28 (2015) PARA 452. Where the regulator is satisfied that an offence under Pt 2 has been committed in respect of a registered provider but by another person (such as a member, employee or agent of the registered provider): (1) Case 6 applies; (2) the regulator may require the other person to pay a penalty; and (3) Pt 2 Ch 7 (ss 218–269B) applies with the substitution of references to that other person for references to the registered provider: s 227(8).
16 Housing and Regeneration Act 2008 s 227(7A) (added by the Welfare Reform and Work Act 2016 s 30(1), (3)). The provisions referred to in the text are the Welfare Reform and Work Act 2016 s 23, regulations under s 27, and Sch 2 Pt 1: see PARA 55.
17 Housing and Regeneration Act 2008 s 228(1). The amount of a penalty imposed on the ground specified in Case 6 may not exceed the maximum amount (if any) of fine that a magistrates' court could impose for the relevant offence: s 229(1) (amended by SI 2015/664). The amount of a penalty imposed on the ground specified in any other case of the Housing and Regeneration Act 2008 s 227 may not exceed £5,000: s 229(2). The Secretary of State may by order amend the amount specified in s 229(2): s 229(3). As to the Secretary of State see PARA 7. As to orders by the Secretary of State see PARA 54.
18 Ie by virtue of the Housing and Regeneration Act 2008 s 234(2): see the text and note 43.
19 Housing and Regeneration Act 2008 s 228(2). The Secretary of State: (1) must make regulations about the period under s 228(2)(d) (head (d) in the text); (2) may make other regulations about the form and content of a penalty notice; and (3) may make regulations about the manner in which a penalty notice is given: s 228(5). See the Housing and Regeneration Act 2008 (Penalty and Compensation Notices) Regulations 2010, SI 2010/662.
20 Housing and Regeneration Act 2008 s 228(3).
21 Ie the effect of the Housing and Regeneration Act 2008 s 234(1), (3) and (6): see the text and notes 41, 44, 46.
22 Ie under the Housing and Regeneration Act 2008 s 235: see the text to note 47.
23 Housing and Regeneration Act 2008 s 228(4).
24 Ie the Housing and Regeneration Act 2008 s 231: see the text and notes 33–37.
25 Ie the Housing and Regeneration Act 2008 s 234(1), (3) and (6).
26 Ie under the Housing and Regeneration Act 2008 s 235.
27 Housing and Regeneration Act 2008 s 230(1).
28 Housing and Regeneration Act 2008 s 230(2) (amended by the Localism Act 2011 ss 178, 195(1), 237, Sch 16 paras 1, 47, Sch 19 paras 46, 59, Sch 25 Pt 26). For the purposes of deciding which other persons it considers appropriate the regulator must consider, in particular, any person who provided information as a result of which the pre-penalty warning is given: Housing and Regeneration Act 2008 s 230(3). As to the Greater London Authority see LONDON GOVERNMENT vol 71 (2013) PARA 67 et seq.
29 Ie the Housing and Regeneration Act 2008 s 125: see PARA 74.
30 Housing and Regeneration Act 2008 s 230(4).
31 Ie the Housing and Regeneration Act 2008 ss 242, 248, 250 and 252: see PARAS 114, 115, 116, 118.
32 Housing and Regeneration Act 2008 s 230(5).

33 As to the meaning of 'representations' see PARA 72 note 18.
34 Housing and Regeneration Act 2008 s 231(1).
35 Housing and Regeneration Act 2008 s 231(2).
36 Housing and Regeneration Act 2008 s 231(3).
37 Housing and Regeneration Act 2008 s 231(4).
38 Housing and Regeneration Act 2008 s 232A (added by the Localism Act 2011 Sch 19 paras 46, 60).
39 Housing and Regeneration Act 2008 s 233(1), (2).
40 Housing and Regeneration Act 2008 s 233(3). As to the HCA see PARA 57 et seq; and PLANNING vol 83 (2010) PARA 1454 et seq. As to the meaning of 'social housing' see PARA 52.
41 Housing and Regeneration Act 2008 s 234(1).
42 Ie under the Housing and Regeneration Act 2008 s 228(2)(d): see head (d) in the text.
43 Housing and Regeneration Act 2008 s 234(2). Regulations under s 234(2)(a) may provide for an interest rate to be: (1) set by a specified person; or (2) determined in accordance with the regulations: s 234(4). As to regulations by the Treasury see PARA 54.
44 Housing and Regeneration Act 2008 s 234(3). It may have the effect of increasing the penalty above a limit set by s 229: see note 16.
45 Housing and Regeneration Act 2008 s 234(5). The date must fall within the period specified under s 228(2)(d) (see head (d) in the text): s 234(5).
46 Housing and Regeneration Act 2008 s 234(6).
47 Housing and Regeneration Act 2008 s 235.

(D)   Compensation

114. Compensation for victims of failure by private registered providers. The provisions noted in this paragraph[1] allow the regulator[2] to award compensation to a victim of a failure on the part of a private registered provider[3].

The regulator may require a private registered provider to pay compensation if the regulator is satisfied that:

(1)   either of the following cases applies; and
(2)   the award of compensation is appropriate (whether or not as part of a response which includes other action)[4].

Case 1 is where the registered provider has failed to meet a standard[5] as to the provision of social housing or the registered provider's management[6].

Case 2 is where the registered provider has given an undertaking[7] and failed to comply with it[8].

Case 3 is where the registered provider has failed to comply with certain provisions of the Welfare Reform and Work Act 2016 or regulations thereunder relating to the reduction in social housing rents[9].

Compensation in respect of a failure may be awarded to one or more persons who have suffered as a result of the failure[10]. However, an award may be made only to:

(a)   a specified tenant[11] of social housing[12] provided by the registered provider;
(b)   each member of a specified class of tenants of social housing provided by the registered provider; or
(c)   each member of the class of tenants of social housing provided by the registered provider[13].

The regulator may not award compensation to a person in respect of a matter if an ombudsman[14] has awarded compensation to the person in respect of the matter[15]; but, in relation to Wales only, if compensation awarded by an ombudsman has not been paid as required, the regulator may award compensation[16].

Compensation is awarded by the regulator giving notice (a 'compensation notice') to the registered provider and the person to be compensated[17]. The notice must specify:

(i)   the grounds on which the compensation is awarded;
(ii)   the amount of the compensation;
(iii)   the person to be compensated;
(iv)   any interest or additional compensation which is payable[18] in the event of late payment; and
(v)   a period within which it must be paid[19].

The notice may require the registered provider to publish information about the compensation award in a specified manner[20]. The notice must explain the effect of the statutory provisions[21] as to enforcement and the right to appeal[22].

When the regulator is considering whether to award compensation or the amount of compensation to award, the regulator must take account of any information available to it about the financial situation of the registered provider[23]. The regulator must consider the likely impact of the compensation on the registered provider's ability to provide services[24]. In particular, the regulator must aim to avoid:

(A)   jeopardising the financial viability of the registered provider;
(B)   preventing the registered provider from honouring financial commitments; or
(C)   preventing the registered provider from taking action to remedy the matters on the grounds of which the compensation might be awarded[25].

Before giving a compensation notice to a private registered provider the regulator must give the provider a notice (a 'pre-compensation warning'):

(I)   specifying grounds on which the regulator thinks compensation could be awarded;
(II)   warning the provider that the regulator is considering awarding compensation to a specified person;
(III)   including any indication that the regulator is able to give of the likely amount of any compensation; and
(IV)   explaining the effect of the statutory provisions[26] as to representations, enforcement and appeals[27].

Before giving a pre-compensation warning the regulator must consult the person appointed[28] as the ombudsman for the scheme of which the registered provider is a member[29]. If the regulator gives a pre-compensation warning it must send a copy to the Greater London Authority (if the pre-compensation warning is given to a registered provider who owns land in Greater London) and any other persons it thinks appropriate[30]. A pre-compensation warning must refer to the statutory provision as to voluntary undertakings and indicate whether or to what extent the regulator would accept a voluntary undertaking instead of, or in mitigation of, awarding compensation[31]. A pre-compensation warning may be combined with notice under one or more of other provisions[32] of the Housing and Regeneration Act 2008[33].

A pre-compensation warning must specify a period during which the registered provider may make representations[34] to the regulator[35]. The period must be a period of at least 28 days and begin with the date on which the registered provider receives the pre-compensation warning[36]. Representations may address whether compensation should be awarded; and the amount of any compensation that may be awarded[37]. After the end of the period specified the regulator must consider any representations made and decide whether to award compensation[38].

Compensation is to be treated as a debt owed to the person to whom it is awarded[39]. The Treasury may make regulations authorising the regulator to award interest on compensation not paid during the period specified[40] and to award additional compensation where compensation is not paid during that period[41]. Interest and additional compensation are to be treated as compensation[42].

A private registered provider who is given a compensation notice may appeal to the High Court against the award of compensation, or its amount, or both[43].

1 Ie the Housing and Regeneration Act 2008 ss 236–245.
2 As to the meaning of 'the regulator' see PARA 57.
3 Housing and Regeneration Act 2008 s 236 (amended by SI 2010/844). As to persons to whom compensation may be awarded see the text to notes 10–13. As to the meaning of 'private registered provider' see PARA 53.
4 Housing and Regeneration Act 2008 s 237(1) (amended by SI 2010/844). As to the meaning of 'action' see PARA 73 note 13.
5 Ie under the Housing and Regeneration Act 2008 s 193 or 194: see PARA 105.
6 Housing and Regeneration Act 2008 s 237(2).
7 Ie under the Housing and Regeneration Act 2008 s 125: see PARA 74.
8 Housing and Regeneration Act 2008 s 237(3).
9 Housing and Regeneration Act 2008 s 237(4) (added by the Welfare Reform and Work Act 2016 s 30(1), (4)). The provisions referred to in the text are the Welfare Reform and Work Act 2016 s 23, regulations under s 27, and Sch 2 Pt 1: see PARA 55.
10 Housing and Regeneration Act 2008 s 238(1).
11 As to the meaning of 'tenant' see PARA 52 note 9.
12 As to the meaning of 'social housing' see PARA 52.
13 Housing and Regeneration Act 2008 s 238(2).
14 Ie appointed by virtue of the Housing and Regeneration Act 2008 s 124: see PARA 130 et seq.
15 Housing and Regeneration Act 2008 s 239(1).
16 Housing and Regeneration Act 2008 s 239(2) (repealed by the Localism Act 2011 ss 180(2), 237, Sch 25 Pt 28; in force in relation to England; in relation to Wales, in force as from a day to be appointed; at the date at which this volume states the law, no such day had been appointed).
17 Housing and Regeneration Act 2008 s 240(1).
18 Ie by virtue of the Housing and Regeneration Act 2008 s 244(2): see the text to notes 40–41.
19 Housing and Regeneration Act 2008 s 240(2). The Secretary of State: (1) must make regulations about the period under s 240(2)(e) (head (v) in the text); (2) may make other regulations about the form and content of a compensation notice; and (3) may make regulations about the manner in which a compensation notice is given: s 240(5). See the Housing and Regeneration Act 2008 (Penalty and Compensation Notices) Regulations 2010, SI 2010/662.
20 Housing and Regeneration Act 2008 s 240(3).
21 Ie the Housing and Regeneration Act 2008 ss 244(1), (3) and 245: see the text and notes 39, 42–43.
22 Housing and Regeneration Act 2008 s 240(4).
23 Housing and Regeneration Act 2008 s 241(1), (2).
24 Housing and Regeneration Act 2008 s 241(3).
25 Housing and Regeneration Act 2008 s 241(4).
26 Ie the Housing and Regeneration Act 2008 ss 243, 244(1), (3) and 245.
27 Housing and Regeneration Act 2008 s 242(1) (amended by SI 2010/844).
28 Ie by virtue of the Housing and Regeneration Act 2008 s 124: see PARA 130 et seq.
29 Housing and Regeneration Act 2008 s 242(2).
30 Housing and Regeneration Act 2008 s 242(3) (amended by the Localism Act 2011 ss 178, 195(1), 237, Sch 16 paras 1, 49, Sch 19 paras 46, 61, Sch 25 Pt 26). For the purposes of considering any other persons it thinks appropriate the regulator must consider, in particular, any person who provided information as a result of which the pre-compensation warning is given: Housing and Regeneration Act 2008 s 242(4). As to the Greater London Authority see LONDON GOVERNMENT vol 71 (2013) PARA 67 et seq.
31 Housing and Regeneration Act 2008 s 242(5). As to the statutory provision as to voluntary undertakings see s 125; and PARA 74.
32 Ie the Housing and Regeneration Act 2008 ss 230, 248, 250 and 252: see PARAS 113, 115, 116, 118.
33 Housing and Regeneration Act 2008 s 242(6).
34 As to the meaning of 'representations' see PARA 72 note 18.
35 Housing and Regeneration Act 2008 s 243(1).
36 Housing and Regeneration Act 2008 s 243(2).
37 Housing and Regeneration Act 2008 s 243(3).

38 Housing and Regeneration Act 2008 s 243(4).
39 Housing and Regeneration Act 2008 s 244(1).
40 Ie under the Housing and Regeneration Act 2008 s 240(2)(e): see head (v) in the text.
41 Housing and Regeneration Act 2008 s 244(2). Regulations under s 244(2)(a) may provide for an interest rate to be: (1) set by a specified person; or (2) determined in accordance with the regulations: s 244(4). As to regulations by the Treasury see PARA 54.
42 Housing and Regeneration Act 2008 s 244(3).
43 Housing and Regeneration Act 2008 s 245 (amended by SI 2010/844).

(E) Management Powers

115. Management tender. The provisions noted in this paragraph and the following paragraphs[1] give the regulator[2] various powers in relation to the management and the constitution[3] of registered providers[4].

The following provisions apply if the regulator is satisfied that: (1) a registered provider has failed to meet a standard applicable to it[5]; (2) a registered provider has failed to comply with certain provisions of the Welfare Reform and Work Act 2016, or regulations thereunder relating to the reduction in social housing rents[6]; or (3) the affairs of a registered provider have been mismanaged[7] in relation to social housing[8]. The regulator may require the registered provider to implement a process specified by the regulator for the purpose of inviting persons to apply to undertake management functions of the registered provider and selecting from the applications and making an appointment[9]. A requirement may relate to: (a) the registered provider's affairs generally in so far as they relate to social housing; or (b) specified affairs relating to social housing[10].

Before taking such action[11] the regulator must give the registered provider a notice: (i) specifying grounds on which action might be taken under the above provisions; (ii) warning the provider that the regulator is considering action under those provisions; and (iii) explaining the effect of the following provisions[12]. The notice must specify a period during which the registered provider may make representations[13] to the regulator[14]. The period must be a period of at least 28 days and begin with the date on which the registered provider receives the notice[15]. The regulator must send a copy of a notice to the Greater London Authority (if the notice is given to a registered provider who owns land in Greater London), the Secretary of State (if the notice is given to a local authority) and any other persons the regulator thinks appropriate[16]. A notice must refer to the statutory provisions as to voluntary undertakings[17] and indicate whether or to what extent the regulator would accept a voluntary undertaking instead of, or in mitigation of, action under the provisions mentioned above[18]. Notice before taking action may be combined with notice under one or more of other provisions[19] of the Housing and Regeneration Act 2008[20]. If the regulator imposes a requirement it must send a copy, in the case of a requirement imposed on a registered provider who owns land in Greater London, to the Greater London Authority and, in the case of a requirement imposed on a local authority, to the Secretary of State[21]. A registered provider may appeal to the High Court against a requirement imposed on it[22].

1 Ie the Housing and Regeneration Act 2008 ss 246–255: see the text and notes 2–22 and PARAS 116–121.
2 As to the meaning of 'the regulator' see PARA 57.
3 As to the meaning of 'constitution' see PARA 71 note 6.
4 Housing and Regeneration Act 2008 s 246. As to the meaning of 'registered provider' see PARA 53.
5 Ie under the Housing and Regeneration Act 2008 s 193 or 194: see PARA 105.
6 Ie the Welfare Reform and Work Act 2016 s 23, regulations under s 27, and Sch 2 Pt 1: see PARA 55.
7 As to the meaning of 'mismanagement' see PARA 108 note 3.

8 Housing and Regeneration Act 2008 s 247(1) (amended by the Welfare Reform and Work Act 2016 s 30(1), (5); and by SI 2010/844). As to the meaning of 'social housing' see PARA 52.
9 Housing and Regeneration Act 2008 s 247(2). In imposing a requirement the regulator must have regard to views of: (1) relevant tenants; (2) the registered provider; (3) the Greater London Authority (if the notice is given to a registered provider who owns land in Greater London); (4) the Secretary of State (if the registered provider is a local authority); and (5) if the regulator thinks it appropriate, any relevant local housing authority: s 248(7) (amended by the Localism Act 2011 ss 178, 195(1), 237, Sch 16 paras 1, 50(1), (3), Sch 19 paras 46, 62(1), (3), Sch 25 Pt 26; and by SI 2010/844). As to the meaning of 'tenant' see PARA 52 note 9; as to the Greater London Authority see LONDON GOVERNMENT vol 71 (2013) PARA 67 et seq; as to the Secretary of State see PARA 7; as to the meaning of 'local authority' see PARA 149 note 4; and as to the meaning of 'local housing authority' see PARA 11 (definitions applied by the Housing and Regeneration Act 2008 s 275).
10 Housing and Regeneration Act 2008 s 247(3). A requirement must include: (1) provision about the constitution of a selection panel (which must include provision for ensuring representation of tenants' interests); (2) provision for ensuring best procurement practice (and consistent with any applicable procurement law); and (3) provision about the terms and conditions on which the manager is to be appointed (including provision about: (a) setting, monitoring and enforcing performance standards; and (b) resources): s 247(4) (amended by SI 2010/844).
11 Ie under the Housing and Regeneration Act 2008 s 247(2).
12 Housing and Regeneration Act 2008 s 248(1).
13 As to the meaning of 'representations' see PARA 72 note 18.
14 Housing and Regeneration Act 2008 s 248(2).
15 Housing and Regeneration Act 2008 s 248(3).
16 Housing and Regeneration Act 2008 s 248(4) (amended by the Localism Act 2011 Sch 16 paras 1, 50(1), (2), Sch 19 paras 46, 62(1), (2), Sch 25 Pt 26; and by SI 2010/844).
17 Ie under the Housing and Regeneration Act 2008 s 125: see PARA 74.
18 Housing and Regeneration Act 2008 s 248(5).
19 Ie the Housing and Regeneration Act 2008 ss 230, 242, 250 and 252: see PARAS 113, 114, 116, 118.
20 Housing and Regeneration Act 2008 s 248(6).
21 Housing and Regeneration Act 2008 s 248(8) (substituted by SI 2010/844; and amended by the Localism Act 2011 Sch 16 paras 1, 50(1), (4), Sch 19 paras 46, 62(1), (4), Sch 25 Pt 26).
22 Housing and Regeneration Act 2008 s 248(9).

116. Management transfer. The following provisions apply if, as a result of an inquiry[1] or an audit[2], the regulator[3] is satisfied that: (1) the affairs of a registered provider[4] have been mismanaged[5] in relation to social housing[6]; or (2) a transfer of certain of a registered provider's management functions would be likely to improve the management of some or all of its social housing[7]. The regulator may require the registered provider to transfer management functions to a specified person[8]. A requirement to transfer management functions may be imposed only with the Secretary of State's consent[9] (both as to the transfer and the terms)[10]. A transferee manager has: (a) any power specified in the requirement; and (b) any other power in relation to the registered provider's affairs required by the manager for the purposes specified in the requirement (including the power to enter into agreements and take other action on behalf of the registered provider)[11].

Before acting under the power to require the transfer of management functions[12] the regulator must give the registered provider a notice: (i) specifying grounds on which action might be taken under the above provisions; (ii) warning the provider that the regulator is considering action under those provisions; and (iii) explaining the effect of the following provisions[13]. The notice must specify a period during which the registered provider may make representations to the regulator[14]. This period must be a period of at least 28 days and begin with the date on which the registered provider receives the notice[15]. The regulator must send a copy of a notice to: (A) in the case of a notice given to a registered provider who owns land in Greater London, the Greater London Authority[16]; (B) in the case of a notice given to a local authority[17], the Secretary of State; and (C) any other persons the regulator thinks appropriate (having regard, in particular, to any person who provided information as a result of which the notice is given)[18]. The notice may be combined with notice under one or more other provisions[19] of the Housing and Regeneration Act 2008[20]. If the regulator imposes a requirement it must send a copy: (I) in the case of a notice given to a registered provider who owns land in Greater London, the Greater London Authority; and (II) in the case of a requirement imposed on a local authority, to the Secretary of State[21]. A registered provider may appeal to the High Court against a requirement imposed[22] on it[23].

1   Ie under the Housing and Regeneration Act 2008 s 206: see PARA 108.
2   Ie under the Housing and Regeneration Act 2008 s 210 or s 210A: see PARA 108.
3   As to the meaning of 'the regulator' see PARA 57.
4   As to the meaning of 'registered provider' see PARA 53.
5   As to the meaning of 'mismanagement' see PARA 108 note 3.
6   As to the meaning of 'social housing' see PARA 52.
7   Housing and Regeneration Act 2008 s 249(1) (amended by the Local Audit and Accountability Act 2014 s 45, Sch 12 paras 89, 96).
8   Housing and Regeneration Act 2008 s 249(2). A requirement may relate to: (1) the registered provider's affairs generally in so far as they relate to social housing; or (2) specified affairs relating to social housing: s 249(4). Transfer is to be on terms and conditions (including as to remuneration) specified in, or determined in accordance with, the requirement: s 249(5). In imposing a requirement the regulator must have regard to views of: (a) relevant tenants; (b) the registered provider; (c) if the requirement would be imposed on a registered provider who owns land in Greater London, the Greater London Authority; (d) if the requirement would be imposed on a local authority, the Secretary of State; and (e) if the regulator thinks it appropriate, any relevant local housing authority: s 250(7) (amended by the Localism Act 2011 ss 178, 195(1), 237, Sch 16 paras 1, 51(1), (3), Sch 19 paras 46, 63(1), (3), Sch 25 Pt 26; and by SI 2010/844). As to the meaning of 'tenant' see PARA 52 note 9; as to the Secretary of State see PARA 7; and as to the meaning of 'local housing authority' see PARA 11 (definition applied by the Housing and Regeneration Act 2008 s 275).
9   As to the meaning of 'consent' see PARA 80 note 29.
10 Housing and Regeneration Act 2008 s 249(3).
11 Housing and Regeneration Act 2008 s 249(6).
12 Ie the Housing and Regeneration Act 2008 s 249(2).
13 Housing and Regeneration Act 2008 s 250(1). A notice under s 250(1) must: (1) refer to s 125 (see PARA 74); and (2) indicate whether or to what extent the regulator would accept a voluntary undertaking under s 125 instead of, or in mitigation of, action under s 249(2): s 250(5).
14 Housing and Regeneration Act 2008 s 250(2).
15 Housing and Regeneration Act 2008 s 250(3).
16 As to the Greater London Authority see LONDON GOVERNMENT vol 71 (2013) PARA 67 et seq.
17 As to the meaning of 'local authority' see PARA 149 note 4 (definition applied by the Housing and Regeneration Act 2008 s 275).
18 Housing and Regeneration Act 2008 s 250(4) (amended by the Localism Act 2011 Sch 16 paras 1, 51(1), (2), Sch 19 paras 46, 63(1), (2), Sch 25 Pt 26; and by SI 2010/844).
19 Ie the Housing and Regeneration Act 2008 ss 230, 242, 248 and 252: see PARAS 113, 114, 115, 118.
20 Housing and Regeneration Act 2008 s 250(6).
21 Housing and Regeneration Act 2008 s 250(8) (substituted by SI 2010/844; and amended by the Localism Act 2011 Sch 16 paras 1, 51(1), (4), Sch 19 paras 46, 63(1), (4), Sch 25 Pt 26).
22 Ie under the Housing and Regeneration Act 2008 s 249(2).
23 Housing and Regeneration Act 2008 s 250(9).

117. Management tender or transfer where registered provider is a local authority. The provisions dealt with in this paragraph[1] make further provision about the application of the statutory powers[2] of the regulator[3] relating to the management of registered providers[4] in a case where the registered provider is a local authority[5]. The regulator may act under those powers even if the local authority already has a management agreement[6] in place[7]. However, while a section 247 or 249 arrangement[8] is in force, the local authority may not give effect to a management agreement as respects functions of the authority which are the subject of the arrangement[9].

Any duty the local authority may have to consult with respect to the exercise of its management functions[10] does not apply so far as it is acting pursuant to a requirement imposed on it under the statutory management powers[11] of the regulator[12].

1 Ie the Housing and Regeneration Act 2008 s 250A (added by SI 2010/844).
2 Ie the Housing and Regeneration Act 2008 ss 247, 249: see PARAS 115–116.
3 As to the meaning of 'the regulator' see PARA 57.
4 As to the meaning of 'registered provider' see PARA 53.
5 Housing and Regeneration Act 2008 s 250A(1) (as added: see note 1). As to the meaning of 'local authority' see PARA 149 note 4 (definition applied by s 275).
6 'Management agreement' has the meaning given by the Housing Act 1985 ss 27(2)(a), 27B(4) (see PARA 457): Housing and Regeneration Act 2008 s 250A(6) (as added: see note 1).
7 Housing and Regeneration Act 2008 s 250A(2) (as added: see note 1).
8 'Section 247 or 249 arrangement' means an arrangement which is entered into pursuant to a requirement imposed on a local authority under the Housing and Regeneration Act 2008 s 247 or 249 and by which functions of the authority are to be exercised by a manager on its behalf: s 250A(6) (as so added). A section 247 or 249 arrangement: (1) is not to be considered a management agreement; but (2) the Housing Act 1985 s 27(13), (15) applies to it as it applies to a management agreement: Housing and Regeneration Act 2008 s 250A(5) (as so added).
9 Housing and Regeneration Act 2008 s 250A(3) (as added: see note 1).
10 Eg a duty arising by virtue of the Housing Act 1985 s 27BA: see PARA 446.
11 Ie the Housing and Regeneration Act 2008 s 247 or s 249.
12 Housing and Regeneration Act 2008 s 250A(4) (as added: see note 1).

118. Appointment of a manager of a private registered provider. The following provisions apply if the regulator[1] is satisfied that: (1) a private registered provider[2] has failed to meet one of the standards in the Housing and Regeneration Act 2008[3]; (2) a private registered provider has failed to comply with certain provisions of the Welfare Reform and Work Act 2016 or regulations thereunder relating to the reduction in social housing rents[4]; or (3) the affairs of a private registered provider have been mismanaged[5] in relation to social housing[6].

The regulator may: (a) appoint an individual as a manager of the registered provider; or (b) require the registered provider to appoint an individual as a manager[7]. A manager has: (i) any power specified in the appointment or requirement; and (ii) any other power in relation to the registered provider's affairs required by the manager for the purposes specified in the appointment or requirement (including the power to enter into agreements and take other action[8] on behalf of the registered provider)[9].

Before acting under the above power[10] the regulator must give the registered provider a notice: (A) specifying grounds on which action might be taken under the provisions above; (B) warning the provider that the regulator is considering action under those provisions; and (C) explaining the effect of the following provisions[11]. The notice must specify a period during which the registered provider may make representations[12] to the regulator[13]. The period must be a period of at least 28 days and begin with the date on which the registered provider receives the notice[14]. The regulator must send a copy of a notice to the Greater London Authority (if the notice is given to a registered provider who owns land in Greater London) and any other persons it thinks appropriate (having regard, in particular, to any person who provided information as a result of which the notice is given)[15]. Notice under these provisions may be combined with notice under one or more other provisions[16] of the Housing and Regeneration Act 2008[17].

The regulator must notify the Greater London Authority of an appointment, or a requirement to appoint[18], a manager in respect of a registered provider who owns land in Greater London[19]. The regulator may require a manager to report to the regulator on the affairs specified[20] in the appointment or requirement[21].

A private registered provider may appeal to the High Court against an appointment of, or a requirement to appoint, a manager[22].

1 As to the meaning of 'the regulator' see PARA 57.
2 As to the meaning of 'private registered provider' see PARA 53.
3 Ie under the Housing and Regeneration Act 2008 s 193 or 194: see PARA 105.
4 Ie the Welfare Reform and Work Act 2016 s 23, regulations under s 27, and Sch 2 Pt 1: see PARA 55.
5 As to the meaning of 'mismanagement' see PARA 108 note 3.
6 Housing and Regeneration Act 2008 s 251(1) (amended by the Welfare Reform and Work Act 2016 s 30(1), (6); and by SI 2010/844). As to the meaning of 'social housing' see PARA 52.
7 Housing and Regeneration Act 2008 s 251(2). An appointment or requirement may relate to a manager: (1) of the registered provider's affairs generally in so far as they relate to social housing; or (2) of specified affairs relating to social housing: s 251(3). Appointment must be on terms and conditions (including as to remuneration) specified in, or determined in accordance with, the appointment or requirement: s 251(4).
8 As to the meaning of 'action' see PARA 73 note 13.
9 Housing and Regeneration Act 2008 s 251(5).
10 Ie under the Housing and Regeneration Act 2008 s 251(2).
11 Housing and Regeneration Act 2008 s 252(1). A notice under s 252(1) must: (1) refer to s 125 (voluntary undertaking: see PARA 74); and (2) indicate whether or to what extent the regulator would accept a voluntary undertaking instead of, or in mitigation of, action under s 251(2): s 252(5).
12 As to the meaning of 'representations' see PARA 72 note 18.
13 Housing and Regeneration Act 2008 s 252(2).
14 Housing and Regeneration Act 2008 s 252(3).
15 Housing and Regeneration Act 2008 s 252(4) (amended by the Localism Act 2011 ss 178, 195(1), 237, Sch 16 paras 1, 52(1), (2), Sch 19 paras 46, 64(1), (2), Sch 25 Pt 26). As to the Greater London Authority see LONDON GOVERNMENT vol 71 (2013) PARA 67 et seq.
16 Ie the Housing and Regeneration Act 2008 ss 230, 242, 248, 250: see PARAS 113, 114, 115, 116.
17 Housing and Regeneration Act 2008 s 252(6).
18 Ie under the Housing and Regeneration Act 2008 s 251(2).
19 Housing and Regeneration Act 2008 s 252(7A) (added by the Localism Act 2011 Sch 19 paras 46, 64(1), (3)).
20 Ie under the Housing and Regeneration Act 2008 s 251(3).
21 Housing and Regeneration Act 2008 s 252(8).
22 Housing and Regeneration Act 2008 s 252(9) (amended by SI 2010/844).

119. Appointment of advisers to local authorities. The following provisions apply to a registered provider[1] which is a local authority[2]. The power set out below is exercisable if the regulator[3] thinks: (1) that it is necessary to exercise it for the proper management of the authority's affairs so far as they relate to the provision of social housing[4] (its 'social housing affairs'); or (2) that it is desirable to exercise it in the interests of securing better services for the authority's tenants[5]. The regulator may: (a) appoint one or more advisers to assist the authority in relation to its social housing affairs (or a particular aspect of those affairs); or (b) require the authority to appoint one or more advisers for that purpose[6]. Appointment is to be on terms and conditions (including as to remuneration) specified in, or determined in accordance with, the appointment or requirement[7]. The authority must cooperate with any advisers appointed by virtue of these provisions[8].

1 As to the meaning of 'registered provider' see PARA 53.
2 Housing and Regeneration Act 2008 s 252A(1) (s 252A added by SI 2010/844). As to the meaning of 'local authority' see PARA 149 note 4 (definition applied by the Housing and Regeneration Act 2008 s 275).

3 As to the meaning of 'the regulator' see PARA 57.
4 As to the meaning of 'social housing' see PARA 52.
5 Housing and Regeneration Act 2008 s 252A(2) (as added: see note 2). As to the meaning of 'tenant' see PARA 52 note 9.
6 Housing and Regeneration Act 2008 s 252A(3) (as added: see note 2). A requirement under s 252A(3)(b) (head (b) in the text) may specify a process which the authority is required to implement for selecting and appointing advisers: s 252A(5) (as so added).
7 Housing and Regeneration Act 2008 s 252A(4) (as added: see note 2).
8 Housing and Regeneration Act 2008 s 252A(6) (as added: see note 2).

120. Transfer of land by private registered provider. The following provisions apply if, as a result of an inquiry[1] or an audit[2], the regulator[3] is satisfied that: (1) the affairs of a private registered provider[4] have been mismanaged[5] in relation to social housing[6]; or (2) a transfer of land by a private registered provider would be likely to improve the management of the land[7].

The regulator may require the registered provider to transfer specified land: (a) to the regulator; or (b) to another specified private registered provider[8]. A requirement may be imposed on a profit-making[9] registered provider only in relation to its social housing and associated land[10]. A requirement may not be imposed on a non-profit registered provider requiring it to transfer land to a profit-making registered provider[11]. A requirement may not be imposed on a registered charity[12]. A requirement may be imposed on a charity which is not registered (C1), but only for transfer to another charity (C2) whose objects the regulator thinks are similar to those of C1[13].

A requirement to transfer land may be imposed only with the Secretary of State's consent[14] (both as to the transfer and the terms)[15].

Where land is transferred to the regulator[16]: (i) the regulator may dispose of it only to a registered provider[17]; and (ii) if it is transferred by a non-profit registered provider, the regulator may dispose of it only to a non-profit registered provider[18].

1 Ie under the Housing and Regeneration Act 2008 s 206: see PARA 108.
2 Ie under the Housing and Regeneration Act 2008 s 210: see PARA 108.
3 As to the meaning of 'the regulator' see PARA 57.
4 As to the meaning of 'private registered provider' see PARA 53.
5 As to the meaning of 'mismanagement' see PARA 108 note 3.
6 As to the meaning of 'social housing' see PARA 52.
7 Housing and Regeneration Act 2008 s 253(1) (amended by SI 2010/844).
8 Housing and Regeneration Act 2008 s 253(2) (amended by SI 2010/844). A transfer under the Housing and Regeneration Act 2008 s 253 must be on terms specified in, or determined in accordance with, the requirement: s 254(1). The price must be not less than an amount certified by the district valuer as the amount the property would fetch if sold by a willing seller to another registered provider: s 254(2). The terms must include provision as to the payment of any debts or liabilities in respect of the land (whether or not secured on it): s 254(3). 'Price' includes premium; and 'district valuer' has the meaning given by the Housing Act 1985 s 622 (see PARA 527 note 14): Housing and Regeneration Act 2008 s 275.
9 As to when a body is a profit-making organisation see PARA 71 note 13.
10 Housing and Regeneration Act 2008 s 253(3) (amended by SI 2010/844). For the purposes of the Housing and Regeneration Act 2008 s 253(3) land is associated with social housing if the regulator thinks that it is used in connection with the social housing or its management: s 253(4).
11 Housing and Regeneration Act 2008 s 253(5).
12 Housing and Regeneration Act 2008 s 253(6). As to the meaning of 'registered charity' see PARA 53 note 2.
13 Housing and Regeneration Act 2008 s 253(7).
14 As to the Secretary of State see PARA 7. As to the meaning of 'consent' see PARA 80 note 29.
15 Housing and Regeneration Act 2008 s 254(4).
16 Ie under the Housing and Regeneration Act 2008 s 253(2)(a).
17 As to the meaning of 'registered provider' see PARA 53.
18 Housing and Regeneration Act 2008 s 254(5).

121. Amalgamation of registered societies. The following provisions apply if as a result of an inquiry[1] or an audit[2] the regulator[3] is satisfied that: (1) the affairs of a non-profit registered provider[4] which is a registered society[5] have been mismanaged[6] in relation to social housing[7]; or (2) the management of social housing owned by a non-profit registered provider which is a registered society would be improved if the provider were amalgamated with another registered society[8].

The regulator may make and execute on behalf of the society an instrument providing for the amalgamation of the society with another registered society[9]. The regulator may so act only with the Secretary of State's consent[10].

An instrument providing for the amalgamation of a society ('S1') with another has the same effect as a resolution by S1 under the Industrial and Provident Societies Act 1965[11] for the amalgamation of societies by special resolution[12]. A copy of an instrument must be sent to and registered by the Financial Conduct Authority[13]. An instrument does not take effect until the copy is registered[14]. The copy must be sent for registration during the period of 14 days beginning with the date of execution; but a copy registered after that period is valid[15].

Any body created by virtue of an amalgamation: (a) must be registered by the regulator and designated as a non-profit organisation; and (b) pending registration, is to be treated as registered and designated as a non-profit organisation[16].

1 Ie under the Housing and Regeneration Act 2008 s 206: see PARA 108.
2 Ie under the Housing and Regeneration Act 2008 s 210: see PARA 108.
3 As to the meaning of 'the regulator' see PARA 57.
4 As to the meaning of 'registered provider' see PARA 53; and as to when a body is a profit-making organisation see PARA 71 note 13.
5 As to the meaning of 'registered society' see PARA 52 note 10.
6 As to the meaning of 'mismanagement' see PARA 108 note 3.
7 As to the meaning of 'social housing' see PARA 52.
8 Housing and Regeneration Act 2008 s 255(1) (amended by the Co-operative and Community Benefit Societies Act 2014 s 151(1), Sch 4 paras 121–123).
9 Housing and Regeneration Act 2008 s 255(2) (amended by the Co-operative and Community Benefit Societies Act 2014 Sch 4 paras 121, 123).
10 Housing and Regeneration Act 2008 s 255(3). As to the Secretary of State see PARA 7. As to the meaning of 'consent' see PARA 80 note 29.
11 Ie under the Co-operative and Community Benefit Societies Act 2014 s 109: see FINANCIAL INSTITUTIONS vol 48 (2015) PARA 1053.
12 Housing and Regeneration Act 2008 s 255(4) (amended by the Co-operative and Community Benefit Societies Act 2014 Sch 4 paras 121, 123).
13 Housing and Regeneration Act 2008 s 255(5) (amended by SI 2013/496).
14 Housing and Regeneration Act 2008 s 255(6).
15 Housing and Regeneration Act 2008 s 255(7).
16 Housing and Regeneration Act 2008 s 255(8).

(F)   Powers in respect of Non-profit Registered Providers

122. Restrictions on dealings by non-profit registered providers. The regulator[1] may make an order under these provisions if: (1) an inquiry[2] is in progress in respect of a non-profit registered provider[3]; and (2) either of the two following cases applies[4].

Case 1 applies if the regulator has reasonable grounds for believing: (a) that the affairs of the registered provider have been mismanaged[5]; and (b) that the interests of tenants[6] of the registered provider, or its assets, require protection[7].

Case 2 applies if as a result of an inquirer's interim report[8] the regulator is satisfied that the affairs of the registered provider have been mismanaged[9].

The regulator may order a bank or other person who holds money or securities on behalf of the registered provider not to part with the money or securities without the regulator's consent[10].

The regulator may make an order restricting: (i) the transactions that may be entered into by the registered provider; or (ii) the nature and amounts of payments that may be made by it[11].

The regulator may make an order in respect of a registered provider that is a registered charity[12] only if it has received public assistance[13].

An order ceases to have effect at the end of the period of six months beginning with the day on which the inquirer's final report[14] is made[15]. However, the regulator may revoke the order before that time or (by order) extend it for a specified period of up to six months[16].

The following provisions apply if as a result of an inquiry[17] or an audit[18] the regulator is satisfied that the affairs of a non-profit registered provider have been mismanaged[19]. The regulator may order a bank or other person who holds money or securities on behalf of the registered provider not to part with the money or securities without the regulator's consent[20]. The regulator may make an order restricting: (A) the transactions that may be entered into by the registered provider; or (B) the nature and amounts of payments that may be made by it[21]. The regulator may make an order in respect of a registered provider that is a registered charity only if it has received public assistance[22]. An order under these provisions has effect until revoked by the regulator[23].

Before making an order under these provisions[24] the regulator must take all reasonable steps to give notice to the registered provider and, in the case of an order to a bank or other person not to part with money or securities without the regulator's consent[25], the person to whom the order is directed[26].

Contravention of an order not to part with money or securities without the regulator's consent[27] is an offence[28].

1 As to the meaning of 'the regulator' see PARA 57.
2 Ie under the Housing and Regeneration Act 2008 s 206: see PARA 108.
3 As to the meaning of 'registered provider' see PARA 53; and as to when a body is a profit-making organisation see PARA 71 note 13.
4 Housing and Regeneration Act 2008 s 256(1).
5 As to the meaning of 'mismanagement' see PARA 108 note 3.
6 As to the meaning of 'tenant' see PARA 52 note 9.
7 Housing and Regeneration Act 2008 s 256(2).
8 Ie under the Housing and Regeneration Act 2008 s 207: see PARA 108.
9 Housing and Regeneration Act 2008 s 256(3).
10 Housing and Regeneration Act 2008 s 256(4).
11 Housing and Regeneration Act 2008 s 256(5). An order under s 256(5) may in particular provide that transactions may not be entered into or payments made without the regulator's consent: s 256(6). As to the meaning of 'consent' see PARA 80 note 29.
12 As to the meaning of 'registered charity' see PARA 53 note 2.
13 Housing and Regeneration Act 2008 s 256(7). As to when a registered charity is considered to have received public assistance see PARA 108 note 21.
14 Ie under the Housing and Regeneration Act 2008 s 207.
15 Housing and Regeneration Act 2008 s 256(8).
16 Housing and Regeneration Act 2008 s 256(9).
17 Ie under the Housing and Regeneration Act 2008 s 206: see PARA 108.
18 Ie under the Housing and Regeneration Act 2008 s 210: see PARA 108.
19 Housing and Regeneration Act 2008 s 257(1).
20 Housing and Regeneration Act 2008 s 257(2).
21 Housing and Regeneration Act 2008 s 257(3). An order under s 257(3) may in particular provide that transactions may not be entered into or payments made without the regulator's consent: s 257(4).
22 Housing and Regeneration Act 2008 s 257(5).

23 Housing and Regeneration Act 2008 s 257(6).

24 Ie the Housing and Regeneration Act 2008 s 256 or s 257.

25 Ie an order under the Housing and Regeneration Act 2008 s 256(4) or s 257(2).

26 Housing and Regeneration Act 2008 s 258(1).

27 Ie an order under the Housing and Regeneration Act 2008 s 256(4) or s 257(2).

28 Housing and Regeneration Act 2008 s 258(2). A person guilty of an offence is liable on summary conviction to a fine not exceeding level 5 on the standard scale: s 258(3). As to the powers of magistrates' courts to issue fines on summary conviction see SENTENCING vol 92 (2015) PARA 176. Proceedings for an offence may be brought only by or with the consent of: (1) the regulator; or (2) the Director of Public Prosecutions: s 258(4). As to the Director of Public Prosecutions see CRIMINAL PROCEDURE vol 27 (2015) PARAS 25, 30 et seq.

123. Suspension and removal of officers of non-profit registered providers. The regulator[1] may make an order under these provisions if: (1) an inquiry[2] is in progress in respect of a non-profit registered provider[3]; and (2) either of the following cases applies[4].

Case 1 applies if the regulator has reasonable grounds for believing: (a) that the affairs of the registered provider have been mismanaged[5]; and (b) that the interests of tenants[6] of the registered provider, or its assets, require protection[7].

Case 2 applies if as a result of an inquirer's interim report[8] the regulator is satisfied that the affairs of the registered provider have been mismanaged[9].

The regulator may by order suspend any officer[10], employee or agent of the registered provider who it thinks has contributed to the failure or mismanagement[11]. The regulator may suspend an officer, employee or agent of a registered charity[12] only if the charity has received public assistance[13].

Such a suspension order ceases to have effect at the end of the period of six months beginning with the day on which the inquirer's final report[14] is made[15]. However, the regulator may revoke an order before the end of that period[16].

The regulator must notify the Charity Commission[17] if it suspends an officer, employee or agent of a registered charity[18].

The following provisions apply if as a result of an inquiry[19] or an audit[20] the regulator is satisfied that the affairs of a non-profit registered provider have been mismanaged[21]. The regulator may by order remove any officer, employee or agent of the registered provider who it thinks has contributed to the failure or mismanagement[22]. Pending a decision whether to remove an officer, employee or agent, the regulator may by order suspend the person for a specified period of up to six months[23]. The regulator may remove or suspend an officer, employee or agent of a registered charity only if the charity has received public assistance[24]. Before making an order the regulator must take all reasonable steps to give at least 14 days' notice to the person and the registered provider[25]. The regulator must notify the Charity Commission if it removes or suspends an officer, employee or agent of a registered charity[26].

Where the regulator suspends an officer, employee or agent of a registered provider[27], the regulator may give directions to the registered provider about: (i) the performance of the suspended person's functions; and (ii) any other matter arising from the suspension[28]. The regulator may appoint a person to perform the suspended person's functions[29].

A person is disqualified from acting as an officer of a registered provider if the person has been removed under specified[30] statutory provisions[31]. The regulator may waive a disqualification either generally or in relation to a particular registered provider or class of registered providers[32]. A waiver may be granted only on an application by the disqualified person[33]. The regulator must notify a person whose disqualification is waived[34]. If a disqualified person acts as an officer of a registered provider, the person's acts are not invalid by reason only of the disqualification[35].

The regulator must maintain a register of disqualified[36] persons[37]. The register must show details of any waivers[38]. The regulator must make the register available for inspection by the public[39].

It is an offence for a person to act as an officer of a registered provider in respect of which the person is disqualified under the provisions above[40]. In addition, where the regulator is satisfied that a person has acted as an officer of a registered provider in respect of which the person is disqualified and, in doing so, has received payments or other benefits from the registered provider, the regulator may require the person to repay the sum or, as the case may be, a specified amount representing the whole or part of the value of the benefit[41]. If a person fails to comply with a requirement the registered provider may recover the sum or specified amount as a debt[42].

The regulator may by order remove an officer of a non-profit registered provider if one of the cases listed below applies to the officer[43].

Case 1 applies to a person who has been made bankrupt[44].

Case 2 applies to a person who has made an arrangement with creditors[45].

Case 3 applies to a person who is subject to a disqualification order or a disqualification undertaking under the Company Directors Disqualification Act 1986 or equivalent legislation in Northern Ireland[46].

Case 4 applies to a person who is subject to an order[47] providing for disabilities on the revocation of a County Court administration order[48].

Case 5 applies to a person who is disqualified[49] from being a charity trustee[50].

Case 6 applies to a person who is incapable of acting by reason of mental disorder[51].

Case 7 applies to a person who is impeding the proper management of the registered provider by reason of absence or failure to act[52].

Before making an order in respect of an officer the regulator must take all reasonable steps to give at least 14 days' notice to the officer and the registered provider[53]. An order may be made in respect of an officer of a registered charity only if the charity has received public assistance[54].

A person removed or suspended[55] may appeal to the High Court[56].

The regulator may by order appoint a person as an officer of a non-profit registered provider: (A) to replace an officer removed by order; (B) where there are no officers; or (C) if the regulator thinks an additional officer is necessary to ensure that the registered provider's affairs are managed in accordance with legal requirements (imposed by or under an Act or otherwise)[57]. The regulator may only appoint more than a minority of the officers of a registered provider if the provider has fewer officers than required by its constitution[58] or its constitution does not specify a minimum number of officers[59]. An order appointing an officer must specify the period for which, and the terms on which, the office is to be held[60]. However, on the expiry of the appointment the regulator may by order renew the appointment and the officer may resign or retire in accordance with the registered provider's constitution[61]. An officer appointed by order has the same rights, powers and obligations as an officer appointed under the registered provider's constitution[62].

1   As to the meaning of 'the regulator' see PARA 57.
2   Ie under the Housing and Regeneration Act 2008 s 206: see PARA 108.

3 As to the meaning of 'registered provider' see PARA 53; and as to when a body is a profit-making organisation see PARA 71 note 13.
4 Housing and Regeneration Act 2008 s 259(1).
5 As to the meaning of 'mismanagement' see PARA 108 note 3.
6 As to the meaning of 'tenant' see PARA 52 note 9.
7 Housing and Regeneration Act 2008 s 259(2).
8 Ie under the Housing and Regeneration Act 2008 s 207: see PARA 108.
9 Housing and Regeneration Act 2008 s 259(3).
10 As to the meaning of 'officer' see PARA 78 note 6.
11 Housing and Regeneration Act 2008 s 259(4).
12 As to the meaning of 'registered charity' see PARA 53 note 2.
13 Housing and Regeneration Act 2008 s 259(5). As to when a registered charity is considered to have received public assistance see PARA 108 note 21.
14 Ie under the Housing and Regeneration Act 2008 s 207: see PARA 108.
15 Housing and Regeneration Act 2008 s 259(6).
16 Housing and Regeneration Act 2008 s 259(7).
17 As to the meaning of 'Charity Commission' see PARA 53 note 3.
18 Housing and Regeneration Act 2008 s 259(8).
19 Ie under the Housing and Regeneration Act 2008 s 206: see PARA 108.
20 Ie under the Housing and Regeneration Act 2008 s 210: see PARA 108.
21 Housing and Regeneration Act 2008 s 260(1).
22 Housing and Regeneration Act 2008 s 260(2).
23 Housing and Regeneration Act 2008 s 260(3).
24 Housing and Regeneration Act 2008 s 260(4).
25 Housing and Regeneration Act 2008 s 260(5).
26 Housing and Regeneration Act 2008 s 260(6).
27 Ie under the Housing and Regeneration Act 2008 s 259 or s 260.
28 Housing and Regeneration Act 2008 s 261(1), (2).
29 Housing and Regeneration Act 2008 s 261(3).
30 Ie under the Housing and Regeneration Act 2008 s 260, the Housing Act 1996 Sch 1 para 24(2)(a) (see PARA 202), the Housing Associations Act 1985 s 30(1)(a) (repealed) or the Housing Act 1974 s 20(1)(a) (repealed) (other similar provisions).
31 Housing and Regeneration Act 2008 s 262(1).
32 Housing and Regeneration Act 2008 s 262(2).
33 Housing and Regeneration Act 2008 s 262(3).
34 Housing and Regeneration Act 2008 s 262(4).
35 Housing and Regeneration Act 2008 s 262(5).
36 Ie under the Housing and Regeneration Act 2008 s 262.
37 Housing and Regeneration Act 2008 s 263(1).
38 Housing and Regeneration Act 2008 s 263(2).
39 Housing and Regeneration Act 2008 s 263(3).
40 Housing and Regeneration Act 2008 s 264(1). A person guilty of an offence is liable: (1) on summary conviction, to imprisonment for a term not exceeding 12 months or a fine not exceeding the statutory maximum or both; (2) on conviction on indictment, to imprisonment for a term not exceeding two years or a fine or both: s 264(2). Proceedings for an offence may be brought only by or with the consent of: (a) the regulator; or (b) the Director of Public Prosecutions: s 264(3). As to the powers of magistrates' courts to issue fines on summary conviction see SENTENCING vol 92 (2015) PARA 176. In relation to an offence committed before the commencement of the Criminal Justice Act 2003 s 282 (short sentences: see SENTENCING vol 92 (2015) PARA 2) the reference in the Housing and Regeneration Act 2008 s 264(2)(a) to 12 months has effect as if it were a reference to six months: s 264(4). At the date at which this volume states the law, no day had been appointed for the commencement of the Criminal Justice Act 2003 s 282. As to the Director of Public Prosecutions see CRIMINAL PROCEDURE vol 27 (2015) PARAS 25, 30 et seq.
41 Housing and Regeneration Act 2008 s 265(1), (2).
42 Housing and Regeneration Act 2008 s 265(3).
43 Housing and Regeneration Act 2008 s 266(1).
44 Housing and Regeneration Act 2008 s 266(2) (amended by SI 2016/481).
45 Housing and Regeneration Act 2008 s 266(3). As to arrangements with creditors see BANKRUPTCY AND INDIVIDUAL INSOLVENCY vol 5 (2013) PARA 852 et seq.
46 Housing and Regeneration Act 2008 s 266(4). As to such disqualification see COMPANIES vol 15A (2016) PARA 1762.
47 Ie under the Insolvency Act 1986 s 429(2): see BANKRUPTCY AND INDIVIDUAL INSOLVENCY vol 5 (2013) PARA 914.

48 Housing and Regeneration Act 2008 s 266(5).
49 Ie under the Charities Act 2011 s 178: see CHARITIES vol 8 (2015) PARA 276.
50 Housing and Regeneration Act 2008 s 266(6) (amended by the Charities Act 2011 s 354(1), Sch 7 para 134).
51 Housing and Regeneration Act 2008 s 266(7). As to mental disorder see MENTAL HEALTH AND CAPACITY vol 75 (2013) PARA 761.
52 Housing and Regeneration Act 2008 s 266(8).
53 Housing and Regeneration Act 2008 s 267(1).
54 Housing and Regeneration Act 2008 s 267(2).
55 Ie under the Housing and Regeneration Act 2008 s 259, 260 or 266.
56 Housing and Regeneration Act 2008 s 268.
57 Housing and Regeneration Act 2008 s 269(1) (amended by the Housing and Planning Act 2016 s 92, Sch 4 paras 36, 37). This overrides any restriction on eligibility or numbers of officers imposed by the body's constitution: Housing and Regeneration Act 2008 s 269(3). The regulator may exercise the power in s 269(1) in respect of a registered charity only if: (1) a condition in s 274 is satisfied (see PARA 108 note 21); and (2) the regulator has consulted the Charity Commission: s 269(6).
58 As to the meaning of 'constitution' see PARA 71 note 6.
59 Housing and Regeneration Act 2008 s 269(2).
60 Housing and Regeneration Act 2008 s 269(4).
61 Housing and Regeneration Act 2008 s 269(4)(a), (b).
62 Housing and Regeneration Act 2008 s 269(5).

(G) Powers in respect of Local Authorities

124. Censure of local authority employees. The regulator[1] may give a censure notice to a local authority[2] if: (1) an inquiry[3] is in progress in respect of the authority; and (2) either of the following cases applies[4].

Case 1 applies if the regulator has reasonable grounds for believing: (a) that the affairs of the authority have been mismanaged[5]; and (b) that the interests of tenants[6] of the authority, or its assets, require protection[7].

Case 2 applies if as a result of an inquirer's interim report[8] the regulator is satisfied that the affairs of the authority have been mismanaged[9].

The regulator may also give a censure notice to a local authority if, as a result of an inquiry[10], the regulator is satisfied that the affairs of the authority have been mismanaged[11].

A censure notice is a notice identifying an employee or agent of the authority who the regulator thinks has contributed to the failure or mismanagement[12]. The notice must include the regulator's reasons[13]. The regulator must send a copy of the notice to the employee or agent concerned[14]. No more than one employee or agent may be identified in a censure notice (but this does not prevent several notices being given in respect of the same failure or mismanagement)[15]. Members of local authorities may not be identified in censure notices[16].

A local authority to which a censure notice is given must respond to the regulator in writing within 28 days of receipt of the notice[17]. The response must: (i) explain what action[18] (if any) the authority has taken or proposes to take in relation to the employee or agent; (ii) explain why the authority does not think the employee or agent has contributed to the failure or mismanagement; or (iii) explain why the authority does not think its affairs have been mismanaged[19].

1 As to the meaning of 'the regulator' see PARA 57.
2 As to the meaning of 'local authority' see PARA 149 note 4 (definition applied by the Housing and Regeneration Act 2008 s 275).
3 Ie under the Housing and Regeneration Act 2008 s 206: see PARA 108.
4 Housing and Regeneration Act 2008 s 269A(1) (s 269A added by SI 2010/844).
5 As to the meaning of 'mismanagement' see PARA 108 note 3.
6 As to the meaning of 'tenant' see PARA 52 note 9.
7 Housing and Regeneration Act 2008 s 269A(2) (as added: see note 4).
8 Ie under the Housing and Regeneration Act 2008 s 207: see PARA 108.

9 Housing and Regeneration Act 2008 s 269A(3) (as added: see note 4).
10 Ie under the Housing and Regeneration Act 2008 s 206.
11 Housing and Regeneration Act 2008 s 269A(4) (as added: see note 4).
12 Housing and Regeneration Act 2008 s 269A(5) (as added: see note 4).
13 Housing and Regeneration Act 2008 s 269A(6) (as added: see note 4).
14 Housing and Regeneration Act 2008 s 269A(7) (as added: see note 4).
15 Housing and Regeneration Act 2008 s 269A(8) (as added: see note 4).
16 Housing and Regeneration Act 2008 s 269A(9) (as added: see note 4).
17 Housing and Regeneration Act 2008 s 269B(1) (s 269B added by SI 2010/844).
18 As to the meaning of 'action' see PARA 73 note 13.
19 Housing and Regeneration Act 2008 s 269B(2) (as added: see note 17).

H.   DUTIES AND POWERS OF HOMES AND COMMUNITIES AGENCY

125. Duties in relation to social housing. If the Homes and Communities Agency ('HCA')[1] acquires, constructs or converts any housing or other land for use as low cost rental accommodation[2], the HCA must ensure that a registered provider of social housing[3] is the landlord of the accommodation when it is made available for rent[4].

If the HCA disposes of any housing or other land to a person on condition that the person provides low cost rental accommodation (whether in the same or different housing or other land), the HCA must impose a further condition that a registered provider of social housing is the landlord of the accommodation when it is made available for rent[5].

If the HCA provides infrastructure to a person on condition that the person provides low cost rental accommodation, the HCA must impose a further condition ensuring that a registered provider of social housing is the landlord of the accommodation when it is made available for rent[6].

If the HCA is proposing to give financial assistance on condition that the recipient provides low cost rental accommodation, the HCA must impose a further condition ensuring that a registered provider of social housing is the landlord of the accommodation when it is made available for rent[7].

For these purposes, a person provides low cost rental accommodation if (and only if) the person acquires, constructs or converts any housing or other land for use as low cost rental accommodation or ensures such acquisition, construction or conversion by another[8].

1 As to the establishment of the Homes and Communities Agency ('HCA') see the Housing and Regeneration Act 2008 s 1, Sch 1; and PLANNING vol 83 (2010) PARA 1454 et seq. As to the exercise of the HCA's housing functions through the Regulation Committee see PARA 57 et seq.
2 As to the meaning of 'low cost rental accommodation' see PARA 52 note 2 (definition applied by the Housing and Regeneration Act 2008 s 31(12)).
3 As to registered providers of social housing see PARA 53. As to the meaning of 'social housing' see PARA 52 (definition applied by s 32(13)).
4 Housing and Regeneration Act 2008 s 31(1), (2) (s 31(2) amended by SI 2010/844). As to the HCA's regulatory role see PARA 57.
5 Housing and Regeneration Act 2008 s 31(3), (4) (s 31(4) amended by SI 2010/844).
6 Housing and Regeneration Act 2008 s 31(5), (6) (s 31(6) amended by SI 2010/844).
7 Housing and Regeneration Act 2008 s 31(7), (8) (s 31(8) amended by SI 2010/844).
8 Housing and Regeneration Act 2008 s 31(11) (amended by the Localism Act 2011 ss 178, 237, Sch 16 paras 1, 4(1), (3)(a), Sch 25 Pt 26).

126. Recovery of social housing assistance. The Homes and Communities Agency ('HCA')[1] may, in such events as it may determine, exercise the powers conferred by the following provisions[2] in relation to a person who has received social housing assistance[3].

The HCA may reduce any grant payable by it or restrict any other social housing assistance due from it[4]. The HCA may suspend or cancel any instalment of any grant payable by it or any aspect of any other social housing assistance due from it[5]. The HCA may direct the recipient of any social housing assistance given by way of grant to: (1) apply or appropriate for such purposes of the recipient as the HCA may specify; or (2) pay to the HCA, such amount as the HCA may specify[6]. The HCA may not specify an amount which exceeds the recoverable amount[7].

In exercising its powers the HCA must act in accordance with such principles as it has determined[8].

A person who has received social housing assistance must notify the HCA if an event of a kind determined by the HCA[9] occurs after the assistance has been given[10]. Such a person must, if required by notice of the HCA, supply the HCA with such particulars of, and information relating to, the event as are specified in the notice[11].

Events and principles determined by the HCA[12] must be determined on or before the time the HCA gives the social housing assistance concerned unless they are determined subsequently with the agreement of the recipient of the assistance[13].

If social housing assistance has been given to a person and at any time the social housing provided as a result of the assistance becomes vested in, or is leased for a term of years to, or reverts to, another person, the statutory provisions[14] have effect in relation to periods after that time as if the assistance, or such element of it as may be determined by the HCA to be appropriate[15], had been given to that other person ('the successor')[16].

The HCA must not make a general determination[17] without the consent of the Secretary of State[18]. Before making such a determination, the HCA must consult such persons as it considers appropriate[19]. If a general determination about relevant events[20] relates to social housing assistance given to a registered provider of social housing, the HCA must, in particular, consult such bodies appearing to it to represent the interests of registered providers of social housing as it considers appropriate[21].

The HCA must publish a general determination in such manner as it considers appropriate for bringing the determination to the attention of those affected by it[22]. A general determination of the HCA may make different provision for different cases or descriptions[23] of case (including different provision for different areas)[24].

A determination of the HCA may be varied or revoked by it (subject to any provision as to the time by which such a determination must be made)[25].

1 As to the HCA see PARA 125 note 1. As to the exercise of the HCA's housing functions through the Regulation Committee see PARA 57 et seq.
2 Ie the Housing and Regeneration Act 2008 s 32(2)–(4).
3 Housing and Regeneration Act 2008 s 32(1). 'Social housing assistance' means financial assistance given under s 19 (see PLANNING vol 83 (2010) PARA 1474) on condition that the recipient provides social housing (whether by itself or as part of a wider project): s 32(13). 'Social housing' has the same meaning as in Pt 2 (ss 59–278A) (see PARA 52) and, for the purposes of Pt 1 (ss 1–58), a person provides social housing if (and only if) the person acquires, constructs, converts, improves or repairs any housing or other land for use as social housing or ensures such acquisition, construction, conversion, improvement or repair by another: s 32(13).
4 Housing and Regeneration Act 2008 s 32(2).
5 Housing and Regeneration Act 2008 s 32(3).
6 Housing and Regeneration Act 2008 s 32(4). A direction by the HCA under s 32(4) may require the application, appropriation or payment, in addition to the specified amount, of one or more of the following: (1) interest on the specified amount; (2) an amount calculated by reference to any increase in the market value of any housing or other land acquired, constructed, converted, improved or repaired as a result of the grant; and (3) interest on the amount falling within head

(2): s 33(1). Any direction falling within head (1) or (3) must specify: (a) the applicable rate or rates of interest (whether fixed or variable); (b) the date from which interest is payable; and (c) any provision for suspended or reduced interest which is applicable: s 33(2). The date specified under head (b) must not be earlier than the date of the event giving rise to the power to give a direction: s 33(3). In head (c): (i) provision for suspended interest means provision to the effect that if the principal amount is applied, appropriated or paid before a date specified in the direction, no interest will be payable for any period after the date of the direction; and (ii) provision for reduced interest means provision to the effect that if the principal amount is so applied, appropriated or paid, any interest payable will be payable at a rate or rates lower than the rate or rates which would otherwise be applicable: s 33(4). Any direction falling within head (2) must specify the housing or other land concerned and the method of calculating the amount concerned: s 33(5).

The matters specified in a direction under s 33(2)(a)–(c) or (5), and the element mentioned in s 33(7) (see the text to note 16), are to be: (A) such as the HCA, acting in accordance with such principles as it may determine, may specify as being appropriate; or (B) such as the HCA may determine to be appropriate in the particular case: s 33(8). Principles determined by the HCA under head (A), and determinations by the HCA under head (B), must be determined on or before the time the HCA gives the social housing assistance concerned unless they are determined subsequently with the agreement of the recipient of the assistance: s 33(9).

7 Housing and Regeneration Act 2008 s 32(5). This is without prejudice to the power of the HCA under s 33(1) (see note 6): s 32(7). The recoverable amount is: (1) the total amount of grant received by the person to whom the direction is given; less (2) the total of any amounts applied, appropriated or paid in accordance with any previous directions given in respect of that grant under s 32(4), and for the purposes of head (2) any amounts provided for by virtue of s 33(1) (see note 6) are to be ignored: s 32(6).

8 Housing and Regeneration Act 2008 s 32(8).

9 Ie under the Housing and Regeneration Act 2008 s 32(1).

10 Housing and Regeneration Act 2008 s 32(9).

11 Housing and Regeneration Act 2008 s 32(10). 'Notice' means notice in writing: s 57(1).

12 Ie under the Housing and Regeneration Act 2008 s 32(1) and (8) respectively.

13 Housing and Regeneration Act 2008 s 32(12).

14 Ie the Housing and Regeneration Act 2008 s 32 and s 33 (including s 33(7)).

15 See note 6.

16 Housing and Regeneration Act 2008 s 33(6), (7) (amended by the Housing and Planning Act 2016 s 94(1), (2), (4)). However, the Housing and Regeneration Act 2008 s 33(7) does not apply if: (1) the successor is a person other than a registered provider of social housing; and (2) at any time since the social housing assistance was given: (a) a person has enforced a security over the social housing; or (b) the social housing has been disposed of by a body while it is being wound up or is in administration (which, for this purpose, includes housing administration under the Housing and Planning Act 2016 Pt 4 Ch 5 (ss 95–117): see PARA 90 et seq): Housing and Regeneration Act 2008 s 33(6A) (added by the Housing and Planning Act 2016 s 94(1), (3).

17 Ie under the Housing and Regeneration Act 2008 s 32 or 33. 'General determination' means a determination which does not relate solely to a particular case: s 34(9).

18 Housing and Regeneration Act 2008 s 34(1). As to the Secretary of State see PARA 7.

19 Housing and Regeneration Act 2008 s 34(2) (amended by the Localism Act 2011 ss 178, 237, Sch 16 paras 1, 6, Sch 25 Pt 26).

20 'Relevant event' means an event of a kind determined by the HCA under the Housing and Regeneration Act 2008 s 32(1): s 34(9).

21 Housing and Regeneration Act 2008 s 34(3), (4).

22 Housing and Regeneration Act 2008 s 34(5).

23 For the purposes of the Housing and Regeneration Act 2008 s 34(6) descriptions may be framed by reference to any matters whatever: s 34(7).

24 Housing and Regeneration Act 2008 s 34(6).

25 Housing and Regeneration Act 2008 s 34(8).

127. Duty to give financial assistance in respect of certain disposals. The Homes and Communities Agency ('HCA')[1] must exercise its powers[2] to give financial assistance by way of grant to a relevant provider of social housing[3] in respect of any discount given by the provider by virtue of a person exercising the right to acquire[4] a dwelling[5].

The amount of the grant given by virtue of the above provisions to a relevant provider of social housing for any year is to be the aggregate value of the discounts given by that provider in that year[6]. The amount of the grant so given to a relevant provider of social housing must not exceed the amount of the discount to which the tenant would have been entitled in respect of the other dwelling[7].

The HCA must specify: (1) the procedure to be followed in relation to applications for a grant by virtue of these provisions; (2) the manner in which, and time or times at which, a grant is to be paid; (3) any other terms or conditions on which such a grant is given[8].

1 As to the HCA see PARA 125 note 1.
2 Ie under the Housing and Regeneration Act 2008 s 19: see PLANNING vol 83 (2010) PARA 1474.
3 'Relevant provider of social housing' means: (1) a private registered provider of social housing; or (2) a registered social landlord: Housing and Regeneration Act 2008 s 35(6) (amended by SI 2010/844). 'Private registered provider of social housing' includes a person falling within the Housing and Regeneration Act 2008 s 180(3) (see PARA 102); and 'registered social landlord' has the same meaning as in the Housing Act 1996 Pt I (ss A1–64) (see PARA 166 et seq): Housing and Regeneration Act 2008 s 35(6) (as so amended). As to the meaning of 'social housing' see PARA 52 (definition applied by s 32(13)).
4 Ie the right conferred by the Housing and Regeneration Act 2008 s 180: see PARAS 102, 240.
5 Housing and Regeneration Act 2008 s 35(1) (substituted by the Housing and Planning Act 2016 s 67(1), (2)). As to the meaning of 'dwelling' see PARA 52 note 8 (definition applied by the Housing and Regeneration Act 2008 s 35(6)).
6 Housing and Regeneration Act 2008 s 35(3).
7 Housing and Regeneration Act 2008 s 35(4) (amended by the Housing and Planning Act 2016 s 67(1), (4)). As to the meaning of 'tenant' see PARA 52 note 9 (definition applied by the Housing and Regeneration Act 2008 s 35(6)).
8 Housing and Regeneration Act 2008 s 35(5) (amended by the Housing and Planning Act 2016 s 67(1), (5)).

128. Information in relation to social housing. The Secretary of State[1] may by order[2] provide for the Homes and Communities Agency ('HCA')[3] to supply such information about:

(1)   which accommodation provided directly or indirectly by it is to be social housing[4];

(2)   the type of social housing to be so provided; and

(3)   the consequences of it being social housing,

as may be specified or described in the order[5].

An order may, in particular, provide for:

(a)   the person or persons to whom the information is to be provided;

(b)   the time at which, or period or frequency within which, the information is to be provided;

(c)   the form and manner in which the information is to be provided[6].

1 As to the Secretary of State see PARA 7.
2 As to orders by the Secretary of State see PARA 54.
3 As to the HCA see PARA 125 note 1.
4 As to the meaning of 'social housing' see PARA 52 (definition applied by the Housing and Regeneration Act 2008 s 32(13)).
5 Housing and Regeneration Act 2008 s 36(1).
6 Housing and Regeneration Act 2008 s 36(2).

129. Further powers of the Regulator of Social Housing with respect to land of certain housing associations. The following provisions apply where the Housing Corporation (which has now been abolished)[1] made a loan to a housing association[2], the Housing Corporation's rights and obligations in respect of the loan have been transferred to the Regulator of Social Housing[3] and the loan has not been repaid[4].

The Regulator of Social Housing may give the association directions with respect to the disposal of land belonging to the association in which the Regulator of Social Housing has an interest as mortgagee under a mortgage, or as creditor in a heritable security[5], entered into by the association to secure the loan[6]. The written consent of the Secretary of State is required for the giving, varying or revoking of directions by the Regulator of Social Housing[7].

If it appears to the Regulator of Social Housing:

(1)   that the association is experiencing difficulty in providing housing accommodation on any land which it has acquired or in managing housing accommodation provided by it on any land, or is in any way failing to perform its functions as a housing association in relation to any land, and that accordingly it is undesirable for the land in question to remain in the hands of the association;

(2)   that there is no other housing association, whether in existence or about to be formed, to which the association's interest in the land in question can suitably be transferred; and

(3)   that the land is capable of being, or continuing to be, used to provide housing accommodation for letting,

the Regulator of Social Housing may prepare and submit to the Secretary of State a scheme[8]. The scheme must be for the Regulator of Social Housing:

(a)   to acquire the association's interest in the land;

(b)   to undertake all such operations as may be required for the provision or continued provision on the land of housing accommodation for letting (including any operation which might have been carried out by a housing association in connection with the provision of housing accommodation); and

(c)   to retain the accommodation and keep it available for letting so long as the scheme has not been terminated in any manner provided for in the scheme[9].

Where such a scheme is submitted to the Secretary of State by the Regulator of Social Housing, the Secretary of State, on being satisfied of:

(i)   the undesirability of the land remaining in the hands of the association; and

(ii)   the lack of any housing association to which it can suitably be transferred,

may, if he thinks fit, approve the scheme[10]. If he does so, the Regulator of Social Housing will have power to acquire for the purposes of the scheme the association's interest in the land and to carry through the provisions of the scheme[11].

1   As to the Housing Corporation (now abolished) see PARA 2.
2   Ie under the Housing Act 1964 s 2 before its repeal by the Housing (Consequential Provisions) Act 1985 s 3, Sch 1 Pt I.
3   Ie by the Transfer of Housing Corporation Functions (Modifications and Transitional Provisions) Order 2008, SI 2008/2839, arts 1(2), 2, 6. As to the Regulator of Social Housing see PARA 57 et seq.
4   Housing Associations Act 1985 s 82, Sch 7 para 1 (s 82 amended by the Government of Wales Act 1998 s 140, Sch 16 para 28(a); the Housing Associations Act 1985 Sch 7 para 1 substituted by SI 2010/866).
5   'Heritable security' is a term of Scots law.
6   Housing Associations Act 1985 Sch 7 para 2(1) (amended by the Government of Wales Act 1998 ss 140, 152, Sch 16 para 53(2)(a), Sch 18 Pt VI; and by SI 2010/866). Directions so given may be varied or revoked by subsequent directions: Housing Associations Act 1985 Sch 7 para 2(2) (amended by the Government of Wales Act 1998 Sch 16 para 53(2)(b), Sch 18 Pt VI). Where the Regulator of Social Housing proposes to give a housing association directions under the Housing Associations Act 1985 Sch 7 para 2 requiring the association to transfer to the Regulator of Social Housing the association's interest in any land, the Secretary of State may not consent to the giving of the directions unless he at the same time approves, or has previously approved, a scheme under Sch 7 para 5 with respect to that land: Sch 7 para 3 (amended by the Government of Wales Act 1998 Sch 16 para 53(3); and by SI 2010/866). Where the Regulator of Social Housing proposes to

give directions under the Housing Associations Act 1985 Sch 7 para 2 to an association whose rules restrict membership to persons entitled or prospectively entitled (whether as tenants or otherwise) to occupy a dwelling provided or managed by the association requiring the association to transfer its interest in any such land to the Regulator of Social Housing, or to any other person, the Secretary of State may not consent to the giving of the directions unless he is satisfied that arrangements have been made which, if the directions are given, will secure that the members of the association receive fair treatment in connection with the transfer: Sch 7 para 4(1) (amended by the Government of Wales Act 1998 Sch 16 para 53(4); and by SI 2010/866). As to the Secretary of State see PARA 7.

7   Housing Associations Act 1985 Sch 7 para 2(3) (added by the Government of Wales Act 1998 Sch 16 para 53(2)(c); and amended by SI 2010/866).
8   Housing Associations Act 1985 Sch 7 para 5(1) (amended by the Government of Wales Act 1998 Sch 16 para 53(3)(a), (5)(a); and by SI 2010/866).
9   Housing Associations Act 1985 Sch 7 para 5(2) (amended by SI 2010/866).
10   Housing Associations Act 1985 Sch 7 para 5(3) (amended by SI 2010/866).
11   Housing Associations Act 1985 Sch 7 para 5(4) (amended by SI 2010/866). A scheme approved by the Secretary of State under the Housing Associations Act 1985 Sch 7 para 5 may be varied from time to time in accordance with proposals in that behalf made by the Regulator of Social Housing and approved by the Secretary of State: Sch 7 para 5(5) (amended by SI 2010/866).

I.   THE HOUSING OMBUDSMAN SERVICE FOR SOCIAL LANDLORD TENANTS IN ENGLAND

130. Introduction. Following consultations[1], a housing association tenants' ombudsman service was created in September 1993 on a non-statutory basis. The service was set up by the Housing Corporation[2] and its powers derived from the Housing Corporation's statutory powers[3]; thus it was not fully independent of the Housing Corporation. There is provision in the Housing Act 1996 for an independent ombudsman scheme in England, under which the Housing Ombudsman Service has been established[4].

1   See the Housing Corporation publication *Resolving Housing Association Tenant Complaints: the Way Forward* (February 1993).
2   As to the Housing Corporation (now abolished) see PARA 2.
3   Eg under the Housing Associations Act 1985 s 27A (repealed).
4   See the Housing Act 1996 s 51, Sch 2; and PARA 131 et seq. See also *Our Future Homes* (Cm 2901) (1995) p 41.
      Amendments to the scheme were made by the Localism Act 2011, including the transfer of functions relating to the investigation of housing complaints to the housing ombudsman from the commissioners for local administration. See eg PARAS 131, 138.
      The Housing Ombudsman Service does not presently handle complaints relating to public housing, and it only operates in England: see further PARAS 9, 131.

131. Provision for a scheme. Provision has been made[1] for the purpose of enabling tenants[2] and other individuals to have complaints against social landlords[3] investigated by a housing ombudsman in accordance with a scheme approved by the Secretary of State[4]. These provisions do not apply, however, in relation to social landlords in Wales[5].

Nothing in the relevant statutory provisions may be construed as restricting membership of an approved scheme to social landlords[6]. Other landlords can become members.

A social landlord, other than a local housing authority, must be a member of an approved scheme covering, or more than one approved scheme which together cover, all his housing activities[7]. A social landlord which is a local housing authority must be a member of an approved scheme covering, or more than one scheme which together cover: (1) action which: (a) is taken by or on behalf of the authority in its capacity as a registered provider of social housing; and (b) is action in connection with its housing activities so far as they relate to the provision or management of social housing[8]; and (2) action taken by or on behalf of the authority in connection with the management of dwellings owned by the authority and let on a long lease[9].

If a social landlord fails to comply with this duty, the Secretary of State may apply to the High Court for an order directing him to comply within a specified period and the High Court may, if it thinks fit, make such an order[10].

1 Ie by the Housing Act 1996 s 51(1), Sch 2: see the text and notes 2–8; and PARA 132 et seq. See also *The Independent Housing Ombudsman Scheme* (December 1996).
2 As to the meaning of 'tenant' see PARA 168 note 16.
3 For these purposes, a 'social landlord' means:
   (1)   a private registered provider of social housing (see PARA 53);
   (2)   a local authority in England which is a registered provider of social housing (as to the meaning of 'local authority' see PARA 149 note 4 (definition applied by the Housing and Regeneration Act 2008 s 275));
   (3)   a transferee of housing pursuant to a large scale disposal, within the meaning of the Housing Act 1985 s 34 (see PARA 524), for which consent was required under s 32 or 43 (see PARAS 522, 531), or a qualifying disposal made under the Leasehold Reform, Housing and Urban Development Act 1993 s 135 (repealed);
   (4)   a body which has acquired dwellings under the Housing Act 1988 Pt IV (ss 93–114) (repealed subject to transitional provisions) (change of landlord, secure tenants: see LANDLORD AND TENANT vol 64 (2016) PARA 1188); or
   (5)   any other body which was at any time registered with the Regulator of Social Housing or the Housing Corporation, or with Housing for Wales, and which owns or manages publicly-funded dwellings,
   and a 'publicly-funded dwelling' means a dwelling which was: (a) provided by means of a grant under the Housing and Regeneration Act 2008 s 19 (financial assistance: see PLANNING vol 83 (2010) PARA 1474) where the grant was made on condition that the recipient provides social housing, or under the Housing Act 1996 s 18 (social housing grant: see PARA 166), the Housing Act 1988 s 50 (repealed in relation to England and Wales), the Housing Associations Act 1985 s 41 (repealed) or the Housing Act 1974 s 29 (repealed) or s 29A (repealed) (housing association grant) or a grant from the Greater London Authority which was a grant made on condition that the recipient provides social housing; or (b) acquired on a disposal by a public sector landlord: Housing Act 1996 s 51(2), (3) (s 51(2) amended by the Government of Wales Act 1998 s 140, Sch 16 paras 81, 90; the Housing and Regeneration Act 2008 ss 124(2), 311, Sch 14 para 4(1), (2); the Localism Act 2011 s 181(2), (3) (in force in relation to England only); and by SI 2010/844; the Housing Act 1996 s 51(3) amended by the Localism Act 2011 ss 195(1), 237, Sch 19 paras 33, 34(1), (2), Sch 25 Pt 31; and by SI 2010/866). 'Provides social housing' has the same meaning as in the Housing and Regeneration Act 2008 Pt 1 (ss 1–58) (see PARA 126 note 3): Housing Act 1996 s 51(3A) (added by the Localism Act 2011 Sch 19 paras 33, 34(1), (3)). As to the Greater London Authority see LONDON GOVERNMENT vol 71 (2013) PARA 67 et seq.
   The Secretary of State may by order add to or amend the descriptions of landlords who are to be treated as social landlords for these purposes: Housing Act 1996 s 51(4). Before making any such order the Secretary of State must consult such persons as he considers appropriate: s 51(5). Any such order must be made by statutory instrument subject to annulment in pursuance of a resolution of either House of Parliament: s 51(6). Section 52 (see PARA 168 note 25) applies to an order under s 51(4) (with any necessary modifications): s 51(8) (added by the Housing and Regeneration Act 2008 s 124(2)). At the date at which this volume states the law, no such order had been made.
   'Public sector landlord' means any of the authorities or bodies within the Housing Act 1985 s 80(1) (the landlord condition for secure tenancies: see LANDLORD AND TENANT vol 63 (2016) PARA 1037): Housing Act 1996 s 63(1). As to the Secretary of State see PARA 7.
4 Housing Act 1996 s 51(1); and see Housing Corporation Circular RS–03/97. The Housing Ombudsman Service has been established under the approved scheme: see PARA 130.
5 Housing Act 1996 s 51(7) (added by the Housing Act 2004 s 228(1); and amended by the Public Services Ombudsman (Wales) Act 2005 s 39(1), Sch 6 paras 56, 57). The Housing Act 1996 s 51(7) refers to social landlords in Wales within the meaning given by the Public Services Ombudsman (Wales) Act 2005 s 41. As to the Public Services Ombudsman for Wales see PARA 9.
6 Housing Act 1996 Sch 2 para 1(3). The Housing Ombudsman Service extends to certain private landlords who are members of the scheme.
7 Housing Act 1996 Sch 2 para 1(1) (amended by the Localism Act 2011 s 181(2), (4)(a) (in force in relation to England only)). As to the meaning of 'housing activities' see PARA 168 note 25.
8 As to the meaning of 'social housing' see PARA 52; definition applied by the Housing Act 1996 Sch 2 para 1(1A)(a)(ii) (Sch 2 para 1(1A) added by the Localism Act 2011 s 181(2), (4)(b) (in force in relation to England only)).

9 Housing Act 1996 Sch 2 para 1(1A) (as added: see note 8). Here 'long lease' has the meaning given by the Landlord and Tenant Act 1987 s 59(3) (see LANDLORD AND TENANT vol 62 (2016) PARA 141 note 1): Housing Act 1996 Sch 2 para 1(1A)(b) (as so added).
10 Housing Act 1996 Sch 2 para 1(2).

132. Matters for which a scheme must provide. A scheme must not be approved[1] unless it makes provision for:

(1)   the establishment or appointment of an independent person to administer the scheme;

(2)   the criteria for membership for social landlords under a duty to be members of an approved scheme, and for membership for other persons[2];

(3)   the manner of becoming or ceasing to be a member;

(4)   the matters about which complaints may be made under the scheme;

(5)   the grounds on which a matter may be excluded from investigation, including that the matter is the subject of court proceedings or was the subject of court proceedings where judgment on the merits was given;

(6)   the descriptions of individual who may make a complaint under the scheme;

(7)   the appointment of an independent individual to be the housing ombudsman under the scheme;

(8)   the appointment of staff to administer the scheme and to assist the housing ombudsman, and the terms upon which they are appointed;

(9)   a duty of the housing ombudsman to investigate any complaint duly made and not withdrawn, and a power to investigate any complaint duly made but withdrawn, and where he investigates to make a determination;

(10)   a power of the housing ombudsman to propose alternative methods of resolving a dispute;

(11)   the powers of the housing ombudsman for the purposes of his investigations, and the procedure to be followed in the conduct of investigations;

(12)   the powers of the housing ombudsman on making a determination;

(13)   the making and publication of annual reports by the housing ombudsman on the discharge of his functions;

(14)   the manner in which determinations are to be communicated to the complainant and the person against whom the complaint was made, and are to be published;

(15)   the manner in which the expenses of the scheme are to be defrayed by the members;

(16)   the keeping and auditing of accounts and the submission of accounts to the Secretary of State[3];

(17)   the making of annual reports on the administration of the scheme;

(18)   the manner of amending the scheme[4].

The Secretary of State may by order amend the above list of requirements by adding to or deleting from it any item or by varying any item for the time being contained in it[5].

1   Ie for the purposes of the Housing Act 1996 Sch 2. The Housing Ombudsman Service has been established under the approved scheme: see PARA 130.
2   As to the meaning of 'social landlord' for these purposes see PARA 131 note 3. The Housing Ombudsman Service extends to certain private landlords who are members of the scheme.
3   As to the Secretary of State see PARA 7.
4   Housing Act 1996 s 51(1), Sch 2 para 2(1); and see Housing Corporation Circular RS–03/97.

5   Housing Act 1996 Sch 2 para 2(2). Such an order must be made by statutory instrument subject to annulment in pursuance of a resolution of either House of Parliament: Sch 2 para 2(3). Section 52 (see PARA 168 note 25) applies to an order of the Secretary of State under Sch 2 (with any necessary modifications): Sch 2 para 12 (added by the Housing and Regeneration Act 2008 s 124(5)). At the date at which this volume states the law, no such order had been made.

133. Approval of scheme, or amendment, and withdrawal of approval. An application to the Secretary of State[1] for approval of a scheme must be made in such manner as the Secretary of State may determine, and must be accompanied by such information as the Secretary of State may require[2]. If it appears to the Secretary of State that the scheme provides for the specified matters[3] and is a satisfactory scheme for the statutory purposes[4], he must approve the scheme[5].

An amendment of an approved scheme is not effective unless approved by the Secretary of State[6].

The Secretary of State may withdraw his approval of a scheme[7]. If, however, he proposes to withdraw his approval of a scheme, he must serve on the person administering the scheme, and on the housing ombudsman under the scheme, a notice stating:

(1)   that he proposes to withdraw his approval;

(2)   the grounds for the proposed withdrawal of his approval; and

(3)   that the person receiving the notice may make representations with respect to the proposed withdrawal of approval within such period of not less than 14 days as is specified in the notice,

and he must, before reaching a decision on whether to withdraw approval, consider any representations duly made to him[8]. The Secretary of State must give notice of his decision on a proposal to withdraw approval of a scheme, together with his reasons, to every person on whom he served a notice as described above[9]. Withdrawal of approval by the Secretary of State has effect from such date as is specified in the notice of his decision[10].

Where the person administering a scheme is given notice of a decision to withdraw approval of the scheme, he must give notice of the decision to every member of the scheme[11].

1   As to the Secretary of State see PARA 7.
2   Housing Act 1996 s 51(1), Sch 2 para 3(1).
3   Ie the matters specified in the Housing Act 1996 Sch 2 para 2: see PARA 132.
4   Ie for the purposes of the Housing Act 1996 Sch 2.
5   Housing Act 1996 Sch 2 para 3(2). The Housing Ombudsman Service has been established under the approved scheme: see PARA 130.
6   Housing Act 1996 Sch 2 para 3(3). Schedule 2 para 3(1) (see the text and note 2) applies in relation to an application for approval of an amendment as it applies to an application for approval of a scheme; and the Secretary of State must approve the amendment if it appears to him that the scheme as amended meets the conditions in Sch 2 para 3(2) (see the text and note 5): Sch 2 para 3(3).
7   Housing Act 1996 Sch 2 para 3(4).
8   Housing Act 1996 Sch 2 para 3(5).
9   Housing Act 1996 Sch 2 para 3(6).
10 Housing Act 1996 Sch 2 para 3(7).
11 Housing Act 1996 Sch 2 para 3(8).

134. Notice of becoming a member of, or of withdrawal from, an approved scheme. A social landlord[1] who:

(1)   becomes a member of an approved scheme[2]; or

(2)   is a member of a scheme which becomes an approved scheme,

must, within the period of 21 days beginning with the date of becoming a member or, as the case may be, of being informed of the Secretary of State's[3] approval of the scheme, give notice of that fact to the Regulator of Social Housing[4]. The Regulator of Social Housing, on receiving the notice, must record his membership of an approved scheme[5].

A person who fails to comply with this notice requirement commits an offence and is liable to a penalty[6]; but proceedings for such an offence may be brought only by or with the consent of the Regulator of Social Housing or the Director of Public Prosecutions[7].

A social landlord wishing to withdraw from membership of an approved scheme must send notice of his proposed withdrawal to the Regulator of Social Housing[8]. The notice must specify:

(a)   the housing activities[9] in relation to which he is subject to investigation under the scheme;

(b)   the approved scheme or schemes of which he is also a member or will, on his withdrawal, become a member; and

(c)   under which scheme or schemes the housing activities mentioned in head (a) will be subject to investigation after his withdrawal[10].

If the Regulator of Social Housing is satisfied that withdrawal by the landlord from the scheme will not result in a failure to comply with his statutory duty to be a member of an approved scheme[11], it must confirm the landlord's withdrawal from the scheme[12]; and if the Regulator of Social Housing is not so satisfied, it must withhold confirmation of the landlord's withdrawal from the scheme; and the landlord continues to be a member of the scheme and bound and entitled under the scheme accordingly[13].

1   As to the meaning of 'social landlord' for these purposes see PARA 131 note 3. The Housing Ombudsman Service extends to certain private landlords who are members of the scheme.

2   As to approval of schemes see PARA 133. The Housing Ombudsman Service has been established under the approved scheme: see PARA 130.

3   As to the Secretary of State see PARA 7.

4   Housing Act 1996 s 51(1), Sch 2 para 4(1) (amended by the Housing and Regeneration Act 2008 s 124(1)). As to the Regulator of Social Housing see PARA 57 et seq.

5   Housing Act 1996 Sch 2 para 4(2) (amended by the Housing and Regeneration Act 2008 s 124(1)).

6   Housing Act 1996 Sch 2 para 4(3) (amended by the Housing and Regeneration Act 2008 s 124(1)). The penalty on summary conviction is a fine not exceeding level 4 on the standard scale: see the Housing Act 1996 Sch 2 para 4(3). As to the powers of magistrates' courts to issue fines on summary conviction see SENTENCING vol 92 (2015) PARA 176.

7   Housing Act 1996 Sch 2 para 4(3) (as amended: see note 6). As to the Director of Public Prosecutions see CRIMINAL PROCEDURE vol 27 (2015) PARAS 25, 30 et seq.

8   Housing Act 1996 Sch 2 para 5(1) (Sch 2 para 5(1), (3), (4) amended by the Housing and Regeneration Act 2008 s 124(1)).

9   As to the meaning of 'housing activities' see PARA 168 note 25.

10 Housing Act 1996 Sch 2 para 5(2).

11 Ie his duty under the Housing Act 1996 Sch 2 para 1: see PARA 131.

12 Housing Act 1996 Sch 2 para 5(3) (as amended: see note 8).

13 Housing Act 1996 Sch 2 para 5(4) (as amended: see note 8).

135. Register of approved schemes. The Regulator of Social Housing[1] must maintain a register of schemes approved by the Secretary of State[2] for the statutory purposes[3] and of the social landlords[4] who are members of those schemes[5]. The Secretary of State must give notice to the Regulator of Social Housing when he grants or withdraws his approval of a scheme, and when he approves an amendment of a scheme; and he must supply the Regulator of Social Housing with copies of any approved scheme or any amendment to a scheme[6].

A member of the public is entitled, upon payment of such fees as the Regulator of Social Housing may determine, to receive a copy of an approved scheme and a list of the social landlords who are members of it[7].

1   As to the Regulator of Social Housing see PARA 57 et seq.
2   As to the Secretary of State see PARA 7.
3   Ie for the purposes of the Housing Act 1996 Sch 2. The Housing Ombudsman Service has been established under the approved scheme: see PARA 130.
4   As to the meaning of 'social landlord' for these purposes see PARA 131 note 3.
5   Housing Act 1996 s 51(1), Sch 2 para 6(1) (amended by the Housing and Regeneration Act 2008 s 124(1)). The Housing Ombudsman Service extends to certain private landlords who are members of the scheme.
6   Housing Act 1996 Sch 2 para 6(2) (amended by Housing and Regeneration Act 2008 s 124(3)).
7   Housing Act 1996 Sch 2 para 6(3) (amended by the Housing and Regeneration Act 2008 s 124(1)).

136. Subscriptions payable in respect of approved schemes. Members of an approved scheme[1] must pay a subscription, calculated as set out in the scheme, to the person administering the scheme[2]. If a change in the method of calculation would result in a member's subscription being more than it would otherwise be, the change may be made only if the Secretary of State approves it[3]. An approved scheme's total defrayable expenses for a period may be more than the scheme's total defrayable expenses[4] for the immediately-preceding corresponding period only if the Secretary of State approves the increase[5].

If a social landlord[6] fails to comply with his statutory duty to be a member of an approved scheme[7], the Secretary of State may determine:

(1)   which approved scheme or schemes he should have joined; and
(2)   what sums by way of subscription he should have paid,

and may require him to pay those amounts to the person administering the scheme or schemes[8]. The person administering an approved scheme may recover sums payable under the above provisions as if they were debts due to him[9].

The Secretary of State may pay grant and provide other financial assistance to a body corporate administering an approved scheme, or, where the scheme does not provide that it is to be administered by a body corporate[10], to the housing ombudsman under an approved scheme, for such purposes and upon such terms as the Secretary of State thinks fit[11].

1   As to the approval of schemes see PARA 133. The Housing Ombudsman Service has been established under the approved scheme: see PARA 130.
2   Housing Act 1996 s 51(1), Sch 2 para 11(1).
3   Housing Act 1996 Sch 2 para 11(1A) (Sch 2 para 11(1A)–(1C) added by the Localism Act 2011 s 181(2), (4)(c); in force in relation to England). As to the Secretary of State see PARA 7.
4   For this purpose, 'defrayable expenses', in relation to a scheme, means expenses of the scheme that are to be defrayed by subscriptions from members of the scheme: Housing Act 1996 Sch 2 para 11(1C) (as added: see note 3).
5   Housing Act 1996 Sch 2 para 11(1B) (as added: see note 3).
6   As to the meaning of 'social landlord' for these purposes see PARA 131 note 3.
7   Ie the duty under the Housing Act 1996 Sch 2 para 1: see PARA 131.
8   Housing Act 1996 Sch 2 para 11(2).
9   Housing Act 1996 Sch 2 para 11(3).
10 Ie in a case where the Housing Act 1996 Sch 2 para 10(2) applies: see PARA 137.
11 Housing Act 1996 Sch 2 para 11(4) (amended by Housing and Regeneration Act 2008 ss 124(4), 321(1), Sch 16).

137. Appointment and status of the housing ombudsman. Where an approved scheme[1] provides that it is to be administered by a body corporate, that body must appoint on such terms as it thinks fit the housing ombudsman for the purposes of the scheme and the appointment and its terms are subject to the approval of the Secretary of State[2]. Where an approved scheme does not so provide:

(1)   the housing ombudsman for the purposes of the scheme must be appointed by the Secretary of State on such terms as the Secretary of State thinks fit;

(2)   the Secretary of State may by order provide that the housing ombudsman for the purposes of the scheme is to be a corporation sole; and

(3)   the staff to administer the scheme and otherwise assist the ombudsman in the discharge of his functions must be appointed and employed by him[3].

The Secretary of State may at any time remove a housing ombudsman from office, whether that ombudsman was appointed by him or otherwise[4].

A housing ombudsman appointed by the Secretary of State or otherwise is not to be regarded as the servant or agent of the Crown or as enjoying any status, privilege or immunity of the Crown or as exempt from any tax, duty, rate, levy or other charge whatsoever, whether general or local, and any property held by him is not to be regarded as property of, or held on behalf of, the Crown[5].

If at any stage in the course of conducting an investigation under the Housing Act 1996 a housing ombudsman forms the opinion that the complaint relates partly to a matter within the jurisdiction of a Local Commissioner[6], the ombudsman may conduct an investigation under that Act jointly with that Commissioner[7]. A housing ombudsman must obtain the consent of the complainant or the complainant's representative before agreeing to a joint investigation[8]. If a housing ombudsman forms the opinion that a complaint which is being investigated by a Local Commissioner relates partly to a matter within the jurisdiction of the ombudsman, the ombudsman may conduct an investigation jointly with that Commissioner[9]. If a housing ombudsman conducts an investigation jointly with a Local Commissioner, the requirements as to determinations[10] may be satisfied by a report made jointly with that person[11]. A joint report made under these provisions must distinguish determinations of a housing ombudsman from other findings or recommendations[12].

1   As to approval of schemes see PARA 133. The Housing Ombudsman Service has been established under the approved scheme: see PARA 130.
2   Housing Act 1996 s 51(1), Sch 2 para 10(1). As to the Secretary of State see PARA 7.
3   Housing Act 1996 Sch 2 para 10(2).
4   Housing Act 1996 Sch 2 para 10(3).
5   Housing Act 1996 Sch 2 para 10(4).
6   As to Local Commissioners see LOCAL GOVERNMENT vol 69 (2009) PARA 839.
7   Housing Act 1996 Sch 2 para 10A(1) (Sch 2 para 10A added by the Localism Act 2011 s 182(8); in force in relation to England).
8   Housing Act 1996 Sch 2 para 10A(2) (as added: see note 7).
9   Housing Act 1996 Sch 2 para 10A(3) (as added: see note 7).
10 Ie the requirements of the Housing Act 1996 Sch 2 para 7: see PARA 139.
11 Housing Act 1996 Sch 2 para 10A(4) (as added: see note 7).
12 Housing Act 1996 Sch 2 para 10A(5) (as added: see note 7).

138. Complaints referred by designated persons. A complaint against a social landlord[1] is not 'duly made' to a housing ombudsman under an approved scheme[2] unless it is made in writing to the ombudsman by a designated person[3] by way of referral of a complaint made to the designated person[4]. This is subject to the provisions[5] relating to complaints that need not be made by way of referral[6].

Before making a referral, a designated person must obtain written consent from the complainant or the complainant's representative[7]. The following provisions apply if a designated person refers a complaint to a housing ombudsman[8]. If the ombudsman decides: (1) not to investigate the complaint; or (2) to discontinue investigation of the complaint, the ombudsman must prepare a statement of reasons for that decision and send a copy of the statement to the designated person[9]. If the ombudsman completes investigation of the complaint, the ombudsman must inform the designated person of: (a) the results of the investigation; and (b) any determination made[10].

The requirement for a complaint to be made by a designated person[11] does not apply in relation to a complaint against a social landlord made to a housing ombudsman under an approved scheme if the ombudsman is satisfied that: (i) the social landlord has procedures for considering complaints against the social landlord; (ii) the matter that forms the subject of the complaint has been submitted to those procedures; (iii) those procedures have been exhausted; and (iv) the complaint has been made to the ombudsman after the end of the eight weeks beginning with the day on which those procedures were exhausted[12].

Nor does the requirement apply in relation to a complaint against a social landlord made to a housing ombudsman under an approved scheme if: (A) the ombudsman is satisfied that a designated person: (I) has refused to refer the complaint to a housing ombudsman under an approved scheme; or (II) has agreed to the complaint being made otherwise than by way of a referral by a designated person; and (B) the refusal, or agreement, is in writing or the ombudsman is satisfied that it has been confirmed in writing[13].

1   As to the meaning of 'social landlord' for these purposes see PARA 131 note 3.
2   As to approval of schemes see PARA 133. The Housing Ombudsman Service has been established under the approved scheme: see PARA 130.
3   For the purposes of the Housing Act 1996 Sch 2 para 7A 'designated person' means: (1) a member of the House of Commons; (2) a member of the local housing authority for the district in which the property concerned is located; or (3) a designated tenant panel (see Sch 2 para 7C(1)) for the social landlord: s 51(1), Sch 2 para 7A(3) (Sch 2 paras 7A–7C added by the Localism Act 2011 s 180(1); in force in relation to England). In head (2) 'district' in relation to a local housing authority has the same meaning as in the Housing Act 1985 (see PARA 11): Housing Act 1996 Sch 2 para 7A(8) (as so added).
    In head (3), 'designated tenant panel' means a group of tenants which is recognised by a social landlord for the purpose of referring complaints against the social landlord: Sch 2 para 7C(1) (as so added). There may be more than one designated tenant panel for a social landlord: Sch 2 para 7C(2) (as so added). Where a social landlord becomes a member of an approved scheme, the social landlord must give to the person administering the scheme contact details for any designated tenant panel for the social landlord: Sch 2 para 7C(3) (as so added). Where a group becomes a designated tenant panel for a social landlord, the social landlord must, as respects each approved scheme of which the social landlord is a member, give to the person administering the scheme contact details for the panel: Sch 2 para 7C(4) (as so added). Where a group ceases to be a designated tenant panel for a social landlord, the social landlord must inform the person administering each approved scheme of which the social landlord is a member: Sch 2 para 7C(5) (as so added). A complaint referred to a housing ombudsman under an approved scheme by a designated tenant panel for a social landlord is not affected by the group concerned ceasing to be a designated tenant panel for the social landlord: Sch 2 para 7C(6) (as so added). As to the meaning of 'tenant' see PARA 168 note 16.
4   Housing Act 1996 Sch 2 para 7A(1) (as added: see note 3).
5   Ie the Housing Act 1996 Sch 2 para 7B: see the text to notes 11–13.
6   Housing Act 1996 Sch 2 para 7A(2) (as added: see note 3).
7   Housing Act 1996 Sch 2 para 7A(4) (as added: see note 3).
8   Housing Act 1996 Sch 2 para 7A(5) (as added: see note 3).
9   Housing Act 1996 Sch 2 para 7A(6) (as added: see note 3).
10 Housing Act 1996 Sch 2 para 7A(7) (as added: see note 3).
11 Ie the Housing Act 1996 Sch 2 para 7A(1).
12 Housing Act 1996 Sch 2 para 7B(1) (as added: see note 3).
13 Housing Act 1996 Sch 2 para 7B(2) (as added: see note 3). Schedule 2 para 7A(3) (meaning of 'designated person': see note 3) applies also for the purposes of Sch 2 para 7B(2): Sch 2 para 7B(3) (as so added).

139. Determinations and reports by the housing ombudsman. A housing ombudsman under an approved scheme[1] must investigate any complaint duly made[2] to him which has not been withdrawn, and the ombudsman may investigate any complaint duly made but withdrawn, and where he investigates a complaint he must determine it by reference to what is, in his opinion, fair in all the circumstances of the case[3]. He may in his determination order the member of a scheme against whom the complaint was made to pay compensation to the complainant, and order that the member or the complainant must not exercise or require the performance of any of the contractual or other obligations or rights existing between them[4]. If the member against whom the complaint was made fails to comply with the determination within a reasonable time, the housing ombudsman may order that member to publish in such manner as the ombudsman sees fit that the member has failed to comply with the determination[5]. Where the member is not a social landlord[6], the housing ombudsman may also order that the member be expelled from the scheme[7], and publish in such manner as the housing ombudsman sees fit that the member has been expelled and the reasons for the expulsion[8].

If a person fails to comply with an order under the above provisions requiring publication of the specified matters[9], the housing ombudsman may take such steps as he thinks appropriate to publish what the member ought to have published and recover from the member the costs of doing so[10].

A member who is ordered by the housing ombudsman to pay compensation or take any other steps has power to do so, except that a member which is also a charity[11] must not do anything contrary to its trusts[12].

A housing ombudsman under an approved scheme may publish his determination on any complaint, and such reports as he thinks fit on the discharge of his functions[13]. He may include in any such determination or report statements, communications, reports, papers or other documentary evidence obtained in the exercise of his functions[14]. In publishing any determination or report, a housing ombudsman must have regard to the need for excluding so far as practicable:

(1) any matter which relates to the private affairs of an individual, where publication would seriously and prejudicially affect the interests of that individual; and

(2) any matter which relates specifically to the affairs of a member of an approved scheme, where publication would seriously and prejudicially affect its interests, unless the inclusion of that matter is necessary for the purposes of the determination or report[15].

For the purposes of the law of defamation, absolute privilege attaches to: (a) any communication between a housing ombudsman under an approved scheme and any person by or against whom a complaint is made to him; (b) any determination by such an ombudsman; and (c) the publication of such a determination or any report under the above provisions[16].

1 As to the approval of schemes see PARA 133. The Housing Ombudsman Service has been established under the approved scheme: see PARA 130.
2 As to when a complaint is duly made see PARA 138.
3 Housing Act 1996 s 51(1), Sch 2 para 7(1).
4 Housing Act 1996 Sch 2 para 7(2).
5 Housing Act 1996 Sch 2 para 7(3).
6 As to the meaning of 'social landlord' for these purposes see PARA 131 note 3.
7 Housing Act 1996 Sch 2 para 7(4)(a).
8 Housing Act 1996 Sch 2 para 7(4)(b).
9 Ie an order under the Housing Act 1996 Sch 2 para 7(3) (see the text and note 5) or Sch 2 para 7(4)(b) (see the text and note 8).

10 Housing Act 1996 Sch 2 para 7(5).
11 As to the meaning of 'charity' see PARA 168 note 3.
12 Housing Act 1996 Sch 2 para 7(6).
13 Housing Act 1996 Sch 2 para 8(1).
14 Housing Act 1996 Sch 2 para 8(2).
15 Housing Act 1996 Sch 2 para 8(3).
16 Housing Act 1996 Sch 2 para 9. As to absolute privilege see DEFAMATION vol 32 (2012) PARA 594 et seq.

140. Enforcement of a housing ombudsman's determinations. The following provisions are not yet in force[1]. The Secretary of State[2] may by order[3] make provision for, or in connection with, authorising a housing ombudsman under an approved scheme[4] to apply to a court or tribunal for an order that a determination made by the ombudsman[5] may be enforced as if it were an order of a court[6]. Before the Secretary of State makes such an order, the Secretary of State must consult: (1) one or more bodies appearing to the Secretary of State to represent the interests of social landlords[7]; (2) one or more bodies appearing to the Secretary of State to represent the interests of other members of approved schemes; (3) one or more bodies appearing to the Secretary of State to represent the interests of tenants[8]; and (4) such other persons as the Secretary of State considers appropriate[9].

1 The Housing Act 1996 Sch 2 para 7D is added, as from a day to be appointed, by the Localism Act 2011 s 180(1); at the date at which this volume states the law, no such day had been appointed.
2 As to the Secretary of State see PARA 7.
3 As to orders by the Secretary of State see PARA 54. The Secretary of State's power to make an order under the Housing Act 1996 Sch 2 para 7D(1) is exercisable by statutory instrument: s 51(1), Sch 2 para 7D(3) (Sch 2 para 7D as added: see note 1). A statutory instrument containing an order made by the Secretary of State under Sch 2 para 7D(1) (as so added) is subject to annulment in pursuance of a resolution of either House of Parliament: Sch 2 para 7D(4) (as so added).
4 As to approval of schemes see PARA 133. The Housing Ombudsman Service has been established under the approved scheme: see PARA 130.
5 As to determinations see PARA 139.
6 Housing Act 1996 Sch 2 para 7D(1) (as added: see note 1).
7 As to the meaning of 'social landlord' for these purposes see PARA 131 note 3.
8 As to the meaning of 'tenant' see PARA 168 note 16.
9 Housing Act 1996 Sch 2 para 7D(2) (as added: see note 1).

(ii) Social Housing in Wales

A.   ROLE OF THE WELSH MINISTERS

(A)   Introduction

141. Role of the Welsh Ministers. Part III of the Housing Associations Act 1985[1] has effect in relation to the Welsh Ministers[2]. The functions in that Part exercisable by the Welsh Ministers may only be exercised in relation to Wales[3].

Part I of the Housing Act 1996[4] also now applies only relation to Wales, and the Welsh Ministers are the appropriate national authority[5].

Under Part 4 of the Housing (Wales) Act 2014[6], the Welsh Ministers have functions concerning the standards of housing provided by local authorities[7].

The Welsh Ministers have functions under the Renting Homes (Wales) Act 2016. Part 2[8] establishes the concept of a 'supplementary provision'; that is, a provision set out in regulations made by the Welsh Ministers which is automatically included as a term of all occupation contracts, or of specified occupation contracts, which replace tenancies and licences[9]. The Welsh Ministers may by regulations provide that a provision of any enactment is a fundamental provision applicable to an occupation contract or that a provision of any enactment that is for the time being a fundamental provision applicable to an occupation contract ceases to be a fundamental provision applicable to an occupation contract[10]. The Welsh Ministers must prescribe model written statements of contracts for such kinds or descriptions of occupation contract as they think fit[11].

1 Ie the Housing Associations Act 1985 Pt III (ss 74–102).
2 Housing Associations Act 1985 s 74(1) (substituted, in relation to England and Wales, by SI 2010/866). As to the Welsh Ministers see PARA 7.
3 Housing Associations Act 1985 s 74(4) (substituted, in relation to England and Wales, by SI 2010/866).
4 Ie the Housing Act 1996 ss A1–64: see PARA 166 et seq.
5 See the Housing and Regeneration Act 2008 ss 60, 61; and PARA 51. References to the Welsh Ministers have been substituted for references to the Secretary of State (see s 62) and references to the National Assembly for Wales have been substituted for references to 'either House of Parliament' (see s 63).
6 Ie the Housing (Wales) Act 2014 Pt 4 (ss 111–130).
7 See PARA 227 et seq.
8 Ie the Renting Homes (Wales) Act 2016 Pt 2 (ss 7–29): see LANDLORD AND TENANT vol 62 (2016) PARAS 45–46.
9 See the Renting Homes (Wales) Act 2016 ss 3(5), 23 (s 3 not in force at the date at which this volume states the law (see PARA 6); s 23 in force for certain purposes from 5 August 2016 (see the Renting Homes (Wales) Act 2016 (Commencement No 1) Order 2016, SI 2016/813, art 2(a), Schedule para 1)).
10 See the Renting Homes (Wales) Act 2016 s 22(1) (not in force at the date at which this volume states the law (see PARA 6)).
11 See the Renting Homes (Wales) Act 2016 s 29 (in force for certain purposes from 5 August 2016 (see the Renting Homes (Wales) Act 2016 (Commencement No 1) Order 2016, SI 2016/813, art 2(a), Schedule para 2)).

142. Functions carried out in relation to housing in Wales by the Welsh Ministers. On 1 December 1988 a body known as Housing for Wales was created by virtue of the Housing Act 1988[1], to exercise functions under the Housing Associations Act 1985[2]. All property in Wales which, immediately before the coming into force of the relevant provisions[3], was held by the Housing Corporation, was on that day transferred to and vested in Housing for Wales[4].

Every registered housing association which immediately before the appointed day[5]:

(1)   was a society registered under the Industrial and Provident Societies Act 1965 and had its registered office in Wales for the purposes of that Act[6]; or

(2)   was a registered charity and had its address in Wales for the purposes of registration by the Charity Commission[7],

on the appointed day ceased to be registered in the register maintained by the Housing Corporation under the Housing Associations Act 1985 and was deemed to be registered in the register maintained by Housing for Wales under that Act[8]. All rights, liabilities and obligations to which, immediately before the appointed day, the Housing Corporation was entitled or subject in relation to any registered housing association[9] and land in Wales held by an unregistered housing association, on that day became rights, liabilities and obligations of Housing for Wales[10].

From 1 November 1998, the functions of Housing for Wales were transferred to the Secretary of State[11]. When he was satisfied that the duties of Housing for Wales in relation to the transfer of functions had been discharged, the Secretary of State was required by order to direct that Housing for Wales was to cease to exist[12]. Housing for Wales ceased to exist on 31 March 1999[13].

The functions that formerly belonged to Housing for Wales were transferred to the National Assembly for Wales and are now exercised by the Welsh Ministers[14].

1   See the Housing Act 1988 s 46(1) (repealed); and the Housing Act 1988 (Commencement No 1) Order 1988, SI 1988/2056. The provisions of the Housing Act 1988 s 46(1), (2) (now repealed) came into force on 1 December 1988; and those of s 46(3)–(5) (now repealed) came into force on 1 April 1989: see the Housing Act 1988 (Commencement No 1) Order 1988, SI 1988/2056; and the Housing Act 1988 (Commencement No 4) Order 1989, SI 1989/404. As to the repeal of the provisions described in this note and in the text and notes 2–10 see the text and notes 12–13.
      As to the constitution and status of Housing for Wales see the Housing Act 1988 s 46, Sch 5 (repealed). The Welsh name for Housing for Wales was Tai Cymru: see the Alternative Names in Welsh Order 1994, SI 1994/2889, art 2, Schedule.
2   See the Housing Act 1988 s 46(3) (repealed). As to powers and functions under the Housing Associations Act 1985 see PARA 143 et seq.
3   Ie the Housing Act 1988 s 46 (repealed). As to the commencement of s 46 (now repealed) see note 1.
4   See the Housing Act 1988 s 46(4) (repealed). Any question whether any property had been transferred to Housing for Wales by virtue of s 46(4) was to be determined by the Secretary of State: s 46(5) (repealed). As to the Housing Corporation (now abolished) see PARA 2.
5   'The appointed day' meant the day appointed for the coming into force of the Housing Act 1988 s 47: s 47(6) (repealed). The provisions of s 47(2), (6) (repealed) came into force on 1 December 1988 (see the Housing Act 1988 (Commencement No 1) Order 1988, SI 1988/2056); and those of the Housing Act 1988 s 47(1), (3)–(5) (repealed) came into force on 1 April 1989 (see the Housing Act 1988 (Commencement No 4) Order 1989, SI 1989/404).
6   Societies registered under the Industrial and Provident Societies Act 1965 are now registered societies under the Co-operative and Community Benefit Societies Act 2014: see FINANCIAL INSTITUTIONS vol 48 (2015) PARA 881 et seq.
7   As to registered charities see CHARITIES vol 8 (2015) PARA 307 et seq; and as to the Charity Commission see CHARITIES vol 8 (2015) PARA 543 et seq.
8   Housing Act 1988 s 47(1), (6) (repealed). As to the notification of transfers and registration see s 47(2), (3) (repealed).
9   Ie a registered housing association to which the Housing Act 1988 s 47(1) (repealed) (see the text and note 8) applied.
10 See the Housing Act 1988 s 47(4) (repealed). Any question whether any rights, liabilities or obligations had become rights, liabilities or obligations of Housing for Wales by virtue of s 47(4) were determined by the Secretary of State: s 47(5) (repealed).
11 See the Government of Wales Act 1998 s 140, Sch 16; and the Government of Wales Act 1998 (Commencement No 1) Order 1998, SI 1998/2244. The provisions relating to the establishment, constitution and status of Housing for Wales (see the text and notes 1–10) were accordingly repealed as from that date: see the Government of Wales Act 1998 s 152, Sch 18 Pt VI. The validity of things done by or in relation to Housing for Wales is not affected: s 141. For transitional and final provisions relating to Housing for Wales see s 142.
      Numerous enactments were amended so as to change references to 'Housing for Wales' to references to the Secretary of State: see Sch 16; and see also s 152, Sch 18 Pt VI. See, however, the text and note 14.
12 See the Government of Wales Act 1998 s 143.
13 See the Housing for Wales (Abolition) Order 1999, SI 1999/781.
14 See the National Assembly for Wales (Transfer of Functions) Order 1999, SI 1999/672, art 2, Sch 1; the Government of Wales Act 2006 s 162, Sch 11 para 30; and PARA 7.

(B)   General Functions

143. General functions of the Welsh Ministers. The Welsh Ministers[1] have the following general functions[2]:

(1)   to facilitate the proper performance of the functions of registered social landlords[3];

(2)   to maintain a register of social landlords and to exercise supervision and control over such persons[4];

(3)   to promote and assist the development of self-build societies[5] (other than registered social landlords) and to facilitate the proper performance of the functions, and to publicise the aims and principles, of such societies[6];

(4)   to undertake, to such extent as the Welsh Ministers consider necessary, the provision (by construction, acquisition, conversion, improvement or otherwise) of dwellings[7] for letting or for sale and of hostels[8], and the management of dwellings or hostels so provided[9].

The Welsh Ministers may do such things and enter into such transactions as are incidental to or conducive to the exercise of any of their functions in relation to housing[10], general or specific[11].

1   As to the Welsh Ministers see PARAS 7, 141.
2   Housing Associations Act 1985 s 75(1) (amended, in relation to England and Wales, by SI 2010/866). The Welsh Ministers must exercise their general functions subject to and in accordance with the provisions of the Housing Associations Act 1985 and the Housing Act 1996 Pt I (ss A1–64): Housing Associations Act 1985 s 75(2) (amended, in relation to England and Wales, by SI 1996/2325 and SI 2010/866). The Housing Associations Act 1985 s 75(1) is without prejudice to specific functions conferred on the Welsh Ministers by or under the Housing Associations Act 1985 or the Housing Act 1996 Pt I: Housing Associations Act 1985 s 75(3) (amended, in relation to England and Wales, by SI 1996/2325 and SI 2010/866).
3   Housing Associations Act 1985 s 75(1)(a) (s 75(1)(a)–(c) substituted by the Housing Act 1996 s 55(1), Sch 3 para 5). As to the meaning of 'registered social landlord' see PARA 13.
4   Housing Associations Act 1985 s 75(1)(b) (as substituted: see note 3).
5   As to the meaning of 'self-build society' see PARA 13.
6   Housing Associations Act 1985 s 75(1)(c) (as substituted: see note 3).
7   'Dwelling' means a building or part of a building occupied or intended to be occupied as a separate dwelling, together with any yard, garden, outhouses and appurtenances belonging to it or usually enjoyed with it: Housing Associations Act 1985 s 106(1).
8   'Hostel' means a building in which is provided for persons generally or for a class or classes of persons: (1) residential accommodation otherwise than in separate and self-contained sets of premises; and (2) either board or facilities for the preparation of food adequate to the needs of those persons, or both: Housing Associations Act 1985 s 106(1).
9   Housing Associations Act 1985 s 75(1)(e) (amended, in relation to England and Wales, by SI 2010/866).
10   Ie under the Housing Associations Act 1985 or the Housing Act 1996 Pt I.
11   Housing Associations Act 1985 s 75(4) (amended, in relation to England and Wales, by SI 1996/2325 and SI 2010/866).

144.   Advisory service. The Welsh Ministers[1] may provide an advisory service for the purpose of giving advice on legal, architectural and other technical matters to registered social landlords[2] or unregistered housing associations[3] and to persons who are forming a housing association or are interested in the possibility of doing so[4]. The Welsh Ministers may make charges for the service[5]. These powers[6] may be exercised by the Welsh Ministers acting jointly with the Regulator of Social Housing[7].

1   As to the Welsh Ministers see PARAS 7, 141.
2   As to the meaning of 'registered social landlord' see PARA 13.
3   As to the meaning of 'housing association' see PARA 13.
4   Housing Associations Act 1985 s 77(1) (amended, in relation to England and Wales, by SI 1996/2325 and SI 2010/866).
5   Housing Associations Act 1985 s 77(2) (amended, in relation to England and Wales, by SI 2010/866).
6   Ie the powers conferred on the Welsh Ministers by the Housing Associations Act 1985 s 77(1), (2): see the text and notes 1–5.
7   Housing Associations Act 1985 s 77(3) (added by the Housing Act 1988 s 59, Sch 6 para 33; and substituted, in relation to England and Wales, by SI 2010/866). As to the Regulator of Social Housing see PARA 57 et seq.

(C) Powers with respect to Grants, Loans and other Financial Assistance

145. Lending powers. The Welsh Ministers[1] may lend to a registered social landlord[2] or an unregistered self-build society[3] for the purpose of enabling the body to meet the whole or part of expenditure incurred or to be incurred by it in carrying out its objects[4].

The Welsh Ministers may lend to an individual for the purpose of assisting him to acquire from the Welsh Ministers, or from a registered social landlord or an unregistered self-build society, a legal estate or interest in a dwelling[5] which he intends to occupy[6].

A loan[7] may be by way of temporary loan or otherwise[8]. The terms of a loan[9] must[10] be such as the Welsh Ministers may determine, either generally or in a particular case[11].

1 As to the Welsh Ministers see PARAS 7, 141.
2 As to the meaning of 'registered social landlord' see PARA 13.
3 As to the meaning of 'self-build society' see PARA 13.
4 Housing Associations Act 1985 s 79(1) (substituted by the Government of Wales Act 1998 s 140, Sch 16 para 35(2); and amended, in relation to England and Wales, by SI 2010/866).
5 As to the meaning of 'dwelling' see PARA 143 note 7.
6 Housing Associations Act 1985 s 79(2) (substituted by the Government of Wales Act 1998 Sch 16 para 35(2); and amended, in relation to England and Wales, by SI 2010/866).
7 Ie made under the Housing Associations Act 1985 s 79.
8 Housing Associations Act 1985 s 79(3) (amended, in relation to England and Wales, by SI 2010/866). The terms of a loan made under the Housing Associations Act 1985 s 79(1) (see the text and notes 1–4) may include terms for preventing repayment of the loan or part of it before a specified date without the consent of the Welsh Ministers, although the terms of a loan made under s 79(2) may not include such terms: s 79(3) (as so amended).
9 Ie made under the Housing Associations Act 1985 s 79.
10 Ie subject to the Housing Associations Act 1985 s 79(3) (see the text and note 9).
11 Housing Associations Act 1985 s 79(4) (substituted, in relation to England and Wales, by SI 2010/866).

146. Security for loans to unregistered self-build societies. Where the Welsh Ministers[1]: (1) make a loan[2] to an unregistered self-build society[3]; and (2) under a mortgage entered into by the society to secure the loan have an interest as mortgagee or creditor in land belonging to the society, they may give the society directions with respect to the disposal of the land[4]. The society must comply with directions so given so long as the Welsh Ministers continue to have such an interest in the land[5]. Directions so given may be varied or revoked by subsequent directions[6]. The Welsh Ministers may not give directions[7] requiring a society to transfer its interest in land to them or any other person, unless they are satisfied that arrangements have been made which will secure that the members of the society receive fair treatment in connection with the transfer[8].

1 As to the Welsh Ministers see PARAS 7, 141.
2 Ie a loan under the Housing Associations Act 1985 s 79(1): see PARA 145.
3 As to the meaning of 'self-build society' see PARA 13.
4 Housing Associations Act 1985 s 80(1) (amended by the Government of Wales Act 1998 ss 140, 152, Sch 16 para 36(2), Sch 18 Pt VI; and, in relation to England and Wales, by SI 2010/866).
5 Housing Associations Act 1985 s 80(2) (amended, in relation to England and Wales, by SI 2010/866).
6 See the Housing Associations Act 1985 s 80(3) (amended by the Government of Wales Act 1998 Sch 16 para 36(3), Sch 18 Pt VI; and, in relation to England and Wales, by SI 2010/866).
7 Ie under the Housing Associations Act 1985 s 80.
8 Housing Associations Act 1985 s 80(4) (amended, in relation to England and Wales, by SI 2010/866).

147. Further advances in case of disposal on shared ownership lease. Where:

(1)   a lease of a dwelling[1], granted otherwise than in pursuance of the right to buy provisions of the Housing Act 1985[2] relating to shared ownership leases, contains a provision to the like effect as that required by provisions of that Act relating to the right of a tenant to acquire additional shares of a shared ownership lease[3]; and

(2)   the Welsh Ministers[4] have, in exercise of any of their powers, left outstanding or advanced any amount on the security of the dwelling,

that power includes power to advance further amounts for the purpose of assisting the tenant to make payments in pursuance of that provision[5]. The right to a shared ownership lease was replaced by the right to acquire on rent to mortgage terms[6], but that was abolished by the Housing Act 2004[7].

1   As to the meaning of 'dwelling' see PARA 143 note 7.
2   Ie the Housing Act 1985 Pt V (ss 118–188): see PARA 230 et seq.
3   Ie required by the Housing Act 1985 Sch 8 para 1 (repealed subject to transitional provisions).
4   As to the Welsh Ministers see PARAS 7, 141.
5   Housing Associations Act 1985 s 81 (amended, in relation to England and Wales, by SI 2010/866).
6   See the Housing Act 1985 ss 143–153; and PARA 318 et seq.
7   See the Housing Act 1985 s 142A (added by the Housing Act 2004 s 190); and PARA 318.

148.   Power to guarantee loans. The Welsh Ministers[1] may guarantee the repayment of the principal of, and the payment of interest on, sums borrowed by registered social landlords[2] or unregistered self-build societies[3].

The aggregate amount outstanding in respect of:

(1)   loans for which the Welsh Ministers (or National Assembly for Wales[4], Secretary of State[5] or Housing for Wales[6]) have given a guarantee[7]; and

(2)   payments made by the Welsh Ministers (or National Assembly for Wales, Secretary of State or Housing for Wales) in meeting an obligation arising by virtue of such a guarantee and not repaid to the Welsh Ministers (or National Assembly for Wales, Secretary of State or Housing for Wales),

may not exceed £30 million or such greater sum not exceeding £50 million as the Welsh Ministers may specify by order[8].

1   As to the Welsh Ministers see PARAS 7, 141.
2   As to the meaning of 'registered social landlord' see PARA 13.
3   Housing Associations Act 1985 s 83(1) (substituted, in relation to England and Wales, by SI 2010/866). A guarantee may be subject to terms and conditions: Housing Associations Act 1985 s 83(2) (substituted, in relation to England and Wales, by SI 2010/866). As to the meaning of 'self-build society' see PARA 13.
4   As to the National Assembly for Wales see CONSTITUTIONAL AND ADMINISTRATIVE LAW vol 20 (2014) PARA 351.
5   As to the Secretary of State see PARA 7.
6   As to Housing for Wales see PARA 142.
7   Ie under the Housing Associations Act 1985 s 83.
8   Housing Associations Act 1985 s 83(3A) (added by the Housing Act 1988 s 59, Sch 6 para 34; and amended, in relation to England and Wales, by SI 2010/866). An order under the Housing Associations Act 1985 s 83(3A) must be made by statutory instrument and may not be made unless a draft of the order has been laid before, and approved by a resolution of, the National Assembly for Wales: s 83(4) (substituted, in relation to England and Wales, by SI 2010/866). At the date at which this volume states the law, no such order had been made.

149.   Agreements to indemnify certain lenders. The Welsh Ministers[1] may enter into an agreement with:

(1)   a building society[2] lending on the security of a house; or

(2)   a recognised body[3] making a relevant advance[4] on the security of a house,

that, in the event of default by the mortgagor, and in circumstances and subject to conditions specified in the agreement, the Welsh Ministers bind themselves to indemnify the society or body in respect of the whole or part of the mortgagor's outstanding indebtedness and any loss or expense falling on the society or body in consequence of the mortgagor's default[5]. The agreement may also, if the mortgagor is made party to it, enable or require the Welsh Ministers in specified circumstances to take a transfer of the mortgage and assume rights and liabilities under it, the building society or recognised body being then discharged in respect of them[6]. The transfer may be made to take effect:

(a)   on terms provided for by the agreement (including terms involving substitution of a new mortgage agreement or modification of the existing one); and

(b)   so that the Welsh Ministers are treated as acquiring (for and in relation to the purposes of the mortgage) the benefit and burden of all preceding acts, omissions and events[7].

The Welsh Ministers must, before entering into an agreement in a form about which they have not previously consulted[8], consult:

(i)   in the case of a form of agreement with a building society, the Financial Conduct Authority[9], the Prudential Regulation Authority[10] and such organisations representative of building societies and local authorities as they think expedient[11]; and

(ii)   in the case of a form of agreement with a recognised body, such organisations representative of such bodies and local authorities as they think expedient[12].

1   As to the Welsh Ministers see PARAS 7, 141.

2   'Building society' means a building society within the meaning of the Building Societies Act 1986 (see FINANCIAL INSTITUTIONS vol 48 (2015) PARA 330 et seq): Housing Associations Act 1985 s 101 (definition substituted by the Building Societies Act 1986 s 120, Sch 18 para 19(4)).

3   For the purposes of the Housing Associations Act 1985 s 84, 'recognised body' means a body specified, or of a class or description specified, in an order made by statutory instrument by the Welsh Ministers: s 85(1), (2) (amended by the Housing Act 1996 ss 222, 227, Sch 18 para 22(1)(d), Sch 19 Pt XIII; and by SI 2009/484). Before making such an order varying or revoking an order previously made, the Welsh Ministers must give an opportunity for representations to be made on behalf of a recognised body which, if the order were made, would cease to be such a body: Housing Associations Act 1985 s 85(3) (amended by SI 2009/484).

4   For the purposes of the Housing Associations Act 1985 s 84, 'relevant advance' means an advance made to a person whose interest in the dwelling is or was acquired by virtue of a conveyance of the freehold or an assignment of a long lease, or a grant of a long lease by: (1) a local authority; (2) a new town corporation; (3) the Welsh Ministers so far as they are or were exercising functions in relation to property transferred (or to be transferred) to them as mentioned in the New Towns Act 1981 s 36(1)(a)(i)–(iii); (4) an urban development corporation; or (5) a registered social landlord, or an advance made to such a person by the Welsh Ministers if the conveyance, assignment or grant was made under the Housing Associations Act 1985 s 90 (see PARA 156): s 85(1), (4) (s 85(4) amended by the Government of Wales Act 1998 ss 140, 152, Sch 16 para 39, Sch 18 Pt IV; and by SI 1996/2325, SI 2008/3002 and SI 2009/484). For the purposes of the Housing Associations Act 1985 s 85(4), 'long lease' has the same meaning as in the Housing Act 1985 Pt V (ss 118–188) (right to buy) (see s 187; and LANDLORD AND TENANT vol 64 (2016) PARA 1503): Housing Associations Act 1985 s 85(5).

'Local authority' means a county, county borough, district, or London borough council, the Common Council of the City of London or the Council of the Isles of Scilly and in s 84(5) includes a joint authority established by the Local Government Act 1985 Pt IV (ss 23–42) (see LOCAL GOVERNMENT vol 69 (2009) PARA 47), an economic prosperity board established under the Local Democracy, Economic Development and Construction Act 2009 s 88 (see TRADE AND INDUSTRY vol 97 (2015) PARA 1086 et seq), a combined authority established under s 103 (see TRADE AND INDUSTRY vol 97 (2015) PARA 1092 et seq) and the London Fire and Emergency Planning Authority; and in the Housing Associations Act 1985 s 85(4) includes such a joint authority, such an economic prosperity board, such a combined authority, the London Fire and

Emergency Planning Authority, a police and crime commissioner (see POLICE AND INVESTIGATORY POWERS vol 84 (2013) PARA 56 et seq) and the Mayor's Office for Policing and Crime (see POLICE AND INVESTIGATORY POWERS vol 84 (2013) PARA 78 et seq): Housing Associations Act 1985 s 106(1) (amended by the Education Reform Act 1988 s 237, Sch 13 Pt I; the Local Government (Wales) Act 1994 s 22(2), Sch 8 para 6(2); the Police and Magistrates' Courts Act 1994 s 43, Sch 4 para 59; the Police Act 1996 s 103, Sch 7 para 1(2)(w); the Greater London Authority Act 1999 s 328, Sch 29 para 43; the Local Democracy, Economic Development and Construction Act 2009 s 119, Sch 6 para 69; and the Police Reform and Social Responsibility Act 2011 s 99, Sch 16 para 169). 'New town corporation' means a development corporation within the meaning of the New Towns Act 1981; and 'urban development corporation' means an urban development corporation established under the Local Government, Planning and Land Act 1980 Pt XVI (ss 134–172) (see PLANNING vol 83 (2010) PARA 1581 et seq): Housing Associations Act 1985 s 106(1) (amended by SI 2008/3002).
As to the meaning of 'registered social landlord' see PARA 13.

5 Housing Associations Act 1985 s 84(1) (amended by the Government of Wales Act 1998 Sch 16 paras 28(a), 38(2), Sch 18 Pt VI; and by SI 2009/484).
6 Housing Associations Act 1985 s 84(2) (amended by SI 2009/484).
7 Housing Associations Act 1985 s 84(3) (amended by SI 2009/484).
8 Ie under the Housing Associations Act 1985 s 84(5).
9 As to the Financial Conduct Authority see FINANCIAL SERVICES REGULATION vol 50 (2016) PARA 5 et seq.
10 As to the Prudential Regulation Authority see FINANCIAL SERVICES REGULATION vol 50 (2016) PARA 20 et seq.
11 Housing Associations Act 1985 s 84(5)(a) (amended by the Government of Wales Act 1998 Sch 16 para 38(4); and by SI 2001/3649, SI 2009/484 and SI 2013/496).
12 Housing Associations Act 1985 s 84(5)(b) (amended by SI 2009/484).

150. Financial assistance with respect to formation, management, etc of certain housing associations. The Welsh Ministers[1] may give financial assistance to any person to facilitate the proper performance of the functions of registered social landlords[2] or co-operative housing associations[3]. Such assistance[4] may take the form of grants[5], loans, guarantees or the incurring of expenditure for the benefit of the person assisted or in such other way as the Welsh Ministers consider appropriate; except that they may not, in giving any form of financial assistance under these provisions, purchase loan or share capital in a company[6].

With respect to such financial assistance:

(1)   the procedure to be followed in relation to applications for assistance;
(2)   the circumstances in which assistance is or is not to be given;
(3)   the method for calculating, and any limitations on, the amount of assistance; and
(4)   the manner in which, and the time or times at which, assistance is to be given,

must be such as may be specified by the Welsh Ministers[7].

In giving assistance, the Welsh Ministers may provide that the assistance is conditional upon compliance by the person to whom the assistance is given with such conditions as they may specify[8].

1 As to the Welsh Ministers see PARAS 7, 141.
2 As to the meaning of 'registered social landlord' see PARA 13.
3 Housing Associations Act 1985 s 87(1) (s 87 substituted, in relation to England and Wales, by the Local Government and Housing Act 1989 s 183; the Housing Associations Act 1985 s 87(1) substituted by the Housing Act 1996 s 55(1), Sch 3 para 7; and amended by SI 2010/866). As to the meaning of 'co-operative housing association' see PARA 13.
4 Ie under the Housing Associations Act 1985 s 87.
5 Where assistance under the Housing Associations Act 1985 s 87 is given in the form of a grant, the Housing Act 1988 s 52(1), (2), (7)–(9) (recovery, etc of grants: see PARA 21) applies as it applies in relation to a grant to which s 52 applies, but with the substitution, for any reference to the relevant housing association to which the grant has been given, of a reference to the person to whom assistance is given under the Housing Associations Act 1985 s 87: s 87(5) (substituted by the Local Government and Housing Act 1989 s 183; and amended by SI 1996/2325 and SI 2010/866).

6 Housing Associations Act 1985 s 87(2) (substituted by the Local Government and Housing Act
   1989 s 183; and amended by the Government of Wales Act 1998 s 140, Sch 16 para 40; and by
   SI 2010/866).
7 Housing Associations Act 1985 s 87(3) (substituted by the Local Government and Housing Act
   1989 s 183; and amended by the Housing Act 2004 ss 218, 266, Sch 11 para 1(a), Sch 16; and by
   SI 2010/866).
8 Housing Associations Act 1985 s 87(4) (substituted by the Local Government and Housing Act
   1989 s 183; and amended by SI 2010/866).

151. Grants to bodies other than registered social landlords. The Welsh
Ministers[1] have power under the Housing Act 1996 to make grants to persons
other than registered social landlords[2]. Such grants may be made for any of the
following purposes[3]:

(1)   acquiring, or repairing and improving, or creating by the conversion of
        houses or other property, houses to be disposed of: (a) under equity
        percentage arrangements; or (b) on shared ownership terms[4];
(2)   constructing houses to be disposed of: (a) under equity percentage
        arrangements; or (b) on shared ownership terms;
(3)   providing loans to be secured by mortgages to assist persons to acquire
        houses for their own occupation;
(4)   providing, constructing or improving houses to be kept available for
        letting[5];
(5)   providing, constructing or improving houses for letting that are to be
        managed by such registered social landlords, and under arrangements
        containing such terms, as are approved by the Welsh Ministers;
(6)   such other purposes as may be specified[6] by the Welsh Ministers[7].

The Welsh Ministers may by order make such provision in connection with the
making of grants under these provisions as they consider appropriate[8]. Such an
order may, in particular, make provision:

(a)   defining 'equity percentage arrangements' for the purposes of these
        provisions;
(b)   specifying or describing the bodies from which loans may be obtained
        by persons wishing to acquire houses for their own occupation;
(c)   dealing with the priority of mortgages entered into by such persons;
(d)   specifying purposes additional to those mentioned in heads (1) to (5)
        above[9].

The Welsh Ministers must specify in relation to grants under these provisions:

(i)   the procedure to be followed in relation to applications for a grant;
(ii)   the circumstances in which a grant is or is not to be payable;
(iii)   the method for calculating, and any limitations on, the amount of a
        grant; and
(iv)   the manner in which, and the time or times at which, a grant is to be
        paid[10].

In making a grant to a person under these provisions the Welsh Ministers may
provide that the grant is conditional on compliance by the person with such
conditions as the Welsh Ministers may specify[11]. The conditions that may be so
specified include conditions requiring the payment to the Welsh Ministers in
specified circumstances of a sum determined by them (with or without interest)[12].

1 As to the Welsh Ministers see PARAS 7, 141.
2 Housing Act 1996 s 27A(1) (s 27A added by the Housing Act 2004 s 220; the Housing Act 1996
   s 27A(1) amended by the Housing and Regeneration Act 2008 s 61(1), (7)). These provisions came
   into force on 18 November 2004 (for the purpose of conferring the power to make an order or
   regulations) (see the Housing Act 2004 s 270(2)(b)), and on 17 February 2005 for remaining
   purposes in relation to England (see the Housing Act 2004 (Commencement No 1) (England)

Order 2005, SI 2005/326, art 2(a)). In relation to Wales they are to come into force for remaining purposes as from a day to be appointed: see the Housing Act 2004 s 270(4), (5)(c). At the date at which this volume states the law, no such day had been appointed. The Housing Act 1996 s 27A no longer applies in relation to England: see the Housing and Regeneration Act 2008 ss 60, 61. As to the meaning of 'registered social landlord' see PARA 13.

3   Housing Act 1996 s 27A(2) (as added: see note 2).
4   As to the meaning of 'disposed of on shared ownership terms' see PARA 168 note 17 (definition applied by the Housing Act 1996 s 27A(11) (as added: see note 2)).
5   'Letting' includes the grant of a licence to occupy: Housing Act 1996 s 27A(11) (as added: see note 2).
6   Ie an order under the Housing Act 1996 s 27A(3): see the text and note 8.
7   Housing Act 1996 s 27A(2)(a)–(f) (as added (see note 2); s 27A(2)(e) amended by the Housing and Regeneration Act 2008 s 61(1), (7)).
8   Housing Act 1996 s 27A(3) (as added (see note 2); amended by the Housing and Regeneration Act 2008 s 62(a), (c), (e)). An order under the Housing Act 1996 s 27A(3) is to be made by statutory instrument which is subject to annulment in pursuance of a resolution of the National Assembly for Wales: s 27A(10) (as so added; amended by the Housing and Regeneration Act 2008 s 63).
9   Housing Act 1996 s 27A(4) (as added: see note 2). See also note 8.
10 Housing Act 1996 s 27A(6) (as added (see note 2); amended by the Housing and Regeneration Act 2008 s 61(1), (7)).
11 Housing Act 1996 s 27A(8) (as added (see note 2); amended by the Housing and Regeneration Act 2008 s 61(1), (7)).
12 Housing Act 1996 s 27A(9) (as added (see note 2); amended by the Housing and Regeneration Act 2008 s 61(1), (7)).

152. Transfer of property funded by grants to persons other than registered social landlords. Where any grant is paid or payable to any person other than a registered social landlord[1], and at any time property to which the grant relates becomes vested in, or is leased for a term of years to, or reverts to, another person who is not a registered social landlord, Part I of the Housing Act 1996[2] has effect, in relation to times falling after that time, as if the grant, or a proportion of it[3], had been paid or (as the case may be) were payable to that other person[4].

Where any amount is so paid or payable to any person by way of grant and at any time property to which the grant relates becomes vested in, or is leased for a term of years to, or reverts to, a registered social landlord, Part I of the Housing Act 1996 has effect, in relation to times falling after that time, as if the grant, or a proportion of it[5], had been paid or (as the case may be) were payable[6] to that other person[7].

The proportion mentioned above is that which in the circumstances of the particular case the Welsh Ministers, acting in accordance with such principles as they may from time to time determine, specify as being appropriate, or which the Welsh Ministers may determine to be appropriate[8].

1   Ie under the Housing Act 1996 s 27A: see PARA 151. As to the meaning of 'registered social landlord' see PARA 13.
2   Ie the Housing Act 1996 ss A1–64: see PARA 166 et seq.
3   Ie such proportion as is determined or specified under the Housing Act 1996 s 27B(4): see the text to note 8.
4   Housing Act 1996 s 27B(1) (s 27B added by the Housing Act 2004 s 220). These provisions came into force on 18 November 2004 (for the purpose of conferring the power to make an order or regulations) (see the Housing Act 2004 s 270(2)(b)), and on 17 February 2005 for remaining purposes in relation to England (see the Housing Act 2004 (Commencement No 1) (England) Order 2005, SI 2005/326, art 2(a)). In relation to Wales they are to come into force for remaining purposes as from a day to be appointed: see the Housing Act 2004 s 270(4), (5)(c). At the date at which this volume states the law, no such day had been appointed. The Housing Act 1996 s 27B no longer applies in relation to England: see the Housing and Regeneration Act 2008 ss 60, 61.
5   Ie such proportion as is determined or specified under the Housing Act 1996 s 27B(4): see the text to note 8.
6   Ie under the Housing Act 1996 s 18 (social housing grants): see PARA 166.

7   Housing Act 1996 s 27B(2) (as added: see note 4). In such a case, the relevant section 18 conditions accordingly apply to that grant or proportion of it, in relation to times falling after that time, in place of those specified under s 27A(8) (see PARA 151): s 27B(3) (as so added). 'The relevant section 18 conditions' means such conditions specified under s 18(3) as would have applied at the time of the making of the grant if it had been made under s 18 to a registered social landlord: s 27B(3) (as so added).
8   Housing Act 1996 s 27B(4) (as added (see note 4); amended by the Housing and Regeneration Act 2008 s 61(1), (7)).

(D)   Provisions in respect of Land and Works

153.   In general. The Welsh Ministers[1] have power to acquire land[2], and may provide dwellings or improve dwellings or hostels on land which is owned by them[3]. The Welsh Ministers also have power to dispose of any interest they own in land[4].

1   As to the Welsh Ministers see PARAS 7, 141.
2   See PARA 154.
3   See PARA 155.
4   See PARA 156.

154.   Acquisition of land. The Welsh Ministers[1] may acquire land by agreement for the purpose of:
   (1)   selling or leasing it to a registered social landlord[2] or an unregistered self-build society[3]; or
   (2)   providing dwellings[4] (for letting or for sale) or hostels[5],
and the Welsh Ministers may acquire land compulsorily[6] for any such purpose[7].

1   As to the Welsh Ministers see PARAS 7, 141.
2   As to the meaning of 'registered social landlord' see PARA 102.
3   Housing Associations Act 1985 s 88(1)(a) (amended, in relation to England and Wales, by SI 1996/2325 and SI 2009/484). As to the meaning of 'self-build society' see PARA 13.
4   As to the meaning of 'dwelling' see PARA 143 note 7.
5   Housing Associations Act 1985 s 88(1)(b). As to the meaning of 'hostel' see PARA 143 note 8.
6   The Acquisition of Land Act 1981 applies to the compulsory purchase of land under the Housing Associations Act 1985 s 88: s 88(3) (substituted, in relation to England and Wales, by SI 2009/484). See generally COMPULSORY ACQUISITION OF LAND vol 18 (2009) PARA 501 et seq.
7   Housing Associations Act 1985 s 88(1) (amended, in relation to England and Wales, by SI 2009/484). Land may be so acquired by the Welsh Ministers notwithstanding that it is not immediately required for any such purpose: Housing Associations Act 1985 s 88(2) (amended, in relation to England and Wales, by SI 2009/484).

155.   Provision of dwellings or hostels and clearance, management and development of land. The Welsh Ministers[1] may provide or improve dwellings[2] or hostels[3] on land belonging to them[4]. The Welsh Ministers may clear land belonging to them and carry out other work on the land to prepare it as a building site or estate, including:
   (1)   the laying out and construction of streets or roads and open spaces; and
   (2)   the provision of sewerage facilities and supplies of gas, electricity and water[5].
The Welsh Ministers may repair, maintain and insure buildings or works on land belonging to them, may generally deal in the proper course of management with such land and buildings or works on it, and may charge for the tenancy or occupation of such land, buildings or works[6]. The Welsh Ministers may carry out such operations on, and do such other things in relation to, land belonging to them as appear to them to be conducive to facilitating the provision or improvement of dwellings or hostels on the land:
   (a)   by the Welsh Ministers themselves; or
   (b)   by a registered social landlord[7] or an unregistered self-build society[8].

1   As to the Welsh Ministers see PARAS 7, 141.

2 As to the meaning of 'dwelling' see PARA 143 note 7.
3 As to the meaning of 'hostel' see PARA 143 note 8.
4 Housing Associations Act 1985 s 89(1) (amended, in relation to England and Wales, by SI 2009/484).
5 Housing Associations Act 1985 s 89(2) (amended, in relation to England and Wales, by SI 2009/484).
6 Housing Associations Act 1985 s 89(3) (amended, in relation to England and Wales, by SI 2009/484).
7 As to the meaning of 'registered social landlord' see PARA 13.
8 Housing Associations Act 1985 s 89(4) (amended, in relation to England and Wales, by SI 1996/2325 and SI 2009/484). As to the meaning of 'self-build society' see PARA 13. In the exercise of their powers under the Housing Associations Act 1985 s 89(4) the Welsh Ministers may carry out any development ancillary to or in connection with the provision of dwellings or hostels, including development which makes provision for buildings or land to be used for commercial, recreational or other non-domestic purposes: s 89(5) (amended, in relation to England and Wales, by SI 2009/484).

156. Disposal of land. The Welsh Ministers[1] may dispose of land in respect of which they have not exercised their powers to provide or improve dwellings or hostels[2] and on which they have not carried out development[3] to a registered social landlord[4] or an unregistered self-build society[5].

The Welsh Ministers may dispose of land on which dwellings or hostels have been provided or improved[6] to a registered social landlord, a local authority, a new town corporation[7] or Scottish Homes[8].

The Welsh Ministers may sell or lease individual dwellings to persons for those persons to occupy[9]. The Welsh Ministers may dispose of a building or land intended for use for commercial, recreational or other non-domestic purposes in respect of which development has been carried out[10]. The Welsh Ministers may dispose of land which is not required for the purposes for which it was acquired[11].

1 As to the Welsh Ministers see PARAS 7, 141.
2 Ie under the Housing Associations Act 1985 s 89(1): see PARA 155.
3 Ie any such development as is mentioned in the Housing Associations Act 1985 s 89(5) (ancillary development): see PARA 155.
4 As to the meaning of 'registered social landlord' see PARA 13.
5 Housing Associations Act 1985 s 90(1) (amended, in relation to England and Wales, by SI 2009/484). As to the meaning of 'self-build society' see PARA 13.
6 Ie in exercise of their powers under the Housing Associations Act 1985 s 89: see PARA 155.
7 As to the meaning of 'new town corporation' see PARA 12.
8 Housing Associations Act 1985 s 90(2) (amended, in relation to England and Wales, by SI 1996/2325 and SI 2009/484).
9 Housing Associations Act 1985 s 90(3) (substituted, in relation to England and Wales, by SI 2009/484).
10 Housing Associations Act 1985 s 90(4) (substituted, in relation to England and Wales, by SI 2009/484). The text refers to development carried out by virtue of the Housing Associations Act 1985 s 89: see PARA 155.
11 Housing Associations Act 1985 s 90(5) (substituted, in relation to England and Wales, by SI 2009/484).

(E) Information, Standards and Guidance

157. Introduction. The Welsh Ministers[1] have a number of powers to monitor and to regulate the performance of registered social landlords[2]. Before the Housing Act 1996, such powers and responsibilities were those of the Housing Corporation, which were contained in the Housing Associations Act 1985 and extended by the Housing Act 1988. This statutory framework was re-enacted by the Housing Act 1996, renewing and extending the powers of the regulator (at the time the Housing Corporation and now the Welsh Ministers) to obtain information from registered social landlords[3], to promulgate performance standards and to monitor compliance with the standards[4]. New powers to enter dwellings which are not properly maintained were introduced by the Housing Act 1996[5] while the regulator's role in the affairs of an insolvent landlord was remodelled[6].

In connection with their functions in relation to registered social landlords, the Welsh Ministers have power to obtain information and documents from registered social landlords, their members and officers and others such as banks[7]. These powers may be enforced by civil and criminal sanctions[8]. There are also specific provisions under which government departments and the Welsh Ministers may provide or receive information on social landlords[9].

1 As to the Welsh Ministers see PARAS 7, 141.
2 See PARA 158 et seq. As to the meaning of 'registered social landlord' see PARA 13.
3 See PARA 158.
4 See PARA 160.
5 See PARA 165.
6 See PARA 206 et seq.
7 See PARA 158.
8 See PARA 158.
9 See PARA 159.

158. General power to obtain information. The Welsh Ministers[1], in the performance of their functions as funders and regulators of registered social landlords[2], may require such a landlord to provide them with a range of different types of information. In order to exercise these powers, the Welsh Ministers may serve a notice[3] on a person requiring him:

(1) to give to the Welsh Ministers, at a time and place and in the form and manner specified in the notice, such information relating to the affairs of a registered social landlord as may be specified or described in the notice; or

(2) to produce to the Welsh Ministers or a person authorised by the Welsh Ministers, at a time and place specified in the notice, any documents[4] relating to the affairs of the registered social landlord which are specified or described in the notice and are in his custody or under his control[5].

For these purposes, a notice may be served on the following persons:

(a) a registered social landlord;

(b) any person who is, or has been an officer, member, employee or agent[6] of a registered social landlord;

(c) a subsidiary or associate of a registered social landlord;

(d) any person who is, or has been, an officer, member, employee or agent of a subsidiary or associate of a registered social landlord; or

(e) any other person whom the Welsh Ministers have reason to believe[7] is or may be in possession[8] of relevant information[9].

There are, however, certain restrictions on the information the Welsh Ministers may seek. The Welsh Ministers may not require the disclosure of anything which a person would be entitled to refuse to disclose on grounds of legal professional privilege in proceedings in the High Court, or the disclosure by a banker of anything in breach of any duty of confidentiality owed by him to a person other than a registered social landlord or a subsidiary or associate of a registered landlord[10].

A person who without reasonable excuse fails to do anything required of him by a notice under these provisions commits an offence and is liable on conviction to a penalty[11]. Further, a person who intentionally alters, suppresses or destroys a document which he has been required by such a notice to produce commits an offence and is liable on conviction to a penalty[12]. Proceedings for an offence for these purposes may be brought only by or with the consent of the Welsh Ministers or the Director of Public Prosecutions[13].

If a person makes default in complying with a notice under these provisions, the High Court may, on the application of the Welsh Ministers, make such order as the court thinks fit for requiring the default to be made good and such an order may provide that all the costs or expenses of and incidental to the application be borne by the person in default or by any officers of a body who are responsible for the default[14].

1   As to the Welsh Ministers see PARAS 7, 141.
2   As to registered social landlords and eligibility for registration as such see the Housing Act 1996 s 2; and PARAS 167–168.
3   A notice under the Housing Act 1996 s 30, if given by the Welsh Ministers, must be given in writing: s 30(5) (substituted by the Government of Wales Act 1998 s 140, Sch 16 para 86; and amended by the Housing and Regeneration Act 2008 s 62(a); and by SI 2010/866).
4   References in the Housing Act 1996 s 30 to a document are references to anything in which information of any description is recorded; and in relation to a document in which information is recorded otherwise than in legible form, references to producing it are references to producing it in legible form: s 30(6).
5   Housing Act 1996 s 30(1) (amended by the Housing and Regeneration Act 2008 s 61(1), (7)). Where by virtue of the Housing Act 1996 s 30 documents are produced to any person, he may take copies of or make extracts from them: s 30(7). 'Custody' means physical custody and 'control' imports the notion of power to direct what is done with the documents in question, and these words are intended to provide a clearer concept than 'possession' which is a technical term of some difficulty: see *Warner v Metropolitan Police Comr* [1969] 2 AC 256, [1968] 2 All ER 356, HL. As to data protection see CONFIDENCE AND INFORMATIONAL PRIVACY vol 19 (2011) PARA 95 et seq.
6   For the purposes of this provision, 'agent' includes banker, solicitor and auditor: see the Housing Act 1996 s 30(2). An 'agent' is a person who has authority, express or implied, to act on behalf of another, called the 'principal', and consents so to act: see *Pole v Leask* (1863) 33 LJ Ch 155 at 161; and AGENCY vol 1 (2008) PARA 1 et seq.
7   The existence of the reason to believe and of the belief founded on it is ultimately a question of fact to be tried on evidence and the grounds on which the person acted must be sufficient to induce the required belief in a reasonable person: see *McArdle v Egan* (1933) 150 LT 412, CA; *Nakkuda Ali v MF De S Jayaratne* [1951] AC 66, PC; *IRC v Rossminster Ltd* [1980] AC 952, [1980] 1 All ER 80, HL.
8   As to the meaning of 'possession' see PERSONAL PROPERTY vol 80 (2013) PARA 834 et seq.
9   Housing Act 1996 s 30(2) (amended by the Housing and Regeneration Act 2008 s 61(1), (7)). No notice, however, may be served upon a person within heads (b)–(e) in the text unless: (1) a notice has been served on the registered social landlord and has not been complied with; or (2) the Welsh Ministers believe that the information or documents in question are not in the possession of the landlord: Housing Act 1996 s 30(3) (amended by the Housing and Regeneration Act 2008 s 61(1), (7)).
10 Housing Act 1996 s 30(4) (amended by the Housing and Regeneration Act 2008 s 61(1), (7)). In a number of cases the courts had allowed statutory inquiries to override the privilege, and so an express protection of privilege has proved to be necessary: see eg *British and Commonwealth Holdings plc (Joint Administrators) v Spicer and Oppenheim* [1993] AC 426, [1992] 4 All ER 876, HL (statutory inquiry into a company's affairs under the Insolvency Act 1986).
11 Housing Act 1996 s 31(1). The penalty on summary conviction is a fine not exceeding level 5 on the standard scale: see s 31(1). As to the powers of magistrates' courts to issue fines on summary conviction see SENTENCING vol 92 (2015) PARA 176.
    Where an offence under the Housing Act 1996 committed by a body corporate is proved to have been committed with the consent or connivance of a director, manager, secretary or other similar officer of the body corporate, or a person purporting to act in such a capacity, he as well as the body corporate is guilty of an offence and liable to be proceeded against and punished accordingly: s 223(1). Where the affairs of a body corporate are managed by its members s 223(1) applies in relation to the acts and defaults of a member in connection with his functions of management as if he were a director of the body corporate: s 223(2).
12 Housing Act 1996 s 31(2). The penalty on summary conviction is a fine not exceeding the statutory maximum, and on conviction on indictment is imprisonment for a term not exceeding two years or a fine or both: see the Housing Act 1996 s 31(2) (amended by the Housing Act 2004 s 218, Sch 11 paras 7, 12(1)). As to the powers of magistrates' courts to issue fines on summary

conviction see SENTENCING vol 92 (2015) PARA 176. As to fines on conviction generally see *Churchill v Walton* [1967] 2 AC 224, [1967] 1 All ER 497, HL; *R v Garner, R v Breeze* [1986] 1 All ER 78, [1986] 1 WLR 73, CA. The statutory power to obtain a compliance order from the High Court overrules the effect of *Ashby v Ebdon* [1985] Ch 394, [1984] 3 All ER 869.

13 Housing Act 1996 s 31(3) (amended by the Housing and Regeneration Act 2008 s 61(1), (7)). As to the Director of Public Prosecutions see CRIMINAL PROCEDURE vol 27 (2015) PARAS 25, 30 et seq.

14 Housing Act 1996 s 31(4) (amended by the Housing and Regeneration Act 2008 s 61(1), (7)).

159. Disclosure of information to and by the Welsh Ministers. Any government department (including a Northern Ireland department), any local authority[1], any constable[2] and any other body or person discharging functions of a public nature (including a body or persons discharging regulatory functions in relation to any description of activities) may disclose to the Welsh Ministers, for the purpose of enabling them to discharge any of their functions relating to registered social landlords, any information received by that body or person under or for the purposes of any enactment[3].

Similarly, the Welsh Ministers may disclose to any government department (including a Northern Ireland department), any local authority, any constable and any other body or person discharging functions of a public nature (including a body or persons discharging regulatory functions in relation to any description of activities)[4] any information received by them relating to a registered social landlord: (1) for any purpose connected with the discharge of the functions of the Welsh Ministers in relation to such landlords; or (2) for the purpose of enabling or assisting that body or person to discharge any of its or his functions[5].

1 In the Housing Act 1996 Pt I (ss A1–64), 'local authority' has the same meaning as in the Housing Associations Act 1985 (see PARA 149 note 4): Housing Act 1996 s 63(1).

2 As to the attestation of every member of a police force as a constable see the Police Act 1996 s 29 (amended by the Greater London Authority Act 1999 ss 325, 423, Sch 27 para 83(a), Sch 34 Pt VII); and as to the jurisdiction of constables see the Police Act 1996 s 30 (amended by the Anti-terrorism, Crime and Security Act 2001 s 101, Sch 7 paras 20, 24; the Police and Justice Act 2006 ss 2, 52, Sch 2 para 21(1)–(3), Sch 15 Pt 1(B); the Policing and Crime Act 2009 s 112(1), Sch 7 paras 1, 7(b); and the Police Reform and Social Responsibility Act 2011 s 99, Sch 16 paras 1, 28). See further POLICE AND INVESTIGATORY POWERS vol 84 (2013) PARA 1 et seq.

3 See the Housing Act 1996 s 32(1), (2) (s 32(1) amended by the Housing and Regeneration Act 2008 s 61(1), (7)). As to the Welsh Ministers see PARAS 7, 141. This provision has effect subject to any express restriction on disclosure imposed by or under any other enactment and it is not to be construed as affecting any power of disclosure exercisable apart from the Housing Act 1996 s 32: see s 32(3), (4). As to data protection see CONFIDENCE AND INFORMATIONAL PRIVACY vol 19 (2011) PARA 95 et seq.

4 This extends to any such body or person in a country or territory outside the United Kingdom: Housing Act 1996 s 33(2). As to the meaning of 'United Kingdom' see PARA 60 note 10.

5 See the Housing Act 1996 s 33(1), (2) (s 33(1) amended by the Housing and Regeneration Act 2008 s 61(1), (7)). Where any information disclosed to the Welsh Ministers under the Housing Act 1966 s 32 (see the text and notes 1–3) is so disclosed subject to any express restriction on the further disclosure of the information, the Welsh Ministers' power of disclosure pursuant to s 33 is exercisable subject to that restriction; and any information disclosed by the Welsh Ministers under s 33 may itself be subject by the Welsh Ministers to any express restriction on the further disclosure of information: see s 33(3), (4) (amended by the Housing and Regeneration Act 2008 s 61(1), (7)). In both these cases, where any restriction is so placed upon the disclosure of information and is contravened, the contravenor commits an offence and is liable on summary conviction to a fine not exceeding level 3 on the standard scale: see the Housing Act 1996 s 33(3), (5). As to the powers of magistrates' courts to issue fines on summary conviction see SENTENCING vol 92 (2015) PARA 176. Proceedings for an offence of contravention of a restriction imposed by the Welsh Ministers may only be brought by or with the consent of the Welsh Ministers or the Director of Public Prosecutions: s 33(5) (amended by the Housing and Regeneration Act 2008 s 61(1), (7)). Nothing in the Housing Act 1996 s 33 is to be construed as affecting any power of disclosure exercisable apart from that provision itself: s 33(6). As to the Director of Public Prosecutions see CRIMINAL PROCEDURE vol 27 (2015) PARAS 25, 30 et seq.

160. Standards of performance relating to housing in Wales. The Welsh Ministers[1] may set standards to be met by registered social landlords[2] in connection with:

(1)   their functions relating to the provision of housing; and

(2)   matters relating to their governance and financial management[3].

In setting standards the Welsh Ministers must have regard to the desirability of registered providers being free to choose how to provide services and conduct business[4]. The standards set may require registered social landlords to comply with rules specified in the standards[5]. The Welsh Ministers may:

(a)   revise the standards by issuing further standards under these provisions;

(b)   withdraw the standards by issuing further standards or by notice[6].

The Welsh Ministers must publish any standards or notice under these provisions[7].

The Welsh Ministers may issue guidance that relates to a matter addressed by a standard and amplifies the standard[8]. In considering whether standards have been met the Welsh Ministers may have regard to the guidance[9]. The Welsh Ministers may:

(i)   revise the guidance by issuing further guidance;

(ii)   withdraw the guidance by issuing further guidance or by notice[10].

The Welsh Ministers must publish any guidance or notice under these provisions[11].

Before setting, revising or withdrawing standards[12], or issuing, revising or withdrawing guidance[13], the Welsh Ministers must consult:

(A)   one or more bodies appearing to them to represent the interests of registered social landlords;

(B)   one or more bodies appearing to them to represent the interests of tenants[14]; and

(C)   one or more bodies appearing to them to represent the interests of local housing authorities[15].

1   As to the Welsh Ministers see PARAS 7, 141.
2   As to the meaning of 'registered social landlord' see PARA 13.
3   Housing Act 1996 s 33A(1) (s 33A added by the Housing (Wales) Measure 2011 s 35). The Housing Act 1996 s 33A does not apply in relation to a registered social landlord's provision of housing in England: s 33A(3) (as so added). As to standards of performance in connection with the provision of housing in England see s 34; and PARA 161.
4   Housing Act 1996 s 33A(2) (as added: see note 3).
5   Housing Act 1996 s 33A(2A) (s 33A(2A)–(2C) added by the Housing (Wales) Act 2014 s 130, Sch 3 para 28(1), (2)).
6   Housing Act 1996 s 33A(2B) (as added: see note 5).
7   Housing Act 1996 s 33A(2C) (as added: see note 5). To 'publish' means to make known to some person other than the originator: see *Dew v DPP* (1920) 89 LJKB 1166; *Ranson v Burgess* (1927) 137 LT 530; *A-G v Walkergate Press Ltd* (1930) 142 LT 408.
8   Housing Act 1996 s 33B(1) (s 33B added by the Housing (Wales) Measure 2011 s 36).
9   Housing Act 1996 s 33B(2) (as added: see note 8).
10 Housing Act 1996 s 33B(3) (as added (see note 8); substituted by the Housing (Wales) Act 2014 Sch 3 para 28(1), (3)(a)).
11 Housing Act 1996 s 33B(4) (as added (see note 8); substituted by the Housing (Wales) Act 2014 Sch 3 para 28(1), (3)(b)).
12 Ie under the Housing Act 1996 s 33A.
13 Ie under the Housing Act 1996 s 33B.
14 As to the meaning of 'tenant' see PARA 168 note 16.
15 Housing Act 1996 s 33C (added by the Housing (Wales) Measure 2011 s 37; and amended by the Housing (Wales) Act 2014 Sch 3 para 28(1), (4)). As to the meaning of 'local housing authority' for these purposes see PARA 11 (definition applied by the Housing Act 1996 s 230).

161. Standards of performance relating to housing in England. The Welsh Ministers[1] may, after consultation with persons or bodies appearing to them to be representative of registered landlords, from time to time[2] determine such standards of performance in connection with the provision of housing in England as, in their opinion, ought to be achieved by such landlords and may arrange for the publication[3], in such form and in such manner as they consider appropriate, of the standards so determined[4].

1 As to the Welsh Ministers see PARAS 7, 141.
2 'From time to time' means 'as the occasion shall arise' or 'as and when it is appropriate so to do': see *Holliday v Wakefield Corpn* (1887) 57 LT 559 at 562–563 per Mathew J; *Re Von Dembinska, ex p the Debtor* [1954] 2 All ER 46 at 48, [1954] 1 WLR 748, CA, per Evershed MR.
3 As to the meaning of 'publish' see PARA 160 note 7.
4 Housing Act 1996 s 34 (amended by the Housing and Regeneration Act 2008 s 61(1), (7); and the Housing (Wales) Measure 2011 s 88, Schedule paras 1, 5).

162. Information about standards of performance. The Welsh Ministers[1] must from time to time[2] collect information as to the levels of performance achieved by registered social landlords[3] in connection with their functions relating to the provision of housing in Wales and with matters relating to their governance and financial management[4].

The Welsh Ministers must from time to time collect information as to the levels of performance achieved by registered social landlords in connection with the provision of housing in England[5].

On or before such date in each year as may be specified in a direction given by the Welsh Ministers, each registered social landlord must provide the Welsh Ministers, as respects each standard determined by the Welsh Ministers pursuant to the relevant provisions[6], with such information as to the level of performance achieved as may be so specified[7]. The Welsh Ministers must at least once in every year arrange for the publication[8], in such form and in such manner as they consider appropriate, of such of the information collected by or provided to them in pursuance of these provisions[9] as appears to them expedient to give to tenants or potential tenants of registered social landlords[10]. In arranging for the publication of any such information the Welsh Ministers must have regard[11] to the need for excluding, so far as that is reasonably practicable: (1) any matter which relates to the affairs of an individual, where publication of that matter would or might, in the opinion of the Welsh Ministers, seriously and prejudicially affect the interests of that individual; and (2) any matter which relates specifically to the affairs of a particular body of persons, whether corporate or unincorporate, where publication of that matter would or might, in the opinion of the Welsh Ministers, seriously and prejudicially affect the interests of that body[12].

1 As to the Welsh Ministers see PARAS 7, 141.
2 As to the meaning of 'from time to time' see PARA 161 note 2.
3 As to the meaning of 'registered social landlord' see PARA 13.
4 Housing and Regeneration Act 2008 s 35(A1) (added, in relation to Wales, by the Housing (Wales) Measure 2011 s 38(1), (2)). A registered social landlord may give the Welsh Ministers an undertaking in respect of any matter concerning housing: Housing Act 1996 s 6A(1) (s 6A added, in relation to Wales, by the Housing (Wales) Measure 2011 s 41). The Welsh Ministers may prescribe a procedure to be followed in giving an undertaking: Housing Act 1996 s 6A(2) (as so added). The Welsh Ministers must have regard to any undertaking offered or given in exercising a regulatory or enforcement power, including a power exercisable under s 35: s 6A(3), (5) (as so added). The Welsh Ministers may base a decision about whether to exercise a regulatory or enforcement power wholly or partly on the extent to which an undertaking has been honoured: s 6A(4) (as so added). Section 6A does not apply in relation to a registered social landlord's provision of housing in England: s 6A(6) (as so added).

5 Housing Act 1996 s 35(1) (amended by the Housing and Regeneration Act 2008 s 61(1), (7); and, in relation to Wales, by the Housing (Wales) Measure 2011 s 38(1), (3)).
6 Ie the Housing Act 1996 s 33A or s 34: see PARAS 160, 161.
7 Housing Act 1996 s 35(2) (amended by the Housing and Regeneration Act 2008 s 61(1), (7); and, in relation to Wales, by the Housing (Wales) Measure 2011 s 38(1), (4)). A registered social landlord who without reasonable excuse fails to do anything required of him by a direction under the Housing Act 1996 s 35(2) commits an offence and is liable on summary conviction to a fine not exceeding level 5 on the standard scale: s 35(3). Proceedings for such an offence may be brought only by or with the consent of the Welsh Ministers or the Director of Public Prosecutions: s 35(3) (amended by the Housing and Regeneration Act 2008 s 61(1), (7)). As to the powers of magistrates' courts to issue fines on summary conviction see SENTENCING vol 92 (2015) PARA 176. As to the Director of Public Prosecutions see CRIMINAL PROCEDURE vol 27 (2015) PARAS 25, 30 et seq.
8 As to the meaning of 'publish' see PARA 160 note 7.
9 Ie the Housing Act 1996 s 35.
10 Housing Act 1996 s 35(4) (amended by the Housing and Regeneration Act 2008 s 61(1), (7)).
11 It has been stated that 'regard' is intended to be a loose and indefinite term: see *Cohen v West Ham Corpn* [1933] Ch 814 at 833, CA, per Lord Hanworth MR.
12 Housing Act 1996 s 35(5) (amended by the Housing and Regeneration Act 2008 s 61(1), (7)). As to corporations generally see COMPANIES vol 14 (2016) PARA 1 et seq; CORPORATIONS.

163. Issue of guidance about complaints about performance. The Welsh Ministers[1] may publish[2] guidance about complaints to the Welsh Ministers about the performance of registered social landlords[3]. The guidance may specify (among other things):

(1)   the procedure to be followed in making a complaint;
(2)   the criteria used by the Welsh Ministers in deciding whether to investigate a complaint;
(3)   periods within which the Welsh Ministers aim to inform complainants of the result of complaints[4].

The Welsh Ministers may revise or withdraw the guidance[5]. These provisions do not apply in relation to complaints about a registered social landlord's provision of housing in England[6].

Before publishing, revising or withdrawing such guidance the Welsh Ministers must consult:

(a)   one or more bodies appearing to them to represent the interests of registered social landlords;
(b)   one or more bodies appearing to them to represent the interests of tenants[7];
(c)   one or more bodies appearing to them to represent the interests of local housing authorities[8]; and
(d)   the Auditor General for Wales[9].

1 As to the Welsh Ministers see PARAS 7, 141.
2 As to the meaning of 'publish' see PARA 160 note 7.
3 Housing Act 1996 s 35A(1) (s 35A added, in relation to Wales, by the Housing (Wales) Measure 2011 s 39). As to the meaning of 'registered social landlord' see PARA 13.
4 Housing Act 1996 s 35A(2) (as added: see note 3).
5 Housing Act 1996 s 35A(3) (as added: see note 3).
6 Housing Act 1996 s 35A(4) (as added: see note 3).
7 As to the meaning of 'tenant' see PARA 168 note 16.'
8 As to the meaning of 'local housing authority' for these purposes see PARA 11 (definition applied by the Housing Act 1996 s 230).
9 Housing Act 1996 s 35B (added, in relation to Wales, by the Housing (Wales) Measure 2011 s 40).

164. Issue of guidance relating to housing in England The Welsh Ministers[1] may issue guidance with respect to the management of housing accommodation[2] in England by registered social landlords[3]. Such guidance[4] may in particular be issued with respect to:

(1)   the housing demands for which provision should be made and the means of meeting those demands;

(2)   the allocation of housing accommodation between individuals;

(3)   the terms of tenancies and the principles upon which levels of rent should be determined;

(4)   standards of maintenance and repair and the means of achieving those standards;

(5)   the services to be provided to tenants;

(6)   the procedures to be adopted to deal with complaints by tenants against a landlord;

(7)   consultation and communication with tenants;

(8)   the devolution to tenants of decisions concerning the management of housing accommodation;

(9)   the policy and procedures a landlord is required[5] to prepare and from time to time revise in connection with anti-social behaviour[6].

Guidance under the above provisions may make different provision in relation to different cases and, in particular, in relation to different areas, different descriptions of housing accommodation and different descriptions of registered social landlord[7].

Before issuing any guidance under these provisions, however, the Welsh Ministers must consult such bodies appearing to the Welsh Ministers to be representative of registered social landlords as the Welsh Ministers consider appropriate; and where the Welsh Ministers issue such guidance it must be issued in such manner as the Welsh Ministers consider appropriate for bringing it to the notice of the landlords concerned[8].

1   As to the Welsh Ministers see PARAS 7, 141.
2   In the Housing Act 1996 Pt I (ss A1–64), 'housing accommodation' includes flats, lodging-houses and hostels; and 'hostel' means a building in which is provided for persons generally, or for a class or classes of persons: (1) residential accommodation otherwise than in separate and self-contained premises; and (2) either board or facilities for the preparation of food adequate to the needs of those persons, or both: s 63(1).
3   Housing Act 1996 s 36(1) (amended by the Housing and Regeneration Act 2008 s 61(1), (7); and, in relation to Wales, by the Housing (Wales) Measure 2011 s 88, Schedule paras 1, 7(a)). In considering whether action needs to be taken to secure the proper management of the affairs of a registered social landlord or whether there has been misconduct or mismanagement, the Welsh Ministers may have regard (among other matters) to the extent to which any guidance under the Housing Act 1996 s 36 is being or has been followed: s 36(7) (amended by the Housing Act 2004 s 218, Sch 11 paras 7, 13(1), (4); and the Housing and Regeneration Act 2008 s 61(1), (7)). As to the meaning of 'registered social landlord' see PARA 13.
4   Ie guidance under the Housing Act 1996 s 36(1): see the text and note 3.
5   Ie under the Housing Act 1996 s 218A: see PARA 28.
6   Housing Act 1996 s 36(2) (amended by the Anti-social Behaviour Act 2003 s 12(2); and the Housing Act 2004 Sch 11 para 13(2)).
7   Housing Act 1996 s 36(6).
8   Housing Act 1996 s 36(3) (substituted by the Government of Wales Act 1998 s 140, Sch 16 para 87; and amended by the Housing and Regeneration Act 2008 s 61(1), (7)). Guidance issued under the Housing Act 1996 s 36 may be revised or withdrawn; and the provisions of s 36(3) apply in relation to the revision of guidance as in relation to its issue: s 36(5) (amended by SI 2010/866).

165. Powers of entry where guidance on maintenance is not followed. Where it appears to the Welsh Ministers[1] that a registered social landlord[2] may be failing to maintain or repair any premises in accordance with standards they have set[3], or guidance they have given[4], a person authorised by the Welsh Ministers may at any reasonable time[5], on giving not less than 28 days' notice[6] of his intention to the landlord concerned, enter any such premises for the purpose of survey and examination[7]. Where such notice is given to the landlord, the landlord must give the occupier or occupiers of the premises not less than seven days' notice of the proposed survey and examination[8].

It is an offence for a registered social landlord or any of its officers or employees to obstruct a person so authorised to enter premises in the performance of anything which he is authorised by these provisions to do[9]. A person who commits such an offence is liable on summary conviction to a fine[10]. Proceedings for such an offence may be brought only by or with the consent of the Welsh Ministers or the Director of Public Prosecutions[11].

A registered social landlord may give the Welsh Ministers an undertaking in respect of any matter concerning housing[12]. The Welsh Ministers must have regard to any undertaking offered or given in exercising a regulatory or enforcement power, including a power of entry[13] under the provisions described above[14]. The Welsh Ministers may base a decision about whether to exercise a regulatory or enforcement power wholly or partly on the extent to which an undertaking has been honoured[15]. These provisions do not apply in relation to a registered social landlord's provision of housing in England[16].

1 As to the Welsh Ministers see PARAS 7, 141.
2 As to the meaning of 'registered social landlord' see PARA 13.
3 Ie under the Housing Act 1996 s 33A. As to the power to set standards see PARA 160.
4 Ie under the Housing Act 1996 s 36. As to the power to issue guidance see PARA 164.
5 What is a reasonable time is a question of fact depending on the particular circumstances of each case: see generally TIME vol 97 (2015) PARA 349.
6 The words 'not less than' indicate that 28 clear days must intervene between the day on which notice is given and that on which the premises are entered: see *R v Turner* [1910] 1 KB 346, 79 LJKB 176, CCA; *Re Hector Whaling Ltd* [1936] Ch 208. As to the calculation of statutory periods see TIME vol 97 (2015) PARAS 334, 335.
7 Housing Act 1996 s 37(1), (2) (amended by the Housing and Regeneration Act 2008 s 61(1), (7); the Housing Act 1996 s 37(1) amended, in relation to Wales, by the Housing (Wales) Measure 2011 s 88, Schedule paras 1, 8). The Welsh Ministers must give a copy of any survey carried out in exercise of the powers conferred by the Housing Act 1996 s 37 to the landlord concerned; and may require the landlord to pay to them such amount as the Welsh Ministers may determine towards the costs of carrying out any such survey: see s 37(6), (7) (amended by the Housing and Regeneration Act 2008 s 61(1), (7)). An authorisation for the purposes of the Housing Act 1996 s 37 must be in writing stating the particular purpose or purposes for which the entry is authorised and, if so required, must be produced for inspection by the occupier or anyone acting on his behalf: s 37(5).
8 Housing Act 1996 s 37(3). A landlord who fails, without reasonable excuse, to give the required notice in relation to premises in Wales, commits an offence and is liable on summary conviction to a fine not exceeding level 3 on the standard scale: s 37(3A) (numbered as such and amended, in relation to Wales, by the Housing (Wales) Measure 2011 s 42(1), (2)(a), (b)). A landlord who fails to give the required notice in relation to premises in England commits an offence and is liable on summary conviction to a fine not exceeding level 3 on the standard scale: Housing Act 1996 s 37(3B) (added, in relation to Wales, by the Housing (Wales) Measure 2011 s 42(1), (2)(c)). Proceedings for an offence under the Housing Act 1996 s 37(3A) or (3B) may be brought only by or with the consent of the Welsh Ministers or the Director of Public Prosecutions: s 37(4) (amended by the Housing and Regeneration Act 2008 s 61(1), (7); and, in relation to Wales, by the Housing (Wales) Measure 2011 s 42(1), (3)). As to the powers of magistrates' courts to issue fines on summary conviction see SENTENCING vol 92 (2015) PARA 176. As to the Director of Public Prosecutions see CRIMINAL PROCEDURE vol 27 (2015) PARAS 25, 30 et seq.
9 Housing Act 1996 s 38(1).
10 Housing Act 1996 s 38(2). The penalty is a fine not exceeding level 3 on the standard scale: see s 38(2). As to the concurrent liability of any director, manager, secretary or other similar officer of a body corporate see s 233; and PARA 158 note 11.
11 Housing Act 1996 s 38(3) (amended by the Housing and Regeneration Act 2008 s 61(1), (7)).
12 Housing Act 1996 s 6A(1) (s 6A added, in relation to Wales, by the Housing (Wales) Measure 2011 s 41). The Welsh Ministers may prescribe a procedure to be followed in giving an undertaking: Housing Act 1996 s 6A(2) (as so added).

13 Ie including a power exercisable under the Housing Act 1996 ss 37, 38.
14 Housing Act 1996 s 6A(3), (5) (as added: see note 11).
15 Housing Act 1996 s 6A(4) (as added: see note 11).
16 Housing Act 1996 s 6A(6) (as added: see note 11).

B. REGISTRATION OF SOCIAL LANDLORDS IN WALES

166. Introduction. Before the Housing Act 1996, only a landlord which was either a registered charity or was registered as a registered society could apply for registration with the Housing Corporation or Housing for Wales[1]. As a result of changes introduced by that Act, a landlord which is registered as a company could also be eligible for registration provided that it was a non-profit making company and met certain other criteria under that Act[2]. The 1996 Act also re-enacted, with some modifications, the provisions governing the registration of housing associations previously contained in the Housing Associations Act 1985[3]. Under the Housing Act 1996, a landlord which was registered with the Housing Corporation was known as a 'registered social landlord'[4]. Registered social landlords became the main providers of new social housing[5], but with the changes brought about by the Housing and Regeneration Act 2008[6], the system of registered social landlords applies only in Wales as from 10 April 2010 and only a 'Welsh body' is eligible for registration[7].

The Welsh Ministers[8] may make grants to registered social landlords in respect of expenditure incurred or to be incurred by them in connection with their housing activities[9]. The Welsh Ministers must specify in relation to such grants: (1) the procedure to be followed in relation to applications for grant; (2) the circumstances in which grant is or is not to be payable; (3) the method for calculating, and any limitations on, the amount of grant; and (4) the manner in which, and time or times at which, grant is to be paid[10]. In making a grant, the Welsh Ministers may provide that the grant is conditional on compliance by the landlord with such conditions as they may specify[11]. The Welsh Ministers may, with the agreement of a local housing authority, appoint the authority to act as their agent in connection with the assessment and payment of grant[12]. The Welsh Ministers have power in certain circumstances to reduce any grants payable by them, or suspend or cancel any instalments of a grant, or recover a grant[13]. A registered social landlord is not entitled to a grant in respect of land comprised in a management agreement[14].

Local authorities may promote the formation of bodies to act as registered social landlords, and the extension of their objects or activities, and may subscribe for their share or loan capital[15]. Local authorities may also make grants or loans to registered social landlords, or guarantee or join in guaranteeing the payment of the principal of, and interest on, money borrowed by them (including money borrowed by the issue of loan capital) or of interest on share capital issued by the landlord[16].

The Public Works Loans Commissioners may lend money to a registered social landlord: (a) for the purpose of constructing or improving, or facilitating or encouraging the construction or improvement of, dwellings; (b) for the purchase of dwellings which the landlord desires to purchase with a view to their improvement; and (c) for the purchase and development of land[17].

A local housing authority[18] may sell or supply under a hire-purchase agreement[19] furniture to the occupants of houses provided by a registered social landlord, and may buy furniture for that purpose[20].

1 As to the Housing Corporation (now abolished) see PARA 2. The functions of Housing for Wales are now exercised by the Welsh Ministers: see PARA 142.

2   See PARA 168 et seq.
3   As to registration see PARA 167 et seq.
4   See PARA 167.
5   As to the policy behind this change see the White Paper *Our Future Homes* (Cm 2901) (1995).
6   See the Housing and Regeneration Act 2008 ss 60–63; and PARA 51 et seq.
7   See the Housing and Regeneration Act 2008 s 60(2); the Housing and Regeneration Act 2008 (Commencement No 7 and Transitional and Saving Provisions) Order 2010, SI 2010/862, art 2; and PARA 52. As to the meaning of 'Welsh body' see PARA 168 note 1.
8   As to the Welsh Ministers see PARAS 7, 141.
9   Housing Act 1996 s 18(1) (amended by the Housing and Regeneration Act 2008 s 61(1), (7)). Where: (1) a grant is payable to a registered social landlord; and (2) at any time property to which the grant relates becomes vested in, or is leased for a term of years to, or reverts to, another registered social landlord, or trustees for another such landlord, these provisions have effect after that time as if the grant, or such proportion of it as is specified or determined, were payable to the other registered social landlord: Housing Act 1996 s 18(6). The relevant proportion is that which, in the circumstances of the particular case: (a) the Welsh Ministers, acting in accordance with such principles as they may from time to time determine, may specify as being appropriate; or (b) the Welsh Ministers may determine to be appropriate: s 18(7) (amended by the Housing and Regeneration Act 2008 s 61(1), (7)). These provisions originally came into force on 1 April 1997. As to social housing grants before that date see the Housing Act 1988 s 50 (repealed in relation to England and Wales).
    As to grants to private developers see PARA 151.
10 Housing Act 1996 s 18(2) (amended by the Housing Act 2004 ss 218, 266, Sch 11 paras 7, 8, Sch 16; and the Housing and Regeneration Act 2008 s 61(1), (7)).
11 Housing Act 1996 s 18(3) (amended by the Housing and Regeneration Act 2008 s 61(1), (7)).
12 Housing Act 1996 s 18(4) (amended by the Housing and Regeneration Act 2008 s 61(1), (7)). The appointment made by the Welsh Ministers must be on such terms as the Welsh Ministers may specify, and the authority must act in accordance with those terms: see the Housing Act 1996 s 18(5) (substituted by the Government of Wales Act 1998 s 140, Sch 16 para 85(2); and amended by the Housing and Regeneration Act 2008 s 62; and by SI 2010/866).
13 See the Housing Act 1996 s 27(1), (2) (amended by the Housing and Regeneration Act 2008 s 61(1), (7)). Where a grant is recovered, interest may be payable (see the Housing Act 1996 s 27(3)–(5) (s 27(3), (4) amended by the Housing and Regeneration Act 2008 s 61(1), (7))), as directed by the Welsh Ministers (see the Housing Act 1996 s 27(7) (amended by the Housing and Regeneration Act 2008 s 61(1), (7))). Where property to which a grant relates becomes vested in, or is leased for a term of years to, or reverts to, another registered social landlord, these provisions have effect after that time as if the grant, or such proportion of it as is specified or determined by the Welsh Ministers, had been made to the other registered social landlord: Housing Act 1996 s 27(6) (amended by the Housing and Regeneration Act 2008 s 61(1), (7)).
14 Housing Act 1996 s 19. As to management agreements see the Housing Act 1985 s 27; and PARA 457.
15 Housing Act 1996 s 22(1), (2).
16 Housing Act 1996 s 22(3).
17 Housing Act 1996 s 23(1). Such a loan, and interest on it, must be secured by a mortgage of the land concerned and other lands (if any) offered, and the money lent may not exceed three quarters (or if the loan is guaranteed by a local authority, nine-tenths) of the value: see s 23(2). If the loan exceeds two-thirds of the value and is not so guaranteed, further security may be required: see s 23(4). Loans may be made by instalments: see s 23(3). In general, the maximum period for repayment of a loan is 40 years (see s 23(5)), but where a loan is made for the purpose of carrying out a scheme for the provision of houses approved by the Welsh Ministers the maximum period is 50 years (see s 23(6) (amended by the Housing and Regeneration Act 2008 s 62(a))).
18 As to local housing authorities see PARA 11.
19 'Hire-purchase agreement' means a hire-purchase agreement or conditional sale agreement within the meaning of the Consumer Credit Act 1974 (see CONSUMER CREDIT vol 21 (2016) PARA 40): Housing Act 1996 s 22(4).
20 Housing Act 1996 s 22(4).

167. The register of social landlords. Chapter 1 of Part I of the Housing Act 1996[1] provides for the registration of social landlords in Wales[2]. The Welsh Ministers[3] must maintain a register of social landlords, which must be open to inspection at all reasonable times[4]. The term 'registered social landlord' is defined in the Housing Act 1985 as a housing association[5] registered[6] in the register maintained under the Housing Act 1996[7] but the term is not defined in the 1996 Act[8].

1   Ie the Housing Act 1996 Pt I Ch I (ss A1–7).
2   Housing Act 1996 s A1 (added by the Housing and Regeneration Act 2008 s 61(1), (2)). As to eligibility for registration see PARA 168.
3   As to the Welsh Ministers see PARAS 7, 141.
4   Housing Act 1996 s 1(1) (amended by the Government of Wales Act 1998 ss 140, 152, Sch 16 paras 81, 82(1)(a), 83(2), Sch 18 Pt VI; and the Housing and Regeneration Act 2008 s 61(3)(a)).
5   As to the meaning of 'housing association' see PARA 13 (definition applied by the Housing Act 1996 s 230).
6   Ie under the Housing Act 1996 s 1.
7   See the Housing Act 1985 s 5(4) (substituted by SI 2010/866); and PARA 13.
8   The Housing Act 1996 s 230 provides that in the Housing Act 1996, 'registered social landlord' has the same meaning as in Pt I; s 64 indicates that 'register, registered and registration (in relation to social landlords)' are defined in s 1, but s 1 does not define those terms.

168. Eligibility for registration. A Welsh body[1] is eligible for registration as a social landlord[2] if it is:

(1)   a registered charity[3] which is a housing association[4];
(2)   a registered society[5] which satisfies specified conditions[6]; or
(3)   a company[7] which satisfies the same conditions[8].

The specified conditions are that the body is principally concerned with Welsh housing[9], is non-profit-making[10] and is established for the purpose of, or has among its objects or powers, the provision, construction, improvement or management of:

(a)   houses[11] to be kept available for letting[12];
(b)   houses for occupation by members of the body, where the rules of the body restrict membership to persons entitled or prospectively entitled (as tenants or otherwise) to occupy a house provided or managed by the body; or
(c)   hostels[13],

and that any additional purposes or objects are among those specified[14]. The permissible additional purposes or objects are:

(i)   providing land, amenities or services, or providing, constructing, repairing or improving buildings, for its residents[15], either exclusively or together with other persons;
(ii)   acquiring, or repairing and improving, or creating by the conversion of houses or other property, houses to be disposed of on sale, on lease[16] or on shared ownership terms[17];
(iii)   constructing houses to be disposed of on shared ownership terms;
(iv)   managing houses held on leases or other lettings[18] or blocks of flats[19];
(v)   providing services of any description for owners or occupiers of houses in arranging or carrying out works of maintenance, repair or improvement, or encouraging or facilitating the carrying out of such works;
(vi)   encouraging and giving advice on the forming of housing associations or providing services for, and giving advice on the running of, such associations and other voluntary organisations[20] concerned with housing, or matters connected with housing[21].

A body is not ineligible for registration as a social landlord by reason only that its powers include power:

(A) to acquire commercial premises or businesses as an incidental part of a project or series of projects undertaken for specified[22] purposes or objects;

(B) to repair, improve or convert commercial premises[23] or to carry on for a limited period any business so acquired;

(C) to repair or improve houses, or buildings in which houses are situated, after a disposal of the houses by the body by way of sale or lease or on shared ownership terms[24].

The Welsh Ministers may by order specify permissible purposes, objects or powers additional to those specified in heads (i) to (vi) and (A) to (C) above[25]. The following have been specified as purposes or objects additional to those specified in heads (i) to (vi):

(I) disposing of houses by way of sale at less than the market value to residents of the social landlord[26];

(II) acquiring, or constructing, or repairing and improving, or creating by the conversion of houses or other property, houses to be disposed of pursuant to equity percentage arrangements[27];

(III) enabling or assisting any residents of the social landlord: (AA) to acquire, or to acquire and enter into occupation of, houses; or (BB) to procure the construction of separate dwellings for occupation by those residents (whether alone or with other persons), or to procure such construction and enter into occupation of the dwellings so constructed, by providing grants to or for such residents or, in a case falling within head (I), by entering into assured percentage arrangements[28] with such residents (or partly in the one way and partly in the other)[29];

(IV) the provision of loans secured by mortgages to assist persons to acquire houses for their own occupation[30];

(V) the carrying out of certain activities, including the provision of land, amenities or services, for persons who are not residents of the body, if any such activity is also being carried out for the body's own residents[31];

(VI) if the body is managing certain accommodation, providing amenities or services for residents both of that accommodation and of other accommodation[32]; and

(VII) carrying out regeneration activities for the benefit of persons all or some of whom are persons benefiting from permissible[33] activities[34].

1 In the Housing Act 1996 Pt I Ch I (ss A1–7) 'Welsh body' means a body which is: (1) a registered charity (see note 3) whose address, for the purposes of registration by the Charity Commission for England and Wales, is in Wales; (2) a registered society within the meaning of the Co-operative and Community Benefit Societies Act 2014 (in the Housing Act 1996 Pt I (ss A1–64), a 'registered society') whose registered office for the purposes of the 2014 Act is in Wales; or (3) a company within the meaning of the Companies Act 2006 which has its registered office for the purposes of that Act in Wales: Housing Act 1996 s 1A (added by the Housing and Regeneration Act 2008 s 61(1), (4); and amended by the Co-operative and Community Benefit Societies Act 2014 s 151(1), Sch 4 paras 55, 57). As to registration under the Companies Act 2006 see COMPANIES vol 14 (2016) PARA 21 et seq.

2 As to the register of social landlords see PARA 167. As to registration see PARA 169.

3 For these purposes, 'registered charity' means a charity which is registered under the Charities Act 2011 s 30 (see CHARITIES vol 8 (2015) PARA 307): Housing Act 1996 s 58(1)(b) (s 58(1) substituted by the Charities Act 2011 s 354(1), Sch 7 para 71).

4 As to the meaning of 'housing association' see PARA 13 (definition applied by the Housing Act 1996 s 230).

5 See note 1; and FINANCIAL INSTITUTIONS vol 48 (2015) PARA 880.

6 Ie the conditions in the Housing Act 1996 s 2(2): see the text and notes 9–14.

7 'Company' means a company registered under the Companies Act 2006: Housing Act 1996 s 63(1) (definition added by SI 2009/1941). References in the Housing Act 1996 Pt I to a company do not include a company which is a registered charity, except where otherwise provided: Housing Act 1996 s 58(2) (amended by SI 2009/1941).

8 Housing Act 1996 s 2(1) (amended by the Housing and Regeneration Act 2008 s 61(1), (5)(a); the Co-operative and Community Benefit Societies Act 2014 Sch 4 paras 55, 58; and SI 2009/1941).

9 A body is principally concerned with Welsh housing if the Welsh Ministers think: (1) that it owns housing only or mainly in Wales; or (2) that its activities are principally undertaken in respect of Wales; and once a body has been registered in reliance on head (1) or (2) it does not cease to be eligible for registration by virtue only of ceasing to satisfy that head: Housing Act 1996 s 2(2A) (added by the Housing and Regeneration Act 2008 s 61(1), (5)(c)). As to the Welsh Ministers see PARAS 7, 141.

10 For the purposes of the Housing Act 1996 s 2, a body is non-profit-making if: (1) it does not trade for profit; or (2) its constitution or rules prohibit the issue of capital with interest or dividend exceeding the rate prescribed by the Treasury for the purposes of the Housing Associations Act 1985 s 1(1)(b): Housing Act 1996 s 2(3). See also *Goodman v Dolphin Square Trust Ltd* (1979) 38 P & CR 257, CA (since housing association's rules prohibited any distribution, direct or indirect, of profits among its members it was unable to trade for profit); *R v Birmingham Housing Benefit Review Board, ex p Ellery* (1989) 21 HLR 398 (housing association which undertakes to make equity share payments is not trading for profit). As to the Treasury see CONSTITUTIONAL AND ADMINISTRATIVE LAW vol 20 (2014) PARA 262 et seq.

11 In the Housing Act 1996 Pt I, 'house' includes: (1) any part of a building occupied or intended to be occupied as a separate dwelling; and (2) any yard, garden, outhouses and appurtenances belonging to it or usually enjoyed with it: s 63(1).

12 In the Housing Act 1996 s 2, 'letting' includes the grant of a licence to occupy: s 2(6).

13 As to the meaning of 'hostel' see PARA 164 note 2.

14 Housing Act 1996 s 2(2) (amended by the Housing and Regeneration Act 2008 s 61(1), (5)(b)). The specified purposes or objects are those specified in the Housing Act 1996 s 2(4) (see the text and notes 15–21): s 2(2).

15 In the Housing Act 1996 s 2, 'residents', in relation to a body, means persons occupying a house or hostel provided or managed by the body: s 2(6).

16 In the Housing Act 1996, 'lease' and 'tenancy' have the same meaning; and both expressions include: (1) a sub-lease or a sub-tenancy; and (2) an agreement for a lease or tenancy (or sub-lease or sub-tenancy): s 229(1), (2). The expressions 'lessor' and 'lessee' and 'landlord' and 'tenant', and references to letting, to the grant of a lease or to covenants or terms, are to be construed accordingly: s 229(3).

17 In the Housing Act 1996 s 2, 'disposed of on shared ownership terms' means disposed of on a lease: (1) granted on a payment of a premium calculated by reference to a percentage of the value of the house or of the cost of providing it; or (2) under which the tenant (or his personal representatives) will or may be entitled to a sum calculated by reference directly or indirectly to the value of the house: s 2(6).

18 Ie not being houses within the Housing Act 1996 s 2(2)(a) or (b): see heads (a)–(b) in the text.

19 In the Housing Act 1996 s 2, 'block of flats' means a building containing two or more flats which are held on leases or other lettings and which are occupied or intended to be occupied wholly or mainly for residential purposes: s 2(6).

20 In the Housing Act 1996 s 2, 'voluntary organisation' means an organisation whose activities are not carried on for profit: s 2(6).

21 Housing Act 1996 s 2(4).

In exercise of the power conferred by s 2(7), (8), the Secretary of State made the Social Landlords (Permissible Additional Purposes or Objects) Order 1996, SI 1996/2256.

22 Ie purposes or objects falling within the Housing Act 1996 s 2(2) or (4).

23 Ie acquired as mentioned in head (A) in the text.

24 Housing Act 1996 s 2(5). See further note 21.

25 Housing Act 1996 s 2(7) (amended by the Housing and Regeneration Act 2008 s 61(1), (5)(d)). The order may (without prejudice to the inclusion of other incidental or supplementary provisions) contain such provision as the Welsh Ministers think fit with respect to the priority of mortgages entered into in pursuance of any additional purposes, objects or powers: Housing Act 1996 s 2(7) (amended by the Housing and Regeneration Act 2008 s 61(1), (5)(d), (7)). An order under the Housing Act 1996 s 2(7) must be made by statutory instrument subject to annulment in pursuance of a resolution of the National Assembly for Wales: s 2(8) (amended by the Housing and Regeneration Act 2008 s 61(1), (5)(e)).

In exercise of the power conferred by the Housing Act 1996 s 2(7), (8), the Secretary of State made the Social Landlords (Permissible Additional Purposes or Objects) Order 1996, SI 1996/2256 (see the text and notes 26–29); the Social Landlords (Additional Purposes or Objects) Order 1999, SI 1999/985 (see the text and note 30); and the Social Landlords (Additional Purposes or Objects) (No 2) Order 1999, SI 1999/1206 (see the text and notes 31–34).

The following provisions apply to any power of the Welsh Ministers under the Housing Act 1996 ss 2, 17, 27A, 39, 50J, 51, 55 or Sch 2 to make an order: s 52(1) (amended by the Government of Wales Act 1998 s 140, Sch 16 para 91; the Housing Act 2004 s 265(1), Sch 15 paras 40, 41; the Housing and Regeneration Act 2008 s 62(a); and the Housing (Wales) Measure 2011 s 88, Schedule paras 1, 11). An order may make different provision for different cases or descriptions of case: Housing Act 1996 s 52(2). This includes power to make different provision for different bodies or descriptions of body, different provision for different housing activities and different provision for different areas: s 52(2). An order may contain such supplementary, incidental, consequential or transitional provisions and savings as the Welsh Ministers consider appropriate: s 52(3) (amended by the Housing and Regeneration Act 2008 s 62(a), (e)).

'Housing activities' means, in relation to a registered social landlord, all its activities in pursuance of the purposes, objects and powers mentioned in or specified under the Housing Act 1996 s 2: s 63(1).

26 Social Landlords (Permissible Additional Purposes or Objects) Order 1996, SI 1996/2256, art 3(a).
27 Social Landlords (Permissible Additional Purposes or Objects) Order 1996, SI 1996/2256, art 3(b). 'Equity percentage arrangements' means arrangements pursuant to which a social landlord conveys a legal estate in a house to an individual (the 'relevant purchaser'), and the relevant purchaser in consideration for that conveyance makes to the landlord a payment (the 'initial payment') expressed to represent a percentage of the initial value of the house and enters into an equity percentage covenant with the landlord; and the liability to make any payment required by the equity percentage covenant is secured by a mortgage: art 2(1) (renumbered by SI 2001/3649). 'Equity percentage covenant' means a covenant requiring the relevant purchaser in the case of the equity percentage arrangements in question to make to the landlord at a date (the 'discharge date') determined in accordance with the covenant a capital payment (the 'discharge payment') determined by reference to that percentage (if any) of the final value of the house which remains after reducing 100% by the sum of the following percentages, ie the percentage of the initial value of the house which the initial payment made pursuant to the equity percentage arrangements in question was expressed to represent and the aggregate of the interim payment percentages (if any); 'final value' of a house, in the case of an assured percentage covenant or, as the case may be, an equity percentage covenant, means the proper value of the estate in question at the time at which the discharge payment required by the covenant falls to be made; 'initial value' of a house means, in the case of assured percentage arrangements, the price required to be paid to or at the direction of the vendor for the conveyance of the estate in question to the participating resident, or, in the case of equity percentage arrangements, an amount agreed between the relevant purchaser and the social landlord, before the conveyance of the estate in question to the relevant purchaser, as being the price for which the estate would have been conveyed at that time, with vacant possession, in an arm's length transaction between a willing buyer and a willing seller on the open market; 'interim payment percentage' means, in relation to an assured percentage covenant or, as the case may be, an equity percentage covenant, the amount of any payment accepted by the landlord before the discharge date, in diminution of the liability to make the discharge payment and in accordance with the terms of the instrument containing the covenant in question, expressed as a percentage of the proper value of the estate in question as at the time of that acceptance; 'proper value', in the case of any estate, means the value of the estate as determined by such person as may be specified or described in, and otherwise in accordance with the terms of, the instrument containing the assured percentage covenant or equity percentage covenant in question; and 'social landlord' means a body which is registered, or is eligible for registration, as a social landlord under the Housing Act 1996 Pt I Ch I (ss A1–7): Social Landlords (Permissible Additional Purposes or Objects) Order 1996, SI 1996/2256, art 2(1) (as so renumbered).
28 For these purposes, 'assured percentage arrangements' means arrangements pursuant to which a social landlord provides a sum (the 'initial capital sum') to a person who, at the time when the landlord offers to provide that sum, is a resident of that landlord (the 'participating resident') for the purpose of enabling or assisting him to acquire a legal estate in a house; the participating resident, in consideration for the provision of the initial capital sum, enters into an assured percentage covenant with the landlord; and the liability to make any payment required by the assured percentage covenant is secured by a mortgage: Social Landlords (Permissible Additional Purposes or Objects) Order 1996, SI 1996/2256, art 2(1) (as renumbered: see note 26). 'Assured percentage covenant' means a covenant requiring the participating resident in the case of the assured percentage arrangements in question to make to the landlord at a date (the 'discharge

date') determined in accordance with the covenant a payment (the 'discharge payment') calculated by reference to the product of: (1) the difference between the initial capital sum, expressed as a percentage of the initial value of the house and the aggregate of the interim payment percentages (if any); and (2) the final value of the house: art 2(1) (as so renumbered).

29 Social Landlords (Permissible Additional Purposes or Objects) Order 1996, SI 1996/2256, art 3(c).
  A mortgage securing a person's liability to make to a registered social landlord any payment required by an assured percentage covenant or equity percentage covenant has priority immediately after any legal charge securing an amount advanced to that person by a qualifying lending institution for the purpose of enabling him to acquire the estate in question or, with the written consent of the social landlord, for the purpose of enabling him to carry out any improvement to the house in question: art 4.

30 See the Social Landlords (Additional Purposes or Objects) Order 1999, SI 1999/985 (amended by SI 2001/3649, SI 2005/2863 and SI 2010/671), which also makes provision as to the priority of certain mortgages entered into under that additional purpose or object.

31 See the Social Landlords (Additional Purposes or Objects) (No 2) Order 1999, SI 1999/1206, art 2(1)(a).

32 See the Social Landlords (Additional Purposes or Objects) (No 2) Order 1999, SI 1999/1206, art 2(1)(b).

33 Ie activities mentioned in or specified by the Housing Act 1996 s 2.

34 See the Social Landlords (Additional Purposes or Objects) (No 2) Order 1999, SI 1999/1206, art 2(1)(c).

169. Registration of social landlords in Wales. The Welsh Ministers[1] may register as a social landlord[2] any Welsh body[3] which is eligible for such registration[4]. An application for registration must be made in such manner, and must be accompanied by such fee (if any), as the Welsh Ministers may determine[5].

As soon as may be after registering a body as a social landlord the Welsh Ministers must give notice[6] of the registration:

(1)   in the case of a registered charity[7], to the Charity Commission;

(2)   in the case of a registered society, to the Financial Conduct Authority[8]; and

(3)   in the case of a company[9] (including a company that is a registered charity), to the registrar of companies[10],

who must record the registration[11].

A Welsh body which at any time is, or was, registered as a social landlord will, for all purposes other than rectification of the register, be conclusively presumed to be, or to have been, at that time a body eligible for registration as a social landlord[12].

Whilst the Welsh Ministers have discretion whether to register an applicant or not, they must have regard to the criteria which they have promulgated[13].

1 As to the Welsh Ministers see PARAS 7, 141.
2 As to the register of social landlords see PARA 167.
3 As to the meaning of 'Welsh body' see PARA 168 note 1.
4 Housing Act 1996 s 3(1) (amended by the Housing and Regeneration Act 2008 s 61(1), (6)(a), (7)). As to the criteria for registration see PARA 171.
5 Housing Act 1996 s 3(2) (amended by the Housing and Regeneration Act 2008 s 61(1), (7)). The following provisions apply to determinations of the Welsh Ministers under the Housing Act 1996 Pt I (ss A1–64): s 53(1) (amended by the Housing and Regeneration Act 2008 s 62(a); and by SI 2010/866). A determination may make different provision for different cases or descriptions of case: Housing Act 1996 s 53(2). This includes power to make:
    (1)   different provision for different registered social landlords or descriptions of registered social landlord; and
    (2)   different provision for different housing activities and different provision for different areas,
and for the purposes of head (2) descriptions may be framed by reference to any matters whatever, including in particular, in the case of housing activities, the manner in which they are financed: s 53(2). For these purposes, a general determination means a determination which does not relate solely to a particular case: s 53(3). Before making a general determination, the Welsh Ministers must consult such bodies appearing to them to be representative of registered social landlords as

they consider appropriate: s 53(4) (amended by the Housing and Regeneration Act 2008 s 62(a); and by SI 2010/866). After making a general determination, the Welsh Ministers must publish the determination in such manner as they consider appropriate for bringing the determination to the notice of the landlords concerned: Housing Act 1996 s 53(5) (amended by the Housing and Regeneration Act 2008 s 62(a); and by SI 2010/866).

6 'Notice' means notice in writing: Housing Act 1996 s 63(1).
7 As to the meaning of 'registered charity' see PARA 168 note 3.
8 As to the Financial Conduct Authority see FINANCIAL SERVICES REGULATION vol 50 (2016) PARAS 5, 6 et seq.
9 As to the meaning of 'company' see PARA 168 note 7.
10 'Registrar of companies' has the same meaning as in the Companies Acts: Housing Act 1996 s 63(1) (amended by SI 2009/1941). See the Companies Act 2006 s 1060; and COMPANIES vol 14 (2016) PARA 126.
11 Housing Act 1996 s 3(3) (amended by the Charities Act 2006 s 75(1), Sch 8 paras 183, 184; the Housing and Regeneration Act 2008 s 61(1), (7); and the Co-operative and Community Benefit Societies Act 2014 s 151(1), Sch 4 paras 55, 56; and by SI 2009/1941 and SI 2013/496).
12 Housing Act 1996 s 3(4) (amended by the Housing and Regeneration Act 2008 s 61(6)(b)).
13 See PARA 171.

170. Removal from the register. A body which has been registered as a social landlord[1] must not be removed from the register except in accordance with the following provisions[2].

If it appears to the Welsh Ministers[3] that a body which is on the register of social landlords:

(1) is no longer a body eligible for such registration[4]; or

(2) has ceased to exist or does not operate,

the Welsh Ministers must, after giving the body at least 14 days' notice[5], remove it from the register[6].

A body which is registered as a social landlord may request the Welsh Ministers to remove it from the register and the Welsh Ministers may do so, subject to the following provisions[7]. Before removing such a body from the register of social landlords[8] the Welsh Ministers must consult the local authorities[9] in whose area the body operates; and the Welsh Ministers must also inform those authorities of their decision[10].

As soon as may be after removing a body from the register of social landlords the Welsh Ministers must give notice of the removal:

(a) in the case of a registered charity[11], to the Charity Commission;

(b) in the case of a registered society[12], to the Financial Conduct Authority[13]; and

(c) in the case of a company[14] (including a company which is a registered charity), to the registrar of companies[15],

who must record the removal[16].

1 As to the register of social landlords see PARA 167. As to registration see PARA 169.
2 Housing Act 1996 s 4(1).
3 As to the Welsh Ministers see PARAS 7, 141.
4 For example, the body may no longer have the requisite purposes, objects or powers. As to eligibility for registration see PARA 168.
5 As to the meaning of 'notice' see PARA 169 note 6. In the case of a body which appears to the Welsh Ministers to have ceased to exist or not to operate, notice under this provision will be deemed to be given to the body if it is served at the address last known to the Welsh Ministers to be the principal place of business of the body: Housing Act 1996 s 4(3) (amended by the Housing and Regeneration Act 2008 s 61(1), (7)).
6 Housing Act 1996 s 4(2) (amended by the Housing and Regeneration Act 2008 s 61(1), (7)).
7 Housing Act 1996 s 4(4) (amended by the Housing and Regeneration Act 2008 s 61(1), (7)).
8 Ie under the Housing Act 1996 s 4(4): see the text and note 7.
9 As to the meaning of 'local authority' for these purposes see PARA 149 note 4 (definition applied by the Housing Act 1996 s 63(1)).
10 Housing Act 1996 s 4(5) (amended by the Housing and Regeneration Act 2008 s 61(1), (7)).

11 As to the meaning of 'registered charity' see PARA 168 note 3.
12 As to the meaning of 'registered society' see PARA 168 note 1.
13 As to the Financial Conduct Authority see FINANCIAL SERVICES REGULATION vol 50 (2016) PARAS 5, 6 et seq.
14 As to the meaning of 'company' see PARA 168 note 7.
15 As to the registrar of companies see PARA 169 note 10.
16 Housing Act 1996 s 4(6) (amended by the Charities Act 2006 s 75(1), Sch 8 paras 183, 185; the Housing and Regeneration Act 2008 s 61(1), (7); and the Co-operative and Community Benefit Societies Act 2014 s 151(1), Sch 4 paras 55, 56; and by SI 2009/1941 and SI 2013/496).

171. Criteria for registration or removal from the register. The Welsh Ministers[1] must establish (and may from time to time vary) criteria which should be satisfied by a body seeking registration as a social landlord[2]. In deciding whether to register a body, the Welsh Ministers must have regard to whether those criteria are met[3]. Also, the Welsh Ministers must establish (and may from time to time vary) criteria which should be satisfied where such a body seeks to be removed from the register of social landlords[4]. In deciding whether to remove a body from the register, the Welsh Ministers must have regard to whether those criteria are met[5]. Before establishing or varying any such criteria the Welsh Ministers must consult such bodies representative of registered social landlords, and such bodies representative of local authorities[6], as they think fit[7].

The Welsh Ministers must publish the criteria for registration and the criteria for removal from the register in such manner as the Welsh Ministers consider appropriate for bringing the criteria to the notice of bodies representative of registered social landlords and bodies representative of local authorities[8].

Where a landlord appears to meet the criteria for registration, there may be an implied obligation to give reasons if registration is refused[9].

1 As to the Welsh Ministers see PARAS 7, 141.
2 Housing Act 1996 s 5(1) (amended by the Housing and Regeneration Act 2008 s 61(1), (7)). As to the register of social landlords see PARA 167. As to registration see PARA 169.
3 Housing Act 1996 s 5(1) (as amended: see note 2).
4 Housing Act 1996 s 5(2) (amended by the Housing and Regeneration Act 2008 s 61(1), (7)). As to removal from the register see PARA 170.
5 Housing Act 1996 s 5(2) (as amended: see note 4).
6 As to the meaning of 'local authority' see PARA 149 note 4 (definition applied by the Housing Act 1996 s 63(1)).
7 Housing Act 1996 s 5(3) (amended by the Housing and Regeneration Act 2008 s 61(1), (7)).
8 Housing Act 1996 s 5(4) (amended by the Housing and Regeneration Act 2008 s 61(1), (7)).
9 As to the duty to give reasons see, by analogy, *R v Secretary of State for the Home Department, ex p Doody* [1994] 1 AC 531, sub nom *Doody v Secretary of State for the Home Department* [1993] 3 All ER 92, HL (Secretary of State should give reasons for departing from judge's recommendations about the period a life prisoner should serve); *R v Kensington and Chelsea Royal London Borough, ex p Grillo* (1995) 28 HLR 94, 94 LGR 144, CA (no general obligation on housing authorities to give reasons for their decisions but such a duty may be implied in appropriate circumstances; there was no such duty in that case).

172. Appeal against a decision concerning registration. A body which is aggrieved by a decision of the Welsh Ministers[1]:
(1)   not to register it as a social landlord[2]; or
(2)   to remove[3] or not to remove it from the register of social landlords,
may appeal against the decision to the High Court[4]. If an appeal is brought against a decision relating to the removal of a body from the register, the Welsh Ministers must not remove the body from the register until the appeal has been finally determined or is withdrawn[5]. As soon as may be after an appeal is brought against a decision relating to the removal of a body from the register, the Welsh Ministers must give notice[6] of the appeal:
(a)   in the case of a registered charity[7], to the Charity Commission;

(b)   in the case of a registered society[8], to the Financial Conduct Authority[9]; and

(c)   in the case of a company[10] (including a company which is a registered charity), to the registrar of companies[11].

1   As to the Welsh Ministers see PARAS 7, 141.
2   As to the register of social landlords see PARA 167. As to registration see PARA 169.
3   As to removal from the register see PARA 170.
4   Housing Act 1996 s 6(1) (amended by the Housing and Regeneration Act 2008 s 61(1), (7)). As to the appeal procedure see CPR Pt 52; *Practice Direction—Appeals* PD 52; and CIVIL PROCEDURE vol 12A (2015) PARA 1548.
5   Housing Act 1996 s 6(2) (amended by the Housing and Regeneration Act 2008 s 61(1), (7)).
6   As to the meaning of 'notice' see PARA 169 note 6.
7   As to the meaning of 'registered charity' see PARA 168 note 3.
8   As to the meaning of 'registered society' see PARA 168 note 1.
9   As to the Financial Conduct Authority see FINANCIAL SERVICES REGULATION vol 50 (2016) PARAS 5, 6 et seq.
10 As to the meaning of 'company' see PARA 168 note 7.
11 Housing Act 1996 s 6(3) (amended by the Charities Act 2006 s 75(1), Sch 8 paras 183, 186; the Housing and Regeneration Act 2008 s 61(1), (7); the Co-operative and Community Benefit Societies Act 2014 s 151(1), Sch 4 paras 55, 56; and by SI 2009/1941 and SI 2013/496). As to the registrar of companies see PARA 169 note 10.

C.   REGULATION OF REGISTERED SOCIAL LANDLORDS IN WALES; IN GENERAL

173. In general. Housing associations were formerly regulated by the Housing Corporation or Housing for Wales[1] under the Housing Associations Act 1985. The relevant provisions of that Act have been repealed and replaced by provisions of the Housing Act 1996, which now apply to registered social landlords in Wales[2], and by the provisions of Part 2 of the Housing and Regeneration Act 2008[3], which apply to regulate the provision of social housing by English bodies. The Housing Act 1996 deals with restrictions on the making of payments or other benefits to members of a registered social landlord[4], constitutional matters[5], accounts and audit[6] and powers under which an inquiry can be made into the affairs of a registered social landlord[7]. It also deals with inspection of a registered social landlord's affairs, save those affairs that relate to the provision of housing in England[8].

In carrying out their functions, registered social landlords must comply with the requirements of the legislation relating to discrimination, particularly those dealing with discrimination on the grounds of disability[9].

1   The Housing Corporation has been abolished and the functions of Housing for Wales are now exercised by the Welsh Ministers: see PARAS 2, 142.
2   As to registered social landlords see PARA 167.
3   Ie the Housing and Regeneration Act 2008 Pt 2 (ss 59–278A): see PARA 51 et seq.
4   See the Housing Act 1996 s 7, Sch 1 Pt I (paras 1–3); and PARA 174.
5   See the Housing Act 1996 Sch 1 Pt II (paras 4–15A); and PARA 175 et seq.
6   See the Housing Act 1996 Sch 1 Pt III (paras 16–19A); and PARA 193.
7   See the Housing Act 1996 Sch 1 Pt IV (paras 20–29); and PARA 200 et seq. As to the enforcement action that Welsh Ministers may take against registered social landlords see PARA 185 et seq. As to additional powers in relation to the management of registered social landlords see PARA 189 et seq
8   See the Housing Act 1996 Sch 1 Pt 3A (paras 19B–19F) (added by the Housing (Wales) Measure 2011 ss 43–49); and PARA 185 et seq.
9   As to discrimination generally see DISCRIMINATION vol 33 (2013) PARA 1 et seq. As to discrimination on the grounds of disability see the Equality Act 2010; and DISCRIMINATION vol 33 (2013) PARA 65 et seq.

174.   Control of payments to members and others. A registered social landlord[1] must not make a gift or pay a sum by way of dividend or bonus to:

(1)   a person who is or has been a member of the body; or
(2)   a person who is a member of the family of a person within head (1); or
(3)   a company of which a person within head (1) or head (2) is a director,
except as is permitted by the following provisions[2].

The payment of a sum which, in accordance with the constitution or rules of the body, is paid as interest on capital lent to the body or subscribed by way of shares in the body is permitted, as is the payment by a fully mutual housing association[3] to a person who has ceased to be a member of the association of a sum which is due to him either under his tenancy[4] agreement with the association or under the terms of the agreement under which he became a member of the association, and the payment of a sum, in accordance with the constitution or rules of the body, to a registered social landlord which is a subsidiary or associate of the body[5].

Where a registered society or a company[6] pays a sum or makes a gift in contravention of these provisions, the society or company may recover the sum or the value of the gift, and proceedings for its recovery must be taken if the Welsh Ministers[7] so direct[8].

A registered social landlord which is a registered society or a company must not make a payment or grant a benefit to:

(a)   an officer[9] or employee of the society or company;
(b)   a person who at any time within the preceding 12 months has been a person within head (a);
(c)   a close relative of a person within head (a) or head (b); or
(d)   a business trading for profit of which a person falling within head (a), head (b) or head (c) is a principal proprietor or in the management of which such a person is directly concerned,

except as permitted by the following provisions[10]. The following payments or grants are permitted for these purposes:

(i)   payments made or benefits granted to an officer or employee of the society or company under his contract of employment with the society or company;
(ii)   the payment of remuneration or expenses to an officer of the society or company who does not have a contract of employment with the society or company;
(iii)   any such payment of interest as is permitted by the provisions relating to payments by way of gift, dividend or bonus[11];
(iv)   the grant or renewal of a tenancy by a co-operative housing association[12];
(v)   where a tenancy of a house has been granted to, or to a close relative of, a person who later became an officer or employee, the grant to that tenant of a new tenancy whether of the same or another house;
(vi)   payments made or benefits granted in accordance with any determination made by the Welsh Ministers[13].

Where a society or company pays a sum or grants a benefit in contravention of these provisions, the society or company may recover the sum or value of the benefit; and proceedings for its recovery must be taken if the Welsh Ministers so direct[14].

The Welsh Ministers may from time to time specify the maximum amounts which may be paid by a registered social landlord which is a registered society or a company by way of fees or other remuneration, or by way of expenses, to a member of the society or company who is not an officer or employee of the society or company, or by way of remuneration or expenses to an officer of the society or company who does not have a contract of employment with the society or company[15]. Different amounts may be so specified for different purposes[16]. Where a society or company makes a payment in excess of the maximum so permitted, the society or company may recover the excess, and proceedings for its recovery must be taken if the Welsh Ministers so direct[17].

1   As to registration as a social landlord see PARA 169.
2   Housing Act 1996 s 7, Sch 1 para 1(1) (s 7 amended, in relation to Wales, by the Housing (Wales) Measure 2011 s 88, Schedule paras 1, 3).
3   As to the meanings of 'fully mutual' and 'housing association' see PARA 13 (definitions applied by the Housing Act 1996 ss 63(1), 230 respectively).
4   As to the meaning of 'tenancy' see PARA 168 note 16.
5   Housing Act 1996 Sch 1 para 1(2) (amended by the Housing Act 2004 s 218, Sch 11 paras 7, 14). As to the meaning of 'subsidiary' see PARA 200 note 8.
6   As to the meaning of 'registered society' see PARA 168 note 1. As to registered societies see FINANCIAL INSTITUTIONS vol 48 (2015) PARA 880 et seq. As to the meaning of 'company' see PARA 168 note 7.
7   As to the Welsh Ministers see PARAS 7, 141.
8   Housing Act 1996 Sch 1 para 1(3) (amended by the Housing and Regeneration Act 2008 s 61(1), (7); the Co-operative and Community Benefit Societies Act 2014 s 151(1), Sch 4 paras 55, 56; and SI 2009/1941). See PARA 166.
9   For these purposes, references to an officer of a registered social landlord are:
    (1)   in the case of a registered charity which is not a company, references to any trustee, secretary or treasurer of the charity;
    (2)   in the case of a registered society, references to any officer of the society as defined in the Co-operative and Community Benefit Societies Act 2014 s 149 (see FINANCIAL INSTITUTIONS vol 48 (2015) PARA 947); and
    (3)   in the case of a company (including a company that is a registered charity), references to any director or other officer of the company within the meaning of the Companies Acts (see the Companies Act 2006 ss 250, 1173(1); and COMPANIES vol 14 (2016) PARA 512, COMPANIES vol 15 (2016) PARA 679),
and any such reference includes, in the case of a registered society, a co-opted member of the committee of the society: Housing Act 1996 s 59(1), (2) (s 59(1) amended by the Co-operative and Community Benefit Societies Act 2014 Sch 4 paras 55, 61; and SI 2009/1941; the Housing Act 1996 s 59(2) amended by the Co-operative and Community Benefit Societies Act 2014 Sch 4 paras 55, 56). As to co-opted members see PARA 175 note 3. As to the meaning of 'registered charity' see PARA 168 note 3.
10 Housing Act 1996 Sch 1 para 2(1) (amended by the Co-operative and Community Benefit Societies Act 2014 Sch 4 paras 55, 56; and SI 2009/1941).
11 Ie any such payment as may be made in accordance with the Housing Act 1996 Sch 1 para 1(2) (interest payable in accordance with the rules and certain sums payable by a fully mutual housing association to a person who has ceased to be a member): see the text to notes 3–5.
12 As to the meaning of 'co-operative housing association' see PARA 13 (definition applied by the Housing Act 1996 s 230).
13 Housing Act 1996 Sch 1 para 2(2) (amended by the Housing and Regeneration Act 2008 s 61(1), (7)). A determination for the purposes of head (vi) in the text may specify the class or classes of case in which a payment may be made or benefit granted and specify the maximum amount: Housing Act 1996 Sch 1 para 2(3).
14 Housing Act 1996 Sch 1 para 2(4) (amended by the Housing and Regeneration Act 2008 s 61(1), (7)).
15 Housing Act 1996 Sch 1 para 3(1) (amended by the Housing and Regeneration Act 2008 s 61(1), (7); the Co-operative and Community Benefit Societies Act 2014 Sch 4 paras 55, 56; and SI 2009/1941).
16 Housing Act 1996 Sch 1 para 3(2).
17 Housing Act 1996 Sch 1 para 3(3) (amended by the Housing and Regeneration Act 2008 s 61(1), (7)).

175. General power to remove an officer. The Welsh Ministers[1] may, in accordance with the following provisions, by order remove an officer[2] of a registered social landlord[3].

The Welsh Ministers may make an order removing any such person if:

(1) he has been made bankrupt or a debt relief order[4] has been made in respect of him, or he or has made an arrangement with his creditors[5];

(2) he is subject to a disqualification order or disqualification undertaking under the Company Directors Disqualification Act 1986[6];

(3) he is subject to an order for failure to pay under a County Court administration order[7];

(4) he is disqualified[8] from being a charity trustee;

(5) he is incapable of acting by reason of mental disorder;

(6) he has not acted; or

(7) he cannot be found or does not act and his absence or failure to act is impeding the proper management of the registered social landlord's affairs[9].

Before making an order the Welsh Ministers must give at least 14 days' notice of their intention to do so to the person whom they intend to remove, and to the registered social landlord[10].

A person who is ordered to be removed under these provisions may appeal against the order to the High Court[11].

This power of removal is additional to the Welsh Ministers' powers of suspension and removal following an inquiry into a registered social landlord[12].

The Welsh Ministers may make an order[13] removing an officer of a registered charity[14] only if the charity has received public assistance[15]. For the purposes of Part I of the Housing Act 1996[16] a registered charity has received public assistance if at least one of the following conditions is satisfied[17]:

(a) the charity has received financial assistance under the Local Government Act 1988[18];

(b) the charity has received financial assistance under the Housing and Regeneration Act 2008[19];

(c) the charity has had housing transferred to it pursuant to:

(i) a large scale disposal[20] for which consent was required[21]; or

(ii) a qualifying disposal that was made under the Leasehold Reform, Housing and Urban Development Act 1993[22];

(d) the charity has received a grant or loan under certain specified[23] statutory provisions[24].

1 As to the Welsh Ministers see PARAS 7, 141.

2 As to the meaning of 'officer' see PARA 174 note 9.

3 Housing Act 1996 s 7, Sch 1 para 4(1) (Sch 1 para 4(1) amended by the Housing and Regeneration Act 2008 s 61(1), (7); in relation to Wales, by the Housing (Wales) Measure 2011 s 84(1), (3); and by SI 2009/1941). As to registration as a social landlord see PARA 169.

4 Ie under the Insolvency Act 1986 Pt VIIA (ss 251A–251X): see BANKRUPTCY AND INDIVIDUAL INSOLVENCY vol 5 (2013) PARA 91 et seq.

5 As to arrangements with creditors see BANKRUPTCY AND INDIVIDUAL INSOLVENCY vol 5 (2013) PARA 852 et seq.

6 See COMPANIES vol 15A (2016) PARA 1762 et seq.

7 Ie an order under the Insolvency Act 1986 s 429(2): see BANKRUPTCY AND INDIVIDUAL INSOLVENCY vol 5 (2013) PARA 905; COMPANY AND PARTNERSHIP INSOLVENCY vol 17 (2011) PARA 1083. As from a day to be appointed, head (3) in the text is substituted with 'he is subject to disabilities on revocation of a County Court administration order': see note 9.

8 Ie under the Charities Act 2011 s 178: see CHARITIES vol 8 (2015) PARA 276.

9 Housing Act 1996 Sch 1 para 4(2) (amended by the Housing and Regeneration Act 2008 s 61(1), (7); the Charities Act 2011 s 354(1), Sch 7 para 72(1), (2); and by SI 2009/1941, SI 2012/2404 and SI 2016/481; and, as from a day to be appointed, by the Tribunals, Courts and Enforcement Act 2007 s 106(2), Sch 16 para 10; at the date at which this volume states the law, no day had been appointed for bringing this amendment into force).

10 Housing Act 1996 Sch 1 para 4(3) (amended by the Housing and Regeneration Act 2008 s 61(1), (7)). That notice may be given by post, and if so given to the person whom the Welsh Ministers

intend to remove may be addressed to his last known address in the United Kingdom: Housing Act 1996 Sch 1 para 4(4) (amended by the Housing and Regeneration Act 2008 s 61(1), (7)).
11 Housing Act 1996 Sch 1 para 4(5).
12 As to the powers referred to in the text see PARAS 201–202.
13 Ie under the Housing Act 1996 Sch 1 para 4.
14 As to the meaning of 'registered charity' see PARA 168 note 3.
15 Housing Act 1996 Sch 1 para 5(1) (amended by the Housing and Regeneration Act 2008 s 61(1), (7); and, in relation to Wales, by the Housing (Wales) Measure 2011 ss 84(1), (4), 88, Schedule paras 1, 13(a)).
16 Ie the Housing Act 1996 Pt I (ss A1–64).
17 Housing Act 1996 s 58(1A) (added, in relation to Wales, by the Housing (Wales) Measure 2011 s 86).
18 Ie under the Local Government Act 1988 s 24 (assistance for privately let housing accommodation: see PARA 378): Housing Act 1996 s 58(1A)(a) (as added: see note 17).
19 Ie under the Housing and Regeneration Act 2008 s 19 (see PLANNING vol 83 (2010) PARA 1474): Housing Act 1996 s 58(1A)(b) (as added: see note 17).
20 Ie within the meaning of the Housing Act 1985 s 34: see PARA 524 note 10.
21 Ie under the Housing Act 1985 s 32 or 43: see PARAS 522, 531.
22 Ie that was made under the Leasehold Reform, Housing and Urban Development Act 1993 s 135 (repealed): Housing Act 1996 s 58(1A)(c) (as added: see note 17).
23 Ie under:
   (1)   the Housing Act 1996 s 18 (social housing grants: see PARA 166);
   (2)   s 22 (assistance from local authorities: see PARA 166);
   (3)   the Housing Associations Act 1985 s 58 (grants or loans by local authorities: see PARA 13);
   (4)   the Housing Act 1980 s 50, the Housing Associations Act 1985 s 41 (repealed) or any enactment replaced by that provision (housing association grant);
   (5)   the Housing Act 1988 s 51 or the Housing Associations Act 1985 s 54 or 55 (both repealed) (revenue deficit grant or hostel deficit grant);
   (6)   the Housing Associations Act 1985 s 79 (loans by Welsh Ministers: see PARA 145);
   (7)   the Housing Act 1974 s 31 (repealed) (management grants); or
   (8)   any enactment mentioned in the Housing Associations Act 1985 Sch 1 para 2 or 3 (pre-1974 grants and certain loans).
24 Housing Act 1996 s 58(1A)(d) (as added: see note 17).

176. Power to appoint a new officer of a company. The Welsh Ministers[1] may by order appoint a person to be an officer[2] of a registered social landlord[3] which is a company[4]: (1) in place of an officer removed by the Welsh Ministers; (2) where there are no officers; or (3) where the Welsh Ministers are of the opinion that it is necessary for the proper management of the company's affairs to have an additional officer[5]. A person may be so appointed whether or not he is a member of the company and notwithstanding anything in the company's articles of association[6]. Where a person is so appointed he holds office for such period and on such terms as the Welsh Ministers may specify, and on the expiry of the appointment the Welsh Ministers may renew the appointment for such period as they may specify; but this does not prevent a person from retiring in accordance with the company's articles of association[7].

A person so appointed is entitled: (a) to receive all such communications relating to a written resolution proposed to be agreed to by the company as are required to be supplied to a member of the company; (b) to receive all notices of, and other communications relating to, any general meeting which a member of the company is entitled to receive, and to attend, speak and vote at any such meeting; (c) to move a resolution at any general meeting of the company; and (d) to require a general meeting of the company to be convened within 21 days of a request to that effect made in writing to the directors of the company[8].

This power is additional to the Welsh Ministers' powers following an inquiry into a registered social landlord[9].

1 As to the Welsh Ministers see PARAS 7, 141.
2 As to the meaning of 'officer' see PARA 174 note 9.

3 As to registration as a social landlord see PARA 169.
4 As to the meaning of 'company' see PARA 168 note 7.
5 Housing Act 1996 s 7, Sch 1 para 7(1) (Sch 1 para 7(1) amended by the Housing and Regeneration Act 2008 s 61(1), (7); in relation to Wales, by the Housing (Wales) Measure 2011 s 85(1), (5); and by SI 2009/1941).
6 Housing Act 1996 Sch 1 para 7(2).
7 Housing Act 1996 Sch 1 para 7(3) (amended by the Housing and Regeneration Act 2008 s 61(1), (7)).
8 Housing Act 1996 Sch 1 para 7(4) (substituted by SI 2007/2194).
9 As to the powers referred to in the text see PARAS 201–202.

177. Power to appoint a new officer of a registered society. The Welsh Ministers[1] may by order appoint a person to be an officer[2] of a registered social landlord[3] which is a registered society[4]: (1) in place of a person removed by the Welsh Ministers; (2) where there are no officers; or (3) where the Welsh Ministers are of the opinion that it is necessary for the proper management of the society's affairs to have an additional officer[5]; and the power conferred in the last-mentioned case may be exercised notwithstanding that it will cause the maximum number of officers permissible under the society's constitution to be exceeded[6].

A person may be so appointed whether or not he is a member of the society and, if he is not, notwithstanding that the rules of the society restrict appointment to members[7]. A person so appointed holds office for such period and on such terms as the Welsh Ministers may specify; and on the expiry of the appointment the Welsh Ministers may renew the appointment for such period as they may specify; but this does not prevent a person so appointed from retiring in accordance with the rules of the society[8]. A person so appointed is entitled: (a) to attend, speak and vote at any general meeting of the society and to receive all notices of and other communications relating to any general meeting which a member of the society is entitled to receive; (b) to move a resolution at any general meeting of the society; and (c) to require a general meeting of the society to be convened within 21 days of a request to that effect made in writing to the committee of the society[9].

This power is additional to the Welsh Ministers' powers following an inquiry into a registered social landlord[10].

1 As to the Welsh Ministers see PARAS 7, 141.
2 As to the meaning of 'officer' see PARA 174 note 9.
3 As to registration as a social landlord see PARA 169.
4 As to the meaning of 'registered society' see PARA 168 note 1.
5 Housing Act 1996 s 7, Sch 1 para 8(1) (Sch 1 para 8(1) amended by the Housing and Regeneration Act 2008 s 61(1), (7); in relation to Wales, by the Housing (Wales) Measure 2011 s 85(1), (7)(a)–(c); and by the Co-operative and Community Benefit Societies Act 2014 s 151(1), Sch 4 paras 55, 56).
6 Housing Act 1996 Sch 1 para 8(1) (amended, in relation to Wales, by the Housing (Wales) Measure 2011 s 85(1), (7)(d)).
7 Housing Act 1996 Sch 1 para 8(2).
8 Housing Act 1996 Sch 1 para 8(3) (amended by the Housing and Regeneration Act 2008 s 61(1), (7)).
9 Housing Act 1996 Sch 1 para 8(4).
10 As to the powers referred to in the text see PARAS 201–202.

178. Power to appoint a new officer of a registered charity. The Welsh Ministers[1] may by order appoint a person to be an officer[2] of a registered social landlord[3] which is a registered charity[4]: (1) in place of a person removed by the Welsh Ministers; (2) where there are no officers; or (3) where the Welsh Ministers are of the opinion that it is necessary for the proper management of the charity's affairs to have an additional officer[5]. The power conferred in the last-mentioned case may be exercised notwithstanding that it will cause the maximum number of officers permissible under the charity's constitution to be exceeded[6].

The Welsh Ministers may, however, only exercise the power to appoint if the charity has, at any time before the power is exercised, received public assistance[7] and the Welsh Ministers have consulted the Charity Commission[8]. A person may be so appointed notwithstanding any restrictions on appointment in the charity's constitution or rules[9].

A person so appointed holds office for such period and on such terms as the Welsh Ministers may specify; and on the expiry of the appointment the Welsh Ministers may renew the appointment for such period as they may specify; but this does not prevent a person so appointed from retiring in accordance with the charity's constitution or rules[10]. A person so appointed as an officer of a registered charity is entitled: (a) to attend, speak and vote at any general meeting of the charity and to receive all notices of and other communications relating to any such meeting which a member is entitled to receive; (b) to move a resolution at any general meeting of the charity; and (c) to require a general meeting of the charity to be convened within 21 days of a request to that effect made in writing to the directors or trustees[11].

This power is additional to the Welsh Ministers' powers which are available following an inquiry into a registered social landlord[12].

1 As to the Welsh Ministers see PARAS 7, 141.
2 As to the meaning of 'officer' see PARA 174 note 9.
3 As to registration as a social landlord see PARA 169.
4 As to the meaning of 'registered charity' see PARA 168 note 3.
5 Housing Act 1996 s 7, Sch 1 para 6(1) (Sch 1 para 6(1) amended by the Housing and Regeneration Act 2008 s 61(1), (7); and, in relation to Wales, by the Housing (Wales) Measure 2011 s 85(1), (3)(a)–(c)).
6 Housing Act 1996 Sch 1 para 6(1) (amended, in relation to Wales, by the Housing (Wales) Measure 2011 s 85(1), (3)(d)).
7 As to the meaning of 'received public assistance' see PARA 175.
8 Housing Act 1996 Sch 1 para 6(2) (amended by the Charities Act 2006 s 75(1), Sch 8 paras 183, 192(1), (2); the Housing and Regeneration Act 2008 s 61(1), (7); and in relation to Wales, by the Housing (Wales) Measure 2011 s 88, Schedule paras 1, 14).
9 Housing Act 1996 Sch 1 para 6(3).
10 Housing Act 1996 Sch 1 para 6(4) (amended by the Housing and Regeneration Act 2008 s 61(1), (7)).
11 Housing Act 1996 Sch 1 para 6(5) (amended, in relation to Wales, by the Housing (Wales) Measure 2011 s 85(1), (3)(e)).
12 As to the powers referred to in the text see PARAS 201–202.

179. Change of rules, etc by a registered society, a charity or a company. Notice must be sent to the Welsh Ministers[1] of any change of the name, or of the situation of the registered office, of a registered society[2] whose registration as a social landlord[3] has been recorded by the Financial Conduct Authority[4]. Any other amendment of the society's rules is not valid unless the Welsh Ministers consent to it[5].

With regard to a registered social landlord which is a registered charity[6] and is not a company[7], and whose registration[8] has been recorded by the Charity Commission[9], no power contained in the provisions establishing the registered social landlord as a charity, or regulating its purposes or administration, to vary or add to its objects may be exercised without the consent of the Charity Commission[10]. Before giving its consent the Charity Commission must consult the Welsh Ministers[11].

In relation to a company (including a company that is a registered charity) whose registration as a social landlord has been recorded by the registrar of companies, notice must be sent to the Welsh Ministers of any change of the company's name or of the address of its registered office[12]; and any other alteration of the company's articles of which notice is required to be given to the registrar of companies is not valid without the Welsh Ministers' consent[13].

1 As to the Welsh Ministers see PARAS 7, 141.
2 As to the meaning of 'registered society' see PARA 168 note 1.
3 As to the register of social landlords see PARA 167.
4 Housing Act 1996 s 7, Sch 1 para 9(1), (2) (Sch 1 para 9(1) amended by the Co-operative and Community Benefit Societies Act 2014 s 151(1), Sch 4 paras 55, 56; and by SI 2013/496; the Housing Act 1996 Sch 1 para 9(2) amended by the Housing and Regeneration Act 2008 s 61(1), (7)). As to the Financial Conduct Authority see FINANCIAL SERVICES REGULATION vol 50 (2016) PARAS 5, 6 et seq.
5 Housing Act 1996 Sch 1 para 9(3) (amended by the Government of Wales Act 1998 ss 140, 152, Sch 16 para 96(2)(a), Sch 18 Pt VI; and the Housing and Regeneration Act 2008 s 61(1), (7)). Consent given by the Welsh Ministers must be given by order in writing: Housing Act 1996 Sch 1 para 9(3A) (added by the Government of Wales Act 1998 Sch 16 para 96(2)(b); and amended by the Housing and Regeneration Act 2008 s 62(a); and by SI 2010/866). A copy of that consent must be sent with the copies of the amendment required by the Co-operative and Community Benefit Societies Act 2014 s 16 (see FINANCIAL INSTITUTIONS vol 48 (2015) PARA 924) to be sent to the Financial Conduct Authority; and the Co-operative and Community Benefit Societies Act 2014 applies in relation to the provisions of the Housing Act 1996 Sch 1 para 9 as if they were contained in the Co-operative and Community Benefit Societies Act 2014 s 16 (amendment of registered rules: see FINANCIAL INSTITUTIONS vol 48 (2015) PARAS 924–925): Housing Act 1996 Sch 1 para 9(4), (5) (Sch 1 para 9(4) amended by the Co-operative and Community Benefit Societies Act 2014 Sch 4 paras 64, 65(1), (4)(a); and by SI 2013/496; the Housing Act 1996 Sch 1 para 9(5) amended by the Co-operative and Community Benefit Societies Act 2014 Sch 4 paras 64, 65(1), (4)(b)).
6 As to the meaning of 'registered charity' see PARA 168 note 3.
7 As to the meaning of 'company' see PARA 168 note 7.
8 Ie under the Housing Act 1996 Pt I (ss A1–64).
9 Ie in accordance with the Housing Act 1996 s 3(3): see PARA 169.
10 Housing Act 1996 Sch 1 para 10(1), (2) (Sch 1 para 10(1), (2) amended by the Charities Act 2006 s 75(1), Sch 8 paras 183, 192(1), (3)(a); the Housing Act 1996 Sch 1 para 10(1) also amended by SI 2009/1941).
11 Housing Act 1996 Sch 1 para 10(2) (amended by the Charities Act 2006 Sch 8 paras 183, 192(1), (3)(a), (b); and the Housing and Regeneration Act 2008 s 61(1), (7)).
12 Housing Act 1996 Sch 1 para 11(1), (2) (Sch 1 para 11(1) amended by SI 2009/1940; the Housing Act 1996 Sch 1 para 11(2) amended by the Housing and Regeneration Act 2008 s 61(1), (7)).
13 Housing Act 1996 Sch 1 para 11(3) (amended by the Government of Wales Act 1998 Sch 16 para 96(2)(a), Sch 18 Pt VI; the Housing and Regeneration Act 2008 s 61(1), (7); and SI 2009/1941). Consent given by the Welsh Ministers must be given by order in writing: Housing Act 1996 Sch 1 para 11(3A) (added by the Government of Wales Act 1998 Sch 16 para 96(2)(b); and amended by the Housing and Regeneration Act 2008 s 62(a); and by SI 2010/866). A copy of that consent must be sent with the copy of the resolution making the alterations that is required to be sent to the registrar of companies under the Companies Act 2006 s 30: Housing Act 1996 Sch 1 para 11(4) (amended by SI 2007/2194).

180. Arrangements, reconstruction etc of company which is a registered social landlord. In the case of a company[1] whose registration as a social landlord[2] has been recorded by the registrar of companies, an order of the court given for certain purposes relating to compromise or arrangement with creditors or members[3] is not effective unless the Welsh Ministers[4] have given their consent to it[5]. Nor is an order of the court given for certain purposes relating to the transfer of the company's undertaking or property for purposes of reconstruction or amalgamation[6] effective without that consent[7].

The registrar of companies must not register any resolution for the conversion of the company into a registered society[8] unless, together with the copy of the resolution, there is sent to him a copy of the Welsh Ministers' consent to the conversion[9].

Where a director, administrator or liquidator of the company proposes to make a voluntary arrangement with the company's creditors[10], the arrangement may not take effect[11] unless the Welsh Ministers have given their consent to the voluntary arrangement[12].

If the company resolves by special resolution that it be wound up voluntarily under the Insolvency Act 1986, the resolution has no effect unless before the resolution was passed the Welsh Ministers gave their consent to its passing, and a copy of the consent is forwarded to the registrar of companies together with a copy of the resolution required[13] to be so forwarded[14].

1   As to the meaning of 'company' see PARA 168 note 7.
2   As to the register of social landlords see PARA 167.
3   Ie an order given for the purposes of the Companies Act 2006 s 899: see COMPANIES vol 15A (2016) PARA 1611.
4   As to the Welsh Ministers see PARAS 7, 141.
5   Housing Act 1996 s 7, Sch 1 para 13(1), (2) (Sch 1 para 13(1) amended by SI 2009/1941; the Housing Act 1996 Sch 1 para 13(2) amended by the Housing and Regeneration Act 2008 s 61(1), (7); and by SI 2008/948). A copy of the consent must be sent to the registrar of companies along with the office copy of the order delivered to him under the Companies Act 2006 s 899 (see COMPANIES vol 15A (2016) PARA 1611): Housing Act 1996 Sch 1 para 13(2). Consent given by the Welsh Ministers must given by order in writing: Sch 1 para 13(7) (amended by the Government of Wales Act 1998, s 140, Sch 16 para 96(3); in relation to Wales, by the Housing (Wales) Measure 2011 s 88, Schedule paras 1, 16; and by SI 2010/866).
6   Ie an order given for the purposes of the Companies Act 2006 s 900: see COMPANIES vol 15A (2016) PARA 1614.
7   Housing Act 1996 Sch 1 para 13(3) (amended by the Housing and Regeneration Act 2008 s 61(1), (7); and by SI 2008/948). A copy of the consent must be sent to the registrar of companies along with the office copy of the order delivered to him under the Companies Act 2006 s 900 (see COMPANIES vol 15A (2016) PARA 1614): Housing Act 1996 Sch 1 para 13(3). Where Sch 1 para 13(3) or (4) applies, the transferee or, as the case may be, any new body created by the conversion is deemed to be registered as a social landlord forthwith upon the transfer or conversion taking effect: Sch 1 para 13(8).
8   Ie under the Co-operative and Community Benefit Societies Act 2014 s 115: see FINANCIAL INSTITUTIONS vol 48 (2015) PARAS 905–908. As to the meaning of 'registered society' see PARA 168 note 1.
9   Housing Act 1996 Sch 1 para 13(4) (amended by the Housing and Regeneration Act 2008 s 61(1), (7); and the Co-operative and Community Benefit Societies Act 2014 s 151(1), Sch 4 paras 55, 65(1), (7)). See note 7.
10 Ie under the Insolvency Act 1986 s 1: see COMPANY AND PARTNERSHIP INSOLVENCY vol 16 (2011) PARA 83 et seq.
11 Ie under the Insolvency Act 1986 s 5: see COMPANY AND PARTNERSHIP INSOLVENCY vol 16 (2011) PARA 143.
12 Housing Act 1996 Sch 1 para 13(5) (amended by the Housing and Regeneration Act 2008 s 61(1), (7)).
13 Ie in accordance with the Companies Act 2006 s 30: see COMPANIES vol 15 (2016) PARA 688.
14 Housing Act 1996 Sch 1 para 13(6) (amended by the Housing and Regeneration Act 2008 s 61(1), (7); and by SI 2007/2194).

181. Amalgamation, dissolution etc of a registered society which is a registered social landlord. In the case of a registered society whose registration as a social landlord[1] has been recorded by the Financial Conduct Authority[2], the Financial Conduct Authority must not register a special resolution which is passed for certain purposes relating to amalgamation, transfer or conversion[3] or transfer its engagements to a company registered under the Companies Act 2006 unless, together with the copy of the resolution, there is sent to it a copy of the consent[4] of the Welsh Ministers[5] to the amalgamation, transfer or conversion[6]. Any new body created by the amalgamation or conversion or, in the case of a transfer of engagements, the transferee is deemed to be registered as a social landlord forthwith upon the amalgamation, conversion or transfer taking effect[7]. If the society resolves by special resolution that it be wound up voluntarily under the

Insolvency Act 1986, the resolution has no effect unless before the resolution was passed the Welsh Ministers gave their consent to its passing, and a copy of the consent is forwarded to the Financial Conduct Authority together with a copy of the resolution required to be so forwarded[8] in accordance with the Co-operative and Community Benefit Societies Act 2014[9]. If the society is to be dissolved by instrument of dissolution, the Financial Conduct Authority must not register the instrument[10] or cause notice of the dissolution to be advertised[11] unless together with the instrument there is sent to it a copy of the Welsh Ministers' consent to its making[12].

1   As to the meaning of 'registered society' see PARA 168 note 1. As to the register of social landlords see PARA 167.
2   As to the Financial Conduct Authority see FINANCIAL SERVICES REGULATION vol 50 (2016) PARAS 5, 6 et seq.
3   Ie for the purposes of the Co-operative and Community Benefit Societies Act 2014 s 109 (amalgamation of societies), s 110 (transfer of engagements between societies), or s 112 (conversion of society into a company etc): see FINANCIAL INSTITUTIONS vol 48 (2015) PARAS 1052–1055.
4   Consent given by the Welsh Ministers under the Housing Act 1996 Sch 1 para 12 must be given by order in writing: s 7, Sch 1 para 12(6) (Sch 1 para 12(6) amended by the Government of Wales Act 1998 s 140, Sch 16 para 96(3); in relation to Wales, by the Housing (Wales) Measure 2011 s 88, Schedule paras 1, 15; and by SI 2010/866).
5   As to the Welsh Ministers see PARAS 7, 141.
6   Housing Act 1996 Sch 1 para 12(1), (2) (Sch 1 para 12(1) amended by the Co-operative and Community Benefit Societies Act 2014 s 151(1), Sch 4 paras 55, 56; and by SI 2013/496; the Housing Act 1996 Sch 1 para 12(2) amended by the Housing and Regeneration Act 2008 s 61(1), (7); the Co-operative and Community Benefit Societies Act 2014 Sch 4 paras 55, 65(1), (6); and by SI 2001/3649 and SI 2013/496).
7   Housing Act 1996 Sch 1 para 12(3).
8   Ie in accordance with the Co-operative and Community Benefit Societies Act 2014 s 123(3)(a): see FINANCIAL INSTITUTIONS vol 48 (2015) PARA 1066.
9   Housing Act 1996 Sch 1 para 12(4) (amended by the Housing and Regeneration Act 2008 s 61(1), (7); the Co-operative and Community Benefit Societies Act 2014 Sch 4 paras 55, 65(1), (6)(b); and by SI 2001/3649 and SI 2009/1941 and SI 2013/496).
10   Ie in accordance with the Co-operative and Community Benefit Societies Act 2014 s 121: see FINANCIAL INSTITUTIONS vol 48 (2015) PARA 1063.
11   Ie in accordance with the Co-operative and Community Benefit Societies Act 2014 s 122: see FINANCIAL INSTITUTIONS vol 48 (2015) PARA 1063.
12   Housing Act 1996 Sch 1 para 12(5) (amended by the Housing and Regeneration Act 2008 s 61(1), (7); the Co-operative and Community Benefit Societies Act 2014 Sch 4 paras 55, 65(1), (6)(c); and by SI 2001/3649 and SI 2013/496). As to the transfer of net assets on dissolution see PARA 183.

182. Power to petition for winding up of a registered social landlord. The Welsh Ministers[1] may present a petition for the winding up under the Insolvency Act 1986 of a registered social landlord[2] which is:

(1)   a company[3] (including a company that is a registered charity[4]); or
(2)   a registered society[5], on either of the following grounds[6]:
    (a)   that the landlord is failing properly to carry out its purposes or objects; or
    (b)   that the landlord is unable to pay its debts[7].

1   As to the Welsh Ministers see PARAS 7, 141.
2   As to the register of social landlords see PARA 167.
3   As to the meaning of 'company' see PARA 168 note 7.
4   As to the meaning of 'registered charity' see PARA 168 note 3.
5   Ie to which the winding-up provisions of the Insolvency Act 1986 apply in accordance with the Co-operative and Community Benefit Societies Act 2014 s 123: see FINANCIAL INSTITUTIONS vol 48 (2015) PARA 1058. As to the meaning of 'registered society' see PARA 168 note 1.
6   Housing Act 1996 s 7, Sch 1 para 14(1) (Sch 1 para 14(1) amended by the Housing and Regeneration Act 2008 s 61(1), (7); the Co-operative and Community Benefit Societies Act 2014

s 151(1), Sch 4 paras 55, 56, 65(1), (8); and by SI 2009/1941). The reference to the landlord being unable to pay its debts is a reference to being unable to pay its debts within the meaning of the Insolvency Act 1986 s 123: see COMPANY AND PARTNERSHIP INSOLVENCY vol 16 (2011) PARA 394. As to insolvency of registered social landlords see PARA 206 et seq.

7   Housing Act 1996 Sch 1 para 14(2).

183.   Transfer of net assets on dissolution or winding up. Where a registered social landlord which is a registered society[1] is dissolved[2] or a registered social landlord which is a company[3] (including a company that is a registered charity[4]) is wound up[5], on such a dissolution or winding up so much of the property of the society or company as remains after meeting the claims of its creditors and any other liabilities arising on or before the dissolution or winding up must be transferred to the Welsh Ministers[6] or, if the Welsh Ministers so direct, to a specified registered social landlord[7]. In order to avoid the necessity for the sale of land belonging to the registered social landlord and thereby secure the transfer of the land, the Welsh Ministers may, if it appears to them appropriate to do so, make payments to discharge such claims or liabilities as are referred to above[8].

Where the registered social landlord which is dissolved or wound up is a charity, the Welsh Ministers may dispose of property transferred to them by virtue of these provisions only to another registered social landlord which is also a charity, and the objects of which appear to the Welsh Ministers to be, as nearly as practicable, akin to those of the body which is dissolved or wound up[9]. In any other case the Welsh Ministers may dispose of property transferred to them by virtue of these provisions to a registered social landlord[10].

Where property transferred to the Welsh Ministers by virtue of these provisions includes land subject to an existing mortgage or charge, whether in favour of the Welsh Ministers or not, the Welsh Ministers may[11] dispose of the land either subject to that mortgage or charge, or subject to a new mortgage or charge in favour of the Welsh Ministers securing such amount as appears to the Welsh Ministers to be appropriate in the circumstances[12].

1   As to the register of social landlords see PARA 167. As to the meaning of 'registered society' see PARA 168 note 1.
2   Ie as mentioned in the Co-operative and Community Benefit Societies Act 2014 s 119 or s 123 (dissolution by instrument of dissolution or by winding up): see FINANCIAL INSTITUTIONS vol 48 (2015) PARA 1058.
3   As to the meaning of 'company' see PARA 168 note 7.
4   As to the meaning of 'registered charity' see PARA 168 note 3.
5   Ie under the Insolvency Act 1986: see generally COMPANY AND PARTNERSHIP INSOLVENCY.
6   As to the Welsh Ministers see PARAS 7, 141.
7   Housing Act 1996 s 7, Sch 1 para 15(1), (2) (Sch 1 para 15(1) amended by the Co-operative and Community Benefit Societies Act 2014 s 151(1), Sch 4 paras 55, 56, 65(1), (9)(a); and SI 2009/1941; the Housing Act 1996 Sch 1 para 15(2) amended by the Housing and Regeneration Act 2008 s 61(1), (7)). This provision has effect notwithstanding anything in the Co-operative and Community Benefit Societies Act 2014, the Companies Act 2006 or the Insolvency Act 1986, or in the rules of the society or, as the case may be, in the articles of the company: Housing Act 1996 Sch 1 para 15(2) (amended by the Co-operative and Community Benefit Societies Act 2014 Sch 4 paras 55, 65(1), (9)(b); and SI 2009/1941).
8   Housing Act 1996 Sch 1 para 15(3) (amended by the Housing and Regeneration Act 2008 s 61(1), (7)).
9   Housing Act 1996 Sch 1 para 15(4) (amended by the Housing and Regeneration Act 2008 s 61(1), (7)). As from a day to be appointed, in such a case any registered social landlord specified in a direction under the Housing Act 1996 Sch 1 para 15(2) must be one to which Sch 1 para 15(4)(a), (b) applies: Sch 1 para 15(4) (prospectively amended by the Housing Act 2004 s 218, Sch 11 para 15(3)). At the date at which this volume states the law, no such day had been appointed.
10 Housing Act 1996 Sch 1 para 15(5) (substituted by SI 2010/866). As to the Housing Corporation (now abolished) see PARA 2.

11 Ie in exercise of its powers under the Housing Associations Act 1985 Pt III (ss 74–102): see PARA 143 et seq.

12 Housing Act 1996 Sch 1 para 15(6) (amended by the Housing and Regeneration Act 2008 s 61(1), (7)).

184. Transfer of net assets on termination of a charity. As from a day to be appointed[1], the Welsh Ministers[2] may by regulations provide for any of the statutory provisions as to the transfer of net assets on dissolution or winding up[3] to apply in relation to a registered social landlord[4] which is a registered charity and is not a registered society which is dissolved or a company which is wound up[5], in such circumstances, and with such modifications, as may be specified in the regulations[6].

Such regulations may in particular provide that any provision of the regulations requiring the transfer of any property of the charity is to have effect notwithstanding: (1) anything in the terms of its trusts; or (2) any resolution, order or other thing done for the purposes of, or in connection with, the termination of the charity in any manner specified in the regulations[7].

1 The Housing Act 1996 Sch 1 para 15A is added by the Housing Act 2004 s 218, Sch 11 paras 7, 16 as from a day to be appointed. At the date at which this volume states the law, no such day had been appointed.
2 As to the Welsh Ministers see PARAS 7, 141.
3 Ie any provisions of the Housing Act 1996 s 7, Sch 1 para 15(2)–(6): see PARA 183.
4 As to the register of social landlords see PARA 167.
5 Ie it does not fall within the Housing Act 1996 Sch 1 para 15(1): see PARA 183.
6 Housing Act 1996 Sch 1 para 15A(1), (2) (as added (see note 1); Sch 1 para 15A(1) amended by the Housing and Regeneration Act 2008 s 62(a)).
7 Housing Act 1996 Sch 1 para 15A(3) (as added: see note 1). Any regulations made under this power must be made by statutory instrument which is to be subject to annulment in pursuance of a resolution of the National Assembly for Wales: Sch 1 para 15A(4) (as so added; amended by the Housing and Regeneration Act 2008 s 63).

D. ENFORCEMENT POWERS OF THE WELSH MINISTERS

185. Exercise of enforcement powers. The following provisions do not apply in relation to a registered social landlord's provision of housing in England[1].

They apply where the Welsh Ministers[2] are deciding whether to exercise an enforcement power[3], which enforcement power to exercise, or how to exercise an enforcement power[4]. The Welsh Ministers must consider: (1) the desirability of registered social landlords being free to choose how to provide services and conduct business; (2) whether the failure or other problem concerned is serious or trivial; (3) whether the failure or other problem is a recurrent or isolated incident; (4) the speed with which the failure or other problem needs to be addressed[5].

A registered social landlord may give the Welsh Ministers an undertaking in respect of any matter concerning housing[6], and the Welsh Ministers must have regard to any undertaking offered or given in exercising their enforcement powers under these provisions[7], and may base a decision about whether to exercise their powers under these provisions wholly or partly on the extent to which the undertaking has been honoured[8].

1 Housing Act 1996 s 50A (added, in relation to Wales, by the Housing (Wales) Measure 2011 s 50). As to the register of social landlords see PARA 167.
2 As to the Welsh Ministers see PARAS 7, 141.
3 For these purposes 'enforcement power' means a power exercisable under the Housing Act 1996 Pt I Ch 4A (ss 50A–50V), Sch 1 Pt II paras 4, 6–8, 14–15B, 15D, 15F and 15H, or Sch 1 Pt IV paras 20–27 (see PARA 200 et seq): s 50B(3) (s 50B added, in relation to Wales, by the Housing (Wales) Measure 2011 s 51).
4 Housing Act 1996 s 50B(1) (as added: see note 3). As to additional powers in relation to the management of registered social landlords see PARA 189 et seq.

5   Housing Act 1996 s 50B(2) (as added: see note 3).
6   Housing Act 1996 s 6A(1) (s 6A added, in relation to Wales, by the Housing (Wales) Measure
    2011 s 41). The Welsh Ministers may prescribe a procedure to be followed in giving an
    undertaking: Housing Act 1996 s 6A(2) (as so added).
7   Ie their powers under the Housing Act 1996 Pt I Ch 4A (see the text to notes 1–5; and
    PARAS 186–188): s 6A(5) (as added: see note 6).
8   Housing Act 1996 s 6A(3), (4) (as added: see note 6). Section 6A does not apply in relation to a
    registered social landlord's provision of housing in England: s 6A(6) (as so added).

186.   Enforcement notice. The following provisions do not apply in relation to a
registered social landlord's provision of housing in England[1].

The Welsh Ministers[2] may give an enforcement notice to a registered social
landlord if they are satisfied that any of the following cases applies and that giving
an enforcement notice is appropriate (whether it is likely to be sufficient in itself
or a prelude to further action)[3].

Case 1 is where the registered social landlord has failed to meet a performance
standard[4] applicable to it[5].

Case 2 is where there has been misconduct[6] or mismanagement in the affairs of
the registered social landlord[7].

Case 3 is where the registered social landlord has failed to comply with an
earlier enforcement notice[8].

Case 4 is where the registered social landlord has failed to publish information
in accordance with a requirement[9] to do so[10].

Case 5 is where the interests of tenants of the registered social landlord require
protection[11].

Case 6 is where the registered social landlord's assets require protection[12].

Case 7 is where the registered social landlord has given an undertaking[13] and
failed to comply with it[14].

Case 8 is where an offence under Part I of the Housing Act 1996 has been
committed by the registered social landlord[15].

Case 9 is where the registered social landlord has failed to implement a
recommendation made by the Public Services Ombudsman for Wales in a report
prepared[16] after an investigation[17].

An enforcement notice must: (1) specify the grounds on which it is given; (2)
specify the action the Welsh Ministers want the registered social landlord to take
in response to the notice; (3) specify when the action is to be taken (which may be
immediately on receipt of the notice); and (4) explain the effect of the provisions[18]
relating to appeal, withdrawal of a notice and sanctions[19]. The action specified in
an enforcement notice may include publishing the notice in a specified manner[20].

A registered social landlord who is given an enforcement notice may appeal to
the High Court[21].

The Welsh Ministers may withdraw an enforcement notice by notice to the
registered social landlord[22].

In the case of an enforcement notice given to a person other than the registered
social landlord[23], the Welsh Ministers may only: (a) exercise the power to issue a
penalty notice to the person[24]; or (b) take steps to have the person prosecuted for
the offence by reference to which the enforcement notice was given[25]. A person to
whom an enforcement notice is given on the ground in Case 8 above may not be
prosecuted for the offence by reference to which the enforcement notice was given
unless the person fails to comply with the enforcement notice[26].

1   Housing Act 1996 s 50A (added, in relation to Wales, by the Housing (Wales) Measure 2011 s 50).
    As to the register of social landlords see PARA 167.
2   As to the Welsh Ministers see PARAS 7, 141.

3 Housing Act 1996 s 50C(1) (ss 50C–50G added, in relation to Wales, by the Housing (Wales) Measure 2011 ss 52–56). As to the meaning of 'notice' see PARA 169 note 6.
4 Ie under the Housing Act 1996 s 33A: see PARA 160.
5 Housing Act 1996 s 50C(2) (as added: see note 3).
6 'Misconduct' includes any failure to comply with the requirements of the Housing Act 1996 Pt I (ss A1–64): s 63(1) (definition added, in relation to Wales, by the Housing (Wales) Measure 2011 s 87).
7 Housing Act 1996 s 50C(3) (as added: see note 3).
8 Housing Act 1996 s 50C(4) (as added: see note 3).
9 Ie under the Housing Act 1996 s 50I(3) (see PARA 187) or s 50Q(3) (see PARA 188).
10 Housing Act 1996 s 50C(5) (as added: see note 3).
11 Housing Act 1996 s 50C(6) (as added: see note 3). As to the meaning of 'tenant' see PARA 168 note 16.
12 Housing Act 1996 s 50C(7) (as added: see note 3).
13 Ie under the Housing Act 1996 s 6A: see PARA 185.
14 Housing Act 1996 s 50C(8) (as added: see note 3).
15 Housing Act 1996 s 50C(9) (as added: see note 3). Where the Welsh Ministers are satisfied that an offence under Pt I has been committed in respect of a registered social landlord but by another person (such as a member, employee or agent of the registered social landlord): (1) Case 8 applies; (2) the Welsh Ministers may give an enforcement notice to the other person; and (3) Pt I Ch 4A (ss 50A–50V) applies with the substitution of references to that other person for references to the registered social landlord: s 50C(11) (as so added).
16 Ie under the Public Services Ombudsman (Wales) Act 2005 s 16: see LOCAL GOVERNMENT vol 69 (2009) PARA 861.
17 Housing Act 1996 s 50C(10) (as added: see note 3).
18 Ie of the Housing Act 1996 ss 50E–50G: see the text to notes 21–26.
19 Housing Act 1996 s 50D(1) (as added: see note 3).
20 Housing Act 1996 s 50D(2) (as added: see note 3).
21 Housing Act 1996 s 50E (as added: see note 3).
22 Housing Act 1996 s 50F (as added: see note 3).
23 Ie by virtue of the Housing Act 1996 s 50C(11): see note 15.
24 Ie in accordance with the Housing Act 1996 ss 50H–50N: see PARA 187.
25 Housing Act 1996 s 50G(1) (as added: see note 3).
26 Housing Act 1996 s 50G(2) (as added: see note 3).

187. Penalty. The following provisions do not apply in relation to a registered social landlord's provision of housing in England[1].

The Welsh Ministers[2] may require a registered social landlord to pay a penalty if they are satisfied that: (1) any of the following cases applies; and (2) the imposition of a penalty is appropriate (whether or not as part of a response including other action)[3].

Case 1 is where the registered social landlord has failed to meet a performance standard[4].

Case 2 is where there has been misconduct[5] or mismanagement in the affairs of the registered social landlord[6].

Case 3 is where the registered social landlord has failed to comply with an enforcement notice[7].

Case 4 is where the registered social landlord has given an undertaking[8] and failed to comply with it[9].

Case 5 is where an offence under Part I of the Housing Act 1996[10] has been committed by the registered social landlord[11]. In order to rely on Case 5 the Welsh Ministers must be satisfied beyond reasonable doubt that it applies[12].

A penalty is imposed by the Welsh Ministers giving notice (a 'penalty notice') to the registered social landlord[13]. The notice must specify: (a) the grounds on which the penalty is imposed; (b) the amount of the penalty; (c) how the penalty must be paid; (d) a period within which it must be paid; and (e) any interest or additional penalty which is payable[14] in the event of late payment[15]. The notice may require the registered social landlord to publish information about the penalty in a specified manner[16]. The notice must explain the effect of certain provisions[17] relating to enforcement of the penalty and appeal against a penalty notice[18].

The amount of a penalty imposed on the ground specified in Case 5 may not exceed the maximum amount (if any) of fine that a magistrates' court could impose for the relevant offence[19]. The amount of a penalty imposed on the ground specified in any other Case may not exceed £5,000[20].

Before giving a penalty notice to a registered social landlord the Welsh Ministers must give the landlord a notice (a 'pre-penalty warning'): (i) specifying grounds on which the Welsh Ministers think a penalty could be imposed; (ii) warning the landlord that the Welsh Ministers are considering imposing a penalty; (iii) including any indication that the Welsh Ministers are able to give of the likely amount of any penalty; and (iv) explaining the effect of certain provisions[21] relating to representations, enforcement and appeal[22].

The Welsh Ministers must send a copy of a pre-penalty warning to any person they think appropriate (having regard, in particular, to any person who provided information as a result of which the pre-penalty warning is given)[23]. A pre-penalty warning must refer to the provision permitting voluntary undertakings[24], and indicate whether or to what extent the Welsh Ministers would accept a voluntary undertaking instead of, or in mitigation of, a penalty[25]. A pre-penalty warning may be combined with notice under one or more of certain other provisions[26] of the Housing Act 1996[27].

A pre-penalty warning must specify a period during which the registered social landlord may make representations[28] to the Welsh Ministers[29]. The period must be a period of at least 28 days, and begin with the date on which the registered social landlord receives the pre-penalty warning[30]. Representations may address whether a penalty should be imposed and the amount of any penalty that may be imposed[31]. After the end of the period specified, the Welsh Ministers must consider any representations made, and decide whether to impose a penalty[32].

A penalty is to be treated as a debt owed to the Welsh Ministers[33]. The Welsh Ministers may charge interest on a penalty not paid during the period specified under head (d) above and impose one or more additional penalties where a penalty is not paid during that period[34]. Interest and additional penalty are to be treated as penalty (and may have the effect of increasing the penalty above a limit set[35] for penalties[36]. A penalty notice may include provision allowing a discount if the penalty is paid on or before a date specified in the notice (falling within the period specified under head (d)[37]. A person to whom a penalty notice is given on the ground in Case 5 may not be prosecuted for the offence by reference to which the penalty notice was given[38].

A registered social landlord who is given a penalty notice may appeal to the High Court against the imposition of the penalty, its amount, or both[39].

1   Housing Act 1996 s 50A (added, in relation to Wales, by the Housing (Wales) Measure 2011 s 50). As to the register of social landlords see PARA 167.
2   As to the Welsh Ministers see PARAS 7, 141.
3   Housing Act 1996 s 50H(1) (ss 50H–50N added, in relation to Wales, by the Housing (Wales) Measure 2011 ss 57–63).
4   Housing Act 1996 s 50H(2) (as added: see note 3). The text refers to a standard under s 33A: see PARA 160.
5   As to the meaning of 'misconduct' see PARA 186 note 6.
6   Housing Act 1996 s 50H(3) (as added: see note 3).
7   Housing Act 1996 s 50H(4) (as added: see note 3). As to enforcement notices see PARA 186.
8   Ie under the Housing Act 1996 s 6A: see PARA 185.
9   Housing Act 1996 s 50H(5) (as added: see note 3).

10 Ie the Housing Act 1996 Pt I (ss A1–64).

11 Housing Act 1996 s 50H(6) (as added: see note 3). Where the Welsh Ministers are satisfied that an offence under Pt I has been committed in respect of a registered social landlord but by another person (such as a member, employee or agent of the registered social landlord): (1) Case 5 applies; (2) the Welsh Ministers may require the other person to pay a penalty; and (3) Pt I Ch 4A (ss 50A–50V) applies with the substitution of references to that other person for references to the registered social landlord: s 50H(7) (as so added).

12 Housing Act 1996 s 50H(8) (as added: see note 3).

13 Housing Act 1996 s 50I(1) (as added: see note 3). As to the meaning of 'notice' see PARA 169 note 6.

14 Ie by virtue of the Housing Act 1996 s 50M: see the text to notes 33–36.

15 Housing Act 1996 s 50I(2) (as added: see note 3).

16 Housing Act 1996 s 50I(3) (as added: see note 3).

17 Ie the Housing Act 1996 ss 50M(1), (3) and (5) and 50N: see the text to notes 33, 36, 38, 39.

18 Housing Act 1996 s 50I(4) (as added: see note 3).

19 Housing Act 1996 s 50J(1) (as added (see note 3); amended by SI 2015/664). As to the powers of magistrates' courts to issue fines on summary conviction see SENTENCING vol 92 (2015) PARA 176.

20 Housing Act 1996 s 50J(2) (as added: see note 3). The Welsh Ministers may by order amend the amount specified in s 50J(2): s 50J(3) (as so added). An order under s 50J(3) is to be made by statutory instrument and must not be made unless a draft of the instrument has been laid before, and approved by a resolution of, the National Assembly for Wales: s 50J(4) (as so added).

21 Ie the Housing Act 1996 ss 50L, 50M(1), (3) and (5) and 50N: see the text to notes 29–33, 36, 38, 39.

22 Housing Act 1996 s 50K(1) (as added: see note 3).

23 Housing Act 1996 s 50K(2) (as added: see note 3).

24 Ie the Housing Act 1996 s 6A: see PARA 185.

25 Housing Act 1996 s 50K(3) (as added: see note 3).

26 Ie the Housing Act 1996 s 50S (see PARA 188), Sch 1 para 15C (see PARA 189), or Sch 1 paras 15E, 15G (see PARAS 190–191).

27 Housing Act 1996 s 50K(4) (as added: see note 3).

28 For these purposes 'representations' means representations in writing: Housing Act 1996 s 63(1) (definition added, in relation to Wales, by the Housing (Wales) Measure 2011 s 87).

29 Housing Act 1996 s 50L(1) (as added: see note 3).

30 Housing Act 1996 s 50L(2) (as added: see note 3).

31 Housing Act 1996 s 50L(3) (as added: see note 3).

32 Housing Act 1996 s 50L(4) (as added: see note 3).

33 Housing Act 1996 s 50M(1) (as added: see note 3).

34 Housing Act 1996 s 50M(2) (as added: see note 3).

35 Ie by the Housing Act 1996 s 50J.

36 Housing Act 1996 s 50M(3) (as added: see note 3).

37 Housing Act 1996 s 50M(4) (as added: see note 3).

38 Housing Act 1996 s 50M(5) (as added: see note 3).

39 Housing Act 1996 s 50N (as added: see note 3).

188. Compensation. The following provisions do not apply in relation to a registered social landlord's provision of housing in England[1].

The Welsh Ministers[2] may require a registered social landlord to pay compensation if they are satisfied that: (1) either of the following cases applies; and (2) the award of compensation is appropriate[3].

Case 1 is where the registered social landlord has failed to meet a performance standard[4].

Case 2 is where the registered social landlord has given an undertaking[5] and failed to comply with it[6].

Compensation in respect of a failure may be awarded to one or more persons who have suffered as a result of the failure[7].

Compensation is awarded by the Welsh Ministers giving notice (a 'compensation notice') to the registered social landlord and the person to be compensated[8]. The notice must specify: (a) the grounds on which the compensation is awarded; (b) the amount of the compensation; (c) the person to be compensated; (d) a period within which it must be paid; and (e) any interest or additional compensation which is payable[9] in the event of late payment[10]. The notice may require the registered social landlord to publish information about the compensation award in a specified manner[11]. The notice must explain the effect of certain provisions[12] as to enforcement and appeal[13].

When the Welsh Ministers are considering whether to award compensation, or the amount of compensation to award, they must take account of any information available to them about the financial situation of the registered social landlord[14]. The Welsh Ministers must also consider the likely impact of the compensation on the registered social landlord's ability to provide services[15]. In particular, the Welsh Minsters must aim to avoid: (i) jeopardising the financial viability of the registered social landlord; (ii) preventing the registered social landlord from honouring financial commitments; or (iii) preventing the registered social landlord from taking action to remedy the matters on the grounds of which the compensation might be awarded[16].

Before giving a compensation notice to a registered social landlord the Welsh Ministers must give the landlord a notice (a 'pre-compensation warning'): (A) specifying grounds on which the Welsh Ministers think compensation could be awarded; (B) warning the landlord that the Welsh Ministers are considering awarding compensation to a specified person; (C) including any indication that the Welsh Ministers are able to give of the likely amount of any compensation; and (D) explaining the effect of certain provisions[17] relating to representations, enforcement and appeal[18].

Before giving a pre-compensation warning the Welsh Ministers must also consult the Public Services Ombudsman for Wales[19]. The Welsh Ministers must send a copy of a pre-compensation warning to any person they think appropriate (having regard, in particular, to any person who provided information as a result of which the pre-compensation warning is given)[20]. A pre-compensation warning must refer to the provision allowing voluntary undertakings[21], and indicate whether or to what extent the Welsh Ministers would accept a voluntary undertaking instead of, or in mitigation of, awarding compensation[22]. A pre-compensation warning may be combined with notice under one or more of certain other provisions[23] of the Housing Act 1996[24].

A pre-compensation warning must specify a period during which the registered social landlord may make representations[25] to the Welsh Ministers[26]. This period must be a period of at least 28 days, and begin with the date on which the registered social landlord receives the pre-compensation warning[27]. Representations may address whether compensation should be awarded and the amount of any compensation that may be awarded[28]. After the end of the period specified, the Welsh Ministers must consider any representations made, and decide whether to award compensation[29].

Compensation is to be treated as a debt owed to the person to whom it is awarded[30]. The Welsh Ministers may award interest on compensation not paid during the period specified under head (d) above, and may award additional compensation where compensation is not paid during that period[31]. Interest and additional compensation are to be treated as compensation[32].

A registered social landlord who is given a compensation notice may appeal to the High Court against the award of compensation, its amount, or both[33].

1   Housing Act 1996 s 50A (added, in relation to Wales, by the Housing (Wales) Measure 2011 s 50). As to the register of social landlords see PARA 167.
2   As to the Welsh Ministers see PARAS 7, 141.

3 Housing Act 1996 s 50O(1) (ss 50O–50V added, in relation to Wales, by the Housing (Wales) Measure 2011 ss 64–71).
4 Housing Act 1996 s 50O(2) (as added: see note 3). The text refers to a standard under s 33A: see PARA 160.
5 Ie under the Housing Act 1996 s 6A: see PARA 185.
6 Housing Act 1996 s 50O(3) (as added: see note 3).
7 Housing Act 1996 s 50P (as added: see note 3).
8 Housing Act 1996 s 50Q(1) (as added: see note 3). As to the meaning of 'notice' see PARA 169 note 6.
9 Ie by virtue of the Housing Act 1996 s 50U(2): see the text to note 31.
10 Housing Act 1996 s 50Q(2) (as added: see note 3).
11 Housing Act 1996 s 50Q(3) (as added: see note 3).
12 Ie the Housing Act 1996 ss 50U(1), (3), 50V: see the text to notes 30, 32, 33.
13 Housing Act 1996 s 50Q(4) (as added: see note 3).
14 Housing Act 1996 s 50R(1), (2) (as added: see note 3).
15 Housing Act 1996 s 50R(3) (as added: see note 3).
16 Housing Act 1996 s 50R(4) (as added: see note 3).
17 Ie the Housing Act 1996 ss 50T, 50U(1), (3), 50V: see the text to notes 26–30, 32, 33.
18 Housing Act 1996 s 50S(1) (as added: see note 3).
19 Housing Act 1996 s 50S(2) (as added: see note 3). As to the Public Services Ombudsman for Wales see CONSTITUTIONAL AND ADMINISTRATIVE LAW vol 20 (2014) PARA 640.
20 Housing Act 1996 s 50S(3) (as added: see note 3).
21 Ie the Housing Act 1996 s 6A: see PARA 185.
22 Housing Act 1996 s 50S(4) (as added: see note 3).
23 Ie the Housing Act 1996 s 50K (see PARA 187), Sch 1 para 15C (see PARA 189), or Sch 1 paras 15E, 15G (see PARAS 190–191).
24 Housing Act 1996 s 50S(5) (as added: see note 3).
25 As to the meaning of 'representations' see PARA 187 note 28.
26 Housing Act 1996 s 50T(1) (as added: see note 3).
27 Housing Act 1996 s 50T(2) (as added: see note 3).
28 Housing Act 1996 s 50T(3) (as added: see note 3).
29 Housing Act 1996 s 50T(4) (as added: see note 3).
30 Housing Act 1996 s 50U(1) (as added: see note 3).
31 Housing Act 1996 s 50U(2) (as added: see note 3).
32 Housing Act 1996 s 50U(3) (as added: see note 3).
33 Housing Act 1996 s 50V (as added: see note 3).

E. MANAGEMENT

189. Management tender. The following provisions apply if the Welsh Ministers[1] are satisfied that a registered social landlord[2] has failed to meet a performance standard[3], or there has been misconduct[4] or mismanagement in the affairs of the registered social landlord[5]. They do not apply where the misconduct or mismanagement relates only to the registered social landlord's provision of housing in England[6].

The Welsh Ministers may require the registered social landlord to implement a process specified by them for the purpose of inviting persons to apply to undertake management functions of the registered social landlord, and selecting from the applications and making an appointment[7]. A requirement may relate to the registered social landlord's affairs generally, or to specified affairs[8]. Such a requirement must include: (1) provision about the constitution of a selection panel (which must include provision for ensuring representation of tenants' interests); (2) provision for ensuring best procurement practice (and consistent with any applicable procurement law); and (3) provision about the terms and conditions on which the manager is to be appointed (including provision about setting, monitoring and enforcing performance standards, and resources)[9].

Before acting under the provision allowing them to require a registered social landlord to implement a specified process[10], the Welsh Ministers must give the registered social landlord a notice: (a) specifying grounds on which action might be taken under that provision; (b) warning the landlord that the Welsh Ministers are considering action under that provision; and (c) explaining the effect of the provisions[11] relating to notice and representations[12]. The notice must specify a period during which the registered social landlord may make representations[13] to the Welsh Ministers[14]. The period must be at least 28 days, beginning with the date on which the registered social landlord receives the notice[15]. The Welsh Ministers must send a copy of such a notice to any person they think appropriate (having regard, in particular, to any person who provided information as a result of which the notice is given)[16]. A notice must refer to the provision allowing voluntary undertakings to be given[17], and indicate whether or to what extent the Welsh Ministers would accept a voluntary undertaking instead of, or in mitigation of, action[18] to implement a specified process[19]. This notice may be combined with notice under one or more of specified[20] other provisions[21]. In imposing a requirement the Welsh Ministers must have regard to views of relevant tenants[22], the registered social landlord, and if they think it appropriate, any relevant local housing authority[23]. A registered social landlord may appeal to the High Court against a requirement to implement a specified process[24].

A registered social landlord may give the Welsh Ministers an undertaking in respect of any matter concerning housing[25], and the Welsh Ministers must have regard to any undertaking offered or given in exercising their powers under these provisions[26], and may base a decision about whether to exercise their powers under these provisions wholly or partly on the extent to which the undertaking has been honoured[27].

1   As to the Welsh Ministers see PARAS 7, 141.
2   As to the register of social landlords see PARA 167.
3   Ie under the Housing Act 1996 s 33A: see PARA 160.
4   As to the meaning of 'misconduct' see PARA 186 note 6.
5   Housing Act 1996 s 7, Sch 1 para 15B(1) (Sch 1 paras 15B, 15C added, in relation to Wales, by the Housing (Wales) Measure 2011 ss 72, 73).
6   Housing Act 1996 Sch 1 para 15B(2) (as added: see note 5).
7   Housing Act 1996 Sch 1 para 15B(3) (as added: see note 5).
8   Housing Act 1996 Sch 1 para 15B(4) (as added: see note 5).
9   Housing Act 1996 Sch 1 para 15B(5) (as added: see note 5).
10 Ie the Housing Act 1996 Sch 1 para 15B(3): see the text to note 7.
11 Ie the Housing Act 1996 Sch 1 para 15C.
12 Housing Act 1996 Sch 1 para 15C(1) (as added: see note 5).
13 As to the meaning of 'representations' see PARA 187 note 28.
14 Housing Act 1996 Sch 1 para 15C(2) (as added: see note 5).
15 Housing Act 1996 Sch 1 para 15C(3) (as added: see note 5).
16 Housing Act 1996 Sch 1 para 15C(4) (as added: see note 5).
17 Ie the Housing Act 1996 s 6A: see the text and notes 24–26.
18 Ie under the Housing Act 1996 Sch 1 para 15B(3).
19 Housing Act 1996 Sch 1 para 15C(5) (as added: see note 5).
20 Ie the Housing Act 1996 s 50K (see PARA 187), s 50S (see PARA 188), Sch 1 paras 15E, 15G (see PARAS 190–191).
21 Housing Act 1996 Sch 1 para 15C(6) (as added: see note 5).
22 As to the meaning of 'tenant' see PARA 168 note 16.
23 Housing Act 1996 Sch 1 para 15C(7) (as added: see note 5). As to the meaning of 'local housing authority' for these purposes see PARA 11 (definition applied by s 230).
24 Housing Act 1996 Sch 1 para 15C(8) (as added: see note 5).
25 Housing Act 1996 s 6A(1) (s 6A added, in relation to Wales, by the Housing (Wales) Measure 2011 s 41). The Welsh Ministers may prescribe a procedure to be followed in giving an undertaking: Housing Act 1996 s 6A(2) (as so added).
26 Ie their powers under the Housing Act 1996 Sch 1 paras 15B–15H (see the text to notes 1–24; and PARAS 190–192): s 6A(5) (as added: see note 25).
27 Housing Act 1996 s 6A(3), (4) (as added: see note 25). Section 6A does not apply in relation to a registered social landlord's provision of housing in England: s 6A(6) (as so added).

190. Management transfer. The following provisions apply if, as a result of an inquiry[1] or an audit[2], the Welsh Ministers[3] are satisfied that there has been misconduct[4] or mismanagement in the affairs of a registered social landlord[5], or that a transfer of certain of a registered social landlord's management functions would be likely to improve the management of some or all of its affairs[6]. These provisions do not, however, apply where: (1) the misconduct or mismanagement relates only to the registered social landlord's provision of housing in England; or (2) the transfer would be likely to improve the registered social landlord's management of its affairs only in relation to the provision of housing in England[7].

The Welsh Ministers may require the registered social landlord to transfer management functions to a specified person[8]. A requirement may relate to the registered social landlord's affairs generally, or to specified affairs[9]. Such a transfer must be on terms and conditions (including those as to remuneration) specified in, or determined in accordance with, the Welsh Ministers' requirement[10]. A transferee manager will have any power specified in the requirement, and any other power in relation to the registered social landlord's affairs required by the manager for the purposes specified in the requirement (including the power to enter into agreements and take other action on behalf of the registered social landlord)[11].

Before acting under the provision allowing them to require the transfer of management functions[12] the Welsh Ministers must give the registered social landlord a notice: (a) specifying grounds on which action might be taken under that provision; (b) warning the landlord that the Welsh Ministers are considering action under that provision; and (c) explaining the effect of the following provisions[13]. The notice must specify a period during which the registered social landlord may make representations[14] to the Welsh Ministers[15]. The period must be a period of at least 28 days, and begin with the date on which the registered social landlord receives the notice[16]. The Welsh Ministers must send a copy of such a notice to any person they think appropriate (having regard, in particular, to any person who provided information as a result of which the notice is given)[17]. A notice must refer to the provision allowing voluntary undertakings to be given[18], and indicate whether or to what extent the social landlord would accept a voluntary undertaking instead of, or in mitigation of, action[19] under the power to require the transfer of management functions to a specified person[20]. Notice under these provisions may be combined with notice under one or more of certain other specified provisions[21] of the Housing Act 1996[22].

In imposing a requirement the Welsh Ministers must have regard to views of relevant tenants[23], the registered social landlord, and if they think it appropriate, any relevant local housing authority[24].

A registered social landlord may appeal to the High Court against a requirement to transfer management functions[25].

1 Ie under the Housing Act 1996 Sch 1 para 20: see PARA 200.
2 Ie under the Housing Act 1996 Sch 1 para 22: see PARA 200.
3 As to the Welsh Ministers see PARAS 7, 141.
4 As to the meaning of 'misconduct' see PARA 186 note 6.
5 As to the register of social landlords see PARA 167.
6 Housing Act 1996 s 7, Sch 1 para 15D(1) (Sch 1 paras 15D, 15E added, in relation to Wales, by the Housing (Wales) Measure 2011 ss 74, 75).
7 Housing Act 1996 Sch 1 para 15D(2) (as added: see note 6).
8 Housing Act 1996 Sch 1 para 15D(3) (as added: see note 6).
9 Housing Act 1996 Sch 1 para 15D(4) (as added: see note 6).
10 Housing Act 1996 Sch 1 para 15D(5) (as added: see note 6).

11 Housing Act 1996 Sch 1 para 15D(6) (as added: see note 6).
12 Ie the Housing Act 1996 Sch 1 para 15D(3).
13 Housing Act 1996 Sch 1 para 15E(1) (as added: see note 6).
14 As to the meaning of 'representations' see PARA 187 note 28.
15 Housing Act 1996 Sch 1 para 15E(2) (as added: see note 6).
16 Housing Act 1996 Sch 1 para 15E(3) (as added: see note 6).
17 Housing Act 1996 Sch 1 para 15E(4) (as added: see note 6).
18 Ie the Housing Act 1996 s 6A: see PARA 189.
19 Ie under the Housing Act 1996 Sch 1 para 15D(3).
20 Housing Act 1996 Sch 1 para 15E(5) (as added: see note 6).
21 Ie the Housing Act 1996 s 50K (see PARA 187), s 50S (see PARA 188), Sch 1 para 15C (see
    PARA 189) or Sch 1 para 15G (see PARA 191).
22 Housing Act 1996 Sch 1 para 15E(6) (as added: see note 6).
23 As to the meaning of 'tenant' see PARA 168 note 16.
24 Housing Act 1996 Sch 1 para 15E(7) (as added: see note 6). As to the meaning of 'local housing
    authority' for these purposes see PARA 11 (definition applied by s 230).
25 Housing Act 1996 Sch 1 para 15E(8) (as added: see note 6).

191. Appointment of manager of registered social landlord. The following provisions apply if the Welsh Ministers[1] are satisfied that a registered social landlord[2] has failed to meet a standard of performance[3], or there has been misconduct[4] or mismanagement in the affairs of the registered social landlord[5]. They do not, however, apply where the misconduct or mismanagement relates only to the registered social landlord's provision of housing in England[6].

The Welsh Ministers may appoint an individual as a manager of the registered social landlord, or require the registered social landlord to appoint an individual as a manager[7]. An appointment or requirement may relate to the management of the registered social landlord's affairs generally, or specified affairs[8]. Appointment is to be on terms and conditions (including as to remuneration) specified in, or determined in accordance with, the appointment or requirement[9]. A manager is to have any power specified in the appointment or requirement, and any other power in relation to the registered social landlord's affairs required by the manager for the purposes specified in the appointment or requirement (including the power to enter into agreements and take other action on behalf of the registered social landlord)[10].

Before acting under the provision giving them power to appoint or require the appointment of a manager[11] the Welsh Ministers must give the registered social landlord a notice: (1) specifying grounds on which action might be taken under that provision; (2) warning the landlord that the Welsh Ministers are considering action under that provision; and (3) explaining the effect of the following provisions[12]. The notice must specify a period during which the registered social landlord may make representations[13] to the Welsh Ministers[14]. The period must be a period of at least 28 days, and begin with the date on which the registered social landlord receives the notice[15]. The Welsh Ministers must send a copy of such a notice to any person they think appropriate (having regard, in particular, to any person who provided information as a result of which the notice is given)[16]. A notice must refer to the provision allowing voluntary undertakings to be given[17], and indicate whether or to what extent the Welsh Ministers would accept a voluntary undertaking instead of, or in mitigation of, action under the power[18] relating to the appointment of a manager[19]. Notice under these provisions may be combined with notice under one or more of certain other provisions[20] of the Housing Act 1996[21]. The Welsh Ministers may require a manager to report to them on the affairs specified in the appointment of, or requirement to appoint, a manager[22].

A registered social landlord may appeal to the High Court against an appointment of, or a requirement to appoint, a manager[23].

1 As to the Welsh Ministers see PARAS 7, 141.
2 As to the register of social landlords see PARA 167.
3 Ie under the Housing Act 1996 s 33A: see PARA 160.
4 As to the meaning of 'misconduct' see PARA 186 note 6.
5 Housing Act 1996 s 7, Sch 1 para 15F(1) (Sch 1 paras 15F, 15G added, in relation to Wales, by the Housing (Wales) Measure 2011 ss 76, 77).
6 Housing Act 1996 Sch 1 para 15F(2) (as added: see note 5).
7 Housing Act 1996 Sch 1 para 15F(3) (as added: see note 5).
8 Housing Act 1996 Sch 1 para 15F(4) (as added: see note 5).
9 Housing Act 1996 Sch 1 para 15F(5) (as added: see note 5).
10 Housing Act 1996 Sch 1 para 15F(6) (as added: see note 5).
11 Ie the Housing Act 1996 Sch 1 para 15F(3).
12 Housing Act 1996 Sch 1 para 15G(1) (as added: see note 5). The notice must explain the effect of Sch 1 para 15G.
13 As to the meaning of 'representations' see PARA 187 note 28.
14 Housing Act 1996 Sch 1 para 15G(2) (as added: see note 5).
15 Housing Act 1996 Sch 1 para 15G(3) (as added: see note 5).
16 Housing Act 1996 Sch 1 para 15G(4) (as added: see note 5).
17 Ie the Housing Act 1996 s 6A: see PARA 189.
18 Ie under the Housing Act 1996 Sch 1 para 15F(3).
19 Housing Act 1996 Sch 1 para 15G(5) (as added: see note 5).
20 Ie the Housing Act 1996 s 50K (see PARA 187), s 50S (see PARA 188), Sch 1 para 15C (see PARA 189), or Sch 1 para 15E (see PARA 190).
21 Housing Act 1996 Sch 1 para 15G(6) (as added: see note 5).
22 Housing Act 1996 Sch 1 para 15G(7) (as added: see note 5).
23 Housing Act 1996 Sch 1 para 15G(8) (as added: see note 5).

192. Amalgamation. The following provisions apply if, as a result of an inquiry[1] or an audit[2], the Welsh Ministers[3] are satisfied that: (1) there has been misconduct[4] or mismanagement in the affairs of a registered social landlord[5] which is a registered society[6]; or (2) the management of the affairs of a registered social landlord which is a registered society would be improved if the landlord were amalgamated with another registered society[7]. They do not, however, apply where: (a) the misconduct or mismanagement relates only to the registered social landlord's provision of housing in England; or (b) the amalgamation would improve the management of the registered social landlord's affairs only in relation to the provision of housing in England by the landlord[8].

The Welsh Ministers may make and execute on behalf of the society an instrument providing for the amalgamation of the society with another registered society[9]. An instrument providing for the amalgamation of a society ('S1') with another has the same effect as a special resolution for amalgamation[10] by S1 under the Co-operative and Community Benefit Societies Act 2014[11]. A copy of an instrument must be sent to and registered by the Financial Conduct Authority[12]. An instrument does not take effect until the copy is registered[13]. The copy must be sent for registration during the period of 14 days beginning with the date of execution, but a copy registered after that period is valid[14]. Any body created by virtue of an amalgamation must be registered as a social landlord by the Welsh Ministers, and pending registration is to be treated as registered[15].

1 Ie under the Housing Act 1996 Sch 1 para 20: see PARA 200.
2 Ie under the Housing Act 1996 Sch 1 para 22: see PARA 200.
3 As to the Welsh Ministers see PARAS 7, 141.
4 As to the meaning of 'misconduct' see PARA 186 note 6.
5 As to the register of social landlords see PARA 167.
6 As to the meaning of 'registered society' see PARA 168 note 1.

7   Housing Act 1996 s 7, Sch 1 para 15H(1) (Sch 1 para 15H added, in relation to Wales, by the Housing (Wales) Measure 2011 s 78; the Housing Act 1996 Sch 1 para 15H(1) amended by the Co-operative and Community Benefit Societies Act 2014 s 151(1), Sch 4 paras 55, 56, 65(1), (10)(a)).
8   Housing Act 1996 Sch 1 para 15H(2) (as added: see note 7).
9   Housing Act 1996 Sch 1 para 15H(3) (as added (see note 7); amended by the Co-operative and Community Benefit Societies Act 2014 Sch 4 paras 55, 65(1), (10)(b)).
10 Ie under the Co-operative and Community Benefit Societies Act 2014 s 109 (amalgamation of societies by special resolution) (see FINANCIAL INSTITUTIONS vol 48 (2015) PARA 1053).
11 Housing Act 1996 Sch 1 para 15H(4) (as added (see note 7); amended by the Co-operative and Community Benefit Societies Act 2014 Sch 4 paras 55, 65(1), (10)(c)).
12 Housing Act 1996 Sch 1 para 15H(5) (as added (see note 7); amended by SI 2013/496). As to the Financial Conduct Authority see FINANCIAL SERVICES REGULATION vol 50 (2016) PARAS 5, 6 et seq.
13 Housing Act 1996 Sch 1 para 15H(6) (as added: see note 7).
14 Housing Act 1996 Sch 1 para 15H(7) (as added: see note 7).
15 Housing Act 1996 Sch 1 para 15H(8) (as added: see note 7). As to registration as a social landlord see PARA 169.

F.   ACCOUNTS, AUDIT AND REPORTS

193. Introduction. Under the Housing Act 1996, the Welsh Ministers[1] are empowered to establish accounting requirements in order to ensure that all registered social landlords[2] prepare their accounts in a proper form which gives a true and fair view of the state of affairs of the landlord so far as its housing activities[3] and a disposition of its funds and assets are concerned[4]. A registered social landlord is required to provide the Welsh Ministers with a copy of the accounts with an auditor's report certifying that there has been compliance with the statutory requirements[5]. Every registered social landlord also has an obligation to prepare and provide accounts, whether it is a registered society[6], a charity or a company[7].

1   As to the Welsh Ministers see PARAS 7, 141.
2   As to registration as a social landlord see PARA 169.
3   As to the meaning of 'housing activities' see PARA 168 note 25.
4   See PARA 194.
5   As to the auditor's report see PARA 194.
6   As to the meaning of 'registered society' see PARA 168 note 1.
7   See further PARAS 194–198.

194. General requirements as to accounts and audit. The Welsh Ministers[1] may from time to time determine accounting requirements for registered social landlords[2] with a view to ensuring that the accounts of every registered social landlord are prepared in a proper form, and give a true and fair view of:

(1)   the state of affairs of the landlord, so far as its housing activities[3] are concerned; and

(2)   the disposition of funds and assets which are, or at any time have been, in its hands in connection with those activities[4].

The Welsh Ministers may, by such a determination, lay down a method by which a registered charity[5] is to distinguish in its accounts between its housing activities and its other activities[6].

The accounts of every registered social landlord must comply with the requirements laid down under these provisions[7]. Every registered social landlord must furnish to the Welsh Ministers, within six months of the end of the period to which they relate:

(a)   a copy of its accounts; and

(b)   (subject to the exceptions below[8]) a copy of the auditor's report in respect of them[9].

The auditor's report must state, in addition to any other matters which it is required to state, whether in the auditor's opinion the accounts comply with the requirements laid down under these provisions[10].

The requirements as to an auditor's report[11] do not apply where, by virtue of any enactment, any accounts of a registered social landlord are not required to be audited and, instead, a report is required to be prepared in respect of them by a person appointed for the purpose ('the reporting accountant')[12]. In such a case:

(i)   the registered social landlord must furnish to the Welsh Ministers a copy of the reporting accountant's report in respect of the accounts within six months of the end of the period to which they relate; and

(ii)   that report must state, in addition to any other matters which it is required to state, whether in the reporting accountant's opinion the accounts comply with the requirements laid down under these provisions[13].

A registered social landlord which is a registered charity is subject, in respect of its housing activities (and separately from its other activities, if any), to specific accounting and audit or reporting requirements[14], but without affecting any obligation of the charity under the provisions of the Charities Act 2011[15] relating to charity accounts[16].

Every responsible person, that is to say, every person who:

(A)   is directly concerned with the conduct and management of the affairs of a registered social landlord; and

(B)   is in that capacity responsible for the preparation and audit of accounts, must ensure that the general requirements as to accounts and audit[17] and, where applicable, the accounting and audit requirements for charities[18], are complied with by the registered social landlord[19]. If those provisions and other related provisions are not complied with[20], every responsible person, and the registered social landlord itself, commits a summary offence and is liable to a penalty[21]. Proceedings for such an offence may be brought only by or with the consent of the Welsh Ministers or the Director of Public Prosecutions[22]. In proceedings for such an offence it is a defence for a responsible person to prove that he did everything that could reasonably have been expected of him by way of discharging the relevant duty and for a registered social landlord to prove that every responsible person did everything that could reasonably have been expected of him by way of discharging the relevant duty in relation to the registered social landlord[23].

A person who is, or has been, an auditor of a registered social landlord does not contravene any duty to which he is subject merely because he gives to the Welsh Ministers information on a matter of which he became aware in his capacity as auditor of the registered social landlord, or his opinion on such a matter, if he is acting in good faith and he reasonably believes that the information or opinion is relevant to any functions of the Welsh Ministers[24]. This applies whether or not the person is responding to a request from the Welsh Ministers[25], and it applies to a person who is, or has been, a reporting accountant[26] as it applies to a person who is, or has been, an auditor[27].

1   As to the Welsh Ministers see PARAS 7, 141.
2   As to the register of social landlords see PARA 167.
3   As to the meaning of 'housing activities' see PARA 168 note 25.
4   Housing Act 1996 s 7, Sch 1 para 16(1) (Sch 1 para 16(1) amended by the Housing and Regeneration Act 2008 s 61(1), (7)).
5   As to the meaning of 'registered charity' see PARA 168 note 3.
6   Housing Act 1996 Sch 1 para 16(2) (amended by the Housing and Regeneration Act 2008 s 61(1), (7)).

7   Housing Act 1996 Sch 1 para 16(3). As to the penalty for non-compliance see the text and notes 20–21.
8   Ie subject to the Housing Act 1996 Sch 1 para 16(7): see the text and note 12.
9   Housing Act 1996 Sch 1 para 16(5) (substituted by the Housing Act 2004 s 218, Sch 11 paras 7, 17(1), (3); and amended by the Housing and Regeneration Act 2008 s 61(1), (7)).
10 Housing Act 1996 Sch 1 para 16(6) (Sch 1 para 16(6)–(8) added by the Housing Act 2004 Sch 11 paras 7, 17(1), (3)).
11 Ie the provisions of the Housing Act 1996 Sch 1 para 16(5)(b) (see head (b) in the text) and Sch 1 para 16(6) (see the text and note 10).
12 Housing Act 1996 Sch 1 para 16(7) (as added: see note 10). As to provisions relating to reports see PARAS 196–198.
13 Housing Act 1996 Sch 1 para 16(8) (as added (see note 10); amended by the Housing and Regeneration Act 2008 s 61(1), (7)).
14 See PARA 195.
15 Ie under the Charities Act 2011 Pt 8 (ss 130–176) (formerly the Charities Act 1993 ss 41–45): see CHARITIES vol 8 (2015) PARA 341 et seq.
16 Housing Act 1996 Sch 1 para 18(1) (amended by the Housing Act 2004 ss 218, 266, Sch 11 paras 7, 20(1), (3), Sch 16).
17 Ie the Housing Act 1996 Sch 1 para 16: see the text and notes 1–13.
18 Ie the Housing Act 1996 Sch 1 para 18: see PARA 195.
19 Housing Act 1996 Sch 1 para 19(1).
20 Ie if: (1) the Housing Act 1996 Sch 1 para 16(5) (furnishing of accounts and auditor's report: see the text and note 9) is not complied with; (2) the accounts furnished to the Welsh Ministers under that provision do not comply with the accounting requirements laid down under Sch 1 para 16(1) (see the text and note 4); (3) Sch 1 para 18 (accounting and audit or reporting requirements for charities: see note 14), where applicable, is not complied with; or (4) any notice under s 26 (information relating to disposal proceeds fund: see PARA 216) is not complied with: see Sch 1 para 19(2)(a)–(e) (amended by the Housing Act 2004 Sch 11 para 22(1), (2)(a), (b), Sch 16; the Housing Act 1996 Sch 1 para 19(2)(b) amended by the Housing and Regeneration Act 2008 s 61(1), (7)).
21 Housing Act 1996 Sch 1 para 19(2). The penalty on conviction is a fine not exceeding level 5 on the standard scale: see Sch 1 para 19(2) (amended by the Housing Act 2004 Sch 11 para 22(2)(c)). As to the powers of magistrates' courts to issue fines on summary conviction see SENTENCING vol 92 (2015) PARA 176.
22 See the Housing Act 1996 Sch 1 para 19(4) (amended by the Housing and Regeneration Act 2008 s 61(1), (7)). As to the Director of Public Prosecutions see CRIMINAL PROCEDURE vol 27 (2015) PARAS 25, 30 et seq. Where any of the provisions of the Housing Act 1996 Sch 1 para 19(2)(a)–(e) (see note 20) applies in respect of any default on the part of a registered social landlord, the High Court may, on the application of the Welsh Ministers, make such order as the court thinks fit for requiring the default to be made good; any such order may provide that all the costs or expenses of and incidental to the application are to be borne by the registered social landlord or by any of its officers who are responsible for the default: Sch 1 para 19(5) (added by the Housing Act 2004 Sch 11 para 22(4); and amended by the Housing and Regeneration Act 2008 s 61(1), (7)).
23 Housing Act 1996 Sch 1 para 19(3).
24 Housing Act 1996 Sch 1 para 19A(1) (Sch 1 para 19A added by the Housing Act 2004 Sch 11 para 23; the Housing Act 1996 Sch 1 para 19A(1) amended by the Housing and Regeneration Act 2008 s 61(1), (7)).
25 Housing Act 1996 Sch 1 para 19A(2) (as added (see note 24); amended by the Housing and Regeneration Act 2008 s 61(1), (7)).
26 A 'reporting accountant' means a person appointed as mentioned in the Housing Act 1996 Sch 1 para 16(7)(b) (see the text to note 12): Sch 1 para 19A(4) (as added: see note 24).
27 Housing Act 1996 Sch 1 para 19A(3) (as added: see note 24).

195. Accounting and audit or reporting requirements for registered charity. A registered social landlord[1] which is a registered charity is subject, in respect of its housing activities[2] (and separately from its other activities, if any), to the following provisions as to accounting and audit or reporting[3]:

(1)   the charity must in respect of its housing activities cause to be kept properly books of account showing its transactions and its assets and liabilities, and establish and maintain a satisfactory system of control of its books of account, its cash holdings and all its receipts and

remittances; and the books of account must be such as to enable a true and fair view to be given of the state of affairs of the charity in respect of its housing activities, and to explain its transactions in the course of those activities[4];

(2)   the charity must for each period of account[5] prepare a revenue account giving a true and fair view of the charity's income and expenditure in the period, so far as arising in connection with its housing activities, and a balance sheet giving a true and fair view as at the end of the period of the state of the charity's affairs; and the revenue account and balance sheet must be signed by at least two directors or trustees of the charity[6];

(3)   the charity must appoint a qualified auditor[7] ('the auditor') to audit the accounts prepared in accordance with head (2) in respect of each period of account in which:

    (a)   the charity's gross income[8] arising in connection with its housing activities exceeds the sum specified[9] for the time being in the Charities Act 2011; or

    (b)   the charity's gross income arising in that connection exceeds the accounts threshold[10] and at the end of that period the aggregate value of its assets (before deduction of liabilities) in respect of its housing activities exceeds the sum for the time being specified[11] in the Charities Act 2011[12];

(4)   where head (3) does not apply in respect of a period of account, the charity must appoint a qualified auditor ('the reporting accountant') to make a report relating to the charity's accounts[13] in respect of the period of account[14];

(5)   the auditor must make a report to the charity on the accounts audited by him, stating whether in his opinion the revenue account gives a true and fair view of the state of income and expenditure of the charity in respect of its housing activities and of any other matters to which it relates, and the balance sheet gives a true and fair view of the state of affairs of the charity as at the end of the period of account[15];

(6)   the auditor in preparing his report must carry out such investigations as will enable him to form an opinion as to the following matters: (a) whether the association has kept, in respect of its housing activities, proper books of account in accordance with these requirements; (b) whether the charity has maintained a satisfactory system of control over its transactions in accordance with these requirements; and (c) whether the accounts are in agreement with the charity's books; and if he is of opinion that the charity has failed in any respect to comply with these requirements, or if the accounts are not in agreement with the books, he must state that fact in his report[16];

(7)   the auditor has a right of access at all times to the books, deeds and accounts of the charity, so far as relating to its housing activities, and to all other documents relating to those activities, and is entitled to require from officers of the charity such information and explanations as he thinks necessary for the performance of his duties; and if he fails to obtain all the information and explanations which, to the best of his knowledge and belief, are necessary for the purposes of his audit, he must state that fact in his report[17].

1   As to the register of social landlords see PARA 167.
2   As to the meaning of 'housing activities' see PARA 168 note 25.

3   Housing Act 1996 Sch 1 para 18(1) (amended by the Housing Act 2004 ss 218, 266, Sch 11 paras 7, 20(1), (3), Sch 16). As to the general accounting requirements for registered social landlords see PARA 194.

4   Housing Act 1996 Sch 1 para 18(2).

5   A period of account for these purposes is 12 months or such other period not less than six months or more than 18 months as the charity may, with the consent of the Welsh Ministers, determine: Housing Act 1996 Sch 1 para 18(8) (amended, in relation to Wales, by the Housing (Wales) Measure 2011 s 88, Schedule paras 1, 17).

6   Housing Act 1996 Sch 1 para 18(3).

7   'Qualified auditor' means a person who is eligible for appointment as a statutory auditor under the Companies Act 2006 Pt 42 (ss 1209–1264) (see COMPANIES vol 15 (2016) PARA 1086) and who, if the appointment were an appointment as a statutory auditor, would not be prohibited from acting by virtue of s 1214 (independence requirement: see COMPANIES vol 15 (2016) PARA 1088): Housing Act 1996 Sch 1 para 18(4B) (added by the Housing Act 2004 Sch 11 para 20(4); substituted by SI 2008/948).

8   For these purposes 'gross income' has the same meaning as in the Charities Act 2011 s 144 (see CHARITIES vol 8 (2015) PARA 356): Housing Act 1996 Sch 1 para 18(4) substituted by the Housing Act 2004 Sch 11 para 20(4); further substituted by the Charities Act 2011 s 354(1), Sch 7 para 72(1), (3)).

9   Ie specified in the Charities Act 2011 s 144(1)(a): see CHARITIES vol 8 (2015) PARA 356.

10   For these purposes 'accounts threshold' has the same meaning as in the Charities Act 2011 s 144 (see CHARITIES vol 8 (2015) PARA 356): Housing Act 1996 Sch 1 para 18(4) (as substituted: see note 8).

11   Ie specified in the Charities Act 2011 s 144(1)(b): see CHARITIES vol 8 (2015) PARA 356.

12   Housing Act 1996 Sch 1 para 18(4) (as substituted: see note 8).

13   Ie such a report as is mentioned in the Housing Act 1996 Sch 1 para 18A(1): see PARA 198.

14   Housing Act 1996 Sch 1 para 18(4A) (added by the Housing Act 2004 Sch 11 para 20(4)).

15   Housing Act 1996 Sch 1 para 18(5).

16   Housing Act 1996 Sch 1 para 18(6).

17   Housing Act 1996 Sch 1 para 18(7).

196. Accountant's report in relation to companies exempt from audit requirements. The following provisions apply in relation to a registered social landlord[1] which is a company[2], which is exempt from the audit requirements of the Companies Act 2006[3] and is not a charity[4]. The directors of the company must cause a report to be prepared[5] and made to the company's members in respect of the company's individual accounts[6] for any year in which the company takes advantage of its exemption from audit[7].

The report required[8] must be prepared by a person ('the reporting accountant') who is eligible[9] for such appointment[10]. The report must state whether in the opinion of the reporting accountant making it: (1) the accounts of the company for the financial year[11] in question are in agreement with the accounting records kept by the company under the Companies Act 2006[12]; and (2) having regard only to, and on the basis of, the information contained in those accounting records, those accounts have been drawn up in a manner consistent with the provisions of Part 15 of that Act[13], so far as applicable to the company[14]. The report must also state that in the opinion of the reporting accountant, having regard only to, and on the basis of, the information contained in the accounting records kept by the company under the Companies Act 2006, the company is entitled to exemption from audit[15] for the financial year in question[16].

The Welsh Ministers[17] may, in respect of any such financial year, give a direction to the company requiring it to appoint a qualified auditor[18] to audit its accounts and balance sheet for that year and to furnish to the Welsh Ministers a copy of the auditor's report by such date as is specified in the direction[19].

1   As to the register of social landlords see PARA 167.

2   In the Housing Act 1996 Sch 1 paras 16A–16D, 'company' means a company registered under the Companies Act 1985: Housing Act 1996 s 7, Sch 1 para 16E (Sch 1 paras 16B–16E added by SI 2008/948).

3 Ie by virtue of the Companies Act 2006 s 477 (small companies' exemption): see COMPANIES vol 15 (2016) PARA 986.
4 Housing Act 1996 Sch 1 para 16A(1) (Sch 1 para 16A added by the Housing Act 2004 s 218, Sch 11 paras 7, 18; and substituted by SI 2008/948).
5 Ie in accordance with the Housing Act 1996 Sch 1 para 16B: see the text and notes 8–16.
6 'Individual accounts' has the meaning given by the Companies Act 2006 s 394 (see COMPANIES vol 15 (2016) PARA 790): Housing Act 1996 Sch 1 para 16E (as added: see note 2).
7 Housing Act 1996 Sch 1 para 16A(2) (as added and substituted: see note 4).
8 Ie for the purposes of the Housing Act 1996 Sch 1 para 16A(2).
9 Ie under the Housing Act 1996 Sch 1 para 16C. The reporting accountant must be either: (1) a member of a body listed in Sch 1 para 16C(4) who, under the rules of the body, is entitled to engage in public practice and who is not ineligible for appointment as a reporting accountant; or (2) any person (whether or not a member of any such body) who is subject to the rules of any such body in seeking appointment or acting as a statutory auditor under the Companies Act 2006 Pt 42 (ss 1209–1264) and who, under those rules, is eligible for such appointment: Housing Act 1996 Sch 1 para 16C(1) (as added: see note 2). In heads (1), (2), references to the rules of a body listed in Sch 1 para 16C(4) are to the rules (whether or not laid down by the body itself) which the body has power to enforce and which are relevant for the purposes of the Companies Act 2006 Pt 42 (statutory auditors) or the Housing Act 1996 Sch 1 para 16C; this includes rules relating to the admission and expulsion of members of the body, so far as relevant for the purposes of the Companies Act 2006 Pt 42 or the Housing Act 1996 Sch 1 para 16C: Sch 1 para 16C(2) (as so added). An individual or a firm may be appointed as a reporting accountant, and the Companies Act 2006 s 1216 (effect of appointment of partnership: see COMPANIES vol 15 (2016) PARA 1089) applies to the appointment as reporting accountant of a partnership constituted under the law of England and Wales or Northern Ireland, or under the law of any other country or territory in which a partnership is not a legal person: Housing Act 1996 Sch 1 para 16C(3) (as so added). 'Firm' has the meaning given by the Companies Act 2006 s 1173(1) (see COMPANIES vol 14 (2016) PARA 1): Housing Act 1996 Sch 1 para 16E (as added: see note 2).
   The bodies referred to in Sch 1 para 16C(1), (2) are: (a) the Institute of Chartered Accountants in England and Wales; (b) the Institute of Chartered Accountants of Scotland; (c) the Institute of Chartered Accountants in Ireland; (d) the Association of Chartered Certified Accountants; (e) the Association of Authorised Public Accountants; (f) the Association of Accounting Technicians; (g) the Association of International Accountants; (h) the Chartered Institute of Management Accountants; and (i) the Institute of Chartered Secretaries and Administrators: Sch 1 para 16C(4) (as so added). The Secretary of State may by order amend Sch 1 para 16C(4) by adding or removing a body to or from the list in that sub-paragraph or by varying any entry for the time being included in that list: Sch 1 para 16C(5) (as so added). An order under Sch 1 para 16C(5) must be made by statutory instrument which is to be subject to annulment in pursuance of a resolution of either House of Parliament: Sch 1 para 16C(6) (as so added). A person may not be appointed by a company as reporting accountant if he would be prohibited from acting as auditor of that company by virtue of the Companies Act 2006 s 1214 (independence requirement: see COMPANIES vol 15 (2016) PARA 1088): Housing Act 1996 Sch 1 para 16C(7) (as so added).
10 Housing Act 1996 Sch 1 para 16B(1) (as added: see note 2). The report must state the name of the reporting accountant and be signed and dated: Sch 1 para 16B(4) (as so added). The report must be signed: (1) where the reporting accountant is an individual, by that individual; (2) where the reporting accountant is a firm, for and on behalf of the firm by an individual authorised to do so: Sch 1 para 16B(5) (as so added).
11 'Financial year' has the meaning given by the Companies Act 2006 s 390 (see COMPANIES vol 15 (2016) PARA 785): Housing Act 1996 Sch 1 para 16E (as added: see note 2).
12 Ie under the Companies Act 2006 s 386: see COMPANIES vol 15 (2016) PARA 782.
13 Ie the Companies Act 2006 Pt 15 (ss 380–474): see COMPANIES vol 15 (2016) PARA 765 et seq.
14 Housing Act 1996 Sch 1 para 16B(2) (as added: see note 2). The provisions of the Companies Act 2006 listed below apply to the reporting accountant and a reporting accountant's report as they apply to an auditor of the company and an auditor's report on the company's accounts, subject to any necessary modifications: Sch 1 para 16D(1) (as so added). The provisions are: (1) the Companies Act 2006 ss 423–425 (duty to circulate copies of annual accounts); (2) ss 431, 432 (right of member or debenture holder to demand copies of accounts); (3) ss 434–436 (requirements in connection with publication of accounts); (4) ss 437, 438 (public companies: laying of accounts before general meeting); (5) ss 441–444 (duty to file accounts with registrar of companies); (6) s 454(4)(b) and regulations made under that provision (functions of auditor in relation to revised accounts); (7) ss 499–501 (auditor's right to information); (8) ss 505, 506 (name of auditor to be stated in published copies of report): Housing Act 1996 Sch 1 para 16D(2) (as so added). See COMPANIES vol 15 (2016) PARAS 935 et seq, 1030 et seq. In the Companies Act 2006 ss 505, 506

(see COMPANIES vol 15 (2016) PARA 1021) as they apply by virtue of the Housing Act 1996 Sch 1 para 16D in a case where the reporting accountant is a firm, any reference to the senior statutory auditor is to be read as a reference to the person who signed the report on behalf of the firm: Sch 1 para 16D(3) (as so added).

15 Ie under the Companies Act 2006 s 477 (small companies' exemption).

16 Housing Act 1996 Sch 1 para 16B(3) (as added: see note 2).

17 As to the Welsh Ministers see PARAS 7, 141.

18 'Qualified auditor', in relation to a company, means a person who: (1) is eligible for appointment as a statutory auditor of the company under the Companies Act 2006 Pt 42 (ss 1209–1264) (see COMPANIES vol 15 (2016) PARA 1086); and (2) is not prohibited from acting as statutory auditor of the company by virtue of s 1214 (independence requirement) (see COMPANIES vol 15 (2016) PARA 1088): Housing Act 1996 Sch 1 para 16E (as added: see note 2).

19 Housing Act 1996 Sch 1 para 16A(3) (as added and substituted (see note 4); and amended by the Housing and Regeneration Act 2008 s 61(1), (7)). A direction under the Housing Act 1996 Sch 1 para 16A(3) may not be given until after the end of the financial year to which it relates: Sch 1 para 16A(4) (as so added and substituted).

197. Accountant's report in relation to registered societies exempt from audit requirements.

The following provisions apply to registered social landlords[1] which are registered societies[2]. The duty to obtain an accountant's report at the end of a society's year of account[3] where the duty to appoint auditors[4] does not apply to the society for the year because of a resolution[5] to disapply the auditing requirements[6], has effect, in its application to such a landlord, with the omission of the provision[7] requiring an accountant's report only where turnover exceeds a specified sum[8]. The Welsh Ministers[9] may, in respect of any relevant year of account[10] of such a landlord, give a direction to the landlord requiring it: (1) to appoint a qualified auditor[11] to audit its accounts and balance sheet for that year; and (2) to furnish to the Welsh Ministers a copy of the auditor's report by such date as is specified in the direction[12].

1 As to the register of social landlords see PARA 167.

2 Housing Act 1996 s 7, Sch 1 para 17(1) (Sch 1 para 17 substituted by the Housing Act 2004 s 218, Sch 11 paras 7, 19; the Housing Act 1996 Sch 1 para 17(1) amended by the Co-operative and Community Benefit Societies Act 2014 s 151(1), Sch 4 paras 55, 65(1), (12)(a)). As to the meaning of 'registered society' see PARA 168 note 1.

3 'Year of account' has the same meaning as in the Co-operative and Community Benefit Societies Act 2014 Pt 7 (ss 75–102) (see ss 77, 78; and FINANCIAL INSTITUTIONS vol 48 (2015) PARA 1003): Housing Act 1996 Sch 1 para 17(5) (as substituted (see note 2); further substituted by the Co-operative and Community Benefit Societies Act 2014 Sch 4 paras 55, 65(1), (12)(d)).

4 Ie the Co-operative and Community Benefit Societies Act 2014 s 83: see FINANCIAL INSTITUTIONS vol 48 (2015) PARA 1004.

5 Ie a resolution under the Co-operative and Community Benefit Societies Act 2014 s 84: see FINANCIAL INSTITUTIONS vol 48 (2015) PARA 1004.

6 Ie the Co-operative and Community Benefit Societies Act 2014 s 85: see FINANCIAL INSTITUTIONS vol 48 (2015) PARA 1004.

7 Ie the Co-operative and Community Benefit Societies Act 2014 s 85(1)(b): see FINANCIAL INSTITUTIONS vol 48 (2015) PARA 1004.

8 Housing Act 1996 Sch 1 para 17(2) (as substituted (see note 2); further substituted by the Co-operative and Community Benefit Societies Act 2014 Sch 4 paras 55, 65(1), (12)(b)).

9 As to the Welsh Ministers see PARAS 7, 141.

10 For the purposes of the Housing Act 1996 Sch 1 para 17(3), a year of account of a landlord is a 'relevant year of account' if: (1) it precedes that in which the direction is given; and (2) the Co-operative and Community Benefit Societies Act 2014 s 83 (duty to appoint auditors) did not apply for the year because of a resolution under s 84 (power to disapply auditing requirements) (see FINANCIAL INSTITUTIONS vol 48 (2015) PARA 1003): Housing Act 1996 Sch 1 para 17(4) (as substituted (see note 2); amended by the Co-operative and Community Benefit Societies Act 2014 Sch 4 paras 55, 65(1), (12)(c)).

11 'Qualified auditor' has the same meaning as in the Co-operative and Community Benefit Societies Act 2014 Pt 7 (see s 91; and FINANCIAL INSTITUTIONS vol 48 (2015) PARA 1004): Housing Act 1996 Sch 1 para 17(5) (as substituted: see notes 2, 3).

12 Housing Act 1996 Sch 1 para 17(3) (as substituted (see note 2); and amended by the Housing and Regeneration Act 2008 s 61(1), (7)).

198. Accountant's report in relation to charities exempt from audit requirements. Where a charity[1] is required to appoint a qualified auditor[2] ('the reporting accountant') to make a report in respect of a period of account[3], the report satisfies the statutory requirements if it is a report:

(1) relating to the charity's accounts prepared in accordance with the statutory provisions[4] in respect of the period of account in question; and

(2) complying with the following provisions[5].

The report must state whether, in the opinion of the reporting accountant:

(a) the revenue account or accounts and the balance sheet are in agreement with the books of account kept by the charity[6];

(b) on the basis of the information contained in those books of account, the revenue account or accounts and the balance sheet comply with the requirements of the Charities Act 2011; and

(c) on the basis of the information contained in those books of account, the requirement to make a report[7] applied to the charity in respect of the period of account in question[8].

The report must also state the name of the reporting accountant and be signed by him[9].

The right of access to the books, deeds, accounts and documents of the charity[10] applies to the reporting accountant and his functions under these provisions as it applies[11] to an auditor and his functions[12].

The Welsh Ministers[13] may, in respect of a relevant period of account[14] of a charity, give a direction to the charity requiring it:

(i) to appoint a qualified auditor to audit its accounts for that period; and

(ii) to furnish to the Welsh Ministers a copy of the auditor's report by such date as is specified in the direction[15].

1 As to the meaning of 'charity' see PARA 168 note 3.
2 As to the meaning of 'qualified auditor' see PARA 195 note 7 head (3) (definition applied by the Housing Act 1996 s 7, Sch 1 para 18A(7) (Sch 1 para 18A added by the Housing Act 2004 s 218, Sch 11 paras 7, 21)).
3 Ie under the Housing Act 1996 Sch 1 para 18(4A): see PARA 195 note 14 head (4). As to the meaning of 'period of account' see PARA 195 note 14 (definition applied by Sch 1 para 18A(7) (as added: see note 2)).
4 Ie in accordance with the Housing Act 1996 Sch 1 para 18(3): see PARA 195 note 6 head (2).
5 Housing Act 1996 Sch 1 para 18A(1) (as added: see note 2).
6 Ie under the Housing Act 1996 Sch 1 para 18(2): see PARA 195 note 4 head (1).
7 Ie the Housing Act 1996 Sch 1 para 18(4A): see PARA 195 note 14 head (4).
8 Housing Act 1996 Sch 1 para 18A(2) (as added (see note 2); amended by the Charities Act 2011 s 354(1), Sch 7 para 72(1), (4)).
9 Housing Act 1996 Sch 1 para 18A(3) (as added: see note 2).
10 Ie the Housing Act 1996 Sch 1 para 18(7): see PARA 195 note 17 head (7).
11 Ie the Housing Act 1996 Sch 1 para 18: see PARA 195 note 14.
12 Housing Act 1996 Sch 1 para 18A(4) (as added: see note 2).
13 As to the Welsh Ministers see PARAS 7, 141.
14 For the purposes of the Housing Act 1996 Sch 1 para 18A(5), a period of account of a charity is a relevant period of account if: (1) it precedes that in which the direction is given; and (2) Sch 1 para 18(4A) (see PARA 195 note 14 head (4)) applied in relation to it: Sch 1 para 18A(6) (as added: see note 2).
15 Housing Act 1996 Sch 1 para 18A(5) (as added (see note 2); amended by the Housing and Regeneration Act 2008 s 61(1), (7)). The provisions of the Housing Act 1996 Sch 1 para 18(5)–(7) (see PARA 195 note 15 heads (5)–(7)) apply to an auditor so appointed as they apply to an auditor appointed under Sch 1 para 18: Sch 1 para 18A(5) (as so added).

G. INSPECTION

199. Inspection of registered social landlord's affairs. The following provisions provide for the inspection of a registered social landlord's affairs[1]. They do not, however, apply in relation to affairs relating only to the provision of housing in England[2].

The Welsh Ministers[3]: (1) may inspect a registered social landlord's affairs; or (2) may arrange for another person to do so[4]. An inspection may be general or specific[5]. If the Welsh Ministers arrange for a person to carry out an inspection, they may direct that person to discontinue it[6]. If the Welsh Ministers arrange for a person to carry out an inspection, the arrangements may include (among other things) provision about payments[7].

The person carrying out the inspection must produce a written report[8]. The Welsh Ministers must give the registered social landlord a copy of the report and may publish the report and related information[9]. If the Welsh Ministers have arranged for a person to carry out the inspection, that person may publish the report and related information (whether or not the Welsh Ministers have done so)[10].

If a registered social landlord is inspected, the Welsh Ministers may charge a fee[11]. A registered social landlord must pay any fee charged to: (a) the person with whom the Welsh Ministers have made an arrangement to carry out an inspection (if any); or (b) the Welsh Ministers[12]. The Welsh Ministers may direct a registered social landlord to pay the fee to one of those persons[13]. If a fee is paid to a person other than the Welsh Ministers, that person must notify the Welsh Ministers about the payment[14].

An inspector[15] may by notice require a person to provide specified documents or information[16]. A requirement may specify: (i) the form and manner in which a document or information is to be provided (which may include the provision of a legible copy of information stored electronically); (ii) when and where it is to be provided[17]. The inspector may copy or record documents or information provided[18]. Failure to comply with a requirement without reasonable excuse is an offence[19]. Intentionally altering, suppressing or destroying a document or information to which a requirement relates is an offence[20]. Proceedings for an offence under these provisions may be brought only by or with the consent of the Welsh Ministers or the Director of Public Prosecutions[21].

If a person fails to comply with a requirement the High Court may, on an application by the inspector, make an order for the purpose of remedying the failure[22].

An inspector[23] may at any reasonable time: (A) enter premises occupied by the registered social landlord which is being inspected; and (B) inspect, copy or take away documents found there[24]. The inspector may not, however, enter residential accommodation[25] (whether the residential accommodation is the whole of, or only part of, premises occupied by the registered social landlord)[26]. An inspector may require any person on the premises to provide such facilities or assistance as the inspector reasonably requests[27]. It is an offence for a person without reasonable excuse to obstruct an inspector exercising the powers conferred by these provisions[28]. Proceedings for an offence may be brought only by or with the consent of the Welsh Ministers or the Director of Public Prosecutions[29].

A registered social landlord may give the Welsh Ministers an undertaking in respect of any matter concerning housing[30], and the Welsh Ministers must have regard to any undertaking offered or given in exercising their powers under the provisions above[31], and may base a decision about whether to exercise their powers under these provisions wholly or partly on the extent to which the undertaking has been honoured[32].

1 Housing Act 1996 s 7, Sch 1 para 19B(1) (Sch 1 paras 19B–19G added, in relation to Wales, by the Housing (Wales) Measure 2011 ss 43–48). As to the register of social landlords see PARA 167.
2 Housing Act 1996 Sch 1 para 19B(2) (as added: see note 1).
3 As to the Welsh Ministers see PARAS 7, 141.
4 Housing Act 1996 Sch 1 para 19C(1) (as added: see note 1).
5 Housing Act 1996 Sch 1 para 19C(2) (as added: see note 1).
6 Housing Act 1996 Sch 1 para 19C(3) (as added: see note 1).
7 Housing Act 1996 Sch 1 para 19C(4) (as added: see note 1).
8 Housing Act 1996 Sch 1 para 19D(1) (as added: see note 1).
9 Housing Act 1996 Sch 1 para 19D(2) (as added: see note 1).
10 Housing Act 1996 Sch 1 para 19D(3) (as added: see note 1).
11 Housing Act 1996 Sch 1 para 19D(4) (as added: see note 1).
12 Housing Act 1996 Sch 1 para 19D(5) (as added: see note 1).
13 Housing Act 1996 Sch 1 para 19D(6) (as added: see note 1).
14 Housing Act 1996 Sch 1 para 19D(7) (as added: see note 1).
15 In the Housing Act 1996 Sch 1 para 19E, 'inspector' means: (1) the Welsh Ministers; or (2) a person authorised in writing by the Welsh Ministers to exercise the powers under Sch 1 para 19E for the purpose of an inspection under Sch 1 para 19C: Sch 1 para 19E(7) (as added: see note 1).
16 Housing Act 1996 Sch 1 para 19E(1) (as added: see note 1). A requirement does not require a person to disclose anything which the person would be entitled to refuse to disclose on grounds of legal professional privilege in proceedings in the High Court: Sch 1 para 19F(1) (as so added). A requirement does not require a banker to breach a duty of confidentiality owed to a person who is not: (1) the registered social landlord to whose affairs or activities the document or information relates; (2) a subsidiary of that landlord; or (3) an associate of that landlord: Sch 1 para 19F(2) (as so added). As to legal professional privilege see CIVIL PROCEDURE vol 12 (2015) PARA 647 et seq. As to the meaning of 'subsidiary' and 'associate' see PARA 200 notes 8, 9.
17 Housing Act 1996 Sch 1 para 19E(2) (as added: see note 1).
18 Housing Act 1996 Sch 1 para 19E(3) (as added: see note 1).
19 Housing Act 1996 Sch 1 para 19E(4) (as added: see note 1). A person guilty of an offence under Sch 1 para 19E(4) is liable on summary conviction to a fine not exceeding level 5 on the standard scale: Sch 1 para 19F(3) (as so added). As to the powers of magistrates' courts to issue fines on summary conviction see SENTENCING vol 92 (2015) PARA 176.
20 Housing Act 1996 Sch 1 para 19E(5) (as added: see note 1). A person guilty of an offence under Sch 1 para 19E(5) is liable: (1) on summary conviction, to a fine not exceeding the statutory maximum; (2) on conviction on indictment, to imprisonment for a term not exceeding two years, a fine or both: Sch 1 para 19F(4) (as so added).
21 Housing Act 1996 Sch 1 para 19F(5) (as added: see note 1). As to the Director of Public Prosecutions see CRIMINAL PROCEDURE vol 27 (2015) PARAS 25, 30 et seq.
22 Housing Act 1996 Sch 1 para 19E(6) (as added: see note 1).
23 In the Housing Act 1996 Sch 1 para 19G, 'inspector' means: (1) the Welsh Ministers; or (2) a person authorised in writing by the Welsh Ministers to exercise the powers under Sch 1 para 19G for the purpose of an inspection under Sch 1 para 19C: Sch 1 para 19G(10) (as added: see note 1).
24 Housing Act 1996 Sch 1 para 19G(1) (as added: see note 1). The reference to documents found on the premises includes (but is not limited to): (1) documents stored on computers or electronic storage devices on the premises; and (2) documents stored elsewhere which can be accessed by computers on the premises: Sch 1 para 19G(3) (as so added). The power to inspect documents includes (but is not limited to) the power to inspect any computer or electronic storage device on which they have been created or stored: Sch 1 para 19G(4) (as so added).
25 For these purposes, 'residential accommodation' means accommodation of any description (including, but not limited to, a dwelling or residential accommodation in a hostel) that is occupied by one or more persons as a permanent or temporary place of residence (whether or not it is also occupied by any person for any other purpose): Housing Act 1996 Sch 1 para 19G(10) (as added: see note 1).
26 Housing Act 1996 Sch 1 para 19G(2) (as added: see note 1).
27 Housing Act 1996 Sch 1 para 19G(5) (as added: see note 1). For the purposes of Sch 1 para 19G(3), (4) (see note 24) an inspector may require any person having charge of a computer to provide any assistance that the inspector reasonably requests: Sch 1 para 19G(6) (as so added).
28 Housing Act 1996 Sch 1 para 19G(7) (as added: see note 1). A person guilty of an offence is liable on summary conviction to a fine not exceeding level 3 on the standard scale: Sch 1 para 19G(8) (as so added).

29 Housing Act 1996 Sch 1 para 19G(9) (as added: see note 1).

30 Housing Act 1996 s 6A(1) (s 6A added, in relation to Wales, by the Housing (Wales) Measure 2011 s 41). The Welsh Ministers may prescribe a procedure to be followed in giving an undertaking: Housing Act 1996 s 6A(2) (as so added).

31 Ie their powers under the Housing Act 1996 Sch 1 Pt 3A (paras 19B–19G) (see the text to notes 1–29): s 6A(5) (as added: see note 30).

32 Housing Act 1996 s 6A(3), (4) (as added: see note 30). Section 6A does not apply in relation to a registered social landlord's provision of housing in England: s 6A(6) (as so added).

H. INQUIRY INTO THE AFFAIRS OF REGISTERED SOCIAL LANDLORDS

200. In general. The Welsh Ministers[1] may direct an inquiry into the affairs of a registered social landlord[2] if it appears to the Welsh Ministers that there may have been misconduct[3] or mismanagement[4]. Any such inquiry must be conducted by one or more persons appointed by the Welsh Ministers[5]. A local authority[6] may, if it thinks fit, contribute to the expenses of the Welsh Ministers in connection with any such inquiry[7].

If the Welsh Ministers so direct, or if during the course of the inquiry the person or persons conducting the inquiry consider it necessary, the inquiry must extend to the affairs of any other body which at any material time is or was a subsidiary[8] or associate[9] of the registered social landlord[10].

The person or persons conducting the inquiry may determine the procedure to be followed in connection with the inquiry[11]. Such person or persons may, if they think fit during the course of the inquiry, make one or more interim reports on such matters as appear to them to be appropriate[12]. On completion of the inquiry the person or persons conducting the inquiry must make a final report on such matters as the Welsh Ministers may specify[13].

For the purposes of an inquiry[14], the person or persons conducting it may serve a notice on an appropriate person[15] directing him to attend at a specified time and place and do either or both of the following, namely: (1) give evidence; and (2) produce any specified documents[16], or documents of a specified description, which are in his custody or under his control and relate to any matter relevant to the inquiry[17]. The person or persons conducting such an inquiry may take evidence on oath and for that purpose may administer oaths or, instead of administering an oath, require the person examined to make and subscribe a declaration of the truth of the matters about which he is examined[18]. The provisions relating to the enforcement of a notice to provide information or produce documents[19] apply in relation to a notice given by the person or persons conducting an inquiry as they apply in relation to a notice given by the Welsh Ministers[20], but subject to specific provision as to penalties[21].

A person appointed by the Welsh Ministers to conduct such an inquiry (or, if more than one person is so appointed, each of those persons) has, for the purposes of the inquiry, the same powers to obtain general information as are conferred[22] on the Welsh Ministers[23].

For the purposes of such an inquiry, the Welsh Ministers may require the accounts and balance sheet of the registered social landlord concerned, or such of them as the Welsh Ministers may specify, to be audited by a qualified auditor[24] appointed by the Welsh Ministers[25]. Such an audit is additional to, and does not affect, any audit made or to be made under any other enactment[26]. On completion of the audit the appointed auditor must make a report to the Welsh Ministers on such matters and in such form as the Welsh Ministers may specify[27]. The expenses of the audit, including the remuneration of the auditor, must be paid by the registered social landlord in respect of which the inquiry is being conducted[28].

1 As to the Welsh Ministers see PARAS 7, 141.
2 As to the register of social landlords see PARA 167.
3 As to the meaning of 'misconduct' see PARA 186 note 6.
4 Housing Act 1996 s 7, Sch 1 para 20(1) (Sch 1 para 20(1) amended by the Housing and Regeneration Act 2008 s 61(1), (7); and, in relation to Wales, by the Housing (Wales) Measure 2011 s 88, Schedule paras 1, 18).
5 Housing Act 1996 Sch 1 para 20(2) (amended by the Housing and Regeneration Act 2008 s 61(1), (7)).
6 As to the meaning of 'local authority' see PARA 149 note 4 (definition applied by the Housing Act 1996 s 63(1)).
7 Housing Act 1996 Sch 1 para 20(8) (added by the Housing Act 2004 s 218, Sch 11 paras 7, 24(1), (4); and amended by the Housing and Regeneration Act 2008 s 61(1), (7)).
8 For these purposes, 'subsidiary', in relation to a registered social landlord, means a company with respect to which one of the following conditions is fulfilled: (1) the landlord is a member of the company and controls the composition of the board of directors; (2) the landlord holds more than half in nominal value of the company's equity share capital; or (3) the company is a subsidiary, within the meaning of the Companies Acts (see the Companies Act 2006 s 1159; and COMPANIES vol 14 (2016) PARA 22) or the Co-operative and Community Benefit Societies Act 2014 Pt 7 (ss 75–102) (see FINANCIAL INSTITUTIONS vol 48 (2015) PARA 1009), of another company which, by virtue of head (1) or head (2), is itself a subsidiary of the landlord: Housing Act 1996 s 60(1) (amended by the Co-operative and Community Benefit Societies Act 2014 s 151(1), Sch 4 paras 55, 62; and by SI 2009/1941). For the purposes of head (1), the composition of a company's board of directors is deemed to be controlled by a registered social landlord if, but only if, the landlord, by the exercise of some power exercisable by him without the consent or concurrence of any other person, can appoint or remove the holders of all or a majority of the directorships: Housing Act 1996 s 60(2). In relation to a company which is a registered society, any reference in s 60 to the board of directors is a reference to the committee of management of the society; and the reference in s 60(2) to the holders of all or a majority of the directorships is a reference: (a) to all or a majority of the members of the committee; or (b) if the landlord is himself a member of the committee, such number as together with him would constitute a majority: s 60(3) (amended by the Co-operative and Community Benefit Societies Act 2014 Sch 4 paras 55, 56). In the case of a registered social landlord which is a body of trustees, references in the Housing Act 1996 s 60 to the landlord are references to the trustees acting as such: s 60(4). As to the meaning of 'registered society' see PARA 168 note 1.
9 For these purposes, 'associate', in relation to a registered social landlord, means: (1) any body of which the landlord is a subsidiary; and (2) any other subsidiary of such a body; and in this definition 'subsidiary' has the same meaning as in the Companies Acts (see the Companies Act 2006 s 1159; and COMPANIES vol 14 (2016) PARA 22) or the Co-operative and Community Benefit Societies Act 2014 Pt 7 (see FINANCIAL INSTITUTIONS vol 48 (2015) PARA 1009) or, in the case of a body which is itself a registered social landlord, has the meaning given by the Housing Act 1996 s 60 (see note 8): s 61(1), (2) (s 61(2) amended by the Co-operative and Community Benefit Societies Act 2014 Sch 4 paras 55, 63; and by SI 2009/1941).
10 Housing Act 1996 Sch 1 para 20(4) (amended by the Housing and Regeneration Act 2008 s 61(1), (7)).
11 Housing Act 1996 Sch 1 para 20(4A) (added by the Housing Act 2004 Sch 11 para 24(2)).
12 Housing Act 1996 Sch 1 para 20(5). An interim or final report must be in such form as the Welsh Ministers may specify, and the Welsh Ministers may arrange for the whole or part of an interim or final report to be published in such manner as they consider appropriate: Sch 1 para 20(7) (amended by the Housing Act 2004 Sch 11 para 24(3); and the Housing and Regeneration Act 2008 s 61(1), (7)).
13 Housing Act 1996 Sch 1 para 20(6) (amended by the Housing Act 2004 Sch 11 para 24(3); and the Housing and Regeneration Act 2008 s 61(7)). As to the form of the report see note 12.
14 Ie an inquiry under the Housing Act 1996 Sch 1 para 20: Housing Act 1996 Sch 1 para 20A(3) (Sch 1 para 20A added by the Housing Act 2004 Sch 11 para 25).
15 'Appropriate person' means a person listed in the Housing Act 1996 s 30(2) (see PARA 158): Housing Act 1996 Sch 1 para 20A(3) (as added: see note 14).
16 As to the meaning of 'document' see PARA 158 note 4 (definition applied by the Housing Act 1996 Sch 1 para 20A(3) (as added: see note 14)).
17 Housing Act 1996 Sch 1 para 20A(1) (as added: see note 14). A person may not be required under Sch 1 para 20A to disclose anything that, by virtue of s 30(4) (see PARA 158), he could not be required to disclose under s 30: Sch 1 para 20A(4) (as so added).
18 Housing Act 1996 Sch 1 para 20A(2) (as added: see note 14).

19 Ie the Housing Act 1996 s 31: see PARA 158.

20 Ie a notice under the Housing Act 1996 s 30: see PARA 158.

21 Housing Act 1996 Sch 1 para 20A(5) (as added (see note 14); amended by the Housing and Regeneration Act 2008 s 61(1), (7)). A person guilty of an offence under the Housing Act 1996 s 31(1) as it applies in accordance with Sch 1 para 20A(5) is liable on summary conviction to a fine not exceeding the statutory maximum, or on conviction on indictment to imprisonment for a term not exceeding two years or a fine or both: Sch 1 para 20A(6) (as so added). As to the powers of magistrates' courts to issue fines on summary conviction see SENTENCING vol 92 (2015) PARA 176. Any person who, in purported compliance with a notice given under Sch 1 para 20A by the person or persons conducting an inquiry, knowingly or recklessly provides any information which is false or misleading in a material particular commits an offence and is liable to the penalties mentioned in Sch 1 para 20A(6): Sch 1 para 20A(7) (as so added). Proceedings for an offence under Sch 1 para 20A(7) may be brought only by or with the consent of the Welsh Ministers or the Director of Public Prosecutions: Sch 1 para 20A(8) (as so added; amended by the Housing and Regeneration Act 2008 s 61(1), (7)). As to the Director of Public Prosecutions see CRIMINAL PROCEDURE vol 27 (2015) PARAS 25, 30 et seq.

22 Ie by the Housing Act 1996 s 30 (general power to obtain information): see PARA 158.

23 Housing Act 1996 Sch 1 para 21(1) (amended by the Housing and Regeneration Act 2008 s 61(1), (7)). Where by virtue of a notice under the Housing Act 1996 s 30 given by an appointed person any documents are produced to any person, the person to whom they are produced may take copies of or make extracts from them: Sch 1 para 21(2). Section 31 (enforcement of notice to provide information etc: see PARA 158) applies in relation to a notice given under this provision by an appointed person as it applies in relation to a notice given under s 30 by the Welsh Ministers, but subject to Sch 1 para 21(4): Sch 1 para 21(3) (amended by the Housing Act 2004 Sch 11 para 26(1), (2); and the Housing and Regeneration Act 2008 s 61(1), (7)). A person guilty of an offence under the Housing Act 1996 s 31(1) as it applies in accordance with Sch 1 para 21(3) is liable on summary conviction to a fine not exceeding the statutory maximum, or on conviction on indictment to imprisonment for a term not exceeding two years or a fine or both: Sch 1 para 21(4) (Sch 1 para 21(4)–(6) added by the Housing Act 2004 Sch 11 para 26(3)). Any person who, in purported compliance with a notice given under this provision by an appointed person, knowingly or recklessly provides any information which is false or misleading in a material particular commits an offence and is liable to the penalties mentioned in the Housing Act 1996 Sch 1 para 21(4): Sch 1 para 21(5) (as so added). Proceedings for an offence under Sch 1 para 21(5) may be brought only by or with the consent of the Welsh Ministers or the Director of Public Prosecutions: Sch 1 para 21(6) (as so added; amended by the Housing and Regeneration Act 2008 s 61(1), (7)).

24 A person is a qualified auditor for this purpose if he would be eligible for appointment as auditor of the ordinary accounts of the registered social landlord: Housing Act 1996 Sch 1 para 22(2). As to persons so qualified see PARA 194. As to the ordinary accounts see PARA 194 et seq.

25 Housing Act 1996 Sch 1 para 22(1) (amended by the Housing and Regeneration Act 2008 s 61(1), (7)).

26 Housing Act 1996 Sch 1 para 22(5).

27 Housing Act 1996 Sch 1 para 22(3) (amended by the Housing and Regeneration Act 2008 s 61(1), (7)).

28 Housing Act 1996 Sch 1 para 22(4) (amended, in relation to Wales, by the Housing (Wales) Measure 2011 s 49).

201. Powers exercisable on an interim basis. The Welsh Ministers[1] may make an order under these provisions:

(1)   where an inquiry has been directed[2] and the Welsh Ministers have reasonable grounds to believe that there has been misconduct[3] or mismanagement in the affairs of the registered social landlord[4] and that immediate action is needed to protect the interests of the tenants of the registered social landlord or to protect the assets of the registered social landlord; or

(2)   where an interim report has been made[5] as a result of which the Welsh Ministers are satisfied that there has been misconduct or mismanagement in the affairs of a registered social landlord[6].

The orders that may be made are:

(a)   an order suspending any officer[7], employee or agent of the registered social landlord who appears to the Welsh Ministers to have been responsible for or privy to the misconduct or mismanagement or by his conduct to have contributed to or facilitated it[8];

(b)   an order directing any bank or other person who holds money or securities on behalf of the registered social landlord not to part with the money or securities without the approval of the Welsh Ministers[9];

(c)   an order restricting the transactions which may be entered into, or the nature or amount of the payments which may be made, by the registered social landlord without the approval of the Welsh Ministers[10].

Before making an order under head (b) or (c) the Welsh Ministers must take all reasonable steps to give notice to the registered social landlord and, in the case of an order under head (b), to the person to whom the order is directed[11].

An order so made, if not previously revoked by the Welsh Ministers, ceases to have effect six months after the making of the final report[12] unless the Welsh Ministers renew it, which they may do for a further period of up to six months[13].

Where a person is suspended by an order under head (a), the Welsh Ministers may give directions with respect to the performance of his functions and otherwise as to matters arising from his suspension and may, in particular, appoint a named person to perform his functions[14]. A person suspended by such an order may appeal against the order to the High Court[15].

A person who contravenes an order under head (b) commits an offence and is liable to a penalty[16]. Proceedings for such an offence may, however, be brought only by or with the consent of the Welsh Ministers or the Director of Public Prosecutions[17].

1   As to the Welsh Ministers see PARAS 7, 141.
2   Ie under the Housing Act 1996 Sch 1 para 20: see PARA 200.
3   As to the meaning of 'misconduct' for these purposes see PARA 186 note 6.
4   As to the register of social landlords see PARA 167.
5   Ie under the Housing Act 1996 Sch 1 para 20(5): see PARA 200.
6   Housing Act 1996 s 7, Sch 1 para 23(1) (Sch 1 para 23(1) amended by the Housing and Regeneration Act 2008 s 61(1), (7)).
7   As to the meaning of 'officer' see PARA 174 note 9.
8   Housing Act 1996 Sch 1 para 23(2)(a) (Sch 1 para 23(2) amended by the Housing and Regeneration Act 2008 s 61(1), (7)).
9   Housing Act 1996 Sch 1 para 23(2)(b) (as amended: see note 8).
10 Housing Act 1996 Sch 1 para 23(2)(c) (as amended: see note 8).
11 Housing Act 1996 Sch 1 para 23(2A) (added, in relation to Wales, by the Housing (Wales) Measure 2011 s 79).
12 Ie under the Housing Act 1996 Sch 1 para 20(6): see PARA 200.
13 Housing Act 1996 Sch 1 para 23(3) (amended by the Housing and Regeneration Act 2008 s 61(1), (7)).
14 Housing Act 1996 Sch 1 para 23(5) (amended by the Housing and Regeneration Act 2008 s 61(1), (7)).
15 Housing Act 1996 Sch 1 para 23(4).
16 Housing Act 1996 Sch 1 para 23(6). The penalty on summary conviction is a fine not exceeding level 5 on the standard scale or imprisonment for a term not exceeding three months, or both: see Sch 1 para 23(6). As to the powers of magistrates' courts to issue fines on summary conviction see SENTENCING vol 92 (2015) PARA 176. As from a day to be appointed, this provision is amended so as to remove the penalty of imprisonment: see Sch 1 para 23(6) (prospectively amended by the Criminal Justice Act 2003 s 332, Sch 37 Pt 9). At the date at which this volume states the law, no such day had been appointed.
17 Housing Act 1996 Sch 1 para 23(6) (amended by the Housing and Regeneration Act 2008 s 61(1), (7)). As to the Director of Public Prosecutions see CRIMINAL PROCEDURE vol 27 (2015) PARAS 25, 30 et seq.

202. Powers exercisable as a result of final report or audit. Where, as the result of an inquiry[1] or an audit[2], the Welsh Ministers[3] are satisfied that there has been misconduct[4] or mismanagement in the affairs of a registered social landlord[5], they may make an order under these provisions[6]. The orders that may be made are:

(1)   an order removing any officer[7], employee or agent of the registered social landlord who appears to the Welsh Ministers to have been responsible for or privy to the misconduct or mismanagement or by his conduct to have contributed to or facilitated it[8];

(2)   an order suspending any such person for up to six months, pending determination whether he should be removed[9];

(3)   an order directing any bank or other person who holds money or securities on behalf of the registered social landlord not to part with the money or securities without the approval of the Welsh Ministers[10];

(4)   an order restricting the transactions which may be entered into, or the nature or amount of the payments which may be made, by the registered social landlord without the approval of the Welsh Ministers[11].

Before making an order under head (1) the Welsh Ministers must give at least 14 days' notice of their intention to do so to the person they intend to remove and to the registered social landlord concerned[12]. Before making an order under head (3) or (4) the Welsh Ministers must take all reasonable steps to give notice to the registered social landlord and, in the case of an order under head (3), to the person to whom the order is directed[13]. An order under head (3) or (4) has effect until it is revoked by the Welsh Ministers[14].

Where a person is suspended under head (2), the Welsh Ministers may give directions with respect to the performance of his functions and otherwise as to matters arising from the suspension and may, in particular, appoint a named person to perform his functions[15]. A person who is ordered to be removed under head (1) or suspended under head (2) may appeal against the order to the High Court[16].

A person who contravenes an order under head (3) commits an offence and is liable to a penalty[17]. Proceedings for such an offence may, however, be brought only by or with the consent of the Welsh Ministers or the Director of Public Prosecutions[18].

1 Ie under the Housing Act 1996 Sch 1 para 20: see PARA 200.
2 Ie under the Housing Act 1996 Sch 1 para 22: see PARA 200.
3 As to the Welsh Ministers see PARAS 7, 141.
4 As to the meaning of 'misconduct' for these purposes see PARA 186 note 6.
5 As to the register of social landlords see PARA 167.
6 Housing Act 1996 s 7, Sch 1 para 24(1) (Sch 1 para 24(1) amended by the Housing and Regeneration Act 2008 s 61(1), (7)).
7 As to the meaning of 'officer' see PARA 174 note 9.
8 Housing Act 1996 Sch 1 para 24(2)(a) (amended by the Housing and Regeneration Act 2008 s 61(1), (7)).
9 Housing Act 1996 Sch 1 para 24(2)(b).
10 Housing Act 1996 Sch 1 para 24(2)(c) (amended by the Housing and Regeneration Act 2008 s 61(1), (7)).
11 Housing Act 1996 Sch 1 para 24(2)(d) (amended by the Housing and Regeneration Act 2008 s 61(1), (7)).
12 Housing Act 1996 Sch 1 para 24(3) (amended by the Housing and Regeneration Act 2008 s 61(1), (7)). Notice may be given by post, and if so given to the person whom the Welsh Ministers intend to remove may be addressed to his last known address in the United Kingdom: Housing Act 1996 Sch 1 para 24(3) (as so amended). As to the meaning of 'United Kingdom' see PARA 60 note 10.
13 Housing Act 1996 Sch 1 para 24(3A) (added, in relation to Wales, by the Housing (Wales) Measure 2011 s 80(1), (2)).

14 Housing Act 1996 Sch 1 para 24(7) (added, in relation to Wales, by the Housing (Wales) Measure 2011 s 80(1), (3)).
15 Housing Act 1996 Sch 1 para 24(5) (amended by the Government of Wales Act 1998 Sch 16 para 82(1)(a)).
16 Housing Act 1996 Sch 1 para 24(4).
17 Housing Act 1996 Sch 1 para 24(6). The penalty on summary conviction is a fine not exceeding level 5 on the standard scale or imprisonment for a term not exceeding three months, or both: see Sch 1 para 24(6). As to the powers of magistrates' courts to issue fines on summary conviction see SENTENCING vol 92 (2015) PARA 176. As from a day to be appointed, this provision is amended so as to remove the penalty of imprisonment: see Sch 1 para 24(6) (prospectively amended by the Criminal Justice Act 2003 s 332, Sch 37 Pt 9). At the date at which this volume states the law, no such day had been appointed.
18 Housing Act 1996 Sch 1 para 24(6) (amended by the Housing and Regeneration Act 2008 s 61(1), (7)). As to the Director of Public Prosecutions see CRIMINAL PROCEDURE vol 27 (2015) PARAS 25, 30 et seq.

203. Disqualification as officer of a registered social landlord. A person is disqualified from being an officer[1] of a registered social landlord[2] if the person has been removed under the provisions relating to removal for misconduct or mismanagement[3] or corresponding statutory provisions[4].

The Welsh Ministers[5] may, on the application of any such person, waive his disqualification either generally or in relation to a particular registered social landlord or particular class of registered social landlord[6]. Any waiver must be notified in writing to the person concerned[7].

For these purposes the Welsh Ministers must keep, in such manner as they think fit, a register of all persons who have been removed from office by the Welsh Ministers under the above-mentioned provisions[8] and the register must be available for public inspection at all reasonable times[9]. The register must show details of any waivers[10].

A person who acts as an officer of a registered social landlord while he is disqualified under these provisions commits an offence[11]. A person guilty of such an offence is liable to a penalty[12]. Proceedings for such an offence may, however, be brought only by or with the consent of the Welsh Ministers or the Director of Public Prosecutions[13].

Acts done as an officer of a registered social landlord by a person who is disqualified under these provisions are not invalid by reason only of that disqualification[14]. Where the Welsh Ministers are satisfied that a person has acted as an officer of a registered social landlord while disqualified, and that while so acting he has received from the registered social landlord any payments or benefits in connection with his so acting, they may by order direct him to repay to the registered social landlord the whole or part of any such sums or, as the case may be, to pay to them the whole or part of the monetary value (as determined by them) of any such benefit[15]. If a person fails to comply with an order directing repayment, the registered social landlord or the Welsh Ministers (as the case may be) may recover the sum or specified amount as a debt[16].

1 As to the meaning of 'officer' see PARA 174 note 9.
2 As to the register of social landlords see PARA 167.
3 Ie under the Housing Act 1996 Sch 1 para 24(2)(a): see PARA 202 head (1).
4 Housing Act 1996 s 7, Sch 1 para 25(1) (Sch 1 para 25(1) substituted by SI 2010/866). The corresponding provisions referred to in the text are those of the Housing and Regeneration Act 2008 s 260 (see PARA 123), the Housing Associations Act 1985 s 30(1)(a) (repealed) and the Housing Act 1974 s 20(1)(a) (repealed), or similar statutory provisions.
5 As to the Welsh Ministers see PARAS 7, 141.
6 Housing Act 1996 Sch 1 para 25(2) (amended by the Housing and Regeneration Act 2008 s 61(1), (7)).
7 Housing Act 1996 Sch 1 para 25(3).

8 Housing Act 1996 Sch 1 para 25(4) (amended by the Housing and Regeneration Act 2008 s 61(1), (7); and, in relation to Wales, by the Housing (Wales) Measure 2011 s 88, Schedule paras 1, 19).
9 Housing Act 1996 Sch 1 para 25(5).
10 Housing Act 1996 Sch 1 para 25(4A) (added, in relation to Wales, by the Housing (Wales) Measure 2011 s 81).
11 Housing Act 1996 Sch 1 para 26(1).
12 Housing Act 1996 Sch 1 para 26(1). The penalty on summary conviction is imprisonment for a term not exceeding 12 months or a fine not exceeding the statutory maximum or both, and on conviction on indictment is imprisonment for a term not exceeding two years or a fine or both: see Sch 1 para 26(1) (amended, in relation to Wales, by the Housing (Wales) Measure 2011 s 82(1), (2)). In relation to an offence committed before the commencement of the Criminal Justice Act 2003 s 282 (short sentences: see SENTENCING vol 92 (2015) PARA 2) the reference above to 12 months has effect as if it were a reference to six months: Housing Act 1996 Sch 1 para 26(1A) (added, in relation to Wales, by the Housing (Wales) Measure 2011 s 82(1), (3)). As to the powers of magistrates' courts to issue fines on summary conviction see SENTENCING vol 92 (2015) PARA 176.
13 Housing Act 1996 Sch 1 para 26(2) (amended by the Housing and Regeneration Act 2008 s 61(1), (7)). As to the Director of Public Prosecutions see CRIMINAL PROCEDURE vol 27 (2015) PARAS 25, 30 et seq.
14 Housing Act 1996 Sch 1 para 26(3).
15 Housing Act 1996 Sch 1 para 26(4) (amended by the Housing and Regeneration Act 2008 s 61(1), (7)).
16 Housing Act 1996 Sch 1 para 26(5) (added, in relation to Wales, by the Housing (Wales) Measure 2011 s 82(1), (4)).

204. Power to direct transfer of land. Where as a result of an inquiry[1] or an audit[2] the Welsh Ministers[3] are satisfied as regards a registered social landlord:

(1)   that there has been misconduct[4] or mismanagement in its administration; or

(2)   that the management of its land would be improved if its land were transferred in accordance with the following provisions,

the Welsh Ministers may direct the registered social landlord to make such a transfer[5]. Where the registered social landlord concerned is a charity[6], the Welsh Ministers may only direct a transfer to be made to another registered social landlord which is also a charity, and the objects of which appear to the Welsh Ministers to be, as nearly as practicable, akin to those of the registered social landlord concerned[7]. In any other case, the Welsh Ministers may direct a transfer to be made to the Welsh Ministers or to another registered social landlord[8].

The transfer must be on such terms as the Welsh Ministers may direct on the basis of principles determined by them[9]. The price must not be less than the amount certified by the district valuer to be the amount the property would command if sold by a willing seller to another registered social landlord[10] and the terms must include provision as to the payment of debts and liabilities (including debts and liabilities secured on the land)[11].

These powers are not exercisable in relation to a landlord which is a registered charity[12].

1 Ie under the Housing Act 1996 Sch 1 para 20: see PARA 200.
2 Ie under the Housing Act 1996 Sch 1 para 22: see PARA 200.
3 As to the Welsh Ministers see PARAS 7, 141.
4 As to the meaning of 'misconduct' for these purposes see PARA 186 note 6.
5 Housing Act 1996 s 7, Sch 1 para 27(1) (Sch 1 para 27(1) amended by the Government of Wales Act 1998 ss 140, 152, Sch 16 para 96(6), Sch 18 Pt VI; the Housing and Regeneration Act 2008 s 61(1), (7); and SI 2010/866). See *R (Clays Lane Housing Co-operative Ltd) v Housing Corpn* [2004] EWCA Civ 1658, [2005] 1 WLR 2229, [2005] HLR 194 (decision to direct transfer of property held not to be a disproportionate interference with rights under the Convention for the Protection of Human Rights and Fundamental Freedoms (Rome, 4 November 1950; TS 71 (1953); Cmd 8969)).
6 As to the meaning of 'charity' see PARA 168 note 3.

7 Housing Act 1996 Sch 1 para 27(2) (amended by the Housing and Regeneration Act 2008 s 61(1),
   (7)).
8 Housing Act 1996 Sch 1 para 27(3) (amended by the Housing and Regeneration Act 2008 s 61(1),
   (7)).
9 Housing Act 1996 Sch 1 para 27(4) (amended by the Housing and Regeneration Act 2008 s 61(1),
   (7); and by SI 2010/866).
10 Housing Act 1996 Sch 1 para 27(5).
11 Housing Act 1996 Sch 1 para 27(6).
12 See PARA 205.

205. Availability of powers in relation to registered charities. The Welsh
Ministers[1] may only exercise their powers to inquire into the affairs of a registered
social landlord[2] in relation to a registered charity[3] if the charity has received public
assistance[4].

For the purposes of the exercise of those powers in relation to a registered
charity, references to the affairs of the registered social landlord are confined to its
housing activities[5] and such other activities (if any) as are incidental to or
connected with its housing activities, and references to its accounts do not include
revenue accounts which do not relate to its housing activities, except so far as such
accounts are necessary for the auditing of revenue accounts which do so relate or
of the balance sheet[6].

The Welsh Ministers must notify the Charity Commission[7] upon the exercise in
relation to a registered charity of their powers to direct an inquiry into the affairs
of a registered social landlord[8], to order the interim suspension of a person in
connection with misconduct or mismanagement[9], to remove a person in
connection with misconduct or mismanagement[10], or to suspend him[11] with a
view to removal[12].

The Welsh Ministers may not exercise their powers to direct a transfer of land[13]
in relation to a registered charity[14].

1 As to the Welsh Ministers see PARAS 7, 141.
2 Ie its powers under the Housing Act 1996 Sch 1 paras 20–26: see PARA 200 et seq.
3 As to the meaning of 'registered charity' see PARA 168 note 3.
4 Housing Act 1996 s 7, Sch 1 para 28(1) (Sch 1 para 28(1) amended by the Housing and
   Regeneration Act 2008 s 61(1), (7); and, in relation to Wales, by the Housing (Wales) Measure
   2011 s 88, Schedule paras 1, 20(a)). As to the meaning of 'received public assistance' see
   PARA 175.
5 As to the meaning of 'housing activities' see PARA 168 note 25.
6 See the Housing Act 1996 Sch 1 para 28(3)(a), (b). In relation to a registered charity, a person is
   a qualified auditor for the purpose of Sch 1 para 22 (extraordinary audit: see PARA 200) only if
   he is an auditor qualified for the purposes of Sch 1 para 18 (accounting and audit requirements for
   charities: see PARA 194 note 14): see Sch 1 para 28(3)(c).
7 As to the Charity Commission see CHARITIES vol 8 (2015) PARA 543 et seq.
8 Ie their powers under the Housing Act 1996 Sch 1 para 20(1): see PARA 200.
9 Ie their powers under the Housing Act 1996 Sch 1 para 23(2)(a): see PARA 201.
10 Ie their powers under the Housing Act 1996 Sch 1 para 24(2)(a): see PARA 202.
11 Ie their powers under the Housing Act 1996 Sch 1 para 24(2)(b): see PARA 202.
12 Housing Act 1996 Sch 1 para 28(4) (amended by the Charities Act 2006 s 75(1), Sch 8 paras 183,
   192(1), (5); and the Housing and Regeneration Act 2008 s 61(1), (7)).
13 Ie their powers under the Housing Act 1996 Sch 1 para 27: see PARA 204.
14 Housing Act 1996 Sch 1 para 29 (amended by the Housing and Regeneration Act 2008 s 61(1),
   (7)).

I.   INSOLVENCY ETC OF REGISTERED SOCIAL LANDLORD

206. Introduction; summary of statutory provisions. Since the enactment of
Part II of the Housing Act 1988[1], most new housing developments by social
landlords have been funded by a combination of public grant and private sector
loan money[2]. Where a private lender takes a charge on dwellings or other property

owned by a registered social landlord[3] to serve as security for the repayment of the loan, there is a statutory power to sell the property in order to realise the security where there has been a default[4]. The exercise of such a power of sale of dwellings owned by a registered social landlord could result in such dwellings being lost to the social rented sector; measures introduced by Part I of the Housing Act 1996 allow the Welsh Ministers[5] to intervene where such a landlord is facing insolvency[6].

Statutory provision has accordingly been made:

(1)   for notice to be given to the Welsh Ministers of any proposal to take certain steps in relation to a registered social landlord[7] and for further notice to be given when any such step is taken[8];

(2)   for a moratorium on the disposal[9] of land, and certain other assets, held by the registered social landlord[10];

(3)   for the appointment of an interim manager during a moratorium[11];

(4)   for proposals by the Welsh Ministers as to the future ownership and management of the land held by the landlord[12] which are binding if agreed[13];

(5)   for the appointment of a manager to implement agreed proposals[14] and as to the powers of such a manager[15];

(6)   for the giving of assistance by the Welsh Ministers[16]; and

(7)   for application to the court to secure compliance with the agreed proposals[17].

The Welsh Ministers may make provision by order defining what is meant by a step to enforce security[18] over land[19].

1   Ie the Housing Act 1988 Pt II (ss 46–59) (repealed).
2   See Hughes and Lowe *Social Housing Law and Policy* (1995) pp 187–191. See also Doolittle *Housing and Regeneration* (2003) and Driscoll *A Guide to the Housing Acct 1988* (1989).
3   As to the meaning of 'registered social landlord' see PARA 13.
4   See the Law of Property Act 1925 s 91; and MORTGAGE vol 77 (2016) PARA 621.
5   As to the Welsh Ministers see PARAS 7, 141.
6   See the Housing Act 1996 ss 39–50; and PARA 207 et seq. See also Driscoll *A Guide to the Housing Act 1996* (1996).
7   See the Housing Act 1996 s 40; and PARA 207.
8   See the Housing Act 1996 s 41; and PARA 208.
9   For these purposes, 'disposal' means sale, lease, mortgage, charge or any other disposition, and includes the grant of an option: Housing Act 1996 s 39(2).
10 See the Housing Act 1996 ss 42, 43; and PARA 209.
11 See the Housing Act 1996 s 43A; and PARA 210.
12 See the Housing Act 1996 s 44; and PARA 211.
13 See the Housing Act 1996 s 45; and PARA 211.
14 See the Housing Act 1996 s 46; and PARA 212.
15 See the Housing Act 1996 ss 47, 48; and PARA 212.
16 See the Housing Act 1996 s 49; and PARA 213.
17 Housing Act 1996 s 39(1) (amended by the Housing and Regeneration Act 2008 s 61(1), (7); and, in relation to Wales, by the Housing (Wales) Measure 2011 s 88, Schedule paras 1, 9). The provision referred to in head (7) in the text is the Housing Act 1996 s 50: see PARA 214.
18 For these purposes, 'security' means any mortgage, charge or other security: Housing Act 1996 s 39(2).
19 Housing Act 1996 s 39(3) (amended by the Housing and Regeneration Act 2008 s 62(a)). Any such order must be made by statutory instrument subject to annulment in pursuance of a resolution of the National Assembly for Wales: Housing Act 1996 s 39(3) (amended by the Housing and Regeneration Act 2008 s 63).

207.   Initial notice to be given to the Welsh Ministers. Notice must be given to the Welsh Ministers[1] before any of the steps mentioned below is taken in relation to a registered social landlord[2]. Before taking any step to enforce any security[3] over land held by the landlord, notice must be given by the person proposing to take the step[4]. Where the registered social landlord is a registered society[5] or a company[6] (including a registered charity[7]), notice before presenting a petition for the winding up of the landlord must be given by the petitioner and notice before passing a resolution for winding up must be given by the landlord[8]. Additionally, where the registered social landlord is a company, notice before applying for an administration order must be given by the applicant[9].

Where the registered social landlord is a registered charity, other than a company, the person proposing to take any step to enforce any security over land held by the landlord must give such a notice[10].

Any step purportedly taken without the requisite notice being given is ineffective[11].

1 As to the Welsh Ministers see PARAS 7, 141.
2 Housing Act 1996 s 40(1) (amended by the Housing and Regeneration Act 2008 s 61(1), (7)). As to the meaning of 'registered social landlord' see PARA 13.
3 As to the meaning of 'security' see PARA 206 note 18.
4 See the Housing Act 1996 s 40(1)–(4) (s 40(1) as amended (see note 2); s 40(2) amended by the Co-operative and Community Benefit Societies Act 2014 s 151(1), Sch 4 paras 55, 56; the Housing Act 1996 s 40(3), (4) amended by SI 2009/1941).
5 As to the meaning of 'registered society' see PARA 168 note 1.
6 As to the meaning of 'company' see PARA 168 note 7.
7 As to the meaning of 'registered charity' see PARA 168 note 3.
8 See the Housing Act 1996 s 40(1)–(3) (s 40(1) as amended (see note 2); s 40(3) as amended (see note 4)). Notice need not, however, be given under s 40 in relation to a resolution for voluntary winding up where the consent of the Welsh Ministers is required (see s 7, Sch 1 paras 12(4), 13(6); and PARAS 181, 180): s 40(5) (amended by the Housing and Regeneration Act 2008 s 61(1), (7)).
9 Housing Act 1996 s 40(3) (as amended: see note 4). In relation to the reference in s 40(3) to applying for an administration order, in a case where an administrator is appointed under the Insolvency Act 1986 s 8, Sch B1 para 14 or 22 (appointment by floating charge holder, company or directors: see COMPANY AND PARTNERSHIP INSOLVENCY vol 16 (2011) PARAS 175 et seq, 183 et seq), the reference includes a reference to appointing an administrator under that provision, and in respect of an appointment under either of those provisions the reference to the applicant is to be taken as a reference to the person making the appointment: Housing Act 1996 s 40(7), (8) (s 40(7)–(9) added by the Enterprise Act 2002 s 248(3), Sch 17 paras 50, 51). In a case where a copy of a notice of intention to appoint an administrator under either the Insolvency Act 1986 Sch B1 para 14 or Sch B1 para 22 is filed with the court, the reference is to be taken to include a reference to the filing of the copy of the notice, and in respect of the filing of a copy of a notice of intention to appoint under either of those provisions the reference to the applicant is to be taken as a reference to the person giving the notice: Housing Act 1996 s 40(9) (as so added).
10 See the Housing Act 1996 s 40(4) (as amended: see note 4).
11 Housing Act 1996 s 40(6).

208. Further notice to be given to the Welsh Ministers. Notice must be given to the Welsh Ministers[1] as soon as may be after any of the steps mentioned below is taken in relation to a registered social landlord[2].

The person taking a step to enforce any security[3] over land held by the registered social landlord must give this notice where the registered social landlord is:

(1) a registered society[4]; or
(2) a company[5] (including a registered charity[6]); or
(3) a registered charity, other than a company[7].

Notice of the making of an order for the winding up of the registered social landlord must be given by the petitioner, and notice of the passing of a resolution for such winding up must be given by the registered social landlord where the registered social landlord is:

(a) a registered society; or
(b) a company (including a registered charity)[8].

Notice of the making of an administration order[9] must be given by the person who applied for the order where the registered social landlord is a company (including a registered charity)[10].

Failure to give such notice does not affect the validity of any step taken; but the statutory 28-day period after which a moratorium on the disposal of land ends[11] does not begin to run until any such requisite notice has been given[12]. In other words, no further steps can be taken until the requisite notice is given.

1 As to the Welsh Ministers see PARAS 7, 141.
2 Housing Act 1996 s 41(1) (amended by the Housing and Regeneration Act 2008 s 61(1), (7)). As to the meaning of 'registered social landlord' see PARA 13.
3 As to the meaning of 'security' see PARA 206 note 18.
4 As to the meaning of 'registered society' see PARA 168 note 1.
5 As to the meaning of 'company' see PARA 168 note 7.
6 As to the meaning of 'registered charity' see PARA 168 note 3.
7 See the Housing Act 1996 s 41(2)–(4) (s 41(2) amended by the Co-operative and Community Benefit Societies Act 2014 s 151(1), Sch 4 paras 55, 56; the Housing Act 1996 s 41(3), (4) amended by SI 2009/1941).
8 See the Housing Act 1996 s 41(2), (3) (as amended: see note 7).
9 The reference to the making of an administration order includes a reference to appointing an administrator under the Insolvency Act 1986 s 8, Sch B1 para 14 or 22 (administration: see COMPANY AND PARTNERSHIP INSOLVENCY vol 16 (2011) PARAS 175 et seq, 183 et seq), and in respect of an appointment under either of those provisions the reference to the applicant is to be taken as a reference to the person making the appointment: Housing Act 1996 s 41(6) (added by the Enterprise Act 2002 s 248(3), Sch 17 paras 50, 52).
10 See the Housing Act 1996 s 41(3) (as amended: see note 7).
11 Ie the period mentioned in the Housing Act 1996 s 43(1): see PARA 209.
12 Housing Act 1996 s 41(5).

209. Moratorium on the disposal of land. Where any of the specified steps[1] is taken in relation to a registered social landlord[2], there is a moratorium on the disposal[3] of land held by the landlord[4]. During the moratorium the consent of the Welsh Ministers[5] is required, subject to certain exceptions[6], for any disposal of land held by the landlord, whether by the landlord itself or any person having a power of disposal in relation to the land[7]. Consent may be given in advance and may be given subject to conditions[8]. A disposal made without the required consent is void[9]. These provisions apply in relation to any existing or future interest of the landlord in rent or other receipts arising from land as they apply to an interest in land[10]. Nothing in these provisions, however, prevents a liquidator from disclaiming any land held by the landlord as onerous property[11].

The moratorium begins when the step in question is taken and ends at the end of the period of 28 days beginning with the day on which notice of its having been taken was given[12] to the Welsh Ministers[13]. However, the taking of any further specified step at a time when a moratorium is already in force does not start a further moratorium or affect the duration of the existing one[14]. A moratorium may be extended from time to time with the consent of all the landlord's secured creditors[15], and notice of any such extension must be given by the Welsh Ministers to the landlord, and to any liquidator, administrative receiver, receiver or administrator appointed in respect of the landlord or any land held by it[16]. If during a moratorium the Welsh Ministers consider that the proper management of the landlord's land can be secured without making proposals as to its ownership and management[17], the Welsh Ministers may direct[18] that the moratorium is to cease to have effect[19].

When a moratorium comes to an end, or ceases to have effect after such a direction, the Welsh Ministers must give notice of that fact to the landlord and the landlord's secured creditors[20]; and when a moratorium comes to an end (but not when it so ceases to have effect), the following provisions apply[21]. If any further specified step is taken within the period of three years after the end of the original period of the moratorium, the moratorium may be renewed with the consent of all the landlord's secured creditors (which may be given before or after the step is taken)[22]; and if a moratorium ends without any proposals being agreed, then for a period of three years the taking of any further specified step does not start a further moratorium except with the consent of the landlord's secured creditors as previously mentioned[23].

1 Ie any of the steps mentioned in the Housing Act 1996 s 41: see PARA 208.
2 As to the meaning of 'registered social landlord' see PARA 13.
3 As to the meaning of 'disposal' see PARA 206 note 9.
4 Housing Act 1996 s 42(1).
5 As to the Welsh Ministers see PARAS 7, 141.
6 Consent is not required under these provisions for any such disposal as is mentioned in the Housing Act 1996 s 10(1), (2) or (3) (lettings and other disposals not requiring consent under s 9: see PARA 218): s 42(3).
7 Housing Act 1996 s 42(2) (amended by the Housing and Regeneration Act 2008 s 61(1), (7)).
8 Housing Act 1996 s 42(2). As to the consent required for the extension of the moratorium see the text and note 15.
9 Housing Act 1996 s 42(4).
10 Housing Act 1996 s 42(6).
11 Housing Act 1996 s 42(5).
12 Ie under the Housing Act 1996 s 41: see PARA 208.
13 See the Housing Act 1996 s 43(1) (amended by the Housing and Regeneration Act 2008 s 61(1), (7)).
14 Housing Act 1996 s 43(2).
15 Housing Act 1996 s 43(3). 'Secured creditor' means a creditor who holds a mortgage or charge (including a floating charge) over land held by the landlord or any existing or future interest of the landlord in rents or other receipts from land: s 39(2).
16 Housing Act 1996 s 43(3) (amended by the Housing and Regeneration Act 2008 s 61(1), (7)).
17 Ie proposals under the Housing Act 1996 s 44: see PARA 211.
18 Before making any such direction the Welsh Ministers must consult the person who took the step which brought about the moratorium: Housing Act 1996 s 43(4) (amended by the Housing and Regeneration Act 2008 s 61(1), (7)).
19 Housing Act 1996 s 43(4) (as amended: see note 18).
20 Housing Act 1996 s 43(5) (amended by the Housing and Regeneration Act 2008 s 61(1), (7)).
21 Housing Act 1996 s 43(6). In such a case the Welsh Ministers' notice must inform the landlord and the landlord's secured creditors of the effect of those provisions: s 43(6) (amended by the Housing and Regeneration Act 2008 s 61(1), (7)).
22 Housing Act 1996 s 43(7). Notice of any such renewal must be given by the Welsh Ministers to the persons to whom notice of an extension is required to be given under s 43(3): s 43(7) (amended by the Housing and Regeneration Act 2008 s 61(1), (7)).
23 Housing Act 1996 s 43(8).

210. Appointment of interim manager. During a moratorium[1] the Welsh Ministers[2] may appoint an interim manager of the registered social landlord[3]. An appointment may relate to the registered social landlord's affairs generally or to affairs specified in the appointment[4]. An appointment may not, however, relate to affairs relating only to the provision of housing in England[5]. Appointment is to be on terms and conditions (including as to remuneration and expenses) specified in, or determined in accordance with, the appointment[6]. An interim manager has any power specified in the appointment, and any other power in relation to the registered social landlord's affairs required by the manager for the purposes specified in the appointment (including the power to enter into agreements and take other action on behalf of the landlord)[7]. But an interim manager may not dispose of land, or grant security over land[8].

The Welsh Ministers may give the interim manager general or specific directions[9]. The Welsh Ministers may revoke or amend any directions given[10]. An appointment under this provision comes to an end with the earliest of: (1) the end of the moratorium; (2) the agreement of proposals as to ownership and management of the landlord's land[11]; or (3) a date specified in the appointment[12]. If a person ceases to be an interim manager before the appointment has come to an end, the Welsh Ministers may appoint a new interim manager in place of that person[13].

1 Ie a moratorium on the disposal of land see the Housing Act 1996 ss 42, 43; and PARA 209.
2 As to the Welsh Ministers see PARAS 7, 141.
3 Housing Act 1996 s 43A(1) (s 43A added, in relation to Wales, by the Housing (Wales) Measure 2011 s 83). As to the meaning of 'registered social landlord' see PARA 13.
4 Housing Act 1996 s 43A(2) (as added: see note 3).
5 Housing Act 1996 s 43A(3) (as added: see note 3).
6 Housing Act 1996 s 43A(4) (as added: see note 3).
7 Housing Act 1996 s 43A(5) (as added: see note 3).
8 Housing Act 1996 s 43A(6) (as added: see note 3).
9 Housing Act 1996 s 43A(7) (as added: see note 3).
10 Housing Act 1996 s 43A(8) (as added: see note 3).
11 Ie proposals made under the Housing Act 1996 s 44: see PARA 211.
12 Housing Act 1996 s 43A(9) (as added: see note 3).
13 Housing Act 1996 s 43A(10) (as added: see note 3).

211. Proposals as to ownership and management of landlord's land. During the period of the moratorium[1] the Welsh Ministers[2] may make proposals as to the future ownership and management of the land held by the registered social landlord[3], designed to secure the continued proper management of the landlord's land by a registered social landlord[4]. In drawing up their proposals the Welsh Ministers must consult the landlord and, so far as is practicable, the tenants concerned[5]. The Welsh Ministers must have regard to the interests of all the landlord's creditors, whether they are secured or unsecured[6]. Where the landlord is a registered society[7], the Welsh Ministers must also consult the Financial Conduct Authority[8]; and where the landlord is a registered charity[9], the Welsh Ministers must also consult the Charity Commission[10].

No proposals may be made under which:
(1)   a preferential debt[11] of the landlord is to be paid otherwise than in priority to debts which are not preferential debts[12];
(2)   an ordinary preferential debt[13] of the landlord is to be paid otherwise than in priority to any secondary preferential debts[14] that the landlord may have[15];
(3)   a preferential creditor[16] is to be paid a smaller proportion of an ordinary preferential debt than another preferential creditor, except with the concurrence of the creditor concerned[17]; or
(4)   a preferential creditor is to be paid a smaller proportion of a secondary preferential debt than another preferential creditor, except with the concurrence of the creditor concerned[18],
and so far as practicable no proposals may be made which have the effect that unsecured creditors of the landlord are in a worse position than they would otherwise be[19].

Where the landlord is a charity[20] the proposals must not require the landlord to act outside the terms of its trusts, and any disposal[21] of housing accommodation[22] occupied under a tenancy[23] or licence from the landlord must be to another charity whose objects appear to the Welsh Ministers to be, as nearly as practicable, akin to those of the landlord[24].

The Welsh Ministers must serve a copy of their proposals on:
(a)   the landlord and its officers[25];

(b) the secured creditors[26] of the landlord; and

(c) any liquidator, administrator, administrative receiver or receiver appointed in respect of the landlord or its land,

and they must make such arrangements as they consider appropriate to see that the members, tenants and unsecured creditors of the landlord are informed of the proposals[27].

If the Welsh Ministers' proposals are agreed, with or without modifications, by all the secured creditors of the registered social landlord, then once agreed they are binding on the Welsh Ministers, the landlord, all the landlord's creditors (whether secured or unsecured) and any liquidator, administrator, administrative receiver or receiver appointed in respect of the landlord or its land[28].

It is the duty of:

(i) the members of the committee where the landlord is a registered society;

(ii) the directors where the landlord is a company[29] (including a company that is a registered charity); and

(iii) the trustees where the landlord is a charitable trust,

to co-operate in the implementation of the proposals; but this does not mean that they have to do anything contrary to any fiduciary or other duty owed by them[30].

The Welsh Ministers must serve a copy of the agreed proposals on:

(A) the landlord and its officers;

(B) the secured creditors of the landlord; and

(C) any liquidator, administrator, administrative receiver or receiver appointed in respect of the landlord or its land; and

(D) where the landlord is a registered society or registered charity, the Financial Conduct Authority or the Charity Commission, as the case may be,

and they must make such arrangements as they consider appropriate to see that the members, tenants and unsecured creditors of the landlord are informed of the proposals[31].

The proposals may subsequently be amended with the consent of the Welsh Ministers and all the landlord's secured creditors[32].

1 As to the moratorium see the Housing Act 1996 ss 42, 43; and PARA 209.

2 As to the Welsh Ministers see PARAS 7, 141.

3 As to the meaning of 'registered social landlord' see PARA 13.

4 Housing Act 1996 s 44(1) (amended by the Housing and Regeneration Act 2008 s 61(1), (7)).

5 See the Housing Act 1996 s 44(2) (amended by the Housing and Regeneration Act 2008 s 61(1), (7)). As to the meaning of 'tenant' see PARA 168 note 16.

6 See the Housing Act 1996 s 44(2) (as amended: see note 5).

7 As to the meaning of 'registered society' see PARA 168 note 1. As to registered societies see FINANCIAL INSTITUTIONS vol 48 (2015) PARA 880 et seq.

8 As to the Financial Conduct Authority see FINANCIAL SERVICES REGULATION vol 50 (2016) PARAS 5, 6 et seq.

9 As to the meaning of 'registered charity' see PARA 168 note 3.

10 Housing Act 1996 s 44(3) (amended by the Charities Act 2006 s 75(1), Sch 8 paras 183, 187; the Housing and Regeneration Act 2008 s 61(1), (7); and the Co-operative and Community Benefit Societies Act 2014 s 151(1), Sch 4 paras 55, 56). As to the Charity Commission see CHARITIES vol 8 (2015) PARA 543 et seq.

11 For these purposes, references to preferential debts have the same meaning as in the Insolvency Act 1986 (see BANKRUPTCY AND INDIVIDUAL INSOLVENCY vol 5 (2013) PARA 591; COMPANY AND PARTNERSHIP INSOLVENCY vol 17 (2011) PARA 721): Housing Act 1996 s 44(4).

12 Housing Act 1996 s 44(4)(a) (amended by SI 2014/3486).

13 For these purposes, references to ordinary preferential debts have the same meaning as in the Insolvency Act 1986 (see BANKRUPTCY AND INDIVIDUAL INSOLVENCY vol 5 (2013) PARA 591; COMPANY AND PARTNERSHIP INSOLVENCY vol 17 (2011) PARA 721): Housing Act 1996 s 44(4) (amended by SI 2014/3486).

14 For these purposes, references to secondary preferential debts have the same meaning as in the Insolvency Act 1986 (see BANKRUPTCY AND INDIVIDUAL INSOLVENCY vol 5 (2013) PARA 591; COMPANY AND PARTNERSHIP INSOLVENCY vol 17 (2011) PARA 721): Housing Act 1996 s 44(4) (amended by SI 2014/3486).

15 Housing Act 1996 s 44(4)(aa) (added by SI 2014/3486).

16 For these purposes, references to preferential creditors have the same meaning as in the Insolvency Act 1986 (see BANKRUPTCY AND INDIVIDUAL INSOLVENCY vol 5 (2013) PARA 591; COMPANY AND PARTNERSHIP INSOLVENCY vol 17 (2011) PARA 721): Housing Act 1996 s 44(4).

17 Housing Act 1996 s 44(4)(b) (amended by SI 2014/3486).

18 Housing Act 1996 s 44(4)(c) (added by SI 2014/3486).

19 Housing Act 1996 s 44(5).

20 As to the meaning of 'charity' see PARA 168 note 3.

21 As to the meaning of 'disposal' see PARA 206 note 9.

22 As to the meaning of 'housing accommodation' see PARA 164 note 2.

23 As to the meaning of 'tenancy' see PARA 168 note 16.

24 Housing Act 1996 s 44(6) (amended by the Housing and Regeneration Act 2008 s 61(1), (7)).

25 As to the meaning of 'officer' see PARA 174 note 9.

26 As to the meaning of 'secured creditor' see PARA 209 note 15.

27 Housing Act 1996 s 44(7) (amended by the Housing and Regeneration Act 2008 s 61(1), (7)).

28 Housing Act 1996 s 45(1), (2) (amended by the Housing and Regeneration Act 2008 s 61(1), (7)).

29 As to the meaning of 'company' see PARA 168 note 7.

30 Housing Act 1996 s 45(3) (amended by the Co-operative and Community Benefit Societies Act 2014 Sch 4 paras 55, 56; and by SI 2009/1941).

31 Housing Act 1996 s 45(4) (amended by the Charities Act 2006 Sch 8 para 188; the Housing and Regeneration Act 2008 s 61(1), (7); the Co-operative and Community Benefit Societies Act 2014 Sch 4 paras 55, 56; and SI 2013/496).

32 Housing Act 1996 s 45(5) (amended by the Housing and Regeneration Act 2008 s 61(1), (7)). The Housing Act 1996 s 44(2)–(7) and s 45(2)–(4) apply in relation to the amended proposals as in relation to the original proposals: s 45(5).

212. Manager to implement agreed proposals; appointment and powers. Where proposals have been agreed[1] they may provide that the Welsh Ministers[2] may by order appoint a manager to implement the proposals or such of them as are specified in the order[3]. If the landlord is a registered charity[4], the Welsh Ministers must give notice of the appointment to the Charity Commission[5]. Where proposals make provision for the appointment of a manager, they must also provide for the payment of his reasonable remuneration and expenses[6].

The Welsh Ministers may give the manager directions in relation to the carrying out of his functions[7] and may amend or revoke any directions given by them[8]. The manager may apply to the High Court for directions in relation to any particular matter arising in connection with the carrying out of his functions and such a direction supersedes any direction of the Welsh Ministers in respect of the same matter[9].

If a vacancy occurs by death, resignation or otherwise in the office of manager, the Welsh Ministers may by further order fill the vacancy[10].

An order appointing a manager to implement agreed proposals must confer on the manager power generally to do all such things as are necessary for carrying out his functions[11] and it may include the following specific powers[12]:

(1)   power to take possession of the land held by the landlord and for that purpose to take any legal proceedings which seem to him expedient;

(2)   power to sell or otherwise dispose[13] of the land by public auction or private contract;

(3)   power to raise or borrow money and for that purpose to grant security[14] over the land;

(4)   power to appoint a solicitor or accountant or other professionally qualified person to assist him in the performance of his functions;

(5) power to bring or defend legal proceedings relating to the land in the name and on behalf of the landlord;

(6) power to refer to arbitration any question affecting the land;

(7) power to effect and maintain insurance in respect of the land;

(8) power where the landlord is a body corporate to use the seal of the body corporate for purposes relating to the land;

(9) power to do all acts and to execute in the name and on behalf of the landlord any deed, receipt or other document relating to the land;

(10) power to appoint an agent to do anything which he is unable to do for himself or which can more conveniently be done by an agent, and power to employ and dismiss any employees;

(11) power to do all such things (including the carrying out of works) as may be necessary in connection with the management or transfer of the land;

(12) power to make any payment which is necessary or incidental to the performance of his functions;

(13) power to carry on the business of the landlord so far as relating to the management or transfer of the land;

(14) power to grant or accept a surrender of a lease or tenancy[15] of any of the land, and to take a lease or tenancy of any property required or convenient for the landlord's housing activities[16];

(15) power to make any arrangement or compromise on behalf of the landlord in relation to the management or transfer of the land;

(16) power to do all other things incidental to the exercise of any of the above powers[17].

In carrying out his functions the manager acts as the landlord's agent and he is not personally liable on a contract which he enters into as manager[18]. So far as practicable he must consult the landlord's tenants about any exercise of his powers which is likely to affect them and inform them about any such exercise of his powers[19]. A person dealing with the manager in good faith and for value is not, however, to be concerned to inquire whether the manager is acting within his powers[20].

Where the landlord is a registered society[21], an order appointing a manager to implement agreed proposals may give the manager power to make and execute on behalf of the society an instrument transferring the engagements of the society[22]. A copy of the instrument, signed by the manager, must be sent to the Financial Conduct Authority[23] and registered by it; and until that copy is so registered the instrument does not take effect[24]. It is the manager's duty to send a copy for registration within 14 days from the day on which the instrument is executed; but this does not invalidate registration after that time[25].

1 Ie agreed as mentioned in the Housing Act 1996 s 45: see PARA 211.

2 As to the Welsh Ministers see PARAS 7, 141.

3 Housing Act 1996 s 46(1) (amended by the Government of Wales Act 1998 ss 140, 152, Sch 16 para 88(1), (2), Sch 18 Pt VI; and the Housing and Regeneration Act 2008 s 61(1), (7)). An order made by the Welsh Ministers under the Housing Act 1996 s 46 must be made in writing: s 46(7) (added by the Government of Wales Act 1998 Sch 16 para 88(3); and amended by the Housing and Regeneration Act 2008 s 62(a); and by SI 2010/866).

4 As to the meaning of 'registered charity' see PARA 168 note 3.

5 Housing Act 1996 s 46(2) (amended by the Charities Act 2006 s 75(1), Sch 8 paras 183, 189; and the Housing and Regeneration Act 2008 s 61(7)). As to the Charity Commission see CHARITIES vol 8 (2015) PARA 543 et seq.

6 Housing Act 1996 s 46(3).

7 Housing Act 1996 s 46(4) (amended by the Housing and Regeneration Act 2008 s 61(1), (7)).

8 Housing Act 1996 s 46(4A) (added, in relation to Wales, by the Housing (Wales) Measure 2011 s 88, Schedule paras 1, 10).

9 See the Housing Act 1996 s 46(5) (amended by the Housing and Regeneration Act 2008 s 61(1), (7)).
10 Housing Act 1996 s 46(6) (amended by the Government of Wales Act 1998 Sch 16 para 88(2), Sch 18 Pt VI; and the Housing and Regeneration Act 2008 s 61(1), (7)). As to requirements for the making of orders see note 3.
11 Housing Act 1996 s 47(1).
12 Housing Act 1996 s 47(2).
13 As to the meaning of 'disposal' see PARA 206 note 9.
14 As to the meaning of 'security' see PARA 206 note 18.
15 As to the meaning of 'tenancy' see PARA 168 note 16.
16 As to the meaning of 'housing activities' see PARA 168 note 25.
17 Housing Act 1996 s 47(2).
18 Housing Act 1996 s 47(3).
19 Housing Act 1996 s 47(5).
20 Housing Act 1996 s 47(4).
21 As to the meaning of 'registered society' see PARA 168 note 1.
22 Housing Act 1996 s 48(1) (amended by the Co-operative and Community Benefit Societies Act 2014 s 151(1), Sch 4 paras 55, 56). Any such instrument has the same effect as a transfer of engagements under the Co-operative and Community Benefit Societies Act 2014 s 110 or s 112 (transfer of engagements by special resolution to another society or a company); and in particular it does not prejudice any right of a creditor of the society: Housing Act 1996 s 48(2) (amended by the Co-operative and Community Benefit Societies Act 2014 Sch 4 paras 55, 59). See further FINANCIAL INSTITUTIONS vol 48 (2015) PARAS 1052–1057.
23 As to the Financial Conduct Authority see FINANCIAL SERVICES REGULATION vol 50 (2016) PARAS 5, 6 et seq.
24 Housing Act 1996 s 48(3) (amended by SI 2001/3649 and SI 2013/496).
25 Housing Act 1996 s 48(4).

213. Assistance by the Welsh Ministers to facilitate agreed proposals. The Welsh Ministers[1] may give such assistance as they think fit:

(1)   to the landlord, for the purpose of preserving the position pending the making of and agreement to proposals[2];

(2)   to the landlord or a manager appointed[3] to implement agreed proposals, for the purpose of carrying out any agreed proposals[4].

The Welsh Ministers may, in particular, lend staff, pay or secure payment of the manager's reasonable remuneration and expenses, and give such financial assistance as appears to the Welsh Ministers to be appropriate[5].

1 As to the Welsh Ministers see PARAS 7, 141.
2 As to making and agreeing proposals see PARA 211.
3 Ie under the Housing Act 1996 s 46: see PARA 212.
4 Housing Act 1996 s 49(1) (amended by the Housing and Regeneration Act 2008 s 61(1), (7)).
5 Housing Act 1996 s 49(2) (amended by the Housing and Regeneration Act 2008 s 61(1), (7)).

214. Application to the court to secure compliance with agreed proposals. The landlord or any creditor of the landlord may apply to the High Court on the ground that an action of the manager appointed to implement agreed proposals[1] is not in accordance with those proposals[2]. On such an application the court may confirm, reverse or modify any act or decision of the manager, give him directions or make such other order as it thinks fit[3].

Similarly, the Welsh Ministers[4] or any other person bound by agreed proposals may apply to the High Court on the ground that any action, or proposed action, by another person bound by the proposals is not in accordance with those proposals[5]. On such an application the court may declare any such action to be ineffective and grant such relief by way of injunction, damages or otherwise as appears to the court to be appropriate[6].

1 Ie the manager appointed under the Housing Act 1996 s 46: see PARA 212.
2 Housing Act 1996 s 50(1).
3 Housing Act 1996 s 50(1).

4   As to the Welsh Ministers see PARAS 7, 141.
5   Housing Act 1996 s 50(2) (amended by the Housing and Regeneration Act 2008 s 61(1), (7)).
6   See the Housing Act 1996 s 50(2)(a), (b).

J.   DISPOSAL OF LAND AND RELATED MATTERS

(A)   *In general*

215.   Introduction. A registered social landlord[1] only has power to dispose of dwellings in accordance with provisions contained in Part I of the Housing Act 1996[2]. In particular, the Welsh Ministers[3] must usually consent to a disposal, and a disposal made without such consent is void[4]. Some types of disposal, however, do not require consent. These include a sale where a tenant exercises the right to buy or the right to acquire a dwelling[5] and a grant of certain tenancies such as assured tenancies[6]. In giving consent to a disposal, the Welsh Ministers may issue general consents as well as considering an application for consent in an individual case[7].

1   As to the register of social landlords see PARA 167.
2   See the Housing Act 1996 s 8; and PARA 216.
3   As to the Welsh Ministers see PARAS 7, 141.
4   See PARA 217.
5   As to the right to acquire a dwelling see PARA 226.
6   See PARA 218.
7   See PARA 217.

216.   Power of a registered social landlord to dispose of land. Subject to the statutory requirement of the Welsh Ministers' consent[1], a registered social landlord[2] has power[3] to dispose, in such manner as it thinks fit, of land held by it[4].

A registered social landlord must show separately in its accounts its net disposal proceeds in the form of a disposal proceeds fund[5]. The sums standing in its disposal proceeds account may only be applied or appropriated by it for such purposes and in such manner as the Welsh Ministers may determine[6]. If any disposal proceeds are not so applied or appropriated within such time as is specified by determination of the Welsh Ministers, the Welsh Ministers may direct that the whole or part of the disposal proceeds must be paid to them[7].

The Welsh Ministers also have power to require registered social landlords to furnish them with information in connection with the treatment of disposal proceeds[8].

1   Ie subject to the Housing Act 1996 s 9: see PARA 217. As to the Welsh Ministers see PARAS 7, 141.
2   As to the register of social landlords see PARA 167.
3   Ie by virtue of the Housing Act 1996 s 8 and not otherwise.
4   Housing Act 1996 s 8(1), (3) (s 8(3) amended by the Housing and Regeneration Act 2008 s 61(1), (7)). The Settled Land Act 1925 s 39 (disposal of land by trustees: see SETTLEMENTS vol 91 (2012) PARAS 729–731) does not apply to the disposal of land by a registered social landlord; and accordingly the disposal need not be for the best consideration in money that can reasonably be obtained: Housing Act 1996 s 8(2). Nothing in s 8(2) is to be taken to authorise any action on the part of a charity which would conflict with the trusts of the charity: s 8(2).
5   See the Housing Act 1996 s 24(1), (4). 'Net disposal proceeds' means: (1) the net proceeds of sale (ie the proceeds of sale less an amount calculated in accordance with a determination by the Welsh Ministers) received in respect of any disposal to a tenant in pursuance of his right to buy under s 16 or under the Housing and Regeneration Act 2008 s 180, or in respect of which a grant was made under the Housing Act 1996 s 21 (see PARA 244), or in respect of which a grant was made under the Housing and Regeneration Act 2008 s 19 (see PLANNING vol 83 (2010) PARA 1474) in respect of discounts given by it on the disposal to the tenant; (2) payments of grant received by the registered social landlord under the Housing Act 1996 s 20 or s 21 (see PARA 244); (3) payments of grant received by it under the Housing and Regeneration Act 2008 s 19 in respect of discounts given by it on disposals of dwellings to tenants; (4) any repayments of discount in respect of which the grant was given; and (5) such other proceeds of sale or grant (if any) as the Welsh Ministers

may determine: Housing Act 1996 s 24(2), (3) (amended by the Housing and Regeneration Act 2008 s 61(1), (7); and by SI 2010/866). The method of constituting the fund and showing it in the landlord's accounts, and the interest to be added, are as determined by the Welsh Ministers: Housing Act 1996 s 24(5), (6) (amended by the Housing and Regeneration Act 2008 s 61(1), (7)). Where the Housing Act 1996 s 24 applies, s 27 (recovery of social housing grants: see PARA 166) and the Housing Act 1988 s 52 (recovery of grants: see PARA 21) do not apply: Housing Act 1996 s 24(7).

6   Housing Act 1996 s 25(1) (s 25 amended by the Housing and Regeneration Act 2008 s 61(1), (7)).
7   Housing Act 1996 s 25(2) (as amended: see note 6).
8   Housing Act 1996 s 26(1) (amended by the Housing and Regeneration Act 2008 s 61(1), (7)). Such a notice may be given by publication in such manner as the Welsh Ministers consider appropriate for bringing it to the attention of the landlords concerned: Housing Act 1996 s 26(2) (as so amended).

217. Consent required for disposal of land by a registered social landlord. The consent of the Welsh Ministers[1] is required for any disposal[2] of land by a registered social landlord[3]. The consent of the Welsh Ministers may be so given:

(1)   generally to all registered social landlords or to a particular landlord or description of landlords;

(2)   in relation to particular land or in relation to a particular description of land,

and may be given subject to conditions[4]. Before giving any consent other than a consent in relation to a particular landlord or particular land, the Welsh Ministers must consult such bodies representative of registered social landlords as they think fit[5].

A disposal of a house[6] by a registered social landlord made without the required consent is void unless:

(a)   the disposal is to an individual (or to two or more individuals);

(b)   the disposal does not extend to any other house; and

(c)   the landlord reasonably believes that the individual or individuals intend to use the house as their principal dwelling[7].

Any other disposal by a registered social landlord which requires consent[8] is valid in favour of a person claiming under the landlord notwithstanding that that consent has not been given; and a person dealing with a registered social landlord, or with a person claiming under such a landlord, is not concerned to see or inquire whether any such consent has been given[9].

Where at the time of its removal from the register of social landlords[10] a body owns land, the above provisions continue to apply to that land after the removal as if the body concerned continued to be a registered social landlord[11].

1   As to the Welsh Ministers see PARAS 7, 141.
2   For the purposes of the Housing Act 1996 s 9, 'disposal' means sale, lease, mortgage, charge or any other disposition: s 9(7). As to the meaning of 'lease' see PARA 168 note 16.
3   Ie under the Housing Act 1996 s 8 (see PARA 216): s 9(1) (amended by the Government of Wales Act 1998 ss 140, 152, Sch 16 para 84(1), (2), Sch 18 Pt VI; and the Housing and Regeneration Act 2008 s 61(1), (7)). Consent given by the Welsh Ministers under the Housing Act 1996 s 9 must be given by order in writing: Housing Act 1996 s 9(1A) (added by the Government of Wales Act 1998 Sch 16 para 84(3); and amended by the Housing and Regeneration Act 2008 s 62(a); and by SI 2010/866). As to lettings and other disposals not requiring the consent of the Welsh Ministers see PARA 218.
4   Housing Act 1996 s 9(2) (amended by the Housing and Regeneration Act 2008 s 61(1), (7)).
5   Housing Act 1996 s 9(3) (amended by the Housing and Regeneration Act 2008 s 61(1), (7)).
6   As to the meaning of 'house' see PARA 168 note 11.
7   Housing Act 1996 s 9(4). 'Dwelling' means a building or part of a building occupied or intended to be occupied as a separate dwelling, together with any yard, garden, outhouses and appurtenances belonging to it or usually enjoyed with it: s 63(1).
8   Ie under the Housing Act 1996 s 9.
9   Housing Act 1996 s 9(5).
10 As to removal from the register see PARA 170.

11 Housing Act 1996 s 9(6). Section 9 has effect subject to s 10 (lettings and other disposals not requiring consent of the Welsh Ministers: see PARA 218): s 9(8) (amended by the Housing and Regeneration Act 2008 s 61(1), (7)).

218. Lettings and other disposals not requiring consent of the Welsh Ministers. A letting by a registered social landlord[1] does not require consent[2] if it is:

(1)   a letting of land under an assured tenancy[3], or an assured agricultural occupancy[4], or what would, except for certain statutory exclusions of business and other tenancies[5], be an assured tenancy or an assured agricultural occupancy; or

(2)   a letting of land under a secure tenancy[6] or what would, except for certain statutory exclusions[7], be a secure tenancy[8].

Certain other disposals, such as a sale under the right to buy[9] or the right to acquire[10], do not require the consent of the Welsh Ministers[11].

1   As to the register of social landlords see PARA 167.
2   Ie under the Housing Act 1996 s 9: see PARA 217.
3   As to the meaning of 'assured tenancy' see LANDLORD AND TENANT vol 63 (2016) PARA 825 (definition applied by the Housing Act 1996 s 230).
4   As to the meaning of 'assured agricultural occupancy' see LANDLORD AND TENANT vol 64 (2016) PARA 1747 (definition applied by the Housing Act 1996 s 230).
5   Ie but for any of the provisions in the Housing Act 1988 s 1(3), Sch 1 paras 4–8 (see LANDLORD AND TENANT vol 63 (2016) PARAS 836–840) or Sch 1 para 12(1)(h) (tenancy under which the interest of the landlord belongs to a fully mutual housing association (see LANDLORD AND TENANT vol 63 (2016) PARA 847)) or Sch 1 paras 12ZA–12ZB (see LANDLORD AND TENANT vol 63 (2016) PARA 848 et seq).
6   As to the meaning of 'secure tenancy' see LANDLORD AND TENANT vol 63 (2016) PARA 1037 (definition applied by the Housing Act 1996 s 230).
7   Ie but for any of the provisions in the Housing Act 1985 s 79, Sch 1 paras 2–12: see LANDLORD AND TENANT vol 63 (2016) PARA 1046 et seq.
8   Housing Act 1996 s 10(1) (amended by SI 2010/866).
9   Consent under the Housing Act 1996 s 9 is not required for a disposal under the Housing Act 1985 Pt V (ss 118–188) (the right to buy: see PARA 239 et seq): Housing Act 1996 s 10(3). Most tenants of registered social landlords do not, however, have this right: see PARA 226.
10 Consent under the Housing Act 1996 s 9 is not required for a disposal under the right conferred by the Housing Act 1996 s 16 (the right to acquire: see PARA 226): s 10(3).
11 Consent under the Housing Act 1996 s 9 is not required in the case of a disposal to which the Housing Act 1988 s 81 or s 133 applies (certain disposals for which the consent of the appropriate national authority is required: see PARAS 532, 556): Housing Act 1996 s 10(2). As to the Welsh Ministers see PARAS 7, 141.

219. Covenant for repayment of discount on disposal. Where on a disposal of a house[1] by a registered social landlord[2], in accordance with a consent given by the Welsh Ministers[3], a discount has been given to the purchaser, and the consent does not provide otherwise, the conveyance, grant or assignment must contain a covenant binding on the purchaser and his successors in title to the following effect[4]. The covenant must be to pay to the landlord such sum (if any) as the landlord may demand[5] on the occasion of the first relevant disposal which is not an exempted disposal[6] and which takes place within the period of five years beginning with the conveyance, grant or assignment[7]. The landlord may demand such sum as he considers appropriate, up to and including the maximum amount statutorily specified[8].

The maximum amount which may be demanded by the landlord is a percentage of the price or premium paid for the first relevant disposal which is equal to the percentage discount given to the purchaser in respect of the disposal of the house by the landlord[9]; but for each complete year which has elapsed after the conveyance, grant or assignment and before the first relevant disposal, the maximum amount which may be demanded by the landlord is reduced by one-fifth[10]. In calculating the maximum amount which may be demanded by the landlord, such amount (if any) of the price or premium paid for the first relevant disposal which is attributable to improvements made to the house by the person by whom the disposal is, or is to be, made, and after the conveyance, grant or assignment and before the disposal, is to be disregarded[11]. The amount to be disregarded is to be such amount as may be agreed between the parties or determined by the district valuer[12]. If the district valuer does not make a determination for this purpose (and in default of an agreement), no amount is required to be disregarded[13].

The liability that may arise under the covenant is a charge on the house, taking effect as if it had been created by deed expressed to be by way of legal mortgage[14]. Where there is a relevant disposal which is an exempted disposal[15]:

(1) the covenant required by virtue of these provisions is not binding on the person to whom the disposal is made or any successor in title of his; and

(2) the covenant and the charge taking effect by virtue of these provisions cease to apply in relation to the property disposed of[16].

1 As to the meaning of 'house' see PARA 168 note 11.
2 As to the register of social landlords see PARA 167.
3 Ie under the Housing Act 1996 s 9: see PARA 217. As to the Welsh Ministers see PARAS 7, 141.
4 Housing Act 1996 s 11(1) (s 11 substituted by the Housing Act 2004 s 199(1); the Housing Act 1996 s 11(1) amended by the Housing and Regeneration Act 2008 s 61(1), (7)).
5 In accordance with the Housing Act 1996 s 11(3).
6 As to the meaning of 'relevant disposal which is not an exempted disposal' see PARA 224.
7 Housing Act 1996 s 11(2) (as substituted: see note 4).
8 Housing Act 1996 s 11(3) (as substituted: see note 4). Section 11(3)–(5) is subject to s 11A (see the text to notes 11–13): s 11(6) (as so substituted).
9 Housing Act 1996 s 11(4) (as substituted: see note 4).
10 Housing Act 1996 s 11(5) (as substituted: see note 4).
11 Housing Act 1996 s 11A(1) (ss 11A, 11B added by the Housing Act 2004 s 199(1)).
12 Housing Act 1996 s 11A(2) (as added: see note 11). The district valuer is not required by virtue of s 11A to make a determination for the purposes of s 11A unless it is reasonably practicable for him to do so and his reasonable costs in making the determination are paid by the person by whom the disposal is, or is to be, made: s 11A(3) (as so added).
13 Housing Act 1996 s 11A(4) (as added: see note 11).
14 Housing Act 1996 s 11B(1) (as added: see note 11).
15 Ie by virtue of the Housing Act 1996 s 15(4)(d) or (e) (compulsory disposal or disposal of yard, garden etc): see PARA 224.
16 Housing Act 1996 s 11B(2) (as added: see note 11).

220. Treatment of deferred resale agreements for purposes of covenant for repayment of discount on disposal. If a purchaser or his successor in title enters into an agreement[1] as specified below[2], any liability arising under the covenant[3] for repayment of discount on a disposal of a house[4] by a registered social landlord[5] must be determined as if a relevant disposal which is not an exempted disposal[6] had occurred at the appropriate time[7]. An agreement is within these provisions if it is an agreement between the purchaser or his successor in title and any other person:

(1) which is made (expressly or impliedly) in contemplation of, or in connection with, a disposal to be made, or made, by a registered social landlord under its power to dispose of land[8];

(2) which is made before the end of the discount repayment period[9]; and

(3) under which a relevant disposal which is not an exempted disposal is or may be required to be made to any person after the end of that period[10].

Such an agreement is within these provisions whether or not the date on which the relevant disposal is to take place is specified in the agreement, and whether or not any requirement to make that disposal is or may be made subject to the fulfilment of any condition[11].

1 'Agreement' includes arrangement: Housing Act 1996 s 15A(7) (s 15A added by the Housing Act 2004 s 201(1)).
2 Ie an agreement within the Housing Act 1996 s 15A(3): see the text and notes 8–10.
3 Ie the covenant required by the Housing Act 1996 s 11: see PARA 219.
4 As to the meaning of 'house' see PARA 168 note 11.
5 As to the register of social landlords see PARA 167.
6 As to the meaning of 'relevant disposal which is not an exempted disposal' see PARA 224.
7 Housing Act 1996 s 15A(1) (as added: see note 1). 'The appropriate time' means: (1) the time when the agreement is entered into; or (2) if it was made before the beginning of the discount repayment period, immediately after the beginning of that period: s 15A(2) (as so added).
8 Ie by virtue of the Housing Act 1996 s 8: see PARA 216.
9 'The discount repayment period' means the period of three or five years that applies for the purposes of the Housing Act 1996 s 11(2) (see PARA 219), depending on whether an offer such as is mentioned in the Housing Act 2004 s 199(3) was made before or on or after the coming into force of that provision (ie 18 January 2005): Housing Act 1996 s 15A(7) (as added: see note 1). The Housing Act 2004 s 199(3) provides that the amendments made by s 199 do not apply in any case where: (1) the purchaser has accepted an offer for the disposal of the house from the landlord; or (2) the landlord has accepted an offer for the disposal of the house from the purchaser, before the day on which s 199 came into force, ie 18 January 2005.
10 Housing Act 1996 s 15A(3) (as added: see note 1). The Welsh Ministers may by order provide for s 15A(1) to apply to agreements of any description specified in the order in addition to those within s 15A(3), or for s 15A(1) not to apply to agreements of any description so specified to which it would otherwise apply: s 15A(5) (as so added; amended by the Housing and Regeneration Act 2008 s 62(a)). Such an order may make different provision with respect to different cases or descriptions of case and must be made by statutory instrument which is subject to annulment in pursuance of a resolution of the National Assembly for Wales: Housing Act 1996 s 15A(6) (as so added; amended by the Housing and Regeneration Act 2008 s 63). As to the Welsh Ministers see PARAS 7, 141.
11 Housing Act 1996 s 15A(4) (as added: see note 1).

221. Priority of charge for repayment of discount. The charge for repayment of a discount[1] has priority immediately after any legal charge securing an amount:

(1) left outstanding by the purchaser; or

(2) advanced to him by an approved lending institution[2] for the purpose of enabling him to acquire the interest disposed of on the first disposal,

subject to the following provisions[3].

An advance which is made for a purpose other than that mentioned in head (2) and which is secured by a legal charge having priority to the charge for repayment of a discount[4], and any further advance which is so secured, will rank in priority to that charge if, and only if, the registered social landlord[5] by notice[6] served on the institution concerned gives consent[7]. The landlord must give consent if the purpose of the advance or further advance is an approved purpose[8].

The following are 'approved purposes':

(a) to enable the purchaser to defray, or to defray on his behalf, any of the following:

(i) the cost of any works to the house[9];

(ii) any service charge[10] payable in respect of the house for works, whether or not to the house; and

(iii) any service charge or other amount payable in respect of the house for insurance, whether or not of the house[11]; and

(b) to enable the purchaser to discharge, or to discharge on his behalf, any of the following:

(i) so much as is still outstanding of any advance or further advance which ranks in priority to the charge for repayment of a discount[12];

    (ii)   any arrears of interest on such an advance or further advance; and

    (iii)   any costs and expenses incurred in enforcing payment of any such interest, or repayment (in whole or in part) of any such advance or further advance[13].

The registered social landlord may at any time by notice served on an approved lending institution postpone the charge for repayment of a discount to an advance or further advance which is made to the purchaser by that institution, and is secured by a legal charge not having priority to that charge; and the landlord must serve such a notice if the purpose of the advance or further advance is an approved purpose[14]. The covenant for repayment of a discount on a disposal[15] does not, by virtue of its binding successors in title of the purchaser, bind a person exercising rights under a charge having priority over the charge for repayment of a discount[16], or a person deriving title under him[17]. A provision of the conveyance, grant or assignment, or of a collateral agreement, is void in so far as it purports to authorise a forfeiture, or to impose a penalty or disability, in the event of any such person failing to comply with that covenant[18].

Where different parts of an advance or further advance are made for different purposes, each of those parts will be regarded as a separate advance or further advance for the above purposes[19].

1 Ie the charge taking effect by virtue of the Housing Act 1996 s 11B: see PARA 219.
2 In the Housing Act 1996 s 12, 'approved lending institution' means: (1) a building society, bank, insurance company or friendly society; (2) the Welsh Ministers; or (3) an authorised mortgage lender (within the meaning of the Housing Act 1985 (see s 622(1); and PARA 527 note 18)): Housing Act 1996 s 12(5) (amended by the Housing and Regeneration Act 2008 ss 61(1), (7), 307(7)). As to the Welsh Ministers see PARAS 7, 141.
3 Housing Act 1996 s 12(1) (amended by the Housing Act 2004 s 199(2)).
4 Ie the charge taking effect by virtue of the Housing Act 1996 s 11B: see PARA 219.
5 As to the register of social landlords see PARA 167.
6 As to the meaning of 'notice' see PARA 169 note 6.
7 Housing Act 1996 s 12(2) (amended by the Housing Act 2004 s 199(2)).
8 Housing Act 1996 s 12(2).
9 As to the meaning of 'house' see PARA 168 note 11.
10 For these purposes, 'service charge' has the meaning given by the Housing Act 1985 s 621A (see PARA 527 note 21): Housing Act 1996 s 12(6).
11 Housing Act 1996 s 12(6)(a).
12 See note 4.
13 Housing Act 1996 s 12(6)(b) (amended by the Housing Act 2004 s 199(2)).
14 Housing Act 1996 s 12(3) (amended by the Housing Act 2004 s 199(2)). As to the meaning of 'an approved purpose' see the text and notes 9–13.
15 Ie the covenant required by the Housing Act 1996 s 11B: see PARA 219.
16 See note 4.
17 Housing Act 1996 s 12(4) (amended by the Housing Act 2004 s 199(2)).
18 Housing Act 1996 s 12(4).
19 Housing Act 1996 s 12(7).

222. Right of first refusal for a registered social landlord. Where on a disposal of a house[1] by a registered social landlord[2], in accordance with a consent given by the Welsh Ministers[3], a discount has been given to the purchaser, and the consent does not provide otherwise, the conveyance, grant or assignment must contain the following covenant, which is binding on the purchaser and his successors in title[4]. The covenant must be to the effect that, until the end of the period of ten years beginning with the conveyance, grant or assignment, there will be no relevant disposal which is not an exempted disposal[5], unless the prescribed conditions[6] have been satisfied in relation to that or a previous such disposal[7]. The limitation imposed by such a covenant is a local land charge[8]. Moreover, the Chief Land

Registrar must enter in the register of title a restriction reflecting the limitation imposed by any such covenant[9]. Where there is a relevant disposal which is an exempted disposal[10], the covenant is not binding on the person to whom the disposal is made or any successor in title of his, and the covenant ceases to apply in relation to the property disposed of[11].

The Welsh Ministers may by regulations prescribe such conditions as they consider appropriate for and in connection with conferring on a registered social landlord which has made a disposal as mentioned above[12], or such other person as is determined in accordance with the regulations, a right of first refusal to have a reconveyance or conveyance of the house or a surrender or assignment of the lease[13] made to him for specified[14] consideration[15].

Such regulations may, in particular, make provision:

(1)   for the purchaser[16] to offer to make such a disposal to such person or persons as may be prescribed;

(2)   for a prescribed recipient of such an offer to be able either to accept the offer or to nominate some other person as the person by whom the offer may be accepted;

(3)   for the person who may be so nominated to be either a person of a prescribed description or a person whom the prescribed recipient considers, having regard to any prescribed matters, to be a more appropriate person to accept the offer;

(4)   for a prescribed recipient making such a nomination to give a notification of the nomination to the person nominated, the purchaser and any other prescribed person;

(5)   for authorising a nominated person to accept the offer and for determining which acceptance is to be effective where the offer is accepted by more than one person;

(6)   for the period within which the offer may be accepted or within which any other prescribed step is to be, or may be, taken;

(7)   for the circumstances in which the right of first refusal lapses (whether following the service of a notice to complete or otherwise) with the result that the purchaser is able to make a disposal on the open market;

(8)   for the manner in which any offer, acceptance or notification is to be communicated[17].

The regulations may make different provision with respect to different cases or descriptions of case and must be made by statutory instrument which is subject to annulment in pursuance of a resolution of the National Assembly for Wales[18].

The consideration for a disposal made in respect of a right of first refusal[19] must be such amount as may be agreed between the parties, or determined by the district valuer, as being the amount which is to be taken to be the value of the house at the time when the offer is made (as determined in accordance with regulations[20] in that regard)[21]. That value is to be taken to be the price which, at that time, the interest to be reconveyed, conveyed, surrendered or assigned would realise if sold on the open market by a willing vendor, on the assumption that any liability under the covenant required[22] as to repayment of discount on early disposal would be discharged by the vendor[23]. If the offer is accepted in accordance with regulations[24], no payment may be required in pursuance of any such covenant as is mentioned above, but the consideration must be reduced[25] by such amount (if any) as, on a disposal made at the time the offer was made, being a relevant disposal which is not an exempted disposal, would fall to be paid under that covenant[26]. Where there is a charge on the house having priority over the charge to secure payment of the sum due under the covenant as to repayment of discount on early disposal, the consideration may not be reduced[27] below the amount necessary to discharge the outstanding sum secured by the first-mentioned charge at the date of the offer (as determined in accordance with regulations)[28].

1 As to the meaning of 'house' see PARA 168 note 11.
2 As to the register of social landlords see PARA 167.
3 Ie under the Housing Act 1996 s 9: see PARA 217. As to the Welsh Ministers see PARAS 7, 141.
4 Housing Act 1996 s 12A(1) (ss 12A, 12B added by the Housing Act 2004 s 200(1); the Housing Act 1996 s 12A(1) amended by the Housing and Regeneration Act 2008 s 61(6), (7)).
5 As to the meaning of 'relevant disposal which is not an exempted disposal' see PARA 224.
6 'The prescribed conditions' means such conditions as are prescribed by regulations under the Housing Act 1996 s 12A at the time when the conveyance, grant or assignment is made: s 12A(3) (as added: see note 4).
7 Housing Act 1996 s 12A(2) (as added: see note 4).
8 Housing Act 1996 s 12A(9) (as added: see note 4).
9 Housing Act 1996 s 12A(10) (as added: see note 4). As to the Chief Land Registrar see REAL PROPERTY AND REGISTRATION vol 87 (2012) PARA 562.
10 Ie by virtue of the Housing Act 1996 s 15(4)(d) or (e) (compulsory disposal or disposal of yard, garden, etc): see PARA 224.
11 Housing Act 1996 s 12A(11) (as added: see note 4).
12 Ie a disposal as mentioned in the Housing Act 1996 s 12A(1).
13 Ie a disposal within the Housing Act 1996 s 12A(5): see the text and note 15.
14 Ie such consideration as is mentioned in the Housing Act 1996 s 12B: see the text and notes 19–28.
15 Housing Act 1996 s 12A(4), (5) (as added (see note 4); s 12A(4) amended by the Housing and Regeneration Act 2008 s 62(a), (c), (e)). As to the regulations that have been made see the Housing (Right of First Refusal) (England) Regulations 2005, SI 2005/1917 (amended by SI 2010/671); and the Housing (Right of First Refusal) (Wales) Regulations 2005, SI 2005/2680 (amended by SI 2010/671); and PARA 328 et seq.
16 In the Housing Act 1996 s 12A(6), any reference to the purchaser is a reference to the purchaser or his successor in title: s 12A(7) (as added: see note 4).
17 Housing Act 1996 s 12A(6) (as added: see note 4). Nothing in s 12A(6) affects the generality of s 12A(4) (see the text and note 15): s 12A(7) (as so added).
18 Housing Act 1996 s 12A(8) (as added (see note 4); amended by the Housing and Regeneration Act 2008 s 63).
19 Ie as mentioned in the Housing Act 1996 s 12A(4): see the text and note 15.
20 As to the regulations see the text and notes 12–18.
21 Housing Act 1996 s 12B(1) (as added: see note 4).
22 Ie required by the Housing Act 1996 s 11: see PARA 219.
23 Housing Act 1996 s 12B(2) (as added: see note 4).
24 Ie regulations under the Housing Act 1996 s 12A: see the text and notes 1–18.
25 Ie subject to the Housing Act 1996 s 12B(4): see the text and note 28.
26 Housing Act 1996 s 12B(3) (as added: see note 4).
27 Ie under the Housing Act 1996 s 12B(3): see the text and note 26.
28 Housing Act 1996 s 12B(4) (as added: see note 4).

223. Restriction on disposal of houses in national parks and other areas. On the disposal by a registered social landlord[1], in accordance with a consent given by the Welsh Ministers[2], of a house[3] situated in:

(1)   a national park;

(2)   an area designated as an area of outstanding natural beauty[4]; or

(3)   an area designated as a rural area[5],

the conveyance, grant or assignment may[6] contain a covenant to the following effect limiting the freedom of the purchaser[7] (including any successor in title of his and any person deriving title under him or such a successor) to dispose of the house[8].

The limitation is that until such time (if any) as may be notified in writing by the registered social landlord to the purchaser, or a successor in title of his, there will be no relevant disposal which is not an exempted disposal[9] without the written consent of the landlord[10]. That consent must not be withheld if the person to whom the disposal is made (or, if it is made to more than one person, at least one of them) has, throughout the period of three years immediately preceding the application for consent:

(a) had his place of work in a region designated by order[11] which, or part of which, is comprised in the national park or area concerned; or

(b) had his only or principal home in such a region,

or if he has had the one in part or parts of that period and the other in the remainder[12].

A disposal in breach of such a covenant as is mentioned above is void[13].

The limitation imposed by such a covenant is a local land charge and, if the first disposal involves registration under the Land Registration Act 2002[14], the Chief Land Registrar[15] must enter in the register of title a restriction reflecting the limitation[16].

1 As to the register of social landlords see PARA 167.
2 Ie under the Housing Act 1996 s 9: see PARA 217. As to the Welsh Ministers see PARAS 7, 141.
3 As to the meaning of 'house' see PARA 168 note 11.
4 Ie under the Countryside and Rights of Way Act 2000 s 82: see OPEN SPACES AND COUNTRYSIDE vol 78 (2010) PARA 658.
5 Ie by order under the Housing Act 1985 s 157: see PARA 333.
6 Ie unless it contains a condition of a kind mentioned in the Housing Act 1985 s 33(2)(b) or (c) (right of pre-emption or restriction on assignment: see PARA 523) or a covenant as mentioned in the Housing Act 1996 s 12A(2) (right of first refusal for registered social landlord: see PARA 222).
7 For these purposes, 'purchaser' means the person acquiring the interest disposed of by the first disposal: Housing Act 1996 s 13(6).
8 Housing Act 1996 s 13(1) (amended by the Countryside and Rights of Way Act 2000 s 93, Sch 15 para 14; the Housing Act 2004 s 200(2); and the Housing and Regeneration Act 2008 s 61(1), (7)).
9 Where there is a relevant disposal which is an exempted disposal by virtue of the Housing Act 1996 s 15(4)(d) or (e) (compulsory disposal or disposal of yard, garden etc: see PARA 224), any such covenant as is mentioned in s 13 ceases to apply in relation to the property disposed of: s 13(7).
10 Housing Act 1996 s 13(2). For these purposes, consent to the grant of an option enabling a person to call for a relevant disposal which is not an exempted disposal is treated as consent to a disposal made in pursuance of the option: see s 14(1), (2). As to the meanings of 'relevant disposal' and 'exempted disposal' see PARA 224.
11 Ie under the Housing Act 1985 s 157(3): see PARA 333.
12 Housing Act 1996 s 13(3). The region need not have been the same throughout the period: s 13(3).
13 Housing Act 1996 s 13(4).
14 See REAL PROPERTY AND REGISTRATION vol 87 (2012) PARA 235 et seq.
15 As to the Chief Land Registrar see REAL PROPERTY AND REGISTRATION vol 87 (2012) PARA 562.
16 Housing Act 1996 s 13(5) (amended by the Land Registration Act 2002 s 133, Sch 11 para 35). See REAL PROPERTY AND REGISTRATION vol 87 (2012) PARA 532.

224. Relevant and exempted disposals. The expression 'relevant disposal which is not an exempted disposal'[1] is to be construed as follows[2].

A disposal, whether of the whole or part of the house[3], is a relevant disposal if it is:

(1) a conveyance of the freehold or an assignment of the lease[4]; or

(2) the grant of a lease or sub-lease (other than a mortgage term) for a term of more than 21 years otherwise than at a rack-rent[5].

A disposal is an exempted disposal if:

(a) it is a disposal of the whole of the house and a conveyance of the freehold or an assignment of the lease and the person or each of the persons to whom it is made is a qualifying person[6];

(b) it is a vesting of the whole of the house in a person taking under a will or on an intestacy;

(c) it is a disposal of the whole of the house in pursuance of a court order[7];

(d) it is a compulsory disposal[8];

(e)   the property disposed of is a yard, garden, outhouses or appurtenances belonging to a house or usually enjoyed with it[9].

1   Ie in the Housing Act 1996 ss 11–14: see PARAS 219–223, 225.
2   Housing Act 1996 s 15(1).
3   As to the meaning of 'house' see PARA 168 note 11.
4   As to the meaning of 'lease' see PARA 168 note 16.
5   Housing Act 1996 s 15(2). For the purposes of head (2) in the text it will be assumed: (1) that any option to renew or extend a lease or sub-lease, whether or not forming part of a series of options, is exercised; and (2) that any option to terminate a lease or sub-lease is not exercised: s 15(3).
6   For these purposes a person is a qualifying person in relation to a disposal if: (1) he is the person or one of the persons by whom the disposal is made; (2) he is the spouse or a former spouse, or the civil partner or a former civil partner, of that person or one of those persons; or (3) he is a member of the family of that person or one of those persons and has resided with him throughout the period of 12 months ending with the disposal: Housing Act 1996 s 15(5) (amended by the Civil Partnership Act 2004 s 81, Sch 8 para 50(1), (2)). A person is a member of another's family within the meaning of the Housing Act 1996 Pt I (ss A1–64) if: (a) he is the spouse or civil partner of that person, or he and that person live together as husband and wife or as if they were civil partners; or (b) he is that person's parent, grandparent, child, grandchild, brother, sister, uncle, aunt, nephew or niece: s 62(1) (amended by the Civil Partnership Act 2004 Sch 8 para 51(1), (2)). For the purpose of head (b): (i) a relationship by marriage or civil partnership will be treated as a relationship by blood; (ii) a relationship of the half-blood will be treated as a relationship of the whole blood; and (iii) the stepchild of a person will be treated as his child: Housing Act 1996 s 62(2) (amended by the Civil Partnership Act 2004 Sch 8 para 51(3)). As to the meaning of 'spouse' see PARA 73 note 2.
7   The orders referred to here are orders under: (1) the Matrimonial Causes Act 1973 s 24 or s 24A (property adjustment orders or orders for the sale of property in connection with matrimonial proceedings: see MATRIMONIAL AND CIVIL PARTNERSHIP LAW vol 73 (2015) PARAS 556 et seq, 578 et seq); (2) the Inheritance (Provision for Family and Dependants) Act 1975 s 2 (orders as to financial provision to be made from estate: see WILLS AND INTESTACY vol 103 (2016) PARAS 591–592); (3) the Matrimonial and Family Proceedings Act 1984 s 17 (property adjustment orders or orders for the sale of property after overseas divorce etc: see MATRIMONIAL AND CIVIL PARTNERSHIP LAW vol 73 (2015) PARA 591); (4) the Children Act 1989 s 15(1), Sch 1 para 1 (orders for financial relief against parents: see CHILDREN AND YOUNG PERSONS vol 9 (2017) PARA 623 et seq); or (5) the Civil Partnership Act 2004 Sch 5 Pt 2 or Pt 3, or Sch 7 para 9 (property adjustment orders, or orders for the sale of property, in connection with civil partnership proceedings or after overseas dissolution of civil partnership, etc: see MATRIMONIAL AND CIVIL PARTNERSHIP LAW vol 73 (2015) PARAS 556 et seq, 591): Housing Act 1996 s 15(6) (amended by the Civil Partnership Act 2004 ss 81, 261(4), Sch 8 para 50(3), Sch 30).
8   For these purposes, a compulsory disposal is a disposal of property which is acquired compulsorily, or is acquired by a person who has made or would have made, or for whom another person has made or would have made, a compulsory purchase order authorising its compulsory purchase for the purposes for which it is acquired: Housing Act 1996 s 15(7).
9   Housing Act 1996 s 15(4).

225. Treatment of options. The grant of an option enabling a person to call for a relevant disposal which is not an exempted disposal[1] is treated[2] as such a disposal made to him[3].

1   As to the meaning of 'relevant disposal which is not an exempted disposal' see PARA 224.
2   Ie for the purposes of the Housing Act 1996 ss 9–13: see PARAS 217–223.
3   Housing Act 1996 s 14(1).

(B)   Tenant's Right to Acquire Dwelling

226. Right of an assured or secure tenant in Wales to acquire dwelling. Prior to the Housing Act 1996, most tenants of registered social landlords[1] did not have a statutory right to buy their homes because of the exclusions contained in the Housing Act 1985[2]. Since the phasing out of secure tenancies after 15 January 1989[3], most new tenants of social housing are granted assured tenancies[4]. An assured tenant does not have the right to buy under the Housing Act 1985[5] although a former secure tenant of a local authority whose dwelling is transferred to the private sector as part of a voluntary transfer becomes an assured tenant following transfer but retains the right to buy under what is called a 'preserved right to buy'[6]. Since 1 April 1996, registered social landlords have been allowed to offer discounts to tenants who wish to buy their homes; this is known as the voluntary purchase scheme[7].

Part I of the Housing Act 1996[8], which no longer applies in England[9], provides that the tenant of a dwelling in Wales has the statutory right to acquire the dwelling, subject to a number of qualifications, if: (1) the landlord is a registered social landlord or a private registered provider of social housing[10]; (2) the tenancy is: (a) an assured tenancy, other than an assured shorthold tenancy or a long tenancy; or (b) a secure tenancy; (3) the dwelling was provided with public money and has remained in the social rented sector; and (4) the tenant satisfies any further qualifying conditions applicable under Part V of the Housing Act 1985 (the right to buy) as it applies in relation to the right conferred by the provision applicable in Wales[11]. This also applies, with modifications, in relation to a dwelling ('a funded dwelling') provided or acquired wholly or in part by means of a grant to a body other than a registered social landlord[12].

Under the Renting Homes (Wales) Act 2016 (which is not fully in force), existing secure tenancies (and assured tenancies granted by housing associations) in Wales will automatically be converted to secure contracts and would therefore appear to be removed from the categories of tenancy to which the right to acquire is applicable[13]. This follows from a White Paper in 2015 in which the Welsh Government sought views on its proposals to change the legislation on the right to buy and right to acquire, whether to reduce the discount or to end the right[14].

1   As to the register of social landlords see PARA 167.
2   See the Housing Act 1985 s 120, Sch 5; and PARA 245 et seq. As to the right to buy see PARA 230 et seq.
3   See the Housing Act 1996 s 80; and LANDLORD AND TENANT vol 63 (2016) PARA 1037.
4   See the Housing Act 1988 s 35; and PARA 242.
5   The right to buy under the Housing Act 1985 is limited to secure tenants: see s 118; and PARA 239.
6   See the Housing Act 1985 ss 171A–171H; and PARA 334 et seq.
7   See Housing Corporation Circular F2–06/96 (March 1996); Circular R2–24/96 (May 1996). See also the Social Landlords (Permissible Additional Purposes or Objects) Order 1996, SI 1996/2256, art 3; and PARA 168.
8   Ie the Housing Act 1996 Pt I (ss A1–64).
9   See PARA 166.
10 As to the meaning of 'private registered provider of social housing' see PARA 53.
11 See the Housing Act 1996 ss 16, 17 (s 16 amended by the Housing Act 2004 s 202(1), (2); the Housing and Regeneration Act 2008 ss 61(1), (7), 185(1); and by SI 2010/844 and SI 2010/866; the Housing Act 1996 s 17 amended by the Housing and Regeneration Act 2008 ss 62(a)–(e), 63); and PARAS 242–243. The Welsh Ministers are required to make grants to registered social landlords and private registered providers of social housing in respect of discounts given by them to persons exercising the right to acquire conferred by the Housing Act 1996 s 16, and may make grants to registered social landlords and private registered providers of social housing in respect of discounts on disposals by them of dwellings in Wales to tenants otherwise than in pursuance of the right conferred by s 16: see ss 20, 21 (s 20 amended by the Housing Act 2004 ss 218, 266, Sch 11 paras 7, 9, Sch 16; the Housing and Regeneration Act 2008 ss 61(1), (7), 185(3); and SI 2010/844; and the Housing Act 1996 s 21 amended by the Housing Act 2004 Sch 11 para 10, Sch 16; the Housing and Regeneration Act 2008 ss 61(1), (7), 185(4); and SI 2010/844); and PARA 244.
12 See the Housing Act 1996 s 16A (added by the Housing Act 2004 s 221; and amended by the Housing and Regeneration Act 2008 ss 61(1), (7), 185(2)); and PARA 242.
13 As to the Renting Homes (Wales) Act 2016 see LANDLORD AND TENANT vol 62 (2016) PARAS 45–46. Most of the provisions of the 2016 Act come into force on a day to be appointed by the Welsh Ministers in an order made by statutory instrument under s 257(2): see PARA 6. At the date at which this volume states the law, no such day had been appointed.
14 See *The Future of Right to Buy and Right to Acquire: A White Paper for Social Housing*, published by the Welsh Government in January 2015. See also *Written Statement — The Future of Right to Buy and Right to Acquire* (Minister for Communities and Tackling Poverty, 22 January 2015).

227. Standards. The Welsh Ministers[1] may set standards to be met by local housing authorities[2] in connection with: (1) the quality of accommodation provided by local housing authorities for housing; (2) rent for such accommodation; (3) service charges for such accommodation[3]. Such standards may require local housing authorities to comply with rules specified in the standards[4]. Standards must be published and may be revised or withdrawn by the Welsh Ministers[5].

The Welsh Ministers may give guidance that relates to a matter addressed by a standard[6] and amplifies the standard[7]. Such guidance must be published and may be revised or withdrawn by the Welsh Ministers[8]. In considering whether standards have been met the Welsh Ministers may have regard to the guidance[9].

Before setting, revising or withdrawing standards or issuing, revising or withdrawing guidance, the Welsh Ministers must consult: (a) one or more bodies appearing to them to represent the interests of local housing authorities; (b) one or more bodies appearing to them to represent the interests of tenants; and (c) any other persons the Welsh Ministers consider it appropriate to consult[10]. A local housing authority must provide the Welsh Ministers with any information they request relating to compliance by the authority with standards set under these provisions[11].

1 As to the Welsh Ministers see PARAS 7, 141.
2 In the Housing (Wales) Act 2014, 'local housing authority' means the council of a county or county borough in Wales: s 143.
3 Housing (Wales) Act 2014 s 111(1). Part 4 (ss 111–130) came into force on 1 December 2014: see the Housing (Wales) Act 2014 (Commencement No 1) Order 2014, 2014/3127, art 2(a), Schedule para 1.
4 Housing (Wales) Act 2014 s 111(2). Rules about rent or service charges may include, among other things, provision for minimum or maximum levels of rent or service charges, and minimum or maximum levels of increase or decrease of rent or service charges: s 111(3).
5 Housing (Wales) Act 2014 s 111(4), (5).
6 Ie a standard under the Housing (Wales) Act 2014 s 111.
7 Housing (Wales) Act 2014 s 112(1).
8 Housing (Wales) Act 2014 s 112(3), (4).
9 Housing (Wales) Act 2014 s 112(2).
10 Housing (Wales) Act 2014 s 113.
11 Housing (Wales) Act 2014 s 114.

228. Powers of entry. Where it appears to the Welsh Ministers[1] that a local housing authority[2] may be failing to maintain or repair any premises in accordance with standards set[3] or guidance given[4] by them, a person authorised in writing by the Welsh Ministers for the purpose of exercising a power of entry may, at any reasonable time, on giving not less than 28 days' notice of his or her intention to the local housing authority concerned, enter any such premises for the purpose of survey and examination[5]. Where such notice is given to the local housing authority, the authority must give the occupier or occupiers of the premises not less than seven days' notice of the proposed survey and examination[6]. The Welsh Ministers must give a copy of any survey carried out in exercise of the powers conferred by these provisions to the local housing authority concerned[7]. The Welsh Ministers may require the local housing authority concerned to pay to them such amount as the Welsh Ministers may determine towards the costs of carrying out any survey under these provisions[8].

1 As to the Welsh Ministers see PARAS 7, 141.
2 As to the meaning of 'local housing authority' see PARA 227 note 2.
3 Ie under the Housing (Wales) Act 2014 s 111: see PARA 227.
4 Ie under the Housing (Wales) Act 2014 s 121: see PARA 227.

5 Housing (Wales) Act 2014 s 115(1), (2), (4).
6 Housing (Wales) Act 2014 s 115(3).
7 Housing (Wales) Act 2014 s 115(5).
8 Housing (Wales) Act 2014 s 115(6).

229. Intervention powers. Where the Welsh Ministers[1] are deciding whether to exercise an intervention power[2], which intervention power to exercise or how to exercise an intervention power, the Welsh Ministers must consider whether the failure or likely failure to meet the standard[3] is, or is likely to be, a recurrent or isolated incident and the speed with which the failure or likely failure to meet the standard needs to be addressed[4]. For the purposes of the Housing (Wales) Act 2014[5], the grounds for intervention are that a local housing authority[6] has failed, or is likely to fail, to meet a standard set by the Welsh Ministers[7] which relates to the quality of accommodation[8].

The Welsh Ministers may give a warning notice to a local housing authority if they are satisfied that the grounds for intervention exist in relation to the authority[9], specifying each of the following in the warning notice:

(1) the reasons why they are satisfied that the grounds exist;
(2) the action they require the authority to take in order to deal with the grounds for intervention;
(3) the period within which the action is to be taken by the authority ('the compliance period');
(4) the action they are minded to take if the authority fails to take the required action[10].

The Welsh Ministers have the power to intervene under Part 4 of the Housing (Wales) Act 2014 if they have given a warning notice and the local housing authority has failed to comply, or secure compliance, with the notice to the Welsh Ministers' satisfaction within the compliance period[11]. Where the Welsh Ministers have the power to intervene, they must keep the circumstances giving rise to the power under review, but they are not limited to taking the action they said they were minded to take in a warning notice[12]. If the Welsh Ministers conclude that the grounds for intervention have been dealt with to their satisfaction or that exercise of their powers under Part 4 would not be appropriate for any other reason, they must notify the local housing authority of their conclusion in writing[13], and their power to intervene continues in effect until they give such a notice[14].

If the Welsh Ministers have the power to intervene, they may:

(a) direct the local housing authority to enter into a contract or other arrangement with a specified[15] person, or a person falling within a specified class, for the provision to the authority, of specified services of an advisory nature[16], and such a direction may require the contract or other arrangement to contain specified terms and conditions[17];
(b) give such directions to the local housing authority or any of its officers as they think are appropriate for securing that the functions to which the grounds for intervention relate are performed on behalf of the authority by a person specified in the direction[18], and such a direction may require that any contract or other arrangement made by the authority with the specified person contains terms and conditions specified in the direction[19];

(c)   direct that the functions to which the grounds for intervention relate are to be exercised by the Welsh Ministers or a person nominated by them[20], and if such a direction is made, the local housing authority must comply with the instructions of the Welsh Ministers or their nominee in relation to the exercise of the functions[21]; and

(d)   if they think it is appropriate in order to deal with the grounds for intervention, give directions to the local housing authority or any of its officers, or take any other steps[22].

A direction: (i) must be in writing; (ii) may be varied or revoked by a later direction; (iii) is enforceable by mandatory order on application by, or on behalf of, the Welsh Ministers[23]. If the Welsh Ministers think it is expedient, a direction under head (b) or (c) above may relate to the performance of functions of the local housing authority in addition to the functions to which the grounds for intervention relate[24].

A local housing authority, or an officer of an authority, subject to a direction or instruction under these provisions must comply with it[25].

A local housing authority must give the Welsh Ministers and other specified persons[26] as much assistance in connection with the exercise of functions under or by virtue of Part 4 of the Housing (Wales) Act 2014 as they are reasonably able to give[27]. A person specified in a direction[28], the Welsh Ministers in pursuance of a direction[29] and a person nominated by direction[30] has, at all reasonable times: (A) a right of entry to the premises of the local housing authority (other than a dwelling) in question; and (B) a right to inspect, and take copies of, any records or other documents[31] kept by the authority, and any other documents containing information relating to the authority, which the person considers relevant to the exercise of his or her functions under or by virtue of Part 4 of the Housing (Wales) Act 2014[32].

1   As to the Welsh Ministers see PARAS 7, 141.
2   Ie a power exercisable under the Housing (Wales) Act 2014 ss 117–127: s 116(3). See the text to notes 8–32.
3   As to the standards see PARA 227.
4   Housing (Wales) Act 2014 s 116(1), (2).
5   Ie the Housing (Wales) Act 2014 Pt 4 (ss 111–130).
6   As to the meaning of 'local housing authority' see PARA 227 note 2.
7   Ie under the Housing (Wales) Act 2014 s 111: see PARA 227.
8   Housing (Wales) Act 2014 s 117.
9   Housing (Wales) Act 2014 s 118(1).
10 Housing (Wales) Act 2014 s 118(2).
11 Housing (Wales) Act 2014 s 119(1).
12 Housing (Wales) Act 2014 s 119(2), (5).
13 Housing (Wales) Act 2014 s 119(3).
14 Housing (Wales) Act 2014 s 119(4).
15 In the Housing (Wales) Act 2014 ss 120, 121 'specified' means specified in a direction: s 120(4).
16 Housing (Wales) Act 2014 s 120(1), (2).
17 Housing (Wales) Act 2014 s 120(3).
18 Housing (Wales) Act 2014 s 121(1), (2).
19 Housing (Wales) Act 2014 s 121(3).
20 Housing (Wales) Act 2014 s 122(1), (2).
21 Housing (Wales) Act 2014 s 122(3).
22 Housing (Wales) Act 2014 s 124.
23 Housing (Wales) Act 2014 s 125(3).
24 Housing (Wales) Act 2014 s 123(1). The Welsh Ministers may have regard (among other things) to financial considerations in deciding whether it is expedient that a direction should relate to the functions of the local housing authority other than functions relating to the grounds for intervention: s 123(2).

25 Housing (Wales) Act 2014 s 125(1). This includes a direction or an instruction to exercise a power or duty that is contingent upon the opinion of the authority or an officer of the authority: s 125(2).

26 The persons are: (1) any person authorised for the purposes of the Housing (Wales) Act 2014 s 126 by the Welsh Ministers; (2) any person acting under directions under Pt 4; (3) any person assisting: (a) the Welsh Ministers; or (b) a person mentioned in head (1) or (2). s 126(2).

27 Housing (Wales) Act 2014 s 126(1).

28 Ie under the Housing (Wales) Act 2014 s 120 or s 121 or, where a direction under s 120 specifies a class of persons, the person with whom the local housing authority enter into the contract or other arrangement required by the direction.

29 Ie under the Housing (Wales) Act 2014 s 122.

30 Ie under the Housing (Wales) Act 2014 s 122.

31 In the Housing (Wales) Act 2014 s 127 'document' and 'records' each include information recorded in any form: s 127(5).

32 Housing (Wales) Act 2014 s 127(1), (2). Any reference in s 127 to a person falling within s 127(2) includes a reference to any person assisting that person: s 127(4).

In exercising the right under s 127(1)(b) (head (B) in the text) to inspect records or other documents, a person ('P'): (1) is entitled to have access to, and inspect and check the operation of, any computer and any associated apparatus or material which is or has been in use in connection with the records or other documents in question; and (2) may require the following persons to provide any assistance P may reasonably require (including, among other things, the making of information available for inspection or copying in a legible form): (a) the person by whom or on whose behalf the computer is or has been so used; (b) any person having charge of, or otherwise concerned with the operation of, the computer, apparatus or material: s 127(3).

(5) SOCIAL HOUSING: RIGHT TO BUY OR ACQUIRE

(i) The Right to Buy or Acquire; in general

230. Tenant's rights; in general. Under Part V of the Housing Act 1985[1] a secure tenant[2] has the right, in certain circumstances and subject to certain conditions and exceptions, to acquire the freehold of the dwelling house[3] which he occupies or to be granted a lease[4] of that dwelling house (the 'right to buy')[5]. The Housing Act 1996[6] introduced a right to acquire extending the right to buy, with modifications, to certain assured tenants[7]. The Housing and Regeneration Act 2008 amended the right to acquire; the amended right under the Housing Act 1996 now only applies in Wales[8] but a similar right under the Housing and Regeneration Act 2008 applies in England[9].

The statutory right to acquire on rent to mortgage terms which was introduced following amendments made to the 1985 Act by the Leasehold Reform, Housing and Urban Development Act 1993 is no longer exercisable, except in transitional cases[10], and the following statutory rights formerly ancillary to the right to buy have been abolished, namely:

(1)   the right to a mortgage[11];

(2)   the right to defer completion[12]; and

(3)   the right[13] to be granted a shared ownership lease[14].

The right to buy may be suspended because of anti-social behaviour by the tenant, a member of his family or a visitor to the dwelling house[15]. In Wales a local housing authority may apply to the Welsh Ministers for a direction suspending the right to buy and related rights in its area for a period of up to five years[16].

In England, the Housing and Planning Act 2016 has made provision to allow grants to be made to private registered providers in respect of right to buy discounts[17].

Certain dwelling houses are excluded from the right to buy or to acquire[18]. It is likely that the Renting Homes (Wales) Act 2016 will exclude tenancies in Wales[19].

1 Ie the Housing Act 1985 Pt V (ss 118–188): see PARA 231 et seq. The 'right to buy' was first introduced by the Housing Act 1980 Pt I Ch I (ss 1–27) (repealed).

2 References in the Housing Act 1985 Pt V to a secure tenancy or a secure tenant in relation to a time before 26 August 1984 are to a tenancy which would have been a secure tenancy if the Housing Act 1980 Pt I Ch II (ss 28–50) (repealed) and the Housing and Building Control Act 1984 Pt I (ss 1–38) (repealed) had then been in force or to a person who would then have been a secure tenant: Housing Act 1985 s 185(1). For the purpose of determining whether a person would have been a secure tenant and his tenancy a secure tenancy: (1) a predecessor of a local authority is to be deemed to have been such an authority; and (2) a housing association is to be deemed to have been registered if it is or was a private registered provider of social housing or registered social landlord at any later time: s 185(2) (amended by SI 1996/2325 and SI 2010/866). As to secure tenants see LANDLORD AND TENANT vol 63 (2016) PARA 1037 et seq; as to housing associations see PARA 13; as to private registered providers of social housing see PARA 53; and as to registered social landlords see PARAS 4, 166 et seq.
    Where the preserved right to buy (see PARA 334 et seq) arises, and the Housing (Preservation of Right to Buy) Regulations 1993, SI 1993/2241, apply, then in the provisions of the Housing Act 1985 Pt V (including ss 122A and 122B added by the Housing (Wales) Measure 2011) for the expressions 'secure tenant' and 'tenant' there is substituted, except in the provisions listed in the Housing (Preservation of Right to Buy) Regulations 1993, SI 1993/2241, Sch 1 para 1(2), the expression 'qualifying person': Sch 1 para 1(1) (amended, in relation to Wales, by SI 2012/2090). See also notes 7, 9.

3 As to the meaning of 'dwelling house' see PARA 231.

4 As to the meaning of 'lease' see PARA 31 note 3.

5 See the Housing Act 1985 s 118(1); and PARA 239 et seq. The right to buy has been extended to tenants of certain houses where there are interests owned by intermediate landlords: see PARA 233.

6 Ie the Housing Act 1996 ss 16–17: see PARAS 242–243.

7 Where the right to acquire conferred by the Housing Act 1996 arises and the Housing (Right to Acquire) Regulations 1997, SI 1997/619 apply, then: (1) in the provisions of the Housing Act 1985 Pt V (including ss 122A and 122B added by the Housing (Wales) Measure 2011) in the expressions 'secure tenant' and 'secure tenancy' the word 'secure' is omitted, except in the provisions listed in the Housing (Right to Acquire) Regulations 1997, SI 1997/619, Sch 1 para 1; and (2) for the expression 'right to buy' there is substituted the expression 'right to acquire', except in the provisions listed in Sch 1 para 2: Sch 1 paras 1, 2 (amended, in relation to Wales, by SI 2012/2090). The Housing Act 1985 Pt V as it applies with modifications to the right to acquire is set out in the Housing (Right to Acquire) Regulations 1997, SI 1997/619, Sch 2 (amended by SI 2006/680, in relation to Wales, by SI 2012/2090, and by SI 2016/481). It is submitted that the Housing (Right to Acquire) Regulations 1997, SI 1997/619, Schs 1, 2 are now to be read in the light of subsequent legislative amendments to the Housing Act 1985 Pt V by eg the Civil Partnership Act 2004 and the Housing Act 2004, even where the 1997 Regulations have not themselves been correspondingly amended, since an alternative interpretation could lead to absurdities, although this is ultimately a matter for the courts.

8 See the Housing Act 1996 ss 16, 16A (amended by the Housing and Regeneration Act 2008 s 185(1), (2)); and PARA 242.

9 See the Housing and Regeneration Act 2008 ss 180–184; and PARAS 240–241. The Housing (Right to Acquire) Regulations 1997, SI 1997/619, Sch 1 paras 1, 2 (see note 7) apply in relation to the right to acquire under the Housing and Regeneration Act 2008 by virtue of s 184, which applies the Housing Act 1996 s 17 (regulations modifying the Housing Act 1985): see PARA 241.

10 See PARA 318.

11 Ie the right conferred by the Housing Act 1985 ss 132–135 (repealed).

12 Ie the right conferred by the Housing Act 1985 s 142 (repealed).

13 Ie the right conferred by the Housing Act 1985 ss 143–151 (as originally enacted).

14 Leasehold Reform, Housing and Urban Development Act 1993 s 107.
    Local authorities and housing associations may, however, participate on a voluntary basis in the Social HomeBuy scheme (launched on 1 April 2006 by the former Office of the Deputy Prime Minister) and thereby enable certain of their tenants to purchase their homes on a shared equity basis. The details of this extra-statutory scheme are set out on the government's website, accessible at the date at which this volume states the law at www.gov.uk/shared-ownership-tenants.

15 See PARA 259.

16 See PARAS 260–266.

17 See the Housing and Planning Act 2016 Pt 4 Ch 1 (ss 64–68); and PARA 238.
18 See PARA 245 et seq.
19 See PARA 226.

231. Meaning of 'house', 'flat' and 'dwelling house'. The following provisions apply to the interpretation of 'house', 'flat' and 'dwelling house' when used in the statutory provisions[1] conferring the right to buy[2].

A dwelling house is a house if, and only if, it or so much of it as does not consist of land included by virtue of the provisions set out below[3] is a structure reasonably so called; so that:

(1)   where a building is divided horizontally, the flats or other units into which it is divided are not houses;

(2)   where a building is divided vertically, the units into which it is divided may be houses;

(3)   where a building is not structurally detached, it is not a house if a material part of it lies above or below the remainder of the structure[4].

A dwelling house which is a commonhold unit[5] is, however, to be treated as a house and not as a flat[6].

A dwelling house which is not a house is a flat[7].

For the statutory purposes[8], land let together with a dwelling house is to be treated as part of the dwelling house, unless the land is agricultural land[9] exceeding two acres[10]. There is also to be treated as included in a dwelling house any land which does not satisfy this condition but is or has been used for the purpose of the dwelling house if:

(a)   the tenant[11], by a written notice served on the landlord[12] at any time before he exercises the right to buy[13], requires the land to be included in the dwelling house; and

(b)   it is reasonable in all the circumstances for the land to be so included[14].

Such a notice may be withdrawn by a written notice served on the landlord at any time before the tenant exercises the right to buy[15]. Where such a notice is served or withdrawn after the service of the landlord's notice of the purchase price etc[16], the parties must, as soon as practicable after the service or withdrawal, take all such steps[17] as may be requisite for the purpose of securing that all parties are, as nearly as may be, in the same position as they would have been in if the notice had been served or withdrawn before the service of that landlord's notice[18].

The above provisions are modified in so far as they apply to:

(i)   the extended right to buy[19];

(ii)   the preserved right to buy[20];

(iii) the right to acquire in Wales conferred by the Housing Act 1996[21]; and

(iv)   the right to acquire in England conferred by the Housing and Regeneration Act 2008[22].

1 Ie in the Housing Act 1985 Pt V (ss 118–188): see PARAS 230, 232 et seq.
2 Housing Act 1985 s 183(1).
3 Ie by virtue of the Housing Act 1985 s 184: see the text and notes 8–18.
4 Housing Act 1985 s 183(1).
5 Ie within the meaning of the Commonhold and Leasehold Reform Act 2002: see COMMONHOLD vol 13 (2009) PARA 330.
6 Housing Act 1985 s 118(3) (added by the Commonhold and Leasehold Reform Act 2002 s 68, Sch 5 para 5).
7 Housing Act 1985 s 183(2).
8 Ie for the purposes of the Housing Act 1985 Pt V.
9 Ie as defined in the General Rate Act 1967 s 26(3)(a) (saved for these purposes): see LANDLORD AND TENANT vol 63 (2016) PARA 712 note 2.
10 Housing Act 1985 s 184(1). Similarly, land owned by the freeholder in fee simple: (1) which is let by the freeholder to the landlord or to an intermediate landlord; (2) in respect of which each of the

intermediate landlords (if any) is an authority or body specified in the Housing (Extension of Right to Buy) Order 1993, SI 1993/2240, art 3(2) (see PARA 233 note 17); and (3) which is let to the tenant together with the dwelling house, is to be treated as part of the dwelling house, unless the land is agricultural land defined as mentioned in note 9 and exceeding two acres: see the Housing (Extension of Right to Buy) Order 1993, SI 1993/2240, Schedule para 63(a), substituting the Housing Act 1985 s 184(1) for these purposes. As to the meanings of 'intermediate landlord' and 'freeholder' see PARA 233 notes 18–19.

11   As to the meaning of 'tenant' see PARA 31 note 3. See also PARA 230 notes 2, 7, 9.

12   As to the meaning of 'landlord' see PARA 31 note 3.

13   Ie or at any time before he exercised the right to acquire on rent to mortgage terms (now only exercisable if claimed before 18 July 2005: see the Housing Act 1985 s 142A; and PARA 318). As to the right to buy see PARA 239 et seq.

14   Housing Act 1985 s 184(2) (s 184(2), (3) amended, to include references to the right to acquire on rent to mortgage terms, by the Leasehold Reform, Housing and Urban Development Act 1993 s 187(1), Sch 21 para 24).

15   Housing Act 1985 s 184(3) (as amended: see note 14). It may also be withdrawn at any time before the tenant exercises the right to acquire on rent to mortgage terms, as to which see note 13: s 184(3) (as so amended).

16   Ie the notice under the Housing Act 1985 s 125: see PARA 276.

17   Ie whether by way of amending, withdrawing or re-serving any notice or extending any period or otherwise: Housing Act 1985 s 184(4).

18   Housing Act 1985 s 184(4).

19   As to the extended right to buy see PARA 233. Where that right arises, and the Housing (Extension of Right to Buy) Order 1993, SI 1993/2240, applies, then the Housing Act 1985 s 184(1) is substituted (see note 10), s 184(2), (3), (4) are amended, and s 184(3A)–(3E) are added, by the Housing (Extension of Right to Buy) Order 1993, SI 1993/2240, Schedule para 63.

20   As to the preserved right to buy see PARA 334 et seq. Where that right arises, and the Housing (Preservation of Right to Buy) Regulations 1993, SI 1993/2241, apply, the references to the right to acquire on rent to mortgage terms in the Housing Act 1985 s 184(2)(a), (3) are omitted: see the Housing (Preservation of Right to Buy) Regulations 1993, SI 1993/2241, Sch 1 para 39.

21   As to the right to acquire under the Housing Act 1996 see PARAS 242–244. Where that right arises, and the Housing (Right to Acquire) Regulations 1997, SI 1997/619, apply, the references to the right to acquire on rent to mortgage terms in the Housing Act 1985 s 184(2)(a), (3) are omitted: see the Housing (Right to Acquire) Regulations 1997, SI 1997/619, Sch 1 para 37.

22   As to the right to acquire under the Housing and Regeneration Act 2008 see PARAS 240–241. Where that right arises, the Housing (Right to Acquire) Regulations 1997, SI 1997/619, Sch 1 para 37 (see note 21) applies in relation to the right to acquire under the Housing and Regeneration Act 2008 by virtue of s 184, which applies the Housing Act 1996 s 17 (regulations modifying the Housing Act 1985): see PARA 241.

232.   Provisions restricting right to buy etc of no effect. A provision of a lease[1] held by the landlord[2] or a superior landlord, or of an agreement, whenever made, is void in so far as it purports to prohibit or restrict:

(1)   the grant of a lease in pursuance of the right to buy[3] or the right to acquire on rent to mortgage terms (where that right is still exercisable)[4]; or

(2)   the subsequent disposal, whether by way of assignment, sublease or otherwise, of a lease so granted,

or to authorise a forfeiture, or impose on the landlord or superior landlord a penalty or disability, in the event of such a grant or disposal[5].

Where a dwelling house[6] let on a secure tenancy[7] is land held:

(a)   for the purposes of pleasure grounds[8]; or

(b)   in accordance with a local authority's duty to maintain open spaces and burial grounds[9],

the dwelling house is deemed[10] to be freed from any trust arising solely by virtue of its being land held in trust for enjoyment by the public[11] or, as the case may be, for[12] an open space or burial ground[13].

1   As to the meaning of 'lease' see PARA 31 note 3.

2   As to the meaning of 'landlord' see PARA 31 note 3.

3   As to the right to buy see PARA 239 et seq. See also PARA 230 notes 7, 9.

4   As to the right to acquire on rent to mortgage terms (now only exercisable if claimed before 18 July 2005: see the Housing Act 1985 s 142A; and PARA 318) see PARA 318.
5   Housing Act 1985 s 179(1) (amended by the Leasehold Reform, Housing and Urban Development Act 1993 s 187(1), Sch 21 para 22). The Housing Act 1985 s 179(1) is: (1) substituted where the Housing (Extension of Right to Buy) Order 1993, SI 1993/2240 (see PARA 233), applies (see Schedule para 60); (2) modified where the Housing (Preservation of Right to Buy) Regulations 1993, SI 1993/2241 (see PARA 334 et seq), apply (see Sch 1 para 35(a)); (3) modified where the Housing (Right to Acquire) Regulations 1997, SI 1997/619, apply (right to acquire conferred by the Housing Act 1996 (see PARAS 242–244) or the Housing and Regeneration Act 2008 (see PARAS 240–241) (see the Housing (Right to Acquire) Regulations 1997, SI 1997/619, Sch 1 para 33(a), applying in relation to the right to acquire under the Housing and Regeneration Act 2008 by virtue of s 184, which applies the Housing Act 1996 s 17 (regulations modifying the Housing Act 1985): see PARA 241).
6   As to the meaning of 'dwelling house' see PARA 231.
7   As to the meaning of 'secure tenancy' and 'secure tenant' for these purposes see PARA 230 note 2; and see also PARA 230 notes 7, 9. As to secure tenants see LANDLORD AND TENANT vol 63 (2016) PARA 1037 et seq.
8   Ie for the purposes of the Public Health Act 1875 s 164: see OPEN SPACES AND COUNTRYSIDE vol 78 (2010) PARA 556.
9   Ie in accordance with the Open Spaces Act 1906 s 10: see OPEN SPACES AND COUNTRYSIDE vol 78 (2010) PARA 577.
10   Ie for the purposes of the Housing Act 1985 Pt V (ss 118–188): see PARAS 230–231, 233 et seq.
11   Ie in accordance with the Public Health Act 1875 s 164.
12   See note 9.
13   Housing Act 1985 s 179(2). Section 179(2) is omitted where: (1) the Housing (Preservation of Right to Buy) Regulations 1993, SI 1993/2241, apply (see Sch 1 para 35(b)); (2) the Housing (Right to Acquire) Regulations 1997, SI 1997/619, apply (see Sch 1 para 33(b); and see note 5).

233. Power to extend right to buy etc. The appropriate national authority may by order provide that, where there are in a dwelling house[1] let on a secure tenancy[2] one or more interests to which these provisions apply, the statutory provisions relating to the right to buy and related rights[3] and the statutory provisions relating to secure tenancies[4] have effect with such modifications as are specified in the order[5].

The above provisions apply to an interest held by:

(1)   a local authority[6];
(2)   a new town corporation[7];
(3)   a housing action trust[8];
(4)   an urban development corporation[9];
(5)   a Mayoral development corporation;
(6)   the Regulator of Social Housing[10];
(7)   a non-profit registered provider of social housing[11]; or
(8)   a registered social landlord[12],

which is immediately superior to the interest of the landlord[13] or to another interest to which these provisions apply[14].

Such an order:

(a)   may make different provision with respect to different cases or descriptions of case;
(b)   may contain such consequential, supplementary or transitional provisions as appear to the appropriate national authority to be necessary or expedient; and
(c)   must be made by statutory instrument[15].

The Housing (Extension of Right to Buy) Order 1993[16] has been made in the exercise of this power. Where, in pursuance of the statutory provisions relating to the right to buy and related rights as modified by that 1993 Order[17], a secure tenant serves a notice claiming to exercise the right to buy and the interest of the landlord, an intermediate landlord[18] or the freeholder[19] in the dwelling house passes to a person other than a specified authority or body[20], the freeholder must as soon as practicable serve on the tenant a notice in writing telling him that he is no longer entitled to acquire the freehold of the dwelling house[21].

The landlord and an intermediate landlord must:

(i)   on written request give the freeholder such information and assistance as it may reasonably require in order to give effect to the relevant statutory provisions[22]; and

(ii)   ensure that all deeds and other documents in its possession or under its control to which the tenant is entitled or which he reasonably requires on the conveyance to him of the freehold of the dwelling house[23] are available for this purpose[24].

In Wales a local housing authority may apply to the Welsh Ministers for a direction suspending the extended right to buy in its area for a period of up to five years[25].

1   As to the meaning of 'dwelling house' see PARA 231.
2   As to the meaning of 'secure tenancy' see PARA 230 note 2.
3   Ie the Housing Act 1985 Pt V (ss 118–188): see PARAS 230–232, 235 et seq. As to the meaning of 'the right to buy' see PARA 239.
4   Ie the Housing Act 1985 Pt IV (ss 79–117): see LANDLORD AND TENANT vol 63 (2016) PARA 1037 et seq.
5   Housing Act 1985 s 171(1). In exercise of the power so conferred, and prior to the transfer of functions in relation to Wales, the Secretary of State made the Housing (Extension of Right to Buy) Order 1993, SI 1993/2240 (amended by SI 2012/2090), which came into force on 11 October 1993 (Housing (Extension of Right to Buy) Order 1993, SI 1993/2240, art 1) and which modifies the provisions of the Housing Act 1985 Pt V (see note 17). At the date at which this volume states the law, no order under s 171 modifying the provisions of Pt IV had been made.
    Section 171 is omitted where: (1) the Housing (Extension of Right to Buy) Order 1993, SI 1993/2240, applies (see Schedule para 55); (2) the Housing (Preservation of Right to Buy) Regulations 1993, SI 1993/2241 (see PARA 334 et seq), apply (see Sch 1 para 26); (3) the Housing (Right to Acquire) Regulations 1997, SI 1997/619 (right to acquire conferred by the Housing Act 1996 (see PARAS 242–244) or the Housing and Regeneration Act 2008 (see PARAS 240–241)), apply (see the Housing (Right to Acquire) Regulations 1997, SI 1997/619, Sch 1 para 26, applying in relation to the right to acquire under the Housing and Regeneration Act 2008 by virtue of s 184, which applies the Housing Act 1996 s 17 (regulations modifying the Housing Act 1985): see PARA 241).
    As to the appropriate national authority, and the transfer of functions under the Housing Act 1985, so far as exercisable in relation to Wales, to the Welsh Ministers see PARA 7.
6   As to the meaning of 'local authority' see PARA 12.
7   As to new town development corporations see PLANNING vol 83 (2010) PARA 1499 et seq.
8   As to the meaning of 'housing action trust' see PARA 12.
9   As to the meaning of 'urban development corporation' see PARA 12. As to Mayoral development corporations see the Localism Act 2011 s 198; and LONDON GOVERNMENT vol 71 (2013) PARA 323.
10 As to the Regulator of Social Housing see PARA 57.
11 As to registered providers of social housing see PARA 53.
12 As to registered social landlords see PARAS 4, 166 et seq.
13 As to the meaning of 'landlord' see PARA 31 note 4.
14 Housing Act 1985 s 171(2) (amended by the Housing Act 1988 ss 83(1), (5); the Government of Wales Act 1998 ss 140, 152, Sch 16 para 13, Sch 18 Pt IV; the Localism Act 2011 s 222, Sch 22 paras 9, 13; and by SI 1996/2325 and SI 2010/866).
15 Housing Act 1985 s 171(3). In the case of an order made by the Secretary of State, the instrument is subject to annulment in pursuance of a resolution of either House of Parliament: see s 171(3). As to the Secretary of State see PARA 7.
16 Ie the Housing (Extension of the Right to Buy) Order 1993, SI 1993/2240: see note 5.
17 Ie the Housing Act 1985 Pt V as modified by the Housing (Extension of the Right to Buy) Order 1993, SI 1993/2240, Schedule. In this title, those modifications are set out in detail if substantive but are otherwise referred to in the notes to the paragraphs in which the relevant provisions of the Housing Act 1985 Pt V are discussed: see eg PARA 232 note 5. The right to acquire on rent to mortgage terms is now only exercisable if claimed before 18 July 2005: see the Housing Act 1985 s 142A; and PARA 318.

Where there are in a dwelling house let on a secure tenancy one or more interests which are interests to which the Housing (Extension of Right to Buy) Order 1993, SI 1993/2240, art 3 applies, and the dwelling house is a house, the Housing Act 1985 Pt V (ss 118–188) has effect with the modifications specified in the Housing (Extension of Right to Buy) Order 1993, SI 1993/2240, Schedule: art 3(1). Article 3(1) applies to an interest held by a local authority, a new town corporation, a housing action trust, an urban development corporation, the Regulator of Social Housing or Welsh Ministers, or a registered housing association, other than one excepted from the right to buy by the Housing Act 1985 Sch 5 para 1 (charities: see PARA 245), Sch 5 para 2 (co-operatives: see PARA 247) or Sch 5 para 3 (associations which have not received grant: see PARA 247), which is immediately superior to the interest of the landlord or to another interest to which the Housing (Extension of Right to Buy) Order 1993, SI 1993/2240, art 3 applies: art 3(2) (amended by SI 2010/671).

18 'Intermediate landlord' means the owner of a lease of the dwelling house (other than one created by way of security) which is immediately superior to the lease of the landlord or to the lease of another intermediate landlord: Housing Act 1985 s 187 (definition added for these purposes by the Housing (Extension of Right to Buy) Order 1993, SI 1993/2240, Schedule para 64).

19 'Freeholder' means the owner of the freehold of the dwelling house: Housing Act 1985 s 187 (definition as added: see note 18).

20 Ie an authority or body to which the Housing (Extension of Right to Buy) Order 1993, SI 1993/2240, art 3(2) applies (see note 17).

21 Housing (Extension of Right to Buy) Order 1993, SI 1993/2240, art 4.

22 Ie the Housing Act 1985 Pt V as modified by the Housing (Extension of the Right to Buy) Order 1993, SI 1993/2240, Schedule.

23 Ie including in the case of registered land the land certificate and any other documents which would be necessary to perfect the tenant's title if the title were not to be registered: Housing Act 1985 s 177A(b) (as added for these purposes: see note 24). However, land certificates are no longer issued although official copies of the register and of the title plan are available as is a 'title information document' explaining why the official copy has been issued and how to obtain further copies: see REAL PROPERTY AND REGISTRATION vol 87 (2012) PARA 620.

24 Housing Act 1985 s 177A (added for these purposes by the Housing (Extension of the Right to Buy) Order 1993, SI 1993/2240, Schedule para 58).

25 See PARAS 260–265.

234. Information to help tenants decide whether to exercise right to buy etc. Every body which lets dwelling houses[1] under secure tenancies[2] must prepare a document that contains information for its secure tenants[3] about such matters as are specified in an order made by the appropriate national authority[4]. The matters that may be so specified are matters which the appropriate national authority considers that it would be desirable for secure tenants to have information about when considering whether to exercise the right to buy or (where still exercisable) the right to acquire on rent to mortgage terms[5]. The information contained in the document must be restricted to information about the specified matters[6], and the information about those matters:

(1)   must be such as the body concerned considers appropriate; but

(2)   must be in a form which the body considers best suited to explaining those matters in simple terms[7].

Once a body has prepared the document so required, it must revise that document as often as it considers necessary in order to ensure that the information contained in it:

(a)   is kept up to date so far as is reasonably practicable; and

(b)   reflects any changes in the matters for the time being specified in an order made under the above provisions[8].

The following provisions set out when the document so prepared by a body is to be published or otherwise made available[9]. The body must:

(i)   publish the document, whether in its original or a revised form; and

(ii)   supply copies of it to the body's secure tenants,

at such times as may be prescribed by, and otherwise in accordance with, an order[10] made by the appropriate national authority[11]. Following publication of the document in accordance with these requirements, a landlord must supply a copy of the document:

(A)   as soon as is reasonably practicable to each of its secure tenants at that time; and

(B)   to each subsequent new secure tenant at the time he signs his tenancy; and a landlord must supply each of its secure tenants with a copy of the current version of the document at least once in every period of five years beginning with the date on which the document was supplied pursuant to head (A) above[12].

The body must make copies of the current version[13] of the document available to be supplied, free of charge, to persons requesting them[14]. The copies must be made available for that purpose at the body's principal offices, and at such other places as it considers appropriate, at reasonable hours[15]. The body must take such steps as it considers appropriate to bring to the attention of its secure tenants the fact that copies of the current version of the document can be obtained free of charge from the places where, and at the times when, they are so made available[16].

1   As to the meaning of 'dwelling house' see PARA 231.
2   As to the meaning of 'secure tenancy' see PARA 230 note 2. See also PARA 230 notes 7, 9. As to secure tenancies see LANDLORD AND TENANT vol 63 (2016) PARA 1037 et seq. Note that under the Renting Homes (Wales) Act 2016 (generally in force as from a day to be appointed: see PARA 6) secure tenancies will be converted to secure contracts and landlords will be either community landlords or private landlords: see LANDLORD AND TENANT vol 62 (2016) PARA 45.
3   As to the meaning of 'secure tenant' see PARA 230 note 2. See also PARA 230 notes 7, 9. As to secure tenants see LANDLORD AND TENANT vol 63 (2016) PARA 1037 et seq.
4   Housing Act 1985 s 121AA(1) (ss 121AA, 121B added by the Housing Act 2004 s 189(1)). As to the appropriate national authority, the Secretary of State and the transfer of functions under the Housing Act 1985, so far as exercisable in relation to Wales, to the Welsh Ministers see PARA 7.
     An order under the Housing Act 1985 s 121AA or s 121B must be made by statutory instrument, subject (if made by the Secretary of State) to annulment in pursuance of a resolution of either House of Parliament: ss 121AA(5), 121B(7) (as so added). In exercise of this power, the Secretary of State has made the Housing (Right to Buy) (Information to Secure Tenants) (England) Order 2005, SI 2005/1735, which came into force on 26 July 2005 and applies in relation to England only (art 1); and the Assembly has made the Housing (Right to Buy) (Information to Secure Tenants) (Wales) Order 2005, SI 2005/2681, which came into force on 28 September 2005 and applies in relation to Wales (art 1). See further notes 6, 11.
5   Housing Act 1985 s 121AA(2) (as added: see note 4). As to the meaning of 'the right to buy' see PARA 239; and see also PARA 230 notes 7, 9. As to the right to acquire on rent to mortgage terms (now only exercisable if claimed before 18 July 2005: see the Housing Act 1985 s 142A; and PARA 318) see PARA 318.
6   The specified matters are the matters set out in the Housing (Right to Buy) (Information to Secure Tenants) (England) Order 2005, SI 2005/1735, art 3, Schedule, and the Housing (Right to Buy) (Information to Secure Tenants) (Wales) Order 2005, SI 2005/2681, art 3, Schedule (Schedule amended by SI 2012/2090), ie the following matters:
     (1)   an outline of the effect of the provisions of the Housing Act 1985 Pt V (ss 118–188) relating to:
            (a)   the circumstances in which the right to buy can and cannot be exercised, including, in relation to Wales, the effect of a suspension of the right to buy under the Housing (Wales) Measure 2011 Pt 1 (ss 1–34);
            (b)   the exceptions to the right to buy set out in the Housing Act 1985 Sch 5 (see PARA 245 et seq);
            (c)   the procedure for claiming to exercise the right to buy (see PARA 273 et seq);
            (d)   the price payable for the dwelling house by a tenant exercising the right to buy (see PARA 283 et seq) in England or the method of calculation of the price payable for the dwelling house by a tenant exercising the right to buy in Wales; and
            (e)   the delay notice procedures for landlords and tenants set out in ss 140, 141, 153A, 153B (see PARAS 316–317, 319–320);

(2)   the fact that initial costs are likely to be incurred by a secure tenant exercising the right to buy; and this reference to initial costs includes costs in respect of stamp duty, legal and survey fees and valuation fees and costs associated with taking out a mortgage;

(3)   the fact that a secure tenant will be likely to have to make regular payments as an owner of a dwelling house; and this reference to regular payments includes payments in respect of:

(a)   any mortgage or charge on the dwelling house;

(b)   building insurance, life assurance, and mortgage payment protection insurance;

(c)   council tax;

(d)   water, sewerage, gas, electricity, or other utility services;

(4)   the risk of repossession of the dwelling house if regular mortgage payments are not made;

(5)   the fact that in order to keep the property maintained and in good repair an owner of a dwelling house will be likely to have to incur expenditure which may include payment of service charges, in respect of major works in England or both annual and in respect of major works in Wales.

7   Housing Act 1985 s 121AA(3) (as added: see note 4).
8   Housing Act 1985 s 121AA(4) (as added: see note 4).
9   Housing Act 1985 s 121B(1) (as added: see note 4).
10 See note 4.
11 Housing Act 1985 s 121B(2) (as added: see note 4). A landlord was to publish the document within two months of 26 July 2005 in England or within two months of 28 September 2005 in Wales; and, where it revises the document, the landlord must publish the document in its revised form within one month of the revision: Housing (Right to Buy) (Information to Secure Tenants) (England) Order 2005, SI 2005/1735, art 4; Housing (Right to Buy) (Information to Secure Tenants) (Wales) Order 2005, SI 2005/2681, art 4.
12 Housing (Right to Buy) (Information to Secure Tenants) (England) Order 2005, SI 2005/1735, art 5; Housing (Right to Buy) (Information to Secure Tenants) (Wales) Order 2005, SI 2005/2681, art 5.
13 For these purposes, any reference to the current version of the document is to the version of the document that was last published by the body in accordance with the Housing Act 1985 s 121B(2)(a) (see head (i) in the text): s 121B(6) (as added: see note 4).
14 Housing Act 1985 s 121B(3) (as added: see note 4).
15 Housing Act 1985 s 121B(4) (as added: see note 4).
16 Housing Act 1985 s 121B(5) (as added: see note 4).

235. Costs. An agreement between the landlord[1] and a tenant[2] claiming to exercise:

(1)   the right to buy[3];

(2)   the right to acquire on rent to mortgage terms, where it is still exercisable[4]; or

(3)   any right to make a final or interim payment on the redemption of a landlord's share[5]; or

(4)   the right to acquire conferred by the Housing Act 1996[6] or the Housing and Regeneration Act 2008[7],

is void in so far as it purports to oblige the tenant to bear any part of the costs incurred by the landlord in connection with the tenant's exercise of that right[8].

1   As to the meaning of 'landlord' see PARA 31 note 3.
2   As to the meaning of 'tenant' see PARA 31 note 3.
3   As to the right to buy see PARA 239 et seq. See also PARA 230 notes 7, 9.
4   As to the right to acquire on rent to mortgage terms see PARA 318. That right is now only exercisable if claimed before 18 July 2005: see the Housing Act 1985 s 142A; and PARA 318.
5   Ie any such right as is mentioned in the Housing Act 1985 Sch 6A para 2(1) or Sch 6A para 6(1) (see PARA 318).
6   See PARAS 242–244.
7   See PARAS 240–241.
8   Housing Act 1985 s 178 (substituted by the Leasehold Reform, Housing and Urban Development Act 1993 s 187(1), Sch 21 para 21; further substituted, for the purposes of the right to acquire mentioned in head (4) in the text, by the Housing (Right to Acquire) Regulations 1997, SI 1997/619, Sch 1 para 32, applying in relation to the right to acquire under the Housing and Regeneration Act 2008 by virtue of s 184, which applies the Housing Act 1996 s 17 (regulations modifying the Housing Act 1985): see PARA 241). The Housing Act 1985 s 178: is (1) modified

where the Housing (Extension of Right to Buy) Order 1993, SI 1993/2240 (see PARA 233), applies (see Schedule para 59); (2) further substituted where the Housing (Preservation of Right to Buy) Regulations 1993, SI 1993/2241 (see PARA 334 et seq), apply (see Sch 1 para 34).

236. Notices and evidence. The appropriate national authority may by regulations prescribe the form of any notice under the statutory provisions relating to the right to buy and related rights[1] and the particulars to be contained in the notice[2]; and such regulations:

(1)   may make different provision with respect to different cases or descriptions of case, including different provision for different areas; and

(2)   must be made by statutory instrument[3].

Where the form of, and the particulars to be contained in, such a notice are so prescribed, a tenant[4] who proposes to claim, or has claimed, to exercise the right to buy may request the landlord[5] to supply him with a form for use in giving such notice; and the landlord must do so within seven days of the request[6].

A notice may be served by sending it by post[7].

Where the landlord is a housing association[8], a notice to be served by the tenant on the landlord may be served by leaving it at, or sending it to, the principal office of the association or the office of the association with which the tenant usually deals[9].

A notice served by a tenant under the statutory provisions relating to the rights referred to above is not invalidated by an error in, or omission from, the particulars which are required[10] to be contained in the notice[11]. Where as a result of such an error or omission:

(a)   the landlord has mistakenly admitted or denied the right to buy[12] or the right to acquire on rent to mortgage terms[13]; or

(b)   the landlord has formed a mistaken opinion as to any matter required to be stated in a notice by any of the specified statutory provisions[14] and has stated that opinion in the notice,

the parties must, as soon as practicable after they become aware of the mistake, take all such steps, whether by way of amending, withdrawing or re-serving any notice or extending any period or otherwise, as may be requisite for the purpose of securing that all parties are, as nearly as may be, in the same position as they would have been if the mistake had not been made[15].

A landlord or the appropriate national authority may, if it thinks fit, accept a statutory declaration[16] made for the purposes of the statutory provisions relating to the rights referred to above as sufficient evidence of the matters declared in it[17].

1   Ie the Housing Act 1985 Pt V (ss 118–188): see PARAS 230 et seq, 237 et seq.
2   Housing Act 1985 s 176(1). For examples of the exercise of this power see the Housing (Right to Buy) (Prescribed Forms) Regulations 1986, SI 1986/2194 (amended by SI 1993/2246, SI 2015/1542 and SI 2015/1736; revoked in relation to Wales by SI 2015/1320); the Housing (Right to Buy Delay Procedure) (Prescribed Forms) Regulations 1989, SI 1989/240 (amended by SI 1993/2245; revoked in relation to Wales by SI 2015/1320); and the Housing (Right to Buy) (Prescribed Forms) (Wales) Regulations 2015, SI 2015/1320 (amended by SI 2015/1795). As to the appropriate national authority, and the transfer of functions under the Housing Act 1985, so far as exercisable in relation to Wales, to the Welsh Ministers see PARA 7.
    The Housing Act 1985 s 176 is modified where: (1) the Housing (Extension of Right to Buy) Order 1993, SI 1993/2240 (see PARA 233), applies (see Schedule para 56); (2) the Housing (Preservation of Right to Buy) Regulations 1993, SI 1993/2241 (see PARA 334 et seq), apply (see Sch 1 para 32); (3) the Housing (Right to Acquire) Regulations 1997, SI 1997/619 (right to acquire conferred by the Housing Act 1996 (see PARAS 242–244) or the Housing and Regeneration Act 2008 (see PARAS 240–241)), apply (see the Housing (Right to Acquire) Regulations 1997, SI 1997/619, Sch 1 para 30, applying in relation to the right to acquire under the Housing and Regeneration Act 2008 by virtue of s 184, which applies the Housing Act 1996 s 17 (regulations modifying the Housing Act 1985): see PARA 241).

3 Housing Act 1985 s 176(5); and see note 2.
4 As to the meaning of 'tenant' see PARA 31 note 3.
5 As to the meaning of 'landlord' see PARA 31 note 3.
6 Housing Act 1985 s 176(2). See also note 2.
7 Housing Act 1985 s 176(3).
8 As to the meaning of 'housing association' see PARA 13.
9 Housing Act 1985 s 176(4). See also note 2.
10 Ie by regulations under the Housing Act 1985 s 176.
11 Housing Act 1985 s 177(1).
12 Ie under the Housing Act 1985 s 124: see PARA 275.
13 Ie under the Housing Act 1985 s 146: see PARA 318. The right to acquire on rent to mortgage terms is now only exercisable if claimed before 18 July 2005: see the Housing Act 1985 s 142A; and PARA 318.
14 The provisions so specified are the Housing Act 1985 s 125 (see PARA 276) and s 146 (see PARA 318): s 177(3) (amended by the Leasehold Reform, Housing and Urban Development Act 1993 s 187(1), (2), Sch 21 para 20(2), Sch 22).
15 Housing Act 1985 s 177(2) (amended by the Leasehold Reform, Housing and Urban Development Act 1993 Sch 21 para 20(1), Sch 22). The Housing Act 1985 s 177(2) does not, however, apply where the tenant has exercised the right to which the notice relates before the parties become aware of the mistake: s 177(4).
    Section 177 is: (1) modified where the Housing (Extension of Right to Buy) Order 1993, SI 1993/2240, applies (see Schedule para 57); (2) omitted where the Housing (Preservation of Right to Buy) Regulations 1993, SI 1993/2241, apply (see Sch 1 para 33); (3) omitted where the Housing (Right to Acquire) Regulations 1997, SI 1997/619, apply (see Sch 1 para 31; and see also note 2).
16 As to statutory declarations see CIVIL PROCEDURE vol 12 (2015) PARA 827.
17 Housing Act 1985 s 180 (amended by the Leasehold Reform, Housing and Urban Development Act 1993 Sch 22). The Housing Act 1985 s 180 is modified where: (1) the Housing (Extension of Right to Buy) Order 1993, SI 1993/2240, applies (see Schedule para 61); (2) the Housing (Preservation of Right to Buy) Regulations 1993, SI 1993/2241, apply (see Sch 1 para 36); (3) the Housing (Right to Acquire) Regulations 1997, SI 1997/619, apply (see Sch 1 para 34; and see note 2).

237. Power to repeal or amend local Acts. The appropriate national authority may by order repeal or amend a provision of a local Act passed before 8 August 1980 where it appears to it that the provision is inconsistent with a statutory provision relating to the right to buy[1]. Before making such an order, the appropriate national authority must consult any local housing authority[2] appearing to it to be concerned[3].

An order so made may contain such transitional, incidental or supplementary provisions as the appropriate national authority considers appropriate[4]; and such an order:

(1) may make different provision with respect to different cases or descriptions of case, including different provision for different areas; and

(2) must be made by statutory instrument[5].

1 Housing Act 1985 s 182(1) (amended by the Leasehold Reform, Housing and Urban Development Act 1993 s 187(2), Sch 22). As to the right to buy see PARA 239 et seq. As to the appropriate national authority, the Secretary of State and the transfer of functions under the Housing Act 1985, so far as exercisable in relation to Wales, to the Welsh Ministers see PARA 7.
2 As to the meaning of 'local housing authority' see PARA 11.
3 Housing Act 1985 s 182(2).
4 Housing Act 1985 s 182(3).
5 Housing Act 1985 s 182(4). If made by the Secretary of State, such an instrument is subject to annulment in pursuance of a resolution of either House of Parliament: see s 182(4). As to the Secretary of State see PARA 7.
    Section 182 is omitted where: (1) the Housing (Preservation of Right to Buy) Regulations 1993, SI 1993/2241 (see PARA 334 et seq), apply (see Sch 1 para 38); (2) the Housing (Right to Acquire) Regulations 1997, SI 1997/619 (right to acquire conferred by the Housing Act 1996 (see PARAS 242–244) or the Housing and Regeneration Act 2008 (see PARAS 240–241)), apply (see the Housing (Right to Acquire) Regulations 1997, SI 1997/619, Sch 1 para 36; applying in relation to

the right to acquire under the Housing and Regeneration Act 2008 by virtue of s 184, which applies the Housing Act 1996 s 17 (regulations modifying the Housing Act 1985): see PARA 241).

238. Implementing the right to buy on a voluntary basis: England. The Secretary of State[1] may make grants to private registered providers[2] in respect of right to buy discounts[3]. A grant may be made on any terms and conditions the Secretary of State considers appropriate[4].

The Greater London Authority may make grants to private registered providers in respect of right to buy discounts for dwellings in London[5]. Such a grant may be made on any terms and conditions the Greater London Authority considers appropriate[6].

The Regulator of Social Housing[7] must, if requested to do so by the Secretary of State, monitor compliance with the home ownership criteria[8]. On making such a request the Secretary of State must publish the home ownership criteria specified in the request[9]. The Regulator must provide such reports or other information as the Secretary of State may request about compliance with the home ownership criteria[10]. The Secretary of State may publish information about a private registered provider that has not met the home ownership criteria[11].

1 As to the Secretary of State see PARA 7.
2 'Private registered provider' means a private registered provider of social housing: Housing and Planning Act 2016 s 68. As to private registered providers of social housing see PARA 53.
3 Housing and Planning Act 2016 s 64(1). 'Right to buy discount' means a discount given to a tenant of a dwelling on the disposal of the dwelling to the tenant otherwise than in the exercise of a right conferred by an Act: s 68. As to the meaning of 'dwelling' see PARA 52 note 8 (definition applied by s 68).
  See also the Housing and Regeneration Act 2008 s 47 (which would allow the Secretary of State to direct the Homes and Communities Agency to use its powers to make grants of the kind mentioned in the text: see PLANNING vol 83 (2010) PARA 1485): Housing and Planning Act 2016 s 64(3).
4 Housing and Planning Act 2016 s 64(2).
5 Housing and Planning Act 2016 s 65(1). As to the Greater London Authority see LONDON GOVERNMENT vol 71 (2013) PARA 67 et seq.
6 Housing and Planning Act 2016 s 65(2).
7 As to the Regulator of Social Housing see PARA 57 et seq.
8 Housing and Planning Act 2016 s 66(1). 'The home ownership criteria' means criteria, specified in the request, that relate to the sale of dwellings by private registered providers to tenants otherwise than in exercise of a right conferred by an Act: s 66(2). The criteria may be expressed by reference to other documents: s 66(3).
9 Housing and Planning Act 2016 s 66(4).
10 Housing and Planning Act 2016 s 66(5).
11 Housing and Planning Act 2016 s 66(6).

(ii) Exercise of the Right to Buy or Acquire

A. THE RELEVANT RIGHTS

(A) Secure Tenants' Rights in England and Wales

239. Right to acquire freehold or lease. A secure tenant[1] has the right to buy, that is to say, the right[2]:

(1) if the dwelling house[3] is a house[4] and the landlord[5] owns the freehold, to acquire the freehold of the dwelling house;

(2) if the landlord does not own the freehold or if the dwelling house is a flat[6], whether or not the landlord owns the freehold, to be granted a lease[7] of the dwelling house[8].

Where a secure tenancy is a joint tenancy, then, whether or not each of the joint tenants occupies the dwelling house as his only or principal home[9], the right to buy belongs jointly to all of them or to such one or more of them as may be agreed between them; but such an agreement is not valid unless the person or at least one of the persons to whom the right to buy is to belong occupies the dwelling house as his only or principal home[10].

The above provisions do not, in themselves, impose any duty, express or implied, on the landlord; they merely state the tenant's right, which is to be established by the procedures under the Housing Act 1985, and which can lead eventually to a duty on the landlord to convey the property, or to grant a lease[11], to the tenant[12].

1　As to the meaning of 'secure tenant' see PARA 230 note 2; and as to the meaning of 'tenant' see PARA 31 note 3. Note that under the Renting Homes (Wales) Act 2016 (generally in force as from a day to be appointed: see PARA 6) secure tenancies in Wales will become secure contracts and tenants under secure contracts are likely to be excluded from the right to buy: see PARA 226.

2　Ie in the circumstances and subject to the conditions and exceptions stated in the Housing Act 1985 Pt V (ss 118–188): see PARA 245 et seq.

3　As to the meaning of 'dwelling house' see PARA 231.

4　As to the meaning of 'house' see PARA 231.

5　As to the meaning of 'landlord' see PARA 31 note 3.

6　As to the meaning of 'flat' see PARA 231.

7　As to the meaning of 'lease' see PARA 31 note 3. As to the circumstances in which a landlord does not have a sufficient interest to grant a lease for these purposes see PARA 248. A lease granted in pursuance of the right to buy is a long lease for the purposes of the Landlord and Tenant Act 1987: see s 59(3)(c); and LANDLORD AND TENANT vol 62 (2016) PARA 141 note 1.

8　Housing Act 1985 s 118(1). See *Haringey London Borough Council v Hines* [2010] EWCA Civ 1111, [2011] HLR 92, [2010] All ER (D) 188 (Oct) (on the facts, the judge found that the defendant's principal home was an alternative property so she was not a secure tenant (because she did not satisfy the tenancy condition set out in LANDLORD AND TENANT vol 63 (2016) PARA 1037) at the time she claimed the right to buy; but that finding did not carry with it the further conclusions that he drew as to her dishonest intention, so the award of damages against her for fraudulent misrepresentation was reversed on appeal).

　　The Housing Act 1985 s 118(1) is substituted where: (1) the Housing (Extension of Right to Buy) Order 1993, SI 1993/2240 (see PARA 233), applies (see Schedule para 1); (2) the Housing (Right to Acquire) Regulations 1997, SI 1997/619 (right to acquire conferred by the Housing Act 1996 (see PARAS 242–244) or the Housing and Regeneration Act 2008 (see PARAS 240–241), apply (see the Housing (Right to Acquire) Regulations 1997, SI 1997/619, Sch 1 para 3; and see PARAS 240, 242).

9　As to the meaning of 'only or principal home' see LANDLORD AND TENANT vol 63 (2016) PARA 1037 note 27.

10　Housing Act 1985 s 118(2). Section 118(2) is omitted where the Housing (Preservation of Right to Buy) Regulations 1993, SI 1993/2241 (see PARA 334 et seq), apply: see Sch 1 para 3.

11　Ie under the Housing Act 1985 s 138: see PARA 291.

12　See *Francis v Southwark London Borough Council* [2011] EWCA Civ 1418, [2012] HLR 241, [2011] All ER (D) 54 (Dec) (nothing in the Housing Act 1985 s 118 suggests that Parliament intended that provision to create a remedy in damages for breach of statutory duty).

(B)　Other Social Housing Tenants' Rights in England

240. Certain tenants' rights to acquire dwelling. Since the phasing out of secure tenancies after 15 January 1989[1], most new tenants of social housing, other than tenants of local housing authorities, have, except for certain transitional cases, been granted assured tenancies[2]. Under the Housing and Regeneration Act 2008, the tenant[3] of a dwelling[4] in England has a right to acquire the dwelling if:

(1)　the landlord is a private registered provider[5] or a registered social landlord[6];

(2)　the tenancy is an assured tenancy[7], other than a long tenancy[8], or a secure tenancy[9];

(3)　the provision of the dwelling was publicly funded[10];

(4)　the dwelling has remained in the social rented sector[11] ever since that provision; and

(5)   the tenant satisfies any applicable[12] qualifying conditions[13].

This right reproduces and replaces the right to acquire a dwelling originally conferred on certain assured tenants by the Housing Act 1996, the relevant provisions of which now only apply in relation to dwellings in Wales[14].

In the circumstances and subject to the statutory conditions and exceptions[15], the right to acquire is the right:

(a)   if the dwelling house[16] is a house[17] and the landlord[18] owns the freehold, to acquire the freehold of the dwelling house;

(b)   if the landlord does not own the freehold (it may have a leasehold interest) or if the dwelling house is a flat[19] (whether or not the landlord owns the freehold), to be granted a lease[20] of the dwelling house[21].

Where a tenancy is a joint tenancy then, whether or not each of the joint tenants occupies the dwelling house as his only or principal home[22], the right to acquire belongs jointly to all of them or to such one or more of them as may be agreed between them; but such an agreement is not valid unless the person or at least one of the persons to whom the right to acquire is to belong occupies the dwelling house as his only or principal home[23].

Regulations under the Town and Country Planning Act 1990 may make provision for securing that in prescribed circumstances:

(i)   the right to acquire social housing under the above provisions is not exercisable in relation to land the development of which is authorised by a community right to build order[24]; or

(ii)   the exercise of that right in relation to that land is subject to modifications provided for by the regulations[25].

The Neighbourhood Planning (General) Regulations 2012 are partly made in the exercise of these powers[26].

1   See the Housing Act 1985 s 80; and LANDLORD AND TENANT vol 63 (2016) PARA 1037 head (8).

2   See the Housing Act 1988 s 35; and LANDLORD AND TENANT vol 63 (2016) PARAS 821, 1031.

3   As to the meaning of 'tenant' in relation to social housing see PARA 52 note 9. As to the meaning of 'social housing' see PARA 52.

4   As to the meaning of 'dwelling' see PARA 52 note 8.

5   As to the meaning of 'private registered provider' see PARA 53. As to the reference in head (1) in the text to a private registered provider see PARA 102 note 3.

6   As to the meaning of 'registered social landlord' for these purposes see PARA 102 note 4. As to registered social landlords see PARAS 4, 166 et seq.

7   As to the meaning of 'assured tenancy' see PARA 80 note 49. The Secretary of State may by regulations provide that an assured shorthold tenancy of a description specified in the regulations is not a tenancy within s 180(2) (see head (2) in the text): s 180(2A) (added by the Localism Act 2011 s 165(1), (3), with effect from 15 January 2012: see the Localism Act 2011 (Commencement No 2 and Transitional and Saving Provision) Order 2012, SI 2012/57, art 4(1)(r)). As to the Secretary of State see PARA 7. As to the exercise of this power see PARA 256.

    Prior to 1 April 2012, when the Localism Act 2011 ss 165(2), Sch 25 Pt 23 (see note 11) came into force (see the Localism Act 2011 (Commencement No 4 and Transitional, Transitory and Saving Provisions) Order 2012, SI 2012/628, art 6(c)), a dwelling let on any assured shorthold tenancy was excluded from the right to acquire: see the Housing and Regeneration Act 2008 s 180(1), (2) as amended by SI 2010/844. The amendments made by the Localism Act 2011 s 165 do not apply in relation to an assured shorthold tenancy that: (1) was granted before the day on which s 165 came into force; or (2) came into being by virtue of the Housing Act 1988 s 5 (periodic tenancy arising on termination of fixed term: see LANDLORD AND TENANT vol 63 (2016) PARA 884) on the coming to an end of an assured shorthold tenancy within head (1) above: Localism Act 2011 s 165(4).

8   As to the meaning of 'long tenancy' for these purposes see PARA 102 note 6. See also PARA 270 note 4.

9   As to the meaning of 'secure tenancy' see PARA 80 note 49.

10   As to when the provision of a dwelling was publicly funded see PARA 102 note 8.

11   As to determining whether a dwelling has remained in the social rented sector PARA 102 note 9.

12 Ie applicable under the Housing Act 1985 Pt V as it applies by virtue of s 184: see PARA 241.

13 Housing and Regeneration Act 2008 s 180(1), (2) (amended by the Localism Act 2011 ss 165(1), (2), Sch 25 Pt 23; and by SI 2010/844).

14 See PARAS 242–244.

15 Ie subject to the conditions and exceptions set out in the Housing Act 1985 ss 118(2)–188 (applied for these purposes by virtue of the Housing and Regeneration Act 2008 s 184, which applies the Housing Act 1996 s 17 (regulations modifying the Housing Act 1985): see PARA 241): see the text and note 21; and PARA 245 et seq.

16 As to the meaning of 'dwelling house' see PARA 231.

17 As to the meaning of 'house' see PARA 231.

18 As to the meaning of 'landlord' see PARA 31 note 3.

19 As to the meaning of 'flat' see PARA 231.

20 As to the meaning of 'lease' see PARA 31 note 3.

21 Housing Act 1985 s 118(1) (substituted for these purposes by the Housing (Right to Acquire) Regulations 1997, SI 1997/619, Sch 1 para 3; and see note 15).

22 As to the meaning of 'only or principal home' see LANDLORD AND TENANT vol 63 (2016) PARA 1037 note 27.

23 Housing Act 1985 s 118(2).

24 As to community right to build orders see the Town and Country Planning Act 1990 Sch 4C (added by the Localism Act 2011 Sch 11); and PLANNING.

25 See the Town and Country Planning Act 1990 Sch 4C para 11 (as added: see note 24); and PLANNING.

26 See the Neighbourhood Planning (General) Regulations 2012, SI 2012/637; LANDLORD AND TENANT vol 64 (2016) PARA 1167; and PLANNING.

241. Supplementary provisions relating to the right to acquire. The following provisions[1] apply in relation to the right to acquire a dwelling conferred by the relevant provisions[2] of the Housing and Regeneration Act 2008[3].

The Secretary of State may by order[4]:

(1) specify the amount or rate of discount to be given on the exercise of the right to acquire[5]; and

(2) designate rural areas in relation to dwellings in which that right does not arise[6].

Before making an order which would have the effect that an area ceased to be designated under head (2) above, the Secretary of State must consult:

(a) the local housing authority[7] or authorities in whose district[8] the area or any part of it is situated or, if the order is general in its effect, local housing authorities in general; and

(b) such bodies appearing to him to be representative of private registered providers[9] as he considers appropriate[10].

The provisions of Part V of the Housing Act 1985[11] apply in relation to the above-mentioned right to acquire[12] subject to any such order and subject to such other exceptions, adaptations and other modifications[13] as may be specified by regulations made by the Secretary of State[14]. The regulations may provide that:

(i) the powers of the Secretary of State to intervene, give directions or assist[15] do not apply;

(ii) the statutory exceptions for charities and certain housing associations[16] and the right of appeal to Secretary of State with regard to dwellings for elderly persons[17] do not apply;

(iii) the statutory provisions relating to the right to acquire on rent to mortgage terms (where still exercisable)[18] do not apply;

(iv) the provisions relating to restrictions on disposals in National Parks etc[19] do not apply; and

(v) the provisions relating to the preserved right to buy[20] do not apply;

but nothing in heads (i) to (v) above affects the generality of the power[21] to make such regulations[22].

1 Ie the Housing Act 1996 s 17, modified for these purposes by the Housing and Regeneration Act 2008 s 184(2).
2 Ie the Housing and Regeneration Act 2008 ss 180–183: see PARA 240.
3 See the Housing and Regeneration Act 2008 s 184(1), (2) (s 184(2)(c) amended by SI 2010/844).
4 An order or regulations under the Housing Act 1996 s 17 may make different provision for different cases or classes of case including different areas, and may contain such incidental, supplementary and transitional provisions as the Secretary of State considers appropriate (s 17(5) (modified by the Housing and Regeneration Act 2008 s 184(2)(b)) and must be made by statutory instrument subject to annulment in pursuance of a resolution of either House of Parliament (Housing Act 1996 s 17(7) (modified by the Housing and Regeneration Act 2008 s 184(2)(b), (d)).
5 Ie the right under the Housing and Regeneration Act 1980 s 180: see PARA 240.
   The Housing (Right to Acquire) (Discount) Order 2002, SI 2002/1091, which prescribes different amounts of discount applicable to dwellings in specified areas in England, subject to a maximum amount of discount of 50% of the value of the dwelling (see art 2, Schedule) is made in the exercise of the power under head (1) in the text.
6 Housing Act 1996 s 17(1) (modified by the Housing and Regeneration Act 1980 s 184(1), (2)). As to the exercise of the power conferred by head (2) in the text see eg the Housing (Right to Acquire or Enfranchise) (Designated Rural Areas in the West Midlands) Order 1997, SI 1997/620; the Housing (Right to Acquire or Enfranchise) (Designated Rural Areas in the South East) Order 1997, SI 1997/625. As to the Secretary of State see PARA 7.
7 As to the meaning of 'local housing authority' see PARA 11 (definition applied by the Housing Act 1996 s 230).
8 As to the meaning of 'district' see PARA 11 (definition applied by the Housing Act 1996 s 230).
9 As to private registered providers of social housing see PARA 53.
10 Housing Act 1996 s 17(6) (modified by the Housing and Regeneration Act 2008 s 184(2)(b), (c) (s 184(2)(c) as amended: see note 3)).
11 Ie the Housing Act 1985 Pt V (ss 118–188): see PARAS 230 et seq, PARA 245 et seq.
12 Ie under the Housing and Regeneration Act 2008 s 180: see PARA 240.
13 For these purposes, 'modifications' includes additions, alterations and omissions and cognate expressions must be construed accordingly: Housing Act 1996 s 63(1).
14 Housing Act 1996 s 17(2) (modified by the Housing and Regeneration Act 2008 s 184(2)(a), (b)). The specified exceptions, adaptations and other modifications must take the form of textual amendments of the provisions of the Housing Act 1985 Pt V as they apply in relation to the right to buy under that Part; and the first regulations, and any subsequent consolidating regulations, must set out the provisions of Pt V as they so apply: Housing Act 1996 s 17(4).
15 Ie under the Housing Act 1985 ss 164–170: see PARA 341 et seq.
16 Ie the Housing Act 1985 Sch 5 paras 1, 3: see PARAS 245–247.
17 Ie the Housing Act 1985 Sch 5 para 11: see PARA 252.
18 As to the right to acquire on rent to mortgage terms (now only exercisable if claimed before 18 July 2005: see the Housing Act 1985 s 142A; and PARA 318) see PARA 318.
19 Ie the Housing Act 1985 s 157: see PARA 333.
20 As to the preserved right to buy see PARA 334 et seq.
21 Ie the power conferred by the Housing Act 1996 s 17(2): see the text and notes 11–14.
22 Housing Act 1996 s 17(3) (modified by the Housing and Regeneration Act 2008 s 184(2)(a), (b)). The Housing (Right to Acquire) Regulations 1997, SI 1997/619, which came into force on 1 April 1997 (reg 1) and are made in the exercise of the power under the Housing Act 1996 s 17 thus apply in relation to the right to acquire under the Housing and Regeneration Act 2008 ss 180–183. By virtue of s 184(1), (2) (see the text and notes 1–3), the Housing Act 1985 Pt V has effect for the purposes of the right to acquire under the Housing and Regeneration Act 2008 ss 180–183 subject to the modifications made by the Housing (Right to Acquire) Regulations 1997, SI 1997/619, reg 2(1), Sch 1, and set out in reg 2(2), Sch 2. It is submitted that Schs 1, 2 are now to be read in the light of subsequent legislative amendments to the Housing Act 1985 Pt V by eg the Civil Partnership Act 2004 and the Housing Act 2004, even where the 1997 Regulations have not themselves been correspondingly amended. In this title, the modifications made by the 1997 Regulations are not all set out in detail but may be referred to in the notes to the paragraphs in which the relevant provisions of the Housing Act 1985 Pt V are discussed: see eg PARA 237 note 5. For exceptions to the right to acquire see the Housing Act 1985 Sch 5 (as so modified). See also the Housing (Right of First Refusal) (England) Regulations 2005, SI 2005/1917, partly made under the powers so conferred); and PARA 328 et seq.

(C)   Other Social Housing Tenants' Rights in Wales

242. Tenants of registered social landlords or private registered providers of social housing in Wales: right to acquire dwelling. Since the phasing out of secure tenancies after 15 January 1989[1], most new tenants of social housing, except tenants of local housing authorities, have been granted assured tenancies[2]. Prior to the Housing Act 1996, most tenants of registered social landlords[3] did not have a statutory right to buy their homes because of the exclusions contained in Schedule 5 to the Housing Act 1985[4]. Registered social landlords[5] in Wales are, however, permitted to offer discounts to the tenants who wish to buy their homes[6]. Further, under the Housing Act 1996 the tenant of a dwelling[7] in Wales has a right to acquire the dwelling if:

(1)   the landlord is a registered social landlord or a private registered provider of social housing[8];

(2)   the tenancy is an assured tenancy[9], other than an assured shorthold tenancy[10] or a long tenancy[11], or is a secure tenancy[12];

(3)   the dwelling was provided with public money[13] and has remained in the social rented sector[14]; and

(4)   the tenant satisfies any further qualifying conditions applicable under the right to buy provisions of the Housing Act 1985[15] as they apply in relation to the right[16] of a tenant to acquire a dwelling[17].

As from a day to be appointed[18], these provisions also apply with modifications in Wales, in relation to a dwelling ('a funded dwelling') provided or acquired wholly or in part by means of a grant[19] to a body other than a registered social landlord[20]. For this purpose, the reference in the above provisions to a registered social landlord includes a reference to any person to whom such a grant has been paid[21].

A tenant of a registered social landlord who satisfies the above conditions has the right to acquire, that is to say, the right, in the circumstances and subject to the conditions and exceptions stated in the relevant provisions of Part V of the Housing Act 1985[22]:

(a)   if the dwelling house[23] is a house and the landlord owns the freehold, to acquire the freehold of the dwelling house;

(b)   if the landlord does not own the freehold or if the dwelling house is a flat, whether or not the landlord owns the freehold, to be granted a lease of the dwelling house[24].

Where a tenancy is a joint tenancy then, whether or not each of the joint tenants occupies the dwelling house as his only or principal home[25], the right to acquire belongs jointly to all of them or to such one or more of them as may be agreed between them; but such an agreement is not valid unless the person or at least one of the persons to whom the right to acquire is to belong occupies the dwelling house as his only or principal home[26].

A local housing authority may apply to the Welsh Ministers for a direction suspending the extended right to buy in its area for a period of up to five years[27].

Under the Renting Homes (Wales) Act 2016, the new forms of tenure are likely to exclude tenants from the right to buy[28].

1   See the Housing Act 1985 s 80; and LANDLORD AND TENANT vol 63 (2016) PARA 1037 head (8).
2   See the Housing Act 1988 s 35; and LANDLORD AND TENANT vol 63 (2016) PARAS 821, 1031.
3   As to the meaning of 'registered social landlord' see PARA 13.
4   See the Housing Act 1985 s 120, Sch 5; and PARA 245 et seq. The right to buy under the Housing Act 1985 is expressed to be limited to secure tenants: see s 118; and PARA 239.
5   As to registered social landlords see PARA 166 et seq.

6　See the Social Landlords (Permissible Additional Purposes or Objects) Order 1996, SI 1996/2256, art 3(a) (made under the Housing Act 1996 s 2(7), (8) and thus now only applying in relation to Wales).

7　As to the meaning of 'dwelling' for these purposes see PARA 217 note 7.

8　As to private registered providers of social housing see PARA 53.

9　As to the meaning of 'assured tenancy' see LANDLORD AND TENANT vol 63 (2016) PARA 825 (definition applied by the Housing Act 1996 s 230).

10　As to the meaning of 'assured shorthold tenancy' see LANDLORD AND TENANT vol 63 (2016) PARA 852 (definition applied by the Housing Act 1996 s 230).

11　As to the meaning of 'long tenancy' see the Housing Act 1985 s 115; and LANDLORD AND TENANT vol 63 (2016) PARA 1042 (definition applied by the Housing Act 1996 s 63(1)).

12　As to the meaning of 'secure tenancy' see LANDLORD AND TENANT vol 63 (2016) PARA 1037 (definition applied by the Housing Act 1996 s 230).

13　For this purpose a dwelling will be regarded as provided with public money if: (1) it was provided or acquired wholly or in part by means of a grant under the Housing Act 1996 s 18 (social housing grant: see PARA 166); (2) it was provided or acquired wholly or in part by applying or appropriating sums standing in the disposal proceeds fund of a registered social landlord (see s 25; and PARA 216); or (3) it was acquired by a registered social landlord or a private registered provider of social housing after 1 April 1997 on a disposal by a public sector landlord at a time when it was capable of being let as a separate dwelling: s 16(2) (amended by the Housing and Regeneration Act 2008 s 185(1)(b); and by SI 2010/844); Housing Act 1996 (Commencement No 10 and Transitional Provisions) Order 1997, SI 1997/618, art 2(1), Schedule para 1. 'Public sector landlord' means any of the authorities or bodies within the Housing Act 1985 s 80(1) (the landlord condition for secure tenancies: see LANDLORD AND TENANT vol 63 (2016) PARA 1037): Housing Act 1996 s 63(1).

A dwelling will be regarded for the purposes of s 16 as provided by means of a grant under s 18 if, and only if, the Welsh Ministers when making the grant notified the recipient that the dwelling was to be so regarded: s 16(4) (amended by the Housing and Regeneration Act 2008 s 61(1), (7)). The Welsh Ministers must before making the grant inform the applicant that they propose to give such a notice and allow him an opportunity to withdraw his application within a specified time: Housing Act 1996 s 16(4) (as so amended). As to the Welsh Ministers see PARA 7.

References in Pt I (ss A1–64) to the provision of a dwelling or house include the provision of a dwelling or house: (a) by erecting the dwelling or house, or converting a building into dwellings or a house; or (b) by altering, enlarging, repairing or improving an existing dwelling or house; and references to a dwelling or house provided by means of a grant or other financial assistance are to its being so provided directly or indirectly: s 63(2).

14　A dwelling will be regarded for the purposes of the Housing Act 1996 s 16 as having remained within the social rented sector if, since it was so provided or acquired: (1) the person holding the freehold interest in the dwelling has been either a registered social landlord, a private registered provider of social housing or a public sector landlord; and (2) any person holding an interest as lessee (otherwise than as mortgagee) in the dwelling has been: (a) an individual holding otherwise than under a long tenancy; or (b) a registered social landlord, a private registered provider of social housing or a public sector landlord: s 16(3) (amended by the Housing and Regeneration Act 2008 s 185(1)(c); and by SI 2010/844). In the Housing Act 1996 s 16(3)(a) (see head (1) above) the reference to the freehold interest in the dwelling includes a reference to such an interest in the dwelling as is held by the landlord under a lease granted in pursuance of the Leasehold Reform, Housing and Urban Development Act 1993 Sch 9 para 3 (mandatory leaseback to former freeholder on collective enfranchisement: see LANDLORD AND TENANT vol 64 (2016) PARA 1428): Housing Act 1996 s 16(3A) (added by the Housing Act 2004 s 202(1), (2)).

15　Ie the Housing Act 1985 Pt V (ss 118–188): see PARAS 230 et seq, 245 et seq.

16　Ie the right conferred by the Housing Act 1996 s 16.

17　Housing Act 1996 s 16(1) (substituted by the Housing and Regeneration Act 2008 s 185(1)(a); and amended by SI 2010/844). As to supplementary provisions with respect to the right of a tenant to acquire a dwelling see PARA 243.

18　Ie as from a day to be appointed under the Housing Act 2004 s 270(4), (5)(c). At the date at which this title states the law, no such day had been appointed.

19　Ie a grant under the Housing Act 1996 s 27A: see PARA 151.

20　Housing Act 1996 s 16A(1) (not yet in force) (s 16A added by the Housing Act 2004 s 221 as from a day to be appointed (see note 18); the Housing Act 1996 s 16A(1) amended by the Housing and Regeneration Act 2008 s 185(2)).

21　Housing Act 1996 s 16A(2) (as added (see note 18); not yet in force). Further, in s 16(2), (4) (see note 3) any reference to s 18 includes a reference to s 27A (see PARA 151): s 16A(3) (as so added; not yet in force). For the purposes of s 16 a funded dwelling is to be regarded as having remained within the social rented sector in relation to any relevant time if, since it was acquired or provided, it was used: (1) by the recipient of the grant mentioned in s 16A(1); or (2) if s 27B applies in relation to the grant (see PARA 152), by each person to whom the grant was, or is treated as having been, paid, exclusively for the purposes for which the grant was made or any other purposes agreed to by the Welsh Ministers: s 16A(4) (as so added (not yet in force); amended by the Housing and Regeneration Act 2008 s 61(1), (7)). 'Relevant time' means a time when the dwelling would not be treated as being within the social rented sector by virtue of the Housing Act 1996 s 16(3) (see note 14): s 16A(5) (as so added; not yet in force).

22 Ie the Housing Act 1985 ss 119–188: see PARAS 231 et seq, 245 et seq.

23 As to the meaning of 'dwelling house' see PARA 231.

24 Housing Act 1985 s 118(1) (substituted for these purposes by the Housing (Right to Acquire) Regulations 1997, SI 1997/619, Sch 1 para 3). Accordingly, for these purposes in the provisions in the Housing Act 1985 Pt V, for the expression 'right to buy' there is substituted the expression 'right to acquire' save for the references to the right to buy in s 122(4) (as added for these purposes: see PARA 273) and s 130(2)(aa) (see PARA 288): Housing (Right to Acquire) Regulations 1997, SI 1997/619, Sch 1 para 2.

25 As to the meaning of 'only or principal home' see LANDLORD AND TENANT vol 63 (2016) PARA 1037 note 27.

26 Housing Act 1985 s 118(2).

27 See PARAS 260–265.

28 See PARA 226. The relevant provisions of the Renting Homes (Wales) Act 2016 are in force as from a day to be appointed: see PARA 6. At the date at which this volume states the law, no such day had been appointed.

243. Supplementary provisions relating to the right to acquire. The Welsh Ministers may by order[1]:

(1)   specify the amount or rate of discount to be given on the exercise of the right of a tenant to acquire a dwelling[2]; and

(2)   designate rural areas in relation to dwellings in which that right does not arise[3].

Before making an order which would have the effect that an area ceased to be designated under head (2) above, the Welsh Ministers must consult:

(a)   the local housing authority[4] or authorities in whose district[5] the area or any part of it is situated or, if the order is general in its effect, local housing authorities in general; and

(b)   such bodies appearing to them to be representative of registered social landlords[6] as they consider appropriate[7].

The provisions of Part V of the Housing Act 1985[8] apply in relation to the right of a tenant to acquire a dwelling[9] subject to any such order and subject to such other exceptions, adaptations and other modifications[10] as may be specified by regulations made by the Welsh Ministers[11]. The regulations may provide that:

(i)   the powers of the Welsh Ministers to intervene, give directions or assist[12] do not apply;

(ii)   the statutory exceptions for charities and certain housing associations[13] and the right of appeal to the Welsh Ministers with regard to dwellings for elderly persons[14] do not apply;

(iii)   the statutory provisions relating to the right to acquire on rent to mortgage terms (where still exercisable)[15] do not apply;

(iv)   the provisions relating to restrictions on disposals in National Parks etc[16] do not apply; and

(v)   the provisions relating to the preserved right to buy[17] do not apply;

but nothing in heads (i) to (v) above affects the generality of the power[18] to make such regulations[19]. Such regulations may also:

(A)   make provision for continuing the effect of a suspension order[20] where the secure tenancy[21] in respect of which the order was made has been replaced by an assured tenancy[22];

(B) make specified provision[23] with regard to the disclosure of information about anti-social behaviour[24].

1 An order or regulations under the Housing Act 1996 s 17 (see the text and notes 2–11) may make different provision for different cases or classes of case including different areas, and may contain such incidental, supplementary and transitional provisions as the Welsh Ministers consider appropriate (s 17(5) (amended by the Housing and Regeneration Act 2008 s 62(a), (e)) and must be made by statutory instrument subject to annulment in pursuance of a resolution of the National Assembly for Wales (Housing Act 1996 s 17(7) (amended by the Housing and Regeneration Act 2008 s 63)).

2 Ie the right conferred by the Housing Act 1996 s 16: see PARA 242. As to the meaning of 'dwelling' see PARA 217 note 7. The Welsh Ministers may make grants to registered social landlords in respect of discounts given by them to persons exercising the right to acquire conferred by s 16 and in respect of discounts on disposals by them of dwellings to tenants otherwise than in pursuance of the right conferred by s 16 (see ss 20, 21; and PARA 244).

   The Housing (Right to Acquire) (Discount) (Wales) Order 1997, SI 1997/569, which prescribes the percentage rate of discount to be given on the exercise of the right to acquire as 25% of the open market value of the dwelling subject to a maximum of £8,000 (art 3 (amended by SI 2015/1249)) and provides that any question arising as to the open market value of a dwelling at the relevant time is to be determined by the district valuer (Housing (Right to Acquire) (Discount) (Wales) Order 1997, SI 1997/569, art 4) is made in the exercise of the power conferred by head (1) in the text.

3 Housing Act 1996 s 17(1) (amended by the Housing and Regeneration Act 2008 s 62(a)). A number of orders have been made in exercise of the power conferred by head (2) in the text: see eg the Leasehold Reform and Housing (Excluded Tenancies) (Designated Rural Areas) (Wales) Order 1997, SI 1997/685; the Housing (Right to Acquire and Right to Buy) (Designated Rural Areas and Designated Regions) (Wales) Order 2003, SI 2003/54 (amended by SI 2003/1147).

4 As to the meaning of local housing authority' see PARA 11 (definition applied by the Housing Act 1996 s 230).

5 As to the meaning of 'district' see PARA 11 (definition applied by the Housing Act 1996 s 230).

6 As to registered social landlords see PARAS 13, 166 et seq.

7 Housing Act 1996 s 17(6) (amended by the Housing and Regeneration Act 2008 s 62(a), (c)–(e)).

8 Ie the Housing Act 1985 Pt V (ss 118–188): see PARAS 230 et seq, 1911 et seq.

9 Ie under the Housing Act 1996 s 16.

10 For these purposes, 'modifications' includes additions, alterations and omissions and cognate expressions must be construed accordingly: Housing Act 1996 s 63(1).

11 Housing Act 1996 s 17(2) (amended by the Housing and Regeneration Act 2008 s 62(a)). The specified exceptions, adaptations and other modifications must take the form of textual amendments of the provisions of the Housing Act 1985 Pt V as they apply in relation to the right to buy under that Part; and the first regulations, and any subsequent consolidating regulations, must set out the provisions of Pt V as they so apply: Housing Act 1996 s 17(4).

12 Ie under the Housing Act 1985 ss 164–170: see PARA 341 et seq.

13 Ie the Housing Act 1985 Sch 5 paras 1, 3: see PARAS 245–247.

14 Ie the Housing Act 1985 Sch 5 para 11: see PARA 252.

15 As to the right to acquire on rent to mortgage terms (now only exercisable if claimed before 18 July 2005: see the Housing Act 1985 s 142A; and PARA 318) see PARA 318.

16 Ie the Housing Act 1985 s 157: see PARA 333.

17 As to the preserved right to buy see PARA 334 et seq.

18 Ie the power conferred by the Housing Act 1996 s 17(2): see the text and notes 8–11.

19 Housing Act 1996 s 17(3). The Housing (Right to Acquire) Regulations 1997, SI 1997/619, are made in the exercise of this power. The Housing Act 1985 Pt V has effect for the purposes of the right to acquire under the Housing Act 1996 Pt I (ss A1–64) subject to the modifications made by the Housing (Right to Acquire) Regulations 1997, SI 1997/619, reg 2(1), Sch 1 (amended by SI 2012/2090), and set out in the Housing (Right to Acquire) Regulations 1997, SI 1997/619, reg 2(2), Sch 2. It is submitted that Schs 1, 2 are now to be read in the light of subsequent legislative amendments to the Housing Act 1985 Pt V by eg the Civil Partnership Act 2004 and the Housing Act 2004, even where the 1997 Regulations have not themselves been correspondingly amended. In this title, the modifications made by the 1997 Regulations are not all set out in detail but may be referred to in the notes to the paragraphs in which the relevant provisions of the Housing Act 1985 Pt V are discussed: see eg PARA 237 note 5. For exceptions to the right to acquire see the Housing Act 1985 Sch 5 (as so modified). See also the Housing (Right of First Refusal) (Wales) Regulations 2005, SI 2005/2680 (amended by SI 2010/671) (partly made under the powers so conferred); and PARA 328 et seq.

20 As to suspension orders see the Housing Act 1985 s 121A; and PARA 259.
21 As to secure tenancies see LANDLORD AND TENANT vol 63 (2016) PARA 1037 et seq.
22 Housing Act 2004 s 192(3)(b). As to assured tenancies see LANDLORD AND TENANT vol 63 (2016) PARA 825 et seq.
23 Ie provision corresponding to the Housing Act 2004 s 194(1)–(3) (see PARA 453) so far as those subsections relate to the Housing Act 1985 s 138(2B) (see PARA 291).
24 Housing Act 2004 s 194(4)(b).

244. Purchase grants to registered social landlords. The Welsh Ministers must make grants to registered social landlords[1] and private registered providers of social housing[2] in respect of discounts given by them to persons exercising the right to acquire conferred[3] by the Housing Act 1996[4]. The amount of the grant for any year must be the aggregate value of the discounts given in that year[5]; and the Welsh Ministers must specify in relation to such grants:

(1)　the procedure to be followed in relation to applications for grant;
(2)　the manner in which, and time or times at which, grant is to be paid[6].

In making such a grant the Welsh Ministers may provide that the grant is conditional on compliance by the registered social landlord or private registered provider of social housing with such conditions as they may specify[7].

The Welsh Ministers may also make grants to registered social landlords and private registered provides of social housing in respect of discounts on disposals by them of dwellings to tenants otherwise than in pursuance of the statutory right[8] to acquire[9]. The Welsh Ministers must make such a grant if the tenant[10] was entitled to exercise the right to acquire[11] in relation to another dwelling[12] of the landlord[13] or provider, as the case may be; but the amount of the grant in such a case must not exceed the amount of the discount to which the tenant would have been entitled in respect of the other dwelling[14]. The Welsh Ministers must specify in relation to such grants:

(a)　the procedure to be followed in relation to applications for grant;
(b)　the circumstances in which grant is or is not to be payable;
(c)　the method for calculating, and any limitations on, the amount of grant; and
(d)　the manner in which, and time or times at which, grant is to be paid[15].

In making such a grant, the Welsh Ministers may provide that the grant is conditional on compliance by the registered social landlord or private registered provider of social housing with such conditions as they may specify[16].

1　As to registered social landlords see PARAS 13, 166 et seq.
2　As to private registered providers of social housing see PARA 53.
3　Ie the right conferred by the Housing Act 1996 s 16: see PARA 242.
4　Housing Act 1996 s 20(1) (ss 20(1), (3)–(4), 21(1)–(4) amended by the Housing and Regeneration Act 2008 s 61(1), (7); the Housing Act 1996 s 20(1) further amended by the Housing and Regeneration Act 2008 s 185(3)(a); and by SI 2010/844). As to housing grants see generally PARA 835 et seq.
5　Housing Act 1996 s 20(2).
6　Housing Act 1996 s 20(3) (as amended (see note 4); further amended by the Housing Act 2004 ss 218, 266, Sch 11 paras 7, 9, Sch 16).
7　Housing Act 1996 s 20(4) (as amended (see note 4); further amended by the Housing and Regeneration Act 2008 s 185(3)(b); and by SI 2010/844).
8　See note 3.
9　Housing Act 1996 s 21(1) (as amended (see note 4); further amended by the Housing and Regeneration Act 2008 s 185(4)(a); and by SI 2010/844).
10　As to the meaning of 'tenant' see PARA 168 note 16.
11　Ie the right conferred by the Housing Act 1996 s 16 (see PARA 242) or by the Housing and Regeneration Act 2008 s 180 (see PARA 240).
12　As to the meaning of 'dwelling' see PARA 217 note 7.
13　As to the meaning of 'landlord' see PARA 168 note 16.

14 Housing Act 1996 s 21(2) (as amended (see note 4); further amended by the Housing and Regeneration Act 2008 s 185(4)(b)).

15 Housing Act 1996 s 21(3) (as amended (see note 4); further amended by the Housing Act 2004 Sch 11 paras 7, 10, Sch 16).

16 Housing Act 1996 s 21(4) (as amended (see note 4); further amended by the Housing and Regeneration Act 2008 s 185(4)(c); and by SI 2010/844).

B. EXCEPTIONS TO, AND SUSPENSION OF, RIGHT TO BUY OR ACQUIRE

(A) Exceptions to the Right to Buy or Acquire

245. Charities. The right to buy[1] does not arise if the landlord[2] is a housing trust[3] or a housing association[4] and is a charity[5]. This exclusion does not, however, apply where the preserved right to buy[6] arises[7]; but its disapplication is not to be taken to authorise any action on the part of a charity which would conflict with the trusts of the charity[8].

This exclusion is also disapplied where the right to acquire conferred by the Housing Act 1996[9] or the Housing and Regeneration Act 2008[10] arises[11].

1 As to the meaning of 'the right to buy' see PARA 239.
2 As to the meaning of 'landlord' see PARA 31 note 3.
3 As to housing trusts see PARA 14.
4 As to housing associations see PARA 13.
5 Housing Act 1985 s 120, Sch 5 para 1.
6 As to the preserved right to buy see PARA 334 et seq.
7 Housing (Preservation of Right to Buy) Regulations 1993, SI 1993/2241, Sch 1 para 41.
8 See the Housing Act 1985 s 171C(5) (added by the Housing Act 1988 s 127(3)).
9 See PARAS 242–244.
10 See PARAS 240–241.
11 Housing (Right to Acquire) Regulations 1997, SI 1997/619, Sch 1 para 40(a), applying in relation to the right to acquire under the Housing and Regeneration Act 2008 by virtue of s 184, which applies the Housing Act 1996 s 17 (regulations modifying the Housing Act 1985): see PARA 241.

246. Dwelling houses in designated rural areas. The right to acquire conferred by the Housing Act 1996[1] or the Housing and Regeneration Act 2008[2] does not arise if the dwelling house[3] is situated in a designated[4] rural area[5].

1 See PARAS 242–244.
2 See PARAS 240–241.
3 As to the meaning of 'dwelling house' see PARA 231.
4 Ie designated by order of the Secretary of State or the Welsh Ministers under the Housing Act 1996 s 17(1)(b): see PARAS 241, 243. As to the Secretary of State and the Welsh Ministers see PARA 7.
5 Housing Act 1985 s 120, Sch 5 para 1A (added for these purposes by the Housing (Right to Acquire) Regulations 1997, SI 1997/619, Sch 1 para 40(a), applying in relation to the right to acquire under the Housing and Regeneration Act 2008 by virtue of s 184, which applies the Housing Act 1996 s 17 (regulations modifying the Housing Act 1985): see PARA 241).

247. Certain housing associations. The right to buy[1] does not arise if the landlord[2] is:

(1) a co-operative housing association[3];

(2) a housing association[4] which at no time received a grant under specified[5] statutory provisions[6].

This exclusion does not, however, apply where the preserved right to buy[7] arises[8]. It is also disapplied where the right to acquire conferred by the Housing Act 1996[9] or the Housing and Regeneration Act 2008[10] arises[11].

1 As to the meaning of 'the right to buy' see PARA 239.
2 As to the meaning of 'landlord' see PARA 31 note 3.
3 Housing Act 1985 s 120, Sch 5 para 2. As to the meaning of 'co-operative housing association' see PARA 13.
4 As to housing associations see PARA 13.

5 Ie at no time received a grant under any enactment mentioned in the Housing Associations Act 1985 Sch 1 para 2, or under the Housing Act 1974 s 31 (repealed), the Housing Associations Act 1985 ss 41, 54 or 55 (all repealed) or s 58, the Housing Act 1988 s 50 or s 51 or the Housing Act 1996 s 18 (social housing grants) or s 22 (grants by local authorities for registered social landlords) or the Housing and Regeneration Act 2008 s 19 (financial assistance: see PLANNING vol 83 (2010) PARA 1474) which was a grant made on condition that the housing association provides social housing) or a grant from the Greater London Authority which was a grant made on condition that the housing association provides social housing: see further PARAS 13, 24, 166, 835. As to the Greater London Authority see LONDON GOVERNMENT vol 71 (2013) PARA 67 et seq.

6 Housing Act 1985 Sch 5 para 3 (amended by the Housing Act 1988 s 140, Sch 17 para 66, Sch 18; the Housing and Regeneration Act 2008 s 56, Sch 8 para 35; the Localism Act 2011 ss 195(1), 237, Sch 19 paras 10, 21, Sch 25 Pt 31; and by SI 1996/2325, SI 1997/627 and SI 2010/866).

7 As to the preserved right to buy see PARA 334 et seq.

8 See the Housing (Preservation of Right to Buy) Regulations 1993, SI 1993/2241, Sch 1 para 41.

9 See PARAS 242–244.

10 See PARAS 240–241.

11 See the Housing (Right to Acquire) Regulations 1997, SI 1997/619, Sch 1 para 40(b), applying in relation to the right to acquire under the Housing and Regeneration Act 2008 by virtue of s 184, which applies the Housing Act 1996 s 17 (regulations modifying the Housing Act 1985): see PARA 241.

248. Landlord with insufficient interest in the property. The right to buy[1] or the right to acquire under the Housing Act 1996[2] or the Housing and Regeneration Act 2008[3] does not arise unless the landlord[4] owns the freehold or has an interest sufficient to grant a lease[5] for:

(1) a term exceeding 21 years, where the dwelling house[6] is a house[7]; or

(2) where the dwelling house is a flat[8], a term of not less than 50 years,

commencing, in either case, with the date on which the tenant's[9] notice claiming to exercise the right to buy is served[10].

1 As to the meaning of 'the right to buy' see PARA 239.
2 See PARAS 242–244.
3 See PARAS 240–241.
4 As to the meaning of 'landlord' see PARA 31 note 3.
5 Ie in pursuance of the Housing Act 1985 Pt V (ss 118–188): see PARAS 230 et seq, 257 et seq. As to the meaning of 'lease' see PARA 31 note 3.
6 As to the meaning of 'dwelling house' see PARA 231.
7 As to the meaning of 'house' see PARA 231.
8 As to the meaning of 'flat' see PARA 231.
9 As to the meaning of 'tenant' see PARA 31 note 3.
10 Housing Act 1985 s 120, Sch 5 para 4; and see PARA 230 notes 7, 9. Schedule 5 para 4 is disapplied where the Housing (Extension of Right to Buy) Order 1993, SI 1993/2240 (see PARA 233), applies: see Schedule para 66(a).

249. Dwelling houses let in connection with employment. The right to buy[1] or the right to acquire under the Housing Act 1996[2] or the Housing and Regeneration Act 2008[3] does not arise if the dwelling house[4]:

(1) forms part of, or is within the curtilage of, a building which, or so much of it as is held by the landlord[5], is held mainly for purposes other than housing purposes[6] and consists mainly of accommodation other than housing accommodation, or is situated in a cemetery[7]; and

(2) was let to the tenant[8] or a predecessor in title of his in consequence of the tenant or predecessor being in the employment of the landlord or of a local authority[9], a development corporation[10], a housing action trust[11], a Mayoral development corporation, an urban development corporation[12] or the governors of an aided school (now known as a 'voluntary aided school')[13].

1 As to the meaning of 'the right to buy' see PARA 239.
2 See PARAS 242–244.

3 See PARAS 240–241.
4 As to the meaning of 'dwelling house' see PARA 231.
5 As to the meaning of 'landlord' see PARA 31 note 3.
6 For these purposes, 'housing purposes' means the purposes for which dwelling houses are held by local housing authorities under the Housing Act 1985 Pt II (ss 8–57) (see PARA 401 et seq) or purposes corresponding to those purposes: s 120, Sch 5 para 5(2). As to the meaning of 'local housing authority' see PARA 11.
7 'Cemetery' has the same meaning as in the Local Government Act 1972 s 214 (see CREMATION AND BURIAL vol 24 (2010) PARA 1108 note 6): Housing Act 1985 s 622(1) (numbered as such by SI 2001/3649).
8 As to the meaning of 'tenant' see PARA 31 note 3.
9 As to the meaning of 'local authority' see PARA 12.
10 As to the meaning of 'development corporation' see PARA 12. As to Mayoral development corporations see the Localism Act 2011 s 198; and LONDON GOVERNMENT vol 71 (2013) PARA 323.
11 As to the meaning of 'housing action trust' see PARA 12.
12 As to the meaning of 'urban development corporation' see PARA 12.
13 Housing Act 1985 Sch 5 para 5(1) (amended by the Housing Act 1988 s 83(1), (6)(d); the Government of Wales Act 1998 s 152, Sch 18 Pt IV; the Localism Act 2011 s 222, Sch 22 paras 9, 20; and by SI 2008/3002); and see PARA 230 notes 7, 9. As to the meaning of 'voluntary aided school' see EDUCATION vol 35 (2015) PARA 106. As to the effect on this exception to the right to buy of the disposal and subsequent leaseback of the public sector landlord's interest in the premises under the Leasehold Reform, Housing and Urban Development Act 1993 Pt I Ch I (ss 1–38) see Sch 10 para 2(4), (5)(a); and LANDLORD AND TENANT vol 64 (2016) PARA 1438.
  The Housing Act 1985 Sch 5 para 5(1) is modified where the Housing (Extension of Right to Buy) Order 1993, SI 1993/2240 (see PARA 233), applies: see Schedule para 66(b).

250. Dwelling houses for the disabled. The right to buy[1] or the right to acquire under the Housing Act 1996[2] or the Housing and Regeneration Act 2008[3] does not arise if:

(1) the dwelling house[4] has features which are substantially different from those of ordinary dwelling houses and are designed to make it suitable for occupation by physically disabled persons[5] and:

  (a) it is one of a group of dwelling houses which it is the practice of the landlord[6] to let for occupation by physically disabled persons; and

  (b) a social service is, or special facilities are, provided in close proximity to the group of dwelling houses wholly or partly for the purpose of assisting those persons[7];

(2) the dwelling house is one of a group of dwelling houses which it is the practice of the landlord to let for occupation by persons who are suffering or have suffered from a mental disorder[8] and a social service is, or special facilities are, provided wholly or partly for the purpose of assisting those persons[9].

1 As to the meaning of 'the right to buy' see PARA 239.
2 See PARAS 242–244.
3 See PARAS 240–241.
4 As to the meaning of 'dwelling house' see PARA 231.
5 A dwelling has features 'designed' to make it suitable for occupation by a disabled person only where the dwelling is built with such features for occupation by a disabled person and not where an ordinary dwelling is merely 'intended', by reason of special features, for occupation by a disabled person: *Freeman v Wansbeck District Council* [1984] 2 All ER 746, (1983) 82 LGR 131, CA.
6 As to the meaning of 'landlord' see PARA 31 note 3.
7 Housing Act 1985 s 120, Sch 5 para 7; and see PARA 230 notes 7, 9. The Housing Act 1985 Sch 5 para 7 is modified where the Housing (Extension of Right to Buy) Order 1993, SI 1993/2240 (see PARA 233), applies: see Schedule para 66(c).
8 For these purposes, 'mental disorder' has the same meaning as in the Mental Health Act 1983 (see MENTAL HEALTH AND CAPACITY vol 75 (2013) PARA 761): Housing Act 1985 Sch 5 para 9(2).

9   Housing Act 1985 Sch 5 para 9(1); and see PARA 230 notes 7, 9. The Housing Act 1985 Sch 5 para 9(1) is modified where the Housing (Extension of Right to Buy) Order 1993, SI 1993/2240, applies: see Schedule para 66(c).

251. Certain dwelling houses for persons with special needs. The right to acquire conferred by the Housing Act 1996[1] or the Housing and Regeneration Act 2008[2] does not arise if the dwelling house[3] is one of a group of dwelling houses which it is the practice of the landlord[4] to let for occupation by persons who have special needs and require intensive housing assistance and such intensive housing assistance is provided, either directly or indirectly, by the landlord[5].

For these purposes, 'persons who have special needs' means persons who are vulnerable as a result of age, physical disability or illness, a mental disorder or impairment of any kind, drug or alcohol addiction, violence or the threat of violence by a member of a person's family, or other special reason[6]. Intensive housing assistance' means the provision by the landlord to persons with special needs of assistance on housing issues which is significantly greater than the assistance which is generally provided by registered social landlords or private registered providers to tenants who do not have special needs[7].

1   See PARAS 242–244.
2   See PARAS 240–241.
3   As to the meaning of 'dwelling house' see PARA 231.
4   As to the meaning of 'landlord' see PARA 31 note 3.
5   Housing Act 1985 s 120, Sch 5 para 9A(1) (Sch 5 para 9A added by the Housing (Right to Acquire) Regulations 1997, SI 1997/619, Sch 1 para 40(c), applying in relation to the right to acquire under the Housing and Regeneration Act 2008 by virtue of s 184, which applies the Housing Act 1996 s 17 (regulations modifying the Housing Act 1985): see PARA 241).
6   Housing Act 1985 Sch 5 para 9A(3) (as added: see note 5).
7   Housing Act 1985 Sch 5 para 9A(2) (as added (see note 5); amended by virtue of the Housing and Regeneration Act 2008 s 184(2)(c)). As to registered social landlords see PARAS 13, 166 et seq; and as to private registered providers of social housing see PARA 53.

252. Certain dwelling houses for elderly persons. The right to buy[1] or the right to acquire conferred by the Housing Act 1996[2] or the Housing and Regeneration Act 2008[3] does not arise if the dwelling house[4] is one of a group of dwelling houses:

(1)   which are particularly suitable, having regard to their location, size, design, heating systems and other features, for occupation by elderly persons; and

(2)   which it is the practice of the landlord[5] to let for occupation by persons aged 60 or more, or for occupation by such persons and physically disabled persons,

and special facilities[6] are provided wholly or mainly for the purposes of assisting those persons[7].

The right to buy does not arise if the dwelling house:

(a)   is particularly suitable[8], having regard to its location, size, design, heating system and other features, for occupation by elderly persons; and

(b)   was let to the tenant or a predecessor in title of his for occupation by a person who was aged 60 or more, whether the tenant or predecessor or another person[9].

The exclusion set out in heads (a) and (b) above does not, however, apply unless the dwelling house concerned was first let before 1 January 1990[10]. Nor does it apply to the right to acquire conferred by the Housing Act 1996 or the Housing and Regeneration Act 2008[11].

1   As to the meaning of 'the right to buy' see PARA 239.

2   See PARAS 242–244.
3   See PARAS 240–241.
4   As to the meaning of 'dwelling house' see PARA 231.
5   As to the meaning of 'landlord' see PARA 31 note 3.
6   The facilities so referred to are facilities which consist of or include: (1) the services of a resident warden; or (2) the services of a non-resident warden, a system for calling him and the use of a common room in close proximity to the group of dwelling houses: Housing Act 1985 s 120, Sch 5 para 10(2).
7   Housing Act 1985 Sch 5 para 10(1) (amended by the Leasehold Reform, Housing and Urban Development Act 1993 s 106(1)); and see PARA 230 notes 7, 9.
    The Housing Act 1985 Sch 5 para 10(1) is modified where the Housing (Extension of Right to Buy) Order 1993, SI 1993/2240 (see PARA 233), applies: see Schedule para 66(d).
8   In determining whether a dwelling is particularly suitable, no regard is to be had to the presence of any feature provided by the tenant or a predecessor in title of his: Housing Act 1985 Sch 5 para 11(2) (Sch 5 para 11 substituted by the Leasehold Reform, Housing and Urban Development Act 1993 s 106(2)).
    Notwithstanding anything in the Housing Act 1985 s 181 (jurisdiction of County Court: see PARA 353), any question arising under Sch 5 para 11 is to be determined as follows: (1) if an application for the purpose is made by the tenant to the appropriate tribunal or authority before the end of the period of 56 days beginning with the service of the landlord's notice under s 124 (see PARA 275), the question must be determined by the appropriate tribunal or authority; and (2) if no such application is so made, the question is deemed to have been determined in favour of the landlord: Sch 5 para 11(3)–(5) (as so substituted; Sch 5 para 11(4) amended by the Housing Act 2004 s 181(1), (2); at the date at which this volume states the law, the latter amendment was in force in relation to England only and in relation to Wales the application was to be made to, and the question determined by, the Welsh Ministers). For these purposes, 'the appropriate tribunal or authority' means: (a) in relation to England, the First-tier Tribunal or, where determined by or under Tribunal Procedure Rules, the Upper Tribunal; and (b) in relation to Wales, the Welsh Ministers: Housing Act 1985 Sch 5 para 11(5A) (Sch 5 para 11(5A), (5B) added by the Housing Act 2004 s 181(1), (3); the Housing Act 1985 Sch 5 para 11(5A) amended by SI 2013/1036). For appeals, see the Tribunals, Courts and Enforcement Act 2007 s 11; and PARA 49 (for decisions of the First-tier Tribunal) and the Rent Act 1977 s 65A; and LANDLORD AND TENANT vol 63 (2016) PARA 737 (for decisions of a rent assessment committee): Housing Act 1985 Sch 5 para 11(5B) (as so added; substituted by SI 2013/1036). At the date at which this volume states the law, the Housing Act 2004 s 181(1), (3) was not yet in force in relation to Wales; those provisions are to come into force as from a day to be appointed under s 270(4), (5)(c). As to the meaning of 'tenant' see PARA 31 note 3.
    The Housing Act 1985 Sch 5 para 11(4), (5) is modified where the Housing (Extension of Right to Buy) Order 1993, SI 1993/2240, applies: see Schedule para 66(e).
9   Housing Act 1985 Sch 5 para 11(1) (as substituted: see note 8). As to the effect on this exception to the right to buy of the disposal and subsequent leaseback of the public sector landlord's interest in the premises under the Leasehold Reform, Housing and Urban Development Act 1993 Pt I Ch I (ss 1–38) see Sch 10 para 2(4), (5)(b); and LANDLORD AND TENANT vol 64 (2016) PARA 1438.
10 Housing Act 1985 Sch 5 para 11(6) (as substituted: see note 8).
11 Housing (Right to Acquire) Regulations 1997, SI 1997/619, Sch 1 para 40(d), applying in relation to the right to acquire under the Housing and Regeneration Act 2008 by virtue of s 184, which applies the Housing Act 1996 s 17 (regulations modifying the Housing Act 1985): see PARA 241.

253.   Dwelling houses held on Crown tenancies. The right to buy[1] or the right to acquire conferred by the Housing Act 1996[2] or the Housing and Regeneration Act 2008[3] does not arise if the dwelling house[4] is held by the landlord[5] on a tenancy from the Crown[6] unless:

(1)   the landlord is entitled to grant a lease[7] without the concurrence of the appropriate authority; or

(2)   the appropriate authority notifies the landlord that as regards any Crown interest affected the authority will give its consent to the granting of such a lease[8].

1   As to the meaning of 'the right to buy' see PARA 239.
2   See PARAS 242–244.
3   See PARAS 240–241.
4   As to the meaning of 'dwelling house' see PARA 231.
5   As to the meaning of 'landlord' see PARA 31 note 3.

6   For these purposes, 'tenancy from the Crown' means a tenancy of land in which there is a Crown
    interest superior to the tenancy; and 'Crown interest' and 'appropriate authority' mean
    respectively: (1) an interest comprised in the Crown Estate, and the Crown Estate Commissioners
    or other government department having the management of the land in question; (2) an interest
    belonging to Her Majesty in right of the Duchy of Lancaster, and the Chancellor of the Duchy; (3)
    an interest belonging to the Duchy of Cornwall, and such person as the Duke of Cornwall or the
    possessor for the time being of the Duchy appoints; (4) any other interest belonging to a
    government department or held on behalf of Her Majesty for the purposes of a government
    department, and that department: Housing Act 1985 s 120, Sch 5 para 12(2). As to the meaning
    of 'tenancy' see PARA 31 note 3. As to the Crown Estate Commissioners see CROWN AND CROWN
    PROCEEDINGS vol 29 (2014) PARA 192 et seq.
7   Ie in pursuance of the Housing Act 1985 Pt V (ss 118–188): see PARAS 230 et seq, 257 et seq. As
    to the meaning of 'lease' see PARA 31 note 3.
8   Housing Act 1985 Sch 5 para 12(1); and see PARA 230 notes 7, 9. Section 179(1) (see PARA 232)
    is to be disregarded for the purposes of Sch 5 para 12(1)(a): Sch 5 para 12(3). The Housing Act
    1985 Sch 5 para 12 is omitted where the Housing (Extension of Right to Buy) Order 1993, SI
    1993/2240 (see PARA 233), applies: see Schedule para 66(f).

254. Dwelling house due to be demolished within 24 months. The right to buy[1]
does not arise if a final demolition notice is in force[2] in respect of the dwelling
house[3]. A 'final demolition notice' is a notice:

(1)   stating that the landlord[4] intends to demolish the dwelling house or, as
        the case may be, the building containing it ('the relevant premises');
(2)   setting out the reasons why the landlord intends to demolish the relevant
        premises;
(3)   specifying the date by which he intends to demolish those premises ('the
        proposed demolition date') and the date when the notice will cease to be
        in force, unless extended[5];
(4)   stating that one of conditions A to C below is satisfied in relation to the
        notice, specifying the condition concerned; and
(5)   stating that the right to buy (or to acquire) does not arise in respect of
        the dwelling house while the notice is in force[6].

If, at the time when the notice is served[7], there is an existing claim to exercise
the right to buy in respect of the dwelling house, the notice must, instead of
complying with head (5) above, state that that claim ceases to be effective on the
notice coming into force, but that there is a statutory right to compensation[8] in
respect of certain expenditure, and the notice must also give details of that right
to compensation and of how it may be exercised[9].

The proposed demolition date must fall within the period of 24 months
beginning with the date of service of the notice on the tenant[10]; and a final
demolition notice is in force for these purposes in respect of the dwelling house
concerned during the period of 24 months so mentioned, subject to compliance
with the requirement, where dwelling house is contained in a building which
contains one or more other dwelling houses and the landlord intends to demolish
the whole of the building, for the landlord to have served a final demolition notice
on the occupier of each of the dwelling houses contained in[11], to the statutory
provisions allowing for an extension of that period[12] and to the statutory
provisions[13] applying where the landlord transfers his interest as landlord to
another person[14].

A final demolition notice may only be served for these purposes if one of
conditions A to C is satisfied in relation to the notice[15]. Condition A is that the
proposed demolition of the dwelling house does not form part of a scheme[16]
involving the demolition of other premises[17].

Condition B is that:

(a)   the proposed demolition of the dwelling house does form part of a scheme involving the demolition of other premises; but

(b)   none of those other premises needs to be acquired by the landlord in order for the landlord to be able to demolish them[18].

Condition C is that:

(i)   the proposed demolition of the dwelling house does form part of a scheme involving the demolition of other premises; and

(ii)   one or more of those premises need to be acquired by the landlord in order for the landlord to be able to demolish them; but

(iii)   in each case arrangements for their acquisition are in place[19].

The appropriate national authority may, on an application by the landlord, give a direction extending or further extending the period during which a final demolition notice is in force in respect of a dwelling house[20]. Such a direction may provide that any extension of that period is not to have effect unless the landlord complies with such requirements relating to the service of further notices as are specified in the direction[21]; and may only be given at a time when the demolition notice is[22] in force[23].

If, while a final demolition notice is in force:

(A)   the landlord decides not to demolish the dwelling house in question, he must, as soon as is reasonably practicable, serve a notice ('a revocation notice') on the tenant which informs him of the landlord's decision and that the demolition notice is revoked as from the date of service of the revocation notice[24];

(B)   it appears to the appropriate national authority that the landlord has no intention of demolishing the dwelling house in question, that authority may serve a notice ('a revocation notice') on the tenant which informs him of the authority's conclusion, and that the demolition notice is revoked as from the date of service of the revocation notice[25]; but the appropriate national authority may not serve a revocation notice unless it has previously served a notice on the landlord which informs him of the intention to serve the revocation notice[26].

Where a revocation notice is served under head (a) or head (b) above, the demolition notice ceases to be in force as from the date of service of the revocation notice[27]. These provisions with regard to revocation notices[28] do not, however, apply if landlord is selling or otherwise transferring his interest as landlord to another person or is offering it for sale or for other transfer[29].

Once a final demolition notice ('the earlier notice') has, for any reason, ceased to be in force in respect of a dwelling house without it being demolished, no further final demolition notice and no initial demolition notice[30] may be served in respect of it by the landlord who served the earlier notice or any landlord who served a continuation notice in respect of the earlier notice during the period of five years following the time when the earlier notice ceases to be in force, unless the further final demolition notice (or, as the case may be, the initial demolition notice) is served with the consent of the appropriate national authority and the notice states that it is so served[31]. Such consent may be given subject to compliance with such conditions as the appropriate national authority may specify[32].

If a final demolition notice is in force in respect of a dwelling house, and the landlord transfers his interest as landlord to another person, then subject to the specified provisions[33], the final demolition notice ('the original notice') continues in force[34]. If the transferee intends to demolish the dwelling house, but has not served a continuation notice[35] and complied with the specified conditions[36] within the period of two months beginning with the date of transfer, the transferee must proceed[37] as if the transferee has decided not to demolish the dwelling house[38].

1 As to the meaning of 'the right to buy' see PARA 239. It is submitted that the provisions set out in the text and notes 2–38 also apply to the right to acquire under the Housing Act 1996 (see PARAS 242–244) or the Housing and Regeneration Act 2008 (see PARAS 240–241): see PARA 230 notes 7, 9.

2 As to when such a notice is in force see the text and notes 11–14.

3 Housing Act 1985 s 120, Sch 5 para 13(1) (Sch 5 paras 13–16 added by the Housing Act 2004 s 182(1)).

4 For the purposes of the Housing Act 1985 Sch 5 paras 13–15, other than Sch 5 para 15(7A) (see the text and notes 28–29), any reference to the landlord, in the context of a reference to an intention or decision on his part to demolish or not to demolish any premises, or of a reference to the acquisition or transfer of any premises, includes a reference to a superior landlord: Sch 5 para 13(9) (as added (see note 3); amended by the Housing and Regeneration Act 2008 s 305, Sch 13 paras 1, 2(1), (3)). As to the meaning of 'landlord' generally see PARA 31 note 3.

5 Ie under the Housing Act 1985 Sch 5 para 15: see the text and notes 20–32.

6 Housing Act 1985 Sch 5 para 13(2) (as added: see note 3).

7 Any notice under the Housing Act 1985 Sch 5 para 13, Sch 5 para 15 or Sch 5 para 15A may be served on a person: (1) by delivering it to him, by leaving it at his proper address or by sending it by post to him at that address; or (2) if the person is a body corporate, by serving it in accordance with head (1) on the secretary of the body: Sch 5 para 16(1) (as added (see note 3); amended by the Housing and Regeneration Act 2008 Sch 13 paras 1, 5). For these purposes and the purposes of the Interpretation Act 1978 s 7 (service of documents by post) the proper address of a person on whom a notice is to be served is: (a) in the case of a body corporate or its secretary, that of the registered or principal office of the body; and (b) in any other case, the last known address of that person: Housing Act 1985 Sch 5 para 16(2) (as so added).

8 Ie that the Housing Act 1985 s 138C confers such a right: see PARA 299.

9 Housing Act 1985 Sch 5 para 13(3) (as added: see note 3).

10 Housing Act 1985 Sch 5 para 13(4) (as added: see note 3). As to the meaning of 'tenant' see PARA 31 note 3.

11 Ie subject to compliance with the Housing Act 1985 Sch 5 para 13(6), (7). If: (1) the dwelling house is contained in a building which contains one or more other dwelling houses; and (2) the landlord intends to demolish the whole of the building, the landlord must have served a final demolition notice on the occupier of each of the dwelling houses contained in it (whether addressed to him by name or just as 'the occupier'); but an accidental omission to serve a final demolition notice on one or more occupiers does not prevent this condition from being satisfied: Sch 5 para 13(6) (as added: see note 3). A notice stating that the landlord intends to demolish the relevant premises must have appeared: (a) in a local or other newspaper circulating in the locality in which those premises are situated (other than one published by the landlord); and (b) in any newspaper published by the landlord; and (c) on the landlord's website (if he has one): Sch 5 para 13(7) (as so added). The notice so mentioned must contain the following information: (i) sufficient information to enable identification of the premises that the landlord intends to demolish; (ii) the reasons why the landlord intends to demolish those premises; (iii) the proposed demolition date; (iv) the date when any final demolition notice or notices relating to those premises will cease to be in force, unless extended or revoked under Sch 5 para 15; (v) that the right to buy will not arise in respect of those premises or (as the case may be) in respect of any dwelling house contained in them; (vi) that there may be a right to compensation under s 138C (see PARA 299) in respect of certain expenditure incurred in respect of any existing claim: Sch 5 para 13(8) (as so added).

12 Ie the provisions of the Housing Act 1985 Sch 5 para 15(1)–(7A): see the text and notes 20–29.

13 Ie the provisions of the Housing Act 1985 Sch 5 para 15A: see the text and notes 33–38.

14 Housing Act 1985 Sch 5 para 13(5) (as added (see note 3); amended by the Housing and Regeneration Act 2008 ss 305, 321(1), Sch 13 paras 1, 2(1), (2), Sch 16).

15 Housing Act 1985 Sch 5 para 14(1) (as added: see note 3).

16 For these purposes, 'scheme' includes arrangements of any description: Housing Act 1985 Sch 5 para 14(6) (as added: see note 3).

17 Housing Act 1985 Sch 5 para 14(2) (as added: see note 3). For these purposes, 'premises' means premises of any description: Sch 5 para 14(6) (as so added).

18 Housing Act 1985 Sch 5 para 14(3) (as added: see note 3).

19 Housing Act 1985 Sch 5 para 14(4) (as added: see note 3). For these purposes, arrangements for the acquisition of any premises are in place if: (1) an agreement under which the landlord is entitled to acquire the premises is in force; or (2) a notice to treat has been given in respect of the premises under the Compulsory Purchase Act 1965 s 5 (see COMPULSORY ACQUISITION OF LAND vol 18

(2009) PARA 616); or (3) a vesting declaration has been made in respect of the premises under the Compulsory Purchase (Vesting Declarations) Act 1981 s 4 (see COMPULSORY ACQUISITION OF LAND vol 18 (2009) PARA 687): Housing Act 1985 Sch 5 para 14(5) (as so added).

20 Housing Act 1985 Sch 5 para 15(1) (as added: see note 3). As to the appropriate national authority, and the transfer of functions under the Housing Act 1985, so far as exercisable in relation to Wales, to the Welsh Ministers see PARA 7.

21 Housing Act 1985 Sch 5 para 15(2) (as added: see note 3).

22 Ie whether by virtue of the Housing Act 1985 Sch 5 para 13 or Sch 5 para 15.

23 Housing Act 1985 Sch 5 para 15(3) (as added: see note 3).

24 Housing Act 1985 Sch 5 para 15(4) (as added: see note 3). See also the text and notes 28–29.

25 Housing Act 1985 Sch 5 para 15(5) (as added: see note 3). Section 169 (see PARA 344) applies in relation to the appropriate national authority's power under this provision as it applies in relation to his or its powers under the provisions mentioned in s 169: see Sch 5 para 15(5) (as so added). See also the text and notes 28–29.

26 Housing Act 1985 Sch 5 para 15(6) (as added: see note 3). See also the text and notes 28–29.

27 Housing Act 1985 Sch 5 para 15(7) (as added: see note 3). See also the text and notes 28–29.

28 Ie the Housing Act 1985 Sch 5 para 15(4)–(7): see the text and notes 24–27.

29 Housing Act 1985 Sch 5 para 15(7A) (added by the Housing and Regeneration Act 2008 Sch 13 paras 1, 3(1), (2)).

30 For these purposes, 'initial demolition notice' has the meaning given by the Housing Act 1985 Sch 5A para 1 (initial demolition notices: see PARA 293): Sch 5 para 15(10) (added by the Housing and Regeneration Act 2008 Sch 13 paras 1, 3(1), (4)).

31 Housing Act 1985 Sch 5 para 15(8) (as added (see note 3); amended by the Housing and Regeneration Act 2008 Sch 13 paras 1, 3(1), (3)). See also PARA 298.

32 Housing Act 1985 Sch 5 para 15(9) (as added: see note 3).

33 Ie subject to the Housing Act 1985 Sch 5 paras 13, 15 (see the text and notes 1–14, 20–32) and Sch 5 para 15A(3)–(11) (see the text and notes 35–38).

34 Housing Act 1985 Sch 5 para 15A(1), (2) (Sch 5 para 15A added by the Housing and Regeneration Act 2008 Sch 13 paras 1, 4).

The Housing Act 1985 Sch 5 para 15A(7)–(10) (see note 36) applies instead of Sch 5 para 13(6)–(8) (see note 11) in relation to a final demolition notice so far as continued in force under Sch 5 para 15A: Sch 5 para 15A(11) (as so added).

35 A continuation notice is a notice: (1) stating that the transferee has acquired the interest concerned, and intends to demolish the dwelling house or (as the case may be) the building containing it ('the relevant premises'); (2) setting out the reasons why the transferee intends to demolish the relevant premises; stating that one of conditions A-C in the Housing Act 1985 Sch 5 para 14 (see the text and notes 16–19) is satisfied in relation to the original notice (specifying the condition concerned); (4) stating that the original notice is to continue in force; and (5) explaining the continued effect of the original notice: Sch 5 para 15A(5) (as added: see note 34). A continuation notice may not vary the proposed demolition date in the original notice nor the date when the original notice will cease to be in force: Sch 5 para 15A(6) (as so added).

36 Ie the conditions in the Housing Act 1985 Sch 5 para 15A(8), (10). Schedule 5 para 15A(8) applies if: (1) the dwelling house is contained in a building which contains one or more other dwelling houses; and (2) the transferee intends to demolish the whole of the building: Sch 5 para 15A(7) (as added: see note 34). The transferee must serve a continuation notice on the occupier of each of the dwelling houses contained in the building (whether addressed to him by name or just as 'the occupier'): Sch 5 para 15A(8) (as so added). An accidental omission to serve a continuation notice on one or more occupiers does not prevent the condition in Sch 5 para 15A(8) from being satisfied: Sch 5 para 15A(9) (as so added). Schedule 5 para 13(7), (8) (see note 11) applies in relation to the transferee's intention to demolish so as to impose a condition on the transferee for a notice to appear within the period of two months beginning with the date of transfer: Sch 5 para 15A(10) (as so added).

37 Ie under the Housing Act 1985 Sch 5 para 15(4): see the text and note 24.

38 Housing Act 1985 Sch 5 para 15A(3), (4) (as added: see note 34). Schedule 5 para 15(5)–(7) (see the text and notes 25–27) applies on the same basis: Sch 5 para 15A(4) (as so added).

255. Dwelling houses where the debt is equal to or greater than the purchase price plus the discount.

The right to acquire conferred by the Housing Act 1996[1] or the Housing and Regeneration Act 2008[2] does not arise if the net debt[3] or the peak debt[4] attributable to the dwelling house[5] on the date of service of the tenant's notice claiming to exercise the right to acquire[6] is equal to or greater than the purchase price plus the discount[7].

1 See PARAS 242–244.
2 See PARAS 240–241.
3 For these purposes, the net debt is the amount of the relevant costs, as defined, less the amount of public subsidy as defined: see the Housing Act 1985 s 120, Sch 5 para 13(2) (Sch 5 para 13 added for these purposes by the Housing (Right to Acquire) Regulations 1997, SI 1997/619, Sch 1 para 40(e), applying in relation to the right to acquire under the Housing and Regeneration Act 2008 by virtue of s 184, which applies the Housing Act 1996 s 17 (regulations modifying the Housing Act 1985): see PARA 241). 'The relevant costs' means the costs incurred by the landlord in respect of the acquisition of the dwelling house, the construction of the dwelling house (including the costs of development works and the acquisition of land) but does not include the costs of: (1) works of repair or maintenance; (2) works to deal with any defect affecting the dwelling house; (3) works of improvement where they are paid for on or after the date of service of the tenant's notice under the Housing Act 1985 s 122 (see PARA 273) unless: (a) the landlord has before that date entered into a written contract for the carrying out of the works; or (b) the tenant has agreed in writing to the carrying out of the works and either the works have been carried out no later than the date of service of the landlord's notice under s 125 (landlord's notice of purchase price and other matters: see PARA 276) or the works will be carried out under the proposed terms of the conveyance: Sch 5 para 13(4) (as so added). 'Public subsidy' means grant or other financial assistance of any kind used by the landlord in whole or in part in connection with the acquisition, construction (including the costs of development and the acquisition of land), repair, maintenance or improvement of the dwelling house where such grant or assistance is received from: (i) the relevant authority (now the Welsh Ministers) under the Housing Act 1996 s 18 (social housing grants: see PARA 166); (ii) the appropriate national authority under the Housing Grants, Construction and Regeneration Act 1996 s 126 (see PLANNING vol 83 (2010) PARA 1653) under the programme designated 'City Challenge' in England and the programmes designated the 'Strategic Development Scheme' and 'Welsh Capital Challenge' in Wales; (iii) a local housing authority where grant is paid pursuant to an application by the landlord under the Local Government and Housing Act 1989 Pt VIII (repealed) or the Housing Grants, Construction and Regeneration Act 1996 Pt I Ch I (ss 1–59) (grants etc for renewal of private sector housing: see PARA 836 et seq); (iv) National Lottery; and (v) a local authority in a case where the local authority has conveyed the freehold or leasehold of land to the landlord at a price which is below the market value of the land at the time of the conveyance: Housing Act 1985 Sch 5 para 13(5) (as so added). As to the appropriate national authority see PARA 7.
4 For these purposes the peak debt is the amount under a loan agreement, ie the portion of the maximum amount which the landlord may borrow under a loan agreement which is attributable to the dwelling house: Housing Act 1985 Sch 5 para 13(3) (as added: see note 3). 'A loan agreement' means an agreement: (1) for a loan between a lender and the landlord which is wholly or partly secured by a charge (however created or arising) on the landlord's interest in the dwelling house; (2) which specifies the portion of the maximum amount which the landlord may borrow in any period which is attributable to the dwelling house; and (3) which is for the purpose of the provision of moneys for use in connection with the acquisition of land held for housing purposes and housing stock pursuant to a disposal under s 32 (see PARA 522); and where a loan is for such a purpose it may include the construction of dwelling houses (including the costs of development works and the acquisition of land) and works of repair, maintenance or improvement to dwelling houses pursuant to such acquisition: Sch 5 para 13(6) (as so added).
5 As to the meaning of 'dwelling house' see PARA 231.
6 Ie the notice under the Housing Act 1985 s 122: see PARA 273.
7 Housing Act 1985 Sch 5 para 13(1) (as added: see note 3). This is similar to the statutory limits on the amount of discount under a right to buy claim: see the Housing Act 1985 s 131; and PARA 289.

256. Certain assured shorthold tenancies. The right to acquire under the Housing Act 1996[1] is not exercisable if the tenancy is an assured shorthold tenancy of any description[2].

The right to acquire under the Housing and Regeneration Act 2008 is not exercisable if the tenancy is:

(1)   an assured shorthold tenancy for a fixed term of less than two years;

(2)   a periodic assured shorthold tenancy; or

(3)   an assured shorthold tenancy where the rent payable under the tenancy is intermediate rent[3] or mortgage rescue rent[4].

1   See PARA 242.
2   See the Housing Act 1996 s 16(1)(b); and PARA 242. As to the meaning of 'assured shorthold tenancy' see LANDLORD AND TENANT vol 63 (2016) PARA 852.
3   As to the meaning of 'intermediate rent' see LANDLORD AND TENANT vol 63 (2016) PARA 904 note 12.
4   See the Transfer of Tenancies and Right to Acquire (Exclusion) Regulations 2012, SI 2012/696, reg 4. As to the meaning of 'mortgage rescue rent' see LANDLORD AND TENANT vol 63 (2016) PARA 904 note 13.

257.   Circumstances in which the right to buy or acquire cannot be exercised. The right to buy[1] or the right to acquire conferred by the Housing Act 1996[2] or the Housing and Regeneration Act 2008[3] cannot be exercised:
   (1)   if the tenant[4] is subject to an order of the court for possession of the dwelling house[5];
   (2)   if the person, or one of the persons, to whom the right to buy or to acquire belongs has made a bankruptcy application that has not been determined or has a bankruptcy petition[6] pending against him, is an undischarged bankrupt[7], has made a composition or arrangement with his creditors[8] the terms of which remain to be fulfilled or is a person in relation to whom a moratorium period under a debt relief order[9] applies[10].

The right to buy cannot be exercised at any time during the suspension period under a suspension order[11] made in respect of the secure tenancy[12].

1   As to the meaning of 'the right to buy' see PARA 239.
2   See PARAS 242–244.
3   See PARAS 240–241.
4   As to the meaning of 'tenant' see PARA 31 note 3.
5   Housing Act 1985 s 121(1) (substituted by the Housing and Regeneration Act 2008 s 304(1)); and see PARA 230 notes 7, 9. As to the meaning of 'dwelling house' see PARA 231. See PARA 258.
6   As to bankruptcy applications and petitions see BANKRUPTCY AND INDIVIDUAL INSOLVENCY vol 5 (2013) PARA 130 et seq.
7   As to discharge from bankruptcy see BANKRUPTCY AND INDIVIDUAL INSOLVENCY vol 5 (2013) PARA 638 et seq.
8   As to compositions and arrangements with creditors see BANKRUPTCY AND INDIVIDUAL INSOLVENCY vol 5 (2013) PARA 852 et seq.
9   Ie under the Insolvency Act 1986 Pt VIIA (ss 251A–251X): see BANKRUPTCY AND INDIVIDUAL INSOLVENCY vol 5 (2013) PARA 91.
10 Housing Act 1985 s 121(2) (amended by the Insolvency Act 1985 s 235, Sch 10 Pt III; and by SI 2012/2494 and SI 2016/481); and see PARA 230 notes 7, 9.
11 Ie an order made under the Housing Act 1985 s 121A: see PARA 259.
12 Housing Act 1985 s 121(3) (added by the Housing Act 2004 s 192(1)). It is submitted that this exclusion also applies to the right to acquire under the Housing Act 1996 or the Housing and Regeneration Act 2008: see PARA 230 notes 7, 9.

258.   Considerations regarding exclusion of right to buy by possession order. If ground on which the right to buy[1] or the right to acquire conferred by the Housing Act 1996[2] or the Housing and Regeneration Act 2008[3] cannot be exercised is that the tenant[4] is subject to an order of the court for possession of the dwelling house[5], there is a potential clash of competing claims, namely that of a landlord for possession and that of the tenant to exercise the right to buy. The conflict is not to be resolved by a race to judgment or to execution of judgment though from a procedural or administrative point of view it may be the best course for the court to hear the possession claim first[6]. The mere fact that the statutory conditions to exercise a right to buy are fulfilled does not dictate the priority of the competing claims[7]. Where a landlord's application for possession and a tenant's application for the right to buy were scheduled together, it was held that the judge was correct to hear the application for possession first[8], and it has since been held that the cases in which it is right not to hear the claims together will be rare; if each claim is arguable it must be right to investigate the merits as a whole which will involve considering both cases at the same time[9]. If a local authority needs to delay the statutory timetable applicable to the right to buy it is preferable for the authority to obtain the court's ruling on the appropriate order for determination of the rival proceedings but a refusal to process a tenant's notice did not require the court to consider the right to buy claim first[10].

The right to buy pursuant to a notice already served[11] by the tenant is not permanently lost once the tenant is obliged to deliver up possession; the effect of the exclusion[12] is to suspend, but not to remove permanently, a secure tenant's right to buy if and so long as the tenant is obliged to give up possession in pursuance of an order of the court[13]. Although the exclusion destroys a tenant's right to buy a dwelling house made subject to a possession order, it does not preclude the right to buy another dwelling house not subject to a possession order of which he becomes the tenant[14].

1   As to the meaning of 'the right to buy' see PARA 239.
2   See PARAS 242–244.
3   See PARAS 240–241.
4   As to the meaning of 'tenant' see PARA 31 note 3.
5   Ie on the ground in the Housing Act 1985 s 121(1): see PARA 257 head (1). As to the meaning of 'dwelling house' see PARA 231.
6   *Bristol City Council v Lovell* [1998] 1 All ER 775, [1998] 1 WLR 446, HL, overruling *Dance v Welwyn Hatfield District Council* [1990] 3 All ER 572, [1990] 1 WLR 1097, CA, and explaining *Taylor v Newham London Borough Council* [1993] 2 All ER 649, [1993] 1 WLR 444.
7   *Basildon District Council v Wahlen* [2006] EWCA Civ 326, [2007] 1 All ER 734, [2006] 1 WLR 2744; and see *Martin v Medina Housing Association Ltd* [2006] EWCA Civ 367, [2006] 15 EG 134 (CS), [2006] All ER (D) 478 (Mar) (where the right to buy had been established but the stage had not been reached at which all matters relating to the grant had been agreed or determined). For guidance in balancing a sound case by a tenant for further implementation of his right to buy the property in question and, on the other hand, a good case for possession being reasonable on the ground that the accommodation afforded by the dwelling house is more extensive than is reasonable required by the tenant (ie the Housing Act 1985 Sch 2 Pt III, Ground 16: see LANDLORD AND TENANT vol 63 (2016) PARA 955) see *Basildon District Council v Wahlen* [2006] EWCA Civ 326, [2007] 1 All ER 734, [2006] 1 WLR 2744; *Kensington and Chelsea London Borough Council v Hislop* [2003] EWHC 2944 (Ch), [2004] 1 All ER 1036, [2003] All ER (D) 113 (Dec); but dicta in those cases were disapproved in *Manchester City Council v Benjamin* [2008] EWCA Civ 189, [2009] 1 All ER 798, [2009] 1 WLR 2202.
8   See *Tandridge District Council v Bickers* (1998) 31 HLR 432, CA.
9   *Basildon District Council v Wahlen* [2006] EWCA Civ 326, [2007] 1 All ER 734, [2006] 1 WLR 2744.
10 See *Tandridge District Council v Bickers* (1998) 31 HLR 432, CA.
11 Ie under the Housing Act 1985 s 122: see PARA 273.
12 Ie in the Housing Act 1985 s 212(1).
13 *Knowsley Housing Trust v White, Honeygan-Green v Islington London Borough Council, Porter v Shepherds Bush Housing Association* [2008] UKHL 70, [2009] AC 636, [2009] 2 All ER 829.
14 *Manchester City Council v Benjamin* [2008] EWCA Civ 189, [2009] 1 All ER 798, [2009] 1 WLR 2202.

(B)   *Suspension of the Right to Buy or Acquire*

(a)   Suspension because of Anti-social Behaviour

259.   Order suspending right to buy because of anti-social behaviour. The court may, on the application of the landlord[1] under a secure tenancy[2], make a suspension order in respect of the tenancy[3]. A suspension order is an order providing that the right to buy[4] may not be exercised in relation to the dwelling house[5] during such period as is specified in the order ('the suspension period')[6].

The court will fix a date for the hearing when it issues the claim form[7]. The defendant must be served with the claim form and the particulars of claim not less than 21 days before the hearing date[8]. Where the defendant does not file a defence within the specified time[9] he may take part in any hearing but the court may take his failure to do so into account when deciding what order to make about costs[10]. The landlord may not obtain a default judgment[11].

At the hearing fixed in accordance with the rules set out above[12] or at any adjournment of that hearing the court may either decide the claim or give case management directions[13]. Where the claim is genuinely disputed on grounds which appear to be substantial, case management directions so given will include the allocation of the claim to a track[14] or directions to enable it to be allocated[15].

The court must not make a suspension order unless it is satisfied:

(1)   that the tenant[16], or a person residing in or visiting the dwelling house, has engaged or threatened to engage in:

    (a)   conduct that is capable of causing nuisance or annoyance to some person (who need not be a particular identified person) and that directly or indirectly relates to or affects the landlord's housing management functions; or

    (b)   conduct that consists of or involves using housing accommodation[17] owned or managed by the landlord for an unlawful purpose[18]; and

(2)   that it is reasonable to make the order[19].

When deciding whether it is reasonable to make the order, the court must consider, in particular:

(i)   whether it is desirable for the dwelling house to be managed by the landlord during the suspension period; and

(ii)   where the conduct mentioned in head (1) above consists of conduct by a person which is capable of causing nuisance or annoyance, the effect that the conduct, or the threat of it, has had on other persons, or would have if repeated[20].

Where a suspension order is made, any existing claim to exercise the right to buy in relation to the dwelling house ceases to be effective as from the beginning of the suspension period[21], and the obligation to complete[22] does not apply to the landlord, in connection with such a claim, at any time after the beginning of that period[23]. The order does not, however, affect the computation[24] of any qualifying period[25].

The court may, on the application of the landlord, make, on one or more occasions, a further order which extends the suspension period under the suspension order by such period as is specified in the further order[26]. The court must not make such a further order unless it is satisfied:

(A)   that, since the making of the suspension order, or the last order extending the suspension period[27], the tenant, or a person residing in or visiting the dwelling house, has engaged or threatened to engage in such conduct as is described in head (1) above; and

(B)   that it is reasonable to make the further order[28].

When deciding whether it is reasonable to make such a further order, the court must consider, in particular:

(I)   whether it is desirable for the dwelling house to be managed by the landlord during the further period of suspension; and

(II)   where the conduct mentioned in head (A) above consists of conduct by a person which is capable of causing nuisance or annoyance, the effect that the conduct, or the threat of it, has had on other persons, or would have if repeated[29].

A suspension order may be claimed in the alternative to a possession order, in which case there are different procedural rules[30].

Regulations[31] which apply Part V of the Housing Act 1985[32] in relation to the right to acquire a dwelling under the Housing Act 1996[33] or the Housing and Regeneration Act 2008[34] may make provision for continuing the effect of a suspension order where the secure tenancy in respect of which the order was made has been replaced by an assured tenancy[35]. At the date at which this volume states the law, however, no such provision had been made.

1   As to the meaning of 'landlord' see PARA 31 note 3.
2   As to the meaning of 'secure tenancy' see LANDLORD AND TENANT vol 63 (2016) PARA 1037.
3   Housing Act 1985 s 121A(1) (s 121A added by the Housing Act 2004 s 192(2)).
4   As to the meaning of 'the right to buy' see PARA 239.
5   As to the meaning of 'dwelling house' see PARA 231.
6   Housing Act 1985 s 121A(2) (as added: see note 3). Where a suspension claim is, or both a suspension and a demotion claim are, made other than in a possession claim, CPR 65.14-CPR 65.19 apply: CPR 65.13. The claim may be made at any County Court hearing centre; the claim will be issued by the hearing centre where the claim is made; and if the claim is not made at the County Court hearing centre which serves the address where the property is situated, the claim, when it is issued, will be sent to that hearing centre: CPR 65.14(1). The claim form and form of defence sent with it must be in the forms set out in Practice Direction PD 65: CPR 65.14(2). The particulars of claim must be filed and served with the claim form: CPR 65.15. See also CPR PD 2C—*Starting Proceedings in the County Court* para 4. As to demotion claims see LANDLORD AND TENANT vol 63 (2016) PARA 1090.
7   CPR 65.16(1). The hearing date will be not less than 28 days from the date of issue of the claim form: CPR 65.16(2). The standard period between the issue of the claim form and the hearing will be not more than eight weeks: CPR 65.16(3). The court may extend or shorten the time for compliance with any rule and may adjourn or bring forward a hearing: see CPR 3.1(2)(a), (b); and CIVIL PROCEDURE vol 12 (2015) PARAS 507, 511.
     The court may use its powers under CPR 3.1(2)(a), (b) to shorten the time periods set out in CPR 65.16(2)–(4): CPR PD 65—*Anti-social Behaviour and Harassment* para 8.1. Particular consideration should be given to the exercise of this power if: (1) the defendant, or a person for whom the defendant is responsible, has assaulted or threatened to assault: (a) the claimant; (b) a member of the claimant's staff; or (c) another resident in the locality; (2) there are reasonable grounds for fearing such an assault; or (3) the defendant, or a person for whom the defendant is responsible, has caused serious damage or threatened to cause serious damage to the property or to the home or property of another resident in the locality: para 8.2. Where para 8.2 applies but the case cannot be determined at the first hearing fixed under CPR 65.16, the court will consider what steps are needed to finally determine the case as quickly as reasonably practicable: CPR PD 65—*Anti-social Behaviour and Harassment* para 8.3.
8   CPR 65.16(4). The claimant must use the appropriate claim form and particulars of claim form set out in CPR PD 4—*Forms* Table 1; and the defence must be in form N11D as appropriate: CPR PD 65—*Anti-social Behaviour and Harassment* para 6.2. The claimant's evidence should include details of the conduct alleged and any other matters relied upon: para 6.3. An acknowledgment of service is not required and CPR Pt 10 (see CIVIL PROCEDURE vol 11 (2015) PARA 311 et seq) does not apply: CPR 65.17(1). Where the claimant serves the claim form and particulars of claim, he must produce at the hearing a certificate of service of those documents, and CPR 6.17(2)(a) (see CIVIL PROCEDURE vol 11 (2015) PARA 257) does not apply: CPR 65.18(5).
     In a suspension claim, the particulars of claim must: (1) state that the suspension claim is a claim under the Housing Act 1985 s 121A; (2) state which of the bodies the claimant's interest belongs to in order to comply with the landlord condition under s 80 (see LANDLORD AND TENANT vol 63 (2016) PARA 1037); (3) identify the property to which the claim relates; (4) state details of the conduct alleged; and (5) explain why it is reasonable to make the order, having regard in particular to the factors set out in s 121A(4) (see heads (i)–(ii) in the text): CPR PD 65—*Anti-social Behaviour and Harassment* para 7.2.

9 Ie the time specified in CPR 15.4: see CIVIL PROCEDURE vol 11 (2015) PARA 315.
10 CPR 65.17(2).
11 See CPR 65.17(3), disapplying CPR Pt 12 (default judgment: see CIVIL PROCEDURE vol 12 (2015) PARA 535 et seq).
12 Ie fixed in accordance with CPR 65.16(1): see the text and note 7.
13 CPR 65.18(1). As to case management see generally CIVIL PROCEDURE vol 12 (2015) PARA 506 et seq. Except where the claim is allocated to the fast track or the multi-track, or the court directs otherwise, any fact that needs to be proved by the evidence of witnesses at a hearing referred to in CPR 65.18(1) may be proved by evidence in writing: CPR 65.18(3). All witness statements must be filed and served at least two days before the hearing: CPR 65.18(4). As to the general rule about evidence, which is subject to any provision to the contrary, see CPR 32.2(1), (2); and CIVIL PROCEDURE vol 12 (2015) PARA 768.
    Each party should wherever possible include all the evidence he wishes to present in his statement of case, verified by a statement of truth: CPR PD 65—*Anti-social Behaviour and Harassment* para 9.1. If: (1) the maker of a witness statement does not attend a hearing; and (2) the other party disputes material evidence contained in the statement, the court will normally adjourn the hearing so that oral evidence can be given: para 9.3.
14 When the court decides the track for the claim, the matters to which it must have regard include: (1) the matters set out in CPR 26.8 (see CIVIL PROCEDURE vol 11 (2015) PARA 208); and (2) the nature and extent of the conduct alleged: CPR 65.19.
15 CPR 65.18(2).
16 For these purposes, any reference to the tenant under a secure tenancy is, in relation to a joint tenancy, a reference to any of the joint tenants: Housing Act 1985 s 121A(9) (as added: see note 3). As to the meaning of 'tenant' generally see PARA 31 note 3.
17 For these purposes, 'housing accommodation' includes: (1) flats, lodging-houses and hostels; (2) any yard, garden, outhouses and appurtenances belonging to the accommodation or usually enjoyed with it; (3) any common areas used in connection with the accommodation: Housing Act 1985 s 121A(10) (added by the Police and Justice Act 2006 Sch 14 para 13(1), (3); and substituted by the Anti-social Behaviour, Crime and Policing Act 2014 s 181(1), Sch 11 para 11(1), (4)).
18 The claimant's evidence should include details of the conduct to which the Housing Act 1996 s 153A or s 153B applies and in respect of which the suspension claim is made: CPR PD 65—*Anti-social Behaviour and Harassment* para 9.2.
19 Housing Act 1985 s 121A(3) (as added (see note 3); amended by the Police and Justice Act 2006 s 52, Sch 14 para 13(1), (2) (in force in relation to England); and the Anti-social Behaviour, Crime and Policing Act 2014 Sch 11 para 11(1), (2)). The amendment made by the Police and Justice Act 2006 Sch 14 para 13(1), (2) is to come into force in Wales as from a day to be appointed under s 53. At the date at which this volume states the law, no such day had been appointed. Accordingly, in Wales, head (1) in the text should read '(1) that the tenant, or a person residing in or visiting the dwelling house, has engaged or threatened to engage in conduct to which the Housing Act 1996 s 153A or 153B applies (anti-social behaviour or use of premises for unlawful purposes); and'. As to the Housing Act 1996 ss 153A, 153B (repealed) see PARA 473.
20 Housing Act 1985 s 121A(4) (as added: see note 3).
21 Housing Act 1985 s 121A(5)(a) (as added: see note 3).
22 Ie the Housing Act 1985 s 138(1): see PARA 291.
23 Housing Act 1985 s 121A(5)(b) (as added: see note 3).
24 Ie in accordance with the Housing Act 1985 ss 119(1), 129(1), Sch 4: see PARA 268 et seq.
25 Housing Act 1985 s 121A(5)(c) (as added: see note 3).
26 Housing Act 1985 s 121A(6) (as added: see note 3).
27 Ie the last order under the Housing Act 1985 s 121A(6).
28 Housing Act 1985 s 121A(7) (as added (see note 3); amended by the Police and Justice Act 2006 Sch 14 para 13(1), (2) (in force in relation to England); and the Anti-social Behaviour, Crime and Policing Act 2014 Sch 11 para 11(1), (3)). As to the position in Wales see note 19.
29 Housing Act 1985 s 121A(8) (as added: see note 3).
30 See CPR 65.12. In such a case the claimant must use the procedure under CPR Pt 55 (see LANDLORD AND TENANT vol 62 (2016) PARA 550 et seq) and CPR Pt 55 Section 1 (CPR 55.2–CPR 55.10A) applies, except that the claim must be made in accordance with CPR 55.3(1): CPR 65.12. If the claim relates to a residential property let on a tenancy and if the claim includes a suspension claim, the particulars of claim must: (1) state that the suspension claim is a claim under the Housing Act 1985 s 121A; (2) state which of the bodies the claimant's interest belongs to in order to comply with the landlord condition under s 80 (see LANDLORD AND TENANT vol 63 (2016) PARA 1037); (3) state details of the conduct alleged; and (4) explain why it is reasonable to make the suspension order, having regard in particular to the factors set out in s 121A(4) (see heads (i)–(ii) in the text): CPR PD 65—*Anti-social Behaviour and Harassment* para 5A.1.

31 Ie regulations under the Housing Act 1996 s 17: see PARAS 241, 243.
32 Ie the Housing Act 1985 Pt V (ss 118–188): see PARAS 230 et seq, 268 et seq.
33 See PARAS 242–244.
34 See PARAS 240–241.
35 See the Housing Act 2004 s 192(3)(b). Regulations under the Housing Act 1985 s 171C
   (modifications of Pt V in relation to the preserved right to buy: see PARA 336) may also make
   provision for continuing the effect of a suspension order where the secure tenancy in respect of
   which the order was made has been replaced by an assured tenancy: see the Housing Act 2004
   s 192(3)(a). At the date at which this volume states the law, no such provision had been made.

(b) Directions Suspending the Right to Buy etc in Wales

260. Application for direction suspending the right to buy and related rights.
With effect from 3 September 2012[1], a local housing authority[2] may apply to the
Welsh Ministers for a direction suspending the right to buy[3] and related rights[4] in
its area for a period of up to five years if, within the period of six months
preceding the application, the authority has completed a consultation exercise[5]
and in the light of that exercise, and having considered any other relevant
information, the authority concludes that the condition described below exists[6].

The consultation exercise must seek views on whether there is a need for the
authority to apply for such a direction[7]. The persons to be consulted are:
(1)   each social housing provider[8] which appears to the authority to be a
        landlord of a dwelling house[9] situated in the authority's area (but the
        authority need not consult itself), and which the authority considers
        would be affected if its application for a direction is granted;
(2)   any body or bodies appearing to the authority to represent the interests
        of tenants of dwelling houses within the authority's area where the
        landlords of those dwelling houses are social housing providers, and the
        authority considers that the tenants of those dwelling houses would be
        affected if its application for a direction is granted;
(3)   any other local housing authority whose area is adjacent to the area to
        which it is proposed that the direction is to apply; and
(4)   such other persons as the authority considers appropriate[10].

The condition referred to above (the 'housing pressure condition') is that:
(a)   within the local housing authority's area, the demand for social housing
        substantially exceeds its supply or is likely to do so; and
(b)   that imbalance between supply and demand is likely to increase as a
        result of the exercise of the right to buy and related rights[11].

A local housing authority may conclude that head (a) above is met:
(i)   in relation to all social housing in its area;
(ii)   in relation to all social housing in a certain part or parts of its area;
(iii)   in relation to a certain type or types of social housing[12], whether
        throughout its area or in a certain part or parts of its area[13].

The requirements to be met by a local housing authority's application to the
Welsh Ministers for a direction suspending the right to buy and related rights are
as follows[14]. The application must:
(A)   include a draft of the direction which:
        (I)   clearly identifies the area to which it is to apply, whether that is
                the whole of the authority's area or one or more parts of its area;
        (II)   states whether or not the direction is to apply to every relevant
                dwelling house[15] within that area;

     (III)   if the direction is not to apply to every relevant dwelling house within that area, clearly describes the type or types of relevant dwelling house to which it is to apply;

     (IV)   states the period for which it is to have effect, which must be no longer than five years from the date on which, if the application were granted, it would be issued;

  (B)   explain why the authority has concluded that the housing pressure condition exists;

  (C)   explain why the authority is of the opinion that the direction is an appropriate response to its having concluded that the housing pressure condition exists;

  (D)   explain what other action the authority proposes to take to reduce the imbalance between the demand for social housing and its supply within its area during the period for which the direction is to have effect, and

  (E)   describe what the authority has done to discharge its obligation[16] to carry out a consultation exercise[17].

The Welsh Ministers may require a local housing authority to provide further information in addition to that provided in an application for such a direction[18]. This power is exercisable if the Welsh Ministers reasonably consider that the further information is required in order for them to decide whether to consider the authority's application or to determine the authority's application[19].

At any time before the Welsh Ministers have made a decision on a local housing authority's application for such a direction, the authority which made the application may by notice in writing withdraw it[20].

1 Ie the date when the Housing (Wales) Measure 2011 Pt 1 (ss 1–34) came into force: see the Housing (Wales) Measure 2011 (Commencement No 2) Order 2012, SI 2012/2091, arts 1(2), 2.

2 For these purposes, 'local housing authority' means a local housing authority in Wales: Housing (Wales) Measure 2011 s 33(2). As to local housing authorities see PARA 11 (definition applied by s 33(2)); and PARA 11.

3 As to meaning of 'the right to buy' see PARA 239 (definition applied by the Housing (Wales) Measure 2011 s 33(1)).

4 For these purposes, the following are rights related to the right to buy: (1) the right to buy as extended under the Housing Act 1985 s 171 (see PARA 233); (2) the preserved right to buy under the Housing Act 1985 s 171A (see PARA 334); (3) the right to acquire under the Housing Act 1996 s 16 (see PARA 242); (4) the right to acquire as extended under the Housing Act 1996 s 16A (see PARA 242): Housing (Wales) Measure 2011 s 1(3).

5 Ie in accordance with the Housing (Wales) Measure 2011 s 2. Section 2 provides for the consultation exercise that a local housing authority must carry out before it may apply to the Welsh Ministers for a direction suspending the right to buy and related rights: s 2(1). See the text to notes 7–10.

6 Housing (Wales) Measure 2011 s 1(1). As to the Welsh Ministers see PARA 7.

7 Housing (Wales) Measure 2011 s 2(2).

8 'Social housing' means any housing provided by a social housing provider; and 'social housing provider' means: (1) a local authority; and (2) a person (other than a local authority) which provides housing to, or has functions relating to allocation of housing to, people whose needs are not adequately served by the commercial housing market; but a local authority or such other person is a social housing provider only in so far as it provides, or has functions relating to allocation of, housing: Housing (Wales) Measure 2011 s 33(2), (4).

9 As to the meaning of 'dwelling house' see PARA 231 (definition applied by s 33(1)).

10 Housing (Wales) Measure 2011 s 2(3).

11 Housing (Wales) Measure 2011 s 1(2).

12 For these purposes, a type of social housing may be identified by reference to any, or any combination of, the following: (1) special needs of tenants; (2) description of dwelling house; (3) type of social housing provider (which may include a particular provider): Housing (Wales) Measure 2011 s 1(5). As to the meaning of 'dwelling house' see PARA 231 (definition applied by s 33(1)).

13 Housing (Wales) Measure 2011 s 1(4).

14 See the Housing (Wales) Measure 2011 s 3(1).
15 For these purposes, 'relevant dwelling house', in relation to an application for a direction, or a direction issued, under the Housing (Wales) Measure 2011 Pt 1 (ss 1–34) means: (1) a dwelling house the landlord of which is a social housing provider, and the tenant of which has the right to buy, or a right related to the right to buy, or would have such a right if he or she met the conditions which give rise to such a right; and (2) includes a dwelling house which meets the requirements of head (1) after the date on which the application for a direction is made: s 33(3).
16 Ie its obligation to carry out a consultation exercise under the Housing (Wales) Measure 2011 s 2: see the text to notes 6–10.
17 Housing (Wales) Measure 2011 s 3(2). In the exercise of its functions under s 3, a local housing authority must have regard to any guidance given from time to time in writing by the Welsh Ministers: s 30.
18 Housing (Wales) Measure 2011 s 27(1).
19 Housing (Wales) Measure 2011 s 27(2).
20 Housing (Wales) Measure 2011 s 26.

261. Consideration of application suspending the right to buy and related rights.
With effect from 3 September 2012[1], if the Welsh Ministers are of the opinion that a local housing authority's[2] application for a direction suspending the right to buy[3] and related rights[4] meets the statutory requirements[5], they must consider the application[6]. If, however, they are of the opinion that an application does not meet those requirements they must refuse to consider it unless, in their opinion, the failure to comply with the requirements is immaterial or insignificant in which case they may consider the application[7]. The Welsh Ministers must notify an authority in writing if they:

(1)   are obliged[8] to consider an application for a direction suspending the right to buy and related rights made by the authority[9];

(2)   decide, where they have discretion to do so[10], to consider such an application[11]; or

(3)   are obliged[12] to refuse to consider an application[13].

If, before the Welsh Ministers have decided to consider an application, a local housing authority provides further information[14], it is to be treated as if it formed part of the application[15].

Where the Welsh Ministers are considering a local housing authority's application for a direction suspending the right to buy and related rights[16], the following provisions apply[17]. The Welsh Ministers may reject the application[18] if they are of the opinion that

(a)   the authority has failed to comply with a requirement for further information[19] in relation to the application; or

(b)   where the authority is required to have a strategy relating to housing under the relevant provision of the Local Government Act 2003[20], the strategy, in so far as it relates to any imbalance between demand for and supply of social housing[21] in the authority's area, is inadequate[22];

but they must not make a decision under head (b) above unless they have considered any statement that the authority is required to prepare[23] and any other information which the Welsh Ministers consider relevant[24]. The Welsh Ministers must grant the application if:

(i)   they agree with the authority's conclusion as to why the housing pressure condition[25] exists;

(ii)   they agree with the authority's opinion that the direction is an appropriate response to the authority having concluded that the housing pressure condition exists;

(iii)   they are satisfied that the authority's proposals included in its application[26] are likely to contribute to a reduction in the imbalance between the demand for social housing and its supply within the authority's area; and

(iv)   they are satisfied that, before making the application, the authority complied with its obligation[27] to carry out a consultation exercise[28].

If any of heads (i) to (iv) above are not met, the Welsh Ministers must reject the application[29]. They must grant or reject an application in accordance with these provisions within six months beginning with the date on which they decided to consider the application[30]; but the validity of their decision is not affected by a failure to comply with this time limit[31].

Where the Welsh Ministers have refused to grant a local housing authority's application for a direction suspending the right to buy and related rights, the local housing authority which made the application must not, during the period of two years beginning with the date of refusal, make an application for a direction that is substantially the same as the direction the application for which was refused[32].

1   Ie the date when the Housing (Wales) Measure 2011 Pt 1 (ss 1–34) came into force: see PARA 260 note 1.
2   As to the meaning of 'local housing authority' see PARA 260 note 2.
3   As to the meaning of 'the right to buy' see PARA 239 (definition applied by the Housing (Wales) Measure 2011 s 33(1)).
4   'Related rights' has the meaning given to 'rights related to the right to buy' (see PARA 260 note 4): Housing (Wales) Measure 2011 s 33(2).
5   Ie the requirements of the Housing (Wales) Measure 2011 3: see PARA 260.
6   Housing (Wales) Measure 2011 s 4(1). As to the Welsh Ministers see PARA 7.
7   Housing (Wales) Measure 2011 s 4(2).
8   Ie under the Housing (Wales) Measure 2011 s 4(1): see the text and notes 2–6.
9   The day after that on which a notice was sent under the Housing (Wales) Measure 2011 s 4(3)(a) or (b) (see heads (1)–(2) in the text) is to be treated as the date on which the Welsh Ministers decided to consider the application: s 4(4).
10   Ie under the Housing (Wales) Measure 2011 s 4(2): see the text and note 7.
11   See note 9.
12   See note 10.
13   See the Housing (Wales) Measure 2011 s 4(3).
14   Ie under the Housing (Wales) Measure 2011 s 27: see PARA 260.
15   Housing (Wales) Measure 2011 s 4(5).
16   Ie in accordance with the Housing (Wales) Measure 2011 s 4(1) or (2): see the text and notes 2–7.
17   Housing (Wales) Measure 2011 s 5(1).
18   Ie without considering whether the Housing (Wales) Measure 2011 s 5(4) (see the text and notes 25–28) requires them to grant it.
19   Ie a requirement imposed under the Housing (Wales) Measure 2011 s 27: see PARA 260.
20   Ie under the Local Government Act 2003 s 87(1): see PARA 366.
21   As to the meaning of 'social housing' see PARA 260 note 8.
22   Housing (Wales) Measure 2011 s 5(2).
23   Ie under the Local Government Act 2003 s 87(2): see PARA 366.
24   Housing (Wales) Measure 2011 s 5(3).
25   As to the meaning of 'the housing pressure condition' see PARA 260.
26   Ie in accordance with the Housing (Wales) Measure 2011 s 3(2)(d): see PARA 260.
27   Ie its obligation to carry out a consultation exercise in accordance with the Housing (Wales) Measure 2011 s 2: see PARA 260 note 5.
28   Housing (Wales) Measure 2011 s 5(4).
29   Housing (Wales) Measure 2011 s 5(5).
30   Housing (Wales) Measure 2011 s 5(6). As to when the Welsh Ministers decide to consider the application see note 9.
31   Housing (Wales) Measure 2011 s 5(7).
32   Housing (Wales) Measure 2011 s 29(1), (2).

262. Issue of direction suspending the right to buy and related rights. With effect from 3 September 2012[1], where the Welsh Ministers grant a local housing authority's[2] application[3] for a direction suspending the right to buy[4] and related rights[5], they must issue in writing a direction which:

(1)   clearly identifies the area to which it applies, whether that is the whole of the authority's area or one or more parts of its area;

(2)   states whether or not the direction applies to every relevant dwelling house[6] within that area;

(3)   if the direction does not apply to every relevant dwelling house within that area, clearly describes the type or types of relevant dwelling house to which it does apply;

(4)   states the period for which it is to have effect, which must be no longer than five years from the date on which it is issued[7].

The Welsh Ministers must not issue a direction under these provisions which differs in any material respect from the draft of the direction included[8] in the local housing authority's application[9].

As soon as reasonably practicable after the issue of such a direction, the local housing authority which applied for the direction must publish it in whatever manner it thinks appropriate[10]. The authority must also take other reasonable steps to bring a direction issued under these provisions to the attention of persons likely to be affected by it[11].

Where the Welsh Ministers have issued a direction under these provisions (the 'relevant direction')[12], the local housing authority must not, during the period which begins on the date that the relevant direction has effect and ends two years from the date on which the relevant direction ceases to have effect, make an application[13] for another direction that is substantially the same as the relevant direction[14].

1   Ie the date when the Housing (Wales) Measure 2011 Pt 1 (ss 1–34) came into force: see PARA 260 note 1.
2   As to the meaning of 'local housing authority' see PARA 260 note 2.
3   Ie under the Housing (Wales) Measure 2011 s 5: see PARA 261.
4   As to the meaning of 'the right to buy' see PARA 239 (definition applied by the Housing (Wales) Measure 2011 s 33(1)).
5   As to the meaning of 'related rights' see PARA 261 note 4.
6   As to the meaning of 'relevant dwelling house' see PARA 260 note 15.
7   Housing (Wales) Measure 2011 s 6(1). As to the Welsh Ministers see PARA 7.
8   Ie in accordance with the Housing (Wales) Measure 2011 s 3(2)(a): see PARA 260.
9   Housing (Wales) Measure 2011 s 6(2).
10   Housing (Wales) Measure 2011 s 28(1).
11   Housing (Wales) Measure 2011 s 28(2).
12   Ie whether or not there has been a variation under the Housing (Wales) Measure 2011 s 13 or s 17 (see PARA 263) or an extension under s 22 (see PARA 264).
13   Ie under the Housing (Wales) Measure 2011 s 1: see PARA 260.
14   Housing (Wales) Measure 2011 s 29(3)–(5). In a case where there has been a variation under s 13 or 17, the references in s 29(4), (5)(b) to the relevant direction are references to the direction having effect after the variation; and in a case where there has been an extension under s 22, the reference in s 29(5)(b) to the time when the relevant direction ceases to have effect is a reference to the time when the direction ceases to have effect in accordance with the extension: s 29(6), (7).

263. Enlarging variation of a direction suspending the right to buy and related rights. With effect from 3 September 2012[1], a local housing authority[2] may apply to the Welsh Ministers for an enlarging variation[3] of a direction issued under Part 1 of the Housing (Wales) Measure 2011[4] if:

(1)   the direction was issued in response to an application made by the authority;

(2)   the application for a variation is made at least six months before the date on which the direction is to cease to have effect;

(3)   within the period of six months preceding the application, the authority has completed a consultation exercise (similar to that on an application for a direction suspending the right to buy)[5]; and

(4)   in the light of that exercise, and having considered any other relevant information, the authority concludes that, in relation to the enlarging elements of the variation, the condition described below exists[6].

That condition is that:

(a)   the demand for social housing falling within the enlarging elements of the variation substantially exceeds its supply or is likely to do so; and

(b)   that imbalance between supply and demand is likely to increase as a result of the exercise of the right to buy[7] and related rights[8].

The following provisions set out the requirements to be met by a local housing authority's application to the Welsh Ministers for an enlarging variation of a direction issued under Part 1 of the 2011 Measure[9]. The application must:

(i)   include a draft of the direction as it would be varied if the application were granted which, if it were included in an application for a direction suspending the right to buy and related rights[10], would comply with the specified requirements[11];

(ii)   explain why the authority has concluded that the condition described in heads (a) and (b) above exists;

(iii)   explain why the authority is of the opinion that the variation is an appropriate response to its having concluded that that condition exists;

(iv)   explain what other action the authority proposes to take to reduce the imbalance between the demand for social housing and its supply within its area during the period for which the direction as varied is to have effect; and

(v)   describe what the authority has done to discharge its obligation[12] to carry out a consultation exercise[13].

If the Welsh Ministers are of the opinion that a local housing authority's application for an enlarging variation meets the requirements of heads (i) to (v) above, they must consider the application[14]. If they are of the opinion that an application does not meet those requirements they must refuse to consider it unless, in their opinion, the failure to comply with the requirements is immaterial or insignificant in which case they may consider the application[15]. If, before the Welsh Ministers have decided to consider an application, a local housing authority provides further information[16], it is to be treated as if it formed part of the application[17].

The Welsh Ministers must notify an authority in writing if they:

(A)   are obliged[18] to consider an application for an enlarging variation[19];

(B)   decide (where they have discretion to do so)[20] to consider such an application[21]; or

(C)   are obliged[22] to refuse to consider an application[23].

The following provisions apply where the Welsh Ministers are considering[24] a local housing authority's application for an enlarging variation[25]. The Welsh Ministers may reject the application[26] if they are of the opinion that the authority has failed to comply with a requirement for further information[27] in relation to the application[28]. They may also reject the application[29] if, where the authority is required to have a strategy relating to housing under the relevant provision of the Local Government Act 2003[30], they are of the opinion that the strategy, in so far as it relates to the imbalance between demand for and supply of social housing in the authority's area, is inadequate[31]; but they must not make such a decision unless they have considered any statement that the authority is required to prepare[32] and any other information which they consider relevant[33]. The Welsh Ministers must grant the application if:

(I)   they agree with the authority's opinion as to why the condition described in heads (a) and (b) above exists;

(II)   they agree with the authority's opinion that the variation is an appropriate response to the authority having concluded that the condition exists;

(III)   they are satisfied that the authority's proposals included in its application in accordance with head (iv) above are likely to contribute to a reduction in the imbalance between the demand for social housing and its supply within the authority's area; and

(IV)   they are satisfied that, before making the application, the authority complied with its obligation[34] to carry out a consultation exercise[35].

If any of heads (I) to (IV) above are not met, the Welsh Ministers must reject the application[36]. The Welsh Ministers must grant or reject an application in accordance with these provisions within six months beginning with the date on which they decided to consider the application[37]; but the validity of their decision is not affected by a failure to comply with this time limit[38].

Where the Welsh Ministers grant a local housing authority's application under the above provisions, they must issue in writing a varied direction which clearly identifies the area to which it applies, which states whether or not the direction applies to every relevant dwelling house within that area and if it does not apply to every relevant dwelling house within that area, clearly describes the type or types of relevant dwelling house to which it does apply, and which states the period for which it is to have effect[39]. They must not issue a direction under these provisions which differs in any material respect from the draft of the direction included in the local housing authority's application in accordance with head (i) above[40].

1   Ie the date when the Housing (Wales) Measure 2011 Pt 1 (ss 1–34) came into force: see PARA 260 note 1.

2   As to the meaning of 'local housing authority' see PARA 260 note 2.

3   For these purposes, an 'enlarging variation' is a variation of a direction issued under the Housing (Wales) Measure 2011 Pt 1 (ss 1–34) (see PARAS 260–262, 264 et seq) which makes either or both of the following changes (and no others): (1) alters the direction so that it applies to an area to which it did not previously apply; (2) alters the direction so that it applies to a type or types of relevant dwelling house to which it did not previously apply; and 'enlarging elements' must be construed accordingly: s 7(1). As to the meaning of 'relevant dwelling house' see PARA 260 note 15.

4   Ie under the Housing (Wales) Measure 2011 Pt 1: see PARAS 260–262, 264 et seq.

5   Ie under the Housing (Wales) Measure 2011 s 9. Section 9 provides for the consultation exercise that a local housing authority must carry out before it may apply to the Welsh Ministers for an enlarging variation of a direction issued under Pt I: s 9(1). The consultation exercise must seek views on whether there is a need to apply for such a variation: s 9(2). The persons to be consulted are: (1) each social housing provider which appears to the authority to be a landlord of a dwelling house situated in the authority's area (but the authority need not consult itself), and which the authority considers would be affected if its application for an enlarging variation of a direction is granted; (2) any body or bodies appearing to the authority to represent the interests of tenants of dwelling houses within the authority's area where the landlords of those dwelling houses are social housing providers, and the authority considers that the tenants of those dwelling houses would be affected if its application for an enlarging variation of a direction is granted; (3) any other local housing authority whose area is adjacent to the area to which it is proposed that the enlarging elements of the direction are to apply; and (4) such other persons as the authority considers

appropriate: s 9(3). As to the meaning of 'social housing provider' see PARA 260 note 8; and as to the meaning of 'dwelling house' see PARA 231 (definition applied by the Housing (Wales) Measure 2011 s 33(1)).

6   Housing (Wales) Measure 2011 s 8(1). As to the Welsh Ministers see PARA 7.

7   As to the meaning of 'the right to buy' see PARA 239 (definition applied by the Housing (Wales) Measure 2011 s 33(1)).

8   Housing (Wales) Measure 2011 s 8(2). As to the meaning of 'related rights' see PARA 261 note 4.

9   Housing (Wales) Measure 2011 s 10(1).

10 Ie an application for a direction under the Housing (Wales) Measure 2011 s 3: see PARA 260.

11 Ie the requirements of the Housing (Wales) Measure 2011 s 3(2)(a): see PARA 260.

12 Ie its obligation to carry out a consultation exercise under the Housing (Wales) Measure 2011 s 9: see note 5.

13 Housing (Wales) Measure 2011 s 10(2). In the exercise of its functions under s 10, a local housing authority must have regard to any guidance given from time to time in writing by the Welsh Ministers: s 30.

14 Housing (Wales) Measure 2011 s 11(1).

15 Housing (Wales) Measure 2011 s 11(2).

16 Ie under the Housing (Wales) Measure 2011 s 27: see PARA 260.

17 Housing (Wales) Measure 2011 s 11(5).

18 Ie under the Housing (Wales) Measure 2011 s 11(1): see the text and note 14.

19 The day after that on which a notice was sent under the Housing (Wales) Measure 2011 s 11(3)(a) or (b) (see heads (A)–(B) in the text) is to be treated as the date on which the Welsh Ministers decided to consider the application: s 11(4).

20 Ie under the Housing (Wales) Measure 2011 s 11(2): see the text and note 15.

21 See note 19.

22 See note 20.

23 See the Housing (Wales) Measure 2011 s 11(3).

24 Ie in accordance with the Housing (Wales) Measure 2011 s 11(1) or (2): see the text and notes 14–15.

25 Housing (Wales) Measure 2011 s 12(1).

26 Ie without considering whether the Housing (Wales) Measure 2011 s 12(4) (see the text and notes 34–35) requires them to grant it.

27 Ie a requirement imposed under the Housing (Wales) Measure 2011 s 27: see PARA 260.

28 Housing (Wales) Measure 2011 s 12(2)(a).

29 See note 26.

30 Ie under the Local Government Act 2003 s 87(1): see PARA 366.

31 Housing (Wales) Measure 2011 s 12(2)(b).

32 Ie under the Local Government Act 2003 s 87(2): see PARA 366.

33 Housing (Wales) Measure 2011 s 12(3).

34 Ie its obligation to carry out a consultation exercise under the Housing (Wales) Measure 2011 s 9: see note 5.

35 Housing (Wales) Measure 2011 s 12(4).

36 Housing (Wales) Measure 2011 s 12(5).

37 Housing (Wales) Measure 2011 s 12(6). As to when the Welsh Ministers decided to consider an application see note 19.

38 See the Housing (Wales) Measure 2011 s 12(7).

39 See the Housing (Wales) Measure 2011 s 13(1).

40 Housing (Wales) Measure 2011 s 13(2). As to publicity for directions see s 28, cited in PARA 262; and as to the restriction on repeat applications see s 29(3)–(7), cited in PARA 262.

264.   Reducing a variation of a direction suspending the right to buy and related rights. With effect from 3 September 2012[1], a local housing authority[2] may apply to the Welsh Ministers for a reducing variation[3] of a direction issued under Part 1 of the Housing (Wales) Measure 2011[4] if the direction was issued in response to an application made by the authority, and the authority concludes that the condition described below exists[5]. That condition is that either:

(1)   the demand for social housing[6] falling within the reducing elements of the variation does not substantially exceed its supply or is not likely to do so; or

(2)   even if demand does substantially exceed supply, or is likely to do so, that imbalance between supply and demand is not likely to increase as a result of the exercise of the right to buy[7] and related rights[8].

The following provision sets out the requirements to be met by a local housing authority's application to the Welsh Ministers for a reducing variation of a direction issued under Part 1 of the 2011 Measure[9]. The application must:

(a)   include a draft of the direction as it would be varied if the application were granted) which, if it were included in an application for a direction suspending the right to buy and related rights[10], would comply with the specified requirements[11]; and

(b)   explain why the authority has concluded that the condition described in heads (1) and (2) above exists[12].

The Welsh Ministers may reject a local housing authority's application for a reducing variation[13] if they are of the opinion that the authority has failed to comply with a requirement for further information[14] in relation to the application[15]. The Welsh Ministers must grant the application if they agree with the authority's opinion as to why the condition described in heads (1) and (2) above exists and, if they do not so agree, they must reject the application[16].

Where the Welsh Ministers grant a local housing authority's application under the above provisions, they must issue in writing a varied direction which:

(i)   clearly identifies the area to which it applies;

(ii)   states whether or not the direction applies to every relevant dwelling house within that area;

(iii)   if the direction does not apply to every relevant dwelling house[17] within that area, clearly describes the type or types of relevant dwelling house to which it does apply;

(iv)   states the period for which it is to have effect[18].

The Welsh Ministers must not issue a direction under these provisions which differs in any material respect from the draft of the direction included in the local housing authority's application in accordance with head (a) above[19].

1   Ie the date when the Housing (Wales) Measure 2011 Pt 1 (ss 1–34) came into force: see PARA 260 note 1.

2   As to the meaning of 'local housing authority' see PARA 260 note 2.

3   For these purposes, a 'reducing variation' is a variation of a direction issued under the Housing (Wales) Measure 2011 Pt 1 (ss 1–34) (see PARAS 260 et seq, 265–267) which makes either or both of the following changes (and no others): (1) alters the direction so that it no longer applies to an area to which it did previously apply; (2) alters the direction so that it no longer applies to a type or types of relevant dwelling house to which it did previously apply; and 'reducing elements' must be construed accordingly: s 7(2).

4   Ie under the Housing (Wales) Measure 2011 Pt 1: see PARAS 260 et seq, 265–267.

5   Housing (Wales) Measure 2011 s 14(1). As to the Welsh Ministers see PARA 7.

6   As to the meaning of 'social housing' see PARA 260 note 8.

7   As to the meaning of 'the right to buy' see PARA 239 (definition applied by the Housing (Wales) Measure 2011 s 33(1)).

8   Housing (Wales) Measure 2011 s 14(2). As to the meaning of 'related rights' see PARA 261 note 4.

9   Housing (Wales) Measure 2011 s 15(1).

10 Ie an application for a direction under the Housing (Wales) Measure 2011 s 3: see PARA 260.

11 Ie the requirements of the Housing (Wales) Measure 2011 s 3(2)(a): see PARA 260.

12 Housing (Wales) Measure 2011 s 15(2). In the exercise of its functions under s 15, a local housing authority must have regard to any guidance given from time to time in writing by the Welsh Ministers: s 30.

13 Ie without considering whether the Housing (Wales) Measure 2011 s 16(2) (see the text and note 16) requires them to grant it.

14 Ie a requirement imposed under the Housing (Wales) Measure 2011 s 27: see PARA 260.

15 Housing (Wales) Measure 2011 s 16(1).

16 Housing (Wales) Measure 2011 s 16(2).
17 As to the meaning of 'relevant dwelling house' see PARA 260 note 12.
18 Housing (Wales) Measure 2011 s 17(1).
19 Housing (Wales) Measure 2011 s 17(2). As to publicity for directions see s 28, cited in PARA 262; and as to the restriction on repeat applications see s 29(3)–(7), cited in PARA 262.

265. Extension of a direction suspending the right to buy and related rights.
With effect from 3 September 2012[1], a local housing authority[2] may apply to the Welsh Ministers for an extension of the period for which a direction issued under Part 1 of the Housing (Wales) Measure 2011[3] is to have effect if within the period of six months preceding the application, the authority has completed a consultation exercise[4], and in the light of that exercise, and having considered any other relevant information, the authority concludes that the housing pressure condition[5] continues to exist[6]. A local housing authority may apply for the extension of a direction which has already been extended but an extended direction may not have effect beyond a period of ten years from the date on which the direction suspending the right to buy[7] and related rights[8] was issued[9].

The requirements to be met by a local housing authority's application to the Welsh Ministers for an extension of a direction issued under Part 1 of the 2011 Measure are as follows[10]. The application must:

(1)   explain why the authority has concluded that the housing pressure condition exists;

(2)   explain why the authority is of the opinion that an extension of the period for which a direction is to have effect would be an appropriate response to its having concluded that the housing pressure condition exists;

(3)   explain what other action the authority has taken to reduce the imbalance between the demand for social housing[11] and its supply within the authority's area since the direction was issued[12];

(4)   explain what other action the authority proposes to take to reduce the imbalance between the demand for social housing and its supply within the authority's area during the proposed period of extension;

(5)   describe what the authority has done to discharge its obligation to consult[13]; and

(6)   state the proposed period of extension, which must not be more than five years from the date on which, but for these provisions[14], the direction would have ceased to have effect[15].

The Welsh Ministers may reject a local housing authority's application for an extension of the period for which a direction issued under Part 1 of the 2011 Measure is to have effect[16] if they are of the opinion that:

(a)   the authority has failed to comply with a requirement for additional information[17] in relation to the application; or

(b)   where the authority is required to have a strategy relating to housing under the relevant provision of the Local Government Act 2003[18], the strategy, in so far as it relates to the imbalance between demand for and supply of social housing in the authority's area, is inadequate[19];

but the Welsh Ministers must not make a decision under head (b) above unless they have considered any statement that the authority is required to prepare[20] and any other information which they consider relevant[21]. The Welsh Ministers must grant the application if:

(i)   they agree with the authority's opinion as to why the housing pressure condition exists;

(ii)   they agree with the authority's opinion that the proposed extension of the period for which the direction is to have effect is an appropriate response to the authority having concluded that the housing pressure condition exists;

(iii)   they are satisfied that, before making the application, the authority complied with their obligation to carry out a consultation exercise[22];

(iv)   they are satisfied that the action taken by the authority to reduce the imbalance between the demand for social housing and its supply since the direction was issued[23] has been adequate, and

(v)   they are satisfied that the authority's proposals included in its application in accordance with head (4) above are likely to contribute to a reduction in the imbalance between the demand for social housing and its supply within the authority's area[24].

If the Welsh Ministers are not satisfied that the action taken by the authority to reduce the imbalance between the demand for social housing and its supply since the direction was issued[25] has been adequate, they may refuse the application[26]; and if any of heads (i) to (iii) or (v) above are not met, they must reject the application[27].

Where the Welsh Ministers grant a local housing authority's application under the above provisions, they must issue in writing an altered direction which states the date on which it is to cease to have effect[28] and in all other respects is identical to the direction in respect of which the application was made (the 'replaced direction')[29]. A direction so issued has effect as from the date on which the replaced direction ceases to have effect[30].

1   Ie the date when the Housing (Wales) Measure 2011 Pt 1 (ss 1–34) came into force: see PARA 260 note 1.
2   As to the meaning of 'local housing authority' see PARA 260 note 2.
3   Ie under the Housing (Wales) Measure 2011 Pt 1 (ss 1–34): see PARAS 260 et seq, 266–267.
4   Ie a consultation exercise in accordance with the Housing (Wales) Measure 2011 s 19. Section 19 provides for the consultation exercise that a local housing authority must carry out before it may make an application to the Welsh Ministers for an extension of the period for which a direction issued under Pt 1 is to have effect: s 19(1). The consultation exercise must seek views on whether there is a need to apply for an extension of the period for which the direction is to have effect: s 19(2). The persons to be consulted are: (1) each social housing provider which appears to the authority to be a landlord of a dwelling house situated in the authority's area (but the authority need not consult itself), and which the authority considers would be affected if its application for an extension of a direction is granted; (2) any body or bodies appearing to the authority to represent the interests of tenants of dwelling houses within the authority's area where the landlords of those dwelling houses are social housing providers, and the authority considers that the tenants of those dwelling houses would be affected if its application for an extension of a direction is granted; (3) any other local housing authority whose area is adjacent to the area to which it is proposed that the extended direction is to apply; and (4) such other persons as the authority considers appropriate: s 19(3). As to the meaning of 'social housing provider' see PARA 260 note 8; and as to the meaning of 'dwelling house' see PARA 231 (definition applied by s 33(1)). As to the Welsh Ministers see PARA 7.
5   As to the meaning of 'the housing pressure condition' see PARA 260.
6   Housing (Wales) Measure 2011 s 18(1).
7   As to the meaning of 'the right to buy' see PARA 239 (definition applied by s 33(1)).
8   As to the meaning of 'related rights' see PARA 261 note 4.
9   See the Housing (Wales) Measure 2011 s 18(2). The direction referred to in the text is the direction issued under s 6: see PARA 262.
10 See the Housing (Wales) Measure 2011 s 20(1).
11 As to the meaning of 'social housing' see PARA 260 note 8.
12 Ie under the Housing (Wales) Measure 2011 s 6: see PARA 262.
13 Ie under the Housing (Wales) Measure 2011 s 19: see note 4.
14 Ie but for the Housing (Wales) Measure 2011 Pt 1 Ch 3 (ss 18–22): see the text and notes 1–13, 15–30.

15 Housing (Wales) Measure 2011 s 20(2). In the exercise of its functions under s 20, a local housing
    authority must have regard to any guidance given from time to time in writing by the Welsh
    Ministers: s 30.
16 Ie without considering whether the Housing (Wales) Measure 2011 s 21(3) (see the text and notes
    22–24) requires them to grant it.
17 Ie a requirement imposed under the Housing (Wales) Measure 2011 s 27: see PARA 260.
18 Ie under the Local Government Act 2003 s 87(1): see PARA 366.
19 Housing (Wales) Measure 2011 s 21(1).
20 Ie under the Local Government Act 2003 s 87(2): see PARA 366.
21 Housing (Wales) Measure 2011 s 21(2).
22 See note 13.
23 See note 12.
24 Housing (Wales) Measure 2011 s 21(3).
25 See note 12.
26 Housing (Wales) Measure 2011 s 21(4).
27 Housing (Wales) Measure 2011 s 21(5).
28 Ie being the date specified in the authority's application under the Housing (Wales) Measure 2011
    s 20(2)(f): see head (6) in the text.
29 Housing (Wales) Measure 2011 s 22(1).
30 Housing (Wales) Measure 2011 s 22(2). As to publicity for directions see s 28, cited in PARA 262;
    and as to the restriction on repeat applications see s 29(3)–(7), cited in PARA 262.

266. Revocation of direction suspending the right to buy and related rights.
With effect from 3 September 2012[1], a local housing authority[2] may apply to the
Welsh Ministers for the revocation of a direction issued under Part 1 of the
Housing (Wales) Measure 2011[3] if the authority concludes that the condition
described below exists[4]. That condition is that either:

(1)   the demand for social housing[5] to which the direction relates does not
        substantially exceed its supply or is not likely to do so; or
(2)   even if demand does substantially exceed supply, or is likely to do so,
        that imbalance between supply and demand is not likely to increase as
        a result of the exercise of the right to buy[6] and related rights[7].

A local housing authority's application to the Welsh Ministers for revocation of
a direction issued under Part 1 of the 2011 Measure must be in writing and must
explain why the authority has concluded that the condition described in heads (1)
and (2) above exists[8]. The Welsh Ministers may require a local housing authority
to provide further information in addition to that provided in an application for
the revocation of such a direction[9]. This power is exercisable if the Welsh
Ministers reasonably consider that the further information is required in order for
them to decide whether to consider the authority's application or to determine the
authority's application[10].

At any time before the Welsh Ministers have made a decision on a local housing
authority's application for the revocation of a direction, the authority which made
the application may by notice in writing withdraw it[11].

The Welsh Ministers may reject a local housing authority's application for the
revocation of a direction[12] if they are of the opinion that the authority has failed
to comply with a requirement for further information[13] in relation to the
application[14]. They must grant the application if they agree with the
authority's conclusion as to why the condition described in heads (1) and (2)
above exists[15]. If the Welsh Ministers grant the application, they must notify the
local housing authority in writing of that fact and the direction ceases to have
effect on the date on which such notice is given[16].

The local housing authority must take reasonable steps to bring the revocation
of a direction to the attention of persons likely to be affected by it[17].

1 Ie the date when the Housing (Wales) Measure 2011 Pt 1 (ss 1–34) came into force: see PARA 260
   note 1.

2   As to the meaning of 'local housing authority' see PARA 260 note 2.
3   Ie under the Housing (Wales) Measure 2011 Pt 1 (ss 1–34): see PARAS 260 et seq, 1938.
4   Housing (Wales) Measure 2011 s 23(1). As to the Welsh Ministers see PARA 7.
5   As to the meaning of 'social housing' see PARA 260 note 8.
6   As to the meaning of 'the right to buy' see PARA 239 (definition applied by the Housing (Wales) Measure 2011 s 33(1)).
7   Housing (Wales) Measure 2011 s 23(2). As to the meaning of 'related rights' see PARA 261 note 4.
8   Housing (Wales) Measure 2011 s 24. In the exercise of its functions under s 24, a local housing authority must have regard to any guidance given from time to time in writing by the Welsh Ministers: s 30.
9   Housing (Wales) Measure 2011 s 27(1).
10 Housing (Wales) Measure 2011 s 27(2).
11 Housing (Wales) Measure 2011 s 26.
12 Ie without considering whether the Housing (Wales) Measure 2011 s 25(2) (see the text and note 15) requires them to grant it.
13 Ie a requirement imposed under the Housing (Wales) Measure 2011 s 27: see the text and notes 9–10.
14 Housing (Wales) Measure 2011 s 25(1).
15 Housing (Wales) Measure 2011 s 25(2).
16 Housing (Wales) Measure 2011 s 25(3).
17 Housing (Wales) Measure 2011 s 28(2).

267. Power to make consequential orders. With effect from 3 September 2012[1], the Welsh Ministers may by order make such provision as they consider appropriate:

(1)   in consequence of, or for giving full effect to, any provision made by Part 1[2] of the Housing (Wales) Measure 2011[3];

(2)   for applying or extending any provision made by that Part, with or without modifications, to any provision about or connected with a right related to the right to buy[4].

The powers under heads (1) and (2) above include, but are not limited to, powers to make provision which amends, repeals or revokes any provision of any Act of Parliament or Measure of the National Assembly for Wales, including the 2011 Measure, and any provision of subordinate legislation[5].

1   Ie the date when the Housing (Wales) Measure 2011 Pt 1 (ss 1–34) came into force: see PARA 260 note 1.
2   Ie under the Housing (Wales) Measure 2011 Pt 1 (ss 1–34): see PARA 260 et seq.
3   Housing (Wales) Measure 2011 s 34(1). As to the Welsh Ministers see PARA 7.
4   Housing (Wales) Measure 2011 s 34(2). As to the meaning of 'the right to buy' see PARA 239 (definition applied by s 33(1)); and as to the meaning of 'rights related to the right to buy' see PARAS 260, 1932 note 4.
5   Housing (Wales) Measure 2011 s 34(3). For these purposes, 'subordinate legislation' has the same meaning as in the Interpretation Act 1978 (see STATUTES AND LEGISLATIVE PROCESS vol 96 (2012) PARA 608): Housing (Wales) Measure 2011 s 34(4).

C.   QUALIFYING PERIOD FOR THE RIGHT TO BUY OR ACQUIRE

268. Qualifying period for the right to buy or acquire; in general. The right to buy[1] does not arise unless the period which is to be taken into account[2] is, in relation to England, at least three years as a tenant[3] or, in relation to Wales, at least five years as a tenant[4]. Where the secure tenancy[5] is a joint tenancy[6], that condition need be satisfied with respect to one only of the joint tenants[7].

A person exercising the right to buy is entitled to a discount of a percentage calculated by reference to the qualifying period for the right to buy[8].

The period to be so taken into account for qualification for the right to buy and the right to a discount is the period qualifying, or the aggregate of the periods qualifying, under the provisions[9] set out in the following paragraphs[10].

1   As to the meaning of 'the right to buy' see PARA 239. See also note 3, and PARA 230 notes 7, 9.
2   Ie in accordance with the Housing Act 1985 s 119(1), Sch 4 (see PARA 269 et seq) for the purposes of s 119.
3   Housing Act 1985 s 119(A1) (added by the Deregulation Act 2015 s 28(1), (2)).
4   Housing Act 1985 s 119(1) (amended by the Housing Act 2004 s 180(1); and the Deregulation Act 2015 s 28(1), (3)). The amendment by the Housing Act 2004 s 180(1) does not, however, apply in relation to a secure tenancy: (1) if the tenancy was entered into before, or in pursuance of an agreement made before, the day on which it came into force (ie 18 January 2005); or (2) if head (1) above does not apply but the tenant is a public sector tenant on that day and does not cease to be such a tenant at any time before serving a notice in respect of the tenancy under the Housing Act 1985 s 122 (see PARA 273); and for these purposes 'public sector tenant' has the same meaning as in Sch 4 (see PARA 270): Housing Act 2004 s 180(5), (6). In such cases, the original time limit of two years applies: see the Housing Act 1985 s 119(1) (as originally enacted). In the case of the right to acquire under the Housing Act 1996 (see PARAS 242–244) or the Housing and Regeneration Act 2008 (see PARAS 240–241) it is submitted that the Housing (Right to Acquire) Regulations 1997, SI 1997/619, Sch 2, where the Housing Act 1985 s 119 as originally enacted is set out with modifications, is now to be read in the light of the Housing Act 2004 s 180 and the Deregulation Act 2015 s 28 so that the time limit will now be three or five years as appropriate: see PARA 230 notes 7, 9.
5   As to the meaning of 'secure tenancy' see PARA 230 note 2. See also PARA 230 notes 7, 9.
6   As to the position where a secure tenancy is a joint tenancy see PARA 239.
7   Housing Act 1985 s 119(2) (amended by the Deregulation Act 2015 s 28(1), (4)). The Housing Act 1985 s 119(2) is modified where the Housing (Preservation of Right to Buy) Regulations 1993, SI 1993/2241 (see PARA 334 et seq), apply: see Sch 1 para 4.
8   See the Housing Act 1985 s 129(1); and PARA 287.
9   Ie the provisions of the Housing Act 1985 Sch 4 paras 2–10: see PARA 269 et seq.
10 Housing Act 1985 Sch 4 para 1. Schedule 4 para 1 is substituted where the right to acquire conferred by the Housing Act 1996 (see PARAS 242–244) or the Housing and Regeneration Act 2008 (see PARAS 240–241) arises, so as to read 'The period to be taken into account for the purposes of s 119 (qualification for the right to acquire) is the period qualifying, or the aggregate of the periods qualifying, under the following provisions of this Schedule': see the Housing (Right to Acquire) Regulations 1997, SI 1997/619, reg 2, Sch 1 para 39(a), applying in relation to the right to acquire under the Housing and Regeneration Act 2008 by virtue of s 184, which applies the Housing Act 1996 s 17 (regulations modifying the Housing Act 1985): see PARA 241.

269. Periods occupying accommodation subject to public sector tenancy. A period qualifies for the right to buy[1] or the right to acquire conferred by the Housing Act 1996[2] or the Housing and Regeneration Act 2008[3] and (in the case of the right to buy) to the right to a discount[4] if it is a period during which, before the relevant time[5], the tenant[6] or his spouse or civil partner, if they are living together at the relevant time, or a deceased spouse or deceased civil partner of his, if they were living together at the time of the death, was a public sector tenant[7] or was the spouse or civil partner of a public sector tenant and occupied as his only or principal home the dwelling house[8] of which the spouse or civil partner was such a tenant[9].

Where the public sector tenant of a dwelling house died or otherwise ceased to be a public sector tenant of the dwelling house and thereupon a child of his[10] who occupied the dwelling house as his only or principal home (the 'new tenant') became the public sector tenant of the dwelling house, whether under the same or another public sector tenancy, then a period during which the new tenant, since reaching the age of 16, occupied as his only or principal home a dwelling house of which a parent of his was a public sector tenant or one of joint tenants under a public sector tenancy, being either:

(1)   the period at the end of which he became the public sector tenant; or

(2)   an earlier period ending two years or less before the period mentioned in head (1) above or before another period within this provision,

is treated[11] as a period during which he was a public sector tenant[12].

1 As to the meaning of 'the right to buy' see PARA 239.
2 See PARAS 242–244.
3 See PARAS 240–241.
4 As to the right to a discount see PARA 287 et seq.
5 For these purposes, 'the relevant time', in relation to the exercise of the right to buy or the right to acquire, means the date on which the notice of claim is served on the landlord, unless, in Wales, the Housing Act 1985 s 122B (see PARA 273) applies: s 122(1), (2) (s 122(1) amended, in relation to Wales, by the Housing (Wales) Measure 2011 s 32(1), (2)); and see PARA 230 notes 7, 9. See further *Copping v Surrey County Council* [2005] EWCA Civ 1604, [2006] 1 EGLR 42, [2005] All ER (D) 340 (Dec), cited in PARA 276 note 11.
6 Ie in the case of the right to buy, the secure tenant, or in the case of the right to acquire, the tenant. As to the meaning of 'secure tenant' for these purposes see PARA 230 note 2.
7 As to the meaning of 'public sector tenant' see PARA 270.
8 As to the meaning of 'dwelling house' see PARA 231.
9 Housing Act 1985 Sch 4 para 2 (amended by the Civil Partnership Act 2004 s 81, Sch 8 para 34(a), (b)); and see PARA 230 notes 7, 9. For these purposes, a person who, as a joint tenant under a public sector tenancy, occupied a dwelling house as his only or principal home is treated as having been the public sector tenant under that tenancy: Housing Act 1985 Sch 4 para 3. As to the meaning of 'only or principal home' see LANDLORD AND TENANT vol 63 (2016) PARA 1037 note 27.
10 For these purposes, two persons are treated as parent and child if they would be so treated under the Housing Act 1985 s 186(2) (see PARA 274 note 5): Sch 4 para 4(3).
11 Ie for the purposes of the Housing Act 1985 Sch 4 para 2.
12 Housing Act 1985 Sch 4 para 4(1), (2); and see PARA 230 notes 7, 9.

270. Meaning of 'public sector tenant'. 'Public sector tenant' means[1] a tenant[2] under a public sector tenancy[3]. A tenancy, other than a long tenancy[4], under which a dwelling house[5] was let as a separate dwelling was a public sector tenancy at a time when the landlord condition[6] and the tenant condition[7] were satisfied[8].

The landlord condition is[9] that the interest of the landlord belonged to, or to a predecessor of, a local authority[10] or other specified body[11]. The other specified bodies are:

(1)   a development corporation[12];
(2)   a housing action trust[13];
(3)   the former Development Board for Rural Wales;
(4)   an urban development corporation[14];
(5)   a Mayoral development corporation[15];
(6)   the former Commission for the New Towns[16];
(7)   the Regulator of Social Housing[17] or the former Housing for Wales;
(8)   a non-profit registered provider of social housing[18] which is not a co-operative housing association[19];
(9)   a registered social landlord[20] which is not a co-operative housing association;
(10)   the appropriate national authority[21] where that interest belonged to it as the result of the exercise by it of specified functions under Part III of the Housing Associations Act 1985[22],

or to, or to a predecessor of, a corresponding authority or other body[23] in Scotland and Northern Ireland[24].

The tenant condition is that the tenant was an individual and occupied the dwelling house as his only or principal home[25] or, where the tenancy was a joint tenancy, that each of the joint tenants was an individual and at least one of them occupied the dwelling house as his only or principal home[26]. The tenant condition is not met during any period when a tenancy is[27] a demoted tenancy[28].

The Renting Homes (Wales) Act 2016 provides for community landlords (that is to say, local authorities, registered social landlords and other kinds of authority)[29].

1 Ie for the purposes of the Housing Act 1985 Sch 4: see PARAS 268–269, 271–272.
2 As to the meaning of 'tenant' see PARA 31 note 3.
3 Housing Act 1985 Sch 4 para 6(1); and see PARA 230 notes 7, 9.
4 For these purposes, 'long tenancy' means a long tenancy within the meaning of the Housing Act 1985 Pt IV (ss 79–117) (see LANDLORD AND TENANT vol 63 (2016) PARA 1042) or a tenancy falling within the Housing (Northern Ireland) Order 1983, SI 1983/1118, Sch 2 para 1; and 'long lease' is to be construed accordingly: Housing Act 1985 s 187 (definition amended by the Housing (Scotland) Act 1987 Sch 23 para 30(2), Sch 24).
5 As to the meaning of 'dwelling house' see PARA 231.
6 Ie the condition described as the landlord condition in the Housing Act 1985 Sch 4 para 7: see the text and notes 9–24.
7 Ie the condition described as the tenant condition in the Housing Act 1985 Sch 4 para 9: see the text and notes 25–26.
8 Housing Act 1985 Sch 4 para 6(2); and see PARA 230 notes 7, 9. The provisions of Sch 4 apply in relation to a licence to occupy a dwelling house, whether or not granted for a consideration, as they apply in relation to a tenancy (Sch 4 para 6(3)); but Sch 4 para 6(3) does not apply to a licence which was granted as a temporary expedient to a person who entered the dwelling house or any other land as a trespasser, whether or not, before the grant of that licence, another licence to occupy that or another dwelling house had been granted to him (Sch 4 para 6(4)).
9 Ie subject to the Housing Act 1985 Sch 4 paras 7A, 7B and to any order under Sch 4 para 8: see note 24.
10 As to the meaning of 'local authority' see PARA 12.
11 Housing Act 1985 Sch 4 para 7(1).
12 See PARA 12.
13 See PARA 12.
14 See PARA 12.
15 See the Localism Act 2011 s 198; and LONDON GOVERNMENT vol 71 (2013) PARA 323.
16 As to the abolition of the Commission for the New Towns and the transfer of its functions, property, rights and liabilities to the Homes and Communities Agency and the Welsh Ministers see PLANNING vol 83 (2010) paras 1452–1453.
17 As to the Regulator of Social Housing see PARA 57.
18 As to private registered providers of social housing see PARA 53. As to when a body is a non-profit organisation see PARA 71 note 13.
19 As to the meaning of 'co-operative housing association' see PARA 13. As to housing associations see PARA 13.
20 As to registered social landlords see PARAS 4, 166 et seq.
21 As to the appropriate national authority, ie the Secretary of State or, where statutory functions have been transferred in relation to Wales, the Welsh Ministers, see PARA 7.
22 Ie the Housing Associations Act 1985 Pt III (ss 74–102) (now only applying in Wales: see PARA 141 et seq).
23 Ie an authority or other body falling within the Housing Act 1985 Sch 4 para 7(2) or (3).
24 Housing Act 1985 Sch 4 para 7(1) (amended by the Housing and Planning Act 1986 s 24(2), (3), Sch 5 para 40(3)(a), Sch 12 Pt I; the Housing Act 1988 s 83(7); the Government of Wales Act 1998 s 140, Sch 16 para 22; the Localism Act 2011 s 222, Sch 22 paras 9, 19; and by SI 1996/2325, SI 1999/61, SI 2008/3002 and SI 2010/866).
   The landlord condition is to be treated as having been satisfied in the case of a dwelling house comprised in a housing co-operative agreement made in England and Wales, by a local housing authority, new town corporation or the former Development Board for Rural Wales, if the interest of the landlord belonged to the housing co-operative: Housing Act 1985 Sch 4 para 7A(1)(a) (Sch 4 para 7A added by the Housing and Planning Act 1986 Sch 5 para 40). For these purposes, 'housing co-operative agreement' and 'housing co-operative', as regards England and Wales, have the same meaning as in the Housing Act 1985 s 27B (agreements with housing co-operatives under superseded provisions: see PARA 457): Sch 4 para 7A(2)(a) (as so added).
   The landlord condition is also to be treated as having been satisfied: (1) in the case of a dwelling house let under a tenancy falling within s 80(2A)–(2E) (see LANDLORD AND TENANT vol 63 (2016) PARA 1037) at any time if, at that time, the interest of the landlord belonged to the Homes and Communities Agency, the Greater London Authority, or the Welsh Ministers (Sch 4 para 7B (added by SI 2008/3002; amended by the Localism Act 2011 s 195(1), Sch 19 paras 10, 20)); and (2) in such circumstances as may be prescribed for these purposes by order of the appropriate national authority, if the interest of the landlord belonged to a person who is so prescribed

(Housing Act 1985 Sch 4 para 8(1)). An order under Sch 4 para 8 may make different provision with respect to different cases or descriptions of case, including different provision for different areas, and must be made by statutory instrument which is subject, if made by the Secretary of State, to annulment in pursuance of a resolution of either House of Parliament: Sch 4 para 8(2). In exercise of the power so conferred the Secretary of State made the Housing (Right to Buy) (Prescribed Persons) Order 1992, SI 1992/1703, which came into force on 17 August 1992: art 1. For the persons and bodies prescribed for these purposes see art 3, Schedule (amended by the Environment Act 1995 s 120, Sch 22 para 233(1); the Countryside and Rights of Way Act 2000 s 73(2); the Police (Northern Ireland) Act 2000 s 2(4), Sch 2 para 6(1); and by SI 1994/2567, SI 1996/2651, SI 2003/1615, SI 2004/696, SI 2004/3168, SI 2005/2929, SI 2012/1659 and SI 2013/755).

For the purpose of determining whether at any time a tenant of a housing association was a public sector tenant and his tenancy a public sector tenancy, the association is deemed to have been registered at that time, under the Housing and Regeneration Act 2008 Pt 2 (ss 59–278A), the Housing Act 1996 Pt I (ss A1–64) or the Housing Associations Act 1985 Pt I (ss 1–40) or the corresponding Northern Ireland legislation, if it was so registered at any later time: Housing Act 1985 Sch 4 para 10 (amended by SI 1996/2325 and SI 2010/866).

25 As to the meaning of 'only or principal home' see LANDLORD AND TENANT vol 63 (2016) PARA 1037 note 27.

26 Housing Act 1985 Sch 4 para 9; and see PARA 230 notes 7, 9.

27 Ie by virtue of the Housing Act 1988 s 20B (see LANDLORD AND TENANT vol 63 (2016) PARA 863) or the Housing Act 1996 s 143A (see LANDLORD AND TENANT vol 63 (2016) PARA 1118).

28 Housing Act 1985 Sch 4 para 9A (added by the Anti-social Behaviour Act 2003 s 14(5), Sch 1 para 2(1), (5)).

29 See the Renting Homes (Wales) Act 2016 s 2(1)(a) (not yet in force: see PARA 6); and LANDLORD AND TENANT vol 62 (2016) PARA 45.

271. Periods occupying forces accommodation. A period qualifies for the right to buy[1] or the right to acquire conferred by the Housing Act 1996[2] or the Housing and Regeneration Act 2008[3] and (in the case of the right to buy) to the right to a discount[4] if it is a period during which before the relevant time[5] the tenant[6] or his spouse[7] or civil partner, if they are living together at the relevant time, or a deceased spouse or deceased civil partner of his, if they were living together at the time of the death, occupied accommodation provided for him as a member of the regular armed forces of the Crown or was the spouse or civil partner of a person occupying accommodation so provided and also occupied that accommodation[8].

1 As to the meaning of 'the right to buy' see PARA 239.

2 See PARAS 242–244.

3 See PARAS 240–241.

4 As to the right to a discount see PARA 287 et seq.

5 As to the meaning of 'the relevant time' see PARA 269 note 5.

6 Ie in the case of the right to buy, the secure tenant, or in the case of the right to acquire, the tenant. As to the meaning of 'secure tenant' for these purposes see PARA 230 note 2.

7 As to the meaning of 'spouse' see PARA 73 note 2.

8 Housing Act 1985 Sch 4 para 5 (amended by the Civil Partnership Act 2004 s 81, Sch 8 para 34(a), (b)); and see PARA 230 notes 7, 9.

272. Periods during which right to buy is preserved. A period qualifies for the right to buy[1] and the right to a discount[2] if it is a period during which, before the relevant time[3]:

(1) the qualifying person[4]; or

(2) his spouse[5] or civil partner, if they are living together at the relevant time; or

(3) a deceased spouse or deceased civil partner of his, if they were living together at the time of the death,

was a qualifying person for the purposes of the preserved right to buy[6] or was the spouse or civil partner of such a person and occupied the qualifying dwelling house[7] as his only or principal home[8].

1 As to the meaning of 'the right to buy' see PARA 239.

2   As to the right to a discount see PARA 287 et seq.
3   As to the meaning of 'the relevant time' see PARA 269 note 5.
4   As to the meaning of 'qualifying person' see PARA 337 note 4.
5   As to the meaning of 'spouse' see PARA 73 note 2.
6   As to the cases in which the right to buy is preserved see PARA 334.
7   As to the meaning of 'qualifying dwelling house' see PARA 337 note 2.
8   Housing Act 1985 Sch 4 para 5A (added by the Housing and Planning Act 1986 s 24(2), Sch 5 para 40(1), (2); amended by the Civil Partnership Act 2004 s 81, Sch 8 para 34(a), (b); and by SI 1992/1709). As to the meaning of 'only or principal home' see LANDLORD AND TENANT vol 63 (2016) PARA 1037 note 27. The Housing Act 1985 Sch 4 para 5A is omitted where the right to acquire conferred by the Housing Act 1996 (see PARAS 242–244) or the Housing and Regeneration Act 2008 (see PARAS 240–241) arises: see the Housing (Right to Acquire) Regulations 1997, SI 1997/619, Sch 1 para 39(b), applying in relation to the right to acquire under the Housing and Regeneration Act 2008 by virtue of s 184, which applies the Housing Act 1996 s 17 (regulations modifying the Housing Act 1985: see PARA 241).

D.   CLAIM TO EXERCISE THE RIGHT TO BUY OR ACQUIRE

(A)   *Tenant's Notice of Claim*

273. Tenant's notice claiming to exercise right. A tenant[1] claims to exercise the right to buy[2] or the right to acquire conferred by the Housing Act 1996[3] or the Housing and Regeneration Act 2008[4] by written notice to that effect served on the landlord[5]. The notice may be withdrawn at any time by notice in writing served on the landlord[6].

Where the extended right to buy arises[7], the notice may be withdrawn by notice in writing served on the landlord or on the freeholder, depending on whether or not the tenant has received the freeholder's notice admitting or denying that right[8]. In such cases, where a notice claiming to exercise the right to buy is served by the tenant, the landlord must, as soon as practicable:

(1)   serve a copy of the notice on the authority or body which is its landlord in relation to the dwelling house; and

(2)   serve on the tenant a notice in writing that this has been done and of the name and address of that authority or body[9].

If the authority or body referred to in head (1) above is an intermediate landlord, it must in turn serve a copy of the notice on the authority or body which is its immediate landlord in relation to the dwelling house, and so on, if that authority or body is also an intermediate landlord (dealing with a case where there is more than one landlord)[10]. The landlord and each of the intermediate landlords, if any, must, at the same time as it serves on its landlord the copy of the tenant's notice, notify that authority or body whether to its knowledge there are any reasons for denying the tenant's right to buy and, if there are, state those reasons[11]. When an intermediate landlord so notifies its immediate landlord whether there are any reasons for denying the tenant's right to buy, it must send with that notification the notification or notifications which it has received[12] from the landlord or from any other intermediate landlord or landlords[13]. An authority or body which serves a copy of the tenant's notice on another authority or body[14] must at the same time notify the landlord and the tenant that this has been done and the name and address of the other authority or body[15].

Where the preserved right to buy arises[16], then where the qualifying dwelling house[17] is occupied by two or more qualifying persons[18] as joint tenants the right to buy may be exercised by such one or more of them as may be agreed between them[19].

Where the right to acquire conferred by the Housing Act 1996[20] or the Housing and Regeneration Act 2008[21] arises, then the tenant must not make an application to acquire the dwelling house under the applicable Act at any time when he has made an application to buy under Part V of the Housing Act 1985[22], as it applies in relation to the right to buy and the preserved right to buy, which has not been withdrawn by the tenant or denied by the landlord; but nothing in this provision prevents the tenant withdrawing such an application and submitting an application[23] under the right to acquire[24].

With effect from 3 September 2012[25], a secure tenant of a dwelling house to which a direction having effect under Part 1 of the Housing (Wales) Measure 2011[26] applies may not claim to exercise the right to buy while that direction has effect[27]. If:

(a) the Welsh Ministers are considering a local housing authority's application for a direction ('the draft direction') in accordance with the specified provisions of the Housing (Wales) Measure 2011[28];

(b) a claim to exercise the right to buy is made[29] in respect of a dwelling house to which either the draft direction applies[30] or the enlarging elements[31] of the draft direction apply[32];

(c) the claim was made after the date on which the Welsh Ministers decided to consider the application for the proposed direction[33]; and

(d) the application has not been determined or withdrawn,

then the claim to exercise the right to buy must be stayed unless withdrawn[34] by the tenant[35]. If the Welsh Ministers refuse to issue the direction, the stay must be lifted on the date of refusal[36]. If the application for the direction is withdrawn, the stay must be lifted on the date of withdrawal[37]. If the Welsh Ministers have not granted or rejected an application for a direction within six months beginning with the date on which they decided to consider the application the stay must be lifted on the day after the end of that period[38]. If a claim to exercise the right to buy is stayed at the time the Welsh Ministers grant an application for a direction, the claim is deemed not to have been made[39].

1 Ie in the case of the right to buy, a secure tenant, or in the case of the right to acquire, a tenant. As to the meaning of 'secure tenant' for these purposes see PARA 230 note 2.

2 As to the meaning of 'the right to buy' see PARA 239.

3 See PARAS 242–244.

4 See PARAS 240–241.

5 Housing Act 1985 s 122(1); and see PARA 230 notes 7, 9. As to the meaning of 'landlord' see PARA 31 note 3. For the prescribed form of notice claiming the right to buy see the Housing (Right to Buy) (Prescribed Forms) Regulations 1986, SI 1986/2194, reg 2, Sch 1, Form RTB1 (substituted in relation to England by SI 2015/1542; the Housing (Right to Buy) (Prescribed Forms) Regulations 1986, SI 1986/2194, revoked in relation to Wales by SI 2015/1320). A form substantially to the like effect may be used: see the Housing (Right to Buy) (Prescribed Forms) Regulations 1986, SI 1986/2194, reg 2. For the prescribed form of notice to be used in Wales see the Housing (Right to Buy) (Prescribed Forms) (Wales) Regulations 2015, SI 2015/1320, reg 2, Sch 1, Form WRTB1 (amended by SI 2015/1795). A form substantially to the like effect may be used: see the Housing (Right to Buy) (Prescribed Forms) (Wales) Regulations 2015, SI 2015/1320, reg 2.

   The prescribed form is properly served when it is received by an agent of the authority who is authorised to receive it on the authority's behalf: *Terry v Tower Hamlets London Borough Council* [2005] EWHC 2783 (QB), [2005] All ER (D) 37 (Dec). As to service of notices see generally PARA 236.

6 Housing Act 1985 s 122(3); and see PARA 230 notes 7, 9. Mere inactivity on the part of the tenant is not sufficient to entitle the landlord to treat the application as withdrawn: see *Hanoman v Southwark London Borough Council* [2004] EWHC 2039 (Ch), [2005] 1 All ER 795, [2004] All ER (D) 243 (Jun) (local housing authority had no power to treat the application to exercise the right to buy as withdrawn because the tenant had failed to provide information requested by the authority in relation to his entitlement within a short period of time under a unilaterally imposed deadline). Where, however, there is not just lengthy inactivity but an express representation to the local authority that the tenant does not intend to proceed with the purchase, this is, in effect, an express release and the authority is entitled to conclude that the claim to buy

has been cancelled: see *Martin v Medina Housing Association Ltd* [2006] EWCA Civ 367, [2007] 1 All ER 813, [2007] 1 WLR 1965. Further, where the tenant does not proceed with the claim for a number of years, the landlord is entitled to interpret his failure to take any further steps as meaning that he has decided not to proceed (even though the claimant has not given notice of withdrawal): see *Copping v Surrey County Council* [2005] EWCA Civ 1604, [2006] 1 EGLR 42, [2005] All ER (D) 340 (Dec), per curiam.

7   See PARA 233.
8   See PARA 275. The Housing Act 1985 s 122(3) does not apply: see the Housing (Extension of Right to Buy) Order 1993, SI 1993/2240, Schedule para 2.
9   Housing Act 1985 s 122A(1) (s 122A as added for these purposes by the Housing (Extension of Right to Buy) Order 1993, SI 1993/2240, Schedule para 3; amended, in relation to Wales, by SI 2012/2090, to renumber the Housing Act 1985 s 122A as s 122AA).
10 Housing Act 1985 s 122A(2) (as added for these purposes: see note 9).
11 Housing Act 1985 s 122A(3) (as added for these purposes: see note 9).
12 Ie under the Housing Act 1985 s 122A(3).
13 Housing Act 1985 s 122A(4) (as added for these purposes: see note 9).
14 Ie in accordance with the Housing Act 1985 s 122A(2): see the text and note 10).
15 Housing Act 1985 s 122A(5) (as added for these purposes: see note 9).
16 See PARA 334 et seq.
17 As to the meaning of 'qualifying dwelling house' see PARA 337 note 2; and as to the meaning of 'dwelling house' see PARA 231.
18 As to the meaning of 'qualifying person' see PARA 337 note 4.
19 Housing Act 1985 s 122(4) (as added for these purposes by the Housing (Preservation of Right to Buy) Regulations 1993, SI 1993/2241, Sch 1 para 5).
20 See PARAS 242–244.
21 See PARAS 240–241.
22 Ie under the Housing Act 1985 Pt V (ss 118–188): see PARAS 231 et seq, 274 et seq.
23 Ie an application under the Housing Act 1996 s 16 (see PARA 242) or the Housing and Regeneration Act 2008 s 180 (see PARA 240).
24 Housing Act 1985 s 122(4) (as added for these purposes by the Housing (Right to Acquire) Regulations 1997, SI 1997/619, Sch 1 para 4, applying in relation to the right to acquire under the Housing and Regeneration Act 2008 by virtue of s 184, which applies the Housing Act 1996 s 17 (regulations modifying the Housing Act 1985): see PARA 241); and see PARA 230 note 9. The provisions of the Housing Act 1985 Pt V would then apply with the prescribed modifications: see PARAS 241, 243.
25 Ie the date when the Housing (Wales) Measure 2011 Pt 1 (ss 1–34) came into force: see PARA 260 note 1.
26 Ie under the Housing (Wales) Measure 2011 Pt 1 (ss 1–34): see PARA 260 et seq.
27 See the Housing Act 1985 s 122B(1), (2) (s 122B added, in relation to Wales, by the Housing (Wales) Measure 2011 s 32(1), (3)). The Housing Act 1985 s 122(1) (see the text and notes 1–5) will accordingly apply unless s 122B applies: see s 122(1) (amended by the Housing (Wales) Measure 2011 s 32(1), (2)).
    The Housing Act 1985 s 122B does not affect the computation of any period in accordance with Sch 4 (see PARAS 268–272): s 122B(3) (as so added).
28 Ie in accordance with the Housing (Wales) Measure 2011 s 4(1) or (2) (see PARA 261) or s 11(1) or (2) (see PARA 263).
29 Ie under the Housing Act 1985 s 122(1): see the text and notes 1–5.
30 Ie in the case of an application which is being considered in accordance with the Housing (Wales) Measure 2011 s 4(1) or (2): see PARA 261.
31 Ie within the meaning of the Housing (Wales) Measure 2011 s 7: see PARA 263.
32 Ie in the case of an application which is being considered in accordance with the Housing (Wales) Measure 2011 s 11(1) or (2): see PARA 263.
33 As to the date on which the Welsh Ministers decide to consider an application see the Housing (Wales) Measure 2011 see ss (4), 11(4); and PARAS 261, 263.
34 Ie under the Housing Act 1985 s 122(3): see the text and note 6.
35 Housing Act 1985 s 122A(1), (2) (s 122A added, in relation to Wales, by the Housing (Wales) Measure 2011 s 31(1), (2)). The Housing Act 1985 s 122A does not affect the computation of any period under Sch 4: s 122A(7) (as so added).
36 Housing Act 1985 s 122A(3) (as added: see note 35).
37 Housing Act 1985 s 122A(4) (as added: see note 35).
38 Housing Act 1985 s 122A(5) (as added: see note 35).
39 Housing Act 1985 s 122A(6) (as added: see note 35).

274. Claim to share right with members of family. A tenant[1] may, in his notice claiming to exercise the right to buy[2] or the right to acquire conferred by the Housing Act 1996[3] or the Housing and Regeneration Act 2008[4], require that not more than three members of his family[5] who are not joint tenants but occupy the dwelling house[6] as their only or principal home[7] should share the right to buy with him[8]. He may validly do so in the case of any such member only if:

(1) that member is his spouse, or is his civil partner, or has been residing with him throughout the period of 12 months ending with the giving of the notice; or

(2) the landlord[9] consents[10].

Where, by such a notice, any members of the tenant's family are validly required to share the right to buy with the tenant, the right belongs to the tenant and those members jointly; and he and they are treated[11] as joint tenants[12].

1 Ie in the case of the right to buy, a secure tenant, or in the case of the right to acquire, a tenant. As to the meaning of 'secure tenant' for these purposes see PARA 230 note 2.

2 Ie his notice under the Housing Act 1985 s 122: see PARA 273. As to the meaning of 'the right to buy' see PARA 239.

3 See PARAS 242–244.

4 See PARAS 240–241.

5 For these purposes, a person is a member of another's family if: (1) he is the spouse or civil partner of that person, or he and that person live together as husband and wife or as if they were civil partners; or (2) he is that person's parent, grandparent, child, grandchild, brother, sister, uncle, aunt, nephew or niece: Housing Act 1985 s 186(1) (s 186(1), (2) amended by the Civil Partnership Act 2004 s 81, Sch 8 para 27(1)–(3)). For the purposes of head (2) above: (a) a relationship by marriage or by civil partnership is treated as a relationship by blood; (b) a relationship of the half-blood is treated as a relationship of the whole blood; (c) the stepchild of a person is treated as his child; and (d) an illegitimate child is treated as the legitimate child of his mother and reputed father: Housing Act 1985 s 186(2) (as so amended). As to the meaning of 'spouse' see PARA 73 note 2.

6 As to the meaning of 'dwelling house' see PARA 231.

7 As to the meaning of 'only or principal home' see LANDLORD AND TENANT vol 63 (2016) PARA 1037 note 27.

8 Housing Act 1985 s 123(1); and see PARA 230 notes 7, 9. See *Harrow London Borough Council v Tonge* [1993] 1 EGLR 49, (1992) 25 HLR 99, CA (tenant holding secure tenancy qualified to exercise right to buy; written notice claiming the right to buy required that the tenant's daughter should share that right; secure tenant died; daughter deemed to be a secure joint tenant and entitled to exercise the right to buy). Cf *Solihull Metropolitan Borough Council v Hickin* [2012] UKSC 39, [2012] 4 All ER 867, [2012] 1 WLR 2295, where the court decided that the common law rights of survivorship applied so that on the death of a secure tenant the tenancy passed to her husband and as he was not living with her at the time of her death the tenancy that passed to him ceased to be secure.

9 As to the meaning of 'landlord' see PARA 31 note 3.

10 Housing Act 1985 s 123(2) (amended by the Civil Partnership Act 2004 Sch 8 para 28); and see PARA 230 notes 7, 9. The Housing Act 1985 123(2) is modified where the Housing (Extension of Right to Buy) Order 1993, SI 1993/2240 (see PARA 233), applies: see Schedule para 4.

11 Ie for the purposes of the Housing Act 1985 Pt V (ss 118–188): see PARAS 230 et seq, 275 et seq.

12 Housing Act 1985 s 123(3); and see PARA 230 notes 7, 9. Section 123(3) is substituted where the Housing (Preservation of Right to Buy) Regulations 1993, SI 1993/2241 (see PARA 334 et seq), apply: see Sch 1 para 6.

(B) Landlord's Notices in Response

275. Landlord's notice admitting or denying right to buy. Where a notice claiming to exercise the right to buy[1] or the right to acquire conferred by the Housing Act 1996[2] or the Housing and Regeneration Act 2008[3] has been served by the tenant[4], the landlord[5] must, unless the notice is withdrawn, serve on the tenant within the specified period[6] a written notice either:

(1) admitting his right; or

(2)   denying it and stating the reasons why, in the opinion of the landlord, the tenant does not have the right to buy[7].

The duty on the landlord is a continuing duty and there is no duty on the tenant to do anything other than wait for the landlord's decision[8]. The duty under head (2) is a qualified duty to state an opinion, not a strict duty such as to found a claim for damages for its breach[9].

Where the right to acquire arises, and the landlord, in his notice under the above provisions, admits the tenant's right to acquire, he may offer to make a disposal to that tenant of an alternative dwelling house[10]. The tenant may refuse the landlord's offer of an alternative dwelling house[11]; but if he accepts it, the provisions of Part V of the Housing Act 1985[12] apply to the alternative dwelling house[13].

Where, however, the extended right to buy arises[14], the following provisions apply in substitution for those set out above. Where the freeholder receives[15] a copy of the secure tenant's notice claiming to exercise right to buy[16], and the notice has not been withdrawn, the freeholder must serve on the tenant, within the specified period[17], a written notice either:

(a)   admitting his right; or
(b)   denying it and stating why, in the opinion of the freeholder, the tenant does not have the right to buy[18].

The freeholder must, as soon as practicable, serve on the landlord and on each of the intermediate landlords, if any, a copy of the notice so served on the tenant[19]. If the tenant wishes to withdraw a notice claiming to exercise the right to buy before he has received the freeholder's notice admitting or denying that right, he may do so by notice in writing served on the landlord[20]. Where the landlord receives the tenant's notice of withdrawal after it has served on its landlord a copy of the tenant's notice claiming to exercise the right to buy, it must, as soon as practicable, serve on its landlord a copy of the notice of withdrawal[21]. An intermediate landlord must, in turn, similarly serve on its immediate landlord a copy of the tenant's notice of withdrawal[22]. If, however, the tenant wishes to withdraw his notice claiming to exercise the right to buy after he has received the freeholder's notice admitting or denying the right, he may do so by a notice in writing served on the freeholder[23]. Where the tenant serves a notice of withdrawal on the freeholder, the freeholder must, as soon as practicable, inform the landlord and the intermediate landlords, if any, of this fact[24].

1   Ie a notice under the Housing Act 1985 s 122: see PARA 273. As to the meaning of 'the right to buy' see PARA 239.
2   See PARAS 242–244.
3   See PARAS 240–241.
4   As to the meaning of 'tenant' see PARA 31 note 3.
5   As to the meaning of 'landlord' see PARA 31 note 3.
6   The period so specified for serving a notice is: (1) four weeks where the requirement of the Housing Act 1985 s 119 (see PARA 268) is satisfied by a period or periods during which the landlord was the landlord on which the tenant's notice under s 122 was served, and eight weeks in any other case (s 124(2); and see PARA 230 notes 7, 9); (2) in a case where the stay of a claim to exercise the right to buy has been lifted under s 122A(3), (4) or (5) (see PARA 273), four weeks beginning with the lifting date where the requirement of s 119 is satisfied by a period or periods during which the landlord was the landlord on which the tenant's notice under s 122 was served, and eight weeks beginning with the lifting date in any other case (Housing Act 1985 s 124(3) (added, in relation to Wales, by the Housing (Wales) Measure 2011 s 31(1), (3)(b)). The reference to the Housing Act 1985 s 122A in this note is to s 122A as added by the Housing (Wales) Measure 2011 s 31(1), (2): see PARA 273 notes 28–39.
7   Housing Act 1985 s 124(1) (amended, in relation to Wales, by the Housing (Wales) Measure 2011 s 31(1), (3)(a)). For the prescribed form of notice in reply to a tenant's right to buy claim see the Housing (Right to Buy) (Prescribed Forms) Regulations 1986, SI 1986/2194, reg 3, Sch 2, Form

RTB2 (England) (substituted in relation to England by SI 2005/1736; the Housing (Right to Buy) (Prescribed Forms) Regulations 1986, SI 1986/2194, revoked in relation to Wales by SI 2015/1320). A form substantially to the like effect may be used: see the Housing (Right to Buy) (Prescribed Forms) Regulations 1986, SI 1986/2194, reg 3. For the prescribed form of notice to be used in Wales see the Housing (Right to Buy) (Prescribed Forms) (Wales) Regulations 2015, SI 2015/1320, reg 3, Sch 2, Form WRTB2. A form substantially to the like effect may be used: see reg 3.

8 See *Hanoman v Southwark London Borough Council* [2004] EWHC 2039 (Ch), [2005] 1 All ER 795, [2004] All ER (D) 243 (Jun) (local housing authority had no power to treat the application to exercise the right to buy as withdrawn because the tenant had failed to provide information requested by the authority in relation to his entitlement within a short period of time under a unilaterally imposed deadline). Cf, however, *Copping v Surrey County Council* [2005] EWCA Civ 1604, [2006] 1 EGLR 42, [2005] All ER (D) 340 (Dec).

9 *Francis v Southwark London Borough Council* [2011] EWCA Civ 1418 at [22], [2012] HLR 241, [2011] All ER (D) 54 (Dec).

10 Housing Act 1985 s 124A(1) (s 124A as added for these purposes by the Housing (Right to Acquire) Regulations 1997, SI 1997/619, Sch 1 para 5, applying in relation to the right to acquire under the Housing and Regeneration Act 2008 by virtue of s 184, which applies the Housing Act 1996 s 17 (regulations modifying the Housing Act 1985): see PARA 241). As to the meaning of 'dwelling house' see PARA 231.

11 Housing Act 1985 s 124A(2) (as added: see note 10).

12 Ie the Housing Act 1985 Pt V (ss 118–188) (as amended and as modified for these purposes): see PARAS 231 et seq, 276 et seq.

13 Housing Act 1985 s 124A(3) (as added: see note 10).

14 See PARA 233.

15 Ie in pursuance of the Housing Act 1985 s 122A or, in Wales, s 122AA (tenant's notice to be served on superior landlords): see PARA 273. As to the meaning of 'freeholder' see PARA 233 note 19. The reference in this note to s 122A is to s 122A as added by SI 1993/2240: see PARA 273 text and notes 7–15.

16 Ie the notice under the Housing Act 1985 s 122: see PARA 273. As to the meaning of 'secure tenant' see LANDLORD AND TENANT vol 63 (2016) PARA 1037.

17 The period for serving such a notice is eight weeks beginning on the day after the date of the service on the freeholder of the copy of the tenant's notice claiming to exercise the right to buy: Housing Act 1985 s 124(2) (s 124 substituted and s 124A added for these purposes by the Housing (Extension of Right to Buy) Order 1993, SI 1993/2240, Schedule paras 5, 6; and amended, in relation to Wales, by SI 2012/2090). However, the period for serving a notice in a case where the stay of a claim to exercise the right to buy has been lifted under the Housing Act 1985 s 122A(3), (4) or (5) is four weeks beginning with the lifting date where the requirement of s 119 is satisfied by a period or periods during which the landlord was the landlord on which the tenant's notice under s 122 was served, and eight weeks beginning with the lifting date in any other case: s 124(3) (added to s 124 as so substituted, in relation to Wales, by SI 2012/2090). The reference to the Housing Act 1985 s 122A is to s 122A as added by the Housing (Wales) Measure 2011 s 31(1), (2): see PARA 273 text and notes 35–39.

18 Housing Act 1985 s 124(1) (as substituted for these purposes and amended in relation to Wales: see note 17).

19 Housing Act 1985 s 124(3) (as substituted for these purposes (see note 17); renumbered, in relation to Wales, as s 124(4) by SI 2012/2090). As to the meaning of 'intermediate landlord' see PARA 233 note 18.

20 Housing Act 1985 s 124A(1) (as added for these purposes: see note 17).

21 Housing Act 1985 s 124A(2) (as added for these purposes: see note 17).

22 Housing Act 1985 s 124A(3) (as added for these purposes: see note 17).

23 Housing Act 1985 s 124A(4) (as added for these purposes: see note 17).

24 Housing Act 1985 s 124A(5) (as added for these purposes: see note 17).

276. Landlord's notice of purchase price and other matters. Where a tenant[1] has claimed to exercise the right to buy[2] or the right to acquire conferred by the Housing Act 1996[3] or the Housing and Regeneration Act 2008[4] and that right has been established, whether by the landlord's[5] admission or otherwise, the landlord must:

(1)   within eight weeks where the right is to acquire the freehold[6]; and

(2)   within 12 weeks where the right is to acquire a leasehold interest[7], serve on the tenant a notice complying with the following provisions[8].

The notice must describe the dwelling house[9], must state the price at which, in the opinion of the landlord, the tenant is entitled to have the freehold conveyed or, as the case may be, the lease[10] granted to him and must, for the purpose of showing how the price has been arrived at, state:

(a)   the value at the relevant time[11];

(b)   the improvements (if any)[12] disregarded[13] in determining value; and

(c)   the discount to which the tenant is entitled, stating (in relation to the right to buy only) the period to be taken into account[14] for the discount and, where applicable, the reduction for previous discount[15] or the limits[16] on the amount of discount[17].

The notice must state the provisions which, in the opinion of the landlord, should be contained in the conveyance or grant[18].

Where the notice states provisions which would enable the landlord to recover from the tenant service charges[19] or improvement contributions (that is, where a lease is to be granted)[20], the notice must contain the estimates and other information[21] required[22].

The notice must contain a description of any structural defect[23] known to the landlord affecting the dwelling house or the building in which it is situated or any other building over which the tenant will have rights under the conveyance or lease[24]. This provision imposes on the landlord an unqualified obligation to give notice of any relevant structural defect known to him, whether or not he wishes to recover from the tenant any part of the cost of putting it right; but there is otherwise no change in the normal relationship between the parties prior to the grant of a long lease and no wider duty of care imposed on the landlord[25].

The notice must also inform the tenant of:

(i)   the effect of the statutory provisions relating to the tenant's notice of intention[26], the landlord's notice in default[27] and the effect of failure to comply[28];

(ii)   his right[29] to have the value of the dwelling house at the relevant time determined or redetermined by the district valuer;

(iii)   the effect of the statutory provisions relating to a change of tenant[30] after service of the tenant's notice of intention;

(iv)   the effect of the statutory provisions relating to the landlord's notices to complete[31] and the effect of failure to comply[32];

(v)   in relation to the right to buy only, the effect of the statutory provisions relating to the right to acquire on rent to mortgage terms, where still exercisable[33]; and

(vi)   in relation to the right to buy only, the relevant amount and multipliers for the time being declared[34] by the appropriate national authority[35].

1   Ie a secure tenant in the case of the right to buy or a tenant in the case of the right to acquire. As to the meaning of 'secure tenant' see PARA 230 note 2; and as to the meaning of 'tenant' see PARA 31 note 3.

2   As to the meaning of 'the right to buy' see PARA 239.

3   See PARAS 242–244.

4   See PARAS 240–241.

5   As to the meaning of 'landlord' see PARA 31 note 3.

6   Ie where the right is that mentioned in the Housing Act 1985 s 118(1)(a): see PARA 239 head (1).

7   Ie where the right is that mentioned in the Housing Act 1985 s 118(1)(b): see PARA 239 head (2).

8   Housing Act 1985 s 125(1); and see PARA 230 notes 7, 9.

9   As to the meaning of 'dwelling house' see PARA 231.

10 As to the meaning of 'lease' see PARA 31 note 3.

11 As to the meaning of 'the relevant time' see PARA 269 note 5. For these purposes, a tenant can only use the date on which his notice claiming the right to buy was served as the valuation date of the property if his right to buy that property is established pursuant to the Housing Act 1985 Pt V

(ss 118–188) in connection with that notice: see *Copping v Surrey County Council* [2005] EWCA Civ 1604, [2006] 1 EGLR 42, [2005] All ER (D) 340 (Dec) (relevant date was date of service of notice in 2001, not date of service of earlier notice of claim in 1991 which had not been proceeded with, although it had not been formally withdrawn).

The landlord has power to correct a clerical mistake in a notice issued under the Housing Act 1985 s 125: see *Nessa v Tower Hamlets London Borough Council* [2010] EWCA Civ 559 at [20], [2010] HLR 604, [2010] All ER (D) 191 (May) where, however, Andrew Morritt C added that the limits to such a power, not least in terms of the time within which it can be exercised, are to be explored in future cases. See also at [26] per Stanley Burnton LJ ('it is clear that the price stated in a notice served under [the Housing Act 1985] s 125 is not set in stone' but the question whether there is any, and if so what, limit on the power of a landlord to vary the price stated in its notice under s 125 was left open).

12 For these purposes, 'improvement' means, in relation to a dwelling house, any alteration in, or addition to, the dwelling house and includes: (1) any addition to, or alteration in, the landlord's fixtures and fittings and any addition to or alteration connected with the provision of services to the dwelling house; (2) the erection of a wireless or television aerial; and (3) the carrying out of external decoration; and is to be similarly construed in relation to any other building or land: Housing Act 1985 s 187 (amended by the Housing and Planning Act 1986 s 24(2), Sch 5 para 30(1), (2)).

13 Ie in pursuance of the Housing Act 1985 s 127: see PARA 284.

14 Ie under the Housing Act 1985 s 129: see PARA 287.

15 Ie the amount mentioned in the Housing Act 1985 s 130(1): see PARA 288.

16 Ie the limits in the Housing Act 1985 s 131(1) or s 131(2): see PARA 289.

17 Housing Act 1985 s 125(2) (modified in relation to the right to acquire by the Housing (Right to Acquire) Regulations 1997, SI 1997/619, Sch 1 para 6(a), applying in relation to the right to acquire under the Housing and Regeneration Act 2008 by virtue of s 184, which applies the Housing Act 1996 s 17 (regulations modifying the Housing Act 1985): see PARA 241); and see PARA 230 notes 7, 9. It has been held that a local authority owes no common law duty of care to the tenant when stating its opinion as to the purchase price in a notice under s 125: see *Blake v Barking and Dagenham London Borough Council* (1996) 30 HLR 963, [1996] EGCS 145.

18 Housing Act 1985 s 125(3); and see PARA 230 notes 7, 9.

19 For these purposes, 'service charge' means an amount payable by a purchaser or lessee of premises: (1) which is payable, directly or indirectly, for services, repairs, maintenance or insurance or the vendor's or lessor's costs of management; and (2) the whole or part of which varies or may vary according to the relevant costs: Housing Act 1985 s 621A(1) (s 621A added by the Housing and Planning Act 1986 s 24(2), Sch 5 para 39). The relevant costs are the costs or estimated costs incurred or to be incurred by or on behalf of the payee or, in the case of a lease, a superior landlord, in connection with the matters for which the service charge is payable: Housing Act 1985 s 621A(2) (as so added). For these purposes, 'costs' includes overheads; and costs are relevant costs in relation to a service charge whether they are incurred, or to be incurred, in the period for which the service charge is payable or in an earlier or later period: s 621A(3) (as so added). In relation to a service charge, the 'payee' means the person entitled to enforce payment of the charge; and the 'payer' means the person liable to pay it: s 621A(4) (as so added).

20 For these purposes, 'improvement contribution' means an amount payable by a tenant of a flat in respect of improvements to the flat, the building in which it is situated or any other building or land, other than works carried out in discharge of any such obligations as are referred to in the Housing Act 1985 Sch 6 para 16A(1) (see PARA 310): s 187 (definition added by the Housing and Planning Act 1986 Sch 5 para 30(1), (3)). As to the meaning of 'flat' see PARA 231.

21 Ie the estimates and other information required by the Housing Act 1985 s 125A (see PARA 277) or s 125B (see PARA 278).

22 Housing Act 1985 s 125(4) (substituted by the Housing and Planning Act 1986 s 4(1)); and see PARA 230 notes 7, 9.

23 Structural defects are defects affecting the structure which require making good as opposed to ordinary items of repair and maintenance: *Payne and Woodland v Barnet London Borough Council* (1997) 76 P & CR 293, 30 HLR 295, CA.

24 Housing Act 1985 s 125(4A) (added by the Housing and Planning Act 1986 Sch 5 para 3); and see PARA 230 notes 7, 9.

25 See *Payne and Woodland v Barnet London Borough Council* (1997) 76 P & CR 293, 30 HLR 295, CA. Failure to disclose this information is a breach of statutory duty but does not give rise to an additional claim for misrepresentation: *Rushton v Worcester City Council* [2001] EWCA Civ 367, [2002] HLR 188, [2001] All ER (D) 195 (Mar).

26 Ie the effect of the Housing Act 1985 s 125D: see PARA 279.

27 Ie the effect of the Housing Act 1985 s 125E(1): see PARA 280.

28 Ie the effect of the Housing Act 1985 s 125E(4): see PARA 280.
29 Ie under the Housing Act 1985 s 128: see PARA 285.
30 Ie the effect of the Housing Act 1985 s 136(2): see PARA 281.
31 Ie the effect of the Housing Act 1985 s 140 (see PARA 316) and s 141(1), (2) (see PARA 317).
32 Ie the effect of the Housing Act 1985 s 141(4): see PARA 317.
33 Ie the effect of the Housing Act 1985 ss 143–153: see PARA 318.
34 Ie for the purposes of the Housing Act 1985 s 143B: see PARA 318.
35 Housing Act 1985 s 125(5) (substituted by the Leasehold Reform, Housing and Urban
    Development Act 1993 s 104; modified by the Housing (Right to Acquire) Regulations 1997, SI
    1997/619, Sch 1 para 6(b); and see note 17). As to the appropriate national authority, and the
    transfer of functions under the Housing Act 1985, so far as exercisable in relation to Wales, to the
    Welsh Ministers see PARA 7.
        The Housing Act 1985 s 125 also is modified where: (1) the Housing (Extension of Right to
    Buy) Order 1993, SI 1993/2240 (see PARA 233), applies (see Schedule para 7); (2) the Housing
    (Preservation of Right to Buy) Regulations 1993, SI 1993/2241 (see PARA 334 et seq), apply (see
    Sch 1 para 7).

277. Estimates and information about service charges where a lease is to be granted. A landlord's notice[1] must state[2] as regards service charges[3]:

(1)   the landlord's estimate of the average annual amount, at current prices, which would be payable in respect of each head of charge in the reference period[4]; and

(2)   the aggregate of those estimated amounts,

and must contain a statement of the reference period adopted for the purpose of the estimates[5].

A landlord's notice given in respect of a flat must, however, as regards service charges in respect of repairs, including works for the making good of structural defects, contain:

(a)   the further estimates required[6], together with a statement of the reference period adopted for the purpose of the estimates; and

(b)   a statement of the effect of the statutory restrictions on service charges[7] by reference to the estimates of the amounts payable by the tenant[8] and (in relation to the right to buy only) the statutory right to a loan[9] in respect of certain service charges[10].

The following further estimates are required for works in respect of which the landlord considers that costs may be incurred in the reference period:

(i)   for works itemised in the notice, estimates of the amount, at current prices, of the likely cost of, and of the tenant's likely contribution in respect of, each item, and the aggregate amounts of those estimated costs and contributions; and

(ii)   for works not so itemised, an estimate of the average annual amount, at current prices, which the landlord considers is likely to be payable by the tenant[11].

1 Ie a notice under the Housing Act 1985 s 125: see PARA 276. As to the meaning of 'landlord' see
   PARA 31 note 3.
2 Ie excluding, in the case of a flat, charges to which the Housing Act 1985 s 125A(2) applies: see
   the text and notes 6–10. As to the meaning of 'flat' see PARA 231.
3 As to the meaning of 'service charge' see PARA 276 note 19.
4 The reference period for the purposes of the estimates required by the Housing Act 1985 s 125A
   and s 125B (see PARA 278) is the period: (1) beginning on such date not more than six months after
   the notice is given as the landlord may reasonably specify as being a date by which the conveyance
   will have been made or the lease granted; and (2) ending five years after that date or, where the
   notice states that the conveyance or lease will provide for a service charge or improvement
   contribution to be calculated by reference to a specified annual period, with the end of the fifth
   such period beginning after that date: s 125C(1) (ss 125A, 125C added by the Housing and
   Planning Act 1986 s 4(2)); and see PARA 230 notes 7, 9. For the purpose of the estimates it is to
   be assumed that the conveyance will be made or the lease granted at the beginning of the reference
   period on the terms stated in the notice: Housing Act 1985 s 125C(2) (as so added). As to the

meaning of 'lease' see PARA 31 note 3; and as to the meaning of 'improvement contribution' see PARA 276 note 20. The Housing Act 1985 s 125C is modified where the Housing (Extension of Right to Buy) Order 1993, SI 1993/2240 (see PARA 233), applies: see Schedule para 10.
5   Housing Act 1985 s 125A(1) (as added: see note 4); and see PARA 230 notes 7, 9. Section 125A is modified where the Housing (Extension of Right to Buy) Order 1993, SI 1993/2240, applies: see Schedule para 8.
6   Ie the estimates required by the Housing Act 1985 s 125A(3): see the text and note 11.
7   Ie the Housing Act 1985 Sch 6 para 16B: see PARA 311.
8   As to the meaning of 'tenant' see PARA 31 note 3.
9   Ie the Housing Act 1985 s 450A: see PARA 923.
10 Housing Act 1985 s 125A(2) (as added (see note 4); modified by the Housing (Right to Acquire) Regulations 1997, SI 1997/619, Sch 1 para 7); and see PARA 230 notes 7, 9. The Housing Act 1985 s 125A(2) is also modified where the Housing (Preservation of Right to Buy) Regulations 1993, SI 1993/2241 (see PARA 334 et seq), apply (see Sch 1 para 8). See also note 5.
11 Housing Act 1985 s 125A(3) (as added: see note 4). See also note 5.

278. Estimates and information about service charges and improvement contributions. A landlord's notice[1] given in respect of a flat[2] must, as regards improvement contributions[3], contain:
  (1)   the estimates required for works in respect of which the landlord considers that costs may be incurred in the reference period[4], together with a statement of the reference period adopted for the purpose of the estimates; and
  (2)   a statement of the effect of the statutory restrictions on service charges[5] by reference to the estimates of the amounts payable by the tenant[6].
The works to which the estimates relate must be itemised and the estimates must show:
  (a)   the amount, at current prices, of the likely cost of, and of the tenant's likely contribution in respect of, each item; and
  (b)   the aggregate amounts of those estimated costs and contributions[7].

1   Ie a notice under the Housing Act 1985 s 125: see PARA 276. As to the meaning of 'landlord' see PARA 31 note 3.
2   As to the meaning of 'flat' see PARA 231.
3   As to the meaning of 'improvement contribution' see PARA 276 note 20.
4   As to the meaning of 'the reference period' see PARA 277 note 4.
5   Ie the Housing Act 1985 Sch 6 para 16C: see PARA 311.
6   Housing Act 1985 s 125B(1), (2) (s 125B added by the Housing and Planning Act 1986 s 4(2)); and see PARA 230 notes 7, 9. As to the meaning of 'tenant' see PARA 31 note 3.
7   Housing Act 1985 s 125B(3) (as added: see note 6); and see PARA 230 notes 7, 9. Section 125B is omitted where the Housing (Extension of Right to Buy) Order 1993, SI 1993/2240 (see PARA 233), applies: see Schedule para 9.

(C)   Tenant's Notice of Intention

279. Tenant's notice of intention. Where a landlord's notice[1] has been served on a tenant[2], he must within the specified period[3] serve a written notice on the landlord stating either that he intends to pursue his claim to exercise the right to buy[4] or the right to acquire conferred by the Housing Act 1996[5] or the Housing and Regeneration Act 2008[6] or that he withdraws that claim[7].

1   Ie a notice under the Housing Act 1985 s 125: see PARA 276. As to the meaning of 'landlord' see PARA 31 note 3.
2   Ie a secure tenant in the case of the right to buy or a tenant in the case of the right to acquire. As to the meaning of 'secure tenant' see PARA 230 note 2; and as to the meaning of 'tenant' see PARA 31 note 3.
3   The period so specified is the period of 12 weeks beginning with whichever of the following is the later: (1) the service of the notice under the Housing Act 1985 s 125; and (2) where the tenant exercises his right to have the value of the dwelling house determined or redetermined by the district valuer, or where the landlord exercises his right to have the value of the dwelling house redetermined by the district valuer, the relevant event: s 125D(2) (s 125D added by the Leasehold

Reform, Housing and Urban Development Act 1993 s 105(1); the Housing Act 1985 s 125D(2) amended by the Housing and Regeneration Act 2008 ss 306(1), (3), 321(1), Sch 16); and see PARA 230 notes 7, 9. 'The relevant event' means: (a) where a review notice was capable of being served under the Housing Act 1985 s 128A (see PARA 285) in relation to the determination or redetermination but no such notice was served during the period permitted by that section, the service of the notice under s 128(5) (see PARA 285) stating the effect of the determination or redetermination; (b) where a review notice was served under s 128A in relation to the determination or redetermination and s 128B(3) applied (see PARA 286), the service on the tenant of the notice under s 128B(3); and (c) where a review notice was served under s 128A in relation to the determination or redetermination and s 128B(5) applied (see PARA 286), the service of the notice under s 128B(7) (see PARA 286): s 125D(3) (added by the Housing and Regeneration Act 2008 s 306(1), (4)). As to the meaning of 'district valuer' see PARA 527 note 14.

4   As to the meaning of 'the right to buy' see PARA 239.
5   See PARAS 242–244.
6   See PARAS 240–241.
7   Housing Act 1985 s 125D(1)(a) (as added (see note 3); substituted and numbered as s 125D(1), where the right to acquire applies, by the Housing (Right to Acquire) Regulations 1997, SI 1997/619, Sch 1 para 8, applying in relation to the right to acquire under the Housing and Regeneration Act 2008 by virtue of s 184, which applies the Housing Act 1996 s 17 (regulations modifying the Housing Act 1985): see PARA 241). The Housing Act 1985 s 125D(1) is also modified where: (1) the Housing (Extension of Right to Buy) Order 1993, SI 1993/2240 (see PARA 233), applies (see Schedule para 11); (2) the Housing (Preservation of Right to Buy) Regulations 1993, SI 1993/2241 (see PARA 334 et seq), apply (see Sch 1 para 9).
    Prior to 18 July 2005 a secure tenant might alternatively serve, within the specified period, a notice under the Housing Act 1985 s 144 claiming to exercise his statutory right to acquire on rent to mortgage terms: see s 125D(1)(b) (as added: see note 3); and see also s 142A (abolition of the right to acquire on rent to mortgage terms, except in pursuance of a notice served before 18 July 2005); and PARA 318.

280. Landlord's notice in default. The landlord[1] may, at any time after the end of the specified period[2], serve on the tenant[3] a written notice:

(1)   requiring him, if he has failed to serve a notice of intention[4], to serve that notice within 28 days; and

(2)   informing him of the effect of these provisions[5] and of the effect of the statutory provisions[6] relating to non-compliance[7].

At any time before the end of the period mentioned in head (1) above, or that period as previously extended, the landlord may by written notice served on the tenant extend it, or further extend it[8].

If, at any time before the end of that period, or that period as extended, the circumstances are such that it would not be reasonable to expect the tenant to comply with a notice under these provisions, that period, or that period as so extended, is extended, or further extended, until 28 days after the time when those circumstances no longer obtain[9].

If the tenant does not comply with a notice under these provisions, the notice claiming to exercise the right to buy[10] or the right to acquire conferred by the Housing Act 1996[11] or the Housing and Regeneration Act 2008[12] is deemed to be withdrawn at the end of that period or, as the case may require, that period as so extended[13].

1   As to the meaning of 'landlord' see PARA 31 note 3.
2   Ie the period specified in the Housing Act 1985 s 125D(2) (see PARA 279) or, as the case may require, s 136(2) (see PARA 281).
3   As to the meaning of 'tenant' see PARA 31 note 3.
4   Ie the notice required by the Housing Act 1985 s 125D(1): see PARA 279.
5   Ie the effect of the Housing Act 1985 s 125E(1) (as added: see note 7).
6   Ie the effect of the Housing Act 1985 s 125E(4) (as added: see note 7).
7   Housing Act 1985 s 125E(1) (s 125E added by the Leasehold Reform, Housing and Urban Development Act 1993 s 105(1)); and see PARA 230 notes 7, 9. The Housing Act 1985 s 125E(1), (2) is modified where the Housing (Extension of Right to Buy) Order 1993, SI 1993/2240 (see PARA 233), applies: see Schedule para 12.

8   Housing Act 1985 s 125E(2) (as added: see note 7); and see PARA 230 notes 7, 9.
9   Housing Act 1985 s 125E(3) (as added: see note 7); and see PARA 230 notes 7, 9.
10 As to the meaning of 'the right to buy' see PARA 239.
11 See PARAS 242–244.
12 See PARAS 240–241.
13 Housing Act 1985 s 125E(4) (as added: see note 7); and see PARA 230 notes 7, 9.

E.   CHANGE OF TENANT OR LANDLORD

281. Change of tenant after notice claiming right to buy or to acquire. Where, after a secure tenant[1] ('the former tenant') has given notice claiming his right to buy[2], another person ('the new tenant'):

(1)   becomes the secure tenant under the same secure tenancy[3], otherwise than on an assignment by way of exchange[4]; or

(2)   becomes the secure tenant under a periodic tenancy arising on the termination of a fixed term[5] on the coming to an end of the secure tenancy,

the new tenant is in the same position as if the notice had been given by him and he had been the secure tenant at the time it was given[6]. This does not confer a benefit upon the new tenant but provides for a continuous process, starting with the original tenant's notice and ending with completion, so that the new tenant is in the same position as if he had been the secure tenant himself, with all his own qualities and characteristics[7].

Where the right to acquire conferred by the Housing Act 1996[8] or the Housing and Regeneration Act 2008[9] arises, then where after an assured tenant[10] ('the former tenant') has given a notice claiming the right to acquire, another person ('the new tenant') becomes

(a)   the assured tenant by succession[11]; or

(b)   the assured tenant under a statutory tenancy arising on the end of a fixed term tenancy[12],

the new tenant is in the same position as if the notice had been given by him and he had been the tenant at the time it was given[13].

If a landlord's notice of the purchase price[14] has been served on the former tenant, then, whether or not the former tenant has served a notice of intention[15], the new tenant must serve such a notice within the specified period[16].

The above provisions do not, however, confer any right on a person required[17] to share the right to buy or to acquire unless he could have been validly so required had the notice claiming to exercise the right to buy been given by the new tenant[18].

The above provisions apply with the necessary modifications if there is a further change in the person who is the secure tenant (or, in a case in which the right to acquire conferred by the Housing Act 1996 arises, the tenant)[19].

1   As to the meaning of 'secure tenant' see PARA 230 note 2.
2   As to the meaning of 'the right to buy' see PARA 239.
3   As to the meaning of 'secure tenancy' see PARA 230 note 2.
4   Ie an assignment made by virtue of the Housing Act 1985 s 92: see LANDLORD AND TENANT vol 63 (2016) PARA 1066.
5   Ie a periodic tenancy arising by virtue of the Housing Act 1985 s 86: see LANDLORD AND TENANT vol 63 (2016) PARA 1039.
6   Housing Act 1985 s 136(1). Section 136 is modified where: (1) the Housing (Extension of Right to Buy) Order 1993, SI 1993/2240 (see PARA 233), applies: see Schedule para 18); (2) the Housing (Preservation of Right to Buy) Regulations 1993, SI 1993/2241 (see PARA 334 et seq), apply (see Sch 1 para 12).
7   *McIntyre v Merthyr Tydfil Borough Council* (1989) 21 HLR 320, CA.
8   See PARAS 242–244.

9　See PARAS 240–241.

10　As to the meaning of 'assured tenant' see LANDLORD AND TENANT vol 63 (2016) PARA 825.

11　Ie by virtue of the Housing Act 1988 s 17: see LANDLORD AND TENANT vol 63 (2016) PARA 901.

12　Ie by virtue of the Housing Act 1988 s 5: see LANDLORD AND TENANT vol 63 (2016) PARAS 884–888.

13　Housing Act 1985 s 136(1A) (added for these purposes by the Housing (Right to Acquire) Regulations 1997, SI 1997/619, Sch 1 para 14, applying in relation to the right to acquire under the Housing and Regeneration Act 2008 by virtue of s 184, which applies the Housing Act 1996 s 17 (regulations modifying the Housing Act 1985): see PARA 241); and see PARA 230 notes 7, 9.

14　Ie a notice under the Housing Act 1985 s 125: see PARA 276.

15　Ie a notice under the Housing Act 1985 s 125D(1): see PARA 279.

16　See the Housing Act 1985 s 136(2) (substituted by the Leasehold Reform, Housing and Urban Development Act 1993 s 105(2)); and see PARA 230 notes 7, 9.

　　　The specified period is 12 weeks beginning with whichever of the following is the later: (1) his becoming the secure tenant (in the case of the right to buy) or the tenant (in the case of the right to acquire); (2) where the right to have the value of the dwelling house determined or redetermined by the district valuer is or has been exercised by him or the former tenant, or where the right to have the value of the dwelling house redetermined by the district valuer is or has been exercised by the landlord, the relevant event: see the Housing Act 1985 s 136(2) (as so substituted; amended by the Housing and Regeneration Act 2008 ss 306(1), (8), 321(1), Sch 16). 'The relevant event' means: (a) where a review notice was capable of being served under the Housing Act 1985 s 128A (see PARA 285) in relation to the determination or redetermination but no such notice was served during the period permitted by s 128A, the service of the notice under s 128(5) (see PARA 285) stating the effect of the determination or redetermination; (b) where a review notice was served under s 128A in relation to the determination or redetermination and s 128B(3) (see LANDLORD AND TENANT vol 63 (2016) PARA 1037) applied, the service on the new tenant or (as the case may be) the former tenant of the notice under s 128B(3); and (c) where a review notice was served under s 128A in relation to the determination or redetermination and s 128B(5) (see LANDLORD AND TENANT vol 63 (2016) PARA 1037) applied, the service of the notice under s 128B(7) (see LANDLORD AND TENANT vol 63 (2016) PARA 1037): s 136(2A) (added by the Housing and Regeneration Act 2008 s 306(1), (9)). As to the meaning of 'dwelling house' see PARA 231; and as to the meaning of 'district valuer' see PARA 527 note 14.

17　Ie in pursuance of the Housing Act 1985 s 123: see PARA 274.

18　Housing Act 1985 s 136(6); and see PARA 230 notes 7, 9. See also note 6.

19　Housing Act 1985 s 136(7); and see PARA 230 notes 7, 9. See also note 6.

282. Change of landlord after notice claiming right to buy or to acquire. Where the interest of the landlord[1] in the dwelling house[2] passes from the landlord to another body after a tenant[3] has given a notice claiming to exercise the right to buy[4] or the right to acquire conferred by the Housing Act 1996[5] or the Housing and Regeneration Act 2008[6], all parties are[7] in the same position as if the other body had become the landlord before the notice was given and had been given that notice and any further notice given by the tenant to the landlord and had taken all steps which the landlord had taken[8]. Where, however, the extended right to buy arises[9], and after a secure tenant has given a notice claiming to exercise the right to buy, the interest of the landlord, an intermediate landlord[10] or the freeholder[11] in the dwelling house passes from it to another person, or the interest comes to an end, then in substitution for the above provision heads (1) to (3) below apply as follows:

(1)　　the landlord, intermediate landlord or freeholder, as the case may be, must forthwith notify its tenant of the change and a landlord or intermediate landlord must similarly notify its landlord;

(2)　　an intermediate landlord so notified by its tenant must, in turn, similarly notify its immediate landlord or, if so notified by its landlord, must similarly notify its tenant; and

(3) all parties are[12] in the same position as if the change had occurred before the notice claiming to exercise the right to buy was given and all other notices given had been given by or to the appropriate parties and all steps had been taken by them[13].

If the circumstances after the disposal differ in any material respect, as for example where:

(a) the interest of the disponee in the dwelling house after the disposal differs from that of the disponor before the disposal; or

(b) any of the exceptions to the right to buy or to acquire[14] becomes or ceases to be applicable,

all those concerned must, as soon as practicable after the disposal, take all such steps, whether by way of amending or withdrawing and re-serving any notice or extending any period or otherwise, as may be requisite for the purpose of securing that all parties are, as nearly as may be, in the same position as they would have been if those circumstances had obtained before the disposal[15].

1 As to the meaning of 'landlord' see PARA 31 note 3.
2 As to the meaning of 'dwelling house' see PARA 231.
3 Ie a secure tenant in the case of the right to buy or a tenant in the case of the right to acquire. As to the meaning of 'secure tenant' see PARA 230 note 2; and as to the meaning of 'tenant' see PARA 31 note 3.
4 As to the meaning of 'the right to buy' see PARA 239.
5 See PARAS 242–244.
6 See PARAS 240–241.
7 Ie subject to the Housing Act 1985 s 137(2): see the text and notes 14–15.
8 Housing Act 1985 s 137(1) (renumbered by the Housing and Planning Act 1986 s 24(1), Sch 5 Pt I para 4(1), (2); amended by the Leasehold Reform, Housing and Urban Development Act 1993 s 187(2), Sch 22); and see PARA 230 notes 7, 9. The Housing Act 1985 s 137(1) is modified where the Housing (Preservation of Right to Buy) Regulations 1993, SI 1993/2241 (see PARA 334 et seq), apply: see Sch 1 para 13).
9 See PARA 233.
10 As to the meaning of 'intermediate landlord' see PARA 233 note 18.
11 As to the meaning of 'freeholder' see PARA 233 note 19.
12 See note 7.
13 Housing Act 1985 s 137(1) (substituted for these purposes by the Housing (Extension of Right to Buy) Order 1993, SI 1993/2240, Schedule para 19).
14 Ie any of the exceptions in the Housing Act 1985 Sch 5: see PARA 245 et seq.
15 Housing Act 1985 s 137(2) (added by the Housing and Planning Act 1986 Sch 5 Pt I para 4(1), (3); amended by the Leasehold Reform, Housing and Urban Development Act 1993 Sch 22); and see PARA 230 notes 7, 9.

F. PURCHASE PRICE

(A) Purchase Price; in general

283. Purchase price payable on a conveyance or grant in pursuance of the right to buy or to acquire. The price payable for a dwelling house[1] on a conveyance or grant in pursuance of the right to buy[2] or the right to acquire conferred by the Housing Act 1996[3] or the Housing and Regeneration Act 2008[4] is:

(1) the amount which is to be taken[5] as its value at the relevant time[6]; less

(2) the discount to which the purchaser is[7] entitled[8].

1 As to the meaning of 'dwelling house' see PARA 231.
2 Ie in pursuance of the Housing Act 1985 Pt V (ss 118–188): see PARAS 230 et seq, 284 et seq. See also PARA 230 notes 7, 9. As to the meaning of 'the right to buy' see PARA 239.
3 See PARAS 242–244.
4 See PARAS 240–241.
5 Ie under the Housing Act 1985 s 127: see PARA 284.
6 As to the meaning of 'the relevant time' see PARA 269 note 5.

7   Ie the discount to which the purchaser is entitled under the Housing Act 1985 Pt V (see PARA 287 et seq) or, in a case in which the right to acquire arises, the discount to which the purchaser is entitled under an order under the Housing Act 1996 s 17 (the right to acquire; supplementary provisions: see PARAS 241, 243). As to the prescribed amount of discount in the latter case see PARA 241 note 5 (discount in the case of the right to acquire under the Housing and Regeneration Act 2008), PARA 243 note 2 (discount in the case of the right to acquire under the Housing Act 1996).

8   Housing Act 1985 s 126(1) (modified in the case of the right to acquire by the Housing (Right to Acquire) Regulations 1997, SI 1997/619, Sch 1 para 9, applying in relation to the right to acquire under the Housing and Regeneration Act 2008 by virtue of s 184, which applies the Housing Act 1996 s 17 (regulations modifying the Housing Act 1985): see PARA 241); and see PARA 230 notes 7, 9. References in the Housing Act 1985 Pt V to the purchase price include references to the consideration for the grant of the lease: s 126(2).

Section 126(1) is modified, and s 126(2) is omitted, where the Housing (Extension of Right to Buy) Order 1993, SI 1993/2240 (see PARA 233), applies: see Schedule para 13.

284. Value of dwelling house. The value of a dwelling house[1] at the relevant time[2] is to be taken to be the price which at that time it would realise if sold on the open market by a willing vendor:

(1)   on the stated assumptions[3];

(2)   disregarding any improvements[4] made by any specified person[5] and any failure to keep the dwelling house in good internal repair; and

(3)   on the assumption that any service charges[6] or improvement contributions[7] payable will not be less than the amounts to be expected in accordance with the estimates contained[8] in the landlord's notice[9].

For a conveyance the assumptions are:

(a)   that the vendor was selling for an estate in fee simple with vacant possession;

(b)   that neither the tenant nor a member of his family residing with him wanted to buy; and

(c)   that the dwelling house was to be conveyed with the same rights and subject to the same burdens as it would be in pursuance of the right to buy[10] or the right to acquire conferred by the Housing Act 1996[11] or the Housing and Regeneration Act 2008[12].

For the grant of a lease[13] the assumptions are:

(i)   that the vendor was granting a lease with vacant possession for the appropriate term[14];

(ii)   that neither the tenant nor a member of his family residing with him wanted to take the lease;

(iii)   that the ground rent would not exceed £10 per annum; and

(iv)   that the grant was to be made with the same rights and subject to the same burdens as it would be in pursuance of the right to buy[15] or to acquire[16].

1   As to the meaning of 'dwelling house' see PARA 231.
2   As to the meaning of 'the relevant time' see PARA 269 note 5.
3   Ie the assumptions stated for a conveyance in the Housing Act 1985 s 127(2) and for a grant in s 127(3): see the text and notes 13–16.
4   As to the meaning of 'improvement' see PARA 276 note 12.
5   In the case of the right to buy, the persons so specified are: (1) the secure tenant; (2) any person who under the same tenancy was a secure tenant or an introductory tenant before him; and (3) any member of his family who, immediately before the secure tenancy was granted (or, where an introductory tenancy has become the secure tenancy, immediately before the introductory tenancy was granted), was a secure tenant or an introductory tenant of the same dwelling house under another tenancy, but do not include, in a case where the secure tenant's tenancy has at any time been assigned by virtue of the Housing Act 1985 s 92 (assignments by way of exchange: see LANDLORD AND TENANT vol 63 (2016) PARA 1066), a person who under that tenancy was a secure tenant or an introductory tenant before the assignment: s 127(4) (amended, and s 127(5) added, by SI 1997/74). For these purposes, 'introductory tenant' and 'introductory tenancy' have

the same meanings as in the Housing Act 1996 Pt V Ch I (ss 124–143) (see LANDLORD AND TENANT vol 63 (2016) PARA 1043 et seq): Housing Act 1985 127(5) (as so added). As to the meanings of 'secure tenant' and 'secure tenancy' see PARA 230 note 2; and as to the meaning of 'member of another's family' see PARA 274 note 5.

Where the right to acquire conferred by the Housing Act 1996 (see PARAS 242–244) or the Housing and Regeneration Act 2008 (see PARAS 240–241) arises and tenant is an assured tenant, the persons so specified are: (a) the assured tenant; (b) any member of his family who was an assured or secure tenant before him under the same tenancy, or who, immediately before the tenancy was granted, was an assured or secure tenant of the same dwelling house under another tenancy: Housing Act 1985 s 127(4A) (added for these purposes by the Housing (Right to Acquire) Regulations 1997, SI 1997/619, Sch 1 para 10(c), applying in relation to the right to acquire under the Housing and Regeneration Act 2008 by virtue of s 184, which applies the Housing Act 1996 s 17 (regulations modifying the Housing Act 1985): see PARA 241). As to the meaning of 'assured tenancy' see LANDLORD AND TENANT vol 63 (2016) PARA 825.

6 As to the meaning of 'service charge' see PARA 276 note 19.
7 As to the meaning of 'improvement contribution' see PARA 276 note 20.
8 Ie contained in the landlord's notice under the Housing Act 1985 s 125: see PARA 276.
9 Housing Act 1985 s 127(1) (amended by the Housing and Planning Act 1986 ss 4(3), (6), 24(2), (3), Sch 5 para 28, Sch 12 Pt I; modified for the purposes of the right to acquire by the Housing (Right to Acquire) Regulations 1997, SI 1997/619, Sch 1 para 10(a); and see note 5). As to the tenant's right to have the value of a dwelling house at the relevant time determined by a district valuer see PARA 285.
The Housing Act 1985 s 127 is also modified where: (1) the Housing (Extension of Right to Buy) Order 1993, SI 1993/2240 (see PARA 233), applies (see Schedule para 14); (2) the Housing (Preservation of Right to Buy) Regulations 1993, SI 1993/2241 (see PARA 334 et seq), apply (see Sch 1 para 10).
10 Ie in pursuance of the Housing Act 1985 Pt V (ss 118–188): see PARAS 230 et seq, 285 et seq.
11 See PARAS 242–244.
12 Housing Act 1985 s 127(2); and see PARA 230 notes 7, 9. See also note 9. As to the right to acquire under the Housing and Regeneration Act 2008 see PARAS 240–241.
13 As to the meaning of 'lease' see PARA 31 note 3.
14 Ie as defined in the Housing Act 1985 Sch 6 para 12, but (in the case of the right to buy only, subject to Sch 6 para 12(3): see PARA 305.
15 See note 10.
16 Housing Act 1985 s 127(3) (modified for the purposes of the right to acquire by the Housing (Right to Acquire) Regulations 1997, SI 1997/619, Sch 1 para 10(b)); and see PARA 230 notes 7, 9. See also notes 5, 9.

285. Determination of value by the district valuer and review notices.

Any question arising[1] as to the value of a dwelling house[2] at the relevant time[3] must be determined by the district valuer[4] in accordance with the following provisions[5].

A tenant[6] may require that value to be determined by a notice in writing served on the landlord[7] not later than three months after the service on him of the landlord's notice of the purchase price[8] or, if proceedings are then pending between the landlord and the tenant for the determination of any other question relating to the right to buy, within three months of the final determination of the proceedings[9].

If such proceedings are begun after a previous determination[10].

(1) the tenant may, by notice in writing served on the landlord within four weeks of the final determination of the proceedings, require the value of the dwelling house at the relevant time to be redetermined; and

(2) the landlord may at any time within those four weeks, whether or not a notice under head (1) is served, require the district valuer to redetermine that value;

and, where the landlord requires a redetermination to be so made, it must serve on the tenant a notice stating that the requirement is being or has been made[11].

Before so making a determination or redetermination, the district valuer must consider any representation made to him by the landlord or the tenant within four weeks from the service of the tenant's notice or, as the case may be, from the service of the landlord's notice[12].

As soon as practicable after a determination or redetermination has been so made, the landlord must serve on the tenant a notice stating:

(a)   the effect of the determination or redetermination;

(b)   the terms for exercise of the right to buy or to acquire[13]; and

(c)   the effect of the statutory right[14] of the district valuer to serve a review notice and of the landlord and tenant to request that such a notice is served[15].

The landlord must as soon as practicable, serve a copy of the notice on the district valuer if the district valuer requests it or the landlord requests a review[16] of the determination or redetermination[17]; and the tenant must, as soon as practicable, serve a copy of the notice on the district valuer if the tenant requests a review[18] of the determination or redetermination[19].

If the value of a dwelling house has been determined or redetermined by the district valuer under the above provisions ('the section 128 determination'), the district valuer may, either:

(i)   on his own initiative; or

(ii)   at the request[20] of the landlord or the tenant of the dwelling house,

serve on the landlord and the tenant a notice of intention to review the section 128 determination giving reasons for the intention ('a review notice')[21].

The landlord or the tenant may not make a request under head (ii) above after the end of the period of 28 days beginning with the day on which the landlord serves a notice on the tenant containing the information set out in heads (a) to (c) above[22] in relation to the section 128 determination (the 'section 128(5) service date')[23]. The district valuer must, before the end of the period of 14 days beginning with the day on which such a request is made, serve on the landlord and the tenant:

(A)   a review notice; or

(B)   a notice stating that the request was made, that the district valuer has decided not to comply with it, and the reasons for the decision[24].

A review notice may not be served:

(I)   after the end of the period of 42 days beginning with the section 128(5) service date[25];

(II)   in relation to a determination which is subject to a redetermination required in pursuance of heads (1) to (3) above; but this does not prevent the service of a review notice in relation to the redetermination[26];

(III)   if the landlord has made a grant of the specified[27] kind[28].

If the district valuer is considering whether to serve a review notice on the valuer's own initiative, the landlord or the tenant must, if requested by the district valuer, inform the valuer whether a grant of the specified kind[29] has been made[30].

1   Ie under the Housing Act 1985 Pt V (ss 118–188): see PARAS 230 et seq, 287 et seq.
2   As to the meaning of 'dwelling house' see PARA 231.
3   As to the meaning of 'the relevant time' see PARA 269 note 5.
4   As to the meaning of 'district valuer' see PARA 527 note 14.
5   Housing Act 1985 s 128(1); and see PARA 230 notes 7, 9.
6   As to the meaning of 'tenant' see PARA 31 note 3.
7   As to the meaning of 'landlord' see PARA 31 note 3.
8   Ie a notice under the Housing Act 1985 s 125: see PARA 276.

9 Housing Act 1985 s 128(2) (amended by the Housing and Regeneration Act 2008 ss 306(1), (5), 321(1), Sch 16); and see PARA 230 notes 7, 9. The Housing Act 1985 s 128(2)–(5) is modified where the Housing (Extension of Right to Buy) Order 1993, SI 1993/2240 (see PARA 233) applies: see Schedule para 15.

10 Ie a previous determination under the Housing Act 1985 s 128.

11 Housing Act 1985 s 128(3); and see PARA 230 notes 7, 9. See also note 9.

12 Housing Act 1985 s 128(4); and see PARA 230 notes 7, 9. See also note 9.

13 Ie the terms mentioned in the Housing Act 1985 s 125(2), (3): see PARA 276.

14 Ie the effect of the Housing Act 1985 s 128A(2): see PARA 286.

15 Housing Act 1985 s 128(5) (amended by the Housing and Regeneration Act 2008, s 306(1), (6)); and see PARA 230 notes 7, 9. See also note 9.

16 Ie under the Housing Act 1985 s 128A(2)(b: see PARA 286.

17 Housing Act 1985 s 128(5A) (s 128(5A)–(5C) added by the Housing and Regeneration Act 2008 s 306(1), (7)). For the purposes of the Housing Act 1985 s 128(5A)–(5B) it does not matter whether the request in question was made before, on or after the service of the notice in accordance with s 128(5): s 128(5C) (as so added).

18 See note 16.

19 Housing Act 1985 s 128(5B) (as added: see note 17).

20 A request under the Housing Act 1985 s 128A(2)(b) (see head (ii) in the text) must: (1) be in writing; (2) state the reason it is being made; and (3) confirm that the landlord has not made to the tenant a grant of the kind mentioned in s 138(1) (see PARA 291) in respect of the claim by the tenant to exercise the right to buy in respect of the dwelling house: s 128A(3) (s 128A added by the Housing and Regeneration Act 2008 s 306(1), (2)). A person who makes a request under the Housing Act 1985 s 128A(2)(b) must inform the district valuer if a grant of the kind mentioned in s 128A(3)(c) (see head (3) above) is made during the period of 14 days mentioned in s 128(5) (see the text and notes 13–15): s 128A(9) (as so added).

21 Housing Act 1985 s 128A(1), (2), (12) (as added: see note 20).

22 Ie a notice under the Housing Act 1985 s 128(5).

23 See the Housing Act 1985 s 128A(4), (12) (as added: see note 20).

24 Housing Act 1985 s 128A(5) (as added: see note 20).

25 Housing Act 1985 s 128A(6) (as added: see note 20).

26 Housing Act 1985 s 128A(7) (as added: see note 20).

27 Ie a grant of the kind mentioned in the Housing Act 1985 s 128A(3)(c): see note 20 head (3).

28 Housing Act 1985 s 128A(8) (as added: see note 20).

29 See note 27.

30 Housing Act 1985 s 128A(10), (11) (as added: see note 20).

286. Review of determination of value. The district valuer[1] must review the section 128 determination[2] as soon as reasonably practicable after serving a review notice[3]. If, following the review, the district valuer decides that neither of the withdrawal conditions[4] is met, he must, as soon as reasonably practicable, serve on the landlord[5] and the tenant[6] a notice stating the decision, the reasons for it; and that no further determination or, as the case may be redetermination is to be made under these provisions[7].

If, following the review, the district valuer decides that either withdrawal condition is met or both are met, he must:

(1) as soon as reasonably practicable, withdraw the section 128 determination by serving a further determination notice[8] on the landlord and the tenant; and

(2) make a further determination or, as the case may be, redetermination of the value of the dwelling house at the relevant time[9].

Before making such a determination or redetermination, the district valuer must consider any representation made to the valuer by the landlord or the tenant before the end of the period of 14 days beginning with the day on which the further determination notice was served[10].

As soon as practicable after such a determination or redetermination has been made, the landlord must serve on the tenant a determination effect notice[11].

1 As to the meaning of 'district valuer' see PARA 527 note 14.

2 As to the meaning of 'section 128 determination notice' see PARA 285.

3   Housing Act 1985 s 128B(1) (s 128B added by the Housing and Regeneration Act 2008 s 306(1), (2)). As to the meaning of 'review notice' see PARA 285.
    The Housing Act 1985 s 128B does not apply to a determination which is subject to a redetermination required in pursuance of s 128(3) (see PARA 285) but this does not prevent s 128B applying to the redetermination: s 128B(10) (as so added).
4   For these purposes, the withdrawal conditions are: (1) that a significant error was made in the section 128 determination; or (2) that the district valuer did not comply with the Housing Act 1985 s 128(4) (see PARA 285) in relation to the section 128 determination: s 128B(9) (as added: see note 3). 'Significant error', in relation to the section 128 determination, means an error of fact, or a number of such errors, made in the section 128 determination as a result of which the value of the dwelling house determined or (as the case may be) redetermined was at least 5% more or less than it would otherwise have been: s 128B(11) (as so added). As to the meaning of 'dwelling house' see PARA 231.
5   As to the meaning of 'landlord' see PARA 31 note 3.
6   As to the meaning of 'tenant' see PARA 31 note 3.
7   Housing Act 1985 s 128B(2), (3) (as added: see note 3).
8   'A further determination notice' is a notice stating: (1) that the section 128 determination is withdrawn; (2) the reasons for the withdrawal; and (3) that a further determination or (as the case may be) redetermination of the value of the dwelling house at the relevant time will be made: Housing Act 1985 s 128B(11) (as added: see note 3).
9   Housing Act 1985 s 128B(4), (5) (as added: see note 3). As to the meaning of 'the relevant time' see PARA 269 note 5.
10 Housing Act 1985 s 128B(6) (as added: see note 3).
11 Housing Act 1985 s 128B(7) (as added: see note 3). A determination effect notice is a notice stating: (1) the effect of the further determination or (as the case may be) redetermination; and (2) the matters mentioned in s 125(2), (3) (see PARA 285): s 128B(8) (as so added).

(B)   Discount

287. Entitlement to discount; in general. A person exercising the right to buy[1] is entitled[2] to a discount of a percentage calculated by reference[3] to the qualifying period[4]. The discount is[5]:

(1)   in the case of a house[6], 35 per cent plus 1 per cent for each complete year by which the qualifying period exceeds five years, up to a maximum of 60 per cent;

(2)   in the case of a flat[7], 50 per cent plus 2 per cent for each complete year by which the qualifying period exceeds five years, up to a maximum of 70 per cent[8].

The appropriate national authority may by order provide, that in such cases as may be specified in the order:

(a)   the minimum percentage discount;

(b)   the percentage increase for each complete year of the qualifying period after the first five; or

(c)   the maximum percentage discount,

shall be such percentage, higher than that specified above, as may be specified in the order[9].

Where, however, the right to acquire conferred by the Housing Act 1996[10] or the Housing and Regeneration Act 2008[11] arises, instead of such a discount as is described above a person exercising that right is entitled to a discount of such amount or at such rate as the appropriate national authority may by order prescribe[12]. Where the tenant has accepted the landlord's offer of an alternative dwelling house[13], the discount to which the tenant is entitled is the discount prescribed[14] in relation to that alternative dwelling house[15].

1   As to the meaning of 'the right to buy' see PARA 239.
2   Ie subject to the Housing Act 1985 s 129(2)–(3) (see the text and notes 5–11) and s 130 et seq (see PARA 288 et seq).
3   Ie by reference to the period which is to be taken into account in accordance with the Housing Act 1985 Sch 4: see PARA 268 et seq. Where joint tenants exercise the right to buy, Sch 4 is to be

construed as if for the secure tenant there were substituted that one of the joint tenants whose substitution will produce the largest discount: s 129(3). As to the meaning of 'secure tenant' see PARA 230 note 2.

4   Housing Act 1985 s 129(1) (s 129(1), (2) substituted, s 129(2A), (2B) added, by the Housing and Planning Act 1986 s 2(1), (2)). As to the reduction of discount where a previous discount is given see PARA 288; as to the limits on the amount of discount see PARA 289; and as to the repayment of discount on early disposal of the freehold or lease see PARA 323.

5   Ie subject to any order under the Housing Act 1985 s 129(2A): see the text and note 9.

6   As to the meaning of 'house' see PARA 231.

7   As to the meaning of 'flat' see PARA 231.

8   Housing Act 1985 s 129(2) (as substituted (see note 4); amended by the Housing Act 2004 s 180(2), (3); for transitional provisions see s 180(5), (6)).
     The Housing Act 1985 s 129(2) is modified where the Housing (Extension of Right to Buy) Order 1993, SI 1993/2240 (see PARA 233), applies: see Schedule para 16. For the modifications to the Housing Act 1985 s 129 which have effect where the right to acquire conferred by the Housing Act 1996 or the Housing and Regeneration Act 2008 arises see the text and notes 11–15.

9   Housing Act 1985 s 129(2A) (as added (see note 4); amended by the Housing Act 2004 s 180(4)). For transitional provisions see note 8. Such an order: (1) may make different provision with respect to different cases or descriptions of case; (2) may contain such incidental, supplementary or transitional provisions as appear to the appropriate national authority to be necessary or expedient; and (3) must be made by statutory instrument and may not, if made by the Secretary of State, be made unless a draft of it has been laid before and approved by resolution of each House of Parliament: Housing Act 1985 s 129(2B) (as so added). See the Housing (Right to Buy) (Maximum Percentage Discount) (England) Order 2014, SI 2014/1915, which applies to England, and specifies the maximum percentage discount in respect of a house as 70%. See also note 12. As to the appropriate national authority, the Secretary of State and the transfer of functions under the Housing Act 1985, so far as exercisable in relation to Wales, to the Welsh Ministers see PARA 7.

10   See PARAS 242–244.

11   See PARAS 240–241.

12   Housing Act 1985 s 129(1) (substituted for these purposes by the Housing (Right to Acquire) Regulations 1997, SI 1997/619, Sch 1 para 11(a), applying in relation to the right to acquire under the Housing and Regeneration Act 2008 by virtue of s 184, which applies the Housing Act 1996 s 17 (regulations modifying the Housing Act 1985): see PARA 241). For the prescribed amount of discount see: (1) the Housing (Right to Acquire) (Discount) (Wales) Order 1997, SI 1997/569 (which extends to dwellings in Wales only (art 1); prescribes the percentage rate of discount to be given on the exercise of the right to acquire as 25% of the open market value of the dwelling subject to a maximum of £8,000 (art 3 (amended by SI 2015/1349)) and provides that any question arising as to the open market value of a dwelling at the relevant time is to be determined by the district valuer (Housing (Right to Acquire) (Discount) (Wales) Order 1997, SI 1997/569, art 4)); and (2) the Housing (Right to Acquire) (Discount) Order 2002, SI 2002/1091, which prescribes different amounts of discount applicable to dwellings in specified areas in England, subject to a maximum amount of discount of 50% of the value of the dwelling (art 2, Schedule).
     The Housing Act 1985 s 129(2), (2A), (2B), (3) is omitted for these purposes: see the Housing (Right to Acquire) Regulations 1997, SI 1997/619, Sch 1 para 11(c).

13   Ie under the Housing Act 1985 s 124A(3) (added for these purposes): see PARA 275.

14   Ie under the Housing Act 1996 s 17: see PARAS 241, 243. As to the discount so prescribed see note 12.

15   Housing Act 1985 s 129(1A) (added for these purposes by the Housing (Right to Acquire) Regulations 1997, SI 1997/619, Sch 1 para 11(b); and see note 12).

288. Reduction of discount where previous discount given. There must be deducted from the discount[1] an amount equal to any previous discount qualifying, or the aggregate of previous discounts qualifying, under the following provisions[2].

For these purposes, 'a previous discount' means a discount given before the relevant time[3]:

(1)   on conveyance of the freehold, or a grant or assignment of a long lease, of a dwelling house[4] by a person meeting the landlord condition[5] or, in such circumstances as may be prescribed by order of appropriate national authority[6], by a person so prescribed; or

(2)   on conveyance of the freehold, or a grant or assignment of a long lease of a dwelling house by a person against whom the preserved right to buy was exercisable[7] to a person who was a qualifying person for the purposes of the preserved right to buy and in relation to whom that dwelling house was the qualifying dwelling house; or

(3)   in pursuance of the provision required in the calculation of the landlord's share and final discount[8]; or

(4)   in pursuance of the provision as to the right to acquire additional shares in the case of a shared ownership lease[9]; or

(5)   in pursuance of any provision of, or required by, Part V of the Housing Act 1985[10] as it has effect[11] in relation to the right to acquire[12].

A previous discount qualifies for these purposes if it was given:

(a)   to the person or one of the persons exercising the right to buy[13] or the right to acquire conferred by the Housing Act 1996[14] or the Housing and Regeneration Act 2008[15]; or

(b)   to the spouse or civil partner of that person or one of those persons, if they are living together at the relevant time; or

(c)   to a deceased spouse or deceased civil partner of that person or one of those persons, if they were living together at the time of the death;

and, where a previous discount was given to two or more persons jointly, these provisions have effect as if each one of them had been given an equal proportion of the discount[16].

Where the whole or part of a previous discount has been recovered by the person by whom it was given, or a successor in title of his:

(i)   by the receipt of a payment determined by reference to the discount; or

(ii)   by a reduction so determined of any consideration given to that person, or a successor in title of his; or

(iii)   in any other way,

then so much of the discount as has been so recovered must be disregarded for these purposes[17].

1   As to the discount to which a person exercising the right to buy or the right to acquire is entitled see PARA 287.
2   Housing Act 1985 s 130(1); and see PARA 230 notes 7, 9.
3   As to the meaning of 'the relevant time' see PARA 269 note 5.
4   For these purposes, 'dwelling house' includes any yard, garden, outhouses and appurtenances belonging to the dwelling house or usually enjoyed with it: Housing Act 1985 s 130(6). For the normal meaning of 'dwelling house' see PARA 231.
5   Ie a person within the Housing Act 1985 Sch 4 para 7 or 7A: see PARA 270.
6   As to the appropriate national authority, the Secretary of State and the transfer of functions under the Housing Act 1985, so far as exercisable in relation to Wales, to the Welsh Ministers see PARA 7.
7   Ie by virtue of the Housing Act 1985 s 171A: see PARA 334.
8   Ie the provision required by the Housing Act 1985 Sch 6A paras 3–5 or Sch 6A para 7: see PARA 318.
9   Ie by the Housing Act 1985 Sch 8 para 1 (repealed) or any other provision to the like effect.
10 Ie by the Housing Act 1985 Pt V (ss 118–188) (see PARAS 230 et seq, 289 et seq).
11 Ie by virtue of the Housing Act 1996 s 17 (the right to acquire: see PARAS 241, 243).
12 Housing Act 1985 s 130(2) (amended by the Housing and Planning Act 1986 s 24(2), Sch 5 para 29; the Leasehold Reform, Housing and Urban Development Act 1993 s 187(1), Sch 21 para 11; and by SI 1997/627; and modified by the Housing (Right to Acquire) Regulations 1997, SI 1997/619, Sch 1 para 12, applying in relation to the right to acquire under the Housing and Regeneration Act 2008 by virtue of s 184, which applies the Housing Act 1996 s 17 (regulations modifying the Housing Act 1985): see PARA 241).
    Section 130(2) is also modified where the Housing (Extension of Right to Buy) Order 1993, SI 1993/2240 (see PARA 233) applies: see Schedule para 17.

An order under the Housing Act 1985 s 130 may make different provision with respect to different cases or descriptions of case, including different provision for different areas, and must be made by statutory instrument which is subject, if made by the Secretary of State, to annulment in pursuance of a resolution of either House of Parliament: see s 130(5). In exercise of the power so conferred, and prior to the transfer of functions in relation to Wales, the Secretary of State made the Housing (Right to Buy) (Prescribed Persons) Order 1992, SI 1992/1703, which came into force on 17 August 1992: art 1. For the persons, bodies and circumstances prescribed for the purposes of head (1) above see arts 3, 4, Schedule (Schedule amended by the Environment Act 1995 s 120, Sch 22 para 233(1); the Countryside and Rights of Way Act 2000 s 73(2); the Police (Northern Ireland) Act 2000 s 2(4), Sch 2 para 6(1); and by SI 1994/2567, SI 1996/2651, SI 2003/1615, SI 2004/696, SI 2004/3168, SI 2005/2929, SI 2012/1659 and SI 2013/755).

13 As to the meaning of 'the right to buy' see PARA 239.
14 See PARAS 242–244.
15 See PARAS 240–241.
16 Housing Act 1985 s 130(3) (amended by the Civil Partnership Act 2004 s 81, Sch 8 para 29); and see PARA 230 notes 7, 9.
17 Housing Act 1985 s 130(4); and see PARA 230 notes 7, 9.

289. Limits on amount of discount; in general. Except where the appropriate national authority so determines, the discount to which a person exercising the right to buy[1] (but not the right to acquire conferred by the Housing Act 1996[2] or the Housing and Regeneration Act 2008[3]) is entitled[4] may not reduce the price below the amount which, in accordance with a determination made by that authority, is to be taken as representing so much of the costs incurred in respect of the dwelling house[5] as, in accordance with the determination:

(1)   is to be treated as incurred at or after the beginning of that period of account[6] of the landlord in which falls the date which is eight years, or such other period of time as may be specified in an order made by the appropriate national authority[7], earlier than the relevant time[8]; and

(2)   is to be treated as relevant for these purposes;

and, if the price before discount is below that amount, there is to be no discount[9]; in other words, the landlord cannot be compelled to sell at a loss. The discount may not in any case reduce the price by more than such sum as the appropriate national authority may by order prescribe[10].

Any such order or determination may make different provision for different cases or descriptions of case, including different provision for different areas[11]; and any such order must be made by statutory instrument[12].

Where the right to acquire conferred by the Housing Act 1996 or the Housing and Regeneration Act 2008 is exercised, the limits on the amount of discount are prescribed in orders made under the Housing Act 1996[13].

1 As to the meaning of 'the right to buy' see PARA 239.
2 See PARAS 242–244.
3 See PARAS 240–241.
4 As to the discount to which a person exercising the right to buy is entitled see PARA 287.
5 As to the meaning of 'dwelling house' see PARA 231.
6 For these purposes, 'period of account', in relation to any costs, means the period for which the landlord made up those of its accounts in which account is taken of those costs: Housing Act 1985 s 131(1A) (added by the Housing Act 1988 s 122(1), (3)). As to the meaning of 'landlord' see PARA 31 note 3.
     The Housing Act 1985 s 131(1), (1A), (3) is modified, and Sch 5A is added and substituted, where the preserved right to buy (see PARA 334 et seq) arises: see PARA 290.
7 The period of time specified for these purposes is: (1) in relation to England, ten years (instead of the period of eight years mentioned in the text) in relation to dwelling houses built or acquired by the landlord prior to 2 April 2012; and (2) 15 years (instead of that period of eight years) in relation to dwelling houses built or acquired by the landlord on or after 2 April 2012 (Housing (Right to Buy) (Limit on Discount) (England) Order 2012, SI 2012/734, art 2; for transitional provisions see art 4) (SI 2012/734 revoked, in relation to dwelling-houses situated within the areas

of London authorities, by SI 2013/677); (2) in relation to Wales, ten years (instead of the period of eight years mentioned in the text) (Housing (Right to Buy) (Limits on Discount) (Wales) Order 1999, SI 1999/292, art 4).

8   As to the meaning of 'the relevant time' see PARA 269 note 5.

9   Housing Act 1985 s 131(1) (amended by the Housing Act 1988 s 122(1), (2)); and see the text and note 13. This is often referred to as the 'cost floor rule'. See also notes 6–7. As to the reduction of discount where a previous discount is given see PARA 288; and as to the repayment of discount on early disposal of the freehold or lease see PARA 323. As to the appropriate national authority, the Secretary of State and the transfer of functions under the Housing Act 1985, so far as exercisable in relation to Wales, to the Welsh Ministers see PARA 7.

    For a case where these provisions were not applied see *Rushton v Worcester City Council* [2001] EWCA Civ 367, [2002] HLR 188, [2001] All ER (D) 195 (Mar) (the Housing (Right to Buy) (Cost Floor) (England) Determination 1998, made under the Housing Act 1985 s 131(1), together with the government circular drawing attention to it, was omitted from the various practitioners' texts and was thus peculiarly within the knowledge of the local authority and ought to have been disclosed prior to trial).

10 Housing Act 1985 s 131(2). In relation to England, the maximum amount of discount is, for dwelling houses situated within the areas of London authorities, £102,700; and, for dwelling houses situated outside of the areas of London authorities, £77,000 for the period from 21 July 2014 to 5 April 2015: Housing (Right to Buy) (Limit on Discount) (England) Order 2014, SI 2014/1378, art 2(1). Thereafter, in relation to each subsequent period of 12 months following the initial period, the prescribed sum is calculated by: (1) increasing the prescribed sum of the previous year by the same percentage as the percentage change in the consumer prices index over the specified period; and (2) rounding down the result from head (1) to the nearest £100: art 2(2). For these purposes, 'consumer prices index' means the general index of consumer prices (for all items) published by the Statistics Board or, if that index is not published for any month, any substituted index or index figures published by that Board; and 'specified period' means the period of 12 months up to and including the September in the previous year referred to in art 2(2): art 2(3). For transitional provision see art 3. In relation to a dwelling house in Wales the prescribed sum for these purposes is £8,000: Housing (Right to Buy) (Limits on Discount) (Wales) Order 1999, SI 1999/292, art 3 (amended by SI 2015/1349, with effect from 14 July 2015).

11 Housing Act 1985 s 131(3).

12 Housing Act 1985 s 131(4). If made by the Secretary of State, the instrument is subject to annulment in pursuance of a resolution of either House of Parliament: see s 131(4).

13 See PARA 287 text and notes 11–15. The Housing Act 1985 s 131 does not apply: see the Housing (Right to Acquire) Regulations 1997, SI 1997/619, Sch 1 para 13, applying in relation to the right to acquire under the Housing and Regeneration Act 2008 by virtue of s 184, which applies the Housing Act 1996 s 17 (regulations modifying the Housing Act 1985): see PARA 241.

290. Limits on amount of discount where the preserved right to buy arises.

Where the preserved right to buy arises[1], then unless the landlord[2] otherwise agrees:

(1)   the discount[3] must not reduce the price below the amount which is to be taken[4] as representing the costs incurred by the landlord in respect of the qualifying dwelling house[5] and is to be treated as relevant for these purposes; and

(2)   if the price before discount is below that amount there is to be no discount[6].

The cost floor (that is, the amount mentioned in head (1)) is an amount equal to the aggregate of the costs which may be treated as relevant costs[7]; and an estimate may be made for the purposes of arriving at the cost floor for a qualifying dwelling house where the amount of any relevant costs or payments for them cannot readily be ascertained[8].

The discount may not in any case reduce the price by more than such sum as the appropriate national authority may by order prescribe[9]. Any such order may make different provision for different cases or descriptions of case, including different provision for different areas[10] and must be made by statutory instrument[11].

1   See PARA 334 et seq.

2   As to the meaning of 'landlord' see PARA 31 note 3.

3   As to the discount to which a person exercising the right to buy is entitled see PARA 287.

4   Ie in accordance with the Housing Act 1985 Sch 5A (substituted for these purposes): see note 6.

5   As to the meaning of 'qualifying dwelling house' see PARA 335.

6   Housing Act 1985 s 131(1) (substituted for these purposes by the Housing (Preservation of Right to Buy) Regulations 1993, SI 1993/2241, Sch 1 para 11(a)). The Housing Act 1985 s 131(1A) (see PARA 289 note 6) is omitted for these purposes; see the Housing (Preservation of Right to Buy) Regulations 1993, SI 1993/2241, Sch 1 para 11(b).

7   Ie under the provisions of the Housing Act 1985 Sch 5A para 2 (as substituted for these purposes: see note 8) or, as the case may be, Sch 5A para 3 (as so substituted), and of Sch 5A para 4 (as so substituted).

8   See the Housing Act 1985 Sch 5A paras 1, 5, 6 (Sch 5A added for these purposes by the Housing (Preservation of Right to Buy) Regulations 1993, SI 1993/2241, Sch 1 para 42, Sch 1 Pt II; substituted in relation to England by SI 1999/1213; and substituted, with minor changes in the wording, in relation to Wales by SI 2001/1301).

Except where a case falls within the Housing Act 1985 Sch 5A para 3 (so substituted for these purposes) and subject to Sch 5A para 4 (as so substituted), the costs which may be treated as relevant costs for the purposes of s 131(1) are the following costs (including VAT) incurred by the landlord: (1) the costs of construction of the dwelling house (including site development works and the acquisition of land); (2) the costs of acquisition of the dwelling house; (3) the costs of works initially required following the acquisition of the dwelling house by the landlord to put it in good repair or to deal with any defect affecting it; (4) where the aggregate of the costs of works of repair or maintenance or works to deal with any defect affecting the dwelling house (except works within head (3)) exceeds the sum of £5,500, the costs in excess of that amount; and (5) the costs of other works to the dwelling house, except costs of the kind mentioned in head (4): Sch 5A paras 1, 2(1) (as so substituted). The following costs are not to be treated as relevant costs for these purposes: (a) any administrative costs; (b) interest; and (c) any costs which are recoverable by the landlord as a service charge or an improvement contribution: Sch 5A para 2(2) (as so substituted). As to the meanings of 'service charge' and 'improvement contribution' see PARA 276 notes 19–20.

Subject to Sch 5A para 4 (substituted for these purposes), where the appropriate national authority consented to the disposal of a qualifying dwelling house under s 32 or s 43 (see PARAS 522, 531) and the sale price attributed to the dwelling house on that disposal was nil, the costs which may be treated as relevant costs are the following costs (including VAT) incurred by the landlord: (i) the costs of works initially required following the acquisition of the dwelling house by the landlord to put it in good repair or to deal with any defect affecting it; (ii) the costs of works of repair or maintenance or works to deal with any defect affecting the dwelling house; (iii) the costs of improvement or other works to the dwelling house; (iv) the costs of works to any garage or parking area where the facility benefits the dwelling house; (v) the costs of works to provide or improve any communal facility provided in particular for the benefit of the dwelling house; (vi) professional fees and consultancy fees; and (vii) administrative costs not exceeding the sum of £2,000: Sch 5A para 3(1) (as so substituted). The following costs are not to be treated as relevant costs for these purposes, ie interest and any costs which are recoverable by the landlord as a service charge or an improvement contribution: Sch 5A para 3(2) (as so substituted).

Costs incurred on any relevant works are not be treated as relevant costs if payment for them was made: (A) in a period of account ending more than 15 years before the date of service of the qualifying person's notice under s 122 (see PARA 273); or (B) on or after the date of service of the qualifying person's notice under s 122 unless: (I) the landlord has before that date entered into a written contract for the carrying out of works; or (II) the qualifying person has agreed in writing to the carrying out of works and the works have been carried out not later than the date of service of the landlord's notice under s 125 (notice of purchase price: see PARA 276) or the works will be carried out under the proposed terms of the conveyance or grant; or (III) the qualifying person was served a notice in writing under Sch 3A para 3(2) (consultation on transfer: see PARA 450) and the costs come within head (3) or head (i) above: Sch 5A para 4 (as so substituted).

In a case where a landlord is a company, references to the landlord in Sch 5A paras 2, 3 and 4 (as so substituted) include references to a connected company: see Sch 5A para 7 (as so substituted).

9   Housing Act 1985 s 131(2); and see PARA 289 note 10. As to the appropriate national authority, and the transfer of functions under the Housing Act 1985, so far as exercisable in relation to Wales, to the Welsh Ministers see PARA 7.

10 Housing Act 1985 s 131(3) (amended for these purposes by the Housing (Preservation of Right to Buy) Regulations 1993, SI 1993/2241, Sch 1 para 11(c)).

11 Housing Act 1985 s 131(4). If made by the Secretary of State, the instrument is subject to annulment in pursuance of a resolution of either House of Parliament: see s 131(4).

G. COMPLETION OF PURCHASE

(A) Completion of Purchase; in general

291. Duty of landlord to convey freehold or grant lease. Where a tenant[1] has claimed to exercise the right to buy[2] or the right to acquire conferred by the Housing Act 1996[3] or the Housing and Regeneration Act 2008[4] and that right has been established, then, as soon as all matters relating to the grant have been agreed or determined, the landlord[5] must make to the tenant:

(1) if the dwelling house[6] is a house[7] and the landlord owns the freehold, a grant of the dwelling house for an estate in fee simple absolute; or

(2) if the landlord does not own the freehold, or if the dwelling house is a flat[8] (whether or not the landlord owns the freehold), a grant of a lease of the dwelling house,

in accordance with[9] the relevant statutory provisions[10]. In the case of the right to buy there is an implicit requirement that the tenant must remain a secure tenant until the conveyance or grant of the lease[11]. The duty to convey the freehold or to grant a lease[12] is enforceable by injunction[13].

The landlord is not, however, bound to comply with the above provisions:

(a) if the tenant has failed to pay the rent or any other payment due from him as a tenant for a period of four weeks after it has been lawfully demanded from him, while the whole or part of that payment remains outstanding[14];

(b) if an application is pending before any court:

(i) for a demotion order[15] or Ground 2 or 2ZA possession order or a section 84A possession order[16] to be made in respect of the tenant; or

(ii) for a suspension order[17] to be made in respect of the tenancy,

(c) until such time, if any, as the application is determined without either a demotion order or an operative Ground 2 or 2ZA possession order or an operative section 84A possession order[18] being made in respect of the tenant, or a suspension order being made in respect of the tenancy, or the application is withdrawn[19];

(d) where a suspension order is made, at any time after the beginning of the suspension period[20];

(e) while an initial demolition notice[21] is in force[22];

(f) where a final demolition notice[23] is served[24].

The tenancy[25] comes to an end on the grant to the tenant of an estate in fee simple, or of a lease, in pursuance of the right to buy; and, if there is then a subtenancy, the statutory provisions relating to the effect of the extinguishment of the reversion[26] apply as on a merger or surrender[27].

1 Ie a secure tenant in the case of the right to buy or a tenant in the case of the right to acquire. As to the meaning of 'secure tenant' see PARA 230 note 2; and as to the meaning of 'tenant' see PARA 31 note 3.
2 As to the meaning of 'the right to buy' see PARA 239.
3 See PARAS 242–244.
4 See PARAS 240–241.
5 As to the meaning of 'landlord' see PARA 31 note 3.
6 As to the meaning of 'dwelling house' see PARA 231.
7 As to the meaning of 'house' see PARA 231.
8 As to the meaning of 'flat' see PARA 231.
9 Ie in accordance with the Housing Act 1985 ss 138(2)–(3), 138A–188: see PARA 292 et seq.
10 Housing Act 1985 s 138(1) (amended by the Leasehold Reform, Housing and Urban Development Act 1993 s 197(2), Sch 22); and see PARA 230 notes 7, 9. Where the extended right to buy (see

PARA 233) arises, the Housing Act 1985 s 138(1) is substituted, s 138(2), (3) is modified, and s 138A is added for those purposes: see PARA 292.

11 *Bradford Metropolitan City Council v McMahon* [1993] 4 All ER 237, [1994] 1 WLR 52, CA (tenant died after the right to buy had been established and a price had been agreed between the parties but no conveyance had taken place; the right to buy disappeared and did not pass under the tenant's estate). Where, however, the tenant ceases to be a secure tenant because of a disposal to a private sector landlord, the right to buy is preserved: see PARA 334 et seq.

12 Ie the duty imposed by the Housing Act 1985 s 138(1): see the text and notes 1–10.

13 Housing Act 1985 s 138(3); and see PARA 230 notes 7, 9. See *Bristol City Council v Lovell* [1998] 1 All ER 775, [1998] 1 WLR 446, HL; *Taylor v Newham London Borough Council* [1993] 2 All ER 649, [1993] 1 WLR 444, CA. A tenant who has exercised his right to buy may be entitled to an injunction, but is not entitled to have his application heard as soon as he can bring it before the court and as an administrative matter the judge is entitled to adjourn the application so that it can be heard together with the local authority's application for a possession order: see *Bristol City Council v Lovell* [1998] 1 All ER 775, [1998] 1 WLR 446, HL As to injunctions generally see CIVIL PROCEDURE vol 12 (2015) PARA 1098 et seq.

A process in four stages can be identified in the provisions of the Housing Act 1985 Pt V (ss 118–188); the first stage is the claim to exercise the right to buy, the fourth and consummating stage that of the grant. Between those stages are the intermediate second and third stages of the establishment of the right and the agreement or determination on, or of, the terms of the grant. A tenant who has ceased to be a secure tenant has no right which he can enforce under s 138(3): *Muir Group Housing Association Ltd v Thornley* (1992) 25 HLR 89, [1993] 1 EGLR 51, CA.

14 Housing Act 1985 s 138(2); and see PARA 230 notes 7, 9.

15 For these purposes, 'demotion order' means a demotion order under the Housing Act 1985 s 82A (see LANDLORD AND TENANT vol 63 (2016) PARA 1090): s 138(2C) (s 138(2A)–(2D) added by the Housing Act 2004 s 193(1)).

16 For these purposes, 'Ground 2 or 2ZA possession order' means an order for possession under the Housing Act 1985 Sch 2 Pt I, Ground 2 or Ground 2ZA (see LANDLORD AND TENANT vol 63 (2016) PARAS 1140, 1141), and 'section 84A possession order' means an order for possession under s 84A (see LANDLORD AND TENANT vol 63 (2016) PARA 1131): s 138(2C) (as added (see note 15); amended by the Anti-social Behaviour, Crime and Policing Act 2014 s 100(1)(c), (e)).

17 For these purposes, 'suspension order' means a suspension order under the Housing Act 1985 s 121A (see PARA 259): s 138(2C) (as added: see note 15).

18 For these purposes, 'operative Ground 2 or 2ZA possession order' means an order made under the Housing Act 1985 Sch 2 Pt I, Ground 2 or Ground 2ZA which requires possession of the dwelling house to be given up on a date specified in the order; and 'operative section 84A possession order' means an order under s 84A which requires possession of the dwelling house to be given up on a date specified in the order: s 138(2C) (as added (see note 15); amended by the Anti-social Behaviour, Crime and Policing Act 2014 s 100(1)(d), (e)).

19 Housing Act 1985 s 138(2A), (2B) (as added (see note 15); amended by the Anti-social Behaviour, Crime and Policing Act 2014 s 100(1)(a), (b)). As to the disclosure of information for the purpose of enabling the landlord to decide whether to invoke this exception see the Housing Act 2004 s 194(1)–(3); and PARA 453.

20 Ie the Housing Act 1985 s 138(1) has effect subject to s 121A(5) (disapplication where suspension order is made: see PARA 259): s 138(2D) (as added: see note 15).

21 As to the meaning of 'initial demolition notice' see PARA 293.

22 Ie the Housing Act 1985 s 138(1) has effect subject to s 138A(2) (operation suspended while initial demolition notice is in force: see PARA 293): s 138(2E)(a) (s 138(2E) added by the Housing Act 2004 s 183(1)).

23 As to the meaning of 'final demolition notice' see PARA 254.

24 Ie the Housing Act 1985 s 138(1) has effect subject to s 138B(2) (disapplication where final demolition notice is served: see PARA 298): s 138(2E)(b) (as added: see note 22).

25 Ie the secure tenancy in the case of the right to buy or the tenancy in the case of the right to acquire. As to the meaning of 'secure tenancy' see PARA 230 note 2.

26 Ie the Law of Property Act 1925 s 139: see LANDLORD AND TENANT vol 62 (2016) PARA 532.

27 Housing Act 1985 s 139(2); and see PARA 230 notes 7, 9. Section 139(2) is: (1) substituted where the extended right to buy (see PARA 233) arises (see PARA 292); (2) modified where the Housing (Preservation of Right to Buy) Regulations 1993, SI 1993/2241 (see PARA 334 et seq), apply (see Sch 1 para 14).

292. Duty to convey freehold and apportionment of purchase price where the extended right to buy arises. Where the extended right to buy arises and the relevant regulations apply[1], a secure tenant[2] has claimed to exercise the right to buy and that right has been established, then, as soon as all matters relating to the grant and to the amount have been agreed or determined, the freeholder[3] must make to the tenant a grant of the dwelling house[4] for an estate in fee simple absolute, in accordance with the relevant[5] statutory provisions[6]. The duty so to convey the freehold is enforceable by injunction[7], subject to the statutory exceptions[8] already set out[9].

On completion the freeholder must pay:

(1)   to the landlord[10] and to each intermediate landlord[11], if any; and

(2)   to the rent owner of a rentcharge[12] charged on or issuing out of the lease of the landlord or an intermediate landlord,

an amount calculated in accordance with the prescribed formula[13]. If that amount, as so calculated, is a negative amount, then on completion a landlord or intermediate landlord in relation to which that amount is a negative amount must pay to the freeholder an amount equal to that amount; and that amount is recoverable as a civil debt due to the freeholder by that landlord or intermediate landlord[14].

The secure tenancy[15], the lease of the landlord and the lease of each of the intermediate landlords, if any, in so far as any such lease relates to the dwelling house, come to an end and are extinguished on the grant to the tenant of an estate in fee simple in pursuance of the right to buy; and if there is then a subtenancy deriving out of the secure tenancy, the statutory provisions relating to the effect of the extinguishment of the reversion[16] apply as on a merger or surrender[17].

1   Ie where the Housing (Extension of Right to Buy) Order 1993, SI 1993/2240, applies: see PARA 233.

2   As to the meaning of 'secure tenant' see PARA 230 note 2.

3   As to the meaning of 'freeholder' see PARA 233 note 19.

4   As to the meaning of 'dwelling house' see PARA 231.

5   Ie in accordance with the Housing Act 1985 ss 138(2)–(3), 138A–188 (amended and modified for these purposes): see PARA 293 et seq.

6   Housing Act 1985 s 138(1) (substituted for these purposes by the Housing (Extension of Right to Buy) Order 1993, SI 1993/2240, Schedule para 20(a)).

7   Housing Act 1985 s 138(3) (modified for these purposes by the Housing (Extension of Right to Buy) Order 1993, SI 1993/2240, Schedule para 20(b)).

8   See PARA 279.

9   See the Housing Act 1985 s 138(2)–(2E); and PARA 291.

10 As to the meaning of 'the landlord' see PARA 31 note 3.

11 As to the meaning of 'intermediate landlord' see PARA 233 note 18.

12 For these purposes, 'rent owner' and 'rentcharge' have the same meanings as in the Rentcharges Act 1977: Housing Act 1985 s 138A(6) (s 138A added for these purposes by the Housing (Extension of Right to Buy) Order 1993, SI 1993/2240, Schedule para 21).

13 See the Housing Act 1985 s 138A(1) (as added for these purposes: see note 12). For the prescribed formula, and as to calculation of the amount under that formula, see s 138A(1), (2), (4), (7) (as so added). No payment is to be made under s 138A(1) (as so added) in relation to a lease of the dwelling house if it is a lease for a term certain and the residue of the term unexpired immediately before completion is a period of less than 12 months or if it is a periodic tenancy: s 138A(5) (as so added).

14 Housing Act 1985 s 138A(3) (as added for these purposes: see note 12).

15 As to the meaning of 'secure tenancy' see PARA 230 note 2.

16 Ie the Law of Property Act 1925 s 139: see LANDLORD AND TENANT vol 62 (2016) PARA 532.

17 Housing Act 1985 s 139(2) (substituted for these purpose by the Housing (Extension of Right to Buy) Order 1993, SI 1993/2240, Schedule para 22(c)).

(B)   Effect of Demolition Notice Served before Completion

(a)   Initial Demolition Notice

293.   Meaning of 'initial demolition notice'; period of validity. An 'initial demolition notice' is[1] a notice served on a secure tenant[2]:

(1)   stating that the landlord[3] intends to demolish the dwelling house[4] or, as the case may be, the building containing it ('the relevant premises');

(2)   setting out the reasons why the landlord intends to demolish the relevant premises;

(3)   specifying the period within which he intends to demolish those premises[5]; and

(4)   stating that, while the notice remains in force, he will not be under any obligation to make a grant of an estate in fee simple or of a lease[6] in respect of any claim made by the tenant to exercise the right to buy[7] in respect of the dwelling house[8].

An initial demolition notice must also state:

(a)   that the notice does not prevent:

    (i)   the making by the tenant of any such claim; or

    (ii)   the taking of steps[9] in connection with any such claim up to the point where the landlord's duty to make a grant[10] would otherwise operate in relation to the claim; or

    (iii)   the operation of that duty in most circumstances where the notice ceases to be in force; but

(b)   that, if the landlord subsequently serves a final demolition notice[11] in respect of the dwelling house, the right to buy will not arise in respect of it while that notice is in force and any existing claim will cease to be effective[12].

If, at the time when an initial demolition notice is served, there is an existing claim to exercise the right to buy in respect of the dwelling house, the notice must:

(A)   state that there is a statutory right to compensation[13] in respect of certain expenditure; and

(B)   give details of that right to compensation and of how it may be exercised[14].

An initial demolition notice comes into force[15] in respect of the dwelling house concerned on the date of service of the notice on the tenant and ceases to be so in force at the end of the period specified in accordance with head (3) above; but this is subject to compliance with the specified statutory conditions with respect to publicity[16] in a case to which they apply, and also to the statutory provisions with regard to the revocation, termination or transfer[17] of initial demolition notices[18].

1   Ie for the purposes of the Housing Act 1985 s 138A, Sch 5A: see the text and notes 2–14; and PARA 294 et seq.

2   The Housing Act 1985 Sch 5 para 16 (service of notices: see PARA 254) applies in relation to notices under Sch 5A as it applies in relation to notices under Sch 5 para 13, Sch 13 para 15 or Sch 5 para 15A: Sch 5A para 5 (Sch 5A added by the Housing Act 2004 s 183(3), Sch 9; the Housing Act 1985 Sch 5A para 5 amended by the Housing and Regeneration Act 2008 ss 305, 310(3), Sch 13 paras 6, 12). As to the meaning of 'secure tenant' see PARA 230 note 2.

3   For these purposes (except in the Housing Act 1985 Sch 5A para 3A: see PARA 296) any reference to the landlord, in the context of a reference to the demolition or intended demolition of any premises, includes a reference to a superior landlord; and 'premises' means premises of any description: Sch 5A para 6(1), (2) (as added (see note 2; amended by the Housing and Regeneration Act 2008 Sch 13 paras 6, 13). As to the meaning of 'landlord' generally see PARA 31 note 3.

4   As to the meaning of 'dwelling house' see PARA 231.

5   The period so specified must not: (1) allow the landlord more than what is, in the circumstances, a reasonable period to carry out the proposed demolition of the relevant premises (whether on their own or as part of a scheme involving the demolition of other premises); or (2) in any case expire more than seven years after the date of service of the notice on the tenant: Housing Act 1985 Sch 5A para 1(4) (as added (see note 2); amended by the Housing and Regeneration Act 2008 Sch 13 paras 6, 7). 'Scheme' includes arrangements of any description: Housing Act 1985 Sch 5A para 6(2) (as so added).

6   Ie such a grant as is mentioned in the Housing Act 1985 s 138(1): see PARA 291.

7   As to the meaning of 'the right to buy' see PARA 239. It is submitted that the Housing Act 1985 Sch 5A also applies to the right to acquire under the Housing Act 1996 or the Housing and Regeneration Act 2008: see PARA 230 notes 7, 9.
8   Housing Act 1985 Sch 5A para 1(1) (as added: see note 2).
9   Ie under the Housing Act 1985 Pt V (ss 118–188): see PARAS 230 et seq, 294 et seq.
10 Ie the Housing Act 1985 s 138(1): see PARA 291.
11 As to the meaning of 'final demolition notice' see PARA 254; definition applied by the Housing Act 1985 Sch 5A para 6(2) (as added: see note 2)
12 Housing Act 1985 Sch 5A para 1(2) (as added: see note 2).
13 Ie state that the Housing Act 1985 s 138C (see PARA 299) confers a right to compensation.
14 Housing Act 1985 Sch 5A para 1(3) (as added: see note 2).
15 Ie for the purposes of the Housing Act 1985 Sch 5A.
16 Ie subject to the conditions mentioned in the Housing Act 1985 Sch 5A para 2(2) and also to Sch 5A para 2(3). The conditions in Sch 5 para 13(6), (7) (publicity for final demolition notices: see PARA 254) apply in relation to an initial demolition notice as they apply in relation to a final demolition notice: Sch 5A para 2(2) (as added: see note 2). The notice mentioned in Sch 5 para 13(7) (as it so applies) must contain the following information (Sch 5A para 2(3) (as so added)), ie:
    (1)   sufficient information to enable identification of the premises that the landlord intends to demolish;
    (2)   the reasons why the landlord intends to demolish those premises;
    (3)   the period within which the landlord intends to demolish those premises;
    (4)   the date when any initial demolition notice or notices relating to those premises will cease to be in force, unless revoked or otherwise terminated under or by virtue of Sch 5A para 3 (see PARA 295);
    (5)   that, during the period of validity of any such notice or notices, the landlord will not be under any obligation to make such a grant as is mentioned in s 138(1) in respect of any claim to exercise the right to buy in respect of any dwelling house contained in those premises;
    (6)   that there may be a right to compensation under s 138C in respect of certain expenditure incurred in respect of any existing claim.
17 Ie subject to the Housing Act 1985 Sch 5A paras 3, 3A: see PARAS 295–296.
18 Housing Act 1985 Sch 5A para 2(1) (as added (see note 2); amended by the Housing and Regeneration Act 2008 Sch 13 paras 6, 8).

294. Effect of initial demolition notice served before completion. In a case where:

(1)   an initial demolition notice[1] is served on a secure tenant[2]; and

(2)   the notice is served on the tenant before the landlord[3] has made to him a grant of the dwelling house for an estate in fee simple absolute or for a lease[4] in respect of a claim by the tenant to exercise the right to buy[5],

the landlord is not bound to comply with the duty to make such a grant as is mentioned in head (2) above[6], in connection with any such claim by the tenant, so long as the initial demolition notice remains[7] in force[8].

There is a right to compensation[9] in certain cases where the above provisions apply[10].

1   As to the meaning of 'initial demolition notice' see PARA 293.
2   As to the meaning of 'secure tenant' see PARA 230 note 2.
3   As to the meaning of 'the landlord' see PARA 31 note 3. See also PARA 293 note 3.
4   Ie such a grant as is required by the Housing Act 1985 s 138(1): see PARA 291.
5   As to the meaning of 'the right to buy' see PARA 239. It is submitted that the Housing Act 1985 s 138A also applies to the right to acquire under the Housing Act 1996 or the Housing and Regeneration Act 2008: see PARA 230 notes 7, 9.
6   Ie he is not bound to comply with the Housing Act 1985 s 138(1).
7   Ie under the Housing Act 1985 Sch 5A: see PARAS 293, 295–297.
8   Housing Act 1985 s 138A(1), (2) (s 138A added by the Housing Act 2004 s 183(2)).
9   Ie the Housing Act 1985 s 138C (see PARA 299) provides such a right.
10 Housing Act 1985 s 138A(3) (as added: see note 8).

295. Revocation or termination of initial demolition notices. If, while an initial demolition notice[1] is in force:

(1)   the landlord[2] decides not to demolish the dwelling house[3] in question, he must, as soon as is reasonably practicable, serve a notice ('a revocation notice') on the tenant which informs him of the landlord's decision, and that the demolition notice is revoked as from the date of service of the revocation notice[4];

(2)   it appears to the appropriate national authority that the landlord has no intention of demolishing the dwelling house in question, that authority may serve a notice ('a revocation notice') on the tenant which informs him of the authority's conclusion and that the demolition notice is revoked as from the date of service of the revocation notice[5]; but the appropriate national authority may not serve a revocation notice unless it has previously served a notice on the landlord which informs him of that authority's intention to serve the revocation notice[6].

Where a revocation notice is served under head (1) or head (2) above, the demolition notice ceases to be in force as from the date of service of the revocation notice[7].

If a compulsory purchase order has been made for the purpose of enabling the landlord to demolish the dwelling house in respect of which he has served an initial demolition notice, whether or not it would enable him to demolish any other premises as well, and:

(a)   a relevant decision to confirm the order with modifications, or not to confirm the whole or part of the order[8], becomes effective while the notice is in force[9]; or

(b)   a relevant decision of the High Court to quash the whole or part of the order[10] becomes final while the notice is in force,

the notice ceases to be in force as from the date when the decision becomes effective[11] or final[12]. Where an initial demolition notice so ceases to be in force, the landlord must, as soon as is reasonably practicable, serve a notice on the tenant which informs him that the notice has ceased to be in force as from the date in question, and of the reason why it has ceased to be in force[13].

If, while an initial demolition notice is in force in respect of a dwelling house, a final demolition notice[14] comes into force[15] in respect of that dwelling house, the initial demolition notice ceases to be in force as from the date when the final demolition notice comes into force[16]. In such a case the final demolition notice must state that it is replacing the initial demolition notice[17].

1   As to the meaning of 'initial demolition notice' see PARA 293.
2   As to the meaning of 'the landlord' see PARA 293 note 3.
3   As to the meaning of 'dwelling house' see PARA 231.
4   Housing Act 1985 s 120, Sch 5 para 15(4) (Sch 5 para 15(4)–(7) added by the Housing Act 2004 s 182(1); applied for these purposes by the Housing Act 1985 Sch 5A para 3(1) (Sch 5A added by the Housing Act 2004 s 183(3), Sch 9; the Housing Act 1985 Sch 5A para 3(1) amended by the Housing and Regeneration Act 2008 s 305, Sch 13 paras 6, 9).
    The Housing Act 1985 Sch 5 para 15(4)–(7) does not apply if the landlord is selling or otherwise transferring his interest as landlord to another person or is offering it for sale or for other transfer: Sch 5 para 15(7A) added by the Housing and Regeneration Act 2008 Sch 13 paras 1, 3(1), (2); applied for these purposes by the Housing Act 1985 Sch 5A para 3(1)).
5   Housing Act 1985 Sch 5 para 15(5) (as added and applied: see note 4). Section 169 (see PARA 344) applies in relation to the appropriate national authority's power under this provision as it applies in relation to his or its powers under the provisions mentioned in s 169(1): Sch 5 para 15(5) (as so added and applied). As to the appropriate national authority, and the transfer of functions under the Housing Act 1985, so far as exercisable in relation to Wales, to the Welsh Ministers see PARA 7.
6   Housing Act 1985 Sch 5 para 15(6) (as added and applied: see note 4).
7   Housing Act 1985 Sch 5 para 15(7) (as added and applied: see note 4).

8   Ie a decision under the Acquisition of Land Act 1981 Pt II (ss 10–15) (see COMPULSORY
    ACQUISITION OF LAND vol 18 (2009) PARA 557 et seq) where the effect of the decision is that
    the landlord will not be able, by virtue of that order, to carry out the demolition of the dwelling
    house.
9   As to the period of validity of an initial demolition notice see PARA 293.
10 Ie a decision of the High Court under the Acquisition of Land Act 1981 s 24 (see COMPULSORY
    ACQUISITION OF LAND vol 18 (2009) PARA 614) where the effect of the decision is that the
    landlord will not be able, by virtue of that order, to carry out the demolition of the dwelling house.
11 A relevant decision within the Housing Act 1985 Sch 5A para 3(3)(a) (see head (a) in the text)
    becomes effective: (1) at the end of the period of 16 weeks beginning with the date of the decision,
    if no application for judicial review is made in respect of the decision within that period; or (2) if
    such an application is so made, at the time when: (a) a decision on the application which upholds
    the relevant decision becomes final; or (b) the application is abandoned or otherwise ceases to have
    effect: Sch 5A para 3(4) (as added: see note 4). See also note 12.
12 Housing Act 1985 Sch 5A para 3(2), (3) (as added: see note 4). A relevant decision within Sch 5A
    para 3(3)(b) (see head (b) in the text), or a decision within Sch 5A para 3(4)(b) (see note 11 head
    (2)), becomes final: (1) if not appealed against, at the end of the period for bringing an appeal; or
    (2) if appealed against, at the time when the appeal (or any further appeal) is disposed of; and for
    these purposes an appeal is disposed of (a) if it is determined and the period for bringing any
    further appeal has ended; or (b) if it is abandoned or otherwise ceases to have effect: Sch 5A
    para 3(5), (6) (as so added).
13 Housing Act 1985 Sch 5A para 3(7) (as added: see note 4).
14 As to the meaning of 'final demolition notice' see PARA 254; definition applied by the Housing Act
    1985 Sch 5A para 6(2) (as added: see note 4).
15 Ie under the Housing Act 1985 Sch 5 para 13: see PARA 254.
16 Housing Act 1985 Sch 5A para 3(8) (as added: see note 4).
17 Housing Act 1985 Sch 5A para 3(9) (as added: see note 4).

296. Transfer of initial demolition notices. If an initial demolition notice[1] is in
force in respect of a dwelling house[2], and the landlord[3] transfers his interest as
landlord to another person, the following provisions apply[4]. The initial
demolition notice ('the original notice') continues in force subject to the
provisions with regard to the period of validity, termination and revocation of
initial demolition notices[5] and to the following provisions[6]. If the transferee
intends to demolish the dwelling house, but has not served a continuation notice,
and complied with the statutory conditions[7], within the period of two months
beginning with the date of transfer, the transferee must proceed[8] as if the
transferee has decided not to demolish the dwelling house[9].

A continuation notice is a notice:

(1)   stating that the transferee has acquired the interest concerned, and
      intends to demolish the dwelling house or (as the case may be) the
      building containing it ('the relevant premises');
(2)   setting out the reasons why the transferee intends to demolish the
      relevant premises;
(3)   stating that the original notice is to continue in force; and
(4)   explaining the continued effect of the original notice[10].

1   As to the meaning of 'initial demolition notice' see PARA 293.
2   As to the meaning of 'dwelling house' see PARA 231.
3   As to the meaning of 'the landlord' see PARA 293 note 3.
4   Housing Act 1985 Sch 5A para 3A(1) (Sch 5A para 3A added by the Housing and Regeneration
    Act 2008 s 305, Sch 13 paras 6, 10).
5   Ie subject to the Housing Act 1985 Sch 5A paras 2, 3: see PARAS 293, 295.
6   Housing Act 1985 Sch 5A para 3A(2) (as added: see note 4).
7   Ie the conditions in the Housing Act 1985 Sch 5A para 3A(8) or (10). Schedule 5A para 3A(8)
    applies if the dwelling house is contained in a building which contains one or more other dwelling
    houses, and the transferee intends to demolish the whole of the building: Sch 5A para 3A(7) (as
    added: see note 4). The transferee must serve a continuation notice on the occupier of each of the
    dwelling houses contained in the building (whether addressed to him by name or just as 'the

occupier'): Sch 5A para 3A(8) (as so added). An accidental omission to serve a continuation notice on one or more occupiers does not, however, prevent this condition from being satisfied: Sch 5A para 3A(9) (as so added).

Schedule 5 para 13(7) (see PARA 254) applies in relation to the transferee's intention to demolish so as to impose a condition on the transferee for a notice to appear within the period of two months beginning with the date of transfer; and Sch 5A para 2(3) (see PARA 293) applies for this purpose: Sch 5A para 3A(10) (as so added).

Schedule 5A para 3A(7)–(10) applies instead of Sch 5A para 2(2), (3) in relation to an initial demolition notice so far as continued in force under Sch 5A para 3A: Sch 5A para 3A(11) (as so added).

8 Ie under the Housing Act 1985 Sch 5 para 15(4) as applied by Sch 5A para 3(1) (see PARA 295) as if the transferee has decided not to demolish the dwelling house (and Sch 5 para 15(5)–(7) as so applied applies on the same basis): see Sch 5A para 3A(4) (as added: see note 4).
9 Housing Act 1985 Sch 5A para 3A(4) (as added: see note 4).
10 Housing Act 1985 Sch 5A para 3A(5) (as added: see note 4). A continuation notice may not vary the period specified in the original notice in accordance with Sch 5A para 1(1)(c) (see PARA 293): Housing Act 1985 Sch 5A para 3A(6) (as so added).

297. Restriction on serving further demolition notices. Where an initial demolition notice[1] ('the relevant notice') has, for any reason, ceased to be in force[2] in respect of a dwelling house[3] without it being demolished, the following provisions apply[4]. No further initial demolition notice may be served in respect of the dwelling house by the landlord[5] who served the relevant notice or any landlord who served a continuation notice[6] in respect of the relevant notice, during the period of five years following the time when the relevant notice ceases to be in force, unless (1) the further notice is served with the consent of the appropriate national authority; and (2) it states that it is so served[7].

No final demolition notice[8] may be served in respect of the dwelling house by the landlord who served the relevant notice or any landlord who served a continuation notice in respect of the relevant notice, during the period of five years following the time when the relevant notice ceases to be in force, unless the final demolition notice is served with the consent of the appropriate national authority and it states that it is so served[9]; but this does not apply to a final demolition notice which is served at a time when an initial demolition notice served in accordance with heads (1) and (2) above is in force[10].

1 As to the meaning of 'initial demolition notice' see PARA 293.
2 As to the period of validity of an initial demolition notice see PARA 293; and as to revocation or termination of such a notice see PARA 295.
3 As to the meaning of 'dwelling house' see PARA 231.
4 Housing Act 1985 Sch 5A para 4(1) (Sch 5A added by the Housing Act 2004 s 183(3), Sch 9).
5 As to the meaning of 'the landlord' see PARA 293 note 3.
6 As to the meaning of 'continuation notice' see PARA 296.
7 Housing Act 1985 Sch 5A para 4(2) (as added (see note 4); amended by the Housing and Regeneration Act 2008 s 305, Sch 13 paras 6, 11(1), (2)). The appropriate national authority's consent under the Housing Act 1985 Sch 5A para 4(2) or Sch 5A para 4(3) may be given subject to compliance with such conditions as the appropriate national authority may specify: Sch 5A para 4(5) (as so added). As to the appropriate national authority, and the transfer of functions under the Housing Act 1985, so far as exercisable in relation to Wales, to the Welsh Ministers see PARA 7.
8 As to the meaning of 'final demolition notice' see PARA 254; definition applied by the Housing Act 1985 Sch 5A para 6(2) (as added: see note 4)
9 Housing Act 1985 Sch 5A para 4(3) (as added (see note 4); amended by the Housing and Regeneration Act 2008 Sch 13 paras 6, 11(1), (3)); and see note 7.
10 Housing Act 1985 Sch 5A para 4(4) (as added: see note 4).

(b)   Final Demolition Notice

298. Effect of final demolition notice served before completion. In a case where:
(1)   a secure tenant[1] has claimed to exercise the right to buy[2]; but

(2)   before the landlord[3] has made to the tenant a grant of the dwelling house for an estate in fee simple absolute or for a lease[4] in respect of the claim,

a final demolition notice[5] is served on the tenant[6], the tenant's claim ceases to be effective as from the time when the final demolition notice comes into force[7] and, accordingly, the duty to make such a grant as is described in head (2) above[8] does not apply to the landlord, in connection with the tenant's claim, at any time after the notice comes into force[9].

There is a statutory right to compensation[10] in certain cases where the above provisions apply[11].

1   As to the meaning of 'secure tenant' see PARA 230 note 2.
2   As to the meaning of 'the right to buy' see PARA 239. It is submitted that the Housing Act 1985 s 138B also applies to the right to acquire under the Housing Act 1996 or the Housing and Regeneration Act 2008: see PARA 230 notes 7, 9.
3   As to the meaning of 'the landlord' see LANDLORD AND TENANT vol 63 (2016) PARA 1037. See also PARA 293 note 3.
4   Ie such a grant as is required by the Housing Act 1985 s 138(1): see PARA 291.
5   As to the meaning of 'final demolition notice' see PARA 254.
6   Ie under the Housing Act 1985 Sch 5 para 13: see PARA 254. As to the restrictions on serving further demolition notices in certain cases see PARA 297.
7   Ie comes into force under the Housing Act 1985 Sch 5 para 13: see PARA 254.
8   Ie the Housing Act 1985 s 138(1).
9   Housing Act 1985 s 138B(1), (2) (s 138B added by the Housing Act 2004 s 183(2)).
10 Ie the Housing Act 1985 s 138C (see PARA 299) provides such a right.
11 Housing Act 1985 s 138B(3) (as added: see note 9).

(c)   Compensation

299. Compensation where demolition notice served. The following provisions apply where:
(1)   a secure tenant[1] has claimed to exercise the right to buy[2];
(2)   before the landlord[3] has made to the tenant a grant of the dwelling house for an estate in fee simple absolute or for a lease[4] in respect of the claim, either an initial demolition notice[5] is served on the tenant[6] or a final demolition notice[7] is served on him[8]; and
(3)   the tenant's claim is established before that notice comes into force[9] under the relevant statutory provision[10].

If, within the period of three months beginning with the date when the notice comes into force ('the operative date'), the tenant serves on the landlord a written notice claiming an amount of compensation in respect of expenditure reasonably incurred by the tenant before the operative date in respect of legal and other fees, and other professional costs and expenses, payable in connection with the exercise by him of the right to buy, the landlord must pay that amount to the tenant[11]. Such a notice must be accompanied by receipts or other documents showing that the tenant incurred the expenditure in question[12].

1   As to the meaning of 'secure tenant' see PARA 230 note 2.
2   As to the meaning of 'the right to buy' see PARA 239. It is submitted that the Housing Act 1985 s 138C also applies to the right to acquire under the Housing Act 1996 or the Housing and Regeneration Act 2008: see PARA 230 notes 7, 9.
3   As to the meaning of 'the landlord' see LANDLORD AND TENANT vol 63 (2016) PARA 1037. See also PARA 293 note 3.
4   Ie such a grant as is required by the Housing Act 1985 s 138(1): see PARA 291. As to the meaning of 'dwelling house' see PARA 231; and as to the meaning of 'lease' see PARA 31 note 3.
5   As to the meaning of 'initial demolition notice' see PARA 293.
6   Ie under the Housing Act 1985 Sch 5A: see PARA 293 et seq.

7   As to the meaning of 'final demolition notice' see PARA 254.
8   Ie under the Housing Act 1985 Sch 5 para 13: see PARA 254.
9   Ie under the Housing Act 1985 Sch 5A or Sch 5 para 13, as the case may be.
10 Housing Act 1985 s 138C(1) (s 138C added by the Housing Act 2004 s 183(2)).
11 Housing Act 1985 s 138C(2), (3) (as added: see note 10).
12 Housing Act 1985 s 138C(4) (as added: see note 10).

(C)   Contents of Conveyance or Lease

(a)   Common Provisions

300.   Contents of conveyance or lease; in general. A conveyance of the freehold
or a grant of a lease executed in pursuance of the right to buy[1] or the right to
acquire conferred by the Housing Act 1996[2] or the Housing and Regeneration Act
2008[3] must conform with the relevant Parts of Schedule 6[4] to the Housing Act
1985[5].

The conveyance or grant may not exclude or restrict the general words implied
in conveyances[6] unless the tenant[7] consents or the exclusion or restriction is made
for the purpose of preserving or recognising an existing interest of the landlord[8]
in tenant's incumbrances[9] or an existing right or interest of another person[10].

A provision of the conveyance or lease[11] is void in so far as it purports to enable
the landlord to charge the tenant a sum for or in connection with the giving of a
consent or approval[12].

1   As to the meaning of 'the right to buy' see PARA 239.
2   See PARAS 242–244.
3   See PARAS 240–241.
4   Ie, in the case of a conveyance of the freehold, with the Housing Act 1985 Sch 6 Pts I, II (paras 1–9)
    (see the text and notes 6–12; and PARAS 301–304) and in the case of a grant of a lease, with Sch 6
    Pts I, III (paras 1–9, 11–19) (see the text and notes 6–12; and PARAS 301–303, 305 et seq).
5   Housing Act 1985 s 139(1); and see PARA 230 notes 7, 9.
6   Ie under the Law of Property Act 1925 s 62: see DEEDS AND OTHER INSTRUMENTS vol 32
    (2012) para 437.
7   As to the meaning of 'tenant' see PARA 31 note 3.
8   As to the meaning of 'landlord' see PARA 31 note 3.
9   For these purposes, 'tenant's incumbrance' means: (1) an incumbrance on the secure tenancy (or,
    in the case of the right to acquire, on the tenancy) which is also an incumbrance on the reversion;
    and (2) an interest derived, directly or indirectly, out of the secure tenancy; and 'incumbrances'
    includes personal liabilities attaching in respect of the ownership of land or an interest in land
    though not charged on the land or interest: Housing Act 1985 Sch 6 para 7. As to the meaning of
    'secure tenancy' see PARA 230 note 2. See also PARA 230 notes 7, 9.
        Section 139(1) and Sch 6 para 7 are modified where the Housing (Extension of Right to Buy)
    Order 1993, SI 1993/2240 (see PARA 233), applies: see Schedule paras 22(a), 67(h). Where that
    Order applies, the freeholder must: (1) execute the conveyance on its own behalf and in the names
    of the landlord and the intermediate landlord or landlords (if any) and it must be binding on those
    authorities or bodies; and (2) secure that the conveyance states that it is a conveyance to which this
    provision applies: Housing Act 1985 s 139(1A) (added for these purposes by the Housing
    (Extension of Right to Buy) Order 1993, SI 1993/2240, Schedule para 22(b)). As to the meanings
    of 'intermediate landlord' and 'freeholder' see PARA 233 notes 18–19. The Housing Act 1985
    Sch 6 para 7 is also modified where the Housing (Preservation of Right to Buy) Regulations 1993,
    SI 1993/2241 (see PARA 334 et seq), apply: see Sch 1 para 43(a)(iii).
10 Housing Act 1985 Sch 6 para 1; and see PARA 230 notes 7, 9. Schedule 6 para 1 is modified where
    the Housing (Extension of Right to Buy) Order 1993, SI 1993/2240, applies: see Schedule
    para 67(a).
11 As to the meaning of 'lease' see PARA 31 note 3.
12 Housing Act 1985 Sch 6 para 6; and see PARA 230 notes 7, 9. Schedule 6 para 6 is modified where
    the Housing (Extension of Right to Buy) Order 1993, SI 1993/2240, applies: see Schedule
    para 67(g). See also *R v Braintree District Council, ex p Halls* (2000) 80 P & CR 266,
    [2000] All ER (D) 511, CA: conveyance in pursuance of the right to buy contained restrictive
    covenant 'to use the property as a single private dwelling house only'; the purchaser later obtained
    planning permission from the vendor authority, in its capacity as local planning authority, to erect
    a further dwelling house within the property's curtilage and sought the authority's consent to the

sale of the building plot. It was held that the authority's offer to release the applicant from the covenant subject to his paying a sum equivalent to 90% of the open market value of the building plot imposed an excessive and unlawful restriction since the ordinary incidents of a sale would not include the reservation of a right in the seller to keep the profits of any enhanced value arising from any potential development and following the exercise of the right to buy the former tenant was now the owner.

301. Rights of support, passage of water etc. As regards:

(1) rights of support for a building or part of a building;

(2) rights to the access of light and air to a building or part of a building;

(3) rights to the passage of water or of gas or other piped fuel, or to the drainage or disposal of water, sewage, smoke or fumes, or to the use or maintenance of pipes or other installations for such passage, drainage or disposal;

(4) rights to the use or maintenance of cables or other installations for the supply of electricity, for the telephone or for the receipt directly or by landline of visual or other wireless transmissions,

the conveyance or grant has effect:

(a) to grant with the dwelling house[1] all such easements and rights over other property, so far as the landlord[2] is capable of granting them, as are necessary to secure to the tenant[3] as nearly as may be the same rights as at the relevant time[4] were available to him under or by virtue of the tenancy[5] or an agreement collateral to it, or under or by virtue of a grant, reservation or agreement made on the severance of the dwelling house from other property then comprised in the same tenancy; and

(b) to make the dwelling house subject to all such easements and rights for the benefit of other property as are capable of existing in law and are necessary to secure to the person interested in the other property as nearly as may be the same rights as at the relevant time were available against the tenant under or by virtue of the secure tenancy or an agreement collateral to it, or under or by virtue of a grant, reservation or agreement made as mentioned in head (a) above[6].

The above provisions:

(i) do not restrict any wider operation which the conveyance or grant may otherwise have; but

(ii) are subject to any provision to the contrary that may be included in the conveyance or grant with the consent of the tenant[7].

1 As to the meaning of 'dwelling house' see PARA 231.
2 As to the meaning of 'landlord' see PARA 31 note 3.
3 As to the meaning of 'tenant' see PARA 31 note 3.
4 As to the meaning of 'the relevant time' see PARA 269 note 5.
5 Ie the secure tenancy in the case of the right to buy or the tenancy in the case of the right to acquire. As to the meaning of 'secure tenancy' see PARA 230 note 2; and as to the meaning of 'tenancy' see PARA 31 note 3.
6 Housing Act 1985 Sch 6 para 2(1), (2); and see PARA 230 notes 7, 9.
   Schedule 6 para 2 is modified where: (1) the Housing (Extension of Right to Buy) Order 1993, SI 1993/2240 (see PARA 233), applies (see Schedule para 67(b)); (2) the Housing (Preservation of Right to Buy) Regulations 1993, SI 1993/2241 (see PARA 334 et seq), apply (see Sch 1 para 43(a)(i)). See also PARA 300 note 9.
7 Housing Act 1985 Sch 6 para 2(3). See also note 6.

302. Rights of way. The conveyance or grant must include:

(1) such provisions, if any, as the tenant[1] may require for the purpose of securing to him rights of way over land not comprised in the dwelling house[2] so far as the landlord[3] is capable of granting them, being rights of way that are necessary for the reasonable enjoyment of the dwelling house; and

(2) such provisions, if any, as the landlord may require for the purpose of making the dwelling house subject to rights of way necessary for the reasonable enjoyment of other property, being property in which at the relevant time the landlord has an interest, or to rights of way granted or agreed to be granted before the relevant time[4] by the landlord or by the person then entitled to the reversion on the tenancy[5].

1 As to the meaning of 'tenant' see PARA 31 note 3.
2 As to the meaning of 'dwelling house' see PARA 231.
3 As to the meaning of 'landlord' see PARA 31 note 3.
4 As to the meaning of 'the relevant time' see PARA 269 note 5.
5 Housing Act 1985 Sch 6 para 3; and see PARA 230 notes 7, 9. Schedule 6 para 3 is modified where the Housing (Extension of Right to Buy) Order 1993, SI 1993/2240 (see PARA 233), applies: see Schedule para 67(c). See also PARA 300 note 9.

303. Covenants and conditions. The conveyance or grant:

(1) must include such provisions, if any, as the landlord[1] may require to secure that the tenant[2] is bound by, or to indemnify the landlord against breaches of, restrictive covenants, that is to say covenants restrictive of the use of any land or premises, which affect the dwelling house[3] otherwise than by virtue of the tenancy[4] or an agreement collateral to it and are enforceable for the benefit of other property[5];

(2) must be expressed to be made by the landlord with full title guarantee, thereby implying the specified covenants[6] for title[7];

(3) may include[8] such other covenants and conditions as are reasonable in the circumstances[9].

1 As to the meaning of 'landlord' see PARA 31 note 3.
2 As to the meaning of 'tenant' see PARA 31 note 3.
3 As to the meaning of 'dwelling house' see PARA 231.
4 Ie the secure tenancy in the case of the right to buy or the tenancy in the case of the right to acquire. As to the meaning of 'secure tenancy' see PARA 230 note 2; and as to the meaning of 'tenancy' see PARA 31 note 3.
5 Housing Act 1985 Sch 6 para 4; and see PARA 230 notes 7, 9. Schedule 6 para 4 is modified: (1) where the Housing (Extension of Right to Buy) Order 1993, SI 1993/2240 (see PARA 233), applies (see Schedule para 67(d)); (2) where the Housing (Preservation of Right to Buy) Regulations 1993, SI 1993/2241 (see PARA 334 et seq), apply (see Sch 1 para 43(a)(ii)). See also PARA 300 note 4.
  Where the Order referred to in head (1) above applies, and the freeholder is aware of an obligation relating to the dwelling house breach of which may expose the landlord or an intermediate landlord to liability to another person, the freeholder must include in the conveyance such provision (if any) as may be reasonable in the circumstances to relieve the landlord or intermediate landlord (as the case may be) from, or to indemnify him against, that liability: Housing Act 1985 Sch 6 para 4A (as added for these purposes by the Housing (Extension of Right to Buy) Order 1993, SI 1993/2240, Schedule para 67(e)). As to the meanings of 'intermediate landlord' and 'freeholder' see PARA 233 notes 18–19.
  The concept of using a property as a private dwelling house involves its use, at least in some way, as a home; thus where a right to buy conveyance contained a restrictive covenant not to use the property or permit it to be used for any use other than that of a private dwelling house, its use for short holiday lettings only was in breach of that covenant: see *Caradon District Council v Paton* [2000] 3 EGLR 57, [2000] All ER (D) 637, CA.
6 Ie the covenants for title specified in the Law of Property (Miscellaneous Provisions) Act 1994 Pt I (ss 1–13): see CONVEYANCING vol 23 (2016) PARA 182.
7 Housing Act 1985 Sch 6 para 4A (added by the Law of Property (Miscellaneous Provisions) Act 1994 s 21(1), Sch 1 para 9(2)); and see PARA 230 notes 7, 9.

8 Ie subject to the Housing Act 1985 Sch 6 para 6 (see PARA 300), Sch 6 Pt II (paras 8–9) (see PARA 304) and Sch 6 Pt III (paras 11–19) (see PARAS 305–312).
9 Housing Act 1985 Sch 6 para 5 (amended by the Law of Property (Miscellaneous Provisions) Act 1994 Sch 1 para 9(3)); and see PARA 230 notes 7, 9. The Housing Act 1985 Sch 6 para 5 is modified where the Housing (Extension of Right to Buy) Order 1993, SI 1993/2240, applies: see Schedule para 67(f).
 A challenge to the reasonableness of the covenant can only be made to the court before the conveyance is executed; after execution, the tenant can only secure his release from the covenant on application to the appropriate national authority made under the Housing Act 1985 ss 167, 168 (see PARA 343) unless the vendor authority agrees to a variation: *Sheffield City Council v Jackson* [1998] 3 All ER 260 [1998] 1 WLR 1591, CA. As to the appropriate national authority, and the transfer of functions under the Housing Act 1985, so far as exercisable in relation to Wales, to the Welsh Ministers see PARA 7.

(b)   Conveyance of Freehold

304.   Conveyance of freehold; in general. The conveyance may not exclude or restrict the implied all estate clause[1] unless the tenant[2] consents to this or the exclusion or restriction is made for the purpose of preserving or recognising an existing interest of the landlord[3] in tenant's incumbrances[4] or an existing right or interest of another person[5].

The conveyance must be of an estate in fee simple absolute, subject to:
(1)   tenant's incumbrances;
(2)   burdens, other than burdens created by the conveyance, in respect of the upkeep or regulation for the benefit of any locality of any land, building, structure, works, ways or watercourses,
but otherwise free from incumbrances[6].

1 Ie the clause implied under the Law of Property Act 1925 s 63: see DEEDS AND OTHER INSTRUMENTS vol 32 (2012) PARA 441.
2 As to the meaning of 'tenant' see PARA 31 note 3.
3 As to the meaning of 'landlord' see PARA 31 note 3.
4 As to the meaning of 'tenant's incumbrances' see PARA 300 note 9.
5 Housing Act 1985 Sch 6 para 8; and see PARA 230 notes 7, 9. Schedule 6 para 8 is modified where the Housing (Extension of Right to Buy) Order 1993, SI 1993/2240 (see PARA 233), applies: see Schedule para 68. See also PARA 300 note 9.
6 Housing Act 1985 Sch 6 para 9(1); and see PARA 230 notes 7, 9. Nothing in Sch 6 para 9(1) is to be taken as affecting the operation of Sch 6 para 5 (see PARA 303): Sch 6 para 9(2). As to the meaning of 'incumbrances' see PARA 300 note 9.

(c)   Leases

305.   Leases; in general. A lease[1] must be for the appropriate term[2] and at a rent not exceeding £10 per annum[3].

If at the time the grant is made the landlord's[4] interest in the dwelling house[5] is not less than a lease for a term of which more than 125 years and five days are unexpired, the appropriate term is a term of not less than 125 years[6]. In any other case the appropriate term is a term expiring five days before the term of the landlord's lease of the dwelling house or, as the case may require, five days before the first date on which the term of any lease under which the landlord holds any part of the dwelling house is to expire[7].

In the case of the right to buy[8] (but not of the right to acquire conferred by the Housing Act 1996[9] or the Housing and Regeneration Act 2008[10]), if the dwelling house is a flat[11] contained in a building which also contains one or more other flats and the landlord has since 8 August 1980 granted a lease of one or more of them for the appropriate term, the lease of the dwelling house may be for a term expiring at the end of the term for which the other lease, or one of the other leases, was granted[12].

1   As to the meaning of 'lease' see PARA 31 note 3.
2   Ie as defined in the Housing Act 1985 Sch 6 para 12 (see the text and notes 4–9) but subject (in the case of the right to buy but not of the right to acquire) to Sch 6 para 12(3) (see the text and notes 8–12).
3   Housing Act 1985 Sch 6 para 11 (modified by the Housing (Right to Acquire) Regulations 1997, SI 1997/619, Sch 1 para 41(a)); and see PARA 230 notes 7, 9. The Housing Act 1985 Sch 6 paras 12–19 (see PARA 306 et seq) have effect with respect to the other terms of the lease: Sch 6 para 11. Schedule 6 Pt III (paras 11–19) is omitted where the Housing (Extension of Right to Buy) Order 1993, SI 1993/2240 (see PARA 233), applies: see Schedule para 69. See also PARA 300 note 9. The Housing Act 1985 Sch 6 para 11 is also modified where the Housing (Preservation of Right to Buy) Regulations 1993, SI 1993/2241 (see PARA 334 et seq), apply: see Sch 1 para 43(b)(i).
    A former tenant who has been granted a lease of a dwelling house which is a flat has, broadly speaking, the same statutory rights as any other leaseholder including the right to challenge service charges under the Landlord and Tenant Act 1985, as to which see LANDLORD AND TENANT vol 63 (2016) PARA 628 et seq.
4   As to the meaning of 'landlord' see PARA 31 note 3.
5   As to the meaning of 'dwelling house' see PARA 231.
6   Housing Act 1985 Sch 6 para 12(1); and see PARA 230 notes 7, 9.
7   Housing Act 1985 Sch 6 para 12(2); and see PARA 230 notes 7, 9.
8   As to the meaning of 'the right to buy' see PARA 239.
9   See PARAS 242–244.
10 See PARAS 240–241.
11 As to the meaning of 'flat' see PARA 231.
12 Housing Act 1985 Sch 6 para 12(3); and see the Housing (Right to Acquire) Regulations 1997, SI 1997/619, Sch 1 para 41(b). The Housing Act 1985 Sch 6 para 12(3) is also omitted where the Housing (Preservation of Right to Buy) Regulations 1993, SI 1993/2241, apply: see Sch 1 para 43(b)(ii).

306. Common use of premises and facilities. Where the dwelling house[1] is a flat[2] and the tenant[3] enjoyed, during the tenancy[4], the use in common with others of any premises, facilities or services, the lease[5] must include rights to the like enjoyment, so far as the landlord[6] is capable of granting them, unless otherwise agreed between the landlord and the tenant[7].

1   As to the meaning of 'dwelling house' see PARA 231.
2   As to the meaning of 'flat' see PARA 231.
3   As to the meaning of 'tenant' see PARA 31 note 3.
4   Ie during the secure tenancy, in the case of the right to buy, or during the tenancy, in the case of the right to acquire. As to the meaning of 'secure tenancy' see PARA 230 note 2; and as to the meaning of 'tenancy' see PARA 31 note 3.
5   As to the meaning of 'lease' see PARA 31 note 3.
6   As to the meaning of 'landlord' see PARA 31 note 3.
7   Housing Act 1985 Sch 6 para 13; and see PARA 230 notes 7, 9. Schedule 6 para 13 is modified where the Housing (Preservation of Right to Buy) Regulations 1993, SI 1993/2241 (see PARA 334 et seq), apply: see Sch 1 para 43(b)(iii). See also PARAS 300 note 9, 305 note 3.

307. Covenants by the landlord in respect of flats. Where the dwelling house[1] is a flat[2], the following provisions apply[3].

There are implied covenants by the landlord[4]:

(1)   to keep in repair the structure and exterior of the dwelling house and of the building in which it is situated, including drains, gutters and external pipes, and to make good any defect affecting the structure;

(2)   to keep in repair any other property over or in respect of which the tenant[5] has rights[6];

(3)   to ensure, so far as practicable, that services which are to be provided by the landlord and to which the tenant is entitled, whether by himself or in common with others, are maintained at a reasonable level and to keep in repair any installations connected with the provision of those services[7].

There is an implied covenant that the landlord is to rebuild or reinstate the dwelling house and the building in which it is situated in the case of destruction or damage by fire, tempest, flood or any other cause against the risk of which it is normal practice to insure[8].

The County Court may, by order made with the consent of the parties, authorise the inclusion in the lease[9] or in an agreement collateral to it of provisions excluding or modifying the obligations of the landlord under the covenants implied by the above provisions, if it appears to the court that it is reasonable to do so[10].

1   As to the meaning of 'dwelling house' see PARA 231.
2   As to the meaning of 'flat' see PARA 231.
3   Housing Act 1985 Sch 6 para 14(1); and see PARA 230 notes 7, 9. See also PARAS 300 note 9, 305 note 3.
4   As to the meaning of 'landlord' see PARA 31 note 3.
5   As to the meaning of 'tenant' see PARA 31 note 3.
6   Ie by virtue of the Housing Act 1985 Sch 6: see PARAS 300 et seq, 308 et seq.
7   Housing Act 1985 Sch 6 para 14(2) (amended by the Housing and Planning Act 1986 s 24(2), (3), Sch 5 para 41(1), (2), Sch 12 Pt I); and see PARA 230 notes 7, 9. The Housing Act 1985 Sch 6 para 14(2), (3) has effect subject to Sch 6 para 15(3) (see PARA 308): Sch 6 para 14(3A) (added by the Housing and Planning Act 1986 Sch 5 para 41(1), (4)).
8   Housing Act 1985 Sch 6 para 14(3) (amended by the Housing and Planning Act 1986 Sch 5 para 41(1), (3)); and see PARA 230 notes 7, 9. See also note 7.
9   As to the meaning of 'lease' see PARA 31 note 3.
10 Housing Act 1985 Sch 6 para 14(4); and see PARA 230 notes 7, 9.

308.   Covenants by the landlord where landlord's interest in the house or flat is leasehold. Where the landlord's[1] interest in the dwelling house[2] is leasehold, the following provisions apply[3].

There is implied a covenant by the landlord to pay the rent reserved by the landlord's lease[4] and, except in so far as they fall to be discharged by the tenant[5], to discharge its obligations under the covenants contained in that lease[6].

A covenant implied where the dwelling house is a flat[7] does not impose on the landlord an obligation which the landlord is not entitled to discharge under the provisions of the landlord's lease or a superior lease[8]. Where the landlord's lease or a superior lease or an agreement collateral to the landlord's lease or a superior lease contains a covenant by a person imposing obligations which would otherwise be imposed by a covenant so implied, there is implied a covenant by the landlord to use its best endeavours to secure that that person's obligations under the first-mentioned covenant are discharged[9].

1   As to the meaning of 'landlord' see PARA 31 note 3.
2   As to the meaning of 'dwelling house' see PARA 231.
3   Housing Act 1985 Sch 6 para 15(1); and see PARA 230 notes 7, 9. See also PARAS 300 note 9, 305 note 3.
4   As to the meaning of 'lease' see PARA 31 note 3.
5   As to the meaning of 'tenant' see PARA 31 note 3.
6   Housing Act 1985 Sch 6 para 15(2); and see PARA 230 notes 7, 9.
7   Ie the covenant implied by the Housing Act 1985 Sch 6 para 14: see PARA 307.
8   Housing Act 1985 Sch 6 para 15(3); and see PARA 230 notes 7, 9.
9   Housing Act 1985 Sch 6 para 15(4); and see PARA 230 notes 7, 9.

309.   Covenant by tenant. Unless otherwise agreed between the landlord[1] and the tenant[2], there is implied a covenant by the tenant:

(1)   where the dwelling house[3] is a house[4], to keep the dwelling house in good repair, including decorative repair;

(2)   where the dwelling house is a flat[5], to keep the interior of the dwelling house in such repair[6].

1   As to the meaning of 'landlord' see PARA 31 note 3.
2   As to the meaning of 'tenant' see PARA 31 note 3.
3   As to the meaning of 'dwelling house' see PARA 231.
4   As to the meaning of 'house' see PARA 231.
5   As to the meaning of 'flat' see PARA 231.
6   Housing Act 1985 Sch 6 para 16; and see PARA 230 notes 7, 9. See also PARAS 300 note 9, 305 note 3.

310. Insurance contributions payable by the tenant. The lease[1] may require the tenant[2] to bear a reasonable part of the costs incurred by the landlord[3]:

(1)   in discharging or insuring against the obligations imposed by the implied covenants relating to repairs, making good structural defects, the provision of services etc[4]; or

(2)   in insuring against the obligations imposed by the implied covenant relating to rebuilding, reinstatement etc[5];

and, to the extent that[6] such obligations are not imposed on the landlord, to bear a reasonable part of the costs incurred by the landlord in contributing to costs incurred by a superior landlord or other person in discharging or, as the case may be, insuring against obligations to the like effect[7].

Where the lease requires the tenant to contribute to the costs of insurance, it must provide that the tenant is entitled to inspect the relevant policy at such reasonable times as may be specified in the lease[8].

Where the landlord does not insure against the obligations imposed by the implied covenant[9] or, as the case may be, the superior landlord or other person does not insure against his obligations to the like effect, the lease may require the tenant to pay a reasonable sum in place of the contribution he could be required to make if there were insurance[10].

1   As to the meaning of 'lease' see PARA 31 note 3.
2   As to the meaning of 'tenant' see PARA 31 note 3.
3   As to the meaning of 'landlord' see PARA 31 note 3.
4   Ie the covenants implied by the Housing Act 1985 Sch 6 para 14(2): see PARA 307. Where in any case the obligations imposed by the covenants implied by virtue of Sch 6 para 14(2) or (3) (see PARA 307) are modified in accordance with Sch 6 para 14(4) (see PARA 307), the references in Sch 6 para 16A are to the obligations as so modified: Sch 6 para 16A(4) (Sch 6 para 14A added by the Housing and Planning Act 1986 s 4(4), (6)); and see PARA 230 notes 7, 9. See also PARAS 300 note 9, 305 note 3.
5   Ie the covenant implied by the Housing Act 1985 Sch 6 para 14(3): see PARA 307. See also note 4.
6   Ie by virtue of the Housing Act 1985 Sch 6 para 15(3): see PARA 308.
7   Housing Act 1985 Sch 6 para 16A(1) (as added: see note 4); and see PARA 230 notes 7, 9. Schedule 6 para 16A has effect subject to Sch 6 para 16B (see PARA 311): Sch 6 para 16A(5) (as so added).
8   Housing Act 1985 Sch 6 para 16A(2) (as added: see note 4); and see PARA 230 notes 7, 9. See *Coventry City Council v Cole* [1994] 1 All ER 997, (1993) 25 HLR 555, CA (clause in a long lease granted under the right to buy providing for the tenant to pay a service charge of a fixed sum plus a sum calculated in accordance with the building cost information service tender price index was held to fall outside the Housing Act 1985 Sch 6 para 16A and Sch 6 para 18 (see PARA 312) and was therefore not void).
9   See note 5.
10 Housing Act 1985 Sch 6 para 16A(3) (as added: see note 4); and see PARA 230 notes 7, 9.

311. Service charges and improvement contributions payable by the tenant. Where a lease[1] of a flat[2] requires the tenant[3] to pay service charges[4] in respect of repairs, including works for the making good of structural defects, his liability in respect of costs incurred in the initial period of the lease[5] is restricted as follows[6].

He is not required to pay in respect of works itemised in the estimates contained in the landlord's notice[7] any more than the amount shown as his estimated contribution in respect of that item, together with an inflation allowance[8]; and he is not required to pay in respect of works not so itemised at a rate exceeding:

(1)   as regards parts of the initial period falling within the reference period[9] for the purposes of the estimates contained in the landlord's notice, the estimated annual average amount shown in the estimates;

(2)   as regards parts of the initial period not falling within that reference period, the average rate produced by averaging over the reference period all works for which estimates are contained in the notice;

together, in each case, with an inflation allowance[10].

Where a lease of a flat requires the tenant to pay improvement contributions[11], his liability in respect of costs incurred in the initial period of the lease[12] is restricted as follows[13]. He is not required to make any payment in respect of works for which no estimate was given[14] in the landlord's notice[15]; nor is he required to pay in respect of works for which an estimate was given in that notice any more than the amount shown as his estimated contribution in respect of that item, together with an inflation allowance[16].

Where a lease of a flat granted in pursuance of the right to acquire on rent to mortgage terms (so far as still exercisable)[17] requires the tenant to pay service charges in respect of repairs (including works for the making good of structural defects), or improvement contributions, his liability in respect of costs incurred at any time before the final payment is made is restricted in accordance with a statutory formula[18].

1   As to the meaning of 'lease' see PARA 31 note 3.
2   As to the meaning of 'flat' see PARA 231.
3   As to the meaning of 'tenant' see PARA 31 note 3.
4   As to the meaning of 'service charge' see PARA 276 note 19.
5   For these purposes, the initial period of the lease begins with the grant of the lease and ends five years after the grant, except that: (1) if the lease includes provision for service charges to be payable in respect of costs incurred in a period before the grant of the lease, the initial period begins with the beginning of that period; and (2) if the lease provides for service charges to be calculated by reference to a specified annual period, the initial period continues until the end of the fifth such period beginning after the grant of the lease: Housing Act 1985 Sch 6 para 16B(4) (Sch 6 paras 16B–16D added by the Housing and Planning Act 1986 s 4(4), (6); the Housing Act 1985 Sch 6 para 16B(4) amended by the Leasehold Reform, Housing and Urban Development Act 1993 s 187(2), Sch 22). See also PARAS 230 notes 7, 9, 300 note 9, 305 note 3.
6   Housing Act 1985 Sch 6 para 16B(1) (as added: see note 5).
7   Ie a notice under the Housing Act 1985 s 125: see PARA 276.
8   Housing Act 1985 Sch 6 para 16B(2) (as added: see note 5). The appropriate national authority may by order prescribe: (1) the method by which inflation allowances for the purposes of Sch 6 para 16B or Sch 6 para 16C are to be calculated by reference to published statistics; and (2) the information to be given to a tenant when he is asked to pay a service charge or improvement contribution to which the provisions of Sch 6 para 16B or Sch 6 para 16C are or may be relevant: Sch 6 para 16D(1) (as added: see note 5). Such an order: (a) may make different provision for different cases or descriptions of case, including different provision for different areas; (b) may contain such incidental, supplementary or transitional provisions as the appropriate national authority thinks appropriate; and (c) must be made by statutory instrument which is subject, if made by the Secretary of State, to annulment in pursuance of a resolution of either House of Parliament: see Sch 6 para 16D(2) (as so added). As to the exercise of the power so conferred see the Housing (Right to Buy) (Service Charges) Order 1986, SI 1986/2195 (amended by SI 2008/533 and SI 2010/2769). As to the appropriate national authority, the Secretary of State and the transfer of functions under the Housing Act 1985, so far as exercisable in relation to Wales, to the Welsh Ministers see PARA 7.
9   As to the meaning of 'reference period' see PARA 277 note 4.
10 Housing Act 1985 Sch 6 para 16B(3) (as added: see note 5).

11 As to the meaning of 'improvement contribution' see PARA 276 note 20.

12 For these purposes, the initial period of the lease begins with the grant of the lease and ends five years after the grant, except that: (1) if the lease includes provision for improvement contributions to be payable in respect of costs incurred in a period before the grant of the lease, the initial period begins with the beginning of that period; and (2) if the lease provides for improvement contributions to be calculated by reference to a specified annual period, the initial period continues until the end of the fifth such period beginning after the grant of the lease: Housing Act 1985 Sch 6 para 16C(4) (as added (see note 4); amended by the Leasehold Reform, Housing and Urban Development Act 1993 Sch 22).

13 Housing Act 1985 Sch 6 para 16C(1) (as added: see note 5).

14 Ie given in the landlord's notice under the Housing Act 1985 s 125: see PARA 276. As to the meaning of 'landlord' see PARA 31 note 3.

15 Housing Act 1985 Sch 6 para 16C(2) (as added: see note 5).

16 Housing Act 1985 Sch 6 para 16C(3) (as added: see note 5). As to the method by which inflation allowances are to be calculated see note 8.

17 As to the right to acquire on rent to mortgage terms, which is now only exercisable if claimed before 18 July 2005, see PARA 318.

18 See the Housing Act 1985 Sch 6 para 16E(1), (2) (added by the Leasehold Reform, Housing and Urban Development Act 1993 s 116(2)). The Housing Act 1985 Sch 6 para 16E is omitted where: (1) the right to acquire conferred by the Housing Act 1996 (see PARAS 242–244) or the Housing and Regeneration Act 2008 (see PARAS 240–241) arises (see the Housing (Right to Acquire) Regulations 1997, SI 1997/619, Sch 1 para 41(c)); (2) the Housing (Preservation of Right to Buy) Regulations 1993, SI 1993/2241 (see PARA 334 et seq), apply (see Sch 1 para 43(b)(iv)).

312. Avoidance of certain provisions. A provision of the lease[1], or of an agreement collateral to it, is void in so far as it purports to prohibit or restrict the assignment of the lease or the subletting, wholly or in part, of the dwelling house[2].

Where the dwelling house is a flat[3], a provision of the lease or of an agreement collateral to it is void in so far as it purports:

(1)   to authorise the recovery of a contribution in respect of repairs etc[4] otherwise than in accordance with the statutory provisions[5]; or

(2)   to authorise the recovery of any charge in respect of costs incurred by the landlord[6]:

    (a)   in discharging the obligations imposed by the implied covenant relating to rebuilding, reinstatement etc[7] or those obligations as modified[8]; or

    (b)   in contributing to costs incurred by a superior landlord or other person in discharging obligations to the like effect; or

(3)   to authorise the recovery of an improvement contribution[9] otherwise than in accordance with[10] the statutory provisions[11].

A provision of the lease, or of an agreement collateral to it, is void in so far as it purports to authorise a forfeiture, or to impose on the tenant[12] a penalty or disability, in the event of his enforcing or relying on the terms to be included[13] in the lease[14].

1   As to the meaning of 'lease' see PARA 31 note 3.

2   Housing Act 1985 Sch 6 para 17(1); and see PARA 230 notes 7, 9. Schedule 6 para 17(1) has effect subject to s 157 (restriction on disposal of dwellings in National Parks, etc: see PARA 333): Sch 6 para 17(2). As to the meaning of 'dwelling house' see PARA 231. Schedule 6 para 17(2) is omitted where the right to acquire conferred by the Housing Act 1996 (see PARAS 242–244) or the Housing and Regeneration Act 2008 (see PARAS 240–241) arises: see the Housing (Right to Acquire) Regulations 1997, SI 1997/619, reg 2, Sch 1 para 41(d), applying in relation to the right to acquire under the Housing and Regeneration Act 2008 by virtue of s 184, which applies the Housing Act 1996 s 17 (regulations modifying the Housing Act 1985): see PARA 241. See also PARAS 300 note 9, 305 note 3.

3   As to the meaning of 'flat' see PARA 231.

4   Ie the recovery of such a charge as is mentioned in the Housing Act 1985 Sch 6 para 16A: see PARA 310.

5   Ie otherwise than in accordance with the Housing Act 1985 Sch 6 para 16A or Sch 6 para 16B: see PARA 310.

6 As to the meaning of 'landlord' see PARA 31 note 3.
7 Ie the covenant implied by the Housing Act 1985 Sch 6 para 14(3): see PARA 307.
8 Ie as modified by the Housing Act 1985 Sch 6 para 14(4): see PARA 307.
9 As to the meaning of 'improvement contribution' see PARA 276 note 20.
10 Ie otherwise than in accordance with the Housing Act 1985 Sch 6 para 16C: see PARA 311.
11 Housing Act 1985 Sch 6 para 18 (added by the Housing and Planning Act 1986 s 4(5), (6)). See *Coventry City Council v Cole* [1994] 1 All ER 997, (1993) 25 HLR 555, CA.
12 As to the meaning of 'tenant' see PARA 31 note 3.
13 Ie in the event of his enforcing or relying on the Housing Act 1985 Sch 6 paras 1–18: see the text and notes 1–12; and PARA 300 et seq.
14 Housing Act 1985 Sch 6 para 19.

(d) Charges

313. Conveyance of freehold. The following provisions apply to a charge, however created or arising, on the freehold where the freehold is conveyed in pursuance of the right to buy[1] or the right to acquire conferred by the Housing Act 1996[2] or the Housing and Regeneration Act 2008[3].

If the charge is not a tenant's incumbrance[4] and is not a rentcharge[5], the conveyance is effective to release the freehold from the charge[6], provided, in the case of the right to acquire, that the statutory conditions[7] are satisfied[8]. The release does not affect the personal liability of the landlord[9] or any other person in respect of any obligation which the charge was created to secure[10].

If the charge is a rentcharge, the conveyance must be made subject to the charge; but, if the rentcharge also affects other land:

(1)   the conveyance must contain a covenant by the landlord to indemnify the tenant[11] and his successors in title in respect of any liability arising under the rentcharge; and

(2)   if the rentcharge is of a kind which may be redeemed under the Rentcharges Act 1977[12], the landlord must immediately after the conveyance take such steps as are necessary to redeem the rentcharge so far as it affects land owned by him[13].

1 As to the meaning of 'the right to buy' see PARA 239.
2 See PARAS 242–244.
3 Housing Act 1985 Sch 6 para 21(1); and see PARA 230 notes 7, 9. As to the right to acquire conferred by the Housing and Regeneration Act 2008 see PARAS 240–241.
4 As to the meaning of 'tenant's incumbrance' see PARA 300 note 9.
5 For these purposes, 'rentcharge' has the same meaning as in the Rentcharges Act 1977 (see REAL PROPERTY AND REGISTRATION vol 87 (2012) PARA 1109): Housing Act 1985 Sch 6 para 21(4).
6 Housing Act 1985 Sch 6 para 21(2); and see the text and notes 7–8. Schedule 6 para 21(2)–(4) is modified where the extended right to buy (see PARA 233) arises: see the Housing (Extension of Right to Buy) Order 1993, SI 1993/2240, Schedule para 69(b). See also PARA 300 note 9. Where that right arises, the Housing Act 1985 Sch 6 para 21A (added for these purposes) applies to a charge (however created or arising) on a lease (including the secure tenancy) extinguished by s 139(2) (terms and effect of conveyance and mortgage: see PARA 291) when the freehold is conveyed in pursuance of the right to buy: Sch 6 para 21A(1) (Sch 6 para 21A added for these purposes by the Housing (Extension of Right to Buy) Order 1993, SI 1993/2240, Schedule para 69(c)). The extinguishment of the lease does not affect the personal liability of the landlord or intermediate landlord (as the case may be) or of any other person in respect of any obligation which the charge was created to secure: Housing Act 1985 Sch 6 para 21A(2) (as so added). As to the meaning of 'intermediate landlord' see PARA 233 note 18.
7 Ie provided that: (1) the landlord has complied with the requirements imposed on the landlord by Sch 6 para 22 (see PARA 315); or (2) the holder of the charge has agreed in writing with the landlord that Sch 6 para 22 is not to apply.
8 See the Housing Act 1985 Sch 6 para 21(2) (modified for these purposes by the Housing (Right to Acquire) Regulations 1997, SI 1997/619, Sch 1 para 41(f), applying in relation to the right to acquire under the Housing and Regeneration Act 2008 by virtue of s 184, which applies the Housing Act 1996 s 17 (regulations modifying the Housing Act 1985): see PARA 241).

9 As to the meaning of 'landlord' see PARA 31 note 3.

10 See notes 6, 8.

11 As to the meaning of 'tenant' see PARA 31 note 3.

12 See REAL PROPERTY AND REGISTRATION vol 87 (2012) PARA 1169 et seq.

13 Housing Act 1985 Sch 6 para 21(3). For the purposes of Sch 6 para 21(3), land is owned by a person if he is the owner of it within the meaning of the Rentcharges Act 1977 s 13(1) (see REAL PROPERTY AND REGISTRATION vol 87 (2012) PARA 1110); and (2) for the purposes of the Housing Act 1985 Sch 6 para 21(3) and the Rentcharges Act 1977 land which has been conveyed by the landlord in pursuance of the right to buy but subject to the rentcharges is to be treated as if it had not been so conveyed but had continued to be owned by him: Housing Act 1985 Sch 6 para 21(4).

314. Grant of lease. A charge, however created or arising, on the interest of the landlord[1] which is not a tenant's incumbrance[2] does not affect a lease[3] granted in pursuance of the right to buy[4] or the right to acquire conferred by the Housing Act 1996[5] or the Housing and Regeneration Act 2008[6], provided, in the case of the right to acquire, that the statutory conditions[7] are satisfied[8].

1 As to the meaning of 'landlord' see PARA 31 note 3.

2 As to the meaning of 'tenant's incumbrance' see PARA 300 note 9.

3 As to the meaning of 'lease' see PARA 31 note 3.

4 As to the meaning of 'the right to buy' see PARA 239.

5 See PARAS 242–244.

6 Housing Act 1985 Sch 6 para 20; and see PARA 230 notes 7, 9. As to the right to acquire conferred by the Housing and Regeneration Act 2008 see PARAS 240–241.

   The Housing Act 1985 Sch 6 para 20 is omitted where the Housing (Extension of Right to Buy) Order 1993, SI 1993/2240 (see PARA 233), applies: see Schedule para 69(a).

7 Ie provided that: (1) the landlord has complied with the requirements imposed on the landlord by the Housing Act 1985 Sch 6 para 22 (see PARA 315); or (2) the holder of the charge has agreed in writing with the landlord that Sch 6 para 22 is not to apply.

8 See the Housing Act 1985 Sch 6 para 20 (modified by the Housing (Right to Acquire) Regulations 1997, SI 1997/619, Sch 1 para 41(e), applying in relation to the right to acquire under the Housing and Regeneration Act 2008 by virtue of s 184, which applies the Housing Act 1996 s 17 (regulations modifying the Housing Act 1985): see PARA 241). The release does not, however, affect the personal liability of the landlord or any other person in respect of any obligation the charge was created to secure: see the Housing Act 1985 Sch 6 para 20 (as so modified).

315. Notice to lenders and discharge of the charge on the landlord's interest in the dwelling house where the right to acquire is exercised. Where the right to acquire conferred by the Housing Act 1996[1] or the Housing and Regeneration Act 2008[2] arises, the following provisions apply to a charge, however created or arising, on the interest of the landlord[3] in the dwelling house[4], unless and until the landlord and the holder of the charge at any time agree otherwise in writing[5]. Within seven days of the landlord receiving the tenant's written notice of intention to pursue his claim to the right to acquire[6], the landlord must serve on the holder of any charge secured against the dwelling house a written notice stating the purchase price of the dwelling house and the amount of discount and whether the landlord intends to redeem the charge in respect of the dwelling house on the grant of the lease or the conveyance of the freehold to the tenant pursuant to the right to acquire[7]. If the landlord's notice states that he intends to redeem the charge then, on the grant of the lease or the conveyance of the freehold, the sum required to redeem the charge must be paid by the landlord to the charge holder and the charge holder must supply to the landlord the necessary documentation to release the charge in respect of the dwelling house[8]. If the landlord does not intend to redeem the charge on the grant of a lease or the conveyance of the freehold the landlord's notice must, in addition, offer to the holder of the sole charge or the charge having priority the option of either:

(1)   taking as alternative security[9] a charge on the interest in a property of the landlord which has a value, excluding any amount secured by a charge with priority on the landlord's interest in the property, equal to or greater than the purchase price of the dwelling house plus the discount; or

(2)   an amount equal to the purchase price of the dwelling house plus the discount[10].

The landlord is not, however, required to offer a property as alternative security unless the landlord owns a freehold or leasehold interest in a property with a value, excluding any amount secured by a charge on the interest which is being offered in the property, equal to or greater than the purchase price plus discount[11].

Where head (1) or head (2) above applies, within 14 days of receipt of the landlord's notice the charge holder must serve on the landlord a written notice stating the option exercised by the charge holder[12].

Where the charge holder exercises the option specified in head (1) above, the landlord must within 14 days of receipt of the charge holder's notice offer the charge holder a specified property in accordance with that head[13]. Where the charge holder accepts the property offered as alternative security the landlord must take all reasonable steps to enable the charge holder to secure a charge against the landlord's interest in the property within whichever is the later of:

(a)   21 days of the date on which the landlord receives notification of the charge holder's acceptance of the property as alternative security; or

(b)   the grant of the lease or the conveyance of the freehold of the dwelling house pursuant to the right to acquire[14].

If the landlord fails to take all reasonable steps to enable the charge holder to secure a charge against the landlord's interest in accordance with head (a) or head (b) above, the charge holder may require the landlord to pay within seven days an amount equal to the purchase price of the dwelling house plus the discount[15]. Where the charge holder rejects the property offered as alternative security the charge holder may require the landlord to pay an amount equal to the purchase price of the dwelling house plus the discount within whichever is the later of:

(i)   21 days of the date on which the landlord receives notification of the charge holder's rejection of the property; or

(ii)   the grant of the lease or the conveyance of the freehold of the dwelling house pursuant to the right to acquire[16].

Where the charge holder exercises the option in head (2) above, the landlord must pay the sum specified in that head on the grant of the lease or the conveyance of the freehold of the dwelling house pursuant to the right to acquire[17].

Where the landlord and the charge holder have agreed in writing that the provisions set out above[18] are not to apply, on the grant of the lease or the conveyance of the freehold pursuant to the right to acquire the landlord must supply to the tenant a certificate confirming the agreement together with a copy of the agreement which is certified as a true copy[19]. Where, however, the provisions set out above apply, then provided that the landlord has complied with the requirements imposed on the landlord by them, any holder of a charge on the landlord's interest in the dwelling house must, on the grant of the lease or the conveyance of the freehold of the dwelling house pursuant to the right to acquire, provide to the landlord such documentation as is necessary to discharge their charge in respect of the dwelling house[20]. Where a charge holder does not so provide the documentation, or where the charge holder has failed to serve a notice stating the option exercised by him[21], the landlord must, on the grant of the lease or the conveyance of the freehold pursuant to the right to acquire, supply to the tenant a certificate stating that the landlord has complied with the requirements imposed on the landlord by the provisions set out above[22].

1   See PARAS 242–244.
2   See PARAS 240–241.
3   As to the meaning of 'landlord' see PARA 31 note 3.
4   As to the meaning of 'dwelling house' see PARA 231.
5   Housing Act 1985 Sch 6 para 22(1) (Sch 6 paras 22, 23 added for these purposes by the Housing (Right to Acquire) Regulations 1997, SI 1997/619, Sch 1 para 41(g), applying in relation to the right to acquire under the Housing and Regeneration Act 2008 by virtue of s 184, which applies the Housing Act 1996 s 17 (regulations modifying the Housing Act 1985): see PARA 241).
6   Ie under the Housing Act 1985 s 125D: see PARA 273.
7   Housing Act 1985 Sch 6 para 22(2) (as added: see note 5).
8   Housing Act 1985 Sch 6 para 22(3) (as added: see note 5).
9   Ie subject to the Housing Act 1985 Sch 6 para 22(5): see the text and note 11.
10 Housing Act 1985 Sch 6 para 22(4) (as added: see note 5).
11 Housing Act 1985 Sch 6 para 22(5) (as added: see note 5).
12 Housing Act 1985 Sch 6 para 22(6) (as added: see note 5).
13 Housing Act 1985 Sch 6 para 22(7) (as added: see note 5).
14 Housing Act 1985 Sch 6 para 22(8) (as added: see note 5).
15 Housing Act 1985 Sch 6 para 22(9) (as added: see note 5).
16 Housing Act 1985 Sch 6 para 22(10) (as added: see note 5).
17 Housing Act 1985 Sch 6 para 22(11) (as added: see note 5).
18 Ie the provisions of the Housing Act 1985 Sch 6 para 22: see the text and notes 1–17.
19 Housing Act 1985 Sch 6 para 23(1) (as added: see note 5). See also note 22.
20 Housing Act 1985 Sch 6 para 23(2) (as added: see note 5).
21 Ie in accordance with the Housing Act 1985 Sch 6 para 22(6): see the text and note 12.
22 Housing Act 1985 Sch 6 para 23(3) (as added: see note 5). A certificate under Sch 6 para 23(1) or (3) is effective to release the dwelling house from the charge on the interest of the landlord to which the certificate applies but does not affect the personal liability of the landlord or any other person in respect of any obligation which such a charge was created to secure: Sch 6 para 23(4) (as so added). As to the form of the certificate see Sch 6 para 23(5) (as so added). The Chief Land Registrar must, for the purpose of registration of title, accept such certificate as sufficient evidence of the facts stated in it, but if as a result he has to meet a claim against him under the Land Registration Act 2002 or its predecessor legislation the landlord is liable to indemnify him: see the Housing Act 1985 Sch 6 para 23(6) (as so added).

(D)   Completion Notices

316. Landlord's first notice to complete. The landlord[1] may serve on the tenant[2] at any time a written notice requiring him:

(1)   if all relevant matters[3] have been agreed or determined, to complete the transaction within a period stated in the notice; or

(2)   if any relevant matters are outstanding, to serve on the landlord within that period a written notice to that effect specifying the matters,

and informing the tenant of the effect of these provisions[4] and of the statutory provisions[5] relating to a landlord's second notice to complete[6]. The period so stated in a notice must be such period, of at least 56 days, as may be reasonable in the circumstances[7].

Such a notice may not, however, be served earlier than three months after:

(a)   the service of the landlord's notice of the purchase price and other matters[8]; or

(b)   in the case of the right to buy[9], but not of the right to acquire conferred by the Housing Act 1996[10] or the Housing and Regeneration Act 2008[11], where a notice has been served by the landlord admitting or denying the tenant's right to acquire on rent to mortgage terms, where still exercisable[12], the service of that notice[13].

Such a notice may not be served if:

(i)   a requirement for the determination or redetermination of the value of the dwelling house[14] by the district valuer[15] has not been complied with;

(ii)   a review notice[16] has been served in relation to such a determination or redetermination, the statutory provisions with regard to carrying out a review[17] apply and the district valuer has neither served a notice of refusal to make a further determination[18], nor served a determination effect notice[19];

(iii)   no such review notice has been served but such a notice may still be served[20];

(iv)   proceedings for the determination of any other relevant matter have not been disposed of; or

(v)   any relevant matter stated to be outstanding in a written notice served on the landlord by the tenant has not been agreed in writing or determined[21].

1   As to the meaning of 'landlord' see PARA 31 note 3.
2   As to the meaning of 'tenant' see PARA 31 note 3.
3   For these purposes, 'relevant matters' means matters relating to the grant: Housing Act 1985 s 140(5) (amended by the Leasehold Reform, Housing and Urban Development Act 1993 s 187(2), Sch 22). A notice by the tenant requesting that the name of a family member who has been nominated as joint purchaser be removed from the application for the right to buy is a relevant outstanding matter if served within the completion period: *Sebanjor v Brent London Borough Council* [2001] 1 WLR 2374, [2001] LGR 339, sub nom *Senbanjo v Brent London Borough Council* (2001) Times, 4 January, [2000] All ER (D) 2393 (tenant's decision to remove the family member's name meant time began to run again and the second notice to complete was invalid).
4   Ie the effect of the Housing Act 1985 s 140.
5   Ie the effect of the Housing Act 1985 s 141(1), (2), (4): see PARA 317.
6   Housing Act 1985 s 140(1); and see PARA 230 notes 7, 9. Section 140 is modified where the Housing (Extension of Right to Buy) Order 1993, SI 1993/2240 (see PARA 233), applies: see Schedule para 23.
7   Housing Act 1985 s 140(2); and see PARA 230 notes 7, 9. See also note 6.
8   Ie the notice under the Housing Act 1985 s 125: see PARA 276.
9   As to the meaning of 'the right to buy' see PARA 239.
10 See PARAS 242–244.
11 See PARAS 240–241.
12 Ie a notice under the Housing Act 1985 s 146: see PARA 318. The right to acquire on rent to mortgage terms is now only exercisable if claimed before 18 July 2005: see s 142A; and PARA 318.
13 Housing Act 1985 s 140(3) (substituted by the Leasehold Reform, Housing and Urban Development Act 1993 s 197(1), Sch 21 para 12; amended by the Housing Act 2004 s 184(1), (2); further substituted for the purposes of the right to acquire by the Housing (Right to Acquire) Regulations 1997, SI 1997/619, Sch 1 para 15, applying in relation to the right to acquire under the Housing and Regeneration Act 2008 by virtue of s 184, which applies the Housing Act 1996 s 17 (regulations modifying the Housing Act 1985): see PARA 241).
    The Housing Act 1985 s 140(3) is further substituted where the Housing (Preservation of Right to Buy) Regulations 1993, SI 1993/2241 (see PARA 334 et seq), apply: see Sch 1 para 15.
14 As to the meaning of 'dwelling house' see PARA 231.
15 As to the meaning of 'district valuer' see PARA 527 note 14.
16 Ie within the meaning of the Housing Act 1985 s 128A: see PARA 285.
17 Ie the Housing Act 1985 s 128B: see PARA 286.
18 Ie a notice under the Housing Act 1985 s 128B(3): see PARA 286.
19 Ie a notice under the Housing Act 1985 s 128B(7): see PARA 286.
20 Ie under the Housing Act 1985 128A: see PARA 285.
21 Housing Act 1985 s 140(4) (amended by the Housing and Regeneration Act 2008 s 306(1), (10)); and see PARA 230 notes 7, 9. See also note 6.

317. Landlord's second notice to complete. If the tenant[1] does not comply with a landlord's first notice to complete[2], the landlord may[3] serve on him a further written notice:

(1)   requiring him to complete the transaction within a period stated in the notice; and

(2)   informing him of the effect of these provisions in the event of his failing to comply[4].

The period stated in such a notice must be such period, of at least 56 days, as may be reasonable in the circumstances[5]; and at any time before the end of that period, or that period as previously extended, the landlord may by a written notice served on the tenant extend it, or further extend it[6].

If the tenant does not comply with such a notice, the notice claiming to exercise the right to buy[7] or the right to acquire conferred by the Housing Act 1996[8] or the Housing and Regeneration Act 2008[9] is deemed to be withdrawn at the end of that period or, as the case may require, that period as so extended[10]. Once this provision has taken effect, the tenant no longer has the protection of the statutory scheme and any extension of time granted by the landlord is at the landlord's discretion[11]. The right to buy is deemed withdrawn even where the landlord's breach of its repairing obligations under the tenancy prevents the tenant from obtaining a mortgage[12].

If such a notice has been served on the tenant and, by virtue of the tenant's failure to pay the rent etc[13], the landlord is not bound to complete, the tenant is deemed not to comply with the notice[14].

1   As to the meaning of 'tenant' see PARA 31 note 3.
2   Ie a notice under the Housing Act 1985 s 140: see PARA 316. As to the meaning of 'landlord' see PARA 31 note 3.
3   The power to serve such a notice is discretionary and does not require the first notice to be followed by a second notice at any given time: *Milne-Berry and Madden v Tower Hamlets London Borough Council* (1997) 30 HLR 229, CA.
4   Housing Act 1985 s 141(1); and see PARA 230 notes 7, 9. Section 141 is modified where the Housing (Extension of Right to Buy) Order 1993, SI 1993/2240 (see PARA 233), applies: see Schedule para 23.
5   Housing Act 1985 s 141(2); and see PARA 230 notes 7, 9.
6   Housing Act 1985 s 141(3); and see PARA 230 notes 7, 9. The requirement that any extension of time must be given in writing: (1) is a formality which can be waived by the individual parties; and (2) does not prevent the doctrine of estoppel operating in favour of the tenant when the landlord has given a verbal extension of time: *Milne-Berry and Madden v Tower Hamlets London Borough Council* (1997) 30 HLR 229, CA, applying *Daejan Properties Ltd v Mahoney* (1995) 28 HLR 498, [1995] 2 EGLR 75, CA.
7   As to the meaning of 'the right to buy' see PARA 239.
8   See PARAS 242–244.
9   See PARAS 240–241.
10 Housing Act 1985 s 141(4); and see PARA 230 notes 7, 9.
11 See *R (on the application of Burrell) v Lambeth London Borough Council* [2006] EWHC 394 (Admin), [2006] RVR 230, [2006] All ER (D) 167 (Feb).
12 *Ryan v Islington London Borough Council* [2009] EWCA Civ 578, [2010] PTSR (CS) 3, [2009] All ER (D) 202 (Jun) (claimant had no right to insist that the completion of the purchase could be deferred until all works of repair and structural rectification had been carried out by the authority).
13 Ie by virtue of the Housing Act 1985 s 138(2): see PARA 291.
14 Housing Act 1985 s 141(5); and see PARA 230 notes 7, 9.

(iii) Transitional Right to Acquire on Rent to Mortgage Terms

318. The former statutory right and the transitional cases in which it may be exercised. Where a secure tenant[1] has claimed to exercise the right to buy[2], his right to buy has been established and his notice claiming to exercise it remains in force, he also has the right[3], in transitional cases, to acquire on rent to mortgage terms in accordance with the relevant statutory provisions[4]. As from 18 July 2005 ('the termination date')[5], that right is not exercisable except in pursuance of a notice served[6] before that date[7]. (Accordingly such claims are probably rare if not obsolete.)

Where the right to buy belongs to two or more persons jointly, the right to acquire on rent to mortgage terms also belongs to them jointly[8].

In the cases in which it may still arise, the right to acquire on rent to mortgage terms cannot be exercised if:

(1)   the exercise of the right to buy is precluded[9] by the existence of the specified circumstances[10]; or

(2)   either it has been determined that the tenant[11] is or was entitled to housing benefit in respect of any part of the relevant period[12], or a claim for housing benefit in respect of any part of that period has been made, or is treated as having been made, by or on behalf of the tenant and has not been determined or withdrawn[13]; or

(3)   the minimum initial payment[14] in respect of the dwelling house exceeds the maximum initial payment[15] in respect of it[16].

The right is not applicable where the preserved right to buy[17] or the right to acquire conferred by the Housing Act 1996[18] or the Housing and Regeneration Act 2008[19] arises[20] and would in any case be excluded from the right under the 2008 Act because of its transitional nature.

It is thought to be unlikely that there are now any cases in which the right to acquire on rent to mortgage terms is still exercisable; but statutory provision is made for:

(a)   the tenant to serve a notice claiming that right[21];

(b)   the landlord to service a notice admitting or denying that right[22];

(c)   the tenant to serve a notice of intention in response to the landlord's notice under head (b) above[23];

(d)   the landlord to serve a notice on the tenant if he is in default of the requirement to serve a notice of intention[24];

(e)   the landlord to serve notice of his share and of the initial discount[25], determined in accordance with the relevant statutory provision[26];

(f)   the effect of a change of landlord after the tenant has given notice claiming to exercise the right to acquire on rent to mortgage terms[27];

(g)   the landlord's duty to convey the freehold or to grant a lease[28];

(h)   the terms and effect of such a conveyance or grant[29];

(i)   redemption of the landlord's share[30];

(j)   the tenant's liability for redemption of the landlord's share to be secured by way of a mortgage[31]; and

(k)   the landlord to serve a first and second notice to complete[32].

1   As to the meaning of 'secure tenant' see PARA 230 note 2.
2   As to the meaning of 'the right to buy' see PARA 239.
3   Ie subject to the Housing Act 1985 s 143(2) (see head (a) in the text) and to s 142A (as added (see the text and notes 5–7), s 143A (see head (b) in the text) and s 143B (see head (c) in the text).
4   See the Housing Act 1985 s 143(1) (s 143 substituted, ss 143A–143C added, by the Leasehold Reform, Housing and Urban Development Act 1993 s 108; the Housing Act 1985 s 143(1) amended by the Housing Act 2004 s 190(2)).
5   For these purposes, 'the termination date' means the date falling eight months after the date of the passing of the Housing Act 2004: Housing Act 1985 s 142A(2) (s 142A added by the Housing Act 2004 s 190(1)).
6   Ie served under the Housing Act 1985 s 144: see the text and note 21.
7   Housing Act 1985 s 142A(1) (as added: see note 5).
8   Housing Act 1985 s 143(3) (as substituted: see note 4).
9   Ie precluded by the Housing Act 1985 s 121: see PARA 257.
10 Housing Act 1985 s 143(2) (as substituted: see note 4).

11 As to the meaning of 'tenant' see PARA 31 note 3.

12 For these purposes, 'the relevant period' means the period: (1) beginning 12 months before the day on which the tenant claims to exercise the right to acquire on rent to mortgage terms; and (2) ending with the day on which the conveyance or grant is executed in pursuance of that right: Housing Act 1985 s 143A(2) (as added: see note 4). Section 143A(2) is modified where the Housing (Extension of Right to Buy) Order 1993, SI 1993/2240 (see PARA 233), applies: see Schedule para 24.

13 Housing Act 1985 s 143A(1) (as added: see note 4). As to housing benefit see WELFARE BENEFITS AND STATE PENSIONS vol 104 (2014) PARA 318 et seq.

14 Where, in the case of a dwelling house which is a house, the weekly rent at the relevant time did not exceed the relevant amount, the minimum initial payment is determined by the formula set out in the Housing Act 1985 s 143B(3); and where, in the case of a dwelling house which is a house, the weekly rent at the relevant time exceeded the relevant amount, the minimum initial payment is determined by the formula set out in s 143B(4). The minimum initial payment in respect of a dwelling house which is a flat is 80% of the amount which would be the minimum initial payment in respect of the dwelling house if it were a house: s 143B(5) (as added: see note 4). As to the meanings of 'dwelling house' and 'flat' see PARA 231.

'Relevant amount' means the amount which at the relevant time was for the time being declared by the appropriate national authority for these purposes; 'relevant time' means the time of the service of the landlord's notice under s 146 (landlord's notice admitting or denying right: see head (b) in the text); and 'rent' means rent payable under the secure tenancy, but excluding any element which is expressed to be payable for services, repairs, maintenance or insurance or the landlord's costs of management: s 143B(8) (as so added). As to the relevant amount and multipliers see further s 143B(6), (7) (as so added).

Section 143B(3), (4), (6), (8) is modified, and s 143B(5) is omitted, where the Housing (Extension of Right to Buy) Order 1993, SI 1993/2240, applies: see Schedule para 25.

15 The maximum initial payment in respect of a dwelling house is 80% per cent of the price which would be payable if the tenant were exercising the right to buy: Housing Act 1985 s 143B(2) (as added: see note 4).

16 Housing Act 1985 s 143B(1) (as added: see note 4).

17 As to the preserved right to buy see PARA 334 et seq.

18 See PARAS 242–244.

19 See PARAS 240–241.

20 See the Housing (Preservation of Right to Buy) Regulations 1993, SI 1993/2241, Sch 1 paras 16, 44; the Housing (Right to Acquire) Regulations 1997, SI 1997/619, Sch 1 paras 16, 42, applying in relation to the right to acquire under the Housing and Regeneration Act 2008 by virtue of s 184, which applies the Housing Act 1996 s 17 (regulations modifying the Housing Act 1985): see PARA 241.

21 See the Housing Act 1985 s 144 (substituted by the Leasehold Reform, Housing and Urban Development Act 1993 s 109; amended by the Housing Act 2004 s 190(3); modified where the Housing (Extension of Right to Buy) Order 1993, SI 1993/2240, applies: see Schedule para 26). Where that Order applies, provision is also made for withdrawal of the tenant's notice: see Schedule para 27, adding the Housing Act 1985 s 144A for those purposes.

22 See the Housing Act 1985 s 146 (substituted by the Leasehold Reform, Housing and Urban Development Act 1993 s 110; modified where the Housing (Extension of Right to Buy) Order 1993, SI 1993/2240, applies: see Schedule para 28).

23 See the Housing Act 1985 s 146A (ss 146A, 146B added by the Leasehold Reform, Housing and Urban Development Act 1993 s 111; modified where the Housing (Extension of Right to Buy) Order 1993, SI 1993/2240, applies: see Schedule para 29).

24 See the Housing Act 1985 s 146B (as added (see note 23); modified where the extended right to buy applies (see note 23)).

25 See the Housing Act 1985 s 147 (substituted by the Leasehold Reform, Housing and Urban Development Act 1993 s 112; modified where the Housing (Extension of Right to Buy) Order 1993, SI 1993/2240, applies: see Schedule para 30).

26 See the Housing Act 1985 s 148 (substituted by the Leasehold Reform, Housing and Urban Development Act 1993 s 113).

27 See the Housing Act 1985 s 149 (substituted by the Leasehold Reform, Housing and Urban Development Act 1993 s 114; modified where the Housing (Extension of Right to Buy) Order 1993, SI 1993/2240, applies: see Schedule para 31).

28 See the Housing Act 1985 s 150 (substituted by the Leasehold Reform, Housing and Urban Development Act 1993 s 115; modified where the Housing (Extension of Right to Buy) Order 1993, SI 1993/2240, applies: see Schedule para 32). Where that Order applies, provision is also

made for apportionment of the initial payment and the power to agree the final apportionment: see Schedule para 33, adding the Housing Act 1985 ss 150A, 150B for those purposes.

29 See the Housing Act 1985 s 151 (substituted by the Leasehold Reform, Housing and Urban Development Act 1993 s 116(1); modified where the Housing (Extension of Right to Buy) Order 1993, SI 1993/2240, applies: see Schedule para 34).

30 See the Housing Act 1985 s 151A, Sch 6A (added by the Leasehold Reform, Housing and Urban Development Act 1993 s 117; modified where the Housing (Extension of Right to Buy) Order 1993, SI 1993/2240, applies: see Schedule paras 35, 70).

31 See the Housing Act 1985 s 151B (added by the Leasehold Reform, Housing and Urban Development Act 1993 s 118; amended by the Government of Wales Act 1998 s 140, Sch 16 para 5; the Housing and Regeneration Act 2008 s 307(5); the Localism Act 2011 s 195(1), Sch 19 paras 10, 14; and by SI 2001/3649 and SI 2010/866; modified where the Housing (Extension of Right to Buy) Order 1993, SI 1993/2240, applies: see Schedule para 36).

32 See the Housing Act 1985 ss 152, 153 (amended by the Leasehold Reform, Housing and Urban Development Act 1993 s 119(1)–(3); modified where the Housing (Extension of Right to Buy) Order 1993, SI 1993/2240, applies: see Schedule para 37).

(iv) Tenant's Sanctions for Landlord's Delays in the Case of the Right to Buy

319. Tenant's notices of delay. Where a secure tenant[1] has claimed to exercise the right to buy[2], he may serve on his landlord[3] a notice (an 'initial notice of delay') in any of the following cases, namely:

(1)   where the landlord has failed to serve a notice[4] within the appropriate period[5];

(2)   where the tenant's right to buy has been established and the landlord has failed to serve a notice[6] within the appropriate period[7];

(3)   where the tenant considers that delays on the part of the landlord are preventing him from exercising expeditiously his right to buy or his right to acquire on rent to mortgage terms[8] (if he has claimed the latter right before 18 July 2005[9]).

An initial notice of delay:

(a)   must specify the most recent action of which the tenant is aware which has been taken by the landlord[10]; and

(b)   must specify a period ('the response period'), not being less than one month, beginning on the date of service of the notice, within which the service by the landlord of a counter-notice will have the effect of cancelling the initial notice of delay[11].

Within the response period specified in an initial notice of delay or at any time thereafter, the landlord may serve on the tenant a counter-notice in either of the following circumstances:

(i)   if the initial notice specifies either of the cases in heads (1) and (2) above and the landlord has served, or is serving together with the counter-notice, the required notice[12]; or

(ii)   if the initial notice specifies the case in head (3) above and there is no action[13] which, at the beginning of the response period, it was for the landlord to take in order to allow the tenant expeditiously to exercise his right to acquire on rent to mortgage terms and which remains to be taken at the time of service of the counter-notice[14].

Such a counter-notice must specify the circumstances by virtue of which it is served[15].

At any time when the response period specified in an initial notice of delay has expired and the landlord has not so served a counter-notice, the tenant may serve on the landlord a notice (an 'operative notice of delay') which must state that the statutory provisions relating to payments of rent attributable to the purchase price[16] will apply to payments of rent made by the tenant on or after the default date or, if the initial notice of delay specified the case in head (3) above, the date of service of the notice[17].

If, after a tenant has served an initial notice of delay, a counter-notice has been so served, then, whether or not the tenant has also served an operative notice of delay, if any of the cases in heads (1) to (3) above again arises, the tenant may serve a further initial notice of delay and the above provisions apply again accordingly[18].

The above provisions do not apply to the right to acquire conferred by the Housing Act 1996[19] or the Housing and Regeneration Act 2008[20].

1   As to the meaning of 'secure tenant' see PARA 230 note 2; and as to the meaning of 'tenant' see PARA 31 note 3.
2   As to the meaning of 'the right to buy' see PARA 239.
3   As to the meaning of 'landlord' see PARA 31 note 3.
4   Ie a notice under the Housing Act 1985 s 124: see PARA 275.
5   Ie within the period appropriate under the Housing Act 1985 s 124(2) or s 124(3): see PARA 275.
6   Ie a notice under the Housing Act 1985 s 125: see PARA 276.
7   Ie the period appropriate under the Housing Act 1985 s 125(1): see PARA 276.
8   Housing Act 1985 s 153A(1) (s 153A added by the Housing Act 1988 s 124; the Housing Act 1985 s 153A(1) amended by the Leasehold Reform, Housing and Urban Development Act 1993 s 187(1), (2), Sch 21 para 13(2), Sch 22; and, in relation to Wales, by the Housing (Wales) Measure 2011 s 31(1), (4)). As to the meaning of 'the right to acquire on rent to mortgage terms' see PARA 318.
    Where an initial notice of delay specifies either of the cases in the Housing Act 1985 s 153A(1)(a), (b) (see heads (1)–(2) in the text), any reference in s 153A or s 153B (see PARA 320) to the default date is a reference to the end of the period referred to in s 153A(1)(a) or, as the case may be s 153A(1)(b) or, if it is later, 10 March 1989: s 153A(1) (as so added and amended). For the prescribed form of an initial notice of delay see the Housing (Right to Buy Delay Procedure) (Prescribed Forms) Regulations 1989, SI 1989/240, reg 2(a), Schedule, Form RTB6 (amended by SI 1993/2245; revoked in relation to Wales by SI 2015/1320). A form substantially to the like effect may be used: see the Housing (Right to Buy Delay Procedure) (Prescribed Forms) Regulations 1989, SI 1989/240, reg 2. In Wales, for the prescribed form see the Housing (Right to Buy) (Prescribed Forms) (Wales) Regulations 2015, SI 2015/1320, under which an initial notice of delay is to be in the form set out in Sch 3, Form WRTB3 or in a form substantially to the like effect (reg 4).
9   See the Housing Act 1985 s 142A; and PARA 318.
10 Ie pursuant to the Housing Act 1985 Pt V (ss 118–188): see PARAS 230 et seq, 1991 et seq.
11 Housing Act 1985 s 153A(2) (as added: see note 8).
12 Ie the required notice under the Housing Act 1985 s 124 or s 125.
13 Ie under the Housing Act 1985 Pt V.
14 Housing Act 1985 s 153A(3) (as added (see note 8); amended by the Leasehold Reform, Housing and Urban Development Act 1993 Sch 21 para 13(3)). For the prescribed form of counter-notice see the Housing (Right to Buy Delay Procedure) (Prescribed Forms) Regulations 1989, SI 1989/240, reg 2(b), Schedule, Form RTB7 (amended by SI 1993/2245; revoked in relation to Wales by SI 2015/1320). In Wales, for the prescribed form see the Housing (Right to Buy) (Prescribed Forms) (Wales) Regulations 2015, SI 2015/1320, reg 5, Sch 4, Form WRTB4. As to the use of a form substantially to the like effect see note 8.
15 Housing Act 1985 s 153A(4) (as added: see note 8).
16 Ie the Housing Act 1985 s 153B: see PARA 320. As to the meaning of references to the purchase price see PARA 283 note 8.
17 Housing Act 1985 s 153A(5) (as added: see note 8). For the prescribed form of operative notice of delay see the Housing (Right to Buy Delay Procedure) (Prescribed Forms) Regulations 1989, SI 1989/240, reg 2(c), Schedule, Form RTB8 (amended by SI 1993/2245 revoked in relation to Wales by SI 2015/1320). In Wales, for the prescribed form see the Housing (Right to Buy) (Prescribed Forms) (Wales) Regulations 2015, SI 2015/1320, reg 6, Sch 6, Form WRTB5. As to the use of a form substantially to the like effect see note 8.
18 Housing Act 1985 s 153A(6) (as added: see note 8). The Housing Act 1985 s 153A (as added and amended) is modified where: (1) the Housing (Extension of Right to Buy) Order 1993, SI 1993/2240 (see PARA 233), applies (see Schedule para 38); (2) the Housing (Preservation of Right to Buy) Regulations 1993, SI 1993/2241 (see PARA 334 et seq), apply (see Sch 1 para 17).
19 See PARAS 242–244.

20 See the Housing (Right to Acquire) Regulations 1997, SI 1997/619, Sch 1 para 17, applying in relation to the right to acquire under the Housing and Regeneration Act 2008 by virtue of s 184, which applies the Housing Act 1996 s 17 (regulations modifying the Housing Act 1985): see PARA 241. As to the right to acquire under the 2008 Act see PARAS 240–241.

320. Payments of rent attributable to purchase price etc. Where a secure tenant[1] has served on his landlord[2] an operative notice of delay[3], the following provisions apply to any payment of rent[4] which is made on or after the default date[5] or, as the case may be, the date of service of the notice and before the occurrence of any of the following events and, if more than one event occurs, before the earliest to occur:

(1)   the service by the landlord of a counter-notice[6];

(2)   the date on which the landlord makes to the tenant the required grant[7];

(3)   the date on which the tenant withdraws or is deemed to have withdrawn the notice claiming to exercise the right to buy[8] or, as the case may be, the notice claiming the right to acquire on rent to mortgage terms[9]; and

(4)   the date on which the tenant ceases to be entitled to exercise the right to buy[10].

Except where these provisions cease to apply on a date determined under head (3) or head (4) above, so much of any payment of rent to which these provisions apply as does not consist of a sum due on account of rates, council tax or a service charge[11] is treated not only as a payment of rent but also a payment on account by the tenant which is to be taken[12] into account[13]; and, in such a case, the amount which would otherwise be the purchase price[14] or, as the case may be, the tenant's initial payment[15] must be reduced by an amount equal to the aggregate of:

(a)   the total of any payments on account treated as having been so paid by the tenant; and

(b)   if those payments on account are derived from payments of rent referable to a period of more than 12 months, a sum equal to the appropriate percentage[16] of the total referred to in head (a) above[17].

The above provisions do not apply to the right to acquire conferred by the Housing Act 1996[18] or the Housing and Regeneration Act 2008[19].

1   As to the meaning of 'secure tenant' see PARA 230 note 2.
2   As to the meaning of 'landlord' see PARA 31 note 3.
3   As to the meaning of 'operative notice of delay' see PARA 319.
4   The crediting of housing benefit to the rent account of a local authority tenant is a payment of rent for these purposes: *Hanoman v Southwark London Borough Council* [2009] UKHL 29, [2009] 4 All ER 585, [2009] 1 WLR 1367.
5   As to the meaning of references to the default date see PARA 319 note 8.
6   Ie under the Housing Act 1985 s 153A(3): see PARA 319.
7   Ie the grant required by the Housing Act 1985 s 138 (see PARA 291) or, as the case may be, s 150 (see PARA 318).
8   As to the meaning of 'the right to buy' see PARA 239.
9   As to the meaning of 'the right to acquire on rent to mortgage terms' see PARA 318. That right is only exercisable if claimed before 18 July 2005: see PARA 318.
10 Housing Act 1985 s 153B(1) (s 153B added by the Housing Act 1988 s 124; the Housing Act 1985 s 153B(1) amended by the Leasehold Reform, Housing and Urban Development Act 1993 s 187(1), (2), Sch 21 para 14(1), Sch 22).
11 Ie as defined in the Housing Act 1985 s 621A: see PARA 276 note 19.
12 Ie taken into account in accordance with the Housing Act 1985 s 153B(3): see the text and notes 14–17.
13 Housing Act 1985 s 153B(2) (as added (see note 10); amended by the Leasehold Reform, Housing and Urban Development Act 1993 Sch 21 para 14(2); and by SI 1993/651).
14 As to the meaning of references to the purchase price see PARA 283 note 8.
15 As to the meaning of 'initial payment' see PARA 318.
16 For these purposes, 'the appropriate percentage' means 50% or such other percentage as may be prescribed: Housing Act 1985 s 153B(4) (as added: see note 10).

17 Housing Act 1985 s 153B(3) (as added (see note 10); amended by the Leasehold Reform, Housing and Urban Development Act 1993 Sch 21 para 14(3)). The Housing Act 1985 s 153B is modified where: (1) the Housing (Extension of Right to Buy) Order 1993, SI 1993/2240 (see PARA 233), applies (see Schedule para 39); (2) the Housing (Preservation of Right to Buy) Regulations 1993, SI 1993/2241 (see PARA 334 et seq), apply (see Sch 1 para 18).

18 See PARAS 242–244.

19 See the Housing (Right to Acquire) Regulations 1997, SI 1997/619, Sch 1 para 17, applying in relation to the right to acquire under the Housing and Regeneration Act 2008 by virtue of s 184, which applies the Housing Act 1996 s 17 (regulations modifying the Housing Act 1985): see PARA 241. As to the right to acquire under the 2008 Act see PARAS 240–241.

(v) Provisions affecting Future Disposals

A. RELEVANT AND EXEMPTED DISPOSALS

321. Meaning of 'relevant disposal'. A disposal, whether of the whole or part of the dwelling house[1], is a relevant disposal for the statutory purposes[2] if it is:

(1)   a further conveyance of the freehold or an assignment of the lease[3]; or

(2)   the grant of a lease, other than a mortgage term, for a term of more than 21 years otherwise than at a rack rent[4].

For the purposes of head (2) above, it is to be assumed:

(a)   that any option to renew or extend a lease or sublease, whether or not forming part of a series of options, is exercised; and

(b)   that any option to terminate a lease or sublease is not exercised[5].

The grant of an option enabling a person to call for a relevant disposal which is not an exempted disposal[6] is treated as such a disposal made to him[7].

1   As to the meaning of 'dwelling house' see PARA 231.

2   Ie for the purposes of the Housing Act 1985 Pt V (ss 118–188): see PARAS 230 et seq, 322 et seq. Should the former tenant who has purchased under Pt V and who was entitled to a discount decide to sell he may have to repay part or all of the discount: see PARA 323 et seq. Some disposals are treated as 'exempted disposals' (see PARA 322) in which case there are no implications for any discount received.

3   As to the meaning of 'lease' see PARA 31 note 3.

4   Housing Act 1985 s 159(1); and see PARA 230 notes 7, 9. 'Rack rent' means a rent of or near the full annual value of the property, determined as at the date of the grant: *Re Sawyer and Withall* [1919] 2 Ch 333; *London Corpn v Cusack-Smith* [1955] AC 337, [1955] 1 All ER 302, HL.

5   Housing Act 1985 s 159(2); and see PARA 230 notes 7, 9. Section 159 is modified where the Housing (Extension of Right to Buy) Order 1993, SI 1993/2240 (see PARA 233), applies: see Schedule para 46.

6   As to the meaning of 'exempted disposal' see PARA 322.

7   Housing Act 1985 s 163(1). For the purposes of s 157(2) (see PARA 333), a consent to such a grant is treated as a consent to a disposal in pursuance of the option: s 163(2). Section 163(2) is omitted where the right to acquire conferred by the Housing Act 1996 (see PARAS 242–244) or the Housing and Regeneration Act 2008 (see PARAS 240–241) arises: see the Housing (Right to Acquire) Regulations 1997, SI 1997/619, Sch 1 para 24, applying in relation to the right to acquire under the Housing and Regeneration Act 2008 by virtue of s 184, which applies the Housing Act 1996 s 17 (regulations modifying the Housing Act 1985): see PARA 241.

   As to the treatment of deferred resale agreements see PARA 325.

322. Meaning of 'exempted disposal'. A disposal is an exempted disposal for the statutory purposes[1] if:

(1)   it is a disposal of the whole of the dwelling house[2] and a further conveyance of the freehold or an assignment of the lease[3] and the person or each of the persons to whom it is made is a qualifying person[4]; or

(2)   it is a vesting of the whole of the dwelling house in a person taking under a will or on an intestacy; or

(3)   it is a disposal of the whole of the dwelling house in pursuance of a property adjustment order or an order for the sale of property made in connection with matrimonial proceedings[5], an order as to financial provision to be made from an estate[6], a property adjustment order or an order for the sale of property after an overseas divorce, etc[7], an order for financial relief against a parent[8] or a property adjustment order or order for the sale of property in connection with civil partnership proceedings or after overseas dissolution of a civil partnership[9]; or

(4)   it is a compulsory disposal[10]; or

(5)   it is a disposal of property consisting of land included in the dwelling house[11], being land let with or used for the purposes of the dwelling house[12].

For the purposes of head (1) above, a person is a qualifying person in relation to a disposal if:

(a)   he is the person, or one of the persons, by whom the disposal is made; or

(b)   he is the spouse or a former spouse, or the civil partner or a former civil partner, of that person or one of those persons; or

(c)   he is a member of the family[13] of that person, or of one of those persons, and has resided with him throughout the period of 12 months ending with the disposal[14].

Where there is a relevant disposal which is an exempted disposal by virtue of head (4) or head (5) above:

(i)   the covenant for repayment of discount on early disposal[15] is not binding on the person to whom the disposal is made or any successor in title of his, and that covenant and the charge[16] on the premises cease to apply in relation to the property disposed of[17];

(ii)   in relation to the right to buy[18]:

    (A)   the covenant required with regard to the right of first refusal for the landlord etc[19] is not binding on the person to whom the disposal is made or any successor in title of his, and that covenant ceases to apply in relation to the property disposed of[20]; and

    (B)   any covenant restricting disposals of dwelling houses in National Parks etc[21] ceases to apply in relation to the property disposed of[22].

1 Ie for the purposes of the Housing Act 1985 Pt V (ss 118–188): see PARAS 230 et seq, 326 et seq.
2 As to the meaning of 'dwelling house' see PARA 231.
3 As to the meaning of 'lease' see PARA 31 note 3.
4 Ie as defined in the Housing Act 1985 s 160(2): see heads (a)–(c) in the text.
5 Ie in pursuance of an order made under the Matrimonial Causes Act 1973 s 24 or s 24A: see MATRIMONIAL AND CIVIL PARTNERSHIP LAW vol 73 (2015) PARA 557 et seq.
6 Ie an order under the Inheritance (Provision for Family and Dependants) Act 1975 s 2: see WILLS AND INTESTACY vol 103 (2016) PARA 591 et seq.
7 Ie in pursuance of an order made under the Matrimonial and Family Proceedings Act 1984 s 17: see MATRIMONIAL AND CIVIL PARTNERSHIP LAW vol 73 (2015) PARA 591.
8 Ie in pursuance of an order made under the Children Act 1989 Sch 1 para 1: see CHILDREN AND YOUNG PERSONS vol 9 (2017) PARA 623 et seq.
9 Ie an order made under the Civil Partnership Act 2004 Sch 5 Pt 2 or Pt 3, or Sch 7 para 9: see MATRIMONIAL AND CIVIL PARTNERSHIP LAW vol 73 (2015) PARAS 556 et seq, 591.
10 For these purposes, a 'compulsory disposal' means a disposal of property which is acquired compulsorily, or is acquired by a person who has made or would have made, or for whom another person has made or would have made, a compulsory purchase order authorising its compulsory purchase for the purposes for which it is acquired: Housing Act 1985 s 161.
11 Ie land included in the dwelling house by virtue of the Housing Act 1985 s 184: see PARA 231.

12 See the Housing Act 1985 s 160(1), (3) (s 160(1) amended, s 160(3) added, by the Housing Act 1996 s 222, Sch 18 para 15(2), (3); the Housing Act 1985 s 160(3) amended by the Civil Partnership Act 2004 s 81, 261(4), Sch 8 para 30, Sch 30).
13 As to the meaning of 'member of a person's family' see PARA 274 note 5.
14 See the Housing Act 1985 s 160(2) (amended by the Civil Partnership Act 2004 Sch 8 para 18). Section 160 is modified where the Housing (Extension of Right to Buy) Order 1993, SI 1993/2240 (see PARA 233) applies: see Schedule para 46.
15 Ie the covenant required by the Housing Act 1985 s 155: see PARA 323.
16 Ie the covenant and charge taking effect by virtue of the Housing Act 1985 s 156: see PARA 326.
17 Housing Act 1985 s 162(a) (s 162 modified by the Housing (Right to Acquire) Regulations 1997, SI 1997/619, Sch 1 para 23 (applying in relation to the right to acquire under the Housing and Regeneration Act 2008 by virtue of s 184, which applies the Housing Act 1996 s 17 (regulations modifying the Housing Act 1985): see PARA 241); and see PARA 230 notes 7, 9.
   The Housing Act 1985 s 162 is also modified where the Housing (Preservation of Right to Buy) Regulations 1993, SI 1993/2241 (see PARA 334 et seq), apply: see Sch 1 para 24.
18 As to the meaning of 'the right to buy' see PARA 239. It is submitted that head (ii)(A) in the text may also apply in relation to the right to acquire conferred by the Housing Act 1996 (see PARAS 242–244) or the Housing and Regeneration Act 2008 (see PARAS 240–241) but that head (ii)(B) in the text does not so apply (see note 21).
19 Ie the covenant required by the Housing Act 1985 s 156A: see PARA 327.
20 Housing Act 1985 s 162(aa) (added by the Housing Act 2004 s 188(4)); and see note 17.
21 Ie any such covenant as is mentioned in the Housing Act 1985 s 157: see PARA 333. Section 157 is omitted in the case of the right to acquire: see PARA 333.
22 Housing Act 1985 s 162(b); and see note 17.

B.   REPAYMENT OF DISCOUNT

323. Repayment of discount on early disposal. A conveyance of the freehold or the grant of a lease[1] in pursuance of Part V of the Housing Act 1985[2] must, unless in the case of a conveyance or grant in pursuance of the right to buy[3] or the right to acquire conferred by the Housing Act 1996[4] or the Housing and Regeneration Act 2008[5] where there is no discount, contain a covenant binding on the tenant[6] and his successors in title to the following effect[7].

In the case of a conveyance or grant in pursuance of the right to buy, the covenant must be to pay the landlord[8] such sum, if any, as the landlord may demand[9] on the occasion of the first relevant disposal[10], other than an exempted disposal[11], which takes place within the period of five years beginning with the conveyance or grant[12]. Where, however, a secure tenant has served on his landlord an operative notice of delay[13], the five years referred to above begin from a date which precedes the date of the conveyance of the freehold or grant of the lease by a period equal to the time, or, if there is more than one such notice, the aggregate of the times, during which any payment of rent falls[14] to be taken[15] into account[16].

In the case of a conveyance or grant in pursuance of the right to acquire on rent to mortgage terms (so far as still exercisable[17]), the covenant must be to pay the landlord such sum, if any, as the landlord may demand[18] on the occasion of the first relevant disposal, other than an exempted disposal, which takes place within the period of five years beginning with the making of the initial payment[19].

In the case of the right to acquire conferred by the 1996 or 2008 Act, the covenant must be to pay to the landlord on demand, if within the statutory period[20] there is a relevant disposal which is not an exempted disposal (but if there is more than one such disposal, then only on the first of them), the discount to which the tenant was entitled, reduced by one third for each complete year which has elapsed after the conveyance or grant and before the disposal[21].

1 As to the meaning of 'lease' see PARA 31 note 3.
2 Ie in pursuance of the Housing Act 1985 Pt V (ss 188–188): see PARAS 230 et seq, 324 et seq.
3 As to the meaning of 'the right to buy' see PARA 239.
4 See PARAS 242–244.

5 See PARAS 240–241.
6 Ie the secure tenant in the case of the right to buy or the tenant in the case of the right to acquire. As to the meaning of 'secure tenant' see PARA 230 note 2; and as to the meaning of 'tenant' see PARA 31 note 3.
7 Housing Act 1985 s 155(1); and see PARA 230 notes 7, 9.
8 As to the meaning of 'landlord' see PARA 31 note 3.
9 Ie in accordance with the Housing Act 1985 s 155A: see PARA 324.
10 As to the meaning of 'relevant disposal' see PARA 321.
11 As to the meaning of 'exempted disposal' see PARA 322.
12 Housing Act 1985 s 155(2) (s 155(2), (3) substituted by the Housing Act 2004 s 185(1), (2); for transitional provisions see s 185(5)–(8)).
13 Ie as defined in the Housing Act 1985 s 153A: see PARA 319.
14 Ie by virtue of the Housing Act 1985 s 153B: see PARA 320.
15 Ie in accordance with the Housing Act 1985 s 153B(3): see PARA 320.
16 Housing Act 1985 s 155(3A)(a) (s 155(3A) added by the Housing Act 1988 s 140, Sch 17 para 41; amended by the Housing Act 2004 s 185(1), (3); for transitional provisions see note 12). The Housing Act 1985 s 155(3A) is omitted where the right to acquire under the Housing Act 1996 or the Housing and Regeneration Act 2008 arises: see the Housing (Right to Acquire) Regulations 1997, SI 1997/619, Sch 1 para 19(b), applying in relation to the right to acquire under the Housing and Regeneration Act 2008 by virtue of s 184, which applies the Housing Act 1996 s 17 (regulations modifying the Housing Act 1985): see PARA 241.
17 As to the meaning of 'the right to acquire on rent to mortgage terms' see PARA 318. That right is only exercisable if the notice of claim was served before 18 July 2005: see the Housing Act 1985 s 142A; and PARA 318.
18 Ie in accordance with the Housing Act 1985 s 155B: see PARA 324.
19 Housing Act 1985 s 155(3) (as substituted (see note 10); omitted where the Housing (Right to Acquire) Regulations 1997, SI 1997/619, apply: see Sch 1 para 19(b). As to the meaning of 'initial payment' see PARA 318. Where a secure tenant has served on his landlord an operative notice of delay, as defined in the Housing Act 1985 s 153A, any reference in s 155(3) to the making of the initial payment is to be construed as a reference to the date which precedes that payment by the period referred to in s 155(3A)(a) (see the text and notes 13–16): s 155(3A)(b) (as added (see note 16); substituted by the Leasehold Reform, Housing and Urban Development Act 1993 s 120(2); and see note 16).
20 Section 155(2) as set out in the Housing (Right to Acquire) Regulations 1997, SI 1997/619, Sch 1 Sch 2 (see note 21) refers to a period of three years but it is submitted that this ought now to be read as a reference to five years: see PARA 230 notes 7, 9.
21 Housing Act 1985 s 155(2) (modified for these purposes by the Housing (Right to Acquire) Regulations 1997, SI 1997/619, Sch 1 para 19(a); and as to the application of those Regulations see note 16).
    The Housing Act 1985 s 155 is also modified where: (1) the Housing (Extension of Right to Buy) Order 1993, SI 1993/2240 (see PARA 233), applies (see Schedule para 41); (2) the Housing (Preservation of Right to Buy) Regulations 1993, SI 1993/2241 (see PARA 334 et seq), apply (see Sch 1 para 20).

324. Amount of discount which may be demanded by the landlord in the case of the right to buy. For the purposes of the covenant to repay discount on an early disposal in the case of a conveyance or grant in pursuance of the right to buy[1], the landlord[2] may demand such sum as it considers appropriate, up to and including the maximum amount specified for these purposes[3]. The maximum amount which may be demanded by the landlord is a percentage of the price or premium paid for the first relevant disposal[4] which is equal to the discount to which the secure tenant[5] was entitled, where the discount is expressed as a percentage of the value which was taken[6] as the value of the dwelling house[7] at the relevant time[8]. For each complete year which has elapsed after the conveyance or grant and before the disposal, however, the maximum amount which may be demanded by the landlord is reduced by one-fifth[9].

In calculating the maximum amount which may be demanded by the landlord, such amount, if any, of the price or premium paid for the disposal which is attributable to improvements made to the dwelling house:

(1) by the person by whom the disposal is, or is to be, made; and

(2)   after the conveyance or grant and before the disposal,

must be disregarded[10]. The amount to be disregarded under this provision is such amount as may be agreed between the parties or determined by the district valuer[11]; but the district valuer is not required[12] to make a determination for these purposes unless:

(a)   it is reasonably practicable for him to do so; and

(b)   his reasonable costs in making the determination are paid by the person by whom the disposal is, or is to be, made[13].

If the district valuer does not make a determination for these purposes, and in default of an agreement, no amount is required to be disregarded under this provision[14].

For the purposes of the covenant to repay discount on an early disposal in the case of a conveyance or grant in pursuance of the right to acquire on rent to mortgage terms, so far as still exercisable[15], the landlord may demand such sum as he considers appropriate, up to and including the maximum amount specified for these purposes[16]. The maximum amount which may be demanded by the landlord is the discount, if any, to which the tenant was entitled on the making of:

(i)   the initial payment[17];

(ii)   any interim payment[18] made before the disposal; or

(iii)   the final payment[19] if so made,

reduced, in each case, by one-fifth for each complete year which has elapsed after the making of the initial payment and before the disposal[20].

1 Ie the covenant mentioned in the Housing Act 1985 s 155(2): see PARA 323.
2 As to the meaning of 'landlord' see PARA 31 note 3.
3 Housing Act 1985 s 155A(1) (ss 155A, 155B added by the Housing Act 2004 s 185(1), (4)). The Housing Act 1985 s 155A is subject to s 155C (see the text and notes 10–14): s 155A(4) (as so added).
4 As to the meaning of 'relevant disposal' see PARA 321.
5 As to the meaning of 'secure tenant' see PARA 230 note 2.
6 Ie under the Housing Act 1985 s 127: see PARA 284.
7 As to the meaning of 'dwelling house' see PARA 231.
8 Housing Act 1985 s 155A(2) (as added: see note 3).
9 Housing Act 1985 s 155A(3) (as added: see note 3).
10 Housing Act 1985 s 155C(1) (s 155C added by the Housing Act 2004 s 186(1)).
11 Housing Act 1985 s 155C(2) (as added: see note 10). As to the meaning of 'district valuer' see PARA 527 note 14.
12 Ie by virtue of the Housing Act 1985 s 155C.
13 Housing Act 1985 s 155C(3) (as added: see note 10).
14 Housing Act 1985 s 155C(4) (as added: see note 10).
15 Ie the covenant mentioned in the Housing Act 1985 s 155(3): see PARA 323.
16 Housing Act 1985 s 155B(1) (as added: see note 3).
17 As to the meaning of 'initial payment' see PARA 318.
18 As to the meaning of 'interim payment' see the Housing Act 1985 Sch 6A para 6 (Sch 6A added by the Leasehold Reform, Housing and Urban Development Act 1993 s 117(2), Sch 16).
19 Ie a payment of the amount required to redeem the landlord's share: see the Housing Act 1985 Sch 6A para 1(1) (as added: see note 18).
20 Housing Act 1985 s 155B(2) (as added: see note 3).

325. Treatment of deferred resale agreements for the purposes of the right to buy. If a secure tenant[1] or his successor in title enters into an agreement[2] to which this provision applies[3], any liability arising under the required covenant to repay discount on an early disposal[4] must be determined as if a relevant disposal[5] which is not an exempted disposal[6] had occurred at the appropriate time[7]; and for these purposes 'the appropriate time' means:

(1)   the time when the agreement is entered into; or

(2)   if it was made before the beginning of the discount repayment period[8], immediately after the beginning of that period[9].

An agreement is one to which these provisions apply if it is an agreement between the secure tenant or his successor in title and any other person:

(a)   which is made, expressly or impliedly, in contemplation of, or in connection with, the tenant exercising, or having exercised, the right to buy[10],

(b)   which is made before the end of the discount repayment period; and

(c)   under which a relevant disposal, other than an exempted disposal, is or may be required to be made to any person after the end of that period[11].

Such an agreement is within heads (a) to (c) above whether or not the date on which the disposal is to take place is specified in the agreement, and whether or not any requirement to make the disposal is or may be made subject to the fulfilment of any condition[12].

The appropriate national authority may by order provide:

(i)   for the above provisions[13] to apply to agreements of any description specified in the order in addition to those within heads (a) to (c) above;

(ii)   for those provisions not to apply to agreements of any description so specified to which they would otherwise apply[14].

Such an order may make different provision with respect to different cases or descriptions of case and must be made by statutory instrument[15].

1   As to the meaning of 'secure tenant' see PARA 230 note 2.
2   For these purposes, 'agreement' includes arrangement: Housing Act 1985 s 163A(7) (s 163A added by the Housing Act 2004 s 187(1)).
3   Ie an agreement within the Housing Act 1985 s 163A(3): see heads (a)–(c) in the text.
4   Ie the covenant required by the Housing Act 1985 s 155: see PARA 323.
5   As to the meaning of 'relevant disposal' see PARA 321.
6   As to the meaning of 'exempted disposal' see PARA 322.
7   Housing Act 1985 s 163A(1) (as added: see note 2).
8   For these purposes 'the discount repayment period' means the period of three or five years that applies for the purposes of the Housing Act 1985 s 155(2) or s 155(3), depending on whether the tenant's notice under s 122 (see PARA 273) was given before, or on or after, the date of the coming into force of the Housing Act 2004 s 185 (see PARA 323 note 12): Housing Act 1985 s 163A(7) (as added: see note 2).
9   Housing Act 1985 s 163A(2) (as added: see note 2).
10 As to the meaning of 'the right to buy' see PARA 239.
11 Housing Act 1985 s 163A(3) (as added: see note 2).
12 Housing Act 1985 s 163A(4) (as added: see note 2).
13 Ie the Housing Act 1985 s 163A(1): see the text and notes 1–7.
14 Housing Act 1985 s 163A(5) (as added: see note 2). As to the appropriate national authority, the Secretary of State and the transfer of functions under the Housing Act 1985, so far as exercisable in relation to Wales, to the Welsh Ministers see PARA 7.
15 Housing Act 1985 s 163A(6) (as added: see note 2). In the case of an order made by the Secretary of State, the instrument is subject to annulment in pursuance of a resolution of either House of Parliament: see s 163A(6) (as so added). At the date at which this volume states the law, no such order had been made.

326. Liability to repay discount is a charge on the premises. The liability that may arise under the covenant to repay discount on an early disposal[1] is a charge on the dwelling house[2], taking effect as if it had been created by deed expressed to be by way of legal mortgage[3].

The charge has priority[4] as follows:

(1)   if it secures the liability that may arise under the covenant to repay discount on an early disposal in the case of a conveyance or grant in pursuance of the right to buy[5], the charge has priority immediately after

any legal charge securing an amount advanced to the secure tenant[6] by an approved lending institution[7] for the purpose of enabling him to exercise the right to buy[8];

(2)   if it secures the liability that may arise under the covenant to repay discount on an early disposal in the case of a conveyance or grant in pursuance of the right to acquire on rent to mortgage terms, where that right is still exercisable[9], the charge has priority immediately after the mortgage which is required[10] for securing the redemption of the landlord's share, and which has priority[11] immediately after any legal charge securing an amount advanced to the secure tenant by an approved lending institution for the purpose of enabling him to exercise the right to acquire on rent to mortgage terms[12];

(3)   in the case of the right to acquire conferred by the Housing Act 1996[13] or the Housing and Regeneration Act 2008[14], the charge has priority immediately after any legal charge securing an amount advanced to the tenant by an approved lending institution for the purpose of enabling him to exercise the right to acquire[15].

The following, namely:

(a)   any advance which is made otherwise than for the purpose mentioned in head (1), head (2) or head (3) above and is secured by a legal charge having priority to the charge taking effect by virtue of these provisions; and

(b)   any further advance which is so secured,

rank in priority to that charge if, and only if, the landlord[16] by written notice served on the institution concerned gives its consent; and the landlord must so give its consent if the purpose of the advance or further advance is an approved purpose[17].

The landlord may at any time by written notice served on an approved lending institution postpone the charge taking effect by virtue of these provisions to any advance or further advance which is made to the tenant by that institution and is secured by a legal charge not having priority to that charge; and the landlord must serve such a notice if the purpose of the advance or further advance is an approved purpose[18].

Provision is made for the apportionment of discount so recovered where the liability arises under the extended right to buy[19].

1   Ie the covenant required by the Housing Act 1985 s 155: see PARA 323.
2   As to the meaning of 'dwelling house' see PARA 231.
3   Housing Act 1985 s 156(1); and see PARA 230 notes 7, 9. The covenant required by s 155 (see PARA 323) does not, by virtue of its binding successors in title of the tenant, bind a person exercising rights under a charge having priority over the charge taking effect by virtue of s 156 (see the text and notes 4–18), or a person deriving title under him; and a provision of the conveyance or grant, or of a collateral agreement, is void in so far as it purports to authorise a forfeiture, or to impose a penalty or disability, in the event of any such person failing to comply with that covenant: s 156(3A) (added by the Housing and Planning Act 1986 s 24(1), Sch 5 para 1(2), (5)). As to the meaning of 'tenant' see PARA 31 note 3.
4   Ie subject to the Housing Act 1985 s 156(2A), (2B): see the text and notes 16–18.
5   Ie the covenant required by the Housing Act 1985 s 155(2): see PARA 323. As to the meaning of 'the right to buy' see PARA 239.
6   As to the meaning of 'secure tenant' see PARA 230 note 2.
7   For these purposes, the approved lending institutions are: (1) the relevant authority; (2) an authorised deposit taker; (3) an authorised insurer; and (4) an authorised mortgage lender: Housing Act 1985 s 156(4) (amended by the Government of Wales Act 1998 s 140, Sch 16 para 5; the Housing and Regeneration Act 2008 s 307(1)(a); and SI 2001/3649). For these purposes, the 'relevant authority' does not include the Regulator of Social Housing but does include the Homes and Communities Agency: Housing Act 1985 s 156(4ZA) (added by SI 2010/866). 'The relevant

authority' also includes the Greater London Authority: Housing Act 1985 s 156(4ZB) (added by the Localism Act 2011 s 195(1), Sch 19 paras 10, 15). As to the relevant authority see PARA 8. As to the Greater London Authority see LONDON GOVERNMENT vol 71 (2013) PARA 67 et seq.

'Authorised deposit taker' means: (a) a person who has permission under the Financial Services and Markets Act 2000 Pt 4A (ss 55A–55Z4) to accept deposits; or (b) an EEA firm of the kind mentioned in Sch 3 para 5(b) who has permission under Sch 3 para 15 (as a result of qualifying for authorisation under Sch 3 para 12) to accept deposits; 'authorised insurer' means: (i) a person who has permission under Pt 4A to effect or carry out contracts of insurance; or (ii) an EEA firm of the kind mentioned in Sch 3 para 5(b) who has permission under Sch 3 para 15 (as a result of qualifying for authorisation under Sch 3 para 12) to effect or carry out contracts of insurance; and 'authorised mortgage lender' means: (A) a person who has permission under Pt 4A to enter into a regulated mortgage contract as lender; (B) an EEA firm of the kind mentioned in Sch 3 para 5(b) who has permission under Sch 3 para 15 (as a result of qualifying for authorisation under Sch 3 para 12) to enter into a regulated mortgage contract as lender; or (C) a Treaty firm within the meaning of Sch 4 who has permission under Sch 4 para 4 (as a result of qualifying for authorisation under Sch 4 para 2) to enter into a regulated mortgage contract as lender: Housing Act 1985 s 622(1) (numbered as such by SI 2001/3649; definitions of 'authorised deposit taker' and 'authorised insurer' added by SI 2001/3649; amended by the Housing and Regeneration Act 2008 s 316; and the Financial Services Act 2012 s 114(1), Sch 18 para 50; definition of 'authorised mortgage lender' added by the Housing and Regeneration Act 2008 s 307(2); amended by the Financial Services Act 2012 Sch 18 para 50). See further FINANCIAL SERVICES REGULATION.

8   Housing Act 1985 s 156(2)(a) (s 156(2) substituted, s 156(2A), (2B) added, by the Leasehold Reform, Housing and Urban Development Act 1993 s 120(3)).

9   Ie the covenant required by the Housing Act 1985 s 155(3): see PARA 323. As to the meaning of 'the right to acquire on rent to mortgage terms' see PARA 318. That right is only exercisable where it has been claimed before 18 July 2005: see s 142A; and PARA 318.

10 Ie by the Housing Act 1985 s 151B: see PARA 318.

11 Ie by virtue of the Housing Act 1985 s 151B(2).

12 Housing Act 1985 s 156(2)(b) (as substituted: see note 8).

13 See PARAS 242–244.

14 See PARAS 240–241.

15 See the Housing Act 1985 s 156(2) (substituted for these purposes by the Housing (Right to Acquire) Regulations 1997, SI 1997/619, Sch 1 para 20(a), applying in relation to the right to acquire under the Housing and Regeneration Act 2008 by virtue of s 184, which applies the Housing Act 1996 s 17 (regulations modifying the Housing Act 1985): see PARA 241).

The Housing Act 1985 s 156 also is modified: (1) where the Housing (Extension of Right to Buy) Order 1993, SI 1993/2240 (see PARA 233), applies (see Schedule para 42); (2) where the Housing (Preservation of Right to Buy) Regulations 1993, SI 1993/2241 (see PARA 334 et seq), apply (Sch 1 para 21).

16 As to the meaning of 'landlord' see PARA 31 note 3.

17 Housing Act 1985 s 156(2A) (as added (see note 8); modified by the Housing (Right to Acquire) Regulations 1997, SI 1997/619, Sch 1 para 20(b)); and see note 15. The approved purposes are:

(1)   in the case of the right to acquire on rent to mortgage terms only (so far as still exercisable), to enable the tenant to make an interim or final payment;

(2)   to enable the tenant to defray, or to defray on his behalf, any of the following:

(a)   the cost of any works to the dwelling house;

(b)   any service charge payable in respect of the dwelling house for works, whether or not to the dwelling house; and

(c)   any service charge or other amount payable in respect of the dwelling house for insurance, whether or not of the dwelling house; and

(3)   to enable the tenant to discharge, or to discharge on his behalf, any of the following:

(a)   so much as is still outstanding of any advance or further advance which ranks in priority to the charge taking effect by virtue of the Housing Act 1985 s 156;

(b)   any arrears of interest on such an advance or further advance; and

(c)   any costs and expenses incurred in enforcing payment of any such interest, or repayment, in whole or in part, of any such advance or further advance: see s 156(4A) (s 156(4A), (4B) added by the Leasehold Reform, Housing and Urban Development Act 1993 s 120(4); modified by the Housing (Right to Acquire) Regulations 1997, SI 1997/619, Sch 1 para 20(c)).

As to interim and final payments see PARA 318; and as to the meaning of 'service charge' see PARA 276 note 19.

Where different parts of an advance or further advance are made for different purposes, each of those parts is be regarded as a separate advance or further advance for these purposes: Housing Act 1985 s 156(4B) (as so added).

18 Housing Act 1985 s 156(2B) (as added: see note 8).

19 Subject in cases of acquisition on rent to mortgage terms to the Housing Act 1985 s 150B (power to agree final apportionment: see PARA 318 note 28), where the whole or any part of any discount obtained by the tenant is recovered by the freeholder (whether by the receipt of a payment determined by reference to the discount or by a reduction so determined of any consideration given by the freeholder or in any other way), the freeholder must pay: (1) to the authority or body which immediately before completion was the landlord or an intermediate landlord; and (2) to the rent owner of any rentcharge which was then charged on or issued out of the lease of any such authority or body, a sum calculated by multiplying the amount of the discount recovered by the freeholder by the apportionment fraction applicable to that authority, body or person (ascertained in accordance with s 138A (added for these purposes: see PARA 292); but no such payment must be made in relation to a lease if it is a lease for a term certain and the residue of the term unexpired immediately before completion was a period of less than 12 months or if it was a periodic tenancy: s 156A(1), (2) (added for these purposes by the Housing (Extension of Right to Buy) Order 1993, SI 1993/2240, Schedule para 43). For these purposes, 'apportionment fraction' has the meaning given by the Housing Act 1985 s 138A(2) (added for these purposes) (apportionment of purchase price: see PARA 292); and 'rentcharge' and 'rent owner' have the same meanings as in the Rentcharges Act 1977: Housing Act 1985 s 156A(3) (as so added for these purposes).

C. LANDLORD'S RIGHT OF FIRST REFUSAL WHERE THE RIGHT TO BUY ETC HAS BEEN EXERCISED

327. Right of first refusal for landlord and related matters. A conveyance of the freehold or grant of a lease[1] in pursuance of the right to buy[2] must[3] contain the following covenant, which is binding on the secure tenant[4] who is exercising the right to buy and his successors in title[5]. The covenant must be to the effect that, until the end of the period of ten years beginning with the conveyance or grant, there will be no relevant disposal[6] which is not an exempted disposal[7], unless the prescribed conditions[8] have been satisfied in relation to that or a previous such disposal[9]. The limitation imposed by such a covenant[10] is a local land charge[11] and the Chief Land Registrar must enter in the register of title[12] a restriction reflecting the limitation imposed by any such covenant[13].

In a case to which the statutory restriction on the disposal of dwelling houses situated in a National Park, an area of outstanding natural beauty or a designated rural area[14] applies, the conveyance or grant may contain a covenant such as is mentioned above instead of a covenant such as is mentioned in the provisions[15] imposing that restriction[16]. The conveyance or grant may, however, do so only if either:

(1) the appropriate national authority; or

(2) where the conveyance or grant is executed by a housing association[17], the relevant authority[18],

consents[19]. Consent may be given in relation to a particular disposal, or disposals by a particular landlord or disposals by landlords generally, and may, in any case, be given subject to conditions[20].

1 As to the meaning of 'lease' see PARA 31 note 3.
2 Ie in pursuance of the right to buy provisions contained in the Housing Act 1985 Pt V (ss 118–188): see PARAS 230 et seq, 328 et seq. As to the meaning of 'the right to buy' see PARA 239. It is submitted that a right of first refusal covenant may also be imposed under s 156A (see the text and notes 3–20) in the case of the right to acquire under the Housing Act 1996 (see PARAS 242–244) or the Housing and Regeneration Act 2008 (see PARAS 240–241): see PARA 230 notes 7, 9. See further PARA 328 note 15.
3 Ie subject to the Housing Act 1985 s 156A(8): see the text and notes 14–19.
4 As to the meaning of 'secure tenant' see PARA 230 note 2.
5 See the Housing Act 1985 s 156A(1) (s 156A added by the Housing Act 2004 s 188(1)). The amendments made by s 188 do not apply in relation to a conveyance of the freehold or grant of a lease in pursuance of the Housing Act 1985 Pt V if the notice under s 122 (tenant's notice

claiming to exercise right to buy: see PARA 273) was served before 18 January 2005 (ie the day on which the Housing Act 2004 came into force: see s 270(3)(a)): s 188(5). Accordingly, nothing in s 188 affects: (1) the operation of a limitation contained in such a conveyance or grant in accordance with the Housing Act 1985 s 157(4) (repealed subject to transitional provisions); or (2) the operation, in relation to such a limitation, of s 157(6) (so far as it renders a disposal in breach of covenant void) or s 158 (consideration payable: see PARA 332): Housing Act 2004 s 188(6).

6　As to the meaning of 'relevant disposal' see PARA 321.

7　As to the meaning of 'exempted disposal' see PARA 322.

8　'The prescribed conditions' means such conditions as are prescribed by regulations under the Housing Act 1985 s 156A at the time when the conveyance or grant is made: s 156A(3) (as added: see note 5). As to the power to prescribe conditions see PARA 328.

9　Housing Act 1985 s 156A(2) (as added: see note 5).

10　Ie a covenant within the Housing Act 1985 s 156A(2), whether the covenant is imposed in pursuance of s 156A(1) (see the text and notes 1–5) or s 156A(8) (see the text and notes 14–19).

11　Housing Act 1985 s 156A(11) (as added: see note 5). As to local land charges see REAL PROPERTY AND REGISTRATION vol 87 (2012) PARA 714 et seq.

12　As to the register of title see REAL PROPERTY AND REGISTRATION vol 87 (2012) PARA 328 et seq.

13　Housing Act 1985 s 156A(12) (as added: see note 5).

14　Ie the restriction imposed by the Housing Act 1985 s 157(1): see PARA 333.

15　Ie as is mentioned in the Housing Act 1985 s 157(1).

16　Housing Act 1985 s 156A(8)(a) (as added: see note 5).

17　Ie a housing association within the Housing Act 1985 s 6A(3) or (4): see PARA 8.

18　As to the relevant authority see PARA 8.

19　Housing Act 1985 s 156A(8)(b) (as added: see note 5). As to the appropriate national authority, and the transfer of functions under the Housing Act 1985, so far as exercisable in relation to Wales, to the Welsh Ministers see PARA 7.

20　Housing Act 1985 s 156A(9) (as added: see note 5).

328. Power to prescribe conditions. The appropriate national authority may by regulations prescribe such conditions as it considers appropriate for and in connection with conferring on:

(1)　a landlord[1] who has conveyed a freehold or granted a lease[2] to a person ('the former tenant') in pursuance of the right to buy[3]; or

(2)　such other person as is determined in accordance with the regulations,

a right of first refusal to have a disposal within head (a) or head (b) below, namely:

(a)　a reconveyance or conveyance of the dwelling house; or

(b)　a surrender or assignment of the lease,

made to him for the specified[4] consideration[5]. Such regulations may, in particular, make provision:

(i)　for the former tenant[6] to offer to make such a disposal to such person or persons as may be prescribed[7];

(ii)　for a prescribed recipient of such an offer to be able either to accept the offer or to nominate some other person as the person by whom the offer may be accepted[8];

(iii)　for the person who may be so nominated to be either a person of a prescribed description or a person whom the prescribed recipient considers, having regard to any prescribed matters, to be a more appropriate person to accept the offer[9];

(iv)　for a prescribed recipient making such a nomination to give a notification of the nomination to the person nominated, the former tenant and any other prescribed person[10];

(v)　for authorising a nominated person to accept the offer and for determining which acceptance is to be effective where the offer is accepted by more than one person[11];

(vi)　for the period within which the offer may be accepted or within which any other prescribed step is to be, or may be, taken[12];

(vii)   for the circumstances in which the right of first refusal lapses, whether following the service of a notice to complete or otherwise, with the result that the former tenant is able to make a disposal on the open market[13];

(viii)   for the manner in which any offer, acceptance or notification is to be communicated[14].

Such regulations may make different provision with respect to different cases or descriptions of case and must be made by statutory instrument[15].

1 As to the meaning of 'landlord' see PARA 31 note 3.
2 As to the meaning of 'lease' see PARA 31 note 3.
3 Ie in pursuance of the right to buy provisions contained in the Housing Act 1985 Pt V (ss 118–188): see PARAS 230 et seq, 332 et seq. As to the meaning of 'the right to buy' see PARA 239. See also PARA 327 note 2.
4 Ie for such consideration as is mentioned in the Housing Act 1985 s 158: see PARA 332.
5 Housing Act 1985 s 156A(4), (5) (s 156A added by the Housing Act 2004 s 188(1)). As to the appropriate national authority, and the transfer of functions under the Housing Act 1985, so far as exercisable in relation to Wales, to the Welsh Ministers see PARA 7.
6 In the Housing Act 1985 s 156A(6) (see heads (i)–(viii) in the text), any reference to the former tenant is a reference to the former tenant or his successor in title: s 156A(7) (as added: see note 5).
7 Housing Act 1985 s 156A(6)(a) (as added: see note 5).
8 Housing Act 1985 s 156A(6)(b) (as added: see note 5).
9 Housing Act 1985 s 156A(6)(c) (as added: see note 5).
10 Housing Act 1985 s 156A(6)(d) (as added: see note 5).
11 Housing Act 1985 s 156A(6)(e) (as added: see note 5).
12 Housing Act 1985 s 156A(6)(f) (as added: see note 5).
13 Housing Act 1985 s 156A(6)(g) (as added: see note 5).
14 Housing Act 1985 s 156A(6)(h) (as added: see note 5). See further PARAS 329–331. Nothing in s 156A affects the generality of s 156A(4): s 156A(7) (as so added).
15 Housing Act 1985 s 156A(10) (as added: see note 5). If made by the Secretary of State, the instrument is subject to annulment in pursuance of a resolution of either House of Parliament: see s 156A(10) (as so added). In exercise of the power so conferred, the Secretary of State has made the Housing (Right of First Refusal) (England) Regulations 2005, SI 2005/1917, which came into force on 10 August 2005 (reg 1(1)); and the National Assembly for Wales has made the Housing (Right of First Refusal) (Wales) Regulations 2005, SI 2005/2680, which came into force on 28 September 2005 (reg 1(1)). Those regulations apply where: (1) a right of first refusal covenant has been imposed in relation to a dwelling house situated in England or in Wales respectively; and (2) there is to be a relevant disposal, other than an exempted disposal, of the owner's interest in the property: Housing (Right of First Refusal) (England) Regulations 2005, SI 2005/1917, regs 1(3), 2(1); Housing (Right of First Refusal) (Wales) Regulations 2005, SI 2005/2680, regs 1(3), 2(1). As to the meanings of 'relevant disposal' and 'exempted disposal' see PARAS 321–322. 'Owner' means the person who is the freehold or leasehold owner of a property and who is bound by a right of first refusal covenant imposed under the Housing Act 1985 s 156A (see PARA 327); and 'property' means a property which is subject to a right of first refusal covenant so imposed: Housing (Right of First Refusal) (England) Regulations 2005, SI 2005/1917, reg 1(2); Housing (Right of First Refusal) (Wales) Regulations 2005, SI 2005/2680, reg 1(2).

    With prescribed exceptions, those regulations also apply if there is to be a relevant disposal, other than an exempted disposal, of the owner's interest in a property: (a) acquired in exercise of the right conferred by the Housing Act 1985 171A (preserved right to buy: see PARA 334 et seq); (b) acquired in exercise of the right conferred by the Housing Act 1996 s 16 (right to acquire in Wales: see PARAS 242–244) or the Housing and Regeneration Act 2008 s 180 (right to acquire in England: see PARAS 240–241); (c) acquired at a discount from a local authority using its power to dispose of land in the Housing Act 1985 s 32 (see PARA 522); (d) acquired at a discount from a registered social landlord using its power to dispose of land in the Housing Act 1996 s 9 (see PARA 217) or from a private registered provider of social housing using its power to dispose of land in the Housing and Regeneration Act 2008 s 171 (see PARA 100); or (e) acquired in England at a discount from a housing action trust using its power to dispose of land in the Housing Act 1988 s 79 (see PARA 575), but subject in cases falling under heads (c)–(e) to prescribed modifications: see the Housing (Right of First Refusal) (England) Regulations 2005, SI 2005/1917, regs 14–18 (regs 15, 17 amended by SI 2010/671); the Housing (Right of First Refusal) (Wales) Regulations 2005, SI 2005/2680, regs 14–17 (reg 17 amended by SI 2010/671). Properties bought under any of these schemes are generally subject to a right of first refusal covenant.

329. Offer notices. Where the owner[1] has a leasehold interest, he must serve an offer notice[2] on:

(1)   the former landlord[3], if it is still the landlord; or

(2)   if the former landlord is not still the landlord, the person in which the reversionary interest is currently vested[4].

Where the owner has a freehold interest, he must serve an offer notice on:

(a)   the former landlord, if that person is still in existence; or

(b)   if the former landlord is not still in existence, the local housing authority[5] for the area in which the property[6] is situated[7].

An offer notice must:

(i)   be in writing;

(ii)   state that the owner wishes to dispose of the property, giving its full postal address;

(iii)   state that there is a covenant requiring him to first offer the property to the recipient of the notice;

(iv)   in relation to the property to which the notice relates:

    (A)   specify whether the property is a house, a flat or a maisonette;

    (B)   specify the number of bedrooms;

    (C)   give details of the heating system;

    (D)   specify any improvements or structural changes which have been made since the purchase; and

(v)   state the address at which the recipient can serve notices upon the owner[8].

The recipient of an offer notice must send an acknowledgment of receipt to the owner as soon as reasonably practicable, which must specify the date of receipt of the offer notice and explain the effect of the provisions relating to acceptance and rejection of the offer[9] in simple terms[10].

1 As to the meaning of 'owner' see PARA 328 note 15.

2 Ie a notice which complies with heads (i)–(v) in the text. Notices under the relevant regulations may be served either by personal delivery, or by post: Housing (Right of First Refusal) (England) Regulations 2005, SI 2005/1917, reg 13; Housing (Right of First Refusal) (Wales) Regulations 2005, SI 2005/2680, reg 13.

3 'Former landlord' means the landlord which disposed of the property under the Housing Act 1985 Pt V (ss 118–188) (see PARAS 230 et seq, 332 et seq): Housing (Right of First Refusal) (England) Regulations 2005, SI 2005/1917, reg 1(2); Housing (Right of First Refusal) (Wales) Regulations 2005, SI 2005/2680, reg 1(2). See also PARA 328 note 15.

4 Housing (Right of First Refusal) (England) Regulations 2005, SI 2005/1917, regs 2(2), 3; Housing (Right of First Refusal) (Wales) Regulations 2005, SI 2005/2680, regs 2(2), 3.

5 For these purposes, 'local housing authority' means, in England, a district council, a London borough council, the Common Council of the City of London or the Council of the Isles of Scilly; or, in Wales, a county council or county borough council: Housing (Right of First Refusal) (England) Regulations 2005, SI 2005/1917, reg 1(2); Housing (Right of First Refusal) (Wales) Regulations 2005, SI 2005/2680, reg 1(2).

6 As to the meaning of 'property' see PARA 328 note 15.

7 Housing (Right of First Refusal) (England) Regulations 2005, SI 2005/1917, regs 2(3), 4; Housing (Right of First Refusal) (Wales) Regulations 2005, SI 2005/2680, regs 2(3), 4.

8 Housing (Right of First Refusal) (England) Regulations 2005, SI 2005/1917, reg 12(1); Housing (Right of First Refusal) (Wales) Regulations 2005, SI 2005/2680, reg 12(1).

9 Ie the effect of regs 6–10 of the relevant regulations: see PARAS 330–331.

10 Housing (Right of First Refusal) (England) Regulations 2005, SI 2005/1917, reg 5(1), (2); Housing (Right of First Refusal) (Wales) Regulations 2005, SI 2005/2680, reg 5(1), (2).

330. Acceptance of the offer. Where the recipient of an offer notice[1] wishes to accept the offer, it must do so within the period of eight weeks[2] beginning with the date of receipt of the notice[3]. Acceptance of an offer must be by giving an acceptance notice[4], in which the recipient of the offer notice must either itself accept the offer or nominate another person[5] to accept the offer[6].

An acceptance notice must:

(1)   be in writing;

(2)   indicate clearly whether the person giving the notice is:

    (a)   accepting the offer; or

    (b)   nominating another person to accept the offer; and

(3)   provide the full postal address and telephone number of any nominee[7].

The service of an acceptance notice by any person entitled to do so does not confer any right on the owner of the property[8] to require that person to purchase the property unless and until that person enters into a binding contract for sale as described below[9].

A person who accepts an offer must enter into a binding contract with the owner for the purchase of the property:

(i)   not later than 12 weeks after the date on which the acceptance notice is served on the owner; or

(ii)   not later than four weeks after the date of receipt of written notification from the owner that he is ready to complete;

whichever is later[10]; and if this time limit is not complied with, the owner may dispose of the property as he sees fit[11].

1   As to the meaning of 'offer notice' see PARA 329.
2   In calculating a period for any purpose of the relevant regulations, with the exception of the 12 month period referred to in PARA 331, Christmas Day, Good Friday, or a day which under the Banking and Financial Dealings Act 1971 is a bank holiday, must be excluded: Housing (Right of First Refusal) (England) Regulations 2005, SI 2005/1917, reg 11; Housing (Right of First Refusal) (Wales) Regulations 2005, SI 2005/2680, reg 11.
3   Housing (Right of First Refusal) (England) Regulations 2005, SI 2005/1917, reg 6(1); Housing (Right of First Refusal) (Wales) Regulations 2005, SI 2005/2680, reg 6(1). As to the application of those regulations see also PARA 328 note 15.
4   Ie a notice which complies with heads (1)–(3) in the text. As to the service of notices see PARA 329 note 2.
5   The recipient of an offer notice may nominate another person to accept the offer, but the only persons who can be nominated to accept an offer are those who either: (1) in England, are private registered providers of social housing; (2) in Wales, are registered as a social landlord under the Housing Act 1996 Pt I (ss A1–64) (see PARA 166 et seq); or (3) in England or Wales, fulfil the landlord condition in the Housing Act 1985 s 80 (see LANDLORD AND TENANT vol 63 (2016) PARA 1037): Housing (Right of First Refusal) (England) Regulations 2005, SI 2005/1917, reg 8(1), (2) (amended by SI 2010/671); Housing (Right of First Refusal) (Wales) Regulations 2005, SI 2005/2680, reg 8(1), (2). Before a person can be nominated to accept a particular offer, that person must have given an unequivocal indication in writing to the recipient of the offer notice that it wishes to be nominated to accept the offer; and for these purposes, 'in writing' includes a document transmitted by facsimile or other electronic means: Housing (Right of First Refusal) (England) Regulations 2005, SI 2005/1917, reg 8(3), (4); Housing (Right of First Refusal) (Wales) Regulations 2005, SI 2005/2680, reg 8(3), (4).
6   Housing (Right of First Refusal) (England) Regulations 2005, SI 2005/1917, reg 6(2); Housing (Right of First Refusal) (Wales) Regulations 2005, SI 2005/2680, reg 6(2).
7   Housing (Right of First Refusal) (England) Regulations 2005, SI 2005/1917, reg 12(2); Housing (Right of First Refusal) (Wales) Regulations 2005, SI 2005/2680, reg 12(2).
8   As to the meanings of 'owner' and 'property' see PARA 328 note 15.
9   Housing (Right of First Refusal) (England) Regulations 2005, SI 2005/1917, reg 6(3); Housing (Right of First Refusal) (Wales) Regulations 2005, SI 2005/2680, reg 6(3).
10 Housing (Right of First Refusal) (England) Regulations 2005, SI 2005/1917, reg 10(1); Housing (Right of First Refusal) (Wales) Regulations 2005, SI 2005/2680, reg 10(1).
    If either or both of the parties request that the district valuer determine the value of the property in accordance with the Housing Act 1985 s 158 (see PARA 332), the time from the date that the request is received by the district valuer until the date that the determined value is notified to the parties must be excluded from the calculation of the period in heads (i)–(ii) in the text:

Housing (Right of First Refusal) (England) Regulations 2005, SI 2005/1917, reg 10(3); Housing (Right of First Refusal) (Wales) Regulations 2005, SI 2005/2680, reg 10(3). As to the meaning of 'district valuer' see PARA 527 note 14.

11 Housing (Right of First Refusal) (England) Regulations 2005, SI 2005/1917, reg 10(2); Housing (Right of First Refusal) (Wales) Regulations 2005, SI 2005/2680, reg 10(2). The relevant regulations do not apply to any subsequent disposal of the property by the owner: Housing (Right of First Refusal) (England) Regulations 2005, SI 2005/1917, reg 10(2); Housing (Right of First Refusal) (Wales) Regulations 2005, SI 2005/2680, reg 10(2).

331. Rejection of the offer. The recipient of an offer notice[1] must serve a rejection notice[2] as soon as it has decided that it does not wish to either:

(1)   accept the offer itself; or

(2)   nominate another person[3] to accept the offer[4].

The rejection notice must be served within eight weeks[5] from the date of receipt of the offer notice[6]. It must be in writing and must state that the person is rejecting the offer to purchase the property[7].

Where an owner[8] has served an offer notice and the recipient:

(a)   has not served either an acceptance notice or a rejection notice within eight weeks from the date of receipt of the offer notice; or

(b)   has served a rejection notice,

then the owner may[9] dispose of the property as he sees fit[10]; but if after the expiry of the period of 12 months[11] the owner retains his interest in the property, the relevant regulations apply[12] if there is to be a relevant disposal[13], other than an exempted disposal[14], of the owner's interest in the property[15].

1   As to the meaning of 'offer notice' see PARA 329.
2   Ie a notice complying with the text to note 7. As to service of notices see PARA 329 note 2.
3   As to such nomination see PARA 330 note 5.
4   Housing (Right of First Refusal) (England) Regulations 2005, SI 2005/1917, reg 7(1); Housing (Right of First Refusal) (Wales) Regulations 2005, SI 2005/2680, reg 7(1). As to the application of those regulations see PARA 328 note 15.
5   As to the computation of this period see PARA 330 note 2.
6   Housing (Right of First Refusal) (England) Regulations 2005, SI 2005/1917, reg 7(2); Housing (Right of First Refusal) (Wales) Regulations 2005, SI 2005/2680, reg 7(2).
7   Housing (Right of First Refusal) (England) Regulations 2005, SI 2005/1917, reg 12(3); Housing (Right of First Refusal) (Wales) Regulations 2005, SI 2005/2680, reg 12(3). As to the meaning of 'property' see PARA 328 note 15.
8   As to the meaning of 'owner' see PARA 328 note 15.
9   Ie subject to the provisions set out in the text to notes 11–15.
10 Housing (Right of First Refusal) (England) Regulations 2005, SI 2005/1917, reg 9(1); Housing (Right of First Refusal) (Wales) Regulations 2005, SI 2005/2680, reg 9(1). The relevant regulations do not apply to any subsequent disposal of the property by the owner: Housing (Right of First Refusal) (England) Regulations 2005, SI 2005/1917, reg 9(1); Housing (Right of First Refusal) (Wales) Regulations 2005, SI 2005/2680, reg 9(1); but see note 9.
11 In the circumstances referred to in head (a) in the text, the 12 month period begins the day after the expiry of the eight week period; and in the circumstances referred to in head (b) in the text, the 12 month period begins the day after that on which the rejection notice is served: Housing (Right of First Refusal) (England) Regulations 2005, SI 2005/1917, reg 9(3), (4); Housing (Right of First Refusal) (Wales) Regulations 2005, SI 2005/2680, reg 9(3), (4).
12 As to the application of those regulations see PARA 328 note 15.
13 As to the meaning of 'relevant disposal' see PARA 321.
14 As to the meaning of 'exempted disposal' see PARA 322.
15 Housing (Right of First Refusal) (England) Regulations 2005, SI 2005/1917, regs 2(1), 9(2); Housing (Right of First Refusal) (Wales) Regulations 2005, SI 2005/2680, regs 2(1), 9(2).

332. Consideration for disposal. The consideration for a disposal in pursuance of the right of first refusal[1] must be such amount as may be agreed between the parties, or determined by the district valuer[2], as being the amount which is to be taken to be the value of the dwelling house[3] at the time when the offer is made[4]. That value is to be taken to be the price which, at that time, the interest to be reconveyed, conveyed, surrendered or assigned would realise if sold on the open market by a willing vendor, on the assumption that any liability under:

(1)   the covenant to repay discount on early disposal[5]; and

(2)   any covenant to redeem the landlord's share where a conveyance or grant is executed in pursuance of the right to acquire on rent to mortgage terms[6]; and

(3)   any covenant to pay for the outstanding share on the disposal of a dwelling house subject to a shared ownership lease[7],

would be discharged by the vendor[8].

If the offer is accepted[9], no payment may be required in pursuance of any such covenant as is mentioned in heads (1) to (3) above; but the consideration must be reduced[10] by such amount, if any, as, on a disposal made at the time the offer was made, being a relevant disposal[11] which is not an exempted disposal[12], would fall to be paid under that covenant[13]. Where, however, there is a charge on the dwelling house having priority over the charge to secure payment of the sum due under the covenant mentioned in heads (1) to (3) above, the consideration may not be so reduced below the amount necessary[14] to discharge the outstanding sum secured by the first-mentioned charge at the date of the offer[15].

1   Ie such a disposal as is mentioned in the Housing Act 1985 s 156A(4): see PARA 328.
2   Ie as determined in accordance with regulations under the Housing Act 1985 s 156A: see PARA 330 note 10. As to the meaning of 'district valuer' see PARA 527 note 14.
3   As to the meaning of 'dwelling house' see PARA 231.
4   Housing Act 1985 s 158(1) (substituted by the Housing Act 2004 s 188(3)(b)). The Housing Act 1985 s 158 is omitted where the Housing (Right to Acquire) Regulations 1997, SI 1997/619 (right to acquire conferred by the Housing Act 1996 or the Housing and Regeneration Act 2008: see PARAS 240–244), apply: see the Housing (Right to Acquire) Regulations 1997, SI 1997/619, Sch 1 para 22).
5   Ie the covenant required by the Housing Act 1985 s 155: see PARA 323.
6   Ie any covenant required by the Housing Act 1985 s 151A, Sch 6A para 1: see PARA 318. As to the meaning of 'the right to acquire on rent to mortgage terms' see PARA 318. That right is now exercisable only where it was claimed before 18 July 2005: see s 142A; and PARA 318.
7   Ie any covenant required by the Housing Act 1985 Sch 8 para 6 (repealed).
8   Housing Act 1985 s 158(2) (amended by the Leasehold Reform, Housing and Urban Development Act 1993 s 187(1), Sch 21 para 15; and the Housing Act 2004 s 188(3)(c)).
9   Ie in accordance with regulations under the Housing Act 1985 s 156A: see PARA 330.
10 Ie subject to the Housing Act 1985 s 158(4): see the text and notes 14–15.
11 As to the meaning of 'relevant disposal' see PARA 321.
12 As to the meaning of 'exempted disposal' see PARA 322.
13 Housing Act 1985 s 158(3) (amended by the Housing and Planning Act 1986 s 24(1)(a), Sch 5 para 1(3), (5); and the Housing Act 2004 s 188(3)(d)).
14 Ie as determined in accordance with regulations under the Housing Act 1985 s 156A: see PARA 330.
15 Housing Act 1985 s 158(4) (added by the Housing and Planning Act 1986 Sch 5 para 1(3), (5); amended by the Housing Act 2004 s 188(3)(e)). The Housing Act 1985 s 158 is modified where: (1) the Housing (Extension of Right to Buy) Order 1993, SI 1993/2240 (see PARA 233), applies (see Schedule para 45); (2) the Housing (Preservation of Right to Buy) Regulations 1993, SI 1993/2241 (see PARA 334 et seq), apply (see Sch 1 para 23).

D.   OTHER RESTRICTIONS ON DISPOSAL WHERE THE RIGHT TO BUY HAS BEEN EXERCISED

333. Restrictions on disposal of dwelling houses in National Parks etc. Where a conveyance or grant is executed in pursuance of the right to buy[1] by a local authority[2] or a housing association[3] ('the landlord') of a dwelling house[4] situated in a National Park, an area designated[5] as an area of outstanding natural beauty or an area designated by order of the appropriate national authority as a rural area[6], the conveyance or grant may[7] contain a covenant limiting the freedom of the tenant[8], including any successor in title of his and any person deriving title under him or such a successor, to dispose of the dwelling house in the following manner[9]. The limitation is that until such time, if any, as may be notified in writing by the landlord to the tenant or a successor in title of his:

(1)   there will be no relevant disposal[10] which is not an exempted disposal[11] without the written consent of the landlord, but that consent may not be withheld if the disposal is to a person satisfying the specified condition[12]; and

(2)   there will be no disposal by way of tenancy[13] or licence[14] without the written consent of the landlord unless the disposal is to a person satisfying that condition or by a person whose only or principal home[15] is, and throughout the duration of the tenancy or licence remains, the dwelling house[16].

The condition is that the person to whom the disposal is made or, if it is made to more than one person, at least one of them, has throughout the period of three years immediately preceding the application for consent or, in the case of a disposal by way of tenancy or licence, preceding the disposal:

(a)   had his place of work in a region designated by order of the appropriate national authority which, or part of which, is comprised in the National Park or area; or

(b)   had his only or principal home in such a region;

or has had the one in part or parts of that period and the other in the remainder; but the region need not have been the same throughout the period[17].

A disposal in breach of such a covenant is void and, so far as it relates to disposals by way of tenancy or licence, such a covenant may be enforced by the landlord as if:

(i)   the landlord were possessed of land adjacent to the house concerned; and

(ii)   the covenant were expressed to be made for the benefit of such adjacent land[18].

Instead of the covenant described above, and subject to the required consent[19], the conveyance or grant may contain a covenant conferring a right of first refusal[20] on the landlord or other prescribed person[21].

The above restrictions do not apply where the right to acquire conferred by the Housing Act 1996[22] or the Housing and Regeneration Act 2008[23] has been exercised[24].

1   Ie in pursuance of the right to buy provisions contained in the Housing Act 1985 Pt V (ss 118–188): see PARAS 230 et seq, 334 et seq. As to the meaning of 'the right to buy' see PARA 239.

2   As to the meaning of 'local authority' see PARA 12.

3   As to housing associations see PARA 13.

4   As to the meaning of 'dwelling house' see PARA 231.

5   Ie designated under the Countryside and Rights of Way Act 2000 s 82: see OPEN SPACES AND COUNTRYSIDE vol 78 (2010) PARA 658.

6   Any such order: (1) may make different provision with respect to different cases or descriptions of case, including different provision for different areas; and (2) if made by the Secretary of State, must be made by statutory instrument which is subject to annulment in pursuance of a resolution of either House of Parliament: see the Housing Act 1985 s 157(8). By virtue of the Housing (Consequential Provisions) Act 1985 s 2(2), a number of orders have effect as if made under these provisions: see eg the Housing (Right to Buy) (Designated Regions) Order 1980, SI 1980/1345. For recent examples of orders made in the exercise of these powers see the Housing (Right to Buy) (Designated Rural Areas and Designated Regions) (England) Order 2005, SI 2005/1995; the Housing (Right to Buy) (Designated Rural Areas and Designated Region) (England) Order 2006, SI 2006/1948; the Housing (Right to Acquire and Right to Buy) (Designated Rural Areas and

Designated Regions) (Wales) Order 2003, SI 2003/54; the Housing (Right to Buy) (Designated Rural Areas and Designated Regions) (England) Order 2016, SI 2016/587.

7 Ie subject to the Housing Act 1985 s 156A(8): see PARA 327.
8 As to the meaning of 'tenant' see PARA 31 note 3.
9 Housing Act 1985 s 157(1) (amended by the Government of Wales Act 1998 s 152, Sch 18 Pt IV; the Countryside and Rights of Way Act 2000 s 93, Sch 15 para 9; and the Housing Act 2004 s 188(2)(a)). As to the appropriate national authority, the Secretary of State and the transfer of functions under the Housing Act 1985, so far as exercisable in relation to Wales, to the Welsh Ministers see PARA 7.
10 As to the meaning of 'relevant disposal' see PARA 321.
11 As to the meaning of 'exempted disposal' see PARA 322.
12 Ie the condition stated in the Housing Act 1985 s 157(3): see the text and note 19.
13 As to the meaning of 'tenancy' see PARA 31 note 3.
14 For these purposes, any reference to a disposal by way of tenancy or licence does not include a reference to a relevant disposal or an exempted disposal: Housing Act 1985 s 157(6A) (added by the Housing Act 1988 s 126(1), (5)).
15 As to the meaning of 'only or principal home' see LANDLORD AND TENANT vol 63 (2016) PARA 1037 note 27.
16 Housing Act 1985 s 157(2) (amended by the Housing Act 1988 s 126(2); and the Housing Act 1988 ss 126(1), (2), 266, Sch 16). Where such a covenant imposes the limitation specified in the Housing Act 1985 s 157(2), the limitation is a local land charge; and the Chief Land Registrar must enter a restriction in the register of title reflecting the limitation: Housing Act 1985 s 157(7) (amended by the Land Registration Act 2002 s 133, Sch 11 para 18(1), (4)). As to local land charges see REAL PROPERTY AND REGISTRATION vol 87 (2012) PARA 714 et seq; and as to the register of title see REAL PROPERTY AND REGISTRATION vol 87 (2012) PARA 328 et seq.
17 Housing Act 1985 s 157(3) (amended by the Housing Act 1988 s 126(1), (3)).
18 Housing Act 1985 s 157(6) (amended by the Housing Act 1988 s 126(1), (4)). The Housing Act 1985 s 157 is modified where: (1) the Housing (Extension of Right to Buy) Order 1993, SI 1993/2240 (see PARA 233), applies (see Schedule para 44); (2) the Housing (Preservation of Right to Buy) Regulations 1993, SI 1993/2241 (see PARA 334 et seq), apply (see Sch 1 para 22).
19 See the Housing Act 1985 s 156A(9); and PARA 327.
20 Ie a covenant such as is described in the Housing Act 1985 s 156A: see PARAS 327–328.
21 See the Housing Act 1985 s 156A(8); and PARA 327.
22 See PARAS 242–244.
23 See PARAS 240–241.
24 See the Housing (Right to Acquire) Regulations 1997, SI 1997/619, Sch 1 para 21, applying in relation to the right to acquire under the Housing and Regeneration Act 2008 by virtue of s 184, which applies the Housing Act 1996 s 17 (regulations modifying the Housing Act 1985): see PARA 241.

(vi) Preservation of Secure Tenant's Right to Buy on Disposal to Certain Types of Landlord

334. Cases in which right to buy is preserved. The right to buy[1] and the right to acquire on rent to mortgage terms[2] (so far as the latter right may still be exercisable[3]) continue to apply where a person ceases to be a secure tenant[4] of a dwelling house[5] by reason of the disposal by the landlord[6] of an interest in the dwelling house to a person who is not an authority or body fulfilling the landlord condition[7] for secure tenancies[8].

The above provisions do not, however, apply:

(1)   where the former landlord[9] was a person against whom the right to buy could not be exercised by virtue of its being a charity or a certain type of housing association[10]; or

(2)   in such other cases as may be excepted from the operation of these provisions by order of the appropriate national authority[11].

Orders made under head (2) above:

(a)　　may relate to particular disposals and may make different provision with respect to different cases or descriptions of case, including different provision for different areas; and

(b)　　must be made by statutory instrument[12].

The preserved right to buy[13] does not apply where the extended right to buy[14], or the right to acquire conferred by the Housing Act 1996[15] or the Housing and Regeneration Act 2008[16] arises and the relevant regulations[17] apply[18].

In Wales a local housing authority may apply to the Welsh Ministers for a direction suspending the preserved right to buy for a period of up to five years[19].

1　As to the meaning of 'the right to buy' see PARA 239.
2　As to the meaning of 'the right to buy on rent to mortgage terms' see PARA 318.
3　The right to buy on rent to mortgage terms is now exercisable only where it was claimed before 18 July 2005: see the Housing Act 1985 s 142A; and PARA 318.
4　As to the meaning of 'secure tenant' see PARA 230 note 2.
5　As to the meaning of 'dwelling house' see PARA 231.
6　As to the meaning of 'landlord' see PARA 31 note 3.
7　Ie a person who is not an authority or body within the Housing Act 1985 s 80: see LANDLORD AND TENANT vol 63 (2016) PARA 1037.
8　Housing Act 1985 s 171A(1) (s 171A added by the Housing and Planning Act 1986 s 8(1)). For the transitional provision made in respect of outstanding applications to exercise a preserved right to buy in relation to an interest in land in England held by an English registered social landlord see the Housing and Regeneration Act 2008 (Consequential Provisions) (No 2) Order 2010, SI 2010/671, art 5, Sch 2 paras 1, 2, 5–8.
9　For these purposes, the 'former landlord' is the person mentioned in the Housing Act 1985 s 171A(1) (see the text and notes 1–8): s 171A(2)(c) (as added: see note 2). Section s 171A(2) is modified where the Housing (Preservation of Right to Buy) Regulations 1993, SI 1993/2241 (see PARA 336 note 3), apply, so as to refer to the provisions of the Housing Act 1985 Pt V (ss 118–188) instead of to the 'following provisions' of Pt V: see the Housing (Preservation of Right to Buy) Regulations 1993, SI 1993/2241, Sch 1 para 27.
10　Ie by virtue of the Housing Act 1985 Sch 5 para 1, 2 or 3: see PARAS 245–247.
11　Housing Act 1985 s 171A(3) (as added: see note 8). As to the appropriate national authority, the Secretary of State and the transfer of functions under the Housing Act 1985, so far as exercisable in relation to Wales, to the Welsh Ministers see PARA 7.
　　Sections 171A–171H are omitted where: (1) the Housing (Extension of Right to Buy) Order 1993, SI 1993/2240 (see PARA 233), applies (see Schedule para 55); (2) the Housing (Right to Acquire) Regulations 1997, SI 1997/619 (right to acquire conferred by the Housing Act 1996 (see PARAS 242–244) or the Housing and Regeneration Act 2008 (see PARAS 240–241), apply (see the Housing (Right to Acquire) Regulations 1997, SI 1997/619, Sch 1 para 27).
12　Housing Act 1985 s 171A(4) (as added: see note 8). If made by the Secretary of State, the instrument is subject to annulment in pursuance of a resolution of either House of Parliament: see s 171A(4) (as so added).
13　Ie the Housing Act 1985 ss 171A–171H: see the text and notes 1–12; and PARA 335 et seq.
14　As to the extended right to buy see PARA 233.
15　See PARAS 242–244.
16　See PARAS 240–241.
17　Ie: (1) the Housing (Extension of Right to Buy) Order 1993, SI 1993/2240; or (2) the Housing (Right to Acquire) Regulations 1997, SI 1997/619, as the case may be.
18　See note 11.
19　See PARAS 260–266.

335. Extent of preserved right; qualifying persons and dwelling houses. Any of the following persons, namely:

(1)　　the former secure tenant[1], or in the case of a joint tenancy, each of them;

(2)　　a qualifying successor[2]; and

(3)　　a person to whom a tenancy[3] of a dwelling house[4] is granted jointly with a person who has the preserved right to buy[5] in relation to that dwelling house,

has the preserved right to buy so long as he occupies the relevant dwelling house as his only or principal home[6], subject to the following provisions[7]. Such a person ceases, however, to have the preserved right to buy if the tenancy of a relevant dwelling house becomes a demoted tenancy[8] by virtue of a demotion order[9].

The following are qualifying successors for these purposes:

(a) where the former secure tenancy was not a joint tenancy and, immediately before his death, the former secure tenant was a tenant under an assured tenancy[10] of a dwelling house in relation to which he had the preserved right to buy, a member of the former secure tenant's family[11] who acquired that assured tenancy under the will or intestacy of the former secure tenant or in whom that assured tenancy vested[12] by way of a statutory succession to the assured tenancy;

(b) where the former secure tenancy was not a joint tenancy, a member of the former secure tenant's family to whom the former secure tenant assigned his assured tenancy of a dwelling house in relation to which, immediately before the assignment, he had the preserved right to buy;

(c) a person who becomes the tenant of a dwelling house, in place of the person who had the preserved right to buy in relation to that dwelling house, in pursuance of a property adjustment order made in connection with matrimonial proceedings[13], an order transferring the tenancy on divorce, separation etc[14], a property adjustment order after an overseas divorce, etc[15], an order for financial relief against a parent[16] or a property adjustment order in connection with civil partnership proceedings[17] or after overseas dissolution of a civil partnership[18].

The relevant dwelling house is in the first instance:

(i) in relation to a person within head (1) above, the dwelling house which was the subject of the qualifying disposal[19];

(ii) in relation to a person within head (2) above, the dwelling house of which he acquired the assured tenancy, became the assignee of the assured tenancy or became the tenant as mentioned in heads (a) to (c) above;

(iii) in relation to a person within head (3) above, the dwelling house of which he became a joint tenant as mentioned in that head[20].

If a person having the preserved right to buy becomes the tenant of another dwelling house in place of the relevant dwelling house, whether the new dwelling house is entirely different or partly or substantially the same as the previous dwelling house, and the landlord is the same person as the landlord of the previous dwelling house or, where that landlord was a company, is a connected company[21], the new dwelling house becomes the relevant dwelling house for the purposes of the preserved right to buy[22].

1   For these purposes, the 'former secure tenant' is the person mentioned in the Housing Act 1985 s 171A(1) (see PARA 334): s 171A(2)(c) (ss 171A, 171B added by the Housing and Planning Act 1986 s 8(1)).

2   Ie as defined in the Housing Act 1985 s 171B(4): see heads (a)–(c) in the text.

3   As to the meaning of 'tenancy' see PARA 31 note 3.

4   As to the meaning of 'dwelling house' see PARA 231.

5   For these purposes, references to the preservation of the right to buy and to a person having the preserved right to buy are to the continued application of the provisions of the Housing Act 1985 Pt V (ss 118–188) (see PARAS 230 et seq, 336 et seq) by virtue of s 171A (see PARA 334) and to a person in relation to whom those provisions so apply: s 171A(2)(a) (as added: see note 1).

6   As to the meaning of 'only or principal home' see LANDLORD AND TENANT vol 63 (2016) PARA 1037 note 27.

7   Housing Act 1985 s 171B(1), (3) (as added: see note 1). For the transitional provision made in respect of outstanding applications to exercise a preserved right to buy in relation to an interest in land in England held by an English registered social landlord see the Housing and Regeneration Act 2008 (Consequential Provisions) (No 2) Order 2010, SI 2010/671, art 5, Sch 2 paras 1, 2, 5–8.

8 Ie by virtue of a demotion order under the Housing Act 1988 s 6A: see LANDLORD AND TENANT vol 63 (2016) PARA 883.
9 Housing Act 1985 s 171B(1A) (added by the Anti-social Behaviour Act 2003 s 14(5), Sch 1 para 2(1), (3)).
10 Ie an assured tenancy under the Housing Act 1988 Pt I (ss 1–45): see LANDLORD AND TENANT vol 63 (2016) PARA 825 et seq.
11 As to the meaning of 'member of a person's family' see PARA 274 note 5.
12 Ie under the Housing Act 1988 s 17: see LANDLORD AND TENANT vol 63 (2016) PARA 901.
13 Ie in pursuance of an order made under the Matrimonial Causes Act 1973 s 24: see MATRIMONIAL AND CIVIL PARTNERSHIP LAW vol 73 (2015) PARA 557 et seq.
14 Ie in pursuance of an order under the Matrimonial Homes Act 1983 Sch 1 (repealed) or the Family Law Act 1996 Sch 7: see MATRIMONIAL AND CIVIL PARTNERSHIP LAW vol 72 (2015) PARA 326 et seq.
15 Ie in pursuance of an order made under the Matrimonial and Family Proceedings Act 1984 s 17(1): see MATRIMONIAL AND CIVIL PARTNERSHIP LAW vol 73 (2015) PARAS 557 et seq, 591.
16 Ie in pursuance of an order made under the Children Act 1989 s 15(1), Sch 1 para 1: see CHILDREN AND YOUNG PERSONS vol 9 (2017) PARA 623 et seq.
17 Ie an order under the Civil Partnership Act 2004 Sch 5 Pt 2, or Sch 7 para 9(2) or (3): see MATRIMONIAL AND CIVIL PARTNERSHIP LAW vol 73 (2015) PARAS 556 et seq, 591.
18 Housing Act 1985 s 171B(4) (as added (see note 1); amended by the Housing Act 1988 s 127(1); the Housing Act 1996 s 222, Sch 18 paras 16, 26(1)(a); the Family Law Act 1996 s 66(1), Sch 8 para 56; and the Civil Partnership Act 2004 s 81, Sch 8 para 31).
19 For these purposes, 'qualifying disposal' means a disposal in relation to which the Housing Act 1985 s 171A (see PARA 334) applies: s 171A(2)(b) (as added: see note 1).
20 Housing Act 1985 s 171B(5) (as added (see note 1); amended by the Housing Act 1996 Sch 18 para 26(1)(b); modified by the Housing (Preservation of Right to Buy) Regulations 1993, SI 1993/2241, Sch 1 para 28). See also PARA 334 note 11.
21 For these purposes, 'connected company' means a subsidiary or holding company within the meaning of the Companies Act 2006 s 1159 (see COMPANIES vol 14 (2016) PARA 22): Housing Act 1985 s 171B(6) (as added (see note 1); amended by SI 2009/1941).
22 Housing Act 1985 s 171B(6) (as added: see note 1).

336. Modification of statutory provisions. Where the right to buy is preserved[1], the statutory provisions relating to that right[2] have effect subject to such exceptions, adaptations and other modifications as may be prescribed by regulations made by the appropriate national authority[3].

The regulations may in particular provide:

(1)   that certain of the exceptions to the right to buy[4] do not apply;
(2)   that the statutory provisions relating to the right to acquire on rent to mortgage terms[5], where that right is still exercisable[6], do not apply; and
(3)   that the landlord[7] is not required to but may include a covenant for the repayment of discount, provided its terms are no more onerous that those of the covenant to be included[8] under the statutory provisions with regard to early disposal[9].

The prescribed exceptions, adaptations and other modifications must take the form of textual amendments of the statutory provisions relating to the right to buy as they apply in cases where the right to buy is preserved; and the first regulations, and any subsequent consolidating regulations, must set out the statutory provisions relating to the right to buy as they so apply[10]. The regulations:

(a)   may make different provision for different cases or descriptions of case, including different provision for different areas;
(b)   may contain such incidental, supplementary and transitional provisions as the appropriate national authority considers appropriate; and
(c)   must be made by statutory instrument[11].

Such regulations may also:

(i)   make provision for continuing the effect of a suspension order[12] where the secure tenancy[13] in respect of which the order was made has been replaced by an assured tenancy[14];

(ii)   make specified provision[15] with regard to the disclosure of information about anti-social behaviour[16].

The specific modifications made by such regulations[17] are set out in the text and notes to the appropriate paragraph of this title if they are substantive, but are otherwise merely referred to in the notes to the appropriate paragraph where relevant[18].

1   As to the cases in which the right to buy is preserved see PARA 334.
2   Ie the Housing Act 1985 Pt V (ss 118–188): see PARAS 230 et seq, 2008 et seq.
3   Housing Act 1985 s 171C(1) (s 171C added by the Housing and Planning Act 1986 s 8(1)). As to the appropriate national authority, the Secretary of State and the transfer of functions under the Housing Act 1985, so far as exercisable in relation to Wales, to the Welsh Ministers see PARA 7.
    In exercise of the power so conferred, and prior to the transfer of functions in relation to Wales, the Secretary of State made the Housing (Preservation of Right to Buy) Regulations 1993, SI 1993/2241, which came into force on 11 October 1993: see reg 1(1). For transitional provisions see regs 1(2), 3, Schs 3, 4. Subject to reg 3, the Housing Act 1985 Pt V, as it applies in the circumstances described in s 171A(1) (cases in which right to buy is preserved: see PARA 334) has effect subject to the exceptions, adaptations and other modifications specified in the Housing (Preservation of Right to Buy) Regulations 1993, SI 1993/2241, Sch 1; and is set out, as it so applies, in Sch 2: reg 2(1), (2). For general modifications to terminology see Sch 1 paras 1, 2. It is submitted that, unless specifically excluded under the 1993 Regulations, later amendments to the Housing Act 1985 Pt V made by eg the Civil Partnership Act 2004 and the Housing Act 2004 also apply with respect to the preserved right to buy, even where the Housing (Preservation of Right to Buy) Regulations 1993, SI 1993/2241, Schs 1, 2 have not been consistently amended in the light of later legislation, since an alternative interpretation could lead to absurdities, although this is ultimately a matter for the courts.
    As to the exercise of that power see also: (1) the Housing (Preservation of Right to Buy) (Amendment) Regulations 1999, SI 1999/1213; the Housing (Preservation of Right to Buy) (Amendment) (Wales) Regulations 2001, SI 2001/1301, cited in PARA 290; (2) the Housing (Right of First Refusal) (England) Regulations 2005, SI 2005/1917, reg 14; the Housing (Right of First Refusal) (Wales) Regulations 2005, SI 2005/2680, reg 14, cited in PARA 328 note 15.
    See also the Local Government Reorganisation (Preservation of Right to Buy) Order 1986, SI 1986/2092, made under the Local Government Act 1985 s 101, which: (a) came into operation on 11 December 1986 (Local Government Reorganisation (Preservation of Right to Buy) Order 1986, SI 1986/2092, art 1); (b) makes provision for preserving the right to buy in certain cases where a landlord which is a successor authority within the meaning of that Order disposes of an interest in the dwelling house to a person which does not fulfil the landlord condition in the Housing Act 1985 s 80 (see LANDLORD AND TENANT vol 63 (2016) PARA 1037) (see the Local Government Reorganisation (Preservation of Right to Buy) Order 1986, SI 1986/2092, arts 2–5 (amended by SI 2000/1553)); and (c) modifies the provisions of the Housing Act 1985 Pt V accordingly (see the Local Government Reorganisation (Preservation of Right to Buy) Order 1986, SI 1986/2092, arts 6–12, Schs 1, 2 (amended by SI 2000/1553, SI 2004/3168, SI 2005/2929, SI 2008/2831 and SI 2012/1659)). That Order is not set out in detail in this work.
    For the transitional provision made in respect of outstanding applications to exercise a preserved right to buy in relation to an interest in land in England held by an English registered social landlord see the Housing and Regeneration Act 2008 (Consequential Provisions) (No 2) Order 2010, SI 2010/671, art 5, Sch 2 paras 1, 2, 5–8.
    The Housing Act 1985 s 171C is omitted where the Housing (Preservation of Right to Buy) Regulations 1993, SI 1993/2241, apply: see Sch 1 para 29. See also PARA 334 note 11.
4   Ie the exceptions in the Housing Act 1985 Sch 5 paras 1, 3, 5–11: see PARAS 245–247, 249–252. The disapplication by the regulations of Sch 5 para 1 is not to be taken to authorise any action on the part of a charity which would conflict with the trusts of the charity: s 171C(5) (added by the Housing Act 1988 s 127(3)). The Housing Act 1985 Sch 5 paras 1, 3 are disapplied where the Housing (Preservation of Right to Buy) Regulations 1993, SI 1993/2241, apply: see Sch 1 para 41.
5   Ie the Housing Act 1985 ss 143–153: see PARA 318 et seq. As to the meaning of 'the right to acquire on rent to mortgage terms' see PARA 318.
6   The right to acquire on rent to mortgage terms is now exercisable only where it was claimed before 18 July 2005: see the Housing Act 1985 s 142A; and PARA 318.
7   As to the meaning of 'landlord' see PARA 31 note 3.
8   Ie the covenant provided for in the Housing Act 1985 s 155: see PARA 323.
9   Housing Act 1985 s 171C(2) (as added (see note 4); amended by the Housing Act 1988 s 127(2), (3); the Leasehold Reform, Housing and Urban Development Act 1993 s 87(1), (2), Sch 21 para 19, Sch 22).
10 Housing Act 1985 s 171C(3) (as added: see note 4).

11 Housing Act 1985 s 171C(4) (as added: see note 4). If made by the Secretary of State, the instrument is subject to annulment in pursuance of a resolution of either House of Parliament: see s 171C(4) (as so added).

12 As to suspension orders see the Housing Act 1985 s 121A; and PARA 259.

13 As to secure tenancies see LANDLORD AND TENANT vol 63 (2016) PARA 1037 et seq.

14 Housing Act 2004 s 192(3)(a). As to assured tenancies see LANDLORD AND TENANT vol 63 (2016) PARA 825 et seq.

15 Ie provision corresponding to the Housing Act 2004 s 194(1)–(3) (see PARA 453) so far as those subsections relate to the Housing Act 1985 s 138(2B) (see PARA 291).

16 Housing Act 2004 s 194(4)(a).

17 Ie those made by the Housing (Preservation of Right to Buy) Regulations 1993, SI 1993/2241, Sch 1 (amended, in relation to Wales, by SI 2012/2090), and set out in the Housing (Preservation of Right to Buy) Regulations 1993, SI 1993/2241, Sch 2 (amended by SI 1999/1213, SI 2006/680 and SI 2016/481; and, in relation to Wales, by SI 2001/1301 and SI 2012/2090).

18 See eg PARA 333 note 18.

337. Disposal of landlord's interest in qualifying dwelling house. The disposal by the landlord[1] of an interest in the qualifying dwelling house[2], whether his whole interest or a lesser interest, does not affect the preserved right to buy, unless:

(1)   as a result of the disposal a specified authority or body[3] becomes the landlord of the qualifying person[4] or persons; or

(2)   the statutory provisions relating to the effect of failure to register an entry protecting a preserved right to buy[5] apply,

in which case the right to buy ceases to be preserved[6].

The disposal by the landlord of a qualifying dwelling house of less than his whole interest as landlord of the dwelling house, or in part of it, requires the consent of the appropriate authority[7], unless the disposal is to the qualifying person or persons[8]. Consent may be given in relation to a particular disposal or generally in relation to disposals of a particular description and may, in either case, be given subject to conditions[9].

A disposal made without the consent so required is void, except in a case where, by reason of a failure to make the entries on the land register or land charges register[10], the preserved right to buy does not bind the person to whom the disposal is made[11].

1 As to the meaning of 'landlord' see PARA 31 note 3.

2 For these purposes, references to a qualifying dwelling house, in relation to the preserved right to buy, are to a dwelling house in relation to which a person has that right: Housing Act 1985 s 171B(2) (ss 171B, 171D added by the Housing and Planning Act 1986 s 8(1)). As to the meaning of 'dwelling house' see PARA 231.

As to the cases in which the right to buy is preserved see PARA 334. For the transitional provision made in respect of outstanding applications to exercise a preserved right to buy in relation to an interest in land in England held by an English registered social landlord see the Housing and Regeneration Act 2008 (Consequential Provisions) (No 2) Order 2010, SI 2010/671, art 5, Sch 2 paras 1, 2, 5–8.

3 Ie an authority or body within the Housing Act 1985 s 80(1): see LANDLORD AND TENANT vol 63 (2016) PARA 1037.

4 For these purposes, references to a qualifying person, in relation to the preserved right to buy, are to a person who has that right: Housing Act 1985 s 171B(2) (as added: see note 2). The rights of a qualifying person under Pt V (ss 118–188) (see PARAS 230 et seq, 338 et seq) in relation to the qualifying dwelling house are not to be regarded as falling within the Land Registration Act 2002 Sch 3 (specified interests overriding registered dispositions: see REAL PROPERTY AND REGISTRATION vol 87 (2012) PARA 482) (and so are liable to be postponed under s 29 (see REAL PROPERTY AND REGISTRATION vol 87 (2012) PARA 455), unless protected by means of a notice in the register): Housing Act 1985 Sch 9A para 6(1) (Sch 9A added by the Housing and Planning Act 1986 s 8(2), (3), Sch 2; the Housing Act 1985 Sch 9A para 6 substituted by the Land Registration Act 2002 s 133, Sch 11 para 18(1), (10)). As to the meaning of references to a person having the preserved right to buy see PARA 335 note 5.

5 Ie the Housing Act 1985 Sch 9A para 6: see note 4; and PARA 349.

6 Housing Act 1985 s 171D(1) (as added: see note 2).

7 'The appropriate authority' means: (1) in relation to a disposal of land in England, the Secretary of State; and (2) in relation to a disposal of land in Wales, the Welsh Ministers: Housing Act 1985 s 171D(2A) (added by the Housing and Regeneration Act 2008 s 191(1)(b)' and amended by the Housing and Planning Act 2016 s 92, Sch 4 para 1(1), (3)). As to the Secretary of State and the Welsh Ministers see PARA 7.

8 Housing Act 1985 s 171D(2) (as added (see note 2); amended by the Housing and Regeneration Act 2008 s 191(1)(a)). The Housing Act 1985 s 171D(2) does not apply to a disposal of land by a private registered provider of social housing: s 171D(2ZA) (added by the Housing and Planning Act 2016 Sch 4 para 1(1), (2)). As to private registered providers of social housing see PARA 53.

9 Housing Act 1985 s 171D(3) (as added: see note 2).

10 Ie the entries required by the Housing Act 1985 Sch 9A: see PARA 347 et seq.

11 Housing Act 1985 s 171D(4) (as added: see note 2). See also PARA 334 note 11.

338. Termination of landlord's interest in qualifying dwelling house. On the termination of the landlord's[1] interest in the qualifying dwelling house[2]:

(1)   on the occurrence of an event determining his estate or interest, or by re-entry on a breach of condition or forfeiture; or

(2)   where the interest is a leasehold interest, by notice given by him or a superior landlord, on the expiry or surrender of the term, or otherwise[3],

the right to buy[4] ceases to be preserved[5].

The termination of the landlord's interest by merger on his acquiring a superior interest, or on the acquisition by another person of the landlord's interest together with a superior interest, does not affect the preserved right to buy, unless:

(a)   as a result of the acquisition a specified authority or body[6] becomes the landlord of the qualifying person[7] or persons; or

(b)   the statutory provisions relating to the effect of failure to register an entry protecting a preserved right to buy[8] apply,

in which case the right to buy ceases to be preserved[9].

Where the termination of the landlord's interest[10] is caused by the act or omission of the landlord, a qualifying person who is thereby deprived of the preserved right to buy is entitled to be compensated by him[11].

1   As to the meaning of 'landlord' see PARA 31 note 3.

2   As to the meaning of 'qualifying dwelling house' see PARA 337 note 2.

3   Ie subject to the Housing Act 1985 s 171E(2): see the text and notes 4–11.

4   As to the meaning of 'the right to buy' see PARA 239.

5   Housing Act 1985 s 171E(1) (s 171E added by the Housing and Planning Act 1986 s 8(1)). As to the cases in which the right to buy is preserved see PARA 334. For the transitional provision made in respect of outstanding applications to exercise a preserved right to buy in relation to an interest in land in England held by an English registered social landlord see the Housing and Regeneration Act 2008 (Consequential Provisions) (No 2) Order 2010, SI 2010/671, art 5, Sch 2 paras 1, 2, 5–8.

6   Ie an authority or body within the Housing Act 1985 s 80(1): see LANDLORD AND TENANT vol 63 (2016) PARA 1037.

7   As to the meaning of 'qualifying person' see PARA 337 note 4.

8   Ie the Housing Act 1985 Sch 9A para 6: see PARAS 337 note 4, 349.

9   Housing Act 1985 s 171E(2) (as added: see note 5).

10 Ie as mentioned in the Housing Act 1985 s 171E(1): see the text and notes 1–5.

11 Housing Act 1985 s 171E(3) (as added: see note 5). See also PARA 334 note 11.

339. Transfer of qualifying person to alternative accommodation. The court may not order a qualifying person[1] to give up possession of the qualifying dwelling house[2] on the grounds that suitable alternative accommodation is available[3] unless the court is satisfied:

(1)   that the preserved right to buy[4] will continue[5] to be exercisable in relation to the dwelling house offered by way of alternative accommodation and that the interest of the landlord[6] in the new dwelling house will be:

(a)   where the new dwelling house is a house[7], not less than the interest of the landlord in the existing dwelling house; or

(b)   where the new dwelling house is a flat[8], not less than the interest of the landlord in the existing dwelling house or a term of years of which 80 years or more remain unexpired, whichever is the less; or

(2)   that the landlord of the new dwelling house will be a specified[9] authority or body[10].

1   As to the meaning of 'qualifying person' see PARA 337 note 4.
2   As to the meaning of 'qualifying dwelling house' see PARA 337 note 2; and as to the meaning of 'dwelling house' see PARA 231.
3   Ie in pursuance of the Rent Act 1977 s 98(1)(a) (see LANDLORD AND TENANT vol 63 (2016) PARAS 920, 921) or the Housing Act 1988 Sch 2 Pt II, Ground 9 (see LANDLORD AND TENANT vol 63 (2016) PARA 946).
4   As to the cases in which the right to buy is preserved see PARA 334. For the transitional provision made in respect of outstanding applications to exercise a preserved right to buy in relation to an interest in land in England held by an English registered social landlord see the Housing and Regeneration Act 2008 (Consequential Provisions) (No 2) Order 2010, SI 2010/671, art 5, Sch 2 paras 1, 2, 5–8.
5   Ie by virtue of the Housing Act 1985 s 171B(6): see PARA 335.
6   As to the meaning of 'landlord' see PARA 31 note 3.
7   As to the meaning of 'house' see PARA 231.
8   As to the meaning of 'flat' see PARA 231.
9   Ie an authority or body within the Housing Act 1985 s 80(1): see LANDLORD AND TENANT vol 63 (2016) PARA 1037.
10 Housing Act 1985 s 171F (added by the Housing and Planning Act 1986 s 8(1); amended by the Housing Act 1988 s 140, Sch 17 para 42). See also PARA 334 note 11.

340.   Disposal after notice claiming to exercise right to buy etc. Where notice has been given in respect of a dwelling house[1] claiming to exercise the right to buy[2] and before completion of the exercise of that right the dwelling house is the subject of:

(1)   a qualifying disposal[3]; or

(2)   a disposal to an authority or body satisfying the landlord condition for secure tenancies[4],

all parties are in the same position as if the disponee had become the landlord[5] before the notice was given and had been given that notice and any further notice given by the tenant[6] to the landlord and had taken all steps which the landlord had taken[7].

If, however, the circumstances after the disposal differ in any material respect, as for example where:

(a)   the interest of the disponee in the dwelling house after the disposal differs from that of the disponor before the disposal; or

(b)   any of the exceptions to the right to buy[8] becomes or ceases to be applicable,

all those concerned must, as soon as practicable, take all such steps, whether by way of amending or withdrawing and re-serving any notice or extending any period or otherwise, as may be requisite for the purpose of securing that all parties are, as nearly as may be, in the same position as they would have been if those circumstances had obtained before the disposal[9].

1   As to the meaning of 'dwelling house' see PARA 231.
2   As to the meaning of 'the right to buy' see PARA 239.
3   As to the meaning of 'qualifying disposal' see PARA 335 note 19.
4   Ie a disposal to which the Housing Act 1985 s 171D(1)(a) (see PARA 337 head (1)) or s 171E(2)(a) (see PARA 338 head (a)) applies.
5   As to the meaning of 'landlord' see PARA 31 note 3.
6   As to the meaning of 'tenant' see PARA 31 note 3.
7   Housing Act 1985 s 171H(1) (s 171H added by the Housing and Planning Act 1986 s 8(1); amended by the Leasehold Reform, Housing and Urban Development Act 1993 s 187(2), Sch 22).

8 Ie any of the provisions of the Housing Act 1985 Sch 5: see PARA 245 et seq.
9 Housing Act 1985 s 171H(2) (as added and amended: see note 7). See also PARA 334 note 11.

(vii) Appropriate National Authority's Powers in relation to the Right to Buy

341. General powers to intervene. The appropriate national authority may use its powers under the provisions set out below where it appears to it that tenants[1] generally, a tenant or tenants of a particular landlord[2], or tenants of a description of landlords, have or may have difficulty in exercising effectively and expeditiously the right to buy[3], or the right to acquire on rent to mortgage terms[4] (so far as the latter right is still exercisable[5]). These powers may, however, be exercised only after the appropriate national authority has given the landlord or landlords notice in writing of its intention to do so and while the notice is in force[6]. Such a notice is deemed to be given 72 hours after it has been sent[7].

Where a notice has been so given to a landlord or landlords, no step taken by the landlord or any of the landlords while the notice is in force or before it was given has any effect in relation to the exercise by a secure tenant[8] of the right to buy or the right to acquire on rent to mortgage terms except in so far as the notice otherwise provides[9].

While such a notice is in force, the appropriate national authority may do all such things as appear to it necessary or expedient to enable secure tenants of the landlord or landlords to which the notice was given to exercise the right to buy and the right to acquire on rent to mortgage terms; and appropriate national authority is not bound to take the steps which the landlord would have been bound[10] to take[11].

Such a notice may be withdrawn by a further notice in writing, either completely or in relation to a particular landlord or a particular case or description of case[12]. The further notice may give such directions as the appropriate national authority may think fit for the completion of a transaction begun before the further notice was given; and such directions are binding on the landlord, and may require the taking of steps different from those which the landlord would have been required to take if the appropriate national authority's powers to intervene[13] had not been used[14].

Where, in consequence of the exercise of its powers to intervene, the appropriate national authority receives sums due to a landlord, it may retain them while a notice is in force in relation to the landlord and it is not bound to account to the landlord for interest accruing on them[15].

Where the appropriate national authority exercises its powers to intervene with respect to secure tenants of a landlord, it may:

(1) calculate, in such manner and on such assumptions as it may determine, the costs incurred by it in doing so; and

(2) certify a sum as representing those costs;

and a sum so certified is a debt from the landlord to the appropriate national authority payable on a date specified in the certificate, together with interest from that date at a rate so specified[16]. Sums so payable may, without prejudice to any other method of recovery, be recovered from the landlord by the withholding of sums due appropriate national authority, including sums payable to the landlord and received by the appropriate national authority in consequence of its exercise of his or its powers to intervene[17].

The powers set out above, and the various powers described in the following paragraphs[18], do not apply:

(a) where the preserved right to buy[19] arises; or

(b)   where the right to acquire conferred by the Housing Act 1996[20] or the
Housing and Regeneration Act 2008[21] arises,

and the relevant regulations[22] apply[23].

1   As to the meaning of 'tenant' see PARA 31 note 3.
2   As to the meaning of 'landlord' see PARA 31 note 3.
3   As to the meaning of 'the right to buy' see PARA 239.
4   Housing Act 1985 s 164(1) (amended by the Leasehold Reform, Housing and Urban Development
Act 1993 s 187(1), Sch 21 para 16(1)). As to the meaning of 'the right to acquire on rent to
mortgage terms' see PARA 318. As to the appropriate national authority, and the transfer of
functions under the Housing Act 1985, so far as exercisable in relation to Wales, to the Welsh
Ministers see PARA 7.
5   The right to acquire on rent to mortgage terms is now only exercisable if claimed before 18 July
2005: see the Housing Act 1985 s 142A; and PARA 318.
6   Housing Act 1985 s 164(2).
7   Housing Act 1985 s 164(3).
8   As to the meaning of 'secure tenant' see PARA 230 note 2.
9   Housing Act 1985 s 164(4) (amended by the Leasehold Reform, Housing and Urban Development
Act 1993 Sch 21 para 16(2)).
10 Ie under the Housing Act 1985 Pt V (ss 118–188): see PARAS 230 et seq, 342 et seq.
11 Housing Act 1985 s 164(5) (amended by the Leasehold Reform, Housing and Urban Development
Act 1993 Sch 21 para 16(3)). Where the Housing (Extension of Right to Buy) Order 1993, SI
1993/2240 (see PARA 233), applies, and where it appears to the appropriate national authority
that the difficulty a tenant or tenants have or may have in exercising effectively and expeditiously
the right to buy or the right to acquire on rent to mortgage terms is due to a particular intermediate
landlord or a description of intermediate landlords or a particular freeholder or a description of
freeholders, the Housing Act 1985 s 164 applies with the necessary modifications as it applies to
a particular landlord or a description of landlords: see s 164(5A) (added for these purposes by the
Housing (Extension of Right to Buy) Order 1993, SI 1993/2240, Schedule para 47). As to the
meaning of 'intermediate landlord' and 'freeholder' see PARA 233 notes 18–19.
12 Housing Act 1985 s 166(1).
13 Ie the powers under the Housing Act 1985 s 164: see the text and notes 1–13.
14 Housing Act 1985 s 166(2).
15 Housing Act 1985 s 166(3).
16 Housing Act 1985 s 166(4).
17 Housing Act 1985 s 166(5). The Housing Act 1985 s 166 is modified where the Housing
(Extension of Right to Buy) Order 1993, SI 1993/2240, applies: see Schedule para 49. Where that
Order applies, the appropriate national authority, on giving to a freeholder, intermediate landlord
or landlord: (1) a notice under the Housing Act 1985 s 164 (notice of intention to intervene); or
(2) a further notice under s 166 (notice withdrawing previous notice), must, as soon as practicable,
send a copy of the notice to any other authority or body which is, to the appropriate national
authority's knowledge, a freeholder, intermediate landlord or landlord of any dwelling house
affected by the notice: see s 166A (added for these purposes by the Housing (Extension of Right
to Buy) Order 1993, SI 1993/2240, Schedule para 50).
18 Ie the Housing Act 1985 ss 164–170: see the text and notes 1–19; and PARAS 342–345.
19 As to the preserved right to buy see PARA 334 et seq.
20 See PARAS 242–244.
21 See PARAS 240–241.
22 Ie either: (1) the Housing (Preservation of Right to Buy) Regulations 1993, SI 1993/2241 (see
PARA 334 et seq); or (2) the Housing (Right to Acquire) Regulations 1997, SI 1997/619 (see
PARAS 241, 243), as the case may be.
23 See the Housing (Preservation of Right to Buy) Regulations 1993, SI 1993/2241, reg 2(1), Sch 1
para 25; the Housing (Right to Acquire) Regulations 1997, SI 1997/619, reg 3, Sch 1 para 25.

342.   Power to execute a vesting order. For the purpose of conveying a freehold
or granting a lease[1] in the exercise of its general powers to intervene[2], the
appropriate national authority may execute a document ('a vesting order'),
containing such provisions as that authority may determine[3].

A vesting order has the like effect, except in so far as it otherwise provides, as
a conveyance or grant duly executed in pursuance of the statutory provisions
relating to the right to buy or (so far as still exercisable[4]) the right to acquire on
rent to mortgage terms[5], and, in particular, binds both the landlord and its

successors in title and the tenant[6] and his successors in title, including any person deriving title under him or them, to the same extent as if the covenants contained in it and expressed to be made on their behalf had been entered into by them[7].

If the landlord's title to the dwelling house[8] in respect of which a vesting order is made is not registered, the vesting order must contain a certificate stating that the freehold conveyed or grant made by it is subject only to such incumbrances, rights and interests as are stated elsewhere in the vesting order or summarised in the certificate[9].

On a vesting order being presented to the Chief Land Registrar, the Registrar must register the tenant as proprietor of the title concerned; and, if the title has not previously been registered:

(1)   he must so register him with an absolute title or, as the case may require, a good leasehold title; and

(2)   he must, for the purpose of registration, accept the certificate in the vesting order as sufficient evidence of the facts stated in it[10].

The power set out above does not apply where the preserved right to buy[11], or the right to acquire conferred by the Housing Act 1996[12] or the Housing and Regeneration Act 2008[13], arises[14].

1   As to the meaning of 'lease' see PARA 31 note 3.
2   Ie in exercise of its powers under the Housing Act 1985 s 164: see PARA 341.
3   Housing Act 1985 s 165(1). As to the appropriate national authority, and the transfer of functions under the Housing Act 1985, so far as exercisable in relation to Wales, to the Welsh Ministers see PARA 7.
    For the purposes of stamp duty, the vesting order is to be treated as a document executed by the landlord (s 165(1)) but such a vesting order cannot now be subject to stamp duty (see the Finance Act 2003 s 125(1)). As to the meaning of 'landlord' see PARA 31 note 3. As to stamp duty land tax with regard to right to buy transactions see PARA 352.
4   The right to acquire on rent to mortgage terms is now only exercisable where claimed before 18 July 2005: seethe Housing Act 1985 s 142A; and PARA 318.
5   Ie the Housing Act 1985 Pt V (ss 118–188): see PARAS 230 et seq, 343 et seq.
6   As to the meaning of 'tenant' see PARA 31 note 3.
7   Housing Act 1985 s 165(2).
8   As to the meaning of 'dwelling house' see PARA 231.
9   Housing Act 1985 s 165(3).
10   Housing Act 1985 s 165(4). If a person suffers loss in consequence of a registration under s 165 in circumstances in which he would have been entitled to be indemnified under the Land Registration Act 2002 Sch 8 (see REAL PROPERTY AND REGISTRATION vol 87 (2012) PARA 500 et seq) by the Chief Land Registrar had the registration of the tenant as proprietor of the title been effected otherwise than under the Housing Act 1985 s 165, he is instead entitled to be indemnified by the appropriate national authority and s 166(4) (see PARA 341) applies accordingly: s 165(6) (amended by the Land Registration Act 2002 s 133, Sch 11 para 18(1), (5)).
    The Housing Act 1985 s 165 is modified where the Housing (Extension of Right to Buy) Order 1993, SI 1993/2240 (see PARA 233), applies: see Schedule para 48.
11   As to the preserved right to buy see PARA 334 et seq.
12   See PARAS 242–244.
13   See PARAS 240–241.
14   See PARA 341 text and notes 19–23.

343. Power to give directions as to covenants and conditions. Where it appears to the appropriate national authority that, if covenants or conditions of any kind were included in conveyances or grants of dwelling houses[1] of any description executed in pursuance of the statutory provisions[2] relating to the right to buy[3] or the right (so far as still exercisable) to acquire on rent to mortgage terms[4]:

(1)   the conveyances would not conform with the provisions to be included in conveyances of freeholds[5];

(2)   the grants would not conform with the provisions to be included in grants of leases[6]; or

(3)   in the case of conveyances or grants executed in pursuance of the right to acquire on rent to mortgage terms, the conveyances or grants would not conform with the provisions relating to redemption of the landlord's share[7],

the appropriate national authority may direct landlords[8] generally, landlords of a particular description or particular landlords not to include covenants or conditions of that kind in such conveyances or grants executed on or after a date specified in the direction[9].

Such a direction may be varied or withdrawn by a subsequent direction[10].

If a direction so given so provides, the following provisions apply in relation to a covenant or condition which:

(a)   was included in a conveyance or grant executed before the date specified in the direction; and

(b)   could not have been so included if the conveyance or grant had been executed on or after that date[11].

The covenant or condition is discharged or, if the direction so provides, modified, as from the specified date, to such extent or in such manner as may be provided by the direction; and the discharge or modification is binding on all person entitled or capable of becoming entitled to the benefit of the covenant or condition[12]. The landlord by whom the conveyance or grant was executed must, within such period as may be specified in the direction:

(i)   serve on the person registered as the proprietor of the dwelling house, and on any person registered as the proprietor of a charge affecting the dwelling house, a written notice informing him of the discharge or modification; and

(ii)   on behalf of the person registered as the proprietor of the dwelling house, apply to the Chief Land Registrar, and pay the appropriate fee, for notice of the discharge or modification to be entered in the register[13].

The power set out above does not apply where the preserved right to buy[14], or the right to acquire conferred by the Housing Act 1996[15] or the Housing and Regeneration Act 2008[16], arises[17].

1   As to the meaning of 'dwelling house' see PARA 231.
2   Ie the Housing Act 1985 Pt V (ss 118–188): see PARAS 230 et seq, 2015 et seq.
3   As to the meaning of 'the right to buy' see PARA 239.
4   The right to acquire on rent to mortgage terms is now only exercisable if claimed before 18 July 2005: see the Housing Act 1985 s 142A; and PARA 318.
5   Ie would not conform with the Housing Act 1985 Sch 6 Pt I (paras 1–7) (see PARAS 300–303) and Sch 6 Pt II (paras 8–9) (see PARA 304).
6   Ie would not conform with the Housing Act 1985 Sch 6 Pt I (paras 1–7) and Sch 6 Pt III (paras 11–19) (see PARAS 305–312).
7   Ie would not conform with the Housing Act 1985 Sch 6A: see PARA 318.
8   As to the meaning of 'landlord' see PARA 31 note 3.
9   Housing Act 1985 s 167(1) (amended by the Leasehold Reform, Housing and Urban Development Act 1993 s 187(1), Sch 21 para 17). As to the appropriate national authority, and the transfer of functions under the Housing Act 1985, so far as exercisable in relation to Wales, to the Welsh Ministers see PARA 7.
       The Housing Act 1985 s 167(1) is modified where the Housing (Extension of Right to Buy) Order 1993, SI 1993/2240 (see PARA 233), applies: see Schedule para 51.
10   Housing Act 1985 s 167(2).
11   Housing Act 1985 s 168(1). Section 168(1), (3) is modified where the Housing (Extension of Right to Buy) Order 1993, SI 1993/2240, applies: see Schedule para 52.
12   Housing Act 1985 s 168(2).
13   Housing Act 1985 s 168(3).
14   As to the preserved right to buy see PARA 334 et seq.
15   See PARAS 242–244.

16 See PARAS 240–241.
17 See PARA 341 text and notes 19–23.

344. Power to obtain information etc. Where it appears to the appropriate national authority necessary or expedient for the purpose of determining whether its general powers to intervene[1] or its power to give directions as to covenants and conditions[2] is or are exercisable, or for or in connection with the exercise of those powers, the appropriate national authority may by notice in writing to a landlord[3] require it:

(1) at such time and at such place as may be specified in the notice, to produce any document; or

(2) within such period as may be so specified or such longer period as the appropriate national authority may allow, to furnish a copy of any document or supply any information[4].

Any officer of the landlord designated in the notice for that purpose or having custody or control of the document or in a position to give that information must, without instructions from the landlord, take all reasonable steps to ensure that the notice is complied with[5].

The power set out above does not apply where the preserved right to buy[6], or the right to acquire conferred by the Housing Act 1996[7] or the Housing and Regeneration Act 2008[8], arises[9].

1 Ie its powers under the Housing Act 1985 s 164 or s 166: see PARA 341.
2 Ie its power under the Housing Act 1985 s 167 or s 168: see PARA 343.
3 For these purposes, references to a landlord include a landlord by whom a conveyance or grant was executed in pursuance of the Housing Act 1985 Pt V (ss 118–188) (see PARAS 230 et seq, 345 et seq): s 169(3) (amended by the Leasehold Reform, Housing and Urban Development Act 1993 s 187(2), Sch 22). As to the meaning of 'landlord' see PARA 31 note 3.
4 Housing Act 1985 s 169(1). As to the appropriate national authority, and the transfer of functions under the Housing Act 1985, so far as exercisable in relation to Wales, to the Welsh Ministers see PARA 7.
  Section 169 is modified where the Housing (Extension of Right to Buy) Order 1993, SI 1993/2240 (see PARA 233), applies: see Schedule para 53.
5 Housing Act 1985 s 169(2). See also note 4.
6 As to the preserved right to buy see PARA 334 et seq.
7 See PARAS 242–244.
8 See PARAS 240–241.
9 See PARA 341 text and notes 19–23.

345. Power to give assistance in connection with legal proceedings. The following provisions apply to:

(1) proceedings under, or to determine a question arising under or in connection with, the right to buy[1] or the right (so far as still exercisable[2]) to acquire on rent to mortgage terms[3];

(2) proceedings to determine a question arising under or in connection with a conveyance or grant executed in pursuance of those rights, other than proceedings to determine a question as to the value of a dwelling house[4] or part of a dwelling house[5].

A party or prospective party to such proceedings or prospective proceedings who has claimed to exercise or has exercised the right to buy or the right to acquire on rent to mortgage terms or is a successor in title of a person who has exercised either of those rights may apply to the appropriate national authority for assistance under these provisions[6]. The appropriate national authority may grant the application, if it thinks fit to do so on the ground:

(a) that the case raises a question of principle; or

(b)   that it is unreasonable, having regard to the complexity of the case, or to any other matter, to expect the applicant to deal with it without such assistance,

or by reason of any other special consideration[7].

Such assistance by the appropriate national authority may include:

(i)   giving advice;

(ii)   procuring or attempting to procure the settlement of the matter in dispute;

(iii) arranging for the giving of advice or assistance by a solicitor[8] or counsel;

(iv)   arranging for representation by a solicitor or counsel, including such assistance as is usually given by a solicitor or counsel in the steps preliminary or incidental to any proceedings, or in arriving at or giving effect to a compromise to avoid or bring to an end any proceedings; and

(v)   any other form of assistance which the appropriate national authority may consider appropriate;

but head (iv) above does not affect the law and practice regulating the descriptions of persons who may appear in, conduct, defend and address the court in any proceedings[9].

In so far as expenses are incurred by the appropriate national authority in providing the applicant with assistance under these provisions, the recovery of those expenses, as taxed or assessed in such manner as may be prescribed by rules of court, constitute a first charge for the benefit of the appropriate national authority:

(A)   on any costs which, whether by virtue of a judgment or order of a court or an agreement or otherwise, are payable to the applicant by any other person in respect of the matter in connection with which the assistance was given; and

(B)   so far as relates to any costs, on his rights under any compromise or settlement arrived at in connection with that matter to avoid or bring to an end any proceedings[10].

The powers set out above do not apply where the preserved right to buy[11], or the right to acquire conferred by the Housing Act 1996[12] or the Housing and Regeneration Act 2008[13], arises[14].

1   As to the meaning of 'the right to buy' see PARA 239.

2   The right to acquire on rent to mortgage terms is now only exercisable if claimed before 18 July 2005: see the Housing Act 1985 s 142A; and PARA 318.

3   Ie proceedings under, or to determine a question arising under or in connection with, the Housing Act 1985 Pt V (ss 118–188): see PARAS 230 et seq, 346 et seq.

4   As to the meaning of 'dwelling house' see PARA 231.

5   Housing Act 1985 s 170(1). Section 170(1) is modified where the Housing (Extension of Right to Buy) Order 1993, SI 1993/2240 (see PARA 233), applies: see Schedule para 54.

6   Housing Act 1985 s 170(2) (amended by the Leasehold Reform, Housing and Urban Development Act 1993 s 187(1), Sch 21 para 18). As to the appropriate national authority, and the transfer of functions under the Housing Act 1985, so far as exercisable in relation to Wales, to the Welsh Ministers see PARA 7.

7   Housing Act 1985 s 170(3).

8   For these purposes, references to a solicitor include the Treasury Solicitor: Housing Act 1985 s 170(6).

9   Housing Act 1985 s 170(4).

10 Housing Act 1985 s 170(5). This is subject to any charge imposed by the Legal Aid, Sentencing and Punishment of Offenders Act 2012 s 25 and any provision in, or made under, Pt I (ss 1–43) for the payment of any sum to the Lord Chancellor: Housing Act 1985 s 170(5) (amended by the Access to Justice Act 1999 s 24, Sch 4 para 37; and the Legal Aid, Sentencing and Punishment of Offenders Act 2012 s 39(1), Sch 5 para 33).

11 As to the preserved right to buy see PARA 334 et seq.

12 See PARAS 242–244.
13 See PARAS 240–241.
14 See PARA 341 text and notes 19–23.

(viii) Registration of Title

A. RIGHT TO BUY OR ACQUIRE

346. Registration of title where the right to buy or the right to acquire is exercised. With regard to the right to buy[1] or the right to acquire conferred by the Housing Act 1996[2] or the Housing and Regeneration Act 2008[3], the following provisions apply.

Where the landlord's[4] title to the dwelling house[5] is not registered, the landlord must give the tenant[6] a certificate stating that the landlord is entitled to convey the freehold or make the grant of the lease subject only to such incumbrances, rights and interests as are stated in the conveyance or grant or summarised in the certificate[7].

Where the landlord's interest in the dwelling house is a lease[8], the certificate must also state particulars of that lease and, with respect to each superior title:

(1)   where it is registered, the title number;

(2)   where it is not registered, whether it was investigated in the usual way on the grant of the landlord's lease[9].

The Chief Land Registrar must, for the purpose of the registration of title, accept such a certificate as sufficient evidence of the facts stated in it; but, if as a result he has to meet a claim against him[10], the landlord is liable to indemnify him[11].

1   As to the meaning of 'the right to buy' see PARA 239.
2   See PARAS 242–244.
3   See PARAS 240–241.
4   As to the meaning of 'landlord' see PARA 31 note 3.
5   As to the meaning of 'dwelling house' see PARA 231.
6   As to the meaning of 'tenant' see PARA 31 note 3.
7   Housing Act 1985 s 154(2); and see PARA 230 notes 7, 9. A certificate under s 154(2) must be in a form approved by the Chief Land Registrar and must be signed by such officer of the landlord or such other person as may be approved by the Chief Land Registrar: s 154(4).
8   As to the meaning of 'lease' see PARA 31 note 3.
9   Housing Act 1985 s 154(3).
10 Ie under the Land Registration Act 2002: see REAL PROPERTY AND REGISTRATION.
11 Housing Act 1985 s 154(5) (amended by the Land Registration Act 2002 s 133, Sch 11 para 18(1), (3)).

    The Housing Act 1985 s 154 is modified where the Housing (Extension of Right to Buy) Order 1993, SI 1993/2240 (see PARA 233), applies: see Schedule para 40. The Housing Act 1985 s 154(1) (now repealed) is stated to be: (1) modified where the Housing (Preservation of Right to Buy) Regulations 1993, SI 1993/2241 (see PARA 334 et seq), apply (see Sch 1 para 19); (2) substituted where the Housing (Right to Acquire) Regulations 1997, SI 1997/619 (right to acquire conferred by the Housing Act 1996: see PARAS 242–244), apply (see the Housing (Right to Acquire) Regulations 1997, SI 1997/619, Sch 1 para 18); but it is apprehended that these provisions have now lapsed with the repeal of the Housing Act 1985 s 154(1) by the Land Registration Act 2002 s 135, Sch 13.

B. PRESERVED RIGHT TO BUY

347. Statement to be contained in instrument effecting qualifying disposal. On a qualifying disposal[1], the disponor must secure that the instrument effecting the disposal:

(1)   states that the disposal is, so far as it relates to dwelling houses[2] occupied by secure tenants[3], a disposal in a case where the right to buy is preserved on a disposal to a private landlord[4]; and

(2)   lists, to the best of the disponor's knowledge and belief, the dwelling houses to which the disposal relates which are occupied by secure tenants[5].

1   As to the meaning of 'qualifying disposal' see PARA 335 note 19. For these purposes, references to a disposal or to the instrument effecting a disposal are to the conveyance, transfer, grant or assignment, as the case may be: Housing Act 1985 s 171G, Sch 9A para 10 (s 171G added by the Housing and Planning Act 1986 s 8(1); the Housing Act 1996 Sch 9A added by the Housing and Planning Act 1986 s 8(2), Sch 2). See also PARA 334 note 11.
2   As to the meaning of 'dwelling house' see PARA 231.
3   As to the meaning of 'secure tenant' see PARA 230 note 2.
4   Ie a disposal to which the Housing Act 1985 s 171A applies: see PARA 334.
5   Housing Act 1985 Sch 9A para 1 (as added: see note 1). The Housing Act 1985 Sch 9A is omitted where: (1) the Housing (Extension of Right to Buy) Order 1993, SI 1993/2240 (see PARA 233), applies (see Schedule para 71); (2) the Housing (Right to Acquire) Regulations 1997, SI 1997/619 (right to acquire conferred by the Housing Act 1996 (see PARAS 242–244) or the Housing and Regeneration Act 2008 (see PARAS 240–241), apply (see the Housing (Right to Acquire) Regulations 1997, SI 1997/619, Sch 1 para 42).

348. Registration of title on qualifying disposal. Where on a qualifying disposal[1] the disponor's title to the dwelling house[2] is not registered, the disponor must give the disponee a certificate stating that the disponor is entitled to effect the disposal subject only to such incumbrances, rights and interests as are stated in the instrument effecting the disposal or summarised in the certificate[3]. Where the disponor's interest in the dwelling house is a lease[4], the certificate must also state particulars of the lease and, with respect to each superior title:

(1)   where it is registered, the title number;

(2)   where it is not registered, whether it was investigated in the usual way on the grant of the disponor's lease[5].

The certificate must be in a form approved by the Chief Land Registrar and it must be signed by such officer of the disponor or such other person as may be approved by the Chief Land Registrar; and the Chief Land Registrar must, for the purpose of registration of title, accept the certificate as sufficient evidence of the facts stated in it[6].

Where the Chief Land Registrar approves an application for registration of a disposition of registered land or, as the case may be, of the disponee's title under a disposition of unregistered land, and the instrument effecting the disposal contains the required statement described above, he must enter in the register:

(a)   a notice in respect of the rights of qualifying persons[7] in relation to dwelling houses comprised in the disposal; and

(b)   a restriction reflecting the statutory limitation[8] on subsequent disposal[9].

Where the registered title to land contains an entry made by virtue of the preserved right to buy[10], the Chief Land Registrar must, for the purpose of removing or amending the entry, accept as sufficient evidence of the facts stated in it a certificate by the registered proprietor that the whole or a specified part of the land is not subject to any right of a qualifying person under the right to buy[11].

1   As to the meaning of 'qualifying disposal' see PARA 335 note 19; and as to the meaning of references to a disposal see PARA 347 note 1.
2   As to the meaning of 'dwelling house' see PARA 231.
3   Housing Act 1985 Sch 9A para 2(2) (Sch 9A added by the Housing and Planning Act 1986 s 8(2), Sch 2; the Housing Act 1985 Sch 9A para 2(2) amended by the Land Registration Act 2002 s 133, Sch 11 para 18(1), (6)).
4   As to the meaning of 'lease' see PARA 31 note 3.
5   Housing Act 1985 Sch 9A para 2(3) (as added: see note 3).

6   Housing Act 1985 Sch 9A para 2(4) (as added: see note 3).
7   Ie under the Housing Act 1985 Pt V (ss 118–188): see PARAS 230 et seq, 349 et seq. As to the meaning of 'qualifying person' see PARA 337 note 4.
8   Ie under the Housing Act 1985 s 171D(2): see PARA 337.
9   Housing Act 1985 Sch 9A para 4 (substituted by the Land Registration Act 2002 Sch 11 para 18(1), (7)).
10 As to when the preserved right to buy arises see PARA 334.
11 Housing Act 1985 Sch 9A para 8 (as added: see note 3). As to the circumstances in which Sch 9A is omitted see PARA 347 note 5.

349. Change of qualifying dwelling house. The following provisions apply where a new dwelling house[1] becomes[2] the qualifying dwelling house[3] which is entirely different from the previous qualifying dwelling house or includes new land, and apply to the new dwelling house or the new land, as the case may be[4].

If the landlord's[5] title is registered, the landlord must apply for the entry in the register of:

(1)   a notice in respect of the rights of the qualifying person[6] or persons[7]; and

(2)   a restriction reflecting the statutory limitation[8] on subsequent disposal[9].

If the landlord's title is not registered, the rights of the qualifying person or persons are registrable under the Land Charges Act 1972 in the same way as an estate contract[10] and the landlord must, and a qualifying person may, apply for such registration[11].

1   As to the meaning of 'dwelling house' see PARA 231.
2   Ie by virtue of the Housing Act 1985 s 171B(6): see PARA 335.
3   As to the meaning of 'qualifying dwelling house' see PARA 337 note 2.
4   Housing Act 1985 Sch 9A para 5(1) (Sch 9A added by the Housing and Planning Act 1986 s 8(2), Sch 2). See also PARA 334 note 11.
5   As to the meaning of 'landlord' see PARA 31 note 3.
6   As to the meaning of 'qualifying person' see PARA 337 note 4.
7   Ie under the provisions of the Housing Act 1985 Pt V (ss 118–188): see PARAS 230 et seq, 350 et seq.
8   Ie under the Housing Act 1985 s 171D(2): see PARA 337.
9   Housing Act 1985 Sch 9A para 5(2) (substituted by the Land Registration Act 2002 s 133, Sch 11 para 18(1), (8)).
10 See REAL PROPERTY AND REGISTRATION vol 87 (2012) PARA 720 et seq.
11 Housing Act 1985 Sch 9A para 5(4) (as added: see note 4). Where, by virtue of Sch 9A para 5(4), the rights of a qualifying person under Pt V in relation to the qualifying dwelling house are registrable under the Land Charges Act 1972 in the same way as an estate contract, s 4(6) (circumstances in which such a contract may be void against a purchaser: see REAL PROPERTY AND REGISTRATION vol 87 (2012) PARA 735) applies accordingly, with the substitution for the reference to the contract being void of a reference to the right to buy ceasing to be preserved: Housing Act 1985 Sch 9A para 6(2) (as so added). As to the circumstances in which Sch 9A is omitted see PARA 347 note 5.

350. Statement required on certain disposals on which right to buy ceases to be preserved. A conveyance of the freehold or the grant of a lease[1] of the qualifying dwelling house[2] to a qualifying person[3] in pursuance of the right to buy[4] must state that it is made in pursuance of the statutory right to buy[5] as that right applies by virtue of the statutory preservation[6] of that right[7].

Where, on a conveyance of the freehold or the grant of a lease of the qualifying dwelling house to a qualifying person otherwise than in pursuance of the right to buy, the dwelling house ceases to be subject to any rights arising under the statutory provisions relating to the right to buy, the conveyance or grant must contain a statement to that effect[8].

Where on a disposal[9] of an interest in a qualifying dwelling house the dwelling house ceases to be subject to the rights of a qualifying person by virtue of that person's becoming the tenant of an authority or body satisfying the landlord condition for secure tenancies[10], the instrument by which the disposal is effected must state that the dwelling house ceases as a result of the disposal to be subject to any rights arising by virtue of the statutory preservation of the right to buy[11].

1 As to the meaning of 'lease' see PARA 31 note 3.
2 As to the meaning of 'qualifying dwelling house' see PARA 337 note 2.
3 As to the meaning of 'qualifying person' see PARA 337 note 4.
4 As to the meaning of 'the right to buy' see PARA 239.
5 Ie the Housing Act 1985 Pt V (ss 118–188): see PARAS 230 et seq, 351, 353.
6 Ie by virtue of the Housing Act 1985 s 171A: see PARA 334.
7 Housing Act 1985 Sch 9A para 7(1) (Sch 9A added by the Housing and Planning Act 1986 s 8(2), Sch 2). See also PARA 334 note 11.
8 Housing Act 1985 Sch 9A para 7(2) (as added: see note 7).
9 As to the meaning of references to a disposal see PARA 347 note 1.
10 Ie by virtue of the Housing Act 1985 s 171D(1)(a) (see PARA 337 head (1)) or s 171E(2)(a) (see PARA 338).
11 Housing Act 1985 Sch 9A para 7(3) (as added: see note 7). As to the circumstances in which Sch 9A is omitted see PARA 347 note 5.

351. Liability to compensate or indemnify. A claim for breach of statutory duty[1] lies where:

(1)   the disponor on a qualifying disposal[2] fails to comply with his duty to secure the inclusion of the required statement in the instrument effecting the disposal[3]; or

(2)   the landlord[4] on a change of the qualifying dwelling house[5] fails to comply with his duty to apply for registration to protect the preserved right to buy[6],

and a qualifying person[7] is deprived of the preserved right to buy by reason of the non-registration of the matters which would have been registered if that duty had been complied with[8].

If the Chief Land Registrar has to meet a claim[9] as a result of acting upon:

(a)   a certificate of title on first registration[10];

(b)   a statement required on a disposal on which the right to buy ceases to be preserved[11]; or

(c)   a certificate that the dwelling house has ceased to be subject to the right to buy[12],

the person who gave the certificate or made the statement must indemnify him[13].

1 As to claims for breach of statutory duty see generally TORT vol 97 (2015) PARA 500 et seq. The statutory wording is 'an action for breach of statutory duty', but an action is now generally referred to as a 'claim': see CIVIL PROCEDURE vol 11 (2015) PARA 117.
2 As to the meaning of 'qualifying disposal' see PARA 335 note 19; and as to the meaning of references to a disposal see PARA 347 note 1.
3 Ie fails to comply with the Housing Act 1985 Sch 9A para 1: see PARA 347.
4 As to the meaning of 'landlord' see PARA 31 note 3.
5 As to the meaning of 'qualifying dwelling house' see PARA 337 note 2.
6 Ie fails to comply with the Housing Act 1985 Sch 9A para 5(2) or Sch 9A para 5(4): see PARA 349.
7 As to the meaning of 'qualifying person' see PARA 337 note 4.
8 Housing Act 1985 Sch 9A para 9(1) (Sch 9A added by the Housing and Planning Act 1986 s 8(2), Sch 2).
9 Ie under the Land Registration Act 2002: see REAL PROPERTY AND REGISTRATION.
10 Ie a certificate given in pursuance of the Housing Act 1985 Sch 9A para 2: see PARA 348.
11 Ie a statement made in pursuance of the Housing Act 1985 Sch 9A para 7: see PARA 350.
12 Ie a certificate given in pursuance of the Housing Act 1985 Sch 9A para 8: see PARA 348.
13 Housing Act 1985 Sch 9A para 9(2) (as added (see note 8); amended by the Land Registration Act 2002 s 133, Sch 11 para 18(1), (11)). As to the circumstances in which the Housing Act 1996 Sch 9A is omitted see PARA 347 note 5.

(ix) Charge to Stamp Duty Land Tax

352. The charge to stamp duty land tax in connection with right to buy etc transactions; in general. The general circumstances in which stamp duty land tax is chargeable on the grant of a lease are discussed elsewhere in this work[1]. Schedule 9 to the Finance Act 2003 makes particular provision with regard to:

(1)   right to buy transactions[2];

(2)   shared ownership leases[3], including those granted under the preserved right to buy[4]; and

(3)   rent to mortgage transactions[5].

Stamp duty land tax is discussed in detail elsewhere in this work[6].

1   See LANDLORD AND TENANT vol 62 (2016) PARA 118.
2   See the Finance Act 2003 Sch 9 para 1; and STAMP TAXES vol 96 (2012) PARA 471.
3   See the Finance Act 2003 Sch 9 paras 2–5; and STAMP TAXES vol 96 (2012) PARA 471. There is now no statutory right to be granted such a lease: see PARA 230.
4   As to the preserved right to buy see PARA 334 et seq.
5   See the Finance Act 2003 Sch 9 para 6; and STAMP TAXES vol 96 (2012) PARA 471. The right to acquire on rent to mortgage terms under the Housing Act 1985 Pt V (ss 118–188) (see PARA 318 et seq) is now only exercisable if claimed before 18 July 2005: see s 142A; and PARA 318.
6   See generally STAMP TAXES vol 96 (2012) PARA 425 et seq. As to stamp duty land tax in connection with right to buy transactions etc see STAMP TAXES vol 96 (2012) PARA 471.

(x) Jurisdiction with regard to the Right to Buy etc

353. Jurisdiction of the County Court. The County Court has jurisdiction:

(1)   to entertain any proceedings brought under the statutory provisions relating to the right to buy[1] (including those provisions as they apply to the right to acquire conferred by the Housing Act 1996[2] or the Housing and Regeneration Act 2008[3]); and

(2)   to determine any question arising under those provisions or under a conveyance or grant executed in pursuance of the right to acquire on rent to mortgage terms[4],

subject to the power of the district valuer[5] to determine matters of valuation of the dwelling[6].

This jurisdiction includes jurisdiction to entertain proceedings on any such question as is mentioned in head (2) above notwithstanding that no other relief is sought than a declaration[7].

1   Ie any proceedings brought under the Housing Act 1985 Pt V (ss 118–188): see PARA 230 et seq. As to the meaning of 'the right to buy' see PARA 239. Note, however, that appeals against a decision of a landlord that the exception from the right to buy under Sch 5 para 11 applies (dwelling house particularly suitable for elderly persons: see PARA 252) now lie to the First-tier Tribunal or the Welsh Ministers: see PARA 252 note 8.
2   See PARAS 242–244.
3   See PARAS 240–241.
4   The right to acquire on rent to mortgage terms is now only exercisable if claimed before 18 July 2005: see the Housing Act 1985 s 142A; and PARA 318.
5   Ie under the Housing Act 1985 s 128 (see PARA 285), or, in the case of the right to buy only, s 128B (see PARA 286) s 155C (see PARA 324) and s 158 (see PARA 332).
6   Housing Act 1985 s 181(1) (amended by the Leasehold Reform, Housing and Urban Development Act 1993 s 187(1), Sch 21 paras 22, 23; the Housing Act 2004 s 186(2); the Housing and Regeneration Act 2008 s 306(1), (11); and the Crime and Courts Act 2013 s 17(5), Sch 9 para 52(1)(a), (2); modified by the Housing (Right to Acquire) Regulations 1997, SI 1997/619, Sch 1 para 35 (applying in relation to the right to acquire under the Housing and Regeneration Act 2008 by virtue of s 184, which applies the Housing Act 1996 s 17 (regulations modifying the Housing Act 1985): see PARA 241)).

The Housing Act 1985 s 181(1) is also modified where: (1) the Housing (Extension of Right to Buy) Order 1993, SI 1993/2240 (see PARA 233), applies (see Schedule para 62); (2) the Housing (Preservation of Right to Buy) Regulations 1993, SI 1993/2241 (see PARA 334 et seq), apply (see Sch 1 para 37).

7   Housing Act 1985 s 181(2). If a person takes proceedings in the High Court which he could, by virtue of s 181, have taken in the County Court, he is not entitled to recover any costs: s 181(3) (prospectively repealed by the Courts and Legal Services Act 1990 s 125(7), Sch 20, as from a day to be appointed; at the date at which this volume states the law, that repeal was not in force). See also *Gregory v Tower Hamlets London Borough Council* [2006] EWCA Civ 1366, [2006] All ER (D) 65 (Jul), CA (where proceedings begun in the County Court are transferred to the Queen's Bench Division of the High Court under CPR 54.20, which provides that 'the court may order a claim to continue as if it had not been started under this Section' and enables claims brought by judicial review to continue as ordinary civil claims under CPR Pt 7, that does not necessarily lead to the conclusion that the proceedings could have been brought in the County Court and are solely proceedings under the Housing Act 1985 Pt V, and s 181(3) does not deprive the court of jurisdiction to make a costs order in favour of the claimant).

(6) HOUSING FINANCE

(i) In general

354. Introduction. Local authority borrowing and expenditure was to a large degree regulated by central government under the Local Government and Housing Act 1989. Part VI of that Act[1] contains provisions dealing with local authority housing finance, which continue to apply; but Part IV of that Act[2] (which has now been repealed[3]) contained provisions under which central government could set some limits to local authority borrowing and the use of capital receipts. Provision as to capital finance and accounts is now made by the Local Government Act 2003, which is dealt with elsewhere in this work[4]. Certain matters particularly relating to housing finance are, however, dealt with in the following paragraphs[5].

Note that local housing authorities now have greater freedom to borrow and to enter into credit agreements, and they may seek to improve their housing stock by making use of the private finance initiative ('PFI') or through partnership arrangements with the private sector[6].

A local authority or development corporation[7] may not incur expenses in providing dwellings[8] by the conversion of houses or other buildings or carrying out works required for the improvement of dwellings, with or without associated works of repair, except in accordance with proposals submitted by the authority or corporation to the appropriate national authority[9] and for the time being approved by it[10].

1   Ie the Local Government and Housing Act 1989 Pt VI (ss 74–88): see PARA 356 et seq; and LOCAL GOVERNMENT FINANCE.

2   Ie the Local Government and Housing Act 1989 Pt IV (ss 39–73) (repealed), which applied to all local authority functions and was not limited to housing.

3   See the Local Government Act 2003 s 127(2), Sch 8. For transitional provisions and savings see the Local Government Act 2003 (Commencement No 1 and Transitional Provisions and Savings) Order 2003, SI 2003/2938 (in relation to England); and the Local Government Act 2003 (Commencement) (Wales) Order 2003, SI 2003/3034 (in relation to Wales). See further the Local Authorities (Capital Finance) (Consequential, Transitional and Saving Provisions) Order 2004, SI 2004/533.

4   See the Local Government Act 2003 Pt 1 (ss 1–24); and LOCAL GOVERNMENT FINANCE vol 70 (2012) PARA 476 et seq.

5   See PARA 355 et seq.

6 As to the funding of local authority housing see eg Doolittle *Housing and Regeneration* (2003). A local authority may borrow for any of the purposes for which borrowing was, before the commencement of the Housing Act 1985, authorised by the Housing Act 1957 s 136, the Housing (Financial Provisions) Act 1958 s 54(1) or the Housing Act 1969 Sch 8 para 19 (all repealed): Housing Act 1985 s 428(1). The maximum period which may be sanctioned as the period for which money may be borrowed for any of those purposes by the Common Council of the City of London is 80 years, notwithstanding the provisions of any Act of Parliament: s 428(2).

7 As to the meaning of 'development corporation' see PARA 12.

8 For these purposes, 'dwelling' means a building or part of a building occupied or intended to be occupied as a separate dwelling, together with any yard, garden, outhouses and appurtenances belonging to it or usually enjoyed with it: Housing Act 1985 s 525 (repealed, as from a day to be appointed, by the Local Government and Housing Act 1989 s 194, Sch 12 Pt II) (definition applied by the Housing Act 1985 s 431(3)). At the date at which this volume states the law, no such day had been appointed.

9 Ie the Secretary of State or, where statutory functions have been transferred in relation to Wales, the Welsh Ministers: see PARA 7.

10 Housing Act 1985 s 431(1) (amended by SI 2008/3002). The appropriate national authority's approval may be given subject to such conditions, and may be varied in such circumstances, as appear to it to be appropriate; but before varying the terms of an approval it must consult the authority or corporation concerned: Housing Act 1985 s 431(2).

355. Housing management grants. The appropriate national authority[1] may give financial assistance to persons managing public sector, or former public sector, housing[2] and to persons seeking to facilitate or encourage improvements in, or providing services in connection with, the management of such housing. The authority may also make payments otherwise than by way of financial assistance in pursuance of such arrangements made with any such person[3].

The appropriate national authority may give financial assistance to persons providing educational or training courses in housing management, persons providing services for those providing such courses, and persons providing financial or other assistance for those attending such courses; and may make payments otherwise than by way of financial assistance in pursuance of arrangements made with any such person[4]. Financial assistance may be given in any form, in particular by way of grants, loans or guarantees or by incurring expenditure for the benefit of the assisted person; although the appropriate national authority must not purchase loan or share capital in a company[5].

A person receiving assistance must comply with the terms on which it is given and compliance may be enforced by the appropriate national authority[6].

1 Ie the Secretary of State or, where statutory functions have been transferred in relation to Wales, the Welsh Ministers: see PARA 7.

2 For this purpose, 'public sector housing' means housing accommodation in which an authority or body within the Housing Act 1985 s 80 (see LANDLORD AND TENANT vol 63 (2016) PARA 1037) or s 429A(2A) (see below) has an interest by virtue of which it receives a rack-rent or would do so if the premises were let at a rack-rent; and 'former public sector housing' means housing accommodation in which an authority, or a predecessor of such an authority or an authority abolished by the Local Government Act 1985 formerly had such an interest: Housing Act 1985 s 429A(2) (s 429A added by the Housing and Planning Act 1986 s 16; the Housing Act 1985 s 429A(2) amended by the Housing Act 1988 s 140, Sch 17 para 54). The reference to a body within the Housing Act 1985 s 429A(2A) includes the appropriate national authority if that authority has the interest as the result of the exercise by that authority (or Housing for Wales) of functions under the Housing Associations Act 1985 Pt III (ss 74–102) (see PARA 141 et seq): Housing Act 1985 s 429A(2B) (added by the Government of Wales Act 1998 s 140, Sch 16 para 15(1), (3)). The functions of Housing for Wales were transferred to the Secretary of State and are now exercised by the Welsh Ministers: see PARAS 7, 142.

The Housing Act 1985 s 429A(2) applies to the following bodies: (1) a housing trust which is a charity; (2) a private registered provider of social housing, or a registered social landlord, other than a co-operative housing association; and (3) a co-operative housing association which is neither a private registered provider of social housing nor a registered social landlord: s 429A(2A) (added by the Housing Act 1988 Sch 17 para 54; and amended by Government of Wales Act 1998 ss 140, 152, Sch 16 para 15(2), Sch 18 Pt VI; and by SI 1996/2325 and SI 2010/866). As to housing trusts see PARA 14. As to the meaning of 'private registered provider of social housing' see PARA 53. As to registered social landlords see PARA 166 et seq.

3   Housing Act 1985 s 429A(1) (as added (see note 2); amended by the Housing Act 1996 ss 222, 227, Sch 18 para 22(1)(c), Sch 19 Pt XIII).

4   Housing Act 1985 s 429A(3) (as added (see note 2); amended by the Housing Act 1996 Sch 18 para 22(1)(c), Sch 19 Pt XIII).

5   Housing Act 1985 s 429A(4) (as added: see note 2). Assistance may be given, and other payments made, on such terms as the appropriate national authority considers appropriate; and the terms may include provision as to repayment: s 429A(5) (as so added; and amended by the Housing Act 1996 Sch 18 para 22(1)(c), Sch 19 Pt XIII).

6   Housing Act 1985 s 429A(6) (as added: see note 2).

(ii) Housing Accounts

356. Duty to keep housing revenue account. A local housing authority[1] must keep, in accordance with proper practices[2], an account, called the 'housing revenue account', of sums falling to be credited or debited in respect of the following matters:

(1)   houses and other buildings which have been provided under Part II of the Housing Act 1985[3];

(2)   land which has been acquired or appropriated for the purposes of that Part[4];

(3)   houses purchased under the former statutory provision for the purchase of a house found on appeal against a repair notice to be unfit and beyond repair at reasonable cost[5];

(4)   dwellings in respect of which a local authority has received assistance under the Housing (Rural Workers) Act 1926[6];

(5)   any property which was brought, whether with the statutory consent[7] or by virtue of having vested in the local authority on the default of another person[8], within the corresponding account kept under Part XIII of the Housing Act 1985[9] for years beginning before 1 April 1990; and

(6)   such land, houses or other buildings not within the heads (1) to (5) as the appropriate national authority[10] may direct[11].

Heads (1) to (5) do not apply to:

(a)   land, houses or other buildings which have been disposed of[12] by the authority;

(b)   land acquired by the authority for the purpose of the disposing of houses provided, or to be provided, on the land, or of disposing of the land to a person who intends to provide housing accommodation on it or facilities which serve a beneficial purpose in connection with the requirements of persons for whom housing accommodation is provided;

(c)   houses provided by the authority on land so acquired; or

(d)   such land, houses or other buildings as the appropriate national authority may direct[13].

In addition, head (1) does not apply to houses and other buildings provided on or before 6 February 1919[14].

A local housing authority which does not possess property to which these provisions apply must nevertheless keep a housing revenue account unless the appropriate national authority consents to the authority's not doing so and the authority complies with such conditions (if any) as may be specified in the consent[15].

Statutory provision is made with respect to credits[16] and debits[17] to the housing revenue account, and also with respect to special cases[18].

The appropriate national authority may, as respects any houses or other property within the housing revenue account, direct that all or any of the provisions of Part VI of the Local Government and Housing Act 1989[19] relating to the account are not to apply, or are to apply subject to such modifications as may be specified in the direction[20]. The appropriate national authority may also direct that the provisions of that Part relating to the housing revenue account are to apply to a local housing authority subject to such modifications as are specified in the direction[21]. A direction may be given for such period and subject to such conditions as may be specified in the direction[22].

A local housing authority, and any officer or employee of a local housing authority concerned with the authority's housing functions, must supply the appropriate national authority with such information as that authority may specify, either generally or in any particular case, for the purpose of enabling that authority to ascertain the state or likely state of the local housing authority's housing revenue account for any year[23]. A local housing authority must supply the appropriate national authority with such certificates supporting the information required by that authority as that authority may specify[24].

1 As to the meaning of 'local housing authority' see PARA 11 (definition applied by the Local Government and Housing Act 1989 s 88(1)(a)).

2 For these purposes, references to 'proper practices' are to be construed in accordance with the Local Government Act 2003 s 21 (see LOCAL GOVERNMENT FINANCE vol 70 (2012) PARA 501): Local Government and Housing Act 1989 s 88(1)(d) (amended by the Local Government Act 2003 s 127(1), Sch 7 paras 28, 32).

3 Ie under the Housing Act 1985 Pt II (ss 8–57): see PARA 401 et seq. In the Local Government and Housing Act 1989 s 74(1) (see heads (1)–(6) in the text) and the other provisions of Pt VI (ss 74–88), references: (1) to provisions of the Housing Act 1985 include, where the context so admits, references to the corresponding provisions of earlier enactments; (2) to the houses or other property of an authority within the authority's housing revenue account are references to the houses, dwellings or other property to which the Local Government and Housing Act 1989 s 74(1) for the time being applies: s 74(2), (5)(a). References to a local housing authority's housing revenue account include, where the context so admits, references to the corresponding account kept by it under the Housing Act 1985 Pt XIII (ss 421–434) (see PARA 372): Local Government and Housing Act 1989 s 88(1)(b).

4 The reference in head (2) in the text to land acquired for the purposes of the Housing Act 1985 Pt II includes: (1) land which a local authority was deemed to have acquired under the Housing Act 1957 Pt V (repealed) by virtue of s 57(6) (land acquired for re-development in pursuance of re-development plan) before the repeal of that provision on 25 August 1969; and (2) any structures on such land which were made available to a local authority under the Housing (Temporary Accommodation) Act 1944 s 1 (repealed) (prefabs): Local Government and Housing Act 1989 s 74(2)(a), (b).

5 Ie purchased under the Housing Act 1985 s 192 (repealed subject to transitional provisions).

6 Ie under the Housing (Rural Workers) Act 1926 s 1 (repealed) or s 4(2A) (repealed).

7 Ie either with the consent of the Secretary of State given under the Housing Act 1985 s 417(1) (repealed) or with the consent of a minister given under the Housing (Financial Provisions) Act 1958 s 50(1)(e) (repealed). As to the Secretary of State see PARA 7.

8 Ie by virtue of the Housing (Financial Provisions) Act 1958 s 50(2) (repealed).

9 Ie under the Housing Act 1985 Pt XIII: see PARA 372.

10 Ie the Secretary of State or, where statutory functions have been transferred in relation to Wales, the Welsh Ministers: see PARA 7.

11 Local Government and Housing Act 1989 s 74(1). For limits on the indebtedness of each local housing authority in England that keeps a housing revenue account see the Localism Act 2011 s 171; and PARA 370.

12 In the Local Government and Housing Act 1989 Pt VI, references (however expressed) to a disposal are references to a conveyance of the freehold, or a grant or assignment of a lease (other than a shared ownership lease) which is a long tenancy within the meaning given by the Housing Act 1985 s 115 (see LANDLORD AND TENANT vol 63 (2016) PARA 1042): Local Government and Housing Act 1989 s 74(5)(b).

13 Local Government and Housing Act 1989 s 74(3)(a)–(d) (amended by the Housing Act 1996 s 222, Sch 18 para 24(2)).

14 Local Government and Housing Act 1989 s 74(3).

15 Local Government and Housing Act 1989 s 74(4).
16 See PARA 357 heads (1)–(9).
17 See PARA 357 heads (i)–(xii).
18 Those special cases are: (1) balance for the year 1989–90 (see the Local Government and Housing Act 1989 Sch 4 Pt III para 1); (2) benefits or amenities shared by the whole community (see Sch 4 Pt III para 3); (3) provision of welfare services (see Sch 4 Pt III para 3A (added by the Leasehold Reform, Housing and Urban Development Act 1993 s 127(b))); (4) land disposed of at less than market value (see the Local Government and Housing Act 1989 Sch 4 Pt III para 4); (5) adjustment of accounts on appropriation of land (see Sch 4 Pt III para 5); (6) transfers of housing stock between authorities in London (see Sch 4 Pt III para 6); and (7) contributions by the appropriate national authority under the Housing Act 1985 s 259 (expenditure on general improvement area: see PARA 832) or under the Local Government and Housing Act 1989 s 96 (expenditure on renewal area: see PARA 827) (see Sch 4 Pt III para 7).
19 See PARA 358 et seq.
20 Local Government and Housing Act 1989 Sch 4 Pt IV para 2(1).
    A determination made or direction given by the appropriate national authority under Pt VI may make different provision for different cases or descriptions of cases, including different provision for different areas, for different local housing authorities or for different descriptions of local housing authorities; it may be made before, during or after the end of the year to which it relates; and it may be varied or revoked by a subsequent determination or direction: s 87(1). Prospectively, the power to vary a determination does not apply to determinations under s 76A(2) (see PARA 359): s 87(1A) (added, as from a day to be appointed, by the Wales Act 2014 s 24(1), (3), (5); at the date at which this volume states the law, no such day had been appointed). Before making a determination or giving a direction under the Local Government and Housing Act 1989 Pt VI relating to all local housing authorities or any description of such authorities, the appropriate national authority must consult such representatives of local government and relevant professional bodies as appear to the authority to be appropriate; and, before making a determination or giving a direction relating to a particular local housing authority, the appropriate national authority must consult that authority: s 87(2). As soon as practicable after making a determination under Pt VI, the appropriate national authority must send a copy of the determination to the local housing authority or authorities to which it relates: s 87(3). For the most recent determination see the Item 8 Credit and Item 8 Debit (General) Determination 2010–2011 (3 February 2010).
    References to sending to a local housing authority a copy of a determination include references to using electronic communications for sending a copy to such address as may for the time being be notified to the appropriate national authority by that local housing authority for that purpose: Local Government and Housing Act 1989 s 87(4) (added, in relation to England, by SI 2000/3056; and, in relation to Wales, by SI 2001/605). 'Electronic communication' means a communication transmitted (whether from one person to another, from one device to another, or from a person to a device or vice versa) by means of an electronic communications network, or by other means but while in an electronic form; and 'address', in relation to electronic communications, includes any number or address used for the purposes of such communications: Local Government and Housing Act 1989 s 88(1)(e) (added, in relation to England, by SI 2000/3056; and, in relation to Wales, by SI 2001/605; and amended by the Communications Act 2003 s 406(1), Sch 17 para 100).
    A copy of a determination is also treated as sent to a local housing authority where:
    (1)   the appropriate national authority and that authority have agreed to the authority instead having access to determinations on a web site;
    (2)   the determination is a determination to which that agreement applies;
    (3)   the appropriate national authority has published the determination on a web site;
    (4)   that authority is notified, in a manner for the time being agreed for the purpose between that authority and the appropriate national authority, of:
          (a)   the publication of the determination on a web site;
          (b)   the address of that web site; and
          (c)   the place on that web site where the determination may be accessed, and how it may be accessed: Local Government and Housing Act 1989 s 87(5) (s 87(5)–(7) added, in relation to England, by SI 2000/3056; and, in relation to Wales, by SI 2001/605).
    A local housing authority which is no longer willing to accept electronic communications for the sending of copies of determinations may withdraw a notification of an address given to the appropriate national authority and such a withdrawal will take effect on a date specified by the local housing authority being a date no less than one month after the date on which the authority informs the appropriate national authority that it wants to withdraw the notification of the address given: Local Government and Housing Act 1989 s 87(6) (as so added). A local housing authority which has entered into an agreement with the appropriate national authority under head (1) may

revoke the agreement; and such a revocation takes effect on a date specified by the local housing authority being a date no less than one month after the date on which the authority informs the appropriate national authority that it wants to revoke the agreement: s 87(7) (as so added).

The text of s 87 refers to 'the Secretary of State'. Prospectively, for references to 'the Secretary of State' there are substituted references to 'the appropriate person', with corresponding grammatical changes: see s 87(1), (2)–(7) (amended, as from a day to be appointed, by the Wales Act 2014 s 24; at the date at which this volume states the law, no such day had been appointed)).

21 Local Government and Housing Act 1989 Sch 4 Pt IV para 2(2).
22 Local Government and Housing Act 1989 Sch 4 Pt IV para 2(3).
23 Local Government and Housing Act 1989 Sch 4 Pt IV para 1(1).
24 Local Government and Housing Act 1989 Sch 4 Pt IV para 1(2).

357. Housing revenue account: credits and debits. For each year a local housing authority[1] which is required to keep a housing revenue account[2] ('the account') must carry to the credit of the account amounts equal to the items listed in heads (1) to (9) below[3]. Those items are:

(1)   rents: the income of the authority for the year from rents and charges in respect of houses and other property within the account; and this includes rent remitted by way of rebate[4];

(2)   charges for services and facilities: the income of the authority for the year in respect of services or facilities provided by the authority in connection with the provision by it of houses and other property within the account:

  (a)   including income in respect of services or facilities provided by the authority[5]; but

  (b)   not including payments for the purchase of furniture or hire-purchase instalments for furniture or income in respect of services provided by the authority[6];

but if the appropriate national authority[7] so directs, this item includes, or does not include, such income as may be determined by or under the direction[8];

(i)   housing revenue account subsidy: housing revenue account subsidy payable to the authority for the year[9];

(ii)   contributions towards expenditure: contributions of any description payable to the authority for the year towards expenditure falling to be debited to the account (for that or any other year); but if the appropriate national authority so directs, this item does not include so much of any such contributions as may be determined by or under the direction[10];

(iii)   transfers from the housing repairs account: sums transferred for the year[11] from the authority's housing repairs account[12];

(iv)   reduced provision for bad or doubtful debts[13];

(v)   sums calculated as determined by the appropriate national authority: sums calculated for the year in accordance with such formulae as the appropriate national authority may from time to time determine; and in determining any formula for these purposes, the appropriate national authority may include variables framed (in whatever way the national authority considers appropriate) by reference to such matters relating to the authority, or to (or to tenants of) houses and other property which are or have been within the account, as he thinks fit[14];

(vi)   sums directed by the Secretary of State or the Welsh Ministers: any sums which for the year the authority is required, by reason of a direction given by the appropriate national authority[15], to carry to the credit of the account from some other revenue account; a direction may require the transfer of sums calculated in accordance with formulae specified in the direction, and any formula so specified may include variables framed (in whatever way the appropriate national authority considers appropriate) by reference to such matters as the appropriate national authority thinks fit[16];

(vii)   credit balance from the previous year: any credit balance shown in the account for the previous year; but this does not include so much of any such balance so shown as is carried to the credit of some other revenue account[17] of the authority[18].

For each year a local housing authority which is required to keep a housing revenue account ('the account') must carry to the debit of the account amounts equal to the items listed in heads (i) to (xii) below[19]. Those items are:

(A)   expenditure on repairs, maintenance and management: the expenditure of the authority for the year in respect of the repair, maintenance, supervision and management of houses and other property within the account, but not including expenditure properly debited to the authority's housing repairs account; but if the appropriate national authority so directs, this item includes, or does not include, such expenditure as may be determined by or under the direction[20];

(B)   capital expenditure: any expenditure of the authority in respect of houses and other property within the account:
(I)   which is capital expenditure[21] for the year; and
(II)   which the authority decides should be charged to a revenue account for the year[22];

(C)   rents, rates, taxes and other charges: the rents, rates, taxes and other charges which the authority is liable to pay for the year in respect of houses and other property within the account[23];

(D)   sums transferred where negative amounts of subsidy are paid to the Welsh Ministers[24]: sums payable for the year to the Welsh Ministers[25], and any interest charged on those sums[26], and any amount charged[27] in respect of costs incurred as a result of late payment of any of those sums[28];

(E)   sums payable for the year to the Secretary of State[29] as a result of late payment of settlement payments[30];

(F)   sums payable for the year to the Welsh Ministers[31] as a result of late payment of settlement payments[32];

(G)   contributions to housing repairs account: sums transferred for the year to the authority's housing repairs account[33];

(H)   provision for bad or doubtful debts[34];

(I)   sums calculated as determined by the appropriate national authority: sums calculated for the year in accordance with such formulae as the appropriate national authority may from time to time determine; and in determining any formula for the purposes of this item, the appropriate national authority may include variables framed (in whatever way that authority considers appropriate) by reference to such matters relating to the local housing authority, or to (or to tenants of) houses or other property which are or have been within the account, as the appropriate national authority thinks fit[35];

(J)   debit balance from previous year: any debit balance shown in the account for the previous year; but this does not include any such balance so shown which is carried[36] to the debit of some other revenue account of the authority[37];

(K)   sums directed by the Secretary of State or Welsh Ministers: any sums which for the year the authority is required, by reason of a direction given by the appropriate national authority, to carry from the account to the credit of some other revenue account; a direction may require the transfer of sums calculated in accordance with formulae specified in the direction, and any formula so specified may include variables framed (in whatever way the appropriate national authority considers appropriate) by reference to such matters as the appropriate national authority thinks fit[38];

(L)   payments in respect of rents for high income social tenants[39]: any sums of increased income payable for the year to the Secretary of State under regulations made in reliance on the relevant statutory provision[40].

1   As to the meaning of 'local housing authority' see PARA 11 (definition applied by the Local Government and Housing Act 1989 s 88(1)(a)).
2   See PARA 356.
3   Local Government and Housing Act 1989 s 75, Sch 4 Pt I. As to the appropriate national authority's power to amend these provisions by order see PARA 362.
4   Local Government and Housing Act 1989 s 75, Sch 4 Pt I item 1.
5   Ie under the Housing Act 1985 ss 10, 11 (power to provide furniture, board and laundry facilities) see PARA 406.
6   Ie under the Housing Act 1985 s 11A (power to provide welfare services): see PARA 407.
7   Ie the Secretary of State or, where statutory functions have been transferred in relation to Wales, the Welsh Ministers: see PARA 7.
8   Local Government and Housing Act 1989 Sch 4 Pt I item 2 (amended by the Leasehold Reform, Housing and Urban Development Act 1993 s 127(a)).
9   Local Government and Housing Act 1989 Sch 4 Pt I item 3 (repealed, relation to Wales, as from a day to be appointed, by the Housing (Wales) Act 2014 s 131(2), (4)(a); at the date at which this volume states the law, no such day had been appointed).
10   Local Government and Housing Act 1989 Sch 4 Pt I item 4.
11   Ie in accordance with the Local Government and Housing Act 1989 s 77(5) (credit balance for year) see PARA 360.
12   Local Government and Housing Act 1989 Sch 4 Pt I item 6.
13   Local Government and Housing Act 1989 Sch 4 Pt I item 7. This head covers: ie: (1) any sums debited to the account for a previous year under Sch 4 Pt II item 7 para (a) which have been recovered by the authority during the year; and (2) any amount by which, in the opinion of the authority, any provision debited to the account for a previous year under Sch 4 Pt II item 7 para (b) should be reduced (see further note 34); but if the appropriate national authority so directs, no sums are to be credited under head (1), and no amount is to be credited under head (2), except (in either case) in such circumstances and to such extent as may be specified in the direction: Sch 4 Pt I item 7.
14   Local Government and Housing Act 1989 Sch 4 Pt I item 8. For the most recent determination see the Item 8 Credit and Item 8 Debit (General) Determination 2010–2011 (3 February 2010).
15   See PARA 362 note 1.
16   Local Government and Housing Act 1989 Sch 4 Pt I item 9 (substituted by the Local Government Act 2003 s 127(1), Sch 7 paras 28, 33(1), (3)).
17   Ie in accordance with Sch 4 Pt III para 1 or 2 (see heads (i), (ii) in the text).
18   Local Government and Housing Act 1989 Sch 4 Pt I item 10.
19   Local Government and Housing Act 1989 Sch 4 Pt II. As to the calculation of the subsidy to be debited to the housing revenue account see *R v Secretary of State for the Environment, ex p Camden London Borough Council* [1998] 1 All ER 937, [1998] 1 WLR 615, HL
20   Local Government and Housing Act 1989 Sch 4 Pt II item 1.
21   In this item 'capital expenditure' means expenditure for capital purposes within the meaning of the Local Government Act 2003 Pt 1 Ch 1 (ss 1–20) (capital finance: see LOCAL GOVERNMENT FINANCE vol 70 (2012) PARA 476 et seq): Local Government and Housing Act 1989 Sch 4 Pt II item 2 (substituted by SI 2004/533))
22   Local Government and Housing Act 1989 Sch 4 Pt II item 2 (as substituted: see note 21).
23   Local Government and Housing Act 1989 Sch 4 Pt II item 3.
24   Ie under the Local Government and Housing Act 1989 s 80ZA.
25   Ie under the Local Government and Housing Act 1989 s 80ZA(1)(b) (housing revenue account subsidy of a negative amount): see PARA 375.

26 Ie under the Local Government and Housing Act 1989 s 80ZA(4).

27 Ie under the Local Government and Housing Act 1989 s 80ZA(5).

28 Local Government and Housing Act 1989 Sch 4 Pt II item 5 (amended by the Localism Act 2011 s 167, Sch 15 paras 1, 11(1), (2); repealed, in relation to Wales, by the Housing (Wales) Act 2014 s 131(2), (4)(b), as from a day to be appointed; at the date at which this volume states the law, no such day had been appointed).

29 Ie under the Localism Act 2011 s 170(4) or (5) (interest etc charged as a result of late payment of settlement payments etc): see PARA 369.

30 Local Government and Housing Act 1989 Sch 4 Pt II item 5A (added by the Localism Act 2011 s 170(9)).

31 Ie under the Housing (Wales) Act 2014 s 134(3) or (4) (interest etc charged as a result of late payment of settlement payments etc): see PARA 369.

32 Local Government and Housing Act 1989 Sch 4 Pt II item 5B (added, in relation to Wales, by the Housing (Wales) Act 2014 s 134(8)).

33 Local Government and Housing Act 1989 Sch 4 Pt II item 6.

34 Local Government and Housing Act 1989 Sch 4 Pt II item 7. This head covers the following: (1) any sums credited to the account for the year or any previous year under Sch 4 Pt I item 1 or item 2 (see heads (1)–(2) in the text) which, in the opinion of the authority, are bad debts which should be written off; and (2) any provision for doubtful debts which, in the authority's opinion, should be made in respect of sums so credited; but if the appropriate national authority so directs, no sums are to be debited under head (1), and no provision is to be debited under head (2), except (in either case) in such circumstances and to such extent as may be specified in the direction: Sch 4 Pt II item 7.

35 Local Government and Housing Act 1989 Sch 4 Pt II item 8. For the most recent determination see the Item 8 Credit and Item 8 Debit (General) Determination 2010–2011 (3 February 2010).

36 Ie in accordance with Local Government and Housing Act 1989 Sch 4 Pt III para 1 (see PARA 356 note 18).

37 Local Government and Housing Act 1989 Sch 4 Pt II item 9.

38 Local Government and Housing Act 1989 Sch 4 Pt II item 10 (added by the Local Government Act 2003 s 127(1), Sch 7 paras 28, 33(1), (5)).

39 Ie under the Housing and Planning Act 2016 s 86 (rents for high income social tenants: payment by local authority of increased income to Secretary of State): see PARA 444.

40 Local Government and Housing Act 1989 Sch 4 Pt II item 11 added by the Housing and Planning Act 2016 s 88(3)).

358. Duty to prevent debit balance on housing revenue account. Where for any year ('the relevant year')[1] a local housing authority[2] which is required to keep a housing revenue account[3] possesses any houses or other property within the account[4], the authority must, during the months of January and February immediately preceding the relevant year, formulate proposals which satisfy the statutory requirements and relate to:

(1)   the income of the authority for the year from rents and other charges in respect of houses and other property within its housing revenue account;

(2)   the expenditure[5] of the authority for the year in respect of the repair, maintenance, supervision and management of such property; and

(3)   such other matters connected with the exercise of the authority's functions in relation to such property as the appropriate national authority[6] may direct[7].

Such proposals satisfy the statutory requirements at any time if implementation of the proposals will secure that the account for that year does not show a debit balance, on the assumption that the following will prove correct, namely:

(a) the best assumptions that the authority is able to make at that time as to all matters which may affect the amounts falling to be credited or debited to the authority's housing revenue account for the relevant year; and (b)	the best estimates that the authority is able to make at that time of the amounts which, on those assumptions, will fall to be so credited or debited[8].

Subject as follows, the authority must implement the proposals so formulated by it[9]. The authority must, however, from time to time determine whether the proposals so formulated satisfy the statutory requirements and if it determines that question in the affirmative, the authority may revise the proposals as it thinks fit, so long as the proposals (as so revised) continue to satisfy those requirements; whereas if it determines that question in the negative, it must make such revisions of the proposals as are reasonably practicable towards securing that the proposals (as so revised) satisfy those requirements[10].

The authority must, within one month of formulating or revising its proposals, prepare a statement setting out those proposals as so formulated or so revised, the estimates made by the authority under head (b) on the basis of which those proposals were so formulated or so revised, and such other particulars relating to those proposals and estimates as the appropriate national authority may direct[11].

The authority must, until the end of the year next following the relevant year, keep copies of the statement which is for the time being the latest statement so prepared available for inspection by the public without charge at all reasonable hours at one or more of the authority's offices; and any person is entitled to take copies of, or extracts from, that statement when so made available[12].

1	As to the meaning of 'year' see PARA 372 note 7 (definition applied by the Local Government and Housing Act 1989 s 88(1)(a)).
2	As to the meaning of 'local housing authority' see PARA 11 (definition applied by the Local Government and Housing Act 1989 s 88(1)(a)).
3	As to the housing revenue account see PARA 356.
4	As to the meaning of 'houses or other property within the housing revenue account' see PARA 356 note 3.
5	References in the Local Government and Housing Act 1989 Pt VI (ss 74–88) to expenditure are to be construed as references to the amount falling to be debited in accordance with directions given under s 78B (see PARA 361): s 78B(3) (added by the Housing Act 1996 s 222, Sch 18 para 4).
6	Ie the Secretary of State or, where statutory functions have been transferred in relation to Wales, the Welsh Ministers: see PARA 7.
7	Local Government and Housing Act 1989 s 76(1), (2).
8	Local Government and Housing Act 1989 s 76(3). No assumptions may be made under s 76(3) as to the exercise by the appropriate national authority of any power except on the basis of information published by or on behalf of the appropriate national authority or supplied by the appropriate national authority to the local housing authority: s 76(4).
9	Local Government and Housing Act 1989 s 76(5).
10	Local Government and Housing Act 1989 s 76(6). Where the proposals formulated under s 76(2) are revised under s 76(6), the provisions of s 76(3)–(6) apply in relation to the proposals as so revised as they applied in relation to the proposals as originally formulated: s 76(7).
11	Local Government and Housing Act 1989 s 76(8)(a)–(c). A direction by the appropriate national authority as to other particulars relating to the proposals and estimates (ie a direction under s 76(8)(c)) may specify the manner in which the particulars are to be set out in the statement: s 76(8).
12	Local Government and Housing Act 1989 s 76(9).

359. Limits on indebtedness: Wales. The following provisions are not yet in force. The Treasury[1] may from time to time make a determination providing for the maximum amount of housing debt[2] that may be held, in aggregate, by local housing authorities[3] in Wales that keep a housing revenue account[4]. The Welsh Ministers may from time to time make a determination providing for the calculation in relation to each such authority of: (1) the amount of housing debt that, at such time and on such assumptions as the Welsh Ministers may determine, is to be treated as held by the authority; and (2) the maximum amount of such housing debt that the authority may hold[5]. The Welsh Ministers must make such a determination in relation to each authority within the period of six months beginning immediately after the day on which the Treasury makes a determination[6]. A local housing authority may not hold debt in contravention of a determination under head (2)[7].

A determination under these provisions may, in particular, provide for all or part of an amount to be calculated in accordance with a formula or formulae[8]. A determination may provide for assumptions to be made in making a calculation whether or not those assumptions are, or are likely to be, borne out by events[9].

As soon as practicable after making a determination, the Treasury must: (a) send a copy of it to the Welsh Ministers; and (b) lay a copy of it before the House of Commons[10].

A local housing authority in Wales, and any officer or employee of a local housing authority in Wales concerned with its housing functions, must supply the Welsh Ministers with such information as the Welsh Ministers may specify, either generally or in any particular case, for the purpose of enabling the Welsh Ministers to exercise their functions in relation to making a determination[11]. A local housing authority must supply the Welsh Ministers with such certificates supporting the information required by them as they may specify[12]. If a local housing authority, or any officer or employee of a local housing authority concerned with its housing functions, fails to comply with these information requirements[13] before the end of such period as the Welsh Ministers may specify, the Welsh Ministers may exercise their functions relating to the amount of housing debt[14] on the basis of such assumptions and estimates as they see fit[15].

1   As to the Treasury see CONSTITUTIONAL AND ADMINISTRATIVE LAW vol 20 (2014) PARA 262 et seq.
2   For these purposes a debt is a 'housing debt', in relation to a local housing authority, if: (1) the debt is held by the authority in connection with the exercise of its functions relating to houses and other property within its Housing revenue account; and (2) interest and other charges in respect of the debt are required to be carried to the debit of that account: Local Government and Housing Act 1989 s 76A(9) (ss 76A, 76B added, as from a day to be appointed, by the Wales Act 2014 s 24(1), (2); at the date at which this volume states the law, no such day had been appointed). As to the housing revenue account see PARA 356.
3   As to the meaning of 'local housing authority' see PARA 11 (definition applied by the Local Government and Housing Act 1989 s 88(1)(a)).
4   Local Government and Housing Act 1989 s 76A(1) (as added: see note 2).
5   Local Government and Housing Act 1989 s 76A(2) (as added: see note 2). The aggregate of the amounts determined under s 76(2)(b) (head (2) in the text) must not exceed the amount determined under s 76A(1): s 76A(4) (as so added).
6   Local Government and Housing Act 1989 s 76A(3) (as added: see note 2).
7   Local Government and Housing Act 1989 s 76A(5) (as added: see note 2).
8   Local Government and Housing Act 1989 s 76A(6) (as added: see note 2).
9   Local Government and Housing Act 1989 s 76A(7) (as added: see note 2).
10 Local Government and Housing Act 1989 s 76A(8) (as added: see note 2).
11 Local Government and Housing Act 1989 s 76B(1) (as added: see note 2).
12 Local Government and Housing Act 1989 s 76B(2) (as added: see note 2).
13 Ie to comply with the Local Government and Housing Act 1989 s 76B(1) or (2).
14 Ie under the Local Government and Housing Act 1989 s 76A: see the text to notes 5–10.
15 Local Government and Housing Act 1989 s 76B(3) (as added: see note 2).

360.   Power to keep housing repairs account. A local housing authority[1] which is required to keep a housing revenue account[2] may also keep, in accordance with proper practices[3], an account called the 'housing repairs account'[4].

An authority which keeps a housing repairs account must carry to the credit of the account for any year[5]:

(1)   sums transferred for the year from its housing revenue account; and

(2) sums receivable by the authority for the year in connection with the repair or maintenance of houses or other property within its housing revenue account[6] (either from the authority's tenants or from the sale of scrapped or salvaged materials)[7].

The authority must carry to the debit of the account for any year:

(a) all expenditure[8] incurred by the authority for the year in connection with the repair or maintenance of houses or other property within its housing revenue account;

(b) such expenditure incurred by the authority for the year in connection with the improvement or replacement of houses or other property within its housing revenue account as may from time to time be determined by the appropriate national authority[9]; and

(c) sums transferred[10] for the year to the housing revenue account[11].

The authority must secure that sufficient credits are carried to the account to secure that no debit balance is shown in the account for any year[12].

1 As to the meaning of 'local housing authority' see PARA 11 (definition applied by the Local Government and Housing Act 1989 s 88(1)(a)).

2 As to the housing revenue account see PARA 356.

3 As to the meaning of 'proper practices' see PARA 356 note 2.

4 Local Government and Housing Act 1989 s 77(1). As to references to a local housing authority's housing repairs account see PARA 356 note 3.

5 As to the meaning of 'year' see PARA 372 note 7 (definition applied by the Local Government and Housing Act 1989 s 88(1)(a)).

6 As to the meaning of 'houses or other property within the housing revenue account' see PARA 356 note 3.

7 Local Government and Housing Act 1989 s 77(2).

8 As to the meaning of 'expenditure' see PARA 358 note 5.

9 Ie the Secretary of State or, where statutory functions have been transferred in relation to Wales, the Welsh Ministers: see PARA 7.

10 Ie in accordance with the Local Government and Housing Act 1989 s 77(5): s 77(3)(c). The authority may carry some or all of any credit balance in the account for any year to the credit of its housing revenue account: s 77(5).

11 Local Government and Housing Act 1989 s 77(3).

12 Local Government and Housing Act 1989 s 77(4). So much of any credit balance shown in an authority's housing repairs account at the end of the year beginning 1 April 1989 as was not carried to the credit of its housing revenue account for that year was to be carried forward and credited to some other revenue account of the authority's for the year beginning 1 April 1990: see s 77(6).

361. Directions by the appropriate national authority. The appropriate national authority[1] may give directions as to the accounting practices (whether actual or prospective) which are to be followed by a local housing authority[2] in the keeping of its housing revenue account[3] or housing repairs account[4]. The appropriate national authority may also give directions as to what items or amounts are to be regarded as referable to property within a local housing authority's housing revenue account[5] where one or more parts of a building have been disposed of but the common parts[6] remain property within that account[7]; and any such direction also has effect for the purposes of any housing repairs account kept by the local housing authority[8].

Where work is carried out by a local housing authority which has successfully bid for the work on a competitive basis, the appropriate national authority may give directions:

(1) to secure that the amount debited to the housing revenue account or any housing repairs account of the local housing authority in respect of the work reflects the amount of the authority's successful bid for the work rather than expenditure[9] actually incurred[10];

(2)   allowing an authority to credit to its housing revenue account any
        surpluses reasonably attributable to work undertaken on or in
        connection with property within that account[11].

1   Ie the Secretary of State or, where statutory functions have been transferred in relation to Wales,
    the Welsh Ministers: see PARA 7.
2   As to the meaning of 'local housing authority' see PARA 11 (definition applied by the Local
    Government and Housing Act 1989 s 88(1)(a)).
3   As to the housing revenue account see PARA 356.
4   Local Government and Housing Act 1989 s 78. As to the housing repairs account see PARA 360.
5   As to the meaning of 'property within the housing revenue account' see PARA 356 note 3.
6   For these purposes, 'common parts' includes the structure and exterior of the building and
    common facilities provided, whether in the building or elsewhere, for persons who include the
    occupiers of one or more parts of the building: Local Government and Housing Act 1989 s 78A(4)
    (ss 78A, 78B added by the Housing Act 1996 s 222, Sch 18 para 4).
7   Local Government and Housing Act 1989 s 78A(1) (as added: see note 6).
8   Local Government and Housing Act 1989 s 78A(2) (as added: see note 6). Directions under s 78A
    may give the authority a discretion as to whether items or amounts are accounted for in the
    housing revenue account or any housing repairs account or in another revenue account: s 78A(3)
    (as so added).
9   As to the meaning of 'expenditure' see PARA 358 note 5.
10 Local Government and Housing Act 1989 s 78B(1), (2)(a) (as added: see note 6). Directions under
    s 78B(2)(a) may make provision for determining the amount to be treated as the amount of the
    authority's successful bid: s 78B(3) (as so added).
11 Local Government and Housing Act 1989 s 78B(1), (2)(b) (as added: see note 6). Directions under
    s 78B(2)(b) may make provision as to the ascertainment of the surpluses and the circumstances in
    which a surplus is or is not to be taken to be attributable to property within an authority's housing
    revenue account: s 78B(4) (as so added).

362. Housing revenue accounts etc: adaptation of enactments. The appropriate
national authority[1] may by order: (1) amend, repeal or re-enact specified
provisions of the Local Government and Housing Act 1989[2]; (2) provide for any
such provisions: (a) not to apply, whether at all or in cases specified by the order or
to authorities so specified; (b) to apply, whether generally or in cases so specified
or to authorities so specified, subject to modifications so specified[3]. Such an
order may: (i) contain such incidental, consequential, transitional or
supplementary provisions (including provisions amending or repealing
enactments), and such savings, as the appropriate national authority considers
appropriate; (ii) make different provision for different cases or authorities[4]. The
power to make an order under these provisions is exercisable by statutory
instrument[5]. In relation to England, the Secretary of State must not make an
order under these provisions unless a draft of the order has been laid before, and
approved by resolution of, each House of Parliament[6].

1   Ie the Secretary of State or, where statutory functions have been transferred in relation to Wales,
    the Welsh Ministers: see PARA 7. The term 'the appropriate person' is used in the Local
    Government and Housing Act 1989 Pt VI (ss 74–88), defined as, in relation to England, the
    Secretary of State and, in relation to Wales, the Welsh Ministers: see s 88(1)(aa) (added by the
    Local Government Act 2003 s 89(6); and amended by the Housing and Regeneration Act 2008
    s 313(2)).
2   Ie the Local Government and Housing Act 1989 ss 74–76, 78, Sch 4: see PARA 356 et seq.
3   Local Government and Housing Act 1989 s 87A(1) (s 87A added by the Local Government Act
    2003 s 91(1)). An order under the Local Government and Housing Act 1989 s 87A may (in
    particular): (1) add items to, or remove items from, Sch 4 Pt I or II, or vary the items; (2) confer
    discretions, or expand, curtail or repeal discretions conferred, on the appropriate national
    authority or any other person; (3) be made before, during or after the end of any year to which it
    relates: s 87A(2) (as so added). In head (2), 'discretion' includes power to make a determination
    or give a direction: s 87A(3) (as so added).
4   Local Government and Housing Act 1989 s 87A(4) (as added: see note 3).
5   Local Government and Housing Act 1989 s 87A(5) (as added: see note 3).

6 Local Government and Housing Act 1989 s 87A(6) (as added: see note 3). As to the Secretary of State see PARA 7.

(iii) Vacant Higher Value Local Authority Housing (England)

363. Payments to Secretary of State. The following matters were introduced by the Housing and Planning Act 2016[1]. The Secretary of State may make a determination requiring a local housing authority[2] in England to make a payment to the Secretary of State in respect of a financial year[3]. The amount of the payment must represent an estimate of the market value of the authority's interest[4] in any higher value housing[5] that is likely to become vacant[6] during the year, less any costs or other deductions of a kind described in the determination[7]. A determination may only be made in respect of a local housing authority that keeps a housing revenue account[8]. A determination must set out the method for calculating the amount of the payment[9]. A determination may, in particular, provide for all or part of the amount to be calculated using a formula[10]. A determination may provide for assumptions to be made in making a calculation whether or not those assumptions are, or are likely to be, borne out by events[11].

Before making a determination that relates to all local housing authorities or a description of local housing authority the Secretary of State must consult such representatives of local government and relevant professional bodies as the Secretary of State thinks appropriate[12]. Before making a determination that relates to a particular local housing authority, the Secretary of State must consult that local housing authority[13]. As soon as possible after making a determination the Secretary of State must send a copy of it to each local housing authority to which it relates[14]. A consultation requirement imposed by these provisions may be satisfied by consultation carried out before the Housing and Planning Act 2016 was passed[15].

A determination must be made before the financial year to which it relates[16]; but the determination may be varied or revoked by a subsequent determination made before, after or during the financial year to which it relates[17]. A determination may relate to one financial year or to more than one financial year[18]. A determination may make provision about how and when a payment is to be made including, in particular, provision for payments by instalment[19]. A determination may provide for interest to be charged in the event of late payment[20]. A determination: (1) may make different provision for different areas; (2) may make different provision for different local housing authorities; (3) may otherwise make different provision for different purposes[21].

1 Ie the Housing and Planning Act 2016 Pt 4 Ch 2 (ss 69–79); in force from 12 May 2016: see s 216(1)(b).
2 As to the meaning of 'local housing authority' see PARA 11 (definition applied by the Housing and Planning Act 2016 s 79(1)).
3 Housing and Planning Act 2016 s 69(1). As to the Secretary of State see PARA 7. 'Financial year' means a period of 12 months beginning with 1 April: s 79(1).
4 'Interest' means a freehold or leasehold interest: Housing Act 1996 Housing and Planning Act 2016 s 79(1).
5 'Higher value', in relation to housing, has the meaning given by regulations under the Housing and Planning Act 2016 s 69; and 'housing' means a building, or part of a building, which is occupied or intended to be occupied as a dwelling or as more than one dwelling: s 79(1). The Secretary of State must by regulations define 'higher value', in relation to housing, for the purposes of Pt 4 Ch 2 (ss 69–79): s 69(8). Regulations under s 69(8) may define 'higher value' in different ways for different kinds of housing, different local housing authorities or different areas: s 69(9). In determining how to define 'higher value', in relation to housing, the Secretary of State may: (1) use any category of housing that the Secretary of State considers appropriate as a comparator (for example, housing in which a local housing authority has an interest or housing in a particular

area); (2) take into account any other factors that the Secretary of State considers appropriate: s 69(10). At the date at which this volume states the law, no regulations had been made under s 69(8).

6 Housing in which a local housing authority has an interest 'becomes vacant' when a tenancy granted by the authority comes to an end and is not renewed expressly or by operation of law: Housing and Planning Act 2016 s 79(1). 'Tenancy' includes a licence to occupy: s 79(1). The Secretary of State may by regulations specify circumstances in which housing is to be treated as not having become vacant for the purposes of Pt 4 (ss 64–121) even if it otherwise would be: s 79(2).

7 Housing and Planning Act 2016 s 69(2). As to the housing to be taken into account under s 69(2) see s 70: see ss 69(3), 70(1). Housing is to be taken into account only if: (1) it appears in the list in the Local Government and Housing Act 1989 s 74(1) (housing revenue account: see PARA 356); and (2) it is not excluded by regulations made by the Secretary of State: Housing and Planning Act 2016 s 70(2). Where a local housing authority disposes of housing under the Housing Act 1985 s 32 or 43 to a private registered provider of social housing (see PARAS 522, 531) the Secretary of State may for the purposes of the Housing and Planning Act 2016 Pt 4 Ch 2: (a) treat the local housing authority as still having that housing; and (b) treat the housing as being likely to become vacant whenever it would have been likely to become vacant if it had not been disposed of: s 70(3). A determination under s 69 must identify any housing that the Secretary of State has taken into account under s 70(3): s 70(4).

Where the Secretary of State is liable to repay an amount that has been overpaid by a local housing authority under s 69, the Secretary of State may set off against the amount of the repayment any amount that the authority is liable to pay the Secretary of State under: (i) s 69; or (ii) the Local Government Act 2003 s 11 (see LOCAL GOVERNMENT FINANCE vol 70 (2012) PARA 485): Housing and Planning Act 2016 s 75.

8 Housing and Planning Act 2016 s 69(4). As to the meaning of 'housing revenue account' see PARA 356 (definition applied by the Housing and Planning Act 2016 s 79(1)).

9 Housing and Planning Act 2016 s 69(5).

10 Housing and Planning Act 2016 s 69(6).

11 Housing and Planning Act 2016 s 69(7).

12 Housing and Planning Act 2016 s 71(1).

13 Housing and Planning Act 2016 s 71(2).

14 Housing and Planning Act 2016 s 71(3). The Local Government and Housing Act 1989 s 87(4)–(7) (electronic communications: see PARA 356 note 20) applies to a determination under the Housing and Planning Act 2016 Pt 4 Ch 2 as it applies to a determination under the Local Government and Housing Act 1989 Pt VI (ss 74–88): Housing and Planning Act 2016 s 71(4).

15 Housing and Planning Act 2016 s 71(5). The Act was passed on 12 May 2016.

16 Housing and Planning Act 2016 s 72(1). If s 69 comes into force part way through a financial year, then, in relation to that financial year: (1) a determination under s 69 may be made at any time (despite s 72(1)); but (2) any reference in s 69 to housing becoming vacant during a financial year is to be read as limited to housing becoming vacant after the determination is made (or, in a case where it is varied in accordance with s 72(2) (see the text to note 15), housing becoming vacant after the original determination in relation to that financial year is made): s 73.

17 Housing and Planning Act 2016 s 72(2).

18 Housing and Planning Act 2016 s 72(3).

19 Housing and Planning Act 2016 s 72(4).

20 Housing and Planning Act 2016 s 72(5).

21 Housing and Planning Act 2016 s 72(6).

364. Reduction of payments by agreement. The Secretary of State[1] and a local housing authority[2] may enter into an agreement to reduce the amount that the authority is required to pay because of a determination[3] relating to vacant higher value housing[4]. The terms and conditions of an agreement must include: (1) the amount of the reduction mentioned above; and (2) any terms and conditions required by the provisions below[5].

Where the agreement is with a local housing authority outside Greater London, it must include terms and conditions requiring the authority to ensure that at least one new affordable home[6] is provided for each old dwelling[7]. Where the agreement is with a local housing authority in Greater London, it must include terms and conditions requiring the authority to ensure that at least two new affordable homes are provided for each old dwelling[8]. However, if the Greater London Authority has agreed to ensure that a number of the new affordable homes are provided, that number is to be deducted from the number for which the local housing authority must be made responsible by terms and conditions in the agreement[9]. The Secretary of State may by regulations create other exceptions to the requirements as to affordable homes in relation to one or more local housing authorities[10].

1   As to the Secretary of State see PARA 7.
2   As to the meaning of 'local housing authority' see PARA 11 (definition applied by the Housing and Planning Act 2016 s 79(1)).
3   Ie under the Housing and Planning Act 2016 Pt 4 Ch 2 (ss 69–79): see PARA 363.
4   Housing and Planning Act 2016 s 74(1). If a determination under Pt 4 Ch 2 relates to more than one financial year: (1) an agreement under s 74 may be made in relation to the determination so far as it relates to a particular financial year; and (2) in the definition of 'old dwelling' in s 74(7) (see note 6) the reference to the determination is to the determination so far as it relates to the financial year to which the agreement relates: s 74(8). As to the meaning of 'financial year' see PARA 363 note 3.
5   Housing and Planning Act 2016 s 74(2).
6   'New affordable home' means a new dwelling in England that: (1) is to be made available for people whose needs are not adequately served by the commercial housing market; or (2) is a starter home as defined by the Housing and Planning Act 2016 s 2 (see PARA 906); 'new dwelling' means a building or part of a building that: (a) has been constructed for use as a single dwelling and has not previously been occupied; or (b) has been adapted for use as a single dwelling and has not been occupied since its adaptation; and 'old dwelling' means a single dwelling taken into account under s 69(2) (see PARA 363) for the purposes of the determination: s 74(7). The Secretary of State may by regulations amend s 74 so as to change the meaning of 'new affordable home': s 74(9).
7   Housing and Planning Act 2016 s 74(3).
8   Housing and Planning Act 2016 s 74(4).
9   Housing and Planning Act 2016 s 74(5).
10 Housing and Planning Act 2016 s 74(6).

365.   Duty to consider selling. A local housing authority[1] in England that keeps a housing revenue account[2] must consider selling its interest in any higher value[3] housing that has become vacant[4]. The Secretary of State[5] may by regulations exclude housing from this duty[6]. In discharging its duty to consider selling, a local housing authority must have regard to any guidance given by the Secretary of State[7].

1   As to the meaning of 'local housing authority' see PARA 11 (definition applied by the Housing and Planning Act 2016 s 79(1)).
2   As to the meaning of 'housing revenue account' see PARA 356 (definition applied by the Housing and Planning Act 2016 s 79(1)). The duty in s 76(1) applies only in relation to housing that appears in the list in the Local Government and Housing Act 1989 s 74(1) (housing revenue account: see PARA 356): Housing and Planning Act 2016 s 76(2).
3   As to the meaning of 'higher value' see PARA 363 note 5.
4   Housing and Planning Act 2016 s 76(1). As to the meaning of 'becomes vacant' see PARA 363 note 6.
5   As to the Secretary of State see PARA 7.
6   Housing and Planning Act 2016 s 76(3).
7   Housing and Planning Act 2016 s 76(4).

(iv) Housing Strategies and Statements (Wales)

366.   Housing strategies and statements and housing revenue account business plans. The Welsh Ministers[1] may: (1) require a local housing authority[2] in Wales to have a strategy in respect of such matters relating to housing[3] as the Welsh Ministers may specify; and (2) impose requirements with respect to: (a) the ends that the strategy is to be designed to achieve; (b) the formulation of policy for the purposes of the strategy; or (c) review of the strategy[4].

The Welsh Ministers may require a local housing authority in Wales, by such time as the Welsh Ministers may specify, to prepare and supply the Welsh

Ministers with a statement setting out such material of either of the following descriptions as the Welsh Ministers may specify: (i) a strategy that the authority is required to have[5]; (ii) other material relating to housing[6]. The Welsh Ministers may, in relation to a statement whose preparation and supply is required[7], impose requirements with respect to: (A) the contents of the statement; (B) the form of the statement; (C) the statement's supply to the Welsh Ministers[8].

1 As to the Welsh Ministers see PARA 7.
2 As to the meaning of 'local housing authority' see PARA 11 (definition applied by the Local Government Act 2003 s 87(4) (substituted by the Housing Act 2004 s 265(1), Sch 15 para 47; the Local Government Act 2003 s 87 repealed, in relation to England, by the Deregulation Act 2015 s 29(1)).
3 'Housing' includes accommodation needs for gypsies and travellers within the meaning of the Housing Act 2004 s 225 (see PARA 475), in the case of a local housing authority in England, or the Housing (Wales) Act 2014 Pt 3 (ss 101–110), in the case of a local housing authority in Wales: Local Government Act 2003 s 87(4) (as substituted (see note 2); definition amended by the Housing (Wales) Act 2014 s 110, Sch 3 para 23(1)).
4 Local Government Act 2003 s 87(1) (amended by the Deregulation Act 2015 s 29(2), (3)).
5 Ie under the Local Government Act 2003 s 87(1): see the text and note 4.
6 Local Government Act 2003 s 87(2) (amended by the Deregulation Act 2015 s 29(2), (4)).
7 Ie under the Local Government Act 2003 s 87(2): see the text and note 6.
8 Local Government Act 2003 s 87(3) (amended by the Deregulation Act 2015 s 29(2), (5)). The power under the Local Government Act 2003 s 87(3) includes (in particular) power to require that material: (1) in a statement; and (2) relating to property within the housing revenue account of the authority preparing the statement, be designated in the statement as being, or forming part of, the authority's housing revenue account business plan: s 88(1). The reference in s 88(1) to property within an authority's housing revenue account has the same meaning as in the Local Government and Housing Act 1989 Pt VI (ss 74–88) (see PARA 356 note 3): Local Government Act 2003 s 88(3). All material that: (a) in accordance with requirements imposed under s 87(3) is so designated in a statement prepared for the purposes of s 87(2) (see the text and note 6) by an authority in Wales; and (b) has not in a subsequent statement so prepared by the authority been declared to be superseded or withdrawn, will collectively be known as the authority's housing revenue account business plan: s 88(2) (amended by the Deregulation Act 2015 s 29(6)(a)).

(v) Housing Subsidies

A. SETTLEMENT PAYMENTS

367. In general. The Secretary of State or the Welsh Ministers[1] may make a determination providing for the calculation of the amount of a payment, referred to[2] as a 'settlement payment' in relation to each local housing authority[3] that keeps a housing revenue account[4]. Such a determination may, in particular, provide for all or part of the amount to be calculated in accordance with a formula or formulae[5]. In determining such a formula in relation to England, the Secretary of State may, in particular, include variables framed by reference to: (1) the amounts (if any) that, during such period and on such assumptions as the Secretary of State may determine, are to be treated as amounts that will be received by the local housing authority in connection with the exercise of its functions relating to houses and other property within its housing revenue account; (2) the amounts (if any) that, during such period and on such assumptions as the Secretary of State may determine, are to be treated as amounts that will be paid by the authority in connection with the exercise of those functions; and (3) the amount (if any) that, at such time and on such assumptions as the Secretary of State may determine, is to be treated as the amount of debt held by the authority in connection with the exercise of those functions[6]. In determining such a formula in relation to Wales, the Welsh Ministers may include variables framed by reference to such matters as they consider appropriate[7].

A determination by the Secretary of State[8] may provide for an assumption to be made about an amount whether or not the assumption is, or is likely to be, borne out by events[9]. A determination by the Secretary of State or the Welsh Ministers[10] may provide that the effect of the calculation in relation to a local housing authority is that: (a) a settlement payment must be made by the Secretary of State or the Welsh Ministers to the local housing authority; (b) a settlement payment must be made by the local housing authority to the Secretary of State or the Welsh Ministers; or (c) the amount of a settlement payment in relation to that authority is nil[11].

1 As to the Secretary of State and the Welsh Ministers see PARA 7.
2 Ie in the Localism Act 2011 Pt 7 Ch 3 (ss 167–175) and the Housing (Wales) Act 2014 Pt 6 (ss 131–136).
3 As to the meaning of 'local housing authority' see PARA 11 (England) (definition applied by the Localism Act 2011 s 175); and PARA 227 note 2 (Wales).
4 Localism Act 2011 s 168(1); Housing (Wales) Act 2014 s 132(1), (2). A determination may make different provision for different cases or descriptions of case, including different provision: (1) for different areas; (2) for different local housing authorities; or (3) for different descriptions of local housing authority: Localism Act 2011 s 173(1); Housing (Wales) Act 2014 s 136(1). Before making a determination that relates to all local housing authorities or a description of local housing authority, the Secretary of State must consult such representatives of local government and relevant professional bodes as the Secretary of State thinks appropriate (Localism Act 2011 s 173(2)), and the Welsh Ministers must consult such representatives of local government in Wales and such other persons, as the Welsh Ministers consider appropriate (Housing (Wales) Act 2014 s 136(2)). Before making a determination relating to a particular local housing authority, the Secretary of State or the Welsh Ministers must consult that local housing authority: Localism Act 2011 s 173(3); Housing (Wales) Act 2014 s 136(3). As soon as practicable after making a determination, the Secretary of State or the Welsh Ministers must send a copy of the determination to the local housing authority or authorities to which it relates: Localism Act 2011 s 173(4); Housing (Wales) Act 2014 s 136(4). The Local Government and Housing Act 1989 s 87(4)–(7) (electronic communications: see PARA 356 note 20) applies to a determination under these provisions as it applies to a determination under Pt VI (ss 74–88) of that Act: Localism Act 2011 s 173(5); Housing (Wales) Act 2014 s 136(5).
5 Localism Act 2011 s 168(2); Housing (Wales) Act 2014 s 132(3).
6 Localism Act 2011 s 168(3).
7 Housing (Wales) Act 2014 s 132(4).
8 Ie under the Localism Act 2011 s 168.
9 Localism Act 2011 s 168(3).
10 Ie under the Localism Act 2011 s 168 or the Housing (Wales) Act 2014 s 132.
11 Localism Act 2011 s 168(5); Housing (Wales) Act 2014 s 132(5). Section 132(3), (4), (5) does not limit the generality of the power conferred by s 132(1): s 132(6).

368. Further payments. If a settlement payment[1] has been made in respect of a local housing authority[2], the Secretary of State or the Welsh Ministers[3] may from time to time make a determination that a further payment calculated in accordance with the determination must be made: (1) by the Secretary of State or the Welsh Ministers to the local housing authority; or (2) by the local housing authority to the Secretary of State or the Welsh Ministers[4]. The Secretary of State or the Welsh Ministers may make such a determination only if there has been a change in any matter that was taken into account in making: (a) the determination relating to the settlement payment or a calculation under that determination; or (b) a previous determination relating to the local housing authority or a calculation under that determination[5]. In addition, the Welsh Ministers may make such a determination if they are satisfied that an error was taken into account in making any such determination or calculation[6]. A determination under these provisions[7] may be varied or revoked by a subsequent determination[8].

1 As to the meaning of 'settlement payment' see PARA 367.

2 As to the meaning of 'local housing authority' see PARA 11 (England) (definition applied by the Localism Act 2011 s 175); and PARA 227 note 2 (Wales).
3 As to the Secretary of State and the Welsh Ministers see PARA 7.
4 Localism Act 2011 s 169(1), (2); Housing (Wales) Act 2014 s 133(1). As to such determinations see PARA 367 note 4.
5 Localism Act 2011 s 169(3); Housing (Wales) Act 2014 s 133(2), (3).
6 Housing (Wales) Act 2014 s 133(4).
7 Ie the Localism Act 2011 s 169 or the Housing (Wales) Act 2014 s 133.
8 Localism Act 2011 s 169(4); Housing (Wales) Act 2014 s 133(5).

369. Further provisions about payments. A settlement payment or a further payment in relation to a housing revenue account[1] must be made in such instalments, at such times and in accordance with such arrangements as the Secretary of State or the Welsh Ministers[2] may determine[3]. A payment by a local housing authority[4] must be accompanied by such information as the Secretary of State or the Welsh Ministers may require[5]. The Secretary of State or the Welsh Ministers may charge a local housing authority interest, at such rates and for such periods as the Secretary of State or Welsh Ministers may determine, on any sum payable by the local housing authority in respect of a settlement payment or further payment[6] that is not paid by a time determined under these provisions[7] for its payment[8]. The Secretary of State or Welsh Ministers may charge a local housing authority an amount equal to any additional costs incurred by the Secretary of State or Welsh Ministers as a result of any such sum payable by the local housing authority not being paid by a time determined under these provisions for its payment[9].

Payments, except in respect of interest or additional costs[10], if made by a local housing authority, are to be treated by the authority[11] as capital expenditure and if made to a local housing authority, are to be treated by the authority[12] as a capital receipt[13]. A determination by the Secretary of State or the Welsh Ministers may require a payment to a local housing authority[14] to be used by the authority for a purpose specified in the determination[15]. A local housing authority to which such a requirement applies must comply with it[16].

1 Ie under the Localism Act 2011 Pt 7 Ch 3 (ss 167–175) or the Housing (Wales) Act 2014 Pt 6 (ss 131–136): see PARAS 367–368.
2 As to the Secretary of State and the Welsh Ministers see PARA 7.
3 Localism Act 2011 s 170(1); Housing (Wales) Act 2014 s 134(1). As to such determinations see PARA 367 note 4. Arrangements under the Localism Act 2011 s 170(1) may include arrangements for payments to be made: (1) by a person or body other than the Secretary of State to a local housing authority; or (2) to a person or body other than the Secretary of State by a local housing authority: s 170(2).
4 As to the meaning of 'local housing authority' see PARA 11 (England) (definition applied by the Localism Act 2011 s 175); and PARA 227 note 2 (Wales).
5 Localism Act 2011 s 170(3); Housing (Wales) Act 2014 s 134(2).
6 Ie under the Localism Act 2011 Pt 7 Ch 3 or the Housing (Wales) Act 2014 Pt 6.
7 Ie under the Localism Act 2011 s 170 or the Housing (Wales) Act 2014 s 134.
8 Localism Act 2011 s 170(4); Housing (Wales) Act 2014 s 134(3).
9 Localism Act 2011 s 170(5); Housing (Wales) Act 2014 s 134(4).
10 Ie a payment under the Localism Act 2011 Pt 7 Ch 3 other than a payment under s 170(4) or (5), or a payment under the Housing (Wales) Act 2014 Pt 6 other than a payment under s 134(3) or (4).
11 Ie for the purposes of the Local Government Act 2003 Pt 1 Ch 1 (ss 1–20): see LOCAL GOVERNMENT FINANCE vol 70 (2012) PARA 476 et seq.
12 Ie for the purposes of the Local Government Act 2003 Pt 1 Ch 1.
13 Localism Act 2011 s 170(6); Housing (Wales) Act 2014 s 134(5).
14 Localism Act 2011 s 170(7); Housing (Wales) Act 2014 s 134(6).
15 Ie under the Localism Act 2011 Pt 7 Ch 3 or the Housing (Wales) Act 2014 Pt 6.
16 Localism Act 2011 s 170(8); Housing (Wales) Act 2014 s 134(7).

370. Limits on indebtedness. The Secretary of State[1] may from time to time make a determination[2] providing for the calculation in relation to each local housing authority[3] in England that keeps a housing revenue account[4] of: (1) the amount of housing debt[5] that, at such time and on such assumptions as the Secretary of State may determine, is to be treated as held by the authority; and (2) the maximum amount of such housing debt that the authority may hold[6].

A determination may, in particular, provide for all or part of an amount to be calculated in accordance with a formula or formulae[7]. A determination may provide for assumptions to be made in making a calculation whether or not those assumptions are, or are likely to be, borne out by events[8]. A determination may be varied or revoked by a subsequent determination[9]. A local housing authority may not hold debt in contravention of a determination[10].

1 As to the Secretary of State see PARA 7.
2 Ie under the Localism Act 2011 Pt 7 Ch 3 (ss 167–175): see PARA 367 note 4.
3 As to the meaning of 'local housing authority' see PARA 11 (definition applied by the Localism Act 2011 s 175).
4 As to the housing revenue account see PARA 356.
5 For these purposes, 'housing debt', in relation to a local housing authority, means debt: (1) which is held by the authority in connection with the exercise of its functions relating to houses and other property within its housing revenue account; and (2) interest and other charges in respect of which are required to be carried to the debit of that account: Localism Act 2011 s 171(6).
6 Localism Act 2011 s 171(1).
7 Localism Act 2011 s 171(2).
8 Localism Act 2011 s 171(3).
9 Localism Act 2011 s 171(4).
10 Localism Act 2011 s 171(5).

371. Power to obtain information. A local housing authority[1] must supply the Secretary of State or Welsh Ministers[2] with such information as the Secretary of State or Welsh Ministers may specify for the purposes of enabling the Secretary of State or Welsh Ministers to exercise functions[3] in respect of settlement payments[4]. The Secretary of State or Welsh Ministers may exercise these powers either generally or in relation to a particular case[5]. If a local housing authority fails to comply with these provisions before the end of such period as the Secretary of State or Welsh Ministers may specify, the Secretary of State or Welsh Ministers may exercise functions in respect of settlement payments on the basis of such assumptions and estimates as the Secretary of State or Welsh Ministers think fit[6].

1 As to the meaning of 'local housing authority' see PARA 11 (England) (definition applied by the Localism Act 2011 s 175); and PARA 227 note 2 (Wales).
2 As to the Secretary of State and the Welsh Ministers see PARA 7.
3 Ie under the Localism Act 2011 Pt 7 Ch 3 (ss 167–175) or the Housing (Wales) Act 2014 Pt 6 (ss 131–136): see PARAS 367–370.
4 Localism Act 2011 s 172(1); Housing (Wales) Act 2014 s 135(1).
5 Localism Act 2011 s 172(2); Housing (Wales) Act 2014 s 135(2).
6 Localism Act 2011 s 172(3); Housing (Wales) Act 2014 s 135(3).

B.   HOUSING SUBSIDY IN RELATION TO NEW TOWNS

372. Housing subsidy. Housing subsidy is payable for each year to a development corporation[1] under Part XIII of the Housing Act 1985[2] and must be credited to the corporation's housing account[3]. The subsidy must be paid by the appropriate national authority[4] at such times, in such manner and subject to such conditions as to records, certificates, audit or otherwise as the authority may, with the agreement of the Treasury, determine[5]. Payment of housing subsidy is subject to the making of a claim for it in such form, and containing such particulars, as the appropriate national authority may from time to time determine[6].

The amount of the housing subsidy payable to a development corporation for a year[7] ('the year of account') is calculated according to a formula based on the corporation's base amount[8], housing costs differential, and local contribution differential for the year[9]. If the amount so calculated is nil or a negative amount, no housing subsidy is payable to the corporation for that year[10].

A development corporation's housing costs differential for a year of account is the amount by which its reckonable expenditure for that year exceeds its reckonable expenditure for the preceding year (and accordingly is nil or, as the case may be, a negative amount if the reckonable expenditure for the year is the same as or less than that for the preceding year)[11]. A development corporation's reckonable expenditure for a year is the aggregate of: (1) so much of the expenditure incurred by the corporation in that year and falling to be debited to the corporation's housing account as the appropriate national authority may determine; and (2) so much of any other expenditure incurred by the corporation in that year, or treated as so incurred in accordance with a determination made by the appropriate national authority, as the appropriate national authority may determine to be taken into account for the purposes of housing subsidy[12].

A development corporation's local contribution differential for a year of account is the amount by which its reckonable income for that year exceeds its reckonable income for the preceding year (and accordingly is nil or, as the case may be, a negative amount if its reckonable income for the year is the same as or less than that for the preceding year)[13]. A corporation's reckonable income for a year is the amount which, in accordance with any determination made by the appropriate national authority, the corporation is assumed to receive for that year as income which it is required to carry to its housing account including: (a) any contribution made by the corporation out of its general revenue account; and (b) any rent rebate subsidy payable[14], but excluding any other subsidy, grant or contribution[15].

1   As to the meaning of 'development corporation' see PARA 12.
2   Ie under the Housing Act 1985 Pt XIII (ss 421–434): see the text and notes 3–12; and PARA 373. Housing subsidy ceased to be payable to local housing authorities under these provisions with effect for years beginning on or after 1 April 1990 and is instead payable to those authorities under the Local Government and Housing Act 1989 ss 79, 80, 80A and 86: see PARAS 374, 377.
3   Housing Act 1985 s 421(1), (2) (amended by the Local Government and Housing Act 1989 s 194, Sch 11 para 77; the Government of Wales Act 1998 s 152, Sch 18 Pt IV; and SI 2008/3002).
4   Ie the Secretary of State or, where statutory functions have been transferred in relation to Wales, the Welsh Ministers: see PARA 7.
5   Housing Act 1985 s 421(3). As to the Treasury see CONSTITUTIONAL AND ADMINISTRATIVE LAW vol 20 (2014) PARA 262 et seq.
6   Housing Act 1985 s 421(4).
7   For these purposes, 'year' means a period of 12 months beginning on 1 April: Housing Act 1985 s 433.
8   A development corporation's base amount for a year of account is, subject to any adjustment under the Housing Act 1985 s 423(2), the amount calculated for the preceding year under s 422, that is to say, the amount of the housing subsidy payable to the corporation for that year or, if none was payable, nil or a negative amount, as the case may be: s 423(1) (amended by the Local Government and Housing Act 1989 Sch 11 para 79(1); and by SI 2008/3002). If the appropriate national authority is of the opinion that particular circumstances require it, the authority may adjust the base amount for any year by increasing or decreasing it, either generally or in relation to any particular body: see the Housing Act 1985 s 423(2) (amended by the Local Government and Housing Act 1989 s 194(4), Sch 11 para 79(2), Sch 12 Pt II).
9   Housing Act 1985 s 422(1) (amended by the Local Government and Housing Act 1989 Sch 11 para 78; and by SI 2008/3002).
10 Housing Act 1985 s 422(2) (amended by the Local Government and Housing Act 1989 Sch 11 para 78).

11 Housing Act 1985 s 424(1) (s 424(1), (2), (4) amended, and s 424(3) substituted, by the Local Government and Housing Act 1989 Sch 11 para 80; the Housing Act 1985 s 424(1)–(4) further amended by SI 2008/3002).

12 Housing Act 1985 s 424(2) (as so amended). A determination may be made for all development corporations or different determinations may be made for individual corporations; and a determination may be varied or revoked in relation to all or any of the corporations for which it was made: s 424(3) (as so substituted and amended). Before making a determination for all development corporations the appropriate national authority must consult organisations appearing to the authority to be representative of development corporations: s 424(4) (as so amended).

The fact that a development corporation has entered into a management agreement, and any letting of land in connection with such an agreement, must be disregarded in determining that corporation's reckonable income or expenditure for the purposes of housing subsidy: s 427A(1) (s 427A added by the Housing and Planning Act 1986 s 24(2), Sch 5 para 32; and amended by the Local Government and Housing Act 1989 Sch 11 para 84; the Government of Wales Act 1998 Sch 18 Pt IV; and SI 2008/3002; the Housing Act 1985 s 427A(1) renumbered as such by SI 2010/844). Reference in the Housing Act 1985 s 427A(1) to a management agreement includes a section 247 or 249 arrangement, as defined by the Housing and Regeneration Act 2008 s 250A(6) (see PARA 117 note 8): Housing Act 1985 s 427A(2) (added by SI 2010/844). As to the meaning of 'management agreement' generally see PARA 457.

13 Housing Act 1985 s 425(1) (amended by the Local Government and Housing Act 1989 Sch 11 para 81; and by SI 2008/3002).

14 Ie under the Social Security Administration Act 1992 s 140A: see WELFARE BENEFITS AND STATE PENSIONS vol 104 (2014) PARA 333.

15 Housing Act 1985 s 425(2) (amended by the Local Government and Housing Act 1989 Sch 11 para 81; the Social Security (Consequential Provisions) Act 1992 s 4, Sch 2 para 70; and the Housing Act 1996 s 123, Sch 13 para 2). A determination must state the assumptions on which it is based and the method of calculation used in it, and in making it the appropriate national authority must have regard, amongst other things, to past and expected movements in incomes, costs and prices: Housing Act 1985 s 425(3). A determination may be made for all development corporations or different determinations may be made for different corporations or groups of corporations: s 425(4) (substituted by the Local Government and Housing Act 1989 Sch 11 para 81; and amended by SI 2008/3002). Before making a determination for all development corporations the appropriate national authority must consult organisations appearing to the authority to be representative of development corporations: Housing Act 1985 s 425(5) (amended by the Local Government and Housing Act 1989 Sch 11 para 81; and by SI 2008/3002). A determination must be made known to the corporations for which it is made in the year preceding the year of account for which it is to have effect: Housing Act 1985 s 425(6) (amended by the Local Government and Housing Act 1989 Sch 11 para 81).

373. Recoupment of subsidy in certain cases. Where housing subsidy has been paid to a development corporation[1] and it appears to the appropriate national authority[2] that the purpose for which it was paid has not been fulfilled or not completely or adequately, or not without unreasonable delay, and that the case falls within rules published by the authority, the appropriate national authority may recover from that corporation the whole or such part of the payment as the authority may determine in accordance with the rules, with interest from such time and at such rates as the authority may so determine[3]. A sum so recoverable may, without prejudice to other methods of recovery, be recovered by withholding or reducing housing subsidy in future[4].

The withholding or reduction under these provisions of housing subsidy for a year[5] does not affect the base amount[6] for the following year[7].

The fact that a development corporation has entered into a management agreement[8], and any letting of land in connection with such an agreement, is not, however, to be regarded as a ground for recovering, withholding or reducing any sum under the above provisions[9].

1 As to the meaning of 'new town corporation' see PARA 12.
2 Ie the Secretary of State or, where statutory functions have been transferred in relation to Wales, the Welsh Ministers: see PARA 7.

3   Housing Act 1985 s 427(1) (amended by the Local Government and Housing Act 1989 s 194(1), Sch 11 para 83; the Government of Wales Act 1998 s 152, Sch 18 Pt IV; and SI 2008/3002).
4   Housing Act 1985 s 427(2).
5   As to the meaning of 'year' for these purposes see PARA 372 note 7.
6   As to the base amount see PARA 372 note 8.
7   Housing Act 1985 s 427(3).
8   As to the meaning of 'management agreement' see PARA 372 note 12; and PARA 457.
9   Housing Act 1985 s 427A(1) (s 427A added by the Housing and Planning Act 1986 s 24(2), Sch 5 para 32; and amended by the Government of Wales Act 1998 Sch 18 Pt IV; the Local Government and Housing Act 1989 Sch 11 para 84; and by SI 2008/3002; the Housing Act 1985 s 427A(1) renumbered as such by SI 2010/844).

C.   IN WALES

374. Housing revenue account subsidy. Housing revenue account subsidy is payable for each year[1] to local housing authorities[2] in Wales and must be paid by the Welsh Ministers[3] in such instalments, at such times and in such manner, and subject to such conditions as to claims, records, certificates, supply of housing revenue account business plans, audit or otherwise, as the Welsh Ministers may determine[4].

The amount of housing revenue account subsidy (if any) payable to a local housing authority in Wales for a year must be calculated in such manner as the Welsh Ministers may from time to time determine[5]. A determination may (in particular):

(1)   provide for all or part of the amount to be calculated in accordance with a formula or formulae;

(2)   provide for the amount, or part of the amount, to be calculated by reference to:

(a)   whether any housing revenue account business plan that the local housing authority is required to prepare by any time has been supplied to the Welsh Ministers or has been supplied to the Welsh Ministers by that time;

(b)   the Welsh Ministers' assessment of any housing revenue account business plan prepared by the local housing authority and supplied to the Welsh Ministers;

(c)   whether conditions are met that relate to, or to the local housing authority's conduct of, the authority's finances or any aspect of those finances;

(d)   an assessment of the state of, or of the authority's conduct of, the authority's finances or any aspect of those finances;

(e)   whether conditions are met that relate to housing provided by the authority, to housing functions of the authority or to the authority's performance in exercising such functions;

(f)   an assessment of, or of the state of, housing provided by the authority;

(g)   an assessment of the authority's performance in exercising functions in relation to housing provided by the authority or in otherwise exercising housing functions;

(h)   whether, as respects housing provided by the authority, management functions exercisable in relation to that housing have been entrusted to a company;

(i)   whether, where such functions have been entrusted to a company, conditions are met that relate to the performance of the company in exercising the functions;

    (j)   an assessment, where such functions have been entrusted to a company, of the performance of the company in exercising those functions;

    (k)   assumptions as to any matter;

(3)   have the effect that the amount, or part of the amount, is nil or a negative amount;

(4)   make different provision for different parts of the amount[6].

The Welsh Ministers may make a determination, or a calculation under such a determination, on the basis of information received by them on or before such date as they think fit[7].

The Welsh Ministers must, as soon as they think fit after the end of the year, make a final decision as to the amount (if any) of housing revenue account subsidy payable to a local housing authority for that year and notify the authority in writing of the decision[8]. Once notified to the local housing authority the decision is conclusive as to the amount (if any) payable by way of subsidy and must not be questioned in any legal proceedings[9]. Where the amount of housing revenue account subsidy paid to a local housing authority is less than the amount finally decided, the authority is entitled to be paid the balance[10], while where housing revenue account subsidy has been paid to an authority in excess of the amount finally decided, the Welsh Ministers may recover the excess, with interest from such time and at such rates as they think fit[11]. Nothing in these provisions, however, affects any power of the Welsh Ministers to vary a determination as to the amount of subsidy before the final decision is made[12].

If an agreement is in force between the Welsh Ministers and a local housing authority for the above provisions[13] not to apply in relation to:

    (i)   the local housing authority; or

    (ii)   specified property[14] or specified descriptions of property, of that authority,

those provisions do not apply in relation to the authority or (as the case may be) property for each year provided for in the agreement[15].

Such an agreement may, in particular, contain terms and conditions about:

    (A)   the period of years for which those provisions are not to apply (whether a fixed or indefinite period);

    (B)   payments to the local housing authority by the Welsh Ministers or by the local housing authority to the Welsh Ministers;

    (C)   the levels of rent for specified property or specified descriptions of property (in the case of an agreement of the kind mentioned in head (ii) above);

    (D)   the provision of information;

    (E)   the variation or termination of the agreement (whether on the occurrence of particular events, at the discretion of the Welsh Ministers or otherwise)[16].

The Welsh Ministers may give directions about supplementary, incidental, consequential or transitional matters relating to the variation or termination of such an agreement[17]. Such directions may not override any provision made on the subject by the agreement unless the directions are given with the consent of the local housing authority concerned[18].

1   As to the meaning of 'year' see PARA 372 note 7 (definition applied by the Local Government and Housing Act 1989 s 88(1)(a)).

2   Local Government and Housing Act 1989 s 79(1) (amended by the Localism Act 2011 s 167, Sch 15 paras 1, 2(1), (2)). The Local Government and Housing Act 1989 ss 79–80B are repealed, as from a day to be appointed, by the Housing (Wales) Act 2014 s 131(2), (3); at the date at which

this volume states the law, no such day had been appointed. As to the meaning of 'local housing authority' see PARA 11 (definition applied by the Local Government and Housing Act 1989 s 88(1)(a)).

As from 1 October 2013 (see the Localism Act 2011 (Commencement No 9) Order 2013, SI 2013/797) the Localism Act 2011 Sch 15 (abolition of housing revenue account subsidy in England) has effect: s 167. Housing revenue account subsidy is prospectively abolished in Wales: see the Housing (Wales) Act 2014 s 131. Housing revenue account subsidy in England and Wales is replaced by a system of settlement payments, to allow councils to keep their rental income and use it locally to maintain their homes: see PARA 367 et seq.

3   As to the Welsh Ministers: see PARA 7. See also PARA 362 note 1.

4   Local Government and Housing Act 1989 s 79(2) (substituted by the Local Government Act 2003 s 89(1); amended by the Localism Act 2011 s 167, Sch 15 paras 1, 2(1), (3); and prospectively repealed (see note 2)).

5   Local Government and Housing Act 1989 s 80(1) (substituted by the Local Government Act 2003 s 89(2); and prospectively repealed (see note 2)). In determining a formula for these purposes for any year, the Welsh Ministers may (in particular) include variables framed (in whatever way they consider appropriate) by reference to:

    (1)   any amounts which fall to be or were credited or debited to the authority's housing revenue account for that year or any previous year;

    (2)   any amounts which, on such assumptions as the Welsh Ministers may determine (whether or not borne out or likely to be borne out of events), would fall to be or would have been so credited or debited; and

    (3)   such other matters relating to the authority, or to (or to tenants of) houses and other property which are or have been within the account, as the Welsh Ministers think fit: Local Government and Housing Act 1989 s 80(3) (amended by the Local Government Act 2003 ss 89(3), (4), 127(2), Sch 8 Pt I; and the Localism Act 2011 Sch 15 paras 1, 3(1), (4); and prospectively repealed (see note 2)).

Without prejudice to the generality of the Local Government and Housing Act 1989 s 80(3), a formula may require it to be assumed that the amount for any year of the rental income or housing expenditure of each authority (or each authority in Wales) is to be determined:

    (a)   by taking the amount which the Welsh Ministers consider (having regard, amongst other things, to past and expected movements in incomes, costs and prices) should be or should have been the aggregate amount for that year of the rental incomes or, as the case may be, the housing expenditure of all of the authorities (or all of the authorities in Wales) taken together; and

    (b)   by apportioning that amount between them in such manner as the Welsh Ministers consider appropriate (which may involve, if the Welsh Ministers think fit, inferring the aggregate values of the houses and other property within the authorities' respective housing revenue accounts from the average values of any of the houses and other property which the authorities have disposed of),

and for these purposes 'rental income' means income falling within s 75, Sch 4 Pt I item 1 (see PARA 357 head (1)) and 'housing expenditure' means expenditure falling within Sch 4 Pt II item 1 (see PARA 357 head (i)) or falling to be debited to the authorities' housing repairs accounts: s 80(4) (amended by the Local Government Act 2003 s 89(4); and the Localism Act 2011 Sch 15 paras 1, 3(1), (5); and prospectively repealed (see note 2)). As to the housing revenue account see PARA 356; and as to the meaning of 'houses or other property within the housing revenue account' see PARA 356 note 3. For the most recent determinations see the Housing Revenue Account Subsidy Determination 2011–2012 (1 April 2011) and the Housing Revenue Account Subsidy (Wales) Determination 2014–2015 (2014 No 4) (4 February 2014).

6   Local Government and Housing Act 1989 s 80(1A) (added by the Local Government Act 2003 s 89(2); amended by the Localism Act 2011 Sch 15 paras 1, 3(1), (3); and prospectively repealed (see note 2)). Nothing in the Local Government and Housing Act 1989 s 80(1A) or s 80(3), (4) is to be taken as limiting the Welsh Ministers' discretion under s 80(1): s 80(5) (added by the Local Government Act 2003 s 89(5); amended by the Localism Act 2011 Sch 15 paras 1, 3(1), (6); and prospectively repealed (see note 2)).

7   Local Government and Housing Act 1989 s 80(6) (added by the Local Government Act 2003 s 89(5); amended by the Localism Act 2011 Sch 15 paras 1, 3(1), (7); and prospectively repealed (see note 2)). See *R v Secretary of State for the Environment, ex p Greenwich London Borough Council* (1990) 22 HLR 543, DC (decided under the Local Government and Housing Act 1989 s 80 as originally enacted, with reference to the Secretary of State).

8   Local Government and Housing Act 1989 s 80A(1) (s 80A added by the Housing Act 1996 s 222, Sch 18 para 5; the Local Government and Housing Act 1989 s 80A(1) amended by the Localism Act 2011 Sch 15 paras 1, 5(1), (2); and prospectively repealed (see note 2)).

Notification in writing of a decision is taken as given to a local housing authority where notice of the decision is sent using electronic communications to such address as may for the time being be notified by that authority to the Welsh Ministers for that purpose: Local Government and Housing Act 1989 s 80A(1A) (s 80A(1A)–(1D) added, in relation to England, by SI 2000/3056; and, in relation to Wales, by SI 2001/605; amended by the Localism Act 2011 Sch 15 paras 1, 5(1)–(6); and prospectively repealed (see note 2)). As to the meanings of 'electronic communication' and 'address' see PARA 356 note 20.

Notification in writing of a decision is also treated as given to a local housing authority where: (1) the Welsh Ministers and that authority have agreed that notifications of decisions required to be given in writing to that authority may instead be accessed by that authority on a web site; (2) the decision is a decision to which that agreement applies; (3) the Welsh Ministers have published the decision on a web site; (4) the local housing authority is notified, in a manner for the time being agreed for the purpose between it and the Welsh Ministers, of: (a) the publication of the decision on a web site; (b) the address of that web site; and (c) the place on that web site where the notice may be accessed, and how it may be accessed: Local Government and Housing Act 1989 s 80A(1B) (as so added, amended and prospectively repealed).

A local housing authority which is no longer willing to accept electronic communications for the notification of decisions, may withdraw a notification of an address given to the Welsh Ministers, and such a withdrawal will take effect on a date specified by the authority being a date no less than one month after the date on which the authority informs the Welsh Ministers that it wants to withdraw the notification of the address given: s 80A(1C) (as so added, amended and prospectively repealed). A local housing authority which has entered into an agreement with the Welsh Ministers under head (1) above may revoke the agreement, and such a revocation will take effect on a date specified by the authority being a date no less than one month after the date on which the authority informs the Welsh Ministers that it wants to revoke the agreement: s 80A(1D) (as so added, amended and prospectively repealed).

9   Local Government and Housing Act 1989 s 80A(2) (as added (see note 8); and prospectively repealed (see note 2)).

10   Local Government and Housing Act 1989 s 80A(3) (as added (see note 8); and prospectively repealed (see note 2)).

11   Local Government and Housing Act 1989 s 80A(4) (as added (see note 8); amended by the Localism Act 2011 Sch 15 paras 1, 5(1), (7); and prospectively repealed (see note 2)). Without prejudice to other methods of recovery, a sum so recoverable may be recovered by withholding or reducing subsidy and if the sum is referable to housing benefit in respect of houses or other property within the authority's housing revenue account, the sum may be recovered by withholding or reducing rent rebate subsidy under the Social Security Administration Act 1992 Pt VIII (ss 134–140G): Local Government and Housing Act 1989 s 80A(4A) (added by the Local Government Act 2003 s 127(1), Sch 7 paras 28, 31; and prospectively repealed (see note 2)).

12   Local Government and Housing Act 1989 s 80A(5) (as added (see note 8); amended by the Localism Act 2011 Sch 15 paras 1, 5(1), (8); and prospectively repealed (see note 2)).

13   Ie the Local Government and Housing Act 1989 ss 79–80A.

14   For these purposes, 'specified', in relation to an agreement, means specified in the agreement; and 'property' means land, houses, dwellings, buildings or property of a kind falling within the Local Government and Housing Act 1989 s 74(1)(a)–(f) (property within the housing revenue account: see PARA 356); and includes future property: Local Government and Housing Act 1989 s 80B(8) (s 80B added by the Housing and Regeneration Act 2008 s 313(1); and prospectively repealed (see note 2)).

15   Local Government and Housing Act 1989 s 80B(1), (2) (as added (see note 14); s 80B(1) amended by the Localism Act 2011 Sch 15 paras 1, 6(1), (2); and prospectively repealed (see note 2)). The Local Government and Housing Act 1989 s 80B does not restrict the circumstances in which housing revenue account subsidy is otherwise not payable to a local housing authority, or in respect of particular property, by virtue of Pt VI (ss 74–88): s 80B(7) (as so added and prospectively repealed).

16   Local Government and Housing Act 1989 s 80B(3) (as added (see note 14); amended by the Localism Act 2011 Sch 15 paras 1, 6(1), (3); and prospectively repealed (see note 2)).

17   Local Government and Housing Act 1989 s 80B(4) (as added (see note 14); amended by the Localism Act 2011 Sch 15 paras 1, 6(1), (4); and prospectively repealed (see note 2)). The provision made by the directions or the agreement may, in particular, include transitional provision about the terms and conditions on which the authority or (as the case may be) property is to become subject to the Local Government and Housing Act 1989 ss 79–80A after the termination of the agreement: s 80B(6) (as so added and prospectively repealed).

18   Local Government and Housing Act 1989 s 80B(5) (as added (see note 14); and prospectively repealed (see note 2)).

375. Housing revenue account subsidy: negative amounts. If calculation in accordance with a determination[1] of the amount of housing revenue account subsidy payable to a local housing authority[2] for a year produces a negative amount, the authority: (1) must for that year debit the equivalent positive amount to its housing revenue account; and (2) must pay that equivalent amount to the Welsh Ministers[3]. Amounts payable to the Welsh Ministers under head (2) must be paid in such instalments, at such times and in such manner as they may determine[4]. A payment in respect of an amount payable under head (2) must be accompanied by such information as the Welsh Ministers may require[5]. The Welsh Ministers may charge a local housing authority interest, at such rates and for such periods as the Welsh Ministers may determine, on any sum payable to the Welsh Ministers under head (2) that is not paid by such time as may be determined[6] for its payment[7]. The Welsh Ministers may charge a local housing authority an amount equal to any additional costs incurred by the Welsh Ministers as a result of any sum payable to them under head (2) not being paid by such time as may be determined[8] for its payment[9].

1 Ie under the Local Government and Housing Act 1989 s 80(1): see PARA 374.
2 As to the meaning of 'local housing authority' see PARA 11 (definition applied by the Local Government and Housing Act 1989 s 88(1)(a)).
3 Local Government and Housing Act 1989 s 80ZA(1) (s 80ZA added by the Local Government Act 2003 s 90(1); repealed, as from a day to be appointed, by the Housing (Wales) Act 2014 s 131(2), (3)(c); at the date at which this volume states the law, no such day had been appointed; the Local Government and Housing Act 1989 s 80ZA(1) amended by the Localism Act 2011 s 167, Sch 15 paras 1, 4(1), (3)). See PARA 374 note 2. As to the Welsh Ministers see PARA 7.
4 Local Government and Housing Act 1989 s 80ZA(2) (as added and prospectively repealed (see note 3); amended by the Localism Act 2011 Sch 15 paras 1, 4(1), (4)).
5 Local Government and Housing Act 1989 s 80ZA(3) (as added and prospectively repealed (see note 3); amended by the Localism Act 2011 Sch 15 paras 1, 4(1), (5)).
6 Ie under the Local Government and Housing Act 1989 s 80ZA(2): see the text and note 4.
7 Local Government and Housing Act 1989 s 80ZA(4) (as added and prospectively repealed (see note 3); amended by the Localism Act 2011 Sch 15 paras 1, 4(1), (6)).
8 Ie under the Local Government and Housing Act 1989 s 80ZA(2): see the text and note 4.
9 Local Government and Housing Act 1989 s 80ZA(5) (as added and prospectively repealed (see note 3); amended by the Localism Act 2011 Sch 15 paras 1, 4(1), (7)).

376. Power to obtain information. A local housing authority[1] in Wales, and any officer or employee of a local housing authority in Wales concerned with its housing functions, must supply the Welsh Ministers[2] with such information as the Welsh Ministers may specify, either generally or in any particular case, for the purpose of enabling the Welsh Ministers to exercise their functions in calculating housing revenue account subsidy[3] or residual debt subsidy[4]. A local housing authority must supply the Welsh Ministers with such certificates supporting the information required by them as they may specify[5].

If a local housing authority, or any officer or employee of a local housing authority concerned with its housing functions, fails to comply with these requirements before the end of such period as the Welsh Ministers may specify, the Welsh Ministers may exercise their functions in calculating the subsidies on the basis of such assumptions and estimates as they see fit[6].

1 As to the meaning of 'local housing authority' see PARA 11 (definition applied by the Local Government and Housing Act 1989 s 88(1)(a)).
2 As to the Welsh Ministers see PARA 7.
3 Ie their functions under the Local Government and Housing Act 1989 s 80: see PARA 374.
4 Local Government and Housing Act 1989 s 85(1) (amended by the Localism Act 2011 ss 167, 237, Sch 15 paras 1, 8(1), (2), Sch 25 Pt 24). Residual debt subsidy was payable under the Local Government and Housing Act 1989 s 83 (repealed) for the year 1989–90. Section 85 is repealed,

as from a day to be appointed, by the Housing (Wales) Act 2014 s 131(2), (3)(f); at the date at which this volume states the law, no such day had been appointed. See PARA 374 note 2.

5   Local Government and Housing Act 1989 s 85(2) (amended by the Localism Act 2011 Sch 15 paras 1, 8(1), (3); prospectively repealed (see note 4)).

6   Local Government and Housing Act 1989 s 85(3) (amended by the Localism Act 2011 Sch 15 paras 1, 8(1), (4); prospectively repealed (see note 4)).

377. Recoupment of subsidy in certain cases. Where housing revenue account subsidy[1] or residual debt subsidy[2] has been paid to a local housing authority[3] and it appears to the Welsh Ministers[4] that the case falls within rules published by them, they may recover from the local housing authority, or any other authority which subsequently exercises the functions of a local housing authority for any part of the same area, the whole or such part of the payment as they may determine in accordance with the rules, with interest from such time and at such rates as they may so determine[5]. Without prejudice to other methods of recovery, a sum so recoverable may be recovered by withholding or reducing subsidy[6].

1   As to housing revenue account subsidy see PARA 374.
2   See PARA 375.
3   As to the meaning of 'local housing authority' see PARA 11 (definition applied by the Local Government and Housing Act 1989 s 88(1)(a)).
4   As to the Welsh Ministers see PARA 7.
5   Local Government and Housing Act 1989 s 86(1) (amended by the Localism Act 2011 ss 167, 237, Sch 15 paras 1, 9, Sch 25 Pt 24; and by SI 1994/2825 and SI 1996/619). The Local Government and Housing Act 1989 s 86 is repealed, as from a day to be appointed, by the Housing (Wales) Act 2014 s 131(2), (3)(g); at the date at which this volume states the law, no such day had been appointed. See PARA 374 note 2.
6   Local Government and Housing Act 1989 s 86(2) (prospectively repealed: see note 5).

(vi) Financial Assistance for Private Landlords

378. Power to provide financial assistance for privately let housing accommodation. The Local Government Act 1988 gives a local housing authority[1] power to provide financial assistance for privately let housing accommodation. Thus a local housing authority has power to provide any person with financial assistance[2] for the purposes of, or in connection with, the acquisition, construction, conversion, rehabilitation, improvement, maintenance or management (whether by that person or by another) of any property which is or is intended to be privately let[3] as housing accommodation[4].

However, a local housing authority or county council must neither exercise this power, nor so exercise any other power[5] as to provide any person, for the purposes of or in connection with the matters mentioned above, with any financial assistance or with any gratuitous benefit[6], except under and in accordance with a consent given by the appropriate national authority[7]. Any transaction entered into in contravention of this provision is void[8]. Nothing in this provision, however, requires the consent of the appropriate national authority to a person's being provided by any local authority with any assistance or benefit if:

    (1)   an obligation to provide that person with that particular assistance or benefit is imposed on the local housing authority by or under any enactment, or, not being an obligation arising as the result of the exercise on or after 6 February 1987 of any option conferred on the authority, has arisen by virtue of an agreement entered into by the authority before that date;

(2)   the assistance or benefit is provided in consequence of, or in connection with, the making by the authority, or by persons who include the authority, of a requirement[9] for the provision of a water main or public sewer;

(3)   the assistance or benefit is provided under the statutory powers[10] to make payments to voluntary organisations out of sums received from health authorities;

(4)   the assistance or benefit is provided in exercise of any power the expenses of exercising which are recoverable[11] as expenses of carrying out works required to be carried out by a repair notice or a notice relating to a house in multiple occupation;

(5)   the assistance or benefit is provided in consequence of, or in connection with, the service of an improvement order under legislation relating to Scotland[12];

(6)   the assistance or benefit is provided in exercise of any power conferred by the statutory provisions relating to the power to cleanse premises of vermin before demolition[13], or the powers exercisable pursuant to the making of a control order[14], or to make loans and grants for, and assistance with, the acquisition, improvement, repair and conversion of housing[15], or the power of local housing authorities[16] to provide assistance[17].

A consent given for these purposes: (a) may be given either unconditionally or subject to conditions; (b) may be given in relation to a particular case or in relation to such description of cases (including cases described by reference to a particular local authority or a particular manner of providing assistance or benefits) as may be specified in the consent; and (c) except in relation to anything already done or agreed to be done on the authority of the consent, may be varied or revoked by a notice given or published by the appropriate national authority in such manner as the appropriate national authority may consider appropriate[18].

In determining whether to give a consent for these purposes in relation to any assistance or benefit or whether to vary or revoke a consent so given, and in determining to what (if any) conditions such a consent should be subject, the appropriate national authority must take into account the extent, if any, to which, and the circumstances in which, it is appropriate, in that authority's opinion, that a local authority should bear the financial burden and risks of acquiring, constructing, converting, rehabilitating, improving, maintaining or managing any of the property in relation to which assistance or benefits might be provided by virtue of the consent[19]. The appropriate national authority may take into account any other matter whatever which that authority considers relevant[20].

Before determining whether to consent under these provisions to the exercise of a power, the Secretary of State must consult the Regulator of Social Housing[21] if: (i) the power is to be exercised by a local authority in England; and (ii) exercise of the power would involve the disposal by the authority of social housing[22].

1   As to the meaning of 'local housing authority' see PARA 11 (definition applied by the Local Government Act 1988 s 24(6)).

2   For these purposes, a local authority (ie a local housing authority or a county council: see the Local Government Act 1988 s 24(6)) provides a person with financial assistance if that local authority does or agrees to do any of the following: (1) makes a grant or loan to that person; (2) guarantees or joins in guaranteeing the performance of any obligation owed to or by that person; (3) indemnifies or joins in indemnifying that person in respect of any liabilities, loss or damage; or (4) if that person is a body corporate, acquires share or loan capital in that person: see s 24(2). 'Loan' includes any form of credit and the remission (whether in whole or in part and whether temporarily or permanently) of any liability or obligation: s 24(6).

3   For these purposes, property is privately let as housing accommodation at any time when: (1) it is occupied as housing accommodation in pursuance of a lease or licence of any description or under a statutory tenancy; and (2) the immediate landlord of the occupier of the property is a person other than a local authority in England and Wales or a public-sector landlord in Scotland: Local Government Act 1988 s 24(3). As to the meaning of 'housing accommodation' see PARA 13 note 1; as to the meaning of 'lease' see PARA 31 note 3; and as to the meaning of 'statutory tenancy' see LANDLORD AND TENANT vol 63 (2016) PARA 673 (definitions applied by s 24(6)). 'Landlord', in relation to a person whose occupation of any property is in pursuance of a lease or statutory tenancy, has the same meaning as in the Landlord and Tenant Act 1985 (see LANDLORD AND TENANT vol 62 (2016) PARA 49) or, in Scotland, the Rent (Scotland) Act 1984 and, in relation to a person whose occupation is in pursuance of a licence, means the person who for the time being owns the interest in right of which the licence was granted: Local Government Act 1988 s 24(6).

4   Local Government Act 1988 s 24(1). Neither the Housing Act 1985 s 438 (local authority mortgage interest rates: see PARA 912) nor the Housing (Scotland) Act 1987 s 219 (local authority home-loan interest rates) applies in relation to anything done under this provision: Local Government Act 1988 s 24(4).

5   Ie whether conferred before or after 24 March 1988.

6   For these purposes, a local authority provides a person with a gratuitous benefit if:

  (1)   the authority provides that person, or agrees to provide that person, with a benefit consisting in the disposal to any person of any land or other property, in the provision to any person of any goods, services or facilities, in the carrying out for any person of any works or in the making to any person of any payment; and

  (2)   that benefit is or is to be provided either for no consideration or for a consideration which has a value in money or money's worth which is significantly less than the value, in money or money's worth, of the benefit which is or is to be provided by the authority: Local Government Act 1988 s 25(5).

   In determining for these purposes whether any benefit is or is to be provided by a local authority for no consideration, and in determining for those purposes the value of any consideration, there must be disregarded:

  (a)   so much (if any) of the consideration for the benefit in question as consists: (i) in the acquisition by any person of any such property as is mentioned in s 24(1) (see the text and note 4) or in a promise that any such property will be acquired by any person; (ii) in the carrying out of any works by any person for the purposes of the construction, conversion, rehabilitation, improvement or maintenance of any such property or in a promise that any works will be carried out by any person for any such purposes; (iii) in the carrying out by any person of any acts of management in relation to any such property or in a promise that any acts of management will be carried out by any person in relation to any such property; or (iv) in the grant of a right to nominate persons to be occupiers of any such property or in a promise to grant any such right (s 25(6)(a)); and

  (b)   without prejudice to head (a), so much of any transaction entered into after 24 March 1988 otherwise than in pursuance of another transaction entered into before that time as provides, in relation to any property which is or is intended to be occupied as housing accommodation, for an obligation which:

    (i)   restricts the occupation of the property as housing accommodation; or

    (ii)   whether because it relates to a matter affecting the suitability of the property for particular purposes or otherwise, has the effect of restricting its occupation as housing accommodation,

   to occupation by persons of a particular description or to occupation by virtue of an interest or agreement of a particular description (s 25(6)(b)).

7   Local Government Act 1988 s 25(1). As to the appropriate national authority, ie the Secretary of State or, where statutory functions have been transferred in relation to Wales, the Welsh Ministers, see PARA 7.

8   Local Government Act 1988 s 25(3). Subject to s 26(3), (4), where at any time on or after 6 February 1987 and before 24 March 1988 a local authority in England and Wales did anything which would have been a contravention of s 25 if it had been in force at that time, the same consequences follow as if s 25 had been in force at that time: s 25(4).

9   Ie under the Water Industry Act 1991 s 41 or s 98: see WATER AND WATERWAYS vol 100 (2009) PARA 332. See also ENVIRONMENTAL QUALITY AND PUBLIC HEALTH vol 46 (2010) PARA 1018.

10 Ie under the National Health Service Act 2006 s 257(3) or the National Health Service (Wales) Act 2006 s 195(3) or the National Health Service (Scotland) Act 1978 s 16A(3)(b): see HEALTH SERVICES vol 54 (2017) PARA 119.

11 Ie the Housing Act 1985 Sch 10 (repealed) or the Housing (Scotland) Act 1987 Sch 9.

12 Ie under the Housing (Scotland) Act 1987 Pt IV.

13 Ie the Housing Act 1985 s 273: see PARA 624.

14 Ie the Housing Act 1985 ss 379–394 (repealed) or corresponding provision relating to Scotland.

15 Ie the Housing Act 1985 Pts XIV–XVI (ss 435–577) (see PARA 908 et seq) or corresponding provisions relating to Scotland.

16 Ie the Regulatory Reform (Housing Assistance) (England and Wales) Order 2002, SI 2002/1860, art 3: see PARA 414.

17 Local Government Act 1988 s 25(2) (amended by the Local Government and Housing Act 1989 s 194(1), (4), Sch 11 para 96, Sch 12 Pt II; the Water Act 1989 s 190(1), Sch 25 para 79(2); the Water Consolidation (Consequential Provisions) Act 1991 s 2(1), Sch 1 para 48; the National Health Service (Consequential Provisions) Act 2006 s 2, Sch 1 paras 102, 103; and SI 2002/1860).

18 Local Government Act 1988 s 26(1).

19 Local Government Act 1988 s 26(2)(a).

20 Local Government Act 1988 s 26(2)(b). Where before 24 March 1988 any statement has been made by or on behalf of the Secretary of State:

    (1)   that, if an enactment were in force requiring his consent to a person's being provided by a local authority with assistance or benefits of any description, he would give his consent for the purposes of that enactment in relation to any matter or would so give his consent subject to certain conditions; and

    (2)   that, if any such enactment is passed, his statement is to be treated as a consent for the purposes of that enactment,

that statement has effect, both for the purposes of s 25(4) (see note 8) and after 24 March 1988, as if it were a consent given for the purposes of s 25 on the conditions (if any) specified in the statement: s 26(3). Where a consent given for the purposes of s 25 or a statement such as is mentioned in s 26(3) relates, in whole or in part, to any assistance or benefits provided before the consent was given or the statement made, that consent or statement has effect for these purposes and the purposes of s 25:

    (a)   as if the consent had been given, or the statement made, before the assistance or benefits were provided; and

    (b)   in the case of a consent relating to any assistance or benefits provided before 24 March 1988, as if the consent had been such a statement,

but a consent or statement having effect in accordance with this provision does not affect any interest deriving from, or impose any liability in respect of, any disposal of property which was made before the giving of the consent or the making of the statement and was made by a person who, apart from heads (a) and (b), had power to make it by virtue of s 25(3) or (4) (see the text and note 8): s 26(4). Where a consent to a disposal of land by a local authority has been given for the purposes of s 25 or any such statement as is mentioned in s 26(3) has effect as such a consent then, if the consent given for the purposes of s 25 so provides, no further consent of the appropriate national authority to that disposal is required, if the disposal is after 24 March 1988, by virtue of the Town and Country Planning Act 1959 s 26(4) or the Local Government (Scotland) Act 1973 s 74(2) (disposal of land for less than the best price etc), the Local Government Act 1972 s 123(2) (disposal of land by certain local authorities: see LOCAL GOVERNMENT vol 69 (2009) PARA 515), or the Housing Act 1985 s 32(2) (see PARA 522) or s 43(1) (see PARA 531) or the Housing (Scotland) Act 1987 s 12 (disposal of land held for housing purposes and of certain other land): Local Government Act 1988 s 26(5) (amended by the Housing Act 1988 s 132(7), (8)).

21 As to the Regulator of Social Housing see PARA 57 et seq.

22 Local Government Act 1988 s 26(2A) (added by SI 2010/844). The text refers to social housing within the meaning of the Housing and Regeneration Act 2008 Pt 2 (ss 59–278A): see PARA 52.

(vii) Housing Benefit

379. Housing benefit and discretionary financial assistance. A statutory scheme is prescribed[1] to provide for housing benefit, under which those who have a low income and who pay a rent for their home may claim benefit whether they are in full-time work or not. This benefit is paid by local authorities and claims are made to the relevant local authority[2]. Exclusions from housing benefit apply if a person's capital or a prescribed part of it exceeds the prescribed amount[3], and provision is made for loss of housing benefit following eviction on certain grounds including anti-social behaviour[4]. Housing benefit subsidy is payable annually by the Secretary of State to each local authority administering housing benefit[5].

Discretionary financial assistance is available (known as 'discretionary housing payments') to persons who are entitled to housing benefit or council tax benefit or to both, and appear to a relevant authority to require some further financial assistance, in addition to the benefit or benefits to which they are entitled, in order to meet housing costs[6]. The Secretary of State may, out of money provided by Parliament, make to a relevant authority such payments as he thinks fit in respect of: (1) the cost to that authority of the making of discretionary housing payments; and (2) the expenses involved in the administration by that authority of any scheme for the making of discretionary housing payments[7].

1 Ie under the Social Security Contributions and Benefits Act 1992 s 123(1)(d), (3). The scheme has been set out in two sets of regulations, one relating to persons who have attained the qualifying age for state pension credit and the other for those who have not (or who have attained that age but are on income support or an income-based jobseeker's allowance): see the Housing Benefit Regulations 2006, SI 2006/213; and the Housing Benefit (Persons who have attained the qualifying age for state pension credit) Regulations 2006, SI 2006/214. In exercise of the powers conferred by the Social Security Contributions and Benefits Act 1992 s 123(1)(d), the Secretary of State has also made the Jobseeker's Allowance (18–21 Work Skills Pilot Scheme) Regulations 2014, SI 2014/3117. See also the Welfare Reform Act 2007 ss 32–34. The Social Security Contributions and Benefits Act 1992 ss 123, 130, 130A–130G, 134, 135, the Social Security Administration Act 1992 Pt VIII (ss 134–140G) and the Welfare Reform Act 2007 ss 32–34 are repealed, as from a day to be appointed, by the Welfare Reform Act 2012 s 147, Sch 14 Pt 1; at the date at which this volume states the law, no such day had been appointed. See further WELFARE BENEFITS AND STATE PENSIONS vol 104 (2014) PARA 318 et seq.
2 See the Social Security Contributions and Benefits Act 1992 ss 1, 130, 130A, 135 (ss 130, 130A, 135 prospectively repealed: see note 1); and WELFARE BENEFITS AND STATE PENSIONS vol 104 (2014) PARA 318 et seq. As to the administration of the scheme see the Social Security Administration Act 1992 Pt VIII (ss 134–140G) (prospectively repealed: see note 1); and WELFARE BENEFITS AND STATE PENSIONS vol 104 (2014) PARA 330 et seq.
3 See the Social Security Contributions and Benefits Act 1992 s 134 (prospectively repealed: see note 1); and WELFARE BENEFITS AND STATE PENSIONS vol 104 (2014) PARA 323.
4 See the Social Security Contributions and Benefits Act 1992 ss 130B–130G (prospectively repealed: see note 1); and WELFARE BENEFITS AND STATE PENSIONS vol 104 (2014) PARA 327.
5 See the Social Security Administration Act 1992 ss 140A–140E (prospectively repealed: see note 1); and WELFARE BENEFITS AND STATE PENSIONS vol 104 (2014) PARA 333.
6 See the Discretionary Financial Assistance Regulations 2001, SI 2001/1167; and WELFARE BENEFITS AND STATE PENSIONS vol 104 (2014) PARA 334.
7 See the Child Support, Pensions and Social Security Act 2000 s 70; and WELFARE BENEFITS AND STATE PENSIONS vol 104 (2014) PARA 334.

(7) ADMINISTRATIVE PROVISIONS OF THE HOUSING ACT 2004

(i) Information

380. Power to require documents to be produced. A person authorised in writing by a local housing authority[1] may exercise the following power[2] in relation to documents[3] reasonably required by the authority: (1) for any purpose connected with the exercise of any of the authority's functions under any of Parts 1 to 4 of the Housing Act 2004[4] in relation to any premises; or (2) for the purpose of investigating whether any offence has been committed under any of those Parts in relation to any premises[5].

A person so authorised may give a notice to a relevant person[6] requiring him: (a) to produce any documents which are specified or described in the notice, or fall within a category of document which is specified or described in the notice, and which are in his custody or under his control; and (b) to produce them at a time and place so specified and to a person so specified[7]. The notice must include information about the possible consequences of not complying with the notice[8]. The person to whom any document is produced in accordance with the notice may copy the document[9]. No person may be required under these provisions to produce any document which he would be entitled to refuse to provide in proceedings in the High Court on grounds of legal professional privilege[10].

1   For the purposes of the Housing Act 2004, 'local housing authority' means, in relation to England: (1) a unitary authority; (2) a district council so far as it is not a unitary authority; (3) a London borough council; (4) the Common Council of the City of London (in its capacity as a local authority); (5) the Sub-Treasurer of the Inner Temple or the Under-Treasurer of the Middle Temple (in his capacity as a local authority); and (6) the Council of the Isles of Scilly: s 261(2). 'Unitary authority' means: (a) the council of a county so far as it is the council for an area for which there are no district councils; (b) the council of any district comprised in an area for which there is no county council: s 261(3). 'Local housing authority', in relation to Wales, means a county council or a county borough council: s 261(4).
2   Ie the power conferred by the Housing Act 2004 s 235(2): see the text and note 7.
3   In the Housing Act 2004 s 235, 'document' includes information recorded otherwise than in legible form; and in relation to information so recorded, any reference to the production of a document is a reference to the production of a copy of the information in legible form: s 235(6).
4   Ie the Housing Act 2004 Pts 1–4 (ss 1–147).
5   Housing Act 2004 s 235(1). As to enforcement of these provisions see PARA 381.
6   For this purpose, 'relevant person' means, in relation to any premises, a person within any of the following heads: (1) a person who is, or is proposed to be, the holder of a licence under the Housing Act 2004 Pt 2 (ss 55–78) (licensing of houses in multiple occupation: see PARA 674 et seq) or Pt 3 (ss 79–100) (selective licensing of other residential accommodation: see PARA 704 et seq) in respect of the premises, or a person on whom any obligation or restriction under such a licence is, or is proposed to be, imposed; (2) a person who has an estate or interest in the premises; (3) a person who is, or is proposing to be, managing or having control of the premises; (4) a person who is, or is proposing to be, otherwise involved in the management of the premises; (5) a person who occupies the premises: s 235(7).
7   Housing Act 2004 s 235(2).
8   Housing Act 2004 s 235(3).
9   Housing Act 2004 s 235(4).
10 Housing Act 2004 s 235(5). As to legal professional privilege see CIVIL PROCEDURE vol 12 (2015) PARA 647 et seq.

381. Enforcement of powers to obtain information. A person commits an offence if he fails to do anything required of him by a notice[1] to produce documents[2]. In proceedings against a person for such an offence, it is a defence that he had a reasonable excuse for failing to comply with the notice[3]. A person who commits such an offence is liable to a penalty[4].

A person commits an offence if he intentionally alters, suppresses or destroys any document which he has been required to produce by a notice[5]. A person who commits such an offence is liable to a penalty[6].

1   Ie a notice under the Housing Act 2004 s 235: see PARA 380.
2   Housing Act 2004 s 236(1). In s 236, 'document' includes information recorded otherwise than in legible form, and in relation to information so recorded: (1) the reference to the production of a document is a reference to the production of a copy of the information in legible form; and (2) the reference to suppressing a document includes a reference to destroying the means of reproducing the information: s 236(6).
3   Housing Act 2004 s 236(2).
4   Housing Act 2004 s 236(3). The penalty on summary conviction is a fine not exceeding level 5 on the standard scale: see s 236(3). As to the powers of magistrates' courts to issue fines on summary conviction see SENTENCING vol 92 (2015) PARA 176.
5   Housing Act 2004 s 236(4). See also note 2.
6   Housing Act 2004 s 236(5). The penalty, on summary conviction, is a fine not exceeding the statutory maximum and, on conviction on indictment, is a fine: see s 236(5). As to the powers of magistrates' courts to issue fines on summary conviction see SENTENCING vol 92 (2015) PARA 176.

382. Use of information obtained for certain other statutory purposes. A local housing authority[1] may use any information which has been obtained by the authority in the exercise of functions relating to housing benefit[2] or council tax[3]:

(1)   for any purpose connected with the exercise of any of the authority's functions under any of Parts 1 to 4 of the Housing Act 2004[4] in relation to any premises; or

(2)   for the purpose of investigating whether any offence has been committed under any of those Parts in relation to any premises[5].

1   As to the meaning of 'local housing authority' see PARA 380 note 1.
2   Ie under the Social Security Administration Act 1992 s 134: see WELFARE BENEFITS AND STATE PENSIONS vol 104 (2014) PARA 330.
3   Ie under the Local Government Finance Act 1992 Pt I (ss 1–69): see LOCAL GOVERNMENT FINANCE vol 70 (2012) PARA 298 et seq.
4   Ie the Housing Act 2004 Pts 1–4 (ss 1–147).
5   Housing Act 2004 s 237(1), (2). Prospectively, the Secretary of State may by regulations amend s 237 so as to change the list of purposes for which a local housing authority in England may use information to which it applies: s 237(3) (added by the Housing and Planning Act 2016 s 129(1), (2)). As to the Secretary of State see PARA 7.

383. False or misleading information. A person commits an offence if:

(1)   he supplies any information to a local housing authority[1] in connection with any of its functions under any of Parts 1 to 4 or Part 7 of the Housing Act 2004[2];

(2)   the information is false or misleading[3]; and

(3)   he knows that it is false or misleading or is reckless as to whether it is false or misleading[4].

A person also commits an offence if:

(a)   he supplies any information to another person which is false or misleading;

(b)   he knows that it is false or misleading or is reckless as to whether it is false or misleading; and

(c)   he knows that the information is to be used for the purpose of supplying information to a local housing authority in connection with any of its functions under any of Parts 1 to 4 or Part 7 of the Housing Act 2004[5].

A person who commits any such offence is liable to a penalty[6].

1   As to the meaning of 'local housing authority' see PARA 380 note 1.
2   Ie the Housing Act 2004 Pts 1–4 (ss 1–147) or Pt 7 (ss 229–270).
3   For this purpose, 'false or misleading' means false or misleading in any material respect: Housing Act 2004 s 238(4).
4   Housing Act 2004 s 238(1).
5   Housing Act 2004 s 238(2).
6   Housing Act 2004 s 238(3). The penalty on summary conviction is a fine not exceeding level 5 on the standard scale: see s 238(3). As to the powers of magistrates' courts to issue fines on summary conviction see SENTENCING vol 92 (2015) PARA 176.

(ii) Enforcement in relation to Housing Authorities' Powers under the Housing Act 2004

384. Powers of entry. The following provisions apply where the local housing authority[1] considers that a survey or examination of any premises is necessary and any of the following conditions is met[2]:

(1)   the authority considers that the survey or examination is necessary in order to carry out an inspection[3] to determine whether any functions under any of Parts 1 to 4 or Part 7 of the Housing Act 2004[4] should be exercised in relation to the premises;

(2)   the premises are specified premises[5] in relation to an improvement notice or prohibition order;

(3)   a management order is in force[6] in respect of the premises[7].

The provisions also apply where the proper officer of the local housing authority considers that a survey or examination of any premises is necessary in order to carry out an inspection[8] following an official complaint about the condition of residential premises[9].

Where these provisions apply, a person authorised by the local housing authority or the proper officer, as the case may be, may enter the premises in question at any reasonable time for the purpose of carrying out a survey or examination of the premises[10]. Before entering any premises in exercise of this power, the authorised person or proper officer must have given at least 24 hours' notice of his intention to do so to the owner[11] of the premises (if known) and to the occupier[12] (if any)[13].

Where the local housing authority considers that any premises need to be entered for the purpose of ascertaining whether a specified offence[14] has been committed, a person authorised by the local housing authority may enter the premises for that purpose at any reasonable time, but without giving any prior notice[15].

A person exercising the power of entry conferred by either of the above provisions may do such of the following as he thinks necessary for the purpose for which the power is being exercised:

(a)   take other persons with him;

(b)   take equipment or materials with him;

(c)   take measurements or photographs or make recordings;

(d)   leave recording equipment on the premises for later collection;

(e)   take samples of any articles or substances found on the premises[16].

If the premises are unoccupied or the occupier is temporarily absent, a person exercising such power of entry must leave the premises as effectively secured against trespassers as he found them[17].

An authorisation for the purposes of these provisions must be in writing and must state the particular purpose or purposes for which the entry is authorised[18]. A person authorised for these purposes must, if required to do so, produce his authorisation for inspection by the owner or any occupier of the premises or anyone acting on his behalf[19].

1   As to the meaning of 'local housing authority' see PARA 380 note 1. References in the Housing Act 2004 to 'the local housing authority', in relation to land, are references to the local housing authority in whose district the land is situated: s 261(5).

2   Housing Act 2004 s 239(1).

3   Ie an inspection under the Housing Act 2004 s 4(1) (to see whether category 1 or category 2 hazards exist) or otherwise: see PARA 565.

4   Ie the Housing Act 2004 Pts 1–4 (ss 1–147) or Pt 7 (ss 229–270).

5   Ie within the meaning of the Housing Act 2004 Pt 1: see PARA 574.

6   Ie under the Housing Act 2004 Pt 4 Ch 1 (ss 101–131), or Ch 2 (ss 132–138): see PARA 745 et seq.

7   Housing Act 2004 s 239(1)(a)–(c).

8   Ie under the Housing Act 2004 s 4(2): see PARA 565.

9   Housing Act 2004 s 239(2).

10 Housing Act 2004 s 239(3). If: (1) an interim or final management order is in force under Pt 4 Ch 1 in respect of any premises consisting of part of a house ('the relevant premises'); and (2) another part of the house is excluded from the order by virtue of s 102(8) (see PARA 746) or s 113(7) (see

PARA 755), the power of entry conferred by s 239(3) is exercisable in relation to any premises comprised in that other part so far as is necessary for the purpose of carrying out a survey or examination of the relevant premises: s 239(4).

11 In the Housing Act 2004, 'owner', in relation to premises: (1) means a person (other than a mortgagee not in possession) who is for the time being entitled to dispose of the fee simple of the premises whether in possession or in reversion; and (2) includes also a person holding or entitled to the rents and profits of the premises under a lease of which the unexpired term exceeds three years: s 262(7).

12 For this purpose, 'occupier', in relation to premises, means a person who occupies the premises, whether for residential or other purposes: Housing Act 2004 s 239(12).

13 Housing Act 2004 s 239(5).

14 Ie an offence under the Housing Act 2004 s 72 (offences in relation to licensing of HMOs: see PARA 693), s 95 (offences in relation to licensing of houses under Pt 3: see PARA 716) or s 234(3) (failure to comply with management regulations in respect of HMOs: see PARA 697).

15 Housing Act 2004 s 239(6), (7).

16 Housing Act 2004 s 239(8).

17 Housing Act 2004 s 239(11).

18 Housing Act 2004 s 239(9). As to warrants to obtain entry see PARA 385.

19 Housing Act 2004 s 239(10).

385. Warrant to authorise entry. Where a justice of the peace is satisfied, on a sworn information in writing, that admission to premises specified in the information is reasonably required for any of the following purposes by a person employed by, or acting on the instructions of, the local housing authority[1], the justice may by warrant under his hand authorise such person to enter on the premises for such of those purposes as may be specified in the warrant[2]. The purposes are:

(1)   surveying or examining premises in order to carry out an inspection[3] to determine whether any functions under any of Parts 1 to 4 or Part 7 of the Housing Act 2004[4] should be exercised in relation to the premises;

(2)   surveying or examining premises:

(a)   which are specified premises[5] in relation to an improvement notice or prohibition order; or

(b)   in respect of which a management order is in force[6];

(3)   ascertaining whether a specified offence[7] has been committed[8].

The justice must not grant the warrant unless he is satisfied:

(i)   that admission to the premises has been sought in accordance with the statutory provisions[9] but has been refused;

(ii)   that the premises are unoccupied or that the occupier[10] is temporarily absent and it might defeat the purpose of the entry to await his return; or

(iii)   that application for admission would defeat the purpose of the entry[11].

The power of entry conferred by a warrant under these provisions includes power to enter by force (if necessary)[12]. A person on whom the power of entry is conferred may do such of the following as he thinks necessary for the purpose for which the power is being exercised:

(A)   take other persons with him;

(B)   take equipment or materials with him;

(C)   take measurements or photographs or make recordings;

(D)   leave recording equipment on the premises for later collection;

(E)   take samples of any articles or substances found on the premises[13].

A warrant must, if so required, be produced for inspection by the owner or any occupier of the premises or anyone acting on his behalf[14]. If the premises are unoccupied or the occupier is temporarily absent, a person entering under the authority of a warrant must leave the premises as effectively secured against trespassers as he found them[15]. A warrant continues in force until the purpose for which the entry is required is satisfied[16].

1 As to the meaning of 'the local housing authority' see PARA 384 note 1.
2 Housing Act 2004 s 240(1), (3). In a case within s 239(4)(a) and (b) (see PARA 384 note 10), the powers conferred by s 240 are exercisable in relation to premises comprised in the excluded part of the house as well as in relation to the relevant premises: s 240(10).
3 Ie under the Housing Act 2004 s 4(1) or (2) (see PARA 565) or otherwise.
4 Ie the Housing Act 2004 Pts 1–4 (ss 1–147) or Pt 7 (ss 229–270).
5 Ie within the meaning of the Housing Act 2004 Pt 1: see PARA 574.
6 Ie under the Housing Act 2004 Pt 4 Ch 1 (ss 101–131) or Ch 2 (ss 132–138): see PARA 745 et seq.
7 Ie an offence under the Housing Act 2004 s 72 (offences in relation to licensing of HMOs), s 95 (offences in relation to licensing of houses under Pt 3) or s 234(3) (failure to comply with management regulations in respect of HMOs: see PARA 697).
8 Housing Act 2004 s 240(2).
9 Ie in accordance with the Housing Act 2004 s 239(5) or (7): see PARA 384.
10 For this purpose, 'occupier', in relation to premises, means a person who occupies the premises, whether for residential or other purposes: Housing Act 2004 s 240(11).
11 Housing Act 2004 s 240(4).
12 Housing Act 2004 s 240(5).
13 Housing Act 2004 s 240(6) (applying s 239(8)).
14 Housing Act 2004 s 240(7).
15 Housing Act 2004 s 240(8).
16 Housing Act 2004 s 240(9).

386. Penalty for obstruction. A person who obstructs a relevant person[1] in the performance of anything which that person is required or authorised[2] to do under the Housing Act 2004 commits an offence[3]. In proceedings against a person for such an offence it is a defence that he had a reasonable excuse for obstructing the relevant person[4]. A person who commits such an offence is liable to a penalty[5].

1 For this purpose, 'relevant person' means an officer of a local housing authority or any person authorised to enter premises by virtue of any of the provisions of the Housing Act 2004 Pts 1–4 (ss 1–147) or s 239 (see PARA 384) or s 240 (see PARA 385): s 241(4). As to the meaning of 'local housing authority' see PARA 380 note 1.
2 Ie by virtue of any provision of the Housing Act 2004 Pts 1–4 or Pt 7 (ss 229–270).
3 Housing Act 2004 s 241(1).
4 Housing Act 2004 s 241(2).
5 Housing Act 2004 s 241(3). The penalty on summary conviction is a fine not exceeding level 4 on the standard scale: see s 241(3). As to the powers of magistrates' courts to issue fines on summary conviction see SENTENCING vol 92 (2015) PARA 176.

387. Additional notice requirements for protection of owners. Where an owner of premises gives a notice to the local housing authority[1] informing it of his interest in the premises, the authority must give him notice of any action taken by it under any of Parts 1 to 4 or Part 7 of the Housing Act 2004[2] in relation to the premises[3].

1 As to the meaning of 'the local housing authority' see PARA 384 note 1.
2 Ie the Housing Act 2004 Pts 1–4 (ss 1–147) or Pt 7 (ss 229–270).
3 Housing Act 2004 s 242.

(iii) Authorisations for Various Purposes

388. Authorisations for enforcement purposes etc. Any authorisation for the following purposes:

(1) the power of entry to carry out work in relation to management orders[1];
(2) the power to require documents to be produced[2];
(3) the powers of entry for survey and examination[3];
(4) the power to enter to carry out work in relation to improvement notices[4]; and

(5)   the power of entry to carry out work in relation to EDMOs[5],
must be given by the appropriate officer[6] of the local housing authority[7].

1   Ie under the Housing Act 2004 s 131: see PARA 778.
2   Ie under the Housing Act 2004 s 235: see PARA 380.
3   Ie under the Housing Act 2004 s 239: see PARA 384.
4   Ie under the Housing Act 2004 Sch 3 para 3(4): see PARA 586.
5   Ie under the Housing Act 2004 Sch 7 para 25: see PARA 804.
6   For this purpose, a person is an 'appropriate officer' of a local housing authority, in relation to an
    authorisation given by the authority, if either: (1) he is a deputy chief officer of the authority
    (within the meaning of the Local Government and Housing Act 1989 s 2: see LOCAL
    GOVERNMENT vol 69 (2009) PARA 122) and the duties of his post consist of or include duties
    relating to the exercise of the functions of the authority in connection with which the authorisation
    is given; or (2) he is an officer of the authority to which such a deputy chief officer reports directly,
    or is directly accountable, as respects duties so relating: Housing Act 2004 s 243(3). As to the
    meaning of 'local housing authority' see PARA 380 note 1.
7   Housing Act 2004 s 243(1), (2).

(iv) Documents

389. Power to prescribe forms. The appropriate national authority[1] may by
regulations prescribe the form of any notice, statement or other document which
is required or authorised to be used under, or for the purposes of, the Housing Act
2004[2]. The power conferred by this provision is not exercisable where specific
provision for prescribing the form of a document is made elsewhere in the Act or
in relation to a document given or made by the First-tier Tribunal or Upper
Tribunal[3].

1   In the Housing Act 2004, 'the appropriate national authority' means: (1) in relation to England,
    the Secretary of State; and (2) in relation to Wales, the National Assembly for Wales: s 261(1). As
    to the Secretary of State see PARA 7.
2   Housing Act 2004 s 244(1).
3   Housing Act 2004 s 244(2) (amended by SI 2013/1036).

390. Power to dispense with notices. The appropriate national authority[1] may
dispense with the service of a notice which is required to be served by a local
housing authority[2] under the Housing Act 2004 if satisfied that it is reasonable to
do so[3]. A dispensation may be given either before or after the time at which the
notice is required to be served[4]; and a dispensation may be given either
unconditionally or on such conditions (whether as to the service of other notices
or otherwise) as the appropriate national authority considers appropriate[5]. Before
giving a dispensation, the appropriate national authority must, in particular, have
regard to the need to ensure, so far as possible, that the interests of any person are
not prejudiced by the dispensation[6].

1   As to the meaning of 'the appropriate national authority' see PARA 389 note 1.
2   As to the meaning of 'local housing authority' see PARA 380 note 1.
3   Housing Act 2004 s 245(1).
4   Housing Act 2004 s 245(2).
5   Housing Act 2004 s 245(3).
6   Housing Act 2004 s 245(4).

391. Service of documents. Where the local housing authority[1] is under a duty[2]
to serve[3] a document[4] on a person who, to the knowledge of the authority, is: (1)
a person having control of premises[5]; (2) a person managing premises[6]; or (3) a
person having an estate or interest in premises[7] or a person who (but for an
interim or final management order[8]) would fall within head (1) or (2), the local
housing authority must take reasonable steps to identify the person or persons
falling within such description[9].

A document required or authorised[10] to be served on a person as: (a) a person having control of premises; (b) a person managing premises; (c) a person having an estate or interest in premises[11]; or (d) a person who (but for an interim or final management order) would fall within head (a) or head (b), may, if it is not practicable after reasonable inquiry to ascertain the name or address of that person, be served in accordance with the following provisions[12]. A person having such a connection with any premises as is mentioned in heads (a) to (d) is served in accordance with these provisions if: (i) the document is addressed to him by describing his connection with the premises (naming them); and (ii) the document is delivered to some person on the premises or, if there is no person on the premises to whom it can be delivered, by fixing it, or a copy of it, to some conspicuous part of the premises[13].

Where a document is to be served[14] on the person having control of premises, the person managing premises, or the owner of premises, and more than one person comes within the description in the provision, the document may be served on more than one of those persons[15].

1   As to the meaning of 'local housing authority' see PARA 380 note 1. The Local Government Act 1972 s 233 (service of notices by local authorities: see LOCAL GOVERNMENT vol 69 (2009) PARA 576) applies in relation to the service of documents for any purposes of the Housing Act 2004 by the authorities mentioned in s 261(2)(d) and (e) (ie the Common Council of the City of London (in its capacity as a local authority) and the Sub-Treasurer of the Inner Temple or the Under-Treasurer of the Middle Temple (in his capacity as a local authority)) as if they were local authorities within the meaning of the Local Government Act 1972 s 233: Housing Act 2004 s 246(9).
2   Ie by virtue of any provision of the Housing Act 2004 Pts 1–4 (ss 1–147) or Pt 7 (ss 229–270).
3   In the Housing Act 2004 s 246, references to serving include references to similar expressions (such as giving or sending): s 246(10)(b).
4   For this purpose, 'document' includes anything in writing: Housing Act 2004 s 246(11).
5   For this purpose, 'premises' means premises however defined: Housing Act 2004 s 246(11). In the Housing Act 2004, 'person having control', in relation to premises, means (unless the context otherwise requires) the person who receives the rack-rent of the premises (whether on his own account or as agent or trustee of another person), or who would so receive it if the premises were let at a rack-rent: s 263(1). 'Rack-rent' means a rent which is not less than two-thirds of the full net annual value of the premises: s 263(2). In *Pollway Nominees Ltd v Croydon London Borough Council* [1987] AC 79, [1986] 2 All ER 349, HL, the landlord who had granted long leases of flats in the building at low rents was not, therefore, receiving a rack-rent and so notice served on it under the Housing Act 1985 s 189 (repealed) was a nullity. In similar circumstances, it has been held that a notice requiring works to the common parts cannot be served on individual leaseholders: see *R v Lambeth London Borough Council, ex p Clayhope Properties Ltd* [1988] QB 563, [1987] 3 All ER 545, CA. In relation to a section 257 HMO (see PARA 669), the Housing Act 2004 s 263 is modified by the Houses in Multiple Occupation (Certain Blocks of Flats) (Modifications to the Housing Act 2004 and Transitional Provisions for section 257 HMOs) (England) Regulations 2007, SI 2007/1904, regs 2, 12; and the Houses in Multiple Occupation (Certain Blocks of Flats) (Modifications to the Housing Act 2004 and Transitional Provisions for section 257 HMOs) (Wales) Regulations 2007, SI 2007/3231, regs 2, 12.
6   'Person managing' means, in relation to premises, the person who, being an owner or lessee of the premises:
    (1)   receives (whether directly or through an agent or trustee) rents or other payments from: (a) in the case of a house in multiple occupation, persons who are in occupation as tenants or licensees of parts of the premises; and (b) in the case of a house to which the Housing Act 2004 Pt 3 applies (see s 79(2); and PARA 704), persons who are in occupation as tenants or licensees of parts of the premises, or of the whole of the premises; or
    (2)   would so receive those rents or other payments but for having entered into an arrangement (whether in pursuance of a court order or otherwise) with another person who is not an owner or lessee of the premises by virtue of which that other person receives the rents or other payments,
and includes, where those rents or other payments are received through another person as agent or trustee, that other person: s 263(3); and see note 5 as to the modification of s 263 in relation to a section 257 HMO. In its application to Pt 1, s 263(3) has effect with the omission of

s 263(3)(a)(ii) (head (1)(b)): s 263(4). In s 246, references to a person managing premises include references to a person authorised to permit persons to occupy premises: s 246(10)(a). References in the Housing Act 2004 to any person involved in the management of a house in multiple occupation (see PARA 667 et seq) or a house to which Pt 3 applies (see s 79(2)) include references to the person managing it: s 263(5).

In the Housing Act 2004, 'lease' and 'tenancy' have the same meaning; and both expressions include a sub-lease or sub-tenancy and an agreement for a lease or tenancy (or sub-lease or sub-tenancy): s 262(1), (2). See also ss 108, 117, Sch 7 paras 3, 11 (which also extend the meaning of references to leases). The expressions 'lessor' and 'lessee' and 'landlord' and 'tenant', and references to letting, to the grant of a lease or to covenants or terms, are to be construed accordingly: s 262(3). 'Lessee' includes a statutory tenant of the premises; and references to a lease or to a person to whom premises are let are to be construed accordingly: s 262(4). As to statutory tenants see LANDLORD AND TENANT vol 63 (2016) PARA 673 et seq. 'Licence', in the context of a licence to occupy premises, includes a licence which is not granted for a consideration, but excludes a licence granted as a temporary expedient to a person who entered the premises as a trespasser (whether or not, before the grant of the licence, another licence to occupy those or other premises had been granted to him); and related expressions are to be construed accordingly: s 262(9). See also ss 108, 117, Sch 7 paras 3, 11 (which also extend the meaning of references to licences).

7   This applies whether the provision requiring or authorising service of the document refers in terms to a person having an estate or interest in premises or instead refers to a class of person having such an estate or interest (such as owners, lessees or mortgagees): Housing Act 2004 s 246(7). A person having an estate or interest in premises may for the purposes of any provision to which s 246(1), (2) applies give notice to the local housing authority of his interest in the premises (s 246(3)) and the local housing authority must enter a notice under s 246(3) in its records (s 246(4)). 'Person having an estate or interest', in relation to premises, includes a statutory tenant of the premises: s 262(8).

8   Ie under the Housing Act 2004 Pt 4 Ch 1 (ss 101–131): see PARA 745 et seq.
9   Housing Act 2004 s 246(1), (2).
10 Ie by any provision of the Housing Act 2004 Pts 1–4, 7.
11 See note 7.
12 Housing Act 2004 s 246(5).
13 Housing Act 2004 s 246(6).
14 Ie under any provision of the Housing Act 2004 Pts 1–4, 7.
15 Housing Act 2004 s 246(8).

392. Licences and other documents in electronic form. A local housing authority[1] may issue a licence to a person under Part 2 or Part 3 of the Housing Act 2004[2] by transmitting the text of the licence to him by electronic means, provided that he has indicated that he is willing to receive documents electronically[3], and the text is received by him in legible form and is capable of being used for subsequent reference[4]. Similarly, a local housing authority may serve a relevant document[5] on a person by transmitting the text of the document to him by electronic means as described above[6].

For the above provisions to apply, the recipient, or the person on whose behalf the recipient receives the document, must have indicated to the local housing authority the recipient's willingness to receive documents transmitted in the form and manner used[7]. Such an indication:

(1)   must be given to the local housing authority in such manner as it may require;

(2)   may be a general indication or one that is limited to documents of a particular description;

(3)   must state the address to be used and must be accompanied by such other information as the local housing authority requires for the making of the transmission; and

(4)   may be modified or withdrawn at any time by a notice given to the local housing authority in such manner as it may require[8].

1   As to the meaning of 'local housing authority' see PARA 380 note 1.

2   Ie the Housing Act 2004 Pt 2 (ss 55–78) (licensing of houses in multiple occupation: see PARA 674
    et seq) or Pt 3 (ss 79–100) (selective licensing of other residential accommodation: see PARA 704
    et seq).
3   See the text and notes 7–8.
4   Housing Act 2004 s 247(1). As to the timing and location of things done electronically see
    PARA 393.
5   For this purpose, 'relevant document' means any document which a local housing authority is, by
    virtue of any provision of the Housing Act 2004 Pts 1–4 (ss 1–147) or Pt 7 (ss 229–270), under
    a duty to serve on any person; and 'document' includes anything in writing: s 247(6). In s 247, any
    reference to serving includes a reference to similar expressions (such as giving or sending): s 247(5).
6   Housing Act 2004 s 247(2).
7   Housing Act 2004 s 247(3).
8   Housing Act 2004 s 247(4).

393.   Timing and location of things done electronically. The Secretary of State[1]
may by regulations make provision specifying, for the purposes of any of Parts 1
to 4 or Part 7 of the Housing Act 2004[2], the manner of determining:

(1)   the times at which things done under any of Parts 1 to 4 or Part 7 by
        means of electronic communications networks[3] are done;
(2)   the places at which things done under any of Parts 1 to 4 or Part 7 by
        means of such networks are done; and
(3)   the places at which things transmitted by means of such networks are
        received[4].

The Secretary of State may by regulations make provision about the manner of
proving in any legal proceedings:

(a)   that something done by means of an electronic communications
        network satisfies any requirements of any of Parts 1 to 4 or Part 7 for
        the doing of that thing; and
(b)   the matters mentioned in heads (1) to (3)[5].

Such regulations may provide for such presumptions to apply (whether
conclusive or not) as the Secretary of State considers appropriate[6].

1   As to the Secretary of State see PARA 7.
2   Ie the Housing Act 2004 Pts 1–4 (ss 1–147) or Pt 7 (ss 229–270).
3   In the Housing Act 2004 s 248, 'electronic communications network' has the meaning given by
    the Communications Act 2003 s 32 (see TELECOMMUNICATIONS vol 97 (2015) PARA 53):
    Housing Act 2004 s 248(4).
4   Housing Act 2004 s 248(1). As to the making of regulations see PARA 395.
5   Housing Act 2004 s 248(2).
6   Housing Act 2004 s 248(3).

394.   Proof of designations. In respect of a copy of: (1) a designation of an area
as subject to additional licensing[1]; or (2) a designation of an area as subject to
selective licensing[2], which purports to be made by a local housing authority[3], a
certificate indorsed on such a copy and purporting to be signed by the proper
officer of the authority stating the matters set out below is prima facie evidence of
the facts so stated without proof of the handwriting or official position of the
person by whom it purports to be signed[4]. Those matters are: (a) that the
designation was made by the authority; (b) that the copy is a true copy of the
designation; and (c) that the designation did not require confirmation by the
confirming authority, or that on a specified date the designation was confirmed by
the confirming authority[5].

1   Ie a designation under the Housing Act 2004 s 56: see PARA 675.
2   Ie a designation under the Housing Act 2004 s 80: see PARA 705.
3   As to the meaning of 'local housing authority' see PARA 380 note 1.
4   Housing Act 2004 s 249(1), (2).
5   Housing Act 2004 s 249(3).

(v) Orders and Regulations

395. Making of orders and regulations. Any power of the Secretary of State[1] or the Welsh Ministers[2] to make an order or regulations under the Housing Act 2004 is exercisable by statutory instrument[3]. Any power of the Secretary of State or the Welsh Ministers to make an order or regulations under that Act may be exercised so as to make different provision for different cases or descriptions of case or different purposes or areas, and includes power to make such incidental, supplementary, consequential, transitory, transitional or saving provision as the Secretary of State considers or (as the case may be) the Welsh Ministers consider appropriate[4].

Subject to certain exceptions[5], any orders or regulations made by the Secretary of State under the Housing Act 2004 are to be subject to annulment in pursuance of a resolution of either House of Parliament[6].

1 As to the Secretary of State see PARA 7.
2 As to the Welsh Ministers see PARA 7.
3 Housing Act 2004 s 250(1).
4 Housing Act 2004 s 250(2).
5 Ie subject to the Housing Act 2004 s 250(5), (6). The requirement does not apply to any order under s 270 (commencement) or Sch 10 para 3 (custodial schemes for tenancy deposits: see LANDLORD AND TENANT vol 63 (2016) PARA 868): s 250(5). Neither does s 250(4) apply to:

    (1)   any order under s 55(3) which makes the provision authorised by s 55(4) (prescribing descriptions of HMOs so that Pt 2 (ss 55–78) applies to all HMOs in the district of a local housing authority: see PARA 674);

    (2)   any order under s 80(5) or (7) (selective licensing areas; adding new matters to be taken into account in deciding whether an area is, or is likely to become, an area of low housing demand (see PARA 705), or prescribing additional sets of conditions to be considered in designating areas as subject to selective licensing (see PARA 705));

    (3)   prospectively, regulations under s 212A (provision of information to local authorities about tenancy deposit schemes: see LANDLORD AND TENANT vol 63 (2016) PARA 866);

    (4)   any order under s 216 (overcrowding: see PARA 698) or s 229(3) (jurisdiction of residential property tribunals: see PARA 34);

    (5)   prospectively, regulations under s 237 (use of information obtained for certain other statutory purposes: see PARA 382);

    (6)   any order under s 265(2) (supplementary, incidental or consequential provision) which modifies any provision of an Act;

    (7)   any regulations under s 254(6) (amendments relating to houses in multiple occupation: see PARA 667);

    (8)   any regulations under Sch 4 para 3 (amending Sch 4 to alter conditions to be included in a licence under Pt 2 and/or Pt 3: see PARA 683 et seq) or orders under Sch 10 para 11 (amending Sch 10 (tenancy deposit schemes): see LANDLORD AND TENANT vol 63 (2016) PARA 867); or

    (9)   any regulations made by virtue of Sch 13 para 11(3)(b) or Sch 13 para 12(3)(b) (amending amount of fees or costs relating to residential property tribunal proceedings: see PARAS 46–47),

and no such order or regulations may be made by the Secretary of State (whether alone or with other provisions) unless a draft of the statutory instrument containing the order or regulations has been laid before, and approved by a resolution of, each House of Parliament: s 250(6) (amended, as from a day to be appointed, by the Housing and Planning Act 2016 ss 128(1), (4), 129(1), (3); at the date at which this volume states the law, no such day had been appointed). 'Modify', in the context of a power to modify an enactment by order or regulations, includes repeal; and 'modifications' has a corresponding meaning: Housing Act 2004 s 250(7).
6 Housing Act 2004 s 250(4).

396. Calculation of numbers of persons. The appropriate national authority[1] may prescribe rules with respect to the calculation of numbers of persons for the purposes of:

    (1)   any provision made by or under the Housing Act 2004 which is specified in the rules; or

(2)   any order or licence made or granted under that Act of any description
          which is so specified[2].

The rules may provide:

(a)   for persons under a particular age to be disregarded for the purposes of
          any such calculation;

(b)   for persons under a particular age to be treated as constituting a fraction
          of a person for the purposes of any such calculation[3].

The rules may be prescribed by order or regulations[4].

1   As to the meaning of 'the appropriate national authority' see PARA 389 note 1.
2   Housing Act 2004 s 264(1). Such calculations may be relevant, for instance, in relation to the
    provisions relating to overcrowding of houses in multiple occupation: see PARA 698 et seq.
3   Housing Act 2004 s 264(2).
4   Housing Act 2004 s 264(3). As to the making or orders and regulations see PARA 395. At the date
    at which this volume states the law, no orders or regulations had been made under s 264.

(vi) Offences and Penalties

397. Financial penalties for certain housing offences in England. The local
housing authority[1] may impose a financial penalty on a person if satisfied, beyond
reasonable doubt, that the person's conduct amounts to a relevant housing
offence[2] in respect of premises in England[3]. For these purposes, a person's conduct
includes a failure to act[4]. Only one financial penalty may be imposed on a person
in respect of the same conduct[5]. The amount of a financial penalty imposed is to
be determined by the local housing authority, but must not be more than
£30,000[6].

The local housing authority may not impose a financial penalty in respect of
any conduct amounting to a relevant housing offence if: (1) the person has been
convicted of the offence in respect of that conduct; or (2) criminal proceedings for
the offence have been instituted against the person in respect of the conduct and
the proceedings have not been concluded[7].

The Secretary of State may by regulations make provision about how local
housing authorities are to deal with financial penalties recovered[8].

1   As to the meaning of 'local housing authority' see PARA 380 note 1.
2   For these purposes, 'relevant housing offence' means an offence under: (1) the Housing Act 2004
    s 30 (failure to comply with improvement notice: see PARA 584); (2) s 72 (licensing of HMOs: see
    PARA 693); (3) s 95 (licensing of houses under Pt 3: see PARA 716); (4) s 139(7) (failure to comply
    with overcrowding notice: see PARA 699); or (5) s 234 (management regulations in respect of
    HMOs: see PARA 697): s 249A(2) (s 249A added by the Housing and Planning Act 2016 s 126,
    Sch 9 paras 1, 7).
3   Housing Act 2004 s 249A(1) (as added: see note 2). Schedule 13A deals with: (1) the procedure for
    imposing financial penalties; (2) appeals against financial penalties; (3) enforcement of financial
    penalties; and (4) guidance in respect of financial penalties: s 249A(6) (as so added). See PARA 398.
4   Housing Act 2004 s 249A(9) (as added: see note 2).
5   Housing Act 2004 s 249A(3) (as added: see note 2).
6   Housing Act 2004 s 249A(4) (as added: see note 2). The Secretary of State may by regulations
    amend the amount specified in s 249A(4) to reflect changes in the value of money: s 249A(8) (as
    so added). As to the Secretary of State see PARA 7.
7   Housing Act 2004 s 249A(5) (as added: see note 2).
8   Housing Act 2004 s 249A(7) (as added: see note 2). See the Rent Repayment Orders and Financial
    Penalties (Amounts Recovered) (England) Regulations 2017, SI 2017/367.

398. Financial penalties: procedure. The following provisions are not yet in
force. Before imposing a financial penalty on a person in respect of a relevant
housing offence[1] the local housing authority[2] must give the person notice of the
authority's proposal to do so (a 'notice of intent')[3]. The notice of intent must be
given before the end of the period of six months beginning with the first day on

which the authority has sufficient evidence of the conduct[4] to which the financial penalty relates[5]. However, if the person is continuing to engage in the conduct on that day, and the conduct continues beyond the end of that day, the notice of intent may be given: (1) at any time when the conduct is continuing; or (2) within the period of six months beginning with the last day on which the conduct occurs[6].

The notice of intent must set out: (a) the amount of the proposed financial penalty; (b) the reasons for proposing to impose the financial penalty; and (c) information about the right to make representations[7]. A person who is given a notice of intent may make written representations to the local housing authority about the proposal to impose a financial penalty[8]. Any representations must be made within the period of 28 days beginning with the day after that on which the notice was given ('the period for representations')[9].

After the end of the period for representations the local housing authority must decide whether to impose a financial penalty on the person and, if it decides to impose a financial penalty, decide the amount of the penalty[10]. If the authority decides to impose a financial penalty on the person, it must give the person a notice (a 'final notice') imposing that penalty[11]. The final notice must require the penalty to be paid within the period of 28 days beginning with the day after that on which the notice was given[12]. The final notice must set out: (i) the amount of the financial penalty; (ii) the reasons for imposing the penalty; (iii) information about how to pay the penalty; (iv) the period for payment of the penalty; (v) information about rights of appeal; and (vi) the consequences of failure to comply with the notice[13].

A local housing authority may at any time withdraw a notice of intent or final notice, or reduce the amount specified in a notice of intent or final notice[14]. This power is to be exercised by giving notice in writing to the person to whom the notice was given[15].

A person to whom a final notice is given may appeal to the First-tier Tribunal[16] against the decision to impose the penalty or the amount of the penalty[17]. If a person appeals under this provision, the final notice is suspended until the appeal is finally determined or withdrawn[18]. An appeal under this provision is to be a re-hearing of the local housing authority's decision but may be determined having regard to matters of which the authority was unaware[19]. On an appeal the First-tier Tribunal may confirm, vary or cancel the final notice[20], but the final notice may not be varied so as to make it impose a financial penalty of more than the local housing authority could have imposed[21].

If a person fails to pay the whole or any part of a financial penalty which, in accordance with these provisions, the person is liable to pay, the local housing authority which imposed the financial penalty may recover the penalty or part on the order of the County Court as if it were payable under an order of that court[22].

A local housing authority must have regard to any guidance given by the Secretary of State[23] about the exercise of its functions[24] in relation to imposing financial penalties[25].

1 Ie under the Housing Act 2004 s 249A: see PARA 397. As to the meaning of 'relevant housing offence' see PARA 397 note 2.
2 As to the meaning of 'local housing authority' see PARA 380 note 1.
3 Housing Act 2004 Sch 13A para 1 (Sch 13A added by the Housing and Planning Act 2016 s 126, Sch 9 paras 1, 8).
4 For these purposes a person's conduct includes a failure to act: Housing Act 2004 Sch 13A para 2(3) (as added: see note 3).
5 Housing Act 2004 Sch 13A para 2(1) (as added: see note 3).

6 Housing Act 2004 Sch 13A para 2(2) (as added: see note 3).
7 Housing Act 2004 Sch 13A para 3 (as added: see note 3). As to the right to make representations see Sch 13A para 4; and the text to notes 8–9.
8 Housing Act 2004 Sch 13A para 4(1) (as added: see note 3).
9 Housing Act 2004 Sch 13A para 4(2) (as added: see note 3).
10 Housing Act 2004 Sch 13A para 5 (as added: see note 3).
11 Housing Act 2004 Sch 13A para 6 (as added: see note 3).
12 Housing Act 2004 Sch 13A para 7 (as added: see note 3).
13 Housing Act 2004 Sch 13A para 8 (as added: see note 3).
14 Housing Act 2004 Sch 13A para 9(1) (as added: see note 3).
15 Housing Act 2004 Sch 13A para 9(2) (as added: see note 3).
16 As to appeals to the First-tier Tribunal see PARAS 32, 33 et seq.
17 Housing Act 2004 Sch 13A para 10(1) (as added: see note 3).
18 Housing Act 2004 Sch 13A para 10(2) (as added: see note 3).
19 Housing Act 2004 Sch 13A para 10(3) (as added: see note 3).
20 Housing Act 2004 Sch 13A para 10(4) (as added: see note 3).
21 Housing Act 2004 Sch 13A para 10(5) (as added: see note 3).
22 Housing Act 2004 Sch 13A para 11(1), (2) (as added: see note 3). In proceedings before the County Court for the recovery of a financial penalty or part of a financial penalty, a certificate which is: (1) signed by the chief finance officer of the local housing authority which imposed the penalty; and (2) states that the amount due has not been received by a date specified in the certificate, is conclusive evidence of that fact: Sch 13A para 11(3) (as so added). A certificate to that effect and purporting to be so signed is to be treated as being so signed unless the contrary is proved: Sch 13A para 11(4) (as so added). In Sch 13A para 11, 'chief finance officer' has the same meaning as in the Local Government and Housing Act 1989 s 5 (see LOCAL GOVERNMENT vol 69 (2009) PARA 428): Housing Act 2004 Sch 13A para 11(5) (as so added).
23 As to the Secretary of State see PARA 7.
24 Ie under the Housing Act 2004 s 249A or Sch 13A.
25 Housing Act 2004 Sch 13A para 12 (as added: see note 3).

399. Offences by bodies corporate. Where an offence under the Housing Act 2004 committed by a body corporate is proved to have been committed with the consent or connivance of, or to be attributable to any neglect on the part of:

(1)   a director, manager, secretary or other similar officer of the body corporate; or

(2)   a person purporting to act in such a capacity,

he as well as the body corporate commits the offence and is liable to be proceeded against and punished accordingly[1]. Where the affairs of a body corporate are managed by its members, the above provision applies in relation to the acts and defaults of a member in connection with his functions of management as if he were a director of the body corporate[2].

1 Housing Act 2004 s 251(1).
2 Housing Act 2004 s 251(2).

400. Power to increase level of fines for certain offences. If the Secretary of State[1] considers that there has been a change in the value of money since the relevant date[2], the Secretary of State may by order substitute for the sum or sums for the time being specified in any specified[3] provision such other sum or sums as he considers to be justified by the change[4]. Nothing in such an order affects the punishment for an offence committed before the order comes into force[5].

1 As to the Secretary of State see PARA 7.
2 For this purpose, 'the relevant date' means: (1) the date of the passing of the Housing Act 2004 (ie 18 November 2004); or (2) where the sums specified in a provision mentioned in s 252(3) (see note 3) have been substituted by an order under s 252(2), the date of that order: s 252(4).
3 Ie a provision mentioned in the Housing Act 2004 s 252(3). Such provisions are s 32(2)(b) (fine for offence of failing to comply with prohibition order etc: see PARA 601), s 35(6) (fine for failure to comply with court order to allow action to be taken on premises: see PARA 588), s 72(6) (fine for offences in connection with licensing HMOs: see PARA 693) and s 95(5) (fine for failure to license house required to be licensed: see PARA 716): s 252(3).

4　Housing Act 2004 s 252(1), (2).
5　Housing Act 2004 s 252(5).

2. OBLIGATION TO PROVIDE AND MANAGE HOUSING

(1) REVIEWS AND RECORDS OF NEED

401. Periodical review of housing needs. Every local housing authority[1] must consider housing conditions in its district[2] and the needs of the district with respect to the provision of further housing accommodation[3]. For that purpose, the authority must review any information which has been brought to its notice, including in particular information brought to its notice as a result of the consideration of the housing conditions in its district required[4] by statute[5]. In the case of a local housing authority in England, the duty includes a duty to consider the needs of people residing in or resorting to its district with respect to the provision of: (1) sites on which caravans[6] can be stationed; or (2) places on inland waterways where houseboats[7] can be moored[8].

In discharging this duty, a local housing authority must have regard to the special needs of chronically sick or disabled persons[9].

1 As to the meaning of 'local housing authority' see PARA 11.
2 As to the meaning of 'district' see PARA 11.
3 Housing Act 1985 s 8(1). As to the meaning of 'housing accommodation' see PARA 13 note 1. See also *Watson v Minister of Local Government and Planning* [1951] 2 KB 779, sub nom *Re Havant and Waterloo UDC Compulsory Purchase Order (No 4) 1950, Application of Watson* [1951] 2 All ER 664 (decided under the Housing Act 1936) (the case decided that it was not outside the purview of a housing authority to have regard to the fact that, in part, it would be making provision for persons living in adjoining districts who desired, or might more easily obtain, housing accommodation in its district).
4 Ie under the Housing Act 2004 s 3: see PARA 402.
5 Housing Act 1985 s 8(2) (amended by the Local Government and Housing Act 1989 s 194(1), Sch 11 para 62; and the Housing Act 2004 s 265(1), Sch 15 paras 10, 11).
6 'Caravan' has the meaning given by the Caravan Sites and Control of Development Act 1960 s 29: Housing Act 1985 s 8(4) (s 8(3), (4) added by the Housing and Planning Act 2016 s 124(1)). See PLANNING vol 83 (2010) PARA 1211.
7 'Houseboat' means a boat or similar structure designed or adapted for use as a place to live: Housing Act 1985 s 8(4) (as added: see note 6).
8 Housing Act 1985 s 8(3) (as added: see note 6).
9 Chronically Sick and Disabled Persons Act 1970 s 3(1) (substituted by the Housing (Consequential Provisions) Act 1985 s 4(1), Sch 2 para 20). 'Chronically sick' and 'disabled' are not defined in the Chronically Sick and Disabled Persons Act 1970. However, where it appears to the Secretary of State to be necessary or expedient to do so for the proper operation of any provision of the Act, he may by regulations made by statutory instrument, which must be subject to annulment in pursuance of a resolution of either House of Parliament, make provision for their interpretation: see s 28. At the date at which this volume states the law no such regulations had been made.
   As to discrimination on the grounds of disability see the Equality Act 2010; and DISCRIMINATION vol 33 (2013) PARA 65 et seq. A local authority, when making decisions of a strategic nature about how to exercise its functions in relation to premises, must have due regard to the desirability of exercising them in a way that is designed to reduce the inequalities of outcome which result from socio-economic disadvantage: see the Equality Act 2010 s 1; and DISCRIMINATION vol 33 (2013) PARAS 289, 290.

402. Review of housing conditions by local housing authorities. A local housing authority[1] must keep the housing conditions in its area under review with a view to identifying any action that may need to be taken by it under any of the statutory provisions relating to housing conditions[2], the licensing of houses in multiple occupation[3], the selective licensing of other houses[4], management orders[5], demolition orders and slum clearance[6], renewal areas[7], and the providing of assistance[8] to improve living conditions[9]. For the purpose of carrying out this duty, a local housing authority and its officers must comply with any directions that may be given by the appropriate national authority[10], and keep such records, and supply the appropriate national authority with such information, as that authority may specify[11].

1 As to the meaning of 'local housing authority' see PARA 380 note 1.
2 Ie under the Housing Act 2004 Pt 1 (ss 1–54): see PARA 563 et seq.
3 Ie under the Housing Act 2004 Pt 2 (ss 55–78): see PARA 674 et seq.
4 Ie under the Housing Act 2004 Pt 3 (ss 79–100): see PARA 704 et seq.
5 Ie under the Housing Act 2004 Pt 4 Ch 1, Ch 2 (ss 101–138): see PARA 745 et seq.
6 Ie under the Housing Act 1985 Pt IX (ss 265–323): see PARA 620 et seq.
7 Ie under the Local Government and Housing Act 1989 Pt VII (ss 89–100): see PARA 820 et seq.
8 Ie under the Regulatory Reform (Housing Assistance) (England and Wales) Order 2002, SI 2002/1860, art 3: see PARA 414.
9 Housing Act 2004 s 3(1), (2).
10 As to the meaning of 'the appropriate national authority' see PARA 389 note 1.
11 Housing Act 2004 s 3(3).

403. Duty to inspect, report and prepare proposals on overcrowding. If it appears to the local housing authority[1] that occasion has arisen for a report on overcrowding[2] in its district[3] or part of it, or if the appropriate national authority[4] so directs, the local housing authority must:

(1)   cause an inspection to be made;

(2)   prepare and submit to the appropriate national authority a report showing the result of the inspection and the number of new dwellings[5] required in order to abate the overcrowding; and

(3)   unless it is satisfied that the dwellings will be otherwise provided, prepare and submit to the appropriate national authority proposals for providing the required number of new dwellings[6].

Where the appropriate national authority gives a direction under these provisions, it may after consultation with the local housing authority fix dates before which the performance of the local housing authority's functions under them is to be completed[7].

1 As to the meaning of 'local housing authority' see PARA 11.
2 As to overcrowding see PARA 649 et seq. As to overcrowding of houses in multiple occupation see PARA 698 et seq.
3 As to the meaning of 'district' see PARA 11.
4 Ie the Secretary of State or, where statutory functions have been transferred in relation to Wales, the Welsh Ministers: see PARA 7.
5 For these purposes, 'dwelling' means premises used or suitable for use as a separate dwelling: Housing Act 1985 s 343.
6 Housing Act 1985 s 334(1).
7 Housing Act 1985 s 334(2).

404. Environmental considerations. A local housing authority[1], in preparing any proposals for the provision of housing accommodation[2], or in taking any action under the Housing Act 1985, must have regard to the beauty of the landscape or countryside, the other amenities[3] of the locality, and the desirability of preserving existing works of architectural, historic or artistic interest; and it must comply with such directions in that behalf as may be given to it by the appropriate national authority[4]. Land which is the site of an ancient monument[5] or other object of archaeological interest may not be acquired for the purposes of slum clearance[6], and may be acquired for the purposes of the provision of housing[7] only by compulsory purchase order[8].

1 As to the meaning of 'local housing authority' see PARA 11.
2 As to the meaning of 'housing accommodation' see PARA 13 note 1.

3   'Amenities' includes pleasant circumstances, or features, or advantages: see *Re Ellis and Ruislip-Northwood UDC* [1920] 1 KB 343 at 370, CA, per Scrutton LJ; *FFF Estates Ltd v Hackney London Borough Council* [1981] QB 503, [1981] 1 All ER 32, CA.
4   Housing Act 1985 s 607. As to the appropriate national authority, ie the Secretary of State or, where statutory functions have been transferred in relation to Wales, the Welsh Ministers, see PARA 7.
5   As to ancient monuments see NATIONAL CULTURAL HERITAGE vol 77 (2016) PARA 1013 et seq.
6   Ie for the purposes of the Housing Act 1985 Pt IX (ss 265–323): see PARA 620 et seq.
7   Ie the purposes of the Housing Act 1985 Pt II (ss 8–57): see PARA 405 et seq.
8   Housing Act 1985 s 608 (amended by the Local Government and Housing Act 1989 ss 165(1), 194(4), Sch 9 para 87, Sch 12 Pt II).

(2) PROVISION OF HOUSING ACCOMMODATION BY LOCAL AUTHORITIES

(i) Provision of Houses and Ancillary Powers

405. Statutory duties. In addition to having statutory duties to review the provision of housing in their districts[1] and to provide accommodation for children in certain circumstances[2], local housing authorities[3] also have powers to provide housing accommodation[4] under Part II of the Housing Act 1985[5], although nothing in the Housing Act 1985 is to be taken to require, or to have at any time required, a local housing authority itself to acquire or hold any houses[6] or other land for the purposes of those powers to provide accommodation[7]. Local housing authorities also have statutory duties to the homeless[8]. Authorities in London have additional powers[9].

1   See PARA 401 et seq. As to the meaning of 'district' see PARA 11.
2   See the Children Act 1989 ss 20–23; and CHILDREN AND YOUNG PERSONS vol 10 (2017) PARA 822 et seq.
3   As to the meaning of 'local housing authority' see PARA 11.
4   As to the meaning of 'housing accommodation' see PARA 13 note 1.
5   See the Housing Act 1985 Pt II (ss 8–57); and PARA 406 et seq.
6   For the purposes of the Housing Act 1985 Pt II, 'house' includes any yard, garden, outhouses and appurtenances belonging to the house or usually enjoyed with it: s 56(1) (numbered as such by SI 2010/844).
7   Housing Act 1985 s 9(5) (added by the Local Government and Housing Act 1989 s 161(1)).
8   See the Housing Act 1996 Pt VII (ss 175–218); and PARA 481 et seq.
9   See the Housing Act 1985 s 15; and LONDON GOVERNMENT vol 71 (2013) PARA 324.

406. Powers to provide housing accommodation and related services. A local housing authority[1] may[2] provide housing accommodation[3]: (1) by erecting houses[4], or converting buildings into houses, on land acquired by the authority for the purposes of Part II of the Housing Act 1985[5]; or (2) by acquiring houses[6]. The authority may alter, enlarge, repair or improve a house so erected, converted or acquired[7]. These powers may also be exercised in relation to land acquired for the purpose of disposing of houses provided, or to be provided, on the land, or of disposing of the land to a person who intends to provide housing accommodation on it[8]. A local housing authority may not, however, provide under these provisions a cottage with a garden of more than one acre[9].

A local housing authority may fit out, furnish and supply a house provided by it under these provisions with all requisite furniture, fittings and conveniences[10] and may sell, or supply under a hire-purchase agreement[11] or a conditional sale agreement[12], furniture to the occupants of houses so provided, and may for that purpose buy furniture[13].

A local housing authority may also provide, in connection with the provision of housing accommodation by it under these provisions, facilities for obtaining meals and refreshments, and facilities for doing laundry and laundry services, such as accord with the needs of the persons for whom the housing accommodation is provided[14]; and it may make reasonable charges for meals and refreshments, and for the use of laundry facilities or laundry services, so provided[15]. In carrying on these activities, a local housing authority is subject to all relevant enactments and rules of law, including enactments relating to the sale of intoxicating liquor or the sale by retail of alcohol[16], in the same manner as other persons carrying on such activities[17].

A local housing authority may only provide permanent accommodation to a person who is qualified for an offer of accommodation under Part VI of the Housing Act 1996[18].

In providing housing accommodation and related services, a local housing authority must comply with the requirements of the legislation relating to discrimination, particularly on the grounds of disability[19].

1 As to the meaning of 'local housing authority' see PARA 11.
2 There is no duty on the local housing authority itself to hold or acquire housing stock: see PARA 405. The decision whether to exercise powers under the Housing Act 1985 s 9 is for the local authority alone, and the court will only interfere on grounds of *Wednesbury* unreasonableness: *R v Lambeth London Borough Council, ex p A1, R v Lambeth London Borough Council, ex p A2* (1997) 30 HLR 933, CA. As to *Wednesbury* unreasonableness see JUDICIAL REVIEW vol 61 (2010) PARA 602.
3 As to the meaning of 'housing accommodation' see PARA 13 note 1.
4 As to the meaning of 'house' see PARA 405 note 6.
5 Ie for the purposes of the Housing Act 1985 Pt II (ss 8–57).
6 Housing Act 1985 s 9(1).
7 Housing Act 1985 s 9(2).
8 Housing Act 1985 s 9(3).
9 Housing Act 1985 s 9(4).
10 Housing Act 1985 s 10(1).
11 For these purposes, 'hire-purchase agreement' has the same meaning as in the Consumer Credit Act 1974 (see CONSUMER CREDIT vol 21 (2016) PARA 40): Housing Act 1985 s 10(3).
12 For these purposes, 'conditional sale agreement' has the same meaning as in the Consumer Credit Act 1974 (see CONSUMER CREDIT vol 21 (2016) PARA 38): Housing Act 1985 s 10(3).
13 Housing Act 1985 s 10(2).
14 Housing Act 1985 s 11(1).
15 Housing Act 1985 s 11(2).
16 Where a premises licence under the Licensing Act 2003 Pt 3 (ss 11–59) authorises the sale by retail of alcohol in connection with the provision of facilities of the kind mentioned in the Housing Act 1985 s 11(1)(a), then, notwithstanding the terms of that licence, it does not have effect so as to authorise the sale by retail of alcohol for consumption otherwise than with a meal: s 11(3) (substituted by the Licensing Act 2003 s 198(1), Sch 6 paras 102, 103(a)). An expression used in the Housing Act 1985 s 11 and in the Licensing Act 2003 has the same meaning in the Housing Act 1985 s 11 as in the Licensing Act 2003: Housing Act 1985 s 11(5) (added by the Licensing Act 2003 Sch 6 para 103(c)).
17 Housing Act 1985 s 11(4) (amended by the Licensing Act 2003 Sch 6 para 103(b)).
18 See the Housing Act 1996 Pt VI (ss 159–174); and PARA 420 et seq.
19 As to discrimination see the Equality Act 2010; and DISCRIMINATION vol 33 (2013) PARA 1 et seq.

407. Provision of welfare services. A local housing authority[1] may provide in connection with the provision of housing accommodation[2] by it, whether or not under Part II of the Housing Act 1985[3], such welfare services[4], that is to say, services for promoting the welfare of the persons for whom the accommodation is so provided, as accord with the needs of those persons[5]. It may make reasonable charges for welfare services so provided[6].

1 As to the meaning of 'local housing authority' see PARA 11.

2　As to the meaning of 'housing accommodation' see PARA 13 note 1. There is no duty on the local housing authority itself to hold or acquire housing stock: see PARA 405.

3　Ie under the Housing Act 1985 Pt II (ss 8–57).

4　For these purposes, 'welfare services' does not include the repair, maintenance, supervision or management of houses or other property: Housing Act 1985 s 11A(3) (s 11A added by the Leasehold Reform, Housing and Urban Development Act 1993 s 126).

5　Housing Act 1985 s 11A(1) (as added: see note 4).

6　Housing Act 1985 s 11A(2) (as added: see note 4). Section 11A reverses the effect of *R v Ealing London Borough Council, ex p Lewis* (1992) 90 LGR 571, 24 HLR 484, CA.

408.　Provision of shops, recreation grounds etc. A local housing authority[1] may, with the consent of the appropriate national authority[2], provide and maintain in connection with housing accommodation[3] provided by it under Part II of the Housing Act 1985[4]:

(1)　buildings adapted for use as shops;

(2)　recreation grounds; and

(3)　other buildings or land which, in the opinion of the appropriate national authority, will serve a beneficial purpose[5] in connection with the requirements of the persons for whom the housing accommodation is provided[6].

This power may be exercised either by the local housing authority itself or jointly with another person[7].

1　As to the meaning of 'local housing authority' see PARA 11.

2　The appropriate national authority may, in giving its consent, by order apply, with any necessary modifications, any statutory provisions which would have been applicable if the land or buildings had been provided under any enactment giving a local authority powers for the purpose: Housing Act 1985 s 12(2). As to the appropriate national authority, ie the Secretary of State or, where statutory functions have been transferred in relation to Wales, the Welsh Ministers, see PARA 7. In relation to England, the Secretary of State must consult the Regulator of Social Housing before deciding whether to consent under s 12 to anything within the Regulator's remit: s 12(4) (added by SI 2010/844). For the purposes of the Housing Act 1985 Pt II (ss 8–57), something is within the remit of the Regulator of Social Housing if it is related to or affects the provision of social housing by a local housing authority, or county council, in England: s 56(2) (added by SI 2010/844). As to the Regulator of Social Housing see PARA 57 et seq. As to the meaning of 'social housing' see PARA 52 (definition applied by the Housing Act 1985 s 56(1) (numbered as such and definition added by SI 2010/844)).

3　As to the meaning of 'housing accommodation' see PARA 13 note 1.

4　Ie under the Housing Act 1985 Pt II (ss 8–57). There is no duty on the local housing authority itself to hold or acquire housing stock: see PARA 405.

5　As to whether the buildings or land will serve a beneficial purpose see *Conron v LCC* [1922] 2 Ch 283; *HE Green & Sons v Minister of Health (No 2)* [1948] 1 KB 34, [1947] 2 All ER 469.

6　Housing Act 1985 s 12(1).

7　Housing Act 1985 s 12(3).

409.　Provision of streets, roads and open spaces and development generally. A local housing authority[1] may lay out and construct public streets[2] or roads and open spaces on land acquired by the authority for the statutory purposes[3]. Where the authority disposes of land to a person who intends to provide housing accommodation[4] on it, the authority may contribute towards the expenses of the development of the land and the laying out and construction of streets on it, subject to the condition that the streets are dedicated to the public[5]. It has been held that this power must be used to build roads which relate to housing accommodation[6].

1　As to the meaning of 'local housing authority' see PARA 11.

2　'Street' includes any court, alley, passage, square or row of houses, whether a thoroughfare or not: Housing Act 1985 s 622(1) (numbered as such by SI 2001/3649). As to the meaning of 'house' see PARA 405 note 6.

3　Housing Act 1985 s 13(1). The purposes referred to in the text are those of Pt II (ss 8–57).

4　As to the meaning of 'housing accommodation' see PARA 13 note 1.

5 Housing Act 1985 s 13(2).
6 See *Meravale Builders Ltd v Secretary of State for the Environment* (1978) 36 P & CR 87, 77 LGR 365 (decided under the similarly worded Housing Act 1957 s 107 (repealed)) (roads must be fairly and reasonably incidental to the provision of housing accommodation).

410. Exercise of powers by local housing authority outside its district. A local housing authority[1] may, for supplying the needs of its district[2], exercise outside its district the powers conferred on it[3] in relation to the provision of housing accommodation[4]. Before doing so, a district council[5] must give notice of its intention to the council of the county in which its district is situated, and, if it proposes to exercise the power outside that county but in England, to the council of the county in which it proposes to exercise the power; but failure to give notice does not invalidate the exercise of the power[6]. Where a Welsh county council or county borough council[7] proposes to exercise the power in England it must before doing so give notice of its intention to the council of the county in which it proposes to exercise the power; but failure to give notice does not invalidate the exercise of the power[8].

Where housing operations under Part II of the Housing Act 1985[9] are being carried out by a local housing authority outside its own district, the authority's power to execute works necessary for the purposes of, or incidental to the carrying out of, the operations, is subject to entering into an agreement with the council of the county, county borough, London borough or district in which the operations are being carried out, as to the terms and conditions on which the works are to be executed[10]. Where housing operations have been carried out by a local housing authority outside its own district, and for the purposes of the operations public streets[11] or roads have been constructed and completed by the authority, the liability to maintain the streets or roads vests in the council which is the local highway authority[12] for the area in which the operations were carried out unless that council is satisfied that the streets or roads have not been properly constructed[13].

Where a local housing authority carries out housing operations outside its own district, any difference arising between that authority and any authority in whose area the operations are carried out may be referred by either authority to the appropriate national authority[14], whose decision is final and binding on them[15].

1 As to the meaning of 'local housing authority' see PARA 11.
2 As to the meaning of 'district' see PARA 11.
3 Ie by the Housing Act 1985 ss 9–13: see PARAS 406–409.
4 Housing Act 1985 s 14(1). As to the meaning of 'housing accommodation' see PARA 13 note 1.
5 As to local government areas and authorities in England see LOCAL GOVERNMENT vol 69 (2009) PARA 22 et seq.
6 Housing Act 1985 s 14(2) (s 14(2), (3) amended, and s 14(2A) added, by the Local Government (Wales) Act 1994 s 22(2), Sch 8 para 5(4)).
7 As to local government areas and authorities in Wales see LOCAL GOVERNMENT vol 69 (2009) PARA 37 et seq.
8 Housing Act 1985 s 14(2A) (as added: see note 6).
9 Ie under the Housing Act 1985 Pt II (ss 8–57).
10 Housing Act 1985 s 14(3) (as amended: see note 6).
11 As to the meaning of 'street' see PARA 409 note 2.
12 As to local highway authorities see HIGHWAYS, STREETS AND BRIDGES vol 55 (2012) PARA 59 et seq.
13 Housing Act 1985 s 14(4).
14 Ie the Secretary of State or, where statutory functions have been transferred in relation to Wales, the Welsh Ministers: see PARA 7.
15 Housing Act 1985 s 14(5).

411. Compliance with minimum standards in erection of houses. A local housing authority[1] by which a house[2] is erected under the enactments relating to housing, whether with or without financial assistance from the government, must secure that, except in so far as the appropriate national authority[3] may, in a particular case, dispense with the observance of this requirement, the house is provided with a fixed bath in a bathroom[4].

1 As to the meaning of 'local housing authority' see PARA 11.
2 As to the meaning of 'house' see PARA 405 note 6.
3 Ie the Secretary of State or, where statutory functions have been transferred in relation to Wales, the Welsh Ministers: see PARA 7.
4 Housing Act 1985 s 52 (amended by the Local Government Act 1988 ss 19(11)(a), 41, Sch 7 Pt I).

412. Special provisions relating to prefabs. 'Prefabs'[1] are deemed to be houses[2] provided by the local housing authority[3] under Part II of the Housing Act 1985[4]. A prefab and the land on which it is situated may, if immediately before 25 August 1972[5] it was deemed to be land acquired for certain statutory purposes[6], be appropriated or disposed of by the local housing authority in the same way as any other land acquired or deemed to be acquired for the purposes of Part II of the Housing Act 1985[7].

These provisions do not affect any obligation of a local housing authority to another person as respects the removal or demolition of a prefab[8].

1 'Prefabs' are structures made available to a local authority under the Housing (Temporary Accommodation) Act 1944 s 1 (repealed); and, for these purposes, references to a prefab include fittings forming part of it: Housing Act 1985 s 53(1), (5).
2 As to the meaning of 'house' see PARA 405 note 6.
3 As to the meaning of 'local housing authority' see PARA 11.
4 Housing Act 1985 s 53(2). As to the provision of houses under Pt II (ss 8–57) see PARAS 401, 406–411. The local housing authority does not have a duty to hold or acquire housing stock itself: see PARA 405.
5 Ie the date on which the Housing (Temporary Accommodation) Act 1944 was repealed.
6 Ie for the purposes of the Housing Act 1957 Pt V (ss 91–134) (repealed).
7 Housing Act 1985 s 53(3).
8 Housing Act 1985 s 53(4).

413. Powers of entry and penalty for obstruction. A person authorised by the local housing authority[1] or the appropriate national authority[2] may at any reasonable time, on giving 24 hours' notice of his intention to the occupier, and to the owner[3] if the owner is known, enter premises for the purpose of survey and examination:

(1)   where it appears to the local housing authority or the appropriate national authority that survey or examination is necessary in order to determine whether any powers under Part II of the Housing Act 1985[4] should be exercised in respect of the premises; or

(2)   in the case of premises which the authority is authorised to purchase compulsorily[5].

An authorisation for these purposes must be in writing stating the particular purpose or purposes for which the entry is authorised and must, if so required, be produced for inspection by the occupier or anyone acting on his behalf[6].

It is a summary offence intentionally to obstruct an officer of the local housing authority or of the appropriate national authority, or any person so authorised to enter premises, in the performance of anything which he is required or authorised[7] to do[8]; and a person committing such an offence is liable on conviction to a penalty[9].

1 As to the meaning of 'local housing authority' see PARA 11.
2 As to the appropriate national authority, ie the Secretary of State or, where statutory functions have been transferred in relation to Wales, the Welsh Ministers, see PARA 7.
3 'Owner', in relation to premises: (1) means a person (other than a mortgagee not in possession) who is for the time being entitled to dispose of the fee simple in the premises, whether in possession

or in reversion; and (2) includes also a person holding or entitled to the rents and profits of the premises under a lease of which the unexpired term exceeds three years: Housing Act 1985 s 56(1) (numbered as such by SI 2010/844).

4   Ie under the Housing Act 1985 Pt II (ss 8–57): see PARA 401 et seq.

5   Housing Act 1985 s 54(1). A person may not be authorised by a local housing authority under s 54(1)(a) (head (1) in the text) to enter and survey or value land in connection with a proposal to acquire an interest in or a right over land (but see the Housing and Planning Act 2016 s 172; and COMPULSORY ACQUISITION OF LAND): Housing Act 1985 s 54(3) (added by the Housing and Planning Act 2016 s 179, Sch 14 para 16).

6   Housing Act 1985 s 54(2) (amended by the Local Government and Housing Act 1989 s 194, Sch 11 para 64).

7   See note 4.

8   Housing Act 1985 s 55(1) (amended by the Local Government and Housing Act 1989 Sch 11 para 65(1)).

9   Housing Act 1985 s 55(2). The penalty is a fine not exceeding level 3 on the standard scale: see s 55(2) (amended by the Local Government and Housing Act 1989 Sch 11 para 65(2)). As to the powers of magistrates' courts to issue fines on summary conviction see SENTENCING vol 92 (2015) PARA 176.

(ii) Provision of Assistance

414. Power of local housing authorities to provide assistance. For the purpose of improving living conditions in its area, a local housing authority[1] may provide, directly or indirectly, assistance[2] to any person for the purpose of enabling him: (1) to acquire living accommodation[3], whether within or outside the authority's area[4]; (2) to adapt or improve living accommodation, whether by alteration, conversion or enlargement, by the installation of any thing or injection of any substance, or otherwise[5]; (3) to repair living accommodation[6]; (4) to demolish buildings comprising or including living accommodation[7]; (5) where buildings comprising or including living accommodation have been demolished, to construct buildings that comprise or include replacement living accommodation[8].

A local housing authority may not exercise such a power in any case unless: (a) it has adopted a policy for the provision of assistance[9]; (b) it has given public notice of the adoption of the policy[10]; (c) it has secured that: (i) a document in which the policy is set out in full is available for inspection, free of charge, at its principal office at all reasonable times[11]; and (ii) copies of a document containing a summary of the policy may be obtained by post on payment, where a reasonable charge is made, of the amount of the charge[12]; and (d) the power is exercised in accordance with the policy[13].

A local housing authority may not provide assistance for a purpose specified in heads (2) to (4) above unless it is also satisfied that the owner[14] of the living accommodation concerned has consented to the carrying out of the assisted work[15]. Where a local housing authority has specified, or approved the specification for, assisted work, it may not vary, or require the variation of, that specification unless it has obtained the consent of every person who, in the authority's opinion, is likely to be affected to any material extent by the variation[16]. A local housing authority may not vary or revoke any condition to which assistance is subject except on the application or with the consent of the person to whom the assistance was provided[17].

A local housing authority may require a person to whom assistance has been provided, or who has applied for assistance, to give to the authority, within such period as it may reasonably specify, such information or evidence, including information or evidence relating to his financial circumstances, as the authority may reasonably require for the purposes of, or purposes connected with, the exercise of its powers[18].

1 'Local housing authority' means a district council, a London borough council, the Common Council of the City of London, a Welsh county council or county borough council, or the Council of the Isles of Scilly: Regulatory Reform (Housing Assistance) (England and Wales) Order 2002, SI 2002/1860, art 2.

2 Assistance may be provided in any form: Regulatory Reform (Housing Assistance) (England and Wales) Order 2002, SI 2002/1860, art 3(3). It may be unconditional or subject to conditions, including conditions as to the repayment of the assistance or of its value, in whole or in part, or the making of a contribution towards the assisted work; but before imposing any such condition, or taking steps to enforce it, a local housing authority must have regard to the ability of the person concerned to make the repayment or contribution: art 3(4). Before a local housing authority provides assistance to any person, it must give that person a statement in writing of the conditions, if any, to which the assistance is subject, and satisfy itself that that person has received appropriate advice or information about the extent and nature of any obligation, whether financial or otherwise, to which he will become subject in consequence of the provision of assistance: art 3(5). A local housing authority may take any form of security in respect of the whole or part of any assistance, and where any such security is taken in the form of a charge on any property, the local housing authority may at any time reduce the priority of the charge or secure its removal: art 3(6), (7).

3 'Living accommodation' means any of: (1) a building or part of a building; (2) a caravan, within the meaning of the Caravan Sites and Control of Development Act 1960 Pt I (ss 1–32), disregarding the amendment made by the Caravan Sites Act 1968 s 13(2) (see PLANNING vol 83 (2010) PARA 1211); and (3) a boat or similar structure, occupied or available for occupation for residential purposes, whether, in the case of a building or part of a building, in single or multiple units, and includes any yard, garden, outhouses and appurtenances belonging to the building or, as the case may be, the caravan, or the boat or similar structure, or usually enjoyed with it: Regulatory Reform (Housing Assistance) (England and Wales) Order 2002, SI 2002/1860, art 2.

4 Regulatory Reform (Housing Assistance) (England and Wales) Order 2002, SI 2002/1860, art 3(1)(a). This power may be exercised to assist a person to acquire living accommodation only where the authority has acquired or proposes to acquire, whether compulsorily or otherwise, his existing living accommodation, or is satisfied that the acquisition of other living accommodation would provide for that person a benefit similar to that which would be provided by the carrying out of work of any description in relation to his existing living accommodation: art 3(2).

5 Regulatory Reform (Housing Assistance) (England and Wales) Order 2002, SI 2002/1860, art 3(1)(b).

6 Regulatory Reform (Housing Assistance) (England and Wales) Order 2002, SI 2002/1860, art 3(1)(c).

7 Regulatory Reform (Housing Assistance) (England and Wales) Order 2002, SI 2002/1860, art 3(1)(d).

8 Regulatory Reform (Housing Assistance) (England and Wales) Order 2002, SI 2002/1860, art 3(1)(e). Nothing in art 3 affects any power of a local housing authority under the Housing Act 1985 Pt XIV (ss 435–459) (see PARA 910 et seq): Regulatory Reform (Housing Assistance) (England and Wales) Order 2002, SI 2002/1860, art 3(9).

9 Regulatory Reform (Housing Assistance) (England and Wales) Order 2002, SI 2002/1860, art 4(a).

10 Regulatory Reform (Housing Assistance) (England and Wales) Order 2002, SI 2002/1860, art 4(b).

11 Regulatory Reform (Housing Assistance) (England and Wales) Order 2002, SI 2002/1860, art 4(c)(i).

12 Regulatory Reform (Housing Assistance) (England and Wales) Order 2002, SI 2002/1860, art 4(c)(ii).

13 Regulatory Reform (Housing Assistance) (England and Wales) Order 2002, SI 2002/1860, art 4(d).

14 For these purposes, 'owner' means, in relation to living accommodation comprising a building or part of a building, the person who:
   (1)   is for the time being entitled to receive from a tenant of the accommodation, or would be so entitled if the accommodation were let, a rent at an annual rate of not less than two-thirds of the net annual value of the accommodation; and
   (2)   is not himself liable as tenant of the accommodation, or of property which includes the accommodation, to pay such a rent to a superior landlord,

and in relation to living accommodation comprising a caravan or a boat or similar structure, the person who is for the time being entitled to dispose of the caravan or boat or similar structure: Regulatory Reform (Housing Assistance) (England and Wales) Order 2002, SI 2002/1860, art 5(2). 'Net annual value', in relation to living accommodation, means the rent at which the accommodation might reasonably be expected to be let from year to year if the tenant undertook to pay all usual tenant's rates and taxes and to bear the cost of repair and insurance and the other expenses, if any, necessary to maintain the accommodation in a state to command that rent: art 5(3). Any dispute arising as to the net annual value of living accommodation must be referred in writing for decision by the district valuer: art 5(4). 'District valuer', in relation to living accommodation in respect of which a person has applied or proposes to apply to a local housing authority for assistance, means an officer appointed by the Commissioners for Her Majesty's Revenue and Customs for the purpose of deciding, in relation to the authority, any dispute under art 5(4): see art 5(5) (amended by virtue of the Commissioners for Revenue and Customs Act 2005 s 50(1), (7)). The Commissioners for Her Majesty's Revenue and Customs are appointed under the Commissioners for Revenue and Customs Act 2005 s 1 and have taken over the functions of the former Commissioners of Inland Revenue and Commissioners of Customs and Excise: see INCOME TAXATION vol 58 (2014) PARAS 33–34.

15 Regulatory Reform (Housing Assistance) (England and Wales) Order 2002, SI 2002/1860, art 5(1). 'Assisted work' means work of any description in relation to the carrying out of which assistance is provided: art 2.

16 Regulatory Reform (Housing Assistance) (England and Wales) Order 2002, SI 2002/1860, art 5(6).

17 Regulatory Reform (Housing Assistance) (England and Wales) Order 2002, SI 2002/1860, art 5(7).

18 Ie its powers under the Regulatory Reform (Housing Assistance) (England and Wales) Order 2002, SI 2002/1860, art 3 (see the text and notes 1–8): art 6.

415. Contributions towards expenditure of local housing authorities in providing assistance. Contributions towards expenditure incurred by a local housing authority[1] in providing assistance[2] may be paid by the appropriate national authority[3]. The rate or rates of the contributions, the calculation of the expenditure to which they relate and the manner of their payment must be determined by the appropriate national authority[4]. Such a determination may be made generally or with respect to a particular local housing authority or description of authority, including a description framed by reference to authorities in a particular area[5], and may make different provision in relation to different cases or descriptions of case[6]. Any such contributions are payable subject to such conditions as to records, certificates, audit or otherwise as the appropriate national authority may impose[7].

Where the appropriate national authority has paid contributions to a local housing authority, it may recover from the authority such amount[8] as it determines to be appropriate in respect of repayments of assistance[9].

1 As to the meaning of 'local housing authority' see PARA 414 note 1.

2 Ie assistance under the Regulatory Reform (Housing Assistance) (England and Wales) Order 2002, SI 2002/1860, art 3: see PARA 414.

3 Regulatory Reform (Housing Assistance) (England and Wales) Order 2002, SI 2002/1860, art 7(1). As to the appropriate national authority, ie the Secretary of State or, where statutory functions have been transferred in relation to Wales, the Welsh Ministers, see art 2; and PARA 7. Where the appropriate national authority is the Secretary of State, the consent of the Treasury is required before any determination is made under art 7(2) or any conditions are imposed under art 7(4): art 7(5). As to the Treasury CONSTITUTIONAL AND ADMINISTRATIVE LAW vol 20 (2014) PARA 262 et seq.

4 Regulatory Reform (Housing Assistance) (England and Wales) Order 2002, SI 2002/1860, art 7(2).

5 Regulatory Reform (Housing Assistance) (England and Wales) Order 2002, SI 2002/1860, art 7(3)(a).

6 Regulatory Reform (Housing Assistance) (England and Wales) Order 2002, SI 2002/1860, art 7(3)(b).

7 Regulatory Reform (Housing Assistance) (England and Wales) Order 2002, SI 2002/1860, art 7(4).

8 The amount is calculated by reference to the amount appearing to the appropriate national authority to represent his contribution to assistance in respect of which repayments have been made to the local housing authority, or assistance in respect of which repayments could have been recovered if reasonable steps had been taken by that authority, together with an appropriate percentage of any interest received by that authority, or which would have been received if reasonable steps had been taken by that authority: Regulatory Reform (Housing Assistance) (England and Wales) Order 2002, SI 2002/1860, art 8(2). The question what steps it would have been reasonable for the local housing authority to take is determined by the appropriate national authority: art 8(3).

9 Regulatory Reform (Housing Assistance) (England and Wales) Order 2002, SI 2002/1860, art 8(1).

(iii) Acquisition and Appropriation of Land

416. Acquisition of land for housing purposes. A local housing authority[1] may for the statutory purposes under the Housing Act 1985[2]:

(1)   acquire land[3] as a site for the erection of houses[4];

(2)   acquire houses, or buildings which may be made suitable as houses, together with any land occupied with the houses or buildings;

(3)   acquire land proposed to be used for any authorised purpose[5]; and

(4)   acquire land in order to carry out on it works for the purpose of, or connected with, the alteration, enlarging, repair or improvement of an adjoining house[6].

This power includes power to acquire land for the purpose of disposing of houses provided, or to be provided, on the land or of disposing of the land to a person who intends to provide housing accommodation[7] on it or facilities which serve a beneficial purpose[8] in connection with the requirements of persons for whom housing accommodation is provided[9].

Land may be acquired by a local housing authority for the statutory purposes by agreement, or the authority may be authorised by the appropriate national authority[10] to acquire it compulsorily[11].

A local housing authority may, with the consent of, and subject to any conditions imposed by, the appropriate national authority, acquire land for the statutory purposes notwithstanding that the land is not immediately required for those purposes; but an authority must not be so authorised to acquire land compulsorily unless it appears to the appropriate national authority that the land is likely to be required for those purposes within ten years from the date on which it confirms the compulsory purchase order[12].

1 As to the meaning of 'local housing authority' see PARA 11.

2 Ie for the purposes of the Housing Act 1985 Pt II (ss 8–57). The local housing authority does not have a duty to hold or acquire housing stock itself: see PARA 405.

     Account may properly be taken of planning considerations: see *Hanks v Minister of Housing and Local Government* [1963] 1 QB 999, [1963] 1 All ER 47 (decided under the Housing Act 1957 s 97 (repealed)).

3 'Land' includes buildings and other structures, land covered with water, and any estate, interest, easement, servitude or right in or over land: see the Interpretation Act 1978 s 5, Sch 1.

4 As to the meaning of 'house' see PARA 405 note 6.

5 Ie any purpose authorised by the Housing Act 1985 ss 11, 12, 15(1): see PARAS 406, 408; and LONDON GOVERNMENT vol 71 (2013) PARA 324.

6 Housing Act 1985 s 17(1). This power may be used to acquire houses which have been left empty for long periods: see *Moore v Minister of Housing and Local Government* [1966] 2 QB 602, [1965] 2 All ER 367 (decided under the similarly worded Housing Act 1957 s 96 (repealed) and ss 91, 92 (both repealed)). The words 'at a reasonable price' cannot be read into the power to acquire: *Charles Terence Estates Ltd v Cornwall Council* [2012] EWCA Civ 1439, [2013] LGR 97.

7 As to the meaning of 'housing accommodation' see PARA 13 note 1.

8 As to the meaning of 'beneficial purpose' see PARA 408 note 5.

9 Housing Act 1985 s 17(2) (amended by the Housing Act 1996 s 222, Sch 18 para 24(1)).

10 Ie the Secretary of State or, where statutory functions have been transferred in relation to Wales, the Welsh Ministers: see PARA 7.

11 Housing Act 1985 s 17(3). As to compulsory purchase see COMPULSORY ACQUISITION OF LAND vol 18 (2009) PARA 501 et seq. See *Ainsdale Investments Ltd v First Secretary of State* [2004] EWHC 1010 (Admin), [2004] HLR 956, [2004] 2 EGLR 9 (land that has been compulsorily acquired must be used for the purpose for which the acquiring authority has been authorised to acquire it, but the authorised purposes include any use which is ancillary to that use).

12 Housing Act 1985 s 17(4); and see *Simpsons Motor Sales (London) Ltd v Hendon Corpn* [1964] AC 1088, [1963] 2 All ER 484, HL (decided under the Housing Act 1936 s 74 (repealed)).

417. Duties with respect to buildings acquired for housing purposes. Where a local housing authority[1] acquires a building which may be made suitable as a house[2], the authority must forthwith proceed to secure that the building is so made suitable either by itself executing any necessary works or by leasing[3] it, or selling it to some person subject to conditions for securing that he will make it suitable[4].

Where a local housing authority acquires a house or acquires a building which may be made suitable as a house and itself carries out any necessary work as mentioned above, the authority must, as soon as practicable after the acquisition or, as the case may be, after the completion of the necessary works, secure that the house or building is used as housing accommodation[5].

1 As to the meaning of 'local housing authority' see PARA 11.

2 As to the meaning of 'house' see PARA 405 note 6.

3 In the Housing Act 1985, 'lease' and 'tenancy' have the same meaning; both expressions include a sublease or subtenancy and an agreement for a lease or tenancy or sublease or subtenancy; and the expressions 'lessor' and 'lessee' and 'landlord' and 'tenant', and references to letting, to the grant of a lease or to covenants or terms are to be construed accordingly: s 621(1)–(3).

4 Housing Act 1985 s 18(1). This duty does not apply where a building is acquired as part of a site for the erection of houses under s 17(1) (see PARA 416): see *Uttoxeter UDC v Clarke* [1952] 1 All ER 1318, [1952] WN 255 (decided under the Housing Act 1936 s 79 (repealed)).

5 Housing Act 1985 s 18(2). As to the meaning of 'housing accommodation' see PARA 13 note 1.

418. Appropriation of land. A local housing authority[1] may appropriate, for the statutory purposes of providing housing accommodation[2], any land for the time being vested in the authority or at its disposal. The authority has the same powers in relation to land so appropriated as it has in relation to land acquired by the authority for those purposes[3].

Where a local housing authority has acquired or appropriated land for those purposes, it must not, without the consent of the appropriate national authority[4], appropriate any part of the land consisting of a house[5] or part of a house for any other purpose[6]. The appropriate national authority's consent may be given either generally to all local housing authorities or to a particular authority or description of authority, and either in relation to particular land or in relation to land of a particular description; and it may be given subject to conditions[7].

In relation to a local housing authority in England, the Secretary of State must consult the Regulator of Social Housing[8] before deciding whether to consent under the provisions above to anything within the Regulator's remit[9].

1 As to the meaning of 'local housing authority' see PARA 11.

2 Ie for the purposes of the Housing Act 1985 Pt II (ss 8–57).

3 Housing Act 1985 s 19(1).

4 Ie the Secretary of State or, where statutory functions have been transferred in relation to Wales, the Welsh Ministers: see PARA 7.

5 As to the meaning of 'house' see PARA 405 note 6.

6 Housing Act 1985 s 19(2).

7 Housing Act 1985 s 19(3).

8 As to the Regulator of Social Housing see PARA 57 et seq.
9 Housing Act 1985 s 19(4) (added by SI 2010/844). As to what is within the regulator's remit see PARA 408 note 2.

419. Exercise of compulsory purchase powers in relation to Crown land. Any power to acquire land compulsorily under the Housing Act 1985, the Housing Associations Act 1985, or the statutory provisions relating to housing action trust areas[1] or renewal areas[2] may be exercised in relation to an interest in Crown land[3] which is for the time being held otherwise than by or on behalf of the Crown, but only with the consent of the appropriate authority[4]. If any question arises as to what authority is the appropriate authority in relation to any land, that question must be referred to the Treasury, whose decision is final[5].

1 Ie the Housing Act 1988 Pt III (ss 60–92): see PARA 537 et seq.
2 Ie the Local Government and Housing Act 1989 Pt VII (ss 89–100): see PARA 820 et seq.
3 For these purposes, 'Crown land' means land in which there is a Crown interest or a Duchy interest; 'Crown interest' means an interest belonging to Her Majesty in right of the Crown or belonging to a government department or held in trust for Her Majesty for the purposes of a government department; and 'Duchy interest' means an interest belonging to Her Majesty in right of the Duchy of Lancaster or belonging to the Duchy of Cornwall: Housing Act 1996 s 221(3).
4 Housing Act 1996 s 221(1), (2). For these purposes, 'the appropriate authority', in relation to Crown land, is: (1) in the case of land belonging to Her Majesty in right of the Crown and forming part of the Crown Estate, the Crown Estate Commissioners; (2) in relation to any other land belonging to Her Majesty in right of the Crown, the government department having the management of that land; (3) in relation to land belonging to Her Majesty in right of the Duchy of Lancaster, the Chancellor of the Duchy; (4) in relation to land belonging to the Duchy of Cornwall, such person as the Duke of Cornwall, or the possessor for the time being of the Duchy of Cornwall, appoints; and (5) in the case of land belonging to a government department or held in trust for Her Majesty for the purposes of a government department, that department: s 221(4).
5 Housing Act 1996 s 221(5). As to the Treasury see CONSTITUTIONAL AND ADMINISTRATIVE LAW vol 20 (2014) PARA 262 et seq.

(iv) Allocation of Housing Accommodation

A. INTRODUCTION

420. Background to the legislation. Since 1935, local housing authorities have been under an obligation to give reasonable preference to certain groups, such as those occupying insanitary or overcrowded houses, when allocating housing[1]. Nonetheless such authorities were relatively free to decide how they selected their tenants and the courts did not interfere with this aspect of local authority decision making except in clear cases of unlawfulness such as, for example, where an authority had applied a strict policy of not granting a tenancy to any applicant who already had an interest in a joint tenancy, thus fettering the authority's discretion and failing to consider the applicant's personal circumstances[2]. Similarly, it has been held that a policy of excluding owner occupiers from being allocated housing, regardless of their circumstances, is unlawful[3]. Local authorities may, however, take account of an applicant's history of rent arrears when refusing to allocate housing[4].

Many authorities used a so-called 'points system' whereby applicants were awarded points according to their housing need, with points being given for such factors as overcrowding or living in a dwelling that suffered from disrepair[5]. Applicants were put on a waiting list of people seeking accommodation[6]. However, each local authority is now required to keep a register of people seeking secure tenancies[7] or nomination to a tenancy with a registered social landlord (which will be an assured tenancy)[8]. All authorities are also required to operate an allocation scheme whose basic principles are set by government, although the details are left to the discretion of each authority[9]. Allocation schemes must be flexible so as to allow the continuing development of common housing registers with registered social landlords[10]. These changes coincided with changes to previous local authority duties to the homeless, so that there is no longer any automatic entitlement to accommodation for unintentionally homeless families or vulnerable individuals[11]. These allocation policies were designed to ensure a single route into social housing[12] and were implemented in Part VI of the Housing Act 1996[13].

In allocating housing, a local housing authority must comply with the requirements of the legislation relating to discrimination, particularly on the grounds of disability[14].

Under the Localism Act 2011, each local housing authority in England has to prepare and publish a strategy (a 'tenancy strategy') setting out the matters to which the registered providers of social housing in its district are to have regard in formulating policies relating to the tenancies to be granted[15].

1 See the Housing Act 1935 s 51 (repealed).
2 See *R v Canterbury City Council, ex p Gillespie* (1986) 19 HLR 7.
3 See *R v Bristol City Council, ex p Johns* (1992) 25 HLR 249 (the council's policy was not in fact unlawful since it had retained a residual discretion).
4 See *R v Wolverhampton Metropolitan Borough Council, ex p Watters* (1997) 29 HLR 931.
5 See Hughes and Lowe *Social Housing Law and Policy* (1995) pp 102–103.
6 See Hughes and Lowe *Social Housing Law and Policy* (1995) pp 100–101.
7 As to the meaning of 'secure tenancy' see LANDLORD AND TENANT vol 63 (2016) PARA 1037.
8 As to the register of social landlords see PARA 167.
9 See PARA 422 et seq.
10 See the White Paper *Our Future Homes* (Cm 2901) (1995). See also the Department of the Environment publication *Allocation of Housing Accommodation by Local Authorities* (January 1996).
11 As to local authority duties to the homeless see the Housing Act 1996 Pt VII (ss 175–218); and PARA 481 et seq.
12 See HC Official Report, SC G (Housing Bill), 12 March 1996, col 614.
13 See the Housing Act 1996 Pt VI (ss 159–174); and PARA 422 et seq. See also s 227, Sch 19, repealing the Housing Act 1985 s 22.
14 As to discrimination see the Equality Act 2010; and DISCRIMINATION vol 33 (2013) PARA 1 et seq.
15 See the Localism Act 2011 s 150; and PARA 421. Consequential amendments are also made to the Housing and Regeneration Act 2008 s 197 (see PARA 105) and the Homelessness Act 2002 s 3 (see PARA 479).

421. Tenancy strategies. A local housing authority[1] in England must prepare and publish a strategy (a 'tenancy strategy') setting out the matters to which the registered providers of social housing for its district[2] are to have regard in formulating policies relating to:

(1)   the kinds of tenancies it grants;
(2)   the circumstances in which it will grant a tenancy of a particular kind;
(3)   where it grants tenancies for a term certain, the lengths of the terms; and
(4)   the circumstances in which it will grant a further tenancy on the coming to an end of an existing tenancy[3].

The strategy must summarise those policies or explain where they may be found[4]. A local housing authority must have regard to its tenancy strategy when exercising its housing management functions[5]. A local housing authority must publish its tenancy strategy before the end of the period of 12 months beginning with 15 January 2012[6].

A local housing authority must keep its tenancy strategy under review, and may modify or replace it from time to time[7]. If a local housing authority modifies its tenancy strategy, it must publish the modifications or the strategy as modified (as it considers appropriate)[8].

A local housing authority must:

(a) make a copy of everything published under these provisions available at its principal office for inspection at all reasonable hours, without charge, by members of the public; and

(b) provide (on payment if required by the authority of a reasonable charge) a copy of anything so published to any member of the public who asks for one[9].

Before adopting a tenancy strategy, or making a modification to it reflecting a major change of policy, the authority must:

(i) send a copy of the draft strategy, or proposed modification, to every private registered provider of social housing for its district; and

(ii) give the private registered provider a reasonable opportunity to comment on those proposals[10].

Before adopting a tenancy strategy, or making a modification to it reflecting a major change of policy, the authority must also consult such other persons as the Secretary of State may by regulations prescribe and, in the case of an authority that is a London borough council, consult the Mayor of London[11].

The authority must, in preparing or modifying a tenancy strategy, have regard to:

(A) its current allocation scheme under the Housing Act 1996[12];

(B) its current homelessness strategy under the Homelessness Act 2002[13]; and

(C) in the case of an authority that is a London borough council, the London housing strategy[14].

1 As to the meaning of 'local housing authority' see PARA 11 (definition applied by the Localism Act 2011 s 150(8)).

2 As to the meaning of 'registered provider of social housing' see PARA 53. In the Localism Act 2011 ss 150, 151: (1) references to a registered provider of social housing for a district are to a registered provider who grants tenancies of dwelling-houses in that district; and (2) 'district' and 'dwelling house' have the same meaning as in the Housing Act 1985 (see PARAS 11, 231): Localism Act 2011 s 150(8).

3 Localism Act 2011 s 150(1).

4 Localism Act 2011 s 150(2).

5 Localism Act 2011 s 150(3).

6 Localism Act 2011 s 150(4). The date in the text is the day on which s 150 came into force: see the Localism Act 2011 (Commencement No 2 and Transitional and Saving Provision) Order 2012, SI 2012/57, art 4(1)(m).

7 Localism Act 2011 s 150(5).

8 Localism Act 2011 s 150(6).

9 Localism Act 2011 s 150(7).

10 Localism Act 2011 s 151(1).

11 Localism Act 2011 s 151(2). As to the Secretary of State see PARA 7. As to regulations by the Secretary of State see PARA 54.

12 Ie under the Housing Act 1996 s 166A: see PARA 427.

13 Ie under the Homelessness Act 2002 s 1: see PARA 479.

14 Localism Act 2011 s 151(3).

422. Allocation under the Housing Act 1996. A local housing authority[1] must comply with the provisions of Part VI of the Housing Act 1996[2] in allocating housing accommodation[3]. A local housing authority allocates housing accommodation when it:

(1) selects a person to be a secure[4] or introductory tenant[5] of housing accommodation held by the authority;

(2)   nominates[6] a person to be a secure or introductory tenant of housing accommodation held by another person; or

(3)   nominates a person to be an assured tenant[7] of housing accommodation held by a private registered provider of social housing or a registered social landlord[8].

The provisions of Part VI of the Housing Act 1996 do not, however, apply to an allocation of housing accommodation by a local housing authority in England to a person who is already: (a) a secure or introductory tenant; or (b) an assured tenant of housing accommodation held by a private registered provider of social housing or a registered social landlord[9].

Nor do the provisions of Part VI apply to an allocation of housing accommodation by a local housing authority in Wales to a person who is already a secure or introductory tenant unless the allocation involves a transfer of housing accommodation for that person and is made on his application[10].

Subject to these statutory provisions, a local housing authority may allocate housing accommodation in such manner as it considers appropriate[11], although it must, of course, comply with the requirements of the legislation relating to discrimination, particularly on the grounds of race or disability[12].

1   As to the meaning of 'local housing authority' see PARA 11 (definition applied by the Housing Act 1996 s 230).
2   Ie the provisions of the Housing Act 1996 Pt VI (ss 159–174): see PARA 423 et seq.
3   Housing Act 1996 s 159(1). Further commentary is to be found in Driscoll *A Guide to the Housing Act 1996* (1996).
4   The reference in head (1) in the text to selecting a person to be a secure tenant includes deciding to exercise any power to notify an existing tenant or licensee that his tenancy or licence is to be a secure tenancy: Housing Act 1996 s 159(3). As to the meanings of 'secure tenancy' and 'secure tenant' see LANDLORD AND TENANT vol 63 (2016) PARA 1037 (definition applied by s 230).
5   As to introductory tenancies see PARA 472.
6   The references in heads (2) and (3) in the text to nominating a person include nominating a person in pursuance of any arrangements (whether legally enforceable or not) to require that housing accommodation, or a specified amount of housing accommodation, is made available to a person or one of a number of persons nominated by the authority: Housing Act 1996 s 159(4).
7   As to the meaning of 'assured tenancy' see LANDLORD AND TENANT vol 63 (2016) PARA 825 (definition applied by the Housing Act 1996 s 230).
8   Housing Act 1996 s 159(2) (amended by SI 2010/866). As to the meaning of 'private registered provider of social housing' see PARA 53; and as to the meaning of 'registered social landlord' see PARA 13.
9   Housing Act 1996 s 159(4A) (s 159(4A), (4B) added by the Localism Act 2011 s 145(1), (2)). The provisions of the Housing Act 1996 Pt VI do apply to an allocation of housing accommodation by a local housing authority in England to a person who falls within s 159(4A)(a) or (b) (heads (a), (b) in the text) if: (1) the allocation involves a transfer of housing accommodation for that person; (2) the application for the transfer is made by that person; and (3) the authority is satisfied that the person is to be given reasonable preference under s 166A(3) (see PARA 427): s 159(4B) (as so added).
10 Housing Act 1996 s 159(5) (substituted by the Homelessness Act 2002 s 13; and amended by the Localism Act 2011 s 145(1), (3)).
11 Housing Act 1996 s 159(7).
12 As to discrimination see the Equality Act 2010; and DISCRIMINATION vol 33 (2013) PARA 1 et seq.

423. Cases where the allocation provisions do not apply. The statutory provisions about the allocation of housing accommodation[1] do not apply in the following circumstances[2]:

(1)   where a secure tenancy[3] vests in a successor on the death of the tenant[4], devolves[5], is assigned[6], is granted in response to a request to transfer the tenancy[7], or vests or is otherwise disposed of in specified[8] circumstances[9];

(2)   where an introductory tenancy[10] becomes a secure tenancy on ceasing to be an introductory tenancy[11], vests in a successor on the death of the tenant[12], is assigned[13], or vests or is otherwise disposed of in specified[14] circumstances[15].

Nor do those provisions apply in such other cases as the appropriate national authority[16] may prescribe by regulations[17]. The regulations may be framed so as to make the exclusion of the statutory provisions about the allocation of housing accommodation subject to such restrictions or conditions as may be specified[18]. In particular, those provisions may be excluded in relation to specified descriptions of persons, or in relation to housing accommodation of a specified description or a specified proportion of housing accommodation of any specified description[19].

The statutory provisions about the allocation of housing accommodation do not apply where a local housing authority secures the provision of suitable alternative accommodation in pursuance of its duty under the compulsory purchase legislation[20] to rehouse residential occupiers who are to lose their home as a result[21]; nor in relation to the grant of a secure tenancy[22] to a former owner-occupier or statutory tenant of a defective dwelling house[23]. In England, the statutory provisions do not apply in relation to the allocation of housing accommodation by a local housing authority to a person who lawfully occupies accommodation let on a family intervention tenancy[24].

1   Ie the Housing Act 1996 Pt VI (ss 159–174).
2   Housing Act 1996 s 160(1).
3   As to the meaning of 'secure tenancy' see LANDLORD AND TENANT vol 63 (2016) PARA 1037 (definition applied by the Housing Act 1996 s 230).
4   Ie under the Housing Act 1985 s 89 (succession to periodic secure tenancy on death of tenant: see LANDLORD AND TENANT vol 63 (2016) PARA 1099): Housing Act 1996 s 160(2)(a).
5   Ie remains a secure tenancy by virtue of the Housing Act 1985 s 90 (devolution of term certain of secure tenancy on death of tenant: see LANDLORD AND TENANT vol 63 (2016) PARA 1100): Housing Act 1996 s 160(2)(b).
6   Ie is assigned under the Housing Act 1985 s 92 (assignment of secure tenancy by way of exchange: see LANDLORD AND TENANT vol 63 (2016) PARA 1066) or is assigned to a person who would be qualified to succeed the secure tenant if the secure tenant died immediately before the assignment: Housing Act 1996 s 160(2)(c), (d).
7   Ie under the Localism Act 2011 s 158 (transfer of tenancy: see LANDLORD AND TENANT vol 63 (2016) PARA 903): Housing Act 1996 s 160(2)(da) (added by virtue of the Localism Act 2011 s 159(7)).
8   Ie in pursuance of an order made under:
    (1)   the Matrimonial Causes Act 1973 s 24 (as amended; prospectively substituted) (property adjustment orders in connection with matrimonial proceedings: see MATRIMONIAL AND CIVIL PARTNERSHIP LAW vol 73 (2015) PARA 556 et seq);
    (2)   the Matrimonial and Family Proceedings Act 1984 s 17(1) (prospectively amended) (property adjustment orders after overseas divorce, etc: see MATRIMONIAL AND CIVIL PARTNERSHIP LAW vol 73 (2015) PARA 591);
    (3)   the Children Act 1989 s 15(1), Sch 1 para 1 (orders for financial relief against parents: see CHILDREN AND YOUNG PERSONS vol 9 (2017) PARA 623 et seq); or
    (4)   the Civil Partnership Act 2004 Sch 5 Pt 2, Sch 7 para 9(2) or Sch 7 para 9(3) (property adjustment orders in connection with civil partnership proceedings or after overseas dissolution of civil partnership, etc).
9   Housing Act 1996 s 160(2)(e) (amended by the Civil Partnership Act 2004 ss 81, 261(4), Sch 8 para 60, Sch 30).
10   As to introductory tenancies see PARA 472.
11   Housing Act 1996 s 160(3)(a).
12   Ie under the Housing Act 1996 s 133(2): see LANDLORD AND TENANT vol 63 (2016) PARA 1117: Housing Act 1996 s 160(3)(b).
13   Ie to a person who would be qualified to succeed the introductory tenant if the introductory tenant died immediately before the assignment: Housing Act 1996 s 160(3)(c).
14   Ie in pursuance of an order made under any of the provisions specified in note 8.
15   Housing Act 1996 s 160(3)(d) (amended by the Civil Partnership Act 2004 Sch 8 para 60, Sch 30).

16 Ie the Secretary of State or, where statutory functions have been transferred in relation to Wales, the Welsh Ministers: see PARA 7.

17 Housing Act 1996 s 160(4). Regulations under Pt VI must be made by statutory instrument subject, except for regulations under s 166A(7) (see PARA 427) or s 167(3) (see PARA 428), to annulment in pursuance of a resolution of either House of Parliament or of the National Assembly for Wales: s 172(1), (3). The regulations may contain such incidental, supplementary and transitional provisions as appear to the appropriate national authority appropriate, and may make different provision for different cases including different provision for different areas: s 172(4).

18 Housing Act 1996 s 160(5).

19 See the Housing Act 1996 s 160(5)(a), (b). As to the exercise of this power see the Allocation of Housing (England) Regulations 2002, SI 2002/3264, reg 3; the Allocation of Housing (Wales) Regulations 2003, SI 2003/239, reg 3; and the text and notes 20–24.

20 Ie the Land Compensation Act 1973 s 39: see COMPULSORY ACQUISITION OF LAND vol 18 (2009) PARA 853.

21 Allocation of Housing (England) Regulations 2002, SI 2002/3264, reg 3(1), (2); Allocation of Housing (Wales) Regulations 2003, SI 2003/239, reg 3(a).

22 Ie under the Housing Act 1985 s 554 or s 555: see PARAS 955–956.

23 Allocation of Housing (England) Regulations 2002, SI 2002/3264, reg 3(1), (3); Allocation of Housing (Wales) Regulations 2003, SI 2003/239, reg 3(b).

24 Allocation of Housing (England) Regulations 2002, SI 2002/3264, reg 3(1), (4) (reg 3(4) added by SI 2008/3015). 'Family intervention tenancy': (1) in relation to a tenancy granted by a local housing authority, has the meaning given by Housing Act 1985 Sch 1 para 4ZA(3) (see LANDLORD AND TENANT); and (2) in relation to a tenancy granted by a registered social landlord, has the meaning given by the Housing Act 1988 Sch 1 Pt I para 12ZA(3) (see LANDLORD AND TENANT): Allocation of Housing (England) Regulations 2002, SI 2002/3264, reg 2 (definition added by SI 2008/3015).

424. Allocation only to eligible persons: England. In England local authorities can only allocate housing to someone who is eligible for it. Thus a local housing authority[1] in England must not allocate housing accommodation: (1) to a person from abroad who is ineligible for an allocation of housing accommodation[2]; or (2) to two or more persons jointly if any of them is a person mentioned in head (1)[3].

A person subject to immigration control[4] is ineligible for an allocation of housing accommodation by a local housing authority in England unless he is of a class prescribed by regulations made by the Secretary of State[5]. No person who is excluded from entitlement to universal credit or housing benefit[6] may be included in any class so prescribed[7]. The Secretary of State may by regulations prescribe other classes of persons from abroad who are ineligible to be allocated housing accommodation by local housing authorities in England[8]. The Secretary of State may by regulations: (a) prescribe classes of persons who are, or are not, to be treated as qualifying persons by local housing authorities in England; and (b) prescribe criteria that may not be used by local housing authorities in England in deciding what classes of persons are not qualifying persons[9].

Except as provided under heads (1) and (2) above, a person may be allocated housing accommodation by a local housing authority in England (whether on his application or otherwise) if that person: (i) is a qualifying person[10]; or (ii) is one of two or more persons who apply for accommodation jointly, and one or more of the other persons is a qualifying person[11].

If a local housing authority in England decides that an applicant for housing accommodation is ineligible for an allocation by it[12] or is not a qualifying person, it must notify the applicant of its decision and the grounds for reaching it[13]. That notice must be given in writing and, if not received by the applicant, is to be treated as having been given if it is made available at the authority's office for a reasonable period for collection by him or on his behalf[14].

A person who is not being treated as a qualifying person may (if he considers that he should be treated as a qualifying person) make a fresh application to the authority for an allocation of housing accommodation by it[15].

1   As to the meaning of 'local housing authority' see PARA 11 (definition applied by the Housing Act 1996 s 230).
2   Ie by virtue of the Housing Act 1996 s 160ZA(2) or (4) (see the text and notes 4–8).
3   Housing Act 1996 s 160ZA(1) (s 160ZA added by the Localism Act 2011 s 146(1)).
4   Ie within the meaning of the Asylum and Immigration Act 1996. As to immigration control see IMMIGRATION AND ASYLUM vol 57 (2012) PARA 5 et seq.
5   Housing Act 1996 s 160ZA(2) (as added: see note 3). As to the Secretary of State see PARA 7.
    The following are classes of persons prescribed for the purposes of s 160ZA(2) (see the Allocation of Housing and Homelessness (Eligibility) (England) Regulations 2006, SI 2006/1294, reg 3):
    (1)   Class A: a person who is recorded by the Secretary of State as a refugee within the definition in the Convention relating to the Status of Refugees (Geneva, 28 July 1951; TS 39 (1954); Cmnd 9171) art 1 (as extended by the Protocol relating to the Status of Refugees (New York, 31 January 1967; TS 15 (1969); Cmnd 3906) art 1(2)) and who has leave to enter or remain in the United Kingdom (Allocation of Housing and Homelessness (Eligibility) (England) Regulations 2006, SI 2006/1294, regs 2(1), 3(a));
    (2)   Class B: a person who has exceptional leave to enter or remain in the United Kingdom granted outside the provisions of the Immigration Rules and who is not subject to a condition requiring him to maintain and accommodate himself, and any person who is dependent on him, without recourse to public funds (reg 3(b));
    (3)   Class C: a person who is habitually resident in the United Kingdom, the Channel Islands, the Isle of Man or the Republic of Ireland and whose leave to enter or remain in the United Kingdom is not subject to any limitation or condition, other than a person: (a) who has been given leave to enter or remain in the United Kingdom upon an undertaking given by his sponsor; (b) who has been resident in the United Kingdom, the Channel Islands, the Isle of Man or the Republic of Ireland for less than five years beginning on the date of entry or the date on which his sponsor gave the undertaking in respect of him, whichever date is the later; and (c) whose sponsor or, where there is more than one sponsor, at least one of whose sponsors, is still alive (reg 3(c));
    (4)   Class D: a person who has humanitarian protection granted under the Immigration Rules (reg 3(d) (substituted by SI 2006/2527; and amended by SI 2016/965));
    (5)   Class E: a person who is habitually resident in the United Kingdom, the Channel Islands, the Isle of Man or the Republic of Ireland and who has limited leave to enter the United Kingdom as a relevant Afghan citizen under the Immigration Rules para 276BA1 (Allocation of Housing and Homelessness (Eligibility) (England) Regulations 2006, SI 2006/1294, reg 3(e) (added by SI 2014/435; and amended by SI 2016/965)); or
    (6)   Class F: a person who has limited leave to enter or remain in the United Kingdom on family or private life grounds under the Human Rights Convention (ie the Convention for the Protection of Human Rights and Fundamental Freedoms, agreed by the Council of Europe at Rome on 4 November 1950 (TS 71 (1953); Cmd 8969) as it has effect for the time being in relation to the United Kingdom) art 8, such leave granted: (a) under the Immigration Rules para 276BE(1), para 276DG or Appendix FM; and (b) who is not subject to a condition requiring that person to maintain and accommodate himself, and any person dependent upon him, without recourse to public funds (Allocation of Housing and Homelessness (Eligibility) (England) Regulations 2006, SI 2006/1294, reg 3(f) (added by SI 2016/965)).
    As to the meaning of 'United Kingdom' see PARA 60 note 10. 'The Immigration Rules' means the rules laid down as mentioned in the Immigration Act 1971 s 3(2) (general provisions for regulation and control: see IMMIGRATION AND ASYLUM vol 57 (2012) PARA 6): Allocation of Housing and Homelessness (Eligibility) (England) Regulations 2006, SI 2006/1294, reg 2(1). 'Sponsor' means a person who has given an undertaking in writing for the purposes of the Immigration Rules to be responsible for the maintenance and accommodation of another person: Allocation of Housing and Homelessness (Eligibility) (England) Regulations 2006, SI 2006/1294, reg 2(1).
6   Ie by the Immigration and Asylum Act 1999 s 115 (exclusion from benefits): see IMMIGRATION AND ASYLUM vol 57 (2012) PARA 335 et seq.
7   Housing Act 1996 s 160ZA(3) (as added (see note 3); amended by SI 2013/630).
8   Housing Act 1996 s 160ZA(4) (as added: see note 3). Nothing in s 150ZA(2) or (4) affects the eligibility of a person who falls within s 159(4B) (see PARA 422 note 9): s 160ZA(5) (as so added).

A person who is not subject to immigration control is to be treated as a person from abroad who is ineligible for an allocation of housing accommodation under Pt VI (ss 159–174) if:

(1) subject to the exceptions below, he is not habitually resident in the United Kingdom, the Channel Islands, the Isle of Man, or the Republic of Ireland;

(2) his only right to reside in the United Kingdom:

  (a) is derived from his status as a jobseeker or the family member of a jobseeker; or

  (b) is an initial right to reside for a period not exceeding three months under the Immigration (European Economic Area) Regulations 2006, SI 2006/1003, reg 13; or

  (c) is a derivative right to reside to which he is entitled under reg 15A(1), but only in a case where the right exists under that regulation because the applicant satisfies the criteria in reg 15A(4A); or

  (d) is derived from the Treaty on the Functioning of the European Union (Rome, 25 March 1957; TS 1 (1973); Cmnd 5179) art 20, in a case where the right to reside arises because a British citizen would otherwise be deprived of the genuine enjoyment of the substance of his or her rights as a European Union citizen; or

(3) his only right to reside in the Channel Islands, the Isle of Man or the Republic of Ireland:

  (a) is a right equivalent to one of those mentioned in head (2)(a), (b) or (c) which is derived from the Treaty on the Functioning of the European Union; or

  (b) is derived from art 20, in a case where the right to reside in the Republic of Ireland arises because an Irish citizen, or in the Channel Islands or the Isle of Man arises because a British citizen also entitled to reside there, would otherwise be deprived of the genuine enjoyment of the substance of his or her rights as a European Union citizen: Allocation of Housing and Homelessness (Eligibility) (England) Regulations 2006, SI 2006/1294, regs 2(1), 4(1) (reg 4(1) amended by SI 2012/2588).

The following are not to be treated as persons from abroad who are ineligible for an allocation of housing accommodation pursuant to head (1) (see the Allocation of Housing and Homelessness (Eligibility) (England) Regulations 2006, SI 2006/1294, reg 4(2)):

(i) a worker (reg 4(2)(a));

(ii) a self-employed person (reg 4(2)(b));

(iii) a person who is treated as a worker for the purpose of the definition of 'qualified person' in the Immigration (European Economic Area) Regulations 2006, SI 2006/1003, reg 6(1) pursuant to the Accession of Croatia (Immigration and Worker Authorisation) Regulations 2013, SI 2013/1460, reg 5 (right of residence of an accession state national subject to worker authorisation) (Allocation of Housing and Homelessness (Eligibility) (England) Regulations 2006, SI 2006/1294, reg 4(2)(c) (substituted by SI 2013/1467; and amended by SI 2014/435));

(iv) a person who is the family member of a person specified in heads (i)–(iii) (Allocation of Housing and Homelessness (Eligibility) (England) Regulations 2006, SI 2006/1294, reg 4(2)(d));

(v) a person with a right to reside permanently in the United Kingdom by virtue of the Immigration (European Economic Area) Regulations 2006, SI 2006/1003, reg 15(1)(c), (d) or (e) (Allocation of Housing and Homelessness (Eligibility) (England) Regulations 2006, SI 2006/1294, reg 4(2)(e) (amended by SI 2014/435)); and

(vi) a person who is in the United Kingdom as a result of his deportation, expulsion or other removal by compulsion of law from another country to the United Kingdom (Allocation of Housing and Homelessness (Eligibility) (England) Regulations 2006, SI 2006/1294, reg 4(2)(g) (amended by SI 2006/2007 and SI 2009/358)).

'Worker', 'self-employed person' and 'jobseeker' have the same meanings as for the purposes of the definition of a 'qualified person' in the Immigration (European Economic Area) Regulations 2006, SI 2006/1003, reg 6(1): Allocation of Housing and Homelessness (Eligibility) (England) Regulations 2006, SI 2006/1294, reg 2(2)(a). References to the family member of a jobseeker, self-employed person or worker are to be construed in accordance with the Immigration (European Economic Area) Regulations 2006, SI 2006/1003, reg 7; but for the purposes of head (d), 'family member' does not include a person who is treated as a family member by virtue of reg 7(3): Allocation of Housing and Homelessness (Eligibility) (England) Regulations 2006, SI 2006/1294, reg 2(2)(b), (3).

9 Housing Act 1996 s 160ZA(8) (as added: see note 3).

See the Allocation of Housing (Qualification Criteria for Armed Forces) (England) Regulations 2012, SI 2012/1869; and the Allocation of Housing (Qualification Criteria for Right to Move) (England) Regulations 2015, SI 2015/967 (made under the Housing Act 1996 s 160ZA(8)(b)).

10 Ie within the meaning of the Housing Act 1996 s 160ZA(7). Subject to s 160ZA(2), (4) and any regulations under s 160ZA(8), a local housing authority may decide what classes of persons are, or are not, qualifying persons: s 160ZA(7) (as added: see note 3).

11 Housing Act 1996 s 160ZA(6) (as added: see note 3).

12 Ie by virtue of the Housing Act 1996 s 160ZA(2) or (4).

13 Housing Act 1996 s 160ZA(9) (as added: see note 3).

14 Housing Act 1996 s 160ZA(10) (as added: see note 3).

15 Housing Act 1996 s 160ZA(11) (as added: see note 3).

425. Allocation only to eligible persons: Wales. Similarly, a local housing authority[1] in Wales must not allocate housing accommodation: (1) to a person from abroad who is ineligible for an allocation of housing accommodation[2]; (2) to a person who the authority has decided is to be treated as ineligible for such an allocation[3]; or (3) to two or more persons jointly if any of them is a person mentioned in head (1) or head (2)[4]. Except as provided above, any person may be allocated housing accommodation by a local housing authority in Wales (whether on his application or otherwise)[5].

A person subject to immigration control[6] is ineligible for an allocation of housing accommodation by a local housing authority in Wales unless he is of a class prescribed by regulations made by the Welsh Ministers[7]. No person who is excluded from entitlement to universal credit or housing benefit[8] may be included in any class so prescribed[9]. The Welsh Ministers may by regulations prescribe other classes of persons from abroad who are[10] ineligible for an allocation of housing accommodation, either in relation to local housing authorities in Wales generally or any particular local housing authority in Wales[11].

A local housing authority in Wales may decide that an applicant is to be treated as ineligible for an allocation of housing accommodation by it if it is satisfied that: (a) he, or a member of his household, has been guilty of unacceptable behaviour[12] serious enough to make him unsuitable to be a tenant of the authority; and (b) in the circumstances at the time his application is considered, he is unsuitable to be a tenant of the authority by reason of that behaviour[13].

If a local housing authority in Wales decides that an applicant for housing accommodation: (i) is ineligible for an allocation by it[14]; or (ii) is to be treated as ineligible for such an allocation[15], it must notify the applicant of its decision and the grounds for reaching it[16]. That notice must be given in writing and, if not received by the applicant, must be treated as having been given if it is made available at the authority's office for a reasonable period for collection by him or on his behalf[17].

A person who is being treated by a local housing authority in Wales as ineligible may (if he considers that he should no longer be treated as ineligible by the authority) make a fresh application to the authority for an allocation of housing accommodation by it[18].

1   As to the meaning of 'local housing authority' see PARA 11 (definition applied by the Housing Act 1996 s 230).

2   Ie by virtue of the Housing Act 1996 s 160A(3) (see the text and note 7) or s 160A(5) (see the text and note 11).

3   Ie by virtue of the Housing Act 1996 s 160A(7) (see the text and note 13).

4   Housing Act 1996 s 160A(1) (s 160A added by the Homelessness Act 2002 s 14(2); the Housing Act 1996 s 160A(1) amended by the Localism Act 2011 s 146(2)(b)).

5   Housing Act 1996 s 160A(2) (as added (see note 4); amended by the Localism Act 2011 s 146(2)(c)).

6   Ie within the meaning of the Asylum and Immigration Act 1996. As to immigration control see IMMIGRATION AND ASYLUM vol 57 (2012) PARA 5 et seq.

7   Housing Act 1996 s 160A(3) (as added (see note 4); amended by the Localism Act 2011 s 146(2)(d)). The Welsh Ministers are the appropriate national authority: see PARA 7. However, nothing in the Housing Act 1996 s 160A(3) or s 160A(5) (see the text and note 11) affects the

eligibility of a person who is already either a secure or introductory tenant or an assured tenant of housing accommodation allocated to him by a local housing authority in Wales: s 160A(6) (as so added; amended by the Localism Act 2011 s 146(2)(f)).

The following are classes of persons prescribed for the purposes of the Housing Act 1996 s 160A(3) who are eligible for an allocation of housing accommodation under Pt VI (ss 159–174) (see the Allocation of Housing and Homelessness (Eligibility) (Wales) Regulations 2014, SI 2014/2603, reg 3):

(1)   Class A: a person recorded by the Welsh Ministers as a refugee within the definition in the Convention relating to the Status of Refugees (Geneva, 28 July 1951; TS 39 (1954); Cmnd 9171) art 1 (as extended by the Protocol relating to the Status of Refugees (New York, 31 January 1967; TS 15 (1969); Cmnd 3906) art 1(2)) and who has leave to enter or remain in the United Kingdom (Allocation of Housing and Homelessness (Eligibility) (Wales) Regulations 2014, SI 2014/2603, regs 2(1), 3(a));

(2)   Class B: a person: (a) who has exceptional leave to enter or remain in the United Kingdom granted outside the provisions of the Immigration Rules; and (b) whose leave to enter or remain is not subject to a condition requiring that person to maintain and accommodate themselves, and any person who is dependant on that person, without recourse to public funds (Allocation of Housing and Homelessness (Eligibility) (Wales) Regulations 2014, SI 2014/2603, reg 3(b));

(3)   Class C: a person who is habitually resident in the United Kingdom, the Channel Islands, the Isle of Man or the Republic of Ireland and whose leave to enter or remain in the United Kingdom is not subject to any limitation or condition, other than a person: (a) who has been given leave to enter or remain in the United Kingdom upon an undertaking given by the person's sponsor; (b) who has been resident in the United Kingdom, the Channel Islands, the Isle of Man or the Republic of Ireland for less than five years beginning on the date of entry or on the date on which the undertaking was given in respect of the person, whichever date is the later; and (c) whose sponsor or, where there is more than one sponsor, at least one of whose sponsors is still alive (reg 3(c));

(4)   Class D: a person who has humanitarian protection granted under the Immigration Rules (Allocation of Housing and Homelessness (Eligibility) (Wales) Regulations 2014, SI 2014/2603, reg 3(d)); and

(5)   Class E: a person who is habitually resident in the United Kingdom, the Channel Islands, the Isle of Man or the Republic of Ireland and who has limited leave to enter the United Kingdom as a relevant Afghan citizen under the Immigration Rules para 276BA1 (Allocation of Housing and Homelessness (Eligibility) (Wales) Regulations 2014, SI 2014/2603, reg 3(e)).

As to the meaning of 'United Kingdom' see PARA 60 note 10. 'The Immigration Rules' means the rules laid down as mentioned in the Immigration Act 1971 s 3(2) (general provisions for regulation and control: see IMMIGRATION AND ASYLUM vol 57 (2012) PARA 5): Allocation of Housing and Homelessness (Eligibility) (Wales) Regulations 2014, SI 2014/2603, reg 2(1). 'Sponsor' means a person who has given an undertaking in writing for the purposes of the Immigration Rules to be responsible for the maintenance and accommodation of another person: Allocation of Housing and Homelessness (Eligibility) (Wales) Regulations 2014, SI 2014/2603, reg 2(1).

8   Ie by the Immigration and Asylum Act 1999 s 115: see IMMIGRATION AND ASYLUM vol 57 (2012) PARA 335 et seq.

9   Housing Act 1996 s 160A(4) (as added (see note 4); amended by SI 2013/630).

10 Ie subject to the Housing Act 1996 s 160A(6): see note 7.

11 Housing Act 1996 s 160A(5) (as added (see note 4); amended by the Localism Act 2011 s 146(2)(e)).

The following persons, not being persons subject to immigration control, are prescribed for the purposes of the Housing Act 1996 s 160A(5) (Allocation of Housing and Homelessness (Eligibility) (Wales) Regulations 2014, SI 2014/2603, reg 4(1)):

(1)   subject to the exceptions below, the person is not habitually resident in the United Kingdom, the Channel Islands, the Isle of Man, or the Republic of Ireland (reg 4(1)(a));

(2)   the person's only right to reside in the United Kingdom:
     (a)   is derived from the person's status as a jobseeker or a family member of a jobseeker; or
     (b)   is an initial right to reside for a period not exceeding three months under the Immigration (European Economic Area) Regulations 2006, SI 2006/1003, reg 13; or
     (c)   is a derivative right to reside to which the person is entitled under reg 15A(1), but only in a case where the right exists under that regulation because the applicant satisfies the criteria in reg 15A(4A); or

(d)   is derived from the Treaty on the Functioning of the European Union (Rome, 25 March 1957; TS 1 (1973); Cmnd 5179) art 20, in a case where the right to reside arises because a British citizen would otherwise be deprived of the genuine enjoyment of the substance of his or her rights as a European Union citizen (Allocation of Housing and Homelessness (Eligibility) (Wales) Regulations 2014, SI 2014/2603, reg 4(1)(b)); or

(3)   the person's only right to reside in the Channel Islands, the Isle of Man or the Republic of Ireland:

        (a)   is a right equivalent to one of those mentioned in head (2)(a), (b) or (c) which is derived from the Treaty on the Functioning of the European Union; or

        (b)   is derived from art 20, in a case where the right to reside in the Republic of Ireland arises because an Irish citizen, or in the Channel Islands or the Isle of Man arises because a British citizen also entitled to reside there, would otherwise be deprived of the genuine enjoyment of the substance of his or her rights as a European Union citizen (Allocation of Housing and Homelessness (Eligibility) (Wales) Regulations 2014, SI 2014/2603, reg 4(1)(c)).

The following are not to be treated as persons from abroad who are ineligible for an allocation of housing accommodation pursuant to head (1) (see the Allocation of Housing and Homelessness (Eligibility) (Wales) Regulations 2014, SI 2014/2603, reg 4(2)):

     (i)   a worker (reg 4(2)(a));

     (ii)   a self-employed person (reg 4(2)(b));

     (iii)   a person who is treated as a worker for the purpose of the definition of 'qualified person' in the Immigration (European Economic Area) Regulations 2006, SI 2006/1003, reg 6(1) pursuant to the Accession of Croatia (Immigration and Worker Authorisation) Regulations 2013, SI 2013/1460, reg 5 (right of residence of an accession state national subject to worker authorisation) (Allocation of Housing and Homelessness (Eligibility) (Wales) Regulations 2014, SI 2014/2603, reg 4(2)(c));

     (iv)   a person who is the family member of a person specified in heads (i)–(iii) (reg 4(2)(d));

     (v)   a person with a right to reside permanently in the United Kingdom by virtue of the Immigration (European Economic Area) Regulations 2006, SI 2006/1003, reg 15(1)(c), (d) or (e) (Allocation of Housing and Homelessness (Eligibility) (Wales) Regulations 2014, SI 2014/2603, reg 4(2)(e)); and

     (vi)   a person who is in the United Kingdom as a result of the person's deportation, expulsion or other removal by compulsion of law from another country to the United Kingdom (reg 4(2)(g)).

'Worker', 'self-employed person' and 'jobseeker' have the same meanings as for the purposes of the definition of a 'qualified person' in the Immigration (European Economic Area) Regulations 2006, SI 2006/1003, reg 6(1): Allocation of Housing and Homelessness (Eligibility) (Wales) Regulations 2014, SI 2014/2603, reg 2(2)(a). References to the family member of a jobseeker, self-employed person or worker are to be construed in accordance with the Immigration (European Economic Area) Regulations 2006, SI 2006/1003, reg 7; but for the purposes of head (iv), 'family member' does not include a person who is treated as a family member by virtue of reg 7(3): Allocation of Housing and Homelessness (Eligibility) (Wales) Regulations 2014, SI 2014/2603, reg 2(2)(b), (3).

12 The only behaviour which may be regarded by the authority as unacceptable for these purposes is: (1) behaviour of the person concerned which would (if he were a secure tenant of the authority) entitle the authority to a possession order under the Housing Act 1985 s 84 (see LANDLORD AND TENANT vol 63 (2016) PARA 1131 et seq) on any ground mentioned in Sch 2 Pt I (other than ground 8); or (2) behaviour of the person concerned which would (if he were a secure tenant of the authority) entitle the authority to a possession order under the Housing Act 1985 s 84A (see LANDLORD AND TENANT vol 63 (2016) PARA 1131); or (3) behaviour of a member of his household which would (if he were a person residing with a secure tenant of the authority) entitle the authority to such a possession order: Housing Act 1996 s 160A(8) (as added (see note 4); amended by SI 2015/1321).

13 Housing Act 1996 s 160A(7) (as added (see note 4); amended by the Localism Act 2011 s 146(2)(g)). The setting of qualification criteria is subject to the reasonable preference duty: *R (on the application of Jakimaviciute) v Hammersmith and Fulham LBC* [2014] EWCA Civ 1438, [2015] HLR 86, [2014] All ER (D) 68 (Nov).

14 Ie by virtue of the Housing Act 1996 s 160A(3) (see the text and note 7) or s 160A(5) (see the text and note 11).

15 Ie by virtue of the Housing Act 1996 s 160A(7) (see the text and note 13).

16 Housing Act 1996 s 160A(9) (as added (see note 4); amended by the Localism Act 2011 s 146(2)(h)).

17 Housing Act 1996 s 160A(10) (as added: see note 4).
18 Housing Act 1996 s 160A(11) (as added (see note 4); amended by the Localism Act 2011
    s 146(2)(i)).

B.   THE HOUSING REGISTER

426. Applications for housing accommodation. A local housing authority[1] must secure that: (1) advice and information is available free of charge to persons in its district[2] about the right to make an application for an allocation of housing accommodation; and (2) any necessary assistance in making such an application is available free of charge to persons in its district who are likely to have difficulty in doing so without assistance[3].

A local housing authority in England must secure that an applicant for an allocation of housing accommodation is informed that he has certain rights[4] in relation to such an allocation[5]. A local housing authority in Wales must secure that an applicant for an allocation of housing accommodation is informed that he has certain rights[6] in relation to such allocation[7]. Every application made to a local housing authority for an allocation of housing accommodation must (if made in accordance with the procedural requirements of the authority's allocation scheme) be considered by the authority[8]. The fact that a person is an applicant for an allocation of housing accommodation may not be divulged (without his consent) to any other member of the public[9].

1 As to the meaning of 'local housing authority' see PARA 11 (definition applied by the Housing Act
   1996 s 230).
2 'District' in relation to a local housing authority has the same meaning as in the Housing Act 1985
   (see PARA 11): Housing Act 1996 s 166(5) (s 166 substituted by the Homelessness Act 2002 s 15).
3 Housing Act 1996 s 166(1) (as substituted: see note 2).
4 Ie the rights mentioned in the Housing Act 1996 s 166A(9) (see PARA 427).
5 Housing Act 1996 s 166(1A) (added by the Localism Act 2011 s 147(1), (2)(a)).
6 Ie the rights mentioned in the Housing Act 1996 s 167(4A) (see PARA 428).
7 Housing Act 1996 s 166(2) (as substituted (see note 2); amended by the Localism Act 2011
   s 147(1), (2)(b)).
8 Housing Act 1996 s 166(3) (as substituted: see note 2).
9 Housing Act 1996 s 166(4) (as substituted: see note 2).

C.   THE ALLOCATION SCHEME

427. Allocation in accordance with allocation scheme in England. Every local housing authority[1] in England must have a scheme (its 'allocation scheme') for determining priorities, and as to the procedure to be followed, in allocating housing accommodation; and for this purpose 'procedure' includes all aspects of the allocation process, including the persons or descriptions of persons by whom decisions are taken[2]. As regards the procedure to be followed, the scheme must be framed in accordance with such principles as the Secretary of State[3] may prescribe by regulations[4].

The scheme must include a statement of the authority's policy on offering people who are to be allocated housing accommodation either a choice of housing accommodation or the opportunity to express preferences about the housing accommodation to be allocated to them[5].

As regards priorities, the scheme must be framed so as to secure that reasonable preference is given to:

(1)   people who are homeless[6];
(2)   people who are owed a duty by any local housing authority[7] or who are occupying accommodation secured by any such authority[8];

(3)   people occupying insanitary or overcrowded housing or otherwise living in unsatisfactory housing conditions;

(4)   people who need to move on medical or welfare grounds (including grounds relating to a disability); and

(5)   people who need to move to a particular locality in the district of the authority, where failure to meet that need would cause hardship (to themselves or to others)[9].

The scheme may also be framed so as to give additional preference to particular descriptions of people within one or more of the categories above (being descriptions of people with urgent housing needs)[10]. The scheme must be framed so as to give additional preference to a person with urgent housing needs who falls within one or more of the categories above and who:

(a)   is serving in the regular forces[11] and is suffering from a serious injury, illness or disability which is attributable (wholly or partly) to the person's service;

(b)   formerly served in the regular forces;

(c)   has recently ceased, or will cease to be entitled, to reside in accommodation provided by the Ministry of Defence following the death of that person's spouse or civil partner who has served in the regular forces and whose death was attributable (wholly or partly) to that service; or

(d)   is serving or has served in the reserve forces[12] and is suffering from a serious injury, illness or disability which is attributable (wholly or partly) to the person's service[13].

The scheme may contain provision for determining priorities in allocating housing accommodation to people in the categories referred to above; and the factors which the scheme may allow to be taken into account include the financial resources available to a person to meet his housing costs, any behaviour of a person (or of a member of his household) which affects his suitability to be a tenant and any local connection[14] which exists between a person and the authority's district[15]. Subject to the requirements as to giving preference to the categories of persons specified above[16], the scheme may also contain provision about the allocation of particular housing accommodation to a person who makes a specific application for that accommodation or to persons of a particular description (whether or not they are within the above categories)[17].

The Secretary of State may by regulations specify further descriptions of people to whom preference is to be given as mentioned above or amend or repeal any part of the relevant provision[18]. The Secretary of State may by regulations specify factors which a local housing authority in England must not take into account in allocating housing accommodation[19].

The scheme must be framed so as to secure that an applicant for an allocation of housing accommodation:

(i)   has the right to request such general information as will enable him to assess how his application is likely to be treated under the scheme (including in particular whether he is likely to be regarded as a member of a group of people who are to be given preference[20]) and whether housing accommodation appropriate to his needs is likely to be made available to him and, if so, how long it is likely to be before such accommodation becomes available for allocation to him;

(ii)   has the right to request the authority to inform him of any decision about the facts of his case which is likely to be, or has been, taken into account in considering whether to allocate housing accommodation to him; and

(iii)   has the right to request a review of a decision mentioned in head (ii), or a decision that he is ineligible or to be treated as ineligible for a housing allocation[21], and to be informed of the decision on the review and the grounds for it[22].

Subject to the above provisions, and to any regulations made under them, the authority may decide on what principles the scheme is to be framed[23]. A local housing authority in England must, in preparing or modifying its allocation scheme, have regard to:

(A)   its current homelessness strategy[24];

(B)   its current tenancy strategy[25]; and

(C)   in the case of an authority that is a London borough council, the London housing strategy[26].

Before adopting an allocation scheme, or making an alteration to its scheme reflecting a major change of policy, a local housing authority in England must send a copy of the draft scheme, or proposed alteration, to every private registered provider of social housing[27] and registered social landlord[28] with which it has nomination arrangements[29] and afford those persons a reasonable opportunity to comment on the proposals[30].

A local housing authority in England must not allocate housing accommodation except in accordance with its allocation scheme[31]. Where a local housing authority so requests, a private registered provider of social housing or registered social landlord must co-operate to such extent as is reasonable in the circumstances in offering accommodation to people with priority under the authority's allocation scheme[32].

1   As to the meaning of 'local housing authority' see PARA 11 (definition applied by the Housing Act 1996 s 230).

2   Housing Act 1996 s 166A(1) (s 166A added by the Localism Act 2011 s 147(1), (4)). See Code of Guidance to Local Authorities on the Allocation of Accommodation and Homelessness 2016 (Department for Communities and Local Government, 24 March 2016). A local housing authority has a wide discretionary power to include in its housing allocation scheme such rules as it feels appropriate: *R (on the application of Giles) v Fareham Borough Council* [2002] EWHC 2951 (Admin), [2003] HLR 524, [2002] All ER (D) 213 (Dec) (policy allowed authority to defer placement on housing list where there had been tenant misconduct). The grant of a secure tenancy to a person to whom accommodation had been allocated inconsistently with an authority's allocation scheme did not render the tenancy void or ineffective: *Birmingham City Council v Qasim* [2009] EWCA Civ 1080, [2010] HLR 327, [2010] LGR 253. See also *R (on the application of HA) v Ealing London Borough Council* [2015] EWHC 2375 (Admin), [2015] All ER (D) 73 (Aug).

3   As to the Secretary of State see PARA 7.

4   Housing Act 1996 s 166A(10) (as added: see note 2). As to the making of regulations generally see PARA 423 note 17. See *R (on the application of Alemi) v Westminster City Council* [2015] EWHC 1765 (Admin), [2015] PTSR 1339, 166 NLJ 7690, [2015] All ER (D) 247 (Jun) (scheme, which suspended applicant's ability to bid for social housing until 12 months after his acceptance as an unintentionally homeless eligible person in priority need, unlawful); *Darby v Richmond upon Thames London Borough Council* [2015] EWHC 909 (QB), [2015] All ER (D) 48 (Apr) (complaint that authority not exercising its statutory duties and powers properly: insufficient to give rise to duty of care).

    As regards the procedure to be followed in England, an authority's allocation scheme must be framed in accordance with the following prescribed principle, ie that a member of an authority who has been elected for the electoral division or ward in which the housing accommodation in relation to which an allocation decision falls to be made is situated, or the person in relation to whom that decision falls to be made has his sole or main residence, must not, at the time the allocation decision is made, be included in the persons constituting the decision-making body:

Allocation of Housing (Procedure) Regulations 1997, SI 1997/483, reg 3. For these purposes, 'allocation decision' means a decision to allocate housing accommodation; 'authority' means a local housing authority in England; and 'decision-making body' means an authority or a committee or sub-committee of an authority: reg 2.

5   Housing Act 1996 s 166A(2) (as added: see note 2). A published scheme does not have to contain every detail as to how a discretion forming a part of such a scheme is to be exercised: *R (on the application of Boolen) v Barking and Dagenham London Borough Council* [2009] EWHC 2196 (Admin), [2009] All ER (D) 347 (Jul).

6   Ie within the meaning of the Housing Act 1996 Pt VII (ss 175–218): see PARA 481 et seq.

7   Ie under the Housing Act 1996 s 190(2) (see PARA 496), s 193(2) (see PARA 498) or s 195(2) (see PARA 499) (or under the Housing Act 1985 s 65(2) or 68(2) (both repealed)).

8   Ie under the Housing Act 1996 s 192(3): see PARA 497.

9   Housing Act 1996 s 166A(3)(a)–(e) (as added: see note 2). However, people are to be disregarded for these purposes if they would not have fallen within head (1) or (2) in the text without the local housing authority having had regard to a restricted person (within the meaning of the Housing Act 1996 Pt VII: see PARA 487 note 11): s 166A(4) (as so added).

In assessing housing needs the fact that there is a joint residence order is highly relevant: *R (on the application of Bibi) v Camden London Borough Council* [2004] EWHC 2527 (Admin), [2005] 1 FLR 413, [2005] HLR 267. See also *R (on the application of Maali) v Lambeth London Borough Council* [2003] EWHC 2231 (Admin), [2004] HLR 178, [2003] All ER (D) 80 (Aug) (refusal to place asthma sufferer in a category equivalent to head (4) in the text unlawful).

10   Housing Act 1996 s 166A(3) (as added (see note 2); amended by SI 2012/2989).

11   For this purpose 'the regular forces' has the meaning given by the Armed Forces Act 2006 s 374 (see ARMED FORCES vol 3 (2011) PARA 327): Housing Act 1996 s 166A(3) (as added (see note 2); amended by SI 2012/2989).

12   For this purpose 'the reserve forces' has the meaning given by the Armed Forces Act 2006 s 374 (see ARMED FORCES vol 3 (2011) PARA 308): Housing Act 1996 s 166A(3) (as added (see note 2); amended by SI 2012/2989).

13   Housing Act 1996 s 166A(3)(i)–(iv) (added by SI 2012/2989).

14   Ie within the meaning of the Housing Act 1996 s 199: see PARA 487.

15   Housing Act 1996 s 166A(5) (as added: see note 2).

16   Ie the Housing Act 1996 s 166A(3): see the text and notes 6–13.

17   Housing Act 1996 s 166A(6) (as added: see note 2).

18   Housing Act 1996 s 166A(7) (as added: see note 2). No such regulations may be made unless a draft of them has been laid before and approved by a resolution of each House of Parliament: s 172(2) (amended by the Localism Act 2011 s 147(1), (6)). The following are specified as further descriptions of people to whom reasonable preference is to be given in the allocation scheme of a local housing authority: (1) people owed a duty by that authority under the Housing Act 1996 s 193 or s 195(2) or their predecessor provisions (ie the Housing Act 1985 s 65(2) or s 68(2) (both repealed)) (main housing duties owed to homeless persons: see PARA 493 et seq); (2) people in respect of whom that authority is exercising its power under the Housing Act 1996 s 194 (power to secure accommodation after minimum period of duty under s 193: see PARA 498); and (3) people: (a) who have within the previous two years been provided with advice and assistance by that authority under s 197(2) (repealed) (duty where other suitable accommodation available); or (b) who are occupying accommodation secured with such advice and assistance: Allocation of Housing (Reasonable and Additional Preference) Regulations 1997, SI 1997/1902, reg 2. See also the Housing Act 1996 (Additional Preference for Armed Forces) (England) Regulations 2012, SI 2012/2989.

19   Housing Act 1996 s 166A(8) (as added: see note 2).

20   Ie by virtue of the Housing Act 1996 s 166A(3).

21   Ie a decision under the Housing Act 1996 s 16ZAA(9): see PARA 424.

22   Housing Act 1996 s 166A(9) (as added: see note 2).

23   Housing Act 1996 s 166A(11) (as added: see note 2).

24   Ie under the Homelessness Act 2002 s 1: see PARA 479.

25   Ie under the Localism Act 2011 s 150: see PARA 421.

26   Housing Act 1996 s 166A(12) (as added: see note 2).

27   As to the meaning of 'private registered provider of social housing' see PARA 53.

28   As to the meaning of 'registered social landlord' see PARA 13.

29   See the Housing Act 1996 s 159(4); and PARA 422 note 6.

30   Housing Act 1996 s 166A(13) (as added: see note 2).

31   Housing Act 1996 s 166A(14) (as added: see note 2).

32   Housing Act 1996 s 170 (amended by the Homelessness Act 2002 s 18(1), Sch 1 paras 2, 5; and by SI 2010/866).

428. Allocation in accordance with allocation scheme in Wales. Similarly, every local housing authority[1] in Wales must have a scheme (its 'allocation scheme') for determining priorities, and as to the procedure to be followed, in allocating housing accommodation; and for this purpose 'procedure' includes all aspects of the allocation process, including the persons or descriptions of persons by whom decisions are to be taken[2]. As regards the procedure to be followed, the scheme must be framed in accordance with such principles as the Welsh Ministers[3] may prescribe by regulations[4].

The scheme must include a statement of the authority's policy on offering people who are to be allocated housing accommodation either a choice of housing accommodation or the opportunity to express preferences about the housing accommodation to be allocated to them[5].

As regards priorities, the scheme must be framed so as to secure that reasonable preference is given to:

(1)   people who are homeless[6];

(2)   people who are owed a duty by any local housing authority[7];

(3)   people occupying insanitary or overcrowded housing or otherwise living in unsatisfactory housing conditions;

(4)   people who need to move on medical or welfare grounds (including grounds relating to a disability); and

(5)   people who need to move to a particular locality in the district of the authority, where failure to meet that need would cause hardship (to themselves or to others)[8].

The scheme may also be framed so as to give additional preference to particular descriptions of people within the categories above (being descriptions of people with urgent housing needs)[9]. The scheme may contain provision for determining priorities in allocating housing accommodation to such people; and the factors which the scheme may allow to be taken into account include the financial resources available to a person to meet his housing costs, any behaviour of a person (or of a member of his household) which affects his suitability to be a tenant and any local connection[10] which exists between a person and the authority's district[11].

The scheme is not, however, required to provide for any preference to be given to people the authority has decided are people to whom the following provision applies[12]. This provision applies to a person if the authority is satisfied that:

(a)   he, or a member of his household, has been guilty of unacceptable behaviour[13] serious enough to make him unsuitable to be a tenant of the authority; and

(b)   in the circumstances at the time his case is considered, he deserves by reason of that behaviour not to be treated as a member of a group of people who are to be given preference by virtue of the provisions[14] described above[15].

Subject to the statutory requirements as to priorities[16], the scheme may contain provision about the allocation of particular housing accommodation to a person who makes a specific application for that accommodation, and to persons of a particular description (whether or not they are within heads (1) to (5))[17].

The Welsh Ministers may by regulations:

(i)   specify further descriptions of people to whom preference is to be given as mentioned in the provisions set out in heads (1) to (5), or amend or repeal any part of those provisions[18];

(ii)   specify factors which a local housing authority in Wales must not take into account in allocating housing accommodation[19].

The scheme must be framed so as to secure that an applicant for an allocation of housing accommodation:

(A)   has the right to request such general information as will enable him to assess how his application is likely to be treated under the scheme (including in particular whether he is likely to be regarded as a member of a group of people who are to be given preference[20]) and whether housing accommodation appropriate to his needs is likely to be made available to him and, if so, how long it is likely to be before such accommodation becomes available for allocation to him;

(B)   is notified in writing of any decision that he is a person who is not to be given preference[21] and the grounds for it;

(C)   has the right to request the authority to inform him of any decision about the facts of his case which is likely to be, or has been, taken into account in considering whether to allocate housing accommodation to him; and

(D)   has the right to request a review of a decision mentioned in head (B) or head (C), or a decision that he is ineligible or to be treated as ineligible for a housing allocation[22], and to be informed of the decision on the review and the grounds for it[23].

Subject to the provisions described above, and to any regulations made under them, the authority may decide on what principles the scheme is to be framed[24]. Before adopting an allocation scheme, or making an alteration to its scheme reflecting a major change of policy, a local housing authority in Wales must send a copy of the draft scheme, or proposed alteration, to every private registered provider of social housing[25] and registered social landlord[26] with which it has nomination arrangements[27] and afford those persons a reasonable opportunity to comment on the proposals[28].

A local housing authority may only allocate housing accommodation in accordance with its allocation scheme[29]. Where a local housing authority so requests, a private registered provider of social housing or registered social landlord must co-operate to such extent as is reasonable in the circumstances in offering accommodation to people with priority under the authority's allocation scheme[30].

1   As to the meaning of 'local housing authority' see PARA 11 (definition applied by the Housing Act 1996 s 230).
2   Housing Act 1996 s 167(1) (amended by the Localism Act 2011 s 147(1), (5)(b)). A local housing authority has a wide discretionary power to include in its housing allocation scheme such rules as it feels appropriate: *R (on the application of Giles) v Fareham Borough Council* [2002] EWHC 2951 (Admin), [2003] HLR 524, [2002] All ER (D) 213 (Dec) (policy allowed authority to defer placement on housing list where there had been tenant misconduct). The grant of a secure tenancy to a person to whom accommodation had been allocated inconsistently with an authority's allocation scheme did not render the tenancy void or ineffective: *Birmingham City Council v Qasim* [2009] EWCA Civ 1080, [2010] HLR 327, [2010] LGR 253. Note that this and the cases cited in notes 4, 5, 8, 9, 24 are decisions on the English law.
3   Ie the appropriate national authority: see PARA 7.
4   Housing Act 1996 s 167(5). As to the making of regulations generally see PARA 423 note 17. See *R (on the application of Alemi) v Westminster City Council* [2015] EWHC 1765 (Admin), [2015] PTSR 1339, 166 NLJ 7690, [2015] All ER (D) 247 (Jun) (scheme, which suspended applicant's ability to bid for social housing until 12 months after his acceptance as an unintentionally homeless eligible person in priority need, unlawful); *Darby v Richmond upon Thames London Borough Council* [2015] EWHC 909 (QB), [2015] All ER (D) 48 (Apr) (complaint that authority not exercising its statutory duties and powers properly: insufficient to give rise to duty of care).

As regards the procedure to be followed in allocating housing accommodation in Wales, the following principles are prescribed as principles in accordance with which an authority's allocation scheme must be framed: Local Housing Authorities (Prescribed Principles for Allocation Schemes) (Wales) Regulations 1997, SI 1997/45, reg 3. In relation to an allocation decision where either: (1) the housing accommodation in question is situated in the electoral division for which a member is elected; or (2) the qualifying person in question has his sole or main residence in the electoral division for which a member is elected, that member must not be included in the persons or descriptions of persons by whom the allocation decision is to be taken: reg 3, Schedule para 1. An officer or a description of officers of the authority must be included in the persons or descriptions of persons by whom allocation decisions, or descriptions of allocation decisions, may be taken, except where the authority or a committee or sub-committee of the authority, as the case may be, has determined that no officer delegation arrangements may be made: Schedule para 2. For these purposes, 'allocation decision' means a decision to allocate housing accommodation; 'allocation scheme' means an allocation scheme within the meaning of the Housing Act 1996 s 167(1) (see the text and notes 1–2); 'authority' means a Welsh local housing authority; 'delegation arrangements' means arrangements made under the Local Government Act 1972 s 101(1) or (2) (see LOCAL GOVERNMENT vol 69 (2009) PARA 370) for the discharge of an authority's function of making allocation decisions; 'officer delegation arrangements' means delegation arrangements which arrange for the discharge (in whole or in part) of an authority's function of making allocation decisions, by an officer or a description of officers of the authority; and 'qualifying person', in relation to an authority, means a person who is qualified to be allocated housing accommodation by that authority: Local Housing Authorities (Prescribed Principles for Allocation Schemes) (Wales) Regulations 1997, SI 1997/45, reg 2.

5   Housing Act 1996 s 167(1A) (added by the Homelessness Act 2002 s 16(1), (2)). A published scheme does not have to contain every detail as to how a discretion forming a part of such a scheme is to be exercised: *R (on the application of Boolen) v Barking and Dagenham London Borough Council* [2009] EWHC 2196 (Admin), [2009] All ER (D) 347 (Jul).

6   Ie within the meaning of the Housing (Wales) Act 2014 Pt 2 (ss 50–100): see PARA 482 et seq.

7   Ie under the Housing (Wales) Act 2014 s 66 (see PARA 490), s 73 (see PARA 501) or s 75 (see PARA 502).

8   Housing Act 1996 s 167(2)(a)–(e) (s 167(2) substituted by the Homelessness Act 2002 s 16(3); and amended by the Housing Act 2004 s 223; the Housing and Regeneration Act 2008 s 314, Sch 15 paras 1, 2(1), (2); and the Housing (Wales) Act 2014 s 100, Sch 3 paras 2, 3(a)). However, people are to be disregarded for these purposes if they would not have fallen within head (1) or (2) in the text without the local housing authority having had regard to a restricted person (within the meaning of the Housing (Wales) Act 2014 Pt 2: see PARA 488 note 13): Housing Act 1996 s 167(2ZA) (added by the Housing and Regeneration Act 2008 Sch 15 para 2(3); and amended by the Housing (Wales) Act 2014 Sch 3 paras 2, 3(b)).

   In assessing housing needs the fact that there is a joint residence order is highly relevant: *R (on the application of Bibi) v Camden London Borough Council* [2004] EWHC 2527 (Admin), [2005] 1 FLR 413, [2005] HLR 267. See also *R (on the application of Maali) v Lambeth London Borough Council* [2003] EWHC 2231 (Admin), [2004] HLR 178, [2003] All ER (D) 80 (Aug) (refusal to place asthma sufferer in a category equivalent to head (4) in the text unlawful).

9   Housing Act 1996 s 167(2) (as substituted: see note 9). In so far as a housing allocation scheme precludes consideration of any categories to which it ought to have given reasonable preference under s 167(2), it is unlawful: *R v Westminster City Council, ex p Al-Khorsan* (1999) 33 HLR 77, [1999] All ER (D) 1428. See also *R (on the application of A) v Lambeth London Borough Council, R (on the application of Lindsay) v Lambeth London Borough Council* [2002] EWCA Civ 1084, [2002] HLR 998, [2002] All ER (D) 324 (Jul). Whether such a preference is reasonable is a matter for the discretion of the local authority: *R (on the application of Lin) v Barnet London Borough Council* [2007] EWCA Civ 132, [2007] LGR 454, [2007] HLR 440, [2007] LGR 454. The fact that the scheme favours certain categories of applicant does not make it irrational: *R (on the application of Yazar) v Southwark London Borough Council* [2008] EWHC 515 (Admin), 152 (No 14) Sol Jo LB 31, [2008] All ER (D) 273 (Mar). A local authority housing allocation scheme which places the majority of applicants into one group and allocates available property to the applicant who has been longest on the waiting list is not unlawful or irrational: *R (on the application of Ahmad) v Newham London Borough Council* [2009] UKHL 14, [2009] 3 All ER 755, [2009] HLR 516.

10 Ie within the meaning of the Housing (Wales) Act 2014 s 81: see PARA 485 note 16.

11 Housing Act 1996 s 167(2A) (s 167(2A)–(2E) added by the Homelessness Act 2002 s 16(3); the Housing Act 1996 s 167(2A) amended by the Housing (Wales) Act 2014 Sch 3 paras 2, 3(c)).

12 Housing Act 1996 s 167(2B) (as added: see note 11).

13 The only behaviour which may be regarded by the authority as unacceptable for this purpose is that specified by the Housing Act 1996 s 160A(8) (see PARA 425 note 12): see s 167(2D) (as added: see note 11).
14 Ie the Housing Act 1996 s 167(2): see the text and notes 6–9.
15 Housing Act 1996 s 167(2B), (2C) (as added: see note 11).
16 Ie the Housing Act 1996 s 167(2): see the text and notes 6–9.
17 Housing Act 1996 s 167(2E) (as added: see note 11).
18 Housing Act 1996 s 167(3). No such regulations may be made unless a draft of them has been laid before and approved by a resolution of the National Assembly for Wales: s 172(2) (amended by the Localism Act 2011 s 147(1), (6)).
19 Housing Act 1996 s 167(4) (amended by the Localism Act 2011 s 147(1), (5)(c)).
20 Ie by virtue of the Housing Act 1996 s 167(2).
21 Ie a person to whom the Housing Act 1996 s 167(2C) applies: see the text and notes 13–15.
22 Ie a decision under the Housing Act 1996 s 160A(9): see PARA 425.
23 Housing Act 1996 s 167(4A) (added by the Homelessness Act 2002 s 16(4)).
24 Housing Act 1996 s 167(6). See eg *R v Newham London Borough Council, ex p Dawson* (1994) 26 HLR 747 (an authority must not adopt a rigid policy); *R v Newham London Borough Council, ex p Miah* (1995) 28 HLR 279 (authority may take account of rent arrears).
25 As to the meaning of 'private registered provider of social housing' see PARA 53.
26 As to the meaning of 'registered social landlord' see PARA 13.
27 See the Housing Act 1996 s 159(4); and PARA 422 note 6.
28 Housing Act 1996 s 167(7) (amended by the Localism Act 2011 s 147(1), (5)(d); and by SI 2010/866).
29 See the Housing Act 1996 s 167(8) (amended by the Localism Act 2011 s 147(1), (5)(e)).
30 Housing Act 1996 s 170 (amended by the Homelessness Act 2002 s 18(1), Sch 1 paras 2, 5; and by SI 2010/866).

429. Information about the allocation scheme. A local housing authority[1] must publish a summary of its allocation scheme[2] and provide a copy of the summary free of charge to any member of the public who asks for a copy[3]. The authority must make the scheme available for inspection at its principal office and must provide a copy of the scheme, on payment of a reasonable fee, to any member of the public who asks for one[4].

When the authority makes an alteration to its scheme reflecting a major change of policy[5], it must within a reasonable period of time take such steps as it considers reasonable to bring the effect of the alteration to the attention of those likely to be affected by it[6].

1 As to the meaning of 'local housing authority' see PARA 11 (definition applied by the Housing Act 1996 s 230).
2 Failure to publish does not, however, make the policy ultra vires: see *R v Newham London Borough Council, ex p Miah* (1995) 28 HLR 279. As to the allocation scheme see PARA 428.
3 Housing Act 1996 s 168(1).
4 Housing Act 1996 s 168(2).
5 As to the consultation required before such a change see PARAS 427 text and notes 27–30, 428 text and notes 25–28.
6 Housing Act 1996 s 168(3) (amended by the Homelessness Act 2002 s 18(1), Sch 1 paras 2, 4).

D.   GUIDANCE

430. Guidance by the appropriate national authority. In the exercise of their statutory functions relating to the allocation of housing[1], local housing authorities[2] must have regard to such guidance as may from time to time be given by the appropriate national authority[3]. The appropriate national authority may give guidance generally or to specified descriptions of authorities[4].

1 Ie their functions under the Housing Act 1996 Pt VI (ss 159–174): see PARA 420 et seq.
2 As to the meaning of 'local housing authority' see PARA 11 (definition applied by the Housing Act 1996 s 230).
3 Housing Act 1996 s 169(1). As to the appropriate national authority, ie the Secretary of State or, where statutory functions have been transferred in relation to Wales, the Welsh Ministers, see PARA 7. As to guidance for local housing authorities in England see Code of Guidance to Local

Authorities on the Allocation of Accommodation and Homelessness 2016 (Department for Communities and Local Government, 24 March 2016). In relation to Wales, see New homelessness legislation (Welsh Government's Website, www.gov.wales, 27 April 2015).

4 Housing Act 1996 s 169(2). An authority must use an up to date version of the code of guidance: see *R v Newham Borough Council, ex p Bones* (1992) 25 HLR 357.

E. OFFENCES RELATING TO THE GIVING OR WITHHOLDING OF INFORMATION

431. False statements and withholding information. A person commits an offence if, in connection with the exercise by a local housing authority[1] of its statutory functions relating to the allocation of housing[2], he knowingly or recklessly makes a statement which is false in a material particular, or he knowingly withholds information which the authority has reasonably required him to give in connection with the exercise of those functions[3]. A person guilty of such an offence is liable to a penalty[4].

1 As to the meaning of 'local housing authority' see PARA 11 (definition applied by the Housing Act 1996 s 230).
2 Ie its functions under the Housing Act 1996 Pt VI (ss 159–174): see PARA 420 et seq.
3 Housing Act 1996 s 171(1).
4 Housing Act 1996 s 171(2). The penalty on summary conviction is a fine not exceeding level 5 on the standard scale: see s 171(2). As to the powers of magistrates' courts to issue fines on summary conviction see SENTENCING vol 92 (2015) PARA 176.

(3) MANAGEMENT OF LOCAL AUTHORITY HOUSING

(i) In general

432. General powers of management. A number of general statutory provisions on housing management matters[1] apply to all houses[2] which are held by a local housing authority[3] for housing purposes[4]. Subject to the provisions relating to management agreements (under which the management, regulation and control of dwellings may be delegated to an approved organisation)[5] and to any requirement imposed on the authority under Part 2 of the Housing and Regeneration Act 2008[6] the general management, regulation and control of a local housing authority's houses is vested in and must be exercised by the authority and the houses must at all times be open to inspection by the authority[7].

1 Ie the Housing Act 1985 ss 20–27BA: see PARA 434 et seq.
2 As to the meaning of 'house' see PARA 405 note 6.
3 As to the meaning of 'local housing authority' see PARA 11.
4 Housing Act 1985 s 20(1) (amended by the Housing and Planning Act 1986 s 24(2), Sch 5 para 21; and the Housing Act 1996 s 222, Sch 18 para 3(1), (3)). References in the Housing Act 1985 ss 20–27BA to an authority's houses are to be construed accordingly: s 20(2).
5 Ie the Housing Act 1985 s 27: see PARA 457.
6 Ie the Housing and Regeneration Act 2008 Pt 2 (ss 59–278A): see PARA 51 et seq.
7 Housing Act 1985 s 21(1), (2) (s 21(2) amended by the Housing and Planning Act 1986 Sch 5 para 22; and by SI 2010/844).

433. 'Best value' requirements. A procedure was introduced by Part III of the Local Government, Planning and Land Act 1980[1] whereby each local authority entering into a works contract[2] whose value exceeded a prescribed amount had first to invite tenders[3]. This procedure, known as 'compulsory competitive tendering', was further extended by the Local Government Act 1988 to 'defined activities'[4] and by the Local Government Act 1992 to professional and other services[5]. However, compulsory competitive tendering was abolished as from 2 January 2000[6].

Now Part I of the Local Government Act 1999[7] makes provision imposing on local and certain other authorities (known as 'best value authorities'[8]) requirements relating to economy, efficiency and effectiveness, which are referred to as 'best value' requirements[9]. A best value authority must make arrangements to secure continuous improvement in the way in which its functions are exercised, having regard to a combination of economy, efficiency and effectiveness, and must consult specified representative persons[10].

1 See the Local Government, Planning and Land Act 1980 Pt III (ss 5–23) (repealed).
2 As to the meaning of 'works contract' see the Local Government, Planning and Land Act 1980 s 5 (repealed).
3 See the Local Government, Planning and Land Act 1980 s 7 (repealed).
4 See the Local Government Act 1988 s 2 (repealed).
5 See the Local Government Act 1992 s 8 (repealed).
6 See the Local Government Act 1999 s 21(1).
7 Ie the Local Government Act 1999 Pt I (ss 1–29).
8 As to best value authorities see the Local Government Act 1999 ss 1(1), 2(1); and LOCAL GOVERNMENT vol 69 (2009) PARA 688.
9 See LOCAL GOVERNMENT vol 69 (2009) PARA 688 et seq.
10 See the Local Government Act 1999 s 3(1), (2); and LOCAL GOVERNMENT vol 69 (2009) PARA 689.

434. Byelaws. A local housing authority[1] may make byelaws:
(1) for the management, use and regulation of its houses[2];
(2) with respect to the use of land held by the authority by virtue of the provisions relating to recreation grounds and other land provided in connection with housing[3], excluding land covered by buildings or included in the curtilage of a building or forming part of a highway[4].

In the case of its lodging-houses[5], a local housing authority must by byelaws make sufficient provision for the following purposes:
(a) for securing that the lodging-houses are under the management and control of persons appointed or employed by the authority for the purpose;
(b) for securing the due separation at night of men and boys above eight years old from women and girls;
(c) for preventing damage, disturbance, interruption and indecent and offensive language and behaviour and nuisances; and
(d) for determining the duties of the persons appointed by the authority[6].

A printed copy or a sufficient abstract of the byelaws relating to lodging-houses must be put up and at all times kept in every room in the lodging-houses[7].

1 As to the meaning of 'local housing authority' see PARA 11.
2 Housing Act 1985 s 23(1). As to the meaning of 'house' see PARA 405 note 6. See also PARA 432 note 4. Byelaws made under s 23 by a local housing authority in England are to be read subject to any requirement imposed on the authority under the Housing and Regeneration Act 2008 Pt 2 (ss 59–278A) (see PARA 51 et seq): Housing Act 1985 s 23(4) (added by SI 2010/844).
3 Ie by virtue of the Housing Act 1985 s 12: see PARA 408.
4 Housing Act 1985 s 23(2).
5 As to the meaning of 'lodging-houses' see PARA 13 note 1.
6 See the Housing Act 1985 s 23(3)(a)–(d).
7 Housing Act 1985 s 23(3).

435. Financial assistance towards tenants' removal expenses. Where a tenant[1] of one of the houses[2] of a local housing authority[3] moves to another house (whether or not that house is also one of the authority's houses), the authority may:
(1) pay any expenses of the removal; and
(2) where the tenant is purchasing the house, pay any expenses incurred by him in connection with the purchase, other than the purchase price[4].

If, however, the house belongs to the same authority, head (2) applies only if the house has never been let[5] and was built expressly with a view to sale or for letting[6].

The appropriate national authority[7] may give directions to authorities in general or to any particular authority as to the expenses which may be treated, whether generally or in any particular case, as incurred in connection with the purchase of a house, and limiting the amount which the authority may pay in respect of such expenses[8].

An authority may make its payment of expenses subject to conditions[9].

1 As to the meaning of 'tenant' see PARA 31 note 3.
2 As to the meaning of 'house' see PARA 405 note 6. See also PARA 249 note 4.
3 As to the meaning of 'local housing authority' see PARA 11. The Housing Act 1985 s 26 applies in relation to a development corporation as it applies in relation to a local housing authority: s 30(1) (amended by SI 2008/3002).
4 Housing Act 1985 s 26(1).
5 As to the meaning of 'let' see PARA 31 note 3.
6 Housing Act 1985 s 26(2).
7 Ie the Secretary of State or, where statutory functions have been transferred in relation to Wales, the Welsh Ministers: see PARA 7.
8 Housing Act 1985 s 26(3).
9 Housing Act 1985 s 26(4).

436. Schemes for payments to assist local housing authority tenants to obtain other accommodation. In accordance with a scheme made by a local housing authority[1] and, where the authority is in Wales, approved by the Welsh Ministers[2], the authority may make grants to or for the benefit of qualifying tenants[3] or licensees of the authority with a view to assisting each person to whom or for whose benefit a grant is made to obtain accommodation, otherwise than as a tenant or licensee of the authority, by:

(1)   acquiring an interest in a dwelling house[4]; or
(2)   carrying out works to a dwelling house to provide additional accommodation; or
(3)   both of those means[5].

Such a scheme must contain such provisions as the local housing authority considers appropriate together with, where the authority is in Wales, any which the Welsh Ministers may require as a condition of their approval; and a scheme may include provisions specifying, or providing for the determination of:

(a)   the persons who are qualifying tenants or licensees for the purposes of the scheme;
(b)   the interests which qualifying tenants or licensees may be assisted to acquire;
(c)   the works for the carrying out of which grants may be made;
(d)   the circumstances in which a grant may be made for the benefit of a qualifying tenant or licensee;
(e)   the amount of the grant which may be made in any particular case and the terms on which it may be made;
(f)   the limits on the total number and amount of grants which may be made; and
(g)   the period within which the scheme is to apply[6].

The Welsh Ministers may approve a scheme made by a local housing authority in Wales under these provisions with or without conditions[7].

Where a scheme has been made and, where the authority is in Wales, approved, a local housing authority must take such steps as it considers appropriate to bring the scheme to the attention of persons likely to be able to benefit from it and must take such other steps, if any, as the appropriate national authority may direct in any particular case to secure publicity for the scheme[8].

The Welsh Ministers may revoke an approval of such a scheme by a notice given to the local housing authority concerned; but, where such a notice is given, the revocation does not affect the operation of the scheme in relation to any grants made or agreed before the date of the notice[9].

Where such a scheme has been made by a local housing authority and, where the authority is in Wales, has been approved, a person dealing with the authority is not to be concerned to see or inquire whether the terms of the scheme have been or are being complied with; and any failure to comply with the terms of a scheme does not invalidate any grant purporting to be made in accordance with the scheme unless the person to whom the grant is made has actual notice of the failure[10].

1   As to the meaning of 'local housing authority' see PARA 11 (definition applied by the Housing Act 1988 s 129(7)(a)).
2   Ie under the Housing Act 1988 s 129: see the text and note 7. As to the Welsh Ministers see PARA 7.
3   For these purposes, 'tenant' does not include a tenant under a long tenancy, as defined in the Housing Act 1985 s 115 (see LANDLORD AND TENANT vol 63 (2016) PARA 1042): Housing Act 1988 s 129(7)(c).
4   For these purposes, 'dwelling house' has the meaning assigned by the Housing Act 1985 s 112 (ie a house or a part of a house: see s 112(1); and LANDLORD AND TENANT vol 63 (2016) PARA 1037): Housing Act 1988 s 129(7)(b).
5   Housing Act 1988 s 129(1) (amended by SI 2003/986).
6   Housing Act 1988 s 129(2) (amended by SI 2003/986).
7   Housing Act 1988 s 129(3) (amended by SI 2003/986).
8   Housing Act 1988 s 129(3) (as amended: see note 7). The appropriate national authority is the Secretary of State or, where statutory functions have been transferred in relation to Wales, the Welsh Ministers: see PARA 7.
9   Housing Act 1988 s 129(4).
10 Housing Act 1988 s 129(6) (amended by SI 2003/986).

437. Services etc for owners and occupiers of houses for work on them. A relevant authority[1] has power to provide professional, technical and administrative services for owners or occupiers of dwellings in connection with their arranging or carrying out relevant works[2] or to encourage or facilitate the carrying out of such works, whether or not on payment of such charges as the authority may determine[3]. It is the duty of a relevant authority exercising any power so conferred to consider whether or not to make a charge for exercising it and to take such measures as are reasonably available to the authority to secure contributions from other persons towards the cost of exercising that power[4].

A relevant authority has power to give financial assistance in any form to any housing association[5], any charity[6], or any body, or a body of any description, approved by the appropriate national authority[7], towards the cost of the provision by that association, charity or body of services of any description for owners or occupiers of dwellings in arranging works of maintenance, repair or improvement or the encouraging or facilitating the carrying out of such works[8]. It is the duty of a relevant authority, in deciding whether to exercise any power so conferred in relation to any association, charity or body, to have regard to the existence and extent of any financial assistance available from other persons to that association, charity or body and, in exercising any power so conferred in relation to any association, charity or body:

(1)   to have regard to whether that association, charity or body has made or will make charges and their amount; and

(2)   to encourage the association, charity or body to take such measures as
        are reasonably available to it to secure contributions from other
        persons[9].

The appropriate national authority may, with the consent of the Treasury, give
financial assistance in any form to any person in respect of expenditure incurred
or to be incurred by that person in connection with the provision, whether or not
by that person, of services of any description for owners or occupiers of dwellings
in arranging or carrying out works of maintenance, repair or improvement, or in
connection with the encouraging or facilitating, whether or not by that person, the
carrying out of such works[10]. The giving of financial assistance under this
provision must be on such terms (which may include terms as to repayment) as the
appropriate national authority with, in relation to England, the consent of the
Treasury, considers appropriate[11]. The person receiving assistance must comply
with the terms on which it is given and compliance may be enforced by the
appropriate national authority[12].

1   For these purposes, 'relevant authority' means a local housing authority or county council; and
    'local housing authority' is to be construed in accordance with the Housing Act 1985 s 1 (see
    PARA 11): Local Government and Housing Act 1989 s 169(9).
2   Works are relevant works in relation to a dwelling or, as the case may be, a dwelling in any area,
    if they are works of any of the following descriptions: (1) works to cause the dwelling to be fit for
    human habitation (see PARA 562 et seq); and (2) where the occupant is disabled, works for any of
    the purposes specified in the Housing Grants, Construction and Regeneration Act 1996 s 23
    (disabled facilities grants) (see PARA 843): Local Government and Housing Act 1989 s 169(2)
    (amended by the Housing Grants, Construction and Regeneration Act 1996 s 103, Sch 1 para 15;
    and by SI 2002/1860).
3   Local Government and Housing Act 1989 s 169(1).
4   See the Local Government and Housing Act 1989 s 169(3).
5   For these purposes, 'housing association' means a housing association within the meaning of the
    Housing Associations Act 1985 s 1(1) (see PARA 13), or a body established by such a housing
    association for the purpose of, or having among its purposes or objects, providing services of any
    description for owners or occupiers of houses in arranging or carrying out works of maintenance,
    repair or improvement, or encouraging or facilitating the carrying out of such works: Local
    Government and Housing Act 1989 s 169(9) (definition amended by SI 1996/2325).
6   As to charities generally see CHARITIES vol 8 (2015) PARA 1 et seq.
7   Ie the Secretary of State or, where statutory functions have been transferred in relation to Wales,
    the Welsh Ministers: see PARA 7.
8   Local Government and Housing Act 1989 s 169(4).
9   Local Government and Housing Act 1989 s 169(5).
10 Local Government and Housing Act 1989 s 169(6). As to the Treasury see CONSTITUTIONAL
    AND ADMINISTRATIVE LAW vol 20 (2014) PARA 262 et seq.
11 Local Government and Housing Act 1989 s 169(7).
12 Local Government and Housing Act 1989 s 169(8).

438.   Secure tenancies. Since 1980, a tenant of a local authority or other public
sector landlord has had the status of secure tenant[1]. The current provisions are
contained in Part IV of the Housing Act 1985[2]. A tenant of such a landlord will,
unless he falls within one of the exceptional cases mentioned in the Act[3], enjoy the
status of a secure tenant for so long as he occupies the dwelling as his only or
principal home[4].

A secure tenant has a number of statutory rights[5]. First, a secure tenant has
security of tenure and the landlord may only recover possession if the landlord can
rely on one or other of the specified statutory grounds[6]. Secondly, a secure tenant
will usually have a statutory right to buy his home[7]. Thirdly, there are a number
of other individual rights including rights for members of a secure tenant's family
to succeed to the tenancy on the death of that tenant[8], the right to be consulted on
matters of housing management[9], and the right to assign subject to the consent of
the landlord[10].

In the case of tenancies granted before 15 January 1989, most tenants of housing associations (now private registered provider of social housing or registered social landlords[11]) held secure tenancies. However, with very limited exceptions, such tenants granted tenancies on or after this date have assured tenancies[12].

The Localism Act 2011 provides that, subject to certain conditions, existing secure and assured tenants will be able to retain a similar level of security on exchanging their property with a social tenant with a less secure tenancy[13].

All these matters except the statutory right of a secure tenant to buy his home are dealt with elsewhere in this work[14].

1   In most cases, this has been true of a licensee as well as a tenant. As to the meanings of 'secure tenancy' and 'secure tenant' see LANDLORD AND TENANT vol 63 (2016) PARA 1037. In Wales, secure tenancies are to be replaced by secure contracts under the Renting Homes (Wales) Act 2016: see LANDLORD AND TENANT vol 62 (2016) PARAS 45–46. The relevant provisions are not in force at the date at which this volume states the law: see PARA 6.
2   See the Housing Act 1985 Pt IV (ss 79–117); and LANDLORD AND TENANT vol 63 (2016) PARA 1037 et seq.
3   See the Housing Act 1985 s 79, Sch 1; and LANDLORD AND TENANT vol 63 (2016) PARA 1037 et seq.
4   See the Housing Act 1985 s 79; and LANDLORD AND TENANT vol 63 (2016) PARA 1037.
5   See LANDLORD AND TENANT vol 63 (2016) PARA 1037 et seq.
6   Ie the grounds specified by the Housing Act 1985 s 84, Sch 2: see LANDLORD AND TENANT vol 63 (2016) PARA 1136 et seq.
7   See the Housing Act 1985 Pt V (ss 118–188); and PARA 230 et seq.
8   See LANDLORD AND TENANT vol 63 (2016) PARA 1097.
9   See LANDLORD AND TENANT vol 63 (2016) PARA 1114.
10 See LANDLORD AND TENANT vol 63 (2016) PARA 1065 et seq.
11 See PARA 51 et seq.
12 See the Housing Act 1988 s 35; and PARA 242. For a commentary, see: Driscoll *A Guide to the Housing Act 1988* (1989).
13 See the Localism Act 2011 ss 158, 159, Sch 14; and LANDLORD AND TENANT vol 63 (2016) PARAS 903–905, 1084.
14 See LANDLORD AND TENANT.

(ii) Rents of Local Authority Houses

A.   IN GENERAL

439. Rents. A local housing authority[1] may make such reasonable charges as it may determine for the tenancy[2] or occupation of the authority's houses[3]. The authority must from time to time review rents and make such changes, either of rents generally or of particular rents, as circumstances may require[4]. In exercising its functions under these provisions, a local housing authority in England must have regard in particular to any relevant standards set[5] for it under the Housing and Regeneration Act 2008[6], and a local housing authority in Wales must comply with any standards relating to rent or service charges which are set for it under the Housing (Wales) Act 2014[7] and have regard to any guidance relating to rent or service charges which is issued[8] under that Act[9].

The lawfulness or otherwise of a local authority's policies on rents may be challenged by judicial review. It has been held that a local housing authority must, so far as it is possible, maintain a reasonable balance between the interests of council tax payers as a whole and those of the authority's council tenants[10] and that it may operate a differential rent scheme whereby different rents are fixed according to the means of a tenant[11].

The onus of showing that rent charges are unreasonable lies with the person who makes the assertion[12]. A tenant who is facing possession proceedings for arrears of rent may challenge the local housing authority's rent policies as a defence to the possession claim[13].

A local housing authority is required to keep a housing revenue account in relation to houses and other buildings which are provided under Part II of the Housing Act 1985[14].

1   As to the meaning of 'local housing authority' see PARA 11.
2   As to the meaning of 'tenancy' see PARA 31 note 3.
3   Housing Act 1985 s 24(1). As to the meaning of 'house' see PARA 405 note 6; and see also PARA 432 note 4.
    Note that the amount charged is now affected by the rent restructuring policy, the aim of which is to gradually introduce a single approach to setting rents for all social landlords.
4   Housing Act 1985 s 24(2).
5   Ie under the Housing and Regeneration Act 2008 s 193: see PARA 105.
6   Housing Act 1985 s 24(5) (added by SI 2010/844). See also the Housing and Planning Act 2016 Pt 4 Ch 3 (ss 80–91); and PARA 441 et seq (rents for high income social tenants in England): Housing Act 1985 s 24(5A) (added by the Housing and Planning Act 2016 s 88(2)).
7   Ie under the Housing (Wales) Act 2014 s 111: see PARA 227.
8   Ie under the Housing (Wales) Act 2014 s 112: see PARA 227.
9   Housing Act 1985 s 24(6) (added by the Housing (Wales) Act 2014 s 130, Sch 3 para 27(b)).
10 *Evans v Collins* [1965] 1 QB 580, [1964] 1 All ER 808 (decided when rates, and not council tax, were payable by local residents); and see *Belcher v Reading Corpn* [1950] Ch 380, [1949] 2 All ER 969 (an action for a declaration that housing committee resolutions imposing rent increases were void, and an injunction to restrain the corporation from collecting increased rents; judgment for the corporation). See also *Summerfield v Hampstead Borough Council* [1957] 1 All ER 221, [1957] 1 WLR 167 (action for declaration that the new rent was unreasonable; it was held that the rent was reasonable and validly charged).
11 *Smith v Cardiff Corpn (No 2)* [1955] Ch 159, [1955] 1 All ER 113 (action for declaration that a differential rent scheme was ultra vires and void; it was held that the scheme was validly made); *Evans v Collins* [1965] 1 QB 580, [1964] 1 All ER 808.
12 *Leeds Corpn v Jenkinson* [1935] 1 KB 168, CA; *Luby v Newcastle-under-Lyme Corpn* [1965] 1 QB 214, [1964] 3 All ER 169, CA.
13 See *Wandsworth London Borough Council v Winder* [1985] AC 461, [1984] 3 All ER 976, HL (such a claim is not an abuse of process).
14 Ie the Housing Act 1985 Pt II (ss 8–57): see PARA 406 et seq. As to the housing revenue account see PARA 356 et seq.

440. Increase of the rent where the tenancy is not secure. Where a house[1] is let by a local housing authority[2] on a weekly or other periodic tenancy[3] which is not a secure tenancy[4] or an introductory tenancy[5], the rent payable under the tenancy may, without the tenancy being terminated, be increased with effect from the beginning of a rental period[6] by a written notice of increase given by the authority to the tenant[7]. The notice is not effective unless:

(1)   it is given at least four weeks before the beginning of the rental period, or any earlier day on which the payment of rent in respect of that period falls to be made;

(2)   it tells the tenant of his right to terminate the tenancy and of the steps to be taken by him if he wishes to do so; and

(3)   it gives him the dates by which, if the increase is not to be effective[8], a notice to quit must be received by the authority and the tenancy be made to terminate[9].

Where the notice is given for the beginning of a rental period and the tenancy continues into that period, the notice does not have effect if:

(a)   the tenancy is terminated by notice to quit given by the tenant in accordance with the provisions (express or implied) of the tenancy;

(b)   the notice to quit is given before the end of the period of two weeks following the date on which the notice of increase is given, or such longer period as may be allowed by the notice of increase; and

(c)   the date on which the tenancy is made to terminate is not later than the earliest day on which the tenancy could be terminated by a notice to quit given by the tenant on the last day of that period[10].

1   As to the meaning of 'house' see PARA 405 note 6.
2   As to the meaning of 'local housing authority' see PARA 11. The Housing Act 1985 s 25 applies in relation to a development corporation as it applies in relation to a local housing authority (s 30(1) (amended by SI 2008/3002)) and in relation to the new towns residuary body as it applies in relation to a local housing authority (Housing Act 1985 s 30(1A) (added by SI 2008/3002)). As to the meanings of 'development corporation' and 'new towns residuary body' see PARA 12.
3   As to the meaning of 'tenancy' see PARA 31 note 3.
4   As to the meaning of 'secure tenancy' see LANDLORD AND TENANT vol 63 (2016) PARA 1037.
5   As to the meaning of 'introductory tenancy' see PARA 472 (definition applied by the Housing Act 1985 s 56(1) (numbered as such by SI 2010/844)).
6   For these purposes, 'rental period' means a period in respect of which a payment of rent falls to be made: Housing Act 1985 s 25(5).
7   Housing Act 1985 s 25(1), (2) (s 25(1) amended by SI 1997/74). As to the meaning of 'tenant' see PARA 31 note 3. As to rent increases for secure tenants see the Housing Act 1985 s 102, s 103; and LANDLORD AND TENANT vol 63 (2016) PARAS 1082–1083. As to rent increases for introductory tenants see ss 102(1), (2), (3)(a), 103, 111A; and LANDLORD AND TENANT vol 63 (2016) PARA 1112.
8   Ie in accordance with the Housing Act 1985 s 25(4): see heads (a)–(c) in the text.
9   Housing Act 1985 s 25(3).
10 Housing Act 1985 s 25(4).

B.   RENTS FOR HIGH INCOME SOCIAL TENANTS IN ENGLAND

441. Mandatory rents. The Secretary of State[1] may by regulations make provision about the levels of rent[2] that an English local housing authority[3] must charge a high income[4] tenant[5] of social housing[6] in England[7]. The regulations may, in particular, require the rent: (1) to be equal to the market rate; (2) to be a proportion of the market rate; or (3) to be determined by reference to other factors[8]. The regulations may, in particular, provide for the rent to be different: (a) for people with different incomes; or (b) for social housing in different areas[9]. The regulations may create exceptions for high income tenants of social housing of a specified description[10]. The regulations may require a local housing authority to have regard to guidance given by the Secretary of State when determining rent in accordance with the regulations[11].

Rent regulations may include provision for the purpose of ensuring that where a requirement about the levels of rent to be charged to high income tenants[12] ceases to apply, the rent is changed to what it would have been if the requirement had never applied[13].

The Secretary of State must use the power[14] to provide by regulations that the requirement in the Welfare Reform and Work Act 2016 for rent reduction[15] does not apply in prescribed cases, to prescribe that that requirement does not apply to a high income tenant of social housing to whom rent regulations apply[16].

1   As to the Secretary of State see PARA 7.
2   'Rent' includes payments under a licence to occupy: Housing and Planning Act 2016 s 91.
3   As to the meaning of 'local housing authority' see PARA 11 (definition applied by the Housing and Planning Act 2016 s 91).
4   In the Housing and Planning Act 2016 Pt 4 Ch 3 (ss 80–91), 'high income' has the meaning given by regulations under s 81: s 91. Rent regulations (see note 6) must: (1) define what is meant by 'high income' for the purposes of Pt 4 Ch 3; and (2) make provision about how a person's income is to be calculated: s 81(1). The regulations may, in particular: (a) define 'high income' in different ways for different areas; (b) specify things that are, or are not, to be treated as income; (c) make

provision about the period by reference to which a person's income is to be calculated (which may be a period in the past); (d) make provision about how a person's income is to be verified; (e) require a person's household income (as defined by the regulations) to be taken into account; (f) require a local housing authority to have regard to guidance given by the Secretary of State when calculating or verifying a person's income: s 81(2).

5 'Tenant' includes a person who has a licence to occupy: Housing and Planning Act 2016 s 91.

6 As to the meaning of 'social housing' see PARA 52 (definition applied by the Housing and Planning Act 2016 s 91).

7 Housing and Planning Act 2016 s 80(1). Regulations under s 80 are referred to in Pt 4 Ch 3 as 'rent regulations': ss 80(6), 91. Part 4 Ch 3 came into force on 1 October 2016: see the Housing and Planning Act 2016 (Commencement No 3) Regulations 2016, SI 2016/956, reg 2(a).

The Government announced on 21 November 2016 that it has decided not to proceed with a compulsory approach introduced by the Housing and Planning Act 2016 which requires local authorities to set higher rents for higher income council tenants. Local authorities and housing associations will continue to have local discretion: see *Social Housing: Written statement* (HCWS274).

8 Housing and Planning Act 2016 s 80(2).

9 Housing and Planning Act 2016 s 80(3).

10 Housing and Planning Act 2016 s 80(4).

11 Housing and Planning Act 2016 s 80(6).

12 Ie a requirement imposed under the Housing and Planning Act 2016 s 80(1): see the text to notes 1–7.

13 Housing and Planning Act 2016 s 84(1).

14 Ie the power in the Welfare Reform and Work Act 2016 s 24(5): See PARA 55.

15 Ie the requirement in the Welfare Reform and Work Act 2016 s 23: See PARA 55.

16 Housing and Planning Act 2016 s 88(1).

442. Information about income. Rent regulations[1] may give a local housing authority[2] the power to require a tenant[3] to provide information or evidence for the purpose of determining whether the local housing authority is obliged by the regulations to charge a specific level of rent[4] and what that level is[5]. Rent regulations may require an English local housing authority to charge the maximum rent[6] to a tenant who has failed to comply with a requirement[7]. Regulations made in reliance on these provisions may, in particular, make provision about: (1) the kind of information or evidence that may be required; (2) the time within which and the manner and form in which the information or evidence is to be provided[8].

The Commissioners for Her Majesty's Revenue and Customs ('HMRC')[9] may disclose information for the purpose of enabling a local housing authority to determine whether it is obliged by rent regulations to charge a tenant[10] a specific level of rent and what that level is[11]. The information may only be disclosed to: (a) a local housing authority; (b) the Secretary of State[12] for the purposes of passing the information to local housing authorities; (c) a public body that has been given the function of passing information between HMRC and local housing authorities by regulations[13]; or (d) a body with which the Secretary of State has made arrangements for the passing of information between HMRC and local housing authorities[14].

The Secretary of State may by regulations: (i) give a public body the function mentioned in head (c); and (ii) make provision about the carrying out of that function[15]. The Secretary of State must obtain HMRC's consent before making such regulations or making arrangements under head (d)[16].

Information disclosed under these provisions to the Secretary of State or to a body mentioned in head (c) or (d) above may be passed on to a local housing authority for which it is intended[17]. Information disclosed under these provisions may not otherwise be further disclosed without authorisation from HMRC[18]. Where a person contravenes this provision by disclosing any revenue and customs information relating to a person[19] whose identity is specified in the disclosure or can be deduced from it, the provision of the Commissioners for Revenue and Customs Act 2005 as to wrongful disclosure[20] applies in relation to that disclosure as it applies in relation to a disclosure of such information in contravention of that Act[21].

Rent regulations may include provision for the purpose of ensuring that where a local housing authority is required[22] to charge the maximum rent because of a tenant's failure to provide information or evidence, and the tenant subsequently provides the necessary information or evidence, the rent is changed to what it would have been if that requirement had never applied[23].

1 As to the meaning of 'rent regulations' see PARA 441 note 7.
2 As to the meaning of 'local housing authority' see PARA 11 (definition applied by the Housing and Planning Act 2016 s 91).
3 As to the meaning of 'tenant' see PARA 441 note 5. In the Housing and Planning Act 2016 s 82(1), 'tenant' includes prospective tenant: s 82(4).
4 As to the meaning of 'rent' see PARA 441 note 2.
5 Housing and Planning Act 2016 s 82(1).
6 'The maximum rent' means the rent that a local housing authority is required to charge a high income tenant of the premises under the Housing and Planning Act 2016 s 80 (see PARA 441) (or, if regulations under s 80(3)(a) provide for different rents for people with different incomes, the rent that a person in the highest income bracket would be required to pay): s 82(5).
7 Housing and Planning Act 2016 s 82(2).
8 Housing and Planning Act 2016 s 82(3).
9 See the Housing and Planning Act 2016 s 83(8). As to the Commissioners for Revenue and Customs see INCOME TAXATION vol 58 (2014) PARAS 33–34.
10 As to the meaning of 'tenant' see PARA 441 note 5. In the Housing and Planning Act 2016 s 83, 'tenant' includes prospective tenant: s 83(8).
11 Housing and Planning Act 2016 s 83(1).
12 As to the Secretary of State see PARA 7.
13 Ie under the Housing and Planning Act 2016 s 83(3).
14 Housing and Planning Act 2016 s 83(2).
15 Housing and Planning Act 2016 s 83(3).
16 Housing and Planning Act 2016 s 83(4).
17 Housing and Planning Act 2016 s 83(5).
18 Housing and Planning Act 2016 s 83(6).
19 'Revenue and customs information relating to a person' has the meaning given by the Commissioners for Revenue and Customs Act 2005 s 19(2) (see INCOME TAXATION vol 59 (2014) PARA 2325 note 5): Housing and Planning Act 2016 s 83(8).
20 Ie the Commissioners for Revenue and Customs Act 2005 s 19: see INCOME TAXATION vol 59 (2014) PARA 2325.
21 Housing and Planning Act 2016 s 83(7). The text refers to contravention of the Commissioners for Revenue and Customs Act 2005 s 20(9): see INCOME TAXATION vol 59 (2014) PARA 2325.
22 Ie by the Housing and Planning Act 2016 s 82(2): see the text to notes 6–7.
23 Housing and Planning Act 2016 s 84(2).

443. Changing rents. Rent regulations[1] may give a local housing authority[2] power to change the rent[3] payable under a tenancy[4] for the purpose of complying with the regulations[5]. Rent regulations may make provision about the procedure for changing rent to comply with the regulations (whether the change is made using a power given by such regulations or otherwise)[6]. Regulations made under the power to provide for procedure may, in particular: (1) make provision about the review of decisions to increase rent; (2) give rights of appeal to the First-tier Tribunal and amend existing rights of appeal[7]. Regulations under these provisions may amend any provision made by or under an Act passed before the Housing and Planning Act 2016[8] or in the same Session[9].

1 As to the meaning of 'rent regulations' see PARA 441 note 7.
2 As to the meaning of 'local housing authority' see PARA 11 (definition applied by the Housing and Planning Act 2016 s 91).
3 As to the meaning of 'rent' see PARA 441 note 2.
4 'Tenancy' includes a licence to occupy: Housing and Planning Act 2016 s 91.

5 Housing and Planning Act 2016 s 85(1).
6 Housing and Planning Act 2016 s 85(2).
7 Housing and Planning Act 2016 s 85(3). As to the First-Tier Tribunal see PARA 36 et seq; and COURTS AND TRIBUNALS vol 24 (2010) PARA 864 et seq.
8 The Housing and Planning Act 2016 was passed on 12 May 2016.
9 Housing and Planning Act 2016 s 85(4).

444. Payment and provision of information to Secretary of State. Rent regulations[1] may require a local housing authority[2] to make a payment or payments to the Secretary of State[3] in respect of any estimated increase in rental income because of the regulations[4]. The amount of a payment is to be calculated in accordance with the regulations[5]. The regulations may provide for deductions to be made to reflect the administrative costs of local authorities in implementing the regulations[6]. The regulations may provide for interest to be charged in the event of late payment[7]. The regulations may provide for assumptions to be made in making a calculation, whether or not those assumptions are, or are likely to be, borne out by events[8]. The regulations may make provision about how and when payments are to be made including, in particular, provision for payments by instalment[9].

Rent regulations may give the Secretary of State a power to require a local housing authority to provide information in connection with the regulations[10].

1 As to the meaning of 'rent regulations' see PARA 441 note 7.
2 As to the meaning of 'local housing authority' see PARA 11 (definition applied by the Housing and Planning Act 2016 s 91).
3 As to the Secretary of State see PARA 7.
4 Housing and Planning Act 2016 s 86(1).
5 Housing and Planning Act 2016 s 86(2).
6 Housing and Planning Act 2016 s 86(3).
7 Housing and Planning Act 2016 s 86(4).
8 Housing and Planning Act 2016 s 86(5).
9 Housing and Planning Act 2016 s 86(6).
10 Housing and Planning Act 2016 s 87.

445. Policies for high income social tenants. A private registered provider of social housing[1] that has a policy about levels of rent[2] for high income[3] social tenants in England must publish that policy[4]. The policy must include provision for requesting reviews of, or appealing, decisions under the policy[5].

The Commissioners for Her Majesty's Revenue and Customs ('HMRC')[6] may disclose information for the purpose of enabling a private registered provider of social housing to apply any relevant[7] policy about levels of rent for high income social tenants[8] in England[9]. The information may only be disclosed to: (1) the private registered provider of social housing; (2) the Secretary of State[10] for the purposes of passing the information to registered providers; (3) a public body that has been given the function of passing information between HMRC and registered providers by regulations[11]; or (4) a body with which the Secretary of State has made arrangements for the passing of information between HMRC and registered providers[12].

The Secretary of State may by regulations: (a) give a public body the function mentioned in head (3); and (b) make provision about the carrying out of that function[13]. The Secretary of State must obtain HMRC's consent before making such regulations or making arrangements under head (4)[14].

Information disclosed under these provisions to the Secretary of State or to a body mentioned in head (3) or (4) above may be passed on to a registered provider for which it is intended[15]. Information disclosed under these provisions may not otherwise be further disclosed without authorisation from HMRC[16]. Where a person contravenes this provision by disclosing any revenue and customs information relating to a person[17] whose identity is specified in the disclosure or can be deduced from it, the provision of the Commissioners for Revenue and Customs Act 2005 as to wrongful disclosure[18] applies in relation to that disclosure as it applies in relation to a disclosure of such information in contravention of that Act[19].

1 As to private registered providers of social housing and as to the meaning of 'registered provider' see PARA 53.
2 As to the meaning of 'rent' see PARA 441 note 2.
3 As to the meaning of 'high income' see PARA 441 note 4.
4 Housing and Planning Act 2016 s 89(1).
5 Housing and Planning Act 2016 s 89(2).
6 See the Housing and Planning Act 2016 s 90(8). As to the Commissioners for Revenue and Customs see INCOME TAXATION vol 58 (2014) PARAS 33–34.
7 'Relevant', in relation to a private registered provider's policy about levels of rent for high income social tenants in England, means a policy that: (1) has been published as required by the Housing and Planning Act 2016 s 89; and (2) complies with any requirements imposed under s 89(2): s 90(8). See the text to notes 1–5.
8 As to the meaning of 'tenant' see PARA 441 note 5. In the Housing and Planning Act 2016 s 90, 'tenant' includes prospective tenant: s 90(8).
9 Housing and Planning Act 2016 s 90(1).
10 As to the Secretary of State see PARA 7.
11 Ie under the Housing and Planning Act 2016 s 90(3).
12 Housing and Planning Act 2016 s 90(2).
13 Housing and Planning Act 2016 s 90(3).
14 Housing and Planning Act 2016 s 90(4).
15 Housing and Planning Act 2016 s 90(5).
16 Housing and Planning Act 2016 s 90(6).
17 'Revenue and customs information relating to a person' has the meaning given by the Commissioners for Revenue and Customs Act 2005 s 19(2) (see INCOME TAXATION vol 59 (2014) PARA 2325 note 5): Housing and Planning Act 2016 s 90(8).
18 Ie the Commissioners for Revenue and Customs Act 2005 s 19: see INCOME TAXATION vol 59 (2014) PARA 2325.
19 Housing and Planning Act 2016 s 90(7). The text refers to contravention of the Commissioners for Revenue and Customs Act 2005 s 20(9): see INCOME TAXATION vol 59 (2014) PARA 2325.

(iii) Consultation and Provision of Information

A. CONSULTATION

(A) Consultation relating to Housing Management

446. Consultation with respect to management. The appropriate national authority[1] may make regulations for imposing requirements on a local housing authority[2] to consult tenants[3], or to consider representations made to the authority by tenants, with respect to the exercise of its management functions[4] (including proposals as to the exercise of those functions), in relation to any of the authority's houses[5] or other land held for a related purpose[6]. The regulations may include provision requiring a local housing authority to consult tenants, or consider representations made by tenants, with respect to:

(1)   the terms of a written specification to be prepared by the authority of functions proposed to be exercised by the authority or another person;
(2)   a proposal of the authority to exercise management functions itself;
(3)   any person whom the authority proposes to invite to submit a bid to exercise any of its management functions;

(4)   the standards of service for the time being achieved by the authority or (as the case may be) the person with whom the authority has entered into a management agreement[7];

(5)   a proposal to enforce the standards of service required by a management agreement[8].

The requirements imposed on a local housing authority by the regulations may include provision with respect to:

(a)   the tenants to be consulted or whose representations are to be considered;

(b)   the means by which consultation is to be effected (including the arrangements to be made for tenants to consider the matters on which they have been consulted);

(c)   the arrangements to be made for tenants to make representations to the authority;

(d)   the action to be taken by the authority where representations are made[9].

The regulations may include provision:

(i)   requiring a local housing authority to consult representatives of tenants, or to consider representations made to the authority by such representatives, as well as, or instead of, the tenants themselves[10];

(ii)   for particular questions arising under them to be determined by a local housing authority on which they impose requirements[11].

1   Ie the Secretary of State or, where statutory functions have been transferred in relation to Wales, the Welsh Ministers: see PARA 7.
2   As to the meaning of 'local housing authority' see PARA 11.
3   As to the meaning of 'tenant' see PARA 31 note 3.
4   References for these purposes to the management functions of a local housing authority in relation to houses or land must be construed in the same way as references to any such functions in the Housing Act 1985 s 27 (see PARA 457): s 27BA(10) (s 27BA added by the Housing Act 1996 s 222, Sch 18 para 3(1), (2)).
5   As to the meaning of 'house' see PARA 405 note 6.
6   Housing Act 1985 s 27BA(1) (as added: see note 4). Nothing in s 27BA(2)–(5) (see the text and notes 7–11) may be taken as prejudicing the generality of s 27BA(1): s 27BA(6) (as so added). Regulations under s 27BA may make different provision with respect to different cases or descriptions of case, including different provision for different areas; may contain such incidental, supplementary or transitional provisions as appear to the appropriate national authority to be necessary or expedient; and must be made by statutory instrument subject to annulment in pursuance of a resolution of either House of Parliament or of the National Assembly for Wales: s 27BA(7) (as so added). Except as otherwise provided by the regulations: (1) in the case of secure tenants, the provisions of the regulations apply in place of the provisions of s 105 (consultation on matters of housing management: see LANDLORD AND TENANT vol 63 (2016) PARA 1114); and (2) in the case of introductory tenants, the provisions of the regulations apply in place of the provisions of the Housing Act 1996 s 137 (consultation on matters of housing management: see LANDLORD AND TENANT vol 63 (2016) PARA 1114): Housing Act 1985 s 27BA(8), (9) (as so added). The provisions of the regulations are, however, themselves disapplied where a local housing authority enters into a management agreement with a tenant management organisation, unless otherwise provided by regulations under s 27AB: see s 27AB(7)(b)(i); and PARA 459 note 15.
7   As to management agreements see PARA 457.
8   Housing Act 1985 s 27BA(2) (as added: see note 4).
9   Housing Act 1985 s 27BA(3) (as added: see note 4). See also the Housing (Right to Manage) (England) Regulations 2012, SI 2012/1821, reg 12 (see PARA 462); and, in relation to houses and authorities in Wales, the Housing (Right to Manage) Regulations 1994, SI 1994/627, reg 3; and PARA 467.
10 Housing Act 1985 s 27BA(4) (as added: see note 4). Accordingly, references in s 27BA(1)–(3) to tenants include references to such representatives: s 27BA(4) (as so added).
11 Housing Act 1985 s 27BA(5) (as added: see note 4).

447. Consultation on matters of housing management: secure tenancies. A landlord authority[1] must maintain such arrangements as it considers appropriate to enable those of its secure tenants[2] who are likely to be substantially affected by a matter of housing management[3] to which these provisions apply[4]:

(1)   to be informed of the authority's proposals in respect of the matter; and

(2)   to make their views known to the authority within a specified period;

and the authority must, before making any decision on the matter, consider any representations made to it in accordance with those arrangements[5].

A landlord authority must publish details of the arrangements which it so makes, and a copy of the documents so published must:

(a)   be made available at the authority's principal office for inspection at all reasonable hours, without charge, by members of the public; and

(b)   be given, on payment of a reasonable fee, to any member of the public who asks for one[6].

A landlord authority which is a private registered provider of social housing[7] or a registered social landlord[8] must, instead of complying with head (a) above, send a copy of any document so published:

(i)   to the relevant authority[9]; and

(ii)   to the council of any district[10], Welsh county or county borough[11] or London borough[12] in which there are dwelling houses let by the landlord authority under secure tenancies;

and a council to which a copy is so sent must make it available at its principal office for inspection at all reasonable hours, without charge, by members of the public[13].

Local housing authorities' powers to enter into management agreements with arm's length management organisations and tenant management organisations, and the relevant consultation requirements, are discussed elsewhere in this title[14].

1   'Landlord authority' means: (1) a local housing authority; (2) a private registered provider of social housing other than a co-operative housing association; (3) a registered social landlord other than a co-operative housing association; (4) a housing trust which is a charity; (5) a development corporation; (6) a Mayoral development corporation; (7) a housing action trust; or (8) an urban development corporation, other than an authority in respect of which an exemption certificate has been issued: Housing Act 1985 s 114(1) (amended by the Housing Act 1988 s 83(4); the Government of Wales Act 1998 ss 129, 152, Sch 15 para 10, Sch 18 Pt IV; the Localism Act 2011 s 222, Sch 22 paras 9, 12; and by SI 1996/2325 and SI 2010/866). The appropriate national authority may, on an application duly made by the authority concerned, issue an exemption certificate to a development corporation, a housing action trust or an urban development corporation, if satisfied that it has transferred, or otherwise disposed of, at least three-quarters of the dwellings which have at any time before the making of the application been vested in it: Housing Act 1985 s 114(2) (amended by the Housing Act 1988 83(4); and the Government of Wales Act 1998 Sch 15 para 10, Sch 18 Pt IV). The application must be in such form and must be accompanied by such information as the appropriate national authority may, either generally or in relation to a particular case, direct: Housing Act 1985 s 114(3). As to the appropriate national authority and the transfer of functions under the Housing Act 1985, so far as exercisable in relation to Wales, to the Welsh Ministers see PARA 7.
      As to the meaning of 'local housing authority' see PARA 11; as to private registered providers of social housing see PARA 53; and as to registered social landlords see PARAS 4, 166 et seq. As to the meaning of 'co-operative housing association' and as to housing associations see PARA 13. As to the meaning of 'development corporation' see PARA 12; as to the meaning of 'housing action trust' see PARA 12; and as to the meaning of 'urban development corporation' see PARA 12. As to the meaning of 'charity' see the Charities Act 2011 s 1; and CHARITIES vol 8 (2015) PARA 1. As to Mayoral development corporations see the Localism Act 2011 s 198; and LONDON GOVERNMENT vol 71 (2013) PARA 323.

2   For these purposes, secure tenants include demoted tenants, and secure tenancies include demoted tenancies, within the meaning of the Housing Act 1996 s 143A (see LANDLORD AND TENANT vol 63 (2016) PARA 1118): Housing Act 1985 s 105(7) (added by the Anti-social Behaviour Act

2003 s 14(5), Sch 1 para 2(1), (2)). As to the meaning of 'secure tenancy' generally see LANDLORD AND TENANT vol 63 (2016) PARAS 1037–1038; and as to the meaning of 'tenant' see PARA 31 note 3.

3 For these purposes, a matter is one of housing management if, in the opinion of the landlord authority, it relates to: (1) the management, maintenance, improvement or demolition of dwelling houses let by the authority under secure tenancies; or (2) the provision of services or amenities in connection with such dwelling houses; but not so far as it relates to the rent payable under a secure tenancy or to charges for services or facilities provided by the authority: Housing Act 1985 s 105(2). In the case of a landlord authority which is a local housing authority, the reference in s 105(2) to the provision of services or amenities is a reference only to the provision of services or amenities by the authority acting in its capacity as landlord of the dwelling houses concerned: s 105(4). For the purposes of Pt IV (ss 79–117) a dwelling house may be a house or a part of a house: s 112(1). Land let together with a dwelling house is to be treated for the purposes of Pt IV as part of the dwelling house unless the land is agricultural land (as defined in the General Rate Act 1967 s 26(3)(a): see LANDLORD AND TENANT vol 63 (2016) PARA 712) exceeding two acres: Housing Act 1985 s 112(2). As to the meaning of 'improvement' see LANDLORD AND TENANT vol 63 (2016) PARA 1075; and as to the meaning of 'local housing authority' see PARA 11.

4 The Housing Act 1985 s 105 applies to matters of housing management which, in the opinion of the landlord authority, represent (1) a new programme of maintenance, improvement or demolition; or (2) a change in the practice or policy of the authority, and are likely substantially to affect either its secure tenants as a whole or a group of them who form a distinct social group or occupy dwelling houses which constitute a distinct class, whether by reference to the kind of dwelling house, or the housing estate or other larger area in which they are situated: s 105(3).

5 Housing Act 1985 s 105(1). Section 105 does not, however, apply to a tenancy when the interest of the landlord belongs to a co-operative housing association: s 109. As to the meaning of 'co-operative housing association' and as to housing associations see PARA 13. In relation to a disposal to which s 106A, Sch 3A (see PARAS 448–451) applies, the provisions of Sch 3A apply in place of the provisions of s 105 (see s 106A(2); and PARA 448 note 1); and in relation to the approval or variation of a redevelopment scheme the provisions of s 84(2)(b), Sch 2 Pt V para 2 apply in place of the provisions of s 105 (see Sch 2 Pt V para 2(3)).

Section 105 does not require an authority to inform every tenant, only to ensure that the tenants are able to be informed of its decisions: *R v Brent London Borough Council, ex p Morris* (1997) 30 HLR 324, CA. There is no legal requirement that a local authority must set out the case against its proposals in its publicity material; the obligation in the Housing Act 1985 s 105(1) is to inform the relevant group of the authority's proposals and not to canvass the disadvantages of its proposals: see *R (on the application of Beale) v Camden London Borough Council* [2004] EWHC 6 (Admin), [2004] HLR 917, [2004] All ER (D) 52 (Jan).

6 Housing Act 1985 s 105(5). See also note 5.

7 As to private registered providers of social housing see PARA 53.

8 As to registered social landlords see PARAS 4, 166 et seq.

9 As to the relevant authority see PARA 8.

10 As to the districts in England and their councils see LOCAL GOVERNMENT vol 69 (2009) PARA 17 et seq.

11 As to the counties and county boroughs in Wales and their councils see LOCAL GOVERNMENT vol 69 (2009) PARA 37 et seq.

12 As to London boroughs see LONDON GOVERNMENT vol 71 (2013) PARA 16 et seq.

13 Housing Act 1985 s 105(6) (amended by the Local Government (Wales) Act 1994 s 22(2), Sch 8 para 5(7); the Government of Wales Act 1998 s 140, Sch 16 para 5; and by SI 1996/2325 and SI 2010/866).

14 See the Housing Act 1985 ss 27, 27AB–27BA; the Housing (Right to Manage) (England) Regulations 2008, SI 2008/2361 (revoked subject to transitional provisions); the Housing (Right to Manage) (England) Regulations 2012, SI 2012/1821; and PARA 457 et seq.

(B) Consultation before Disposal to Private Sector Landlord

448. Consultation before disposal; in general. The following provisions[1] have effect with respect to the duties:

(1) of a local authority[2] proposing to dispose of dwelling houses[3] subject to secure tenancies[4] or introductory tenancies[5]; and

(2) of the appropriate national authority in considering whether to give its consent to such a disposal[6],

to have regard to the views of tenants[7] liable as a result of the disposal to cease to be secure tenants or introductory tenants[8]. Such disposals are sometimes referred to as 'large-scale voluntary transfers'. These provisions do not, however, apply in relation to any disposal of an interest in land by a local authority if:

(a)   the interest has been acquired by the authority, whether compulsorily or otherwise, following the making of an order for compulsory purchase under any enactment, other than under the statutory provision relating to the acquisition of land for clearance[9];

(b)   the order provides that the interest is being acquired for the purpose of disposal to a private registered provider of social housing[10] or a registered social landlord[11]; and

(c)   such a disposal is made within one year of the acquisition[12].

The disposals to which those provisions apply are disposals by a local authority of an interest in land as a result of which a secure tenant or an introductory tenant of the authority will become the tenant of a private sector landlord[13]. The grant of an option which, if exercised, would result in a secure tenant or an introductory tenant of a local authority becoming the tenant of a private sector landlord is treated as a disposal of the interest which is the subject of the option[14].

Disposals which are proposed by a tenant group are discussed elsewhere in this title[15].

1   Ie the provisions of the Housing Act 1985 s 106A, Sch 3A: see the text and notes 2–12; and PARAS 449–451. In relation to a disposal to which Sch 3A applies, the provisions of Sch 3A apply in place of the provisions of s 105 (consultation on matters of housing management: see PARA 447) in the case of secure tenants and the Housing Act 1996 s 137 (consultation on matters of housing management: see LANDLORD AND TENANT vol 63 (2016) PARA 1114) in the case of introductory tenants: Housing Act 1985 s 106A(2) (s 106A(1), (2) added by the Housing and Planning Act 1986 s 6(1); amended by SI 1997/74).
2   As to the meaning of 'local authority' see PARA 12.
3   As to the meaning of 'dwelling house' see PARA 447 note 3.
4   As to the meaning of 'secure tenancy' see LANDLORD AND TENANT vol 63 (2016) PARA 1037.
5   As to the meaning of 'introductory tenancy' see LANDLORD AND TENANT vol 63 (2016) PARA 1043.
6   References for these purposes to the appropriate national authority's consent to a disposal are to the consent required by the Housing Act 1985 s 32 or s 43 (requirement of consent for disposal of houses or land held for housing purposes, which may be granted either generally or in relation to specific cases: see PARAS 522, 531): see Sch 3A para 2(3) (Sch 3A added by the Housing and Planning Act 1986 s 6(2), (3), Sch 1). As to the appropriate national authority and the transfer of functions under the Housing Act 1985, so far as exercisable in relation to Wales, to the Welsh Ministers see PARA 7.
    The appropriate national authority's consent to a disposal is not invalidated by a failure on its part or that of the local authority to comply with the requirements of the Housing Act 1985 Sch 3A: see Sch 3A para 6 (as so added).
7   As to the meaning of 'tenant' see PARA 31 note 3.
8   Housing Act 1985 s 106A(1) (as added and amended: see note 1). Section 106A does not, however, apply to a tenancy when the interest of the landlord belongs to a co-operative housing association: s 109. As to the meaning of 'co-operative housing association' and as to housing associations see PARA 13.
9   Ie other than under the Housing Act 1985 s 290: see PARA 633.
10 As to private registered providers of social housing see PARA 53.
11 For these purposes, 'registered social landlord' has the same meaning as in the Housing Act 1996 Pt I (ss A1–64) (see PARAS 4, 166 et seq): Housing Act 1985 s 106A(4) (s 106A(3), (4) added by the Housing Act 1996 Sch 18 para 23).
12 Housing Act 1985 s 106A(3) (as added (see note 11); amended by SI 2010/866).
13 Housing Act 1985 Sch 3A para 1(1) (as added (see note 6); Sch 3A para 1(1), (2) amended by SI 1997/74). For these purposes, 'private sector landlord' means a person other than an authority or body within the Housing Act 1985 s 80 (see LANDLORD AND TENANT vol 63 (2016) PARA 1037): Sch 3A para 1(4) (as so added).
    Where a disposal of land by a local authority is in part a disposal to which Sch 3A applies, the provisions of Sch 3A apply to that part as to a separate disposal: Sch 3A para 1(3) (as so added).

14 Housing Act 1985 Sch 3A para 1(2) (as added and amended: see notes 6, 13).
15 See the Housing Act 1985 s 34A; and PARA 525.

449. Application for the appropriate national authority's consent. The appropriate national authority may not entertain an application for its consent to a disposal[1] unless the local authority[2] certifies either:

    (1)   that the statutory requirements as to consultation[3] have been complied with; or

    (2)   that those requirements as to consultation have been complied with except in relation to tenants[4] expected to have vacated the dwelling house[5] in question before the disposal;

and the certificate must be accompanied by a copy of the notices given[6] by the local authority[7].

Where the certificate is in the latter form, the appropriate national authority may not determine the application until the local authority certifies as regards the tenants not originally consulted:

    (a)   that they have vacated the dwelling house in question; or

    (b)   that the requirements as to consultation have been complied with;

and a certificate under head (b) above must be accompanied by a copy of the notices given[8] by the local authority[9].

1 Ie a disposal to which the Housing Act 1985 s 106A, Sch 3A applies: see PARA 448. As to the meaning of references to the appropriate national authority's consent to a disposal see PARA 448 note 6. As to the appropriate national authority and the transfer of functions under the Housing Act 1985, so far as exercisable in relation to Wales, to the Welsh Ministers see PARA 7.
2 As to the meaning of 'local authority' see PARA 12.
3 Ie the requirements of the Housing Act 1985 Sch 3A para 3: see PARA 450.
4 As to the meaning of 'tenant' see PARA 31 note 3.
5 As to the meaning of 'dwelling house' see PARA 447 note 3.
6 Ie in accordance with the Housing Act 1985 Sch 3A para 3: see PARA 450.
7 Housing Act 1985 Sch 3A para 2(1) (Sch 3A added by the Housing and Planning Act 1986 s 6(2), (3), Sch 1).
8 See note 6.
9 Housing Act 1985 Sch 3A para 2(2) (as added: see note 7).

450. Requirements as to consultation. The statutory requirements as to consultation[1] are as follows[2]. The local authority[3] must serve a notice in writing on the tenant[4] informing him of:

    (1)   such details of its proposal as the authority considers appropriate, but including the identity of the person to whom the disposal is to be made;

    (2)   the likely consequences of the disposal for the tenant; and

    (3)   the effect of the statutory provisions as to consultation[5] and, in the case of a secure tenant[6], of the statutory preservation of the right to buy on a disposal to a private sector landlord[7],

and informing him that he may, within such reasonable period as may be specified in the notice, make representations to the local authority[8].

The local authority must consider any representations made to it within that period and must serve a further written notice on the tenant informing him:

    (a)   of any significant changes in the authority's proposal; and

    (b)   that he may within such period as is specified, which must be at least 28 days after the service of the notice, communicate to the appropriate national authority his objection to the proposal,

and, in the case of a secure tenant, informing him of the effect of the statutory provision[9] requiring consent to be withheld if the majority of the tenants are opposed[10]. When a notice has been so served, the local authority must arrange a ballot of the tenants[11] to establish whether or not the tenants wish the disposal to proceed[12]. After the ballot has been held the local authority must serve a notice on each tenant, whether or not he voted in the ballot, informing him:

(i)   of the ballot result; and

(ii)   if the local authority intends to proceed with the disposal, that he may within 28 days after the service of the notice make representations to the appropriate national authority[13].

The appropriate national authority may require the local authority to carry out such further consultation with its tenants, and to give the appropriate national authority such information as to the results of that consultation, as the appropriate national authority may direct[14].

1   Ie as referred to in the Housing Act 1985 Sch 3A para 2: see PARA 449.
2   Housing Act 1985 Sch 3A para 3(1) (Sch 3A added by the Housing and Planning Act 1986 s 6(2), (3), Sch 1).
    The appropriate national authority (referred to in the Housing Act 1985 Sch 3A para 5A as 'the appropriate person') must give guidance to local authorities about complying with the requirements of Sch 3A para 3: see Sch 3A para 5A(1), (6) (Sch 3A para 5A added by the Housing and Regeneration Act 2008 s 294(1), (4)). For these purposes, references to giving guidance include references to giving guidance by varying existing guidance: Housing Act 1985 Sch 3A para 5A(5) (as so added). The appropriate national authority must publish guidance so given as soon as reasonably practicable after giving it: see Sch 3A para 5A(2) (as so added). Local authorities must, in complying with the requirements of Sch 3A para 3 (see the text and notes 3–13) as to consultation, have regard to the guidance for the time being in force under Sch 3A para 5A: Sch 3A para 5A(3) (as so added). The appropriate national authority may revoke guidance so given: Sch 3A para 5A(4) (as so added). As to the appropriate national authority and the transfer of functions under the Housing Act 1985, so far as exercisable in relation to Wales, to the Welsh Ministers see PARA 7.
    Statutory guidance under Sch 3A para 5A in relation to England was published by the Department for Communities and Local Government in July 2009 and was available, at the date at which this volume states the law, on the department's website at www.gov.uk/government/organisations/department-for-communities-and-local-government.
3   As to the meaning of 'local authority' see PARA 12.
4   As to the meaning of 'tenant' see PARA 31 note 3.
5   Ie the effect of the Housing Act 1985 Sch 3A: see PARAS 448–449; the text and notes 6–12; and PARA 451.
6   As to the meaning of 'secure tenancy' see LANDLORD AND TENANT vol 63 (2016) PARA 1037.
7   Ie the effect of the Housing Act 1985 ss 171A–171H: see PARA 334 et seq. As to the meaning of 'private sector landlord' see PARA 448 note 13.
8   Housing Act 1985 Sch 3A para 3(2) (as added (see note 2); amended by SI 1997/74).
9   Ie the effect of the Housing Act 1985 Sch 3A para 5: see PARA 451.
10 Housing Act 1985 Sch 3A para 3(3) (as added: see note 2). As to the appropriate national authority and the transfer of functions under the Housing Act 1985, so far as exercisable in relation to Wales, to the Welsh Ministers see PARA 7.
11 The local authority must: (1) make arrangements for such person as it considers appropriate to conduct the ballot in such manner as that person considers appropriate; or (2) conduct the ballot itself: Housing Act 1985 Sch 3A para 3(5) (Sch 3A para 3(4)–(6) added by the Housing and Regeneration Act 2008 s 294(1), (2)).
12 Housing Act 1985 Sch 3A para 3(4) (as added: see note 11).
13 Housing Act 1985 Sch 3A para 3(6) (as added: see note 11).
14 Housing Act 1985 Sch 3A para 4 (as added: see note 2).

451.   Consent to be withheld if majority of tenants are opposed. The appropriate national authority may not give its consent to a disposal[1] if the result of a ballot arranged under the relevant statutory provisions[2] shows that a majority of the tenants[3] of the dwelling houses[4] to which the application relates who voted in the ballot do not wish the disposal to proceed[5]. This does not affect the appropriate national authority's general discretion to refuse consent on grounds relating to whether a disposal has the support of the tenants or on any other ground[6].

In making its decision, the appropriate national authority may have regard to any information available to it; and the local authority[7] must give the appropriate national authority such information as to the representations made to that local authority by tenants and others, and other relevant maters, as the appropriate national authority may require[8].

1 As to the meaning of references to the appropriate national authority's consent to a disposal see PARA 448 note 6. As to the appropriate national authority and the transfer of functions under the Housing Act 1985, so far as exercisable in relation to Wales, to the Welsh Ministers see PARA 7.
2 Ie a ballot arranged under the Housing Act 1985 Sch 3A para 3(4): see PARA 450.
3 As to the meaning of 'tenant' see PARA 31 note 3.
4 As to the meaning of 'dwelling house' see PARA 447 note 3.
5 Housing Act 1985 Sch 3A para 5(1) (Sch 3A added by the Housing and Planning Act 1986 s 6(2), (3), Sch 1; the Housing Act 1985 Sch 3A para 5(1) amended by the Housing and Regeneration Act 2008 s 294(1), (3)).
6 Housing Act 1985 Sch 3A para 5(1) (as added: see note 5).
7 As to the meaning of 'local authority' see PARA 12.
8 Housing Act 1985 Sch 3A para 5(2) (as added: see note 5).

B. PROVISION OF INFORMATION

452. Secure tenancies: provision of information. Every body which lets dwelling houses[1] under secure tenancies[2] must from time to time publish information about its secure tenancies, in such form as it considers best suited to explain in simple terms, and so far as it considers appropriate, the effect of:

(1)   the express terms[3] of its secure tenancies;
(2)   the statutory provisions relating to secure tenancies[4]; and
(3)   the statutory provisions relating to a landlord's repairing obligations[5]; and must ensure that, so far as is reasonably practicable, the information so published is kept up to date[6].

The landlord[7] under a secure tenancy must supply the tenant[8] with:

(a)   a copy of the information for secure tenants so published by it; and
(b)   a written statement of the terms of the tenancy, so far as they are neither expressed in the lease[9] or written tenancy agreement, if any, nor implied by law;

and the statement required by head (b) above must be supplied when the secure tenancy arises or as soon as practicable afterwards[10].

A local authority[11] which is the landlord under a secure tenancy must supply the tenant, at least once in every relevant year[12], with a copy of such information relating to the provisions in head (2) and (3) above as was last published by it[13].

Among other new requirements under the Localism Act 2011, local housing authorities in England are to prepare and publish tenancy strategies[14].

1 As to the meaning of 'dwelling house' see PARA 447 note 3.
2 As to the meaning of 'secure tenancy' see LANDLORD AND TENANT vol 63 (2016) PARA 1037.
3 As to the meaning of 'term' see LANDLORD AND TENANT vol 63 (2016) PARA 1039 note 10.
4 Ie the Housing Act 1985 Pt IV (ss 79–117): see PARA 447 et seq; and LANDLORD AND TENANT vol 63 (2016) PARA 1037 et seq.
5 Ie the Landlord and Tenant Act 1985 ss 11–16: see LANDLORD AND TENANT vol 62 (2016) PARAS 300–307.
6 Housing Act 1985 s 104(1) (amended by the Housing Act 2004 ss 189(2), 266, Sch 16). The Housing Act 1985 s 104 does not, however, apply to a tenancy when the interest of the landlord belongs to a co-operative housing association: s 109. As to the meaning of 'co-operative housing association' and as to housing associations see PARA 13.
7 As to the meaning of 'landlord' see PARA 31 note 3.
8 As to the meaning of 'tenant' see PARA 31 note 3.
9 As to the meaning of 'lease' see PARA 31 note 3.
10 Housing Act 1985 s 104(2) (amended by the Housing Act 1996 s 141(1), Sch 14 para 2). See also note 6.
11 As to the meaning of 'local authority' see PARA 12.

12 For these purposes, 'relevant year' means any period of 12 months beginning with the anniversary of the date of such publication: Housing Act 1985 s 104(3) (added by the Leasehold Reform, Housing and Urban Development Act 1993 s 123).

13 Housing Act 1985 s 104(3) (as added: see note 12). See also note 7.

14 See the Localism Act 2011 ss 150, 151; and PARA 421.

453. Disclosure of information as to orders etc in respect of anti-social behaviour. Any person may disclose relevant information[1] to a landlord under a secure tenancy[2] if the information is disclosed for the purpose of enabling the landlord:

(1)   to decide whether either of the specified provisions (set out below) of the Housing Act 1985[3] can be invoked in relation to the tenant under the tenancy[4]; or

(2)   to take any appropriate action in relation to the tenant in reliance on either of those provisions[5].

The specified provisions for these purposes are:

(a)   the provision allowing the landlord to withhold consent to an assignment by way of mutual exchange where an order is in force or an application is pending in connection with anti-social behaviour[6]; and

(b)   the provision suspending the landlord's obligation to complete a purchase in pursuance of the right to buy[7] while an application is pending in connection with such behaviour[8].

1 For these purposes, 'relevant information' means information relating to any order or application relevant for the purposes of either of the provisions mentioned in the Housing Act 2004 s 194(2) (see heads (a)–(b) in the text), including (in particular) information identifying the person in respect of whom any such order or application has been made: s 194(3)(a).

2 As to the meaning of 'secure tenancy' see LANDLORD AND TENANT vol 63 (2016) PARA 1037 (definition applied by the Housing Act 2004 s 194(3)(b)).

3 Ie the provisions mentioned in the Housing Act 2004 s 194(2): see heads (a)–(b) in the text.

4 For these purposes, any reference to the tenant under a secure tenancy is, in relation to a joint tenancy, a reference to any of the joint tenants: Housing Act 2004 s 194(3)(c).

5 Housing Act 2004 s 194(1).

6 Ie the Housing Act 1985 Sch 3, Ground 2A: see LANDLORD AND TENANT vol 63 (2016) PARA 1067 head (4).

7 Ie the Housing Act 2004 s 138(2B): see PARA 291.

8 Housing Act 2004 s 194(2).

454. Information about housing allocation. A landlord authority[1] must publish a summary of its rules on the following matters:

(1)   for determining priority as between applicants in the allocation of its housing accommodation; and

(2)   governing cases where secure tenants[2] wish to move, whether or not by way of exchange of dwelling houses[3], to other dwelling houses let under secure tenancies by that authority or another body[4].

A landlord authority must:

(a)   maintain a set of such rules and of the rules which it has laid down governing the procedure to be followed in allocating its housing accommodation; and

(b)   make them available at its principal office for inspection at all reasonable hours, without charge, by members of the public[5].

A landlord authority which is a private registered provider of social housing or a registered social landlord must, however, instead of complying with head (b) above, send a set of the rules referred to in head (a) above:

(i)   to the relevant authority[6]; and

(ii)   to the council of any district[7], Welsh county or county borough[8] or London borough[9] in which there are dwelling houses let or to be let by the landlord authority under secure tenancies;

and a council to which a set of the rules is so sent must make it available at its principal office for inspection at all reasonable hours, without charge, by members of the public[10].

At the request of a person who has applied to it for housing accommodation, a landlord authority must make available to him, at all reasonable times and without charge, details of the particulars which he has given to the authority about himself and his family and which the authority has recorded as being relevant to his application for accommodation[11].

1   As to the meaning of 'landlord authority' see PARA 447 note 1.
2   As to the meaning of 'secure tenancy' see LANDLORD AND TENANT vol 63 (2016) PARA 1037.
3   As to the meaning of 'dwelling house' see PARA 447 note 3.
4   Housing Act 1985 s 106(1). A copy of the summary so published must be given without charge to any member of the public who asks for one: s 106(4).

     The provisions of s 106 do not, however, apply to a landlord authority which is a local housing authority so far as they impose requirements corresponding to those to which such an authority is subject under the Housing Act 1996 s 168 (provision of information about allocation schemes: see PARA 429): Housing Act 1985 s 106(6) (added by the Housing Act 1996 s 173, Sch 16 para 1; and amended by the Homelessness Act 2002 s 18(1), (2), Sch 1 para 1, Sch 2). Nor does the Housing Act 1985 s 106 apply to a tenancy when the interest to the landlord belongs to a co-operative housing association: s 109.
5   Housing Act 1985 s 106(2). A copy of the set of rules so maintained must be given on payment of a reasonable fee to any member of the public who asks for one: s 106(4). See also note 4.
6   As to the relevant authority see PARA 8.
7   As to the districts in England and their councils see LOCAL GOVERNMENT vol 69 (2009) PARA 17 et seq.
8   As to the counties and county boroughs in Wales and their councils see LOCAL GOVERNMENT vol 69 (2009) PARA 37 et seq.
9   As to London boroughs see LONDON GOVERNMENT vol 71 (2013) PARA 16 et seq.
10   Housing Act 1985 s 106(3) (amended by the Local Government (Wales) Act 1994 s 22(2), Sch 8 para 5(7); the Government of Wales Act 1998 s 140, Sch 16 para 5; and by SI 1996/2325 and SI 2010/866). See also note 4.
11   Housing Act 1985 s 106(5). See also note 4.

C.   HEATING CHARGES

455. Heating charges. The following provisions apply to secure tenants[1] of dwelling houses[2] to which a heating authority[3] supplies heat produced at a heating installation[4].

The appropriate national authority may by regulations[5] require heating authorities to adopt such methods for determining heating charges[6] payable by such tenants as will secure that the proportion of heating costs[7] borne by each of those tenants is no greater than is reasonable[8].

The appropriate national authority may also by regulations make provision for entitling such tenants, subject to and in accordance with the regulations, to require the heating authority:

(1)   to give them, in such form as may by prescribed by the regulations, such information as to heating charges and heating costs as may be so prescribed; and

(2)   where such information has been given, to afford them reasonable facilities for inspecting the accounts, receipts and other documents supporting the information and for taking copies or extracts from them[9].

The statutory provisions relating to information about heating charges to be provided to secure tenants[10] apply in relation to introductory tenancies as they apply in relation to secure tenancies[11].

1 As to the meaning of 'secure tenancy' see LANDLORD AND TENANT vol 63 (2016) PARA 1037; and as to the meaning of 'tenant' see PARA 31 note 3.
2 As to the meaning of 'dwelling house' see PARA 447 note 3.
3 For these purposes, 'heating authority' means a housing authority or housing action trust which operates a heating installation and supplies to premises heat produced at the installation; 'heating installation' means a generating station or other installation for producing heat; and references to heat produced at an installation include steam produced from, and air and water heated by, heat so produced: Housing Act 1985 s 108(5)(a)–(c) (amended by the Housing Act 1988 s 83(1), (3)). As to the meaning of 'housing authority' see PARA 12. As to the meaning of 'housing action trust' see PARA 12 head (6).
4 Housing Act 1985 s 108(1). Section 108 does not, however, apply to a tenancy when the interest of the landlord belongs to a co-operative housing association: s 109. As to the meaning of 'co-operative housing association' and as to housing associations see PARA 13.
5 Regulations under the Housing Act 1985 s 108 must be made by statutory instrument and may: (1) make different provision with respect to different cases or descriptions of case, including different provision for different areas; (2) make such procedural, incidental, supplementary and transitional provision as appears to the appropriate national authority to be necessary or expedient; and may in particular provide for any question arising under the regulations to be referred to and determined by the county court: see s 108(4). If made by the Secretary of State, the statutory instrument by which the regulations are made is subject to annulment in pursuance of a resolution of either House of Parliament: see s 108(4). As to the appropriate national authority, the Secretary of State and the transfer of functions under the Housing Act 1985, so far as exercisable in relation to Wales, to the Welsh Ministers see PARA 7.
6 For these purposes, 'heating charge' means an amount payable to a heating authority in respect of heat produced at a heating installation and supplied to premises, including in the case of heat supplied to premises let by the authority such an amount payable as part of the rent: Housing Act 1985 s 108(5)(d).
7 For these purposes, 'heating costs' means expenses incurred by a heating authority in operating a heating installation: Housing Act 1985 s 108(5)(e).
8 Housing Act 1985 s 108(2). At the date at which this title states the law, no such regulations had been made and none had effect as if so made. See also notes 4–5.
9 Housing Act 1985 s 108(3). See also notes 4–5, 8.
10 Ie the Housing Act 1985 s 108: see the text and notes 1–9.
11 Housing Act 1985 s 111A (added by SI 1997/74). As to the meaning of 'introductory tenancy' see LANDLORD AND TENANT vol 63 (2016) PARA 1043.

(iv) Repairs

456. In general. A local authority or other public sector landlord will almost invariably have a responsibility for repairs to, and maintenance of, the dwelling which has been let. This is because of the provisions in the Landlord and Tenant Act 1985 under which the landlord is responsible for keeping in repair and proper working order the structure and the exterior of the dwelling let[1], as well as certain installations for the supply of gas and electricity[2] and certain other matters[3].

All these matters are considered elsewhere in this work[4].

In addition, local authorities now have duties and rights to take enforcement action under the Housing Health and Safety Rating System ('HHSRS') provided for by the Housing Act 2004, based on categories of hazards to be assessed by prescribed methods[5]. It appears that a local housing authority cannot be forced to use these procedures in relation to its own housing stock[6].

1 See the Landlord and Tenant Act 1985 ss 8, 11–17; and LANDLORD AND TENANT vol 62 (2016) PARA 303 et seq.
2 See the Landlord and Tenant Act 1985 s 11(1); and LANDLORD AND TENANT vol 62 (2016) PARA 303.

3 See the Landlord and Tenant Act 1985 s 11; and LANDLORD AND TENANT vol 62 (2016) PARA 303.
4 See LANDLORD AND TENANT.
5 See PARA 562 et seq. For a commentary see Driscoll *Housing: the New Law* (2007).
6 See *R v Cardiff City Council, ex p Cross* (1982) 81 LGR 105, 6 HLR 1, CA.

(v) Management Agreements

A. IN GENERAL

457. General power to enter into management agreement. The power for local authorities to set up arm's length management organisations ('ALMO's) to manage their housing services was introduced by the Housing Act 1980 and retained in the Housing Act 1985. More recently, the government's decision to encourage local authorities in England to set up ALMOs has resulted in substantial changes to the legislation, with the overall objective of delivering better housing services to council tenants and others, and of providing all social housing tenants with decent homes by 2010. The policy was reaffirmed in the Sustainable Communities Plan in February 2003, and since then there have been further steps taken to improve sustainability.

A local housing authority[1] may agree that another person is to exercise in relation to such of the authority's houses[2] as are specified in the agreement, and any other land so specified which is held for a related purpose, such of the authority's management functions[3] as are so specified[4]. A management agreement[5] must set out the terms on which the authority's functions are exercisable by a manager[6] and must contain such provisions as may be prescribed by regulations made by the appropriate minister[7]. A management agreement may: (1) include provision authorising a manager, with the consent of the authority, to agree that another person is to exercise any management function exercisable by the manager under the agreement; and (2) where a body or association is a manager, provide that the management functions of the body or association under the agreement may be performed by a committee, sub-committee, officer or employee of the body or association[8].

The approval of the appropriate authority[9] is required for the making of any management agreement and the variation of a provision of a management agreement, if the provision is specified, or is of a description specified, by the appropriate authority in giving approval to the making of a management agreement[10]. The appropriate authority may, in giving approval to the making of an agreement: (a) specify a moratorium period[11] and the circumstances in which it is to apply; (b) specify circumstances in which the appropriate authority's approval is not required for the making of a sub-agreement under the agreement[12].

The appropriate authority's approval for the making of an agreement or the variation of such an agreement may be given generally or to a particular local housing authority or description of local housing authority[13]. The appropriate authority's approval may be given in relation to a particular case or description of case, and may be given unconditionally or subject to conditions[14].

Anything done, or not done, by a manager in connection with the exercise (or purported exercise) of a relevant function[15] is to be treated as done, or not done, by the authority, and anything done, or not done, in relation to a manager in connection with the exercise (or purported exercise) of a relevant function is to be treated as done, or not done, in relation to the authority[16]. This does not apply, however, to the extent that a management agreement provides otherwise as between the parties to it, or for the purposes of any criminal proceedings brought in respect of anything done or not done by the manager[17].

A housing co-operative[18] agreement made with a local housing authority which was in force immediately before 7 January 1987 has effect as if made under these provisions, so that, in particular, any terms of the agreement providing for the letting of land to the housing co-operative no longer have effect except in relation to lettings made before that date, and a housing co-operative agreement made with a new town corporation[19] which was in force immediately before that date remains in force notwithstanding that the above provisions do not apply to such authorities[20].

As from a day to be appointed[21], an employee of a housing management body[22] who is authorised[23] by that body for the purposes of the relevant statutory provisions[24] has a right of audience[25] in relation to any proceedings to which those provisions apply and a right to conduct litigation[26] in relation to any such proceedings[27]. Those proceedings are 'relevant housing proceedings'[28] in the County Court that are not excluded by rules of court and are brought: (i) in the name of a local housing authority; and (ii) by the housing management body in the exercise of functions of that local housing authority delegated to that body under a housing management agreement[29].

1   As to the meaning of 'local housing authority' see PARA 11.
2   As to the meaning of 'house' see PARA 405 note 6.
3   References for these purposes to the management functions of a local housing authority in relation to houses or land do not include such functions as may be prescribed by regulations made by the appropriate national authority, but, subject to that, include functions conferred by any statutory provision and the powers and duties of the authority as holder of an estate or interest in the houses or land in question: Housing Act 1985 s 27(16) (s 27 substituted by SI 2003/940; the Housing Act 1985 s 27(16) amended by SI 2010/844). The appropriate national authority is the Secretary of State or, where statutory functions have been transferred in relation to Wales, the Welsh Ministers: see PARA 7. As to the approval of the appropriate national authority see the text and notes 12–14. Regulations under the Housing Act 1985 s 27 may make different provision with respect to different cases or descriptions of case, including different provision for different areas; may contain such incidental, supplementary or transitional provisions as appear to the appropriate national authority to be necessary or expedient; and must be made by statutory instrument subject to annulment in pursuance of, in the case of regulations made by the Secretary of State, a resolution of either House of Parliament and, in the case of regulations made by the Welsh Ministers, a resolution of the National Assembly for Wales: s 27(17) (as so substituted; amended by SI 2010/844).
     In exercise of the power so conferred, the appropriate national authority has made the Housing (Right to Manage) Regulations 1994, SI 1994/627, which came into force on 1 April 1994 (reg 1(1)); and the Housing (Right to Manage) (England) Regulations 2012, SI 2012/1821, which came into force on 6 August 2012 (see reg 1(1)) and apply in relation to houses and authorities in England only (reg 1(2)); the Housing (Right to Manage) Regulations 1994, SI 1994/627, were revoked in so far as they relate to houses and local authorities in England by the Housing (Right to Manage) (England) Regulations 2008, SI 2008/2361, reg 2 (revoked).
4   Housing Act 1985 s 27(1) (as substituted: see note 3). A company set up by a local authority to manage some or all of its housing stock is often referred to as an arm's length management organisation (or 'ALMO').
5   In the Housing Act 1985, 'management agreement' means an agreement under s 27 or a sub-agreement: s 27(2)(a) (as substituted: see note 3). For the purposes of s 27, 'sub-agreement' means an agreement made by a manager and another person pursuant to a provision included in an agreement by virtue of s 27(5)(a) (see head (1) in the text): s 27(18) (substituted by SI 2010/844). See, however, note 19.
6   Housing Act 1985 s 27(3) (as substituted: see note 3). For the purposes of the Housing Act 1985, 'manager', in relation to a management agreement, means a person by whom management functions are exercisable under the agreement: s 27(2)(b) (as so substituted). See, however, note 19.
7   Housing Act 1985 s 27(4) (as substituted (see note 3); amended by SI 2010/844). 'The appropriate Minister' means: (1) in relation to a local housing authority in England, the Secretary of State; (2)

in relation to a local housing authority in Wales, the Welsh Ministers: Housing Act 1985 s 27(18) (as substituted: see note 5). As to terms to be included see PARA 458.

8   Housing Act 1985 s 27(5) (as substituted: see note 3).

9   'The appropriate authority' means: (1) in relation to a local housing authority in England which is a registered provider of social housing, the Regulator of Social Housing; (2) in relation to any other local housing authority in England, the Secretary of State; (3) in relation to a local housing authority in Wales, the Welsh Ministers: Housing Act 1985 s 27(18) (as substituted: see note 5).

10 Housing Act 1985 s 27(6) (as substituted (see note 3); amended by SI 2010/844).

11 A moratorium period so specified must not exceed six months: Housing Act 1985 s 27(9) (as substituted: see note 3). If a moratorium period applies in relation to a management agreement: (1) during the moratorium period the approval of the appropriate authority is not required for the making of a sub-agreement under the agreement; (2) any sub-agreement made under the agreement during the moratorium period without the approval of the appropriate authority is not valid unless it is approved by the appropriate authority immediately after the end of the moratorium period: s 27(8) (as so substituted; amended by SI 2010/844). Where a sub-agreement has been made during a moratorium period without the approval of the appropriate authority, the appropriate authority may extend the moratorium period if it is satisfied that it will not give its approval to that sub-agreement immediately after the end of that period; and this provision may apply more than once: Housing Act 1985 s 27(10) (as so substituted; amended by SI 2010/844).

12 Housing Act 1985 s 27(7) (as substituted (see note 3); amended by SI 2010/844).

13 Housing Act 1985 s 27(11) (as substituted (see note 3); amended by SI 2010/844).

14 Housing Act 1985 s 27(12) (as substituted (see note 3); amended by SI 2010/844).

15 For this purpose, 'relevant function' means a management function of the authority exercisable by the manager under a management agreement: Housing Act 1985 s 27(14) (as substituted: see note 3).

16 Housing Act 1985 s 27(13) (as substituted: see note 3).

17 Housing Act 1985 s 27(15) (as substituted: see note 3).

18 For these purposes, 'housing co-operative' means a society, company or body of trustees with which a housing co-operative agreement was made, ie: (1) an agreement to which the Housing Rents and Subsidies Act 1975 Sch 1 para 9 (repealed) or the Housing Act 1980 Sch 20 (repealed) applied; or (2) an agreement made under the Housing Act 1985 s 27 (as originally enacted) before 7 January 1987: see s 27B(1) (s 27B added by the Housing and Planning Act 1986 s 10).

19 As to the meaning of 'new town corporation' see PARA 12.

20 See the Housing Act 1985 s 27B(2), (3) (as added (see note 18); s 27B(3) amended by the Government of Wales Act 1998 s 152, Sch 18 Pt IV). In the Housing Act 1985 (except in s 27), the expressions 'management agreement' and 'manager', in relation to such an agreement, include a housing co-operative agreement to which s 27B(2) or s 27B(3) applies and the housing co-operative with which the agreement is made: s 27B(4) (as so added).

21 The County Courts Act 1984 s 60A is added by the Legal Services Act 2007 s 191 as from a day to be appointed by order under s 211(2). At the date at which this volume states the law, no such day had been appointed.

22 'Housing management body' means a person who exercises management functions of a local housing authority by virtue of a housing management agreement; and 'local housing authority' has the same meaning as in the Housing Act 1985 s 27 (see PARA 11): County Courts Act 1984 s 60A(7) (as added: see note 21). 'Housing management agreement' means: (1) an agreement under the Housing Act 1985 s 27 (including an agreement to which s 27B(2) or (3) applies (see the text and notes 18–20)); or (2) a section 247 or 249 arrangement, as defined by the Housing and Regeneration Act 2008 s 250A(6) (see PARA 117 note 8): County Courts Act 1984 s 60A(7) (as so added; definition substituted by SI 2010/844).

23 An authorisation for the purposes of the County Courts Act 1984 s 60A must be in writing: s 60A(4) (as added: see note 21).

24 Ie the purposes of the County Courts Act 1984 s 60A.

25 'Right of audience' means the right to appear before and address a court, including the right to call and examine witnesses: County Courts Act 1984 s 60A(7) (as added: see note 21). See COURTS AND TRIBUNALS vol 24 (2010) PARA 612.

26 'Right to conduct litigation' means the right: (1) to issue proceedings before any court in England and Wales; (2) to commence, prosecute and defend such proceedings; and (3) to perform any ancillary functions in relation to such proceedings (such as entering appearances to actions): County Courts Act 1984 s 60A(7) (as added: see note 21). See COURTS AND TRIBUNALS vol 24 (2010) PARA 613.

27 County Courts Act 1984 s 60A(1) (as added: see note 21).

28 'Relevant housing proceedings' are: (1) proceedings under the Housing Act 1985 s 82A (demotion because of anti-social behaviour) (see PARA 471; and LANDLORD AND TENANT vol 63 (2016)

PARA 1090); (2) proceedings for possession of a dwelling house subject to a secure tenancy, where possession is sought on Sch 2 Pt I ground 2 (anti-social behaviour) (see LANDLORD AND TENANT vol 63 (2016) PARA 1140); (3) proceedings for possession of a dwelling house subject to a demoted tenancy (see PARA 474; and LANDLORD AND TENANT vol 63 (2016) PARAS 1163–1165); (4) proceedings for a suspension order under the Housing Act 1985 s 121A (suspension of right to buy) (see PARA 259); (5) proceedings under the Housing Act 1996 s 153A, 153B or 153D (injunctions against anti-social behaviour) (repealed); (6) proceedings for the attachment of a power of arrest to an injunction by virtue of the Anti-social Behaviour Act 2003 s 91(2) (repealed) or the Police and Justice Act 2006 s 27(2) (proceedings under the Local Government Act 1972 s 222: power of arrest attached to injunction) (see LOCAL GOVERNMENT vol 69 (2009) PARA 573); (7) at a hearing at which a decision is made in relation to proceedings within heads (1)–(6), proceedings for permission to appeal against that decision; (8) such other proceedings as the Lord Chancellor may prescribe by order: County Courts Act 1984 s 60A(3) (as added: see note 21). 'Dwelling house' and 'secure tenancy' have the same meanings as in the Housing Act 1985 Pt IV (ss 79–117) (secure tenancies: see PARA 447 note 3; and LANDLORD AND TENANT vol 63 (2016) PARA 1037 et seq): County Courts Act 1984 s 60A(7) (as so added). The power to make an order under s 60A(3)(h) is exercisable by statutory instrument subject to annulment by resolution of either House of Parliament: s 60A(5) (as so added). In head (5) the reference to the Housing Act 1996 s 153A is a reference to that section: (a) as inserted by the Anti-social Behaviour Act 2003 s 13; or (b) as substituted by the Police and Justice Act 2006 s 26: County Courts Act 1984 s 60A(6) (as so added).

29 County Courts Act 1984 s 60A(2) (as added (see note 21); amended by the Crime and Courts Act 2013 s 17(5), Sch 9 paras 1, 10(1)(b), (17)).

458. Break clause to be included in management agreements. In England, every management agreement[1] between an authority[2] and a manager after 6 August 2012, where the agreement relates to the same houses[3] and the same management functions[4] in relation to those houses, that are the subject of a subsequent TMO agreement[5], must contain the following terms: (1) that the authority must determine the agreement where it is required to enter into a TMO agreement; and (2) that on the determination of the agreement, the authority and the manager must make arrangements for the transfer of the management functions from the manager to the TMO, if such arrangements are necessary[6]. An agreement to which these provisions apply that, when made, does not contain the terms specified, is to be treated as if it had always contained those terms[7]. An authority must determine the agreement as soon as reasonably practicable after the date it is required[8] to enter into a TMO agreement[9]. The authority and the manager must make arrangements in accordance with head (2) within three months of the determination of the agreement[10].

In England, a management agreement entered into after 1 April 2010[11] must provide that where a requirement to put the management out to tender or transfer the management is imposed[12]: (a) the authority and the manager must make arrangements for the transfer of management functions from the manager; and (b) the authority and the manager must determine the agreement, so far as necessary to ensure that the agreement does not continue to have effect as respects management functions which are the subject of the requirement[13].

In Wales, a management agreement (other than an agreement with a tenant management organisation) entered into by a local housing authority after 1 April 1994 must contain a provision (a 'break clause') enabling the authority to determine it to the extent that it overlaps[14] with any subsequent management agreement entered into with a tenant management organisation[15]. A break clause contained in a management agreement in accordance with this provision must provide that the authority may exercise the rights conferred by it at different times in relation to different overlapping provisions and that it must determine the provisions in relation to which it is exercised within three months of it being exercised[16]. Nothing in these provisions, however, requires an agreement (or any part of an agreement) to be determined otherwise than in accordance with provisions contained in that agreement[17].

1   Ie any agreement made under the Housing Act 1985 s 27(1): see PARA 457.
2   'Authority' means the local housing authority on which a proposal notice is served: Housing (Right to Manage) (England) Regulations 2012, SI 2012/1821, reg 3. 'Proposal notice' means a notice which complies with reg 9 (see PARA 461): reg 3. As to the meaning of 'local housing authority' see PARA 11.
3   'House' includes: (1) part of a house; (2) land let together with a house; and (3) land held for a purpose related to the house: Housing (Right to Manage) (England) Regulations 2012, SI 2012/1821, reg 3.
4   As to the meaning of 'management functions' see PARA 457 note 3.
5   'TMO agreement' means an agreement required to be made between an authority and a tenant management organisation under the Housing (Right to Manage) (England) Regulations 2012, SI 2012/1821, reg 16 (see PARA 464): reg 3.
6   Housing (Right to Manage) (England) Regulations 2012, SI 2012/1821, reg 19(1), (2).
7   Housing (Right to Manage) (England) Regulations 2012, SI 2012/1821, reg 19(3).
8   Ie under the Housing (Right to Manage) (England) Regulations 2012, SI 2012/1821, reg 16 (see PARA 464):
9   Housing (Right to Manage) (England) Regulations 2012, SI 2012/1821, reg 19(4).
10 Housing (Right to Manage) (England) Regulations 2012, SI 2012/1821, reg 19(5).
11 Ie the date of commencement of the Housing and Regeneration Act 2008 s 111 (as to which see PARAS 21 note 2, 70).
12 Ie under the Housing and Regeneration Act 2008 s 247(2) or 249(2): see PARAS 115, 116.
13 See the Housing Management Agreements (Break Clause) (England) Regulations 2010, SI 2010/663, regs 1, 2.
14 For these purposes, two management agreements overlap when and to the extent that they contain provisions which relate to the exercise of the same management functions in relation to the same houses or land; and 'overlapping provisions' is to be construed accordingly: Housing (Right to Manage) Regulations 1994, SI 1994/627, reg 1(3).
15 Housing (Right to Manage) Regulations 1994, SI 1994/627, reg 8(1). As to the meaning of 'tenant management organisation' see PARA 460.
16 Housing (Right to Manage) Regulations 1994, SI 1994/627, reg 8(2).
17 Housing (Right to Manage) Regulations 1994, SI 1994/627, reg 8(6).

B.   AGREEMENTS WITH TENANT MANAGEMENT ORGANISATIONS

(A)   In general

459. Regulations relating to agreements with tenant management organisations. The appropriate national authority[1] may make regulations for imposing requirements on a local housing authority[2] in any case where a tenant management organisation[3] serves written notice on the authority proposing that the authority should enter into a management agreement[4] with that organisation[5]. The regulations may make provision requiring the authority:

(1)   to provide or finance the provision of such office accommodation and facilities, and such training, as the organisation reasonably requires for the purpose of pursuing the proposal;

(2)   to arrange for such feasibility studies with respect to the proposal as may be determined by or under the regulations to be conducted by such persons as may be so determined;

(3)   to provide to the organisation such information or descriptions of information, in connection with the proposal, as may be prescribed in the regulations;

(4)   to take, in circumstances prescribed in the regulations, such other steps as may be so prescribed to co-operate with the organisation in connection with the proposal;

(5)   to arrange for such ballots or polls with respect to the proposal as may be determined by or under the regulations to be conducted of such persons as may be so determined; and

(6)   in such circumstances as may be prescribed by the regulations (which must include the organisation becoming registered[6] if it has not already done so), to enter into a management agreement with the organisation[7].

The regulations may make provision with respect to any management agreement which is to be entered into in pursuance of the regulations:

(a)   for determining the houses[8] and land to which the agreement should relate, and the amounts which should be paid under the agreement to the organisation;

(b)   requiring the agreement to be in such form as may be approved by the appropriate national authority and to contain such provisions as may be prescribed by the regulations;

(c)   requiring the agreement to take effect immediately after the expiry or other determination of any previous agreement[9]; and

(d)   where any previous agreement contains provisions for its determination by the authority, requiring the authority to determine it as soon as may be after the agreement is entered into[10].

The regulations may also make such procedural, incidental, supplementary and transitional provisions as may appear to the appropriate national authority necessary or expedient[11], and may in particular make provision:

(i)   for particular questions arising under the regulations to be determined by the local housing authority or the person making the regulations;

(ii)   for other questions so arising to be determined by an arbitrator agreed to by the parties or, in default of agreement, appointed by the appropriate national authority[12];

(iii)   setting time-limits for the carrying out of requirements under the regulations;

(iv)   requiring any person exercising functions under the regulations to act in accordance with any guidance or directions given by the appropriate national authority[13]; and

(v)   for enabling the local housing authority, if invited to do so by the organisation concerned, to nominate one or more persons to be directors or other officers of any tenant management organisation with which the local housing authority has entered into, or proposes to enter into, a management agreement[14].

Except as otherwise provided by such regulations, a local housing authority must not enter into a management agreement with a tenant management organisation otherwise than in pursuance of the regulations[15]; and the provisions of the regulations apply in relation to the entering into of such an agreement with such an organisation in place of specified statutory provisions[16].

1   Ie the Secretary of State or, where statutory functions have been transferred in relation to Wales, the Welsh Ministers: see PARA 7.

2   As to the meaning of 'local housing authority' see PARA 11.

3   As to the meaning of 'tenant management organisation' see PARA 460.

4   As to the meaning of 'management agreement' see PARA 457 note 5.

5   Housing Act 1985 s 27AB(1) (as added: see note 3). Nothing in s 27AB(2)–(4) (see heads (1)–(6), (a)–(d), (i)–(v) in the text) may be taken as prejudicing the generality of s 27AB(1): s 27AB(5) (as so added). Such regulations may make different provision with respect to different cases or descriptions of case, including different provision for different areas; and must be made by statutory instrument subject to annulment in pursuance of a resolution of either House of Parliament or of the National Assembly for Wales, as appropriate: s 27AB(6) (as so added). In

exercise of the power so conferred, the Secretary of State made the Housing (Right to Manage) Regulations 1994, SI 1994/627, which came into force on 1 April 1994 (see reg 1(1)); and the Housing (Right to Manage) (England) Regulations 2012, SI 2012/1821, which came into force on 6 August 2012 (see reg 1(1)) and apply in relation to houses and authorities in England only (reg 1(2)); the Housing (Right to Manage) Regulations 1994, SI 1994/627, were revoked in so far as they relate to houses and local authorities in England by the Housing (Right to Manage) (England) Regulations 2008, SI 2008/2361, reg 2 (revoked). See further the text and notes 10–15; and PARAS 461 et seq, 466 et seq.

6 'Registered' means registered under the Co-operative and Community Benefit Societies Act 2014 (see FINANCIAL INSTITUTIONS vol 48 (2015) PARA 898 et seq) or the Companies Act 2006 (see COMPANIES vol 14 (2016) PARA 21 et seq): Housing Act 1985 s 27AB(8) (as added (see note 3); amended by the Co-operative and Community Benefit Societies Act 2014 s 151(1), Sch 4 paras 32, 35; and by SI 2009/1941).

7 Housing Act 1985 s 27AB(2) (as added see note 3); amended by the Housing and Regeneration Act 2008 s 295(1), (2)).

8 As to the meaning of 'house' see PARA 405 note 6.

9 'Previous agreement', in relation to an agreement entered into in pursuance of the regulations, means a management agreement, or a section 247 or 249 arrangement, previously entered into in relation to the same houses and land: Housing Act 1985 s 27AB(8) (as added (see note 3); amended by SI 2010/844). 'Section 247 or 249 arrangement' has the meaning given by the Housing and Regeneration Act 2008 s 250A(6) (see PARA 117 note 8): Housing Act 1985 s 27AB(8) (as so added; definition added by SI 2010/844).

10 Housing Act 1985 s 27AB(3) (as added: see note 3). In Wales, where a local housing authority enters into a management agreement with a tenant management organisation in pursuance of the regulations and: (1) at the time of entering into that agreement a previous agreement is in operation; and (2) the two agreements overlap when the management agreement is entered into or the two agreements subsequently overlap on the variation of either; and (3) the previous agreement contains provisions which allow the authority to determine the overlapping provisions (whether by determining the whole of that agreement or otherwise), then, subject as follows, the local housing authority must determine the overlapping provisions in the previous agreement (whether by determining the whole of that agreement or otherwise) as soon as possible after the two agreements overlap: Housing (Right to Manage) Regulations 1994, SI 1994/627, reg 8(3), (4). If, however, the tenant management organisation agrees in writing, the local housing authority may postpone the determination of the overlapping provisions (or some of them, if the previous agreement allows the authority to determine the provisions at different times) until such time as may be agreed: reg 8(5). Nothing in reg 8 requires an agreement (or any part of an agreement) to be determined otherwise than in accordance with provisions contained in that agreement: reg 8(6). As to the requirement for a management agreement which is not with a tenant management organisation to contain a break clause see reg 8(1), (2); and PARA 458. As to the meaning of 'overlapping provisions' see PARA 458 note 14.

11 For transitional provisions see the Housing (Right to Manage) (England) Regulations 2012, SI 2012/1821, regs 22–25 (in relation to England); and the Housing (Right to Manage) Regulations 1994, SI 1994/627, reg 10 (in relation to Wales).

12 See the Housing (Right to Manage) (England) Regulations 2012, SI 2012/1821, regs 8, 12(4)–(6) (in relation to England); and the Housing (Right to Manage) Regulations 1994, SI 1994/627, reg 1(5) (in relation to Wales). 'Arbitrator' means a member of a panel approved for the purposes of the regulations by the appropriate national authority: Housing Act 1985 s 27AB(8) (as added: see note 3).

13 See the Housing (Right to Manage) (England) Regulations 2012, SI 2012/1821, reg 18 (in relation to England); and the Housing (Right to Manage) Regulations 1994, SI 1994/627, reg 7 (in relation to Wales).

14 Housing Act 1985 s 27AB(4) (as added (see note 3); amended by the Housing and Regeneration Act 2008 s 295(3)); and see the Housing (Right to Manage) (England) Regulations 2012, SI 2012/1821, reg 20 (in relation to England); and the Housing (Right to Manage) Regulations 1994, SI 1994/627, reg 9 (in relation to Wales).

15 Housing Act 1985 s 27AB(7)(a) (as added: see note 3). In England, a local housing authority may enter into a TMO agreement otherwise than in accordance with the Housing (Right to Manage) (England) Regulations 2012, SI 2012/1821, where that agreement is in such form as is approved by the Secretary of State and the requirements of the Housing Act 1985 s 27(see PARA 457) are satisfied: Housing (Right to Manage) (England) Regulations 2012, SI 2012/1821, reg 21. In Wales, a local housing authority may enter into a management agreement with a tenant management organisation otherwise than in pursuance of the Housing (Right to Manage) Regulations 1994, SI 1994/627, regs 1–10 where that agreement is in such form as is approved by the Welsh Ministers

for the purposes of the regulations and the requirements of the Housing Act 1985 s 27 (see PARA 457) are satisfied: see the Housing (Right to Manage) Regulations 1994, SI 1994/627, reg 11.

16 Housing Act 1985 s 27AB(7)(b) (as added: see note 3). The specified statutory provisions are: (1) the provisions of regulations under s 27BA (consultation with respect to management: see PARA 446); (2) in the case of secure tenants, the provisions of s 105 (consultation on matters of housing management: see LANDLORD AND TENANT vol 63 (2016) PARA 1114); and (3) in the case of introductory tenants, the provisions of the Housing Act 1996 s 137 (consultation on matters of housing management: see LANDLORD AND TENANT vol 63 (2016) PARA 1114): Housing Act 1985 s 27AB(b)(i)–(iv) (as so added; amended by the Housing Act 1996 s 222, Sch 18 para 3(1), (5); the Local Government Act 2003 s 127(2), Sch 8 Pt 1; and SI 1977/74).

460. Tenant management organisations. For the purposes of the provisions relating to management agreements with tenant management organisations[1], 'tenant management organisation' means a body which satisfies such conditions as may be determined by or under regulations made by the appropriate national authority[2].

In relation to England, a tenant management organisation, referred to[3] as a TMO, is an organisation which satisfies the following conditions:

(1)   it has a constitution in written form;

(2)   its constitution specifies an area in relation to which it seeks to enter into a TMO agreement with an authority[4];

(3)   its constitution provides that any tenant[5] of a house in that area may become a member of the TMO;

(4)   its constitution provides that, in conducting its affairs, the TMO must avoid any unlawful discrimination;

(5)   its constitution provides that the affairs of the TMO must be conducted either by the members of the TMO at a general meeting or by a committee or board of directors elected by members of the TMO[6].

For the purposes of the regulations, a TMO is not disqualified from being a TMO if its constitution contains provision for matters other than those specified in heads (1) to (5) and does not cease to be a TMO if its constitution is at any time amended to contain such provision[7].

In exercising its functions under the regulations, a TMO must act in accordance with the provisions of its constitution relevant to the exercise of its functions under the regulations and must have regard to any guidance provided from time to time by the Secretary of State relevant to the exercise of its functions under the regulations[8].

In Wales, the conditions which a body must satisfy are that its constitution:

(a)   specifies an area as being the area of the organisation in relation to which it may serve a proposal notice[9];

(b)   provides that any tenant[10] of a dwelling house[11] in relation to which the organisation could serve a proposal notice may become a member of the organisation;

(c)   provides that in conducting its affairs the organisation must avoid discrimination against any person on grounds of racial origin, gender, sexuality, disability or religion; and

(d)   provides either that the affairs of the organisation must be conducted by the members of the organisation at general meeting, or that they must be conducted by a committee or board of directors elected by the members of the organisation[12].

1   Ie the Housing Act 1985 s 27AB: see PARA 457.
2   See the Housing Act 1985 s 27AB(8) (s 27AB added by the Leasehold Reform, Housing and Urban Development Act 1993 s 132(1)). As to the relevant authority, ie the Secretary of State or, where statutory functions have been transferred in relation to Wales, the Welsh Ministers: see PARA 7.

3 Ie in the Housing (Right to Manage) (England) Regulations 2012, SI 2012/1821, regs 4(2)–25.
4 As to the meaning of 'authority' see PARA 458 note 2.
5 'Tenant' means a person who holds a secure tenancy (within the meaning of the Housing Act 1985 s 79: see LANDLORD AND TENANT vol 63 (2016) para 1037), or other tenancy of a house from an authority; and 'house' includes part of a house, land let together with a house and land held for a purpose related to the house: Housing (Right to Manage) (England) Regulations 2012, SI 2012/1821, reg 3. See further PARA 461 et seq.
6 Housing (Right to Manage) (England) Regulations 2012, SI 2012/1821, reg 4(1). See further PARA 461 et seq.
7 Housing (Right to Manage) (England) Regulations 2012, SI 2012/1821, reg 4(2).
8 Housing (Right to Manage) (England) Regulations 2012, SI 2012/1821, reg 4(3).
9 'Proposal notice' means a notice served by a tenant management organisation on a local housing authority which complies with the Housing (Right to Manage) Regulations 1994, SI 1994/627, reg 2 (see PARA 466) and, in relation to a particular proposal for a management agreement, references to a proposal notice refer to the notice containing that proposal: reg 1(2).
10 'Tenant' means a person who holds a secure tenancy or other tenancy of a dwelling house from a local housing authority; and 'secure tenancy' has the same meaning as in the Housing Act 1985 s 79 (see LANDLORD AND TENANT vol 63 (2016) PARA 1037): Housing (Right to Manage) Regulations 1994, SI 1994/627, reg 1(2).
11 'Dwelling house' has the same meaning as in the Housing Act 1985 s 112 (see LANDLORD AND TENANT vol 63 (2016) PARA 1037): Housing (Right to Manage) Regulations 1994, SI 1994/627, reg 1(2).
12 Housing (Right to Manage) Regulations 1994, SI 1994/627, reg 1(4). See further PARA 466 et seq.

(B) Procedure in England

461. Proposal notice. A notice is a proposal notice if it complies with the provisions below and is served on an authority[1] by a TMO[2]. The notice must contain the following:

(1) a statement that the authority on which it is served should enter into a TMO agreement[3] with the TMO serving the notice;

(2) a statement that the subject of the proposed TMO agreement is to be the management of houses[4] within the TMO's area[5] of which, at the time the notice is served, at least 25 are let under secure tenancies[6]; and

(3) a statement that those houses to which the proposed TMO agreement relates are within the TMO's area[7].

The notice must be accompanied by evidence demonstrating that the requirements as to consultation[8] have been complied with[9]. A proposal notice must not contain a proposal relating to houses already included in an existing management agreement between a TMO and an authority unless:

(a) all of those houses are included in the proposal and the TMO which serves the notice is a party to that existing management agreement; or

(b) the number of houses which are the subject of the existing agreement is greater than 2,500[10].

A TMO must:

(i) before serving a proposal notice on an authority, use its best endeavours to deliver a copy of the notice to every house which is identified in the proposal notice;

(ii) before serving a proposal notice, be satisfied that a majority of members of the TMO voted in favour of serving the notice at a ballot[11] of all members or that a majority of members of the TMO in attendance at a properly constituted general meeting voted in favour of a resolution to serve a notice;

(iii) at the time the notice is served, ensure that the membership of the TMO includes at least 20 per cent of the tenants[12] and at least 20 per cent of the secure tenants, of the houses identified in the proposal notice[13].

In general, an authority on which a proposal notice is served must accept it[14]. An authority may, however, refuse to accept a proposal notice if it contains a similar proposal to one contained in a previous proposal notice, and:

(A)   at least half of the houses identified in the current proposal notice were also identified in the previous proposal notice; and

(B)   within the two years preceding the date on which the current notice is received, the previous proposal notice was withdrawn voluntarily, by the TMO, or was deemed[15] to be withdrawn[16].

An authority may refuse to accept a proposal notice if it has reasonable grounds for believing that the TMO which serves the notice has failed to comply with the requirements in head (i) or (ii)[17], or that the requirements in head (iii)[18] have not been met[19].

An authority must notify[20] the TMO within 28 days of receiving the proposal notice whether it has accepted or refused the proposal notice and, where it has refused, the reasons for the refusal[21]. Where an authority accepts a proposal notice, it must at the time of notification inform the TMO of any other management organisation or person which already exercises management functions in relation to the houses identified in the proposal notice and provide a copy of the proposal notice to any other such management organisation or person[22].

1   As to the meaning of 'authority' see PARA 458 note 2.
2   Housing (Right to Manage) (England) Regulations 2012, SI 2012/1821, reg 9(1). As to the meaning of 'TMO' see PARA 460.
3   As to the meaning of 'TMO agreement' see PARA 458 note 5.
4   As to the meaning of 'house' see PARA 460 note 5.
5   'Area' in relation to a tenant management organisation, means the area specified in its constitution in accordance with the Housing (Right to Manage) (England) Regulations 2012, SI 2012/1821, reg 4(1)(b) (see PARA 460): reg 3.
6   As to the meaning of 'secure tenancy' see LANDLORD AND TENANT vol 63 (2016) PARA 1037.
7   Housing (Right to Manage) (England) Regulations 2012, SI 2012/1821, reg 9(2).
8   Ie the requirements in the Housing (Right to Manage) (England) Regulations 2012, SI 2012/1821, reg 10. See heads (i)–(iii) in the text.
9   Housing (Right to Manage) (England) Regulations 2012, SI 2012/1821, reg 9(3).
10 Housing (Right to Manage) (England) Regulations 2012, SI 2012/1821, reg 9(4).
11 Any ballot held under the Housing (Right to Manage) (England) Regulations 2012, SI 2012/1821, must be organised so that the vote cast by any individual is kept secret: reg 6.
12 As to the meaning of 'tenant' see PARA 460 note 5.
13 Housing (Right to Manage) (England) Regulations 2012, SI 2012/1821, reg 10. As to the meaning of 'secure tenant' see LANDLORD AND TENANT vol 63 (2016) PARA 1037.
14 Housing (Right to Manage) (England) Regulations 2012, SI 2012/1821, reg 11(1). As to exceptions see reg 11(4), (5); and the text and notes 15–19.
15 Ie as mentioned in the Housing (Right to Manage) (England) Regulations 2012, SI 2012/1821, reg 13(8) (competence of TMO: see PARA 463 text and notes 15–16), reg 15(4) (refusal of offer to tenants: see PARA 463 text and note 27) or reg 17 (failure to register TMO: see PARA 464 text and note 11).
16 Housing (Right to Manage) (England) Regulations 2012, SI 2012/1821, reg 11(4).
17 Ie the requirements of the Housing (Right to Manage) (England) Regulations 2012, SI 2012/1821, reg 10(a), (b).
18 Ie the requirements of the Housing (Right to Manage) (England) Regulations 2012, SI 2012/1821, reg 10(c).
19 Housing (Right to Manage) (England) Regulations 2012, SI 2012/1821, reg 11(5).
20 Any requirement under the Housing (Right to Manage) (England) Regulations 2012, SI 2012/1821, to make, prepare, provide or send a notification, request, referral, report, plan, offer or other communication, is a requirement to do so in writing: reg 7.
21 Housing (Right to Manage) (England) Regulations 2012, SI 2012/1821, reg 11(2).
22 Housing (Right to Manage) (England) Regulations 2012, SI 2012/1821, reg 11(3).

462. Local authority support following proposal notice. Where an authority[1] has accepted a proposal notice[2], the TMO[3] which served the notice may make a request[4] to the authority for such support[5] as is specified in the request, being support that is reasonably required for the purposes of pursuing the proposal notice[6]. On receipt of such a request, the authority must determine the support which it considers the TMO reasonably requires for the purposes of pursuing the proposal notice and notify[7] the TMO of the determination within 28 days of receipt of the request[8]. Unless the proposal notice is withdrawn voluntarily by the TMO, or is deemed to be withdrawn[9], the authority must provide support in accordance with the determination[10].

1 As to the meaning of 'authority' see PARA 458 note 2.
2 As to the meaning of 'proposal notice' see PARA 458 note 2; and as to such notices see PARA 461.
3 As to the meaning of 'TMO' see PARA 460.
4 As to the requirements for a request see PARA 461 note 20.
5 'Support' means the provision or financing by an authority of office accommodation, facilities or training: Housing (Right to Manage) (England) Regulations 2012, SI 2012/1821, reg 3.
6 Housing (Right to Manage) (England) Regulations 2012, SI 2012/1821, reg 12(1). As to disputes see PARA 465.
7 As to the requirements for notification see PARA 461 note 20.
8 Housing (Right to Manage) (England) Regulations 2012, SI 2012/1821, reg 12(2). Where any person is required or authorised to exercise any function under the regulations within a specified period, the TMO and the authority concerned may by agreement before the expiry of that period, extend the period for a further specified period: reg 5.
9 See the Housing (Right to Manage) (England) Regulations 2012, SI 2012/1821, reg 12(8). As to withdrawal and deemed withdrawal of a proposal notice see PARA 463 text and notes 15–16.
10 Housing (Right to Manage) (England) Regulations 2012, SI 2012/1821, reg 12(3). This is subject to reg 12(7), (8). As to reg 12(7) see PARA 465.

463. Competence of TMO and offer to tenants. Where an authority[1] has accepted a proposal notice[2], the TMO[3] must within three months[4] of the acceptance date apply to the approved assessor service to appoint an approved assessor[5] to report on the competence[6] of the TMO to exercise the management functions[7] set out in the proposal[8]. The authority must arrange for the approved assessor to produce the report[9]. The report must: (1) state whether or not the approved assessor concludes that the TMO is competent; and (2) if the approved assessor concludes that the TMO is not competent, suggest the action the authority and the TMO should take to ensure that the TMO becomes competent[10].

The approved assessor must, within 15 months of the acceptance date, complete the report and provide it to the authority and the TMO[11]. The authority and the TMO must: (a) use all reasonable efforts to take the action suggested by the approved assessor in accordance with head (2); and (b) jointly agree an action plan to enable them to do so[12]. The authority must notify the approved assessor within seven days of the action being completed[13]. The approved assessor must within 35 days of receipt of the authority's notification reassess whether or not the TMO is competent and notify the authority and the TMO of his conclusion[14].

The proposal notice is deemed to be withdrawn: (i) if a TMO and authority fail to comply with the requirements of these provisions; or (ii) if the approved assessor concludes in his reassessment[15] that the TMO is not competent[16].

Within 15 months of the acceptance date[17], the TMO and the authority must jointly prepare an offer notice[18]. The offer notice must contain a statement describing: (A) the management functions the TMO proposes to exercise; (B) the funding or budget to be allocated by the authority to enable the TMO to exercise those functions; (C) the financial accountability and control procedures which the authority and the TMO will have in place; and (D) the management and governance arrangements of the TMO[19]. In preparing the offer notice, the TMO and the authority must have regard to any guidance issued from time to time by the Secretary of State[20].

Where the approved assessor concludes[21] that the TMO is competent, the authority must within three months of receiving his conclusion, make to the tenants[22] of each house identified in the proposal notice, an offer containing the offer notice, the conclusion of the approved assessor and information submitted by the TMO concerning the proposal[23]. The authority must arrange for a ballot to be carried out within three months of making the offer, with a view to establishing whether those tenants wish to accept the offer[24]. The authority must within 14 days of carrying out the ballot notify the TMO of whether a majority of the tenants who voted and a majority of the secure tenants who voted accepted the offer or refused the offer[25].

The proposal notice is deemed to be withdrawn if the offer is refused by a majority of the tenants who voted in the ballot or a majority of the secure tenants[26] who voted in the ballot[27].

1   As to the meaning of 'authority' see PARA 458 note 2.
2   As to the meaning of 'proposal notice' see PARA 458 note 2; and as to such notices see PARA 461.
3   As to the meaning of 'TMO' see PARA 460.
4   As to extension of time by agreement see PARA 462 note 8.
5   'Approved assessor service' means a person designated by the Secretary of State to appoint an approved assessor on the application of a tenant management organisation under the Housing (Right to Manage) (England) Regulations 2012, SI 2012/1821, reg 13(1); and 'approved assessor' means a person approved by the Secretary of State for the purposes of assessing the competence of tenant management organisations under reg 13(1): reg 3. As to the Secretary of State see PARA 7.
6   'Competence' means the competence of a tenant management organisation to exercise the management functions set out in the offer notice: Housing (Right to Manage) (England) Regulations 2012, SI 2012/1821, reg 3.
7   'Management functions' has the same meaning as in the Housing Act 1985 s 27 (see PARA 457 note 3): Housing (Right to Manage) (England) Regulations 2012, SI 2012/1821, reg 3.
8   Housing (Right to Manage) (England) Regulations 2012, SI 2012/1821, reg 13(1).
9   Housing (Right to Manage) (England) Regulations 2012, SI 2012/1821, reg 13(2).
10   Housing (Right to Manage) (England) Regulations 2012, SI 2012/1821, reg 13(3).
11   Housing (Right to Manage) (England) Regulations 2012, SI 2012/1821, reg 13(4). As to extension of time by agreement see PARA 462 note 8.
12   Housing (Right to Manage) (England) Regulations 2012, SI 2012/1821, reg 13(5).
13   Housing (Right to Manage) (England) Regulations 2012, SI 2012/1821, reg 13(6).
14   Housing (Right to Manage) (England) Regulations 2012, SI 2012/1821, reg 13(7). As to extension of time by agreement see PARA 462 note 8.
15   Ie under the Housing (Right to Manage) (England) Regulations 2012, SI 2012/1821, reg 13(7).
16   Housing (Right to Manage) (England) Regulations 2012, SI 2012/1821, reg 13(8).
17   'Acceptance date' means the date on which a tenant management organisation receives a notice under the Housing (Right to Manage) (England) Regulations 2012, SI 2012/1821, reg 11(2)(a) (see PARA 461) that an authority has accepted its proposal notice: reg 3.
18   Housing (Right to Manage) (England) Regulations 2012, SI 2012/1821, reg 14(1).
19   Housing (Right to Manage) (England) Regulations 2012, SI 2012/1821, reg 14(2).
20   Housing (Right to Manage) (England) Regulations 2012, SI 2012/1821, reg 14(3).
21   Ie under the Housing (Right to Manage) (England) Regulations 2012, SI 2012/1821, reg 13.
22   As to the meaning of 'tenant' see PARA 460 note 5.
23   Housing (Right to Manage) (England) Regulations 2012, SI 2012/1821, reg 15(1).
24   Housing (Right to Manage) (England) Regulations 2012, SI 2012/1821, reg 15(2). As to voting at ballots see PARA 461 note 11.
25   Housing (Right to Manage) (England) Regulations 2012, SI 2012/1821, reg 15(3).
26   As to the meaning of 'secure tenant' see LANDLORD AND TENANT vol 63 (2016) PARA 1037.
27   Housing (Right to Manage) (England) Regulations 2012, SI 2012/1821, reg 15(4).

464. Implementation stage. Where a majority of the tenants[1] who voted in the ballot on the authority's offer[2] and a majority of the secure tenants[3] who voted in that ballot, have accepted the offer, the authority must within nine months of the date of the authority's notification of the result of the ballot[4], enter into a TMO agreement[5] with the TMO[6]. That TMO agreement must take into account any guidance issued from time to time by the Secretary of State relating to TMO agreements[7].

However, the authority is not required to enter into a TMO agreement unless within nine months of the local authority's notification[8], the TMO is registered as either a co-operative or community benefit society under the Co-operative and Community Benefit Societies Act 2014[9] or a company under the Companies Act 2006[10]. The proposal notice is deemed to be withdrawn if the TMO fails to satisfy these requirements[11].

1   As to the meaning of 'tenant' see PARA 460 note 5.
2   Ie under the Housing (Right to Manage) (England) Regulations 2012, SI 2012/1821, reg 15(2): see PARA 463. As to the meaning of 'authority' see PARA 458 note 2. As to voting at ballots see PARA 461 note 11.
3   As to the meaning of 'secure tenant' see LANDLORD AND TENANT vol 63 (2016) PARA 1037.
4   Ie under the Housing (Right to Manage) (England) Regulations 2012, SI 2012/1821, reg 15(3): see PARA 463. As to extension of time by agreement see PARA 462 note 8.
5   As to the meaning of 'TMO agreement' see PARA 458 note 5.
6   Housing (Right to Manage) (England) Regulations 2012, SI 2012/1821, reg 16(1). As to the meaning of 'TMO' see PARA 460.
7   Housing (Right to Manage) (England) Regulations 2012, SI 2012/1821, reg 16(2). As to the Secretary of State see PARA 7.
8   Ie under the Housing (Right to Manage) (England) Regulations 2012, SI 2012/1821, reg 15(3): see PARA 463. As to extension of time by agreement see PARA 462 note 8.
9   As to societies registered under the Co-operative and Community Benefit Societies Act 2014 see FINANCIAL INSTITUTIONS vol 48 (2015) PARA 880 et seq.
10 Housing (Right to Manage) (England) Regulations 2012, SI 2012/1821, reg 17 (amended by SI 2014/1815). As to companies registered under the Companies Act 2006 see COMPANIES vol 14 (2016) PARA 21 et seq.
11 Housing (Right to Manage) (England) Regulations 2012, SI 2012/1821, reg 17.

465. Determination of disputes. Where an authority[1] and a TMO[2] cannot resolve a dispute that has arisen between them concerning the application or interpretation of any provision of the Housing (Right to Manage) (England) Regulations 2012[3] or the TMO agreement[4], or a determination made under those Regulations, either party may refer[5] the matter for determination to an arbitrator[6] appointed by agreement between them or, in default of agreement, appointed by the Secretary of State[7]. In making such a referral, the authority and the TMO must have regard to any guidance provided from time to time by the Secretary of State as to the procedure and conduct of the arbitration[8].

If a TMO is dissatisfied with an authority's determination of the support[9] which it considers the TMO reasonably requires for the purposes of pursuing a proposal notice[10], it may, within 28 days of being notified of the determination, refer the request for support to an arbitrator[11]. Where a TMO makes a referral to an arbitrator it must at the same time give notice of that referral to the authority[12]. Within 28 days of a referral the arbitrator must determine the support which the arbitrator considers the TMO reasonably requires for the purposes of pursuing the proposal notice and notify the authority and the TMO of the determination[13]. Where a determination has been so notified, the authority must provide support in accordance with that determination[14].

1   As to the meaning of 'authority' see PARA 458 note 2.
2   As to the meaning of 'TMO' see PARA 460.
3   Ie the Housing (Right to Manage) (England) Regulations 2012, SI 2012/1821.
4   As to the meaning of 'TMO agreement' see PARA 458 note 5.
5   As to the requirements for referral see PARA 461 note 20.
6   As to the meaning of 'arbitrator' see PARA 459 note 12.

7   Housing (Right to Manage) (England) Regulations 2012, SI 2012/1821, reg 8(1). As to the Secretary of State see PARA 7.
8   Housing (Right to Manage) (England) Regulations 2012, SI 2012/1821, reg 8(2).
9   As to the meaning of 'support' see PARA 462 note 5.
10 Ie under the Housing (Right to Manage) (England) Regulations 2012, SI 2012/1821, reg 12(2)(a): see PARA 462. As to the meaning of 'proposal notice' see PARA 458 note 2; and as to such notices see PARA 461.
11 Housing (Right to Manage) (England) Regulations 2012, SI 2012/1821, reg 12(4). As to agreement to extend time see PARA 462 note 8.
12 Housing (Right to Manage) (England) Regulations 2012, SI 2012/1821, reg 12(5).
13 Housing (Right to Manage) (England) Regulations 2012, SI 2012/1821, reg 12(6). As to agreement to extend time see PARA 462 note 8. As to the requirements for notification see PARA 461 note 20.
14 Housing (Right to Manage) (England) Regulations 2012, SI 2012/1821, reg 12(7).

(C)   Procedure in Wales

466. Proposal notice. Subject as follows, a notice served by a tenant management organisation[1] on a local housing authority[2] complies with the statutory requirements[3] if it contains a proposal that the local housing authority should enter into a management agreement[4] with the tenant management organisation in relation to such of the authority's houses[5], including not less than 25 dwelling houses[6] which at the time the notice is served are let[7] under secure tenancies[8], and such other land held by the authority for a related purpose, as are identified in the notice[9]. The other requirements are that:

(1)   none of those houses or that land is outside the area of the tenant management organisation which has served the notice[10];

(2)   none of those houses or that land is identified in any notice which complies with these requirements and which has previously been served on the authority and not withdrawn; and

(3)   if any of those houses or that land is already included in a management agreement with a tenant management organisation, all of those houses or that land are so included, and either the tenant management organisation which has served the notice is a party to that agreement or the number of dwelling houses to which that agreement relates is greater than 2,500[11].

A local housing authority may decline to accept a notice (a 'further notice') served on the authority by a tenant management organisation proposing a management agreement if that further notice contains a similar proposal to the proposal contained in a previous proposal notice[12] which was withdrawn within a period of two years ending on the date on which the further notice is received[13]. Where an authority declines to accept a further notice in those circumstances, that notice must not be treated as complying with the statutory requirements[14]. The authority may also decline to accept the notice where, within one month of receiving a notice served on the authority by a tenant management organisation proposing a management agreement, it has requested the organisation to demonstrate to the authority that:

(a)   before the notice was served, the organisation had used its best endeavours to secure that a copy of the notice was delivered to every dwelling house to which the notice relates; and

(b)   before the notice was served, both a majority of tenants and a majority of secure tenants of the houses to which the notice relates who were at the time members of the organisation, and who voted (either in a ballot or poll of all members, or on a resolution put before a properly constituted general meeting of the organisation), voted in favour of a proposal to serve the notice; and

(c)   at the time the notice was served, the membership of the organisation included both at least 20 per cent of the tenants and at least 20 per cent of the secure tenants of the houses to which the notice relates,

and the organisation has failed within one month to comply with that request in relation to one or more of these matters[15]. Where an authority declines to accept a notice, that notice is not to be treated as complying with the statutory requirements[16]. An authority must not, however, be treated as having declined to accept a notice in accordance with the above provisions unless it has, within the specified period[17], informed the tenant management organisation concerned in writing that the authority has not accepted the notice and of the reason for its decision not to accept the notice[18].

A tenant management organisation may by notice in writing to the local housing authority withdraw a proposal notice served by it at any time[19]. Where a proposal notice is withdrawn no further action may be taken[20] in relation to that notice[21].

1   As to the meaning of 'tenant management organisation' see PARA 460.
2   As to the meaning of 'local housing authority' see PARA 11.
3   Ie the requirements of the Housing (Right to Manage) Regulations 1994, SI 1994/627, reg 2. A notice which complies with these requirements is referred to as a 'proposal notice': see reg 1(2). As to the application of the Housing (Right to Manage) Regulations 1994, SI 1994/627, to Wales only see PARA 459 note 5.
4   As to the meaning of 'management agreement' see PARA 457 note 5.
5   As to the meaning of 'house' see PARA 405 note 6.
6   As to the meaning of 'dwelling house' for these purposes see PARA 460 note 11.
7   As to the meaning of 'let' see PARA 31 note 3.
8   As to the meanings of 'secure tenancy' and 'secure tenant' see LANDLORD AND TENANT vol 63 (2016) PARA 1037.
9   Housing (Right to Manage) Regulations 1994, SI 1994/627, reg 2(1).
10 Ie as specified in the constitution of that organisation in accordance with the Housing (Right to Manage) Regulations 1994, SI 1994/627, reg 1(4): see PARA 460.
11 See the Housing (Right to Manage) Regulations 1994, SI 1994/627, reg 2(1)(a)–(c).
12 For these purposes, a further notice contains a similar proposal to the proposal contained in a previous proposal notice if at least half of the houses identified in it were also identified in the previous proposal notice: Housing (Right to Manage) Regulations 1994, SI 1994/627, reg 2(3).
13 See the Housing (Right to Manage) Regulations 1994, SI 1994/627, reg 2(2).
14 See note 13.
15 See the Housing (Right to Manage) Regulations 1994, SI 1994/627, reg 2(4), (5).
16 Housing (Right to Manage) Regulations 1994, SI 1994/627, reg 2(4).
17 The period referred to is, where the Housing (Right to Manage) Regulations 1994, SI 1994/627, reg 2(5) applies (see the text to note 15), six weeks from the date on which the authority made the request under reg 2(5), and, where reg 2(5) does not apply, one month from the date on which the notice was served: reg 2(7). Except in relation to the period specified in reg 4(16) (see PARA 468), where any person is required or permitted to exercise any function under the Housing (Right to Manage) Regulations 1994, SI 1994/627, within a specified period, the tenant management organisation and local housing authority concerned may by agreement in writing before the expiry of that period extend the period for a further specified period: reg 1(6), (7).
18 Housing (Right to Manage) Regulations 1994, SI 1994/627, reg 2(6).
19 Housing (Right to Manage) Regulations 1994, SI 1994/627, reg 6(1).
20 Ie under the Housing (Right to Manage) Regulations 1994, SI 1994/627.
21 Housing (Right to Manage) Regulations 1994, SI 1994/627, reg 6(2).

467. Local authority support following proposal notice. A tenant management organisation[1] which has served a proposal notice[2] on a local housing authority[3] may, at any time after the service of the notice, request the authority to provide or finance the provision of such office accommodation and facilities, and such training, as the organisation reasonably requires at the time of the request for the purpose of pursuing the proposal contained in the notice[4]. Such a request must be in writing and must specify the provision which the tenant management organisation considers it reasonably requires at that time for that purpose[5].

On receipt of such a request, the authority must determine the provision which it considers the organisation reasonably requires and notify the organisation of its determination within two months[6] of receipt of the request[7]. The authority must provide support in accordance with its determination[8].

If a tenant management organisation is dissatisfied with an authority's determination under these provisions, it may, within 28 days of being notified of the determination, refer the request to an arbitrator[9]. A tenant management organisation which refers a request to an arbitrator must, at the same time, give notice of that referral to the authority[10].

Where a request is so referred to an arbitrator:

(1)   the arbitrator must determine the provision which he considers the organisation reasonably requires for the purpose of pursuing the proposal at the time of the request and notify the authority and the organisation of his determination within two months of the request being referred to him[11]; and

(2)   the authority must provide support in accordance with the determination notified by him under head (1)[12].

Any requirement on an authority to provide support under these provisions ceases if a proposal notice is withdrawn[13].

1   As to the meaning of 'tenant management organisation' see PARA 460.
2   As to the meaning of 'proposal notice' see PARA 466 note 3.
3   As to the meaning of 'local housing authority' see PARA 11.
4   Housing (Right to Manage) Regulations 1994, SI 1994/627, reg 3(1). As to the application of the
    Housing (Right to Manage) Regulations 1994, SI 1994/627, to Wales only see PARA 459 note 5.
5   Housing (Right to Manage) Regulations 1994, SI 1994/627, reg 3(2).
6   As to the extension of time limits see PARA 466 note 17.
7   Housing (Right to Manage) Regulations 1994, SI 1994/627, reg 3(3).
8   Housing (Right to Manage) Regulations 1994, SI 1994/627, reg 3(4). This duty is subject to
    reg 3(8): see head (2) in the text.
9   Housing (Right to Manage) Regulations 1994, SI 1994/627, reg 3(5). As to the meaning of
    'arbitrator' see PARA 459 note 12.
10 Housing (Right to Manage) Regulations 1994, SI 1994/627, reg 3(6).
11 Housing (Right to Manage) Regulations 1994, SI 1994/627, reg 3(7). See note 6.
12 Housing (Right to Manage) Regulations 1994, SI 1994/627, reg 3(8).
13 See the Housing (Right to Manage) Regulations 1994, SI 1994/627, reg 3(9). As to withdrawal of
    a proposal notice see PARA 466.

468. Procedure following proposal notice. If a tenant management organisation[1] has not, within three months[2] of serving a proposal notice[3], appointed an approved person[4] to carry out an initial feasibility study[5] and notified the Welsh Ministers and the local housing authority[6] of the appointment, the proposal notice is deemed to have been withdrawn[7].

The authority must arrange for an initial feasibility study to be conducted by the approved person appointed[8] and that person must, within nine months of his appointment, send a report of the study to the Welsh Ministers, the authority and the tenant management organisation, which must include his conclusion[9] as to whether or not it is reasonable to proceed with a full feasibility study[10]. Where the approved person concludes that it is not reasonable to proceed with a full feasibility study, the proposal notice is deemed to have been withdrawn[11]. Where the approved person concludes that it is reasonable to proceed with a full feasibility study, the authority must, within one month of the approved person submitting his report to the authority, give to the tenants of each house[12] identified in the proposal notice a description prepared by the approved person of the proposal, and arrange for a ballot[13] or poll to be carried out within that period of those tenants with a view to establishing their opinion about the proposal[14]. If it appears from a ballot or poll so carried out that either a majority of the tenants or a majority of the secure tenants[15] who, on that ballot or poll, express an opinion about the proposal are opposed to it, the authority must notify the tenant management organisation accordingly, and the proposal notice is deemed to have been withdrawn[16]. If it appears otherwise, the authority must notify the Welsh Ministers and the tenant management organisation accordingly[17].

Where all of the houses which are identified in a proposal notice are already included in a management agreement[18] to which the tenant management organisation which served the notice is a party, an approved person is deemed to have been appointed to carry out an initial feasibility study and is deemed to have concluded that it is reasonable to proceed with a full feasibility study, and the authority is deemed to have complied with the relevant requirements[19].

If the tenant management organisation has not, within six months of receiving the notification[20] or, where appropriate[21], within six months of serving a proposal notice, appointed an approved person to carry out a full feasibility study and notified the Welsh Ministers and the authority of the appointment, the proposal notice is deemed to have been withdrawn[22]. The authority must arrange for a full feasibility study to be conducted by the approved person so appointed[23] and that person must, within two years of his appointment, submit a report of the full feasibility study to the Welsh Ministers, the authority and the tenant management organisation, which must include his conclusion as to whether it is reasonable to proceed with the proposed management agreement and, if so, on what terms the agreement should be entered into[24]. Where the approved person concludes that it is not reasonable to proceed with the proposed agreement, and this conclusion is not referred to an arbitrator[25], the proposal notice is deemed to have been withdrawn[26].

Where the approved person concludes that it is reasonable to proceed with the proposed agreement, and neither this conclusion nor his conclusion as to the terms to be included in the agreement are referred to an arbitrator[27], the authority must, within a period of two months beginning on the day on which the approved person submitted his report to the authority:

(1)   serve a notice prepared by the approved person on the tenants of each house identified in the proposal notice which summarises the terms of the proposed agreement set out in his report and contains the address of a place within the locality of the identified houses at which a copy of that report, containing those terms, may be inspected; and

(2)   arrange for a ballot (using a ballot paper prepared by the approved person) to be carried out within such period of those tenants with a view to establishing their opinion about the proposal to enter into a management agreement on those terms[28].

If it does not appear from a ballot carried out in accordance with head (2) that both a majority of the tenants and a majority of the secure tenants are in favour of the proposal, the authority must notify the Welsh Ministers and the tenant management organisation and the proposal notice is deemed to have been withdrawn[29]. If it does appear that both a majority of the tenants and a majority of the secure tenants are in favour of the proposal, the authority must within one month notify the Welsh Ministers and the tenant management organisation[30]. Within two months of that notification (or within one month of the registration of that organisation[31], if later) the authority must enter into a management agreement with the tenant management organisation on the terms made available for inspection, or on those terms subject to such modifications as may be agreed by the tenant management organisation[32].

Within 14 days of entering into a management agreement, an authority must submit a copy of the agreement to the Welsh Ministers[33].

1   As to the meaning of 'tenant management organisation' see PARA 460.
2   As to the extension of time limits see PARA 466 note 17.
3   As to the meaning of 'proposal notice' see PARA 466 note 3.
4   'Approved person' means a member of a panel of persons approved by the Welsh Ministers for the purpose of conducting initial or full feasibility studies (see notes 5, 10) under the Housing (Right to Manage) Regulations 1994, SI 1994/627, and the Welsh Ministers may approve a person to act in a specified area only: reg 1(2). As to the Welsh Ministers see PARA 7. As to the application of the Housing (Right to Manage) Regulations 1994, SI 1994/627, to Wales only see PARA 459 note 5.
5   'Initial feasibility study' means, in relation to a particular proposal for a management agreement, a study carried out by an approved person to determine whether it is reasonable to proceed with a full feasibility study: Housing (Right to Manage) Regulations 1994, SI 1994/627, reg 1(2).
6   As to the meaning of 'local housing authority' see PARA 11.
7   Housing (Right to Manage) Regulations 1994, SI 1994/627, reg 4(1)(a).
8   Housing (Right to Manage) Regulations 1994, SI 1994/627, reg 4(1)(b).
9   As to guidance by the Welsh Ministers see the Housing (Right to Manage) Regulations 1994, SI 1994/627, reg 7; and PARA 459.
10   Housing (Right to Manage) Regulations 1994, SI 1994/627, reg 4(2). 'Full feasibility study' means, in relation to a particular proposal for a management agreement, a study carried out by an approved person to determine whether it is reasonable to proceed with the agreement and, if so, the terms on which the agreement should be entered into: reg 1(2).
11   Housing (Right to Manage) Regulations 1994, SI 1994/627, reg 4(3).
12   As to the meaning of 'tenant' see PARA 31 note 3; and as to the meaning of 'house' see PARA 405 note 6.
13   Any ballot held under the Housing (Right to Manage) Regulations 1994, SI 1994/627, must be organised so that the vote cast by any individual is kept secret: reg 1(8).
14   Housing (Right to Manage) Regulations 1994, SI 1994/627, reg 4(4).
15   As to the meaning of 'secure tenant' see LANDLORD AND TENANT vol 63 (2016) PARA 1037 (definition applied by the Housing (Right to Manage) Regulations 1994, SI 1994/627, reg 1(2)).
16   Housing (Right to Manage) Regulations 1994, SI 1994/627, reg 4(5).
17   See the Housing (Right to Manage) Regulations 1994, SI 1994/627, reg 4(6).
18   As to the meaning of 'management agreement' see PARA 457 note 5.
19   See the Housing (Right to Manage) Regulations 1994, SI 1994/627, reg 4(7). The relevant requirements are those of reg 4(4)(a), (b), (6) (see the text and notes 14, 17): see reg 4(7).
20   Ie the notification mentioned in the Housing (Right to Manage) Regulations 1994, SI 1994/627, reg 4(6): see the text and note 17.
21   Ie where the Housing (Right to Manage) Regulations 1994, SI 1994/627, reg 4(7) applies: see the text and notes 18–19.
22   Housing (Right to Manage) Regulations 1994, SI 1994/627, reg 4(8)(a).
23   Housing (Right to Manage) Regulations 1994, SI 1994/627, reg 4(8)(b).
24   Housing (Right to Manage) Regulations 1994, SI 1994/627, reg 4(9). The terms of a management agreement set out in a report submitted under reg 4(9) and the terms as modified in accordance with reg 4(14) (see the text to notes 30–32) must be in such form as may be approved by the Welsh Ministers for the purpose of the Housing (Right to Manage) Regulations 1994, SI 1994/627: reg 4(10).
25   Ie under the Housing (Right to Manage) Regulations 1994, SI 1994/627, reg 5: see PARA 469.
26   Housing (Right to Manage) Regulations 1994, SI 1994/627, reg 4(11).
27   See note 25.
28   Housing (Right to Manage) Regulations 1994, SI 1994/627, reg 4(12).
29   Housing (Right to Manage) Regulations 1994, SI 1994/627, reg 4(13).
30   Housing (Right to Manage) Regulations 1994, SI 1994/627, reg 4(14).
31   An authority must not enter into a management agreement under the Housing (Right to Manage) Regulations 1994, SI 1994/627, reg 4(14) unless the tenant management organisation is registered as a registered society under the Co-operative and Community Benefit Societies Act 2014 (see FINANCIAL INSTITUTIONS vol 48 (2015) PARA 880 et seq) or as a company under the Companies Act 2006 (see COMPANIES vol 14 (2016) PARA 21 et seq); and where the organisation is not so

registered nor has applied to be so registered on the expiry of the two month period mentioned in the Housing (Right to Manage) Regulations 1994, SI 1994/627, reg 4(14), the proposal notice is deemed to have been withdrawn: reg 4(15); Co-operative and Community Benefit Societies Act 2014 s 150(1).
32 See the Housing (Right to Manage) Regulations 1994, SI 1994/627, reg 4(14).
33 Housing (Right to Manage) Regulations 1994, SI 1994/627, reg 4(16). The period of 14 days may not be extended: see reg 1(7).

469. Determination of disputes. Where an approved person[1] submits a report of the full feasibility study[2], the local housing authority[3] or the tenant management organisation[4] may refer any of the conclusions set out in the report with which it disagrees to an arbitrator[5]. This must be done within two months[6] of the report being submitted to the body which makes the reference[7]. Where the approved person's conclusion as to whether it is reasonable to proceed with the proposed management agreement[8] is referred to an arbitrator, the arbitrator must decide whether it is reasonable so to proceed and notify the Welsh Ministers[9], the local housing authority, the tenant management organisation and the approved person of his decision within two months of the matter being referred to him[10]. Where the arbitrator decides that it is not reasonable to proceed with the agreement, the proposal notice[11] is deemed to have been withdrawn[12].

Where the arbitrator decides that it is reasonable to proceed with the agreement, this decision accords with the approved person's conclusion, and the approved person's conclusion as to the terms on which the agreement should be entered into has not been referred to the arbitrator, the local housing authority must proceed further[13]. Within two months of being notified of the arbitrator's decision, the authority must:

(1) serve a notice prepared by the approved person on the tenants of each house[14] identified in the proposal notice which summarises the terms of the proposed agreement set out in his report and contains the address of a place within the locality of the identified houses at which a copy of that report, containing those terms, may be inspected; and

(2) arrange for a ballot[15] (using a ballot paper prepared by the approved person) to be carried out within such period of those tenants with a view to establishing their opinion about the proposal to enter into a management agreement on those terms[16].

Where the arbitrator decides that it is reasonable to proceed with the agreement but this decision does not accord with the approved person's conclusion, the matter must be referred back to the approved person, who must, within three months of the matter being referred back to him, resubmit his report[17]. That report must be in accordance with the decision of the arbitrator and must include the terms on which the agreement should be entered into[18]. Where a report is resubmitted, the approved person's conclusion in the resubmitted report as to whether it is reasonable to proceed with the agreement is not to be referred to an arbitrator[19].

Where the approved person's conclusion as to the terms on which the agreement should be entered into is referred to an arbitrator, the arbitrator must, within two months of the matter being referred to him (or, where he has given notice[20] of his decision that it is reasonable to proceed with the agreement, within two months of giving that notice):

(a) determine the terms on which the agreement should be entered into[21]; and

(b) notify the Welsh Ministers, the local housing authority, the tenant management organisation and the approved person of his determination, setting out those terms in his notification[22].

Where an authority is so notified of a determination it must comply with heads (1) and (2) within two months of being so notified[23].

1   As to the meaning of 'approved person' see PARA 468 note 4.
2   Ie a report under the Housing (Right to Manage) Regulations 1994, SI 1994/627, reg 4(9): see PARA 468. As to the meaning of 'full feasibility study' see PARA 468 note 10. As to the application of the Housing (Right to Manage) Regulations 1994, SI 1994/627, to Wales only see PARA 459 note 5.
3   As to the meaning of 'local housing authority' see PARA 11.
4   As to the meaning of 'tenant management organisation' see PARA 460.
5   Housing (Right to Manage) Regulations 1994, SI 1994/627, reg 5(1). This is subject to reg 5(6): see the text to note 19. As to the choice of arbitrator see PARA 459 note 12.
6   As to the extension of time limits see PARA 466 note 17.
7   See the Housing (Right to Manage) Regulations 1994, SI 1994/627, reg 5(1). This is subject to reg 5(6): see the text to note 19.
8   As to the meaning of 'management agreement' see PARA 457 note 5.
9   As to the Welsh Ministers see PARA 7.
10 Housing (Right to Manage) Regulations 1994, SI 1994/627, reg 5(2).
11 As to the meaning of 'proposal notice' see PARA 466 note 3.
12 Housing (Right to Manage) Regulations 1994, SI 1994/627, reg 5(3).
13 See the Housing (Right to Manage) Regulations 1994, SI 1994/627, reg 5(4).
14 As to the meaning of 'tenant' see PARA 31 note 3; and as to the meaning of 'house' see PARA 405 note 6.
15 As to organisation of the ballot see PARA 468 note 13.
16 See the Housing (Right to Manage) Regulations 1994, SI 1994/627, reg 4(12)(a), (b) (applied by reg 5(4)).
17 Housing (Right to Manage) Regulations 1994, SI 1994/627, reg 5(5). The report must be resubmitted under reg 4(9): see PARA 468.
18 Housing (Right to Manage) Regulations 1994, SI 1994/627, reg 5(5).
19 Housing (Right to Manage) Regulations 1994, SI 1994/627, reg 5(6).
20 Ie under the Housing (Right to Manage) Regulations 1994, SI 1994/627, reg 5(2): see the text and notes 8–10.
21 The terms must be in such form as may be approved by the Welsh Ministers for the purpose of the Housing (Right to Manage) Regulations 1994, SI 1994/627: see reg 5(7)(a).
22 Housing (Right to Manage) Regulations 1994, SI 1994/627, reg 5(7).
23 Housing (Right to Manage) Regulations 1994, SI 1994/627, reg 5(8). For the purpose of such compliance, the reference in head (1) in the text to the terms of the agreement as set out in the approved person's report and to that report must be construed as a reference to the terms of the agreement as set out in the determination notified under reg 5(7) (see the text and notes 20–22) and to that determination: see reg 5(8).

(vi) Recovery of Possession and Grounds for Possession

470. In general. A secure tenant[1] of a local authority or other public sector landlord has security of tenure[2]. This means that the landlord may only recover possession by bringing court proceedings in a manner prescribed by the Housing Act 1985[3]. Before starting proceedings, the landlord must usually serve a notice of intended possession proceedings on the tenant which sets out the ground or grounds on which the landlord will rely as well as giving particulars of those grounds[4]. The grounds for possession which are set out in the Housing Act 1985[5] fall into three categories: (1) grounds where the landlord must also satisfy the court that it is reasonable to make an order[6]; (2) grounds where the landlord must also satisfy the court that suitable alternative accommodation is available[7]; and (3) grounds where the landlord must satisfy the court that it is reasonable to make an order and that suitable alternative accommodation is available[8].

These matters are dealt with elsewhere in this work[9].

1   As to the meanings of 'secure tenancy' and 'secure tenant' see LANDLORD AND TENANT vol 63 (2016) PARA 1037. Note the prospective changes to tenure in Wales under the Renting Homes (Wales) Act 2016: see PARAS 6, 226.

2 See the Housing Act 1985 s 82; and LANDLORD AND TENANT vol 63 (2016) PARA 1085.
3 See the Housing Act 1985 ss 83, 83A; and LANDLORD AND TENANT vol 63 (2016) PARA 1113.
4 See note 3.
5 See the Housing Act 1985 s 84, Sch 2; and LANDLORD AND TENANT vol 63 (2016) PARA 1139 et seq.
6 See the Housing Act 1985 Sch 2 Pt I (grounds 1–8); and LANDLORD AND TENANT vol 63 (2016) PARAS 1139–1148.
7 See the Housing Act 1985 Sch 2 Pt II (grounds 9–11); and LANDLORD AND TENANT vol 63 (2016) PARAS 1149–1153. As to suitable alternative accommodation see LANDLORD AND TENANT vol 63 (2016) PARA 1137.
8 See the Housing Act 1985 Sch 2 Pt III (grounds 12–16); and LANDLORD AND TENANT vol 63 (2016) PARAS 1154–1159.
9 See LANDLORD AND TENANT.

(vii) Dealing with Anti-social Behaviour

A. MEASURES AVAILABLE

471. Background to the legislation. Under Part V of the Housing Act 1996[1], local housing authorities[2] and other social landlords have powers to deal with anti-social behaviour by tenants, their families or visitors. A three-pronged approach was adopted by the Housing Act 1996. First, a local housing authority or housing action trust may elect to operate an introductory tenancy regime[3]. Secondly, the right of local authorities and other social landlords to recover possession in cases of anti-social behaviour is extended; in particular, nuisance as a ground for possession is broadened and now applies to behaviour in the locality of a tenant's home and to misbehaviour by the tenant's visitors and towards the landlord[4]. Landlords may start proceedings as soon as a notice of possession proceedings has been issued where nuisance or other anti-social behaviour is alleged[5]. Thirdly, it was possible to seek a power of arrest when applying for an injunction to prevent anti-social behaviour[6]. This last has been replaced by a general power for the court to grant an injunction against anti-social behaviour[7].

Provision has also been made for the demotion of tenancies as an additional measure for dealing with anti-social behaviour; a demoted tenancy becomes a secure tenancy only at the end of the period of one year (the demotion period) starting with the day on which the demotion order takes effect[8].

1 Ie the Housing Act 1996 Pt V (ss 124–151): see PARA 472. For the background see: Driscoll *A Guide to the Housing Act 1996* (1996).
2 As to the meaning of 'local housing authority' see PARA 11.
3 See PARA 472. As to housing action trusts see PARA 537 et seq.
4 See the Housing Act 1985 s 84, Sch 2 Pt I ground 2 (substituted by the Housing Act 1996 s 144; and amended by the Serious Organised Crime and Police Act 2005 s 111, Sch 7 para 45; the Anti-social Behaviour, Crime and Policing Act 2014 s 98(1)); and LANDLORD AND TENANT vol 63 (2016) PARA 1140.
5 See the Housing Act 1985 s 83 (substituted by the Housing Act 1996 s 147(1); and amended by the Anti-social Behaviour Act 2003 s 14(3); the Anti-social Behaviour, Crime and Policing Act 2014 s 181(1), Sch 11, para 7; and the Housing and Planning Act 2016 ss 118, 119(1), (3), Sch 7 para 33(2)); and LANDLORD AND TENANT vol 63 (2016) PARA 1134.
6 See the Housing Act 1996 Pt V Ch III (ss 153A–158) (repealed by the Anti-social Behaviour, Crime and Policing Act 2014 s 181(1), Sch 11 para 22 as from 23 March 2015). The Anti-social Behaviour Act 2003 amended the provisions relating to injunctions and other matters, and like changes were made to the powers of registered social landlords in relation to their assured tenants, but these provisions have been replaced by a general power to grant an injunction against anti-social behaviour in the Anti-social Behaviour, Crime and Policing Act 2014 s 1 as from 23 March 2015: see PARA 473.
7 See PARA 473.
8 See the Housing Act 1985 s 82A (added by the Anti-social Behaviour Act 2003 s 14(2); and amended by the Police and Justice Act 2006 s 52, Sch 14 para 12(1), (2); the Crime and Courts Act

2013 s 17(5), Sch 9 para 52(1)(b), (2); the Anti-social Behaviour, Crime and Policing Act 2014 s 181(1), Sch 11 para 6(1), (2); and SI 2010/866; and, as from a day to be appointed, by the Housing and Planning Act 2016 s 118, Sch 7 paras 2, 7; at the date at which this volume states the law, no such day had been appointed); the Housing Act 1996 Pt V Ch 1A (ss 143A–143P) (added by the Anti-social Behaviour Act 2003 Sch 1); PARA 474; and LANDLORD AND TENANT vol 63 (2016) PARA 1118 et seq.

B.   INTRODUCTORY TENANCIES

472. Introductory tenancy regime. It is important to emphasise that the use of introductory tenancies is not mandatory and each local housing authority or housing action trust can decide whether or not it wishes to introduce such a regime[1]. When considering the introduction of such a regime, landlords may have to consider consulting their secure tenants under the statutory procedures laid down in the Housing Act 1985[2]. When such an election is in force, every periodic tenancy[3] of a dwelling house[4] entered into or adopted by the authority or trust must, with certain exceptions[5], if it would otherwise be a secure tenancy[6], be an introductory tenancy[7].

Under an introductory tenancy, the tenant will not become a secure tenant[8] until 12 months after the start of the tenancy; he has no security of tenure during this 12-month period and the landlord can recover possession if the landlord believes that the tenant's conduct is unsatisfactory[9]. Unless proceedings for possession are begun, a tenancy remains an introductory tenancy until the end of the trial period, unless a specified event occurs before the end of that period[10]. If both of the specified conditions are met in relation to an introductory tenancy, the trial period is extended by six months[11].

The landlord may only bring an introductory tenancy to an end by obtaining an order of the court[12] for the possession of the dwelling house, and the court may not make such an order unless the requirements relating to notice are satisfied[13]. Where the court makes an order for possession of the dwelling house, the tenancy comes to an end when the order is executed[14]. A request for review of the landlord's decision to seek an order for possession of a dwelling house let under an introductory tenancy must be made before the end of the period of 14 days beginning with the day on which the notice of proceedings is served[15]. On a request being duly made, the landlord must review the decision[16]. Where the landlord has begun proceedings for the possession of a dwelling house let under an introductory tenancy and the trial period ends, or any of the specified events occurs, then subject to specified exceptions, the tenancy remains an introductory tenancy until the tenancy comes to an end on the execution of an order of the court, or until the proceedings are otherwise finally determined[17].

Provision is made as to the person qualified to succeed the tenant under an introductory tenancy[18], and as to succession to an introductory tenancy[19]. There is a general prohibition (with some exceptions) on assignment of an introductory tenancy[20].

Every local housing authority or housing action trust which lets dwelling houses under introductory tenancies must from time to time publish information about its introductory tenancies[21], and must maintain such arrangements as it considers appropriate to enable those of its introductory tenants who are likely to be substantially affected by a relevant matter of housing management to be informed of the proposals of the authority or trust in respect of the matter, and to make their views known to the authority or trust within a specified period; and the authority or trust must, before making a decision on the matter, consider any representations made to it in accordance with those arrangements[22].

The appropriate national authority[23] may by regulations apply to introductory tenants any provision made under the right to repair provisions[24] of the Housing Act 1985 in relation to secure tenants[25].

Amendments made by the Localism Act 2011 provide that certain introductory tenancies should become flexible tenancies[26]. Flexible tenancies are a new category of less secure tenancy introduced by the Localism Act 2011 with effect from 1 April 2012[27]. However, because the flexible tenancies regime did not alter the use of social housing stock to the extent that was intended, the Housing and Planning Act 2016 contains provisions abolishing them[28].

1　See the Housing Act 1996 s 124(1); and LANDLORD AND TENANT vol 63 (2016) PARA 1103. Advocating the use of introductory tenancies, a consultation document stated that 'A probationary tenancy, to be converted automatically on its satisfactory completion, will give a clear signal to new tenants that anti-social behaviour is unacceptable and that it will result in the loss of their homes. It would also give reassurance to existing tenants that their authority would take prompt action to remove any new tenants acting in this way': see Department of the Environment consultation document *Anti-social Behaviour on Council Estates* para 3.2 (April 1995). See now Tackling anti-social behaviour: tools and powers for social landlords (Department for Communities and Local Government, 1 April 2010). As to the meaning of 'local housing authority' see PARA 11 (definition applied by the Housing Act 1996 s 230). As to housing action trusts see PARA 537 et seq.

2　See HL Official Report, 10 July 1996, col 411. The statutory procedures referred to are those laid down in the Housing Act 1985 s 105: see PARA 447.

3　As to the meaning of 'tenancy' see PARA 168 note 16.

4　As to the meaning of 'dwelling house' for these purposes see the Housing Act 1996 s 139; and LANDLORD AND TENANT vol 63 (2016) PARA 1103.

5　See the Housing Act 1996 s 124(3); and LANDLORD AND TENANT vol 63 (2016) PARA 1103.

6　As to the meanings of 'secure tenancy' and 'secure tenant' see LANDLORD AND TENANT vol 63 (2016) PARA 1037 (definitions applied by the Housing Act 1996 s 230).

7　See the Housing Act 1996 s 124(1A), (2), (2A); and LANDLORD AND TENANT vol 63 (2016) PARA 1103. Prospectively, an introductory tenancy must be granted for a fixed term of at least two years and in general not more than ten years: see ss 124A, 124B (added, as from a day to be appointed, by the Housing and Planning Act 2016 s 118, Sch 7 paras 19, 21; at the date at which this volume states the law, no such day had been appointed); and LANDLORD AND TENANT vol 63 (2016) PARAS 1104–1105.

　　The statutory provisions relating to introductory tenancies apply in relation to a licence to occupy a dwelling house, whether or not granted for a consideration, as they apply in relation to a tenancy (see the Housing Act 1996 s 126(1); and LANDLORD AND TENANT vol 63 (2016) PARA 1108), but there are exceptions to this (see s 126(2); and LANDLORD AND TENANT vol 63 (2016) PARA 1108) and in view of the decision of the House of Lords in *Street v Mountford* [1985] AC 809, [1985] 2 All ER 289, HL, it is unlikely that valid licences will be granted.

8　As to the meaning of 'secure tenancy' see LANDLORD AND TENANT vol 63 (2016) PARA 1037.

9　See the Housing Act 1996 s 127; and LANDLORD AND TENANT vol 63 (2016) PARA 1160. It is settled law that the introductory tenancy schemes and the homelessness legislation are compliant with the Convention for the Protection of Human Rights and Fundamental Freedoms (Rome, 4 November 1950; TS 71 (1953); Cmd 8969) arts 6 and 8 (as set out in the Human Rights Act 1998 Sch 1 Pt I) and it will thus only be in highly exceptional cases that any defence to possession proceedings on the ground that the court's decision to recover possession was a decision that no reasonable person would consider justifiable can be established: *Salford City Council v Mullen (Secretary of State for Communities and Local Government, intervening)* [2010] EWCA Civ 336, [2011] 1 All ER 119, [2010] HLR 555.

10　See the Housing Act 1996 s 125; and LANDLORD AND TENANT vol 63 (2016) PARA 1106.

11　See the Housing Act 1996 s 125A; and LANDLORD AND TENANT vol 63 (2016) PARA 1107. The conditions relate to the giving of notice and, if requested by the tenant, the holding of a review of the landlord's decision to extend the trial period: see ss 125A, 125B; and LANDLORD AND TENANT vol 63 (2016) PARA 1107.

12　Ie the County Court: see the Housing Act 1996 s 138(1); and LANDLORD AND TENANT vol 63 (2016) PARA 1161.

13　See the Housing Act 1996 ss 127, 128; and LANDLORD AND TENANT vol 63 (2016) PARA 1160.

14　See the Housing Act 1996 s 127(1A); and LANDLORD AND TENANT vol 63 (2016) PARA 1160.

15　See the Housing Act 1996 s 129(1); and LANDLORD AND TENANT vol 63 (2016) PARA 1161.

16　See the Housing Act 1996 s 129(2); and LANDLORD AND TENANT vol 63 (2016) PARA 1161. See also the Introductory Tenants (Review) Regulations 1997, SI 1997/72.

17 See the Housing Act 1996 s 130; and LANDLORD AND TENANT vol 63 (2016) PARA 1162.
18 See the Housing Act 1996 ss 130A, 131, 132; and LANDLORD AND TENANT vol 63 (2016) PARA 1116.
19 See the Housing Act 1996 s 133; and LANDLORD AND TENANT vol 63 (2016) PARA 1117.
20 See the Housing Act 1996 s 134; and LANDLORD AND TENANT vol 63 (2016) PARA 1110.
21 See the Housing Act 1996 s 136; and LANDLORD AND TENANT vol 63 (2016) PARA 1113.
22 See the Housing Act 1996 s 137; and LANDLORD AND TENANT vol 63 (2016) PARA 1114.
23 Ie the Secretary of State or, where statutory functions have been transferred in relation to Wales, the Welsh Ministers: see PARA 7.
24 Ie under the Housing Act 1985 s 96: see LANDLORD AND TENANT vol 63 (2016) PARA 1074.
25 See the Housing Act 1996 s 135; the Secure Tenants of Local Housing Authorities (Right to Repair) (Amendment) Regulations 1997, SI 1997/73; and LANDLORD AND TENANT vol 63 (2016) PARA 1111.
26 See the Housing Act 1996 s 137A (added by the Localism Act 2011 s 155(6)); and LANDLORD AND TENANT vol 63 (2016) PARA 1109.
27 See the Housing Act 1985 ss 107A–107E (added by the Localism Act 2011 s 154; repealed, as from a day to be appointed, by the Housing and Planning Act 2016 s 118, Sch 7, paras 2, 14, 33(1)); and LANDLORD AND TENANT vol 63 (2016) PARA 1059 et seq.
28 See LANDLORD AND TENANT vol 63 (2016) PARA 1059.

C.   INJUNCTIONS AGAINST ANTI-SOCIAL BEHAVIOUR

473. Power to grant injunctions against anti-social behaviour. The provisions of the Housing Act 1996 under which in England, the court on the application of a relevant landlord could grant an anti-social behaviour injunction[1], have been replaced by a general power applying in England and Wales under which a court may grant an injunction against a person aged ten or over ('the respondent') if the court is satisfied, on the balance of probabilities, that the respondent has engaged or threatens to engage in anti-social behaviour, or the court considers it just and convenient to grant the injunction for the purpose of preventing the respondent from engaging in anti-social behaviour[2].

For these purposes, 'anti-social behaviour' means:

(1)   conduct that has caused, or is likely to cause, harassment, alarm or distress to any person;

(2)   conduct capable of causing nuisance or annoyance to a person in relation to that person's occupation of residential premises; or

(3)   conduct capable of causing housing-related[3] nuisance or annoyance to any person[4].

Head (2) applies only where the injunction is applied for by: (a) a housing provider[5]; (b) a local authority[6]; or (c) a chief officer of police[7]. An application for an injunction must be made: (i) to a youth court, in the case of a respondent aged under 18; or (ii) the High Court or the County Court, in any other case[8].

Prohibitions and requirements in an injunction under these provisions must, so far as practicable, be such as to avoid: (i) any interference with the times, if any, at which the respondent normally works or attends school or any other educational establishment; (ii) any conflict with the requirements of any other court order or injunction to which the respondent may be subject[9]. An injunction must either specify the period for which it has effect, or state that it has effect until further order[10]. An injunction may specify periods for which particular prohibitions or requirements have effect[11]. The court may grant an interim injunction[12]. The court may vary or discharge an injunction on the application of the person who applied for it or the respondent[13].

Breach of an injunction may result in arrest without warrant, or in the issue of a warrant of arrest[14]. In the case of a young person under 18, a youth court may make a supervision order in respect of a person who it is satisfied beyond reasonable doubt is in breach of a provision of an injunction[15], and where it is satisfied that a defaulter has failed to comply with the requirements of a supervision order, a youth court may make a detention order[16].

1 Ie the Housing Act 1996 Pt V Ch III (ss 153A–158) (repealed by the Anti-social Behaviour, Crime and Policing Act 2014 s 181(1), Sch 11 para 22 as from 23 March 2015).

2 See the Anti-social Behaviour, Crime and Policing Act 2014 s 1(1)–(3). An injunction under s 1 may for the purpose of preventing the respondent from engaging in anti-social behaviour: (1) prohibit the respondent from doing anything described in the injunction; (2) require the respondent to do anything described in the injunction: s 1(4). See generally SENTENCING vol 92 (2015) PARA 371 et seq.

3 'Housing-related' means directly or indirectly relating to the housing management functions of a housing provider or a local authority: Anti-social Behaviour, Crime and Policing Act 2014 s 2(3). For the purposes of s 2(3) the housing management functions of a housing provider or a local authority include: (1) functions conferred by or under an enactment; (2) the powers and duties of the housing provider or local authority as the holder of an estate or interest in housing accommodation: s 2(4).

4 Anti-social Behaviour, Crime and Policing Act 2014 s 2(1).

5 'Housing provider' means: (1) a housing trust, within the meaning given by the Housing Associations Act 1985 s 2 (see PARA 14), that is a charity; (2) a housing action trust established under the Housing Act 1988 s 62 (see PARA 539); (3) in relation to England, a non-profit private registered provider of social housing; (4) in relation to Wales, a Welsh body registered as a social landlord under the Housing Act 1996 s 3 (see PARA 169); (5) any body (other than a local authority or a body within heads (1) to (4)) that is a landlord under a secure tenancy within the meaning given by the Housing Act 1985 s 79 (see LANDLORD AND TENANT vol 63 (2016) PARA 1037): Anti-social Behaviour, Crime and Policing Act 2014 s 20(1).
As to registered providers of social housing see PARA 53; as to when a provider is 'non-profit' see PARA 71.

6 'Local authority' means: (1) in relation to England, a district council, a county council, a London borough council, the Common Council of the City of London or the Council of the Isles of Scilly; (2) in relation to Wales, a county council or a county borough council: Anti-social Behaviour, Crime and Policing Act 2014 s 20(1). As to local government areas and authorities in England and Wales see LOCAL GOVERNMENT vol 69 (2009) PARA 22 et seq. As to the London boroughs and the City of London see LONDON GOVERNMENT vol 71 (2013) PARAS 15, 16.

7 Anti-social Behaviour, Crime and Policing Act 2014 s 2(2).

8 Anti-social Behaviour, Crime and Policing Act 2014 s 1(8). Section 1(8)(b) (head (ii) in the text) is subject to any rules of court made under s 18(2): s 1(8). As to applications see the Anti-social Behaviour, Crime and Policing Act 2014 ss 5, 6, 14; and SENTENCING vol 92 (2015) PARAS 373, 376.

9 Anti-social Behaviour, Crime and Policing Act 2014 s 1(5). As to prohibitions and requirements which may be imposed see the Anti-social Behaviour, Crime and Policing Act 2014 ss 3, 4; and SENTENCING vol 92 (2015) PARA 374. As to exclusion of the respondent from his home see the Anti-social Behaviour, Crime and Policing Act 2014 s 13; and SENTENCING vol 92 (2015) PARA 375.

10 Anti-social Behaviour, Crime and Policing Act 2014 s 1(6). In the case of an injunction granted before the respondent has reached the age of 18, a period must be specified and it must be no more than 12 months: s 1(6).

11 Anti-social Behaviour, Crime and Policing Act 2014 s 1(7).

12 See the Anti-social Behaviour, Crime and Policing Act 2014 s 12; and SENTENCING vol 92 (2015) PARA 377.

13 See the Anti-social Behaviour, Crime and Policing Act 2014 s 8; and SENTENCING vol 92 (2015) PARA 378.

14 See the Anti-social Behaviour, Crime and Policing Act 2014 ss 9, 10; and SENTENCING vol 92 (2015) PARAS 379–380. See also, as to remand, the Anti-social Behaviour, Crime and Policing Act 2014 s 11, Sch 1; and SENTENCING vol 92 (2015) PARAS 381–382.

15 See the Anti-social Behaviour, Crime and Policing Act 2014 s 12, Sch 2 Pt 2 (paras 2–13); and SENTENCING vol 92 (2015) PARAS 384–389.

16 See the Anti-social Behaviour, Crime and Policing Act 2014 s 12, Sch 2 Pt 3 (paras 14–15); and SENTENCING vol 92 (2015) PARAS 390–391.

D.   DEMOTED TENANCIES

474. Provisions relating to demoted tenancies. A demoted tenancy is a periodic tenancy of a dwelling house[1] where

(1)   the landlord is either a local housing authority[2] or a housing action trust[3];

(2)   the tenant condition[4] is satisfied; and

(3)   the tenancy is created by virtue of a demotion order[5].

A demoted tenancy becomes a secure tenancy[6] at the end of the period of one year (the demotion period) starting with the day the demotion order takes effect[7]. In general, a tenancy ceases to be a demoted tenancy if:

(a)   either head (1) or head (2) above ceases to be satisfied;

(b)   the demotion order is quashed; or

(c)   the tenant dies and no one is entitled to succeed to the tenancy[8].

A tenancy does not come to an end merely because it ceases to be a demoted tenancy[9].

The landlord may only bring a demoted tenancy to an end by obtaining an order of the court for possession of the dwelling house; if the court makes such an order, the tenancy comes to an end on the date on which the order is executed[10]. The tenant may request the landlord to review its decision to seek an order for possession and, if such a request is made, the landlord must review the decision[11].

If the landlord has begun proceedings for the possession of a dwelling house let under a demoted tenancy and the demotion period ends, or any of the circumstances in which a tenancy ceases to be a demoted tenancy apply, and if a tenancy ceases to be a demoted tenancy and becomes a secure tenancy, the tenant is not entitled to exercise the right to buy[12] unless the proceedings are finally determined, and he is not required to give up possession of the dwelling house[13].

Specific provision is made as to succession to a demoted tenancy[14]. Except in defined circumstances, a demoted tenancy is not capable of being assigned[15].

The appropriate national authority[16] may by regulations apply to demoted tenants any provision relating to the right of secure tenants to carry out repairs[17].

The landlord of a demoted tenancy which is a local housing authority or a housing action trust is required to publish and keep up to date information about the demoted tenancy in such form as it thinks best suited to explain in simple terms and so far as it considers appropriate the effect of:

(i)   the express terms of the demoted tenancy;

(ii)   the statutory provisions relating to demoted tenancies; and

(iii)   the landlord's repairing obligations,

and must supply the tenant with a copy of such information and a written statement of the terms of the tenancy, so far as they are neither expressed in the lease or written tenancy agreement, if any, nor implied by law[18].

A demoted tenancy may become flexible tenancy in certain circumstances; when a flexible tenancy is demoted, the tenancy reverts to being a flexible tenancy on successful completion of the period of demotion[19].

The County Court has jurisdiction in relation to demoted tenancies[20]. Under the Housing Act 1988, a registered provider of social housing[21] or a registered social landlord[22] may apply to the County Court for a demotion order; and, for the court to make such an order, it must be satisfied that the tenant or a person residing in or visiting the dwelling house has engaged or has threatened to engage in anti-social behaviour or use of the premises for unlawful purposes, and that it is reasonable to make the order[23]. A demotion order has the effect that: (A) the assured tenancy is terminated with effect from the date specified in the order; (B) if the tenant remains in occupation of the dwelling house after that date a demoted tenancy[24] is created with effect from that date, with statutorily specified terms[25].

1 As to the meaning of 'dwelling house' for this purpose see the Housing Act 1996 s 143O; and LANDLORD AND TENANT vol 63 (2016) PARA 1118.
2 As to the meaning of 'local housing authority' for these purposes see LANDLORD AND TENANT vol 63 (2016) PARA 1046.
3 As to housing action trusts see PARA 537 et seq.
4 Ie the tenant condition in the Housing Act 1985 s 81: see LANDLORD AND TENANT vol 63 (2016) PARA 1037.
5 See the Housing Act 1996 s 143A; and LANDLORD AND TENANT vol 63 (2016) PARA 1118. As to the new tenure under the Renting Homes (Wales) Act 2016 see PARAS 6, 226.
6 As to secure tenancies see LANDLORD AND TENANT vol 63 (2016) PARA 1037.
7 See the Housing Act 1996 s 143B(1); and LANDLORD AND TENANT vol 63 (2016) PARA 1118.
8 See the Housing Act 1996 s 143B(2); and LANDLORD AND TENANT vol 63 (2016) PARA 1118. As to the position where at any time before the end of the demotion period the landlord serves a notice of proceedings for possession of the dwelling house see s 143B(3), (4); and LANDLORD AND TENANT vol 63 (2016) PARA 1118.
9 See the Housing Act 1996 s 143B(5); and LANDLORD AND TENANT vol 63 (2016) PARA 1118. As to continuation of a demoted tenancy where the interest of the landlord is transferred see s 143C; and LANDLORD AND TENANT vol 63 (2016) PARA 1120.
10 See the Housing Act 1996 ss 143D, 143E; and LANDLORD AND TENANT vol 63 (2016) PARA 1163. See also *Manchester City Council v Pinnock (No 2)* [2011] UKSC 6, [2011] 2 AC 104, [2011] 2 All ER 586.
11 See the Housing Act 1996 s 143F; and LANDLORD AND TENANT vol 63 (2016) PARA 1164.
12 As to the right to buy see PARA 230 et seq.
13 See the Housing Act 1996 s 143G; and LANDLORD AND TENANT vol 63 (2016) PARA 1165.
14 See the Housing Act 1996 ss 143GA, 143GB, 143H, 143I, 143J, 143P; and LANDLORD AND TENANT vol 63 (2016) PARA 1123.
15 See the Housing Act 1996 s 143K; and LANDLORD AND TENANT vol 63 (2016) PARA 1125.
16 Ie the Secretary of State or, where statutory functions have been transferred in relation to Wales, the Welsh Ministers: see PARA 7.
17 See the Housing Act 1996 s 143L; and LANDLORD AND TENANT vol 63 (2016) PARA 1121.
18 See the Housing Act 1996 s 143M; and LANDLORD AND TENANT vol 63 (2016) PARA 1122.
19 See the Housing Act 1996 ss 143MA, 143MB (s 143MA added by the Localism Act 2011 s 155(7); the Housing Act 1996 s 143MB added, as from a day to be appointed, by the Housing and Planning Act 2016 s 118, Sch 7, paras 19, 28; at the date at which this volume states the law, no such day had been appointed); and LANDLORD AND TENANT vol 63 (2016) PARA 1119. As to flexible tenancies see the Housing Act 1985 s 107A (added by the Localism Act 2011 s 154; repealed, as from a day to be appointed, by the Housing and Planning Act 2016 Sch 7 paras 2, 14, 33(1); at the date at which this volume states the law, no such day had been appointed); and LANDLORD AND TENANT vol 63 (2016) PARAS 1040, 1059 et seq.
20 See the Housing Act 1996 s 143N; and LANDLORD AND TENANT vol 63 (2016) PARAS 1129, 1163.
21 As to the meaning of 'registered provider of social housing' see PARA 53.
22 As to the meaning of 'registered social landlord' see PARA 13.
23 See the Housing Act 1988 s 6A; and LANDLORD AND TENANT vol 63 (2016) PARA 883.
24 For these purposes, a 'demoted tenancy' is a tenancy to which the Housing Act 1988 s 20B applies, ie a demoted assured shorthold tenancy: see the Housing Act 1988 s 6A(11); and LANDLORD AND TENANT vol 63 (2016) PARA 863.
25 See the Housing Act 1988 s 6A(3); and LANDLORD AND TENANT vol 63 (2016) PARA 883.

(4) ACCOMMODATION NEEDS OF GYPSIES AND TRAVELLERS

475. Consideration of accommodation needs of gypsies and travellers: England. In the case of a local housing authority[1] in England, the duty to undertake a review of housing needs in its district includes[2] a duty to consider the needs of people residing in or resorting to its district with respect to the provision of: (1) sites on which caravans[3] can be stationed; or (2) places on inland waterways where houseboats[4] can be moored[5]. The former specific provisions relating to the duty of local housing authorities in relation to the accommodation needs of gypsies and travellers have been repealed[6].

1 As to the meaning of 'local housing authority' see PARA 11.
2 Ie under the Housing Act 1985 s 8: see PARA 401.
3 As to the meaning of 'caravan' see PARA 401 note 6.
4 As to the meaning of 'houseboat' see PARA 401 note 7.
5 Housing Act 1985 s 8(3) (added by the Housing and Planning Act 2016 s 124(1)).
6 Ie the Housing Act 1985 ss 225, 226 (repealed by the Housing and Planning Act 2016 s 124(2)).

476. Meeting accommodation needs of gypsies and travellers: Wales. A local housing authority[1] in Wales must carry out an assessment of the accommodation needs[2] of gypsies and travellers[3] residing in or resorting to its area[4]. In carrying out such an assessment, a local housing authority must consult such persons as it considers appropriate[5]. After carrying out an assessment a local housing authority must prepare a report which: (1) details how the assessment was carried out; (2) contains a summary of the consultation it carried out in connection with the assessment and the responses (if any) it received to that consultation; (3) details the accommodation needs identified by the assessment[6].

A local housing authority must submit the report to the Welsh Ministers for approval of the authority's assessment[7]. The Welsh Ministers may: (a) approve the assessment as submitted; (b) approve the assessment with modifications; (c) reject the assessment[8]. If the Welsh Ministers reject the assessment, the local housing authority must either revise and resubmit its assessment for approval by the Welsh Ministers or conduct another assessment[9]. A local housing authority must publish an assessment approved by the Welsh Ministers under these provisions[10].

If a local housing authority's most recent assessment of accommodation needs approved by the Welsh Ministers[11] identifies needs within the authority's area with respect to the provision of sites on which mobile homes may be stationed the authority must exercise its powers under the Mobile Homes (Wales) Act 2013[12] to provide sites for mobile homes so far as may be necessary to meet those needs[13]. This does not require a local housing authority to provide, in or in connection with sites for the stationing of mobile homes, working space and facilities for the carrying on of activities normally carried out by gypsies and travellers[14].

If satisfied that a local housing authority has failed to comply with the duty to meet assessed needs[15], the Welsh Ministers may direct the authority to exercise its powers under the Mobile Homes (Wales) Act 2013 to provide sites for mobile homes so far as may be necessary to meet the needs identified in the authority's approved assessment[16]. Before giving a direction the Welsh Ministers must consult the local housing authority to which the direction would relate[17]. A local housing authority must comply with a direction given to it[18].

A local housing authority must provide the Welsh Ministers with such information (and at such times) as they may require in connection with the exercise of their functions under Part 3[19] of the Housing (Wales) Act 2014[20]. In exercising its functions under Part 3, a local housing authority must have regard to any guidance given by the Welsh Ministers[21].

Where a local housing authority is required[22] to have a strategy in respect of meeting the accommodation needs of gypsies and travellers residing in or resorting to its area, the authority must have regard to any guidance given by the Welsh Ministers in preparing its strategy and take the strategy into account in exercising its functions (including functions exercisable other than as a local housing authority)[23].

1 As to the meaning of 'local housing authority' see PARA 227 note 2.
2 'Accommodation needs' includes, but is not limited to, needs with respect to the provision of sites on which mobile homes (within the meaning of the Mobile Homes (Wales) Act 2013 s 60: see LANDLORD AND TENANT vol 64 (2016) PARA 1762 note 1) may be stationed: Housing (Wales) Act 2014 s 108.
3 'Gypsies and travellers' means: (1) persons of a nomadic habit of life, whatever their race or origin, including: (a) persons who, on grounds only of their own or their family's or dependant's educational or health needs or old age, have ceased to travel temporarily or permanently; and (b) members of an organised group of travelling show people or circus people (whether or not travelling together as such); and (2) all other persons with a cultural tradition of nomadism or of living in a mobile home: Housing (Wales) Act 2014 s 108. The Welsh Ministers may by order amend the definition of 'gypsies and travellers' by: (i) adding a description of persons; (ii) modifying a description of persons; (iii) removing a description of persons: s 109(1). An order under s 109 may also make such amendments of the Mobile Homes (Wales) Act 2013 as the Welsh Ministers consider necessary or appropriate in consequence of a change to this definition: s 109(2).
4 Housing (Wales) Act 2014 s 101(1). The first assessment must be carried out before 25 February 2016 and further assessments must be carried out within a period of five years from the date of the previous assessment: s 101(3); Housing (Wales) Act 2014 (Commencement No 2) Order 2015, SI 2015/380, art 2(a). The Welsh Ministers may amend the subsequent assessment period by order: Housing (Wales) Act 2014 s 101(4). As to the Welsh Ministers see PARA 7.
5 Housing (Wales) Act 2014 s 101(2).
6 Housing (Wales) Act 2014 s 102(1).
7 Housing (Wales) Act 2014 s 102(2).
8 Housing (Wales) Act 2014 s 102(3).
9 Housing (Wales) Act 2014 s 102(4). In that case s 101(2) and s 102 apply again, as if the assessment were carried out under s 101(1): s 102(4)(b).
10 Housing (Wales) Act 2014 s 102(5).
11 Ie under the Housing (Wales) Act 2014 s 102(3).
12 Ie in the Mobile Homes (Wales) Act 2013 s 56: see PARA 518.
13 Housing (Wales) Act 2014 s 103(1), (3).
14 Housing (Wales) Act 2014 s 103(2).
15 Ie the duty imposed by the Housing (Wales) Act 2014 s 103.
16 Housing (Wales) Act 2014 s 104(1). A direction given under s 104: (1) must be in writing; (2) may be varied or revoked by a subsequent direction; (3) is enforceable by mandatory order on application by, or on behalf of, the Welsh Ministers: s 104(4).
17 Housing (Wales) Act 2014 s 104(2).
18 Housing (Wales) Act 2014 s 104(3).
19 Ie the Housing (Wales) Act 2014 Pt 3 (ss 101–110).
20 Housing (Wales) Act 2014 s 105(1). The Welsh Ministers may exercise their powers under s 105 generally or in relation to a particular case: s 105(2).
21 Housing (Wales) Act 2014 s 106(1). The Welsh Ministers may: (1) give guidance either generally or to specified descriptions of authorities; (2) revise the guidance by giving further guidance under s 106; (3) withdraw the guidance by giving further guidance under s 106 or by notice: s 106(2). The Welsh Ministers must publish any such guidance or notice: s 106(3).
22 Ie under the Local Government Act 2003 s 87: see PARA 366.
23 Housing (Wales) Act 2014 s 107.

(5) LOCAL HOUSING AUTHORITY DUTIES TO THE HOMELESS

(i) In general

477. General background. Local housing authorities were given specific statutory responsibilities for the homeless following the passage of the Housing (Homeless Persons) Act 1977. In summary, a local authority owed a duty to someone who was either homeless or threatened with homelessness. These duties included the responsibility to secure that accommodation was available to a homeless person who had a priority need; but only limited duties were owed to those who, although homeless, had become intentionally homeless. These statutory provisions were amended by the Housing and Planning Act 1986 with the effect of providing that someone could be considered homeless where the accommodation occupied was such that it was not reasonable for the person to remain in occupation of it[1]. Local authority statutory duties to the homelessness were consolidated in the Housing Act 1985[2] and amendments were then made by the Asylum and Immigration Appeals Act 1993 restricting local authority duties in relation to asylum seekers[3].

A local housing authority may now owe duties to someone who is homeless or threatened with homelessness under Part VII of the Housing Act 1996[4]. In addition to these duties a local authority social services department may have responsibility for the housing of children and young persons, as every local authority must provide accommodation for any child in need within its area who appears to require accommodation as a result of his being lost or having been abandoned or there being no parent or carer[5]. Authorities must also provide accommodation for any child in need who has reached the age of 16 years and whose welfare the authority considers is likely to be seriously prejudiced if it does not provide him with accommodation[6]; and a local authority social services department also has responsibilities in relation to children and young persons in order to safeguard their welfare[7]. These duties are owed to the child and not automatically to his parents, particularly where they are intentionally homeless[8]. Local authorities in England also have powers to provide residential accommodation for persons aged 18 years or over who by reason of age, infirmity or other circumstances are in need of care and attention which is not otherwise available to them[9].

1   This reverses the effect of the decision in *Puhlhofer v Hillingdon London Borough Council*, [1986] AC 484, [1986] 1 All ER 467, HL.
2   See the Housing Act 1985 Pt III (ss 58–78) (repealed).
3   See the Asylum and Immigration Appeals Act 1993 ss 4, 5, Sch 1 (repealed).
4   Ie the Housing Act 1996 Pt VII (ss 175–218): see PARAS 478, 481 et seq. The duties of a local housing authority in Wales in relation to someone who is homeless or threatened with homelessness are set out in the Housing (Wales) Act 2014 Pt 2 (ss 50–100); see PARA 480 et seq.
5   See the Children Act 1989 s 20(1); and CHILDREN AND YOUNG PERSONS vol 10 (2017) PARA 822.
6   See the Children Act 1989 s 20(3); and CHILDREN AND YOUNG PERSONS vol 10 (2017) PARA 822.
7   See the Children Act 1989 s 20(4), (5); and CHILDREN AND YOUNG PERSONS vol 10 (2017) PARA 823.
8   See *R v Tower Hamlets London Borough Council, ex p Byas* (1992) 25 HLR 105, [1993] 2 FLR 605, CA. As to intentional homelessness see PARA 483.
    In *R v Northavon District Council, ex p Smith* [1994] 2 AC 402, [1994] 3 All ER 313, HL, the local housing authority had decided that a family seeking assistance under the local authority's general duties to the homeless was intentionally homeless. A local authority social service department accepted responsibilities for the family since they had children, exercising its powers under the Children Act 1989, and then sought financial assistance from the housing authority. It was held by the House of Lords that the housing authority had discharged its duties and could not be required to assist further.
9   See the National Assistance Act 1948 s 21 (repealed, in relation to Wales, by SI 2016/413); and SOCIAL SERVICES vol 95 (2017) PARA 3. See also *R (on the application of Hughes) v Liverpool City Council* [2005] EWHC 428 (Admin), [2005] LGR 531, [2005] All ER (D) 320 (Mar).

478. Current framework. Local housing authority duties to the homeless in England are now contained in Part VII of the Housing Act 1996[1]. These provisions came fully into force on 20 January 1997[2]. They replace the provisions in the Housing Act 1985 but there are several similarities between the new and the old legislation such as the concepts and definitions of 'homelessness', 'threatened with homelessness', 'priority need', and 'intentionality'. These revised statutory duties (and the statutory provisions governing local authority allocation of housing contained in Part VI of the Housing Act 1996[3]) represent policies proposed in a Consultation Paper[4] and in a White Paper on Housing published in 1995[5]. In accordance with these policies local authority duties to the homeless have been curtailed and the new regulatory system limits a local authority's right to allocate a tenancy to those who appear in a housing register[6]. Another aspect of the policy is that local authorities are required to provide (or assist in the provision of) assistance for those who are looking for accommodation[7].

The main changes between the homelessness provisions in the Housing Act 1996 as opposed to those in the Housing Act 1985 are as follows:

(1)   an individual may not now be considered homeless if he has accommodation either in England and Wales or elsewhere[8];

(2)   the definition of intentionality has been widened[9];

(3)   a local housing authority's duty to the unintentionally homeless who have a priority need is reduced to securing that temporary accommodation for a period of up to two years (which is renewable) is available[10];

(4)   applicants for assistance from a local housing authority who are dissatisfied with the authority's decision have the right to seek an administrative review of the decision by the authority concerned, and applicants have a statutory right of appeal to the County Court against what they consider to be an adverse decision[11]; and

(5)   local housing authorities are now under a duty to secure that advisory services are available in their area[12].

Apart from these changes, a local housing authority's statutory duties to the homeless under the Housing Act 1996 are similar in many respects to those under the Housing Act 1985. In summary, a local housing authority's duties commence when an application is made by someone who appears to be homeless or threatened with homelessness[13]. If that person is eligible for assistance and has a defined priority need, the authority must secure that temporary accommodation is made available while the authority carries out its duties to consider the eligibility of the application for assistance[14]. Where, on completing these inquiries, the authority decides that the applicant is not in fact homeless or threatened with homelessness, or does not in fact have a priority need, or that a homeless applicant with a priority need became homeless intentionally, the duties are limited to giving advice, with a duty to secure temporary accommodation for those applicants who have a priority need[15]. Where a local housing authority decides that an applicant who is homeless has a priority need and did not become homeless intentionally, the authority must secure that temporary accommodation is made available for a period of up to two years unless, in the opinion of the authority, there is sufficient accommodation available in the area suitable to the needs of the applicant[16]. An authority may also refer the application for assistance to another authority if it concludes that the applicant has a connection with that authority[17]. An applicant who wishes to challenge an adverse decision may first seek an administrative review by the local authority and may then appeal against an adverse decision to the County Court on a point of law[18].

The Homelessness Act 2002 makes provision for a local housing authority to carry out homelessness reviews and to formulate and adopt homelessness strategies for its district based on the results of such reviews[19].

Separate provision is made as to homelessness in Wales by the Housing (Wales) Act 2014[20].

1 Ie the Housing Act 1996 Pt VII (ss 175–218) (amended by the Housing (Wales) Act 2014 s 100, Sch 3 Pt 1 to apply in relation to England only): see PARA 481 et seq.
2 See the Housing Act 1996 (Commencement No 5 and Transitional Provisions) Order 1996, SI 1996/2959.
3 See the Housing Act 1996 Pt VI (ss 159–174); and PARA 422 et seq.
4 Ie the Department of the Environment publication *Access to Local Authority and Housing Association Tenancies* (1994).
5 Ie *Our Future Homes* (1995) (Cm 2901).
6 See the Housing Act 1996 Pt VI; and PARA 422 et seq.
7 See PARA 485.
8 See PARA 481.
9 See PARA 483.
10 See PARA 498.
11 See PARAS 507–509.
12 See PARA 485.
13 See PARA 487.
14 See PARA 493.
15 See PARAS 496–497, 499–505.
16 See PARA 498.
17 See PARA 503.
18 See PARAS 507–509.
19 See PARA 479.
20 See PARA 480.

479. Homelessness reviews and strategies: England. A local housing authority[1] in England may from time to time: (1) carry out a homelessness review[2] for its district[3]; and (2) formulate and publish a homelessness strategy[4] based on the results of that review[5]. The social services authority[6] for the district of the local housing authority (where that is a different local authority) must give such assistance in connection with the exercise of that power as the local housing authority may reasonably require[7]. The local housing authority must exercise that power so as to ensure that the first homelessness strategy for its district is published within a specified period[8]. The local housing authority must exercise that power so as to ensure that a new homelessness strategy for its district is published within the period of five years beginning with the day on which its last homelessness strategy was published[9]. A local housing authority in England must take its homelessness strategy into account in the exercise of its functions[10]. A social services authority must take the homelessness strategy for the district of a local housing authority into account in the exercise of its functions in relation to that district[11].

'Homelessness review' means a review by a local housing authority of: (a) the levels, and likely future levels, of homelessness[12] in its district; (b) the activities which are carried out for any of a number of specified purposes (or which contribute to their achievement); and (c) the resources available to the authority, the social services authority for its district, other public authorities, voluntary organisations[13] and other persons for such activities[14]. The specified purposes are preventing homelessness in the district of the authority, securing that accommodation is or will be available for people in the district who are or may become homeless[15], and providing support[16] for people in the district who are or may become homeless, or who have been homeless and need support to prevent them becoming homeless again[17]. A local housing authority must, after completing a homelessness review: (i) arrange for the results of the review to be available at its principal office for inspection at all reasonable hours, without charge, by members of the public; and (ii) provide (on payment of a reasonable charge, if required by the authority) a copy of those results to any member of the public who asks for one[18].

'Homelessness strategy' means a strategy formulated by a local housing authority for: (A) preventing homelessness in its district; (B) securing that sufficient accommodation is and will be available for people in its district who are or may become homeless; (C) securing the satisfactory provision of support for people in its district who are or may become homeless, or who have been homeless and need support to prevent them becoming homeless again[19]. A homelessness strategy may include specific objectives to be pursued, and specific action planned to be taken, in the course of the exercise of the functions of the authority as a local housing authority, or the functions of the social services authority for the district[20]. A homelessness strategy may also include provision relating to specific action which the authority expects to be taken by any public authority with functions[21] which are capable of contributing to the achievement of any of the specified objectives[22] or by any voluntary organisation or other person whose activities are capable of contributing to the achievement of any of those objectives[23]. The inclusion in a homelessness strategy of any provision relating to such action requires the approval of the body or person concerned[24]. In formulating a homelessness strategy, the authority must consider (among other things) the extent to which any of the specified objectives can be achieved through action involving two or more bodies or other persons[25]. The authority must keep its homelessness strategy under review and may modify it from time to time[26]. If the authority modifies its homelessness strategy, it must publish the modifications or the strategy as modified (as it considers most appropriate)[27]. Before adopting or modifying a homelessness strategy the authority must consult such public or local authorities, voluntary organisations or other persons as it considers appropriate[28]. The authority must make a copy of everything published under the provisions described above[29] available at its principal office for inspection at all reasonable hours, without charge, by members of the public[30]. It must also provide (on payment of a reasonable charge, if required by the authority) a copy of anything so published to any member of the public who asks for one[31].

1   For these purposes, 'local housing authority' has the same meaning as in the Housing Act 1985 (see PARA 11): Homelessness Act 2002 s 4.
2   See the text and notes 12–18.
3   For these purposes, 'district' has the same meaning as in the Housing Act 1985 (see PARA 11): Homelessness Act 2002 s 4.
4   See the text and notes 19–31.
5   Homelessness Act 2002 s 1(1) (amended, in relation to Wales, by the Housing (Wales) Act 2014 s 100, Sch 3 paras 15, 17(a)).
6   'Social services authority' means a local authority for the purposes of the Local Authority Social Services Act 1970 (see SOCIAL SERVICES vol 95 (2017) PARA 1 et seq) or the Social Services and Well-being (Wales) Act 2014 Pt 8 (ss 143–161): Homelessness Act 2002 s 4 (amended by SI 2016/413).
7   Homelessness Act 2002 s 1(2).
8   Ie the period of 12 months beginning with the day on which the Homelessness Act 2002 s 1 comes into force: s 1(3). Section 1 came into force on 31 July 2002 in relation to England, and on 30 September 2002 in relation to Wales: see the Homelessness Act 2002 (Commencement No 1) (England) Order 2002, SI 2002/1799; and the Homelessness Act 2002 (Commencement) (Wales) Order 2002, SI 2002/1736.
9   Homelessness Act 2002 s 1(4).
10 Homelessness Act 2002 s 1(5) (amended, in relation to Wales, by the Housing (Wales) Act 2014 Sch 3 paras 15, 17(a)). This does not affect any duty or requirement arising apart from s 1: s 1(7).

11 Homelessness Act 2002 s 1(6). This does not affect any duty or requirement arising apart from s 1: s 1(7).
12 For these purposes, 'homelessness' has the same meaning as in the Housing Act 1996 Pt VII (ss 175–218) (see PARA 481): Homelessness Act 2002 s 4.
13 For these purposes, 'voluntary organisation' has the same meaning as in the Housing Act 1996 s 180(3) (see PARA 485 note 7): Homelessness Act 2002 s 4.
14 Homelessness Act 2002 s 2(1).
15 For these purposes, 'homeless' has the same meaning as in the Housing Act 1996 Pt VII (see PARA 481): Homelessness Act 2002 s 4.
16 'Support' means advice, information or assistance: Homelessness Act 2002 s 4.
17 Homelessness Act 2002 s 2(2).
18 Homelessness Act 2002 s 2(3).
19 Homelessness Act 2002 s 3(1). In formulating or modifying a homelessness strategy, a local housing authority must have regard to: (1) its current allocation scheme under the Housing Act 1996 s 166A (see PARA 427); (2) its current tenancy strategy under the Localism Act 2011 s 150 (see PARA 421); and (3) in the case of an authority that is a London borough council, the current London housing strategy: Homelessness Act 2002 s 3(7A) (added by the Localism Act 2011 s 153; and amended, in relation to Wales, by the Housing (Wales) Act 2014 Sch 3 paras 15, 18).
20 Homelessness Act 2002 s 3(2).
21 Ie functions not being functions mentioned in the Homelessness Act 2002 s 3(2) (see the text and note 20).
22 Ie the objectives mentioned in the Homelessness Act 2002 s 3(1) (see the text and note 19).
23 Homelessness Act 2002 s 3(3).
24 Homelessness Act 2002 s 3(4).
25 Ie two or more of the bodies or other persons mentioned in the Homelessness Act 2002 s 3(2), (3) (see the text and notes 20–23): s 3(5).
26 Homelessness Act 2002 s 3(6).
27 Homelessness Act 2002 s 3(7).
28 Homelessness Act 2002 s 3(8).
29 Ie under the Homelessness Act 2002 s 1: see the text and notes 1–11.
30 Homelessness Act 2002 s 3(9)(a) (amended by the Local Government Act 2003 s 127(1), Sch 7 para 81(a)).
31 Homelessness Act 2002 s 3(9)(b) (amended by the Local Government Act 2003 Sch 7 para 81(b)).

480. Homelessness reviews and strategies: Wales. A local housing authority[1] in Wales must carry out a homelessness review for its area, and formulate and adopt a homelessness strategy based on the results of that review[2]. The authority must adopt a homelessness strategy in 2018 and a new homelessness strategy in every fourth year after 2018[3]. A council of a county or county borough in Wales must take its homelessness strategy into account in the exercise of its functions (including functions other than its functions as local housing authority)[4].

A homelessness review must include a review of:

(1)   the levels, and likely future levels, of homelessness[5] in the authority's area;

(2)   the activities which are carried out in the authority's area for the achievement of, or which contribute to the achievement of:

     (a)   the prevention of homelessness;

     (b)   that suitable accommodation is or will be available for people who are or may become homeless;

     (c)   that satisfactory support is available for people who are or may become homeless;

(3)   the resources available to the authority (including the resources available in exercise of functions other than its functions as local housing authority), other public authorities, voluntary organisations and other persons for such activities[6].

After completing a homelessness review, a local housing authority must publish the results of the review by:

     (i)   making the results of the review available on its website (if it has one);

(ii)   making a copy of the results of the review available at its principal office for inspection at all reasonable hours, without charge, by members of the public;

(iii)   providing (on payment if required by the authority of a reasonable charge) a copy of those results to any member of the public who asks for one[7].

A homelessness strategy is a strategy for achieving the following objectives in the local housing authority's area:

(A)   the prevention of homelessness;

(B)   that suitable accommodation is and will be available for people who are or may become homeless;

(C)   that satisfactory support is available for people who are or may become homeless[8].

A homelessness strategy may specify more detailed objectives to be pursued, and action planned to be taken, in the exercise of any functions of the authority (including functions other than its functions as local housing authority)[9]. A homelessness strategy may also include provision relating to specific action which the authority expects to be taken by any public authority with functions which are capable of contributing to the achievement of any of the objectives mentioned in heads (A) to (C), or by any voluntary organisation or other person whose activities are capable of contributing to the achievement of any of those objectives[10]. The inclusion in a homelessness strategy of any such provision relating to action requires the approval of the body or person concerned[11].

A homelessness strategy must include provision relating to action planned by the authority to be taken in the exercise of its functions, and specific action expected by the authority to be taken by public authorities, voluntary organisations and other persons[12], in relation to those who may be in particular need of support if they are or may become homeless, including in particular people leaving prison or youth detention accommodation, young people leaving care, people leaving the regular armed forces of the Crown, people leaving hospital after medical treatment for mental disorder as an inpatient and people receiving mental health services in the community[13].

A local housing authority must keep its homelessness strategy under review and may modify it[14]. Before adopting or modifying a homelessness strategy a local housing authority must consult such public or local authorities, voluntary organisations or other persons as it considers appropriate[15]. After adopting or modifying a homelessness strategy, a local housing authority must publish the strategy by:

(I)   making a copy of the strategy available on its website (if it has one);

(II)   making a copy of the strategy available at its principal office for inspection at all reasonable hours, without charge, by members of the public;

(III)   providing (on payment if required by the authority of a reasonable charge) a copy of the strategy to any member of the public who asks for one[16].

If the authority modifies its homelessness strategy, it may publish the modifications or the strategy as modified (as it considers most appropriate)[17]. Where the authority decides to publish only the modifications, the references to the homelessness strategy in heads (I) to (III) are to be interpreted as references to the modifications[18].

1   As to the meaning of 'local housing authority' see PARA 227 note 2.

2   Housing (Wales) Act 2014 s 50(1).
3   Housing (Wales) Act 2014 s 50(2). The Welsh Ministers may amend s 50(2) by order: s 50(3). As
    to the Welsh Ministers see PARA 7.
4   Housing (Wales) Act 2014 s 50(4). Nothing in s 50(4) affects any duty or requirement arising apart
    from s 50: s 50(5).
5   In the Housing (Wales) Act 2014 Pt 2 Ch 1 (ss 50–52) 'homeless' has the meaning given by s 55
    (see PARA 482) and 'homelessness' is to be interpreted accordingly: s 50(6).
6   Housing (Wales) Act 2014 s 51(1).
7   Housing (Wales) Act 2014 s 51(2).
8   Housing (Wales) Act 2014 s 52(1).
9   Housing (Wales) Act 2014 s 52(2).
10 Housing (Wales) Act 2014 s 52(3). In formulating a homelessness strategy, the authority must
    consider (among other things) the extent to which any of the objectives mentioned in s 52(1) can
    be achieved through action involving two or more of the bodies or other persons mentioned in
    s 52(2), (3): s 52(5).
11 Housing (Wales) Act 2014 s 52(4).
12 Ie within the Housing (Wales) Act 2014 s 52(3): see the text to note 10.
13 Housing (Wales) Act 2014 s 52(6).
14 Housing (Wales) Act 2014 s 52(7).
15 Housing (Wales) Act 2014 s 52(8).
16 Housing (Wales) Act 2014 s 52(9).
17 Housing (Wales) Act 2014 s 52(10).
18 Housing (Wales) Act 2014 s 52(11).

(ii) Persons who are Homeless

481. Homelessness and threatened homelessness: England. A person is homeless
if he has no accommodation available for his occupation[1], in the United Kingdom[2]
or elsewhere[3], which he:

(1)   is entitled to occupy by virtue of an interest in it or by virtue of an
         order of a court;

(2)   has an express or implied licence to occupy; or

(3)   occupies as a residence by virtue of any enactment or rule of law giving
         him the right to remain in occupation or restricting the right of another
         person to recover possession[4].

A person who has accommodation may also be homeless if he cannot secure
entry to it, or if it consists of a movable structure, vehicle or vessel designed or
adapted for human habitation and there is no place where he is entitled or
permitted both to place it and to reside in it[5].

However, a person is not to be treated as having accommodation unless it is
accommodation which it would be reasonable for him to continue to occupy[6]. It
is not reasonable for a person to continue to occupy accommodation if it is
probable that this will lead to domestic violence or other violence against him, or
against a person who normally resides with him as a member of his family, or any
other person who might reasonably be expected to reside with him[7]. For this
purpose, 'violence' means:

(a)   violence from another person; or

(b)   threats of violence from another person which are likely to be carried
         out,

and violence is 'domestic violence' if it is from a person who is associated with the
victim[8].

In determining whether it would be, or would have been, reasonable for a
person to continue to occupy accommodation, regard may be had to the general

circumstances prevailing in relation to housing in the district[9] of the local housing authority[10] to which he has applied for accommodation or for assistance in obtaining accommodation[11].

The Secretary of State[12] may by order specify:

(i)   other circumstances in which it is to be regarded as reasonable or not reasonable for a person to continue to occupy accommodation; and

(ii)   other matters to be taken into account or disregarded in determining whether it would be, or would have been, reasonable for a person to continue to occupy accommodation[13].

A person is threatened with homelessness if it is likely that he will become homeless within 28 days[14].

1   Accommodation must be regarded as available for a person's occupation only if it is available for occupation by him together with any other person who normally resides with him as a member of his family, or any other person who might reasonably be expected to reside with him; and references in the Housing Act 1996 Pt VII (ss 175–218) (see PARA 485 et seq) to securing that accommodation is available for a person's occupation must be construed accordingly: s 176. In *R v Brent London Borough Council, ex p Awua* [1996] AC 55, sub nom *Awua v Brent London Borough Council* [1995] 3 All ER 493, HL, it was held that 'accommodation' means a place which can fairly be described as accommodation and which it is reasonable, having regard to the general housing conditions in the area, for a person to continue to occupy; there is no additional requirement that this accommodation is in any sense settled or permanent. Prison does not constitute 'accommodation' for the purposes of the Housing Act 1996 s 175: *R (on the application of B) v Southwark London Borough Council* [2003] EWHC 1678 (Admin), [2004] HLR 18, [2003] All ER (D) 75 (Jul). See also *R v Hackney London Borough Council, ex p Tonnicodi* (1997) 30 HLR 916 (council failed to consider need of applicant to live with a friend who helped him cope with physical and mental disabilities); and *R (on the application of Ogbeni) v Tower Hamlets London Borough Council* [2008] EWHC 2444 (Admin), [2008] All ER (D) 67 (Aug).

2   As to the meaning of 'United Kingdom' see PARA 60 note 10.

3   This means that an applicant who has accommodation available in another country may not be treated as either homeless or threatened with homelessness.

4   Housing Act 1996 s 175(1). The reference in head (1) in the text to a person who is entitled to occupy includes an owner of a dwelling, a tenant or someone who has the right to occupy by an order of the court made under the Matrimonial Causes Act 1973, the Domestic Violence and Matrimonial Proceedings Act 1976, the Matrimonial Homes Act 1983 or the Family Law Act 1996. The reference to occupying under an express or an implied licence obviously includes such licensees as a lodger or a service occupancy where an employee is required to occupy a premises for the better performance of his duties (see eg *Norris v Checksfield* [1991] 4 All ER 327, [1991] 1 WLR 1241, CA). See *Hemans v Windsor and Maidenhead Royal Borough Council* [2011] EWCA Civ 374; [2011] HLR 405 (joint application for accommodation amounted to implicit licence to occupy for husband reconciling with wife). The language of the Housing Act 1996 s 175(1), being in the present tense, does not cover a situation where another local authority has indicated that it would be willing to provide unspecified accommodation in its area: *Johnston v City of Westminster* [2015] EWCA Civ 554, [2015] All ER (D) 29 (Jun).

This statutory definition also applies to someone who occupies by virtue of an enactment or rule of law either allowing him to remain in occupation or restricting the right of another person to recover possession. Examples of this category are a tenant whose tenancy is protected by the Rent Act 1977, an agricultural worker in tied accommodation enjoying rights under the Rent (Agriculture) Act 1976 or the holder of a long lease whose lease has expired but who now enjoys statutory rights under the Rent Act 1977 or under the Housing Act 1988: see generally LANDLORD AND TENANT. See also the Landlord and Tenant Act 1954 Pt I (ss 1–22); the Local Government and Housing Act 1989 s 186, Sch 10; and LANDLORD AND TENANT vol 63 (2016) PARAS 968 et seq, 1015 et seq. The Protection from Eviction Act 1977 prohibits the eviction of those who do not have protection (other than those who have an excluded tenancy or an excluded licence) and so it is possible that occupiers falling within this category also have 'accommodation for occupation' for this purpose.

5   Housing Act 1996 s 175(2). There are several reported cases on the Housing Act 1985 which illustrate how difficult questions can arise when housing authorities have to judge whether somebody is actually homeless or not. It has been held eg that a woman living in a women's refuge should be considered homeless: *R v Ealing London Borough Council, ex p Sidhu* (1982) 80 LGR 534. Similarly, a man living in a night shelter has been considered homeless (*R v Medina*

Borough Council, ex p Dee (1992) 24 HLR 562), as has a pregnant woman living in a prefabricated beach hut which was in poor condition (*R v Waveney District Council, ex p Bowers* [1983] QB 238, [1982] 3 All ER 727, CA).

6　　Housing Act 1996 s 175(3). This also applies to asylum-seekers: see *Lismane v Hammersmith and Fulham London Borough Council* (1998) 31 HLR 427, CA. A person who has accommodation which is legally and practically available for his occupation anywhere in the world is not homeless, unless it is accommodation in which he was living but cannot reasonably continue to live: *Begum (Nipa) v Tower Hamlets London Borough Council* [2000] 1 WLR 306, CA. See also *R (on the application of Ali) v Birmingham City Council; Manchester City Council v Moran* [2009] UKHL 36, [2009] 4 All ER 161; *Harouki v Kensington and Chelsea Royal London Borough Council* [2007] EWCA Civ 1000, [2008] LGR 605 (accommodation not so overcrowded that continued occupation unreasonable); *Maloba v Waltham Forest London Borough Council* [2007] EWCA Civ 1281, [2008] 2 All ER 701, [2008] 1 WLR 2079 (accommodation not reasonable for particular family to occupy disregarded for all purposes); *Hemans v Windsor and Maidenhead Royal Borough Council* [2011] EWCA Civ 374; [2011] HLR 405 (joint application for accommodation amounted to implicit licence to occupy for husband reconciling with wife).

7　　Housing Act 1996 s 177(1) (amended by the Homelessness Act 2002 s 10(1)(a)). See also *Yemshaw v Hounslow London Borough Council* [2011] UKSC 3, [2011] 1 All ER 912. 'Other violence' in the Housing Act 1996 s 177(1) covers not only physical violence (actual or threatened) but other threatening or intimidating behaviour or abuse, if of such seriousness that it might give rise to psychological harm: *Hussain v Waltham Forest London Borough Council* [2015] EWCA Civ 14, [2015] 1 WLR 2912.

8　　Housing Act 1996 s 177(1A) (added by the Homelessness Act 2002 s 10(1)(b)).
　　　A person is associated with another person if: (1) they are or have been married to each other; (2) they are or have been civil partners of each other; (3) they are cohabitants or former cohabitants; (4) they live or have lived in the same household; (5) they are relatives; (6) they have agreed to marry one another (whether or not that agreement has been terminated); (7) they have entered into a civil partnership agreement between them (whether or not that agreement has been terminated); (h) in relation to a child, each of them is a parent of the child or has, or has had, parental responsibility for the child: Housing Act 1996 s 178(1) (amended by the Civil Partnership Act 2004 s 81, Sch 8 para 61(1)–(3)). If a child has been adopted or falls within the Housing Act 1996 s 178(2A), two persons are also associated with each other for these purposes if: (a) one is a natural parent of the child or a parent of such a natural parent; and (b) the other is the child or a person: (i) who has become a parent of the child by virtue of an adoption order or who has applied for an adoption order; or (ii) with whom the child has at any time been placed for adoption: s 178(2) (amended by the Adoption and Children Act 2002 s 139(1), Sch 3 paras 89, 90). A child falls within the Housing Act 1996 s 178(2A) if an adoption agency, within the meaning of the Adoption and Children Act 2002 s 2 (see CHILDREN AND YOUNG PERSONS vol 9 (2017) PARAS 473 note 1), is authorised to place him for adoption under s 19 (placing children with parental consent: see CHILDREN AND YOUNG PERSONS vol 9 (2017) PARA 407) or he has become the subject of an order under s 21 (placement orders: see CHILDREN AND YOUNG PERSONS vol 9 (2017) PARA 410 et seq), or he is freed for adoption by virtue of an order made, in England and Wales, under the Adoption Act 1976 s 18, or, in Scotland, under the Adoption (Scotland) Act 1978 s 18 or, in Northern Ireland, under the Adoption (Northern Ireland) Order 1987, SI 1987/2203, art 17(1) or art 18(1): Housing Act 1996 s 178(2A) (added by the Adoption and Children Act 2002 Sch 3 para 91). See further CHILDREN AND YOUNG PERSONS.
　　　'Adoption order' means an adoption order within the meaning of the Adoption Act 1976 s 72(1) or the Adoption and Children Act 2002 s 46(1) (see CHILDREN AND YOUNG PERSONS vol 9 (2017) PARA 436); 'child' means a person under the age of 18 years; 'cohabitants' means a man and a woman who, although not married to each other, are living together as husband and wife, or two people of the same sex who, although not civil partners of each other, are living together as if they were civil partners (and 'former cohabitants' must be construed accordingly); 'parental responsibility' has the same meaning as in the Children Act 1989 (see CHILDREN AND YOUNG PERSONS vol 9 (2017) PARA 150); 'relative', in relation to a person, means: (I) the father, mother, stepfather, stepmother, son, daughter, stepson, stepdaughter, grandfather, grandmother, grandson or granddaughter of that person or of that person's spouse, civil partner, former spouse or former civil partner; or (II) the brother, sister, uncle, aunt, niece or nephew (whether of the full blood or of the half blood or by marriage or civil partnership) of that person or of that person's spouse, civil partner, former spouse or former civil partner, and includes, in relation to a person who is living or has lived with another person as husband and wife, a person who would fall within head (I) or head (II) if the parties were married to each other; and 'civil partnership agreement' has the meaning given by the Civil Partnership Act 2004 s 73: Housing Act 1996 s 178(3) (amended by the Adoption and Children Act 2002 Sch 3 para 92; and the Civil Partnership Act 2004 s 81, Sch 8 para 61(4)–(7)).

Marriage includes marriage of a same sex couple; and a person who is married includes a person who is married to a person of the same sex: see the Marriage (Same Sex Couples) Act 2013 s 11, Sch 3 para 1(1)(a), (c), (2), (3); and MATRIMONIAL AND CIVIL PARTNERSHIP LAW vol 72 (2015) para 2.

9 As to the meaning of 'district' see PARA 11 (definition applied by the Housing Act 1996 s 217(3)).

10 As to the meaning of 'local housing authority' see PARA 11 (definition applied by the Housing Act 1996 s 230).

11 Housing Act 1996 s 177(2).

12 As to the Secretary of State see PARA 7.

13 Housing Act 1996 s 177(3). In determining whether accommodation is suitable for a person, the local housing authority must have regard to the Housing Act 1985 Pts IX, X (ss 264–344) (slum clearance and overcrowding: see PARAS 620 et seq, 649 et seq) and the Housing Act 2004 Pts 1–4 (ss 1–147) (housing conditions; licensing of houses in multiple occupation and other residential accommodation; additional controls: see PARAS 563 et seq, 666 et seq, 704 et seq, 745 et seq): Housing Act 1996 s 210(1) (amended by the Housing Act 2004 s 265(1), Sch 15 paras 40, 43).

The Secretary of State may by order specify circumstances in which accommodation is or is not to be regarded as suitable for a person and matters to be taken into account or disregarded in determining whether accommodation is suitable for a person: Housing Act 1996 s 210(2). Under the Homelessness (Suitability of Accommodation) Order 1996, SI 1996/3204, art 2 (revoked, in relation to Wales, by SI 2015/1268), a number of matters must be considered in determining whether it would be, or would have been, reasonable for a person to continue to occupy accommodation and whether accommodation is suitable or affordable for that person. These are:

(1) the financial resources available to that person (including, but not limited to: (a) salary, fees and other remuneration; (b) social security benefits; (c) payments due under a court order for the making of periodical payments to a spouse or a former spouse, or to, or for the benefit of, a child; (d) payments of child support maintenance due under the Child Support Act 1991; (e) pensions; (f) contributions to the costs in respect of the accommodation which are or were made or which might reasonably be expected to be, or have been, made by other members of his household; (g) financial assistance towards the costs in respect of the accommodation, including loans, provided by a local authority, voluntary organisation or other body; (h) benefits derived from a policy of insurance; (i) savings and other capital sums);

(2) the costs of the accommodation (including, but not limited to: (a) payments of, or by way of, rent; (b) payments in respect of a licence or permission to occupy the accommodation; (c) mortgage costs; (d) payments of, or by way of, service charges; (e) mooring charges payable for a houseboat; (f) where the accommodation is a caravan or a mobile home, payments in respect of the site on which it stands; (g) the amount of council tax payable in respect of the accommodation; (h) payments by way of deposit or security in respect of the accommodation; (i) payments required by an accommodation agency);

(3) payments which that person is required to make under a court order for the making of periodical payments to a spouse or a former spouse, or to, or for the benefit of, a child and payments of child support maintenance required to be made under the Child Support Act 1991; and

(4) that person's other reasonable living expenses.

In relation to England, subject to the exceptions contained in the Homelessness (Suitability of Accommodation) (England) Order 2003, SI 2003/3326, art 4, B & B accommodation is not to be regarded as suitable for an applicant with family commitments where accommodation is made available for occupation: (i) under the Housing Act 1996 s 188(1) (see PARA 493), s 190(2) (see PARA 496), s 193(2) (see PARA 498) or s 200(1) (see PARA 505); or (ii) under s 195(2) (see PARA 499), where the accommodation is other than that occupied by the applicant at the time of making his application: Homelessness (Suitability of Accommodation) (England) Order 2003, SI 2003/3326, art 3. 'B & B accommodation' means accommodation (whether or not breakfast is included), which is not separate and self-contained premises and in which a toilet, personal washing facilities, or cooking facilities are shared by more than one household, but it does not include accommodation which is owned or managed by a local housing authority, a non-profit registered provider of social housing (as to registered providers of social housing see PARA 51 et seq; as to when such a body is a non-profit organisation see PARA 71 note 13) or a voluntary organisation as defined in the Housing Act 1996 s 180(3) (see PARA 485 note 7): Homelessness (Suitability of Accommodation) (England) Order 2003, SI 2003/3326, art 2 (definition amended by SI 2010/671). 'Applicant with family commitments' means an applicant who is pregnant, or with whom a pregnant woman resides or might reasonably be expected to reside, or with whom dependant children reside or might reasonably be expected to reside: Homelessness (Suitability of Accommodation) (England) Order 2003, SI 2003/3326, art 2. Article 3 does not apply: (A) where no accommodation other than B & B accommodation is available for occupation by an applicant with family commitments; and (B) where the applicant occupies B & B accommodation for a period, or a total of periods, which does not exceed six weeks: art 4(1). In calculating such period, or such total period, of an applicant's occupation of B & B accommodation for these purposes, there is to be disregarded any period before April 2004 and, where a local housing authority is subject to the duty under the Housing Act 1996 s 193 (see PARA 498) by virtue of s 200(4) (see PARA 505), any period before that authority became subject to that duty: Homelessness (Suitability of Accommodation) (England) Order 2003, SI 2003/3326, art 4(2).

The location of housing is relevant to the assessment of its suitability *R v Newham London Borough Council, ex p Sacupima* [2001] 1 WLR 563, [2000] All ER (D) 1947, CA. See also the Homelessness (Suitability of Accommodation) (England) Order 2012, SI 2012/2601, art 2.

See *Samuels v Birmingham City Council* [2015] EWCA Civ 1051, [2015] All ER (D) 230 (Oct) (benefits income did not have any special status or treatment in the exercise of establishing whether accommodation was affordable). Short-term bed and breakfast accommodation was held to be suitable for the claimant and her family, who were traditional gypsies, where the local authority was unable to find a site for them to pitch their caravans: *Codona v Mid-Bedfordshire District Council* [2004] EWCA Civ 925, [2005] HLR 1, [2005] LGR 241.

14 Housing Act 1996 s 175(4).

482. Homelessness and threatened homelessness: Wales. A person is homeless if there is no accommodation available for the person's occupation[1], in the United Kingdom[2] or elsewhere[3], which the person:

(1)   is entitled to occupy by virtue of an interest in it or by virtue of an order of a court;

(2)   has an express or implied licence to occupy; or

(3)   occupies as a residence by virtue of any enactment or rule of law giving the person the right to remain in occupation or restricting the right of another person to recover possession[4].

A person is also homeless if the person has accommodation but cannot secure entry to it, or it consists of a movable structure, vehicle or vessel designed or adapted for human habitation and there is no place where the person is entitled or permitted both to place it and to reside in it[5].

A person is not to be treated as having accommodation unless it is accommodation which it would be reasonable for the person to continue to occupy[6]. It is not reasonable for a person to continue to occupy accommodation if it is probable that it will lead to the person, or a member of the person's household[7], being subjected to abuse[8]. In determining whether it would be, or would have been, reasonable for a person to continue to occupy accommodation, a local housing authority[9]:

(a)   may have regard to the general circumstances prevailing in relation to housing in the area of the local housing authority to which the person has applied for help in securing accommodation; and

(b)   must have regard to whether or not the accommodation is affordable for that person[10].

The Welsh Ministers[11] may by order specify:

(i)   other circumstances in which it is to be regarded as reasonable or not reasonable for a person to continue to occupy accommodation; and

(ii)   other matters to be taken into account or disregarded in determining whether it would be, or would have been, reasonable for a person to continue to occupy accommodation[12].

A person is threatened with homelessness if it is likely that the person will become homeless within 56 days[13].

1   Accommodation may only be regarded as available for a person's occupation if it is available for occupation by that person together with: (1) any other person who normally resides with that person as a member of his or her family; or (2) any other person who might reasonably be expected

to reside with that person: Housing (Wales) Act 2014 s 56(1). A reference in Pt 2 Ch 2 (ss 53–100) to securing that accommodation is available for a person's occupation is to be interpreted accordingly: s 56(2). See also PARA 481 note 1.

2   As to the meaning of 'United Kingdom' see PARA 60 note 10.

3   See PARA 481 note 2.

4   Housing (Wales) Act 2014 s 55(1).

5   Housing (Wales) Act 2014 s 55(2).

6   Housing (Wales) Act 2014 s 55(3).

7   In the Housing (Wales) Act 2014 s 57, 'member of a person's household' means: (1) a person who normally resides with him or her as member of his or her family; or (2) any other person who might reasonably be expected to reside with that person: s 57(2).

8   Housing (Wales) Act 2014 s 57(1). 'Abuse' means physical violence, threatening or intimidating behaviour and any other form of abuse which, directly or indirectly, may give rise to the risk of harm; and abuse is 'domestic abuse' where the victim is associated with the abuser: s 58(1). A person is associated with another person if:

   (1)   they are or have been married to each other;
   (2)   they are or have been civil partners of each other;
   (3)   they live or have lived together in an enduring family relationship (whether they are of different sexes or the same sex);
   (4)   they live or have lived in the same household;
   (5)   they are relatives;
   (6)   they have agreed to marry one another (whether or not that agreement has been terminated);
   (7)   they have entered into a civil partnership agreement between them (whether or not that agreement has been terminated);
   (8)   they have or have had an intimate personal relationship with each other which is or was of significant duration;
   (9)   in relation to a child, each of them is a parent of the child or has, or has had, parental responsibility for the child: s 58(2).

   If a child has been adopted or falls within s 58(4), two persons are also associated with each other for the purposes of Pt 2 Ch 2 if: (a) one is a natural parent of the child or a parent of such a natural parent; and (b) the other is: (i) the child; or (ii) a person who has become a parent of the child by virtue of an adoption order, who has applied for an adoption order or with whom the child has at any time been placed for adoption: s 58(3).

   A child falls within s 48(4) if: (A) an adoption agency, within the meaning of the Adoption and Children Act 2002 s 2 (see CHILDREN AND YOUNG PERSONS vol 9 (2017) PARAS 473 note 1), is authorised to place the child for adoption under s 19 (placing children with parental consent: see CHILDREN AND YOUNG PERSONS vol 9 (2017) PARA 407) or the child has become the subject of an order under s 21 (placement orders: see CHILDREN AND YOUNG PERSONS vol 9 (2017) PARA 410 et seq); or (B) the child is freed for adoption by virtue of an order made, in England and Wales, under the Adoption Act 1976 s 18 or, in Northern Ireland, under the Adoption (Northern Ireland) Order 1987, SI 1987/2203, art 17(1) or 18(1); or (C) the child is the subject of a Scottish permanence order which includes granting authority to adopt: Housing (Wales) Act 2014 s 58(4). See further CHILDREN AND YOUNG PERSONS.

   'Adoption order' means an adoption order within the meaning of the Adoption Act 1976 s 72(1) or the Adoption and Children Act 2002 s 46(1) (see CHILDREN AND YOUNG PERSONS vol 9 (2017) PARA 436); 'civil partnership agreement' has the meaning given by the Civil Partnership Act 2004 s 73; 'parental responsibility' has the meaning given by the Children Act 1989 s 3 (see CHILDREN AND YOUNG PERSONS vol 9 (2017) PARA 150); and 'relative', in relation to a person, means that person's parent, grandparent, child, grandchild, brother, half-brother, sister, half-sister, uncle, aunt, nephew, niece (including any person who is or has been in that relationship by virtue of a marriage or civil partnership or an enduring family relationship): Housing (Wales) Act 2014 s 58(5). As to the meaning of 'marriage' see PARA 481 note 8.

9   In the Housing (Wales) Act 2014 Pt 2 Ch 2, 'local housing authority' means: (1) in relation to Wales, the council of a county or county borough; and (2) in relation to England, a district council, a London borough council, the Common Council of the City of London or the Council of the Isles of Scilly, but a reference to a 'local housing authority' is to be interpreted as a reference to a local housing authority for an area in Wales only, unless Pt 2 Ch 2 expressly provides otherwise: s 99.

10   Housing (Wales) Act 2014 s 57(3).

11   As to the Welsh Ministers see PARA 7.

12   Housing (Wales) Act 2014 s 57(4). In determining whether accommodation is suitable for a person, a local housing authority must have regard to the Housing Act 1985 Pts IX, X (ss 264–344) (slum clearance and overcrowding: see PARAS 620 et seq, 649 et seq), the Housing Act 2004 Pts 1–4 (ss 1–147) (housing conditions; licensing of houses in multiple occupation and

other residential accommodation; additional controls: see PARAS 563 et seq, 666 et seq, 704 et seq, 745 et seq) and the Housing (Wales) Act 2014 Pt 1 (ss 1–49) (regulation of private rented housing: see PARA 729 et seq): s 59(1). In determining whether accommodation is suitable for a person, a local housing authority must have regard to whether or not the accommodation is affordable for that person: s 59(2).

The Welsh Ministers may by order specify: (1) circumstances in which accommodation is or is not to be regarded as suitable for a person; and (2) matters to be taken into account or disregarded in determining whether accommodation is suitable for a person: s 59(3). The Homelessness (Suitability of Accommodation) (Wales) Order 2015, SI 2015/1268, specifies matters local housing authorities must take into account in determining the suitability of accommodation for persons who are or may be in priority need (Pt 1 (art 3)), circumstances in which B&B and shared accommodation are not suitable to be used for temporary accommodation (Pt 2 (arts 4–7), Schedule), and when private rented sector accommodation is not suitable for discharging duties under the Housing (Wales) Act 2014 s 75 (see PARA 502) (Homelessness (Suitability of Accommodation) (Wales) Order 2015, SI 2015/1268, Pt 3 (art 8).
13 Housing (Wales) Act 2014 s 55(4).

483. Becoming homeless intentionally: England and Wales. Where a local housing authority decides that an otherwise eligible applicant became homeless intentionally, its duties are usually limited to providing advice and assistance[1]. Local authority decisions on this issue were often the subject of challenge through judicial review by disappointed applicants under the corresponding provisions in the Housing Act 1985; similar challenges are possible under the Housing Act 1996 in England and the Housing (Wales) Act 2014 in Wales, although applicants now have a statutory right to appeal against a decision on a point of law to the County Court[2].

The concept of 'intentionality' is now wider than it was under the Housing Act 1985. Under the Housing Act 1996 and the Housing (Wales) Act 2014, a person becomes homeless intentionally if he deliberately does or fails to do anything in consequence of which he ceases to occupy accommodation which is available for his occupation and which it would have been reasonable for him to continue to occupy[3]. For this purpose, an act or omission in good faith on the part of a person who was unaware of any relevant fact is not to be treated as deliberate[4]. A person who enters into an arrangement which requires him to cease to occupy accommodation which it would have been reasonable for him to continue to occupy is intentionally homeless where the purpose of such an arrangement was to obtain assistance under Part VII of the Housing Act 1996[5] or to help under Chapter 2 of Part 2 of the Housing (Wales) Act 2014[6] and there is no other good reason why the person is homeless[7].

The correct question to determine whether conduct has been the cause of a person's homelessness, is whether a likely consequence of the conduct could reasonably be regarded as being that the person would cease to occupy his accommodation[8]. A prisoner who, as a result of serving a custodial sentence, is unable to pay rent and, therefore, is evicted, is to be regarded as having become homeless intentionally[9]. The test for assessing whether a person is intentionally homeless in cases of domestic violence is one of probability[10]. It is for the authority to determine whether it would be reasonable for a person to continue to occupy the accommodation[11]. Occupation of accommodation for six months on an assured shorthold tenancy is not always sufficient to constitute settled accommodation so as to break the chain of causation from previous intentional homelessness[12]. Whether an applicant was intentionally homeless depends on the cause of the homelessness existing at the date of the decision; a later event constituting an involuntary cause of homelessness could be regarded as superseding an earlier deliberate conduct where in view of the later event it could not reasonably be said that, but for the applicant's deliberate conduct, he would not have become homeless[13].

In Wales, the Welsh Ministers[14] must, by regulations, specify a category or categories of applicant in relation to which a local housing authority[15] may not have regard[16] to whether or not an applicant has become homeless intentionally unless: (1) the applicant falls within a specified category[17] in respect of which the authority has decided to have regard to whether or not applicants in that category have become homeless intentionally; and (2) the authority has published a notice of its decision which specifies the category[18]. Where a local housing authority has published such a notice, unless the authority has: (a) decided to stop having regard to whether or not applicants falling into the category specified in the notice have become homeless intentionally; and (b) published a notice of its decision specifying the category, then[19] a local housing authority must have regard to whether or not an applicant has become homeless intentionally if the applicant falls within a category specified in the notice published by the authority under head (2)[20].

1 See PARA 496.
2 See PARA 509.
3 Housing Act 1996 s 191(1); Housing (Wales) Act 2014 s 77(1), (2).
4 Housing Act 1996 s 191(2); Housing (Wales) Act 2014 s 77(3). Thus an applicant who believed her husband's assurance that they would be rehoused under a union agreement was unaware of a relevant fact when this assurance proved subsequently to be false: see *R v Mole Valley District Council, ex p Burton* (1988) 20 HLR 479. The act or omission which led to the loss of accommodation must usually be that of the applicant and not of a spouse or partner: see *Lewis v North Devon District Council* [1981] 1 All ER 27, sub nom *R v North Devon District Council, ex p Lewis* [1981] 1 WLR 328. Hence an applicant who believed that her husband had cleared rent arrears could not be regarded as having become homeless intentionally when she and her husband (who were joint tenants) were evicted for rent arrears: see *R v East Northamptonshire District Council, ex p Spruce* (1988) 20 HLR 508. Similarly, an applicant's genuine misunderstanding about her family's entitlement to rehousing (her husband having voluntarily resigned from a job which carried tied accommodation) did not mean that she had become homeless intentionally: see *R v Mole Valley District Council, ex p Burton*. The Homelessness code of guidance for councils (Department for Communities and Local Government, 24 July 2006) (see PARA 486) advises that an applicant who has lost his home through rent or mortgage arrears should not automatically be treated as intentionally homeless as such arrears may have been caused by genuine financial difficulties, such as illness or unemployment: see para 11.18; and see also *R v Wandsworth London Borough Council, ex p Hawthorne* [1995] 2 All ER 331, [1994] 1 WLR 1442, CA; *R v Brent London Borough Council, ex p Baruwa* (1997) 29 HLR 915, CA. See further *O'Connor v Kensington and Chelsea Royal London Borough Council* [2004] EWCA Civ 394, [2004] HLR 601, [2004] All ER (D) 552 (Mar) (tenant ignorant of accrual of rent arrears and commencement of possession proceedings); and *Ugiagbe v Southwark London Borough Council* [2009] EWCA Civ 31, [2009] PTSR 1465, [2009] All ER (D) 95 (Feb) (no bad faith where claimant refused to attend Homeless Persons Unit).
5 'Assistance under Part VII of the Housing Act 1996' means the benefit of any function under ss 184–218 relating to accommodation or assistance in obtaining accommodation: s 183(2).
6 'Help under this Chapter' (ie the Housing (Wales) Act 2014 Pt 2 Ch 2 (ss 53–100)) means the benefit of any function under s 66, 68, 73, or 75I: s 99.
7 Housing Act 1996 s 191(3); Housing (Wales) Act 2014 s 77(1), (4). According to the Homelessness code of guidance for councils, this might include collusive arrangements not only between the applicant and friends and family but also with landlords: see para 11.28.
8 *Stewart v Lambeth London Borough Council* [2002] EWCA Civ 753, [2002] HLR 747, [2002] All ER (D) 260 (Apr).
9 *Minchin v Sheffield City Council* (2000) Times, 26 April, CA. See also *Goodger v Ealing London Borough Council* [2003] EWCA Civ 751, [2003] HLR 51, [2002] All ER (D) 203 (Apr) (person deemed intentionally homeless following eviction from flat after conviction for possession of cannabis).
10 *Bond v Leicester City Council* [2001] EWCA Civ 1544, [2002] HLR 158.

11　*Noh v Hammersmith and Fulham London Borough Council* [2001] EWCA Civ 905, [2002] HLR 960, [2001] All ER (D) 201 (Apr).

12　*Knight v Vale Royal Borough Council* [2003] EWCA Civ 1258, [2004] HLR 106, [2003] All ER (D) 11 (Aug). See also *Denton v Southwark London Borough Council* [2007] EWCA Civ 623, [2008] HLR 161, [2007] All ER (D) 56 (Jul) (person who left family home after breakdown of relationship with mother was not intentionally homeless).

13　*Haile v Waltham Forest London Borough* [2015] UKSC 34, [2015] AC 1471, [2015] All ER (D) 173 (May) (applicant's surrender of single occupancy accommodation superseded by her giving birth).

14　As to the Welsh Ministers see PARA 7.

15　As to the meaning of 'local housing authority' see PARA 482 note 9.

16　Ie for the purposes of the Housing (Wales) Act 2014 s 68 (see PARA 494) and s 75 (see PARA 502).

17　Ie specified under the Housing (Wales) Act 2014 s 78(1).

18　Housing (Wales) Act 2014 s 78(1), (2). As to regulations made under s 78(1) see the Homelessness (Intentionality) (Specified Categories) (Wales) Regulations 2015, SI 2015/1265, which specify a list of categories of applicants for the purposes of the Housing (Wales) Act 2014 s 78.

19　Ie for the purposes of the Housing (Wales) Act 2014 s 68 and s 75.

20　Housing (Wales) Act 2014 s 78(3), (4).

484. Becoming threatened with homelessness intentionally: England. In England, a person becomes threatened with homelessness intentionally if he deliberately does, or fails to do anything, the likely result of which is that he will be forced to leave accommodation which is available for his occupation[1] and which it would have been reasonable for him to continue to occupy[2]. However, an act or omission in good faith on the part of a person who was unaware of any relevant fact is not treated as deliberate for these purposes[3].

A person is treated as becoming threatened with homelessness intentionally if he enters into an arrangement under which he is required to cease to occupy accommodation which it would have been reasonable for him to continue to occupy, and the purpose of the arrangement is to enable him to become entitled to assistance under Part VII of the Housing Act 1996[4], and there is no other good reason why he is threatened with homelessness[5].

1　As to the meaning of 'available for his occupation' see PARA 481 note 1.

2　Housing Act 1996 s 196(1). See *R v Harrow London Borough Council, ex p Fahia* [1998] 4 All ER 137, [1998] 1 WLR 1396, HL; *R v Brighton Borough Council, ex p Harvey* (1997) 30 HLR 670; *R v Wandsworth London Borough Council, ex p Dodia* (1997) 30 HLR 562; *R v Hackney London Borough Council, ex p Ajayi* (1997) 30 HLR 473; *R v Camden London Borough Council, ex p Aranda* (1997) 30 HLR 76, CA; *R v Hounslow London Borough Council, ex p R* (1997) 29 HLR 939. As to whether it is reasonable to continue to occupy accommodation see PARA 481.

3　Housing Act 1996 s 196(2).

4　As to the meaning of 'assistance under Part VII of the Housing Act 1996' (ss 175–218) see PARA 483 note 5.

5　Housing Act 1996 s 196(3).

485. Advisory services; assistance to voluntary organisations: England and Wales. Every local housing authority[1] in England must secure that advice and information about homelessness[2], and the prevention of homelessness, is available free of charge to any person in its district[3]. The authority may give to any person by whom such advice and information is provided on behalf of the authority assistance by way of grant or loan[4], and may also assist any such person by permitting him to use premises belonging to the authority, by making available furniture or other goods, whether by way of gift, loan or otherwise, and by making available the services of staff employed by the authority[5].

The Secretary of State[6] or a local housing authority in England may give assistance by way of grant or loan to voluntary organisations[7] concerned with homelessness or matters relating to homelessness[8]. A local housing authority may also assist any such organisation by permitting it to use premises belonging to the authority, by making available furniture or other goods, whether by way of gift, loan or otherwise, and by making available the services of staff employed by the authority[9].

Assistance given under these provisions must be on such terms, and subject to such conditions, as the person giving the assistance may determine[10]. In all cases these conditions must require the person to whom the assistance is given:

(1)   to keep proper books of account and have them audited in such manner as may be specified;

(2)   to keep records indicating how he has used the money, furniture or other goods or premises; and

(3)   to submit the books of account and records for inspection by the person giving the assistance[11].

No assistance may be given unless the person to whom it is given undertakes to use the money, furniture or other goods or premises for a specified purpose, and to provide such information as may reasonably be required as to the manner in which the assistance is being used[12]. If it appears to the person giving the assistance that the recipient has failed to carry out his undertaking as to the purpose for which the assistance was to be used, all reasonable steps must be taken to recover from that person an amount equal to the amount of the assistance[13]. Before doing so, a notice must be given specifying the amount which is recoverable and the basis on which that amount has been calculated[14].

A local housing authority[15] in Wales must secure the provision, without charge, of a service providing people in its area, or people who have a local connection[16] with its area, with:

(a)   information and advice relating to preventing homelessness, securing accommodation when homeless, accessing any other help available for people who are homeless or may become homeless; and

(b)   assistance in accessing help under Chapter 2 of Part 2 of the Housing (Wales) Act 2014[17] or any other help for people who are homeless or may become homeless[18].

The local housing authority must, in particular by working with other public authorities, voluntary organisations[19] and other persons, ensure that the service is designed to meet the needs of groups at particular risk of homelessness, including in particular: (i) people leaving prison or youth detention accommodation[20]; (ii) young people leaving care; (iii) people leaving the regular armed forces of the Crown[21]; (iv) people leaving hospital after medical treatment for mental disorder as an inpatient; and (v) people receiving mental health services in the community[22].

1   As to the meaning of 'local housing authority' in relation to England see PARA 11 (definition applied by the Housing Act 1996 s 230).

2   As to when a person is homeless see PARAS 481, 482.

3   Housing Act 1996 s 179(1). As to the meaning of 'district' see PARA 11 (definition applied by s 217(3)). As to the scope of the duty and the freedom of local housing authorities to provide services themselves or to invite other agencies to act as the provider see 574 HL Official Report (5th series), 8 July 1996 cols 87–88.

4   Housing Act 1996 s 179(2).

5   Housing Act 1996 s 179(3).

6   As to the Secretary of State see PARA 7.

7   A 'voluntary organisation' means a body (other than a public or local authority) whose activities are not carried on for profit: Housing Act 1996 s 180(3).

8   Housing Act 1996 s 180(1) (amended, in relation to Wales, by the Housing (Wales) Act 2014 s 100, Sch 3 paras 2, 6).

9   Housing Act 1996 s 180(2).

10 Housing Act 1996 s 181(1), (2).

11 Housing Act 1996 s 181(4).

12 Housing Act 1996 s 181(3). The person giving the assistance may require such information by notice in writing, which must be complied with within 21 days beginning with the date on which the notice is served: s 181(3).

13 Housing Act 1996 s 181(5).

14 Housing Act 1996 s 181(6).

15 As to the meaning of 'local housing authority' in relation to Wales see PARA 482 note 9. Two or more local housing authorities may jointly secure the provision of a service under the Housing (Wales) Act 2014 s 60 for their areas; and where they do so: (1) references in s 60 to a local housing authority are to be read as references to the authorities acting jointly; and (2) references in s 60 to a local housing authority's area are to be read as references to the combined area: s 60(5).

16 For the purposes of the Housing (Wales) Act 2014 Pt 2 Ch 2 (ss 53–100), a person has a local connection with the area of a local housing authority in Wales or England if the person has a connection with it: (1) because the person is, or in the past was, normally resident there, and that residence is or was of the person's own choice; (2) because the person is employed there; (3) because of family associations; or (4) because of special circumstances: s 81(1), (2). Residence in an area is not of a person's own choice if the person, or a person who might reasonably be expected to reside with that person, becomes resident there because the person is detained under the authority of an enactment: s 81(3). The Welsh Ministers may by order specify circumstances in which: (a) a person is not to be treated as employed in an area; or (b) residence in an area is not to be treated as of a person's own choice: s 81(4). As to the Welsh Ministers see PARA 7.

   A person has a local connection with the area of a local housing authority in Wales or England if the person was (at any time) provided with accommodation in that area under the Immigration and Asylum Act 1999 s 95 (support for asylum seekers: see IMMIGRATION AND ASYLUM vol 57 (2012) PARA 344 et seq): Housing (Wales) Act 2014 s 81(5). This does not apply, however: (i) to the provision of accommodation for a person in an area of a local housing authority if the person was subsequently provided with accommodation in the area of another local housing authority under the Immigration and Asylum Act 1999 s 95; or (ii) to the provision of accommodation in an accommodation centre by virtue of the Nationality, Immigration and Asylum Act 2002 s 22 (use of accommodation centres for section 95 support: see IMMIGRATION AND ASYLUM vol 57 (2012) PARA 350): Housing (Wales) Act 2014 s 81(6). An asylum-seeker who has been provided with accommodation in a local authority's district under the Immigration and Asylum Act 1999 s 95 has a local connection there, even if he has no friends or family there and does not want to live there: *Ozbek v Ipswich Borough Council* [2006] EWCA Civ 534, [2006] HLR 777, [2006] LGR 853.

17 As to the meaning of 'help under the Housing (Wales) Act 2014 Pt 2 Ch 2' see PARA 483 note 6.

18 Housing (Wales) Act 2014 s 60(1). In relation to head (a) in the text, the service must include, in particular, the publication of information and advice on the following matters: (1) the system provided for by Pt 2 Ch 2 and how the system operates in the authority's area; (2) whether any other help for people who are homeless or may become homeless (whether or not the person is threatened with homelessness within the meaning of Pt 2 Ch 2) is available in the authority's area; (3) how to access the help that is available: s 60(2). In relation to head (b) in the text, the service must include, in particular, assistance in accessing help to prevent a person becoming homeless which is available whether or not the person is threatened with homelessness within the meaning of Pt 2 Ch 2: s 60(3).

   The service required by s 60 may be integrated with the service required by the Social Services and Well-being (Wales) Act 2014 s 17 (see SOCIAL SERVICES vol 95 (2017) PARA 392): Housing (Wales) Act 2014 s 60(6).

19 'Voluntary organisation' means a body (other than a public or local authority) whose activities are not carried on for profit: Housing (Wales) Act 2014 s 99.

20 'Prison' has the same meaning as in the Prison Act 1952 (see s 53(1); and PRISONS AND PRISONERS vol 85 (2012) PARA 403 note 1); and 'youth detention accommodation' means: (1) a secure children's home; (2) a secure training centre; (3) a young offender institution; (4) accommodation provided, equipped and maintained by the Welsh Ministers under the Children Act 1989 s 82(5) for the purpose of restricting the liberty of children; (5) accommodation, or accommodation of a description, for the time being specified by order under the Powers of Criminal Courts (Sentencing) Act 2000 s 107(1)(e) (youth detention accommodation for the purposes of detention and training orders): Housing (Wales) Act 2014 s 99.

21 'Regular armed forces of the Crown' means the regular forces as defined by the Armed Forces Act 2006 s 374 (see ARMED FORCES vol 3 (2011) PARA 327): Housing (Wales) Act 2014 s 99.

22 Housing (Wales) Act 2014 s 60(4).

486. Guidance by the appropriate national authority. In the exercise of its functions relating to homelessness and the prevention of homelessness[1], a local housing authority[2] or social services authority[3] in England must have regard to such guidance as may from time to time be given by the Secretary of State[4]. The Secretary of State may give guidance either generally or to specified descriptions of authorities[5].

In the exercise of its functions relating to homelessness, a council of a county or county borough in Wales must have regard to guidance given by the Welsh Ministers[6]. The Welsh Ministers may: (1) give guidance either generally or to specified descriptions of authorities; (2) revise the guidance by giving further guidance under Part 2 of the Housing (Wales) Act 2014; (3) withdraw the guidance by giving further guidance or by notice[7]. The Welsh Ministers must publish any guidance or notice given under Part 2[8].

Whilst a local housing authority must have regard to the guidance, it is not required to follow it to the letter, and it may be appropriate, therefore, to depart from the guidance provided that such a departure can be justified[9].

1 As to when a person is homeless see PARA 481.
2 As to the meaning of 'local housing authority' see PARA 11 (definition applied by the Housing Act 1996 s 230).
3 'Social services authority' means, in relation to England, a local authority for the purposes of the Local Authority Social Services Act 1970 as defined in s 1 (see SOCIAL SERVICES vol 95 (2017) PARA 1), and in relation to Wales, a local authority exercising social services functions for the purposes of the Social Services and Well-being (Wales) Act 2014: Housing Act 1996 s 217(1) (amended by SI 2016/413).
4 Housing Act 1996 s 182(1) (amended, in relation to Wales, by the Housing (Wales) Act 2014 s 100, Sch 3 paras 2, 7). As to the Secretary of State see PARA 7. As to such guidance see Homelessness code of guidance for councils (Department for Communities and Local Government, 24 July 2006); Intentional homelessness: guidance for councils (Department for Communities and Local Government, 5 August 2009).
5 Housing Act 1996 s 182(2).
6 Housing (Wales) Act 2014 s 98(1). This applies in relation to functions under Pt 2 (ss 50–100) and any other enactment: s 98(2). As to the Welsh Ministers see PARA 7.
7 Housing (Wales) Act 2014 s 98(3).
8 Housing (Wales) Act 2014 s 98(4). As to such guidance see Code of Guidance to Local Authorities on the Allocation of Accommodation and Homelessness 2016 (Welsh Government, 24 March 2016).
9 See eg *De Falco v Crawley Borough Council* [1980] QB 460, [1980] 1 All ER 913, CA. It is the authority's duty to follow the most up-to-date version of the guidance: see *R v Newham Borough Council, ex p Bones* (1992) 25 HLR 357.

(iii) Applications and Eligibility for Assistance

487. Application for assistance in case of homelessness or threatened homelessness: England. The following procedure applies (under Part VII of the Housing Act 1996[1]) where a person applies to a local housing authority in England for accommodation, or for assistance in obtaining accommodation, and the authority has reason to believe that he is or may be homeless or threatened with homelessness[2].

If the local housing authority has reason to believe that an applicant[3] may be homeless or threatened with homelessness, it must make such inquiries as are necessary to satisfy itself whether he is eligible for assistance[4], and if so, whether any duty, and if so what duty, is owed to him under the statutory homelessness provisions[5]. The authority may also make inquiries whether he has a local connection[6] with the district of another local housing authority in England, Wales or Scotland[7]. On completing its inquiries, the authority must notify the applicant of its decision and, so far as any issue is decided against his interests, inform him of the reasons for its decision[8]. If the authority decides that a duty is owed to the applicant to secure that accommodation is available for occupation by him[9] or that accommodation does not cease to be available for his occupation[10] but would not have done so without having had regard to a restricted person[11], the notice must also: (1) inform the applicant that its decision was reached on that basis; (2) include the name of the restricted person; (3) explain why the person is a restricted person; and (4) explain the effect of the relevant legislation[12] which applies in a restricted case[13]. The notice must be given to the applicant in writing and, if not received by him, is treated as having been given to him if it is made available at the authority's office for a reasonable period for collection by him or on his behalf[14].

1   Ie the Housing Act 1996 Pt VII (ss 175–218) (amended by the Housing (Wales) Act 2014 s 100, Sch 3 Pt 1 to apply in relation to England only). See generally the *Homelessness Code of Guidance for Local Authorities* (Department for Communities and Local Government, 2006)

2   Housing Act 1996 s 183(1) (amended, in relation to Wales, by the Housing (Wales) Act 2014 Sch 3 paras 2, 8). Nothing in the Housing Act 1996 ss 183–218 affects a person's entitlement to advice and information under s 179 (see PARA 485): s 183(3). It is not possible to circumvent s 183 by invoking the general power of a local authority to provide housing pursuant to the National Assistance Act 1948 s 21 (see PARA 477 text and note 9): *R (on the application of PB) v Haringey London Borough Council* [2006] EWHC 2255 (Admin), [2007] HLR 175, [2006] All ER (D) 82 (Sep).

3   'Applicant' means a person making an application under the Housing Act 1996 s 183(1) (see the text to note 1): s 183(2). Subject to any transitional provision contained in a commencement order under s 232(4), the provisions of Pt VII do not apply in relation to an applicant whose application for accommodation or assistance in obtaining accommodation was made before the commencement of those provisions (ie 20 January 1997): see the Housing Act 1996 (Commencement No 5 and Transitional Provisions) Order 1996, SI 1996/2959): Housing Act 1996 s 216(2).

4   'Eligible for assistance' means not excluded from such assistance by the Housing Act 1996 s 185 (persons from abroad not eligible for housing assistance: see PARA 491) or s 186 (asylum seekers and their dependants: see PARA 492): s 183(2). As from a day to be appointed, this provision is amended so as to omit the reference to s 186 (prospectively repealed): see s 183(2) (prospectively amended by the Immigration and Asylum Act 1999 s 169(1), (3), Sch 14 para 116, Sch 16). At the date at which this volume states the law, no such day had been appointed.

5   Housing Act 1996 s 184(1). See *R v Wandsworth London Borough Council, ex p Dodia* (1997) 30 HLR 562. See also *R v Newham London Borough Council, ex p Khan* (2001) 33 HLR 269 (authority is under a duty to take immediate action where an order for possession is in force but not yet enforced); applied in *R v Newham London Borough Council, ex p Sacupima* [2001] 1 WLR 563, [2000] All ER (D) 1947, CA. See also *Begum v Tower Hamlets London Borough Council* [2005] EWCA Civ 340, [2005] 1 WLR 2103, [2005] All ER (D) 393 (Mar). The inquiry should not be delayed by the local authority seeking mediation between the homeless person and the person who is responsible for their exclusion from their home: *Robinson v Hammersmith and Fulham London Borough Council* [2006] EWCA Civ 1122, [2006] 1 WLR 3295, [2006] LGR 822, applied in *R (on the application of Aweys) v Birmingham City Council* [2007] EWHC 52 (Admin), [2007] HLR 394, [2007] 1 FLR 2066. See also *Hanton-Rhouila v Westminster City Council* [2010] EWCA Civ 1334, [2011] HLR 204, [2010] All ER (D) 259 (Nov) (claimant obtained assured shorthold tenancy in property while application for housing on ground of homelessness pending; claimant not homeless).

6   A person has a local connection with the district of a local housing authority if he has a connection with it: (1) because he is, or in the past was, normally resident there, and that residence is or was of his own choice; (2) because he is employed there; (3) because of family associations; or (4) because of special circumstances: Housing Act 1996 s 199(1). As to the meaning of 'district' see PARA 11 (definition applied by s 217(3)). Residence in a district is not of a person's own choice if he, or a person who might reasonably be expected to reside with him, becomes resident there because he is detained under the authority of an Act of Parliament (s 199(3) (amended by the Housing and Regeneration Act 2008 ss 315(b), 321(1), Sch 16).

     The Secretary of State may by order specify circumstances in which a person is not to be treated as employed in a district, or residence in a district is not to be treated as of a person's own choice: Housing Act 1996 s 199(5) (amended by the Housing and Regeneration Act 2008 ss 315(d), 321(1), Sch 16). At the date at which this volume states the law, no such order had been made. As to the Secretary of State see PARA 7.

     A person has a local connection with the district of a local housing authority if he was (at any time) provided with accommodation in that district under the Immigration and Asylum Act 1999 s 95 (support for asylum seekers) (see IMMIGRATION AND ASYLUM vol 57 (2012) PARA 344 et seq): Housing Act 1996 s 199(6) (added by the Asylum and Immigration (Treatment of Claimants, etc) Act 2004 s 11(1)). However, this does not apply: (i) to the provision of accommodation for a person in a district of a local housing authority if he was subsequently provided with accommodation in the district of another local housing authority under the Immigration and Asylum Act 1999 s 95; or (ii) to the provision of accommodation in an accommodation centre by virtue of the Nationality, Immigration and Asylum Act 2002 s 22 (use of accommodation centres for s 95 support) (see IMMIGRATION AND ASYLUM vol 57 (2012) PARA 350): Housing Act 1996 s 199(7) (added by the Asylum and Immigration (Treatment of Claimants, etc) Act 2004 s 11(1)). An asylum-seeker who has been provided with accommodation in a local authority's district under the Immigration and Asylum Act 1999 s 95 has a local connection there, even if he has no friends or family there and does not want to live there: *Ozbek v Ipswich Borough Council* [2006] EWCA Civ 534, [2006] HLR 777, [2006] LGR 853.

7   Housing Act 1996 s 184(2).
8   Housing Act 1996 s 184(3). A notice under s 184(3) must also inform the applicant of his right to request a review of the decision and of the time within which such a request must be made (see PARA 507): s 184(5).
9   Ie under the Housing Act 1996 s 193(2): see PARA 498.
10 Ie under the Housing Act 1996 s 195(2): see PARA 499.
11 In the Housing Act 1996 Pt VII 'a restricted person' means a person: (1) who is not eligible for assistance under Pt VII; (2) who is subject to immigration control within the meaning of the Asylum and Immigration Act 1996; and (3) either: (a) who does not have leave to enter or remain in the United Kingdom; or (b) whose leave to enter or remain in the United Kingdom is subject to a condition to maintain and accommodate himself, and any dependants, without recourse to public funds: Housing Act 1996 s 184(7) (added by the Housing and Regeneration Act 2008 s 314, Sch 15 paras 1, 3(1), (3)). As to immigration control and leave to enter or remain in the United Kingdom see IMMIGRATION AND ASYLUM vol 57 (2012) PARA 5 et seq.
12 Ie the Housing Act 1996 s 193(7AD) or (as the case may be) s 195(4A): see PARAS 498, 499.
13 Housing Act 1996 s 184(3A) (added by the Housing and Regeneration Act 2008 Sch 15 para 3(2)).
14 Housing Act 1996 s 184(6). If the authority has notified or intends to notify another local housing authority under s 198 (referral of cases: see PARA 503), it must at the same time notify the applicant of that decision and inform him of the reasons for it: s 184(4). A notice under s 184(4) must also inform the applicant of his right to request a review of the decision and of the time within which such a request must be made (see PARA 507): s 184(5).

488.   Applications for help in case of homelessness or threatened homelessness: Wales. Under the Housing (Wales) Act 2014, a local housing authority[1] must carry out an assessment of a person's case if the person has applied to a local housing authority for accommodation or help in retaining or obtaining accommodation and it appears to the authority that the person may be homeless or threatened with homelessness, unless the person has previously been assessed and the person's circumstances have not changed materially[2]. The authority must assess whether or not the applicant[3] is eligible for help[4] under the Housing (Wales) Act 2014[5]. If the applicant is eligible for such help, the assessment must include an assessment of:

(1)   the circumstances that have caused the applicant to be homeless[6] or threatened with homelessness;

(2)   the housing needs of the applicant and any person with whom the applicant lives or might reasonably be expected to live;

(3)   the support needed for the applicant and any person with whom the applicant lives or might reasonably be expected to live to retain accommodation which is or may become available;

(4)   whether or not the authority has any duty under the relevant provisions of the Housing (Wales) Act 2014[7] to the applicant[8].

In carrying out an assessment, the local housing authority must:

(a)   seek to identify the outcome the applicant wishes to achieve from the authority's help; and

(b)   assess whether the exercise of any function under Chapter 2 of Part 2 of the Housing (Wales) Act 2014 could contribute to the achievement of that outcome[9].

A local housing authority must keep its assessment under review during the period in which the authority considers that it owes a duty to the applicant under the relevant provisions[10] or that it may do so[11]. A local housing authority must review its assessment in two specific cases[12].

The local housing authority must notify the applicant of the outcome of its assessment (or any review of its assessment) and, in so far as any issue is decided against the applicant's interests, inform the applicant of the reasons for its decision[13]. If the authority has notified or intends to notify another local housing authority[14], it must at the same time notify the applicant of that decision and inform him of the reasons for it[15]. A notice under these provisions must be given in writing and must inform the applicant of his right to request a review of the decision and of the time within which such a request must be made[16].

1 As to the meaning of 'local housing authority' in relation to Wales see PARA 482 note 9.
2 Housing (Wales) Act 2014 s 62(1), (2).
3 Ie a person to whom the duty in the Housing (Wales) Act 2014 s 62(1) applies: s 62(3).
4 Ie the Housing (Wales) Act 2014 Pt 2 Ch 2. 'Eligible for help' means not excluded from help under the Housing (Wales) Act 2014 Pt 2 Ch 2 (ss 53–100) by Sch 2 (see PARAS 491–492): s 99.
5 Housing (Wales) Act 2014 s 62(4).
6 As to when a person is homeless see PARA 482.
7 Ie the Housing (Wales) Act 2014 ss 62(6)–100.
8 Housing (Wales) Act 2014 s 62(5). A local housing authority may carry out its assessment of the matters mentioned in s 62(5) and (6) (see the text to note 9) before it has concluded that the applicant is eligible for help under Pt 2 Ch 2: s 62(7).
9 Housing (Wales) Act 2014 s 62(6). See note 8.
10 See note 7.
11 Housing (Wales) Act 2014 s 62(8).
12 Housing (Wales) Act 2014 s 62(9). Those cases are: case 1—where an applicant has been notified under s 63 (see the text and notes 13–16) that a duty is owed to the applicant under s 66 (duty to help to prevent an applicant from becoming homeless: see PARA 490) and subsequently it appears to the authority that the duty under s 66 has or is likely to come to an end because the applicant is homeless; case 2—where an applicant has been notified under s 63 that a duty is owed to the applicant under s 73 (duty to help to secure accommodation for homeless applicants: see PARA 501) and subsequently it appears to the authority that the duty in s 73 has or is likely to come to an end in circumstances where a duty may be owed to the applicant under s 75 (duty to secure accommodation for applicants in priority need when the duty in s 73 ends: see PARA 502): s 62(9) cases 1, 2.
    The duty in s 62(5)(d) (head (4) in the text) does not require a local housing authority to assess whether or not a duty would be owed to the applicant under s 75 unless and until it reviews its assessment in accordance with s 62(9) in the circumstances described in s 62 case 2; but it may do so before then: s 62(10). Section 62(9), (10) do not affect the generality of s 62(8): s 62(11).
13 Housing (Wales) Act 2014 s 63(1). If the authority decides that a duty is owed to the applicant under s 75 (securing accommodation for certain persons in priority need: see PARA 502), but would not have done so without having had regard to a restricted person, the notice under s 63(1) must also: (1) inform the applicant that its decision was reached on that basis; (2) include the name of the restricted person; (3) explain why the person is a restricted person; and (4) explain the effect of s 76(5): s 63(2).
    In Pt 2 Ch 2, 'a restricted person' means a person: (a) who is not eligible for help under Pt 2 Ch 2; (b) who is subject to immigration control within the meaning of the Asylum and Immigration Act 1996; and (c) who either: (i) does not have leave to enter or remain in the United Kingdom; or (ii) has leave to enter or remain in the United Kingdom subject to a condition to maintain and accommodate himself or herself, and any dependants, without recourse to public funds: Housing (Wales) Act 2014 s 63(5). As to immigration control and leave to enter or remain in the United Kingdom see IMMIGRATION AND ASYLUM vol 57 (2012) PARA 5 et seq. As to the meaning of 'United Kingdom' see PARA 60 note 10.
14 Ie under the Housing (Wales) Act 2014 s 80 (referral of cases: see PARA 503).
15 Housing (Wales) Act 2014 s 63(3).
16 Housing (Wales) Act 2014 s 63(4). As to the time within which such a request must be made see s 85; and PARA 508. If not received, a notice is to be treated as having been given if it is made available at the authority's office for a reasonable period for collection by the applicant or on the applicant's behalf: s 63(4)(b).

489. Securing or helping to secure the availability of accommodation: Wales.
Examples of the ways in which a local housing authority[1] may secure or help to
secure that suitable accommodation is available, or does not cease to be available,
for occupation by an applicant[2] are: (1) by arranging for a person other than the
authority to provide something; (2) by itself providing something; (3) by
providing something, or arranging for something to be provided, to a person other
than the applicant[3].

Examples of what may be provided or arranged to secure or help to secure that
suitable accommodation is available, or does not cease to be available, for
occupation by an applicant are: (a) mediation; (b) payments by way of grant or
loan; (c) guarantees that payments will be made; (d) support in managing debt,
mortgage arrears or rent arrears; (e) security measures for applicants at risk of
abuse; (f) advocacy or other representation; (g) accommodation; (h) information
and advice; (i) other services, goods or facilities[4].

The Welsh Ministers[5] must give guidance to local housing authorities in
relation to how they may secure or help to secure that suitable accommodation is
available, or does not cease to be available, for occupation by an applicant[6].

Where a local housing authority is required[7] to help to secure (rather than 'to
secure') that suitable accommodation is available, or does not cease to be
available, for occupation by an applicant, the authority: (i) is required to take
reasonable steps to help, having regard (among other things) to the need to make
the best use of the authority's resources; (ii) is not required to secure an offer of
accommodation[8]; (iii) is not required to otherwise provide accommodation[9].

1　As to the meaning of 'local housing authority' in relation to Wales see PARA 482 note 9.
2　As to the meaning of 'applicant' see PARA 488 note 3.
3　Housing (Wales) Act 2014 s 64(1). See also Code of Guidance to Local Authorities on the
　　Allocation of Accommodation and Homelessness (Welsh Government; last updated 24 March
　　2016).
4　Housing (Wales) Act 2014 s 64(2).
5　As to the Welsh Ministers see PARA 7.
6　Housing (Wales) Act 2014 s 64(3).
7　Ie by the Housing (Wales) Act 2014 Pt 2 Ch 2 (ss 53–100).
8　Ie under the Housing Act 1996 Pt VI (ss 159–174) (allocation of housing): see PARA 420 et seq.
9　Housing (Wales) Act 2014 s 65.

490. Duty to prevent an applicant becoming homeless: Wales. A local housing
authority[1] must help to secure[2] that suitable accommodation does not cease to be
available for occupation by an applicant[3] if it is satisfied that the applicant is:
(1)　threatened with homelessness[4]; and
(2)　eligible for help[5].
This duty does not affect any right the authority may have, whether by virtue of
a contract, enactment or rule of law, to secure vacant possession of any
accommodation[6].

If the applicant has been notified by the local housing authority that it no
longer regards itself as being subject to the duty[7], this duty comes to an end in the
following circumstances[8]:
(a)　where the local authority is satisfied that the applicant has become
　　　homeless[9];
(b)　where the local housing authority is satisfied (whether as a result of the
　　　steps it has taken or not) that the applicant is no longer threatened with
　　　homelessness and that suitable accommodation is likely to be available
　　　for occupation by the applicant for a period of at least six months,
　　　beginning on the day the notice by the authority is sent or first made
　　　available for collection[10];

(c)   where the applicant, having been notified in writing of the possible consequences of refusal or acceptance of the offer, refuses an offer of accommodation from any person which the authority is satisfied is suitable for the applicant, and the authority is satisfied that the accommodation offered is likely to be available for occupation by the applicant for a period of at least six months, beginning on the day the notice by the authority is sent or first made available for collection[11];

(d)   where the local housing authority is no longer satisfied that the applicant is eligible for help[12];

(e)   where the local housing authority is satisfied that a mistake of fact led to the applicant being notified[13] that the duty was owed to the applicant[14];

(f)   where the local authority is satisfied that the applicant has withdrawn his or her application[15];

(g)   where the local housing authority is satisfied that the applicant is unreasonably failing to co-operate with the authority in connection with the exercise of its functions under the relevant provisions of the Housing (Wales) Act 2014[16] as they apply to the applicant[17].

1   As to the meaning of 'local housing authority' in relation to Wales see PARA 482 note 9.
2   As to the meaning of 'help to secure' see PARA 489.
3   As to the meaning of 'applicant' see PARA 488 note 3.
4   As to the meaning of 'threatened with homelessness' see PARA 488.
5   Housing (Wales) Act 2014 s 66(1). As to the meaning of 'eligible for help' see PARA 488 note 4.
6   Housing (Wales) Act 2014 s 66(2).
7   Ie in accordance with the Housing (Wales) Act 2014 s 84: see PARA 501.
8   Housing (Wales) Act 2014 ss 67(1), 79(1).
9   Housing (Wales) Act 2014 s 67(2).
10 Housing (Wales) Act 2014 s 67(3), (5).
11 Housing (Wales) Act 2014 s 67(4), (5).
12 Housing (Wales) Act 2014 s 79(2).
13 Ie under the Housing (Wales) Act 2014 s 63: see PARA 488.
14 Housing (Wales) Act 2014 s 79(3).
15 Housing (Wales) Act 2014 s 79(4).
16 Ie the Housing (Wales) Act 2014 Pt 2 Ch 2 (ss 53–100): see PARA 482 et seq.
17 Housing (Wales) Act 2014 s 79(5).

491. Persons from abroad not eligible for assistance: England and Wales. A person is not eligible for assistance[1] under Part VII of the Housing Act 1996[2] or for help under the Housing (Wales) Act 2014[3] if he is a person from abroad who is ineligible for housing assistance[4]. A person who is subject to immigration control[5] is not eligible for housing assistance unless he is of a class prescribed by regulations made by the appropriate national authority[6]. No person who is excluded from entitlement to universal credit or housing benefit by the Immigration and Asylum Act 1999[7] may be included in any class so prescribed[8].

The appropriate national authority has made provision by regulations as to other descriptions of persons who are to be treated for these purposes as persons from abroad who are ineligible for housing assistance[9].

A person from abroad who is not eligible for housing assistance must be disregarded in determining whether a person falling within specified categories[10] is homeless or threatened with homelessness[11], or has a priority need for accommodation[12].

1   As to the meaning of 'eligible for assistance' see PARA 487 note 4.
2   Ie under the Housing Act 1996 Pt VII (ss 175–218). As to the meaning of 'assistance under Part VII' see PARA 483 note 5.
3   Ie under the Housing (Wales) Act 2014 s 66, 68, 73 or 75.

4   Housing Act 1996 s 185(1); Housing (Wales) Act 2014 s 61, Sch 2 para 1(1). As to the position
     in a case where the Housing Act 1996 came into force while inquiries were pending see *R v
     Southwark London Borough Council, ex p Bediako* (1997) 30 HLR 22; *R v Hackney London
     Borough Council, ex p K* (1997) 30 HLR 760, CA.
5   Ie within the meaning of the Asylum and Immigration Act 1996: see IMMIGRATION AND
     ASYLUM vol 57 (2012) PARA 5 et seq. The ineligibility of persons subject to immigration control
     for housing assistance is justifiable in the context of leave to enter being conditional on having no
     recourse to public funds and in view of the legitimate aim of allocating a scarce resource fairly
     between different categories of claimant: Application 56328/07 *Bah v United Kingdom*
     (2011) 31 BHRC 609, 54 EHRR 773, [2011] 39 LS Gaz R 19, (2011) Times, 15 November,
     ECtHR.
6   Housing Act 1996 s 185(2); Housing (Wales) Act 2014 Sch 2 para 1(2). 'Prescribed' means
     prescribed by regulations made by the Secretary of State (Housing Act 1996 s 215(1)) or in
     regulations made by the Welsh Ministers (Housing (Wales) Act 2014 s 99). As to the Secretary
     of State and the Welsh Ministers ('the appropriate national authority') see PARA 7. Regulations or
     an order under the Housing Act 1996 Pt VII may make different provision for different purposes,
     including different provision for different areas: s 215(2). They must be made by statutory
     instrument and, unless required to be approved in draft, are subject to annulment in pursuance of
     a resolution of either House of Parliament: s 215(3), (4). A power to make an order or regulations
     under the Housing (Wales) Act 2014 is to be exercised by statutory instrument: s 142(1). A power
     to make an order or regulations under the Housing (Wales) Act 2014 includes power to make
     different provision for different cases or classes of case, different areas or different purposes; to
     make different provision generally or subject to specified exemptions or exceptions or only in
     relation to specific cases or classes of case; to make such incidental, supplementary, consequential,
     transitory, transitional or saving provision as the person making the order or regulations considers
     appropriate: s 142(2). In general, a statutory instrument containing an order or regulations made
     by the Welsh Ministers under the Housing (Wales) Act 2014 other than an order made under
     s 40(7) is subject to annulment in pursuance of a resolution of the National Assembly for Wales:
     s 142(4).
         The classes of persons are prescribed for the purposes of the Housing Act 1996 s 185(2), in
     relation to England, by the Allocation of Housing and Homelessness (Eligibility) (England)
     Regulations 2006, SI 2006/1294 (amended by SI 2006/2007, SI 2006/2527, SI 2006/3340, SI
     2009/358, SI 2012/1809, SI 2012/2588, SI 2013/1467, SI 2014/435 and SI 2016/965), and, for the
     purposes of the Housing (Wales) Act 2014 Sch 2 para 1 in relation to Wales, by the Allocation of
     Housing and Homelessness (Eligibility) (Wales) Regulations 2014, SI 2014/2603, which now have
     effect under the Housing (Wales) Act 2014 Sch 2 para 1; see the Housing (Wales) Act 2014
     (Commencement No 3 and Transitory, Transitional and Saving Provisions) Order 2015, SI
     2015/1272, art 5.
         The prescribed classes in relation to England are as follows (see the Allocation of Housing and
     Homelessness (Eligibility) (England) Regulations 2006, SI 2006/1294, reg 5(1) (amended by SI
     2006/2527)):
     (1)   Class A: a person recorded by the Secretary of State as a refugee within the definition in
           the Refugee Convention, ie the Convention relating to the Status of Refugees (Geneva,
           28 July 1951; TS 39 (1954); Cmnd 9171) art 1 (as extended by the Protocol relating to
           the Status of Refugees (New York, 31 January 1967; TS 15 (1969); Cmnd 3906))
           (Allocation of Housing and Homelessness (Eligibility) (England) Regulations 2006, SI
           2006/1294, regs 2(1), 5(1)(a));
     (2)   Class B: a person who has exceptional leave to enter or remain in the United Kingdom
           granted outside the provisions of the Immigration Rules and whose leave to enter or
           remain is not subject to a condition requiring him to maintain and accommodate
           himself, and any person who is dependent on him, without recourse to public funds
           (reg 5(1)(b));
     (3)   Class C: a person who is habitually resident in the United Kingdom, the Channel Islands,
           the Isle of Man or the Republic of Ireland and whose leave to enter or remain in the
           United Kingdom is not subject to any limitation or condition, other than a person:
           (a)   who has been given leave to enter or remain in the United Kingdom upon an
                  undertaking given by his sponsor;
           (b)   who has been resident in the United Kingdom, the Channel Islands, the Isle of
                  Man or the Republic of Ireland for less than five years beginning on the date of
                  entry or the date on which his sponsor gave the undertaking in respect of him,
                  whichever date is the later; and
           (c)   whose sponsor or, where there is more than one sponsor, at least one of whose
                  sponsors, is still alive (reg 5(1)(c));
     (4)   Class D: a person who has humanitarian protection granted under the Immigration
           Rules (reg 5(1)(d) (substituted by SI 2006/2527));

(5)   Class F: a person who is habitually resident in the United Kingdom, the Channel Islands, the Isle of Man or the Republic of Ireland and who has limited leave to enter the United Kingdom as a relevant Afghan citizen under the Immigration Rules para 276BA1 (Allocation of Housing and Homelessness (Eligibility) (England) Regulations 2006, SI 2006/1294, reg 5(1)(f) (added by SI 2014/435; amended by SI 2016/965)); and

(6)   Class G: a person who has limited leave to enter or remain in the United Kingdom on family or private life grounds under the Human Rights Convention (ie the Convention for the Protection of Human Rights and Fundamental Freedoms, agreed by the Council of Europe at Rome on 4 November 1950 (TS 71 (1953); Cmd 8969) as it has effect for the time being in relation to the United Kingdom) art 8, such leave granted:

(a)   under the Immigration Rules para 276BE(1), para 276DG or Appendix FM; and

(b)   who is not subject to a condition requiring that person to maintain and accommodate himself, and any person dependent upon him, without recourse to public funds (Allocation of Housing and Homelessness (Eligibility) (England) Regulations 2006, SI 2006/1294, reg 5(1)(g) (added by SI 2016/965)).

As to the meaning of 'United Kingdom' and 'Great Britain see PARA 60 note 10. As to the meaning of 'Immigration Rules' and 'sponsor' see PARA 424 note 5.

The prescribed classes in relation to Wales are as follows (see the Allocation of Housing and Homelessness (Eligibility) (Wales) Regulations 2014, SI 2014/2603, reg 5(1)):

(i)   Class A: a person who is recorded by the Welsh Ministers as a refugee within the definition in the Refugee Convention, ie the Convention relating to the Status of Refugees (Geneva, 28 July 1951; TS 39 (1954); Cmnd 9171) art 1 (as extended by the Protocol relating to the Status of Refugees (New York, 31 January 1967; TS 15 (1969); Cmnd 3906) art 1(2)) (Allocation of Housing and Homelessness (Eligibility) (Wales) Regulations 2014, SI 2014/2603, regs 2(1), 5(1)(a));

(ii)   Class B: a person:

(A)   who has exceptional leave to enter or remain in the United Kingdom granted outside the provisions of the Immigration Rules; and

(B)   whose leave to enter or remain is not subject to a condition requiring that person to maintain and accommodate themselves, and any person who is dependent on that person, without recourse to public funds (Housing and Homelessness (Eligibility) (Wales) Regulations 2014, SI 2014/2603, reg 5(1)(b));

(iii)   Class C: a person who is habitually resident in the United Kingdom, the Channel Islands, the Isle of Man or the Republic of Ireland and whose leave to enter or remain in the United Kingdom is not subject to any limitation or condition, other than a person:

(A)   who has been given leave to enter or remain in the United Kingdom upon an undertaking given by the person's sponsor;

(B)   who has been resident in the United Kingdom, the Channel Islands, the Isle of Man or the Republic of Ireland for less than five years beginning on the date of entry or on the date on which the undertaking was given in respect of the person, whichever date is the later; and

(C)   whose sponsor or, where there is more than one sponsor, at least one of whose sponsors is still alive (reg 5(1)(c));

(iv)   Class D: a person who has humanitarian protection granted under the Immigration Rules (reg 5(1)(d));

(v)   Class E: a person who is an asylum-seeker whose claim for asylum is recorded by the Welsh Ministers as having been made before 3 April 2000 and in the circumstances mentioned in one of the following heads:

(A)   on arrival (other than on the person's re-entry) in the United Kingdom from a country outside the United Kingdom, the Channel Islands, the Isle of Man or the Republic of Ireland;

(B)   within three months from the day on which the Welsh Ministers made a relevant declaration, and the applicant was in Great Britain on the day on which the declaration was made; or

(C)   on or before 4 February 1996 by an applicant who was on 4 February 1996 entitled to benefit under the Housing Benefit (General) Regulations 1987, SI 1987/1971, reg 7A (persons from abroad) (revoked) (Housing and Homelessness (Eligibility) (Wales) Regulations 2014, SI 2014/2603, reg 5(1)(e)); and

(vi)   Class F: a person who is habitually resident in the United Kingdom, the Channel Islands, the Isle of Man or the Republic of Ireland and who has limited leave to enter the United Kingdom as a relevant Afghan citizen under the Immigration Rules para 276BA1 (Housing and Homelessness (Eligibility) (Wales) Regulations 2014, SI 2014/2603, reg 5(1)(f));

For the purpose of reg 5(1)(e), 'asylum-seeker' means a person who is at least 18 years old, who is in the United Kingdom and who has made a claim for asylum; 'claim for asylum' means a claim that it would be contrary to the United Kingdom's obligations under the Refugee Convention for the claimant to be removed from, or required to leave the United Kingdom; 'relevant declaration' means a declaration to the effect that the country of which the applicant is a national is subject to such fundamental change of circumstances that the Welsh Ministers would not normally order the return of a person to that country; and subject to reg 5(3), a person ceases to be an asylum-seeker when his claim for asylum is recorded by the Welsh Ministers as having been decided (other than on appeal) or abandoned: reg 5(2). For the purposes of reg 5(1)(e)(iii) (head (v)(C) above), a person does not cease to be an asylum-seeker as mentioned in reg 5(2)(d) while he is eligible for housing benefit by virtue of the Housing Benefit Regulations 2006, SI 2006/213, reg 10(6) or the Housing Benefit (Persons who have attained the qualifying age for state pension credit) Regulations 2006, SI 2006/214, reg 10(6), as modified in both cases by the Housing Benefit and Council Tax Benefit (Consequential Provisions) Regulations 2006, SI 2006/217, Sch 3 para 6: Housing and Homelessness (Eligibility) (Wales) Regulations 2014, SI 2014/2603, reg 5(3).

As to the meaning of 'Immigration Rules' and 'sponsor' see PARA 425 note 7.

7 Ie by the Immigration and Asylum Act 1999 s 115 (exclusion from benefits): see IMMIGRATION AND ASYLUM vol 57 (2012) PARA 335.

8 Housing Act 1996 s 185(2A) (added by the Immigration and Asylum Act 1999 s 117(4); substituted by the Homelessness Act 2002 s 18(1), Sch 1 paras 2, 7(1); and amended by SI 2013/630); Housing (Wales) Act 2014 Sch 2 para 1(3).

9 Housing Act 1996 s 185(3); Housing (Wales) Act 2014 Sch 2 para 1(4). In relation to England, a person who is not subject to immigration control is to be treated as a person from abroad who is ineligible for housing assistance under the Housing Act 1996 Pt VII if:

(1) subject to the exceptions below, he is not habitually resident in the United Kingdom, the Channel Islands, the Isle of Man, or the Republic of Ireland (Allocation of Housing and Homelessness (Eligibility) (England) Regulations 2006, SI 2006/1294, reg 6(1)(a));

(2) his only right to reside in the United Kingdom:
   (a) is derived from his status as a jobseeker or the family member of a jobseeker;
   (b) is an initial right to reside for a period not exceeding three months under the Immigration (European Economic Area) Regulations 2006, SI 2006/1003, reg 13;
   (c) is a derivative right to reside to which he is entitled under reg 15A(1), but only in a case where the right exists under that regulation because the applicant satisfies the criteria in reg 15A(4A); or
   (d) is derived from the Treaty on the Functioning of the European Union (Rome, 25 March 1957; TS 1 (1973); Cmnd 5179) art 20 in a case where the right to reside arises because a British citizen would otherwise be deprived of the genuine enjoyment of the substance of the rights attaching to the status of European Union citizen (Allocation of Housing and Homelessness (Eligibility) (England) Regulations 2006, SI 2006/1294, regs 2(1), 6(1)(b) (reg 6(1)(b) amended by SI 2012/2588)); or

(3) his only right to reside in the Channel Islands, the Isle of Man or the Republic of Ireland:
   (a) is a right equivalent to one of those mentioned in head (2)(a), (b) or (c) which is derived from the Treaty on the Functioning of the European Union; or
   (b) is derived from art 20 in a case where the right to reside in the Republic of Ireland arises because an Irish citizen, or in the Channel Islands or the Isle of Man arises because a British citizen also entitled to reside there, would otherwise be deprived of the genuine enjoyment of the substance of their rights as a European Union citizen (Allocation of Housing and Homelessness (Eligibility) (England) Regulations 2006, SI 2006/1294, reg 6(1)(c) (amended by SI 2012/2588)).

However, the following are not to be treated as persons from abroad who are ineligible for housing assistance pursuant to the Allocation of Housing and Homelessness (Eligibility) (England) Regulations 2006, SI 2006/1294, reg 6(1)(a) (head (1) above) (see reg 6(2)):

(i) a worker (reg 6(2)(a));

(ii) a self-employed person (reg 6(2)(b));

(iii) a person who is treated as a worker for the purpose of the definition of 'qualified person' in the Immigration (European Economic Area) Regulations 2006, SI 2006/1003, reg 6(1) pursuant to the Accession of Croatia (Immigration and Worker Authorisation) Regulations 2013, SI 2013/1460, reg 5 (right of residence of an accession state national subject to worker authorisation) (Allocation of Housing and Homelessness (Eligibility) (England) Regulations 2006, SI 2006/1294, regs 2(1), 6(2)(c) (amended and substituted respectively by SI 2013/1467; reg 6(2)(c) amended by SI 2014/435));

(iv)   a person who is the family member of a person specified in heads (i)–(iii) (Allocation of Housing and Homelessness (Eligibility) (England) Regulations 2006, SI 2006/1294, reg 6(2)(d));

(v)   a person with a right to reside permanently in the United Kingdom by virtue of the Immigration (European Economic Area) Regulations 2006, SI 2006/1003, reg 15(1)(c), (d) or (e) (Allocation of Housing and Homelessness (Eligibility) (England) Regulations 2006, regs 2(1), 6(2)(e) (reg 6(2)(e) amended by SI 2014/435)); and

(vi)   a person who is in the United Kingdom as a result of his deportation, expulsion or other removal by compulsion of law from another country to the United Kingdom (Allocation of Housing and Homelessness (Eligibility) (England) Regulations 2006, reg 6(2)(g) (amended by SI 2006/2007 and SI 2009/358)).

As to the meaning of 'worker', 'self-employed person' and 'family member' see PARA 424 note 8. For the purposes of head (iv), 'family member' does not include a person who is treated as a family member by virtue of the Immigration (European Economic Area) Regulations 2006, SI 2006/1003, reg 7(3): Allocation of Housing and Homelessness (Eligibility) (England) Regulations 2006, SI 2006/1294, reg 2(2)(b), (3).

In relation to Wales, a person who is not subject to immigration control is to be treated as a person from abroad who is ineligible for housing assistance under the Housing (Wales) Act 2014 Pt 2 Ch 2 (ss 53–100) (see the Allocation of Housing and Homelessness (Wales) Regulations 2014, SI 2014/2603, reg 6(1)) if:

(A)   subject to the exceptions below, the person is not habitually resident in the United Kingdom, the Channel Islands, the Isle of Man or the Republic of Ireland (reg 6(1)(a));

(B)   the person's only right to reside in the United Kingdom: (I) is derived from the person's status as a jobseeker or a family member of a jobseeker; or (II) is an initial right to reside for a period not exceeding three months under the Immigration (European Economic Area) Regulations 2006, SI 2006/1003, reg 13; or (III) is a derivative right to reside to which the person is entitled under reg 15A(1), but only in a case where the right exists under that regulation because the applicant satisfies the criteria in reg 15A(4A); or (IV) is derived from the Treaty on the Functioning of the European Union art 20 in a case where the right to reside arises because a British citizen would otherwise be deprived of the genuine enjoyment of the substance of their rights as a European Union citizen (Allocation of Housing and Homelessness (Wales) Regulations 2014, SI 2014/2603, regs 2, 6(1)(b)); or

(C)   the person's only right to reside in the Channel Islands, the Isle of Man or the Republic of Ireland: (I) is a right equivalent to one of those mentioned in head (B)(I), (II) or (III) which is derived from the Treaty on the Functioning of the European Union; or (II) is derived from the Treaty of the Functioning of the European Union art 20 in a case where the right to reside, in the Republic of Ireland arises because an Irish citizen, or in the Channel Islands or the Isle of Man arises because a British citizen also entitled to reside there, would otherwise be deprived of the genuine enjoyment of the substance of their rights as a European Union citizen (Allocation of Housing and Homelessness (Wales) Regulations 2014, SI 2014/2603, reg 6(1)(c)).

The following persons will not, however, be treated as persons from abroad who are ineligible pursuant to head (A):

(I)   a worker (reg 6(2)(a));

(II)   a self-employed person (reg 6(2)(b));

(III) a person who is treated as a worker for the purpose of the definition of 'qualified person' in the Immigration (European Economic Area) Regulations 2006, SI 2006/1003, reg 6(1) pursuant to the Accession of Croatia (Immigration and Worker Authorisation) Regulations 2013, SI 2013/1460, reg 5 (right of residence of an accession state national subject to worker authorisation) (Allocation of Housing and Homelessness (Wales) Regulations 2014, SI 2014/2603, reg 6(2)(c));

(IV)   a person who is the family member of a person specified in heads (I)–(III) (reg 6(2)(d));

(V)   a person with a right to reside permanently in the United Kingdom by virtue of the Immigration (European Economic Area) Regulations 2006, SI 2006/1003, reg 15(1)(c), (d) or (e) (Allocation of Housing and Homelessness (Wales) Regulations 2014, SI 2014/2603, reg 6(2)(e)); and

(VI)   a person who is in the United Kingdom as a result of the person's deportation, expulsion or other removal by compulsion of law from another country to the United Kingdom (reg 6(2)(f)).

As to the meaning of 'family member' see PARA 425 note 11. For the purposes of head (DD), 'family member' does not include a person who is treated as a family member by virtue of the Immigration (European Economic Area) Regulations 2006, SI 2006/1003, reg 7(3): Allocation of Housing and Homelessness (Eligibility) (Wales) Regulations 2014, SI 2014/2603, reg 2(2)(b), (3).

10 Ie a person falling within the Housing Act 1996 s 185(5) or the Housing (Wales) Act 2014 Sch 2 para 1(6). A person falls within those provisions if the person: (1) falls within a class prescribed by regulations made under the Housing Act 1996 s 185(2) or the Housing (Wales) Act 2014 Sch 2 para 1(2); but (2) is not a national of an EEA state or Switzerland: Housing Act 1996 s 185(5) (added by the Housing and Regeneration Act 2008 s 314, Sch 15 paras 1, 4(1), (3)); Housing (Wales) Act 2014 Sch 2 para 1(6).

11 As to the meanings of 'homeless' and 'threatened with homelessness' see PARAS 481, 482.

12 Housing Act 1996 s 185(4) (amended by the Housing and Regeneration Act 2008 Sch 15 para 4(2)); Housing (Wales) Act 2014 Sch 2 para 1(5). It had been held that the Housing Act 1996 s 185(4) before its amendment was incompatible with the Convention for the Protection of Human Rights and Fundamental Freedoms (Rome, 4 November 1950; TS 71 (1953); Cmd 8969) art 14 (enacted in the Human Rights Act 1998 Sch 1 art 14) to the extent that it required a dependant child of a British citizen, if both were habitually resident in the United Kingdom, to be disregarded when determining whether the British citizen had a priority need for accommodation, when that child was subject to immigration control: see *R (on the application of Morris) v Westminster City Council, R (on the application of Badhu) v Lambeth London Borough Council* [2005] EWCA Civ 1184, [2006] 1 WLR 505, [2006] HLR 122.

492. Asylum-seekers and their dependants: England and Wales. An asylum-seeker, or a dependant of an asylum-seeker[1], who is not a person from abroad who is ineligible for housing assistance[2], is not eligible for assistance[3] under Part VII of the Housing Act 1996[4] if he has any accommodation in the United Kingdom[5], however temporary, available for his occupation[6]. For these purposes, a person who makes a claim for asylum[7] becomes an asylum-seeker at the time when his claim is recorded by the appropriate national authority as having been made, and ceases to be an asylum-seeker at the time when his claim is recorded by the appropriate national authority as having been finally determined or abandoned[8].

The appropriate national authority must, at the request of a local housing authority[9], provide the authority with such information as it may require as to whether a person is excluded from social security benefits[10], and to enable the authority to determine whether such a person is eligible[11] for assistance[12]. If it appears to the appropriate national authority that any application, decision or other change of circumstances has affected the status of a person about whom information was previously provided by it to a local housing authority under this provision, it must inform that authority in writing of that fact, the reason for it and the date on which the previous information became inaccurate[13].

1 In relation to an asylum-seeker, 'dependant' means a person who is his spouse or a child of his under the age of 18, and who has neither a right of abode in the United Kingdom (see IMMIGRATION AND ASYLUM vol 57 (2012) PARA 12) nor indefinite leave under the Immigration Act 1971 to enter or remain in the United Kingdom (see IMMIGRATION AND ASYLUM vol 57 (2012) PARA 5): Housing Act 1996 s 186(4). As to the prospective repeal of s 186 see note 6. For these purposes, a person becomes a dependant of an asylum-seeker at the time when he is recorded by the appropriate national authority as being a dependant of the asylum-seeker, and ceases to be a dependant of an asylum-seeker at the time when the person whose dependant he is ceases to be an asylum-seeker or, if it is earlier, at the time when he is recorded by the appropriate national authority as ceasing to be a dependant of the asylum-seeker: s 186(3). The appropriate national authority is the Secretary of State or, where statutory functions have been transferred in relation to Wales, the Welsh Ministers: see PARA 7. Functions of the Secretary of State under the Housing Act 1996 ss 186, 187 have not been transferred, but s 186 applies for the purposes of the Housing (Wales) Act 2014 Pt 2 Ch 2 (ss 53–100): see note 6.

2 Ie by virtue of the Housing Act 1996 s 185 or the Housing (Wales) Act 2014 Sch 2 para 1: see PARA 491.

3 As to the meaning of 'eligible for assistance' see PARA 487 note 4.

4 As to the meaning of 'assistance under Part VII of the Housing Act 1996' see PARA 483 note 5.

5 As to the meaning of 'United Kingdom' see PARA 60 note 10.

6 Housing Act 1996 s 186(1). The application of s 175(3) is not excluded (see PARA 481), so the accommodation must be that which it is reasonable for the asylum-seeker to occupy: *Lismane v Hammersmith and Fulham London Borough Council* (1998) 31 HLR 427, CA. As to the meaning of 'accommodation available for occupation' see PARA 481 note 1.

The Housing Act 1996 s 186 is prospectively repealed by the Immigration and Asylum Act 1999 ss 117(5), 169(3), Sch 16, as from a day to be appointed under s 170(4). At the date at which this volume states the law, no such day had been appointed. Until the commencement of the repeal of the Housing Act 1996 s 196, that section applies to the Housing (Wales) Act 2014 Pt 2 Ch 2 as it applies to the Housing Act 1996 Pt VII (ss 175–218): Housing (Wales) Act 2014 s 61, Sch 2 para 2(1). For this purpose, in the Housing Act 1996 s 186, the reference to s 185 is to be interpreted as a reference to the Housing (Wales) Act 2014 Sch 2 para 1 (see PARA 491) and the reference to 'Pt VII' is to be interpreted as a reference to the Housing (Wales) Act 2014 Pt 2 Ch 2 and not the Housing Act 1996 Pt VII: Housing (Wales) Act 2014 Sch 2 para 2(2).

7   A 'claim for asylum' means a claim made by a person that it would be contrary to the United Kingdom's obligations under the Convention relating to the Status of Refugees (Geneva, 28 July 1951; TS 39 (1954); Cmnd 9171) and the Protocol relating to the Status of Refugees (New York, 31 January 1967; TS 15 (1969); Cmnd 3906) for him to be removed from, or required to leave, the United Kingdom: Housing Act 1996 s 186(5).

8   Housing Act 1996 s 186(2).

9   As to the meaning of 'local housing authority' see PARA 11 (definition applied by the Housing Act 1996 s 230).

10 Ie under the Immigration and Asylum Act 1999 s 115: see IMMIGRATION AND ASYLUM vol 57 (2012) PARAS 335, 349.

11 Ie under the Housing Act 1996 s 185 or the Housing (Wales) Act 2014 Sch 2 para 1: see PARA 491.

12 Housing Act 1996 s 187(1) (amended by the Immigration and Asylum Act 1999 s 117(6); and, in relation to Wales, by the Housing (Wales) Act 2014 s 100, Sch 3 paras 2, 9); Housing (Wales) Act 2014 Sch 2 para 3(1). Where that information is given otherwise than in writing, the appropriate national authority must confirm it in writing if a written request is made to it by the local housing authority: Housing Act 1996 s 187(2); Housing (Wales) Act 2014 Sch 2 para 3(2).

13 Housing Act 1996 s 187(3); Housing (Wales) Act 2014 Sch 2 para 3(3).

(iv) Duty to Secure Accommodation

493. Interim duty to accommodate in case of apparent priority need: England. If the local housing authority[1] has reason to believe that an applicant[2] may be homeless[3], eligible for assistance[4] and have a priority need[5], the authority must secure that accommodation is available for his occupation[6] pending a decision as to the duty (if any) owed to him under the homelessness provisions[7]. There is no obligation for the decision maker to be a different decision maker to the one who has made a previous decision[8] on an application for assistance[9]. If a housing authority has secured an offer of suitable temporary accommodation, ordinarily, it will have performed its statutory duty under these provisions, notwithstanding an applicant's refusal of the offer[10].

However, if the local housing authority has reason to believe that the duty to secure accommodation for a person with priority need who is not homeless intentionally[11] may apply in relation to an applicant re-applying after a private rented sector offer[12], it must secure that accommodation is available for the applicant's occupation pending a decision of the kind referred to above regardless of whether the applicant has a priority need[13].

This duty arises irrespective of any possibility of the referral of the applicant's case to another local housing authority[14], and ceases when the authority's decision is notified to the applicant even if the applicant requests a review[15] of the decision[16].

The authority may secure that accommodation is available for the applicant's occupation pending a decision on a review, although there is no duty to do so[17]. An authority therefore has a discretion to continue to secure that such accommodation remains available but it is unlawful to adopt a rigid policy or a policy which simply allows an officer to make the decision without having to give reasons[18].

1 As to the meaning of 'local housing authority' see PARA 11 (definition applied by the Housing Act 1996 s 230).
2 As to the meaning of 'applicant' see PARA 487 note 3.
3 As to the meaning of 'homeless' see PARA 481.
4 As to the meaning of 'eligible for assistance' see PARA 487 note 4.
5 As to priority need see PARA 495.
6 As to the meaning of 'accommodation available for his occupation' see PARA 481 note 1. A local housing authority must provide accommodation sufficient to enable a family to live together as a unit: *R v Ealing London Borough Council, ex p Surdonja* [1999] 1 All ER 566, 31 HLR 686.
7 Housing Act 1996 s 188(1). See *R v Lambeth London Borough Council, ex p Ekpo-Wedderman* (1998) 31 HLR 498 (decided under the Housing Act 1985 s 65(2) (repealed)); *R v Newham London Borough Council, ex p Sacupima* [2001] 1 WLR 563, (2000) Times, 1 December, [2000] All ER (D) 1947, CA; *R (on the application of M) v Hammersmith and Fulham London Borough Council* [2008] UKHL 14, [2008] 4 All ER 271, [2008] 1 WLR 535; *R (on the application of TG) v Lambeth London Borough Council* [2011] EWCA Civ 526, [2011] 4 All ER 453. In relation to England, certain accommodation made available for occupation under the Housing Act 1996 s 188(1) is to be regarded as unsuitable where there is a family commitment: see the Homelessness (Suitability of Accommodation) (England) Order 2003, SI 2003/3326; and PARA 481 note 13.
8 Ie under the Housing Act 1996 s 184: see PARA 487.
9 *R (on the application of Abdi) v Lambeth London Borough Council* [2007] EWHC 1565 (Admin), [2008] HLR 73, [2008] LGR 676. See also *R (on the application of IA) v Westminster City Council* [2013] EWHC 1273 (QB), 177 CL&J 397, [2013] All ER (D) 355 (May) (claimant with prospect of showing unlawfulness of decision finding him homeless and eligible for assistance but not in priority need: interim accommodation had to be provided pending judicial review of decision).
10 *R (on the application of Brooks) v Islington London Borough Council* [2015] EWHC 2657 (Admin), [2015] All ER (D) 103 (Sep).
11 Ie under the Housing Act 1996 s 193(2): see PARA 498.
12 Ie in the circumstances referred to in the Housing Act 1996 s 195A(1): see PARA 500.
13 Housing Act 1996 s 188(1A) (added by the Localism Act 2011 s 149(1), (2); in force in relation to England; in force in relation to Wales as from a day to be appointed; at the date at which this volume states the law, no such day had been appointed).
14 Housing Act 1996 s 188(2). As to such referral see ss 198–200; and PARAS 503–505.
15 Ie under the Housing Act 1996 s 202: see PARA 507.
16 Housing Act 1996 s 188(3). Where a local authority has provided accommodation under s 188(1), it does not need to initiate court proceedings to recover possession: *Desnousse v Newham London Borough Council* [2006] EWCA Civ 547, [2006] QB 831, [2007] 2 All ER 218. See also *R (on the application of N) v Lewisham London Borough Council, R (on the application of H) v Newham London Borough Council* [2014] UKSC 62, [2015] AC 1259, [2014] LGR 842 (court order not required before possession taken of interim accommodation).
17 Housing Act 1996 s 188(3) (amended by the Homelessness Act 2002 s 18(1), Sch 1 paras 2, 8). Where the authority decides not to exercise this discretion in the applicant's favour, the County Court has no jurisdiction under the Housing Act 1996 s 204 (see PARA 509) to override the authority's discretionary power by means of a mandatory interim injunction requiring it to continue to provide accommodation for a person proceeding with an appeal: see *Ali v Westminster City Council, Nairne v Camden London Borough Council* [1999] 1 All ER 450, [1999] 1 WLR 384, CA.
18 See *R v Lambeth London Borough Council, ex p Trabi* (1997) 30 HLR 975. See also *R v Camden London Borough Council, ex p Mohammed* (1997) 30 HLR 315; *R v Hammersmith and Fulham London Borough Council, ex p Fleck* (1998) 30 HLR 679.

494. Interim duty to secure accommodation for homeless applicants in priority need: Wales. A local housing authority[1] must secure that suitable accommodation is available for the occupation of an applicant[2] who the authority:

(1)   has reason to believe may be homeless, eligible for help[3] and have a priority need for accommodation, in circumstances where the authority is not yet satisfied that the applicant is homeless, eligible for help and in priority need for accommodation[4];

(2)   has reason to believe or is satisfied has a priority need or whose case has been referred from a local housing authority in England[5], and to whom the duty to help to end homelessness[6] applies[7].

This duty arises irrespective of any possibility of the referral of the applicant's case to another local housing authority[8].

If the applicant has been notified by the local housing authority that its duty has ended[9], this duty comes to an end in the following circumstances[10], namely where:

(a)   the local authority has decided that no duty to help to secure accommodation is owed to the applicant[11] and the applicant is notified of that decision[12];

(b)   in the case of an applicant to whom the duty under head (2) applies, the local housing authority has decided that the duty owed to the applicant to help to secure accommodation has come to an end and that a duty to secure accommodation thereafter[13] is or is not owed to the applicant, and has notified the applicant of that decision (subject to an exception where the local housing authority has decided that no duty is owed to the applicant)[14];

(c)   the applicant, having been notified of the possible consequence of refusal, refuses an offer of accommodation[15] which the local housing authority is satisfied is suitable for the applicant[16];

(d)   the local housing authority is satisfied that the applicant has become homeless intentionally from suitable interim accommodation made available[17] for the applicant's occupation[18];

(e)   the local housing authority is satisfied that the applicant voluntarily ceased to occupy as his only or principal home suitable interim accommodation made available[19] for the applicant's occupation[20];

(f)   the local housing authority is no longer satisfied that the applicant is eligible for help[21];

(g)   the local housing authority is satisfied that a mistake of fact led to the applicant being notified[22] that the duty was owed to the applicant[23];

(h)   the local authority is satisfied that the applicant has withdrawn his application[24];

(i)   the local housing authority is satisfied that the applicant is unreasonably failing to co-operate with the authority in connection with the exercise of its functions under the Chapter 2 of Part 2 of the Housing (Wales) Act 2014[25] as they apply to the applicant[26].

The duty comes to an end in accordance with these provisions even if the applicant requests a review of any decision that has led to the duty coming to an end[27]. The authority may secure that suitable accommodation is available for the applicant's occupation pending a decision on a review[28].

1   As to the meaning of 'local housing authority' in relation to Wales see PARA 482 note 9.
2   As to the meaning of 'applicant' see PARA 488 note 3.
3   As to the meaning of 'eligible for help' see PARA 488 note 4.
4   Housing (Wales) Act 2014 s 68(1), (2). As to priority need see PARA 495.
5   Ie under the Housing Act 1996 s 198(1): see PARA 503.
6   Ie in the Housing (Wales) Act 2014 s 73 (duty to help to end homelessness: see PARA 501.
7   Housing (Wales) Act 2014 s 68(1), (3).
8   Housing (Wales) Act 2014 s 68(4). As to such duty see ss 80–82; and PARA 503.
9   Ie in accordance with the Housing (Wales) Act 2014 s 84: see PARA 501.
10 Housing (Wales) Act 2014 ss 69(1), (12), 79(1).
11 Ie under the Housing (Wales) Act 2014 s 73: see PARA 501.
12 Housing (Wales) Act 2014 s 69(2).
13 Ie under the Housing (Wales) Act 2014 s 75: see PARA 502.

14 Housing (Wales) Act 2014 s 69(3). This is subject to s 69(4), (5): s 69(3). Where a local housing authority has decided that no duty is owed to the applicant under s 75 on the basis that the authority: (1) is satisfied that the applicant became homeless intentionally in the circumstances which gave rise to the application; or (2) has previously secured an offer of accommodation of the kind described in s 75(3)(f) (see PARA 502 head (f)), the duty under s 68 does not come to an end in the circumstances described in s 69(3) until the authority is also satisfied that the accommodation it has secured under s 68 has been available to the applicant for a sufficient period, beginning on the day on which he or she is notified that s 75 does not apply, to allow the applicant a reasonable opportunity of securing accommodation for his or her occupation: s 69(4), (5). The period mentioned in s 69(5) is not sufficient for the purposes of that subsection if it ends on a day during the period of 56 days beginning with the day on which the applicant was notified that the duty in s 73 applied: s 69(6).

15 Ie secured under the Housing (Wales) Act 2014 s 68.

16 Housing (Wales) Act 2014 s 69(7).

17 Ie under the Housing (Wales) Act 2014 s 68.

18 Housing (Wales) Act 2014 s 69(8).

19 Ie under the Housing (Wales) Act 2014 s 68.

20 Housing (Wales) Act 2014 s 69(9).

21 Housing (Wales) Act 2014 s 79(2).

22 Ie under the Housing (Wales) Act 2014 s 63.

23 Housing (Wales) Act 2014 s 79(3).

24 Housing (Wales) Act 2014 s 79(4).

25 Ie the Housing (Wales) Act 2014 Pt 2 Ch 2 (ss 53–100).

26 Housing (Wales) Act 2014 s 79(5).

27 Housing (Wales) Act 2014 s 69(10). As to review of a decision see s 85; and PARA 508.

28 Housing (Wales) Act 2014 s 69(11).

495. Priority need: England and Wales. The following have a priority need for accommodation in England:

(1)   a pregnant woman or a person with whom she resides or might reasonably be expected to reside;

(2)   a person with whom dependant children[1] reside or might reasonably be expected to reside;

(3)   a person who is vulnerable as a result of old age, mental illness or handicap or physical disability[2] or other special reason[3], or with whom such a person resides or might reasonably be expected to reside; and

(4)   a person who is homeless or threatened with homelessness as a result of an emergency such as flood, fire, or other disaster[4].

The Secretary of State[5] has power by order to specify further descriptions of persons who would have a priority need and may also by order amend or repeal any of the categories described above[6].

In Wales, the following have a priority need for accommodation:

(a)   a pregnant woman or a person with whom she resides or might reasonably be expected to reside;

(b)   a person with whom a dependant child resides or might reasonably be expected to reside;

(c)   a person who is vulnerable[7] as a result of some special reason (for example old age, physical or mental illness or physical or mental disability), or a person with whom such a person resides or might reasonably be expected to reside;

(d)   a person who is homeless or threatened with homelessness as a result of an emergency such as flood, fire or other disaster, or a person with whom such a person resides or might reasonably be expected to reside;

(e)   a person who is homeless as a result of being subject to domestic abuse[8], or a person with whom such a person resides (other than the abuser) or might reasonably be expected to reside;

(f)   a person who is aged 16 or 17 when the person applies to a local housing authority for accommodation or help in obtaining or retaining accommodation, or a person with whom such a person resides or might reasonably be expected to reside;

(g)   a person who has attained the age of 18, when the person applies to a local housing authority for accommodation or help in obtaining or retaining accommodation, but not the age of 21, who is at particular risk of sexual or financial exploitation, or a person with whom such a person resides (other than an exploiter or potential exploiter) or might reasonably be expected to reside;

(h)   a person who has attained the age of 18, when the person applies to a local housing authority for accommodation or help in obtaining or retaining accommodation, but not the age of 21, who was looked after, accommodated or fostered[9] at any time while under the age of 18, or a person with whom such a person resides or might reasonably be expected to reside;

(i)   a person who has served in the regular armed forces of the Crown who has been homeless since leaving those forces, or a person with whom such a person resides or might reasonably be expected to reside;

(j)   a person who has a local connection with the area of the local housing authority[10] and who is vulnerable as a result of:

       (i)   having served a custodial sentence[11];

       (ii)   having been remanded in or committed to custody by an order of a court; or

       (iii)   having been remanded to youth detention accommodation[12], or a person with whom such a person resides or might reasonably be expected to reside[13].

The Welsh Ministers may by order:

(A)   make provision for and in connection with removing any condition that a local housing authority must have reason to believe or be satisfied that an applicant is in priority need for accommodation before any power or duty to secure accommodation under Chapter 2 of Part 2 of the Housing (Wales) Act 2014[14] applies;

(B)   amend or omit the descriptions of persons as having a priority need for accommodation for the purposes of that Chapter;

(C)   specify further descriptions of persons as having a priority need for accommodation for the purposes of that Chapter[15].

1   Once a child has gone into full-time employment he can no longer be considered as a dependant and for this purpose a young person who is on a youth training scheme can be considered to be in gainful employment and therefore not dependant: *R v Royal Borough of Kensington and Chelsea, ex p Amarfio* (1995) 27 HLR 543, CA. Where the child's parents are separated it may still be possible for the child to be considered to reside and be dependent on more than one person. Where, however, the mother has been given day to day care and control of the child, the father having periodic contact, the child cannot be held to be dependent on the father: see *R v Lambeth London Borough Council, ex p Vagliviello* (1990) 22 HLR 392, CA; *R v Port Talbot Borough Council, ex p McCarthy* (1990) 23 HLR 207, CA. A child spouse is not a dependant child: *Hackney London Borough Council v Ekinci* [2001] EWCA Civ 776, [2002] HLR 12. The provision of suitable temporary accommodation to a claimant with dependant children reduces the claimant's priority need: *R (on the application of Ibrahim) v Redbridge London Borough Council* [2002] EWHC 2756 (Admin), (2002) Times, 27 December, [2002] All ER (D) 246 (Dec). A housing authority is not obliged to regard a homeless person as having a priority need on the ground that dependant children might reside with him when they already have a home with their other parent: *Holmes-Moorhouse v Richmond-upon-Thames London Borough Council* [2009] UKHL 7, [2009] 3 All ER 277, [2009] 1 WLR 413.

2   An applicant with drug or alcohol dependence may be considered vulnerable if he is less able to fend for himself as a result of that dependence: see *R v Camden London Borough Council, ex p Pereira* (1998) 31 HLR 317, CA; *Ortiz v City of Westminster* (1993) 27 HLR 364, CA. See, however, *Tetteh v Kingston upon Thames Royal London Borough Council* [2004] EWCA Civ 1775, [2005] HLR 313, [2004] All ER (D) 241 (Dec). A local authority's decision was quashed where it decided that a young single woman was not vulnerable even though she had been excluded from a parental home, and had been living in transient accommodation where she had been the victim of sexual assault, which left her anxious and unable to cope: *Wilson v Nithsdale District Council* 1992 SLT 1131, Ct of Sess. As to old age, mental illness and physical disability, the ministerial guidance (see PARA 486) recommends that careful considerable be given to applications from anyone who is aged 60 years or over; and in relation to vulnerability because of a mental or physical disability, authorities should have regard to medical advice and in some cases seek advice from social services. Particular care should be taken with those with mental health problems who have been discharged from hospital or a local authority hostel and also with those who are chronically sick. In the case of an applicant who suffers from epilepsy, the needs of such a person must be reassessed from time to time: *R v Reigate and Banstead Borough Council, ex p Di Dominico* (1987) 20 HLR 153, [1989] Fam Law 69. A local authority must make its own evaluation of every medical opinion received on the question of the applicant's priority need, and not merely select advice to provide or back up its own reasons for refusing an application: *Shala v Birmingham City Council* [2007] EWCA Civ 624, [2008] LGR 23, [2007] All ER (D) 347 (Jun). See also *Hotak v Southwark London Borough Council; Kanu v Southwark London Borough Council; Johnson v Solihull Metropolitan Borough Council* [2015] UKSC 30, [2015] 3 All ER 1053, [2015] LGR 530 (determination of correct comparator group in assessment of vulnerability); *Poshteh v Royal Borough of Kensington and Chelsea* [2015] EWCA Civ 711, [2015] HLR 729, [2015] All ER (D) 95 (Jul).

3   As to other special reasons, the ministerial guidance recommends that young people (ie those aged 16 years or more) can in some circumstances be considered at risk and would therefore have a priority need. The inability of a person to fend for himself while homeless constitutes a priority need where his situation will result in injury or detriment to him which would not be suffered by an ordinary homeless person who is able to cope: *R v Camden London Borough Council, ex p Periera* (1998) 31 HLR 317, CA (likelihood of rehabilitated drug user relapsing if housed with other drug users constituted priority need); applied in *Griffin v Westminster City Council* [2004] EWCA Civ 108, [2004] HLR 536, [2004] All ER (D) 262 (Jan). See also *Crossley v Westminster City Council* [2006] EWCA Civ 140, [2006] All ER (D) 321 (Feb); and *Simms v Islington London Borough Council* [2008] EWCA Civ 1083, [2009] HLR 343, [2008] All ER (D) 146 (Oct).

4   Housing Act 1996 s 189(1). It has been held that the expression 'other disaster' means a disaster similar to flood or fire: *R v Kensington and Chelsea London Borough Council, ex p Kihara* (1996) 29 HLR 147. Thus a person who became homeless because the dwelling was the subject of a demolition order under the Housing Act 1985 Pt IX (ss 265–323) had not become homeless as a result of some other disaster: *Noble v South Herefordshire District Council* (1983) 17 HLR 80, CA (note, however, that in this case the occupiers had moved into the accommodation after the demolition order had been made). It should also be noted that where premises are made subject to a demolition order any occupiers will usually be entitled to be rehoused under the provisions in the Land Compensation Act 1973: see s 39; and COMPULSORY ACQUISITION OF LAND vol 18 (2009) PARA 853. An impecunious asylum seeker may have a priority need: see *R v Kensington and Chelsea London Borough Council, ex p Kihara*. The emergency must be the cause of the person's homelessness: *Higgs v Brighton and Hove City Council* [2003] EWCA Civ 895, [2003] 3 All ER 753, [2003] 1 WLR 2241 (claimant's mobile caravan disappeared; as there was nowhere where claimant had been entitled to place and reside in his caravan, he was homeless before its disappearance by virtue of the Housing Act 1996 s 175(2)(b) (see PARA 481)).

5   Ie the Secretary of State or, where statutory functions have been transferred in relation to Wales, the Welsh Ministers: see PARA 7.

6   Housing Act 1996 s 189(2). Before making such an order the appropriate national authority must consult such associations representing relevant authorities, and such other persons, as it considers appropriate; and no such order may be made unless a draft of it has been approved by resolution of each House of Parliament or, as appropriate, the National Assembly for Wales: s 189(3), (4). 'Relevant authority' means a local housing authority or a social services authority: s 217(1). As to the meaning of 'social services authority' see PARA 486 note 3. As to the orders that have been made under s 189(2) see the Homeless Persons (Priority Need) (Wales) Order 2001, SI 2001/607 (amended by SI 2004/696 and SI 2010/1142) (see note 15); and the Homelessness (Priority Need for Accommodation) (England) Order 2002, SI 2002/2051 (amended by SI 2016/211).

In relation to England, the following are also specified as having a priority need for accommodation: (1) a person, other than a person to whom a local authority owes a duty to provide accommodation under the Children Act 1989 s 20 or, as the case may be, the Social Services and Well-being (Wales) Act 2014 s 76, aged 16 or 17 who is not a relevant child for the purposes of the Children Act 1989 s 23A (see CHILDREN AND YOUNG PERSONS vol 10 (2017) PARA 849) or, as the case may be, is not a category 2 young person within the meaning of the Social Services and Well-being (Wales) Act 2014 s 104(2); (2) a person (other than a relevant student) who is under 21 and at any time after reaching the age of 16, but while still under 18, was, but is no longer, looked after, accommodated or fostered; (3) a person (other than a relevant student) who has reached the age of 21 and who is vulnerable as a result of having been looked after, accommodated or fostered; (4) a person who is vulnerable as a result of having been a member of Her Majesty's regular naval, military or air forces; (5) a person who is vulnerable as a result of having served a custodial sentence (within the meaning of the Powers of Criminal Courts (Sentencing) Act 2000 s 76: see SENTENCING vol 92 (2015) PARA 9 note 15), having been committed for contempt of court or any other kindred offence, or having been remanded in custody (within the meaning of s 88(1)(b), (c) or (d) (now repealed)); (6) a person who is vulnerable as a result of ceasing to occupy accommodation by reason of violence from another person or threats of violence from another person which are likely to be carried out: Homelessness (Priority Need for Accommodation) (England) Order 2002, SI 2002/2051, arts 2–6 (art 2 amended by SI 2016/211). 'Relevant student' means a person to whom the Children Act 1989 s 24B(3) or, as the case may be, the Social Services and Well-being (Wales) Act 2014 s 114(5) or 115(6) applies who is in full-time further or higher education, and whose term-time accommodation is not available to him during a vacation: Homelessness (Priority Need for Accommodation) (England) Order 2002, SI 2002/2051, art 1(3) (amended by SI 2016/211).

7   A person is vulnerable as a result of a reason mentioned in head (c) or (j) in the text if, having regard to all the circumstances of the person's case: (1) the person would be less able to fend for himself (as a result of that reason) if the person were to become street homeless than would an ordinary homeless person who becomes street homeless; and (2) this would lead to the person suffering more harm than would be suffered by the ordinary homeless person: Housing (Wales) Act 2014 s 71(1). This applies regardless of whether or not the person whose case is being considered is, or is likely to become, street homeless: s 71(1). 'Street homeless', in relation to a person, means that the person has no accommodation available for the person's occupation in the United Kingdom or elsewhere, which the person: (a) is entitled to occupy by virtue of an interest in it or by virtue of an order of a court; (b) has an express or implied licence to occupy; or (c) occupies as a residence by virtue of any enactment or rule of law giving the person the right to remain in occupation or restricting the right of another person to recover possession: s 71(2). Sections 55 and 56 (see PARA 482) do not apply to this definition: s 71(2).

8   As to the meaning of 'domestic abuse' see PARA 482 note 8.

9   'Looked after, accommodated or fostered' means: (1) looked after by a local authority (within the meaning of the Social Services and Well-Being (Wales) Act 2014 s 74 or the Children Act 1989 s 22); (2) accommodated by or on behalf of a voluntary organisation; (3) accommodated in a private children's home; (4) accommodated for a continuous period of at least three months: (a) by any Local Health Board or Special Health Authority; (b) by or on behalf of a clinical commissioning group or the National Health Service Commissioning Board; (c) by or on behalf of a county or county borough council in Wales in the exercise of education functions; (d) by or on behalf of a local authority in England in the exercise of education functions; (e) in any care home or independent hospital; or (f) in any accommodation provided by or on behalf of an NHS Trust or by or on behalf of an NHS Foundation Trust; or (5) privately fostered (within the meaning of the Children Act 1989 s 66): Housing (Wales) Act 2014 s 70(2).

For these purposes, 'Local Health Board' means a Local Health Board established under the National Health Service (Wales) Act 2006 s 11; 'clinical commissioning group' means a body established under the National Health Service Act 2006 s 14D; 'education functions' has the meaning given by the Education Act 1996 s 597(1); 'local authority in England' means: (i) a county council in England; (ii) a district council for an area in England for which there is no county council; (iii) a London borough council; or (iv) the Common Council of the City of London; 'care home' has the same meaning as in the Care Standards Act 2000; and 'independent hospital': (A) in relation to Wales, has the meaning given by the Care Standards Act 2000 s 2; and (B) in relation to England, means a hospital as defined by the National Health Service Act 2006 s 275 that is not a health service hospital as defined by s 275: Housing (Wales) Act 2014 s 70(3).

10 As to when a person has a local connection with the area of the local housing authority see PARA 485 note 16.

11 Ie within the meaning of the Powers of Criminal Courts (Sentencing) Act 2000 s 76: see SENTENCING vol 92 (2015) PARA 9 note 15.

12 Ie under the Legal Aid, Sentencing and Punishment of Offenders Act 2012 s 91(4): see CHILDREN AND YOUNG PERSONS.

13 Housing (Wales) Act 2014 s 70(1).

14 Ie the Housing (Wales) Act 2014 Pt 2 Ch 2 (ss 53–100).

15 Housing (Wales) Act 2014 s 72(1). An order under s 72(1) may amend or repeal any provision of Pt 2 (ss 50–100): s 72(2). Before making an order under s 72 the Welsh Ministers must consult such associations representing councils of counties and county boroughs in Wales, and such other persons, as they consider appropriate: s 72(3).

The following are also specified as having a priority need for accommodation: (1) a care leaver or person at particular risk of sexual or financial exploitation, who is 18 years or over but under the age of 21; (2) a person who is 16 or 17 years old; (3) a person fleeing domestic violence or threatened domestic violence; (4) a person homeless after leaving the armed forces; and (5) a former prisoner homeless after being released from custody: Homeless Persons (Priority Need) (Wales) Order 2001, SI 2001/607, arts 3–7 (art 3 amended by SI 2004/696 and SI 2010/1142).

496. Limited duty to persons becoming homeless intentionally: England. Where the local housing authority[1] in England is satisfied that an applicant[2] is homeless[3] and eligible for assistance[4], but is also satisfied that he became homeless intentionally[5], then if the authority is satisfied that the applicant has a priority need[6] it must:

(1)   secure that accommodation is available for his occupation for such period as it considers will give him a reasonable opportunity of securing accommodation for his occupation; and

(2)   provide him with (or secure that he is provided with) advice and assistance in any attempts he may make to secure that accommodation becomes available for his occupation[7].

If, however, the authority is not satisfied that the applicant has a priority need, it must merely provide him with (or secure that he is provided with) advice and assistance in any attempts he may make to secure that accommodation becomes available for his occupation[8]. The applicant's housing needs must in either case be assessed before advice and assistance are provided[9]. The advice and assistance provided must include information about the likely availability in the authority's district of types of accommodation appropriate to the applicant's housing needs (including, in particular, the location and sources of such types of accommodation)[10].

1   As to the meaning of 'local housing authority' see PARA 11 (definition applied by the Housing Act 1996 s 230).
2   As to the meaning of 'applicant' see PARA 487 note 3.
3   As to the meaning of 'homeless' see PARA 481.
4   As to the meaning of 'eligible for assistance' see PARA 487 note 4.
5   As to the meaning of 'homeless intentionally' see PARA 483.
6   As to persons in priority need see PARA 495.
7   Housing Act 1996 s 190(1), (2) (s 190(2) amended by the Homelessness Act 2002 s 18(1), Sch 1 paras 2, 9). See *R (on the application of Conville) v Richmond-upon-Thames London Borough Council* [2006] EWCA Civ 718, [2006] 4 All ER 917, [2006] 1 WLR 2808. As to when accommodation is available for occupation see PARA 481 note 1. In relation to England, certain accommodation made available for occupation under the Housing Act 1996 s 190(2) is to be regarded as unsuitable where there is a family commitment: see the Homelessness (Suitability of Accommodation) (England) Order 2003, SI 2003/3326; and PARA 481 note 13.
    As to the duty of a local housing authority for an area in Wales to help to secure that suitable accommodation is available for occupation by a homeless person, see the Housing (Wales) Act 2014 ss 73–76; and PARAS 501–502.
8   Housing Act 1996 s 190(3) (amended by the Homelessness Act 2002 Sch 1 para 9).
9   Housing Act 1996 s 190(4) (s 190(4), (5) added by the Homelessness Act 2002 Sch 1 para 10).
10 Housing Act 1996 s 190(5) (as added: see note 9).

497. Duty to persons not in priority need who are not homeless intentionally: England. Where the local housing authority[1] is satisfied that an applicant[2] is homeless[3] and eligible for assistance[4], and is not satisfied that he became homeless intentionally[5], but where the authority is not satisfied that he has a priority need[6], the authority must provide the applicant with (or secure that he is provided with) advice and assistance in any attempts he may make to secure that accommodation becomes available for his occupation[7]. The authority may secure that accommodation is available for occupation by the applicant[8]. The applicant's housing needs must be assessed before such advice and assistance are provided[9]. The advice and assistance provided must include information about the likely availability in the authority's district of types of accommodation appropriate to the applicant's housing needs (including, in particular, the location and sources of such types of accommodation)[10].

1   As to the meaning of 'local housing authority' see PARA 11 (definition applied by the Housing Act 1996 s 230).
2   As to the meaning of 'applicant' see PARA 487 note 3.
3   As to the meaning of 'homeless' see PARA 481.
4   As to the meaning of 'eligible for assistance' see PARA 487 note 4.
5   As to the meaning of 'homeless intentionally' see PARA 483.
6   As to persons in priority need see PARA 495.
7   Housing Act 1996 s 192(1), (2) (s 192(2) amended by the Homelessness Act 2002 s 18(1), Sch 1 paras 2, 11). As to when accommodation is available for occupation see PARA 481 note 1.
     As to the duty of a local housing authority for an area in Wales to help to secure that suitable accommodation is available for occupation by a homeless person, see the Housing (Wales) Act 2014 ss 73–76; and PARAS 501–502.
8   Housing Act 1996 s 192(3) (added by the Homelessness Act 2002 s 5(1)).
9   Housing Act 1996 s 192(4) (s 192(4), (5) added by the Homelessness Act 2002 s 18(1), Sch 1 paras 2, 12).
10 Housing Act 1996 s 192(5) (as added: see note 9).

498. Duty to persons with priority need who are not homeless intentionally: England. Where the local housing authority[1] is satisfied that an applicant[2] is homeless[3], is eligible for assistance[4], has a priority need[5], and did not become homeless intentionally[6], then, unless the authority refers the application to another local housing authority[7], it must secure that accommodation is available for occupation[8] by the applicant[9]. It is unlawful for the local housing authority to impose any further condition once these criteria are met[10]. The authority is subject to this duty until it ceases by virtue of any of the following provisions[11].

The local housing authority ceases to be subject to the duty to secure accommodation if:

(1)   the applicant, having been informed by the authority of the possible consequence of refusal or acceptance and of the right to request a review of the suitability of the accommodation, refuses an offer of accommodation which the authority is satisfied is suitable for the applicant;

(2)   that offer of accommodation is not an offer of accommodation under the allocation provisions[12] or a private rented sector offer[13]; and

(3)   the authority notifies the applicant that it regards itself as ceasing to be subject to the duty to secure accommodation[14];

The local housing authority also ceases to be subject to the duty to secure accommodation if the applicant:

(a)   ceases to be eligible for assistance, or becomes homeless intentionally from the accommodation made available for his occupation, or accepts an offer of accommodation under the allocation provisions, or accepts an offer of an assured tenancy[15] (other than an assured shorthold tenancy) from a private landlord[16], or otherwise voluntarily ceases to occupy as his only or principal home the accommodation made available for his occupation[17];

(b)   having been informed of the possible consequence of refusal or acceptance and of his right to request a review of the suitability of the accommodation, refuses a final offer of accommodation under the allocation provisions[18];

(c)   having been informed in writing: (i) of the possible consequence of refusal or acceptance of the offer; and (ii) that the applicant has the right to request a review of the suitability of the accommodation: and (iii) in a case which is not a restricted case[19], of the effect[20] of a further application to a local housing authority within two years of acceptance of the offer[21], accepts a private rented sector offer or refuses such an offer[22].

A person who ceases to be owed the duty under these provisions may make a fresh application to the authority for accommodation or assistance in obtaining accommodation[23].

1   As to the meaning of 'local housing authority' see PARA 11 (definition applied by the Housing Act 1996 s 230).
2   As to the meaning of 'applicant' see PARA 487 note 3.
3   As to the meaning of 'homeless' see PARA 481.
4   As to the meaning of 'eligible for assistance' see PARA 487 note 4.
5   As to persons in priority need see PARA 495.
6   As to the meaning of 'homeless intentionally' see PARA 483. Where the local housing authority's review officer had been entitled to find that accommodation occupied by the claimant and her family was not settled accommodation, he had been right to conclude that the causal link between the claimant's present homelessness and her earlier status as intentionally homeless had not been broken, and that the defendant was not under a duty to provide her with accommodation under the Housing Act 1996: *Mohamed v Westminster City Council* [2005] BLD 1606052597.
7   Ie under the Housing Act 1996 s 198: see PARA 503.
8   As to the meaning of 'available for occupation' see PARA 481 note 1. A housing authority must take all reasonable steps to ensure that suitable accommodation is provided: *R v Newham London Borough Council, ex p Begum* [2000] 2 All ER 72, 32 HLR 808.
9   Housing Act 1996 s 193(1), (2) (s 193(1) amended by the Homelessness Act 2002 s 18(2), Sch 2). In relation to England, certain accommodation made available for occupation under the Housing Act 1996 s 193(2) is to be regarded as unsuitable where there is a family commitment: see the Homelessness (Suitability of Accommodation) (England) Order 2003, SI 2003/3326; and PARA 481 note 13. A housing authority must take all reasonable steps to ensure that suitable accommodation is provided: *R v Newham London Borough Council, ex p Begum* [2000] 2 All ER 72, 32 HLR 808. The authority is not obliged to take into account an applicant's views on the suitability of the accommodation, or to provide him with an opportunity to view the accommodation in advance: *R (on the application of Khatun) v Newham London Borough Council* [2004] EWCA Civ 55, [2005] QB 37, [2004] LGR 696. In making determinations under the Housing Act 1996 Pt VII (ss 175–218) in areas in which a person's disability could be of relevance, a local authority should have due regard to the need to take steps to take account of disabled persons' disabilities; in circumstances in which a reviewing officer under s 202, or the initial decision maker under s 184, was not invited to consider an alleged disability, it would be wrong in the light of the discrimination legislation (see DISCRIMINATION vol 33 (2013) PARA 1 et seq) to say that he should consider disability only if it was obvious: *Pieretti v Enfield London Borough Council* [2010] EWCA Civ 1104, [2011] 2 All ER 642, [2010] LGR 944. See *Aster Communities Ltd (formerly Flourish Homes Ltd) v Akerman-Livingstone* [2015] UKSC 15, [2015] AC 1399, [2015] All ER (D) 118 (Mar) (eviction of disabled person to alternative housing to suit housing stock needs proportionate means of achieving legitimate aim: no discrimination).
    Having made a lawful decision that it owes a duty under the Housing Act 1996 s 193(2), a local housing authority may not reconsider its decision in the light of a subsequent change of circumstances which takes place before accommodation is found for the applicant: *R v Brent London Borough Council, ex p Sadiq* (2000) 33 HLR 525. See also *Deugi v Tower Hamlets London Borough Council* [2006] EWCA Civ 159 [2006] All ER (D) 87 (Mar); *Osseily v Westminster City Council* [2007] EWCA Civ 1108, [2008] HLR 301, [2008] LGR 260; and *Boreh v Ealing London Borough Council* [2008] EWCA Civ 1176, [2009] 2 All ER 383, [2009] HLR 379.

As to the duty of a local housing authority for an area in Wales to help to secure that suitable accommodation is available for occupation by a homeless person, see the Housing (Wales) Act 2014 ss 73–76; and PARAS 501–502.

10 *R (on the application of Hammia) v Wandsworth London Borough Council* [2005] HLR 735, [2005] All ER (D) 244 (May).

11 Housing Act 1996 s 193(3) (substituted by the Homelessness Act 2002 s 6(1)).

12 Ie the Housing Act 1996 Pt VI (ss 159–174): see PARA 420 et seq.

13 For these purposes an offer is a private rented sector offer if: (1) it is an offer of an assured shorthold tenancy made by a private landlord to the applicant in relation to any accommodation which is, or may become, available for the applicant's occupation; (2) it is made, with the approval of the authority, in pursuance of arrangements made by the authority with the landlord with a view to bringing the authority's duty under the Housing Act 1996 s 193 to an end; and (3) the tenancy being offered is a fixed term tenancy (within the meaning of the Housing Act 1988 Pt I (ss 1–45): see LANDLORD AND TENANT vol 63 (2016) PARA 852 note 3) for a period of at least 12 months: Housing Act 1996 s 193(7AC) (s 193(7AA)–(7AD) added by the Housing and Regeneration Act 2008 s 314, Sch 15 para 5(4); the Housing Act 1996 s 193(7AC) amended by the Localism Act 2011 s 148(1), (7)).

The Secretary of State may provide by regulations that the Housing Act 1996 s 193(7AC)(c) (head (3) above) is to have effect as if it referred to a period of the length specified in the regulations: s 193(10) (s 193(10), (11) added by the Localism Act 2011 s 148(1), (11); the Housing Act 1996 s 193(10) amended by the Housing (Wales) Act 2014 s 100, Sch 3 paras 2, 10(a)). Regulations under the Housing Act 1996 s 193(10) may not specify a period of less than 12 months and may not apply to restricted cases: s 193(11) (as so added).

14 Housing Act 1996 s 193(5) (substituted by the Localism Act 2011 s 148(1), (3)). See *R v Islington London Borough Council, ex p Thomas* (1997) 30 HLR 111. See also *Griffiths v St Helen's Metropolitan Borough Council* [2006] EWCA Civ 160, [2006] 1 WLR 2233, [2006] All ER (D) 94 (Mar) (the Housing Act 1996 s 193(5) is capable of applying to any offer of suitable accommodation). Following a refusal of an offer of suitable accommodation, the authority is not required to consider a further application from another member of the same household: *R v Camden London Borough Council, ex p Hersi* (2000) 3 HLR 577, CA. See also *Vilvarasa v Harrow London Borough Council* [2010] EWCA Civ 1278, [2011] HLR 191; *Sharif v Camden London Borough Council* [2013] UKSC 10, [2013] 2 All ER 309. As to when accommodation is suitable see PARA 481 note 13.

15 As to the meaning of 'assured tenancy' see LANDLORD AND TENANT vol 63 (2016) PARA 825.

16 As to the meaning of 'private landlord' see PARA 512 note 3.

17 Housing Act 1996 s 193(6) (amended by the Homelessness Act 2002 s 7(1), (2)).

18 Housing Act 1996 s 193(7) (substituted by the Homelessness Act 2002 s 7(3); amended by the Localism Act 2011 s 148(1), (4)). An offer of accommodation under the Housing Act 1996 Pt VI is a final offer for the purposes of s 193(7) if it is made in writing and states that it is a final offer for the purposes of s 193(7): s 193(7A) (added by the Homelessness Act 2002 s 7(3)). The local housing authority must not make a final offer of accommodation under the Housing Act 1996 Pt VI for the purposes of s 193(7) or approve a private rented sector offer unless it is satisfied that the accommodation is suitable for the applicant and that s 193(8) does not apply to the applicant: s 193(7F) (added by the Homelessness Act 2002 s 7(4); amended by the Housing and Regeneration Act 2008 Sch 15 paras 1, 5(1), (6); and the Localism Act 2011 ss 148(1), (9), 237, Sch 25 Pt 22). The Housing Act 1996 s 193(8) applies to an applicant if: (1) the applicant is under contractual or other obligations in respect of the applicant's existing accommodation; and (2) the applicant is not able to bring those obligations to an end before being required to take up the offer: s 193(8) (substituted by the Localism Act 2011 s 148(1), (10)).

It is not necessary for a letter offering accommodation to a person with priority need who is not intentionally homeless, to state specifically that the offer of accommodation is a final offer, where it is already clear that it is a final offer: *Omar v Birmingham City Council* [2007] EWCA Civ 610, [2007] HLR 639, [2007] All ER (D) 245 (Jul). The word 'inform' requires information to be conveyed in understandable English, it is not to be judged by extent to which recipient understood the content: *Ali v Birmingham City Council* [2009] EWCA Civ 1279, [2011] HLR 271, [2009] All ER (D) 150 (Oct) (local authority had set out what was required by statute). The Court of Appeal has issued guidance on the application of the Housing Act 1996 s 193(7), (7F): see *Ravichandran v Lewisham London Borough Council* [2010] EWCA Civ 755, (2010) Times, 19 July, [2010] All ER (D) 32 (Jul).

19 For these purposes, 'a restricted case' means a case where the local housing authority would not be satisfied as mentioned in the Housing Act 1996 s 193(1) without having had regard to a restricted person: s 193(3B) (added by the Housing and Regeneration Act 2008 Sch 15 paras 1, 5(1), (3)). As to the meaning of 'a restricted person' see PARA 487 note 11. In a restricted case the

authority must, so far as reasonably practicable, bring its duty under the Housing Act 1996 s 193 to an end as mentioned in s 193(7AA) (see head (c) in the text): s 193(7AD) (as added: see note 12).

20 Ie under the Housing Act 1996 s 195A: see PARA 500.

21 See the Housing Act 1996 s 193(7AB) (as added (see note 12); amended by the Localism Act 2011 s 148(1), (6)).

22 Housing Act 1996 s 193(7AA) (as added (see note 12); amended by the Localism Act 2011 s 148(1), (5), Sch 25 Pt 22).

23 Housing Act 1996 s 193(9).

499. Duties in cases of threatened homelessness: England. Where the local housing authority[1] is satisfied that an applicant[2] is threatened with homelessness[3] and is eligible for assistance[4], then provided the authority is satisfied that he has a priority need[5], and did not become threatened with homelessness intentionally[6], it must take reasonable steps to secure that accommodation does not cease to be available for his occupation[7]. This provision does not, however, affect any right of the authority, whether by virtue of a contract, enactment or rule of law, to secure vacant possession of any accommodation[8].

Where, in a case which is not a restricted threatened homelessness case[9], in pursuance of this duty the authority secures that accommodation is available for occupation by the applicant other than that occupied by him when he made his application, the statutory provisions relating to the period for which the duty is owed[10] apply, with any necessary modifications, as they do in relation to the duty owed[11] when an applicant is homeless in a case which is not a restricted case (within the meaning of those provisions)[12]. Where, in a restricted threatened homelessness case, in pursuance of the duty to secure accommodation for the applicant, the authority secures that accommodation other than that occupied by the applicant when he made his application is available for occupation by him, the statutory provisions relating to the period for which the duty is owed[13] apply, with any necessary modifications, as they apply in relation to the duty owed[14] in a restricted case (within the meaning of those provisions)[15].

If, however, the authority is not satisfied that the applicant has a priority need, or is so satisfied but is also satisfied that he became threatened with homelessness intentionally, it must provide him with (or secure that he is provided with) advice and assistance in any attempts he may make to secure that accommodation does not cease to be available for his occupation[16]. The applicant's housing needs must be assessed before such advice and assistance are provided[17]. The advice and assistance provided must include information about the likely availability in the authority's district of types of accommodation appropriate to the applicant's housing needs (including, in particular, the location and sources of such types of accommodation)[18]. If the authority decides that it owes the applicant the duty of providing advice and assistance by virtue of being satisfied that the applicant has a priority need but that he became threatened with homelessness intentionally[19], it may, pending a decision on a review of that decision: (1) secure that accommodation does not cease to be available for his occupation; and (2) if he becomes homeless, secure that accommodation is so available[20].

If the authority: (a) is not satisfied that the applicant has a priority need; and (b) is not satisfied that he became threatened with homelessness intentionally, it may take reasonable steps to secure that accommodation does not cease to be available for the applicant's occupation[21].

1 As to the meaning of 'local housing authority' see PARA 11 (definition applied by the Housing Act 1996 s 230).

2 As to the meaning of 'applicant' see PARA 487 note 3.

3 As to the meaning of 'threatened with homelessness' see PARA 481.

4 As to the meaning of 'eligible for assistance' see PARA 487 note 4.
5 As to persons with priority need see PARA 495.
6 As to the meaning of 'threatened with homelessness intentionally' see PARA 484.
7 Housing Act 1996 s 195(1), (2) (s 195(2) amended by the Homelessness Act 2002 s 18(2), Sch 2).
   As to the meaning of 'available for occupation' see PARA 481 note 1. In relation to England, certain accommodation made available for occupation under the Housing Act 1996 s 195(2) is to be regarded as unsuitable where there is a family commitment: see the Homelessness (Suitability of Accommodation) (England) Order 2003, SI 2003/3326; and PARA 481 note 13.
   As to the duty of a local housing authority for an area in Wales to help to secure that suitable accommodation is available for occupation by a homeless person, see the Housing (Wales) Act 2014 ss 73–76; and PARAS 501–502.
8 Housing Act 1996 s 195(3).
9 In the Housing Act 1996 s 195(4), (4A) 'a restricted threatened homelessness case' means a case where the local housing authority would not be satisfied as mentioned in s 195(1) without having had regard to a restricted person: s 195(4B) (s 195(4A), (4B) added by the Housing and Regeneration Act 2008 s 314, Sch 15 paras 1, 6(1), (4); the Housing Act 1996 s 195(4B) amended by the Localism Act 2011 s 149(1), (3)(b)). As to the meaning of 'a restricted person' see PARA 487 note 11.
10 Ie the Housing Act 1996 s 193(3)–(9): see PARA 498.
11 Ie the duty under the Housing Act 1996 s 193: see PARA 498.
12 Housing Act 1996 s 195(4) (amended by the Homelessness Act 2002 Sch 2; and the Housing and Regeneration Act 2008 Sch 15 para 6(3)). As to the meaning of 'a restricted case' see PARA 498 note 19.
13 See note 10.
14 See note 11.
15 Housing Act 1996 s 195(4A) (as added: see note 9).
16 Housing Act 1996 s 195(5) (amended by the Homelessness Act 2002 Sch 1 para 14(b)).
17 Housing Act 1996 s 195(6) (s 195(6), (7) added by the Homelessness Act 2002 Sch 1 para 14(c)).
18 Housing Act 1996 s 195(7) (as added: see note 17).
19 Ie the Housing Act 1996 s 195(5)(b) is satisfied.
20 Housing Act 1996 s 195(8) (added by the Homelessness Act 2002 Sch 1 para 14(d)).
21 Housing Act 1996 s 195(9) (added by the Homelessness Act 2002 s 5(2)).

500. Duty on re-application after private rented sector offer: England. If within two years beginning with the date on which an applicant[1] accepts a private rented sector offer[2], the applicant re-applies for accommodation, or for assistance in obtaining accommodation, and the local housing authority[3]: (1) is satisfied that the applicant is homeless and eligible for assistance[4]; and (2) is not satisfied that the applicant became homeless intentionally[5], the duty to secure accommodation[6] applies regardless of whether the applicant has a priority need[7].

If within two years beginning with the date on which an applicant accepts an private rented sector offer, the applicant re-applies for accommodation, or for assistance in obtaining accommodation, and the local housing authority: (a) is satisfied that the applicant is threatened with homelessness[8] and eligible for assistance; and (b) is not satisfied that the applicant became threatened with homelessness intentionally[9], the duty to secure accommodation[10] applies regardless of whether the applicant has a priority need[11].

These provisions do not apply to a case where the local housing authority would not be satisfied as mentioned without having regard to a restricted person[12]. Nor do they apply to a re-application by an applicant for accommodation, or for assistance in obtaining accommodation, if the immediately preceding application made by that applicant was one to which heads (1) and (2) or (a) and (b) applied[13].

1 As to the meaning of 'applicant' see PARA 487 note 3.
2 Ie an offer under the Housing Act 1996 s 193(7AA): see PARA 498 head (c).
3 As to the meaning of 'local housing authority' see PARA 11 (definition applied by the Housing Act 1996 s 230).
4 As to the meaning of 'eligible for assistance' see PARA 487 note 4.
5 As to the meaning of 'homeless intentionally' see PARA 483.

6   Ie under the Housing Act 1996 s 193(2): see PARA 498.
7   Housing Act 1996 s 195A(1) (s 195A added by the Localism Act 2011 s 149(1), (4)). As to persons
    with priority need see PARA 495. For the purpose of the Housing Act 1996 s 195A(1), an applicant
    in respect of whom a valid notice under the Housing Act 1988 s 21 (orders for possession on expiry
    or termination of assured shorthold tenancy: see LANDLORD AND TENANT vol 63 (2016)
    PARA 926) has been given is to be treated as homeless from the date on which that notice expires:
    Housing Act 1996 s 195A(2) (as so added).
8   As to the meaning of 'threatened with homelessness' see PARA 481.
9   As to the meaning of 'threatened with homelessness intentionally' see PARA 484.
10 Ie under the Housing Act 1996 s 195(2): see PARA 499.
11 Housing Act 1996 s 195A(3) (as added: see note 7). For the purpose of s 195A(3), an applicant in
    respect of whom a valid notice under the Housing Act 1988 s 21 has been given is to be treated
    as threatened with homelessness from the date on which that notice is given: Housing Act 1996
    s 195A(4) (as so added).
12 Housing Act 1996 s 195A(5) (as added: see note 7). As to the meaning of 'a restricted person' see
    PARA 487 note 11.
13 Housing Act 1996 s 195A(6) (as added: see note 7).

501. Duty to help to secure suitable accommodation: Wales. A local housing
authority[1] must help to secure that suitable accommodation is available[2] for
occupation by an applicant[3] if the authority is satisfied that the applicant is
homeless and eligible for help[4]. This duty does not apply if the authority refers the
application to another local housing authority[5].

Where a local housing authority concludes that its duty to an applicant[6] has
come to an end (including where the authority has referred the applicant's case to
another authority or decided that the conditions for referral are met), it must
notify the applicant in writing:

(1)   that it no longer regards itself as being subject to the relevant duty;
(2)   of the reasons why it considers that the duty has come to an end;
(3)   of the right to request a review; and
(4)   of the time within which such a request must be made[7].

Where a notice is not received by an applicant, the applicant may be treated as
having been duly notified under if the notice is made available at the
authority's office for a reasonable period for collection by the applicant or on the
applicant's behalf[8].

If the applicant has been notified in accordance with these provisions, the
authority's duty comes to an end in the following circumstances[9]:

(a)   at the end of a period of 56 days[10];
(b)   before the end of a period of 56 days the local housing authority is
       satisfied that reasonable steps have been taken to help to secure that
       suitable accommodation is available for occupation by the applicant[11];
(c)   the local housing authority is satisfied (whether as a result of the steps
       it has taken or not) that the applicant has suitable accommodation
       available for occupation and the accommodation is likely to be available
       for occupation by the applicant for a period of at least six months[12];
(d)   the applicant, having been notified of the possible consequence of
       refusal or acceptance of the offer, refuses an offer of accommodation
       from any person which the authority is satisfied is suitable for the
       applicant, and the authority is satisfied that the accommodation offered
       is likely to be available for occupation by the applicant for a period of
       at least six months[13];
(e)   the local housing authority is no longer satisfied that the applicant is
       eligible for help[14];
(f)   the local housing authority is satisfied that a mistake of fact led to the
       applicant being notified[15] that the duty was owed to the applicant[16];

(g)   the local authority is satisfied that the applicant has withdrawn his application[17];

(h)   the local housing authority is satisfied that the applicant is unreasonably failing to co-operate with the authority in connection with the exercise of its functions under Chapter 2 of Part 2 of the Housing (Wales) Act 2014[18] as they apply to the applicant[19].

1   As to the meaning of 'local housing authority' in relation to Wales see PARA 482 note 9.
2   As to the meaning of 'help to secure' that suitable accommodation is available for occupation see PARA 489.
3   As to the meaning of 'applicant' see PARA 488 note 3.
4   Housing (Wales) Act 2014 s 73(1). As to the meaning of 'eligible for help' see PARA 488 note 4. As to the duty to secure accommodation for persons in priority need see PARA 502.
5   Housing (Wales) Act 2014 s 73(2). As to such referral see s 80; and PARA 504.
6   Ie under the Housing (Wales) Act 2014 s 66 (see PARA 490), s 68 (see PARA 494), s 73 (see PARA 501) or s 75 (see PARA 502).
7   Housing (Wales) Act 2014 s 84(1), (3). Where such a notice relates to the duty in s 73 coming to an end in the circumstances described in s 74(2) or (3) (see the text to notes 10–11), it must include notice of the steps taken by the local housing authority to help to secure that suitable accommodation would be available for occupation by the applicant: s 84(2).
8   Housing (Wales) Act 2014 s 84(4).
9   Housing (Wales) Act 2014 ss 74(1), (8), 79(1).
10 Housing (Wales) Act 2014 s 74(2). The period of 56 days mentioned in s 74(2), (3) begins on the day the applicant is notified under s 63 (see PARA 488) and for this purpose the applicant is to be treated as notified on the day the notice is sent or first made available for collection: s 74(6).
11 Housing (Wales) Act 2014 s 74(3).
12 Housing (Wales) Act 2014 s 74(4). The period of six months mentioned in s 74(4)(b) and (5)(b) (heads (c), (d) in the text) begins on the day the notice under s 84 (see the text to notes 6–7) is sent or first made available for collection: s 74(7).
13 Housing (Wales) Act 2014 s 74(5).
14 Housing (Wales) Act 2014 s 79(2).
15 Ie under the Housing (Wales) Act 2014 s 63: see PARA 488.
16 Housing (Wales) Act 2014 s 79(3).
17 Housing (Wales) Act 2014 s 79(4).
18 Ie the Housing (Wales) Act 2014 Pt 2 Ch 2 (ss 53–100).
19 Housing (Wales) Act 2014 s 79(5).

502. Further duty to secure accommodation for persons in priority need: Wales.
When the duty to help to secure accommodation for homeless applicants[1] comes to an end in respect of an applicant, the local housing authority[2] must secure that suitable accommodation is available for occupation by the applicant[3] where either of the two sets of circumstances set out below applies[4].

The first set of circumstances is where the authority is required to secure that suitable accommodation is available is where the local housing authority:

(1)   is satisfied that the applicant does not have suitable accommodation available for occupation, or has suitable accommodation, but it is not likely that the accommodation will be available for occupation by the applicant for a period of at least six months starting on the day the applicant is notified[5] that the authority's duty to help secure accommodation[6] does not apply;

(2)   is satisfied that the applicant is eligible for help[7];

(3)   is satisfied that the applicant has a priority need[8] for accommodation; and

(4)   if the authority is having regard to whether or not the applicant is homeless intentionally[9], is not satisfied that the applicant became homeless intentionally in the circumstances which gave rise to the application[10].

The second set of circumstances where the authority is required to secure that suitable accommodation is available is where the local housing authority is having regard to whether or not the applicant is homeless intentionally and is satisfied that:

(a)   the applicant became homeless intentionally in the circumstances which gave rise to the application;

(b)   the applicant does not have suitable accommodation available for occupation, or has suitable accommodation, but it is not likely that the accommodation will be available for occupation by the applicant for a period of at least six months starting on the day on which the applicant is notified[11] that the authority's duty to help secure accommodation[12] does not apply;

(c)   the applicant is eligible for help;

(d)   the applicant has a priority need for accommodation;

(e)   the applicant is: (i) a pregnant woman or a person with whom she resides or might reasonably be expected to reside; (ii) a person with whom a dependant child resides or might reasonably be expected to reside; (iii) a person who had not attained the age of 21 when the application for help was made or a person with whom such a person resides or might reasonably be expected to reside; or (iv) a person who had attained the age of 21, but not the age of 25, when the application for help was made and who was looked after, accommodated or fostered[13] at any time while under the age of 18, or a person with whom such a person resides or might reasonably be expected to reside; and

(f)   the authority has not previously secured an offer of accommodation to the applicant under these provisions[14] following a previous application for help under the Chapter 2 of Part 2 of the Housing (Wales) Act 2014[15], where that offer was made:

        (i)   at any time within the period of five years before the day on which the applicant was notified[16] that a duty was owed to him under these provisions; and

        (ii)   on the basis that the applicant fell within heads (a) to (f)[17].

If the applicant has been notified[18], this duty comes to an end in the following circumstances[19], namely where:

(A)   the applicant accepts an offer of suitable accommodation under the allocation of housing provisions[20] or an offer of suitable accommodation under an assured tenancy[21] (including an assured shorthold tenancy)[22];

(B)   the applicant, having been given notice in writing of the possible consequence of refusal or acceptance of the offer, refuses:(I) an offer of suitable interim accommodation[23]; (II) a private rented sector offer[24]; or (III) an offer of accommodation under the allocation provisions[25], which the authority is satisfied is suitable for the applicant[26];

(C)   the local housing authority is satisfied that the applicant has become homeless intentionally[27] from suitable interim accommodation made available[28] for the applicant's occupation[29];

(D)   the local housing authority is satisfied that the applicant has voluntarily ceased to occupy as his only or principal home, suitable interim accommodation made available[30] for the applicant's occupation[31];

(E)   the local housing authority is no longer satisfied that the applicant is eligible for help[32];

(F)   the local housing authority is satisfied that a mistake of fact led to the applicant being notified[33] that the duty was owed to the applicant[34];

(G)   the local authority is satisfied that the applicant has withdrawn his application[35];

(H)   the local housing authority is satisfied that the applicant is unreasonably failing to co-operate with the authority in connection with the exercise of its functions under Chapter 2 of Part 2 of the Housing (Wales) Act 2014 as they apply to the applicant[36].

1   Ie the duty in the Housing (Wales) Act 2014 s 73: see PARA 501.
2   As to the meaning of 'local housing authority' in relation to Wales see PARA 482 note 9.
3   As to the meaning of 'applicant' see PARA 488 note 3.
4   Housing (Wales) Act 2014 s 75(1).
5   Ie in accordance with the Housing (Wales) Act 2014 s 84: see PARA 501. For this purpose, the applicant is to be treated as notified on the day the notice is sent or first made available for collection: s 75(4).
6   Ie the Housing (Wales) Act 2014 s 73.
7   As to the meaning of 'eligible for help' see PARA 488 note 4.
8   As to persons in priority need see PARA 495.
9   See the Housing (Wales) Act 2014 s 77; and PARA 483.
10 Housing (Wales) Act 2014 s 75(2).
11 Ie in accordance with the Housing (Wales) Act 2014 s 84: see PARA 501. For this purpose, the applicant is to be treated as notified on the day the notice is sent or first made available for collection: s 75(4).
12 Ie the Housing (Wales) Act 2014 s 73.
13 As to the meaning of 'looked after, accommodated or fostered' see PARA 495 note 9.
14 Ie under the Housing (Wales) Act 2014 s 75.
15 Ie the Housing (Wales) Act 2014 Pt 2 Ch 2 (ss 53–100).
16 Ie under the Housing (Wales) Act 2014 s 63: see PARA 488.
17 Housing (Wales) Act 2014 s 75(3).
18 Ie in accordance with the Housing (Wales) Act 2014 s 84.
19 Housing (Wales) Act 2014 ss 76(1), (8), 79(1).
20 Ie the Housing Act 1996 Pt VI (ss 159–174): see PARA 420 et seq.
21 As to the meaning of 'assured tenancy' see LANDLORD AND TENANT vol 63 (2016) PARA 825.
22 Housing (Wales) Act 2014 s 76(2). For the purposes of s 76, accommodation must not be regarded as suitable where the authority is of the view that it is not in reasonable physical condition, it does not comply with all the statutory requirements or the landlord is not a fit and proper person to act as landlord: Homelessness (Suitability of Accommodation) (Wales) Order 2015, SI 2015/1268, reg 8.
23 Ie under the Housing (Wales) Act 2014 s 75.
24 For the purposes of the Housing (Wales) Act 2014 s 76 an offer is a private rented sector offer if: (1) it is an offer of an assured shorthold tenancy made by a private landlord to the applicant in relation to any accommodation which is available for the applicant's occupation; (2) it is made, with the approval of the authority, in pursuance of arrangements made by the authority with the landlord with a view to bringing the authority's duty under s 75 to an end; and (3) the tenancy being offered is a fixed term tenancy for a period of at least six months: s 76(4). In a restricted case, the local housing authority must, so far as reasonably practicable, bring its duty to an end by securing a private rented sector offer; for this purpose, a 'restricted case' means a case where the local housing authority would not be satisfied as mentioned in s 75(1) without having regard to a restricted person: s 76(5). 'Fixed term tenancy' has the meaning given by the Housing Act 1988 Pt I (ss 1–45) (see LANDLORD AND TENANT vol 63 (2016) PARA 852 note 3): Housing (Wales) Act 2014 s 76(9). As to the meaning of 'a restricted person' see PARA 488 note 13.
25 See note 20.
26 Housing (Wales) Act 2014 s 76(3).
27 As to the meaning of 'homeless intentionally' see PARA 483.
28 Ie: (1) under the Housing (Wales) Act 2014 s 68 (interim duty to secure accommodation for homeless applicants in priority need: see PARA 494) and which continues to be made available under s 75; or (2) under s 75.
29 Housing (Wales) Act 2014 s 76(6).
30 Ie: (1) under the Housing (Wales) Act 2014 s 68 and which continues to be made available under s 75; or (2) under s 75.
31 Housing (Wales) Act 2014 s 76(7).

32 Housing (Wales) Act 2014 s 79(2).
33 Ie under the Housing (Wales) Act 2014 s 63: see PARA 488.
34 Housing (Wales) Act 2014 s 79(3).
35 Housing (Wales) Act 2014 s 79(4).
36 Housing (Wales) Act 2014 s 79(5).

503.   Referral of case to another local housing authority: England. If the local housing authority[1] would be subject to the statutory duty to secure that accommodation is available[2], but considers that the conditions for referral of the case to another local housing authority are met, it may notify that other authority of its opinion[3]. The conditions for referral of the case to another authority are met if:

(1)   neither the applicant[4] nor any person who might reasonably be expected to reside with him has a local connection with the district[5] of the authority to which his application was made;

(2)   the applicant or a person who might reasonably be expected to reside with him has a local connection with the district of that other authority; and

(3)   neither the applicant nor any person who might reasonably be expected to reside with him will run the risk of domestic violence[6] in that other district[7].

The conditions for referral of the case to another authority are also met if the application is made within the period of two years beginning with the date on which the applicant accepted a private rented sector offer[8] from the other authority, and neither the applicant nor any person who might reasonably be expected to reside with the applicant will run the risk of domestic violence in the district of the other authority[9].

The conditions for referral of the case to another authority are also met if the applicant was, on a previous application made to that other authority, placed[10] in accommodation in the district of the authority to which his application is now made, and the previous application was within such period as may be prescribed of the present application[11].

The question whether the conditions for referral of a case which does not involve a referral to a local housing authority in Wales are satisfied must be decided by agreement between the notifying authority and the notified authority or, in default of agreement, in accordance with such arrangements as the Secretary of State[12] may direct by order[13]. The question whether the conditions for referral of a case involving a referral to a local housing authority in Wales must be decided by agreement between the notifying authority and the notified authority or, in default of agreement, in accordance with such arrangements as the Secretary of State and the Welsh Ministers may jointly direct by order[14]. An order may direct that the arrangements are to be those agreed by any relevant authorities[15] or associations of relevant authorities, or, in default of such agreement, such arrangements as appear to the Secretary of State or, in the case of an order involving a referral to a local housing authority in Wales, to the Secretary of State and the Welsh Ministers, to be suitable, after consultation with such associations representing relevant authorities, and such other persons, as he thinks appropriate[16].

1   As to the meaning of 'local housing authority' see PARA 11 (definition applied by the Housing Act 1996 s 230).
2   Ie the duty under the Housing Act 1996 s 193: see PARA 498. As to persons with priority need see PARA 495; and as to the meaning of 'homeless intentionally' see PARA 483. There is no statutory right of review of a local housing authority's decision to refuse to refer an application to another

local housing authority: *Hackney London Borough Council v Sareen* [2003] EWCA Civ 351, [2003] HLR 800, [2003] All ER (D) 274 (Mar).

3   Housing Act 1996 s 198(1) (amended by the Homelessness Act 2002 s 18(2), Sch 2). As to when accommodation is suitable see PARA 481 note 13.

4   As to the meaning of 'applicant' see PARA 487 note 3.

5   As to when a person has a local connection with the district of a local housing authority see the Housing Act 1996 s 199; and PARA 487 note 6. As to the meaning of 'district' see PARA 11 (definition applied by s 217(3)). The material date for determining whether an eligible applicant or member of his household has a local connection is the date of review of the housing authority's decision; in assessing whether there is a local connection, interim residence within a local housing authority's area can be taken into account: *Mohamed v Hammersmith and Fulham London Borough Council* [2001] UKHL 57, [2002] 1 AC 547, [2002] 1 All ER 176. An asylum-seeker does not have a local connection to a locality where he has been given accommodation under a support service dispersal scheme: *Osmani v Harrow London Borough Council* [2004] UKHL 4, [2004] 2 AC 159, [2004] 1 All ER 1104.

6   The conditions for referral mentioned in the Housing Act 1996 s 198(2) or (2ZA) (see the text to notes 8–9) are not met if: (1) the applicant or any person who might reasonably be expected to reside with him has suffered violence (other than domestic violence) in the district of the other authority; and (2) it is probable that the return to that district of the victim will lead to further violence of a similar kind against him: s 198(2A) (added by the Homelessness Act 2002 s 10(2); and amended by the Localism Act 2011 s 149(1), (5), (7)). For the purposes of the Housing Act 1996 s 198(2), (2ZA), (2A), 'violence' means violence from another person, or threats of violence from another person which are likely to be carried out; and violence is 'domestic violence' if it is from a person who is associated with the victim: s 198(3) (substituted by the Homelessness Act 2002 s 10(2); and amended by the Localism Act 2011 s 149(1), (5), (8)). As to the meaning of 'associated person' see PARA 481 note 8. 'Violence' means physical violence and not common assault; the probability of further violence is to be assessed objectively: *Danesh v Kensington and Chelsea Royal London Borough Council* [2006] EWCA Civ 1404, [2007] 1 WLR 69, [2007] HLR 263.

7   Housing Act 1996 s 198(2).

8   Ie under the Housing Act 1996 s 193(7AA): see PARA 498 head (c).

9   Housing Act 1996 s 198(2A) (added by the Localism Act 2011 s 149(1), (5), (6)).

10   Ie in pursuance of that authority's functions under the Housing Act 1996 Pt VII (ss 175–218). In a case where the other authority is an authority in Wales, this is to be construed as if the reference were a reference to that authority's functions under the Housing (Wales) Act 2014 Pt 2 (ss 50–100): Housing Act 1996 s 198(4A) (added by the Housing (Wales) Act 2014 s 100, Sch 3 paras 2, 11(a)).

11   Housing Act 1996 s 198(4). The prescribed period is, in relation to England, the aggregate of: (1) five years; and (2) the period beginning on the date of the previous application and ending on the date on which the applicant was first placed in pursuance of that application in accommodation in the district of the authority to which the application is now made: Allocation of Housing and Homelessness (Miscellaneous Provisions) (England) Regulations 2006, SI 2006/2527, reg 3.

12   As to the Secretary of State see PARA 7.

13   Housing Act 1996 s 198(5) (amended by the Housing (Wales) Act 2014 Sch 3 paras 2, 11(b)).

14   Housing Act 1996 s 198(5A) (added by the Housing (Wales) Act 2014 Sch 3 paras 2, 11(c)). As to the Welsh Ministers see PARA 7. As to the meaning of 'local housing authority' in relation to Wales see PARA 482 note 9.

15   As to the meaning of 'relevant authority' see PARA 495 note 6.

16   Housing Act 1996 s 198(6) (amended by the Housing (Wales) Act 2014 Sch 3 paras 2, 11(d)). An order under the Housing Act 1996 s 198 may not be made unless a draft of the order has been approved by a resolution of each House of Parliament and, in the case of a joint order, a resolution of the National Assembly for Wales: s 198(7) (amended by the Housing (Wales) Act 2014 Sch 3 paras 2, 11(e)). See the Homelessness (Decisions on Referrals) Order 1998, SI 1998/1578.
    As to the application of the Housing Act 1996 s 198 to cases arising in Scotland see s 201.

504. Referral of case to another local housing authority: Wales. Where:

(1)   a local housing authority[1] considers that the conditions for referral to another local housing authority (whether in Wales or England) are met; and

(2)   the local housing authority would, if the case is not referred, be subject to the duty to help to secure accommodation in respect of an applicant who is in priority need of accommodation and unintentionally homeless[2],

the local housing authority may notify the other authority of its opinion that the conditions for referral are met in respect of the applicant[3].

The conditions for referral of the case to another local housing authority (whether in Wales or England) are met if:

(a)   neither the applicant nor any person who might reasonably be expected to reside with the applicant has a local connection with the area[4] of the authority to which the application was made;

(b)   the applicant or a person who might reasonably be expected to reside with the applicant has a local connection with the area of that other authority; and

(c)   neither the applicant nor any person who might reasonably be expected to reside with the applicant will run the risk of domestic abuse[5] in that other area[6].

The question of whether the conditions for referral of a case are satisfied is to be decided: (i) by agreement between the notifying authority and the notified authority; or (ii) in default of agreement, in accordance with such arrangements: (A) as the Welsh Ministers may direct by order, where both authorities are in Wales; or (B) as the Welsh Ministers and the Secretary of State may jointly direct by order, where the notifying authority is in Wales and the notified authority is in England[7]. Such an order may direct that the arrangements are to be either those agreed by any relevant authorities[8] or associations of relevant authorities or, in default of such agreement, such arrangements as appear to the Welsh Ministers or, in the case of an order under head (ii)(B), to the Welsh Ministers and the Secretary of State, to be suitable, after consultation with such associations representing relevant authorities, and such other persons, as they think appropriate[9].

The Welsh Ministers may by order specify other circumstances in which the conditions are or are not met for referral of the case to another local housing authority[10].

1   As to the meaning of 'local housing authority' in relation to Wales see PARA 482 note 9. As to the meaning of 'local housing authority' in relation to England see PARA 11.
2   Ie the duty in the Housing (Wales) Act 2014 s 73: see PARA 501.
3   Housing (Wales) Act 2014 s 80(1), (2). As to the meaning of 'applicant' see PARA 488 note 3.
4   As to when a person has a local connection with the area of the local housing authority see PARA 485 note 16.
5   As to the meaning of 'domestic abuse' see PARA 482 note 8. The conditions for referral mentioned in the Housing (Wales) Act 2014 s 80(3) are not met if: (1) the applicant or any person who might reasonably be expected to reside with the applicant has suffered abuse (other than domestic abuse) in the area of the other authority; and (2) it is probable that the return to that area of the victim will lead to further abuse of a similar kind against him or her: s 80(4).
6   Housing (Wales) Act 2014 s 80(3).
7   Housing (Wales) Act 2014 s 80(5). As to the Secretary of State and the Welsh Ministers see PARA 7.
8   'Relevant authority' means a local housing authority or a social services authority; and it includes, in so far as the Housing (Wales) Act 2014 s 80(6) applies to arrangements under s 80(5)(b)(ii) (head (ii)(B) in the text), such authorities in Wales and England: s 80(7). 'Social services authority' means: (1) in relation to Wales, the council of a county or county borough council in the exercise of its social services functions, within the meaning of the Social Services and Well-being (Wales) Act 2014 s 119; and (2) in relation to England, a local authority for the purposes of the Local Authority Social Services Act 1970, as defined in s 1 of that Act, but a reference to a 'social services authority' is to be interpreted as a reference to a social services authority for an area in Wales only, unless the Housing (Wales) Act 2014 Pt 2 Ch 2 (ss 53–100) expressly provides otherwise: s 99.
9   Housing (Wales) Act 2014 s 80(6).
10 Housing (Wales) Act 2014 s 80(8).

505.   Duties to an applicant whose case is considered for referral or is referred: England. Where a local housing authority[1] notifies an applicant[2] that it intends to notify (or has notified) another local housing authority of its opinion that the conditions are met for the referral of his case to that other authority[3], the first-mentioned authority ceases to be subject to any interim duty to accommodate that person in the case of apparent priority need[4], and is not subject to the main housing duty[5]. However, it must secure that accommodation is available for occupation[6] by the applicant until he is notified of the decision whether the conditions for referral of his case are met[7].

When it has been decided whether the conditions for referral are met, the notifying authority must notify the applicant of the decision and inform him of the reasons for it. This notice must also inform the applicant of his right to request a review of the decision and of the time within which such a request must be made[8].

If it is decided that the conditions for referral are not met, the notifying authority is subject to the main housing duty[9]. If it is decided that those conditions are met and the notified authority is not an authority in Wales, the notified authority is subject to the main housing duty[10].

The duty under these provisions[11] ceases as provided above even if the applicant requests a review of the authority's decision[12], but the authority may secure that accommodation is available for the applicant's occupation pending the decision on a review[13].

Where an application has been referred by a local housing authority in Wales to a local housing authority in England[14], if it is decided that the conditions for referral of the case are met, the notified authority is subject to the main housing duty[15] in respect of the person whose case is referred[16].

1   As to the meaning of 'local housing authority' see PARA 11 (definition applied by the Housing Act 1996 s 230).
2   Notice required to be given to an applicant under these provisions must be given in writing and, if not received by him, must be treated as having been given to him if it is made available at the authority's office for a reasonable period for collection by him or on his behalf: Housing Act 1996 s 200(6). As to the meaning of 'applicant' see PARA 487 note 3.
3   As to when the conditions referred to in the text are met see PARA 503.
4   Ie any duty under the Housing Act 1996 s 188: see PARA 493. As to persons in priority need see PARA 495.
5   Ie the duty under the Housing Act 1996 s 193: see PARA 498.
6   As to when accommodation is available for occupation see PARA 481 note 1.
7   Housing Act 1996 s 200(1). In relation to England, certain accommodation made available for occupation under the Housing Act 1996 s 200(1) is to be regarded as unsuitable where there is a family commitment: see the Homelessness (Suitability of Accommodation) (England) Order 2003, SI 2003/3326; and PARA 481 note 13.
8   Housing Act 1996 s 200(2).
9   Housing Act 1996 s 200(3) (substituted by the Homelessness Act 2002 s 18(1), Sch 1 paras 2, 15(a)).
10 Housing Act 1996 s 200(4) (substituted by the Homelessness Act 2002 Sch 1 para 15(a); and amended by the Housing (Wales) Act 2014 s 100, Sch 3 paras 2, 12). For provision about cases where it is decided that those conditions are met and the notified authority is an authority in Wales, see the Housing (Wales) Act 2014 s 83; and PARA 506.
11 Ie under the Housing Act 1996 s 200(1): see the text and note 7.
12 Ie under the Housing Act 1996 s 202: see PARA 507.
13 Housing Act 1996 s 200(5) (amended by the Homelessness Act 2002 s 18(1), (2), Sch 1 para 15(b), Sch 2). As to accommodation which is not regarded as suitable where accommodation is made available by local housing authorities in England under the Housing Act 1996 s 200(1) see note 7.
        As to the application of s 200 to cases arising in Scotland see s 201.
14 Ie under the Housing (Wales) Act 2014 s 80: PARA 504. As to the meaning of 'local housing authority' in relation to Wales see PARA 482 note 9.
15 Ie the duty under the Housing Act 1996 s 193: see PARA 498.
16 Housing Act 1996 s 201A(1), (2) (s 201A added by the Housing (Wales) Act 2014 s 100, Sch 3 paras 2, 13). For provision about cases where it is decided that the conditions for referral are not

met, see the Housing (Wales) Act 2014 s 82; and PARA 506. References in the Housing Act 1996 Pt VII (ss 175–218) to an applicant include a reference to a person to whom a duty is owed by virtue of s 201A(2): s 201A(3) (as so added).

506. Duties to an applicant whose case is considered for referral or is referred: Wales. Where a local housing authority[1] notifies an applicant[2] that it intends to notify or has notified another local housing authority in Wales or England of its opinion that the conditions are met for the referral of the applicant's case to that other authority[3]: (1) it ceases to be subject to any duty[4] to secure accommodation for homeless applicants in priority need; and (2) it is not subject to any duty[5] to help to secure accommodation for homeless applicants[6]; but it must secure that suitable accommodation is available for occupation by the applicant until the applicant is notified of the decision whether the conditions for referral of the case are met[7].

When it has been decided whether the conditions for referral are met, the notifying authority must notify the applicant[8]. If it is decided that the conditions for referral are not met, the notifying authority is subject to the duty[9] to help to secure accommodation[10]. If it is decided that those conditions are met and the notified authority is an authority in Wales, the notified authority is subject to the duty[11] to help to secure accommodation[12].

The duty under these provisions[13] ceases as provided above even if the applicant requests a review of the authority's decision[14]; but the authority may secure that suitable accommodation is available for the applicant's occupation pending the decision on a review[15].

Where an application has been referred by a local housing authority in England to a local housing authority in Wales[16], if it is decided that the conditions for referral of the case are met the notified authority is subject to the following duties in respect of the person whose case is referred: (a) the interim duty[17] to secure accommodation for homeless applicants in priority need; (b) the duty[18] to help to secure accommodation for homeless applicants[19].

1 As to the meaning of 'local housing authority' in relation to Wales see PARA 482 note 9. As to the meaning of 'local housing authority' in relation to England see PARA 11.
2 Ie in accordance with the Housing (Wales) Act 2014 s 84 (see PARA 501). If notice required to be given to an applicant under s 82 is not received by the applicant, it is to be treated as having been given if it is made available at the authority's office for a reasonable period for collection by the applicant or on the applicant's behalf: s 82(7). As to the meaning of 'applicant' see PARA 488 note 3.
3 As to when the conditions referred to in the text are met see PARA 504.
4 Ie under the Housing (Wales) Act 2014 s 68: see PARA 494.
5 Ie under the Housing (Wales) Act 2014 s 73: see PARA 501.
6 Housing (Wales) Act 2014 s 82(1)(a), (b).
7 Housing (Wales) Act 2014 s 82(1). As to when accommodation is available for occupation see PARA 481 note 1.
8 Housing (Wales) Act 2014 s 82(2). As to notification see note 2.
9 Ie under the Housing (Wales) Act 2014 s 73.
10 Housing (Wales) Act 2014 s 82(3).
11 See note 9.
12 Housing (Wales) Act 2014 s 82(4). For provision about cases where it is decided that those conditions are met and the notified authority is an authority in England, see the Housing Act 1996 s 201A (cases referred from a local housing authority in Wales); and PARA 505.
13 Ie under the Housing (Wales) Act 2014 s 82(1).
14 Housing (Wales) Act 2014 s 82(5). As to review of a decision see s 85; and PARA 508.
15 Housing (Wales) Act 2014 s 82(6).
16 Ie under the Housing Act 1996 s 198(1): see PARA 503.
17 Ie under the Housing (Wales) Act 2014 s 68: see PARA 494.
18 Ie under the Housing (Wales) Act 2014 s 73: see PARA 501.
19 Housing (Wales) Act 2014 s 83(1), (2). For provision about cases where it is decided that the conditions for referral are not met, see the Housing Act 1996 s 200; and PARA 505. Accordingly,

references in the Housing (Wales) Act 2014 Pt 2 Ch 2 (ss 53–100) to an applicant include a reference to a person to whom the duties mentioned in s 83(2) are owed by virtue of s 83: s 83(3).

507. Right to request review of a decision: England. An applicant[1] has the right to have a review of:

(1)   any decision of a local housing authority[2] as to his eligibility for assistance[3];

(2)   any decision of a local housing authority as to what duty (if any) is owed to him under the provisions relating to duties to persons found to be homeless or threatened with homelessness[4];

(3)   any decision of a local housing authority to notify another authority of its opinion that the conditions are met for the referral of his case to that other authority[5];

(4)   any decision[6] whether the conditions are met for the referral of his case[7];

(5)   any decision as to the duty owed to the applicant if his case is considered for referral or referred[8];

(6)   any decision of a local housing authority as to the suitability of accommodation offered to him in discharge of any of its duties under head (2) or head (5) or as to the suitability of accommodation offered to him[9] where, having been informed of the possible consequence of refusal and of his right to request a review of the suitability of the accommodation, he refuses a final offer of accommodation under the allocation provisions for persons with priority need who are not homeless intentionally[10]; or

(7)   any decision of a local housing authority as to the suitability of accommodation offered to him by way of a private rented sector offer[11].

There is, however, no right to request a review of the decision reached following an earlier review[12].

An applicant must request a review within 21 days of the day on which he is notified of the authority's decision (or such longer period as the authority may in writing allow)[13]. The authority must then review the decision[14].

The Secretary of State[15] may by regulations[16] prescribe the procedure to be followed[17]. Provision may be made by regulations:

(a)   requiring the review to be undertaken by a person of appropriate seniority who was not involved in the original decision[18]; as to the circumstances in which the applicant is entitled to an oral hearing; and by whom he may be represented at such a hearing[19]; and

(b)   as to the period within which the review must be carried out and notice given of the decision[20].

The authority must notify the applicant of the outcome of the review[21]. If the decision is:

(i)   to confirm the original decision; or

(ii)   to confirm a previous decision to notify another authority under the provisions relating to referral of cases[22], or that the conditions are met for the referral of his case,

it must also notify him of the reasons for the decision[23]. He must also be informed of his right to appeal to the County Court on a point of law[24], and as to the period within which such an appeal must be made[25].

1   As to the meaning of 'applicant' see PARA 487 note 3; and see PARA 505 note 16.
2   As to the meaning of 'local housing authority' see PARA 11 (definition applied by the Housing Act 1996 s 230). A local housing authority is in principle empowered to contract out the function of reviewing eligibility decisions: *De-Winter Heald v Brent London Borough Council; Al-Jarah v Brent London Borough Council* [2009] EWCA Civ 930, [2010] 1 WLR 990, [2009] LGR 937.

3 As to the meaning of 'eligible for assistance' see PARA 487 note 4.

4 Ie under the Housing Act 1996 ss 190–193, 195, 196: see PARAS 483–484, 497–499. See also note 2. As to the meanings of 'homeless' and 'threatened with homelessness' see PARA 481. The right to request a review of a decision as to the duty owed by a local housing authority to persons found to be homeless or threatened with homelessness includes the right to request a review of the decision that such a duty has ceased to exist: *Warsame v Hounslow London Borough Council* [2000] 1 WLR 696, 32 HLR 335, CA. Where a local authority's decision is amenable to review under the Housing Act 1996 s 202, it is inappropriate to seek judicial review to challenge that decision and the procedure in the Housing Act 1996 is to be followed: *R v Merton London Borough Council, ex p Sembi* (1999) Times, 9 June. As to the independence and impartiality of the review procedure see *Adan v Newham London Borough Council* [2001] EWCA Civ 1916, [2002] 1 All ER 931, [2002] 1 WLR 2120; *Runa Begum v Tower Hamlets London Borough Council* [2003] UKHL 5, [2003] 2 AC 430, [2003] 1 All ER 731; *Feld v Barnet London Borough Council, Pour v Westminster City Council* [2004] EWCA Civ 1307, [2005] LGR 411, [2004] All ER (D) 208 (Oct). See also *R (on the application of Ali) v Birmingham City Council; Manchester City Council v Moran* [2009] UKHL 36, [2009] 4 All ER 161, [2009] 1 WLR 1506.

5 Ie any decision under the Housing Act 1996 s 198(1): see PARA 503.

6 Ie under the Housing Act 1996 s 198(5): see PARA 503.

7 As to when those conditions are met see PARA 503.

8 Ie any decision under the Housing Act 1996 s 200(3) or (4): see PARA 505.

9 Ie as mentioned in the Housing Act 1996 s 193(7): see PARA 498.

10 Ie within the meaning of the Housing Act 1996 s 193: see PARA 498.

11 Housing Act 1996 s 202(1) (amended by Homelessness Act 2002 ss 8(2)(a), 18(1), Sch 1 paras 2, 16; the Housing and Regeneration Act 2008 ss 314, 321(1), Sch 15 paras 1, 7(1), (2), Sch 16; and the Localism Act 2011 s 149(1), (9)). An applicant who is offered accommodation as mentioned in the Housing Act 1996 s 193(5), (7) or (7AA) may under s 202(1)(f) or (g) request a review of the suitability of the accommodation offered to him whether or not he has accepted the offer: s 202(1A) (added by the Homelessness Act 2002 s 8(2)(b); and amended by the Housing and Regeneration Act 2008 Sch 15 para 7(3)). See *R v Lambeth London Borough Council, ex p Woodburne* (1997) 29 HLR 836.

12 Housing Act 1996 s 202(2).

13 Housing Act 1996 s 202(3). A local authority's discretion under s 202(3) to grant extra time to an applicant to request a review will generally be decided on the particular facts of each case, but the length of the delay in requesting such review and the reasons for it will play an important role: *R (on the application of C) v Lewisham London Borough Council* [2003] EWCA Civ 927, [2003] 3 All ER 1277, [2004] HLR 27.

14 See the Housing Act 1996 s 202(4). A request for a review under s 202 must be made to the local housing authority, where the original decision falls within s 202(1)(a), (b), (c), (e) or (f) (see heads (1)–(3), (5), (6) in the text): Allocation of Housing and Homelessness (Review Procedures) Regulations 1999, SI 1999/71, reg 6(1)(a). The authority must then notify the applicant that he, or someone acting on his behalf, may make representations in writing to the authority in connection with the review; and, if it has not already done so, it must notify the applicant of the procedure to be followed in connection with the review: reg 6(2). At the review, the authority must, subject to compliance with reg 9 (see note 20), consider any such representations: reg 8(1)(a). If the reviewer considers that there is a deficiency or irregularity in the original decision, or in the manner in which it was made, but is minded nonetheless to make a decision which is against the interests of the applicant on one or more issues, the reviewer must notify the applicant that it is so minded and why: reg 8(2)(a). It must also notify the applicant that he, or someone acting on his behalf, may make representations to the reviewer orally or in writing or both: reg 8(2)(b). The authority must then consider any such representations: reg 8(1)(b). See *Hall v Wandsworth London Borough Council, Carter v Wandsworth London Borough Council* [2004] EWCA Civ 1740, [2005] 2 All ER 192, [2005] LGR 350; *Gibbons v Bury Metropolitan Borough Council* [2010] EWCA Civ 327, [2010] HLR 527, [2010] All ER (D) 254 (Mar). As to the discretion to conduct sequential reviews of the same decision see *Crawley Borough Council v B* (2000) 32 HLR 636, [2000] All ER (D) 220, CA. The material date for the purposes of a review, and any subsequent challenge to the review decision, is the date of the review: *Omar v Westminster City Council* [2008] EWCA Civ 421, [2008] HLR 581, [2008] All ER (D) 38 (Mar). Cf *Banks v Royal Borough of Kingston upon Thames* [2008] EWCA Civ 1443, [2009] HLR 482, [2009] LGR 536 (subsequent change of circumstances can be relevant). The reviewer, if mindful to find against the applicant, has no discretion under the Allocation of Housing and Homelessness (Review Procedures) Regulations 1999, SI 1999/71, reg 8(2)(a) to dispense with giving notice of his grounds for doing so: *Johnston v Lambeth London Borough Council* [2008] EWCA Civ 690, (2008) Times, 30 June, [2008] All ER (D) 242 (Jun). The Allocation of Housing and Homelessness (Review Procedures) Regulations 1999, SI 1999/71, reg 8(2)(b) confers on an applicant the right

to an oral hearing, and not merely the right to make oral representations by any means the authority so chooses, such as by telephone: *Makisi v Birmingham City Council; Yosief v Birmingham City Council; Nagi v Birmingham City Council* [2011] EWCA Civ 355, [2011] PTSR 1545, [2011] All ER (D) 12 (Apr).

A request for a review under the Housing Act 1996 s 202 must be made to the notifying body, where the original decision falls within s 202(1)(d) (a decision under s 198(5): see head (4) in the text): Allocation of Housing and Homelessness (Review Procedures) Regulations 1999, SI 1999/71, reg 6(1)(b). See also Code of Guidance to Local Authorities on the Allocation of Accommodation and Homelessness 2016 (Department for Communities and Local Government, 24 March 2016). Except where the original decision under the Housing Act 1996 s 198(5) was made under the Homelessness (Decisions on Referrals) Order 1998, SI 1998/1578 (see PARA 503), the notifying body must then notify the applicant of the matters set out in the Allocation of Housing and Homelessness (Review Procedures) Regulations 1999, SI 1999/71, reg 6(2). Where, however, the original decision under the Housing Act 1996 s 198(5) was made under the Decisions on Referrals Order 1998, SI 1998/1578, the Allocation of Housing and Homelessness (Review Procedures) Regulations 1999, SI 1999/71, reg 7 applies and a person must be appointed to carry out the review, in accordance with the procedures laid down by that provision: see reg 7(1)–(3). The appointed person must not be the same person as the person who made the original decision: reg 7(6). Within five working days of the appointment, the notifying authority and the notified authority (see PARA 503) must provide the appointed person with the reasons for the original decision and the information and evidence on which that decision is based: reg 7(4). The appointed person must then notify the applicant that he, or someone else acting on his behalf, may make representations in writing to that person in connection with the review, and notify the applicant of the procedure to be followed in connection with the review: reg 6(3). The appointed person must send to the notifying authority and the notified authority any such representations, and invite those authorities to respond to them: reg 7(5)(a), (b). Where the review is carried out by a person appointed under reg 7, the appointed person must also consider any responses provided to him under reg 7(5)(b): reg 8(1)(a).

15 As to the Secretary of State see PARA 7.
16 As to the making of regulations generally see PARA 491 note 6.
17 Housing Act 1996 s 203(1). As to the exercise of this power see the Allocation of Housing and Homelessness (Review Procedures) Regulations 1999, SI 1999/71.
18 Where the decision of the authority on a review of an original decision made by an officer of the authority is also to be made by an officer, that officer must be someone who was not involved in the original decision and who is senior to the officer who made the original decision: Allocation of Housing and Homelessness (Review Procedures) Regulations 1999, SI 1999/71, reg 2.
19 Housing Act 1996 s 203(2). See note 14. Notice required to be given to a person under s 203 must be given in writing and, if not received by him, will be treated as having been given if it is made available at the authority's office for a reasonable period for collection by him or on his behalf: s 203(8).
20 Housing Act 1996 s 203(7). Where the original decision falls within s 202(1)(a), (b), (c), (e) or (f) (see heads (1)–(3), (5), (6) in the text), notice of the decision on a review must be given under s 203(3) to the applicant eight weeks from the day on which the request for the review is made or such longer period as the authority and the applicant may agree in writing: Allocation of Housing and Homelessness (Review Procedures) Regulations 1999, SI 1999/71, reg 9(1)(a), (2). Where the original decision falls within the Housing Act 1996 s 202(1)(d) (see head (4) in the text), notice of the decision on a review must be given under s 203(3) to the applicant: (1) within ten weeks from the day on which the request for the review is made, where the original decision falls within s 202(1)(d) and the review is carried out by the notifying authority and the notified authority; or (2) within 12 weeks from the day on which the request for a review is made in a case falling within the Allocation of Housing and Homelessness (Review Procedures) Regulations 1999, SI 1999/71, reg 7 (see note 14); or (3) within such longer period as the reviewer and the applicant may agree in writing: reg 9(1)(b), (c), (2). In a case falling within reg 7, the appointed person must also notify his decision on the review, and his reasons for it, in writing to the notifying authority and the notified authority within 11 weeks from the day on which the request for the review is made, or within a period commencing on that day which is one week shorter than that agreed in accordance with reg 9(2): reg 9(3).
21 Housing Act 1996 s 203(3). The decision may be less favourable than the original one: *T v Hackney London Borough Council* [2014] EWCA Civ 877, [2014] LGR 689.
22 Ie under the Housing Act 1996 s 198: see PARA 503.
23 Housing Act 1996 s 203(4). As to the giving of reasons see *R v Haringey London Borough Council, ex p Sampaio* (1999) 31 HLR 1. See also *Bernard v Enfield London Borough Council* [2001] EWCA Civ 1831, [2002] HLR 860, [2001] All ER (D) 27 (Dec) (notice

of decision on review did not have to contain arithmetical calculations of expenses of applicant); and *Akhtar v Birmingham City Council* [2011] EWCA Civ 383, [2011] HLR 474, [2011] All ER (D) 111 (Apr).

24 Ie under the Housing Act 1996 s 204: see PARA 509.

25 Housing Act 1996 s 203(5) (amended by the Crime and Courts Act 2013 s 17(5), Sch 9 para 52(1)(b), (2)). Notice of the decision must not be treated as given unless and until the provisions of the Housing Act 1996 s 203(5) and, where applicable, s 203(4) (see the text and note 23) are complied with: s 203(6).

508. Right to request review of a decision: Wales. An applicant[1] has the right to request a review of the following decisions:

(1)   a decision of a local housing authority[2] as to the applicant's eligibility for help;

(2)   a decision of a local housing authority that a duty is not owed to the applicant under the statutory provisions relating to duties to applicants who are homeless or threatened with homelessness[3];

(3)   a decision of a local housing authority that such a duty owed to the applicant[4] has come to an end (including where the authority has referred the applicant's case to another authority or decided that the conditions for referral are met)[5].

Where the duty owed to an applicant[6] to help secure accommodation has come to an end either at the end of a period of 56 days or, before the end of a period of 56 days if the local housing authority is satisfied that reasonable steps have been taken to help to secure that suitable accommodation is available for occupation by the applicant[7], an applicant has the right to request a review of whether or not reasonable steps were taken during the period in which the duty was owed to help to secure that suitable accommodation would be available for his occupation[8].

An applicant who is offered accommodation in, or in connection with, the discharge of any duty under Chapter 2 of Part 2 of the Housing (Wales) Act 2014[9] may request a review of the suitability of the accommodation offered to the applicant (whether or not he or she has accepted the offer)[10]. There is, however, no right to request a review of the decision reached on an earlier review[11]. A request for review must be made before the end of the period of 21 days (or such longer period as the authority may in writing allow) beginning with the day on which the applicant is notified of the authority's decision[12]. On a request being made to them, the authority or authorities concerned must review their decision[13].

The Welsh Ministers[14] may make provision by regulations as to the procedure to be followed in connection with a review under the provisions above[15]. Regulations may, for example:

(a)   require the decision on review to be made by a person of appropriate seniority who was not involved in the original decision; and

(b)   provide for the circumstances in which the applicant is entitled to an oral hearing, and whether and by whom the applicant may be represented at such a hearing; and

(c)   provide for the period within which the review must be carried out and notice given of the decision[16].

The authority, or as the case may be either of the authorities, concerned must notify[17] the applicant of the decision on the review[18]. The authority must also notify the applicant of the reasons for the decision, if the decision is:

(i)   to confirm the original decision on any issue against the interests of the applicant; or

(ii)   to confirm that reasonable steps were taken[19].

In any case they must inform the applicant of his right to appeal to the County Court on a point of law[20], and of the period within which such an appeal must be made[21].

Where it is decided on review of whether or not reasonable steps were taken to help to secure that suitable accommodation would be available for the applicant's occupation[22] or on an appeal of a decision[23] that reasonable steps were not taken, the duty to help secure accommodation[24] applies to the applicant again, with the modification that the 56-day period mentioned above is to be interpreted as starting on the day the authority notifies the applicant of its decision on review or, on an appeal, on such date as the court may order[25].

1 As to the meaning of 'applicant' see PARA 488 note 3; and see PARA 506 note 19.
2 As to the meaning of 'local housing authority' in relation to Wales see PARA 482 note 9. As to the meaning of 'local housing authority' in relation to England see PARA 11.
3 Ie under the Housing (Wales) Act 2014 s 66, 68, 73, or 75: see PARAS 490, 494, 501, 502.
4 Ie under the Housing (Wales) Act 2014 s 66, 68, 73, or 75.
5 Housing (Wales) Act 2014 s 85(1). As to where the authority has referred the applicant's case to another authority or decided that the conditions for referral are met see PARAS 504, 506.
6 Ie under the Housing (Wales) Act 2014 s 73.
7 Ie in the circumstances described in the Housing (Wales) Act 2014 s 74(2) or (3): see PARA 501.
8 Housing (Wales) Act 2014 s 85(2).
9 Ie the Housing (Wales) Act 2014 Pt 2 Ch 2 (ss 53–100).
10 Housing (Wales) Act 2014 s 85(3).
11 Housing (Wales) Act 2014 s 85(4).
12 Housing (Wales) Act 2014 s 85(5).
13 Housing (Wales) Act 2014 s 85(6).
14 As to the Welsh Ministers see PARA 7.
15 Housing (Wales) Act 2014 s 86(1). Such provision is made by the Homelessness (Review Procedure) (Wales) Regulations 2015, SI 2015/1266, which largely correspond to the Allocation of Housing and Homelessness (Review Procedures) Regulations 1999, SI 1999/71 (see PARA 507) (which are revoked in relation to Wales: see the Homelessness (Review Procedure) (Wales) Regulations 2015, SI 2015/1266, reg 8).
16 Housing (Wales) Act 2014 s 86(2).
     A request for a review under s 85 must be made to the authority, ie the local housing authority which made the decision whose review under s 85 has been requested, or the notifying authority if the decision was made under s 80(5) (a decision as to whether the conditions are met for the referral of a case to another local housing authority): Homelessness (Review Procedure) (Wales) Regulations 2015, SI 2015/1266, regs 1(3), 2(1). Except where a case falls within reg 4, the authority to which a request for a review has been made must within five working days of receipt of a request: (a) invite the applicant, and where relevant, the applicant's representative, to make representations orally or in writing or both orally and in writing; and (b) if it has not already done so, notify the applicant of the procedure to be followed in connection with the review: reg 2(2). Where a case falls within reg 4, the person appointed in accordance with that regulation must within five working days of appointment: (i) invite the applicant, and where relevant, the applicant's representative, to make representations orally or in writing or both orally and in writing; and (ii) notify the applicant of the procedure to be followed in connection with the review: reg 2(3). Where the decision of the authority on a review of an original decision made by an officer of the authority is also to be made by an officer, that officer must be someone who was not involved in the original decision: Homelessness (Review Procedure) (Wales) Regulations 2015, SI 2015/1266, reg 3.
     Where the original decision under the Housing (Wales) Act 2014 80(5) (whether the conditions are met for the referral of a case) was made under the Homelessness (Decisions on Referrals) Order 1998, SI 1998/1578 (see PARA 503), a review of that decision is (subject to the Homelessness (Review Procedure) (Wales) Regulations 2015, SI 2015/1266, reg 4(2)) to be carried out by a person appointed by the notifying authority and the notified authority: reg 4(1). If a person is not appointed in accordance with reg 4(1) within five working days from the day on which the request for a review is made, then the review is to be carried out by a person from the panel constituted in accordance with the Homelessness (Decisions on Referrals) Order 1998, SI 1998/1578, Schedule para 3 ('the panel') and appointed in accordance with the Homelessness (Review Procedure) (Wales) Regulations 2015, SI 2015/1266, reg 4(3): reg 4(2). The notifying authority must within five working days from the end of the period specified in reg 4(2) request the chair of the Welsh Local Government Association or the chair's nominee ('the proper officer') to appoint a person

from the panel and the proper officer must do so within seven days of the request: reg 4(3). The notifying authority and the notified authority must within five working days of the appointment of the person appointed ('the appointed person') provide the appointed person with the reasons for the original decision and the information and evidence on which that decision was based: reg 4(4). The appointed person must: (A) send to the notifying authority and the notified authority any representations made under reg 2; and (B) invite those authorities to respond to those representations: reg 4(5). The appointed person must not be the same person as the person who made the original decision: reg 4(6). The Homelessness (Decisions on Referrals) Order 1998, SI 1998/1578, has effect for the purpose of the Homelessness (Review Procedure) (Wales) Regulations 2015, SI 2015/1266, as if made under the powers conferred by the Housing (Wales) Act 2014 s 80(5)(b), (6)(b), and references in that Order to the Housing Act 1996 are to be construed as if referring to the equivalent provisions of the Housing (Wales) Act 2014: Homelessness (Review Procedure) (Wales) Regulations 2015, SI 2015/1266, reg 7.

In any case, the reviewer must, subject to compliance with the provisions of reg 6 (see note 17), consider any representations made under reg 2, and in a case falling within reg 4, any responses to them, and any representations made under reg 5(2): reg 5(1). If the reviewer considers there is a deficiency or irregularity in the original decision, or in the manner in which it was made, but is minded nonetheless to make a decision which is against the interests of the applicant on one or more issues, the reviewer must notify the applicant: (I) that the reviewer is so minded and the reasons why; and (II) that the applicant, or someone acting on the applicant's behalf, may make representations to the reviewer orally or in writing or both orally and in writing: reg 5(2).

'The reviewer' means, where the original decision is not made under the Housing (Wales) Act 2014 s 80(5), the authority; where the original decision is made under s 80(5) (a decision whether the conditions are met for the referral of a case), the notifying authority and the notified authority, where the review is carried out by those authorities or the person appointed to carry out the review in accordance with the Homelessness (Review Procedure) (Wales) Regulations 2015, SI 2015/1266, reg 4, where a case falls within reg 4: reg 1(3).

17 Notice required to be given to a person under the Housing (Wales) Act 2014 s 86 must be given in writing and, if not received by that person, is to be treated as having been given if it is made available at the authority's office for a reasonable period for collection by the person or on his behalf: s 86(7).

18 Housing (Wales) Act 2014 s 86(3). Notice of the decision is not to be treated as given unless and until s 86(5) (see the text to note 21), and where applicable s 86(4) (see the text to note 19), is complied with: s 86(6). The period within which notice of the decision on a review under s 85 must be given to the applicant is to be: (1) eight weeks from the day on which the request for the review is made, except where the original decision falls within heads (2) and (3); (2) ten weeks from the day on which the request for the review is made, where the original decision falls within s 80(5) and the review is carried by a person appointed by the notified and notifying authorities; (3) 12 weeks from the day on which the request for the review is made in a case falling within the Homelessness (Review Procedure) (Wales) Regulations 2015, SI 2015/1266, reg 4: reg 6(1). The period specified in reg 6(1) may be such longer period as the applicant and the reviewer may agree in writing: reg 6(2). In a case falling within head (3), the appointed person must notify the decision on the review, and the reasons for it, in writing to the notifying authority and the notified authority within a period of 11 weeks from the day on which the request for the review is made, or within a period commencing on that day which is one week shorter than that agreed in accordance with reg 6(2): reg 6(3).

19 Housing (Wales) Act 2014 s 86(4).

20 Ie under the Housing (Wales) Act 2014 s 88: see PARA 509.

21 Housing (Wales) Act 2014 s 86(5).

22 Ie under the Housing (Wales) Act 2014 s 85(2): see the text to notes 6–8.

23 Ie under the Housing (Wales) Act 2014 s 85.

24 Ie in the Housing (Wales) Act 2014 s 73.

25 Housing (Wales) Act 2014 s 87.

509. Right of appeal to County Court on a point of law. If an applicant[1] who has requested a review[2] is dissatisfied with the decision on the review, or is not notified of the decision on the review within the prescribed time[3], he may appeal to the County Court on any point of law arising from the decision or, as the case may be, the original decision[4]. An appeal must be brought within 21 days of the applicant being notified of the decision or, as the case may be, of the date on which he should have been notified of a decision on review[5].

On appeal the court may make such order confirming, quashing or varying the decision as it thinks fit[6].

Where the local housing authority[7] was under a duty[8] to secure that accommodation (or in Wales, suitable accommodation) is available for the applicant's occupation[9], or (in England) had the power to do so[10], the authority may secure that accommodation is so available during the period for appealing against the authority's decision, and, if an appeal is brought, until the appeal (and any further appeal) is finally determined[11].

The following provisions apply where an applicant has the right to appeal to the County Court against a local housing authority's decision on a review[12]. If the applicant is dissatisfied with a decision by the authority: (1) not to exercise its power to secure that accommodation (or suitable accommodation) is available during the appeal[13] in his case; (2) to exercise that power for a limited period ending before the final determination[14] by the County Court of his appeal ('the main appeal'); or (3) to cease exercising that power before that time, he may appeal to the County Court against the decision[15]. Such an appeal may not be brought after the final determination by the County Court of the main appeal[16]. On an appeal the court: (a) may order the authority to secure that accommodation is available for the applicant's occupation until the determination of the appeal (or such earlier time as the court may specify); and (b) must confirm or quash the decision appealed against[17], and in considering whether to confirm or quash the decision the court must apply the principles applied by the High Court on an application for judicial review[18]. If the court quashes the decision it may order the authority to exercise the power to secure accommodation in the applicant's case for such period as may be specified in the order[19]. Such an order may only be made if the court is satisfied that failure to exercise the power in accordance with the order would substantially prejudice the applicant's ability to pursue the main appeal, and may not specify any period ending after the final determination by the County Court of the main appeal[20].

1   As to the meaning of 'applicant' see PARAS 487 note 3, 505 note 16 (England); PARAS 488 note 3, 506 note 19 (Wales).
2   Ie under the Housing Act 1996 s 202 (see PARA 507) or the Housing (Wales) Act 2014 s 85 (see PARA 508).
3   Ie the time prescribed under the Housing Act 1996 s 203 (see PARA 507) or the Housing (Wales) Act 2014 s 86 (see PARA 508).
4   Housing Act 1996 s 204(1); Housing (Wales) Act 2014 s 88(1). As to the procedure applicable to appeals under the Housing Act 1996 s 204 see *Practice Direction—Statutory Appeals and Appeals subject to Special Provision* PD 52D para 28.1. As to appeals on a point of law generally see CIVIL PROCEDURE vol 12A (2015) PARA 1548 et seq. The right to appeal against review decisions taken under the Housing Act 1996 s 202 relating to when a local authority's duties arise in relation to persons who are homeless or threatened with homelessness includes the right to appeal against a review decision as to when such duties cease to exist: *Warsame v Hounslow London Borough Council* [2000] 1 WLR 696, 32 HLR 335, CA. There is no need for further review where a local authority appeals against a decision to quash a review of a decision that the applicant is intentionally homeless: *William v Wandsworth London Borough Council*; *Bellamy v Hounslow London Borough Council* [2006] EWCA Civ 535, [2006] HLR 809, [2006] All ER (D) 61 (May). See also *Richmond upon Thames Borough Council v Kubicek* [2012] EWCA Civ 3292 (QB), [2012] All ER (D) 321 (Nov).
5   Housing Act 1996 s 204(2); Housing (Wales) Act 2014 s 88(2). The court may give permission for an appeal to be brought after the end of the period allowed by these provisions, but only if it is satisfied: (1) where permission is sought before the end of that period, that there is a good reason for the applicant to be unable to bring the appeal in time; or (2) where permission is sought after that time, that there was a good reason for the applicant's failure to bring the appeal in time and for any delay in applying for permission: s 204(2A) (added by the Homelessness Act 2002 s 18(1), Sch 1 paras 2, 17(a)); Housing (Wales) Act 2014 s 88(3). The 21-day time limit runs from the date of the decision of the original review, even where there has been a subsequent review of the original review: *Demetri v Westminster City Council* [2000] 1 WLR 772, [1999] All ER (D) 1218, CA. When a County Court office is closed on the expiry of the 21-day time limit, the time limit is extended until the next day the office is open: *Aadan v Brent London Borough Council* (1999) 32

HLR 848, Times, 3 December, CA. Under CPR 2.3(1), the appeal is filed on its delivery at court, regardless of whether or not the court is open: *Van Aken v Camden London Borough Council* [2002] EWCA Civ 1724, [2003] 1 All ER 552, [2003] 1 WLR 684. The court's discretion to grant permission for an appeal to be brought out of time only arises where it is satisfied that there is a good reason for the delay: *Short v Birmingham City Council* [2004] EWHC 2112 (QB), [2005] HLR 66, [2004] All ER (D) 67 (Sep).

6 Housing Act 1996 s 204(3); Housing (Wales) Act 2014 s 88(4). See *Cramp v Hastings London Borough Council, Phillips v Camden London Borough Council* [2005] EWCA Civ 1005, [2005] 4 All ER 1014n, [2005] HLR 786 (it had not been open to the judge on either of two appeals to the County Court to hold that no reasonable authority would have refrained from making further inquiries as to whether the claimants were in priority need which the claimants contended that they should have made).

7 As to the meaning of 'local housing authority' in relation to England see PARA 11. As to the meaning of 'local housing authority' in relation to Wales see PARA 482 note 9.

8 Ie under the Housing Act 1996 s 188 (see PARA 493), s 190 (see PARA 496) or s 200 (see PARA 505) or under the Housing (Wales) Act 2014 s 68 (see PARA 494), s 75 (see PARA 502) or s 82 (see PARA 506).

9 As to the meaning of 'available for occupation' see PARAS 481 note 1. As to when accommodation is suitable see PARA 482 note 12.

10 Ie under the Housing Act 1996 s 195(8): see PARA 499.

11 Housing Act 1996 s 204(4) (amended by the Homelessness Act 2002 Sch 1 para 17(b)); Housing (Wales) Act 2014 s 88(5). Where, however, the authority decides not to exercise its discretion under the Housing Act 1996 s 188 in the applicant's favour, the County Court has no jurisdiction under s 204 to override the authority's discretionary power by means of a mandatory interim injunction requiring it to continue to provide accommodation for a person proceeding with an appeal: see *Ali v Westminster City Council, Nairne v Camden London Borough Council* [1999] 1 All ER 450, [1999] 1 WLR 384, CA. It is not normally appropriate to seek judicial review of a refusal to continue to secure accommodation pending the outcome of an appeal: *Ex p Nacion* (1999) Times, 3 February, CA. The provision of accommodation under the Housing Act 1996 s 204(4) is not necessary in order to enable a national of an accession state who has ceased work to look for new work in exercise of his rights under the Treaty on the Functioning of the European Union art 39: *Putans v Tower Hamlets London Borough Council* [2006] EWHC 1634 (Ch), [2007] HLR 126.

12 Housing Act 1996 s 204A(1) (s 204A added by the Homelessness Act 2002 s 11); Housing (Wales) Act 2014 s 89(1). As to the procedure applicable to appeals under the Housing Act 1996 s 204A see *Practice Direction—Statutory Appeals and Appeals subject to Special Provision* PD 52D para 28.1.

13 Ie under the Housing Act 1996 s 204(4) or the Housing (Wales) Act 2014 s 88(5): see the text to notes 7–11.

14 Ie under the Housing Act 1996 s 204(1) or the Housing (Wales) Act 2014 s 88(1): see the text to notes 1–4.

15 Housing Act 1996 s 204A(2) (as added: see note 12); Housing (Wales) Act 2014 s 89(2).

16 Housing Act 1996 s 204A(3) (as added: see note 12); Housing (Wales) Act 2014 s 89(3).

17 Housing Act 1996 s 204A(4) (as added: see note 12); Housing (Wales) Act 2014 s 89(4).

18 Housing Act 1996 s 204A(4) (as added: see note 12); Housing (Wales) Act 2014 s 89(5). When exercising its power under s 204A(4), the court must only consider whether the local authority has correctly directed itself in reaching its decision; it is not to consider the merits of the main appeal: *Francis v Kensington and Chelsea Royal London Borough Council* [2003] EWCA Civ 443, [2003] 2 All ER 1052, [2003] 1 WLR 2248. The exercise carried out in the County Court under the Housing Act 1996 s 204 is in substance the same as that of the High Court in judicial review and there is no jurisdiction for the court to act as a finder of the relevant primary facts for itself: *Bubb v Wandsworth London Borough Council* [2011] EWCA Civ 1285, [2012] LGR 94.

19 Housing Act 1996 s 204A(5) (as added: see note 12); Housing (Wales) Act 2014 s 89(6).

20 Housing Act 1996 s 204A(6) (as added: see note 12); Housing (Wales) Act 2014 s 89(7).

(v) Types of Accommodation to be Secured

510. In general: England and Wales. A local housing authority[1] in England may discharge its duty to secure accommodation only in one or other of the following ways:

(1)   by securing that suitable accommodation[2] provided by the authority is available[3];

(2)   by securing that the applicant obtains suitable accommodation from some other person[4]; or

(3)   by giving the applicant such advice and assistance as will secure that suitable accommodation is available from some other person[5].

The authority may require a person who is so accommodated to pay such reasonable charges as it may determine in respect of the accommodation secured for his occupation (either by making it available itself or otherwise), or to pay such reasonable amount as it may determine in respect of sums payable by it for accommodation made available by another person[6].

A local housing authority[7] in Wales may require a person in relation to whom it is discharging its functions under Chapter 2 of Part 2 of the Housing (Wales) Act 2014[8] to pay reasonable charges determined by the authority in respect of accommodation which it secures for the person's occupation (either by making it available itself or otherwise), or to pay a reasonable amount determined by the authority in respect of sums payable by it for accommodation made available by another person[9].

1   As to the meaning of 'local housing authority' see PARA 11 (definition applied by the Housing Act 1996 s 230).
2   As to when accommodation is suitable see PARA 481 note 13.
3   Housing Act 1996 ss 205, 206(1)(a) (s 205 amended by the Homelessness Act 2002 s 18(1), (2), Sch 1 paras 2, 18, Sch 2).
4   Housing Act 1996 s 206(1)(b).
5   Housing Act 1996 s 206(1)(c).
6   Housing Act 1996 s 206(2).
7   As to the meaning of 'local housing authority' in relation to Wales see PARA 482 note 9.
8   Ie the Housing (Wales) Act 2014 Pt 2 Ch 2 (ss 53–100).
9   Housing (Wales) Act 2014 s 90.

511. Out-of-area placements: England and Wales. So far as reasonably practicable, a local housing authority[1] in England must, in discharging its housing functions in respect of the homeless,[2] secure that accommodation is available for the occupation[3] of the applicant[4] in its district[5]. If the authority secures that accommodation is available for occupation outside its district, it must give notice to the local housing authority in whose district the accommodation is situated[6].

A local housing authority in Wales[7] must in discharging its functions relating to the homeless[8] secure or help to secure[9] that suitable accommodation[10] is available for the occupation[11] of the applicant[12] in its area, so far as is reasonably practicable[13]. If the authority secures that accommodation is available for the occupation of the applicant outside its area in Wales or England, it must give notice to the local housing authority (whether in Wales or England) in whose area the accommodation is situated[14].

This notice must state:

(1)   the name of the applicant;

(2)   the number and description of other persons who normally reside with him as a member of his family or might reasonably be expected to reside with him;

(3)   the address of the accommodation;

(4)   the date on which the accommodation was made available to him; and

(5)   which statutory function[15] the authority was discharging in securing that the accommodation is available for his occupation[16].

The notice must be in writing, and must be given within 14 days of the day on which the accommodation was made available to the applicant[17].

1 As to the meaning of 'local housing authority' see PARA 11 (definition applied by the Housing Act 1996 s 230).
2 Ie under the Housing Act 1996 Pt VII (ss 175–218).
3 As to when accommodation is available for occupation see PARA 481 note 1.
4 As to the meaning of 'applicant' see PARA 487 note 3.
5 Housing Act 1996 s 208(1). See *R (on the application of Calgin) v Enfield London Borough Council* [2005] EWHC 1716 (Admin), [2006] 1 All ER 112, [2006] LGR 1. See also *Nzolameso v City of Westminster* [2015] UKSC 22, [2015] 2 All ER 942 (authority could not show that offer of property out of district sufficient to discharge obligations under the Housing Act 1996) (discussed in Local News, Nicholas Dobson: 165 NLJ 7668, p 13).
6 Housing Act 1996 s 208(2).
7 As to the meaning of 'local housing authority' in relation to Wales see PARA 482 note 9.
8 Ie its functions under the Housing (Wales) Act 2014 Pt 2 Ch 2 (ss 53–100).
9 As to the meaning of 'help to secure' see PARA 489.
10 As to when accommodation is suitable see PARA 482 note 12.
11 As to when accommodation is available for occupation see PARA 482 note 1.
12 As to the meaning of 'applicant' see PARA 488 note 3; and see PARA 506 note 19.
13 Housing (Wales) Act 2014 s 91(1).
14 Housing (Wales) Act 2014 s 91(2).
15 Ie under the Housing Act 1996 Pt VII or the Housing (Wales) Act 2014 Pt 2 Ch 2.
16 Housing Act 1996 s 208(3); Housing (Wales) Act 2014 s 91(3).
17 Housing Act 1996 s 208(4); Housing (Wales) Act 2014 s 91(4).

512. Arrangements with private landlord: England and Wales. In pursuance of its interim duties in respect of the homeless[1], a local housing authority[2] may make arrangements with a private landlord[3] to provide accommodation[4]. In such a case, a tenancy granted to the applicant in pursuance of the arrangements cannot be an assured tenancy[5] before the end of the period of 12 months beginning with the date on which the applicant was notified of the authority's decision[6] or, if there is a review of that decision[7] or an appeal to the court[8], the date on which he is notified of the decision on review or the appeal is finally determined, unless, before or during that period, the tenant is notified by the landlord (or in the case of joint landlords, at least one of them) that the tenancy is to be regarded as an assured shorthold tenancy[9] or an assured tenancy other than an assured shorthold tenancy (that is a fully assured tenancy)[10].

1 Ie under the Housing Act 1996 s 188 (see PARA 493), s 190 (see PARA 496), s 200 (see PARA 505) or s 204(4) (see PARA 509) or the Housing (Wales) Act 2014 s 68 (see PARA 494), s 82 (see PARA 506) or s 88(5) (see PARA 509).
2 As to the meaning of 'local housing authority' in relation to England see PARA 11. As to the meaning of 'local housing authority' in relation to Wales see PARA 482 note 9.
3 'Private landlord' means a landlord who is not within the Housing Act 1985 s 80(1) (see LANDLORD AND TENANT vol 63 (2016) PARA 1037): Housing Act 1996 s 217(1) (amended by the Homelessness Act 2002 s 18(1), Sch 1 paras 2, 20); Housing (Wales) Act 2014 s 99.
4 See the Housing Act 1996 s 209(1) (s 209 substituted by the Homelessness Act 2002 s 18(1), Sch 1 paras 2, 19); and the Housing (Wales) Act 2014 s 92(1).
5 As to the meaning of 'assured tenancy' see LANDLORD AND TENANT vol 63 (2016) PARA 825.
6 Ie under the Housing Act 1996 s 184(3) (see PARA 487) or s 198(5) (see PARA 503) or the Housing (Wales) Act 2014 s 63(1) (see PARA 488) or s 80(5) (see PARA 504).
7 Ie under the Housing Act 1996 s 202 (see PARA 507) or the Housing (Wales) Act 2014 s 85 (see PARA 508).
8 Ie under the Housing Act 1996 s 204 or the Housing (Wales) Act 2014 s 88: see PARA 509.
9 As to the meaning of 'assured shorthold tenancy' see LANDLORD AND TENANT vol 63 (2016) PARA 852.
10 Housing Act 1996 s 209(2) (as substituted: see note 4); Housing (Wales) Act 2014 s 92(2).

513. Protection of property of homeless persons and persons threatened with homelessness: England and Wales. Where a local housing authority has reason to believe that there is danger of loss of, or damage to, any personal property[1] of an applicant by reason of his inability to protect it or deal with it, and that no other suitable arrangements have been or are being made, it may take certain steps for the protection of such property[2]. If the authority has become subject to a duty to accommodate the applicant[3], then, whether or not it is still subject to the duty, it must take reasonable steps to prevent the loss of the property or prevent or mitigate damage to it[4]. In England, if the authority has not become subject to such a duty, it may take any steps it considers reasonable for the purpose[5].

In Wales, a local housing authority may take any steps it considers reasonable for the purpose of protecting the personal property of an applicant who is eligible for help or prevent or mitigate damage to it if the authority has reason to believe that there is danger of loss of, or damage to, the property by reason of the applicant's inability to protect it or deal with it, and no other suitable arrangements have been or are being made[6].

For the above purposes, the authority may: (1) enter, at all reasonable times, any premises which are the usual place of residence of the applicant or which were his last usual place of residence; and (2) deal with any personal property of the applicant in any way which is reasonably necessary, in particular by storing it or arranging for its storage[7]. If the applicant asks the authority to move his property to a particular location, the authority may, if it appears to it that his request is reasonable, do so, but must inform him that this discharges the authority's duty in relation to that property[8]. If no such request is made (or, if made, is not acted upon), the authority ceases to have any duty or power to take action under these provisions when, in its opinion, there is no longer any reason to believe that there is a danger of loss of or damage to a person's personal property by reason of his inability to protect it or deal with it; but property stored by virtue of the authority's having taken such action may be kept in store and any conditions upon which it was taken into store continue to have effect, with any necessary modifications[9].

Where the authority ceases to be subject to a duty to take action under these provisions in respect of an applicant's property, or, having previously taken such action, ceases to have power to do so, the authority must notify the applicant of that fact and of the reason for it[10].

1   For this purpose, 'personal property' includes personal property of any person who might reasonably be expected to reside with the applicant: Housing Act 1996 ss 211(5), 212(6); Housing (Wales) Act 2014 ss 93(6), 94(10). See *Deadman v Southwark London Borough Council* (2000) 33 HLR 865 (decided under the similar provisions of the Housing Act 1985 s 70 (repealed)).

2   Housing Act 1996 s 211(1); Housing (Wales) Act 2014 s 93(1). See *Deadman v Southwark London Borough Council* (2000) 33 HLR 865 (decided under the similar provisions of the Housing Act 1985 s 70 (repealed)).

3   Ie under the Housing Act 1996 s 188 (see PARA 493), s 190 (see PARA 496), s 193 (see PARA 498), s 195 (see PARA 499) or s 200 (see PARA 505) or the Housing (Wales) Act 2014 s 66 (see PARA 490), s 68 (see PARA 494), s 75 (see PARA 502) or s 82 (see PARA 506). See *Deadman v Southwark London Borough Council* (2000) 33 HLR 865 (decided under the similar provisions of the Housing Act 1985 s 70 (repealed)).

4   Housing Act 1996 s 211(2); Housing (Wales) Act 2014 s 93(1)–(3). See *Deadman v Southwark London Borough Council* (2000) 33 HLR 865 (decided under the similar provisions of the Housing Act 1985 s 70 (repealed)).

    However, the authority may decline to take action under the Housing Act 1996 s 211 except upon such conditions as it considers appropriate in the particular case: s 211(4). The conditions may include the making and recovery by the authority of reasonable charges for the action taken, or the disposal by the authority, in such circumstances as may be specified, of property in relation to which it has taken action: s 211(4). The duty of a local housing authority under the Housing (Wales) Act 2014 s 93(1) is subject to any conditions it considers appropriate in the particular case, which may include conditions as to: (1) the making and recovery by the authority of reasonable charges for the action taken; or (2) the disposal by the authority, in such circumstances as may be specified, of property in relation to which it has taken action: s 93(4).

5   Housing Act 1996 s 211(3).
6   Housing (Wales) Act 2014 s 93(5).
7   Housing Act 1996 ss 211(6), 212(1); Housing (Wales) Act 2014 s 94(1). Where a local authority is proposing to exercise the power in s 94(1)(a) (head (1) in the text), the officer it authorises to do so must, upon request, produce valid documentation setting out the authorisation to do so: s 94(2). A person who, without reasonable excuse, obstructs the exercise of the power under s 94(1)(a) commits an offence and is liable on summary conviction to a fine not exceeding level 4 on the standard scale: s 94(3). As to the powers of magistrates' courts to issue fines on summary conviction see SENTENCING vol 92 (2015) PARA 176.
8   Housing Act 1996 s 212(2); Housing (Wales) Act 2014 s 94(4), (5).
9   Housing Act 1996 s 212(3); Housing (Wales) Act 2014 s 94(6), (7).
10 Housing Act 1996 s 212(4); Housing (Wales) Act 2014 s 94(8). The notification must be given to the applicant by delivering it to him, or by leaving it, or sending it to him, at his last known address: Housing Act 1996 s 212(5); Housing (Wales) Act 2014 s 94(9).

514. Co-operation between relevant housing authorities and bodies: England. Where a local housing authority[1] in England requests another relevant housing authority or body[2], in England, Wales or Scotland, to assist it in the discharge of its functions under Part VII of the Housing Act 1996[3], or requests a social services authority[4], in England, Wales or Scotland, to exercise any of its functions in relation to a case which the local housing authority is dealing with under that Part, the authority or body to whom the request is made must co-operate in rendering such assistance in the discharge of the functions to which the request relates as is reasonable in the circumstances[5].

1   As to the meaning of 'local housing authority' see PARA 11 (definition applied by the Housing Act 1996 s 230).
2   For these purposes, 'relevant housing authority or body' means:
    (1)   in relation to England and Wales, a local housing authority, a new town corporation, a private registered provider of social housing, a registered social landlord or a housing action trust;
    (2)   in relation to Scotland, a local authority, a development corporation, a registered housing association or Scottish Homes,
    and expressions used in head (1) have the same meaning as in the Housing Act 1985 and expressions used in head (2) have the same meaning as in the Housing (Scotland) Act 1987: Housing Act 1996 s 213(2) (amended by SI 2010/866). As to the meaning of 'new town corporation' see PARA 12; as to the meaning of 'private registered provider of social housing' see PARA 53; as to the meaning of 'registered social landlord' see PARA 13; and as to housing action trusts see PARA 537 et seq.
3   Ie under the Housing Act 1996 ss 175–218: see PARA 481 et seq.
4   As to the meaning of 'social services authority' see PARA 486 note 3. The functions of a social services authority under this provision are to be referred to a social services committee established under the Local Authority Social Services Act 1970 s 2: see s 2(1), Sch 1.
5   Housing Act 1996 s 213(1) (amended by the Housing (Wales) Act 2014 s 100, Sch 3 paras 2, 14). The Housing Act 1996 s 213(1) applies to a request by a local authority in Scotland under the Housing (Scotland) Act 1987 s 38 as it applies to a request by a local housing authority in England and Wales (the references to the Housing Act 1996 Pt VII being construed, in relation to such a request, as references to the Housing (Scotland) Act 1987 Pt II): Housing Act 1996 s 213(3). As to co-operation in certain cases involving children see PARA 516.

515. Co-operation between relevant housing authorities and bodies: Wales. A council of a county or county borough in Wales must make arrangements to promote co-operation between the officers of the authority who exercise its social services functions and those who exercise its functions as the local housing authority with a view to achieving the following objectives in its area:
    (1)   the prevention of homelessness;
    (2)   that suitable accommodation[1] is or will be available[2] for people who are or may become homeless[3];

(3)   that satisfactory support is available for people who are or may become homeless; and

(4)   the effective discharge of its functions[4] relating to homelessness[5].

The provisions set out below apply in relation to the following persons, whether in Wales or England:

(a)   a local housing authority[6];

(b)   a social services authority[7];

(c)   a registered social landlord[8];

(d)   a new town corporation[9];

(e)   a private registered provider of social housing[10];

(f)   a housing action trust[11].

The Welsh Ministers[12] may by order omit or add a person, or a description of a person, to this list (but may not add a minister of the Crown)[13].

If a local housing authority requests the co-operation of a specified person in the exercise of its functions relating to homelessness[14], or requests that a specified person provides it with information it requires for the purpose of the exercise of any of those functions, the person must comply with the request unless the person considers that doing so would be incompatible with the person's own duties or otherwise have an adverse effect on the exercise of the person's functions[15]. A person who decides not to comply with any such request must give the authority which made the request written reasons for the decision[16].

1   As to when accommodation is suitable see PARA 482 note 12.
2   As to when accommodation is available for occupation see PARA 482 note 1.
3   As to homelessness and threatened homelessness see PARA 482.
4   Ie under the Housing (Wales) Act 2014 Pt 2 (ss 50–100).
5   Housing (Wales) Act 2014 s 95(1).
6   As to the meaning of 'local housing authority' in relation to England see PARA 11. As to the meaning of 'local housing authority' in relation to Wales see PARA 482 note 9.
7   As to the meaning of 'social services authority' see PARA 486 note 3 (England); PARA 504 note 8 (Wales).
8   Ie within the meaning given by the Housing Act 1996 Pt I (ss A1–64): see PARA 13.
9   Ie within the meaning given in the Housing Act 1985 Pt I (ss 1–7): PARA 12.
10 Ie within the meaning given by the Housing and Regeneration Act 2008 Pt 2 (ss 59–278A): see PARA 53.
11 Housing (Wales) Act 2014 s 95(5), (8). The text refers to a housing action trust established under the Housing Act 1988 Pt III (ss 60–92): see PARA 537 et seq.
12 As to the Welsh Ministers see PARA 7.
13 Housing (Wales) Act 2014 s 95(6), (7).
14 Ie under the Housing (Wales) Act 2014 Pt 2.
15 Housing (Wales) Act 2014 s 95(2), (3).
16 Housing (Wales) Act 2014 s 95(4).

516. Co-operation in certain cases involving children: England and Wales. Where a local housing authority[1] has reason to believe that an applicant[2] with whom a person under the age of 18 normally resides, or might reasonably be expected to reside:

(1)   in relation to England, may be ineligible for assistance, may be homeless and may have become so intentionally, or may be threatened with homelessness intentionally; or

(2)   in relation to Wales, may be ineligible for help, may be homeless and that a duty to secure or help to secure accommodation[3] is not likely to apply to the applicant, or may be threatened with homelessness and that a duty to help to prevent the applicant from becoming homeless[4] is not likely to apply to the applicant,

the authority must make arrangements for ensuring that:

(a)   the applicant is invited to consent to the referral of the essential facts of his case to (in England) the social services authority for the district of the housing authority (where that is a different authority) or (in Wales), to the social services department[5]; and

(b)   if the applicant has given that consent, the social services authority or the social services department is made aware of those facts and of the subsequent decision of the housing authority in respect of his case[6].

In England, where the local housing authority and the social services authority for a district is the same authority (a 'unitary authority'), that authority must make arrangements for ensuring that, where these provisions apply, the applicant is invited to consent to the referral to the social services department[7] of the essential facts of his case and, if the applicant has given that consent, that the social services department is made aware of those facts and of the subsequent decision of the authority in respect of his case[8].

Nothing in the provisions described above[9] affects any other power to disclose information relating to the applicant's case to the social services authority or to the social services department (as the case may be) without the consent of the applicant[10].

In England, where a social services authority: (i) is aware of a decision of a local housing authority that the applicant is ineligible for assistance, became homeless intentionally or became threatened with homelessness intentionally; and (ii) requests the local housing authority to provide it with advice and assistance in the exercise of its social services functions[11], the local housing authority must provide it with such advice and assistance as is reasonable in the circumstances[12]. A unitary authority must make arrangements for ensuring that, where it makes a decision of a kind mentioned in head (i), the housing department[13] provides the social services department with such advice and assistance as the social services department may reasonably request[14].

In Wales, a council of a county or county borough must make arrangements for ensuring that, where it makes a decision as local housing authority that an applicant is ineligible for help, became homeless intentionally or became threatened with homelessness intentionally, its housing department[15] provides the social services department with such advice and assistance as the social services department may reasonably request[16].

1   As to the meaning of 'local housing authority' in relation to England see PARA 11. As to the meaning of 'local housing authority' in relation to Wales see PARA 482 note 9.
2   As to the meaning of 'applicant' see PARAS 487 note 3, 505 note 16 (England); PARAS 488 note 3, 506 note 19 (Wales).
3   Ie under the Housing (Wales) Act 2014 s 68 (se PARA 494), s 73 (see PARA 501) or s 75 (see PARA 502).
4   Ie under the Housing (Wales) Act 2014 s 66: see PARA 490.
5   'The social services department', in relation to the council of a county or county borough, means those persons responsible for the exercise of its social services functions under the Social Services and Well-being (Wales) Act 2014 Pt 3 (ss 19–31): Housing (Wales) Act 2014 s 96(5).
6   Housing Act 1996 s 213A(1), (2) (s 213A added by the Homelessness Act 2002 s 12; amended by SI 2016/413); Housing (Wales) Act 2014 s 96(1), (2).
7   In relation to a unitary authority, 'the social services department' means those persons responsible for the exercise of its social services functions under the Children Act 1989 Pt III (ss 17–30) or the Social Services and Well-being (Wales) Act 2014 Pt 6 (ss 74–125D): Housing Act 1996 s 213A(7) (as added (see note 6); amended by SI 2016/413).
8   Housing Act 1996 s 213A(3) (as added: see note 6).
9   Ie the Housing Act 1996 s 213A(2) or (3) or the Housing (Wales) Act 2014 s 96(2): see the text and notes 1–8.
10 Housing Act 1996 s 213A(4) (as added: see note 6); Housing (Wales) Act 2014 s 96(3). Local authorities do not have an additional duty under the Children Act 2004 s 11 to conduct an

assessment of the needs of children: *Mohamoud v Royal Borough of Kensington and Chelsea; Saleem v The Mayor and Burgesses of the London Borough of Wandsworth* [2015] EWCA Civ 780, [2015] All ER (D) 243 (Jul).

11 Ie under the Children Act 1989 Pt III or the Social Services and Well-being (Wales) Act 2014 Pt 6.
12 Housing Act 1996 s 213A(5) (as added (see note 6); amended by SI 2016/413).
13 In relation to a unitary authority, 'the housing department' means those persons responsible for the exercise of its housing functions: Housing Act 1996 s 213A(7) (as added: see note 6).
14 Housing Act 1996 s 213A(6) (as added: see note 6).
15 'The housing department', in relation to the council of a county or county borough, means those persons responsible for the exercise of its functions as local housing authority: Housing (Wales) Act 2014 s 96(5).
16 Housing (Wales) Act 2014 s 96(4).

(vi) Information

517. False statements, withholding information and failure to disclose change of circumstances. It is an offence for a person, with intent to induce a local housing authority[1] to believe in connection with the exercise of its functions relating to homelessness[2] that he or another person is entitled to accommodation or assistance in accordance with the relevant statutory provisions, or is entitled to accommodation or assistance of a particular description:

(1)   knowingly or recklessly to make a statement which is false in a material particular; or

(2)   knowingly to withhold information which the authority has reasonably required him to give in connection with the exercise of those functions[3].

If before an applicant[4] receives notification of the local housing authority's decision on his application there is any change of facts material to his case, he must notify the authority as soon as possible[5], and a person who fails to comply with this duty commits an offence unless he shows that he was not given the explanation required by statute or that he had some other reasonable excuse for non-compliance[6]. The authority must explain to every applicant, in ordinary language, the duty imposed on him by this provision and the effect of his failure to comply[7].

A person guilty of an offence under these provisions is liable to a penalty[8].

1 As to the meaning of 'local housing authority' in relation to England see PARA 11. As to the meaning of 'local housing authority' in relation to Wales see PARA 482 note 9.
2 Ie under the Housing Act 1996 Pt VII (ss 175–218) or the Housing (Wales) Act 2014 Pt 2 Ch 2 (ss 53–100): see PARA 481 et seq.
3 Housing Act 1996 s 214(1); Housing (Wales) Act 2014 s 97(1).
4 As to the meaning of 'applicant' see PARAS 487 note 3, 505 note 16 (England); PARAS 488 note 3, 506 note 19 (Wales).
5 Housing Act 1996 s 214(2); Housing (Wales) Act 2014 s 97(2).
6 Housing Act 1996 s 214(3); Housing (Wales) Act 2014 s 97(4), (5).
7 Housing Act 1996 s 214(2); Housing (Wales) Act 2014 s 97(3). Note also that the landlord may seek possession where a tenancy was granted as a result of a false statement made by the tenant: see the Housing Act 1985 s 84(2)(a), Sch 2, Ground 5; and LANDLORD AND TENANT vol 63 (2016) PARA 1145.
8 Housing Act 1996 s 214(4); Housing (Wales) Act 2014 s 97(6). The penalty on summary conviction is a fine not exceeding level 5 on the standard scale: see the Housing Act 1996 s 214(4); and the Housing (Wales) Act 2014 s 97(6). As to the powers of magistrates' courts to issue fines on summary conviction see SENTENCING vol 92 (2015) PARA 176.

(6) SITES FOR MOBILE HOMES: WALES

518. Power of local authorities to provide sites. A local authority[1] may within its area provide sites where mobile homes[2] may be brought, whether for holidays or other temporary purposes or for use as permanent residences, and may manage the sites or lease them to another person[3]. A local authority has power to do anything appearing to it desirable in connection with the provision of such sites and the things which it has power to do include (but are not limited to): (1) acquiring land which is in use as a mobile home site or which has been laid out as a mobile home site; (2) providing for the use of those occupying mobile home sites any services for their health or convenience; and (3) providing, in or in connection with sites for the accommodation of gypsies and travellers[4], working space and facilities for the carrying on of activities normally carried on by them[5]. In exercising its powers under these provisions a local authority must have regard to any standards specified[6] by the Welsh Ministers[7].

Before exercising the power to provide a site the local authority must consult the fire and rescue authority[8]: (a) as to measures to be taken for preventing and detecting the outbreak of fire on the site; and (b) as to the provision and maintenance of means of fighting fire on it[9].

A local authority must make in respect of sites managed by it, and of any services or facilities provided or made available under these provisions, such reasonable charges as it may determine[10]. A local authority may make available the services and facilities provided under these provisions for persons whether or not they normally reside in its area[11].

A local authority may, where it appears to it that a mobile home site or an additional mobile home site in needed in its area, or that land which is in use as a mobile home site should in the interests of the users of mobile homes be taken over by the local authority, acquire land, or any interest in land, compulsorily[12]. This power is exercisable in any particular case only if the local authority is authorised by the Welsh Ministers to exercise it[13].

A local authority does not have power under these provisions to provide mobile homes[14].

1 'Local authority' means the council of a Welsh county or county borough: Mobile Homes (Wales) Act 2013 s 62.
2 As to the meaning of 'mobile home' see the Mobile Homes (Wales) Act 2013 s 60; and LANDLORD AND TENANT vol 64 (2016) PARA 1762 note 1.
3 Mobile Homes (Wales) Act 2013 s 56(1).
4 'Gypsies and travellers' means: (1) persons of a nomadic habit of life, whatever their race or origin, including: (a) persons who, on grounds only of their own or their family's or dependant's educational needs or old age, have ceased to travel temporarily or permanently; and (b) members of an organised group of travelling show people or circus people (whether or not travelling together as such); and (2) all other persons with a cultural tradition of nomadism or of living in a mobile home: Mobile Homes (Wales) Act 2013 s 62 (definition amended by the Housing (Wales) Act 2014 s 110, Sch 3 para 26(1), (2)).
5 Mobile Homes (Wales) Act 2013 s 56(2).
6 Ie under the Mobile Homes (Wales) Act 2013 s 10: see PLANNING.
7 Mobile Homes (Wales) Act 2013 s 56(3). As to the Welsh Ministers see PARA 7.
8 'Fire and rescue authority', in relation to any land, means the fire and rescue authority under the Fire and Rescue Services Act 2004 for the area in which the land is situated: Mobile Homes (Wales) Act 2013 s 62 (definition added by the Housing (Wales) Act 2014 s 141, Sch 3 para 30(1), (4)).
9 Mobile Homes (Wales) Act 2013 s 56(4).
10 Mobile Homes (Wales) Act 2013 s 56(5).
11 Mobile Homes (Wales) Act 2013 s 56(6).
12 Mobile Homes (Wales) Act 2013 s 56(7). The Acquisition of Land Act 1981 (see COMPULSORY ACQUISITION OF LAND vol 18 (2009) PARA 501 et seq) has effect in relation to the acquisition of land, or an interest in land, under the Mobile Homes (Wales) Act 2013 s 56(7): s 56(9).
13 Mobile Homes (Wales) Act 2013 s 56(8).
14 Mobile Homes (Wales) Act 2013 s 56(10).

519. Power to prohibit mobile homes on commons. The following provisions apply to any land in Wales which is or forms part of a common[1] and is not: (1) land subject to public access rights[2]; (2) land subject to a scheme for its regulation and management[3]; or (3) land as respects which a site licence[4] is for the time being in force[5]. A local authority[6] may make with respect to land to which these provisions apply and which is in its area an order prohibiting, either absolutely or except in such circumstances as may be specified in the order, the stationing of mobile homes[7] on the land for the purposes of human habitation[8].

A person who stations a mobile home on any land in contravention of such an order for the time being in force with respect to the land commits an offence[9]. A local authority must take all reasonable steps to secure that copies of any order which is for the time being in force with respect to any land in its area are displayed on the land so as to give persons entering the land warning of the existence of the order[10]. A local authority has the right to place on the land the notices that it considers necessary for the performance of this duty[11].

An order made by a local authority prohibiting the stationing of mobile homes may be revoked at any time by a subsequent order made[12] by the local authority or may be varied so as to exclude any land from the operation of the order or so as to introduce any exception, or further exception, from the prohibition imposed by the order[13]. Where the whole or part of any land to which an order is in force ceases to be land to which these provisions apply, the order ceases to have effect with respect to the land or that part of it[14]. Where an order ceases to have effect with respect to part only of any land, the local authority must cause any copy of the order which is displayed on that part of the land with respect to which the order remains in force to be amended accordingly[15].

1   In the Mobile Homes (Wales) Act 2013 s 57, 'common' includes any land subject to be enclosed under the Inclosure Acts 1845 to 1882 and any town or village green: Mobile Homes (Wales) Act 2013 s 57(11). See generally COMMONS.
2   Ie land to which the Law of Property Act 1925 s 193 (see COMMONS vol 13 (2009) PARA 581) applies.
3   Ie under the Commons Act 1899 Pt I (ss 1–15): see COMMONS vol 13 (2009) PARAS 427, 590 et seq.
4   Ie a licence under the Mobile Homes (Wales) Act 2013 Pt 2 (ss 4–39): see ss 5(1), 62; and PLANNING.
5   Mobile Homes (Wales) Act 2013 s 57(1).
6   As to the meaning of 'local authority' see PARA 518 note 1.
7   As to the meaning of 'mobile home' see the Mobile Homes (Wales) Act 2013 s 60; and LANDLORD AND TENANT vol 64 (2016) PARA 1762 note 1.
8   Mobile Homes (Wales) Act 2013 s 57(2). Schedule 3 makes further provision with respect to orders under s 57(2): s 57(10). See Sch 3 paras 1–6.
9   Mobile Homes (Wales) Act 2013 s 57(3). A person guilty of an offence under s 57(3) is liable on summary conviction to a fine not exceeding level 1 on the standard scale: s 57(4). As to the powers of magistrates' courts to issue fines on summary conviction see SENTENCING vol 92 (2015) PARA 176.
10 Mobile Homes (Wales) Act 2013 s 57(5).
11 Mobile Homes (Wales) Act 2013 s 57(6).
12 Ie under the Mobile Homes (Wales) Act 2013 s 57(2).
13 Mobile Homes (Wales) Act 2013 s 57(7).
14 Mobile Homes (Wales) Act 2013 s 57(8).
15 Mobile Homes (Wales) Act 2013 s 57(9).

3. LARGE SCALE VOLUNTARY TRANSFERS

520. In general. Under powers contained in the Housing Act 1985, local authorities may dispose of or sell land and dwellings with the consent of the appropriate national authority[1]. Following amendments made by the Housing and Planning Act 1986 and further amendments made by the Housing Act 1988, a local authority which is contemplating such a disposal must carry out a consultation exercise with the tenants who will be affected by the disposal[2]. These disposals are known as 'large scale voluntary transfers'. In the case of transfers on or after 15 January 1989, the tenants transferred cease to be secure tenants and become assured tenants of the new landlord instead with a preserved right to buy[3]. Following amendments made by the Housing and Regeneration Act 2008 a requirement to co-operate with a tenant group may be imposed on a local housing authority in relation to certain disposals[4].

As well as the powers to sell dwellings which are held by a local authority for housing purposes under Part II of the Housing Act 1985[5], local authorities which own dwellings which were not built or acquired under Part II also have a separate power to sell[6].

Further changes were made with the passage of the Leasehold Reform, Housing and Urban Development Act 1993, which by amendments provides for central government to have a 20 per cent levy on the net proceeds of sale of housing under these powers[7].

1   See the Housing Act 1985 ss 32–34, 43; and PARA 522 et seq. As to the appropriate national authority, ie the Secretary of State or, where statutory functions have been transferred in relation to Wales, the Welsh Ministers, see PARA 7.
2   See PARA 524.
3   The preserved right to buy provisions are contained in the Housing Act 1985 ss 171A–171H: see PARA 334 et seq.
4   See the Housing Act 1985 s 34A; and PARA 525. See also Housing Transfer Manual Period to 31 March 2016 (Department for Communities and Local Government, HCA and Mayor of London, 2014).
5   Ie the Housing Act 1985 Pt II (ss 8–57).
6   As to the power to sell dwellings held for housing purposes see the Housing Act 1985 ss 32–34A; and as to the power to sell dwellings not built or acquired under Pt II see s 43. See further PARAS 522 et seq, 531.
7   See PARA 526.

521. Power of bodies corporate to sell or let land for housing purposes. A body corporate holding land may sell, exchange or lease[1] the land for the purpose of providing housing of any description at such price, or for such consideration, or for such rent, as having regard to all the circumstances of the case is the best that can reasonably be obtained, notwithstanding that a higher price, consideration or rent might have been obtained if the land were sold, exchanged or leased for the purpose of providing housing of another description or for a purpose other than the provision of housing[2].

1   As to the meaning of 'lease' see PARA 31 note 3.
2   Housing Act 1985 s 31.

522. Power to dispose of land held for housing purposes. Without prejudice to the statutory provisions relating to the right to buy[1], a local authority[2] has power by these provisions, and not otherwise, to dispose of land which is held by the authority for certain housing purposes[3]. Such a disposal may be effected in any manner but may not be made without the consent of the appropriate national authority, whether general or specific[4]. No consent is, however, required for the letting[5] of land under a secure tenancy[6] or an introductory tenancy[7] or under what would be a secure tenancy but for certain statutory provisions[8].

The grant of an option to purchase the freehold of, or any other interest in, land is a disposal for these purposes and a consent given to such a disposal extends to a disposal made in pursuance of the option[9].

The statutory requirements[10] whereby surplus land is first to be offered to the original owner and to adjoining land-owners do not apply to the sale by a local authority of land held by the authority for the relevant housing purposes[11].

On the disposal of a house under these provisions by way of sale or by the grant or assignment of a lease[12] at a premium, the local authority may agree to the price or premium, or part of it, and any expenses incurred by the purchaser, being secured by a mortgage of the premises[13].

A disposal made without the consent of the appropriate national authority is void unless it is to an individual (or to two or more individuals) and the disposal does not extend to any other house[14].

1 Ie the Housing Act 1985 Pt V (ss 118–188): see PARA 230 et seq.
2 As to the meaning of 'local authority' see PARA 12.
3 Housing Act 1985 s 32(1) (amended by the Housing Act 1988 s 140(1), Sch 17 para 38; and the Housing Act 1996 s 227, Sch 19 Pt IX). The purposes referred to in the text are those of the Housing Act 1985 Pt II (ss 8–57).
4 Housing Act 1985 s 32(2). As to consents see PARA 524. As to the appropriate national authority, ie the Secretary of State or, where statutory functions have been transferred in relation to Wales, the Welsh Ministers, see PARA 7. In relation to England, the Secretary of State must consult the Regulator of Social Housing before deciding whether to consent under s 32 to anything within the regulator's remit: s 32(6) (added by SI 2010/844). As to the Regulator of Social Housing see PARA 57 et seq. As to what is within the regulator's remit see PARA 408 note 2.
5 As to the meaning of 'letting' see PARA 31 note 3.
6 As to the meaning of 'secure tenancy' see LANDLORD AND TENANT vol 63 (2016) PARA 1037.
7 As to introductory tenancies see PARA 472.
8 See the Housing Act 1985 s 32(3) (amended by SI 1997/74). The statutory provisions referred to in the text are any of the provisions of the Housing Act 1985 Sch 1 paras 2–12: see LANDLORD AND TENANT vol 63 (2016) PARA 1046 et seq.
9 Housing Act 1985 s 32(4).
10 Ie the Lands Clauses Consolidation Act 1845 ss 128–132: see COMPULSORY ACQUISITION OF LAND vol 18 (2009) PARA 901 et seq.
11 Housing Act 1985 s 32(5). The purposes referred to in the text are those of Pt II.
12 As to the meaning of 'lease' see PARA 31 note 3.
13 Housing Act 1985 s 437.
14 Housing Act 1985 s 44(1). See also PARA 524 note 10.

523. Covenants and conditions which may be imposed. On a disposal of land held for housing purposes[1] the local authority[2] may impose such covenants and conditions as it thinks fit[3], but, with certain exceptions[4], a condition of any of the following kinds may be imposed only with the consent of the appropriate national authority[5]:

(1) a condition limiting the price or premium which may be obtained on a further disposal of a house[6];

(2) in the case of a sale, a condition reserving a right of pre-emption[7];

(3) in the case of a lease[8], a condition precluding the lessee from assigning the lease or granting a sub-lease[9].

1 Ie a disposal under the Housing Act 1985 s 32: see PARA 522.
2 As to the meaning of 'local authority' see PARA 12.
3 Housing Act 1985 s 33(1).
4 Ie subject to the Housing Act 1985 s 36A (right of first refusal for local authority: see PARA 529) and s 37 (restriction on disposal of dwelling houses in national parks, etc: see PARA 530).
5 Housing Act 1985 s 33(2) (amended by the Housing Act 2004 s 197(2)). As to consents see PARA 524. As to the appropriate national authority, ie the Secretary of State or, where statutory functions have been transferred in relation to Wales, the Welsh Ministers, see PARA 7. In relation to England, the Secretary of State must consult the Regulator of Social Housing before deciding whether to consent under the Housing Act 1985 s 33 to anything within the regulator's remit:

s 33(5) (added by SI 2010/844). As to the Regulator of Social Housing see PARA 57 et seq. As to what is within the regulator's remit see PARA 408 note 2.

A restrictive covenant by a local authority which effectively prevents the authority from creating any new lettings on that part of the estate retained by it, except by the grant of long leases on payment of premium, does not constitute an impermissible fetter on the authority's duty to provide public housing accommodation in its district: *R v Hammersmith and Fulham London Borough Council, ex p Beddowes* [1987] QB 1050, [1987] 1 All ER 369, CA. Where a condition is a right of pre-emption, it is registrable as a Class C(iv) land charge, and if it is so registered it takes priority over a mortgage granted subsequent to the registration: *First National Securities Ltd v Chiltern District Council* [1975] 2 All ER 766, [1975] 1 WLR 1075.

6   Housing Act 1985 s 33(2)(a). As to the meaning of 'house' see PARA 405 note 6.

7   Housing Act 1985 s 33(2)(b). For these purposes, a condition reserving a right of pre-emption means a condition precluding the purchaser from selling or leasing the land unless: (1) he first notifies the authority of the proposed sale or lease and offers to sell or lease the land to the authority; and (2) the authority refuses the offer or fails to accept it within one month after it is made: s 33(3). References in s 33 to the purchaser or lessee include references to his successors in title and any person deriving title under him or his successors in title: s 33(4).

8   As to the meaning of 'lease' see PARA 31 note 3.

9   Housing Act 1985 s 33(2)(c).

524. Consents required on disposal of land held for housing purposes. The appropriate national authority's consent[1] may be given either generally to all local authorities[2] or to a particular authority or description of authority[3], and either in relation to particular land or in relation to land of a particular description[4]. Consent may be given subject to conditions[5] and may, in particular, be given subject to conditions as to the price, premium or rent to be obtained on the disposal, including conditions as to the amount by which on the disposal of a house[6] by way of sale or by the grant or assignment of a lease[7] at a premium, the price or premium is to be, or may be, discounted by the local authority[8].

The matters to which the appropriate national authority may have regard in determining whether to give consent and, if so, to what conditions consent should be subject include:

(1)   the extent (if any) to which the person to whom the proposed disposal is to be made ('the intending purchaser') is, or is likely to be, dependent upon, controlled by or subject to influence from the local authority making the disposal or any members or officers of that authority;

(2)   the extent (if any) to which the proposed disposal would result in the intending purchaser becoming the predominant or a substantial owner in any area of housing accommodation[9] let on tenancies or subject to licences;

(3)   the terms of the proposed disposal;

(4)   in the case of a proposed large scale disposal[10], the appropriate national authority's estimate of the exchequer costs[11] of the large scale disposal;

(5)   any reduction in the amount that the local authority may be required to pay to the Secretary of State in respect of vacant higher value housing in England[12] as a result of the disposal; and

(6)   any other matters whatsoever which the appropriate national authority considers relevant[13].

A disposal of a house by a local authority made without the required consent is void, unless the disposal is to an individual (or to two or more individuals), and the disposal does not extend to any other house[14].

A local authority which is disposing of an interest in land as a result of which a secure tenant[15] or an introductory tenant[16] of the authority will become the tenant of a private sector landlord is first required to consult with that tenant[17].

1 Ie under the Housing Act 1985 s 32 (see PARA 522) or s 33 (see PARA 523). As to the appropriate national authority, ie the Secretary of State or, where statutory functions have been transferred in relation to Wales, the Welsh Ministers, see PARA 7.

2 As to the meaning of 'local authority' see PARA 12.

3 A description of an authority may be framed by reference to any circumstances whatever: Housing Act 1985 s 34(4AC)(c) (s 34(4AA)–(4AE) added by the Housing and Regeneration Act 2008 s 311, Sch 14 para 1(1), (2)(c)).

4 Housing Act 1985 s 34(1), (2) (s 34(1) amended by the Housing and Regeneration Act 2008 Sch 14 para 1(2)(a)).

5 Housing Act 1985 s 34(3).

6 As to the meaning of 'house' see PARA 405 note 6.

7 As to the meaning of 'lease' see PARA 31 note 3.

8 Housing Act 1985 s 34(4).

9 As to the meaning of 'housing accommodation' see PARA 13 note 1.

10 'Large scale disposal' means a disposal of one or more dwelling houses by a local authority to a person where:

   (1) the number of dwelling houses included in the disposal; and

   (2) the number of dwelling houses which, in the relevant period, have previously been disposed of by the authority to that person, or that person and any of the person's associates taken together,

   exceeds 499 or, if the appropriate national authority by order so provides, such other number as may be specified in the order: Housing Act 1985 s 34(4AB) (as added: see note 3). 'Dwelling house' has the same meaning as in Pt V (ss 118–188) (see PARA 231) except that it does not include a hostel or any part of a hostel: s 34(4AB) (as so added). 'The relevant period', in relation to a large scale disposal means the period of five years ending with the date of the disposal or, if the appropriate national authority by order so provides, such other period ending with that date as may be specified in the order: s 34(4AB) (as so added). Two persons are associates of each other if: (a) one of them is a subsidiary of the other; (b) they are both subsidiaries of some other person; or (c) there exists between them such relationship or other connection as may be specified in a determination made by the appropriate national authority: s 34(4AC)(b) (as so added). 'Subsidiary' has the same meaning as in the Housing Act 1996 s 61 (see PARA 200 note 9) but as if references in s 61(2) and s 60 to registered social landlords and landlords were references to housing associations (within the meaning of the Housing Associations Act 1985): Housing Act 1985 s 34(4AB) (as so added). An order made by the appropriate national authority under s 34: (i) is to be made by statutory instrument which, in the case of an order made by the Secretary of State, is subject to annulment in pursuance of a resolution of either House of Parliament and, in the case of an order made by the Welsh Ministers, is subject to annulment in pursuance of a resolution of the National Assembly for Wales; (ii) may make different provision for different cases or descriptions of case, or for different authorities or descriptions of authority; and (iii) may contain such transitional and supplementary provisions as appear to the appropriate national authority to be necessary or expedient: s 34(4AD) (as so added). A determination under s 34 may make different provision for different cases or descriptions of case, or for different authorities or descriptions of authority, and may be varied or revoked by a subsequent determination: s 34(4AE) (as so added).

   For the purposes of s 34, a disposal of any dwelling house is to be disregarded if at the time of the disposal the local authority's interest in the dwelling house is or was subject to a long lease: s 34(4AC)(a) (as so added). 'Long lease' means a lease for a term of years certain exceeding 21 years other than a lease which is terminable before the end of that term by notice given by or to the landlord: s 34(4AB) (as so added).

11 'The exchequer costs', in relation to a large scale disposal, means any increase which is or may be attributable to the disposal in the aggregate of any housing subsidies; and 'housing subsidies' means any subsidies payable under the Social Security Administration Act 1992 s 140A (subsidy: see WELFARE BENEFITS AND STATE PENSIONS vol 104 (2014) PARA 333) or the Local Government and Housing Act 1989 s 79 (housing revenue account subsidy: see PARA 374): Housing Act 1985 s 34(4AB) (as added: see note 3). The estimate is to be based on such assumptions (including as to the period during which housing subsidies may be payable) as the appropriate national authority may determine, regardless of whether those assumptions are, or are likely to be, borne out by events: s 34A(4AA) (as so added).

12 Ie under the Housing and Planning Act 2016 s 69: see PARA 363.

13 Housing Act 1985 s 34(4A) (added by the Housing Act 1988 s 132(1), (2), (8); and amended by the Housing and Regeneration Act 2008 Sch 14 para 1(2)(b); and the Housing and Planning Act

2016 s 77(1), (2)). See *Swords v Secretary of State for Communities and Local Government* [2007] EWCA Civ 795, [2008] HR 271, [2007] LGR 757 (not unreasonable for Secretary of State to consider views of leaseholders but then attach no weight to them).

14 Housing Act 1985 s 44(1). Section 44(1) has effect notwithstanding the Town and Country Planning Act 1959 s 29 and the Local Government Act 1972 s 128(2) (protection of purchasers dealing with authority: see LOCAL GOVERNMENT vol 69 (2009) PARA 529): Housing Act 1985 s 44(2). For the purposes of s 44, 'house' does not have the extended meaning applicable by virtue of the definition of 'housing accommodation' in s 56 (see PARA 13 note 1), but includes a flat: s 44(3).

15 As to the meaning of 'secure tenancy' see LANDLORD AND TENANT vol 63 (2016) PARA 1037.

16 As to introductory tenancies see PARA 472.

17 See the Housing Act 1985 s 106A(1), Sch 3A (added by the Housing and Planning Act 1986 s 6(2), (3), Sch 1); and PARA 448 et seq.

525. Requirements to co-operate in relation to certain disposals. The appropriate national authority[1] may make regulations for imposing requirements on a local housing authority[2] in any case where a tenant group[3] serves written notice on the authority proposing that the authority should dispose of particular land held by it for the purposes of Part II of the Housing Act 1985[4], or a particular description of such land, to a relevant housing provider[5].

The regulations may make provision requiring the local housing authority:

(1)   to provide, or finance the provision of, such office accommodation and facilities, and such training, as the tenant group reasonably requires for the purpose of pursuing the proposal;

(2)   to arrange for such feasibility studies with respect to the proposal as may be determined by or under the regulations to be conducted by such persons as may be so determined;

(3)   to provide to the tenant group such information or descriptions of information, in connection with the proposal, as may be prescribed in the regulations;

(4)   to take, in circumstances prescribed in the regulations, such other steps as may be so prescribed to co-operate with the tenant group in connection with the proposal;

(5)   to arrange for such ballots or polls with respect to the proposal as may be determined by or under the regulations to be conducted by such persons as may be so determined; and

(6)   in such circumstances as may be prescribed by the regulations, to enter into an agreement for the disposal[6].

The regulations may make provision:

(a)   for determining the houses[7] and other land to which the disposal should relate, and the amounts which should be paid in respect of the disposal;

(b)   requiring the agreement for the disposal to be in such form as may be approved by the appropriate national authority and to contain such provisions as may be prescribed by the regulations[8].

1   Ie the Secretary of State or, where statutory functions have been transferred in relation to Wales, the Welsh Ministers: see PARA 7.

2   As to the meaning of 'local housing authority' see PARA 11.

3   'Tenant group' means a body or other person which satisfies such conditions as may be determined by or under the regulations mentioned in the text: Housing Act 1985 s 34A(9) (s 34A added by the Housing and Regeneration Act 2008 s 296).

4   Ie the Housing Act 1985 Pt II (ss 8–57).

5   Housing Act 1985 s 34A(1) (as added: see note 3). 'Relevant housing provider' means: (1) in relation to England, a private registered provider of social housing; and (2) in relation to Wales, a registered social landlord: s 34A(9) (definition amended by SI 2010/844). As to the meaning of 'private registered provider of social housing' see PARA 53; and as to the meaning of 'registered

social landlord' see PARA 13. The Housing Act 1985 s 34A does not affect any requirement under s 32 (see PARA 522) or s 33 (see PARA 523) for the consent of the Secretary of State or the Welsh Ministers: s 34A(7) (as so added).

Regulations under s 34A: (a) may make different provision with respect to different cases or descriptions of case, including different provision for different areas; and (b) are to be made by statutory instrument which, in the case of an instrument made by the Secretary of State, is subject to annulment in pursuance of a resolution of either House of Parliament and, in the case of an instrument made by the Welsh Ministers, is subject to annulment in pursuance of a resolution of the National Assembly for Wales: s 34A(8) (as so added).

As to regulations made under s 34A see the Housing (Right to Transfer from a Local Authority Landlord) (England) Regulations 2013, SI 2013/2898.

6   Housing Act 1985 s 34A(2) (as added: see note 3).
7   As to the meaning of 'house' see PARA 405 note 6.
8   Housing Act 1985 s 34A(3) (as added: see note 3). The regulations may make such procedural, incidental, supplementary and transitional provisions as may appear to the appropriate national authority necessary or expedient, and may in particular make provision: (1) for particular questions arising under the regulations to be determined by the local housing authority or the appropriate national authority; (2) setting time-limits for the carrying out of requirements under the regulations; (3) requiring any person exercising functions under the regulations to act in accordance with any guidance or directions given by the appropriate national authority: s 34A(4) (as so added). Nothing in s 34A(2)–(4) is to be taken as prejudicing the generality of s 34A(1): s 34A(5) (as so added). Any regulations which provide for the appropriate national authority to approve a proposal for a local housing authority to dispose of land must ensure that the authority has the opportunity to make representations to the appropriate national authority before the appropriate national authority decides whether or not to approve the proposal: s 34A(6) (as so added).

526. Levy on disposals. A local authority[1] which makes a disposal after 20 July 1993 which is or includes, or which subsequently becomes or includes, a qualifying disposal[2] is liable to pay to the appropriate national authority a levy of an amount calculated[3] in accordance with the statutory formula[4]. The administrative arrangements for the payment of any such levy are such as may be specified in a determination made by the appropriate national authority[5], and such a determination may in particular make provision as to:

(1)   the information to be supplied by authorities;
(2)   the form and manner in which, and the time within which, the information is to be supplied;
(3)   the payment of the levy in stages in such circumstances as may be provided in the determination;
(4)   the date on which payment of the levy (or any stage payment of the levy) is to be made;
(5)   the adjustment of any levy which has been paid in such circumstances as may be provided in the determination;
(6)   the payment of interest in such circumstances as may be provided in the determination; and
(7)   the rate or rates (whether fixed or variable, and whether or not calculated by reference to some other rate) at which such interest is to be payable[6].

Any such administrative arrangements are binding on local authorities[7] and any amounts by way of levy or interest which are not paid to the appropriate national authority as required by those arrangements are recoverable in a court of competent jurisdiction[8].

Any sums received by the appropriate national authority under these provisions must be paid into the Consolidated Fund and any sums paid by the appropriate national authority by way of adjustment of levies paid thereunder must be paid out of money provided by Parliament[9].

1 As to the meaning of 'local authority' see PARA 12 (definition applied by the Leasehold Reform, Housing and Urban Development Act 1993 s 136(14) (substituted by the Housing and Regeneration Act 2008 s 311, Sch 14 para 3(1), (3))).

2 For these purposes, a disposal of one or more dwelling houses by a local authority to any person (a 'disposal') is a qualifying disposal if: (1) it requires the consent of the appropriate national authority under the Housing Act 1985 s 32 (power to dispose of land held for the purposes of Pt II (ss 8–57): see PARA 522) or s 43 (consent required for certain disposals not within s 32: see PARA 531); and (2) the aggregate of the following, namely: (a) the number of dwelling houses included in the disposal; and (b) the number of dwelling houses which, within the relevant period, have been previously disposed of by the authority to that person, or that person and any associates of his taken together, exceeds 499 or, if the appropriate national authority by order so provides, such other number as may be specified in the order: Leasehold Reform, Housing and Urban Development Act 1993 s 136(1). For these purposes, 'relevant period' means: (i) any period of five years beginning after 20 July 1993 and including the date of the disposal; or (ii) if the appropriate national authority by order so provides, any such other period beginning after 20 July 1993 and including that disposal date as may be specified in the order: s 136(2). For the purposes of s 136, two persons are associates of each other if: (A) one of them is a subsidiary of the other; (B) they are both subsidiaries of some other person; or (C) there exists between them such relationship or other connection as may be specified in a determination made by the appropriate national authority: s 136(15)(b) (s 136(15) added by the Housing and Regeneration Act 2008 Sch 14 para 3(3)). See also, as to references to the Secretary of State, the Housing and Regeneration Act 2008 Sch 14 para 3(5). 'Subsidiary' has the same meaning as in the Housing Act 1996 s 61 (see PARA 200 note 9) but as if references in s 61(2) and s 60 to registered social landlords and landlords were references to housing associations (within the meaning of the Housing Associations Act 1985): Leasehold Reform, Housing and Urban Development Act 1993 s 136(14) (as substituted: see note 1). As to the appropriate national authority, ie the Secretary of State or, where statutory functions have been transferred in relation to Wales, the Welsh Ministers, see PARA 7.

Before making an order under s 136, the appropriate national authority must consult such representatives of local government as appear to it to be appropriate: s 136(11). An order under s 136 must be made by statutory instrument subject to annulment in pursuance of a resolution of either House of Parliament or, in relation to Wales, of the National Assembly for Wales, may make different provision for different cases or descriptions of case, or for different authorities or descriptions of authority, and may contain such transitional and supplementary provisions as the appropriate national authority considers necessary or expedient: s 136(12) (amended by SI 2004/533). A description of authority may be framed by reference to any circumstances whatever: see the Leasehold Reform, Housing and Urban Development Act 1993 s 136(15)(c) (as so added). A disposal of any dwelling house is to be disregarded if at the time of the disposal the local authority's interest in the dwelling house is or was subject to a long lease: s 135(15)(a) (as so added). 'Dwelling house' has the same meaning as in the Housing Act 1985 Pt V (ss 118–188) (see PARA 231) except that it does not include a hostel (as defined in s 622) or any part of a hostel; and 'long lease' means a lease for a term of years certain exceeding 21 years other than a lease which is terminable before the end of that term by notice given by or to the landlord: Leasehold Reform, Housing and Urban Development Act 1993 s 136(14) (as so substituted).

3 As to the statutory formula see the Leasehold Reform, Housing and Urban Development Act 1993 s 136(3), (4), (4A) (s 136(3) amended by SI 2004/533; the Leasehold Reform, Housing and Urban Development Act 1993 s 136(4A) added by the Finance Act 1997 s 109).

4 Leasehold Reform, Housing and Urban Development Act 1993 s 136(3). The levy was suspended but was introduced in 1999: see DETR letter '1999 Housing Transfer Programme', 20 August 1998.

5 Leasehold Reform, Housing and Urban Development Act 1993 s 136(5). Before making a determination under s 136, the appropriate national authority must consult such representatives of local government as appear to it to be appropriate: s 136(11). Any such determination may make different provision for different cases or descriptions of case, or for different authorities or descriptions of authority, and may be varied or revoked by a subsequent determination: s 136(13).

6 Leasehold Reform, Housing and Urban Development Act 1993 s 136(5)(a)–(g).

7 Leasehold Reform, Housing and Urban Development Act 1993 s 136(5).

8 Leasehold Reform, Housing and Urban Development Act 1993 s 136(6).

9 Leasehold Reform, Housing and Urban Development Act 1993 s 136(10). As to the Consolidated Fund see CONSTITUTIONAL AND ADMINISTRATIVE LAW vol 20 (2014) PARA 480; PARLIAMENT vol 78 (2010) PARA 1028 et seq.

527. Repayment of discount on early disposal. Where, on a disposal of a house[1], a discount is given to the purchaser by the local authority[2] in accordance with a consent given by the appropriate national authority[3], the conveyance, grant or assignment on the disposal must contain a covenant binding on the purchaser and his successors in title to the following effect, unless the consent provides otherwise[4]. The covenant must be to pay to the authority such sum (if any) as the authority may demand[5] on the occasion of the first relevant disposal[6] (other than an exempted disposal[7]) which takes place within the period of five years beginning with the conveyance, grant or assignment[8]. The authority may demand such sum as it considers appropriate, up to and including the maximum amount specified[9]. The maximum amount which may be demanded by the authority is a percentage of the price or premium paid for the first relevant disposal which is equal to the percentage discount given to the purchaser in respect of the disposal of the house[10]; but for each complete year which has elapsed after the conveyance, grant or assignment and before the first relevant disposal the maximum amount which may be demanded by the landlord is reduced by one-fifth[11].

The provisions as to price are subject to those relating to the disregarding of the value of improvements to the house[12]. In calculating the maximum amount which may be demanded by the authority, such amount (if any) of the price or premium paid for the first relevant disposal which is attributable to improvements made to the house by the person by whom the disposal is or is to be made, and after the conveyance, grant or assignment and before the disposal, must be disregarded[13]. The amount to be so disregarded is to be such amount as may be agreed between the parties or determined by the district valuer[14]. The district valuer may not be required by virtue of these provisions to make such a determination unless it is reasonably practicable for him to do so and his reasonable costs in making the determination are paid by the person by whom the disposal is or is to be made[15]. If the district valuer does not make a determination (and in default of an agreement), no amount is required to be disregarded[16].

The liability that may arise under the covenant required by these provisions is a charge on the house, taking effect as if it had been created by deed expressed to be by way of legal mortgage[17]. Subject as follows, the charge has priority immediately after any legal charge securing an amount:

(1) left outstanding by the purchaser; or

(2) advanced to him by an approved lending institution[18] for the purpose of enabling him to acquire the interest disposed of on the first disposal[19].

Any advance which is made otherwise than for the purpose mentioned in head (2) and is secured by a legal charge having priority to the charge taking effect by virtue of these provisions, and any further advance which is so secured, rank in priority to that charge if, and only if, the local authority by written notice served on the institution concerned gives its consent; and the local authority must so give its consent if the purpose of the advance or further advance is an approved purpose[20]. The approved purposes are:

(a) to enable the purchaser to defray, or to defray on his behalf, any of the following:

(i) the cost of any works to the house;

(ii) any service charge[21] payable in respect of the house for works, whether or not to the house; and

(iii) any service charge or other amount payable in respect of the house for insurance, whether or not of the house; and

(b) to enable the purchaser to discharge, or to discharge on his behalf, any of the following:

(i) so much as is still outstanding of any advance or further advance which ranks in priority to the charge taking effect by virtue of these provisions;

(ii) any arrears of interest on such an advance or further advance; and

(iii) any costs and expenses incurred in enforcing payment of any such interest or repayment, in whole or in part, of any such advance or further advance[22].

The local authority may at any time by written notice served on an approved lending institution postpone the charge taking effect by virtue of these provisions to any advance or further advance which is made to the purchaser by that institution and is secured by a legal charge not having priority to that charge[23]. The local authority must serve such a notice if the purpose of the advance or further advance is an approved purpose[24].

The required covenant for repayment of discount does not, by virtue of its binding successors in title of the purchaser, bind a person exercising rights under a charge having priority over the charge taking effect by virtue of these provisions, or a person deriving title under him; and a provision of the conveyance, grant or assignment, or of a collateral agreement, is void in so far as it purports to authorise a forfeiture, or to impose a penalty or disability, in the event of any such person failing to comply with the covenant[25].

1   Ie under the Housing Act 1985 s 32: see PARA 522. As to the meaning of 'house' see PARA 405 note 6.
2   As to the meaning of 'local authority' see PARA 12.
3   Ie under the Housing Act 1985 s 32(2): see PARA 522. As to the appropriate national authority, ie the Secretary of State or, where statutory functions have been transferred in relation to Wales, the Welsh Ministers, see PARA 7; and as to consents see PARA 524.
4   Housing Act 1985 s 35(1), (2) (s 35(2) amended by the Housing Act 2004 s 195(1), (2)). Where there is a relevant disposal which is an exempted disposal by virtue of the Housing Act 1985 s 39(1)(d) or (e) (compulsory disposal or disposal of yard, garden, etc: see note 7 heads (4)–(5)), the covenant required by s 35 is not binding on the person to whom the disposal is made or any successor in title of his, and that covenant and the charge taking effect by virtue of s 36 (liability to repay a charge on the premises: see the text and notes 17–25) cease to apply in relation to the property disposed of: s 41(a).
5   Ie in accordance with the Housing Act 1985 s 35(4) (see the text and note 9).
6   A disposal, whether of the whole or part of the house, is a relevant disposal for the purposes of the Housing Act 1985 Pt II (ss 8–57) if it is: (1) a conveyance of the freehold or an assignment of the lease; or (2) the grant of a lease or sub-lease (other than a mortgage term) for a term of more than 21 years otherwise than at a rack rent: s 38(1). For the purposes of head (2) it must be assumed: (a) that any option to renew or extend a lease or sub-lease, whether or not forming part of a series of options, is exercised; and (b) that any option to terminate a lease or sub-lease is not exercised: s 38(2). The grant of an option enabling a person to call for a relevant disposal which is not an exempted disposal (see note 7) is to be treated as such a disposal made to him: s 42(1).
7   A disposal is an exempted disposal for these purposes if: (1) it is a disposal of the whole of the house and a conveyance of the freehold or an assignment of the lease and the person or each of the persons to whom it is made is a qualifying person; (2) it is a vesting of the whole of the house in a person taking under a will or on an intestacy; (3) it is a disposal of the whole of the house in pursuance of any such order as is mentioned in heads (i)–(v) below; (4) it is a compulsory disposal; or (5) the property disposed of is property included with the house by virtue of the definition of 'house' in the Housing Act 1985 s 56 (ie yard, garden, outhouses, etc): s 39(1) (amended by the Housing Act 1996 s 222, Sch 18 para 8(2)). For the purposes of head (1), a person is a qualifying person in relation to a disposal if: (a) he is the person or one of the persons by whom the disposal is made; (b) he is the spouse or a former spouse, or the civil partner or a former civil partner, of that person or one of those persons; or (c) he is a member of the family of that person or one of those persons and has resided with him throughout the period of 12 months ending with the

disposal: Housing Act 1985 s 39(2) (amended by the Civil Partnership Act 2004 s 81, Sch 8 para 18). The orders referred to in head (3) are orders under: (i) the Matrimonial Causes Act 1973 s 24 or s 24A (property adjustment orders or orders for the sale of property in connection with matrimonial proceedings); (ii) the Inheritance (Provision for Family and Dependants) Act 1975 s 2 (orders as to financial provision to be made from estate: see WILLS AND INTESTACY vol 103 (2016) PARA 591 et seq); (iii) the Matrimonial and Family Proceedings Act 1984 s 17 (property adjustment orders or orders for the sale of property after overseas divorce, etc: see MATRIMONIAL AND CIVIL PARTNERSHIP LAW vol 73 (2015) PARA 591); (iv) the Children Act 1989 Sch 1 para 1 (orders for financial relief against parents: see CHILDREN AND YOUNG PERSONS vol 9 (2017) PARA 623 et seq); or (v) the Civil Partnership Act 2004 Sch 5 Pt 2, Sch 5 Pt 3 or Sch 7 para 9 (property adjustment orders, or orders for the sale of property, in connection with civil partnership proceedings or after overseas dissolution of civil partnership, etc): Housing Act 1985 s 39(3) (added by the Housing Act 1996 Sch 18 para 8(3); amended by the Civil Partnership Act 2004 ss 81, 261(4), Sch 8 para 19, Sch 30).

A 'compulsory disposal' means a disposal of property which is acquired compulsorily, or is acquired by a person who has made or would have made, or for whom another person has made or would have made, a compulsory purchase order authorising its compulsory purchase for the purposes for which it is acquired: Housing Act 1985 s 40.

8 Housing Act 1985 s 35(3) (s 35(3)–(7) added by the Housing Act 2004 s 195(3)).

9 Housing Act 1985 s 35(4) (as added: see note 8).

10 Housing Act 1985 s 35(5) (as added: see note 8).

11 Housing Act 1985 s 35(6) (as added: see note 8).

12 Ie the Housing Act 1985 s 35A (see the text and notes 13–16): s 35(7) (as added: see note 8).

13 Housing Act 1985 s 35A(1) (s 35A added by the Housing Act 2004 s 196).

14 Housing Act 1985 s 35A(2) (as added: see note 13). 'District valuer', in relation to any land in the district of a local housing authority, means an officer of the Commissioners for Her Majesty's Revenue and Customs appointed by them for the purpose of exercising, in relation to that district, the functions of the district valuer under the Housing Act 1985: s 622(1) (s 622(1) numbered as such by SI 2001/3649; definition substituted by SI 1990/434; and amended by virtue of the Commissioners for Revenue and Customs Act 2005 s 50(1), (7)). The Commissioners for Her Majesty's Revenue and Customs are appointed under the Commissioners for Revenue and Customs Act 2005 s 1 and have taken over the functions of the former Commissioners of Inland Revenue and Her Majesty's Customs and Excise: see INCOME TAXATION vol 58 (2014) PARAS 33–34. See also VALUE ADDED TAX vol 99 (2012) PARA 421.

15 Housing Act 1985 s 35A(3) (as added: see note 13).

16 Housing Act 1985 s 35A(4) (as added: see note 13).

17 Housing Act 1985 s 36(1).

18 The approved lending institutions for these purposes are an authorised deposit taker, an authorised insurer, and an authorised mortgage lender: Housing Act 1985 s 36(4) (amended by the Housing and Regeneration Act 2008 s 307(4); and by SI 2001/3649). 'Authorised deposit taker' means: (1) a person who has permission under the Financial Services and Markets Act 2000 Pt 4A (ss 55A–55Z4) to accept deposits; or (2) an EEA firm of the kind mentioned in Sch 3 para 5(b) who has permission under Sch 3 para 15 (as a result of qualifying for authorisation under Sch 3 para 12) to accept deposits (see FINANCIAL SERVICES REGULATION vol 50 (2016) PARA 462): Housing Act 1985 s 622(1) (renumbered, and definition added, by SI 2001/3649; amended by the Housing and Regeneration Act 2008 s 316(a); and the Financial Services Act 2012 s 114(1), Sch 18 para 50). 'Authorised insurer' means: (a) a person who has permission under the Financial Services and Markets Act 2000 Pt 4A to effect or carry out contracts of insurance; or (b) an EEA firm of the kind mentioned in Sch 3 para 5(b) who has permission under Sch 3 para 15 (as a result of qualifying for authorisation under Sch 3 para 12) to effect or carry out contracts of insurance (see FINANCIAL SERVICES REGULATION vol 50 (2016) PARA 462): Housing Act 1985 s 622(1) (as so renumbered; definition added by SI 2001/3649; and amended by the Housing and Regeneration Act 2008 s 316(b); and the Financial Services Act 2012 Sch 18 para 50). 'Authorised mortgage lender' means: (i) a person who has permission under the Financial Services and Markets Act 2000 Pt 4A to enter into a regulated mortgage contract as lender; (ii) an EEA firm of the kind mentioned in Sch 3 para 5(b) who has permission under Sch 3 para 15 (as a result of qualifying for authorisation under Sch 3 para 12) to enter into a regulated mortgage contract as lender; or (iii) a Treaty firm within the meaning of Sch 4 who has permission under Sch 4 para 4 (as a result of qualifying for authorisation under Sch 4 para 2) to enter into a regulated mortgage contract as lender: Housing Act 1985 s 622(1) (as so renumbered; definition added by the Housing and Regeneration Act 2008 s 307(2); and amended by the Financial Services Act 2012 Sch 18 para 50).

19 Housing Act 1985 s 36(2) (substituted by the Leasehold Reform, Housing and Urban Development Act 1993 s 133).

20 Housing Act 1985 s 36(2A) (s 36(2A), (2B), (5), (6) added by the Leasehold Reform, Housing and Urban Development Act 1993 s 133). Where different parts of an advance or further advance are

made for different purposes, each of those parts must be regarded as a separate advance or further advance for the purposes of these provisions: Housing Act 1985 s 36(6) (as so added).

21 'Service charge' means an amount payable by a purchaser or lessee of premises:

(1) which is payable, directly or indirectly, for services, repairs, maintenance or insurance or the vendor's or lessor's costs of management; and

(2) the whole or part of which varies or may vary according to the relevant costs,

and the relevant costs are the costs or estimated costs incurred or to be incurred by or on behalf of the payee, or (in the case of a lease) a superior landlord, in connection with the matters for which the service charge is payable: Housing Act 1985 s 621A(1), (2) (s 621A added by the Housing and Planning Act 1986 s 24(2), Sch 5 para 39). For this purpose, 'costs' includes overheads; and costs are relevant costs in relation to a service charge whether they are incurred, or to be incurred, in the period for which the service charge is payable or in an earlier or later period: Housing Act 1985 s 621A(3) (as so added). In relation to a service charge, the 'payee' means the person entitled to enforce payment of the charge; and the 'payer' means the person liable to pay it: s 621A(4) (as so added). Section 621A does not apply in relation to Pt XIV (ss 435–459) (see PARA 910 et seq): s 621A(5) (s 621A as so added; and s 621A(5) added by the Commonhold and Leasehold Reform Act 2002 s 150, Sch 9 paras 1, 6).

22 Housing Act 1985 s 36(5) (as added: see note 20).

23 Housing Act 1985 s 36(2B)(a), (b) (as added: see note 20).

24 Housing Act 1985 s 36(2B) (as added: see note 20).

25 Housing Act 1985 s 36(3A) (added by the Housing and Planning Act 1986 s 24(1), Sch 5 Pt 1 para 1).

528. Treatment of deferred resale agreements for purposes of repayment of discount on early disposal. If a purchaser or a successor in title enters into an agreement[1] of the following nature[2], any liability arising under the covenant required under the provision as to repayment of discount on early disposal[3] must be determined as if a relevant disposal[4] which is not an exempted disposal[5] had occurred at the appropriate time[6]. Such an agreement is an agreement between the purchaser or his successor in title and any other person: (1) which is made (expressly or impliedly) in contemplation of, or in connection with, a disposal to be made, or made, under the statutory power to dispose of land held for housing purposes[7]; (2) which is made before the end of the discount repayment period[8]; and (3) under which a relevant disposal (other than an exempted disposal) is or may be required to be made to any person after the end of that period[9]. An agreement falls within these provisions whether or not the date on which the relevant disposal is to take place is specified in the agreement, and whether or not any requirement to make that disposal is or may be made subject to the fulfilment of any condition[10].

1 'Agreement' includes arrangement: Housing Act 1985 s 39A(7) (s 39A added by the Housing Act 2004 s 198(1)).

2 Ie an agreement within the Housing Act 1985 s 39A(3) (see the text and note 9). The appropriate national authority may by order provide: (1) for s 39A(1) (see the text and note 6) to apply to agreements of any description specified in the order in addition to those within s 39A(3); (2) for s 39A(1) not to apply to agreements of any description so specified to which it would otherwise apply: s 39A(5) (as added: see note 1). Such an order may make different provision with respect to different cases or descriptions of case, and must be made by statutory instrument subject to annulment in pursuance of a resolution of either House of Parliament or, in relation to Wales, of the National Assembly for Wales: s 39A(6) (as so added). As to the appropriate national authority, ie the Secretary of State or, where statutory functions have been transferred in relation to Wales, the Welsh Ministers, see PARA 7.

3 Ie by the Housing Act 1985 s 35: see PARA 527.

4 As to the meaning of 'relevant disposal' see PARA 527 note 6.

5 As to the meaning of 'exempted disposal' see PARA 527 note 7.

6 Housing Act 1985 s 39A(1) (as added: see note 1). For this purpose, 'the appropriate time' means the time when the agreement is entered into or, if it was made before the beginning of the discount repayment period, immediately after the beginning of that period: s 39A(2) (as so added).

7 Ie under the Housing Act 1985 s 32: see PARA 522.

8 'The discount repayment period' means the period of three years that applies for the purposes of the Housing Act 1985 s 35(2) before its amendment by the Housing Act 2004 s 195(1), (2) or the

period of five years that applies for the purposes of the Housing Act 1985 s 35(3) (depending on whether an offer such as is mentioned in the Housing Act 2004 s 195(4) was made before or on or after the coming into force of that provision): Housing Act 1985 s 39A(7) (as added: see note 1). Under the Housing Act 2004 s 195(4), the amendments made by s 195 do not apply in any case where: (1) the purchaser accepted an offer for the disposal of the house from the authority; or (2) the authority accepted an offer for the disposal of the house from the purchaser, before the day on which s 195 came into force (ie 18 January 2005: see s 270(3)(a)).

9   Housing Act 1985 s 39A(3) (as added: see note 1).

10 Housing Act 1985 s 39A(4) (as added: see note 1).

529. Right of first refusal for local authority. The voluntary transfer provisions were amended by the Housing Act 2004 and the following provisions now apply where, on a disposal of a house[1], a discount is given to the purchaser by the local authority in accordance with a consent given by the appropriate national authority[2]; but they do not apply in any such case if the consent so provides[3]. On the disposal the conveyance, grant or assignment must contain the following covenant, which is to be binding on the purchaser and his successors in title[4]. The covenant must be to the effect that, until the end of the period of ten years beginning with the conveyance, grant or assignment, there will be no relevant disposal[5] which is not an exempted disposal[6], unless the prescribed conditions[7] have been satisfied in relation to that or a previous such disposal[8].

The appropriate national authority[9] may by regulations prescribe such conditions as he considers appropriate for and in connection with conferring on a local authority[10] which has made a disposal of a house at a discount, or such other person as is determined in accordance with the regulations, a right of first refusal to have a reconveyance or conveyance of the house or a surrender or assignment of the lease made to it or him for such consideration as is mentioned below[11].

Regulations made under this power may in particular (but without affecting the generality of the power[12]) make provision:

(1)   for the purchaser[13] to offer to make such a disposal to such person or persons as may be prescribed;

(2)   for a prescribed recipient of such an offer to be able either to accept the offer or to nominate some other person as the person by whom the offer may be accepted;

(3)   for the person who may be so nominated to be either a person of a prescribed description or a person whom the prescribed recipient considers, having regard to any prescribed matters, to be a more appropriate person to accept the offer;

(4)   for a prescribed recipient making such a nomination to give a notification of the nomination to the person nominated, the purchaser and any other prescribed person;

(5)   for authorising a nominated person to accept the offer and for determining which acceptance is to be effective where the offer is accepted by more than one person;

(6)   for the period within which the offer may be accepted or within which any other prescribed step is to be, or may be, taken;

(7)   for the circumstances in which the right of first refusal lapses (whether following the service of a notice to complete or otherwise) with the result that the purchaser is able to make a disposal on the open market;

(8)   for the manner in which any offer, acceptance or notification is to be communicated[14].

Such regulations may make different provision with respect to different cases or descriptions of case, and must be made by statutory instrument subject to annulment in pursuance of a resolution of either House of Parliament[15].

The consideration for a disposal made in respect of a right of first refusal is to be such amount as may be agreed between the parties, or determined by the district valuer, as being the amount which is to be taken to be the value of the house at the time when the offer is made[16]. That value is to be taken to be the price which, at that time, the interest to be reconveyed, conveyed, surrendered or assigned would realise if sold on the open market by a willing vendor, on the assumption that any liability under the covenant required under the provision as to repayment of discount on early disposal[17] would be discharged by the vendor[18]. If the offer is accepted in accordance with regulations, no payment may be required in pursuance of any such covenant, but the consideration must be reduced by such amount (if any) as, on a disposal made at the time the offer was made (being a relevant disposal which is not an exempted disposal), would fall to be paid under that covenant[19]. Where there is a charge on the house having priority over the charge to secure payment of the sum due under the covenant, the consideration must not be reduced below the amount necessary to discharge the outstanding sum secured by the first-mentioned charge at the date of the offer[20].

1   Ie under the Housing Act 1985 s 32: see PARA 522. As to the meaning of 'house' see PARA 405 note 6.
2   Ie under the Housing Act 1985 s 32(2): see PARA 522.
3   Housing Act 1985 s 36A(1) (ss 36A, 36B added by the Housing Act 2004 s 197(1)).
4   Housing Act 1985 s 36A(2) (as added: see note 3). Where there is a relevant disposal which is an exempted disposal by virtue of s 39(1)(d) or (e) (compulsory disposal or disposal of yard, garden, etc: see PARA 527 note 7 heads (4)–(5)), the covenant required by s 36A is not binding on the person to whom the disposal is made or any successor in title of his, and that covenant ceases to apply in relation to the property disposed of: s 41(aa) (added by the Housing Act 2004 s 197(4)).
5   As to the meaning of 'relevant disposal' see PARA 527 note 6.
6   As to the meaning of 'exempted disposal' see PARA 527 note 7.
7   For this purpose, 'the prescribed conditions' means such conditions as are prescribed by regulations under the Housing Act 1985 s 36A at the time when the conveyance, grant or assignment is made: s 36A(4) (as added: see note 3). As to such regulations see the text and notes 9–15.
8   Housing Act 1985 s 36A(3) (as added: see note 3). The limitation imposed by such a covenant is a local land charge: s 36A(10) (as so added). The Chief Land Registrar must enter in the register of title a restriction reflecting the limitation imposed by any such covenant: s 36A(11) (as so added). See REAL PROPERTY AND REGISTRATION vol 87 (2012) PARAS 532, 764. As to the Chief Land Registrar see REAL PROPERTY AND REGISTRATION vol 87 (2012) PARA 562.
9   As to the appropriate national authority, ie the Secretary of State or, where statutory functions have been transferred in relation to Wales, the Welsh Ministers, see PARA 7.
10 As to the meaning of 'local authority' see PARA 12.
11 Housing Act 1985 s 36A(5), (6) (as added: see note 3). As to regulations made under this power see the Housing (Right of First Refusal) (England) Regulations 2005, SI 2005/1917; and the Housing (Right of First Refusal) (Wales) Regulations 2005, SI 2005/2680.
12 Housing Act 1985 s 36A(8) (as added: see note 3).
13 For this purpose, any reference to the purchaser is a reference to the purchaser or his successor in title: Housing Act 1985 s 36A(8) (as added: see note 3).
14 Housing Act 1985 s 36A(7) (as added: see note 3).
15 Housing Act 1985 s 36A(9) (as added: see note 3).
16 Ie as determined in accordance with regulations made under the Housing Act 1985 s 36A: s 36B(1) (as added: see note 3). As to the meaning of 'district valuer' see PARA 527 note 14.
17 Ie by the Housing Act 1985 s 35: see PARA 527.
18 Housing Act 1985 s 36B(2) (as added: see note 3).
19 Housing Act 1985 s 36B(3) (as added: see note 3).
20 Ie as determined in accordance with regulations under the Housing Act 1985 s 36A: s 36B(4) (as added: see note 3).

530. Restriction on disposal of dwelling houses in national parks, etc. Where a conveyance, grant or assignment executed under the statutory power to dispose of land held for housing purposes[1] is of a house[2] situated in:

(1)   a national park[3]; or

(2)   an area designated[4] as an area of outstanding natural beauty; or

(3)   an area designated by order[5] as a rural area,

the conveyance, grant or assignment may, unless it contains a condition reserving a right of pre-emption[6] or a restriction on assignment[7] or a covenant reserving a right of first refusal for the local authority[8], contain a covenant limiting the freedom of the purchaser[9] (including any successor in title of his and any person deriving title under him or such a successor) to dispose of the house[10]. The limitation is that until such time, if any, as may be notified in writing by the local authority to the purchaser or a successor in title of his:

(a)   there will be no relevant disposal[11] which is not an exempted disposal[12] without the written consent of the authority[13]; but that consent must not be withheld if the disposal is to a person satisfying the condition that the person to whom the disposal is made (or, if it is made to more than one person, at least one of them) has throughout the period of three years immediately preceding the application for consent or, in the case of a disposal by way of tenancy or licence[14], preceding the disposal had his place of work in a region designated by order as a rural area[15] which, or part of which, is comprised in the national park or designated area, or had his only or principal home in such a region, or has had the one in part or parts of that period and the other in the remainder; but the region need not have been the same throughout the period[16]; and

(b)   there will be no disposal by way of tenancy or licence without the written consent of the authority unless the disposal is to a person satisfying the condition mentioned in head (a) or by a person whose only or principal home is and, throughout the duration of the tenancy or licence, remains the house[17].

A disposal in breach of such a covenant is void and, so far as it relates to disposals by way of tenancy or licence, such a covenant may be enforced by the local authority as if the authority were possessed of land adjacent to the house concerned and the covenant were expressed to be made for the benefit of such adjacent land[18].

The limitation imposed by such a covenant is a local land charge[19].

1   Ie under the Housing Act 1985 s 32: see PARA 522.

2   As to the meaning of 'house' see PARA 405 note 6.

3   As to national parks see OPEN SPACES AND COUNTRYSIDE vol 78 (2010) PARA 636 et seq.

4   Ie under the Countryside and Rights of Way Act 2000 s 82: see OPEN SPACES AND COUNTRYSIDE vol 78 (2010) PARA 658.

5   Ie under the Housing Act 1985 s 157 (which makes provision in relation to disposals in pursuance of the right to buy corresponding to that made by s 37): see PARA 333.

6   Ie a condition of a kind mentioned in the Housing Act 1985 s 33(2)(b): see PARA 523 head (2).

7   Ie a condition of a kind mentioned in the Housing Act 1985 s 33(2)(c): see PARA 523 head (3).

8   Ie a covenant of a kind mentioned in the Housing Act 1985 s 36A: see PARA 529. As to the meaning of 'local authority' see PARA 12.

9   For these purposes, 'purchaser' means the person acquiring the interest disposed of by the first disposal: Housing Act 1985 s 37(6).

10 Housing Act 1985 s 37(1) (amended by the Countryside and Rights of Way Act 2000 s 93, Sch 15 para 8; and the Housing Act 2004 s 197(3)).

11 As to the meaning of 'relevant disposal' see PARA 527 note 6.

12 As to the meaning of 'exempted disposal' see PARA 527 note 7. Where there is a relevant disposal which is an exempted disposal by virtue of the Housing Act 1985 s 39(1)(d) or (e) (compulsory

disposal or disposal of yard, garden, etc: see PARA 527 note 7 heads (4), (5)), any such covenant as is mentioned in s 37 ceases to apply in relation to the property disposed of: s 41(b).

13 For the purposes of heads (a) and (b) in the text, a consent to the grant of an option enabling a person to call for a relevant disposal which is not an exempted disposal is treated as a consent to a disposal made in pursuance of the option: see the Housing Act 1985 s 42(1), (2).

14 Any reference in the Housing Act 1985 s 37(1)–(4) to a disposal by way of tenancy or licence does not include a reference to a relevant disposal or an exempted disposal: s 37(4A) (added by the Housing Act 1988 s 125).

15 See note 5.

16 Housing Act 1985 s 37(2)(a), (3) (s 37(2)–(4) amended by the Housing Act 1988 s 125).

17 Housing Act 1985 s 37(2)(b) (as amended: see note 16).

18 Housing Act 1985 s 37(4) (as amended: see note 16).

19 Housing Act 1985 s 37(5) (amended by the Land Registration Act 2002 s 133, Sch 11 para 18(1), (2)). Where the Chief Land Registrar approves an application for registration of a disposition of registered land, or the disponee's title under a disposition of unregistered land, and the instrument effecting the disposition contains a covenant of the kind mentioned in the Housing Act 1985 s 37(1), he must enter in the register a restriction reflecting the limitation imposed by the covenant: s 37(5A) (added by the Land Registration Act 2002 Sch 11 para 18(2)). See further REAL PROPERTY AND REGISTRATION vol 87 (2012) PARAS 532, 764. As to the Chief Land Registrar see REAL PROPERTY AND REGISTRATION vol 87 (2012) PARA 562.

531. Consent required for certain other disposals. The provisions dealing with large scale voluntary transfers[1] apply in respect of land and dwellings which are held for housing purposes by local housing authorities under the provisions of Part II of the Housing Act 1985[2]. A local authority may wish to dispose of land and dwellings which are not acquired or appropriated under Part II and provision is made giving authorities power to sell in these circumstances with the consent of the appropriate national authority.

Thus the consent of the appropriate national authority[3] is required for the disposal[4] by a local authority[5], otherwise than in pursuance of the right to buy[6], of a house belonging to the authority which is let on a secure tenancy[7] or an introductory tenancy[8], or of which a lease[9] has been granted in pursuance of the right to buy[10], but which has not been acquired or appropriated by the authority for the purposes of Part II[11]. Consent may be given:

(1) either generally to all local authorities or to any particular local authority or description of authority, and either generally in relation to all houses or in relation to any particular house or description of house[12];

(2) subject to conditions[13] and, in particular, subject to conditions as to the price, premium or rent to be obtained on a disposal of the house, including conditions as to the amount by which, on a disposal of the house by way of sale or by the grant or assignment of a lease at a premium, the price or premium is to be, or may be, discounted by the local authority[14].

The matters to which the appropriate national authority may have regard in determining whether to give consent and, if so, to what conditions consent should be subject include:

(a) the extent (if any) to which the person to whom the proposed disposal is to be made ('the intending purchaser') is, or is likely to be, dependent upon, controlled by or subject to influence from the local authority making the disposal or any members or officers of that authority;

(b) the extent (if any) to which the proposed disposal would result in the intending purchaser becoming the predominant or a substantial owner in any area of housing accommodation[15] let on tenancies or subject to licences;

(c) the terms of the proposed disposal;

(d)   in the case of a proposed disposal which is part of a proposed large scale disposal, the appropriate national body's estimate of the exchequer costs of the large scale disposal[16];

(e)   any reduction in the amount that the local authority may be required to pay to the Secretary of State in respect of vacant higher value housing in England[17] as a result of the disposal; and

(f)   any other matters whatsoever which the appropriate national authority considers relevant[18].

A disposal of a house by a local authority made without the consent so required is void, unless the disposal is to an individual (or to two or more individuals), and the disposal does not extend to any other house[19].

1 See PARA 520 et seq.
2 Ie the Housing Act 1985 Pt II (ss 8–57).
3 As to the appropriate national authority, ie the Secretary of State or, where statutory functions have been transferred in relation to Wales, the Welsh Ministers, see PARA 7.
4 For these purposes, the grant of an option to purchase the freehold of, or any other interest in, a house to which the Housing Act 1985 s 43 applies is a disposal; and a consent given under s 43 to such a disposal extends to a disposal made in pursuance of the option: s 43(5). As to the meaning of 'house' see PARA 405 note 6.
5 For these purposes, references in the Housing Act 1985 s 43 (other than in s 43(4A)(ca) and in s 34(4AB)–(4AE) as applied for the purposes of s 43 (see note 17)) and s 44 to a local authority include references to a national park authority: Housing Act 1985 s 43(5A) (added by the Environment Act 1995 s 78, Sch 10 para 24(1); and amended by the Housing and Regeneration Act 2008 s 311, Sch 14 para 1(1), (3)(d)). As to national park authorities see OPEN SPACES AND COUNTRYSIDE vol 78 (2010) PARA 526 et seq. As to the meaning of 'local authority' generally see PARA 12.
6 Ie otherwise than in pursuance of the Housing Act 1985 Pt V (ss 118–188): see PARA 230 et seq.
7 As to the meaning of 'secure tenancy' see LANDLORD AND TENANT vol 63 (2016) PARA 1037.
8 As to introductory tenancies see PARA 472.
9 As to the meaning of 'lease' see PARA 31 note 3.
10 Ie in pursuance of the Housing Act 1985 Pt V: see PARA 230 et seq.
11 Housing Act 1985 s 43(1) (amended by the Housing Act 1988 s 140, Sch 17 para 39; the Housing Act 1996 s 227, Sch 19 Pt IX; the Housing and Regeneration Act 2008 Sch 14 para 1(3)(a); and SI 1997/74). In relation to England, the Secretary of State must consult the Regulator of Social Housing before deciding whether to consent under the Housing Act 1985 s 43 to anything within the regulator's remit: s 43(6) (added by SI 2010/844). As to the Regulator of Social Housing see PARA 57 et seq. As to what is within the regulator's remit see PARA 408 note 2.
12 Housing Act 1985 s 43(2).
13 Housing Act 1985 s 43(3).
14 Housing Act 1985 s 43(4).
15 As to the meaning of 'housing accommodation' see PARA 13 note 1.
16 The estimate mentioned in head (d) in the text is to be based on such assumptions (including as to the period during which housing subsidies may be payable) as the appropriate national authority may determine, regardless of whether those assumptions are, or are likely to be, borne out by events: Housing Act 1985 s 43(4AA) (added by the Housing and Regeneration Act 2008 Sch 14 para 1(3)(c)).
17 Ie under the Housing and Planning Act 2016 s 69: see PARA 363.
18 Housing Act 1985 s 43(4A) (added by the Housing Act 1988 s 132(1), (2), (8); and amended by the Housing and Regeneration Act 2008 Sch 14 para 1(3)(b); and the Housing and Planning Act 2016 s 77(1), (3)). The Housing Act 1985 s 34(4AB)–(4AE) (see PARA 524) applies for the purposes of s 43 as it applies for the purposes of s 34: s 43(4AB) (added by the Housing and Regeneration Act 2008 Sch 14 para 1(3)(c)).
19 Housing Act 1985 s 44(1). Section 44(1) has effect notwithstanding the Town and Country Planning Act 1959 s 29 and the Local Government Act 1972 s 128(2) (protection of purchasers dealing with authority: see LOCAL GOVERNMENT vol 69 (2009) PARA 529): Housing Act 1985 s 44(2). For the purposes of s 44, 'house' does not have the extended meaning applicable by virtue of the definition of 'housing accommodation' in s 56 (see PARA 13 note 1), but includes a flat: s 44(3).

532. Consent required for certain subsequent disposals. Where consent is required for a disposal[1] ('the original disposal') and that consent does not provide otherwise, the person who acquires the land or house on the disposal must not dispose of it except with the consent of the appropriate authority[2]; but these provisions do not apply in relation to an exempt disposal[3], nor if the original disposal was made to a private registered provider of social housing[4].

Where an estate or interest of the person who acquired the land or house on the original disposal has been mortgaged or charged, the prohibition above applies also to a disposal by the mortgagee or chargee in exercise of a power of sale or leasing, whether or not the disposal is in the name of the person who so acquired the land or house; and in any case where, by operation of law or by virtue of an order of a court, the land or house which has been acquired passes or is transferred from the person who so acquired it to another person and that passing or transfer does not constitute a disposal for which consent is required, these provisions[5] apply as if the other person to whom the land or house passes or is transferred were the person who acquired it on the original disposal[6].

Consent required for the purposes of these provisions may be given either generally to all persons who may require such consent or to any particular person or description of person who may require such consent[7].

Before giving any consent required by virtue of these provisions, the appropriate authority:

(1)　　must satisfy itself that the person who is seeking the consent has taken appropriate steps to consult every tenant of any land or house proposed to be disposed of; and

(2)　　must have regard to the responses of any such tenants to that consultation[8].

However, a person seeking any such consent is not required to consult a tenant of the land or house proposed to be disposed of if:

(a)　　consent is sought for the disposal of the land or house to that tenant or to persons including that tenant; or

(b)　　consent is sought subject to the condition that the land or house is vacant at the time of the disposal[9].

Where the title of the authority to the land or house which is disposed of by the original disposal is not registered, and the original disposal is a transfer or grant falling within the provisions as to compulsory registration of title[10]:

(i)　　the authority must give to the person to whom the original disposal is made a certificate in a form approved by the Chief Land Registrar stating that the authority is entitled to make the disposal subject only to such encumbrances, rights and interests as are stated in the instrument by which the original disposal is effected or summarised in the certificate; and

(ii)　　for the purpose of registration of title, the Chief Land Registrar must accept such a certificate as evidence of the facts stated in it, but if as a result he has to meet a claim against him under the Land Registration Act 2002 the authority by which the original disposal was made is liable to indemnify him[11].

Where the Chief Land Registrar approves an application for registration of a disposition of registered land or a person's title under a disposition of unregistered land, and the instrument effecting the original disposal contains a statement that the requirement as to consent applies to a subsequent disposal of the land[12], he must enter in the register a restriction reflecting the limitation under the provisions above on subsequent disposal[13].

1 Ie by virtue of the Housing Act 1985 s 32 or 43: see PARAS 522, 531. In every case where the consent of the appropriate national authority is required for the original disposal by virtue of s 32 or 43 (whether or not consent is required under the Housing Act 1988 s 133 to a subsequent disposal), the authority by which the original disposal is made must furnish to the person to whom it is made a copy of that consent: s 133(10). As to the appropriate national authority, ie the Secretary of State or, where statutory functions have been transferred in relation to Wales, the Welsh Ministers, see PARA 7.

2 For these purposes, 'the appropriate authority' means: (1) in relation to a disposal of land in England, the Secretary of State; and (2) in relation to a disposal of land in Wales, the Welsh Ministers: Housing Act 1988 s 133(1ZA) (added by the Housing and Regeneration Act 2008 s 191(3)(b); and amended by the Housing and Planning Act 2016 s 92, Sch 4 paras 2, 4(1), (2)). As to the Secretary of State and the Welsh Ministers see PARA 7.

3 Housing Act 1988 s 133(1) (amended by the Housing and Regeneration Act 2008 s 191(3)(a)). As to the meaning of 'exempt disposal' see PARA 556 note 13. The Housing Act 1988 s 133 does not apply if the original disposal was made before the date on which s 133 came into force (ie 15 November 1988): s 133(1A) (added with retrospective effect by the Housing Act 1996 s 22, Sch 18 para 21(1)).

Where the Housing Act 1988 s 133(1) applies: (1) if the Housing Act 1985 s 34 applies to the consent given to the original disposal (see PARA 524), s 34(2)(b), (3), (4), (4A)(a)–(c), (d) also applies to any consent required by virtue of the Housing Act 1988 s 133; (2) if the consent to the original disposal was given under the Housing Act 1985 s 43 (see PARA 531), s 43(2)(b), (3), (4), (4A)(a)–(c), (d) also applies to any consent required by virtue of the Housing Act 1988 s 133; (3) in the application of the Housing Act 1985 s 34(4A)(a)–(c), (d) or s 43(4A)(a)–(c), (d) to any consent required by virtue of the Housing Act 1988 s 133, any reference to the appropriate national body is to be construed as a reference to the appropriate authority and any reference to the local authority making the disposal is to be construed as a reference to the local authority making the original disposal; and (4) the instrument by which the original disposal is effected must contain a statement in a form approved by the Chief Land Registrar that the requirement of s 133 as to consent applies to a subsequent disposal of the land or house by the person to whom the original disposal was made: s 133(3) (amended by the Housing and Regeneration Act 2008 ss 191(3)(d), 311, Sch 14 para 2). As to the Chief Land Registrar see REAL PROPERTY AND REGISTRATION vol 87 (2012) PARA 562.

The Housing Act 1985 s 32(4) or, as the case may be, s 43(5) (options to purchase as disposals: see PARAS 522, 531) applies for the purposes of the Housing Act 1988 s 133: s 133(4).

4 Housing Act 1988 s 133(1B) (added by the Housing and Regeneration Act 2008 s 191(3)(c); and substituted by the Housing and Planning Act 2016 s 92, Sch 4 paras 2, 4(1), (3)). As to the meaning of 'private registered provider of social housing' see PARA 53.

No consent is required under the Housing Act 1996 s 9 or s 42 (see PARAS 217, 209 respectively) or the Housing Associations Act 1985 s 9 (see PARA 24) for any disposal in respect of which consent is given under the Housing Act 1988 s 133: s 133(7) (amended by the Government of Wales Act 1998 s 140, Sch 16 para 71(b); the Housing and Planning Act 2016 Sch 4 paras 2, 4(1), (4); and SI 1996/2325).

5 Ie the Housing Act 1988 s 133, including, where there is more than one such passing or transfer, s 133(2).

6 Housing Act 1988 s 133(2).

7 Housing Act 1988 s 133(2A) (added by the Housing Act 1996 Sch 18 para 21(3)).

8 Housing Act 1988 s 133(5) (amended by the Housing and Regeneration Act 2008 s 191(3)(e), (f)).

9 Housing Act 1988 s 133(5A)(a), (b) (s 133(5A) added by the Housing Act 1996 Sch 18 para 21(4)). Accordingly, the Housing Act 1988 s 133(5) does not apply in either case: s 133(5A) (as so added).

10 Ie a transfer or grant mentioned in the Land Registration Act 2002 s 4: see REAL PROPERTY AND REGISTRATION vol 87 (2012) PARA 345.

11 Housing Act 1988 s 133(8) (amended by the Land Registration Act 1997 s 4(2), Sch 2 Pt I; and the Land Registration Act 2002 s 133, Sch 11 para 23(1), (5)).

12 Ie the statement required by the Housing Act 1988 s 133(3)(d): see note 3 head (4).

13 Housing Act 1988 s 133(9) (substituted by the Land Registration Act 2002 Sch 11 para 23(6)).

533. Limitation of service charges payable after disposal of house. Where the freehold of a house[1] has been conveyed by a public sector authority[2] and the conveyance enabled the vendor to recover from the purchaser a service charge[3], relevant costs[4] must be taken into account in determining the amount of a service charge payable for a period only to the extent that they are reasonably incurred, and where they are incurred on the provision of services or the carrying out of works, only if the services or works are of a reasonable standard, and the amount payable is to be limited accordingly[5]. Where the service charge is payable before the relevant costs are incurred, no greater amount than is reasonable is so payable; and after the relevant costs have been incurred any necessary adjustment must be made by repayment, reduction of subsequent charges or otherwise[6]. An agreement by the payer[7], other than an arbitration agreement[8], is void in so far as it purports to provide for a determination in a particular manner or on particular evidence of any question:

(1)   whether an amount payable before costs for services, repairs, maintenance, insurance or management are incurred is reasonable;

(2)   whether such costs were reasonably incurred; or

(3)   whether services or works for which costs were incurred are of a reasonable standard[9].

Where relevant costs are incurred or to be incurred on the carrying out of works in respect of which a grant has been or is to be paid by way of assistance for the provision of a separate service pipe for a water supply[10] or under any provision of Part I of the Housing Grants, Construction and Regeneration Act 1996[11] or any corresponding earlier enactment, the amount of the grant must be deducted from the costs and the amount of the service charge payable must be reduced accordingly[12].

The appropriate national authority's statutory power[13] to give assistance in connection with legal proceedings and the statutory provisions relating to the jurisdiction of the County Court[14] apply to proceedings and questions arising under these provisions as they apply to proceedings and questions arising under the right to buy[15].

1   As to the meaning of 'house' see PARA 405 note 6.
2   For these purposes, 'public sector authority' means a local authority, a national park authority, a development corporation, an urban development corporation, a Mayoral development corporation, the Homes and Communities Agency, the Greater London Authority so far as exercising its housing or regeneration functions or its new towns and urban development functions, the Welsh Ministers so far as exercising functions in relation to anything transferred (or to be transferred) to them as mentioned in the New Towns Act 1981 s 36(1)(a)(i)–(iii), a housing action trust, the Regulator of Social Housing or Scottish Homes, a non-profit registered provider of social housing or a registered social landlord: Housing Act 1985 s 45(2) (amended by the Landlord and Tenant Act 1987 s 61, Sch 5; the Housing Act 1988 ss 79(11), 140(1), Sch 17 para 106; the Environment Act 1995 s 78, Sch 10 para 24(2); the Government of Wales Act 1998 ss 140, 152, Sch 16 para 8(2), Sch 18 Pt IV; and the Localism Act 2011 ss 195(1), 222, Sch 19 paras 10, 12, Sch 22 paras 9, 10; and by SI 1996/2325, SI 2008/3002 and SI 2010/866). As to the meaning of 'local authority' see PARA 12. As to national park authorities see OPEN SPACES AND COUNTRYSIDE vol 78 (2010) PARA 526 et seq. As to the meaning of 'development corporation' see PARA 12. As to urban development corporations see PLANNING vol 83 (2010) PARA 1581 et seq. As to Mayoral development corporations see LONDON GOVERNMENT vol 71 (2013) PARA 323. As to the Homes and Communities Agency see PARA 57 et seq; and PLANNING vol 83 (2010) PARA 1454 et seq. As to housing action trusts see PARA 537 et seq. As to the Regulator of Social Housing see PARA 57 et seq. As to registered providers of social housing see PARA 51 et seq; as to when such a body is a non-profit organisation see PARA 71 note 13. As to the meaning of 'registered social landlord' see PARA 13.
        'Public sector authority' also includes the Welsh Ministers if the freehold has been conveyed by them (or by the National Assembly for Wales, the Secretary of State (or Housing for Wales)) under the Housing Associations Act 1985 s 90 (see PARA 156): Housing Act 1985 s 45(2A) (added by the Government of Wales Act 1998 Sch 16 para 8(3); and amended by SI 2008/3002); and 'public sector authority' also includes a profit-making registered provider of social housing in respect of

any house which, before the conveyance, was social housing within the meaning of the Housing and Regeneration Act 2008 Pt 2 (ss 59–278A) (see PARA 52): Housing Act 1985 s 45(2B) (added by SI 2010/866).

3 As to the meaning of 'service charge' see PARA 527 note 21.
4 As to the meaning of 'relevant costs' see PARA 527 note 21.
5 Housing Act 1985 ss 45(1), 47(1) (s 45(1) amended by the Landlord and Tenant Act 1987 Sch 4 para 4).
6 Housing Act 1985 s 47(2).
7 As to the meaning of 'payer' see PARA 527 note 21.
8 Ie within the meaning of the Arbitration Act 1996 Pt I (ss 1–84): see ARBITRATION vol 2 (2017) PARA 509.
9 Housing Act 1985 s 47(3) (amended by the Arbitration Act 1996 s 107(1), Sch 3 para 42).
10 Ie under the Housing Act 1985 s 523: see WATER AND WATERWAYS vol 100 (2009) PARA 399.
11 Ie under any provision of the Housing Grants, Construction and Regeneration Act 1996 Pt I (ss 1–103): see PARA 835 et seq.
12 Housing Act 1985 s 47(4) (added by the Housing and Planning Act 1986 s 24(1)(i), Sch 5 para 9(3); and amended by the Housing Grants, Construction and Regeneration Act 1996 s 103, Sch 1 para 2).
13 Ie the Housing Act 1985 s 170: see PARA 345. As to the appropriate national authority, ie the Secretary of State or, where statutory functions have been transferred in relation to Wales, the Welsh Ministers, see PARA 7.
14 Ie the Housing Act 1985 s 181: see PARA 353.
15 Housing Act 1985 s 45(3). As to the right to buy see Pt V (ss 118–188): see PARA 230 et seq.

534. Information as to relevant costs. Where the freehold of a house[1] has been conveyed by a public sector authority[2] and the conveyance enabled the vendor to recover from the purchaser a service charge[3], the payer may require the payee[4] in writing to supply him with a written summary of the costs[5] incurred:

(1)   if the relevant accounts are made up for periods of 12 months, in the last such period ending not later than the date of the request; or

(2)   if the accounts are not so made up, in the period of 12 months ending with the date of the request,

and which are relevant to the service charges payable or demanded as payable in that or any other period[6]. The payee must comply with the request within one month of the request or within six months of the end of the period referred to in head (1) or head (2), whichever is the later[7]. A disposal of the house by the payer does not affect the validity of a request made under these provisions before the disposal but a person is not obliged to provide a summary more than once for the same house and for the same period[8].

The summary must set out those costs in a way showing how they are or will be reflected in demands for service charges and must be certified by a qualified accountant[9] as in his opinion a fair summary complying with this requirement and as being sufficiently supported by accounts, receipts and other documents which have been produced to him[10]. It must also state whether any of the costs relate to works in respect of which a grant has been or is to be paid by way of assistance for the provision of a separate service pipe for a water supply[11] or under any provision of Chapter I of Part I of the Housing Grants, Construction and Regeneration Act 1996[12] or any corresponding earlier enactment[13].

Where the payer has obtained such a summary, whether in pursuance of these provisions or otherwise, he may within six months of obtaining it require the payee to afford him reasonable facilities for inspecting the accounts, receipts and other documents supporting the summary, and for taking copies or extracts from them, and the payee must then make such facilities available to the payer for a period of two months beginning not later than one month after the request is made[14]. A person is not, however, obliged to make the facilities available more than once for the same house and for the same period[15].

If a person fails without reasonable excuse to perform a duty imposed on him by these provisions he commits a summary offence and is liable to a penalty[16] except where the payee is a local authority, a development corporation or the Welsh Ministers[17].

The appropriate national authority's statutory power[18] to give assistance in connection with legal proceedings and the statutory provisions relating to the jurisdiction of the County Court[19] apply to proceedings and questions arising under these provisions as they apply to proceedings and questions arising under the right to buy[20].

1 As to the meaning of 'house' see PARA 405 note 6.
2 As to the meaning of 'public sector authority' see PARA 533 note 2.
3 As to the meaning of 'service charge' see PARA 527 note 21.
4 A request under these provisions is deemed to be served on the payee if it is served on a person who receives the service charge on behalf of the payee; and a person on whom a request is so served must forward it as soon as possible to the payee: Housing Act 1985 s 48(5). As to the meanings of 'payer' and 'payee' see PARA 527 note 21.
5 As to the meaning of 'costs' see PARA 527 note 21.
6 Housing Act 1985 ss 45(1), 48(1) (s 45(1) amended by the Landlord and Tenant Act 1987 s 61(1), Sch 4 para 4).
7 Housing Act 1985 s 48(2).
8 Housing Act 1985 s 48(6).
9 This reference to a 'qualified accountant' is a reference to a person who, in accordance with the following provisions, has the necessary qualification and is not disqualified from acting: Housing Act 1985 s 51(1). A person has the necessary qualification only if he is eligible for appointment as a statutory auditor under the Companies Act 2006 Pt 42 (ss 1209–1264) (see COMPANIES vol 15 (2016) PARA 1086): Housing Act 1985 s 51(2) (substituted by SI 1991/1997; and amended by SI 2008/948). The following are disqualified from acting:
    (1)   where the payee is a company, the payee or any associated company of the payee;
    (2)   an officer or employee of the payee or, where the payee is a company, of an associated company;
    (3)   a person who is a partner or employee of any such officer or employee,
and a company is associated with the payee company for these purposes if it is (within the meaning of the Companies Act 2006 s 1159: see COMPANIES vol 14 (2016) PARA 22) the payee's holding company or subsidiary or is a subsidiary of the payee's holding company: Housing Act 1985 s 51(4), (5) (amended by SI 1991/1997; and the Housing Act 1985 s 51(5) amended by SI 2009/1941). Where the payee is a local authority or a development corporation, the persons who have the necessary qualification include members of the Chartered Institute of Public Finance and Accountancy, and head (2) does not apply: Housing Act 1985 s 51(6) (amended by the Government of Wales Act 1998 s 129, Sch 15 para 9; and by SI 2008/3002). As to the meaning of 'local authority' see PARA 12; and as to development corporations see PARA 12.
10 Housing Act 1985 s 48(3).
11 Ie under the Housing Act 1985 s 523: see WATER AND WATERWAYS vol 100 (2009) PARA 399.
12 Ie under any provision of the Housing Grants, Construction and Regeneration Act 1996 Pt I Ch I (ss 1–103): see PARA 835 et seq.
13 Housing Act 1985 s 48(3A) (added by the Housing and Planning Act 1986 s 24(1)(i), Sch 5 para 9(4); and amended by the Housing Grants, Construction and Regeneration Act 1996 s 103, Sch 1 para 3).
14 Housing Act 1985 s 48(4). The request must be made in writing: see s 48(4).
15 See the Housing Act 1985 s 48(6).
16 Housing Act 1985 s 50(1) (amended by the Landlord and Tenant Act 1987 s 61, Sch 4 para 6, Sch 5). The penalty on conviction is a fine not exceeding level 4 on the standard scale: see the Housing Act 1985 s 50(1). As to the powers of magistrates' courts to issue fines on summary conviction see SENTENCING vol 92 (2015) PARA 176.
17 Housing Act 1985 s 50(2) (amended by the Government of Wales Act 1998 s 152, Sch 18 Pt IV; and by SI 2008/3002).
18 Ie the Housing Act 1985 s 170: see PARA 345. As to the appropriate national authority, ie the Secretary of State or, where statutory functions have been transferred in relation to Wales, the Welsh Ministers, see PARA 7.
19 Ie the Housing Act 1985 s 181: see PARA 353.
20 Housing Act 1985 s 45(3). As to the right to buy see Pt V (ss 118–188); and PARA 230 et seq.

535. Contributions towards costs of housing mobility arrangements. The appropriate national authority[1] may (in relation to England, with the consent of the Treasury[2]) make grants or loans towards the cost of arrangements for enabling or assisting persons to move and become tenants[3] or licensees of dwellings[4]. The grants or loans may be made subject to such conditions as the appropriate national authority may determine and may be made so as to be repayable or, as the case may be, repayable earlier if there is a breach of such a condition[5].

1 As to the appropriate national authority, ie the Secretary of State or, where statutory functions have been transferred in relation to Wales, the Welsh Ministers, see PARA 7.
2 As to the Treasury see CONSTITUTIONAL AND ADMINISTRATIVE LAW vol 20 (2014) PARA 262 et seq.
3 For these purposes, 'tenant' does not include a tenant under a long lease within the meaning of the Landlord and Tenant Act 1987 (see LANDLORD AND TENANT vol 62 (2016) PARA 141): see the Local Government and Housing Act 1989 s 168(3).
4 Local Government and Housing Act 1989 s 168(1). For these purposes, 'dwelling' means a building or a part of a building occupied or intended to be occupied as a separate dwelling: s 168(3). As to separate dwellings cf LANDLORD AND TENANT vol 63 (2016) PARAS 661–669.
5 Local Government and Housing Act 1989 s 168(2).

536. The improvement for sale scheme. The appropriate national authority[1] may (with, in relation to England, the consent of the Treasury[2]) make schemes for making contributions to the net cost (as determined under the schemes) to local housing authorities[3] of disposing of dwellings where the authority:

(1) disposes of a house[4] as one dwelling;
(2) divides a house into two or more separate dwellings and disposes of them; or
(3) combines two houses to form one dwelling and disposes of it,

after carrying out works of repair, improvement or conversion[5].

The cost towards which contributions may be made under such a scheme must not exceed, for any one dwelling, £10,000 in respect of a dwelling in Greater London or £7,500 in respect of a dwelling elsewhere, or such other amount as may be prescribed by order of the appropriate national authority made, in relation to England, with the consent of the Treasury[6]. Such an order may make different provision in respect of different cases or descriptions of case, including different provision for different areas, and must be made by statutory instrument subject to annulment in pursuance of a resolution of either House of Parliament[7].

1 As to the appropriate national authority, ie the Secretary of State or, where statutory functions have been transferred in relation to Wales, the Welsh Ministers, see PARA 7.
2 As to the Treasury see CONSTITUTIONAL AND ADMINISTRATIVE LAW vol 20 (2014) PARA 262 et seq. In relation to Wales, the functions of the Treasury under the Housing Act 1985 s 429 were transferred to the National Assembly for Wales by the National Assembly for Wales (Transfer of Functions) Order 1999, SI 1999/672, art 2, Sch 1 and following the transfer of functions of the Assembly to the Welsh Ministers (see PARA 7) consent is no longer required in relation to Wales.
3 As to the meaning of 'local housing authority' see PARA 11.
4 For these purposes, 'house' includes a flat: Housing Act 1985 s 429(4).
5 Housing Act 1985 s 429(1).
6 Housing Act 1985 s 429(2). See note 2.
7 Housing Act 1985 s 429(3).

4. HOUSING ACTION TRUSTS

(1) AREAS AND TRUSTS

537. Background and general introduction. The Housing Act 1988 provides for the establishment of housing action trusts, set up and funded by central government, whose functions are to improve housing in the worst areas of deprivation[1]. The appropriate national authority[2] has power to define their tasks and appoint their members. These trusts, which are to have a limited life span, have power to take over local authority housing, renovate it and dispose of it to a range of different landlords.

Housing action trusts are governed by Part III of the Housing Act 1988[3]. These provisions give central government wide powers to set up housing action trusts in any part of England and Wales and to take over all or part of the local authority responsibilities in the area affected. These powers and responsibilities can include those relating to planning and public health functions, and highways, as well as those relating to housing[4].

In practice, only six housing action trusts were set up, and all of them have now been dissolved. Stonebridge Housing Action Trust was the last operational trust but it closed in 2007. After completing regeneration of their estates, the housing action trusts transferred ownership of the tenanted housing estates to other social landlords and their residuary assets and undertakings passed to English Partnerships, the national regeneration agency. On 1 December 2008 English Partnerships became part of the Homes and Communities Agency[5].

1   Cf the urban development corporations which were set up under the Local Government, Planning and Land Act 1980 Pt XVI (ss 134–172) (see PLANNING vol 83 (2010) PARA 1575 et seq), allowing central government to intervene directly to regenerate the local economy in areas of urban deprivation. See generally Driscoll *A Guide to the Housing Act 1988* (1989).
2   As to the appropriate national authority, ie the Secretary of State or, where statutory functions have been transferred in relation to Wales, the Welsh Ministers, see PARA 7.
3   Ie the Housing Act 1988 Pt III (ss 60–92). See PARA 538 seq.
4   See PARA 542 et seq.
5   As to the Homes and Communities Agency see PARA 57 et seq; and PLANNING vol 83 (2010) PARA 1454 et seq.

538. Housing action trust areas. The appropriate national authority[1] has power to designate, by order[2], an area of land for which, in its opinion, it is expedient that a housing action trust, having the functions specified by statute[3], should be established[4]. An area designated by such an order is known as a housing action trust area[5]. In deciding whether to make such an order designating any area of land, the appropriate national authority must have regard to such matters as it thinks fit[6].

Before a designation order is made, the statutory requirements as to consultation and publicity must be followed[7].

In principle, a decision made by the appropriate national authority under these provisions is subject to judicial review but the courts will only intervene in highly restricted cases[8].

The appropriate national authority may require a local authority[9] to produce specified documents or provide specified information for any of the following purposes, namely:

(1)   determining whether the appropriate national authority should make a designation order in respect of any area;

(2)   where a designation order is to be or has been made, determining whether, and to what extent, the appropriate national authority should exercise any of its other relevant statutory powers[10];

(3)   enabling the appropriate national authority to provide information to a housing action trust the better to enable it to carry out its functions[11].

1   As to the appropriate national authority, ie the Secretary of State or, where statutory functions have been transferred in relation to Wales, the Welsh Ministers, see PARA 7.
2   An order under these provisions must be made by statutory instrument but no such order may be made unless a draft of it has been laid before, and approved by a resolution of, each House of Parliament or, as appropriate, the National Assembly for Wales: Housing Act 1988 s 60(3). In ss 61–92, such an order is referred to as a 'designation order': ss 60(6)(b), 92(1)(a).
3   Ie the functions specified in the Housing Act 1988 Pt III (ss 60–92).
4   Housing Act 1988 s 60(1). This is subject to s 61 (see the text and note 8): s 60(1). The area designated by such an order may comprise two or more parcels of land which need not be contiguous and need not be in the district of the same local housing authority: s 60(2). 'Local housing authority' has the same meaning as in the Housing Act 1985 (see PARA 11), and s 2 (the district of a local housing authority: see PARA 11) has effect in relation to the Housing Act 1988 Pt III as it has effect in relation to the Housing Act 1985: Housing Act 1988 s 92(1)(d). As to the meaning of 'district' see PARA 11.
5   Housing Act 1988 s 60(6). In ss 61–92, such an area is referred to as a 'designated area': ss 60(6)(a), 92(1)(a).
6   Housing Act 1988 s 60(4). As to matters to be taken into consideration without prejudice to the generality of s 60(4) see s 60(5).
7   See the Housing Act 1988 s 61 (amended by the Deregulation Act 2015 s 103(3), Sch 22 para 9; and by SI 1997/74); and the Housing Action Trust Areas (Tenant Notification) Regulations 1989, SI 1989/1246. As to the meaning of consultation see eg *R v Secretary of State for Social Services, ex p Association of Metropolitan Authorities* [1986] 1 All ER 164, [1986] 1 WLR 1.
8   See eg *Nottinghamshire County Council v Secretary of State for the Environment* [1986] AC 240, [1986] 1 All ER 199, HL.
9   For these purposes, 'local authority' has the same meaning as in the Housing Act 1988 s 74 (see PARA 551 note 8): s 90(7).
10 Ie his other powers under the Housing Act 1988 Pt III.
11 See the Housing Act 1988 s 90 (amended by the Land Registration Act 2002 s 133, Sch 11 para 23(1), (4)). As to the functions of a housing action trust see PARA 542 et seq.

539. Establishment of housing action trusts. Subject as follows, where the appropriate national authority[1] makes a designation order[2], it must in that order or by a separate order[3] either establish a housing action trust for the designated area[4] or specify as the housing action trust for the designated area a housing action trust already established for another designated area[5]. A housing action trust is not to be regarded as the servant or agent of the Crown or as enjoying any status, immunity or privilege of the Crown and the trust's property is not to be regarded as the property of, or property held on behalf of, the Crown[6].

Detailed provision is made as to the constitution and staff[7] of housing action trusts, and as to their finances, including requirements as to accounts and reports[8].

1   As to the appropriate national authority, ie the Secretary of State or, where statutory functions have been transferred in relation to Wales, the Welsh Ministers, see PARA 7.
2   As to the meaning of 'designation order' see PARA 538 note 2.
3   Such a separate order must be made by statutory instrument but no such order may be made unless a draft of it has been laid before, and approved by a resolution of, each House of Parliament or, as appropriate, the National Assembly for Wales: Housing Act 1988 s 62(2).
4   As to the meaning of 'designated area' see PARA 538 note 5.
5   Housing Act 1988 s 62(1). A housing action trust is to be a body corporate by such name as may be prescribed by the order establishing it (s 62(3)), but where the appropriate national authority specifies as the housing action trust for the designated area a housing action trust already established for another designated area, the housing action trust specified in the order must, by virtue of the order, be treated as established for the new designated area as well as for any designated area for which it is already established and the order may alter the name of the trust to take account of the addition of the new designated area (s 62(4)).

6   Housing Act 1988 s 62(6).
7   See the Housing Act 1988 s 62(5), Sch 7 (Sch 7 amended by the Housing Act 1996 ss 222, 227, Sch 18 para 22(1)(e), Sch 19 Pt XIII; and by SI 2012/2404).
8   See the Housing Act 1988 Sch 8 (amended by the Government of Wales Act 2006 s 160(1), Sch 10 para 33; and by SI 1991/1997 and SI 2008/948). The requirements for Treasury approval under the Housing Act 1988 Sch 8 paras 2, 4, 6, 7 and Treasury consent under Sch 8 para 10 have not been transferred in relation to Wales: see the National Assembly for Wales (Transfer of Functions) Order 1999, SI 1999/672, art 2, Sch 1. Housing action trusts were expected to attract private capital into the designated area. In addition, they received central government funding. A housing action trust would also have a rental income from the housing it managed and it is possible that the transferring local authority might be required to make a payment on the transfer if the dwellings transferred had negative value. It was also possible that a trust would receive capital receipts on the sale of housing to other landlords or where a tenant exercised the right to buy. Subject to the statutory provisions a housing action trust had power to borrow money to finance its operation.

540.   Objects and general powers of housing action trusts. The primary objects of a housing action trust[1] in relation to the designated area[2] for which it is established are:

(1)   to secure the repair or improvement of housing accommodation[3] for the time being held by the trust;

(2)   to secure the proper and effective management and use of that housing accommodation;

(3)   to encourage diversity in the interests by virtue of which housing accommodation in the area is occupied and, in the case of accommodation which is occupied under tenancies, diversity in the identity of the landlords; and

(4)   generally to secure or facilitate the improvement of living conditions of those living in the area and the social conditions and general environment of the area[4].

Without prejudice to heads (1) to (4), a housing action trust may provide and maintain housing accommodation and facilitate the provision of shops, advice centres and other facilities for the benefit of the community or communities who live in the designated area[5]. It is immaterial for these purposes whether action taken by a housing action trust for achieving its objects or exercising the powers so conferred on it also benefits persons who do not live in the designated area or improves the social conditions or general environment of an area outside the designated area[6].

For the protection of those dealing with a housing action trust, it is provided that a transaction between any person and a housing action trust is not invalidated by reason of any failure by the trust to observe the statutory objects[7] or the requirement that the trust must exercise the statutory powers conferred on it[8] for the specified purpose[9].

With the approval of the appropriate national authority[10], a housing action trust may enter into an agreement with another person under which that person exercises specified functions of the trust as its agent[11].

A housing action trust and an urban development corporation[12], or a housing action trust and a Mayoral development corporation[13], may enter into any agreement with each other for all or any of the specified purposes[14] of the Local Authorities (Goods and Services) Act 1970 as if they were local authorities within the meaning[15] of that Act[16].

1   As to the establishment and constitution of housing action trusts see PARA 539.
2   As to the meaning of 'designated area' see PARA 538 note 5.
3   'Housing accommodation' includes flats, lodging-houses and hostels: Housing Act 1988 s 92(1)(c).

4   Housing Act 1988 s 63(1) (amended by the Housing Act 1996 s 222, Sch 18 para 25(1)). As to the achieving by a housing action trust of its objects and the exercise of its powers see further the Housing Act 1988 s 63(3), (4). In carrying out its functions, a housing action trust must comply with the requirements of the legislation relating to discrimination, particularly on the grounds of race or disability. As to discrimination see the Equality Act 2010; and DISCRIMINATION vol 33 (2013) PARA 65 et seq.
5   Housing Act 1988 s 63(2).
6   Housing Act 1988 s 63(2A) (added by the Housing Act 1996 Sch 18 para 25(1)).
7   Ie the objects in the Housing Act 1988 s 63(1): see heads (1)–(4) in the text.
8   Ie by the Housing Act 1988 s 63(2) or (3): see note 4.
9   Housing Act 1988 s 63(6). The specified purpose is that referred to in s 63(2) or (3): s 63(6).
10 As to the appropriate national authority, ie the Secretary of State or, where statutory functions have been transferred in relation to Wales, the Welsh Ministers, see PARA 7.
11 See the Housing Act 1988 s 87.
12 Ie an urban development corporation established by an order under the Local Government, Planning and Land Act 1980 s 135: see PLANNING vol 83 (2010) PARA 1581.
13 As to Mayoral development corporations see LONDON GOVERNMENT vol 71 (2013) PARA 323.
14 Ie the purposes set out in the Local Authorities (Goods and Services) Act 1970 s 1(1): see LOCAL GOVERNMENT vol 69 (2009) PARA 495.
15 Ie within the meaning of the Housing Act 1988 s 1: see LOCAL GOVERNMENT vol 69 (2009) PARA 495.
16 Housing Act 1988 s 89(1) (amended by the Localism Act 2011 s 222, Sch 22 paras 25, 28).

541. The housing action trust's proposals for its area. As soon as practicable after a housing action trust has been established[1] for a designated area[2], the trust must prepare a statement of its proposals with regard to the exercise of its functions in relation to the area[3]. In doing so, the trust must consult every local housing authority[4] or county council, any part of whose area lies within the designated area, with regard to the proposals contained in the statement[5].

A housing action trust must take such steps as it considers appropriate to secure:

(1)   that adequate publicity is given in the designated area to the proposals contained in the statement;

(2)   that those who live in the designated area are made aware that they have an opportunity to make, within such time as the trust may specify, representations to the trust with respect to those proposals; and

(3)   that those who live in the designated area are given an adequate opportunity of making such representations,

and the trust must consider any such representations as may be made within the time specified[6].

As soon as may be after a housing action trust has complied with these requirements, it must send to the appropriate national authority[7] a copy of the statement so prepared together with a report of the steps the trust has taken to consult as mentioned above and to secure the matters referred to in heads (1) to (3) and the consideration it has given to points raised in the course of consultation and to representations received[8].

At such times as a housing action trust considers appropriate or as it may be directed by the appropriate national authority, the trust must prepare a further statement of its proposals with regard to the exercise of its functions in relation to its area; in which case the consultation and reporting requirements set out above again apply as they applied in relation to the first statement[9].

1   As to the establishment and constitution of housing action trusts see PARA 539.
2   As to the meaning of 'designated area' see PARA 538 note 5.
3   Housing Act 1988 s 64(1) (amended by the Housing Act 1996 s 222, Sch 18 para 25(2)). As to the functions of a housing action trust see PARA 542 et seq.
4   As to the meaning of 'local housing authority' see PARA 538 note 4.

5 Housing Act 1988 s 64(2).
6 Housing Act 1988 s 64(3).
7 As to the appropriate national authority, ie the Secretary of State or, where statutory functions have been transferred in relation to Wales, the Welsh Ministers, see PARA 7.
8 Housing Act 1988 s 64(4).
9 Housing Act 1988 s 64(5) (amended by the Housing Act 1996 Sch 18 para 25(2)).

(2) FUNCTIONS OF HOUSING ACTION TRUSTS

542. Background and general introduction. The transfer of local authority housing to a housing action trust necessarily involves a transfer of the housing management obligations which are conferred on a landlord by the Housing Act 1985[1]. During its period of ownership, the housing action trust will act as the landlord of the tenants whose dwellings have been transferred to it and these tenants will remain secure tenants. In effect, the housing action trust has much the same role as does a local authority acting as a landlord under the Housing Act 1985. Although that Act contains a wide range of local authority powers and duties, from the provision of housing to dealing with overcrowding and slum clearance, not all these powers and duties will necessarily be transferred. In practice, the specific role of a housing action trust and the extent of its powers are shaped by factors such as its size, scale of operation and its relationship with the relevant local authorities.

1 See PARA 543.

543. Housing action trust as housing authority etc. If the appropriate national authority[1] so provides by order[2], in a designated area[3] or, as the case may be, in such part of the area as may be specified in the order, the housing action trust[4] for the area is to have such of the statutory functions[5] as may be specified in the order[6]. On the coming into force of the order, as respects that area any function conferred on a housing action trust by the order is exercisable, according to the terms of the order, either: (1) by the trust instead of by the authority by which, apart from the order, the function would be exercisable; or (2) by the trust concurrently with that authority[7].

Any enactment under which a housing action trust is to exercise a function by virtue of an order so made has effect: (a) in relation to the trust; and (b) where the trust is to have the function concurrently with another authority, in relation to that authority, subject to such modifications (if any) as may be specified in the order[8].

Where a housing action trust is to exercise functions conferred[9] on a local housing authority, the statutory provisions for the recovery by local authorities of establishment charges[10] apply to the housing action trust as if it were a local authority[11].

Such (if any) of the provisions of Parts XVII and XVIII of the Housing Act 1985[12] as may be specified in an order under these provisions have effect in relation to a housing action trust subject to such modifications as may be specified in the order[13].

1 As to the appropriate national authority, ie the Secretary of State or, where statutory functions have been transferred in relation to Wales, the Welsh Ministers, see PARA 7.
2 As to the making of an order under these provisions see the Housing Act 1988 s 65(7).
3 As to the meaning of 'designated area' see PARA 538 note 5.
4 As to the establishment and constitution of housing action trusts see PARA 539.
5 The functions referred to in the text are: (1) the functions conferred on a local housing authority by the Housing Act 1985 Pt II (ss 8–57) (see PARA 520 et seq), Pt VI (ss 189–208) (repealed), Pt VII

(ss 209–238) (repealed), Pts IX–XI (ss 264–400) (see PARA 620 et seq), Pt XVI (ss 527–577) (see PARA 928 et seq), and the Chronically Sick and Disabled Persons Act 1970 s 3(1) (see PARA 401); (2) the functions conferred by the Housing Associations Act 1985 Pt II (ss 41–73) (see PARA 13) on a local authority, within the meaning of that Act; and (3) the functions conferred by the Land Compensation Act 1973 ss 39–41 on the authority which is 'the relevant authority' for the purposes of s 39 (see COMPULSORY ACQUISITION OF LAND vol 18 (2009) PARA 853): Housing Act 1988 s 65(2) (amended by the Housing Act 1996 s 80(2)(b)). As to the meaning of 'local housing authority' see PARA 538 note 4.

6   Housing Act 1988 s 65(1).
7   Housing Act 1988 s 65(3).
8   Housing Act 1988 s 65(4).
9   Ie by any of the Housing Act 1985 Pts VI, VII, IX and XI.
10 Ie the Local Government Act 1974 s 36: see LOCAL GOVERNMENT vol 69 (2009) PARA 583.
11 Housing Act 1988 s 65(5).
12 Ie the Housing Act 1985 ss 578–624 (compulsory purchase, land compensation and miscellaneous and general provisions): see PARA 812 et seq.
13 Housing Act 1988 s 65(6).

544. Planning control. A housing action trust[1] may submit to the appropriate national authority[2] proposals for the development of land within its designated area[3] and the appropriate national authority, after consultation with the local planning authority[4] within whose area the land is situated and with any other local authority which appears to it to be concerned, may approve any such proposals either with or without modification[5]. Without prejudice to the generality of the statutory powers to make development orders[6], a special development order made by the appropriate national authority[7] may grant permission for any development of land in accordance with proposals approved under these provisions, subject to such conditions, if any[8], as may be specified in the order[9].

The appropriate national authority must give to a housing action trust such directions with regard to the disposal of land held by it and with respect to the development by it of such land as appear to him to be necessary or expedient for securing, so far as practicable, the preservation of any features of special architectural or historical interest and, in particular, of any buildings included in any list compiled or approved or having effect as if compiled or approved by him under the relevant provision[10] of the Planning (Listed Buildings and Conservation Areas) Act 1990[11].

1   As to the establishment and constitution of housing action trusts see PARA 539.
2   As to the appropriate national authority, ie the Secretary of State or, where statutory functions have been transferred in relation to Wales, the Welsh Ministers, see PARA 7.
3   As to the meaning of 'designated area' see PARA 538 note 5.
4   Any reference for these purposes to the local planning authority is a reference: (1) in relation to land in Wales, Greater London or a metropolitan county, to the authority which is the local planning authority as ascertained in accordance with the Town and Country Planning Act 1990 ss 1, 2 (see PLANNING vol 81 (2010) PARA 43 et seq); and (2) in relation to other land, to the district planning authority and also (in relation to proposals for any development which is a county matter, as defined in s 1(5), Sch 1 para 1: see PLANNING vol 81 (2010) PARA 53) to the county planning authority: Housing Act 1988 s 66(4) (amended by the Planning (Consequential Provisions) Act 1990 s 4, Sch 2 para 79(2); and the Local Government (Wales) Act 1994 s 22(2), Sch 8 para 9(1)).
5   Housing Act 1988 s 66(1).
6   Ie under the Town and Country Planning Act 1990 ss 59–61: see PLANNING vol 81 (2010) PARA 387 et seq.
7   Ie under the Housing Act 1988 s 59: see PLANNING vol 81 (2010) PARA 387.
8   Ie including conditions requiring details of any proposed development to be submitted to the local planning authority: Housing Act 1988 s 66(2).
9   Housing Act 1988 s 66(2) (s 66(2), (3) amended by the Planning (Consequential Provisions) Act 1990 Sch 2 para 79(2)).

10 Ie under the Planning (Listed Building and Conservation Areas) Act 1990 s 1 (which relates to the compilation or approval by the appropriate national authority of lists of buildings of special architectural or historical interest: see PLANNING vol 83 (2010) PARA 1248).
11 Housing Act 1988 s 66(3) (as amended: see note 9).

545. Housing action trust as planning authority. The appropriate national authority[1] may by order[2] provide that, for such statutory planning control purposes[3], and kinds of development, as are specified in the order, a housing action trust[4] is to be the local planning authority[5] for the whole or such part as may be so specified of its designated area[6]. An order so made may provide that any enactment relating to local planning authorities is not to apply to the trust and that any such enactment which applies to the trust is to apply to it subject to such modifications as may be specified in the order[7].

An order made by the appropriate national authority may provide:

(1)   that, subject to any modifications specified in the order, a housing action trust specified in the order is to have, in the whole or any part of its designated area, such of the functions conferred by certain planning provisions[8] as may be so specified; and

(2)   that such of the provisions relating to planning[9] as are mentioned in the order are to have effect, in relation to the housing action trust specified in the order and to land in the trust's area, subject to the modifications there specified[10].

1   As to the appropriate national authority, ie the Secretary of State or, where statutory functions have been transferred in relation to Wales, the Welsh Ministers, see PARA 7.
2   As to the making of an order under the Housing Act 1988 s 67 (see the text and notes 3–11) see s 67(7).
3   Ie for purposes of the Town and Country Planning Act 1990 Pt III (ss 55–106C) and of the Planning (Listed Buildings and Conservation Areas) Act 1990 ss 67, 73: see PLANNING vol 81 (2010) PARA 292 et seq; PLANNING vol 83 (2010) PARAS 1261, 1322.
4   As to the establishment and constitution of housing action trusts see PARA 539.
5   As to local planning authorities see PLANNING vol 81 (2010) PARA 43 et seq.
6   Housing Act 1988 s 67(1) (s 67(1), (3) amended, and s 67(3A) added, by the Planning (Consequential Provisions) Act 1990 ss 3, 4, Sch 1 Pt I, Sch 2 para 79(3)).
7   Housing Act 1988 s 67(2).
8   The statutory provisions referred to are the Town and Country Planning Act 1990 ss 96, 100, 104, 171C, 171D, 172–185, 187–202, 206–222, 224, 225, 231, 320–336, Sch 9 para 11; the Planning (Listed Buildings and Conservation Areas) Act 1990 Pt I Chs I, II, IV ss 54–56, 59–61, 66, 68–72, 74–76, 88; and the Planning (Hazardous Substances) Act 1990 ss 4–15, 17–21, 23–26AA, 36, 36A: Housing Act 1988 s 67(3A) (as added (see note 6); amended by the Planning and Compensation Act 1991 ss 25, 32, Sch 3 para 18, Sch 7 para 7). See further PLANNING.
9   Ie the provisions of the Town and Country Planning Act 1990 Pt VI (ss 137–171), ss 249–251, 258, and the Planning (Listed Buildings and Conservation Areas) Act 1990 ss 32–37: see PLANNING.
10 Housing Act 1988 s 67(3) (as amended: see note 6). The order may also provide that, for the purposes of any of the provisions specified in the order, any enactment relating to local planning authorities is to apply to the housing action trust specified in the order subject to such modifications as may be so specified: s 67(4).

546. Public health. The appropriate national authority[1] may by order[2] provide that, in relation to premises comprising or consisting of housing accommodation[3], a housing action trust[4] is to have in its designated area[5] (or in such part of its designated area as may be specified in the order) the functions conferred on a local authority by certain statutory provisions[6] relating to public health[7]. On the order coming into force, the trust has the functions conferred in relation to the designated area (or part) instead of or concurrently with any such authority, depending on the terms of the order[8]. The order may provide that any enactment under which the trust is to exercise functions by virtue of the order is to have effect in relation to the trust and, where the trust is to have any function concurrently with another authority, in relation to that authority, as modified by the order[9].

Where such an order provides that a housing action trust is to have the functions conferred upon a local authority by the statutory provisions relating to nuisances and offensive trades[10], the provision for the recovery by local authorities of establishment charges[11] applies to the housing action trust as if it were a local authority[12].

1   As to the appropriate national authority, ie the Secretary of State or, where statutory functions have been transferred in relation to Wales, the Welsh Ministers, see PARA 7.
2   As to such orders see the Housing Act 1988 s 68(5), (6).
3   As to the meaning of 'housing accommodation' see PARA 540 note 3.
4   As to the establishment and constitution of housing action trusts see PARA 539.
5   As to the meaning of 'designated area' see PARA 538 note 5.
6   Ie: (1) the Public Health Act 1936 ss 83, 84 and the Public Health Act 1961 s 36 (filthy or verminous premises or articles); (2) any enactment contained in the Public Health Act 1936 Pt III (repealed) (nuisances and offensive trades); (3) so much of Pt XII (ss 275–347) as relates to any of the enactments mentioned in heads (1)–(2); and (4) the Prevention of Damage by Pests Act 1949 Pt I (ss 1–12) (rats and mice): see further ENVIRONMENTAL QUALITY AND PUBLIC HEALTH.
7   Housing Act 1988 s 68(1).
8   Housing Act 1988 s 68(2).
9   Housing Act 1988 s 68(3).
10 Ie the Public Health Act 1936 Pt III (repealed) (nuisances and offensive trades).
11 Ie the Local Government Act 1974 s 36: see LOCAL GOVERNMENT vol 69 (2009) PARA 583.
12 Housing Act 1988 s 68(4).

547. Highways. When any street works have been executed on any land in a designated area[1] which was then or has since become a private street[2] (or part of a private street), the housing action trust[3] may serve a notice on the street works authority[4] requiring it to declare the street (or part) to be a highway which for the purposes of the Highways Act 1980 is a highway maintainable at the public expense[5]. Within the period of two months beginning on the date of the service of such a notice, the street works authority may appeal against the notice to the appropriate national authority[6]. After considering any representations made to it by the housing action trust and the street works authority, the appropriate national authority must determine such an appeal by setting aside or confirming the notice with or without modifications[7]. Where the appropriate national authority confirms a notice under these provisions:

(1)   it may at the same time impose conditions (including financial conditions) upon the housing action trust with which the trust must comply in order for the notice to take effect; and

(2)   the highway (or part) becomes a highway maintainable at the public expense with effect from such date as the appropriate national authority may specify[8].

Where a street works authority neither complies with the notice nor appeals under these provisions, the street (or part) concerned becomes a highway maintainable at the public expense upon the expiry of the specified two-month period[9].

1   As to the meaning of 'designated area' see PARA 538 note 5.
2   For these purposes, 'private street' has the same meaning as in the Highways Act 1980 Pt XI (ss 203–237) (see HIGHWAYS, STREETS AND BRIDGES vol 55 (2012) PARA 10): Housing Act 1988 s 69(6).
3   As to the establishment and constitution of housing action trusts see PARA 539.
4   For these purposes, 'street works authority' has the same meaning as in the Highways Act 1980 Pt XI (see HIGHWAYS, STREETS AND BRIDGES vol 55 (2012) PARA 144): Housing Act 1988 s 69(6).

5 Housing Act 1988 s 69(1) (amended by the Leasehold Reform, Housing and Urban Development Act 1993 s 182(1)). As to the service of a notice required or authorised by the Housing Act 1988 Pt III (ss 60–92) to be served on any person by a housing action trust see s 91.

As to highways maintainable at the public expense see HIGHWAYS, STREETS AND BRIDGES vol 55 (2012) PARA 250 et seq.

6 Housing Act 1988 s 69(2) (amended by the Leasehold Reform, Housing and Urban Development Act 1993 ss 182(2), 187(2), Sch 22).
7 Housing Act 1988 s 69(3).
8 Housing Act 1988 s 69(4).
9 Housing Act 1988 s 69(5).

548. Power to give financial assistance. For the purpose of achieving its objects[1] a housing action trust[2] may, with the consent of the appropriate national authority[3], give financial assistance to any person[4]. Such financial assistance may be given in any form and, in particular, may be given by way of:

(1) grants;
(2) loans;
(3) guarantees;
(4) incurring expenditure for the benefit of the person assisted; or
(5) purchasing loan or share capital in a company[5],

and may be given on such terms as the housing action trust, with the consent of the appropriate national authority, considers appropriate[6].

Any person receiving such assistance must comply with the terms on which it is given and compliance may be enforced by the housing action trust[7].

1 As to the objects of a housing action trust see PARA 540.
2 As to the establishment and constitution of housing action trusts see PARA 539.
3 As to consent under these provisions see the Housing Act 1988 s 71(4). As to the appropriate national authority, ie the Secretary of State or, where statutory functions have been transferred in relation to Wales, the Welsh Ministers, see PARA 7.
4 Housing Act 1988 s 71(1).
5 Housing Act 1988 s 71(2).
6 Housing Act 1988 s 71(3). Those terms may, in particular, include provision as to: (1) the circumstances in which the assistance must be repaid or otherwise made good to the housing action trust and the manner in which that is to be done; or (2) the circumstances in which the housing action trust is entitled to recover the proceeds or part of the proceeds of any disposal of land or buildings in respect of which assistance was provided: s 71(5). The consent of the appropriate national authority must be given with the approval of the Treasury: see s 71(4). As to the Treasury see CONSTITUTIONAL AND ADMINISTRATIVE LAW vol 20 (2014) PARA 262 et seq.
7 Housing Act 1988 s 71(6).

549. Directions as to the exercise of functions. In the exercise of its functions[1], a housing action trust[2] must comply with any directions given by the appropriate national authority[3]. Directions given by the appropriate national authority may be of a general or particular character and may be varied or revoked by subsequent directions[4]. The appropriate national authority must publish any such direction[5].

A transaction between any person and a housing action trust acting in purported exercise of its statutory powers[6] is not void by reason only that the transaction was carried out in contravention of a direction so given; and a person dealing with a housing action trust is not to be concerned to see or inquire whether such a direction has been given or complied with[7].

1 As to the functions of a housing action trust see PARA 542 et seq.
2 As to the establishment and constitution of housing action trusts see PARA 539.
3 Housing Act 1988 s 72(1). As to the appropriate national authority, ie the Secretary of State or, where statutory functions have been transferred in relation to Wales, the Welsh Ministers, see PARA 7.
4 Housing Act 1988 s 72(2).
5 Housing Act 1988 s 72(3).

6 Ie its powers under the Housing Act 1988 Pt III (ss 60–92).
7 Housing Act 1988 s 72(4).

550. Transfer of functions. If, in the case of any designated area[1], it appears to the appropriate national authority[2] that it is expedient that the functions of a housing action trust established for the area[3] should be transferred: (1) to the housing action trust established for another designated area; or (2) to a new housing action trust to be established for the area, it may by order provide for the dissolution of the first-mentioned trust and for the transfer of its functions, property, rights and liabilities to that other trust, or, as the case may be, to a new housing action trust established for the area by the order[4]. Before making such an order the appropriate national authority must consult the housing action trust whose functions are to be transferred and also, where the transfer is to an existing trust, the housing action trust to which the functions are to be transferred[5].

Where such an order provides for the functions of a housing action trust established for a designated area to be transferred to the housing action trust established for another designated area the latter trust is, by virtue of the order, to be treated as established for the first-mentioned designated area (as well as its own designated area) and the order may alter the name of the latter trust in such manner as appears to the appropriate national authority to be expedient[6].

1 As to the meaning of 'designated area' see PARA 538 note 5.
2 As to the appropriate national authority, ie the Secretary of State or, where statutory functions have been transferred in relation to Wales, the Welsh Ministers, see PARA 7.
3 As to the establishment and constitution of housing action trusts see PARA 539.
4 Housing Act 1988 s 73(1). As to orders under s 73 see s 73(4).
5 Housing Act 1988 s 73(3).
6 Housing Act 1988 s 73(2).

(3) TRANSFER OF HOUSING ACCOMMODATION; VESTING AND ACQUISITION OF LAND

551. Transfer of land and other property to housing action trusts. The appropriate national authority[1] may by order[2] provide for the transfer from a local housing authority[3] to a housing action trust[4] of all or any of the authority's local authority housing[5] situated in the designated area[6] and any other land held or provided in connection with that local authority housing[7]. If in the opinion of the appropriate national authority a housing action trust requires for the purposes of its functions any land which, though not falling within provision described above, is situated in the designated area and held (for whatever purpose) by a local authority[8], the appropriate national authority may by order provide for the transfer of that land to the trust[9]. The appropriate national authority may also by order transfer from a local housing authority or other local authority to a housing action trust so much as appears to it to be appropriate of any property[10] which is held or used by the authority in connection with any local authority housing or other land transferred to the trust under these powers[11].

Such a transfer of any local authority housing or other land or property is to be on such terms, including financial terms[12], as the appropriate national authority thinks fit[13].

Before making a transfer order, the appropriate national authority must comply with the statutory requirements as to consultation and publicity[14].

1 As to the appropriate national authority, ie the Secretary of State or, where statutory functions have been transferred in relation to Wales, the Welsh Ministers, see PARA 7.

2   As to the making of orders under these provisions see the Housing Act 1988 s 74(7); and as to such orders see further s 75(4). An order under s 74(1)–(3) is referred to as a 'transfer order': see s 75(1). Such orders are local in effect and are not recorded in this work.
3   As to the meaning of 'local housing authority' see PARA 538 note 4.
4   As to the establishment and constitution of housing action trusts see PARA 539.
5   For these purposes, 'local authority housing' means housing accommodation provided by a local housing authority, whether in its own district or not: Housing Act 1988 s 92(1)(e). As to the meaning of 'housing accommodation' see PARA 540 note 3.
6   As to the meaning of 'designated area' see PARA 538 note 5.
7   Housing Act 1988 s 74(1).
8   For the purposes of the Housing Act 1988 s 74, 'local authority' means any of the following: (1) a local housing authority; (2) the council of a county; (3) the former Inner London Education Authority (abolished with effect from 1 April 1990: see the Education Reform Act 1988 s 162 (repealed)); (4) an authority established by an order under the Local Government Act 1985 s 10(1) (waste disposal: see LOCAL GOVERNMENT vol 69 (2009) PARA 17); (5) a joint authority established by Pt IV (ss 23–42) (see LOCAL GOVERNMENT vol 69 (2009) PARA 47); (6) a residuary body established by Pt VII (ss 57–67) (see LOCAL GOVERNMENT vol 69 (2009) PARA 17); (7) an economic prosperity board established under the Local Democracy, Economic Development and Construction Act 2009 s 88 (see TRADE AND INDUSTRY vol 97 (2015) PARA 1086 et seq); (8) a combined authority established under s 103 (see TRADE AND INDUSTRY vol 97 (2015) PARA 1092 et seq); and (9) the London Fire and Emergency Planning Authority: Housing Act 1988 s 74(8) (amended by the Greater London Authority Act 1999 s 328, 423, Sch 29 para 52, Sch 34 Pt VIII; and the Local Democracy, Economic Development and Construction Act 2009 s 119, Sch 6 para 79(1), (2)). As to local authorities see further LOCAL GOVERNMENT vol 69 (2009) PARA 22 et seq. As to the London Fire and Emergency Planning Authority see FIRE AND RESCUE SERVICES vol 51 (2013) PARA 17.
9   Housing Act 1988 s 74(2).
10 For this purpose, 'property' includes chattels of any description and rights and liabilities, whether arising by contract or otherwise: Housing Act 1988 s 74(3).
11 Housing Act 1988 s 74(3).
12 As to the financial terms see the Housing Act 1988 s 74(5), (6) (s 74(6) amended by the Local Government and Public Involvement in Health Act 2007 s 238(1); and by SI 1990/778).
13 Housing Act 1988 s 74(4). An order under s 74 may provide that, notwithstanding anything in the Law of Property Act 1925 s 141 (rent and the benefit of lessee's covenants to run with the reversion: see LANDLORD AND TENANT vol 62 (2016) PARA 458), any rent or other sum which arises under a tenancy of any local authority housing or other land transferred to the housing action trust under these powers and which falls due before the date of the transfer is to continue to be recoverable by the local housing authority or, as the case may be, the local authority to the exclusion of the trust and of any other person in whom the reversion on the tenancy may become vested: Housing Act 1988 s 74(4).
14 See the Housing Act 1988 s 75(1)–(3).

552. Vesting of land by order in housing action trust. The appropriate national authority[1] may by order[2] provide that land specified in the order which is vested in statutory undertakers[3] or any other public body or in a wholly-owned subsidiary[4] of a public body is to vest in a housing action trust[5] established or to be established for the designated area[6] in which the land is situated[7]. Such an order may not, however, specify land vested in statutory undertakers which is used for the purpose of carrying on their statutory undertakings[8] or which is held for that purpose[9]; and, in the case of land vested in statutory undertakers, the power to make such an order is exercisable by the appropriate national authority and the appropriate minister[10].

An order under these provisions has the same effect as a declaration under the Compulsory Purchase (Vesting Declarations) Act 1981 except that, in relation to such an order, certain provisions of the Land Compensation Act 1961[11] have effect subject to modifications[12]. Compensation under the Land Compensation Act 1961, as so applied, must be assessed by reference to values current on the date the vesting order under these provisions comes into force[13].

1   As to the appropriate national authority, ie the Secretary of State or, where statutory functions have been transferred in relation to Wales, the Welsh Ministers, see PARA 7.

2   As to the making of an order under the Housing Act 1988 s 76 see s 76(7).
3   As to the meaning of 'statutory undertakers' for these purposes see the Housing Act 1988 s 76(4), Sch 9 paras 1, 2(1), 4, 5 (Sch 9 para 4 amended by the Planning (Consequential Provisions) Act 1990 s 4, Sch 2 para 79(5); the British Technology Group Act 1991 s 17(2), Sch 2 Pt I; the Coal Industry Act 1994 s 67(1), (8), Sch 9 para 37, Sch 11 Pt II; and by SI 2001/1149 and SI 2013/687).
4   'Wholly-owned subsidiary' has the meaning given by the Companies Act 2006 s 1159 (see COMPANIES vol 14 (2016) PARA 22): Housing Act 1988 Sch 9 para 2(2) (amended by SI 2009/1941).
5   As to the establishment and constitution of housing action trusts see PARA 539.
6   As to the meaning of 'designated area' see PARA 538 note 5.
7   Housing Act 1988 s 76(1). No order, however, may be made under s 76 in relation to a universal service provider (within the meaning of the Postal Services Act 2011 Pt 3 (ss 27–67): see POSTAL SERVICES vol 85 (2012) PARA 252): Housing Act 1988 s 76(6A) (added by SI 2001/1149; and amended by the Postal Services Act 2011 s 91(1), (2), Sch 12 paras 128, 129).
8   'Statutory undertaking' is to be construed in accordance with the Housing Act 1988 Sch 9 para 4(a)–(d) (see note 3): Sch 9 para 4.
9   Housing Act 1988 s 76(2).
10 Housing Act 1988 s 76(3). As to the reference in the text to the appropriate national authority and the appropriate minister see Sch 9 para 3 (Sch 9 para 3(1) amended by the Planning (Consequential Provisions) Act 1990 Sch 2 para 79(5)). The Treasury function under the Housing Act 1988 Sch 9 para 3(2) has not been transferred in relation to Wales: see the National Assembly for Wales (Transfer of Functions) Order 1999, SI 1999/672, art 2, Sch 1.
11 Ie those mentioned in the Housing Act 1988 Sch 9 Pt II (paras 6–12): see note 12.
12 Housing Act 1988 s 76(5). As to vesting declarations under the Compulsory Purchase (Vesting Declarations) Act 1981 (Sch 2 para 1 of which is modified to include a reference to the Housing Act 1988 s 76(5) by Sch 9 para 12(1)) see COMPULSORY ACQUISITION OF LAND vol 18 (2009) PARA 686 et seq. As to the modification of the provisions of the Land Compensation Act 1961 (see COMPULSORY ACQUISITION OF LAND vol 18 (2009) PARA 501 et seq) in relation to orders under the Housing Act 1988 s 76 see Sch 9 paras 6–11 (Sch 9 para 8 amended by the Localism Act 2011 s 232(7)).
13 Housing Act 1988 s 76(6). As to compensation see further COMPULSORY ACQUISITION OF LAND vol 18 (2009) PARA 753 et seq.

553. Acquisition of land by housing action trust. For the purposes of achieving its objects[1] and performing any of its functions[2], a housing action trust[3] may acquire land within its designated area[4] by agreement[5] or, on being authorised to do so by the appropriate national authority[6], compulsorily[7]. A housing action trust may similarly acquire land adjacent to the designated area which the trust requires for purposes connected with the discharge of its functions in the area, and land outside the designated area, whether or not adjacent to it, which the trust requires for the provision of services in connection with the discharge of its functions in the area[8]. Where a housing action trust exercises its powers under either of these provisions in relation to land which forms part of a common[9] or open space[10] or fuel or field garden allotment[11], the trust may acquire[12] land for giving in exchange for the land acquired[13].

A housing action trust may be authorised by the appropriate national authority, by means of a compulsory purchase order[14], to purchase compulsorily such new rights[15] as are specified in the order, being rights over land:

(1)   in the designated area and which the trust requires for the purposes of its functions;

(2)   adjacent to the designated area and which the trust requires for purposes connected with the discharge of its functions in the area; and

(3)   outside the designated area, whether or not adjacent to it, and which the trust requires for the provision of services in connection with the discharge of its functions in the area[16].

Specific provision is made as to the extinguishment of rights over land vested in or acquired by a housing action trust[17], as to the extinguishment of public rights of way over such land[18] and as to the rights and apparatus of statutory undertakers on land acquired by a housing action trust[19]. Special provision is made as to consecrated land and burial grounds[20] and open spaces[21] vested in or acquired by a housing action trust. If the appropriate national authority certifies that possession of a house which has been vested in or acquired by a housing action trust for the statutory purposes and is for the time being held by that trust for the purposes for which it was acquired, is immediately required for those purposes, nothing in the Rent (Agriculture) Act 1976 or the Rent Act 1977 or the Housing Act 1988 is to prevent that trust from obtaining possession of the house[22].

1 As to the objects of a housing action trust see PARA 540.
2 As to the functions of a housing action trust see PARA 542 et seq.
3 As to the establishment and constitution of housing action trusts see PARA 539.
4 As to the meaning of 'designated area' see PARA 538 note 5.
5 The provisions of the Compulsory Purchase Act 1965 Pt I (ss 1–32) (so far as applicable), other than s 31 (ecclesiastical property), apply in relation to the acquisition of land by agreement under these provisions; and in Pt I as so applied 'land' has the meaning given by the Interpretation Act 1978 (see STATUTES AND LEGISLATIVE PROCESS vol 96 (2012) PARA 1215): Housing Act 1988 s 77(7). See further COMPULSORY ACQUISITION OF LAND vol 18 (2009) PARA 501 et seq.
6 As to the appropriate national authority, ie the Secretary of State or, where statutory functions have been transferred in relation to Wales, the Welsh Ministers, see PARA 7.
7 Housing Act 1988 s 77(1). The Acquisition of Land Act 1981 applies in relation to the compulsory acquisition of land in pursuance of the Housing Act 1988 s 77(1)–(3): s 77(4). The Acquisition of Land Act 1981, as so applied, has effect as if the reference in s 17(3) to statutory undertakers included a reference to a housing action trust: Housing Act 1988 s 78(1), Sch 10 Pt I (paras 1–3) (amended by the Planning and Compulsory Purchase Act 2004 ss 118(2), 120, Sch 7 para 15(1), Sch 9). See further COMPULSORY ACQUISITION OF LAND vol 18 (2009) PARA 501 et seq.
8 Housing Act 1988 s 77(2). See also notes 5, 7.
9 As to commons see COMMONS vol 13 (2009) PARA 401 et seq.
10 As to open spaces see OPEN SPACES AND COUNTRYSIDE vol 78 (2010) PARA 501 et seq.
11 As to fuel or field garden allotments see AGRICULTURAL LAND vol 1 (2008) PARA 511 et seq.
12 Ie by agreement or, on being authorised to do so by the appropriate national authority, compulsorily: Housing Act 1988 s 77(3).
13 Housing Act 1988 s 77(3).
14 For these purposes, 'compulsory purchase order' has the same meaning as in the Acquisition of Land Act 1981 (see COMPULSORY ACQUISITION OF LAND vol 18 (2009) PARA 557); and Sch 3 (see COMPULSORY ACQUISITION OF LAND vol 18 (2009) PARA 606 et seq) applies to a compulsory purchase of a right by virtue of heads (1)–(3) in the text: Housing Act 1988 s 77(6)(b).
15 For these purposes, 'new rights' means rights which are not in existence when the order specifying them is made: Housing Act 1988 s 77(6)(a).
16 Housing Act 1988 s 77(5). The Compulsory Purchase Act 1965 has effect with the modifications necessary to make it apply to the compulsory purchase of rights by virtue of the Housing Act 1988 s 77(5) as it applies to the compulsory purchase of land so that, in appropriate contexts, references in the Compulsory Purchase Act 1965 to land are to be read as referring, or as including references, to the rights or to land over which the rights are or are to be exercisable, according to the requirements of the particular context; and without prejudice to the generality of this, in relation to the purchase of rights in pursuance of the Housing Act 1988 s 77(5), the Compulsory Purchase Act 1965 Pt I (ss 1–32) (which relates to compulsory purchases under the Acquisition of Land Act 1981: see COMPULSORY ACQUISITION OF LAND vol 18 (2009) PARA 501 et seq) has effect with the modifications specified in the Housing Act 1988 Sch 10 paras 21–23, and the enactments relating to compensation for the compulsory purchase of land apply with the necessary modifications as they apply to such compensation: Sch 10 para 20(1), (2).
17 See the Housing Act 1988 s 78(2)(a), Sch 10 para 4 (amended by the Communications Act 2003 s 406(1), Sch 17 para 94(1), (2)).
18 See the Housing Act 1988 Sch 10 paras 9, 10 (Sch 10 para 9(7) amended by the Postal Services Act 2011 s 91(1), (2), Sch 12 paras 128, 130; and by SI 2001/1149). Specific provision is made as to telegraphic lines (see the Housing Act 1988 Sch 10 para 11 (amended by the Communications Act 2003 Sch 17 para 94(1), (2))).
19 See the Housing Act 1988 Sch 10 paras 12–18 (Sch 10 paras 12, 14 amended by the Planning (Consequential Provisions) Act 1990 s 4, Sch 2 para 79(5); and the Communications Act 2003 Sch 17 para 94(1), (2)).

20 See the Housing Act 1988 Sch 10 para 6 (amended by the Housing and Planning Act 2016 s 206, Sch 19 para 7(1), (3)).
21 See the Housing Act 1988 Sch 10 para 7 (amended by the Housing and Planning Act 2016 Sch 19 para 7(1), (4)).
22 See the Housing Act 1988 Sch 10 para 8.

(4) DISPOSALS OF LAND

554. Background and general introduction. The primary task of a housing action trust is to renovate and improve the dwellings it has acquired with a view to selling them to a range of different landlords[1]. While a housing action trust is improving its dwellings, it is the landlord of the tenants concerned. Once the works have been completed a housing action trust will wish to sell or transfer the improved dwellings. However, secure tenants may only be transferred to a landlord which has been approved by the appropriate national authority, such as a non-profit registered provider of social housing or a registered social landlord[2], and a majority of the tenants can require the housing action trust to transfer their dwellings to the local authority from which they were originally acquired[3]. Disposals of land by a housing action trust may only take place if they have been approved by the appropriate national authority[4]; and, if the transfer is to a landlord other than a local authority, that landlord must also carry out a consultation exercise and obtain the appropriate national authority's consent before a further disposal[5]. However, some disposals are exempt from these requirements; in particular, a sale to a secure tenant under the right to buy provisions in the Housing Act 1985 does not require the approval of the appropriate national authority[6].

1 See PARA 540.
2 As to registered social landlords see PARA 166 et seq.
3 See PARA 558.
4 See PARAS 555–558.
5 See PARA 556.
6 See PARA 558.

555. Disposal of land. Subject as follows, and subject to any directions given by the appropriate national authority[1], a housing action trust[2] may, with the consent of the appropriate national authority[3], dispose of any land[4] for the time being held by it to such persons, in such manner and on such terms as it considers expedient for the purpose of achieving its objects[5]. A housing action trust may not, however, dispose of a house[6] which is for the time being subject to a secure tenancy[7] or an introductory tenancy[8] except to:

(1)   a non-profit registered provider of social housing[9];
(2)   a registered social landlord[10]; or
(3)   a local housing authority[11] or other local authority,

unless the disposal is made under the right to buy provisions[12].

Any disposal of a house by a housing action trust which is made without the required consent is void unless the disposal is to an individual (or to two or more individuals), and the disposal does not extend to any other house[13]. Subject to this, a disposal of any land made by a housing action trust is not invalid by reason only that it is made without the required consent, and a person dealing with a housing action trust or with a person claiming under such a trust is not to be concerned to see or inquire whether any such consent has been obtained[14].

A housing action trust is treated as a local authority for the purposes of the statutory provisions relating to limitations on service charges and requests for information about costs[15], and those provisions do not, therefore, apply to a service charge payable by a tenant of a housing action trust unless the tenancy is a long tenancy[16].

Where, on the disposal of a house under the statutory provisions[17], a discount is given to the purchaser by the housing action trust in accordance with a consent given by the appropriate national authority[18] and that consent does not exclude the application of the relevant statutory provisions, the trust or another person may be given a right of first refusal, until the end of the period of ten years beginning with the conveyance, grant or assignment, to have a disposal of the house made to it or him for a specified consideration[19].

Specific provision is made as to the treatment of deferred resale agreements[20].

1   As to the appropriate national authority, ie the Secretary of State or, where statutory functions have been transferred in relation to Wales, the Welsh Ministers, see PARA 7.
2   As to the establishment and constitution of housing action trusts see PARA 539.
3   As to such consent see the Housing Act 1988 s 79(4), (5).
4   This reference to disposing of land includes a reference to granting an interest in or right over land, and, in particular, the granting of an option to purchase the freehold of, or any other interest in, land is a disposal for these purposes; and a consent under the Housing Act 1988 s 79(1) given to such a disposal extends to a disposal made in pursuance of the option: s 79(3). For the purposes of Sch 11, which deals with certain specific disposals of houses (see note 5), the grant of an option enabling a person to call for a relevant disposal which is not an exempted disposal must be treated as such a disposal made to him: s 79(13), Sch 11 para 7. A disposal, whether of the whole or part of the house, is a relevant disposal for those purposes if it is a conveyance of the freehold or an assignment of the lease, or the grant of a lease or sub-lease (other than a mortgage term) for a term of more than 21 years otherwise than at a rack rent (assuming that any option to renew or extend a lease or sub-lease, whether or not forming part of a series of options, is exercised and that any option to terminate a lease or sub-lease is not exercised): see Sch 11 para 3(1), (2).
      Certain disposals are exempted disposals for these purposes: see Sch 11 para 4 (amended by the Housing Act 1996 s 222, Sch 18 para 19; and the Civil Partnership Act 2004 ss 81, 261(4), Sch 8 para 45, Sch 30). A 'compulsory disposal' means a disposal of property which is acquired compulsorily, or is acquired by a person who has made or would have made, or for whom another person has made or would have made, a compulsory purchase order authorising its compulsory purchase for the purposes for which it is acquired: Housing Act 1988 Sch 11 para 5.
5   Housing Act 1988 s 79(1). As to the objects of a housing action trust see PARA 540.
      Specific provision is made by Sch 11 as to repayment of discount on early disposal, taking account of any increase in value of the house attributable to home improvements (see Sch 11 paras 1, 1A (amended and added respectively by the Housing Act 2004 s 203)) and the obligation to repay a charge on the house (see the Housing Act 1988 Sch 11 para 2 (amended by the Land Registration Act 2002 s 135, Sch 13; and the Housing and Regeneration Act 2008 s 307(6))). Provision is also made as to exempted disposals ending obligations under covenants (see the Housing Act 1988 Sch 11 para 6 (amended by the Housing Act 2004 s 204(2))).
6   For these purposes, any reference to a house includes a reference to a flat and to any yard, garden, outhouses and appurtenances belonging to the house or flat or usually enjoyed with it: Housing Act 1988 s 92(1)(b).
7   'Secure tenancy' has the meaning assigned by the Housing Act 1985 s 79 and 'secure tenant' is to be construed accordingly: Housing Act 1988 s 92(1)(f); see LANDLORD AND TENANT vol 63 (2016) PARA 1037.
8   'Introductory tenancy' has the same meaning as in the Housing Act 1996 Pt V Ch I (ss 152–158) and 'introductory tenant' is to be construed accordingly: Housing Act 1988 s 92(1)(ca) (added by SI 1997/74). As to introductory tenancies see PARA 472.
9   As to registered providers of social housing see PARA 51 et seq; as to when such a body is a non-profit organisation see PARA 71 note 13.
10 Ie within the meaning of the Housing Act 1996 Pt I (ss A1–64): see PARA 167.
11 As to the meaning of 'local housing authority' see PARA 538 note 4.
12 Housing Act 1988 s 79(2) (amended by the Leasehold Reform, Housing and Urban Development Act 1993 ss 124(1), 187(2), Sch 22; the Housing Act 1996 ss 55(1), 227, Sch 3 para 11, Sch 19 Pt I; and SI 1997/74 and SI 2010/866). As to the right to buy see the Housing Act 1985 Pt V (ss 118–188); and PARA 230 et seq. The Housing Act 1988 s 79(2) has effect as if the saving effected by the Housing Act 1996 (Commencement No 3 and Transitional Provisions) Order 1996,

SI 1996/2402, Schedule para 9 related also to disposals of houses subject to introductory tenancies: Housing Act 1988 s 79(5A) (added by SI 1997/74).

13 Housing Act 1988 s 80(1).

14 Housing Act 1988 s 80(2).

15 Housing Act 1988 s 79(12). The statutory provisions referred to in the text are those of the Landlord and Tenant Act 1985 ss 18–30: see LANDLORD AND TENANT vol 63 (2016) PARA 613 et seq.

16 See the Housing Act 1988 s 26; and LANDLORD AND TENANT vol 63 (2016) PARA 613.

17 Ie under the Housing Act 1988 s 79.

18 Ie under the Housing Act 1988 s 79(1).

19 See the Housing Act 1988 Sch 11 paras 2A, 2B (added by the Housing Act 2004 s 204(1)).

20 See the Housing Act 1988 Sch 11 para 8 (added by the Housing Act 2004 s 205(1)).

556. Consent required for certain subsequent disposals. If, by a material disposal[1], a housing action trust[2] disposes of a house[3] which is for the time being subject to a secure tenancy[4] or an introductory tenancy[5] to a non-profit registered provider of social housing[6] or a registered social landlord[7] (an 'approved person')[8], the conveyance[9] must contain a statement[10] that the following requirement as to consent applies to a subsequent disposal of the house by the approved person[11]. An approved person who acquires a house on such a material disposal must not dispose of it except with the consent of the appropriate authority[12] which may be given either unconditionally or subject to conditions; but nothing in this prohibition applies in relation to an exempt disposal[13].

Where an estate or interest in a house acquired by an approved person on such a material disposal has been mortgaged or charged, the above prohibition applies also to a disposal by the mortgagee or chargee in exercise of a power of sale or leasing, whether or not the disposal is in the name of the approved person; and in any case where:

(1)   by operation of law or by virtue of an order of a court, property which has been acquired by an approved person passes or is transferred to another person; and

(2)   that passing or transfer does not constitute a disposal for which consent is required,

these provisions[14] apply as if the other person to whom the property passes or is transferred were the approved person[15].

Before giving consent in respect of a disposal to which the above prohibition applies, the appropriate authority must satisfy itself that the person who is seeking the consent has taken appropriate steps to consult every tenant of any house proposed to be disposed of and must have regard to the responses of any such tenants to that consultation[16].

Where the title of a housing action trust to a house which is disposed of by a material disposal falling within the above provisions is not registered:

(a)   the housing action trust must give the approved person a certificate[17] stating that it is entitled to make the disposal subject only to such incumbrances, rights and interests as are stated in the conveyance or summarised in the certificate; and

(b)   for the purpose of registration of title, the Chief Land Registrar must accept such a certificate as evidence of the facts stated in it, but if as a result he has to meet a claim against him under the Land Registration Act 2002 the housing action trust is liable to indemnify him[18].

Where the Chief Land Registrar approves an application for registration of a disposition of registered land or the approved person's title under a disposition of unregistered land, and the instrument effecting the disposition contains the required statement concerning consent to a subsequent disposal[19], he must enter in the register a restriction reflecting the limitation under these provisions on subsequent disposal[20].

1   For these purposes, a 'material disposal' is the transfer of the fee simple, the transfer of an existing lease, or the grant of a new lease: Housing Act 1988 s 81(2)(a)–(c).

2   As to the establishment and constitution of housing action trusts see PARA 539.

3   For these purposes, references to disposing of a house include references to: (1) granting or disposing of any interest in the house; (2) entering into a contract to dispose of the house or to grant or dispose of any such interest; and (3) granting an option to acquire the house or any such interest: Housing Act 1988 s 81(11)(a)–(c). As to the meaning of 'house' see PARA 555 note 6.

4   As to the meaning of 'secure tenancy' see PARA 555 note 7; and LANDLORD AND TENANT vol 63 (2016) PARA 1037.

5   As to introductory tenancies see PARA 555 note 8; and PARA 472.

6   As to registered providers of social housing see PARA 51 et seq; as to when such a body is a non-profit organisation see PARA 71 note 13.

7   As to the meaning of 'registered social landlord' see PARA 13.

8   Ie such a person as is mentioned in the Housing Act 1988 s 79(2)(a) (see PARA 555 head (2)).

9   For these purposes, 'the conveyance' means the instrument by which a material disposal is effected: Housing Act 1988 s 81(2).

10 For these purposes, any reference to a statement is a reference to a statement in a form approved by the Chief Land Registrar: Housing Act 1988 s 81(11). As to the Chief Land Registrar see REAL PROPERTY AND REGISTRATION vol 87 (2012) PARA 562.

11 Housing Act 1988 s 81(1) (amended by the Housing and Planning Act 2016 s 92, Sch 4 paras 2, 3(1), (2); and by SI 1997/74 and SI 2010/866).

12 For these purposes, 'the appropriate authority' means: (1) in relation to a disposal of land in England, the Secretary of State; and (2) in relation to a disposal of land in Wales, the Welsh Ministers: Housing Act 1988 s 81(3A) (added by the Housing and Regeneration Act 2008 s 191(2)(b); and amended by the Housing and Planning Act 2016 Sch 4 paras 2, 3(1), (3)).

13 Housing Act 1988 s 81(3) (amended by the Housing and Regeneration Act 2008 s 191(2)(a)). For these purposes, an 'exempt disposal' means: (1) the disposal of a dwelling house to a person having the right to buy under the Housing Act 1985 Pt V (ss 118–188) (see PARA 230 et seq), whether the disposal is in fact made under Pt V or otherwise; (2) the disposal of a dwelling house to a person having the right to acquire it under the Housing and Regeneration Act 2008 s 180 (see PARA 102) or the Housing Act 1996 Pt I (ss A1–64) (see ss 16, 17; and PARA 226), whether or not the disposal is in fact made under provisions having effect by virtue of s 17; (3) a compulsory disposal, within the meaning of the Housing Act 1985 Pt V (see s 161); (4) the disposal of an easement or rentcharge; (5) the disposal of an interest by way of security for a loan; (6) the grant of a secure tenancy (see LANDLORD AND TENANT vol 63 (2016) PARA 1037) or what would be a secure tenancy but for any of the provisions of Sch 1 paras 2–12 (see LANDLORD AND TENANT vol 63 (2016) PARA 1046 et seq); (7) the grant of an assured tenancy or an assured agricultural occupancy, within the meaning of the Housing Act 1988 Pt I (ss 1–45) (see LANDLORD AND TENANT vol 63 (2016) PARA 825 et seq; LANDLORD AND TENANT vol 64 (2016) PARA 1747 et seq), or what would be such a tenancy or occupancy but for any of the provisions of Sch 1 paras 4–8 (see LANDLORD AND TENANT vol 63 (2016) PARA 836 et seq); and (8) the transfer of an interest held on trust for any person where the disposal is made in connection with the appointment of a new trustee or in connection with the discharge of any trustee: s 81(8) (amended by SI 1997/672 and SI 2010/866).

14 Ie including, where there is more than one such passing or transfer, the Housing Act 1988 s 81(4): see the text and note 15.

15 Housing Act 1988 s 81(4).

16 Housing Act 1988 s 81(5) (amended by the Housing and Regeneration Act 2008 s 191(2)(c), (d)). No consent is required under the Housing Act 1996 s 9 or 42, or the Housing Associations Act 1985 s 9 for any disposal in respect of which consent is given under the Housing Act 1988 s 81: s 81(7) (amended by the Government of Wales Act 1998 Sch 16 para 68(b); the Housing and Planning Act 2016 Sch 4 paras 2, 3(1), (4); and SI 1996/2325).

17 For these purposes, any reference to a certificate is a reference to a certificate in a form approved by the Chief Land Registrar: Housing Act 1988 s 81(11). As to the Chief Land Registrar see REAL PROPERTY AND REGISTRATION vol 87 (2012) PARA 562.

18 Housing Act 1988 s 81(9) (amended by the Land Registration Act 1997 s 4(2), Sch 2 Pt I; and the Land Registration Act 2002 s 133, Sch 11 para 23(1), (2)). See further REAL PROPERTY AND REGISTRATION vol 87 (2012) PARA 532.

19 Ie the statement required by the Housing Act 1988 s 81(1): see the text and notes 1–11.
20 Housing Act 1988 s 81(10) (substituted by the Land Registration Act 2002 Sch 11 para 23(3)).

557. Provision of legal assistance to tenants after disposal. Where a house[1] has been disposed of by a disposal made by a housing action trust[2] to a non-profit registered provider of social housing[3], a registered social landlord[4], a local housing authority[5] or other local authority[6], then on an application by a transferred tenant[7] of a house who is a party or a prospective party to proceedings or prospective proceedings to determine any dispute between himself and the person who acquired the house on that disposal, the appropriate authority[8] may give assistance to the transferred tenant if it thinks fit to do so:

(1)   on the ground that the case raises a question of principle; or

(2)   on the ground that it is unreasonable, having regard to the complexity of the case, or to any other matter, to expect the transferred tenant to deal with it without assistance; or

(3)   by reason of any other special consideration[9].

Assistance so given by the appropriate authority may include:

(a)   giving advice;

(b)   procuring or attempting to procure the settlement of the matter in dispute;

(c)   arranging for the giving of advice or assistance by a solicitor[10] or counsel;

(d)   arranging for representation by a solicitor or counsel, including such assistance as is usually given by a solicitor or counsel in the steps preliminary or incidental to any proceedings, or in arriving at or giving effect to a compromise to avoid or bring to an end any proceedings[11]; and

(e)   any other form of assistance which the appropriate authority may consider appropriate[12].

In so far as expenses are incurred by the appropriate authority in providing a transferred tenant with such assistance, the recovery of those expenses (as taxed or assessed in such manner as may be prescribed by rules of court) constitutes a first charge for the benefit of the appropriate authority: (i) on any costs which (whether by virtue of a judgment or order of a court or an agreement or otherwise) are payable to the tenant by any other person in respect of the matter in connection with which the assistance was given; and (ii) so far as relates to any costs, on his rights under any compromise or settlement arrived at in connection with that matter to avoid or bring to an end any proceedings, but subject to any charge on recovered property imposed by the Legal Aid, Sentencing and Punishment of Offenders Act 2012[13] and any provision in, or made under, Part 1 of that Act[14] for the payment of any sum to the Lord Chancellor[15].

1   As to the meaning of 'house' see PARA 555 note 6.
2   As to the establishment and constitution of housing action trusts see PARA 539.
3   As to registered providers of social housing see PARA 51 et seq; as to when such a body is a non-profit organisation see PARA 71 note 13.
4   As to the meaning of 'registered social landlord' see PARA 13.
5   As to the meaning of 'local housing authority' see PARA 538 note 4.
6   Ie a disposal falling within the Housing Act 1988 s 79(2): see PARA 555.
7   In relation to a house which has been disposed of as described in the text, a 'transferred tenant' means a tenant of it who was the secure tenant or the introductory tenant of the house immediately before the disposal or who is the widow, widower or surviving civil partner of the person who was then the secure tenant or the introductory tenant of it: Housing Act 1988 s 82(1) (amended by the Civil Partnership Act 2004 s 81, Sch 8 para 42; and by SI 1997/74). As to the meaning of 'secure

tenant' see PARA 555 note 7; and LANDLORD AND TENANT vol 63 (2016) PARA 1037. As to introductory tenants see PARA 555 note 8; and PARA 472.

8   For these purposes, 'the appropriate authority' means: (1) in a case where the disposal referred to in the text was to a private registered provider of social housing, the Regulator of Social Housing; and (2) in a case where the disposal was to a registered social landlord, the Welsh Ministers: Housing Act 1988 s 82(5) (substituted by SI 2010/866). As to the meaning of 'private registered provider of social housing' see PARA 53. As to the Regulator of Social Housing see PARA 57 et seq. As to the Welsh Ministers see PARA 7.

9   Housing Act 1988 s 82(2) (amended by SI 2010/866).

10 For these purposes, 'solicitor' includes a body recognised by the Council of the Law Society under the Administration of Justice Act 1985 s 9 (see LEGAL PROFESSIONS vol 65 (2015) PARA 496 et seq): see the Solicitors' Recognised Bodies Order 1991, SI 1991/2684, arts 2–5, Sch 1 (amended by SI 2001/645 and SI 2009/500).

11 Head (d) in the text does not affect the law and practice regulating the descriptions of persons who may appear in, conduct, defend and address the court in any proceedings: Housing Act 1988 s 82(3).

12 Housing Act 1988 s 82(3)(a)–(e) (amended by SI 2010/866).

13 Ie by the Legal Aid, Sentencing and Punishment of Offenders Act 2012 s 25: see LEGAL AID vol 65 (2015) PARA 150.

14 Ie the Legal Aid, Sentencing and Punishment of Offenders Act 2012 Pt 1 (ss 1–43).

15 Housing Act 1988 s 82(4) (amended by the Access to Justice Act 1999 s 24, Sch 4 paras 42, 43; the Legal Aid, Sentencing and Punishment of Offenders Act 2012 s 39(1), Sch 5 para 37; and SI 2010/866).

558. Disposals of dwelling houses subject to secure tenancies. The following provisions apply in any case where a housing action trust[1] proposes to make a disposal of one or more houses[2] let on secure tenancies[3] or introductory tenancies[4] which would result in a person who, before the disposal, is a secure tenant or an introductory tenant of the trust becoming, after the disposal, the tenant of another person, and that other person is not a local housing authority[5] or other local authority[6]. Before applying to the appropriate national authority[7] for consent to the proposed disposal or serving notice of its intentions on the tenant[8], the housing action trust must serve notice in writing[9] on any local housing authority in whose area any such houses are situated:

(1)   informing the authority of the proposed disposal and specifying the houses concerned; and

(2)   requiring the authority within such period, being not less than 28 days, as may be specified in the notice, to serve on the trust a notice informing the trust, with respect to each of the houses specified in the notice served by the trust which is in the authority's area, of the likely consequences for the tenant if the house were to be acquired by the authority[10].

Before applying to the appropriate national authority for consent to the proposed disposal, and after the expiry of the period specified in the notice so served on the local housing authority, the housing action trust must serve notice in writing on the secure tenant or, as the case may be, introductory tenant:

(a)   informing him of the proposed disposal and of the name of the person to whom the disposal is to be made;

(b)   containing such other details of the disposal as seem to the trust to be appropriate;

(c)   informing him of the likely consequences of the disposal on his position as a secure tenant or an introductory tenant and, if appropriate, of the effect of the statutory provisions preserving the right to buy on a disposal to a private sector landlord[11];

(d)   if the local housing authority in whose area the house of which he is tenant is situated has served notice on the trust as mentioned in head (2), informing him, in accordance with the information given in the notice, of the likely consequences for him if the house were to be acquired by that authority;

(e)   informing him, if he wishes to become a tenant of that authority, of his right to make representations to that effect[12] and of the rights conferred under the provisions relating to transfer orders[13]; and

(f)   informing him of his right to make representations to the trust with respect to the proposed disposal within such period, being not less than 28 days, as may be specified in the notice[14].

If, by virtue of any representations made to the housing action trust in accordance with head (f), the provisions relating to transfer orders apply in relation to any house or block of flats[15], the trust must serve notice of that fact on the appropriate national authority, on the local housing authority and on the tenant of the house or each of the tenants of the block, and so amend its proposals with respect to the disposal as to exclude the house or block[16]. The housing action trust must consider any other representations so made and, if it considers it appropriate to do so having regard to any of those representations, may amend (or further amend) its proposals with respect to the disposal; and, in such a case, it must serve a further notice under heads (a) to (f)[17].

When applying to the appropriate national authority for consent to the proposed disposal[18] the housing action trust must furnish to it a copy of any notice served on the trust[19] or by it[20] under the above provisions, a copy of any representations received by the trust and a statement of the consideration given by the trust to those representations[21]. Where an application is made to the appropriate national authority for consent to a disposal to which these provisions apply, or to which they would apply if the disposal were not to a local housing authority or other local authority[22], the appropriate national authority may[23] require the housing action trust to carry out such further consultation, or, as the case may be, such consultation, with respect to the proposed disposal as may be specified in the direction and to furnish to it such information as may be so specified with respect to the results of that consultation[24].

If, in the case of a house specified in a notice served in accordance with head (1), the tenant makes representations in accordance with head (f) to the effect that he wishes to become a tenant of the local housing authority in whose area the house is situated, or if, in the case of a block of flats so specified, the majority of the tenants who make representations in accordance with head (f) make representations to the effect that they wish to become tenants of the local housing authority in whose area the block is situated, the appropriate national authority must by order provide for the transfer of the house or block of flats from the housing action trust to the local housing authority[25]. The appropriate national authority may also by order transfer from the housing action trust to the local housing authority so much as appears to the appropriate national authority to be appropriate of any property[26] belonging to or usually enjoyed with the house or, as the case may be, the block or any flat contained in it[27]. A transfer of any house, block of flats or other property under these provisions must be on such terms, including financial terms[28], as the appropriate national authority thinks fit; and an order so made may provide that, notwithstanding anything in the statutory provision whereby rent and the benefit of the lessee's covenants are to run with the reversion[29], any rent or other sum which arises under the tenant's tenancy or any of the tenants' tenancies and falls due before the date of the transfer is to continue to be recoverable by the housing action trust to the exclusion of the authority[30].

1 As to the establishment and constitution of housing action trusts see PARA 539.
2 As to the meaning of 'house' see PARA 555 note 6.
3 As to the meaning of 'secure tenancy' see PARA 555 note 7; and LANDLORD AND TENANT vol 63 (2016) PARA 1037.
4 As to introductory tenancies see PARA 555 note 8; and PARA 472.
5 As to the meaning of 'local housing authority' see PARA 538 note 4.
6 Housing Act 1988 s 84(1) (s 84(1)–(3), (4)(d), (e), (5) substituted, s 84(5A) added, and s 84(6), (7) amended by the Leasehold Reform, Housing and Urban Development Act 1993 ss 124(2), (3), 125(1)–(4); the Housing Act 1988 s 84(1) amended by SI 1997/74).
   Notwithstanding the application to a housing action trust of the Housing Act 1985 Pt IV (ss 79–117) (secure tenancies: see LANDLORD AND TENANT vol 63 (2016) PARA 1037 et seq) and of the Housing Act 1996 Pt V Ch I (ss 124–143) (introductory tenancies: see PARA 472), a disposal falling within the Housing Act 1988 s 84(1) is to be treated as not being a matter of housing management to which the Housing Act 1985 s 105 (see LANDLORD AND TENANT vol 63 (2016) PARA 1114) applies (in the case of secure tenants) or the Housing Act 1996 s 137 (see PARA 472) applies (in the case of introductory tenants): Housing Act 1988 s 84(8) (substituted by SI 1997/74).
7 As to the appropriate national authority, ie the Secretary of State or, where statutory functions have been transferred in relation to Wales, the Welsh Ministers, see PARA 7.
8 Ie under the Housing Act 1988 s 84(4): see heads (a)–(f) in the text.
9 As to service of notice see the Housing Act 1988 s 91.
10 Housing Act 1988 s 84(2), (3) (as substituted: see note 6).
11 Ie the Housing Act 1985 ss 171A–171H: see PARA 334 et seq.
12 Ie under head (f) in the text.
13 Ie the Housing Act 1988 s 84A: see the text and notes 25–30.
14 Housing Act 1988 s 84(4) (as amended (see note 6); and further amended by SI 1997/74).
15 For these purposes, 'flat' and 'house' have the meanings given by the Housing Act 1985 s 183 (see PARA 231); 'block of flats' means a building containing two or more flats; and any reference to a block of flats specified in a notice under the Housing Act 1988 s 84(2) is a reference to a block in the case of which each flat which is let on a secure tenancy or an introductory tenancy is so specified: ss 84(5), 84A(6) (s 84(5) as substituted (see note 6); s 84A added by the Leasehold Reform, Housing and Urban Development Act 1993 s 125(5); the Housing Act 1988 s 84A(6), (7) amended by SI 1997/74). For these purposes, a building which contains:
   (1)   one or more flats which are let, or available for letting, on secure tenancies or introductory tenancies by the housing action trust concerned; and
   (2)   one or more flats which are not so let or so available,
must be treated as if it were two separate buildings, the one containing the flat or flats mentioned in head (1) and the other containing the flat or flats mentioned in head (2) and any common parts; and 'common parts', in relation to a building containing two or more flats, means any parts of the building which the tenants of the flats are entitled under the terms of their tenancies to use in common with each other: Housing Act 1988 s 84A(6), (7) (as so added and amended).
16 Housing Act 1988 s 84(5) (as substituted: see note 6).
17 Housing Act 1988 s 84(5A) (as added: see note 6). In relation to the further notice referred to in the text s 84(5A) will again apply: s 84(5A) (as so added).
18 Ie the proposed disposal as amended, where appropriate, by virtue of the Housing Act 1988 s 84(5) (see the text and note 16) or s 84(5A) (see the text to note 17).
19 Ie under the Housing Act 1988 s 84(3) (see the text to note 10).
20 Ie under the Housing Act 1988 s 84(4) (see the text to note 14).
21 Housing Act 1988 s 84(6).
22 Ie a disposal which would be such a disposal if the Housing Act 1988 s 84(1)(b) (see the text to note 6) were omitted: s 84(7) (as amended: see note 6).
23 Ie by a direction under the Housing Act 1988 s 72 (see PARA 549) and without prejudice to the generality of s 72: s 84(7).
24 Housing Act 1988 s 84(7) (as amended: see note 6).
25 Housing Act 1988 s 84A(1), (2) (as added: see note 15).
26 For this purpose, 'property' includes chattels of any description and rights and liabilities, whether arising by contract or otherwise: Housing Act 1988 s 84A(3) (as added: see note 15).
27 Housing Act 1988 s 84A(3) (as added: see note 15).
28 Without prejudice to the generality of the Housing Act 1988 s 84A(4) (see the text and notes 28–30), the financial terms referred to in the text may include provision for payments to a local housing authority (as well as or instead of payments by a local housing authority); and the transfer

from a housing action trust of any house, block of flats or other property by virtue of this provision must not be taken to give rise to any right to compensation: s 84A(5) (as added: see note 15).

29 Ie the Law of Property Act 1925 s 141: see LANDLORD AND TENANT vol 62 (2016) PARAS 458, 461.

30 Housing Act 1988 s 84A(4) (as added: see note 15).

(5) RENTS

559. In general. A housing action trust[1] may make such reasonable charges as it may determine for the tenancy or occupation of housing accommodation[2] for the time being held by it[3]. The trust must from time to time review rents and make such changes, either of rents generally or of particular rents, as circumstances may require[4]. This is academic now that the six housing action trusts have been dissolved.

1 As to the establishment and constitution of housing action trusts see PARA 539.
2 As to the meaning of 'housing accommodation' see PARA 540 note 3.
3 Housing Act 1988 s 85(1).
4 Housing Act 1988 s 85(2). See further PARA 560.

560. Increase of rent where tenancy is not secure or introductory. Some tenants who are transferred to a housing action trust may not have either a secure or introductory tenancy status[1]. For example, temporary accommodation provided for the homeless, and certain student lettings, cannot be secure or introductory[2]. As with non-secure lettings by local authorities, there is special provision for dealing with increases in rent.

Thus where a dwelling house is let by a housing action trust[3] on a periodic tenancy which is not a secure tenancy or an introductory tenancy, the rent payable under the tenancy may, without the tenancy being terminated, be increased with effect from the beginning of a rental period[4] by a written notice of increase given by the housing action trust to the tenant[5]. Such a notice is not effective unless:

(1) it is given at least four weeks before the first day of the rental period, or any earlier day on which the payment of rent in respect of that period falls to be made;

(2) it tells the tenant of his right to terminate the tenancy and of the steps to be taken by him if he wishes to do so; and

(3) it gives him the dates by which, if the increase is not to be effective[6], a notice to quit must be received by the trust and the tenancy be made to terminate[7].

Where such a notice is given specifying an increase in rent with effect from the beginning of a rental period and the tenancy continues into that period, the notice does not have effect if:

(a) the tenancy is terminated by notice to quit given by the tenant in accordance with the express or implied provisions of the tenancy;

(b) the notice to quit is given before the expiry of the period of two weeks beginning on the day following the date on which the notice of increase is given, or before the expiry of such longer period as may be allowed by the notice of increase; and

(c) the date on which the tenancy is made to terminate is not later than the earliest day on which the tenancy could be terminated by a notice to quit given by the tenant on the last day of that rental period[8].

1 As to the meaning of 'secure tenancy' see PARA 555 note 7; and LANDLORD AND TENANT vol 63 (2016) PARA 1037. As to introductory tenancies see PARA 555 note 8; and PARA 472.
2 See LANDLORD AND TENANT vol 63 (2016) PARAS 1048, 1055.

3   As to the establishment and constitution of housing action trusts see PARA 539.
4   For these purposes, 'rental period' means a period in respect of which a payment of rent falls to
    be made: Housing Act 1988 s 86(5).
5   Housing Act 1988 s 86(1), (2) (s 86(1) amended by SI 1997/74).
6   Ie by virtue of the Housing Act 1988 s 86(4): see heads (a)–(c) in the text.
7   Housing Act 1988 s 86(3).
8   Housing Act 1988 s 86(4).

(6) DISSOLUTION

561. Dissolution of housing action trust. Housing action trusts[1] have a limited
life span and once a trust's objects have been substantially achieved it must take
steps to be dissolved. In such a case the following provisions apply. All housing
action trusts have now been dissolved.

A housing action trust must use its best endeavours to secure that its objects are
achieved as soon as practicable[2]. Where it appears to a trust that its objects have
been substantially achieved, it must so far as practicable, dispose or arrange to
dispose of any remaining property, rights or liabilities of the trust[3], and submit
proposals to the appropriate national authority[4] for:

(1)   the dissolution of the trust;
(2)   the disposal to any person of any remaining property, rights or liabilities
        of the trust which it has not been able to dispose of or arrange to dispose
        of as described above; and
(3)   the transfer of any function exercisable by the trust to another person
        (including, where appropriate, a person with whom the trust has
        entered into an agency agreement)[5].

The appropriate national authority may by order provide for the dissolution of
a housing action trust and for any such disposal as is mentioned in head (2),
whether by way of giving effect (with or without modifications) to any proposals
submitted to him by the trust or otherwise[6]. Where such an order provides for any
such disposal or transfer as is mentioned in heads (1) to (3), it may be on such
terms, including financial terms, as the appropriate national authority thinks fit;
and it may create or impose such new rights or liabilities in respect of what is
transferred as appear to him to be necessary or expedient[7]. It may also contain
provisions establishing new bodies corporate to receive the disposal or transfer or
amending, repealing or otherwise modifying any enactment[8] for the purpose of
enabling any body established under any enactment to receive the disposal or
transfer[9].

1   As to the establishment and constitution of housing action trusts see PARA 539.
2   Housing Act 1988 s 88(1).
3   Ie in accordance with the Housing Act 1988 ss 60–87: see PARA 538 et seq.
4   As to the appropriate national authority, ie the Secretary of State or, where statutory functions
    have been transferred in relation to Wales, the Welsh Ministers, see PARA 7.
5   Housing Act 1988 s 88(2). The reference to an agency agreement is a reference to an agreement
    under s 87: see PARA 540.
6   Housing Act 1988 s 88(3). An order under s 88 may contain such supplementary and transitional
    provisions as the appropriate national authority thinks necessary or expedient, including
    provisions amending, repealing or otherwise modifying any enactment: s 88(4)(b) (amended by the
    Housing Grants, Construction and Regeneration Act 1996 s 144). An order is to be made by
    statutory instrument subject to annulment in pursuance of a resolution of either House of
    Parliament or, as appropriate, the National Assembly for Wales: Housing Act 1988 s 88(4)(c).
7   Housing Act 1988 s 88(4)(a).
8   For these purposes, 'enactment' includes any instrument made under any enactment: Housing Act
    1988 s 88(5) (added by the Housing Grants, Construction and Regeneration Act 1996 s 144).

9   Housing Act 1988 s 88(4)(aa) (added by the Housing Grants, Construction and Regeneration Act 1996 s 144).

5. HOUSING CONDITIONS AND HOUSING STANDARDS

(1) IN GENERAL

562. General introduction. Local housing authorities formerly had powers and duties under the Housing Act 1985 to deal with dwelling houses which were not fit for human habitation[1]. In discharging these powers and duties local housing authorities were required to carry out inspections of dwellings in their areas[2]. Where a local housing authority concluded that a dwelling was unfit for human habitation it was required to take the most satisfactory course of action, namely either by serving a repairs notice or by serving a closing or demolition order. However, an authority had the right to defer action in relation to an unfit dwelling. In exercising these powers, local housing authorities had to consider guidance given by the Secretary of State.

The system under the Housing Act 1985 has been replaced by new provisions made by the Housing Act 2004[3], which substitutes tests based on categories of hazards to be assessed by prescribed methods and thus largely removes the element of subjectivity inherent in the classification of buildings as unfit for human habitation. Part 1 of the Housing Act 2004[4] introduces the Housing Health and Safety Rating System ('HHSRS'), which is an evidence-based system for assessing housing conditions. The Housing Act 2004 imposes a duty on local authorities to take enforcement action where a category 1 hazard exists and gives discretion to take action where a category 2 hazard exists[5]. The action to be taken by an authority may, depending on the circumstances, be by serving an improvement notice[6], making a prohibition order[7], serving a hazard awareness notice[8] or taking specified emergency measures[9]. There is still power to make a demolition order or a slum clearance order (under the Housing Act 1985)[10]. Provision is made for appeals to be made to the First-tier Tribunal or a residential property tribunal against the serving of notices[11]. Under the new system, local housing authorities have to consider guidance given by the appropriate national authorities[12].

Local housing authorities were also responsible for ensuring that housing met the Decent Homes Standard, which required that by 2010 all social housing should be in a reasonable state of repair and have modern facilities and services[13].

1   Ie under the Housing Act 1985 Pt VI (ss 189–208) (repealed). Local housing authorities still have additional powers in relation to the overcrowding of dwellings (see Pt X (ss 324–344); and PARA 649 et seq), and houses in multiple occupation (see the Housing Act 2004 Pt 4 Ch 3 (ss 139–144); and PARA 698 et seq). The results of research surveys continue to show that there are a substantial number of unfit dwellings in England and Wales: see eg Leather and Morris *The State of UK Housing* (1997); Sharp 'Housing Conditions' in *The Great Divide* (2005). See also Driscoll *Housing: the New Law, A Guide to the Housing Act 2004* (2006). Authorities still also have powers as to area improvement and the making of demolition orders under the Housing Act 1985 Pt VIII (ss 239–263) and Pt IX (ss 265–323): see PARAS 620 et seq, 831 et seq.
2   See the Housing Act 1985 s 605 (repealed).
3   See PARA 563 et seq. The Housing Act 2004 largely came into force on 6 April 2004: see PARA 3.
4   Ie the Housing Act 2004 Pt 1 (ss 1–54).
5   See PARAS 564–565.
6   See PARA 571 et seq.
7   See PARA 590 et seq. As to when emergency remedial works may be more appropriate than a prohibition order see *Luton Borough Council v Universal Group* HA/6/2007, Lands Tribunal (this was the first appeal of a residential property tribunal (RPT) decision on the provisions in the Housing Act 2004 Pt 1 to the Lands Tribunal (now the Upper Tribunal) and concerned a case where a landlord had cut off electricity and water supplies to force tenants to leave their accommodation; the local authority had pursued emergency remedial works; the landlord appealed to the RPT, which decided that an emergency prohibition order was the proper course of action and criticised other aspects of the local authority's approach and procedures; the local

authority appealed, and the Lands Tribunal upheld the appeal and generally confirmed the local authority's position, in particular confirming that remedial works were the appropriate course of action and indicating that in emergency situations, a degree of latitude was reasonable in relation to procedural matters).

8 See PARAS 608–609.
9 See PARA 613 et seq.
10 See PARAS 620 et seq, 631 et seq.
11 See eg PARA 616. As to appeals to tribunals see PARA 32 et seq.
12 See PARA 569.
13 The government introduced the Decent Homes standard in 2000.

563. The new system for assessing housing conditions and enforcing housing standards. Part 1 of the Housing Act 2004[1] introduced a new system of assessing the condition of residential premises, and for that system to be used in the enforcement of housing standards in relation to such premises[2]. The new system operates by reference to the existence of category 1 or category 2 hazards on residential premises[3], and it replaces the existing system based on the test of fitness for human habitation[4] contained in the Housing Act 1985[5]. The new system is to be used in relation to:

(1)   the new kinds of enforcement action[6], comprising improvement notices, prohibition orders and hazard awareness notices;

(2)   the new emergency measures[7], comprising emergency remedial action and emergency prohibition orders; and

(3)   certain existing kinds of enforcement action[8], namely demolition orders and slum clearance declarations[9].

For these purposes, 'residential premises' means: (a) a dwelling[10]; (b) an HMO[11]; (c) unoccupied HMO accommodation[12]; and (d) any common parts[13] of a building containing one or more flats[14]. In Part 1 of the Housing Act 2004, any reference to a dwelling, an HMO or a building containing one or more flats includes (where the context permits) any yard, garden, outhouses and appurtenances belonging to, or usually enjoyed with, the dwelling, HMO or building (or any part of it)[15].

1 Ie the Housing Act 2004 Pt 1 (ss 1–54).
2 Housing Act 2004 s 1(1). This system is known as the Housing Health and Safety Rating System (HHSRS).
3 See the Housing Act 2004 s 2; and PARA 564.
4 Ie the test contained in the Housing Act 1985 s 604 (repealed).
5 Housing Act 2004 s 1(2).
6 Ie those contained in the Housing Act 2004 Pt 1 Ch 2 (ss 11–39): see PARAS 571–612.
7 Ie those contained in the Housing Act 2004 Pt 1 Ch 3 (ss 40–45): see PARA 613 et seq.
8 Ie those dealt with in the Housing Act 2004 Pt 1 Ch 4 (ss 46–48): see PARA 620 et seq.
9 Housing Act 2004 s 1(3).
10 'Dwelling' means a building or part of a building occupied or intended to be occupied as a separate dwelling: Housing Act 2004 s 1(5).
11 'HMO' means a house in multiple occupation as defined by the Housing Act 2004 ss 254–259 (see PARA 667 et seq), as they have effect for the purposes of Pt 1 (ie without the exclusions contained in Sch 14: see PARA 668): s 1(5).
12 'Unoccupied HMO accommodation' means a building or part of a building constructed or adapted for use as a house in multiple occupation but for the time being either unoccupied or only occupied by persons who form a single household: Housing Act 2004 s 1(5).
13 'Common parts', in relation to a building containing one or more flats, includes the structure and exterior of the building, and common facilities provided (whether or not in the building) for persons who include the occupiers of one or more of the flats; 'building containing one or more flats' does not include an HMO; and 'flat' means a separate set of premises (whether or not on the same floor) which forms part of a building, which is constructed or adapted for use for the purposes of a dwelling, and either the whole or a material part of which lies above or below some other part of the building: Housing Act 2004 s 1(5). In the Housing Act 2004, 'occupier', in relation to premises, means a person who occupies the premises as a residence, and (subject to the context) so occupies them whether as a tenant or other person having an estate or interest in the

premises or as a licensee; and related expressions are to be construed accordingly: s 262(6). This definition has effect subject to any other provision defining 'occupier' for any purposes of the Housing Act 2004: s 262(6) (amended by the Localism Act 2011 s 237, Sch 25 Pt 29). As to the meaning of 'tenant' see PARA 391 note 6; and as to the meaning of 'person having an estate or interest' see PARA 391 note 7.

14 Housing Act 2004 s 1(4). Part 1 applies to flats as follows: references to a dwelling or an HMO include a dwelling or HMO which is a flat (as defined by s 1(5)); and s 1(6) applies in relation to such a dwelling or HMO as it applies in relation to other dwellings or HMOs (but it is not to be taken as referring to any common parts of the building containing the flat): s 1(7). Part 1 applies to unoccupied HMO accommodation as it applies to an HMO; and references to an HMO in s 1(6), (7) and in ss 2–54 are to be read accordingly: s 1(8).

15 Housing Act 2004 s 1(6).

(2) HOUSING STANDARDS

(i) Category 1 and Category 2 Hazards and Inspection

564. Meanings of 'category 1 hazard' and 'category 2 hazard'. Under the Housing Act 2004, local housing authorities must seek to deal with certain housing hazards which are either category 1 or category 2 hazards[1].

In the Housing Act 2004:

(1)   'category 1 hazard' means a hazard of a prescribed[2] description which falls within a prescribed band[3] as a result of achieving, under a prescribed method for calculating the seriousness of hazards of that description, a numerical score of or above a prescribed amount;

(2)   'category 2 hazard' means a hazard of a prescribed description which falls within a prescribed band as a result of achieving, under a prescribed method for calculating the seriousness of hazards of that description, a numerical score below the minimum amount prescribed for a category 1 hazard of that description; and

(3)   'hazard' means any risk of harm[4] to the health[5] or safety of an actual or potential occupier[6] of a dwelling[7] or an HMO which arises from a deficiency in the dwelling or HMO or in any building[8] or land in the vicinity (whether the deficiency arises as a result of the construction of any building, an absence of maintenance or repair, or otherwise)[9].

1   See PARA 563.
2   'Prescribed' means prescribed by regulations made by the appropriate national authority: Housing Act 2004 s 2(2). As to the meaning of 'appropriate national authority' see s 261(1); and PARA 389 note 1. Regulations under s 2 may, in particular, prescribe a method for calculating the seriousness of hazards which takes into account both the likelihood of the harm occurring and the severity of the harm if it were to occur: s 2(3). As to the regulations so made in relation to residential premises in England see the Housing Health and Safety Rating System (England) Regulations 2005, SI 2005/3208; and in relation to residential premises in Wales see the Housing Health and Safety Rating System (Wales) Regulations 2006, SI 2006/1702. A hazard is of a prescribed description for the purposes of the Housing Act 2004 where the risk of harm is associated with the occurrence of any of the matters or circumstances listed in the Housing Health and Safety Rating System (England) Regulations 2005, SI 2005/3208, Sch 1 (reg 3(1)) or in the Housing Health and Safety Rating System (Wales) Regulations 2006, SI 2006/1702, Sch 1 (see reg 3(1)). The matters and circumstances so listed are:
    (1)   damp and mould growth: exposure to house dust mites, damp, mould or fungal growths;
    (2)   excess cold: exposure to low temperatures;
    (3)   excess heat: exposure to high temperatures;
    (4)   asbestos and MMF: exposure to asbestos fibres or manufactured mineral fibres;
    (5)   biocides: exposure to chemicals used to treat timber and mould growth;
    (6)   carbon monoxide and fuel combustion products: exposure to:
        (a)   carbon monoxide;
        (b)   nitrogen dioxide;

   (c) sulphur dioxide and smoke;

(7) lead: the ingestion of lead;

(8) radiation: exposure to radiation;

(9) uncombusted fuel gas: exposure to uncombusted fuel gas;

(10) volatile organic compounds: exposure to volatile organic compounds;

(11) crowding and space: a lack of adequate space for living and sleeping;

(12) entry by intruders: difficulties in keeping the dwelling or HMO secure against unauthorised entry;

(13) lighting: a lack of adequate lighting;

(14) noise: exposure to noise;

(15) domestic hygiene, pests and refuse:

   (a) poor design, layout or construction such that the dwelling or HMO cannot readily be kept clean;

   (b) exposure to pests;

   (c) an inadequate provision for the hygienic storage and disposal of household waste;

(16) food safety: an inadequate provision of facilities for the storage, preparation and cooking of food;

(17) personal hygiene, sanitation and drainage: an inadequate provision of:

   (a) facilities for maintaining good personal hygiene;

   (b) sanitation and drainage;

(18) water supply: an inadequate supply of water free from contamination, for drinking and other domestic purposes;

(19) falls associated with baths etc: falls associated with toilets, baths, showers or other washing facilities;

(20) falling on level surfaces etc: falling on any level surface or falling between surfaces where the change in level is less than 300 mm;

(21) falling on stairs etc: falling on stairs, steps or ramps where the change in level is 300 mm or more;

(22) falling between levels: falling between levels where the difference in levels is 300 mm or more;

(23) electrical hazards: exposure to electricity;

(24) fire: exposure to uncontrolled fire and associated smoke;

(25) flames, hot surfaces etc: contact with:

   (a) controlled fire or flames;

   (b) hot objects, liquid or vapours;

(26) collision and entrapment: collision with, or entrapment of body parts in, doors, windows or other architectural features;

(27) explosions: an explosion at the dwelling or HMO;

(28) position and operability of amenities etc: the position, location and operability of amenities, fittings and equipment;

(29) structural collapse and falling elements: the collapse of the whole or part of the dwelling or HMO: Housing Health and Safety Rating System (England) Regulations 2005, SI 2005/3208, Sch 1 paras 1–29; Housing Health and Safety Rating System (Wales) Regulations 2006, SI 2006/1702, Sch 1 paras 1–29.

As to the meaning of 'HMO' see PARA 563 note 11. In the list above, a reference to a matter or circumstance is, unless otherwise stated, to a matter or circumstance in or, as the case may be, at the dwelling or HMO in question, or in any building or land in the vicinity of the dwelling or HMO: Housing Health and Safety Rating System (England) Regulations 2005, SI 2005/3208, reg 3(2); Housing Health and Safety Rating System (Wales) Regulations 2006, SI 2006/1702, reg 3(2). The matters and circumstances listed above reflect the profiles of hazards set out in Annex D of the operating guidance given by the appropriate national authority under the Housing Act 2004 s 9(1)(a) (see PARA 569).

'Harm' means harm which is within any of Classes I to IV as set out in the Housing Health and Safety Rating System (England) Regulations 2005, SI 2005/3208, Sch 2 (see reg 2) or the Housing Health and Safety Rating System (Wales) Regulations 2006, SI 2006/1702, Sch 2 (see reg 2). The classes of harm so set out are as follows (Housing Health and Safety Rating System (England) Regulations 2005, SI 2005/3208, Sch 2; Housing Health and Safety Rating System (Wales) Regulations 2006, SI 2006/1702, Sch 2):

Class I: a Class I harm is such extreme harm as is reasonably foreseeable as a result of the hazard in question, including:

   (i) death from any cause;

   (ii) lung cancer;

   (iii) mesothelioma and other malignant tumours;

   (iv) permanent paralysis below the neck;

   (v) regular severe pneumonia;

   (vi) permanent loss of consciousness;

   (vii) 80% burn injuries.

Class II: a Class II harm is such severe harm as is reasonably foreseeable as a result of the hazard in question, including:

(i)   cardio-respiratory disease;
(ii)   asthma;
(iii)   non-malignant respiratory diseases;
(iv)   lead poisoning;
(v)   anaphylactic shock;
(vi)   cryptosporidiosis;
(vii)   legionnaires disease;
(viii) myocardial infarction;
(ix)   mild stroke;
(x)   chronic confusion;
(xi)   regular severe fever;
(xii)   loss of a hand or foot;
(xiii) serious fractures;
(xiv)   serious burns;
(xv)   loss of consciousness for days.

Class III: a Class III harm is such serious harm as is reasonably foreseeable as a result of the hazard in question, including:

(i)   eye disorders;
(ii)   rhinitis;
(iii)   hypertension;
(iv)   sleep disturbance;
(v)   neuropsychological impairment;
(vi)   sick building syndrome;
(vii)   regular and persistent dermatitis, including contact dermatitis;
(viii) allergy;
(ix)   gastro-enteritis;
(x)   diarrhoea;
(xi)   vomiting;
(xii)   chronic severe stress;
(xiii) mild heart attack;
(xiv)   malignant but treatable skin cancer;
(xv)   loss of a finger;
(xvi)   fractured skull and severe concussion;
(xvii) serious puncture wounds to head or body;
(xviii) severe burns to hands;
(xix)   serious strain or sprain injuries;
(xx)   regular and severe migraine.

Class IV: a Class IV harm is such moderate harm as is reasonably foreseeable as a result of the hazard in question, including:

(i)   pleural plaques;
(ii)   occasional severe discomfort;
(iii)   benign tumours;
(iv)   occasional mild pneumonia;
(v)   broken finger;
(vi)   slight concussion;
(vii)   moderate cuts to face or body;
(viii) severe bruising to body;
(ix)   regular serious coughs or colds.

See also *HHSRS Operating Guidance — Housing Act 2004: Guidance about inspections and assessment of hazards given under Section 9* (published 27 February 2006).

3   'Prescribed band' means a band so prescribed for a category 1 hazard or a category 2 hazard, as the case may be: Housing Act 2004 s 2(2). For the purposes of the Housing Act 2004, in relation to residential premises in England, a hazard falls within a band identified by a letter in the Housing Health and Safety Rating System (England) Regulations 2005, SI 2005/3208, reg 7 Table 3 column 1 where it achieves a numerical score calculated in accordance with reg 6(5) (see PARA 565 note 10) which is within the range corresponding to that letter in reg 7 Table 3 column 2 (reg 7); and, in relation to residential premises in Wales, a hazard falls within a band identified by a letter in the Housing Health and Safety Rating System (Wales) Regulations 2006, SI 2006/1702, reg 7 Table 3 column 1 where it achieves a numerical score calculated in accordance with reg 6(5) (see PARA 565 note 10) which is within the range corresponding to that letter in reg 7 Table 3 column 2 (reg 7).

4 For this purpose, 'harm' includes temporary harm: Housing Act 2004 s 2(4).
5 For these purposes of the Housing Act 2004, 'health' includes mental health: s 2(5).
6 As to the meaning of 'occupier' see PARA 563 note 13.
7 As to the meaning of 'dwelling' see PARA 563 note 10.
8 For this purpose, 'building' includes part of a building: Housing Act 2004 s 2(4).
9 Housing Act 2004 s 2(1). For the purposes of the Act, in relation to England: (1) a hazard falling within the Housing Health and Safety Rating System (England) Regulations 2005, SI 2005/3208, reg 7 Table 3 band A, B or C is a category 1 hazard; and (2) a hazard falling within any other band in that Table is a category 2 hazard (reg 8); and, in relation to Wales: (a) a hazard falling within the Housing Health and Safety Rating System (Wales) Regulations 2006, SI 2006/1702, reg 7 Table 3 band A, B or C is a category 1 hazard; and (b) a hazard falling within any other band in that Table is a category 2 hazard (reg 8). See further PARA 565.

565. Inspections by local housing authorities to see whether category 1 or category 2 hazards exist. If a local housing authority[1] considers, either as a result of any matters of which it has become aware in carrying out its duty to review housing conditions in its district[2] or for any other reason, that it would be appropriate for any residential premises[3] in its district to be inspected with a view to determining whether any category 1 or category 2 hazard[4] exists on those premises, the authority must arrange for such an inspection to be carried out[5]. If an official complaint[6] about the condition of any residential premises in the district of a local housing authority is made to the proper officer of the authority, and the circumstances complained of indicate that any category 1 or category 2 hazard may exist on those premises, or that an area in the district should be dealt with as a clearance area[7], the proper officer must inspect the premises or the area[8].

An inspection of any premises under these provisions is to be carried out in accordance with regulations made by the appropriate national authority[9], and is to extend to so much of the premises as the local housing authority or proper officer (as the case may be) considers appropriate in the circumstances having regard to any applicable provisions of the regulations[10]. Where such an inspection has been carried out and the proper officer of a local housing authority is of the opinion that a category 1 or category 2 hazard exists on any residential premises in the authority's district, or that an area in its district should be dealt with as a clearance area, the officer must, without delay, make a report in writing to the authority which sets out his opinion together with the facts of the case[11]. The authority must consider any such report made to it as soon as possible[12].

1 As to the meaning of 'local housing authority' see PARA 380 note 1.
2 Ie under the Housing Act 2004 s 3: see PARA 402.
3 As to the meaning of 'residential premises' see PARA 563.
4 As to the meanings of 'category 1 hazard' and 'category 2 hazard' see PARA 564.
5 Housing Act 2004 s 4(1).
6 For this purpose, 'an official complaint' means a complaint in writing made by a justice of the peace having jurisdiction in any part of the district, or the parish or community council for a parish or community within the district: Housing Act 2004 s 4(3).
7 As to clearance areas see PARA 632.
8 Housing Act 2004 s 4(2).
9 As to the meaning of 'appropriate national authority' see PARA 389 note 1.
10 Housing Act 2004 s 4(4). Regulations under s 4(4) may in particular make provision about the manner in which, and the extent to which, premises are to be inspected under s 4(1) (see the text and note 5) or s 4(2) (see the text and note 8), and the manner in which the assessment of hazards is to be carried out: s 4(5). Regulations have been made in relation to England and Wales separately, which provide that an inspector must: (1) have regard to any guidance for the time being given under s 9 (see PARA 569) in relation to the inspection of residential premises; (2) inspect any residential premises with a view to preparing an accurate record of their state and condition; and (3) prepare and keep such a record in written or in electronic form: Housing Health and Safety Rating System (England) Regulations 2005, SI 2005/3208, reg 5; Housing Health and Safety Rating System (Wales) Regulations 2006, SI 2006/1702, reg 5. 'Inspector' means a person carrying out an inspection under the Housing Act 2004 s 4: Housing Health and Safety Rating

System (England) Regulations 2005, SI 2005/3208, reg 2; Housing Health and Safety Rating System (Wales) Regulations 2006, SI 2006/1702, reg 2.

Where, following an inspection of residential premises under the Housing Act 2004 s 4, the inspector: (a) determines that a hazard of a prescribed description (see PARA 564 note 2) exists; and (b) considers, having regard to any guidance for the time being given under s 9 in relation to the assessment of hazards, that it is appropriate to calculate the seriousness of that hazard, the seriousness of that hazard must be calculated in accordance with the provisions of the Housing Health and Safety Rating System (England) Regulations 2005, SI 2005/3208, reg 6(2)–(4) (reg 6(1)), or the Housing Health and Safety Rating System (Wales) Regulations 2006, SI 2006/1702, reg 6(2)–(4) (reg 6(1)), as appropriate. The inspector must assess the likelihood, during the period of 12 months beginning with the date of the assessment, of a relevant occupier suffering any harm as a result of that hazard as falling within one of the range of ratios of likelihood set out in the Housing Health and Safety Rating System (England) Regulations 2005, SI 2005/3208, reg 6(2) Table 1 column 1 (reg 6(2)), or the Housing Health and Safety Rating System (Wales) Regulations 2006, SI 2006/1702, reg 6(2) Table 1 column 1 (reg 6(2)). The inspector must assess which of the four classes of harm (see the Housing Health and Safety Rating System (England) Regulations 2005, SI 2005/3208, Sch 2; the Housing Health and Safety Rating System (Wales) Regulations 2006, SI 2006/1702, Sch 2; and PARA 564 note 2) a relevant occupier is most likely to suffer during the period mentioned above: Housing Health and Safety Rating System (England) Regulations 2005, SI 2005/3208, reg 6(3); Housing Health and Safety Rating System (Wales) Regulations 2006, SI 2006/1702, reg 6(3). The inspector must then: (i) assess the possibility of each of the other classes of harm occurring as a result of that hazard, as falling within one of the range of percentages of possibility set out in reg 6(4) Table 2 column 1 of the respective regulations; (ii) record each possibility so assessed as the corresponding RSPRR set out in reg 6(4) Table 2 column 2; and (iii) record the possibility (which is to be known, for the purposes of the formula in reg 6(5), as the RSPPR) of the most likely class of harm occurring as a percentage calculated using the prescribed formula: see the Housing Health and Safety Rating System (England) Regulations 2005, SI 2005/3208, reg 6(4); and the Housing Health and Safety Rating System (Wales) Regulations 2006, SI 2006/1702, reg 6(4). 'RSPPR' means the representative scale point of the percentage range: Housing Health and Safety Rating System (England) Regulations 2005, SI 2005/3208, reg 6(7); Housing Health and Safety Rating System (Wales) Regulations 2006, SI 2006/1702, reg 6(7). When the inspector has assessed likelihood under reg 6(2) of the respective regulations and assessed the possibility of each harm occurring under reg 6(3), the seriousness of that hazard must be expressed by a numerical score calculated using the prescribed formula: see the Housing Health and Safety Rating System (England) Regulations 2005, SI 2005/3208, reg 6(5), (6); and the Housing Health and Safety Rating System (Wales) Regulations 2006, SI 2006/1702, reg 6(5), (6).

Except in the Housing Health and Safety Rating System (England) Regulations 2005, SI 2005/3208, reg 6(7)(e), and the Housing Health and Safety Rating System (Wales) Regulations 2006, SI 2006/1702, reg 6(7)(e) (see head (E) below), 'occupier' includes potential occupier: Housing Health and Safety Rating System (England) Regulations 2005, SI 2005/3208, reg 2; Housing Health and Safety Rating System (Wales) Regulations 2006, SI 2006/1702, reg 2. In reg 6 of the respective regulations, 'relevant occupier' means, where the risk of harm concerned is associated with the occurrence of any of the matters or circumstances listed in: (A) Sch 1 para 1, an occupier under the age of 15 years; (B) Sch 1 para 2, 3 or 6(a), an occupier aged 65 years or over; (C) Sch 1 para 7, an occupier under the age of 3 years; (D) Sch 1 para 8, an occupier aged 60 years or over who has been exposed to radon since birth; (E) Sch 1 para 11, the actual occupier; (F) Sch 1 para 17, 22, 23 or 25, an occupier under the age of 5 years; (G) Sch 1 para 19, 20, 21, 24 or 28, an occupier aged 60 years or over; (H) Sch 1 para 26, except where a collision is with low architectural features, an occupier under the age of 5 years, and where a collision is with low architectural features, an occupier aged 16 years or over; (I) any other paragraph of Sch 1, any occupier: Housing Health and Safety Rating System (England) Regulations 2005, SI 2005/3208, reg 6(7); Housing Health and Safety Rating System (Wales) Regulations 2006, SI 2006/1702, reg 6(7). In making assessments under these provisions, an inspector must have regard to any guidance for the time being given under the Housing Act 2004 s 9 (see PARA 569): Housing Health and Safety Rating System (England) Regulations 2005, SI 2005/3208, reg 6(8); Housing Health and Safety Rating System (Wales) Regulations 2006, SI 2006/1702, reg 6(8).

See also *HHSRS Operating Guidance — Housing Act 2004: Guidance about inspections and assessment of hazards given under Section 9* (published 27 February 2006).

11 Housing Act 2004 s 4(6).
12 Housing Act 2004 s 4(7).

(ii) Enforcement of Housing Standards

566. General duty to take enforcement action in relation to category 1 hazards. If a local housing authority[1] considers that a category 1 hazard[2] exists on any residential premises[3], it must take the appropriate enforcement action in relation to the hazard[4]. 'The appropriate enforcement action' means whichever of the following courses of action is indicated[5]. If only one course of action is available[6] to the authority in relation to the hazard, it must take that course of action[7]. If two or more courses of action are available to the authority in relation to the hazard, it must take the course of action which it considers to be the most appropriate of those available to it[8]. The available courses of action are:

(1) serving an improvement notice[9];
(2) making a prohibition order[10];
(3) serving a hazard awareness notice[11];
(4) taking emergency remedial action[12];
(5) making an emergency prohibition order[13];
(6) making a demolition order[14];
(7) declaring the area in which the premises concerned are situated to be a clearance area[15].

The taking by the authority of a course of action as mentioned above does not prevent it being required[16] to take in relation to the same hazard:

(a) either the same course of action again or another such course of action, if it considers that the action taken by it so far has not proved satisfactory; or

(b) another such course of action, where the first course of action is that mentioned in head (7) and its eventual decision[17] means that the premises concerned are not to be included in a clearance area[18].

1   As to the meaning of 'local housing authority' see PARA 380 note 1.
2   As to the meaning of 'category 1 hazard' see PARA 564.
3   As to the meaning of 'residential premises' see PARA 563.
4   Housing Act 2004 s 5(1). Section 6 (see notes 10, 12–15) applies for the purposes of s 5 to explain how the duty under s 5 operates in certain cases: s 5(7). Under previous legislation, it was held that in reaching a decision on such matters, authorities should act in a judicial spirit: see *Hall v Manchester Corpn* (1915) 84 LJ Ch 732, HL.
5   Ie by the Housing Act 2004 s 5(3) (see the text and note 7) or s 5(4) (see the text and note 8): s 5(2). As to the serving of improvement notices as an available course of action see PARA 571.
6   To determine whether a course of action mentioned in any of the paragraphs of the Housing Act 2004 s 5(2)(a)–(g) is 'available' to the authority in relation to the hazard, see the provision mentioned in that paragraph (see notes 9–15): s 5(6).
7   Housing Act 2004 s 5(3).
8   Housing Act 2004 s 5(4). The courses of action in heads (1)–(5) in the text are new courses of action introduced under the Housing Act 2004.
9   Ie under the Housing Act 2004 s 11 (see PARA 571): s 5(2)(a).
10 Ie under the Housing Act 2004 s 20 (see PARA 590): s 5(2)(b). The reference to making such an order is to be read as a reference to making instead a determination under the Housing Act 1985 s 300(1) or (2) (power to purchase for temporary housing use: see PARA 638) in a case where the authority considers the latter course of action to be the better alternative in the circumstances: Housing Act 2004 s 6(1), (2).
11 Ie under the Housing Act 2004 s 28 (see PARA 608): s 5(2)(c).
12 Ie under the Housing Act 2004 s 40 (see PARA 613): s 5(2)(d). In this case, the authority may regard the taking of emergency remedial action under s 40 followed by the service of an improvement notice under s 11 (see PARA 571) as a single course of action: s 6(1), (3).
13 Ie under the Housing Act 2004 s 43 (see PARA 615): s 5(2)(e). In this case, the authority may regard the making of an emergency prohibition order under s 43 followed by the service of a prohibition order under s 20 (see PARA 590) as a single course of action: s 6(1), (4).
14 Ie under the Housing Act 1985 s 265(1) or (2) (see PARA 621): Housing Act 2004 s 5(2)(f). The reference to making such an order is to be read as a reference to making instead a determination under the Housing Act 1985 s 300(1) or (2) (power to purchase for temporary housing use: see PARA 638) in a case where the authority considers the latter course of action to be the better alternative in the circumstances: Housing Act 2004 s 6(1), (2).
15 Ie by virtue of the Housing Act 1985 s 289(2) (see PARA 632): Housing Act 2004 s 5(2)(g). In this case, any duty to take the course of action mentioned is subject to the operation of the Housing

Act 1985 s 289(2B)–(4) (procedural and other restrictions relating to slum clearance declarations: see PARA 632), and the Housing Act 2004 s 5(2)(g) does not apply in a case where the authority has already declared the area in which the premises concerned are situated to be a clearance area in accordance with the Housing Act 1985 s 289, but the premises have been excluded by virtue of s 289(2F)(b): Housing Act 2004 s 6(1), (5).

16 Ie under the Housing Act 2004 s 5(1): see the text and note 4.
17 Ie under the Housing Act 1985 s 289(2F): see PARA 632.
18 Housing Act 2004 s 5(5).

567. Powers to take enforcement action in relation to category 2 hazards. A local housing authority[1] has powers (but not a duty) to take particular kinds of enforcement action in cases where it considers that a category 2 hazard[2] exists on residential premises[3]. These powers are:

(1)   the power to serve an improvement notice[4];
(2)   the power to make a prohibition order[5];
(3)   the power to serve a hazard awareness notice[6];
(4)   the power to make a demolition order[7]; and
(5)   the power to make a slum clearance declaration[8].

The taking by the authority of one of these kinds of enforcement action in relation to a particular category 2 hazard does not prevent it from taking either the same kind of action again, or a different kind of enforcement action, in relation to the hazard, where it considers that the action taken by it so far has not proved satisfactory[9].

1 As to the meaning of 'local housing authority' see PARA 380 note 1.
2 As to the meaning of 'category 2 hazard' see PARA 564.
3 Housing Act 2004 s 7(1). As to the meaning of 'residential premises' see PARA 563.
4 Ie under the Housing Act 2004 s 12 (see PARA 572): s 7(2)(a).
5 Ie under the Housing Act 2004 s 21 (see PARA 591): s 7(2)(b).
6 Ie under the Housing Act 2004 s 29 (see PARA 609): s 7(2)(c).
7 Ie under the Housing Act 1985 s 265(3), (4) (see PARA 621): Housing Act 2004 s 7(2)(d).
8 Ie under the Housing Act 1985 s 289(2ZB) (see PARA 632): Housing Act 2004 s 7(2)(e).
9 Housing Act 2004 s 7(3).

568. Reasons for decision to take enforcement action. The following provisions apply where a local housing authority[1] decides to take one of the specified kinds of enforcement action[2] ('the relevant action')[3]. The authority must prepare a statement of the reasons for its decision to take the relevant action[4]. Those reasons must include the reasons why the authority decided to take the relevant action rather than any other kind (or kinds) of enforcement action available[5] to it[6]. A copy of the statement of reasons must accompany every notice, copy of a notice, or copy of an order which is served in accordance with the provisions as to the service of improvement notices etc[7], the service of copies of prohibition orders etc[8], or the service of copies of demolition orders[9], in or in connection with the taking of the relevant action[10].

If the relevant action consists of declaring an area to be a clearance area, the statement of reasons must be published as soon as possible after the relevant resolution is passed[11], and in such manner as the authority considers appropriate[12].

1 As to the meaning of 'local housing authority' see PARA 380 note 1.
2 Ie under the Housing Act 2004 s 5(2) (see PARA 566) or s 7(2) (see PARA 567).
3 Housing Act 2004 s 8(1).
4 Housing Act 2004 s 8(2).
5 Ie under the provisions mentioned in the Housing Act 2004 s 5(2) (see PARA 566) or s 7(2) (see PARA 567).
6 Housing Act 2004 s 8(3).

7 Ie the Housing Act 2004 s 18, Sch 1 Pt 1 (paras 1–5): see PARA 574. The reference to Sch 1 Pt 1 includes a reference to that Part as applied by s 28(7) or s 29(7) (hazard awareness notice: see PARAS 608–609) or to s 40(7) (emergency remedial action: see PARA 613): s 8(5)(a).
8 Ie the Housing Act 2004 s 27, Sch 2 Pt 1 (paras 1–2): see PARA 593. The reference to Sch 2 Pt 1 includes a reference to that Part as applied by s 43(4) (emergency prohibition orders: see PARA 615): s 8(5)(b).
9 Ie the Housing Act 1985 s 268: see PARA 621.
10 Housing Act 2004 s 8(4).
11 Ie under the Housing Act 1985 s 289: see PARA 632.
12 Housing Act 2004 s 8(6).

569. Guidance about inspections and enforcement action. The appropriate national authority[1] may give guidance to local housing authorities[2] about exercising: (1) their functions[3] in relation to the inspection of premises and the assessment of hazards; (2) their functions[4] in relation to improvement notices, prohibition orders or hazard awareness notices; (3) their functions[5] in relation to emergency remedial action and emergency prohibition orders; or (4) their functions[6] in relation to demolition orders and slum clearance[7]. A local housing authority must have regard to any guidance for the time being so given[8].

The appropriate national authority may give different guidance for different cases or descriptions of case or different purposes (including different guidance to different descriptions of local housing authority or to local housing authorities in different areas)[9]. In relation to England, before giving such guidance, or revising guidance already given, the Secretary of State[10] must lay a draft of the proposed guidance or alterations before each House of Parliament[11]. The Secretary of State must not give or revise the guidance before the end of the period of 40 days beginning with the day on which the draft is laid before each House of Parliament (or, if copies are laid before each House of Parliament on different days, the later of those days)[12]. The Secretary of State must not proceed with the proposed guidance or alterations if, within that period of 40 days, either House resolves that the guidance or alterations be withdrawn[13].

1 As to the meaning of 'appropriate national authority' see PARA 389 note 1.
2 As to the meaning of 'local housing authority' see PARA 380 note 1.
3 Ie under the Housing Act 2004 Pt 1 Ch 1 (ss 1–10).
4 Ie under the Housing Act 2004 Pt 1 Ch 2 (ss 11–39): see PARAS 571–612.
5 Ie under the Housing Act 2004 Pt 1 Ch 3 (ss 40–45): see PARA 613 et seq.
6 Ie under the Housing Act 1985 Pt IX (ss 265–323): see PARA 620 et seq.
7 Housing Act 2004 s 9(1). As to the guidance that has been issued see eg *HHSRS Operating Guidance — Housing Act 2004: Guidance about inspections and assessment of hazards given under Section 9* (published 27 February 2006); and *Housing Act 2004 — Enforcement Guidance: Part 1, Housing Conditions* (published 27 February 2006).
8 Housing Act 2004 s 9(2).
9 Housing Act 2004 s 9(3).
10 As to the Secretary of State see PARA 7.
11 Housing Act 2004 s 9(4).
12 Housing Act 2004 s 9(5). In calculating the period of 40 days, no account is to be taken of any time during which Parliament is dissolved or prorogued or during which both Houses are adjourned for more than four days: s 9(8).
13 Housing Act 2004 s 9(6). This is without prejudice to the possibility of laying a further draft of the guidance or alterations before each House of Parliament: s 9(7).

570. Consultation with fire and rescue authorities. The following provisions apply where a local housing authority[1] is satisfied that a prescribed fire hazard[2] exists in an HMO[3] or in any common parts[4] of a building containing one or more flats[5], and intends to take in relation to the hazard one of the specified[6] kinds of enforcement action[7]. Before taking the enforcement action in question, the authority must consult the fire and rescue authority[8] for the area in which the HMO or building is situated[9]. In the case of any proposed emergency measures[10], the authority's duty is a duty to consult that fire and rescue authority so far as it is practicable to do so before taking those measures[11].

1 As to the meaning of 'local housing authority' see PARA 380 note 1.
2 For this purpose, 'prescribed fire hazard' means a category 1 or category 2 hazard which is prescribed as a fire hazard for the purposes of the Housing Act 2004 s 10 by regulations under s 2: s 10(4). As to the meanings of 'category 1 hazard' and 'category 2 hazard' see PARA 564. For the purposes of s 10 a category 1 or 2 hazard is a prescribed fire hazard if the risk of harm is associated with exposure to uncontrolled fire and associated smoke: Housing Health and Safety Rating System (England) Regulations 2005, SI 2005/3208, reg 4; Housing Health and Safety Rating System (Wales) Regulations 2006, SI 2006/1702, reg 4.
3 As to the meaning of 'HMO' see PARA 563 note 11.
4 As to the meaning of 'common parts' see PARA 563 note 13.
5 As to the meaning of 'building containing one or more flats' see PARA 563 note 13.
6 Ie under the Housing Act 2004 s 5(2) (see PARA 566) or s 7(2) (see PARA 567).
7 Housing Act 2004 s 10(1).
8 'Fire and rescue authority' means a fire and rescue authority under the Fire and Rescue Services Act 2004: Housing Act 2004 s 10(4). See FIRE AND RESCUE SERVICES.
9 Housing Act 2004 s 10(2).
10 'Emergency measures' means emergency remedial action under the Housing Act 2004 s 40 (see PARA 613) or an emergency prohibition order under s 43 (see PARA 615): s 10(4).
11 Housing Act 2004 s 10(3).

(iii) Methods of Enforcement

A.   IMPROVEMENT NOTICES

(A)   *Service, Suspension and Revocation of Improvement Notices*

571. Duty of authority to serve improvement notice relating to category 1 hazard. If the local housing authority[1] is satisfied that a category 1 hazard[2] exists on any residential premises[3], and no management order is in force[4] in relation to the premises, serving an improvement notice[5] in respect of the hazard is a course of action available to the authority in relation to the hazard for the purposes of the authority's general duty[6] to take enforcement action in relation to category 1 hazards[7]. An improvement notice under these provisions is a notice requiring the person on whom it is served to take such remedial action[8] in respect of the hazard concerned as is specified[9] in the notice[10].

The notice may require remedial action to be taken in relation to the following premises:

(1)   if the residential premises on which the hazard exists are a dwelling[11] or HMO[12] which is not a flat[13], it may require such action to be taken in relation to the dwelling or HMO;

(2)   if those premises are one or more flats, it may require such action to be taken in relation to the building containing the flat or flats (or any part of the building) or any external common parts[14];

(3)   if those premises are the common parts of a building containing one or more flats, it may require such action to be taken in relation to the building (or any part of the building) or any external common parts[15].

The notice may not, in a case under head (2) or head (3)[16], require any remedial action to be taken in relation to any part of the building or its external common parts that is not included in any residential premises on which the hazard exists, unless the authority is satisfied that the deficiency from which the hazard arises is situated there, and that it is necessary for the action to be so taken in order to protect the health or safety of any actual or potential occupiers[17] of one or more of the flats[18]. The remedial action required to be taken by the notice must, as a minimum, be such as to ensure that the hazard ceases to be a category 1 hazard, but may extend beyond such action[19].

An improvement notice may relate to more than one category 1 hazard on the same premises or in the same building containing one or more flats[20].

The operation of an improvement notice may be suspended[21].

1 As to the meaning of 'local housing authority' see PARA 380 note 1.
2 As to the meaning of 'category 1 hazard' see PARA 564.
3 As to the meaning of 'residential premises' see PARA 563.
4 Ie under the Housing Act 2004 Pt 4 Ch 1 (ss 101–131) or Ch 2 (ss 132–138): see PARA 745 et seq. As to the effect of the making of a management order see PARA 612.
5 Ie under the Housing Act 2004 s 11.
6 Ie for the purposes of the Housing Act 2004 s 5: see PARA 566.
7 Housing Act 2004 s 11(1).
8 In the Housing Act 2004 Pt 1 (ss 1–54), 'remedial action', in relation to a hazard, means action (whether in the form of carrying out works or otherwise) which, in the opinion of the local housing authority, will remove or reduce the hazard: s 11(8).
9 Ie in accordance with the Housing Act 2004 s 11(3)–(5) (see the text and notes 11–19) and s 13 (see PARA 573).
10 Housing Act 2004 s 11(2).
11 As to the meaning of 'dwelling' see PARA 563 note 10.
12 As to the meaning of 'HMO' see PARA 563 note 11.
13 As to the meaning of 'flat' see PARA 563 note 13.
14 'External common parts', in relation to a building containing one or more flats, means common parts of the building which are outside it: Housing Act 2004 s 1(5). As to the meaning of 'building containing one or more flats', and as to the meaning of 'common parts', see PARA 563 note 13.
15 Housing Act 2004 s 11(3). Heads (2), (3) in the text are subject to s 11(4) (see the text to note 18): s 11(3).
16 Ie by virtue of the Housing Act 2004 s 11(3)(b) or (c) (see heads (2), (3) in the text).
17 As to the meaning of 'occupier' see PARA 563 note 13.
18 Housing Act 2004 s 11(4).
19 Housing Act 2004 s 11(5).
20 Housing Act 2004 s 11(6).
21 Ie in accordance with the Housing Act 2004 s 14 (see PARA 575): s 11(7).

572. Power of authority to serve improvement notice relating to category 2 hazard. If the local housing authority[1] is satisfied that a category 2 hazard[2] exists on any residential premises[3], and no management order is in force[4] in relation to the premises, the authority may serve an improvement notice[5] in respect of the hazard[6]. Such an improvement notice is a notice requiring the person on whom it is served to take such remedial action[7] in respect of the hazard concerned as is specified[8] in the notice[9].

The notice may require remedial action to be taken in relation to the following premises:

(1)   if the residential premises on which the hazard exists are a dwelling[10] or an HMO[11] which is not a flat[12], it may require such action to be taken in relation to the dwelling or HMO;

(2)   if those premises are one or more flats, it may require such action to be taken in relation to the building containing the flat or flats (or any part of the building) or any external common parts[13];

(3)   if those premises are the common parts of a building containing one or more flats, it may require such action to be taken in relation to the building (or any part of the building) or any external common parts[14].

The notice may not, in a case under head (2) or head (3)[15], require any remedial action to be taken in relation to any part of the building or its external common parts that is not included in any residential premises on which the hazard exists, unless the authority is satisfied that the deficiency from which the hazard arises is situated there, and that it is necessary for the action to be so taken in order to protect the health or safety of any actual or potential occupiers[16] of one or more of the flats[17].

An improvement notice under these provisions may relate to more than one category 2 hazard on the same premises or in the same building containing one or more flats[18]. Such an improvement notice may be combined in one document with a notice in respect of a category 1 hazard[19] where they require remedial action to be taken in relation to the same premises[20].

The operation of an improvement notice under these provisions may be suspended[21].

1   As to the meaning of 'local housing authority' see PARA 380 note 1.
2   As to the meaning of 'category 2 hazard' see PARA 564.
3   As to the meaning of 'residential premises' see PARA 563.
4   Ie under the Housing Act 2004 Pt 4 Ch 1 (ss 101–131) or Ch 2 (ss 132–138): see PARA 745 et seq. As to the effect of the making of a management order see PARA 612.
5   Ie under the Housing Act 2004 s 12.
6   Housing Act 2004 s 12(1).
7   As to the meaning of 'remedial action' see PARA 571 note 8.
8   Ie in accordance with the Housing Act 2004 s 12(3) (see the text and notes 10–14) and s 13 (see PARA 573).
9   Housing Act 2004 s 12(2).
10 As to the meaning of 'dwelling' see PARA 563 note 10.
11 As to the meaning of 'HMO' see PARA 563 note 11.
12 As to the meaning of 'flat' see PARA 563 note 13.
13 As to the meaning of 'external common parts' see PARA 571 note 14. As to the meaning of 'building containing one or more flats', and as to the meaning of 'common parts', see PARA 563 note 13.
14 Housing Act 2004 s 11(3) (applied by s 12(3)).
15 Ie by virtue of the Housing Act 2004 s 11(3)(b) or (c): see heads (2), (3) in the text.
16 As to the meaning of 'occupier' see PARA 563 note 13.
17 Housing Act 2004 s 11(4) (applied by s 12(3)).
18 Housing Act 2004 s 12(4).
19 Ie a notice under the Housing Act 2004 s 11: see PARA 571. As to the meaning of 'category 1 hazard' see PARA 564.
20 Housing Act 2004 s 12(5).
21 Ie in accordance with the Housing Act 2004 s 14 (see PARA 575): s 12(6).

573. Contents of improvement notices. An improvement notice[1] must comply with the following provisions[2]. The notice must specify, in relation to the hazard[3] (or each of the hazards) to which it relates[4]:

(1)   whether the notice is served under the statutory provision relating to category 1 hazards[5] or under that relating to category 2 hazards[6];
(2)   the nature of the hazard and the residential premises[7] on which it exists[8];
(3)   the deficiency giving rise to the hazard[9];
(4)   the premises in relation to which remedial action[10] is to be taken in respect of the hazard and the nature of that remedial action[11];
(5)   the date when the remedial action is to be started[12]; and
(6)   the period within which the remedial action is to be completed or the periods within which each part of it is to be completed[13].

The notice must contain information about the right of appeal against the decision[14] and the period within which an appeal may be made[15].

1   Ie under the Housing Act 2004 s 11 (see PARA 571) or s 12 (see PARA 572).
2   Housing Act 2004 s 13(1).
3   As to the meaning of 'hazard' see PARA 564.
4   Housing Act 2004 s 13(2).
5   Ie the Housing Act 2004 s 11. As to the meaning of 'category 1 hazard' see PARA 564.
6   Ie the Housing Act 2004 s 12: s 13(2)(a). As to the meaning of 'category 2 hazard' see PARA 564.

7 As to the meaning of 'residential premises' see PARA 563.

8 Housing Act 2004 s 13(2)(b).

9 Housing Act 2004 s 13(2)(c).

10 As to the meaning of 'remedial action' see PARA 571 note 8.

11 Housing Act 2004 s 13(2)(d). Under the previous legislation, it was held that the notice must specify the works to be carried out so as to enable a reasonably competent builder to carry out the works: see *Our Lady of Hal Church v Camden London Borough Council* (1980) 40 P & CR 472, 79 LGR 103, CA.

12 Housing Act 2004 s 13(2)(e). The notice may not require any remedial action to be started earlier than the 28th day after that on which the notice is served: s 13(3).

13 Housing Act 2004 s 13(2)(f).

14 Ie under the Housing Act 2004 s 18, Sch 1 Pt 3 (paras 10–20): see PARA 580 et seq.

15 Housing Act 2004 s 13(4).

574. Service of improvement notices and copies. Where the specified premises[1] in the case of an improvement notice[2] are a dwelling[3] which is licensed under Part 3 of the Housing Act 2004[4] or an HMO[5] which is licensed under Part 2 or Part 3 of that Act[6], the local housing authority[7] must serve the notice on the holder of the licence under that Part[8].

Where the specified premises in the case of an improvement notice are a dwelling which is not licensed under Part 3 of the Housing Act 2004 or an HMO which is not licensed under Part 2 or Part 3 of that Act, and which (in either case) is not a flat[9], the local housing authority must serve the notice (in the case of a dwelling) on the person having control of the dwelling[10], and (in the case of an HMO) either on the person having control of the HMO or on the person managing it[11].

Where any specified premises in the case of an improvement notice are a dwelling which is not licensed under Part 3 of the Housing Act 2004 or an HMO which is not licensed under Part 2 or Part 3 of that Act, and which (in either case) is a flat: (1) in the case of dwelling which is a flat, the local housing authority must serve the notice on a person who is an owner[12] of the flat and in the authority's opinion ought to take the action specified in the notice; and (2) in the case of an HMO which is a flat, the local housing authority must serve the notice either on a person who is an owner of the flat (that is, the leaseholder), and in the authority's opinion ought to take the action specified in the notice, or on the person managing the flat[13].

Where any specified premises in the case of an improvement notice are common parts[14] of a building containing one or more flats[15] or any part of such a building which does not consist of residential premises[16], the local housing authority must serve the notice on a person who is an owner of the specified premises concerned and who in the authority's opinion ought to take the action specified in the notice[17].

In addition to serving an improvement notice in accordance with these provisions, the local housing authority must serve a copy of the notice on every other person who, to its knowledge, has a relevant interest[18] in any specified premises or is an occupier[19] of any such premises[20]. Such copies must be served within the period of seven days beginning with the day on which the notice is served[21].

1 In the Housing Act 2004 Pt 1 (ss 1–54), 'specified premises', in relation to an improvement notice, means premises specified in the notice, in accordance with s 13(2)(d) (see PARA 573), as premises in relation to which remedial action is to be taken in respect of the hazard: s 13(5). As to the meaning of 'hazard' see PARA 564. As to the meaning of 'remedial action' see PARA 571 note 8.

2 Ie a notice under the Housing Act 2004 s 11 (see PARA 571) or s 12 (see PARA 572).

3 As to the meaning of 'dwelling' see PARA 563 note 10.

4   Ie the Housing Act 2004 Pt 3 (ss 79–100) (selective licensing of other residential accommodation): see PARA 704 et seq.

5   As to the meaning of 'HMO' see PARA 563 note 11.

6   Ie the Housing Act 2004 Pt 2 (ss 55–78) (licensing of houses in multiple occupation: see PARA 674 et seq) or Pt 3 (ss 79–100) (selective licensing of other residential accommodation: see PARA 704 et seq).

7   As to the meaning of 'local housing authority' see PARA 380 note 1.

8   Housing Act 2004 s 18, Sch 1 para 1.

9   As to the meaning of 'flat' see PARA 563 note 13.

10 As to the meaning of 'person having control' see PARA 391 note 5.

11 Housing Act 2004 Sch 1 para 2. As to the meaning of 'person managing' see PARA 391 note 6.

12 As to the meaning of 'owner' see PARA 384 note 11.

13 Housing Act 2004 Sch 1 para 3.

14 As to the meaning of 'common parts' see PARA 563 note 13.

15 As to the meaning of 'building containing one or more flats' see PARA 563 note 13.

16 As to the meaning of 'residential premises' see PARA 563.

17 Housing Act 2004 Sch 1 para 4(1), (2). For the purposes of Sch 1 para 4, a person is an owner of any common parts of a building if he is an owner of the building or part of the building concerned, or (in the case of external common parts) of the particular premises in which the common parts are comprised: Sch 1 para 4(3). As to the meaning of 'external common parts' see PARA 571 note 14.

18 A 'relevant interest' means an interest as freeholder, mortgagee or lessee: Housing Act 2004 Sch 1 para 5(2). For the purposes of Sch 1 para 5, a person has a relevant interest in any common parts of a building if he has a relevant interest in the building or part of the building concerned, or (in the case of external common parts) in the particular premises in which the common parts are comprised: Sch 1 para 5(3).

19 As to the meaning of 'occupier' see PARA 563 note 13.

20 Housing Act 2004 Sch 1 para 5(1).

21 Housing Act 2004 Sch 1 para 5(4).

575. Suspension of improvement notices. An improvement notice[1] may provide for the operation of the notice to be suspended until a time, or the occurrence of an event, specified in the notice[2]. The time so specified may, in particular, be the time when a person of a particular description begins, or ceases, to occupy any premises[3]. The event so specified may, in particular, be a notified breach[4] of an undertaking accepted by the local housing authority for the purposes of this provision from the person on whom the notice is served[5]. If an improvement notice does provide for the operation of the notice to be suspended, any periods specified in the notice[6] are to be fixed by reference to the day when the suspension ends[7]; and the notice may not require any remedial action to be started earlier than the twenty-first day after that on which the suspension ends[8].

The local housing authority may at any time review an improvement notice whose operation is suspended[9]. The local housing authority must review an improvement notice whose operation is suspended not later than one year after the date of service of the notice and at subsequent intervals of not more than one year[10]. Copies of the authority's decision on a review must be served on the person on whom the improvement notice was served, and on every other person on whom a copy of the notice was required to be served[11].

1   Ie a notice under the Housing Act 2004 s 11 (see PARA 571) or s 12 (see PARA 572).

2   Housing Act 2004 s 14(1).

3   Housing Act 2004 s 14(2).

4   For this purpose, a 'notified breach', in relation to such an undertaking, means an act or omission by the person on whom the notice is served, which the local housing authority considers to be a breach of the undertaking, and which is notified to that person in accordance with the terms of the undertaking: Housing Act 2004 s 14(4). As to the meaning of 'local housing authority' see PARA 380 note 1.

5   Housing Act 2004 s 14(3).

6   Ie under the Housing Act 2004 s 13: see PARA 573.

7   Housing Act 2004 s 14(5).

8 Housing Act 2004 s 14(5) (modifying s 13(3): see PARA 573).
9 Housing Act 2004 s 17(1).
10 Housing Act 2004 s 17(2).
11 Housing Act 2004 s 17(3). As to service of improvement notices see PARA 574.

576. Operation of improvement notices. The general rule is that an improvement notice[1] becomes operative at the end of the period of 21 days beginning with the day on which it is served[2] (which is the period of time for appealing[3] against the notice)[4]. This is subject to the following provisions regarding suspended notices and appeals[5].

If the notice is suspended[6], the notice becomes operative at the time when the suspension ends[7].

If an appeal against the notice is made[8], the notice does not become operative until such time (if any) as is the statutory operative time[9]. If no appeal against an improvement notice is made within the period for appealing against it, the notice is final and conclusive as to matters which could have been raised on an appeal[10].

1 Ie a notice under the Housing Act 2004 s 11 (see PARA 571) or s 12 (see PARA 572).
2 Ie under the Housing Act 2004 s 18, Sch 1 Pt 1 (paras 1–5): see PARA 574.
3 Ie under the Housing Act 2004 Sch 1 Pt 3 (paras 10–20): see PARA 580 et seq.
4 Housing Act 2004 s 15(1), (2). As to the position where an appeal is brought see the text and notes 8–10. Note, however, that this will not apply to a defective notice: see *Graddage v Haringey London Borough Council* [1975] 1 All ER 224, [1975] 1 WLR 241; *Pollway Nominees Ltd v Croydon London Borough Council* [1987] AC 79, [1986] 2 All ER 849, HL. There is, therefore, no obligation to appeal against such a notice (though it may be prudent to do so until the authority accepts that the notice is defective).
5 Housing Act 2004 s 15(3).
6 Ie the Housing Act 2004 s 14: see PARA 575.
7 Housing Act 2004 s 15(4). This is subject to s 15(5) (see the text to notes 8–9): s 15(4).
8 Ie under the Housing Act 2004 Sch 1 Pt 3: see PARA 580 et seq.
9 Housing Act 2004 s 15(5). If an appeal is made under Sch 1 para 10 (see PARA 580) against an improvement notice which is not suspended, and a decision on the appeal is given which confirms the notice, 'the operative time' is as follows: (1) if the period within which an appeal to the Upper Tribunal may be brought expires without such an appeal having been brought, 'the operative time' is the end of that period; (2) if an appeal to the Upper Tribunal is brought, 'the operative time' is the time when a decision is given on the appeal which confirms the notice: Sch 1 para 19(1), (2) (Sch 1 para 19(2) amended by SI 2009/1307). If an appeal is made under the Housing Act 2004 Sch 1 para 10 against an improvement notice which is suspended, and a decision is given on the appeal which confirms the notice, 'the operative time' is: (a) the time that would be the operative time under Sch 1 para 19(2) if the notice were not suspended; or (b) if later, the time when the suspension ends: Sch 1 para 19(3). For this purpose, the withdrawal of an appeal has the same effect as a decision which confirms the notice, and references to a decision which confirms the notice are references to a decision which confirms it with or without variation: Sch 1 para 19(4). As to appeals to the Upper Tribunal, ie the Upper Tribunal (Lands Chamber), the successor to the Lands Tribunal, see PARAS 49–50.
10 Housing Act 2004 s 15(6).

577. Revocation and variation of improvement notices. The local housing authority[1] must revoke an improvement notice[2] if it is satisfied that the requirements of the notice have been complied with[3]. The local housing authority may revoke an improvement notice if: (1) in the case of a notice relating to a category 1 hazard[4], it considers that there are any special circumstances making it appropriate to revoke the notice; or (2) in the case of a notice relating to a category 2 hazard[5], it considers that it is appropriate to revoke the notice[6]. A revocation comes into force at the time when it is made[7].

Where an improvement notice relates to a number of hazards, the requirement as to revocation[8] is to be read as applying separately in relation to each of those hazards, and if, as a result, the authority is required to revoke only part of the notice, it may vary the remainder as it considers appropriate[9]. The local housing authority may vary an improvement notice with the agreement of the person on whom the notice was served or, in the case of a notice whose operation is suspended, so as to alter the time or events by reference to which the suspension is to come to an end[10]. If it is made with the agreement of the person on whom the improvement notice was served, such a variation comes into force at the time when it is made[11]; otherwise a variation does not come into force until such time (if any) as is the operative time for this purpose[12] in relation to the expiry of the time for appealing[13].

The power to revoke or vary an improvement notice under these provisions is exercisable by the authority either on an application made by the person on whom the improvement notice was served[14], or on the authority's own initiative[15].

1 As to the meaning of 'local housing authority' see PARA 380 note 1.
2 Ie a notice under the Housing Act 2004 s 11 (see PARA 571) or s 12 (see PARA 572).
3 Housing Act 2004 s 16(1).
4 Ie a notice served under the Housing Act 2004 s 11: see PARA 571. As to the meaning of 'category 1 hazard' see PARA 564.
5 Ie a notice served under the Housing Act 2004 s 12: see PARA 572. As to the meaning of 'category 2 hazard' see PARA 564.
6 Housing Act 2004 s 16(2).
7 Housing Act 2004 s 16(5).
8 Ie the Housing Act 2004 s 16(1): see the text and note 3.
9 Housing Act 2004 s 16(3).
10 Housing Act 2004 s 16(4).
11 Housing Act 2004 s 16(6).
12 Ie under the Housing Act 2004 s 18, Sch 1 para 20. If no appeal is made under Sch 1 para 13 (see PARA 581) before the end of the period of 28 days mentioned in Sch 1 para 14(2) (see PARA 581), 'the operative time' is the end of that period: Sch 1 para 20(1), (2). If an appeal is made under Sch 1 para 13 before the end of that period and a decision is given on the appeal which confirms the variation, 'the operative time' is as follows: (1) if the period within which an appeal to the Upper Tribunal may be brought expires without such an appeal having been brought, 'the operative time' is the end of that period; (2) if an appeal to the Upper Tribunal is brought, 'the operative time' is the time when a decision is given on the appeal which confirms the variation: Sch 1 para 20(3) (amended by SI 2009/1307). For this purpose, the withdrawal of an appeal has the same effect as a decision which confirms the variation, and references to a decision which confirms the variation are references to a decision which confirms it with or without variation: Housing Act 2004 Sch 1 para 20(4). As to appeals to the Upper Tribunal, ie the Upper Tribunal (Lands Chamber), the successor to the Lands Tribunal, see PARAS 49–50.
13 Housing Act 2004 s 16(7).
14 If the application is refused, an appeal may be brought: see PARA 581.
15 Housing Act 2004 s 16(8).

578. Service of notices relating to variation or revocation of improvement notices. Where the local housing authority[1] decides to revoke or vary[2] an improvement notice[3], the authority must serve a notice, and copies of that notice, on the persons on whom it would be required[4] to serve an improvement notice and copies in respect of the specified premises[5]. If, in so doing, the authority serves a notice under this provision on a person who is not the person on whom the improvement notice was served ('the original recipient'), the authority must serve a copy of the notice on the original recipient unless it considers that it would not be appropriate to do so[6]. The notice and copies[7] must be served within the period of seven days beginning with the day on which the decision is made[8].

A notice under these provisions must set out: (1) the authority's decision to revoke or vary the improvement notice; (2) the reasons for the decision and the date on which it was made; and (3) if the decision is to vary the notice: (a) the right of appeal against the decision[9]; and (b) the period within which an appeal may be made[10].

Where the local housing authority, having been asked to, refuses to revoke or vary an improvement notice, the authority must serve a notice, and copies of that notice, on the persons on whom it would be required to serve an improvement notice and copies in respect of the specified premises[11]. If, in so doing, the authority serves a notice under this provision on a person who is not the person on whom the improvement notice was served ('the original recipient'), the authority must serve a copy of the notice on the original recipient unless it considers that it would not be appropriate to do so[12]. The notice and copies[13] must be served within the period of seven days beginning with the day on which the decision is made[14].

Such a notice must set out: (i) the authority's decision not to revoke or vary the improvement notice; (ii) the reasons for the decision and the date on which it was made; (iii) the right of appeal against the decision[15]; and (iv) the period within which an appeal may be made[16].

1 As to the meaning of 'local housing authority' see PARA 380 note 1.
2 As to revocation and variation see PARA 577.
3 Ie a notice under the Housing Act 2004 s 11 (see PARA 571) or s 12 (see PARA 572).
4 Ie under the Housing Act 2004 s 18, Sch 1 Pt 1 (paras 1–5): see PARA 574.
5 Housing Act 2004 Sch 1 para 6(1), (2). As to the meaning of 'specified premises' see PARA 574 note 1.
6 Housing Act 2004 Sch 1 para 6(3), (4).
7 Ie the documents required to be served under the Housing Act 2004 Sch 1 para 6(2): see the text and note 5.
8 Housing Act 2004 Sch 1 para 6(5).
9 Ie under the Housing Act 2004 Sch 1 Pt 3 (paras 10–20): see PARA 580 et seq.
10 Housing Act 2004 Sch 1 para 7. See also Sch 1 para 14(2); and PARA 581.
11 Housing Act 2004 Sch 1 para 8(1), (2).
12 Housing Act 2004 Sch 1 para 8(3), (4).
13 Ie the documents required to be served under the Housing Act 2004 Sch 1 para 8(2): see the text and note 11.
14 Housing Act 2004 Sch 1 para 8(5).
15 Ie under the Housing Act 2004 Sch 1 Pt 3: see PARA 580 et seq.
16 Housing Act 2004 Sch 1 para 9. See also Sch 1 para 14(2); and PARA 581.

579. Change in person liable to comply with improvement notice. Where an improvement notice[1] has been served on any person ('the original recipient') in respect of any premises, and at a later date ('the changeover date') that person ceases to be a person of the relevant category[2] in respect of the premises, then, as from the changeover date, the liable person[3] in respect of the premises is to be in the same position as if the improvement notice had originally been served on him, and he had taken all relevant steps[4] which the original recipient had taken[5]. The effect of this is that, inter alia, any period for compliance with the notice or for bringing any appeal is unaffected[6]. However, where the original recipient has become subject to any liability arising by virtue of Part 1 of the Housing Act 2004 before the changeover date, this provision does not have the effect of relieving him of the liability, or making the new liable person subject to it[7]. This provision applies with any necessary modifications where a person to whom it applies[8] ceases to be the liable person in respect of the premises[9].

1 Ie a notice under the Housing Act 2004 s 11 (see PARA 571) or s 12 (see PARA 572).
2 The reference to a person ceasing to be a 'person of the relevant category' is a reference to his ceasing to fall within the description of person (eg the holder of a licence under the Housing Act 2004 Pt 2 (ss 55–78) or Pt 3 (ss 79–100) or the person managing a dwelling) by reference to which the improvement notice was served on him: s 19(2).
3 Unless the Housing Act 2004 s 19(8) or (9) applies, the person who is at any time the 'liable person' in respect of any premises is the person having control of the premises: s 19(7). However, if the original recipient was served as the person managing the premises, and there is a new person managing the premises as from the changeover date, that new person is the 'liable person': s 19(8). If the original recipient was served as an owner of the premises, the 'liable person' is the owner's successor in title on the changeover date: s 19(9). As to the meaning of 'owner' see PARA 384 note 11.

4   Ie for the purposes of the Housing Act 2004 Pt 1 (ss 1–54).
5   Housing Act 2004 s 19(1), (3).
6   Housing Act 2004 s 19(4).
7   Housing Act 2004 s 19(5).
8   Ie by virtue of any provision of the Housing Act 2004 s 19.
9   Housing Act 2004 s 19(6).

(B)   Appeals relating to Improvement Notices

580. Appeal against improvement notice. The person on whom an improvement notice[1] is served may appeal to the appropriate tribunal[2] against the notice[3]. Two specific grounds on which an appeal may be made are mentioned in the Housing Act 2004[4], but they do not affect the generality of the right to appeal[5]. Thus an appeal may be made by a person on the ground that:

(1)   one or more other persons, as an owner[6] or owners of the specified premises[7], ought either to take the action concerned or to pay the whole or part of the cost of taking that action[8];

(2)   one of the following courses of action is the best course of action in relation to the hazard[9] in respect of which the notice was served[10]:

         (a)   making a prohibition order[11];

         (b)   serving a hazard awareness notice[12]; or

         (c)   making a demolition order[13].

Where the grounds on which an appeal is made consist of or include the ground mentioned in head (1), the appellant must serve a copy of his notice of appeal on the other person or persons concerned[14].

Any appeal against an improvement notice must be made within the period of 21 days beginning with the date on which the improvement notice was served[15]. The appropriate tribunal may allow an appeal to be made to it after the end of such period if it is satisfied that there is a good reason for the failure to appeal before the end of that period (and for any delay since then in applying for permission to appeal out of time)[16].

1   Ie a notice under the Housing Act 2004 s 11 (see PARA 571) or s 12 (see PARA 572).
2   In the Housing Act 2004, 'appropriate tribunal' means: (1) in relation to premises in England, the First-tier Tribunal or, where determined by or under Tribunal Procedure Rules, the Upper Tribunal; and (2) in relation to premises in Wales, a residential property tribunal: s 261(8) (added by SI 2013/1036). As to appeals to the appropriate tribunal see PARA 32 et seq. As to the powers of the tribunal on an appeal see PARA 582.
3   Housing Act 2004 s 18, Sch 1 para 10(1) (amended by SI 2013/1036).
4   Ie in the Housing Act 2004 Sch 1 paras 11, 12: see the text and notes 6–14.
5   Housing Act 2004 Sch 1 para 10(2).
6   As to the meaning of 'owner' see PARA 384 note 11.
7   As to the meaning of 'specified premises' see PARA 574 note 1.
8   Housing Act 2004 Sch 1 para 11(1).
9   As to the meaning of 'hazard' see PARA 564.
10 Housing Act 2004 Sch 1 para 12(1).
11 Ie under the Housing Act 2004 s 20 (see PARA 590) or s 21 (see PARA 591): Sch 1 para 12(2)(a).
12 Ie under the Housing Act 2004 s 28 (see PARA 608) or s 29 (see PARA 609): Sch 1 para 12(2)(b).
13 Ie under the Housing Act 1985 s 265 (see PARA 621): Housing Act 2004 Sch 1 para 12(2)(c).
14 Housing Act 2004 Sch 1 para 11(2).
15 Ie in accordance with the Housing Act 2004 Sch 1 Pt 1 (paras 1–5) (see PARA 574): Sch 1 para 14(1).
16 Housing Act 2004 Sch 1 para 14(3) (amended by SI 2013/1036).

581. Appeal against decision relating to variation or revocation of improvement notice. The relevant person[1] may appeal to the appropriate tribunal[2] against a decision by the local housing authority[3] to vary an improvement notice[4] or a decision by the authority to refuse to revoke or vary an improvement notice[5].

Any appeal against such a decision must be made within the period of 28 days beginning with the date specified in the notice as to variation or revocation[6] as the date on which the decision concerned was made[7]. The appropriate tribunal may allow an appeal to be made to it after the end of such period if it is satisfied that there is a good reason for the failure to appeal before the end of that period (and for any delay since then in applying for permission to appeal out of time)[8].

1   For this purpose, 'the relevant person' means in relation to a decision to vary an improvement notice, the person on whom the notice was served, and in relation to a decision to refuse to revoke or vary an improvement notice, the person who applied for the revocation or variation: Housing Act 2004 s 18, Sch 1 para 13(2).
2   As to the meaning of 'appropriate tribunal' see PARA 580 note 2. As to appeals to the appropriate tribunal see PARA 32 et seq. As to the powers of the tribunal on an appeal see PARA 582.
3   As to the meaning of 'local housing authority' see PARA 380 note 1.
4   See PARA 577. As to improvement notices see PARA 571 et seq.
5   Housing Act 2004 Sch 1 para 13(1) (amended by SI 2013/1036).
6   Ie under the Housing Act 2004 Sch 1 para 6 or 8: see PARA 578.
7   Housing Act 2004 Sch 1 para 14(2).
8   Housing Act 2004 Sch 1 para 14(3) (amended by SI 2013/1036).

582. Powers of tribunal on appeal against improvement notice. An appeal to the appropriate tribunal[1] against an improvement notice[2] is to be by way of a re-hearing, and it may be determined having regard to matters of which the authority was unaware when it took the decision[3]. The tribunal may by order confirm, quash or vary the improvement notice[4].

Where the grounds of appeal consist of or include the ground that one or more other persons, as an owner[5] or owners of the specified premises[6], ought to take the action concerned or to pay the whole or part of the cost of taking that action[7], on the hearing of the appeal the tribunal may vary the improvement notice so as to require the action to be taken by any such owner mentioned in the notice of appeal, or make such order as it considers appropriate with respect to the payment to be made by any such owner to the appellant or, where the action is taken by the local housing authority[8], to the authority[9]. Where, by virtue of the exercise of these powers of the tribunal, a person other than the appellant is required to take the action specified in an improvement notice, so long as that other person remains an owner of the premises to which the notice relates, he is to be regarded for the purposes of Part 1 of the Housing Act 2004[10] as the person on whom the notice was served (in place of any other person)[11].

Where the grounds of appeal consist of or include the ground that another specific course of action is the best course of action in relation to the hazard[12], the tribunal when deciding whether one of the other courses of action is the best course of action in relation to a particular hazard must have regard to any guidance given[13] to the local housing authority[14]. Where an appeal is allowed against an improvement notice in respect of a particular hazard, and the reason, or one of the reasons, for allowing the appeal is that one of the other courses of action is the best course of action in relation to that hazard, the tribunal must, if requested to do so by the appellant or the local housing authority, include in its decision a finding to that effect and identifying the course of action concerned[15].

1   Ie under the Housing Act 2004 s 18, Sch 1 para 10: see PARA 580. As to the meaning of 'appropriate tribunal' see PARA 580 note 2. As to appeals to the appropriate tribunal see PARA 32 et seq.
2   As to improvement notices see PARA 571 et seq.
3   Housing Act 2004 Sch 1 para 15(1), (2) (Sch 1 para 15(1) amended by SI 2013/1036).

4 Housing Act 2004 Sch 1 para 15(3). Special provision is made in connection with the grounds of appeal set out in Sch 1 paras 11, 12 (see PARA 580): Sch 1 para 15(4). See also *Hillbank Properties Ltd v Hackney London Borough Council* [1978] QB 998, [1978] 3 All ER 343, CA (decided under previous legislation).
5 As to the meaning of 'owner' see PARA 384 note 11.
6 As to the meaning of 'specified premises' see PARA 574 note 1.
7 Ie the ground set out in the Housing Act 2004 Sch 1 para 11: see PARA 580.
8 As to the meaning of 'local housing authority' see PARA 380 note 1.
9 Housing Act 2004 Sch 1 para 16(1), (2). In the exercise of these powers, the tribunal must take into account, as between the appellant and any such owner: (1) their relative interests in the premises concerned (considering both the nature of the interests and the rights and obligations arising under or by virtue of them); (2) their relative responsibility for the state of the premises which gives rise to the need for the taking of the action concerned; and (3) the relative degree of benefit to be derived from the taking of the action concerned: Sch 1 para 16(3).
10 Ie the Housing Act 2004 Pt 1 (ss 1–54).
11 Housing Act 2004 Sch 1 para 16(4), (5).
12 Ie the ground set out in the Housing Act 2004 Sch 1 para 12: see PARA 580. As to the meaning of 'hazard' see PARA 564.
13 Ie under the Housing Act 2004 s 9: see PARA 569.
14 Housing Act 2004 Sch 1 para 17(1), (2).
15 Housing Act 2004 Sch 1 para 17(3), (4). It may be possible to seek a finding later if the authority omitted to ask for it at the original hearing: see *Victoria Square Property Co Ltd v Southwark London Borough Council* [1978] 2 All ER 281, [1978] 1 WLR 463, CA (decided under previous legislation).

583. Powers of tribunal on appeal against a decision relating to variation or revocation of improvement notice. On an appeal to the appropriate tribunal[1] against a decision by a local housing authority[2] to vary, or to refuse to revoke or vary, an improvement notice[3], the appeal is to be by way of a re-hearing, and it may be determined having regard to matters of which the authority was unaware[4]. The tribunal may by order confirm, quash or vary the improvement notice[5]. If the appeal is against a decision of the authority to refuse to revoke an improvement notice, the tribunal may make an order revoking the notice as from a date specified in the order[6].

1 Ie under the Housing Act 2004 s 18, Sch 1 para 13: see PARA 581. As to the meaning of 'appropriate tribunal' see PARA 580 note 2. As to appeals to the appropriate tribunal see PARA 32 et seq.
2 As to the meaning of 'local housing authority' see PARA 380 note 1.
3 As to improvement notices see PARA 571 et seq.
4 Housing Act 2004 Sch 1 para 15(2) (applied by Sch 1 para 18(1), (2) (Sch 1 para 18(1) amended by SI 2013/1036)).
5 Housing Act 2004 Sch 1 para 18(3).
6 Housing Act 2004 Sch 1 para 18(4).

(C) Enforcement of Improvement Notices

584. Offence of failing to comply with an improvement notice. Where an improvement notice[1] has become operative[2], the person on whom the notice was served[3] commits an offence if he fails to comply with it[4]. For this purpose, compliance with an improvement notice means, in relation to each hazard[5], beginning and completing any remedial action[6] specified in the notice:
  (1) if no appeal is brought against the notice, not later than the date when the remedial action is required to be started[7] and within the period or periods specified[8] for its completion;
  (2) if an appeal is brought against the notice and is not withdrawn, not later than such date and within such period as may be fixed by the tribunal determining the appeal; and

(3)   if an appeal brought against the notice is withdrawn, not later than the twenty-first day after the date on which the notice becomes operative and within the period (beginning on that twenty-first day) specified[9] in the notice[10].

In proceedings against a person for an offence under these provisions, it is a defence that he had a reasonable excuse for failing to comply with the notice[11].

The obligation to take any remedial action specified in the notice in relation to a hazard continues despite the fact that the period for completion of the action has expired[12].

1   As to improvement notices see PARA 571 et seq.
2   As to the operation of improvement notices see PARA 576.
3   As to service of improvement notices see PARA 574.
4   Housing Act 2004 s 30(1). A person who commits such an offence is liable on summary conviction to a fine not exceeding level 5 on the standard scale: s 30(3). As to the powers of magistrates' courts to issue fines on summary conviction see SENTENCING vol 92 (2015) PARA 176.
    As to the imposition of a financial penalty instead of a fine for certain housing offences in England see s 249A; and PARA 397: s 30(7) (s 30(7), (8) added by the Housing and Planning Act 2016 s 126, Sch 9 paras 1, 2). If a local housing authority has imposed a financial penalty on a person under the Housing Act 2004 s 249A in respect of conduct amounting to an offence under s 30 the person may not be convicted of an offence under s 30 in respect of the conduct: s 30(8) (as so added).
5   As to the meaning of 'hazard' see PARA 564.
6   As to the meaning of 'remedial action' see PARA 571 note 8. In the Housing Act 2004 s 30, any reference to any remedial action specified in a notice includes a reference to any part of any remedial action which is required to be completed within a particular period specified in the notice: s 30(6).
7   Ie the date specified under the Housing Act 2004 s 13(2)(e): see PARA 573 head (5).
8   Ie within the period specified under the Housing Act 2004 s 13(2)(f): see PARA 573 head (6).
9   See note 8.
10 Housing Act 2004 s 30(2).
11 Housing Act 2004 s 30(4).
12 Housing Act 2004 s 30(5).

585.   Enforcement action by local housing authorities by agreement. The local housing authority[1] may, by agreement with the person on whom an improvement notice[2] has been served[3], take (instead of that person) any action which that person is required to take in relation to any premises in pursuance of the notice[4]. For that purpose, the authority has all the rights which that person would have against any occupying tenant[5] of, and any other person having an interest in, the premises (or any part of the premises)[6]. Any action taken by the local housing authority under these provisions is to be taken at the expense of the person on whom the notice is served[7].

1   As to the meaning of 'local housing authority' see PARA 380 note 1.
2   For this purpose, 'improvement notice' means an improvement notice which has become operative under the Housing Act 2004 Pt 1 Ch 2 (ss 11–39): s 31, Sch 3 para 1(3). As to improvement notices see PARA 571 et seq; and as to the operation of improvement notices see PARA 576.
3   As to service of improvement notices see PARA 574.
4   Housing Act 2004 Sch 3 para 1(1). As to the authority's power to take action without agreement see PARA 586.
5   'Occupying tenant', in relation to any premises, means a person (other than an owner-occupier) who: (1) occupies or is entitled to occupy the premises as a lessee; (2) is a statutory tenant of the premises; (3) occupies the premises under a restricted contract; (4) is a protected occupier within the meaning of the Rent (Agriculture) Act 1976; or (5) is a licensee under an assured agricultural occupancy: Housing Act 2004 Sch 3 para 1(3). 'Owner-occupier', in relation to any premises, means the person who occupies or is entitled to occupy the premises as owner or lessee under a long tenancy (within the meaning of the Leasehold Reform Act 1967 Pt I (ss 1–37): see LANDLORD AND TENANT vol 64 (2016) PARA 1167 et seq): Housing Act 2004 Sch 3 para 1(3). As to the meaning of 'owner' see PARA 384 note 11. As to the meaning of 'occupies' see PARA 563 note 13. As to the meaning of 'tenant' see PARA 391 note 6.

6   Housing Act 2004 Sch 3 para 1(2).
7   Housing Act 2004 Sch 3 para 2.

586. Enforcement action by local housing authorities without agreement. The local housing authority[1] may itself take the action required to be taken in relation to a hazard[2] by an improvement notice[3] if one of the following provisions applies[4], namely:

(1)   if the notice is not complied with in relation to that hazard[5]; or

(2)   if, before the end of the period which is appropriate for completion of the action specified in the notice in relation to the hazard[6], it considers that reasonable progress is not being made towards compliance with the notice in relation to the hazard[7].

Any person authorised in writing by the authority may enter any part of the specified premises for the purposes of the taking of any action which the authority is authorised to take under these provisions[8]. The right of entry may be exercised at any reasonable time[9]. The local housing authority must serve a notice before it enters any premises[10] for the purpose of taking action in relation to a hazard[11]. The notice must identify the improvement notice to which it relates and state:

(a)   the premises and hazard concerned;

(b)   that the authority intends to enter the premises;

(c)   the action which the authority intends to take on the premises; and

(d)   the power under which the authority intends to enter the premises and take the action[12].

The notice must be served on the person on whom the improvement notice was served[13], and a copy of the notice must be served on any other person who is an occupier[14] of the premises[15]. The notice and any such copy must be served sufficiently in advance of the time when the authority intends to enter the premises as to give the recipients reasonable notice of the intended entry[16]. A copy of the notice may also be served on any owner[17] of the premises[18].

If, at any relevant time[19], the person on whom the notice was served is on the premises for the purpose of carrying out any works, or any workman employed by that person, or by any contractor employed by that person, is on the premises for that purpose, that person is to be taken to have committed an offence[20] of obstruction[21]. In proceedings for such an offence it is a defence that there was an urgent necessity to carry out the works in order to prevent danger to persons occupying the premises[22].

Provision is made[23] with respect to the recovery by the local housing authority of expenses incurred by it in taking action under these provisions[24]. Where, after a local housing authority has given notice of its intention to enter premises and take action, the action is in fact taken by the person on whom the improvement notice is served, any administrative and other expenses incurred by the authority with a view to itself taking the action are to be treated for this purpose as expenses incurred by it in taking enforcement action without agreement[25].

1   As to the meaning of 'local housing authority' see PARA 380 note 1.
2   As to the meaning of 'hazard' see PARA 564.
3   For this purpose, 'improvement notice' means an improvement notice which has become operative under the Housing Act 2004 Pt 1 Ch 2 (ss 11–39): s 31, Sch 3 para 3(7). As to improvement notices see PARA 571 et seq; and as to the operation of improvement notices see PARA 576.
4   Housing Act 2004 Sch 3 para 3(1).
5   Housing Act 2004 Sch 3 para 3(2).
6   Ie under the Housing Act 2004 s 30(2): see PARA 584.
7   Housing Act 2004 Sch 3 para 3(3).

8 Housing Act 2004 Sch 3 para 3(4). Any reference in Sch 3 Pt 2 (paras 3–6) (of whatever nature) to a local housing authority entering any premises under Sch 3 para 3 is a reference to its doing so in accordance with Sch 3 para 3(4): Sch 3 para 3(6).
9 Housing Act 2004 Sch 3 para 3(5).
10 Ie under the Housing Act 2004 Sch 3 para 3.
11 Housing Act 2004 Sch 3 para 4(1).
12 Housing Act 2004 Sch 3 para 4(2).
13 As to service of improvement notices see PARA 574.
14 As to the meaning of 'occupier' see PARA 563 note 13.
15 Housing Act 2004 Sch 3 para 4(3).
16 Housing Act 2004 Sch 3 para 4(4).
17 As to the meaning of 'owner' see PARA 384 note 11.
18 Housing Act 2004 Sch 3 para 4(5).
19 For this purpose, 'relevant time' means: (1) any time after the end of the period of seven days beginning with the date of service of the notice under the Housing Act 2004 Sch 3 para 4; and (2) any time when any workman or contractor employed by the local housing authority is taking action on the premises which has been mentioned in the notice in accordance with Sch 3 para 4(2)(c) (see head (c) in the text): Sch 3 para 5(3).
20 Ie under the Housing Act 2004 s 241(1): see PARA 386.
21 Housing Act 2004 Sch 3 para 5(1).
22 Housing Act 2004 Sch 3 para 5(2).
23 Ie by the Housing Act 2004 Sch 3 Pt 3 (paras 7–14): see PARA 587.
24 See the Housing Act 2004 Sch 3 para 6(1).
25 Housing Act 2004 Sch 3 para 6(2), (3).

587. Recovery of expenses incurred in taking enforcement action without agreement. Where a local housing authority[1] has taken enforcement action without agreement[2] in relation to a hazard[3] it is entitled to recover expenses reasonably incurred by it in taking such action[4].

The expenses are recoverable by the local housing authority from the person on whom the improvement notice was served ('the relevant person')[5]. Where the relevant person receives the rent of the premises as agent or trustee for another person, the expenses are also recoverable by the local housing authority from the other person, or partly from him and partly from the relevant person[6].

Where the relevant person proves in connection with a demand served on him[7] that he receives the rent of the premises as agent or trustee for another person, and that he has not, and since the date of the service on him of the demand has not had, in his hands on behalf of the other person sufficient money to discharge the whole demand of the local housing authority, the liability of the relevant person is limited to the total amount of the money which he has, or has had, in his hands[8].

Expenses are not recoverable under these provisions so far as they are, by any direction given by the appropriate tribunal[9] on an appeal to the tribunal[10], recoverable under an order of the tribunal[11].

A demand for expenses recoverable under these provisions, together with interest[12], must be served on each person from whom the local housing authority is seeking to recover them[13]. If no appeal is brought, the demand becomes operative at the end of the period of 21 days beginning with the date of service of the demand[14]. A demand which so becomes operative is final and conclusive as to matters which could have been raised on an appeal[15]. Expenses in respect of which a demand is served carry interest, at such reasonable rate as the local housing authority may determine, from the date of service until payment of all sums due under the demand[16].

A person on whom a demand for the recovery of expenses has been served may appeal to the appropriate tribunal against the demand[17]. An appeal must be made within the period of 21 days beginning with the date of service of the demand or copy of it[18]. The appropriate tribunal may allow an appeal to be made to it after the end of such period if it is satisfied that there is a good reason for the failure to appeal before the end of that period (and for any delay since then in applying for permission to appeal out of time)[19]. Where the demand relates to action taken because the authority considers that reasonable progress is not being made towards compliance with the notice in relation to the hazard[20], an appeal may be brought on the ground that reasonable progress was being made towards compliance with the improvement notice when the local housing authority gave notice[21] of its intention to enter and take the action[22]. The tribunal may, on an appeal, make such order confirming, quashing or varying the demand as it considers appropriate[23]. No question may be raised on appeal which might have been raised on an appeal against the improvement notice[24].

A demand against which an appeal is brought becomes operative as follows:

(1)   if a decision is given on the appeal which confirms the demand and the period within which an appeal to the Upper Tribunal[25] may be brought expires without such an appeal having been brought, the demand becomes operative at the end of that period;

(2)   if an appeal to the Upper Tribunal is brought and a decision is given on the appeal which confirms the demand, the demand becomes operative at the time of that decision[26].

For this purpose, the withdrawal of an appeal has the same effect as a decision which confirms the demand, and references to a decision which confirms the demand are references to a decision which confirms it with or without variation[27].

Where a demand becomes operative[28], the local housing authority may serve a recovery notice on any person who occupies the premises concerned, or part of those premises, as the tenant or licensee[29] of the person on whom the demand was served and who, by virtue of his tenancy or licence, pays rent or any sum in the nature of rent to the person on whom the demand was served[30]. A recovery notice is a notice stating the amount of expenses recoverable by the local housing authority and requiring all future payments by the tenant or licensee of rent or sums in the nature of rent (whether already accrued due or not) to be made direct to the authority until the expenses recoverable by the authority, together with any accrued interest on them, have been duly paid[31]. The effect of a recovery notice, once served, is to transfer to the local housing authority the right to recover, receive and give a discharge for the rent or sums in the nature of rent[32]. This is subject to any direction to the contrary contained in a further notice served by the local housing authority on the tenant or licensee[33]. In addition, the right to recover, receive and give a discharge for any rent or sums in the nature of rent is postponed to any right in respect of that rent or those sums which may at any time be vested in a superior landlord by virtue of a notice under the Law of Distress Amendment Act 1908[34].

Until recovered, the expenses recoverable by the local housing authority, together with any accrued interest on them, are a charge on the premises to which the improvement notice related[35]. The charge takes effect when the demand for the expenses and interest becomes operative[36]. For the purpose of enforcing the charge, the local housing authority has the same powers and remedies[37] as if it was a mortgagee by deed having powers of sale and lease, of accepting surrenders of leases and of appointing a receiver[38]. The power of appointing a receiver is exercisable at any time after the end of one month beginning with the date when the charge takes effect[39]. If, on an application to the appropriate tribunal, the local housing authority satisfies the tribunal that the expenses and interest have not been and are unlikely to be recovered, and that a person is profiting by the taking of the enforcement action in respect of which the expenses were incurred in that he is obtaining rents or other payments which would not have been obtainable if the number of persons living in the premises was limited to that appropriate for the premises in their state before the action was taken, the tribunal may, if satisfied that the person concerned has had proper notice of the application, order him to make such payments to the local housing authority as the tribunal considers to be just[40].

1 As to the meaning of 'local housing authority' see PARA 380 note 1.
2 Ie under the Housing Act 2004 s 31, Sch 3 para 3: see PARA 586.
3 As to the meaning of 'hazard' see PARA 564.
4 Ie under the Housing Act 2004 Sch 3 Pt 3 (paras 7–14): see Sch 3 para 7.
5 Housing Act 2004 Sch 3 para 8(1). As to improvement notices see PARA 571 et seq; and as to the service of improvement notices see PARA 574.
6 Housing Act 2004 Sch 3 para 8(2).
7 Ie under the Housing Act 2004 Sch 3 para 9: see the text and notes 12–15.
8 Housing Act 2004 Sch 3 para 8(3), (4).
9 As to the meaning of 'appropriate tribunal' see PARA 580 note 2. As to appeals to the appropriate tribunal see PARA 32 et seq.
10 Ie under the Housing Act 2004 Sch 3 para 11: see the text and notes 17–27.
11 Housing Act 2004 Sch 3 para 8(5) (amended by SI 2013/1036).
12 Ie in accordance with the Housing Act 2004 Sch 3 para 10: see the text and note 16.
13 Housing Act 2004 Sch 3 para 9(1).
14 Housing Act 2004 Sch 3 para 9(2). As to appeals see Sch 3 para 11 (see the text and notes 17–27); applied by Sch 3 para 9(4).
15 Housing Act 2004 Sch 3 para 9(3).
16 Housing Act 2004 Sch 3 para 10.
17 Housing Act 2004 Sch 3 para 11(1) (amended by SI 2013/1036).
18 Housing Act 2004 Sch 3 para 11(2).
19 Housing Act 2004 Sch 3 para 11(3) (amended by SI 2013/1036).
20 Ie by virtue of the Housing Act 2004 Sch 3 para 3(3): see PARA 586 head (2).
21 Ie under the Housing Act 2004 Sch 3 para 4: see PARA 586.
22 Housing Act 2004 Sch 3 para 11(4). This does not affect the generality of Sch 3 para 11(1) (see the text and note 17): Sch 3 para 11(4).
23 Housing Act 2004 Sch 3 para 11(5).
24 Housing Act 2004 Sch 3 para 11(8). As to appeals against improvement notices see PARA 580.
25 As to appeals to the Upper Tribunal see PARAS 49–50.
26 Housing Act 2004 Sch 3 para 11(6) (amended by SI 2009/1307).
27 Housing Act 2004 Sch 3 para 11(7).
28 Ie by virtue of the Housing Act 2004 Sch 3 para 9(2) (see the text to note 14) or Sch 3 para 11(6) (see the text to notes 25–26).
29 As to the meaning of 'occupies' see PARA 563 note 13. As to the meanings of 'tenant' and 'licensee' see PARA 391 note 6.
30 Housing Act 2004 Sch 3 para 12(1). In the case of a demand which was served on any person as agent or trustee for another person ('the principal'), Sch 3 para 12(1) has effect as if the references to the person on whom the demand was served were references to that person or the principal: Sch 3 para 12(3).
31 Housing Act 2004 Sch 3 para 12(2).
32 Housing Act 2004 Sch 3 para 12(4).
33 Housing Act 2004 Sch 3 para 12(5).
34 Ie the Law of Distress Amendment Act 1908 s 6: Housing Act 2004 Sch 3 para 12(6).
35 Housing Act 2004 Sch 3 para 13(1).
36 Ie by virtue of the Housing Act 2004 Sch 3 para 9(2) (see the text to note 14) or Sch 3 para 11(6) (see the text to notes 25–26): Sch 3 para 13(2).
37 Ie under the Law of Property Act 1925 and otherwise: see MORTGAGE vol 77 (2016) PARA 518 et seq.
38 Housing Act 2004 Sch 3 para 13(3).
39 Housing Act 2004 Sch 3 para 13(4).
40 Housing Act 2004 Sch 3 para 14 (amended by SI 2013/1036).

588. Power of court to order occupier or owner to allow action to be taken on premises. Where an improvement notice[1] has become operative[2], then, if the occupier[3] of any specified premises[4] has received reasonable notice of any intended action[5] in relation to the premises, but is preventing a relevant person[6], or any representative[7] of a relevant person or of the local housing authority, from taking that action in relation to the premises, a magistrates' court may order the occupier to permit to be done on the premises anything which the court considers is necessary or expedient for the purpose of enabling the intended action to be taken[8]. If a relevant person has received reasonable notice of any intended action in relation to any specified premises, but is preventing a representative of the local housing authority from taking that action in relation to the premises, a magistrates' court may order the relevant person to permit to be done on the premises anything which the court considers is necessary or expedient for the purpose of enabling the intended action to be taken[9]. A person who fails to comply with an order of the court under these provisions commits an offence[10]. In proceedings for such an offence it is a defence that the person had a reasonable excuse for failing to comply with the order[11].

1   As to improvement notices see PARA 571 et seq.
2   As to as to when an improvement notice becomes operative see PARA 576.
3   As to the meaning of 'occupier' see PARA 563 note 13.
4   As to the meaning of 'specified premises' see PARA 574 note 1.
5   For this purpose, 'intended action', in relation to any specified premises, means, where an improvement notice has become operative, any action which the person on whom that notice has been served is required by the notice to take in relation to the premises and which: (1) in the context of the Housing Act 2004 s 35(2) (see the text and note 8), is proposed to be taken by or on behalf of that person or on behalf of the local housing authority in pursuance of Sch 3 (see PARA 585 et seq); or (2) in the context of s 35(3) (see the text and note 9), is proposed to be taken on behalf of the local housing authority in pursuance of Sch 3: s 35(7).
6   For this purpose, 'relevant person', in relation to any premises, means a person who is an owner of the premises, a person having control of or managing the premises, or the holder of any licence under the Housing Act 2004 Pt 2 (ss 55–78) (see PARA 674 et seq) or Pt 3 (ss 79–100) (see PARA 704 et seq) in respect of the premises: s 35(8). As to the meaning of 'owner' see PARA 384 note 11.
7   'Representative', in relation to a relevant person or a local housing authority, means any officer, employee, agent or contractor of that person or authority: Housing Act 2004 s 35(8). As to the meaning of 'local housing authority' see PARA 380 note 1.
8   Housing Act 2004 s 35(1), (2).
9   Housing Act 2004 s 35(3).
10 Housing Act 2004 s 35(4). A person who commits such an offence is liable on summary conviction to a fine not exceeding £20 in respect of each day or part of a day during which the failure continues: s 35(6). As to the power of the Secretary of State to increase the fine for this offence see PARA 400.
11 Housing Act 2004 s 35(5).

589. Power of court to authorise action by one owner on behalf of another. Where an improvement notice[1] has become operative[2], an owner[3] of any specified premises[4] may apply to a magistrates' court for an order in the following terms[5]. A magistrates' court may, on such an application, make an order enabling the applicant immediately to enter on the premises and to take any required action[6] within a period fixed by the order[7]. No order may be made unless the court is satisfied that the interests of the applicant will be prejudiced as a result of a failure by another person to take any required action[8]. No order may be made unless notice of the application has been given to the local housing authority[9]. If it considers that it is appropriate to do so, the court may make an order in favour of any other owner of the premises which is similar to the order that it is making in relation to the premises under these provisions[10].

1   As to improvement notices see PARA 571 et seq.
2   As to as to when an improvement notice becomes operative see PARA 576.
3   As to the meaning of 'owner' see PARA 384 note 11.

4 As to the meaning of 'specified premises' see PARA 574 note 1.
5 Housing Act 2004 s 36(1).
6 'Required action' means any remedial action which is required to be taken by the notice: Housing Act 2004 s 36(3).
7 Housing Act 2004 s 36(2).
8 Housing Act 2004 s 36(4).
9 Housing Act 2004 s 36(5). As to the meaning of 'local housing authority' see PARA 380 note 1.
10 Housing Act 2004 s 36(6).

B.   PROHIBITION ORDERS

(A)   Making, Suspension and Revocation of Prohibition Orders

590. Duty of authority to make prohibition orders relating to category 1 hazards. If the local housing authority[1] is satisfied that a category 1 hazard[2] exists on any residential premises[3], and no management order is in force[4] in relation to the premises, making a prohibition order[5] in respect of the hazard is a course of action available to the authority in relation to the hazard for the purposes of the authority's general duty[6] to take enforcement action in relation to category 1 hazards[7]. A prohibition order under these provisions is an order imposing such prohibition or prohibitions on the use of any premises as is or are specified[8] in the order[9].

The order may prohibit use of the following premises:
(1)   if the residential premises on which the hazard exists are a dwelling[10] or an HMO[11] which is not a flat[12], it may prohibit use of the dwelling or the HMO;
(2)   if those premises are one or more flats, it may prohibit use of the building containing the flat or flats (or any part of the building) or any external common parts[13];
(3)   if those premises are the common parts of a building containing one or more flats, it may prohibit use of the building (or any part of the building) or any external common parts[14].

The order may not, by virtue of head (2) or head (3)[15], prohibit use of any part of the building or its external common parts that is not included in any residential premises on which the hazard exists, unless the authority is satisfied that the deficiency from which the hazard arises is situated there, and that it is necessary for such use to be prohibited in order to protect the health or safety of any actual or potential occupiers[16] of one or more of the flats[17].

A prohibition order may relate to more than one category 1 hazard on the same premises or in the same building containing one or more flats[18].

The operation of a prohibition order may be suspended[19].

1 As to the meaning of 'local housing authority' see PARA 380 note 1.
2 As to the meaning of 'category 1 hazard' see PARA 564.
3 As to the meaning of 'residential premises' see PARA 563.
4 Ie under the Housing Act 2004 Pt 4 Ch 1 (ss 101–131) or Ch 2 (ss 132–138): see PARA 745 et seq. As to the effect of the making of a management order see PARA 612.
5 Ie under the Housing Act 2004 s 20.
6 Ie for the purposes of the Housing Act 2004 s 5: see PARA 566.
7 Housing Act 2004 s 20(1). See also the guidance that has been issued; and PARA 569. As to when emergency remedial works may be more appropriate than a prohibition order see *Luton Borough Council v Universal Group* HA/6/2007, Lands Tribunal; and PARA 562 note 7.
8 Ie in accordance with the Housing Act 2004 s 22(3), (4): see PARA 592.
9 Housing Act 2004 s 20(2).
10 As to the meaning of 'dwelling' see PARA 563 note 10.
11 As to the meaning of 'HMO' see PARA 563 note 11.
12 As to the meaning of 'flat' see PARA 563 note 13.

13 As to the meaning of 'external common parts' see PARA 571 note 14.
14 Housing Act 2004 s 20(3). As to the meaning of 'building containing one or more flats', and as to the meaning of 'common parts', see PARA 563 note 13. Heads (2), (3) in the text are subject to s 20(4) (see the text and note 17): s 20(3).
15 Ie by virtue of the Housing Act 2004 s 20(3)(b) or (c): see heads (2), (3) in the text.
16 As to the meaning of 'occupier' see PARA 563 note 13.
17 Housing Act 2004 s 20(4). This provision refers to a 'notice', but it is submitted that the reference should be to an order.
18 Housing Act 2004 s 20(5).
19 Ie in accordance with the Housing Act 2004 s 23 (see PARA 594): s 20(6).

591. Power of authority to make prohibition orders relating to category 2 hazards. If the local housing authority[1] is satisfied that a category 2 hazard[2] exists on any residential premises[3], and no management order is in force[4] in relation to the premises, the authority may make a prohibition order[5] in respect of the hazard[6]. Such a prohibition order is an order imposing such prohibition or prohibitions on the use of any premises as is or are specified[7] in the order[8].

The order may prohibit use of the following premises:

(1)   if the residential premises on which the hazard exists are a dwelling[9] or an HMO[10] which is not a flat[11], it may prohibit use of the dwelling or HMO;

(2)   if those premises are one or more flats, it may prohibit use of the building containing the flat or flats (or any part of the building) or any external common parts[12];

(3)   if those premises are the common parts of a building containing one or more flats, it may prohibit use of the building (or any part of the building) or any external common parts[13].

The order may not, in a case under head (2) or head (3)[14], require any remedial action to be taken in relation to any part of the building or its external common parts that is not included in any residential premises on which the hazard exists, unless the authority is satisfied that the deficiency from which the hazard arises is situated there, and that it is necessary for the action to be so taken in order to protect the health or safety of any actual or potential occupiers[15] of one or more of the flats[16].

A prohibition order under these provisions may relate to more than one category 2 hazard on the same premises or in the same building containing one or more flats[17]. Such a prohibition order may be combined in one document with an order in respect of a category 1 hazard[18] where they impose prohibitions on the use of the same premises or on the use of premises in the same building containing one or more flats[19].

The operation of a prohibition order under these provisions may be suspended[20].

1   As to the meaning of 'local housing authority' see PARA 380 note 1.
2   As to the meaning of 'category 2 hazard' see PARA 564.
3   As to the meaning of 'residential premises' see PARA 563.
4   Ie under the Housing Act 2004 Pt 4 Ch 1 (ss 101–131) or Ch 2 (ss 132–138): see PARA 745 et seq. As to the effect of the making of a management order see PARA 612.
5   Ie under the Housing Act 2004 s 21.
6   Housing Act 2004 s 21(1).
7   Ie in accordance with the Housing Act 2004 s 21(3) (see the text and notes 9–13) and s 22 (see PARA 592).
8   Housing Act 2004 s 21(2).
9   As to the meaning of 'dwelling' see PARA 563 note 10.
10 As to the meaning of 'HMO' see PARA 563 note 11.
11 As to the meaning of 'flat' see PARA 563 note 13.

12 As to the meaning of 'external common parts' see PARA 571 note 14. As to the meaning of 'building containing one or more flats', and as to the meaning of 'common parts', see PARA 563 note 13.
13 Housing Act 2004 s 20(3) (applied by s 21(3)).
14 Ie by virtue of the Housing Act 2004 s 21(3)(b) or (c): see heads (2), (3) in the text.
15 Housing Act 2004 s 20(4) (applied by s 21(3)).
16 As to the meaning of 'occupier' see PARA 563 note 13.
17 Housing Act 2004 s 21(4).
18 Ie a notice under the Housing Act 2004 s 20: see PARA 590. As to the meaning of 'category 1 hazard' see PARA 564.
19 Housing Act 2004 s 21(5).
20 Ie in accordance with the Housing Act 2004 s 23 (see PARA 594): s 21(6).

592. Contents of prohibition orders. A prohibition order[1] must comply with the following provisions[2]. The order must specify, in relation to the hazard[3] (or each of the hazards) to which it relates[4]:

(1)   whether the order is made under the statutory provision relating to category 1 hazards[5] or category 2 hazards[6];
(2)   the nature of the hazard concerned and the residential premises[7] on which it exists[8];
(3)   the deficiency giving rise to the hazard[9];
(4)   the premises in relation to which prohibitions are imposed by the order[10];
(5)   any remedial action[11] which the authority considers would, if taken in relation to the hazard, result in its revoking[12] the order[13].

The order may impose such prohibition or prohibitions on the use of any premises as comply with the relevant statutory provisions[14], and as the local housing authority[15] considers appropriate in view of the hazard or hazards in respect of which the order is made[16]. Any such prohibition may prohibit use of any specified premises[17], or of any part of those premises, either for all purposes or for any particular purpose[18], except (in either case) to the extent to which any use of the premises or part is approved by the authority[19].

The order must also contain information about the right to appeal against the order[20], and the period within which an appeal may be made, and specify the date on which the order is made[21].

1   Ie an order under the Housing Act 2004 s 20 (see PARA 590) or s 21 (see PARA 591).
2   Housing Act 2004 s 22(1).
3   As to the meaning of 'hazard' see PARA 564.
4   Housing Act 2004 s 22(2).
5   Ie the Housing Act 2004 s 20. As to the meaning of 'category 1 hazard' see PARA 564.
6   Ie the Housing Act 2004 s 21: s 22(2)(a). As to the meaning of 'category 2 hazard' see PARA 564.
7   As to the meaning of 'residential premises' see PARA 563.
8   Housing Act 2004 s 22(2)(b).
9   Housing Act 2004 s 22(2)(c).
10 Housing Act 2004 s 22(2)(d). See the text and notes 14–19.
11 As to the meaning of 'remedial action' see PARA 571 note 8.
12 Ie under the Housing Act 2004 s 25: see PARA 596.
13 Housing Act 2004 s 22(2)(e).
14 Ie the Housing Act 2004 s 20(3), (4): see PARA 590.
15 As to the meaning of 'local housing authority' see PARA 380 note 1.
16 Housing Act 2004 s 22(3).
17 'Specified premises', in relation to a prohibition order, means premises specified in the order, in accordance with the Housing Act 2004 s 22(2)(d) (see head (4) in the text), as premises in relation to which prohibitions are imposed by the order: s 22(10).
18 A prohibition imposed by virtue of the Housing Act 2004 s 22(4)(b) as to any particular purpose may, in particular, relate to occupation of the premises or part by more than a particular number of households or persons, or to occupation of the premises or part by particular descriptions of persons: s 22(5).

19 Housing Act 2004 s 22(4). Any approval of the authority for the purposes of s 22(4) must not be unreasonably withheld: s 22(7). If the authority does refuse to give any such approval, it must, within the period of seven days beginning with the day on which the decision was made, notify the person applying for the approval of: (1) its decision; (2) the reasons for it and the date on which it was made; (3) the right to appeal against the decision under s 22(9); and (4) the period within which an appeal may be made: s 22(8). The person applying for the approval may appeal to the appropriate tribunal against the decision within the period of 28 days beginning with the date specified in the notice as the date on which it was made: s 22(9) (amended by SI 2013/1036). The appropriate tribunal is either the First-tier Tribunal (or the Upper Tribunal) (in relation to England) or a residential property tribunal (in relation to Wales): see PARA 32 et seq.

20 Ie under the Housing Act 2004 s 27, Sch 2 Pt 3 (paras 7–16): see PARA 598 et seq.

21 Housing Act 2004 s 22(6).

593. Service of copies of prohibition orders. Where the specified premises[1] are a dwelling[2] or an HMO[3] which is not a flat[4], the local housing authority[5] must serve copies of the prohibition order[6] on every person who, to its knowledge, is: (1) an owner[7] or occupier[8] of the whole or part of the specified premises; (2) authorised to permit persons to occupy the whole or part of those premises; or (3) a mortgagee of the whole or part of those premises[9]. The copies so required to be served must be served within the period of seven days beginning with the day on which the order is made[10]. A copy of the order is to be regarded as having been served on every occupier in accordance with these provisions if a copy of the order is fixed to some conspicuous part of the specified premises within the specified period of seven days[11].

Where the specified premises consist of or include the whole or any part of a building containing one or more flats[12] or any common parts[13] of such a building, the authority must serve copies of the order on every person who, to its knowledge, is: (a) an owner or occupier of the whole or part of the building; (b) authorised to permit persons to occupy the whole or part of the building; or (c) a mortgagee of the whole or part of the building[14]. Where the specified premises consist of or include any external common parts[15] of such a building, the authority must, in addition to complying with heads (a) to (c), serve copies of the order on every person who, to its knowledge, is an owner or mortgagee of the premises in which the common parts are comprised[16]. The copies required to be served under these provisions must be served within the period of seven days beginning with the day on which the order is made[17]. A copy of the order is to be regarded as having been duly served on every occupier if a copy of the order is fixed to some conspicuous part of the building within the specified period of seven days[18].

1 As to the meaning of 'specified premises' see PARA 592 note 17.
2 As to the meaning of 'dwelling' see PARA 563 note 10.
3 As to the meaning of 'HMO' see PARA 563 note 11.
4 As to the meaning of 'flat' see PARA 563 note 13.
5 As to the meaning of 'local housing authority' see PARA 380 note 1.
6 Ie an order under the Housing Act 2004 s 20 (see PARA 590) or s 21 (see PARA 591).
7 As to the meaning of 'owner' see PARA 384 note 11.
8 As to the meaning of 'occupier' see PARA 563 note 13.
9 Housing Act 2004 s 27, Sch 2 para 1(1), (2).
10 Housing Act 2004 Sch 2 para 1(3).
11 Housing Act 2004 Sch 2 para 1(4).
12 As to the meaning of 'building containing one or more flats' see PARA 563 note 13.
13 As to the meaning of 'common parts' see PARA 563 note 13.
14 Housing Act 2004 Sch 2 para 2(1), (2).
15 As to the meaning of 'external common parts' see PARA 571 note 14.
16 Housing Act 2004 Sch 2 para 2(3).
17 Housing Act 2004 Sch 2 para 2(4).
18 Housing Act 2004 Sch 2 para 2(5).

594. Suspension of prohibition orders. A prohibition order[1] may provide for the operation of the order to be suspended until a time, or the occurrence of an event, specified in the order[2]. The time so specified may, in particular, be the time when a person of a particular description begins, or ceases, to occupy any premises[3]. The event so specified may, in particular, be a notified breach[4] of an undertaking accepted by the local housing authority for this purpose from a person on whom a copy of the order is served[5].

The local housing authority may at any time review a prohibition order whose operation is suspended[6]. The local housing authority must review a prohibition order whose operation is suspended not later than one year after the date on which the order was made and at subsequent intervals of not more than one year[7]. Copies of the authority's decision on such a review must be served on every person on whom a copy of the order was required[8] to be served[9].

1 Ie an order under the Housing Act 2004 s 20 (see PARA 590) or s 21 (see PARA 591).
2 Housing Act 2004 s 23(1).
3 Housing Act 2004 s 23(2).
4 For this purpose a 'notified breach', in relation to such an undertaking, means an act or omission by such a person which the local housing authority considers to be a breach of the undertaking, and which is notified to that person in accordance with the terms of the undertaking: Housing Act 2004 s 23(4). As to the meaning of 'local housing authority' see PARA 380 note 1.
5 Housing Act 2004 s 23(3).
6 Housing Act 2004 s 26(1).
7 Housing Act 2004 s 26(2).
8 Ie under the Housing Act 2004 s 27, Sch 2 Pt 1 (paras 1–2): see PARA 593.
9 Housing Act 2004 s 26(3).

595. Operation of prohibition orders. The general rule is that a prohibition order becomes operative at the end of the period of 28 days beginning with the date specified in the notice as the date on which it is made[1]. The general rule is subject to the following provisions as to suspended orders and appeals[2]. If the order is suspended[3], the order becomes operative at the time when the suspension ends[4]. However, if an appeal is brought against the order[5], the order does not become operative until such time (if any) as is the statutory operative time[6]. If no appeal against a prohibition order is made within the period for appealing against it, the order is final and conclusive as to matters which could have been raised on an appeal[7]. Compensation is payable when a prohibition order becomes operative[8].

1 Housing Act 2004 s 24(1), (2). The Housing Act 1985 ss 584A, 584B provide for the payment of compensation where certain prohibition orders become operative, and for the repayment of such compensation in certain circumstances: see the Housing Act 2004 s 24(7); and PARAS 606–607.
2 Housing Act 2004 s 24(3).
3 Ie under the Housing Act 2004 s 23: see PARA 594.
4 Housing Act 2004 s 24(4).
5 Ie under the Housing Act 2004 s 27, Sch 2 Pt 3 (paras 7–16): see PARA 598 et seq.
6 Housing Act 2004 s 24(5). If an appeal is made under Sch 2 para 7 (see PARA 598) against a prohibition order which is not suspended, and a decision on the appeal is given which confirms the order, 'the operative time' is as follows: (1) if the period within which an appeal to the Upper Tribunal may be brought expires without such an appeal having been brought, 'the operative time' is the end of that period; (2) if an appeal to the Upper Tribunal is brought, 'the operative time' is the time when a decision is given on the appeal which confirms the order: Sch 2 para 14(1), (2) (Sch 2 para 14(2) amended by SI 2009/1307). If an appeal is made under the Housing Act 2004 Sch 2 para 7 against a prohibition order which is suspended, and a decision is given on the appeal which confirms the order, 'the operative time' is: (a) the time that would be the operative time under Sch 2 para 14(2) if the order were not suspended; or (b) if later, the time when the suspension ends: Sch 2 para 14(3). For these purposes, the withdrawal of an appeal has the same effect as a decision which confirms the notice, and references to a decision which confirms the

order are references to a decision which confirms it with or without variation: Sch 2 para 14(4). As to appeals to the Upper Tribunal, ie the Upper Tribunal (Lands Chamber), the successor to the Lands Tribunal, see PARAS 49–50.

7   Housing Act 2004 s 24(6).
8   See PARAS 606–607.

596. Revocation and variation of prohibition orders. The local housing authority[1] must revoke a prohibition order[2] if at any time it is satisfied that the hazard[3] in respect of which the order was made does not then exist on the residential premises[4] specified[5] in the order[6]. The local housing authority may revoke a prohibition order if: (1) in the case of an order relating to a category 1 hazard[7], it considers that there are any special circumstances making it appropriate to revoke the order; or (2) in the case of an order relating to a category 2 hazard[8], it considers that it is appropriate to do so[9]. A revocation comes into force at the time when it is made[10].

Where a prohibition order relates to a number of hazards, the requirement as to revocation[11] is to be read as applying separately in relation to each of those hazards, and if, as a result, the authority is required to revoke only part of the order, it may vary the remainder as it considers appropriate[12]. The local housing authority may vary a prohibition order: (a) with the agreement of every person on whom copies of the notice were required to be served[13]; or (b) in the case of an order whose operation is suspended, so as to alter the time or events by reference to which the suspension is to come to an end[14]. If it is made with the agreement of every person within head (a), such a variation comes into force at the time when it is made[15]. Otherwise a variation does not come into force until such time (if any) as is the operative time[16] for this purpose[17].

The power to revoke or vary a prohibition order is exercisable by the authority either on an application made by a person on whom a copy of the order was required to be served[18] or on the authority's own initiative[19].

1   As to the meaning of 'local housing authority' see PARA 380 note 1.
2   Ie an order under the Housing Act 2004 s 20 (see PARA 590) or s 21 (see PARA 591).
3   As to the meaning of 'hazard' see PARA 564.
4   As to the meaning of 'residential premises' see PARA 563.
5   Ie in accordance with the Housing Act 2004 s 22(2)(b): see PARA 592 head (2).
6   Housing Act 2004 s 25(1).
7   Ie an order under the Housing Act 2004 s 20: see PARA 590. As to the meaning of 'category 1 hazard' see PARA 564.
8   Ie an order under the Housing Act 2004 s 21: see PARA 591. As to the meaning of 'category 2 hazard' see PARA 564.
9   Housing Act 2004 s 25(2).
10   Housing Act 2004 s 25(5).
11   Ie the Housing Act 2004 s 25(1): see the text and note 6.
12   Housing Act 2004 s 25(3).
13   Ie under the Housing Act 2004 s 27, Sch 2 Pt 1 (paras 1–2): see PARA 593.
14   Housing Act 2004 s 25(4).
15   Housing Act 2004 s 25(6).
16   If no appeal is made under the Housing Act 2004 Sch 2 para 9 (see PARA 598) before the end of the period of 28 days mentioned in Sch 2 para 10(2) (see PARA 599), 'the operative time' is the end of that period: Sch 2 para 15(1), (2). If an appeal is made under Sch 2 para 10 within that period and a decision is given on the appeal which confirms the variation, 'the operative time' is as follows: (1) if the period within which an appeal to the Upper Tribunal may be brought expires without such an appeal having been brought, 'the operative time' is the end of that period; (2) if an appeal to the Upper Tribunal is brought, 'the operative time' is the time when a decision is given on the appeal which confirms the variation: Sch 2 para 15(3) (amended by SI 2009/1307). For this purpose, the withdrawal of an appeal has the same effect as a decision which confirms the variation; and references to a decision which confirms the variation are references to a decision which confirms it with or without variation: Housing Act 2004 Sch 2 para 15(4). As to appeals to the Upper Tribunal, ie the Upper Tribunal (Lands Chamber), the successor to the Lands Tribunal, see PARAS 49–50.

17 Housing Act 2004 s 25(7).
18 Ie under the Housing Act 2004 Sch 2 Pt 1: see PARA 593.
19 Housing Act 2004 s 25(8).

597. Service of notices relating to revocation or variation of prohibition orders. Where the local housing authority[1] decides to revoke or vary[2] a prohibition order[3], the authority must serve a notice on each of the persons on whom it would be required[4] to serve copies of a prohibition order in respect of the specified premises[5]. The notices so required to be served must be served within the period of seven days beginning with the day on which the decision is made[6]. A copy of the notice is to be regarded as having been served on every occupier[7] in accordance with these provisions if a copy of the notice is fixed to some conspicuous part of the specified premises within the specified period of seven days[8]. A notice under these provisions must set out: (1) the authority's decision to revoke or vary the order; (2) the reasons for the decision and the date on which it was made; (3) if the decision is to vary the order: (a) the right of appeal[9] against the decision; and (b) the period within which an appeal may be made[10].

Where the local housing authority, having been asked to, refuses to revoke or vary a prohibition order, the authority must serve a notice on each of the persons on whom it would be required to serve copies of a prohibition order in respect of the specified premises[11]. The notices so required to be served must be served within the period of seven days beginning with the day on which the decision is made[12]. A copy of the notice is to be regarded as having been served on every occupier in accordance with these provisions if a copy of the notice is fixed to some conspicuous part of the specified premises within the specified period of seven days[13]. A notice under these provisions must set out: (i) the authority's decision not to revoke or vary the notice; (ii) the reasons for the decision and the date on which it was made; (iii) the right of appeal against the decision[14]; and (iv) the period within which an appeal may be made[15].

1 As to the meaning of 'local housing authority' see PARA 380 note 1.
2 See PARA 596.
3 Ie an order under the Housing Act 2004 s 20 (see PARA 590) or s 21 (see PARA 591).
4 Ie under the Housing Act 2004 s 27, Sch 2 Pt 1 (paras 1–2): see PARA 593.
5 Housing Act 2004 Sch 2 para 3(1), (2). As to the meaning of 'specified premises' see PARA 592 note 17.
6 Housing Act 2004 Sch 2 para 3(3).
7 As to the meaning of 'occupier' see PARA 563 note 13.
8 Housing Act 2004 Sch 2 para 1(4) (applied by Sch 2 para 3(4)).
9 Ie under the Housing Act 2004 Sch 2 Pt 3 (paras 7–16): see PARA 598 et seq.
10 Housing Act 2004 Sch 2 para 4. As to the period within which an appeal may be made see Sch 2 para 10(2); and PARA 599.
11 Housing Act 2004 Sch 2 para 5(1), (2).
12 Housing Act 2004 Sch 2 para 5(3).
13 Housing Act 2004 Sch 2 para 1(4) (applied by Sch 2 para 5(4)).
14 Ie under the Housing Act 2004 Sch 2 Pt 3.
15 Housing Act 2004 Sch 2 para 6. As to the period within which an appeal may be made see Sch 2 para 10(2); and PARA 599.

(B) Appeals relating to Prohibition Orders

598. Appeal relating to prohibition order. A relevant person[1] may appeal to the appropriate tribunal[2] against a prohibition order[3]. The Housing Act 2004 mentions a specific ground on which an appeal may be made[4], but it does not affect the generality the right of appeal[5]. Thus an appeal may be made by a person on the ground that one of the following courses of action is the best course of action in relation to the hazard in respect of which the order was made[6]. The courses of action are: (1) serving an improvement notice[7]; (2) serving a hazard awareness notice[8]; and (3) making a demolition order[9].

A relevant person may appeal to the appropriate tribunal against a decision by the local housing authority to vary[10] a prohibition order, or a decision by the authority to refuse to revoke or vary[11] a prohibition order[12].

1 For the purposes of the Housing Act 2004 Sch 2 Pt 3 (paras 7–16), 'relevant person', in relation to a prohibition order, means a person who is: (1) an owner or occupier of the whole or part of the specified premises; (2) authorised to permit persons to occupy the whole or part of those premises; or (3) a mortgagee of the whole or part of those premises: s 27, Sch 2 para 16(1). If any specified premises are common parts of a building containing one or more flats, then in relation to those specified premises, 'relevant person' means every person who is an owner or mortgagee of the premises in which the common parts are comprised: Sch 2 para 16(2). As to prohibition orders see PARA 590 et seq. As to the meaning of 'owner' see PARA 384 note 11. As to the meaning of 'occupier' see PARA 563 note 13. As to the meaning of 'specified premises' see PARA 592 note 17. As to the meaning of 'common parts', and as to the meaning of 'building containing one or more flats', see PARA 563 note 13.
2 As to the meaning of 'appropriate tribunal' see PARA 580 note 2. As to the powers of the tribunals on an appeal see PARA 600.
3 Housing Act 2004 Sch 2 para 7(1) (amended by SI 2013/1036). As to the time limit for appeal see PARA 599.
4 Ie in the Housing Act 2004 Sch 2 para 8: see the text and notes 6–9.
5 Housing Act 2004 Sch 2 para 7(2).
6 Housing Act 2004 Sch 2 para 8(1).
7 Ie under the Housing Act 2004 s 11 (see PARA 571) or s 12 (see PARA 572): Sch 2 para 8(2)(a).
8 Ie under the Housing Act 2004 s 28 (see PARA 608) or s 29 (see PARA 609): Sch 2 para 8(2)(b).
9 Ie under the Housing Act 1985 s 265 (see PARA 621): Housing Act 2004 Sch 2 para 8(2)(c).
10 As to variation of a prohibition order see PARA 596.
11 As to refusal to revoke or vary a prohibition order see PARA 596.
12 Housing Act 2004 Sch 2 para 9 (amended by SI 2013/1036). As to the powers of the tribunals on an appeal see PARA 600.

599. Time limit for appeal. Any appeal against a prohibition order[1] must be made within the period of 28 days beginning with the date specified in the prohibition order as the date on which the order was made[2]. Any appeal against a decision to vary, or to refuse to revoke or vary, a prohibition order[3] must be made within the period of 28 days beginning with the date specified in the notice of revocation or variation, or of refusal to revoke or vary[4], as the date on which the decision concerned was made[5]. The appropriate tribunal[6] may allow an appeal to be made to it after the end of the specified period if it is satisfied that there is a good reason for the failure to appeal before the end of that period (and for any delay since then in applying for permission to appeal out of time)[7].

1 Ie under the Housing Act 2004 s 27, Sch 2 para 7: see PARA 598. As to prohibition orders see PARA 590 et seq.
2 Housing Act 2004 Sch 2 para 10(1).
3 Ie under the Housing Act 2004 Sch 2 para 9: see PARA 598.
4 Ie under the Housing Act 2004 Sch 2 para 3 or 5: see PARA 597.
5 Housing Act 2004 Sch 2 para 10(2).
6 As to the meaning of 'appropriate tribunal' see PARA 580 note 2. As to appeals to the appropriate tribunal see PARA 32 et seq. As to the powers of the tribunal on an appeal see PARA 600.
7 Housing Act 2004 Sch 2 para 10(3) (amended by SI 2013/1036).

600. Powers of tribunal on an appeal. An appeal to the appropriate tribunal[1] against a prohibition order[2] is to be by way of a re-hearing, and may be determined having regard to matters of which the local housing authority[3] was unaware when it took the decision[4]. The tribunal may by order confirm, quash or vary the prohibition order[5]. Where the grounds of appeal consist of or include the ground that another course of action is more appropriate[6], then when deciding whether one of the courses of action specified is the best course of action in relation to a particular hazard[7], the tribunal must have regard to any guidance given[8] to the local housing authority[9]. Where an appeal is allowed against a prohibition order made in respect of a particular hazard and the reason, or one of the reasons, for allowing the appeal is that one of the specified courses of action is the best course of action in relation to that hazard, the tribunal must, if requested to do so by the appellant or the local housing authority, include in its decision a finding to that effect and identifying the course of action concerned[10].

Where the appeal is against a decision to vary, or to refuse to revoke or vary, a prohibition order[11], the appeal is to be by way of a re-hearing, and may be determined having regard to matters of which the local housing authority was unaware[12]. The tribunal may by order confirm, reverse or vary the decision of the local housing authority[13]. If the appeal is against a decision of the authority to refuse to revoke a prohibition order, the tribunal may make an order revoking the prohibition order as from a date specified in its order[14].

1   As to the meaning of 'appropriate tribunal' see PARA 580 note 2. As to appeals to the appropriate tribunal see PARA 32 et seq.
2   Ie under the Housing Act 2004 s 27, Sch 2 para 7: see PARA 598. As to prohibition orders see PARA 590 et seq.
3   As to the meaning of 'local housing authority' see PARA 380 note 1.
4   Housing Act 2004 Sch 2 para 11(1), (2) (Sch 2 para 11(1) amended by SI 2013/1036).
5   Housing Act 2004 Sch 2 para 11(3).
6   Ie the ground set out in the Housing Act 2004 Sch 2 para 8: see PARA 598.
7   As to the meaning of 'hazard' see PARA 564.
8   Ie under the Housing Act 2004 s 9: see PARA 569.
9   Housing Act 2004 Sch 2 paras 11(4), 12(1), (2).
10 Housing Act 2004 Sch 2 para 12(3), (4).
11 Ie under the Housing Act 2004 Sch 2 para 9: see PARA 598.
12 Housing Act 2004 Sch 2 para 11(2) (applied by Sch 2 para 13(1), (2) (Sch 2 para 13(1) amended by SI 2013/1036)).
13 Housing Act 2004 Sch 2 para 13(3).
14 Housing Act 2004 Sch 2 para 13(4).

(C)   Enforcement of Prohibition Orders

601.   Offence of failing to comply with prohibition order etc. A person commits an offence if, knowing that a prohibition order[1] has become operative[2] in relation to any specified premises[3], he uses the premises in contravention of the order or permits the premises to be so used[4]. In proceedings against a person for such an offence, it is a defence that he had a reasonable excuse for using the premises, or (as the case may be) permitting them to be used, in contravention of the order[5].

1   As to prohibition orders see PARA 590 et seq.
2   As to when a prohibition order becomes operative see PARA 595.
3   As to the meaning of 'specified premises' see PARA 592 note 17.
4   Housing Act 2004 s 32(1). A person who commits an offence under s 32(1) is liable on summary conviction to a fine not exceeding level 5 on the standard scale, and to a further fine not exceeding £20 for every day or part of a day on which he so uses the premises, or permits them to be so used, after conviction: s 32(2). As to the powers of magistrates' courts to issue fines on summary conviction see SENTENCING vol 92 (2015) PARA 176. As to the power of the Secretary of State to increase the fine for this offence see PARA 400.
5   Housing Act 2004 s 32(3).

602.   Recovery of possession of premises in order to comply with order. Nothing in the Rent Act 1977 or the Rent (Agriculture) Act 1976[1] or Part I of the Housing Act 1988[2] prevents possession being obtained by the owner[3] of any specified premises[4] in relation to which a prohibition order[5] is operative[6] if possession of the premises is necessary for the purpose of complying with the order[7].

1   Ie the Rent Acts: see LANDLORD AND TENANT vol 63 (2016) PARAS 653 et seq, 861 et seq.

2   Ie the Housing Act 1988 Pt I (ss 1–45): see LANDLORD AND TENANT vol 63 (2016) PARA 825 et seq.
3   As to the meaning of 'owner' see PARA 384 note 11.
4   As to the meaning of 'specified premises' see PARA 592 note 17.
5   As to prohibition orders see PARA 590 et seq.
6   As to when a prohibition order becomes operative see PARA 595.
7   Housing Act 2004 s 33.

603. Power of tribunal to determine or vary lease. Where a prohibition order[1] has become operative[2] and the whole or part of any specified premises[3] form the whole or part of the subject matter of a lease[4], the lessor or the lessee[5] may apply to the appropriate tribunal[6] for an order determining or varying the lease[7]. On such an application the tribunal may make an order determining or varying the lease, if it considers it appropriate to do so[8]. Before making such an order, the tribunal must give any sub-lessee an opportunity of being heard[9]. An order may be unconditional or subject to such terms and conditions as the tribunal considers appropriate[10]. The conditions may, in particular, include conditions about the payment of money by one party to the proceedings to another by way of compensation, damages or otherwise[11]. In deciding what is appropriate for these purposes, the tribunal must have regard to the respective rights, obligations and liabilities of the parties under the lease and to all the other circumstances of the case[12].

1   As to prohibition orders see PARA 590 et seq.
2   As to when a prohibition order becomes operative see PARA 595.
3   As to the meaning of 'specified premises' see PARA 592 note 17.
4   As to the meaning of 'lease' see PARA 391 note 6.
5   For the purposes of the Housing Act 2004 s 34, 'lessor' and 'lessee' include a person deriving title under a lessor or lessee: s 34(8). As to the meanings of 'lessor' and 'lessee' in the Housing Act 2004 generally see PARA 391 note 6.
6   As to the meaning of 'appropriate tribunal' see PARA 580 note 2. As to appeals to the appropriate tribunal see PARA 32 et seq.
7   Housing Act 2004 s 34(1), (2) (s 34(2) amended by SI 2013/1036).
8   Housing Act 2004 s 34(3).
9   Housing Act 2004 s 34(4).
10   Housing Act 2004 s 34(5).
11   Housing Act 2004 s 34(6).
12   Housing Act 2004 s 34(7).

604. Power of court to order occupier or owner to allow action to be taken on premises. Where a prohibition order[1] has become operative[2], then, if the occupier[3] of any specified premises[4] has received reasonable notice of any intended action[5] in relation to the premises, but is preventing a relevant person[6], or any representative[7] of a relevant person or of the local housing authority, from taking that action in relation to the premises, a magistrates' court may order the occupier to permit to be done on the premises anything which the court considers is necessary or expedient for the purpose of enabling the intended action to be taken[8]. If a relevant person has received reasonable notice of any intended action in relation to any specified premises, but is preventing a representative of the local housing authority from taking that action in relation to the premises, a magistrates' court may order the relevant person to permit to be done on the premises anything which the court considers is necessary or expedient for the purpose of enabling the intended action to be taken[9]. A person who fails to comply with an order of the court under these provisions commits an offence[10]. In proceedings for such an offence it is a defence that the person had a reasonable excuse for failing to comply with the order[11].

1   As to prohibition orders see PARA 590 et seq.

2 As to when a prohibition order becomes operative see PARA 595.

3 As to the meaning of 'occupier' see PARA 563 note 13.

4 As to the meaning of 'specified premises' see PARA 592 note 17.

5 For this purpose, 'intended action', in relation to any specified premises, means, where a prohibition order has become operative, any action which is proposed to be taken and which either is necessary for the purpose of giving effect to the order or is remedial action specified in the order in accordance with the Housing Act 2004 s 22(2)(e) (see PARA 592): s 35(7).

6 For this purpose, 'relevant person', in relation to any premises, means a person who is an owner of the premises, a person having control of or managing the premises, or the holder of any licence under the Housing Act 2004 Pt 2 (ss 55–78) (see PARA 674 et seq) or Pt 3 (ss 79–100) (see PARA 704 et seq) in respect of the premises: s 35(8). As to the meaning of 'owner' see PARA 384 note 11.

7 As to the meaning of 'representative' see PARA 588 note 7.

8 Housing Act 2004 s 35(1), (2).

9 Housing Act 2004 s 35(3).

10 Housing Act 2004 s 35(4). A person who commits such an offence is liable on summary conviction to a fine not exceeding £20 in respect of each day or part of a day during which the failure continues: s 35(6). As to the power of the Secretary of State to increase the fine for this offence see PARA 400.

11 Housing Act 2004 s 35(5).

605. Power of court to authorise action by one owner on behalf of another. Where a prohibition order[1] has become operative[2], an owner[3] of any specified premises[4] may apply to a magistrates' court for an order in the following terms[5]. A magistrates' court may, on such an application, make an order enabling the applicant immediately to enter on the premises and to take any required action[6] within a period fixed by the order[7]. No order may be made unless the court is satisfied that the interests of the applicant will be prejudiced as a result of a failure by another person to take any required action[8]. No order may be made unless notice of the application has been given to the local housing authority[9]. If it considers that it is appropriate to do so, the court may make an order in favour of any other owner of the premises which is similar to the order that it is making in relation to the premises under these provisions[10].

1 As to prohibition orders see PARA 590 et seq.

2 As to as to when a prohibition order becomes operative see PARA 595.

3 As to the meaning of 'owner' see PARA 384 note 11.

4 As to the meaning of 'specified premises' see PARA 592 note 17.

5 Housing Act 2004 s 36(1).

6 'Required action' means any action necessary for the purpose of complying with the order or any remedial action specified in the order in accordance with the Housing Act 2004 s 22(2)(e) (see PARA 592): s 36(3).

7 Housing Act 2004 s 36(2).

8 Housing Act 2004 s 36(4).

9 Housing Act 2004 s 36(5). As to the meaning of 'local housing authority' see PARA 380 note 1.

10 Housing Act 2004 s 36(6).

(D) *Compensation in respect of Prohibition Orders*

606. Compensation payable. Where a relevant prohibition order[1] becomes operative[2] in respect of any premises, the local housing authority[3] must pay to every owner[4] of the premises an amount determined in accordance with the following provisions[5]. The amount to be paid is the diminution in the compulsory purchase value[6] of the owner's interest in the premises as a result of the coming into operation of the relevant prohibition order, and that amount must be determined:

(1)   as at the date of the coming into operation of the order in question; and

(2)   in default of agreement, as if it were compensation payable in respect of the compulsory purchase of the interest in question and must be dealt with accordingly[7].

1 'Relevant prohibition order' means a prohibition order under the Housing Act 2004 s 20 (see PARA 590) or s 21 (see PARA 591) which imposes in relation to the whole of any premises a prohibition on their use for all purposes other than any purpose approved by the authority: Housing Act 1985 s 584A(4) (s 584A added by the Local Government and Housing Act 1989 s 165(1), Sch 9 para 75; and substituted by the Housing Act 2004 s 265(1), Sch 15 paras 10, 30). 'Premises', in relation to a prohibition order, means premises which are specified premises in relation to the order within the meaning of the Housing Act 2004 Pt 1 (ss 1–54) (see PARA 592 note 17): Housing Act 1985 s 584A(4) (as so substituted).
2 As to when a prohibition order becomes operative see PARA 595.
3 As to the meaning of 'local housing authority' see PARA 11.
4 For these purposes, 'owner', in relation to premises: (1) means a person (other than a mortgagee not in possession) who is for the time being entitled to dispose of the fee simple in the premises, whether in possession or in reversion; and (2) includes also a person holding or entitled to the rents and profits of the premises or part of the premises under a lease of which the unexpired term exceeds three years: Housing Act 1985 s 602 (definition amended by the Local Government and Housing Act 1989 Sch 9 para 81).
5 Housing Act 1985 s 584A(1) (as added and substituted: see note 1). A person entitled to a payment under s 584A(1) is not also entitled to a disturbance payment under the Land Compensation Act 1973 s 37: see COMPULSORY ACQUISITION OF LAND vol 18 (2009) PARA 838.
6 For these purposes, 'compulsory purchase value', in relation to an owner's interest in premises, means the compensation which would be payable in respect of the compulsory purchase of that interest if it fell to be assessed in accordance with the Land Compensation Act 1961 (see COMPULSORY ACQUISITION OF LAND vol 18 (2009) PARA 753 et seq): Housing Act 1985 s 584A(4) (as added and substituted: see note 1).
7 Housing Act 1985 s 584A(2) (as added and substituted: see note 1).

607. Repayment of compensation on revocation or variation of prohibition order. Where a payment in respect of any premises[1] has been made by a local housing authority[2] in connection with a relevant prohibition order[3] and the relevant prohibition order is revoked[4], then, if at that time the person to whom the payment was made has the same interest in the premises as he had at the time the payment was made, he must on demand repay to the authority the amount of the payment[5].

In any case where:

(1)   a payment in respect of any premises has been made by a local housing authority[6] in connection with a relevant prohibition order; and

(2)   the order is revoked as respects part of the premises[7] and not varied; and

(3)   the person to whom the payment was made ('the recipient') had, at the time the payment was made, an owner's interest in the part of the premises concerned (whether or not he had such an interest in the rest of the premises),

then, if at the time of the revocation of the relevant prohibition order the recipient has the same interest in the premises as he had at the time the payment was made, he must on demand pay to the authority an amount determined in accordance with the following provisions[8].

In any case where a payment in respect of any premises has been made by a local housing authority in connection with a relevant prohibition order, and the order is varied[9], then, if at the time of the variation of the order the recipient has the same interest in the premises as he had at the time the payment was made, he must on demand pay to the authority an amount determined in accordance with the following provisions[10].

That amount is whichever is the less of:

(a)   the amount by which the value of the interest of the recipient in the premises increases as a result of the revocation or variation of the relevant prohibition order[11]; and

(b)   the amount paid to the recipient[12] in respect of his interest in the premises[13].

1   As to the meaning of 'premises' see PARA 606 note 1 (definition applied by the Housing Act 1985 s 584B(7) (s 584B added by the Local Government and Housing Act 1989 s 165(1), Sch 9 para 75; and substituted by the Housing Act 2004 s 265(1), Sch 15 paras 10, 31)).
2   Ie under the Housing Act 1985 s 584A(1): see PARA 606. As to the meaning of 'local housing authority' see PARA 11.
3   As to the meaning of 'relevant prohibition order' see PARA 606 note 1 (definition applied by the Housing Act 1985 s 584B(7) (as added: see note 1)).
4   Ie under the Housing Act 2004 s 25(1) or (2): see PARA 596.
5   Housing Act 1985 s 584B(1) (as added and substituted: see note 1).
6   Ie under the Housing Act 1985 s 584A(1): see PARA 606.
7   Ie by virtue of the Housing Act 2004 s 25(3): see PARA 596.
8   Housing Act 1985 s 584B(2) (as added and substituted: see note 1).
9   Ie by virtue of the Housing Act 2004 s 25(4): see PARA 596.
10 Housing Act 1985 s 584B(3) (as added and substituted: see note 1).
11 The amount referred to in head (a) in the text must be determined as at the date of the revocation or variation of the relevant prohibition order: Housing Act 1985 s 584B(4) (as added and substituted: see note 1). For the purpose of assessing that amount, the rules set out in the Land Compensation Act 1961 s 5 (see COMPULSORY ACQUISITION OF LAND vol 18 (2009) PARA 753 et seq), so far as applicable and subject to any necessary modifications, have effect as they have effect for the purpose of assessing compensation for the compulsory acquisition of an interest in land: Housing Act 1985 s 584B(5) (as so added and substituted). Any dispute as to that amount must be referred to and determined by the Upper Tribunal; and the Land Compensation Act 1961 ss 2, 4(1)(a), (4), (5) apply, subject to any necessary modifications, for these purposes as they apply for the purposes of that Act: Housing Act 1985 s 584B(6) (as so added and substituted; amended by SI 2009/1307). See further COMPULSORY ACQUISITION OF LAND vol 18 (2009) PARA 724 et seq.
12 See note 9.
13 Housing Act 1985 s 584B(4) (as added and substituted: see note 1).

C.   HAZARD AWARENESS NOTICES

608. Duty of authority to serve hazard awareness notice relating to category 1 hazard. If the local housing authority[1] is satisfied that a category 1 hazard[2] exists on any residential premises[3], and that no management order is in force[4] in relation to the premises, serving a hazard awareness notice in respect of the hazard is a course of action available to the authority in relation to the hazard for the purposes of the authority's general duty[5] to take enforcement action[6]. A hazard awareness notice is a notice advising the person on whom it is served of the existence of a category 1 hazard on the residential premises concerned which arises as a result of a deficiency on the premises in respect of which the notice is served[7]. The notice may be served in respect of the following premises:

(1)   if the residential premises on which the hazard exists are a dwelling[8] or an HMO[9] which is not a flat[10], it may be served in respect of the dwelling or HMO;

(2)   if those premises are one or more flats, it may be served in respect of the building containing the flat or flats (or any part of the building) or any external common parts[11];

(3)   if those premises are the common parts of a building containing one or more flats[12], it may be served in respect of the building (or any part of the building) or any external common parts[13].

The notice may not, by virtue of head (2) or head (3)[14], be served in respect of any part of the building or its external common parts that is not included in any residential premises on which the hazard exists, unless the authority is satisfied that the deficiency from which the hazard arises is situated there, and that it is desirable for the notice to be so served in the interests of the health or safety of any actual or potential occupiers[15] of one or more of the flats[16].

A notice may relate to more than one category 1 hazard on the same premises or in the same building containing one or more flats[17]. A notice must specify, in relation to the hazard (or each of the hazards) to which it relates:

(a)   the nature of the hazard and the residential premises on which it exists;

(b)   the deficiency giving rise to the hazard;

(c)   the premises on which the deficiency exists;

(d)   the authority's reasons for deciding to serve the notice, including its reasons for deciding that serving the notice is the most appropriate course of action; and

(e)   details of the remedial action[18] (if any) which the authority considers that it would be practicable and appropriate to take in relation to the hazard[19].

The statutory provisions as to the service of improvement notices and copies of such notices[20] apply to a hazard awareness notice as if it were an improvement notice[21].

There appears to be no right of appeal against a hazard awareness notice.

1   As to the meaning of 'local housing authority' see PARA 380 note 1.
2   As to the meaning of 'category 1 hazard' see PARA 564.
3   As to the meaning of 'residential premises' see PARA 563.
4   Ie under the Housing Act 2004 Pt 4 Ch 1 (ss 101–131) or Ch 2 (ss 132–138): see PARA 745 et seq. As to the effect of the making of a management order see PARA 612.
5   Ie under the Housing Act 2004 s 5: see PARA 566.
6   Housing Act 2004 s 28(1).
7   Housing Act 2004 s 28(2).
8   As to the meaning of 'dwelling' see PARA 563 note 10.
9   As to the meaning of 'HMO' see PARA 563 note 11.
10 As to the meaning of 'flat' see PARA 563 note 13.
11 As to the meaning of 'external common parts' see PARA 571 note 14.
12 As to the meaning of 'common parts', and as to the meaning of 'building containing one or more flats', see PARA 563 note 13.
13 Housing Act 2004 s 28(3). Heads (2) and (3) in the text are subject to s 28(4) (see the text and note 16): s 28(3).
14 Ie by virtue of the Housing Act 2004 s 28(3)(b) or (c) (see heads (2), (3) in the text).
15 As to the meaning of 'occupier' see PARA 563 note 13.
16 Housing Act 2004 s 28(4).
17 Housing Act 2004 s 28(5).
18 As to the meaning of 'remedial action' see PARA 571 note 8.
19 Housing Act 2004 s 28(6).
20 Ie the Housing Act 2004 s 18, Sch 1 Pt 1 (paras 1–5): see PARA 574.
21 Housing Act 2004 s 28(7). For that purpose, any reference in Sch 1 Pt 1 to 'the specified premises' is, in relation to a hazard awareness notice under s 28, a reference to the premises specified under s 28(6)(c) (see head (c) in the text): s 28(8).

609.   Power of authority to serve hazard awareness notice relating to category 2 hazard. If the local housing authority[1] is satisfied that a category 2 hazard[2] exists on any residential premises[3], and that no management order is in force[4] in relation to the premises, the authority may serve a hazard awareness notice under these provisions in respect of the hazard[5]. Such a hazard awareness notice is a notice advising the person on whom it is served of the existence of a category 2 hazard on the residential premises concerned which arises as a result of a deficiency on the premises in respect of which the notice is served[6]. The notice may be served in respect of the following premises:

(1) if the residential premises on which the hazard exists are a dwelling[7] or an HMO[8] which is not a flat[9], it may be served in respect of the dwelling or HMO;

(2) if those premises are one or more flats, it may be served in respect of the building containing the flat or flats (or any part of the building) or any external common parts[10];

(3) if those premises are the common parts of a building containing one or more flats[11], it may be served in respect of the building (or any part of the building) or any external common parts[12].

The notice may not, by virtue of head (2) or head (3)[13], be served in respect of any part of the building or its external common parts that is not included in any residential premises on which the hazard exists, unless the authority is satisfied that the deficiency from which the hazard arises is situated there, and that it is desirable for the notice to be so served in the interests of the health or safety of any actual or potential occupiers[14] of one or more of the flats[15].

A notice may relate to more than one category 2 hazard on the same premises or in the same building containing one or more flats[16]. A notice must specify, in relation to the hazard (or each of the hazards) to which it relates:

(a) the nature of the hazard and the residential premises on which it exists;

(b) the deficiency giving rise to the hazard;

(c) the premises on which the deficiency exists;

(d) the authority's reasons for deciding to serve the notice, including its reasons for deciding that serving the notice is the most appropriate course of action; and

(e) details of the remedial action[17] (if any) which the authority considers that it would be practicable and appropriate to take in relation to the hazard[18].

A notice relating to a category 2 hazard may be combined in one document with a notice relating to a category 1 hazard[19] where they are served in respect of the same premises[20].

The statutory provisions as to the service of improvement notices and copies of such notices[21] apply to a hazard awareness notice as if it were an improvement notice[22].

There appears to be no right of appeal against a hazard awareness notice.

1 As to the meaning of 'local housing authority' see PARA 380 note 1.
2 As to the meaning of 'category 2 hazard' see PARA 564.
3 As to the meaning of 'residential premises' see PARA 563.
4 Ie under the Housing Act 2004 Pt 4 Ch 1 (ss 101–131) or Ch 2 (ss 132–138): see PARA 745 et seq. As to the effect of the making of a management order see PARA 612.
5 Housing Act 2004 s 29(1).
6 Housing Act 2004 s 29(2).
7 As to the meaning of 'dwelling' see PARA 563 note 10.
8 As to the meaning of 'HMO' see PARA 563 note 11.
9 As to the meaning of 'flat' see PARA 563 note 13.
10 As to the meaning of 'external common parts' see PARA 571 note 14.
11 As to the meaning of 'common parts', and as to the meaning of 'building containing one or more flats', see PARA 563 note 13.
12 Housing Act 2004 s 28(3) (applied by s 29(3)). Heads (2) and (3) in the text are subject to s 28(4) (see the text and note 15): s 28(3) (as so applied).
13 Ie by virtue of the Housing Act 2004 s 28(3)(b) or (c) (as applied by s 29(3)).
14 As to the meaning of 'occupier' see PARA 563 note 13.
15 Housing Act 2004 s 28(4) (applied by s 29(3)).
16 Housing Act 2004 s 29(4).
17 As to the meaning of 'remedial action' see PARA 571 note 8.
18 Housing Act 2004 s 29(5).

19 Ie a notice under the Housing Act 2004 s 28: see PARA 608. As to the meaning of 'category 1 hazard' see PARA 564.
20 Housing Act 2004 s 29(6).
21 Ie the Housing Act 2004 s 18, Sch 1 Pt 1 (paras 1–5): see PARA 574.
22 Housing Act 2004 s 29(7). For that purpose, any reference in Sch 1 Pt 1 to 'the specified premises' is, in relation to a hazard awareness notice under s 29, a reference to the premises specified under s 29(5)(c) (see head (c) in the text): s 29(8).

D.   EFFECT OF IMPROVEMENT NOTICES AND PROHIBITION ORDERS ETC

610. Effect of improvement notices and prohibition orders as local land charges. An improvement notice[1] or a prohibition order[2] is a local land charge if one of the following provisions applies[3]:

(1)   if the notice or order has become operative[4];

(2)   if the notice or order is suspended[5], and the period for appealing against it[6] has expired without an appeal having been brought[7];

(3)   if the notice or order is suspended, an appeal has been brought against it and, were it not suspended: (a) the notice would have become operative[8] by virtue of the provisions relating to confirmation of improvement notices on appeal or expiry of the period for further appeal; or (b) the order would have become operative[9] by virtue of the provisions relating to confirmation of prohibition orders on appeal or expiry of the period for further appeal[10].

1   As to improvement notices see PARA 571 et seq.
2   As to prohibition orders see PARA 590 et seq.
3   Housing Act 2004 s 37(1). As to local land charges see the Local Land Charges Act 1975; and REAL PROPERTY AND REGISTRATION vol 87 (2012) PARA 763 et seq.
4   Housing Act 2004 s 37(2). As to as to when an improvement notice becomes operative see PARA 576; and as to when a prohibition order becomes operative see PARA 595.
5   Ie under the Housing Act 2004 s 14 (see PARA 575) or s 23 (see PARA 594).
6   Ie under the Housing Act 2004 s 18, Sch 1 Pt 3 (paras 10–20) (see PARA 580 et seq) or s 27, Sch 2 Pt 3 (paras 7–16) (see PARA 598 et seq).
7   Housing Act 2004 s 37(3).
8   Ie under the Housing Act 2004 s 15(5) by virtue of Sch 1 para 19(2): see PARA 576 note 9.
9   Ie under the Housing Act 2004 s 24(5) by virtue of Sch 2 para 14(2): see PARA 595 note 6.
10 Housing Act 2004 s 37(4).

611. Savings for rights arising from breach of covenant. Nothing in the housing standards provisions of the Housing Act 2004[1] affects any remedy of an owner[2] for breach of any covenant or contract entered into by a tenant[3] in connection with any premises which are specified premises[4] in relation to an improvement notice[5] or prohibition order[6]. If an owner is obliged to take possession of any premises in order to comply with an improvement notice or prohibition order, the taking of possession does not affect his right to take advantage of any such breach which occurred before he took possession[7]. No action taken under those provisions affects any remedy available to the tenant of any premises against his landlord (whether at common law or otherwise)[8].

1   Ie the Housing Act 2004 Pt 1 Ch 2 (ss 11–39).
2   As to the meaning of 'owner' see PARA 384 note 11.
3   As to the meaning of 'tenant' see PARA 391 note 6.
4   As to the meaning of 'specified premises' in relation to improvement notices see PARA 574 note 1; and as to the meaning of 'specified premises' in relation to prohibition orders see PARA 592 note 17.
5   As to improvement notices see PARA 571 et seq.
6   Housing Act 2004 s 38(1). As to prohibition orders see PARA 590 et seq.
7   Housing Act 2004 s 38(2).
8   Housing Act 2004 s 38(3). As to the meaning of 'landlord' see PARA 391 note 6.

612. Effect of management orders and redevelopment proposals. If an improvement notice[1] or prohibition order[2] has been served[3] or made[4], and a management order[5] comes into force in relation to the specified premises[6], the improvement notice or prohibition order if operative[7] at the time when the management order comes into force, ceases to have effect at that time, and otherwise is to be treated as from that time as if it had not been served or made[8]. This does not affect any right acquired or liability (civil or criminal) incurred before the improvement notice or prohibition order ceases to have effect[9].

Where the local housing authority[10] has approved proposals for the redevelopment of land[11], no action is to be taken under the housing standards provisions of the Housing Act 2004[12] in relation to the land if, and so long as, the redevelopment is being proceeded with (subject to any variation or extension approved by the authority) in accordance with the proposals and within the time limits specified by the local housing authority[13].

1 As to improvement notices see PARA 571 et seq.
2 As to prohibition orders see PARA 590 et seq.
3 As to service of improvement notices see PARA 574.
4 As to making prohibition orders see PARAS 590–591.
5 Ie under the Housing Act 2004 Pt 4 Ch 1 (ss 101–131) or Ch 2 (ss 132–138): see PARA 745 et seq.
6 As to the meaning of 'specified premises' in relation to improvement notices see PARA 574 note 1; and as to the meaning of 'specified premises' in relation to prohibition orders see PARA 592 note 17.
7 As to when an improvement notice becomes operative see PARA 576; and as to when a prohibition order becomes operative see PARA 595.
8 Housing Act 2004 s 39(1), (2).
9 Housing Act 2004 s 39(3).
10 As to the meaning of 'local housing authority' for this purpose see PARA 380 note 1.
11 Ie under the Housing Act 1985 s 308: see PARA 645.
12 Ie the Housing Act 2004 Pt 1 Ch 2 (ss 11–39): see PARA 571 et seq.
13 Housing Act 2004 s 39(4), (5).

(iv) Emergency Measures

A. EMERGENCY REMEDIAL ACTION

613. Emergency remedial action. If the local housing authority[1] is satisfied that a category 1 hazard[2] exists on any residential premises[3], and it is further satisfied that the hazard involves an imminent risk of serious harm to the health or safety of any of the occupiers of those or any other residential premises[4], and no management order is in force in relation to the premises on which the hazard exists[5], the taking by the authority of emergency remedial action[6] in respect of the hazard is a course of action available to the authority in relation to the hazard for the purposes of the authority's general duty[7] to take enforcement action[8]. Emergency remedial action may be taken by the authority in relation to any premises in relation to which remedial action could be required[9] to be taken by an improvement notice[10]. Emergency remedial action may be taken by the authority in respect of more than one category 1 hazard on the same premises or in the same building containing one or more flats[11].

The statutory provisions as to enforcement action by local authorities[12] apply in connection with the taking of emergency remedial action as they apply in connection with the taking of the remedial action required by an improvement notice which has become operative[13] but has not been complied with, but with modifications[14].

Within the period of seven days beginning with the date when the authority starts taking emergency remedial action, the authority must serve a notice of the action[15] and copies of such a notice on the persons on whom the authority would be required[16] to serve an improvement notice and copies of it[17]. The notice so required is a notice which complies with the following requirements[18]. The notice must specify, in relation to the hazard[19] (or each of the hazards) to which it relates:

(1) the nature of the hazard and the residential premises on which it exists;

(2) the deficiency giving rise to the hazard;

(3) the premises in relation to which emergency remedial action has been (or is to be) taken by the authority[20] and the nature of that remedial action;

(4) the power under which that remedial action has been (or is to be) taken by the authority; and

(5) the date when that remedial action was (or is to be) started[21].

The notice must contain information about the right to appeal[22] against the decision of the authority to make the order, and the period within which an appeal may be made[23].

The provisions as to warrants to authorise entry[24] apply for the purpose of enabling a local housing authority to enter any premises to take emergency remedial action in relation to the premises, as if that purpose were mentioned in those provisions[25], and the circumstances as to which the justice of the peace must be satisfied[26] were that there are reasonable grounds for believing that the authority will not be able to gain admission to the premises without a warrant[27].

1   As to the meaning of 'local housing authority' see PARA 380 note 1.
2   As to the meaning of 'category 1 hazard' see PARA 564.
3   Housing Act 2004 s 40(1)(a). As to the meaning of 'residential premises' see PARA 563.
4   Housing Act 2004 s 40(1)(b). As to the meaning of 'occupier' see PARA 563 note 13.
5   Housing Act 2004 s 40(1)(c). As to management orders see Pt 4 Ch 1 (ss 101–131) or Ch 2 (ss 132–138): see PARA 745 et seq.
6   'Emergency remedial action' means such remedial action in respect of the hazard concerned as the authority considers immediately necessary in order to remove the imminent risk of serious harm within the Housing Act 2004 s 40(1)(b) (see the text and note 4): s 40(2).
7   Ie for the purposes of the Housing Act 2004 s 5: see PARA 566.
8   Housing Act 2004 s 40(1). See also the guidance that has been issued; and PARA 569.
9   Ie under the Housing Act 2004 s 11: see s 11(3), (4); and PARA 571.
10 Housing Act 2004 s 40(3). As to improvement notices see PARA 571 et seq. For the purposes of the operation of any provision relating to improvement notices as it applies by virtue of s 40 in connection with emergency remedial action or a notice under s 41, any reference in that provision to the specified premises is to be read as a reference to the premises specified, in accordance with s 41(2)(c) (see head (3) in the text), as those in relation to which emergency remedial action has been (or is to be) taken: s 40(9).
11 Housing Act 2004 s 40(4). As to the meaning of 'building containing one or more flats' see PARA 563 note 13.
12 Ie the Housing Act 2004 s 31, Sch 3 paras 3–5: see PARA 586.
13 As to as to when an improvement notice becomes operative see PARA 576.
14 Housing Act 2004 s 40(5). The modifications are as follows: (1) the right of entry conferred by Sch 3 para 3(4) may be exercised at any time; and (2) the notice required by Sch 3 para 4 (notice before entering premises) must (instead of being served in accordance with that provision) be served on every person who, to the authority's knowledge, is an occupier of the premises in relation to which the authority proposes to take emergency remedial action or, if those premises are common parts of a building containing one or more flats, is an occupier of any part of the building; but (3) that notice is to be regarded as so served if a copy of it is fixed to some conspicuous part of the premises or building: s 40(6). As to the meaning of 'common parts' see PARA 563 note 13.
15 Ie under the Housing Act 2004 s 41: see the text and notes 18–23.
16 Ie under the Housing Act 2004 s 18, Sch 1 Pt 1 (paras 1–5): see PARA 574.
17 Housing Act 2004 s 40(7).
18 Housing Act 2004 s 41(1).
19 As to the meaning of 'hazard' see PARA 564.

20 Ie under the Housing Act 2004 s 40: see the text and notes 1–17.
21 Housing Act 2004 s 41(2).
22 Ie under the Housing Act 2004 s 45: see PARA 616.
23 Housing Act 2004 s 41(3).
24 Ie the Housing Act 2004 s 240: see PARA 385.
25 Ie in the Housing Act 2004 s 240(2): see PARA 385.
26 Ie under the Housing Act 2004 s 240(4): see PARA 385.
27 Housing Act 2004 s 40(8).

614. Recovery of expenses of taking emergency remedial action. The following provisions relate to the recovery by a local housing authority[1] of expenses reasonably incurred in taking emergency remedial action[2] ('emergency expenses')[3]. The statutory provisions as to the recovery of expenses of taking enforcement action by local authorities in relation to improvement notices[4] apply for the purpose of enabling a local housing authority to recover emergency expenses as they apply for the purpose of enabling such an authority to recover expenses incurred in taking remedial action[5], but with certain modifications[6].

1 As to the meaning of 'local housing authority' see PARA 380 note 1.
2 Ie under the Housing Act 2004 s 40: see PARA 613. As to the meaning of 'emergency remedial action' see PARA 613 note 6.
3 Housing Act 2004 s 42(1).
4 Ie the Housing Act 2004 s 31, Sch 3 paras 6–14: see PARAS 586–587. As to improvement notices see PARA 571 et seq.
5 Ie under the Housing Act 2004 Sch 3 para 3: see PARA 586.
6 Housing Act 2004 s 42(2). The modifications are as follows: (1) any reference to the improvement notice is to be read as a reference to the notice under s 41 (see PARA 613); and (2) no amount is recoverable in respect of any emergency expenses until such time (if any) as is the operative time for this purpose: s 42(3). For the purposes of s 42(3): (a) if no appeal against the authority's decision to take the emergency remedial action is made under s 45 (see PARA 616) before the end of the period of 28 days mentioned in s 45(3)(a), 'the operative time' is the end of that period; (b) if an appeal is made under s 45 within that period and a decision is given on the appeal which confirms the authority's decision, 'the operative time' is as follows: (i) if the period within which an appeal to the Upper Tribunal may be brought expires without such an appeal having been brought, 'the operative time' is the end of that period; (ii) if an appeal to the Upper Tribunal is brought, 'the operative time' is the time when a decision is given on the appeal which confirms the authority's decision: s 42(4) (amended by SI 2009/1307). For the purposes of the Housing Act 2004 s 42(4), the withdrawal of an appeal has the same effect as a decision which confirms the authority's decision; and references to a decision which confirms the authority's decision are references to a decision which confirms it with or without variation: s 42(5). As to appeals to the Upper Tribunal, ie the Upper Tribunal (Lands Chamber), the successor to the Lands Tribunal, see PARAS 49–50.

B. EMERGENCY PROHIBITION ORDERS

615. Emergency prohibition orders. If the local housing authority[1] is satisfied that a category 1 hazard[2] exists on any residential premises[3], and is further satisfied that the hazard involves an imminent risk of serious harm to the health or safety of any of the occupiers[4] of those or any other residential premises, and no management order is in force[5] in relation to the premises on which the hazard[6] exists, making an emergency prohibition order in respect of the hazard is a course of action available to the authority in relation to the hazard for the purposes of the authority's general duty[7] to take enforcement action[8]. An emergency prohibition order is an order imposing, with immediate effect, such prohibition or prohibitions on the use of any premises as are specified[9] in the order[10].

As regards the imposition of any such prohibition or prohibitions, specified statutory provisions[11] apply to an emergency prohibition order as they apply to a prohibition order[12]. The provisions as to service of copies of prohibition orders[13] also apply in relation to an emergency prohibition order as they apply to a prohibition order, but any requirement to serve copies within a specified period of seven days is to be read as a reference to serve them on the day on which the emergency prohibition order is made (or, if that is not possible, as soon after that day as is possible)[14].

The provisions as to revocation and variation[15], enforcement[16], effect[17], notices relating to revocation or variation[18], appeals (so far as they relate to any decision to vary, or to refuse to revoke or vary, a prohibition order)[19], and payment, and repayment, of compensation[20] also apply to an emergency prohibition order as they apply to a prohibition order (or to a prohibition order which has become operative[21], as the case may be)[22].

An emergency prohibition order must comply with the following requirements[23]. The order must specify, in relation to the hazard (or each of the hazards) to which it relates:

(1)   the nature of the hazard concerned and the residential premises on which it exists;

(2)   the deficiency giving rise to the hazard;

(3)   the premises in relation to which prohibitions are imposed by the order[24]; and

(4)   any remedial action which the authority considers would, if taken in relation to the hazard, result in its revoking[25] the order[26].

The order must contain information about the right to appeal against the order[27], and the period within which an appeal may be made, and specify the date on which the order is made[28].

1   As to the meaning of 'local housing authority' see PARA 380 note 1.
2   As to the meaning of 'category 1 hazard' see PARA 564.
3   As to the meaning of 'residential premises' see PARA 563.
4   As to the meaning of 'occupier' see PARA 563 note 13.
5   Ie under the Housing Act 2004 Pt 4 Ch 1 (ss 101–131) or Ch 2 (ss 132–138): see PARA 745 et seq.
6   As to the meaning of 'hazard' see PARA 564.
7   Ie for the purposes of the Housing Act 2004 s 5: see PARA 566.
8   Housing Act 2004 s 43(1).
9   Ie in accordance with the Housing Act 2004 s 43(3) (see the text and notes 11–12) and s 44 (see the text and notes 23–28). For the purposes of the operation of any provision relating to prohibition orders as it applies in connection with emergency prohibition orders by virtue of s 43 or s 45 (see PARA 616), any reference in that provision to the specified premises is to be read as a reference to the premises specified, in accordance with s 44(2)(c) (see head (3) in the text), as the premises in relation to which prohibitions are imposed by the order: s 43(6).
10 Housing Act 2004 s 43(2).
11 Ie the Housing Act 2004 ss 20(3)–(5), 22(3)–(5), (7)–(9): see PARAS 590, 592.
12 Housing Act 2004 s 43(3). As to prohibition orders see PARA 590 et seq.
13 Ie the Housing Act 2004 s 27, Sch 2 Pt 1 (paras 1–2): see PARA 593.
14 Housing Act 2004 s 43(4).
15 Ie the Housing Act 2004 s 25: see PARA 596.
16 Ie the Housing Act 2004 ss 32–36: see PARAS 601–605.
17 Ie the Housing Act 2004 ss 37–39: see PARAS 610–612.
18 Ie the Housing Act 2004 Sch 2 Pt 2 (paras 3–6): see PARA 597.
19 Ie the Housing Act 2004 Sch 2 Pt 3 (paras 7–16): see PARAS 598–600.
20 Ie the Housing Act 1985 ss 584A, 584B: see PARAS 606–607.
21 As to when a prohibition order becomes operative see PARA 595.
22 Housing Act 2004 s 43(5).
23 Housing Act 2004 s 44(1).
24 See the Housing Act 2004 s 22(3), (4) (as applied by s 43(3)); and PARA 592.
25 Ie under the Housing Act 2004 s 25 (as applied by s 43(5)): see PARA 596.
26 Housing Act 2004 s 44(2).
27 Ie under the Housing Act 2004 s 45: see PARA 616.
28 Housing Act 2004 s 44(3).

616. Appeals relating to emergency measures. A person on whom a notice[1] has been served in connection with the taking of emergency remedial action[2] may appeal to the appropriate tribunal[3] against the decision of the local housing authority[4] to take that action[5]. A relevant person[6] may also appeal to the appropriate tribunal against an emergency prohibition order[7]. An appeal under these provisions must be made within the period of 28 days beginning with the date specified in the notice as the date when the emergency remedial action was (or was to be) started, or the date specified in the emergency prohibition order as the date on which the order was made[8]. The appropriate tribunal may allow an appeal to be made to it after the end of that period if it is satisfied that there is a good reason for the failure to appeal before the end of that period (and for any delay since then in applying for permission to appeal out of time)[9]. An appeal is to be by way of a re-hearing, and may be determined having regard to matters of which the authority was unaware when it made the order[10]. The tribunal may in the case of an appeal in connection with the taking of emergency remedial action, confirm, reverse or vary the decision of the authority and in the case of an appeal against an emergency prohibition order, confirm or vary the emergency prohibition order or make an order revoking it as from a date specified in that order[11].

1   Ie under the Housing Act 2004 s 41: see PARA 613.
2   Ie under the Housing Act 2004 s 40: see PARA 613.
3   As to the meaning of 'appropriate tribunal' see PARA 580 note 2. As to appeals to the appropriate tribunal see PARA 32 et seq.
4   As to the meaning of 'local housing authority' see PARA 380 note 1.
5   Housing Act 2004 s 45(1) (amended by SI 2013/1036).
6   The Housing Act 2004 s 27, Sch 2 para 16 (see PARA 598 note 1) applies for the purpose of identifying who is a relevant person for the purposes of s 45(2) in relation to an emergency prohibition order as it applies for the purpose of identifying who is a relevant person for the purposes of Sch 2 Pt 3 (paras 7–16) (see PARAS 598–600) in relation to a prohibition order: s 45(7). As to prohibition orders see PARA 590 et seq.
7   Housing Act 2004 s 45(2) (amended by SI 2013/1036). As to emergency prohibition orders see PARA 615.
8   Housing Act 2004 s 45(3).
9   Housing Act 2004 s 45(4) (amended by SI 2013/1036).
10 Housing Act 2004 s 45(5).
11 Housing Act 2004 s 45(6).

(v) Protection against Retaliatory Eviction

617. Protection for assured shorthold tenants against retaliatory eviction. Where a relevant notice[1] is served in relation to a dwelling house[2] in England, a notice ('a section 21 notice')[3] may not be given in relation to an assured shorthold tenancy[4] of the dwelling house:

(1)   within six months beginning with the day of service of the relevant notice; or

(2)   where the operation of the relevant notice has been suspended, within six months beginning with the day on which the suspension ends[5].

A section 21 notice given in relation to an assured shorthold tenancy of a dwelling house in England is invalid where:

(a)   before the section 21 notice was given, the tenant made a complaint in writing to the landlord[6] regarding the condition of the dwelling house at the time of the complaint;

(b)   the landlord:

(i)   did not provide a response to the complaint within 14 days beginning with the day on which the complaint was given;

(ii)   provided a response to the complaint that was not an adequate response[7]; or

(iii)   gave a section 21 notice in relation to the dwelling house following the complaint;

(c)   the tenant then made a complaint to the relevant local housing authority[8] about the same, or substantially the same, subject matter as the complaint to the landlord;

(d)   the relevant local housing authority served a relevant notice in relation to the dwelling house in response to the complaint; and

(e)   if the section 21 notice was not given before the tenant's complaint to the local housing authority, it was given before the service of the relevant notice[9].

This applies despite the requirement in head (a) for a complaint to be in writing not having been met where the tenant does not know the landlord's postal or e-mail address[10]; and despite the requirements in heads (a) and (b) not having been met where the tenant made reasonable efforts to contact the landlord to complain about the condition of the dwelling house but was unable to do so[11].

The court must strike out proceedings for an order for possession on the expiry or termination of an assured shorthold tenancy[12] in relation to a dwelling house in England if, before the order is made, the section 21 notice that would otherwise require the court to make an order for possession in relation to the dwelling house has become invalid under heads (a) to (e) above[13]. An order for possession of a dwelling house in England[14] must not be set aside on the ground that a relevant notice was served in relation to the dwelling house after the order for possession was made[15].

The prohibition on giving a section 21 notice within the time specified in heads (1) or (2)[16] does not apply where the section 21 notice is given after:

(A)   the relevant notice has been wholly revoked[17] as a result of the notice having been served in error;

(B)   the relevant notice has been quashed[18];

(C)   a decision of the relevant local housing authority to refuse to revoke the relevant notice has been reversed[19]; or

(D)   a decision of the relevant local housing authority to take the action to which the relevant notice relates has been reversed[20].

A section 21 notice is not invalid[21] where the operation of the relevant notice has been suspended[22].

The provisions as to timing and invalidity of a section 21 notice[23] do not apply:

(I)   where the condition of the dwelling house or common parts that gave rise to the service of the relevant notice is due to a breach by the tenant of the duty to use the dwelling house in a tenant-like manner or of an express term of the tenancy to the same effect[24];

(II)   where at the time the section 21 notice is given the dwelling house is genuinely on the market for sale[25];

(III)   where the landlord is a private registered provider of social housing[26];

(IV)   where the dwelling house is subject to a mortgage[27] granted before the beginning of the tenancy, the mortgagee[28] is entitled to exercise a power of sale conferred on the mortgagee by the mortgage or by statute[29] and, at the time the section 21 notice is given the mortgagee requires possession of the dwelling house for the purpose of disposing of it with vacant possession in exercise of that power[30].

1 'Relevant notice' means: (1) a notice served under the Housing Act 2004 s 11 (improvement notices relating to category 1 hazards: see PARA 571); (2) a notice served under s 12 (improvement notices relating to category 2 hazards: see PARA 572); or (3) a notice served under s 40(7) (emergency remedial action: see PARA 613): Deregulation Act 2015 s 33(13).

2 'Dwelling house' has the meaning given by the Housing Act 1988 s 45 (see LANDLORD AND TENANT vol 63 (2016) PARA 819 note 11): Deregulation Act 2015 s 33(13). References in s 33 and s 34 to a relevant notice served, or complaint made, in relation to a dwelling house include a relevant notice served, or complaint made, in relation to any common parts of the building of which the dwelling house forms a part; but this applies only if the landlord has a controlling interest in the common parts in question and the condition of those common parts is such as to affect the tenant's enjoyment of the dwelling house or of any common parts which the tenant is entitled to use: s 33(10), (11). 'Common parts', in relation to a building, includes the structure and exterior of the building, and common facilities provided (whether or not in the building) for persons who include one or more of the occupiers of the building; and 'controlling interest' means an interest which is such as to entitle the landlord to decide whether action is taken in relation to a complaint within s 33 or a relevant notice: s 33(13).

3 'Section 21 notice' means a notice given under the Housing Act 1988 s 21(1)(b) or (4)(a) (recovery of possession on termination of shorthold tenancy: see LANDLORD AND TENANT vol 63 (2016) PARA 926): Deregulation Act 2015 s 33(13).

4 'Assured shorthold tenancy' means a tenancy within the Housing Act 1988 s 19A or 20 (see LANDLORD AND TENANT vol 63 (2016) PARA 852 et seq): Deregulation Act 2015 s 33(13).

5 Deregulation Act 2015 s 33(1). Subject to s 41(2), (3), a provision of ss 33, 34 applies only to an assured shorthold tenancy of a dwelling house in England granted on or after the day on which the provision comes into force: s 41(1). Subject to s 41(3), a provision of ss 33, 34 does not apply to an assured shorthold tenancy that came into being under the Housing Act 1988 s 5(2) after the commencement of that provision and on the coming to an end of an assured shorthold tenancy that was granted before the commencement of that provision: Deregulation Act 2015 s 41(2). At the end of the period of three years beginning with the coming into force of a provision of ss 33, 34, that provision also applies to any assured shorthold tenancy of a dwelling house in England: (1) which is in existence at that time; and (2) to which that provision does not otherwise apply by virtue of s 41(1) or (2): s 41(3). Sections 33, 34 came into force on 1 October 2015: see the Deregulation Act 2015 (Commencement No 1 and Transitional and Saving Provisions) Order 2015, SI 2015/994, art 11(g), (h).

6 In the Deregulation Act 2015 ss 33, 34 a reference to a complaint to a landlord includes a complaint made to a person acting on behalf of the landlord in relation to the tenancy: s 33(12).

7 The reference here to an adequate response by the landlord is to a response in writing which provides a description of the action that the landlord proposes to take to address the complaint, and sets out a reasonable timescale within which that action will be taken: Deregulation Act 2015 s 33(3).

8 'Relevant local housing authority', in relation to a dwelling house, means the local housing authority as defined in the Housing Act 2004 s 261(2), (3) (see PARA 380 note 1) within whose area the dwelling house is located: Deregulation Act 2015 s 33(13).

9 Deregulation Act 2015 s 33(2).

10 Deregulation Act 2015 s 33(4).

11 Deregulation Act 2015 s 33(5).

12 Ie under the Housing Act 1988 s 21: see LANDLORD AND TENANT vol 63 (2016) PARA 926.

13 Deregulation Act 2015 s 33(6).

14 Ie made under the Housing Act 1988 s 21.

15 Deregulation Act 2015 s 33(7).

16 Ie the Deregulation Act 2015 s 33(1).

17 Ie under the Housing Act 2004 s 16: see PARA 577.

18 Ie under the Housing Act 2004 Sch 1 para 15: see PARA 582.

19 Ie under the Housing Act 2004 Sch 1 para 18: see PARA 583.

20 Deregulation Act 2015 s 33(8). As to reversal of a decision to take action see the Housing Act 2004 s 45; and PARA 616.

21 Ie the Deregulation Act 2015 s 33(2) does not apply.

22 Deregulation Act 2015 s 33(9).

23 Ie the Deregulation Act 2015 s 33(1), (2).

24 Deregulation Act 2015 s 34(1).

25 Deregulation Act 2015 s 34(2). For the purposes of s 34(2), a dwelling house is not genuinely on the market for sale if, in particular, the landlord intends to sell the landlord's interest in the dwelling house to: (1) a person associated with the landlord; (2) a business partner of the landlord; (3) a person associated with a business partner of the landlord; or (4) a business partner of a person associated with the landlord: s 34(3). In s 34(3), references to a person who is associated with another person are to be read in accordance with the Housing Act 1996 s 178 (see PARA 481 note 8): Deregulation Act 2015 s 34(4). For the purposes of s 34(3), a business partner of a person ('P') is a person who is: (a) a director, secretary or other officer of a company of which P is also a director, secretary or other officer; (b) a director, secretary or other officer of a company in which P has a shareholding or other financial interest; (c) a person who has a shareholding or other financial interest in a company of which P is a director, secretary or other officer; (d) an employee of P; (e) a person by whom P is employed; or (f) a partner of a partnership of which P is also a partner: s 34(5).

26 Deregulation Act 2015 s 34(6). As to the meaning of 'private registered provider of social housing' see PARA 53.

27 For this purpose, 'mortgage' includes a charge: Deregulation Act 2015 s 34(8)(a).

28 For this purpose, 'mortgagee' includes a receiver appointed by the mortgagee under the terms of the mortgage or in accordance with the Law of Property Act 1925: Deregulation Act 2015 s 34(8)(b).

29 Ie by the Law of Property Act 1925 s 101: see MORTGAGE vol 77 (2016) PARA 479.

30 Deregulation Act 2015 s 34(7).

(vi) Recovery of Expenses relating to Enforcement Action

618. Power to charge for certain enforcement action. A local housing authority[1] may make such reasonable charge as it considers appropriate as a means of recovering certain administrative and other expenses incurred by it[2] in:

(1)   serving an improvement notice[3];

(2)   making a prohibition order[4];

(3)   serving a hazard awareness notice[5];

(4)   taking emergency remedial action[6];

(5)   making an emergency prohibition order[7]; or

(6)   making a demolition order[8].

The expenses are:

(a)   in the case of the service of an improvement notice or a hazard awareness notice, the expenses incurred in determining whether to serve the notice, identifying any action to be specified in the notice, and serving the notice[9];

(b)   in the case of emergency remedial action, the expenses incurred in determining whether to take such action, and in serving the required[10] notice[11];

(c)   in the case of a prohibition order, an emergency prohibition order or a demolition order, the expenses incurred in determining whether to make the order and in serving copies of the order on persons as owners of premises[12].

A local housing authority may make such reasonable charge as it considers appropriate as a means of recovering expenses incurred by it in carrying out any review of an improvement notice or a prohibition order whose operation is suspended[13], or serving copies of the authority's decision on such a review[14]. The amount of the charge may not exceed such amount as is specified by order of the appropriate national authority[15].

Where a tribunal allows an appeal against the underlying notice or order mentioned in heads (1) to (6) above, it may make such order as it considers appropriate reducing, quashing, or requiring the repayment of, any charge under these provisions made in respect of the notice or order[16].

1 As to the meaning of 'local housing authority' see PARA 380 note 1.
2 Housing Act 2004 s 49(1).
3 Ie under the Housing Act 2004 s 11 (see PARA 571) or s 12 (see PARA 572).
4 Ie under the Housing Act 2004 s 20 (see PARA 590) or s 21 (see PARA 591).
5 Ie under the Housing Act 2004 s 28 (see PARA 608) or s 29 (see PARA 609).
6 Ie under the Housing Act 2004 s 40: see PARA 613.
7 Ie under the Housing Act 2004 s 43: see PARA 615.
8 Housing Act 2004 s 49(1)(a)–(f). The text refers to the making of a demolition order under the Housing Act 1985 s 265: see PARA 621.
9 Housing Act 2004 s 49(2).
10 Ie required by the Housing Act 2004 s 40(7): see PARA 613.
11 Housing Act 2004 s 49(3).
12 Housing Act 2004 s 49(4). As to the meaning of 'owner' see PARA 384 note 11.
13 Ie under the Housing Act 2004 s 17 (see PARA 575) or s 26 (see PARA 594).
14 Housing Act 2004 s 49(5). As to recovery of any charge see PARA 619.
15 Housing Act 2004 s 49(6). As to the meaning of 'appropriate national authority' see PARA 389 note 1. At the date at which this volume states the law, no such order had been made.
16 Housing Act 2004 s 49(7).

619. Recovery of charge. Where a local housing authority[1] has made a charge in respect of expenses incurred by it in taking enforcement action[2], the authority may recover the charge as follows[3]. In the case of an improvement notice[4], or a hazard awareness notice[5], the charge may be recovered from the person on whom the notice is served[6]. In the case of emergency remedial action[7], the charge may be recovered from the person served with the required[8] notice[9]. In the case of a prohibition order under[10], an emergency prohibition order[11], or a demolition order[12], the charge may be recovered from any person on whom a copy of the order is served as an owner of the premises[13]. A demand for payment of the charge must be served on the person from whom the authority seeks to recover it[14].

The demand becomes operative, if no appeal is brought against the underlying notice or order, at the end of the period of 21 days beginning with the date of service of the demand[15]. If such an appeal is brought and a decision is given on the appeal which confirms the underlying notice or order, the demand becomes operative at the time when the period within which an appeal to the Upper Tribunal[16] may be brought expires without such an appeal having been brought, or a decision is given on such an appeal which confirms the notice or order[17].

As from the time when the demand becomes operative, the sum recoverable by the authority is, until recovered, a charge on the premises concerned[18]; the charge takes effect at that time as a legal charge which is a local land charge[19]. For the purpose of enforcing the charge the authority has the same powers and remedies[20] as if it was a mortgagee by deed having powers of sale and lease, of accepting surrenders of leases and of appointing a receiver[21]. The power of appointing a receiver is exercisable at any time after the end of the period of one month beginning with the date on which the charge takes effect[22].

1 As to the meaning of 'local housing authority' see PARA 380 note 1.
2 Ie under the Housing Act 2004 s 49: see PARA 618.
3 Housing Act 2004 s 50(1). The appropriate national authority may by regulations prescribe the form of, and the particulars to be contained in, a demand for payment of any charge under s 49: s 50(13). At the date at which this volume states the law, no such regulations had been made. As to the meaning of 'appropriate national authority' see PARA 389 note 1.
4 Ie under the Housing Act 2004 s 11 (see PARA 571) or s 12 (see PARA 572).
5 Ie under the Housing Act 2004 s 28 (see PARA 608) or s 29 (see PARA 609).
6 Housing Act 2004 s 50(2). As to the persons on whom improvement notices and hazard awareness notices are served see PARA 574.

7   Ie under the Housing Act 2004 s 40: see PARA 613.
8   Ie required by the Housing Act 2004 s 40(7): see PARA 613.
9   Housing Act 2004 s 50(3).
10 Ie under the Housing Act 2004 s 20 (see PARA 590) or s 21 (see PARA 591).
11 Ie under the Housing Act 2004 s 43: see PARA 615.
12 Ie under the Housing Act 1985 s 265: see PARA 621.
13 Housing Act 2004 s 50(4). As to the persons on whom copies of the order are served see
    PARAS 593, 621. As to the meaning of 'owner' see PARA 384 note 11.
14 Housing Act 2004 s 50(5).
15 Housing Act 2004 s 50(6).
16 As to appeals to the Upper Tribunal see PARAS 49–50.
17 Housing Act 2004 s 50(7) (amended by SI 2009/1307). For this purpose, the withdrawal of an
    appeal has the same effect as a decision which confirms the notice or order; and references to a
    decision which confirms the notice or order are references to a decision which confirms it with or
    without variation: Housing Act 2004 s 50(8).
18 Housing Act 2004 s 50(9).
19 Housing Act 2004 s 50(10). As to local land charges see the Local Land Charges Act 1975; and
    REAL PROPERTY AND REGISTRATION vol 87 (2012) PARA 763 et seq.
20 Ie under the Law of Property Act 1925 and otherwise.
21 Housing Act 2004 s 50(11). As to such powers see MORTGAGE vol 77 (2016) PARA 518 et seq.
22 Housing Act 2004 s 50(12).

(3) HOUSES INCAPABLE OF BEING MADE FIT

(i) Demolition of Unfit Premises; in general

620. In general. Where a local housing authority[1] is satisfied that a category 1 hazard[2] or, in defined circumstances, a category 2 hazard[3], exists in a dwelling[4], the authority has power to order its demolition, provided that the relevant statutory provision has not been disapplied and that no management order is in force[5] in relation to the dwelling[6]. The owner of the dwelling, and others who have an interest in it, have a right to appeal to a tribunal against the service of a demolition order[7].

1   As to the meaning of 'local housing authority' see PARA 11.
2   As to the meaning of 'category 1 hazard' see PARA 564.
3   As to the meaning of 'category 2 hazard' see PARA 564.
4   As to the meaning of 'dwelling' see PARA 563 note 10.
5   Ie under the Housing Act 2004 Pt 4 Ch 1 (ss 101–131) or Ch 2 (ss 132–138): see PARA 745 et seq.
6   See PARA 621.
7   See PARA 622. As to appeals to tribunals see PARA 32 et seq.

621. Demolition orders. If the local housing authority[1] is satisfied that a category 1 hazard[2] exists in a dwelling[3] or an HMO[4] which is not a flat[5], and this provision is not disapplied[6], making a demolition order in respect of the dwelling or HMO is a course of action available to the authority in relation to the hazard for the purposes of the general duty[7] to take enforcement action[8]. Similarly, if, in the case of any building containing one or more flats[9], the local housing authority is satisfied that a category 1 hazard exists in one or more of the flats contained in the building or in any common parts[10] of the building, and this provision is not disapplied[11], making a demolition order in respect of the building is a course of action available to the authority in relation to the hazard for the purposes of the general duty to take enforcement action[12].

A demolition order is an order requiring that the premises[13]:

(1)   be vacated within a specified period of at least 28 days from the date on which the order becomes operative[14]; and

(2)   be demolished within six weeks after the end of that period or, if it is not
        vacated before the end of that period, after the date on which it is
        vacated or, in either case, within such longer period as in the
        circumstances the local housing authority considers it reasonable to
        specify[15].

The local housing authority may make a demolition order in respect of a
dwelling or an HMO which is not a flat if it is satisfied that a category 2 hazard[16]
exists in the dwelling or HMO, and this provision is not disapplied and the
circumstances of the case are circumstances specified or described in an
order made by the appropriate national authority[17]. Likewise, the local housing
authority may make a demolition order in respect of any building containing one
or more flats if it is satisfied that a category 2 hazard exists in one or more of the
flats contained in the building or in any common parts of the building, and this
provision is not disapplied and the circumstances of the case are circumstances
specified or described in an order made by the appropriate national authority[18].

None of the above provisions applies if a management order under the Housing
Act 2004[19] is in force in relation to the premises concerned[20]. The provisions
above also have effect subject to the prohibition[21] on making a demolition order in
respect of listed buildings[22].

A local housing authority which has made a demolition order must serve[23] a
copy of the order on every person who, to its knowledge, is an owner[24] or occupier
of the whole or part of the premises to which the order relates, or is authorised to
permit persons to occupy the whole or part of those premises, or is a mortgagee
of the whole or part of the premises[25]. The copies required to be served must be
served within the period of seven days beginning with the day on which the
order is made[26]. A copy of the order is to be regarded as having been duly served
on every occupier if a copy of the order is fixed to some conspicuous part of the
premises within the period of seven days[27].

A demolition order which has been made in respect of any premises ceases to
have effect if a management order under the Housing Act 2004 comes into force
in relation to the premises[28].

1   As to the meaning of 'local housing authority' see PARA 11.
2   As to the meanings of 'category 1 hazard' and 'hazard' see PARA 564 (definition applied by the
    Housing Act 1985 s 322(1) (s 322 substituted by the Housing Act 2004 s 265(1), Sch 15 paras 10,
    26)).
3   As to the meaning of 'dwelling' see PARA 563 note 10 (definition applied by the Housing Act 1985
    s 322(1) (as substituted: see note 2)).
4   For the purposes of the Housing Act 1985 s 265, 'HMO' means house in multiple occupation:
    s 265(7) (s 265 substituted by the Housing Act 2004 s 46). For the purposes of the Housing Act
    1985 Pt IX (ss 265–323), 'house in multiple occupation' means a house in multiple occupation as
    defined by the Housing Act 2004 ss 254–259 (see PARAS 667–671) as they have effect for the
    purposes of Pt 1 (ss 1–54) (ie without the exclusions contained in Sch 14) (see PARA 668): Housing
    Act 1985 s 322(2) (as substituted: see note 2). The Housing Act 1985 Pt IX applies to unoccupied
    HMO accommodation (as defined by the Housing Act 2004 s 1(5): see PARA 563 note 12) as it
    applies to a house in multiple occupation; and references to a house in multiple occupation in the
    Housing Act 1985 Pt IX are to be read accordingly: s 322(3) (as so substituted).
5   As to the meaning of 'flat' see PARA 563 note 13 (definition applied by the Housing Act 1985
    s 322(1) (as substituted: see note 2)).
6   Ie by the Housing Act 1985 s 265(5): see the text to notes 19–20.
7   Ie for the purposes of the Housing Act 2004 s 5: see PARA 566.
8   Housing Act 1985 s 265(1) (as substituted: see note 4); and see PARA 620 note 6.
9   As to the meaning of 'building containing one or more flats' see PARA 563 note 13 (definition
    applied by the Housing Act 1985 s 322(1) (as substituted: see note 2)).
10 As to the meaning of 'common parts' see PARA 563 note 13 (definition applied by the Housing Act
    1985 s 322(1) (as substituted: see note 2)).
11 Ie by the Housing Act 1985 s 265(5): see the text to notes 19–20.

12 Housing Act 1985 s 265(2) (as substituted: see note 4).

13 'Premises', in relation to a demolition order, means the dwelling, house in multiple occupation or building in respect of which the order is made: Housing Act 1985 s 322(2) (as substituted: see note 2).

14 A demolition order against which no appeal is brought becomes operative at the end of the period of 28 days beginning with the day on which the order is made and is final and conclusive as to matters which could be raised on an appeal: see the Housing Act 1985 s 268(4) (s 268 substituted by the Housing Act 2004 Sch 15 para 13). As to appeals see PARA 622. The requirement that the premises are to be vacated must be made even though the premises are vacant when the order was made: see *Pocklington v Melksham UDC* [1964] 2 QB 673, [1964] 2 All ER 862, CA; *R v Epsom and Ewell Corpn, ex p RB Property Investment (Eastern) Ltd* [1964] 2 All ER 832, [1964] 1 WLR 1060.

15 Housing Act 1985 s 267(1).

16 As to the meaning of 'category 2 hazard' see PARA 564 (definition applied by the Housing Act 1985 s 322(1) (as substituted: see note 2)).

17 Housing Act 1985 s 265(3) (as substituted: see note 4). As to the appropriate national authority, ie the Secretary of State or, where statutory functions have been transferred in relation to Wales, the Welsh Ministers, see PARA 7. An order made under s 265(3) or (4) may make different provision for different cases or descriptions of case (including different provision for different areas), may contain such incidental, supplementary, consequential, transitory, transitional or saving provision as the appropriate national authority considers appropriate, and must be made by statutory instrument subject to annulment in pursuance of a resolution of either House of Parliament or, in relation to Wales, of the National Assembly for Wales: s 265(8) (as so substituted). Sections 584A, 584B (see PARAS 628–629) provide for the payment of compensation where demolition orders are made under s 265, and for the repayment of such compensation in certain circumstances: see s 265(9) (as so substituted).

18 Housing Act 1985 s 265(4) (as substituted: see note 4).

19 Ie under the Housing Act 2004 Pt 4 Ch 1 (ss 101–131) or Ch 2 (ss 132–138): see PARA 745 et seq.

20 Housing Act 1985 s 265(5) (as substituted: see note 4).

21 Ie the Housing Act 1985 s 304(1): see PARA 641.

22 Housing Act 1985 s 265(6) (as substituted: see note 4). For these purposes, 'listed building' means a building included in a list of buildings of special architectural or historic interest under the Planning (Listed Buildings and Conservation Areas) Act 1990 s 1 (see PLANNING vol 83 (2010) PARA 1248): Housing Act 1985 s 303 (amended by the Planning (Consequential Provisions) Act 1990 s 4, Sch 2 para 71(2)).

23 The Housing Act 2004 s 246 (service of notices: see PARA 391) applies in relation to copies required to be served under the Housing Act 1985 s 268 (instead of s 617 (see PARA 17)), and so applies as it applies in relation to documents required to be served under any provision of the Housing Act 2004 Pts 1–4 (ss 1–147): Housing Act 1985 s 268(5) (as substituted: see note 14).

24 'Owner', in relation to premises: (1) means a person (other than a mortgagee not in possession) who is for the time being entitled to dispose of the fee simple in premises, whether in possession or reversion; and (2) includes also a person holding or entitled to the rents and profits of the premises under a lease of which the unexpired term exceeds three years: Housing Act 1985 s 322(2) (as substituted: see note 2).

25 Housing Act 1985 s 268(1) (as substituted: see note 14). As to service on an owner etc of premises see PARA 17.

26 Housing Act 1985 s 268(2) (as substituted: see note 14).

27 Housing Act 1985 s 268(3) (as substituted: see note 14).

28 Housing Act 1985 s 274A (added by the Housing Act 2004 Sch 15 para 17).

622. Right of appeal against a demolition order. A person aggrieved[1] by a demolition order[2] may, within the period of 28 days beginning with the day on which the order is made, appeal to the appropriate tribunal[3]. No appeal lies, however, at the instance of a person who is in occupation of the premises[4] or part of the premises under a lease or agreement with an unexpired term of three years or less[5].

On an appeal the tribunal may make such order confirming or quashing or varying the order as it thinks fit[6].

If an appeal is brought the demolition order does not become operative until:

(1)   a decision on the appeal confirming the order, with or without variation, is given and the period within which an appeal to the Upper Tribunal[7] may be brought expires without any such appeal having been brought; or

(2)   if a further appeal to the Upper Tribunal is brought, a decision on that appeal is given confirming the order, with or without variation,

and for this purpose the withdrawal of an appeal has the same effect as a decision confirming the order or decision appealed against[8].

One ground of appeal in relation to a demolition order is that one of the following courses of action is the best course of action in relation to the hazard concerned[9]. The courses of action are:

(a)   serving an improvement notice under the Housing Act 2004[10];
(b)   making a prohibition order under that Act[11];
(c)   serving a hazard awareness notice under that Act[12]; or
(d)   declaring the area in which the premises concerned are situated to be a clearance area[13] in accordance with the Housing Act 1985[14].

Where the appropriate tribunal is hearing an appeal in relation to a demolition order and the grounds on which the appeal is brought are or include the ground that a course of action mentioned in heads (a) to (d) is the best course of action in relation to each hazard concerned, the tribunal must have regard to any guidance given[15] to the local housing authority under the Housing Act 2004[16].

Where an appeal is allowed against a demolition order and the reason, or one of the reasons, for allowing the appeal is that a course of action mentioned in heads (a) to (d) is the best course of action in relation to the hazard concerned, the tribunal must, if requested to do so by the appellant or the local housing authority[17], include in its decision a finding to that effect and identifying the course of action concerned[18].

1   As to persons aggrieved see JUDICIAL REVIEW vol 61 (2010) PARA 656.
2   As to demolition orders see PARA 621.
3   Housing Act 1985 s 269(1) (amended by the Housing Act 2004 ss 48(1), (2)(a), 265(1), Sch 15 paras 10, 14; and by SI 2013/1036). In the Housing Act 1985 Pt IX (ss 264–322), 'appropriate tribunal' means: (1) in relation to premises in England the First-tier Tribunal or, where determined by or under Tribunal Procedure Rules, the Upper Tribunal; and (2) in relation to premises in Wales, a residential property tribunal: s 322(4) (added by SI 2013/1036). As to appeals to those tribunals see PARA 32 et seq.
4   As to the meaning of 'premises' see PARA 621 note 13.
5   Housing Act 1985 s 269(2) (amended by the Local Government and Housing Act 1989 s 165(1)(b), Sch 9 para 17(1)).
6   Housing Act 1985 s 269(3) (amended by the Local Government and Housing Act 1989 s 194, Sch 9 para 17(3), Sch 12 Pt II; and by the Housing Act 2004 s 48(2)(b)).
7   As to appeals to the Upper Tribunal see PARAS 49–50.
8   Housing Act 1985 s 269(6) (amended by the Housing Act 2004 s 48(2)(c); and by SI 2009/1307).
9   Housing Act 1985 s 269A(1) (s 269A added by the Housing Act 2004 Sch 15 para 15). The Housing Act 1985 s 269A(1) is without prejudice to the generality of s 269: s 269A(7) (as so added). As to the meaning of 'hazard' see PARA 564 (definition applied by s 322(1) (substituted by the Housing Act 2004 Sch 15 para 26)).
10 Ie under the Housing Act 2004 s 11 (see PARA 571) or s 12 (see PARA 572).
11 Ie under the Housing Act 2004 s 20 (see PARA 590) or s 21 (see PARA 591).
12 Ie under the Housing Act 2004 s 28 (see PARA 608) or s 29 (see PARA 609).
13 Ie in accordance with the Housing Act 1985 s 289: see PARA 632.
14 Housing Act 1985 s 269A(2) (as added: see note 9).
15 Ie under the Housing Act 2004 s 9: see PARA 569.
16 Housing Act 1985 s 269A(3), (4) (as added (see note 9); s 269A(3) amended by SI 2013/1036). See Housing Health and Safety Rating System—Enforcement Guidance (Office of the Deputy Prime Minister (now Department for Communities and Local Government), February 2006), paras 5.44–5.46.

17 As to the meaning of 'local housing authority' see PARA 11.
18 Housing Act 1985 s 269A(5), (6) (as added: see note 9).

(ii) Demolition Order Procedure

623. Recovery of possession of building to be demolished. Where a demolition order[1] has become operative[2] with respect to any premises[3], the local housing authority[4] must serve on any occupier of the premises or any part of the premises a notice:

(1) stating the effect of the order;

(2) specifying the date by which the order requires the premises to be vacated; and

(3) requiring him to quit the premises before that date or before the expiration of 28 days from the service of the notice, whichever may be the later[5].

If any person is in occupation of the premises, or any part of them, at any time after the date on which the notice requires the premises to be vacated, the local housing authority or an owner[6] of the premises may apply to the County Court which must thereupon order vacant possession of the premises or part to be given to the applicant within such period, of not less than two or more than four weeks, as the court may determine[7]. Expenses incurred by the local housing authority under these provisions in obtaining possession of any premises, or part of any premises, may be recovered by the authority by action from the owner, or from any of the owners, of the premises[8].

A person who, knowing that a demolition order has become operative and applies to any premises, either enters into occupation of the premises, or a part of them, after the date by which the order requires them to be vacated, or permits another person to enter into such occupation after that date, commits a summary offence and is liable on conviction to a penalty[9].

1 As to the making of demolition orders see PARA 621.
2 As to when the order becomes operative see PARAS 621 note 14, 408.
3 As to the meaning of 'premises' see PARA 621 note 13.
4 As to the meaning of 'local housing authority' see PARA 11.
5 Housing Act 1985 s 270(1) (s 270(1)–(5) amended by the Local Government and Housing Act 1989 s 165(1)(b), Sch 9 para 18). The notice must be served at a time which will allow the occupier to leave: see *R v Epsom and Ewell Corpn, ex p RB Property Investment (Eastern) Ltd* [1964] 2 All ER 832, [1964] 1 WLR 1060. Nothing in the Rent Acts (ie the Rent Act 1977 or the Rent (Agriculture) Act 1976: see LANDLORD AND TENANT vol 63 (2016) PARA 653 et seq; LANDLORD AND TENANT vol 64 (2016) PARA 1699 et seq) or in the Housing Act 1988 Pt I (ss 1–45) (see LANDLORD AND TENANT vol 63 (2016) PARA 825 et seq) affects the provisions set out in the text relating to obtaining possession of any premises: Housing Act 1985 s 270(3) (as so amended; further amended by the Housing Act 1988 s 140(1), Sch 17 para 47). The Housing Act 1985 s 270 does not confer a right to damages for breach of statutory duty: see *R v Lambeth London Borough Council, ex p Sarbrook Ltd* (1994) 27 HLR 380; and see also *R v Forest of Dean District Council, ex p Trigg* (1989) 22 HLR 167, [1990] 2 EGLR 29.
6 As to the meaning of 'owner' see PARA 621 note 24.
7 Housing Act 1985 s 270(2) (as amended: see note 5).
8 Housing Act 1985 s 270(4) (as amended: see note 5).
9 Housing Act 1985 s 270(5) (as amended: see note 5). The penalty is a fine not exceeding level 5 on the standard scale and a further fine not exceeding £5 for every day or part of a day on which the occupation continues after conviction: see s 270(5). As to the powers of magistrates' courts to issue fines on summary conviction see SENTENCING vol 92 (2015) PARA 176.

624. Cleansing before demolition. If it appears to the local housing authority[1] that premises[2] to which a demolition order[3] applies require to be cleansed from vermin, the authority may, at any time between the date on which the order is made and the date on which it becomes operative[4], serve notice in writing on the owner[5] or owners of the premises that the authority intends to cleanse the premises before they are demolished[6]. Where the authority has served such a notice:

(1) the authority may, at any time after the order has become operative and the premises have been vacated, enter and carry out such work as the authority may think requisite for the purpose of destroying or removing vermin; and

(2) the demolition must not be begun or continued by an owner after service of the notice on him, except as mentioned below, until the authority has served on him a further notice authorising him to proceed with the demolition[7].

An owner on whom a notice that the authority intends to cleanse the premises has been so served may, at any time after the premises have been vacated, serve notice in writing on the authority requiring it to carry out the work within 14 days from the receipt of the notice served by him, and at the end of that period is at liberty to proceed with the demolition whether the work has been completed or not[8].

Where the local housing authority serves a notice that it intends to cleanse the premises before demolition, it must not take action to demolish the premises[9] until the expiration of six weeks from the date on which the owner or owners become entitled[10] to proceed with the demolition[11].

1 As to the meaning of 'local housing authority' see PARA 11; and see PARA 620 note 6.
2 As to the meaning of 'premises' see PARA 621 note 13.
3 As to the making of demolition orders see PARA 621.
4 As to when the order becomes operative see PARAS 621 note 14, 622.
5 As to the meaning of 'owner' see PARA 621 note 24.
6 Housing Act 1985 s 273(1). As to service of notice on the owner etc of premises see PARA 17.
7 Housing Act 1985 s 273(2).
8 Housing Act 1985 s 273(3).
9 Ie under the Housing Act 1985 s 271: see PARA 625.
10 Ie by virtue of the Housing Act 1985 s 273(2) or (3): see the text to notes 7–8.
11 Housing Act 1985 s 273(4) (amended by the Local Government and Housing Act 1989 s 165, Sch 9 para 19).

625. Execution of a demolition order. When a demolition order[1] has become operative[2] (and subject to the statutory provisions relating to cleansing before demolition[3], the power to permit reconstruction[4], and use otherwise than for human habitation[5]), the owner[6] of the premises[7] to which the order applies must demolish the premises within the time limited by the order, and if the premises are not demolished within that time the local housing authority[8] must enter and demolish them and sell the materials[9].

Expenses incurred by the local housing authority in executing the demolition order, after giving credit for any amount realised by the sale of materials, may be recovered by the authority from the owner of the premises[10]. If there is more than one owner, the expenses may be recovered by the local housing authority from the owners in such shares as the appropriate tribunal[11] may determine to be just and equitable[12], and an owner who pays to the authority the full amount of its claim may recover from any other owner such contribution, if any, as the appropriate tribunal may determine to be just and equitable[13].

A surplus in the hands of the authority must be paid by the authority to the owner of the premises or, if there is more than one owner, as the owners may agree[14]; and if there is more than one owner and the owners do not agree as to the division of the surplus, the authority is trustee of the surplus for the owners of the premises[15].

1   As to the making of demolition orders see PARA 621.
2   As to when the order becomes operative see PARAS 621 note 14, 622.
3   Ie the Housing Act 1985 s 273: see PARA 624.
4   Ie the Housing Act 1985 s 274: see PARA 626.
5   Ie the Housing Act 1985 s 275: see PARA 627.
6   As to the meaning of 'owner' see PARA 621 note 24.
7   As to the meaning of 'premises' see PARA 621 note 13.
8   As to the meaning of 'local housing authority' see PARA 11; and see PARA 620 note 6.
9   Housing Act 1985 s 271(1), (2).
10 Housing Act 1985 s 272(1).
11 As to the meaning of 'appropriate tribunal' see PARA 622 note 3. As to appeals to the appropriate tribunal see PARA 32 et seq.
12 The appropriate tribunal has jurisdiction to hear and determine proceedings under the Housing Act 1985 s 272(1), (2): s 272(5) (amended by the Housing Act 2004 s 48(1), (3)(b); and by SI 2013/1036). In determining for these purposes the shares in which expenses are to be paid or contributed by, or a surplus divided between, two or more owners of premises, a tribunal or court must have regard to all the circumstances of the case, including: (1) their respective interests in the premises; and (2) their respective obligations and liabilities in respect of maintenance and repair under any covenant or agreement, whether express or implied: Housing Act 1985 s 272(6) (amended by the Housing Act 2004 s 48(3)(c)).
13 Housing Act 1985 s 272(2) (amended by the Housing Act 2004 s 48(3)(a); and by SI 2013/1036).
14 Housing Act 1985 s 272(3).
15 Housing Act 1985 s 272(4). The Trustee Act 1925 s 63 (which relates to payment into court by trustees: see TRUSTS AND POWERS vol 98 (2013) PARA 357) has effect accordingly; and the County Court has jurisdiction thereunder in relation to such a surplus as is referred to in the text: see the Housing Act 1985 s 272(4), (5) (s 272(5) amended by the Crime and Courts Act 2013 s 17(5), Sch 9 para 52(1)(b), (2)). See also note 12.

626. Power to permit reconstruction of condemned house. Where a demolition order[1] has become operative[2], the owner[3] of the premises[4], or any other person who in the opinion of the local housing authority[5] is or will be in a position to put his proposals into effect, may submit proposals to the authority for the execution by him of works designed to secure the reconstruction, enlargement or improvement of the premises, or of buildings including the premises[6].

If the authority is satisfied that the result of the works will be: (1) in the case of a demolition order relating to a category 1 hazard[7], that the hazard concerned ceases to be a category 1 hazard; or (2) in the case of a demolition order relating to a category 2 hazard[8], that a prescribed state of affairs[9] exists, it may, in order that the person submitting the proposals may have an opportunity of carrying out the works, extend for such period as it may specify the time within which the owner of the premises is required[10] to demolish them[11]. That time may be further extended by the authority, once or more often as the case may require, if the works have begun and appear to the authority to be making satisfactory progress or if, though they have not begun, the authority thinks there has been no unreasonable delay[12]. Where the authority determines to extend, or further extend, the time within which the owner of any premises is required to demolish them, notice of the determination must be served by the authority on every person having an interest in the premises or part of the premises, whether as freeholder, mortgagee or otherwise[13].

If the works are completed to the satisfaction of the authority, it must then revoke the demolition order[14].

1   As to the making of demolition orders see PARA 621.
2   As to when the order becomes operative see PARAS 621 note 14, 622.
3   As to the meaning of 'owner' see PARA 621 note 24.
4   As to the meaning of 'premises' see PARA 621 note 13.

5   As to the meaning of 'local housing authority' see PARA 11.
6   Housing Act 1985 s 274(1) (amended by the Local Government and Housing Act 1989 s 165(1)(b), Sch 9 para 20).
7   Ie a demolition order made under the Housing Act 1985 s 265(1) or (2): see PARA 621. As to the meanings of 'category 1 hazard' and 'hazard' see PARA 564; definitions applied by s 322(1) (substituted by the Housing Act 2004 s 265(1), Sch 15 paras 10, 26).
8   Ie a demolition order made under the Housing Act 1985 s 265(3) or (4): see PARA 621. As to the meaning of 'category 2 hazard' see PARA 564 (definition applied by s 322(1) (as substituted: see note 7)).
9   'Prescribed state of affairs' means such state of affairs as may be specified or described in an order made by the appropriate national authority: Housing Act 1985 s 274(3) (s 274(2)–(5) substituted by the Housing Act 2004 Sch 15 para 16). Such an order may make different provision for different cases or descriptions of case (including different provision for different areas), may contain such incidental, supplementary, consequential, transitory, transitional or saving provision as the appropriate national authority considers appropriate, and must be made by statutory instrument subject to annulment in pursuance of a resolution of either House of Parliament or, in relation to Wales, of the National Assembly for Wales: Housing Act 1985 s 274(4) (as so substituted). As to the appropriate national authority, ie the Secretary of State or, where statutory functions have been transferred in relation to Wales, the Welsh Ministers, see PARA 7.
10 Ie under the Housing Act 1985 s 271: see PARA 625.
11 Housing Act 1985 s 274(2) (as substituted: see note 9); and see PARA 620 note 6.
12 Housing Act 1985 s 274(5) (as substituted: see note 9).
13 Housing Act 1985 s 274(6) (s 274(6), (7) added by the Housing Act 2004 Sch 15 para 16).
14 Housing Act 1985 s 274(7) (as added: see note 13). This is without prejudice to any subsequent proceedings under the Housing Act 1985 Pt IX (ss 265–323) or the Housing Act 2004 Pt 1 (ss 1–54): Housing Act 1985 s 274(7) (as so added).

627. Substitution of prohibition order to permit use otherwise than for human habitation. If an owner[1] of any premises[2] in respect of which a demolition order[3] has become operative[4], or any other person who has an interest in the premises, submits proposals to the local housing authority[5] for the use of the premises for a purpose other than human habitation, the authority may, if it thinks fit, determine the demolition order and make a prohibition order[6] in respect of the hazard[7] concerned[8]. The authority must serve notice that the demolition order has been determined, and a copy of the prohibition order, on every person on whom it is required[9] to serve a copy of the prohibition order[10].

1   As to the meaning of 'owner' see PARA 621 note 24.
2   As to the meaning of 'premises' see PARA 621 note 13.
3   As to the making of demolition orders see PARA 621.
4   As to when the order becomes operative see PARAS 621 note 14, 622.
5   As to the meaning of 'local housing authority' see PARA 11.
6   Ie under the Housing Act 2004 s 20 (see PARA 590) or s 21 (see PARA 591).
7   As to the meaning of 'hazard' see PARA 564 (definition applied by the Housing Act 1985 s 322(1) (substituted by the Housing Act 2004 s 265(1), Sch 15 paras 10, 26)).
8   Housing Act 1985 s 275(1) (s 275 substituted by the Housing Act 2004 Sch 15 para 18); and see PARA 620 note 6.
9   Ie by the Housing Act 2004 s 27, Sch 2 Pt 1 (paras 1–2): see PARA 593.
10 Housing Act 1985 s 275(2) (as substituted: see note 8). As to service of notice on a person in control of premises see PARA 17.

(iii) Compensation in respect of Demolition Orders

628. Compensation payable. Where a demolition order[1] is made in respect of any premises[2], the local housing authority[3] must pay to every owner[4] of the premises an amount which must be determined in accordance with the following provisions[5]. The amount to be paid is the diminution in the compulsory purchase value[6] of the owner's interest in the premises as a result of the making of the demolition order, and that amount must be determined:

(1)   as at the date of the making of the order in question; and

(2)   in default of agreement, as if it were compensation payable in respect of the compulsory purchase of the interest in question and must be dealt with accordingly[7].

In any case where a relevant prohibition order[8] has been made in respect of any premises[9] and that order is revoked and a demolition order is made in its place, the amount payable to the owner in connection with the demolition order must be reduced by the amount (if any) paid to the owner or a previous owner in connection with the relevant prohibition order[10].

1 Ie an order under the Housing Act 1985 s 265: see PARA 621. As to compensation where a building is demolished on the execution of an obstructive building order see PARA 630.
2 As to the meaning of 'premises' in relation to a demolition order see PARA 621 note 13 (definition applied by the Housing Act 1985 s 584A(4) (s 584A added by the Local Government and Housing Act 1989 s 165(1), Sch 9 para 75; and substituted by the Housing Act 2004 s 265(1), Sch 15 paras 10, 30).
3 As to the meaning of 'local housing authority' see PARA 11.
4 As to the meaning of 'owner' for these purposes see PARA 606 note 4.
5 Housing Act 1985 s 584A(1) (as added and substituted: see note 2). A person entitled to a payment under s 584A(1) is not also entitled to a disturbance payment under the Land Compensation Act 1973 s 37: see COMPULSORY ACQUISITION OF LAND vol 18 (2009) PARA 838.
6 As to the meaning of 'compulsory purchase value' for these purposes see PARA 606 note 6.
7 Housing Act 1985 s 584A(2) (as added and substituted: see note 2).
8 As to the meaning of 'relevant prohibition order' see PARA 606 note 1.
9 As to the meaning of 'premises', in relation to a prohibition order, see PARA 606 note 1.
10 Housing Act 1985 s 584A(3) (as added and substituted: see note 2).

629. Repayment of compensation on revocation of demolition order. Where a payment in respect of any premises[1] has been made by a local housing authority[2] in connection with a demolition order[3] and the demolition order is later revoked[4], then, if at that time the person to whom the payment was made has the same interest in the premises as he had at the time the payment was made, he must on demand repay to the authority the amount of the payment[5].

1 As to the meaning of 'premises' see PARA 628 note 2 (definition applied by the Housing Act 1985 s 584B(7) (s 584B added by the Local Government and Housing Act 1989 s 165(1), Sch 9 para 75; and substituted by the Housing Act 2004 s 265(1), Sch 15 paras 10, 31)).
2 Ie under the Housing Act 1985 s 584A(1): see PARA 628. As to the meaning of 'local housing authority' see PARA 11.
3 As to demolition orders see PARA 621.
4 Ie under the Housing Act 1985 s 274: see PARA 626.
5 Housing Act 1985 s 584B(1) (as added and substituted: see note 1).

(iv) Obstructive Buildings

630. Compensation payable on demolition of obstructive building. Where a building is demolished on the execution of an obstructive building order[1], whether by the owner[2] or by the local housing authority[3], compensation must be paid by the authority to the owner in respect of loss arising from the demolition[4]. The compensation must be assessed in accordance with Part I of the Land Compensation Act 1961[5], but in assessing the compensation no allowance may be made on account of the demolition being compulsory[6].

1 Ie under the Housing Act 1985 s 287 (repealed by the Housing Act 2004 ss 52, 266, Sch 16).
2 As to the meaning of 'owner' see PARA 621 note 24.
3 As to the meaning of 'local housing authority' see PARA 11.
4 Housing Act 1985 s 597(1). As to compensation when a demolition order is made see PARAS 628–629.
5 Ie the Land Compensation Act 1961 Pt I (ss 1–4): see COMPULSORY ACQUISITION OF LAND vol 18 (2009) PARA 753 et seq.
6 Housing Act 1985 s 597(2), (3).

(v) Clearance Areas

631. Background and general introduction. A local housing authority has powers to use a clearance area procedure where, after a survey, it is satisfied that this is the most satisfactory way of dealing with housing conditions in the area[1]. A consultation exercise with those who will be directly affected by the making of a clearance area order, such as freeholders, lessees and mortgagees of the buildings affected, must be undertaken before the clearance area is declared[2]. It has been clear policy for some time that the clearance and compulsory purchase area procedures should only be used where there is a very compelling case for their use on the grounds of public interest, and the burden of justification lies with the acquiring authority[3].

1 See PARA 632 et seq; and PARA 620 note 6.
2 See PARA 632.
3 See eg DETR Circular 17/96 Annex B para 68; DOE Circular 5/93 para 1. See also Hughes and Lowe *Social Housing Law and Policy* (1995) pp 331–332. And see also CIR 05/01 Housing Grants, Construction and Regeneration Act 1996: Part I—Amendments to the renovation grant system (2001).

632. Declaration of clearance area. A clearance area is an area which is to be cleared of all buildings in accordance with the relevant statutory provisions[1]. If the local housing authority[2] is satisfied, in relation to any area, that each of the residential buildings[3] in the area contains a category 1 hazard[4], and that the other buildings (if any) in the area are dangerous or harmful to the health or safety of the inhabitants of the area, declaring the area to be a clearance area is a course of action available to the authority in relation to the hazard or hazards for the purposes of the general duty under the Housing Act 2004[5] to take enforcement action[6].

The local housing authority may declare an area to be a clearance area if it is satisfied that the residential buildings in the area are dangerous or harmful to the health or safety of the inhabitants of the area as a result of their bad arrangement or the narrowness or bad arrangement of the streets[7], and that the other buildings (if any) in the area are dangerous or harmful to the health or safety of the inhabitants of the area[8].

The local housing authority may declare an area to be a clearance area if it is satisfied that each of the residential buildings in the area contains a category 2 hazard[9], that the other buildings (if any) in the area are dangerous or harmful to the health or safety of the inhabitants of the area, and the circumstances of the case are circumstances specified or described in an order made by the appropriate national authority[10].

Before declaring an area to be a clearance area, the authority must:

(1)   serve notice of its intention to include a building in the clearance area on every person who has an interest in the building (whether as freeholder, lessee or mortgagee) and also, in the case of a residential building, on every person who has such an interest in any flat in the building, inviting representations from such a person within such reasonable period[11] as may be specified in the notice[12]; and

(2)   take reasonable steps to inform any occupiers of a residential building who do not have such an interest in the building or a flat in the building as is referred to in head (1) of the authority's intention to include the building in the clearance area, inviting representations from those occupiers within such reasonable period[13] as may be specified by the authority[14]; and

(3)   publish in two or more newspapers circulating in the locality (of which one at least must, if practicable, be a local newspaper) notice of the authority's intention to declare the area to be a clearance area, inviting representations from any interested persons within such reasonable period[15] as may be specified in the notice[16].

The authority must consider all representations duly made and, in the light of the representations, must take whichever of the following decisions the authority thinks appropriate, that is to say it may:

(a)   decide to declare the area to be a clearance area; or

(b)   decide to declare the area to be a clearance area but exclude such residential buildings which contain category 1 or category 2 hazards as the authority thinks fit; or

(c)   decide not to declare the area to be a clearance area[17].

Where the authority decides to declare an area to be a clearance area in accordance with head (a) or head (b), it must cause the area to be defined on a map in such manner as to exclude from the area:

(i)   any residential building which is not dangerous or harmful to health or safety;

(ii)   any other building which is not dangerous or harmful to health or safety; and

(iii)   any residential buildings which, by virtue of head (b), the authority has decided to exclude from the area,

and must pass a resolution declaring the area so defined to be a clearance area[18]. However, before passing such a resolution, the authority must satisfy itself that, in so far as suitable accommodation does not already exist for the persons who will be displaced by the clearance of the area, the authority can provide, or secure the provision of, such accommodation in advance of the displacements which will from time to time become necessary as the demolition of the buildings in the area, or in different parts of it, proceeds, and that the resources of the authority are sufficient for the purposes of carrying the resolution into effect[19]. The authority must forthwith transmit to the appropriate national authority a copy of any resolution so passed, together with a statement of the number of persons who on a day specified in the statement were occupying the buildings comprised in the clearance area[20].

The local housing authority may include in a clearance area land belonging to the authority which it might have included in the area if it had not belonged to the authority, and the clearance area provisions[21] apply to land so included as they apply to land purchased by the authority as being comprised in the clearance area[22].

1   Housing Act 1985 s 289(1). The statutory provisions referred to are those of ss 290–323: see PARA 633 et seq.

2   As to the meaning of 'local housing authority' see PARA 11.

3   For the purposes of the Housing Act 1985 s 289, 'residential buildings' means buildings which are dwellings or houses in multiple occupation or contain one or more flats: s 289(2ZC) (s 289(2ZA)–(2ZE) added by the Housing Act 2004 s 47). As to the meaning of 'house in multiple occupation' see PARA 621 note 4. As to the meaning of 'flat' see PARA 563 note 13 (definition applied by the Housing Act 1985 s 322(1) (substituted by the Housing Act 2004 s 265(1), Sch 15 paras 10, 26)). This is subject to the Housing Act 1985 s 289(2ZD): s 289(2ZC) (as so added). For the purposes of s 289(2) or (2ZB), s 289(2ZC) applies as if 'two or more flats' were substituted for 'one or more flats'; and a residential building containing two or more flats is only to be treated as containing a category 1 or category 2 hazard if two or more of the flats within it contain such a hazard: s 289(2ZD) (as so added).

4   As to the meaning of 'category 1 hazard' see PARA 564 (definition applied by the Housing Act 1985 s 322(1) (as substituted: see note 3)).

5 Ie under the Housing Act 2004 s 5: see PARA 566.
6 Housing Act 1985 s 289(2) (substituted by the Housing Act 2004 s 47); and see PARA 620 note 6. The provisions of the Housing Act 1985 s 289(2), (2ZA), (2ZB) are subject to those of s 289(2B)–(2F), (3), (4) and (5B): s 289(2ZE) (as added: see note 3).
7 As to the meaning of 'street' see PARA 409 note 2.
8 Housing Act 1985 s 289(2ZA) (as added: see note 3). See note 6.
9 As to the meaning of 'category 2 hazard' see PARA 564 (definition applied by the Housing Act 1985 s 322(1) (as substituted: see note 3)).
10 Housing Act 1985 s 289(2ZB) (as added: see note 3). See note 6. As to the appropriate national authority, ie the Secretary of State or, where statutory functions have been transferred in relation to Wales, the Welsh Ministers, see PARA 7. The provision as to the making of orders (ie s 265(8): see PARA 621 note 17) applies in relation to an order under s 289(2ZB) as it applies in relation to an order under s 265(3) or (4) (see PARA 621): s 289(2ZB) (as so added).
11 A notice so served must invite representations from the person on whom the notice was served within such reasonable period, being not less than 28 days after the date on which the notice is served, as may be specified in the notice: Housing Act 1985 s 289(2C) (s 289(2A)–(2F), (5A), (5B) added, and s 289(2), (3) amended, by the Local Government and Housing Act 1989 ss 165(1)(b), 194(1), Sch 9 para 25, Sch 11 para 70; the Housing Act 1985 s 289(2A) substituted by the Housing Act 2004 s 47).
12 See the Housing Act 1985 s 289(2B)(a), (2C) (as added: see note 11). As to service of notice on a person having an interest in premises see PARA 17.
13 The authority must, by the steps taken in relation to occupiers of a residential building as mentioned in head (b) in the text, invite representations from those occupiers within such reasonable period, expiring not less than 28 days after the date on which the steps are taken, as may be specified by the authority: Housing Act 1985 s 289(2D) (as added: see note 11).
14 See the Housing Act 1985 s 289(2)(b), (2D) (as added: see note 11).
15 A notice published in accordance with head (3) in the text must invite representations from any interested persons within such reasonable period, being not less than 28 days after the date on which the notice is published, as may be specified in the notice: Housing Act 1985 s 289(2E) (as added: see note 11).
16 See the Housing Act 1985 s 289(2)(c), (2E) (as added: see note 11).
17 Housing Act 1985 s 289(2F) (as added (see note 11); amended by the Housing Act 2004 Sch 15 para 19(1), (2)).
18 Housing Act 1985 s 289(3) (as amended (see note 11); further amended by the Housing Act 2004 Sch 15 para 19(3)). Subject to the Housing Act 1985 s 578A (see below), a clearance area may not include any parcel of land which is not contiguous with another parcel of land within the area; and, where the effect of s 289(3) would otherwise be that a clearance area would comprise two or more separate and distinct areas s 289(3)(b) has effect with modifications: see s 289(5B) (as added: see note 11). Where the local housing authority makes a compulsory purchase order, within the meaning of the Acquisition of Land Act 1981, in respect of land it has determined to purchase under the Housing Act 1985 s 290 (acquisition of land comprised, surrounded by or adjoining a clearance area: see PARA 633), the appropriate national authority may, in accordance with the Acquisition of Land Act 1981 s 13 and ss 13A–13C (confirmation of order: see COMPULSORY ACQUISITION OF LAND vol 18 (2009) PARA 565 et seq), confirm the order with modifications notwithstanding that the effect of the modifications made by him in excluding any land or buildings from the clearance area concerned is to sever the area into two or more separate and distinct areas; and, in such a case, the severance does not prevent those areas from continuing to be treated as one clearance area for the purposes of the provisions of the Housing Act 1985 Pt IX (ss 265–323): s 578A(1), (2) (added by the Local Government and Housing Act 1989 Sch 9 para 72; the Housing Act 1985 s 578A(2) amended by the Planning and Compulsory Purchase Act 2004 s 118(2), Sch 7 para 13).
19 Housing Act 1985 s 289(4). 'Suitable accommodation' means suitable dwelling accommodation: *Re Gateshead County Borough (Barn Close) Clearance Order 1931* [1933] 1 KB 429.
20 Housing Act 1985 s 289(5).
21 Ie the provisions of the Housing Act 1985 Pt IX.
22 Housing Act 1985 s 293(1).

633. Acquisition of land for clearance. As soon as the local housing authority[1] has declared an area to be a clearance area[2], it must proceed to secure the clearance of the area[3] by purchasing the land comprised in the area and itself undertaking, or otherwise securing, the demolition of the buildings on the land[4]. Where the authority determines to purchase land comprised in a clearance area, it may also purchase:

(1)   land which is surrounded by the clearance area and the acquisition of which is reasonably necessary for the purpose of securing a cleared area of convenient shape and dimensions; and

(2)   adjoining land the acquisition of which is reasonably necessary for the satisfactory development or use of the cleared area[5].

Where the authority has so determined to purchase land, it may purchase it by agreement or be authorised by the appropriate national authority[6] to purchase the land compulsorily[7] and the powers so conferred are exercisable notwithstanding that any of the buildings within the area have been demolished since the area was declared to be a clearance area[8].

Where land belonging to the local housing authority is surrounded by or adjoins a clearance area and might, had it not previously been acquired by the authority, have been purchased by the authority under the powers set out in heads (1) and (2), the clearance area provisions[9] apply to that land as they apply to land purchased by the authority as being surrounded by or adjoining the clearance area[10].

1 As to the meaning of 'local housing authority' see PARA 11.
2 As to the meaning of 'clearance area' see PARA 632.
3 Ie subject to and in accordance with the provisions of the Housing Act 1985 Pt IX (ss 265–323).
4 Housing Act 1985 s 290(1); and see PARA 620 note 6.
5 Housing Act 1985 s 290(2). See *Coleen Properties Ltd v Minister of Housing and Local Government* [1971] 1 All ER 1049, [1971] 1 WLR 433, CA; *Gosling v Secretary of State for the Environment* [1975] JPL 406; *Bass Charrington (North) Ltd v Minister of Housing and Local Government* (1970) 22 P & CR 31 (land must be partially contiguous with land in the clearance area); and see also *Sheffield Burgesses v Minister of Health* (1935) 154 LT 183.
6 As to the appropriate national authority, ie the Secretary of State or, where statutory functions have been transferred in relation to Wales, the Welsh Ministers, see PARA 7.
7 Housing Act 1985 s 290(3). As to compulsory purchase see PARA 812 et seq.
8 Housing Act 1985 s 290(4). See *Rowe v First Secretary of State, Burnley Borough Council v First Secretary of State* [2006] EWHC 798 (Admin), [2006] All ER (D) 149 (Mar).
9 Ie the provisions of the Housing Act 1985 Pt IX.
10 Housing Act 1985 s 293(2).

634. Method of dealing with land acquired for clearance and power to discontinue proceedings. A local housing authority[1] which has purchased land for clearance[2] must, so soon as may be, cause every building on the land to be vacated and deal with the land in one or other of the following ways, or partly in one of those ways and partly in the other, that is to say:

(1)   itself demolish every building on the land within the period of six weeks from the date on which the building is vacated or such longer period as in the circumstances the authority considers reasonable, and thereafter appropriate or dispose of the land[3], subject to such restrictions and conditions, if any, as the authority thinks fit; or

(2)   dispose of the land as soon as may be subject to a condition that the buildings on it be demolished forthwith, and subject to such restrictions and other conditions, if any, as the authority thinks fit[4].

These provisions have effect subject to the statutory power to retain premises for temporary housing use[5] and the statutory suspension of the clearance procedure[6] on a building becoming listed[7].

Where the local housing authority has submitted to the appropriate national authority[8] an order for the compulsory purchase of land in a clearance area and the appropriate national authority, on an application being made to him by the owner[9] or owners of the land and the authority, is satisfied:

(a)   that the owner or owners of the land, with the concurrence of any
          mortgagee of the land, agree to the demolition of the buildings on the
          land; and

(b)   that the authority can secure the proper clearance of the area without
          acquiring the land,

the appropriate national authority may authorise the authority to discontinue
proceedings for the purchase of the land on the authority's being satisfied that
such covenants have been or will be entered into by all necessary parties as may
be requisite for securing that the buildings will be demolished, and the land
become subject to the like restrictions and conditions, as if the authority had dealt
with the land in accordance with the above provisions[10].

1   As to the meaning of 'local housing authority' see PARA 11.
2   Ie under the Housing Act 1985 s 290: see PARA 633.
3   These references to appropriation or disposal are references to appropriation or disposal under the
    general powers conferred by the Local Government Act 1972 s 122 or s 123 (see LOCAL
    GOVERNMENT vol 69 (2009) PARAS 513, 515): Housing Act 1985 s 291(4).
4   Housing Act 1985 s 291(1), (2); and see PARA 620 note 6. See *A-G (at the relation of Martin) v
    Finsbury Borough Council* [1939] Ch 892, [1939] 3 All ER 995.
5   Ie the Housing Act 1985 s 301: see PARA 639.
6   Ie the Housing Act 1985 ss 305, 306: see PARAS 642–643.
7   Housing Act 1985 s 291(3) (amended by the Local Government and Housing Act 1989
    ss 165(1)(b), 194(4), Sch 9 para 26, Sch 12 Pt II).
8   As to the appropriate national authority, ie the Secretary of State or, where statutory functions
    have been transferred in relation to Wales, the Welsh Ministers, see PARA 7.
9   As to the meaning of 'owner' see PARA 621 note 24.
10 Housing Act 1985 s 292.

635. Extinguishment of public rights of way over land acquired. The local
housing authority[1] may, with the approval of the appropriate national authority[2],
by order extinguish any public right of way over land acquired by the authority
for clearance[3] as from such date as the appropriate national authority in
approving the order may direct[4]. Where the authority has resolved to purchase
land for clearance over which a public right of way exists, an order made by the
authority in advance of the purchase and approved by the appropriate national
authority (whether before or after the purchase) extinguishes that right as from
such date as the appropriate national authority in approving the order may
direct[5]. The order must be published in such manner as may be prescribed[6], and
if objection to the order is made to the appropriate national authority before the
expiration of four weeks from its publication then the order must not be approved
until the appropriate national authority has caused a public local inquiry to be
held into the matter[7], although such an inquiry may be dispensed with if the
appropriate national authority is satisfied that in the special circumstances of the
case the holding of such an inquiry is unnecessary[8].

Where a public right of way over land is extinguished by such an order and
immediately before the order comes into operation there is under, in, on, over,
along or across the land electronic communications apparatus[9] kept installed for
the purposes of an electronic communications code network[10], the powers of the
operator[11] of the network in respect of the apparatus are not affected by the
order[12]. However, any person entitled to the land over which the right of way
subsisted may require the alteration of the apparatus, and the procedure in the
electronic communications code[13] for exercise of right to require removal of
apparatus[14] applies[15].

1   As to the meaning of 'local housing authority' see PARA 11.

2   As to the appropriate national authority, ie the Secretary of State or, where statutory functions have been transferred in relation to Wales, the Welsh Ministers, see PARA 7.

3   Ie acquired under the Housing Act 1985 s 290: see PARA 633.

4   Housing Act 1985 s 294(1) (s 294(1)–(3) amended by the Local Government and Housing Act 1989 s 165(1)(b), Sch 9 para 27); and see PARA 620 note 6.

5   Housing Act 1985 s 294(2) (as amended: see note 4).

6   For the prescribed form of the order and of notice of the making of the order see the Housing (Prescribed Forms) Regulations 1990, SI 1990/447, reg 2(1), Schedule, Forms 1, 2 (Form 2 amended by SI 1997/2971).

7   Housing Act 1985 s 294(3) (as amended: see note 4).

8   Housing Act 1985 s 294(4) (added by the Local Government and Housing Act 1989 Sch 9 para 27).

9   As to the meaning of 'electronic communications apparatus' see TELECOMMUNICATIONS vol 97 (2015) PARA 168 note 6.

10 As to the meaning of 'electronic communications code network' see TELECOMMUNICATIONS vol 97 (2015) PARA 179 note 3.

11 As to the meaning of 'operator' see TELECOMMUNICATIONS vol 97 (2015) PARA 179 note 4.

12 Housing Act 1985 s 298(2) (amended by the Communications Act 2003 s 406(1), Sch 17 para 79(1), (3)).

13 As to the meaning of 'electronic communications code' see TELECOMMUNICATIONS vol 97 (2015) PARA 155 note 1.

14 Ie the Telecommunication Act 1984 Sch 2 para 21: see TELECOMMUNICATIONS vol 97 (2015) PARA 189.

15 Housing Act 1985 s 298(2) (as amended: see note 12).

636. Extinguishment of other rights over land acquired. Upon the completion by the local housing authority[1] of the purchase by it of land acquired for clearance[2], all private rights of way over the land, all rights of laying down, erecting, continuing or maintaining apparatus on, under or over the land, and all other rights or easements in or relating to the land, are extinguished and any such apparatus vests in the authority, subject to any agreement which may be made between the local housing authority and the person in or to whom the right or apparatus is vested or belongs, and subject also to the statutory provisions regarding the rights and apparatus of statutory undertakers[3] and certain operators of electronic communications networks[4]. A person who suffers loss by the extinguishment of any right or the vesting of any apparatus under this provision is entitled to be paid compensation[5] by the local housing authority[6].

These extinguishment and vesting provisions do not apply to:

(1)   any right vested in statutory undertakers[7] of laying down, erecting, continuing or maintaining any apparatus[8]; or

(2)   any apparatus belonging to statutory undertakers[9]; or

(3)   any right conferred by or in accordance with the electronic communications code[10] on the operator[11] of an electronic communications code network[12]; or

(4)   electronic communications apparatus[13] kept installed for the purposes of such a network[14].

Where, however, the removal or alteration of apparatus[15] belonging to statutory undertakers on, under or over land purchased by a local housing authority for clearance, or on, under or over a street[16] running over, or through, or adjoining any such land, is reasonably necessary for the purpose of enabling the authority to exercise any of the powers conferred on it by the statutory provisions relating to clearance areas[17], the authority may execute works for the removal or alteration of the apparatus[18], subject to and in accordance with the following provisions[19].

A local housing authority which intends to remove or alter apparatus in exercise of the power so conferred:

(a) must serve on the undertakers notice in writing of the authority's intention with particulars of the proposed works and of the manner in which they are to be executed and plans and sections of them; and

(b) must not commence any works until the expiration of the period of 28 days from the date of service of that notice,

and within that period the undertakers may, by notice in writing served on the authority, make objections to, or state requirements with respect to, the proposed works as follows[20]. The undertakers may object to the execution of the works, or any of them, on the ground that they are not reasonably necessary for the specified purpose[21]; and if objection is so made to any works and not withdrawn, the authority must not execute the works unless they are determined by arbitration to be so necessary[22]. The undertakers may state requirements to which, in their opinion, effect ought to be given as to the manner of, or the conditions to be observed in, the execution of the works, or as to the execution of other works for the protection of other apparatus belonging to the undertakers or for the provision of substituted apparatus, whether permanent or temporary; and if any such requirement is so made and not withdrawn, the authority must give effect to it unless it is determined by arbitration to be unreasonable[23]. At least seven days before commencing any works which it is authorised or required by the above provisions to execute, the local housing authority must, except in cases of emergency, serve on the undertakers notice in writing of its intention to do so; and the works must be executed by the authority under the superintendence (at the expense of the authority) and to the reasonable satisfaction of the undertakers[24]. If, however, within seven days from the date of service on them of such a notice the undertakers so elect, they must themselves execute the works in accordance with the reasonable directions and to the reasonable satisfaction of the authority; and the reasonable costs of the works must be repaid to the undertakers by the authority[25].

The local housing authority must make reasonable compensation to statutory undertakers for any damage sustained by the undertakers by reason of the execution by the authority of works under these powers and not made good by the provision of substituted apparatus; and any question as to the right of undertakers to recover such compensation or as to its amount must be referred to and determined by the Upper Tribunal[26].

1 As to the meaning of 'local housing authority' see PARA 11.
2 Ie under the Housing Act 1985 s 290: see PARA 633.
3 Ie subject to the Housing Act 1985 ss 296, 298: see the text and notes 8–14.
4 See the Housing Act 1985 s 295(1), (2) (s 295(2) amended by the Communications Act 2003 s 406(1), Sch 17 para 79(1), (2)). It was held under corresponding earlier legislation that this provision applied to ancient lights in buildings adjoining the purchased lands: *Badham v Marris* (1881) 52 LJ Ch 237n. See also *Swainston v Finn and Metropolitan Board of Works* (1883) 52 LJ Ch 235 (rights of support); *Barlow v Ross* (1890) 24 QBD 381, CA; *Re Harvey and LCC* [1909] 1 Ch 528 (rights to light).
5 The compensation is to be determined under and in accordance with the Land Compensation Act 1961 (see COMPULSORY ACQUISITION OF LAND vol 18 (2009) PARA 753 et seq): Housing Act 1985 s 295(3).
6 Housing Act 1985 s 295(3).
7 For these purposes, 'statutory undertakers' means persons authorised by an enactment, or by an order, rule or regulation made under an enactment, to construct, work or carry on a railway, canal, inland navigation, dock, harbour, tramway, gas or other public undertaking; and 'apparatus' means sewers, drains, culverts, water-courses, mains, pipes, valves, tubes, cables, wires, transformers and other apparatus laid down or used for or in connection with the carrying, conveying or supplying to any premises of a supply of water, water for hydraulic power, gas or

electricity, and standards and brackets carrying street lamps: Housing Act 1985 s 296(4)(a), (b) (amended by the Water Act 1989 s 190(3), Sch 27 Pt I; and the Electricity Act 1989 s 112(4), Sch 18).

8   Housing Act 1985 s 296(1)(a).

9   Housing Act 1985 s 296(1)(b).

10   As to the meaning of 'electronic communications code' see TELECOMMUNICATIONS vol 97 (2015) PARA 151 note 1.

11   As to the meaning of 'operator' see TELECOMMUNICATIONS vol 97 (2015) PARA 179 note 4.

12   Housing Act 1985 s 298(3)(a) (s 298(3) amended by the Communications Act 2003 Sch 17 para 79(3)). As to the meaning of 'electronic communications code network' see TELECOMMUNICATIONS vol 97 (2015) PARA 179 note 3.

13   As to the meaning of 'electronic communications apparatus' see TELECOMMUNICATIONS vol 97 (2015) PARA 168 note 6.

14   Housing Act 1985 s 298(3)(b) (as amended: see note 12). However, where it is reasonably necessary for the purpose of enabling the local housing authority to exercise any of the powers conferred on the authority by the clearance area provisions, the authority may execute works for the alteration of such apparatus, and the procedure in the electronic communications code for works involving alteration of apparatus (ie the Telecommunications Act 1984 Sch 2 para 23: see TELECOMMUNICATIONS vol 97 (2015) PARAS 190–191) applies: Housing Act 1985 s 298(3) (as so amended).

15   For these purposes, references to the alteration of apparatus include references to diversion and to the alteration of position or level: Housing Act 1985 s 296(4)(c).

16   As to the meaning of 'street' see PARA 409 note 2.

17   Ie any of the provisions of the Housing Act 1985 Pt IX (ss 265–323): see PARAS 621 et seq, 638 et seq.

18   Ie subject to the Housing Act 1985 s 297: see the text and notes 20–25.

19   Housing Act 1985 s 296(2); and see PARA 620 note 6.

20   Housing Act 1985 s 297(1).

21   Ie the purpose mentioned in the Housing Act 1985 s 296(2): see the text to notes 15–19.

22   Housing Act 1985 s 297(2). Any matter which by virtue of s 297(2) or (3) (see the text and note 23) is to be determined by arbitration, and any difference arising between statutory undertakers and a local housing authority under s 297(4) (see the text and note 24) or s 297(5) (see the text and note 25), must be referred to and determined by an arbitrator to be appointed, in default of agreement, by the appropriate national authority: s 297(6).

23   Housing Act 1985 s 297(3). See note 22.

24   Housing Act 1985 s 297(4). See note 22.

25   Housing Act 1985 s 297(5). See note 22.

26   Housing Act 1985 s 296(3) (amended by SI 2009/1307). As to the Upper Tribunal, ie the Upper Tribunal (Lands Chamber), the successor to the Lands Tribunal, see COMPULSORY ACQUISITION OF LAND vol 18 (2009) PARA 720 et seq.

637. Power to compensate shop-keepers in areas affected by clearance. Where, as a result of action taken by a local housing authority[1] under the provisions of Part IX of the Housing Act 1985[2] relating to clearance areas[3], the population of the locality is materially decreased, the authority may pay to any person carrying on a retail shop in the locality such reasonable allowance as it thinks fit towards any loss involving personal hardship which in the authority's opinion he will thereby sustain, but in estimating any such loss the authority must have regard to the probable future development of the locality[4].

1   As to the meaning of 'local housing authority' see PARA 11.

2   Ie under the provisions of the Housing Act 1985 Pt IX (ss 265–323).

3   As to clearance areas see PARA 631 et seq.

4   Housing Act 1985 s 596.

(vi) Use of Condemned Houses for Temporary Housing Accommodation

638. Purchase of houses liable to be demolished or to be subject to a prohibition order. Where the local housing authority[1] would be required[2] to make a demolition order[3] relating to a category 1 hazard[4] in respect of a dwelling[5], a house in multiple occupation[6] or a building containing one or more flats[7], and it appears to the authority that the dwelling, house in multiple occupation or, as the case may be, building is or can be rendered capable of providing accommodation of a standard which is adequate for the time being, it may purchase it instead, with a view to letting it[8].

Where an authority has so determined to purchase any premises, it must serve a notice of its determination on the persons on whom it would have been required[9] to serve a copy of a demolition order, and the statutory provisions as to the operative date[10] and the right of appeal[11] apply to such a notice as they apply to a demolition order[12].

Where the local housing authority would be required[13] to make a relevant prohibition order[14] in respect of a dwelling, a house in multiple occupation or a building containing one or more flats, and it appears to the authority that the dwelling, house in multiple occupation or, as the case may be, building is or can be rendered capable of providing accommodation of a standard which is adequate for the time being, it may purchase it instead, with a view to letting it[15].

Where an authority has so determined to purchase any premises, it must serve a notice of its determination on the persons on whom it would have been required[16] to serve a copy of the relevant prohibition order, and the statutory provisions as to the operative date[17] and the right of appeal[18] apply to such a notice as they apply to a prohibition order which is not suspended or to appeals against such an order (as the case may be)[19].

At any time after a notice of a determination to purchase has become operative the authority may purchase the dwelling, house in multiple occupation or building by agreement or be authorised by the appropriate national authority[20] to purchase it compulsorily[21], unless it is a listed building[22] or a building which is protected pending listing[23].

1   As to the meaning of 'local housing authority' see PARA 11.
2   Ie under the Housing Act 2004 s 5: see PARA 566.
3   As to demolition orders see PARA 621.
4   Ie under the Housing Act 1985 s 265(1) or (2): see PARA 621. As to the meaning of 'category 1 hazard' see PARA 564 (definition applied by s 322(1) (substituted by the Housing Act 2004 s 265(1), Sch 15 paras 10, 26)).
5   As to the meaning of 'dwelling' see PARA 563 note 10 (definition applied by the Housing Act 1985 s 322(1) (as substituted: see note 4)).
6   As to the meaning of 'house in multiple occupation' see PARA 621 note 4.
7   As to the meaning of 'building containing one or more flats' see PARA 563 note 13 (definition applied by the Housing Act 1985 s 322(1) (as substituted: see note 4)).
8   Housing Act 1985 s 300(1) (s 300 substituted by the Housing Act 2004 Sch 15 para 20); and see PARA 620 note 6. This power to purchase is to provide temporary accommodation pending demolition, not to acquire permanent additions to the authority's housing stock: *Victoria Square Property Co Ltd v Southwark London Borough Council* [1978] 2 All ER 281, [1978] 1 WLR 463, CA (decided under previous legislation).
9   Ie by the Housing Act 1985 s 268(1): see PARA 621.
10 Ie the Housing Act 1985 s 268(4): see PARA 621 note 14.
11 Ie the Housing Act 1985 s 269(1)–(3), (6): see PARA 622.
12 Housing Act 1985 s 300(4) (as substituted: see note 8).
13 See note 2.
14 'Relevant prohibition order' means a prohibition order under the Housing Act 2004 s 20 (see PARA 590) which imposes in relation to the whole of the dwelling, house in multiple occupation or building a prohibition on its use for all purposes other than any purpose approved by the authority: Housing Act 1985 s 300(3) (as substituted: see note 8).
15 Housing Act 1985 s 300(2) (as substituted: see note 8).
16 Ie by the Housing Act 2004 s 27, Sch 2 Pt 1 (paras 1–2): see PARA 593.
17 Ie the Housing Act 2004 s 24: see PARA 595.
18 Ie the Housing Act 2004 Sch 2 Pts 1, 3 (paras 1–2, 7–16): see PARAS 593, 598 et seq.
19 Housing Act 1985 s 300(5) (as substituted: see note 8).

20 As to the appropriate national authority, ie the Secretary of State or, where statutory functions have been transferred in relation to Wales, the Welsh Ministers, see PARA 7.
21 Housing Act 1985 s 300(6) (as substituted: see note 8).
22 As to the meaning of 'listed building' see PARA 621 note 22.
23 Housing Act 1985 s 300(7) (as substituted: see note 8), disapplying s 300 where s 304(1) (see PARA 641) applies.

639. Retention of houses acquired for clearance. Having declared an area to be a clearance area[1], a local housing authority[2] may postpone for such period as it may determine the demolition of residential buildings[3] on land purchased by it within the area if, in the authority's opinion, the residential buildings are or can be rendered capable of providing accommodation of a standard which is adequate for the time being[4]. Where the local housing authority is satisfied that a residential building on land purchased by it within a clearance area which is not retained by the authority for temporary use for housing purposes is required for the support of a residential building which is so retained, or should not be demolished for the time being for some other special reason connected with the exercise in relation to the clearance area of the authority's powers, the authority may retain the residential building for the time being and is not required to demolish it so long as it is required for that purpose or, as the case may be, so long as those powers are being exercised by the authority in relation to that area[5].

Where the demolition of any residential buildings in a clearance area is postponed under these provisions, the local housing authority may also postpone the taking of proceedings under the statutory power of acquisition of land for clearance[6] in respect of buildings other than residential buildings within the area[7].

1 As to the meaning of 'clearance area' see PARA 632.
2 As to the meaning of 'local housing authority' see PARA 11.
3 For these purposes, 'residential building' has the same meaning as it has in the Housing Act 1985 s 289 (see PARA 632 note 3): s 301(4) (s 301(1)–(3) amended, and s 301(4) added, by the Local Government and Housing Act 1989 s 165(1)(b), Sch 9 para 30).
4 Housing Act 1985 s 301(1) (as amended: see note 3); and see PARA 620 note 6.
5 Housing Act 1985 s 301(2) (as amended: see note 3). As to how long demolition may be postponed see *R v Birmingham City Corpn, ex p Sale* (1983) 9 HLR 33. Properties retained under these provisions may be below the standard of fitness but must not be in such a condition as to be prejudicial to health or a statutory nuisance: see *Nottingham Corpn v Newton, Nottingham Friendship Housing Association Ltd v Newton* [1974] 2 All ER 760, [1974] 1 WLR 923; *Salford City Council v McNally* [1976] AC 379, [1975] 2 All ER 860, HL (both cases decided under previous legislation).
6 Ie under the Housing Act 1985 s 290(1): see PARA 633.
7 Housing Act 1985 s 301(3) (as amended: see note 3).

640. Management and repair of houses acquired or retained. Where a residential building[1] is acquired by a local housing authority[2] or retained by a local housing authority[3] for temporary use for housing purposes, the authority has the like powers in respect of that building as it has in respect of dwellings provided by the authority under its statutory powers[4] to provide housing accommodation[5]. The authority may carry out such works as may from time to time be required for rendering and keeping the residential building capable of providing accommodation of a standard which is adequate for the time being pending its demolition[6]. The implied condition of fitness for human habitation[7] does not, however, apply to a contract for the letting of the residential building or any flat[8] in the building by the authority[9].

1 For these purposes, 'residential building' has the same meaning as it has in the Housing Act 1985 s 289 (see PARA 632 note 3): s 301(4) (added by the Local Government and Housing Act 1989 s 165(1)(b), Sch 9 para 30).
2 Ie under the Housing Act 1985 s 300: see PARA 638. As to the meaning of 'local housing authority' see PARA 11.

3 Ie under the Housing Act 1985 s 301: see PARA 639.
4 Ie under the Housing Act 1985 Pt II (ss 8–57): see PARA 405 et seq.
5 Housing Act 1985 s 302(a) (s 302 amended by the Local Government and Housing Act 1989 Sch 9 para 31); and see PARA 620 note 6.
6 Housing Act 1985 s 302(b) (as amended: see note 5).
7 Ie under the Landlord and Tenant Act 1985 s 8: see LANDLORD AND TENANT vol 62 (2016) PARA 311. However, the effect of *Salford City Council v McNally* [1976] AC 379, [1975] 2 All ER 860, HL, should be noted.
8 As to the meaning of 'flat' see PARA 563 note 13 (definition applied by the Housing Act 1985 s 322(1) (substituted by the Housing Act 2004 s 265(1), Sch 15 paras 10, 26)).
9 Housing Act 1985 s 302(c) (as amended: see note 5).

(vii) Listed Buildings

641. Prohibition on making of demolition order in respect of listed building. A local housing authority[1] must not make a demolition order[2] in respect of a listed building (that is under the Planning (Listed Buildings and Conservation Areas) Act 1990)[3].

Where a dwelling[4], house in multiple occupation[5] or building in respect of which a demolition order has been made becomes a listed building, the local housing authority must determine the order (whether or not it has become operative)[6]. The local housing authority must serve notice that the demolition order has been determined on every person on whom it would be required[7] to serve a copy of a new demolition order in relation to the premises[8].

The appropriate national authority[9] may give notice in respect of a dwelling, house in multiple occupation or building to the local housing authority stating that its architectural or historic interest is sufficient to render it inexpedient that it should be demolished pending determination of the question whether it should be a listed building; and the above provisions apply to a dwelling, house in multiple occupation or building in respect of which such a notice is in force as they apply to a listed building[10].

1 As to the meaning of 'local housing authority' see PARA 11.
2 Ie under the Housing Act 1985 s 265: see PARA 621.
3 Housing Act 1985 s 304(1) (s 304 substituted by the Housing Act 2004 s 265(1), Sch 15 paras 10, 21); and see PARA 620 note 6. As to the meaning of 'listed building' see PARA 621 note 22.
4 As to the meaning of 'dwelling' see PARA 563 note 10 (definition applied by the Housing Act 1985 s 322(1) (substituted by the Housing Act 2004 Sch 15 para 26)).
5 As to the meaning of 'house in multiple occupation' see PARA 621 note 4.
6 Housing Act 1985 s 304(2) (as substituted: see note 3). As to when the order becomes operative see PARAS 621 note 14, 622.
7 Ie by the Housing Act 1985 s 268: see PARA 621.
8 Housing Act 1985 s 304(3) (as substituted: see note 3). As to service of notice on a person in control of premises etc see PARA 17.
9 As to the appropriate national authority, ie the Secretary of State or, where statutory functions have been transferred in relation to Wales, the Welsh Ministers, see PARA 7.
10 Housing Act 1985 s 304(4) (as substituted: see note 3).

642. Building becoming listed when it is subject to compulsory purchase for clearance. Where a building to which a compulsory purchase order[1] under the power of acquisition of land for clearance applies becomes a listed building[2] at any time after the making of the order, the authority making the order may, within the period of three months beginning with the date on which the building becomes a listed building, apply to the appropriate national authority[3] (and only to that authority) for its consent[4] to the demolition of the building[5]. If the authority making the order has not served notice to treat[6] in respect of the building it must not do so unless and until the appropriate national authority gives that consent[7].

Where an application for such consent is made and refused, or the period for making an application expires without the authority having made an application, then if at the date of the refusal or, as the case may be, the expiry of that period ('the relevant date'), the building has not vested in the authority, and no notice to treat has been served by the authority[8] in respect of an interest in the building, the compulsory purchase order ceases to have effect in relation to the building and, where applicable, the building ceases to be comprised in a clearance area[9]. Where this does not apply, the authority ceases to be subject to the statutory duty[10] to demolish the building, and:

(1)   if the building or an interest in it is vested in the authority at the relevant date, it must be treated in the case of a residential building[11] as appropriated to the purposes of the provision of housing accommodation[12] and in any other case as appropriated to planning purposes[13];

(2)   in relation to an interest in the building which has not at the relevant date vested in the authority, the compulsory purchase order has effect in the case of a residential building as if made and confirmed under Part II of the Housing Act 1985[14] and in any other case as if made and confirmed under Part IX of the Town and Country Planning Act 1990[15].

1   Ie under the Housing Act 1985 s 290: see PARA 633.
2   As to the meaning of 'listed building' see PARA 621 note 22.
3   As to the appropriate national authority, ie the Secretary of State or, where statutory functions have been transferred in relation to Wales, the Welsh Ministers, see PARA 7.
4   Ie under the Planning (Listed Buildings and Conservation Areas) Act 1990 s 8: see PLANNING vol 83 (2010) PARA 1262.
5   Housing Act 1985 s 305(1) (s 305(1), (6) amended by the Planning (Consequential Provisions) Act 1990 s 4, Sch 2 para 71(3)(a), (b)); and see PARA 620 note 6.
6   Ie under the Compulsory Purchase Act 1965 s 5: see COMPULSORY ACQUISITION OF LAND vol 18 (2009) PARA 616.
7   Housing Act 1985 s 305(2). No account may be taken for the purposes of the Compulsory Purchase Act 1965 s 4 (time limit for completing compulsory purchase: see COMPULSORY ACQUISITION OF LAND vol 18 (2009) PARA 617) of any period during which an authority is prevented by this provision from serving a notice to treat under s 5 (see COMPULSORY ACQUISITION OF LAND vol 18 (2009) PARA 616): Housing Act 1985 s 305(7).
8   See note 6.
9   Housing Act 1985 s 305(4).
10 Ie the duty imposed by the Housing Act 1985 s 291: see PARA 634.
11 For these purposes, 'residential building' has the same meaning as in the Housing Act 1985 s 289 (see PARA 632 note 3): s 305(8) (added by the Local Government and Housing Act 1989 s 165, Sch 9 para 33; and amended by the Housing Act 2004 s 266, Sch 16).
12 Ie the purposes of the Housing Act 1985 Pt II (ss 8–57): see PARA 405 et seq.
13 Ie the purposes of the Town and Country Planning Act 1990 Pt IX (ss 226–246): see PLANNING vol 83 (2010) PARA 1112 et seq.
14 As to the Housing Act 1985 Pt II see PARA 405 et seq.
15 Housing Act 1985 s 305(6) (as amended (see note 5); further amended by the Local Government and Housing Act 1989 Sch 9 para 33). As to the Town and Country Planning Act 1990 Pt IX see PLANNING vol 83 (2010) PARA 1112 et seq.

643. Building becoming listed when acquired by agreement for clearance. Where the statutory method of dealing with land acquired for clearance[1] applies to a building purchased by the local housing authority[2] by agreement and the building becomes a listed building[3], the authority may, within the period of three months beginning with the date on which the building becomes a listed building, apply to the appropriate national authority[4] (and only to it) for its consent[5] to demolition[6]. Where such an application is made and is refused, or the period for making such an application expires without the local housing authority making an application, the authority ceases to be subject to the duty[7] to demolish the building, and the building must be treated, in the case of a residential building[8], as appropriated to the purposes of the provision of housing accommodation[9] and in any other case as appropriated to planning[10] purposes[11].

1 Ie the Housing Act 1985 s 291: see PARA 634.
2 As to the meaning of 'local housing authority' see PARA 11.
3 As to the meaning of 'listed building' see PARA 621 note 22.
4 As to the appropriate national authority, ie the Secretary of State or, where statutory functions have been transferred in relation to Wales, the Welsh Ministers, see PARA 7.
5 Ie under the Planning (Listed Buildings and Conservation Areas) Act 1990 s 8: see PLANNING vol 83 (2010) PARA 1262.
6 Housing Act 1985 s 306(1) (s 306(1), (2) amended by the Planning (Consequential Provisions) Act 1990 s 4, Sch 2 para 71(4)(a), (b)); and see PARA 620 note 6.
7 Ie the duty imposed by the Housing Act 1985 s 291: see PARA 634.
8 Ie within the meaning of the Housing Act 1985 s 289: see PARA 632.
9 Ie the purposes of the Housing Act 1985 Pt II (ss 8–57): see PARA 405 et seq.
10 Ie appropriated to the purposes of the Town and Country Planning Act 1990 Pt IX (ss 226–246): see PLANNING vol 83 (2010) PARA 1112 et seq.
11 Housing Act 1985 s 306(2) (as amended (see note 6); further amended by the Local Government and Housing Act 1989 Sch 9 para 34).

(viii) Protective Provisions

644. Savings for rights arising from breach of covenant etc. Nothing in the provisions of Part IX of the Housing Act 1985[1] relating to the demolition or purchase of unfit premises[2] prejudices or interferes with the rights or remedies of an owner[3] for breach of any covenant or contract entered into by a lessee[4] in reference to premises in respect of which an order is made by the local housing authority[5] under those provisions[6]. If an owner is obliged to take possession of premises in order to comply with such an order, the taking possession does not affect his right to avail himself of any such breach which occurred before he so took possession[7].

1 Ie the provisions of the Housing Act 1985 Pt IX (ss 265–323): see PARA 620 et seq.
2 As to the meaning of 'premises' see PARA 621 note 13.
3 As to the meaning of 'owner' see PARA 621 note 24.
4 As to the meaning of 'lessee' see PARA 31 note 3.
5 As to the meaning of 'local housing authority' see PARA 11.
6 Housing Act 1985 s 307(1) (amended by the Housing Act 2004 s 265(1), Sch 15 paras 10, 22).
7 Housing Act 1985 s 307(2).

645. Approval of owner's proposals for redevelopment. A person proposing to undertake the redevelopment of land may submit particulars of his proposals to the local housing authority[1] for approval[2]. The authority must consider the proposals and if they appear to the authority to be satisfactory, the authority must give notice to that effect to the person by whom they were submitted, specifying times within which the several parts of the redevelopment are to be carried out[3]. Where the authority has so given notice of its satisfaction with proposals, no action must be taken in relation to the land under any of the powers conferred by the provisions of Part IX of the Housing Act 1985[4] or Chapter 2 of Part 1 of the Housing Act 2004[5] relating to the demolition or purchase of premises[6] or the prohibition of uses of premises, or to clearance areas, if and so long as the redevelopment is being proceeded with in accordance with the proposals and within the specified time limits, subject to any variation or extension approved by the authority[7]. These provisions do not, however, apply to premises in respect of which a demolition order[8] has become operative[9] or which are comprised in a compulsory purchase order of land for clearance[10] which has been confirmed by the appropriate national authority[11].

Where proposals for premises in a clearance area are submitted to the local housing authority under these provisions, the local housing authority may, instead of proceeding thereunder, transmit the proposals to the appropriate national authority[12]. The appropriate national authority must deal with the proposals in connection with its consideration of the compulsory purchase order relating to the premises as if the proposals had been objections to the order made on the date on which they were submitted to the local housing authority[13]. If in confirming the order the appropriate national authority excludes the premises from the clearance area, the local housing authority must then proceed in relation to the proposals under the above provisions[14].

1   As to the meaning of 'local housing authority' see PARA 11.
2   Housing Act 1985 s 308(1).
3   Housing Act 1985 s 308(2); and see PARA 620 note 6.
4   Ie the provisions of the Housing Act 1985 Pt IX (ss 265–323): see PARA 620 et seq.
5   Ie the provisions of the Housing Act 2004 Pt 1 Ch 2 (ss 11–39): see PARAS 571–612.
6   As to the meaning of 'premises' see PARA 621 note 13.
7   Housing Act 1985 s 308(3) (amended by the Housing Act 2004 s 265(1), Sch 15 paras 10, 23). Application may be made for an order restraining the authority from taking action under these procedures: *Boyce v Paddington Borough Council* [1903] 1 Ch 109.
8   As to the making of demolition orders see PARA 621.
9   As to when the order becomes operative see PARAS 621 note 14, 622.
10 Ie an order under the Housing Act 1985 s 290: see PARA 633.
11 Housing Act 1985 s 308(4). Section 308 has effect subject to s 311 (see the text and notes 12–14) in a case where proposals are submitted with respect to premises in a clearance area: s 308(4). As to the appropriate national authority, ie the Secretary of State or, where statutory functions have been transferred in relation to Wales, the Welsh Ministers, see PARA 7.
12 Housing Act 1985 s 311(1) (amended by the Housing Act 2004 s 266, Sch 16).
13 Housing Act 1985 s 311(2).
14 Housing Act 1985 s 311(3) (amended by the Housing Act 2004 Sch 16).

646. Recovery of possession of premises for purposes of approved redevelopment. Where the local housing authority[1] has given notice of its satisfaction with an owner's proposals for redevelopment submitted to the authority[2] and it is satisfied:

(1)   that it is necessary for the purpose of enabling redevelopment to be carried out in accordance with the proposals that a dwelling house[3] let on or subject to a protected tenancy[4] or statutory tenancy[5] or let on or subject to an assured tenancy[6] or assured agricultural occupancy[7] should be vacated; and

(2)   that alternative accommodation complying with the specified requirements is available for the tenant[8] or will be available for him at a future date,

the authority may issue to the landlord[9] a certificate, which is conclusive evidence for the statutory purposes[10] that suitable alternative accommodation is available for the tenant or will be available for him by that future date[11].

The requirements with which the alternative accommodation must comply are:

(a)   that it must be a dwelling house in which the tenant and his family can live without causing it to be overcrowded[12];

(b)   that it must be certified by the local housing authority to be suitable to the needs of the tenant and his family as respects security of tenure, proximity to place of work and otherwise, and to be suitable in relation to his means; and

(c)   that if the dwelling house belongs to the local housing authority it must
        be certified by the authority to be suitable to the needs of the tenant and
        his family as regards accommodation, for this purpose treating a
        dwelling house containing two bedrooms as providing accommodation
        for four persons, a dwelling house containing three bedrooms as
        providing accommodation for five persons and a dwelling house
        containing four bedrooms as providing accommodation for seven
        persons[13].

1   As to the meaning of 'local housing authority' see PARA 11.
2   Ie under the Housing Act 1985 s 308: see PARA 645. As to the meaning of 'owner' see PARA 621
    note 24.
3   For the purposes of the Housing Act 1985 Pt IX (ss 265–323) (see PARA 620 et seq), 'dwelling
    house' was defined to include any yard, garden, outhouses and appurtenances belonging to it or
    usually enjoyed with it: see s 322(1), (2) (s 322(1) amended, and s 322(2) added, by the Local
    Government and Housing Act 1989 ss 165(1)(b), Sch 9 para 42); however, the definition is now
    omitted (see the Housing Act 1985 s 322(1), (2) (substituted by the Housing Act 2004 s 265(1),
    Sch 15 paras 10, 26)), and only a definition of 'dwelling' is given.
4   Ie within the meaning of the Rent Act 1977: see LANDLORD AND TENANT vol 63 (2016)
    PARA 660 et seq.
5   Ie within the meaning of the Rent Act 1977: see LANDLORD AND TENANT vol 63 (2016)
    PARA 673 et seq.
6   As to the meaning of 'assured tenancy' see LANDLORD AND TENANT vol 63 (2016) PARA 825.
7   As to the meaning of 'assured agricultural occupancy' see LANDLORD AND TENANT vol 64 (2016)
    PARA 1747.
8   As to the meaning of 'tenant' see PARA 31 note 3.
9   As to the meaning of 'landlord' see PARA 31 note 3.
10 Ie for the purposes of the Rent Act 1977 s 98(1)(a) or the Housing Act 1988 s 7 (grounds for
    possession): see LANDLORD AND TENANT vol 63 (2016) PARAS 920, 921.
11 Housing Act 1985 s 309(1) (amended by the Housing Act 1988 s 140(1), Sch 17 para 48); and see
    PARA 620 note 6.
12 Ie overcrowded within the meaning of the Housing Act 1985 Pt X (ss 324–344): see PARA 649.
13 Housing Act 1985 s 309(2) (amended by the Local Government and Housing Act 1989 Sch 9
    para 35).

(ix) Enforcement

647. Powers of the court. If a person, after receiving notice of the intended
action:

(1)   being the occupier of premises[1], prevents the owner[2] of the premises, or
        his officers, servants or agents, from carrying into effect with respect to
        the premises any of the provisions of Part IX of the Housing Act 1985[3];
        or

(2)   being the occupier, or owner of premises, prevents an officer, servant or
        agent of the local housing authority[4] from so doing,

a magistrates' court may order him to permit to be done on the premises all things
requisite for carrying those provisions into effect[5]. A person who fails to comply
with such a court order commits a summary offence and is liable on conviction to
a penalty[6].

If it appears to a magistrates' court, on the application of an owner of premises
in respect of which a demolition order[7] has been made, that owing to the default
of another owner of the premises in demolishing the premises, the interests of the
applicant will be prejudiced, the court may make an order empowering the
applicant forthwith to enter on the premises, and, within a period fixed by the
order, demolish them[8]. Before such an order is made, notice of the application

must be given to the local housing authority[9]. Where the court makes such an order, the court may, where it seems to the court just to do so, make a like order in favour of any other owner[10].

Where premises in respect of which a demolition order has become operative[11] form the subject matter of a lease[12], the lessor or the lessee[13] may apply to the appropriate tribunal[14] for an order determining or varying the lease[15]. On the application the tribunal may make such an order if it thinks fit, after giving any sub-lessee an opportunity of being heard[16]. The order may be unconditional or subject to such terms and conditions, including conditions with respect to the payment of money by one party to the proceedings to another by way of compensation, damages or otherwise, as the tribunal may think just and equitable to impose, having regard to the respective rights, obligations and liabilities of the parties under the lease and to all the other circumstances of the case[17].

Where, on an application made by a person entitled to any interest in land used in whole or in part as a site for dwellings[18] or houses in multiple occupation[19] or both, the appropriate tribunal is satisfied:

(a)   that the premises on the land are, or are likely to become, dangerous or injurious to health or harmful to health or safety and the interests of the applicant are thereby prejudiced; or

(b)   that the applicant should be entrusted with the carrying out of a scheme of improvement or reconstruction approved by the local housing authority,

the tribunal may make an order empowering the applicant forthwith to enter on the land and within a period fixed by the order execute such works as may be necessary[20]. Where the tribunal makes such an order, it may order that any lease held from the applicant and any derivative lease must be determined, subject to such conditions and the payment of such compensation as the court may think just[21]; and the tribunal must include in its order provisions to secure that the proposed works are carried out and may authorise the local housing authority to exercise such supervision or take such action as may be necessary for the purpose[22].

1   As to the meaning of 'premises' see PARA 621 note 13.
2   As to the meaning of 'owner' see PARA 621 note 24.
3   Ie the provisions of the Housing Act 1985 Pt IX (ss 265–323): see PARA 620 et seq.
4   As to the meaning of 'local housing authority' see PARA 11.
5   Housing Act 1985 s 315(1) (amended by the Local Government and Housing Act 1989 ss 165(1)(b), 194(4), Sch 9 para 37, Sch 12 Pt II).
6   Housing Act 1985 s 315(2). The penalty is a fine not exceeding £20 in respect of each day during which the failure continues: see s 315(2).
7   As to the making of demolition orders see PARA 621.
8   Housing Act 1985 s 316(1) (amended by the Housing Act 2004 s 266, Sch 16).
9   Housing Act 1985 s 316(3).
10 Housing Act 1985 s 316(2).
11 As to when the order becomes operative see PARAS 621 note 14, 622.
12 As to the meaning of 'lease' see PARA 31 note 3.
13 For these purposes, 'lessor' and 'lessee' include a person deriving title under a lessor or lessee: Housing Act 1985 s 317(4). As to the meanings of 'lessor' and 'lessee' generally see PARA 31 note 3.
14 As to the meaning of 'appropriate tribunal' see PARA 622 note 3. As to appeals to the appropriate tribunal see PARA 32 et seq.
15 Housing Act 1985 s 317(1) (amended by the Housing Act 2004 s 48(1), (4)(a), Sch 16; and by SI 2013/1036).
16 Housing Act 1985 s 317(2) (amended by the Housing Act 2004 s 48(4)(b)).
17 Housing Act 1985 s 317(3) (amended by the Housing Act 2004 s 48(4)(b)).

18 As to the meaning of 'dwelling' see PARA 563 note 10 (definition applied by the Housing Act 1985 s 322(1) (substituted by the Housing Act 2004 s 265(1), Sch 15 paras 10, 26)).
19 As to the meaning of 'house in multiple occupation' see PARA 621 note 4.
20 Housing Act 1985 s 318(1) (amended by the Housing Act 2004 s 48(5)(b), Sch 15 para 25; and by SI 2013/1036).
21 Housing Act 1985 s 318(2) (amended by the Housing Act 2004 s 48(5)(c)).
22 Housing Act 1985 s 318(3) (amended by the Housing Act 2004 s 48(5)(c)).

648. Powers of entry and penalty for obstruction. A person authorised by the local housing authority[1] or the appropriate national authority[2] may at any reasonable time, on giving seven days' notice of his intention to the occupier, and to the owner[3] if the owner is known, enter premises[4]:

(1)　for the purpose of survey and examination where it appears to the local housing authority or the appropriate national authority that survey or examination is necessary in order to determine whether any powers under Part IX of the Housing Act 1985[5] should be exercised in respect of the premises; or

(2)　for the purpose of survey and examination where a demolition order[6] has been made in respect of the premises; or

(3)　for the purpose of survey or valuation where the authority is authorised[7] to purchase the premises compulsorily[8].

An authorisation for these purposes must be in writing stating the particular purpose or purposes for which the entry is authorised and must, if so required, be produced for inspection by the occupier or anyone acting on his behalf[9].

It is a summary offence intentionally to obstruct an officer of the local housing authority or of the appropriate national authority, or any person so authorised to enter premises, in the performance of anything which he is required or authorised[10] to do[11]; and a person committing such an offence is liable on conviction to a penalty[12].

1　As to the meaning of 'local housing authority' see PARA 11.
2　As to the appropriate national authority, ie the Secretary of State or, where statutory functions have been transferred in relation to Wales, the Welsh Ministers, see PARA 7.
3　As to the meaning of 'owner' see PARA 621 note 24.
4　As to the meaning of 'premises' see PARA 621 note 13.
5　Ie under the Housing Act 1985 Pt IX (ss 265–323): see PARA 620 et seq.
6　As to the making of demolition orders see PARA 621.
7　Ie by the Housing Act 1985 Pt IX: see PARA 621 et seq.
8　Housing Act 1985 s 319(1) (amended by the Local Government and Housing Act 1989 s 165(1)(b), Sch 9 para 39; and the Housing Act 2004 s 266, Sch 16).
9　Housing Act 1985 s 319(2) (amended by the Local Government and Housing Act 1989 Sch 9 para 39).
10　See note 7.
11　Housing Act 1985 s 320(1) (amended by the Local Government and Housing Act 1989 Sch 9 para 40).
12　Housing Act 1985 s 320(2). The penalty is a fine not exceeding level 3 on the standard scale: see s 320(2) (amended by the Local Government and Housing Act 1989 Sch 9 para 40). As to the powers of magistrates' courts to issue fines on summary conviction see SENTENCING vol 92 (2015) PARA 176.

6. OVERCROWDING

(1) IN GENERAL

649. Introduction. Part X of the Housing Act 1985[1] makes provision for the regulation of overcrowding in dwellings. These provisions are not to be confused with those in Chapter 3 of Part 4 of the Housing Act 2004[2], which deals specifically with the overcrowding of certain houses in multiple occupation[3]. The 1985 Act overcrowding provisions apply to all dwellings.

A dwelling[4] is overcrowded for the purposes of Part X of the Housing Act 1985 when the number of persons sleeping in the dwelling is such as to contravene either the room standard[5] or the space standard[6]. There are certain relaxations of these standards in relation to younger children[7], cases where a family has a visitor for a limited period[8] and cases where a local housing authority[9] licenses overcrowding for a temporary period[10]. These relaxations apart, certain offences may be committed by an occupier or a landlord who permits overcrowding[11]. In addition, a landlord must supply in a rent book a statement about overcrowding[12] and he is under a duty to inform the local housing authority if the dwelling has become overcrowded[13].

In regulating overcrowding, local housing authorities have powers to inspect and to prepare reports[14], to acquire information about persons sleeping in the dwelling[15], to require production of a rent books[16], to enter to find out whether there is overcrowding in a dwelling[17] and to serve a notice on the occupier to abate overcrowding[18]. Provision is made for enforcement of these powers[19].

The Housing Act 2004, as well as dealing with the overcrowding of houses in multiple occupation, also provides for orders to be made for determining whether a dwelling is overcrowded for the purposes of Part X of the Housing Act 1985 and for harmonising the concept of overcrowding in both Acts[20].

1   Ie the Housing Act 1985 Pt X (ss 324–344): see PARA 650 et seq.
2   Ie the Housing Act 2004 Pt 4 Ch 3 (ss 139–144): see PARA 699 et seq.
3   As to the meaning of 'house in multiple occupation' see PARA 667.
4   As to the meaning of 'dwelling' see PARA 403 note 5.
5   As to the room standard see PARA 651.
6   Housing Act 1985 s 324. As to the space standard see PARA 652.
7   See the Housing Act 1985 s 328; and PARA 654.
8   See the Housing Act 1985 s 329; and PARA 655.
9   As to the meaning of 'local housing authority' see PARA 11.
10   See the Housing Act 1985 s 330; and PARA 656.
11   See the Housing Act 1985 ss 327, 341; and PARAS 653, 663. See also PARA 650.
12   See the Housing Act 1985 s 332; and PARA 658.
13   See the Housing Act 1985 s 333; and PARA 659.
14   See the Housing Act 1985 s 334; and PARA 403.
15   See the Housing Act 1985 s 335; and PARA 661.
16   See the Housing Act 1985 s 336; and PARA 662.
17   See the Housing Act 1985 s 337; and PARA 663.
18   See the Housing Act 1985 s 338; and PARA 664.
19   See the Housing Act 1985 s 339; and PARA 665.
20   See the Housing Act 2004 s 216; and PARA 698.

650. Recovery of possession where dwelling is overcrowded. An occupier who causes or permits a dwelling to be overcrowded is guilty of an offence[1].

Under the Rent Act 1977, a landlord is entitled to recover possession of a dwelling which is occupied by a tenant who is otherwise protected under that Act where the occupation is such as to render the occupier guilty of such an offence[2]. It has been held that the offence must exist at the date of the hearing of the possession claim[3]. It would appear that a landlord is entitled to recover possession in these circumstances even though he may himself have been at fault[4].

A local housing authority[5] can itself take proceedings for possession where occupation is such that the occupier is guilty of overcrowding[6].

In the case of a letting on a secure tenancy[7], where the dwelling is overcrowded the landlord is entitled to recover possession without establishing that it is reasonable for the court to make an order, although the landlord must provide the occupier with suitable alternative accommodation[8].

In the case of an introductory tenancy[9], no specific provision with regard to overcrowding is made but proceedings for possession may be brought once the statutory notice[10] has been served on the tenant[11].

In the case of an assured shorthold tenancy[12] the landlord may recover possession provided the statutory notice requirements[13] are fulfilled[14]. Alternatively, possession may be recovered on one of the statutory grounds[15] applying to assured tenancies[16]. Overcrowding is not specifically provided for as a ground for possession but possession may be obtained either on the ground that suitable alternative accommodation is or will be available for the tenant[17] or on the ground that the tenant is in breach of any obligation of the tenancy[18].

The recovery of possession by landlords is dealt with in detail elsewhere in this work[19].

1 See the Housing Act 1985 s 327; and PARA 653.
2 See the Rent Act 1977 s 101; and LANDLORD AND TENANT vol 63 (2016) PARA 770.
3 See *Zbytniewski v Broughton* [1956] 2 QB 673, [1956] 3 All ER 348, CA.
4 See by analogy *Buswell v Goodwin* [1971] 1 All ER 418, [1971] 1 WLR 92, CA (decided under the provisions relating to closing orders).
5 As to the meaning of 'local housing authority' see PARA 11.
6 See the Housing Act 1985 s 338; and PARA 664.
7 As to the meanings of 'secure tenancy' and 'secure tenant' see LANDLORD AND TENANT vol 63 (2016) PARA 1037.
8 See the Housing Act 1985 s 84, Sch 2 Ground 9; and LANDLORD AND TENANT vol 63 (2016) PARA 1149. As to suitable alternative accommodation see LANDLORD AND TENANT vol 63 (2016) PARA 1137.
9 As to the meaning of 'introductory tenancy' see PARA 472.
10 Ie notice under the Housing Act 1996 s 128: see PARA 472.
11 See the Housing Act 1996 s 127; and PARA 472.
12 As to the meaning of 'assured shorthold tenancy' see LANDLORD AND TENANT vol 63 (2016) PARA 852.
13 Ie the requirements of the Housing Act 1988 s 21 (which requires not less than two months' notice to be given): see LANDLORD AND TENANT vol 63 (2016) PARA 926.
14 See the Housing Act 1988 s 21; and LANDLORD AND TENANT vol 63 (2016) PARA 926.
15 See the Housing Act 1988 ss 7–9, Sch 2; and LANDLORD AND TENANT vol 63 (2016) PARA 920 et seq. As to the meaning of 'assured tenancy' see LANDLORD AND TENANT vol 63 (2016) PARA 825.
16 See the Housing Act 1988 s 21(1); and LANDLORD AND TENANT vol 63 (2016) PARA 926.
17 See the Housing Act 1988 Sch 2 Ground 9; and LANDLORD AND TENANT vol 63 (2016) PARA 946.
18 See the Housing Act 1988 Sch 2 Ground 12; and LANDLORD AND TENANT vol 63 (2016) PARA 949.
19 See LANDLORD AND TENANT.

651. The room standard. The room standard is contravened when the number of persons sleeping in a dwelling[1] and the number of rooms available as sleeping accommodation is such that two persons of opposite sexes who are not living together as husband and wife must sleep in the same room[2]. For this purpose:

  (1) children under the age of ten[3] must be left out of account[4]; and

(2)   a room is available as sleeping accommodation if it is of a type normally used in the locality either as a bedroom or as a living room[5].

1 As to the meaning of 'dwelling' see PARA 403 note 5.
2 Housing Act 1985 s 325(1). A daughter away at boarding school must be taken into account, although not a nephew who sleeps in the house only occasionally: *Zaitzeff v Olmi* (1952) 102 L Jo 416.
3 A person attains a particular age expressed in years at the commencement of the relevant anniversary of the date of his birth: see the Family Law Reform Act 1969 s 9.
4 Housing Act 1985 s 325(2)(a).
5 Housing Act 1985 s 325(2)(b).

652.   The space standard. The space standard is contravened when the number of persons sleeping in a dwelling[1] is in excess of the permitted number, having regard to the number and floor area of the rooms of the dwelling available as sleeping accommodation[2]. For this purpose:
(1)   no account must be taken of a child under the age of one[3] and a child aged one or over but under ten must be reckoned as one-half of a unit[4]; and
(2)   a room is available as sleeping accommodation if it is of a type normally used in the locality either as a living room or as a bedroom[5].
The permitted number[6] of persons in relation to a dwelling is whichever is the less of:
(a)   the number specified in Table I[7] in relation to the number of rooms in the dwelling available as sleeping accommodation[8]; and
(b)   the aggregate for all such rooms in the dwelling of the numbers specified in column 2 of Table II[9] in relation to each room of the floor area specified in column 1 of Table II[10].
No account may be taken for the purposes of either Table of a room having a floor area of less than 50 square feet[11].

The appropriate national authority[12] may by regulations[13] prescribe the manner in which the floor area of a room is to be ascertained for these purposes; and the regulations may provide for the exclusion from computation, or the bringing into computation at a reduced figure, of floor space in a part of the room which is of less than a specified height not exceeding eight feet[14].

A certificate of the local housing authority stating the number and floor areas of the rooms in a dwelling, and that the floor areas have been ascertained in the prescribed manner, is prima facie evidence for the purposes of legal proceedings of the facts stated in it[15].

1 As to the meaning of 'dwelling' see PARA 403 note 5.
2 Housing Act 1985 s 326(1).
3 A person attains a particular age expressed in years at the commencement of the relevant anniversary of the date of his birth: see the Family Law Reform Act 1969 s 9.
4 Housing Act 1985 s 326(2)(a).
5 Housing Act 1985 s 326(2)(b).
6 As to the power of a local housing authority to authorise a number of persons in excess of the permitted number to sleep in a dwelling see PARA 656. Where a rent book is used in relation to a dwelling it must contain a statement of the permitted number of persons: see PARA 658. As to the meaning of 'local housing authority' see PARA 11.
7 The number of rooms and number of persons specified in the Housing Act 1985 s 326(3), Table I are as follows: for one room, two persons; for two rooms, three persons; for three rooms, five persons; for four rooms, seven and one half persons; and for five or more rooms, two persons for each room: s 326(3), Table I.
8 Housing Act 1985 s 326(3)(a).
9 The floor area of room and number of persons specified in the Housing Act 1985 s 326(3), Table II cols 1, 2 are as follows: for a floor area of: (1) 110 sq ft or more, two persons; (2) 90 sq ft or

more but less than 110 sq ft, one and one half persons; (3) 70 sq ft or more but less than 90 sq ft, one person; and (4) 50 sq ft or more but less than 70 sq ft, one half person: s 326(3), Table II.

10 Housing Act 1985 s 326(3)(b).

11 Housing Act 1985 s 326(3).

12 As to the appropriate national authority, ie the Secretary of State or, where statutory functions have been transferred in relation to Wales, the Welsh Ministers, see PARA 7.

13 Regulations under the Housing Act 1985 s 326(4) must be made by statutory instrument subject to annulment in pursuance of a resolution of either House of Parliament or, in relation to Wales, of the National Assembly for Wales: s 326(5). At the date at which this volume states the law, no such regulations had been made.

14 Housing Act 1985 s 326(4).

15 Housing Act 1985 s 326(6). As to legal proceedings in relation to overcrowding see PARAS 653 (penalty for overcrowding), 664 (abatement and possession proceedings), 665 (enforcement).

(2) RESPONSIBILITY OF OCCUPIER

653. Penalty for occupier causing or permitting overcrowding. The occupier of a dwelling[1] who causes or permits it to be overcrowded[2] commits a summary offence[3]. He is not, however, guilty of such an offence:

(1)   if the overcrowding is within the permitted exceptions for children attaining a specified age[4] or visiting relatives[5]; or

(2)   by reason of anything done under the authority of, and in accordance with any conditions specified in, a licence granted[6] by the local housing authority[7].

1   As to the meaning of 'dwelling' see PARA 403 note 5.

2   As to when a dwelling is overcrowded see PARA 649. As to overcrowding of houses in multiple occupation see PARA 698 et seq. As to control by London borough councils of overcrowding in certain hostels see the Greater London Council (General Powers) Act 1981 Pt IV (ss 8–16).

3   Housing Act 1985 s 327(1). A person committing such an offence is liable on conviction to a fine not exceeding level 2 on the standard scale and to a further fine not exceeding one-tenth of the amount corresponding to that level in respect of every day subsequent to the date on which he is convicted on which the offence continues: s 327(3) (amended by the Local Government and Housing Act 1989 s 194(1), Sch 11 para 71). As to the powers of magistrates' courts to issue fines on summary conviction see SENTENCING vol 92 (2015) PARA 176.

4   Ie the exception specified in the Housing Act 1985 s 328: see PARA 654.

5   Ie the exception specified in the Housing Act 1985 s 329: see PARA 655.

6   Ie under the Housing Act 1985 s 330: see PARA 656.

7   Housing Act 1985 s 327(2). As to the meaning of 'local housing authority' see PARA 11.

654. Exception: children attaining age of one or ten. Where a dwelling[1] which would not otherwise be overcrowded[2] becomes overcrowded by reason of a child attaining the age[3] of one or ten, then if the occupier:

(1)   applies to the local housing authority[4] for suitable alternative accommodation[5]; or

(2)   has so applied before the date when the child attained the age in question[6],

he does not commit an offence of causing or permitting overcrowding[7], so long as the statutory condition is met and the occupier does not fail to take action in the circumstances specified in head (a) or head (b) below[8]. The statutory condition is that all the persons sleeping in the dwelling are persons who were living there when the child attained that age and thereafter continuously live there, or children born after that date of any of those persons[9].

The exception provided by these provisions ceases to apply if:

(a)　　　suitable alternative accommodation is offered to the occupier on or after the date on which the child attains that age, or, if he has applied before that date, is offered at any time after the application, and he fails to accept it[10]; or

(b)　　　the removal from the dwelling of some person not a member of the occupier's family is on that date, or thereafter becomes, reasonably practicable having regard to all the circumstances (including the availability of suitable alternative accommodation for that person), and the occupier fails to require his removal[11].

1　As to the meaning of 'dwelling' see PARA 403 note 5.
2　As to when a dwelling is overcrowded see PARA 649.
3　A person attains a particular age expressed in years at the commencement of the relevant anniversary of the date of his birth: see the Family Law Reform Act 1969 s 9.
4　As to the meaning of 'local housing authority' see PARA 11.
5　Housing Act 1985 s 328(1)(a). For the purposes of Pt X (ss 324–344), 'suitable alternative accommodation', in relation to the occupier of a dwelling, means a dwelling as to which the following conditions are satisfied: (1) he and his family can live in it without causing it to be overcrowded; (2) it is certified by the local housing authority to be suitable to his needs and those of his family as respects security of tenure, proximity to place of work and otherwise, and to be suitable in relation to his means; (3) where the dwelling belongs to the local housing authority, it is certified by the authority to be suitable to his needs and those of his family as respects accommodation: s 342(1)(a)–(c). For the purpose of head (3), a dwelling containing two bedrooms must be treated as providing accommodation for four persons, a dwelling containing three bedrooms must be treated as providing accommodation for five persons and a dwelling containing four bedrooms must be treated as providing accommodation for seven persons: s 342(2).
6　Housing Act 1985 s 328(1)(b).
7　Ie an offence under the Housing Act 1985 s 327 (occupier causing or permitting overcrowding): see PARA 653.
8　Housing Act 1985 s 328(1).
9　Housing Act 1985 s 328(2).
10　Housing Act 1985 s 328(3)(a).
11　Housing Act 1985 s 328(3)(b).

655. Exception: visiting member of family. Where the persons sleeping in an overcrowded dwelling[1] include a member of the occupier's family who does not live there but is sleeping there temporarily, the occupier is not guilty of an offence of causing or permitting overcrowding[2] unless the circumstances are such that he would be so guilty if that member of his family were not sleeping there[3].

1　As to when a dwelling is overcrowded see PARA 649. As to the meaning of 'dwelling' see PARA 403 note 5.
2　Ie an offence under the Housing Act 1985 s 327 (occupier causing or permitting overcrowding): see PARA 653.
3　Housing Act 1985 s 329.

656. Licence granted by local housing authority. The occupier or intending occupier of a dwelling[1] may apply to the local housing authority[2] for a licence[3] authorising him to permit a number of persons in excess of the permitted number to sleep in the dwelling[4]. The authority may grant such a licence if it appears to the authority that there are exceptional circumstances (which may include a seasonal increase of population) and that it is expedient to do so; and it must specify in the licence the number of persons authorised in excess of the permitted number[5]. The licence must be in the prescribed form[6] and may be granted either unconditionally or subject to conditions specified in it[7].

The local housing authority may revoke the licence at its discretion by notice[8] in writing served on the occupier and specifying a period (at least one month from the date of service) at the end of which the licence will cease to be in force[9]. Unless previously revoked, the licence continues in force for such period not exceeding

12 months as may be specified in it[10]. A copy of the licence and of any notice of revocation must, within seven days of the issue of the licence or the service of the notice on the occupier, be served by the local housing authority on the landlord (if any) of the dwelling[11].

1　As to the meaning of 'dwelling' see PARA 403 note 5.
2　As to the meaning of 'local housing authority' see PARA 11.
3　An occupier is not guilty of an offence under the Housing Act 1985 s 327 (see PARA 653) where he acts under the authority of, and in accordance with any conditions specified in, a licence granted under s 330: see PARA 653 head (2). A landlord is excepted from the obligation to notify the local authority of overcrowding where the use of the dwelling is in accordance with a licence under s 330: see PARA 659.
4　Housing Act 1985 s 330(1); and see PARA 649 note 1. As to the meaning of 'permitted number' see PARA 652.
5　Housing Act 1985 s 330(2).
6　For the prescribed form see the Housing (Prescribed Forms) Regulations 1990, SI 1990/447, reg 2(1)(b), Schedule, Form 3.
7　Housing Act 1985 s 330(3).
8　For the prescribed form of notice see the Housing (Prescribed Forms) (No 2) Regulations 1990, SI 1990/1730, reg 2(1)(t), Schedule, Form 23, or the equivalent Welsh form prescribed by the Housing (Prescribed Forms) (No 2) (Welsh Forms) Regulations 1991, SI 1991/974.
9　Housing Act 1985 s 330(4).
10　Housing Act 1985 s 330(5).
11　Housing Act 1985 s 330(6).

(3) RESPONSIBILITIES OF THE LANDLORD

657. Penalty for landlord causing or permitting overcrowding. The landlord[1] of a dwelling commits a summary offence if he causes or permits it to be overcrowded[2]. He is deemed to cause or permit it to be overcrowded in the following circumstances, and not otherwise:

(1)　if he, or a person effecting the letting on his behalf, had reasonable cause to believe that the dwelling would become overcrowded in circumstances rendering the occupier guilty of an offence[3];

(2)　if he, or a person effecting the letting on his behalf, failed to make inquiries of the proposed occupier as to the number, age and sex of the persons who would be allowed to sleep in the dwelling[4];

(3)　if notice[5] is served on him or his agent[6] by the local housing authority[7] that the dwelling is overcrowded in such circumstances as to render the occupier guilty of an offence[8] and he fails to take such steps as are reasonably open to him for securing the abatement of the overcrowding, including if necessary legal proceedings for possession of the dwelling[9].

A person who commits such an offence is liable on conviction to a fine, and he is liable to a further fine in respect of every day subsequent to the day on which he is convicted on which the offence continues[10].

1　For these purposes, 'landlord', in relation to a dwelling: (1) means the immediate landlord of an occupier of the dwelling; and (2) in the case of a dwelling occupied under a contract of employment under which the provision of the dwelling for his occupation forms part of the occupier's remuneration, includes the occupier's employer: Housing Act 1985 s 343. As to the meaning of 'dwelling' see PARA 403 note 5.
2　Housing Act 1985 s 331(1). As to when a dwelling is overcrowded see PARA 649.
3　Housing Act 1985 s 331(2)(a). As to when an occupier is guilty of an offence in relation to overcrowding see s 327; and PARA 653.
4　Housing Act 1985 s 331(2)(b).
5　For the prescribed form of notice see the Housing (Prescribed Forms) (No 2) Regulations 1990, SI 1990/1730, reg 2(1)(u), Schedule, Form 24, or the equivalent Welsh form prescribed by the Housing (Prescribed Forms) (No 2) (Welsh Forms) Regulations 1991, SI 1991/974.

6   'Agent', in relation to the landlord of a dwelling: (1) means a person who collects rent in respect of the dwelling on behalf of the landlord, or is authorised by him to do so; and (2) in the case of a dwelling occupied under a contract of employment under which the provision of the dwelling for his occupation forms part of the occupier's remuneration, includes a person who pays remuneration on behalf of the employer, or is authorised by him to do so: Housing Act 1985 s 343.

7   As to the meaning of 'local housing authority' see PARA 11.

8   See note 3.

9   Housing Act 1985 s 331(2)(c). As to proceedings for possession see PARAS 650, 664.

10 Housing Act 1985 s 331(3). The penalty is a fine not exceeding level 2 on the standard scale, and the penalty for a continuing offence is a further fine not exceeding one-tenth of the amount corresponding to that level in respect of every day subsequent to the day on which he is convicted on which the offence continues: see s 331(3) (amended by the Local Government and Housing Act 1989 s 194(1), Sch 11 para 72). As to the powers of magistrates' courts to issue fines on summary conviction see SENTENCING vol 92 (2015) PARA 176.

658. Information to be contained in rent book. A landlord who lets under a weekly tenancy is under a statutory obligation to provide the tenant with a rent book[1].

Every rent book or similar document used in relation to a dwelling[2] by or on behalf of the landlord[3] must contain:

(1)   a summary in the prescribed form[4] of certain provisions of Part X of the Housing Act 1985[5]; and

(2)   a statement of the permitted number[6] of persons in relation to the dwelling[7].

If a rent book or similar document not containing such a summary and statement is used by or on behalf of the landlord, the landlord is guilty of a summary offence and liable on conviction to a penalty[8]. The local housing authority[9] must on the application of the landlord or the occupier of a dwelling inform him in writing of the permitted number of persons in relation to the dwelling; and a statement inserted in a rent book or similar document which agrees with information so given is deemed to be a sufficient and correct statement[10].

1   As to the obligation to provide a rent book see the Landlord and Tenant Act 1985 s 4; and LANDLORD AND TENANT vol 62 (2016) PARA 247. As to other information contained in such a rent book see s 5; and LANDLORD AND TENANT vol 62 (2016) PARA 248. As to the power to require production of a rent book see PARA 662.

2   As to the meaning of 'dwelling' see PARA 403 note 5.

3   As to the meaning of 'landlord' see PARA 657 note 1.

4   For the prescribed form see the Housing (Prescribed Forms) Regulations 1990, SI 1990/447, reg 2(1)(c), Schedule, Form 4.

5   Ie certain provisions of the Housing Act 1985 Pt X (ss 324–344), namely ss 324–331 (see PARAS 649–657): s 332(1)(a).

6   As to the meaning of 'permitted number' see PARA 652.

7   Housing Act 1985 s 332(1)(b).

8   Housing Act 1985 s 332(2). The penalty is a fine not exceeding level 1 on the standard scale: see s 332(2). As to the powers of magistrates' courts to issue fines on summary conviction see SENTENCING vol 92 (2015) PARA 176.

9   As to the meaning of 'local housing authority' see PARA 11.

10 Housing Act 1985 s 332(3); and see PARA 649 note 1.

659. Duty to inform local housing authority of overcrowding. Where it comes to the knowledge of the landlord[1] of a dwelling[2], or of his agent[3], that the dwelling is overcrowded[4], then, except in the cases mentioned in heads (1) to (3) below, the landlord or, as the case may be, the agent must give notice of the fact of overcrowding to the local housing authority[5] within seven days after that fact first comes to his knowledge[6]. This obligation to notify does not, however, arise in the case of overcrowding which:

(1)   has already been notified to the local housing authority[7];

(2)   has been notified to the landlord or his agent by the local housing authority[8]; or

(3)   is constituted by the use of the dwelling for sleeping by such number of persons as the occupier is authorised by a local housing authority licence[9] to permit to sleep there[10].

A landlord or agent who fails to give notice in accordance with these provisions commits a summary offence and is liable on conviction to a penalty[11].

1   As to the meaning of 'landlord' see PARA 657 note 1. See also *R v Cardiff City Council, ex p Cross* (1982) 81 LGR 105, 6 HLR 1, CA (a local authority is not required to serve notices on itself in relation to its own housing stock).
2   As to the meaning of 'dwelling' see PARA 403 note 5.
3   As to the meaning of 'agent' see PARA 657 note 6.
4   As to when a dwelling is overcrowded see PARA 649.
5   As to the meaning of 'local housing authority' see PARA 11.
6   Housing Act 1985 s 333(1).
7   Housing Act 1985 s 333(2)(a).
8   Housing Act 1985 s 333(2)(b).
9   Ie a licence under the Housing Act 1985 s 330: see PARA 656.
10 Housing Act 1985 s 333(2)(c).
11 Housing Act 1985 s 333(3). The penalty is a fine not exceeding level 1 on the standard scale: see s 333(3). As to the powers of magistrates' courts to issue fines on summary conviction see SENTENCING vol 92 (2015) PARA 176.

(4) POWERS AND DUTIES OF THE LOCAL HOUSING AUTHORITY

660.   Duty to inspect, report and prepare proposals. A local housing authority[1] has a statutory duty in certain circumstances to cause an inspection of overcrowding in its area to be made, to prepare a report and to submit proposals to the appropriate national authority[2] to abate the overcrowding[3]. This duty is dealt with elsewhere in this title[4].

1   As to the meaning of 'local housing authority' see PARA 11.
2   As to the appropriate national authority, ie the Secretary of State or, where statutory functions have been transferred in relation to Wales, the Welsh Ministers, see PARA 7.
3   See the Housing Act 1985 s 334; and PARA 403.
4   See PARA 403.

661.   Power to require information about persons sleeping in dwelling. The local housing authority[1] may, for the purpose of enabling it to discharge its duties under Part X of the Housing Act 1985[2], serve notice[3] on the occupier of a dwelling[4] requiring him to give the authority within 14 days a written statement of the number, ages and sexes of the persons sleeping in the dwelling[5]. The occupier commits a summary offence if he makes default in complying with this requirement[6] or if he gives a statement which to his knowledge is false in a material particular[7], and is liable on conviction to a penalty[8].

1   As to the meaning of 'local housing authority' see PARA 11.
2   Ie the Housing Act 1985 Pt X (ss 324–344).
3   For the prescribed form of notice see the Housing (Prescribed Forms) (No 2) Regulations 1990, SI 1990/1730, reg 2(1)(v), Schedule, Form 25, or the equivalent Welsh form prescribed by the Housing (Prescribed Forms) (No 2) (Welsh Forms) Regulations 1991, SI 1991/974.
4   As to the meaning of 'dwelling' see PARA 403 note 5.
5   Housing Act 1985 s 335(1).
6   Housing Act 1985 s 335(2)(a).
7   Housing Act 1985 s 335(2)(b).

8 Housing Act 1985 s 335(2). The penalty is a fine not exceeding level 1 on the standard scale: see s 335(2). As to the powers of magistrates' courts to issue fines on summary conviction see SENTENCING vol 92 (2015) PARA 176.

662. Power to require production of rent book. A duly authorised officer of the local housing authority[1] may require an occupier of a dwelling[2] to produce for inspection any rent book[3] or similar document which is being used in relation to the dwelling and is in his custody or under his control[4]. On being so required, or within seven days thereafter, the occupier must produce any such book or document to the officer or at the offices of the authority[5]. An occupier who fails to do so commits a summary offence and is liable on conviction to a penalty[6].

1 As to the meaning of 'local housing authority' see PARA 11.
2 As to the meaning of 'dwelling' see PARA 403 note 5.
3 For information which is to be contained in a rent book for these purposes see PARA 658. As to rent books generally see LANDLORD AND TENANT vol 62 (2016) PARA 247 et seq.
4 Housing Act 1985 s 336(1); and see PARA 649 note 1.
5 Housing Act 1985 s 336(2).
6 Housing Act 1985 s 336(3). The penalty is a fine not exceeding level 1 on the standard scale: see s 336(3). As to the powers of magistrates' courts to issue fines on summary conviction see SENTENCING vol 92 (2015) PARA 176.

663. Powers of entry. A person authorised by the local housing authority[1] may at any reasonable time, on giving 24 hours' notice[2] of his intention to the occupier, and to the owner[3] if the owner is known, enter premises for the purposes of measuring the rooms of a dwelling[4] in order to ascertain for the purposes of Part X of the Housing Act 1985[5] the number of persons permitted[6] to use the dwelling for sleeping[7]. An authorisation for these purposes must be in writing stating the particular purpose for which the entry is authorised[8].

In addition to the specific power described above, a person authorised by the local housing authority may also, at all reasonable times, on giving 24 hours' notice[9] to the occupier, and to the owner if the owner is known, enter any premises for the purpose of survey and examination where it appears to the authority that survey or examination is necessary in order to determine whether any powers under Part X should be exercised[10]. An authorisation for these purposes must be in writing stating the particular purpose for which it is given and must, if so required, be produced for inspection by the occupier or anyone acting on his behalf[11].

It is a summary offence intentionally to obstruct an officer of the local housing authority, or any person authorised to enter premises in pursuance of these provisions, in the performance of anything which he is required or authorised to do[12]. A person committing such an offence is liable on conviction to a penalty[13].

1 As to the meaning of 'local housing authority' see PARA 11.
2 For the prescribed form of notice see the Housing (Prescribed Forms) (No 2) Regulations 1990, SI 1990/1730, reg 2(1)(f), Schedule, Form 9 (amended by SI 1997/892), or the equivalent Welsh form prescribed by the Housing (Prescribed Forms) (No 2) (Welsh Forms) Regulations 1991, SI 1991/974.
3 For these purposes, 'owner', in relation to premises: (1) means a person (other than a mortgagee not in possession) who is for the time being entitled to dispose of the fee simple, whether in possession or in reversion; and (2) includes a person holding or entitled to the rents and profits of the premises under a lease of which the unexpired term exceeds three years: Housing Act 1985 s 343.
4 As to the meaning of 'dwelling' see PARA 403 note 5.
5 Ie the Housing Act 1985 Pt X (ss 324–344).
6 As to the number of persons permitted etc see PARA 652.
7 Housing Act 1985 s 337(1).
8 Housing Act 1985 s 337(2).
9 As to the form of notice see note 2.

10 Housing Act 1985 s 340(1).

11 Housing Act 1985 s 340(2) (amended by the Local Government and Housing Act 1989 s 194(1), Sch 11 para 73).

12 Housing Act 1985 s 341(1) (s 341 amended by the Local Government and Housing Act 1989 Sch 11 para 74).

13 Housing Act 1985 s 341(2) (as amended: see note 12). The penalty is a fine not exceeding level 3 on the standard scale: see s 341(2) (as so amended). As to the powers of magistrates' courts to issue fines on summary conviction see SENTENCING vol 92 (2015) PARA 176.

 Where an offence under the Housing Act 1985 committed by a body corporate is proved to have been committed with the consent or connivance of, or to be attributable to any neglect on the part of, a director, manager, secretary or other similar officer of the body corporate, or a person purporting to act in any such capacity, he, as well as the body corporate, is guilty of an offence and liable to be proceeded against and punished accordingly: s 613(1). Where the affairs of a body corporate are managed by its members, this applies in relation to the acts and defaults of a member in connection with his functions of management as if he were a director of the body corporate: s 613(2).

664. Notice to abate overcrowding. Where a dwelling[1] is overcrowded[2] in circumstances such as to render the occupier guilty of an offence[3], the local housing authority[4] may serve on the occupier notice[5] in writing requiring him to abate the overcrowding within 14 days from the date of service of the notice[6].

If at any time within three months from the end of that period:

(1) the dwelling is in the occupation of the person on whom the notice was served or of a member of his family[7]; and

(2) it is overcrowded in circumstances such as to render the occupier guilty of an offence[8],

the local housing authority may apply to the County Court which must order vacant possession of the dwelling to be given to the landlord[9] within such period, not less than 14 or more than 28 days, as the court may determine[10].

Any expenses incurred by the local housing authority under these provisions in securing the giving of possession of a dwelling to the landlord may be recovered by the authority from him[11].

1 As to the meaning of 'dwelling' see PARA 403 note 5.
2 As to when a dwelling is overcrowded see PARA 649.
3 As to the circumstances in which the occupier is guilty of an offence in relation to overcrowding see PARA 653.
4 As to the meaning of 'local housing authority' see PARA 11.
5 For the prescribed form of notice see the Housing (Prescribed Forms) (No 2) Regulations 1990, SI 1990/1730, reg 2(1)(w), Schedule, Form 26, or the equivalent Welsh form prescribed by the Housing (Prescribed Forms) (No 2) (Welsh Forms) Regulations 1991, SI 1991/974.
6 Housing Act 1985 s 338(1); and see PARA 649 note 1.
7 Housing Act 1985 s 338(2)(a).
8 Housing Act 1985 s 338(2)(b).
9 As to the meaning of 'landlord' see PARA 657 note 1.
10 Housing Act 1985 s 338(2).
11 See the Housing Act 1985 s 338(3).

665. Enforcement. A local housing authority[1] must enforce the provisions of Part X[2] of the Housing Act 1985[3]. A prosecution for an offence against those provisions may be brought only:

(1) by the local housing authority[4]; or

(2) in the case of a prosecution against the authority itself, with the consent of the Attorney General[5].

1 As to the meaning of 'local housing authority' see PARA 11.
2 Ie the Housing Act 1985 Pt X (ss 324–344).
3 Housing Act 1985 s 339(1); and see PARA 649 note 1.
4 Housing Act 1985 s 339(2)(a).

5 Housing Act 1985 s 339(2)(b). In certain cases, the functions of the Attorney General may be discharged by the Solicitor General: see CONSTITUTIONAL AND ADMINISTRATIVE LAW vol 20 (2014) PARA 273. As to arrest, remand, etc where the consent of the Attorney General has not yet been given, and as to evidence of such consent, see the Prosecution of Offences Act 1985 ss 25, 26; and CRIMINAL PROCEDURE vol 27 (2015) PARA 51; CRIMINAL PROCEDURE vol 28 (2015) PARA 560.

7. HOUSES IN MULTIPLE OCCUPATION

(1) INTRODUCTION

666. In general. Many families and individuals live in buildings where they share such accommodation as kitchens, bathrooms and toilets with other households; hostels and bed and breakfast establishments are two common examples. In other cases, private landlords let rooms where the occupants share some of the facilities. Facilities in housing in multiple occupation are often poor and below statutory standards and in some cases fire escape arrangements are unsatisfactory or unsafe[1]. Provision was made for the regulation of houses in multiple occupation[2] by local housing authorities[3] under Part XI of the Housing Act 1985[4], and a number of amendments to this body of legislation were made by Part II of the Housing Act 1996 (including the introduction of registration schemes)[5].

The Housing Act 2004 repealed those provisions and replaced them with a new regime[6]. This provides, inter alia, for the making of HMO declarations and the licensing of certain houses in multiple occupation[7], and also for the selective licensing of houses let by private landlords[8].

1 See eg *The Physical and Social Survey of Houses in Multiple Occupation* (Department of the Environment, 1985); *Death Trap Housing* (National Consumer Council, 1991); *Healthy Housing; the Role of Environmental Health Services* (Audit Commission, 1991); *Houses in Multiple Occupation* (Campaign for Bedsit Rights, 1993); and HC research paper 96/11 *Houses in Multiple Occupation*.
2 Note that under the Housing Act 2004, houses in multiple occupation are often referred to as 'HMOs'. As to the meaning of 'house in multiple occupation' for the purposes of the Housing Act 2004 see PARA 667. See Driscoll *Housing: the New Law, A Guide to the Housing Act 2004* (2007) Chs 4, 5, 6.
3 As to the meaning of 'local housing authority' see PARA 11.
4 See the Housing Act 1985 Pt XI (ss 345–400) (repealed by the Housing Act 2004 s 266, Sch 16).
5 See the Housing Act 1996 Pt II (ss 65–80) (repealed by the Housing Act 2004 s 266, Sch 16).
6 See PARA 667 et seq.
7 See PARA 672 et seq.
8 See the Housing Act 2004 Pt 3 (ss 79–100); and PARA 704 et seq. As to the regulation of the letting and management of dwellings under domestic tenancies in Wales see the Housing (Wales) Act 2014 Pt 1 (ss 1–49); and PARA 729 et seq.

667. Meaning of 'house in multiple occupation'. For the purposes of the Housing Act 2004, a building or a part of a building is a 'house in multiple occupation' (or 'HMO') if:

(1)   it meets the conditions of the standard test[1];
(2)   it meets the conditions of the self-contained flat test[2];
(3)   it meets the conditions of the converted building test[3];
(4)   an HMO declaration is in force in respect of it[4]; or
(5)   it is a converted block of flats[5].

A building or a part of a building meets the standard test if:

(a)   it consists of one or more units of living accommodation not consisting of a self-contained flat[6] or flats;
(b)   the living accommodation is occupied by persons who do not form a single household[7];
(c)   the living accommodation is occupied by those persons as their only or main residence or they are to be treated as so occupying it[8];
(d)   their occupation of the living accommodation constitutes the only use of that accommodation;

(e)   rents are payable or other consideration is to be provided in respect of at least one of those persons' occupation of the living accommodation; and

(f)   two or more of the households who occupy the living accommodation share one or more basic amenities or the living accommodation is lacking in one or more basic amenities[9].

A part of a building meets the self-contained flat test if it consists of a self-contained flat and heads (b) to (f) apply (reading references to the living accommodation concerned as references to the flat)[10].

A building or a part of a building meets the converted building test if:

(i)   it is a converted building[11];

(ii)   it contains one or more units of living accommodation that do not consist of a self-contained flat or flats (whether or not it also contains any such flat or flats);

(iii)   the living accommodation is occupied by persons who do not form a single household[12];

(iv)   the living accommodation is occupied by those persons as their only or main residence or they are to be treated as so occupying it[13];

(v)   their occupation of the living accommodation constitutes the only use of that accommodation; and

(vi)   rents are payable or other consideration is to be provided in respect of at least one of those persons' occupation of the living accommodation[14].

The appropriate national authority[15] may by regulations make such amendments of the relevant statutory provisions[16] as the authority considers appropriate with a view to securing that any building or part of a building of a description specified in the regulations is or is not to be a house in multiple occupation for any specified purposes of the Housing Act 2004; it may provide for such amendments to have effect also for the purposes of definitions in other enactments that operate by reference to the Housing Act 2004; and it may make such consequential amendments of any provision of the Housing Act 2004, or any other enactment[17], as the authority considers appropriate[18].

1   Ie the conditions in the Housing Act 2004 s 254(2): see the text and notes 6–9.
    Certain issues relating to the licensing of HMOs have been decided by the residential property tribunal (RPT) (now the First-tier Tribunal (Property Chamber)). In *33 Coptic Street, London, WC1A 1NP* (LON/OOAG/HMV/2009/0002), the RPT determined that the local authority was correct in granting an HMO licence in relation to premises that were occupied by students (not only was the building correctly designated as an HMO under the standard test in the Housing Act 2004 s 254 but it was on the facts one that required to be licensed under the Licensing of Houses in Multiple Occupation (Prescribed Regulations) (England) Order 2006, SI 2006/371 (see PARA 674); the requirement that an occupier must occupy as their only or main home applies to the basic definition in the Housing Act 2004 s 254, but the Licensing of Houses in Multiple Occupation (Prescribed Regulations) (England) Order 2006, SI 2006/371, which provides (amongst other things) that an HMO requires a licence for occupation by five or more persons, does not require all of them to be in occupation as their only or main residence). See also a similar determination by the RPT in *79 Bayham Street London NW1 0AA* (LON/OOAG/HMA/2008/0001). As to whether a maisonette falls within the categories of property needing to be licensed under the Licensing of Houses in Multiple Occupation (Prescribed Regulations) (England) Order 2006, SI 2006/371, see *Bristol City Council v DIGS (Bristol) Ltd* [2014] EWHC 869, [2014] HLR 453, [2014] All ER (D) 02 (Apr).
2   Ie the conditions in the Housing Act 2004 s 254(3): see the text and note 10.
3   Ie the conditions in the Housing Act 2004 s 254(4): see the text and notes 11–13.
4   Ie under the Housing Act 2004 s 255: see PARA 672.
5   Ie to which the Housing Act 2004 s 257 applies (see PARA 669): s 254(1). However, for any purposes of the Housing Act 2004 (other than those of Pt 1 (ss 1–54) (housing conditions)), a building or part of a building within s 254(1) is not a house in multiple occupation if it is listed in Sch 14 (see PARA 668): s 254(5).

6 'Self-contained flat' means a separate set of premises (whether or not on the same floor): (1) which forms part of a building; (2) either the whole or a material part of which lies above or below some other part of the building; and (3) in which all three basic amenities are available for the exclusive use of its occupants: Housing Act 2004 s 254(8). 'Basic amenities' means a toilet, personal washing facilities, or cooking facilities: s 254(8).

7 As to persons to be regarded as not forming a single household see the Housing Act 2004 s 258; and PARA 670.

8 See the Housing Act 2004 s 259; and PARA 671.

9 Housing Act 2004 s 254(2). See also *33 Coptic Street, London, WC1A 1NP* (LON/OOAG/HMV/2009/0002); and note 1.

10 Housing Act 2004 s 254(3).

11 'Converted building' means a building or part of a building consisting of living accommodation in which one or more units of such accommodation have been created since the building or part was constructed: Housing Act 2004 s 254(8).

12 See note 7.

13 See note 8.

14 Housing Act 2004 s 254(4).

15 As to the meaning of 'the appropriate national authority' see PARA 389 note 1.

16 Ie the Housing Act 2004 ss 254–259.

17 'Enactment' includes an enactment comprised in subordinate legislation (within the meaning of the Interpretation Act 1978: see STATUTES AND LEGISLATIVE PROCESS vol 96 (2012) PARA 609): Housing Act 2004 s 254(8).

18 Housing Act 2004 s 254(6). Regulations under s 254(6) may frame any description by reference to any matters or circumstances whatever: s 254(7).

668. Buildings which are not houses in multiple occupation. The following are buildings[1] which are not houses in multiple occupation[2] for any purposes of the Housing Act 2004 other than those of Part 1 (that is, the housing conditions provisions)[3]:

(1) buildings controlled or managed by public sector bodies etc, namely:
   (a) a building where the person managing[4] or having control[5] of it is:
   (b) a local housing authority[6];
   (c) a non-profit registered provider of social housing[7];
   (d) a body which is registered as a social landlord[8];
   (e) a police and crime commissioner[9];
   (f) the Mayor's Office for Policing and Crime[10];
   (g) a fire and rescue authority[11]; or
   (h) a health service body[12]; and
   (i) a building:
   (j) which is social housing within the meaning of Part 2 of the Housing and Regeneration Act 2008[13]; and
   (k) where the person managing or having control of it is a profit-making registered provider of social housing[14];

(2) a building where:
   (a) the person managing or having control of it is a co-operative society[15] whose rules are such as to secure that each of the statutory conditions[16] is met; and
   (b) no person who occupies premises in the building does so by virtue of an assured tenancy, a secure tenancy or a protected tenancy[17];

(3) any building whose occupation is regulated otherwise than by or under the Housing Act 2004 and which is of a description specified for this purpose in regulations made by the appropriate national authority[18];

(4) buildings occupied by students, namely any building:

(a)   which is occupied solely or principally by persons who occupy it
        for the purpose of undertaking a full-time course of further or
        higher education at a specified[19] educational establishment or at
        an educational establishment of a specified description; and

(b)   where the person managing or having control of it is the
        educational establishment in question or a specified person or a
        person of a specified description[20];

(5)   buildings occupied by religious communities, namely any building
        (except certain converted blocks of flats[21]) which is occupied principally
        for the purposes of a religious community whose principal occupation is
        prayer, contemplation, education or the relief of suffering[22];

(6)   buildings occupied by owners, namely any building (except certain
        converted blocks of flats[23]) which is occupied only by persons within the
        following heads:

        (a)   one or more persons who have, whether in the whole or any part
                of it, either the freehold estate or a leasehold interest granted for
                a term of more than 21 years;

        (b)   any member of the household of such a person or persons;

        (c)   no more than such number of other persons as is specified for this
                purpose in regulations made by the appropriate national
                authority[24];

(7)   any building which is occupied only by two persons who form two
        households[25].

1   For the purposes of the Housing Act 2004 Sch 14, 'building' includes a part of a building: s 254(5),
    Sch 14 para 1(2).
2   Ie even if they otherwise would be. As to the meaning of 'house in multiple occupation' see
    PARA 667.
3   Housing Act 2004 Sch 14 para 1(1). As to Pt 1 (ss 1–54) see PARA 563 et seq.
4   As to the meaning of 'person managing' see PARA 391 note 6.
5   As to the meaning of 'person having control' see PARA 391 note 5.
6   As to the meaning of 'local housing authority' see PARA 380 note 1.
7   As to registered providers of social housing see PARA 51 et seq; as to when such a body is a
    non-profit organisation see PARA 71 note 13.
8   Ie under the Housing Act 1996 Pt I (ss A1–64): see PARA 166 et seq.
9   As to police and crime commissioners see POLICE AND INVESTIGATORY POWERS vol 84 (2013)
    PARA 56 et seq
10 As to the Mayor's Office for Policing and Crime see POLICE AND INVESTIGATORY POWERS
    vol 84 (2013) PARA 78 et seq.
11 'Fire and rescue authority' means a fire and rescue authority under the Fire and Rescue Services Act
    2004 (see FIRE AND RESCUE SERVICES): Housing Act 2004 Sch 14 para 2(2).
12 Housing Act 2004 Sch 14 para 2(1) (amended by the National Health Service (Consequential
    Provisions) Act 2006 s 2, Sch 1 para 269; the Police Reform and Social Responsibility Act 2011
    s 99, Sch 16 para 355; and SI 2010/866). The text refers to a health service body within the
    meaning of the National Health Service Act 2006 s 9: see HEALTH SERVICES vol 54 (2017)
    PARA 274.
13 Ie within the meaning of the Housing and Regeneration Act 2008 Pt 2 (ss 59–278A): see PARA 52.
14 Housing Act 2004 Sch 14 para 2A (added by SI 2010/866). As to when a registered provider of
    social housing is profit-making see PARA 71 note 13.
15 For these purposes, 'co-operative society' means a body that: (1) is registered as a co-operative
    society under the Co-operative and Community Benefit Societies Act 2014 or is a
    pre-commencement society (within the meaning of that Act) that meets the condition in s 2(2)(a)(i)
    (see FINANCIAL INSTITUTIONS vol 48 (2015) PARA 890); and (2) is neither: (a) a non-profit
    registered provider of social housing; nor (b) registered as a social landlord under the Housing Act
    1996 Pt I: Housing Act 2004 Sch 14 para 2B(3), (4) (Sch 14 para 2B added by the Localism Act
    2011 s 185(1); and amended by the Co-operative and Community Benefit Societies Act 2014
    s 151(1), Sch 4 para 91).
16 The conditions are: (1) that membership of the society is restricted to persons who are occupiers
    or prospective occupiers of buildings managed or controlled by the society; (2) that all

management decisions of the society are made by the members (or a specified quorum of members) at a general meeting which all members are entitled to, and invited to, attend; (3) that each member has equal voting rights at such a meeting; and (4) that, if a person occupies premises in the building and is not a member, that person is an occupier of the premises only as a result of sharing occupation of them with a member at the member's invitation: Housing Act 2004 Sch 14 para 2(2) (as added: see note 15).

17 Housing Act 2004 Sch 14 para 2B(1) (as added: see note 15). As to the meaning of 'assured tenancy' see LANDLORD AND TENANT vol 63 (2016) PARA 825; as to the meaning of 'protected tenancy' see LANDLORD AND TENANT vol 63 (2016) PARA 660; and as to the meaning of 'secure tenancy' see LANDLORD AND TENANT vol 63 (2016) PARA 1037 (definitions applied by Sch 14 para 2B(4) (as so added).

18 Housing Act 2004 Sch 14 para 3. As to the meaning of 'the appropriate national authority' see PARA 389 note 1. As to the regulations made see the Licensing and Management of Houses in Multiple Occupation and Other Houses (Miscellaneous Provisions) (England) Regulations 2006, SI 2006/373, reg 6(1), Sch 1 (Sch 1 amended by SI 2015/541); and the Licensing and Management of Houses in Multiple Occupation and Other Houses (Miscellaneous Provisions) (Wales) Regulations 2006, SI 2006/1715, reg 6(1), Sch 1.

19 'Specified' means specified for the purposes of the Housing Act 2004 Sch 14 para 4 in regulations made by the appropriate national authority: Sch 14 para 4(2). As to the regulations that have been made see the Houses in Multiple Occupation (Specified Educational Establishments) (England) Regulations 2016, SI 2016/420; and the Houses in Multiple Occupation (Specified Educational Establishments) (Wales) Regulations 2006, SI 2006/1707. In connection with any decision by the appropriate national authority as to whether to make, or revoke, any regulations specifying a particular educational establishment or a particular description of educational establishments, the appropriate national authority may have regard to the extent to which, in its opinion: (1) the management by or on behalf of the establishment in question of any building or buildings occupied for connected educational purposes is in conformity with any code of practice for the time being approved under the Housing Act 2004 s 233 (see PARA 696) which appears to the authority to be relevant; or (2) the management of such buildings by or on behalf of establishments of the description in question is in general in conformity with any such code of practice, as the case may be: Sch 14 para 4(3), (4). 'Occupied for connected educational purposes', in relation to a building managed by or on behalf of an educational establishment, means occupied solely or principally by persons who occupy it for the purpose of undertaking a full-time course of further or higher education at the establishment: Sch 14 para 4(5).

20 Housing Act 2004 Sch 14 para 4(1).

21 Ie a converted block of flats to which the Housing Act 2004 s 257 applies (see PARA 669): Sch 14 para 5(2).

22 Housing Act 2004 Sch 14 para 5(1).

23 Ie a converted block of flats to which the Housing Act 2004 s 257 applies (see PARA 669): Sch 14 para 6(2).

24 Housing Act 2004 Sch 14 para 6(1). The number of persons specified in regulations is two: see the Licensing and Management of Houses in Multiple Occupation and Other Houses (Miscellaneous Provisions) (England) Regulations 2006, SI 2006/373, reg 6(2); and the Licensing and Management of Houses in Multiple Occupation and Other Houses (Miscellaneous Provisions) (Wales) Regulations 2006, SI 2006/1715, reg 6(2). As to rules for counting the number of persons see PARA 396.

25 Housing Act 2004 Sch 14 para 7.

669. Converted blocks of flats: section 257 HMOs. Certain blocks of flats are widely known as 'section 257 HMOs' if they fall within the following description. The relevant statutory provisions[1] apply to a converted block of flats[2] if: (1) building work undertaken in connection with the conversion did not comply with the appropriate building standards[3] and still does not comply with them; and (2) less than two-thirds of the self-contained flats are owner-occupied[4]. The fact that these provisions apply to a converted block of flats (with the result that it is a house in multiple occupation[5]), does not affect the status of any flat in the block as a house in multiple occupation[6].

1 Ie the Housing Act 2004 s 257. This has the consequence that specific provisions of the Act may be applied with modifications in relation to such blocks of flats. See the Houses in Multiple Occupation (Certain Converted Blocks of Flats) (Modifications to the Housing Act 2004 and Transitional Provisions for section 257 HMOs) (England) Regulations 2007, SI 2007/1904; and

the Houses in Multiple Occupation (Certain Blocks of Flats) (Modifications to the Housing Act 2004 and Transitional Provisions for section 257 HMOs) (Wales) Regulations 2007, SI 2007/3231.

2   For the purposes of the Housing Act 2004 s 257, a 'converted block of flats' means a building or part of a building which has been converted into, and consists of self-contained flats: s 257(1). As to the meaning of 'self-contained flat' see PARA 667 note 6 (definition applied by s 257(6)).

3   'Appropriate building standards' means: (1) in the case of a converted block of flats, on which building work was completed before 1 June 1992 or which is dealt with by the Building Regulations 1991, SI 1991/2768, reg 20 (revoked) and which would not have been exempt under those Regulations, building standards equivalent to those imposed, in relation to a building or part of a building to which those Regulations applied, by those Regulations as they had effect on 1 June 1992; and (2) in the case of any other converted block of flats, the requirements imposed at the time in relation to it by regulations under the Building Act 1984 s 1: Housing Act 2004 s 257(3).

4   Housing Act 2004 s 257(2). For the purposes of s 257(2), a flat is 'owner-occupied' if it is occupied: (1) by a person who has a lease of the flat which has been granted for a term of more than 21 years; (2) by a person who has the freehold estate in the converted block of flats; or (3) by a member of the household of a person within head (1) or head (2): s 257(4).

5   Ie under the Housing Act 2004 s 254(1)(e): see PARA 667.

6   Housing Act 2004 s 257(5).

670. Persons not forming a single household. Persons are to be regarded as not forming a single household for the purposes of the statutory definition of houses in multiple occupation[1] unless:

(1)   they are all members of the same family; or

(2)   their circumstances are circumstances of a description specified for this purpose in regulations made by the appropriate national authority[2].

For these purposes, a person is a member of the same family as another person if:

(a)   those persons are married[3] to each other or live together as husband and wife (or in an equivalent relationship in the case of persons of the same sex);

(b)   one of them is a relative[4] of the other; or

(c)   one of them is, or is a relative of, one member of a couple[5] and the other is a relative of the other member of the couple[6].

1   Ie the Housing Act 2004 s 254: see PARA 667.

2   Housing Act 2004 s 258(1), (2). As to the meaning of 'the appropriate national authority' see PARA 389 note 1. Regulations under s 258(2)(b) may, in particular, secure that a group of persons are to be regarded as forming a single household only where (as the regulations may require) each member of the group has a prescribed relationship, or at least one of a number of prescribed relationships, to any one or more of the others: s 258(5). 'Prescribed relationship' means any relationship of a description specified in the regulations: s 258(6). Persons to be regarded as forming a single household for these purposes are specified in the Licensing and Management of Houses in Multiple Occupation and Other Houses (Miscellaneous Provisions) (England) Regulations 2006, SI 2006/373, regs 3, 4; and the Licensing and Management of Houses in Multiple Occupation and Other Houses (Miscellaneous Provisions) (Wales) Regulations 2006, SI 2006/1715, regs 3, 4.

3   A married couple includes a married same sex couple: see the Marriage (Same Sex Couples) Act 2013 s 11, Sch 3 para 1(1)(b), (2), (3); and MATRIMONIAL AND CIVIL PARTNERSHIP LAW vol 72 (2015) PARA 1 et seq.

4   For this purpose, 'relative' means parent, grandparent, child, grandchild, brother, sister, uncle, aunt, nephew, niece or cousin: Housing Act 2004 s 258(4)(b). A relationship of the half-blood is to be treated as a relationship of the whole blood, and the stepchild of a person is to be treated as his child: s 258(4)(c), (d).

5   For this purpose, 'couple' means two persons who are married to each other or otherwise fall within the Housing Act 2004 s 258(3)(a) (see head (a) in the text): s 258(4)(a).

6   Housing Act 2004 s 258(3).

671. Persons treated as occupying premises as only or main residence. For the purposes of the statutory definition of houses in multiple occupation[1], a person is to be treated as occupying a building or part of a building as his only or main residence if it is occupied by the person: (1) as the person's residence for the purpose of undertaking a full-time course of further or higher education; (2) as a refuge[2]; or (3) in any other circumstances which are circumstances of a description specified for this purpose in regulations made by the appropriate national authority[3].

1   Ie the Housing Act 2004 s 254: PARA 453.
2   For this purpose, 'refuge' means a building or part of a building managed by a voluntary organisation and used wholly or mainly for the temporary accommodation of persons who have left their homes as a result of: (1) physical violence or mental abuse; or (2) threats of such violence or abuse, from persons to whom they are or were married or with whom they are or were co-habiting: Housing Act 2004 s 259(3). As to the meaning of 'married' see PARA 670 note 3.
3   Housing Act 2004 s 259(1), (2). As to the meaning of 'the appropriate national authority' see PARA 389 note 1. Circumstances have been specified for this purpose: see the Licensing and Management of Houses in Multiple Occupation and Other Houses (Miscellaneous Provisions) (England) Regulations 2006, SI 2006/373, reg 5; and the Licensing and Management of Houses in Multiple Occupation and Other Houses (Miscellaneous Provisions) (Wales) Regulations 2006, SI 2006/1715, reg 5.

(2) HMO DECLARATIONS

672. HMO declarations. If a local housing authority[1] is satisfied that the following provisions apply to a building or part of a building in its area, it may serve a notice (an 'HMO declaration') declaring the building or part to be a house in multiple occupation[2]. The statutory provisions apply to a building or part of a building if the building or part meets any of the following tests (as it applies without the sole use condition[3]) and the occupation, by persons who do not form a single household, of the living accommodation or flat referred to in the test in question constitutes a significant use of that accommodation or flat[4]. The tests are the standard test[5], the self-contained flat test[6] or the converted building test[7].

The notice must: (1) state the date of the authority's decision to serve the notice; (2) be served[8] on each relevant person[9] within the period of seven days beginning with the date of that decision; (3) state the day on which it will come into force if no appeal is made[10] against the authority's decision[11]; and (4) set out the right to appeal against the decision and the period within which an appeal may be made[12].

If no appeal is made before the end of the period of 28 days after the date of the authority's decision to serve the notice[13], the notice comes into force on the day stated in the notice[14]. If such an appeal is made before the end of that period of 28 days, the notice does not come into force unless and until a decision is given on the appeal which confirms the notice and either the period within which an appeal to the Upper Tribunal[15] may be brought expires without such an appeal having been brought or, if an appeal to the Upper Tribunal is brought, a decision is given on the appeal which confirms the notice[16].

Any relevant person may appeal to the appropriate tribunal[17] against a decision of the local housing authority to serve an HMO declaration[18]. The appeal must be made within the period of 28 days beginning with the date of the authority's decision[19]. Such an appeal is to be by way of a re-hearing, but may be determined having regard to matters of which the authority was unaware[20]. The tribunal may confirm or reverse the decision of the authority, and if it reverses the decision, may revoke the HMO declaration[21].

1   As to the meaning of 'local housing authority' see PARA 380 note 1.
2   Housing Act 2004 s 255(1). As to the meaning of 'house in multiple occupation' see PARA 667.

3 'The sole use condition' means the condition contained in either the Housing Act 2004 s 254(2)(d) (see PARA 667 head (d)) (as it applies for the purposes of the standard test or the self-contained flat test) or s 254(4)(e) (see PARA 667 head (v)), as the case may be: s 255(3). As to the presumption that the sole use condition is met see note 4.

4 Housing Act 2004 s 255(2). Where a question arises in any proceedings as to whether either the sole use condition or the significant use condition is met in respect of a building or part of a building, it must be presumed, for the purposes of the proceedings, that the condition is met unless the contrary is shown: s 260(1). For this purpose, 'the sole use condition' means the condition contained in either s 254(2)(d) (see PARA 667 head (d)) (as it applies for the purposes of the standard test or the self-contained flat test) or s 254(4)(e) (see PARA 667 head (v)), as the case may be (s 260(2)(a)); and 'the significant use condition' means the condition contained in s 255(2) that the occupation of the living accommodation or flat referred to in that provision by persons who do not form a single household constitutes a significant use of that accommodation or flat (s 260(2)(b)).

5 Ie the test in the Housing Act 2004 s 254(2): see PARA 667 text and notes 6–9.

6 Ie the test in the Housing Act 2004 s 254(3): see PARA 667 text and note 10.

7 Ie the test in the Housing Act 2004 s 254(4): see PARA 667 text and notes 11–14.

8 As to service of documents see PARA 391.

9 For the purposes of the Housing Act 2004 ss 255, 256, 'relevant person', in relation to an HMO declaration, means any person who, to the knowledge of the local housing authority, is: (1) a person having an estate or interest in the building or part of the building concerned (but is not a tenant under a lease with an unexpired term of three years or less); or (2) a person managing or having control of that building or part (and not falling within head (1)): s 255(12). As to the meaning of 'person having control' see PARA 391 note 5; and as to the meaning of 'person managing' see PARA 391 note 6. As to the meaning of 'person having an estate or interest' see PARA 391 note 7. In the Housing Act 2004, any reference to a person who is a tenant under a lease with an unexpired term of three years or less includes a statutory tenant as well as a tenant under a yearly or other periodic tenancy: s 262(5). As to statutory tenants see LANDLORD AND TENANT vol 64 (2016) PARA 1711 et seq.

10 Ie under the Housing Act 2004 s 255(9): see the text and notes 17–18.

11 The day stated in the notice must be not less than 28 days after the date of the authority's decision to serve the notice: Housing Act 2004 s 255(5).

12 Housing Act 2004 s 255(4).

13 See note 10.

14 Housing Act 2004 s 255(6).

15 As to appeals to the Upper Tribunal see PARAS 49–50.

16 Housing Act 2004 s 255(7) (amended by SI 2009/1307). For the purposes of the Housing Act 2004 s 255(7), the withdrawal of an appeal has the same effect as a decision which confirms the notice appealed against: s 255(8).

17 For the purposes of the Housing Act 2004 ss 255, 256, 'appropriate tribunal' means: (1) in relation to a building in England, the First-tier Tribunal or, where determined by or under Tribunal Procedure Rules, the Upper Tribunal; and (2) in relation to a building in Wales, a residential property tribunal: s 255(13) (added by SI 2013/1036). As to appeals to the appropriate tribunal see PARA 32 et seq.

18 Housing Act 2004 s 255(9) (amended by SI 2013/1036).

19 Housing Act 2004 s 255(9).

20 Housing Act 2004 s 255(10).

21 Housing Act 2004 s 255(11).

673. Revocation of HMO declarations. A local housing authority[1] may revoke an HMO declaration[2] at any time if it considers that the statutory provisions[3] no longer apply to the building or part of the building in respect of which the declaration was served[4]. The power to revoke an HMO declaration is exercisable by the authority either on an application made by a relevant person[5] or on the authority's own initiative[6]. If, on an application by such a person, the authority decides not to revoke the HMO declaration, it must without delay serve on him a notice informing him of the decision, the reasons for it and the date on which it was made, the right to appeal against it[7], and the period within which an appeal may be made[8].

A person who applies to a local housing authority for the revocation of an HMO declaration may appeal to the appropriate tribunal[9] against a decision of the authority to refuse to revoke the notice[10]. The appeal must be made within the period of 28 days beginning with the date specified[11] as the date on which the decision was made[12]. Such an appeal is to be by way of a re-hearing, and may be determined having regard to matters of which the authority was unaware[13]. The tribunal may confirm or reverse the decision of the authority, and if it reverses the decision, it may revoke the HMO declaration[14].

1　As to the meaning of 'local housing authority' see PARA 380 note 1.
2　Ie a declaration served under the Housing Act 2004 s 255: see PARA 672.
3　Ie the Housing Act 2004 s 255(2): see PARA 672.
4　Housing Act 2004 s 256(1).
5　As to the meaning of 'relevant person' see PARA 672 note 9.
6　Housing Act 2004 s 256(2).
7　Ie under the Housing Act 2004 s 256(4): see the text and notes 9–12.
8　Housing Act 2004 s 256(3).
9　As to the meaning of 'appropriate tribunal' see PARA 672 note 17.
10　Housing Act 2004 s 256(4) (amended by SI 2013/1036).
11　Ie under the Housing Act 2004 s 256(3): see the text and notes 7–8.
12　Housing Act 2004 s 256(4).
13　Housing Act 2004 s 256(5).
14　Housing Act 2004 s 256(6).

(3) LICENSING OF HOUSES IN MULTIPLE OCCUPATION

(i) Licensing Requirement

674. Licensing of houses in multiple occupation. Part 2 of the Housing Act 2004[1] provides for HMOs[2] to be licensed by local housing authorities[3] where they are HMOs to which that Part applies[4] and they are required[5] to be licensed under that Part[6]. The appropriate national authority[7] may by order prescribe descriptions of HMOs as being HMOs to which Part 2 applies[8].

Every local housing authority has the following general duties:

(1)　to make such arrangements as are necessary to secure the effective implementation in its district of the licensing regime provided for by Part 2;

(2)　to ensure that all applications for licences and other issues falling to be determined by it under Part 2 are determined within a reasonable time; and

(3)　to satisfy itself, as soon as is reasonably practicable, that there are no Part 1 functions[9] that ought to be exercised by it in relation to the premises in respect of which such applications are made[10].

1　Ie the Housing Act 2004 Pt 2 (ss 55–78).
2　In the Housing Act 2004 Pt 2, 'HMO' means a house in multiple occupation as defined by ss 254–259 (see PARAS 667–673); and references to an HMO include (where the context permits) any yard, garden, outhouses and appurtenances belonging to, or usually enjoyed with, it (or any part of it): s 77.
3　As to the meaning of 'local housing authority' see PARA 380 note 1.
4　The Housing Act 2004 Pt 2 applies to the following HMOs in the case of each local housing authority: (1) any HMO in the authority's district which falls within any prescribed description of HMO (see note 8); and (2) if an area is for the time being designated by the authority under s 56 (see PARA 675) as subject to additional licensing, any HMO in that area which falls within any description of HMO specified in the designation: s 55(2). References in the Housing Act 2004 to the district of a local housing authority are references to the area of the council concerned, that is to say: (a) in the case of a unitary authority, the area or district; (b) in the case of a district council so far as it is not a unitary authority, the district; (c) in the case of a London borough council, the Common Council of the City of London (in its capacity as a local authority), the Sub-Treasurer

of the Inner Temple or the Under-Treasurer of the Middle Temple (in his capacity as a local authority) and the Council of the Isles of Scilly, the London borough, the City of London, the Inner or Middle Temple or the Isles of Scilly (as the case may be); and (d) in the case of a Welsh county council or a county borough council, the Welsh county or county borough: s 261(6). As to local government areas and authorities see LOCAL GOVERNMENT vol 69 (2009) PARA 22 et seq.

5 Ie under the Housing Act 2004 s 61(1): see PARA 679.

6 Housing Act 2004 s 55(1). As to the regulation of the letting and management of dwellings under domestic tenancies in Wales see the Housing (Wales) Act 2014 Pt 1 (ss 1–49); and PARA 729 et seq.

7 As to the meaning of 'the appropriate national authority' see PARA 389 note 1.

8 Housing Act 2004 s 55(3). The power conferred by s 55(3) may be exercised in such a way that Pt 2 applies to all HMOs in the district of a local housing authority: s 55(4). As to the orders that have been made see the Licensing of Houses in Multiple Occupation (Prescribed Descriptions) (England) Order 2006, SI 2006/371; and the Licensing of Houses in Multiple Occupation (Prescribed Descriptions) (Wales) Order 2006, SI 2006/1712.

9 'Part 1 function' means any duty under the Housing Act 2004 s 5 to take any course of action to which that provision applies (general duty to take enforcement action in relation to category 1 hazards: see PARA 566) or any power to take any course of action to which s 7 applies (powers to take enforcement action in relation to category 2 hazards: see PARA 567): s 55(6)(a).

10 Housing Act 2004 s 55(5). The authority may take such steps as it considers appropriate (whether or not involving an inspection) to comply with its duty under s 55(5)(c) (see head (3) in the text) in relation to each of the premises in question, but it must in any event comply with it within the period of five years beginning with the date of the application for a licence: s 55(6)(b).

675. Designation of areas subject to additional licensing. A local housing authority[1] may extend licensing beyond the scope of mandatory licensing by designating either the area of its district[2], or an area in its district, as subject to additional licensing in relation to a description of HMOs[3] specified in the designation, if the following requirements are met[4]. The authority must consider that a significant proportion of the HMOs of that description in the area are being managed sufficiently ineffectively as to give rise, or to be likely to give rise, to one or more particular problems either for those occupying the HMOs or for members of the public[5].

Before making a designation the authority must take reasonable steps to consult persons who are likely to be affected by the designation, and consider any representations made in accordance with the consultation and not withdrawn[6].

The power to make such a designation may be exercised in such a way that Part 2 of the Housing Act 2004[7] applies to all HMOs in the area in question[8].

In making such a designation, the authority must ensure that any exercise of the power is consistent with the authority's overall housing strategy[9]. The authority must also seek to adopt a co-ordinated approach in connection with dealing with homelessness[10], empty properties[11] and anti-social behaviour[12] affecting the private rented sector, both as regards combining licensing under of HMOs with other courses of action available to it, and as regards combining such licensing with measures taken by other persons[13].

The authority must not make a particular designation unless: (1) it has considered whether there are any other courses of action available to it (of whatever nature) that might provide an effective method of dealing with the problem or problems in question; and (2) it considers that making the designation will significantly assist it to deal with the problem or problems (whether or not it takes any other course of action as well)[14].

1 As to the meaning of 'local housing authority' see PARA 380 note 1.

2 As to the area of a local housing authority's district see PARA 674 note 4.

3 As to the meaning of 'HMO' see PARA 674 note 2.

4 Housing Act 2004 s 56(1); and see PARA 674 note 4. In addition, s 57 (see the text and notes 9–14) applies for the purposes of s 56: s 56(6).

5 Housing Act 2004 s 56(2). In forming an opinion as to this matter, the authority must have regard to any information regarding the extent to which any codes of practice approved under s 233 (see

PARA 696) have been complied with by persons managing HMOs in the area in question: s 56(5). As to the meaning of 'person managing' see PARA 391 note 6.
6   Housing Act 2004 s 56(3).
7   Ie the Housing Act 2004 Pt 2 (ss 55–78).
8   Housing Act 2004 s 56(4).
9   Housing Act 2004 s 57(1), (2). As to housing strategy see PARA 366.
10   As to a local housing authority's duties to the homeless see PARA 477 et seq.
11   As to a local housing authority's duties in relation to empty houses see PARA 781 et seq.
12   In the Housing Act 2004, 'anti-social behaviour' means conduct on the part of occupiers of, or visitors to, residential premises which causes or is likely to cause a nuisance or annoyance to persons residing, visiting or otherwise engaged in lawful activities in the vicinity of such premises, or which involves or is likely to involve the use of such premises for illegal purposes: s 57(5). As to anti-social behaviour see PARA 471 et seq. As to the meaning of 'occupy' see PARA 563 note 13.
13   Housing Act 2004 s 57(3).
14   Housing Act 2004 s 57(4).

676. Confirmation or general approval of designation. A designation of an area as subject to additional licensing[1] cannot come into force unless: (1) it has been confirmed by the appropriate national authority[2]; or (2) it falls within a description of designations in relation to which that authority has given[3] a general approval[4].

The appropriate national authority may either confirm, or refuse to confirm, a designation as it considers appropriate[5]. If the appropriate national authority confirms a designation, the designation comes into force on the date specified for this purpose by that authority[6]. That date must be no earlier than three months after the date on which the designation is confirmed[7].

A general approval may be given in relation to a description of designations framed by reference to any matters or circumstances[8]. Accordingly, a general approval may (in particular) be given in relation to: (a) designations made by a specified[9] local housing authority[10]; (b) designations made by a local housing authority falling within a specified description of such authorities; (c) designations relating to HMOs of a specified description[11].

If, by virtue of a general approval, a designation does not need to be confirmed before it comes into force, the designation comes into force on the date specified for this purpose in the designation[12]. That date must be no earlier than three months after the date on which the designation is made[13].

1   Ie under the Housing Act 2004 s 57: see PARA 675.
2   As to the meaning of 'the appropriate national authority' see PARA 389 note 1.
3   Ie in accordance with the Housing Act 2004 s 58(6).
4   Housing Act 2004 s 58(1). See the Housing Act 2004: Licensing of Houses in Multiple Occupation and Selective Licensing of Other Residential Accommodation (England) General Approval 2015 (Department for Communities and Local Government, 26 March 2015).
5   Housing Act 2004 s 58(2).
6   Housing Act 2004 s 58(3).
7   Housing Act 2004 s 58(4).
8   Housing Act 2004 s 58(5).
9   'Specified' means specified by the appropriate national authority in the approval: Housing Act 2004 s 58(6).
10   As to the meaning of 'local housing authority' see PARA 380 note 1.
11   Housing Act 2004 s 58(6).
12   Housing Act 2004 s 58(7).
13   Housing Act 2004 s 58(8).

677. Notification requirements. As soon as the designation of an area as subject to additional licensing is confirmed[1] or (if it is not required to be so confirmed) as soon as it is made by the local housing authority[2], the authority must publish in the prescribed[3] manner a notice stating:
    (1)   that the designation has been made;

(2) whether or not the designation was required to be confirmed and either that it has been confirmed or that a general approval[4] applied to it (giving details of the approval in question);

(3) the date on which the designation is to come into force[5]; and

(4) any other information which may be prescribed[6].

After publication of such a notice, and for as long as the designation is in force, the local housing authority must make available to the public in accordance with any prescribed requirements copies of the designation, and such information relating to the designation as is prescribed[7].

1 Ie under the Housing Act 2004 s 58: see PARA 676. As to designations see PARA 675.
2 As to the meaning of 'local housing authority' see PARA 380 note 1.
3 'Prescribed' means prescribed by regulations made by the appropriate national authority: Housing Act 2004 s 59(4). As to the meaning of 'the appropriate national authority' see PARA 389 note 1. Regulations have been made prescribing the publication requirements: see the Licensing and Management of Houses in Multiple Occupation and Other Houses (Miscellaneous Provisions) (England) Regulations 2006, SI 2006/373, reg 9; and the Licensing and Management of Houses in Multiple Occupation and Other Houses (Miscellaneous Provisions) (Wales) Regulations 2006, SI 2006/1715, reg 9.
4 Ie under the Housing Act 2004 s 58: see PARA 676.
5 As to the coming into force of designations see PARA 676.
6 Housing Act 2004 s 59(1), (2); and see PARA 674 note 4. See also note 3.
7 Housing Act 2004 s 59(3). See note 3.

678. Duration, review and revocation of designations. Unless previously revoked[1], a designation of an area as subject to additional licensing[2] ceases to have effect at the time that is specified for this purpose in the designation[3]. That time must be no later than five years after the date on which the designation comes into force[4]. A local housing authority[5] must from time to time review the operation of any designation made by it[6]. If following a review it considers it appropriate to do so, the authority may revoke the designation[7]. If it does revoke the designation, the designation ceases to have effect at the time that is specified by the authority for this purpose[8]. On revoking a designation the authority must publish notice of the revocation in such manner as is prescribed by regulations made by the appropriate national authority[9].

1 Ie under the Housing Act 2004 s 60(4).
2 Ie a designation under the Housing Act 2004 s 57: see PARA 675.
3 Housing Act 2004 s 60(1).
4 Housing Act 2004 s 60(2).
5 As to the meaning of 'local housing authority' see PARA 380 note 1.
6 Housing Act 2004 s 60(3); and see PARA 674 note 4.
7 Housing Act 2004 s 60(4).
8 Housing Act 2004 s 60(5).
9 Housing Act 2004 s 60(6). As to the meaning of 'the appropriate national authority' see PARA 389 note 1. Regulations have been made prescribing the publication requirements: see the Licensing and Management of Houses in Multiple Occupation and Other Houses (Miscellaneous Provisions) (England) Regulations 2006, SI 2006/373, reg 10; and the Licensing and Management of Houses in Multiple Occupation and Other Houses (Miscellaneous Provisions) (Wales) Regulations 2006, SI 2006/1715, reg 10.

679. Houses in multiple occupation required to be licensed. Every HMO[1] to which Part 2 of the Housing Act 2004[2] applies must be licensed[3] unless: (1) a temporary exemption notice is in force in relation to it[4]; or (2) an interim or final management order is in force[5] in relation to it[6]. A licence under Part 2 of the Housing Act 2004 is a licence authorising occupation of the house concerned by not more than a maximum number of households or persons specified in the licence[7].

The local housing authority[8] must take all reasonable steps to secure that applications for licences are made to it in respect of HMOs in its area[9] which are required to be licensed but are not[10].

The appropriate national authority[11] may by regulations provide for specified provisions[12] to have effect in relation to a section 257 HMO[13] with such modifications as are prescribed by the regulations[14].

1 As to the meaning of 'HMO' see PARA 674 note 2.
2 Ie the Housing Act 2004 Pt 2 (ss 55–78).
3 Unless the context otherwise requires, references in the Housing Act 2004 Pt 2 to an HMO being (or not being) licensed under that Part are to its being (or not being) an HMO in respect of which a licence is in force under that Part: s 61(6)(c).
4 Ie under the Housing Act 2004 s 62: see PARA 680.
5 Ie under the Housing Act 2004 Pt 4 Ch 1 (ss 101–131): see PARA 745 et seq.
6 Housing Act 2004 s 61(1).
7 Housing Act 2004 s 61(2). Applications for licences, the granting or refusal of licences and the imposition of licence conditions are dealt with in ss 63–67 (see PARAS 682–683): s 61(3). As to rules for counting the number of persons see PARA 396.
8 As to the meaning of 'local housing authority' see PARA 380 note 1.
9 As to the area of a local housing authority's district see PARA 674 note 4.
10 Housing Act 2004 s 61(4); and see PARA 674 note 4.
11 As to the meaning of 'the appropriate national authority' see PARA 389 note 1.
12 Ie any provision of the Housing Act 2004 Pt 2, or s 263 (definitions, etc) in its operation for the purposes of any such provision.
13 A 'section 257 HMO' is an HMO which is a converted block of flats to which the Housing Act 2004 s 257 applies (see PARA 669): s 61(5).
14 Housing Act 2004 s 61(5). As to regulations made see the Houses in Multiple Occupation (Certain Converted Blocks of Flats) (Modifications to the Housing Act 2004 and Transitional Provisions for section 257 HMOs) (England) Regulations 2007, SI 2007/1904; and the Houses in Multiple Occupation (Certain Blocks of Flats) (Modifications to the Housing Act 2004 and Transitional Provisions for section 257 HMOs) (Wales) Regulations 2007, SI 2007/3231, which modify the Housing Act 2004 s 61 and other provisions in relation to section 257 HMOs.

680. Temporary exemption from licensing requirement. Where a person having control of or managing[1] an HMO[2] which is required[3] to be licensed under Part 2 of the Housing Act 2004[4], but which is not so licensed, notifies the local housing authority[5] of his intention to take particular steps with a view to securing that the house is no longer required to be licensed, the authority may, if it thinks fit, serve on that person a notice (a 'temporary exemption notice') in respect of the house[6]. If a temporary exemption notice is served, the house is[7] not required to be licensed under Part 2 or, where relevant, under Part 3[8] of the Housing Act 2004 during the period for which the notice is in force[9]. A temporary exemption notice is in force either for the period of three months beginning with the date on which it is served, or (in the case of a second temporary exemption notice[10]) for the period of three months after the date when the first notice ceases to be in force[11].

If the authority receives a further notification, and considers that there are exceptional circumstances that justify the service of a second temporary exemption notice in respect of the house that would take effect from the end of the period of three months applying to the first notice, the authority may serve a second such notice on the person having control of or managing the house (but no further notice may be served by virtue of this provision)[12].

If the authority decides not to serve a temporary exemption notice in response to a notification, it must without delay serve on the person concerned a notice informing him of: (1) the decision; (2) the reasons for it and the date on which it was made; (3) the right to appeal against the decision[13]; and (4) the period within which an appeal may be made[14].

The person concerned may appeal to the appropriate tribunal[15] against the decision within the period of 28 days beginning with the date specified[16] as the date on which it was made[17]. Such an appeal is to be by way of a re-hearing, and may be determined having regard to matters of which the authority was unaware[18]. The tribunal may confirm or reverse the decision of the authority and, if it reverses the decision, must direct the authority to serve a temporary exemption notice that comes into force on such date as the tribunal directs[19].

1   As to the meaning of 'person having control' see PARA 391 note 5; and as to the meaning of 'person managing' see PARA 391 note 6.
2   As to the meaning of 'HMO' see PARA 674 note 2.
3   Ie under the Housing Act 2004 s 61(1): see PARA 679.
4   Ie the Housing Act 2004 Pt 2 (ss 55–78).
5   As to the meaning of 'local housing authority' see PARA 380 note 1.
6   Housing Act 2004 s 62(1), (2); and see PARA 674 note 4. As to service of documents see PARA 391.
7   Ie in accordance with the Housing Act 2004 s 61(1) and s 85(1): see PARAS 679, 709.
8   Ie the Housing Act 2004 Pt 3 (ss 79–100): see PARA 704 et seq.
9   Housing Act 2004 s 62(3).
10   Ie a notice served by virtue of the Housing Act 2004 s 62(5): see the text to note 12.
11   Housing Act 2004 s 62(4).
12   Housing Act 2004 s 62(5).
13   Ie under the Housing Act 2004 s 62(7): see the text and notes 15–17.
14   Housing Act 2004 s 62(6).
15   As to the meaning of 'appropriate tribunal' see PARA 580 note 2. As to appeals to the appropriate tribunal see PARA 32 et seq.
16   Ie under the Housing Act 2004 s 62(6).
17   Housing Act 2004 s 62(7) (amended by SI 2013/1036).
18   Housing Act 2004 s 62(8).
19   Housing Act 2004 s 62(9).

681. Transitional arrangements relating to introduction and termination of licensing. Where an order[1] which prescribes a particular description of HMOs[2] comes into force, or a designation of an area subject to additional licensing[3] comes into force in relation to HMOs of a particular description, Part 2 of the Housing Act 2004[4] applies in relation to the occupation by persons or households of such HMOs on or after the coming into force of the order or designation even if their occupation began before, or in pursuance of a contract made before, it came into force[5].

Where an HMO which is licensed under Part 2, or a part of such an HMO, is occupied by more households or persons than the number permitted by the licence[6], and the occupation of all or any of those households or persons began before, or in pursuance of a contract made before, the licence came into force, in proceedings against a person for an offence of overcrowding[7] it is a defence that at the material time he was taking all reasonable steps to try to reduce the number of households or persons occupying the house to the number permitted by the licence[8]. This does not apply if the licence came into force immediately after a previous licence in respect of the same HMO unless the occupation in question began before, or in pursuance of a contract made before, the coming into force of the original licence[9].

Provision may be made[10] as regards the licensing under Part 2 of HMOs which are registered immediately before the appointed day[11] under a scheme containing control provisions[12] or special control provisions[13] under the Housing Act 1985, or in respect of which applications for registration under such a scheme are then pending[14].

1   Ie an order under the Housing Act 2004 s 55(3): see PARA 674.
2   As to the meaning of 'HMO' see PARA 674 note 2.

3 Ie under the Housing Act 2004 s 56: see PARA 675.
4 Ie the Housing Act 2004 Pt 2 (ss 55–78).
5 Housing Act 2004 s 76(1), (2).
6 As to the maximum number of persons or households permitted see PARA 682.
7 Ie under the Housing Act 2004 s 72(2): see PARA 693.
8 Housing Act 2004 s 76(3), (4).
9 Housing Act 2004 s 76(5).
10 Ie in a commencement order under the Housing Act 2004 s 270.
11 For this purpose, 'the appointed day' means the day appointed for the coming into force of the Housing Act 2004 s 61 (see PARA 679): s 76(7). Section 61 came fully into force on 6 April 2006 in relation to England and on 16 June 2006 in relation to Wales: see the Housing Act 2004 (Commencement No 5 and Transitional Provisions and Savings) (England) Order 2006, SI 2006/1060, arts 1(3)(c), 2(1)(a); and the Housing Act 2004 (Commencement No 3 and Transitional Provisions and Savings) (Wales) Order 2006, SI 2006/1535, arts 1(2)(c), 2(a).
12 Ie a scheme to which the Housing Act 1985 s 347 (repealed) applied.
13 Ie a scheme to which the Housing Act 1985 s 348B (repealed) applied.
14 Housing Act 2004 s 76(6).

(ii) HMO Licences

682. Application for licence. Where a dwelling is an HMO, and one which requires a licence[1], an application for a licence must be made to the local housing authority[2], and must be made in accordance with such requirements as the authority may specify[3]. The authority may, in particular, require the application to be accompanied by a fee fixed by the authority[4].

The appropriate national authority[5] may by regulations make provision about the making of applications for licences[6]. Such regulations may, in particular:

(1)   specify the manner and form in which applications are to be made;
(2)   require the applicant to give copies of the application, or information about it, to particular persons;
(3)   specify the information or, as from a day to be appointed, evidence which is to be supplied in connection with applications;
(4)   specify the maximum fees which are to be charged (whether by specifying amounts or methods for calculating amounts);
(5)   specify cases in which no fees are to be charged or fees are to be refunded[7].

Where an application in respect of an HMO is made to the local housing authority, the authority must either grant a licence in accordance with the following provisions[8], or refuse to grant a licence[9]. If the authority is satisfied as to the matters mentioned below, it may grant a licence either to the applicant or to some other person, if both he and the applicant agree to this[10]. Those matters are:

(a)   that the house is reasonably suitable for occupation by not more than the maximum number of households or persons specified[11] or that it can be made so suitable by the imposition of conditions[12];
(b)   prospectively, that no banning order[13] is in force against a person who: (i) owns an estate or interest in the house or part of it; and (ii) is a lessor or licensor of the house or part;
(c)   that the proposed licence holder[14]: (i) is a fit and proper person to be the licence holder[15]; and (ii) is, out of all the persons reasonably available to be the licence holder in respect of the house, the most appropriate person to be the licence holder[16];
(d)   that the proposed manager of the house is either: (i) the person having control of the house[17]; or (ii) a person who is an agent or employee of the person having control of the house;

(e) that the proposed manager of the house is a fit and proper person to be the manager of the house[18]; and

(f) that the proposed management arrangements for the house are otherwise satisfactory[19].

The local housing authority cannot be satisfied that the house is reasonably suitable for occupation by a particular maximum number of households or persons if it considers that it fails to meet prescribed standards for occupation by that number of households or persons[20]. However, the authority may decide that the house is not reasonably suitable for occupation by a particular maximum number of households or persons even if it does meet prescribed standards for occupation by that number of households or persons[21].

1   See PARA 674. As to the meaning of 'HMO' see PARA 674 note 2. Unless the context otherwise requires, references in the Housing Act 2004 Pt 2 (ss 55–78) to a licence are references to a licence under that Part: s 61(6)(a). As to the conditions to be included in licences see PARA 683. As to procedural requirements see PARA 687 et seq. As to the duration and transferability of licences see PARA 684. As to variation of licences see PARA 685. As to revocation of licences see PARA 686.

2   As to the meaning of 'local housing authority' see PARA 380 note 1.

3   Housing Act 2004 s 63(1), (2); and see PARA 674 note 4. The power of the authority to specify requirements under s 63 is subject to any regulations made under s 63(5) (see the text and note 6): s 63(4).

4   Housing Act 2004 s 63(3). When fixing fees under s 63, the local housing authority may (subject to any regulations made under s 63(5): see the text and note 6) take into account all costs incurred by the authority in carrying out its functions under Pt 2, and all costs incurred by it in carrying out its functions under Pt 4 Ch 1 (ss 101–131) in relation to HMOs (so far as they are not recoverable under or by virtue of any provision of that Chapter): s 63(7). As to the meaning of 'HMO' see PARA 674 note 2.

5   As to the meaning of 'the appropriate national authority' see PARA 389 note 1.

6   Housing Act 2004 s 63(5). As to the regulations made see the Licensing and Management of Houses in Multiple Occupation and Other Houses (Miscellaneous Provisions) (England) Regulations 2006, SI 2006/373, reg 7, Sch 2 (reg 7 amended by SI 2012/2111; the Licensing and Management of Houses in Multiple Occupation and Other Houses (Miscellaneous Provisions) (England) Regulations 2006, SI 2006/373, Sch 2 amended by SI 2007/1903 and SI 2012/2111); and the Licensing and Management of Houses in Multiple Occupation and Other Houses (Miscellaneous Provisions) (Wales) Regulations 2006, SI 2006/1715, reg 7, Sch 2 (Sch 2 amended by SI 2007/3229).

7   Housing Act 2004 s 63(6) (amended, as from a day to be appointed, by the Housing and Planning Act 2016 s 125(1), (2); at the date at which this volume states the law, no such day had been appointed). See note 6.

8   Ie in accordance with the Housing Act 2004 s 63(2): see the text and note 3.

9   Housing Act 2004 s 64(1). In relation to a section 257 HMO (see PARA 669), s 64 is modified by the Houses in Multiple Occupation (Certain Converted Blocks of Flats) (Modifications to the Housing Act 2004 and Transitional Provisions for section 257 HMOs) (England) Regulations 2007, SI 2007/1904, regs 2, 4; and the Houses in Multiple Occupation (Certain Blocks of Flats) (Modifications to the Housing Act 2004 and Transitional Provisions for section 257 HMOs) (Wales) Regulations 2007, SI 2007/3231, regs 2, 4.

10 Housing Act 2004 s 64(2).

11 The maximum number of households or persons is either the maximum number specified in the application, or some other maximum number decided by the authority: Housing Act 2004 s 64(4). As to rules for counting the number of persons see PARA 396.

12 Ie under the Housing Act 2004 s 67: see PARA 683. See also the text to notes 20–21.

13 Ie under the Housing and Planning Act 2016 s 16: see PARA 719 et seq.

14 Unless the context otherwise requires, references in the Housing Act 2004 Pt 2 to a licence holder are references to the holder of a licence under that Part: s 61(6)(b).

15 In deciding for the purposes of the Housing Act 2004 s 64(3)(b) or (d) (see heads (c) and (e) in the text) whether a person ('P') is a fit and proper person to be the licence holder or (as the case may be) the manager of the house, the local housing authority must have regard (among other things) to any evidence within s 66(2) or (3): ss 64(5), 66(1). Evidence is within s 66(2) if it shows that P has: (1) committed any offence involving fraud or other dishonesty, or violence or drugs, or any offence listed in the Sexual Offences Act 2003 Sch 3 (offences attracting notification requirements: see SENTENCING vol 92 (2015) PARA 329); (2) practised unlawful discrimination on grounds of sex, colour, race, ethnic or national origins or disability in, or in connection with, the carrying on

of any business (see DISCRIMINATION vol 33 (2013) PARA 65 et seq); (3) contravened any provision of the law relating to housing or of landlord and tenant law (see LANDLORD AND TENANT) including, as from a day to be appointed, the Immigration Act 2014 Pt 3 (ss 20–47); or (4) acted otherwise than in accordance with any applicable code of practice approved under the Housing Act 2004 s 233 (see PARA 696): s 66(2) (amended, as from a day to be appointed, by the Housing and Planning Act 2016 s 125(1), (3)(b); at the date at which this volume states the law, no such day had been appointed). Evidence is within the Housing Act 2004 s 66(3) if: (a) it shows that any person associated or formerly associated with P (whether on a personal, work or other basis) has done any of the things set out in heads (1) to (4); and (b) it appears to the authority that the evidence is relevant to the question whether P is a fit and proper person to be the licence holder or (as the case may be) the manager of the house: s 66(3).

Prospectively, a local housing authority in England must also have regard to any evidence within s 66(3A) or (3B): s 66(1A) (s 66(1A), (3A), (3B) added, as from a day to be appointed, by the Housing and Planning Act 2016 s 125(1), (3)(a), (c); at the date at which this volume states the law, no such day had been appointed). Evidence is within the Housing Act 2004 s 66(3A) if it shows that P: (i) requires leave to enter or remain in the United Kingdom but does not have it; or (ii) is insolvent or an undischarged bankrupt: s 66(3A) (as so added). Evidence is within s 66(3B) if: (A) it shows that any person associated or formerly associated with P (whether on a personal, work or other basis) is a person to whom head (i) or (ii) applies; and (B) it appears to the authority that the evidence is relevant to the question whether P is a fit and proper person to be the licence holder or (as the case may be) the manager of the house: s 66(3B) (as so added).

Prospectively, a person is not a fit and proper person for the purposes of s 64(3)(b) or (d) if a banning order under the Housing and Planning Act 2016 s 16 is in force against the person: Housing Act 2004 s 66(3C) (added, as from a day to be appointed, by the Housing and Planning Act 2016 s 25, Sch 2 paras 1, 3; at the date at which this volume states the law, no such day had been appointed).

16 For the purposes of the Housing Act 2004 s 64(3)(b) (see head (c) in the text), the local housing authority must assume, unless the contrary is shown, that the person having control of the house is a more appropriate person to be the licence holder than a person not having control of it: s 66(4). Any reference in s 66(4) or s 64(3)(c)(i) or (ii) (see note 16) to a person having control of the house, or to being a person of any other description, includes a reference to a person who is proposing to have control of the house, or (as the case may be) to be a person of that description, at the time when the licence would come into force: s 66(7).

17 As to the meaning of 'person having control' see PARA 391 note 5. See also note 16.

18 See notes 15–16.

19 Housing Act 2004 s 64(3) (amended, as from a day to be appointed, by the Housing and Planning Act 2016 Sch 2 paras 1, 2; at the date at which this volume states the law, no such day had been appointed). In deciding for the purposes of the Housing Act 2004 s 64(3)(e) (see head (f) in the text) whether the proposed management arrangements for the house are otherwise satisfactory, the local housing authority must have regard (among other things) to the considerations mentioned in s 66(6): s 66(5). The considerations are: (1) whether any person proposed to be involved in the management of the house has a sufficient level of competence to be so involved; (2) whether any person proposed to be involved in the management of the house (other than the manager) is a fit and proper person to be so involved; and (3) whether any proposed management structures and funding arrangements are suitable: s 66(6).

20 Housing Act 2004 ss 64(5), 65(1).

21 Housing Act 2004 s 65(2). 'Prescribed standards' means standards prescribed by regulations made by the appropriate national authority: s 65(3). The standards that may be so prescribed include: (1) standards as to the number, type and quality of: (a) bathrooms, toilets, washbasins and showers; (b) areas for food storage, preparation and cooking; and (c) laundry facilities, which should be available in particular circumstances; and (2) standards as to the number, type and quality of other facilities or equipment which should be available in particular circumstances: s 65(4). As to the regulations made see the Licensing and Management of Houses in Multiple Occupation and Other Houses (Miscellaneous Provisions) (England) Regulations 2006, SI 2006/373, reg 8, Sch 3 (reg 8 substituted and Sch 3 amended by SI 2007/1903); and the Licensing and Management of Houses in Multiple Occupation and Other Houses (Miscellaneous Provisions) (Wales) Regulations 2006, SI 2006/1715, reg 8, Sch 3 (reg 8 substituted and Sch 3 amended by SI 2007/3229).

In relation to a section 257 HMO (see PARA 669), the Housing Act 2004 s 65 is modified by the Houses in Multiple Occupation (Certain Converted Blocks of Flats) (Modifications to the Housing Act 2004 and Transitional Provisions for section 257 HMOs) (England) Regulations 2007, SI 2007/1904, regs 2, 5; and the Houses in Multiple Occupation (Certain Blocks of Flats) (Modifications to the Housing Act 2004 and Transitional Provisions for section 257 HMOs) (Wales) Regulations 2007, SI 2007/3231, regs 2, 5.

683. Licence conditions. There are certain conditions which must be included in a licence[1], whilst others may be included at the discretion of the local housing authority[2].

A licence may include such conditions as the local housing authority considers appropriate for regulating all or any of the following:

(1) the management, use and occupation of the house concerned; and

(2) its condition and contents[3].

Those conditions may, in particular, include (so far as appropriate in the circumstances):

(a) conditions imposing restrictions or prohibitions on the use or occupation of particular parts of the house by persons occupying it;

(b) conditions requiring the taking of reasonable and practicable steps to prevent or reduce anti-social behaviour[4] by persons occupying or visiting the house;

(c) conditions requiring facilities and equipment to be made available in the house for the purpose of meeting prescribed[5] standards;

(d) conditions requiring such facilities and equipment to be kept in repair and proper working order;

(e) conditions requiring, in the case of any works needed in order for any such facilities or equipment to be made available or to meet any such standards, that the works are carried out within such period or periods as may be specified in, or determined under, the licence;

(f) conditions requiring the licence holder[6] or the manager of the house to attend training courses in relation to any applicable approved[7] code of practice[8].

A licence must include the following conditions[9]:

(i) conditions requiring the licence holder, if gas is supplied to the house[10], to produce to the local housing authority annually for its inspection a gas safety certificate obtained in respect of the house within the last 12 months[11];

(ii) conditions requiring the licence holder: (A) to keep electrical appliances and furniture made available by him in the house in a safe condition; (B) to supply the authority, on demand, with a declaration by him as to the safety of such appliances and furniture[12];

(iii) conditions requiring the licence holder: (A) where the house is in England, to ensure that a smoke alarm is installed on each storey of the house on which there is a room used wholly or partly as living accommodation[13] and to keep each such alarm in proper working order; (B) where the house is in Wales, to ensure that smoke alarms are installed in the house and to keep them in proper working order; (C) in either case, to supply the authority, on demand, with a declaration by him as to the condition and positioning of such alarms[14];

(iv) where the house is in England, conditions requiring the licence holder: (A) to ensure that a carbon monoxide alarm is installed in any room[15] in the house which is used wholly or partly as living accommodation and contains a solid fuel burning combustion appliance; (B) to keep any such alarm in proper working order; and (C) to supply the authority, on demand, with a declaration by him as to the condition and positioning of any such alarm[16];

(v) conditions requiring the licence holder to supply to the occupiers[17] of the house a written statement of the terms on which they occupy it[18].

As regards the relationship between the authority's power to impose conditions in a licence and functions exercisable by it under or for the purposes of Part 1 of the Housing Act 2004[19] ('Part 1 functions')[20], the authority must proceed on the basis that, in general, it should seek to identify, remove or reduce category 1 or category 2 hazards[21] in the house by the exercise of Part 1 functions and not by means of licence conditions[22]. The fact that licence conditions are imposed for a particular purpose that could be achieved by the exercise of Part 1 functions does not affect the way in which Part 1 functions can be subsequently exercised by the authority[23].

A licence may not include conditions imposing restrictions or obligations on a particular person other than the licence holder unless that person has consented to the imposition of the restrictions or obligations[24]. A licence may not include conditions requiring (or intended to secure) any alteration in the terms of any tenancy or licence[25] under which any person occupies the house[26].

1 See the text and notes 9–18. As to the meaning of 'licence' see PARA 682 note 1. As to applications for a licence see PARA 682. As to the duration and transferability of licences see PARA 684. As to variation of licences see PARA 685. As to revocation of licences see PARA 686.
2 See the text and notes 3–8. As to the meaning of 'local housing authority' see PARA 380 note 1; and see PARA 674 note 4.
3 Housing Act 2004 s 67(1). In relation to a section 257 HMO (see PARA 669), s 67, Sch 4 (see the text and notes 9–15) are modified by the Houses in Multiple Occupation (Certain Converted Blocks of Flats) (Modifications to the Housing Act 2004 and Transitional Provisions for section 257 HMOs) (England) Regulations 2007, SI 2007/1904, regs 2, 6, 10; and the Houses in Multiple Occupation (Certain Blocks of Flats) (Modifications to the Housing Act 2004 and Transitional Provisions for section 257 HMOs) (Wales) Regulations 2007, SI 2007/3231, regs 2, 6, 10.
4 As to the meaning of 'anti-social behaviour' see PARA 675 note 12.
5 Ie prescribed under the Housing Act 2004 s 65: see PARA 682 note 12.
6 As to the meaning of 'licence holder' see PARA 682 note 14.
7 Ie approved under the Housing Act 2004 s 233: see PARA 696.
8 Housing Act 2004 s 67(2).
9 Housing Act 2004 s 67(3), Sch 4. The appropriate national authority may by regulations amend Sch 4 so as to alter (by the addition or removal of conditions) the conditions which must be included in a licence under Pt 2 (ss 55–78) or Pt 3 (ss 79–100), or only in a licence under one of those Parts: Sch 4 para 3. See the Smoke and Carbon Monoxide Alarm (England) Regulations 2015, SI 2015/1693. As to the meaning of 'the appropriate national authority' see PARA 389 note 1.
10 For this purpose, 'the house' means the HMO in respect of which the licence is granted: Housing Act 2004 Sch 4 para 4. As to the meaning of 'HMO' see PARA 674 note 2.
11 Housing Act 2004 Sch 4 para 1(1), (2).
12 Housing Act 2004 Sch 4 para 1(3).
13 For the purposes of the Housing Act 2004 Sch 4 para 1(4), (4A) (see head (iv) in the text), a bathroom or lavatory is to be treated as a room used as living accommodation: Sch 4 para 1(7) (added, in relation to England, by SI 2015/1693).
14 Housing Act 2004 Sch 4 para 1(4) (amended, in relation to England, by SI 2015/1693).
15 For these purposes, 'room' includes a hall or landing: Housing Act 2004 Sch 4 para 1(6) (added, in relation to England, by SI 2015/1693).
16 Housing Act 2004 Sch 4 para 1(4A) (added, in relation to England, by SI 2015/1693).
17 As to the meaning of 'occupier' see PARA 563 note 13.
18 Housing Act 2004 Sch 4 para 1(5).
19 Ie the Housing Act 2004 Pt 1 (ss 1–54): see PARA 563 et seq.
20 As to Part 1 functions see also PARA 674 note 9.
21 As to the meanings of 'category 1 hazard' and 'category 2 hazard' see PARA 564.
22 Housing Act 2004 s 67(4)(a). This does not, however, prevent the authority from imposing licence conditions relating to the installation or maintenance of facilities or equipment within s 67(2)(c) (see head (c) in the text), even if the same result could be achieved by the exercise of Part 1 functions: s 67(4)(b).
23 Housing Act 2004 s 67(4)(c).
24 Housing Act 2004 s 67(5).

25 As to the meanings of 'tenancy' and 'licence' see PARA 391 note 6.
26 Housing Act 2004 s 67(6).

684. General requirements and duration. A licence[1] may not relate to more than one HMO[2]. A licence may be granted before the time when it is required by virtue of Part 2 of the Housing Act 2004[3] but, if so, the licence cannot come into force until that time[4]. A licence comes into force at the time that is specified in or determined under the licence for this purpose, and unless previously terminated[5] or revoked[6], continues in force for the period that is so specified or determined[7]. That period must not end more than five years after: (1) the date on which the licence was granted; or (2) if the licence was granted in advance, the date when the licence comes into force[8].

A licence may not be transferred to another person[9]. If the holder of the licence dies while the licence is in force, the licence ceases to be in force on his death[10]. However, during the period of three months beginning with the date of the licence holder's death, the house is to be treated for the purposes of Part 2[11] as if on that date a temporary exemption notice had been served[12] in respect of the house[13]. If, at any time during that period ('the initial period'), the personal representatives of the licence holder request the local housing authority[14] to do so, the authority may serve on them a notice which, during the period of three months after the date on which the initial period ends, has the same effect as a temporary exemption notice[15].

1 As to the meaning of 'licence' see PARA 682 note 1. As to applications for and the conditions to be included in licences see PARAS 682–683. As to variation of licences see PARA 685. As to revocation of licences see PARA 686.
2 Housing Act 2004 s 68(1). Thus the owner of two or more HMOs needs a licence for each one. As to the meaning of 'HMO' see PARA 674 note 2.
3 Ie by virtue of the Housing Act 2004 Pt 2 (ss 55–78). As to when a licence is required see PARA 674.
4 Housing Act 2004 s 68(2).
5 Ie by the Housing Act 2004 s 68(7): see the text to note 10.
6 Ie under the Housing Act 2004 s 70 or, prospectively, s 70A: see PARA 686.
7 Housing Act 2004 s 68(3) (amended, as from a day to be appointed, by the Housing and Planning Act 2016 s 25, Sch 2 paras 1, 4; at the date at which this volume states the law, no such day had been appointed). This applies even if, at any time during that period, the HMO concerned subsequently ceases to be one to which the Housing Act 2004 Pt 2 applies: s 68(5). As to HMOs to which Pt 2 applies see PARA 674.
8 Housing Act 2004 s 68(4).
9 Housing Act 2004 s 68(6).
10 Housing Act 2004 s 68(7). As to the meaning of 'licence holder' see PARA 682 note 14.
11 And also for the purposes of the Housing Act 2004 Pt 3 (ss 79–100) (see PARA 704 et seq).
12 Ie under the Housing Act 2004 s 62: see PARA 680.
13 Housing Act 2004 s 68(8).
14 As to the meaning of 'local housing authority' see PARA 380 note 1.
15 Housing Act 2004 s 68(9). As to service of documents see PARA 391. The provisions as to notification and appeal in s 62(6)–(8) (see PARA 680) apply (with any necessary modifications) in relation to a decision by the authority not to serve such a notice as they apply in relation to a decision not to serve a temporary exemption notice: s 68(10).

685. Variation of licences. The local housing authority[1] may vary the terms and conditions of a licence[2]: (1) if it does so with the agreement of the licence holder[3]; or (2) if it considers that there has been a change of circumstances[4] since the time when the licence was granted[5]. Where the authority is considering whether to vary a licence under head (2) and is considering: (a) what number of households or persons is appropriate as the maximum number authorised to occupy the HMO[6] to which the licence relates; or (b) the standards applicable to occupation by a particular number of households or persons[7], the authority must apply the same standards in relation to the circumstances existing at the time when it is considering whether to vary the licence as were applicable at the time when it was granted[8]. However, if the standards statutorily prescribed[9] and applicable at the time when the licence was granted have subsequently been revised or superseded by provisions of regulations[10], the authority may apply the new standards[11].

A variation made with the agreement of the licence holder takes effect at the time when it is made[12]. Otherwise, a variation does not come into force until such time, if any, as is the operative time[13] for this purpose[14].

The power to vary a licence is exercisable by the authority either on an application made by the licence holder or a relevant person[15], or on the authority's own initiative[16]. If the local housing authority refuses to vary the licence, the licence holder or relevant person may bring an appeal[17].

1　As to the meaning of 'local housing authority' see PARA 380 note 1.
2　As to the meaning of 'licence' see PARA 682 note 1. As to applications for and the conditions to be included in licences see PARAS 682–683. As to the duration and transferability of licences see PARA 684. As to revocation of licences see PARA 686.
3　Housing Act 2004 s 69(1)(a). As to the meaning of 'licence holder' see PARA 682 note 14.
4　For this purpose 'change of circumstances' includes any discovery of new information: Housing Act 2004 s 69(1).
5　Housing Act 2004 s 69(1)(b); and see PARA 674 note 4. As to procedural requirements see PARA 687 et seq.
6　See PARA 682 notes 11–12. As to the meaning of 'HMO' see PARA 674 note 2. As to rules for counting the number of persons see PARA 396.
7　See PARA 682 note 12.
8　Housing Act 2004 s 69(3). This is subject to s 69(4) (see the text and notes 9–11): s 69(3).
9　Ie by the Housing Act 2004 s 65: see PARA 682 note 12.
10　Ie regulations under the Housing Act 2004 s 65: see PARA 682.
11　Housing Act 2004 s 69(4).
12　Housing Act 2004 s 69(5).
13　Ie under the Housing Act 2004 Sch 5 para 35. If the period of 28 days mentioned in Sch 5 para 33(2) (see PARA 691) has expired without an appeal having been made under Sch 5 para 32 (see PARA 691), 'the operative time' is the end of that period: s 71, Sch 5 para 35(1), (2). If an appeal is made under Sch 5 para 32 within that period and a decision is given on the appeal which confirms the variation or revocation, 'the operative time' is as follows: (1) if the period within which an appeal to the Upper Tribunal may be brought expires without such an appeal having been brought, 'the operative time' is the end of that period; (2) if an appeal to the Upper Tribunal is brought, 'the operative time' is the time when a decision is given on the appeal which confirms the variation or revocation: Sch 5 para 35(3) (amended by SI 2009/1307). For this purpose, the withdrawal of an appeal has the same effect as a decision confirming the variation or revocation appealed against; and references to a decision which confirms a variation are references to a decision which confirms it with or without variation: Housing Act 2004 Sch 5 para 35(4). As to appeals to the Upper Tribunal, ie the Upper Tribunal (Lands Chamber), the successor to the Lands Tribunal, see PARAS 49–50.
14　Housing Act 2004 s 69(6).
15　For this purpose, 'relevant person' means any person (other than the licence holder): (1) who has an estate or interest in the HMO concerned (but is not a tenant under a lease with an unexpired term of three years or less); or (2) who is a person managing or having control of the house (and does not fall within head (1)); or (3) on whom any restriction or obligation is imposed by the licence in accordance with the Housing Act 2004 s 67(5) (see PARA 683): s 69(8). As to the meaning of 'person having an estate or interest' see PARA 391 note 7. As to the meaning of 'tenant' see PARA 391 note 6; and as to references to a tenant under a lease with an unexpired term of three years or less see PARA 672 note 9. As to the meaning of 'person managing' see PARA 391 note 6; and as to the meaning of 'person having control' see PARA 391 note 5.
16　Housing Act 2004 s 69(7).
17　See PARA 691.

686. Revocation of licences. The local housing authority[1] may revoke a licence[2]:
(1)　if it does so with the agreement of the licence holder[3];
(2)　in any of the following cases:

> (a) where the authority considers that the licence holder or any other person has committed a serious breach of a condition of the licence or repeated breaches of such a condition[4];
>
> (b) where the authority no longer considers that the licence holder is a fit and proper person to be the licence holder[5]; and
>
> (c) where the authority no longer considers that the management of the house is being carried on by persons who are in each case fit and proper persons to be involved in its management[6];
>
> (3) in any of the following cases:
>
> (a) where the HMO[7] to which the licence relates ceases to be an HMO to which Part 2 of the Housing Act 2004 applies[8]; and
>
> (b) where the authority considers at any time that, were the licence to expire at that time, it would, for a particular reason relating to the structure of the HMO, refuse to grant a new licence to the licence holder on similar terms in respect of it[9]; or
>
> (4) in any other circumstances prescribed by regulations made by the appropriate national authority[10].

A revocation made with the agreement of the licence holder takes effect at the time when it is made[11]. Otherwise, a revocation does not come into force until such time, if any, as is the operative time[12] for this purpose[13].

The power to revoke a licence is exercisable by the authority either on an application made by the licence holder or a relevant person[14], or on the authority's own initiative[15].

As from a day to be appointed, the local housing authority must revoke a licence if a banning order (under the Housing and Planning Act 2016)[16] is made against the licence holder[17]. The local housing authority must revoke a licence if a banning order is made against a person who: (i) owns an estate or interest in the house or part of it; and (ii) is a lessor or licensor of the house or part[18]. The notice served by the local housing authority[19] must specify when the revocation takes effect[20]. The revocation must not take effect earlier than the end of the period of seven days beginning with the day on which the notice is served[21].

1 As to the meaning of 'local housing authority' see PARA 380 note 1; and see PARA 674 note 4.
2 As to the meaning of 'licence' see PARA 682 note 1. As to procedural requirements see PARA 687 et seq. As to applications for a licence see PARA 682. As to the duration and transferability of licences see PARA 684. As to variation of licences see PARA 685.
3 Housing Act 2004 s 70(1)(a). As to the meaning of 'licence holder' see PARA 682 note 14.
4 As to the conditions to be included in licences see PARA 683.
5 The Housing Act 2004 s 66(1) (and prospectively s 66(1A)) (see PARA 682 note 15) applies in relation to head (2)(b) or head (2)(c) in the text as it applies in relation to s 64(3)(b) or (d): s 70(2) (amended, as from a day to be appointed, by the Housing and Planning Act 2016 s 125(1), (4); at the date at which this volume states the law, no such day had been appointed). See PARA 682.
6 Housing Act 2004 s 70(1)(b), (2). See note 5.
7 As to the meaning of 'HMO' see PARA 674 note 2.
8 As to HMOs to which the Housing Act 2004 Pt 2 (ss 55–78) applies see PARA 674.
9 Housing Act 2004 s 70(1)(c), (3). Where the authority is considering whether to revoke a licence by virtue of s 70(3)(b) on the grounds that the HMO is not reasonably suitable for the number of households or persons specified in the licence as the maximum number authorised to occupy the house (see PARA 682 notes 11–12), the authority must apply the same standards in relation to the circumstances existing at the time when it is considering whether to revoke the licence as were applicable at the time when it was granted: s 70(4), (5). However, if the standards prescribed under s 65 (see PARA 682 note 12) and applicable at the time when the licence was granted have subsequently been revised or superseded by provisions of regulations under that provision, the authority may apply the new standards: s 70(6).
10 Housing Act 2004 s 70(1)(d). As to the meaning of 'the appropriate national authority' see PARA 389 note 1.
11 Housing Act 2004 s 70(7).

12 Ie under the Housing Act 2004 s 71, Sch 5 para 35: see PARA 685 note 13.
13 Housing Act 2004 s 70(8).
14 For this purpose, 'relevant person' means any person (other than the licence holder): (1) who has an estate or interest in the HMO concerned (but is not a tenant under a lease with an unexpired term of three years or less); or (2) who is a person managing or having control of that house (and does not fall within head (1)); or (3) on whom any restriction or obligation is imposed by the licence in accordance with s 67(5) (see PARA 683): s 70(10). As to the meaning of 'person having an estate or interest' see PARA 391 note 7. As to the meaning of 'tenant' see PARA 391 note 6; and as to references to a tenant under a lease with an unexpired term of three years or less see PARA 672 note 9. As to the meaning of 'person managing' see PARA 391 note 6; and as to the meaning of 'person having control' see PARA 391 note 5.
15 Housing Act 2004 s 70(9). As to appeals against revocation of a licence see PARA 691.
16 'Banning order' means a banning order under the Housing and Planning Act 2016 s 16 (see PARA 719 et seq): Housing Act 2004 s 70A(5) (s 70A added, as from a day to be appointed, by the Housing and Planning Act 2016 s 25, Sch 2 paras 1, 6).
17 Housing Act 2004 s 70A(1) (as added: see note 16).
18 Housing Act 2004 s 70A(2) (as added: see note 16). As to the meanings of 'lessor' and 'licensor' see PARA 391 note 6.
19 Ie under the Housing Act 2004 Sch 5 para 24: see PARA 690.
20 Housing Act 2004 s 70A(3) (as added: see note 16).
21 Housing Act 2004 s 70A(4) (as added: see note 16).

(iii) Licensing Procedure

687. Procedure relating to grant or refusal of licence. Before granting a licence[1], the local housing authority[2] must serve[3] a notice in the following terms, together with a copy of the proposed licence, on the applicant for the licence and each relevant person[4], and consider any representations made in accordance with the notice and not withdrawn[5]. The notice must state that the authority is proposing to grant the licence and set out:

(1) the reasons for granting the licence;
(2) the main terms of the licence; and
(3) the end of the consultation period[6].

If, having considered representations made in accordance with such a notice or a notice in the following terms, the local housing authority proposes to grant a licence with modifications, then before granting the licence the authority must serve a notice on the applicant for the licence and each relevant person, and consider any representations made in accordance with the notice and not withdrawn[7].

Such a notice must set out:

(a) the proposed modifications;
(b) the reasons for them; and
(c) the end of the consultation period[8].

Before refusing to grant a licence, the local housing authority must serve a notice in the following terms on the applicant for the licence and each relevant person, and consider any representations made in accordance with the notice and not withdrawn[9]. The notice must state that the local housing authority is proposing to refuse to grant the licence and set out:

(i) the reasons for refusing to grant the licence; and
(ii) the end of the consultation period[10].

1 'Licence', in the Housing Act 2004 Sch 5 Pt 1 (paras 1–13), means a licence under Pt 2 (ss 55–78) or Pt 3 (ss 79–100): ss 71, 94, Sch 5 para 13(1). The licensing procedure applies to licences granted under Pt 3 as well as to those granted under Pt 2. As to licences under Pt 2 see PARA 674 et seq; as to licences under Pt 3 see PARA 704 et seq. As to the granting of licences see PARAS 682, 711.
2 As to the meaning of 'local housing authority' see PARA 380 note 1.
3 As to service of documents see PARA 391.

4   For this purpose, 'relevant person', in relation to a licence under the Housing Act 2004 Pt 2 or Pt 3, means any person (other than a person excluded by Sch 5 para 13(3)): (1) who, to the knowledge of the local housing authority concerned, is: (a) a person having an estate or interest in the HMO or Part 3 house in question; or (b) a person managing or having control of that HMO or Part 3 house (and not falling within head (1)(a)); or (2) on whom any restriction or obligation is or is to be imposed by the licence in accordance with s 67(5) or s 90(6) (see PARAS 683, 712): Sch 5 para 13(2). As to the meaning of 'person having an estate or interest' see PARA 391 note 7. As to the meaning of 'HMO' see PARA 674 note 2; and as to the meaning of 'Part 3 house' see PARA 705 note 7. As to the meaning of 'person managing' see PARA 391 note 6; and as to the meaning of 'person having control' see PARA 391 note 5.

   The persons excluded by Sch 5 para 13(3) are: (i) the applicant for the licence and (if different) the licence holder; and (ii) any tenant under a lease with an unexpired term of three years or less: Sch 5 para 13(3). As to the meaning of 'tenant' see PARA 391 note 6; and as to references to a tenant under a lease with an unexpired term of three years or less see PARA 672 note 9.

5   Housing Act 2004 Sch 5 para 1. See note 7.

6   Housing Act 2004 Sch 5 para 2. For the purposes of Sch 5 Pt 1, 'the end of the consultation period' means the last day for making representations in respect of the matter in question: Sch 5 para 12(1). The end of the consultation period must be: (1) in the case of a notice under Sch 5 para 1 (see the text and note 5) or Sch 5 para 5 (see the text and note 9), a day which is at least 14 days after the date of service of the notice; and (2) in the case of a notice under Sch 5 para 3 (see the text and note 7), a day which is at least seven days after the date of service of the notice: Sch 5 para 12(2). 'The date of service' of a notice means, in a case where more than one notice is served, the date on which the last of the notices is served: Sch 5 para 12(3).

7   Housing Act 2004 Sch 5 para 3(1), (2). The requirements of Sch 5 para 3 (and Sch 5 para 1: see the text and note 5) do not apply if the local housing authority has already served a notice under Sch 5 para 1 but not under Sch 5 para 3 in relation to the proposed licence, and considers that the modifications which are now being proposed are not material in any respect: Sch 5 para 9. Nor do the requirements of Sch 5 para 3 (and Sch 5 para 1) apply if the local housing authority has already served notices under Sch 5 para 1 and Sch 5 para 3 in relation to the matter concerned, and considers that the further modifications which are now being proposed do not differ in any material respect from the modifications in relation to which a notice was last served under Sch 5 para 3: Sch 5 para 10.

8   Housing Act 2004 Sch 5 para 4. See note 6.

9   Housing Act 2004 Sch 5 para 5. Schedule 5 paras 5, 6 do not apply to a refusal to grant a licence on particular terms if the local housing authority is proposing to grant the licence on different terms: Sch 5 para 11. Prospectively, the requirements of Sch 5 para 5 do not apply where the refusal to grant the licence was because of s 66(3C) or s 89(3C) (person with banning order not a fit and proper person: see PARAS 682 note 15, 711 note 13): Sch 5 para 11A (added, as from a day to be appointed, by the Housing and Planning Act 2016 s 25, Sch 2 paras 1, 12(1), (2); at the date at which this volume states the law, no such day had been appointed).

10   Housing Act 2004 Sch 5 para 6. See notes 6, 9.

688. Requirements following grant or refusal of licence. Where the local housing authority[1] decides to grant a licence[2], it must serve[3] on the applicant for the licence (and, if different, the licence holder) and each relevant person[4]: (1) a copy of the licence; and (2) a notice setting out: (a) the reasons for deciding to grant the licence and the date on which the decision was made; (b) the right of appeal against the decision[5]; and (c) the period within which an appeal may be made[6]. The documents required to be so served must be served within the period of seven days beginning with the day on which the decision is made[7].

Where the local housing authority refuses to grant a licence, it must serve on the applicant for the licence and each relevant person a notice setting out: (i) the authority's decision not to grant the licence; (ii) the reasons for the decision and the date on which it was made; (iii) the right of appeal against the decision[8]; and (iv) the period within which an appeal may be made[9]. The notice so required to be served must be served within the period of seven days beginning with the day on which the decision is made[10].

1   As to the meaning of 'local housing authority' see PARA 380 note 1.

2   As to the meaning of 'licence' for this purpose see PARA 687 note 1. As to the granting of licences see PARAS 682, 711.

3   As to service of documents see PARA 391.
4   As to the meaning of 'relevant person' for this purpose see PARA 687 note 4.
5   Ie under the Housing Act 2004 ss 71, 94, Sch 5 Pt 3 (paras 31–36): see PARA 691.
6   Housing Act 2004 Sch 5 para 7(1), (2); and see PARA 687 note 1. As to the period within which an appeal may be made see Sch 5 para 33(1); and PARA 691.
7   Housing Act 2004 Sch 5 para 7(3).
8   Ie under the Housing Act 2004 Sch 5 Pt 3: see PARA 691.
9   Housing Act 2004 Sch 5 para 8(1), (2). As to the period within which an appeal may be made see Sch 5 para 33(1); and PARA 691. Schedule 5 para 8 does not apply to a refusal to grant a licence on particular terms if the local housing authority is proposing to grant the licence on different terms: Sch 5 para 11.
10 Housing Act 2004 Sch 5 para 8(3). See note 9.

689. Procedure relating to variation of licence. Before varying a licence[1], the local housing authority[2] must serve[3] a notice on the licence holder and each relevant person[4], and consider any representations made in accordance with the notice and not withdrawn[5]. The notice must state that the local housing authority is proposing to make the variation and set out: (1) the effect of the variation; (2) the reasons for the variation; and (3) the end of the consultation period[6].

Where the local housing authority decides to vary a licence, it must serve on the licence holder and each relevant person a copy of the authority's decision to vary the licence, and a notice setting out: (a) the reasons for the decision and the date on which it was made; (b) the right of appeal against the decision[7]; and (c) the period within which an appeal may be made[8]. The documents so required to be served must be served within the period of seven days beginning with the day on which the decision is made[9].

Before refusing to vary a licence, the local housing authority must serve a notice on the licence holder and each relevant person, and consider any representations made in accordance with the notice and not withdrawn[10]. The notice must state that the authority is proposing to refuse to vary the licence and set out the reasons for refusing to vary the licence, and the end of the consultation period[11].

Where the local housing authority refuses to vary a licence, it must serve on the licence holder and each relevant person a notice setting out: (i) the authority's decision not to vary the licence; (ii) the reasons for the decision and the date on which it was made; (iii) the right of appeal against the decision[12]; and (iv) the period within which an appeal may be made[13]. The notice so required to be served must be served within the period of seven days beginning with the day on which the decision is made[14].

1   'Licence', in the Housing Act 2004 Sch 5 Pt 2 (paras 14–30), means a licence under Pt 2 (ss 55–78) or Pt 3 (ss 79–100): ss 71, 94, Sch 5 para 30(1). As to licences under Pt 2 see PARA 674 et seq; and as to licences under Pt 3 see PARA 704 et seq. As to the variation of licences see PARAS 685, 714.
2   As to the meaning of 'local housing authority' see PARA 380 note 1.
3   As to service of documents see PARA 391.
4   For this purpose, 'relevant person', in relation to a licence under the Housing Act 2004 Pt 2 or Pt 3, means any person (other than a person excluded by Sch 5 para 30(3)): (1) who, to the knowledge of the local housing authority concerned, is: (a) a person having an estate or interest in the HMO or Part 3 house in question; or (b) a person managing or having control of that HMO or Part 3 house (and not falling within head (1)(a)); or (2) on whom any restriction or obligation is or is to be imposed by the licence in accordance with s 67(5) or s 90(6) (see PARAS 683, 712): Sch 5 para 30(2). As to the meaning of 'person having an estate or interest' see PARA 391 note 7. As to the meaning of 'HMO' see PARA 674 note 2; and as to the meaning of 'Part 3 house' see PARA 705 note 7. As to the meaning of 'person managing' see PARA 391 note 6; and as to the meaning of 'person having control' see PARA 391 note 5.
    The persons excluded by Sch 5 para 30(3) are: (i) licence holder; and (ii) any tenant under a lease with an unexpired term of three years or less: Sch 5 para 30(3). As to the meaning of 'tenant' see PARA 391 note 6; and as to references to a tenant under a lease with an unexpired term of three years or less see PARA 672 note 9.

5 Housing Act 2004 Sch 5 para 14; and see PARA 687 note 1. The requirements of Sch 4 para 14 do not apply: (1) if the local housing authority considers that the variation is not material, or if the variation is agreed by the licence holder and the local housing authority considers that it would not be appropriate to comply with the requirements (Sch 5 para 17); or (2) if the local housing authority has already served a notice under Sch 5 para 14 in relation to a proposed variation, and considers that the variation which is now being proposed is not materially different from the previous proposed variation (Sch 5 para 18).

6 Housing Act 2004 Sch 5 para 15. For the purposes of Sch 5 Pt 2, 'the end of the consultation period' means the last day on which representations may be made in respect of the matter in question: Sch 5 para 29(1). That date must be at least 14 days after the date of service of the notice in question: Sch 5 para 29(2). 'The date of service' of a notice means, in a case where more than one notice is served, the date on which the last of the notices is served: Sch 5 para 29(3).

7 Ie under the Housing Act 2004 Sch 5 Pt 3 (paras 31–36): see PARA 691.

8 Housing Act 2004 Sch 5 para 16(1), (2). As to the period within which an appeal may be made see Sch 5 para 33(2); and PARA 691.

9 Housing Act 2004 Sch 5 para 16(3).

10 Housing Act 2004 Sch 5 para 19.

11 Housing Act 2004 Sch 5 para 20.

12 Ie under the Housing Act 2004 Sch 5 Pt 3: see PARA 691.

13 Housing Act 2004 Sch 5 para 21(1), (2). As to the period within which an appeal may be made see Sch 5 para 33(2); and PARA 691.

14 See the Housing Act 2004 Sch 5 para 21(3).

690. Procedure relating to revocation of licence. Before revoking a licence[1], the local housing authority[2] must serve[3] a notice on the licence holder and each relevant person[4], and consider any representations made in accordance with the notice and not withdrawn[5]. The notice must state that the authority is proposing to revoke the licence, and set out the reasons for the revocation and the end of the consultation period[6].

Where the local housing authority decides to revoke a licence, it must serve on the licence holder and each relevant person: (1) a copy of the authority's decision to revoke the licence; and (2) a notice setting out: (a) the reasons for the decision and the date on which it was made; (b) the right of appeal against the decision[7]; and (c) the period within which an appeal may be made[8]. The documents so required to be served must be served within the period of seven days beginning with the day on which the decision is made[9].

Before refusing to revoke a licence, the local housing authority must serve a notice on the licence holder and each relevant person, and consider any representations made in accordance with the notice and not withdrawn[10]. The notice must state that the authority is proposing to refuse to revoke the licence, and set out the reasons for refusing to revoke the licence and the end of the consultation period[11].

Where the local housing authority refuses to revoke a licence, it must serve on the licence holder and each relevant person a notice setting out: (i) the authority's decision not to revoke the licence; (ii) the reasons for the decision and the date on which it was made; (iii) the right of appeal against the decision[12]; and (iv) the period within which an appeal may be made[13]. The notice so required to be served must be served within the period of seven days beginning with the day on which the decision is made[14].

1 As to the meaning of 'licence' for this purpose see PARA 689 note 1. As to the revocation of licences see PARAS 686, 715.

2 As to the meaning of 'local housing authority' see PARA 380 note 1.

3 As to service of documents see PARA 391.

4 As to the meaning of 'relevant person' for this purpose see PARA 689 note 4.

5 Housing Act 2004 ss 71, 94, Sch 5 para 22; and see PARA 687 note 1. The requirements of Sch 5 para 22 do not apply if the revocation is agreed by the licence holder and the local housing authority considers that it would not be appropriate to comply with those requirements: Sch 5 para 25. Prospectively, the requirements of Sch 5 para 22 do not apply if the revocation is required

by s 70A or s 93A (duty to revoke licence in banning order cases: see PARAS 686, 715): Sch 5 para 25A (added, as from a day to be appointed, by the Housing and Planning Act 2016 s 25, Sch 2 paras 1, 12(1), (3); at the date at which this volume states the law, no such day had been appointed).

6 Housing Act 2004 Sch 5 para 23. As to the meaning of 'the end of the consultation period' see PARA 689 note 6.

7 Ie under the Housing Act 2004 Sch 5 Pt 3 (paras 31–36): see PARA 691.

8 Housing Act 2004 Sch 5 para 24(1), (2). As to the period within which an appeal may be made see Sch 5 para 33(2); and PARA 691.

9 Housing Act 2004 Sch 5 para 24(3).

10 Housing Act 2004 Sch 5 para 26.

11 Housing Act 2004 Sch 5 para 27.

12 Ie under the Housing Act 2004 Sch 5 Pt 3: see PARA 691.

13 Housing Act 2004 Sch 5 para 28(1), (2). As to the period within which an appeal may be made see Sch 5 para 33(2); and PARA 691.

14 Housing Act 2004 Sch 5 para 28(3).

691. Appeals against licence decisions. The applicant or any relevant person[1] may appeal to the appropriate tribunal[2] against a decision by the local housing authority[3] on an application for a licence[4] either to refuse to grant the licence or to grant the licence[5]. The licence holder or any relevant person may appeal to the appropriate tribunal against a decision by the local housing authority either to vary or revoke a licence or to refuse to vary or revoke a licence[6]; but this does not apply to the licence holder in a case where the decision to vary or revoke the licence was made with his agreement[7].

Any appeal against a decision to grant, or (as the case may be) to refuse to grant, a licence must be made within the period of 28 days beginning with the date specified in the notice of the decision[8] as the date on which the decision was made[9]. Any appeal against a decision to vary or revoke, or (as the case may be) to refuse to vary or revoke, a licence must be made within the period of 28 days beginning with the date specified in the notice of the decision[10] as the date on which the decision was made[11]. The appropriate tribunal may allow an appeal to be made to it after the end of either period if it is satisfied that there is a good reason for the failure to appeal before the end of that period (and for any delay since then in applying for permission to appeal out of time)[12].

An appeal under these provisions to the appropriate tribunal is to be by way of a re-hearing, and may be determined having regard to matters of which the authority was unaware[13]. The tribunal may confirm, reverse or vary the decision of the local housing authority[14]. On an appeal against a decision to refuse to grant or to grant a licence, the tribunal may direct the authority to grant a licence to the applicant for the licence on such terms as the tribunal may direct[15].

1 For this purpose, 'relevant person', in relation to a licence under the Housing Act 2004 Pt 2 (ss 55–78) or Pt 3 (ss 79–100), means any person (other than a person excluded by Sch 5 para 36(3)): (1) who is (a) a person having an estate or interest in the HMO or Part 3 house concerned; or (b) a person managing or having control of that HMO or Part 3 house (and not falling within head (1)(a)); or (2) on whom any restriction or obligation is or is to be imposed by the licence in accordance with s 67(5) or 90(6) (see PARAS 683, 712): ss 71, 94, Sch 5 para 36(2). As to the meaning of 'person having an estate or interest' see PARA 391 note 7. As to the meaning of 'HMO' see PARA 674 note 2; and as to the meaning of 'Part 3 house' see PARA 705 note 7. As to the meaning of 'person managing' see PARA 391 note 6; and as to the meaning of 'person having control' see PARA 391 note 5.

    The persons excluded by Sch 5 para 36(3) are: (i) the applicant for the licence and (if different) licence holder; and (ii) any tenant under a lease with an unexpired term of three years or less: Sch 5 para 36(3). As to the meaning of 'tenant' see PARA 391 note 6; and as to references to a tenant under a lease with an unexpired term of three years or less see PARA 672 note 9.

2 As to the meaning of 'appropriate tribunal' see PARA 580 note 2. As to appeals to the appropriate tribunal see PARA 32 et seq.

3 As to the meaning of 'local housing authority' see PARA 380 note 1.

4 'Licence', in the Housing Act 2004 Sch 5 Pt 3 (paras 31–36), means a licence under Pt 2 or Pt 3: Sch 5 para 36(1). As to licences under Pt 2 see PARA 674 et seq; and as to licences under Pt 3 see PARA 704 et seq.

5 Housing Act 2004 Sch 5 para 31(1) (amended by SI 2013/1036). See PARA 682. An appeal against a decision to grant a licence may, in particular, relate to any of the terms of the licence: Housing Act 2004 Sch 5 para 31(2). Prospectively, the right of appeal under Sch 5 para 31(1)(a) does not apply where a licence is refused because of s 66(3A) or s 89(3A) (person with banning order not a fit and proper person: see PARAS 682 note 15, 711 note 13): Sch 5 para 32A(1) (Sch 5 para 32A added, as from a day to be appointed, by the Housing and Planning Act 2016 s 25, Sch 2 paras 1, 12(1), (4); at the date at which this volume states the law, no such day had been appointed).

6 Housing Act 2004 Sch 5 para 32(1) (amended by SI 2013/1036). Prospectively, the right of appeal under the Housing Act 2004 Sch 5 para 32(1)(a) does not apply in relation to the revocation of a licence required by s 70A or s 93A (duty to revoke licence in banning order cases: see PARAS 686, 715): Sch 5 para 32A(2) (as added: see note 5).

7 Housing Act 2004 Sch 5 para 32(2).

8 Ie under the Housing Act 2004 Sch 5 para 7 or Sch 5 para 8: see PARA 688.

9 Housing Act 2004 Sch 5 para 33(1).

10 Ie under the Housing Act 2004 Sch 5 para 16, 21, 24 or 28: see PARAS 689–690.

11 Housing Act 2004 Sch 5 para 33(2).

12 Housing Act 2004 Sch 5 para 33(3) (amended by SI 2013/1036).

13 Housing Act 2004 Sch 5 para 34(1), (2) (Sch 5 para 34(1) amended by SI 2013/1036).

14 Housing Act 2004 Sch 5 para 34(3).

15 Housing Act 2004 Sch 5 para 34(4).

692. Register of licences and management orders. Every local housing authority[1] must establish and maintain a register of: (1) all licences granted by it under Part 2 or Part 3 of the Housing Act 2004[2] which are in force; (2) all temporary exemption notices served by it[3] which are in force; and (3) all management orders made by it[4] which are in force[5]. The register may, subject to any requirements that may be prescribed[6], be in such form as the authority considers appropriate[7]. Each entry in the register is to contain such particulars as may be prescribed[8].

The authority must ensure that the contents of the register are available at the authority's head office for inspection by members of the public at all reasonable times[9]. If requested by a person to do so and subject to payment of such reasonable fee (if any) as the authority may determine, a local housing authority must supply the person with a copy (certified to be true) of the register or of an extract from it[10]. A copy so certified is prima facie evidence of the matters mentioned in it[11].

1 As to the meaning of 'local housing authority' see PARA 380 note 1.

2 Ie under the Housing Act 2004 Pt 2 (ss 55–78) or Pt 3 (ss 79–100). As to licences under Pt 2 see PARA 674 et seq; and as to licences under Pt 3 see PARA 704 et seq.

3 Ie under the Housing Act 2004 s 62 (see PARA 680) or s 86 (see PARA 710).

4 Ie under the Housing Act 2004 Pt 4 Ch 1 (ss 101–131) or Pt 4 Ch 2 (ss 132–138): see PARA 745 et seq.

5 Housing Act 2004 s 232(1).

6 For this purpose, 'prescribed' means prescribed by regulations made by the appropriate national authority: Housing Act 2004 s 232(7). As to the meaning of 'the appropriate national authority' see PARA 389 note 1.

7 Housing Act 2004 s 232(2).

8 Housing Act 2004 s 232(3). As to the particulars prescribed see the Licensing and Management of Houses in Multiple Occupation and Other Houses (Miscellaneous Provisions) (England) Regulations 2006, SI 2006/373, reg 11 (amended by SI 2007/1903, SI 2009/1307 and SI 2013/1036); and the Licensing and Management of Houses in Multiple Occupation and Other Houses (Miscellaneous Provisions) (Wales) Regulations 2006, SI 2006/1715, reg 11 (amended by SI 2007/3229).

9 Housing Act 2004 s 232(4).

10 Housing Act 2004 s 232(5).

11 Housing Act 2004 s 232(6).

(iv) Enforcement

A.   OFFENCES AND PENALTIES

693. Offences in relation to licensing of houses in multiple occupation. A person commits an offence if he is a person having control of or managing an HMO[1] which is required to be licensed under Part 2 of the Housing Act 2004[2] but is not so licensed[3]. In proceedings against a person for such an offence it is a defence that, at the material time, a notification of his intention to take particular steps with a view to securing that the house is no longer required to be licensed had been duly given in respect of the house[4], or that an application for a licence had been duly made in respect of the house[5], and that that notification or application was still effective[6].

A person commits an offence if: (1) he is a person having control of or managing an HMO[7] which is licensed under Part 2; (2) he knowingly permits another person to occupy the house; and (3) the other person's occupation results in the house being occupied by more households or persons than is authorised by the licence[8].

A person also commits an offence if he is a licence holder[9] or a person on whom restrictions or obligations under a licence are imposed[10], and he fails to comply with any condition of the licence[11].

In proceedings against a person for an offence under any of the above provisions it is a defence that he had a reasonable excuse: (a) for having control of or managing the house which was required to be, but was not, licensed; or (b) for permitting the person to occupy the house; or (c) for failing to comply with the condition of the licence, as the case may be[12].

1   As to the meaning of 'HMO' see PARA 674 note 2.
2   As to HMOs which are required to be licensed under the Housing Act 2004 Pt 2 (ss 55–78) see s 61(1); and PARA 679.
3   Housing Act 2004 s 72(1). A person who commits such an offence is liable on summary conviction to a fine: s 72(6) (amended by SI 2015/664). In relation to England, the provisions of the Housing Act 2004 s 72(1), (4), (8)–(10) have effect as from 6 July 2006 and the provisions of s 72(2), (3), (5)–(7) have effect as from 6 April 2006: see the Housing Act 2004 (Commencement No 5 and Transitional Provisions and Savings) (England) Order 2006, SI 2006/1060, arts 1(3)(c), (d), 2(1)(b), (2)(b). In relation to Wales, the Housing Act 2004 s 72 has effect as from 16 June 2006: see the Housing Act 2004 (Commencement No 3 and Transitional Provisions and Savings) (Wales) Order 2006, SI 2006/1535, art 1(2)(c), 2(a). As to the power of the Secretary of State to increase the fine for this offence see PARA 400. As to offences by bodies corporate see PARA 399. Prospectively, see also the Housing Act 2004 s 249A (financial penalties as alternative to prosecution for certain housing offences in England); and PARA 397: s 72(7A) (s 72(7A), (7B) added by the Housing and Planning Act 2016 s 126, Sch 9 paras 1, 3). If a local housing authority has imposed a financial penalty on a person under the Housing Act 2004 s 249A in respect of conduct amounting to an offence under s 72 the person may not be convicted of an offence under s 72 in respect of the conduct: s 72(7B) (as so added).
4   Ie under the Housing Act 2004 s 62(1): see PARA 680.
5   Ie under the Housing Act 2004 s 63: see PARA 682.
6   Housing Act 2004 s 72(4). For the purposes of s 72(4), a notification or application is 'effective' at a particular time if at that time it has not been withdrawn, and: (1) the local housing authority has not decided whether to serve a temporary exemption notice or (as the case may be) grant a licence in pursuance of the notification or application; or (2) if it has decided not to do so, one of the following conditions is met: s 72(8). Those conditions are: (a) that the period for appealing against the decision of the authority not to serve or grant such a notice or licence (or against any relevant decision of the appropriate tribunal) has not expired; or (b) that an appeal has been brought against the authority's decision (or against any relevant decision of such a tribunal) and the appeal has not been determined or withdrawn: s 72(9) (amended by SI 2013/1036). 'Relevant decision' means a decision which is given on an appeal to the tribunal and confirms the authority's decision (with or without variation): Housing Act 2004 s 72(10). As to the meaning of

'local housing authority' see PARA 380 note 1. As to appeals and the time for appealing see PARAS 680, 691. As to the meaning of 'appropriate tribunal' see PARA 580 note 2. As to appeals to the appropriate tribunal see PARA 32 et seq.

7   As to the meaning of 'person having control' see PARA 391 note 5; and as to the meaning of 'person managing' see PARA 391 note 6.

8   Housing Act 2004 s 72(2). A person who commits such an offence is liable on summary conviction to a fine: s 72(6) (as amended: see note 3); and see note 3. As to the maximum number of households or persons see PARA 682 note 11.

9   As to the meaning of 'licence holder' see PARA 682 note 14.

10 Ie in accordance with the Housing Act 2004 s 67(5): see PARA 683.

11 Housing Act 2004 s 72(3). As to licence conditions see PARA 683. A person who commits such an offence is liable on summary conviction to a fine not exceeding level 5 on the standard scale: s 72(7). See also note 3. As to the powers of magistrates' courts to issue fines on summary conviction see SENTENCING vol 92 (2015) PARA 176.

12 Housing Act 2004 s 72(5).

B.   OTHER CONSEQUENCES OF OPERATING UNLICENSED HOUSES IN MULTIPLE OCCUPATION

694.   Rent repayment orders. In addition to the criminal penalties, there are two other sanctions against operating an HMO without a licence under Part 2 of the Housing Act 2004[1]. First, rent repayment orders may be made; second, there are restrictions on recovery of possession[2].

For the purposes of the following provisions, an HMO is an 'unlicensed HMO' if it is required to be licensed under Part 2 of the Housing Act 2004 but is not so licensed, and neither of the following conditions is satisfied[3]. Those conditions are:

(1)   that a notification of intention to take particular steps with a view to securing that the house is no longer required to be licensed has been duly given in respect of the HMO[4] and that notification is still effective[5]; and

(2)   that an application for a licence has been duly made in respect of the HMO[6] and that application is still effective[7].

No rule of law relating to the validity or enforceability of contracts in circumstances involving illegality[8] is to affect the validity or enforceability of any provision requiring the payment of rent or the making of any other periodical payment in connection with any tenancy or licence[9] of a part of an unlicensed HMO, or any other provision of such a tenancy or licence[10]. Nevertheless, amounts paid in respect of rent or other periodical payments payable in connection with such a tenancy or licence may be recovered in accordance with the following provisions[11].

If an application in respect of an HMO in Wales is made to the appropriate tribunal[12] by the local housing authority[13] or an occupier[14] of a part of the HMO, and the tribunal is satisfied as to the matters mentioned below[15], the tribunal may make an order (a 'rent repayment order') requiring the appropriate person[16] to pay to the applicant such amount in respect of the relevant award or awards of universal credit or the housing benefit paid[17] or (as the case may be) the periodical payments paid[18], as is specified in the order[19].

If the application is made by the local housing authority, the tribunal must be satisfied as to the following matters[20]:

(a)   that, at any time within the period of 12 months ending with the date of the notice of intended proceedings[21], the appropriate person has committed an offence of not having a licence[22] in relation to the HMO (whether or not he has been charged or convicted);

(b)   that one or more relevant awards of universal credit[23] have been paid (to any person) or housing benefit has been paid (to any person) in respect of periodical payments payable in connection with the occupation of a part or parts of the HMO during any period during which it appears to the tribunal that such an offence was being committed; and

(c)   that the requirements as to notice of the intended proceedings[24] have been complied with in relation to the application[25].

If the application is made by an occupier of a part of the HMO, the tribunal must be satisfied as to the following matters[26]:

(i)   that the appropriate person has been convicted of an offence of not having a licence[27] in relation to the HMO, or has been required by a rent repayment order to make a payment in respect of one or more relevant awards of universal credit or housing benefit paid in connection with occupation of a part or parts of the HMO;

(ii)   that the occupier paid, to a person having control of or managing[28] the HMO, periodical payments in respect of occupation of part of the HMO during any period during which it appears to the tribunal that such an offence was being committed in relation to the HMO; and

(iii)   that the application is made within the period of 12 months beginning with the date of the conviction or order or, if such a conviction was followed by such an order (or vice versa), the date of the later of them[29].

Where a local housing authority serves a notice of intended proceedings on any person, it must ensure that a copy of the notice is received by the department of the authority responsible for administering the housing benefit to which the proceedings would relate and that that department is subsequently kept informed of any matters relating to the proceedings that are likely to be of interest to it in connection with the administration of housing benefit[30].

Where, on an application by the local housing authority for a rent repayment order, the tribunal is satisfied:

(A)   that a person has been convicted of an offence of not having a licence in relation to the HMO; and

(B)   that:

    (I)   one or more relevant awards of universal credit were paid (whether or not to the appropriate person); or

    (II)   housing benefit was paid (whether or not to the appropriate person) in respect of periodical payments payable in connection with occupation of a part or parts of the HMO,

    during any period during which it appears to the tribunal that such an offence was being committed in relation to the HMO in question,

the tribunal must make a rent repayment order requiring the appropriate person to pay to the authority a specified amount[31]. However, if the total of the amounts received by the appropriate person in respect of periodical payments payable as mentioned in head (B) above ('the rent total') is less than the specified amount, the amount required to be paid by virtue of a rent repayment order made in accordance with these provisions is limited to the rent total[32]. A rent repayment order so made may not require the payment of any amount which the tribunal is satisfied that, by reason of any exceptional circumstances, it would be unreasonable for that person to be required to pay[33]. In a case where head (A) or head (B) above does not apply, the amount required to be paid by virtue of a rent repayment order[34] is to be such amount as the tribunal considers reasonable in the circumstances[35].

Any amount payable to a local housing authority under a rent repayment order does not, when recovered by the authority, constitute an amount of universal credit or housing benefit recovered by it, and until recovered by it, is a legal charge on the HMO which is a local land charge[36].

If the authority subsequently grants a licence[37] in respect of the HMO to the appropriate person or any person acting on his behalf, the conditions contained in the licence may include a condition requiring the licence holder to pay to the authority any amount payable to it under the rent repayment order and not so far recovered by it, and to do so in such instalments as are specified in the licence[38].

If the authority subsequently makes a management order[39] in respect of the HMO, the order may contain such provisions as the authority considers appropriate for the recovery of any amount payable to it under the rent repayment order and not so far recovered by it[40].

Any amount payable to an occupier by virtue of a rent repayment order is recoverable by the occupier as a debt due to him from the appropriate person[41].

The appropriate national authority[42] may by regulations make such provision as it considers appropriate for supplementing these provisions, and in particular for securing that persons are not unfairly prejudiced by rent repayment orders (whether in cases where there have been over-payments of universal credit or housing benefit or otherwise), and for requiring or authorising amounts received by local housing authorities by virtue of rent repayment orders to be dealt with in such manner as is specified in the regulations[43].

1   As to the meaning of 'HMO' see PARA 674 note 2. As to HMOs which are required to be licensed under the Housing Act 2004 Pt 2 (ss 55–78) see s 61(1); and PARA 679.
2   As to restrictions on recovery of possession see PARA 695.
3   Housing Act 2004 s 73(1). The provisions of ss 73, 74 have effect in relation to England as from 6 July 2006 (see the Housing Act 2004 (Commencement No 5 and Transitional Provisions and Savings) (England) Order 2006, SI 2006/1060, arts 1(3)(d), 2(2)(a), (b)); and in relation to Wales as from 16 June 2006 (see the Housing Act 2004 (Commencement No 3 and Transitional Provisions and Savings) (Wales) Order 2006, SI 2006/1535, arts 1(2)(c), 2(a)).
4   Ie under the Housing Act 2004 s 62(1): see PARA 680.
5   Ie as defined by the Housing Act 2004 s 72(8): see PARA 693 note 6.
6   Ie under the Housing Act 2004 s 63: see PARA 682.
7   Housing Act 2004 s 73(2).
8   See CONTRACT vol 22 (2012) PARA 424 et seq.
9   As to the meanings of 'tenancy' and 'licence' see PARA 391 note 6.
10 Housing Act 2004 s 73(3).
11 Housing Act 2004 s 73(4). Prospectively, such amounts may be recovered in accordance with s 73(5) and s 74 (in the case of an HMO in Wales) or in accordance with the Housing and Planning Act 2016 Pt 2 Ch 4 (ss 40–52) (in the case of an HMO in England) (see PARA 727): Housing Act 2004 s 73(4) (amended by the Housing and Planning Act 2016 s 50(1), (2)(a)).
    In relation to a section 257 HMO (see PARA 669), a definition of 'rent' is added ('rent' does not include ground rent, service charges or insurance charges paid under the terms of a lease in respect of a flat within a section 257 HMO) by the Houses in Multiple Occupation (Certain Converted Blocks of Flats) (Modifications to the Housing Act 2004 and Transitional Provisions for section 257 HMOs) (England) Regulations 2007, SI 2007/1904, regs 2, 7; and the Houses in Multiple Occupation (Certain Blocks of Flats) (Modifications to the Housing Act 2004 and Transitional Provisions for section 257 HMOs) (Wales) Regulations 2007, SI 2007/3231, regs 2, 7.
12 As to the meaning of 'appropriate tribunal' see PARA 580 note 2. As to appeals to the appropriate tribunal see PARA 32 et seq.
13 As to the meaning of 'local housing authority' see PARA 380 note 1.
14 'Occupier', in relation to any periodical payment, means a person who was an occupier at the time of the payment, whether under a tenancy or licence or otherwise (and 'occupation' has a corresponding meaning): Housing Act 2004 s 73(10). This applies also for the purposes of s 74: s 74(16). As to the meaning of 'occupier' generally see PARA 563 note 13.
15 Ie the matters mentioned in the Housing Act 2004 s 73(6), (8).

16 'The appropriate person', in relation to any payment of universal credit or housing benefit or periodical payment payable in connection with occupation of a part of an HMO, means the person who at the time of the payment was entitled to receive on his own account periodical payments payable in connection with such occupation: Housing Act 2004 s 73(10) (definition amended in relation to England by SI 2013/630; and in relation to Wales by SI 2013/1788). This applies also for the purposes of s 74: s 74(16). In relation to a section 257 HMO (see PARA 669), the definition of 'the appropriate person' is substituted by the Houses in Multiple Occupation (Certain Converted Blocks of Flats) (Modifications to the Housing Act 2004 and Transitional Provisions for section 257 HMOs) (England) Regulations 2007, SI 2007/1904, regs 2, 7; and the Houses in Multiple Occupation (Certain Blocks of Flats) (Modifications to the Housing Act 2004 and Transitional Provisions for section 257 HMOs) (Wales) Regulations 2007, SI 2007/3231, regs 2, 7.

17 Ie as mentioned in the Housing Act 2004 s 73(6)(b) (see head (b) in the text). 'Housing benefit' means housing benefit provided by virtue of a scheme under the Social Security Contributions and Benefits Act 1992 s 123 (see WELFARE BENEFITS AND STATE PENSIONS vol 104 (2014) PARA 249 et seq): Housing Act 2004 s 73(10). This applies also for the purposes of s 74: s 74(16).

18 Ie as mentioned in the Housing Act 2004 s 73(8)(b) (see head (ii) in the text). 'Periodical payments' means: (1) payments in respect of which an amount under the Welfare Reform Act 2012 s 11 may be included in the calculation of an award of universal credit, as referred to in the Universal Credit Regulations 2013, SI 2013/376, Sch 4 para 3 ('relevant payments') or any corresponding provision replacing that paragraph (see WELFARE BENEFITS AND STATE PENSIONS vol 104 (2014) PARA 72 et seq); and (2) periodical payments in respect of which housing benefit may be paid by virtue of the Housing Benefit Regulations 2006, SI 2006/213, reg 12 or any corresponding provision replacing that regulation (see WELFARE BENEFITS AND STATE PENSIONS vol 104 (2014) PARA 320): Housing Act 2004 s 73(10) (definition substituted in relation to England by SI 2013/630; and in relation to Wales by SI 2013/1788). For the purposes of the Housing Act 2004 s 73, an amount which is not actually paid by an occupier but is used by him to discharge the whole or part of his liability in respect of a periodical payment (eg by offsetting the amount against any such liability), and is not an amount of universal credit or housing benefit, is to be regarded as an amount paid by the occupier in respect of that periodical payment: s 73(11) (amended in relation to England by SI 2013/630; and in relation to Wales by SI 2013/1788). These provisions apply also for the purposes of the Housing Act 2004 s 74: s 74(16).

19 Housing Act 2004 s 73(5) (amended by SI 2013/1036; and in relation to England by SI 2013/630; and in relation to Wales by SI 2013/1788; and by the Housing and Planning Act 2016 s 50(1), (2)(b)). See the Housing Act 2004 s 74(2)–(8); and the text and notes 31–35. As to the purposes for which money received by a local housing authority under a rent repayment order may be applied, see the Rent Repayment Orders (Supplementary Provisions) (England) Regulations 2007, SI 2007/572, regs 3, 4 (reg 3 amended by SI 2013/1036); and the Rent Repayment Orders (Supplementary Provisions) (Wales) Regulations 2008, SI 2008/254, regs 3, 4.

If, in the course of proceedings on an application under the Housing Act 2004 s 73(5), it comes to the notice of the local housing authority that in respect of periodical payments payable in connection with occupation of the part or parts of the HMO or of the whole or part of the house to which the application applies there may have been a payment of housing benefit or of a relevant award of universal credit that was not properly payable, a local housing authority may apply to the First-tier Tribunal (in England) or the residential property tribunal (in Wales) for leave to amend its application by substituting for the total amount of housing benefit paid, such part of that amount as it believes is properly payable: Rent Repayment Orders (Supplementary Provisions) (England) Regulations 2007, SI 2007/572, reg 2(1), (2) (amended by SI 2013/630 and SI 2013/1036); Rent Repayment Orders (Supplementary Provisions) (Wales) Regulations 2008, SI 2008/254, reg 2(1), (2) (amended by SI 2013/1788). For these purposes, an amount of housing benefit is properly payable if the person to whom, or in respect of whom, it is paid is entitled to it under the Housing Benefit Regulations 2006, SI 2006/213, or the Housing Benefit (Persons who have attained the qualifying age for state pension credit) Regulations 2006, SI 2006/214 (whether on the initial decision or as subsequently revised or superseded or further revised or superseded): Rent Repayment Orders (Supplementary Provisions) (England) Regulations 2007, SI 2007/572, reg 2(3) (amended by SI 2013/630); Rent Repayment Orders (Supplementary Provisions) (Wales) Regulations 2008, SI 2008/254, reg 2(3) (substituted by SI 2013/1788). In relation to England, 'overpayment of housing benefit' has the meaning given by the Housing Benefit Regulations 2006, SI 2006/213, reg 99 or, as the case may be, the Housing Benefit (Persons who have attained the qualifying age for state pension credit) Regulations 2006, SI 2006/214, reg 80; and in relation to England and Wales, a relevant award of universal credit is properly payable if the person to whom, or in respect of whom, it is paid is entitled to it under the Universal Credit Regulations 2013, SI 2013/376 (whether on the initial decision or as subsequently revised or superseded or further revised or superseded: Rent Repayment Orders (Supplementary Provisions) (England) Regulations

2007, SI 2007/572, reg 2(3) (amended by SI 2013/630); Rent Repayment Orders (Supplementary Provisions) (Wales) Regulations 2008, SI 2008/254, reg 2(3) (as so substituted).

20 Housing Act 2004 s 73(6).

21 Ie the notice required by the Housing Act 2004 s 73(7): see note 24.

22 Ie under the Housing Act 2004 s 72(1): see PARA 693.

23 'Relevant award of universal credit' means an award of universal credit the calculation of which included an amount under the Welfare Reform Act 2012 s 11, calculated in accordance with the Universal Credit Regulations 2013, SI 2013/376, Sch 4 or any corresponding provision replacing that Schedule, in respect of periodical payments payable in connection with the occupation of a part or parts of the HMO: Housing Act 2004 s 73(6A) (added in relation to England by SI 2013/630; and in relation to Wales by SI 2013/1788). See WELFARE BENEFITS AND STATE PENSIONS vol 104 (2014) PARAS 72–76.

24 Those requirements are as follows: (1) the authority must have served on the appropriate person a notice (a 'notice of intended proceedings'): (a) informing him that the authority is proposing to make an application under the Housing Act 2004 s 73(5) (see the text and notes 12–19); (b) setting out the reasons why it proposes to do so; (c) stating the amount that it will seek to recover under s 73(5) and how that amount is calculated; and (d) inviting him to make representations to the authority within a period specified in the notice of not less than 28 days; (2) that period must have expired; and (3) the authority must have considered any representations made to it within that period by the appropriate person: s 73(7). As to service of documents see PARA 391.

25 Housing Act 2004 s 73(6)(a)–(c) (s 73(6)(b) substituted in relation to England by SI 2013/630; and in relation to Wales by SI 2013/1788).

26 Housing Act 2004 s 73(8).

27 See note 22.

28 As to the meaning of 'person having control' see PARA 391 note 5; and as to the meaning of 'person managing' see PARA 391 note 6.

29 Housing Act 2004 s 73(8)(a)–(c) (s 73(8)(a) amended in relation to England by SI 2013/630; and in relation to Wales by SI 2013/1788).

30 Housing Act 2004 s 73(9).

31 Housing Act 2004 s 74(1), (2) (s 74(2) amended, s 74(2A) added, in relation to England by SI 2013/630; and in relation to Wales by SI 2013/1788). As to the commencement of the Housing Act 2004 s 74 see note 3. The amount to be paid is that mentioned in the Housing Act 2004 s 74(2A): see s 74(2) (as so amended). The amount referred to in s 74(2) is: (1) an amount equal to: (a) where one relevant award of universal credit was paid as mentioned in s 74(2)(b)(i) (see head (B)(I) in the text), the amount included in the calculation of that award under the Welfare Reform Act 2012 s 11, calculated in accordance with the Universal Credit Regulations 2013, SI 2013/376, Sch 4 (housing costs element for renters) or any corresponding provision replacing that Schedule, or the amount of the award if less; or (b) if more than one such award was paid as mentioned in s 74(2)(b)(i), the sum of the amounts included in the calculation of those awards as referred to in head (1)(a) above, or the sum of the amounts of those awards if less; or (2) an amount equal to the total amount of housing benefit paid as mentioned in s 74(2)(b)(ii) (see head (B)(bb) in the text) (as the case may be): s 74(2A) (as so added).

32 Housing Act 2004 s 74(3) (amended in relation to England by SI 2013/630; and in relation to Wales by SI 2013/1788).

33 Housing Act 2004 s 74(4).

34 Ie under the Housing Act 2004 s 73(5): see the text and notes 12–19.

35 Housing Act 2004 s 74(5). In such a case the tribunal must, in particular, take into account the following matters: (1) the total amount of relevant payments paid in connection with occupation of the HMO during any period during which it appears to the tribunal that an offence was being committed by the appropriate person in relation to the HMO under s 72(1) (see PARA 693); (2) the extent to which that total amount consisted of, or derived from, payments of relevant awards of universal credit or housing benefit, and was actually received by the appropriate person; (3) whether the appropriate person has at any time been convicted of an offence under s 72(1) in relation to the HMO; (4) the conduct and financial circumstances of the appropriate person; and (5) where the application is made by an occupier, the conduct of the occupier: s 74(6) (amended in relation to England by SI 2013/630; and in relation to Wales by SI 2013/1788). 'Relevant payments' means: (a) in relation to an application by a local housing authority, payments of relevant awards of universal credit, housing benefit or periodical payments payable by occupiers; (b) in relation to an application by an occupier, periodical payments payable by the occupier, less: (i) where one or more relevant awards of universal credit were payable during the period in question, the amount mentioned in the Housing Act 2004 s 74(2A)(a) (see note 31 head (1)) in respect of the award or awards that related to the occupation of the part of the HMO occupied by him during that period; or (ii) any amount of housing benefit payable in respect of the occupation of the part of the HMO occupied by him during the period in question: s 74(7) (amended in

relation to England by SI 2013/630; and in relation to Wales by SI 2013/1788). A rent repayment order may not require the payment of any amount which (where the application is made by a local housing authority) is in respect of any time falling outside the period of 12 months mentioned in the Housing Act 2004 s 73(6)(a) (see head (a) in the text) or (where the application is made by an occupier) is in respect of any time falling outside the period of 12 months ending with the date of the occupier's application under s 73(5) (see the text and notes 12–19), and the period to be taken into account under head (1) is restricted accordingly: s 74(8).

36 Housing Act 2004 s 74(9) (amended in relation to England by SI 2013/630; and in relation to Wales by SI 2013/1788). As to the meaning of 'local land charge', and as to the effect of such a charge, see the Local Land Charges Act 1975; and REAL PROPERTY AND REGISTRATION vol 87 (2012) PARA 763 et seq. For the purpose of enforcing that charge the authority has the same powers and remedies under the Law of Property Act 1925 and otherwise as if it was a mortgagee by deed having powers of sale and lease, and of accepting surrenders of leases and of appointing a receiver: Housing Act 2004 s 74(10). See MORTGAGE vol 77 (2016) PARA 518 et seq. The power of appointing a receiver is exercisable at any time after the end of the period of one month beginning with the date on which the charge takes effect: s 74(11).

37 Ie under the Housing Act 2004 Pt 2 or Pt 3 (ss 79–100). As to licences under Pt 3 see PARA 704 et seq.

38 Housing Act 2004 s 74(12).

39 Ie under the Housing Act 2004 Pt 4 Ch 1 (ss 101–131): see PARA 745 et seq.

40 Housing Act 2004 s 74(13).

41 Housing Act 2004 s 74(14).

42 As to the meaning of 'the appropriate national authority' see PARA 389 note 1.

43 Housing Act 2004 s 74(15) (amended in relation to England by SI 2013/630; and in relation to Wales by SI 2013/1788). See the Rent Repayment Orders and Financial Penalties (Amounts Recovered) (England) Regulations 2017, SI 2017/367.

695. Restrictions on terminating tenancies. A landlord under an assured shorthold tenancy[1] has all of the grounds for possession set out in Schedule 2 to the Housing Act 1988[2]. In addition, the landlord has the right[3] to recover possession, on or after the coming to an end of an assured shorthold tenancy which was a fixed term tenancy, on the giving of a two month notice to the tenant stating that possession is required (a 'section 21 notice')[4]. No section 21 notice may be given in relation to a shorthold tenancy[5] of a part of an unlicensed HMO[6] so long as it remains such an HMO[7].

1 As to the meaning of 'assured shorthold tenancy' see LANDLORD AND TENANT vol 63 (2016) PARA 852.

2 See LANDLORD AND TENANT vol 63 (2016) PARA 934 et seq.

3 Ie under the Housing Act 1988 s 21.

4 See LANDLORD AND TENANT vol 63 (2016) PARA 926. For the purposes of the Housing Act 2004 s 75, a 'section 21 notice' means a notice under the Housing Act 1988 s 21(1)(b) or s 21(4)(a) (recovery of possession on termination of shorthold tenancy): Housing Act 2004 s 75(2).

5 A 'shorthold tenancy' means an assured shorthold tenancy within the meaning of the Housing Act 1988 Pt I Ch II (ss 19A–23) (see LANDLORD AND TENANT vol 63 (2016) PARA 852): Housing Act 2004 s 75(2).

6 As to the meaning of 'unlicensed HMO' see PARA 694 (definition applied by the Housing Act 2004 s 75(2)). As to the meaning of 'HMO' see PARA 674 note 2.

7 Housing Act 2004 s 75(1). In relation to a section 257 HMO (see PARA 669), s 75 is modified by the Houses in Multiple Occupation (Certain Converted Blocks of Flats) (Modifications to the Housing Act 2004 and Transitional Provisions for section 257 HMOs) (England) Regulations 2007, SI 2007/1904, regs 2, 8; and the Houses in Multiple Occupation (Certain Blocks of Flats) (Modifications to the Housing Act 2004 and Transitional Provisions for section 257 HMOs) (Wales) Regulations 2007, SI 2007/3231, regs 2, 8. Cf the restriction on the recovery of possession on expiry or termination of an assured shorthold tenancy under the Housing Act 1988 s 21: see LANDLORD AND TENANT vol 63 (2016) PARA 926.

(4) MANAGEMENT OF HOUSES IN MULTIPLE OCCUPATION

696. Approval of codes of practice with regard to management of houses in multiple occupation etc. The appropriate national authority[1] may by order: (1)

approve a code of practice (whether prepared by that authority or another person) laying down standards of conduct and practice to be followed with regard to the management of houses in multiple occupation[2] or of excepted accommodation[3]; (2) approve a modification of such a code; or (3) withdraw the authority's approval of such a code or modification[4].

Before approving a code of practice or a modification of a code of practice under these provisions, the appropriate national authority must take reasonable steps to consult: (a) persons involved in the management of houses in multiple occupation or (as the case may be) excepted accommodation of the kind in question and persons occupying such houses or accommodation; or (b) persons whom the authority considers to represent the interests of those persons[5].

The appropriate national authority may only approve a code of practice or a modification of a code if satisfied that: (i) the code or modification has been published (whether by the authority or by another person) in a manner that the authority considers appropriate for the purpose of bringing the code or modification to the attention of those likely to be affected by it; or (ii) arrangements have been made for the code or modification to be so published[6]. The appropriate national authority may approve a code of practice which makes different provision in relation to different cases or descriptions of case (including different provision for different areas)[7].

A failure to comply with a code of practice for the time being approved under these provisions does not of itself make a person liable to any civil or criminal proceedings[8].

1   As to the meaning of 'the appropriate national authority' see PARA 389 note 1.
2   As to the meaning of 'house in multiple occupation' see PARA 667.
3   For this purpose, 'excepted accommodation' means such description of living accommodation falling within any provision of the Housing Act 2004 s 254(5), Sch 14 (buildings which are not HMOs for purposes of provisions other than Pt 1 (ss 1–54): see PARA 668) as is specified in an order under s 233(1): s 233(6).
4   Housing Act 2004 s 233(1). As to the codes that have been approved see the Housing (Codes of Management Practice) (Student Accommodation) (England) Order 2010, SI 2010/2615; and the Housing (Approval of Codes of Management Practice) (Student Accommodation) (Wales) Order 2006, SI 2006/1709.
5   Housing Act 2004 s 233(2).
6   Housing Act 2004 s 233(3).
7   Housing Act 2004 s 233(4).
8   Housing Act 2004 s 233(5). As to offences in connection with the licensing of houses in multiple occupation see PARA 693.

697. Management regulations in respect of houses in multiple occupation. The appropriate national authority[1] may by regulations make provision for the purpose of ensuring that, in respect of every house in multiple occupation[2] of a description specified in the regulations, there are in place satisfactory management arrangements and satisfactory standards of management are observed[3]. The regulations may in particular: (1) impose duties on the person managing[4] a house in respect of the repair, maintenance, cleanliness and good order of the house and facilities and equipment in it; (2) impose duties on persons occupying a house for the purpose of ensuring that the person managing the house can effectively carry out any duty imposed on him by the regulations[5].

A person commits an offence if he fails to comply with such a regulation[6]. In proceedings against a person for such an offence it is a defence that he had a reasonable excuse for not complying with the regulation[7].

1   As to the meaning of 'the appropriate national authority' see PARA 389 note 1.
2   As to the meaning of 'house in multiple occupation' see PARA 667.

3 Housing Act 2004 s 234(1). As to the regulations that have been made see the Management of Houses in Multiple Occupation (England) Regulations 2006, SI 2006/372 (amended by SI 2009/724); the Management of Houses in Multiple Occupation (Wales) Regulations 2006, SI 2006/1713 (amended by SI 2009/1915); the Licensing and Management of Houses in Multiple Occupation (Additional Provisions) (England) Regulations 2007, SI 2007/1903 (amended by SI 2009/724); and the Licensing and Management of Houses in Multiple Occupation (Additional Provisions) (Wales) Regulations 2007, SI 2007/3229 (amended by SI 2009/1915).

4 As to the meaning of 'person managing' see PARA 391 note 6.

5 Housing Act 2004 s 234(2). See note 3.

6 Housing Act 2004 s 234(3). A person who commits an offence under s 234(3) is liable on summary conviction to a fine not exceeding level 5 on the standard scale: s 234(5). As to the powers of magistrates' courts to issue fines on summary conviction see SENTENCING vol 92 (2015) PARA 176. As to the imposition of a financial penalty instead of a fine see s 249A; and PARA 397: see s 234(6) (s 234(6), (7) added by the Housing and Planning Act 2016 s 126, Sch 9 paras 1, 6). If a local housing authority has imposed a financial penalty on a person under the Housing Act 2004 s 249A in respect of conduct amounting to an offence under s 234 the person may not be convicted of an offence under s 234 in respect of the conduct: s 234(7) (as so added).

7 Housing Act 2004 s 234(4).

(5) OVERCROWDING IN RELATION TO CERTAIN HOUSES IN MULTIPLE OCCUPATION

698. Overcrowding. The appropriate national authority[1] may by order make such provision as it considers appropriate for and in connection with:

(1)   determining whether a dwelling is overcrowded for the purposes of Part X of the Housing Act 1985[2];

(2)   introducing for the purposes of Chapter 3 of Part 4 of the Housing Act 2004[3] a concept of overcrowding similar to that applying for the purposes of Part X of the Housing Act 1985 (and accordingly removing the discretion of local housing authorities[4] to decide particular issues arising under those provisions);

(3)   securing that overcrowding in premises to which Chapter 3 of Part 4 of the Housing Act 2004 would otherwise apply, or any description of such premises, is regulated only by provisions of Part X of the Housing Act 1985[5].

Such an order may, in particular, make provision for regulating the making by local housing authorities of determinations as to whether premises are overcrowded, including provision prescribing:

(a)   factors that must be taken into account by such authorities when making such determinations;

(b)   the procedure that is to be followed by them in connection with making such determinations[6].

Such an order may modify any enactment[7] (including the Housing Act 2004)[8].

1 As to the meaning of 'the appropriate national authority' see PARA 389 note 1.

2 Ie the Housing Act 1985 Pt X (ss 324–344), which deals with overcrowding of dwellings generally: see PARA 649 et seq. For the purposes of the Housing Act 2004 s 216, any reference to the Housing Act 1985 Pt X includes a reference to Pt X as modified by an order under the Housing Act 2004 s 216: s 216(4).

3 Ie the Housing Act 2004 Pt 4 Ch 3 (ss 139–144), which deals with overcrowding of houses in multiple occupation: see PARA 699 et seq.

4 As to the meaning of 'local housing authority' see PARA 380 note 1.

5 Housing Act 2004 s 216(1). At the date at which this volume states the law, no order had been made under s 216.

6 Housing Act 2004 s 216(2).

7   For these purposes, 'enactment' includes an enactment comprised in subordinate legislation (ie within the meaning of the Interpretation Act 1978: see STATUTES AND LEGISLATIVE PROCESS vol 96 (2012) PARA 609): Housing Act 2004 s 216(4).
8   Housing Act 2004 s 216(3).

699. Service of overcrowding notice. Chapter 3 of Part 4 of the Housing Act 2004[1] applies to any HMO[2] in relation to which no interim or final management order is in force[3] and which is not required to be licensed under Part 2[4] of the Act[5].

The local housing authority[6] may serve[7] an overcrowding notice on one or more relevant persons[8] if, having regard to the rooms available, it considers that an excessive number of persons is being, or is likely to be, accommodated in the HMO concerned[9]. The authority must, at least seven days before serving an overcrowding notice, inform in writing every relevant person (whether or not the person on whom the authority is to serve the notice) of its intention to serve the notice, and ensure that, so far as is reasonably possible, every occupier of the HMO concerned is informed of the authority's intention[10]. The authority must also give the persons so informed an opportunity of making representations about the proposal to serve an overcrowding notice[11].

An overcrowding notice becomes operative, if no appeal is brought[12], at the end of the period of 21 days from the date of service of the notice[13]. If no appeal is brought, an overcrowding notice is final and conclusive as to matters which could have been raised on such an appeal[14].

A person who contravenes an overcrowding notice commits an offence and is liable to a penalty[15]. In proceedings for such an offence it is a defence that the person had a reasonable excuse for contravening the notice[16].

1   Ie the Housing Act 2004 Pt 4 Ch 3 (ss 139–144).
2   As to the meaning of 'HMO' see PARA 745 note 5.
3   As to interim and final management orders see PARA 745 et seq.
4   As to HMOs required to be licensed under the Housing Act 2004 Pt 2 (ss 55–78) see PARA 674 et seq.
5   Housing Act 2004 s 139(1). Overcrowding in licensable HMOs is covered in the Housing Act 2004 Pt 2, since a licence only permits a limited number of occupants: see PARA 679. As to the provisions of the Housing Act 1985 relating to overcrowding see PARA 649 et seq. In relation to a section 257 HMO (see PARA 669), the Housing Act 2004 s 139 is modified by the Houses in Multiple Occupation (Certain Converted Blocks of Flats) (Modifications to the Housing Act 2004 and Transitional Provisions for section 257 HMOs) (England) Regulations 2007, SI 2007/1904, regs 2, 11; and the Houses in Multiple Occupation (Certain Blocks of Flats) (Modifications to the Housing Act 2004 and Transitional Provisions for section 257 HMOs) (Wales) Regulations 2007, SI 2007/3231, regs 2, 11.
6   As to the meaning of 'local housing authority' see PARA 380 note 1.
7   As to service of documents under the Housing Act 2004 see PARA 391.
8   For these purposes, 'relevant person' means a person who is, to the knowledge of the local housing authority, a person having an estate or interest in the HMO concerned or a person managing or having control of it: Housing Act 2004 s 139(9). As to the meaning of 'person having an estate or interest' see PARA 391 note 7. As to the meaning of 'person managing' see PARA 391 note 6; and as to the meaning of 'person having control' see PARA 391 note 5.
9   Housing Act 2004 s 139(2). As to the contents of an overcrowding notice see PARA 700.
10 Housing Act 2004 s 139(3).
11 Housing Act 2004 s 139(4).
12 Ie under the Housing Act 2004 s 143: see PARA 702.
13 Housing Act 2004 s 139(5).
14 Housing Act 2004 s 139(6).
15 Housing Act 2004 s 139(7). The penalty on summary conviction is a fine not exceeding level 4 on the standard scale: see s 139(7). Prospectively, the reference to a fine in s 139(7) is removed, and a person who commits an offence under s 139(7) in relation to premises in England is liable on summary conviction to a fine; and a person who commits an offence under s 139(7) in relation to premises in Wales is liable on summary conviction to a fine not exceeding level 4 on the standard

scale: see s 139(7), (7A), (7B) (s 139(7) amended and s 139(7A), (7B) added, as from a day to be appointed, by the Housing and Planning Act 2016 s 127; at the date at which this volume states the law, no such day had been appointed).

As to the powers of magistrates' courts to issue fines on summary conviction see SENTENCING vol 92 (2015) PARA 176. As to the imposition of a financial penalty instead of a fine see the Housing Act 2004 s 249A; and PARA 397: see s 139(10) (s 139(10), (11) added by the Housing and Planning Act 2016 s 126, Sch 9 paras 1, 5). If a local housing authority has imposed a financial penalty on a person under the Housing Act 2004 s 249A in respect of conduct amounting to an offence under s 139 the person may not be convicted of an offence under s 139 in respect of the conduct: s 139(11) (as so added).

16 Housing Act 2004 s 139(8).

700. Contents of overcrowding notice. An overcrowding notice[1] must state in relation to each room in the HMO[2] concerned:

(1) what the local housing authority[3] considers to be the maximum number of persons by whom the room is suitable to be occupied as sleeping accommodation at any one time; or

(2) that the local housing authority considers that the room is unsuitable to be occupied as sleeping accommodation[4].

An overcrowding notice may specify special maxima applicable where some or all of the persons occupying a room are under such age as may be specified in the notice[5].

An overcrowding notice must contain:

(a) the prescribed[6] requirement not to permit an excessive number of persons to sleep in the HMO; or

(b) the prescribed[7] requirement not to admit new residents if the number of persons is excessive[8].

The local housing authority may at any time withdraw an overcrowding notice which has been served on any person and which contains the requirement in head (b), and serve on him instead an overcrowding notice containing the requirement in head (a)[9].

1 As to the service of an overcrowding notice see PARA 699.
2 As to the meaning of 'HMO' see PARA 745 note 5.
3 As to the meaning of 'local housing authority' see PARA 380 note 1.
4 Housing Act 2004 s 140(1); and see PARA 699 note 5.
5 Housing Act 2004 s 140(2).
6 Ie prescribed by the Housing Act 2004 s 141: see PARA 701 heads (1)–(2).
7 Ie prescribed by the Housing Act 2004 s 142: see PARA 701 heads (a)–(b).
8 Housing Act 2004 s 140(3).
9 Housing Act 2004 s 140(4).

701. Requirements as to overcrowding. The general requirement as to overcrowding is that the person on whom the overcrowding notice is served[1] must refrain from:

(1) permitting a room to be occupied as sleeping accommodation otherwise than in accordance with the notice; or

(2) permitting persons to occupy the HMO[2] as sleeping accommodation in such numbers[3] that it is not possible to avoid persons of opposite sexes who are not living together as husband and wife sleeping in the same room[4].

The requirement not to admit new residents[5] is that the person on whom the notice is served must refrain from:

(a) permitting a room to be occupied by a new resident as sleeping accommodation otherwise than in accordance with the notice; or

(b) permitting a new resident to occupy any part of the HMO as sleeping accommodation if that is not possible without persons of opposite sexes who are not living together as husband and wife sleeping in the same room[6].

1 As to the service of an overcrowding notice see PARA 699.
2 As to the meaning of 'HMO' see PARA 745 note 5.
3 For the purposes of head (2) in the text: (1) children under the age of ten are to be disregarded; and (2) it must be assumed that the persons occupying the HMO as sleeping accommodation sleep only in rooms for which a maximum is set by the notice and that the maximum set for each room is not exceeded: Housing Act 2004 s 141(2).
4 Housing Act 2004 s 141(1).
5 'New resident' means a person who was not an occupier of the HMO immediately before the notice was served: Housing Act 2004 s 142(2).
6 Housing Act 2004 s 142(1). For the purposes of head (b) in the text: (1) children under the age of ten are to be disregarded; and (2) it must be assumed that the persons occupying any part of the HMO as sleeping accommodation sleep only in rooms for which a maximum is set by the notice and that the maximum set for each room is not exceeded: s 142(3).

702. Appeals against overcrowding notices. A person aggrieved[1] by an overcrowding notice[2] may appeal to the appropriate tribunal[3] within the period of 21 days beginning with the date of service of the notice[4]. Such an appeal is to be by way of a re-hearing, and may be determined having regard to matters of which the local housing authority[5] was unaware[6]. On an appeal the tribunal may by order confirm, quash or vary the notice[7].

The appropriate tribunal may allow an appeal to be made to it after the end of the period mentioned above if it is satisfied that there is good reason for the failure to appeal before the end of that period (and for any delay since then in applying for permission to appeal out of time)[8].

If an appeal is brought, the notice does not become operative until: (1) a decision is given on the appeal which confirms the notice and the period within which an appeal to the Upper Tribunal[9] may be brought expires without any such appeal having been brought; or (2) if an appeal is brought to the Upper Tribunal, a decision is given on the appeal which confirms the notice[10].

1 As to the meaning of 'person aggrieved' see JUDICIAL REVIEW vol 61 (2010) PARA 656.
2 As to the service of an overcrowding notice see PARA 699.
3 As to the meaning of 'appropriate tribunal' see PARA 580 note 2. As to appeals to the appropriate tribunal see PARA 32 et seq.
4 Housing Act 2004 s 143(1) (amended by SI 2013/1036).
5 As to the meaning of 'local housing authority' see PARA 380 note 1.
6 Housing Act 2004 s 143(2).
7 Housing Act 2004 s 143(3).
8 Housing Act 2004 s 143(6) (amended by SI 2013/1036).
9 As to appeals to the Upper Tribunal, ie the Upper Tribunal (Lands Chamber), the successor to the Lands Tribunal, see PARAS 49–50.
10 Housing Act 2004 s 143(4) (amended by SI 2009/1307). For this purpose, the withdrawal of an appeal has the same effect as a decision which confirms the notice appealed against; and references to a decision which confirms the notice are references to a decision which confirms it with or without variation: Housing Act 2004 s 144(5).

703. Revocation and variation of overcrowding notices. The local housing authority[1] may at any time, on the application of a relevant person[2]: (1) revoke an overcrowding notice[3]; or (2) vary it so as to allow more people to be accommodated in the HMO concerned[4].

The applicant may appeal to the appropriate tribunal[5] if the local housing authority: (a) refuses an application for revocation or variation of an overcrowding notice; or (b) does not notify the applicant of its decision within the period of 35 days beginning with the making of the application (or within such further period as the applicant may in writing allow)[6].

Such an appeal must be made within: (i) the period of 21 days beginning with the date when the applicant is notified by the authority of its decision to refuse the application; or (ii) the period of 21 days immediately following the end of the period (or further period) applying for the purposes of head (b), as the case may be[7]. The appropriate tribunal may allow an appeal to be made to it after the end of the 21-day period mentioned above if it is satisfied that there is good reason for the failure to appeal before the end of that period (and for any delay since then in applying for permission to appeal)[8].

An appeal is to be by way of a re-hearing, and may be determined having regard to matters of which the local housing authority was unaware[9]. On an appeal the tribunal may revoke the notice or vary it in any manner in which it might have been varied by the local housing authority[10].

1 As to the meaning of 'local housing authority' see PARA 380 note 1.
2 For this purpose, 'relevant person' means any person who has an estate or interest in the HMO concerned, or any other person who is a person managing or having control of it: Housing Act 2004 s 144(7). As to the meaning of 'person having an estate or interest' see PARA 391 note 7. As to the meaning of 'HMO' see PARA 745 note 5. As to the meaning of 'person managing' see PARA 391 note 6; and as to the meaning of 'person having control' see PARA 391 note 5.
3 As to the service of an overcrowding notice see PARA 699.
4 Housing Act 2004 s 144(1); and see PARA 699 note 5.
5 As to the meaning of 'appropriate tribunal' see PARA 580 note 2. As to appeals to the appropriate tribunal see PARA 32 et seq.
6 Housing Act 2004 s 144(2) (amended by SI 2013/1036).
7 Housing Act 2004 s 144(3).
8 Housing Act 2004 s 144(6) (amended by SI 2013/1036).
9 Housing Act 2004 s 143(2) (applied by s 144(4)).
10 Housing Act 2004 s 144(5).

8. SELECTIVE LICENSING OF PRIVATE LANDLORDS

(1) APPLICATION OF LICENSING PROVISIONS

704. Houses to which licensing provisions apply. Part 3 of the Housing Act 2004[1] provides for houses[2] to be licensed by local housing authorities[3] where: (1) they are houses to which that Part applies[4]; and (2) they are required to be licensed[5] under that Part[6]. Part 3 applies to a house if: (a) it is in an area that is for the time being designated[7] as subject to selective licensing; and (b) the whole of it is occupied either under a single tenancy or licence[8] that is not an exempt tenancy or licence[9], or under two or more tenancies or licences in respect of different dwellings contained in it, none of which is an exempt tenancy or licence[10].

A tenancy or licence is an exempt tenancy or licence if: (i) it is granted by a non-profit registered provider of social housing[11]; (ii) it is granted by a profit-making registered provider of social housing in respect of social housing[12], or it is granted by a body which is registered[13] as a social landlord[14]. In addition, the appropriate national authority[15] may by order provide for a tenancy or licence to be an exempt tenancy or licence if it falls within any description of tenancy or licence specified in the order or in any other circumstances so specified[16].

Every local housing authority has the following general duties: (A) to make such arrangements as are necessary to secure the effective implementation in its district[17] of the licensing regime provided for by Part 3; and (B) to ensure that all applications for licences and other issues falling to be determined by it under that Part are determined within a reasonable time[18].

1 Ie the Housing Act 2004 Pt 3 (ss 79–100). Whereas Pt 2 (ss 55–78) (see PARA 674 et seq) introduces a mandatory licensing scheme for certain houses in multiple occupation, Pt 3 provides a power for selective licensing aimed at dealing with particular problems in a particular area. See Driscoll *Housing: the New Law, A Guide to the Housing Act 2004* (2007) Ch 7.
2 For the purposes of the Housing Act 2004 Pt 3, 'house' means a building or part of a building consisting of one or more dwellings; and references to a house include (where the context permits) any yard, garden, outhouses and appurtenances belonging to, or usually enjoyed with, it (or any part of it): s 99. 'Dwelling' means a building or part of a building occupied or intended to be occupied as a separate dwelling: s 99.
3 As to the meaning of 'local housing authority' see PARA 380 note 1.
4 See the Housing Act 2004 s 79(2); and text and notes 7–10.
5 See the Housing Act 2004 s 85(1); and PARA 709.
6 Housing Act 2004 s 79(1).
7 Ie under the Housing Act 2004 s 80: see PARA 705.
8 As to the meanings of 'tenancy' and 'licence' see PARA 391 note 6.
9 Ie under the Housing Act 2004 s 79(3) (see the text and note 14) or s 79(4) (see the text and note 16).
10 Housing Act 2004 s 79(2).
11 As to registered providers of social housing see PARA 51 et seq; as to when such a body is a non-profit organisation see PARA 71 note 13.
12 Ie within the meaning of the Housing and Regeneration Act 2008 Pt 2 (ss 59–278A): see PARA 52. As to when a registered provider of social housing is profit-making see PARA 71 note 13.
13 Ie under the Housing Act 1996 Pt I (ss A1–64): see PARA 166 et seq.
14 Housing Act 2004 s 79(3) (amended by SI 2010/866).
15 As to the meaning of 'the appropriate national authority' see PARA 389 note 1.
16 Housing Act 2004 s 79(4). As to the orders that have been made see the Selective Licensing of Houses (Specified Exemptions) (England) Order 2006, SI 2006/370; and the Selective Licensing of Houses (Specified Exemptions) (Wales) Order 2006, SI 2006/2824 (amended by SI 2014/107).
17 As to the area of a local housing authority's district see PARA 674 note 4.
18 Housing Act 2004 s 79(5).

(2) SELECTIVE LICENSING AREAS

705. Designation of selective licensing areas. A local housing authority[1] may designate either the area of its district[2] or an area in its district as subject to selective licensing, if the following requirements[3] are met[4]. The authority must consider that the first or second set of general conditions[5], or any conditions specified[6] as an additional set of conditions are satisfied in relation to the area, as set out below[7].

The first set of general conditions are:

(1)   that the area is, or is likely to become, an area of low housing demand[8]; and

(2)   that making a designation will, when combined with other measures taken in the area by the local housing authority, or by other persons together with the local housing authority, contribute to the improvement of the social or economic conditions in the area[9].

The second set of general conditions are:

(a)   that the area is experiencing a significant and persistent problem caused by anti-social behaviour[10];

(b)   that some or all of the private sector landlords[11] who have let premises in the area (whether under leases or licences[12]) are failing to take action to combat the problem that it would be appropriate for them to take; and

(c)   that making a designation will, when combined with other measures taken in the area by the local housing authority, or by other persons together with the local housing authority, lead to a reduction in, or the elimination of, the problem[13].

Before making a designation the local housing authority must:

(i)   take reasonable steps to consult persons who are likely to be affected by the designation; and

(ii)   consider any representations made in accordance with the consultation and not withdrawn[14].

The authority must ensure that any exercise of the power to make a designation is consistent with the authority's overall housing strategy[15]. The authority must also seek to adopt a co-ordinated approach in connection with dealing with homelessness[16], empty properties[17] and anti-social behaviour, both as regards combining licensing under Part 3 of the Housing Act 2004 with other courses of action available to it, and as regards combining such licensing with measures taken by other persons[18].

The authority must not make a particular designation unless it has considered whether there are any other courses of action available to it (of whatever nature) that might provide an effective method of achieving the objective or objectives that the designation would be intended to achieve, and the authority considers that making the designation will significantly assist it to achieve the objective or objectives (whether or not it takes any other course of action as well)[19].

1   As to the meaning of 'local housing authority' see PARA 380 note 1.
2   As to the area of a local housing authority's district see PARA 674 note 4.
3   Ie the requirements of the Housing Act 2004 s 80(2), (9) (see the text and notes 7, 14).
4   Housing Act 2004 s 80(1); and see PARA 704 note 1. In addition, s 81 (see the text and notes 15–19) applies for the purposes of s 80: s 80(10).
5   Ie the conditions mentioned in the Housing Act 2004 s 80(3) (see the text and note 9) or s 80(6) (see the text and note 13).
6   Ie in an order under the Housing Act 2004 s 80(7): see note 7.

7   Housing Act 2004 s 80(2). The appropriate national authority may by order provide for any conditions specified in the order to apply as an additional set of conditions for the purposes of s 80(2): s 80(7). As to the meaning of 'the appropriate national authority' see PARA 389 note 1. The conditions that may be specified include, in particular, conditions intended to permit a local housing authority to make a designation for the purpose of dealing with one or more specified problems affecting persons occupying Part 3 houses in the area: s 80(8). 'Specified' means specified in an order under s 80(7): s 80(8). In Pt 3 (ss 79–100), references to a Part 3 house are references to a house to which Pt 3 applies (see s 79(2); and PARA 704): s 85(5)(a). As to the meaning of 'house' for this purpose see PARA 704 note 2. As to the additional set of conditions specified see the Selective Licensing of Houses (Additional Conditions) (England) Order 2015, SI 2015/977; and the Selective Licensing of Houses (Additional Conditions) (Wales) Order 2006, SI 2006/2825.

8   In deciding whether an area is, or is likely to become, an area of low housing demand a local housing authority must take into account (among other matters): (1) the value of residential premises in the area, in comparison to the value of similar premises in other areas which the authority considers to be comparable (whether in terms of types of housing, local amenities, availability of transport or otherwise); (2) the turnover of occupiers of residential premises; (3) the number of residential premises which are available to buy or rent and the length of time for which they remain unoccupied: Housing Act 2004 s 80(4). The appropriate national authority may by order amend s 80(4) by adding new matters to those for the time being mentioned therein: s 80(5).

9   Housing Act 2004 s 80(3).

10   As to the meaning of 'anti-social behaviour' see PARA 675 note 12.

11   'Private sector landlord' does not include a non-profit registered provider of social housing or a registered social landlord within the meaning of the Housing Act 1996 Pt I (ss A1–64) (see PARA 166 et seq): Housing Act 2004 s 80(6) (amended by SI 2010/866). As to registered providers of social housing see PARA 51 et seq; as to when such a body is a non-profit organisation see PARA 71 note 13.

12   As to the meanings of 'lease' and 'licence' see PARA 391 note 6.

13   Housing Act 2004 s 80(6).

14   Housing Act 2004 s 80(9).

15   Housing Act 2004 s 81(1), (2).

16   As to a local housing authority's duties to the homeless see PARA 477 et seq.

17   As to a local housing authority's duties in relation to empty houses see PARA 781 et seq.

18   Housing Act 2004 s 81(3).

19   Housing Act 2004 s 81(4).

706. Confirmation or general approval of designation. A designation of an area as subject to selective licensing[1] cannot come into force unless: (1) it has been confirmed by the appropriate national authority[2]; or (2) it falls within a description of designations in relation to which that authority has given[3] a general approval[4]. The appropriate national authority may either confirm, or refuse to confirm, a designation as it considers appropriate[5]. If the appropriate national authority confirms a designation, the designation comes into force on a date specified for this purpose by that authority[6]. That date must be no earlier than three months after the date on which the designation is confirmed[7].

A general approval may be given in relation to a description of designations framed by reference to any matters or circumstances[8]. Accordingly, a general approval may (in particular) be given in relation to: (a) designations made by a specified[9] local housing authority[10]; (b) designations made by a local housing authority falling within a specified description of such authorities; (c) designations relating to Part 3 houses[11] of a specified description[12]. If, by virtue of a general approval, a designation does not need to be confirmed before it comes into force, the designation comes into force on the date specified for this purpose in the designation[13]. That date must be no earlier than three months after the date on which the designation is made[14].

Where a designation comes into force, Part 3 of the Housing Act 2004[15] applies in relation to the occupation by persons of houses in the area on or after the coming into force of the designation even if their occupation began before, or in pursuance of a contract made before, it came into force[16].

1 Ie under the Housing Act 2004 s 80: see PARA 705.
2 As to the meaning of 'the appropriate national authority' see PARA 389 note 1.
3 Ie in accordance with the Housing Act 2004 s 82(6): see the text and note 12.
4 Housing Act 2004 s 82(1).
5 Housing Act 2004 s 82(2).
6 Housing Act 2004 s 82(3).
7 Housing Act 2004 s 82(4).
8 Housing Act 2004 s 82(5). See the Housing Act 2004: Licensing of Houses in Multiple Occupation and Selective Licensing of Other Residential Accommodation (England) General Approval 2015 (Department for Communities and Local Government, 26 March 2015).
9 'Specified' means specified by the appropriate national authority in the approval: Housing Act 2004 s 82(6).
10 As to the meaning of 'local housing authority' see PARA 380 note 1.
11 As to the meaning of 'Part 3 house' see PARA 705 note 7. As to the meaning of 'house' for this purpose see PARA 704 note 2.
12 Housing Act 2004 s 82(6)(a)–(c).
13 Housing Act 2004 s 82(7).
14 Housing Act 2004 s 82(8).
15 Ie the Housing Act 2004 Pt 3 (ss 79–100).
16 Housing Act 2004 s 82(9).

707. Notification requirements. When a designation of an area as subject to selective licensing[1] is confirmed[2], or (if it is not required to be so confirmed) when it is made by the local housing authority[3], then as soon as the designation is confirmed or made, the authority must publish in the prescribed[4] manner a notice stating:

(1)   that the designation has been made;
(2)   whether or not the designation was required to be confirmed and either that it has been confirmed or that a general approval[5] applied to it (giving details of the approval in question);
(3)   the date on which the designation is to come into force[6]; and
(4)   any other information which may be prescribed[7].

After publication of such a notice, and for as long as the designation is in force, the local housing authority must make available to the public in accordance with any prescribed requirements: (a) copies of the designation; and (b) such information relating to the designation as is prescribed[8].

1 Ie under the Housing Act 2004 s 80: see PARA 705.
2 Ie under the Housing Act 2004 s 82: see PARA 706.
3 As to the meaning of 'local housing authority' see PARA 380 note 1.
4 'Prescribed' means prescribed by regulations made by the appropriate national authority: Housing Act 2004 s 83(4). As to the meaning of 'the appropriate national authority' see PARA 389 note 1. As to the prescribed publication requirements see the Licensing and Management of Houses in Multiple Occupation and Other Houses (Miscellaneous Provisions) (England) Regulations 2006, SI 2006/373, reg 9; and the Licensing and Management of Houses in Multiple Occupation and Other Houses (Miscellaneous Provisions) (Wales) Regulations 2006, SI 2006/1715, reg 9.
5 Ie under the Housing Act 2004 s 82: see PARA 706.
6 As to the coming into force of a designation see PARA 706.
7 Housing Act 2004 s 83(1), (2); and see PARA 704 note 1. See also note 4.
8 Housing Act 2004 s 83(3).

708. Duration, review and revocation of designations. Unless previously revoked[1], a designation of an area as subject to selective licensing[2] ceases to have effect at the time that is specified for this purpose in the designation[3]. That time must be no later than five years after the date on which the designation comes into force[4]. A local housing authority[5] must from time to time review the operation of any designation made by it[6]. If, following a review, it considers it appropriate to do so, the authority may revoke the designation[7]. If it does revoke the designation, the designation ceases to have effect on the date that is specified by the authority for this purpose[8]. On revoking a designation, the authority must publish notice of the revocation in such manner as is prescribed by regulations made by the appropriate national authority[9].

1   Ie under the Housing Act 2004 s 84(4): see the text and note 7.
2   Ie under the Housing Act 2004 s 80: see PARA 705.
3   Housing Act 2004 s 84(1).
4   Housing Act 2004 s 84(2).
5   As to the meaning of 'local housing authority' see PARA 380 note 1.
6   Housing Act 2004 s 84(3); and see PARA 704 note 1.
7   Housing Act 2004 s 84(4).
8   Housing Act 2004 s 84(5).
9   Housing Act 2004 s 84(6). As to the meaning of 'the appropriate national authority' see PARA 389 note 1. As to the prescribed publication requirements see the Licensing and Management of Houses in Multiple Occupation and Other Houses (Miscellaneous Provisions) (England) Regulations 2006, SI 2006/373, reg 10; and the Licensing and Management of Houses in Multiple Occupation and Other Houses (Miscellaneous Provisions) (Wales) Regulations 2006, SI 2006/1715, reg 10.

(3) PART 3 LICENCES

(i) Licensing Requirement

709. Houses required to be licensed. Every Part 3 house[1] must be licensed under Part 3 of the Housing Act 2004[2] unless: (1) it is an HMO[3] to which Part 2 of the Act[4] applies[5]; or (2) a temporary exemption notice[6] is in force in relation to it; or (3) a management order[7] is in force in relation to it[8]. A licence under Part 3 is a licence authorising occupation of the house concerned under one or more tenancies or licences[9]. The local housing authority[10] must take all reasonable steps to secure that applications for licences are made to it in respect of houses in its area which are required to be licensed under Part 3 but are not so licensed[11].

1   As to the meaning of 'Part 3 house' see PARA 705 note 7.
2   Ie under the Housing Act 2004 Pt 3 (ss 79–90). As to licences under Pt 3 see PARA 711 et seq. In Pt 3, unless the context otherwise requires, references to a house being (or not being) licensed under Pt 3 are references to its being (or not being) a house in respect of which a licence is in force under Pt 3: s 85(5)(d).
3   As to HMOs see PARA 666 et seq. As to the meaning of 'HMO' in the Housing Act 2004 Pt 2 see PARA 674 note 2.
4   Ie the Housing Act 2004 Pt 2 (ss 55–78).
5   See the Housing Act 2004 s 55(2); and PARA 674.
6   Ie under the Housing Act 2004 s 86: see PARA 710.
7   Ie under the Housing Act 2004 Pt 4 Ch 1 (ss 101–131) or Pt 4 Ch 2 (ss 132–138): see PARAS 745 et seq, 781 et seq.
8   Housing Act 2004 s 85(1). As to applications for licences, the granting or refusal of licences, and the imposition of licence conditions see ss 87–90; and PARAS 711–712: s 85(3).
9   Ie within the Housing Act 2004 s 79(2)(b) (see PARA 704): s 85(2). As to the meanings of 'tenancy' and 'licence' see PARA 391 note 6.
10 As to the meaning of 'local housing authority' see PARA 380 note 1.
11 Housing Act 2004 s 85(4); and see PARA 704 note 1.

710. Temporary exemption from licensing requirement. Where a person having control of or managing[1] a Part 3 house[2] which is required to be licensed under Part 3 of the Housing Act 2004[3], but is not so licensed, notifies the local housing authority[4] of his intention to take particular steps with a view to securing that the house is no longer required to be licensed, the authority may, if it thinks fit, serve on that person a notice ('a temporary exemption notice') in respect of the house[5].

If a temporary exemption notice is served[6], the house is not required[7] to be licensed under Part 3 during the period for which the notice is in force[8]. A temporary exemption notice is in force for the period of three months beginning with the date on which it is served, or (in the case of a second temporary exemption notice[9]) for the period of three months after the date when the first notice ceases to be in force[10].

If the authority receives a further notification and considers that there are exceptional circumstances that justify the service of a second temporary exemption notice in respect of the house that would take effect from the end of the period of three months applying to the first notice, the authority may serve a second such notice on the person having control of or managing the house (but no further notice may be served by virtue of this provision)[11].

If the authority decides not to serve a temporary exemption notice in response to a notification, it must without delay serve on the person concerned a notice informing him of: (1) the decision; (2) the reasons for it and the date on which it was made; (3) the right to appeal against the decision[12]; and (4) the period within which an appeal may be made[13].

The person concerned may appeal to the appropriate tribunal[14] against the decision within the period of 28 days beginning with the date specified[15] as the date on which it was made[16]. Such an appeal is to be by way of a re-hearing, and may be determined having regard to matters of which the authority was unaware[17]. The tribunal may confirm or reverse the decision of the authority, and if it reverses the decision, must direct the authority to issue a temporary exemption notice with effect from such date as the tribunal directs[18].

1   As to the meaning of 'person having control' see PARA 391 note 5; and as to the meaning of 'person managing' see PARA 391 note 6.
2   As to the meaning of 'Part 3 house' see PARA 705 note 7.
3   Ie under the Housing Act 2004 Pt 3 (ss 79–100): see s 85(1); and PARA 709.
4   As to the meaning of 'local housing authority' see PARA 380 note 1.
5   Housing Act 2004 s 86(1), (2); and see PARA 704 note 1.
6   As to service of documents see PARA 391.
7   Ie in accordance with the Housing Act 2004 s 85(1): see PARA 709.
8   Housing Act 2004 s 86(3).
9   Ie a notice served by virtue of the Housing Act 2004 s 86(5): see the text to note 11.
10 Housing Act 2004 s 86(4).
11 Housing Act 2004 s 86(5).
12 Ie under the Housing Act 2004 s 86(7): see the text and note 16.
13 Housing Act 2004 s 86(6).
14 As to the meaning of 'appropriate tribunal' see PARA 580 note 2. As to appeals to the appropriate tribunal see PARA 32 et seq.
15 Ie under the Housing Act 2004 s 86(6).
16 Housing Act 2004 s 86(7) (amended by SI 2013/1036).
17 Housing Act 2004 s 86(8).
18 Housing Act 2004 s 86(9).

(ii) Licences

711. Application for licence. An application for a licence[1] must be made to the local housing authority[2], and must be made in accordance with such requirements as the authority may specify[3]. The authority may, in particular, require the application to be accompanied by a fee fixed by the authority[4].

The appropriate national authority[5] may by regulations make provision about the making of applications for licences[6]. Such regulations may, in particular:

(1)   specify the manner and form in which applications are to be made;

(2) require the applicant to give copies of the application, or information about it, to particular persons;

(3) specify the information or, prospectively, evidence which is to be supplied in connection with applications;

(4) specify the maximum fees which are to be charged (whether by specifying amounts or methods for calculating amounts);

(5) specify cases in which no fees are to be charged or fees are to be refunded[7].

Where an application in respect of a house[8] is made to the local housing authority[9], the authority must either grant a licence in accordance with the following provisions[10], or refuse to grant a licence[11]. If the authority is satisfied as to the matters mentioned below, it may grant a licence either to the applicant or to some other person, if both he and the applicant agree[12]. Those matters are:

(a) that the proposed licence holder is a fit and proper person to be the licence holder[13], and is, out of all the persons reasonably available to be the licence holder in respect of the house, the most appropriate person to be the licence holder[14];

(b) prospectively, that no banning order under the Housing and Planning Act 2016[15] is in force against a person who: (i) owns an estate or interest in the house or part of it; and (ii) is a lessor or licensor of the house or part;

(c) that the proposed manager of the house is either the person having control of the house[16], or a person who is an agent or employee of the person having control of the house;

(d) that the proposed manager of the house is a fit and proper person to be the manager of the house[17]; and

(e) that the proposed management arrangements for the house are otherwise satisfactory[18].

1 In the Housing Act 2004 Pt 3 (ss 79–100), unless the context otherwise requires, references to a licence are references to a licence under Pt 3; and references to a licence holder are to be read accordingly: s 85(5)(b), (c). As to the conditions to be included in licences see PARA 712. As to the procedural requirements, which are the same as those for licences granted under Pt 2 (ss 55–78), see PARA 687 et seq. As to the duration and transferability of licences see PARA 713. As to variation of licences see PARA 714. As to revocation of licences see PARA 715.

2 Housing Act 2004 s 87(1). As to the meaning of 'local housing authority' see PARA 380 note 1.

3 Housing Act 2004 s 87(2); and see PARA 704 note 1. As to the procedure see further PARA 687 et seq.

4 Housing Act 2004 s 87(3). The power of the authority to specify requirements under s 87 is subject to any regulations made under s 87(5) (see the text and note 6): s 87(4).

5 As to the meaning of 'the appropriate national authority' see PARA 389 note 1.

6 Housing Act 2004 s 87(5). As to the regulations made see the Licensing and Management of Houses in Multiple Occupation and Other Houses (Miscellaneous Provisions) (England) Regulations 2006, SI 2006/373, reg 7, Sch 2 (reg 7 amended by SI 2012/2111; the Licensing and Management of Houses in Multiple Occupation and Other Houses (Miscellaneous Provisions) (England) Regulations 2006, SI 2006/373, Sch 2 amended by SI 2007/1903 and SI 2012/2111); and the Licensing and Management of Houses in Multiple Occupation and Other Houses (Miscellaneous Provisions) (Wales) Regulations 2006, SI 2006/1715, reg 7, Sch 2 (Sch 2 amended by SI 2007/3229).

7 Housing Act 2004 s 87(6) (amended, as from a day to be appointed, by the Housing and Planning Act 2016 s 125(1), (5); at the date at which this volume states the law, no such day had been appointed). See note 6. When fixing fees under the Housing Act 2004 s 87, the local housing authority may (subject to any regulations made under s 87(5): see the text and note 6) take into account: (1) all costs incurred by the authority in carrying out its functions under Pt 3; and (2) all costs incurred by it in carrying out its functions under Pt 4 Ch 1 (ss 101–131) (see PARA 745 et seq) in relation to Part 3 houses (so far as they are not recoverable under or by virtue of any provision of Pt 4 Ch 1): s 87(7). As to the meaning of 'Part 3 house' see PARA 705 note 7.

8   As to the meaning of 'house' for this purpose see PARA 704 note 2.
9   Ie under the Housing Act 2004 s 87.
10 Ie the Housing Act 2004 s 88(2).
11 Housing Act 2004 s 88(1).
12 Housing Act 2004 s 88(2).
13 In deciding for the purposes of the Housing Act 2004 s 88(3)(a) or (c) (see heads (a), (d) in the text) whether a person ('P') is a fit and proper person to be the licence holder or (as the case may be) the manager of the house, the local housing authority must have regard (among other things) to any evidence within s 89(2) or (3): ss 88(4), 89(1).
    Evidence is within s 89(2) if it shows that P has: (1) committed any offence involving fraud or other dishonesty, or violence or drugs, or any offence listed in the Sexual Offences Act 2003 Sch 3 (offences attracting notification requirements: see SENTENCING vol 92 (2015) PARA 329); (2) practised unlawful discrimination on grounds of sex, colour, race, ethnic or national origins or disability in, or in connection with, the carrying on of any business (see DISCRIMINATION vol 33 (2013) PARA 65 et seq); or (3) contravened any provision of the law relating to housing or of landlord and tenant law (including, prospectively, the Immigration Act 2014 Pt 3 (ss 20–47): Housing Act 2004 s 89(2) (amended, as from a day to be appointed, by the Housing and Planning Act 2016 s 125(1), (6)(b); at the date at which this volume states the law, no such day had been appointed).
    Evidence is within the Housing Act 2004 s 89(3) if: (a) it shows that any person associated or formerly associated with P (whether on a personal, work or other basis) has done any of the things set out in heads (1)–(3); and (b) it appears to the authority that the evidence is relevant to the question whether P is a fit and proper person to be the licence holder or (as the case may be) the manager of the house: s 89(3).
    Prospectively, a local housing authority in England must also have regard to any evidence within s 89(3A) or (3B): s 89(1A) (s 89(1A), (3A), (3B) added as from a day to be appointed, by the Housing and Planning Act 2016 s 125(1), (6)(a), (c); at the date at which this volume states the law, no such day had been appointed). Evidence is within the Housing Act 2004 s 89(3A) if it shows that P: (i) requires leave to enter or remain in the United Kingdom but does not have it; or (ii) is insolvent or an undischarged bankrupt: s 89(3A) (as so added). Evidence is within s 89(3B) if: (A) it shows that any person associated or formerly associated with P (whether on a personal, work or other basis) is a person to whom s 89(3A)(a) or (b) (see heads (i), (ii)) applies; and (B) it appears to the authority that the evidence is relevant to the question whether P is a fit and proper person to be the licence holder or (as the case may be) the manager of the house: s 89(3B) (as so added).
    Prospectively, a person is not a fit and proper person for the purposes of s 88(3)(a) or (c) if a banning order under the Housing and Planning Act 2016 s 16 (see PARA 719 et seq) is in force against the person: Housing Act 2004 s 89(3C) (added, as from a day to be appointed, by the Housing and Planning Act 2016 s 25, Sch 2 paras 1, 8; at the date at which this volume states the law, no such day had been appointed).
14 For the purposes of the Housing Act 2004 s 88(3)(a) (see head (a) in the text), the local housing authority must assume, unless the contrary is shown, that the person having control of the house is a more appropriate person to be the licence holder than a person not having control of it: s 89(4). Any reference in s 88(3)(b)(i) or (ii) or s 89(4) to a person having control of the house, or to being a person of any other description, includes a reference to a person who is proposing to have control of the house, or (as the case may be) to be a person of that description, at the time when the licence would come into force: s 89(7).
15 Ie under the Housing and Planning Act 2016 s 16: see PARA 719 et seq.
16 As to the meaning of 'person having control' see PARA 391 note 5. See also note 13.
17 See note 13.
18 Housing Act 2004 s 88(3) (amended, as from a day to be appointed, by the Housing and Planning Act 2016 Sch 2 paras 1, 7; at the date at which this volume states the law, no such day had been appointed). In deciding for the purposes of the Housing Act 2004 s 88(3)(d) (see head (e) in the text) whether the proposed management arrangements for the house are otherwise satisfactory, the local housing authority must have regard (among other things) to the considerations mentioned in s 89(6): s 89(5). The considerations are: (1) whether any person proposed to be involved in the management of the house has a sufficient level of competence to be so involved; (2) whether any person proposed to be involved in the management of the house (other than the manager) is a fit and proper person to be so involved; and (3) whether any proposed management structures and funding arrangements are suitable: s 89(6).

712. Licence conditions. There are certain conditions which must be included in a licence[1], whilst others may be included at the discretion of the local housing authority[2].

A licence may include such conditions as the local housing authority considers appropriate for regulating the management, use or occupation of the house[3] concerned[4]. Those conditions may, in particular, include (so far as appropriate in the circumstances):

(1) conditions imposing restrictions or prohibitions on the use or occupation of particular parts of the house by persons occupying it;

(2) conditions requiring the taking of reasonable and practicable steps to prevent or reduce anti-social behaviour[5] by persons occupying or visiting the house[6].

A licence may also include:

(a) conditions requiring facilities and equipment to be made available in the house for the purpose of meeting standards prescribed for this purpose by regulations made by the appropriate national authority[7];

(b) conditions requiring such facilities and equipment to be kept in repair and proper working order;

(c) conditions requiring, in the case of any works needed in order for any such facilities or equipment to be made available or to meet any such standards, that the works are carried out within such period or periods as may be specified in, or determined under, the licence[8].

A licence must include the following conditions[9]:

(i) conditions requiring the licence holder, if gas is supplied to the house[10], to produce to the local housing authority annually for its inspection a gas safety certificate obtained in respect of the house within the last 12 months[11];

(ii) conditions requiring the licence holder: (A) to keep electrical appliances and furniture made available by him in the house in a safe condition; (B) to supply the authority, on demand, with a declaration by him as to the safety of such appliances and furniture[12];

(iii) conditions requiring the licence holder: (A) where the house is in England, to ensure that a smoke alarm is installed on each storey of the house on which there is a room used wholly or partly as living accommodation[13] and to keep each such alarm in proper working order; (B) where the house is in Wales, to ensure that smoke alarms are installed in the house and to keep them in proper working order; (C) in either case, to supply the authority, on demand, with a declaration by him as to the condition and positioning of such alarms[14];

(iv) where the house is in England, conditions requiring the licence holder: (A) to ensure that a carbon monoxide alarm is installed in any room[15] in the house which is used wholly or partly as living accommodation and contains a solid fuel burning combustion appliance; (B) to keep any such alarm in proper working order; and (C) to supply the authority, on demand, with a declaration by him as to the condition and positioning of any such alarm[16];

(v) conditions requiring the licence holder to supply to the occupiers[17] of the house a written statement of the terms on which they occupy it[18];

(vi) conditions requiring the licence holder to demand references from persons who wish to occupy the house[19].

As regards the relationship between the authority's power to impose conditions in a licence and functions exercisable by it under or for the purposes of Part 1 of the Housing Act 2004[20] ('Part 1 functions'), the authority must proceed on the basis that, in general, it should seek to identify, remove or reduce category 1 or category 2 hazards[21] in the house by the exercise of Part 1 functions and not by means of licence conditions[22]. The fact that licence conditions are imposed for a particular purpose that could be achieved by the exercise of Part 1 functions does not affect the way in which Part 1 functions can be subsequently exercised by the authority[23].

A licence may not include conditions imposing restrictions or obligations on a particular person other than the licence holder unless that person has consented to the imposition of the restrictions or obligations[24]. A licence may not include conditions requiring (or intended to secure) any alteration in the terms of any tenancy or licence[25] under which any person occupies the house[26].

1   See the text and notes 9–19. As to the meaning of 'licence' see PARA 711 note 1. As to applications for licences see PARA 711. As to the duration and transferability of licences see PARA 713. As to variation of licences see PARA 714. As to revocation of licences see PARA 715.
2   See the text and notes 3–8. As to the meaning of 'local housing authority' see PARA 380 note 1.
3   As to the meaning of 'house' for this purpose see PARA 704 note 2.
4   Housing Act 2004 s 90(1).
5   As to the meaning of 'anti-social behaviour' see PARA 675 note 12.
6   Housing Act 2004 s 90(2).
7   As to the meaning of 'the appropriate national authority' see PARA 389 note 1. At the date at which this volume states the law, no such regulations had been made.
8   Housing Act 2004 s 90(3).
9   Housing Act 2004 s 90(4), Sch 4. The appropriate national authority may by regulations amend Sch 4 so as to alter (by the addition or removal of conditions) the conditions which must be included in a licence under Pt 2 (ss 55–78) or Pt 3 (ss 79–100), or only in a licence under one of those Parts: Sch 4 para 3. See the Smoke and Carbon Monoxide Alarm (England) Regulations 2015, SI 2015/1693. In relation to a section 257 HMO (see PARA 669), the Housing Act 2004 Sch 4 is modified by the Houses in Multiple Occupation (Certain Converted Blocks of Flats) (Modifications to the Housing Act 2004 and Transitional Provisions for section 257 HMOs) (England) Regulations 2007, SI 2007/1904, regs 2, 10; and the Houses in Multiple Occupation (Certain Blocks of Flats) (Modifications to the Housing Act 2004 and Transitional Provisions for section 257 HMOs) (Wales) Regulations 2007, SI 2007/3231, regs 2, 10.
10 For this purpose, 'the house' means the Part 3 house in respect of which the licence is granted: Housing Act 2004 Sch 4 para 4. As to the meaning of 'Part 3 house' see PARA 705 note 7.
11 Housing Act 2004 Sch 4 para 1(1), (2).
12 Housing Act 2004 Sch 4 para 1(3).
13 For the purposes of the Housing Act 2004 Sch 4 para 1(4), (4A) (see head (iv) in the text), a bathroom or lavatory is to be treated as a room used as living accommodation: Sch 4 para 1(7) (added, in relation to England, by SI 2015/1693).
14 Housing Act 2004 Sch 4 para 1(4) (amended, in relation to England, by SI 2015/1693).
15 For these purposes, 'room' includes a hall or landing: Housing Act 2004 Sch 4 para 1(6) (added, in relation to England, by SI 2015/1693).
16 Housing Act 2004 Sch 4 para 1(4A) (added, in relation to England, by SI 2015/1693).
17 As to the meaning of 'occupier' see PARA 563 note 13.
18 Housing Act 2004 Sch 4 para 1(5).
19 Housing Act 2004 Sch 4 para 2.
20 Ie the Housing Act 2004 Pt 1 (ss 1–54): see PARA 563 et seq.
21 As to the meanings of 'category 1 hazard' and 'category 2 hazard' see PARA 564.
22 Housing Act 2004 s 90(5)(a). This does not, however, prevent the authority from imposing (in accordance with s 90(3): see the text and note 8) licence conditions relating to the installation or maintenance of facilities or equipment within s 90(3)(a) (see head (a) in the text), even if the same result could be achieved by the exercise of Part 1 functions: s 90(5)(b).
23 Housing Act 2004 s 90(5)(c).
24 Housing Act 2004 s 90(6).
25 As to the meanings of 'tenancy' and 'licence' see PARA 391 note 6.
26 Housing Act 2004 s 90(7).

713.   General requirements and duration. A licence[1] may not relate to more than one Part 3 house[2]. A licence may be granted before the time when it is required[3] but, if so, the licence cannot come into force until that time[4]. A licence comes into force at the time that is specified in or determined under the licence for this purpose and, unless previously terminated[5] or revoked[6], continues in force for the period that is so specified or determined[7]. That period must not end more than five years after: (1) the date on which the licence was granted; or (2) if the licence was granted in advance[8], the date when the licence comes into force[9].

A licence may not be transferred to another person[10]. If the holder of the licence dies while the licence is in force, the licence ceases to be in force on his death[11]. However, during the period of three months beginning with the date of the licence holder's death, the house is to be treated for the purposes of Part 3 of the Housing Act 2004 as if on that date a temporary exemption notice had been served[12] in respect of the house[13]. If, at any time during that period ('the initial period'), the personal representatives of the licence holder request the local housing authority[14] to do so, the authority may serve on them a notice which, during the period of three months after the date on which the initial period ends, has the same effect as a temporary exemption notice[15].

1 As to the meaning of 'licence' see PARA 711 note 1. As to applications for licences see PARA 711. As to the conditions to be included in licences see PARA 712. As to the duration and transferability of licences see the text and notes 3–11. As to variation of licences see PARA 714. As to revocation of licences see PARA 715.
2 Housing Act 2004 s 91(1). Thus the owner of two or more Part 3 houses needs a licence for each one. As to the meaning of 'Part 3 house' see PARA 705 note 7.
3 Ie by virtue of the Housing Act 2004 Pt 3 (ss 79–100). As to when a licence is so required see PARA 709.
4 Housing Act 2004 s 91(2).
5 Ie under the Housing Act 2004 s 91(7): see the text to note 11.
6 Ie under the Housing Act 2004 s 93 or prospectively s 93A: see PARA 715.
7 Housing Act 2004 s 91(3) (amended, as from a day to be appointed, by the Housing and Planning Act 2016 s 25, Sch 2 paras 1, 9; at the date at which this volume states the law, no such day had been appointed). This applies even if, at any time during that period, the house concerned subsequently ceases to be a Part 3 house or becomes an HMO to which the Housing Act 2004 Pt 2 (ss 55–78) applies: s 91(5). As to HMOs to which Pt 2 applies see s 55(2); and PARA 674. As to the meaning of 'HMO' in Pt 2 see PARA 674 note 2.
8 Ie under the Housing Act 2004 s 91(2): see the text and note 4.
9 Housing Act 2004 s 91(4).
10 Housing Act 2004 s 91(6).
11 Housing Act 2004 s 91(7). As to the meaning of 'licence holder' see PARA 711 note 1.
12 Ie under the Housing Act 2004 s 86: see PARA 710. As to service of documents see PARA 391.
13 Housing Act 2004 s 91(8). As to the meaning of 'house' for this purpose see PARA 704 note 2.
14 As to the meaning of 'local housing authority' see PARA 380 note 1.
15 Housing Act 2004 s 91(9). The provisions as to notification and appeal in s 86(6)–(8) (see PARA 710) apply (with any necessary modifications) in relation to a decision by the authority not to serve such a notice as they apply in relation to a decision not to serve a temporary exemption notice: s 91(10).

714. Variation of licences. The local housing authority[1] may vary a licence[2]: (1) if it does so with the agreement of the licence holder[3]; or (2) if it considers that there has been a change of circumstances[4] since the time when the licence was granted[5]. A variation made with the agreement of the licence holder takes effect at the time when it is made[6]. Otherwise, a variation does not come into force until such time, if any, as is the operative time[7] for this purpose[8]. The power to vary a licence is exercisable by the authority either on an application made by the licence holder or a relevant person[9], or on the authority's own initiative[10].

1 As to the meaning of 'local housing authority' see PARA 380 note 1.
2 As to the meaning of 'licence' see PARA 711 note 1. As to applications for licences see PARA 711. As to the conditions to be included in licences see PARA 712.
3 As to the meaning of 'licence holder' see PARA 711 note 1.
4 For this purpose, 'change of circumstances' includes any discovery of new information: Housing Act 2004 s 92(1).
5 Housing Act 2004 s 92(1); and see PARA 704 note 1. As to procedural requirements see PARA 687 et seq.
6 Housing Act 2004 s 92(2).

7 Ie under the Housing Act 2004 Sch 5 para 35. If the period of 28 days mentioned in Sch 5
    para 33(2) (see PARA 691) has expired without an appeal having been made under Sch 5 para 32
    (see PARA 691), 'the operative time' is the end of that period: s 94, Sch 5 para 35(1), (2). If an
    appeal is made under Sch 5 para 32 within that period and a decision is given on the appeal which
    confirms the variation or revocation, 'the operative time' is as follows: (1) if the period within
    which an appeal to the Upper Tribunal may be brought expires without such an appeal having
    been brought, 'the operative time' is the end of that period; (2) if an appeal to the Upper Tribunal
    is brought, 'the operative time' is the time when a decision is given on the appeal which confirms
    the variation or revocation: Sch 5 para 35(3) (amended by SI 2009/1307). For this purpose, the
    withdrawal of an appeal has the same effect as a decision confirming the variation or revocation
    appealed against; and references to a decision which confirms a variation are references to a
    decision which confirms it with or without variation: Sch 5 para 35(4). As to appeals to the Upper
    Tribunal, ie the Upper Tribunal (Lands Chamber), the successor to the Lands Tribunal, see
    PARAS 49–50.
8 Housing Act 2004 s 92(3).
9 If the local housing authority refuses to vary the licence, the licence holder or relevant person may
    bring an appeal: see PARA 691. For this purpose, 'relevant person' means any person (other than
    the licence holder): (1) who has an estate or interest in the house concerned (but is not a tenant
    under a lease with an unexpired term of three years or less); or (2) who is a person managing or
    having control of the house (and does not fall within head (1)), or on whom any restriction or
    obligation is imposed by the licence in accordance with the Housing Act 2004 s 90(6) (see
    PARA 712): s 92(5). As to the meaning of 'person having an estate or interest' see PARA 391 note
    7. As to the meaning of 'tenant' see PARA 391 note 6; and as to references to a tenant under a lease
    with an unexpired term of three years or less see PARA 672 note 9. As to the meaning of 'person
    managing' see PARA 391 note 6; and as to the meaning of 'person having control' see PARA 391
    note 5.
10 Housing Act 2004 s 92(4).

715. Revocation of licences. The local housing authority[1] may revoke a licence[2]:

(1)   if it does so with the agreement of the licence holder[3];
(2)   in any of the following cases:
   (a)   where the authority considers that the licence holder or any other
           person has committed a serious breach of a condition of the
           licence[4] or repeated breaches of such a condition;
   (b)   where the authority no longer considers that the licence holder is
           a fit and proper person to be the licence holder[5]; and
   (c)   where the authority no longer considers that the management of
           the house is being carried on by persons who are in each case fit
           and proper persons to be involved in its management[6];
(3)   in any of the following cases:
   (a)   where the house[7] to which the licence relates ceases to be a Part 3
           house[8];
   (b)   where a licence has been granted under Part 2 of the Housing Act
           2004[9] in respect of the house;
   (c)   where the authority considers at any time that, were the licence
           to expire at that time, it would, for a particular reason relating to
           the structure of the house, refuse to grant a new licence to the
           licence holder on similar terms in respect of it[10]; or
(4)   in any other circumstances prescribed by regulations made by the
         appropriate national authority[11].

A revocation made with the agreement of the licence holder takes effect at the
time when it is made[12]. Otherwise, a revocation does not come into force until
such time, if any, as is the operative time[13] for this purpose[14].

The power to revoke a licence is exercisable by the authority either on an
application made by the licence holder or a relevant person[15], or on the
authority's own initiative[16].

As from a day to be appointed, the local housing authority must revoke a
licence if a banning order under the Housing and Planning Act 2016[17] is made

against the licence holder[18]. The local housing authority must revoke a licence if a banning order is made against a person who: (i) owns an estate or interest in the house or part of it; and (ii) is a lessor or licensor of the house or part[19]. The notice served by the local housing authority[20] must specify when the revocation takes effect[21]. The revocation must not take effect earlier than the end of the period of seven days beginning with the day on which the notice is served[22].

1 As to the meaning of 'local housing authority' see PARA 380 note 1; and see PARA 704 note 1.
2 As to the meaning of 'licence' see PARA 711 note 1. As to procedural requirements see PARA 687 et seq.
3 Housing Act 2004 s 93(1)(a). As to the meaning of 'licence holder' see PARA 711 note 1.
4 As to conditions in the licence see PARA 712.
5 The Housing Act 2004 s 89(1) (and prospectively s 89(1A)) (see PARA 711 note 13) applies in relation to head (2)(b) or head (2)(c) in the text as it applies in relation to s 88(3)(a) or (c): s 93(2) (amended, as from a day to be appointed, by the Housing and Planning Act 2016 s 125(1), (7); at the date at which this volume states the law, no such day had been appointed). See PARA 711.
6 Housing Act 2004 s 93(1)(b), (2).
7 As to the meaning of 'house' for this purpose see PARA 704 note 2.
8 As to the meaning of 'Part 3 house' see PARA 705 note 7.
9 As to licences granted under the Housing Act 2004 Pt 2 (ss 55–78) see PARA 674 et seq.
10 Housing Act 2004 s 93(1)(c), (3).
11 Housing Act 2004 s 93(1)(d).
12 Housing Act 2004 s 93(4).
13 Ie under the Housing Act 2004 s 94, Sch 5 para 35: see PARA 714 note 7.
14 Housing Act 2004 s 93(5). A revocation made in a case within s 93(3)(b) (see head (3)(b) in the text) cannot come into force before such time as would be the operative time for the purposes of s 93(5) under Sch 5 para 35 (see PARA 714 note 7) on the assumption that Sch 5 para 35 applied: (1) to an appeal against the Part 2 licence under Sch 5 para 31 as it applies to an appeal under Sch 5 para 32; and (2) to the period for appealing against the Part 2 licence mentioned in Sch 5 para 33(1) as it applies to the period mentioned in Sch 5 para 33(2): s 93(6). See PARA 691.
15 For this purpose, 'relevant person' means any person (other than the licence holder): (1) who has an estate or interest in the house concerned (but is not a tenant under a lease with an unexpired term of three years or less); or (2) who is a person managing or having control of the house (and does not fall within head (1)); or (3) on whom any restriction or obligation is imposed by the licence in accordance with the Housing Act 2004 s 90(6) (see PARA 712): s 93(8). As to the meaning of 'person having an estate or interest' see PARA 391 note 7. As to the meaning of 'tenant' see PARA 391 note 6; and as to references to a tenant under a lease with an unexpired term of three years or less see PARA 672 note 9. As to the meaning of 'person managing' see PARA 391 note 6; and as to the meaning of 'person having control' see PARA 391 note 5.
16 Housing Act 2004 s 93(7).
17 'Banning order' means a banning order under the Housing and Planning Act 2016 s 16 (see PARA 719 et seq): Housing Act 2004 s 93A(5) (s 93A added, as from a day to be appointed, by the Housing and Planning Act 2016 s 25, Sch 2 paras 1, 11; at the date at which this volume states the law, no such day had been appointed).
18 Housing Act 2004 s 93A(1) (as added: see note 17).
19 Housing Act 2004 s 93A(2) (as added: see note 17). As to the meanings of 'lessor' and 'licensor' see PARA 391 note 6.
20 Ie under the Housing Act 2004 Sch 5 para 24: see PARA 690.
21 Housing Act 2004 s 93A(3) (as added: see note 17).
22 Housing Act 2004 s 93A(4) (as added: see note 17).

(4) ENFORCEMENT

(i) Offences and Penalties

716. Offences in relation to licensing of Part 3 houses. A person commits an offence if he is a person having control of or managing[1] a house[2] which is required to be licensed under Part 3 of the Housing Act 2004[3] but which is not so licensed[4]. In proceedings against a person for such an offence it is a defence that, at the material time, a notification of his intention to take particular steps with a view to securing that the house is no longer required to be licensed had been duly given in respect of the house[5], or an application for a licence had been duly made in respect of the house[6], and that that notification or application was still effective[7].

A person commits an offence if he is a licence holder[8] or a person on whom restrictions or obligations under a licence are imposed[9], and he fails to comply with any condition of the licence[10].

In proceedings against a person for either offence it is a defence that he had a reasonable excuse for having control of or managing the house which was required to be, but was not, licensed, or for failing to comply with the condition of the licence, as the case may be[11].

1   As to the meaning of 'person having control' see PARA 391 note 5; and as to the meaning of 'person managing' see PARA 391 note 6.
2   As to the meaning of 'house' for this purpose see PARA 704 note 2.
3   As to houses required to be licensed under the Housing Act 2004 Pt 3 (ss 79–100) see s 85(1); and PARA 709.
4   Housing Act 2004 s 95(1). A person who commits such an offence is liable on summary conviction to a fine: s 95(5) (amended by SI 2015/664). In relation to England, the provisions of the Housing Act 2004 s 95(2), (4), (6) have effect as from 6 April 2006 and those of s 95(1), (3), (5), (7)–(9) have effect as from 6 July 2006: see the Housing Act 2004 (Commencement No 5 and Transitional Provisions and Savings) (England) Order 2006, SI 2006/1060, arts 1(3)(c), (d), 2(1)(c), (2)(b). In relation to Wales, the Housing Act 2004 s 95 has effect as from 16 June 2006: see the Housing Act 2004 (Commencement No 3 and Transitional Provisions and Savings) (Wales) Order 2006, SI 2006/1535, arts 1(2)(c), 2(a).
    As to the power of the Secretary of State to increase the fine for this offence see PARA 400. As to offences by bodies corporate see PARA 399. As to the imposition of a financial penalty instead of a fine see the Housing Act 2004 s 249A; and PARA 397: see s 95(6A) (s 96(6A), (6B) added by the Housing and Planning Act 2016 s 126, Sch 9 paras 1, 4). If a local housing authority has imposed a financial penalty on a person under the Housing Act 2004 s 249A in respect of conduct amounting to an offence under s 95 the person may not be convicted of an offence under s 95 in respect of the conduct: s 95(6B) (as so added).
5   Ie under the Housing Act 2004 s 62(1) (see PARA 680) or s 86(1) (see PARA 710).
6   Ie under the Housing Act 2004 s 87: see PARA 711.
7   Housing Act 2004 s 95(3). For this purpose, a notification or application is 'effective' at a particular time if at that time it has not been withdrawn, and either: (1) the local housing authority has not decided whether to serve a temporary exemption notice or (as the case may be) grant a licence in pursuance of the notification or application; or (2) if it has decided not to do so, one of the following conditions is met: s 95(7). Those conditions are: (a) that the period for appealing against the decision of the authority not to serve or grant such a notice or licence (or against any relevant decision of the appropriate tribunal) has not expired; or (b) that an appeal has been brought against the authority's decision (or against any relevant decision of such a tribunal) and the appeal has not been determined or withdrawn: s 95(8) (amended by SI 2013/1036). 'Relevant decision' means a decision which is given on an appeal to the tribunal and confirms the authority's decision (with or without variation): Housing Act 2004 s 95(9). As to the meaning of 'local housing authority' see PARA 380 note 1. As to appeals and the time for appealing see PARAS 680, 691, 710. As to the meaning of 'appropriate tribunal' see PARA 580 note 2. As to appeals to the appropriate tribunal see PARA 32 et seq.
8   As to the meaning of 'licence holder' see PARA 711 note 1.
9   Ie in accordance with the Housing Act 2004 s 90(6): see PARA 712.
10 Housing Act 2004 s 95(2). As to conditions in the licence see PARA 712. A person who commits such an offence is liable on summary conviction to a fine not exceeding level 5 on the standard scale: s 95(6). As to the imposition of a financial penalty instead of a fine see note 4. As to the powers of magistrates' courts to issue fines on summary conviction see SENTENCING vol 92 (2015) PARA 176.
11 Housing Act 2004 s 95(4).

(ii) Other Consequences of Operating Unlicensed Houses

717. Rent repayment orders. As with HMO licences (in Part 2 of the Housing Act 2004)[1] there are, in addition to criminal penalties, other consequences for failing to comply with the requirement to obtain a licence under Part 3 of the Housing Act 2004[2]. These are the powers to make rent repayment orders and certain restrictions on recovering possession[3].

Dealing first with rent repayment orders, for the purposes of the following provisions, a house[4] is an 'unlicensed house' if it is required to be licensed under Part 3 of the Housing Act 2004 but is not so licensed, and neither of the following conditions is satisfied[5]. Those conditions are:

(1)   that a notification of intention to take particular steps with a view to securing that the house is no longer required to be licensed has been duly given in respect of the house[6] and that notification is still effective[7]; and

(2)   that an application for a licence has been duly made in respect of the house[8] and that application is still effective[9].

No rule of law relating to the validity or enforceability of contracts in circumstances involving illegality[10] is to affect the validity or enforceability of any provision requiring the payment of rent or the making of any other periodical payment in connection with any tenancy or licence[11] of the whole or a part of an unlicensed house, or any other provision of such a tenancy or licence[12]. Nevertheless, amounts paid in respect of rent or other periodical payments payable in connection with such a tenancy or licence may be recovered in accordance with the following provisions[13].

If an application in respect of a house in Wales is made to the appropriate tribunal[14] by the local housing authority[15] or an occupier[16] of the whole or part of the house, and the tribunal is satisfied as to the matters mentioned below[17], the tribunal may make an order (a 'rent repayment order') requiring the appropriate person[18] to pay to the applicant such amount in respect of the relevant award or awards of universal credit or the housing benefit paid[19], or (as the case may be) the periodical payments paid[20], as is specified in the order[21].

If the application is made by the local housing authority, the tribunal must be satisfied as to the following matters[22]:

(a)   that, at any time within the period of 12 months ending with the date of the notice of intended proceedings[23], the appropriate person has committed an offence of not having a licence in relation to the house[24] (whether or not he has been charged or convicted);

(b)   that one or more relevant awards of universal credit[25] have been paid (to any person) or housing benefit has been paid (to any person) in respect of periodical payments payable in connection with the occupation of a part or parts of the HMO during any period during which it appears to the tribunal that such an offence was being committed; and

(c)   that the requirements as to notice of the intended proceedings[26] have been complied with in relation to the application[27].

If the application is made by an occupier of the whole or part of the house, the tribunal must be satisfied as to the following matters[28]:

(i)   that the appropriate person has been convicted of an offence of not having a licence in relation to the house[29], or has been required by a rent repayment order to make a payment in respect of one or more relevant awards of universal credit, or housing benefit paid in connection with occupation of the whole or any part or parts of the house;

(ii)   that the occupier paid, to a person having control of or managing[30] the house, periodical payments in respect of occupation of the whole or part of the house during any period during which it appears to the tribunal that such an offence was being committed in relation to the house; and

(iii)   that the application is made within the period of 12 months beginning with the date of the conviction or order or, if such a conviction was followed by such an order (or vice versa), the date of the later of them[31].

Where a local housing authority serves a notice of intended proceedings on any person, it must ensure that a copy of the notice is received by the department of the authority responsible for administering the housing benefit to which the proceedings would relate; and that that department is subsequently kept informed of any matters relating to the proceedings that are likely to be of interest to it in connection with the administration of housing benefit[32].

Where, on an application by the local housing authority for a rent repayment order, the tribunal is satisfied:

(A)   that a person has been convicted of an offence of not having a licence in relation to the house; and

(B)   that:

    (I)   one or more relevant awards of universal credit were paid (whether or not to the appropriate person); or

    (II)   housing benefit was paid (whether or not to the appropriate person) in respect of periodical payments payable in connection with occupation of the whole or any part or parts of the house,

during any period during which it appears to the tribunal that such an offence was being committed in relation to the house,

the tribunal must make a rent repayment order requiring the appropriate person to pay to the authority a specified amount[33]. However, if the total of the amounts received by the appropriate person in respect of periodical payments payable as mentioned in head (B) ('the rent total') is less than the specified amount, the amount required to be paid by virtue of a rent repayment order made in accordance with these provisions is limited to the rent total[34]. A rent repayment order so made may not require the payment of any amount which the tribunal is satisfied that, by reason of any exceptional circumstances, it would be unreasonable for that person to be required to pay[35].

In a case where head (A) or head (B) does not apply, the amount required to be paid by virtue of a rent repayment order[36] is to be such amount as the tribunal considers reasonable in the circumstances[37]. Any amount payable to a local housing authority under a rent repayment order does not, when recovered by the authority, constitute an amount of universal credit or housing benefit recovered by it, and is, until recovered by it, a legal charge on the house which is a local land charge[38].

If the authority subsequently grants a licence under Part 2[39] or Part 3 of the Housing Act 2004 in respect of the house to the appropriate person or any person acting on his behalf, the conditions contained in the licence may include a condition requiring the licence holder to pay to the authority any amount payable to it under the rent repayment order and not so far recovered by it, and to do so in such instalments as are specified in the licence[40]. If the authority subsequently makes a management order[41] in respect of the house, the order may contain such provisions as the authority considers appropriate for the recovery of any amount payable to it under the rent repayment order and not so far recovered by it[42]. Any amount payable to an occupier by virtue of a rent repayment order is recoverable by the occupier as a debt due to him from the appropriate person[43].

The appropriate national authority[44] may by regulations make such provision as it considers appropriate for supplementing these provisions, and in particular for securing that persons are not unfairly prejudiced by rent repayment orders (whether in cases where there have been over-payments of universal credit or housing benefit or otherwise), and for requiring or authorising amounts received by local housing authorities by virtue of rent repayment orders to be dealt with in such manner as is specified in the regulations[45].

1   Ie under the Housing Act 2004 Pt 2 (ss 55–78). See PARAS 694–695.
2   Ie the Housing Act 2004 Pt 3 (ss 79–100). As to houses required to be licensed under Pt 3 see s 85(1); and PARA 709.
3   As to restrictions on recovering possession see PARA 718.
4   As to the meaning of 'house' for this purpose see PARA 704 note 2.
5   Housing Act 2004 s 96(1). The provisions of ss 96, 97 have effect in relation to England as from 6 July 2006 (see the Housing Act 2004 (Commencement No 5 and Transitional Provisions and Savings) (England) Order 2006, SI 2006/1060, arts 1(3)(d), 2(2)(a), (b)); and in relation to Wales as from 16 June 2006 (see the Housing Act 2004 (Commencement No 3 and Transitional Provisions and Savings) (Wales) Order 2006, SI 2006/1535, arts 1(2)(c), 2(a)).
6   Ie under the Housing Act 2004 s 62(1) (see PARA 680) or s 86(1) (see PARA 710).
7   Ie as defined by the Housing Act 2004 s 95(7): see PARA 716 note 7.
8   Ie under the Housing Act 2004 s 87: see PARA 711.
9   Housing Act 2004 s 96(2).
10 See CONTRACT vol 22 (2012) PARA 424 et seq.
11 As to the meanings of 'tenancy' and 'licence' see PARA 391 note 6.
12 Housing Act 2004 s 96(3).
13 Housing Act 2004 s 96(4). Prospectively, such amounts may be recovered in accordance with s 96(5) and s 97 (in the case of an HMO in Wales) or in accordance with the Housing and Planning Act 2016 Pt 2 Ch 4 (ss 40–52) (in the case of an HMO in England) (see PARA 727): Housing Act 2004 s 96(4) (amended by the Housing and Planning Act 2016 s 50(1), (3)(a)).
14 As to the meaning of 'appropriate tribunal' see PARA 580 note 2. As to appeals to the appropriate tribunal see PARA 32 et seq.
15 As to the meaning of 'local housing authority' see PARA 380 note 1.
16 'Occupier', in relation to any periodical payment, means a person who was an occupier at the time of the payment, whether under a tenancy or licence (and 'occupation' has a corresponding meaning): Housing Act 2004 s 96(10). This applies also for the purposes of s 97: s 97(16). As to the meaning of 'occupier' generally see PARA 563 note 13.
17 Ie the matters mentioned in the Housing Act 2004 s 96(6) (see the text and note 27) or s 96(8) (see the text and note 31).
18 'The appropriate person', in relation to any payment of universal credit or housing benefit or periodical payment payable in connection with occupation of the whole or a part of a house, means the person who at the time of the payment was entitled to receive on his own account periodical payments payable in connection with such occupation: Housing Act 2004 s 96(10) (definition amended in relation to England by SI 2013/630; and in relation to Wales by SI 2013/1788). This applies also for the purposes of the Housing Act 2004 s 97: s 97(16).
19 Ie as mentioned in the Housing Act 2004 s 96(6)(b) (see head (b) in the text). 'Housing benefit' means housing benefit provided by virtue of a scheme under the Social Security Contributions and Benefits Act 1992 s 123 (see WELFARE BENEFITS AND STATE PENSIONS vol 104 (2014) PARA 249 et seq): Housing Act 2004 s 96(10). This applies also for the purposes of s 97: s 97(16).
20 Ie as mentioned in the Housing Act 2004 s 96(8)(b) (see head (ii) in the text). 'Periodical payments' means: (1) payments in respect of which an amount under the Welfare Reform Act 2012 s 11 may be included in the calculation of an award of universal credit, as referred to in the Universal Credit Regulations 2013, SI 2013/376, Sch 4 para 3 ('relevant payments') or any corresponding provision replacing that paragraph (see WELFARE BENEFITS AND STATE PENSIONS vol 104 (2014) PARA 72 et seq); and (2) periodical payments in respect of which housing benefit may be paid by virtue of the Housing Benefit Regulations 2006, SI 2006/213, reg 12 or any corresponding provision replacing that regulation (see WELFARE BENEFITS AND STATE PENSIONS vol 104 (2014) PARA 320): Housing Act 2004 s 96(10) (definition substituted in relation to England by SI 2013/630; and in relation to Wales by SI 2013/1788). For the purposes of the Housing Act 2004 s 96, an amount which is not actually paid by an occupier but is used by him to discharge the whole or part of his liability in respect of a periodical payment (eg by offsetting the amount against any

such liability), and is not an amount of universal credit or housing benefit, is to be regarded as an amount paid by the occupier in respect of that periodical payment: s 96(11) (amended in relation to England by SI 2013/630; and in relation to Wales by SI 2013/1788). These provisions apply also for the purposes of the Housing Act 2004 s 97: s 97(16).

21 Housing Act 2004 s 96(5) (amended by SI 2013/1036; in relation to England by SI 2013/630; in relation to Wales by SI 2013/1788; and by the Housing and Planning Act 2016 s 50(1), (3)(b)). See the Housing Act 2004 s 97(2)–(8); and the text and notes 33–37. As to the purposes for which money received by a local housing authority under a rent repayment order may be applied, see the Rent Repayment Orders (Supplementary Provisions) (England) Regulations 2007, SI 2007/572, regs 3, 4 (reg 3 amended by SI 2013/1036); and the Rent Repayment Orders (Supplementary Provisions) (Wales) Regulations 2008, SI 2008/254, regs 3, 4.

If, in the course of proceedings on an application under the Housing Act 2004 s 96(5), it comes to the notice of the local housing authority that in respect of periodical payments payable in connection with occupation of the part or parts of the HMO or of the whole or part of the house to which the application applies there may have been a payment of housing benefit that was not properly payable, a local housing authority may apply to the First-tier Tribunal (in England) or the residential property tribunal (in Wales) for leave to amend its application by substituting for the total amount of housing benefit paid, such part of that amount as it believes is properly payable: Rent Repayment Orders (Supplementary Provisions) (England) Regulations 2007, SI 2007/572, reg 2(1), (2) (amended by SI 2013/630 and SI 2013/1036); Rent Repayment Orders (Supplementary Provisions) (Wales) Regulations 2008, SI 2008/254, reg 2(1), (2) (amended by SI 2013/1788). For these purposes, an amount of housing benefit is properly payable if the person to whom, or in respect of whom, it is paid is entitled to it under the Housing Benefit Regulations 2006, SI 2006/213, or the Housing Benefit (Persons who have attained the qualifying age for state pension credit) Regulations 2006, SI 2006/214 (whether on the initial decision or as subsequently revised or superseded or further revised or superseded): Rent Repayment Orders (Supplementary Provisions) (England) Regulations 2007, SI 2007/572, reg 2(3) (amended by SI 2013/630); Rent Repayment Orders (Supplementary Provisions) (Wales) Regulations 2008, SI 2008/254, reg 2(3) (substituted by SI 2013/1788). In relation to England, 'overpayment of housing benefit' has the meaning given by the Housing Benefit Regulations 2006, SI 2006/213, reg 99 or, as the case may be, the Housing Benefit (Persons who have attained the qualifying age for state pension credit) Regulations 2006, SI 2006/214, reg 80; and in relation to England and Wales, a relevant award of universal credit is properly payable if the person to whom, or in respect of whom, it is paid is entitled to it under the Universal Credit Regulations 2013, SI 2013/376 (whether on the initial decision or as subsequently revised or superseded or further revised or superseded): Rent Repayment Orders (Supplementary Provisions) (England) Regulations 2007, SI 2007/572, reg 2(3) (amended by SI 2013/630); Rent Repayment Orders (Supplementary Provisions) (Wales) Regulations 2008, SI 2008/254, reg 2(3) (as so substituted).

22 Housing Act 2004 s 96(6).

23 Ie the notice required by the Housing Act 2004 s 96(7): see note 26.

24 Ie under the Housing Act 2004 s 95(1): see PARA 716.

25 'Relevant award of universal credit' means an award of universal credit the calculation of which included an amount under the Welfare Reform Act 2012 s 11, calculated in accordance with the Universal Credit Regulations 2013, SI 2013/376, Sch 4 or any corresponding provision replacing that Schedule, in respect of periodical payments payable in connection with the occupation of a part or parts of the HMO: Housing Act 2004 s 96(6A) (added in relation to England by SI 2013/630; and in relation to Wales by SI 2013/1788).

26 Those requirements are as follows: (1) the authority must have served on the appropriate person a notice (a 'notice of intended proceedings'): (a) informing him that the authority is proposing to make an application under the Housing Act 2004 s 96(5); (b) setting out the reasons why it proposes to do so; (c) stating the amount that it will seek to recover under s 96(5) and how that amount is calculated; and (d) inviting him to make representations to the authority within a period specified in the notice of not less than 28 days; (2) that period must have expired; and (3) the authority must have considered any representations made to it within that period by the appropriate person: s 96(7). As to service of documents see PARA 391.

27 Housing Act 2004 s 96(6)(a)–(c) (s 96(6)(b) substituted in relation to England by SI 2013/630; and in relation to Wales by SI 2013/1788).

28 Housing Act 2004 s 96(8).

29 See note 24.

30 As to the meaning of 'person having control' see PARA 391 note 5, and as to the meaning of 'person managing' see PARA 391 note 6.

31 Housing Act 2004 s 96(8)(a)–(c) (s 96(8)(a) amended in relation to England by SI 2013/630; and in relation to Wales by SI 2013/1788).

32 Housing Act 2004 s 96(9).
33 Housing Act 2004 s 97(1), (2) (s 97(2) amended, s 97(2A) added, in relation to England by SI 2013/630; and in relation to Wales by SI 2013/1788). As to the commencement of the Housing Act 2004 s 97 see note 5. The amount to be paid is that mentioned in the Housing Act 2004 s 97(2A): see s 97(2) (as so amended). The amount referred to in s 97(2) is: (1) an amount equal to: (a) where one relevant award of universal credit was paid as mentioned in s 97(2)(b)(i) (see head (B)(I) in the text), the amount included in the calculation of that award under the Welfare Reform Act 2012 s 11, calculated in accordance with the Universal Credit Regulations 2013, SI 2013/376, Sch 4 (housing costs element for renters) or any corresponding provision replacing that Schedule, or the amount of the award if less; or (b) if more than one such award was paid as mentioned in s 97(2)(b)(i), the sum of the amounts included in the calculation of those awards as referred to in head (1)(a) above, or the sum of the amounts of those awards if less; or (2) an amount equal to the total amount of housing benefit paid as mentioned in s 97(2)(b)(ii) (see head (B)(bb) in the text) (as the case may be): s 97(2A) (as so added).
34 Housing Act 2004 s 97(3) (amended in relation to England by SI 2013/630; and in relation to Wales by SI 2013/1788).
35 Housing Act 2004 s 97(4).
36 Ie under the Housing Act 2004 s 96(5): see the text and note 21.
37 Housing Act 2004 s 97(5). In such a case the tribunal must, in particular, take into account the following matters:
  (1)   the total amount of relevant payments paid in connection with occupation of the house during any period during which it appears to the tribunal that an offence was being committed by the appropriate person in relation to the house under s 95(1) (see PARA 716);
  (2)   the extent to which that total amount consisted of, or derived from, payments of relevant awards of universal credit or housing benefit, and was actually received by the appropriate person;
  (3)   whether the appropriate person has at any time been convicted of an offence under s 95(1) in relation to the house;
  (4)   the conduct and financial circumstances of the appropriate person; and
  (5)   where the application is made by an occupier, the conduct of the occupier: s 97(6) (amended in relation to England by SI 2013/630; and in relation to Wales by SI 2013/1788).
'Relevant payments' means:
  (a)   in relation to an application by a local housing authority, payments of relevant awards of universal credit or housing benefit or periodical payments payable by occupiers;
  (b)   in relation to an application by an occupier, periodical payments payable by the occupier, less:
    (i)   where one or more relevant awards of universal credit were payable during the period in question, the amount mentioned in the Housing Act 2004 s 97(2A)(a) (see note 33 head (1)) in respect of the award or awards that related to the occupation of the part of the HMO occupied by him during that period; or
    (ii)   any amount of housing benefit payable in respect of the occupation of the part of the HMO occupied by him during the period in question: s 97(7) (amended in relation to England by SI 2013/630; and in relation to Wales by SI 2013/1788).
A rent repayment order may not require the payment of an amount which:
  (A)   where the application is made by a local housing authority, is in respect of any time falling outside the period of 12 months mentioned in the Housing Act 2004 s 96(6)(a) (see head (a) in the text); or
  (B)   where the application is made by an occupier, is in respect of any time falling outside the period of 12 months ending with the date of the occupier's application under s 96(5) (see the text and note 21),
and the period to be taken into account under head (1) is restricted accordingly: s 97(8).
38 Housing Act 2004 s 97(9) (amended in relation to England by SI 2013/630; and in relation to Wales by SI 2013/1788). As to the meaning of 'local land charge', and as to the effect of such a charge, see the Local Land Charges Act 1975; and REAL PROPERTY AND REGISTRATION vol 87 (2012) PARA 763 et seq. For the purpose of enforcing that charge the authority has the same powers and remedies under the Law of Property Act 1925 and otherwise as if it was a mortgagee by deed having powers of sale and lease, and of accepting surrenders of leases and of appointing a receiver (see MORTGAGE vol 77 (2016) PARA 518 et seq): Housing Act 2004 s 97(10). The power of appointing a receiver is exercisable at any time after the end of the period of one month beginning with the date on which the charge takes effect: s 97(11).
39 As to licences granted under the Housing Act 2004 Pt 2 (ss 55–78) see PARA 674 et seq.
40 Housing Act 2004 s 97(12).

41 Ie under the Housing Act 2004 Pt 4 Ch 1 (ss 101–131): see PARA 745 et seq.
42 Housing Act 2004 s 97(13).
43 Housing Act 2004 s 97(14).
44 As to the meaning of 'the appropriate national authority' see PARA 389 note 1.
45 Housing Act 2004 s 97(15) (amended in relation to England by SI 2013/630; and in relation to
    Wales by SI 2013/1788). As to the regulations made under this power see the Rent Repayment
    Orders (Supplementary Provisions) (England) Regulations 2007, SI 2007/572; the Rent
    Repayment Orders (Supplementary Provisions) (Wales) Regulations 2008, SI 2008/254; and the
    Rent Repayment Orders and Financial Penalties (Amounts Recovered) (England) Regulations
    2017, SI 2017/367.

718. Restriction on recovery of possession. Where a landlord grants an assured
shorthold tenancy[1] all of the grounds for possession set out in Schedule 2 to the
Housing Act 1988 may in principle be used to recover possession[2]. There is an
additional mandatory ground which may be used after giving the tenant a notice
(a 'section 21 notice') that possession is required[3]. No section 21 notice[4], however,
may be given in relation to a shorthold tenancy[5] of a part of an unlicensed house[6]
so long as it remains such a house[7].

1 As to the meaning of 'assured shorthold tenancy' see LANDLORD AND TENANT vol 63 (2016)
   PARA 852.
2 See LANDLORD AND TENANT vol 63 (2016) PARA 934 et seq.
3 Ie under the Housing Act 1988 s 21: see LANDLORD AND TENANT vol 63 (2016) PARA 926.
4 For the purposes of the Housing Act 2004 s 98, a 'section 21 notice' means a notice under the
   Housing Act 1988 s 21(1)(b) or s 21(4)(a) (recovery of possession on termination of shorthold
   tenancy): Housing Act 2004 s 98(2).
5 A 'shorthold tenancy' means an assured shorthold tenancy within the meaning of the Housing Act
   1988 Pt I Ch II (ss 19A–23) (see LANDLORD AND TENANT vol 63 (2016) PARA 852): Housing
   Act 2004 s 98(2).
6 As to the meaning of 'unlicensed house' see PARA 717 (definition applied by the Housing Act 2004
   s 98(2)).
7 Housing Act 2004 s 98(1). Cf the restriction on the recovery of possession on expiry or termination
   of an assured shorthold tenancy under the Housing Act 1988 s 21: see LANDLORD AND TENANT
   vol 63 (2016) PARA 926.

9. BANNING ORDERS AND RENT REPAYMENT ORDERS IN ENGLAND

(1) BANNING ORDERS

719. Application for a banning order. The following are introduced by Part 2 of the Housing and Planning Act 2016[1]. They have been introduced to discourage bad practice or unlawful behaviour by private landlords[2]. They allow local housing authorities to apply to the First-tier Tribunal (Property Chamber) for a banning order against landlords and managing agents where a landlord or property agent has been convicted of a banning order offence[3], requires a database of rogue landlords and property agents to be established[4] and allows a rent repayment order to be made against a landlord[5] who has committed a specified[6] offence[7].

A local housing authority[8] in England may apply for a banning order against a person who has been convicted of a banning order offence[9]. A 'banning order' is an order, made by the First-tier Tribunal, banning a person from: (1) letting housing[10] in England; (2) engaging in English letting agency work[11]; (3) engaging in English property management work[12]; or (4) doing two or more of those things[13]. If a local housing authority in England applies for a banning order against a body corporate that has been convicted of a banning order offence, it must also apply for a banning order against any officer[14] who has been convicted of the same offence in respect of the same conduct[15].

Before applying for a banning order, the authority must give the person a notice of intended proceedings: (a) informing the person that the authority is proposing to apply for a banning order and explaining why; (b) stating the length of each proposed ban; and (c) inviting the person to make representations within a period specified in the notice of not less than 28 days ('the notice period')[16]. The authority must consider any representations made during the notice period[17]. The authority must wait until the notice period has ended before applying for a banning order[18]. A notice of intended proceedings may not be given after the end of the period of six months beginning with the day on which the person was convicted of the offence to which the notice relates[19].

A local housing authority may require a person to provide specified information for the purpose of enabling the authority to decide whether to apply for a banning order against the person[20]. It is an offence for the person to fail to comply with a requirement, unless the person has a reasonable excuse for the failure[21]. It is an offence for the person to provide information that is false or misleading if the person knows that the information is false or misleading or is reckless as to whether it is false or misleading[22].

1 The Housing and Planning Act 2016 Pt 2 (ss 13–56) is to come into force as from a day to be appointed under s 216(3); at the date at which this volume states the law, the Housing and Planning Act 2016 (Commencement No 5, Transitional Provisions and Savings) Regulations 2017, SI 2017/281, has been made. Regulation 3 brought into force on 10 March 2017 the Housing and Planning Act 2016 s 47(3), Sch 9 para 7 (and s 126 insofar as it relates to Sch 9 para 7 for the purpose of making regulations under the Housing Act 2004 s 249A(7)). The Housing and Planning Act 2016 (Commencement No 5, Transitional Provisions and Savings) Regulations 2017, SI 2017/281, reg 4(a)-(f) brought into force on 6 April 2017 the Housing and Planning Act 2016 ss 40-46, 48 (all for certain purposes only), s 47(1), (2), ss 49-56, and s 126, Sch 9 insofar as not already in force. As to transitional provisions and savings see the Housing and Planning Act 2016 (Commencement No 5, Transitional Provisions and Savings) Regulations 2017, SI 2017/281, reg 5.
2 See the Housing and Planning Act 2016 s 13(1).

3   See the Housing and Planning Act 2016 Pt 2 Ch 2 (ss 14–27); the text to notes 8–22; and
    PARAS 720–723.
4   See the Housing and Planning Act 2016 Pt 2 Ch 3 (ss 28–39); and PARAS 724–726.
5   See the Housing and Planning Act 2016 Pt 2 Ch 4 (ss 40–52); and PARA 727.
6   Ie an offence to which the Housing and Planning Act 2016 Pt 2 Ch 4 applies: see PARA 727 note
    3.
7   See the Housing and Planning Act 2016 s 13(2).
8   As to the meaning of 'local housing authority' see PARA 11 (definition applied by the Housing and
    Planning Act 2016 s 56).
9   Housing and Planning Act 2016 s 15(1). 'Banning order offence' means an offence of a description
    specified in regulations made by the Secretary of State: s 14(3). Regulations under s 14(3) may, in
    particular, describe an offence by reference to: (1) the nature of the offence; (2) the characteristics
    of the offender; (3) the place where the offence is committed; (4) the circumstances in which it is
    committed; (5) the court sentencing a person for the offence; or (6) the sentence imposed: s 14(4).
    As to the Secretary of State see PARA 7. As to the making of a banning order see PARA 720.
        The government has issued a consultation paper on what should constitute banning
    order offences, suggesting that they should include the following: illegally evicting a tenant; renting
    out a property decided to be unsafe as a dwelling by local authorities; failing to carry out works
    required by local authorities to prevent health and safety risk to tenants; renting out a property to
    an illegal migrant; using violence, or threatening violence against a tenant; making fraudulent
    applications for housing benefit, or committing identity theft; using the property to cultivate
    cannabis; theft or criminal damage; colluding with the tenant to commit a criminal offence, such
    as tax evasion or the supply of illegal drugs. See Proposed Banning Order Offences under the
    Housing and Planning Act 2016 (Department for Communities and Local Government, December
    2016).
10 'Letting': (1) includes the grant of a licence; but (2) except in the Housing and Planning Act 2016
    Pt 2 Ch 4, does not include the grant of a tenancy or licence for a term of more than 21 years, and
    'let' is to be read accordingly: s 56. 'Housing' means a building, or part of a building, occupied or
    intended to be occupied as a dwelling or as more than one dwelling: s 56.
11 'English letting agency work' means letting agency work that relates to housing in England:
    Housing and Planning Act 2016 s 54(5). 'Letting agency work' means things done by a person in
    the course of a business in response to instructions received from: (1) a person ('a prospective
    landlord') seeking to find another person to whom to let housing; or (2) a person ('a prospective
    tenant') seeking to find housing to rent: s 54(3). But 'letting agency work' does not include any of
    the following things when done by a person who does nothing else within s 54(3): (a) publishing
    advertisements or disseminating information; (b) providing a means by which a prospective
    landlord or a prospective tenant can, in response to an advertisement or dissemination of
    information, make direct contact with a prospective tenant or a prospective landlord; (c) providing
    a means by which a prospective landlord and a prospective tenant can communicate directly with
    each other: s 54(4).
12 'English property management work' means things done by a person in the course of a business in
    response to instructions received from another person ('the client') where: (1) the client wishes the
    person to arrange services, repairs, maintenance, improvements or insurance in respect of, or to
    deal with any other aspect of the management of, premises on the client's behalf; and (2) the
    premises consist of housing in England let under a tenancy: Housing and Planning Act 2016
    s 55(3). 'Tenancy' in Pt 2: (a) includes a licence; but (b) except in Pt 2 Ch 4, does not include a
    tenancy or licence for a term of more than 21 years: s 56.
13 Housing and Planning Act 2016 s 14(1). Section 18 enables a banning order to include a ban on
    involvement in certain bodies corporate (see PARA 720): s 14(2).
14 'Officer', in relation to a body corporate, means: (1) any director, secretary or other similar officer
    of the body corporate; or (2) any person who was purporting to act in any such capacity; and 'body
    corporate' includes a body incorporated outside England and Wales: Housing and Planning Act
    2016 s 56.
15 Housing and Planning Act 2016 s 15(2). As to the First-tier Tribunal see COURTS AND
    TRIBUNALS vol 24 (2010) PARA 864 et seq.
16 Housing and Planning Act 2016 s 15(3).
17 Housing and Planning Act 2016 s 15(4).
18 Housing and Planning Act 2016 s 15(5).
19 Housing and Planning Act 2016 s 15(6).
20 Housing and Planning Act 2016 s 19(1).

21 Housing and Planning Act 2016 s 19(2). A person who commits an offence under s 19 is liable on summary conviction to a fine: s 19(4). As to the powers of magistrates' courts to issue fines on summary conviction see SENTENCING vol 92 (2015) PARA 176.
22 Housing and Planning Act 2016 s 19(3). See note 21.

720. Making and effect of a banning order. Part 2 of the Housing and Planning Act 2016[1] provides that the First-tier Tribunal[2] may make a banning order[3] against a person who: (1) has been convicted of a banning order offence[4]; and (2) was a residential landlord[5] or a property agent[6] at the time the offence was committed[7]. A banning order may only be made on an application by a local housing authority[8] in England that has complied with the statutory requirements[9] as to application and notice[10]. Where an application is made[11] against an officer of a body corporate[12], the First-tier Tribunal may make a banning order against the officer even if the condition in head (2) is not met[13]. In deciding whether to make a banning order against a person, and in deciding what order to make, the Tribunal must consider: (a) the seriousness of the offence of which the person has been convicted; (b) any previous convictions that the person has for a banning order offence; (c) whether the person is or has at any time been included in the database of rogue landlords and property agents[14]; and (d) the likely effect of the banning order on the person and anyone else who may be affected by the order[15].

A banning order must specify the length of each ban imposed by the order[16]. A ban must last at least 12 months[17]. A banning order may contain exceptions to a ban for some or all of the period to which the ban relates and the exceptions may be subject to conditions[18].

A banning order may include provision banning the person against whom it is made from being involved in any body corporate that carries out an activity that the person is banned by the order from carrying out[19].

A person who is subject to a banning order that includes a ban on letting may not make an unauthorised transfer[20] of an estate in land to a prohibited person[21]. A disposal in breach of this prohibition is void[22].

A banned person may not hold an HMO licence[23] or a licence under Part 3 of the Housing Act 2004[24], in respect of a house, and an HMO licence or Part 3 licence must be revoked if a banning order is made against the licence holder or against a person who owns an estate or interest in the house or part of it and is a lessor or licensor of the house or part[25]. Interim and final management orders may be made in cases where a banning order has been made and property has been let in breach of the banning order[26].

1 At the date at which this volume states the law, the Housing and Planning Act 2016 Pt 2 (ss 13–56) was not fully in force: see PARA 719 note 1.
2 As to the First-tier Tribunal see COURTS AND TRIBUNALS vol 24 (2010) PARA 864 et seq.
3 As to the meaning of 'banning order' see PARA 719.
4 As to the meaning of 'banning order offence' see PARA 719 note 9.
5 'Residential landlord' means a landlord of housing: Housing and Planning Act 2016 s 56. As to the meaning of 'housing' see PARA 719 note 10.
6 'Property agent' means a letting agent or property manager: Housing and Planning Act 2016 s 56. 'Letting agent' means a person who engages in letting agency work (whether or not that person engages in other work): s 54(1). However, a person is not a letting agent for the purposes of Pt 2 (ss 13–56) if the person engages in letting agency work in the course of that person's employment under a contract of employment: s 54(2). 'Property manager' means a person who engages in English property management work: s 55(1). However, a person is not a property manager for the purposes of Pt 2 if the person engages in English property management work in the course of that person's employment under a contract of employment: 55(2). As to the meaning of 'letting agency work' see PARA 719 note 11. As to the meaning of 'English property management work' see PARA 719 note 12.
7 Housing and Planning Act 2016 s 16(1). As to appeals from the First-tier Tribunal see PARA 728.

8   As to the meaning of 'local housing authority' see PARA 11 (definition applied by the Housing and Planning Act 2016 s 56).
9   Ie the Housing and Planning Act 2016 s 15: see PARA 719.
10 Housing and Planning Act 2016 s 16(2).
11 Ie under the Housing and Planning Act 2016 s 15(1): see PARA 719.
12 As to the meanings of 'officer' and 'body corporate' see PARA 719 note 14.
13 Housing and Planning Act 2016 s 16(3).
14 As to the database of rogue landlords and property agents see PARAS 724–726.
15 Housing and Planning Act 2016 s 16(4).
16 Housing and Planning Act 2016 s 17(1).
17 Housing and Planning Act 2016 s 17(2).
18 Housing and Planning Act 2016 s 17(3). A banning order may, for example, contain exceptions: (1) to deal with cases where there are existing tenancies and the landlord does not have the power to bring them to an immediate end; or (2) to allow letting agents to wind down current business: s 17(4). As to the meaning of 'tenancy' see PARA 719 note 12.
19 Housing and Planning Act 2016 s 18(1). For this purpose, a person is 'involved' in a body corporate if the person acts as an officer of the body corporate or directly or indirectly takes part in or is concerned in the management of the body corporate: s 18(2).
20 A transfer is 'unauthorised' for these purposes unless it is authorised by the First-tier Tribunal on an application by the person who is subject to the banning order: Housing and Planning Act 2016 s 27(3).
21 Housing and Planning Act 2016 s 27(1). In s 27(1), 'prohibited person' means: (1) a person associated with the landlord; (2) a business partner of the landlord; (3) a person associated with a business partner of the landlord; (4) a business partner of a person associated with the landlord; (5) a body corporate of which the landlord or a person mentioned in heads (1) to (4) is an officer; (6) a body corporate in which the landlord has a shareholding or other financial interest; or (7) in a case where the landlord is a body corporate, any body corporate that has an officer in common with the landlord: s 27(4). In s 27(4), 'associated person' is to be read in accordance with the Housing Act 1996 s 178 (see PARA 481 note 1); and 'business partner' is to be read in accordance with the Deregulation Act 2015 s 34(5) (see PARA 617 note 25): Housing and Planning Act 2016 s 27(5).
22 Housing and Planning Act 2016 s 27(2).
23 See PARA 682.
24 Ie under the Housing Act 2004 Pt 3 (ss 79–100): see PARA 711.
25 See PARAS 686, 715.
26 See PARAS 745, 746, 755.

721. Revocation or variation of a banning order. Part 2 of the Housing and Planning Act 2016[1] provides that a person against whom a banning order is made[2] may apply to the First-tier Tribunal[3] for an order under revoking or varying the order[4]. If the banning order was made on the basis of one or more convictions all of which are overturned on appeal, the First-tier Tribunal must revoke the banning order[5]. If the banning order was made on the basis of more than one conviction and some of them (but not all) have been overturned on appeal, the First-tier Tribunal may: (1) vary the banning order; or (2) revoke the banning order[6]. If the banning order was made on the basis of one or more convictions that have become spent[7], the First-tier Tribunal may: (a) vary the banning order; or (b) revoke the banning order[8].

The power to vary a banning order under head (1) or (a) may be used to add new exceptions to a ban or to vary: (i) the banned activities; (ii) the length of a ban; or (iii) existing exceptions to a ban[9].

1   At the date at which this volume states the law, the Housing and Planning Act 2016 Pt 2 (ss 13–56) was not fully in force: see PARA 719 note 1.
2   As to the meaning of 'banning order' see PARA 719 and as to the making of a banning order see PARA 720.
3   As to the First-tier Tribunal see COURTS AND TRIBUNALS vol 24 (2010) PARA 864 et seq.
4   Housing and Planning Act 2016 s 20(1).
5   Housing and Planning Act 2016 s 20(2).
6   Housing and Planning Act 2016 s 20(3). As to appeals from the First-tier Tribunal see PARA 728.

7 'Spent', in relation to a conviction, means spent for the purposes of the Rehabilitation of Offenders Act 1974 (see SENTENCING vol 92 (2015) PARA 594): Housing and Planning Act 2016 s 20(6).
8 Housing and Planning Act 2016 s 20(4).
9 Housing and Planning Act 2016 s 20(5). As to the banned activities, the length of the ban and exceptions to the ban see PARA 720.

722. Offence of breach of a banning order. Part 2 of the Housing and Planning Act 2016[1] provides that a person who breaches a banning order[2] commits an offence[3]. If a financial penalty[4] has been imposed in respect of the breach, the person may not be convicted of an offence under these provisions[5].

Where a person is convicted of breaching a banning order and the breach continues after conviction, the person commits a further offence[6]. In proceedings for such an offence it is a defence to show that the person had a reasonable excuse for the continued breach[7].

Where an offence of breach of a banning order committed by a body corporate[8] is proved to have been committed with the consent or connivance of, or to be attributable to any neglect on the part of, an officer[9] of a body corporate, the officer as well as the body corporate commits the offence and is liable to be proceeded against and punished accordingly[10]. Where the affairs of a body corporate are managed by its members, this applies in relation to the acts and defaults of a member in connection with the member's functions of management as if the member were an officer of the body corporate[11].

A breach of a banning order does not affect the validity or enforceability of any provision of a tenancy or other contract entered into by a person despite any rule of law relating to the validity or enforceability of contracts in circumstances involving illegality[12].

1 At the date at which this volume states the law, the Housing and Planning Act 2016 Pt 2 (ss 13–56) was not fully in force: see PARA 719 note 1.
2 As to the meaning of 'banning order' see PARA 719 and as to the making of a banning order see PARA 720.
3 Housing and Planning Act 2016 s 21(1). A person guilty of an offence under s 21(1) is liable on summary conviction to imprisonment for a period not exceeding 51 weeks or to a fine or to both: s 21(2). In relation to an offence committed before the Criminal Justice Act 2003 s 281(5) comes into force in force as from a day to be appointed), the reference in the Housing and Planning Act 2016 s 21(2) to 51 weeks is to be read as a reference to six months: s 21(6). As to the powers of magistrates' courts to issue fines on summary conviction see SENTENCING vol 92 (2015) PARA 176.
4 Ie under the Housing and Planning Act 2016 s 23: see PARA 723.
5 Housing and Planning Act 2016 s 21(3).
6 Housing and Planning Act 2016 s 21(4). Such a person is liable on summary conviction to a fine not exceeding one-tenth of level 2 on the standard scale for each day or part of a day on which the breach continues: s 21(4).
7 Housing and Planning Act 2016 s 21(5).
8 As to the meaning of 'body corporate' see PARA 719 note 14.
9 As to the meaning of 'officer' see PARA 719 note 14.
10 Housing and Planning Act 2016 s 22(1).
11 Housing and Planning Act 2016 s 22(2).
12 Housing and Planning Act 2016 s 24. As to the meaning of 'tenancy' see PARA 719 note 12.

723. Financial penalty for breach of a banning order. Part 2 of the Housing and Planning Act 2016[1] provides that the responsible local housing authority[2] may impose a financial penalty[3] on a person if satisfied, beyond reasonable doubt, that the person's conduct amounts to an offence[4] of breach of a banning order[5]. Only one financial penalty may be imposed in respect of the same conduct unless the following provision allows another penalty to be imposed[6]. If a breach continues for more than six months, a financial penalty may be imposed for each additional six month period for the whole or part of which the breach continues[7]. The amount of a financial penalty imposed under these provisions is to be determined by the authority imposing it, but must not be more than £30,000[8]. The responsible local housing authority may not impose a financial penalty in respect of any conduct amounting to an offence of breach of a banning order if: (1) the person has been convicted of an offence in respect of the conduct; or (2) criminal proceedings for the offence have been instituted against the person in respect of the conduct and the proceedings have not been concluded[9].

Before imposing a financial penalty on a person a local housing authority must give the person notice of its proposal to do so (a 'notice of intent')[10]. The notice of intent must be given before the end of the period of six months beginning with the first day on which the authority has sufficient evidence of the conduct to which the financial penalty relates[11]. However, if the person is continuing to engage in the conduct on that day, and the conduct continues beyond the end of that day, the notice of intent may be given: (a) at any time when the conduct is continuing; or (b) within the period of six months beginning with the last day on which the conduct occurs[12].

A person who is given a notice of intent may make written representations to the local housing authority about the proposal to impose a financial penalty[13]. Any representations must be made within the period of 28 days beginning with the day after that on which the notice was given ('the period for representations')[14].

After the end of the period for representations the local housing authority must decide whether to impose a financial penalty on the person and, if it decides to impose a financial penalty, decide the amount of the penalty[15]. If the authority decides to impose a financial penalty on the person, it must give the person a notice (a 'final notice') imposing that penalty[16]. The final notice must require the penalty to be paid within the period of 28 days beginning with the day after that on which the notice was given[17].

A local housing authority may at any time: (i) withdraw a notice of intent or final notice; or (ii) reduce the amount specified in a notice of intent or final notice[18]. This power is to be exercised by giving notice in writing to the person to whom the notice was given[19].

A person to whom a final notice is given may appeal to the First-tier Tribunal against: (A) the decision to impose the penalty; or (B) the amount of the penalty[20]. Such an appeal must be brought within the period of 28 days beginning with the day after that on which the final notice was sent[21]. If a person appeals under these provisions, the final notice is suspended until the appeal is finally determined or withdrawn[22]. An appeal: (I) is to be a re-hearing of the local housing authority's decision; but (II) may be determined having regard to matters of which the authority was unaware[23]. On an appeal the First-tier Tribunal may confirm, vary or cancel the final notice[24]. The final notice may not be varied so as to make it impose a financial penalty of more than the local housing authority could have imposed[25].

If a person fails to pay the whole or any part of a financial penalty which[26] the person is liable to pay, the local housing authority which imposed the financial penalty may recover the penalty or part on the order of the County Court as if it were payable under an order of that court[27]. In proceedings before the County Court for the recovery of a financial penalty or part of a financial penalty, a certificate which is signed by the chief finance officer[28] of the local housing authority which imposed the penalty and states that the amount due has not been received by a date specified in the certificate, is conclusive evidence of that fact[29]. A certificate to that effect and purporting to be so signed is to be treated as being so signed unless the contrary is proved[30].

The Secretary of State may by regulations make provision about how local housing authorities are to deal with financial penalties recovered[31]. A local housing authority must have regard to any guidance given by the Secretary of State about the exercise of its functions under the provisions[32] relating to financial penalties[33].

1   At the date at which this volume states the law, the Housing and Planning Act 2016 Pt 2 (ss 13–56) was not fully in force: see PARA 719 note 1.
2   'Responsible local housing authority' means the local housing authority for the area in which the housing to which the conduct relates is situated: Housing and Planning Act 2016 s 23(2). As to the meaning of 'local housing authority' see PARA 11 (definition applied by s 56). As to the meaning of 'housing' see PARA 719 note 10.
3   'Financial penalty' means a penalty that: (1) is imposed in respect of conduct that amounts to an offence; but (2) is imposed otherwise than following the person's conviction for the offence: Housing and Planning Act 2016 s 56.
4   Ie under the Housing and Planning Act 2016 s 21: see PARA 722.
5   Housing and Planning Act 2016 s 23(1). As to the meaning of 'banning order' see PARA 719 and as to the making of a banning order see PARA 720.
6   Housing and Planning Act 2016 s 23(3).
7   Housing and Planning Act 2016 s 23(4).
8   Housing and Planning Act 2016 s 23(5). The Secretary of State may by regulations amend the amount specified in s 23(5) to reflect changes in the value of money: s 23(9). As to the Secretary of State see PARA 7.
9   Housing and Planning Act 2016 s 23(6).
10   Housing and Planning Act 2016 s 23(7), Sch 1 para 1. The notice of intent must set out: (1) the amount of the proposed financial penalty; (2) the reasons for proposing to impose the financial penalty; and (3) information about the right to make representations under Sch 1 para 14 (see the text to notes 13–14): Sch 1 para 3.
11   Housing and Planning Act 2016 Sch 1 para 2(1).
12   Housing and Planning Act 2016 Sch 1 para 2(2).
13   Housing and Planning Act 2016 Sch 1 para 4(1).
14   Housing and Planning Act 2016 Sch 1 para 4(2).
15   Housing and Planning Act 2016 Sch 1 para 5.
16   Housing and Planning Act 2016 Sch 1 para 6. The final notice must set out: (1) the amount of the financial penalty; (2) the reasons for imposing the penalty; (3) information about how to pay the penalty; (4) the period for payment of the penalty; (5) information about rights of appeal; and (6) the consequences of failure to comply with the notice: Sch 1 para 8.
17   Housing and Planning Act 2016 Sch 1 para 7.
18   Housing and Planning Act 2016 Sch 1 para 9(1).
19   Housing and Planning Act 2016 Sch 1 para 9(2).
20   Housing and Planning Act 2016 Sch 1 para 10(1). As to the First-tier Tribunal see COURTS AND TRIBUNALS vol 24 (2010) PARA 864 et seq. As to appeals to the First-tier Tribunal see PARA 36 et seq.
21   Housing and Planning Act 2016 Sch 1 para 10(2).
22   Housing and Planning Act 2016 Sch 1 para 10(3).
23   Housing and Planning Act 2016 Sch 1 para 10(4).
24   Housing and Planning Act 2016 Sch 1 para 10(5). As to appeals from the First-tier Tribunal see PARA 728.
25   Housing and Planning Act 2016 Sch 1 para 10(6).
26   Ie in accordance with the Housing and Planning Act 2016 Sch 1.
27   Housing and Planning Act 2016 Sch 1 para 11(1), (2).
28   'Chief finance officer' has the same meaning as in the Local Government and Housing Act 1989 s 5 (see LOCAL GOVERNMENT vol 69 (2009) PARA 429): Housing and Planning Act 2016 Sch 1 para 11(5).
29   Housing and Planning Act 2016 Sch 1 para 11(3).
30   Housing and Planning Act 2016 Sch 1 para 11(4).
31   Housing and Planning Act 2016 s 23(8).
32   Ie the Housing and Planning Act 2016 s 23, Sch 1.
33   Housing and Planning Act 2016 s 23(10).

(2) DATABASE OF ROGUE LANDLORDS AND PROPERTY AGENTS

724. Duties as to database and entries. Part 2 of the Housing and Planning Act 2016[1] provides that in addition to the new powers for local authorities to take action against rogue landlords and managing agents[2], there are also new powers that supplement these by requiring databases of those against whom action has been taken. Thus the Secretary of State must establish and operate a database of rogue landlords and property agents for the purposes of Chapter 3 of Part 4[3] of the Housing and Planning Act 2016[4]. Local housing authorities[5] in England have responsibility for maintaining the content of the database[6]. The Secretary of State must ensure that local housing authorities are able to edit the database for the purpose of carrying out their functions as to its content and of updating the database[7].

A local housing authority in England must make an entry in the database in respect of a person if:

(1)   a banning order[8] has been made against the person following an application by the authority; and

(2)   no entry was made[9], before the banning order was made, on the basis of a conviction for the offence to which the banning order relates[10].

An entry made under this provision must be maintained for the period for which the banning order has effect and must then be removed[11].

A local housing authority in England may make an entry in the database in respect of a person:

(a)   if the person has been convicted of a banning order offence[12] and the offence was committed at a time when the person was a residential landlord[13] or a property agent[14];

(b)   who has, at least twice within a period of 12 months, received a financial penalty[15] in respect of a banning order offence committed at a time when the person was a residential landlord or a property agent[16].

An entry made under head (a) or (b): (i) must be maintained for the period specified in the decision notice given[17] before the entry was made (or that period as reduced on variation[18]); and (ii) must be removed at the end of that period[19]. The Secretary of State must publish guidance setting out criteria to which local housing authorities must have regard in deciding whether to make an entry in the database under these provisions and the period to specify in a decision notice[20].

If a local housing authority decides to make an entry in the database in respect of a person under head (a) or (b) it must give the person a decision notice before the entry is made[21]. The decision notice must: (A) explain that the authority has decided to make the entry in the database after the end of the period of 21 days beginning with the day on which the notice is given ('the notice period'); and (B) specify the period for which the person's entry will be maintained, which must be at least two years beginning with the day on which the entry is made[22]. The decision notice must also summarise the person's appeal rights[23]. The authority must wait until the notice period has ended before making the entry in the database[24]. If a person appeals within the notice period the local housing authority may not make the entry in the database until the appeal has been determined or withdrawn and there is no possibility of further appeal (ignoring the possibility of an appeal out of time)[25]. A decision notice may not be given after the end of the period of six months beginning with the day on which the person was convicted of the banning order offence to which the notice relates or received the second of the financial penalties to which the notice relates[26].

A person who has been given a decision notice[27] may appeal to the First-tier Tribunal against: (I) the decision to make the entry in the database in respect of the person; or (II) the decision as to the period for which the person's entry is to be maintained[28]. An appeal must be made before the end of the notice period specified[29] in the decision notice[30]. The Tribunal may allow an appeal to be made to it after the end of the notice period if satisfied that there is a good reason for the person's failure to appeal within the period (and for any subsequent delay)[31]. On an appeal the Tribunal may confirm, vary or cancel the decision notice[32].

The Secretary of State must give every local housing authority in England access to information in the database[33].

1   At the date at which this volume states the law, the Housing and Planning Act 2016 Pt 2 (ss 13–56) was not fully in force: see PARA 719 note 1.
2   See PARAS 719–723.
3   Ie the Housing and Planning Act 2016 Pt 4 Ch 3 (ss 28–39).
4   Housing and Planning Act 2016 s 28(1). As to the Secretary of State see PARA 7.
5   As to the meaning of 'local housing authority' see PARA 11 (definition applied by the Housing and Planning Act 2016 s 56).
6   Housing and Planning Act 2016 s 28(2). See ss 29, 30; and the text and notes 8–20. As to information to be included in the database see PARA 725.
7   Housing and Planning Act 2016 s 28(3). As to updating the database see s 34; and PARA 725.
8   As to the meaning of 'banning order' see PARA 719 and as to the making of a banning order see PARA 720.
9   Ie under the Housing and Planning Act 2016 s 30.
10 Housing and Planning Act 2016 s 29(1).
11 Housing and Planning Act 2016 s 29(2). As to the period for which the banning order has effect see PARA 720.
12 As to the meaning of 'banning order offence' see PARA 719 note 9.
13 As to the meaning of 'residential landlord' see PARA 720 note 5.
14 Housing and Planning Act 2016 s 30(1). As to the meaning of 'property agent' see PARA 720 note 6. Section 31 imposes procedural requirements that must be met before an entry may be made in the database under s 30: s 30(4). See the text to notes 21–26.
15 See PARA 723. As to the meaning of 'financial penalty' see PARA 723 note 3.
16 Housing and Planning Act 2016 s 30(2). A financial penalty is to be taken into account for the purposes of s 30(2) only if the period for appealing the penalty has expired and any appeal has been finally determined or withdrawn: s 30(3).
17 Ie under the Housing and Planning Act 2016 s 31.
18 Ie in accordance with the Housing and Planning Act 2016 s 36: see PARA 726.
19 Housing and Planning Act 2016 s 30(5). Section 30(5)(a) (see head (i) in the text) does not prevent an entry being removed early in accordance under s 36: s 30(6).
20 Housing and Planning Act 2016 s 30(7).
21 Housing and Planning Act 2016 s 31(1).
22 Housing and Planning Act 2016 s 31(2).
23 Housing and Planning Act 2016 s 31(3). As to appeals see s 32; and the text to notes 27–32.
24 Housing and Planning Act 2016 s 31(4).
25 Housing and Planning Act 2016 s 31(5).
26 Housing and Planning Act 2016 s 31(6).
27 Ie under the Housing and Planning Act 2016 s 31.
28 Housing and Planning Act 2016 s 32(1). As to the First-tier Tribunal see COURTS AND TRIBUNALS vol 24 (2010) PARA 864 et seq.
29 Ie under the Housing and Planning Act 2016 s 31(2).
30 Housing and Planning Act 2016 s 32(2).
31 Housing and Planning Act 2016 s 32(3).
32 Housing and Planning Act 2016 s 32(4). As to appeals from the First-tier Tribunal see PARA 728.
33 Housing and Planning Act 2016 s 38.

725.   Information in the database. Part 2 of the Housing and Planning Act 2016[1] provides that the Secretary of State[2] may by regulations make provision about the information that must be included in a person's entry in the database of rogue landlords and letting agents ('the database')[3]. The regulations may, in particular, require a person's entry to include: (1) the person's address or other contact details; (2) the period for which the entry is to be maintained; (3) details of properties owned, let or managed by the person; (4) details of any banning order offences[4] of which the person has been convicted; (5) details of any banning orders[5] made against the person, whether or not still in force; (6) details of financial penalties[6] that the person has received[7]. In relation to a case where a body corporate[8] is entered in the database, the regulations may also require information to be included about its officers[9].

A local housing authority[10] must take reasonable steps to keep information in the database up-to-date[11].

A local housing authority may require a person to provide specified information for the purpose of enabling the authority to decide whether to make an entry in the database in respect of the person[12]. A local housing authority that makes an entry in the database in respect of a person, or that is proposing to make an entry in the database in respect of a person, may require the person to provide any information needed to complete the person's entry or keep it up-to-date[13]. It is an offence for the person to fail to comply with a requirement, unless the person has a reasonable excuse for the failure[14]. It is an offence for the person to provide information that is false or misleading if the person knows that the information is false or misleading or is reckless as to whether it is false or misleading[15].

The Secretary of State may use information in the database for statistical or research purposes[16]. The Secretary of State may disclose information in the database to any person if the information is disclosed in an anonymised form[17].

A local housing authority in England may only use information obtained from the database: (a) for purposes connected with its functions under the Housing Act 2004[18]; (b) for the purposes of a criminal investigation or proceedings relating to a banning order offence; (c) for the purposes of an investigation or proceedings relating to a contravention of the law relating to housing or landlord and tenant; (d) for the purposes of promoting compliance with the law relating to housing or landlord and tenant by any person in the database; or (e) for statistical or research purposes[19].

For the purposes of the statutory data-gathering powers of Her Majesty's Revenue and Customs[20], the database is to be treated as being maintained by the Secretary of State[21].

1 At the date at which this volume states the law, the Housing and Planning Act 2016 Pt 2 (ss 13–56) was not fully in force: see PARA 719 note 1.
2 As to the Secretary of State see PARA 7.
3 Housing and Planning Act 2016 ss 33(1), 56. As to the database see PARA 724.
4 As to the meaning of 'banning order offence' see PARA 719 note 9.
5 As to the meaning of 'banning order' see PARA 719 and as to the making of a banning order see PARA 720.
6 See PARA 723. As to the meaning of 'financial penalty' see PARA 723 note 3.
7 Housing and Planning Act 2016 s 33(2).
8 As to the meaning of 'body corporate' see PARA 719 note 14.
9 Housing and Planning Act 2016 s 33(3). As to the meaning of 'officer' see PARA 719 note 14.
10 As to the meaning of 'local housing authority' see PARA 11 (definition applied by the Housing and Planning Act 2016 s 56).
11 Housing and Planning Act 2016 s 34.
12 Housing and Planning Act 2016 s 35(1).
13 Housing and Planning Act 2016 s 35(2).
14 Housing and Planning Act 2016 s 35(3). A person who commits an offence under s 35 is liable on summary conviction to a fine: s 35(5). As to the powers of magistrates' courts to issue fines on summary conviction see SENTENCING vol 92 (2015) PARA 176.
15 Housing and Planning Act 2016 s 35(4). As to the penalty see note 14.
16 Housing and Planning Act 2016 s 39(1).

17 Housing and Planning Act 2016 s 39(2). Information is disclosed in an anonymised form if no individual or other person to whom the information relates can be identified from the information: s 39(3).
18 See eg PARAS 562 et seq, 666 et seq, 698 et seq, 704 et seq, 745 et seq.
19 Housing and Planning Act 2016 s 39(4).
20 Ie the Finance Act 2011 Sch 23 para 17: see INCOME TAXATION vol 59 (2014) PARA 2189.
21 Housing and Planning Act 2016 s 39(5).

726. Removal or variation of entries. Part 2 of the Housing and Planning Act 2016[1] provides that an entry made in the database of rogue landlords and letting agents ('the database')[2] relating to a person convicted of a banning order offence[3] may be removed or varied in accordance with the following provisions[4].

If the entry was made on the basis of one or more convictions all of which are overturned on appeal, the responsible local housing authority[5] must remove the entry[6].

If the entry was made on the basis of more than one conviction and some of them (but not all) have been overturned on appeal, the responsible local housing authority may: (1) remove the entry; or (2) reduce the period for which the entry must be maintained[7]. If the entry was made on the basis of one or more convictions that have become spent[8], the responsible local housing authority may: (a) remove the entry; or (b) reduce the period for which the entry must be maintained[9].

If the entry was made on the basis that the person has received two or more financial penalties[10] and at least one year has elapsed since the entry was made, the responsible local housing authority may: (i) remove the entry; or (ii) reduce the period for which the entry must be maintained[11].

The power to remove or reduce an entry[12] may even be used: (A) to remove an entry before the end of the two-year minimum period[13]; or (B) to reduce the period for which an entry must be maintained to less than the two-year minimum period[14].

If a local housing authority removes an entry in the database, or reduces the period for which it must be maintained, it must notify the person to whom the entry relates[15].

A person in respect of whom an entry is made in the database relating to conviction of a banning order offence[16] may request the responsible local housing authority to use its powers described above to: (I) remove the entry; or (II) reduce the period for which the entry must be maintained[17]. The request must be in writing[18]. Where a request is made, the local housing authority must decide whether to comply with the request and give the person notice of its decision[19]. If the local housing authority decides not to comply with the request the notice must include reasons for that decision and a summary of the appeal rights conferred by these provisions[20].

Where a person is given notice that the responsible local housing authority has decided not to comply with the request the person may appeal to the First-tier Tribunal against that decision[21]. An appeal to the First-tier Tribunal must be made before the end of the period of 21 days beginning with the day on which the notice was given[22]. The First-tier Tribunal may allow an appeal to be made to it after the end of that period if satisfied that there is a good reason for the person's failure to appeal within the period (and for any subsequent delay)[23]. On an appeal the Tribunal may order the local housing authority either to remove the entry or to reduce the period for which the entry must be maintained[24].

1 At the date at which this volume states the law, the Housing and Planning Act 2016 Pt 2 (ss 13–56) was not fully in force: see PARA 719 note 1.

2 Housing and Planning Act 2016 s 56. As to the database see PARA 724.

3 Ie under the Housing and Planning Act 2016 s 30: see PARA 724 heads (a), (b).

4 Housing and Planning Act 2016 s 36(1).

5 'Responsible local housing authority' means the local housing authority by which the entry was made: Housing and Planning Act 2016 s 36(8). As to the meaning of 'local housing authority' see PARA 11 (definition applied by s 56).

6 Housing and Planning Act 2016 s 36(2).

7 Housing and Planning Act 2016 s 36(3).

8 'Spent', in relation to a conviction, means spent for the purposes of the Rehabilitation of Offenders Act 1974 (see SENTENCING vol 92 (2015) PARA 594): Housing and Planning Act 2016 s 36(8).

9 Housing and Planning Act 2016 s 36(4).

10 See PARA 723. As to the meaning of 'financial penalty' see PARA 723 note 3.

11 Housing and Planning Act 2016 s 36(5).

12 Ie under the Housing and Planning Act 2016 s 36(3), (4) or (5).

13 Ie the period mentioned in the Housing and Planning Act 2016 s 31(2)(b): see PARA 724 head (B).

14 Housing and Planning Act 2016 s 36(6).

15 Housing and Planning Act 2016 s 36(7).

16 Ie under the Housing and Planning Act 2016 s 30: see PARA 724 heads (a), (b).

17 Housing and Planning Act 2016 s 37(1).

18 Housing and Planning Act 2016 s 37(2).

19 Housing and Planning Act 2016 s 37(3).

20 Housing and Planning Act 2016 s 37(4).

21 Housing and Planning Act 2016 s 37(5). As to the First-tier Tribunal see COURTS AND TRIBUNALS vol 24 (2010) PARA 864 et seq.

22 Housing and Planning Act 2016 s 37(6).

23 Housing and Planning Act 2016 s 37(7).

24 Housing and Planning Act 2016 s 37(8). As to appeals from the First-tier Tribunal see PARA 728.

(3) RENT REPAYMENT ORDERS

727. Rent repayment orders under the Housing and Planning Act 2016. Part 2 of the Housing and Planning Act 2016[1] supplements the new rogue landlord provisions[2] by allowing for the making of rent repayment orders against certain landlords. Chapter 4 of Part 2 of the Housing and Planning Act 2016[3] confers power on the First-tier Tribunal to make a rent repayment order where a landlord has committed an offence to which that Chapter applies[4]. Such offences are offences of the following descriptions which are committed by a landlord in relation to housing in England let by that landlord[5]: (1) using violence for securing entry[6]; (2) eviction or harassment of occupiers[7]; (3) failure to comply with an improvement notice[8]; (4) failure to comply with a prohibition order[9]; (5) control or management of an unlicensed HMO[10]; (6) control or management of unlicensed house[11]; and (7) breach of a banning order[12].

A rent repayment order is an order requiring the landlord under a tenancy[13] of housing[14] in England to: (a) repay an amount of rent[15] paid by a tenant; or (b) pay a local housing authority[16] an amount in respect of a relevant award of universal credit[17] paid (to any person) in respect of rent under the tenancy[18].

A tenant or a local housing authority may apply to the First-tier Tribunal for a rent repayment order against a person who has committed an offence to which Chapter 4 of Part 2 of the Housing and Planning Act 2016 applies[19]. A tenant may apply for a rent repayment order only if: (i) the offence relates to housing that, at the time of the offence, was let to the tenant; and (ii) the offence was committed in the period of 12 months ending with the day on which the application is made[20]. A local housing authority may apply for a rent repayment order only if: (A) the offence relates to housing in the authority's area; and (B) the authority has complied with the requirements as to notice[21]. In deciding whether to apply for a rent repayment order a local housing authority must have regard to any guidance given by the Secretary of State[22].

The First-tier Tribunal may make a rent repayment order if satisfied, beyond reasonable doubt, that a landlord has committed an offence to which Chapter 4 of Part 2 of the Housing and Planning Act 2016 applies (whether or not the landlord has been convicted)[23]. A rent repayment order under this provision may be made only on an application under the provisions above[24]. The amount of a rent repayment order is to be determined in accordance with the relevant provisions, depending on whether the application is made by a tenant[25], the application is made by a local housing authority[26] or in certain cases[27] whether the landlord has been convicted of an offence[28].

An amount payable to a tenant or local housing authority under a rent repayment order is recoverable as a debt[29]. An amount payable to a local housing authority under a rent repayment order does not, when recovered by the authority, constitute an amount of universal credit recovered by the authority[30]. The Secretary of State may by regulations make provision about how local housing authorities are to deal with amounts recovered under rent repayment orders[31].

If a local housing authority becomes aware that a person has been convicted of an offence to which Chapter 4 of Part 2 of the Housing and Planning Act 2016 applies in relation to housing in its area, the authority must consider applying for a rent repayment order[32]. A local housing authority in England may help a tenant to apply for a rent repayment order[33]. A local housing authority may, for example, help the tenant to apply by conducting proceedings or by giving advice to the tenant[34].

1 At the date at which this volume states the law, the Housing and Planning Act 2016 Pt 2 (ss 13–56) was not fully in force: see PARA 719 note 1.
2 Ie in the Housing and Planning Act 2016 ss 14–39. See PARAS 719–726.
3 Ie the Housing and Planning Act 2016 Pt 2 Ch 4 (ss 40–52).
4 Housing and Planning Act 2016 s 40(1). A reference to 'an offence to which Pt 2 Ch 4 applies' is to an offence, of a description specified in the table to s 40(3), that is committed by a landlord in relation to housing in England let by that landlord: ss 40(3), 52(1).
5 Housing and Planning Act 2016 s 40(3), Table. For the purposes of the Housing and Planning Act 2016 s 40(3), an offence under the Housing Act 2004 s 30(1) or 32(1) (see the text and notes 8–9) is committed in relation to housing in England let by a landlord only if the improvement notice or prohibition order mentioned in s 30 or s 32 was given in respect of a hazard on the premises let by the landlord (as opposed, for example, to common parts): Housing and Planning Act 2016 s 40(4).
6 Ie under the Criminal Law Act 1977 s 6(1): see CRIMINAL LAW vol 26 (2016) PARA 643; LANDLORD AND TENANT vol 62 (2016) PARA 542.
7 Ie under the Protection from Eviction Act 1977 s 1(2), (3) or (3A): see CRIMINAL LAW vol 26 (2016) PARA 651.
8 Ie under the Housing Act 2004 s 30(1): see PARA 584.
9 Ie under the Housing Act 2004 s 32(1): see PARA 601.
10 Ie under the Housing Act 2004 s 72(1): see PARA 693.
11 Ie under the Housing Act 2004 s 95(1): see PARA 716.
12 Ie under the Housing and Planning Act 2016 s 21: see PARA 722.
13 'Tenancy' in the Housing and Planning Act 2016 Pt 2 (ss 13–56): (1) includes a licence; but (2) except in Pt 2 Ch 4, does not include a tenancy or licence for a term of more than 21 years: s 56.
14 As to the meaning of 'housing' see PARA 719 note 10.
15 'Rent' includes any payment in respect of which an amount under the Welfare Reform Act 2012 s 11 (see WELFARE BENEFITS AND STATE PENSIONS vol 104 (2014) PARAS 72–76) may be included in the calculation of an award of universal credit: Housing and Planning Act 2016 s 52(1). For the purposes of Pt 2 Ch 4 an amount that a tenant does not pay as rent but which is offset against rent is to be treated as having been paid as rent: s 52(2).

16 As to the meaning of 'local housing authority' see PARA 11 (definition applied by the Housing and Planning Act 2016 s 56).

17 'Relevant award of universal credit' means an award of universal credit the calculation of which included an amount under the Welfare Reform Act 2012 s 11: Housing and Planning Act 2016 s 52(1). In Pt 2 Ch 4 a reference to universal credit or a relevant award of universal credit includes housing benefit under the Social Security Contributions and Benefits Act 1992 Pt VII (ss 123–137): Housing and Planning Act 2016 s 51(1). Where a local authority applies for a rent repayment order in relation to housing benefit, a reference in Pt 2 Ch 4 to 'rent' includes any payment in respect of which housing benefit may be paid: s 51(2).

18 Housing and Planning Act 2016 ss 40(2), 52(1).

19 Housing and Planning Act 2016 s 41(1). As to the First-tier Tribunal see COURTS AND TRIBUNALS vol 24 (2010) PARA 864 et seq.

20 Housing and Planning Act 2016 s 41(2).

21 Housing and Planning Act 2016 s 41(3). Before applying for a rent repayment order a local housing authority must give the landlord a notice of intended proceedings: s 42(1). A notice of intended proceedings must: (1) inform the landlord that the authority is proposing to apply for a rent repayment order and explain why; (2) state the amount that the authority seeks to recover; and (3) invite the landlord to make representations within a period specified in the notice of not less than 28 days ('the notice period'): s 42(2). The authority must consider any representations made during the notice period: s 42(3). The authority must wait until the notice period has ended before applying for a rent repayment order: s 42(4). A notice of intended proceedings may not be given after the end of the period of 12 months beginning with the day on which the landlord committed the offence to which it relates: s 42(5).

22 Housing and Planning Act 2016 s 41(4). As to the Secretary of State see PARA 7.

23 Housing and Planning Act 2016 s 43(1). As to appeals from the First-tier Tribunal see PARA 728.

24 Housing and Planning Act 2016 s 43(2).

25 Ie under the Housing and Planning Act 2016 s 44. Where the First-tier Tribunal decides to make a rent repayment order under s 43 in favour of a tenant, the amount is to be determined in accordance with s 44: s 44(1). The amount must relate to rent paid during the period mentioned in s 44(2), Table: s 44(2). If the order is made: (1) on the ground that the landlord has committed an offence mentioned in head (1) or (2) in the text, the amount must relate to rent paid by the tenant in respect of the period of 12 months ending with the date of the offence; (2) on the ground that the landlord has committed an offence mentioned in head (3), (4), (5), (6) or (7) in the text, the amount must relate to rent paid by the tenant in respect of a period, not exceeding 12 months, during which the landlord was committing the offence: s 44(2), Table. The amount that the landlord may be required to repay in respect of a period must not exceed: (a) the rent paid in respect of that period; less (b) any relevant award of universal credit paid (to any person) in respect of rent under the tenancy during that period: s 44(3). In determining the amount the tribunal must, in particular, take into account: (i) the conduct of the landlord and the tenant; (ii) the financial circumstances of the landlord; and (iii) whether the landlord has at any time been convicted of an offence to which Pt 2 Ch 4 applies: s 44(4).

26 Ie under the Housing and Planning Act 2016 s 45. Where the First-tier Tribunal decides to make a rent repayment order under s 43 in favour of a local housing authority, the amount is to be determined in accordance with s 45: s 45(1). The amount must relate to universal credit paid during the period mentioned in s 45(2), Table: s 45(2). If the order is made: (1) on the ground that the landlord has committed an offence mentioned in head (1) or (2) in the text, the amount must relate to universal credit paid in respect of the period of 12 months ending with the date of the offence; (2) on the ground that the landlord has committed an offence mentioned in head (3), (4), (5), (6) or (7) in the text, the amount must relate to universal credit paid in respect of a period, not exceeding 12 months, during which the landlord was committing the offence: s 45(2), Table. The amount that the landlord may be required to repay in respect of a period must not exceed the amount of universal credit that the landlord received (directly or indirectly) in respect of rent under the tenancy for that period: s 45(3). In determining the amount the tribunal must, in particular, take into account: (a) the conduct of the landlord; (b) the financial circumstances of the landlord; and (c) whether the landlord has at any time been convicted of an offence to which Pt 2 Ch 4 applies: s 45(4).

27 Ie under the Housing and Planning Act 2016 s 46. Where the First-tier Tribunal decides to make a rent repayment order under s 43 and both of the following conditions are met, the amount is to be the maximum that the tribunal has power to order in accordance with s 44 or 45 (see notes 25, 26) (but disregarding ss 44(4), 45(4)): s 46(1). Condition 1 is that the order: (1) is made against a landlord who has been convicted of the offence; or (2) is made against a landlord who has received a financial penalty in respect of the offence and is made at a time when there is no prospect of appeal against that penalty: s 46(2). Condition 2 is that the order is made: (a) in favour of a

tenant on the ground that the landlord has committed an offence mentioned in head (1), (2), (3), (4) or (7) in the text; or (b) in favour of a local housing authority: s 46(3). For the purposes of head (2) above, there is 'no prospect of appeal', in relation to a penalty, when the period for appealing the penalty has expired and any appeal has been finally determined or withdrawn: s 46(4). Nothing in s 46 requires the payment of any amount that, by reason of exceptional circumstances, the tribunal considers it would be unreasonable to require the landlord to pay: s 46(5). As to the imposition of a financial penalty instead of a fine in relation to certain offences in England see PARA 397.

28 Housing and Planning Act 2016 s 43(3).
29 Housing and Planning Act 2016 s 47(1).
30 Housing and Planning Act 2016 s 47(2).
31 Housing and Planning Act 2016 s 47(3). See the Rent Repayment Orders and Financial Penalties (Amounts Recovered) (England) Regulations 2017, SI 2017/367.
32 Housing and Planning Act 2016 s 48.
33 Housing and Planning Act 2016 s 49(1).
34 Housing and Planning Act 2016 s 49(2).

(4) APPEALS

728. Appeals from First-tier Tribunal. Part 2 of the Housing and Planning Act 2016[1] provides that a person aggrieved by a decision of the First-tier Tribunal made under Part 2 of the Housing and Planning Act 2016[2] may appeal to the Upper Tribunal[3]. An appeal may not be brought in relation to a decision on a point of law, although a different statutory provision makes provision for such an appeal[4]. An appeal may not be brought if the decision is set aside[5] on a review of the decision[6]. An appeal may be brought only if, on an application made by the person concerned, the First-tier Tribunal or Upper Tribunal has first given its permission for the appeal to be brought[7].

1 At the date at which this volume states the law, the Housing and Planning Act 2016 Pt 2 (ss 13–56) was not fully in force: see PARA 719 note 1.
2 Ie the Housing and Planning Act 2016 Pt 2 (ss 13–56). As to decisions of the First-tier Tribunal under Pt 2 see PARAS 719–721, 723, 726, 727.
3 Housing and Planning Act 2016 s 53(1). In any case where the Upper Tribunal is determining an appeal under s 53(1), the Tribunals, Courts and Enforcement Act 2007 s 12(2)–(4) (proceedings on appeal to the Upper Tribunal: see COURTS AND TRIBUNALS vol 24 (2010) PARA 928) applies: Housing and Planning Act 2016 s 53(5).
4 Housing and Planning Act 2016 s 53(2). See instead the Tribunals, Courts and Enforcement Act 2007 s 11 (right of appeal to Upper Tribunal); and COURTS AND TRIBUNALS vol 24 (2010) PARA 928.
5 Ie under the Tribunals, Courts and Enforcement Act 2007 s 9: see COURTS AND TRIBUNALS vol 24 (2010) PARA 926.
6 Housing and Planning Act 2016 s 53(3).
7 Housing and Planning Act 2016 s 53(4).

10. REGULATION OF LANDLORDS AND AGENTS OF DWELLINGS IN WALES

(1) SYSTEM OF REGULATION

729. Domestic tenancies in Wales: regulation of letting and management of dwellings. Part 1 of the Housing (Wales) Act 2014[1] regulates the letting of dwellings[2] under domestic tenancies[3] and the management of dwellings subject to domestic tenancies by requiring landlords[4] to be registered in respect of their dwellings and to be licensed to carry out lettings activities or property management activities, and requiring agents to be licensed to carry out lettings work or property management work[5]. A licensing authority or number of licensing authorities will administer and enforce the system of registration and licensing and the Welsh Ministers must issue a code of practice setting standards relating to letting and managing rental properties[6] and may give guidance or directions to the licensing authority or authorities[7].

No rule of law relating to the validity or enforceability of contracts in circumstances involving illegality is to affect the validity or enforceability of any provision of a domestic tenancy of a dwelling in respect of which a contravention of Part 1 of the Housing (Wales) Act 2014 occurred[8]. However, periodical payments: (1) payable in connection with such a tenancy may be stopped[9]; and (2) paid in connection with such a tenancy may be recovered[10].

1 Ie the Housing (Wales) Act 2014 Pt 1 (ss 1–49).
2 'Dwelling' means a building or part of a building occupied or intended to be occupied as a separate dwelling, together with any yard, garden, outhouses and appurtenances belonging to it or usually enjoyed with it, where the whole of the dwelling is in Wales: ss 2(1), 49(1).
3 'Domestic tenancy' means: (1) a tenancy which is an assured tenancy for the purposes of the Housing Act 1988 (which includes an assured shorthold tenancy) (see LANDLORD AND TENANT vol 63 (2016) PARA 819 et seq), except where the tenancy: (a) is a long lease for the purposes of the Leasehold Reform, Housing and Urban Development Act 1993 Pt I Ch I (ss 1–38); or (b) in the case of a shared ownership lease (within the meaning given by s 7(7)), would be such a lease if the tenant's share (within the meaning given by s 7) were 100 per cent; (2) a regulated tenancy for the purposes of the Rent Act 1977 (see LANDLORD AND TENANT vol 63 (2016) PARA 692); or (3) a tenancy under which a dwelling is let as a separate dwelling and which is of a description specified for the purposes of the Housing (Wales) Act 2014 Pt 1 in an order made by the Welsh Ministers: s 2(1). Cf now, however, the new system of occupation contracts under the Renting Homes (Wales) Act 2016: see LANDLORD AND TENANT vol 62 (2016) PARAS 45–46. As to the Welsh Ministers see PARA 7.
4 'Landlord' means: (1) in relation to a dwelling subject to a domestic tenancy, the immediate landlord or, in relation to a statutory tenant, the person who, apart from the statutory tenancy, would be entitled to possession of the dwelling subject to the tenancy; and (2) in relation to a dwelling that is not subject to a domestic tenancy, the person who would be the immediate landlord if the dwelling were let under a domestic tenancy: Housing (Wales) Act 2014 s 2(1). 'Statutory tenant' and 'statutory tenancy' mean a statutory tenant or statutory tenancy within the meaning of the Rent Act 1977 (see LANDLORD AND TENANT vol 63 (2016) PARA 673 : Housing (Wales) Act 2014 s 2(2).
5 Housing (Wales) Act 2014 s 1.
6 'Rental property' means a dwelling subject to, or marketed or offered for let under, a domestic tenancy: Housing (Wales) Act 2014 s 2(1).
7 See the Housing (Wales) Act 2014 ss 4–13; and PARA 730 et seq. See the Housing (Wales) Act 2014 ss 3, 14–35, 40–42, 46–48, Sch 1; and PARAS 733–738, 744.
8 Housing (Wales) Act 2014 s 43(1).
9 Ie in accordance with the Housing (Wales) Act 2014 s 30 (see PARA 741).
10 Housing (Wales) Act 2014 s 43(2). Such payments may be recovered in accordance with ss 32, 33 (see PARA 742): s 43(2).

(2) REGISTRATION AND LICENSING REQUIREMENTS

730. Requirement for a landlord to be registered. The landlord[1] of a dwelling[2] subject to, or marketed or offered for let under, a domestic tenancy[3] must be registered under Part 1 of the Housing (Wales) Act 2014[4] in respect of the dwelling[5], unless an exception[6] applies[7]. A landlord who contravenes this requirement commits an offence[8], but in proceedings against a landlord for such an offence it is a defence that the landlord has a reasonable excuse for not being registered[9].

The requirement to be registered does not apply: (1) if the landlord has applied to the licensing authority[10] to be registered in relation to that dwelling and the application has not been determined; (2) for a period of 28 days beginning with the date the landlord's interest in the dwelling is assigned to the landlord; (3) if the landlord takes steps to recover possession of the dwelling within a period of 28 days beginning with the date the landlord's interest in the dwelling is assigned to the landlord, for so long as the landlord continues to diligently pursue the recovery of possession; (4) to a landlord who is a registered social landlord[11]; (5) to a landlord who is a fully mutual housing association[12]; (6) to a person of a description specified for these purposes in an order made by the Welsh Ministers[13].

1 As to the meaning of 'landlord' see PARA 729 note 4.
2 As to the meaning of 'dwelling' see PARA 729 note 2.
3 As to the meaning of 'domestic tenancy' see PARA 729 note 3.
4 Ie the Housing (Wales) Act 2014 Pt 1 (ss 1–49).
5 See the Housing (Wales) Act 2014 ss 14–17; and PARA 735.
6 Ie in the Housing (Wales) Act 2014 s 5: see the text to notes 10–13.
7 Housing (Wales) Act 2014 s 4(1).
8 Housing (Wales) Act 2014 s 4(2). The landlord is liable on summary conviction to a fine not exceeding level 3 on the standard scale: s 4(2). As to the powers of magistrates' courts to issue fines on summary conviction see SENTENCING vol 92 (2015) PARA 176.
9 Housing (Wales) Act 2014 s 4(3).
10 As to licensing authorities see PARA 733.
11 As to registered social landlords see PARAS 13, 166 et seq.
12 As to the meaning of 'fully mutual housing association' see PARA 13 (definition applied by the Housing (Wales) Act 2014 s 49(1)).
13 Housing (Wales) Act 2014 s 5. As to the Welsh Ministers see PARA 7.

731. Landlords to be licensed to carry out lettings or property management activities. A landlord[1] must not do any of the things described in heads (a) to (d), (i) to (vi) below[2] in respect of a dwelling[3] subject to a domestic tenancy[4], or any of the things described in heads (A) and (B) below[5] in respect of a dwelling formerly subject to a domestic tenancy, unless: (1) the landlord is licensed to do so[6] for the area in which the dwelling is located; (2) the thing done is arranging for an authorised agent[7] to do something on the landlord's behalf; or (3) an exception[8] applies[9].

The landlord of a dwelling marketed or offered for let under a domestic tenancy must not do any of the following things unless any of heads (1) to (3) applies: (a) arranging or conducting viewings with prospective tenants; (b) gathering evidence for the purpose of establishing the suitability of prospective tenants[10]; (c) preparing, or arranging the preparation of, a tenancy agreement; (d) preparing, or arranging the preparation of, an inventory for the dwelling or schedule of condition for the dwelling[11].

The landlord of a dwelling subject to a domestic tenancy must not do any of the following things unless any of heads (1) to (3) applies: (i) collecting rent; (ii) being the principal point of contact for the tenant in relation to matters arising under the tenancy; (iii) making arrangements with a person to carry out repairs or maintenance; (iv) making arrangements with a tenant or occupier of the dwelling to secure access to the dwelling for any purpose; (v) checking the contents or condition of the dwelling, or arranging for them to be checked; (vi) serving notice to terminate a tenancy[12].

The landlord of a dwelling that was subject to a domestic tenancy, but is no longer subject to that domestic tenancy, must not: (A) check the contents or condition of the dwelling' or (B) arrange for them to be checked, for any purpose connected with that tenancy unless any of heads (1) to (3) applies[13].

A landlord who contravenes the provisions above[14] commits an offence[15], but in proceedings against a landlord for such an offence it is a defence that the landlord has a reasonable excuse for not being licensed[16].

The requirements above do not apply: (I) if the landlord has applied to the licensing authority[17] to be licensed, for the period from the date of the application until it is determined by the authority or (if the authority refuses the application) until all means of appealing against a decision to refuse an application have been exhausted and the decision is upheld; (II) for a period of 28 days beginning with the date the landlord's interest in the dwelling is assigned to the landlord; (III) if the landlord takes steps to recover possession of the dwelling within a period of 28 days beginning with the date the landlord's interest in the dwelling is assigned to the landlord, for so long as the landlord continues to diligently pursue the recovery of possession; (IV) to a landlord who is a registered social landlord[18]; (V) to a landlord who is a fully mutual housing association[19]; (VI) in cases specified for these purposes in an order made by the Welsh Ministers[20].

1   As to the meaning of 'landlord' see PARA 729 note 4.
2   Ie described in the Housing (Wales) Act 2014 s 6(2) or s 7(2).
3   As to the meaning of 'dwelling' see PARA 729 note 2.
4   As to the meaning of 'domestic tenancy' see PARA 729 note 3.
5   Ie any of the things described in the Housing (Wales) Act 2014 s 7(3).
6   Ie under the Housing (Wales) Act 2014 Pt 1 (ss 1–49).
7   'Authorised agent' in the Housing (Wales) Act 2014 s 6(1) means: (1) a person licensed to carry out lettings work and property management work under Pt 1 for the area in which the dwelling is located; (2) a local housing authority (whether or not in exercise of its functions as a local housing authority); or (3) in relation to preparing, or arranging the preparation of a tenancy agreement only, a qualified solicitor (within the meaning of the Solicitors Act 1974 Pt I (ss 1–30)), a person acting on behalf of such a solicitor or any person of a description specified in an order made by the Welsh Ministers: Housing (Wales) Act 2014 s 6(6). In s 7(1), 'authorised agent' means: (a) a person licensed to carry out lettings work and property management work under Pt 1 for the area in which the dwelling is located; (b) a local housing authority (whether or not in exercise of its functions as a local housing authority); or (c) in relation to serving notice to terminate a tenancy only, a qualified solicitor (within the meaning of the Solicitors Act 1974 Pt I), a person acting on behalf of such a solicitor or any person of a description specified in an order made by the Welsh Ministers: Housing (Wales) Act 2014 s 7(7). As to the Welsh Ministers see PARA 7. As to the meaning of 'local housing authority' see PARA 227 note 2.
8   Ie in the Housing (Wales) Act 2014 s 8: see the text to notes 17–20.
9   Housing (Wales) Act 2014 ss 6(1), 7(1), (3).
10 For example, by confirming character references, undertaking credit checks or interviewing a prospective tenant: see the Housing (Wales) Act 2014 s 6(2)(b).
11 Housing (Wales) Act 2014 s 6(2). The Welsh Ministers may by order: (1) amend or omit the descriptions of things in s 6(2) (including things added under head (2)); (2) add further descriptions of things to s 6(2): s 6(3).
12 Housing (Wales) Act 2014 s 7(2). The Welsh Ministers may by order: (1) amend or omit the descriptions of things in s 7(2) or (3) (including things added under head (2)) that a landlord must not do unless any of s 7(1)(a)–(c) or of s 7(3)(a)–(c) applies (as the case may be); (2) add further descriptions of things for the purposes of s 7 (including by way of amendment to Pt 1): s 7(4).
13 Housing (Wales) Act 2014 s 7(3). See note 12.
14 Ie under the Housing (Wales) Act 2014 s 6(1) or s 7(1) or (3).

15 Housing (Wales) Act 2014 ss 6(4), 7(5). A person who commits such an offence is liable on conviction to a fine: ss 6(4), 7(5).
16 Housing (Wales) Act 2014 ss 6(5), 7(6).
17 As to licensing authorities see PARA 733.
18 As to registered social landlords see PARAS 13, 166 et seq.
19 As to the meaning of 'fully mutual housing association' see PARA 13.
20 Housing (Wales) Act 2014 s 8.

732. Agents to be licensed to carry out lettings work and property management work. A person acting on behalf of the landlord[1] of a dwelling[2] marketed or offered for let under a domestic tenancy[3] must not carry out lettings work[4] in respect of the dwelling unless the person is licensed to do so under Part 1 of the Housing (Wales) Act 2014[5] for the area in which the dwelling is located[6]. A person who contravenes this provision commits an offence[7], but in proceedings against a person for such an offence it is a defence that the person has a reasonable excuse for not being licensed[8].

A landlord of a dwelling marketed or offered for let under a domestic tenancy who appoints or continues to allow a person to undertake lettings work without a licence commits an offence if the landlord knows or should know that the person does not hold such a licence[9].

A person acting on behalf of the landlord of a dwelling subject to a domestic tenancy must not carry out property management work[10] in respect of the dwelling unless the person is licensed to do so under Part 1 of the Housing (Wales) Act 2014 for the area in which the dwelling is located[11].

Where a dwelling was subject to a domestic tenancy, but is no longer subject to that domestic tenancy, a person acting on behalf of the landlord of the dwelling must not check the contents or condition of the dwelling, or arrange for them to be checked, for any purpose connected with that tenancy unless: (1) the person is licensed to do so under Part 1 of the Housing (Wales) Act 2014 for the area in which the dwelling is located; (2) the person does no other thing in respect of the dwelling falling within the definition of 'lettings work'[12] (except preparing, or arranging the preparation of, any inventory or schedule of condition) or the definition of 'property management work'[13]; or (3) the activity would not, by virtue of specified exceptions[14], be property management work[15].

A person who contravenes the provisions as to property management work[16] commits an offence[17], but in proceedings against a person for such an offence it is a defence that the person has a reasonable excuse for not being licensed[18].

A landlord of a dwelling subject to a domestic tenancy who appoints or continues to allow a person to undertake property management work without a licence commits an offence if the landlord knows or should know that the person does not hold such a licence[19].

1 As to the meaning of 'landlord' see PARA 729 note 4.
2 As to the meaning of 'dwelling' see PARA 729 note 2.
3 As to the meaning of 'domestic tenancy' see PARA 729 note 3.
4 'Lettings work' means things done by any person in response to instructions received from:
   (1)   a person seeking to find another person wishing to rent a dwelling under a domestic tenancy and, having found such a person, to grant such a tenancy ('a prospective landlord');
   (2)   a person seeking to find a dwelling to rent under a domestic tenancy and, having found such a dwelling, to obtain such a tenancy of it ('a prospective tenant'): Housing (Wales) Act 2014 s 10(1).
However, the following are excluded from the definition of 'lettings work':
   (a)   when done by a person who does no other thing within s 10(1) and does no property management work in respect of the property:
       (i)   publishing advertisements or disseminating information;

    (ii)   providing a means by which:
        (A)   a prospective landlord (or the prospective landlord's agent) or a prospective tenant can, in response to an advertisement or dissemination of information, make direct contact with a prospective tenant or (as the case may be) prospective landlord (or the prospective landlord's agent); or
        (B)   a prospective landlord (or the prospective landlord's agent) and a prospective tenant can continue to communicate directly with each other (s 10(2));

  (b)   when done by a person who does no other thing in heads (i) to (iii) below or anything else within s 10(1) and does nothing within s 12(1) (see note 10) in respect of the property:
    (i)   arranging and conducting viewings with prospective tenants;
    (ii)   preparing, or arranging the preparation of, the tenancy agreement; (iii) preparing, or arranging the preparation of, any inventory or schedule of condition (s 10(3));
  (c)   doing things under a contract of service or apprenticeship with a landlord (s 10(4)(a));
  (d)   doing things under a contract of service or apprenticeship, or a contract for services, with a person who is: (i) instructed to carry out the work by a landlord; and (ii) licensed to do so under Pt 1 (s 10(4)(b));
  (e)   anything done by a local housing authority (whether or not in exercise of its functions as a local housing authority) (s 10(4)(c));
  (f)   things of a description, or things done by a person of a description, specified for the purposes of s 10 in an order made by the Welsh Ministers (s 10(4)(d)).
As to the meaning of 'local housing authority' see PARA 227 note 2. As to the Welsh Ministers see PARA 7.

5 Ie the Housing (Wales) Act 2014 Pt 1 (ss 1–49).
6 Housing (Wales) Act 2014 s 9(1).
7 Housing (Wales) Act 2014 s 9(2). A person who commits such an offence is liable on summary conviction to a fine: s 9(2).
8 Housing (Wales) Act 2014 s 9(3).
9 Housing (Wales) Act 2014 s 13(1). A person who commits such an offence is liable on summary conviction to a fine not exceeding level 4 on the standard scale: s 13(3). As to the powers of magistrates' courts to issue fines on summary conviction see SENTENCING vol 92 (2015) PARA 176.
10 'Property management work' means doing any of the following things: (1) collecting rent; (2) being the principal point of contact for the tenant in relation to matters arising under the tenancy; (3) making arrangements with a person to carry out repairs or maintenance; (4) making arrangements with a tenant or occupier of the dwelling to secure access to the dwelling for any purpose; (5) checking the contents or condition of the dwelling, or arranging for them to be checked; (6) serving notice to terminate a tenancy: Housing (Wales) Act 2014 s 12(1). However, 'property management work' does not include: (a) doing any one of the things in heads (2) to (6) when done by a person who does no other thing within s 12(1) and does nothing within s 10(1) (see note 4) in respect of the dwelling (s 12(2)); (b) doing things under a contract of service or apprenticeship with a landlord (s 12(3)(a)); (c) doing things under a contract of service or apprenticeship, or a contract for services, with a person who is instructed to carry out the work by a landlord and licensed to do so under Pt 1 (s 12(3)(b)); (d) anything done by a local housing authority (whether or not in exercise of its functions as a local housing authority) (s 12(3)(c)); (e) things of a description, or things done by a person of a description, specified for the purposes of s 12 in an order made by the Welsh Ministers (s 12(3)(d)).
11 Housing (Wales) Act 2014 s 11(1).
12 Ie within the Housing (Wales) Act 2014 s 10(1): see note 4.
13 Ie within the Housing (Wales) Act 2014 s 12(1): see note 10.
14 Ie by virtue of the Housing (Wales) Act 2014 s 12(3): see note 10.
15 Housing (Wales) Act 2014 s 11(2).
16 Ie the Housing (Wales) Act 2014 s 11(1) or (2).
17 Housing (Wales) Act 2014 s 11(3). A person convicted of such an offence is liable on summary conviction to a fine: s 11(3).
18 Housing (Wales) Act 2014 s 11(4).
19 Housing (Wales) Act 2014 s 13(2). A person convicted of such an offence is liable on summary conviction to a fine not exceeding level 4 on the standard scale: s 13(3).

(3) ADMINISTRATION OF REGISTRATION AND LICENSING.

733. Licensing authorities. For the purposes of Part 1 of the Housing (Wales) Act 2014[1] the Welsh Ministers must by order designate one person as the licensing authority for the whole of Wales or designate different persons as licensing authorities for different areas of Wales specified in the order, provided that each area has no more than one licensing authority and that all of the areas taken together comprise the whole of Wales[2]. The Welsh Ministers may only designate a person who exercises functions of a public nature wholly or mainly in relation to Wales, may designate themselves, and may not designate a minister of the Crown[3]. The Welsh Ministers may by order make any provision they consider necessary or expedient in connection with the designation of a person as a licensing authority[4]. Before making a designation order, the Welsh Ministers must consult any person whom they propose to designate (except themselves) and such other persons as the Welsh Ministers consider appropriate[5].

1 Ie the Housing (Wales) Act 2014 Pt 1 (ss 1–49).
2 Housing (Wales) Act 2014 s 3(1). As to the Welsh Ministers see PARA 7. The County Council of the City and County of Cardiff is designated as the licensing authority for the whole of Wales: see the Regulation of Private Rented Housing (Designation of Licensing Authority) (Wales) Order 2015, SI 2015/1026.
3 Housing (Wales) Act 2014 s 3(2).
4 Housing (Wales) Act 2014 s 3(3).
5 Housing (Wales) Act 2014 s 3(4).

734. Licensing authority's duty to maintain register. A licensing authority[1] must establish and maintain a register for its area containing specified information[2], which includes the landlord's name[3], the address of the landlord's rental properties[4], details about the landlord's licence, about any refusals to a licence, and details about agents[5]. If trustees constitute a landlord, the landlord may be registered for the purposes of Part 1 of the Housing (Wales) Act 2014[6] under a name which is a collective description of the trustees as the trustees of the trust in question[7]. Provision is made relating to public access to information held on the register[8].

1 'Licensing authority' means a person designated by order under the Housing (Wales) Act 2014 s 3: s 49(1). See PARA 733.
2 Ie the information set out in the Housing (Wales) Act 2014 Sch 1 Pt 1 (paras 1, 2).
3 As to the meaning of 'landlord' see PARA 729 note 4.
4 As to the meaning of 'rental property' see PARA 729 note 6.
5 Housing (Wales) Act 2014 s 14(1), Sch 1 paras 1, 2.
6 Ie the Housing (Wales) Act 2014 Pt 1 (ss 1–49).
7 Housing (Wales) Act 2014 s 45.
8 See the Housing (Wales) Act 2014 Sch 1 Pt 2 (paras 3–5).

735. Registration of landlords. An application for registration[1] is to be made to the licensing authority[2] for the area in which the dwelling[3] to which the application relates is located; and the authority must register the landlord within four weeks of receipt if it is satisfied that the application: (1) is made in the form required by the authority; (2) includes such information as is prescribed; (3) includes such other information as the authority requires; and (4) is accompanied by the prescribed fee[4].

A licensing authority must publish information about its requirements relating to the form and content of applications to be registered, and information to be provided when making applications[5]. If the landlord is registered, the licensing authority must notify the landlord that the landlord is registered and of the registration number assigned to the landlord[6]. A licensing authority may charge the landlord a further prescribed fee for continued registration every five years[7].

A registered landlord must give the licensing authority written notification of specified changes within 28 days beginning with the first day on which the landlord knew, or should have known, of the change[8]. A person who contravenes this provision commits an offence[9], but in proceedings against a person for such an offence it is a defence that the person had a reasonable excuse for failing to comply[10].

Provision is made as to the giving of notifications or documents pursuant to Part 1 of the Housing (Wales) Act 2014 to a licensing authority, a local housing authority[11] or a person exercising functions on behalf of a licensing authority or a local housing authority[12].

A licensing authority may revoke the registration of any landlord who: (a) provides false or misleading information in an application for registration[13] or in notifying a change[14]; (b) contravenes the provision imposing the duty to update information[15]; (c) fails to pay any further fee charged[16]. Before revoking a landlord's registration a licensing authority must: (i) notify the landlord of its intention to revoke the registration and the reasons for this; and (ii) consider any representations made by the landlord before the end of the period of 21 days beginning with the date the landlord was notified[17]. After revoking a landlord's registration a licensing authority must notify the landlord of the revocation and the reasons for doing so, and of the landlord's right of appeal[18].

A person whose registration is revoked may appeal against the decision to a residential property tribunal[19]: (i) must be made before the end of the period of 28 days beginning with the date on which the person was notified of the decision (the 'appeal period'); (ii) may be determined having regard to matters of which the licensing authority was unaware[20]. The tribunal may allow an appeal to be made to it after the end of the appeal period if it is satisfied that there is a good reason for the failure to appeal before the end of that period (and for any delay in applying for permission to appeal out of time)[21]. The tribunal may confirm the decision of the licensing authority or direct the authority to register the landlord[22].

Revocation of a landlord's registration takes effect on the day whichever of the following first occurs: (A) where the landlord does not appeal against the decision to revoke the registration within the appeal period, the expiry of that period; (B) where the landlord appeals within the appeal period but later withdraws the appeal, the date of the withdrawal; (C) where the landlord appeals within the appeal period and the residential property tribunal confirms the decision of the licensing authority, subject to head (D), the date of the tribunal's decision; (D) where the landlord makes a further appeal, the date on which all means of appealing against the decision have been exhausted and the licensing authority's decision is upheld[23]. Where a landlord's registration is revoked, the licensing authority must notify any person recorded on the register as having been appointed by the landlord to carry out lettings work[24] or property management work[25] on behalf of the landlord, and notify the tenants or occupiers of rental properties registered under the landlord's name[26].

1   Ie under the Housing (Wales) Act 2014 Pt 1 (ss 1–49).
2   As to the meaning of 'licensing authority' see PARA 734 note 1. As to licensing authorities see PARA 733.
3   As to the meaning of 'dwelling' see PARA 729 note 2.
4   Housing (Wales) Act 2014 s 15(1); Regulation of Private Rented Housing (Information, Periods and Fees for Registration and Licensing) (Wales) Regulations 2015, SI 2015/1368, regs 3, 4, 7, 9, 10. Regulations made under the Housing (Wales) Act 2014 Pt 1 which prescribe the amount of a

fee payable by a person in connection with applications to be registered or licensed may provide that the fee is to be: (1) an amount stated in the regulations; (2) determined by a person or means specified in the regulations: s 46(1). Such regulations may prescribe a different fee for different persons: s 46(2).

5 Housing (Wales) Act 2014 s 47.

6 Housing (Wales) Act 2014 s 15(2). On the first occasion a landlord is registered a licensing authority must assign a registration number to the landlord: s 15(3).

7 Housing (Wales) Act 2014 s 15(4); Regulation of Private Rented Housing (Information, Periods and Fees for Registration and Licensing) (Wales) Regulations 2015, SI 2015/1368, reg 9.

8 Housing (Wales) Act 2014 s 16(1), (2); Regulation of Private Rented Housing (Information, Periods and Fees for Registration and Licensing) (Wales) Regulations 2015, SI 2015/1368, reg 5.

9 Housing (Wales) Act 2014 s 16(3). A person who commits such an offence is liable on summary conviction to a fine not exceeding level 1 on the standard scale: s 16(3). As to the powers of magistrates' courts to issue fines on summary conviction see SENTENCING vol 92 (2015) PARA 176.

10 Housing (Wales) Act 2014 s 16(4).

11 As to the meaning of 'local housing authority' see PARA 227 note 2.

12 See the Housing (Wales) Act 2014 s 48.

13 Ie under the Housing (Wales) Act 2014 s 15.

14 Ie under the Housing (Wales) Act 2014 s 16.

15 Ie the Housing (Wales) Act 2014 s 16.

16 Housing (Wales) Act 2014 s 17(1). Ie a further fee charged under s 15.

17 Housing (Wales) Act 2014 s 17(2).

18 Housing (Wales) Act 2014 s 17(3).

19 Housing (Wales) Act 2014 s 17(4). As to appeals to residential property tribunals see PARA 34.

20 Housing (Wales) Act 2014 s 17(5).

21 Housing (Wales) Act 2014 s 17(6).

22 Housing (Wales) Act 2014 s 17(7).

23 Housing (Wales) Act 2014 s 17(8).

24 As to the meaning of 'lettings work' see PARA 732 note 4.

25 As to the meaning of 'property management work' see PARA 732 note 10.

26 Housing (Wales) Act 2014 s 17(9). As to the meaning of 'rental property' see PARA 729 note 6.

736. Licences. A licensing authority[1] may only grant the following kinds of licence under Part 1 of the Housing (Wales) Act 2014[2]: (1) a licence for its area for the purpose of compliance with the requirements[3] for landlords to be licensed to carry out lettings activities and property management activities; (2) a licence for its area for the purpose of compliance with the requirements[4] for agents to be licensed to carry out lettings activities and property management activities[5].

If trustees constitute a landlord[6], the landlord may be licensed for the purposes of Part 1 of the Housing (Wales) Act 2014 under a name which is a collective description of the trustees as the trustees of the trust in question[7].

An application for a licence must (a) be made in such form as is required by the licensing authority[8]; (b) provide such information as is prescribed[9]; (c) provide such other information as the authority requires[10]; and (d) be accompanied by the prescribed fee[11]. A licensing authority must publish information about its requirements relating to the form and content of applications to be licensed, and information to be provided when making applications[12].

Before granting a licence a licensing authority must be satisfied: (i) that the applicant is a fit and proper person to be licensed[13]; (ii) that requirements in relation to training specified in or under regulations made by the Welsh Ministers are met or will be met (as the case may be)[14]. The licensing authority must determine an application for a licence within eight weeks of receipt of an application for a licence which it is satisfied meets the requirements for an application[15].

Where a licensing authority is satisfied that the applicant meets the application requirements, it must grant a licence[16], assign and record a licence number, record the date of the grant and give the licence to the licence holder[17]. The licence is to be granted subject to a condition that the licence holder complies with any code of practice issued by the Welsh Ministers[18], and such further conditions as the licensing authority considers appropriate[19]. Where a licensing authority refuses an application, it must notify the applicant of that refusal, the reasons why and of the applicant's right to appeal[20]. Provision is made as to the giving of notifications or documents pursuant to Part 1 of the Housing (Wales) Act 2014 to a licensing authority, a local housing authority or a person exercising functions on behalf of a licensing authority or a local housing authority[21].

A licence holder must notify the licensing authority in writing of any change in the name under which the licence holder is licensed, the correspondence address, the contact telephone number (if provided), the e-mail address (if provided), any other contact information provided in the application, any material change that would constitute evidence relating to the fit and proper person requirement, and any changes in identity of any connected person[22]. A licence holder must comply with that duty within 28 days beginning with the first day on which the licence holder knew, or should have known, of the change[23]. A person who contravenes this provisions commits an offence[24], but in proceedings against a person for such an offence it is a defence that the person had a reasonable excuse for failing to comply[25].

1   As to the meaning of 'licensing authority' see PARA 734 note 1. As to licensing authorities see PARA 733.
2   Ie under the Housing (Wales) Act 2014 Pt 1 (ss 1–49).
3   Ie compliance with the Housing (Wales) Act 2014 ss 6, 7: see PARA 731. As to the meaning of 'lettings work' see PARA 732 note 4; and as to the meaning of 'property management work' see PARA 732 note 10.
4   Ie compliance with the Housing (Wales) Act 2014 ss 9, 11: see PARA 732.
5   Housing (Wales) Act 2014 s 18.
6   As to the meaning of 'landlord' see PARA 729 note 4.
7   Housing (Wales) Act 2014 s 45.
8   Housing (Wales) Act 2014 s 19(1)(a); Regulation of Private Rented Housing (Information, Periods and Fees for Registration and Licensing) (Wales) Regulations 2015, SI 2015/1368, reg 10.
9   Housing (Wales) Act 2014 s 19(1)(b); Regulation of Private Rented Housing (Information, Periods and Fees for Registration and Licensing) (Wales) Regulations 2015, SI 2015/1368, reg 7.
10   Housing (Wales) Act 2014 s 19(1)(c).
11   Housing (Wales) Act 2014 ss 19(1)(d), 46; Regulation of Private Rented Housing (Information, Periods and Fees for Registration and Licensing) (Wales) Regulations 2015, SI 2015/1368, reg 9.
12   Housing (Wales) Act 2014 s 47.
13   Housing (Wales) Act 2014 s 19(2)(a). See s 20. In deciding whether a person is a fit and proper person to be licensed as required by s 19(2)(a), a licensing authority must have regard to all matters it considers appropriate: s 20(1). Among the matters to which the licensing authority must have regard is any evidence within s 20(3)–(5): s 20(2). Evidence is within s 20(3) if it shows that the person has: (1) committed any offence involving fraud or other dishonesty, violence, firearms or drugs or any offence listed in the Sexual Offences Act 2003 Sch 3 (offences attracting notification requirements: see SENTENCING vol 92 (2015) PARA 329); (2) practised unlawful discrimination or harassment on the grounds of any characteristic which is a protected characteristic under the Equality Act 2010 s 4 (see DISCRIMINATION vol 33 (2013) PARA 48), or victimised another person contrary to that Act, in or in connection with the carrying on of any business; or (3) contravened any provision of the law relating to housing or landlord and tenant: Housing (Wales) Act 2014 s 20(3). Evidence is within s 20(4) if: (a) it shows that any other person associated or formerly associated with the person (whether on a personal, work or other basis) has done any of the things set out in s 20(3); and (b) it appears to the licensing authority that the evidence is relevant to the question whether the person is a fit and proper person to be licensed: s 20(4). Evidence is within s 20(5) if it shows the person has previously failed to comply with a condition of a licence granted under Pt 1 by a licensing authority: s 20(5). The Welsh Ministers must give guidance to licensing authorities about deciding whether a person is a fit and proper person to be licensed as required by s 19(2)(a): Housing (Wales) Act 2014 s 20(6). The Welsh Ministers may amend s 20 by order to vary the evidence to which a licensing authority must have regard in deciding whether a person is a fit and proper person to be licensed: s 20(7). As to the Welsh Ministers see PARA 7.

14 Housing (Wales) Act 2014 s 19(2)(b). As to such regulations, see the Regulation of Private Rented Housing (Training Requirements) (Wales) Regulations 2015, SI 2015/1366.
15 Housing (Wales) Act 2014 s 21(4); Regulation of Private Rented Housing (Information, Periods and Fees for Registration and Licensing) (Wales) Regulations 2015, SI 2015/1368, reg 6.
16 Housing (Wales) Act 2014 s 21(1).
17 Housing (Wales) Act 2014 s 21(2).
18 Ie under the Housing (Wales) Act 2014 s 40: see PARA 744.
19 Housing (Wales) Act 2014 s 22.
20 Housing (Wales) Act 2014 s 21(3). As to the right to appeal see s 27; and PARA 738.
21 See the Housing (Wales) Act 2014 s 48. As to the meaning of 'local housing authority' see PARA 227 note 2.
22 Housing (Wales) Act 2014 s 23(1); Regulation of Private Rented Housing (Information, Periods and Fees for Registration and Licensing) (Wales) Regulations 2015, SI 2015/1368, reg 8.
23 Housing (Wales) Act 2014 s 23(2).
24 Housing (Wales) Act 2014 s 23(3). A person guilty of such an offence is liable on summary conviction to a fine not exceeding level 4 on the standard scale: s 23(3). As to the powers of magistrates' courts to issue fines on summary conviction see SENTENCING vol 92 (2015) PARA 176.
25 Housing (Wales) Act 2014 s 23(4).

737. Amendment, revocation, expiry and renewal of licences. A licensing authority[1] may amend any licence granted by it[2]. A licence may be amended to: (1) impose new conditions; (2) remove or change existing conditions (other than the requirement to comply with any code of practice issued by the Welsh Ministers)[3]. Before deciding to amend a licence a licensing authority must notify the licence holder of its intention to amend the licence and the reasons for this and consider any representations made by the licence holder before the end of the period of 21 days beginning with the date the licence holder was notified[4]. After amending a licence, the licensing authority must notify the licence holder of: (a) the amendment and the reasons for it; (b) except where the licence holder has consented to the amendment, information about the licence holder's right of appeal[5]. An amendment to a licence takes effect on the day whichever of the following first occurs: (i) where the licence holder has consented, when the licensing authority notifies the licence holder[6]; (ii) where the licence holder does not appeal against the decision to amend the licence within the appeal period[7], the expiry of that period; (iii) where the licence holder appeals within the appeal period but later withdraws the appeal, the date of the withdrawal; (iv) where the licence holder appeals within the appeal period and the residential property tribunal confirms the decision of the licensing authority to amend the licence, subject to head (v), the date of the tribunal's decision; (v) where the licence holder makes a further appeal, the date on which all means of appealing against the decision have been exhausted and the licensing authority's decision is upheld[8].

A licensing authority may revoke a licence if: (A) the licence holder has breached a condition of the licence; (B) the authority is no longer satisfied that the licence holder is a fit and proper person to hold a licence; (C) the licence holder has contravened the requirement to update information[9]; (D) the licence holder and the licensing authority have agreed that the licence should be revoked[10]. Before revoking a licence, a licensing authority must notify the licence holder of its intention to revoke the licence and the reasons for this, and consider any representations made by the licence holder before the end of the period of 21 days beginning with the date the licence holder was notified[11].

Revocation of a licence takes effect on the day whichever of the following first occurs: (I) the licence holder contacts the licensing authority consenting to the revocation; (II) where the licence holder does not appeal against the decision to revoke the licence within the appeal period[12], the expiry of that period; (III) where the licence holder appeals within the appeal period but later withdraws the appeal, the date of the withdrawal; (IV) where the licence holder appeals within the appeal period and the residential property tribunal confirms the decision of the licensing authority to revoke the licence, subject to head (V), the date of the tribunal's decision; (V) where the licence holder makes a further appeal, the date on which all means of appealing against the decision have been exhausted and the licensing authority's decision is upheld[13].

After revoking a licence, the licensing authority must notify the licence holder of the revocation and the reasons for it, and of the licence holder's right of appeal[14]. Where a person's licence to carry out lettings work[15] and property management work[16] on behalf of a landlord[17] is revoked, the licensing authority must notify any landlord recorded on its register as having appointed that person[18]. Where a landlord's licence is revoked, the licensing authority must notify the tenants or occupiers of rental property[19] registered under the landlord's name[20].

A licence expires at the end of a period of five years beginning with the date it was granted, unless the licence holder makes an application to renew the licence during the period of 84 days before the licence's expiry date[21], in which case the licence does not expire until the application is decided and expires only if the application is refused[22]. A licence expires and any renewal application made by the licence holder is treated as having been withdrawn where a licence holder dies or, in the case of a body corporate, is dissolved[23].

1   As to the meaning of 'licensing authority' see PARA 734 note 1. As to licensing authorities see PARA 733.
2   See the Housing (Wales) Act 2014 s 24(1). As to the grant of licences see PARA 736.
3   Housing (Wales) Act 2014 s 24(2). As to codes of practice see the Housing (Wales) Act 2014 s 40; and PARA 744.
4   Housing (Wales) Act 2014 s 24(3). The requirement to consider representations does not apply to an amendment if: (1) the licence holder consents to it; or (2) the licensing authority considers that there are exceptional circumstances which mean that it needs to be made without delay: s 24(4).
5   Housing (Wales) Act 2014 s 24(5). As to the right of appeal see s 27; and PARA 738.
6   Ie under the Housing (Wales) Act 2014 s 24(5).
7   The 'appeal period' for the purposes of the Housing (Wales) Act 2014 s 24(6) is the period mentioned in s 27(3)(a) (licensing appeals: see PARA 738): s 24(7).
8   Housing (Wales) Act 2014 s 24(6).
9   Ie the Housing (Wales) Act 2014 s 23: see PARA 736.
10 Housing (Wales) Act 2014 s 25(1).
11 Housing (Wales) Act 2014 s 25(2). The requirement to consider representations does not apply: (1) if the licence holder consents to the revocation; or (2) where the licensing authority considers that there are exceptional circumstances which mean that it needs to be revoked without delay: s 25(3).
12 The 'appeal period' for the purposes of the Housing (Wales) Act 2014 s 25(5) is the period mentioned in s 27(3)(a) (licensing appeals: see PARA 738): s 25(6).
13 Housing (Wales) Act 2014 s 25(5).
14 Housing (Wales) Act 2014 s 25(4). As to appeals see PARA 738.
15 As to the meaning of 'lettings work' see PARA 732 note 4.
16 As to the meaning of 'property management work' see PARA 732 note 10.
17 As to the meaning of 'landlord' see PARA 729 note 4.
18 Housing (Wales) Act 2014 s 25(7).
19 As to the meaning of 'rental property' see PARA 729 note 6.
20 Housing (Wales) Act 2014 s 25(8).
21 Housing (Wales) Act 2014 s 26(1), (2). An application for renewal of a licence is to be made and determined in accordance with ss 19–21 (see PARA 736), but where a licensing authority renews a licence, the requirement in s 21(2)(a) to assign a licence number to the licence holder does not apply: s 26(4), (5).
22 Housing (Wales) Act 2014 s 26(3). If an application to renew a licence is refused, the existing licence expires on whichever of the following dates first occurs: (1) where the licence holder does not appeal against the refusal within the appeal period, the date of expiry of that period; (2) where the licence holder appeals within the appeal period but later withdraws the appeal, the date of the

withdrawal; (3) where the licence holder appeals within the appeal period and the residential property tribunal confirms the decision of the licensing authority, the date of the tribunal's decision (subject to head (4)); (4) where the licence holder makes a further appeal, the date on which all means of appealing against the decision have been exhausted and the licensing authority's decision is upheld: s 26(6). The 'appeal period' for the purposes of s 26(6) is the period mentioned in s 27(3)(a) (licensing appeals: see PARA 738): s 26(7).

23 Housing (Wales) Act 2014 s 26(8).

738. Licensing appeals. An applicant for a licence or, as the case may be, the holder of a licence[1] may appeal to a residential property tribunal[2] against a decision to: (1) grant a licence subject to a condition, other than the requirement to comply with any code of practice issued by the Welsh Ministers; (2) refuse an application for a licence; (3) amend a licence; or (4) revoke a licence[3]. An appeal must be made before the end of the period of 28 days beginning with the date the applicant was notified of the decision (the 'appeal period'), and may be determined having regard to matters of which the licensing authority was unaware[4]. The tribunal may allow an appeal to be made to it after the end of the appeal period if it is satisfied that there is a good reason for the failure to appeal before the end of that period (and for any delay in applying for permission to appeal out of time)[5].

The tribunal may confirm the decision of the licensing authority or alternatively: (a) in the case of a decision to grant a licence subject to a condition, direct the authority to grant a licence on such terms as the tribunal considers appropriate; (b) in the case of a decision to refuse an application for a licence, direct the authority to grant a licence on such terms as the tribunal considers appropriate; (c) in the case of a decision to amend a licence, direct the authority not to amend the licence or to amend the licence on such terms as the tribunal considers appropriate; (d) in the case of a decision to revoke a licence, quash that decision[6]. A licence granted by a licensing authority following a direction of a tribunal under these provisions is to be treated as having been granted by the authority[7] on an application for a licence[8].

1 As to licences see PARA 736.
2 As to residential property tribunals see PARA 34 et seq.
3 Housing (Wales) Act 2014 s 27(1), (2). As to the grant of licences see PARA 736; as to amendment or revocation of licences see PARA 737.
4 Housing (Wales) Act 2014 s 27(3). As to the meaning of 'licensing authority' see PARA 734 note 1. As to licensing authorities see PARA 733.
5 Housing (Wales) Act 2014 s 27(4).
6 Housing (Wales) Act 2014 s 27(5).
7 Ie under the Housing (Wales) Act 2014 s 21(1): see PARA 736.
8 Housing (Wales) Act 2014 s 27(6).

(4) INFORMATION

739. Information. A licensing authority[1] may, for the purpose of exercising its functions under Part 1 of the Housing (Wales) Act 2014[2], require a local housing authority[3] to provide it with any information it has obtained in the exercise of its functions as the local housing authority or functions in relation to council tax[4]. The local housing authority must comply with the request unless the local housing authority considers that doing so would be incompatible with the local housing authority's own duties or otherwise have an adverse effect on the exercise of the local housing authority's functions[5]. A licensing authority may, for the purpose of exercising its functions under Part 1, require another licensing authority to provide it with information obtained in the exercise of its functions under Part 1 and the other authority must comply with the request unless the other authority considers that doing so would be incompatible with its own duties or otherwise have an adverse effect on the exercise of its functions[6]. A local housing authority may, for the purpose of exercising its functions under Part 1, require a licensing authority to provide it with information obtained in the exercise of the licensing authority's functions under Part 1, and the licensing authority must comply with the request unless the licensing authority considers that doing so would be incompatible with its own duties or otherwise have an adverse effect on the exercise of its functions[7].

A licensing authority may use any such information[8] for any purpose connected with the exercise of the authority's functions under Part 1[9] and a local housing authority may use any information provided to it[10] for any purpose connected with the exercise of the authority's functions under Part 1[11].

A person authorised in writing by a licensing authority may exercise the powers described below[12] in relation to documents[13] or information (as the case may be) reasonably required by the authority for any purpose connected with the exercise of any of the authority's functions under Part 1 of the Housing (Wales) Act 2014 or for the purpose of investigating whether any offence has been committed under Part 1[14]. A person so authorised may give a notice to a relevant person[15]:

(1)   requiring that person:
   (a)   to produce any documents which: (i) are specified or described in the notice, or fall within a category of document which is specified or described in the notice; and (ii) are in the person's custody or under the person's control; and
   (b)   to produce them at a time and place, and to a person, specified in the notice[16];
(2)   requiring that person:
   (a)   to give any information which: (i) is specified or described in the notice, or falls within a category of information which is specified or described in the notice; and (ii) is known to the person; and
   (b)   to give it in a form and manner specified in the notice[17].

The notice under head (1) or (2) must include information about the possible consequences of not complying with the notice[18]. The person to whom any document is produced in accordance with a notice may copy the document[19]. No person may be required under these provisions to produce any document or give any information which the person would be entitled to refuse to provide in proceedings in the High Court on grounds of legal professional privilege[20].

A person who fails to do anything required of that person by a notice under head (1) or (2) commits an offence[21], but in proceedings against a person for such an offence it is a defence that the person had a reasonable excuse for failing to comply with the notice[22]. A person who intentionally alters, suppresses or destroys any document[23] which the person has been required to produce by such a notice commits an offence[24].

A person who supplies any information to a licensing authority in connection with any of its functions under Part 1 of the Housing (Wales) Act 2014 which is false or misleading in any material respect, and knows that it is so false or misleading or is reckless as to whether it is so false or misleading, commits an offence[25]. A person who: (A) supplies any information to another person which is false or misleading in any material respect; (B) knows that it is false or misleading in any material respect or is reckless as to whether it is so false or misleading; and

(C) knows that the information is to be used for the purpose of supplying information to a licensing authority in connection with any of its functions under Part 1 of the Housing (Wales) Act 2014, commits an offence[26].

1   As to the meaning of 'licensing authority' see PARA 734 note 1. As to licensing authorities see PARA 733.
2   Ie the Housing (Wales) Act 2014 Pt 1 (ss 1–49): see PARA 729 et seq.
3   As to the meaning of 'local housing authority' see PARA 227 note 2.
4   Housing (Wales) Act 2014 s 36(1), (2). The text refers to functions under the Local Government Finance Act 1992 Pt I (ss 1–69): see LOCAL GOVERNMENT FINANCE vol 70 (2012) PARA 298 et seq.
5   Housing (Wales) Act 2014 s 36(1). Information obtained by a local housing authority under the Social Security Administration Act 1992 s 134 (housing benefit: see WELFARE BENEFITS AND STATE PENSIONS vol 104 (2014) PARA 323) before the repeal of s 134 by the Welfare Reform Act 2012 Sch 14 is to be treated as information to which the Housing (Wales) Act 2014 s 36(2) applies: s 36(3).
6   Housing (Wales) Act 2014 s 36(4), (5).
7   Housing (Wales) Act 2014 s 36(7).
8   Ie any information to which the Housing (Wales) Act 2014 s 36(2) or (5) applies (whether or not obtained under s 36(1) or (4)).
9   Housing (Wales) Act 2014 s 36(6).
10 Ie any information to which the Housing (Wales) Act 2014 s 36(2) or (5) applies (whether or not obtained under s 36(7)).
11 Housing (Wales) Act 2014 s 36(8).
12 Ie the powers conferred by the Housing (Wales) Act 2014 s 37(2), (3).
13 In the Housing (Wales) Act 2014 s 37 'document' includes information recorded otherwise than in legible form, and in relation to information so recorded, any reference to the production of a document is a reference to the production of a copy of the information in legible form: s 37(7).
14 Housing (Wales) Act 2014 s 37(1).
15 'Relevant person' means a person within any of the following heads: (1) a person who applies for a licence under the Housing (Wales) Act 2014 Pt 1 or who is the holder of a licence under Pt 1 (see PARA 736); (2) a person who has an estate or interest in rental property; (3) a person who is, or is proposing to be, involved in the letting or management of a rental property; (4) a person who occupies a rental property: s 37(8). As to the meaning of 'rental property' see PARA 729 note 6.
16 Housing (Wales) Act 2014 s 37(2).
17 Housing (Wales) Act 2014 s 37(3).
18 Housing (Wales) Act 2014 s 37(4).
19 Housing (Wales) Act 2014 s 37(5).
20 Housing (Wales) Act 2014 s 37(6). As to legal professional privilege generally see CIVIL PROCEDURE vol 12 (2015) PARAS 647–662.
21 Housing (Wales) Act 2014 s 38(1). A person who commits such an offence is liable on summary conviction to a fine not exceeding level 4 on the standard scale: s 38(3). As to the powers of magistrates' courts to issue fines on summary conviction see SENTENCING vol 92 (2015) PARA 176.
22 Housing (Wales) Act 2014 s 38(2).
23 For this purpose, 'document' includes information recorded otherwise than in legible form, and in relation to information so recorded: (1) the reference to the production of a document is a reference to the production of a copy of the information in legible form; and (2) the reference to suppressing a document includes a reference to destroying the means of reproducing the information: Housing (Wales) Act 2014 s 38(6).
24 Housing (Wales) Act 2014 s 38(4). A person who commits such an offence is liable on summary conviction to a fine: s 38(5).
25 Housing (Wales) Act 2014 s 39(1), (4). A person who commits such an offence is liable on summary conviction to a fine: s 39(3).
26 Housing (Wales) Act 2014 s 39(2). A person who commits such an offence is liable on summary conviction to a fine: s 39(3).

(5) ENFORCEMENT

740. Prosecution and fixed penalty notices. A licensing authority[1] may bring criminal proceedings in respect of an offence under specified provisions of the

Housing (Wales) Act 2014 in specified circumstances[2]. A local housing authority[3] that is not the licensing authority for its area may, with the consent of the licensing authority for the area, bring criminal proceedings in respect of certain offences[4], if the alleged offence arises in respect of a dwelling in its area[5]. These provisions do not affect any other power of the person designated[6] to bring legal proceedings or the power[7] of local authorities to prosecute or defend legal proceedings[8].

Where on any occasion a person authorised in writing for the purpose by a licensing authority[9] has reason to believe that a person has committed an offence under Part 1 of the Housing (Wales) Act 2014[10] (subject to two exceptions[11]), the authorised person may, by notice, offer the person the opportunity of discharging any liability to conviction for that offence by payment of a fixed penalty to the authority[12]. Where a person is given such a notice in respect of an offence: (1) no proceedings may be issued for that offence before the expiration of the period of 21 days following the date of the notice; (2) the person may not be convicted of the offence if the person pays the fixed penalty before the end of that period[13].

A notice must: (a) give such particulars of the circumstances alleged to constitute the offence as are necessary for giving reasonable information of the offence; (b) state the period during which proceedings will not be taken for the offence; (c) state the amount of the fixed penalty; and (d) state the person to whom and the address at which the fixed penalty may be paid[14]. The fixed penalty payable to a licensing authority under these provisions is £150 unless the offence is an offence attracting an unlimited fine; in which case, the fixed penalty payable is £250[15].

Payment of a fixed penalty may be made by pre-paying and posting a letter containing the amount of the penalty (in cash or otherwise) to the person specified in the notice at the address specified[16]; but this does not prevent payment by another method[17]. Where a letter is posted in accordance with this provision, payment is to be regarded as having been made at the time at which the letter would be delivered in the ordinary course of post[18]. In any proceedings a certificate: (i) which purports to be signed on behalf of a person authorised for this purpose by the licensing authority; and (ii) states that payment of a fixed penalty was or was not received by a date specified in the certificate, is evidence of the facts stated[19].

A licensing authority may use its fixed penalty receipts only for the purposes of its functions relating to the enforcement of Part 1 of the Housing (Wales) Act 2014[20].

Where an offence under Part 1 of the Housing (Wales) Act 2014 committed by a body corporate is proved to have been committed with the consent and connivance of, or to be attributable to any neglect on the part of, a director, manager or secretary of the body corporate[21], or a person purporting to act in such a capacity, that person, as well as the body corporate commits the offence and is liable to be proceeded against and punished accordingly[22].

1   As to the meaning of 'licensing authority' see PARA 734 note 1. As to licensing authorities see PARA 733.
2   Ie: (1) under the Housing (Wales) Act 2014 s 4(2), 6(4), 7(5), 9(2), 11(3) or 13(3) (see PARAS 730–732) if the alleged offence arises in respect of a dwelling in the area for which it is the licensing authority; (2) under s 16(3) (see PARA 735) or 23(3) (see PARA 736), in respect of information to be provided to the licensing authority; (3) under s 38(1) or (4) (see PARA 739), in respect of anything required by a notice given by a person authorised by the authority; (4) under s 39(1) or (2) (see PARA 739), in respect of information supplied to the authority: s 28(1). As to the meaning of 'dwelling' see PARA 729 note 2.
3   As to the meaning of 'local housing authority' see PARA 227 note 2.

4 Ie an offence under the Housing (Wales) Act 2014 s 4(2), 6(4), 7(5), 9(2), 11(3) or 13(3): see PARAS 730–732.
5 Housing (Wales) Act 2014 s 28(2). A licensing authority may give its consent under s 28(2) generally or in specific cases: s 28(3).
6 Ie under the Housing (Wales) Act 2014 s 3: see PARA 733.
7 Ie under the Local Government Act 1972 s 222: see LOCAL GOVERNMENT vol 69 (2009) PARA 573.
8 Housing (Wales) Act 2014 s 28(4).
9 In the Housing (Wales) Act 2014 s 29, 'licensing authority' means: (1) in the case of an offence under s 4(2), 6(4), 7(5), 9(2) or 11(3), the licensing authority for the area in which the dwelling to which the offence relates is located; (2) in the case of an offence under s 16(3) or 23(3), the licensing authority to which the information to which the offence relates was provided; (3) in the case of an offence under s 38(1), the licensing authority which authorised the person who gave the relevant notice; (4) in the case of an offence under s 39(1) or (2), the licensing authority to which the information was supplied: s 29(10). A local housing authority that is not the licensing authority for its area may, with the consent of the licensing authority for the area, exercise the functions of the licensing authority under s 29 concurrently with the licensing authority; but only in respect of the offences mentioned in head (1) above: s 29(11). Where a local housing authority exercises functions under s 29 by virtue of s 29(11), the references in s 29(1), (4), (8), (9) and (10)(a) to 'licensing authority' are to be read as if they were references to the local housing authority: s 29(12).
10 Ie the Housing (Wales) Act 2014 Pt 1 (ss 1–49): see PARA 729 et seq.
11 Ie other than an offence under the Housing (Wales) Act 2014 s 13(3) (see PARA 732) or s 38(4) (see PARA 739).
12 Housing (Wales) Act 2014 s 29(1).
13 Housing (Wales) Act 2014 s 29(2).
14 Housing (Wales) Act 2014 s 29(3).
15 Housing (Wales) Act 2014 s 29(4). The Welsh Ministers may amend s 29(4) by order: s 29(5). As to the Welsh Ministers see PARA 7.
16 See head (d) in the text.
17 Housing (Wales) Act 2014 s 29(6).
18 Housing (Wales) Act 2014 s 29(7).
19 Housing (Wales) Act 2014 s 29(8).
20 Housing (Wales) Act 2014 s 29(9).
21 The reference to the director, manager or secretary of the body corporate includes a reference to any similar officer of the body and, where the body is a body corporate whose affairs are managed by its members, to any officer or member of the body: s 35(2).
22 Housing (Wales) Act 2014 s 35(1).

741. Rent stopping orders. A residential property tribunal[1] may make an order (a 'rent stopping order') in relation to a dwelling[2] subject to a domestic tenancy[3] on an application made to it by the licensing authority[4] for the area in which the dwelling is located or the local housing authority[5] for the area in which the dwelling is located (which must be made with the consent of the licensing authority)[6]. This is a new procedure, introduced by the Housing (Wales) Act 2014. An application cannot be made by a tenant, unlike an application for a rent repayment order[7].

Where the tribunal makes a rent stopping order:
(1)   periodical payments payable in connection with a domestic tenancy of the dwelling which relate to a period, or part of a period, falling between a date specified in the order (the 'stopping date') and a date specified by the tribunal when the order is revoked are stopped[8];
(2)   an obligation under a domestic tenancy to pay an amount stopped by the order is treated as being met;
(3)   all other rights and obligations under such a tenancy continue unaffected;
(4)   any periodical payments stopped by the order but made by a tenant of the dwelling (whether before or after the stopping date) must be repaid by the landlord[9]; and

(5)   the authority which made the application for the order must give a copy of it to the landlord of the dwelling to which the order relates and the tenant of the dwelling[10].

The tribunal may make a rent stopping order only if it is satisfied that:

(a)   an offence of carrying out property management activities without a licence[11] or of appointing an unlicensed agent[12] is being committed in relation to the dwelling (whether or not a person has been convicted or charged for the offence); and

(b)   the authority making the application has given the landlord and the tenant a notice of intended proceedings[13], the period for making representations has expired and the authority has considered any representations made to it within that period by the landlord[14].

On an application by: (i) the licensing authority for the area in which the dwelling is located; (ii) with the consent of the licensing authority, the local housing authority for the area in which the dwelling is located; or (iii) the landlord of the dwelling, a residential property tribunal may revoke a rent stopping order in relation to the dwelling if it is satisfied that an offence specified in head (a)[15] is no longer being committed[16]. Where the tribunal revokes a rent stopping order, periodical payments in connection with a domestic tenancy of the dwelling become payable from a date specified by the tribunal (which may, if the tribunal considers it appropriate, be a date earlier than the date on which the order is revoked)[17]. However, revocation of a rent stopping order does not make a person liable to pay any periodical payments which, by virtue of the order, were stopped in respect of the period beginning with the stopping date and ending with the date specified by the tribunal when revoking the order[18]. If a rent stopping order is revoked following an application made by the licensing authority or the local housing authority[19], the authority which made the application must notify any tenant or occupier of the dwelling, and the landlord of the dwelling that the order is revoked and of the effect of the revocation[20]. Where revocation occurs following an application made by a landlord, the licensing authority for the area in which the dwelling is located must ensure that any tenant or occupier of the dwelling is notified that the order is revoked and of the effect of the revocation[21].

1   As to residential property tribunals see PARA 34 et seq.
2   As to the meaning of 'dwelling' see PARA 729 note 2.
3   As to the meaning of 'domestic tenancy' see PARA 729 note 3.
4   As to the meaning of 'licensing authority' see PARA 734 note 1. As to licensing authorities see PARA 733.
5   As to the meaning of 'local housing authority' see PARA 227 note 2.
6   Housing (Wales) Act 2014 s 30(1), (2). Consent is required unless the local housing authority is the licensing authority, and consent for this purpose may be given generally or in respect of a particular application: s 30(2).
7   As to rent repayment orders see PARA 742.
8   The tribunal may not specify a stopping date for the purpose of head (1) in the text which precedes the date on which the rent stopping order is made: Housing (Wales) Act 2014 s 30(7).
9   As to the meaning of 'landlord' see PARA 729 note 4. An amount payable by virtue of head (4) in the text which is not repaid is recoverable by the tenant as a debt due to the tenant from the landlord: Housing (Wales) Act 2014 s 30(8).
10   Housing (Wales) Act 2014 s 30(3).
11   Ie under the Housing (Wales) Act 2014 s 7(5): see PARA 731.
12   Ie under the Housing (Wales) Act 2014 s 13(3): see PARA 732. The reference to an offence committed under s 13(3) does not include an offence committed in consequence of a contravention of s 13(1): s 30(9).
13   The notice must: (1) explain that the authority is proposing to apply for a rent stopping order; (2) set out the reasons why it proposes to do so; (3) explain the effect of a rent stopping order; (4) explain how a rent stopping order may be revoked; and (5) in the case of a notice given to a

landlord, invite the landlord to make representations to the authority within a period of not less than 28 days specified in the notice: Housing (Wales) Act 2014 s 30(6)(a).

14 Housing (Wales) Act 2014 s 30(4)–(6).

15 Ie an offence under the Housing (Wales) Act 2014 s 7(5) or 13(3). For this purpose, the reference to an offence under s 7(5) does not include an offence committed in consequence of a contravention of s 7(3), and the reference to an offence committed under s 13(3) does not include an offence committed in consequence of a contravention of s 13(1): s 31(8).

16 Housing (Wales) Act 2014 s 31(1)–(3). Consent is required unless the local housing authority is the licensing authority, and consent for this purpose may be given generally or in respect of a particular application: s 31(3).

17 Housing (Wales) Act 2014 s 31(4).

18 Housing (Wales) Act 2014 s 31(5).

19 Ie an application under the Housing (Wales) Act 2014 s 31(2)(a)(i) or (ii).

20 Housing (Wales) Act 2014 s 31(6).

21 Housing (Wales) Act 2014 s 31(7).

742. Rent repayment orders. A residential property tribunal[1] may make an order (a 'rent repayment order') in relation to a dwelling[2] on an application by: (1) the licensing authority[3] for the area in which the dwelling is located; (2) the local housing authority[4] for the area in which the dwelling is located (which must be made with the consent of the licensing authority); or (3) the tenant of the dwelling[5]. A 'rent repayment order' is an order made in relation to a dwelling which requires the appropriate person[6] to pay to the applicant such amount in respect of the relevant award or awards of universal credit[7] or the housing benefit paid, or (as the case may be) the periodical payments paid, as is specified in the order[8].

Where the applicant is the licensing authority or a local housing authority, the tribunal may make a rent repayment order only if it is satisfied: (a) that the applicant authority has given the appropriate person a notice of intended proceedings[9]; (b) that an offence of carrying out property management activities without a licence[10] or of appointing an unlicensed agent[11] has been committed in relation to the dwelling at any time within the period of 12 months ending with the date of the notice of intended proceedings; and (c) that one or more relevant awards of universal credit or housing benefit has been paid in respect of periodical payments payable in connection with a domestic tenancy of the dwelling during any period during which it appears to the tribunal that such an offence was being committed[12].

Where the applicant is the tenant[13], the tribunal may make a rent repayment order only if it is satisfied that: (i) a person has been convicted of an offence of carrying out property management activities without a licence or of appointing an unlicensed agent in relation to the dwelling, or that a rent repayment order has required a person to make a payment in respect of one or more relevant awards of universal credit or in respect of housing benefit paid in connection with a tenancy of the dwelling; (ii) the tenant paid to the appropriate person (whether directly or otherwise) periodical payments in respect of the tenancy of the dwelling during any period during which it appears to the tribunal that such an offence was being committed in relation to the dwelling[14]; and (iii) the application is made within the period of 12 months beginning with the date of the conviction or order or, if such a conviction was followed by such an order (or vice versa), the date of the later of them[15].

Where, on an application by the licensing authority or a local housing authority (as the case may be) for a rent repayment order, the tribunal is satisfied: (A) that a person has been convicted of an offence of carrying out property management activities without a licence or of appointing an unlicensed agent[16] in relation to the dwelling to which the application relates; and (B) that one or more relevant awards of universal credit were paid (whether or not to the appropriate person), or that housing benefit was paid (whether or not to the appropriate person) in respect of periodical payments payable in connection with a domestic tenancy of the dwelling during any period during which it appears to the tribunal that such an offence was being committed in relation to the dwelling in question, the tribunal must make a rent repayment order requiring the appropriate person to pay to the authority which made the application the specified amount[17]. A rent repayment order made in accordance with these provisions may not require the payment of any amount which the tribunal is satisfied that, by reason of any exceptional circumstances, it would be unreasonable for that person to be required to pay[18].

In a case where heads (A) and (B) do not apply, the amount required to be paid by virtue of a rent repayment order is to be such amount as the tribunal considers reasonable in the circumstances[19].

Any amount payable by virtue of a rent repayment order is recoverable as a debt due to the licensing authority, local housing authority or tenant (as the case may be) from the appropriate person[20]; and an amount payable to the licensing authority or a local housing authority by virtue of such an order does not, when recovered by it, constitute an amount of universal credit or housing benefit (as the case may be) recovered by the authority[21].

The Welsh Ministers may by regulations make such provision as they consider appropriate for supplementing the provisions above[22].

1   As to residential property tribunals see PARA 34 et seq.
2   As to the meaning of 'dwelling' see PARA 729 note 2.
3   As to the meaning of 'licensing authority' see PARA 734 note 1. As to licensing authorities see PARA 733.
4   As to the meaning of 'local housing authority' see PARA 227 note 2.
5   Housing (Wales) Act 2014 s 32(1), (2). Consent is required unless the local housing authority is the licensing authority, and consent for this purpose may be given generally or in respect of a particular application: s 32(2). Compare rent stopping orders: see PARA 741.
6   'Appropriate person', in relation to any payment of universal credit or housing benefit or periodical payment in connection with a domestic tenancy of a dwelling, means the person who at the time of the payment was entitled to receive, on that person's own account, periodical payments in connection with the tenancy: Housing (Wales) Act 2014 s 32(9). 'Housing benefit' means housing benefit provided by virtue of a scheme under the Social Security Contributions and Benefits Act 1992 s 123 (see WELFARE BENEFITS AND STATE PENSIONS vol 104 (2014) PARA 249 et seq): Housing (Wales) Act 2014 s 32(9).
7   'Relevant award of universal credit' means an award of universal credit the calculation of which included an amount under the Welfare Reform Act 2012 s 11 (see WELFARE BENEFITS AND STATE PENSIONS vol 104 (2014) PARAS 72–76), calculated in accordance with the Universal Credit Regulations 2013, SI 2013/376, Sch 4 (housing costs element for renters) or any corresponding provision replacing that Schedule, in respect of periodical payments in connection with a domestic tenancy of the dwelling: Housing (Wales) Act 2014 s 32(9). As to the meaning of 'domestic tenancy' see PARA 729 note 3.
8   Housing (Wales) Act 2014 s 32(3).
9   The notice must: (1) inform the person that the authority is proposing to make an application for a rent repayment order; (2) set out the reasons why it proposes to do so; (3) state the amount that it will seek to recover and how that amount is calculated; and (4) invite the person to make representations to the authority within a period of not less than 28 days specified in the notice: Housing (Wales) Act 2014 s 32(6)(a). The tribunal must be satisfied that that period has expired and that the authority has considered any representations made to it within that period by the appropriate person: s 32(6)(b), (c).
10 Ie under the Housing (Wales) Act 2014 s 7(5): see PARA 731. References in s 32 to an offence under s 7(5) do not include an offence committed in consequence of a contravention of s 7(3): s 32(8)(a).
11 Ie under the Housing (Wales) Act 2014 s 13(3): see PARA 732. References in s 32 to an offence committed under s 13(3) do not include an offence committed in consequence of a contravention of s 13(1): s 32(b)(b).

12 Housing (Wales) Act 2014 s 32(4)(a), (5), (6).

13 'Tenant', in relation to any periodical payment, means a person who was a tenant at the time of the payment (and 'tenancy' has a corresponding meaning): Housing (Wales) Act 2014 s 32(9).

14 For the purposes of the Housing (Wales) Act 2014 s 32, an amount which: (1) is not actually paid by a tenant but is used to discharge the whole or part of the tenant's liability in respect of a periodical payment (for example, by offsetting the amount against any such liability); and (2) is not an amount of universal credit or housing benefit, is to be regarded as an amount paid by the tenant in respect of that periodical payment: s 32(10).

15 Housing (Wales) Act 2014 s 32(4)(b), (7), (8).

16 Ie under the Housing (Wales) Act 2014 s 7(5) or 13(3). See notes 10, 11.

17 Housing (Wales) Act 2014 s 33(1). This is subject to s 33(3), (4), (8): s 33(1). Section 32(8), (9), (10) applies for the purposes of s 33 as it applies for the purposes of s 32: s 33(11).

The amount is: (1) an amount equal to: (a) where one relevant award of universal credit was paid as mentioned in s 33(1)(b)(i), the amount included in the calculation of that award under the Welfare Reform Act 2012 s 11, calculated in accordance with the Universal Credit Regulations 2013, SI 2013/376, Sch 4 (housing costs element for renters) or any corresponding provision replacing that Schedule, or the amount of the award if less; or (b) if more than one such award was paid as mentioned in s 33(1)(b)(i), the sum of the amounts included in the calculation of those awards as referred to in head (a), or the sum of the amounts of those awards if less; or (2) an amount equal to the total amount of housing benefit paid as mentioned in s 33(1)(b)(ii) (as the case may be): s 33(2). If the total of the amounts received by the appropriate person in respect of periodical payments payable as mentioned in s 33(1)(b) ('the rent total') is less than the amount mentioned in s 33(2), the amount required to be paid by virtue of a rent repayment order made in accordance with s 33(1) is limited to the rent total: s 33(3).

18 Housing (Wales) Act 2014 s 33(4).

19 Housing (Wales) Act 2014 s 33(5). This is subject to s 33(6)–(8): s 33(5). In such a case, the tribunal must take into account the following matters: (1) the total amount of relevant payments paid in connection with a tenancy of the dwelling during any period during which it appears to the tribunal that an offence was being committed in relation to the dwelling under s 7(5) or 13(3); (2) the extent to which that total amount: (a) consisted of, or derived from, payments of relevant awards of universal credit or housing benefit; and (b) was actually received by the appropriate person; (3) whether the appropriate person has at any time been convicted of an offence under s 7(5) or 13(3); (4) the conduct and financial circumstances of the appropriate person; and (5) where the application is made by a tenant, the conduct of the tenant: s 33(6). In s 33(6) 'relevant payments' means: (a) in relation to an application by the licensing authority or a local housing authority (as the case may be), payments of relevant awards of universal credit, housing benefit or periodical payments payable by tenants; (b) in relation to an application by a tenant, periodical payments payable by the tenant, less: (i) where one or more relevant awards of universal credit were payable during the period in question, the amount mentioned in s 33(2)(a) in respect of the award or awards that related to the tenancy during that period; or (ii) any amount of housing benefit payable in respect of the tenancy of the dwelling during the period in question: s 33(7). A rent repayment order may not require the payment of any amount which: (A) where the application is made by the licensing authority or a local housing authority (as the case may be), is in respect of any time falling outside the period of 12 months ending with the date of the notice of intended proceedings given under s 32(6); or (B) where the application is made by a tenant, is in respect of any time falling outside the period of 12 months ending with the date of the tenant's application under s 32(1), and the period to be taken into account under s 33(6)(a) is restricted accordingly: s 33(8).

20 Housing (Wales) Act 2014 s 33(9).

21 Housing (Wales) Act 2014 s 33(10).

22 Housing (Wales) Act 2014 s 34(1). Regulations made under s 34(1) may, for example, make provision: (1) for securing that persons are not unfairly prejudiced by rent repayment orders (whether in cases where there have been over-payments of universal credit or housing benefit or otherwise); (2) requiring or authorising amounts received by the licensing authority or local housing authorities by virtue of rent repayment orders to be dealt with in such manner as is specified in the regulations: s 34(2). As to regulations made under s 34 see the Regulation of Private Rented Housing (Rent Repayment Orders) (Supplementary Provisions) (Wales) Regulations 2016, SI 2016/1022.

743. Restrictions on terminating tenancies. A section 21 notice[1] may not be given in relation to a dwelling[2] subject to a domestic tenancy[3] which is an assured shorthold tenancy[4] if: (1) the landlord[5] is not registered[6] in respect of the dwelling;

or (2) the landlord is not licensed under Part 1 of the Housing (Wales) Act 2014[7] for the area in which the dwelling is located and the landlord has not appointed a person who is licensed under Part 1 to carry out all property management work[8] in respect of the dwelling on the landlord's behalf[9]. However, this restriction does not apply for the period of 28 days beginning with the day on which the landlord's interest in the dwelling is assigned to the landlord[10].

1   Ie a notice under the Housing Act 1988 s 21(1)(b) or (4)(a) (recovery of possession on termination of shorthold tenancy: see LANDLORD AND TENANT vol 63 (2016) PARA 926): Housing (Wales) Act 2014 s 44(3).
2   As to the meaning of 'dwelling' see PARA 729 note 2.
3   As to the meaning of 'domestic tenancy' see PARA 729 note 3.
4   As to assured shorthold tenancies see LANDLORD AND TENANT vol 63 (2016) PARA 852 et seq.
5   As to the meaning of 'landlord' see PARA 729 note 4.
6   As to registered landlords see PARAS 13, 166 et seq.
7   Ie under the Housing (Wales) Act 2014 Pt 1 (ss 1–49): see PARA 729 et seq.
8   As to the meaning of 'property management work' see PARA 732 note 10
9   Housing (Wales) Act 2014 s 44(1).
10   Housing (Wales) Act 2014 s 44(2).

(6) CODE OF PRACTICE, GUIDANCE AND DIRECTIONS

744. Powers of the Welsh Ministers. The Welsh Ministers[1] must issue a code of practice setting standards relating to letting and managing rental properties[2]. Those standards may (among other things) be set in relation to training[3]. The Welsh Ministers may issue a code of practice which, in part or in whole, applies only to specified persons or cases, or applies differently to different persons or cases, and may amend or withdraw such a code[4]. Before issuing or amending a code of practice the Welsh Ministers must take reasonable steps to consult persons involved in letting and managing rental properties and persons occupying such properties under a tenancy, or persons whom the Welsh Ministers consider to represent the interests of those persons on a draft of the code or a draft of an amended code ('the proposed code')[5].

If the Welsh Ministers wish to proceed with the proposed code (with or without modifications) they must lay a copy before the National Assembly for Wales[6]. The Welsh Ministers must not issue the proposed code in the form of that draft unless it is approved by resolution of the National Assembly for Wales[7]. Once approved the code or amended code comes into force on the date appointed by order of the Welsh Ministers[8].

The Welsh Ministers may withdraw a code in an amended code or by direction[9]. A code approved by the National Assembly for Wales may not be withdrawn unless a proposal to that effect is approved by resolution of the National Assembly[10].

The Welsh Ministers must publish each code or amended code issued under these provisions[11].

In exercising its functions under Part 1 of the Housing (Wales) Act 2014, a licensing authority[12] must have regard to any guidance given by the Welsh Ministers[13]. In exercising functions under that Part other than as a licensing authority, a local housing authority[14] must have regard to any guidance given by the Welsh Ministers[15]. The Welsh Ministers may: (1) give guidance under that Part generally or to authorities of a specified description; (2) revise guidance given under that Part by giving further guidance; (3) revoke guidance given under that Part by giving further guidance or by notice[16]. The Welsh Ministers must publish any guidance or notice under these provisions[17]. Before giving, revising or revoking guidance under Part 1 of the Housing (Wales) Act 2014, the Welsh Ministers must consult such persons as the Welsh Ministers consider appropriate[18].

In exercising its functions under Part 1 of the Housing (Wales) Act 2014, a licensing authority must comply with any directions given by the Welsh Ministers[19]. In exercising functions under Part 1 other than as a licensing authority, a local housing authority must comply with any directions given by the Welsh Ministers[20], which may be given generally or to authorities of a specified description[21]. A direction given under these provisions may be varied or revoked by a subsequent direction and must be published[22].

1   As to the Welsh Ministers see PARA 7.
2   Housing (Wales) Act 2014 s 40(1). As to the meaning of 'rental property' see PARA 729 note 6.
3   Housing (Wales) Act 2014 s 40(2).
4   Housing (Wales) Act 2014 s 40(3).
5   Housing (Wales) Act 2014 s 40(4).
6   Housing (Wales) Act 2014 s 40(5).
7   Housing (Wales) Act 2014 s 40(6).
8   Housing (Wales) Act 2014 s 40(7).
9   Housing (Wales) Act 2014 s 40(8).
10 Housing (Wales) Act 2014 s 40(9).
11 Housing (Wales) Act 2014 s 40(10). See the Code of Practice for Landlords and Agents licensed under Part 1 of the Housing (Wales) Act 2014 (brought into force by the Code of Practice for Landlords and Agents licensed under Part 1 of the Housing (Wales) Act 2014, (Appointed Date) Order 2015, SI 2015/1932).
12 As to the meaning of 'licensing authority' see PARA 734 note 1. As to licensing authorities see PARA 733.
13 Housing (Wales) Act 2014 s 41(1).
14 As to the meaning of 'local housing authority' see PARA 227 note 2.
15 Housing (Wales) Act 2014 s 41(2).
16 Housing (Wales) Act 2014 s 41(3).
17 Housing (Wales) Act 2014 s 41(4).
18 Housing (Wales) Act 2014 s 41(5). Consultation undertaken before the coming into force of s 41 may satisfy the requirement in s 41(5): s 41(6).
19 Housing (Wales) Act 2014 s 42(1).
20 Housing (Wales) Act 2014 s 42(2).
21 Housing (Wales) Act 2014 s 42(3).
22 Housing (Wales) Act 2014 s 42(4).

11. MANAGEMENT ORDERS UNDER THE HOUSING ACT 2004

(1) INTERIM AND FINAL MANAGEMENT ORDERS

(i) Nature of Orders

745. Nature of interim and final management orders. Chapter 1 of Part 4 of the Housing Act 2004[1] introduces provisions which enable a local housing authority[2] to make an interim management order[3], or a final management order[4], in respect of an HMO[5] or a Part 3 house[6] or, prospectively, property let in breach of a banning order under the Housing and Planning Act 2016[7].

An interim management order is an order (expiring not more than 12 months after it is made) which is made for the purpose of securing that the following steps are taken in relation to the house[8]:

(1)   any immediate steps which the authority considers necessary to protect the health, safety or welfare of persons occupying the house, or persons occupying or having an estate or interest in any premises in the vicinity[9]; and

(2)   any other steps which the authority thinks appropriate with a view to the proper management of the house pending the grant of a licence under Part 2 or Part 3 of the Housing Act 2004[10] in respect of the house or the making of a final management order in respect of it (or, if appropriate, the revocation of the interim management order)[11].

A final management order is an order (expiring not more than five years after it is made) which is made for the purpose of securing the proper management of the house on a long-term basis in accordance with a management scheme contained in the order[12].

1   Ie the Housing Act 2004 Pt 4 Ch 1 (ss 101–131).
2   As to the meaning of 'local housing authority' see PARA 380 note 1.
3   See the Housing Act 2004 s 102; and PARA 746. Section 103 deals with the making of a special interim management order in respect of a house to which that provision applies: see s 101(2); and PARA 747.
4   See the Housing Act 2004 s 113; and PARA 755.
5   For the purposes of the Housing Act 2004 Pt 4 (ss 101–147), 'HMO' means a house in multiple occupation as defined by ss 254–259 (see PARAS 667–671): s 146(1). See also note 6. The appropriate national authority may by regulations provide for any provision of Pt 4 or s 263 (in its operation for the purposes of any such provision) (see PARA 391 notes 5–6), to have effect in relation to a section 257 HMO with such modifications as are prescribed by the regulations: s 146(3). A 'section 257 HMO' is an HMO which is a converted block of flats to which s 257 applies (see PARA 669): s 146(4). As to the meaning of 'the appropriate national authority' see PARA 389 note 1. As to regulations made under s 146(3) see the Houses in Multiple Occupation (Certain Converted Blocks of Flats) (Modifications to the Housing Act 2004 and Transitional Provisions for section 257 HMOs) (England) Regulations 2007, SI 2007/1904; and the Houses in Multiple Occupation (Certain Converted Blocks of Flats) (Modifications to the Housing Act 2004 and Transitional Provisions for section 257 HMOs) (Wales) Regulations 2007, SI 2007/3231.
6   For the purposes of the Housing Act 2004 Pt 4, 'Part 3 house' means a house to which Pt 3 (ss 79–100) applies (see s 79(2); and PARA 704): s 146(1). Any reference to an HMO or Part 3 house includes (where the context permits) a reference to any yard, garden, outhouses and appurtenances belonging to, or usually enjoyed with, it (or any part of it): s 146(1).
7   Housing Act 2004 s 101(1) (amended, as from a day to be appointed, by the Housing and Planning Act 2016 s 26, Sch 3 paras 1, 2(1), (2); at the date at which this volume states the law, no such day had been appointed). The text refers to a banning order under the Housing and Planning Act 2016 s 16: see PARA 719 et seq. In the Housing Act 2004 Pt 4 Ch 1, any reference to property that is let in breach of a banning order under the Housing and Planning Act 2016 s 16 includes property in respect of which a breach is (or would be) caused by a licence to occupy: Housing Act 2004

s 101(6B) (s 101(6A)–(6C) added, as from a day to be appointed, by the Housing and Planning Act 2016 Sch 3 paras 1, 2(1), (5); at the date at which this volume states the law, no such day had been appointed). When determining for the purposes of the Housing Act 2004 Pt 4 Ch 1 whether property is let in breach of a banning order any exception included in the banning order in reliance on the Housing and Planning Act 2016 s 17 (see PARA 720) should be disregarded: Housing Act 2004 s 101(6C) (as so added).

8   Housing Act 2004 s 101(3). For the purposes of Pt 4 Ch 1, any reference to 'the house', in relation to an interim or final management order (other than an order under s 102(7) or prospectively s 102(7A): see PARA 746 head (ii)), is a reference to the HMO or Part 3 house to which the order relates: s 101(5) (amended, as from a day to be appointed, by the Housing and Planning Act 2016 Sch 3 paras 1, 2(1), (4); at the date at which this volume states the law, no such day had been appointed). This has effect subject to the Housing Act 2004 s 102(8) and s 113(7) (exclusion of part occupied by resident landlord: see PARAS 746, 755): s 101(6). Prospectively, in Pt 4 Ch 1, any reference to 'the house', in relation to an interim or final management order that relates to property let in breach of a banning order under the Housing and Planning Act 2016 s 16, means the property let in breach of that order: Housing Act 2004 s 101(6A) (as added: see note 7). See also PARA 747 note 9.

9   Housing Act 2004 s 101(3)(a). As to the meaning of 'occupy' see PARA 563 note 13; and as to the meaning of 'person having an estate or interest' see PARA 391 note 7.

10   The reference to the grant of a licence under the Housing Act 2004 Pt 2 or Pt 3 in respect of the house includes a reference to serving a temporary exemption notice under s 62 (see PARA 680) or s 86 (see PARA 710) in respect of it (whether or not a notification is given under s 62(1) or s 86(1)): s 106(6).

11   Housing Act 2004 s 101(3)(b).

12   Housing Act 2004 s 101(4). As to management schemes see PARA 760.

(ii) Interim Management Orders

A.   MAKING AND OPERATION

746. Making of interim management orders. A local housing authority[1] is under a duty to make an interim management order[2] in respect of a house in a case within head (1) or head (2) below, and, in addition, has the power to make an interim management order in respect of a house in a case within head (i) or head (ii) or, prospectively (iii) below[3].

The authority must make an interim management order in respect of a house if:

(1)   it is an HMO[4] or a Part 3 house[5] which is required to be licensed under the Housing Act 2004 Part 2 or Part 3[6] but is not so licensed, and the authority considers either that there is no reasonable prospect of its being so licensed in the near future, or that the health and safety condition is satisfied[7]; or

(2)   it is an HMO or a Part 3 house which is required to be licensed[8] and is so licensed, and:

(a)   the authority has revoked the licence concerned but the revocation is not yet in force; and

(b)   it considers either that, on the revocation coming into force, there will be no reasonable prospect of the house being so licensed in the near future, or that, on the revocation coming into force, the health and safety condition will be satisfied[9].

The authority may also make an interim management order:

(i)   in respect of a house if it is an HMO other than one that is required to be licensed[10], and, on an application by the authority to the appropriate tribunal[11], the tribunal by order authorises it to make such an order, either in the terms of a draft order submitted by it or in those terms as varied by the tribunal[12]; or

(ii)   in respect of a house if it is a house to which the provisions as to special interim management orders[13] apply, and, on an application by the authority to the appropriate tribunal, the tribunal by order authorises the authority to make such an order, either in the terms of a draft order submitted by it or in those terms as varied by the tribunal[14]; or

(iii)   as from a day to be appointed, in respect of any property let in breach of a banning order[15].

The authority may make an interim management order which is expressed not to apply to a part of the house that is occupied by a person who has an estate or interest[16] in the whole of the house[17].

Nothing in these provisions requires or authorises the making of an interim management order in respect of a house if an interim management order has been previously made in respect of it and the authority has not exercised any relevant function[18] in respect of the house at any time after the making of the interim management order[19].

1   As to the meaning of 'local housing authority' see PARA 380 note 1.
2   As to the meaning of 'interim management order' see PARA 745.
3   Housing Act 2004 s 102(1) (amended, as from a day to be appointed, by the Housing and Planning Act 2016 s 26, Sch 3 paras 1, 3(1), (2); at the date at which this volume states the law, no such day had been appointed); and see PARA 745 note 1.
4   As to the meaning of 'HMO' see PARA 745 note 5.
5   As to the meaning of 'Part 3 house' see PARA 745 note 6.
6   Ie under the Housing Act 2004 Pt 2 (ss 55–78) (see s 61(1); and PARA 679) or Pt 3 (ss 79–100) (see s 85(1); and PARA 709).
7   Housing Act 2004 s 102(2)(a), (b). The health and safety condition for the purposes of s 102 is that the making of an interim management order is necessary for the purpose of protecting the health, safety or welfare of persons occupying the house, or persons occupying or having an estate or interest in any premises in the vicinity: s 104(1), (2). As to the meaning of 'occupy' see PARA 563 note 13. A threat to evict persons occupying a house in order to avoid the house being required to be licensed under Pt 2 may constitute a threat to the welfare of those persons for the purposes of s 104(2), but this does not affect the generality of s 104(2): s 104(3). The health and safety condition is not to be regarded as satisfied for the purposes of s 102(2)(b)(ii) or s 102(3)(c)(ii) (see heads (1), (2) in the text) where both of the following conditions are satisfied: s 104(4). The first condition is that the local housing authority either: (1) in a case within s 102(2)(b)(ii), is required by s 5 (general duty to take enforcement action in respect of category 1 hazards: see PARA 566) to take a course of action within s 5(2) in relation to the house; or (2) in a case within s 102(3)(c)(ii), considers that on the revocation coming into force it will be required to take such a course of action: s 104(5). As to the meaning of 'category 1 hazard' see PARA 564. The second condition is that the local housing authority considers that the health, safety or welfare of the persons in question would be adequately protected by taking that course of action: s 104(6).
8   See note 6.
9   Housing Act 2004 s 102(3)(a)–(c). See also note 7.
10 Ie under the Housing Act 2004 Pt 2. As to HMOs which are required to be licensed under Pt 2 see PARA 674.
11 As to the meaning of 'appropriate tribunal' see PARA 580 note 2. As to appeals to the appropriate tribunal see PARA 32 et seq.
12 Housing Act 2004 s 102(4)(a), (b) (s 102(4)(b) amended by SI 2013/1036). The authority may make such an order despite any pending appeal against the order of the tribunal which authorised it (but this is without prejudice to any order that may be made on the disposal of any such appeal): Housing Act 2004 s 102(4). The tribunal may only authorise the authority to make an interim management order under s 102(4) if it considers that the health and safety condition is satisfied: s 102(5). In determining whether to authorise the authority to make an interim management order in respect of an HMO under s 102(4), the tribunal must have regard to the extent to which any applicable code of practice approved under s 233 (see PARA 696) has been complied with in respect of the HMO in the past: s 102(6).
13 Ie the Housing Act 2004 s 103: see PARA 747.
14 Housing Act 2004 s 102(7)(a), (b) (s 102(7)(b) amended by SI 2013/1036). The authority may make such an order despite any pending appeal against the order of the tribunal which authorised it (but this is without prejudice to any order that may be made on the disposal of any such appeal):

s 102(7). The provisions of s 103(2)–(6) (see PARA 747) apply in relation to the power of a tribunal to authorise the making of an interim management order under s 102(7): s 102(7).

15 Housing Act 2004 s 102(7A) (added, as from a day to be appointed, by the Housing and Planning Act 2016 Sch 3 paras 1, 3(1), (3); at the date at which this volume states the law, no such day had been appointed). The text refers to a banning order under the Housing and Planning Act 2016 s 16: see PARA 719 et seq.

16 As to the meaning of 'person having an estate or interest' see PARA 391 note 7.

17 Housing Act 2004 s 102(8). In relation to such an order, a reference in Pt 4 Ch 1 (ss 101–131) to 'the house' does not include the part so excluded (unless the context requires otherwise, such as where the reference is to the house as an HMO or a Part 3 house): s 102(8).

18 For this purpose, 'relevant function' means the function of: (1) granting a licence under the Housing Act 2004 Pt 2 or Pt 3 (see PARAS 682, 711); (2) serving a temporary exemption notice under s 62 or s 86 (see PARAS 680, 710); or (3) making a final management order under s 113 (see PARA 755): s 102(10). As to the meaning of 'final management order' see PARA 745.

19 Housing Act 2004 s 102(9) (amended, as from a day to be appointed, by the Housing and Planning Act 2016 Sch 3 paras 1, 3(1), (4) to refer to the making of an interim management order under the Housing Act 2004 s 102(2), (3), (4) or (7); at the date at which this volume states the law, no such day had been appointed).

747. Special interim management orders. The following provisions apply to a house[1] if the whole of it is occupied[2] either under a single tenancy or licence[3] that is not an exempt tenancy or licence[4], or under two or more tenancies or licences in respect of different dwellings contained in it, none of which is an exempt tenancy or licence[5]. The appropriate tribunal[6] may only authorise the local housing authority[7] to make an interim management order[8] in respect of such a house if it considers that both of the following conditions are satisfied[9].

The first condition is that the circumstances relating to the house[10] fall within any category of circumstances prescribed[11] for this purpose[12]. The second condition is that the making of the order is necessary for the purpose of protecting the health, safety or welfare of persons occupying, visiting or otherwise engaging in lawful activities in the vicinity of the house[13].

1 As to the meaning of 'house' for these purposes see PARA 704 note 2 (definition applied by the Housing Act 2004 s 103(7)).

2 As to the meaning of 'occupy' see PARA 563 note 13.

3 As to the meanings of 'tenancy' and 'licence' see PARA 391 note 6.

4 Ie under the Housing Act 2004 s 79(3) or (4): see PARA 704.

5 Housing Act 2004 s 103(1). Section 103 allows a special interim management order to be made in relation to a house that is potentially licensable under Pt 3 (ss 79–100) (see PARA 704 et seq), although no designation has been made under that Part.

6 As to the meaning of 'appropriate tribunal' see PARA 580 note 2.

7 As to the meaning of 'local housing authority' see PARA 380 note 1.

8 Ie under the Housing Act 2004 s 102(7): see PARA 746.

9 Housing Act 2004 s 103(3) (amended by SI 2013/1036).

10 For the purposes of the Housing Act 2004 Pt 4 Ch 1 (ss 101–131), any reference to 'the house', in relation to an interim management order under s 102(7) is a reference to the house to which the order relates, and any such reference includes (where the context permits) a reference to any yard, garden, outhouses and appurtenances belonging to, or usually enjoyed with, it (or any part of it): s 103(8).

11 Ie by an order under the Housing Act 2004 s 103(5): see note 10.

12 Housing Act 2004 s 103(3). The appropriate national authority may by order prescribe categories of circumstances for the purposes of s 103(3), and provide for any of the provisions of the Housing Act 2004 to apply in relation to houses to which s 103 applies, or interim or final management orders made in respect of them, with any modifications specified in the order: s 103(5). As to the meaning of 'the appropriate national authority' see PARA 389 note 1. The categories prescribed by such an order are to reflect one or more of the following: (1) the first or second set of general conditions mentioned in s 80(3) or (6) (see PARA 705 text and notes 8–14); or (2) any additional set of conditions specified under s 80(7) (see PARA 705 note 7), but (in each case) with such modifications as the appropriate national authority considers appropriate to adapt them to the circumstances of a single house: s 103(6). As to the orders that have been made see the Housing

(Interim Management Orders) (Prescribed Circumstances) (England) Order 2006, SI 2006/369; and the Housing (Interim Management Orders) (Prescribed Circumstances) (Wales) Order 2006, SI 2006/1706.
13 Housing Act 2004 s 103(4).

748. Operation of interim management orders. An interim management order[1] comes into effect when it is made, except in a case where the local housing authority[2] has revoked the licence relating to a house but the revocation is not yet in force[3], in which case it comes into effect when the revocation of the licence comes into force[4]. The order ceases to have effect at the end of the period of 12 months beginning with the date on which it is made, unless it ceases to have effect at some other time as mentioned below[5]. If the order provides that it is to cease to have effect on a date falling before the end of that period, it accordingly ceases to have effect on that date[6]. If the order is made pursuant to the revocation of a licence it must include a provision for determining the date on which it will cease to have effect, and it accordingly ceases to have effect on the date so determined[7]. That date must be no later than 12 months after the date on which the order comes into force[8].

Provision is made for where a final management order has been made[9] so as to replace the interim management order, but the final management order has not come into force because of an appeal to the appropriate tribunal[10] against the making of it. If the house[11] would (but for the interim management order being in force) be required to be licensed under Part 2 or Part 3 of the Housing Act 2004[12], and the date on which the final management order, any licence under Part 2 or Part 3, or another interim management order, comes into force in relation to the house (or part of it) following the disposal of the appeal is later than the date on which the interim management order would cease to have effect apart from this provision, the interim management order continues in force until that later date[13]. If, on the application of the authority, the tribunal makes an order providing for the interim management order to continue in force, pending the disposal of the appeal, until a date later than that on which the interim management order would cease to have effect apart from this provision, the interim management order accordingly continues in force until that later date[14].

These provisions have effect subject to the provisions as to variation or revocation of orders by the authority[15] and subject to the power of revocation exercisable by the appropriate tribunal on an appeal made[16] to it[17].

1 As to the meaning of 'interim management order' see PARA 745.
2 As to the meaning of 'local housing authority' see PARA 380 note 1.
3 Ie under the Housing Act 2004 s 102(3): see PARA 746 head (2).
4 Housing Act 2004 s 105(1)–(3).
5 Housing Act 2004 s 105(4).
6 Housing Act 2004 s 105(5).
7 Housing Act 2004 s 105(6).
8 Housing Act 2004 s 105(7). An order under s 102(7A) (see PARA 746 head (iii)) ceases to have effect (if it has not already ceased to have effect) when the ban on letting housing in England ceases to have effect: s 105(7A) (s 105(7A), (7B) added, as from a day to be appointed, by the Housing and Planning Act 2016 s 26, Sch 3 paras 1, 4(1), (2); at the date at which this volume states the law, no such day had been appointed). 'The ban on letting housing in England' means the ban on letting contained in the banning order mentioned in the Housing Act 2004 s 102(7A): s 105(7B) (as so added).
9 Ie under the Housing Act 2004 s 113: see PARA 755. As to the meaning of 'final management order' see PARA 745.
10 Ie under the Housing Act 2004 Sch 6 para 24: see PARA 770. As to the meaning of 'appropriate tribunal' see PARA 580 note 2. As to appeals to the appropriate tribunal see PARA 32 et seq.
11 As to the meaning of 'the house' see PARA 745 note 8.
12 Ie under the Housing Act 2004 Pt 2 (ss 55–78) (see s 61(1); and PARA 679) or Pt 3 (ss 79–100) (see s 85(1); and PARA 709).

13 Housing Act 2004 s 105(8), (9) (s 105(8) amended by SI 2013/1036; and, as from a day to be appointed, by the Housing and Planning Act 2016 Sch 3 paras 1, 4(1), (3); at the date at which this volume states the law, no such day had been appointed). If the IMO was made under the Housing Act 2004 s 102(7A) (see PARA 746 head (iii)) and the date on which the FMO or another interim management order comes into force in relation to the house (or part of it) following the disposal of the appeal is later than the date on which the IMO would cease to have effect apart from this provision, the IMO continues in force until that later date: s 105(9A) (added, as from a day to be appointed, by the Housing and Planning Act 2016 Sch 3 paras 1, 4(1), (4); at the date at which this volume states the law, no such day had been appointed).
14 Housing Act 2004 s 105(8), (10) (s 105(8) as amended: see note 13).
15 Ie the Housing Act 2004 ss 111, 112: see PARAS 753–754.
16 Ie under the Housing Act 2004 Sch 6 para 24 or 28: see PARAS 770, 772.
17 Housing Act 2004 s 105(11) (amended by SI 2013/1036).

749. Local housing authority's duties once interim management order is in force. A local housing authority[1] which has made an interim management order[2] in respect of a house must comply with the following provisions as soon as practicable after the order has come into force[3]. The authority must first take any immediate steps which it considers to be necessary for the purpose of protecting the health, safety or welfare of persons occupying[4] the house, or persons occupying or having an estate or interest[5] in any premises in the vicinity[6]. The authority must also take such other steps as it considers appropriate with a view to the proper management of the house[7] pending the grant of a licence[8] or the making of a final management order[9] in respect of the house, or the revocation[10] of the interim management order[11].

If the house would (but for the order being in force) be required to be licensed under Part 2 or Part 3 of the Housing Act 2004[12], the authority must, after considering all the circumstances of the case, decide to take one of the following courses of action:

(1) to grant a licence under that Part[13] in respect of the house; or
(2) to make a final management order[14] in respect of it[15].

If the house does not require to be licensed, the authority must, after considering all the circumstances of the case, decide to take one of the following courses of action:

(a) to make a final management order[16] in respect of the house; or
(b) to revoke the order[17] without taking any further action[18].

1 As to the meaning of 'local housing authority' see PARA 380 note 1.
2 As to the meaning of 'interim management order' see PARA 745. As to the making of such an order see PARA 746.
3 Housing Act 2004 s 106(1); and see PARA 745 note 1. As to the coming into force of an order see PARA 748.
4 As to the meaning of 'occupy' see PARA 563 note 13.
5 As to the meaning of 'person having an estate or interest' see PARA 391 note 7.
6 Housing Act 2004 s 106(2).
7 As to the meaning of 'the house' see PARA 745 note 8.
8 Ie as mentioned in the Housing Act 2004 s 106(4): see head (1) in the text.
9 Ie as mentioned in the Housing Act 2004 s 106(5): see head (a) in the text. As to the meaning of 'final management order' see PARA 745.
10 Ie as mentioned in the Housing Act 2004 s 106(5): see head (b) in the text.
11 Housing Act 2004 s 106(3). For the avoidance of doubt, the authority's duty under s 106(3) includes taking such steps as are necessary to ensure that, while the order is in force, reasonable provision is made for insurance of the house against destruction or damage by fire or other causes: s 106(7). As to when an order is in force see PARA 748.
12 Ie under the Housing Act 2004 Pt 2 (ss 55–78) (see s 61(1); and PARA 679) or Pt 3 (ss 79–100) (see s 85(1); and PARA 709).
13 In the Housing Act 2004 s 106(3), (4), the reference to the grant of a licence under Pt 2 or Pt 3 in respect of the house includes a reference to serving a temporary exemption notice under s 62 (see PARA 680) or s 86 (see PARA 710) in respect of it (whether or not a notification is given under s 62(1) or s 86(1)): s 106(6).

14 Ie under the Housing Act 2004 s 113(1): see PARA 755.
15 Housing Act 2004 s 106(4).
16 Ie under the Housing Act 2004 s 113(3): see PARA 755.
17 Ie under the Housing Act 2004 s 112: see PARA 754.
18 Housing Act 2004 s 106(5).

750. General effect of interim management orders. The following provisions apply while an interim management order[1] is in force in relation to a house[2]. The following rights and powers conferred[3] on a local housing authority[4] are exercisable by the authority in performing its duties[5] in respect of the house[6]. The authority:

(1)   has the right to possession of the house (subject to the rights of existing occupiers[7]);

(2)   has the right to do (and authorise a manager or other person to do) in relation to the house anything which a person having an estate or interest in the house[8] would (but for the order) be entitled to do;

(3)   may create one or more of the following: (a) an interest in the house which, as far as possible, has all the incidents of a leasehold[9]; or (b) a right in the nature of a licence[10] to occupy part of the house[11].

The authority: (i) does not under these provisions acquire any estate or interest in the house[12]; and (ii) accordingly is not entitled by virtue of such provisions to sell, lease[13], charge or make any other disposition of any such estate or interest[14]; but, where the immediate landlord[15] of the house or part of it is a lessee under a lease of the house or part, the authority is to be treated (subject to head (i)) as if it were the lessee instead[16]. Any enactment[17] or rule of law relating to landlords and tenants or leases applies in relation to a lease in relation to which the authority is to be treated as the lessee[18], or a lease to which the authority becomes a party[19], as if the authority were the legal owner of the premises[20].

Neither the authority nor any person authorised by it[21] is liable to any person having an estate or interest in the house for anything done or omitted to be done in the performance (or intended performance) of the authority's duties[22] unless the act or omission is due to the negligence of the authority or any such person[23].

References in any enactment to housing accommodation provided or managed by a local housing authority do not include a house in relation to which an interim management order is in force[24].

An interim management order which has come into force is a local land charge[25], and the authority may apply to the Chief Land Registrar for the entry of an appropriate restriction in the register of title in respect of such an order[26].

1   As to the meaning of 'interim management order' see PARA 745. As to the making of such an order see PARA 746.
2   Housing Act 2004 s 107(1). As to when an interim management order is in force see PARA 748.
3   Ie by the Housing Act 2004 s 107(3): see the text and note 11.
4   As to the meaning of 'local housing authority' see PARA 380 note 1.
5   Ie under the Housing Act 2004 s 106(1)–(3): see PARA 749.
6   Housing Act 2004 s 107(2); and see PARA 745 note 1. As to the meaning of 'the house' see PARA 745 note 8.
7   Ie rights preserved by the Housing Act 2004 s 124(3): see PARA 774. As to the meaning of 'occupier' see PARA 563 note 13.
8   As to the meaning of 'person having an estate or interest' see PARA 391 note 7.
9   See LANDLORD AND TENANT vol 62 (2016) PARA 1 et seq; REAL PROPERTY AND REGISTRATION vol 87 (2012) PARA 75 et seq.
10 As to the meaning of 'licence' see PARA 391 note 6.
11 Housing Act 2004 s 107(3). The authority may not, however, under s 107(3)(c) (see head (3) in the text) create any interest or right in the nature of a lease or licence unless consent in writing has been given by the person who (but for the order) would have power to create the lease or licence in question: s 107(4). In relation to any interest or right created by the authority under s 107(3)(c),

for the purposes of any enactment or rule of law: (1) any interest created by the authority under s 107(3)(c)(i) (see head (3)(a) in the text) is to be treated as if it were a legal lease; and (2) any right created by the authority under s 107(3)(c)(ii) (see head (3)(b) in the text) is to be treated as if it were a licence to occupy granted by the legal owner of the premises, despite the fact that the authority has no legal estate in the premises (see s 107(5)(a); and head (i) in the text): s 108(1), (2). For these purposes, 'enactment' has the meaning given by s 107(11) (see note 17): s 108(7). 'Legal lease' means a term of years absolute (ie within the Law of Property Act 1925 s 1(1)(b): see REAL PROPERTY AND REGISTRATION vol 87 (2012) PARA 76): Housing Act 2004 s 108(7).

Any enactment or rule of law relating to landlords and tenants or leases accordingly applies in relation to any interest created by the authority under s 107(3)(c)(i) as if the authority were the legal owner of the premises: s 108(3). References to leases and licences in Pt 4 Ch 1 (ss 101–131) and in any other enactment accordingly include (where the context permits) interests and rights created by the authority under s 107(3)(c): s 108(4). The provisions of s 108(1)–(4) have effect subject to s 124(7)–(9) (see PARA 774), and subject to any provision to the contrary contained in an order made by the appropriate national authority: s 108(5). As to the meaning of 'the appropriate national authority' see PARA 389 note 1.

12 Housing Act 2004 s 107(5)(a).
13 The reference in the Housing Act 2004 s 107(5)(b) to leasing does not include the creation of interests under s 107(3)(c)(i) (see head (3)(a) in the text and note 11): s 108(6).
14 Housing Act 2004 s 107(5)(b).
15 Ie within the meaning of the Housing Act 2004 s 109: see PARA 751.
16 Housing Act 2004 s 107(5). The appropriate national authority may by regulations make such provision as it considers appropriate for supplementing the provisions of Pt 4 Ch 1 in relation to cases where a local housing authority is to be treated as the lessee under a lease under s 107(5): s 145(1). Such regulations may, in particular, make provision: (1) as respects rights and liabilities in such cases of: (a) the authority; (b) the person who (apart from s 107(5)) is the lessee under the lease; or (c) other persons having an estate or interest in the premises demised under the lease; (2) requiring the authority to give copies to the person mentioned in head (1)(b) of notices and other documents served on it in connection with the lease; (3) for treating things done by or in relation to the authority as done by or in relation to that person, or vice versa: s 145(2). As to the regulations that have been made see the Housing (Management Orders and Empty Dwelling Management Orders) (Supplemental Provisions) (England) Regulations 2006, SI 2006/368; and the Housing (Management Orders and Empty Dwelling Management Orders) (Supplemental Provisions) (Wales) Regulations 2006, SI 2006/2822.
17 For these purposes, 'enactment' includes an enactment comprised in subordinate legislation (within the meaning of the Interpretation Act 1978: see STATUTES AND LEGISLATIVE PROCESS vol 96 (2012) PARA 609): Housing Act 2004 s 107(11).
18 Ie under the Housing Act 2004 s 107(5): see the text and notes 12–16.
19 Ie under the Housing Act 2004 s 124(4): see PARA 774 text to note 8.
20 Housing Act 2004 s 107(6). This is subject, however, to s 124(7)–(9): see PARA 774.
21 Ie under the Housing Act 2004 s 107(3)(b): see head (2) in the text.
22 Ie under the Housing Act 2004 s 106(1)–(3): see PARA 749.
23 Housing Act 2004 s 107(7).
24 Housing Act 2004 s 107(8).
25 Housing Act 2004 s 107(9). As to local land charges see REAL PROPERTY AND REGISTRATION vol 87 (2012) PARA 763 et seq.
26 Housing Act 2004 s 107(10). As to the Chief Land Registrar see REAL PROPERTY AND REGISTRATION vol 87 (2012) PARA 562.

751. Effect of interim management orders on immediate landlords, mortgagees and others. The following provisions apply in relation to immediate landlords[1] and other persons with an estate or interest[2] in the house, while an interim management order is in force in relation to a house[3].

A person who is an immediate landlord of the house or a part of it:

(1)   is not entitled to receive any rents or other payments from persons occupying the house or part which are payable to the local housing authority[4], or any rents or other payments from persons occupying the house or part which are payable to the authority by virtue of any leases or licences granted by it[5];

(2)   may not exercise any rights or powers with respect to the management of the house or part; and

(3)   may not create any leasehold interest in the house or part (other than a lease of a reversion[6]) or any licence[7] or other right to occupy it[8].

However (subject to head (3)) nothing in the relevant statutory provisions[9] affects the ability of a person having an estate or interest in the house to make any disposition of that estate or interest[10]. Nothing in those provisions affects: (a) the validity of any mortgage relating to the house or any rights or remedies available to the mortgagee under such a mortgage[11]; or (b) the validity of any lease of the house or part of it under which the immediate landlord is a lessee, or any superior lease, or any rights or remedies available to the lessor under such a lease[12], except to the extent that any of those rights or remedies would prevent the local housing authority from exercising its power[13] to create an interest or a right equivalent to a lease or a licence[14]. In proceedings for the enforcement of any such rights or remedies the court may make such order as it thinks fit as regards the operation of the interim management order (including an order quashing it)[15].

1   For the purposes of the Housing Act 2004 Pt 4 Ch 1 (ss 101–131), as it applies in relation to an interim management order, a person is an 'immediate landlord' of the house or a part of it if: (1) he is an owner or lessee of the house or part; and (2) but for the order, he would be entitled to receive the rents or other payments from persons occupying the house or part which are payable to the local housing authority by virtue of s 124(4) (see PARA 774): s 109(6). As to the meaning of 'interim management order' see PARA 745. As to the making and effect of such an order see PARA 746 et seq. As to the meaning of 'owner' see PARA 384 note 11. As to the meaning of 'lessee' see PARA 391 note 6. As to the meaning of 'the house' see PARA 745 note 8. As to the meaning of 'occupy' see PARA 563 note 13. As to the meaning of 'local housing authority' see PARA 380 note 1.
2   As to the meaning of 'person having an estate or interest' see PARA 391 note 7.
3   Housing Act 2004 s 109(1). As to when an interim management order is in force see PARA 748.
4   Ie by virtue of the Housing Act 2004 s 124(4) (under which the local housing authority is treated as the landlord): see PARA 774.
5   Ie under the Housing Act 2004 s 107(3)(c): see PARA 750 head (3).
6   As to a lease of a reversion see LANDLORD AND TENANT vol 62 (2016) PARA 98.
7   As to the meaning of 'licence' see PARA 391 note 6.
8   Housing Act 2004 s 109(2).
9   Ie the Housing Act 2004 s 107 (see PARA 750) or s 109.
10   Housing Act 2004 s 109(3).
11   See MORTGAGE vol 77 (2016) PARA 518 et seq. For the purposes of the Housing Act 2004 Pt 4 (ss 101–147), 'mortgage' includes a charge or lien; and 'mortgagee' is to be read accordingly: s 146(2).
12   Ie subject to the Housing Act 2004 s 107(5): see PARA 750.
13   Ie under the Housing Act 2004 s 107(3)(c): see PARA 750 head (3).
14   Housing Act 2004 s 109(4).
15   Housing Act 2004 s 109(5).

752. Financial arrangements while order is in force. The following provisions apply to relevant expenditure[1] of a local housing authority[2] which has made an interim management order[3]. Rent or other payments[4] which the authority has collected or recovered[5] from persons occupying[6] the house may be used by the authority to meet relevant expenditure and any amounts of compensation payable to a third party[7] by virtue of a decision[8] of the authority[9]. The authority must pay to such relevant landlord[10], or to such relevant landlords in such proportions, as it considers appropriate: (1) any amount of rent or other payments collected or recovered as mentioned above that remains after deductions to meet relevant expenditure and any amounts of compensation payable; and (2) where appropriate, interest on that amount at a reasonable rate fixed by the authority, and such payments are to be made at such intervals as the authority considers appropriate[11].

The authority must keep full accounts of its income and expenditure in respect of the house, and afford to each relevant landlord, and to any other person who has an estate or interest in the house, all reasonable facilities for inspecting, taking copies of and verifying those accounts[12].

A relevant landlord may apply to the appropriate tribunal[13] for an order: (a) declaring that an amount shown in the accounts as expenditure of the authority does not constitute expenditure reasonably incurred[14] by the authority; (b) requiring the authority to make such financial adjustments (in the accounts and otherwise) as are necessary to reflect the tribunal's declaration[15].

1 'Relevant expenditure' means expenditure reasonably incurred by the authority in connection with performing its functions under the Housing Act 2004 s 106(1)–(3) (see PARA 749) in respect of the house (including any premiums paid for insurance of the premises): s 110(2). 'Expenditure' includes administrative costs: s 110(8). As to the meaning of 'the house' see PARA 745 note 8.
2 As to the meaning of 'local housing authority' see PARA 380 note 1.
3 Housing Act 2004 s 110(1); and see PARA 745 note 1. As to the meaning of 'interim management order' see PARA 745. As to the making and effect of such an order see PARA 746 et seq.
4 'Rent or other payments' means rents or other payments payable under leases or licences or in respect of furniture within the Housing Act 2004 s 126(1) (see PARA 776): s 110(8).
5 Ie by virtue of the Housing Act 2004 Pt 4 Ch 1 (ss 101–131).
6 As to the meaning of 'occupy' see PARA 563 note 13.
7 For the purposes of the Housing Act 2004 Pt 4 Ch 1, 'third party', in relation to a house, means any person who has an estate or interest in the house (other than an immediate landlord and any person who is a tenant under a lease granted under s 107(3)(c) or s 116(3)(c) (see PARAS 750 head (3), 758 head (3))): s 101(7). As to the meaning of 'person having an estate or interest' see PARA 391 note 7. As to the meanings of 'landlord', 'tenant' and 'lease' see PARA 391 note 6.
8 Ie under the Housing Act 2004 s 128: see PARA 777.
9 Housing Act 2004 s 110(3).
10 'Relevant landlord' means any person who is an immediate landlord of the house or part of it (see PARA 751 note 1): Housing Act 2004 s 110(8).
11 Housing Act 2004 s 110(4) (amended, as from a day to be appointed, to provide that s 110(4) applies only if the interim management order is not made under s 102(7A), by the Housing and Planning Act 2016 s 26, Sch 3 paras 1, 5(1), (2); at the date at which this volume states the law, no such day had been appointed). The interim management order may provide for: (1) the rate of interest which is to apply for the purposes of the Housing Act 2004 s 110(4)(b); and (2) the intervals at which payments are to be made under s 110(4): s 110(5). Schedule 6 para 24(3) enables an appeal to be brought where the order does not provide for both of those matters: see s 110(5); and PARA 770. As from a day to be appointed, the Secretary of State may by regulations make provision about how local authorities are to deal with any surplus in a case where the interim management order was made under s 102(7A) (see PARA 746 head (iii)): s 110(5A) (s 110(5A), (5B) added, as from a day to be appointed, by the Housing and Planning Act 2016 Sch 3 paras 1, 5(1), (3); at the date at which this volume states the law, no such day had been appointed). For this purpose, 'surplus' means any amount of rent or other payments collected or recovered as mentioned in the Housing Act 2004 s 110(3) that remains after deductions to meet relevant expenditure and any amounts of compensation payable as mentioned in s 110(3): s 110(5B) (as so added).
12 Housing Act 2004 s 110(6).
13 As to the meaning of 'appropriate tribunal' see PARA 580 note 2. As to appeals to the appropriate tribunal see PARA 32 et seq.
14 Ie as mentioned in the Housing Act 2004 s 110(2): see note 1.
15 Housing Act 2004 s 110(7) (amended by SI 2013/1036).

B. VARIATION AND REVOCATION

753. Variation of order. The local housing authority[1] may vary an interim management order[2] if it considers it appropriate to do so[3]. A variation does not come into force until such time, if any, as is the operative time[4] for this purpose[5]. The power to vary an order is exercisable by the authority either on an application made by a relevant person (such as the owner)[6] or on the authority's own initiative[7].

1 As to the meaning of 'local housing authority' see PARA 380 note 1.
2 As to the meaning of 'interim management order' see PARA 745. As to the making and effect of such an order see PARA 746 et seq.

3 Housing Act 2004 s 111(1); and see PARA 745 note 1.
4 If no appeal is made under the Housing Act 2004 Sch 6 para 28 (see PARA 772) before the end of the period of 28 days mentioned in Sch 6 para 29(2) (see PARA 772), 'the operative time' for this purpose is the end of that period: s 123, Sch 6 para 31(1), (2). If an appeal is made under Sch 6 para 28 within that period, and a decision is given on the appeal which confirms the variation or revocation, 'the operative time' is as follows: (1) if the period within which an appeal to the Upper Tribunal may be brought expires without such an appeal having been brought, 'the operative time' is the end of that period; (2) if an appeal to the Upper Tribunal is brought, 'the operative time' is the time when a decision is given on the appeal which confirms the variation or revocation: Sch 6 para 31(3) (amended by SI 2009/1307). For this purpose, the withdrawal of an appeal has the same effect as a decision which confirms the variation or revocation appealed against; and references to a decision which confirms a variation are references to a decision which confirms it with or without variation: Housing Act 2004 Sch 6 para 31(4). As to appeals to the Upper Tribunal, ie the Upper Tribunal (Lands Chamber), the successor to the Lands Tribunal, see PARAS 49–50.
5 Housing Act 2004 s 111(2).
6 The relevant person may appeal against a refusal to vary the interim management order: see PARA 772. For this purpose, 'relevant person' means: (1) any person who has an estate or interest in the house or part of it (but is not a tenant under a lease with an unexpired term of three years or less); or (2) any other person who (but for the order) would be a person managing or having control of the house or part of it: Housing Act 2004 s 111(4). As to the meaning of 'person having an estate or interest' see PARA 391 note 7. As to the meaning of 'the house' see PARA 745 note 8. As to the meaning of 'tenant' see PARA 391 note 6; and as to references to a tenant under a lease with an unexpired term of three years or less see PARA 672 note 9. As to the meaning of 'person managing' see PARA 391 note 6; and as to the meaning of 'person having control' see PARA 391 note 5.
7 Housing Act 2004 s 111(3).

754. Revocation of order. The local housing authority[1] may revoke an interim management order[2] in the following cases[3]:

(1) if the order was made[4] in respect of a house which needs to be licensed[5] and the house[6] has ceased to be an HMO[7] to which Part 2 of the Housing Act 2004 applies or a Part 3 house[8] (as the case may be)[9];

(2) if the order was so made and a licence granted by the authority[10] in respect of the house is due to come into force under Part 2 or Part 3 on the revocation of the order[11];

(3) if a final management order[12] has been made by it in respect of the house so as to replace the order[13];

(4) if in any other circumstances the authority considers it appropriate to revoke the order[14].

Prospectively, an interim management order may not be revoked under these provisions if: (a) the immediate landlord is subject to a banning order under the Housing and Planning Act 2016[15]; (b) there is in force an agreement which[16] has effect as a lease or licence granted by the authority; and (c) revoking the interim management order would cause the immediate landlord to breach[17] the banning order[18].

A revocation does not come into force until such time, if any, as is the operative time[19] for this purpose[20]. The power to revoke an order under these provisions is exercisable by the authority either on an application made by a relevant person[21] or on the authority's own initiative[22].

1 As to the meaning of 'local housing authority' see PARA 380 note 1.
2 As to the meaning of 'interim management order' see PARA 745. As to the making and effect of such an order see PARA 746 et seq.
3 Housing Act 2004 s 112(1); and see PARA 745 note 1.
4 Ie under the Housing Act 2004 s 102(2) or (3): see PARA 746 heads (1), (2).
5 Ie under the Housing Act 2004 Pt 2 (ss 55–78) (see s 61(1); and PARA 679) or Pt 3 (ss 79–100) (see s 85(1); and PARA 709).
6 As to the meaning of 'the house' see PARA 745 note 8.
7 As to the meaning of 'HMO' see PARA 745 note 5.
8 As to the meaning of 'Part 3 house' see PARA 745 note 6.
9 Housing Act 2004 s 112(1)(a).

10 As to references to the grant of a licence see PARA 745 note 10.

11 Housing Act 2004 s 112(1)(b).

12 As to the meaning of 'final management order' see PARA 745.

13 Housing Act 2004 s 112(1)(c).

14 Housing Act 2004 s 112(1)(d).

15 Ie a banning order under the Housing and Planning Act 2016 s 16: see PARA 719 et seq.

16 Ie under the Housing Act 2004 s 108: see PARA 750.

17 Ie because of the effect of the Housing Act 2004 s 130(2)(b): see PARA 780.

18 Housing Act 2004 s 112(2A) (added, as from a day to be appointed, by the Housing and Planning Act 2016 s 26, Sch 3 paras 1, 6; at the date at which this volume states the law, no such day had been appointed).

19 Ie under the Housing Act 2004 Sch 6 para 31: see PARA 753 note 4.

20 Housing Act 2004 s 112(2).

21 For this purpose, 'relevant person' means: (1) any person who has an estate or interest in the house or part of it (but is not a tenant under a lease with an unexpired term of three years or less); or (2) any other person who (but for the order) would be a person managing or having control of the house or part of it: Housing Act 2004 s 112(4). As to the meaning of 'person having an estate or interest' see PARA 391 note 7. As to the meaning of 'tenant' see PARA 391 note 6; and as to references to a tenant under a lease with an unexpired term of three years or less see PARA 672 note 9. As to the meaning of 'person managing' see PARA 391 note 6; and as to the meaning of 'person having control' see PARA 391 note 5.

22 Housing Act 2004 s 112(3).

(iii) Final Management Orders

A. MAKING AND OPERATION

755. Making of final management orders. A local housing authority[1] which has made an interim management order[2] in respect of a house has a duty to make a final management order in respect of the house[3] in a case within heads (1) and (2)[4] below, and has power to make such an order in a case within heads (a) and (b)[5] below[6].

The authority must make a final management order[7] so as to replace the interim management order as from its expiry date[8] if:

(1)   on that date the house would be required to be licensed under Part 2 or Part 3 of the Housing Act 2004[9]; and

(2)   the authority considers that it is unable to grant a licence[10] under Part 2 or Part 3 in respect of the house that would replace the interim management order as from that date[11].

The authority may make a final management order so as to replace the interim management order as from its expiry date if:

(a)   on that date the house will not be one that would be required to be licensed as mentioned in head (1); and

(b)   the authority considers that making the final management order is necessary for the purpose of protecting, on a long-term basis, the health, safety or welfare of persons occupying[12] the house, or persons occupying or having an estate or interest[13] in any premises in the vicinity[14].

A local housing authority which has made a final management order in respect of a house under the provisions described above ('the existing order') has a duty to make a final management order in respect of the house in a case within heads (i) and (ii)[15] below, and has power to make such an order in a case within heads (A) and (B)[16] below[17].

The authority must make a new final management order so as to replace the existing order as from its expiry date if:

(i)   on that date the condition in head (1) will be satisfied in relation to the house; and

(ii)   the authority considers that it is unable to grant a licence under Part 2 or Part 3 in respect of the house that would replace the existing order as from that date[18].

The authority may make a new final management order so as to replace the existing order as from its expiry date if:

(A)   on that date the condition in head (a) will be satisfied in relation to the house; and

(B)   the authority considers that making the new order is necessary for the purpose of protecting, on a long-term basis, the health, safety or welfare of persons mentioned in head (b)[19].

As from a day to be appointed, a local housing authority which has made an interim management order in respect of any property let in breach of a banning order[20] may make a final management order so as to replace the interim management order as from its expiry date if the authority considers that making the final management order is necessary for the purpose of protecting, on a long-term basis, the health, safety or welfare of persons occupying the house, or persons occupying or having an estate or interest in any premises in the vicinity[21]. A local housing authority which has made a final management order in respect of a house let in breach of a banning order[22] ('the existing order') may make a new final management order so as to replace the existing order as from its expiry date if the authority considers that making the new order is necessary for the purpose of protecting, on a long-term basis, the health, safety or welfare of persons occupying the house, or persons occupying or having an estate or interest in any premises in the vicinity[23].

The authority may make a final management order which is expressed not to apply to a part of the house that is occupied by a person who has an estate or interest in the whole of the house[24].

1   As to the meaning of 'local housing authority' see PARA 380 note 1.
2   Ie under the Housing Act 2004 s 102 (prospectively, any provision of s 102 other than s 102(7A): see PARA 746. As to the meaning of 'interim management order' see PARA 745.
3   As to the meaning of 'the house' see PARA 745 note 8.
4   Ie in a case within the Housing Act 2004 s 113(2).
5   Ie in a case within the Housing Act 2004 s 113(3).
6   Housing Act 2004 s 113(1) (amended, as from a day to be appointed, by the Housing and Planning Act 2016 s 26, Sch 3 paras 1, 7(1), (2); at the date at which this volume states the law, no such day had been appointed); and see PARA 745 note 1.
7   As to the meaning of 'final management order' see PARA 745.
8   'Expiry date', in relation to an interim or final management order, means: (1) where the order is revoked (see PARAS 754, 763), the date as from which it is revoked; and (2) otherwise, the date on which the order ceases to have effect under the Housing Act 2004 s 105 (see PARA 748) or s 114 (see PARA 756), and nothing in s 113 applies in relation to an interim or final management order which has been revoked on an appeal under Sch 6 Pt 3 (paras 24–35) (see PARA 770 et seq): s 113(8).
9   Ie under the Housing Act 2004 Pt 2 (ss 55–78) (see s 61(1); and PARA 679) or Pt 3 (ss 79–100) (see s 85(1); and PARA 709).
10   As to references to the grant of a licence see PARA 745 note 10.
11   Housing Act 2004 s 113(2).
12   As to the meaning of 'occupy' see PARA 563 note 13.
13   As to the meaning of 'person having an estate or interest' see PARA 391 note 7.
14   Housing Act 2004 s 113(3).
15   Ie in a case within the Housing Act 2004 s 13(5).
16   Ie in a case within the Housing Act 2004 s 13(6).

17 Housing Act 2004 s 113(4). As from a day to be appointed, s 113(4) refers to a final management order under s 113(2), (3), (5) or (6): s 113(4) (amended, as from a day to be appointed, by the Housing and Planning Act 2016 Sch 3 paras 1, 7(1), (4); at the date at which this volume states the law, no such day had been appointed).

18 Housing Act 2004 s 113(5).

19 Housing Act 2004 s 113(6).

20 Ie under the Housing Act 2004 s 102(7A): see PARA 746. As to banning orders under the Housing and Planning Act 2016 s 16 see PARA 719 et seq.

21 Housing Act 2004 s 113(3A) (added, as from a day to be appointed, by the Housing and Planning Act 2016 Sch 3 paras 1, 7(1), (3); at the date at which this volume states the law, no such day had been appointed).

22 Ie under the Housing Act 2004 s 113(3A) or (6A).

23 Housing Act 2004 s 113(6A) (added, as from a day to be appointed, by the Housing and Planning Act 2016 Sch 3 paras 1, 7(1), (5); at the date at which this volume states the law, no such day had been appointed).

24 Housing Act 2004 s 113(7). In relation to such an order, a reference in Pt 4 Ch 1 (ss 101–131) to 'the house' does not include the part so excluded (unless the context requires otherwise, such as where the reference is to the house as an HMO or a Part 3 house): s 113(7). As to the meaning of 'HMO' see PARA 745 note 5; and as to the meaning of 'Part 3 house' see PARA 745 note 6.

756. Operation of final management orders. A final management order[1] does not come into force until such time (if any) as is the operative time (which allows, for example, for an appeal)[2] for this purpose[3]. The order ceases to have effect at the end of the period of five years beginning with the date on which it comes into force, unless it ceases to have effect at some other time as mentioned below[4]. If the order provides that it is to cease to have effect on a date falling before the end of that period, it accordingly ceases to have effect on that date[5].

Where a new final management order ('the new order') has been made so as to replace an order ('the existing order'), but the new order has not come into force because of an appeal to the appropriate tribunal[6] against the making of that order, then if: (1) the house[7] would (but for the existing order being in force) be required to be licensed under Part 2 or Part 3 of the Housing Act 2004[8]; and (2) the date on which the new order, or any licence under Part 2 or Part 3, or a temporary exemption notice[9] comes into force in relation to the house (or part of it) following the disposal of the appeal is later than the date on which the existing order would cease to have effect apart from this provision, the existing order continues in force until that later date[10]. If, on the application of the authority, the tribunal makes an order providing for the existing order to continue in force, pending the disposal of the appeal, until a date later than that on which it would cease to have effect apart from this provision, the existing order accordingly continues in force until that later date[11].

These provisions have effect subject to the provisions as to variation or revocation of orders[12] and subject to the power of revocation exercisable by the appropriate tribunal on an appeal made[13] to it[14].

1 As to the meaning of 'final management order' see PARA 745. As to the making of such an order see PARA 755.

2 If no appeal is made under the Housing Act 2004 Sch 6 para 24 (see PARA 770) before the end of the period of 28 days mentioned in Sch 6 para 25(2) (see PARA 770), 'the operative time' for this purpose is the end of that period: s 123, Sch 6 para 27(1), (2). If an appeal is made under Sch 6 para 24 before the end of that period, and a decision is given on the appeal which confirms the order, 'the operative time' is as follows: (1) if the period within which an appeal to the Upper Tribunal may be brought expires without such an appeal having been brought, 'the operative time' is the end of that period; (2) if an appeal to the Upper Tribunal is brought, 'the operative time' is the time when a decision is given on the appeal which confirms the order: Sch 6 para 27(3) (amended by SI 2009/1307). For this purpose, the withdrawal of an appeal has the same effect as a decision which confirms the order; and references to a decision which confirms the order are references to a decision which confirms it with or without variation: Housing Act 2004 Sch 6 para 27(4). As to appeals to the Upper Tribunal, ie the Upper Tribunal (Lands Chamber), the successor to the Lands Tribunal, see PARAS 49–50.

3 Housing Act 2004 s 114(1), (2).
4 Housing Act 2004 s 114(3). As from a day to be appointed, an order under s 113(3A) or (6A) (see PARA 755 text to notes 21–23) ceases to have effect (if it has not already ceased to have effect) when the relevant ban on letting housing in England ceases to have effect: s 114(4A) (s 114(4A), (4B) added, as from a day to be appointed, by the Housing and Planning Act 2016 s 26, Sch 3 paras 1, 8(1), (2); at the date at which this volume states the law, no such day had been appointed). 'The relevant ban on letting housing in England' means the ban on letting contained in the banning order mentioned in the Housing Act 2004 s 102(7A) (see PARA 746): s 114(4B) (as so added).
5 Housing Act 2004 s 114(4).
6 Ie under the Housing Act 2004 Sch 6 para 24: see PARA 770. As to the meaning of 'appropriate tribunal' see PARA 580 note 2. As to appeals to the appropriate tribunal see PARA 32 et seq.
7 As to the meaning of 'the house' see PARA 745 note 8.
8 Ie under the Housing Act 2004 Pt 2 (ss 55–78) (see s 61(1); and PARA 679) or Pt 3 (ss 79–100) (see s 85(1); and PARA 709).
9 Ie under the Housing Act 2004 s 62 (see PARA 680) or s 86 (see PARA 710).
10 Housing Act 2004 s 114(5), (6) (s 114(5) amended by SI 2013/1036; and, as from a day to be appointed, by the Housing and Planning Act 2016 Sch 3 paras 1, 8(1), (3); at the date at which this volume states the law, no such day had been appointed). Prospectively, if: (1) the existing order was made under the Housing Act 2004 s 113(3A) or (6A); and (2) the date on which the new order comes into force in relation to the house (or part of it) following the disposal of the appeal is later than the date on which the existing order would cease to have effect apart from this provision, the existing order continues in force until that later date: s 114(6A) (added, as from a day to be appointed, by the Housing and Planning Act 2016 Sch 3 paras 1, 8(1), (4); at the date at which this volume states the law, no such day had been appointed).
11 Housing Act 2004 s 114(7).
12 Ie the Housing Act 2004 ss 121, 122: see PARAS 762–763.
13 Ie under the Housing Act 2004 Sch 6 para 24 or Sch 6 para 28: see PARAS 770, 772.
14 Housing Act 2004 s 114(8) (amended by SI 2013/1036).

757. Local housing authority's duties once a final management order is in force.
A local housing authority[1] which has made a final management order[2] in respect of a house must comply with the following provisions once the order has come into force[3]. The local housing authority must take such steps as it considers appropriate with a view to the proper management of the house[4] in accordance with the management scheme contained in the order[5]. The local housing authority must from time to time review the operation of the order and in particular the management scheme contained within it, and whether keeping the order in force in relation to the house (with or without making any variations[6]) is the best alternative available to it[7]. If on a review the authority considers that any variations should be made, it must proceed to make those variations[8]. If on a review the authority considers that either granting a licence under Part 2 or Part 3 of the Housing Act 2004[9] in respect of the house, or revoking the order[10] and taking no further action, is the best alternative available to it, the authority must grant such a licence or revoke the order (as the case may be)[11].

1 As to the meaning of 'local housing authority' see PARA 380 note 1.
2 As to the meaning of 'final management order' see PARA 745. As to the making of such an order see PARA 755.
3 Housing Act 2004 s 115(1); and see PARA 745 note 1.
4 As to the meaning of 'the house' see PARA 745 note 8.
5 Housing Act 2004 s 115(2). As to the management scheme see s 119; and PARA 760. For the avoidance of doubt, the authority's duty under s 115(2) includes taking such steps as are necessary to ensure that, while the order is in force, reasonable provision is made for insurance of the house against destruction or damage by fire or other causes: s 115(6).
6 Ie under the Housing Act 2004 s 121: see PARA 762.
7 Housing Act 2004 s 115(3).
8 Housing Act 2004 s 115(4).
9 Ie under the Housing Act 2004 Pt 2 (ss 55–78) (see s 61(1); and PARA 679) or Pt 3 (ss 79–100) (see s 85(1); and PARA 709).
10 Ie under the Housing Act 2004 s 122: see PARA 763.
11 Housing Act 2004 s 115(5).

758. General effect of final management orders. While a final management order[1] is in force[2] in relation to a house, the following rights and powers are exercisable by the local housing authority[3] in performing its duty to ensure proper management[4] in respect of the house[5]. The authority:

(1)   has the right to possession of the house (subject to the rights of existing and other occupiers[6]);

(2)   has the right to do (and authorise a manager or other person to do) in relation to the house anything which a person having an estate or interest in the house[7] would (but for the order) be entitled to do;

(3)   may create one or more of the following: (a) an interest in the house which, as far as possible, has all the incidents of a leasehold[8]; or (b) a right in the nature of a licence[9] to occupy part of the house[10].

The authority does not under these provisions: (i) acquire any estate or interest in the house[11]; and (ii) accordingly is not entitled by virtue of such provisions to sell, lease[12], charge or make any other disposition of any such estate or interest[13]. However, where the immediate landlord of the house or part of it[14] is a lessee under a lease of the house or part, the authority is to be treated (subject to head (i)) as if it were the lessee instead[15].

Any enactment[16] or rule of law relating to landlords and tenants or leases applies in relation to a lease in relation to which the authority is to be treated as the lessee[17], or a lease to which the authority becomes a party[18], as if the authority were the legal owner of the premises[19].

Neither the authority, nor any person authorised by it[20], is liable to any person having an estate or interest in the house for anything done or omitted to be done in the performance (or intended performance) of the authority's duty as to the proper management of the house unless the act or omission is due to the negligence of the authority or any such person[21].

References in any enactment to housing accommodation provided or managed by a local housing authority do not include a house in relation to which a final management order is in force[22].

A final management order which has come into force is a local land charge[23], and the authority may apply to the Chief Land Registrar for the entry of an appropriate restriction in the register in respect of such an order where the title to the property is registered[24].

1   As to the meaning of 'final management order' see PARA 745. As to the making of such an order see PARA 755.
2   As to when a final management order is in force see PARA 756.
3   As to the meaning of 'local housing authority' see PARA 380 note 1.
4   Ie under the Housing Act 2004 s 115(2): see PARA 757.
5   Housing Act 2004 s 116(1), (2); and see PARA 745 note 1. As to the meaning of 'the house' see PARA 745 note 8.
6   Ie rights preserved by the Housing Act 2004 s 124(3), (6): see PARA 774. As to the meaning of 'occupier' see PARA 563 note 13.
7   As to the meaning of 'person having an estate or interest' see PARA 391 note 7.
8   See LANDLORD AND TENANT vol 62 (2016) PARA 1 et seq; REAL PROPERTY AND REGISTRATION vol 87 (2012) PARA 75 et seq.
9   As to the meaning of 'licence' see PARA 391 note 6.
10 Housing Act 2004 s 116(3). The powers of the authority under s 116(3)(c) (see head (3) in the text) are restricted as follows: (1) it may not create any interest or right in the nature of a lease or licence which is for a fixed term expiring after the date on which the management order is due to expire, or (subject to head (2)) which is terminable by notice to quit, or an equivalent notice, of more than four weeks, unless consent in writing has been given by the person who would (but for the order) have power to create the lease or licence in question; (2) it may create an interest in the nature of an assured shorthold tenancy without any such consent so long as it is created before the beginning of the period of six months that ends with the date on which the order is due to expire: s 116(4).

As to the meaning of 'lease' see PARA 391 note 6. As to assured shorthold tenancies see LANDLORD AND TENANT vol 63 (2016) PARA 852 et seq.

In relation to any interest or right created by the authority under s 116(3)(c), for the purposes of any enactment or rule of law: (a) any interest created by the authority under s 116(3)(c)(i) (see head (3)(a) in the text) is to be treated as if it were a legal lease; and (b) any right created by the authority under s 116(3)(c)(ii) (see head (3)(b) in the text) is to be treated as if it were a licence to occupy granted by the legal owner of the premises, despite the fact that the authority has no legal estate in the premises (see s 116(5)(a); and head (i) in the text): s 117(1), (2). For these purposes, 'enactment' has the meaning given by s 116(11) (see note 16); and 'legal lease' means a term of years absolute (ie within the Law of Property Act 1925 s 1(1)(b): see REAL PROPERTY AND REGISTRATION vol 87 (2012) PARA 76): Housing Act 2004 s 117(7). Any enactment or rule of law relating to landlords and tenants or leases accordingly applies in relation to any interest created by the authority under s 116(3)(c)(i) as if the authority were the legal owner of the premises: s 117(3). References to leases and licences in Pt 4 Ch 1 (ss 101–131) and in any other enactment accordingly include (where the context permits) interests and rights created by the authority under s 116(3)(c): s 117(4). The provisions of s 117(1)–(4) have effect subject to s 124(7)–(9) (see PARA 774), and subject to any provision to the contrary contained in an order made by the appropriate national authority: s 117(5). As to the meaning of 'the appropriate national authority' see PARA 389 note 1.

11 Housing Act 2004 s 116(5)(a).

12 In the Housing Act 2004 s 116(5)(b) (see head (ii) in the text), the reference to leasing does not include the creation of interests under s 116(3)(c)(i) (see head (3)(a) in the text and note 10): s 117(6).

13 Housing Act 2004 s 116(5)(b).

14 Ie within the meaning of the Housing Act 2004 s 118: see PARA 759.

15 Housing Act 2004 s 116(5). The appropriate national authority may by regulations make such provision as it considers appropriate for supplementing the provisions of Pt 4 Ch 1 in relation to cases where a local housing authority is to be treated as the lessee under a lease under s 116(5): s 145(1). Such regulations may, in particular, make provision: (1) as respects rights and liabilities in such cases of: (a) the authority; (b) the person who (apart from s 116(5)) is the lessee under the lease; or (c) other persons having an estate or interest in the premises demised under the lease; (2) requiring the authority to give copies to the person mentioned in head (1)(b) of notices and other documents served on it in connection with the lease; (3) for treating things done by or in relation to the authority as done by or in relation to that person, or vice versa: s 145(2). As to the regulations that have been made see the Housing (Management Orders and Empty Dwelling Management Orders) (Supplemental Provisions) (England) Regulations 2006, SI 2006/368; and the Housing (Management Orders and Empty Dwelling Management Orders) (Supplemental Provisions) (Wales) Regulations 2006, SI 2006/2822.

16 For these purposes, 'enactment' includes an enactment comprised in subordinate legislation (within the meaning of the Interpretation Act 1978: see STATUTES AND LEGISLATIVE PROCESS vol 96 (2012) PARA 609): Housing Act 2004 s 116(11).

17 Ie under the Housing Act 2004 s 116(5): see the text and notes 11–15.

18 Ie under the Housing Act 2004 s 124(4): see PARA 774.

19 Housing Act 2004 s 116(6). This is, however, subject to s 124(7)–(9): see PARA 774.

20 Ie under the Housing Act 2004 s 116(3)(b): see head (2) in the text.

21 Housing Act 2004 s 116(7).

22 Housing Act 2004 s 116(8).

23 Housing Act 2004 s 116(9). As to local land charges see REAL PROPERTY AND REGISTRATION vol 87 (2012) PARA 763 et seq.

24 Housing Act 2004 s 116(10). As to the Chief Land Registrar see REAL PROPERTY AND REGISTRATION vol 87 (2012) PARA 562.

759. Effect of final management orders on immediate landlords, mortgagees and others. The following provisions apply in relation to immediate landlords[1], and to other persons with an estate or interest[2] in the house, while a final management order[3] is in force in relation to a house[4].

A person who is an immediate landlord of the house or a part of it:

(1)   is not entitled to receive any rents or other payments from persons occupying[5] the house or part which are payable to the local housing authority[6], or any rents or other payments from persons occupying the house or part which are payable to the authority by virtue of any leases or licences granted by it[7];

(2) may not exercise any rights or powers with respect to the management of the house or part; and

(3) may not create any leasehold interest in the house or part (other than a lease of a reversion), or any licence[8] or other right to occupy it[9].

However (subject to head (3)) nothing in the relevant statutory provisions[10] affects the ability of a person having an estate or interest in the house to make any disposition of that estate or interest[11]. Nothing in those provisions affects: (a) the validity of any mortgage relating to the house or any rights or remedies available to the mortgagee under such a mortgage[12]; or (b) the validity of any lease of the house or part of it under which the immediate landlord is a lessee, or any superior lease, or any rights or remedies available to the lessor under such a lease[13], except to the extent that any of those rights or remedies would prevent the local housing authority from exercising its power[14] to create an interest or a right equivalent to a lease or a licence[15].

In proceedings for the enforcement of any such rights or remedies the court may make such order as it thinks fit as regards the operation of the final management order (including an order quashing it)[16].

1 For the purposes of the Housing Act 2004 Pt 4 Ch 1 (ss 101–131), as it applies in relation to a final management order, a person is an 'immediate landlord' of the house or a part of it if: (1) he is an owner or lessee of the house or part; and (2) but for the order, he would be entitled to receive the rents or other payments from persons occupying the house or part which are payable to the local housing authority by virtue of s 124(4) (see PARA 774): s 118(6). As to the meaning of 'the house' see PARA 745 note 8. As to the meaning of 'owner' see PARA 384 note 11; and as to the meaning of 'lessee' see PARA 391 note 6. As to the meaning of 'local housing authority' see PARA 380 note 1.

2 As to the meaning of 'person having an estate or interest' see PARA 391 note 7.

3 As to the meaning of 'final management order' see PARA 745. As to the making of such an order see PARA 755.

4 Housing Act 2004 s 118(1). As to when a final management order is in force see PARA 756.

5 As to the meaning of 'occupy' see PARA 563 note 13.

6 Ie by virtue of the Housing Act 2004 s 124(4): see PARA 774.

7 Ie under the Housing Act 2004 s 107(3)(c) (see PARA 750 head (3)) or s 116(3)(c) (see PARA 758 head (3)).

8 As to the meaning of 'licence' see PARA 391 note 6.

9 Housing Act 2004 s 118(2).

10 Ie the Housing Act 2004 s 116 (see PARA 758) or s 118.

11 Housing Act 2004 s 118(3).

12 See MORTGAGE vol 77 (2016) PARA 518 et seq. As to the meaning of 'mortgage' see PARA 751 note 11.

13 Ie subject to the Housing Act 2004 s 116(5): see PARA 758 text to notes 11-13.

14 Ie under the Housing Act 2004 s 116(3)(c): see PARA 758 head (3).

15 Housing Act 2004 s 118(4).

16 Housing Act 2004 s 118(5).

760. Management schemes and accounts. A final management order[1] must contain a management scheme[2]. A 'management scheme' is a scheme setting out how the local housing authority[3] is to carry out its duty[4] as respects the management of the house[5]. A management scheme is to be divided into two parts[6].

Part 1 must contain a plan giving details of the way in which the authority proposes to manage the house[7], which must (in particular) include:

(1) details of any works that the authority intends to carry out in connection with the house;

(2) an estimate of the capital and other expenditure to be incurred by the authority in respect of the house while the order is in force;

(3) the amount of rent or other payments[8] that the authority will seek to obtain having regard to the condition or expected condition of the house at any time while the order is in force;

(4)   the amount of any compensation that is payable to a third party[9] by virtue of a decision of the authority[10] in respect of any interference in consequence of the final management order with the rights of that person;

(5)   provision as to the payment of any such compensation;

(6)   provision as to the payment by the authority to a relevant landlord[11], from time to time, of amounts of rent or other payments that remain after the deduction of:

(a)   relevant expenditure[12]; and

(b)   any amounts of compensation payable as mentioned in head (4);

(7)   provision as to the manner in which the authority is to pay to a relevant landlord, on the termination of the final management order, any amounts of rent or other payments that remain after the deduction of:

(a)   relevant expenditure; and

(b)   any amounts of compensation payable as mentioned in head (4);

(8)   provision as to the manner in which the authority is to pay, on the termination of the final management order, any outstanding balance of compensation payable to a third party[13].

Part 1 may also state:

(i)   the authority's intentions as regards the use of rent or other payments to meet relevant expenditure;

(ii)   the authority's intentions as regards the payment to a relevant landlord (where appropriate) of interest on amounts within heads (6) and (7);

(iii)   that statutory provisions as to payment on termination of the agreement[14] are not to apply in relation to an interim or (as the case may be) final management order that immediately preceded the final management order, and that instead the authority intends to use any balance or amount such as is mentioned in those provisions to meet relevant expenditure incurred during the currency of the final management order, and any compensation that may become payable to a third party;

(iv)   that statutory provisions as to recovery of sums on termination of the agreement[15] are not to apply in relation to an interim or (as the case may be) final management order that immediately preceded the final management order, and that instead the authority intends to use rent or other payments collected during the currency of the order to reimburse the authority in respect of any deficit or amount such as is mentioned in those provisions;

(v)   the authority's intentions as regards the recovery from a relevant landlord, with or without interest, of any amount of relevant expenditure that cannot be reimbursed out of the total amount of rent or other payments[16].

Part 2 must describe in general terms how the authority intends to address the matters which caused it to make the final management order and may, for example, include:

(A)   descriptions of any steps that the authority intends to take to require persons occupying[17] the house to comply with their obligations under any lease or licence[18] or under the general law;

(B)   descriptions of any repairs that are needed to the property and an explanation as to why those repairs are necessary[19].

The authority must keep full accounts of its income and expenditure in respect of the house, and afford to each relevant landlord, and to any other person who has an estate or interest[20] in the house, all reasonable facilities for inspecting, taking copies of and verifying those accounts[21].

1 As to the meaning of 'final management order' see PARA 745. As to the making of such an order see PARA 755.
2 Housing Act 2004 s 119(1). In the provisions of Pt 4 Ch 1 (ss 101–131) relating to varying, revoking or appealing against decisions relating to a final management order, any reference to such an order includes (where the context permits) a reference to the management scheme contained in it: s 119(9).
3 As to the meaning of 'local housing authority' see PARA 380 note 1.
4 Ie under the Housing Act 2004 s 115(2): see PARA 757.
5 Housing Act 2004 s 119(2); and see PARA 745 note 1.
6 Housing Act 2004 s 119(3).
7 As to the meaning of 'the house' see PARA 745 note 8.
8 'Rent or other payments' means rent or other payments which are payable under leases or licences or in respect of furniture within the Housing Act 2004 s 126(1) (see PARA 776) and which the authority has collected or recovered by virtue of Pt 4 Ch 1: s 119(8).
9 As to the meaning of 'third party' see PARA 752 note 7.
10 Ie under the Housing Act 2004 s 128: see PARA 777.
11 'Relevant landlord' means any person who is an immediate landlord of the house or part of it (see PARA 759 note 1): Housing Act 2004 s 119(8).
12 'Relevant expenditure' means expenditure reasonably incurred by the authority in connection with performing its duties under the Housing Act 2004 s 115(2) in respect of the house (including any reasonable administrative costs and any premiums paid for insurance of the premises): s 119(8).
13 Housing Act 2004 s 119(4). Prospectively, s 119(4)(f), (g) (see heads (6), (7) in the text) does not apply in a case where the final management order was made under s 113(3A) or (6A) (see PARA 755 text to notes 21–23): s 119(4A) (s 119(4A)–(4C) added, as from a day to be appointed, by the Housing and Planning Act 2016 s 26, Sch 3 paras 1, 9; at the date at which this volume states the law, no such day had been appointed). The Secretary of State may by regulations make provision about how local authorities are to deal with any surplus in a case where the final management order was made under the Housing Act 2004 s 113(3A) or (6A): s 119(4B) (as so added). In s 119(4B) 'surplus' means any amount of rent or other payments that the authority has collected or recovered, by virtue of Pt 4 Ch 1, that remains after deductions to meet relevant expenditure and any amounts of compensation payable as mentioned in s 119(4)(d) (see head (4) in the text): s 119(4C) (as so added).
14 Ie the Housing Act 2004 s 129(2) or (4): see PARA 779.
15 Ie the Housing Act 2004 s 129(3) or (5): see PARA 779.
16 Housing Act 2004 s 119(5).
17 As to the meaning of 'occupy' see PARA 563 note 13.
18 As to the meanings of 'lease' and 'licence' see PARA 391 note 6.
19 Housing Act 2004 s 119(6).
20 As to the meaning of 'person having an estate or interest' see PARA 391 note 7.
21 Housing Act 2004 s 119(7).

761. Enforcement of management scheme by relevant landlord. An affected person[1] may apply to the appropriate tribunal[2] for an order requiring the local housing authority to manage the whole or part of a house in accordance with the management scheme[3] contained in a final management order[4] made in respect of the house[5]. On such an application the tribunal may, if it considers it appropriate to do so, make an order: (1) requiring the local housing authority to manage the whole or part of the house in accordance with the management scheme; or (2) revoking the final management order as from a date specified in the tribunal's order[6]. Such an order may: (a) specify the steps which the authority is to take to manage the whole or part of the house in accordance with the management scheme; (b) include provision varying the final management order; (c) require the payment of money to an affected person by way of damages[7].

1 'Affected person' means: (1) a relevant landlord (within the meaning of the Housing Act 2004 s 119: see PARA 760 note 11); and (2) any third party to whom compensation is payable by virtue

of a decision of the local housing authority under s 128 (see PARA 777): s 120(4). As to the meaning of 'third party' see PARA 752 note 7. As to the meaning of 'local housing authority' see PARA 380 note 1.

2   As to the meaning of 'appropriate tribunal' see PARA 580 note 2. As to appeals to the appropriate tribunal see PARA 32 et seq.

3   As to the contents of management schemes see PARA 760.

4   As to the meaning of 'final management order' see PARA 745. As to the making of such an order see PARA 755.

5   Housing Act 2004 s 120(1) (amended by SI 2013/1036). As to the meaning of 'the house' see PARA 745 note 8.

6   Housing Act 2004 s 120(2).

7   Housing Act 2004 s 120(3).

B.   VARIATION AND REVOCATION OF A FINAL MANAGEMENT ORDER

762. Variation of order. The local housing authority[1] may vary a final management order[2] if it considers it appropriate to do so[3]. A variation does not come into force until such time, if any, as is the operative time[4] for this purpose[5]. The power to vary an order under these provisions is exercisable by the authority either on an application made by a relevant person[6] or on the authority's own initiative[7].

1   As to the meaning of 'local housing authority' see PARA 380 note 1.

2   As to the meaning of 'final management order' see PARA 745; and see PARA 760 note 2. As to the making of such an order see PARA 755.

3   Housing Act 2004 s 121(1); and see PARA 745 note 1.

4   Ie under the Housing Act 2004 Sch 6 para 31: see PARA 753 note 4.

5   Housing Act 2004 s 121(2).

6   If the local housing authority refuses to vary the order, the relevant person may bring an appeal: see PARA 772. For this purpose, 'relevant person' means: (1) any person who has an estate or interest in the house or part of it (but is not a tenant under a lease with an unexpired term of three years or less); or (2) any other person who (but for the order) would be a person managing or having control of the house or part of it: Housing Act 2004 s 121(4). As to the meaning of 'person having an estate or interest' see PARA 391 note 7. As to the meaning of 'tenant' see PARA 391 note 6; and as to references to a tenant under a lease with an unexpired term of three years or less see PARA 672 note 9. As to the meaning of 'person managing' see PARA 391 note 6; and as to the meaning of 'person having control' see PARA 391 note 5.

7   Housing Act 2004 s 121(3).

763. Revocation of order. The local housing authority[1] may revoke a final management order[2] in the following cases[3]:

(1)   if the order was made[4] in respect of a house requiring to be licensed[5] and the house[6] has ceased to be an HMO[7] to which Part 2 of the Housing Act 2004 applies or a Part 3 house[8] (as the case may be)[9];

(2)   if the order was so made and a licence granted[10] by the authority in respect of the house is due to come into force under Part 2 or Part 3 as from the revocation of the order[11];

(3)   if a further final management order has been made by it in respect of the house so as to replace the order[12];

(4)   if in any other circumstances the authority considers it appropriate to revoke the order[13].

Prospectively, a final management order may not be revoked under these provisions at a time when: (a) the immediate landlord is subject to a banning order under the Housing and Planning Act 2016[14]; (b) there is in force an agreement which[15] has effect as a lease or licence granted by the authority; and (3) revoking the final management order would cause the immediate landlord to breach[16] the banning order[17].

A revocation does not come into force until such time, if any, as is the operative time[18] for this purpose[19]. The power to revoke an order under these provisions is exercisable by the authority either on an application made by a relevant person[20] or on the authority's own initiative[21].

1 As to the meaning of 'local housing authority' see PARA 380 note 1.
2 As to the meaning of 'final management order' see PARA 745; and see PARA 760 note 2. As to the making of such an order see PARA 755.
3 Housing Act 2004 s 122(1); and see PARA 745 note 1.
4 Ie under the Housing Act 2004 s 113(2) or (5): see PARA 755.
5 Ie under the Housing Act 2004 Pt 2 (ss 55–78) (see s 61(1); and PARA 679) or Pt 3 (ss 79–100) (see s 85(1); and PARA 709).
6 As to the meaning of 'the house' see PARA 745 note 8.
7 As to the meaning of 'HMO' see PARA 745 note 5.
8 As to the meaning of 'Part 3 house' see PARA 745 note 6.
9 Housing Act 2004 s 122(1)(a).
10 As to references to the grant of a licence see PARA 745 note 10.
11 Housing Act 2004 s 122(1)(b).
12 Housing Act 2004 s 122(1)(c).
13 Housing Act 2004 s 122(1)(d).
14 Ie a banning order under the Housing and Planning Act 2016 s 16: see PARA 719 et seq.
15 Ie under the Housing Act 2004 s 117: see PARA 758 note 10.
16 Ie because of the effect of the Housing Act 2004 s 130(2)(b): see PARA 780.
17 Housing Act 2004 s 122(2A) (added, as from a day to be appointed, by the Housing and Planning Act 2016 s 26, Sch 3 paras 1, 10; at the date at which this volume states the law, no such day had been appointed).
18 Ie under the Housing Act 2004 Sch 6 para 31: see PARA 753 note 4.
19 Housing Act 2004 s 122(2).
20 If the local housing authority refuses to revoke the order, the relevant person may bring an appeal: see PARA 772. For this purpose, 'relevant person' means: (1) any person who has an estate or interest in the house or part of it (but is not a tenant under a lease with an unexpired term of three years or less); or (2) any other person who (but for the order) would be a person managing or having control of the house or part of it: Housing Act 2004 s 122(4). As to the meaning of 'person having an estate or interest' see PARA 391 note 7. As to the meaning of 'tenant' see PARA 391 note 6; and as to references to a tenant under a lease with an unexpired term of three years or less see PARA 672 note 9. As to the meaning of 'person managing' see PARA 391 note 6; and as to the meaning of 'person having control' see PARA 391 note 5.
21 Housing Act 2004 s 122(3).

(iv) Procedure and Appeals

A. PROCEDURE RELATING TO MAKING OF MANAGEMENT ORDERS

764. Requirements before making final management order. Before making a final management order[1], the local housing authority[2] must serve[3] a copy of the proposed order, together with a notice in the following terms, on each relevant person[4], and consider any representations made in accordance with the notice and not withdrawn[5]. The notice must state that the authority is proposing to make a final management order and set out:

(1)   the reasons for making the order;
(2)   the main terms of the proposed order (including those of the management scheme[6] to be contained in it); and
(3)   the end of the consultation period[7].

If, having considered representations made in accordance with such a notice or a notice in the following terms, the local housing authority proposes to make a final management order with modifications, the authority must, before making the order, serve a notice on each relevant person and consider any representations made in accordance with the notice and which are not withdrawn[8]. The notice must set out:

(a)　　the proposed modifications;

(b)　　the reasons for them; and

(c)　　the end of the consultation period[9].

1　As to the meaning of 'local housing authority' see PARA 380 note 1.

2　As to the meaning of 'final management order' see PARA 745. As to the making of such an order see PARA 755.

3　As to service of documents see PARA 391.

4　In the Housing Act 2004 Sch 6 Pt 1 (paras 1–8), 'relevant person' means any person who, to the knowledge of the local housing authority, is: (1) a person having an estate or interest in the house or part of it (but who is not a tenant under a lease with an unexpired term of three years or less); or (2) any other person who (but for the order) would be a person managing or having control of the house or part of it: s 123, Sch 6 para 8(4). As to the meaning of 'person having an estate or interest' see PARA 391 note 7. As to the meaning of 'the house' see PARA 745 note 8. As to the meaning of 'tenant' see PARA 391 note 6; and as to references to a tenant under a lease with an unexpired term of three years or less see PARA 672 note 9. As to the meaning of 'person managing' see PARA 391 note 6; and as to the meaning of 'person having control' see PARA 391 note 5.

5　Housing Act 2004 Sch 6 para 1; and see PARA 745 note 1. See also note 8.

6　As to management schemes see PARA 760.

7　Housing Act 2004 Sch 6 para 2. For the purposes of Sch 6 Pt 1, 'the end of the consultation period' means the last day for making representations in respect of the matter in question: Sch 6 para 8(1). The end of the consultation period must be: (1) in the case of a notice under Sch 6 para 1, a day which is at least 14 days after the date of service of the notice; and (2) in the case of a notice under Sch 6 para 3, a day which is at least seven days after the date of service of the notice: Sch 6 para 8(2). For this purpose, 'the date of service' of a notice means, in a case where more than one notice is served, the date on which the last of the notices is served: Sch 6 para 8(3).

8　Housing Act 2004 Sch 6 para 3(1), (2). The requirements of Sch 6 para 3 (and those of Sch 6 para 1: see the text and note 5) do not apply if the local housing authority has already served notice under Sch 6 para 1 but not under Sch 6 para 3 in relation to the proposed final management order, and considers that the modifications which are now being proposed are not material in any respect: Sch 6 para 5. Nor do the requirements of Sch 6 para 3 (and those of Sch 6 para 1) apply if the local housing authority has already served notices under Sch 6 paras 1, 3 in relation to the matter concerned, and considers that the further modifications which are now being proposed do not differ in any material respect from the modifications in relation to which a notice was last served under Sch 6 para 3: Sch 6 para 6.

9　Housing Act 2004 Sch 6 para 4. See note 7.

765.　Requirements following making of an interim or a final management order. Where the local housing authority[1] makes an interim management order[2] or a final management order[3], the authority must, as soon as practicable after the order is made, serve on the occupiers[4] of the house[5] a copy of the order, and a notice in the following terms[6]. The notice must set out:

(1)　　the reasons for making the order and the date on which it was made;

(2)　　the general effect of the order; and

(3)　　the date on which the order is to cease to have effect[7],

and (if it is a final management order) give a general description of the way in which the house is to be managed by the authority in accordance with the management scheme contained in the order[8].

The authority must also serve a copy of the order, together with a notice in the following terms, on each relevant person[9]. The notice must comply with the requirements above and also contain information about: (a) the right of appeal against the order[10]; and (b) the period within which any such appeal may be made[11].

1　As to the meaning of 'local housing authority' see PARA 380 note 1.

2　As to the meaning of 'interim management order' see PARA 745. As to the making of such an order see PARA 746.

3   As to the meaning of 'final management order' see PARA 745. As to the making of such an order see PARA 755.

4   As to the meaning of 'occupier' see PARA 563 note 13.

5   As to the meaning of 'the house' see PARA 745 note 8.

6   Housing Act 2004 s 123, Sch 6 para 7(1), (2); and see PARA 745 note 1. Those documents are to be regarded as having been served on the occupiers if they are fixed to a conspicuous part of the house: Sch 6 para 7(3). As to service of documents under the Housing Act 2004 generally see PARA 391.

7   Ie in accordance with the Housing Act 2004 s 105(4), (5) (see PARA 748) or s 114(3), (4) (prospectively, s 105(4), (5) or (7A) or s 114(3), (4) or (4A)) (see PARA 756) (or, if applicable, setting out how the date mentioned in s 105(6) (see PARA 748 text to note 7) is to be determined).

8   Housing Act 2004 Sch 6 para 7(4) (amended, as from a day to be appointed, by the Housing and Planning Act 2016 s 26, Sch 3 paras 1, 12(1), (2); at the date at which this volume states the law, no such day had been appointed). As to management schemes see PARA 760.

9   Housing Act 2004 Sch 6 para 7(5). The documents required to be served on each relevant person under Sch 6 para 7(5) must be served within the period of seven days beginning with the day on which the order is made: Sch 6 para 7(7). As to the meaning of 'relevant person' see PARA 764 note 4.

10 Ie under the Housing Act 2004 Sch 6 Pt 3 (paras 24–35): see PARA 770 et seq.

11 Housing Act 2004 Sch 6 para 7(6). As to the period within which an appeal may be made see Sch 6 para 25(2); and PARA 770.

B.   PROCEDURE RELATING TO VARIATION OR REVOCATION

766. Variation of management orders. Before varying an interim or final management order[1], the local housing authority[2] must serve[3] a notice in the following terms on each relevant person[4], and consider any representations made in accordance with the notice and which are not withdrawn[5]. The notice must state that the authority is proposing to make the variation and specify:

(1)   the effect of the variation;

(2)   the reasons for the variation; and

(3)   the end of the consultation period[6].

Where the local housing authority decides to vary an interim or final management order, it must serve on each relevant person, within the period of seven days beginning with the day on which the decision is made[7]:

(a)   a copy of the authority's decision to vary the order; and

(b)   a notice setting out:

(i)   the reasons for the decision and the date on which it was made;

(ii)   the right of appeal against the decision[8]; and

(iii) the period within which an appeal may be made[9].

1   As to the meaning of 'interim management order' see PARA 745; and as to the variation of such an order see PARA 753. As to the meaning of 'final management order' see PARA 745; and as to the variation of such an order see PARA 762.

2   As to the meaning of 'local housing authority' see PARA 380 note 1.

3   As to service of documents under the Housing Act 2004 see PARA 391.

4   For the purposes of the Housing Act 2004 Sch 6 Pt 2 (paras 9–23), 'relevant person' means any person who, to the knowledge of the local housing authority, is: (1) a person having an estate or interest in the house or part of it (but who is not a tenant under a lease with an unexpired term of three years or less); or (2) any other person who (but for the order) would be a person managing or having control of the house or part of it: s 123, Sch 6 para 23(4). As to the meaning of 'person having an estate or interest' see PARA 391 note 7. As to the meaning of 'the house' see PARA 745 note 8. As to the meaning of 'tenant' see PARA 391 note 6; and as to references to a tenant under a lease with an unexpired term of three years or less see PARA 672 note 9. As to the meaning of 'person managing' see PARA 391 note 6; and as to the meaning of 'person having control' see PARA 391 note 5.

5   Housing Act 2004 Sch 6 para 9; and see PARA 745 note 1. The requirements of Sch 6 para 9 do not apply: (1) if the local housing authority considers that the variation is not material (Sch 6 para 12); or (2) if the local housing authority has already served a notice under that provision in relation to a proposed variation and considers that the variation which is now being proposed is not materially different from the previous proposed variation (Sch 6 para 13).

6	Housing Act 2004 Sch 6 para 10. For the purposes of Sch 6 Pt 2, 'the end of the consultation period' means the last day for making representations in respect of the matter in question: Sch 6 para 23(1). The end of the consultation period must be a day which is at least 14 days after the date of service of the notice: Sch 6 para 23(2). For this purpose, 'the date of service' of a notice means, in a case where more than one notice is served, the date on which the last of the notices is served: Sch 6 para 23(3).
7	See the Housing Act 2004 Sch 6 para 11(3).
8	Ie under the Housing Act 2004 Sch 6 Pt 3 (paras 24–35): see PARA 770 et seq.
9	Housing Act 2004 Sch 6 para 11(1), (2). As to the period within which an appeal may be made see Sch 6 para 29(2); and PARA 772.

767. Refusal to vary a management order. Before refusing to vary an interim or final management order[1], the local housing authority[2] must serve[3] a notice in the following terms on each relevant person[4], and consider any representations made in accordance with the notice and not withdrawn[5]. The notice must state that the authority is proposing to refuse vary the order, and set out:

(1)	the reasons for refusing to make the variation; and
(2)	the end of the consultation period[6].

Where the local housing authority refuses to vary an interim or final management order, it must serve on each relevant person, within the period of seven days beginning with the day on which the decision is made[7], a notice setting out:

(a)	the authority's decision not to vary the order;
(b)	the reasons for the decision and the date on which it was made;
(c)	the right of appeal against the decision[8]; and
(d)	the period within which an appeal may be made[9].

1	As to the meaning of 'interim management order' see PARA 745; and as to the variation of such an order see PARA 753. As to the meaning of 'final management order' see PARA 745; and as to the variation of such an order see PARA 762.
2	As to the meaning of 'local housing authority' see PARA 380 note 1.
3	As to service of documents under the Housing Act 2004 see PARA 391.
4	As to the meaning of 'relevant person' see PARA 766 note 4.
5	Housing Act 2004 s 123, Sch 6 para 14; and see PARA 745 note 1.
6	Housing Act 2004 Sch 6 para 15. As to the meaning of 'the end of the consultation period' see PARA 766 note 6.
7	See the Housing Act 2004 Sch 6 para 16(3).
8	Ie under the Housing Act 2004 Sch 6 Pt 3 (paras 24–35): see PARA 770 et seq.
9	Housing Act 2004 Sch 16 para 16(1), (2). As to the period within which an appeal may be made see Sch 6 para 29(2); and PARA 772.

768. Revocation of management orders. Before revoking an interim or final management order[1], the local housing authority[2] must serve[3] a notice in the following terms on each relevant person[4], and consider any representations made in accordance with the notice and not withdrawn[5]. The notice must state that the authority is proposing to revoke the order and specify:

(1)	the reasons for the revocation; and
(2)	the end of the consultation period[6].

Where the authority decides to revoke an interim or final management order, it must, within the period of seven days beginning with the day on which the decision is made[7], serve on each relevant person:

(a)	a copy of the authority's decision to revoke the order; and
(b)	a notice setting out:
	(i)	the reasons for the decision and the date on which it was made;
	(ii)	the right of appeal against the decision[8]; and

(iii)   the period within which an appeal may be made[9].

1   As to the meaning of 'interim management order' see PARA 745; and as to the revocation of such
     an order see PARA 754. As to the meaning of 'final management order' see PARA 745; and as to
     the revocation of such an order see PARA 763.
2   As to the meaning of 'local housing authority' see PARA 380 note 1.
3   As to service of documents under the Housing Act 2004 see PARA 391.
4   As to the meaning of 'relevant person' see PARA 766 note 4.
5   Housing Act 2004 s 123, Sch 6 para 17; and see PARA 745 note 1.
6   Housing Act 2004 Sch 6 para 18. As to the meaning of 'the end of the consultation period' see
     PARA 766 note 6.
7   See the Housing Act 2004 Sch 6 para 19(3).
8   Ie under the Housing Act 2004 Sch 6 Pt 3 (paras 24–35): see PARA 770 et seq.
9   Housing Act 2004 Sch 16 para 19(1), (2). As to the period within which an appeal may be made
     see Sch 6 para 29(2); and PARA 772.

769. Refusal to revoke a management order. Before refusing to revoke an
interim or final management order[1], the local housing authority[2] must serve[3] a
notice in the following terms on each relevant person[4] and consider any
representations made in accordance with the notice and not withdrawn[5]. The
notice must state that the authority is proposing to refuse to revoke the order and
set out:

(1)   the reasons for refusing to revoke the order; and
(2)   the end of the consultation period[6].

Where the local housing authority refuses to revoke an interim or a final
management order, it must, within the period of seven days beginning with the
day on which the decision is made[7], serve[8] on each relevant person a notice setting
out:

(a)   the authority's decision not to revoke the order;
(b)   the reasons for the decision and the date on which it was made;
(c)   the right of appeal against the decision[9]; and
(d)   the period within which an appeal may be made[10].

1   As to the meaning of 'interim management order' see PARA 745; and as to the revocation of such
     an order see PARA 754. As to the meaning of 'final management order' see PARA 745; and as to
     the revocation of such an order see PARA 763.
2   As to the meaning of 'local housing authority' see PARA 380 note 1.
3   As to service of documents under the Housing Act 2004 see PARA 391.
4   As to the meaning of 'relevant person' see PARA 766 note 4.
5   Housing Act 2004 s 123, Sch 6 para 20; and see PARA 745 note 1.
6   Housing Act 2004 Sch 6 para 21.
7   See the Housing Act 2004 Sch 6 para 22(3).
8   As to service of documents under the Housing Act 2004 see PARA 391.
9   Ie under the Housing Act 2004 Sch 6 Pt 3 (paras 24–35): see PARA 770 et seq.
10   Housing Act 2004 Sch 6 para 22(1), (2). As to the period within which an appeal may be made see
     Sch 6 para 29(2); and PARA 772.

C.   APPEALS AGAINST DECISIONS RELATING TO MANAGEMENT ORDERS

770. Right to appeal against making of order etc. A relevant person[1] may appeal
to the appropriate tribunal[2] against: (1) a decision of the local housing authority[3]
to make an interim or final management order[4]; or (2) the terms of such an
order (including, if it is a final management order, those relating to the
management scheme[5] contained in it)[6].

An appeal may be made under head (2) on the grounds that the terms of an
interim management order do not provide[7], in relation to payments of surplus rent
and interest on such payments, for one or both of the rate of interest which is to
apply and the intervals at which payments are to be made[8]. Where an appeal is
made only on those grounds, the appeal may be brought at any time while the

order is in force[9]; and the powers of the appropriate tribunal[10] are limited to determining whether the order should be varied by the tribunal so as to include a term providing for the matter or matters in question, and (if so) what provision should be made by that term[11].

An appeal in respect of the making or terms of an interim or final management order must usually be made within the period of 28 days beginning with the date specified in the notice served on each relevant person[12] as the date on which the order was made[13]. The appropriate tribunal may, however, allow an appeal to be made to it after the end of the period mentioned above if it is satisfied that there is a good reason for the failure to appeal before the end of that period (and for any delay since then in applying for permission to appeal out of time)[14].

If no appeal is brought against an interim or final management order under these provisions within the time allowed[15] for making such an appeal, the order is final and conclusive as to the matters which could have been raised on appeal[16].

1   In the Housing Act 2004 Sch 6 Pt 3 (paras 24–35), 'relevant person' means: (1) any person who has an estate or interest in the house or part of it (but is not a tenant under a lease with an unexpired term of three years or less); or (2) any other person who (but for the order) would be a person managing or having control of the house or part of it: s 123, Sch 6 para 35. As to the meaning of 'person having an estate or interest' see PARA 391 note 7. As to the meaning of 'the house' see PARA 745 note 8. As to the meaning of 'tenant' see PARA 391 note 6; and as to references to a tenant under a lease with an unexpired term of three years or less see PARA 672 note 9. As to the meaning of 'person managing' see PARA 391 note 6; and as to the meaning of 'person having control' see PARA 391 note 5.
2   As to the meaning of 'appropriate tribunal' see PARA 580 note 2. As to appeals to the appropriate tribunal see PARA 32 et seq.
3   As to the meaning of 'local housing authority' see PARA 380 note 1.
4   As to the meaning of 'interim management order' see PARA 745; and as to the making of such an order see PARA 746. As to the meaning of 'final management order' see PARA 745; and as to the making of such an order see PARA 755.
5   As to management schemes see PARA 760.
6   Housing Act 2004 Sch 6 para 24(1) (amended by SI 2013/1036). Except to the extent that an appeal may be made in accordance with the Housing Act 2004 Sch 6 para 24(3), (4) (see the text and notes 7–11), Sch 6 para 24(1) does not apply to an interim management order made under s 102(4) or (7) (see PARA 746 heads (i), (ii)) or in accordance with a direction given under Sch 6 para 26(5) (see PARA 771): Sch 6 para 24(2).
7   Ie in accordance with the Housing Act 2004 s 110(5)(a), (b): see PARA 752 note 11.
8   Housing Act 2004 Sch 6 para 24(3).
9   Ie with the result that nothing in the Housing Act 2004 Sch 6 para 24(5) (see the text and note 16) or Sch 6 para 25 (see the text to notes 12–14) applies in relation to the appeal: Sch 6 para 24(4)(a). As to when an interim management order is in force see PARA 748; and as to when a final management order is in force see PARA 756.
10 Ie under the Housing Act 2004 Sch 6 para 26: see PARA 771.
11 Housing Act 2004 Sch 6 para 24(4) (amended by SI 2013/1036).
12 Ie under the Housing Act 2004 Sch 6 para 7(5): see PARA 765.
13 Housing Act 2004 Sch 6 para 25(1), (2).
14 Housing Act 2004 Sch 6 para 25(3) (amended by SI 2013/1036).
15 Ie by the Housing Act 2004 Sch 6 para 25: see the text and notes 12–14.
16 Housing Act 2004 Sch 6 para 24(5).

771. Powers of tribunal on appeal against order. An appeal[1] to the appropriate tribunal[2] against the making or terms of an interim or final management order[3] by a local housing authority[4] is to be by way of a re-hearing, and it may be determined having regard to matters of which the authority was unaware when it made its decision[5]. The tribunal may confirm or vary the order or revoke it:

(1)   in the case of an interim management order, as from a date specified in the tribunal's order; or

(2)   in the case of a final management order, as from the date of the
       tribunal's order[6]. Prospectively, an interim management order may not
       be revoked under these provisions if:
       (a)   the immediate landlord is subject to a banning order under the
              Housing and Planning Act[7];
       (b)   there is in force an agreement which[8] has effect as a lease or
              licence granted by the authority; and
       (c)   revoking the interim management order specified in the
              order would cause the immediate landlord to breach[9] the
              banning order[10].
   If:
   (i)   the tribunal revokes an interim or a final management order;
   (ii)   it appears to the tribunal that, on the revocation of the order, the house
          will be required to be licensed under Part 2 or Part 3 of the Housing Act
          2004[11]; and
   (iii) the tribunal does not give a direction as mentioned below[12],
the tribunal must direct the local housing authority to grant such a licence to such
person and on such terms as the tribunal may direct[13].

If the tribunal revokes a final management order, the tribunal may direct the
local housing authority to make an interim management order in respect of the
house[14] or part of it on such terms as the tribunal may direct[15]. If the tribunal
revokes a final management order, the tribunal may direct the local housing
authority to serve a temporary exemption notice[16] in respect of the house that
comes into force on such date as the tribunal directs[17].

The revocation of an interim management order by the tribunal does not affect
the validity of anything previously done in pursuance of the order[18].

1   Ie under the Housing Act 2004 Sch 6 para 24: see PARA 770.
2   As to the meaning of 'appropriate tribunal' see PARA 580 note 2. As to appeals to the appropriate
    tribunal see PARA 32 et seq.
3   As to the meaning of 'interim management order' see PARA 745; and as to the making of such an
    order see PARA 746. As to the meaning of 'final management order' see PARA 745; and as to the
    making of such an order see PARA 755.
4   As to the meaning of 'local housing authority' see PARA 380 note 1.
5   Housing Act 2004 s 123, Sch 6 para 26(1), (2) (Sch 6 para 26(1) amended by SI 2013/1036).
6   Housing Act 2004 Sch 6 para 26(3).
7   Ie under the Housing and Planning Act 2016 s 16: see PARA 719 et seq.
8   Ie under the Housing Act 2004 s 108: see PARA 750.
9   Ie because of the effect of the Housing Act 2004 s 130(2)(b): see PARA 780.
10 Housing Act 2004 Sch 6 para 26(4A) (Sch 6 para 26(4A), (4B) added, as from a day to be
    appointed, by the Housing and Planning Act 2016 s 26, Sch 3 paras 1, 12(1), (3); at the date at
    which this volume states the law, no such day had been appointed). In a case where the Housing
    Act 2004 Sch 6 para 26(4A) would otherwise prevent the tribunal from revoking the order with
    effect from a particular date, the tribunal may require the local housing authority to exercise any
    power it has to bring an agreement mentioned in that provision to an end: Sch 6 para 26(4B) (as
    so added).
11 Ie under the Housing Act 2004 Pt 2 (ss 55–78) (see s 61(1); and PARA 679) or Pt 3 (ss 79–100) (see
    s 85(1); and PARA 709).
12 Ie under the Housing Act 2004 Sch 6 para 26(5) (see the text and note 15) or Sch 6 para 26(6) (see
    the text and note 13).
13 Housing Act 2004 Sch 6 para 26(4).
14 As to the meaning of 'the house' see PARA 745 note 8.
15 Housing Act 2004 Sch 6 para 26(5). This applies despite s 102(9) (see PARA 746): Sch 6
    para 26(5).
16 Ie under the Housing Act 2004 s 62 (see PARA 680) or s 86 (see PARA 710). As to service of
    documents under the Housing Act 2004 see PARA 391.
17 Housing Act 2004 Sch 6 para 26(6).
18 Housing Act 2004 Sch 6 para 26(7).

772. Appeal in relation to variation or revocation of interim or final management orders. A relevant person[1] may appeal to the appropriate tribunal[2] against: (1) a decision of a local housing authority[3] to vary or revoke an interim or final management order[4]; or (2) a refusal of a local housing authority to vary or revoke an interim or final management order[5]. Any such appeal must be made before the end of the period of 28 days beginning with the date specified in the notice of the decision[6] as the date on which the decision concerned was made[7]. The appropriate tribunal may allow an appeal to be made to it after the end of the period mentioned above if it is satisfied that there is a good reason for the failure to appeal before the end of that period (and for any delay since then in applying for permission to appeal out of time)[8].

Such an appeal is to be by way of a re-hearing, and may be determined having regard to matters of which the authority was unaware when it made the decision[9]. The tribunal may confirm, reverse or vary the decision of the local housing authority[10]. If the appeal is against a decision of the authority to refuse to revoke the order, the tribunal may make an order revoking the order as from a date specified in its order[11].

1   As to the meaning of 'relevant person' see PARA 770 note 1.
2   As to the meaning of 'appropriate tribunal' see PARA 580 note 2. As to appeals to the appropriate tribunal see PARA 32 et seq.
3   As to the meaning of 'local housing authority' see PARA 380 note 1.
4   As to the meaning of 'interim management order' see PARA 745; and as to the revocation or variation of such an order see PARAS 753–754. As to the meaning of 'final management order' see PARA 745; and as to the revocation or variation of such an order see PARAS 762–763.
5   Housing Act 2004 s 123, Sch 6 para 28 (amended by SI 2013/1036).
6   Ie under the Housing Act 2004 Sch 6 para 11, 16, 19 or 22: see PARAS 766–769.
7   Housing Act 2004 Sch 6 para 29(1), (2).
8   Housing Act 2004 Sch 6 para 29(3) (amended by SI 2013/1036).
9   Housing Act 2004 Sch 6 para 26(2) (applied by Sch 6 para 30(1), (2) (Sch 6 para 30(1) amended by SI 2013/1036)).
10 Housing Act 2004 Sch 6 para 30(3).
11 Housing Act 2004 Sch 6 para 30(4). Prospectively, in a case where s 112(2A) (see PARA 754) or s 122(2A) (see PARA 763) would otherwise prevent the tribunal from revoking the order with effect from a particular date, the tribunal may require the local housing authority to exercise any power it has to bring an agreement mentioned in that provision to an end: Sch 6 para 30(5) (added, as from a day to be appointed, by the Housing and Planning Act 2016 s 26, Sch 3 paras 1, 12(1), (4); at the date at which this volume states the law, no such day had been appointed).

773. Appeal against decision in respect of compensation payable to third parties. Where a local housing authority[1] has made a decision[2] as to whether compensation should be paid to a third party in respect of any interference with his rights in consequence of an interim or final management order[3], the third party may appeal to the appropriate tribunal[4] against: (1) a decision by the authority not to pay compensation to him; or (2) a decision of the authority so far as relating to the amount of compensation that should be paid[5].

Any such appeal must be made within the period of 28 days beginning with the date the authority notifies[6] the third party of its decision[7]. The appropriate tribunal may allow an appeal to be made to it after the end of the period mentioned above if it is satisfied that there is good reason for the failure to appeal before the end of that period (and for any delay since then in applying for permission to appeal out of time)[8].

The appeal is to be by way of re-hearing, and may be determined having regard to matters of which the authority was unaware when it took the decision[9]. The tribunal may confirm, reverse or vary the decision of the local housing authority[10]. Where the tribunal reverses or varies a decision of the authority in respect of a final management order, it must make an order varying the management scheme contained in the final management order accordingly[11].

1 As to the meaning of 'local housing authority' see PARA 380 note 1.
2 Ie under the Housing Act 2004 s 128: see PARA 777.
3 As to the meaning of 'interim management order' see PARA 745; and as to the making of such an order see PARA 746. As to the meaning of 'final management order' see PARA 745; and as to the making of such an order see PARA 755.
4 As to the meaning of 'appropriate tribunal' see PARA 580 note 2. As to appeals to the appropriate tribunal see PARA 32 et seq.
5 Housing Act 2004 s 123, Sch 6 para 32(1), (2) (Sch 6 para 32(2) amended by SI 2013/1036).
6 Ie under the Housing Act 2004 s 128(2): see PARA 777.
7 Housing Act 2004 Sch 6 para 33(1), (2).
8 Housing Act 2004 Sch 6 para 33(3) (amended by SI 2013/1036).
9 Housing Act 2004 Sch 6 para 34(1), (2).
10 Housing Act 2004 Sch 6 para 34(3).
11 Housing Act 2004 Sch 6 para 34(4). As to management schemes see PARA 760.

(v) Effect of Interim and Final Management Orders

774. Effect on occupiers. The following provisions apply to both existing and new occupiers[1] of a house in relation to which an interim or final management order[2] is in force[3]. The statutory provisions as to the rights and powers of the local housing authority[4] while an order is in force do not affect the rights or liabilities of an existing occupier under a lease or licence[5] (whether in writing or not) under which he is occupying the whole or part of the house[6] at the commencement date[7].

Where the lessor or licensor under such a lease or licence has an estate or interest in the house, and is not an existing occupier, the lease or licence has effect while the order is in force as if the local housing authority was substituted in it for the lessor or licensor[8]. Such a lease continues to have effect, as far as possible, as a lease despite the fact that the rights of the local housing authority, as substituted for the lessor, do not amount to an estate in law in the premises[9].

The statutory provisions as to the rights and powers of a local authority under a final management order[10] do not affect the rights or liabilities of a new occupier who, in the case of a final management order, is occupying the whole or part of the house at the time when the order comes into force[11].

The statutory provisions which exclude local authority lettings from the Rent Acts[12] and from Part I[13] of the Housing Act 1988[14] do not apply to a lease or agreement under which an existing or new occupier is occupying the whole or part of the house[15] (so the occupier could, for example, be an assured shorthold tenant).

Nothing in the statutory provisions as to management orders[16] has the result that the local authority is to be treated as the legal owner of any premises for the purposes of such statutory provisions as to the landlord condition for secure tenancies[17] or as to introductory tenancies[18]. If, immediately before the coming into force of an interim or final management order, an existing occupier was occupying the whole or part of the house under a protected or statutory tenancy[19], or an assured tenancy or an assured agricultural occupancy[20], nothing in those provisions prevents the continuance of that tenancy or occupancy or affects the continued operation of any other Acts in relation to the tenancy or occupancy after the coming into force of the order (although the local authority is treated as the landlord)[21].

1 As to the meaning of 'occupier' see PARA 563 note 13. For these purposes, 'existing occupier' means a person who, at the time when the order comes into force, either: (1) in the case of an HMO or a Part 3 house, is occupying part of the house and does not have an estate or interest in

the whole of the house; or (2) in the case of a Part 3 house, is occupying the whole of the house, but is not a new occupier within the Housing Act 2004 s 124(6) (see the text to notes 10–11); and 'new occupier' means a person who, at a time when the order is in force, is occupying the whole or part of the house under a lease or licence granted under s 107(3)(c) (see PARA 750 head (3)) or s 116(3)(c) (see PARA 758 head (3)): s 124(2). As to the meaning of 'HMO' see PARA 745 note 5; and as to the meaning of 'Part 3 house' see PARA 745 note 6. As to the meaning of 'person having an estate or interest' see PARA 391 note 7.

2   As to the meaning of 'interim management order' see PARA 745; and as to the making of such an order see PARA 746. As to the meaning of 'final management order' see PARA 745; and as to the making of such an order see PARA 755.

3   Housing Act 2004 s 124(1). As to when an interim management order is in force see PARA 748; and as to when a final management order is in force see PARA 756.

4   Ie the Housing Act 2004 ss 107, 116: see PARAS 750, 758. As to the meaning of 'local housing authority' see PARA 380 note 1.

5   As to the meanings of 'lease' and 'licence' see PARA 391 note 6.

6   As to the meaning of 'the house' see PARA 745 note 8.

7   Housing Act 2004 s 124(3). For the purposes of s 124, 'the commencement date' means the date on which the order came into force (or, if that order was preceded by one or more orders under Pt 4 Ch 1 (ss 101–131), the date when the first order came into force): s 124(11).

8   Housing Act 2004 s 124(4).

9   Housing Act 2004 s 124(5). As to estates in law see REAL PROPERTY AND REGISTRATION vol 87 (2012) PARA 75 et seq.

10   Ie the Housing Act 2004 s 116: see PARA 758.

11   Housing Act 2004 s 124(6).

12   Ie the Rent Act 1977 ss 14–16 and those provisions as applied by the Rent (Agriculture) Act 1976 s 5(2)–(4), Sch 2: see AGRICULTURAL PRODUCTION AND MARKETING vol 1 (2008) PARA 1295; LANDLORD AND TENANT vol 63 (2016) PARA 706 et seq. As to the Rent Acts (ie the Rent Act 1977 and the Rent (Agriculture) Act 1976) see LANDLORD AND TENANT vol 63 (2016) PARAS 653 et seq, 940 et seq.

13   Ie the Housing Act 1988 Pt I (ss 1–45): see LANDLORD AND TENANT vol 63 (2016) PARA 825 et seq.

14   Ie the Housing Act 2004 s 1(2), Sch 1 para 12: see LANDLORD AND TENANT vol 63 (2016) PARA 847.

15   Housing Act 2004 s 124(7), (8).

16   Ie the Housing Act 2004 Pt 4 Ch 1 (ss 101–131).

17   Ie the Housing Act 1985 s 80: see LANDLORD AND TENANT vol 63 (2016) PARA 1037.

18   Housing Act 2004 s 124(9). As to introductory tenancies see the Housing Act 1996 s 124; PARA 472; and LANDLORD AND TENANT vol 63 (2016) PARA 1102 et seq.

19   Ie within the meaning of the Rent Act 1977 or the Rent (Agriculture) Act 1976: see LANDLORD AND TENANT vol 63 (2016) PARA 673 et seq.

20   Ie within the meaning of the Housing Act 1988 Pt I: see LANDLORD AND TENANT vol 64 (2016) PARA 1747. As to the meaning of 'assured tenancy' see LANDLORD AND TENANT vol 63 (2016) PARA 825.

21   Housing Act 2004 s 124(10).

775. Effect on agreements and legal proceedings. An agreement[1] or instrument which satisfies the following criteria has effect, while an interim or final management order is in force[2], as if any rights or liabilities of the immediate landlord[3] under the agreement or instrument were instead rights or liabilities of the local housing authority[4]. An agreement or instrument is within these provisions if:

(1)   it is effective on the commencement date[5];

(2)   one of the parties to it is a person who is the immediate landlord of the house[6] or a part of the house ('the relevant premises');

(3)   it relates to the house, whether in connection with any management activities[7] with respect to the relevant premises, or to the provision of any services or facilities for persons occupying[8] those premises, or otherwise;

(4)   it is specified for this purpose in the order or falls within a description of agreements or instruments so specified; and

(5)   the authority serves a notice in writing on all the parties to it stating that these provisions are to apply to it[9].

An agreement or instrument is not within these provisions if:

(a)   it is a lease under which the local authority is treated as the lessee[10]; or

(b)   it relates to any disposition by the immediate landlord which is not precluded by the statutory provisions[11] while the order is in force; or

(c)   it is one under which the local housing authority is treated as the lessor or licensor[12] in place of a lessor or licensor who is not an existing occupier[13].

Proceedings in respect of any cause of action to which the following provision applies may, while an interim or final management order is in force, be instituted or continued by or against the local housing authority instead of by or against the immediate landlord[14]. A cause of action is within this provision if:

(i)   it is a cause of action (of any nature) which accrued to or against the immediate landlord of the house (or a part of the house) before the commencement date;

(ii)   it relates to the house as mentioned in head (3);

(iii) it is specified for the purposes of this provision in the order or falls within a description of causes of action so specified; and

(iv)   the authority serves a notice in writing on all interested parties stating that this provision is to apply to it[15].

If, by virtue of these provisions, the authority becomes subject to any liability to pay damages in respect of anything done (or omitted to be done) before the commencement date by or on behalf of the immediate landlord of the house or a part of it, the immediate landlord is liable to reimburse to the authority an amount equal to the amount of the damages paid by it[16].

1   For this purpose, 'agreement' includes arrangement: Housing Act 2004 s 125(7).
2   As to the meaning of 'interim management order' see PARA 745; and as to the making of such an order see PARA 746. As to the meaning of 'final management order' see PARA 745; and as to the making of such an order see PARA 755. As to when an interim management order is in force see PARA 748; and as to when a final management order is in force see PARA 756.
3   As to the meaning of 'landlord' see PARA 391 note 6.
4   Housing Act 2004 s 125(1). As to the meaning of 'local housing authority' see PARA 380 note 1.
5   For this purpose, 'the commencement date' means the date on which the order comes into force (or, if that order was preceded by one or more orders under the Housing Act 2004 Pt 4 Ch 1 (ss 101–131), the date when the first order came into force): s 125(7).
6   As to the meaning of 'the house' see PARA 745 note 8.
7   'Management activities' includes repair, maintenance, improvement and insurance: Housing Act 2004 s 125(7).
8   As to the meaning of 'occupy' see PARA 563 note 13.
9   Housing Act 2004 s 125(2). As to service of documents under the Housing Act 2004 see PARA 391.
10 Ie it is a lease within the Housing Act 2004 s 107(5) (see PARA 750) or s 116(5) (see PARA 758). As to the meanings of 'lease' and 'lessee' see PARA 391 note 6.
11 Ie by the Housing Act 2004 s 109(2) (see PARA 751 heads (1)–(3)) or s 118(2) (see PARA 759 heads (1)–(3)).
12 Ie under the Housing Act 2004 s 124(4): see PARA 774. As to the meaning of 'licensor' see PARA 391 note 6.
13 Housing Act 2004 s 125(3).
14 Housing Act 2004 s 125(4).
15 Housing Act 2004 s 125(5).
16 Housing Act 2004 s 125(6).

776. Possession and supply of furniture. The following provisions apply where, on the date on which an interim or final management order comes into force[1], there is furniture[2] in the house[3] which a person occupying[4] the house has the right to use in consideration of periodical payments to a person who is an immediate landlord of the house or a part of it (whether the payments are included in the rent payable by the occupier or not)[5]. The right to possession of the furniture against all persons other than the occupier vests in the local housing authority[6] on that date and remains vested in the authority while the order is in force[7].

The local housing authority may renounce the right to possession of the furniture conferred on it by the legislation if: (1) an application in writing has been made to it for the purpose by the person owning the furniture; and (2) it renounces the right by notice in writing served on that person not less than two weeks before the notice takes effect[8].

If the authority's right to possession of furniture is a right exercisable against more than one person interested in the furniture, any of those persons may apply to the appropriate tribunal[9] for an adjustment of their respective rights and liabilities as regards the furniture[10]. On such an application the tribunal may make an order for such an adjustment of rights and liabilities, either unconditionally or subject to such terms and conditions, as it considers appropriate[11]. The terms and conditions may, in particular, include terms and conditions about the payment of money by a party to the proceedings to another party to the proceedings by way of compensation, damages or otherwise[12].

The local housing authority may supply the house to which an interim or final management order relates with such furniture[13] as it considers to be required[14].

For the purposes of the statutory provisions as to financial arrangements[15] or a management scheme[16], any expenditure incurred by the authority under this provision constitutes expenditure incurred by the authority in connection with performing its duty[17] as to proper management of the house[18].

1   As to the meaning of 'interim management order' see PARA 745; and as to the making of such an order see PARA 746. As to the meaning of 'final management order' see PARA 745; and as to the making of such an order see PARA 755. As to when an interim management order is in force see PARA 748; and as to when a final management order is in force see PARA 756.
2   For these purposes, 'furniture' includes fittings and other articles: Housing Act 2004 s 126(7).
3   As to the meaning of 'the house' see PARA 745 note 8.
4   As to the meaning of 'occupy' see PARA 563 note 13.
5   Housing Act 2004 s 126(1).
6   As to the meaning of 'local housing authority' see PARA 380 note 1.
7   Housing Act 2004 s 126(2).
8   Housing Act 2004 s 126(3). As to service of documents under the Housing Act 2004 see PARA 391.
9   As to the meaning of 'appropriate tribunal' see PARA 580 note 2. As to appeals to the appropriate tribunal see PARA 32 et seq.
10 Housing Act 2004 s 126(4) (amended by SI 2013/1036).
11 Housing Act 2004 s 126(5).
12 Housing Act 2004 s 126(6).
13 For this purpose, 'furniture' includes fittings and other articles: Housing Act 2004 s 127(3).
14 Housing Act 2004 s 127(1).
15 Ie the Housing Act 2004 s 110: see PARA 752.
16 Ie under the Housing Act 2004 s 119: see PARA 760.
17 Ie under the Housing Act 2004 s 106(3) (see PARA 749) or s 115(2) (see PARA 757).
18 Housing Act 2004 s 127(2).

777. Compensation payable to third parties. If a third party[1] requests it to do so at any time, the local housing authority[2] must consider whether an amount by way of compensation should be paid to him in respect of any interference with his rights in consequence of an interim or final management order[3]. The authority must notify the third party of its decision as soon as practicable[4]. Where the local housing authority decides that compensation ought to be paid to a third party in consequence of a final management order, it must vary the management scheme[5] contained in the order so as to specify the amount of the compensation to be paid and to make provision as to its payment[6].

1 As to the meaning of 'third party' see PARA 752 note 7.
2 As to the meaning of 'local housing authority' see PARA 380 note 1.
3 Housing Act 2004 s 128(1); and see PARA 745 note 1. As to the meaning of 'interim management order' see PARA 745; and as to the making of such an order see PARA 746. As to the meaning of 'final management order' see PARA 745; and as to the making of such an order see PARA 755.
4 Housing Act 2004 s 128(2).
5 As to management schemes see PARA 760.
6 Housing Act 2004 s 128(3).

778. Power of entry to carry out work. The following entry right is exercisable by the local housing authority[1], or any person authorised in writing by it, at any time when an interim or final management order[2] is in force[3]. That right is the right at all reasonable times to enter any part of the house[4] for the purpose of carrying out works, and is exercisable as against any person having an estate or interest[5] in the house[6]. Where part of a house is excluded from the provisions of an interim or final management order[7], the right is exercisable as respects that part so far as is reasonably required for the purpose of carrying out works in the part of the house which is subject to the order[8].

If, after receiving reasonable notice of the intended action, any occupier[9] of the whole or part of the house prevents any officer, employee, agent or contractor of the local housing authority from carrying out work in the house, a magistrates' court may order him to permit to be done on the premises anything which the authority considers to be necessary[10]. A person who fails to comply with such an order of the court commits an offence[11].

1 As to the meaning of 'local housing authority' see PARA 380 note 1.
2 As to the meaning of 'interim management order' see PARA 745; and as to the making of such an order see PARA 746. As to the meaning of 'final management order' see PARA 745; and as to the making of such an order see PARA 755.
3 Housing Act 2004 s 131(1); and see PARA 745 note 1. As to when an interim management order is in force see PARA 748; and as to when a final management order is in force see PARA 756.
4 As to the meaning of 'the house' see PARA 745 note 8.
5 As to the meaning of 'person having an estate or interest' see PARA 391 note 7.
6 Housing Act 2004 s 131(2).
7 Ie under the Housing Act 2004 s 102(8) (see PARA 746) or s 113(7) (see PARA 755).
8 Housing Act 2004 s 131(3).
9 As to the meaning of 'occupier' see PARA 563 note 13.
10 Housing Act 2004 s 131(4).
11 Housing Act 2004 s 131(5). A person who commits an offence under s 131(5) is liable on summary conviction to a fine not exceeding level 5 on the standard scale: s 131(6). As to the powers of magistrates' courts to issue fines on summary conviction see SENTENCING vol 92 (2015) PARA 176.

(vi) Termination of Management Orders

779. Financial arrangements on termination. The following provisions apply where an interim or final management order[1] ceases to have effect for any reason (such as it has reached the end of the term specified in the order)[2].

If, on the termination date[3] for an interim management order, the total amount of rent or other payments[4] collected or recovered by a local housing authority[5] from persons occupying[6] the house[7] exceeds the total amount of the local housing authority's relevant expenditure[8], and any amounts of compensation payable to third parties[9] by virtue of decisions of the authority[10], the authority must, as soon as practicable after the termination date, pay the balance to such relevant landlord[11], or to such relevant landlords in such proportions, as it considers appropriate[12]. If, on the termination date for an interim management order, the total amount of rent or other payments collected or recovered by the authority[13] is less than the total amount of the authority's relevant expenditure and any amounts of compensation payable as mentioned above, the difference is recoverable by the authority from such relevant landlord, or such relevant landlords in such proportions, as it considers appropriate[14].

If, on the termination date for a final management order, any amount is payable to a third party or to any relevant landlord in accordance with the management scheme[15], that amount must be paid to that person by the local housing authority in the manner provided by the scheme[16]. If, on the termination date for a final management order, any amount is payable to the local housing authority in accordance with the management scheme, that amount is recoverable by the local housing authority from such relevant landlord, or from such relevant landlords in such proportions, as is provided by the scheme[17].

Any of the provisions described above do not, however, apply in relation to the order if the order is followed by a final management order and the management scheme contained in that final management order provides[18] for that provision not to apply in relation to the order[19].

Any sum recoverable by the authority[20] is, until recovered, a charge on the house[21]. The charge takes effect on the termination date for the order as a legal charge which is a local land charge[22].

If the order is to be followed by a licence granted under Part 2 or Part 3 of the Housing Act 2004[23] in respect of the house, the conditions contained in the licence may include a condition requiring the licence holder to repay to the authority any amount recoverable by it from relevant landlords, and to do so in such instalments as are specified in the licence[24].

1   As to the meaning of 'interim management order' see PARA 745; and as to the making of such an order see PARA 746. As to the meaning of 'final management order' see PARA 745; and as to the making of such an order see PARA 755. As to when an interim management order is in force see PARA 748; and as to when a final management order is in force see PARA 756.
2   Housing Act 2004 s 129(1).
3   For these purposes, 'the termination date' means the date on which the order ceases to have effect: Housing Act 2004 s 129(12).
4   For these purposes, 'rent or other payments' means rents or other payments payable under leases or licences or in respect of furniture within the Housing Act 2004 s 126(1) (see PARA 776): s 129(12).
5   As to the meaning of 'local housing authority' see PARA 380 note 1.
6   As to the meaning of 'occupy' see PARA 563 note 13.
7   Ie as mentioned in the Housing Act 2004 s 110(3): see PARA 752. As to the meaning of 'the house' see PARA 745 note 8.
8   As to the meaning of 'relevant expenditure' see PARA 752 note 1 (definition applied by the Housing Act 2004 s 129(12)).
9   As to the meaning of 'third party' see PARA 752 note 7.
10 Ie under the Housing Act 2004 s 128: see PARA 777.
11 'Relevant landlord' means a person who was the immediate landlord of the house or part of it immediately before the termination date or his successor in title for the time being: Housing Act 2004 s 129(12).
12 Housing Act 2004 s 129(2). Prospectively, s 129(2) applies in respect of an interim management order that is not made under s 102(7A) (see PARA 746 head (ii)): s 129(2) (amended, as from a day to be appointed, by the Housing and Planning Act 2016 s 26, Sch 3 paras 1, 11; at the date at which this volume states the law, no such day had been appointed).
13 See note 7.
14 Housing Act 2004 s 129(3).
15 Ie under the Housing Act 2004 s 119: see PARA 760.
16 Housing Act 2004 s 129(4).
17 Housing Act 2004 s 129(5).
18 See the Housing Act 2004 s 119(5)(c), (d); and PARA 760 heads (iii), (iv).

19 Housing Act 2004 s 129(6).
20 Ie under the Housing Act 2004 s 129(3) (see the text and note 14) or s 129(5) (see the text and note 17).
21 Housing Act 2004 s 129(7).
22 Housing Act 2004 s 129(8). As to local land charges see REAL PROPERTY AND REGISTRATION vol 87 (2012) PARA 763 et seq. For the purpose of enforcing the charge the authority has the same powers and remedies under the Law of Property Act 1925 and otherwise as if it were a mortgagee by deed having powers of sale and lease, of accepting surrenders of leases and of appointing a receiver (see MORTGAGE vol 77 (2016) PARA 518 et seq): Housing Act 2004 s 129(9). The power of appointing a receiver is exercisable at any time after the end of the period of one month beginning with the date on which the charge takes effect: s 129(10).
23 Ie under the Housing Act 2004 Pt 2 (ss 55–78) (see s 61(1); and PARA 679) or Pt 3 (ss 79–100) (see s 85(1); and PARA 709).
24 Housing Act 2004 s 129(11).

780. Effect of termination on leases, agreements and proceedings. The following provisions apply where an interim or final management order[1] ceases to have effect for any reason[2], and the order is not immediately followed by a further order[3] under the statutory provisions as to management orders[4]. As from the termination date[5], a lease or licence[6] in which the local housing authority[7] was substituted for another party[8] has effect with the substitution of the original party, or his successor in title, for the authority, and an agreement[9] which has effect[10] as a lease or licence granted by the authority[11] has effect with the substitution of the relevant landlord[12] for the authority[13].

If the relevant landlord is a lessee, nothing in a superior lease imposes liability on him or any superior lessee in respect of anything done before the termination date in pursuance of the terms of an agreement as mentioned above[14].

If the authority serves[15] a notice on the other party or parties to the agreement stating that this provision applies to the agreement, any other agreement entered into by the authority in the performance of its duties[16] in respect of the house has effect, as from the termination date, with the substitution of the relevant landlord for the authority[17].

If the authority serves a notice on all interested parties stating that this provision applies to the rights or liabilities or (as the case may be) the proceedings, any rights or liabilities that were rights or liabilities of the authority immediately before the termination date by virtue of any of the statutory provisions as to management orders[18] or under any agreement in which the relevant landlord has been substituted for the authority[19] are rights or liabilities of the relevant landlord instead[20]. Any proceedings instituted or continued by or against the authority by virtue of any such provision or agreement may be continued by or against the relevant landlord instead, as from the termination date[21].

If by virtue of these provisions a relevant landlord becomes subject to any liability to pay damages in respect of anything done (or omitted to be done) before the termination date by or on behalf of the authority, the authority is liable to reimburse to the relevant landlord an amount equal to the amount of the damages paid by him[22].

1 As to the meaning of 'interim management order' see PARA 745; and as to the making of such an order see PARA 746. As to the meaning of 'final management order' see PARA 745; and as to the making of such an order see PARA 755.
2 As to when an interim management order ceases to have effect see PARA 748; and as to when a final management order ceases to have effect see PARA 756.
3 Ie under the Housing Act 2004 Pt 4 Ch 1 (ss 101–131).
4 Housing Act 2004 s 130(1).
5 For these purposes, 'the termination date' means the date on which the order ceases to have effect: Housing Act 2004 s 130(11).
6 As to the meanings of 'lease' and 'licence' see PARA 391 note 6.

7 As to the meaning of 'local housing authority' see PARA 380 note 1.
8 Ie by virtue of the Housing Act 2004 s 124(4): see PARA 774.
9 For these purposes, 'agreement' includes arrangement: Housing Act 2004 s 130(11). Section 130 applies to instruments as it applies to agreements: s 130(10).
10 Ie in accordance with the Housing Act 2004 s 108 or s 117: see PARAS 750, 758.
11 Ie under the Housing Act 2004 s 107 or s 116: see PARAS 750, 758.
12 For these purposes, 'relevant landlord' means a person who was the immediate landlord of the house immediately before the termination date or his successor in title for the time being: Housing Act 2004 s 130(11). As to the meaning of 'the house' see PARA 745 note 8. Where two or more persons are relevant landlords in relation to different parts of the house, any reference in s 130 to 'the relevant landlord' is to be taken to refer to such one or more of them as is determined by agreement between them or (in default of agreement) by the appropriate tribunal on an application made by any of them: s 130(9) (amended by SI 2013/1036). As to the meaning of 'appropriate tribunal' see PARA 580 note 2. As to appeals to the appropriate tribunal see PARA 32 et seq.
13 Housing Act 2004 s 130(2).
14 Housing Act 2004 s 130(3).
15 As to service of documents under the Housing Act 2004 see PARA 391.
16 Ie under the Housing Act 2004 s 106(1)–(3) or s 115(2): see PARAS 749, 757.
17 Housing Act 2004 s 130(4), (5).
18 Ie the Housing Act 2004 Pt 4 Ch 1.
19 Ie any agreement to which the Housing Act 2004 s 130(4) (see the text and note 17) applies.
20 Housing Act 2004 s 130(6)(a), (7).
21 Housing Act 2004 s 130(6)(b).
22 Housing Act 2004 s 130(8).

(2) INTERIM AND FINAL EMPTY DWELLING MANAGEMENT ORDERS

(i) In general

781. Empty dwelling management orders (EDMOs). Chapter 2 of Part 4 of the Housing Act 2004[1] deals with the making by a local housing authority[2] of an interim empty dwelling management order (an 'interim EDMO'), or a final empty dwelling management order (a 'final EDMO'), in respect of a dwelling[3].

An interim EDMO is an order made to enable a local housing authority, with the consent of the relevant proprietor[4], to take steps for the purpose of securing that a dwelling[5] becomes and continues to be occupied[6]. A final EDMO is an order made, in succession to an interim EDMO or a previous final EDMO, for the purpose of securing that a dwelling is occupied[7].

1 Ie the Housing Act 2004 Pt 4 Ch 2 (ss 132–138). See Driscoll *Housing: the New Law, A Guide to the Housing Act 2004* (2007) Ch 10.
2 As to the meaning of 'local housing authority' see PARA 380 note 1.
3 Housing Act 2004 s 132(1).
4 'Relevant proprietor', in relation to a dwelling, means: (1) if the dwelling is let under one or more leases with an unexpired term of seven years or more, the lessee under whichever of those leases has the shortest unexpired term; or (2) in any other case, the person who has the freehold estate in the dwelling: Housing Act 2004 s 132(4)(c). As to the meanings of 'lessee' and 'lease' see PARA 391 note 6. In s 132(4)(c), the reference to an unexpired term of seven years or more of a lease of a dwelling is: (a) in relation to a dwelling in respect of which the local housing authority is considering making an interim EDMO, a reference to the unexpired term of the lease at the time the authority begins taking steps under s 133(3) (see PARA 782); (b) in relation to a dwelling in respect of which an interim EDMO has been made, a reference to the unexpired term of the lease at the time the application for authorisation to make the interim EDMO was made under s 133(1) (see PARA 782); or (c) in relation to a dwelling in respect of which a local housing authority is considering making or has made a final EDMO, a reference to the unexpired term of the lease at the time the application for authorisation to make the preceding interim EDMO was made under s 133(1): s 132(5)(a)–(c). 'Preceding interim EDMO', in relation to a final EDMO, means the

interim EDMO that immediately preceded the final EDMO or, where there has been a succession of final EDMOs, the interim EDMO that immediately preceded the first of them: s 132(5).

5　For these purposes, 'dwelling' means: (1) a building intended to be occupied as a separate dwelling; or (2) a part of a building intended to be occupied as a separate dwelling which may be entered otherwise than through any non-residential accommodation in the building: Housing Act 2004 s 132(4)(a). Any reference to 'the dwelling', in relation to an interim EDMO or a final EDMO, is a reference to the dwelling to which the order relates: s 132(4)(b).

6　Housing Act 2004 s 132(2). See further PARA 782 et seq.

7　Housing Act 2004 s 132(3). See further PARA 790 et seq.

(ii) Interim Empty Dwelling Management Orders

782. Making of interim EDMOs. A local housing authority[1] may make an interim EDMO[2] in respect of a dwelling[3] if it is a dwelling to which these provisions apply, and on an application by the authority to the appropriate tribunal[4], the tribunal by order authorises it[5] to make such an order, either in the terms of a draft order submitted by it or in those terms as varied by the tribunal[6]. These provisions apply to a dwelling if: (1) the dwelling is wholly unoccupied[7]; and (2) the relevant proprietor[8] is not a public sector body[9].

Before determining whether to make an application to the appropriate tribunal for an authorisation to make an interim EDMO, the authority must make reasonable efforts to notify the relevant proprietor that it is considering making an interim EDMO in respect of the dwelling, and to ascertain what steps (if any) he is taking, or is intending to take, to secure that the dwelling is occupied[10]. In determining whether to make an application to the appropriate tribunal for an authorisation, the authority must take into account the rights of the relevant proprietor of the dwelling and the interests of the wider community[11]. The authority may make an interim EDMO in respect of the dwelling despite any pending appeal against the order of the tribunal (but this is without prejudice to any order that may be made on the disposal of any such appeal)[12].

An application to the appropriate tribunal for authorisation to make an interim EDMO in respect of a dwelling may include an application for an order[13] determining a lease or licence of the dwelling[14].

The statutory provisions as to the procedure for making management orders[15] apply in relation to the making of an interim EDMO in respect of a dwelling as they apply in relation to the making of an interim management order in respect of a house, subject to modifications[16].

1　As to the meaning of 'local housing authority' see PARA 380 note 1.

2　As to the meaning of 'interim EDMO' see PARA 781.

3　As to the meaning of 'dwelling' see PARA 781 note 5.

4　As to the meaning of 'appropriate tribunal' see PARA 580 note 2. As to appeals to the appropriate tribunal see PARA 32 et seq.

5　Ie under the Housing Act 2004 s 134: see PARA 783.

6　Housing Act 2004 s 133(1) (amended by SI 2013/1036); and see PARA 781 note 1.

7　'Wholly unoccupied' means that no part is occupied, whether lawfully or unlawfully: Housing Act 2004 s 133(2).

8　As to the meaning of 'relevant proprietor' see PARA 781 note 4.

9　Housing Act 2004 s 133(2)(a), (b). For the purposes of s 133, 'public sector body' means a body mentioned in any of Sch 14 para 2(1)(a)–(f) (see PARA 668): s 133(7).

10　Housing Act 2004 s 133(3) (amended by SI 2013/1036).

11　Housing Act 2004 s 133(4) (amended by SI 2013/1036).

12　Housing Act 2004 s 133(5).

13　Ie under the Housing Act 2004 Sch 7 para 22: see PARA 801.

14　Housing Act 2004 s 133(6) (amended by SI 2013/1036).

15　Ie the Housing Act 2004 s 123, Sch 6 Pt 1 (paras 1–8): see PARAS 764–765.

16 Housing Act 2004 s 133(8). The modifications are that: (1) Sch 6 para 7(2) (serving copy of order and notice: see PARA 765) does not apply; (2) Sch 6 para 7(4)(c) (requirement to set out date on which order is to cease to have effect: see PARA 765) is to be read as referring instead to the date on which the order is to cease to have effect in accordance with Sch 7 para 1(3), (4) or Sch 7 para 9(3)–(5); (3) in Sch 6 para 7(6) (requirement to set out information as to appeals: see PARA 765), Sch 6 para 7(6)(a) is to be read as referring instead to Sch 7 Pt 4, and Sch 6 para 7(6)(b) does not apply; (4) Sch 6 para 8(4) (see PARA 764) is to be read as defining 'relevant person' as any person who, to the knowledge of the local housing authority, is a person having an estate or interest in the dwelling (other than a person who is a tenant under a lease granted under Sch 7 para 2(3)(c): see PARA 786 head (3)): s 133(8)(a)–(d). As to the meaning of 'person having an estate or interest' see PARA 391 note 7. As to the meanings of 'tenant' and 'lease' see PARA 391 note 6.

783. Authorisation to make interim EDMOs. The appropriate tribunal[1] may authorise a local housing authority[2] to make an interim EDMO[3] in respect of a dwelling[4] if the tribunal is satisfied as to the matters mentioned below, and is not satisfied that the case falls within one of the prescribed exceptions[5]. The matters as to which the tribunal must be satisfied are:

(1)   that the dwelling has been wholly unoccupied[6] for at least six months or such longer period as may be prescribed;

(2)   that there is no reasonable prospect that the dwelling will become occupied in the near future;

(3)   that, if an interim order is made, there is a reasonable prospect that the dwelling will become occupied;

(4)   that the authority has complied with the requirements as to notifying the relevant proprietor[7]; and

(5)   that any prescribed requirements have been complied with[8].

In deciding whether to authorise a local housing authority to make an interim EDMO in respect of a dwelling, the tribunal must take into account the interests of the community and the effect that the order will have on the rights of the relevant proprietor and may have on the rights of third parties[9]. On authorising a local housing authority to make an interim EDMO in respect of a dwelling, the tribunal may, if it thinks fit, make an order requiring the authority (if it makes the EDMO) to pay to any third party specified in the order an amount of compensation in respect of any interference in consequence of the order with the rights of the third party[10].

The appropriate national authority[11] may by order:

(a)   prescribe exceptions for the purposes of authorising the making of an EDMO;

(b)   prescribe a period of time for which the dwelling must have been wholly unoccupied; and

(c)   prescribe requirements for the purposes of head (5)[12].

An order prescribing exceptions may in particular include exceptions in relation to:

(i)   dwellings that have been occupied solely or principally by the relevant proprietor who is at the material time temporarily resident elsewhere;

(ii)   dwellings that are holiday homes or that are otherwise occupied by the relevant proprietor or his guests on a temporary basis from time to time;

(iii)   dwellings undergoing repairs or renovation;

(iv)   dwellings in respect of which an application for planning permission[13] or building control approval[14] is outstanding;

(v)   dwellings which are genuinely on the market for sale or letting;

(vi)   dwellings where the relevant proprietor has died not more than the
         prescribed number of months before the material time[15].

1   As to the meaning of 'appropriate tribunal' see PARA 580 note 2. As to appeals to the appropriate
    tribunal see PARA 32 et seq.
2   As to the meaning of 'local housing authority' see PARA 380 note 1.
3   As to the meaning of 'interim EDMO' see PARA 781.
4   Ie a dwelling to which the Housing Act 2004 s 133 applies: see PARA 782. As to the meaning of
    'dwelling' see PARA 781 note 5.
5   Housing Act 2004 s 134(1) (amended by SI 2013/1036). 'Prescribed' means prescribed by an
    order under the Housing Act 2004 s 134(5) (see the text and notes 11–12): s 134(7).
6   'Wholly unoccupied' means that no part is occupied, whether lawfully or unlawfully: Housing Act
    2004 s 134(7).
7   Ie under the Housing Act 2004 s 133(3): see PARA 782. As to the meaning of 'relevant proprietor'
    see PARA 781 note 4.
8   Housing Act 2004 s 134(2). Proposals were announced on 7 January 2011 to restrict the use of
    EDMOs. Their use will be limited to empty properties which have become magnets for vandalism,
    squatters and other forms of anti-social behaviour, and a property will have to stand empty for at
    least two years before an EDMO can be obtained, and property owners will have to be given at
    least three months' notice before the order can be issued. See the Department for Communities and
    Local Government press notice published on 7 January 2011.
9   Housing Act 2004 s 134(3). 'Third party', in relation to a dwelling, means any person who has an
    estate or interest in the dwelling (other than the relevant proprietor and any person who is a tenant
    under a lease granted under Sch 7 para 2(3)(c) (see PARA 786 head (3)) or Sch 7 para 10(3)(c) (see
    PARA 793 head (3)): s 132(4)(d). As to the meaning of 'person having an estate or interest' see
    PARA 391 note 7. As to the meanings of 'tenant' and 'lease' see PARA 391 note 6.
10 Housing Act 2004 s 134(4).
11 As to the meaning of 'the appropriate national authority' see PARA 389 note 1.
12 Housing Act 2004 s 134(5). As to the orders that have been made under heads (a) and (c) in the
    text see the Housing (Empty Dwelling Management Orders) (Prescribed Exceptions and
    Requirements) (England) Order 2006, SI 2006/367 (amended by SI 2012/2625 and SI 2013/1036);
    and the Housing (Empty Dwelling Management Orders) (Prescribed Exceptions and
    Requirements) (Wales) Order, SI 2006/2823.
13 'Planning permission' has the meaning given by the Town and Country Planning Act 1990 s 336(1)
    (see PLANNING vol 81 (2010) PARA 54): Housing Act 2004 s 134(7).
14 'Building control approval' means approval for the carrying out of any works under building
    regulations (see BUILDING): Housing Act 2004 s 134(7).
15 Housing Act 2004 s 134(6). See note 12.

784. Local housing authority's duties once interim EDMO is in force. A local
housing authority[1] which has made an interim EDMO[2] in respect of a dwelling[3]
must comply with the following provisions as soon as practicable after the
order has come into force[4]. The authority must take such steps as it considers
appropriate for the purpose of securing that the dwelling becomes and continues
to be occupied[5]. The authority must also take such other steps as it considers
appropriate with a view to the proper management of the dwelling pending the
making of a final EDMO in respect of the dwelling[6] or the revocation of the
interim EDMO[7].

If the local housing authority concludes that there are no steps which it could
appropriately take under the order for the purpose of securing that the dwelling
becomes occupied, the authority must either make a final EDMO in respect of the
dwelling or revoke the order[8] without taking any further action[9].

1   As to the meaning of 'local housing authority' see PARA 380 note 1.
2   As to the meaning of 'interim EDMO' see PARA 781. As to the making of such an order see
    PARA 782.
3   As to the meaning of 'dwelling' see PARA 781 note 5.
4   Housing Act 2004 s 135(1); and see PARA 781 note 1. As to when the order comes into force see
    s 132(6), Sch 7 para 1; and PARA 785.
5   Housing Act 2004 s 135(2).

6   Ie under the Housing Act 2004 s 136: see PARA 790. As to the meaning of 'final EDMO' see
    PARA 781. As to the making of such an order see PARA 790.
7   Housing Act 2004 s 135(3). As to revocation see PARA 789. For the avoidance of doubt, the
    authority's duty under s 135(3) includes taking such steps as are necessary to ensure that, while the
    order is in force, reasonable provision is made for insurance of the dwelling against destruction or
    damage by fire or other causes: s 135(5).
8   Ie under the Housing Act 2004 Sch 7 para 7: see PARA 789.
9   Housing Act 2004 s 135(4).

785. Operation of interim EDMOs. An interim EDMO[1] comes into force when
it is made[2]. The order ceases to have effect at the end of the period of 12 months
beginning with the date on which it is made, unless it ceases to have effect at some
other time as mentioned below[3]. If the order provides that it is to cease to have
effect on a date falling before the end of that period, it accordingly ceases to have
effect on that date[4]. Where a final EDMO[5] has been made[6] so as to replace the
interim EDMO, but the final EDMO has not come into force because of an appeal
to the appropriate tribunal[7] against the making of the final EDMO, then if the
date on which the final EDMO comes into force in relation to the dwelling[8]
following the disposal of the appeal is later than the date on which the interim
EDMO would cease to have effect apart from this provision, the interim EDMO
continues in force until that later date[9]. If, on the application of the authority, the
tribunal makes an order providing for the interim EDMO to continue in force,
pending the disposal of the appeal, until a date later than that on which the
interim EDMO would cease to have effect apart from this provision, the interim
EDMO will therefore continue in force until that later date[10].

These provisions have effect subject to the provisions on the variation or
revocation of orders by the local housing authority[11] and subject also to the power
of revocation exercisable by the appropriate tribunal[12] on an appeal[13] made to it[14].

1   As to the meaning of 'interim EDMO' see PARA 781.
2   Housing Act 2004 s 132(6), Sch 7 para 1(1), (2). As to the making of interim EDMOs see
    PARA 782.
3   Housing Act 2004 Sch 7 para 1(1), (3).
4   Housing Act 2004 Sch 7 para 1(4).
5   As to the meaning of 'final EDMO' see PARA 781. As to the making of such an order see
    PARA 790.
6   Ie under the Housing Act 2004 s 136: see PARA 790.
7   Ie under the Housing Act 2004 Sch 7 para 26: see PARA 806.
8   As to the meaning of 'dwelling' see PARA 781 note 5.
9   Housing Act 2004 Sch 7 para 1(5), (6) (Sch 7 para 1(5) amended by SI 2013/1036).
10 Housing Act 2004 Sch 7 para 1(5), (7) (Sch 7 para 1(5) as amended: see note 9).
11 Ie the Housing Act 2004 Sch 7 paras 6, 7: see PARA 789. As to the meaning of 'local housing
    authority' see PARA 380 note 1.
12 As to the meaning of 'appropriate tribunal' see PARA 580 note 2. As to appeals to the appropriate
    tribunal see PARA 32 et seq.
13 Ie under the Housing Act 2004 Sch 7 para 30: see PARA 808.
14 Housing Act 2004 Sch 7 para 1(8).

786. General effect of interim EDMOs. The following provisions have effect
while an interim EDMO is in force[1] in relation to a dwelling[2]. The rights and
powers conferred on the local housing authority[3] are exercisable by the authority
in performing its duties[4] to secure the occupation and proper management of the
dwelling[5]. The authority:

(1)   has (subject to the rights of existing occupiers[6]) the right to possession
      of the dwelling[7];
(2)   has the right to do (and authorise a manager or other person to do) in
      relation to the dwelling anything which the relevant proprietor[8] of the
      dwelling would (but for the order) be entitled to do[9];

(3) may create one or more of the following:
    (a) an interest in the dwelling which, as far as possible, has all the incidents of a leasehold[10]; or
    (b) a right in the nature of a licence[11] to occupy part of the dwelling[12];
(4) may apply to the appropriate tribunal[13] for an order[14] determining a lease or licence of the dwelling[15].

The authority, however:
(i) does not under these provisions acquire any estate or interest in the dwelling; and
(ii) accordingly is not entitled by virtue of such provisions to sell, lease[16], charge or make any other disposition of any such estate or interest[17].

But, where the relevant proprietor of the dwelling is a lessee under a lease of the dwelling, the authority is to be treated (subject to head (i)) as if it were the lessee instead[18]. Any enactment[19] or rule of law relating to landlords and tenants or leases applies in relation to a lease in relation to which the authority is to be treated as the lessee[20], or a lease to which the authority becomes a party[21], as if the authority were the legal owner of the premises[22].

Neither the authority nor any person authorised by it[23] is liable to any person having an estate or interest[24] in the dwelling for anything done or omitted to be done in the performance (or intended performance) of the authority's duties to secure the occupation and proper management of the dwelling unless the act or omission is due to negligence of the authority or any such person[25].

An interim EDMO which has come into force is a local land charge[26]. The authority may apply to the Chief Land Registrar for the entry of an appropriate restriction in the register of title in respect of such an order[27].

1 As to the meaning of 'interim EDMO' see PARA 781. As to when an interim EDMO is in force see PARA 785.
2 Housing Act 2004 s 132(6), Sch 7 para 2(1).
3 Ie by the Housing Act 2004 Sch 7 para 2(3). As to the meaning of 'local housing authority' see PARA 380 note 1.
4 Ie under the Housing Act 2004 s 135(1), (3): see PARA 784.
5 Housing Act 2004 Sch 7 para 2(2); and see PARA 781 note 1. As to the meaning of 'dwelling' see PARA 781 note 5.
6 Ie rights preserved by the Housing Act 2004 Sch 7 para 18(3): see PARA 798.
7 Housing Act 2004 Sch 7 para 2(3)(a).
8 As to the meaning of 'relevant proprietor' see PARA 781 note 4.
9 Housing Act 2004 Sch 7 para 2(3)(b).
10 See LANDLORD AND TENANT vol 62 (2016) PARA 1 et seq; REAL PROPERTY AND REGISTRATION vol 87 (2012) PARA 75 et seq.
11 As to the meaning of 'licence' see PARA 391 note 6.
12 Housing Act 2004 Sch 7 para 2(3)(c). The authority may not, however, under Sch 7 para 2(3)(c) create any interest or right in the nature of a lease or licence unless: (1) consent in writing has been given by the relevant proprietor of the dwelling; and (2) where the relevant proprietor is a lessee under a lease of the dwelling, the interest or right is created for a term that is less than the term of that lease: Sch 7 para 2(4). In relation to any interest or right created by the authority under Sch 7 para 2(3)(c), for the purposes of any enactment or rule of law, any interest created by the authority under Sch 7 para 2(3)(c)(i) (see head (3)(a) in the text) is to be treated as if it were a legal lease, and any right created by the authority under Sch 7 para 2(3)(c)(ii) (see head (3)(b) in the text) is to be treated as if it were a licence to occupy granted by the legal owner of the dwelling, despite the fact that the authority has no legal estate in the dwelling (see Sch 7 para 2(5)(a); and head (i) in the text): Sch 7 para 3(1), (2). For these purposes, 'enactment' has the meaning given by Sch 7 para 2(11) (see note 19); and 'legal lease' means a term of years absolute (ie within the Law of Property Act 1925 s 1(1)(b): see REAL PROPERTY AND REGISTRATION vol 87 (2012) PARA 76): Housing Act 2004 Sch 7 para 3(7). Any enactment or rule of law relating to landlords and tenants or leases accordingly applies in relation to any interest created by the authority under Sch 7 para 2(3)(c)(i) as if the authority were the legal owner of the dwelling: Sch 7 para 3(3). References

to leases and licences in Pt 4 Ch 2 (ss 132–138) and in any other enactment accordingly include (where the context permits) interests and rights created by the authority under Sch 7 para 2(3)(c): Sch 7 para 3(4). The provisions of Sch 7 para 3(1)–(4) have effect subject to Sch 7 para 4(4)–(6) (see PARA 787), and subject to any provision to the contrary contained in an order made by the appropriate national authority: Sch 7 para 3(5). As to the meaning of 'the appropriate national authority' see PARA 389 note 1.

13 As to the meaning of 'appropriate tribunal' see PARA 580 note 2. As to appeals to the appropriate tribunal see PARA 32 et seq.

14 Ie under the Housing Act 2004 Sch 7 para 22: see PARA 801.

15 Housing Act 2004 Sch 7 para 2(3)(d) (amended by SI 2013/1036).

16 In the Housing Act 2004 Sch 7 para 2(5)(b) the reference to leasing does not include the creation of interests under Sch 7 para 2(3)(c)(i) (see head (3)(a) in the text and note 12): Sch 7 para 3(6).

17 Housing Act 2004 Sch 7 para 2(5).

18 Housing Act 2004 Sch 7 para 2(6). The appropriate national authority may by regulations make such provision as it considers appropriate for supplementing the provisions of Pt 4 Ch 2 in relation to cases where a local housing authority is to be treated as the lessee under a lease under Sch 7 para 2(6): s 145(1). Such regulations may, in particular, make provision: (1) as respects rights and liabilities in such cases of: (a) the authority; (b) the person who (apart from Sch 7 para 2(6)) is the lessee under the lease; or (c) other persons having an estate or interest in the premises demised under the lease; (2) requiring the authority to give copies to the person mentioned in head (1)(b) of notices and other documents served on it in connection with the lease; (3) for treating things done by or in relation to the authority as done by or in relation to that person, or vice versa: s 145(2). As to the regulations that have been made see the Housing (Management Orders and Empty Dwelling Management Orders) (Supplemental Provisions) (England) Regulations 2006, SI 2006/368; and the Housing (Management Orders and Empty Dwelling Management Orders) (Supplemental Provisions) (Wales) Regulations 2006, SI 2006/2822.

19 For these purposes, 'enactment' includes an enactment comprised in subordinate legislation (within the meaning of the Interpretation Act 1978: see STATUTES AND LEGISLATIVE PROCESS vol 96 (2012) PARA 609): Housing Act 2004 Sch 7 para 2(11).

20 Ie under the Housing Act 2004 Sch 7 para 2(6).

21 Ie under the Housing Act 2004 Sch 7 para 4(2): see PARA 787.

22 Housing Act 2004 Sch 7 para 2(7). This is subject, however, to Sch 7 para 4(4)–(6): see PARA 787.

23 Ie under the Housing Act 2004 Sch 7 para 2(3)(b): see head (2) in the text.

24 As to the meaning of 'person having an estate or interest' see PARA 391 note 7.

25 Housing Act 2004 Sch 7 para 2(8).

26 Housing Act 2004 Sch 7 para 2(9).

27 Housing Act 2004 Sch 7 para 2(10). As to the Chief Land Registrar see REAL PROPERTY AND REGISTRATION vol 87 (2012) PARA 562.

787. Effect on relevant proprietor, mortgagees etc. The following provisions apply to the relevant proprietor[1] and other persons with an estate or interest[2] in the dwelling[3], while an interim EDMO is in force[4] in relation to a dwelling[5]. Where the relevant proprietor is a lessor or licensor under a lease or licence[6] of the dwelling, the lease or licence has effect while the order is in force as if the local housing authority[7] were substituted in it for the lessor or licensor[8]. Such a lease continues to have effect, as far as possible, as a lease despite the fact that the rights of the local housing authority, as substituted for the lessor, do not amount to an estate in law in the dwelling[9]. The statutory provisions[10] which exclude local authority lettings from the Rent Acts[11] and from Part I[12] of the Housing Act 1988[13] do not apply to such a lease or licence[14] (so an assured shorthold tenancy, for example, could be granted under the Housing Act 1988).

Nothing in the statutory provisions relating to empty dwelling management orders[15] has the result that the authority is to be treated as the legal owner of any premises for the purposes of the statutory provisions as to the landlord condition for secure tenancies[16] or as to introductory tenancies[17].

On the making of an EDMO, the relevant proprietor of the dwelling:

(1) is not entitled to receive any rents or other payments made in respect of occupation of the dwelling;

(2)   may not exercise any rights or powers with respect to the management of the dwelling; and

(3)   may not create any of the following:

 (a)   any leasehold interest in the dwelling or a part of it (other than a lease of a reversion); or

 (b)   any licence or other right to occupy it[18].

However (subject to head (3) above) nothing in these provisions or in those relating to the general effect of interim empty dwelling management orders[19] affects the ability of a person having an estate or interest in the dwelling to make any disposition of that estate or interest[20]. Neither does anything in those provisions affect:

(i)   the validity of any mortgage[21] relating to the dwelling or any rights or remedies available to the mortgagee under such a mortgage; or

(ii)   the validity of any lease of the dwelling under which the relevant proprietor is a lessee, or any superior lease, or (subject to the local housing authority being treated as the lessee[22]) any rights or remedies available to the lessor under such a lease,

except to the extent that any of those rights or remedies would prevent the local housing authority from exercising its power[23] to create an interest or right in the dwelling[24].

In proceedings for the enforcement of any such rights or remedies the court may make such order as it thinks fit as regards the operation of the interim EDMO (including an order quashing it)[25].

1   As to the meaning of 'relevant proprietor' see PARA 781 note 4.
2   As to the meaning of 'person having an estate or interest' see PARA 391 note 7.
3   As to the meaning of 'dwelling' see PARA 781 note 5.
4   As to the meaning of 'interim EDMO' see PARA 781. As to when an interim EDMO is in force see PARA 785.
5   Housing Act 2004 s 132(6), Sch 7 para 4(1).
6   As to the meanings of 'lessor', 'licensor', 'lease' and 'licence' see PARA 391 note 6.
7   As to the meaning of 'local housing authority' see PARA 380 note 1.
8   Housing Act 2004 Sch 7 para 4(2).
9   Housing Act 2004 Sch 7 para 4(3).
10 Ie the Rent Act 1977 ss 14–16 and those provisions as applied by the Rent (Agriculture) Act 1976 s 5(2)–(4), Sch 2: see AGRICULTURAL PRODUCTION AND MARKETING vol 1 (2008) PARA 1295; LANDLORD AND TENANT vol 63 (2016) PARA 706 et seq; LANDLORD AND TENANT vol 64 (2016) PARA 1706.
11 Ie the Rent Act 1977 and the Rent (Agriculture) Act 1976: see LANDLORD AND TENANT vol 63 (2016) PARA 653 et seq; LANDLORD AND TENANT vol 64 (2016) PARA 1699 et seq.
12 Ie the Housing Act 1988 Pt I (ss 1–45): see LANDLORD AND TENANT vol 63 (2016) PARA 825 et seq.
13 Ie the Housing Act 2004 s 1(2), Sch 1 para 12: see LANDLORD AND TENANT vol 63 (2016) PARA 847.
14 Housing Act 2004 Sch 7 para 4(4), (5).
15 Ie the Housing Act 2004 Pt 4 Ch 2 (ss 132–138).
16 Ie the Housing Act 1985 s 80: see LANDLORD AND TENANT vol 63 (2016) PARA 1037.
17 Housing Act 2004 Sch 7 para 4(6). As to introductory tenancies see the Housing Act 1996 s 124; PARA 472; and LANDLORD AND TENANT vol 63 (2016) PARA 1102 et seq.
18 Housing Act 2004 Sch 7 para 4(7).
19 Ie the Housing Act 2004 Sch 7 para 2: see PARA 786.
20 Housing Act 2004 Sch 7 para 4(8).
21 As to the meaning of 'mortgage' see PARA 751 note 11.
22 Ie under the Housing Act 2004 Sch 7 para 2(6): see PARA 786.
23 Ie under the Housing Act 2004 Sch 7 para 2(3)(c): see PARA 786 head (3).
24 Housing Act 2004 Sch 7 para 4(9).
25 Housing Act 2004 Sch 7 para 4(10).

788. Financial arrangements while order is in force. The following provisions apply to relevant expenditure[1] of a local housing authority[2] which has made an interim EDMO[3]. Rent or other payments which the authority has collected or recovered, by virtue of the statutory provisions relating to empty dwelling management orders[4], from persons occupying[5] or having the right to occupy the dwelling may be used by the authority to meet the following expenditure: (1) relevant expenditure; and (2) any amounts of compensation payable to a third party[6] or to a dispossessed landlord or tenant[7] by virtue of an order for compensation in respect of the determination of the lease or licence[8].

The authority must pay to the relevant proprietor any amount of rent or other payments collected or recovered as mentioned above that remains after deductions to meet relevant expenditure and any amounts of compensation payable as mentioned above, and (where appropriate) interest on that amount at a reasonable rate fixed by the authority, and such payments are to be made at such intervals as the authority considers appropriate[9].

The interim EDMO may provide for: (a) the rate of interest which is to apply for these purposes; and (b) the intervals at which such payments are to be made[10].

The authority must keep full accounts of its income and expenditure in respect of the dwelling, and afford to the relevant proprietor, and to any other person who has an estate or interest[11] in the dwelling, all reasonable facilities for inspecting, taking copies of and verifying those accounts[12].

The relevant proprietor may apply to the appropriate tribunal[13] for an order: (i) declaring that an amount shown in the accounts as expenditure of the authority does not constitute relevant expenditure; (ii) requiring the authority to make such financial adjustments (in the accounts and otherwise) as are necessary to reflect the tribunal's declaration[14].

1 For these purposes, 'relevant expenditure' means expenditure incurred by the local housing authority with the consent of the relevant proprietor, or any other expenditure reasonably incurred by the authority, in connection with performing its duties under the Housing Act 2004 s 135(1)–(3) (see PARA 784) in respect of the dwelling (including any premiums paid for insurance of the premises): s 132(6), Sch 7 para 5(2). 'Expenditure' includes administrative costs: Sch 7 para 5(8). As to the meaning of 'relevant proprietor' see PARA 781 note 4. As to the meaning of 'dwelling' see PARA 781 note 5.
2 As to the meaning of 'local housing authority' see PARA 380 note 1.
3 Housing Act 2004 Sch 7 para 5(1); and see PARA 781 note 1. As to the meaning of 'interim EDMO' see PARA 781. As to the making of interim EDMOs see PARA 782.
4 Ie the Housing Act 2004 Pt 4 Ch 2 (ss 132–138). In Pt 4 Ch 2, any reference (however expressed) to rent or other payments in respect of occupation of a dwelling, includes any payments that the authority receives from persons in respect of unlawful occupation of the dwelling: s 132(4)(e).
5 As to the meaning of 'occupy' see PARA 563 note 13.
6 Ie by virtue of an order under the Housing Act 2004 s 134(4) or s 138(2): see PARAS 783, 805. As to the meaning of 'third party' see PARA 783 note 9.
7 Ie by virtue of an order under the Housing Act 2004 Sch 7 para 22(5): see PARA 801. 'Dispossessed landlord or tenant' means a person who was a lessor, lessee, licensor or licensee under a lease or licence determined by an order under Sch 7 para 22: Sch 7 para 5(8). As to the meanings of 'lessor', 'lessee', 'licensor' and 'licensee' see PARA 391 note 6.
8 Housing Act 2004 Sch 7 para 5(3).
9 Housing Act 2004 Sch 7 para 5(4).
10 Housing Act 2004 Sch 7 para 5(5). An appeal may be brought where the order does not provide for both of those matters: see Sch 7 para 26(1)(c); and PARA 806.
11 As to the meaning of 'person having an estate or interest' see PARA 391 note 7.
12 Housing Act 2004 Sch 7 para 5(6).
13 As to the meaning of 'appropriate tribunal' see PARA 580 note 2. As to appeals to the appropriate tribunal see PARA 32 et seq.
14 Housing Act 2004 Sch 7 para 5(7) (amended by SI 2013/1036).

789. Variation or revocation of interim EDMOs. The local housing authority[1] may vary an interim EDMO[2] if it considers it appropriate to do so[3]. A variation does not come into force until such time, if any, as is the operative time[4] for this purpose, which depends on whether there is an appeal[5]. The power to vary an order is exercisable by the authority either on an application made by a relevant person[6] or on the authority's own initiative[7].

The local housing authority may revoke an interim EDMO in the following cases:

(1)   where the authority concludes that there are no steps which it could appropriately take for the purpose of securing that the dwelling is occupied[8];

(2)   where the authority is satisfied that: (a) the dwelling will either become or continue to be occupied, despite the order being revoked; or (b) the dwelling is to be sold;

(3)   where a final EDMO[9] has been made by the authority in respect of the dwelling so as to replace the order;

(4)   where the authority concludes that it would be appropriate to revoke the order in order to prevent or stop interference with the rights of a third party[10] in consequence of the order; and

(5)   where in any other circumstances the authority considers it appropriate to revoke the order[11].

In a case where the dwelling is occupied, however, the local housing authority may not revoke an interim EDMO under head (2), (4) or (5) unless the relevant proprietor[12] consents[13].

A revocation does not come into force until such time, if any, as is the operative time[14] for this purpose[15].

The power to revoke an order is exercisable by the authority either on an application made by a relevant person[16] or on the authority's own initiative[17].

Where a relevant person applies to the authority for the revocation of an order, the authority may refuse to revoke it unless the relevant proprietor (or some other person) agrees to pay to the authority any deficit[18] on termination[19].

The provisions as to the variation or revocation of an interim management order[20] apply in relation to the variation or revocation of an interim EDMO as they do in relation to the variation or revocation of an interim management order, subject to variations[21].

1   As to the meaning of 'local housing authority' see PARA 380 note 1.
2   As to the meaning of 'interim EDMO' see PARA 781. As to the making of interim EDMOs see PARA 782.
3   Housing Act 2004 s 132(6), Sch 7 para 6(1); and see PARA 781 note 1.
4   Ie under the Housing Act 2004 Sch 7 para 33: see note 5.
5   Housing Act 2004 Sch 7 para 6(2). If no appeal is made under Sch 7 para 30 (see PARA 808) before the end of the period of 28 days mentioned in Sch 7 para 31(2) (see PARA 808), 'the operative time' is the end of that period: Sch 7 para 33(1), (2). If an appeal is made under Sch 7 para 30 before the end of that period, and a decision is given on the appeal which confirms the variation or revocation, 'the operative time' is as follows: (1) if the period within which an appeal to the Upper Tribunal may be brought expires without such an appeal having been brought, 'the operative time' is the end of that period; (2) if an appeal to the Upper Tribunal is brought, 'the operative time' is the time when a decision is given on the appeal which confirms the variation or revocation: Sch 7 para 33(3) (amended by SI 2009/1307). For this purpose, the withdrawal of an appeal has the same effect as a decision which confirms the variation or revocation appealed against; and references to a decision which confirms a variation are references to a decision which confirms it with or without variation: Housing Act 2004 Sch 7 para 33(4). As to appeals to the Upper Tribunal, ie the Upper Tribunal (Lands Chamber), the successor to the Lands Tribunal, see PARAS 49–50.
6   The relevant person may appeal against a refusal to vary the order: see PARA 808. For this purpose, 'relevant person' means any person who has an estate or interest in the dwelling (other than a person who is a tenant under a lease granted under the Housing Act 2004 Sch 7 para 2(3)(c): see

PARA 786 head (3)): Sch 7 para 6(4). As to the meaning of 'person having an estate or interest' see PARA 391 note 7. As to the meaning of 'dwelling' see PARA 781 note 5. As to the meanings of 'tenant' and 'lease' see PARA 391 note 6.

7   Housing Act 2004 Sch 7 para 6(3).
8   See the Housing Act 2004 s 135(4); and PARA 784.
9   As to the meaning of 'final EDMO' see PARA 781. As to the making of such an order see PARA 790.
10 As to the meaning of 'third party' see PARA 783 note 9.
11 Housing Act 2004 Sch 7 para 7(1).
12 As to the meaning of 'relevant proprietor' see PARA 781 note 4.
13 Housing Act 2004 Sch 7 para 7(2).
14 Ie under the Housing Act 2004 Sch 7 para 33: see note 5.
15 Housing Act 2004 Sch 7 para 7(3).
16 For this purpose, 'relevant person' means any person who has an estate or interest in the dwelling (other than a person who is a tenant under a lease granted under the Housing Act 2004 Sch 7 para 2(3)(c): see PARA 786 head (3)): Sch 7 para 7(6).
17 Housing Act 2004 Sch 7 para 7(4).
18 Ie as mentioned in the Housing Act 2004 Sch 7 para 23(4): see PARA 802.
19 Housing Act 2004 Sch 7 para 7(5).
20 Ie the Housing Act 2004 s 123, Sch 6 Pt 2 (paras 9–23): see PARAS 766–769.
21 Housing Act 2004 Sch 7 para 8(1). The provisions of Sch 6 Pt 2 apply: (1) as if references to the right of appeal under Sch 6 Pt 3 (paras 24–35) and to Sch 6 para 29(2) were references to the right of appeal under Sch 7 Pt 4 (paras 26–37) and to Sch 7 para 31(2) (see PARA 808); and (2) as if Sch 6 para 23(4) defined 'relevant person' as any person who, to the knowledge of the local housing authority, is a person having an estate or interest in the dwelling (other than a person who is a tenant under a lease granted under Sch 7 para 2(3)(c): see PARA 786 head (3)): Sch 7 para 8(2).

(iii) Final Empty Dwelling Management Orders

790.   Making of final EDMOs. A local housing authority[1] may make a final EDMO[2] to replace an interim EDMO[3] if:

(1)   it considers that, unless a final EDMO is made in respect of the dwelling[4], the dwelling is likely to become or remain unoccupied;

(2)   where the dwelling is unoccupied, the authority has taken all such steps as it was appropriate for it to take under the interim EDMO with a view to securing the occupation of the dwelling[5].

A local housing authority may make a new final EDMO so as to replace an existing final EDMO made under these provisions if:

(a)   it considers that unless a new final EDMO is made in respect of the dwelling, the dwelling is likely to become or remain unoccupied; and

(b)   where the dwelling is unoccupied, the authority has taken all such steps as it was appropriate for it to take under the existing final EDMO with a view to securing the occupation of the dwelling[6].

In deciding whether to make a final EDMO in respect of a dwelling, the authority must take into account the interests of the community, and the effect that the order will have on the rights of the relevant proprietor[7] and may have on the rights of third parties[8].

Before making a final EDMO, the authority must consider whether compensation should be paid by it to any third party in respect of any interference in consequence of the order with the rights of the third party[9].

The statutory provisions as to the procedure for making management orders[10] apply in relation to the making of a final EDMO in respect of a dwelling as they apply in relation to the making of a final management order in respect of a house, subject to modifications[11].

1   As to the meaning of 'local housing authority' see PARA 380 note 1.
2   As to the meaning of 'final EDMO' see PARA 781.

3   As to the meaning of 'interim EDMO' see PARA 781. As to the making of interim EDMOs see PARA 782.
4   As to the meaning of 'the dwelling' see PARA 781 note 5.
5   Housing Act 2004 s 136(1); and see PARA 781 note 1.
6   Housing Act 2004 s 136(2).
7   As to the meaning of 'relevant proprietor' see PARA 781 note 4.
8   Housing Act 2004 s 136(3). As to the meaning of 'third party' see PARA 783 note 9.
9   Housing Act 2004 s 136(4).
10 Ie the Housing Act 2004 s 123, Sch 6 Pt 1 (paras 1–8): see PARAS 764–765.
11 Housing Act 2004 s 136(5). The modifications are that: (1) Sch 6 para 7(2) (serving copy of order and notice: see PARA 765) does not apply; (2) Sch 6 para 7(4)(c) (requirement to set out date on which order is to cease to have effect: see PARA 765) is to be read as referring instead to the date on which the order is to cease to have effect in accordance with Sch 7 para 1(3), (4) or Sch 7 para 9(3)–(5); (3) in Sch 6 para 7(6) (requirement to set out information as to appeals: see PARA 765), Sch 6 para 7(6)(a) is to be read as referring instead to Sch 7 Pt 4, and Sch 6 para 7(6)(b) is to be read as referring instead to Sch 7 para 27(2); (4) Sch 6 para 7(6) is to be read as requiring the notice under Sch 6 para 7(5) also to contain: (a) the decision of the authority as to whether to pay compensation to any third party; (b) the amount of any such compensation to be paid; and (c) information about the right of appeal against the decision under Sch 7 para 34; (5) Sch 6 para 8(4) (see PARA 764) is to be read as defining 'relevant person' as any person who, to the knowledge of the local housing authority, is a person having an estate or interest in the dwelling (other than a person who is a tenant under a lease granted under Sch 7 para 2(3)(c) (see PARA 786 head (3)) or Sch 7 para 10(3)(c) (see PARA 793 head (3))): s 136(5)(a)–(e). As to the meaning of 'person having an estate or interest' see PARA 391 note 7. As to the meanings of 'tenant' and 'lease' see PARA 391 note 6.

791. Local housing authority's duties once final EDMO is in force. A local housing authority[1] which has made a final EDMO[2] in respect of a dwelling[3] must comply with the following provisions once the order has come into force[4]. The authority must take such steps as it considers appropriate for the purpose of securing that the dwelling is occupied[5]. The authority must also take such other steps as it considers appropriate with a view to the proper management of the dwelling in accordance with the management scheme[6] contained in the order[7]. The authority must from time to time review:

(1)   the operation of the order and in particular the management scheme contained in it;

(2)   whether, if the dwelling is unoccupied, there are any steps which the authority could appropriately take under the order for the purpose of securing that the dwelling becomes occupied; and

(3)   whether keeping the order in force in relation to the dwelling (with or without making any variations[8]) is necessary to secure that the dwelling becomes or remains occupied[9].

If on a review the authority considers that any variations should be made to the order, it must proceed to make those variations[10]. If the dwelling is unoccupied and on a review the authority concludes that either there are no steps which it could appropriately take as mentioned in head (2), or keeping the order in force is not necessary as mentioned in head (3), it must proceed to revoke the order[11].

1   As to the meaning of 'local housing authority' see PARA 380 note 1.
2   As to the meaning of 'final EDMO' see PARA 781. As to the making of such an order see PARA 790.
3   As to the meaning of 'dwelling' see PARA 781 note 5.
4   Housing Act 2004 s 137(1); and see PARA 781 note 1. As to when the order comes into force see Sch 7 para 9; and PARA 792.
5   Housing Act 2004 s 137(2).
6   As to management schemes see PARA 795.
7   Housing Act 2004 s 137(3). See Sch 7 para 13; and PARA 795. For the avoidance of doubt, the authority's duty under s 137(3) includes taking such steps as are necessary to ensure that, while the order is in force, reasonable provision is made for insurance of the dwelling against destruction or damage by fire or other causes: s 137(7).

8　Ie under the Housing Act 2004 Sch 7 para 15: see PARA 797.
9　Housing Act 2004 s 137(4).
10　Housing Act 2004 s 137(5).
11　Housing Act 2004 s 137(6).

792. Operation of final EDMOs. A final EDMO[1] does not come into force until such time (if any) as is the operative time[2] for these purposes, which depends on whether there is an appeal[3]. The order ceases to have effect at the end of the period of seven years beginning with the date on which it comes into force, unless it ceases to have effect at some other time as mentioned below[4]. If the order provides that it is to cease to have effect on a date falling before the end of that period, it accordingly ceases to have effect on that date[5]. If the order provides that it is to cease to have effect on a date falling after the end of that period and the relevant proprietor[6] of the dwelling[7] has consented to that provision, the order accordingly ceases to have effect on that date[8].

Where a new final EDMO ('the new order') has been made so as to replace the order ('the existing order'), but the new order has not come into force because of an appeal to the appropriate tribunal[9] against the making of that order, then:

(1)　　if the date on which the new order comes into force in relation to the dwelling following the disposal of the appeal is later than the date on which the existing order would cease to have effect apart from this provision, the existing order continues in force until that later date[10];

(2)　　if, on the application of the local housing authority[11], the tribunal makes an order providing for the existing order to continue in force, pending the disposal of the appeal, until a date later than that on which it would cease to have effect apart from this provision, the existing order accordingly continues in force until that later date[12].

These provisions have effect subject to the provisions as to variation or revocation of orders[13] and subject to the power of revocation exercisable by the appropriate tribunal on an appeal made[14] to it[15].

1　As to the meaning of 'final EDMO' see PARA 781. As to the making of such an order see PARA 790.
2　Ie under the Housing Act 2004 Sch 7 para 29: see note 3.
3　Housing Act 2004 s 132(6), Sch 7 para 9(1), (2). If no appeal is made under Sch 7 para 26 (see PARA 806) before the end of the period of 28 days mentioned in Sch 7 para 27(2) (see PARA 806), 'the operative time' is the end of that period: Sch 7 para 29(1), (2). If an appeal is made under Sch 7 para 26 before the end of that period, and a decision is given on the appeal which confirms the order, 'the operative time' is as follows: (1) if the period within which an appeal to the Upper Tribunal may be brought expires without such an appeal having been brought, 'the operative time' is the end of that period; (2) if an appeal to the Upper Tribunal is brought, 'the operative time' is the time when a decision is given on the appeal which confirms the order: Sch 7 para 29(3) (amended by SI 2009/1307). For this purpose, the withdrawal of an appeal has the same effect as a decision which confirms the order; and references to a decision which confirms the order are references to a decision which confirms it with or without variation: Housing Act 2004 Sch 7 para 29(4). As to appeals to the Upper Tribunal, ie the Upper Tribunal (Lands Chamber), the successor to the Lands Tribunal, see PARAS 49–50.
4　Housing Act 2004 Sch 7 para 9(3).
5　Housing Act 2004 Sch 7 para 9(4).
6　As to the meaning of 'relevant proprietor' see PARA 781 note 4.
7　As to the meaning of 'dwelling' see PARA 781 note 5.
8　Housing Act 2004 Sch 7 para 9(5).
9　Ie under the Housing Act 2004 Sch 7 para 26: see PARA 806. As to the meaning of 'appropriate tribunal' see PARA 580 note 2. As to appeals to the appropriate tribunal see PARA 32 et seq.
10　Housing Act 2004 Sch 7 para 9(6), (7) (Sch 7 para 9(6) amended by SI 2013/1036).
11　As to the meaning of 'local housing authority' see PARA 380 note 1.
12　Housing Act 2004 Sch 7 para 9(6), (8) (Sch 7 para 9(6) as amended: see note 10).
13　Ie the Housing Act 2004 Sch 7 paras 15, 16: see PARA 797.

14 Ie the Housing Act 2004 Sch 7 para 26 or Sch 7 para 30: see PARAS 806, 808.
15 Housing Act 2004 Sch 7 para 9(9) (amended by SI 2013/1036).

793. General effect of final EDMOs. While a final EDMO is in force[1] in relation to a dwelling[2], the following rights and powers are exercisable by the local housing authority[3] in performing its duties to secure occupation and proper management[4] in respect of the dwelling[5]. The authority:

(1) has (subject to the rights of existing and other occupiers[6]) the right to possession of the dwelling[7];

(2) has the right to do (and authorise a manager or other person to do) in relation to the dwelling anything which the relevant proprietor[8] of the dwelling would (but for the order) be entitled to do[9];

(3) may create one or more of the following: (a) an interest in the dwelling which, as far as possible, has all the incidents of a leasehold[10]; or (b) a right in the nature of a licence[11] to occupy part of the dwelling[12];

(4) may apply to the appropriate tribunal[13] for an order[14] determining a lease or licence of the dwelling[15].

The authority: (i) does not under these provisions acquire any estate or interest in the dwelling; and (ii) accordingly is not entitled by virtue of such provisions to sell, lease[16], charge or make any other disposition of any such estate or interest[17]. However, where the relevant proprietor of the dwelling is a lessee under a lease of the dwelling, the authority is to be treated (subject to head (i)) as if it were the lessee instead[18]. Any enactment[19] or rule of law relating to landlords and tenants or leases applies in relation to a lease in relation to which the authority is to be treated as the lessee[20], or a lease to which the authority becomes a party[21], as if the authority were the legal owner of the premises[22].

Neither the authority nor any person authorised by it[23] is liable to any person having an estate or interest[24] in the dwelling for anything done or omitted to be done in the performance (or intended performance) of the authority's duties to secure the occupation and proper management of the dwelling unless the act or omission is due to negligence of the authority or any such person[25].

A final EDMO which has come into force is a local land charge[26]. The authority may apply to the Chief Land Registrar for the entry of an appropriate restriction in the register of title in respect of such an order[27].

1 As to the meaning of 'final EDMO' see PARA 781. As to when such an order is in force see PARA 792.
2 As to the meaning of 'dwelling' see PARA 781 note 5.
3 As to the meaning of 'local housing authority' see PARA 380 note 1.
4 Ie under the Housing Act 2004 s 137(1)–(3): see PARA 791.
5 Housing Act 2004 s 132(6), Sch 7 para 10(1), (2); and see PARA 781 note 1.
6 Ie rights preserved by the Housing Act 2004 Sch 7 para 18(3), (4): see PARA 798.
7 Housing Act 2004 Sch 7 para 10(3)(a).
8 As to the meaning of 'relevant proprietor' see PARA 781 note 4.
9 Housing Act 2004 Sch 7 para 10(3)(b).
10 See LANDLORD AND TENANT vol 62 (2016) PARA 1 et seq; REAL PROPERTY AND REGISTRATION vol 87 (2012) PARA 75 et seq.
11 As to the meaning of 'licence' see PARA 391 note 6.
12 Housing Act 2004 Sch 7 para 10(3)(c). The powers of the authority under Sch 7 para 10(3)(c) are restricted as follows: (1) it may not create any interest or right in the nature of a lease or licence which is for a fixed term expiring after the date on which the order is due to expire, or (subject to head (2)) which is terminable by notice to quit, or an equivalent notice, of more than four weeks, unless consent in writing has been given by the relevant proprietor; (2) it may create an interest in the nature of an assured shorthold tenancy without any such consent so long as it is created before the beginning of the period of six months that ends with the date on which the order is due to expire: Sch 7 para 10(4). As to the meaning of 'assured shorthold tenancy' see LANDLORD AND TENANT vol 63 (2016) PARA 852. In relation to any interest or right created by the authority under

Sch 7 para 10(3)(c), for the purposes of any enactment or rule of law, any interest created by the authority under Sch 7 para 10(3)(c)(i) (see head (3)(a) in the text) is to be treated as if it were a legal lease, and any right created by the authority under Sch 7 para 10(3)(c)(ii) (see head (3)(b) in the text) is to be treated as if it were a licence to occupy granted by the legal owner of the dwelling, despite the fact that the authority has no legal estate in the dwelling (see Sch 7 para 10(5)(a); and head (i) in the text): Sch 7 para 11(1), (2). For these purposes, 'enactment' has the meaning given by Sch 7 para 10(11) (see note 19); and 'legal lease' means a term of years absolute (ie within the Law of Property Act 1925 s 1(1)(b): see REAL PROPERTY AND REGISTRATION vol 87 (2012) PARA 76): Housing Act 2004 Sch 7 para 11(7). Any enactment or rule of law relating to landlords and tenants or leases accordingly applies in relation to any interest created by the authority under Sch 7 para 10(3)(c)(i) as if the authority were the legal owner of the dwelling: Sch 7 para 11(3). References to leases and licences in Pt 4 Ch 2 (ss 132–138) and in any other enactment accordingly include (where the context permits) interests and rights created by the authority under Sch 7 para 10(3)(c): Sch 7 para 11(4). The provisions of Sch 7 para 11(1)–(4) have effect subject to Sch 7 para 12(4)–(6) (see PARA 794), and subject to any provision to the contrary contained in an order made by the appropriate national authority: Sch 7 para 11(5). As to the meaning of 'the appropriate national authority' see PARA 389 note 1.

13 As to the meaning of 'appropriate tribunal' see PARA 580 note 2. As to appeals to the appropriate tribunal see PARA 32 et seq.
14 Ie under the Housing Act 2004 Sch 7 para 22: see PARA 801.
15 Housing Act 2004 Sch 7 para 10(3)(d) (amended by SI 2013/1036).
16 In the Housing Act 2004 Sch 7 para 10(5)(b) the reference to leasing does not include the creation of interests under Sch 7 para 10(3)(c)(i) (see head (3)(a) in the text and note 12): Sch 7 para 11(6).
17 Housing Act 2004 Sch 7 para 10(5).
18 Housing Act 2004 Sch 7 para 10(6). The appropriate national authority may by regulations make such provision as it considers appropriate for supplementing the provisions of Pt 4 Ch 2 in relation to cases where a local housing authority is to be treated as the lessee under a lease under Sch 7 para 10(6): s 145(1). Such regulations may, in particular, make provision: (1) as respects rights and liabilities in such cases of: (a) the authority; (b) the person who (apart from Sch 7 para 10(6)) is the lessee under the lease; or (c) other persons having an estate or interest in the premises demised under the lease; (2) requiring the authority to give copies to the person mentioned in head (1)(b) of notices and other documents served on it in connection with the lease; (3) for treating things done by or in relation to the authority as done by or in relation to that person, or vice versa: s 145(2). As to the regulations that have been made see the Housing (Management Orders and Empty Dwelling Management Orders) (Supplemental Provisions) (England) Regulations 2006, SI 2006/368; and the Housing (Management Orders and Empty Dwelling Management Orders) (Supplemental Provisions) (Wales) Regulations 2006, SI 2006/2822.
19 For these purposes, 'enactment' includes an enactment comprised in subordinate legislation (within the meaning of the Interpretation Act 1978: see STATUTES AND LEGISLATIVE PROCESS vol 96 (2012) PARA 609): Housing Act 2004 Sch 7 para 10(11).
20 Ie under the Housing Act 2004 Sch 7 para 10(6): see the text and note 18.
21 Ie under the Housing Act 2004 Sch 7 para 12(2): see PARA 794.
22 Housing Act 2004 Sch 7 para 10(7). This is subject, however, to Sch 7 para 12(4)–(6): see PARA 794.
23 Ie under the Housing Act 2004 Sch 7 para 10(3)(b): see head (2) in the text.
24 As to the meaning of 'person having an estate or interest' see PARA 391 note 7.
25 Housing Act 2004 Sch 7 para 10(8).
26 Housing Act 2004 Sch 7 para 10(9).
27 Housing Act 2004 Sch 7 para 10(10). As to the Chief Land Registrar see REAL PROPERTY AND REGISTRATION vol 87 (2012) PARA 562.

794. Effect on relevant proprietor, mortgagees and others. The following provisions apply to the relevant proprietor[1] and other persons with an estate or interest[2] in the dwelling[3], while a final EDMO is in force[4] in relation to a dwelling[5].

Where the relevant proprietor is a lessor or licensor under a lease or licence[6] of the dwelling, the lease or licence has effect while the order is in force as if the local housing authority[7] were substituted in it for the lessor or licensor[8]. Such a lease continues to have effect, as far as possible, as a lease despite the fact that the rights of the local housing authority, as substituted for the lessor, do not amount to an estate in law in the dwelling[9]. The statutory provisions[10] which exclude local authority lettings from the Rent Acts[11] and from Part I[12] of the Housing Act

1988[13] do not apply to such a lease or licence[14] (so an assured shorthold tenancy, for example, could be granted under the 1988 Act).

However, nothing in the statutory provisions relating to empty dwelling management orders[15] has the result that the authority is to be treated as the legal owner of any premises for the purposes of the statutory provisions as to the landlord condition for secure tenancies[16] or as to introductory tenancies[17].

Once the order has been made, the relevant proprietor of the dwelling:

(1)　is not entitled to receive any rents or other payments made in respect of occupation of the dwelling;

(2)　may not exercise any rights or powers with respect to the management of the dwelling; and

(3)　may not create any of the following: (a) any leasehold interest in the dwelling or a part of it (other than a lease of a reversion); or (b) any licence or other right to occupy it[18].

However (subject to head (3)) nothing in these provisions or in those relating to the general effect of final empty dwelling management orders[19] affects the ability of a person having an estate or interest in the dwelling to make any disposition of that estate or interest[20]. Neither does anything in those provisions affect: (i) the validity of any mortgage[21] relating to the dwelling or any rights or remedies available to the mortgagee under such a mortgage; or (ii) the validity of any lease of the dwelling under which the relevant proprietor is a lessee, or any superior lease, or (subject to the local housing authority being treated as the lessee[22]) any rights or remedies available to the lessor under such a lease, except to the extent that any of those rights or remedies would prevent the local housing authority from exercising its power[23] to create an interest or right in the dwelling[24].

In proceedings for the enforcement of any such rights or remedies the court may make such order as it thinks fit as regards the operation of the final EDMO (including an order quashing it)[25].

1　As to the meaning of 'relevant proprietor' see PARA 781 note 4.
2　As to the meaning of 'person having an estate or interest' see PARA 391 note 7.
3　As to the meaning of 'dwelling' see PARA 781 note 5.
4　As to the meaning of 'final EDMO' see PARA 781. As to when such an order is in force see PARA 792.
5　Housing Act 2004 s 132(6), Sch 7 para 12(1).
6　As to the meanings of 'lessor', 'licensor', 'lease' and 'licence' see PARA 391 note 6.
7　As to the meaning of 'local housing authority' see PARA 380 note 1.
8　Housing Act 2004 Sch 7 para 12(2).
9　Housing Act 2004 Sch 7 para 12(3).
10　Ie the Rent Act 1977 ss 14–16 and those provisions as applied by the Rent (Agriculture) Act 1976 s 5(2)–(4), Sch 2: see AGRICULTURAL PRODUCTION AND MARKETING vol 1 (2008) PARA 1295; LANDLORD AND TENANT vol 63 (2016) PARA 706 et seq; LANDLORD AND TENANT vol 64 (2016) PARA 1706.
11　Ie the Rent Act 1977 and the Rent (Agriculture) Act 1976: see LANDLORD AND TENANT vol 63 (2016) PARA 653 et seq; LANDLORD AND TENANT vol 64 (2016) PARA 1699 et seq.
12　Ie the Housing Act 1988 Pt I (ss 1–45): see LANDLORD AND TENANT vol 63 (2016) PARA 825 et seq.
13　Ie the Housing Act 2004 s 1(2), Sch 1 para 12: see LANDLORD AND TENANT vol 63 (2016) PARA 847.
14　Housing Act 2004 Sch 7 para 12(4), (5).
15　Ie the Housing Act 2004 Pt 4 Ch 2 (ss 132–138).
16　Ie the Housing Act 1985 s 80: see LANDLORD AND TENANT vol 63 (2016) PARA 1037.
17　Housing Act 2004 Sch 7 para 12(6). Thus the occupiers cannot become secure or introductory tenants under these provisions. As to introductory tenancies see the Housing Act 1996 s 124; PARA 472; and LANDLORD AND TENANT vol 63 (2016) PARA 1102 et seq.
18　Housing Act 2004 Sch 7 para 12(7).

19 Ie the Housing Act 2004 Sch 7 para 10: see PARA 793.
20 Housing Act 2004 Sch 7 para 12(8).
21 As to the meaning of 'mortgage' see PARA 751 note 11.
22 Ie under the Housing Act 2004 Sch 7 para 10(6): see PARA 793.
23 Ie under the Housing Act 2004 Sch 7 para 10(3)(c): see PARA 793 head (3).
24 Housing Act 2004 Sch 7 para 12(9).
25 Housing Act 2004 Sch 7 para 12(10).

795. Management scheme and accounts. A final EDMO[1] must contain a management scheme[2]. A 'management scheme' is a scheme setting out how the local housing authority[3] is to carry out its duties to secure occupation and proper management[4] as respects the dwelling[5]. The scheme is to contain a plan giving details of the way in which the authority proposes to manage the dwelling, which must (in particular) include:

(1)   details of any works that the authority intends to carry out in connection with the dwelling;

(2)   an estimate of the capital and other expenditure to be incurred by the authority in respect of the dwelling while the order is in force;

(3)   the amount of rent which, in the opinion of the authority, the dwelling might reasonably be expected to fetch on the open market at the time the management scheme is made;

(4)   the amount of rent or other payments[6] that the authority will seek to obtain;

(5)   the amount of any compensation that is payable to a third party[7] by virtue of a decision of the authority[8] in respect of any interference in consequence of the final EDMO with the rights of that person;

(6)   provision as to the payment of any such compensation and of any compensation payable to a dispossessed landlord or tenant[9] by virtue of an order[10] for compensation in respect of the determination of the lease or licence;

(7)   where the amount of rent payable to the authority in respect of the dwelling for a period is less than the amount of rent mentioned in head (3) in respect of a period of the same length, provision as to the following:

(a)   the deduction from the difference of relevant expenditure[11] and any amounts of compensation payable to a third party or dispossessed landlord or tenant;

(b)   the payment of any remaining amount to the relevant proprietor;

(c)   the deduction from time to time of any remaining amount from any amount that the authority is entitled to recover from the proprietor[12];

(8)   provision as to the payment by the authority to the relevant proprietor from time to time of amounts of rent or other payments that remain after the deduction of:

(a)   relevant expenditure; and

(b)   any amount of compensation payable to a third party or dispossessed landlord or tenant;

(9)   provision as to the manner in which the authority is to pay to the relevant proprietor, on the termination of the final EDMO, the balance of any amounts of rent or other payments that remain after the deduction of relevant expenditure and any amounts of compensation payable to a third party or dispossessed landlord or tenant;

(10) provision as to the manner in which the authority is to pay, on the termination of the final EDMO, any outstanding amount of compensation payable to a third party or dispossessed landlord or tenant[13].

The scheme may also state:

(i) the authority's intentions as regards the use of rent or other payments to meet relevant expenditure;

(ii) the authority's intentions as regards the payment to the relevant proprietor (where appropriate) of interest on amounts within heads (8) and (9);

(iii) that the provision for payment of any balance on the termination of an interim EDMO[14] or, where the relevant proprietor consents, on the termination of a final EDMO[15], is not to apply in relation to an interim EDMO or (as the case may be) final EDMO that immediately preceded the final EDMO, and that instead the authority intends to use any balance to meet: (A) relevant expenditure incurred during the currency of that final EDMO; and (B) any compensation that may become payable to a third party or a dispossessed landlord or tenant;

(iv) that the provisions for the recovery of deficit from the relevant proprietor[16] are not to apply in relation to an interim EDMO or, where the relevant proprietor consents, a final EDMO that immediately preceded the final EDMO, and that instead the authority intends to use rent or other payments collected during the currency of that final EDMO to reimburse the authority in respect of any deficit;

(v) the authority's intentions as regards the recovery from the relevant proprietor, with or without interest, of any amount of relevant expenditure incurred under a previous interim EDMO or final EDMO that the authority is entitled to recover[17] from the proprietor[18].

The authority must keep full accounts of its income and expenditure in respect of the dwelling and afford to the relevant proprietor, and to any other person who has an estate or interest[19] in the dwelling, all reasonable facilities for inspecting, taking copies of and verifying those accounts[20].

1 As to the meaning of 'final EDMO' see PARA 781. As to the making of such an order see PARA 790; and as to when such an order is in force see PARA 792.
2 Housing Act 2004 s 132(6), Sch 7 para 13(1). As to making an application in respect of breach of a management scheme see PARA 796.
3 As to the meaning of 'local housing authority' see PARA 380 note 1.
4 Ie under the Housing Act 2004 s 137(1)–(3): see PARA 791.
5 Housing Act 2004 Sch 7 para 13(2); and see PARA 781 note 1. As to the meaning of 'dwelling' see PARA 781 note 5. In any provision of Pt 4 Ch 2 (ss 132–138) relating to varying, revoking or appealing against decisions relating to a final EDMO, any reference to such an order includes (where the context permits) a reference to the management scheme contained in it: Sch 7 para 13(7).
6 For these purposes, 'rent or other payments' means rent or other payments collected or recovered, by virtue of the Housing Act 2004 Pt 4 Ch 2, from persons occupying or having the right to occupy the dwelling: Sch 7 para 13(6). As to the meaning of 'occupy' see PARA 563 note 13.
7 As to the meaning of 'third party' see PARA 783 note 9.
8 Ie under the Housing Act 2004 s 136(4) or s 138(3): see PARAS 790, 805.
9 For these purposes, 'dispossessed landlord or tenant' means a person who was a lessor, lessee, licensor or licensee under a lease or licence determined by an order under the Housing Act 2004 Sch 7 para 22 (see PARA 801): Sch 7 para 13(6).
10 Ie under the Housing Act 2004 Sch 7 para 22(5): see PARA 801.
11 'Relevant expenditure' means: (1) expenditure incurred by the authority with the consent of the relevant proprietor; or (2) any other expenditure reasonably incurred by the authority, in connection with performing its duties under s 135(1)–(3) (see PARA 784) or s 137(1)–(3) (see

PARA 791) in respect of the dwelling (including any reasonable administrative costs and any premiums paid for insurance of the premises): Sch 7 para 13(6). As to the meaning of 'relevant proprietor' see PARA 781 note 4.

12 Ie under the Housing Act 2004 Sch 7 para 23(5) or (6): see PARA 802.
13 Housing Act 2004 Sch 7 para 13(3)(a)–(j).
14 Ie the Housing Act 2004 Sch 7 para 23(2): see PARA 802. As to the meaning of 'interim EDMO' see PARA 781. As to termination of such an order see PARA 785.
15 Ie the Housing Act 2004 Sch 7 para 23(3)(c): see PARA 802.
16 Ie the Housing Act 2004 Sch 7 para 23(4)–(6): see PARA 802.
17 Ie under the Housing Act 2004 Sch 7 para 23(5) or (6): see PARA 802.
18 Housing Act 2004 Sch 7 para 13(4)(a)–(e).
19 As to the meaning of 'person having an estate or interest' see PARA 391 note 7.
20 Housing Act 2004 Sch 7 para 13(5).

796. Application to tribunal in respect of breach of management scheme. An affected person (such as the proprietor)[1] may apply to the appropriate tribunal for an order requiring the local housing authority to manage a dwelling[2] in accordance with the management scheme[3] contained in a final EDMO[4] made in respect of the dwelling[5]. On such an application the tribunal may, if it considers it appropriate to do so, make an order: (1) requiring the authority to manage the dwelling in accordance with the management scheme; or (2) revoking the final EDMO as from a date specified in the tribunal's order[6]. Such an order may: (a) set out the steps which the authority is to take to manage the dwelling in accordance with the management scheme; (b) include provision varying the final EDMO; and (c) require the payment of money to an affected person by way of damages[7].

1 For this purpose, 'affected person' means: (1) the relevant proprietor; and (2) any third party to whom compensation is payable by virtue of an order under the Housing Act 2004 s 134(4) or s 138(2) (see PARAS 783, 805) or a decision of the local housing authority under s 136(4) or s 138(3) (see PARAS 790, 805) or who was a lessor, lessee, licensor or licensee under a lease or licence determined by an order of the appropriate tribunal under Sch 7 para 22 and to whom compensation is payable by virtue of an order under Sch 7 para 22 (see PARA 801): s 132(6), Sch 7 para 14(4) (amended by SI 2013/1036). As to the meaning of 'relevant proprietor' see PARA 781 note 4. As to the meaning of 'third party' see PARA 783 note 9. As to the meaning of 'local housing authority' see PARA 380 note 1. As to the meanings of 'lessor', 'licensor', 'lease' and 'licence' see PARA 391 note 6. As to the meaning of 'appropriate tribunal' see PARA 580 note 2. As to appeals to the appropriate tribunal see PARA 32 et seq.
2 As to the meaning of 'dwelling' see PARA 781 note 5.
3 As to management schemes see PARA 795.
4 As to the meaning of 'final EDMO' see PARA 781. As to the making of such an order see PARA 790.
5 Housing Act 2004 Sch 7 para 14(1) (amended by SI 2013/1036).
6 Housing Act 2004 Sch 7 para 14(2).
7 Housing Act 2004 Sch 7 para 14(3).

797. Variation or revocation of final EDMOs. The local housing authority[1] may vary a final EDMO[2] if it considers it appropriate to do so[3]. A variation does not come into force until such time, if any, as is the operative time[4] for this purpose[5]. The power to vary an order is exercisable by the authority either on an application made by a relevant person[6] or on the authority's own initiative[7].

The local housing authority may revoke a final EDMO in the following cases:
(1)   where the authority concludes that there are no steps which it could appropriately take under the order for the purpose of securing that the dwelling becomes occupied[8] or that keeping the order in force is not necessary to secure that the dwelling becomes or remains occupied[9];
(2)   where the authority is satisfied that: (a) the dwelling will either become or continue to be occupied, despite the order being revoked; or (b) the dwelling is to be sold;

(3)   where a further final EDMO has been made by the authority in respect of the dwelling so as to replace the order;

(4)   where the authority concludes that it would be appropriate to revoke the order in order to prevent or stop interference with the rights of a third party[10] in consequence of the order; and

(5)   where in any other circumstances the authority considers it appropriate to revoke the order[11].

In a case where the dwelling is occupied, however, the local housing authority may not revoke a final EDMO under head (2), (4) or (5) unless the relevant proprietor[12] consents[13].

A revocation does not come into force until such time, if any, as is the operative time[14] for this purpose[15].

The power to revoke an order under these provisions is exercisable by the authority either on an application made by a relevant person[16], or on the authority's own initiative[17]. Where a relevant person applies to the authority for the revocation of an order, the authority may refuse to revoke the order unless the relevant proprietor (or some other person) agrees to pay to the authority any deficit[18] on termination[19].

The provisions as to the variation or revocation of a final management order[20] apply in relation to the variation or revocation of a final EDMO as they do in relation to the variation or revocation of a final management order, subject to variations[21].

1   As to the meaning of 'local housing authority' see PARA 380 note 1.
2   As to the meaning of 'final EDMO' see PARA 781. As to the making of such an order see PARA 790.
3   Housing Act 2004 s 132(6), Sch 7 para 15(1); and see PARA 781 note 1.
4   Ie under the Housing Act 2004 Sch 7 para 33: see PARA 789 note 5.
5   Housing Act 2004 Sch 7 para 15(2).
6   For this purpose, 'relevant person' means any person who has an estate or interest in the dwelling (other than a person who is a tenant under a lease granted under the Housing Act 2004 Sch 7 para 2(3)(c) (see PARA 786 head (3)) or Sch 7 para 10(3)(c) (see PARA 793 head (3))): Sch 7 para 15(4). As to the meaning of 'person having an estate or interest' see PARA 391 note 7. As to the meaning of 'dwelling' see PARA 781 note 5. As to the meanings of 'tenant' and 'lease' see PARA 391 note 6.
7   Housing Act 2004 Sch 7 para 15(3).
8   Ie as mentioned in the Housing Act 2004 s 137(4)(b): see PARA 791 head (2).
9   Ie as mentioned in the Housing Act 2004 s 137(4)(c): see PARA 791 head (3).
10 As to the meaning of 'third party' see PARA 783 note 9.
11 Housing Act 2004 Sch 7 para 16(1)(a)–(e).
12 As to the meaning of 'relevant proprietor' see PARA 781 note 4.
13 Housing Act 2004 Sch 7 para 16(2).
14 Ie under the Housing Act 2004 Sch 7 para 33: see PARA 789 note 5.
15 Housing Act 2004 Sch 7 para 16(3).
16 For this purpose, 'relevant person' means any person who has an estate or interest in the dwelling (other than a person who is a tenant under a lease granted under the Housing Act 2004 Sch 7 para 2(3)(c) or Sch 7 para 10(3)(c)): Sch 7 para 16(6).
17 Housing Act 2004 Sch 7 para 16(4).
18 Ie such as is mentioned in the Housing Act 2004 Sch 7 para 23(4): see PARA 802.
19 Housing Act 2004 Sch 7 para 16(5).
20 Ie the Housing Act 2004 s 123, Sch 6 Pt 2 (paras 9–23): see PARAS 766–769.
21 Housing Act 2004 Sch 7 para 17(1). The provisions of Sch 6 Pt 2 apply: (1) as if references to the right of appeal under Sch 6 Pt 3 (paras 24–35) and to Sch 6 para 29(2) were references to the right of appeal under Sch 7 Pt 4 (paras 26–37) and to Sch 7 para 31(2) (see PARA 808); and (2) as if Sch 6 para 23(4) defined 'relevant person' as any person who, to the knowledge of the local housing authority, is a person having an estate or interest in the dwelling (other than a person who is a tenant under a lease granted under Sch 7 para 2(3)(c) or Sch 7 para 10(3)(c)): Sch 7 para 17(2).

(iv) General Provisions as to Interim and Final Empty Dwelling Management Orders

798. Effect on persons occupying or having a right to occupy the dwelling. The following provisions apply to existing and new occupiers[1] of a dwelling[2] in relation to which an interim EDMO[3] or final EDMO[4] is in force[5]. The provisions as to the general effect of EDMOs[6] do not affect the rights or liabilities of an existing occupier under a lease or licence (whether in writing or not) under which he has the right to occupy the dwelling at the commencement date[7]; and the provisions as to the general effect of a final EDMO[8] do not affect the rights and liabilities of a new occupier who, in the case of a final EDMO, is occupying the dwelling at the time when the order comes into force[9].

The statutory provisions[10] which exclude local authority lettings from the Rent Acts[11] and from Part I[12] of the Housing Act 1988[13] do not apply to a lease or agreement under which a new occupier has the right to occupy or is occupying the dwelling[14] (and so the letting can be under an assured shorthold tenancy granted under the 1988 Act). If, immediately before the coming into force of an interim EDMO or final EDMO, an existing occupier had the right to occupy the dwelling under a protected or statutory tenancy[15] or an assured tenancy or assured agricultural occupancy[16], nothing in the provisions relating to empty dwelling management orders[17] (except an order determining a lease or licence[18]) prevents the continuance of that tenancy or occupancy or affects the continued operation of any other Acts in relation to the tenancy or occupancy after the coming into force of the order[19].

1 As to the meaning of 'occupier' see PARA 563 note 13. For these purposes, 'existing occupier' means a person other than the relevant proprietor who, at the time when the order comes into force, has the right to occupy the dwelling, but is not a new occupier within the Housing Act 2004 Sch 7 para 18(4) (see the text to notes 8–9); and 'new occupier' means a person who, at a time when the order is in force, is occupying the dwelling under a lease or licence granted under Sch 7 para 2(3)(c) (see PARA 786 head (3)) or Sch 7 para 10(3)(c) (see PARA 793 head (3)): s 132(6), Sch 7 para 18(2). As to the meaning of 'relevant proprietor' see PARA 781 note 4. As to the meaning of 'dwelling' see PARA 781 note 5. As to the meanings of 'lease' and 'licence' see PARA 391 note 6.
2 As to the meaning of 'dwelling' see PARA 781 note 5.
3 As to the meaning of 'interim EDMO' see PARA 781; and as to when such an order is in force see PARA 785.
4 As to the meaning of 'final EDMO' see PARA 781; and as to when such an order is in force see PARA 792.
5 Housing Act 2004 Sch 7 para 18(1).
6 Ie the Housing Act 2004 Sch 7 paras 2, 10: see PARAS 786, 793.
7 Housing Act 2004 Sch 7 para 18(3). 'The commencement date' means the date on which the order came into force (or, if that order was preceded by one or more orders under Pt 4 Ch 2 (ss 132–138), the date when the first order came into force): Sch 7 para 18(8).
8 Ie the Housing Act 2004 Sch 7 para 10: see PARA 793.
9 Housing Act 2004 Sch 7 para 18(4).
10 Ie the Rent Act 1977 ss 14–16 and those provisions as applied by the Rent (Agriculture) Act 1976 s 5(2)–(4), Sch 2: see AGRICULTURAL PRODUCTION AND MARKETING vol 1 (2008) PARA 1295; LANDLORD AND TENANT vol 63 (2016) PARA 706 et seq; LANDLORD AND TENANT vol 64 (2016) PARA 1706.
11 Ie the Rent Act 1977 and the Rent (Agriculture) Act 1976: see LANDLORD AND TENANT vol 63 (2016) PARA 653 et seq; LANDLORD AND TENANT vol 64 (2016) PARA 1699 et seq.
12 Ie the Housing Act 1988 Pt I (ss 1–45): see LANDLORD AND TENANT vol 63 (2016) PARA 825 et seq.
13 Ie the Housing Act 2004 s 1(2), Sch 1 para 12: see LANDLORD AND TENANT vol 63 (2016) PARA 852.
14 Housing Act 2004 Sch 7 para 18(5), (6).
15 Ie within the meaning of the Rent Act 1977 or the Rent (Agriculture) Act 1976: see LANDLORD AND TENANT vol 63 (2016) PARA 673 et seq.

16 Ie within the meaning of the Housing Act 1988 Pt I: see LANDLORD AND TENANT vol 64 (2016) PARA 1747. As to the meaning of 'assured tenancy' see LANDLORD AND TENANT vol 63 (2016) PARA 825.
17 Ie the Housing Act 2004 Pt 4 Ch 2.
18 Ie under the Housing Act 2004 Sch 7 para 22: see PARA 801.
19 Housing Act 2004 Sch 7 para 18(7).

799. Effect on agreements and on legal proceedings. An agreement[1] or instrument which satisfies the following criteria has effect, while an interim EDMO[2] or final EDMO[3] is in force, as if any rights or liabilities of the relevant proprietor[4] under the agreement or instrument were instead rights or liabilities of the local housing authority[5]. An agreement or instrument is within these provisions if:

(1)   it is effective on the commencement date[6];
(2)   one of the parties to it is the relevant proprietor of the dwelling[7];
(3)   it relates to the dwelling, whether in connection with any management activities[8] with respect to it, or otherwise;
(4)   it is specified for these purposes in the order or falls within a description of agreements or instruments so specified; and
(5)   the authority serves a notice in writing on all the parties to it stating that these provisions are to apply to it[9].

An agreement or instrument is not within these provisions if:

(a)   it is a lease or licence under which the local authority is treated as the lessee[10]; or
(b)   it relates to any disposition by the relevant proprietor which is not precluded[11] by the statutory provisions as to EDMOs[12].

Proceedings in respect of any cause of action within the following provision may, while an interim EDMO or final EDMO is in force, be instituted or continued by or against the local housing authority instead of by or against the relevant proprietor[13]. A cause of action is within this provision if:

(i)   it is a cause of action (of any nature) which accrued to or against the relevant proprietor of the dwelling before the commencement date;
(ii)   it relates to the dwelling as mentioned in head (3);
(iii)   it is specified for the purposes of this provision in the order or falls within a description of causes of action so specified; and
(iv)   the authority serves a notice in writing on all interested parties stating that this provision is to apply to it[14].

If, by virtue of these provisions, the authority becomes subject to any liability to pay damages in respect of anything done (or omitted to be done) before the commencement date by or on behalf of the relevant proprietor of the dwelling, the relevant proprietor is liable to reimburse to the authority an amount equal to the amount of damages paid by it[15].

1 For this purpose, 'agreement' includes arrangement: Housing Act 2004 s 132(6), Sch 7 para 19(7).
2 As to the meaning of 'interim EDMO' see PARA 781; and as to when such an order is in force see PARA 785.
3 As to the meaning of 'final EDMO' see PARA 781; and as to when such an order is in force see PARA 792.
4 As to the meaning of 'relevant proprietor' see PARA 781 note 4.
5 Housing Act 2004 Sch 7 para 19(1); and see PARA 781 note 1. As to the meaning of 'local housing authority' see PARA 380 note 1.
6 For this purpose, 'the commencement date' means the date on which the order comes into force (or, if that order was preceded by one or more orders under the Housing Act 2004 Pt 4 Ch 2 (ss 132–138), the date when the first order came into force): Sch 7 para 19(7).
7 As to the meaning of 'dwelling' see PARA 781 note 5.

8 'Management activities' includes repair, maintenance, improvement and insurance: Housing Act 2004 Sch 7 para 19(7).
9 Housing Act 2004 Sch 7 para 19(2)(a)–(e). As to service of documents under the Housing Act 2004 see PARA 391.
10 Ie it is within the Housing Act 2004 Sch 7 para 2(6) (see PARA 786) or Sch 7 para 10(6) (see PARA 793).
11 Ie by the Housing Act 2004 Sch 7 para 4(7) (see PARA 787) or Sch 7 para 12(7) (see PARA 794).
12 Housing Act 2004 Sch 7 para 19(3).
13 Housing Act 2004 Sch 7 para 19(4).
14 Housing Act 2004 Sch 7 para 19(5).
15 Housing Act 2004 Sch 7 para 19(6).

800. Possession and supply of furniture. The following provisions apply where, on the date on which an interim EDMO[1] or final EDMO[2] comes into force, there is furniture[3] owned by the relevant proprietor[4] in the dwelling[5]. The right to possession of the furniture against all persons vests in the local housing authority[6] on that date and remains vested in the authority while the order is in force[7]. However, the right of the local housing authority to possession of the furniture is subject to the rights of any person who, on the date on which the interim EDMO or final EDMO comes into force, has the right to possession of the dwelling[8]. Also, where the local housing authority has the right to possession of the furniture, and it has not granted a right to possession of the furniture to any other person, it must, on a request by the relevant proprietor, give up possession of the furniture to him[9].

The local housing authority may renounce the right to possession of the furniture by serving notice on the relevant proprietor not less than two weeks before the renunciation is to have effect[10]. Where the local housing authority renounces the right to possession of the furniture, it must make appropriate arrangements for storage of the furniture at its own cost[11].

The local housing authority may supply the dwelling to which an interim EDMO or final EDMO relates with such furniture[12] as it considers to be required[13]. For the purposes of the financial arrangements while an order is in force[14], any expenditure incurred by the authority in so supplying furniture constitutes expenditure incurred by the authority in connection with performing its duties[15] to secure the occupation and proper management of the dwelling[16].

1 As to the meaning of 'interim EDMO' see PARA 781; and as to when such an order is in force see PARA 785.
2 As to the meaning of 'final EDMO' see PARA 781; and as to when such an order is in force see PARA 792.
3 For these purposes, 'furniture' includes fittings and other articles: Housing Act 2004 s 132(6), Sch 7 para 20(7).
4 As to the meaning of 'relevant proprietor' see PARA 781 note 4.
5 Housing Act 2004 Sch 7 para 20(1). As to the meaning of 'dwelling' see PARA 781 note 5.
6 As to the meaning of 'local housing authority' see PARA 380 note 1.
7 Housing Act 2004 Sch 7 para 20(2).
8 Housing Act 2004 Sch 7 para 20(3).
9 Housing Act 2004 Sch 7 para 20(4).
10 Housing Act 2004 Sch 7 para 20(5). As to service of documents under the Housing Act 2004 see PARA 391.
11 Housing Act 2004 Sch 7 para 20(6).
12 For this purpose, 'furniture' includes fittings and other articles: Housing Act 2004 Sch 7 para 21(3).
13 Housing Act 2004 Sch 7 para 21(1).
14 Ie the Housing Act 2004 Sch 7 para 5 or Sch 7 para 13: see PARAS 788, 795.
15 Ie its duties under the Housing Act 2004 s 135(1)–(3) (see PARA 784) or s 137(1)–(3) (see PARA 791).
16 Housing Act 2004 Sch 7 para 21(2).

801. Power of tribunal to determine certain leases and licences. The appropriate tribunal[1] may make an order determining a lease or licence[2] to which these provisions apply if the case falls within head (a) or head (b) below and the tribunal is satisfied that the dwelling is not being occupied and that the local housing authority[3] needs to have the right to possession of the dwelling[4] in order to secure that the dwelling becomes so occupied[5]. These provisions apply to the following leases and licences of a dwelling:

(1) a lease of the dwelling in respect of which the relevant proprietor[6] is the lessor;

(2) a sub-lease of any such lease; and

(3) a licence of the dwelling[7].

The tribunal may make such an order in a case where either:

(a) an interim or final EDMO[8] is in force in respect of the dwelling, and the local housing authority has applied[9] for an order determining the lease or licence[10]; or

(b) the local housing authority has applied[11] to the appropriate tribunal for an order authorising it to make an interim EDMO in respect of the dwelling and an order determining the lease or licence, and the appropriate tribunal has decided to authorise the authority to make an interim EDMO in respect of the dwelling[12].

An order under these provisions may include provision requiring the local housing authority to pay such amount or amounts to one or more of the lessor, lessee, licensor or licensee by way of compensation in respect of the determination of the lease or licence as the tribunal determines[13].

Where a final EDMO is in force in respect of a dwelling, and the tribunal makes an order requiring the local housing authority to pay an amount of compensation to a lessor, lessee, licensor or licensee in respect of the determination of a lease or licence of the dwelling, the tribunal must make an order varying the management scheme[14] contained in the final EDMO so as to make provision as to the payment of that compensation[15].

1 As to the meaning of 'appropriate tribunal' see PARA 580 note 2. As to appeals to the appropriate tribunal see PARA 32 et seq.
2 As to the meanings of 'lease' and 'licence' see PARA 391 note 6.
3 As to the meaning of 'local housing authority' see PARA 380 note 1.
4 As to the meaning of 'dwelling' see PARA 781 note 5.
5 Housing Act 2004 s 132(6), Sch 7 para 22(1) (amended by SI 2013/1036).
6 As to the meaning of 'relevant proprietor' see PARA 781 note 4.
7 Housing Act 2004 Sch 7 para 22(2).
8 As to the meaning of 'interim EDMO' see PARA 781; and as to when such an order is in force see PARA 785. As to the meaning of 'final EDMO' see PARA 781; and as to when such an order is in force see PARA 792.
9 Ie under the Housing Act 2004 Sch 7 para 2(3)(d) or Sch 7 para 10(3)(d): see PARAS 786, 793.
10 Housing Act 2004 Sch 7 para 22(3).
11 Ie under the Housing Act 2004 s 133: see PARA 782.
12 Housing Act 2004 Sch 7 para 22(4) (amended by SI 2013/1036).
13 Housing Act 2004 Sch 7 para 22(5).
14 As to management schemes see PARA 795.
15 Housing Act 2004 Sch 7 para 22(6).

802. Financial arrangements on termination of EDMOs. The following provisions apply where an interim EDMO[1] or final EDMO[2] ceases to have effect for any reason[3]. If, on the termination date[4] for an interim EDMO, the total amount of rent or other payments[5] collected or recovered[6] by the local housing authority[7] exceeds the total amount of the authority's relevant expenditure[8], and any amounts of compensation payable to third parties[9], the authority must, as soon as possible after the termination date, pay the balance to the relevant proprietor[10]. If, on the termination date for a final EDMO, any balance is payable to a third party, a dispossessed landlord or tenant[11] or the relevant proprietor in accordance with the management scheme[12], that amount must be paid to that person by the local housing authority in the manner provided by the scheme[13].

The following provisions apply where, on the termination date for an interim EDMO or final EDMO, the total amount of rent or other payments collected or recovered by the authority[14] is less than the total amount of the authority's relevant expenditure together with any such amounts of compensation payable to third parties[15]. The authority may recover from the relevant proprietor the amount of the shortfall, that is any relevant expenditure (not exceeding the deficit mentioned above) which he has agreed in writing to pay either as a condition of revocation of the order or otherwise and, where the relevant proprietor is a tenant under a lease in respect of the dwelling[16], the amount of any outstanding service charges[17] payable under the lease[18].

In the case of an interim EDMO ceasing to have effect, the authority may recover the deficit mentioned above from the relevant proprietor if, in its opinion, he unreasonably refused to consent to the creation of an interest or right in the dwelling[19] while the order was in force[20].

None of the provisions above, however, applies in relation to the order if the order is followed by a final EDMO, and the management scheme contained in that final EDMO provides[21] for those provisions not to apply in relation to the order[22].

Any sum recoverable by the authority under these provisions is, until recovered, a charge on the dwelling[23]. The charge takes effect on the termination date for the order as a legal charge which is a local land charge[24]. For the purpose of enforcing the charge the authority has the same powers and remedies under the Law of Property Act 1925 and otherwise as if it were a mortgagee by deed having powers of sale and lease, of accepting surrenders of leases and of appointing a receiver[25].

1 As to the meaning of 'interim EDMO' see PARA 781; and as to when such an order is in force see PARA 785.
2 As to the meaning of 'final EDMO' see PARA 781; and as to when such an order is in force see PARA 792.
3 Housing Act 2004 s 132(6), Sch 7 para 23(1).
4 'The termination date' means the date on which the order ceases to have effect: Housing Act 2004 Sch 7 para 23(12).
5 As to the meaning of 'rent or other payments' see PARA 788 note 4.
6 Ie as mentioned in the Housing Act 2004 Sch 7 para 5(3): see PARA 788.
7 As to the meaning of 'local housing authority' see PARA 380 note 1.
8 As to the meaning of 'relevant expenditure', in relation to an interim EDMO, see PARA 788 note 1; and, in relation to a final EDMO, see PARA 795 note 11 (definitions applied by the Housing Act 2004 Sch 7 para 23(12)).
9 Ie by virtue of orders under the Housing Act 2004 s 134(4) or s 138(2) (see PARAS 783, 805) or decisions of the authority under s 136(4) or s 138(3) (see PARAS 790, 805). As to the meaning of 'third party' see PARA 783 note 9.
10 Housing Act 2004 Sch 7 para 23(2); and see PARA 781 note 1. As to the meaning of 'relevant proprietor' see PARA 781 note 4.
11 'Dispossessed landlord or tenant' means a person who was a lessor, lessee, licensor or licensee under a lease or licence determined by an order under the Housing Act 2004 Sch 7 para 22 (see PARA 801): Sch 7 para 23(12). As to the meanings of 'lessor', 'lessee', 'licensor', 'licensee', 'lease' and 'licence' see PARA 391 note 6.
12 As to management schemes see PARA 795.
13 Housing Act 2004 Sch 7 para 23(3).
14 See note 6.
15 Housing Act 2004 Sch 7 para 23(4).
16 As to the meaning of 'dwelling' see PARA 781 note 5.

17 'Service charge' has the meaning given by the Landlord and Tenant Act 1985 s 18 (see LANDLORD
   AND TENANT vol 63 (2016) PARA 614): Housing Act 2004 Sch 7 para 23(12).
18 Housing Act 2004 Sch 7 para 23(5).
19 Ie as mentioned in the Housing Act 2004 Sch 7 para 2(3)(c): see PARA 786 head (3).
20 Housing Act 2004 Sch 7 para 23(6).
21 See the Housing Act 2004 Sch 7 para 13(4)(c), (d); and PARA 795.
22 Housing Act 2004 Sch 7 para 23(7).
23 Housing Act 2004 Sch 7 para 23(8).
24 Housing Act 2004 Sch 7 para 23(9). As to local land charges see REAL PROPERTY AND
   REGISTRATION vol 87 (2012) PARA 763 et seq.
25 Housing Act 2004 Sch 7 para 23(10). As to the meaning of 'mortgage' see PARA 751 note 11. See
   MORTGAGE vol 77 (2016) PARA 518 et seq. The power of appointing a receiver is exercisable at
   any time after the end of the period of one month beginning with the date on which the charge
   takes effect: Sch 7 para 23(11).

803. Leases, agreements and proceedings following termination of an EDMO.
The following provisions apply where an interim EDMO[1] or final EDMO[2] ceases
to have effect for any reason and the order is not immediately followed by a
further EDMO[3]. As from the termination date[4], an agreement[5] which has effect[6]
as a lease or licence[7] granted by the local housing authority[8] has effect with the
substitution of the relevant proprietor[9] for the authority[10]. If the relevant
proprietor is a lessee, nothing in a superior lease imposes liability on him or any
superior lessee in respect of anything done before the termination date in
pursuance of the terms of such an agreement[11].

If the following condition is met, namely that the authority serves[12] a notice on
the other party or parties to the agreement stating that this provision applies to the
agreement, any other agreement entered into by the authority in the performance
of its duties in respect of the dwelling to secure its occupation and proper
management[13] has effect, as from the termination date, with the substitution of
the relevant proprietor for the authority[14].

If the following condition is met, namely that the authority serves a notice on
all interested parties stating that this provision applies to the rights or liabilities or
(as the case may be) the proceedings, then, as from the termination date: (1) any
rights or liabilities that were rights or liabilities of the authority immediately
before the termination date by virtue of any provision relating to empty dwelling
management orders[15], or under any agreement in relation to which the relevant
proprietor has been substituted for the authority[16], are rights or liabilities of the
relevant proprietor instead; and (2) any proceedings instituted or continued by or
against the authority by virtue of any such provision or agreement may be
continued by or against the relevant proprietor instead[17].

If by virtue of these provisions a relevant proprietor becomes subject to any
liability to pay damages in respect of anything done (or omitted to be done) before
the termination date by or on behalf of the authority, the authority is liable to
reimburse to the relevant proprietor an amount equal to the amount of the
damages paid by him[18].

1 As to the meaning of 'interim EDMO' see PARA 781; and as to when such an order is in force see
  PARA 785.
2 As to the meaning of 'final EDMO' see PARA 781; and as to when such an order is in force see
  PARA 792.
3 Housing Act 2004 s 132(6), Sch 7 para 24(1).
4 'The termination date' means the date on which the order ceases to have effect: Housing Act 2004
  Sch 7 para 24(10).
5 'Agreement' includes arrangement (Housing Act 2004 Sch 7 para 24(10)); and Sch 7 para 24
  applies to instruments as it applies to agreements (Sch 7 para 24(9)).
6 Ie in accordance with the Housing Act 2004 Sch 7 para 3 or Sch 7 para 11: see PARAS 786, 793.
7 As to the meanings of 'lease' and 'licence' see PARA 391 note 6.

8 Ie under the Housing Act 2004 Sch 7 para 2 or Sch 7 para 10: see PARAS 786, 793. As to the meaning of 'local housing authority' see PARA 380 note 1.
9 As to the meaning of 'relevant proprietor' see PARA 781 note 4.
10 Housing Act 2004 Sch 7 para 24(2).
11 Housing Act 2004 Sch 7 para 24(3).
12 As to service of documents under the Housing Act 2004 see PARA 391.
13 Ie its duties under the Housing Act 2004 s 135(1)–(3) (see PARA 784) or s 137(1)–(3) (see PARA 791). As to the meaning of 'dwelling' see PARA 781 note 5.
14 Housing Act 2004 Sch 7 para 24(4), (5).
15 See the Housing Act 2004 Pt 4 Ch 2 (ss 132–138).
16 Ie any agreement to which the Housing Act 2004 Sch 7 para 24(4) applies: see the text and notes 12–14.
17 Housing Act 2004 Sch 7 para 24(6), (7).
18 Housing Act 2004 Sch 7 para 24(8).

804. Power of entry to carry out work. The following right is exercisable by the local housing authority[1], or any person authorised in writing by it, at any time when an interim EDMO or final EDMO is in force[2]. That right is the right at all reasonable times to enter any part of the dwelling[3] for the purpose of carrying out works, and is exercisable as against any person having an estate or interest[4] in the dwelling[5]. If, after receiving reasonable notice of the intended action, any occupier[6] of the dwelling prevents any officer, employee, agent or contractor of the local housing authority from carrying out work in the dwelling, a magistrates' court may order him to permit to be done on the premises anything which the authority considers to be necessary[7]. A person who fails to comply with such an order of the court commits an offence[8].

1 As to the meaning of 'local housing authority' see PARA 380 note 1.
2 Housing Act 2004 s 132(6), Sch 7 para 25(1); and see PARA 781 note 1. As to the meaning of 'interim EDMO' see PARA 781; and as to when such an order is in force see PARA 785. As to the meaning of 'final EDMO' see PARA 781; and as to when such an order is in force see PARA 792.
3 As to the meaning of 'dwelling' see PARA 781 note 5.
4 As to the meaning of 'person having an estate or interest' see PARA 391 note 7.
5 Housing Act 2004 Sch 7 para 25(2).
6 As to the meaning of 'occupier' see PARA 563 note 13.
7 Housing Act 2004 Sch 7 para 25(3).
8 Housing Act 2004 Sch 7 para 25(4). A person who commits such an offence is liable on summary conviction to a fine not exceeding level 5 on the standard scale: Sch 7 para 25(5). As to the powers of magistrates' courts to issue fines on summary conviction see SENTENCING vol 92 (2015) PARA 176.

805. Compensation payable to third parties. A third party[1] may, while an interim EDMO[2] is in force in respect of a dwelling[3], apply to the appropriate tribunal[4] for an order requiring the local housing authority[5] to pay to him compensation in respect of any interference in consequence of the order with his rights in respect of the dwelling[6]. On such an application, the tribunal may, if it thinks fit, make an order requiring the authority to pay to the third party an amount by way of compensation in respect of any such interference[7].

If a third party requests it to do so at any time, the local housing authority must consider whether an amount by way of compensation should be paid to him in respect of any interference in consequence of a final EDMO[8] with his rights[9]. The authority must notify the third party of its decision as soon as practicable[10]. Where the local housing authority decides that compensation ought to be paid to a third party, it must vary the management scheme[11] contained in the order so as to specify the amount of the compensation to be paid and to make provision as to its payment[12].

1 As to the meaning of 'third party' see PARA 783 note 9.

2 As to the meaning of 'interim EDMO' see PARA 781. As to when an interim EDMO is in force see PARA 785.

3 As to the meaning of 'dwelling' see PARA 781 note 5.

4 As to the meaning of 'appropriate tribunal' see PARA 580 note 2. As to appeals to the appropriate tribunal see PARA 32 et seq.

5 As to the meaning of 'local housing authority' see PARA 380 note 1.

6 Housing Act 2004 s 138(1) (amended by SI 2013/1036).

7 Housing Act 2004 s 138(2).

8 As to the meaning of 'final EDMO' see PARA 781. As to when a final EDMO is in force see PARA 792.

9 Housing Act 2004 s 138(3).

10 Housing Act 2004 s 138(4).

11 As to management schemes see PARA 795.

12 Housing Act 2004 s 138(5).

(v) Appeals

806. Appeals against decisions relating to EDMOs. A relevant person[1] may appeal to the appropriate tribunal[2] against:

(1)   a decision of the local housing authority[3] to make a final EDMO[4];

(2)   the terms of a final EDMO (including the terms of the management scheme[5] contained in it); or

(3)   the terms of an interim EDMO[6] on the grounds that they do not provide for one or both of the specified matters[7] relating to payments of surplus rent etc[8].

Where an appeal is made under head (3), the appeal may be brought at any time while the order is in force[9], and the powers of the appropriate tribunal[10] are limited to determining whether the order should be varied by the tribunal so as to include a term providing for the matter or matters in question, and (if so) what provision should be made by the term[11].

Any appeal against a final EDMO must generally be made within the period of 28 days beginning with the date specified in the notice[12] given by the authority as the date on which the order was made[13]. The appropriate tribunal may, however, allow an appeal to be made to it after the end of the period mentioned above if it is satisfied that there is a good reason for the failure to appeal before the end of that period (and for any delay since then in applying for permission to appeal out of time)[14].

If no appeal is brought under these provisions in respect of a final EDMO within the time allowed[15] for making such an appeal, the order is final and conclusive as to the matters which could have been raised on appeal[16].

1 For the purposes of the Housing Act 2004 Sch 7 Pt 4 (paras 26–37), 'relevant person' means any person who has an estate or interest in the dwelling (other than a person who is a tenant under a lease granted under Sch 7 para 2(3)(c) (see PARA 786 head (3)) or Sch 7 para 10(3)(c) (see PARA 793 head (3))): s 132(6), Sch 7 para 37. As to the meaning of 'person having an estate or interest' see PARA 391 note 7. As to the meaning of 'dwelling' see PARA 781 note 5. As to the meanings of 'tenant' and 'lease' see PARA 391 note 6.

2 As to the meaning of 'appropriate tribunal' see PARA 580 note 2. As to appeals to the appropriate tribunal see PARA 32 et seq.

3 As to the meaning of 'local housing authority' see PARA 380 note 1.

4 As to the meaning of 'final EDMO' see PARA 781. As to the making of such an order see PARA 790.

5 As to management schemes see PARA 795.

6 As to the meaning of 'interim EDMO' see PARA 781. As to the making of such an order see PARA 782.

7 Ie the matters mentioned in the Housing Act 2004 Sch 7 para 5(5)(a), (b) (the rate of interest which is to apply and the intervals at which payments are to be made): see PARA 788.

8 Housing Act 2004 Sch 7 para 26(1) (amended by SI 2013/1036).

9   Ie with the result that nothing in the Housing Act 2004 Sch 7 para 26(3) (see the text and notes 15–16) or Sch 7 para 27 (see the text and notes 12–14) applies in relation to the appeal.

10   Ie under the Housing Act 2004 Sch 7 para 28: see PARA 807.

11   Housing Act 2004 Sch 7 para 26(2) (amended by SI 2013/1036).

12   Ie under the Housing Act 2004 Sch 6 para 7(5) (as applied by s 136(5)): see PARA 790 note 11.

13   Housing Act 2004 Sch 7 para 27(1), (2).

14   Housing Act 2004 Sch 7 para 27(3) (amended by SI 2013/1036).

15   Ie by the Housing Act 2004 Sch 7 para 27: see the text and notes 12–14.

16   Housing Act 2004 Sch 7 para 26(3).

807. Powers of tribunal on appeal against decisions relating to EDMOs. An appeal to the appropriate tribunal[1] in respect of an interim EDMO[2] or a final EDMO[3] is to be by way of a re-hearing, and may be determined having regard to matters of which the local housing authority[4] was unaware when it made the decision[5].

The tribunal may:

(1)   in the case of an interim EDMO, vary the order to provide for the matters in question[6]; or

(2)   in the case of a final EDMO, confirm or vary the order or revoke it as from the date of the tribunal's order[7].

1   Ie under the Housing Act 2004 Sch 7 para 26: see PARA 806. As to the meaning of 'appropriate tribunal' see PARA 580 note 2. As to appeals to the appropriate tribunal see PARA 32 et seq.

2   As to the meaning of 'interim EDMO' see PARA 781. As to the making of such an order see PARA 782.

3   As to the meaning of 'final EDMO' see PARA 781. As to the making of such an order see PARA 790.

4   As to the meaning of 'local housing authority' see PARA 380 note 1.

5   Housing Act 2004 s 132(6), Sch 7 para 28(1), (2) (Sch 7 para 28(1) amended by SI 2013/1036).

6   Ie as mentioned in the Housing Act 2004 Sch 7 para 26(2)(b): see PARA 806.

7   Housing Act 2004 Sch 7 para 28(3).

808. Appeals against decision or refusal to vary or revoke EDMO. Similarly, a relevant person[1] may appeal to the appropriate tribunal[2] against:

(1)   a decision of a local housing authority[3] to vary or revoke an interim EDMO[4] or a final EDMO[5]; or

(2)   a refusal of a local housing authority to vary or revoke an interim EDMO or a final EDMO[6].

Any such appeal must be made before the end of the period of 28 days beginning with the date specified in the notice given by the authority[7] as the date on which the decision concerned was made[8]. The appropriate tribunal may allow an appeal to be made to it after the end of the period mentioned above if it is satisfied that there is a good reason for the failure to appeal before the end of that period (and for any delay since then in applying for permission to appeal out of time)[9].

1   As to the meaning of 'relevant person' see PARA 806 note 1.

2   As to the meaning of 'appropriate tribunal' see PARA 580 note 2. As to appeals to the appropriate tribunal see PARA 32 et seq.

3   As to the meaning of 'local housing authority' see PARA 380 note 1.

4   As to the meaning of 'interim EDMO' see PARA 781. As to the variation or revocation of such an order see PARA 789.

5   As to the meaning of 'final EDMO' see PARA 781. As to the variation or revocation of such an order see PARA 797.

6   Housing Act 2004 s 132(6), Sch 7 para 30 (amended by SI 2013/1036).

7   Ie under the Housing Act 2004 Sch 6 para 11, 16, 19 or 22 (as applied by Sch 7 para 8 or 17 (as the case may be)): see PARAS 789 note 21, 797 note 21.

8   Housing Act 2004 Sch 7 para 31(1), (2).

9   Housing Act 2004 Sch 7 para 31(3) (amended by SI 2013/1036).

809. Powers of tribunal on appeal relating to variation or revocation of EDMO. The following provisions apply to an appeal to the appropriate tribunal[1] against a decision to vary or revoke, or (as the case may be) to refuse to vary or revoke, an interim EDMO[2] or final EDMO[3]. The appeal is to be by way of a re-hearing, and may be determined having regard to matters of which the local housing authority[4] was unaware when it made the decision[5]. The tribunal may confirm, reverse or vary the decision of the local housing authority[6]. If the appeal is against a decision of the authority to refuse to revoke the order, the tribunal may make an order revoking the order as from a date specified in its order[7].

1 Ie under the Housing Act 2004 Sch 7 para 30: see PARA 808. As to the meaning of 'appropriate tribunal' see PARA 580 note 2. As to appeals to the appropriate tribunal see PARA 32 et seq.
2 As to the meaning of 'interim EDMO' see PARA 781. As to the variation or revocation of such an order see PARA 789.
3 Housing Act 2004 s 132(6), Sch 7 para 32(1) (amended by SI 2013/1036). As to the meaning of 'final EDMO' see PARA 781. As to the variation or revocation of such an order see PARA 797.
4 As to the meaning of 'local housing authority' see PARA 380 note 1.
5 Housing Act 2004 Sch 7 para 32(2).
6 Housing Act 2004 Sch 7 para 32(3).
7 Housing Act 2004 Sch 7 para 32(4).

810. Appeal against a decision on compensation payable to third parties. The following provisions apply where a local housing authority[1] has made a decision[2] as to whether compensation should be paid to a third party[3] in respect of any interference with his rights in consequence of a final EDMO[4]. The third party may appeal to the appropriate tribunal[5] against:

(1) a decision by the authority not to pay compensation to him; or
(2) a decision of the authority so far as relating to the amount of compensation that should be paid[6].

Any such appeal must be made:

(a) where the decision is made before the final EDMO is made, within the period of 28 days beginning with the date specified in the notice given by the authority[7] as the date on which the order was made; or
(b) in any other case, within the period of 28 days beginning with the date on which the authority notifies[8] the third party[9].

The appropriate tribunal may allow an appeal to be made to it after the end of the period mentioned above if it is satisfied that there is good reason for the failure to appeal before the end of that period (and for any delay since then in applying for permission to appeal out of time)[10].

1 As to the meaning of 'local housing authority' see PARA 380 note 1.
2 Ie under the Housing Act 2004 s 136(4) or s 138(3): see PARAS 790, 805.
3 As to the meaning of 'third party' see PARA 783 note 9.
4 Housing Act 2004 s 132(6), Sch 7 para 34(1). As to the meaning of 'final EDMO' see PARA 781. As to the making of such an order see PARA 790.
5 As to the meaning of 'appropriate tribunal' see PARA 580 note 2. As to appeals to the appropriate tribunal see PARA 32 et seq.
6 Housing Act 2004 Sch 7 para 34(2) (amended by SI 2013/1036).
7 Ie under the Housing Act 2004 Sch 6 para 7(5) (as applied by s 136(5)): see PARA 790 note 11.
8 Ie under the Housing Act 2004 s 138(4): see PARA 805.
9 Housing Act 2004 Sch 7 para 35(1), (2).
10 Housing Act 2004 Sch 7 para 35(3) (amended by SI 2013/1036).

811. Powers of tribunal on an appeal on compensation. An appeal to the appropriate tribunal[1] against a decision of a local housing authority[2] not to pay compensation to a third party[3], or as to the amount of compensation to be paid, is to be by way of re-hearing, and may be determined having regard to matters of which the authority was unaware when it took the decision[4]. The tribunal may confirm, reverse or vary the decision of the local housing authority[5]. Where the tribunal reverses or varies the decision of the authority, it must make an order varying the management scheme[6] contained in the final EDMO[7] accordingly[8].

1 Ie under the Housing Act 2004 Sch 7 para 34: see PARA 810. As to the meaning of 'appropriate tribunal' see PARA 580 note 2. As to appeals to the appropriate tribunal see PARA 32 et seq. An appeal lies to the Upper Tribunal: see PARAS 49–50.
2 As to the meaning of 'local housing authority' see PARA 380 note 1.
3 As to the meaning of 'third party' see PARA 783 note 9. As to compensation see PARAS 790, 805.
4 Housing Act 2004 s 132(6), Sch 7 para 36(1), (2).
5 Housing Act 2004 Sch 7 para 36(3).
6 As to management schemes see PARA 795.
7 As to the meaning of 'final EDMO' see PARA 781.
8 Housing Act 2004 Sch 7 para 36(4).

12. COMPULSORY PURCHASE AND RELATED PROVISIONS

812. Introduction. Under the Housing Act 1985, local housing authorities have power to make orders authorising the compulsory purchase of land[1].

The Acquisition of Land Act 1981, the Compulsory Purchase Act 1965 and the Land Compensation Act 1961 apply to the compulsory purchase of land under the Housing Act 1985 subject to the provisions of Part XVII of that Act[2].

1 As to compulsory purchase generally see COMPULSORY ACQUISITION OF LAND vol 18 (2009) PARA 501 et seq. For a decision on the compensation payable see *Nelson v Burnley Borough Council* (unreported, 13 October 2005), Lands Tribunal.
2 See the Housing Act 1985 s 578. As to the provisions of Pt XVII (ss 578–603) see PARAS 627 et seq, 813 et seq. As to Crown land see PARA 419.

813. Restriction on recovery of possession after making of compulsory purchase order. Where a local housing authority[1] has made a compulsory purchase order authorising:

(1) the acquisition of a house in multiple occupation[2] under the statutory powers relating to the provision of housing[3] or the purchase of a condemned house for temporary housing use[4]; or

(2) the acquisition of land in a renewal area[5] on which there are premises consisting of or including housing accommodation,

and within the specified period[6] proceedings for possession of premises forming part of the house or land in question are brought in the County Court against a person who was the lessee[7] of the premises when the order was made, or became the lessee after the order was made, but is no longer the lessee, the court may suspend the execution of any order for possession for such period, and subject to such conditions, as it thinks fit[8]. The period of suspension ordered by the court must not, however, extend beyond the end of the period of three years beginning with the date on which the court makes its order or, if earlier, the date on which the compulsory purchase order became operative[9]. The court may from time to time vary the period of suspension[10] or terminate it, or vary the terms of the order in other respects[11].

If at any time:

(a) the appropriate national authority notifies the authority that he declines to confirm the compulsory purchase order, or the order is quashed by a court; or

(b) the authority decides, whether before or after the order has been submitted to the appropriate national authority for confirmation, not to proceed with it,

the authority must notify the person entitled to the benefit of the order for possession; and that person is entitled, on applying to the court, to obtain an order terminating the period of suspension, but subject to the exercise of the same discretion in fixing the date on which possession is to be given as the court might exercise if it were then making an order for possession for the first time[12].

These provisions do not apply where the person entitled to possession of the premises is the local housing authority[13].

1 As to the meaning of 'local housing authority' see PARA 11.
2 In the Housing Act 1985 s 582, 'house in multiple occupation' has the meaning given by the Housing Act 2004 ss 254–259 for the purposes of that Act (other than Pt 1) (ss 1–54) (see PARA 667): Housing Act 1985 s 582(8) (substituted by the Housing Act 2004 s 265(1), Sch 15 paras 10, 29).
3 Ie under the Housing Act 1985 s 17: see PARA 416.
4 Ie under the Housing Act 1985 s 300: see PARA 638.
5 Ie under the Local Government and Housing Act 1989 s 93(2): see PARA 824.

6　The period referred to in the text is the period beginning with the making of the compulsory purchase order and ending with: (1) the third anniversary of the date on which the order became operative; or (2) any earlier date on which the appropriate national authority notifies the local housing authority that it declines to confirm the order or the order is quashed by a court: Housing Act 1985 s 582(2). As to the appropriate national authority, ie the Secretary of State or, where statutory functions have been transferred in relation to Wales, the Welsh Ministers, see PARA 7.
7　As to the meaning of 'lessee' see PARA 31 note 3.
8　Housing Act 1985 s 582(1), (3) (s 582(1) amended by the Local Government and Housing Act 1989 ss 165(1), 194(1), (4), Sch 9 para 74, Sch 11 para 85, Sch 12 Pt II).
9　Housing Act 1985 s 582(4).
10　However, the period may not be enlarged beyond the end of the period of three years referred to in the Housing Act 1985 s 582(4) (see the text and note 9): see s 582(5).
11　Housing Act 1985 s 582(5).
12　Housing Act 1985 s 582(6).
13　Housing Act 1985 s 582(7) (amended by SI 1991/724).

814. Continuance of tenancies of houses compulsorily acquired and to be used for housing purposes. Where a local housing authority[1] is authorised to purchase compulsorily a house[2] which is to be used for housing purposes, and has acquired the right to enter on and take possession of the house by virtue of having served a notice of intended entry[3], the authority may, instead of exercising that right by taking actual possession of the house, proceed by serving notice on any person then in occupation of the house, or part of it, authorising him to continue in occupation upon terms specified in the notice or on such other terms as may be agreed[4].

Where the authority proceeds in this way, the same consequences follow with respect to the determination of the rights and liabilities of any person arising out of any interest of his in the house, or a part of it, and the authority may deal with the premises in all respects, as if the authority had taken actual possession on the date of the notice[5].

A person who ceases to be entitled to receive rent in respect of the premises by virtue of these provisions is deemed for the purposes of statutory compensation[6] to have been required to give up possession of the premises[7].

1　As to the meaning of 'local housing authority' see PARA 11.
2　For these purposes, 'house' includes: (1) any part of a building which is occupied as a separate dwelling; and (2) any yard, garden, outhouses and appurtenances belonging to the house or usually enjoyed with it: Housing Act 1985 s 583(4).
3　Ie a notice under the Compulsory Purchase Act 1965 s 11: see COMPULSORY ACQUISITION OF LAND vol 18 (2009) PARA 645.
4　Housing Act 1985 s 583(1).
5　Housing Act 1985 s 583(2).
6　Ie for the purposes the Compulsory Purchase Act 1965 s 20: see COMPULSORY ACQUISITION OF LAND vol 18 (2009) PARA 699.
7　Housing Act 1985 s 583(3).

815. Power to enter and determine short tenancies of land acquired or appropriated. Where a local housing authority[1] has agreed to purchase or has determined to appropriate land for the purposes of the provision of:

(1)　housing[2];
(2)　area improvement[3];
(3)　the provisions relating to clearance areas[4]; or
(4)　the provisions relating to renewal areas[5],

then, subject to the interest of the person in possession of the land, if that person's interest is not greater than that of a tenant[6] for a year, or from year to year, the authority may, after giving him not less than 14 days' notice, enter on and take possession of the land, or such part of the land as is specified in the notice, without previous consent[7]. This power may be exercised at any time after the making of the agreement or the determination, except where the appropriation requires ministerial consent in which case the power is not exercisable until that consent has been given[8].

The exercise of the local housing authority's power under these provisions is subject to the payment to the person in possession of the like compensation, and interest on the compensation awarded, as would be payable if the authority had been authorised to acquire the land compulsorily, and that person had been required in pursuance of the authority's powers in that behalf to quit possession before the expiry of his term or interest in the land, but without any necessity for compliance with the statutory prohibition[9] of entry on the land acquired before the compensation has been ascertained and paid or secured[10].

1   As to the meaning of 'local housing authority' see PARA 11.
2   Ie for the purposes of the Housing Act 1985 Pt II (ss 8–57): see PARA 405 et seq.
3   Ie for the purposes of the Housing Act 1985 Pt VIII (ss 239–263): see PARAS 7, 830 et seq.
4   Ie the provisions of the Housing Act 1985 Pt IX (ss 265–323): see PARA 620 et seq. As to clearance areas see PARA 631 et seq.
5   Ie the provisions of the Local Government and Housing Act 1989 Pt VII (ss 89–100): see PARA 820 et seq.
6   As to the meaning of 'tenant' see PARA 31 note 3.
7   Housing Act 1985 s 584(1), (2) (s 584(1) amended by the Local Government and Housing Act 1989 s 194(1), Sch 11 para 86).
8   Housing Act 1985 s 584(3).
9   Ie the Compulsory Purchase Act 1965 s 11: see COMPULSORY ACQUISITION OF LAND vol 18 (2009) PARA 645.
10 Housing Act 1985 s 584(4).

816. Application of compensation due to another local authority. Compensation payable in respect of land of another local authority[1] in pursuance of a compulsory purchase under the statutory powers relating to the provision of housing[2], the acquisition of land for clearance[3] or the purchase of a condemned house for temporary housing use[4] which would otherwise be paid into court[5] may, if the appropriate national authority[6] consents, instead be paid and applied as it may determine[7].

1   As to the meaning of 'local authority' see PARA 12.
2   Ie under the Housing Act 1985 s 17: see PARA 416.
3   Ie under the Housing Act 1985 s 290: see PARA 633.
4   Ie under the Housing Act 1985 s 300: see PARA 638.
5   Ie in accordance with the Compulsory Purchase Act 1965 Sch 1 (purchase from persons not having power to dispose): see COMPULSORY ACQUISITION OF LAND vol 18 (2009) PARAS 553–555.
6   As to the appropriate national authority, ie the Secretary of State or, where statutory functions have been transferred in relation to Wales, the Welsh Ministers, see PARA 7.
7   Housing Act 1985 s 599 (amended by the Local Government and Housing Act 1989 ss 165(1), 194(4), Sch 9 para 78, Sch 12 Pt II).

817. Powers of entry and penalty for obstruction. A person authorised by the local housing authority[1] or the appropriate national authority[2] may at any reasonable time, on giving seven days' notice of his intention to the occupier, and to the owner[3] if the owner is known, enter premises for the purpose of survey and examination where it appears to the local housing authority or the appropriate national authority that survey or examination is necessary in order to determine whether any powers under Part XVII of the Housing Act 1985[4] should be exercised in respect of the premises[5].

An authorisation for these purposes must be in writing, stating the particular purpose or purposes for which the entry is authorised[6]. It must, if so required, be produced for inspection by the occupier or anyone acting on his behalf[7].

It is a summary offence intentionally to obstruct an officer of the local housing authority or of the appropriate national authority, or any person authorised[8] to enter premises, in the performance of anything which he is required or authorised to do by Part XVII[9].

1 As to the meaning of 'local housing authority' see PARA 11.
2 As to the appropriate national authority, ie the Secretary of State or, where statutory functions have been transferred in relation to Wales, the Welsh Ministers, see PARA 7.
3 As to the meaning of 'owner' see PARA 606 note 4.
4 Ie the Housing Act 1985 Pt XVII (ss 578–603).
5 Housing Act 1985 s 600(1) (s 600(1), (2) amended by the Local Government and Housing Act 1989 s 165(1), Sch 9 para 79).
6 Housing Act 1985 s 600(2) (as amended: see note 5).
7 Housing Act 1985 s 600(2) (as amended: see note 5).
8 Ie in pursuance of the Housing Act 1985 Pt XVII.
9 Housing Act 1985 s 601(1) (s 601(1), (2) amended by the Local Government and Housing Act 1989 Sch 9 para 80). A person committing such an offence is liable on conviction to a fine not exceeding level 3 on the standard scale: Housing Act 1985 s 601(2) (as so amended). As to the powers of magistrates' courts to issue fines on summary conviction see SENTENCING vol 92 (2015) PARA 176.

818. Removal or alteration of apparatus of statutory undertakers. Where by reason of the stopping up, diversion or alteration of the level or width of a street[1] by a local housing authority[2] under powers exercisable by the authority by virtue of the Housing Act 1985:

(1)   the removal or alteration of apparatus[3] belonging to statutory undertakers[4]; or

(2)   the execution of works for the provision of substituted apparatus, whether permanent or temporary,

is reasonably necessary for the purposes of their undertaking, the statutory undertakers may by notice in writing served on the authority require the authority to remove or alter the apparatus or to execute the works[5]. Where such a requirement is made (and not withdrawn), the authority must give effect to it unless the authority serves notice in writing on the undertakers of its objection to the requirement within 28 days of the service of the notice upon the authority and the requirement is determined by arbitration[6] to be unreasonable[7].

At least seven days before commencing any works which the authority is so required to execute, the authority must, except in case of emergency, serve on the undertakers notice in writing of its intention to do so; and if the undertakers so elect within seven days from the date of service of the notice on them, they must themselves execute the works[8]. If the works are executed by the authority, they must be executed at the authority's expense and under superintendence (also at the authority's expense) and to the reasonable satisfaction of the undertakers; and if the works are executed by the undertakers, they must be executed in accordance with the reasonable directions and to the reasonable satisfaction of the authority, and the reasonable costs of the works must be repaid to the undertakers by the authority[9].

1 As to the meaning of 'street' see PARA 409 note 2.
2 As to the meaning of 'local housing authority' see PARA 11.
3 For these purposes, 'apparatus' means sewers, drains, culverts, watercourses, mains, pipes, valves, tubes, cables, wires, transformers and other apparatus laid down or used for or in connection with the carrying, conveying or supplying to premises of a supply of water, water for hydraulic power, gas or electricity, and standards and brackets carrying street lamps; and references to the alteration of apparatus include diversion and the alteration of position or level: Housing Act 1985 s 611(6)(b), (c).
4 For these purposes, 'statutory undertakers' means any persons authorised by an enactment, or by an order, rule or regulation made under an enactment, to construct, work or carry on a railway,

canal, inland navigation, dock, harbour, tramway, gas or other public undertaking: Housing Act 1985 s 611(6)(a) (amended by the Water Act 1989 s 190(3), Sch 27 Pt I; and the Electricity Act 1989 s 112(4), Sch 18).

5 Housing Act 1985 s 611(1).

6 Any difference arising between statutory undertakers and a local housing authority under the Housing Act 1985 s 611(3) (see the text and note 8) or s 611(4) (see the text and note 9), and any matter which by virtue of s 611(2)(b) is to be determined by arbitration, must be referred to and determined by an arbitrator to be appointed, in default of agreement, by the appropriate national authority: s 611(5). As to the appropriate national authority, ie the Secretary of State or, where statutory functions have been transferred in relation to Wales, the Welsh Ministers, see PARA 7.

7 Housing Act 1985 s 611(2).

8 Housing Act 1985 s 611(3).

9 Housing Act 1985 s 611(4).

819. Exclusion of statutory protection for residential occupiers. Nothing in the Rent (Agriculture) Act 1976, the Rent Act 1977, or Part I of the Housing Act 1988[1] prevents possession being obtained of a dwelling house[2] of which possession is required for the purpose of enabling a local housing authority[3] to exercise its powers under any enactment relating to housing[4].

1 Ie the Housing Act 1988 Pt I (ss 1–45): see LANDLORD AND TENANT vol 63 (2016) PARA 825 et seq. As to the Rent Act 1977 and the Rent (Agriculture) Act 1976 (both largely repealed subject to transitional provisions and savings) see LANDLORD AND TENANT vol 63 (2016) PARA 653 et seq; LANDLORD AND TENANT vol 64 (2016) PARA 1699 et seq.

2 For the purposes of the Housing Act 1985 Pt XVIII (ss 604–625), 'dwelling house' includes any yard, garden, outhouses and appurtenances belonging to it or usually enjoyed with it and s 183 (see PARA 231) has effect to determine whether a dwelling house is a flat: s 623(1), (2) (amended by the Local Government and Housing Act 1989 s 165, Sch 9 para 90; and the Housing Act 2004 s 266, Sch 16).

3 As to the meaning of 'local housing authority' see PARA 11.

4 Housing Act 1985 s 612 (amended by the Housing Act 1988 s 140(1), Sch 17 para 63; and the Local Government and Housing Act 1989 s 165(1), Sch 9 para 89). Thus any occupier loses his security of tenure. As to rehousing and compensation see the Land Compensation Act 1973; and COMPULSORY ACQUISITION OF LAND vol 18 (2009) PARA 853 et seq.

13. AREA IMPROVEMENT

(1) INTRODUCTION

820. In general. Since 1969, the improvement of poor housing conditions on an area basis has been an option available to local housing authorities.

The Housing Act 1969 introduced the concept of a general improvement area[1] whilst the Housing Act 1974 introduced the notion of a housing action area[2]. The relevant provisions were codified as part of the Housing Act 1985[3] but the law was often criticised in that it did not provide one single, comprehensive way of dealing with poor housing and also because it did not allow for housing conditions to be considered in the broader context of employment, education and other poor facilities and amenities[4]. Following changes made by the Local Government and Housing Act 1989, local authorities no longer have power to declare either a general improvement or a housing action area[5], but the legislation relating to those powers remains on the statute book[6].

Part VII of the Local Government and Housing Act 1989 now provides a framework to facilitate the revitalisation of areas suffering from poor housing conditions by the declaration of a renewal area[7]. Where a local housing authority declares a renewal area it has the power to acquire land and to carry out or assist in carrying out works of improvement or repair[8]. This renewal area strategy is designed to deal with private sector housing and different provisions are available to deal with a local housing authority's own housing[9].

1 See the Housing Act 1969 Pt II (ss 28–41) (repealed).
2 See the Housing Act 1974 Pt IV (ss 36–49) (repealed).
3 See the Housing Act 1985 Pt VIII (ss 239–263) (as originally enacted).
4 See Hughes and Lowe *Social Housing Law and Policy* (1995) p 335.
5 Local Government and Housing Act 1989 s 98(1).
6 See the Housing Act 1985 Pt VIII; and PARA 831 et seq.
7 See the Local Government and Housing Act 1989 Pt VII (ss 89–100); and PARA 821 et seq.
8 See the Local Government and Housing Act 1989 s 93; and PARA 824.
9 See PARA 405 et seq.

(2) RENEWAL AREAS

821. Declaration of a renewal area. Where upon consideration of a report containing particulars of specified matters[1] and of any other matters which the authority considers relevant, a local housing authority[2] is satisfied:

(1)   that the living conditions in an area within its district[3] consisting primarily of housing accommodation[4] are unsatisfactory[5]; and

(2)   that those conditions can most effectively be dealt with by declaring the area to be a renewal area[6],

then, subject to the following provisions[7], it may cause the area to be defined on a map and by resolution[8] declare it to be a renewal area for the period specified in the declaration[9].

Subject to the power of a local housing authority to declare that an area is to cease to be a renewal area[10], an area which is declared to be a renewal area is such an area either:

(a)   until the end of the period specified in the declaration; or

(b)   if at any time during that period the local housing authority by resolution extends the period for which the area is to be a renewal area, until the end of the period specified in the resolution, unless further extended under this provision[11].

In considering whether to declare an area to be a renewal area, or to extend the period for which an area is to be a renewal area, a local housing authority must have regard to such guidance[12] as may from time to time be given by the appropriate national authority[13].

Before exercising its power to declare an area to be a renewal area or to extend (or further extend) the period for which an area is to be a renewal area, a local housing authority must take such steps as appear to the authority best designed to secure:

(i)   that the detailed proposals for the exercise of the authority's powers during the period that the area will be a renewal area[14] or, where the authority is considering the extension of the period for which an area is to be a renewal area, such of those proposals as remain to be implemented, are brought to the attention of persons residing or owning property in the area; and

(ii)   that those persons are informed of the name and address of the person to whom should be addressed inquiries and representations concerning those proposals[15].

The provisions of the Housing Act 1985 relating to compulsory purchase and land compensation[16] apply as if Part VII of the Local Government and Housing Act 1989 were contained in the Housing Act 1985[17].

1   The matters of which particulars must be included in the report are:
   (1)   the living conditions in the area concerned;
   (2)   the ways in which those conditions may be improved (whether by the declaration of a renewal area or otherwise);
   (3)   the powers available to the authority (including powers available apart from the Local Government and Housing Act 1989);
   (4)   the authority's detailed proposals for the exercise of those powers during the period that the area will be a renewal area (if so declared);
   (5)   the cost of those proposals;
   (6)   the financial resources available, or likely to be available, to the authority (from whatever source) for implementing those proposals; and
   (7)   the representations (if any) made to the authority in relation to those proposals,
   and the report must contain a recommendation, with reasons, as to whether a renewal area should be declared and, if so, the period for which the area should be a renewal area: Local Government and Housing Act 1989 s 89(3) (s 89(3)–(7) substituted, and s 89(8) added, by SI 2002/1860). For the powers available to the local housing authority see the Local Government and Housing Act 1989 s 93; and PARA 824.
2   As to the meaning of 'local housing authority' and any reference to the district of such an authority see PARA 11 (definitions applied by the Local Government and Housing Act 1989 s 100(1)).
3   See note 2.
4   'Housing accommodation' means dwellings, houses in multiple occupation and hostels: Local Government and Housing Act 1989 s 100(1); and see *R v Camden London Borough Council, ex p Comyn Ching & Co (London) Ltd* (1983) 47 P & CR 417, [1984] JPL 661 (decided under the Housing Act 1974 s 43 (repealed)). 'Dwelling' means a building or part of a building occupied or intended to be occupied as a separate dwelling, together with any yard, garden, outhouses and appurtenances belonging to or usually enjoyed with it: Local Government and Housing Act 1989 s 100(1). 'House in multiple occupation' means a house in multiple occupation as defined by the Housing Act 2004 ss 254–259, as they have effect for the purposes of Pt 1 (ss 1–54) (ie, without the exclusions contained in Sch 14) (see PARA 668), but does not include any part of such a house which is occupied as a separate dwelling by persons who form a single household: Local Government and Housing Act 1989 s 100(1) (definition substituted by the Housing Act 2004 s 265(1), Sch 15 paras 10, 34). See PARA 667.
5   Local Government and Housing Act 1989 s 89(1)(a).

6 Local Government and Housing Act 1989 s 89(1)(b).
7 Ie the provisions in the Local Government and Housing Act 1989 ss 89–100: see PARA 822 et seq.
8 A resolution declaring an area to be a renewal area has effect from the day on which it is passed, and is a local land charge: Local Government and Housing Act 1989 s 89(8) (as added: see note 1). As to local land charges see REAL PROPERTY AND REGISTRATION vol 87 (2012) PARA 763 et seq.
9 Local Government and Housing Act 1989 s 89(1) (amended by SI 2002/1860).
10 Ie the provisions in the Local Government and Housing Act 1989 s 95: see PARA 826.
11 Local Government and Housing Act 1989 s 89(4) (as substituted: see note 1).
12 As to guidance generally see the Local Government and Housing Act 1989 s 99; and PARA 830. See also Department of the Environment Circular 17/96, Annex B.
13 Local Government and Housing Act 1989 s 89(5) (as substituted: see note 1). As to the appropriate national authority, ie the Secretary of State or, where statutory functions have been transferred in relation to Wales, the Welsh Ministers, see PARA 7.
14 Ie the proposals referred to in the Local Government and Housing Act 1989 s 89(3)(d): see note 1 head (4).
15 Local Government and Housing Act 1989 s 89(6), (7) (as substituted: see note 1). See also Department of the Environment Circular 17/96, Annex C; and see Doolittle *Housing and Regeneration* (2003).
16 Ie the Housing Act 1985 Pt XVII (ss 578–603) (compulsory purchase and land compensation): see PARA 812 et seq.
17 Local Government and Housing Act 1989 s 100(2).

822. Steps to be taken after declaration of a renewal area. As soon as may be after declaring an area to be a renewal area[1], or extending (or further extending) the period for which an area is to be a renewal area[2], a local housing authority[3] must take such steps as appear to the authority to be best designed to secure:

  (1)   that the resolution to which the declaration, or extension (or further extension) of the period, relates is brought to the attention of persons residing or owning property in the area; and

  (2)   that those persons are informed of the name and address of the person to whom should be addressed inquiries and representations concerning action to be taken with respect to the renewal area[4].

1 As to the declaration of a renewal area see PARA 821.
2 See PARA 821.
3 As to the meaning of 'local housing authority' see PARA 11 (definition applied by the Local Government and Housing Act 1989 s 100(1)).
4 Local Government and Housing Act 1989 s 91 (substituted by SI 2002/1860).

823. Duty to publish information. Where a local housing authority[1] has declared an area to be a renewal area[2], it must from time to time publish, in such manner as appears to it best designed to secure that the information is brought to the attention of persons residing or owning property in the area, information with respect to:

  (1)   the action it proposes to take in relation to the area[3];
  (2)   the action it has taken in relation to the area[4]; and
  (3)   the assistance available for the carrying out of works in the area[5].

This information must be such as appears to the authority best designed to further the purpose for which the area was declared a renewal area[6].

1 As to the meaning of 'local housing authority' see PARA 11 (definition applied by the Local Government and Housing Act 1989 s 100(1)).
2 As to the declaration of a renewal area see PARA 821.
3 Local Government and Housing Act 1989 s 92(1)(a).
4 Local Government and Housing Act 1989 s 92(1)(b).
5 Local Government and Housing Act 1989 s 92(1)(c).
6 Local Government and Housing Act 1989 s 92(1). Land indicated by information published under s 92(1) falls within the Town and Country Planning Act 1990 s 149, Sch 13 (see Sch 13 para 12) and as such is affected by Pt VI Ch II ss 149–171 (blighted land): see PLANNING vol 83 (2010) PARA 1154 et seq.

824. General powers of local housing authority. Where a local housing authority[1] has declared an area to be a renewal area[2], the authority may exercise a number of statutory powers[3]. Under these powers, it may:

(1) for the purpose of securing or assisting in securing all or any of the specified objectives[4], acquire by agreement[5], or be authorised by the appropriate national authority[6] to acquire compulsorily[7], any land[8] in the area on which there are premises consisting of or including housing accommodation[9] or which forms part of the curtilage of any such premises; and the authority may provide housing accommodation on such land acquired[10];

(2) for the purpose of effecting or assisting the improvement of the amenities in the area, acquire by agreement, or be authorised by the appropriate national authority to acquire compulsorily, any land in the area (including land which the authority proposes to dispose of to another person who intends to effect or assist the improvement of those amenities)[11];

(3) carry out works (including works of demolition) on land owned by the authority in the area[12]; and

(4) enter into an agreement with a housing association[13] or other person under which, in accordance with the terms of the agreement, certain of the authority's functions[14] are to be exercisable by that association or other person[15].

1 As to the meaning of 'local housing authority' see PARA 11 (definition applied by the Local Government and Housing Act 1989 s 100(1)).

2 As to the declaration of a renewal area see PARA 821.

3 Local Government and Housing Act 1989 s 93(1). The powers conferred by s 93 are without prejudice to any power which a local housing authority may have under or by virtue of any other enactment: s 93(8).

4 The specified objectives are: (1) the improvement or repair of the premises, either by the authority or by a person to whom it proposes to dispose of the premises; (2) the proper and effective management and use of the housing accommodation, either by the authority or by a person to whom it proposes to dispose of the premises comprising the accommodation; and (3) the well-being of the persons for the time being residing in the area: Local Government and Housing Act 1989 s 93(3)(a)–(c).

5 As to the determination of short tenancies of land which a local housing authority has agreed to purchase, or has determined to appropriate, for the purposes of the Local Government and Housing Act 1989 Pt VII (ss 89–100) subject to the interest of the person in possession see the Housing Act 1985 s 584; and PARA 815.

6 As to the appropriate national authority, ie the Secretary of State or, where statutory functions have been transferred in relation to Wales, the Welsh Ministers, see PARA 7.

7 Ie authorised to acquire compulsorily under the Housing Act 1985 s 578 (see PARA 812). See also the Acquisition of Land Act 1981, the Compulsory Purchase Act 1965, the Land Compensation Act 1961; and COMPULSORY ACQUISITION OF LAND vol 18 (2009) PARA 501 et seq. See *Varsani v Secretary of State for the Environment* (1980) 40 P & CR 354, 255 Estates Gazette 457 (a case on compulsory acquisition within a housing action area (see PARA 831 et seq)).

8 As to the meaning of 'land' see PARA 416 note 3.

9 As to the meaning of 'housing accommodation' see PARA 821 note 4. See also *R v Camden London Borough Council, ex p Comyn Ching & Co (London) Ltd* (1983) 47 P & CR 417, [1984] JPL 661 (decided under the Housing Act 1974 s 43 (repealed)).

10 Local Government and Housing Act 1989 s 93(2). As to the meaning of 'curtilage' see *Dyer v Dorset County Council* [1989] QB 346, 86 LGR 686, CA (a decision under the right to buy provisions of the Housing Act 1980 (repealed: see now the Housing Act 1985 Pt V (ss 118–188); and PARA 239 et seq).

11 Local Government and Housing Act 1989 s 93(4). If after: (1) the authority has entered into a contract for the acquisition of land under s 93(2) (see the text and note 10) or s 93(4); or (2) a compulsory purchase order authorising the acquisition of land under either of those provisions has been confirmed, the renewal area concerned ceases to be such an area or the land is excluded from the area, the provision in question continues to apply as if the land continued to be in a renewal

area: s 93(7). As to the duration of a renewal area see PARA 821; and as to the exclusion of land from, and the termination of, such an area see PARA 826.

12 Local Government and Housing Act 1989 s 93(5)(a) (s 93(5) amended by SI 2002/1860).

13 As to the meaning of 'housing association' see PARA 13.

14 Ie the authority's functions under the Local Government and Housing Act 1989 s 93(5) (see the text and note 12): s 93(6).

15 Local Government and Housing Act 1989 s 93(6) (amended by SI 2002/1860).

825. Power to apply for orders extinguishing right to use vehicles on highway. A local housing authority[1] which has declared a renewal area[2] may exercise the powers of a local planning authority[3] under the Town and Country Planning Act 1990[4] with respect to a highway in that area even though it is not the local planning authority, but this is subject to the following provisions[5]. The local housing authority may not make an application to the appropriate national authority[6] to make or revoke an order extinguishing the right to use vehicles[7] except with the consent of the local planning authority[8]. If the local housing authority is not also the highway authority[9], any such application made by it must in the first place be sent to the highway authority, which must transmit it to the appropriate national authority[10]. Where an order extinguishing the right to use vehicles[11] has been made on an application made by a local housing authority, any compensation for loss of access to the highway[12] is payable by it instead of by the local planning authority[13].

1   As to the meaning of 'local housing authority' see PARA 11 (definition applied by the Local Government and Housing Act 1989 s 100(1)).

2   As to the declaration of a renewal area see PARA 821.

3   As to local planning authorities see PLANNING vol 81 (2010) PARA 43 et seq.

4   Ie the powers under the Town and Country Planning Act 1990 ss 249, 250 (extinguishment of right to use vehicles on certain highways): see HIGHWAYS, STREETS AND BRIDGES vol 55 (2012) PARA 824.

5   Local Government and Housing Act 1989 s 94(1) (s 94(1), (2), (4) amended by the Planning (Consequential Provisions) Act 1990 s 4, Sch 2 para 84).

6   As to the appropriate national authority, ie the Secretary of State or, where statutory functions have been transferred in relation to Wales, the Welsh Ministers, see PARA 7.

7   Ie an application under the Town and Country Planning Act 1990 s 249(2) or (6): see HIGHWAYS, STREETS AND BRIDGES vol 55 (2012) PARA 824.

8   Local Government and Housing Act 1989 s 94(2) (as amended: see note 5).

9   As to highway authorities see HIGHWAYS, STREETS AND BRIDGES vol 55 (2012) PARA 52 et seq.

10 Local Government and Housing Act 1989 s 94(3).

11 Ie an order under the Town and Country Planning Act 1990 s 249(2): see HIGHWAYS, STREETS AND BRIDGES vol 55 (2012) PARA 824.

12 Ie compensation under the Town and Country Planning Act 1990 s 250(1): see HIGHWAYS, STREETS AND BRIDGES vol 55 (2012) PARA 824.

13 Local Government and Housing Act 1989 s 94(4) (as amended: see note 5).

826. Exclusion of land from, or termination of, a renewal area. A local housing authority[1] may by resolution[2]:

(1)   exclude land[3] from a renewal area[4]; or

(2)   declare that an area is to cease to be a renewal area[5].

Before exercising these powers, an authority must take such steps as appear to the authority best designed to secure:

(a)   that the proposed exclusion or cessation, as the case may be, is brought to the attention of persons residing or owning property in the area; and

(b)   that those persons are informed of the name and address of the person to whom should be addressed representations concerning the proposed exclusion or cessation[6], and as soon as may be after passing such a resolution the authority must take such steps as appear to it best designed to secure that the resolution is brought to the attention of persons residing or owning property in the renewal area[7].

1　As to the meaning of 'local housing authority' see PARA 11 (definition applied by the Local Government and Housing Act 1989 s 100(1)).

2　A resolution under the Local Government and Housing Act 1989 s 95(1) has effect from the day on which it is passed: s 95(6). Such a resolution does not affect the continued operation of the provisions of Pt VII (ss 89–100), or any other enactment relating to renewal areas, in relation to works begun before the date on which the exclusion or cessation takes effect; but the resolution does have effect with respect to works which have not been begun before that date, notwithstanding that expenditure in respect of the works has been approved before that date: s 95(7).

3　As to the meaning of 'land' see PARA 416 note 3.

4　Local Government and Housing Act 1989 s 95(1)(a). As to the declaration of a renewal area see PARA 821.

5　Local Government and Housing Act 1989 s 95(1)(b).

6　Local Government and Housing Act 1989 s 95(2) (substituted by SI 2002/1860).

7　Local Government and Housing Act 1989 s 95(1), (5) (amended by SI 2002/1860). See also Department of the Environment Circular 17/96, Annex C1.

827. Contributions by the appropriate national authority. Subsidy is available to defray a local housing authority's costs in dealing with a renewal area. Thus the appropriate national authority[1] may pay contributions[2] to local housing authorities[3] towards such expenditure incurred by them under Part VII of the Local Government and Housing Act 1989[4] as it may determine[5]. The rate or rates of the contributions, the calculation of the expenditure to which they relate and the manner of their payment is determined by the appropriate national authority with, in relation to England, the consent of the Treasury; and any such determination may be made generally, or with respect to a particular local housing authority or description of authority, including a description framed by reference to authorities in a particular area[6].

If, before the declaration of a renewal area[7], a local housing authority is satisfied that the rate of contributions which, in accordance with such a determination, would otherwise be applicable to the authority will not be adequate, bearing in mind the action it proposes to take with regard to the area, it may, before making the declaration, apply to the appropriate national authority for contributions at a higher rate in respect of that area[8]. Where such an application is made, the local housing authority may not declare the area concerned to be a renewal area until the application is approved, refused or withdrawn[9]. If such an application is approved, the appropriate national authority may pay contributions in respect of the area concerned at such higher rate as it may determine[10].

1　As to the appropriate national authority, ie the Secretary of State or, where statutory functions have been transferred in relation to Wales, the Welsh Ministers, see PARA 7.

2　Contributions under the Local Government and Housing Act 1989 s 96 are payable subject to such conditions as to records, certificates, audit or otherwise as the appropriate national authority may (with, in relation to England, the approval of the Treasury) impose: s 96(3). As to the commutation of contributions see s 157; and LOCAL GOVERNMENT FINANCE vol 70 (2012) PARA 25. As to the Treasury CONSTITUTIONAL AND ADMINISTRATIVE LAW vol 20 (2014) PARA 262 et seq.

3　As to the meaning of 'local housing authority' see PARA 11 (definition applied by the Local Government and Housing Act 1989 s 100(1)).

4　Ie the Local Government and Housing Act 1989 Pt VII (ss 89–100).

5　Local Government and Housing Act 1989 s 96(1). As to works which are eligible, or ineligible, see Department of the Environment Circular 17/96, Annex C para 8.

6　See the Local Government and Housing Act 1989 s 96(2).

7　As to the declaration of a renewal area see PARA 821.

8 Local Government and Housing Act 1989 s 96(4); and see Department of the Environment Circular 17/96, Annex C. Such an application must be made in such form and must contain such particulars as the appropriate national authority may determine: Local Government and Housing Act 1989 s 96(5).
9 Local Government and Housing Act 1989 s 96(5).
10 Local Government and Housing Act 1989 s 96(6).

828. Powers of entry and penalty for obstruction. A person authorised by the local housing authority[1] or the appropriate national authority[2] may at any reasonable time, on giving not less than seven days' notice of his intention to the occupier, and to the owner[3] if the owner is known, enter premises:

(1) for the purpose of survey and examination where it appears to the local housing authority or the appropriate national authority that survey or examination is necessary in order to determine whether any powers should be exercised[4]; or

(2) for the purpose of survey or valuation where the local housing authority is authorised to acquire the premises compulsorily[5].

An authorisation for these purposes:

(a) must be in writing stating the particular purpose or purposes for which the entry is authorised[6]; and

(b) must, if so required, be produced[7] for inspection by the occupier or anyone acting on his behalf[8].

It is a summary offence[9] intentionally to obstruct an officer of the local housing authority or of the appropriate national authority, or a person authorised to enter premises under the Local Government and Housing Act 1989, in the performance of anything which that officer, authority or person is required or authorised to do[10].

1 As to the meaning of 'local housing authority' see PARA 11 (definition applied by the Local Government and Housing Act 1989 s 100(1)).
2 As to the appropriate national authority, ie the Secretary of State or, where statutory functions have been transferred in relation to Wales, the Welsh Ministers, see PARA 7.
3 'Owner', in relation to premises: (1) means a person (other than a mortgagee not in possession) who is for the time being entitled to dispose of the fee simple in the premises, whether in possession or reversion; and (2) includes also a person holding or entitled to the rents and profits of the premises under a lease of which the unexpired term exceeds three years: Local Government and Housing Act 1989 s 97(5).
4 Local Government and Housing Act 1989 s 97(1)(a). A person may not be authorised by a local housing authority under s 97(1)(a) to enter and survey or value land in connection with a proposal to acquire an interest in or a right over land (but see the Housing and Planning Act 2016 s 172; and COMPULSORY ACQUISITION OF LAND): Local Government and Housing Act 1989 s 97(1A) (added by the Housing and Planning Act 2016 s 179, Sch 14 para 17).
5 Local Government and Housing Act 1989 s 97(1)(b). As to compulsory acquisition see PARA 812 et seq.
6 Local Government and Housing Act 1989 s 97(2)(a).
7 This does not mean that the right of entry can only be exercised if there is someone to whom the authority can be produced: see *Grove v Eastern Gas Board* [1952] 1 KB 77, [1951] 2 All ER 1051, CA.
8 Local Government and Housing Act 1989 s 97(2)(b).
9 A person who commits such an offence is liable on conviction to a fine not exceeding level 3 on the standard scale: Local Government and Housing Act 1989 s 97(4). As to the powers of magistrates' courts to issue fines on summary conviction see SENTENCING vol 92 (2015) PARA 176.
10 Local Government and Housing Act 1989 s 97(3). However, it has been held in a different context that no offence is committed if a written authority is unavailable at the time of entry: see *Stroud v Bradbury* [1952] 2 All ER 76, [1952] WN 306, DC (a decision on the powers of entry under the Public Health Act 1936 ss 287, 288).

829. Transitional provisions. The provisions of Part VII of the Local Government and Housing Act 1989[1] have effect in place of the provisions relating to housing action and general improvement areas contained in Part VIII of the Housing Act 1985[2] and, accordingly, after 1 April 1990[3], a local housing authority[4] no longer has power under the Housing Act 1985 to declare an area a housing action area[5] or a general improvement area[6]. If a general improvement area would otherwise have remained in existence on 1 April 1991, the area ceased to be a general improvement area on that date[7]. In any case where, immediately before 1 April 1990, the period for which a housing action area had effect exceeded two years, the duration of that area ended, subject to certain exceptions[8], on 1 April 1991[9].

1 Ie the Local Government and Housing Act 1989 Pt VII (ss 89–100): see PARA 821 et seq.
2 Ie the Housing Act 1985 Pt VIII (ss 239–263): see PARA 831 et seq.
3 Ie the appointed day: see the Local Government and Housing Act 1989 s 98(7); and the Local Government and Housing Act 1989 (Commencement No 5 and Transitional Provisions) Order 1990, SI 1990/431.
4 As to the meaning of 'local housing authority' see PARA 11 (definition applied by the Local Government and Housing Act 1989 s 100(1)).
5 As to the meaning of 'housing action area' see PARA 831. In the application of the Housing Act 1985 s 245 (contributions by appropriate national authority towards expenditure of local housing authorities relating to environmental works in housing action areas) in relation to expenditure which was incurred on or after 14 June 1989 and in respect of which no contribution under s 245 was paid before the appointed day, s 245(2) is substituted by the Local Government and Housing Act 1989 s 98(5): see PARA 831.
6 Local Government and Housing Act 1989 s 98(1). As to the meaning of 'general improvement area' see PARA 832. In the application of the Housing Act 1985 s 259 (contributions by appropriate national authority towards expenditure of local housing authorities relating to general improvement areas) in relation to expenditure which was incurred on or after 14 June 1989 and in respect of which no contribution under s 259 was paid before the appointed day, s 259(2) is substituted by the Local Government and Housing Act 1989 s 98(6): see PARA 832.
7 Local Government and Housing Act 1989 s 98(2).
8 Nothing in the Local Government and Housing Act 1989 s 98(3) affects the power of a local housing authority: (1) by resolution under the Housing Act 1985 s 250(1)(b) to bring a housing action area to an end (see PARA 831); or (2) by resolution under s 251 to extend, on one occasion only, the duration of a housing action area by a period of two years (see PARA 831): Local Government and Housing Act 1989 s 98(4)(a), (b).
9 Local Government and Housing Act 1989 s 98(3).

830. Exercise of power to give guidance. Any power under Part VII of the Local Government and Housing Act 1989[1] to give guidance may be so exercised as to make different provision for different cases, different descriptions of cases and different areas and, in particular, with respect to different local housing authorities[2] or descriptions of authority (including a description framed by reference to authorities in a particular area)[3].

1 Ie under the Local Government and Housing Act 1989 Pt VII (ss 89–100): see PARA 821 et seq.
2 As to the meaning of 'local housing authority' see PARA 11 (definition applied by the Local Government and Housing Act 1989 s 100(1)).
3 Local Government and Housing Act 1989 s 99 (amended by SI 2002/1860).

(3) HOUSING ACTION AREAS AND GENERAL IMPROVEMENT AREAS

(i) Housing Action Areas

831. Effect of declaration of housing action area. Although the legislation relating to housing action areas and general improvement areas[1] remains in force, local authorities no longer have power to declare either a general improvement area or a housing action area[2]. A housing action area could be declared in the following circumstances. Where a report with respect to an area within its district[3] consisting primarily of housing accommodation[4] was submitted to the local housing authority[5] by a person appearing to the authority to be suitably qualified (who could be an officer of the authority), and the authority, upon consideration of the report and of any other information in its possession, was satisfied, having regard to:

    (1)   the physical state of the housing accommodation in the area as a whole[6]; and

    (2)   social conditions in the area,

that the statutory requirement[7] was fulfilled with respect to the area[8], it could cause the area to be defined on a map[9] and by resolution declare it to be a housing action area[10]. In considering whether to take such action the local housing authority had to have regard to such guidance as might from time to time be given by the appropriate national authority[11], either generally or with respect to a particular authority or description of authority or in any particular case, with regard to the identification of areas suitable to be declared housing action areas[12].

As soon as might be after declaring an area to be a housing action area the local housing authority had to take certain steps to publicise the declaration and notify the appropriate national authority[13], which had power to reject or amend the declaration or require more time to consider it[14]. If a local housing authority proposed to declare as a housing action area an area which consisted of or included land which was comprised in a general improvement area[15], it was required to indicate on the required map the land which was so comprised and the land would be deemed to have been excluded from the general improvement area or to have ceased to be such an area[16].

Where a local housing authority declared an area to be a housing action area, it could exercise statutory powers for the purpose of securing or assisting in securing all or any of the required objectives[17]. For the purposes of improving the amenities in a housing action area, the local housing authority was given power to carry out environmental works[18] on land[19] belonging to it and to give assistance towards the carrying out of environmental works by others[20]. The appropriate national authority had power to pay contributions to a local housing authority towards expenditure incurred by it in relation to environmental works[21].

A local housing authority had a statutory duty to publish information designed to further the purpose for which the area was declared a housing action area[22].

Changes of ownership or occupation of the land in a housing action area had to be notified to the local housing authority[23], and a penalty could be imposed for failure to notify such changes[24].

The local housing authority could by resolution exclude land from a housing action area or declare that an area was to cease to be a housing action area, and as soon as might be after passing such a resolution the authority had to take certain required steps to publicise the resolution[25]. The local housing authority could by resolution extend the duration of a housing action area by a period of two years, and could do so more than once, subject to notifying the appropriate national authority and obtaining its approval[26].

Subject to certain transitional provisions[27], these powers have been replaced by the power to declare a renewal area[28].

1   Ie the Housing Act 1985 Pt VIII (ss 239–263).
2   See PARA 820.
3   As to the meaning of 'district' see PARA 11.
4   'Housing accommodation' means dwellings, houses in multiple occupation and hostels: Housing Act 1985 s 252(a). 'Dwelling' means a building or part of a building occupied or intended to be

occupied as a separate dwelling, together with any yard, garden, outhouses and appurtenances belonging to or usually enjoyed with that building or part: s 252(b). 'House in multiple occupation' means a house in multiple occupation as defined by the Housing Act 2004 ss 254–259, as they have effect for the purposes of Pt 1 (ss 1–54) (ie without the exclusions contained in Sch 14) (see PARA 668), but does not include any part of such a house which is occupied as a separate dwelling by persons who form a single household (see PARA 667): Housing Act 1985 s 252(c) (substituted by the Housing Act 2004 s 265(1), Sch 15 paras 10, 12). 'Hostel' means a building in which is provided, for persons generally or for a class or classes of persons: (1) residential accommodation otherwise than in separate and self-contained sets of premises; and (2) either board or facilities for the preparation of food adequate to the needs of those persons, or both: Housing Act 1985 s 622(1) (numbered as such by SI 2001/3649).

5   As to the meaning of 'local housing authority' see PARA 11.
6   Housing Act 1985 s 239(1)(a).
7   The requirement was that the living conditions in the area were unsatisfactory and could most effectively be dealt with within a period of five years so as to secure: (1) the improvement of the housing accommodation in the area as a whole; (2) the well-being of the persons for the time being resident in the area; and (3) the proper and effective management and use of that accommodation, by declaring the area to be a housing action area: Housing Act 1985 s 239(2).
8   Housing Act 1985 s 239(1)(b).
9   Where the area proposed as a housing action area consisted of or included land which was comprised in a general improvement area, the land involved had to be indicated on the map prepared under the Housing Act 1985 s 239(1): see s 242(1).
10 Housing Act 1985 s 239(1). An area which was declared to be a housing action area had to be such an area for the period of five years subject to: (1) the power of the appropriate national authority to overrule a declaration under s 241(2)(a); (2) the power of a local housing authority to terminate housing action area under s 250(1)(b); and (3) the provision for extension of the duration of a housing action area under s 251: s 239(4) (amended by the Housing and Planning Act 1986 s 21(2)(a)).
11 As to the appropriate national authority, ie the Secretary of State or, where statutory functions have been transferred in relation to Wales, the Welsh Ministers, see PARA 7.
12 Housing Act 1985 s 239(3). A resolution declaring an area to be a housing action area is a local land charge: s 239(5). As to local land charges see REAL PROPERTY AND REGISTRATION vol 87 (2012) PARA 763 et seq.
13 See the Housing Act 1985 s 240 (amended by the Housing and Planning Act 1986 s 21(2); and by SI 1996/2325 and SI 2010/866).
14 See the Housing Act 1985 s 241.
15 As to the declaration of such areas see the Housing Act 1985 s 253; and PARA 831. See also, however, PARA 580.
16 See the Housing Act 1985 s 242 (amended by the Housing and Planning Act 1986 s 21(2)).
17 See the Housing Act 1985 s 243.
18 'Environmental works' means any works other than works to the interior of housing accommodation: Housing Act 1985 s 244(5). When taking any action under the Housing Act 1985, the local housing authority must have regard to environmental considerations: see s 607; and PARA 404.
19 As to the meaning of 'land' see PARA 416 note 3.
20 See the Housing Act 1985 s 244 (amended by SI 2002/1860).
21 See the Housing Act 1985 s 245 (amended by SI 1988/1258). In the application of the Housing Act 1985 s 245 in relation to expenditure: (1) which was incurred on or after 14 June 1989; and (2) in respect of which no contribution under s 245 was paid before 1 April 1990 ('the appointed day': see PARA 829 note 3), s 245(2) is substituted by the Local Government and Housing Act 1989 s 98(5).
22 See the Housing Act 1985 s 246.
23 See the Housing Act 1985 ss 247, 248 (s 247 amended by the Housing Act 1988 s 140, Sch 17 para 45).
24 See the Housing Act 1985 s 249.
25 See the Housing Act 1985 s 250 (amended by the Housing and Planning Act 1986 s 21(2)).
26 See the Housing Act 1985 s 251 (amended by the Housing and Planning Act 1986 s 24(1)(j), Sch 5 para 10(3), (9)).
27 See the Local Government and Housing Act 1989 s 98(2)–(4); and PARA 829.
28 See PARA 820 et seq.

(ii) General Improvement Areas

832. Effect of declaration of general improvement area. Where a report with respect to a predominantly residential area within its district[1] was submitted to the local housing authority[2] by a person appearing to the authority to be suitably qualified (who could be an officer of the authority), and it appeared to the authority, upon consideration of the report and of any other information in its possession:

(1) that living conditions in the area could most appropriately be improved by the improvement of the amenities of the area or of dwellings in the area, or both; and

(2) that such an improvement might be effected or assisted by the exercise of its powers relating to general improvement areas,

the authority had power to cause the area to be defined on a map and by resolution declare it to be a general improvement area[3]. A general improvement area could not be defined so as to include, but might be defined so as to surround, land[4] which was comprised in a housing action area[5]. A general improvement area could not (unless the land had been cleared of buildings) be so defined as to include, but might be so defined as to surround:

(a) land comprised in a clearance area[6];

(b) land purchased by the local housing authority, that was surrounded by or adjoining a clearance area[7]; or

(c) land included in a clearance area that was a local housing authority's own property[8],

and where the appropriate national authority[9] on confirming a compulsory purchase order[10] modified the order by excluding from a clearance area land adjoining a general improvement area, the land was, unless the appropriate national authority otherwise directed, to be taken to be included in the general improvement area[11].

As soon as may be after declaring an area to be a housing action area the local housing authority had to take certain steps to publicise the declaration and notify the appropriate national authority[12]. Where a local housing authority declared an area to be a general improvement area, it could, for the purpose of effecting or assisting the improvement of the amenities of the area, or of the dwellings in the area, or both: (i) carry out works on land owned by it and assist (by grants, loans or otherwise) in the carrying out of works on land not owned by it; (ii) acquire any land by agreement; and (iii) let or otherwise dispose of land for the time being owned by it[13].

A local housing authority which declared a general improvement area could exercise the powers of a local planning authority[14] to extinguish the right to use vehicles with respect to a highway in that area notwithstanding that it was not the local planning authority, but subject to certain statutory restrictions[15].

Where a local housing authority passed a resolution declaring an area to be a general improvement area it had a statutory duty to publish information designed to further the objects of the statutory provisions[16] under which the declaration was made[17]. The local housing authority could by resolution exclude land from a general improvement area or declare that an area should cease to be a general improvement area[18].

The appropriate national authority had power to pay annual contributions for a period of 20 years to a local housing authority towards expenditure incurred by it relating to general improvement areas[19].

Subject to certain transitional provisions[20], these powers have been replaced by the power to declare a renewal area[21].

1　As to the meaning of 'district' see PARA 11.
2　As to the meaning of 'local housing authority' see PARA 11.
3　Housing Act 1985 s 253(1).
4　As to the meaning of 'land' see PARA 416 note 3.
5　Housing Act 1985 s 253(2). As to the meaning of 'housing action area' see PARA 831.
6　Housing Act 1985 s 253(3)(a). As to the meaning of 'clearance area' see PARA 632.
7　Housing Act 1985 s 253(3)(b). As to the meaning of 'land surrounded by or adjoining clearance area' see s 290(2); and PARA 633.
8　Housing Act 1985 s 253(3)(c). As to the meaning of 'local housing authority's own property' see s 293(1); and PARA 632.
9　As to the appropriate national authority, ie the Secretary of State or, where statutory functions have been transferred in relation to Wales, the Welsh Ministers, see PARA 7.
10　Ie an order under the Housing Act 1985 Sch 22 (repealed) (acquisition of land for clearance).
11　Housing Act 1985 s 253(3).
12　See the Housing Act 1985 s 254.
13　See the Housing Act 1985 s 255 (amended by the Local Government and Housing Act 1989 s 194, Sch 11 para 69; the Housing Grants, Construction and Regeneration Act 1996 ss 103, 147, Sch 1 para 8(2), Sch 3 Pt I; and SI 2002/1860). 'Disposal', in relation to land, includes a conveyance of, or contract to convey, an estate or interest not previously in existence: Housing Act 1985 s 262.
14　As to local planning authorities see PLANNING vol 81 (2010) PARA 43 et seq. For the powers available see the Town and Country Planning Act 1990 ss 249, 250 (extinguishment of right to use vehicles on certain highways); and HIGHWAYS, STREETS AND BRIDGES vol 55 (2012) PARA 824.
15　See the Housing Act 1985 s 256 (amended by the Planning (Consequential Provisions) Act 1990 ss 3, 4, Sch 1 Pt I, Sch 2 para 71(1)).
16　Ie the Housing Act 1985 Pt VIII (ss 239–263).
17　See the Housing Act 1985 s 257 (amended by the Housing and Planning Act 1986 s 21(2)).
18　See the Housing Act 1985 s 258 (amended by the Housing and Planning Act 1986 s 21(2)).
19　See the Housing Act 1985 s 259 (amended by SI 1988/1258). See also the Housing (Contributions Towards Expenditure for Area Improvement) Order 1988, SI 1988/1258. In the application of the Housing Act 1985 s 259 in relation to expenditure: (1) which was incurred on or after 14 June 1989; and (2) in respect of which no contribution under s 259 was paid before 1 April 1990 ('the appointed day': see PARA 829 note 3), s 259(2) is substituted by the Local Government and Housing Act 1989 s 98(6).
20　See the Local Government and Housing Act 1989 s 98(2)–(4); and PARA 829.
21　See PARA 820 et seq.

(iii)　Effect of Resolutions

833.　Effect of resolutions relating to a housing action area or general improvement area. A resolution of a local housing authority[1] passed after 7 November 1986[2]:

(1)　declaring an area to be a housing action area[3], excluding land from a housing action area or declaring that an area was to cease to be a housing action area[4]; or

(2)　declaring an area to be a general improvement area[5], excluding land from a general improvement area or declaring that an area was to cease to be a general improvement area[6],

had effect from the day on which the resolution was passed[7]. A resolution declaring an area to be a general improvement area could be expressed to have effect from a future date, not later than four weeks after the passing of the resolution, on which the whole or part of that area would cease to be, or be included in, a housing action area[8].

Where before 7 November 1986 a local housing authority passed a resolution of any of the descriptions mentioned above expressed to have effect from a date after that on which it was passed:

(a)   anything done before 7 November 1986 in reliance on the view that the resolution was invalid had effect as if the resolution had not been passed[9]; but

(b)   otherwise, the resolution was taken for all purposes, both before and after 7 November 1986, to have been validly passed and to have had effect from the date on which it was expressed to have had effect[10].

Subject to certain transitional provisions[11], no such resolutions may now be passed[12].

1   As to the meaning of 'local housing authority' see PARA 11.
2   Ie the commencement date of the Housing Act 1985 ss 259A, 259B.
3   As to the meaning of 'housing action area', as to exclusion of land from a housing action area and as to an area ceasing to be a housing action area see PARA 831.
4   Housing Act 1985 s 259A(1)(a) (ss 259A, 259B added by the Housing and Planning Act 1986 s 21(1)).
5   As to the meaning of 'general improvement area', as to exclusion of land from a general improvement area, and as to an area ceasing to be a general improvement area, see PARA 832.
6   Housing Act 1985 s 259A(1)(b) (as added: see note 4).
7   Housing Act 1985 s 259A(1) (as added: see note 4).
8   Housing Act 1985 s 259A(2) (as added: see note 4).
9   Housing Act 1985 s 259B(1)(a) (as added: see note 4).
10   Housing Act 1985 s 259B(1)(b) (as added: see note 4). However, a person must not be proceeded against in respect of anything done or omitted before 7 November 1986 which would not have been an offence if the resolution had not been passed: s 259B(2) (as so added). Where the resolution declared a housing action area or general improvement area and, before 7 November 1986, the local housing authority passed a further resolution making the like declaration in relation to the whole or part of the area to which the first resolution then related: (1) both resolutions were effective, notwithstanding that they related in whole or in part to the same area; (2) the area covered by both resolutions was a housing action area or general improvement area by virtue of the joint effect of the two resolutions, and in the case of a housing action area continued to be such an area until the end of the period of five years beginning with the date on which the second resolution was passed; (3) it was immaterial whether steps taken before 7 November 1986 were taken in reliance on the first resolution or the second, but steps taken in reliance on the first were not to be proceeded with to the extent that they had been superseded by, or were inconsistent with, steps taken in reliance on the second; and (4) the areas declared by the two resolutions could be treated as one for the purposes of s 245(3) or s 259(3) (limit on aggregate expenditure qualifying for contributions by appropriate national authority: see PARAS 831, 832): s 259B(3) (as so added). The provisions of s 259B(3) do not affect the powers of the appropriate national authority under s 241(2)(a), (b) (power to overrule declaration of housing action area or exclude land from area) and, so far as they relate to the duration of a housing action area, have effect subject to s 241(4) (effect of appropriate national authority's decision in such a case): s 259B(4) (as so added). As to the appropriate national authority, ie the Secretary of State or, where statutory functions have been transferred in relation to Wales, the Welsh Ministers, see PARA 7.
11   See the Local Government and Housing Act 1989 s 98(2)–(4); and PARA 829.
12   See PARA 820 et seq.

(iv) Powers of Entry and Penalties for Obstruction

834. Powers of entry and penalty for obstruction. A person who is authorised by the local housing authority[1] or the appropriate national authority[2] may at any reasonable time, on giving 24 hours' notice of his intention to the occupier, and to the owner[3] if the owner is known, enter premises:

(1)   for the purpose of survey and examination where it appears to the authority or the appropriate national authority that survey or examination is necessary in order to determine whether any relevant powers should be exercised[4]; or

(2)   for the purpose of survey or valuation where the authority is authorised to purchase the premises compulsorily[5].

An authorisation for these purposes must be in writing stating the particular purpose or purposes for which the entry is authorised[6].

It is a summary offence[7] to obstruct an officer of the local housing authority or of the appropriate national authority, or a person authorised under the Housing Act 1985[8] to enter premises, in the performance of anything which that officer, authority or person is required or authorised to do by that Act[9].

However, following the replacement of the power to declare housing action areas and general improvement areas with the power to declare renewal areas, the provisions described above are for practical purposes obsolete[10].

1   As to the meaning of 'local housing authority' see PARA 11.
2   As to the appropriate national authority, ie the Secretary of State or, where statutory functions have been transferred in relation to Wales, the Welsh Ministers, see PARA 7.
3   'Owner', in relation to premises: (1) means a person (other than a mortgagee not in possession) who is for the time being entitled to dispose of the fee simple in the premises, whether in possession or reversion; and (2) includes also a person holding or entitled to the rents and profits of the premises under a lease of which the unexpired term exceeds three years: Housing Act 1985 s 262.
4   Housing Act 1985 s 260(1)(a).
5   Housing Act 1985 s 260(1)(b).
6   Housing Act 1985 s 260(2).
7   A person who commits such an offence is liable on conviction to a fine not exceeding level 2 on the standard scale: Housing Act 1985 s 261(2). As to the powers of magistrates' courts to issue fines on summary conviction see SENTENCING vol 92 (2015) PARA 176. As to offences by bodies corporate see s 613; and PARA 663 note 13.
8   See the Housing Act 1985 Pt VIII (ss 239–263); and PARA 831 et seq.
9   Housing Act 1985 s 261(1).
10 See PARA 820 et seq.

14. HOUSING GRANTS

(1) IN GENERAL

835. Introduction to the legislation. Prior to the Housing Grants, Construction and Regeneration Act 1996, most of which was brought into force on 17 December 1996[1], mandatory grants for dwellings falling below defined standards were available to enable the owners to carry out works and improvements to render the dwellings habitable. Such grants were first introduced in 1959[2] and a new approach to the making of grants was introduced by the Housing Act 1974[3] which was subsequently consolidated into the Housing Act 1985[4] and later replaced by Part VIII of the Local Government and Housing Act 1989[5].

Under the Housing Act 1985, five main housing grants were available: improvement grants for the conversion of premises for dwellings or for certain defined major works of improvement; intermediate grants for the improvement of dwellings lacking standard amenities; repairs grants for works of repair or replacement; special grants for works to be undertaken to houses in multiple occupation; and common parts grants for the repair or improvement of the common parts of buildings containing flats[6].

The Local Government and Housing Act 1989 introduced a means test for grants so that even if an applicant was eligible for a mandatory grant he would have to make a contribution to the cost depending on his means[7]. The five main grants were replaced by four: renovation grants for the improvement or repair of a dwelling or the provision of dwellings by works of conversion; common parts grants for the improvement or repair of the common parts of a building; disabled facilities grants for the provision of facilities for disabled persons; and grants for works of improvement or repair to houses in multiple occupation[8]. A new provision enabled grants to be paid for minor works such as thermal insulation to a dwelling[9].

The availability of grants was a major source of expenditure for local authorities[10] and, as a result, a policy decision was taken to make renovation grants for owner occupier property discretionary, with assistance for landlords also available on a discretionary basis but only in renewal areas as provided for in the Local Government and Housing Act 1989[11]. Certain grants made to the improvement of facilities for dwellings owned or occupied by the disabled are, however, still mandatory[12]. These changes were introduced by Part I of the Housing Grants, Construction and Regeneration Act 1996[13], which retained the four principal grants which were available under the Local Government and Housing Act 1989 and replaced the minor works grant with a new type of grant known as a home repair assistance grant[14]; of these, following further amendments made by order[15] and by the Housing Act 2004, only grants for providing facilities for disabled persons now remain but such grants are available in respect of qualifying houseboats, caravans and the common parts of buildings containing flats[16]. Part IV of the Housing Grants, Construction and Regeneration Act 1996 introduced relocation grants, which were designed to keep local communities together[17].

Grants may also be available under the Social Security Act 1990 to assist in the improvement of energy efficiency in certain dwellings[18].

1   See the Housing Grants, Construction and Regeneration Act 1996 s 150(3), (4); and the Housing Grants, Construction and Regeneration Act 1996 (Commencement No 2 and Revocation, Savings, Supplementary and Transitional Provisions) Order 1996, SI 1996/2842.

2   See the Housing Act 1959 Pt II (ss 4–18) (repealed).

3   See the Housing Act 1974 Pt VII (ss 56–84) (repealed).

4   See the Housing Act 1985 Pt XV (ss 460–526) (now repealed with the exception of s 523 (assistance for provision of separate service pipe for water supply: see WATER AND WATERWAYS vol 100 (2009) PARA 399)).

5   See the Local Government and Housing Act 1989 Pt VIII (ss 101–138) (repealed). See also *Brent London Borough Council v Patel* [2001] 1 WLR 897, [2001] LGR 285 (interpretation of the Local Government and Housing Act 1989 ss 106, 122).

6   See note 4.

7   See the Local Government and Housing Act 1989 s 109 (repealed).

8   See note 5.

9   See the Local Government and Housing Act 1989 s 131 (repealed).

10 See the White Paper *Our Future Homes* (Cm 2901) (1995) p 16. See also Hughes and Lowe *Social Housing Law and Policy* (1995) Ch 7.

11 See *The Future of Private Renewal Housing Programmes* (Department of the Environment, June 1995). See also *Our Future Homes* (Cm 2901) (1995) p 17. As to renewal areas see PARA 820 et seq.

12 See the Housing Grants, Construction and Regeneration Act 1996 s 23; and PARA 843.

13 See the Housing Grants, Construction and Regeneration Act 1996 Pt I (ss 1–103): and PARA 836 et seq.

14 See the Housing Grants, Construction and Regeneration Act 1996 Pt I Ch III (ss 76–80) (repealed).

15 Ie by the Regulatory Reform (Housing Assistance) (England and Wales) Order 2002, SI 2002/1860.

16 See PARA 836 et seq; and www.gov.uk/disabled-facilities-grants.

17 See the Housing Grants, Construction and Regeneration Act 1996 Pt IV (ss 131–140) (repealed).

18 See PARA 896 et seq.

836. Availability of grants for provision of facilities for disabled persons.

Grants[1] are available from local housing authorities[2] towards the cost of works required for the provision of facilities for disabled persons[3] in dwellings[4], qualifying houseboats[5] and caravans[6], and in the common parts[7] of buildings containing one or more flats[8].

1   In the provisions of the Housing Grants, Construction and Regeneration Act 1996 Pt I Ch I (ss 1–59), 'grant' means a grant under s 1(1): s 1(6) (amended by SI 2002/1860).

2   As to the meaning of 'local housing authority' see PARA 11 (definition applied by the Housing Grants, Construction and Regeneration Act 1996 s 101).

3   For these purposes, a person is disabled if: (1) his sight, hearing or speech is substantially impaired; (2) he has a mental disorder or impairment of any kind; or (3) he is physically substantially disabled by illness, injury, impairment present since birth, or otherwise: Housing Grants, Construction and Regeneration Act 1996 s 100(1). Nothing in s 100(1) is, however, to be construed as affecting the persons who are to be regarded as having a disability for the purposes of the Care Act 2014 s 77 or as disabled under the Children Act 1989 s 17(11) or the Social Services and Well-being (Wales) Act 2014 s 3: Housing Grants, Construction and Regeneration Act 1996 s 100(5) (amended by SI 2015/914 and SI 2016/413).

    A person aged 18 or over is taken to be disabled if: (a) the person is registered in a register maintained under the Care Act 2014 s 77(1) or (3) (registers of sight-impaired adults, disabled adults, etc: see SOCIAL SERVICES vol 95 (2017) PARA 328); (b) in the opinion of the social services authority, the person falls within a category mentioned in s 77(4) (persons for whom register may be maintained); (c) the person is registered in a register maintained under the Social Services and Well-being (Wales) Act 2014 s 18(5) (register of disabled adults and adults with an impairment or who have needs for care and support); or (d) in the opinion of the social services authority, the person falls within a category mentioned in s 18(6): Housing Grants, Construction and Regeneration Act 1996 s 100(2) (amended by SI 2015/914 and SI 2016/413).

    A person under the age of 18 is taken to be disabled if: (i) he is registered in a register of disabled children maintained under the Children Act 1989 Sch 2 para 2 (see CHILDREN AND YOUNG PERSONS vol 10 (2017) PARA 790); or (ii) he is in the opinion of the social services authority a disabled child as defined for the purposes of Pt III (ss 17–30) (local authority support for children and their families: see CHILDREN AND YOUNG PERSONS vol 10 (2017) PARA 789 et seq); or (iii) the person is registered as disabled in a register maintained under the Social Services and Well-being (Wales) Act 2014 s 18(4); or (iv) the person is, in the opinion of the social services authority, disabled as defined for the purposes of the Social Services and Well-being (Wales) Act 2014 s 3: Housing Grants, Construction and Regeneration Act 1996 s 100(3) (amended by SI 2016/413).

For these purposes, 'social services authority' means: (A) in England, the council which is the local authority for the purposes of the Local Authority Social Services Act 1970; and (B) in Wales, the council which is the local authority for the purposes of the Social Services and Well-being (Wales) Act 2014, for the area in which the dwelling or building is situated: Housing Grants, Construction and Regeneration Act 1996 s 100(4) (substituted by SI 2016/413). As to those authorities see SOCIAL SERVICES vol 95 (2017) PARA 1 et seq.

As to discrimination on the grounds of disability see the Equality Act 2010; and DISCRIMINATION vol 33 (2013) PARA 65 et seq.

4 'Dwelling' means a building or part of a building occupied or intended to be occupied as a separate dwelling, together with any yard, garden, outhouses and appurtenances belonging to it or usually enjoyed with it: Housing Grants, Construction and Regeneration Act 1996 s 101.

5 'Qualifying houseboat' means a boat or similar structure designed or adapted for use as a place of permanent habitation which: (1) has its only or main mooring within the area of a single local housing authority; (2) is moored in pursuance of a right to that mooring; and (3) is a dwelling for the purposes of the Local Government Finance Act 1992 Pt I (ss 1–69) (council tax: see LOCAL GOVERNMENT FINANCE vol 70 (2012) PARA 298 et seq), and includes any yard, garden, outhouses and appurtenances belonging to it or usually enjoyed with it: Housing Grants, Construction and Regeneration Act 1996 s 58 (definition added by SI 2002/1860).

6 'Caravan' means a caravan within the meaning of the Caravan Sites and Control of Development Act 1960 Pt I (ss 1–32) (see PLANNING vol 83 (2010) PARA 1211), disregarding the amendment made by the Caravan Sites Act 1968 s 13(2), and includes any yard, garden, outhouses and appurtenances belonging to it or usually enjoyed with it: Housing Grants, Construction and Regeneration Act 1996 s 58 (definition added by the Housing Act 2004 s 224(1), (7)(a)).

7 'Common parts', in relation to a building, includes the structure and exterior of the building and common facilities provided, whether in the building or elsewhere, for persons who include the occupiers of one or more flats in the building; and 'flat' means a dwelling which is a separate set of premises, whether or not on the same floor, divided horizontally from some other part of the building: Housing Grants, Construction and Regeneration Act 1996 s 58.

8 Housing Grants, Construction and Regeneration Act 1996 s 1(1) (amended by the Housing Act 2004 s 224(1), (2); and by SI 2002/1860). See PARA 839 et seq. A local authority is not entitled to have regard to its financial resources when determining whether to approve an application for a disabled facilities grant: *R v Birmingham City Council, ex p Mohammed* [1998] 3 All ER 788; [1999] 1 WLR 33.

837. Applications for grants. An application for a grant[1] must be in writing[2] and must specify the premises to which it relates and contain the following:

(1)   particulars of the works in respect of which the grant is sought (the 'relevant works')[3];

(2)   (unless the local housing authority otherwise directs[4] in any particular case) at least two estimates from different contractors of the cost of carrying out the relevant works[5];

(3)   particulars of any preliminary or ancillary services and charges[6] in respect of the cost of which the grant is also sought[7]; and

(4)   such other particulars as may be prescribed[8].

The appropriate national authority may by regulations prescribe a form of application for a grant and an application for a grant to which any such regulations apply is not validly made unless it is in the prescribed form[9].

1 No grant may be paid unless an application for it is made to the local housing authority in accordance with the provisions of the Housing Grants, Construction and Regeneration Act 1996 Pt I Ch I (ss 1–59) and is approved by it: s 2(1). As to the meaning of 'grant' see PARA 836 note 1. As to the meaning of 'local housing authority' see PARA 11 (definition applied by s 101). As to approval see PARA 844.

2 Unless the contrary intention appears, this includes other modes of representing or reproducing words in a visible form: see the Interpretation Act 1978 s 5, Sch 1.

3 Housing Grants, Construction and Regeneration Act 1996 s 2(2)(a).

4 Directions under the Housing Grants, Construction and Regeneration Act 1996 may make different provision for different cases or descriptions of case, including different provision for different areas: s 146(1).

5 Housing Grants, Construction and Regeneration Act 1996 s 2(2)(b).

6 'Preliminary or ancillary services and charges', in relation to an application for a grant, means services and charges which relate to the application and the preparation for and the carrying out of works and are specified for these purposes by order of the appropriate national authority: Housing Grants, Construction and Regeneration Act 1996 s 2(3)(a), (b). The services and charges specified for these purposes are those for which the applicant is liable in respect of: (1) confirmation, if sought by the local authority, that the applicant has an owner's interest; (2) technical and structural surveys; (3) design and preparation of plans and drawings; (4) preparation of schedules of relevant works; (5) assistance in completing forms; (6) advice on financing the costs of the relevant works which are not met by grant; (7) applications for building regulations approval (including application fee and preparation of related documents); (8) applications for planning permission (including application fee and preparation of related documents); (9) applications for listed building consent (including application fee and preparation of related documents); (10) applications for conservation area consent (including application fee and preparation of related documents); (11) obtaining of estimates; (12) advice on contracts; (13) consideration of tenders; (14) supervision of the relevant works; (15) disconnection and reconnection of electricity, gas, water or drainage utilities where this is necessitated by the relevant works; and (16) payment of contractors: Housing Renewal Grants (Services and Charges) Order 1996, SI 1996/2889, art 2(1). In a case where the application is for disabled facilities grant, the services and charges of an occupational therapist in relation to the relevant works are also specified for those purposes: art 2(2). As to the appropriate national authority, ie the Secretary of State or, where statutory functions have been transferred in relation to Wales, the Welsh Ministers, see PARA 7.

Orders and regulations under the Housing Grants, Construction and Regeneration Act 1996 may make different provision for different cases or descriptions of case, including different provision for different areas, and may contain such incidental supplementary or transitional provisions and savings as the authority making them considers appropriate: s 146(1), (2) (s 146(2) amended by the Local Democracy, Economic Development and Construction Act 2009 s 138(1), (4)(a)). They must be made by statutory instrument; and, except for: (a) regulations which only prescribe forms or particulars to be contained in forms; and (b) orders and regulations subject to affirmative resolution procedure (see the Housing Grants, Construction and Regeneration Act 1996 ss 104(4), 105(4), 106(4), 106A, 114(5); and BUILDING CONTRACTS vol 6 (2011) PARA 211 et seq) or orders under s 150(3) (commencement), are subject to annulment in pursuance of a resolution of either House of Parliament: s 146(3) (amended by the Local Democracy, Economic Development and Construction Act 2009 s 138(4)(b)).

7 Housing Grants, Construction and Regeneration Act 1996 s 2(2)(c).

8 Housing Grants, Construction and Regeneration Act 1996 s 2(2)(d). 'Prescribed' means prescribed by regulations made by the appropriate national authority: Housing Grants, Construction and Regeneration Act 1996 s 101. For the prescribed particulars see the Housing Renewal Grants Regulations 1996, SI 1996/2890, reg 4A (added, in relation to England, by SI 2000/531, and, in relation to Wales, by virtue of SI 2000/973).

9 Housing Grants, Construction and Regeneration Act 1996 s 2(4).

838. Ineligible applicants. No grant[1] is payable unless the applicant is aged[2] 18 or over on the date of the application; and, in the case of a joint application, any applicant under the age of 18 years on the date of the application must be left out of account[3]. No main grant[4] is payable if the person who would otherwise qualify as the applicant for the grant is:

(1)   a local authority[5];

(2)   a development corporation[6];

(3)   an urban development corporation[7];

(4)   a housing action trust[8];

(5)   the National Health Service Commissioning Board, a clinical commissioning group, local health board, special health authority[9], NHS trust or NHS foundation trust[10];

(6)   a police and crime commissioner[11];

(7)   a joint authority[12];

(8)   a residuary body[13];
(9)   a waste disposal authority[14];
(10)   an economic prosperity board[15];
(11)   a combined authority[16]; or
(12)   the London Fire and Emergency Planning Authority[17].

No main grant is payable if the applicant is of a description excluded from entitlement to grant aid by regulations[18] made by the appropriate national authority[19].

1   As to the meaning of 'grant' see PARA 836 note 1.
2   A person attains a particular age expressed in years at the commencement of the relevant anniversary of the date of birth: Family Law Reform Act 1969 s 9.
3   Housing Grants, Construction and Regeneration Act 1996 s 3(1).
4   Ie grant under the Housing Grants, Construction and Regeneration Act 1996 Pt I Ch I (ss 1–59): see PARAS 836–837.
5   Housing Grants, Construction and Regeneration Act 1996 s 3(2)(a). As to the meaning of 'local housing authority' see PARA 11 (definition applied by s 101).
6   Housing Grants, Construction and Regeneration Act 1996 s 3(2)(b) (amended by SI 2008/3002). As to the meaning of 'development corporation' see PARA 12 (definition applied by the Housing Grants, Construction and Regeneration Act 1996 s 101 (amended by SI 2008/3002)).
7   Housing Grants, Construction and Regeneration Act 1996 s 3(2)(c). As to the meaning of 'urban development corporation' see PARA 12 (definition applied by s 101).
8   Housing Grants, Construction and Regeneration Act 1996 s 3(2)(d). 'Housing action trust' means a housing action trust established under the Housing Act 1988 Pt III (ss 60–92) (see PARA 537 et seq) and includes any body established by order under s 88 (see PARA 561): Housing Grants, Construction and Regeneration Act 1996 s 101.
9   As to the National Health Service Commissioning Board, clinical commissioning groups, local health boards and special health authorities see HEALTH SERVICES vol 54 (2017) PARA 98 et seq.
10 Housing Grants, Construction and Regeneration Act 1996 s 3(2)(f) (amended by the Health and Social Care (Community Health and Standards) Act 2003 s 34, Sch 4 paras 102, 103; the Health and Social Care Act 2012 s 55(5), Sch 5 para 76; and SI 2000/90 and SI 2007/961). As to NHS trusts and NHS foundation trusts see HEALTH SERVICES vol 54 (2017) PARA 234 et seq.
11 Housing Grants, Construction and Regeneration Act 1996 s 3(2)(g) (substituted by the Police Reform and Social Responsibility Act 2011 s 99, Sch 16 para 220). As to police and crime commissioners see POLICE AND INVESTIGATORY POWERS vol 84 (2013) PARA 56 et seq.
12 Housing Grants, Construction and Regeneration Act 1996 s 3(2)(h). The authority referred to in the text is a joint authority established by the Local Government Act 1985 Pt IV (ss 23–42): see LOCAL GOVERNMENT vol 69 (2009) PARA 47 et seq.
13 Housing Grants, Construction and Regeneration Act 1996 s 3(2)(i) (amended by the Greater London Authority Act 1999 s 423, Sch 34 Pt VIII). The body referred to in the text is a residuary body established by the Local Government Act 1985 Pt VII (ss 57–67): see LOCAL GOVERNMENT vol 69 (2009) PARA 17.
14 Housing Grants, Construction and Regeneration Act 1996 s 3(2)(j). The authority referred to in the text is a waste disposal authority established under the Local Government Act 1985 s 10(1): see ENVIRONMENTAL QUALITY AND PUBLIC HEALTH vol 46 (2010) PARA 620.
15 Housing Grants, Construction and Regeneration Act 1996 s 3(2)(jb) (added by the Local Democracy, Economic Development and Construction Act 2009 s 119, Sch 6 para 88). The board referred to in the text is an economic prosperity board established under the Local Democracy, Economic Development and Construction Act 2009 s 88: see TRADE AND INDUSTRY vol 97 (2015) PARA 1086 et seq.
16 Housing Grants, Construction and Regeneration Act 1996 s 3(2)(jc) (added by the Local Democracy, Economic Development and Construction Act 2009 Sch 6 para 88). The authority referred to in the text is a combined authority established under the Local Democracy, Economic Development and Construction Act 2009 s 103: see TRADE AND INDUSTRY vol 97 (2015) PARA 1092 et seq.
17 Housing Grants, Construction and Regeneration Act 1996 s 3(2)(k) (added by the Greater London Authority Act 1999 s 328, Sch 29 para 60). As to the London Fire and Emergency Planning Authority see LONDON GOVERNMENT vol 71 (2013) PARA 315.
18 Regulations under the Housing Grants, Construction and Regeneration Act 1996 s 3(3) may proceed wholly or in part by reference to the provisions relating to entitlement to housing benefit, universal credit, or any other form of assistance, as they have effect from time to time: s 3(4A)

(added by SI 2013/630; and amended by SI 2013/1788). As to the making of regulations see PARA 837 note 6; and as to housing benefit see WELFARE BENEFITS AND STATE PENSIONS vol 104 (2014) PARA 318 et seq.

19 Housing Grants, Construction and Regeneration Act 1996 s 3(3). As to the appropriate national authority, ie the Secretary of State or, where statutory functions have been transferred in relation to Wales, the Welsh Ministers, see PARA 7. No grant is payable under the Housing Grants, Construction and Regeneration Act 1996 Pt I Ch I if the applicant, or any of the applicants, or any person who is not an applicant but is entitled to make an application and lives or intends to live in the dwelling or, as the case may be, a flat in the building, is a person from abroad within the meaning of the Housing Benefit Regulations 2006, SI 2006/213, reg 10 or, as the case may be, the Housing Benefit (Persons who have attained the qualifying age for state pension credit) Regulations 2006, SI 2006/214, reg 10, as those regulations have effect from time to time (see WELFARE BENEFITS AND STATE PENSIONS vol 104 (2014) PARA 320): Housing Renewal Grants Regulations 1996, SI 1996/2890, reg 3(1) (amended, in relation to England, by SI 2000/531, and, in relation to Wales, by SI 2000/973; and further amended by SI 2006/217). 'Applicant' means a person who applies, or who joins in an application, for a grant under the Housing Grants, Construction and Regeneration Act 1996 Pt I Ch I: Housing Renewal Grants Regulations 1996, SI 1996/2890, reg 3(2).

(2) GRANTS

839. Owner's, tenant's and occupier's applications. A grant[1] for providing facilities for disabled persons[2] is a mandatory grant[3]. However, a local housing authority[4] must not entertain an application for such a grant unless it is satisfied[5]:

(1)   that the applicant has, or proposes to acquire, an owner's interest[6] in every parcel of land on which the relevant works[7] are to be carried out[8]; or

(2)   that the applicant is a tenant[9] (alone or jointly with others):

(a)   of the dwelling, in the case of an application in respect of works to a dwelling[10]; or

(b)   of a flat in the building, in the case of a common parts application[11],

(3)   and, in either case, does not have or propose to acquire such an owner's interest[12]; or

(4)   that the applicant is an occupier (alone or jointly with others) of a qualifying houseboat[13] or a caravan[14] and, in the case of a caravan, that at the time the application was made the caravan was stationed on land within the authority's area[15].

These requirements do not apply to an application for a grant in respect of glebe land or the residence house of an ecclesiastical benefice, or to an application made by a charity[16] or on behalf of a charity by the charity trustees of the charity[17].

1   As to the meaning of 'grant' see PARA 836 note 1.
2   As to the meaning of 'disabled person' see PARA 836 note 3. As to discrimination on the grounds of disability see the Equality Act 2010; and DISCRIMINATION vol 33 (2013) PARA 65 et seq.
3   See PARAS 835, 843.
4   As to the meaning of 'local housing authority' see PARA 11 (definition applied by the Housing Grants, Construction and Regeneration Act 1996 s 101).
5   Housing Grants, Construction and Regeneration Act 1996 s 19(1) (amended by SI 2002/1860).
6   'Owner's interest', in relation to any premises, means: (1) an estate in fee simple absolute in possession; or (2) a term of years absolute of which not less than five years remain unexpired at the date of the application, whether held by the applicant alone or jointly with others: Housing Grants, Construction and Regeneration Act 1996 s 101.
7   As to the meaning of 'relevant works' see PARA 837.
8   Housing Grants, Construction and Regeneration Act 1996 s 19(1)(a). In accordance with directions given by the appropriate national authority, a local housing authority may treat this condition as met by a person who has, or proposes to acquire, an owner's interest in only part of the land concerned: s 19(3). In Pt I Ch I (ss 1–59), in relation to an application for a grant,

'qualifying owner's interest' means an owner's interest meeting the condition in s 19(1)(a) or treated by virtue of s 19(3) as meeting that condition: s 19(4) (amended by SI 2002/1860). As to the appropriate national authority, ie the Secretary of State or, where statutory functions have been transferred in relation to Wales, the Welsh Ministers, see PARA 7. As to the giving of directions see PARA 837 note 6.

9 'Tenant', in relation to a grant, includes:
    (1)   a secure tenant, introductory tenant or statutory tenant;
    (2)   a protected occupier under the Rent (Agriculture) Act 1976 (see LANDLORD AND TENANT vol 64 (2016) PARA 1706 et seq) or a person in occupation under an assured agricultural occupancy within the meaning of the Housing Act 1988 Pt I (ss 1–45) (see LANDLORD AND TENANT vol 64 (2016) PARA 1747 et seq);
    (3)   an employee (whether full-time or part-time) who occupies the dwelling or flat concerned for the better performance of his duties (ie, as a licensee); and
    (4)   a person having a licence to occupy the dwelling or flat concerned which satisfies such conditions as may be specified by order of the appropriate national authority,
and other expressions relating to tenancies, in the context of an application for disabled facilities grant, must be construed accordingly: Housing Grants, Construction and Regeneration Act 1996 s 19(5) (amended by the SI 2002/1860). As to the meaning of 'dwelling' see PARA 836 note 4. As to the meaning of 'flat' see PARA 836 note 7. As to the meaning of 'secure tenant' see LANDLORD AND TENANT vol 63 (2016) PARA 1037; as to the meaning of 'introductory tenant' see PARA 472; and as to the meaning of 'statutory tenant' see LANDLORD AND TENANT vol 63 (2016) PARA 673 (definitions applied by the Housing Grants, Construction and Regeneration Act 1996 s 101).
    An employee who falls within head (3) has a licence: see eg *Redbank Schools Ltd v Abdullahzadeh* (1995) 95 LGR 176, 28 HLR 431, CA.

10 Housing Grants, Construction and Regeneration Act 1996 s 19(1)(b)(i).

11 Housing Grants, Construction and Regeneration Act 1996 s 19(1)(b)(ii). In Pt I Ch I, in relation to an application for a grant, 'qualifying tenant' means a tenant who meets the conditions in s 19(1)(b): s 19(4). 'Common parts application', in relation to an application for a grant, means an application in respect of works to the common parts of a building containing one or more flats: s 58 (amended by SI 2002/1860). As to the meaning of 'common parts' see PARA 836 note 7.

12 Housing Grants, Construction and Regeneration Act 1996 s 19(1)(b). References in Pt I Ch I to an 'owner's application', a 'tenant's application' or an 'occupier's application', in relation to a grant, are to be construed accordingly: s 19(2) (amended by SI 2002/1860).

13 As to the meaning of 'qualifying houseboat' see PARA 836 note 5.

14 As to the meaning of 'caravan' see PARA 836 note 6.

15 Housing Grants, Construction and Regeneration Act 1996 s 19(1)(c) (added by SI 2002/1860; and substituted by the Housing Act 2004 s 224(1), (3)).

16 For these purposes, 'charity' does not include a private registered provider of social housing or a registered social landlord but otherwise has the same meaning as it has under the Charities Act 2011 s 10 (see CHARITIES vol 8 (2015) PARA 1): Housing Grants, Construction and Regeneration Act 1996 s 95(6) (amended by the Charities Act 2011 s 354(1), Sch 7 para 73; and by SI 2010/866). As to the meaning of 'private registered provider of social housing' see PARA 53. As to the meaning of 'registered social landlord' see PARA 13 (definition applied by the Housing Grants, Construction and Regeneration Act 1996 s 101).

17 Housing Grants, Construction and Regeneration Act 1996 s 95(1) (amended by SI 2002/1860). As to glebe land and houses of ecclesiastical benefices see ECCLESIASTICAL LAW vol 34 (2011) PARA 956 et seq.

840. Certificate required in case of owner's application. A local housing authority[1] must not entertain an owner's application[2] for a grant[3] unless it is accompanied by an owner's certificate[4] in respect of the dwelling to which the application relates or, in the case of a common parts application[5], in respect of each flat in the building occupied or proposed to be occupied by a disabled occupant[6].

This restriction does not apply to an application for a grant in respect of glebe land or the residence house of an ecclesiastical benefice[7], or to an application made by a charity[8] or on behalf of a charity by the charity trustees of the charity[9].

1 As to the meaning of 'local housing authority' see PARA 11 (definition applied by the Housing Grants, Construction and Regeneration Act 1996 s 101).

2 As to an owner's application see PARA 839.

3 As to the meaning of 'grant' see PARA 836 note 1.

4 An 'owner's certificate', for the purposes of an application for a grant, certifies that the applicant: (1) has or proposes to acquire a qualifying owner's interest; and (2) intends that the disabled occupant will live in the dwelling or flat as his only or main residence throughout the grant condition period or for such shorter period as his health and other relevant circumstances permit: Housing Grants, Construction and Regeneration Act 1996 s 21(2)(a), (b) (amended by SI 2002/1860). As to the meaning of 'dwelling' see PARA 836 note 4. As to the meaning of 'flat' see PARA 836 note 7. As to the meaning of 'qualifying owner's interest' see PARA 839 note 8. The 'grant condition period' means the period of five years, or such other period as the appropriate national authority may by order specify or as may be imposed by the local housing authority with the consent of the appropriate national authority, beginning with the certified date; and the 'certified date' means the date certified by the local housing authority as the date on which the execution of the eligible works is completed to the authority's satisfaction: Housing Grants, Construction and Regeneration Act 1996 s 44(3). As to the meaning of 'eligible works' see PARA 871. As to the appropriate national authority, ie the Secretary of State or, where statutory functions have been transferred in relation to Wales, the Welsh Ministers, see PARA 7.

The 'disabled occupant', in relation to an application for grant, means the disabled person for whose benefit it is proposed to carry out any of the relevant works: s 20 (amended by SI 2002/1860). As to the meaning of 'disabled person' see PARA 836 note 3.

5 As to the meaning of 'common parts application' see PARA 839 note 11.

6 Housing Grants, Construction and Regeneration Act 1996 s 21(1).

7 As to glebe land and houses of ecclesiastical benefices see ECCLESIASTICAL LAW vol 34 (2011) PARA 956 et seq.

8 As to the meaning of 'charity' see PARA 839 note 16.

9 See the Housing Grants, Construction and Regeneration Act 1996 s 95(1) (amended by SI 2002/1860).

841. Certificates required in case of tenant's application. A local housing authority[1] must not entertain a tenant's application for a grant[2] unless it is accompanied by a tenant's certificate[3]. Except where the authority considers it unreasonable in the circumstances to require such a certificate, it must not entertain a tenant's application for a grant unless it is also accompanied by an owner's certificate[4] from the person who at the time of the application is the landlord under the tenancy[5].

This restriction does not apply to an application for a grant in respect of glebe land or the residence house of an ecclesiastical benefice[6], or to an application made by a charity[7] or on behalf of a charity by the charity trustees of the charity[8].

1 As to the meaning of 'local housing authority' see PARA 11 (definition applied by the Housing Grants, Construction and Regeneration Act 1996 s 101).

2 As to the meaning of 'grant' see PARA 836 note 1.

3 Housing Grants, Construction and Regeneration Act 1996 s 22(1) (s 22 amended by SI 2002/1860). A 'tenant's certificate', for the purposes of an application for a grant, certifies: (1) that the application is a tenant's application; and (2) that the applicant intends that he (if he is the disabled occupant) or the disabled occupant will live in the dwelling or flat as his only or main residence throughout the grant condition period or for such shorter period as his health and other relevant circumstances permit: Housing Grants, Construction and Regeneration Act 1996 s 22(2)(a), (b) (as so amended). As to the tenant's application see PARA 839; and as to the grant condition period see PARA 840 note 4. As to the meaning of 'disabled occupant' see PARA 840 note 4. As to the meaning of 'dwelling' see PARA 836 note 4. As to the meaning of 'flat' see PARA 836 note 7.

4 As to the meaning of 'owner's certificate' see PARA 840 note 4.

5 Housing Grants, Construction and Regeneration Act 1996 s 22(3) (as amended: see note 3). As to the meaning of 'tenancy' see PARA 839 note 9.

6 As to glebe land and houses of ecclesiastical benefices see ECCLESIASTICAL LAW vol 34 (2011) PARA 956 et seq.

7 As to the meaning of 'charity' see PARA 839 note 16.

8 See the Housing Grants, Construction and Regeneration Act 1996 s 95(1) (amended by SI 2002/1860).

842. Certificates required in case of occupier's application. A local housing authority[1] must not entertain an occupier's application for a grant unless it is accompanied by an occupier's certificate[2]. Except where the authority considers it unreasonable in the circumstances to require such a certificate, it may not entertain an occupier's application for a grant unless such an application is also accompanied by a consent certificate[3] from each person, other than the applicant, who, at the time of the application: (1) is entitled to possession of the premises[4] at which the qualifying houseboat is moored or, as the case may be, the land on which the caravan is stationed[5]; or (2) is entitled to dispose of the qualifying houseboat or, as the case may be, the caravan[6].

This restriction does not apply to an application for a grant in respect of glebe land or the residence house of an ecclesiastical benefice[7], or to an application made by a charity[8] or on behalf of a charity by the charity trustees of the charity[9].

1 As to the meaning of 'local housing authority' see PARA 11 (definition applied by the Housing Grants, Construction and Regeneration Act 1996 s 101).
2 Housing Grants, Construction and Regeneration Act 1996 s 22A(1) (s 22A added by SI 2002/1860). An 'occupier's certificate', for the purposes of an application for a grant, certifies that the application is an occupier's application, and that the applicant intends that he (if he is the disabled occupant) or the disabled occupant will live in the qualifying houseboat or caravan, as the case may be, as his only or main residence throughout the grant condition period or for such shorter period as his health and other relevant circumstances permit: Housing Grants, Construction and Regeneration Act 1996 s 22A(2) (as so added; amended by the Housing Act 2004 s 224(1), (4)(a)). As to the meaning of 'disabled occupant' see PARA 840 note 4. As to the meaning of 'qualifying houseboat' see PARA 836 note 5; and as to the meaning of 'caravan' see PARA 836 note 6. As to the grant condition period see PARA 840 note 4.
3 A 'consent certificate', for these purposes, certifies that the person by whom the certificate is given consents to the carrying out of the relevant works: Housing Grants, Construction and Regeneration Act 1996 s 22A(4) (as added: see note 2).
4 'Premises' includes a qualifying houseboat or a caravan: Housing Grants, Construction and Regeneration Act 1996 s 58 (definition added by SI 2002/1860; and amended by the Housing Act 2004 s 224(7)(b)).
5 Housing Grants, Construction and Regeneration Act 1996 s 22A(3)(a) (as added (see note 2); amended by the Housing Act 2004 s 224(4)(a), (b)).
6 Housing Grants, Construction and Regeneration Act 1996 s 22A(3)(b) (as added (see note 2); amended by the Housing Act 2004 s 224(4)(a)).
7 As to glebe land and houses of ecclesiastical benefices see ECCLESIASTICAL LAW vol 34 (2011) PARA 956 et seq.
8 As to the meaning of 'charity' see PARA 839 note 16.
9 See the Housing Grants, Construction and Regeneration Act 1996 s 95(1) (amended by SI 2002/1860).

843. Purposes for which grant must be given. The mandatory purposes for which an application for a grant[1] is to be approved are as follows[2]:

(1) facilitating access by the disabled occupant[3] to and from the dwelling[4], qualifying houseboat[5] or caravan[6] or the building in which the dwelling or, as the case may be, flat[7] is situated[8];

(2) making the dwelling, qualifying houseboat or caravan, or the building, safe for the disabled occupant and other persons residing with him[9];

(3) facilitating access by the disabled occupant to a room used or usable as the principal family room[10];

(4) facilitating access by the disabled occupant to, or providing for the disabled occupant, a room used or usable for sleeping[11];

(5) facilitating access by the disabled occupant to, or providing for the disabled occupant, a room in which there is a lavatory, or facilitating the use by the disabled occupant of such a facility[12];

(6) facilitating access by the disabled occupant to, or providing for the disabled occupant, a room in which there is a bath or shower (or both), or facilitating the use by the disabled occupant of such a facility[13];

(7) facilitating access by the disabled occupant to, or providing for the disabled occupant, a room in which there is a wash hand-basin, or facilitating the use by the disabled occupant of such a facility[14];

(8) facilitating the preparation and cooking of food by the disabled occupant[15];

(9) improving any heating system in the dwelling, qualifying houseboat or caravan to meet the needs of the disabled occupant or, if there is no existing heating system there or any such system is unsuitable for use by the disabled occupant, providing a heating system suitable to meet his needs[16];

(10) facilitating the use by the disabled occupant of a source of power, light or heat by altering the position of one or more means of access to or control of that source or by providing additional means of control[17];

(11) facilitating access and movement by the disabled occupant around the dwelling, qualifying houseboat or caravan in order to enable him to care for a person who is normally resident there and is in need of such care[18];

(12) such other purposes as may be specified by order of the appropriate national authority[19].

If in the opinion of the local housing authority[20] the relevant works[21] are more or less extensive than is necessary to achieve any of the mandatory purposes, it may, with the consent of the applicant, treat the application as varied so that the relevant works are limited to or, as the case may be, include such works as seem to the authority to be necessary for that purpose[22].

1 As to the meaning of 'grant' see PARA 836 note 1.
2 Housing Grants, Construction and Regeneration Act 1996 s 23(1) (amended by SI 2002/1860).
3 As to the meaning of 'disabled occupant' see PARA 840 note 4.
4 As to the meaning of 'dwelling' see PARA 836 note 4.
5 As to the meaning of 'qualifying houseboat' see PARA 836 note 5.
6 As to the meaning of 'caravan' see PARA 836 note 6.
7 As to the meaning of 'flat' see PARA 836 note 7.
8 Housing Grants, Construction and Regeneration Act 1996 s 23(1)(a) (amended by the Housing Act 2004 s 224(1), (5)(a); and by SI 2002/1860).
9 Housing Grants, Construction and Regeneration Act 1996 s 23(1)(b) (amended by the Housing Act 2004 s 224(5)(a); and by SI 2002/1860). To qualify for a grant under the Housing Grants, Construction and Regeneration Act 1996 s 23(1)(b), the proposed works must pass a threshold of safety so that they minimise the material risk, as far as is reasonably practicable; it is not necessary that the dwelling be made entirely safe: *R (on the application of B) v Calderdale Metropolitan Borough Council* [2004] EWCA Civ 134, [2004] 1 WLR 2017, [2004] HLR 276.
10 Housing Grants, Construction and Regeneration Act 1996 s 23(1)(c).
11 Housing Grants, Construction and Regeneration Act 1996 s 23(1)(d).
12 Housing Grants, Construction and Regeneration Act 1996 s 23(1)(e).
13 Housing Grants, Construction and Regeneration Act 1996 s 23(1)(f).
14 Housing Grants, Construction and Regeneration Act 1996 s 23(1)(g).
15 Housing Grants, Construction and Regeneration Act 1996 s 23(1)(h).
16 Housing Grants, Construction and Regeneration Act 1996 s 23(1)(i) (amended by the Housing Act 2004 s 224(5)(a); and by SI 2002/1860).
17 Housing Grants, Construction and Regeneration Act 1996 s 23(1)(j).
18 Housing Grants, Construction and Regeneration Act 1996 s 23(1)(k) (amended by the Housing Act 2004 s 224(5)(a); and by SI 2002/1860).
19 Housing Grants, Construction and Regeneration Act 1996 s 23(1)(l). See *R v Birmingham City Council, ex p Mohammed* [1998] 3 All ER 788, [1999] 1 WLR 33. As to the appropriate national authority, ie the Secretary of State or, where statutory functions have been transferred in relation to Wales, the Welsh Ministers, see PARA 7. As to the making of orders see PARA 837 note 6. Additional purposes have been specified by the Disabled Facilities Grants (Maximum Amounts and Additional Purposes) (England) Order 2008, SI 2008/1189, art 3; and the Disabled Facilities Grants (Maximum Amounts and Additional Purposes) (Wales) Order 2008, SI 2008/2370, art 3.

20 As to the meaning of 'local housing authority' see PARA 11 (definition applied by the Housing Grants, Construction and Regeneration Act 1996 s 101).
21 As to the meaning of 'relevant works' see PARA 837.
22 Housing Grants, Construction and Regeneration Act 1996 s 23(3) (amended by SI 2002/1860).

844. Approval of application. The local housing authority[1] must approve an application for a grant[2] for one of the mandatory purposes[3]. Approval is subject to the following provisions[4]:

(1) where an authority entertains an owner's application[5] for a grant made by a person who proposes to acquire a qualifying owner's interest[6], it must not approve the application until it is satisfied that he has done so[7];

(2) a local housing authority must not approve an application for a grant unless it is satisfied:

(a) that the relevant works[8] are necessary and appropriate to meet the needs of the disabled occupant[9]; and

(b) that it is reasonable and practicable to carry out the relevant works having regard to the age and condition of the dwelling[10], qualifying houseboat[11] or caravan[12], or the building[13];

(3) a local housing authority must not approve a common parts application[14] for a grant unless it is satisfied that the applicant has a power or is under a duty to carry out the relevant works[15].

1 As to the meaning of 'local housing authority' see PARA 11 (definition applied by the Housing Grants, Construction and Regeneration Act 1996 s 101).
2 As to the meaning of 'grant' see PARA 836 note 1.
3 Housing Grants, Construction and Regeneration Act 1996 s 24(1) (substituted by SI 2002/1860). The text refers to one of the purposes within the Housing Grants, Construction and Regeneration Act 1996 s 23(1): see PARA 843 heads (1)–(12).
4 Housing Grants, Construction and Regeneration Act 1996 s 24(1) (as substituted: see note 3).
5 As to an owner's application see PARA 839.
6 As to the meaning of 'qualifying owner's interest' see PARA 839 note 8.
7 Housing Grants, Construction and Regeneration Act 1996 s 24(2) (amended by SI 2002/1860).
8 As to the meaning of 'relevant works' see PARA 837.
9 Housing Grants, Construction and Regeneration Act 1996 s 24(3)(a). In considering the matters mentioned in s 24(3)(a), a local housing authority which is not itself a social services authority must consult the social services authority: s 24(3). As to the meaning of 'social services authority' see PARA 836 note 3; and as to the meaning of 'disabled occupant' see PARA 840 note 4.
10 As to the meaning of 'dwelling' see PARA 836 note 4.
11 As to the meaning of 'qualifying houseboat' see PARA 836 note 5.
12 As to the meaning of 'caravan' see PARA 836 note 6.
13 Housing Grants, Construction and Regeneration Act 1996 s 24(3)(b) (amended by the Housing Act 2004 s 224(1), (5)(b); and by SI 2002/1860).
14 As to the meaning of 'common parts application' see PARA 839 note 11.
15 Housing Grants, Construction and Regeneration Act 1996 s 24(5) (amended by SI 2002/1860).

(3) RESTRICTIONS ON GRANT AID

(i) In general

845. Restriction on grants for works already begun. A local housing authority[1] must not approve[2] an application for a grant[3] if the relevant works[4] have been begun before the application has been approved[5]. However, where the relevant works have been begun but have not been completed, the authority may approve the application for a grant if it is satisfied that there were good reasons for beginning the works before the application was approved[6].

A local housing authority must not approve an application for a grant if the relevant works have been completed[7].

1 As to the meaning of 'local housing authority' see PARA 11 (definition applied by the Housing Grants, Construction and Regeneration Act 1996 s 101).
2 As to approval see PARA 844.
3 As to the meaning of 'grant' see PARA 836 note 1.
4 As to the meaning of 'relevant works' see PARA 837.
5 Housing Grants, Construction and Regeneration Act 1996 s 29(1).
6 Housing Grants, Construction and Regeneration Act 1996 s 29(2). Where an authority decides to approve an application in accordance with s 29(2), it may, with the consent of the applicant, treat the application as varied so that the relevant works do not include any that are completed: s 29(3). However, in determining for the purposes of the application the physical condition of the dwelling, qualifying houseboat, caravan or common parts concerned, it must consider the condition of the premises at the date of the application: s 29(3) (amended by the Housing Act 2004 s 224(1), (5)(c); and by SI 2002/1860). As to the meaning of 'dwelling' see PARA 836 note 4. As to the meaning of 'qualifying houseboat' see PARA 836 note 5. As to the meaning of 'caravan' see PARA 836 note 6. As to the meaning of 'common parts' see PARA 836 note 7.
7 Housing Grants, Construction and Regeneration Act 1996 s 29(4) (amended by SI 2002/1860).

846. Determination of amount of grant in case of landlord's application. Provision is made for local housing authorities[1] to consider an owner's application[2] for a grant[3] in respect of works to a dwelling[4] which is or is intended to be let, or the common parts[5] of a building in which a flat[6] is or is intended to be let[7].

The amount of the grant (if any) must be determined by the local housing authority, having regard to:

(1) the extent to which the landlord is able to charge a higher rent[8] for the premises because of the works[9]; and

(2) such other matters as the appropriate national authority[10] may direct[11].

1 As to the meaning of 'local housing authority' see PARA 11 (definition applied by the Housing Grants, Construction and Regeneration Act 1996 s 101).
2 As to an owner's application for a grant see PARA 839.
3 As to the meaning of 'grant' see PARA 836 note 1.
4 As to the meaning of 'dwelling' see PARA 836 note 4.
5 As to the meaning of 'common parts' see PARA 836 note 7.
6 As to the meaning of 'flat' see PARA 836 note 7.
7 Housing Grants, Construction and Regeneration Act 1996 s 31(1) (substituted by SI 2002/1860).
8 The authority may, if it thinks it appropriate, seek and act upon the advice of rent officers as to any matter: Housing Grants, Construction and Regeneration Act 1996 s 31(4). As to the appointment of rent officers see the Rent Act 1977 s 63; and LANDLORD AND TENANT vol 63 (2016) PARA 738. Although an authority cannot delegate its duty to determine likely rent increases to a rent officer, it is entitled to act on the basis of his advice: see *R v Bolsover District Council and Rent Officer for Derbyshire Registration Area, ex p East Midlands Development Ltd* (1995) 28 HLR 329.
9 Housing Grants, Construction and Regeneration Act 1996 s 31(3)(a).
10 The appropriate national authority may by regulations make provision requiring any information or evidence needed for the determination of any matter under the Housing Grants, Construction and Regeneration Act 1996 s 31 to be furnished by such person as may be prescribed: s 31(5). In the case of any application to which s 31 applies, a local housing authority may require a pension fund holder to provide the authority with the information specified in the Housing Renewal Grants Regulations 1996, SI 1996/2890, reg 31(8) (details of deferred income under personal pension scheme or retirement annuity contract: see PARA 862 note 19) for the purpose of determining as described in reg 31(4), (5) the amount of any income foregone under a personal pension scheme or retirement annuity contract by an applicant, or a partner of an applicant, who is aged not less than 60: reg 4. As to the appropriate national authority, ie the Secretary of State or, where statutory functions have been transferred in relation to Wales, the Welsh Ministers, see PARA 7.
11 Housing Grants, Construction and Regeneration Act 1996 s 31(3)(b). As to the giving of directions generally see PARA 837 note 4. It may be appropriate for an authority to depart from such directions: cf *De Falco v Crawley Borough Council* [1980] QB 460, [1980] 1 All ER 913, CA.

847. Power to specify maximum amount of grant. The appropriate national authority[1] may, if it thinks fit, by order[2] specify a maximum amount[3] or a formula for calculating a maximum amount of grant[4] which a local housing authority[5] may pay in respect of an application for a grant[6]. An authority may not pay an amount of grant in excess of a specified maximum amount[7].

1 As to the appropriate national authority, ie the Secretary of State or, where statutory functions have been transferred in relation to Wales, the Welsh Ministers, see PARA 7.
2 An order under the Housing Grants, Construction and Regeneration Act 1996 s 33 may make different provision for different circumstances: s 33(2) (amended by SI 2002/1860). As to the exercise of this power see the Disabled Facilities Grants and Home Repair Assistance (Maximum Amounts) Order 1996, SI 1996/2888; the Disabled Facilities Grants (Maximum Amounts and Additional Purposes) (England) Order 2008, SI 2008/1189; the Disabled Facilities Grants (Maximum Amounts and Additional Purposes) (Wales) Order 2008, SI 2008/2370; and note 3.
3 Where a local housing authority has to approve an application for disabled facilities grant by virtue of the Housing Grants, Construction and Regeneration Act 1996 s 23(1) (mandatory disabled facilities grant), the maximum amount which the authority may pay in respect of the application is £30,000 if the dwelling or building is in England (Disabled Facilities Grants (Maximum Amounts and Additional Purposes) (England) Order 2008, SI 2008/1189, art 2), and £36,000 if it is in Wales (Disabled Facilities Grants (Maximum Amounts and Additional Purposes) (Wales) Order 2008, SI 2008/2370, art 2).
4 As to the meaning of 'grant' see PARA 836 note 1.
5 As to the meaning of 'local housing authority' see PARA 11 (definition applied by the Housing Grants, Construction and Regeneration Act 1996 s 101).
6 Housing Grants, Construction and Regeneration Act 1996 s 33(1).
7 Housing Grants, Construction and Regeneration Act 1996 s 33(4) (amended by SI 2002/1860).

(ii) Means Testing

A. IN GENERAL

848. Means testing; in general. In the case of an application for a grant[1] by either an owner-occupier or a tenant the applicant must be means tested[2]. However, a landlord's application for a grant is not means tested, although the local housing authority[3] has a statutory discretion as to whether to approve the grant or not and, if so, as to how much is to be paid[4].

Where an applicant for grant has to be means tested, the applicant's income and capital are calculated in accordance with regulations[5] dealing with, inter alia:

(1) general definitions of 'relevant person'[6], 'non-dependant'[7] and 'remunerative work'[8], the circumstances in which a person is treated as responsible or not responsible for another[9] or as being or not being a member of the household[10], the applicable amount[11] and financial resources[12];
(2) reduction in the amount of grant[13];
(3) applicable amounts[14];
(4) income and capital[15], including the determination of income on a weekly basis[16] and treatment of child care charges[17];
(5) employed earners[18] and self-employed earners[19]; and
(6) students[20].

1 As to the meaning of 'grant' see PARA 836 note 1.
2 See PARA 849.
3 As to the meaning of 'local housing authority' see PARA 11.
4 See PARAS 606, 631.
5 As to the making of regulations generally see PARA 837 note 6. The relevant regulations are the Housing Renewal Grants Regulations 1996, SI 1996/2890. The regulations came into force on 17 December 1996: see reg 1.
6 See PARA 850.

7   See PARA 851.
8   See PARA 852.
9   See PARA 853.
10 See PARA 853.
11 See PARA 854.
12 See PARA 854.
13 See PARAS 856–857.
14 See PARA 855 et seq.
15 See PARA 855.
16 See PARA 858 et seq.
17 See PARA 858.
18 See PARA 859.
19 See PARA 860.
20 See PARAS 867–870.

849. Means testing in case of application by owner-occupier or tenant. If in the case of an application for a grant[1] the financial resources of any person of a description specified by regulations[2] exceed the applicable amount, the amount of any grant which may be paid must, in accordance with regulations, be reduced from what it would otherwise have been[3].

Provision may be made by regulations:

(1)   for the determination of the amount which is to be taken to be the financial resources of any person[4];

(2)   for the determination of the applicable amount[5]; and

(3)   as to circumstances in which the financial resources of a person are to be assumed (by reason of his receiving a prescribed benefit or otherwise) not to exceed the applicable amount[6].

Regulations[7] may, in particular:

(a)   make provision for account to be taken of the income, assets, needs and outgoings not only of the person himself but also of his spouse, his civil partner, any person living with him or intending to live with him and any person on whom he is dependent or who is dependent on him[8];

(b)   make provision for amounts specified in or determined under the regulations to be taken into account for particular purposes[9].

Regulations may also make provision requiring any information or evidence needed for the determination of any such matter to be furnished by such person as may be prescribed[10].

Apart from the provisions described above, there is no residual discretion to approve a grant at a lower amount[11].

1   As to the meaning of 'grant' see PARA 836 note 1.
2   For these purposes, 'regulations' means regulations made by the appropriate national authority with, in relation to England, the consent of the Treasury: Housing Grants, Construction and Regeneration Act 1996 s 30(9). In exercise of the power so conferred, the appropriate national authority has made the Housing Renewal Grants Regulations 1996, SI 1996/2890: see PARAS 848, 850 et seq. As to the appropriate national authority, ie the Secretary of State or, where statutory functions have been transferred in relation to Wales, the Welsh Ministers, see PARA 7; and as to the making of regulations see PARA 837 note 6. As to the Treasury see CONSTITUTIONAL AND ADMINISTRATIVE LAW vol 20 (2014) PARA 262 et seq.
3   Housing Grants, Construction and Regeneration Act 1996 s 30(4) (amended by SI 2002/1860).
4   See the Housing Grants, Construction and Regeneration Act 1996 s 30(5)(a); and PARA 854.
5   Ie the amount referred to in the Housing Grants, Construction and Regeneration Act 1996 s 30(4) (see the text and note 3): s 30(5)(b) (amended by SI 2002/1860). As to the applicable amount see PARA 854.
6   Housing Grants, Construction and Regeneration Act 1996 s 30(5)(c).
7   Regulations may apply for the purposes of the Housing Grants, Construction and Regeneration Act 1996 s 30, subject to such modifications as may be prescribed, any other statutory

means-testing regime as it has effect from time to time: s 30(7). As to the meaning of 'prescribed' see PARA 837 note 8.

8 See the Housing Grants, Construction and Regeneration Act 1996 s 30(6)(a) (amended by the Civil Partnership Act 2004 s 81, Sch 8 para 62).
9 See the Housing Grants, Construction and Regeneration Act 1996 s 30(6)(b).
10 See the Housing Grants, Construction and Regeneration Act 1996 s 30(8).
11 See *R v Sunderland City Council, ex p Redezeus Ltd* (1994) 94 LGR 105, 27 HLR 477.

850. Meaning of 'relevant person'. In respect of an application[1] for a grant[2], a relevant person is any person who:

(1)   is the disabled occupant[3], or one of the disabled occupants, of the dwelling[4]; or

(2)   is the partner[5], or a partner, of the disabled occupant or of one of the disabled occupants of the dwelling,

and is not a young person[6] or child[7] or the partner of a young person[8].

Where head (1) or head (2) applies to both members of a couple[9] or to two or more members of a polygamous marriage[10], only one member of that couple or marriage will be the relevant person in respect of that application[11].

1 'Application', without more, means an application for grant other than an application to which the Housing Grants, Construction and Regeneration Act 1996 s 31 (see PARA 846) applies; and 'applicant' is to be construed accordingly: Housing Renewal Grants Regulations 1996, SI 1996/2890, reg 2(1) (definition substituted, in relation to England, by SI 2003/2504; and, in relation to Wales, by SI 2004/253).
2 As to the meaning of 'grant' see PARA 836 note 1.
3 As to the meaning of 'disabled occupant' see PARA 840 note 4.
4 'Dwelling' includes a qualifying houseboat and a caravan: Housing Renewal Grants Regulations 1996, SI 1996/2890, reg 2(1) (definition added, in relation to England, by SI 2003/2504; and, in relation to Wales, by SI 2004/253; and amended, in relation to England, by SI 2005/3323; and, in relation to Wales by SI 2006/2801).
5 In relation to England, 'partner' means: (1) where a person is a member of a couple, the other member of that couple; or (2) where a person is polygamously married to two or more members of his household, any such member: Housing Renewal Grants Regulations 1996, SI 1996/2890, reg 2(1) (amended by SI 2005/3323).

   In relation to Wales, 'partner' means: (a) where a person is a member of a couple or of a civil partnership, the other member of that couple; or (b) where a person is polygamously married to two or more members of his household, any such member: Housing Renewal Grants Regulations 1996, SI 1996/2890, reg 2(1) (amended by SI 2005/3302 and SI 2006/2801). The definition of 'partner' does not apply to the Housing Renewal Grants Regulations 1996, SI 1996/2890, reg 38(4) (see PARA 864): reg 2(1) (definition amended, in relation to England, by SI 2005/3323 and, in relation to Wales, by SI 2006/2801).

   As to polygamous marriage see note 8; and as to members of a household see PARA 853.
6 'Child' means a person under the age of 16: Housing Renewal Grants Regulations 1996, SI 1996/2890, reg 2(1).
7 'Young person' means a person who is: (1) a qualifying young person within the meaning of the Social Security Contributions and Benefits Act 1992 s 142(2)(a); and (2) not in receipt of income support, jobseeker's allowance, incapacity benefit, or employment and support allowance: Housing Renewal Grants Regulations 1996, SI 1996/2890, reg 2(1) (definition substituted, in relation to England, by SI 2009/1807; and, in relation to Wales, by SI 2010/297). 'Jobseeker's allowance' means an allowance payable under the Jobseekers Act 1995; and 'employment and support allowance' means an employment and support allowance payable under the Welfare Reform Act 2007 Pt 1 (ss 1–29): Housing Renewal Grants Regulations 1996, SI 1996/2890, reg 2(1) (definitions added, in relation to England, by SI 2009/1807; and, in relation to Wales, by SI 2010/297). As to the benefits and allowances mentioned see WELFARE BENEFITS AND STATE PENSIONS vol 104 (2014) PARAS 252 et seq, 262 et seq.
8 Housing Renewal Grants Regulations 1996, SI 1996/2890, reg 5(1) (reg 5 substituted, in relation to England, by SI 2008/1190; and, in relation to Wales, by SI 2008/2377).
9 'Couple' means: (1) two people who are married to, or civil partners of, each other and are members of the same household; or (2) two people who are not married to, or civil partners of, each other but are living together as a married couple: Housing Renewal Grants Regulations 1996, SI 1996/2890, reg 2(1) (definition added, in relation to England, by SI 2005/3323; and, in relation to Wales, by SI 2006/2801; substituted by SI 2014/107). A married couple includes a married same

sex couple: see the Marriage (Same Sex Couples) Act 2013 s 11, Sch 3 para 1(1)(b), (2), (3); and
MATRIMONIAL AND CIVIL PARTNERSHIP LAW vol 72 (2015) PARA 1 et seq.
10 'Polygamous marriage' means any marriage during the subsistence of which a party to it is married
to more than one person and the ceremony of marriage took place under the law of a country
which permits polygamy: Housing Renewal Grants Regulations 1996, SI 1996/2890, reg 2(1).
11 Housing Renewal Grants Regulations 1996, SI 1996/2890, reg 5(2) (as substituted: see note 7).

851. Meaning of 'non-dependant'. For the purposes of the means test for
owner-occupier's and tenant's applications[1], 'non-dependant' means any person
who normally resides[2] with a relevant person[3] or with whom a relevant person
normally resides[4], except:

(1)   any member of the relevant person's family[5];
(2)   if the relevant person is polygamously married[6], any partner[7] of his and
        any child[8] or young person[9] who is a member of his household and for
        whom he or one of his partners is responsible[10];
(3)   a child or young person who is living with the relevant person but who
        is not a member of his household[11];
(4)   a person who jointly occupies the relevant person's dwelling[12] and is
        either a co-owner of that dwelling with the relevant person or his
        partner (whether or not there are other co-owners) or is liable with the
        relevant person or his partner to make payments[13] in respect of his
        occupation of the dwelling[14];
(5)   any person who is liable to make payments on a commercial basis to the
        relevant person or the relevant person's partner in respect of the
        occupation of the dwelling[15];
(6)   any person to whom or to whose partner the relevant person or the
        relevant person's partner is liable to make payments on a commercial
        basis in respect of the occupation of the dwelling[16];
(7)   any other member of the household of the person to whom or to whose
        partner the relevant person or the relevant person's partner is liable to
        make payments on a commercial basis in respect of the occupation of
        the dwelling[17];
(8)   a person who lives with the relevant person in order to care for him or
        a partner of his and who is engaged by a charitable or voluntary
        organisation[18] which makes a charge to the relevant person or his
        partner for the services provided by that person[19].

Except for persons to whom heads (1) to (3) and (6) apply, a person is a
non-dependant if he resides with a relevant person to whom he is liable to make
payments in respect of the dwelling and either that relevant person is a close
relative[20] of his or his partner[21], or the tenancy or other agreement between them
is other than on a commercial basis[22].

1   See PARAS 848–849.
2   A person resides with another only if they share any accommodation except a bathroom, a
    lavatory or a communal area, but not if each person is separately liable to make payments in
    respect of his occupation of the dwelling to the landlord: Housing Renewal Grants Regulations
    1996, SI 1996/2890, reg 6(4)(a). 'Communal area' means an area, other than a room or rooms, of
    common access (including halls and passageways): reg 6(4)(b).
3   As to the meaning of 'relevant person' see PARA 850.
4   Housing Renewal Grants Regulations 1996, SI 1996/2890, reg 6(1).
5   Housing Renewal Grants Regulations 1996, SI 1996/2890, reg 6(2)(a). 'Family', in relation to
    England, means: (1) a couple; (2) a couple and a member of the same household for whom one of
    the couple is or both are responsible and who is a child or a young person; (3) a person who is not
    a member of a couple and a member of the same household for whom that person is responsible
    and who is a child or a young person; and, in relation to Wales, means: (a) a couple or both
    members of a civil partnership; (b) a couple or both members of a civil partnership and a member

of the same household for whom one of them is or both are responsible and who is a child or a young person; (c) a person who is not a member of a couple or of a civil partnership and a member of the same household for whom that person is responsible and who is a child or a young person: reg 2(1) (amended, in relation to England, by SI 2005/3323; and, in relation to Wales, by SI 2005/3302 and SI 2006/2801). As to members of the same household see PARA 853.

6 As to the meaning of 'polygamous marriage' see PARA 850 note 10.

7 As to the meaning of 'partner' see PARA 850 note 5.

8 As to the meaning of 'child' see PARA 850 note 6.

9 As to the meaning of 'young person' see PARA 850 note 7.

10 Housing Renewal Grants Regulations 1996, SI 1996/2890, reg 6(2)(b). Subject to the following provisions, a person is treated as responsible for a child or young person who is normally living with him: reg 8(1). Where there is a question as to which person a child or young person is normally living with, the child or young person is treated for these purposes as normally living with: (1) the person who is receiving child benefit in respect of him or, if no-one is in that position, with whom he has been placed under the Children Act 1989 s 23(2) or, as the case may be, the Social Services and Well-being (Wales) Act 2014 s 81 (see CHILDREN AND YOUNG PERSONS vol 10 (2017) PARA 886 et seq); or (2) if there is no such person: (a) where only one claim for child benefit has been made in respect of him, the person who made that claim; or (b) in any other case, the person who has the primary responsibility for him: Housing Renewal Grants Regulations 1996, SI 1996/2890, reg 8(2) (amended, in relation to England, by SI 2001/739; and, in relation to Wales, by SI 2001/2073 and SI 2016/211). For these purposes, any person other than the one treated as responsible for the child or young person under the Housing Renewal Grants Regulations 1996, SI 1996/2890, reg 8 is treated as not so responsible: reg 8(3). 'Child benefit' means child benefit under the Social Security Contributions and Benefits Act 1992 Pt IX (ss 141–147) (see WELFARE BENEFITS AND STATE PENSIONS vol 104 (2014) PARA 160 et seq): Housing Renewal Grants Regulations 1996, SI 1996/2890, reg 2(1).

11 Housing Renewal Grants Regulations 1996, SI 1996/2890, reg 6(2)(c). For the circumstances in which a person is treated as being not part of a household see reg 9; and PARA 853.

12 As to the meaning of 'dwelling' see PARA 850 note 4.

13 'Payment' includes part of a payment: Housing Renewal Grants Regulations 1996, SI 1996/2890, reg 2(1).

14 Housing Renewal Grants Regulations 1996, SI 1996/2890, reg 6(2)(d).

15 Housing Renewal Grants Regulations 1996, SI 1996/2890, reg 6(2)(e)(i).

16 Housing Renewal Grants Regulations 1996, SI 1996/2890, reg 6(2)(e)(ii).

17 Housing Renewal Grants Regulations 1996, SI 1996/2890, reg 6(2)(e)(iii).

18 'Charity' has the meaning given by the Charities Act 1993 s 96 (repealed: see now the Charities Act 2011 s 10) (see CHARITIES vol 8 (2015) PARA 1); and 'charitable body' must be construed accordingly: Housing Renewal Grants Regulations 1996, SI 1996/2890, reg 2(1). 'Voluntary organisation' has the meaning given by the Children Act 1989 s 105(1) (see CHILDREN AND YOUNG PERSONS vol 9 (2017) PARA 171 note 8): Housing Renewal Grants Regulations 1996, SI 1996/2890, reg 2(1).

19 Housing Renewal Grants Regulations 1996, SI 1996/2890, reg 6(2)(f).

20 'Close relative' means a parent, parent-in-law, son, son-in-law, daughter, daughter-in-law, step-parent, step-son, step-daughter, brother, sister, or, if any of the preceding persons is one member of a couple, the other member of that couple: Housing Renewal Grants Regulations 1996, SI 1996/2890, reg 2(1) (amended, in relation to England, by SI 2005/3323; and, in relation to Wales, by SI 2006/2801). As to the meaning of 'couple' see PARA 850 note 9.

21 Housing Renewal Grants Regulations 1996, SI 1996/2890, reg 6(3)(a).

22 Housing Renewal Grants Regulations 1996, SI 1996/2890, reg 6(3)(b).

852. Meaning of 'remunerative work'. For the purposes of the means test for owner-occupier's and tenant's applications[1], a person is treated as engaged in remunerative work if he is engaged for not less than 16 hours a week, or, where his hours of work fluctuate, for not less than 16 hours a week on average, in work for which payment[2] is made or which is done in expectation of payment[3]. In determining the number of hours for which a person is engaged in work where his hours of work fluctuate, regard must be had to the average of hours worked in one of the following ways:

(1)   if there is a recognisable cycle of work, over the period of one complete cycle (including, where the cycle involves periods in which the person does not work, those periods but disregarding any other absences)[4]; or

(2)   in any other case, over the period of five weeks immediately prior to the
        date of the application[5], or such other length of time as may, in the
        particular case, enable the person's weekly average of hours of work to
        be determined more accurately[6].

Where no recognisable cycle has been established in respect of a person's work,
regard must be had to the number of hours or, where those hours fluctuate, the
average of the hours, which he is expected to work in a week[7]. A person in receipt
of income support[8], state pension credit[9] or an income-based
jobseeker's allowance[10] for more than three days in any period of seven
consecutive days commencing upon a Monday and ending on a Sunday is treated
as not being in remunerative work in that week[11]. A person is not treated as
engaged in remunerative work for any period during which he is participating in
the intensive activity period (New Deal) programme[12]. A person is not treated as
engaged in remunerative work on any day on which that person is on parental
leave[13] or is absent from work because he is ill[14]. A person is not treated as
engaged in remunerative work on any day on which that person is engaged in an
activity in respect of which: (a) a sports award[15] has been made, or is to be made,
to him; and (b) no other payment is made or is expected to be made to him[16].

1   See PARAS 608–609.
2   As to the meaning of 'payment' see PARA 851 note 13.
3   Housing Renewal Grants Regulations 1996, SI 1996/2890, reg 7(1). A person is treated as engaged
    in remunerative work during any period for which he is absent from work referred to in reg 7(1)
    if the absence is either without good cause or by reason of a recognised, customary or other
    holiday: reg 7(5).
4   Housing Renewal Grants Regulations 1996, SI 1996/2890, reg 7(2)(a). Where a
    person's recognisable cycle of work at a school, other educational establishment or other place of
    employment is one year and includes periods of school holidays or similar vacations during which
    he does not work, those periods and any other periods not forming part of such holidays or
    vacations during which he is not required to work must be disregarded in establishing the average
    hours for which he is engaged in work: reg 7(3).
5   As to the meaning of 'application' see PARA 850 note 1.
6   Housing Renewal Grants Regulations 1996, SI 1996/2890, reg 7(2)(b).
7   Housing Renewal Grants Regulations 1996, SI 1996/2890, reg 7(4).
8   'Income support' means income support under the Social Security Contributions and Benefits Act
    1992 Pt VII (ss 123–137) (see WELFARE BENEFITS AND STATE PENSIONS vol 104 (2014)
    PARA 292 et seq): Housing Renewal Grants Regulations 1996, SI 1996/2890, reg 2(1).
9   'State pension credit' has the same meaning as in the State Pension Credit Act 2002 (see WELFARE
    BENEFITS AND STATE PENSIONS vol 104 (2014) PARAS 236–247): Housing Renewal Grants
    Regulations 1996, SI 1996/2890, reg 2(1) (definition added, in relation to England, by SI
    2003/2504; and, in relation to Wales, by SI 2004/253).
10 'Income-based jobseeker's allowance' and 'a joint-claim jobseeker's allowance' have the same
    meanings as in the Jobseekers Act 1995 s 1(4) (see WELFARE BENEFITS AND STATE PENSIONS
    vol 104 (2014) PARAS 264): Housing Renewal Grants Regulations 1996, SI 1996/2890, reg 2(1)
    (amended, in relation to England, by SI 2002/530; and, in relation to Wales, by SI 2002/2798).
11 Housing Renewal Grants Regulations 1996, SI 1996/2890, reg 7(6) (amended by SI 1988/808; and
    further amended, in relation to England, by SI 2003/2504; and, in relation to Wales, by SI
    2004/253).
12 Housing Renewal Grants Regulations 1996, SI 1996/2890, reg 7(6A) (added by SI 1999/1523).
    'Intensive activity period (New Deal) programme' means the programme known as the intensive
    activity period of the New Deal pilot for 25 plus as defined for the purposes of the Social Security
    (New Deal Pilot) Regulations 1998, SI 1998/2825: Housing Renewal Grants Regulations 1996, SI
    1996/2890, reg 2(1) (definition added by SI 1999/1523). The Social Security (New Deal Pilot)
    Regulations 1998, SI 1998/2825, ceased to have effect on 29 November 1999: see reg 1(2).
13 'Parental leave' means maternity leave, paternity leave or adoption leave: Housing Renewal Grants
    Regulations 1996, SI 1996/2890, reg 2(1) (definition added, in relation to England, by SI
    2003/2504; and, in relation to Wales, by SI 2004/253). 'Maternity leave' means a period during
    which a woman is absent from work because she is pregnant or has given birth to a child, and at
    the end of which she has a right to return to work either under the terms of her contract of

employment or under the Employment Rights Act 1996 Pt VIII (ss 71–85) (see EMPLOYMENT vol 40 (2014) PARA 354 et seq): Housing Renewal Grants Regulations 1996, SI 1996/2890, reg 2(1). 'Paternity leave' means a period of absence from work on leave under the Employment Rights Act 1996 s 80A or s 80B (see EMPLOYMENT vol 40 (2014) PARA 368 et seq); and 'adoption leave' means a period of absence from work on ordinary or additional adoption leave under s 75A or s 75B (see EMPLOYMENT vol 40 (2014) PARA 377 et seq): Housing Renewal Grants Regulations 1996, SI 1996/2890, reg 2(1) (definitions added, in relation to England, by SI 2003/2504; and, in relation to Wales, by SI 2004/253).

14 Housing Renewal Grants Regulations 1996, SI 1996/2890, reg 7(7) (amended, in relation to England, by SI 2003/2504; and, in relation to Wales, by SI 2004/253).

15 'Sports award' means an award made by one of the Sports Councils named in the National Lottery etc Act 1993 s 23(2) (see LEISURE AND ENTERTAINMENT vol 67 (2016) PARA 581) out of sums allocated to it for distribution under s 23: Housing Renewal Grants Regulations 1996, SI 1996/2890, reg 2(1) (amended, in relation to England, by SI 2000/531; and, in relation to Wales, by virtue of SI 2000/973).

16 Housing Renewal Grants Regulations 1996, SI 1996/2890, reg 7(8) (added, in relation to England, by SI 2000/531; and, in relation to Wales, by virtue of SI 2000/973).

853. Circumstances in which a person is to be treated as being or not being a member of the household. A relevant person[1] and any partner[2] and, where the relevant person or his partner is treated as responsible[3] for a child[4] or young person[5], that child or young person and any child of that child or young person, must be treated as members of the same household notwithstanding that any of them is temporarily living away from the other members of his family[6].

This does not, however, apply to:

(1) a person who is living away from the other members of his family where:

 (a) that person does not intend to resume living with the other members of his family[7]; or

 (b) his absence from the other members of his family is likely to exceed 52 weeks, unless there are exceptional circumstances (for example, where the person is in hospital or otherwise has no control over the length of his absence) and the absence is unlikely to be substantially more than 52 weeks[8]; or

(2) a child or young person[9] where he is:

 (a) placed with the relevant person or his partner by a local authority[10] under the Children Act 1989[11] or by a voluntary organisation[12] under that Act[13]; or

 (b) placed with the relevant person or his partner prior to adoption[14]; or

 (c) placed for adoption with the relevant person or his partner pursuant to a decision under the Adoption Agencies Regulations 1983[15] or the Adoption Agencies (Scotland) Regulations 2009[16]; or

(3) a child or young person who is not living with the relevant person and who:

 (a) is being looked after by a local authority under a relevant enactment[17]; or

 (b) has been placed with a person other than the relevant person prior to adoption[18]; or

 (c) has been placed for adoption pursuant to a decision under the Adoption Agencies Regulations 1983[19] or the Adoption Agencies (Scotland) Regulations 2009[20].

1 As to the meaning of 'relevant person' see PARA 850.
2 As to the meaning of 'partner' see PARA 850 note 5.

3 As to responsibility for a child or young person see the Housing Renewal Grants Regulations 1996, SI 1996/2890, reg 8; and PARA 851 note 10.
4 As to the meaning of 'child' see PARA 850 note 6.
5 As to the meaning of 'young person' see PARA 850 note 7.
6 Housing Renewal Grants Regulations 1996, SI 1996/2890, reg 9(1). As to the meaning of 'family' see PARA 851 note 5.
7 Housing Renewal Grants Regulations 1996, SI 1996/2890, reg 9(2)(a).
8 Housing Renewal Grants Regulations 1996, SI 1996/2890, reg 9(2)(b).
9 The Housing Renewal Grants Regulations 1996, SI 1996/2890, reg 9(3) does not apply to cases where a child or young person has been placed with the relevant person or his partner by a local authority under the Children Act 1989 s 23(2)(a) or, as the case may be, the Social Services and Well-being (Wales) Act 2014 s 81 (see CHILDREN AND YOUNG PERSONS vol 10 (2017) PARA 888 et seq) and, in accordance with the Housing Renewal Grants Regulations 1996, SI 1996/2890, reg 8(2)(a) (see PARA 851 note 10), is to be treated as normally living with the relevant person or his partner: reg 9(3A) (added, in relation to England, by SI 2002/530; and, in relation to Wales, by SI 2002/2798; and amended by SI 2016/211).
10 'Local authority' and 'local housing authority', in relation to England and Wales, have the same meanings as in the Housing Act 1985 (see PARAS 11, 12); and 'local authority', in relation to Scotland, means a council constituted under the Local Government etc (Scotland) Act 1994 s 2: Housing Renewal Grants Regulations 1996, SI 1996/2890, reg 2(1).
11 Ie under the Children Act 1989 s 23(2)(a).
12 As to the meaning of 'voluntary organisation' see PARA 851 note 18.
13 Ie under the Children Act 1989 s 59(1)(a) (see CHILDREN AND YOUNG PERSONS vol 10 (2017) PARA 930) or, as the case may be, the Social Services and Well-being (Wales) Act 2014 s 81: Housing Renewal Grants Regulations 1996, SI 1996/2890, reg 9(3)(a) (amended by SI 2016/211).
14 Housing Renewal Grants Regulations 1996, SI 1996/2890, reg 9(3)(b).
15 Ie the Adoption Agencies Regulations 1983, SI 1983/1964.
16 Ie the Adoption Agencies (Scotland) Regulations 2009, SSI 2009/154: Housing Renewal Grants Regulations 1996, SI 1996/2890, reg 9(3)(c) (amended by SI 2011/1740).
17 Housing Renewal Grants Regulations 1996, SI 1996/2890, reg 9(4)(a). A child or young person to whom reg 9(4)(a) applies is treated as being a member of the relevant person's household in any period of seven consecutive days commencing upon a Monday and ending on a Sunday where: (1) that child or young person lives with the relevant person for part or all of that period; and (2) it is reasonable to do so taking into account the nature and frequency of that child's or young person's visits: reg 9(5)(a), (b).

For these purposes, 'relevant enactment' means the Army Act 1955, the Air Force Act 1955, the Naval Discipline Act 1957, the Adoption Act 1958, the Matrimonial Proceedings (Children) Act 1958, the Social Work (Scotland) Act 1968, the Family Law Reform Act 1969, the Children and Young Persons Act 1969, the Matrimonial Causes Act 1973, the Guardianship Act 1973, the Children Act 1975, the Domestic Proceedings and Magistrates' Courts Act 1978, the Adoption (Scotland) Act 1978, the Child Care Act 1980, the Family Law Act 1986 and the Children Act 1989: Housing Renewal Grants Regulations 1996, SI 1996/2890, reg 9(6).
18 Housing Renewal Grants Regulations 1996, SI 1996/2890, reg 9(4)(b).
19 Ie the Adoption Agencies Regulations 1983, SI 1983/1964.
20 Housing Renewal Grants Regulations 1996, SI 1996/2890, reg 9(4)(c) (amended by SI 2011/1740).

854. The applicable amount and financial resources. The 'applicable amount' in respect of any one application[1] is the aggregate of:
(1)   the total of the weekly applicable amounts[2] of all those persons who are relevant persons in the case of that application[3]; and
(2)   £61.30[4].
The weekly applicable amount of a relevant person is the aggregate of such of the following amounts as may apply in his case:
(a)   an amount in respect of himself or, if he is a member of a couple[5], an amount in respect of both of them[6];
(b)   an amount[7] in respect of any child[8] or young person[9] who is a member of his family;
(c)   if he is a member of a family of which at least one member is a child or young person, an amount of family premium[10];
(d)   the amount of any premiums which may be applicable[11] to him[12].

Where a relevant person is a member of a polygamous marriage[13], his weekly applicable amount is the aggregate of such of the following amounts as may apply in his case:

(i)   the highest amount applicable to him and one of his partners[14] determined[15] as if he and that partner were a couple;

(ii)   an amount equal to the difference between the amounts specified[16] in respect of each of his other partners;

(iii)   an amount determined[17] in respect of any child or young person for whom he or a partner of his is responsible and who is a member of the same household;

(iv)   if he or another partner of the polygamous marriage is responsible for a child or young person who is a member of the same household, the amount specified[18] for family premium;

(v)   the amount of any premiums which may be applicable[19] to him[20].

The applicable amount of a relevant person who has attained or whose partner has attained the qualifying age for state pension credit is the aggregate of such of the following amounts as apply in his case:

(A)   an amount in respect of his personal allowance[21];

(B)   an amount in respect of any child or young person who is a member of his family[22];

(C)   if he is a member of a family of which at least one member is a child or young person, an amount[23] for family premium;

(D)   the amount of any premiums which may be applicable[24] to him[25].

In respect of any one application, the amount which is to be taken to be the financial resources of the applicant or applicants is the total of the incomes of all those persons who are relevant persons in the case of that application[26], and the income[27] of each relevant person must be determined on a weekly basis by aggregating:

(I)   his average weekly earnings[28] from employment as an employed earner[29];

(II)   his average weekly earnings from employment as a self-employed earner[30];

(III)   his average weekly income other than earnings[31];

(IV)   the weekly tariff income determined from his capital[32],

and by then deducting the average weekly relevant child care charge[33] from the aggregated weekly income or, in a case where specified[34] conditions are met, from the aggregated weekly income plus whichever credit is appropriate[35], up to a maximum deduction in respect of the relevant person's family of whichever of the specified sums[36] applies in his case[37].

1   As to the meaning of 'application' see PARA 850 note 1.
2   For these purposes, the weekly applicable amount as regards any of the following persons:
    (1)   a relevant person who is in receipt of, and entitled to be in receipt of: (a) housing benefit; (b) income-based jobseeker's allowance; (c) income-related employment and support allowance; (d) income support; or (e) universal credit;
    (2)   a relevant person who: (a) is in receipt of guarantee credit; or (b) is a member of a couple, and the other member is in receipt of guarantee credit;
    (3)   a relevant person: (a) who is in receipt of working tax credit or child tax credit; and (b) whose annual income for the purposes of assessing his entitlement to working tax credit or child tax credit has been calculated as being less than £15,050; or
    (4)   subject to the Housing Renewal Grants Regulations 1996, SI 1996/2890, reg 10(5), a relevant person who has a partner, where the partner is entitled to universal credit,
    is £1: reg 10(2), (3) (reg 10 substituted, in relation to England, by SI 2008/1190; and, in relation to Wales, by SI 2008/2377; the Housing Renewal Grants Regulations 1996, SI 1996/2890, reg 10(3) amended, in relation to England, by SI 2009/1807, SI 2013/458 and SI 2013/630; and,

in relation to Wales, by SI 2010/297, SI 2013/552 and SI 2013/1788). As regards any other relevant person the weekly applicable amount is the amount determined in his case in accordance with the Housing Renewal Grants Regulations 1996, SI 1996/2890, reg 14 (applicable amounts: see the text to notes 5–12): reg 10(4) (as so substituted; renumbered as such by SI 2013/630). As to the meaning of 'relevant person' see PARA 850. For the purposes of head (4) and the Housing Renewal Grants Regulations 1996, SI 1996/2890, reg 11(2)(b) (see note 26), where the relevant person and a partner of that person are parties to a polygamous marriage, the fact that they are partners will be disregarded if one of them is a party to an earlier marriage that still subsists and the other party to that earlier marriage is living in the same household: reg 10(5) (added, in relation to England by SI 2013/630; and, in relation to Wales, by SI 2013/1788).

For these purposes, a person is on an income-based jobseeker's allowance on any day in respect of which an income-based jobseeker's allowance is payable to him and on any day: (i) in respect of which he satisfies the conditions for entitlement to an income based jobseeker's allowance but where the allowance is not paid in accordance with the Jobseekers Act 1995 s 19 (circumstances in which a jobseeker's allowance is not payable: see WELFARE BENEFITS AND STATE PENSIONS vol 104 (2014) PARA 280); or (ii) which is a waiting day for the purposes of the Jobseekers' Act 1995 Sch 1 para 4 (see WELFARE BENEFITS AND STATE PENSIONS vol 104 (2014) PARA 420) and which falls immediately before a day in respect of which an income-based jobseeker's allowance is payable to him but for s 19: Housing Renewal Grants Regulations 1996, SI 1996/2890, reg 2(3). As to the meaning of 'income-based jobseeker's allowance' see PARA 852 note 10. 'Universal credit' means universal credit under the Welfare Reform Act 2012 Pt 1 (ss 1–43) (see WELFARE BENEFITS AND STATE PENSIONS vol 104 (2014) PARAS 72–76): Housing Renewal Grants Regulations 1996, SI 1996/2890, reg 2(1) (definition added, in relation to England, by SI 2013/630; and, in relation to Wales, by SI 2013/1788). 'Guarantee credit' is to be construed in accordance with the State Pension Credit Act 2002 ss 1, 2 (see WELFARE BENEFITS AND STATE PENSIONS vol 104 (2014) PARAS 236, 238): Housing Renewal Grants Regulations 1996, SI 1996/2890, reg 2(1) (definition added, in relation to England, by SI 2003/2504; and, in relation to Wales, by SI 2004/253). 'Working tax credit' means a working tax credit under the Tax Credits Act 2002 s 10 (see WELFARE BENEFITS AND STATE PENSIONS vol 104 (2014) PARA 337); and 'child tax credit' means a child tax credit under s 8: Housing Renewal Grants Regulations 1996, SI 1996/2890, reg 2(1) (definitions added, in relation to England, by SI 2003/2504; and, in relation to Wales, by SI 2004/253).

3   Housing Renewal Grants Regulations 1996, SI 1996/2890, reg 10(1)(a) (as substituted: see note 2).

4   Housing Renewal Grants Regulations 1996, SI 1996/2890, reg 10(1)(b) (as substituted: see note 2).

5   As to the meaning of 'couple' see PARA 850 note 9.

6   Ie determined in accordance with the Housing Renewal Grants Regulations 1996, SI 1996/2890, Sch 1 para 1(1), (2) or (3), as the case may be.

7   Ie determined in accordance with the Housing Renewal Grants Regulations 1996, SI 1996/2890, Sch 1 para 2.

8   As to the meaning of 'child' see PARA 850 note 6.

9   As to the meaning of 'young person' see PARA 850 note 7.

10 Ie determined in accordance with the Housing Renewal Grants Regulations 1996, SI 1996/2890, Sch 1 Pt II. As to the meaning of 'family' see PARA 851 note 5.

11 Ie as determined in accordance with the Housing Renewal Grants Regulations 1996, SI 1996/2890, Sch 1 Pts III, IV.

12 Housing Renewal Grants Regulations 1996, SI 1996/2890, reg 14 (amended, in relation to England, by SI 2005/3323; and, in relation to Wales, by SI 2006/2801).

13 As to the meaning of 'polygamous marriage' see PARA 850 note 10.

14 As to the meaning of 'partner' see PARA 850 note 5.

15 Ie in accordance with the Housing Renewal Grants Regulations 1996, SI 1996/2890, Sch 1 para 1(3).

16 Ie in the Housing Renewal Grants Regulations 1996, SI 1996/2890, Sch 1 para 1(3)(b) and Sch 1 para 1(1)(b).

17 Ie in accordance with the Housing Renewal Grants Regulations 1996, SI 1996/2890, Sch 1 para 2.

18 Ie in the Housing Renewal Grants Regulations 1996, SI 1996/2890, Sch 1 Pt II.

19 Ie as determined in accordance with the Housing Renewal Grants Regulations 1996, SI 1996/2890, Sch 1 Pts III, IV.

20 Housing Renewal Grants Regulations 1996, SI 1996/2890, reg 15 (amended, in relation to England, by SI 2005/3323; and, in relation to Wales, by SI 2006/2801).

21 Ie determined in accordance with the Housing Renewal Grants Regulations 1996, SI 1996/2890, Sch 1A para 1.

22 Ie determined in accordance with the Housing Renewal Grants Regulations 1996, SI 1996/2890, Sch 1A para 2.

23 Ie determined in accordance with the Housing Renewal Grants Regulations 1996, SI 1996/2890, Sch 1A Pt II.
24 Ie as determined in accordance with the Housing Renewal Grants Regulations 1996, SI 1996/2890, Sch 1A Pts III, IV.
25 Housing Renewal Grants Regulations 1996, SI 1996/2890, reg 14(1) (reg 14 substituted for regs 14, 15 in relation to any person who has attained the qualifying age for state pension credit, in relation to England, by SI 2005/3323; and, in relation to Wales, by SI 2006/2801).
26 Housing Renewal Grants Regulations 1996, SI 1996/2890, reg 11(1) (numbered as such and amended, in relation to England by SI 2013/630; and, in relation to Wales, by SI 2013/1788). However, subject to the Housing Renewal Grants Regulations 1996, SI 1996/2890, reg 10(5) (see note 2), where a relevant person in the case of the application is entitled to universal credit or is not entitled to universal credit but their partner is so entitled, then the income of that relevant person for the purposes of reg 11(1) is to be taken to be nil: reg 11(2) (added, in relation to England by SI 2013/630; and, in relation to Wales, by SI 2013/1788).
27 Income is determined in accordance with the Housing Renewal Grants Regulations 1996, SI 1996/2890, reg 18 (determination of income on a weekly basis): reg 11(1) (as so numbered: see note 26). For the purposes of reg 18(1), 'income' includes income to which reg 30 (annuity treated as income), reg 31 (notional income), reg 43 (determination of grant income) and reg 46 (treatment of student loans) refer: reg 18(2).
28 'Earnings' has the meaning given by the Housing Renewal Grants Regulations 1996, SI 1996/2890, reg 24 (see PARA 859) or, as the case may be, reg 26 (see PARA 860): reg 2(1).
29 'Employed earner' is to be construed in accordance with the Social Security Contributions and Benefits Act 1992 s 2(1)(a) (see WELFARE BENEFITS AND STATE PENSIONS vol 104 (2014) PARA 381) and also includes a person who is in receipt of a payment which is payable under any enactment having effect in Northern Ireland and which corresponds to statutory sick pay or statutory maternity pay: Housing Renewal Grants Regulations 1996, SI 1996/2890, reg 2(1). The earnings of such a person are to be determined in accordance with Pt II Ch V (regs 18–23) and Pt II Ch VI (regs 24–25) (see PARA 859): reg 18(1)(a).
30 'Self-employed earner' is to be construed in accordance with the Social Security Contributions and Benefits Act 1992 s 2(1)(b) (see WELFARE BENEFITS AND STATE PENSIONS vol 104 (2014) PARA 381): Housing Renewal Grants Regulations 1996, SI 1996/2890, reg 2(1). The earnings of such a person are to be determined in accordance with Pt II Ch V and Pt II Ch VII (regs 26–28) (see PARA 860): reg 18(1)(b).
31 Ie determined in accordance with the Housing Renewal Grants Regulations 1996, SI 1996/2890, Pt II Ch V and Pt II Ch VIII (regs 29–32): reg 18(1)(c).
32 Ie under the Housing Renewal Grants Regulations 1996, SI 1996/2890, reg 40 (see PARA 866): reg 18(1)(d).
33 Ie in accordance with the Housing Renewal Grants Regulations 1996, SI 1996/2890, reg 19: see PARA 858.
34 Ie the conditions in the Housing Renewal Grants Regulations 1996, SI 1996/2890, reg 18(1ZA). Those conditions are that: (1) the relevant person's average weekly earnings from employment as an employed earner and from employment as a self-employed earner are less than the lower of either his relevant child care charges or whichever of the deductions specified in reg 18(1A) otherwise applies in his case; and (2) that relevant person or, if he is a member of a couple, either the relevant person or his partner, is in receipt of working tax credit or child tax credit: reg 18(1ZA) (added, in relation to England, by SI 2001/739; and, in relation to Wales, by SI 2001/2073; and amended, in relation to England, by SI 2003/2504; and, in relation to Wales, by SI 2004/253). As to working tax credit and child tax credit see WELFARE BENEFITS AND STATE PENSIONS vol 104 (2014) PARA 335 et seq.
35 Ie either working tax credit or child tax credit.
36 The maximum deduction for these purposes is: (1) where the relevant person's family includes only one child in respect of whom relevant child care charges are paid, £175 per week; and (2) where the relevant person's family includes more than one child in respect of whom relevant child care charges are paid, £300 per week: Housing Renewal Grants Regulations 1996, SI 1996/2890, reg 18(1A) (added by SI 1998/808; and amended, in relation to England, by SI 2005/3323; and, in relation to Wales, by SI 2006/2801).
37 Housing Renewal Grants Regulations 1996, SI 1996/2890, regs 11(1), 18(1) (reg 11(1) as renumbered and amended (see note 26); reg 18(1) amended by SI 1998/808).

855. General provisions relating to income and capital. For grant purposes, where a relevant person[1] is a member of a family[2], the income and capital of any member of that family must, except where otherwise provided, be treated as the income and capital of that person[3].

The income and capital of a relevant person's partner[4] which is to be treated as income and capital of the relevant person is determined in the same manner as for the relevant person[5]; and any reference to the relevant person is to be construed, for the purposes of the regulations relating to income and capital[6] (and except where the context otherwise requires) as if it were a reference to his partner[7].

Where a relevant person or the partner of that person is married polygamously[8] to two or more members of his household[9]:

(1)   the relevant person is treated as possessing capital and income belonging to each such member[10]; and

(2)   the income and capital of that member is to be calculated in like manner as for the relevant person[11].

The income and capital of a child[12] or young person[13] are not to be treated as the income and capital of the relevant person[14].

1   As to the meaning of 'relevant person' see PARA 850.
2   As to the meaning of 'family' see PARA 851 note 5.
3   Housing Renewal Grants Regulations 1996, SI 1996/2890, reg 16.
4   As to the meaning of 'partner' see PARA 850 note 5.
5   Ie in accordance with the Housing Renewal Grants Regulations 1996, SI 1996/2890, Pt II Ch IV (regs 16–17) and Pt II Ch V–Ch IX (regs 18–40) (see PARA 858 et seq).
6   Ie for the purposes of the Housing Renewal Grants Regulations 1996, SI 1996/2890, regs 17(3), (4), 18–40: see PARA 858 et seq.
7   Housing Renewal Grants Regulations 1996, SI 1996/2890, reg 17(1) (amended, in relation to England, by SI 2005/3323; and, in relation to Wales, by SI 2006/2801).
8   As to the meaning of 'polygamous marriage' see PARA 850 note 10.
9   As to members of the same household see PARA 853.
10   Housing Renewal Grants Regulations 1996, SI 1996/2890, reg 17(3)(a) (reg 17(3)(a), (b) substituted, in relation to England, by SI 2005/3323; and, in relation to Wales by SI 2006/2801).
11   Housing Renewal Grants Regulations 1996, SI 1996/2890, reg 17(3)(b) (as substituted: see note 10).
12   As to the meaning of 'child' see PARA 850 note 6.
13   As to the meaning of 'young person' see PARA 850 note 7.
14   Housing Renewal Grants Regulations 1996, SI 1996/2890, reg 17(4) (added, in relation to England, by SI 2005/3323; and, in relation to Wales, by SI 2006/2801).

B.   REDUCTION IN AMOUNT OF GRANT

856.   Calculation of reduction. The amount of any grant[1] which may be paid in respect of an application[2] which is accompanied by an owner's certificate[3] must, if the financial resources of the applicant or applicants exceed the applicable amount[4], be reduced from what it would otherwise have been by an amount equal to the aggregate of the amounts determined in accordance with the relevant regulations[5].

The amount of any grant which may be paid in respect of an application which is accompanied by a tenant's certificate[6] or occupier's certificate[7] must also, if the financial resources of the applicant or applicants exceed the applicable amount, be reduced from what it would otherwise have been by an amount equal to the aggregate of the amounts determined in the prescribed manner[8].

1   As to the meaning of 'grant' see PARA 836 note 1.
2   As to the meaning of 'application' see PARA 850 note 1.
3   As to the meaning of 'owner's certificate' see PARA 840 note 4.
4   As to the meanings of 'financial resources' and 'applicable amount' see PARA 854.
5   Housing Renewal Grants Regulations 1996, SI 1996/2890, reg 12(1) (amended, in relation to England, by SI 2003/2504; and, in relation to Wales, by SI 2004/253). As to determination of the amount of the reduction see the Housing Renewal Grants Regulations 1996, SI 1996/2890, reg 12(1)(a)–(d) (amended by SI 1997/977; and further amended, in relation to England, by SI 2008/1190; and, in relation to Wales, by SI 2008/2377).
6   As to the meaning of 'tenant's certificate' see PARA 841 note 3.

7   As to the meaning of 'occupier's certificate' see PARA 842 note 2.
8   Housing Renewal Grants Regulations 1996, SI 1996/2890, reg 12(2) (amended, in relation to England, by SI 2003/2504; and, in relation to Wales, by SI 2004/253). As to determination of the amount of the reduction see the Housing Renewal Grants Regulations 1996, SI 1996/2890, reg 12(2)(a)–(d) (amended by SI 1977/977; and further amended, in relation to England, by SI 2008/1190; and, in relation to Wales, by SI 2008/2377).

857. Successive applications. Special provisions apply where a person makes more than one application for a grant[1]. Thus in any of the following cases where:

(1)   within the ten years preceding the date of approval of the current application[2], at least one application, accompanied by an owner-occupation certificate for a renovation grant or disabled facilities grant under the Local Government and Housing Act 1989[3], an owner-occupation certificate for a renovation grant under the Housing Grants, Construction and Regeneration Act 1996[4] or an owner's certificate[5] for a grant under the Housing Grants, Construction and Regeneration Act 1996[6], relating to the same dwelling[7] or building was made, in respect of which at least one of the relevant persons[8] is a relevant person in the current application[9]; or

(2)   within the five years preceding the date of approval of the current application, at least one application, accompanied by a tenant's certificate[10] or occupier's certificate[11] relating to the same dwelling or building was made, in respect of which at least one of the relevant persons is a relevant person in the current application[12]; or

(3)   within the ten years preceding the date of approval of the current application, at least one tenants' common parts application[13] relating to the same building was made, in respect of which at least one of the relevant persons in the current application was an occupying tenant[14] in relation to a flat[15] in the building by virtue of a fixed term tenancy of which not less than five years remained unexpired at the date of the application and was also an applicant[16]; or

(4)   within the five years preceding the date of approval of the current application, at least one tenants' common parts application relating to the same building was made, in respect of which at least one of the relevant persons in the current application was an occupying tenant in relation to a flat in the building by virtue of a specified interest[17], and was also an applicant[18],

the amount by which a grant[19] in respect of a current application is reduced must be abated by the amount by which any grant paid in respect of any previous application referred to in heads (1) to (4) was itself reduced by virtue of the relevant statutory provisions[20]. These special provisions do not, however, apply in any case where, by reason of such a reduction, no grant was paid in respect of the application, except where the eligible works[21] in respect of which the application was approved were executed to a satisfactory standard[22].

Similarly, where within the ten years preceding the date of approval of the current application, at least one of the relevant persons in the current application signified scheme consent under the Local Government and Housing Act 1989[23], or under the Housing Grants, Construction and Regeneration Act 1996[24], in respect of at least one group repair scheme[25] in relation to which the same dwelling, building or flat was, or was part of, a qualifying building[26], the amount by which a grant in respect of a current application is reduced must be abated by the amount of any participant's contribution notified[27] to any person who is a relevant person in the current application[28].

1 See the Housing Renewal Grants Regulations 1996, SI 1996/2890, reg 13; and the text and notes 2–28.
2 For these purposes, 'current application' means an application to which the Housing Renewal Grants Regulations 1996, SI 1996/2890, reg 12 (see PARA 856) refers: reg 13(1). As to the meaning of 'application' see PARA 850 note 1.
3 Ie under the Local Government and Housing Act 1989 s 106(2) (repealed).
4 Ie under the Housing Grants, Construction and Regeneration Act 1996 s 8(2) (repealed).
5 As to the meaning of 'owner's certificate' see PARA 840 note 4.
6 Ie under the Housing Grants, Construction and Regeneration Act 1996 s 21(2): see PARA 840.
7 As to the meaning of 'dwelling' see PARA 850 note 4.
8 As to the meaning of 'relevant person' see PARA 850.
9 Housing Renewal Grants Regulations 1996, SI 1996/2890, reg 13(3)(a) (amended, in relation to England, by SI 2003/2504; and, in relation to Wales, by SI 2004/253).
10 As to the meaning of 'tenant's certificate' see PARA 841 note 3.
11 As to the meaning of 'occupier's certificate' see PARA 842 note 2.
12 Housing Renewal Grants Regulations 1996, SI 1996/2890, reg 13(3)(b) (amended, in relation to England, by SI 2003/2504; and, in relation to Wales, by SI 2004/253).
13 As to the meaning of 'common parts application' see PARA 839 note 11.
14 Ie as defined in the Housing Grants, Construction and Regeneration Act 1996 s 14 (repealed).
15 As to the meaning of 'flat' see PARA 836 note 7.
16 Housing Renewal Grants Regulations 1996, SI 1996/2890, reg 13(3)(c).
17 Ie such an interest as is mentioned in the Local Government and Housing Act 1989 s 105(4)(c)–(e) (repealed) or in the Housing Grants, Construction and Regeneration Act 1996 s 14(2)(a)–(d) (repealed).
18 Housing Renewal Grants Regulations 1996, SI 1996/2890, reg 13(3)(d).
19 As to the meaning of 'grant' see PARA 836 note 1.
20 See the Housing Renewal Grants Regulations 1996, SI 1996/2890, reg 13(2) (amended by SI 1988/808; and further amended, in relation to England, by SI 2003/2504; and, in relation to Wales, by SI 2004/253). The reduction must be abated: (1) in a case to which head (1) or head (2) in the text applies, by the amount by which any grant paid in respect of any application there referred to was itself reduced by virtue of the Housing Renewal Grants Regulations 1996, SI 1996/2890, reg 12, reg 13, or the corresponding predecessor provisions; (2) in a case to which head (3) or head (4) in the text applies, by the amount by which any grant paid in respect of any application there referred to was itself reduced, by virtue of the Local Government and Housing Act 1989 s 111(4) (repealed), by reference to persons (other than participating landlords) who are relevant persons in the current application: see the Housing Renewal Grants Regulations 1996, SI 1996/2890, reg 13(2)(a), (b) (as so amended).
21 As to the works eligible for grant see PARA 837.
22 Housing Renewal Grants Regulations 1996, SI 1996/2890, reg 13(4).
23 Ie under the Local Government and Housing Act 1989 s 129(1) (repealed).
24 Ie the Housing Grants, Construction and Regeneration Act 1996 s 65(1) (repealed).
25 Ie a scheme under the Housing Grants, Construction and Regeneration Act 1996 s 60 (repealed).
26 Ie a qualifying building under the Housing Grants, Construction and Regeneration Act 1996 s 61(2) (repealed).
27 Ie under the Local Government and Housing Act 1989 s 129(1) (repealed) or the Housing Grants, Construction and Regeneration Act 1996 s 67(1) (repealed).
28 Housing Renewal Grants Regulations 1996, SI 1996/2890, reg 13(2)(c), (3)(e).

C. INCOME

858. Treatment of child care charges. In determining income for the means test for owner-occupier's and tenant's applications for grant[1], a deduction is made for child care charges[2]. Where a relevant person[3] incurs relevant child care charges and:

(1)	is a lone parent[4] and is engaged in remunerative work[5];
(2)	is a member of a couple[6] both of whom are engaged in remunerative work; or

(3)   is a member of a couple where one member is engaged in remunerative work and the other is incapacitated[7], is an in-patient in hospital or is in prison (whether serving a custodial sentence or remanded in custody awaiting trial or sentence),

relevant child care charges are determined over such period, not exceeding a year, as is appropriate in order that the average weekly charge may be estimated accurately having regard to information as to the amount of the charge provided by the child minder or person providing the care[8].

'Relevant child care charges' means those charges for care to which the following provisions[9] apply, and they must be calculated[10] on a weekly basis[11]:

(a)   charges paid by the relevant person for care which is provided: (i) in the case of any child[12] of the relevant person's family[13] who is not disabled[14], in respect of the period beginning on that child's date of birth and ending on the day preceding the first Monday in September following that child's fifteenth birthday; (ii) in the case of any child of the relevant person's family who is disabled, in respect of the period beginning on that child's date of birth and ending on the day preceding the first Monday in September following that child's sixteenth birthday[15];

(b)   charges paid for care which is provided in defined circumstances[16] but not paid: (i) in respect of the child's compulsory education; (ii) by a relevant person to a partner or by a partner to a relevant person in respect of any child for whom either of them is responsible[17]; or (iii) in respect of care provided by a relative of a child wholly or mainly in the child's home[18].

1   As to the means test see PARAS 848–849.
2   See the Housing Renewal Grants Regulations 1996, SI 1996/2890, reg 18; and PARA 854.
3   As to the meaning of 'relevant person' see PARA 850.
4   'Lone parent' means a person who has no partner and who is responsible for and a member of the same household as a child or young person: Housing Renewal Grants Regulations 1996, SI 1996/2890, reg 2(1). As to the meaning of 'partner' see PARA 850 note 5; as to the meaning of 'child' see PARA 850 note 6; as to the meaning of 'young person' see PARA 850 note 7; and as to members of the same household see PARA 853.
5   As to the meaning of 'remunerative work' see PARA 852.
6   As to the meaning of 'member of a couple' see PARA 850 note 9.
7   For these purposes, the other member of a couple is incapacitated where:
     (1)   the relevant person's applicable amount includes a disability premium or a higher pensioner premium by virtue of the satisfaction of the Housing Renewal Grants Regulations 1996, SI 1996/2890, Sch 1 para 10(2)(b) on account of the other member's incapacity;
     (2)   the relevant person's applicable amount would include a disability premium or a higher pensioner premium on account of the other member's incapacity, but for that other member being treated as capable of work by virtue of a determination made in accordance with regulations made under the Social Security Contributions and Benefits Act 1992 s 171E (incapacity for work, disqualification, etc: see WELFARE BENEFITS AND STATE PENSIONS vol 104 (2014) PARA 472) or the Employment and Support Allowance Regulations 2008, SI 2008/794 or the Employment and Support Allowance Regulations 2013, SI 2013/379 (see WELFARE BENEFITS AND STATE PENSIONS vol 104 (2014) PARA 443);
     (3)   the relevant person: (a) is or is treated as incapable of work, and has been incapable or treated as incapable of work in accordance with the provisions of, and regulations made under, the Social Security Contributions and Benefits Act 1992 Pt XIIA (ss 171A–171G) (incapacity for work: see WELFARE BENEFITS AND STATE PENSIONS vol 104 (2014) PARA 472) for a continuous period of not less than 196 days, and for this purpose any two or more periods separated by a break of not more than 56 days are to be treated as one continuous period; or (b) has, or is being treated as having, limited capability for work and has had, or been treated as having, limited capability for work in accordance with the Employment and Support Allowance Regulations 2008, SI 2008/794, or the Employment and Support Allowance Regulations 2013, SI 2013/379, for a continuous

period of not less than 196 days, and for this purpose any two or more periods separated by a break of not more than 84 days are to be treated as one continuous period;

(4)   there is payable in respect of him one or more of the following:

(a)   long-term incapacity benefit, or short-term incapacity benefit at the higher rate, under the Social Security Contributions and Benefits Act 1992 Sch 4 (rates of benefits, etc: see WELFARE BENEFITS AND STATE PENSIONS vol 104 (2014) PARAS 122, 154, 193, 198, 201, 510);

(b)   attendance allowance under s 64 (entitlement to an attendance allowance: see WELFARE BENEFITS AND STATE PENSIONS vol 104 (2014) PARA 147);

(c)   severe disablement allowance under s 68 (severe disablement allowance, entitlement and rate);

(d)   disability living allowance under s 71 (disability living allowance: see WELFARE BENEFITS AND STATE PENSIONS vol 104 (2014) PARA 144);

(e)   increase of disablement pension under s 104 (increase where constant attendance needed: see WELFARE BENEFITS AND STATE PENSIONS vol 104 (2014) PARA 199);

(f)   a pension increase under a war pension scheme or an industrial injuries scheme which is analogous to an allowance or increase of disablement pension under head (b), (d) or (e);

(g)   main phase employment and support allowance;

(h)   personal independence payment;

(i)   armed forces independence payment;

(5)   a pension or allowance to which head (4)(b), (d), (e) or (f) refers was payable on account of his incapacity but has ceased to be payable in consequence of his becoming a patient within the meaning of the Housing Benefit Regulations 2006, SI 2006/213, reg 24(2);

(6)   head (4) or head (5) would apply to him if the legislative provisions referred to therein were provisions under any corresponding enactment having effect in Northern Ireland;

(7)   he has an invalid carriage or other vehicle provided to him by the appropriate national authority under the National Health Service Act 1977 s 5(2)(a), Sch 2 (provision of vehicles for those suffering disability: see HEALTH SERVICES vol 54 (2017) PARA 62) or under the National Health Service (Scotland) Act 1978 s 46 or provided by the Department of Health and Social Services for Northern Ireland under the relevant Northern Ireland legislation; or

(8)   personal independence payment would be payable but for regulations under the Welfare Reform Act 2012 s 85 (care home residents: see WELFARE BENEFITS AND STATE PENSIONS vol 104 (2014) PARA 138) or s 86(1) (hospital in-patients: see WELFARE BENEFITS AND STATE PENSIONS vol 104 (2014) PARA 139).

See the Housing Renewal Grants Regulations 1996, SI 1996/2890, reg 19(3) (amended by SI 2006/217; and, in relation to England, by SI 2009/1807, SI 2013/388, SI 2013/591 and SI 2013/630; and, in relation to Wales, by SI 2010/297, SI 2013/552, SI 2013/1788 and SI 2013/3138). 'Long-term incapacity benefit' means long-term incapacity benefit under the Social Security Contributions and Benefits Act 1992 Pt II (ss 20–62) (see WELFARE BENEFITS AND STATE PENSIONS vol 104 (2014) PARA 409 et seq); 'short-term incapacity benefit' means short-term incapacity benefit under Pt II (see WELFARE BENEFITS AND STATE PENSIONS vol 104 (2014) PARA 409 et seq); 'attendance allowance' means: (i) an attendance allowance under Pt III (ss 63–79) (see WELFARE BENEFITS AND STATE PENSIONS vol 104 (2014) PARA 147 et seq); (ii) an increase of disablement pension under s 104 or s 105 (see WELFARE BENEFITS AND STATE PENSIONS vol 104 (2014) PARAS 199, 201); (iii) a payment under regulations made in exercise of the power conferred by Sch 8 para 7(2)(b) (constant attendance allowance); (iv) an increase of an allowance which is payable in respect of constant attendance under a scheme under, or having effect under Sch 8 para 4 (industrial diseases benefit schemes); (v) a payment by virtue of the Personal Injuries (Civilians) Scheme 1983, SI 1983/686, art 14, 15, 16, 43 or 44 (see ARMED FORCES vol 3 (2011) PARA 721) or any analogous payment; (vi) any payment based on need for attendance which is paid as part of a war disablement pension: Housing Renewal Grants Regulations 1996, SI 1996/2890, reg 2(1) (amended, in relation to England by SI 2002/530; and, in relation to Wales, by SI 2002/2798). 'War disablement pension' and 'war widow's pension' have the meanings given by the Social Security Contributions and Benefits Act 1992 s 150(2) (see WELFARE BENEFITS AND STATE PENSIONS vol 104 (2014) PARA 36); and 'disability living allowance' means a disability living allowance under Pt III (see WELFARE BENEFITS AND STATE PENSIONS vol 104 (2014) PARA 144 et seq): Housing Renewal Grants Regulations 1996, SI 1996/2890, reg 2(1). 'Invalid carriage or other vehicle' means a vehicle propelled by petrol engine or electric power supplied for use on the road and to be controlled by the occupant: reg 2(1). 'Main phase employment and support allowance' means an employment and support allowance where the calculation of the amount payable in respect of the claimant includes an addition under the Welfare Reform Act 2007 s 2(1)(b) or s 4(2)(b) (see WELFARE BENEFITS AND STATE PENSIONS vol 104 (2014) PARAS 252, 466): Housing Renewal Grants Regulations 1996, SI 1996/2890, reg 2(1) (definition added, in relation to England, by SI 2009/1807; and, in relation to Wales, by SI 2010/297).

8   Housing Renewal Grants Regulations 1996, SI 1996/2890, reg 19(1), (2) (reg 19(1) amended, in relation to England, by SI 2005/3323; and, in relation to Wales by SI 2006/2801). A person who was in remunerative work immediately before: (1) the first day of the period in respect of which he was first paid statutory sick pay, short-term incapacity benefit, employment and support allowance or income support on the grounds of incapacity for work; or (2) the first day of the period in respect of which earnings are credited, as the case may be, is be treated as engaged in remunerative work for a period not exceeding 28 weeks during which he: (a) is paid statutory sick pay; (b) is paid short-term incapacity benefit at the lower rate under the Social Security Contributions and Benefits Act 1992 ss 30A–30E (see WELFARE BENEFITS AND STATE PENSIONS vol 104 (2014) PARA 472); (c) is paid income support on the grounds of incapacity for work under the Income Support (General) Regulations 1987, SI 1987/1967, reg 4ZA, Sch 1B para 7 or 14 (see WELFARE BENEFITS AND STATE PENSIONS vol 104 (2014) PARA 294); (d) is credited with earnings on the grounds of incapacity for work or limited capability for work under the Social Security (Credits) Regulations 1975, SI 1975/566, reg 8B; or (e) is paid employment and support allowance: Housing Renewal Grants Regulations 1996, SI 1996/2890, reg 19(1A), (1B) (added, in relation to England, by SI 2005/3323; and, in relation to Wales, by SI 2006/2801; and amended, in relation to England, by SI 2009/1807; and, in relation to Wales, by SI 2010/297). In a case to which head (c) or (d) applies, the period of 28 weeks begins on the day on which the person is first paid income support or on the first day of the period in respect of which earnings are credited, as the case may be: Housing Renewal Grants Regulations 1996, SI 1996/2890, reg 19(1C) (added, in relation to England, by SI 2005/3323; and, in relation to Wales, by SI 2006/2801). 'Employment and support allowance' means an employment and support allowance payable under the Welfare Reform Act 2007 Pt 1 (ss 1–29) (see WELFARE BENEFITS AND STATE PENSIONS vol 104 (2014) PARA 443 et seq): Housing Renewal Grants Regulations 1996, SI 1996/2890, reg 2(1) (definition added, in relation to England, by SI 2009/1807; and, in relation to Wales, by SI 2010/297).
      A person on parental leave must be treated as if engaged in remunerative work for the relevant period where: (i) in the week before the period of leave began the person was in remunerative work; (ii) the relevant person is incurring relevant child care charges; and (iii) the person on leave is entitled to parental support: Housing Renewal Grants Regulations 1996, SI 1996/2890, reg 19(9) (added, in relation to England, by SI 2002/530; and substituted by SI 2003/2504; added, in relation to Wales, by SI 2002/2798; and substituted by SI 2004/253; and amended, in relation to England, by SI 2005/3323; and, in relation to Wales, by SI 2006/2801). The relevant period begins on the day on which the person's parental leave commences and ends on: (A) the date that leave ends; (B) if no child care element of working tax credit is in payment on the date that entitlement to parental support ends, the date that entitlement ends; or (C) if a child care element of working tax credit is in payment on the date that entitlement to parental support ends, the date that entitlement to that award of the tax credit ends, whichever occurs first: Housing Renewal Grants Regulations 1996, SI 1996/2890, reg 19(9A) (added, in relation to England, by SI 2003/2504; and, in relation to Wales, by SI 2004/253; and amended, in relation to England, by SI 2005/3323; and, in relation to Wales, by SI 2006/2801).
      For these purposes, 'parental support' means: (I) statutory maternity pay under the Social Security Contributions and Benefits Act 1992 s 164 (see EMPLOYMENT vol 40 (2014) PARA 401 et seq); (II) statutory paternity pay under s 171ZA or s 171ZB (see EMPLOYMENT vol 40 (2014) PARA 443 et seq); (III) statutory adoption pay under s 171ZA (see EMPLOYMENT vol 40 (2014) PARA 488 et seq); (IV) maternity allowance under s 35 (see WELFARE BENEFITS AND STATE PENSIONS vol 104 (2014) PARA 473–475); or (V) income support to which that person is entitled by virtue of the Income Support (General) Regulations 1987, SI 1987/1967, Sch 1B para 14B (see WELFARE BENEFITS AND STATE PENSIONS vol 104 (2014) PARA 294): Housing Renewal Grants Regulations 1996, SI 1996/2890, reg 19(9B) (added, in relation to England, by SI 2003/2504; and, in relation to Wales, by SI 2004/253; and amended, in relation to England, by SI 2005/3323 and SI 2014/1829; and, in relation to Wales, by SI 2006/2801). As to the meaning of 'working tax credit' see PARA 854 note 2. Any child care charges in respect of the child to whom the parental leave relates are not to be treated as relevant child care charges for the purposes of the Housing Renewal Grants Regulations 1996, SI 1996/2890, regs 18, 19: reg 19(10) (added, in relation to England, by SI 2002/530; and added by SI 2003/2504; and added, in relation to Wales, by SI 2002/2798; and amended by SI 2004/253).

9   Ie the provisions of the Housing Renewal Grants Regulations 1996, SI 1996/2890, reg 19(5), (6).

10 Ie in accordance with the Housing Renewal Grants Regulations 1996, SI 1996/2890, reg 19(2) (see the text and note 8).

11 Housing Renewal Grants Regulations 1996, SI 1996/2890, reg 19(4) (definition substituted, in relation to England, by SI 1999/2568; and, in relation to Wales, by SI 1999/3468).

12 For the purposes of the Housing Renewal Grants Regulations 1996, SI 1996/2890, reg 19(5)–(7), a person is to be treated as a child in respect of the period commencing on his sixteenth birthday and ending on the day preceding the first Monday in September following his sixteenth birthday: Housing Renewal Grants Regulations 1996, SI 1996/2890, reg 19(8)(a) (reg 19(5)–(8) added, in relation to England, by SI 1999/2568; and, in relation to Wales, by SI 1999/3468).

13 As to the meaning of 'family' see PARA 851 note 5.

14 For the purposes of the Housing Renewal Grants Regulations 1996, SI 1996/2890, reg 19(5)–(7), a child is disabled if he is a child: (1) in respect of whom disability living allowance is payable, or has ceased to be payable solely because he is a patient; (2) who is registered as blind in a register compiled under the National Assistance Act 1948 s 29 (welfare services), or is registered as severely sight-impaired in a register kept by a local authority in Wales under the Social Services and Well-being (Wales) Act 2014 s 18(1); (3) who ceased to be registered as blind or severely sight-impaired in such a register within the 28 weeks immediately preceding the date of claim; (4) in respect of whom personal independence payment is payable, or would, but for regulations made under the Welfare Reform Act 2012 s 85 (care home residents: see WELFARE BENEFITS AND STATE PENSIONS vol 104 (2014) PARA 138) or s 86(1) (hospital in-patients: see WELFARE BENEFITS AND STATE PENSIONS vol 104 (2014) PARA 139), be payable; or (5) in respect of whom armed forces independence payment is payable: Housing Renewal Grants Regulations 1996, SI 1996/2890, reg 19(8)(b) (as added (see note 12); amended, in relation to England by SI 2013/388 and SI 2013/591; in relation to Wales by SI 2013/552 and SI 2013/3138; and by SI 2016/211). 'Personal independence payment' means personal independence payment under the Welfare Reform Act 2012 Pt 4 (ss 77–95): Housing Renewal Grants Regulations 1996, SI 1996/2890, reg 2(1) (definition added, in relation to England by SI 2013/388; and in relation to Wales by SI 2013/552). 'Armed forces independence payment' means armed forces independence payment under the Armed Forces and Reserve Forces (Compensation Scheme) Order 2011, SI 2011/517 (see ARMED FORCES vol 3 (2011) PARA 731 et seq): Housing Renewal Grants Regulations 1996, SI 1996/2890, reg 2(1) (definition added, in relation to England, by SI 2013/591; and, in relation to Wales by SI 2013/3138).

For these purposes, 'local authority' means, in relation to England and Wales, the council of a county or district, a metropolitan district, a London borough, the Common Council of the City of London or the Council of the Isles of Scilly or, in relation to Scotland, a council constituted under the Local Government etc (Scotland) Act 1994 s 2; and 'Crown property' means property held by Her Majesty in right of the Crown or by a government department or which is held in trust for Her Majesty for the purposes of a government department, except (in the case of an interest held by Her Majesty in right of the Crown) where the interest is under the management of the Crown Estate Commissioners: Housing Renewal Grants Regulations 1996, SI 1996/2890, reg 19(4).

15 Housing Renewal Grants Regulations 1996, SI 1996/2890, reg 19(5) (as added: see note 12).

16 The care to which the Housing Renewal Grants Regulations 1996, SI 1996/2890, reg 19(6) refers is provided: (1) out of school hours, by a school on school premises or by a local authority for a child who is not disabled in respect of the period beginning on his eighth birthday and ending on the day preceding the first Monday in September following his fifteenth birthday, or for a child who is disabled in respect of the period beginning on his eighth birthday and ending on the day preceding the first Monday in September following his sixteenth birthday; (2) by a child care provider approved by an organisation accredited by the appropriate national authority under the scheme established by the Tax Credit (New Category of Child Care Provider) Regulations 1999, SI 1999/3110; (3) by persons registered under the Children Act 1989 Pt XA (ss 79A–79X) (repealed) or the Children and Families (Wales) Measure 2010 Pt 2 (ss 19–56); (4) in schools or establishments which are exempted from registration under the Children Act 1989 Pt XA by virtue of Sch 9A para 1 or 2 or by a person who is excepted from registration under the Children and Families (Wales) Measure 2010 Pt 2 because the child care that person provides is in a school or establishment referred to in the Child Minding and Day Care Exceptions (Wales) Order 2010, SI 2010/2838, art 11, 12 or 14; or (5) by a person prescribed in regulations made pursuant to the Tax Credits Act 2002 s 12(4) (see WELFARE BENEFITS AND STATE PENSIONS vol 104 (2014) PARA 344): Housing Renewal Grants Regulations 1996, SI 1996/2890, reg 19(7) (as added (see note 12); amended, in relation to England, by SI 2001/739 and SI 2005/3323; and, in relation to Wales, by SI 2001/2073, SI 2006/2801 and SI 2010/2582).

17 Ie in accordance with the Housing Renewal Grants Regulations 1996, SI 1996/2890, reg 8: see PARA 851 note 10.

18 Housing Renewal Grants Regulations 1996, SI 1996/2890, reg 19(6) (as added (see note 12); amended, in relation to England, by SI 2005/3323; and, in relation to Wales, by SI 2006/2801).

859. Employed earners. Where the income of a relevant person[1] consists of or includes earnings[2] from employment as an employed earner, his average weekly earnings from such employment must be determined by reference to his earnings from it over the period of 52 weeks immediately preceding the application[3] or, where his earnings fluctuate, over such other lesser period immediately preceding the application as may enable his average weekly earnings to be determined more accurately[4].

Where the period in respect of which a payment is made:

(1)   does not exceed a week, the weekly amount is the amount of that payment[5];

(2)   exceeds a week, the weekly amount is determined:

    (a)   in a case where that period is a month, by multiplying the amount of the payment by 12 and dividing the product by 52[6];

    (b)   in any other case, by dividing the amount of the payment by the number equal to the number of days in the period to which it relates and multiplying the quotient by seven[7].

For these purposes the earnings of a relevant person derived from employment as an employed earner to be taken into account are his net earnings[8], subject to the statutory disregards[9].

1   As to the meaning of 'relevant person' see PARA 850.
2   For these purposes, the Housing Renewal Grants Regulations 1996, SI 1996/2890, reg 24(1) (amended, in relation to England, by SI 2000/531 and SI 2003/2504; and, in relation to Wales, by SI 2000/973 and SI 2004/253) provides that 'earnings' means any remuneration or profit derived from employment as an employed earner and includes:

    (1)   any bonus or commission;
    (2)   any payment in lieu of remuneration except any periodic sum paid to a relevant person on account of the termination of his employment by reason of redundancy;
    (3)   any payment in lieu of notice or any lump sum payment intended as compensation for the loss of employment but only to the extent that it represents loss of income;
    (4)   any holiday pay except any payable more than four weeks after termination or interruption of the employment;
    (5)   any payment by way of a retainer;
    (6)   any payment made by the relevant person's employer in respect of expenses not wholly, exclusively and necessarily incurred in the performance of the duties of the employment, including any payment made by the employer in respect of: (a) travelling expenses incurred by the relevant person between his home and place of employment; (b) expenses incurred by the relevant person under arrangements made for the care of a member of his family owing to the relevant person's absence from home;
    (7)   any award of compensation made under the Employment Rights Act 1996 s 112(1), (4) or s 117(3)(a) (remedies and compensation for unfair dismissal: see EMPLOYMENT vol 41 (2014) PARAS 810, 813);
    (8)   any such sum as is referred to in the Social Security Contributions and Benefits Act 1992 s 112(3) (certain sums to be earnings for social security purposes: see WELFARE BENEFITS AND STATE PENSIONS vol 104 (2014) PARA 382);
    (9)   any statutory sick pay under Pt XI (ss 151–163) (see EMPLOYMENT vol 40 (2014) PARA 558 et seq) or statutory maternity pay under Pt XII (ss 164–171) (see EMPLOYMENT vol 40 (2014) PARA 401 et seq), or a corresponding payment under any enactment having effect in Northern Ireland;
    (10)   any remuneration paid by or on behalf of an employer to the relevant person who for the time being is on parental leave or is absent from work because he is ill;
    (11)   the amount of any payment by way of a non-cash voucher which has been taken into account in the computation of a person's earnings in accordance with the Social Security (Contributions) Regulations 2001, SI 2001/1004, reg 24 (see WELFARE BENEFITS AND STATE PENSIONS vol 104 (2014) PARA 382); and
    (12)   where a relevant person qualifies for the national minimum wage under the National Minimum Wage Act 1998 s 1 (see EMPLOYMENT vol 39 (2014) PARA 176 et seq), any amount which under s 17 (see EMPLOYMENT vol 39 (2014) PARA 242) that person is taken to be entitled to be paid under his contract as additional remuneration in respect of any pay reference period falling within the 52 weeks immediately preceding the application.

As to the meaning of 'employed earner' see PARA 854 note 29. 'Any pay reference period' means the period prescribed by the Secretary of State in regulations made under the National Minimum Wage Act 1998 s 1(4) (see EMPLOYMENT vol 39 (2014) PARA 202): Housing Renewal Grants Regulations 1996, SI 1996/2890, reg 24(4) (added, in relation to England, by SI 2000/531; and, in relation to Wales, by virtue of SI 2000/973).

For these purposes, earnings do not include any payment in kind, any payment in respect of expenses wholly, exclusively and necessarily incurred in the performance of the duties of the employment, or any occupational pension: Housing Renewal Grants Regulations 1996, SI 1996/2890, reg 24(2) (amended, in relation to England, by SI 2000/531; and, in relation to Wales, by virtue of SI 2000/973). For the purposes of head (11), however, 'earnings' do include payments in kind: Housing Renewal Grants Regulations 1996, SI 1996/2890, reg 24(3) (added, in relation to England, by SI 2000/531; and, in relation to Wales, by virtue of SI 2000/973). 'Occupational pension' means any pension or other periodical payment under an occupational pension scheme but does not include any discretionary payment out of a fund established for relieving hardship in particular cases: Housing Renewal Grants Regulations 1996, SI 1996/2890, reg 2(1).

3 As to the meaning of 'application' see PARA 850 note 1.
4 Housing Renewal Grants Regulations 1996, SI 1996/2890, reg 20.
5 Housing Renewal Grants Regulations 1996, SI 1996/2890, reg 23(1)(a). As to the meaning of 'payment' see PARA 851 note 13.
6 Housing Renewal Grants Regulations 1996, SI 1996/2890, reg 23(1)(b)(i).
7 Housing Renewal Grants Regulations 1996, SI 1996/2890, reg 23(1)(b)(ii).
8 Housing Renewal Grants Regulations 1996, SI 1996/2890, reg 25(1). Net earnings must be determined by taking into account the gross earnings of the relevant person from that employment over the assessment period, less: (1) any amount deducted from those earnings by way of income tax and primary Class 1 contributions under the Social Security Contributions and Benefits Act 1992 Pt I (ss 1–19) (see WELFARE BENEFITS AND STATE PENSIONS vol 104 (2014) PARA 387); (2) one-half of any sum paid by the relevant person by way of a contribution towards an occupational pension scheme; (3) one-half of the amount calculated in respect of any qualifying contribution payable by the relevant person; and (4) where those earnings include a payment which is payable under any enactment having effect in Northern Ireland and which corresponds to statutory sick pay or statutory maternity pay, statutory paternity pay or statutory adoption pay, any amount deducted from those earnings by way of any contributions which are payable under any enactment having effect in Northern Ireland and which correspond to primary Class 1 contributions under the Social Security Contributions and Benefits Act 1992 Pt I: Housing Renewal Grants Regulations 1996, SI 1996/2890, reg 25(3) (amended, in relation to England, by SI 2005/3323; and, in relation to Wales, by SI 2006/2801). The amount in respect of any qualifying contribution must be calculated by multiplying the daily amount of the qualifying contribution by the number equal to the number of days in the assessment period; and for these purposes the daily amount of the qualifying contribution is determined: (a) where the qualifying contribution is payable monthly, by multiplying the amount of the qualifying contribution by 12 and dividing the product by 365; and (b) in any other case, by dividing the amount of the qualifying contribution by the number equal to the number of days in the period to which the qualifying contribution relates: Housing Renewal Grants Regulations 1996, SI 1996/2890, reg 25(4). 'Assessment period' means such period as is prescribed in regs 20–22 over which income falls to be determined: reg 2(1). 'Qualifying contribution' means any sum which is payable periodically as a contribution towards a personal pension scheme: reg 25(5). 'Personal pension scheme' has the same meaning as in the Pension Schemes Act 1993 s 1 (see PERSONAL AND OCCUPATIONAL PENSIONS vol 80 (2013) PARA 780); and, in the case of a self-employed earner, includes a scheme approved under the Income and Corporation Taxes Act 1988 Pt XIV Ch IV (ss 630–655) (now repealed): Housing Renewal Grants Regulations 1996, SI 1996/2890, reg 2(1).
9 There must be disregarded from a relevant person's net earnings, any sum, where applicable, specified in the Housing Renewal Grants Regulations 1996, SI 1996/2890, Sch 2 paras 1–16, 18 (sums to be disregarded in the determination of earnings): reg 25(2) (amended, in relation to England, by SI 1999/2568; and, in relation to Wales, by SI 1999/3468).

860. Self-employed earners. Where the income of a relevant person[1] consists of or includes earnings[2] from employment as a self-employed earner, his average weekly earnings from such employment must be determined by reference to his earnings from it over the period of 52 weeks immediately preceding the application[3] or, where his earnings from such employment fluctuate, over such other lesser period immediately preceding the application as may enable his average weekly income to be determined more accurately[4].

For these purposes, the weekly amount must be determined by dividing the relevant person's earnings during the assessment period by a number equal to the number of days in the assessment period and multiplying the quotient by seven[5]. The earnings of a relevant person to be taken into account, subject to any sums to be disregarded[6], are:

(1)   in the case of a self-employed earner who is engaged in employment on his own account, the net profit[7] derived from that employment[8];

(2)   in the case of a self-employed earner whose employment is carried on in partnership or is that of a share fisherman[9], his share of the net profit[10] derived from that employment, less:

(a)   an amount in respect of income tax and of social security contributions payable under the Social Security Contributions and Benefits Act 1992[11]; and

(b)   one-half of the amount calculated in respect of any qualifying premium[12].

For the avoidance of doubt, where a relevant person is engaged in employment as a self-employed earner and he is also engaged in one or more other employments as a self-employed earner or employed earner[13], any loss incurred in any one of his employments is not to be offset against his earnings in any other of his employments[14].

1   As to the meaning of 'relevant person' see PARA 850.
2   'Earnings', in the case of employment as a self-employed earner, means the gross income of the employment and: (1) includes any allowance paid under the Employment and Training Act 1973 s 2 (see EMPLOYMENT vol 40 (2014) PARA 634) or the Enterprise and New Towns (Scotland) Act 1990 s 2 to the relevant person for the purpose of assisting him in carrying on his business, unless at the date of the application the allowance has been terminated; but (2) does not include any payment to which the Housing Renewal Grants Regulations 1996, SI 1996/2890, Sch 3 para 23 or Sch 3 para 24 refers (payments in respect of a person accommodated with the relevant person under arrangements made by a local authority or voluntary organisation and payments made to the relevant person by a health authority, a clinical commissioning group, the National Health Service Commissioning Board, a local authority or a voluntary organisation in respect of persons temporarily in the relevant person's care), nor any sports award (see PARA 852): reg 26 (amended by SI 1998/808, SI 2002/2469 and SI 2013/235; and further amended, in relation to England, by SI 2000/531; and, in relation to Wales, by SI 2000/973). 'Health authority' means a health authority under the National Health Service Act 1977 s 8 (see HEALTH SERVICES vol 54 (2017) PARA 98 et seq): Housing Renewal Grants Regulations 1996, SI 1996/2890, reg 2(1). In relation to Wales, references to a health authority are to be treated as references to a local health board: see the References to Health Authorities Order 2007, SI 2007/961. 'Clinical commissioning group' means a body established under the National Health Service Act 2006 s 14D (see HEALTH SERVICES): Housing Renewal Grants Regulations 1996, SI 1996/2890, reg 2(1) (definition added by SI 2013/235). As to the National Health Service Commissioning Board see HEALTH SERVICES. As to the meaning of 'voluntary organisation' see PARA 851 note 18. As to the meaning of 'self-employed earner' see PARA 854 note 30.
        For the purposes of the Housing Renewal Grants Regulations 1996, SI 1996/2890, if during any period or periods commencing with or falling after 13 September 2001 a person is participating in the New Deal for Lone Parents within the self-employment route and that person receives either a top-up payment or other payment made to him in order to assist with the expenses of participation, such a payment is to be treated as a training premium: see the New Deal (Lone Parents) (Miscellaneous Provisions) Order 2001, SI 2001/2915. 'The self-employment route' means the Employment Option of the New Deal as specified in the Jobseeker's Allowance Regulations 1996, SI 1996/207, reg 75(1)(a)(ii), (aa)(ii), or assistance in pursuing self-employed earner's employment while participating in: (a) an employment zone programme; (b) a course of training or instruction funded by or on behalf of the Secretary of State for Work and Pensions, the National Assembly for Wales, Scottish Enterprise or Highland and Islands Enterprise; (c) the Intensive Activity Period specified in reg 75(1)(a)(iv); (d) the Intensive Activity Period for 50 plus; or (e) a scheme prescribed in the Jobseeker's Allowance (Schemes for Assisting Persons to Obtain Employment) Regulations 2013, SI 2013/276, reg 3: Housing Renewal Grants Regulations 1996, SI 1996/2890, reg 2(1) (definition added, in relation to England, by SI 2001/739; and, in relation to Wales, by SI 2001/2073; and amended, in relation to England, by SI 2002/350; and, in relation to Wales, by SI 2002/2798; further amended by SI 2013/276). 'The New Deal options' means the employment programmes specified in the Jobseeker's Allowance Regulations 1996, SI 1996/207,

reg 75(1)(a)(ii) and the training scheme specified in reg 75(1)(b)(ii): Housing Renewal Grants Regulations 1996, SI 1996/2890, reg 2(1) (definition added, in relation to England, by SI 2002/530; and, in relation to Wales, by SI 2002/2798).

3   As to the meaning of 'application' see PARA 850 note 1.

4   Housing Renewal Grants Regulations 1996, SI 1996/2890, reg 21.

5   Housing Renewal Grants Regulations 1996, SI 1996/2890, reg 23(2).

6   There must be disregarded from a relevant person's net profit, any sum, where applicable, specified in the Housing Renewal Grants Regulations 1996, SI 1996/2890, Sch 2 paras 1–16 or 18 (sums to be disregarded in the determination of earnings): reg 27(2) (amended, in relation to England, by SI 1999/2568; and, in relation to Wales, by SI 1999/3468).

7   For these purposes, except where the relevant person is engaged in employment as a child minder, the net profit of the employment is determined by taking into account the earnings of the employment over the assessment period less: (1) subject to the Housing Renewal Grants Regulations 1996, SI 1996/2890, reg 27(5)–(7) (see note 10), any expenses wholly and exclusively incurred in that period for the purposes of that employment; (2) an amount in respect of income tax and social security contributions payable under the Social Security Contributions and Benefits Act 1992, determined in accordance with the Housing Renewal Grants Regulations 1996, SI 1996/2890, reg 28 (deduction for tax and contributions for self-employed earners); and (3) one-half of the amount calculated in accordance with reg 27(12) in respect of any qualifying premium: reg 27(3).

Where a relevant person is engaged in employment as a child minder the net profit of the employment is one-third of the earnings of that employment, less: (a) an amount in respect of income tax and social security contributions payable under the Social Security Contributions and Benefits Act 1992, determined in accordance with the Housing Renewal Grants Regulations 1996, SI 1996/2890, reg 28; and (b) one-half of the amount calculated in accordance with reg 27(12) in respect of any qualifying premium: reg 27(9).

For these purposes, 'qualifying premium' means any premium which at the date of the application is payable periodically in respect of a retirement annuity contract or a personal pension scheme; and the amount in respect of any qualifying premium is calculated by multiplying the daily amount of the qualifying premium by the number equal to the number of days in the assessment period: reg 27(11), (12). The daily amount of the qualifying premium is determined: (i) where the qualifying premium is payable monthly, by multiplying the amount of the qualifying premium by 12 and dividing the product by 365; (ii) in any other case, by dividing the amount of the qualifying premium by the number equal to the number of days in the period to which the qualifying premium relates: reg 27(12). 'Retirement annuity contract' means a contract or trust scheme approved under the Income and Corporation Taxes Act 1988 Pt XIV Ch III (ss 618–629) (see PERSONAL AND OCCUPATIONAL PENSIONS vol 80 (2013) PARAS 336, 441 et seq): Housing Renewal Grants Regulations 1996, SI 1996/2890, reg 2(1). As to the meaning of 'personal pension scheme' see PARA 859 note 8.

The amount to be deducted in respect of income tax under reg 27(1)(b)(i), reg 27(3)(b)(i) or reg 27(9)(a)(i) is determined on the basis of the amount of chargeable income and as if that income were assessable to income tax at the lower rate or, as the case may be, the lower rate and the basic rate or the basic rate and higher rate of tax in the year of assessment in which the application was made less only the personal relief to which the relevant person is entitled under the Income and Corporation Taxes Act 1988 s 257 (repealed) (personal reliefs: see now the Income Tax Act 2007 ss 23, 46; and INCOME TAXATION vol 58A (2014) PARA 1258 et seq) as is appropriate to his circumstances; but, if the assessment period is less than a year, the earnings to which the lower rate and, if appropriate, the basic rate and the higher rate of tax is to be applied and the amount of the personal relief deductible are to be calculated on a pro-rata basis: Housing Renewal Grants Regulations 1996, SI 1996/2890, reg 28(1). The amount to be deducted in respect of social security contributions is the total of: (A) the amount of Class 2 contributions payable under the Social Security Contributions and Benefits Act 1992 s 11(1) or, as the case may be s 11(3) (liability for Class 2 contributions: see WELFARE BENEFITS AND STATE PENSIONS vol 104 (2014) PARA 393) at the rate applicable at the date of the application except where the relevant person's chargeable income is less than the amount for the time being specified in s 11(4) (small earnings exception) for the tax year in which the date of the application falls; but if the assessment period is less than a year, the amount specified for that tax year is reduced pro rata; and (B) the amount of Class 4 contributions (if any) which would be payable under s 15 (Class 4 contributions recoverable under the Income Tax Acts: see WELFARE BENEFITS AND STATE PENSIONS vol 104 (2014) PARA 396) at the percentage rate applicable at the date of the application on so much of the chargeable income as exceeds the lower limit but does not exceed the upper limit of profits and gains applicable for the tax year in which the date of the application falls; but if the assessment period is less than a year, those limits are reduced pro rata: Housing Renewal Grants Regulations 1996, SI 1996/2890, reg 28(2). For these purposes, 'chargeable income' means, in the case of employment as a child minder, one-third of the earnings of that employment; and, in any other case, the earnings derived from the employment less any expenses deducted under reg 27(3)(a) or, as the case may be, reg 27(4) (see note 10): reg 28(3).

8 Housing Renewal Grants Regulations 1996, SI 1996/2890, reg 27(1)(a).

9 As to the meaning of 'share fisherman' see the Social Security (Mariners' Benefits) Regulations 1975, SI 1975/529; and WELFARE BENEFITS AND STATE PENSIONS vol 104 (2014) PARA 30.

10 For these purposes, the net profit of the employment is determined by taking into account the earnings of the employment over the assessment period less, subject to the Housing Renewal Grants Regulations 1996, SI 1996/2890, reg 27(5)–(7), any expenses wholly and exclusively incurred in that period for the purposes of the employment: reg 27(4).

No deduction is to be made under reg 27(3)(a) (see note 7) or reg 27(4) in respect of any capital expenditure, any depreciation of any capital asset, any sum employed or intended to be employed in the setting up or expansion of the employment, any loss incurred before the beginning of the assessment period, the repayment of capital on any loan taken out for the purposes of the employment, any expenses incurred in providing business entertainment and any debts, except bad debts proved to be such, but this does not apply to any expenses incurred in the recovery of a debt: reg 27(5). A deduction must, however, be made under reg 27(3)(a) or reg 27(4) in respect of the repayment of capital on any loan used for the replacement in the course of business of equipment or machinery and the repair of an existing business asset except to the extent that any sum is payable under an insurance policy for its repair: reg 27(6). No deduction is to be made in respect of any expenses under reg 27(3)(a) or (4) where, given the nature and the amount of the expense, it has been unreasonably incurred: reg 27(7). For the avoidance of doubt: (1) a deduction may not be made under reg 27(3)(a) or (4) in respect of any sum unless it has been expended for the purposes of the business; (2) a deduction must, however, be made thereunder in respect of: (a) the excess of any value added tax paid by the relevant person in respect of taxable supplies made to him, over any such tax received by him in respect of taxable supplies made by him, calculated with reference to the assessment period; (b) any income expended in the repair of an existing business asset except to the extent that any sum is payable under an insurance policy for its repair; (c) any payment of interest on a loan taken out for the purposes of the employment: reg 27(8) (amended by SI 1988/808).

11 Ie determined in accordance with the Housing Renewal Grants Regulations 1996, SI 1996/2890, reg 28 (deduction of tax and contributions for self-employed earners): see note 7.

12 Housing Renewal Grants Regulations 1996, SI 1996/2890, reg 27(1)(b).

13 As to the meaning of 'employed earner' see PARA 854 note 29.

14 Housing Renewal Grants Regulations 1996, SI 1996/2890, reg 27(10).

861. Other income. Any part of a relevant person's[1] income which does not consist of earnings as defined for these purposes[2] must be determined by reference to such income over the period of 52 weeks immediately preceding the application[3] or, where such income fluctuates, over such other lesser period immediately preceding the application as may enable his average weekly income to be determined more accurately[4].

Where the period in respect of which a payment is made:

(1)   does not exceed a week, the weekly amount is the amount of that payment[5];

(2)   exceeds a week, the weekly amount is determined:

(a)   in a case where that period is a month, by multiplying the amount of the payment by 12 and dividing the product by 52[6];

(b)   in any other case, by dividing the amount of the payment by the number equal to the number of days in the period to which it relates and multiplying the quotient by seven[7].

For these purposes, the income of a relevant person which does not consist of earnings to be taken into account is, subject to certain exceptions[8], his gross income and any capital treated[9] as income[10]. For the avoidance of doubt, there must be included as income to be taken into account any payments which are not earnings[11].

1   As to the meaning of 'relevant person' see PARA 850.

2   As to the meaning of 'earnings' see PARAS 859 note 2, 860 note 2.

3   As to the meaning of 'application' see PARA 850 note 1.

4	Housing Renewal Grants Regulations 1996, SI 1996/2890, reg 22.
5	Housing Renewal Grants Regulations 1996, SI 1996/2890, reg 23(1)(a). As to the meaning of 'payment' see PARA 851 note 13.
6	Housing Renewal Grants Regulations 1996, SI 1996/2890, reg 23(1)(b)(i).
7	Housing Renewal Grants Regulations 1996, SI 1996/2890, reg 23(1)(b)(ii).
8	There must be disregarded from the determination of a relevant person's gross income any sum, where applicable, specified in the Housing Renewal Grants Regulations 1996, SI 1996/2890, Sch 3: reg 29(2). Where the payment of any benefit under the Social Security Contributions and Benefits Act 1992 is subject to any deduction by way of recovery, the amount to be taken into account is the gross amount payable: Housing Renewal Grants Regulations 1996, SI 1996/2890, reg 29(3). As to the recovery of social security benefits in personal injury cases see DAMAGES vol 29 (2014) PARA 459 et seq.
9	Ie under the Housing Renewal Grants Regulations 1996, SI 1996/2890, reg 30. Any payment received under an annuity, any career development loan paid pursuant to the Employment and Training Act 1973 s 2 (see EMPLOYMENT vol 40 (2014) PARA 634), and any payment made in consequence of any personal injury to a relevant person pursuant to any agreement or court order, where such payments are to be made, wholly or partly, by way of periodical payments, must be treated as income: Housing Renewal Grants Regulations 1996, SI 1996/2890, reg 30 (substituted by SI 1998/808; and amended, in relation to England, by SI 2003/2504; and, in relation to Wales, by SI 2004/253).
10	Housing Renewal Grants Regulations 1996, SI 1996/2890, reg 29(1) (amended by SI 1998/808; and, in relation to England, by SI 2005/3323; and, in relation to Wales, by SI 2006/2801).
11	Housing Renewal Grants Regulations 1996, SI 1996/2890, reg 29(4). The payments referred to in the text are payments to which reg 24(2) applies: see PARA 859.

862. Notional income. A relevant person[1] must be treated as possessing income[2] of which he has deprived himself for the purpose of increasing the amount of grant[3]. Except in the case of:

(1)	a discretionary trust[4];
(2)	a trust derived from a payment made in consequence of a personal injury[5];
(3)	a personal pension scheme[6] or retirement annuity contract[7] where the relevant person is aged under 60[8]; or
(4)	any sum of capital administered on behalf of a person under the age of 18 by the High Court, the County Court or the Court of Protection where that sum derives from an award of damages for a personal injury to that person, or compensation for the death of one or both parents[9],

any income which would have become available to the relevant person upon application for that income being made, but which has not been acquired by him, is treated as possessed by the relevant person but only from the date on which it could be expected to have been acquired had an application been made[10].

Where a person, aged not less than 60, is a member of, or a person deriving entitlement to a pension under, a personal pension scheme, or is a party to, or a person deriving entitlement to a pension under, a retirement annuity contract, and:

(a)	in the case of a personal pension scheme, he fails to purchase an annuity with the funds available in that scheme where:
    (i)	he defers, in whole or in part, the payment of any income which would have been payable to him by his pension fund holder[11];
    (ii)	he fails to take any necessary action to secure that the whole of any income which would be payable to him by his pension fund holder upon his applying for it, is so paid[12]; or
    (iii)	income withdrawal is not available to him under that scheme[13]; or
(b)	in the case of a retirement annuity contract, he fails to purchase an annuity with the funds available under that contract[14],

the amount of any income foregone is treated as possessed by him, but only from the date on which it could be expected to be acquired were an application for it to be made[15].

Where a relevant person or any partner[16] is aged not less than 60 and is a member of, or a person deriving entitlement to a pension under, a personal pension scheme, or is a party to, or a person deriving entitlement to a pension under, a retirement annuity contract, he must, where the authority[17] so requires, furnish the name and address of the pension fund holder and such other information, including any reference or policy number, as is needed to enable the personal pension scheme or retirement annuity contract to be identified[18]. If the pension fund holder receives from the authority a request for details concerning a personal pension scheme or retirement annuity contract relating to a person or any such partner, the pension fund holder must provide the authority with the specified information[19].

Subject to certain exceptions[20], any payment of income made:

(A)   to a third party in respect of a single relevant person or a member of his family (but not a member of the third party's family[21]) is, where that payment is a payment of an occupational pension or is a pension or other periodical payment made under a personal pension scheme, to be treated as possessed by that single relevant person or, as the case may be, by that member[22];

(B)   to a third party in respect of a relevant person who is a single person[23] or in respect of a member of the family (but not a member of the third party's family) is, where it is not a payment referred to in head (A), to be treated as possessed by that single person or by that member to the extent that it is used for the food, ordinary clothing or footwear[24], household fuel or rent[25] of that single person or, as the case may be, of any member of that family, or is used for any council tax, personal community charge, collective community charge contribution or water charges[26] for which that relevant person or member is liable[27];

(C)   to a relevant person who is a single person or a member of the family in respect of a third party (but not in respect of another member of that family) is to be treated as possessed by that single person or, as the case may be, that member of the family to the extent that it is kept or used by him or used by or on behalf of any member of the family[28].

Where a relevant person is treated as possessing any income under any of the provisions above, the provisions as to means testing[29] apply for the purposes of determining the amount of that income as if a payment had actually been made and as if it were actual income which he does possess[30].

Where a relevant person performs a service for another person and that person makes no payment of earnings[31], or pays less than that paid for a comparable employment in the area, the relevant person is to be treated as possessing such earnings (if any) as is reasonable for that employment unless the relevant person satisfies the local housing authority that the means of that person are insufficient for him to pay or to pay more for the service[32]. This does not, however, apply to a relevant person who is engaged by a charitable or voluntary organisation[33] or is a volunteer if the local authority[34] is satisfied that it is reasonable for him in any of those cases to provide his services free of charge[35]. Nor does it apply to a service performed in connection with the relevant person's participation[36] in an employment or training programme approved by the Secretary of State or in the intensive activity period (New Deal) programme[37], or to the relevant person's or the relevant person's partner's participation in an employment or training programme[38] for which a training allowance is not payable or, where such an allowance is payable, it is payable for the sole purpose of reimbursement of travelling or meal expenses to the person participating in that programme[39].

1　As to the meaning of 'relevant person' see PARA 850.
2　As to the determination of income generally see PARAS 858–861.
3　Housing Renewal Grants Regulations 1996, SI 1996/2890, reg 31(1). As to the meaning of 'grant' see PARA 836 note 1.
4　Housing Renewal Grants Regulations 1996, SI 1996/2890, reg 31(2)(a).
5　Housing Renewal Grants Regulations 1996, SI 1996/2890, reg 31(2)(b) (amended by SI 1998/808).
6　As to the meaning of 'personal pension scheme' see PARA 859 note 8.
7　As to the meaning of 'retirement annuity contract' see PARA 860 note 7.
8　Housing Renewal Grants Regulations 1996, SI 1996/2890, reg 31(2)(c).
9　Housing Renewal Grants Regulations 1996, SI 1996/2890, reg 31(2)(d) (added by SI 1998/808). The sums referred to in head (4) in the text are sums to which the Housing Renewal Grants Regulations 1996, SI 1996/2890, Sch 4 para 46 or Sch 4 para 47 refers.
10　Housing Renewal Grants Regulations 1996, SI 1996/2890, reg 31(2). For the purposes of reg 31(1), (2), a person is not to be regarded as deprived of income where his rights to benefits under a registered pension scheme are extinguished, in consequence of which a payment is received by him from the scheme, and the payment is a trivial commutation lump sum within the meaning given by the Finance Act 2004 Sch 29 para 7 (see PERSONAL AND OCCUPATIONAL PENSIONS vol 80 (2013) PARA 447): Housing Renewal Grants Regulations 1996, SI 1996/2890, reg 31(2A) (reg 31(2A), (2B) added, in relation to England, by SI 2008/1190; and, in relation to Wales, by SI 2008/2377). For these purposes 'registered pension scheme' has the meaning given in the Finance Act 2004 s 150(2) (see PERSONAL AND OCCUPATIONAL PENSIONS vol 80 (2013) PARA 441): Housing Renewal Grants Regulations 1996, SI 1996/2890, reg 31(2B) (as so added).
11　Housing Renewal Grants Regulations 1996, SI 1996/2890, reg 31(3)(a)(i). See note 12. 'Pension fund holder' means, with respect to a personal pension scheme or retirement annuity contract, the trustees, managers or scheme administrators, as the case may be, of the scheme or contract concerned: reg 2(1).
12　Housing Renewal Grants Regulations 1996, SI 1996/2890, reg 31(3)(a)(ii). The amount of any income foregone in a case to which either reg 31(3)(a)(i) (see the text and note 11) or reg 31(3)(a)(ii) applies is the maximum amount of income which may be withdrawn from the fund and must be determined taking account of information provided by the pension fund holder in accordance with reg 31(7) (see the text and note 19): reg 31(4).
13　Housing Renewal Grants Regulations 1996, SI 1996/2890, reg 31(3)(a)(iii). See note 14.
14　Housing Renewal Grants Regulations 1996, SI 1996/2890, reg 31(3)(b). The amount of any income foregone in a case to which either reg 31(3)(a)(iii) (see the text and note 13) or reg 31(3)(b) applies is the income that the relevant person could have received without purchasing an annuity had the funds held under the relevant personal pension scheme or retirement annuity contract been held under a personal pension scheme where income withdrawal was available, and must be determined in the manner specified in reg 31(4) (see note 12): reg 31(5).
15　Housing Renewal Grants Regulations 1996, SI 1996/2890, reg 31(3).
16　As to the meaning of 'partner' see PARA 850 note 5.
17　Ie the local housing authority: see PARA 11.
18　Housing Renewal Grants Regulations 1996, SI 1996/2890, reg 31(6).
19　Housing Renewal Grants Regulations 1996, SI 1996/2890, reg 31(7). The specified information is: (1) where the purchase of an annuity under a personal pension scheme has been deferred, the amount of any income which is being withdrawn from the personal pension scheme; (2) in the case of: (a) a personal pension scheme where income withdrawal is available, the maximum amount of income which may be withdrawn from the scheme; or (b) a personal pension scheme where income withdrawal is not available or a retirement annuity contract, the maximum amount of income which might be withdrawn from the fund if the fund were held under a personal pension scheme where income withdrawal was available, calculated by or on behalf of the pension fund holder by means of tables prepared from time to time by the Government Actuary which are appropriate for this purpose: reg 31(8).
20　Ie any of the payments referred to in the Housing Renewal Grants Regulations 1996, SI 1996/2890, reg 31(9A): reg 31(9) (amended by SI 1998/808). The payments for the purposes of the exclusion referred to in the text are any payment of income: (1) made under the MacFarlane Trusts, the Fund, the Eileen Trust or the Independent Living Funds; (2) made pursuant to the Coal Industry Act 1994 s 19(1)(a) (concessionary coal: see MINES, MINERALS AND QUARRIES vol 76 (2013) PARA 81); (3) made pursuant to the Employment and Training Act 1973 s 2 (see

EMPLOYMENT vol 40 (2014) PARA 634) in respect of a person's participation: (a) in an employment programme specified in the Jobseeker's Allowance Regulations 1996, SI 1996/207, reg 75(1)(a)(ii); (b) in a training scheme specified in reg 75(1)(b)(ii) (see WELFARE BENEFITS AND STATE PENSIONS vol 104 (2014) PARA 281); (c) in the Intensive Activity Period specified in reg 75(1)(a)(iv) or in the Intensive Activity Period for 50 plus; or (d) in a qualifying course within the meaning specified in reg 17A(7); or (e) in the intensive activity period (New Deal) programme (see PARA 852) but only to the extent that it is not used for a purpose specified in the Housing Renewal Grants Regulations 1996, SI 1996/2890, reg 31(9)(a) (see the text and note 27); (4) in respect of a person's participation in the Mandatory Work Activity Scheme; (5) in respect of a claimant's participation in a scheme prescribed in the Jobseeker's Allowance (Schemes for Assisting Persons to Obtain Employment) Regulations 2013, SI 2013/276, reg 3; (6) in respect of a person's participation in a scheme prescribed in the Jobseeker's Allowance (Supervised Jobsearch Pilot Scheme) Regulations 2014, SI 2014/1913, reg 3; (7) in respect of a person's participation in a scheme prescribed in the Jobseekers Allowance (18–21 Work Skills Pilot Scheme) Regulations 2014, SI 2014/3117, reg 3; (8) made under an occupational pension scheme or in respect of a pension or other periodical payment made under a personal pension scheme where: (a) a bankruptcy order has been made in respect of the person in respect of whom the payment has been made; (b) the payment is made to the trustee in bankruptcy or any other person acting on behalf of the creditors; and (c) the person referred to in head (a) and any member of his family does not possess, or is not treated as possessing, any other income apart from that payment: reg 31(9A) (added by SI 1998/808; substituted by SI 1999/1523; and amended, in relation to England, by SI 2000/531 and SI 2002/530; and, in relation to Wales, by SI 2000/973 and SI 2002/2798; further amended by SI 2011/688, SI 2013/276, SI 2014/1913 and SI 2014/3117).

'The MacFarlane Trusts' means the MacFarlane Trust, the MacFarlane (Special Payments) Trust and the MacFarlane (Special Payments) (No 2) Trust; 'the MacFarlane Trust' means the charitable trust, established partly out of funds provided by the Secretary of State to the Haemophilia Society, for the relief of poverty or distress among those suffering from haemophilia; 'the MacFarlane (Special Payments) Trust' means the trust of that name, established on 29 January 1990, partly out of funds provided by the Secretary of State, for the benefit of certain persons suffering from haemophilia; and 'the MacFarlane (Special Payments) (No 2) Trust' means the trust of that name, established on 3 May 1991, partly out of funds provided by the Secretary of State, for the benefit of certain persons suffering from haemophilia and other beneficiaries: Housing Renewal Grants Regulations 1996, SI 1996/2890, reg 2(1) (amended by SI 1998/808). 'The Eileen Trust' means the charitable trust of that name established on 29 March 1993 out of funds provided by the Secretary of State for the benefit of persons eligible for payment in accordance with its provisions: Housing Renewal Grants Regulations 1996, SI 1996/2890, reg 2(1) (definition added by SI 1999/1523). 'The Independent Living Funds' means the Independent Living Fund, the Independent Living (Extension) Fund, the Independent Living (1993) Fund and the Independent Living Fund (2006); 'the Independent Living Fund' means the charitable trust established out of funds provided by the Secretary of State for the purpose of providing financial assistance to those persons incapacitated by or otherwise suffering from very severe disablement who are in need of such assistance to enable them to live independently; 'the Independent Living (Extension) Fund' means the Trust of that name established by a deed dated 25 February 1993 and made between the Secretary of State for Social Security of the one part and Robin Glover Wendt and John Fletcher Shepherd of the other part; 'the Independent Living (1993) Fund' means the trust of that name established by a deed dated 25 February 1993 and made between the Secretary of State for Social Security of the one part and Robin Glover Wendt and John Fletcher Shepherd of the other part; and 'the Independent Living Fund (2006)' means the trust of that name established by a deed dated 10 April 2006 and made between the Secretary of State for Work and Pensions of the one part and Margaret Rosemary Cooper, Michael Beresford Boyall and Marie Theresa Martin of the other part: Housing Renewal Grants Regulations 1996, SI 1996/2890, reg 2(1) (amended by SI 2007/2538). 'The Fund' means money made available from time to time by the Secretary of State for the benefit of persons eligible for payment in accordance with the provisions of a scheme established by him on 24 April 1992, or, in Scotland, on 10 April 1992: Housing Renewal Grants Regulations 1996, SI 1996/2890, reg 2(1). 'Intensive Activity Period for 50 plus' means the programme of that name provided in pursuance of arrangements made by, or on behalf of, the Secretary of State under the Employment and Training Act 1973 s 2 (see EMPLOYMENT vol 40 (2014) PARA 634), lasting for up to 52 weeks for any one individual aged 50 years or over on the day that he first joined any such programme, and consisting for that individual of any one or more of the following elements, namely assistance in pursuing self-employed earner's employment, education and training, work experience, assistance with job search, motivation and skills training: Housing Renewal Grants Regulations 1996, SI 1996/2890, reg 2(1) (definition added, in relation to England, by SI 2002/530; and, in relation to Wales, by SI 2002/2798). 'The Mandatory Work Activity Scheme' means a scheme within the Jobseekers Act 1995 s 17A (schemes for assisting persons to obtain employment: 'work for your benefit' schemes etc: see WELFARE BENEFITS AND

STATE PENSIONS vol 104 (2014) PARA 288) known by that name and provided pursuant to arrangements made by the Secretary of State that is designed to provide work or work-related activity for up to 30 hours per week over a period of four consecutive weeks with a view to assisting claimants to improve their prospects of obtaining employment: Housing Renewal Grants Regulations 1996, SI 1996/2890, reg 2(1) (definition added by SI 2011/688).

21 As to members of a family see PARA 851 note 5.

22 Housing Renewal Grants Regulations 1996, SI 1996/2890, reg 31(9)(za) (added, in relation to England, by SI 2000/531; and, in relation to Wales, by SI 2000/973).

23 'Single person' means a person who neither has a partner nor is a lone parent: Housing Renewal Grants Regulations 1996, SI 1996/2890, reg 2(1).

24 'Ordinary clothing or footwear' means clothing or footwear for normal daily use, but does not include school uniforms, or clothing or footwear used solely for sporting activities: Housing Renewal Grants Regulations 1996, SI 1996/2890, reg 31(14)(a).

25 'Rent' means eligible rent determined in accordance with: (1) in the case of a person who has not attained the qualifying age for state pension credit to whom head (3) does not apply, the Housing Benefit Regulations 2006, SI 2006/213, reg 12B (eligible rent), 12C (eligible rent and maximum rent) or 12D (eligible rent and maximum rent (LHA)) or any of regs 12E–12K (transitional protection for former pathfinder authorities), as the case may require, less any deductions in respect of non-dependants which fall to be made under reg 74 (non-dependant deductions); (2) in the case of a person who has attained the qualifying age for state pension credit to whom head (3) does not apply, the Housing Benefit (Persons who have attained qualifying age for state pension credit) Regulations 2006, SI 2006/214, reg 12B (eligible rent), 12C (eligible rent and maximum rent) or 12D (eligible rent and maximum rent (LHA)) or any of regs 12E–12K (transitional protection for former pathfinder authorities) as the case may require, less any deductions in respect of non-dependants which fall to be made under reg 55 (non-dependant deductions); or (3) where the Housing Benefit and Council Tax Benefit (Consequential Provisions) Regulations 2006, SI 2006/217, Sch 3 para 4 applies, the Housing Benefit Regulations 2006, SI 2006/213, regs 12 (rent) and 13 (restrictions on unreasonable payments) or the Housing Benefit (Persons who have attained qualifying age for state pension credit) Regulations 2006, SI 2006/214, regs 12 (rent) and 13 (restrictions on unreasonable payments) as set out in the Housing Benefit and Council Tax Benefit (Consequential Provisions) Regulations 2006, SI 2006/217, Sch 3 para 5 less any deductions which fall to be made in respect of non-dependants under the Housing Benefit Regulations 2006, SI 2006/213, reg 74 (non-dependant deductions) or the Housing Benefit (Persons who have attained the qualifying age for state pension credit) Regulations 2006, SI 2006/214, reg 55 (non-dependant deductions), as the case may be: Housing Renewal Grants Regulations 1996, SI 1996/2890, reg 31(14)(b) (substituted by SI 2007/2870). As to housing benefit see WELFARE BENEFITS AND STATE PENSIONS vol 104 (2014) PARA 318 et seq.

26 'Water charges' means any water and sewerage charges under the Water Industry Act 1991 Pt V Ch I (ss 142–150A) (see ENVIRONMENTAL QUALITY AND PUBLIC HEALTH vol 46 (2010) PARA 1038; WATER AND WATERWAYS vol 100 (2009) PARA 417 et seq), in so far as such charges are in respect of the dwelling which a person occupies as his only or main residence: Housing Renewal Grants Regulations 1996, SI 1996/2890, reg 2(1). As to the meaning of 'dwelling' see PARA 850 note 4.

27 Housing Renewal Grants Regulations 1996, SI 1996/2890, reg 31(9)(a) (amended, in relation to England, by SI 2000/531; and, in relation to Wales, by virtue of SI 2000/973).

28 Housing Renewal Grants Regulations 1996, SI 1996/2890, reg 31(9)(b).

29 Ie the provisions of the Housing Renewal Grants Regulations 1996, SI 1996/2890, regs 5–30: see PARAS 850–861.

30 Housing Renewal Grants Regulations 1996, SI 1996/2890, reg 31(12) (amended, in relation to England, by SI 2003/2504; and, in relation to Wales, by SI 2004/253).

31 As to the meaning of 'earnings' see PARAS 859 note 2, 860 note 2.

32 Housing Renewal Grants Regulations 1996, SI 1996/2890, reg 31(10) (amended by SI 1999/1523).

33 As to the meanings of 'charity' and 'voluntary organisation' see PARA 851 note 18.

34 As to the meaning of 'local authority' see PARA 853 note 10.

35 Housing Renewal Grants Regulations 1996, SI 1996/2890, reg 31(10A)(a) (reg 31(10A) added by SI 1999/1523; the Housing Renewal Grants Regulations 1996, SI 1996/2890, reg 31(10A)(a) amended, in relation to England, by SI 2001/739; and, in relation to Wales, by SI 2001/2073).

36 Ie in accordance with the Jobseeker's Allowance Regulations 1996, SI 1996/207, reg 19(1)(q): see WELFARE BENEFITS AND STATE PENSIONS vol 104 (2014) PARA 273.

37 As to the meaning of 'intensive activity period (New Deal) programme' see PARA 852 note 12.

38 Ie as defined in the Jobseeker's Allowance Regulations 1996, SI 1996/207, reg 19(3).

39 Housing Renewal Grants Regulations 1996, SI 1996/2890, reg 31(10A)(b) (as added (see note 35); and amended, in relation to England, by SI 2001/739, SI 2002/530 and SI 2013/630; and, in relation to Wales, by SI 2001/2073, SI 2002/2798 and SI 2013/1788). Where a relevant person is treated as possessing any earnings under the Housing Renewal Grants Regulations 1996, SI 1996/2890, reg 31(10), regs 5–30 (see PARA 850 et seq) apply for the purposes of determining the amount of those earnings as if a payment had actually been made and as if they were actual earnings which he does possess except that reg 25(3) (determination of net earnings of employed earners: see PARA 859) does not apply and his net earnings must be determined by taking into account those earnings which he is treated as possessing, less: (1) an amount in respect of income tax equivalent to an amount determined by applying to those earnings the lower rate or, as the case may be, the lower and the basic rate or the basic rate and higher rate of tax in the year of assessment in which the application was made less only the personal relief to which the relevant person is entitled under the Income and Corporation Taxes Act 1988 s 257 (repealed) (see now the Income Tax Act 2007 ss 23, 46; and INCOME TAXATION vol 58A (2014) PARA 1258 et seq) as is appropriate to his circumstances (but if the assessment period is less than a year the earnings to which the lower rate and, if appropriate, the basic rate and the higher rate of tax is to be applied and the amount of the personal relief so deductible must be determined on a pro-rata basis); (2) an amount equivalent to the amount of primary Class 1 contributions which would be payable under the Social Security Contributions and Benefits Act 1992 in respect of those earnings if those earnings were actual earnings and the rate of any primary percentage (within the meaning of that Act) applicable to those earnings under that Act were the rate applicable at the date of application (see further WELFARE BENEFITS AND STATE PENSIONS vol 104 (2014) PARA 387); and (3) one-half of any sum payable by the relevant person by way of a contribution towards an occupational or personal pension scheme: see the Housing Renewal Grants Regulations 1996, SI 1996/2890, reg 31(13)(a)–(c).

D.   CAPITAL

863. Determination of capital for the purposes of grants. The capital of a relevant person[1] to be taken into account must be the whole of his capital determined in accordance with the relevant regulations[2], and any income treated[3] as capital[4]; except that specified capital[5] must, where applicable, be disregarded from the determination of a relevant person's capital[6].

Capital which a relevant person possesses in the United Kingdom[7] is determined at its current market or surrender value less:

(1)   where there would be expenses attributable to sale, 10 per cent; and

(2)   the amount of any incumbrance secured on it[8].

In the case of a National Savings Certificate, however, the capital is determined:

(a)   if purchased from an issue the sale of which ceased before 1 July last preceding the date of the application, at the price which it would have realised on that 1 July had it been purchased on the last day of that issue[9];

(b)   in any other case, at its purchase price[10].

Capital which a relevant person possesses in a country outside the United Kingdom is determined:

(i)   in a case where there is no prohibition in that country against the transfer to the United Kingdom of an amount equal to its current market or surrender value in that country, at that value[11];

(ii)   in a case where there is such a prohibition, at the price which it would realise if sold in the United Kingdom to a willing buyer[12],

less, where there would be expenses attributable to sale, 10 per cent, and the amount of any incumbrance secured on it[13].

1   As to the meaning of 'relevant person' see PARA 850.
2   Ie determined in accordance with the Housing Renewal Grants Regulations 1996, SI 1996/2890, Pt II (regs 5–48): see the text and notes 3–14; and PARA 849 et seq.
3   Ie under the Housing Renewal Grants Regulations 1996, SI 1996/2890, reg 35. Any bounty derived from employment to which Sch 2 para 8 applies and paid at intervals of at least one year is treated as capital, as is any amount by way of a refund of income tax deducted from profits of emoluments chargeable to income tax under the Income and Corporation Taxes Act 1988 s 18,

Schedule D or s 19, Schedule E (repealed) (see now the Income Tax (Trading and Other Income) Act 2005; the Income Tax (Earnings and Pensions) Act 2003; and INCOME TAXATION vol 58 (2014) PARAS 92 et seq, 730 et seq) and any holiday pay which is not earnings under the Housing Renewal Grants Regulations 1996, SI 1996/2890, reg 24(1)(d) (earnings of employed earners: see PARA 859): reg 35(1)–(3). Except any income derived from capital disregarded under Sch 4 paras 1, 2, 3, 5, 8, 14, 25 or 26, any income derived from capital is treated as capital but only from the date it is normally due to be credited to the relevant person's account: reg 35(4). In the case of employment as an employed earner, any advance of earnings or any loan made by the relevant person's employer is treated as capital except in so far as the advance or loan is spent; and thereupon the advance or loan, so far as it is spent, is not treated as income: reg 35(5). Finally, any charitable or voluntary payment which is not made or due to be made at regular intervals, other than a payment which is made under any of the MacFarlane Trusts, the Independent Living Funds or the Fund (as to which see PARA 862 note 20), is treated as capital: reg 35(6).

There must be treated as capital the gross receipts of any commercial activity carried on by a person in respect of which assistance is received under the self-employment route, but only in so far as those receipts were payable into a special account during the period in which that person was receiving such assistance: reg 35(7) (added by SI 1999/1523; and amended, in relation to England, by SI 2001/739; and, in relation to Wales, by SI 2001/2073). As to the meaning of 'the self-employment route' see PARA 860 note 2. Any arrears of subsistence allowance which are paid to a relevant person as a lump sum are to be treated as capital: Housing Renewal Grants Regulations 1996, SI 1996/2890, reg 35(8) (added, in relation to England, by SI 2001/739; and, in relation to Wales, by SI 2001/2073). 'Subsistence allowance' means an allowance which an employment zone contractor has agreed to pay to a person who is participating in an employment zone programme: Housing Renewal Grants Regulations 1996, SI 1996/2890, reg 2(1) (definition added, in relation to England, by SI 2001/739; and, in relation to Wales, by SI 2001/2073).

4 Housing Renewal Grants Regulations 1996, SI 1996/2890, reg 33(1).
5 Ie any capital specified in the Housing Renewal Grants Regulations 1996, SI 1996/2890, Sch 4: reg 33(2).
6 Housing Renewal Grants Regulations 1996, SI 1996/2890, reg 33(2).
7 As to the meaning of 'United Kingdom' see PARA 60 note 10.
8 Housing Renewal Grants Regulations 1996, SI 1996/2890, reg 36(a).
9 Housing Renewal Grants Regulations 1996, SI 1996/2890, reg 36(b)(i).
10 Housing Renewal Grants Regulations 1996, SI 1996/2890, reg 36(b)(ii).
11 Housing Renewal Grants Regulations 1996, SI 1996/2890, reg 37(a).
12 Housing Renewal Grants Regulations 1996, SI 1996/2890, reg 37(b).
13 Housing Renewal Grants Regulations 1996, SI 1996/2890, reg 37.

864. Notional capital. A relevant person[1] must be treated as possessing capital of which he has deprived himself for the purpose of increasing the amount of grant[2]. Except in any of the following cases:

(1)   a discretionary trust[3];
(2)   a trust derived from a payment made in consequence of a personal injury[4];
(3)   any loan which would be obtained only if secured against disregarded capital[5];
(4)   a personal pension scheme[6] or retirement annuity contract[7];
(5)   any sum of capital administered on behalf of a person under the age of 18 by the High Court, the County Court or the Court of Protection where that sum derives from an award of damages for a personal injury to that person, or compensation for the death of one or both parents[8]; or
(6)   any rehabilitation allowance[9],

any capital which would have become available to the relevant person upon application for that income being made, but which has not been acquired by him, must be treated as possessed by him but only from the date on which it could be expected to have been acquired had an application been made[10].

Any payment[11] of capital, other than a payment:

(a)   made under any of the MacFarlane Trusts[12], the Fund[13], the Eileen Trust[14] or the Independent Living Funds[15];

(b)   made[16] in respect of a person's participation in an employment programme[17], a training scheme[18], the Intensive Activity Period[19] or the Intensive Activity Period for 50 plus[20], a qualifying course[21], or the intensive activity period (New Deal) programme[22] but only to the extent that it is not used for a purpose specified in head (B) below;

(c)   in respect of a person's participation in the Mandatory Work Activity Scheme[23];

(d)   in respect of a claimant's participation in a scheme prescribed[24] for assisting persons to obtain employment;

(e)   in respect of a person's participation in a supervised jobsearch pilot scheme[25];

(f)   in respect of a person's participation in a work skills pilot scheme[26];

(g)   made under an occupational pension scheme or in respect of a pension or other periodical payment made under a personal pension scheme where:

     (i)   a bankruptcy order has been made in respect of the person in respect of whom the payment has been made;

     (ii)   the payment is made to the trustee in bankruptcy or any other person acting on behalf of the creditors; and

     (iii)   the person referred to in head (i) and any member of his family does not possess, or is not treated as possessing, any other income apart from that payment[27]:

         (A)   if made to a third party in respect of a single relevant person or a member of his family[28] (but not a member of the third party's family) is, where that payment is a payment of an occupational pension or is a pension or other periodical payment made under a personal pension scheme, to be treated as possessed by that single relevant person or, as the case may be, by that member[29];

         (B)   if made to a third party in respect of a single relevant person or in respect of a member of the family (but not a member of the third party's family) is, where it is not a payment referred to in head (A), to be treated as possessed by that single person[30] or by that member to the extent that it is used for the food, ordinary clothing or footwear[31], household fuel or rent[32] of that single person or, as the case may be, of any member of that family, or is used for any council tax, personal community charge, collective community charge contribution or water charges for which that relevant person or member is liable[33];

         (C)   if made to a single relevant person or a member of the family in respect of a third party (but not in respect of another member of that family), is to be treated as possessed by that single person or, as the case may be, that member of the family to the extent that it is kept or used by him or used by or on behalf of any member of the family[34].

Where a relevant person stands in relation to a company in a position analogous to that of a sole owner or partner in the business of that company, he may be treated as if he were such sole owner or partner[35]. In such a case, the value of his holding in that company must, notwithstanding the general rule as to the determination of capital[36], be disregarded[37] and he is treated as possessing an amount of capital equal to the value or, as the case may be, his share of the value of the capital of that company, and the relevant regulations[38] apply for the purposes of determining that amount as if it were actual capital which he does possess[39].

1 As to the meaning of 'relevant person' see PARA 850.
2 Housing Renewal Grants Regulations 1996, SI 1996/2890, reg 38(1). As to the meaning of 'grant' see PARA 836 note 1.
3 Housing Renewal Grants Regulations 1996, SI 1996/2890, reg 38(2)(a) (amended by SI 1998/808).
4 Housing Renewal Grants Regulations 1996, SI 1996/2890, reg 38(2)(b) (amended by SI 1998/808).
5 Housing Renewal Grants Regulations 1996, SI 1996/2890, reg 38(2)(c) (amended by SI 1998/808). The capital referred to in head (3) in the text is capital disregarded under the Housing Renewal Grants Regulations 1996, SI 1996/2890, Sch 4: reg 38(2)(c).
6 As to the meaning of 'personal pension scheme' see PARA 859 note 8.
7 Housing Renewal Grants Regulations 1996, SI 1996/2890, reg 38(2)(d) (amended by SI 1999/1523). As to the meaning of 'retirement annuity contract' see PARA 860 note 7.
8 Housing Renewal Grants Regulations 1996, SI 1996/2890, reg 38(2)(e) (added by SI 1998/808). The sums referred to in head (5) in the text are sums to which the Housing Renewal Grants Regulations 1996, SI 1996/2890, Sch 4 para 46 or Sch 4 para 47 refers.
9 Ie made under the Employment and Training Act 1973 s 2 (see EMPLOYMENT vol 40 (2014) PARA 634): Housing Renewal Grants Regulations 1996, SI 1996/2890, reg 38(2)(f) (added by SI 1999/1523).
10 Housing Renewal Grants Regulations 1996, SI 1996/2890, reg 38(2).
11 As to the meaning of 'payment' see PARA 851 note 13.
12 As to the meaning of 'the MacFarlane Trusts' see PARA 862 note 20.
13 As to the meaning of 'the Fund' see PARA 862 note 20.
14 As to the meaning of 'the Eileen Trusts' see PARA 862 note 20.
15 As to the meaning of 'the Independent Living Funds' see PARA 862 note 20.
16 Ie made pursuant to the Employment and Training Act 1973 s 2: see EMPLOYMENT vol 40 (2014) PARA 634.
17 Ie an employment programme specified in the Jobseeker's Allowance Regulations 1996, SI 1996/207, reg 75(1)(a)(ii): see WELFARE BENEFITS AND STATE PENSIONS vol 104 (2014) PARA 281.
18 Ie a training scheme specified in the Jobseeker's Allowance Regulations 1996, SI 1996/207, reg 75(1)(b)(ii): see WELFARE BENEFITS AND STATE PENSIONS vol 104 (2014) PARA 281.
19 Ie the scheme specified in the Jobseeker's Allowance Regulations 1996, SI 1996/207, reg 75(1)(a)(iv): see WELFARE BENEFITS AND STATE PENSIONS vol 104 (2014) PARA 281.
20 As to the Intensive Activity Period for 50 plus see PARA 862 note 20.
21 Ie within the meaning specified in the Jobseeker's Allowance Regulations 1996, SI 1996/207, reg 17A(7).
22 As to the intensive activity period (New Deal) programme see PARA 852 note 12.
23 As to the Mandatory Work Activity Scheme see PARA 862 note 20.
24 Ie in the Jobseeker's Allowance (Schemes for Assisting Persons to Obtain Employment) Regulations 2013, SI 2013/276, reg 3.
25 Ie a scheme prescribed in the Jobseeker's Allowance (Supervised Jobsearch Pilot Scheme) Regulations 2014, SI 2014/1913, reg 3.
26 Ie a scheme prescribed in the Jobseekers Allowance (18–21 Work Skills Pilot Scheme) Regulations 2014, SI 2014/3117, reg 3.
27 Housing Renewal Grants Regulations 1996, SI 1996/2890, reg 38(3), (3A) (reg 38(3) amended by SI 1999/1523; the Housing Renewal Grants Regulations 1996, SI 1996/2890, reg 38(3A) added by SI 1999/1523; and amended, in relation to England, by SI 2000/531; SI 2002/530; and, in relation to Wales, by virtue of SI 2000/973 and by SI 2002/2798; further amended by SI 2011/688, SI 2013/276, SI 2014/1913 and SI 2014/3117).
28 As to members of a family see PARA 851 note 5.
29 Housing Renewal Grants Regulations 1996, SI 1996/2890, reg 38(3)(za) (added, in relation to England, by SI 2000/531; and, in relation to Wales, by virtue of SI 2000/973).
30 As to the meaning of 'single person' see PARA 862 note 23.
31 'Ordinary clothing or footwear' means clothing or footwear for normal daily use, but does not include school uniforms, or clothing or footwear used solely for sporting activities: Housing Renewal Grants Regulations 1996, SI 1996/2890, reg 38(7)(a).
32 'Rent' means eligible rent determined in accordance with: (1) in the case of a person who has not attained the qualifying age for state pension credit to whom head (3) does not apply, the Housing

Benefit Regulations 2006, SI 2006/213, reg 12B (eligible rent), 12C (eligible rent and maximum rent) or 12D (eligible rent and maximum rent (LHA)) or any of regs 12E–12K (transitional protection for former pathfinder authorities), as the case may require, less any deductions in respect of non-dependants which fall to be made under reg 74 (non-dependant deductions); (2) in the case of a person who has attained the qualifying age for state pension credit to whom head (3) does not apply, the Housing Benefit (Persons who have attained qualifying age for state pension credit) Regulations 2006, SI 2006/214, reg 12B (eligible rent), 12C (eligible rent and maximum rent) or 12D (eligible rent and maximum rent (LHA)) or any of regs 12E–12K (transitional protection for former pathfinder authorities), as the case may require, less any deductions which fall to be made under reg 55; or (3) where the Housing Benefit and Council Tax Benefit (Consequential Provisions) Regulations 2006, SI 2006/217, Sch 3 para 4 applies, the Housing Benefit Regulations 2006, SI 2006/213, regs 12 (rent) and 13 (restrictions on unreasonable payments) the Housing Benefit (Persons who have attained qualifying age for state pension credit) Regulations 2006, SI 2006/214, regs 12 (rent) and 13 (restrictions on unreasonable payments) as set out in the Housing Benefit and Council Tax Benefit (Consequential Provisions) Regulations 2006, SI 2006/217, Sch 3 para 5 less any deductions which fall to be made in respect of non-dependants under the Housing Benefit Regulations 2006, SI 2006/213, reg 74 (non-dependant deductions) or the Housing Benefit (Persons who have attained the qualifying age for state pension credit) Regulations 2006, SI 2006/214, reg 55 (non-dependant deductions), as the case may be: Housing Renewal Grants Regulations 1996, SI 1996/2890, reg 38(7)(b) (substituted by SI 2007/2870). As to housing benefit see WELFARE BENEFITS AND STATE PENSIONS vol 104 (2014) PARA 318 et seq.

33 Housing Renewal Grants Regulations 1996, SI 1996/2890, reg 38(3)(a) (amended, in relation to England, by SI 2000/531; and, in relation to Wales, by virtue of SI 2000/973).

34 Housing Renewal Grants Regulations 1996, SI 1996/2890, reg 38(3)(b). Where a relevant person is treated as possessing capital under reg 38(1)–(3), the provisions of regs 33–37 (see PARA 863) and reg 38(5) (see note 39) apply for the purposes of determining its amount as if it were actual capital which he does possess: reg 38(6).

35 Housing Renewal Grants Regulations 1996, SI 1996/2890, reg 38(4).

36 Ie the Housing Renewal Grants Regulations 1996, SI 1996/2890, reg 33: see PARA 863.

37 Housing Renewal Grants Regulations 1996, SI 1996/2890, reg 38(4)(a).

38 Ie the Housing Renewal Grants Regulations 1996, SI 1996/2890, regs 33–37 (see PARA 863) and reg 38(1)–(3) (see the text and notes 1–34).

39 Housing Renewal Grants Regulations 1996, SI 1996/2890, reg 38(4)(b). For so long as the relevant person undertakes activities in the course of the business of the company, the amount which he is treated as possessing under reg 38(4) must be disregarded: reg 38(5).

865. Capital held jointly. Except where a relevant person[1] possesses capital which is disregarded under the rules relating to notional capital[2], where a relevant person and one or more persons are beneficially entitled in possession to any capital asset they must be treated as if each of them were entitled in possession to the whole beneficial interest in the asset in an equal share[3].

1 As to the meaning of 'relevant person' see PARA 850.

2 Ie under the Housing Renewal Grants Regulations 1996, SI 1996/2890, reg 38(4): see PARA 864.

3 Housing Renewal Grants Regulations 1996, SI 1996/2890, reg 39 (amended by SI 1999/1523). The provisions of the Housing Renewal Grants Regulations 1996, SI 1996/2890, regs 33–38 (see PARAS 863–864) apply for the purposes of calculating the amount of capital which the relevant person is treated as possessing as if it were actual capital which the relevant person does possess: reg 39.

866. Determination of tariff income received from capital. Where the relevant person's capital[1] exceeds £6,000 it must be treated as equivalent to a weekly tariff income of: (1) where the relevant person is aged under 60, £1 for each complete £250 in excess of £6,000; and (2) where the relevant person is aged 60 or over, £1 for each complete £500 in excess of £6,000[2]. Where, however, any part of the excess is not a complete £250 or £500, that part must be treated as equivalent to a weekly tariff income of £1[3]. For these purposes, capital includes any income treated[4] as capital[5].

1 Ie his capital determined in accordance with the Housing Renewal Grants Regulations 1996, SI 1996/2890, Pt II Chs IV–IX (regs 16–40): see PARAS 853–854, 857 et seq. As to the meaning of 'relevant person' see PARA 850.

2 Housing Renewal Grants Regulations 1996, SI 1996/2890, reg 40(1) (substituted, in relation to England, by SI 2003/2504; and, in relation to Wales, by SI 2004/253).
3 Housing Renewal Grants Regulations 1996, SI 1996/2890, reg 40(2) (amended, in relation to England, by SI 2003/2504; and, in relation to Wales, by SI 2004/253).
4 Ie under the Housing Renewal Grants Regulations 1996, SI 1996/2890, reg 35: see PARA 863.
5 Housing Renewal Grants Regulations 1996, SI 1996/2890, reg 40(3).

E. STUDENTS

867. Determination of grant income. A number of provisions in the Housing Renewal Grants Regulations 1996[1] are directed specifically at students[2]. The amount of a student's grant income[3] to be taken into account must be the whole of his grant income[4]. There must, however, be excluded from a student's grant income any payment:

(1) intended to meet tuition fees or examination fees[5];
(2) in respect of the student's disability[6];
(3) intended to meet additional expenditure connected with term time residential study away from the student's educational establishment[7];
(4) on account of the student maintaining a home at a place other than that at which he resides during his course[8];
(5) on account of any other person but only if that person is residing outside the United Kingdom and there is no applicable amount in respect of him[9];
(6) intended to meet the cost of books and equipment[10];
(7) intended to meet travel expenses incurred as a result of his attendance on the course[11].

Where a student does not have a student loan[12] and is not treated as possessing such a loan, there must be excluded from the student's grant income:

(a) the sum of £275 in respect of travel costs; and
(b) the sum of £343 towards the costs of books and equipment, whether or not any such costs are incurred[13].

There is also excluded from a student's grant income:

(i) any grant of £250 for an only or eldest dependant child[14];
(ii) any grant of £500 in respect of expenditure on travel, books and equipment for the purpose of attending his course[15];
(iii) any grant for child care costs[16];
(iv) any grant in respect of a lone parent's child care costs specified to be payable[17];
(v) and any grant paid under specified[18] regulations[19].

A student's grant income is generally to be apportioned either equally between the weeks in the student's study period or equally between the weeks in the period in respect of which the grant income is payable[20].

1 Ie the Housing Renewal Grants Regulations 1996, SI 1996/2890, Pt II Ch X (regs 41–47): see the text and notes 2–12; and PARAS 868–870.
2 See the Housing Renewal Grants Regulations 1996, SI 1996/2890, reg 42. 'Student' means a person, other than a person in receipt of a training allowance, who is attending or undertaking: (1) a course of study at an educational establishment; or (2) a qualifying course: reg 41 (definition substituted, in relation to England, by SI 2001/739; and, in relation to Wales, by SI 2001/2073).
  'Training allowance' has the meaning given by the Housing Benefit Regulations 2006, SI 2006/213, reg 2(1): Housing Renewal Grants Regulations 1996, SI 1996/2890, reg 2(1) (definition amended by SI 2006/217). 'Course of study' means any course of study, whether or not it is a sandwich course and whether or not a grant is made for undertaking or attending it: Housing Renewal Grants Regulations 1996, SI 1996/2890, reg 41 (amended, in relation to England, by SI 2001/739; and, in relation to Wales, by SI 2001/2073). 'Sandwich course' has the meaning prescribed in the Education (Student Support) Regulations 2000, SI 2000/1121, reg 5(2) (revoked:

see now the Education (Student Support) Regulations 2009, SI 2009/1555, reg 2(1), (10) (reg 2(10) amended by SI 2010/2546)) or, as the case may be, in the corresponding provisions of Scottish or Northern Ireland legislation: see the Housing Renewal Grants Regulations 1996, SI 1996/2890, reg 41 (definition substituted, in relation to England, by SI 2001/739; and, in relation to Wales, by SI 2001/2073).

'Grant' (except in the definition of 'access funds': see PARA 870) means any kind of educational grant or award and includes any scholarship, studentship, exhibition, allowance or bursary but does not include a payment from access funds: Housing Renewal Grants Regulations 1996, SI 1996/2890, reg 41 (definition substituted, in relation to England, by SI 2001/739; and, in relation to Wales, by SI 2001/2073). 'Qualifying course' has the meaning given in the Jobseeker's Allowance Regulations 1996, SI 1996/207, reg 17A(7): Housing Renewal Grants Regulations 1996, SI 1996/2890, reg 41 (definition added, in relation to England, by SI 2001/739; and, in relation to Wales, by SI 2001/2073). As to the phasing out of local authority grants to students see EDUCATION vol 36 (2015) PARA 1095 et seq.

3   'Grant income' means: (1) any income by way of a grant; (2) any contribution whether or not it is paid: Housing Renewal Grants Regulations 1996, SI 1996/2890, reg 41. 'Contribution' means any contribution (including one which is not paid) in respect of the income of a student or of any other person which the appropriate national authority, the Scottish Ministers or an education authority takes into account in ascertaining the amount of the student's grant or student loan; or any sums, which in determining the amount of a student's allowance or bursary in Scotland under the Further and Higher Education (Scotland) Act 1992, the Scottish Ministers or the education authority takes into account being sums which the Scottish Ministers or the education authority consider that the holder of the allowance or bursary, the holder's parents and the holder's spouse or civil partner can reasonably be expected to contribute towards the holder's expenses: Housing Renewal Grants Regulations 1996, SI 1996/2890, reg 41 (amended by SI 1999/1523; and further amended, in relation to England, by SI 2000/531, SI 2002/530 and SI 2005/3323; and, in relation to Wales, by virtue of SI 2000/973; and by SI 2002/2798 and SI 2006/2801). 'Education authority' means a government department, a local education authority as defined in the Education Act 1996 s 579 (see EDUCATION vol 35 (2015) PARA 25), a local education authority as defined in the Local Government (Scotland) Act 1973 s 123, an education and library board established under the Education and Libraries (Northern Ireland) Order 1986, SI 1986/594, art 3, any body which is a research council for the purposes of the Science and Technology Act 1965 (see NATIONAL CULTURAL HERITAGE vol 77 (2016) PARA 963 et seq) or any analogous government department, authority, board or body of the Channel Islands, Isle of Man or any other country outside Great Britain: Housing Renewal Grants Regulations 1996, SI 1996/2890, reg 41 (amended by SI 2010/1172).

4   Housing Renewal Grants Regulations 1996, SI 1996/2890, reg 43(1).

5   Housing Renewal Grants Regulations 1996, SI 1996/2890, reg 43(2)(a).

6   Housing Renewal Grants Regulations 1996, SI 1996/2890, reg 43(2)(b).

7   Housing Renewal Grants Regulations 1996, SI 1996/2890, reg 43(2)(c).

8   Housing Renewal Grants Regulations 1996, SI 1996/2890, reg 43(2)(d).

9   Housing Renewal Grants Regulations 1996, SI 1996/2890, reg 43(2)(e). As to the meaning of 'United Kingdom' see PARA 60 note 10; and as to the meaning of 'applicable amount' see PARA 854.

10 See the Housing Renewal Grants Regulations 1996, SI 1996/2890, reg 43(2)(f) (amended, in relation to England, by SI 2000/531; and, in relation to Wales, by virtue of SI 2000/973).

11 Housing Renewal Grants Regulations 1996, SI 1996/2890, reg 43(2)(g).

12 'Student loan' means a loan towards a student's maintenance pursuant to any regulations made under the Teaching and Higher Education Act 1998 s 22, the Education (Scotland) Act 1980 s 73 or the Education (Student Support) (Northern Ireland) Order 1998, SI 1998/1760, art 3, and includes, in Scotland, a young student's bursary paid under the Students' Allowances (Scotland) Regulations 1999, SI 1999/1131, reg 4(1)(c) (revoked): Housing Renewal Grants Regulations 1996, SI 1996/2890, reg 41 (definition added, in relation to England by SI 2000/531; and, in relation to Wales, by virtue of SI 2000/973; and amended, in relation to England, by SI 2002/530; and, in relation to Wales, by SI 2002/2798).

13 Housing Renewal Grants Regulations 1996, SI 1996/2890, reg 43(3) (substituted, in relation to England, by SI 2000/531; and, in relation to Wales, by virtue of SI 2000/973; and amended, in relation to England, by SI 2002/530, SI 2003/2504 and SI 2005/3323; and, in relation to Wales, by SI 2002/2798, SI 2004/253 and SI 2006/2801).

14 Ie payable under the Education (Student Support) Regulations 2001, SI 2001/951, reg 15(1)(c) (revoked). See now the Education (Student Support) Regulations 2011, SI 2011/1986; and EDUCATION vol 36 (2015) PARA 1096.

15 Ie which is payable under the Education (Student Support) Regulations 2001, SI 2001/951, reg 15(8) (revoked). See note 14.

16 Ie which is payable under the Education (Student Support) Regulations 2001, SI 2001/951, reg 16 (revoked). See note 14.

17 Ie which is payable under the Students' Allowances (Scotland) Regulations 1999, SI 1999/1131, reg 4(1)(c) (revoked) and which is specified as such on the student's award notice. See now the Students' Allowances (Scotland) Regulations 2007, SSI 2007/153.

18 Ie under the Education (Assembly Learning Grant Scheme) (Wales) Regulations 2002, SI 2002/1857, Schedule and under the Education (Student Support) (No 2) Regulations 2002, SI 2002/3200, reg 15(7) (revoked).

19 Housing Renewal Grants Regulations 1996, SI 1996/2890, reg 43(3A) (added, in relation to England, by SI 2002/530; and, in relation to Wales, by SI 2002/2798; and amended, in relation to England, by SI 2003/2504; and, in relation to Wales, by SI 2004/253).

20 See the Housing Renewal Grants Regulations 1996, SI 1996/2890, reg 43(4)–(7) (added, in relation to England, by SI 2001/739; and, in relation to Wales, by SI 2001/2073; the Housing Renewal Grants Regulations 1996, SI 1996/2890, reg 43(5) amended, in relation to England, by SI 2002/530; and, in relation to Wales, by SI 2002/2798).

868. Amounts to be disregarded. No part of a student's[1] grant income[2] may be disregarded in the determination of income other than earnings[3]. For the purposes of ascertaining income other than grant income and loans treated as income[4], any amounts intended for any expenditure necessary as a result of his attendance on the course[5] must be disregarded but only if, and to the extent that, the necessary expenditure exceeds or is likely to exceed the amount of the sums disregarded[6] on like expenditure[7]. Where a grant for school meals for dependant children or a grant for meals for dependant children aged three or four is paid[8], that payment is to be disregarded as income[9].

Where the relevant person[10] or his partner[11] is a student and the income of one is taken into account for the purposes of assessing the amount of the student's grant[12] or the student's loan[13], an amount equal to the contribution[14] (whether or not the contribution is paid) must be disregarded in determining the income of the other[15].

Where any part of a student's income has already been taken into account for the purposes of assessing his entitlement to a student grant or student loan, the amount taken into account must be disregarded in assessing that student's income[16].

1 As to the meaning of 'student' see PARA 867 note 2.
2 As to the meaning of 'grant income' see PARA 867 note 3.
3 Ie under the Housing Renewal Grants Regulations 1996, SI 1996/2890, Sch 3 para 12: reg 44.
4 Ie in accordance with the Housing Renewal Grants Regulations 1996, SI 1996/2890, reg 46 (treatment of student loans): see PARA 869.
5 Ie expenditure specified in the Housing Renewal Grants Regulations 1996, SI 1996/2890, reg 43(2): see PARA 867.
6 Ie under the Housing Renewal Grants Regulations 1996, SI 1996/2890, reg 43(2) or (3) or reg 46(5): see PARAS 867, 869.
7 Housing Renewal Grants Regulations 1996, SI 1996/2890, reg 45(1) (renumbered, in relation to England, by SI 2001/739; and, in relation to Wales, by SI 2001/2073; amended, relation to England by SI 2000/531; and in relation to Wales by virtue of SI 2000/973).
8 Ie pursuant to any regulations made under the Teaching and Higher Education Act 1998 s 22: see EDUCATION vol 36 (2015) PARA 1096.
9 Housing Renewal Grants Regulations 1996, SI 1996/2890, reg 45(2) (added, in relation to England, by SI 2001/739; and, in relation to Wales, by SI 2001/2073).
10 As to the meaning of 'relevant person' see PARA 850.
11 As to the meaning of 'partner' see PARA 850 note 5.
12 As to the meaning of 'grant' see PARA 867 note 2.
13 As to the meaning of 'student loan' see PARA 867 note 12.
14 As to the meaning of 'contribution' see PARA 867 note 3.
15 Housing Renewal Grants Regulations 1996, SI 1996/2890, reg 47 (amended, in relation to England by SI 2000/531; and, in relation to Wales, by virtue of SI 2000/973). As to the phasing out of local authority grants to students see EDUCATION vol 36 (2015) PARA 1095 et seq.

16 Housing Renewal Grants Regulations 1996, SI 1996/2890, reg 47A (added by SI 1999/1523; and amended, in relation to England, by SI 2000/531; and, in relation to Wales, by virtue of SI 2000/973).

869. Treatment of student loans. A student loan[1] must be treated as income unless it is a hardship loan[2], in which case it must be disregarded[3]. In calculating the weekly amount of the loan to be taken into account as income:

(1) a loan which is payable in respect of a course that is of a single academic year's duration or less is to be apportioned equally between the weeks in the period beginning with:

    (a) the start of the single academic year[4]; or

    (b) where the course is of less than an academic year's duration, the first day of the course,

and ending with the last day of the course[5];

(2) in respect of an academic year of a course which starts other than on 1 September, a loan which is payable in respect of that academic year is to be apportioned equally between the weeks in the period beginning with the benefit week[6] immediately following that which includes the first day of that academic year and ending with the benefit week which includes the last day of that academic year but excluding any benefit weeks falling entirely within the quarter[7] during which, in the opinion of the appropriate national authority, the longest of any vacation is taken[8];

(3) a loan which is payable in respect of the final academic year of a course (not being a course of a single year's duration) is to be apportioned equally between the weeks in the period beginning with the earlier of:

    (a) the first day of the first benefit week in September; or

    (b) the first day of the first benefit week following the beginning of the autumn term,

and ending with the last day of the last benefit week before the last day of the course[9];

(4) in any other case, the loan is to be apportioned equally between the weeks in the period beginning with the earlier of:

    (a) the first day of the first benefit week in September; or

    (b) the first day of the first benefit week following the beginning of the autumn term,

and ending with the last day of the last benefit week in June[10],

and in all cases, from the weekly amount so apportioned there is to be disregarded £10[11].

For these purposes, a student[12] is treated as possessing a student loan in respect of an academic year where either a student loan has been made to him in respect of that year, or he could acquire such a loan in respect of that year by taking reasonable steps to do so[13]. Where a student is treated as possessing a student loan, the amount of the student loan to be taken into account as income is:

(i) in the case of a student to whom a student loan is made in respect of an academic year, a sum equal to:

    (A) the maximum student loan he is able to acquire in respect of that year by taking reasonable steps to do so; and

    (B) any contribution whether or not it has been paid;

(ii) in the case of a student to whom a student loan is not made in respect of an academic year, the maximum student loan that would be made to the student if:

(A) he took all reasonable steps to obtain the maximum student loan he is able to acquire in respect of that year; and

(B) no deduction in that loan was made by virtue of the application of a means test[14].

There is to be deducted from the amount of a student's loan income the sum of £260 in respect of travel costs and the sum of £319 towards the costs of books and equipment[15].

1 As to the meaning of 'student loan' see PARA 867 note 12. As to treatment of payments from access funds, and refunds of tax deducted from a student's covenant income, see PARA 870.

2 'Hardship loan' means a loan made under the Education (Student Support) Regulations 2000, SI 2000/1121, reg 21 (revoked and not reproduced in the Education (Student Support) Regulations 2011, SI 2011/1986) or under the corresponding provisions of Scottish or Northern Ireland legislation: Housing Renewal Grants Regulations 1996, SI 1996/2890, reg 46(1A) (added, in relation to England, by SI 2001/739; and, in relation to Wales, by SI 2001/2073). See further EDUCATION vol 36 (2015) PARA 1095 et seq.

3 Housing Renewal Grants Regulations 1996, SI 1996/2890, reg 46(1) (substituted, in relation to England, by SI 2001/739; and, in relation to Wales, by SI 2001/2073).

4 'Academic year' means the period of 12 months beginning on 1 January, 1 April, 1 July or 1 September according to whether the course in question begins in the winter, the spring, the summer or the autumn respectively; but if students are required to begin attending the course during August or September and to continue attending through the autumn, the academic year of the course is considered to begin in the autumn rather than the summer: Housing Renewal Grants Regulations 1996, SI 1996/2890, reg 41 (definition added, in relation to England, by SI 2002/530; and, in relation to Wales, by SI 2002/2798).

5 Housing Renewal Grants Regulations 1996, SI 1996/2890, reg 46(2)(a) (reg 46(2) substituted, in relation to England, by SI 2001/739; and, in relation to Wales, by SI 2001/2073). 'Last day of the course' means the date on which the last day of the final academic term falls in respect of the course in which the student is enrolled: Housing Renewal Grants Regulations 1996, SI 1996/2890, reg 41.

6 'Benefit week' means a period of seven consecutive days commencing upon a Monday and ending on a Sunday: Housing Renewal Grants Regulations 1996, SI 1996/2890, reg 2(1) (definition added, in relation to England, by SI 2001/739; and, in relation to Wales, by SI 2001/2073).

7 For these purposes, 'quarter' has the same meaning as that given by the definition in the Education (Student Support) Regulations 2001, SI 2001/951, reg 2 (revoked; definition not reproduced in the Education (Student Support) Regulations 2009, SI 2009/1555) (see EDUCATION vol 36 (2015) PARA 1096): Housing Renewal Grants Regulations 1996, SI 1996/2890, reg 46(2)(aa) (reg 46(2) as substituted (see note 5); and reg 46(2)(aa) added, in relation to England, by SI 2002/530; and, in relation to Wales, by SI 2002/2798).

8 Housing Renewal Grants Regulations 1996, SI 1996/2890, reg 46(2)(aa) (as added: see note 7).

9 Housing Renewal Grants Regulations 1996, SI 1996/2890, reg 46(2)(b) (as substituted: see note 5).

10 Housing Renewal Grants Regulations 1996, SI 1996/2890, reg 46(2)(c) (as substituted: see note 5).

11 Housing Renewal Grants Regulations 1996, SI 1996/2890, reg 46(2) (as substituted: see note 5).

12 As to the meaning of 'student' see PARA 867 note 2.

13 Housing Renewal Grants Regulations 1996, SI 1996/2890, reg 46(3) (substituted, in relation to England, by SI 2000/531; and, in relation to Wales, by virtue of SI 2000/973).

14 Housing Renewal Grants Regulations 1996, SI 1996/2890, reg 46(4) (added, in relation to England, by SI 2000/531; and, in relation to Wales, by virtue of SI 2000/973).

15 Housing Renewal Grants Regulations 1996, SI 1996/2890, reg 46(5) (added, in relation to England, by SI 2000/531; and, in relation to Wales, by virtue of SI 2000/973; and amended, in relation to England, by SI 2002/530; and, in relation to Wales, by SI 2002/2798).

870. Treatment of refunds of tax deducted from a student's covenant income and payments from access funds. Any amount by way of a refund of tax deducted from a student's covenant income must be treated as capital[1]. An amount paid from access funds[2] as a single lump sum must be treated as capital[3]. An amount paid from access funds as a single lump sum which is intended and used for an item other than food, household fuel or rent or ordinary clothing or footwear[4], of a single relevant person[5] or, as the case may be, of the relevant person or any other member of his family, or which is used for any council tax or water charges for which that relevant person or member is liable, must be disregarded as capital, but only for a period of 52 weeks from the date of payment[6].

An amount paid from access funds other than as a single lump sum[7] must be disregarded as income where it is made:

(1) on or after 1 September or the first day of the course, whichever first occurs, but before receipt of any student loan in respect of the academic year beginning on 1 September and that payment is intended for the purpose of bridging the period until receipt of the student loan; or

(2) before the first day of the course to a person in anticipation of that person becoming a student[8].

Subject to heads (1), (2), an amount paid from access funds other than as a single lump sum which is intended and used for food, household fuel or rent or ordinary clothing or footwear[9], of a single relevant person or any other member of his family, and any payment from access funds which is used for any council tax or water charges for which that relevant person or member is liable, must be disregarded as income to the extent of £20 per week[10].

Any other payment from access funds other than as a single lump sum must be disregarded as income[11].

1 Housing Renewal Grants Regulations 1996, SI 1996/2890, reg 46B(1) (reg 46B added, in relation to England, by SI 2001/739; and, in relation to Wales, by SI 2001/2073). As to a student's covenant income see WELFARE BENEFITS AND STATE PENSIONS vol 104 (2014) PARA 317.
2 As to the grants and payments included in the definition of 'access funds' see the Housing Renewal Grants Regulations 1996, SI 1996/2890, reg 41 (definition added, in relation to England, by SI 2001/739; and, in relation to Wales, by SI 2001/2073; and amended, in relation to England, by SI 2002/530; and, in relation to Wales, by SI 2002/2798, SI 2005/3238 and SI 2010/297; further amended by SI 2010/1941, SI 2012/956 and SI 2015/971).
3 Housing Renewal Grants Regulations 1996, SI 1996/2890, reg 46B(2) (as added: see note 1).
4 For these purposes, 'rent' and 'ordinary clothing or footwear' have the same meanings as in the Housing Renewal Grants Regulations 1996, SI 1996/2890, Sch 3 para 12(2): reg 46B(3) (as added: see note 1).
5 As to the meaning of 'relevant person' see PARA 850.
6 Housing Renewal Grants Regulations 1996, SI 1996/2890, reg 46B(3) (as added: see note 1).
7 Ie payments from access funds that are not payments to which the provisions of the Housing Renewal Grants Regulations 1996, SI 1996/2890, reg 46B(2), (3) apply: reg 46A(1) (reg 46A added, in relation to England, by SI 2001/739; and, in relation to Wales, by SI 2001/2073).
8 Housing Renewal Grants Regulations 1996, SI 1996/2890, reg 46A(4) (as added: see note 7).
9 For these purposes, 'rent' and 'ordinary clothing or footwear' have the same meanings as in the Housing Renewal Grants Regulations 1996, SI 1996/2890, Sch 3 para 12(2): reg 46A(3) (as added: see note 7).
10 Housing Renewal Grants Regulations 1996, SI 1996/2890, reg 46A(3) (as added: see note 7).
11 Housing Renewal Grants Regulations 1996, SI 1996/2890, reg 46A(2) (as added: see note 7).

(4) DECISION AND NOTIFICATION

871. In general. A local housing authority[1] must by notice in writing notify an applicant[2] for a grant[3] as soon as reasonably practicable, and, in any event, not later than six months[4] after the date of the application concerned, whether the application is approved[5] or refused[6]. Where an authority decides to approve an application for a grant, it must determine:

(1) which of the relevant works[7] are eligible for grant (such works being referred to as 'the eligible works')[8];

(2) the amount of the expenses which in its opinion are properly to be incurred in the execution of the eligible works[9];

(3) the amount of the costs which in its opinion have been properly incurred, or are properly to be incurred, with respect to preliminary or ancillary services and charges[10]; and

(4) the amount of grant the authority has decided to pay, taking into account all the relevant statutory provisions[11].

If the authority notifies the applicant that the application is approved, it must also specify in the notice:

(a) the eligible works[12];

(b) the estimated expense[13], and how those amounts have been calculated[14]; and

(c) the amount of the grant[15].

If the authority notifies the applicant that the application is refused, it must at the same time notify him of the reasons for the refusal[16].

If after an application for a grant has been approved the authority is satisfied that owing to circumstances beyond the control of the applicant:

(i) the eligible works cannot be, or could not have been, carried out on the basis of the estimated expense[17];

(ii) the amount of the costs which have been or are to be incurred with respect to preliminary or ancillary services and charges has increased[18]; or

(iii) the eligible works cannot be, or could not have been, carried out without carrying out additional works which could not have been reasonably foreseen at the time the application was made[19],

the authority may re-determine the estimated expense and the amount of the grant[20].

1 As to the meaning of 'local housing authority' see PARA 11 (definition applied by the Housing Grants, Construction and Regeneration Act 1996 s 101).
2 As to the meanings of 'applicant' and 'application' see PARA 850 note 1.
3 As to the meaning of 'grant' see PARA 836 note 1.
4 'Month' means calendar month: see the Interpretation Act 1978 s 5, Sch 1.
5 As to approval see PARA 844.
6 Housing Grants, Construction and Regeneration Act 1996 s 34(1).
7 As to the meaning of 'relevant works' see PARA 837.
8 Housing Grants, Construction and Regeneration Act 1996 s 34(2)(a).
9 Housing Grants, Construction and Regeneration Act 1996 s 34(2)(b).
10 Housing Grants, Construction and Regeneration Act 1996 s 34(2)(c). As to the meaning of 'preliminary or ancillary services and charges' see PARA 837 note 6.
11 Housing Grants, Construction and Regeneration Act 1996 s 34(2)(d).
12 Housing Grants, Construction and Regeneration Act 1996 s 34(3)(a).
13 The total of the amounts referred to in the Housing Grants, Construction and Regeneration Act 1996 s 34(2)(b), (c) (see heads (2)–(3) in the text) is referred to as 'the estimated expense': s 34(2).
14 Housing Grants, Construction and Regeneration Act 1996 s 34(3)(b).
15 Housing Grants, Construction and Regeneration Act 1996 s 34(3)(c). Where an application for a grant is approved, the local housing authority may not impose any condition in relation to the approval or payment of the grant, except as provided by ss 35–59 (see PARA 872 et seq) or with the consent of the appropriate national authority, and this applies whether the condition purports to operate as a condition, a personal covenant or otherwise: s 34(6). As to the appropriate national authority, ie the Secretary of State or, where statutory functions have been transferred in relation to Wales, the Welsh Ministers, see PARA 7.
16 Housing Grants, Construction and Regeneration Act 1996 s 34(4). In a different statutory context, it has been held that the purpose of requiring an authority to give reasons is to enable the recipient to see whether the decision can be challenged in law: see *Thornton v Kirklees Metropolitan Borough Council* [1979] QB 626, [1979] 2 All ER 349, CA. See also eg *R v Brent London Borough Council, ex p Baruwa* (1995) 28 HLR 361.
17 Housing Grants, Construction and Regeneration Act 1996 s 34(5)(a).
18 Housing Grants, Construction and Regeneration Act 1996 s 34(5)(b).

19 Housing Grants, Construction and Regeneration Act 1996 s 34(5)(c).
20 Housing Grants, Construction and Regeneration Act 1996 s 34(5).

(5) PAYMENT OF GRANTS

872. In general. Where the local housing authority[1] has approved[2] an application for a grant[3], it must pay the grant[4]. The grant may be paid:

(1)   in whole after the completion of the eligible works[5]; or

(2)   in part by instalments as the works progress and the balance after completion of the works[6].

Where a grant is paid by instalments, the aggregate of the instalments paid before the completion of the eligible works must not at any time exceed nine-tenths of the amount of the grant[7].

1   As to the meaning of 'local housing authority' see PARA 11 (definition applied by the Housing Grants, Construction and Regeneration Act 1996 s 101).
2   As to approval see PARA 844.
3   As to the meaning of 'application' see PARA 850 note 1; and as to the meaning of 'grant' see PARA 836 note 1.
4   Housing Grants, Construction and Regeneration Act 1996 s 35(1).
5   As to the meaning of 'eligible works' see PARA 871.
6   Housing Grants, Construction and Regeneration Act 1996 s 35(2).
7   Housing Grants, Construction and Regeneration Act 1996 s 35(3).

873. Delayed payment of a mandatory grant. The local housing authority[1] may approve[2] an application for a grant[3] on terms that payment of the grant, or part of it, will not be made before a date[4] specified in the notification of the authority's decision on the application[5].

1   As to the meaning of 'local housing authority' see PARA 11 (definition applied by the Housing Grants, Construction and Regeneration Act 1996 s 101).
2   As to approval see PARA 844.
3   As to the meaning of 'grant' see PARA 836 note 1.
4   That date must not be more than 12 months, or such other period as may be specified by order of the appropriate national authority, after the date of the application: Housing Grants, Construction and Regeneration Act 1996 s 36(2). As to the making of orders see PARA 837 note 6. At the date at which this volume states the law, no such order had been made. As to the appropriate national authority, ie the Secretary of State or, where statutory functions have been transferred in relation to Wales, the Welsh Ministers, see PARA 7.
5   Housing Grants, Construction and Regeneration Act 1996 s 36(1) (amended by SI 2002/1860). This provision allows a local housing authority to budget where it has received a number of applications for mandatory grants.

874. Conditions as to carrying out of the works. It is a condition of payment of every grant[1] that the eligible works[2] are carried out within 12 months[3] from:

(1)   the date of approval of the application concerned[4]; or

(2)   in the case of delayed payment of a mandatory grant[5], the date specified in the notification of the authority's decision,

or, in either case, such further period as the local housing authority may allow[6].

The authority may, in particular, allow further time where it is satisfied that the eligible works cannot be, or could not have been, carried out without carrying out other works which could not have been reasonably foreseen at the time when the application was made[7].

The payment of a grant, or part of a grant, is conditional upon:

(a)   the eligible works or the corresponding part of the works being executed to the satisfaction of the authority[8]; and

(b) the authority being provided with an acceptable invoice, demand or receipt[9] for payment for the works and any preliminary or ancillary services or charges[10] in respect of which the grant or part of the grant is to be paid[11].

It has been held in a similar statutory context that the purpose of such statutory conditions is the protection of public funds and that no duty of care is thereby imposed on the authority as to the quality of the works that have been carried out (that is, it has no liability for any defects which may emerge)[12].

1 As to the meaning of 'grant' see PARA 836 note 1.
2 In approving an application for a grant a local housing authority may require as a condition of payment of the grant that the eligible works are carried out in accordance with such specifications as it determines: Housing Grants, Construction and Regeneration Act 1996 s 37(3). As to the meaning of 'eligible works' see PARA 871. As to the meaning of 'local housing authority' see PARA 11 (definition applied by s 101).
3 As to the meaning of 'month' see PARA 871 note 4.
4 As to approval see PARA 844.
5 Ie where the Housing Grants, Construction and Regeneration Act 1996 s 36 (delayed payment of mandatory grant) applies: see PARA 873.
6 Housing Grants, Construction and Regeneration Act 1996 s 37(1).
7 Housing Grants, Construction and Regeneration Act 1996 s 37(2).
8 Housing Grants, Construction and Regeneration Act 1996 s 37(4)(a).
9 For this purpose, an invoice, demand or receipt is acceptable if it satisfies the authority and is not given by the applicant or a member of his family: Housing Grants, Construction and Regeneration Act 1996 s 37(4).
10 As to the meaning of 'preliminary or ancillary services or charges' see PARA 837 note 6.
11 Housing Grants, Construction and Regeneration Act 1996 s 37(4)(b).
12 See *Curran v Northern Ireland Co-ownership Housing Association Ltd* [1987] AC 718, [1987] 2 All ER 13, HL.

875. Conditions as to contractors to be employed. It is a condition of payment of every grant[1], unless the local housing authority[2] directs otherwise in any particular case, that the eligible works[3] are carried out by the contractor whose estimate accompanied the application or, where two or more estimates were submitted, by one of those contractors[4]. The appropriate national authority[5] may by regulations[6] make provision as to the establishing and maintaining by local housing authorities of lists of contractors approved by them for the purpose of carrying out grant-aided works[7].

The local housing authority may pay a grant or part of a grant:
(1) by payment direct to the contractor[8]; or
(2) by delivering to the applicant an instrument of payment in a form made payable to the contractor[9].

It must not, however, do so unless the applicant was informed before the grant application was approved that this would or might be the method of payment[10].

Where an amount of grant is payable, but the works in question have not been executed to the satisfaction of the applicant, the local housing authority may at the applicant's request, and if it considers it appropriate to do so, withhold payment from the contractor[11] and may, if it does so, make the payment to the applicant instead[12].

1 As to the meaning of 'grant' see PARA 836 note 1.
2 As to the meaning of 'local housing authority' see PARA 11 (definition applied by the Housing Grants, Construction and Regeneration Act 1996 s 101).
3 As to the meaning of 'eligible works' see PARA 871.
4 Housing Grants, Construction and Regeneration Act 1996 s 38(1).
5 As to the appropriate national authority, ie the Secretary of State or, where statutory functions have been transferred in relation to Wales, the Welsh Ministers, see PARA 7.
6 The regulations may provide that it is to be a condition of payment of every grant by a local housing authority by which such a list is maintained that, except in such cases as may be prescribed

and unless the local housing authority directs otherwise in any particular case, the eligible works are carried out by a contractor who is on the authority's list of approved contractors: Housing Grants, Construction and Regeneration Act 1996 s 38(3). As to the meaning of 'prescribed' see PARA 837 note 8. As to the making of regulations see PARA 837 note 6. At the date at which this volume states the law, no such regulations had been made.

7 Housing Grants, Construction and Regeneration Act 1996 s 38(2).
8 Housing Grants, Construction and Regeneration Act 1996 s 39(1)(a).
9 Housing Grants, Construction and Regeneration Act 1996 s 39(1)(b).
10 Housing Grants, Construction and Regeneration Act 1996 s 39(1).
11 Housing Grants, Construction and Regeneration Act 1996 s 39(2).
12 Housing Grants, Construction and Regeneration Act 1996 s 39(2).

876. Applicant ceasing to be entitled before payment of grant. Where an application for a grant[1] is approved[2] but before the certified date[3] the applicant ceases to be a person entitled to a grant[4] or, in the case of a joint application, all the applicants cease to be so entitled[5], then:

(1)   no grant is to be paid or, as the case may be, no further instalments are to be paid[6]; and

(2)   the authority may demand that any instalment of the grant which has been paid be repaid forthwith, together with interest from the date on which it was paid until repayment, at such reasonable rate as the authority may determine[7].

1 As to the meaning of 'grant' see PARA 836 note 1.
2 As to approval see PARA 844.
3 As to the meaning of 'certified date' see PARA 840 note 4.
4 For these purposes, an applicant ceases to be a person entitled to a grant: (1) in the case of an owner's application, if he ceases to have a qualifying owner's interest, or if he ceases to have the intention specified in the owner's certificate which accompanied the application; (2) in the case of a tenant's application, if he ceases to be a qualifying tenant of the dwelling, or if the application was accompanied by an owner's certificate and the landlord ceases to have the intention specified in the certificate: Housing Grants, Construction and Regeneration Act 1996 s 40(4)(a), (b) (amended by SI 2002/1860). If, however, the case falls within the Housing Grants, Construction and Regeneration Act 1996 s 41 (change of circumstances affecting disabled occupant: see PARA 877), the authority must act under s 41: s 40(4). As to the meanings of 'owner's application' and 'tenant's application' see PARA 839; as to the meaning of 'qualifying tenant' see PARA 839 note 11; as to the meaning of 'qualifying owner's interest' see PARA 839 note 8; and as to the meaning of 'owner's certificate' see PARA 840 note 4.
5 See the Housing Grants, Construction and Regeneration Act 1996 s 40(1) (amended by SI 2002/1860). The Housing Grants, Construction and Regeneration Act 1996 s 40 has effect subject to s 56 (provisions relating to death of applicant: see PARA 884): s 40(7).
6 Housing Grants, Construction and Regeneration Act 1996 s 40(2)(a) (substituted by SI 2002/1860).
7 Housing Grants, Construction and Regeneration Act 1996 s 40(2)(b) (renumbered by SI 2002/1860).

877. Change of circumstances affecting disabled occupant. The following provisions apply where an application[1] for a grant[2] has been approved[3] and before the certified date[4]:

(1)   the works cease to be necessary or appropriate to meet the needs of the disabled occupant[5]; or

(2)   the disabled occupant ceases to occupy the dwelling[6], qualifying houseboat[7], caravan[8] or flat[9] concerned or it ceases to be the intention that he should occupy it[10]; or

(3)   the disabled occupant dies[11].

The local housing authority[12] may take such action as appears to it appropriate and may decide:

(a)   that no grant is to be paid or, as the case may be, no further instalments are to be paid[13];

(b) that the relevant works[14] or some of them should be completed and the grant or an appropriate proportion of it paid[15]; or

(c) that the application should be redetermined in the light of the new circumstances[16].

In making its decision, the authority must have regard to all the circumstances of the case[17]. If it decides that no grant is to be paid or that no further instalments are to be paid, it may demand that any instalment of the grant which has been paid is to be repaid forthwith, together with interest from the date on which it was paid until its repayment, at such reasonable rate as the authority may determine[18].

1 The Housing Grants, Construction and Regeneration Act 1996 s 41 (see the text and notes 2–18) applies whether or not the disabled occupant (or any of them) is the applicant (or one of them): s 41(2). As to the meaning of 'disabled occupant' see PARA 840 note 4.

2 As to the meaning of 'grant' see PARA 836 note 1.

3 As to approval see PARA 844.

4 Housing Grants, Construction and Regeneration Act 1996 s 41(1) (amended by SI 2002/1860). As to the meaning of 'certified date' see PARA 840 note 4.

5 Housing Grants, Construction and Regeneration Act 1996 s 41(1)(a).

6 As to the meaning of 'dwelling' see PARA 836 note 4.

7 As to the meaning of 'qualifying houseboat' see PARA 836 note 5.

8 As to the meaning of 'caravan' see PARA 836 note 6.

9 As to the meaning of 'flat' see PARA 836 note 7.

10 Housing Grants, Construction and Regeneration Act 1996 s 41(1)(b) (amended by the Housing Act 2004 s 224(1), (5)(d); and by SI 2002/1860).

11 Housing Grants, Construction and Regeneration Act 1996 s 41(1)(c). Where the application related to more than one disabled occupant s 41 applies if any of heads (1)–(3) in the text applies in relation to any of them: s 41(1).

12 As to the meaning of 'local housing authority' see PARA 11 (definition applied by the Housing Grants, Construction and Regeneration Act 1996 s 101).

13 Housing Grants, Construction and Regeneration Act 1996 s 41(3)(a).

14 As to the meaning of 'relevant works' see PARA 837.

15 Housing Grants, Construction and Regeneration Act 1996 s 41(3)(b).

16 Housing Grants, Construction and Regeneration Act 1996 s 41(3)(c).

17 Housing Grants, Construction and Regeneration Act 1996 s 41(4).

18 Housing Grants, Construction and Regeneration Act 1996 s 41(5). This entitlement to interest continues until payment and does not end in the judgment: see *Ealing London Borough Council v El Isaac* [1980] 2 All ER 548, [1980] 1 WLR 932, CA.

878. Cases in which grants may be recalculated, withheld or repaid. Where an application for a grant[1] has been approved[2] by the local housing authority[3] and one of the following cases applies:

(1) the authority ascertains that the amount was determined[4] on the basis of inaccurate or incomplete information and exceeds that to which the applicant was entitled[5];

(2) the authority ascertains that without its knowledge the eligible works[6] were started before the application was approved[7];

(3) the eligible works are not completed to the satisfaction of the authority within the period specified[8] or such extended period as the authority may allow[9];

(4) the authority ascertains that the aggregate of the cost of completing the eligible works and the costs incurred with respect to preliminary or ancillary services and charges[10] is, or is likely to be, lower than the estimated expense[11]; or

(5) the authority ascertains that without its knowledge the eligible works were carried out otherwise than as required by the statutory conditions[12] as to contractors employed[13],

then the authority may either refuse to pay the grant or any further instalment of grant which remains to be paid, or may make a reduction in the grant which, in a case falling within head (4), is to be a reduction proportionate to the reduction in the estimated expense[14]. The authority may also demand repayment by the applicant forthwith, in whole or part, of the grant or any instalment of the grant paid, together with interest at such reasonable rate as the authority may determine from the date of payment until repayment[15].

1 As to the meaning of 'grant' see PARA 836 note 1.
2 As to approval see PARA 844.
3 As to the meaning of 'local housing authority' see PARA 11 (definition applied by the Housing Grants, Construction and Regeneration Act 1996 s 101).
4 Ie determined under the Housing Grants, Construction and Regeneration Act 1996 s 30 (see PARA 849) or s 31 (see PARA 846).
5 Housing Grants, Construction and Regeneration Act 1996 s 42(1)(a).
6 As to the meaning of 'eligible works' see PARA 871.
7 Housing Grants, Construction and Regeneration Act 1996 s 42(1)(b).
8 Ie the period specified under the Housing Grants, Construction and Regeneration Act 1996 s 37(1): see PARA 874.
9 Housing Grants, Construction and Regeneration Act 1996 s 42(1)(c). The extended period referred to in head (3) in the text is such extended period as the authority may allow under s 37(1): see PARA 874.
10 As to the meaning of 'preliminary or ancillary services and charges' see PARA 837 note 6.
11 Housing Grants, Construction and Regeneration Act 1996 s 42(1)(d). As to the meaning of 'estimated expense' see PARA 871 note 13.
12 Ie otherwise than as required by the Housing Grants, Construction and Regeneration Act 1996 s 38: see PARA 875.
13 Housing Grants, Construction and Regeneration Act 1996 s 42(1)(e).
14 Housing Grants, Construction and Regeneration Act 1996 s 42(1), (2)(a), (b).
15 Housing Grants, Construction and Regeneration Act 1996 s 42(2). As to interest see PARA 877 note 18.

879. Repayment where applicant not entitled to grant. Where an application for a grant[1] is approved[2] but it subsequently appears to the local housing authority[3] that the applicant (or, in the case of a joint application, any of the applicants) was not, at the time the application was approved, entitled to a grant[4], then:

(1)   no grant is to be paid or, as the case may be, no further instalments are to be paid; and

(2)   the authority may demand that any grant which has been paid be repaid forthwith, together with interest from the date on which it was paid until repayment, at such reasonable rate as the authority may determine[5].

1 As to the meaning of 'grant' see PARA 836 note 1.
2 As to approval see PARA 844.
3 As to the meaning of 'local housing authority' see PARA 11 (definition applied by the Housing Grants, Construction and Regeneration Act 1996 s 101).
4 See the Housing Grants, Construction and Regeneration Act 1996 s 43(1) (amended by SI 2002/1860). For these purposes an applicant is not entitled to a grant: (1) in the case of an owner's application, if he does not have a qualifying owner's interest, or he does not have the intention specified in the owner-occupation certificate or certificate of intended letting which accompanied the application; (2) in the case of a tenant's application, if he is not a qualifying tenant of the dwelling, or if the application was accompanied by a certificate of intended letting and the landlord does not have the intention specified in the certificate; or (3) in the case of an occupier's application, if he does not have the intention specified in the occupier's certificate which accompanied the application: Housing Grants, Construction and Regeneration Act 1996 s 43(4) (amended by SI 2002/1860). As to the meanings of 'owner's application', 'tenant's application' and 'occupier's application' see PARA 839; as to the meaning of 'qualifying owner's interest' see PARA 839 note 8; as to the meaning of 'qualifying tenant' see PARA 839 note 11; as to the meaning of 'owner's certificate' see PARA 840 note 4; and as to the meaning of 'occupier's certificate' see PARA 842 note 2.

5 Housing Grants, Construction and Regeneration Act 1996 s 43(2) (amended by SI 2002/1860). As to interest see PARA 877 note 18.

(6) GRANT CONDITIONS AND REPAYMENT

(i) Introduction

880. In general. Provision is made for the imposition of conditions when making a grant which a local housing authority[1] is entitled to enforce by seeking repayment[2]. In this way authorities can recover grant where a condition has been broken[3]. A local housing authority may not, however, impose any condition requiring a grant[4] to be repaid except in accordance with the relevant statutory provisions[5]; and this applies whether the condition purports to operate as a condition of the grant, as a personal covenant or otherwise[6].

Except as otherwise provided, a grant condition[7] imposed under the power to impose other conditions with the consent of the appropriate national authority[8] has effect for such period as may be specified in, or in accordance with, the appropriate national authority's consent[9].

1 As to the meaning of 'local housing authority' see PARA 11 (definition applied by the Housing Grants, Construction and Regeneration Act 1996 s 101).
2 See the Housing Grants, Construction and Regeneration Act 1996 s 44(1) (amended by SI 2002/1860).
3 See PARAS 881–882.
4 As to the meaning of 'grant' see PARA 836 note 1.
5 Ie in accordance with the Housing Grants, Construction and Regeneration Act 1996 ss 51, 52: see PARAS 881–882.
6 Housing Grants, Construction and Regeneration Act 1996 s 44(4) (amended by SI 2002/1860).
7 'Grant condition' means a condition having effect in accordance with either the Housing Grants, Construction and Regeneration Act 1996 s 51 (see PARA 881) or s 52 (see PARA 882): s 44(1) (as amended: see note 2).
8 Ie under the Housing Grants, Construction and Regeneration Act 1996 s 52: see PARA 882. As to the appropriate national authority, ie the Secretary of State or, where statutory functions have been transferred in relation to Wales, the Welsh Ministers, see PARA 7.
9 Housing Grants, Construction and Regeneration Act 1996 s 44(2) (amended by SI 2002/1860).

(ii) Conditions

881. Conditions as to repayment in case of other compensation, etc. Where a local housing authority[1] approves[2] an application for a grant[3] it may, with the consent of the appropriate national authority[4], impose a condition requiring the applicant to take reasonable steps to pursue any relevant claim and to repay the grant, so far as appropriate, out of the proceeds of such a claim[5].

The claims to which this applies are:
(1)   an insurance claim, or a legal claim against another person, in respect of damage to the premises to which the grant relates[6]; or
(2)   a legal claim for damages in which the cost of the works to premises to which the grant relates is part of the claim[7],
and a claim is a relevant claim to the extent that works to make good the damage, or the cost of which is claimed, are works to which the grant relates[8].

In the event of a breach of such a condition, the applicant must on demand pay to the local housing authority the amount of the grant so far as relating to any such works, together with compound interest as from such date as may be prescribed[9] by or determined in accordance with the regulations[10], calculated at such reasonable rate as the authority may determine and with yearly rests[11]. However, the local housing authority may determine not to make such a demand or to demand a lesser amount[12].

1 As to the meaning of 'local housing authority' see PARA 11 (definition applied by the Housing Grants, Construction and Regeneration Act 1996 s 101).
2 As to approval see PARA 844.
3 As to the meaning of 'grant' see PARA 836 note 1.
4 As to the appropriate national authority, ie the Secretary of State or, where statutory functions have been transferred in relation to Wales, the Welsh Ministers, see PARA 7.
5 Housing Grants, Construction and Regeneration Act 1996 s 51(1).
6 Housing Grants, Construction and Regeneration Act 1996 s 51(2)(a).
7 Housing Grants, Construction and Regeneration Act 1996 s 51(2)(b).
8 Housing Grants, Construction and Regeneration Act 1996 s 51(2).
9 As to the meaning of 'prescribed' see PARA 837 note 8.
10 At the date at which this volume states the law, no such regulations had been made. As to the making of regulations generally see PARA 837 note 6.
11 Housing Grants, Construction and Regeneration Act 1996 s 51(3). As to interest see PARA 877 note 18.
12 Housing Grants, Construction and Regeneration Act 1996 s 51(4).

882. Power to impose other conditions with consent of appropriate national authority. Where a local housing authority[1] approves[2] an application for a grant[3] it may, with the consent of the appropriate national authority[4], impose such conditions as it thinks fit:

(1) relating to things done or omitted before the certified date[5] and requiring the repayment to the local housing authority on demand of any instalments of grant paid[6]; or

(2) relating to things done or omitted on or after that date and requiring the payment to the local housing authority on demand of a sum equal to the amount of the grant paid[7],

and, in either case, that amount may be required to be paid together with compound interest on that amount as from the date of payment, calculated at such reasonable rate as the authority may determine and with yearly rests[8]. Where, however, the authority has the right to demand repayment of an amount, it may determine not to demand payment or to demand a lesser amount[9].

A condition under these provisions is a local land charge and is binding on:

(a) any person who is for the time being an owner of the dwelling or building[10]; and

(b) such other persons (if any) as the authority may specify with the consent of the appropriate national authority[11].

1 As to the meaning of 'local housing authority' see PARA 11 (definition applied by the Housing Grants, Construction and Regeneration Act 1996 s 101).
2 As to approval see PARA 844.
3 As to the meaning of 'grant' see PARA 836 note 1.
4 As to the appropriate national authority, ie the Secretary of State or, where statutory functions have been transferred in relation to Wales, the Welsh Ministers, see PARA 7.
5 As to the meaning of 'certified date' see PARA 840 note 4.
6 Housing Grants, Construction and Regeneration Act 1996 s 52(1)(a).
7 Housing Grants, Construction and Regeneration Act 1996 s 52(1)(b).
8 Housing Grants, Construction and Regeneration Act 1996 s 52(1). As to interest see PARA 877 note 18.
9 Housing Grants, Construction and Regeneration Act 1996 s 52(4). Any conditions imposed under s 52 are in addition to the conditions provided for by s 51 (see PARA 881): s 52(5) (amended by SI 2002/1860).
10 As to the meaning of 'dwelling' see PARA 836 note 4. For the purposes of the Housing Grants, Construction and Regeneration Act 1996 Pt I (ss 1–103), 'owner', in relation to a dwelling, means the person who: (1) is for the time being entitled to receive from a lessee of the dwelling (or would be so entitled if the dwelling were let) a rent at an annual rate of not less than two-thirds of the

net annual value of the dwelling; and (2) is not himself liable as lessee of the dwelling, or of property which includes the dwelling, to pay such a rent to a superior landlord: s 99(1). For this purpose the net annual value of a dwelling means the rent at which the dwelling might reasonably be expected to be let from year to year if the tenant undertook to pay all usual tenant's rates and taxes and to bear the cost of repair and insurance and the other expenses, if any, necessary to maintain the dwelling in a state to command that rent: s 99(2). Any dispute arising as to the net annual value of a dwelling is to be referred in writing for decision by the district valuer: s 99(3). 'District valuer' has the same meaning as in the Housing Act 1985 (see PARA 527 note 14): Housing Grants, Construction and Regeneration Act 1996 s 99(3).

11 Housing Grants, Construction and Regeneration Act 1996 s 52(2) (amended by SI 2002/1860). As to local land charges see REAL PROPERTY AND REGISTRATION vol 87 (2012) PARA 763 et seq.

(iii) Cessation of Conditions on Repayment

883. In general. If at any time while a grant condition[1] remains in force with respect to a dwelling[2] or building:

(1) the owner[3] of the dwelling or building to which the condition relates pays the amount of the grant[4] to the local housing authority[5] by which the grant was made[6];

(2) a mortgagee of the interest of the owner in that dwelling or building (being a mortgagee entitled to exercise a power of sale) makes such a payment[7];

(3) the local housing authority determines not to demand repayment on the breach of a grant condition[8]; or

(4) the authority demands repayment in whole or in part on the breach of a grant condition and that demand is satisfied[9],

that grant condition and any other grant conditions cease to be in force with respect to that dwelling or building[10].

1 As to the meaning of 'grant condition' see PARA 880 note 7.
2 As to the meaning of 'dwelling' see PARA 836 note 4.
3 As to the meaning of 'owner' see PARA 882 note 10.
4 As to the meaning of 'grant' see PARA 836 note 1.
5 As to the meaning of 'local housing authority' see PARA 11 (definition applied by the Housing Grants, Construction and Regeneration Act 1996 s 101).
6 Housing Grants, Construction and Regeneration Act 1996 s 55(1)(a) (s 55(1) amended by SI 2002/1860). See *R v Hackney London Borough Council, ex p Gransils Investments Ltd* (1988) 20 HLR 313.
7 Housing Grants, Construction and Regeneration Act 1996 s 55(1)(b) (as amended: see note 6). An amount paid by a mortgagee under s 55(1)(b) is treated as part of the sums secured by the mortgage and may be discharged accordingly: s 55(3).
8 Housing Grants, Construction and Regeneration Act 1996 s 55(1)(c).
9 Housing Grants, Construction and Regeneration Act 1996 s 55(1)(d).
10 Housing Grants, Construction and Regeneration Act 1996 s 55(1) (as amended: see note 6). The purposes authorised for the application of capital money by the Settled Land Act 1925 s 73 (see SETTLEMENTS vol 91 (2012) PARA 709) and the Universities and College Estates Act 1925 s 26 (see EDUCATION vol 36 (2015) PARA 1329) include the making of payments under the Housing Grants, Construction and Regeneration Act 1996 s 55: s 55(4) (amended by the Trusts of Land and Appointment of Trustees Act 1996 s 25(2), Sch 4).

(iv) Supplementary Provisions

884. Provisions relating to death of an applicant. References to the applicant, in relation to a grant[1] or an application for a grant, are to be construed in relation to any time after his death as a reference to his personal representatives[2]. Where the applicant dies after liability has been incurred for any preliminary or ancillary services or charges[3], the local housing authority[4] may, if it thinks fit, pay grant in respect of some or all of those matters[5]. Where the applicant dies after the relevant works[6] have been begun and before the certified date[7], the local housing authority may, if it thinks fit, pay grant in respect of some or all of the works already carried out and other relevant works covered by the application[8].

1 As to the meaning of 'grant' see PARA 836 note 1.
2 Housing Grants, Construction and Regeneration Act 1996 s 56(1).
3 As to the meaning of 'preliminary or ancillary services or charges' see PARA 837 note 6.
4 As to the meaning of 'local housing authority' see PARA 11 (definition applied by the Housing Grants, Construction and Regeneration Act 1996 s 101).
5 Housing Grants, Construction and Regeneration Act 1996 s 56(2). See note 8.
6 As to the meaning of 'relevant works' see PARA 837.
7 As to the meaning of 'certified date' see PARA 840 note 4.
8 Housing Grants, Construction and Regeneration Act 1996 s 56(3). Nothing in s 56 may be construed as preventing the provisions as to grant conditions (ie ss 44–55) (see PARA 880 et seq) applying in relation to any payment of grant under s 56(2) (see the text and note 5) or s 56(3): s 56(4). As to the meaning of 'grant condition' see PARA 880 note 7.

885. Power of local housing authority to carry out works which would attract grant. A local housing authority[1] may by agreement with a person having the requisite interest[2] execute at his expense:

(1) any works towards the cost of which a grant[3] is payable or might be paid on an application duly made and approved[4]; and

(2) any further works which it is in its opinion necessary or desirable to execute together with the works mentioned above[5].

1 As to the meaning of 'local housing authority' see PARA 11 (definition applied by the Housing Grants, Construction and Regeneration Act 1996 s 101).
2 The reference in the Housing Grants, Construction and Regeneration Act 1996 s 57(1) to a person having the requisite interest is a reference to: (1) in the case of a qualifying houseboat or caravan, the person who is entitled to possession of the premises at which the qualifying houseboat is moored or the land on which the caravan is stationed, or who is entitled to dispose of the qualifying houseboat or caravan; or (2) in any other case, the person who has an owner's interest: s 57(2) (substituted by SI 2002/1860; and amended by the Housing Act 2004 s 224(1), (6)). As to the meaning of 'qualifying houseboat' see PARA 836 note 5; and as to the meaning of 'caravan' see PARA 836 note 6. As to the meaning of 'qualifying owner's interest' see PARA 839 note 8. As to the meaning of 'premises' see PARA 842 note 4.
3 As to the meaning of 'grant' see PARA 836 note 1.
4 Housing Grants, Construction and Regeneration Act 1996 s 57(1)(a). As to approval see PARA 844.
5 Housing Grants, Construction and Regeneration Act 1996 s 57(1)(b).

(7) HOME ENERGY EFFICIENCY AND CONSERVATION

(i) In general

886. Energy efficiency of residential accommodation. A number of statutory provisions have been enacted to promote energy efficiency in residential accommodation, including the Sustainable Energy Act 2003 which will be repealed in due course by the Energy Act 2011[1].

Until a day to be appointed, the Secretary of State must designate at least one energy efficiency aim[2] in relation to residential accommodation[3], and may at any time after such designation designate a further energy efficiency aim or aims[4]. The Secretary of State must take reasonable steps to achieve any aim so designated[5], and, in deciding which steps to take for that purpose, must consider steps relating to the heating, cooling, ventilation, lighting and insulation of the residential accommodation[6]. A designation may be withdrawn but not if its withdrawal would result in there being no designated energy efficiency aim[7]. In relation to Wales, similar provisions apply to the Welsh Ministers[8].

In relation to England, the Secretary of State was required to take reasonable steps to ensure that by 2010 the general level of energy efficiency of residential accommodation[9] in England had increased by at least 20 per cent compared with the general level of such energy efficiency in 2000[10].

1 The Sustainable Energy Act 2003 s 2 is repealed by the Energy Act 2011 s 110(3) as from a day to be appointed under s 121(1); at the date at which this volume states the law, no such day had been appointed. As to the financing and facilitation of the installation of energy efficiency measures in homes under the green deal plan see the Energy Act 2011 Pt 1 Ch 1 (ss 1–41); and PARA 889 et seq. As to energy efficiency in the private rented sector see Pt 1 Ch 2 (ss 42–53); and LANDLORD AND TENANT vol 62 (2016) PARA 317 et seq.

2 'Energy efficiency aim' means an aim which: (1) is contained in a published document; (2) relates to the energy efficiency of residential accommodation in England; and (3) is compatible with EU obligations and any other international obligations of the United Kingdom: Sustainable Energy Act 2003 s 2(2) (amended by SI 2011/1043). As to the meaning of 'United Kingdom' see PARA 60 note 10. If a designated energy efficiency aim ceases to meet the condition in head (3), it ceases to be designated under the Sustainable Energy Act 2003 s 2 but if this results in there being no energy efficiency aim so designated, the Secretary of State must without delay designate a new energy efficiency aim: s 2(7). As to the Secretary of State see PARA 7.

3 Sustainable Energy Act 2003 s 2(1). For these purposes, 'residential accommodation' has the meaning given by the Home Energy Conservation Act 1995 s 1 (see PARA 901 note 6): Sustainable Energy Act 2003 s 2(9).

4 Sustainable Energy Act 2003 s 2(3). An aim or a withdrawal or cessation of an aim must be published in such a way as the appropriate national authority considers appropriate, and a designation may be contained in the same document as the aim itself: s 2(8).

5 Sustainable Energy Act 2003 s 2(4).

6 Sustainable Energy Act 2003 s 2(5).

7 Sustainable Energy Act 2003 s 2(6).

8 See the Sustainable Energy Act 2003 s 3 (amended by SI 2011/1043). This provision is not repealed.

9 For these purposes, 'residential accommodation' has the meaning given by the Home Energy Conservation Act 1995 s 1 (see PARA 901 note 6): Housing Act 2004 s 217(3) (repealed: see note 10).

10 Housing Act 2004 s 217(1) (s 217 repealed by the Energy Act 2011 s 118(5) as from 21 March 2012). Nothing in the Housing Act 2004 s 217 affected the duties of the Secretary of State under the Sustainable Energy Act 2003 s 2 (see the text and notes 1–6): Housing Act 2004 s 217(2) (repealed).

887. Reducing fuel poverty: England. The Secretary of State[1] must make regulations setting out an objective for addressing the situation of persons in England who live in fuel poverty, and those regulations must specify a target date for achieving the objective[2]. A person is to be regarded as living 'in fuel poverty' if he is a member of a household living on a lower income in a home which cannot be kept warm at reasonable cost[3]. The objective is to ensure that as many as is reasonably practicable of the homes in which such persons live have a minimum energy efficiency rating of Band C as determined by the Fuel Poverty Energy Efficiency Rating Methodology[4]. This objective is to be achieved by 31 December 2030[5].

The Secretary of State must prepare and publish a strategy setting out his policies for achieving the objective above by the target date specified in the regulations[6]. The strategy must be published within six months of the day on which the first regulations come into force[7]. The strategy must: (1) describe the households to which it applies; (2) specify a comprehensive package of measures for achieving the objective by the target date; and (3) specify interim objectives to be achieved and target dates for achieving them[8]. The Secretary of State must take such steps as are in his opinion necessary to implement the strategy[9].

The Secretary of State must: (a) from time to time assess the impact of steps taken and the progress made in achieving the objectives and meeting the target dates; (b) make any revision of the strategy which the Secretary of State thinks appropriate in consequence of the assessment; and (c) from time to time publish reports on such assessments[10]. If further regulations are made revising an objective or the target date for achieving it, and the Secretary of State considers that changes to the strategy are necessary or desirable as a result of those regulations, the Secretary of State must revise the strategy within six months of the day on which those regulations come into force[11]. If the Secretary of State revises the strategy, he must publish the strategy as revised[12]. In preparing the strategy or any revision of the strategy, the Secretary of State must consult: (i) local authorities[13] or associations of local authorities; (ii) persons appearing to the Secretary of State to represent the interests of persons living in fuel poverty; (iii) the Gas and Electricity Markets Authority; and (iv) such other persons as the Secretary of State thinks fit[14].

1 As to the Secretary of State see PARA 7.
2 Warm Homes and Energy Conservation Act 2000 s 1A(1), (2) (ss 1A, 1B added by the Energy Act 2013 s 145(1), (2)). As to reducing fuel poverty in Wales see PARA 888. Regulations under the Warm Homes and Energy Conservation Act 2000 s 1A must be made by statutory instrument; and a statutory instrument containing such regulations may not be made unless a draft of the instrument has been laid before and approved by a resolution of each House of Parliament: s 1A(3) (as so added). The Secretary of State must lay a draft of the instrument before each House of Parliament within six months of the day on which the Energy Act 2013 s 145 comes into force (ie 18 February 2014: see the Energy Act 2013 s 156(2)(i)): Warm Homes and Energy Conservation Act 2000 s 1A(3) (as so added). For regulations made under s 1A see the Fuel Poverty (England) Regulations 2014, SI 2014/3220.
    As to reducing fuel poverty in Wales see PARA 888. As to the financing and facilitation of the installation of energy efficiency measures in homes under the green deal plan see the Energy Act 2011 Pt 1 Ch 1 (ss 1–41); and PARA 889 et seq. As to energy efficiency in the private rented sector see Pt 1 Ch 2 (ss 42–53); and LANDLORD AND TENANT vol 62 (2016) PARA 317 et seq.
3 Warm Homes and Energy Conservation Act 2000 s 1(1). The Secretary of State (as respects England) or the Welsh Ministers (as respects Wales) may, after consulting persons appearing to the Secretary of State or the Welsh Ministers to represent the interests of persons living in fuel poverty and such other persons as the Secretary of State or the Assembly thinks fit, by regulations: (1) specify what is to be regarded as a lower income or a reasonable cost or the circumstances in which a home is to be regarded for those purposes as being warm; or (2) substitute for the definition of 'in fuel poverty' such other definition as may be specified in the regulations: s 1(2), (3). Regulations made under s 1(2) must be made by statutory instrument and a statutory instrument containing such regulations made by the by the Secretary of State is subject to annulment in pursuance of a resolution of either House of Parliament: s 1(4).
4 Fuel Poverty (England) Regulations 2014, SI 2014/3220, reg 2(1), (2). The Fuel Poverty Energy Efficiency Rating Methodology is that dated 17 July 2014.
5 Fuel Poverty (England) Regulations 2014, SI 2014/3220, reg 2(3).
6 Warm Homes and Energy Conservation Act 2000 s 1B(1) (as added: see note 2).
7 Warm Homes and Energy Conservation Act 2000 s 1B(2) (as added: see note 2). The Fuel Poverty (England) Regulations 2014, SI 2014/3220, came into force on 5 December 2014: see reg 1.
8 Warm Homes and Energy Conservation Act 2000 s 1B(3) (as added: see note 2).
9 Warm Homes and Energy Conservation Act 2000 s 1B(4) (as added: see note 2). See *R (on the application of Friends of the Earth) v Secretary of State for Business Enterprise and Regulatory Reform* [2008] EWHC 2518 (Admin), [2009] PTSR 529, [2008] All ER (D) 232 (Oct) (government able to have regard to its overall budget and other calls on resources in deciding steps to take to implement strategy); affd in part [2009] EWCA Civ 810, [2010] HLR 313, [2009] All ER (D) 331 (Jul). Any expenses of the Secretary of State under the Warm Homes and Energy Conservation Act 2000, and any increase attributable to that Act in the sums payable under any other Act, are to be paid out of money provided by Parliament: s 3.
10 Warm Homes and Energy Conservation Act 2000 s 1B(5) (as added: see note 2).
11 Energy Conservation Act 2000 s 1B(6) (as added: see note 3).
12 Warm Homes and Energy Conservation Act 2000 s 1B(7) (as added: see note 2).
13 'Local authority' means, in relation to England, the council of a county, district or London borough, the Common Council of the City of London or the Council of the Isles of Scilly: Warm Homes and Energy Conservation Act 2000 s 4(1)(a).
14 Warm Homes and Energy Conservation Act 2000 s 1B(8) (as added: see note 2).

888. Strategy for reducing fuel poverty: Wales. It is the duty of the appropriate authority[1] to prepare and publish, before the end of the period of 12 months beginning with the relevant commencement[2], a strategy setting out its policies for ensuring, by means including the taking of measures to ensure the efficient use of energy, that as far as is reasonably practicable persons do not live in fuel poverty[3]. The strategy must: (1) describe the households to which it applies; (2) specify a comprehensive package of measures for ensuring the efficient use of energy, such as the installation of appropriate equipment or insulation; (3) specify interim objectives to be achieved and target dates for achieving them; and (4) specify a target date[4] for achieving the objective of ensuring that as far as is reasonably practicable persons in Wales do not live in fuel poverty[5].

In preparing the strategy or any revision of the strategy, the appropriate authority must consult: (a) local authorities[6] or associations of local authorities; (b) persons appearing to the appropriate authority to represent the interests of persons living in fuel poverty; (c) the Gas and Electricity Markets Authority and Citizens Advice; and (d) such other persons as it thinks fit[7].

The appropriate authority must take such steps as are in its opinion necessary to implement the strategy[8]. The appropriate authority must: (i) from time to time assess the impact of steps taken to implement the strategy and the progress made in achieving the objectives and meeting the target dates; (ii) make any revision of the strategy which it considers appropriate in consequence of the assessment; and (iii) from time to time publish reports on such assessments[9]. If the appropriate authority revises the strategy, it must publish the strategy as revised[10].

1 'The appropriate authority' means, as respects Wales, the Welsh Ministers: Warm Homes and Energy Conservation Act 2000 s 2(8) (amended by the Energy Act 2013 s 145(1), (3)(d)(i)); Government of Wales Act 2006 s 162, Sch 11 para 30. As to the Welsh Ministers see PARA 7.
2 'The relevant commencement' means, as respects Wales, 1 April 2002: Warm Homes and Energy Conservation Act 2000 s 2(8) (amended by the Energy Act 2013 s 145(1), (3)(d)(ii)).
3 Warm Homes and Energy Conservation Act 2000 s 2(1) (amended by the Energy Act 2013 s 145(1), (3)(b)). As to when a person is to be regarded as living 'in fuel poverty' see PARA 887 note 2.
    As to reducing fuel poverty in England see PARA 887. As to the financing and facilitation of the installation of energy efficiency measures in homes under the green deal plan see the Energy Act 2011 Pt 1 Ch 1 (ss 1–41); and PARA 889 et seq. As to energy efficiency in the private rented sector see Pt 1 Ch 2 (ss 42–53); and LANDLORD AND TENANT vol 62 (2016) PARA 317 et seq.
4 The target date specified must be not more than 15 years after the date on which the strategy is published: Warm Homes and Energy Conservation Act 2000 s 2(3).
5 Warm Homes and Energy Conservation Act 2000 s 2(2) (amended by the Energy Act 2013 s 145(1), (3)(c)).
6 'Local authority' means, in relation to Wales, the council of a county or county borough: Warm Homes and Energy Conservation Act 2000 s 4(1)(b).
7 Warm Homes and Energy Conservation Act 2000 s 2(4) (amended by SI 2014/631).
8 Warm Homes and Energy Conservation Act 2000 s 2(5). See *R (on the application of Friends of the Earth) v Secretary of State for Business Enterprise and Regulatory Reform* [2008] EWHC 2518 (Admin), [2009] PTSR 529, [2008] All ER (D) 232 (Oct) (government able to have regard to its overall budget and other calls on resources in deciding steps to take to implement strategy); affd in part [2009] EWCA Civ 810, [2010] HLR 313, [2009] All ER (D) 331 (Jul).
9 Warm Homes and Energy Conservation Act 2000 s 2(6).
10 Warm Homes and Energy Conservation Act 2000 s 2(7).

(ii) Green Deal

889. Green deal plans. For the purposes of Chapter 1 of Part 1 of the Energy Act 2011[1], an energy plan is an arrangement made by the occupier or owner of a property for a person to make energy efficiency improvements to the property[2]. An energy plan is a green deal plan if the energy efficiency improvements are to be paid for wholly or partly in instalments, and all of the requirements listed in heads (1)–(5) below are met in relation to the plan at the time when it is made[3]. The requirements are:

(1) the property is an eligible property[4];

(2) the energy efficiency improvements fall within a description specified in an order made by the Secretary of State ('qualifying energy improvements')[5];

(3) the conditions as to assessment of the property[6] and other matters have been met;

(4) the conditions as to the terms of the plan[7] and other matters are met; and

(5) a relevant energy supplier[8] supplies, or is to supply, energy to the property[9].

The following provisions apply to a green deal plan from the time when:

(a) improvements have been installed[10];

(b) the plan is confirmed[11]; and

(c) the requirements of any supplementary provision imposed as to documents[12] are met[13].

The payments in instalments agreed in the plan are to be:

(i) made by the person who is for the time being liable to pay the energy bills[14] for the property;

(ii) made to the relevant energy supplier through the energy bills for the property;

(iii) recoverable as a debt by the relevant energy supplier from the person referred to in head (i); and

(iv) recovered and held by the relevant energy supplier as agent and trustee for the person who made the improvements (unless the relevant energy supplier is also that person)[15].

This applies irrespective of whether the person referred to in head (i) is the person who entered into the plan[16].

The occupier or owner who makes the arrangement for a person to make energy efficiency improvements is the 'improver' and the person who makes the improvements is the 'green deal provider'[17]. The person referred to in head (i) is the 'bill payer'[18]. References to energy efficiency improvements, in relation to a property, are to measures for improving efficiency in the use in the property of electricity, gas conveyed through pipes or any other source of energy which is specified in an order made by the Secretary of State, or measures falling within head (A) or (B) below[19], namely if they are:

(A) any of the following: (I) measures for increasing the amount of electricity generated, or heat produced, by microgeneration[20]; (II) any other measures for increasing the amount of electricity generated, or heat produced, using low-emissions sources or technologies[21]; or (III) measures for reducing the consumption of such energy as is mentioned above[22], and they are specified in an order made by the Secretary of State[23];

(B) they are: (I) installed at the property for the purpose of supplying to it any of the following types of energy: electricity generated by a generating station operated for the purposes of producing heat, or a cooling effect, in association with electricity; heat produced in association with electricity or steam produced from (or air or water heated by) such heat; any gas or liquid subjected to a cooling effect produced in association with electricity; and (II) specified in an order made by the Secretary of State[24].

The Secretary of State may by order make such amendments to the Consumer Credit Act 1974, the Financial Services and Markets Act 2000 and any statutory instrument made under that Act as the Secretary of State considers appropriate in consequence of provision made by or under the Chapter 1 of Part 1 of the Energy Act 2011[25]. Before exercising this power, the Secretary of State must consult the Financial Conduct Authority, and such other persons as the Secretary of State considers appropriate[26].

1   The following provisions apply for the purposes of the Energy Act 2011 Pt 1 Ch 1 (ss 1–41): ss 1(1), 2(1). That Chapter applies to England and Wales: see s 120(1), (2)(a)–(c). These provisions bind the Crown: s 41.
2   Energy Act 2011 s 1(2). 'Energy' (except in s 2), 'occupier' and 'owner' have the meaning given in regulations made by the Secretary of State: s 2(9). As to such regulations see the Green Deal Framework (Disclosure, Acknowledgment, Redress etc) Regulations 2012, SI 2012/2079 (amended by SI 2012/3021, SI 2013/139, SI 2013/1881 and SI 2014/549). 'Energy', except in the Energy Act 2011 s 2 and the Green Deal Framework (Disclosure, Acknowledgment, Redress etc) Regulations 2012, SI 2012/2079, reg 28(2), means electricity: 'occupier' means, in respect of a property, a person who lawfully occupies a property but is not an owner of it; and 'owner', except in regs 36 and 37 and Pt 8 (regs 51–85), means, in respect of a property, a person who is: (1) a relevant title holder; (2) a tenant under a lease of the property; or (3) a licensee under a licence of the property, but does not include a mortgagee not in possession of the property: reg 4(1), (2). 'Relevant title holder' means a person who, in respect of a property in England or Wales, is entitled to dispose of the fee simple of the property whether in possession or reversion: reg 2(1). As to the Secretary of State see PARA 7. The Secretary of State here concerned is the Secretary of State for Business, Energy and Industrial Strategy.
3   Energy Act 2011 s 1(3). As to the obligation on those selling and letting out green deal properties to disclose information about the green deal plan see the Energy Act 2011 ss 12–16; and LANDLORD AND TENANT vol 62 (2016) PARAS 315-316.
4   For this purpose, a property is an eligible property unless it falls within a description specified in an order made by the Secretary of State: s 1(9).
5   As to energy efficiency improvements specified for the purposes of head (2) in the text as qualifying energy improvements see the Green Deal (Qualifying Energy Improvements) Order 2012, SI 2012/2105 (amended by SI 2014/2020).
6   Ie the conditions mentioned in the Energy Act 2011 s 4: see PARA 891.
7   Ie the conditions mentioned in the Energy Act 2011 s 5: see PARA 892.
8   'Relevant energy supplier' has the meaning given in regulations made by the Secretary of State, ie: (1) a person who: (a) supplies energy to a property; (b) holds a licence issued under the Electricity Act 1989 s 6(1)(d) (electricity supply licences); and (c) is a party to the Green Deal Arrangements Agreement; or (2) where no electricity is supplied to a green deal property, the person who last satisfied head (1) in respect of that property: Energy Act 2011 s 2(9); Green Deal Framework (Disclosure, Acknowledgment, Redress etc) Regulations 2012, SI 2012/2079, reg 4(2). 'Green Deal Arrangements Agreement' means the agreement with persons licensed under the Electricity Act 1989 s 6(1)(d) (electricity supply licences) to be entered into by green deal providers under the Green Deal Framework (Disclosure, Acknowledgment, Redress etc) Regulations 2012, SI 2012/2079, reg 24(1)(b), regarding the collection of green deal instalments by electricity suppliers; and 'green deal instalments' means payments in instalments which are payable under a green deal plan: reg 2(1).
9   Energy Act 2011 s 1(4).
10 Ie in accordance with the Energy Act 2011 s 7: see PARA 893.
11 Ie in accordance with the Energy Act 2011 s 8: see PARA 894.
12 Ie by virtue of the Energy Act 2011 s 9: see PARA 894 note 10.
13 Energy Act 2011 s 1(5).
14 'Energy bill' has the meaning given in regulations made by the Secretary of State, ie except in the Energy Act 2011 s 4(4) and the Green Deal Framework (Disclosure, Acknowledgment, Redress etc) Regulations 2012, SI 2012/2079, Pt 5 (regs 27–37): (1) where electricity is supplied to a green deal property, a demand for payment issued by the relevant energy supplier to the bill payer in respect of the supply of electricity to the property; (2) where no electricity is supplied to a green deal property, a demand by the relevant energy supplier for payment of green deal instalments:

Energy Act 2011 s 2(9); Green Deal Framework (Disclosure, Acknowledgment, Redress etc) Regulations 2012, SI 2012/2079, reg 4(2). For the purpose of the Energy Act 2011 s 4(4) and the Green Deal Framework (Disclosure, Acknowledgment, Redress etc) Regulations 2012, SI 2012/2079, Pt 5, 'energy bill' means a charge for the supply of any one or more of: (a) electricity to a property; (b) heat or hot water to the property; (c) fuel, other than electricity, used to heat a property or to heat water at a property: reg 5.

15 Energy Act 2011 s 1(6). Section 1(6) is subject to provision made in regulations under s 34 (see note 18; and PARA 895), and any suspension or cancellation, by virtue of provision made in regulations under s 3(3)(h) or (i) (see PARA 890 heads (h) and (i)), s 6(4) (see PARA 890), s 16 (see LANDLORD AND TENANT vol 62 (2016) PARAS 315-316) or s 35 (see PARA 890), of liability to make payments: s 1(8).

16 Energy Act 2011 s 1(7).

17 Energy Act 2011 s 2(2).

18 Energy Act 2011 s 2(3). Regulations under s 2(9) may also make provision as to the circumstances in which a person who is not a bill payer for these purposes may be treated as a bill payer for those purposes: s 2(10). As to such regulations see the Green Deal Framework (Disclosure, Acknowledgment, Redress etc) Regulations 2012, SI 2012/2079, reg 6. 'Bill payer' is the person described in the Energy Act 2011 s 1(6)(a) and, where no electricity is supplied to a green deal property, has the meaning given by the Green Deal Framework (Disclosure, Acknowledgment, Redress etc) Regulations 2012, SI 2012/2079, reg 6: reg 2(1).

19 Energy Act 2011 s 2(4).

20 Ie within the meaning given by the Climate Change and Sustainable Energy Act 2006 s 26(1): see ENERGY AND CLIMATE CHANGE vol 42 (2011) PARA 114.

21 For the purposes of head (A)(bb) in the text, electricity is generated, or heat is produced, using low-emissions sources or technologies if it is generated, or produced, by plant which relies wholly or mainly on a source of energy or a technology mentioned in the Climate Change and Sustainable Energy Act 2006 s 26(2) (see ENERGY AND CLIMATE CHANGE vol 42 (2011) PARA 114): Energy Act 2011 s 2(7).

22 Ie such energy as is mentioned in the Energy Act 2011 s 2(4).

23 Energy Act 2011 s 2(5). As to the order made under s 2(4), (5) see the Green Deal (Energy Efficiency Improvements) Order 2012, SI 2012/2106.

24 Energy Act 2011 s 2(6). For the purposes of s 2(6) 'generating station' and 'supplying' are to be read in accordance with the Electricity Act 1989 s 64(1): Energy Act 2011 s 2(8). See ENERGY AND CLIMATE CHANGE vol 43 (2011) PARA 507.

25 Energy Act 2011 s 30(1) (amended by SI 2013/1881). See the Consumer Credit Act 1974 (Green Deal) (Amendment) Order 2014, SI 2014/436; and the Financial Services and Markets Act 2000 (Regulated Activities) (Green Deal) (Amendment) Order 2014, SI 2014/1850. As to the Financial Conduct Authority see FINANCIAL SERVICES REGULATION vol 50 (2016) PARAS 5, 6 et seq.

26 Energy Act 2011 s 30(2) (amended by SI 2013/1881).

890. Framework regulations. The Secretary of State[1] must by regulations ('the framework regulations'[2]) establish a scheme making provision for the Secretary of State:

(1) to authorise persons to act as green deal assessors, green deal providers or green deal installers in connection with green deal plans[3] (either individually or through membership of a body specified in, or authorised under, the scheme); and

(2) to regulate the conduct of those assessors, providers or installers ('green deal participants')[4].

The scheme established by the framework regulations may, in particular, make provision:

(a) requiring the payment of a fee in connection with initial or continued authorisation under the scheme;

(b) for the establishment and maintenance of a register of green deal participants and of persons from whom authorisation under the scheme has been withdrawn;

(c) requiring green deal participants to provide the information required under the scheme;

(d) for the issuing, revision or revocation of a code of practice[5];

(e) requiring green deal participants to comply with the code of practice as a condition of their authorisation;

(f) requiring green deal providers to enter into an agreement with the holder of a gas or electricity supply licence[6] and to comply with that agreement as a condition of their authorisation;

(g) requiring that an agreement mentioned in head (f) be approved by the Secretary of State before being entered into;

(h) for securing compliance with any condition or any other requirement of the scheme, code or agreement;

(i) as to the consequences of non-compliance with any such condition or requirement[7].

The code of practice issued for the purposes of the scheme may, in particular, make provision:

(i) as to the qualification and training of green deal participants;

(ii) as to their handling of queries or complaints;

(iii) requiring green deal participants to have such arrangements for insurance as are specified in the code;

(iv) as to the payment of green deal assessors by green deal providers or green deal installers and the payment of green deal installers by green deal providers;

(v) as to the circumstances in which green deal assessors may charge customers for qualifying assessments of properties and as to the amount of any such charge;

(vi) requiring green deal assessors to act with impartiality;

(vii) as to the provision of information by green deal providers to improvers and bill payers and prospective improvers and bill payers;

(viii) as to marketing in connection with green deal plans[8].

The code may include provision for regulating a body specified in head (1) or authorised as a green deal participant[9].

The scheme and the code may make different provision for different circumstances or cases or for different purposes[10]. The provision made by the scheme or code in relation to green deal participants may also extend to matters in connection with any energy plans which are not green deal plans[11]. The provision made for the purposes of head (h) or (i) may, in particular, include provision enabling the Secretary of State to: (A) cancel any liability to pay for a qualifying assessment[12] of a property; (B) require a green deal provider to suspend or cancel the liability of a bill payer[13] to make payments under a green deal plan; (C) require a green deal participant to rectify a qualifying energy improvement or its installation; (D) require a green deal participant to pay compensation or a financial penalty; (E) withdraw, or require a body specified or authorised to withdraw, an authorisation to act as a green deal participant; (F) withdraw authorisation from a body authorised for the purposes of head (1) as a body whose members are authorised to act as green deal participants[14].

The framework regulations may make provision for dealing with cases where, at the time when a plan is entered into the improver and the bill payer are different persons or the bill payer at the time when a plan is entered into is a different person from the bill payer at any subsequent time (a 'subsequent bill payer')[15]. The framework regulations may make provision for the purpose of providing redress in cases where a permission or consent in respect of the improvements[16] was not obtained or was improperly obtained[17].

The Secretary of State may by order provide for any function conferred on the Secretary of State in connection with the scheme established by the framework regulations, and any function exercisable under the framework regulations by virtue of the power to provide redress where permission or consent was not obtained[18], to be exercised instead by a public body specified in the order[19].

If provision is included in a scheme or regulations by virtue of heads (h) and (i) above[20], the Secretary of State must by regulations provide for a right of appeal to a court or tribunal against any sanction imposed, or other action taken, by the Secretary of State or any public body specified in an order[21] as able to exercise functions of the Secretary of State[22].

Before making the first framework regulations, the Secretary of State must lay before Parliament a report on what, if any, steps the Secretary of State has taken to encourage green deal installation apprenticeships[23].

1 As to the Secretary of State see PARAS 7, 889 note 2.
2 Energy Act 2011 s 3(2).
3 As to the meaning of 'green deal plan' see PARA 889.
4 Energy Act 2011 s 3(1). As to such regulations see the Green Deal Framework (Disclosure, Acknowledgment, Redress etc) Regulations 2012, SI 2012/2079; and PARA 889. The Energy Act 2011 s 3 is without prejudice to the powers conferred on the Secretary of State by other provisions of Pt 1 Ch 1 (ss 1–41) to make provision in or under the framework regulations: s 3(10). For general provision as to the making of regulations and orders under Pt 1 Ch 1 see s 40.
5 As to the parliamentary procedure in relation to code of practice see the Energy Act 2011 s 39. In Pt 1 Ch 1, references to a code of practice include references to a code of practice which has been revised by virtue of s 3(3)(d): s 3(11).
6 Ie a licence under the Gas Act 1986 s 7 or 7A (gas transporter, shipper or supply licences: see ENERGY AND CLIMATE CHANGE vol 42 (2011) PARAS 264, 266) or the Electricity Act 1989 s 6(1)(c) or (d) (electricity distributor and supply licences: see ENERGY AND CLIMATE CHANGE vol 43 (2011) PARA 539).
7 Energy Act 2011 s 3(3). See the Green Deal Framework (Disclosure, Acknowledgment, Redress etc) Regulations 2012, SI 2012/2079, Pt 2 (regs 8–10), Pt 3 (regs 11–18).
8 Energy Act 2011 s 3(4). See the Green Deal Code of Practice (Version 4), dated 23 June 2014.
9 Energy Act 2011 s 3(5).
10 Energy Act 2011 s 3(6).
11 Energy Act 2011 s 3(7).
12 For these purposes references to a qualifying assessment are to an energy efficiency assessment which meets the requirements specified in the framework regulations and deals with such other matters as may be so specified: Energy Act 2011 s 3(9). See the Green Deal Framework (Disclosure, Acknowledgment, Redress etc) Regulations 2012, SI 2012/2079, reg 7.
13 As to the meaning of 'bill payer' see PARA 889.
14 Energy Act 2011 s 3(8).
15 Energy Act 2011 s 6(1). Provision which may be made by virtue of s 6(1) includes: (1) provision requiring the term included in the plan by virtue of s 5(2)(a)(i) (see PARA 892 head (a)(i)) to be one to which the bill payer different from the improver (ie mentioned in s 6(1)(a)) has consented; and (2) provision as to the terms of the plan which are to bind or benefit that bill payer or a subsequent bill payer: s 6(2). Section 6(1) is subject to s 1(6) (see PARA 889): s 6(3).
16 Ie a condition or consent mentioned in the Energy Act 2011 s 5(2)(b): see PARA 892 head (b).
17 Energy Act 2011 s 6(4). Provision included in framework regulations by virtue of s 6(4) may, in particular, enable the Secretary of State to: (1) require a green deal provider to suspend or cancel the liability of a bill payer to make payments under a green deal plan; (2) require a green deal provider to refund any such payments that have already been made; (3) require an improver to pay compensation to the green deal provider in respect of the suspension, cancellation or refund: s 6(5).
18 Ie under the Energy Act 2011 s 6(4).
19 See the Energy Act 2011 s 31. As to the exercise of scheme functions on behalf of the Secretary of State or the public body so specified in an order under s 31, see s 32. Where a function is delegated to a public body, the Secretary of State may make regulations which require the public body to collect information on specified matters and provide the Secretary of State with a report on those matters at a specified time: see s 33.
20 Ie by virtue of the Energy Act 2011 s 3(3)(h) or (i).
21 Ie an order made by virtue of the Energy Act 2011 s 31: see s 35(7)(a).

22 Energy Act 2011 s 35(1), (2). Regulations under s 35(2) may, in particular, include provision: (1) as to the jurisdiction of the court or tribunal to which an appeal may be made; (2) as to the persons who may make an appeal; (3) as to the grounds on which an appeal may be made; (4) as to the procedure for making an appeal (including any fee which may be payable); (5) suspending the effect of a sanction or other action being appealed against, pending determination of the appeal; (6) as to the powers of the court or tribunal to which an appeal is made; (7) as to how any sum payable in pursuance of a decision of the court or tribunal is to be recoverable: s 35(3). The provision referred to in head (6) includes provision conferring on the court or tribunal to which an appeal is made power: (a) to confirm the sanction imposed or action taken; (b) to withdraw the sanction or action; (c) to impose a different sanction or take different action; (d) to remit the decision whether to confirm the sanction or other action, or any matter relating to that decision, to the person who imposed the sanction or took the action; (e) to award costs: s 35(4). If the Secretary of State considers it appropriate for the purpose of, or in consequence of, any provision falling within head (1), (4), (6) or (7), regulations under s 35(2) may revoke or amend any subordinate legislation: s 35(5). 'Subordinate legislation' has the meaning given in the Interpretation Act 1978 s 2(1) and includes an instrument made under a Measure or Act of the National Assembly for Wales: Energy Act 2011 s 35(7)(b). See the Green Deal Framework (Disclosure, Acknowledgment, Redress etc) Regulations 2012, SI 2012/2079, reg 87, providing for appeal to the First-tier Tribunal.

23 Energy Act 2011 s 38(1). A 'green deal installation apprenticeship' is an apprenticeship which provides training on how to install energy efficiency improvements at properties: s 38(2).

891. Assessment of the property and other matters. The conditions as to assessment of the property and other matters which are required to be met for an energy plan to be a green deal plan[1] are the conditions set out below, and such other conditions (whether relating to the green deal assessor, the green deal provider[2], the improver[3] or any other person) as are specified in the framework regulations[4]. The first condition is that a qualifying assessment[5] of the property has been carried out by a person authorised by virtue of the framework regulations to act as a green deal assessor[6]. The second condition is that the green deal assessor has recommended the energy efficiency improvements[7]. The third condition is that the green deal provider has given an estimate, on the basis specified in the framework regulations, of the savings likely to be made on the energy bills for the property if the improvements are carried out[8]. The fourth condition is that the green deal provider has given an estimate, on the basis specified in the framework regulations, of the period over which such savings are likely to be made[9]. The fifth condition is that the green deal provider is authorised by virtue of the framework regulations to act as a green deal provider[10]. The sixth condition is that the green deal provider has offered to carry out the improvements on the basis that the whole or part of the cost will be repaid in instalments over a period after the improvements have been made[11]. The seventh condition is that the green deal provider meets any requirement specified in the framework regulations as to the relationship between the estimated total of the proposed instalments, and the estimate of the savings likely to be made[12]. The eighth condition is that the green deal provider meets any requirement specified in the framework regulations as to the relationship between the period for which the instalments are proposed to be paid, and the estimated period over which the savings are likely to be made[13].

1 Ie for the purposes of the Energy Act 2011 s 1(4)(c): see PARA 889 head (3). As to the meaning of 'energy plan' and 'green deal plan' see PARA 889.

2 As to the meaning of 'green deal provider' see PARA 889.

3 As to the meaning of 'improver' see PARA 889.

4 Energy Act 2011 s 4(1). As to the meaning of 'framework regulations' see PARA 890. See the Green Deal Framework (Disclosure, Acknowledgment, Redress etc) Regulations 2012, SI 2012/2079; and PARA 890.

5 The reference to a qualifying assessment is to be read in accordance with the Energy Act 2011 s 3(9) (see PARA 890 note 12): s 4(10).

6 Energy Act 2011 s 4(2).
7 Energy Act 2011 s 4(3). As to the meaning of 'energy efficiency improvements' see PARA 889.
8 Energy Act 2011 s 4(4). See the Green Deal Framework (Disclosure, Acknowledgment, Redress etc) Regulations 2012, SI 2012/2079, reg 27.
9 Energy Act 2011 s 4(5). See the Green Deal Framework (Disclosure, Acknowledgment, Redress etc) Regulations 2012, SI 2012/2079, reg 28.
10 Energy Act 2011 s 4(6).
11 Energy Act 2011 s 4(7).
12 Energy Act 2011 s 4(8). See the Green Deal Framework (Disclosure, Acknowledgment, Redress etc) Regulations 2012, SI 2012/2079, regs 29–37 (reg 30 amended by SI 2013/139).
13 Energy Act 2011 s 4(9). See the Green Deal Framework (Disclosure, Acknowledgment, Redress etc) Regulations 2012, SI 2012/2079, reg 31.

892. Terms of the plan and related matters. The conditions as to the terms of the plan and other matters which are required to be met for an energy plan to qualify as a green deal plan[1] are:
(1)   the conditions set out in below; and
(2)   such other conditions as are specified in the framework regulations[2].
The first condition is that the plan includes the following terms:
(a)   a term in which the improver[3] agrees to:
    (i)   the amounts of the payments in instalments and the intervals at which, and period for which, they are payable; and
    (ii)   such other matters as are specified in the regulations;
(b)   a term in which the improver confirms that any necessary permissions or consents have been obtained in respect of the improvements;
(c)   a term providing that the green deal provider[4] may not take a charge over any person's property by way of security for payments;
(d)   a term providing that the green deal plan does not prevent the bill payer[5] from changing the intervals at which energy bills are to be paid[6].
The second condition is that the plan does not include any of the following terms:
(A)   a term making a person liable to make any payments under the green deal plan otherwise than in respect of the period for which the person is the bill payer in relation to the property;
(B)   a term requiring the bill payer to make in any circumstances an early repayment of the whole or part of the amount outstanding under the green deal plan (except in accordance with the framework regulations or regulations dealing with special circumstances[7], or provision made under them);
(C)   a term providing for money to be advanced to the improver (except in accordance with the framework regulations or provision made under them)[8].
The third condition is that the agreements mentioned in head (a) and the permissions and consents mentioned in head (b) have not been withdrawn before the end of the period of 14 days beginning with the last day on which they were given[9].
The conditions which may be specified in the framework regulations by virtue of head (2) include, in particular:
(I)   a condition that the plan includes a term so specified enabling the early repayment of the whole or part of the amount outstanding under the plan and making provision as to the calculation of the amount payable and any fee;

(II)   a condition that the plan includes a term so specified guaranteeing the improvements and making provision as to who is to benefit from the guarantee;

(III)   a condition that the plan includes a term so specified as to how any problems with the improvements installed, or arising in connection with the installation of them, are to be dealt with; and

(IV)   a condition requiring the agreements mentioned in head (a) to be in the form specified in the framework regulations[10].

1 Ie for the purposes of the Energy Act 2011 s 1(4)(d): see PARA 889 head (4). As to the meaning of 'energy plan' and 'green deal plan' see PARA 889.
2 Energy Act 2011 s 5(1). As to the meaning of 'framework regulations' see PARA 890. See the Green Deal Framework (Disclosure, Acknowledgment, Redress etc) Regulations 2012, SI 2012/2079; and PARA 890.
3 As to the meaning of 'improver' see PARA 889.
4 As to the meaning of 'green deal provider' see PARA 889.
5 As to the meaning of 'bill payer' see PARA 889.
6 Energy Act 2011 s 5(2).
7 Ie regulations under the Energy Act 2011 s 34: see PARA 895.
8 Energy Act 2011 s 5(3).
9 Energy Act 2011 s 5(4). References in s 5 to the agreements mentioned in head (a) in the text include references to the consent required by virtue of s 6(2)(a) (see PARA 890 note 15 head (1)): s 5(6).
10 Energy Act 2011 s 5(5).

893. Installation of improvements. For the purposes of the application of a green deal plan[1], improvements[2] are installed in accordance with the following provisions if the following three conditions are met[3]. The first condition is that the person carrying out the installation of the improvements is authorised by virtue of the framework regulations[4] to act as a green deal installer[5]. The second condition is that any product installed in making the improvements: (1) meets the standard specified in the code of practice[6] in relation to the product or description of product; or (2) is listed in a document which: (a) is issued by the Secretary of State or a person authorised by the Secretary of State in connection with the code; and (b) is referred to in the code as listing the products which are to be taken as meeting the required standard[7]. The third condition is that the carrying out of the installation meets the standard specified in the code of practice[8].

1 Ie for the purposes of the Energy Act 2011 s 1(5)(a): see PARA 889 head (a). As to the meaning of 'green deal plan' see PARA 889.
2 See PARA 889.
3 Energy Act 2011 s 7(1).
4 As to the meaning of 'framework regulations' see PARA 890. See the Green Deal Framework (Disclosure, Acknowledgment, Redress etc) Regulations 2012, SI 2012/2079; and PARA 890.
5 Energy Act 2011 s 7(2).
6 For these purposes references to the code of practice are to the code of practice issued for the purposes of the scheme under the framework regulations: Energy Act 2011 s 7(6). As to the parliamentary procedure in relation to any such code of practice see s 39. In specifying the standard in relation to a product or description of product for the purposes of head (1) in the text, the code of practice may make provision as to the testing and certification of the product or description of product: s 7(4).
7 Energy Act 2011 s 7(3). As to the Secretary of State see PARAS 7, 889 note 2.
8 Energy Act 2011 s 7(5).

894. Confirmation of plan. For the purposes of the application of a green deal plan[1], an arrangement is confirmed[2] if the following two conditions are met[3]. The first condition is that the relevant energy supplier[4] notifies the bill payer[5]: (1) that payments for the energy efficiency improvements[6] to the property are to be included in the energy bills[7] for the property from the date specified in the notification; and (2) of the amounts of those payments and the period for which they are to be made[8]. The second condition is that, as soon as practicable after the improvements have been installed, the green deal provider[9] takes one or more of the following actions as required by the framework regulations in the circumstances: (a) producing a document containing such information in connection with the plan as is specified in the regulations in the form so specified; (b) securing that a document of a description specified in the regulations is produced; or (c) securing that a document of such a description is updated[10].

The framework regulations may make provision as to the circumstances in which a document produced for the purposes of head (a) is required to be updated in accordance with the regulations[11].

Those selling and letting out a green deal property must disclose the document required to be produced or updated under the second condition, or each such document, to prospective buyers, tenants and licensees[12].

1   Ie for the purposes of the Energy Act 2011 s 1(5)(b): see PARA 889 head (b). As to the meaning of 'green deal plan' see PARA 889.
2   Ie in accordance with the Energy Act 2011 s 8.
3   Energy Act 2011 s 8(1).
4   As to the meaning of 'relevant energy supplier' see PARA 889 note 8.
5   As to the meaning of 'bill payer' see PARA 889.
6   See PARA 889.
7   As to the meaning of 'energy bill' see PARA 889 note 14.
8   Energy Act 2011 s 8(2). The date mentioned in head (1) in the text must not fall earlier than the end of the period specified in the framework regulations: s 8(3). As to the meaning of 'framework regulations' see PARA 890. See the Green Deal Framework (Disclosure, Acknowledgment, Redress etc) Regulations 2012, SI 2012/2079; and PARA 890. As to the specified period under the Energy Act 2011 s 8(3) see the Green Deal Framework (Disclosure, Acknowledgment, Redress etc) Regulations 2012, SI 2012/2079, reg 41.
9   As to the meaning of 'green deal provider' see PARA 889.
10 Energy Act 2011 s 8(4). The reference in s 8 to securing that a document is updated includes a reference to securing that a document is replaced by a document of the same description: s 8(5). As to supplementary provision in relation to the second condition see s 9: s 8(6).
    If, by virtue of s 8(4)(b) or (c), the framework regulations specify a document of a description which is required to be produced under the Energy Performance of Buildings (Certificates and Inspections) (England and Wales) Regulations 2007, SI 2007/991, or the Building Regulations 2010, SI 2010/2214, the Secretary of State may by regulations make provision amending the 2007 Regulations or the 2010 Regulations or both (as the case may require) in connection with a document required to be produced or updated by virtue of the Energy Act 2011 s 8(4)(b) or (c): s 9(1), (2), (4). The amendments made by virtue of s 9(2) may, in particular, include amendments for the purpose of requiring a document to contain additional or updated information in connection with the plan or the improvements installed under the plan: s 9(3). As to the action to be taken under s 8(4) and the specified description of document for the purposes of s 8(4)(b) see the Green Deal Framework (Disclosure, Acknowledgment, Redress etc) Regulations 2012, SI 2012/2079, reg 42. As to the Secretary of State see PARAS 7, 889 note 2.
11 See the Energy Act 2011 s 11 (amended by SI 2012/3170). As to the updating of documents see the Green Deal Framework (Disclosure, Acknowledgment, Redress etc) Regulations 2012, SI 2012/2079, regs 42A–42C (added by SI 2013/139).
12 See the Energy Act 2011 ss 12–16; and LANDLORD AND TENANT vol 62 (2016) PARAS 315–316.

895. Power of Secretary of State to deal with special circumstances. The Secretary of State[1] may by regulations make provision as to:

(1)   the circumstances in which a bill payer's[2] liability to make green deal payments to the relevant energy supplier[3] is suspended or cancelled;
(2)   the circumstances in which any suspension of liability ends;
(3)   the consequences of any suspension or cancellation;
(4)   the circumstances in which the green deal provider may require the early repayment of the whole or part of the total of the payments outstanding under a green deal plan[4].

The regulations may, in particular, include provision:

(a)   as to the procedure to be followed for securing a suspension or cancellation (including the payment of an administration fee calculated in accordance with the regulations);

(b)   as to how any payments due under a green deal plan during a period of suspension are to be paid;

(c)   as to the making of payments due under a green deal plan after a period of suspension;

(d)   as to the calculation of the amount payable on early repayment (including a fee calculated in accordance with the regulations)[5].

1   As to the Secretary of State see PARAS 7, 889 note 2.
2   As to the meaning of 'bill payer' see PARA 889. For these purposes 'bill payer' includes the person who would be the bill payer if the supply from the relevant energy supplier were not temporarily disconnected or the liability to make green deal payments were not suspended; and payments are green deal payments if they are made under a green deal plan: Energy Act 2011 s 34(3).
3   As to the meaning of 'relevant energy supplier' see PARA 889 note 8.
4   Energy Act 2011 s 34(1). As to the meaning of 'green deal plan' see PARA 889.
5   Energy Act 2011 s 34(2). As to such regulations see the Green Deal Framework (Disclosure, Acknowledgment, Redress etc) Regulations 2012, SI 2012/2079, regs 38–40.

(iii) Grants for Improvement of Energy Efficiency

896. Introduction. Under the Social Security Act 1990, grants may be payable for the improvement of energy conservation in certain dwellings[1]. Minor amendments to take account of technological advances were made by the Housing Grants, Construction and Regeneration Act 1996[2].

1   See the Social Security Act 1990 s 15; and PARA 897. There must be paid out of money provided by Parliament: (1) any expenses incurred under the Social Security Act 1990 by a Minister of the Crown; and (2) any increase attributable to the provisions of that Act in the sums payable out of such money under any other Act: s 18(1)(a), (b). A power conferred by the Social Security Act 1990 to make any regulations or an order, where the power is not expressed to be exercisable with the consent of the Treasury, is exercisable, if the Treasury so directs, only in conjunction with the Treasury: s 19(3). As to the Treasury see CONSTITUTIONAL AND ADMINISTRATIVE LAW vol 20 (2014) PARA 262 et seq. As to the power to make regulations under s 15 see PARA 897 note 5. As to the financing and facilitation of the installation of energy efficiency measures in homes under the green deal plan see the Energy Act 2011 Pt 1 Ch 1 (ss 1–41); and PARA 889 et seq.
2   See the Housing Grants, Construction and Regeneration Act 1996 s 142; and PARA 897.

897. Grants for the improvement of energy efficiency in certain dwellings etc. The appropriate national authority[1] may make or arrange for the making of grants:

(1)   towards the cost of carrying out work for the purpose of improving the thermal insulation of dwellings[2] or otherwise reducing or preventing the wastage of energy in dwellings (whether in connection with space or water heating, lighting, the use of domestic appliances or otherwise)[3]; and

(2)   where any such work is, or is to be, carried out, towards the cost of providing persons with advice on reducing or preventing the wastage of energy in dwellings[4].

However, no grants may be made under these provisions except in accordance with regulations[5] made by the appropriate national authority[6]. The regulations may make provision with respect to:

(a)   the descriptions of dwelling and work in respect of which a grant may be made[7];

(b)   the nature and extent of the advice with respect to the provision of which grants may be made[8];

(c)　　　the descriptions of person from whom an application for a grant may be entertained[9];

(d)　　　the persons to whom such an application is to be made[10];

(e)　　　the payment of such grants to persons other than the applicant[11];

(f)　　　the conditions on which such a grant may be made[12].

The regulations may specify, or make provision for determining, the amount or maximum amount of any such grant and may include provision requiring work to comply with standards of materials[13] and workmanship (whether prescribed[14] standards, or standards otherwise laid down from time to time by a prescribed person) if it is to be eligible for a grant[15]. Without prejudice to the generality of the powers conferred by these provisions, the regulations may make provision[16] for any of the following matters:

(i)　　　for appointing for any particular area a person or body of persons (an 'administering agency') to perform in that area such functions as the appropriate national authority may confer upon that person or body for the purposes of, or otherwise in connection with, these provisions (whether those functions are prescribed, or specified otherwise than in regulations)[17];

(ii)　　for the administering agency for any area to select, in accordance with criteria (whether prescribed criteria, or criteria otherwise laid down from time to time by a prescribed person), and register as the network installer for any particular locality within its area, a person or body of persons capable of carrying out, or arranging for the carrying out of, work in respect of which grants may be made, to perform in that locality such functions as the appropriate national authority or that agency may confer upon that person or body for the purposes of, or otherwise in connection with, these provisions (whether those functions are prescribed, or specified otherwise than in regulations)[18];

(iii)　　for the allocation by the appropriate national authority to an administering agency of the sums which are to be available to that agency in any period for the purpose of making grants under these provisions in that period, and for the re-allocation of any sums so allocated[19];

(iv)　　for the allocation by an administering agency to a network installer of an amount which represents the total amount of grant under these provisions which the agency determines is, or is to be, available for any period in respect of work carried out, and advice given, by that installer and any sub-contractors of his in that period, and for the re-allocation of any amount so allocated[20].

1　　The appropriate national authority may delegate any of its functions in relation to grants under the Social Security Act 1990 s 15 to such persons or bodies of persons as it may determine, and may pay to any person or body of persons to whom functions are so delegated, or upon whom functions are otherwise conferred under or by virtue of s 15, such fees as may be agreed: s 15(5). 'Functions' means powers and duties and includes the exercise of a discretion with respect to any matter: s 15(10). As to the appropriate national authority see further PARA 7.

2　　Social Security Act 1990 s 15(1)(a)(i) (s 15(1) substituted by the Housing Grants, Construction and Regeneration Act 1996 s 142). There is no statutory definition of 'dwelling' for these purposes; but cf PARA 836 note 4.

3　　Social Security Act 1990 s 15(1)(a)(ii) (as substituted: see note 2).

4　　Social Security Act 1990 s 15(1)(b) (as substituted: see note 2).

5　　The power to make regulations under the Social Security Act 1990 s 15 is exercisable by statutory instrument made, in relation to England, with the consent of the Treasury; and any statutory instrument containing such regulations is subject to annulment in pursuance of a resolution of the House of Commons or, as appropriate, the National Assembly for Wales: s 15(8). Regulations made under s 15 may make different provision with respect to any labour involved, materials used or other items comprised in the carrying out of work and may make different provision for different cases and different areas: s 15(9)(a), (b). As to the meaning of 'materials' see note 13. As to the Treasury see CONSTITUTIONAL AND ADMINISTRATIVE LAW vol 20 (2014) PARA 262 et seq. As to the regulations that have been made in relation to England see the Home Energy Efficiency Scheme (England) Regulations 2005, SI 2005/1530 (which came into force on 1 July 2005: see reg 1(1)); and PARA 898. As to the regulations that have been made in relation to Wales see the Home Energy Efficiency Schemes (Wales) Regulations 2011, SI 2011/656 (which came into force on 1 April 2011: see reg 1(1)); and PARA 899.

6 Social Security Act 1990 s 15(1) (as substituted: see note 2).
7 Social Security Act 1990 s 15(2)(a).
8 Social Security Act 1990 s 15(2)(b).
9 Social Security Act 1990 s 15(2)(c).
10 Social Security Act 1990 s 15(2)(d).
11 Social Security Act 1990 s 15(2)(e).
12 Social Security Act 1990 s 15(2)(f).
13 'Materials' includes space and water heating systems: Social Security Act 1990 s 15(10) (definition added by the Housing Grants, Construction and Regeneration Act 1996 s 142).
14 'Prescribed' means specified in, or determined in accordance with regulations under the Social Security Act 1990 s 15: s 15(10). See note 5.
15 Social Security Act 1990 s 15(3). The provisions of s 15(1)–(3) apply in relation to any building in multiple occupation as they apply in relation to a dwelling; and for this purpose 'building in multiple occupation' means a building which is occupied by persons who do not form a single household, exclusive of any part of the building which is occupied as a separate dwelling by persons who form a single household: s 15(4).
16 Regulations made by virtue of the Social Security Act 1990 s 15(6) may include provision: (1) for the making of appointments, or the conferring of functions, under s 15(6) to be effected in whole or in part by or under a contract made between prescribed persons and for requiring any such contract to contain prescribed terms and conditions or terms and conditions with respect to prescribed matters; (2) for terminating any appointment as an administering agency or any registration as a network installer; (3) for conferring upon network installers the exclusive right to apply for grants by virtue of s 15(4) (see note 15); (4) for conferring upon administering agencies functions relating to the general oversight of network installers and the verification of claims made, and information supplied, by them: s 15(7)(a)–(d). See note 5.
17 Social Security Act 1990 s 15(6)(a).
18 Social Security Act 1990 s 15(6)(b).
19 Social Security Act 1990 s 15(6)(c).
20 Social Security Act 1990 s 15(6)(d).

898. Home energy efficiency scheme in England. In order to improve energy efficiency, a works application[1] may in certain circumstances be made by a householder[2] of a dwelling in England for a grant in respect of the dwelling if he occupies the dwelling as his only or main residence and if he or his partner is in receipt of certain benefits[3]. The dwelling in respect of which the works application is made must, except where the dwelling is a mobile home[4], have a SAP rating of 63 or less[5]. A works application must be made to the administering agency for the area in which the dwelling is situated[6]. A works application must be in writing, signed either by the person making the application or by a person specified or of a description specified by the administering agency and must be in such form and contain such particulars[7], as are laid down by the administering agency[8]. A works application must be refused where the sums allocated or re-allocated by the Secretary of State to the administering agency for the financial year in which the application falls to be determined have, in the opinion of the Secretary of State, been provisionally allocated in respect of works applications which have already been allocated or approved in accordance with the regulations[9]. An administering agency may not pay a total amount of grant in respect of a works application exceeding the following amounts: (1) except where head (2) applies, the amount properly charged for the works or £3,500, whichever is the less; (2) where the work approved is to install oil fired central heating, or is to provide space or water heating systems which use renewable or near renewable energy sources[10], or includes the treatment or removal of asbestos, the amount properly charged for the works or £6,000, whichever is the less[11].

A person may apply for an additional grant in respect of a dwelling for which grant has already been paid[12], whether or not there has been a change of freeholder or leaseholder since grant was last paid, if the person meets the eligibility requirements[13] and, if applicable, satisfies the following condition[14]. The condition referred is that if the works application for additional grant is in respect of any one or more of certain specified purposes[15], the person has not previously received grant[16] for that or those purposes[17]. The amount of the additional grant in respect of that dwelling is to be determined at the date of the works application for additional grant and calculated as the grant maximum determined under heads (1) and (2) above less the amount of grant already paid in respect of the dwelling[18] (whether to the person or a previous freeholder or leaseholder)[19].

The Secretary of State may impose such conditions on which grants may be made as he sees fit[20]. The Secretary of State must appoint one or more persons or bodies of persons, each such person or body to be known as an 'administering agency', to perform in an area specified in the appointment (which may be the whole of England) such functions as he may determine in connection with the making of grants, and must exercise this function so that an administering agency is in place for each area in England[21].

1 'Works application' means an application in which the applicant proposes that an administering agency will arrange for the carrying out of the works in respect of which a grant is sought: Home Energy Efficiency Scheme (England) Regulations 2005, SI 2005/1530, reg 2. 'Administering agency' means, except in reg 3(2) (see the text to note 5), the scheme manager, person or body of persons for the time being appointed and responsible for the area in question under reg 3 (see the text and note 21): reg 2.
2 'Householder' means a person who, alone or jointly with others, is a freeholder or a leaseholder with a term of 21 years or more unexpired at the time of making the application for grant or a tenant; and 'tenant' includes a sub-tenant and a person who has: (1) a protected occupancy or statutory tenancy under the Rent (Agriculture) Act 1976 (see LANDLORD AND TENANT vol 64 (2016) PARAS 1709, 1711); (2) a statutory tenancy under the Rent Act 1977 (see LANDLORD AND TENANT vol 63 (2016) PARA 673 et seq); (3) a secure tenancy under the Housing Act 1985 Pt IV (ss 79–117) (see LANDLORD AND TENANT vol 63 (2016) PARA 1037) or an introductory tenancy under the Housing Act 1996 Pt V Ch I (ss 124–143) (see PARA 472; and LANDLORD AND TENANT vol 63 (2016) PARA 1102 et seq); (4) a licence to occupy which meets the conditions in the Housing Act 1985 Sch 1 paras 12(a), (b) (almshouse licences: see LANDLORD AND TENANT vol 63 (2016) PARA 1058); or (5) an assured agricultural occupancy under the Housing Act 1988 Pt I (ss 1–45) (see LANDLORD AND TENANT vol 64 (2016) PARA 1747 et seq): Home Energy Efficiency Scheme (England) Regulations 2005, SI 2005/1530, reg 4(4).
3 See the Home Energy Efficiency Scheme (England) Regulations 2005, SI 2005/1530, reg 4(1), (3), (3A) (reg 4(1)–(3) substituted, and reg 4(3A) added, by SI 2011/833 and substituted by SI 2012/2140). See also the Home Energy Efficiency Scheme (England) Regulations 2005, SI 2005/1530, reg 4(4) (amended by SI 2011/833); and the Home Energy Efficiency Scheme (England) Regulations 2005, SI 2005/1530, reg 4(5) (substituted by SI 2006/1953; and amended by SI 2011/833).
4 'Mobile home' means a caravan within the meaning of the Caravan Sites and Control of Development Act 1960 Pt I (ss 1–32) (disregarding the amendment made by the Caravan Sites Act 1968 s 13(2)) (see PLANNING vol 83 (2010) PARA 1211) which is a dwelling for the purposes of the Local Government Finance Act 1992 Pt I (ss 1–69) (see LOCAL GOVERNMENT FINANCE vol 70 (2012) PARA 298 et seq): Home Energy Efficiency Scheme (England) Regulations 2005, SI 2005/1530, reg 2 (definition added by SI 2012/2140).
5 Home Energy Efficiency Scheme (England) Regulations 2005, SI 2005/1530, reg 4(1), (2) (as substituted (see note 3); reg 4(2) amended by SI 2012/2140). 'SAP rating' means the energy efficiency rating of a building determined in accordance with the Reduced Data Standard Assessment Procedure contained in the Government's Standard Assessment Procedure for Energy Rating of Dwellings published by or on behalf of the Department for Energy and Climate Change and in force on 13 April 2011: Home Energy Efficiency Scheme (England) Regulations 2005, SI

2005/1530, reg 4(4) (definition added by SI 2013/833). As to the purposes for which a grant may be approved see the Home Energy Efficiency Scheme (England) Regulations 2005, SI 2005/1530, reg 5 (amended by SI 2006/1953 and SI 2011/833).

6 Home Energy Efficiency Scheme (England) Regulations 2005, SI 2005/1530, reg 9(1).

7 Ie subject to the Home Energy Efficiency Scheme (England) Regulations 2005, SI 2005/1530, reg 9(3). The works application must contain the following: (1) particulars of the dwelling in respect of which the grant is sought; (2) information about the person making the application sufficient for the administering agency to check whether the person meets the criteria of eligibility set out in reg 4; (3) a statement of the purposes for which the grant is sought; (4) a statement that reasonable access to the dwelling in respect of which the works application is made will be given to a representative of the administering agency to inspect the dwelling and carry out the works; (5) where the person wishes to receive grant over a period of time, a statement to that effect and the suggested period: reg 9(3) (amended by SI 2011/833).

8 Home Energy Efficiency Scheme (England) Regulations 2005, SI 2005/1530, reg 9(2) (amended by SI 2011/833).

9 Home Energy Efficiency Scheme (England) Regulations 2005, SI 2005/1530, reg 9(4) (substituted by SI 2010/1893; and amended by SI 2011/833 and SI 2012/2140). As to the Secretary of State see PARAS 7, 897 note 1. As to the allocation of sums see note 21.

10 Ie is for one or more of the purposes listed in the Home Energy Efficiency Scheme (England) Regulations 2005, SI 2005/1530, reg 5(1)(m) (to provide space or water heating systems which use energy from renewable sources including solar, wind and hydro-electric power and near renewable resources including ground and air heat).

11 Home Energy Efficiency Scheme (England) Regulations 2005, SI 2005/1530, reg 6 (amended by SI 2006/1953, SI 2009/1816 and SI 2011/833).

12 Ie under either the Home Energy Efficiency Scheme (England) Regulations 2000, SI 2000/1280 (revoked), or the Home Energy Efficiency Scheme (England) Regulations 2005, SI 2005/1530.

13 Ie the requirements of the Home Energy Efficiency Scheme (England) Regulations 2005, SI 2005/1530, reg 4.

14 Home Energy Efficiency Scheme (England) Regulations 2005, SI 2005/1530, reg 7(1) (amended by SI 2011/833).

15 Ie the purposes in the Home Energy Efficiency Scheme (England) Regulations 2005, SI 2005/1530, reg 5(1)(a), (b), (e), (f), (fa), (g), (j), (l) or (m).

16 Ie under either the Home Energy Efficiency Scheme (England) Regulations 2000, SI 2000/1280 (revoked), or the Home Energy Efficiency Scheme (England) Regulations 2005, SI 2005/1530.

17 Home Energy Efficiency Scheme (England) Regulations 2005, SI 2005/1530, reg 7(2) (amended by SI 2011/833).

18 Ie under either or both of the Home Energy Efficiency Scheme (England) Regulations 2000, SI 2000/1280 (revoked), and the Home Energy Efficiency Scheme (England) Regulations 2005, SI 2005/1530.

19 Home Energy Efficiency Scheme (England) Regulations 2005, SI 2005/1530, reg 7(3) (amended by SI 2011/833).

20 Home Energy Efficiency Scheme (England) Regulations 2005, SI 2005/1530, reg 3(1).

21 Home Energy Efficiency Scheme (England) Regulations 2005, SI 2005/1530, reg 3(2). Such an appointment may be terminated by the Secretary of State: reg 3(3). For each financial year, the Secretary of State must allocate to an administering agency the sums which are to be available to that agency for the purpose of making grants in accordance with the Home Energy Efficiency Scheme (England) Regulations 2005, SI 2005/1530, in that year: reg 3(4) (added by SI 2010/1893). In respect of an amount allocated to an administering agency under this provision, the Secretary of State: (1) may re-allocate any such amount within a financial year; but (2) must not re-allocate any amounts which have already been allocated or provisionally allocated for the purpose of making grants in accordance with the Home Energy Efficiency Scheme (England) Regulations 2005, SI 2005/1530: reg 3(5) (added by SI 2012/2140).

899. Home energy efficiency scheme in Wales. In order to improve energy efficiency, an advice application[1] or a works application[2] may in certain circumstances be made by an occupant[3] of a dwelling in Wales for a grant in respect of the dwelling[4]. An advice application may be entertained from a person who is an occupant of the dwelling in respect of which the application is made[5]. A works application may be entertained in respect of a dwelling if: (1) the dwelling is in private occupancy[6]; (2) the applicant is an occupant of the dwelling and is in receipt of a means-tested benefit[7]; and (3) the area agency is satisfied that the asset rating[8] of the dwelling is 38 or less[9]. A partial grant application may be entertained in respect of a dwelling which is in private occupancy from an occupant of the dwelling who: (a) is aged 60 or over; (b) is disabled or chronically ill; (c) is pregnant; or (d) occupies the dwelling with a child or young person under the age of 25[10]. The eligibility criteria[11] may be modified, replaced or supplemented by the area agency with the consent of the Welsh Ministers[12].

An application for a grant is to be made to the area agency for the area in which the dwelling is situated[13]. An application must be in writing, signed either by the applicant or by a person specified or of a description specified by the area agency and must be in such form[14], as is laid down by the area agency[15].

An area agency may not pay a total amount of grant in respect of a works application which exceeds the lower of: (i) the amount properly charged for the works carried out; or (ii) the maximum amount of grant as determined from time to time by the Welsh Ministers in accordance with: (A) the cost and/or availability of works and materials of the types required by or in connection with the purposes for which a grant may be approved[16]; and (B) the current policy and priorities of the Welsh Ministers in relation to energy conservation[17]. The Welsh Ministers may determine different maximum amounts: (I) for grants in respect of dwellings in multiple occupation; (II) by reference to any category or combination of categories of works for which a grant may be approved[18]; and (III) by reference to whether the works application is a partial grant application[19]. Subject to the above, an area agency may, with the consent of the Welsh Ministers, specify a maximum amount of grant which may be paid and a grant-calculation basis, expressed in terms of amounts per unit of measurement, for any category or combination of categories of works[20] for which a grant may be approved[21].

On making any grant, the area agency must impose conditions relating to specified[22] matters and may impose such conditions relating to such further, additional or modified matters as may be specified by the area agency with the consent of the Welsh Ministers[23].

The Welsh Ministers may appoint one or more person or persons, each such person to be known as an area agency, to perform in relation to Wales or any area of Wales such functions as the Welsh Ministers may confer by means of a contract upon that person or persons for the purpose of, or otherwise in connection with, providing advice, the making or administering of grants and arranging for the carrying out of works[24].

1   'Advice application' means an application which is for a grant in relation to advice and in which the applicant proposes that an area agency will arrange for the giving of advice; and 'advice' means advice on reducing or preventing the wastage of energy in dwellings in respect of which any works are carried out or contemplated: Home Energy Efficiency Schemes (Wales) Regulations 2011, SI 2011/656, reg 2. 'Area agency' means, except in reg 4(1) (see the text to note 24), the person or body of persons for the time being appointed and responsible for the area in question under reg 4 (see the text and note 24): reg 2.

2   'Works application' means an application in which the applicant proposes that an area agency will arrange for the carrying out of the works in respect of which a grant is sought: Home Energy Efficiency Schemes (Wales) Regulations 2011, SI 2011/656, reg 2.

3   'Occupant' means a person who lawfully occupies a dwelling as his or her only or main residence and who intends to continue in occupation of the dwelling in the long term: Home Energy Efficiency Schemes (Wales) Regulations 2011, SI 2011/656, reg 2.

4   'Dwelling' includes any building in multiple occupation; and for this purpose 'building in multiple occupation' means a building which is occupied by persons who do not form a single household, exclusive of any part of the building which is occupied as a separate dwelling by persons who form a single household: Home Energy Efficiency Schemes (Wales) Regulations 2011, SI 2011/656, reg 2. As to the purposes for which a grant may be approved see reg 6.

5   Home Energy Efficiency Schemes (Wales) Regulations 2011, SI 2011/656, reg 5(1).

6 'Private occupancy' means occupancy of a dwelling such that none of the occupants occupies that dwelling as a tenant or licensee of a county council, county borough council or registered social landlord: Home Energy Efficiency Schemes (Wales) Regulations 2011, SI 2011/656, reg 2 (definition amended by SI 2013/2843). As to registered social landlords see PARA 13.

7 'Means-tested benefit' means: (1) income support and housing benefit (each as defined in the Social Security Contributions and Benefits Act 1992 Pt VII (ss 123–137)); (2) council tax reduction scheme (as defined in Local Government Finance Act 1992); (3) state pension credit (as defined in the State Pension Credit Act 2002); (4) working tax credit and child tax credit (each as defined in the Tax Credits Act 2002) provided that in each case the income of the applicant does not exceed the relevant income threshold; (5) income-related employment and support allowance (as defined in the Welfare Reform Act 2007); and (6) universal credit (as defined in the Welfare Reform Act 2012): Home Energy Efficiency Schemes (Wales) Regulations 2011, SI 2011/656, reg 2 (definition substituted by SI 2013/2843).

8 'Asset rating' has the meaning given in the Energy Performance of Buildings (Certificates and Inspections) (England and Wales) Regulations 2007, SI 2007/991, reg 2(1) (revoked: see now the Energy Performance of Buildings (Certificates and Inspections) (England and Wales) Regulations 2012, SI 2012/3118, reg 2(1) (definition substituted by SI 2016/284): Home Energy Efficiency Schemes (Wales) Regulations 2011, SI 2011/656, reg 2. See BUILDING.

9 Home Energy Efficiency Schemes (Wales) Regulations 2011, SI 2011/656, reg 5(2).

10 Home Energy Efficiency Schemes (Wales) Regulations 2011, SI 2011/656, reg 5(3).

11 'Eligibility criteria' means the criteria determined for the time being by or (as the case may be) in accordance with the Home Energy Efficiency Schemes (Wales) Regulations 2011, SI 2011/656, reg 5: reg 2.

12 Home Energy Efficiency Schemes (Wales) Regulations 2011, SI 2011/656, reg 5(4). As to the Welsh Ministers see PARA 7.

13 Home Energy Efficiency Schemes (Wales) Regulations 2011, SI 2011/656, reg 8(1).
    Where a person has applied for a grant under the Home Energy Efficiency Schemes (Wales) Regulations 2007, SI 2007/375 (now revoked), but the application had not been approved or refused before the Home Energy Efficiency Schemes (Wales) Regulations 2011, SI 2011/656, came into force, or if the application had been approved but none of the works had been commenced, the application will be treated as having been made under the Home Energy Efficiency Schemes (Wales) Regulations 2011, SI 2011/656: reg 3(2). The Home Energy Efficiency Schemes (Wales) Regulations 2011, SI 2011/656, came into force on 1 April 2011: reg 1(1).

14 Ie subject to the Home Energy Efficiency Schemes (Wales) Regulations 2011, SI 2011/656, reg 8(3). The application must contain: (1) particulars of the dwelling in respect of which the grant is sought and if the applicant is not the freehold owner, the name and address of the freehold owner or landlord; (2) information about the applicant sufficient for the area agency to determine whether the applicant meets the eligibility criteria; (3) a statement that reasonable access to the dwelling in respect of which an application is made will be given to a representative of the area agency to inspect the dwelling and carry out the works; (4) a statement as to whether the applicant or, to the applicant's knowledge, any other person has received or applied for a grant or assistance under these Regulations or any other legislation or scheme in respect of the dwelling which is the subject of the application; and (5) such further particulars as may be specified from time to time by the area agency with the consent of the Welsh Ministers: reg 8(3).

15 Home Energy Efficiency Schemes (Wales) Regulations 2011, SI 2011/656, reg 8(2).

16 Ie determined in accordance with the Home Energy Efficiency Schemes (Wales) Regulations 2011, SI 2011/656, reg 6.

17 Home Energy Efficiency Schemes (Wales) Regulations 2011, SI 2011/656, reg 7(1).

18 Ie works specified by or (as the case may be) pursuant to the Home Energy Efficiency Schemes (Wales) Regulations 2011, SI 2011/656, reg 6.

19 Home Energy Efficiency Schemes (Wales) Regulations 2011, SI 2011/656, reg 7(2).

20 Ie works specified by or (as the case may be) pursuant to the Home Energy Efficiency Schemes (Wales) Regulations 2011, SI 2011/656, reg 6.

21 Home Energy Efficiency Schemes (Wales) Regulations 2011, SI 2011/656, reg 7(3).

22 Ie (subject to any modification made pursuant to the Home Energy Efficiency Schemes (Wales) Regulations 2011, SI 2011/656, reg 9(1)(b)) as the area agency considers relevant to the circumstances of the grant: (1) the circumstances in which any grant or part of a grant made under the regulations may become repayable by the person in respect of whose application it was made; (2) the means for securing repayment of such sums as become repayable, including (but not limited to) requiring an applicant or owner of a dwelling to enter into a charge or other security over the dwelling; (3) (where the applicant is a tenant) obtaining agreement of a landlord not to increase

rent for a specified period (save in line with inflation), or not to take into account the work carried out pursuant to a grant made under the regulations when conducting any rent review: reg 9(1)(a)(i)–(iii).

23 Home Energy Efficiency Schemes (Wales) Regulations 2011, SI 2011/656, reg 9(1). In the event of termination of the appointment of an area agency, the conditions imposed on the making of any grant by the Welsh Ministers must be in accordance with reg 9(1) as it applied to the area agency immediately prior to the termination of its appointment: reg 9(2).

24 Home Energy Efficiency Schemes (Wales) Regulations 2011, SI 2011/656, reg 4(1). An appointment under reg 4(1) may be terminated by the Welsh Ministers: reg 4(2). The Welsh Ministers may allocate to the area agency sums which are to be available to that agency in any period for the purpose of making grants under the Home Energy Efficiency Schemes (Wales) Regulations 2011, SI 2011/656, in that period, and for the re-allocation of sums so allocated: reg 4(3). Where the Welsh Ministers have made an arrangement with a person other than the applicant, for financing works in respect of which a grant is payable, they may pay all or part of any grant to that other person: reg 4(4).

(iv) Conservation of Energy (England)

900. Introduction. As part of the policy of encouraging households to reduce energy consumption at home, the Home Energy Conservation Act 1995 allows for the drawing up of local energy conservation reports in relation to residential accommodation[1]. This Act also confers functions on the appropriate national authority[2] in relation to these reports[3] and powers to give guidance to energy conservation authorities[4]. Amendments to this Act were made by the Energy Conservation Act 1996[5] and it was repealed in relation to energy conservation authorities in Wales by the Energy Act 2011[6].

The Home Energy Conservation Act 1995 extends to Northern Ireland[7].

1 See PARA 901 et seq. As to energy efficiency see PARA 886 et seq; and as to energy conservation see also ENERGY AND CLIMATE CHANGE vol 42 (2011) PARA 7 et seq. As to the financing and facilitation of the installation of energy efficiency measures in homes under the green deal plan see the Energy Act 2011 Pt 1 Ch 1 (ss 1–41); and PARA 889 et seq.
2 As to the appropriate national authority see PARAS 7, 897 note 1.
3 See PARA 902.
4 See PARA 903.
5 See PARA 901 et seq.
6 See the Energy Act 2011 s 118(1).
7 Home Energy Conservation Act 1995 s 8(1). As to the application of the Act to Northern Ireland see s 8(2).

901. Energy conservation reports. Subject to special provisions in relation to houses in multiple occupation and houseboats[1], it is the duty of every energy conservation authority[2] to prepare a report[3] in accordance with the following requirements[4]. The report must set out energy conservation measures[5] that the authority considers practicable, cost-effective and likely to result in significant improvement in the energy efficiency of residential accommodation[6] in its area[7]. The report must include:

(1) an assessment of the cost of the energy conservation measures set out in it[8];

(2) an assessment of the extent to which carbon dioxide emissions into the atmosphere would be decreased as a result of those measures[9]; and

(3) a statement of any policy of the authority for taking into account, in deciding whether to exercise any power in connection with those measures, the personal circumstances of any person[10],

but nothing in heads (1) to (3) is to be taken as requiring the authority to set out in the report energy conservation measures to be taken in relation to any particular dwelling or building[11].

Further, the report may, if the energy conservation authority considers it desirable, include:

(a)   an assessment of the extent of decreases in emissions into the atmosphere of oxides of nitrogen and sulphur dioxide which would result from the implementation of the measures set out in the report[12];

(b)   an assessment of the number of jobs which would result from the implementation of those measures[13];

(c)   an assessment of the average savings in fuel bills and in kilowatt hours of fuel used that might be expected to result from the measures by different types of household in different types of accommodation[14];

(d)   such other matters as it considers appropriate[15].

In preparing the report, an energy conservation authority may consult such persons as it considers appropriate[16].

An energy conservation authority may prepare a report on houses in multiple occupation or houseboats which is separate from the report on other residential accommodation[17].

When an energy conservation authority has prepared a report in accordance with these provisions, it must publish it and send a copy to the appropriate national authority[18].

1   Ie subject to the Home Energy Conservation Act 1995 s 2(7): see the text and note 17.

2   'Energy conservation authority' means: (1) in England and Wales, a local housing authority within the meaning of the Housing Act 1985 (see PARA 11); and (2) in Northern Ireland, the Northern Ireland Housing Executive: Home Energy Conservation Act 1995 s 1(1). As to the repeal of the Home Energy Conservation Act 1995 in relation to energy conservation authorities in Wales see PARA 900.

3   As to the appropriate national authority's functions in relation to such reports see PARA 902. As to the appropriate national authority see PARAS 7, 897 note 1.

4   Home Energy Conservation Act 1995 s 2(1) (amended by SI 1997/47).

5   'Energy conservation measures' includes information, advice, education, promotion, any available financial assistance, making grants and loans and carrying out works: Home Energy Conservation Act 1995 s 1(1) (definition amended by the Energy Act 2011 s 118(2)).

6   'Residential accommodation' means: (1) premises occupied or intended to be occupied as a separate dwelling and forming the whole or part of a building; or (2) a house in multiple occupation (that is, in England and Wales, as defined by the Housing Act 2004 ss 254–259, as they have effect for the purposes of Pt 1 (ss 1–54) (ie, without the exclusions contained in Sch 14) (see PARAS 667–668) and, in Northern Ireland, a house in multiple occupation as defined by the Housing (Northern Ireland) Order 1992, SI 1992/1725, art 75); or (3) a houseboat (that is, a boat or other floating decked structure: (a) designed or adapted for use solely as a place of permanent habitation; and (b) not having means of, or capable of being readily adapted for, self-propulsion, which is a dwelling for the purposes of the Local Government Finance Act 1992 Pt I (ss 1–69) (see LOCAL GOVERNMENT FINANCE vol 70 (2012) PARA 298 et seq) or, as the case may be, the purposes of the Rates (Northern Ireland) Order 1977, SI 1977/2157); or (4) a mobile home (that is: (a) in England and Wales or Scotland, a caravan within the meaning of the Caravan Sites and Control of Development Act 1960 Pt I (ss 1–32) (disregarding the amendment made by the Caravan Sites Act 1968 s 13(2)) (see PLANNING vol 83 (2010) PARA 1211) which is a dwelling for the purposes of the Local Government Finance Act 1992 Pt I or Pt II (ss 70–99); (b) in Northern Ireland, a caravan within the meaning of the Caravans Act (Northern Ireland) 1963 which is a dwelling house for the purposes of the Rates (Northern Ireland) Order 1977, SI 1977/2157): Home Energy Conservation Act 1995 s 1(1) (definition amended by the Energy Conservation Act 1996 s 1; and the Housing Act 2004 s 265(1), Sch 15 para 38). As to houses in multiple occupation see PARA 666 et seq.

7   Home Energy Conservation Act 1995 s 2(2). Any reference to the area of an energy conservation authority is: (1) in the case of a local housing authority in England and Wales, to the area of that authority within the meaning of the Housing Act 1985 (see PARA 11); (2) in the case of the Northern Ireland Housing Executive, to Northern Ireland: Home Energy Conservation Act 1995 s 1(2).

8   Home Energy Conservation Act 1995 s 2(3)(a).

9   Home Energy Conservation Act 1995 s 2(3)(b).

10   Home Energy Conservation Act 1995 s 2(3)(c).

11   Home Energy Conservation Act 1995 s 2(3).

12 Home Energy Conservation Act 1995 s 2(4)(a).
13 Home Energy Conservation Act 1995 s 2(4)(b).
14 Home Energy Conservation Act 1995 s 2(4)(c).
15 Home Energy Conservation Act 1995 s 2(4)(d).
16 Home Energy Conservation Act 1995 s 2(5).
17 Home Energy Conservation Act 1995 s 2(7) (added by SI 1997/47). As to the appropriate national authority's power to make such adaptations of the Home Energy Conservation Act 1995 ss 2–4 as are necessary to enable an energy conservation authority to prepare such a separate report see PARA 902 note 1.
18 Home Energy Conservation Act 1995 s 2(6).

902. Functions of the appropriate national authority in relation to reports. The appropriate national authority[1] must give directions as to the date by which the required reports[2] are to be sent to it by energy conservation authorities[3]. The directions may set different dates for different authorities, different descriptions of authority and different areas[4]. It may also set different dates for reports on houses in multiple occupation or houseboats or reports on other residential accommodation[5].

Where the appropriate national authority has received a report from an energy conservation authority, and it appears to it that the report has been duly prepared in accordance with the statutory requirements, it must:

(1)   notify the energy conservation authority of a timetable[6] in accordance with which that authority must prepare, publish and send to the appropriate national authority reports on the progress made in implementing the measures set out in the report[7]; and

(2)   take such steps as it considers desirable in order to assist with and to encourage other persons to assist with the measures set out in any such report[8].

The appropriate national authority must from time to time prepare a report on the progress made by energy conservation authorities in implementing the measures set out in the required reports prepared by them, and any steps it has taken pursuant to head (2), and must lay any such report before Parliament or, as appropriate, the National Assembly for Wales[9].

1 The appropriate national authority may by order under the Energy Conservation Act 1996 s 2(2) make such transitional provision as appears to it to be appropriate; and it may, in particular, make such adaptations of the Home Energy Conservation Act 1995 ss 2–4 as are necessary to enable an energy conservation authority to prepare a separate report under s 2 (see PARA 901) on houses in multiple occupation or houseboats: Energy Conservation Act 1996 s 2(3). As to the exercise of this power see the Energy Conservation Act 1996 (Commencement No 3 and Adaptations) Order 1997, SI 1997/47, art 3; note 5; and PARA 901. As to the meanings of 'house in multiple occupation' and 'houseboat' see PARA 901 note 6. As to the appropriate national authority see PARAS 7, 897 note 1.
2 Ie the report required under the Home Energy Conservation Act 1995 s 2: see PARA 901.
3 Home Energy Conservation Act 1995 s 3(1). As to the meaning of 'energy conservation authority' see PARA 901 note 2. As to the repeal of the Home Energy Conservation Act 1995 in relation to energy conservation authorities in Wales see PARA 900.
4 Home Energy Conservation Act 1995 s 3(1). As to the meaning of 'area of an energy conservation authority' see PARA 901 note 7.
5 Home Energy Conservation Act 1995 s 3(1) (amended by SI 1997/47). As to the meaning of 'residential accommodation' see PARA 901 note 6.
6 The appropriate national authority may vary any timetable set by it under the Home Energy Conservation Act 1995 s 3(2) (see the text and notes 7–8): s 3(3).
7 Home Energy Conservation Act 1995 s 3(2)(a).
8 Home Energy Conservation Act 1995 s 3(2)(b).
9 Home Energy Conservation Act 1995 s 3(4).

903. Guidance from the appropriate national authority. The appropriate national authority[1] may, from time to time, give to energy conservation authorities² such guidance as it considers appropriate in relation to the preparation of reports³. It may, in particular, give guidance as to what improvements in energy efficiency are to be regarded as significant⁴. An energy conservation authority must have regard to any such guidance given by the appropriate national authority⁵.

1 As to the appropriate national authority see PARAS 7, 897 note 1.
2 As to the meaning of 'energy conservation authority' see PARA 901 note 2. As to the repeal of the Home Energy Conservation Act 1995 in relation to energy conservation authorities in Wales see PARA 900.
3 The reports referred to in the text are reports under the Home Energy Conservation Act 1995 s 2 (see PARA 901) or reports under s 3(2)(a) (see PARA 902): s 4(1). As to the power to make a separate report in relation to houses in multiple occupation or houseboats see s 2(7); and PARA 901. As to the appropriate national authority's power to make such adaptations of s 4 as are necessary to enable an energy conservation authority to prepare such a report see PARA 902 note 1. As to the meanings of 'house in multiple occupation' and 'houseboat' see PARA 901 note 6.
4 Home Energy Conservation Act 1995 s 4(2).
5 Home Energy Conservation Act 1995 s 4(3).

904. Modification of a report and further reports. An energy conservation authority¹ may, and, if so directed by the appropriate national authority², must:

(1) modify the prepared report³; or

(2) prepare further reports setting out additional or modified energy conservation measures⁴.

1 As to the meaning of 'energy conservation authority' see PARA 901 note 2. As to the repeal of the Home Energy Conservation Act 1995 in relation to energy conservation authorities in Wales see PARA 900.
2 As to the functions of the appropriate national authority in relation to reports see PARA 902. As to the appropriate national authority see PARAS 7, 897 note 1.
3 Ie the report prepared under the Home Energy Conservation Act 1995 s 2: see PARA 901.
4 Home Energy Conservation Act 1995 s 5(1). The provisions of s 2(2)–(6), s 3(2)–(4) (see PARA 902), s 4 (see PARA 903) and s 5(1) apply in relation to any such modified or further report: s 5(2). As to the meaning of 'energy conservation measures' see PARA 901 note 5.

905. Supplementary provisions. There must be paid out of money provided by Parliament or the National Assembly for Wales, as appropriate:

(1) any expenses of the appropriate national authority¹ under the Home Energy Conservation Act 1995²; and

(2) any increase attributable to that Act in the sums payable out of such money under any other Act³.

Nothing in the Home Energy Conservation Act 1995 may be taken as conferring:

(a) any power to make grants or loans⁴;

(b) any power of entry⁵; or

(c) any power to carry out works, or require any person to carry out works⁶;

and nothing in that Act requires an energy conservation authority⁷ to inspect any premises or requires any person to give any information to an energy conservation authority⁸.

1 As to the appropriate national authority see PARAS 7, 897 note 1.
2 Home Energy Conservation Act 1995 s 7(a).
3 Home Energy Conservation Act 1995 s 7(b).
4 Home Energy Conservation Act 1995 s 6(1)(a).
5 Home Energy Conservation Act 1995 s 6(1)(b).
6 Home Energy Conservation Act 1995 s 6(1)(c).
7 As to the meaning of 'energy conservation authority' see PARA 901 note 2. As to the repeal of the Home Energy Conservation Act 1995 in relation to energy conservation authorities in Wales see PARA 900.
8 Home Energy Conservation Act 1995 s 6(2).

15. STARTER HOMES IN ENGLAND

906. Definition of starter home. New statutory provisions to promote home ownership through 'starter homes' have been made by Chapter 1 of Part 1 of the Housing and Planning Act 2016[1], in force as from a day to be appointed. The purpose of this chapter is to promote the supply of starter homes in England[2]. For this purpose, 'starter home' means a building or part of a building that: (1) is a new dwelling[3]; (2) is available for purchase[4] by qualifying first-time buyers[5] only; (3) is to be sold at a discount of at least 20 per cent of the market value; (4) is to be sold for less than the price cap[6]; and (5) is subject to any restrictions on sale or letting specified in regulations made by the Secretary of State[7].

The Secretary of State may by regulations: (a) amend the definition of 'first-time buyer'; (b) disapply the age requirement for first time buyers[8] in relation to specified categories of people; (c) specify circumstances in which a dwelling may still be a starter home even if it is available for purchase by joint purchasers not all of whom meet the age requirement[9]. The Secretary of State may by regulations amend the price cap; and the regulations may provide for different price caps to apply: (i) for starter homes in different areas in Greater London; (ii) for starter homes in different areas outside Greater London[10]. Before making regulations amending the price cap the Secretary of State must consult each local planning authority[11] in England, the Mayor of London and any other person the Secretary of State thinks appropriate[12]. Regulations under these provisions may amend Chapter 1 of Part 1 of the Housing and Planning Act 2016[13].

1 Ie the Housing and Planning Act 2016 Pt 1 Ch 1 (ss 1–8), in force as from a day to be appointed under s 216(3). At the date at which this volume states the law, no such day had been appointed.
  In addition, Pt 1 Ch 2 (ss 9–12) makes amendments to the Self-build and Custom Housebuilding Act 2015, to require local authorities to meet the demand for custom-built and self-built homes by granting permissions for suitable sites. See LOCAL GOVERNMENT. The Housing and Planning Act 2016 s 159 adds the Town and Country Planning Act 1990 s 106ZA, which empowers the Secretary of State to make regulations restricting, or imposing other conditions on, the enforceability of planning obligations which relate to the provision of affordable housing. See PLANNING.
2 Housing and Planning Act 2016 s 1. As to implementation of the policy see PARA 907.
3 'New dwelling' means a building or part of a building that: (1) has been constructed for use as a single dwelling and has not previously been occupied; or (2) has been adapted for use as a single dwelling and has not been occupied since its adaptation: Housing and Planning Act 2016 s 2(2).
4 'Purchase': the reference to a building or part of a building being available for purchase is to a freehold or a leasehold interest in the building or part being available for purchase: Housing and Planning Act 2016 s 2(5).
5 'Qualifying first-time buyer' means an individual who: (1) is a first-time buyer; (2) is at least 23 years old but has not yet reached the age of 40; and (3) meets any other criteria specified in regulations made by the Secretary of State (for example, relating to nationality): Housing and Planning Act 2016 s 2(3). 'First-time buyer' has the meaning given by the Finance Act 2003 s 57AA(2) (see STAMP TAXES vol 96 (2012) PARA 456): Housing and Planning Act 2016 s 2(4).
6 Where the starter home is in Greater London, the price cap is £450,000; and where the starter home is outside Greater London, the price cap is £250,000: Housing and Planning Act 2016 s 2(6).
7 Housing and Planning Act 2016 s 2(1). The restrictions on sale that may be specified by regulations under s 2(1)(e) (see head (5) in the text) in relation to a dwelling that has been sold to a qualifying first-time buyer include, in particular, restrictions: (1) requiring a person who sells the dwelling within a specified period to make a payment to a specified person in respect of the starter homes discount; or (2) prohibiting a person from selling the dwelling within a specified period unless the dwelling is sold to a qualifying first-time buyer at a discount: s 3(1). Regulations made by virtue of s 3(1) must: (a) set out how the amount of the payment or discount is to be determined; and (b) provide for reductions in the amount of the payment or discount according to the length of time since the dwelling was first sold to a qualifying first-time buyer: s 3(2). The person specified in regulations under s 3(1)(a) (see head (1) above) may be the Secretary of State, a local planning authority in England or any other person: s 3(3). Regulations under s 2(1)(e) may impose restrictions that require a person selling the dwelling to sell it subject to any restrictions to which

he or she is subject: s 3(4). Regulations under s 2(1)(e) may include provision about the legal mechanism by which any requirement is to be imposed: s 3(5). The Secretary of State may by regulations make provision about the use of sums that are paid to a person in accordance with a requirement imposed by regulations made by virtue of s 3(1)(a) (including provision permitting or requiring the payment of sums into the Consolidated Fund): s 3(6). In s 3(1)(a) 'starter homes discount' means the discount mentioned in s 2(1)(c) or s 3(1)(b): s 3(7). As to the Secretary of State see PARA 7.

8　Ie in the Housing and Planning Act 2016 s 2(3)(b) (see note 5 head (2)).

9　Housing and Planning Act 2016 s 2(7).

10 Housing and Planning Act 2016 s 2(8).

11 'Local planning authority' means a person who is a local planning authority for the purposes of any provision of the Town and Country Planning Act 1990 Pt III (ss 55–106C): Housing and Planning Act 2016 s 8. See PLANNING vol 81 (2010) PARA 43 et seq.

12 Housing and Planning Act 2016 s 2(9).

13 Housing and Planning Act 2016 s 2(10).

907. Promoting the supply of starter homes in England. The following provisions are not yet in force[1]. An English planning authority[2] must carry out its relevant planning functions[3] with a view to promoting the supply of starter homes in England[4]. A local planning authority in England must have regard to any guidance given by the Secretary of State in carrying out that duty[5].

The Secretary of State may by regulations provide that an English planning authority[6] may only grant planning permission[7] for a residential development[8] of a specified description if the starter homes requirement is met[9]. Where the Secretary of State makes such regulations, the regulations must give an English planning authority power to dispense with the condition requiring the starter homes requirement to be met where: (1) an application is made for planning permission in respect of a rural exception site; and (2) the application falls to be determined wholly or partly on the basis of a policy contained in a development plan for the provision of housing on rural exception sites[10].

Regulations under these provisions may, for example, provide that an English planning authority may grant planning permission only if a person has entered into a planning obligation to provide a certain number of starter homes or to pay a sum to be used by the authority for providing starter homes[11]. The regulations may confer discretions on an English planning authority[12]. The regulations may make different provision for different areas[13].

A local planning authority in England must prepare reports containing information about the carrying out of its functions in relation to starter homes[14]. The Secretary of State may by regulations make provision about such reports, including: (a) provision about their form and content; (b) provision about their timing; (c) provision requiring them to be combined with annual reports as to local development[15] by the authority[16]. The regulations may require a report to contain information about applications to which regulations as to granting planning permission only where the starter home requirement is met[17] apply and details of how those applications have been dealt with[18]. An authority must make its reports available to the public[19].

The Secretary of State may make a compliance direction if satisfied that: (i) a local planning authority has failed to carry out its functions in relation to starter homes[20] or has failed to carry them out adequately; and (ii) a policy contained in a local development document[21] for the authority is incompatible with those functions[22]. A 'compliance direction' is a direction that no regard is to be had to the policy for the purposes of any determination to be made under the planning Acts[23]. A compliance direction remains in force until revoked by a further direction given by the Secretary of State[24]. A direction must include the Secretary of State's reasons for making it[25]. The Secretary of State must publish any direction under these provisions and give a copy to the local planning authority[26].

1 See PARA 906 note 1.
2 'English planning authority' means: (1) a local planning authority in England; or (2) the Secretary of State when exercising a function relating to the grant of planning permission on an application in respect of land in England: Housing and Planning Act 2016 s 4(3). As to the meaning of 'local planning authority' see PARA 906 note 11. As to the Secretary of State see PARA 7. The Secretary of State may by regulations amend the definition of 'English planning authority' in s 4(3): s 4(5)(a);
3 'Relevant planning functions' means: (1) functions under the Town and Country Planning Act 1990 Pt III (ss 55–106C) (see PLANNING vol 81 (2010) PARA 292 et seq), other than functions relating to the grant of permission in principle; (2) functions under the Greater London Authority Act 1999 Pt VIII (ss 334–350) (see LONDON GOVERNMENT vol 71 (2013) PARA 327); (3) functions under the Planning and Compulsory Purchase Act 2004 Pt 2 (ss 13–37) (see PLANNING vol 81 (2010) PARA 87 et seq): Housing and Planning Act 2016 s 4(4). The Secretary of State may by regulations amend the definition of 'relevant planning functions' in s 4(4): s 4(5)(b).
4 Housing and Planning Act 2016 s 4(1). As to the meaning of 'starter home' see PARA 906 (definition applied by s 8).
5 Housing and Planning Act 2016 s 4(2).
6 'English planning authority' means: (1) a local planning authority in England; or (2) the Secretary of State when exercising a function relating to the grant of planning permission on an application in respect of land in England: Housing and Planning Act 2016 s 5(3).
7 'Planning permission' has the meaning given by the Town and Country Planning Act 1990 s 336 (see PLANNING vol 81 (2010) PARA 54 note 6): Housing and Planning Act 2016 s 8.
8 'Residential development' means a development that includes at least one dwelling; and 'development' has the meaning given by the Town and Country Planning Act 1990 s 336 (see PLANNING vol 81 (2010) PARA 292): Housing and Planning Act 2016 s 8.
9 Housing and Planning Act 2016 s 5(1). 'The starter homes requirement' means a requirement, specified in the regulations, relating to the provision of starter homes in England s 5(4).
10 Housing and Planning Act 2016 s 5(2).
11 Housing and Planning Act 2016 s 5(5). 'Planning obligation' means a planning obligation under the Town and Country Planning Act 1990 s 106 (see PLANNING vol 81 (2010) PARA 335): Housing and Planning Act 2016 s 8.
12 Housing and Planning Act 2016 s 5(6).
13 Housing and Planning Act 2016 s 5(7).
14 Housing and Planning Act 2016 s 6(1).
15 Ie under the Planning and Compulsory Purchase Act 2004 s 35: see PLANNING vol 81 (2010) PARA 92.
16 Housing and Planning Act 2016 s 6(2).
17 Ie regulations under the Housing and Planning Act 2016 s 5.
18 Housing and Planning Act 2016 s 6(3).
19 Housing and Planning Act 2016 s 6(4).
20 'Functions in relation to starter homes', in relation to a local planning authority, means the authority's functions under the Housing and Planning Act 2016 s 4 and regulations under s 5: s 8.
21 'Local development document' is to be read in accordance with the Planning and Compulsory Purchase Act 2004 ss 17, 18(3) (see PLANNING vol 81 (2010) PARAs 100, 102): Housing and Planning Act 2016 s 8.
22 Housing and Planning Act 2016 s 7(1).
23 Housing and Planning Act 2016 s 7(2). 'The planning Acts' has the meaning given by the Planning and Compulsory Purchase Act 2004 s 117(4) (see PLANNING vol 81 (2010) PARA 2): Housing and Planning Act 2016 s 8.
24 Housing and Planning Act 2016 s 7(3).
25 Housing and Planning Act 2016 s 7(4).
26 Housing and Planning Act 2016 s 7(5).

16. LOANS FOR THE ACQUISITION OR IMPROVEMENT OF HOUSING

(1) IN GENERAL

908. Introduction. Local housing authorities[1] formerly had power to give a mortgage to a secure tenant[2] seeking to exercise the right to buy under Part V of the Housing Act 1985[3]. However, this right to a mortgage was abolished by amendments made by the Leasehold Reform, Housing and Urban Development Act 1993, which introduced a new right to acquire on rent to mortgage terms (through amendments to the Housing Act 1985)[4]. This right itself has now been abolished by amendments made by the Housing Act 2004[5].

However, since 1899 local housing authorities have had a more general power to make advances to assist those who wish to purchase their homes[6]. These powers, now contained in Part XIV of the Housing Act 1985[7], allow authorities to make advances to someone who wishes to acquire a house, construct a house, convert another building into a house, or enlarge, repair or improve a house[8].

The general provisions relating to housing finance are dealt with elsewhere in this title[9].

1 As to the meaning of 'local housing authority' see PARA 11.
2 As to the meanings of 'secure tenancy' and 'secure tenant' see LANDLORD AND TENANT vol 63 (2016) PARA 1037.
3 As to the right to buy see the Housing Act 1985 Pt V (ss 118–188); and PARA 239 et seq.
4 As to the right to acquire on rent to mortgage terms see the Housing Act 1985 ss 143–153; and PARA 318 et seq.
5 See the Housing Act 1985 s 142A (added by the Housing Act 2004 s 190(1)); and PARA 318 et seq.
6 Advances might be made under the Small Dwellings Acquisition Acts 1899 to 1923 before the repeal of those Acts by the Housing (Consequential Provisions) Act 1985. For transitional provisions see the Housing Act 1985 s 456, Sch 18.
7 See the Housing Act 1985 Pt XIV (ss 435–459); and PARA 910 et seq.
8 See the Housing Act 1985 s 435; and PARA 910.
9 See PARA 354 et seq.

909. Loans by Public Works Loan Commissioners. The Public Works Loan Commissioners[1] may lend money for the purpose of constructing or improving houses[2], or facilitating or encouraging the construction or improvement of houses, to any person entitled to land[3] for an estate in fee simple absolute in possession or for a term of years absolute[4] of which not less than 50 years remains unexpired[5]. A loan for any of those purposes, and interest on the loan, must be secured by a mortgage of:

(1)   the land in respect of which the purpose is to be carried out[6]; and
(2)   such other land, if any, as may be offered as security for the loan[7],

and the money lent must not exceed three-quarters of the value, to be ascertained to the satisfaction of the Public Works Loan Commissioners, of the estate or interest in the land proposed to be mortgaged in this way[8]. Loans may be made by instalments from time to time as the building or other work on the mortgaged land progresses[9]; and a mortgage may be accordingly made to secure such loans so made[10]. If the loan exceeds two-thirds of the value of the land, the Public Works Loan Commissioners must require, in addition to such a mortgage, such further security as they may think fit[11]. The period for repayment of the loan must not exceed 40 years, and no money must be lent on a mortgage of land or houses unless the estate proposed to be mortgaged is either a fee simple absolute in possession or an estate for a term of years absolute of which not less than 50 years are unexpired at the date of the loan[12].

1 As to the Public Works Loan Commissioners see FINANCIAL INSTRUMENTS AND TRANSACTIONS vol 49 (2015) PARA 160.
2 For these purposes, 'house' includes: (1) any yard, garden, outhouses and appurtenances belonging to the house or usually enjoyed with it; and (2) any part of a building which is occupied or intended to be occupied as a separate dwelling including, in particular, a flat; and 'house property' is to be construed accordingly: Housing Act 1985 s 457.
3 As to the meaning of 'land' see PARA 416 note 3.
4 As to the meanings of 'fee simple absolute' and 'term of years absolute' see REAL PROPERTY AND REGISTRATION vol 87 (2012) PARAS 66, 76.
5 Housing Act 1985 s 451(1).
6 Housing Act 1985 s 451(2)(a).
7 Housing Act 1985 s 451(2)(b).
8 Housing Act 1985 s 451(2).
9 The total amount lent must not, however, at any time exceed the amount specified in the Housing Act 1985 s 451(2): s 451(3).
10 Housing Act 1985 s 451(3).
11 Housing Act 1985 s 451(4).
12 Housing Act 1985 s 451(5). Section 451 does not apply to housing associations; but corresponding provision is made by the Housing Act 1996 s 23 (see PARA 166): Housing Act 1985 s 451(6) (amended by SI 1996/2325). As to the meaning of 'housing association' see PARA 13.

(2) LOCAL AUTHORITY MORTGAGES

910. Power of local authorities to advance money. A local authority[1] may advance money[2] to a person for the purpose of:

(1)   acquiring a house[3];
(2)   constructing a house[4];
(3)   converting another building into a house or acquiring another building and converting it into a house[5],

or for the purpose of facilitating the repayment of an amount outstanding on a previous loan[6] made for any of those purposes[7]. A local authority which is not a local housing authority[8] may advance money to a person for the purpose of altering, enlarging, repairing or improving a house, or for the purpose of facilitating the repayment of an amount outstanding on a previous loan made for any of those purposes[9].

The authority may make an advance notwithstanding that it is intended that some part of the premises will be used, or continue to be used, otherwise than as a dwelling if it appears to the authority that the principal effect of making the advance would be to meet the applicant's housing needs[10]. In such a case the premises are treated as a building to be converted into a house[11].

The authority may make such advances whether or not the houses or buildings are in its area[12]. An advance may be made in addition to assistance given by the authority in respect of the same house under any other Act or any other provision of the Housing Act 1985[13].

1 As to the meaning of 'local authority' see PARA 12.
2 For the terms on which money may be advanced see PARA 911; and as to the interest charged see PARA 912.
3 Housing Act 1985 s 435(1)(a). As to the meaning of 'house' see PARA 909 note 2.
4 Housing Act 1985 s 435(1)(b).
5 Housing Act 1985 s 435(1)(c).
6 Money may only be advanced for the repayment of a previous loan if the local authority is satisfied that the primary effect of the advance will be to meet the housing needs of the applicant: see PARA 913.

7   Housing Act 1985 s 435(1) (amended SI 2002/1860).
8   As to the meaning of 'local housing authority' see PARA 11.
9   Housing Act 1985 s 435(1A) (added by SI 2002/1860).
10   Housing Act 1985 s 435(2).
11   Housing Act 1985 s 435(2).
12   Housing Act 1985 s 435(3).
13   Housing Act 1985 s 435(4). This provision enables an authority to take over an existing mortgage.

911. Terms of the advance. Provision is made with respect to the terms of advances by local authorities[1]. The advance, together with the interest on it, must be secured by a mortgage of the land concerned; and an advance must not be made unless the estate proposed to be mortgaged is either:

(1)   an estate in fee simple absolute[2] in possession[3]; or
(2)   an estate for a term of years absolute[4] of which a period of not less than ten years in excess of the period fixed for the repayment of the advance remains unexpired on the date on which the mortgage is executed[5].

The amount of the principal of the advance must not exceed the value of the mortgaged security or, as the case may be, the value which it is estimated the mortgaged security will bear when the construction, conversion, alteration, enlargement, repair or improvement has been carried out; and the advance must not be made except after a valuation duly made on behalf of the authority[6]. Where the advance is for construction, conversion, alteration, enlargement, repair or improvement[7], it may be made by instalments from time to time as the works progress[8].

The mortgage deed must provide:

(a)   for repayments of the principal either by instalments of equal or unequal amounts, beginning on the date of the advance or at a later date, or at the end of a fixed period (with or without a provision allowing the authority to extend the period) or on the happening of a specified event before the end of that period[9]; and
(b)   for the payment of instalments of interest throughout the period beginning on the date of the advance and ending when the whole of the principal is repaid[10].

This is subject to the statutory provisions for waiver or reduction of payments in the case of a property requiring repair or improvement[11] and to the provision for assistance for first-time buyers[12] whereby part of the loan may be interest-free for up to five years[13].

The mortgage deed must also provide that, notwithstanding the statutory provisions referred to above, the balance for the time being unpaid:

(i)   becomes repayable on demand by the authority in the event of any of the conditions subject to which the advance is made not being complied with[14]; and
(ii)   may, in any event, be repaid on one of the usual quarter-days by the person for the time being entitled to the equity of redemption after one month's written notice of intention to repay has been given to the authority[15].

Where the authority is selling a property which is held for housing purposes it has power to grant a mortgage by leaving an amount outstanding on the disposal[16].

1   Housing Act 1985 s 436(1). As to the meaning of 'local authority' see PARA 12. The advances referred to in the text are advances under s 435: see PARA 910. As to the meaning of 'mortgage' see *Santley v Wilde* [1899] 2 Ch 474, CA.
2   As to the meaning of 'fee simple absolute' see REAL PROPERTY AND REGISTRATION vol 87 (2012) PARA 66.

3   Housing Act 1985 s 436(2)(a).
4   As to the meaning of 'term of years absolute' see REAL PROPERTY AND REGISTRATION vol 87 (2012) PARA 76.
5   Housing Act 1985 s 436(2)(b).
6   Housing Act 1985 s 436(3).
7   Ie for any of the purposes specified in the Housing Act 1985 s 435(1)(b), (c) (see PARA 910 heads (2), (3)) or s 435(1A) (see PARA 910).
8   Housing Act 1985 s 436(4) (amended by SI 2002/1860).
9   Housing Act 1985 s 436(5)(a).
10 Housing Act 1985 s 436(5)(b).
11 Ie the Housing Act 1985 s 441: see PARA 915.
12 Ie the Housing Act 1985 s 446(1)(b): see PARA 920.
13 Housing Act 1985 s 436(5).
14 Housing Act 1985 s 436(6)(a). As to the general rights of a mortgagee to possession and sale in the event of non-payment of the instalments or other breach of the mortgage see the Law of Property Act 1925 ss 87(1), 101–107; and MORTGAGE vol 77 (2016) PARAS 165, 404 et seq.
15 Housing Act 1985 s 436(6)(b).
16 See the Housing Act 1985 s 437; and PARA 522.

912. Local authority mortgage interest rates. Where after 3 October 1980[1] a local authority[2]:

(1)   advances money for any of the statutory purposes[3]; or

(2)   on the disposal of a house[4] allows, or has to allow, a sum to be left outstanding on the security of the house[5]; or

(3)   takes a transfer of a mortgage[6] in pursuance of an agreement by a local authority to indemnify a mortgagee[7],

the provision made by the authority with respect to interest on the sum advanced or remaining outstanding must comply with the following provisions[8].

The rate of interest must be whichever is for the time being the higher[9] of:

(a)   the standard national rate[10]; or

(b)   the applicable local average rate[11].

The rate must be capable of being varied[12] by the local authority whenever a change in either or both of those rates requires it; and the amount of the periodic payments must be capable of being changed accordingly[13].

1   Ie the date on which the corresponding provision in the earlier legislation came into operation: see the Housing Act 1980 (Commencement No 1) Order 1980, SI 1980/1406.
2   As to the meaning of 'local authority' see PARA 12.
3   Housing Act 1985 s 438(1)(a). The purposes referred to in head (1) in the text are the purposes of s 435: see PARA 910.
4   As to the meaning of 'house' see PARA 909 note 2.
5   Housing Act 1985 s 438(1)(b).
6   As to transfers of mortgages generally see MORTGAGE vol 77 (2016) PARA 366 et seq.
7   Housing Act 1985 s 438(1)(c). The agreement referred to in head (3) in the text is an agreement in pursuance of s 442: see PARA 916.
8   Housing Act 1985 s 438(1). Section 438 does not prevent a local authority from giving assistance in the manner provided by s 441 (waiver or reduction of payments in case of property requiring repair or improvement: see PARA 915) or s 446(1)(b) (assistance for first-time buyers, part of loan interest-free for up to five years: see PARA 920): s 438(2). Nor does s 438 apply to loans made by local authorities under s 228 (repealed) (former duty to make loans for improvements required by improvement notice) or under the Housing Act 1996 s 22 (see PARA 166) or the Housing Associations Act 1985 s 58 (financial assistance for housing associations: see PARA 13): Housing Act 1985 s 438(3) (amended by SI 1996/2325).
    The Housing Act 1985 s 438 does not apply to anything done under the Local Government Act 1988 s 24 (power to give financial assistance for privately let housing accommodation): see PARA 378.
9   The appropriate national authority may by notice in writing to a local authority direct it to treat a rate specified in the notice as being the higher of the two rates mentioned in the Housing Act 1985 Sch 16 para 1, either for a period specified in the notice or until further notice; and Sch 1 paras 1–6 have effect accordingly: s 438(1), Sch 16 para 7(1). A direction so given may be varied

or withdrawn by a further notice in writing: Sch 16 para 7(2). As to the appropriate national authority, ie the Secretary of State or, where statutory functions have been transferred in relation to Wales, the Welsh Ministers, see PARA 7.

10   Housing Act 1985 Sch 16 para 1(1)(a). The standard national rate is the rate for the time being declared as such by the appropriate national authority after taking into account interest rates charged by building societies in the United Kingdom and any movement in those rates: Sch 16 para 2. As to the meaning of 'United Kingdom' see PARA 60 note 10.

11   Housing Act 1985 Sch 16 para 1(1)(b). A local authority must for every period of six months declare, on a date falling within the month immediately preceding that period: (1) a rate applicable to the advances and transfers mentioned in s 438(1)(a), (c) (see heads (1), (3) in the text); and (2) a rate applicable to sums left outstanding as mentioned in s 438(1)(b) (see head (2) in the text): Sch 16 para 3(a), (b). The rate declared under Sch 16 para 3(a) or (b) must be a rate calculated in such manner as the appropriate national authority may determine: Sch 16 para 4(1) (Sch 16 para 4 substituted by the Local Government and Housing Act 1989 s 194(1), Sch 11 para 88). Such a determination: (a) may make different provision for different cases or descriptions of cases, including different provision for different areas, for different local authorities or for different descriptions of local authorities; and (b) may be varied or withdrawn by a subsequent determination: Housing Act 1985 Sch 16 para 4(2)(a), (b) (as so substituted). As soon as practicable after making such a determination, the appropriate national authority must send a copy of the determination to the local authority or authorities to which it relates: Sch 16 para 4(3) (as so substituted).

12   Where on a change of the standard national rate or the applicable local average rate a rate of interest is capable of being varied, the local authority must vary it: Housing Act 1985 Sch 16 para 5(1). The authority must serve on the person liable to pay the interest notice in writing of the variation not later than two months after the change: Sch 16 para 5(2). The variation takes effect with the first payment of interest due after a date specified in the notice, which: (1) if the variation is a reduction, must be not later than one month after the change; and (2) if the variation is an increase, must not be earlier than one month nor later than three months after the service of the notice: Sch 16 para 5(3)(a), (b).

On a variation of the rate of interest, the local authority may make a corresponding variation of the periodic payments: Sch 16 para 6(1). The authority must do so if the period over which the repayment of principal is to be made would otherwise be reduced below the period fixed when the mortgage was effected: Sch 16 para 6(2). The variation must be notified and must take effect together with the variation of the rate of interest: Sch 16 para 6(3).

13   Housing Act 1985 Sch 16 para 1(2).

913.   Requirements as to fitness of premises and related matters. An advance must not be made for the repayment of a previous loan[1], unless the local authority[2] satisfies itself that the primary effect of the advance will be to meet the housing needs of the applicant by enabling him either:

(1)   to retain an interest in the house concerned[3]; or

(2)   to carry out such works in relation to the building or house concerned as would be eligible for an advance for conversion[4] or improvement[5],

as the case may be[6].

1   Ie an advance under the closing words of the Housing Act 1985 s 435(1) (repayment of previous loan) or under s 435(1A)(b) (repayment of previous loan for improvements etc): see PARA 910.
2   As to the meaning of 'local authority' see PARA 12.
3   Housing Act 1985 s 439(3)(a) (amended by SI 2002/1860).
4   Ie under the Housing Act 1985 s 435(1)(c): see PARA 910 head (3).
5   Ie under the Housing Act 1985 s 435(1A)(a): see PARA 910.
6   Housing Act 1985 s 439(3)(b) (amended SI 2002/1860).

914.   Deposits in respect of maintenance or repair of mortgaged premises. A local authority[1] by which money has been advanced on the mortgage of a house[2] in pursuance of any enactment[3] may accept the deposit by the mortgagor of the sums estimated to be required for the maintenance or repair of the mortgaged premises, and may pay interest on sums so deposited[4].

1   As to the meaning of 'local authority' see PARA 12.
2   As to the meaning of 'house' see PARA 909 note 2.

3 For the powers of a local authority to advance money on the mortgage of a house see the Housing Act 1985 s 435, s 437; and PARAS 522, 910.
4 Housing Act 1985 s 440.

915. Waiver or reduction of payments there the property requires repairs or improvement. Where a local authority[1]:

(1)   advances money for the acquisition of a house[2] which is in need of repair or improvement[3]; or

(2)   on the disposal of a house which is in need of repair or improvement, allows, or has to allow, a sum to be left outstanding[4] on the security of the house[5],

it may, if certain conditions[6] are satisfied, give assistance to the person acquiring the house[7]. The assistance must take the form of making provision for waiving or reducing the interest payable on the sum advanced or remaining outstanding, and for dispensing with the repayment of principal, for a period ending not later than five years after the date of the advance or, as the case may be, the date of the disposal[8].

1 As to the meaning of 'local authority' see PARA 12.
2 As to such an advance see the Housing Act 1985 s 435; and PARA 910. As to the meaning of 'house' see PARA 909 note 2.
3 Housing Act 1985 s 441(1)(a).
4 This may be done under the Housing Act 1985 s 437: see PARA 522.
5 Housing Act 1985 s 441(1)(b).
6 The conditions are: (1) that the assistance is given in accordance with a scheme which either has been approved by the appropriate national authority or conforms with such requirements as may be prescribed; and (2) that the person acquiring the house has entered into an agreement with the local authority to carry out, within a period specified in the agreement, such works of repair or improvement as are so specified: Housing Act 1985 s 441(2)(a), (b). 'Prescribed' means prescribed by order of the appropriate national authority made, in relation to England, with the consent of the Treasury: s 441(4). As to the appropriate national authority, ie the Secretary of State or, where statutory functions have been transferred in relation to Wales, the Welsh Ministers, see PARA 7. As to the Treasury see CONSTITUTIONAL AND ADMINISTRATIVE LAW vol 20 (2014) PARA 262 et seq. An order: (a) may make different provision with respect to different cases or descriptions of case, including different provision for different areas; and (b) must be made by statutory instrument subject to annulment in pursuance of a resolution of either House of Parliament or, as the case may be, the National Assembly for Wales: s 441(5)(a), (b). At the date at which this volume states the law, no such order had been made and none had effect thereunder by virtue of the Housing (Consequential Provisions) Act 1985 s 2(2).
7 Housing Act 1985 s 441(1). Section 436(5) (repayments of principal and payment of interest), and s 438 (local authority mortgage interest rates) are made subject to s 441: see PARAS 911–912.
8 Housing Act 1985 s 441(3).

(3) LOCAL AUTHORITY ASSISTANCE IN CONNECTION WITH MORTGAGES

916. Agreement by local authority to indemnify mortgagee. A local authority[1] may enter into an agreement with a person or body making an advance on the security of a house[2] (or a building to be converted into a house) whereby, in the event of default by the mortgagor, and in the circumstances and subject to conditions specified in the agreement, the authority binds itself to indemnify the mortgagee in respect of the whole or part of the mortgagor's outstanding indebtedness and any loss or expense falling on the mortgagee in consequence of the mortgagor's default[3]. The local authority may only enter into such an agreement if the advance is for one or more of the specified purposes[4].

The agreement may also, if the mortgagor is made party to it, enable or require the authority in specified circumstances to take a transfer of the mortgage[5] and assume rights and liabilities under it, the mortgagee being then discharged in respect of them[6]. The transfer may be made to take effect:

(1)   on terms provided for by the agreement (including terms involving the substitution of a new mortgage agreement or modification of the existing one)[7]; and

(2)   so that the authority is treated as acquiring (for and in relation to the purposes of the mortgage) the benefit and burden of all preceding acts, omissions and events[8].

These powers are designed to support loans on an unimproved property so that the mortgagee might be willing to lend on the basis of the improved value of a currently unimproved dwelling[9].

1   As to the meaning of 'local authority' see PARA 12. The residuary bodies (which replaced the councils abolished by the Local Government Act 1985 (see LOCAL GOVERNMENT vol 69 (2009) PARA 17)) were local authorities for these purposes: Local Government Reorganisation (Property etc) Order 1986, SI 1986/148, art 10(1).
2   As to the meaning of 'house' see PARA 909 note 2.
3   Housing Act 1985 s 442(1) (amended by the Housing Act 1996 s 222, Sch 18 para 27(2)).
4   Housing Act 1985 s 442(1A) (added by the Housing Act 1996 Sch 18 para 27(3); and amended by SI 2002/1860). The purposes referred to in the text are those specified in the Housing Act 1985 s 435(1) or (1A): see PARA 910. The provisions of s 435(2)–(4) (see PARA 910) apply in relation to the power to enter into such an agreement as they apply to the power to make an advance under s 435: s 442(1A) (as so added).
5   If the authority takes a transfer of the mortgage, the provision made by it regarding interest must comply with the Housing Act 1985 s 438(1), Sch 16: see s 438(1)(c); and PARA 912.
6   Housing Act 1985 s 442(2) (amended by the Housing Act 1996 Sch 18 para 27(2)).
7   Housing Act 1985 s 442(3)(a).
8   Housing Act 1985 s 442(3)(b).
9   See Department of the Environment Circular 5/81 paras 7–10.

917.   Local authority contributions to mortgage costs. A local authority[1] may contribute towards costs incurred by a person in connection with a legal charge which secures, or a proposed legal charge which is intended to secure, a relevant advance[2] made or proposed to be made to him by any person or body[3].

1   As to the meaning of 'local authority' see PARA 12.
2   'Relevant advance' means an advance made to a person whose interest in the house (or building to be converted into a house) on the security of which the advance is made is, or was, acquired by virtue of a conveyance of the freehold, or a grant or assignment of a long lease, by a housing authority: Housing Act 1985 s 444 (substituted by the Housing Act 1996 s 222, Sch 18 para 29(1)). 'Housing authority' includes any local authority, an urban development corporation, a Mayoral development corporation, the Homes and Communities Agency, the Greater London Authority, the relevant authority, a private registered provider of social housing and a registered social landlord: Housing Act 1985 s 458(1) (definition added by the Housing and Planning Act 1986 s 24(2), Sch 5 para 37; and amended by the Government of Wales Act 1998 s 140, Sch 16 paras 5, 18(2); the Localism Act 2011 ss 195(1), 222, Sch 19 paras 10, 10, Sch 22 paras 9, 14; and by SI 1996/2325, SI 2008/3002 and SI 2010/866). A profit-making registered provider of social housing is a housing authority for the purposes of the Housing Act 1985 Pt XIV only in relation to social housing within the meaning of the Housing and Regeneration Act 2008 Pt 2 (ss 59–278A) (see PARA 52): Housing Act 1985 s 458(1A) (added by SI 2010/866). As to registered providers of social housing see PARA 51 et seq; as to when such a body is a profit-making organisation see PARA 71 note 13. In the Housing Act 1985 s 444, 'housing authority' does not include the Welsh Ministers unless the interest in the house is or was acquired on a disposal by them under the Housing Associations Act 1985 s 90 (see PARA 156): Housing Act 1985 s 458(2) (added by the Government of Wales Act 1998 Sch 16 para 18(3)). As to the meaning of 'house' see PARA 909 note 2. 'Long lease' means a lease creating a long tenancy within the meaning of the Housing Act 1985 s 115 (see LANDLORD AND TENANT vol 63 (2016) PARA 1042): s 458(1). As to the meaning of 'urban development corporation' see PARA 12; as to Mayoral development corporations see LONDON GOVERNMENT vol 71 (2013) PARA 323); as to the Homes and Communities Agency see PARA 57 et seq; and PLANNING vol 83 (2010) PARA 1454 et seq; as to the Greater London Authority see LONDON GOVERNMENT vol 71 (2013) PARA 67 et seq; as to the meaning of 'the

relevant authority' see PARA 8; as to the meaning of 'private registered provider of social housing' see PARA 53; and as to the meaning of 'registered social landlord' see PARA 13. As to the Welsh Ministers see PARA 7.

3 Housing Act 1985 s 443(1) (amended by the Housing Act 1996 s 222, Sch 18 para 28).

918. Further advances in case of disposal on a shared ownership lease. Where:

(1)   a lease[1] of a house[2], granted otherwise than in pursuance of the right to buy provisions[3] relating to shared ownership leases, contains a provision concerning the right of a tenant to acquire additional shares[4]; and

(2)   a housing authority[5] (other than the Homes and Communities Agency[6] or the Greater London Authority[7]) has, in the exercise of any of its powers, left outstanding or advanced any amount on the security of the house[8],

that power includes power to advance further amounts for the purpose of assisting the tenant to make payments in pursuance of that provision[9].

The statutory right to be granted a shared ownership lease has been abolished[10]. The above provisions, however, apply to voluntary shared ownership leases and allow local housing authorities to make further advances to the lessee wishing to purchase further tranches of equity.

1 As to the meaning of 'lease' see PARA 31 note 3.
2 As to the meaning of 'house' see PARA 909 note 2.
3 Ie the Housing Act 1985 Pt V (ss 118–188): see PARA 239 et seq.
4 Ie a provision to the like effect as that required by the Housing Act 1985 Sch 8 para 1 (repealed) (terms of shared ownership lease; right of a tenant to acquire additional shares): s 453(1)(a). 'Shared ownership lease' means a lease: (1) granted on payment of a premium calculated by reference to a percentage of the value of the dwelling or of the cost of providing it; or (2) under which the tenant (or his personal representatives) will or may be entitled to a sum calculated by reference, directly or indirectly, to the value of the dwelling: s 622(1) (numbered as such by SI 2001/3649).
5 As to the meaning of 'housing authority' see PARA 11.
6 As to the Homes and Communities Agency see PARA 57 et seq; and PLANNING vol 83 (2010) PARA 1454 et seq.
7 As to the Greater London Authority see LONDON GOVERNMENT vol 71 (2013) PARA 67 et seq.
8 Housing Act 1985 s 453(1)(b) (amended by the Localism Act 2011 s 195(1), Sch 19 paras 10, 18; and by SI 2008/3002).
9 Housing Act 1985 s 453(1).
10 See PARA 230.

(4) ASSISTANCE FOR FIRST-TIME BUYERS

919. Advances to recognised lending institutions to assist first-time buyers. The appropriate national authority[1] was empowered make advances[2] to recognised lending institutions[3] enabling them to provide assistance to first-time purchasers[4] of house property[5] in Great Britain[6] where:

(1)   the purchaser intended to make his home in the property[7];

(2)   finance for the purchase of the property (and improvements, if any) was obtained by means of a secured loan from the lending institution[8]; and

(3)   the purchase price was within the prescribed[9] limits[10].

Under the Local Government and Housing Act 1989, however, the appropriate national authority was given power by order to make provision for the purpose of bringing this scheme for assistance for first-time buyers[11] to an end[12]. Since

1 April 1993, account has no longer been taken under the assistance legislation of the making of any application for assistance[13].

1   As to the appropriate national authority, ie the Secretary of State or, where statutory functions have been transferred in relation to Wales, the Welsh Ministers, see PARA 7.

2   For the forms in which assistance could be given and the qualifying conditions see the Housing Act 1985 s 446; and PARA 920. For the terms of advances and administration see s 449; and PARA 921.

3   The lending institutions recognised for these purposes were: authorised deposit takers, authorised insurers, local authorities and development corporations: Housing Act 1985 s 447(1) (amended by SI 2001/3649 and SI 2008/3002). The appropriate national authority could by order made, in the case of an order relating to England, with the consent of the Treasury either: (1) add to this list; or (2) direct that a named body was no longer to be a recognised lending institution: Housing Act 1985 s 447(2). Such an order had to be made by statutory instrument (s 447(3)); and before making an order under head (2) the appropriate national authority had to give an opportunity for representations to be made on behalf of the body concerned (s 447(2)). As to the meanings of 'authorised deposit taker' and 'authorised insurer' see the Housing Act 1985 s 622(1); and PARA 527 note 18. As to the meaning of 'development corporation' see PARA 12. As to the Treasury see CONSTITUTIONAL AND ADMINISTRATIVE LAW vol 20 (2014) PARA 262 et seq.

4   For the considerations by reference to which a person was treated as a first-time buyer see PARA 921.

5   As to the meaning of 'house property' see PARA 909 note 2.

6   As to the meaning of 'Great Britain' see PARA 60 note 10.

7   Housing Act 1985 s 445(1)(a).

8   Housing Act 1985 s 445(1)(b).

9   'Prescribed' means prescribed by order of the appropriate national authority: Housing Act 1985 s 445(2). An order: (1) could prescribe different limits for properties in different areas; and (2) had to be made by statutory instrument subject to annulment in pursuance of a resolution of the House of Commons: s 445(3)(a), (b).

10 Housing Act 1985 s 445(1)(c). The Home Purchase Assistance (Price-limits) Order 1991, SI 1991/819 (spent) specified the price-limits for these purposes, which ranged from £83,600 in Greater London to £38,500 in Cleveland, Durham, Northumberland and Tyne and Wear.

11 Ie the scheme contained in the Housing Act 1985 ss 445–450: see the text and notes 1–10; and PARAS 920–921.

12 Local Government and Housing Act 1989 s 171(1)(a). The enactments specified in s 171(1)(a), together with any orders and directions made under them, are referred to as 'the assistance legislation': s 171(1).

Without prejudice to the generality of the power conferred by s 171, an order thereunder could: (1) specify a date or dates with effect from which account would no longer be taken under the assistance legislation of matters specified in the order; (2) vary the terms of advances to lending institutions so as to commute what would otherwise be a number of payments or repayments to or by such an institution into a single payment or a smaller number of payments of such amount and payable at such time or times as might be determined in accordance with the order; and (3) provide for the amendment or repeal, in whole or in part, of the assistance legislation with effect from such date or dates and subject to such transitional provisions as might be specified in the order: s 171(2). The powers conferred on the appropriate national authority by the Housing Act 1985 s 446(3) (see PARA 920) to relax or modify the conditions of s 446(2) and any power to make an order under any provision of the assistance legislation could be so exercised as to make provision for the purpose referred to in the Local Government and Housing Act 1989 s 171(1): s 171(3). The power to make an order under s 171(1) was exercisable by statutory instrument subject to annulment in pursuance of a resolution of either House of Parliament: s 171(4).

As to the exercise of these powers see the Home Purchase Assistance (Winding Up of Scheme) Order 1990, SI 1990/374 (see note 13); and the Home Purchase Assistance (Commutation of Repayments) Order 1994, SI 1994/548. The terms of relevant advances were varied so as to commute what would otherwise be a number of repayments by an institution into a single repayment calculated in accordance with the formula set out in art 2(2) and that single repayment was to be paid by each institution to the appropriate national authority on 29 April 1994 ('the repayment date'): arts 1(2), 2(1). 'Relevant advance' means an advance which would otherwise have been repayable on or after the repayment date and which the appropriate national authority made to an institution under the Housing Act 1985 s 445(1) for providing assistance under s 446(1)(a) or (b): Home Purchase Assistance (Commutation of Repayments) Order 1994, SI 1994/548, art 1(2).

13 Home Purchase Assistance (Winding Up of Scheme) Order 1990, SI 1990/374, art 3. Moreover, 1 April 1990 is specified as the date from which account would no longer be taken under the assistance legislation of: (1) any notice given on or after that date under the Home Purchase Assistance Directions 1978 para 34(5); or (2) any period of two years as described in the Home Purchase Assistance Directions 1978 para 34(8) which starts to run on or after that date: Home Purchase Assistance (Winding Up of Scheme) Order 1990, SI 1990/374, art 2.

As to assistance for buying a home see now eg the Help to Buy equity loan and the Help to Buy ISA operated on behalf of the government, which help eligible people who could not otherwise afford to buy a home, and the provisions as to starter homes in the Housing and Planning Act 2016 Pt 1 Ch 1 (ss 1–8): see PARAS 906–907.

920. Forms of assistance and qualifying conditions. Assistance for first-time buyers[1] could be given in the following ways:

(1)   the secured loan could be financed by the appropriate national authority[2] to the extent of the specified amount[3] (that amount being normally additional to that which the institution[4] would otherwise have lent, but not so that the total loan exceeded the loan value of the property)[5];

(2)   a specified amount[6] of the total loan could be made free of interest, and of any obligation to repay principal[7], for up to five years from the date of purchase[8]; and

(3)   the institution could provide the purchaser with a bonus on his savings[9] (which bonus was to be tax-exempt) up to a maximum amount[10], payable towards the purchase or expenses arising in connection with it[11].

The purchaser qualified for assistance[12] in the form of an interest-free loan[13] by satisfying the following conditions with respect to his own savings[14]:

(a)   that he had been saving with a recognised savings institution[15] for at least two years[16] preceding the date of his application for assistance[17];

(b)   that throughout the 12 months[18] preceding that date he had savings of at least the required amount[19]; and

(c)   that by that date he had accumulated at least the specified amount[20] of such savings[21],

and he qualified for assistance in the form of a bonus on savings[22] by satisfying the conditions specified in heads (a) and (b)[23].

The appropriate national authority could allow for the conditions to be relaxed or modified in particular classes of case[24]. No assistance was to be given in any case unless the amount of the secured loan was at least that required[25] and amounted to not less than the required percentage[26] of the purchase price of the property[27].

As from 1 April 1993, however, account will no longer be taken under the assistance legislation[28] of the making of any application for assistance[29].

1 Ie assistance under the Housing Act 1985 s 445: see PARA 919.
2 As to the appropriate national authority, ie the Secretary of State or, where statutory functions have been transferred in relation to Wales, the Welsh Ministers, see PARA 7.
3 Ie £600: see the Housing Act 1985 s 446(1)(a). However, the appropriate national authority was given power, by order made, in the case of an order relating to England, with the consent of the Treasury, to alter any of the money sums specified in s 446: s 446(5)(a). Any order under s 446 had to be made by statutory instrument subject to annulment in pursuance of a resolution of the House of Commons: s 446(6). As to the Treasury see CONSTITUTIONAL AND ADMINISTRATIVE LAW vol 20 (2014) PARA 262 et seq.
4 Ie a recognised lending institution: see PARA 919 note 3.
5 Housing Act 1985 s 446(1)(a). As to the determination of the loan value of the property see s 449(2)(b); and PARA 921.
6 Ie £600: see the Housing Act 1985 s 446(1)(b). See also note 3.

7 The Housing Act 1985 s 436(5) (repayments of principal and payment of interest) and s 438 (local authority mortgage interest rates) are made subject to s 446(1)(b): see PARAS 911–912.
8 Housing Act 1985 s 446(1)(b).
9 For the method of quantifying bonus by reference to savings see the Housing Act 1985 s 449(2)(c); and PARA 921.
10 Ie £110: see the Housing Act 1985 s 446(1)(c). See also note 3.
11 Housing Act 1985 s 446(1)(c).
12 For the supporting evidence and declarations which had to be furnished in order to establish qualification see the Housing Act 1985 s 449(2)(f); and PARA 921.
13 Ie a loan under the Housing Act 1985 s 446(1)(a) or (b): see heads (1)–(2) in the text.
14 For the satisfaction of such conditions see the Housing Act 1985 s 449(2)(e); and PARA 921.
15 For these purposes, the recognised savings institutions were: authorised deposit takers, local authorities, friendly societies and the Director of Savings: Housing Act 1985 s 448(1) (amended by SI 2001/1149 and SI 2001/3649). The appropriate national authority could by order made, in the case of an order relating to England, with the consent of the Treasury either: (1) add to this list; or (2) direct that a named body was no longer to be a recognised savings institution: Housing Act 1985 s 448(2). Such an order had to be made by statutory instrument (s 448(3)); and before making an order under head (2) the appropriate national authority had to give an opportunity for representations to be made on behalf of the body concerned (s 448(2)). As to the meaning of 'local authority' see PARA 12. As to the meaning of 'authorised deposit taker' see the Housing Act 1985 s 622(1); and PARA 527 note 18.
    The Home Purchase Assistance (Recognised Savings Institutions) Order 1986, SI 1986/1490 (spent), was made for these purposes; and, by virtue of the Housing (Consequential Provisions) Act 1985 s 2(2), the Home Purchase Assistance (Recognised Savings Institutions) Order 1978, SI 1978/1785 (spent), had effect as if so made. Various other orders were made, the most recent being the Home Purchase Assistance (Recognised Savings Institutions) Order 1990, SI 1990/1387, but all are now spent.
16 The appropriate national authority could by order made by statutory instrument and, in the case of an order relating to England, with the consent of the Treasury substitute a longer or shorter period for this period: Housing Act 1985 s 446(5)(b), (6).
17 Housing Act 1985 s 446(2)(a).
18 The appropriate national authority could by order made by statutory instrument and, in the case of an order relating to England, with the consent of the Treasury substitute a longer or shorter period for this period: Housing Act 1985 s 446(5)(b), (6).
19 Housing Act 1985 s 446(2)(b). The required amount was £300: see s 446(2)(b). See also note 3.
20 Ie £600: see the Housing Act 1985 s 446(2)(c). See also note 3. The appropriate national authority could by order made, in the case of an order relating to England, with the consent of the Treasury alter the condition in head (c) in the text so as to enable the purchaser to satisfy it with lesser amounts of savings and to enable assistance to be given in such a case according to reduced scales specified in the order: s 446(5)(c).
21 Housing Act 1985 s 446(2)(c).
22 Ie under the Housing Act 1985 s 446(1)(c): see head (1) in the text.
23 Housing Act 1985 s 446(2).
24 Housing Act 1985 s 446(3).
25 Ie £1,600: see the Housing Act 1985 s 446(4). See also note 3.
26 Ie 25%: see the Housing Act 1985 s 446(4). The appropriate national authority could by order made, in the case of an order relating to England, with the consent of the Treasury alter the percentage mentioned in head (d) in the text: s 446(5)(d).
27 Housing Act 1985 s 446(4).
28 As to the meaning of 'the assistance legislation' see PARA 919 note 12.
29 See PARA 919.

921. Terms of advances and administration. Advances to lending institutions[1] to assist first-time buyers[2] were to be on such terms as to repayment and otherwise as might be settled by the appropriate national authority with, in relation to England, the consent of the Treasury[3], after consultation with lending and savings institutions or organisations representative of them; and the terms were to be embodied in directions issued by the appropriate national authority[4]. The following matters, among others, could be dealt with in directions issued by the appropriate national authority:

(1)   the cases in which assistance was to be provided[5];

(2)   the method of determining the loan value of property[6];
(3)   the method of quantifying bonus by reference to savings[7];
(4)   the considerations by reference to which a person was or was not to be treated as a first-time purchaser of house property[8];
(5)   the steps which were to be taken with a view to satisfying the conditions as to a purchaser's own savings[9], and the circumstances in which those conditions were or were not to be treated as satisfied[10];
(6)   the supporting evidence and declarations which were to be furnished by a person applying for assistance, in order to establish his qualification for it, and the means of ensuring that restitution was made in the event of it being obtained by false representations[11];
(7)   the way in which amounts paid over by way of assistance were to be repaid to the lending institutions and to the appropriate national authority[12].

The appropriate national authority had power, to the extent that it thought proper for safeguarding the lending institutions, to include in the terms an undertaking to indemnify the institutions in respect of loss suffered in cases where assistance had been given[13].

As from 1 April 1993, however, account will no longer be taken under the assistance legislation[14] of the making of any application for assistance[15].

1   As to the lending institutions recognised for these purposes see PARA 919 note 3.
2   Ie under the Housing Act 1985 s 445: see PARA 919.
3   As to the appropriate national authority, ie the Secretary of State or, where statutory functions have been transferred in relation to Wales, the Welsh Ministers, see PARA 7. As to the Treasury see CONSTITUTIONAL AND ADMINISTRATIVE LAW vol 20 (2014) PARA 262 et seq.
4   Housing Act 1985 s 449(1).
5   Housing Act 1985 s 449(2)(a).
6   Ie for the purpose of the Housing Act 1985 s 446(1)(a) (limit on total loan: see PARA 920): s 449(2)(b).
7   Housing Act 1985 s 449(2)(c).
8   Housing Act 1985 s 449(2)(d). As to the meaning of 'house property' see PARA 909 note 2.
9   Ie the conditions within the Housing Act 1985 s 446(2): see PARA 920.
10 Housing Act 1985 s 449(2)(e).
11 Housing Act 1985 s 449(2)(f). Information may be false on account of what it omits even though it is literally true: see *R v Lord Kylsant* [1932] 1 KB 442, 101 LJKB 97, CCA; *R v Bishirgian* [1936] 1 All ER 586, 154 LT 499, CCA; cf *Curtis v Chemical Cleaning and Dyeing Co Ltd* [1951] 1 KB 805 at 808–809, [1951] 1 All ER 631 at 634, CA.
12 Housing Act 1985 s 449(2)(g).
13 Housing Act 1985 s 449(3).
14 As to the meaning of 'the assistance legislation' see PARA 919 note 12.
15 See PARA 919.

(5) LOANS IN RESPECT OF SERVICE CHARGES

922. Introduction. Provision is made for a right to be granted to former secure tenants[1] to a loan in respect of service charges where the tenant, in exercising the right to buy[2], has purchased a lease of a flat[3]. In a case where one of the local housing authority's[4] former secure tenants has exercised the right to buy, the right is a right to leave the whole or part of the service charge outstanding, whilst in the case of a tenant of a housing association or other registered social landlord[5], the right is to an advance from the Homes and Communities Agency[6].

Such a loan may not be sufficient to meet the whole of the service charge, or the lessee may no longer be entitled because, for example, the ten year statutory period which applies has elapsed[7]. There is, however, an additional power to make loans in such cases[8], and a power to enable the landlord to purchase an equitable interest in the flat for the purpose of assisting the tenant to meet some or all of the service charge payments[9].

1   As to the meanings of 'secure tenancy' and 'secure tenant' see LANDLORD AND TENANT vol 63 (2016) PARA 1037.
2   As to the right to buy see PARA 239 et seq.
3   See the Housing Act 1985 s 450A; and PARA 923.
4   As to the meaning of 'local housing authority' see PARA 11.
5   As to the meaning of 'registered social landlord' see PARA 13.
6   See PARA 923. As to the Homes and Communities Agency see PARA 57 et seq; and PLANNING vol 83 (2010) PARA 1454 et seq.
7   As to the ten year period see PARA 923.
8   See the Housing Act 1985 s 450B; and PARA 924.
9   See the Housing Act 1985 s 450D; and PARA 925.

923. Right to a loan in certain cases after exercise of right to buy. The appropriate national authority[1] may by regulations[2] provide that where:

(1)   a lease[3] of a flat[4] has been granted in pursuance of the right to buy under Part V of the Housing Act 1985[5]; and

(2)   the landlord[6] is the housing authority[7] which granted the lease or another housing authority[8],

the tenant[9] has, in such circumstances as may be prescribed, a right to a loan[10] in respect of service charges[11] to which these provisions apply[12]. The regulations may provide that the right:

(a)   arises only in respect of so much of a service charge as exceeds a minimum qualifying amount and does not exceed a maximum qualifying amount[13]; and

(b)   does not arise unless the amount thus qualifying for a loan itself exceeds a minimum amount[14],

the amounts[15] being either prescribed or ascertained in a prescribed manner[16]. The regulations must provide that the right is:

(i)   where the landlord is a housing association, a right to an advance from the relevant authority[17]; and

(ii)   in any other case, a right to leave the whole or part of the service charge outstanding[18].

The regulations may, as regards the procedure for exercising the right, provide:

(A)   that a demand for service charges in respect of repairs or improvements must inform the tenant whether, in the landlord's opinion, he is entitled to a loan and, if he is, what he must do to claim it[19];

(B)   that the right must be claimed within a prescribed period of the demand[20]; and

(C)   that on the right being claimed the lender must inform the tenant of the terms of the loan and of the prescribed period within which the tenant may accept the offer[21].

1   As to the appropriate national authority, ie the Secretary of State or, where statutory functions have been transferred in relation to Wales, the Welsh Ministers, see PARA 7.
2   These provisions apply to regulations under the Housing Act 1985 s 450A (see the text and notes 3–21) or s 450B (see PARA 924) conferring the right to a loan, or the power to make a loan, in respect of service charges: s 450C(1) (ss 450A–450C added by the Housing and Planning Act 1986 s 5). The regulations may provide that the right or, as the case may be, the power does not arise in the case of any prescribed description of landlord: Housing Act 1985 s 450C(2) (as so added). The regulations must provide that the loan:
    (1)   in the case of a loan made in pursuance of regulations under s 450A, must be on such terms as may be prescribed; and
    (2)   in the case of a loan made by virtue of regulations under s 450B, must be on such terms as the lender may determine subject to any provision made by the regulations,

and must, in either case, be secured by a mortgage of the flat in question, but may be made whether or not the flat is adequate security for the loan: s 450C(3) (as so added). The regulations may: (a) in relation to England, in a case where a rate of interest is payable on some or all of the loan or, in relation to Wales, as regards the rate of interest payable on the loan, either prescribe the rate or provide that the rate is to be such reasonable rate as may be determined by the lender or, where the lender is a local authority, provide that s 438(1), Sch 16 (local authority mortgage interest rates: see PARA 912) applies; (b) in a case where amounts calculated by reference to the market value of the flat are payable instead of (or as well as) interest, make provision about calculating the market value of the flat (including imposing charges for the services of district valuers); (c) as regards administrative expenses of the lender in connection with a loan, provide that the lender may charge such expenses to the borrower, to the extent that they do not exceed such amount as may be prescribed, and that the expenses so charged may, at the option of the borrower (in the case of a loan under s 450A) or at the option of the lender (in the case of a loan under s 450B), be added to the amount of the loan: s 450C(4) (as so added; amended by the Housing and Regeneration Act 2008 s 308(1)). See further the Housing and Regeneration Act 2008 s 308(2), (3). As to the meaning of 'district valuer' see PARA 527 note 14.

The regulations may apply whenever the lease in question was granted or assigned and whenever the service charge in question became payable: Housing Act 1985 s 450C(5) (as so added). The regulations: (i) may make different provision for different cases or descriptions of case, including different provision for different areas; (ii) may contain such incidental, supplementary and transitional provisions as the appropriate national authority considers appropriate; and (iii) must be made by statutory instrument subject to annulment in pursuance of a resolution of either House of Parliament or, as appropriate, the National Assembly for Wales: s 450C(6) (as so added).

See also Department of the Environment Circular 21/92.

3   As to the meaning of 'lease' see PARA 31 note 3.
4   As to the meaning of 'flat' cf PARA 563 note 13.
5   Housing Act 1985 s 450A(1)(a) (as added: see note 2). As to the right to buy see Pt V (ss 118–188); and PARA 239 et seq.
6   As to the meaning of 'landlord' see PARA 31 note 3.
7   For these purposes, 'housing authority': (1) does not include a private registered provider of social housing, or a registered social landlord, which is a co-operative housing association; (2) includes a co-operative housing association which is neither a private registered provider of social housing nor a registered social landlord: Housing Act 1985 s 450A(6) (as added (see note 2); definition substituted by SI 2010/866). As to the meaning of 'private registered provider of social housing' see PARA 53; as to the meaning of 'co-operative housing association' see PARA 13; and as to the meaning of 'registered social landlord' see PARA 13. As to the meaning of 'housing authority' generally see PARA 11.
8   Housing Act 1985 s 450A(1)(b) (as added: see note 2).
9   As to the meaning of 'tenant' see PARA 31 note 3.
10 The loan must be secured by a mortgage of the flat in question but may be made whether or not the flat is adequate security for the loan: Housing (Service Charge Loans) Regulations 1992, SI 1992/1708, reg 7.
11 For these purposes, 'service charge' has the meaning given by the Landlord and Tenant Act 1985 s 18(1) (see LANDLORD AND TENANT vol 63 (2016) PARA 614): Housing Act 1985 s 458(1) (definition added by the Commonhold and Leasehold Reform Act 2002 s 150, Sch 9 paras 1, 4). The Housing Act 1985 s 450A applies to service charges in respect of repairs or improvements (whether to the flat, the building in which it is situated or any other building or land) which are payable in the period beginning with the grant of the lease and ending with the tenth anniversary of the grant or, where the lease provides for service charges to be payable by reference to a specified annual period, with the end of the tenth such period beginning after the grant of the lease: s 450A(2) (as added (see note 2); amended by the Commonhold and Leasehold Reform Act 2002 Sch 9 para 2(2)). 'Repairs' includes works for making good a structural defect: Housing Act 1985 s 450A(6) (as so added).

Any part of the service charge which does not qualify for a loan under these provisions may qualify under s 450B: see s 450B(3); and PARA 924.
12 Housing Act 1985 s 450A(1) (as added: see note 2). Except for cases where it is the landlord as the result of the exercise of functions under the Housing Associations Act 1985 Pt III (ss 74–102) (see PARA 141 et seq), regulations may not contain provision for cases where the appropriate national authority is the landlord: Housing Act 1985 s 450A(1A) (added by the Government of Wales Act 1998 s 140, Sch 16 para 16). Subject to the Housing (Service Charge Loans) Regulations 1992, SI 1992/1708, regs 3, 4 (see notes 15–21), a tenant has a right to a loan in respect of service charges to which the Housing Act 1985 s 450A(2) applies (see note 11) where: (1) a lease of a flat has been granted in pursuance of Pt V (the right to buy), except in a case where the grant is in pursuance of the preserved right to buy within the meaning of Pt V (see PARA 334 et seq); (2) the landlord

is the housing authority which granted the lease or another housing authority; and (3) a demand for such charges is made on or after 17 August 1992: Housing (Service Charge Loans) Regulations 1992, SI 1992/1708, regs 1(1), 2(1).

13 Housing Act 1985 s 450A(3)(a) (as added: see note 2).

14 Housing Act 1985 s 450A(3)(b) (as added: see note 2).

15 The right to a loan under the Housing (Service Charge Loans) Regulations 1992, SI 1992/1708, reg 2 (see notes 12, 18): (1) arises only in respect of so much of a service charge to which the Housing Act 1985 s 450A applies as: (a) exceeds £1,500 less the amount of any service charge already demanded under the lease in respect of the same accounting period as that charge; and (b) does not exceed £20,000 less the amount of any outstanding loan which has been made in pursuance of the right to a loan under the Housing (Service Charge Loans) Regulations 1992, SI 1992/1708, reg 2; and (2) does not arise unless the amount thus qualifying for a loan itself exceeds £500: reg 3(1)(a), (b). If the retail prices index for January immediately preceding an index linked period is higher than it was for January 1992, then reg 3(1) applies in relation to any demand for service charges made during that index linked period as if for each amount there specified ('the specified amount') there were substituted the amount arrived at by increasing the specified amount by the same percentage as the percentage increase in the retail prices index between January 1992 and the January immediately preceding that index linked period; and, if the amount arrived at is not a multiple of £10, it must be rounded up to the nearest amount which is such a multiple: reg 3(3). 'Accounting period' means: (i) where the lease provides for service charges to be payable by reference to a specified annual period, the first such period and any subsequent specified annual period, ending with the end of the tenth specified annual period beginning after the grant of the lease; or (ii) in any other case, the period of 12 months beginning with the grant of the lease and any of the next nine consecutive periods of 12 months each of which begins on an anniversary of that grant: reg 3(2).

Repayment of the amount secured must be made in equal instalments of principal and interest combined: reg 6(1), Sch 1 para 1. The period over which repayment is to be made must be three years, in respect of a loan of less than £1,500; five years, in respect of a loan of £1,500 or above but less than £5,000; and ten years, in respect of a loan of £5,000 or above, or, at the option of the borrower, a shorter period: Sch 1 para 2(1). For ascertaining the period of repayment, the amount of the loan is the aggregate of the amount of the loan made in pursuance of the right to a loan under reg 2 and the amount of any loan made under reg 5 (see PARA 924) in respect of any part of the service charge which does not qualify for a loan in pursuance of the right: Sch 1 para 2(2).

'Index linked period' means a period of 12 months beginning on 1 April 1993 and each subsequent period of 12 months: reg 3(4)(a). 'The retail prices index' means the United Kingdom General Index of Retail Prices (for all items) compiled by the Central Statistical Office: reg 3(4)(b).

16 Housing Act 1985 s 450A(3) (as added: see note 2).

17 Housing Act 1985 s 450A(4)(a) (as added (see note 2); amended by the Government of Wales Act 1998 Sch 16 para 5); and see the Housing (Service Charge Loans) Regulations 1992, SI 1992/1708, reg 2(2)(a) (amended by SI 2008/2831 and SI 2012/702). For these purposes, 'the relevant authority', in relation to a housing association falling within the Housing Act 1985 s 6A(4) (see PARA 8) and in the case of a property outside Greater London, means the Homes and Communities Agency: s 450A(5A) (added by SI 2008/3002; and amended by the Localism Act 2011 s 195(1), Sch 19 paras 10, 16(1), (2)). In the Housing Act 1985 s 450A(4)(a) 'the relevant authority', in relation to a housing association falling within s 6A(4) and in the case of a property in Greater London, means the Greater London Authority: s 450A(5B) (added by the Localism Act 2011 Sch 19 paras 10, 16(1), (3)). As to the Homes and Communities Agency see PARA 57 et seq; and PLANNING vol 83 (2010) PARA 1454 et seq. As to the Greater London Authority see LONDON GOVERNMENT vol 71 (2013) PARA 67 et seq.

18 Housing Act 1985 s 450A(4)(b) (as added: see note 2); and see the Housing (Service Charge Loans) Regulations 1992, SI 1992/1708, reg 2(2)(b).

19 Housing Act 1985 s 450A(5)(a) (as added (see note 2); amended by the Commonhold and Leasehold Reform Act 2002 Sch 9 para 2(3)). A demand for service charges in respect of repairs or improvements must inform the tenant whether, in the landlord's opinion, the tenant is entitled to a loan under the Housing (Service Charge Loans) Regulations 1992, SI 1992/1708, reg 2; and, if he is, what he must do to claim it: reg 4(1).

20 Housing Act 1985 s 450A(5)(b) (as added: see note 2). Any claim by the tenant to the right to such a loan must be made by notifying the lender in writing to that effect within the period of six weeks beginning on the date the demand for service charges in respect of repairs to which the claim relates was given: Housing (Service Charge Loans) Regulations 1992, SI 1992/1708, reg 4(2).

21 Housing Act 1985 s 450A(5)(c) (as added: see note 2). On the right being claimed the lender must inform the tenant of the terms of the loan and of the period within which the tenant may accept the offer: Housing (Service Charge Loans) Regulations 1992, SI 1992/1708, reg 4(3). The tenant

may accept the offer by notifying the lender in writing to that effect within the period of four weeks beginning on the date on which the lender informed the tenant as mentioned in reg 4(3): reg 4(4).

924. Power to make loans in other cases. The appropriate national authority[1] may by regulations[2] provide that where:

(1)   a housing authority (other than the Homes and Communities Agency or the Greater London Authority)[3] is the landlord[4] of a flat[5] under a long lease[6] granted or assigned by the authority or by another housing authority[7]; and

(2)   the tenant[8] is liable under the terms of the lease[9] to pay service charges[10] in respect of repairs[11] or improvements (whether to the flat, the building in which it is situated or any other building or land)[12],

the landlord or, where the landlord is a housing association[13], the relevant authority[14] may, in such circumstances as may be prescribed, make a loan[15] to the tenant in respect of the service charges[16]. The regulations must provide that the power is:

(a)   where the landlord is a housing association, a power of the relevant authority to make an advance[17]; and

(b)   in any other case, a power of the landlord to leave the whole or part of the service charge outstanding[18].

These provisions do not affect any other power of the landlord or the relevant authority to make loans[19].

1   As to the appropriate national authority, ie the Secretary of State or, where statutory functions have been transferred in relation to Wales, the Welsh Ministers, see PARA 7.

2   As to regulations under the Housing Act 1985 s 450B see s 450C; and PARA 923 note 2.

3   For these purposes, 'housing authority': (1) does not include a private registered provider of social housing, or a registered social landlord, which is a co-operative housing association; (2) includes a co-operative housing association which is neither a private registered provider of social housing nor a registered social landlord: Housing Act 1985 s 450B(4) (s 450B added by the Housing and Planning Act 1986 s 5; definition substituted by SI 2010/866). The Housing Act 1985 s 450B does not apply to a landlord which is a housing association falling within s 6A(4) (housing associations which are not Welsh or Scottish housing associations: see PARA 8): s 450B(6) (added by SI 2008/3002). As to the meaning of 'private registered provider of social housing' see PARA 53; as to the meaning of 'co-operative housing association' see PARA 13; and as to the meaning of 'registered social landlord' see PARA 13. As to the meaning of 'housing authority' generally see PARA 12. As to the Homes and Communities Agency see PARA 57 et seq; and PLANNING vol 83 (2010) PARA 1454 et seq. As to the Greater London Authority see LONDON GOVERNMENT vol 71 (2013) PARA 67 et seq.

4   As to the meaning of 'landlord' see PARA 31 note 3.

5   As to the meaning of 'flat' cf PARA 563 note 13.

6   As to the meaning of 'long lease' see PARA 917 note 2. For the purposes of the Housing Act 1985 s 450B, a long lease granted or assigned by the appropriate national authority may only be taken to have been granted or assigned by a housing authority if the appropriate national authority granted or assigned it in exercise of its powers under the Housing Associations Act 1985 s 90 (see PARA 156): Housing Act 1985 s 450B(3A) (s 450B as added (see note 3); s 450B(3A) added by the Government of Wales Act 1998 s 140, Sch 16 para 17(3)).

7   Housing Act 1985 s 450B(1)(a) (as added (see note 3); amended by the Localism Act 2011 s 195(1), Sch 19 paras 10, 17; and by SI 2008/3002).

8   As to the meaning of 'tenant' see PARA 31 note 3.

9   As to the meaning of 'lease' see PARA 31 note 3.

10   As to the meaning of 'service charge' see PARA 923 note 11. Where the tenant is entitled to a loan in pursuance of regulations under the Housing Act 1985 s 450A (see PARA 923), the power conferred by regulations under s 450B may be exercised in respect of any part of the service charge which does not qualify for a loan under s 450A: s 450B(3) (as added: see note 3).

11   For these purposes, 'repairs' includes works for making good a structural defect: Housing Act 1985 s 450B(4) (as added: see note 3).

12   Housing Act 1985 s 450B(1)(b) (as added (see note 3); amended by the Commonhold and Leasehold Reform Act 2002 s 150, Sch 9 paras 1, 3).

13   As to the meaning of 'housing association' see PARA 13.

14 As to the relevant authority see PARA 8.
15 Subject to the Housing (Service Charge Loans) Regulations 1992, SI 1992/1708, regs 6, 7 (see notes 16–19), a landlord or, where the landlord is a housing association, the Welsh Ministers, may make a loan to a tenant in respect of service charges in respect of repairs where: (1) a housing authority is the landlord of a flat under a long lease granted or assigned by the authority or by another housing authority; and (2) the tenant is liable under the terms of the lease to pay those charges (whether the repairs are to the flat, the building in which it is situated or any other building or land): reg 5(1) (amended by SI 2008/2831).
16 Housing Act 1985 s 450B(1) (as added (see note 3); amended by the Government of Wales Act 1998 Sch 16 para 5). Except for cases where it is the landlord as the result of the exercise of functions under the Housing Associations Act 1985 Pt III (ss 74–102) (see PARA 141 et seq), regulations may not contain provision for cases where the appropriate national authority is the landlord: Housing Act 1985 s 450B(1A) (added by the Government of Wales Act 1998 Sch 16 para 17(2)). A loan made by virtue of this power may be made on terms that: (1) do not require the payment of interest; or (2) require the payment of interest only on part of the loan, and must otherwise, subject to the Housing (Service Charge Loans) Regulations 1992, SI 1992/1708, reg 6(3), be on such terms as the lender may determine: reg 6(2) (substituted, in relation to England, by SI 2009/602; and, in relation to Wales, by SI 2011/1864). A loan under the Housing (Service Charge Loans) Regulations 1992, SI 1992/1708, must, as regards the rate of interest payable on it and the administrative expenses of the lender in connection with it, be subject to the provisions of Sch 2: reg 6(3). It must be secured by a mortgage of the flat in question but may be made whether or not the flat is adequate security for the loan: reg 7.
17 Housing Act 1985 s 450B(2)(a) (as added (see note 3); amended by the Government of Wales Act 1998 Sch 16 para 5); and see the Housing (Service Charge Loans) Regulations 1992, SI 1992/1708, reg 5(2)(a) (amended by SI 2008/2831).
18 Housing Act 1985 s 450B(2)(b) (as added: see note 3); and see the Housing (Service Charge Loans) Regulations 1992, SI 1992/1708, reg 5(2)(b).
19 Housing Act 1985 s 450B(5) (as added (see note 3); amended by the Government of Wales Act 1998 Sch 16 para 5).

925. Purchase of equitable interests. The appropriate national authority[1] may by regulations[2] provide that where:

(1)   a housing authority[3] is the landlord[4] of a flat[5] under a long lease[6] granted or assigned by the housing authority or another housing authority[7]; and

(2)   the tenant[8] is liable under the terms of the lease[9] to pay service charges[10] in respect of repairs[11] or improvements (whether to the flat, the building in which it is situated or any other building or land)[12],

the landlord may, with the agreement of the tenant and in such circumstances as may be prescribed, purchase an equitable interest in the flat for the purpose of assisting the tenant to meet some or all of the service charge payments[13].

Regulations must ensure that the purchase price is to be met by the landlord reducing or (as the case may be) cancelling the service charge payable to the landlord by the tenant to such extent as corresponds to the amount concerned[14].

Regulations may, in particular:

(a)   provide that the power to purchase an equitable interest does not arise in the case of particular descriptions of landlord[15];

(b)   make provision about calculating the purchase price (including provision about any discounts and about imposing charges for the services of district valuers)[16];

(c)   provide for: (i) the tenant to be liable for the administrative expenses of the landlord in connection with the purchase; (ii) such expenses not to exceed such amount (if any) as may be specified in the regulations; (iii) the purchase price to include, at the option of the purchaser, a deduction for such expenses[17];

(d)   provide for an alteration, as a result of the purchase of the equitable interest, in the liability of the tenant for future service charges or improvement contributions[18].

Regulations may apply whenever the lease concerned was granted or assigned and whenever the service charge concerned became payable[19].

1   As to the appropriate national authority, ie the Secretary of State or, where statutory functions have been transferred in relation to Wales, the Welsh Ministers, see the Housing Act 1985 s 450D(10) (s 450D added by the Housing and Regeneration Act 2008 s 309); and PARA 7.

2   Regulations under the Housing Act 1985 s 450D: (1) are to be made by statutory instrument; (2) may make different provision for different cases or descriptions of case including different provision for different areas; (3) may contain such incidental, supplementary and transitional provisions as the appropriate national authority considers appropriate: s 450D(8) (as added: see note 1). An instrument containing regulations made under s 450D: (a) by the Secretary of State is subject to annulment in pursuance of a resolution of either House of Parliament; (b) by the Welsh Ministers is subject to annulment in pursuance of a resolution of the National Assembly for Wales: s 450D(9) (as so added).

3   For these purposes, 'housing authority': (1) does not include a registered provider of social housing, or a registered social landlord, which is a co-operative housing association; (2) includes a co-operative housing association which is neither a registered provider of social housing nor a registered social landlord: Housing Act 1985 s 450D(10) (as added: see note 1). As to the meaning of 'private registered provider of social housing' see PARA 53; as to the meaning of 'co-operative housing association' see PARA 13; and as to the meaning of 'registered social landlord' see PARA 13. As to the meaning of 'housing authority' generally see PARA 12.

4   As to the meaning of 'landlord' see PARA 31 note 3.

5   As to the meaning of 'flat' cf PARA 563 note 13.

6   As to the meaning of 'long lease' see PARA 917 note 2. For the purposes of the Housing Act 1985 s 450D, a long lease granted or assigned by the Welsh Ministers or, in a case falling within s 450D(4)(b) (see note 13 head (2)), the former National Assembly for Wales, the Secretary of State, Housing for Wales or the Housing Corporation, is to be taken to have been granted or assigned by a housing authority if (but only if) the person concerned granted or assigned it in exercise of its powers under the Housing Associations Act 1985 s 90 (see PARA 156): Housing Act 1985 s 450D(5) (as added: see note 1).

7   Housing Act 1985 s 450D(1)(a) (as added: see note 1).

8   As to the meaning of 'tenant' see PARA 31 note 3.

9   As to the meaning of 'lease' see PARA 31 note 3.

10 As to the meaning of 'service charge' see PARA 923 note 11.

11 For these purposes, 'repairs' includes works for making good a structural defect: Housing Act 1985 s 450D(10) (as added: see note 1).

12 Housing Act 1985 s 450D(1)(b) (as added: see note 1).

13 Housing Act 1985 s 450D(1) (as added: see note 1). Section 450D does not affect any other power of the landlord to purchase an equitable interest in the flat for the purpose of assisting the tenant to meet some or all of the service charge payments: s 450D(6) (as so added). Regulations under s 450D may not contain provision for cases where the Secretary of State or the Welsh Ministers are the landlord unless the Welsh Ministers are the landlord: (1) as the result of the exercise by them of functions under the Housing Associations Act 1985 Pt III (ss 74–102) (see PARA 141 et seq); or (2) as the result of: (a) the exercise by the former National Assembly for Wales, the Secretary of State, Housing for Wales or the Housing Corporation of functions under Pt III; and (b) the transfer of the flat to the Welsh Ministers by virtue of the Government of Wales Act 2006 Sch 11 para 39: Housing Act 1985 s 450D(4) (as so added). 'Former National Assembly for Wales' means the Assembly constituted by the Government of Wales Act 1998: Housing Act 1985 s 450A(10) (as so added).

A housing authority ('the landlord') may with the agreement of the tenant purchase an equitable interest in a flat where the conditions below are satisfied: Housing (Purchase of Equitable Interests) (England) Regulations 2009, SI 2009/601, reg 2(1); Housing (Purchase of Equitable Interests) (Wales) Regulations 2011, SI 2011/1865, reg 2(1). Those conditions mentioned are that: (1) a long lease of the flat was granted or assigned by the landlord or another housing authority; (2) the tenant is liable under the terms of the lease to pay service charges to the landlord in respect of repairs or improvement contributions (whether to the flat, the building in which it is situated or any other building or land); and (3) the purpose of the purchase is to assist the tenant to meet some or all of the service charge payments: Housing (Purchase of Equitable Interests) (England) Regulations 2009, SI 2009/601, reg 2(2); Housing (Purchase of Equitable Interests) (Wales) Regulations 2011, SI 2011/1865, reg 2(2).

14 Housing Act 1985 s 450D(2) (as added: see note 1). The cost of the equitable interest purchased ('purchase price') must be met by the landlord reducing or (as the case may be) cancelling the service charge payable to the landlord by the tenant to such extent as corresponds to the amount concerned, but this is subject to the Housing (Purchase of Equitable Interests) (England)

Regulations 2009, SI 2009/601, reg 4(2) or the Housing (Purchase of Equitable Interests) (Wales) Regulations 2011, SI 2011/1865, reg 4(2): Housing (Purchase of Equitable Interests) (England) Regulations 2009, SI 2009/601, reg 4(1); Housing (Purchase of Equitable Interests) (Wales) Regulations 2011, SI 2011/1865, reg 4(1). Where, in accordance with a term agreed as mentioned in reg 5 of the respective regulations (see note 17), the tenant is liable to pay the landlord's administrative expenses, the purchase price may, at the option of the landlord, be reduced by the amount of those expenses: Housing (Purchase of Equitable Interests) (England) Regulations 2009, SI 2009/601, reg 4(2); Housing (Purchase of Equitable Interests) (Wales) Regulations 2011, SI 2011/1865, reg 4(2).

15 Housing Act 1985 s 450D(3)(a) (as added: see note 1).
16 Housing Act 1985 s 450D(3)(b) (as added: see note 1). As to the meaning of 'district valuer' see PARA 527 note 14.
17 Housing Act 1985 s 450D(3)(c) (as added: see note 1). It may be a term of the agreement for a purchase that the tenant be liable for the administrative expenses of the landlord in connection with the purchase: Housing (Purchase of Equitable Interests) (England) Regulations 2009, SI 2009/601, reg 5; Housing (Purchase of Equitable Interests) (Wales) Regulations 2011, SI 2011/1865, reg 5.
18 Housing Act 1985 s 450D(3)(d) (as added: see note 1). 'Improvement contribution' has the same meaning as in Pt V (see s 187; and PARA 276): s 450D(10) (as so added).
19 Housing Act 1985 s 450D(7) (as added: see note 1). In England, the landlord may make a purchase under the Housing (Purchase of Equitable Interests) (England) Regulations 2009, SI 2009/601, reg 2 (see note 13) notwithstanding that the lease concerned was granted or assigned, or the service charge concerned became payable, before the coming into force of those regulations (ie 6 April 2009: see reg 1(1)): reg 3. In Wales, the landlord may make a purchase under the Housing (Purchase of Equitable Interests) (Wales) Regulations 2011, SI 2011/1865, reg 2 (see note 13) notwithstanding that the lease concerned was granted or assigned, or the service charge concerned became payable, before the coming into force of those regulations (ie 19 August 2011: see reg 1(1)): reg 3.

926. Interest and administrative expenses of lender. In England, the rate of interest payable on a loan in respect of service charges[1] or the part of it on which interest is payable is to be such reasonable rate as may be determined by the lender[2], but in the case of a loan after the exercise of the right to buy[3] where the lender is a local authority[4], the statutory provisions relating to local authority mortgage interest rates[5] apply[6].

In Wales, the rate of interest payable on a loan in respect of service charges or the part of it on which interest is payable is to be such reasonable rate as may be determined by the lender, except where the lender is a local authority, in which case the statutory provisions relating to local authority mortgage interest rates[7] apply[8].

The administrative expenses of the lender, or any part of them, in connection with a loan may be charged by the lender to the borrower[9], but where a loan is made solely in pursuance of the right to a loan[10] the administrative expenses so charged may not exceed £100[11].

At the option of the borrower in the case of a loan made under the right to a loan[12], and at the option of the lender in the case of a discretionary loan[13], the administrative expenses charged by the lender may be added to the amount of the loan[14].

1 Ie a loan under the Housing (Service Charge Loans) Regulations 1992, SI 1992/1708: see PARAS 923–924.
2 Housing (Service Charge Loans) Regulations 1992, SI 1992/1708, reg 6(3), Sch 2 para 1(a) (Sch 2 para 1 substituted, in relation to England, by SI 2000/1963; the Housing (Service Charge Loans) Regulations 1992, SI 1992/1708, Sch 2 para 1(a) amended by SI 2009/602).
3 Ie under the Housing (Service Charge Loans) Regulations 1992, SI 1992/1708, reg 2: see PARA 923.
4 As to the meaning of 'local authority' see PARA 12.
5 Ie the Housing Act 1985 s 438(1), Sch 16: see PARA 912.
6 Housing (Service Charge Loans) Regulations 1992, SI 1992/1708 Sch 2 para 1(b) (as substituted, in relation to England: see note 2).

7 See note 5.
8 Housing (Service Charge Loans) Regulations 1992, SI 1992/1708, Sch 2 para 1 (amended, in relation to Wales, by SI 2011/1864).
9 Housing (Service Charge Loans) Regulations 1992, SI 1992/1708, Sch 2 para 2.
10 Ie in pursuance of the Housing (Service Charge Loans) Regulations 1992, SI 1992/1708, reg 2: see PARA 923.
11 Housing (Service Charge Loans) Regulations 1992, SI 1992/1708, Sch 2 para 3.
12 See note 10.
13 Ie a loan under the Housing (Service Charge Loans) Regulations 1992, SI 1992/1708, reg 5 (power to make a loan): see PARA 924.
14 Housing (Service Charge Loans) Regulations 1992, SI 1992/1708, Sch 2 para 4.

(6) EXERCISE OF POWER OF SALE

927. Vesting of house in authority entitled to exercise power of sale. Where there has been a disposal[1] of a house[2] by a housing authority[3] and:

(1)   the authority is a mortgagee of the house[4];

(2)   the conveyance or grant contains a pre-emption provision[5] in favour of the authority[6]; and

(3)   within the period during which the pre-emption provision has effect the authority becomes entitled as mortgagee to exercise the power of sale conferred by the Law of Property Act 1925[7] or the mortgage deed[8],

the following provisions[9] apply with respect to the vesting of the house in the authority[10].

The authority[11] may, if the County Court[12] gives it leave to do so, by deed vest the house[13] in itself for the estate and interest in the house which is the subject of the mortgage and which the authority would be authorised to sell or convey on exercising its power of sale[14], and freed from all estates, interests and rights to which the mortgage has priority[15], but subject to all estates, interests and rights which have priority to the mortgage[16]. On the vesting of the house, the authority's mortgage term or charge by way of legal mortgage, and any subsequent mortgage term or charge, merges or is extinguished as respects the house[17]. Where the house is registered under the Land Registration Act 2002[18], the Chief Land Registrar[19] must, on application being made to him by the authority, register the authority as the proprietor of the house free from all estates, interests and rights to which its mortgage had priority, and he is not to be concerned to inquire whether any of the relevant requirements[20] were complied with[21]. Where the authority conveys the house, or part of it, to a person, he is not to be concerned to inquire whether any of these provisions were complied with[22] and his title is not impeachable on the ground that the house was not properly vested in the authority or that those provisions were not complied with[23].

Where the authority has vested the house in itself, it must appropriate a fund equal to the aggregate of:

(a)   the amount agreed between the authority and the mortgagor or determined by the district valuer[24] as being the amount which is to be taken as the value of the house at the time of the vesting[25]; and

(b)   interest on that amount, for the period beginning with the vesting and ending with the appropriation, at the rate prescribed for that period under the Land Compensation Act 1961[26].

The fund must be applied in the following order:

(i)   in discharging, or paying sums into court for meeting, any prior incumbrances to which the vesting is not made subject[27];

(ii)   in recovering the costs, charges, and expenses properly incurred by the authority as incidental to the vesting of the house[28];

(iii)   in recovering the mortgage money, interest, costs and other money (if any) due under the mortgage[29];

(iv)   in recovering any amount which falls to be paid under the covenant required by the statutory provisions relating to the repayment of discount or the payment of the outstanding share on disposal[30] or any provision of the conveyance or grant to the like effect[31],

and any residue then remaining in the fund must be paid to the person entitled to the mortgaged house, or who would have been entitled to give receipts for the proceeds of sale of the house if it had been sold in the exercise of the power of sale[32].

Where a conveyance or grant executed before 26 August 1984[33] contains both a pre-emption provision[34] and a covenant concerning the repayment of discount on early disposal[35] or any other provision to the like effect[36], the latter covenant or provision has effect as from that date with such modifications as may be necessary to bring it into conformity with these provisions[37].

Where before 8 August 1980[38] a local authority sold property under the powers of the Housing Act 1957[39] and:

(A)   part of the price was secured by a mortgage of the property[40];

(B)   a condition was imposed on the sale[41]; and

(C)   within the period during which the authority has the right to re-acquire the property it becomes entitled to exercise the power of sale conferred by the Law of Property Act 1925[42] or by the mortgage deed[43],

the statutory provisions with respect to the vesting of the property in the authority apply with modifications[44].

1   'Disposal' means a conveyance of the freehold or a grant or assignment of a long lease: Housing Act 1985 s 452(2). As to the meaning of 'long lease' see PARA 917 note 2.

2   As to the meaning of 'house' see PARA 909 note 2.

3   In the Housing Act 1985 s 452, 'housing authority' does not include the Welsh Ministers unless the disposal was under the Housing Associations Act 1985 s 90 (see PARA 156): Housing Act 1985 s 458(2) (added by the Government of Wales Act 1998 s 140, Sch 16 para 18(3)). As to the Welsh Ministers see PARA 7.

4   Housing Act 1985 s 452(1)(a).

5   'Pre-emption provision' means a covenant imposing a condition of the kind mentioned in the Housing Act 1985 s 33(2)(b) or (c) (right of pre-emption or prohibition of assignment: see PARA 523), the limitation specified in s 157(4) (restriction on disposal of dwellings in national parks, etc: see PARA 239), or any other provision to the like effect: s 452(2).

6   Housing Act 1985 s 452(1)(b).

7   Ie conferred by the Law of Property Act 1925 s 101: see MORTGAGE vol 77 (2016) PARA 446 et seq.

8   Housing Act 1985 s 452(1)(c).

9   Ie the Housing Act 1985 Sch 17: see the text and notes 11–32. The vesting of a house under Sch 17 is treated as a relevant disposal for the purposes of: (1) the provisions of Pt II (ss 8–57) (see PARA 401 et seq) and Pt V (ss 118–188) (see PARA 239 et seq) relating to the covenant required by s 35 (see PARA 527) or s 155 (see PARA 323) (repayment of discount on early disposal); and (2) any provision of the conveyance or grant to the like effect as the covenant required by those statutory provisions: s 452(3)(a), (b).

10   Housing Act 1985 s 452(1). See note 38. Prior to the enactment of the predecessor provision, such a vesting in an authority had been held to be a nullity: see *Williams v Wellingborough Borough Council* [1975] 3 All ER 462, [1975] 1 WLR 1327, CA. Special provision may be made by regulations under the Housing Act 1985 s 568(4) (see PARA 941) for a payment on the vesting in the housing authority of a defective dwelling by virtue of such regulations or under Sch 17 (see the text and notes 11–32).

11   Ie the housing authority: see note 3.

12   Where application for leave under the Housing Act 1985 Sch 17 para 1 is made to the County Court, the court may adjourn the proceedings or postpone the date for the execution

of the authority's deed for such period as the court thinks reasonable: Sch 17 para 1(2). An adjournment or postponement may be made subject to such conditions with regard to payment by the mortgagor of any sum secured by the mortgage or the remedy of any default as the court thinks fit; and the court may from time to time vary or revoke any such conditions: Sch 17 para 1(3).

13 A house which is vested under the Housing Act 1985 Sch 17 in a local housing authority must be treated as acquired under Pt II (ss 8–57) (provision of housing: see PARA 401 et seq): Sch 17 para 2(4).

14 Housing Act 1985 Sch 17 para 1(1)(a).

15 Housing Act 1985 Sch 17 para 1(1)(b). As to priorities with regard to mortgages see MORTGAGE vol 77 (2016) PARA 260 et seq.

16 Housing Act 1985 Sch 17 para 1(1).

17 Housing Act 1985 Sch 17 para 2(1).

18 As to registration of title see generally REAL PROPERTY AND REGISTRATION vol 87 (2012) PARA 232 et seq.

19 As to the Chief Land Registrar see REAL PROPERTY AND REGISTRATION vol 87 (2012) PARA 562.

20 Ie the requirements of the Housing Act 1985 Sch 17.

21 Housing Act 1985 Sch 17 para 2(2) (amended by the Land Registration Act 2002 s 133, Sch 11 para 18(1), (12)).

22 Housing Act 1985 Sch 17 para 2(3)(a).

23 Housing Act 1985 Sch 17 para 2(3)(b).

24 As to the meaning of 'district valuer' see PARA 527 note 14.

25 Housing Act 1985 Sch 17 para 3(1)(a). The value of the house at the time of the vesting must be taken to be the price which, at that time, the interest vested in the authority would realise if sold on the open market by a willing vendor on the assumption that any prior incumbrances to which the vesting is not made subject would be discharged by the vendor: Sch 17 para 3(2).

26 Housing Act 1985 Sch 17 para 3(1)(b). For the prescribed rate see the Land Compensation Act 1961 s 32 (rate prescribed for compulsory purchase cases where entry is made before compensation is paid); and COMPULSORY ACQUISITION OF LAND vol 18 (2009) PARA 641.

27 Housing Act 1985 Sch 17 para 3(3)(a).

28 Housing Act 1985 Sch 17 para 3(3)(b).

29 Housing Act 1985 Sch 17 para 3(3)(c).

30 Ie a covenant required by the Housing Act 1985 s 35 (see PARA 527) or s 155 (see PARA 323) (repayment of discount, etc on disposal) or Sch 8 para 6 (repealed) (terms of shared ownership lease; payment for outstanding share on disposal): Sch 17 para 3(3)(d).

31 Housing Act 1985 Sch 17 para 3(3)(d).

32 Housing Act 1985 Sch 17 para 3(3). The Law of Property Act 1925 s 107(1) (mortgagee's written receipt sufficient discharge for money arising under power of sale: see MORTGAGE vol 77 (2016) PARA 471) applies to money payable under the Housing Act 1985 Sch 17 as it applies to money arising under the power of sale conferred by the Law of Property Act 1925: Housing Act 1985 Sch 17 para 3(4).

33 Ie the date on which the corresponding provisions of the earlier legislation came into operation.

34 Housing Act 1985 s 452(4)(a).

35 See note 30.

36 Housing Act 1985 s 452(4)(b).

37 Housing Act 1985 s 452(4).

38 Ie the date on which the Housing Act 1980 received Royal Assent. The provisions of the Housing Act 1985 s 452(1)–(4) (see the text and notes 1–10, 33–37) do not apply where the conveyance or grant was executed before 8 August 1980: s 452(5).

39 Ie the powers contained in the Housing Act 1957 s 104(1) (repealed) (disposal of houses provided under Pt V (ss 91–134) (repealed)).

40 Housing Act 1985 s 452(6)(a).

41 Housing Act 1985 s 452(6)(b). The condition referred to in head (B) in the text is such a condition as was mentioned in the Housing Act 1957 s 104(3)(c) (repealed).

42 Ie the power of sale conferred by the Law of Property Act 1925 s 101: see MORTGAGE vol 77 (2016) PARA 446 et seq.

43 Housing Act 1985 s 452(6)(c).

44 Housing Act 1985 s 452(6). For the relevant modifications see Sch 17 para 4.

17. ASSISTANCE FOR OWNERS OF DEFECTIVE HOUSING

(1) ASSISTANCE IN GENERAL

928. Eligibility for assistance. Since 1945, some public sector housing has proved to be seriously defective[1]. Former tenants of local authorities who bought such dwellings under the right to buy provisions in the Housing Act 1985 found that in many cases the value of their property had fallen significantly. Such persons may be eligible for assistance under Part XVI of that Act[2].

A person is eligible for such assistance in respect of a dwelling[3] if:

(1)   he is an individual who is not a trustee, or he is a trustee for beneficiaries who are all individuals or a personal representative[4];

(2)   the dwelling is a defective dwelling[5] within the meaning of Part XVI[6];

(3)   he holds a relevant interest[7] in the dwelling[8]; and

(4)   the specified conditions[9] are satisfied[10].

However, a person who holds a relevant interest in a defective dwelling is not eligible for assistance in respect of the dwelling at any time when that interest is subject to the rights of a person who is a protected occupier or statutory tenant within the meaning of the Rent (Agriculture) Act 1976[11] or who occupies the dwelling under an assured agricultural occupancy which is not an assured tenancy[12]. Further, a person is not eligible for assistance in respect of a defective dwelling if the local housing authority[13] is of the opinion:

(a)   that work to the building which consists of or includes the dwelling has been carried out in order to deal with the qualifying defect[14]; and

(b)   that on the completion of the work, no further work relating to the dwelling was required to be done to the building in order to deal satisfactorily with the qualifying defect[15].

1   See *Hodge v Newport Borough Council* (2001) 33 HLR 187, [2001] LGR 20, CA, per Roch LJ.
2   See the Housing Act 1985 Pt XVI (ss 527–577), replacing the Housing Defects Act 1984 (repealed). See also *Hodge v Newport Borough Council* (2001) 33 HLR 187, [2001] LGR 20, CA.
3   For the purposes of the Housing Act 1985 Pt XVI, 'dwelling' means any house, flat or other unit designed or adapted for living in: s 575(1). For the purposes of Pt XVI, a building so designed or adapted is a 'house' if it is a structure reasonably so called; so that where a building is divided into units so designed or adapted: (1) if it is so divided horizontally, or a material part of a unit lies above or below another unit, the units are not houses (though the building as a whole may be); and (2) if it is so divided vertically, the units may be houses: s 575(2)(a), (b).
4   Housing Act 1985 s 527(a).
5   As to the meaning of 'defective dwelling' see PARA 929.
6   Housing Act 1985 s 527(b).
7   'Relevant interest', in relation to a dwelling, means the freehold or a long tenancy, not being in either case subject to a long tenancy: Housing Act 1985 s 530(1).
    A tenancy is a long tenancy for this purpose, if it is: (1) a tenancy granted for a term certain exceeding 21 years, whether or not it is (or may become) terminable before the end of that term by notice given by or to the tenant or by re-entry, forfeiture or otherwise; (2) a tenancy granted in pursuance of Pt V (ss 118–188) (the right to buy); or (3) a tenancy for a term fixed by law under a grant with a covenant or obligation for perpetual renewal, unless it is a tenancy by sub-demise from one which is not a long tenancy: s 530(2)(a)–(c).
    A tenancy is not a long tenancy for this purpose if it is: (a) an interest created by way of security and liable to termination by the exercise of a right of redemption or otherwise; or (b) a secure tenancy: s 530(3)(a), (b).
    References to an interest in a dwelling are references to an interest in land which is or includes the dwelling: s 530(4). As to the meaning of 'secure tenancy' see LANDLORD AND TENANT vol 63 (2016) PARA 1037.
8   Housing Act 1985 s 527(c).
9   Ie the conditions specified in the Housing Act 1985 s 531 (conditions of eligibility; disposal by public sector authority, etc): see PARA 931.

10 Housing Act 1985 s 527(d). Part XVI may in certain circumstances be extended by regulations to mortgagees of defective dwellings: see PARA 941.
11 As to the meanings of 'protected occupier' and 'statutory tenant' see the Rent (Agriculture) Act 1976 ss 2–5; and LANDLORD AND TENANT vol 64 (2016) PARAS 1709, 1711.
12 Housing Act 1985 s 533(1) (amended by the Housing Act 1988 s 140(1), Sch 17 para 59). As to the meaning of 'assured tenancy' see the Housing Act 1988 s 1; and LANDLORD AND TENANT vol 63 (2016) PARA 825. As to the meaning of 'assured agricultural occupancy' see the Housing Act 1988 s 24; and LANDLORD AND TENANT vol 64 (2016) PARA 1747.
13 As to the meaning of 'local housing authority' see PARA 11.
14 Housing Act 1985 s 533(2)(a). As to the meaning of 'qualifying defect' see PARA 929 note 9.
15 Housing Act 1985 s 533(2)(b).

929. Designation of defective dwellings by appropriate national authority. The appropriate national authority[1] may designate as a class buildings[2] each of which consists of or includes one or more dwellings[3] if it appears to it that:

(1)   buildings in the proposed class are defective by reason of their design or construction[4]; and

(2)   by virtue of these circumstances having become generally known, the value of some or all of the dwellings concerned has been substantially reduced[5].

A dwelling which is, or is included in, a building in a class so designated is referred to in Part XVI of the Housing Act 1985[6] as a 'defective dwelling'[7]. A designation[8] must describe the qualifying defect[9] and specify:

(a)   the cut-off date[10];

(b)   the date (being a date falling on or after the cut-off date) on which the designation is to come into operation[11]; and

(c)   the period within which persons may seek assistance in respect of the defective dwellings concerned[12].

The appropriate national authority may vary a designation, but not so as to vary the cut-off date[13]; or it may revoke such a designation[14]. The appropriate national authority may also by a variation of the designation extend the period within which assistance must be applied for whether or not it has expired[15]. The variation or revocation of a designation does not affect the operation of the defective housing provisions in relation to a dwelling if, before the variation or revocation comes into operation, the dwelling is a defective dwelling by virtue of the designation in question and an application for assistance has been made[16].

1   As to the appropriate national authority, ie the Secretary of State or, where statutory functions have been transferred in relation to Wales, the Welsh Ministers, see PARA 7.
2   Any question arising as to whether a building is or was at any time in a class designated under the Housing Act 1985 s 528 must be determined by the appropriate national authority: s 528(6). Where a dwelling, house or building is or forms part of a class designated under s 528 or s 559, no grant is payable under the Housing Grants, Construction and Regeneration Act 1996 Pt I Ch I (ss 1–59): see PARA 835 et seq.
3   As to the meaning of 'dwelling' see PARA 928 note 3.
4   Housing Act 1985 s 528(1)(a).
5   Housing Act 1985 s 528(1)(b).
6   Ie the Housing Act 1985 Pt XVI (ss 527–577).
7   Housing Act 1985 s 528(2). As to the Housing Health and Safety Rating System ('HHSRS') under the Housing Act 2004, and category 1 and category 2 hazards, see PARA 562 et seq.
8   A designation may make different provision in relation to England and Wales; subject to that, a designated class must not be described by reference to the area in which the buildings concerned are situated: Housing Act 1985 s 528(4). Notice of a designation must be published in the London Gazette: s 528(5). As to the publication of notices see also PARA 685.
9   'The qualifying defect' means what, in the opinion of the appropriate national authority, is wrong with the buildings in that class: Housing Act 1985 s 528(2)(a).
10 Housing Act 1985 s 528(3)(a). The 'cut-off date' means the date by which, in the opinion of the appropriate national authority, the circumstances mentioned in s 528(1)(a) (see the text and note 4) became generally known: s 528(2)(b).

11 Housing Act 1985 s 528(3)(b).
12 Housing Act 1985 s 528(3)(c).
13 Housing Act 1985 s 529(1)(a).
14 Housing Act 1985 s 529(1)(b).
15 Housing Act 1985 s 529(2).
16 Housing Act 1985 s 529(3). Notice of the variation or revocation of a designation must be published in the London Gazette: s 529(4). As to the publication of notices see also PARA 935.

930. Contributions by appropriate national authority. The appropriate national authority[1] may, if it thinks fit in any case, contribute towards the expense incurred by a local housing authority[2]:

(1)   in giving assistance by way of reinstatement grant[3];

(2)   in giving assistance by way of repurchase[4] of a dwelling[5] which is a defective dwelling[6] by virtue of a designation by the appropriate national authority[7]; or

(3)   in making payments in respect of the making up of consideration on disposal[8] in pursuance of a right of pre-emption, etc[9] or in respect of the making up[10] of compulsory purchase compensation[11].

The contributions must be equal to the relevant percentage[12] of the amount of the expense incurred[13]. Payment of these contributions is subject to the making of a claim in such form, and containing such particulars, as the appropriate national authority may determine; and the contributions are payable at such times, in such manner and subject to such conditions as to records, certificates, audit or otherwise as the appropriate national authority may (in relation to England, with the agreement of the Treasury) determine[14].

The appropriate national authority may by order[15] made, in relation to England, with the consent of the Treasury, vary all or any of the relevant percentages for the purposes of contribution to the expenditure of the local housing authority[16] in respect of assistance or payments, or a class of assistance or payments, specified in the order[17]. An order applies to assistance given or payments made in pursuance of applications made after such date as may be specified in the order, and the specified date must not be earlier than the date of the laying of the draft[18].

1   As to the appropriate national authority, ie the Secretary of State or, where statutory functions have been transferred in relation to Wales, the Welsh Ministers, see PARA 7.
2   As to the meaning of 'local housing authority' see PARA 11. The rights and duties of an abolished authority in respect of payments under the Housing Act 1985 s 569 are to be treated as the rights and duties of the designated authority: see the Local Government Changes for England (Finance) Regulations 1994, SI 1994/2825, reg 54A (added by SI 1995/2862; and amended by SI 1996/563).
3   Housing Act 1985 s 569(1)(a). As to assistance by way of reinstatement grant see PARA 942 et seq.
4   As to assistance by way of repurchase see PARA 946 et seq.
5   As to the meaning of 'dwelling' see PARA 928 note 3.
6   As to the meaning of 'defective dwelling' see PARA 929.
7   Housing Act 1985 s 569(1)(b).
8   As to the meaning of 'disposal' see PARA 931 note 2.
9   Ie payments under the Housing Act 1985 s 549 (making up of consideration on disposal in pursuance of right of pre-emption, etc): see PARA 950.
10 Ie under the Housing Act 1985 s 550: see PARA 951.
11 Housing Act 1985 s 569(1)(c).
12 The relevant percentage is:
    (1)   90% in the case of reinstatement grant (Housing Act 1985 s 569(3)(a));
    (2)   75% in the case of repurchase or a payment under s 549 (see PARA 950) or s 550 (see PARA 951) where there has at any time been a disposal of a relevant interest in the defective dwelling by the local housing authority or a predecessor of that authority (s 569(3)(b)); and
    (3)   100% in the case of repurchase or a payment under s 549 (see PARA 950) or s 550 (see PARA 951) not within s 569(3)(b) (see head (2)) (s 569(3)(c)),

or such other percentage as, in any of those cases, may be provided by order under s 570 (see the text and notes 15–18): s 569(3).

13 Housing Act 1985 s 569(2) (amended by the Local Government and Housing Act 1989 s 157(8), (10)). The amount of the expense incurred is:

    (1)   in the case of reinstatement grant, the amount of the grant (Housing Act 1985 s 569(4)(a));

    (2)   in the case of repurchase, the price paid for the acquisition, together with any amount reimbursed under s 552 (incidental expenses: see PARA 953), less the value of the interest at the relevant time determined in accordance with Sch 20 para 8 (value for purposes of repurchase: see PARA 947) but without the assumption required by Sch 20 para 8(1)(a) (assumption that dwelling is defect free: see PARA 947) (s 569(4)(b));

    (3)   in the case of a payment under s 549 (see PARA 950) or s 550 (see PARA 951), the amount of the payment (s 569(4)(c)).

14 Housing Act 1985 s 569(6). As to the Treasury see CONSTITUTIONAL AND ADMINISTRATIVE LAW vol 20 (2014) PARA 262 et seq.

15 An order: (1) may make different provision for assistance given or payments made in respect of defective dwellings in different areas or under different provisions or for different purposes of the same provision; (2) must be made by statutory instrument; and (3) must not be made unless a draft of it has been laid before and approved by a resolution of the House of Commons or, as appropriate, the National Assembly for Wales: Housing Act 1985 s 570(2)(a)–(c). At the date at which this volume states the law no such order had been made.

16 Ie the percentages specified in the Housing Act 1985 s 569(3): see note 12.

17 Housing Act 1985 s 570(1).

18 Housing Act 1985 s 570(3). At the date at which this volume states the law, no such order had been made.

931. Conditions of eligibility: disposal by public sector authority, etc. The conditions as to eligibility for assistance[1] are that there has been a disposal[2] by a public sector authority[3] of a relevant interest[4] in the dwelling[5] and that either of the following two sets of conditions is satisfied[6]. The first set of conditions is that:

    (1)   the disposal by a public sector authority was made before the cut-off date[7]; and

    (2)   there has been no disposal for value[8] by any person of a relevant interest in the dwelling on or after that date[9].

The second set of conditions is that:

    (a)   an eligible person[10] acquired a relevant interest in the dwelling on a disposal for value occurring within the period of 12 months beginning with the cut-off date[11];

    (b)   he was unaware on the date of the disposal of the association of the dwelling with the qualifying defect[12];

    (c)   the value by reference to which the price for the disposal was calculated did not take any, or any adequate, account of the qualifying defect[13]; and

    (d)   if the cut-off date had fallen immediately after the date of the disposal, the first set of conditions[14] would have been satisfied[15].

1 Ie the conditions referred to in the Housing Act 1985 s 527(d): see PARA 928.

2 References in the Housing Act 1985 Pt XVI (ss 527–577) to a disposal include a part disposal; but for these purposes a disposal of an interest in a dwelling is a disposal of a relevant interest in the dwelling only if on the disposal the person to whom it is made acquires a relevant interest in the dwelling: s 532(1). Where an interest in land is disposed of under a contract, the time at which the disposal is made is, for these purposes:

    (1)   if the contract is unconditional, the time at which the contract is made; and

    (2)   if the contract is conditional (and in particular if it is conditional on the exercise of an option), the time when the condition is satisfied,

and not, if different, the time at which the interest is conveyed: s 532(2). In relation to a person holding an interest in a dwelling formed by the conversion of another dwelling, references in Pt XVI to a previous disposal of an interest in the dwelling include a previous disposal on which an interest in land which included that part of the original dwelling in which his interest subsists was acquired: s 532(4).

3 For these purposes, where a public sector authority holds an interest in a dwelling a disposal of the interest by or under an enactment must be treated as a disposal by the authority: Housing Act 1985 s 531(4). References in Pt XVI to a disposal of an interest in a dwelling by a public sector authority include a disposal of: (1) an interest belonging to Her Majesty in right of the Crown; (2) an interest belonging to, or held in trust for Her Majesty for the purposes of, a government department or Minister of the Crown; or (3) an interest belonging to Her Majesty in right of the Duchy of Lancaster or belonging to the Duchy of Cornwall: s 574. As to the meaning of 'public sector authority' see PARA 933.

4 As to the meaning of 'relevant interest' see PARA 928 note 7.

5 As to the meaning of 'dwelling' see PARA 928 note 3. As to the meaning of 'interest in a dwelling' see PARA 928 note 7.

6 Housing Act 1985 s 531(1).

7 Housing Act 1985 s 531(2)(a). As to the meaning of 'cut-off date' see PARA 929 note 10.

8 References to a disposal of an interest for value are references to a disposal for money or money's worth, whether or not representing full value for the interest disposed of: Housing Act 1985 s 532(3).

9 Housing Act 1985 s 531(2)(b).

10 Ie a person to whom the Housing Act 1985 s 527 applies: see PARA 928.

11 Housing Act 1985 s 531(3)(a).

12 Housing Act 1985 s 531(3)(b). As to the meaning of 'qualifying defect' see PARA 929 note 9.

13 Housing Act 1985 s 531(3)(c).

14 Ie the conditions in the Housing Act 1985 s 531(2): see heads (1) and (2) in the text.

15 Housing Act 1985 s 531(3)(d).

932. Duties of public sector authority when disposing of a defective dwelling. A public sector authority[1] must, where a person is to acquire a relevant interest[2] in a defective dwelling[3] on a disposal by the authority[4], give him notice in writing[5] before the time of the disposal:

(1) specifying the qualifying defect[6]; and

(2) stating that he will not be eligible for assistance[7] under Part XVI of the Housing Act 1985[8] in respect of the dwelling[9].

A public sector authority must, before it conveys a relevant interest in a defective dwelling in pursuance of a contract to a person on whom the required notice has not been served, give him notice in writing:

(a) specifying the qualifying defect[10];

(b) stating, where the time of disposal of the interest falls after the cut-off date[11], that he will not be eligible for assistance under Part XVI[12]; and

(c) stating the effect of other relevant provisions[13].

A person on whom such a notice is served is not obliged to complete the conveyance before the expiry of the period of six months beginning with the service of that notice on him[14], and he may within that period withdraw from the transaction by notice in writing to the authority to that effect[15]. Upon such a notice of withdrawal being given to the authority the parties to the contract are discharged from any obligations in connection with it and any deposit paid must be repaid[16].

1 As to the meaning of 'public sector authority' see PARA 933.

2 As to the meaning of 'relevant interest' see PARA 928 note 7.

3 As to the meaning of 'defective dwelling' see PARA 929.

4 As to the meaning of 'disposal of an interest in a dwelling by a public sector authority' see PARA 931 note 3. As to the meaning of 'disposal' see PARA 931 note 2.

5 Where a public sector authority is required to serve a notice under the Housing Act 1985 s 124 (landlord's response to notice claiming to exercise right to buy: see PARA 275) in respect of a defective dwelling, the notice under s 563(1) must be served with that notice: s 563(4).

A notice under s 563(1) or (2) must (except in the case of a notice under s 563(1) which is served in accordance with s 563(4)) be served at the earliest date at which it is reasonably practicable to do so: s 563(5).

6 Housing Act 1985 s 563(1)(a). As to the meaning of 'qualifying defect' see PARA 929 note 9.

7 As to eligibility for assistance see PARA 928.

8 Ie the Housing Act 1985 Pt XVI (ss 527–577).
9 Housing Act 1985 s 563(1)(b). As to the meaning of 'dwelling' see PARA 928 note 3. As to
   damages for breach of the authority's duty under s 563(1) see *Berry v Newport Borough Council*
   (2000) 33 HLR 197, [2000] 2 EGLR 26, CA.
10 Housing Act 1985 s 563(2)(a).
11 As to the meaning of 'cut-off date' see PARA 929 note 10.
12 Housing Act 1985 s 563(2)(b).
13 Ie the effect of the provisions contained in the Housing Act 1985 s 563(3) (see the text and notes
   14–16): s 563(2)(c).
14 Housing Act 1985 s 563(3)(a).
15 Housing Act 1985 s 563(3)(b).
16 Housing Act 1985 s 563(3).

933. Meaning of 'public sector authority'. In Part XVI of the Housing Act 1985[1]
'public sector authority' means a local authority[2] (or a predecessor of a local
authority); a joint board of which every constituent member is, or is appointed by,
a local authority (or a predecessor of a local authority); a national park authority[3]
(or a predecessor of such an authority); a Welsh planning board[4]; the Natural
Resources Body for Wales[5]; the Environment Agency[6]; the relevant authority[7]; a
non-profit registered provider of social housing[8] other than a co-operative housing
association[9] (or a predecessor housing association of such a provider); a registered
social landlord[10] other than a co-operative housing association (or a predecessor
housing association of such a landlord)[11]; a new town corporation[12]; the
British Coal Corporation, the Coal Authority[13], or the United Kingdom Atomic
Energy Authority[14]; or a body corporate or housing association specified by
order of the appropriate national authority[15].
   The appropriate national authority may provide that a body corporate is to be
treated as a public sector authority if it is satisfied:
   (1)   that the affairs of the body are managed by its members[16]; and
   (2)   that its members hold office by virtue of appointment (to that or another
          office) by a Minister of the Crown under an enactment[17],
or if it is satisfied that it is a subsidiary[18] of such a body[19]. Where the appropriate
national authority is satisfied that a body or association met the specified
requirements[20] during any period, it may, whether or not it makes an order in
respect of the body or association, provide that it is to be treated as having been
a public sector authority during that period[21].
   If the appropriate national authority is satisfied that a body or association
specified in an order has ceased to meet the requirements on any date, it may by
order provide that it is to be treated as having ceased to be a public sector
authority on that date[22].

1 Ie the Housing Act 1985 Pt XVI (ss 527–577).
2 As to the meaning of 'local authority' see PARA 12. References to a local authority include
   references to the councils abolished by the Local Government Act 1985: Housing (Consequential
   Provisions) Act 1985 s 5(1), Sch 3 para 5(2), (3).
3 As to national park authorities see OPEN SPACES AND COUNTRYSIDE vol 78 (2010) PARA 526
   et seq.
4 For the purposes of the Housing Act 1985 s 573(1), 'Welsh planning board' means a board
   constituted under the Town and Country Planning Act 1990 s 2(1B) (see PLANNING vol 81 (2010)
   PARA 45): Housing Act 1985 s 573(1A) (added by the Local Government (Wales) Act 1994
   s 20(4)(b), Sch 6 para 19; and amended by the Environment Act 1995 s 120, Sch 24).
5 As to the Natural Resources Body for Wales see ENVIRONMENTAL QUALITY AND PUBLIC
   HEALTH.
6 The National Rivers Authority was abolished and its functions were transferred to the
   Environment Agency by the Environment Act 1995 s 2: see WATER AND WATERWAYS vol 100
   (2009) PARA 12.
7 As to the relevant authority see PARA 8.

8 As to registered providers of social housing see PARA 51 et seq; as to when such a body is a non-profit organisation see PARA 71 note 13.
9 As to the meaning of 'co-operative housing association' see PARA 13.
10 As to the meaning of 'registered social landlord' see PARA 13.
11 The appropriate national authority may provide that a housing association is to be treated as a public sector authority if it is satisfied that the objects or powers of the association include the provision of housing accommodation for individuals employed at any time by a public sector authority or dependants of such individuals: Housing Act 1985 s 573(3). As to the meaning of 'housing association' see PARA 13. As to the appropriate national authority, ie the Secretary of State or, where statutory functions have been transferred in relation to Wales, the Welsh Ministers, see PARA 7.
12 As to the meaning of 'new town corporation' see PARA 12.
13 The British Coal Corporation was established under the name 'the National Coal Board' by the Coal Industry Nationalisation Act 1946 ss 1, 2, and it was renamed by the Coal Industry Act 1987 s 1: see MINES, MINERALS AND QUARRIES vol 76 (2013) PARA 49. As to the British Coal Corporation and its replacement by the Coal Authority see MINES, MINERALS AND QUARRIES vol 76 (2013) PARA 74 et seq.
14 The United Kingdom Atomic Energy Authority is constituted under the Atomic Energy Authority Act 1954 s 1, Sch 1: see ENERGY AND CLIMATE CHANGE vol 44 (2011) PARA 787 et seq.
15 Housing Act 1985 s 573(1) (amended by the Coal Industry Act 1987 s 1(2), Sch 1 para 47; the Housing Act 1988 s 140(1), Sch 17 para 106; the Water Act 1989 s 190(1), Sch 25 para 74(1); the Coal Industry Act 1994 s 67(1), Sch 9 para 33; the Local Government (Wales) Act 1994 s 20(4)(b), Sch 6 para 19; the Environment Act 1995 ss 78, 120(3), Sch 10 para 24(3), Sch 24; the Government of Wales Act 1998 ss 140, 152, Sch 16 para 5, Sch 18 Pt IV; and by SI 1996/2325, SI 2010/866 and SI 2013/755).
16 Housing Act 1985 s 573(2)(a).
17 Housing Act 1985 s 573(2)(b).
18 As to the meaning of 'subsidiary' see the Companies Act 2006 s 1159; and COMPANIES vol 14 (2016) PARA 22.
19 Housing Act 1985 s 573(2).
20 Ie the requirements of the Housing Act 1985 s 573(2) (see the text and notes 16–19) or s 573(3) (see note 11).
21 Housing Act 1985 s 573(4).
22 Housing Act 1985 s 573(5). An order under s 573 must be made by statutory instrument: s 573(6). At the date at which this volume states the law, no such order had been made.

934. Reinstatement of a defective dwelling by a local housing authority. Remedial works to a defective dwelling may be carried out on behalf of its owner. Where a relevant interest[1] in a defective dwelling[2] has been disposed of by a public sector authority[3], the local housing authority[4] may, before the end of the period within which a person may seek assistance[5] under Part XVI of the Housing Act 1985[6] in respect of the dwelling[7], enter into an agreement with:

(1)   any person holding an interest in the dwelling[8]; or

(2)   any person who is a statutory tenant[9] of it[10],

to execute at his expense any of the work required to reinstate the dwelling[11]. For these purposes, a disposal by or under an enactment of an interest in a dwelling held by a public sector authority is to be treated as a disposal of the interest by the authority[12].

1 As to the meaning of 'relevant interest' see PARA 928 note 7.
2 As to the meaning of 'defective dwelling' see PARA 929.
3 As to the meaning of 'disposal by a public sector authority' see PARA 931 note 3. As to the meaning of 'public sector authority' see PARA 933.
4 As to the meaning of 'local housing authority' see PARA 11.
5 As to the period in which a person may seek assistance see PARA 936.
6 Ie the Housing Act 1985 Pt XVI (ss 527–577).
7 As to the meaning of 'dwelling' see PARA 928 note 3.
8 Housing Act 1985 s 564(1)(a).
9 As to the meaning of 'statutory tenant' see LANDLORD AND TENANT vol 63 (2016) PARA 673.
10 Housing Act 1985 s 564(1)(b).

11 Housing Act 1985 s 564(1). As to the meaning of 'work required to reinstate a defective dwelling' see PARA 937 note 10.
12 Housing Act 1985 s 564(2).

935. Duty of a local housing authority to publicise availability of assistance.
Local authorities have a duty to publicise the availability of defective housing assistance whether the designation is local or national.

A local housing authority[1] must, within the period of three months beginning with the coming into operation of:

(1)   a designation of defective dwellings[2] by the appropriate national authority[3] or a designation of defective dwellings under a local scheme[4]; or

(2)   a variation of such a designation[5],

publish in a newspaper circulating in its district notice suitable for the purpose of bringing the effect of the designation or variation to the attention of persons who may be eligible for assistance[6] in respect of such of the dwellings concerned as are situated within their district[7]. No such notice need be published by a local housing authority which is of the opinion:

(a)   that none of the dwellings concerned are situated in its district[8]; or

(b)   that no one is likely to be eligible for assistance in respect of the dwellings concerned which are situated in its district[9].

If at any time it becomes apparent to a local housing authority that a person is likely to be eligible for assistance in respect of a defective dwelling within its district, it must forthwith take such steps as are reasonably practicable to inform him of the fact that assistance is available[10].

1   As to the meaning of 'local housing authority' see PARA 11.
2   As to the meaning of 'defective dwelling' see PARA 929.
3   Ie a designation under the Housing Act 1985 s 528 (designation of defective dwellings by appropriate national authority): see PARA 929.
4   Ie a designation under the Housing Act 1985 s 559 (see PARA 959): s 562(1)(a).
5   Housing Act 1985 s 562(1)(b).
6   As to a person's eligibility for assistance in respect of a defective dwelling see PARA 928.
7   Housing Act 1985 s 562(1).
8   Housing Act 1985 s 562(2)(a).
9   Housing Act 1985 s 562(2)(b).
10   Housing Act 1985 s 562(3). The duty is not owed to persons who purchase their houses privately after the cut-off date envisaged by the Housing Act 1985: *Hodge v Newport Borough Council* (2001) 33 HLR 187, [2001] LGR 20, CA. As to the designation of the cut-off date see PARA 929.

936. Application for assistance. A person seeking assistance in respect of a defective dwelling[1] must make a written application to the local housing authority[2] within the period specified in the relevant designation[3].

The local housing authority may not entertain an application for assistance if:

(1)   an application has been made in respect of the defective dwelling (whether before or after the relevant designation came into operation) for renovation grant or common parts grant under the legislation[4] as to grants for renewal of private sector housing[5]; and

(2)   the relevant works[6] in relation to that grant include the whole or part of the work required to reinstate the dwelling[7],

unless the grant application has been refused or has been withdrawn or the relevant works have been completed[8]. Where a person has applied for such a grant in respect of a dwelling and:

(a)   the dwelling is a defective dwelling; and

(b)   the relevant works include the whole or part of the work required to reinstate it, he may withdraw his application, whether or not it has been approved, if the relevant works have not been begun[9].

1   As to the meaning of 'defective dwelling' see PARA 929.
2   As to the meaning of 'local housing authority' see PARA 11.
3   Housing Act 1985 s 534.
4   Ie the Housing Grants, Construction and Regeneration Act 1996 Pt I Ch I (ss 1–59): see PARA 835 et seq.
5   Housing Act 1985 s 535(1)(a) (amended by the Housing Grants, Construction and Regeneration Act 1996 s 103, Sch 1 para 9).
6   The Housing Act 1985 s 535(3) provides that 'relevant works', in relation to a grant, has the same meaning as in Pt XV (ss 460–526), but these provisions have largely been repealed (see PARA 835). As to the meaning of 'relevant works' see now PARA 837.
7   Housing Act 1985 s 535(1)(b). As to the meaning of 'dwelling' see PARA 928 note 3.
8   Housing Act 1985 s 535(1).
9   Housing Act 1985 s 535(2).

937. Determination of eligibility and form of assistance to be made.

A local housing authority[1] receiving an application for assistance[2] must as soon as reasonably practicable give notice[3] in writing to the applicant stating whether in its opinion he is eligible for assistance[4] in respect of the defective dwelling[5]. If the authority is of the opinion that he is not so eligible, the notice must state the reasons for its view[6]. If it is of the opinion that the applicant is so eligible, the notice must inform him of his right to make such a claim[7].

If the applicant is eligible for assistance, then the local housing authority must determine as soon as reasonably practicable whether he is entitled to assistance by way of reinstatement grant[8] or by way of repurchase[9]. If the authority is satisfied, on a claim by the applicant to that effect, that it would be unreasonable to expect him to secure or await the carrying out of the work required to reinstate the defective dwelling[10], the applicant is entitled to assistance by way of repurchase[11]. Subject to this, the applicant is entitled to assistance by way of reinstatement grant if the authority is satisfied that the conditions for such assistance are met, and otherwise to assistance by way of repurchase[12].

1   As to the meaning of 'local housing authority' see PARA 11.
2   As to applications for assistance see PARA 936.
3   As to service of notices see PARA 963.
4   As to a person's eligibility for assistance see PARA 931.
5   Housing Act 1985 s 536(1). As to the meaning of 'defective dwelling' see PARA 929.
6   Housing Act 1985 s 536(2). See eg *R v Gloucester City Council, ex p Miles* (1985) 17 HLR 292, 83 LGR 607, CA.
7   Housing Act 1985 s 536(3).
8   As to assistance by way of a reinstatement grant see PARA 942 et seq.
9   Housing Act 1985 s 537(1) (amended by the Local Government and Housing Act 1989 s 166(1), (2)). As to assistance by way of repurchase see PARA 946 et seq.
10   For these purposes, the work required to reinstate a defective dwelling is the work relating to the dwelling that is required to be done to the building that consists of or includes the dwelling in order to deal satisfactorily with the qualifying defect, together with any further work: (1) required to be done, in order to deal satisfactorily with the qualifying defect, to any garage or outhouse designed or constructed as that building is designed or constructed, being a garage or outhouse in which the interest of the person eligible for assistance subsists and which is occupied with and used for the purposes of the dwelling or any part of it; or (2) reasonably required in connection with other work falling within this provision: Housing Act 1985 s 539(1).
      In any case where:
    (1)   the most satisfactory way of dealing with the qualifying defect is substantially to demolish the building that consists of or includes the defective dwelling or a part of that building; and
    (2)   it is practicable to rebuild the building or part concerned on, or substantially on, its existing foundations and reconstruct the dwelling to the same, or substantially the same, plan,

the work required to carry out those operations is regarded for the purposes of Pt XVI (ss 527–577) as work required to reinstate the defective dwelling: s 539(1A) (added by the Local Government and Housing Act 1989 s 166(3)).

11 Housing Act 1985 s 537(2). It appears that the presumption is in favour of reinstatement, and it has been held that an applicant's age and infirmity are not sufficient to displace an authority's decision that it is reasonable to expect such an individual to await reinstatement works, particularly where the individual wishes to remain in the premises in any event: see *R v Metropolitan Borough of Sandwell, ex p Cashmore* (1993) 25 HLR 544. A challenge to an authority's decision should be pursued by way of appeal to the County Court as provided for in the Housing Act 1985 s 572 (see PARA 964), and not by judicial review, save in exceptional circumstances: see *R v Metropolitan Borough of Sandwell, ex p Cashmore* (1993) 25 HLR 544.

12 Housing Act 1985 s 537(3).

938. Notice of the determination. Where an applicant is eligible for assistance[1], the authority to which the application was made must as soon as reasonably practicable give him notice in writing[2] (a 'notice of determination') stating the form of assistance[3] to which he is entitled[4]. If, on a claim by an applicant that assistance by way of reinstatement grant is inappropriate in his case[5], the authority is not satisfied that it would be unreasonable to expect him to secure or await the carrying out of the work required to reinstate the defective dwelling[6], the notice must state the reasons for the authority's view[7].

A notice stating that the applicant is entitled to assistance by way of reinstatement grant[8] must also state:

(1)   the grounds for the authority's determination[9];

(2)   the work which, in its opinion, is required to reinstate the defective dwelling[10];

(3)   the amount of expenditure which, in its opinion, may properly be incurred in executing the work[11];

(4)   the amount of expenditure which, in its opinion, may properly be incurred in entering into an associated arrangement[12];

(5)   the required condition as to the execution of work to the satisfaction of the authority within the specified period[13], including the period within which the work is to be carried out[14]; and

(6)   the authority's estimate of the amount of grant payable in respect of the dwelling in pursuance of these provisions[15].

A notice stating that the applicant is entitled to assistance by way of repurchase[16] must also state the grounds for the authority's determination and the effect of:

(a)   a request[17] for notice of the proposed terms of repurchase[18]; and

(b)   the statutory provisions[19] as to the grant of a tenancy to a former owner-occupier of a repurchased dwelling[20].

1   As to a person's eligibility for assistance in respect of a defective dwelling see PARA 928. References to a person entitled to assistance by way of reinstatement grant or, as the case may be, by way of repurchase are references to a person who is eligible for assistance in respect of the dwelling and on whom a notice of determination has been served stating that he is entitled to that form of assistance: Housing Act 1985 s 540(5). See also *R v Thurrock Borough Council, ex p Wellham* (1991) 23 HLR 434 (applicant is only entitled to one determination of the application and to one notice).

2   As to service of notices see PARA 963.

3   As to the form of assistance to which an applicant is entitled see PARA 937.

4   Housing Act 1985 s 540(1).

5   Ie a claim under the Housing Act 1985 s 537(2): see PARA 937.

6   As to the meaning of 'work required to reinstate a defective dwelling' see PARA 937 note 10. As to the meaning of 'defective dwelling' see PARA 929. As to the meaning of 'dwelling' see PARA 928 note 3.

7   Housing Act 1985 s 540(2).

8   As to assistance by way of reinstatement grant see PARA 942 et seq.

9   Housing Act 1985 s 540(3)(a).

10 Housing Act 1985 s 540(3)(b).
11 Housing Act 1985 s 540(3)(c).
12 Housing Act 1985 s 540(3)(d). 'Associated arrangement' means an arrangement which is entered into in connection with the execution of the work required to reinstate a defective dwelling and is likely to contribute towards the dwelling being regarded as an acceptable security by a lending institution: s 539(2). For the purposes of Pt XVI (ss 527–577), 'lending institution' means an authorised deposit taker or an authorised insurer: s 576 (amended by SI 2001/3649). As to the meanings of 'authorised deposit taker' and 'authorised insurer' see the Housing Act 1985 s 622(1); and PARA 527 note 18.
13 Ie the condition required by the Housing Act 1985 s 542: see PARA 943.
14 Housing Act 1985 s 540(3)(e).
15 Housing Act 1985 s 540(3)(f).
16 As to assistance by way of repurchase see PARA 946 et seq.
17 Ie a request under the Housing Act 1985 Sch 20 paras 1–3: see PARA 946.
18 Housing Act 1985 s 540(4)(a).
19 Ie the provisions contained in the Housing Act 1985 ss 554, 556 and 557(1): see PARAS 955, 957–958.
20 Housing Act 1985 s 540(4)(b).

939. Dwellings included in more than one designation. Provision is made to deal with cases in which a dwelling is subject to more than one designation as a defective dwelling, for example where a dwelling which has been designated locally is subsequently designated nationally by the appropriate national authority. Thus the following provisions apply in relation to a defective dwelling[1] where the building that the dwelling[2] consists of or includes falls within two or more designations[3].

Where a person is already eligible for assistance[4] in respect of a defective dwelling at a time when another designation comes into operation, the later designation must be disregarded if:

(1)   he would not be eligible for assistance in respect of the dwelling by virtue of that designation[5]; or

(2)   he is by virtue of an earlier designation entitled to assistance by way of repurchase[6] in respect of the dwelling[7].

Where a person is eligible for assistance in respect of a defective dwelling and there are two or more applicable designations, Part XVI of the Housing Act 1985[8] has effect in relation to the dwelling as if:

(a)   references to the designation were references to any applicable designation[9];

(b)   references to the provision by virtue of which it is a defective dwelling were references to any provision under which an applicable designation was made[10];

(c)   references to the qualifying defect[11] were references to any qualifying defect described in an applicable designation[12];

(d)   references to the period within which persons may seek assistance under Part XVI were references to any period specified for that purpose in any applicable designation[13]; and

(e)   the reference in the provisions concerning the amount of reinstatement grant[14] to the maximum amount permitted to be taken into account for the purposes of those provisions was a reference to the aggregate of the maximum amounts for each applicable designation[15].

The following provisions[16] apply where:

(i)   notice concerning the determination of eligibility[17] has been given to a person stating that he is in the opinion of the local housing authority[18] eligible for assistance in respect of a defective dwelling[19]; and

(ii) after the notice has been given another designation comes into operation designating a class within which the building that consists of or includes the dwelling falls[20].

In these circumstances, the local housing authority must, as soon as reasonably practicable, give him notice in writing[21] stating whether in its opinion the new designation falls to be disregarded[22]. If in its opinion it is to be disregarded the notice must state the reasons for its view[23]. Where it appears to the authority that the new designation does not fall to be disregarded[24], it must forthwith give him notice in writing stating the effect of the new designation, how it may be relied on and whether the entitlement is to be redetermined[25], and informing him that he has the right to make a claim that assistance by way of a reinstatement grant[26] is inappropriate in his case[27]. It must as soon as reasonably practicable make a further determination of the form of assistance to which the person is entitled[28], taking account of the new designation[29]; and give a further notice of determination in place of the previous notice[30], and where the determination is that he is entitled to assistance by way of repurchase, the notice must state the effect of cases where reinstatement work has already begun or been contracted for[31].

Where a person entitled to assistance by way of reinstatement grant is given a further notice of entitlement[32] stating that he is entitled to assistance by way of repurchase[33], and:

(A) he satisfies the authority that he has, before the further notice was received, entered into a contract for the provision of services or materials for any of the reinstatement work[34]; or

(B) any such work has been carried out before the further notice was received, and has been carried out to the satisfaction of the appropriate authority[35],

the previous notice (and any notice concerning the change of work required[36]) continues to have effect for the purposes of reinstatement grant in relation to the reinstatement work, or such of that work as has been carried out before further notice was received, and the authority must pay reinstatement grant accordingly[37].

1 As to the meaning of 'defective dwelling' see PARA 929.
2 As to the meaning of 'dwelling' see PARA 928 note 3.
3 Ie designations under the Housing Act 1985 s 528 (designation by appropriate national authority: see PARA 929) or s 559 (designation under local scheme: see PARA 959): s 566, Sch 21 para 1.
4 As to eligibility for assistance in respect of a defective dwelling see PARA 928.
5 Housing Act 1985 Sch 21 para 2(a).
6 As to the meaning of 'person entitled to assistance by way of repurchase' see PARA 938 note 1.
7 Housing Act 1985 Sch 21 para 2(b).
8 Ie the Housing Act 1985 Pt XVI (ss 527–577).
9 Housing Act 1985 Sch 21 para 3(a).
10 Housing Act 1985 Sch 21 para 3(b).
11 As to the meaning of 'qualifying defect' see PARA 929 note 9.
12 Housing Act 1985 Sch 21 para 3(c).
13 Housing Act 1985 Sch 21 para 3(d).
14 Ie the Housing Act 1985 s 543(1)(c): see PARA 944.
15 Housing Act 1985 Sch 21 para 3(e).
16 Ie the Housing Act 1985 Sch 21 paras 5–7: see the text and notes 21–37.
17 Ie a notice under the Housing Act 1985 s 536: see PARA 937.
18 As to the meaning of 'local housing authority' see PARA 11.
19 Housing Act 1985 Sch 21 para 4(a).
20 Housing Act 1985 Sch 21 para 4(b).
21 As to the giving of notices see PARA 963.
22 Ie disregarded under the Housing Act 1985 Sch 21 para 2 (see the text and notes 1–7): Sch 21 para 5(1).

23 Housing Act 1985 Sch 21 para 5(2).

24 Housing Act 1985 Sch 21 para 6(1).

25 Housing Act 1985 Sch 21 para 6(2)(a).

26 As to the meaning of 'person entitled to assistance by way of reinstatement grant' see PARA 938 note 1.

27 Ie a claim under the Housing Act 1985 s 537(2) (see PARA 937): Sch 21 para 6(2)(b).

28 Ie a determination under the Housing Act 1985 s 537(1): see PARA 937.

29 Housing Act 1985 Sch 21 para 6(3)(a).

30 Housing Act 1985 Sch 21 para 6(3)(b).

31 Ie the effect of the Housing Act 1985 Sch 21 para 7: Sch 21 para 6(3).

32 Ie a notice under the Housing Act 1985 Sch 21 para 6: see the text and notes 24–31.

33 Housing Act 1985 Sch 21 para 7(1).

34 Housing Act 1985 Sch 21 para 7(2)(a). 'The reinstatement work' means the work stated in the previous notice or in a notice under s 544 (change of work required: see PARA 945): Sch 21 para 7(1).

35 Housing Act 1985 Sch 21 para 7(2)(b).

36 Ie a notice under the Housing Act 1985 s 544 (change of work required): see PARA 945.

37 Housing Act 1985 Sch 21 para 7(2). Where in a case within Sch 21 para 7(2) the reinstatement work is not completed but part of the work is carried out to the satisfaction of the appropriate authority within the period stated in the notice in question: (1) the amount of reinstatement grant payable in respect of that part of the work must be an amount equal to the maximum instalment of grant payable under s 545(2) (instalments not to exceed appropriate percentage of cost of work completed: see PARA 944); and (2) s 546 (repayment of grant in event of failure to complete work: see PARA 944) does not apply in relation to reinstatement grant paid in respect of that part of the work: Sch 21 para 7(3)(a), (b).

940. Modifications of defective housing legislation in relation to shared ownership leases. If it appears to a local housing authority[1] that the interest of a person eligible for assistance[2] in respect of a defective dwelling[3] in its area is:

(1)   a shared ownership lease[4]; or

(2)   the freehold acquired under the terms of a shared ownership lease[5],

the authority must prepare and submit to the appropriate national authority[6] a scheme providing for the provisions of Part XVI of the Housing Act 1985[7] to have effect, in their application to such a case, subject to such modifications as may be specified in the scheme[8]. Such a scheme must not have effect unless approved by the appropriate national authority; and any such approval may be made conditional upon compliance with requirements specified by the appropriate national authority[9].

1 As to the meaning of 'local housing authority' see PARA 11.

2 As to eligibility for assistance in respect of a defective dwelling see PARA 928.

3 As to the meaning of 'defective dwelling' see PARA 929.

4 Housing Act 1985 s 567(1)(a) (s 567(1), (2) substituted by the Local Government and Housing Act 1989 s 166(6)). For the purposes of the Housing Act 1985 s 567, 'shared ownership lease' means:

    (1)   a shared ownership lease granted in pursuance of Pt V (ss 118–188) (the right to buy: see PARA 239 et seq) (s 567(4)(a));

    (2)   a lease of a dwelling house granted otherwise than in pursuance of Pt V which contains provision to the like effect as that required by Sch 8 paras 1, 2 (repealed) (terms of shared ownership lease; right to acquire additional shares and to acquire freehold) (s 567(4)(b));

    (3)   a lease determined, or of a class or description determined, by the appropriate national authority to be a shared ownership lease (s 567(4)(d) (amended by the Local Government and Housing Act 1989 ss 166(7), 194, Sch 12 Pt II)).

The right to be granted a shared ownership lease under the Housing Act 1985 ss 143–151 (as originally enacted) was abolished by the Leasehold Reform, Housing and Urban Development Act 1993 s 107(c). The fact that a lease becomes a shared ownership lease by virtue of a determination under the Housing Act 1985 s 567(4)(d) (see head (3)) does not affect the operation of the provisions of Pt XVI (ss 527–577) in relation to a case where an application for assistance under Pt XVI has previously been made: s 567(5) (amended by the Local Government and Housing Act 1989 Sch 12 Pt II).

5 Housing Act 1985 s 567(1)(b) (as substituted: see note 4).

6 As to the appropriate national authority, ie the Secretary of State or, where statutory functions have been transferred in relation to Wales, the Welsh Ministers, see PARA 7.

7 Ie the Housing Act 1985 Pt XVI.
8 Housing Act 1985 s 567(1) (as substituted: see note 4).
9 Housing Act 1985 s 567(2) (as substituted: see note 4).

941. Extension of assistance to mortgagees. The appropriate national authority[1] may by regulations[2] make provision for conferring rights and obligations on a mortgagee of a defective dwelling[3] where:

(1)   a power of sale (whether conferred by the Law of Property Act 1925[4] or otherwise) is exercisable by the mortgagee[5]; and

(2)   the mortgagor[6] is eligible for assistance[7] in respect of the defective dwelling[8].

The rights that may be so conferred are:

(a)   rights corresponding to those conferred by Part XVI of the Housing Act 1985 on a person holding a relevant interest[9] in the defective dwelling[10];

(b)   the right to require the purchasing authority[11] to acquire in accordance with the regulations any interest in the defective dwelling to be disposed of in exercise of the power of sale[12]; and

(c)   where the mortgagee is the purchasing authority, the right by deed to vest the dwelling[13] in itself[14],

and those rights may be conferred in place of rights conferred by Part XVI of the Housing Act 1985 on any other person[15].

Where a defective dwelling is vested in a mortgagee in pursuance of:

(i)   regulations under these provisions[16]; or

(ii)   the provisions[17] vesting a dwelling house in an authority entitled to exercise the power of sale[18],

the regulations may provide for the payment in respect of the vesting of an amount calculated on the assumption that none of the defective dwellings to which the designation in question relates is affected by the qualifying defect[19]; and those enactments have effect subject to any such provisions[20].

1 As to the appropriate national authority, ie the Secretary of State or, where statutory functions have been transferred in relation to Wales, the Welsh Ministers, see PARA 7.
2 Regulations under these provisions: (1) may make different provision for different cases and may make incidental and consequential provision; and (2) must be made by statutory instrument which is subject to annulment in pursuance of a resolution of either House of Parliament: Housing Act 1985 s 568(5)(a), (b). See the Defective Dwellings (Mortgagees) Regulations 1986, SI 1986/797, which extend the Housing Act 1985 Pt XVI (ss 527–577), with modifications, to mortgagees of defective dwellings.
3 As to the meaning of 'defective dwelling' see PARA 929.
4 Ie the Law of Property Act 1925 s 101: see MORTGAGE vol 77 (2016) PARA 446 et seq.
5 Housing Act 1985 s 568(1)(a). See note 8. 'Mortgagee' has the same meaning as in the Law of Property Act 1925 s 205(1)(xvi) (see MORTGAGE vol 77 (2016) PARA 104): Housing Act 1985 s 568(6).
6 'Mortgagor' has the same meaning as in the Law of Property Act 1925 s 205(1)(xvi) (see MORTGAGE vol 77 (2016) PARA 104): Housing Act 1985 s 568(6).
7 As to eligibility for assistance in respect of a defective dwelling see PARA 928.
8 Housing Act 1985 s 568(1)(b). The regulations may provide that where the conditions in s 568(1)(a) (see the text and note 5) and s 568(1)(b) are or have been satisfied, Pt XVI, the power of sale in question and any enactment relating to the power of sale are to have effect subject to such modifications as may be specified in the regulations: s 568(3).
9 As to the meaning of 'relevant interest' see PARA 928 note 7.
10 Housing Act 1985 s 568(2)(a).
11 As to the meaning of 'purchasing authority' see PARA 949 note 15.
12 Housing Act 1985 s 568(2)(b).
13 As to the meaning of 'dwelling' see PARA 928 note 3.
14 Housing Act 1985 s 568(2)(c).
15 Housing Act 1985 s 568(2).
16 Housing Act 1985 s 568(4)(a).

17 Ie the Housing Act 1985 s 452, Sch 17: see PARA 927.
18 Housing Act 1985 s 568(4)(b).
19 As to the meaning of 'qualifying defect' see PARA 929 note 9.
20 Housing Act 1985 s 568(4).

(2) REINSTATEMENT GRANT

942. Conditions for assistance by way of reinstatement grant. The conditions for assistance by way of reinstatement grant are:

(1)   that the dwelling[1] is a house[2];

(2)   that if the work required to reinstate the dwelling (together with any other work which the local housing authority[3] is satisfied the applicant proposes to carry out) were carried out:

    (a)   the dwelling would be likely to provide satisfactory housing accommodation for a period of at least 30 years; and

    (b)   an individual acquiring the freehold of the dwelling with vacant possession would be likely to be able to arrange a mortgage on satisfactory terms with a lending institution[4];

(3)   that giving assistance by way of a reinstatement grant is justified having regard, on the one hand, to the amount of reinstatement grant that would be payable in respect of the dwelling and, on the other hand, to the likely value of the freehold of the dwelling with vacant possession after the work required to reinstate it has been carried out[5].

The appropriate national authority may by order[6] amend these conditions so as to modify or omit any of the conditions or to add or substitute for any of the conditions other conditions[7].

1   As to the meaning of 'dwelling' see PARA 928 note 3.
2   Housing Act 1985 s 538(1)(a). Where a house which is divided into flats or other units is a defective dwelling, and a person is eligible for assistance in respect of that dwelling, the fact that it is so divided must be disregarded for the purposes of s 538(1)(a): s 575(3). As to the meaning of 'house' see PARA 928 note 3.
3   As to the meaning of 'local housing authority' see PARA 11.
4   Housing Act 1985 s 538(1)(b). As to the meaning of 'lending institution' see PARA 938 note 12.
5   Housing Act 1985 s 538(1)(c). See *R v Thamesdown Borough Council, ex p Pritchard* (1988) 20 HLR 633; *Kenny v Kingston-upon-Thames Royal London Borough Council* (1985) 17 HLR 344, [1985] 1 EGLR 26, CA.
6   An order may make different provision for different classes of case, must be made by statutory instrument, and may not be made unless a draft of it has been laid before and approved by a resolution of each House of Parliament or, as appropriate, the National Assembly for Wales: Housing Act 1985 s 538(3). An order does not affect an application for assistance made before the order comes into force: s 538(4). As to the appropriate national authority, ie the Secretary of State or, where statutory functions have been transferred in relation to Wales, the Welsh Ministers, see PARA 7.
7   Housing Act 1985 s 538(2). As to the order that has been made see the Housing Defects (Reinstatement Grant) (Amendment of Conditions for Assistance) Order 1988, SI 1988/884 (which amended the Housing Act 1985 s 538 by repealing the former s 538(1)(d)).

943. Reinstatement grant and conditions of payment. Where a person is entitled to assistance by way of reinstatement grant[1], the local housing authority[2] must pay reinstatement grant to him in respect of: (1) the qualifying work[3]; and (2) any associated arrangement[4]. However, it is a condition of payment of reinstatement grant that the qualifying work is carried out to the satisfaction of the local housing authority[5] and within the period specified[6] in the notice of determination, or that period as extended[7]. If there are reasonable grounds for doing so, the authority must, by notice in writing[8] served on the person entitled to assistance, extend or further extend the period[9] for carrying out the qualifying work (whether or not the period has expired)[10]. Payment of reinstatement grant must not be subject to any other condition, however expressed[11].

1 See PARA 937 et seq.
2 As to the meaning of 'local housing authority' see PARA 11.
3 Housing Act 1985 s 541(1)(a). 'Qualifying work' means the work stated in the notice of determination, or in a notice under s 544 (notice of change of work required: see PARA 945), to be the work which in the opinion of the local housing authority is required to reinstate the dwelling: s 541(2). As to the meaning of 'dwelling' see PARA 928 note 3. As to the notice of determination see PARA 938.
4 Housing Act 1985 s 541(1)(b). As to the meaning of 'associated arrangement' see PARA 938 note 12.
5 Housing Act 1985 s 542(1)(a).
6 The period so specified must be such reasonable period (of at least 12 months), beginning with service of the notice, as the authority may determine: Housing Act 1985 s 542(2).
7 Housing Act 1985 s 542(1)(b).
8 As to service of notices see PARA 963.
9 As to the County Court's power to extend or further extend the period of carrying out the qualifying work where the local housing authority has failed to do so see PARA 964.
10 Housing Act 1985 s 542(3).
11 Housing Act 1985 s 542(4).

944. Amount and payment of a reinstatement grant. The amount of reinstatement grant[1] payable is the appropriate percentage[2] of whichever is the least of:

(1)   the amount stated in the notice of determination[3], or in a notice of change in work required or expenditure permitted[4], to be the amount of expenditure which, in the opinion of the local housing authority[5], may properly be incurred in executing the qualifying work[6] and entering into any associated arrangement[7];

(2)   the expenditure actually incurred in executing the qualifying work and entering into any associated arrangement[8]; and

(3)   the expenditure which is the maximum amount permitted to be taken into account for these purposes[9].

The maximum amount of expenditure permitted to be taken into account for these purposes is the amount specified as the expenditure limit by order made by the appropriate national authority, except in a case or description of case in which the appropriate national authority, on the application of a local housing authority, approves a higher amount[10].

The local housing authority may pay reinstatement grant in respect of the qualifying work in a single sum on completion of the work, or by instalments[11]. However, no instalment is to be paid if the instalment, together with any amount previously paid, would exceed the appropriate percentage[12] of the cost of so much of the qualifying work as has been executed at that time[13]. The authority must pay reinstatement grant in respect of an associated arrangement[14] when payment in respect of the expenditure incurred in entering into the arrangement falls to be made[15].

Where an amount of reinstatement grant has been paid in one or more instalments and the qualifying work is not completed within the period for carrying out the work, the local housing authority may, if it thinks fit, require the person who was entitled to assistance to repay that amount to it forthwith[16].

1 As to reinstatement grants see PARA 942 et seq.
2 The appropriate percentage is currently 90% or, in a case where the authority is satisfied that the person entitled to assistance would suffer financial hardship unless a higher percentage of the expenditure referred to in the Housing Act 1985 s 543(1) were paid to him, 100 per cent: s 543(2).

As to the meaning of 'person entitled to assistance by way of reinstatement grant' see PARA 938 note 1. The appropriate national authority may by order vary either or both of the percentages mentioned in s 543(2): s 543(3). As to the appropriate national authority, ie the Secretary of State or, where statutory functions have been transferred in relation to Wales, the Welsh Ministers, see PARA 7.

3   As to the meaning of 'notice of determination' see PARA 938.

4   Ie a notice under the Housing Act 1985 s 544 (notice of change in work required or expenditure permitted): see PARA 945.

5   As to the meaning of 'local housing authority' see PARA 11.

6   As to the meaning of 'qualifying work' see PARA 943 note 3.

7   Housing Act 1985 s 543(1)(a).

8   Housing Act 1985 s 543(1)(b). As to the meaning of 'associated arrangement' see PARA 938 note 12.

9   Housing Act 1985 s 543(1)(c).

10   Housing Act 1985 s 543(4). An order under s 543(4) may make different provision for different areas, different designated classes and different categories of dwelling: s 543(5). As to the meaning of 'dwelling' see PARA 928 note 3. An order under s 543 is made by statutory instrument which is subject to annulment in pursuance of a resolution of the House of Commons or, as appropriate, the National Assembly for Wales: s 543(6). As to the order that has been made see the Housing Defects (Expenditure Limits) Order 1992, SI 1992/446, which specifies expenditure limits ranging from £14,000 to £40,000 for various categories of defective dwelling.

11   Housing Act 1985 s 545(1).

12   As to the appropriate percentage see note 2.

13   Housing Act 1985 s 545(2).

14   As to the meaning of 'associated arrangement' see PARA 938 note 12.

15   Housing Act 1985 s 545(3).

16   Housing Act 1985 s 546(1). The amount required to be repaid (or, if it was paid in more than one instalment, the amount of each instalment) must carry interest, at such reasonable rate as the authority may determine, from the date on which it was paid until repayment: s 546(2).

945. Changes in work or expenditure. Where the local housing authority[1] is satisfied that:

(1)   the work required to reinstate the defective dwelling[2] is more extensive than that stated in the notice of determination[3] or in a previous notice under these provisions[4]; or

(2)   the amount of the expenditure which may properly be incurred in executing that work is greater than that so stated[5]; or

(3)   there is an amount of expenditure which may properly be incurred in entering into an associated arrangement[6] but no such amount is stated in the notice of determination or a previous notice under these provisions[7]; or

(4)   where such an amount is so stated, the amount of expenditure which may be properly so incurred is greater than that amount[8],

the authority must by notice in writing[9] served on the person entitled to assistance[10] state its opinion as to that amount or, as the case may be, that work and that amount; and the amount of reinstatement grant must be adjusted accordingly[11].

1   As to the meaning of 'local housing authority' see PARA 11.

2   As to the meaning of 'work required to reinstate a defective dwelling' see PARA 937 note 10. As to the meaning of 'defective dwelling' see PARA 929.

3   As to the meaning of 'notice of determination' see PARA 938.

4   Housing Act 1985 s 544(a).

5   Housing Act 1985 s 544(b).

6   As to the meaning of 'associated arrangement' see PARA 938 note 12.

7   Housing Act 1985 s 544(c).

8   Housing Act 1985 s 544(d).

9   As to the service of notices see PARA 963.

10 As to the meaning of 'person entitled to assistance by way of a reinstatement grant' see PARA 938 note 1.
11 Housing Act 1985 s 544.

(3) REPURCHASE

946. Assistance by way of repurchase. A person who is entitled to assistance by way of repurchase[1] may, within the period of three months beginning with the service of the notice of determination[2] (or that period as extended), request the purchasing authority[3] in writing to notify him of the proposed terms and conditions for its acquisition of the interest to be acquired[4]. The authority must, if there are reasonable grounds for doing so, by notice in writing served on the person so entitled, extend, or further extend, the period within which he may make a request under these provisions (whether or not that period has expired)[5].

Within the period of three months beginning with the making of such a request, the purchasing authority must serve on the person so entitled a notice in writing specifying the proposed terms and conditions and stating:

(1) the authority's opinion as to the value of the interest to be acquired[6]; and
(2) the effect of the statutory provisions[7] as to agreement to repurchase[8].

Subject to the provisions as to the price payable and valuation[9], an agreement for the acquisition by the purchasing authority of the interest to be acquired is to contain such provisions as the parties agree or, in default of agreement, as are determined in accordance with Part XVI of the Housing Act 1985[10] to be reasonable[11]. Within three months of all the provisions to be included in the agreement being agreed or determined, the authority must:

(a) draw up for execution by the parties an agreement embodying those provisions[12]; and
(b) serve a copy of the agreement on the person entitled to assistance[13].

The person entitled to assistance may, at any time within the period of six months beginning with the service of the copy of the agreement, or within that period as extended, notify the authority in writing that he requires it to enter into an agreement embodying those provisions and the authority must comply with the requirement[14]. If there are reasonable grounds for doing so, the authority must by notice in writing served on the person so entitled extend, or further extend, the period within which such a notice may be given (whether or not the period has expired)[15].

1 As to when a person is entitled to assistance by way of repurchase see PARA 937.
2 As to service of notices see PARA 963. As to the meaning of 'notice of determination' see PARA 938.
3 As to the meaning of 'purchasing authority' see PARA 949 note 15.
4 Housing Act 1985 s 547, Sch 20 para 2(1). In Sch 20, 'the interest to be acquired' means the interest of the person entitled to assistance by way of repurchase, so far as subsisting in the defective dwelling, and any garage, outhouse, garden, yard and appurtenances occupied and used for the purposes of the dwelling or a part of it: Sch 20 para 1. As to the meaning of 'defective dwelling' see PARA 929. As to the meaning of 'dwelling' see PARA 928 note 3.
5 Housing Act 1985 Sch 20 para 2(2).
6 Housing Act 1985 Sch 20 para 3(a).
7 Ie the provisions contained in the Housing Act 1985 Sch 20 paras 4–6: see the text and notes 9–15.
8 Housing Act 1985 Sch 20 para 3(b).
9 Ie the provisions in the Housing Act 1985 Sch 20 Pt II (paras 7–10): see PARA 947.
10 Ie the Housing Act 1985 Pt XVI (ss 527–577).
11 Housing Act 1985 Sch 20 para 4.
12 Housing Act 1985 Sch 20 para 5(a).
13 Housing Act 1985 Sch 20 para 5(b).

14 Housing Act 1985 Sch 20 para 6(1).
15 Housing Act 1985 Sch 20 para 6(2).

947. Price payable and valuation. The price payable for the acquisition of an interest in pursuance of Part XVI of the Housing Act 1985[1] is 95 per cent of the value of the interest[2] at the relevant time[3]. Where the value of an interest falls to be considered at a time later than the relevant time and there has been since the relevant time a material change in the circumstances affecting the value of the interest, the value at the relevant time must be determined on the further assumption that the change had occurred before the relevant time[4].

Any question arising under these provisions[5] as to the value of an interest in a defective dwelling[6] must be determined by the district valuer[7]. The person entitled to assistance or the purchasing authority[8] may require that value to be determined or redetermined by notice in writing[9] served on the district valuer:

(1) within the period beginning with the service on the person entitled to assistance of an authority's notice of the proposed terms of acquisition[10] and ending with the service[11] of the copy of the agreement drawn up for execution by the parties[12]; or

(2) after the end of that period but before the parties enter into an agreement for the acquisition of the interest of the person so entitled, if there is a material change in the circumstances affecting the value of the interest[13].

A person serving notice on the district valuer must serve notice in writing of that fact on the other party[14]. Before making a determination, the district valuer must consider any representation made to him, within four weeks of the service of the required notice, by the person entitled to assistance or the purchasing authority[15].

Where the value of an interest is determined, or redetermined, in pursuance of a notice given after the service of a draft agreement[16]:

(a) the purchasing authority must comply again with provisions concerning the service of the draft agreement within three months of terms being settled[17]; and

(b) the requirements concerning a notice to enter into agreement[18] apply in relation to that agreement instead of the earlier one[19].

1 Ie the Housing Act 1985 Pt XVI (ss 527–577).
2 For these purposes, the value of an interest at the relevant time is the amount which, at that time, would be realised by a disposal of the interest on the open market by a willing seller to a person other than the purchasing authority on the following assumptions: (1) that none of the defective dwellings to which the designation in question relates is affected by the qualifying defect; (2) that no liability has arisen or will arise under a covenant required by the Housing Act 1985 s 35 or s 155 (covenant to repay discount: see PARAS 527, 323) or Sch 8 para 6(1) (repealed) (terms of shared ownership lease; covenant to pay for outstanding share), or any covenant to the like effect; (3) that no obligation to acquire the interest arises under Pt XVI; and (4) that (subject to heads (1)–(3)) the seller is selling with and subject to the rights and burdens with and subject to which the disposal is to be made: s 547, Sch 20 para 8(1)(a)–(d).
   'The relevant time' means the time at which the notice under Sch 20 para 3 (authority's notice of proposed terms of acquisition: see PARA 946) is served on the person entitled to assistance: Sch 20 para 7(2). In determining the value of an interest no account must be taken of any right to the grant of a tenancy under s 554 (former owner-occupier: see PARA 955) or s 555 (former statutory tenant: see PARA 956): Sch 20 para 8(3).
3 Housing Act 1985 Sch 20 para 7(1).
4 Housing Act 1985 Sch 20 para 8(2).
5 Ie the Housing Act 1985 Sch 20.
6 As to the meaning of 'defective dwelling' see PARA 929. As to the meaning of 'interest in a dwelling' see PARA 928 note 7.
7 Housing Act 1985 Sch 20 para 9(1). As to the meaning of 'district valuer' see PARA 527 note 14.

8   As to the meaning of 'purchasing authority' see PARA 949 note 15.
9   As to service of notices see PARA 963.
10 Ie a notice under the Housing Act 1985 Sch 20 para 3: see PARA 946.
11 Ie in accordance with the provisions of the Housing Act 1985 Sch 20 para 5: see PARA 946.
12 Housing Act 1985 Sch 20 para 9(2)(a).
13 Housing Act 1985 Sch 20 para 9(2)(b).
14 Housing Act 1985 Sch 20 para 9(3).
15 Housing Act 1985 Sch 20 para 9(4).
16 Ie a notice served in pursuance of the Housing Act 1985 Sch 20 para 9(2)(b) (notice given after service of draft agreement: see head (2) in the text).
17 Ie comply again with the Housing Act 1985 Sch 20 para 5 (service of draft agreement within three months of terms being settled: see PARA 946): Sch 20 para 10(a).
18 Ie the requirements contained in the Housing Act 1985 Sch 20 para 6 (notice to enter into agreement): see PARA 946.
19 Housing Act 1985 Sch 20 para 10(b).

948. Supplementary provisions. The conveyance[1] executed under an agreement to repurchase is effective:

(1)   to discharge the interest acquired[2] from any relevant charge[3];

(2)   to discharge the interest acquired from the operation of any order made by a court for the enforcement of such a charge[4]; and

(3)   to extinguish any term of years created for the purposes of such a charge[5],

without the persons entitled to or interested in such a charge, order or term of years becoming parties to or executing the conveyance[6]. The effect of this is restricted to discharging the interest acquired from the charge and does not affect any personal liabilities[7].

The acquiring authority[8] must apply the purchase price in the first instance in or towards the redemption of any relevant charge securing the payment of money (and if there is more than one, then according to their priorities)[9]. This is subject to the following provisions:

(a)   a person entitled to a charge may not exercise a right to consolidate the charge with a separate charge on other property[10];

(b)   a person may be required to accept three months' or longer notice of the intention to repay the principal or any part of it secured by the charge, together with interest to the date of payment, notwithstanding that this differs from the terms of the security as to the time and manner of payment[11];

(c)   a charge to which the vendor[12] or the authority itself is entitled ranks for payment as it would if another person were entitled to it[13]; and

(d)   where a person, without payment or for less payment than he would otherwise be entitled to, joins in the conveyance for the purpose of discharging the interest acquired from a charge, the persons to whom the purchase price ought to be paid must be determined accordingly[14].

If the authority does not apply an amount which it is required to apply[15] in or towards the redemption of a charge (and does not pay that amount into court in accordance with other requirements[16]), the charge is not discharged and the interest acquired remains subject to the charge as security for that amount[17].

Where a person is or may be entitled to receive, in respect of a relevant charge, the whole or part of the purchase price and:

(i)   for any reason difficulty arises in ascertaining how much is payable in respect of the charge[18]; or

(ii)   for any specified reason[19] difficulty arises in making a payment in respect of the charge[20], the authority may pay into court on account of the purchase price the amount, if known, of the payment to be made in respect of the charge or, if the amount is not known, the whole of the purchase price or such lesser amount as the authority thinks right in order to provide for that payment[21].

The authority must pay the purchase price into court if, before the execution of the conveyance, written notice[22] is given to it that the vendor, or a person entitled to a charge on the interest to be acquired, so requires either for the purpose of protecting the rights of persons so entitled or for reasons related to the bankruptcy or winding up of the vendor[23], or that steps have been taken to enforce a charge on the interest to be acquired by the bringing of proceedings in a court, by the appointment of a receiver or otherwise[24]. Where a payment into court is made by reason only of such a notice and the notice is given with reference to proceedings in a specified court (other than the County Court), payment must be made into that court[25].

For the purposes of registration of title to the land acquired by the authority:

(A)   the authority must give to the Chief Land Registrar[26] a certificate[27] stating that the person from whom the relevant interest[28] was acquired was entitled to convey the interest subject only to such incumbrances, rights and interests as are stated in the conveyance or summarised in the certificate[29]; and

(B)   the Chief Land Registrar must accept the certificate as sufficient evidence of the facts stated in it[30],

but if, as a result, he has to meet a claim against him under the Land Registration Act 2002, the authority must indemnify him[31].

1   For the purposes of the Housing Act 1985 Sch 20 Pt III (paras 11–20), 'the conveyance' means the conveyance executed under the agreement; and 'the agreement' means the agreement entered into in pursuance of Sch 20 Pts I and II (paras 1–10): s 547, Sch 20 para 11(1).

2   In the Housing Act 1985 Sch 20 Pt III, 'the interest acquired' means the interest in the dwelling concerned of which the vendor disposes under the agreement: Sch 20 para 11(1). As to the meaning of 'dwelling' see PARA 928 note 3.

        Where the interest acquired is or includes a dwelling in relation to which an improvement grant, intermediate grant, special grant or repairs grant has been paid under Pt XV (ss 460–526) (largely repealed) (see PARA 226): (1) any grant condition imposed under or by virtue of that Part ceases to be in force with respect to the dwelling with effect from the time of disposal of the interest; and (2) the owner for the time being of the dwelling is not liable to make in relation to the grant any payment under s 506 (repealed) (repayment of grant for breach of condition) except in pursuance of a demand made before the time of disposal of the interest: Sch 20 para 19(1)(a), (b). In Sch 20 para 19, 'dwelling' and 'owner' have the same meanings as in Pt XV (largely repealed): Sch 20 para 19(2).

3   Housing Act 1985 Sch 20 para 12(1)(a). 'Relevant charge' means a charge to which the interest acquired is subject immediately before the conveyance and which secures the performance of an obligation but is not either a local land charge or a charge which is, or would be, otherwise overreached by the conveyance: Sch 20 para 11(2)(b). References to a charge include a mortgage or lien, but not a rentcharge within the meaning of the Rentcharges Act 1977 (see REAL PROPERTY AND REGISTRATION vol 87 (2012) PARAS 1105, 1119): Housing Act 1985 Sch 20 para 11(2)(a).

4   Housing Act 1985 Sch 20 para 12(1)(b).

5   Housing Act 1985 Sch 20 para 12(1)(c).

6   Housing Act 1985 Sch 20 para 12(1). The conveyance also has effect under the Law of Property Act 1925 s 2(1) (conveyances overreaching certain equitable interests and powers: see REAL PROPERTY AND REGISTRATION vol 87 (2012) PARA 260 et seq) to overreach any incumbrance capable of being overreached under s 2: (1) as if the requirements to which s 2 refers as to the payment of capital money allowed any part of the purchase price paid under the Housing Act 1985 Sch 20 para 13, 15 or 16 (payment in satisfaction of charge or into court: see the text and notes 10–26) to be so paid; and (2) where the interest conveyed is settled land, as if the conveyance were made under the powers of the Settled Land Act 1925 (see SETTLEMENTS vol 91 (2012) PARA 579 et seq): Housing Act 1985 Sch 20 para 20(a), (b).

7 Housing Act 1985 Sch 20 para 12(2). Further, these provisions do not prevent a person from joining in the conveyance for the purpose of discharging the interest acquired from a charge: Sch 20 para 12(3). The operation of these provisions is subject to Sch 20 para 14 (see the text to note 17): Sch 20 para 12(4).

8 If the authority is a local housing authority, the interest acquired by it must be treated as acquired by it under the Housing Act 1985 s 17 (acquisition of land for purposes of Pt II (ss 8–57) (provision of housing): see PARA 416): Sch 20 para 18. In Sch 20 Pt III, 'the authority' means the authority acquiring an interest in a defective dwelling under the agreement: Sch 20 para 11(1). As to the meaning of 'local housing authority' see PARA 11.

9 Housing Act 1985 Sch 20 para 13(1). Schedule 20 para 13 does not apply to a charge in favour of the holders of a series of debentures issued by a body, or a charge in favour of trustees for such debenture holders which at the date of the conveyance is a floating charge and the authority must disregard such charges in performing its duty under these provisions: Sch 20 para 13(3).

10 Housing Act 1985 Sch 20 para 13(2)(a).

11 Housing Act 1985 Sch 20 para 13(2)(b).

12 In the Housing Act 1985 Sch 20 Pt III, 'the vendor' means the person with whom the authority enters into the agreement: Sch 20 para 11(1).

13 Housing Act 1985 Sch 20 para 13(2)(c).

14 Housing Act 1985 Sch 20 para 13(2)(d).

15 Ie required under the Housing Act 1985 Sch 20 para 13: see the text and notes 8–14.

16 Ie the requirements of the Housing Act 1985 Sch 20 para 15: see the text and notes 18–21.

17 Housing Act 1985 Sch 20 para 14.

18 Housing Act 1985 Sch 20 para 15(1)(a).

19 The specified reasons are: (1) that a person who is or may be entitled to receive payment cannot be found or ascertained; (2) that any such person refuses or fails to make out a title, or to accept payment and give a proper discharge, or to take any step reasonably required of him to enable the sum payable to be ascertained and paid; or (3) that a tender of the sum payable cannot, by reason of complications in the entitlement to payment or the want of two or more trustees or for other reasons, be effected, or not without incurring or involving unreasonable cost or delay: Housing Act 1985 Sch 20 para 15(2).

20 Housing Act 1985 Sch 20 para 15(1)(b).

21 Housing Act 1985 Sch 20 para 15(1).

22 As to service of notices see PARA 963.

23 Housing Act 1985 Sch 20 para 16(1)(a).

24 Housing Act 1985 Sch 20 para 16(1)(b).

25 Housing Act 1985 Sch 20 para 16(2).

26 As to the Chief Land Registrar see REAL PROPERTY AND REGISTRATION vol 87 (2012) PARA 562.

27 A certificate under the Housing Act 1985 Sch 20 para 17(2) must be in a form approved by the Chief Land Registrar and must be signed by such officer of the authority, or such other person, as may be approved by the Chief Land Registrar: Sch 20 para 17(3).

28 As to the meaning of 'relevant interest' see PARA 928 note 7.

29 Housing Act 1985 Sch 20 para 17(2)(a).

30 Housing Act 1985 Sch 20 para 17(2)(b).

31 Housing Act 1985 Sch 20 para 17(2) (amended by the Land Registration Act 2002 s 133, Sch 11 para 18(1), (13)).

949. Repurchase by an authority other than a local housing authority. Where the local housing authority[1] gives a notice of determination[2] to a person stating that he is entitled to assistance by way of repurchase[3] and it is of the opinion that:

(1)   a relevant interest[4] in the dwelling[5] was disposed of by a specified public sector authority[6] (or a predecessor of such an authority)[7];

(2)   there has been no such disposal since the time of that disposal[8]; and

(3)   any of the specified conditions[9] in relation to the authority are met[10],

it must forthwith give that other authority a notice in writing[11], together with a copy of the notice of determination, stating that the authority may acquire, in accordance with these provisions, the interest of the person entitled to assistance[12].

The other authority may, within the period of four weeks beginning with the service of the notice on it, give notice in writing to the local housing authority:

(a)   stating that it wishes to acquire the interest[13]; and

(b)   specifying the address of the principal office of the authority and any other address which may also be used as an address for service[14],

and the local housing authority must forthwith give to the person entitled to assistance a transfer notice, that is, a notice in writing of the contents of the notice received by that authority and its effect[15].

1   As to the meaning of 'local housing authority' see PARA 11.
2   As to the meaning of 'notice of determination' see PARA 938.
3   As to the meaning of 'person entitled to assistance by way of repurchase' see PARA 938 note 1.
4   As to the meaning of 'relevant interest' see PARA 928 note 7.
5   As to the meaning of 'dwelling' see PARA 928 note 3.
6   Ie a non-profit registered provider of social housing (other than a co-operative housing association) or a predecessor housing association of that provider, a registered social landlord (other than a co-operative housing association) or a predecessor housing association of that registered social landlord, a development corporation, another local housing authority or a predecessor of that authority, or any other public sector authority prescribed by order of the appropriate national authority, or a predecessor so prescribed: Housing Act 1985 s 548(1) (amended by the Government of Wales Act 1998 s 152, Sch 18 Pt IV; and by SI 1996/2325 and SI 2010/866). As to registered providers of social housing see PARA 51 et seq; as to when such a body is a non-profit organisation see PARA 71 note 13. As to the meaning of 'co-operative housing association' see PARA 13; as to the meaning of 'registered social landlord' see PARA 13; and as to the meaning of 'development corporation' see PARA 12.
7   Housing Act 1985 s 548(1)(a).
8   Housing Act 1985 s 548(1)(b).
9   The specified conditions are: (1) (for a development corporation) that no interests have at any time been transferred from the corporation in pursuance of a scheme made or having effect as if made under the New Towns Act 1981 s 42 (repealed) (transfer of housing to district council); (2) (for another local housing authority or a predecessor of that authority) that the local housing authority provides housing accommodation in the vicinity of the defective dwelling with which the dwelling may conveniently be managed; (3) (for any other public sector authority prescribed by order of the appropriate national authority) any conditions prescribed in the order; (4) (for a non-profit registered provider of social housing or a registered social landlord) none: Housing Act 1985 s 548(1) (as amended: see note 6). An order under s 548 must be made by statutory instrument: s 548(4). As to the meaning of 'defective dwelling' see PARA 929.
10 Housing Act 1985 s 548(1)(c).
11 As to service of notices see PARA 963.
12 Housing Act 1985 s 548(1).
13 Housing Act 1985 s 548(2)(a).
14 Housing Act 1985 s 548(2)(b).
15 Housing Act 1985 s 548(2). After a transfer notice has been given to the person entitled to assistance, the other authority must be treated as the appropriate authority for the purposes of anything done or falling to be done under Pt XVI (ss 527–577), except that: (1) a request under Sch 20 para 2 (request for notice of proposed terms of acquisition: see PARA 946) may be made either to the local housing authority or to the other authority; and (2) any such request given to the local housing authority (whether before or after the notice) must be forwarded by it to the other authority, and references in Pt XVI to 'the purchasing authority' are to be construed accordingly: s 548(3).

950. Interest subject to right of pre-emption and other matters. Dwellings sold under the right to buy in certain areas, such as a designated rural area or an area of natural beauty, must be sold subject to a pre-emption clause limiting the freedom of the purchaser and his successors in title to sell, and there are also other cases where dwellings sold under the right to buy contain pre-emption and similar clauses[1]. Provision is made to deal with such pre-emption rights where there is a repurchase by a different authority.

Thus where a person ('the owner'[2]) is entitled to assistance by way of repurchase in respect of a defective dwelling[3] and there is a covenant[4] relating to his interest in the dwelling[5] whereby:

(1)   before disposing of the interest he must offer to dispose of it to a public sector authority[6]; or

(2)   in the case of a leasehold interest, he may require a public sector authority who is his landlord to accept a surrender of the lease but is otherwise prohibited from disposing of it[7],

provision is made as follows. If the public sector authority is not the local housing authority, the provisions of Part XVI of the Housing Act 1985[8] as to repurchase do not apply so long as there is such a covenant; but if:

(a)   the owner disposes of his interest to the public sector authority in pursuance of the covenant or lease[9]; and

(b)   the interest acquired by that authority on the disposal subsists only in the land affected, that is to say, the defective dwelling and any garage, outhouse, garden, yard and appurtenances occupied with and used for the purposes of the dwelling or part of it[10],

the owner is entitled to be paid by the local housing authority[11] the amount (if any) by which 95 per cent of the defect-free value[12] exceeds the consideration for the disposal[13].

1   As to the right to buy see PARA 239 et seq. Note that the Housing Act 2004 makes some amendment to the right to buy provisions, eg by introducing a right of first refusal on a disposal (see the Housing Act 1985 s 156A; and PARAS 326–328).

2   References in the Housing Act 1985 s 549 to the owner of an interest in a defective dwelling include his personal representatives: s 565(2).

3   As to the meaning of 'person entitled to assistance by way of repurchase' see PARA 938 note 1. As to the meaning of 'defective dwelling' see PARA 929.

4   If the public sector authority is the local housing authority, the covenant must be disregarded for the purposes of the Housing Act 1985 Sch 20 (repurchase: see PARA 946 et seq): s 549(2). As to the meaning of 'local housing authority' see PARA 11. As to the meaning of 'public sector authority' see PARA 933.

5   As to the meaning of 'dwelling' see PARA 928 note 3.

6   Housing Act 1985 s 549(1)(a).

7   Housing Act 1985 s 549(1)(b).

8   Ie the Housing Act 1985 Pt XVI (ss 527–577).

9   Housing Act 1985 s 549(3)(a).

10 Housing Act 1985 s 549(3)(b).

11 As to the power of the appropriate national authority to contribute towards the expense incurred by a local housing authority in making payments under the Housing Act 1985 s 549 see s 569, s 570; and PARA 930.

12 'Defect-free value' means the amount that would have been the consideration for the disposal if none of the defective dwellings to which the designation in question related had been affected by the qualifying defect: Housing Act 1985 s 549(4)(b). As to the meaning of 'qualifying defect' see PARA 929 note 9.

13 Housing Act 1985 s 549(3). 'Consideration for the disposal' means the amount before any reduction required by s 158(3) (reduction corresponding to amount of discount repayable or amount payable for outstanding share under shared ownership lease: see PARA 332) or any provision to the like effect: s 549(4)(a).

951. Compulsory purchase compensation to be made up to 95 per cent of defect-free value. Where a person ('the owner'[1]) has disposed of an interest in a defective dwelling[2] (other than by repurchase[3]) to an authority possessing compulsory purchase powers[4] and:

(1)   immediately before the time of the disposal[5] he was eligible for assistance under these provisions in respect of the dwelling[6];

(2)   the amount paid as consideration for the disposal[7] did not include any amount attributable to his right to apply for such assistance[8]; and

(3)   on the disposal the authority acquired an interest in any of the affected land, that is to say, the defective dwelling and any garage, outhouse, garden, yard and appurtenances occupied with and used for the purposes of the dwelling or part of it[9],

he is entitled, subject to certain provisions, to be paid by the local housing authority[10] the amount (if any) by which 95 per cent of the defect-free value[11] exceeds the amount of the compensation for the disposal[12]. Where the compensation for the disposal fell to be assessed by reference to the value of the land as a site cleared of buildings and available for development, it must be assumed for the purposes of determining the defect-free value that it did not fall to be so assessed[13]. The amount payable by the local housing authority under these provisions must be reduced by the amount of any payments for well-maintained houses[14] made in respect of the defective dwelling[15].

1   References in the Housing Act 1985 s 550 to the owner of an interest in a defective dwelling include his personal representatives: s 565(2).
2   As to the meaning of 'defective dwelling' see PARA 929. As to the meaning of 'dwelling' see PARA 928 note 3.
3   Ie otherwise than in pursuance of the Housing Act 1985 Sch 20 (repurchase): see PARAS 946–948.
4   'Authority possessing compulsory purchase powers' has the same meaning as in the Land Compensation Act 1961 s 39(1) (see COMPULSORY ACQUISITION OF LAND vol 18 (2009) PARA 763): Housing Act 1985 s 550(6).
5   For these purposes, it must be assumed that the disposal occurred on a compulsory acquisition (in cases where it did not in fact do so): Housing Act 1985 s 550(3).
6   Housing Act 1985 s 550(1)(a).
7   'Amount of compensation for the disposal' means the amount that would have been the proper amount of compensation for the disposal (having regard to any relevant determination of the Upper Tribunal) or, if greater, the amount paid as the consideration for the disposal, but excluding any amount payable for disturbance or for any other matter not directly based on the value of land: Housing Act 1985 s 550(2)(a) (amended by SI 2009/1307).
8   Housing Act 1985 s 550(1)(b).
9   Housing Act 1985 s 550(1)(c).
10   As to the meaning of 'local housing authority' see PARA 11.
11   'Defect-free value' means the amount that would have been the proper amount of compensation for the disposal if none of the defective dwellings to which the designation in question related had been affected by the qualifying defect, but excluding any amount payable for disturbance or for any other matter not directly based on the value of land: Housing Act 1985 s 550(2)(b). As to the meaning of 'qualifying defect' see PARA 929 note 9.
12   Housing Act 1985 s 550(1).
13   Housing Act 1985 s 550(4).
14   Ie payments made under the Housing Act 1985 Sch 23 (repealed).
15   Housing Act 1985 s 550(5).

952. Supplementary provisions as to payments. The local housing authority[1] is not required to make a payment to a person, except in certain circumstances[2], unless he makes a written application to it for payment before the end of the period of two years beginning with the time of the disposal[3].

Where the authority:

(1)   refuses an application for a pre-emption right compensation payment[4] on any grounds[5]; or

(2)   refuses an application for a compulsory purchase compensation payment[6] on the grounds that the owner was not eligible for assistance[7] in respect of the defective dwelling[8],

it must give the applicant written notice[9] of the reasons for its decision[10]. Any question arising as to the defect-free value[11], or as to the amount of compensation for the disposal[12], must be determined by the district valuer[13] if the owner or the local housing authority so requires by notice in writing served on the district valuer[14].

1 As to the meaning of 'local housing authority' see PARA 11.
2 Ie except under the Housing Act 1985 s 549 (making-up of consideration on disposal in pursuance of right of pre-emption, etc: see PARA 950), or s 550 (making up of compulsory purchase compensation: see PARA 951): s 551(1)(a), (b).
3 Housing Act 1985 s 551(1).
4 Ie a payment under the Housing Act 1985 s 549: see PARA 950.
5 Housing Act 1985 s 551(2)(a).
6 Ie a payment under the Housing Act 1985 s 550: see PARA 951.
7 As to eligibility for assistance see PARA 942 et seq.
8 Housing Act 1985 s 551(2)(b). As to the meaning of 'defective dwelling' see PARA 929.
9 As to service of notices see PARA 963.
10 Housing Act 1985 s 551(2).
11 Ie under the Housing Act 1985 s 549 (see PARA 950) or s 550 (see PARA 951): s 551(3)(a). As to the meaning of 'defect-free value' see PARA 950 note 12.
12 Ie under the Housing Act 1985 s 550 (see PARA 951): s 551(3)(b).
13 As to the meaning of 'district valuer' see PARA 527 note 14.
14 Housing Act 1985 s 551(3). A person serving a notice on the district valuer in pursuance of s 551(3) must serve notice in writing of that fact on the other party: s 551(4). Before making a determination in pursuance of s 551(3), the district valuer must consider any representation by the owner or the authority made to him within four weeks from the service of the notice under that provision: s 551(5). References in s 551 to the owner of an interest in a defective dwelling include his personal representatives: s 565(2).

953. Reimbursement of expenses incidental to repurchase. A person whose interest in a defective dwelling[1] is acquired by the purchasing authority[2] as a result of repurchase[3] is entitled to be reimbursed by the purchasing authority the proper amount of:

(1) expenses in respect of legal services provided in connection with the authority's acquisition[4]; and

(2) other expenses in connection with negotiating the terms of that acquisition[5],

being in each case expenses which are reasonably incurred by him after receipt of an authority's notice of proposed terms of acquisition[6]. An agreement between a person and the purchasing authority is void in so far as it purports to oblige him to bear any part of the costs or expenses incurred by the authority in connection with the exercise by him of his rights under the defective housing provisions[7].

1 As to the meaning of 'defective dwelling' see PARA 929.
2 As to the meaning of 'purchasing authority' see PARA 949 note 15.
3 Ie in pursuance of the Housing Act 1985 Sch 20: see PARAS 946–948.
4 Housing Act 1985 s 552(1)(a).
5 Housing Act 1985 s 552(1)(b).
6 Ie a notice under the Housing Act 1985 Sch 20 para 3 (authority's notice of proposed terms of acquisition: see PARA 946): s 552(1).
7 Housing Act 1985 s 552(2).

954. Effect of repurchase on certain existing tenancies. Where a dwelling is purchased under Part XVI of the Housing Act 1985[1], it is possible that the dwelling is occupied by a tenant who has either protection under the Rent Act 1977 (if the tenancy was granted before 15 January 1989) or an assured tenancy under the Housing Act 1988. In such cases there is, subject to a number of qualifications, a right for the tenant concerned to acquire a secure tenancy from the acquiring local authority under the provisions contained in the Housing Act 1985.

Thus where an authority satisfying the landlord condition for a secure tenancy[2] acquires an interest in a defective dwelling[3] as a result of repurchase[4] and:

(1)　　　the land in which the interest subsists is or includes a dwelling house occupied as a separate dwelling[5]; and

(2)　　　the interest of the person entitled to assistance by way of repurchase[6] is, immediately before the completion of the authority's acquisition, subject to a tenancy[7] of the dwelling house[8],

the tenancy does not, on or after the acquisition, become a secure tenancy unless the required conditions are met[9]. The required conditions are:

(a)　　　that the tenancy was a protected tenancy[10] or an assured tenancy[11] throughout the period beginning with the making of an application for assistance under these provisions in respect of the defective dwelling and ending immediately before the authority's acquisition[12]; and

(b)　　　no notice that possession might be recovered under the Rent Act 1977[13] was given in respect of the tenancy nor a notice that the tenancy is to be a protected shorthold tenancy[14], nor a notice that possession might be recovered under the Housing Act 1988[15]; and

(c)　　　the tenancy is not by virtue of any provision of the Part I of the Housing Act 1988[16] an assured shorthold tenancy[17].

1　Ie the Housing Act 1985 Pt XVI (ss 527–577).
2　Ie any of the authorities or bodies within the Housing Act 1985 s 80(1) (the landlord condition for secure tenancies: see LANDLORD AND TENANT vol 63 (2016) PARA 1037).
3　As to the meaning of 'defective dwelling' see PARA 929. As to the meaning of 'dwelling' see PARA 928 note 3.
4　Ie in pursuance of the Housing Act 1985 Sch 20 (repurchase): see PARAS 946–948.
5　Housing Act 1985 s 553(1)(a). 'Dwelling house' has the same meaning as in Pt IV (ss 79–117) (secure tenancies: see PARA 436 note 4): s 558(a).
6　As to the meaning of 'person entitled to assistance by way of repurchase' see PARA 938 note 1.
7　As to the meaning of 'tenancy' see PARA 31 note 3.
8　Housing Act 1985 s 553(1)(b).
9　Housing Act 1985 s 553(1).
10　As to the meaning of 'protected tenancy' see LANDLORD AND TENANT vol 63 (2016) PARA 660 (definition applied by the Housing Act 1985 s 622).
11　As to the meaning of 'assured tenancy' see LANDLORD AND TENANT vol 63 (2016) PARA 825 (definition applied by the Housing Act 1985 s 622).
12　Housing Act 1985 s 553(2)(a) (amended by the Housing Act 1988 s 140(1), Sch 17 para 60).
13　Ie a notice under the Rent Act 1977 Sch 15 Cases 11–18, 20 (notice that possession might be recovered under that Case): see LANDLORD AND TENANT vol 63 (2016) PARA 816 et seq.
14　Ie a notice under the Housing Act 1980 s 52(1)(b) (repealed by the Housing Act 1988 s 140(2), Sch 18, except with respect to any tenancy entered into before 15 January 1989, or any tenancy which, having regard to s 34, can be a protected shorthold tenancy).
15　Ie a notice under the Housing Act 1988 Sch 2 Grounds 1, 3–5 (see LANDLORD AND TENANT vol 63 (2016) PARA 934 et seq): Housing Act 1985 s 553(2)(b) (amended by the Housing Act 1988 Sch 17 para 60; and the Housing Act 1996 ss 104, 227, Sch 8 para 1, Sch 19 Pt IV).
16　Ie the Housing Act 1988 Pt I (ss 1–45).
17　Housing Act 1985 s 553(2)(c) (added by the Housing Act 1988 Sch 17 para 60; and substituted by the Housing Act 1996 Sch 8 para 1). As to the meaning of 'assured shorthold tenancy' see LANDLORD AND TENANT vol 63 (2016) PARA 852.

955. Grant of tenancy to former owner-occupier. Where an authority acquires an interest in a defective dwelling[1] as a result of repurchase[2], or in the exercise of right of pre-emption[3], and:

(1)　　　the land in which the interest subsists is or includes a dwelling house[4] occupied as a separate dwelling[5]; and

(2)　　　an individual is an occupier[6] of the dwelling house throughout the period beginning with the making of an application for assistance under these provisions in respect of the dwelling and ending immediately before the completion of the authority's acquisition[7]; and

(3)　　he is a person entitled to assistance by way of repurchase[8] in respect of the defective dwelling, or the persons so entitled are in relation to the interest concerned his trustees[9],

the authority must either grant, or arrange for him to be granted, a tenancy (of that dwelling house or another[10]) on the completion of its acquisition of the interest concerned[11]. If the authority is a public sector authority capable of granting secure tenancies[12] its obligation is to grant a secure tenancy[13]. If the authority is the new towns residuary body[14] or a private registered provider of social housing[15] or a registered social landlord[16], other than a housing co-operative[17], its obligation is to grant a secure tenancy if the individual to whom a tenancy is to be granted:

(a)　　is a person who, immediately before he acquired his interest in the dwelling house, was a secure tenant of it[18]; or

(b)　　is the spouse or civil partner, or a former spouse or former civil partner, or the surviving spouse or surviving civil partner, of such a person[19]; or

(c)　　is a member of the family[20] of such a person who has died, and was residing with that person in the dwelling house at the time of and for the period of 12 months before his death[21].

In any other case its obligation is to grant or arrange for the grant of either:

(i)　　a secure tenancy[22]; or

(ii)　　a protected tenancy other than one under which the landlord[23] might recover possession under the Rent Act 1977[24]; or

(iii)　　an assured tenancy which is neither an assured shorthold tenancy, within the meaning of the Part I of the Housing Act 1988[25], nor a tenancy under which the landlord might recover possession[26] under that Act[27].

Where two or more persons qualify for the grant of a tenancy under these provisions in respect of the same dwelling house, the authority must grant the tenancy, or arrange for it to be granted, to such one or more of them as they may agree among themselves or (if there is no such agreement) to all of them[28].

1　As to the meaning of 'defective dwelling' see PARA 929.
2　Ie in pursuance of the Housing Act 1985 Sch 20: see PARAS 946–948.
3　Ie the circumstances described in the Housing Act 1985 s 549(3) (exercise of right of pre-emption etc): see PARA 950.
4　As to the meaning of 'dwelling house' see PARA 954 note 5.
5　Housing Act 1985 s 554(1)(a).
6　'Occupier', in relation to a dwelling house, means a person who occupies the dwelling house as his only or principal home or (in the case of a statutory tenant) as his residence: Housing Act 1985 s 558(b).
7　Housing Act 1985 s 554(1)(b).
8　As to the meaning of 'person entitled to assistance by way of repurchase' see PARA 938 note 1.
9　Housing Act 1985 s 554(1)(c).
10　As to alternative accommodation see the Housing Act 1985 s 556; and PARA 957.
11　Housing Act 1985 s 554(1).
12　Ie an authority mentioned in the Housing Act 1985 s 80(1): see LANDLORD AND TENANT vol 63 (2016) PARA 1037.
13　Housing Act 1985 s 554(2). References in ss 553–557 to the grant of a secure tenancy are references to the grant of a tenancy which would be a secure tenancy assuming that the tenant under the tenancy occupies the dwelling house as his only or principal home: s 558(c). As to the meaning of 'secure tenancy' see LANDLORD AND TENANT vol 63 (2016) PARA 1037.
14　As to the new towns residuary body see PARA 12.
15　As to the meaning of 'private registered provider of social housing' see PARA 53.
16　As to the meaning of 'registered social landlord' see PARA 13.
17　Ie a housing co-operative within the meaning of the Housing Act 1985 s 27B: see PARA 457 note 18.

18 Housing Act 1985 s 554(2A)(a) (s 554(2A) added by the Housing Act 1988 s 140(1), Sch 17 para 61; and amended by SI 1996/2325, SI 2008/3002 and SI 2010/866).
19 Housing Act 1985 s 554(2A)(b) (as added (see note 18); substituted by the Civil Partnership Act 2004 s 81, Sch 8 para 32). As to the meaning of 'spouse' see PARA 73 note 2.
20 Ie member of the family of that person within the meaning of the Housing Act 1985 s 186 (see PARA 274).
21 Housing Act 1985 s 554(2A)(c) (as added: see note 18).
22 Housing Act 1985 s 554(3)(a).
23 As to the meaning of 'landlord' see PARA 31 note 3.
24 Housing Act 1985 s 554(3)(b).
25 Ie the Housing Act 1988 ss 1–45: see LANDLORD AND TENANT vol 63 (2016) PARA 825 et seq.
26 Ie under the Housing Act 1985 Sch 2 Grounds 1–5: see LANDLORD AND TENANT vol 63 (2016) PARAS 934–939.
27 Housing Act 1985 s 554(3)(c) (added by the Housing Act 1988 Sch 17 para 61).
28 Housing Act 1985 s 554(4).

956. Grant of tenancy to former statutory tenant. Where an authority, as a public sector authority capable of granting secure tenancies[1], acquires an interest in a defective dwelling[2] as a result of repurchase[3] and:

(1)   the land in which the interest subsists is or includes a dwelling house[4] occupied as a separate dwelling[5]; and

(2)   an individual is an occupier[6] of a dwelling house throughout the period beginning with the making of an application for assistance[7] in respect of the dwelling and ending immediately before the completion of the authority's acquisition[8]; and

(3)   he is a statutory tenant[9] of the dwelling house at the end of that period[10]; and

(4)   no notice was given in respect of the original tenancy[11] in accordance with the Rent Act 1977[12] or under the Housing Act 1980[13]; and

(5)   the interest of the person entitled to assistance would, if the statutory tenancy were a contractual tenancy, be subject to the tenancy at the end of the period beginning with the making of an application for assistance in respect of the dwelling and ending immediately before the completion of the authority's acquisition[14],

the authority must grant him a secure tenancy (of that dwelling house or another[15]) on the completion of its acquisition of the interest concerned[16]. Where two or more persons qualify for the grant of a tenancy in respect of the same dwelling house, the authority must grant the tenancy to such one or more of them as they may agree among themselves or (if there is no such agreement) to all of them[17].

If at any time after the service of a notice of determination[18] it appears to the purchasing authority that a person may be entitled to request it to grant him a secure tenancy, it must forthwith give him notice in writing[19] of that fact[20].

1 Ie an authority mentioned in the Housing Act 1985 s 80(1) (public sector authorities capable of granting secure tenancies): see LANDLORD AND TENANT vol 63 (2016) PARA 1037. As to the meaning of 'secure tenancy' see LANDLORD AND TENANT vol 63 (2016) PARA 1037.
2 As to the meaning of 'defective dwelling' see PARA 929.
3 Ie in pursuance of the Housing Act 1985 Sch 20 (repurchase): see PARAS 946–948.
4 As to the meaning of 'dwelling house' see PARA 954 note 5.
5 Housing Act 1985 s 555(1)(a). As to the meaning of 'dwelling' see PARA 928 note 3.
6 As to the meaning of 'occupier' see PARA 955 note 6.
7 As to applications for assistance see PARA 936.
8 Housing Act 1985 s 555(1)(b).
9 As to the meaning of 'statutory tenant' see LANDLORD AND TENANT vol 63 (2016) PARA 673.
10 Housing Act 1985 s 555(1)(c).
11 As to the meaning of 'tenancy' see PARA 31 note 3.

12 Ie the Rent Act 1977 Sch 15 Cases 11–18, 20: see LANDLORD AND TENANT vol 63 (2016) PARA 934 et seq.
13 Ie the Housing Act 1980 s 52(1)(b) (repealed) (notice that tenancy is to be a protected shorthold tenancy: see PARA 954 note 14): Housing Act 1985 s 555(1)(d).
14 Housing Act 1985 s 555(1)(e).
15 As to alternative accommodation see PARA 957.
16 Housing Act 1985 s 555(1).
17 Housing Act 1985 s 555(2).
18 As to the meaning of 'notice of determination' see PARA 938.
19 As to service of notices see PARA 963.
20 Housing Act 1985 s 555(3).

957. Alternative accommodation and requests for tenancy. The dwelling house[1] to be let under the tenancy granted, or arranged to be granted[2], to a former owner-occupier or statutory tenant of a defective dwelling house is to be the dwelling house of which he is the occupier[3] immediately before the completion of the authority's acquisition (the 'current dwelling house')[4].

However, this does not apply where:

(1)   by reason of the condition of any building of which the current dwelling house consists or of which it forms part, the dwelling house may not safely be occupied for residential purposes[5];

(2)   the authority intends, within a reasonable time of the completion of its acquisition of the interest concerned:

(a)   to demolish or reconstruct the building which consists of or includes the defective dwelling in question; or

(b)   to carry out work on any building or land in which the interest concerned subsists,

and cannot reasonably do so if the current dwelling house remains in residential occupation[6].

In those cases, the dwelling house to be let must be another dwelling house which, so far as is reasonably practicable in the case of that authority, affords accommodation which is:

(i)   similar as regards extent and character to the accommodation afforded by the current dwelling house[7];

(ii)   reasonably suitable to the means of the prospective tenant[8] and his family[9]; and

(iii)   reasonably suitable to the needs of the prospective tenant and his family as regards proximity to place of work and place of education[10].

1 As to the meaning of 'dwelling house' see PARA 954 note 5.
2 Ie under the Housing Act 1985 s 554 or s 555 or under arrangements made for the purposes of s 554: see PARAS 955–956.
3 As to the meaning of 'occupier' see PARA 955 note 6.
4 Housing Act 1985 s 556(1).
5 Housing Act 1985 s 556(1) case 1.
6 Housing Act 1985 s 556(1) case 2.
7 Housing Act 1985 s 556(2)(a).
8 As to the meaning of 'tenant' see PARA 31 note 3.
9 Housing Act 1985 s 556(2)(b).
10 Housing Act 1985 s 556(2)(c).

958. Request for tenancy. An authority is not required to grant, or arrange for the grant of, a tenancy to a former owner-occupier or statutory tenant of a defective dwelling house[1] unless he requests it to do so in writing before:

(1)   in the case of an acquisition by repurchase[2], the service on the person entitled to assistance of a copy of the agreement[3]; or

(2)   in the case of an acquisition in pursuance of a right of pre-emption[4], the time of the disposal[5].

An authority receiving such a request must, as soon as reasonably practicable, give notice in writing to the person making the request stating whether in its opinion either of the cases for alternative accommodation[6] apply[7]. If its opinion is that either case does apply, the notice must also state which of the cases is applicable and the consequent effect[8].

1   Ie under the Housing Act 1985 s 554 or s 555: see PARAS 955–956.
2   Ie an acquisition under the Housing Act 1985 Sch 20 (repurchase): see PARAS 946–948.
3   Ie the agreement drawn up under the Housing Act 1985 Sch 20 para 5 (see PARA 946): s 557(1)(a).
4   Ie an acquisition under the Housing Act 1985 s 549: see PARA 950.
5   Housing Act 1985 s 557(1)(b). As to the meaning of 'disposal' see PARA 931 note 2.
6   Ie the cases in the Housing Act 1985 s 556(1): see PARA 957.
7   Housing Act 1985 s 557(2).
8   Housing Act 1985 s 557(3).

(4) LOCAL SCHEMES

959. Designation of defective dwellings under local schemes. A local housing authority[1] may by resolution designate as a class buildings in its district[2] each of which consists of or includes one or more dwellings[3] if it appears to it that:

(1)   buildings in the proposed class are defective by reason of their design or construction[4]; and

(2)   by virtue of these circumstances having become generally known, the value of some or all of the dwellings concerned has been substantially reduced[5].

A dwelling which is, or is included in, a building in a class so designated is referred to in Part XVI of the Housing Act 1985[6] as a 'defective dwelling'[7]. A designation must describe the qualifying defect[8] and specify:

(a)   the cut-off date[9];

(b)   the date (being a date falling on or after the cut-off date) on which the designation is to come into operation[10]; and

(c)   the period within which persons may seek assistance under these provisions in respect of the defective dwellings concerned[11].

A designation may not describe a designated class by reference to the area (other than the authority's district) in which the buildings concerned are situated; but a designated class may be so described that within the authority's district there is only one building in the class[12].

1   As to the meaning of 'local housing authority' see PARA 11.
2   As to the meaning of 'district' see PARA 11.
3   As to the meaning of 'dwelling' see PARA 928 note 3.
4   Housing Act 1985 s 559(1)(a).
5   Housing Act 1985 s 559(1)(b). Section 559 does not apply to a building in a class designated under s 528 (designation by appropriate national authority: see PARA 929); but a building does not cease to be included in a class designated under s 559 by virtue of its inclusion in a class designated under s 528: s 559(2). Any question arising as to whether a building is or was at any time in a class designated under s 559 is to be determined by the local housing authority concerned: s 559(6).
6   Ie the Housing Act 1985 Pt XVI (ss 527–577).
7   Housing Act 1985 s 559(3). As to the Housing Health and Safety Rating System ('HHSRS') under the Housing Act 2004, and category 1 and category 2 hazards, see PARA 562 et seq.
8   'The qualifying defect' means what, in the opinion of the authority, is wrong with the buildings in that class: Housing Act 1985 s 559(3)(a).
9   Housing Act 1985 s 559(4)(a). The 'cut-off date' means the date by which, in the opinion of the authority, the circumstances mentioned in s 559(1)(a) (see head (1) in the text) became generally known: s 559(3)(b).

10 Housing Act 1985 s 559(4)(b).
11 Housing Act 1985 s 559(4)(c).
12 Housing Act 1985 s 559(5).

960. Variation or revocation of a designation under a local scheme. The local housing authority[1] may by resolution:

(1) vary a designation[2], but not so as to vary the cut-off date[3]; or

(2) revoke such a designation[4].

The authority may by a variation of the designation extend the assistance application period[5] whether or not it has expired[6]. The variation or revocation of a designation does not affect the operation of the provisions of Part XVI of the Housing Act 1985[7] in relation to a dwelling[8] if, before the variation or revocation comes into operation, the dwelling is a defective dwelling[9] by virtue of the designation in question and application for assistance has been made[10].

1 As to the meaning of 'local housing authority' see PARA 11.
2 Ie a designation under the Housing Act 1985 s 559: see PARA 959.
3 Housing Act 1985 s 560(1)(a). As to the meaning of 'cut-off date' see PARA 959 note 9.
4 Housing Act 1985 s 560(1)(b).
5 Ie the period referred to in the Housing Act 1985 s 559(4)(c): see PARA 959 head (c).
6 Housing Act 1985 s 560(2).
7 Ie the Housing Act 1985 Pt XVI (ss 527–577).
8 As to the meaning of 'dwelling' see PARA 928 note 3.
9 As to the meaning of 'defective dwelling' see PARA 959.
10 Housing Act 1985 s 560(3).

961. Appropriate national authority's control over designation, variation or revocation. Where a local housing authority[1] has passed a resolution designating defective dwellings or varying or revoking such a designation[2], it must give written notice[3] to the appropriate national authority[4] of the resolution before the expiry of the period of 28 days beginning with the date on which it is passed[5]. The designation, variation or revocation must not come into operation before the cut-off date[6] or, if it is later, the expiry of the period of two months or such longer period[7] as the appropriate national authority may direct for these purposes beginning with the receipt by the appropriate national authority of the required notice[8]. If before the cut-off date or, if it is later, the expiry of the relevant period[9] the appropriate national authority serves notice in writing to that effect on the authority, the designation, revocation or variation is not to come into operation[10].

1 As to the meaning of 'local housing authority' see PARA 11.
2 Ie a resolution under either the Housing Act 1985 s 559 (see PARA 959) or s 560 (see PARA 960).
3 As to the giving of notices see PARA 963.
4 As to the appropriate national authority, ie the Secretary of State or, where statutory functions have been transferred in relation to Wales, the Welsh Ministers, see PARA 7.
5 Housing Act 1985 s 561(1).
6 As to the meaning of 'cut-off date' see PARA 959 note 9.
7 If, within the period for the time being specified in or (by virtue of the previous operation of this provision) for the purposes of the Housing Act 1985 s 561(2), the appropriate national authority is satisfied that it does not have reasonably sufficient information to enable it to come to a decision with respect to the resolution concerned, it may direct for the purposes of that s 561(2) that it must have effect as if for the period so specified there were substituted such longer period as is specified in the direction: s 561(2A) (added by the Local Government and Housing Act 1989 s 166(1), (4)).
8 Ie the notice required under the Housing Act 1985 s 561(1) (see the text and note 5): s 561(2) (amended by the Local Government and Housing Act 1989 s 166(4)).
9 Ie the period for the time being specified in or for the purposes of the Housing Act 1985 s 561(2): see the text and notes 6–8.
10 Housing Act 1985 s 561(3) (amended by the Local Government and Housing Act 1989 s 166(4)).

(5) ADMINISTRATIVE PROVISIONS

962. Death of person eligible for assistance and other matters. Where a person who is eligible for assistance[1] in respect of a defective dwelling[2]: (1) dies[3]; or (2) disposes of his interest in the dwelling[4] (otherwise than on a disposal for value) to another person qualifying for assistance[5], Part XVI of the Housing Act 1985[6] applies as if anything done (or treated by virtue of these provisions as done) by or in relation to the person so eligible had been done by or in relation to his personal representatives or, as the case may be, the person acquiring his interest[7].

1   As to eligibility for assistance in respect of a defective dwelling see PARA 928.
2   As to the meaning of 'defective dwelling' see PARAS 929, 959.
3   Housing Act 1985 s 565(1)(a).
4   As to the meaning of 'interest in a dwelling' see PARA 928 note 7.
5   Ie a person mentioned in the Housing Act 1985 s 527(a) (individuals, trustees for individuals and personal representatives: see PARA 928): s 565(1)(b).
6   Ie the Housing Act 1985 Pt XVI (ss 527–577).
7   Housing Act 1985 s 565(1). In ss 549–551 (see PARAS 950–952) references to the owner of an interest in a defective dwelling include his personal representatives: s 565(2).

963. Service of notices. A notice or other document under Part XVI of the Housing Act 1985[1] may be given to or served[2] on a person, and an application or written request under that Part may be made to a person:

(1)   by delivering it to him or leaving it at his proper address[3]; or
(2)   by sending it to him by post[4],

and also, where the person concerned is a body corporate, by giving or making it to or serving it on the secretary of that body[5].

1   Ie the Housing Act 1985 Pt XVI (ss 527–577).
2   As this provision is permissive only, it is clear that, where a notice is served in a different manner and is received, this constitutes good service: see *Sharpley v Manby* [1942] 1 KB 217, sub nom *Re Sharpley's and Manby's Arbitration* [1942] 1 All ER 66, CA; *Stylo Shoes Ltd v Prices Tailors Ltd* [1960] Ch 396, [1959] 3 All ER 901.
3   Housing Act 1985 s 571(1)(a). For the purposes s 571, and the Interpretation Act 1978 s 7 (see note 4) as it applies for the purposes of the Housing Act 1985 s 571, the proper address of a person is: (1) in the case of a body corporate or its secretary, the address of the principal office of the body; (2) in any other case, his last known address, and also, where an additional address for service has been specified by that person in a notice under s 548(2) (notice of intention to assume responsibility for repurchase: see PARA 949), that address: s 571(2).
4   Housing Act 1985 s 571(1)(b). This provision brings into operation the provisions of the Interpretation Act 1978 s 7, to the effect that service is deemed to be effected by properly addressing, prepaying and posting a letter containing the document and, unless the contrary is proved, is deemed to have been effected at the time at which the letter would be delivered in the ordinary course of post.
5   Housing Act 1985 s 571(1).

964. Jurisdiction of County Court. The County Court[1] has jurisdiction:

(1)   to determine any question arising under Part XVI of the Housing Act 1985[2] notwithstanding that a declaration is the only relief sought[3]; and
(2)   to entertain any proceedings brought in connection with the performance or discharge of obligations arising under that Part, including proceedings for the recovery of damages in the event of the obligations not being performed[4].

Where an authority fails to extend or further extend a period when required to do so[5], the County Court may by order extend or further extend that period until such date as may be specified in the order[6].

1   As to the County Court see generally COURTS AND TRIBUNALS vol 24 (2010) PARA 758 et seq.
2   Ie the Housing Act 1985 Pt XVI (ss 527–577).
3   Housing Act 1985 s 572(1)(a).

4　Housing Act 1985 s 572(1)(b). Section 572(1) has effect subject to: (1) s 528(6) (see PARA 929) and s 559(6) (see PARA 959) (questions of designation to be decided by designating authority); and (2) s 551(3) (see PARA 952) and Sch 20 para 9 (see PARA 947) (questions of valuation to be determined by district valuer): s 572(2). As to the relationship between this jurisdiction and judicial review see *R v Metropolitan Borough of Sandwell, ex p Cashmore* (1993) 25 HLR 544.

5　Ie when required to do so by: (1) the Housing Act 1985 s 542(3) (reinstatement grant; period within which work is to be completed: see PARA 943); or (2) Sch 20 para 2(2) or Sch 20 para 6(2) (repurchase; period for service of request or notice by person entitled to assistance: see PARA 946): s 572(3)(a), (b).

6　Housing Act 1985 s 572(3).

INDEX

Housing

References are to paragraph numbers; superior figures refer to notes

ENERGY CONSERVATION AND
　CONTROL—*continued*
energy conservation report—*continued*
　supplementary provisions 905
ENERGY EFFICIENCY
green deal—
　meaning 889
　assessment of property, conditions
　　as to 891
　confirmation of plan 894
　energy bill: meaning $889n^{14}$
　framework regulations 890
　improvement, installation of 893
　occupier: meaning $889n^2$
　owner: meaning $889n^2$
　relevant energy supplier: meaning
　　$889n^8$
　relevant title holder: meaning $889n^2$
　Secretary of State, power of 895
　terms of plan 892
GENERAL IMPROVEMENT AREA
declaration of 832
penalty for obstruction 834
powers of entry 834
resolutions relating to 833
GYPSY
meaning $476n^2$
accommodation needs—
　local housing authority's duties 476
HOME ENERGY CONSERVATION
fuel poverty, reduction of—
　England 887
　Wales 888
grants for improving energy
　efficiency—
　administering agency: meaning
　　$899n^1$
　advice: meaning $899n^1$
　advice application: meaning $899n^1$
　appropriate national authority, role
　　of 897
　area agency: meaning $899n^1$
　asset rating: meaning $899n^8$
　building in multiple occupation:
　　meaning $897n^{15}$
　dwelling: meaning $899n^4$
　eligibility criteria: meaning $899n^{11}$
　England, scheme in 898
　householder: meaning $899n^2$
　materials: meaning $897n^{13}$
　means-tested benefit: meaning
　　$899n^7$
　mobile home: meaning $899n^4$
　occupant: meaning $899n^3$
　private occupancy: meaning $899n^6$

HOME ENERGY
　CONSERVATION—*continued*
grants for improving energy
　efficiency—*continued*
　SAP rating: meaning $899n^5$
　statutory provisions 896
　tenant: meaning $899n^2$
　Wales, scheme in 899
　works application:
　　meaning $899n^{1, 2}$
residential accommodation, efficiency
　of 886
HOMELESSNESS
assistance: meaning $483n^5$
England—
　advisory services 485
　application for assistance 487
　appropriate national authority,
　　guidance by 486
　asylum-seekers and their
　　dependants, assistance for 492
　cases involving children, co-
　　operation in 516
　co-operation between housing
　　authorities 514, 516
　current framework 478
　failure to disclose change of
　　circumstances, offences as to
　　517
　false statements, offences as to 517
　general background 477
　homelessness: meaning 481
　intentional homelessness 483
　interim duty to secure
　　accommodation 493
　limited duty to intentionally
　　homeless 496
　out-of-area placements 511
　priority need—
　　meaning 495
　　duty to persons with 498
　　duty to persons without 497
　private landlord, arrangements
　　with 512
　protection of property of homeless
　　persons or persons threatened
　　with homelessness 513
　re-application after private rented
　　sector offer, duty on 499, 500
　referral to another authority—
　　appeal on point of law, right to
　　　509
　　conditions for 503
　　duties to applicant 505

References are to paragraph numbers; superior figures refer to notes

HOUSING—*continued*
　orders and regulations, making of 395
　registered social landlords 10, 13
　regulator: meaning 57
　residential property tribunals—
　　meaning 34
　　additional relief 43
　　appeals 50
　　costs 47
　　determination without hearing 45
　　dismissal powers of 44
　　enforcement of decisions 48
　　fees 46
　　information, regulations as to 41
　　interim orders 43
　　parties 39
　　powers of 35
　　pre-trial reviews 42
　　procedure regulations 39
　　transfer of proceedings 40
　temporary use, management and
　　　repair of houses acquired or
　　　retained for 640
　tribunals (England)—
　　First-tier Tribunal and Upper
　　　Tribunal, jurisdiction of. *See*
　　　First-tier Tribunal and Upper
　　　Tribunal *above*
　　rent assessment committees 32
　　Upper Tribunal, jurisdiction of. *See*
　　　First-tier Tribunal and Upper
　　　Tribunal *above*
　tribunals (Wales)—
　　residential property tribunals. *See*
　　　residential property tribunals
　　　above
HOUSING ACCOMMODATION
　allocation of—
　　eligible persons, only to 424, 425
　　false statements 431
　　guidance on 430
　　Housing Act 1996, under 422
　　information, withholding 431
　　legislative background 420
　　provisions not applying, where 423
　　tenancy strategies 421
　housing register 426
　scheme—
　　England, in 427
　　information about 429
　　Wales, in 428
HOUSING ACTION AREA
　declaration of 831

HOUSING ACTION AREA—*continued*
　dwelling: meaning 831n[4]
　environmental works: meaning
　　831n[18]
　hostel: meaning 831n[4]
　house in multiple occupation:
　　meaning 831n[4]
　housing accommodation: meaning
　　831n[4]
　penalty for obstruction 834
　powers of entry 834
　publicising declaration of 832
　resolutions relating to 833
HOUSING ACTION TRUST
　meaning 12
　acquisition of land by 553
　areas—
　　meaning 538
　　proposals for 541
　disposal of land—
　　background 554
　　consent to 555, 556
　　dwelling houses subject to secure
　　　tenancies, of 558
　　legal assistance to tenants, provision
　　　of 557
　　subsequent disposals, consent to
　　　556
　dissolution of 561
　establishment of 539
　functions—
　　background 542
　　directions as to exercise of 549
　　financial assistance, power to give
　　　548
　　highways, as to 547
　　housing authority, as 543
　　planning authority, as 545
　　planning control 544
　　public health 546
　　transfer of 550
　legislative background 537
　objects and general powers of 540
　rent 559, 560
　transfer of land to 553
　vesting of land in 552
HOUSING ASSOCIATION
　meaning 13
　appropriate authority: meaning 21n[3]
　county councils, provision of land by
　　25
　dispositions of land, control as to 24
　fully mutual: meaning 13

References are to paragraph numbers; superior figures refer to notes

HOUSING LOAN
acquisition or improvement of
 housing, for—
 house: meaning 909n^2
 local housing authorities, powers
  of 908
 Public Works Loan Commissioners,
  by 909
first-time buyers, assistance to—
 administration 921
 forms of 920
 indemnification of lending
  institutions 921
 prescribed: meaning 919n^9
 qualifying conditions 920
 recognised lending institutions,
  advances to 919
 terms of advances 921
service charges, in respect of—
 administrative expenses 926
 appropriate national authority
  regulations 924, 925
 equitable interests, purchase of 925
 housing authority: meaning 923n^7,
  924n^3
 index linked period: meaning
  923n^{15}
 interest on loan 926
 provision for 922, 924
 right to loan after exercise of right
  to buy 923
HOUSING OMBUDSMAN SERVICE
appointment and status of 137
approved scheme—
 amendment of 133
 approval of 133
 notices as to 134
 provision for 131
 register of 135
 requirements 132
 subscriptions payable in respect of
  136
 withdrawal of 133
designated person—
 meaning 138n^3
 complaints referred by 138
designated tenant panel: meaning
 138n^3
determinations and reports by 139
duly made complaints 138
enforcement of determinations 140
establishment of 130
public sector landlord: meaning 131n^3
publicly-funded dwelling: meaning
 131n^3
social landlord: meaning 131n^3

HOUSING STANDARDS
Decent Homes Standard 562
emergency remedial action—
 meaning 613n^6
 appeals 616
 expenses, recovery of 614
 power to take 613
enforcement—
 charge, recovery of 619
 decision to take enforcement
  actions, reasons for 568
 expenses, recovery of 618
 guidance about enforcement
  actions 569
new system of assessment 563
hazard—
 category 1—
  meaning 564
  enforcement, general duty of 566
  inspections as to existence of 565
 category 2—
  meaning 564
  enforcement actions 567
  inspections as to existence of 565
 consultation with fire and rescue
  authorities 570
 decision to take enforcement
  actions, reasons for 568
 guidance about enforcement
  actions 569
 guidance about inspections 569
hazard awareness notice—
 category 1 hazard, relating to 608
 category 2 hazard, relating to 609
improvement notice—
 appeal against—
  generally 580
  tribunal, powers of 582, 583
  variation or revocation of notice,
   decision as to 581, 583
 category 1 hazard, relating to 571
 category 2 hazard, relating to 572
 contents of 573
 enforcement—
  expenses, recovery of 587
  failing to comply, offence of 584
  local housing authorities, action
   by 585, 586
  power of court as to 588, 589
 local land charges, effect as 610
 management order, effect of 612
 operation of 576
 person liable to comply with,
  change in 579

References are to paragraph numbers; superior figures refer to notes

MANAGEMENT ORDER—*continued*
appeal against empty dwelling
　　management order—*continued*
compensation, against decision on
　　810, 811
general procedure 806
powers of tribunal on appeal 807,
　　809, 811
relevant person: meaning 806n[1]
vary or revoke order, against
　　decision or refusal to 808
final empty dwelling management
　　order—
meaning 781
accounts 795
appeals against. *See* appeal against
　　empty dwelling management
　　order *above*
application to tribunal as to breach
　　of management scheme 796
compensation payable to third
　　party 805
dwelling: meaning 781n[5]
effect of—
　　agreements and legal proceedings,
　　　　on 799
　　furniture, on possession and
　　　　supply of 800
　　order determining lease or licence,
　　　　power of tribunal to make
　　　　801
　　order determining lease or licence,
　　　　power of tribunal to make
　　　　801
　　persons occupying or having right
　　　　to occupy dwelling, on 798
general effect of 793
local housing authority's duties 791
making of 790
management scheme 795, 796
mortgagees, effect on 794
operation of 792
power of entry to carry out work
　　804
preceding interim order: meaning
　　781n[4]
relevant proprietor—
meaning 781n[4]
effect on 794
revocation of 797
termination of—
　　financial arrangements on 802
　　leases, agreements and
　　　　proceedings following 803
variation of 797

MANAGEMENT ORDER—*continued*
final order—
meaning 745
accounts: meaning 760
appeal against. *See* appeal against
　　above
effect of—
　　agreements and legal proceedings,
　　　　on 775
　　compensation to third parties,
　　　　on 777
　　furniture, on possession and
　　　　supply of 752
　　general effect 758
　　immediate landlords, on 759
　　mortgagees, on 759
　　occupiers, on 774
　　persons occupying or having right
　　　　to occupy dwelling, on 798
　　possession and supply of
　　　　furniture 776
　　powers of entry to carry out
　　　　work, on 778
empty dwelling management order.
　　See final empty dwelling
　　management order *above*
expiry date: meaning 755n[8]
local housing authority, duties of
　　757
making of 755
management scheme—
meaning 760
affected person: meaning 761n[1]
enforcement by relevant landlord
　　761
operation of 756
refusal to revoke 769
refusal to vary 767
requirements after making 765
requirements before making 764
revocation of 763, 769
variation of 762
improvement notice, effect on 612
interim empty dwelling management
　　order—
meaning 781
appeals against. *See* appeal against
　　empty dwelling management
　　order *above*
authorisation to make 783
compensation payable to third
　　party 805
dwelling: meaning 781n[5]

References are to paragraph numbers; superior figures refer to notes

References are to paragraph numbers; superior figures refer to notes

References are to paragraph numbers; superior figures refer to notes

References are to paragraph numbers; superior figures refer to notes